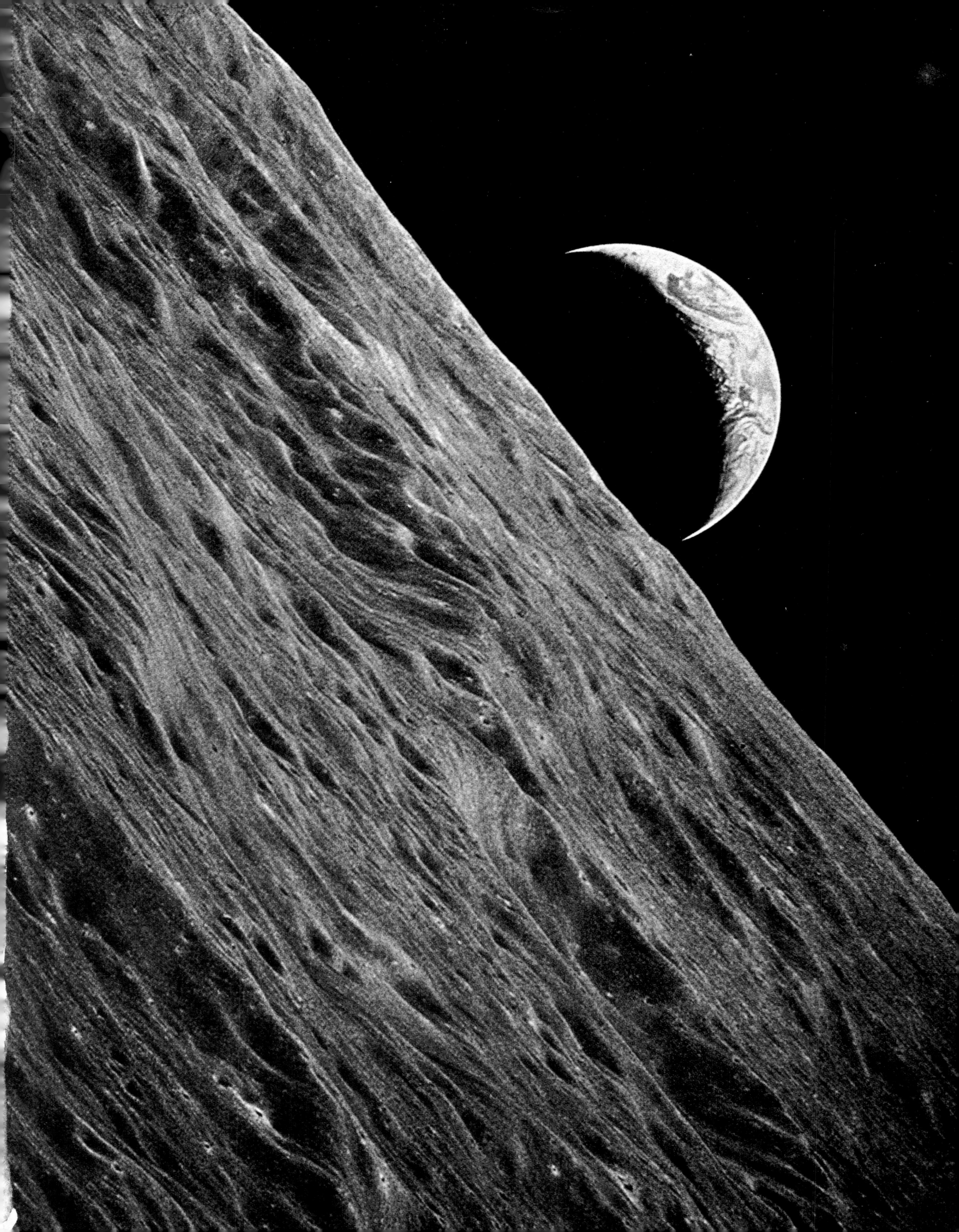

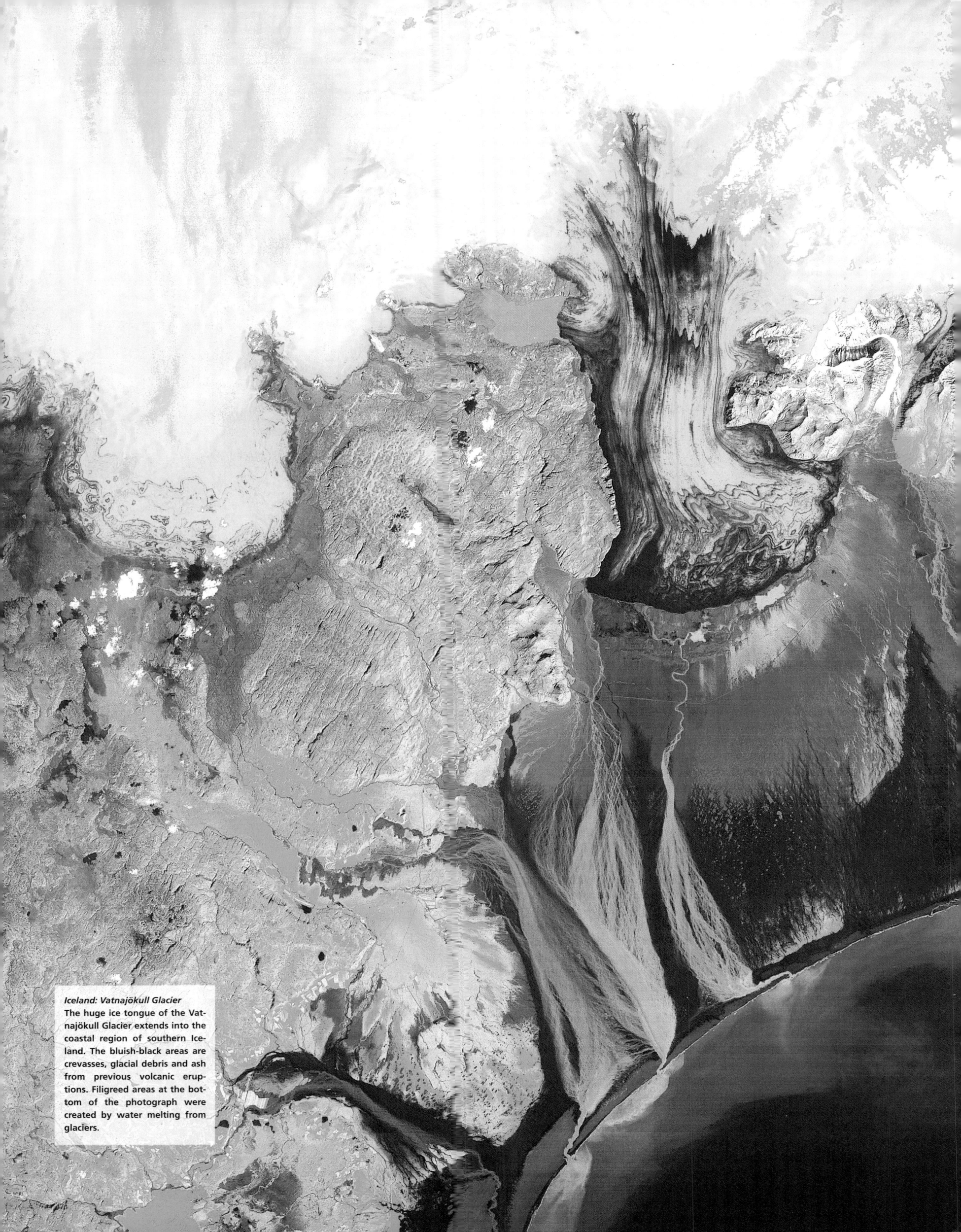

Iceland: Vatnajökull Glacier
The huge ice tongue of the Vatnajökull Glacier extends into the coastal region of southern Iceland. The bluish-black areas are crevasses, glacial debris and ash from previous volcanic eruptions. Filigreed areas at the bottom of the photograph were created by water melting from glaciers.

THE
GREAT
WORLD
ATLAS

U.S.A.: New York City
The Greater New York area is one of the world's largest metropolitan areas. Between the Hudson River and the East River lies the borough of Manhattan with the green rectangle of famous Central Park. Brooklyn, the most populous borough, lies on the western tip of Long Island. Sandbars line the southern coast of Long Island.

The Earth is our home, both in the region where we happen to live and on the entire planet. We travel to Antarctica or Bali, have friends in Brisbane and Yokohama, place telephone calls to Johannesburg or perhaps even to Tierra del Fuego. Our stereo system was manufactured in Korea, our whiskies were distilled in Scotland or Kentucky. The planet is fast becoming a global village.

For millions of years humankind has been wandering across the face of the Earth, and today global travel has become a familiar feature of life. An increasingly large number of people are spending ever more time and money visiting foreign places. Three decades ago, only seventy million people were counted at international frontier crossings; that number has since increased sevenfold: the world has become mobile.

Modern communications technologies add another dimension to this mobility. An event happening right now in Beijing appears without delay on video screens around the world. No spectacular event can occur without immediately attracting the attention of the world community. Distances have become irrelevant as the continents seem to move closer together. And yet, far too much of the world still remains unknown and foreign to us. The vast expanses of Siberia and Australia, the island world of Oceania, the landscapes of central Africa, the far north and the extreme south of the two American continents: who can claim to have a clear, detailed mental image of these fascinating regions of our planet?

The Great World Atlas is designed to meet the changing needs of a changing world. Although it follows in the tradition of Mercator and other cartographers, this new volume is a revolutionary innovation, a trailblazing geographic and cartographic databank. Its fundamental concept reflects two essential goals. First, it is a precise and detailed reference designed to meet the information needs of a contemporary people. It has been created with travelers, both business and leisure, in mind, and it also serves as an invaluable resource for families and students, politicians, scientists, and businesspeople. The maps in this volume have been drawn to depict the actual state of today's world with unprecedented fidelity.

But beyond all that, *The Great World Atlas* hopes to communicate a dream and a fascination: the fascination of our wonderful blue spaceship, a place where life is precious and worthwhile, a threatened oasis whose continued survival depends upon the cooperation and commitment of people around the world.

This book is the creation of the distinguished Bertelsmann Cartographic Institute, which has invested many years and many millions of dollars to create a revolutionary digital cartographic database for a major new atlas series. The 80 to 100 staff members and their expert advisers who have spent years designing (and who continually update) the cartographic database are passionately committed to the goals that define this atlas program. Worldwide cooperation is the guiding principle in all their work. To give just two examples: Chinese geographers and cartographers at the University of Nanking designed the cartography of China; and former employees of Sojus Karta in Moscow helped create the maps of the Commonwealth of Independent States that were born after the collapse of the Soviet Union. These collaborations are all the more remarkable in view of the fact that mapmakers have always been strongly influenced by the complex interplays of military and political forces.

The worldview embodied by *The Great World Atlas* provides other examples of cartographic collaboration as well. New techniques and innovations in cartography have been harnessed in a variety of ways. The revolutionary technique of computer cartography – all map designs were digitally scanned, and all individual map elements are stored in a central databank – permits rapid reaction to changes of every sort. This is a milestone on the path to creating a truly up-to-date cartography commensurate with the actual state of the world.

In creating *The Great World Atlas,* some antiquated cartographic conventions have been abandoned, new methods of representation have been developed, and different informational features have been emphasized. The most obvious example of these improvements lies in the new, more realistic use of color. Subtle gradations of color represent fine distinctions in the world's ecological zones, which are depicted according to their particular climates and characteristic vegetation. Unlike the deserts and mountains in traditional atlases, where color is almost exclusively a function of elevation, the deserts in *The Great World Atlas* are not green and mountains are not brown. Rather, coloration reflects more closely what you would see if you looked down at the Earth from an orbiting spaceship.

The inclusion of a detailed network of transportation arteries is another important feature, and one that will no doubt prove useful to leisure travelers and businesspeople alike. For the first time ever, *The Great World Atlas* presents the world's entire continental network of roads and railways, complete with their exact routes, classifications and numbers. Emphasis has also been given to major cultural or natural sites that are likely to be of interest to tourists.

But perhaps the most important innovation of all has to do with the way we perceive the countries of the world in relation to one another. Previous atlases compel their readers to cope with maps whose scales vary from one page to the next. *The Great World Atlas* puts an end to that by depicting our planet's land surfaces in a single, unified and detailed scale of 1:4.5 million. The scale is the same everywhere, from Nordkapp to Capetown, from Siberia to Australia and Oceania. In order to satisfy the desire for precise and detailed information, *The Great World Atlas* also provides additional larger-scale maps depicting regions of particular interest to its primary audience: a detailed series of maps showing the United States and southern Canada in a scale of 1:2.25 million. As its users will quickly recognize, the policy of treating the continents and their countries with cartographic equality offers obvious practical advantages. Most of us grew up with atlases in which the map of England was nearly as big as the map of China and in which Europe was emphasized at the expense of marginally treated non-European continents. Cartographic misinformation has misled generations of atlas users into forming mistaken notions about the relative sizes of the world's nations and cultural regions.

To deepen our understanding of our home planet and its topographic structures, *The Great World Atlas* offers much more than mere cartography. Selected satellite photographs at the beginning of the volume provide fascinating insights into the world's characteristic natural and cultural landscapes. These images also show the actual models which the map colorations endeavor to represent faithfully.

The Great World Atlas is conceived to serve as the ideal tool for discriminating people with global perspectives in their professional work and personal lifestyles. The atlas sets new standards in graphic design, information density and practical usability. The foundation for this new worldview is an enlightened perspective on humankind's responsibility to the universe. This responsibility involves both an ecologically sensitive attitude and a respect for the fundamental equality of human rights throughout the world. What may seem like a utopia today can and must become a reality – step by step. We hope that the *The Great World Atlas* will help to carry this message.

Table of Contents

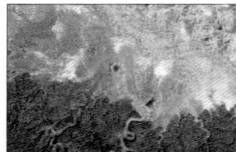

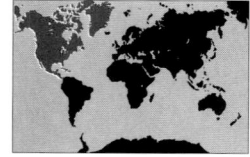
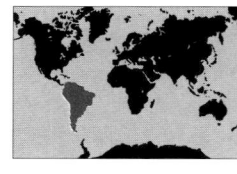
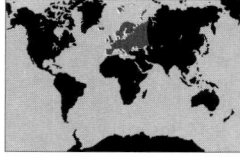

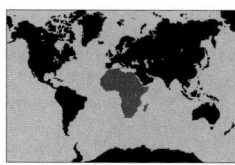
VII

Key to Maps: Continents

North and Middle America · 1:4,500,000

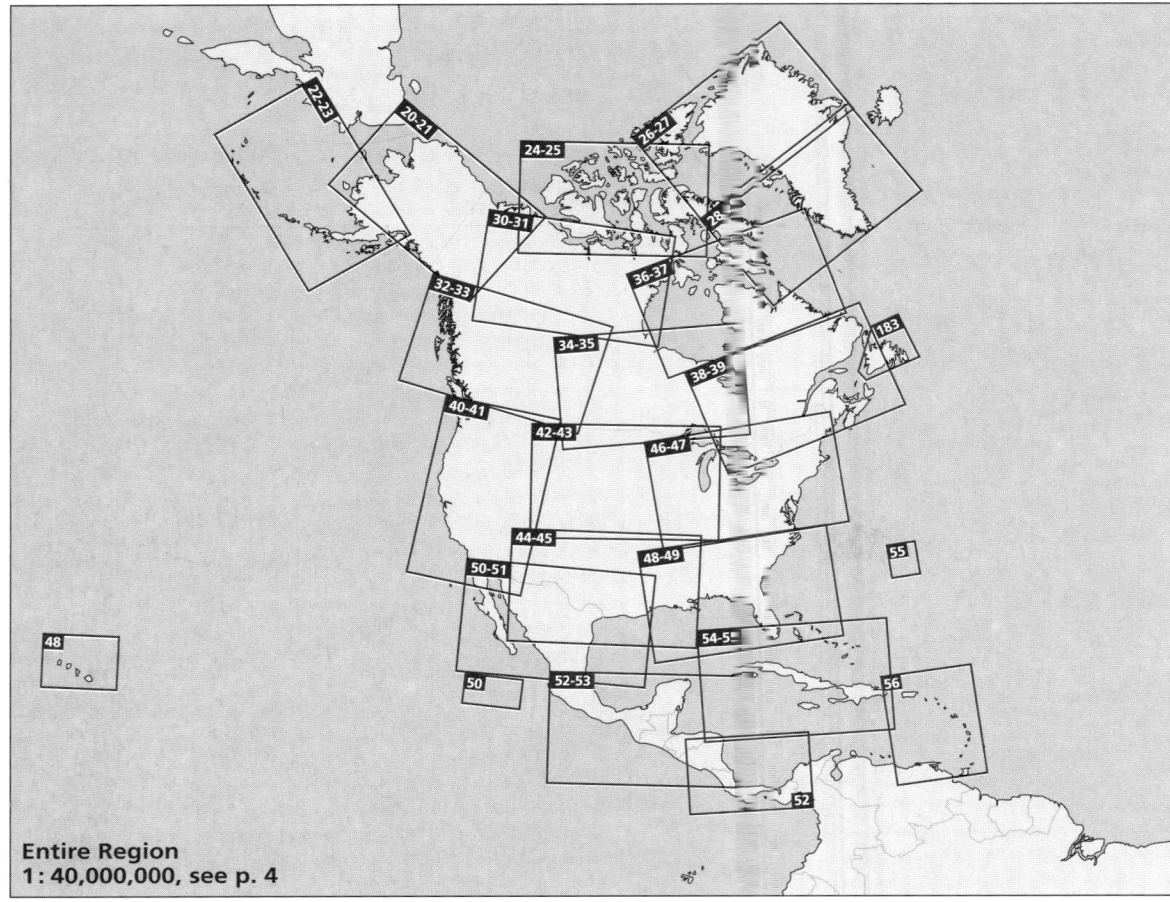

Entire Region
1:40,000,000, see p. 4

Europe · 1:4,500,000

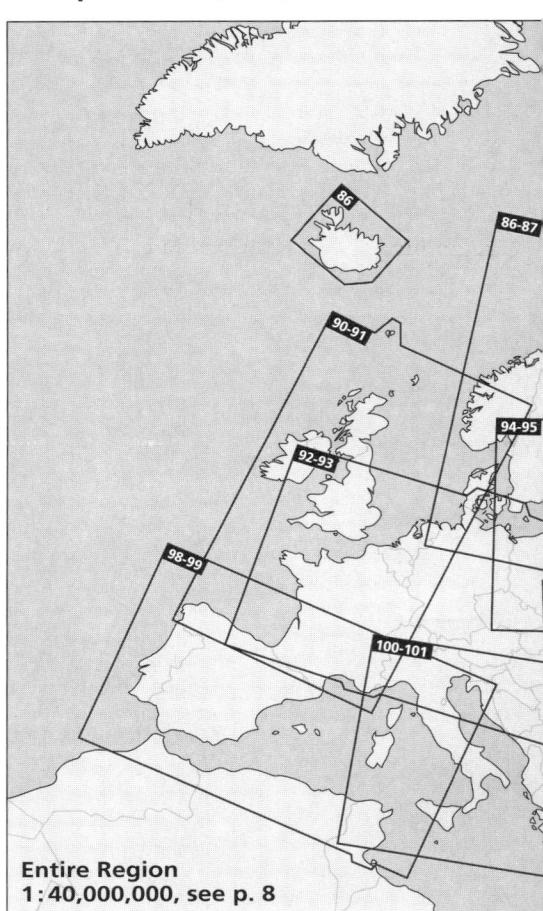

Entire Region
1:40,000,000, see p. 8

South America · 1:4,500,000

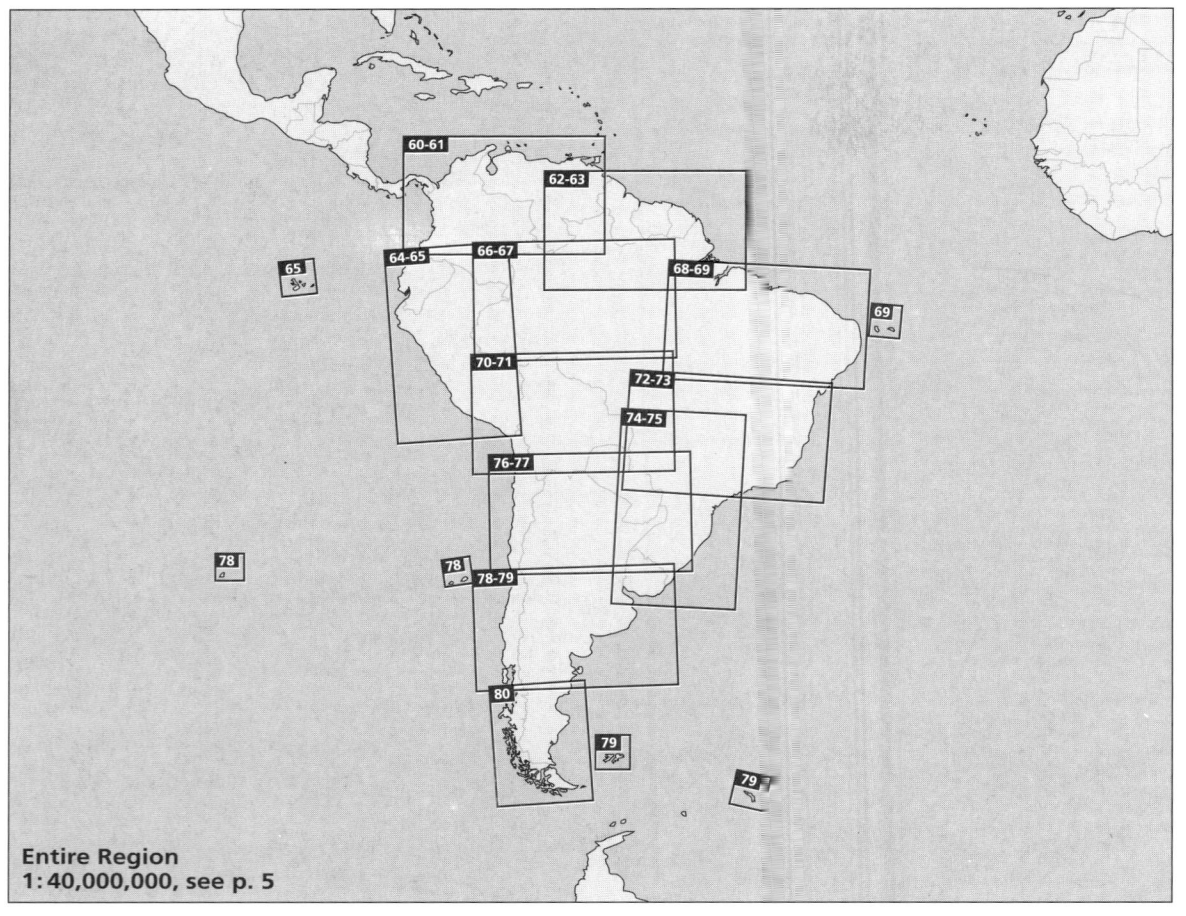

Entire Region
1:40,000,000, see p. 5

Asia · 1:4,500,000

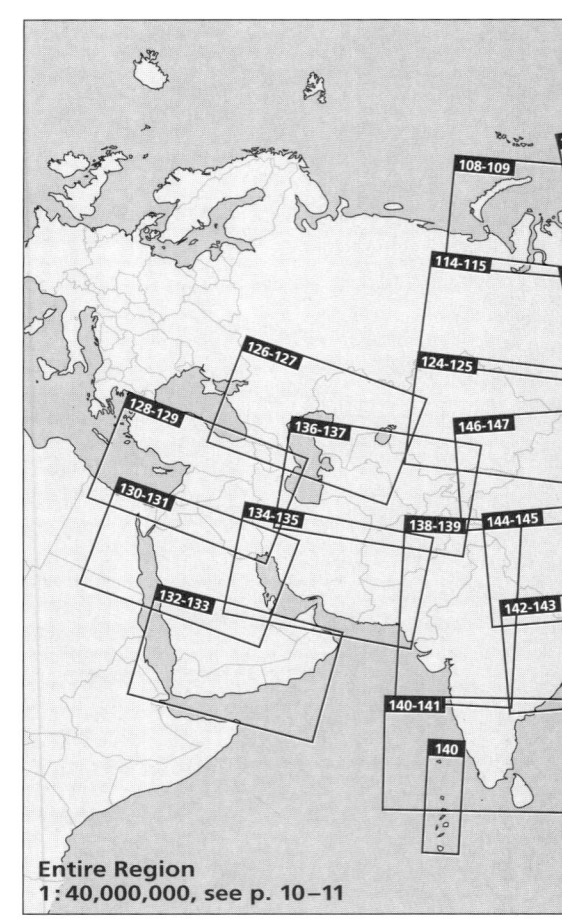

Entire Region
1:40,000,000, see p. 10–11

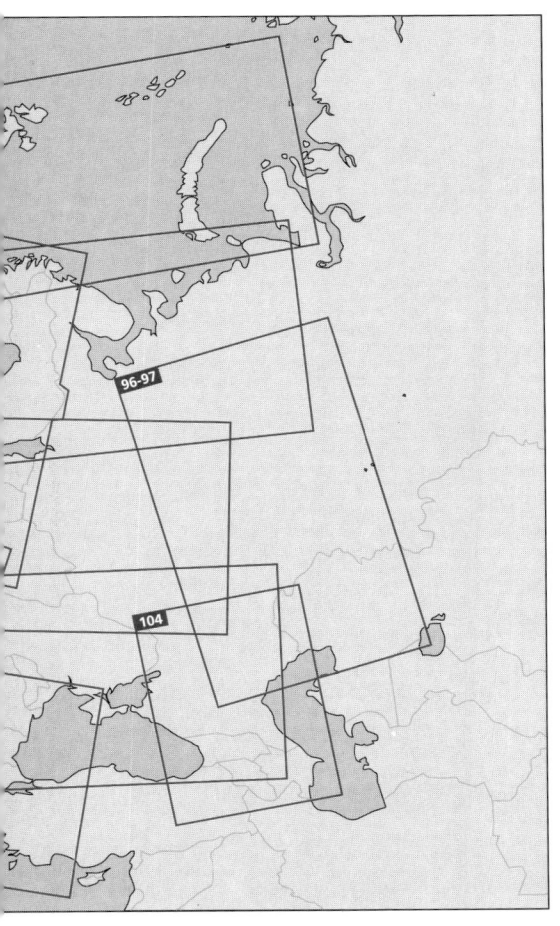

Australia and Oceania · 1:4,500,000

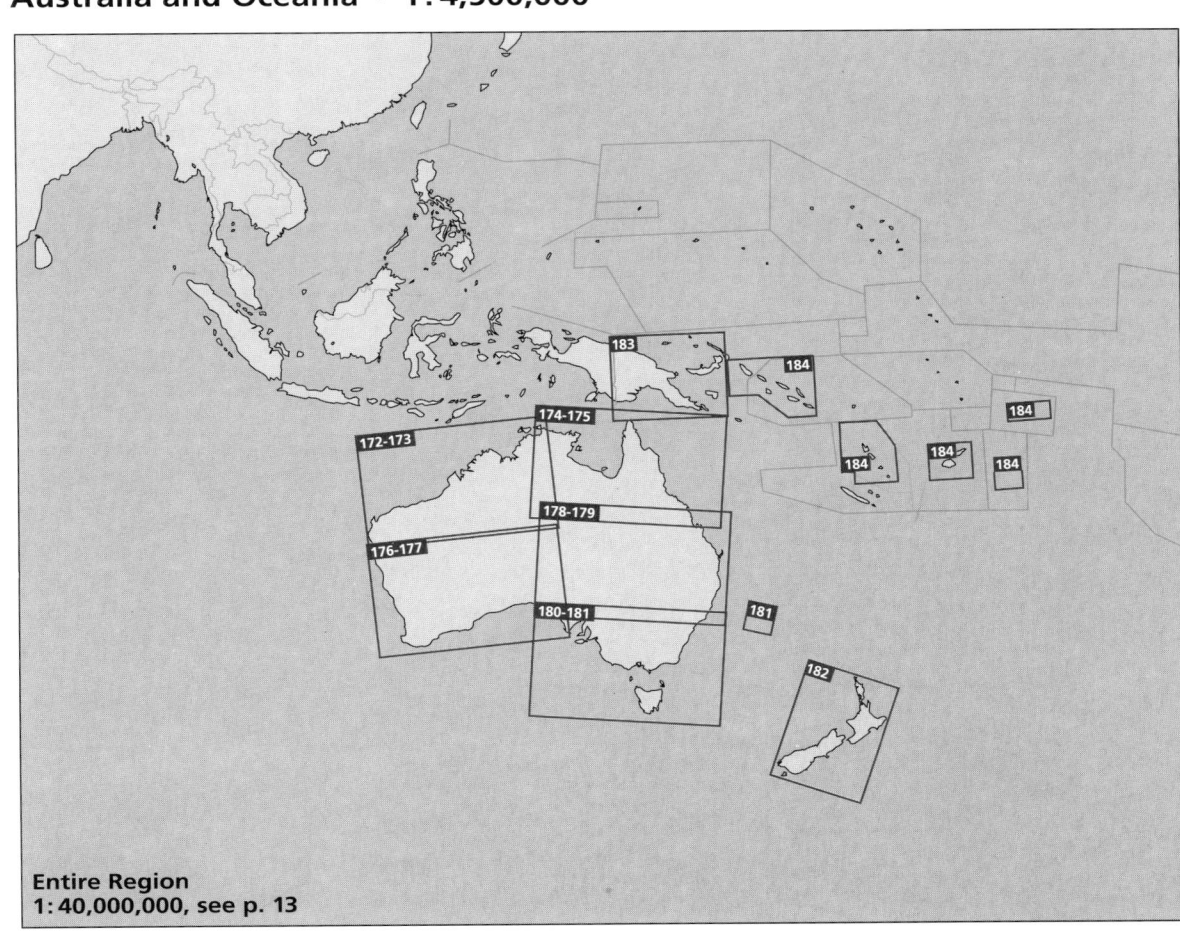

183
184
184
184
172-173
174-175
184
184
176-177
178-179
180-181
181
182

Entire Region
1:40,000,000, see p. 13

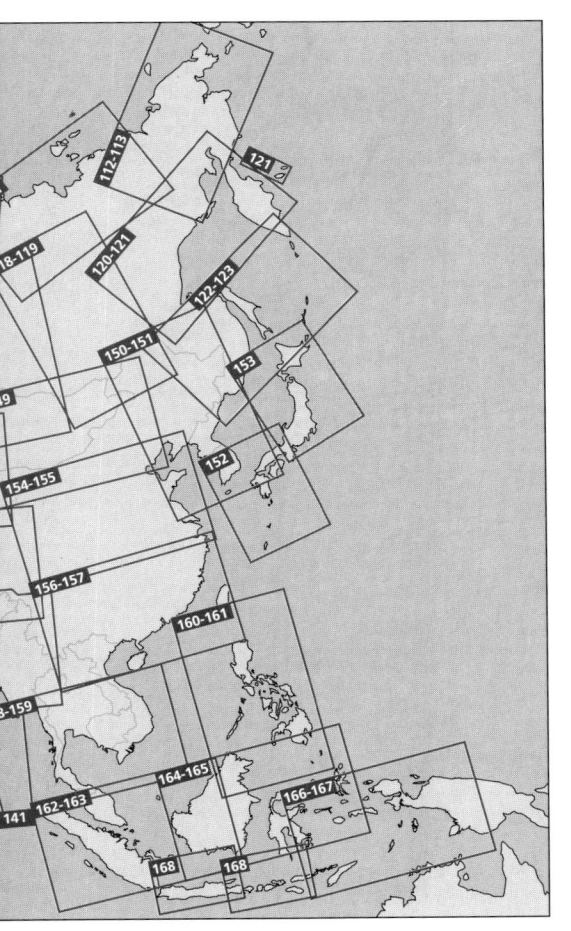

Africa · 1:4,500,000

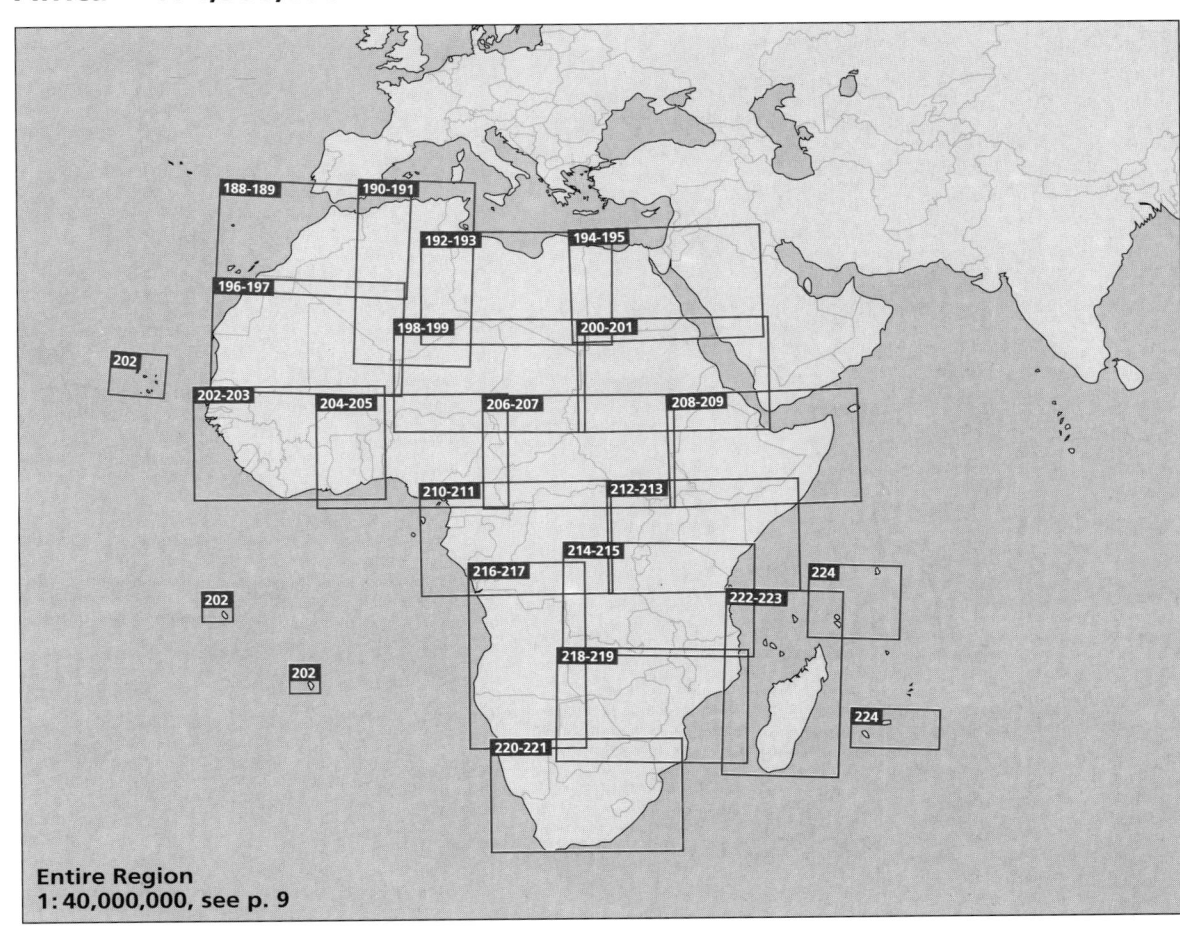

188-189
190-191
192-193
194-195
196-197
198-199
200-201
202
202-203
204-205
206-207
208-209
210-211
212-213
214-215
216-217
224
222-223
202
218-219
224
220-221

Entire Region
1:40,000,000, see p. 9

Map Samples

Satellite Imagery

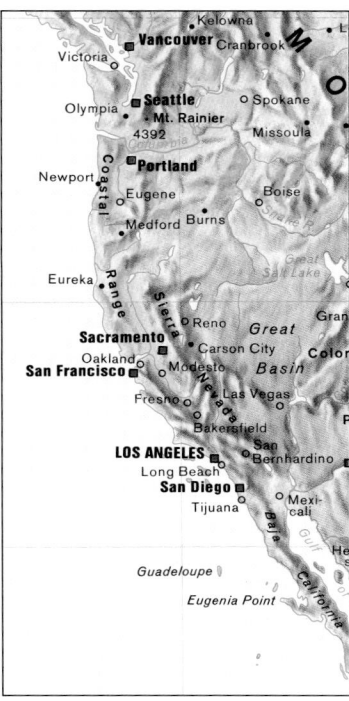

Scale 1 : 40,000,000

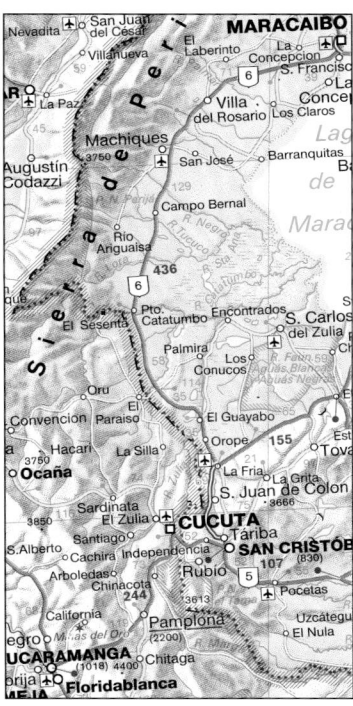

Scale 1 : 4,500,000

Space travel has provided us with a new image of the Earth. Earth-observation satellites like those in the LANDSAT series orbit the Earth at an altitude of approximately 400 miles (700 kilometers). Sensors on board these satellites detect electromagnetic radiation reflected by the Earth, then transmit this information as photographic data to a global network of ground stations. But to arrive at brilliant satellite images like those selected for inclusion in this book, photographic data received from satellites must first be enhanced in a variety of ways.

Computers help make the gradations of color in the satellite images faithful renditions of their counterparts in nature. Various computer-assisted combinations of individually received spectral bands are used to achieve this accuracy. Filtering and contrast manipulation further enhance the images. Favorable photographic conditions are essential: optimum sunlight, ideal climatic conditions, and a minimum of cloud cover.

Of course, satellite photographs are no substitute for maps, but their multifaceted images do serve as a valuable complement to the cartographic information expressed in maps. Their brilliance is fascinating, and they provide views of the Earth from new and fantastic perspectives.

Space probes can photograph the whole Earth in its entirety as a heavenly body. Satellites in orbit closer to the Earth can photograph areas the size of continents or subcontinents. The view from an airplane reveals individual landscapes. A map's scale expresses the distance between the Earth and an imaginary observer. It determines the extent and contents of the map.

The scale of 1:40,000,000 is suitable for representing the Earth as a whole. The world map shows the Earth's major structures, its division into oceans and landmasses, the continents and their relative positions.

The various colors on the continents indicate major zones of vegetation. Bluish violet and yellowish red represent cold and dry deserts, green tones stand for various kinds of plant life. Since vegetation is largely a function of climate, a bluish green color indicates both coniferous forests and the colder climate of higher latitudes. Deep green, on the other hand, represents tropical rain forests in the hot, humid climate near the equator.

Shadings depict major topographic features of the Earth's crust: chains of folded mountains, highlands and basins, lowlands and low-mountain regions.

The majority of maps in this book are drawn in the scale of 1:4,500,000. All continents are thoroughly depicted in this scale, with the exception of Antarctica and some of the world's smaller islands. Maps on individual pages show parts of the continents. Settlements, transportation routes and political boundaries of various kinds are clearly visible against a color-coded background denoting the various topographies, climates and vegetation zones.

The spatial distribution and extent of settlements reflects population density. The few, widely spaced urban settlements in sparsely settled regions contrast with the urban sprawl of more densely populated regions. Maps also show the density of transportation networks, the presence or absence of roads and the accessibility of various places, as well as the distances between major intersections and the locations of railroads and airports. Political boundaries indicate international frontiers and national administrative subdivisions.

The representation of cultural sights is more than just an aid to tourists and leisure travelers. These sites are often focal points of ethno-cultural traditions, important places of religious worship or national identity.

Explanation of Map Symbols Physical Aspects of the Earth

The Ocean

① Coastline, shoreline
② Island(s), archipelago
③ Tidal flat
④ Mangrove coast
⑤ Coral reef

Bathymetric Tints

⑥ 0 – 200 meters
⑦ 200 – 2,000 meters
⑧ 2000 – 4,000 meters
⑨ 4000 – 6,000 meters
⑩ 6000 – 8,000 meters
⑪ 8000 – 10,000 meters
⑫ Deeper than 10,000 meters
⑬ Water depth in meters

Coastlines are drawn with detail and precision in this atlas. As tides ebb and flow, certain sections of coast alternately belong to the mainland and the ocean. This is especially true of tidal flats and mangrove coasts, both of which are specially labeled on the maps.

Coral reefs in tropical oceans are remarkable features. Because of their low tolerance for changes in water temperature, salinity and deterioration in water quality, coral reefs are sensitive indicators of the quality of marine ecosystems.

Ocean depths are represented by bathymetric tints. The epicontinental shelf seas, which attain depths of 656 feet (200 m), are particularly important both politically and economically. During earlier geologic eras, some parts of these zones were dry land. Also known as continental shelves, these regions are rich in economically important resources. The ocean's deepest points are found near the edges of the continents. These deep sea trenches are depicted on individual map pages. Trenches are critical interfaces in the ongoing process of continental genesis and disappearance.

Hydrographic Features

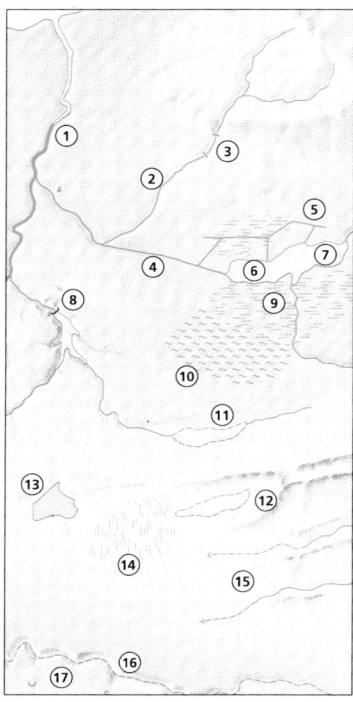

① Perennial stream or river
② Tributary river with headwaters
③ Waterfall, rapids
④ Navigable canal
⑤ Non-navigable canal
⑥ Freshwater lake
⑦ Elevation of lake above sea level and depth of Lake
⑧ Reservoir with dam
⑨ Marsh, moor
⑩ Flood plain
⑪ Lake with variable shoreline

Mostly in Arid Regions

⑫ Seasonal lake
⑬ Salt lake
⑭ Salt swamp
⑮ River, drying up
⑯ Intermittent stream (wadi, arroyo)
⑰ Spring, well

The network of rivers and lakes provides a natural framework for the structures created by human beings in the process of developing and cultivating the land. Rivers and their mouths, bays and lake shores are preferred sites for human settlements. Rivers provide transportation routes, a source of hydroelectric power and water for irrigation. Above all, they supply us with our most basic need - potable water.

The maps depict the catchment areas of larger rivers with the treelike branching of their tributaries. Line thicknesses used in drawing the rivers correspond to their various sizes and to the hierarchy of main artery, major tributaries and headwaters. The paths of the blue lines represent the predominant characteristics of each natural watercourse with its meanders, branches, lakelike widenings and oxbows, as well as the comparatively rigid course of artificial waterways (canals). Agricultural and recreational uses are indicated by reservoirs and dams. The network of rivers and lakes reflects the world's gradient of water resources from abundance to aridity.

Glaciation

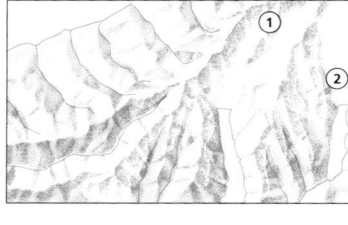

① Glacier in high-mountain range
② Glacial tongue

③ Continental ice sheet, icecap
④ Mean pack ice limit in summer
⑤ Mean pack ice limit in winter

The most recent ice age came to an end about 10,000 years ago. Its traces are still visible on roughly one-third of the Earth's landmasses, 11 percent of which are still covered by ice. The depiction of glaciers in the maps shows the worldwide distribution of these icy deserts. Continental ice sheets occupy by far the largest area, covering all of Antarctica and Greenland with sheets of ice as much as 10,000 feet (3,000 m) thick. Extensive surfaces of ocean, especially around the North Pole, are covered by sea or pack ice, and shelf ice is distributed along the edge of the Antarctic ice

sheet. Alpine glaciers cover only a relatively insignificant 1 percent of the landmasses.

Glaciers are almost always in motion, usually at a very slow pace. Glacial tongues tend to move more rapidly. Sometimes reaching lengths of more than 125 miles (200 km), these tongues of ice stretch from continental glaciers to the ocean, where they calve icebergs. Glacial tongues are often the most impressive features of alpine glaciers; larger examples of these ice tongues are shown on the maps.

The Topography of the Earth's Surface

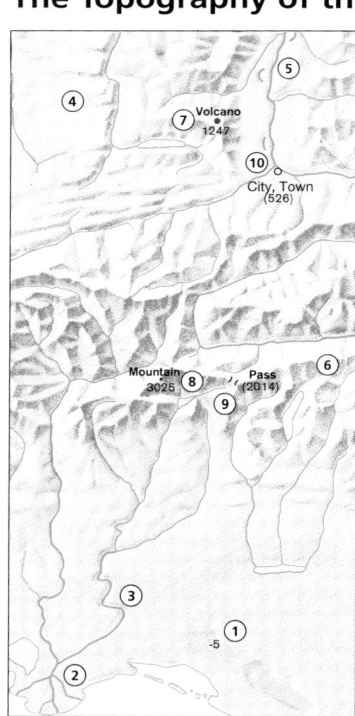

① Depressed region (land below sea level with depth in meters below sea level)
② River delta
③ Plain with depressed river valley
④ Hill country and highlands
⑤ Rift valley
⑥ Mountain range
⑦ Active volcano
⑧ Mountain (with elevation)
⑨ Pass (with elevation)
⑩ Approximate elevation of a city above sea level

Representing the third dimension – the topographic relief of the Earth's surface – is a special challenge for cartographers. The maps in this atlas derive their extraordinary plasticity from "relief shading." Gradations from pale to dark on the two-dimensional surface of the page help users visualize the Earth's actual three-dimensional topography. This impression is quantified with precise information about the elevations above sea level of mountains, passes and major cities.

The network of lakes and rivers is the counterpart to the relief depicted on the map. Waterways mark the locations of valleys that divide the topography. These two phenomena combine to provide an expressive picture of the major geographic regions and their underlying tectonic structures.

Particularly clear examples include the Great Rift Valley (which runs from the Near East to southern East Africa), the gigantic basins and high plateaus of central Asia (surrounded by the world's highest mountains), the generously watered lowlands of North and South America, and the mighty ranges of corrugated mountains that form the Andes.

The Biosphere: Continental Ecological Zones

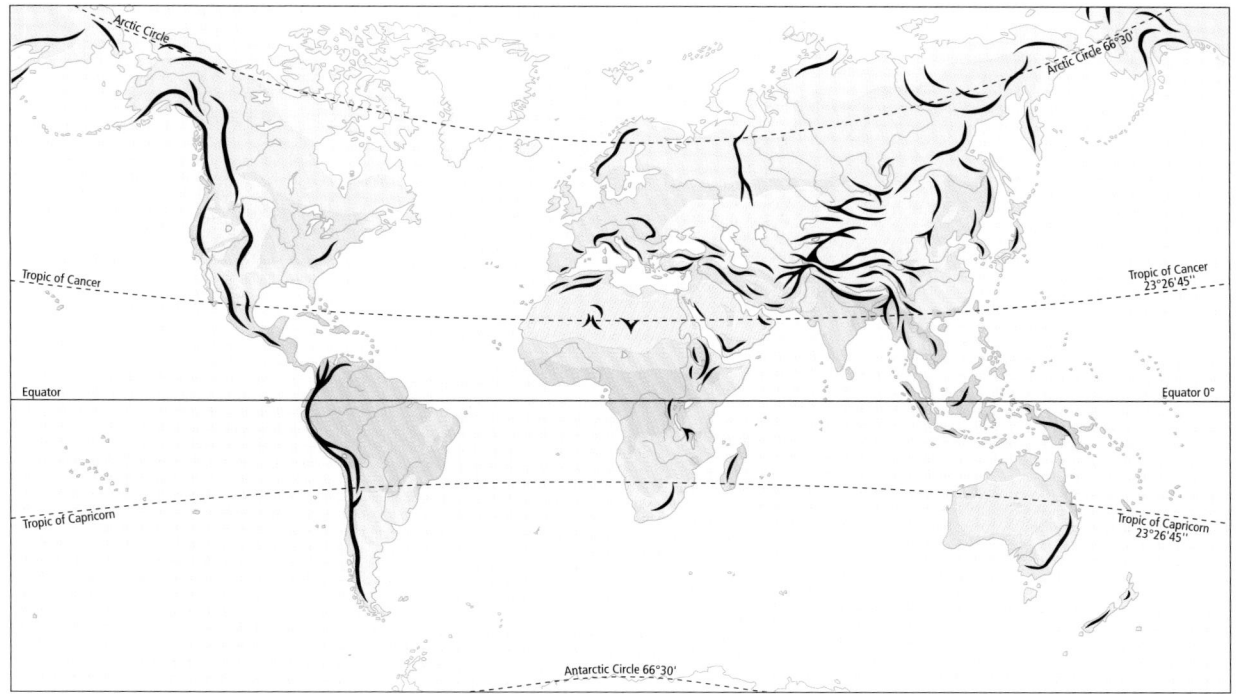

Tropics

I — Perennially humid climates
Tropical rain forest, moist savanna

II — Moist summer climates
Moist and dry savannas,
deciduous forests

Subtropics

III — Subtropical-tropical semidesert and
desert climates
Thorny scrub, desert

IV — Summer-humid to perennially moist
climates
Monsoon forest, shrubs

V — Mediterranean climates with dry
summers and moist winters
Shrubs, broadleaved evergreen forests

Temperature zones (middle latitudes)

VI — Winter-cold steppes, semidesert and
desert climates
Grasslands (steppe, prairie), desert

VII — Maritime to continental moist climates
Broadleaved deciduous forests, mixed
forests

Boreal zone

VIII — Taiga (needleleaved evergreen forests)

Polar and subpolar zone

IX — a: continental ice, ice cap
b: tundra (lichens, mosses, dwarf
shrubs)

High Mountains

Vertical arrangement of plant
communities by altitude

Macroclimates are among the most significant of the many factors affecting the distribution of life on earth. Macroclimates influence soil formation and help shape surface topography, as well as affecting plant growth and animal communities, which in turn determine the suitability of a given geographic region for human habitation. All of these biotic and abiotic factors combine to create a complex web in which each factor influences the others in a variety of ways.

Based on climatic conditions and on the prevailling plant communities determined by those con-ditions, the earth's landmasses can be subdivided into various habitats and ecozones. The boundaries between these zones, however, are not sharply defined. Instead, each zone emanates from a central region with characteristics typical of that zone, makes a transition across a boundary belt, and then more or less gradually changes into the adjacent landscape zone.

Although the limits of continental ecozones generally correspond to latitude, these zones exhibit two important asymmetries: regions of winter rainfall (Mediterranean climate) occur only along the western edges of the continents; regions with moist summers (or perennially moist tropics) are located exclusively on the eastern edges (so-called "Shanghai climates").

Trees in Eurasia and America cannot grow beyond about 70 degrees of latitude; in South America tree-line occurs at 57 degrees, in New Zealand and Oceania at 48 degrees. The boreal or "northern" band of coniferous forests is entirely absent in the Southern Hemisphere because of the relatively limited extent of land area and the associated dominance of the ocean.

Arrangement of Ecological Zones by Altitude

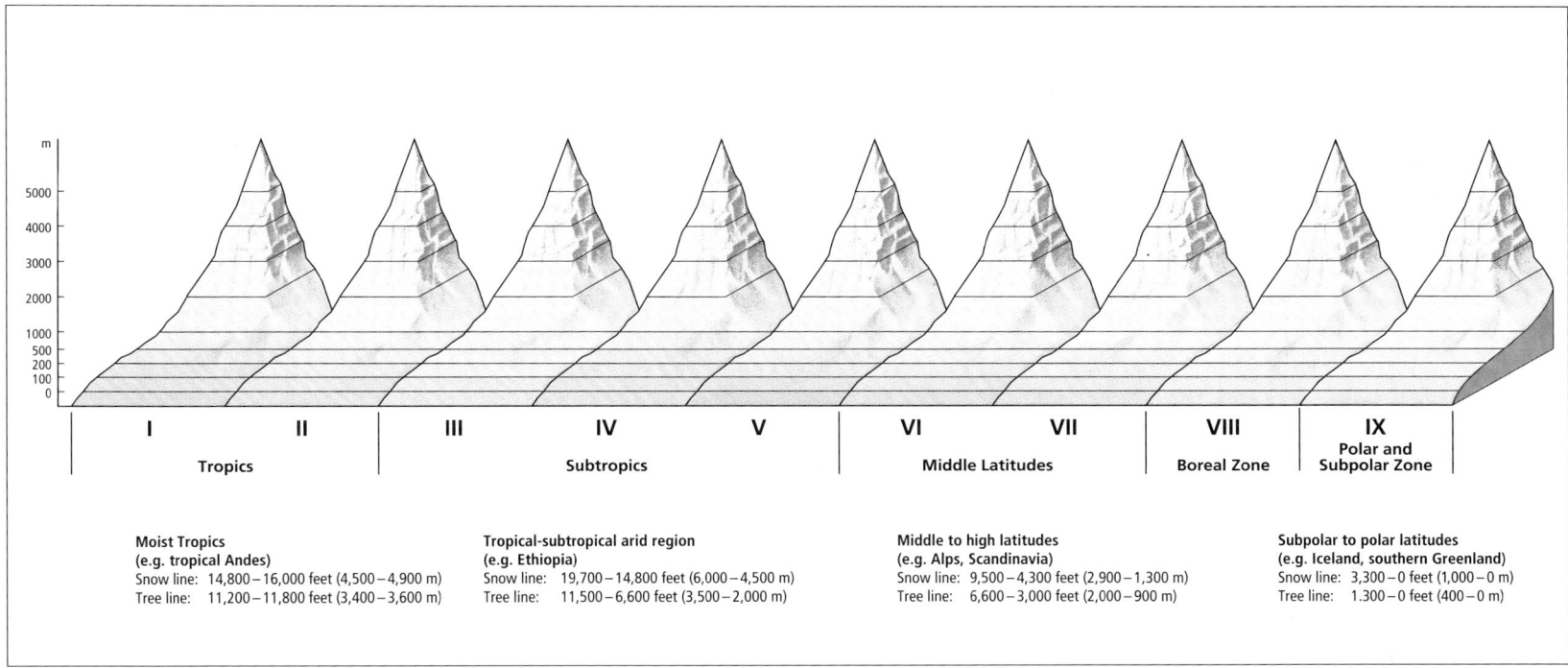

Moist Tropics
(e.g. tropical Andes)
Snow line: 14,800 – 16,000 feet (4,500 – 4,900 m)
Tree line: 11,200 – 11,800 feet (3,400 – 3,600 m)

Tropical-subtropical arid region
(e.g. Ethiopia)
Snow line: 19,700 – 14,800 feet (6,000 – 4,500 m)
Tree line: 11,500 – 6,600 feet (3,500 – 2,000 m)

Middle to high latitudes
(e.g. Alps, Scandinavia)
Snow line: 9,500 – 4,300 feet (2,900 – 1,300 m)
Tree line: 6,600 – 3,000 feet (2,000 – 900 m)

Subpolar to polar latitudes
(e.g. Iceland, southern Greenland)
Snow line: 3,300 – 0 feet (1,000 – 0 m)
Tree line: 1.300 – 0 feet (400 – 0 m)

An essential feature of geographic landscapes is their three-dimensional structure. The maps in this atlas provide clearly legible depictions of heights and depths on the face of the Earth. The arrangement of ecological zones is largely dependent upon latitude. This pattern, however, is overlaid by mountain ranges, which cut across latitudinally oriented climatic zones to create their own ecosystems where altitude creates characteristic ecological arrangements. A visible expression of the fact that biological conditions vary with altitude is the vertical arrangement of typical plant commu-nities: generally forest (grassland) – meadows – cliffs (or talus) – ice (or glacier). This arrangement also creates characteristic ecological boundary lines: above, the tree line and the (climatic) snow line; and in arid regions, the lower tree line as well.

Elevations show typical climatic characteristics depending on a mountain range's location in the overall pattern of global climatic zones. Tropical mountains, for example, experience the same diurnal climatic variations typical of their neighboring lowlands.

The upper tree line in mountainous regions is caused by the lack of adequate warmth. The low-er tree line found in arid regions is related to the lack of adequate moisture. This combination restricts the growth of forests in arid regions to more or less wide bands along the slopes of mountains.

Where a lower tree line is now found in humid high mountain regions, or where the band of forest is entirely absent in certain places, the causes of this deforestation are likely to be manmade.

Forests in mountainous regions provide abso-lutely essential protection against avalanches and slope erosion.

The cultivation of crops in mountainous regions is likewise limited by prevailing climatic factors which, in turn, are primarily a function of elevation. In the Andes, for example, grains cannot be cultivated above 5,000 feet (1,500 m), although in the tropical Andes millet can be grown at elevations as high as 14,400 feet (4,400 m). With the exception of mining camps and settlements of shepherds at still higher elevations, these heights mark the upper limits of permanent human settlement.

Explanation of Map Symbols Manmade Features on Earth

The Map Margins

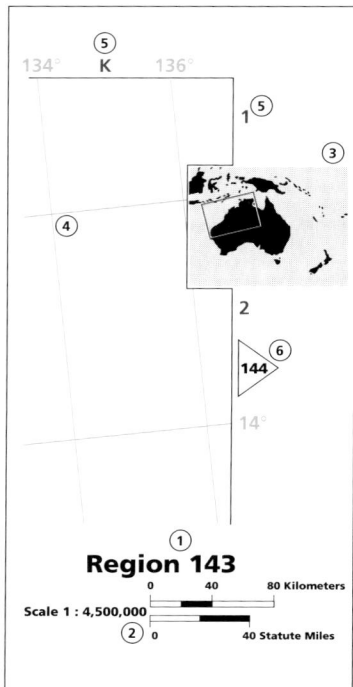

① Page number and short title

② Numeric and graphic map scales
(scales in kilometers and miles)

③ Locator map showing the position and extent
continental area covered by that particular m
page

④ Map grid (graticule) and its designation

.0 degrees longitude
(Meridian of Greenwich) = Gr.

Longitude 180 degrees to 1 degree west of Gr.	Longitude 1 degree to 180 degrees east of Gr.

Latitude 1 degree to 90 degrees north of the equator	Latitu 1 degree to 90 degre north of the equa

Equator 0 degrees — Equator 0 degre

Latitude 1 degree to 90 degrees south of the Equator	Latitu 1 degree to 90 degre south of the Equa

Longitude 180 degrees to 1 degree west of Gr.	Longitude 1 degree to 180 degrees east of Gr.

0 degrees longitude of
Greenwich = Gr.

⑤ Grid search key as specified for each index entry
Letters at top/bottom
Numbers at left/right
with graticule as searching grid

⑥ Page number of adjacent map page

Along with the short title and the page number, further aid in using the atlas is provided by the map overviews in the preface and by the locator maps at the beginning of each series of maps of individual continents. The number inside a small triangle on each map indicates the page where a map of the adjacent region can be found.

A locator map at the top right-hand corner of each double-page spread shows the area within the particular continent depicted by that particular map page. The scale notations in the lower margin are essential for determining geographic distances. They express the relationship between a given distance on the map and a corresponding distance in the real world.

For centuries, the degree-calibrated latitude and longitude grid system has been used to define locations and plot courses on the face of the globe. The red letters along the top and bottom, together with the red numbers along the left and right margins, identify individual fields within the blue search grid.

Political and Other Boundaries

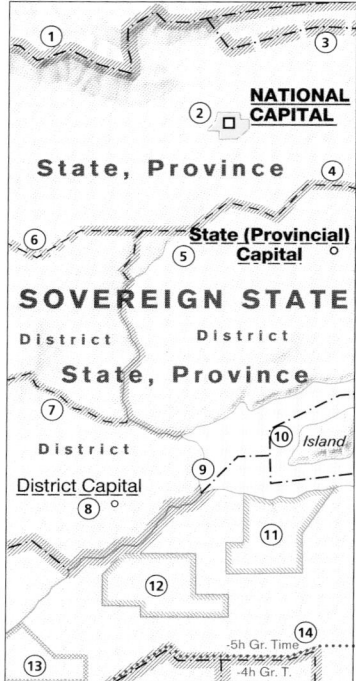

① International boundary

② Capital of a sovereign state

③ Disputed international boundary

④ 1st-order administrative boundary
(e.g. region, state, autonomous region, province)

⑤ Capital city (1st-order administrative seat)

⑥ Disputed 1st-order administrative boundary

⑦ 2nd-order administrative boundary
(e.g. region, area, province, country)

⑧ 2nd-order administrative seat

⑨ Boundary along watercourses or across bodies of water

⑩ Dependent region and specification of nation with jurisdiction

⑪ National park, national monument

⑫ Reservation

⑬ Restricted area

⑭ Boundary of a time zone with difference between local time and Greenwich Mean Time (GMT)

The documentation of territorial possessions was one of the reasons maps were invented. Maps play a central political role in border disputes and are an indispensable aid in interpreting or representing spatially related statistical data. The vast majority of statistical studies are based on national units or on regions within nations. Regardless of whether population distribution, buying power or cancer-incidence rates are measured, maps are the most convincing method of visually presenting and interpreting data.

International boundaries occupy first place in the hierarchy of political boundaries. They are therefore clearly marked in this atlas. First-order administrative boundaries, which define the limits of the major administrative units within a nation, come next in rank. Secondary boundaries are drawn when their political status merits it, providing their average surface area permits graphic representation on the scale involved. The maps also show capital cities or administrative seats of the depicted administrative entities.

Settlements and Transportation Routes

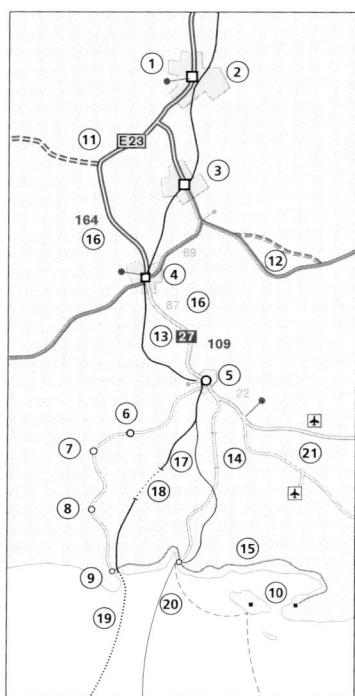

Town Symbols

① Urban area
(normally surrounding cities with populations over 100,000)

② Population over 5 million

③ 1,000,000 – 5,000,000

④ 500,000 – 1,000,000

⑤ 100,000 – 500,000

⑥ 50,000 – 100,000

⑦ 10,000 – 50,000

⑧ 5,000 – 10,000

⑨ Population less than 5,000

⑩ Settlement, hamlet, research station
(in remote areas often seasonally inhabited only)

Transportation Routes

⑪ Superhighway, four or more lanes, with number in blue

⑫ Highway under construction

⑬ Main road with number

⑭ Other road – road tunnel

⑮ Unpaved road, track

⑯ Distance in kilometers

⑰ Railway: main track – other track

⑱ Railway tunnel

⑲ Railway ferry

⑳ Car ferry – shipping line

㉑ International airport
Domestic airport

Town symbols correspond to the populations of their respective places. The density of these symbols on the map combines with their relative values to indicate a region's population density and settlement structure (urban area or smaller, equally distributed towns).

The representation of urban areas sheds light on the increasing concentration of humanity in major metropolitan areas. According to UNESCO, by the year 2000 approximately half of the world's population will live in cities occupying only about four percent of the Earth's total land area.

In the depiction of transportation routes, special emphasis has been given to the representation of continental road networks. This corresponds to the importance of such networks on the threshold of the 21st century. Transportation of economically important goods, tourism, and the migrations of people searching for work or fleeing disasters all take place primarily over roads. These routes have been classified and numbered according to their relative importance. Distance specifications help map users make accurate calculations of distances.

Places and Points of Interest

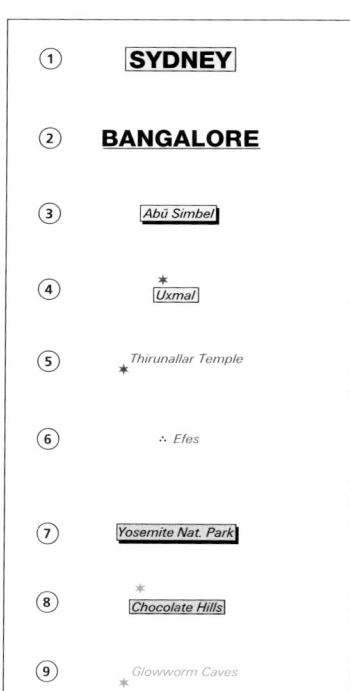

① Place of special interest

② Place of interest

③ UNESCO World Cultural Heritage Site

④ Cultural monument of special interest

⑤ Interesting cultural monument

⑥ Ancient monument or excavation

⑦ UNESCO World Natural Heritage Site

⑧ Natural monument of special interest

⑨ Interesting natural monument

The maps in this atlas provide the reader with a global view of the Blue Planet's most remarkable places and points of interest. These include exceptional monuments of natural or historico-cultural developments. Many of these places are important to national, ethnic or religious identity. This atlas places such sites in their geographical contexts. Graphic distinctions are made between natural and cultural monuments and according to their significance as magnets for tourism. UNESCO, a suborganization of the United Nations, has designated selected cultural sites and natural monuments worldwide as part of the "heritage of mankind" and urged their special preservation. These sites are specially marked in the atlas. The volume thus provides not only an informative manual for globetrotters with widely ranging interests, but also serves as a helpful supplement for students of travel and nature guides or of relevant artistic and historico-cultural literature.

Lettering of Cities and Towns

① **TEHRĀN**
MONTEVIDEO

② **MIAMI**
LE HAVRE

③ MANHATTAN
VAIHINGEN

④ **Darwin**
Thimphu

⑤ Gallipolis
Grindelwald
Laugarvatn

⑥ **BOLZANO**
BOZEN

⑦ **HALAP**
(ALEPPO)

⑧ **FRANKFURT**
am Main

Type size indicates the relative importance and population of the town

① City with a population over one million
② Large city
③ Boroughs of large cities or of cities with populations over one million
④ Medium-sized city
⑤ Small town, rural community
⑥ Place names in region with two official languages
⑦ Place name, alternate or earlier form
⑧ Official supplement to a place name

This atlas includes carefully selected place names. Type size corresponds to the number of inhabitants; type face indicates the particular significance or function of the place. Place names in capital letters indicate large cities with more than 100,000 inhabitants.

Some names of important places, landscape features and bodies of water are written in the accepted American form, but as a general rule, place names are written in the official national spelling. In the case of countries having two official languages, both versions are given. This rule also applies to all other geographic names.

Letter-oriented transliteration or phonetic transcription is used to spell names from languages with non-Roman alphabets. Wherever possible, the atlas has followed accepted standards for such procedures.

Geographic names can offer valuable insights into historical developments and relationships.

Topographic Typography

① **CHILE**   Réunion   (France)

② *GOBI* *Cappadocia* *Kimberley*

③ **ANDES** Nan Ling   Tibesti

④ Mt. McKinley   Simplonpass (2005)   Cabo de Hornos
6194

⑤ *JAVA*   *Galápagos Islands*   *York Peninsula*

⑥ *PACIFIC OCEAN*
Finskij zaliv   *The Channel*

⑦ *Niger*   *Panama Canal*   *Taj Hu*   *Niagara Falls*

⑧ *Yucatán Basin*   *Cayman Trench*

⑨ Nazca Ridge   Aves Ridge

⑩ *Aboriginal Land*   *Military Training Area*

⑪ 8848   *10540*   398

① Nation, administrative unit, designation of sovereignty
② Landscape, historical landscape
③ Mountains, mountain range, highland
④ Mountain with elevation above sea level, pass with elevation above sea level, cape
⑤ Island, archipelago, peninsula
⑥ Ocean, sea, gulf, bay, strait
⑦ River, canal, lake, waterfall
⑧ Undersea landscapes, trenches
⑨ Undersea mountains
⑩ Reservation, restricted areas
⑪ Elevation in meters above sea level
Depth in oceans and lakes, elevation of lake surface

Lettering and typeface help explain the various features on a map. They also serve to structure geographic data according to significance and rank. These distinctions are reflected by the use of either all capital letters or mixtures of capital and lower-case letters, and by various type faces and sizes. Color also supports these distinctions: for example, rivers are labeled in blue, political units in gray, and sites of natural interest in green. Colored backgrounds or colored underlining indicates sites of interest to tourists.

Geographic names are one of the ways human beings express their possession of the land. People have given names to the remotest islands, to minor coves in the inhospitable Antarctic and to barely defined coastal promontories. The maps in this atlas, as in any other atlas, can include only the most important of these geographic names. All of them are listed in alphabetical order in the index of geographic names, together with search-grid designations that make it easy to pinpoint them on individual maps.

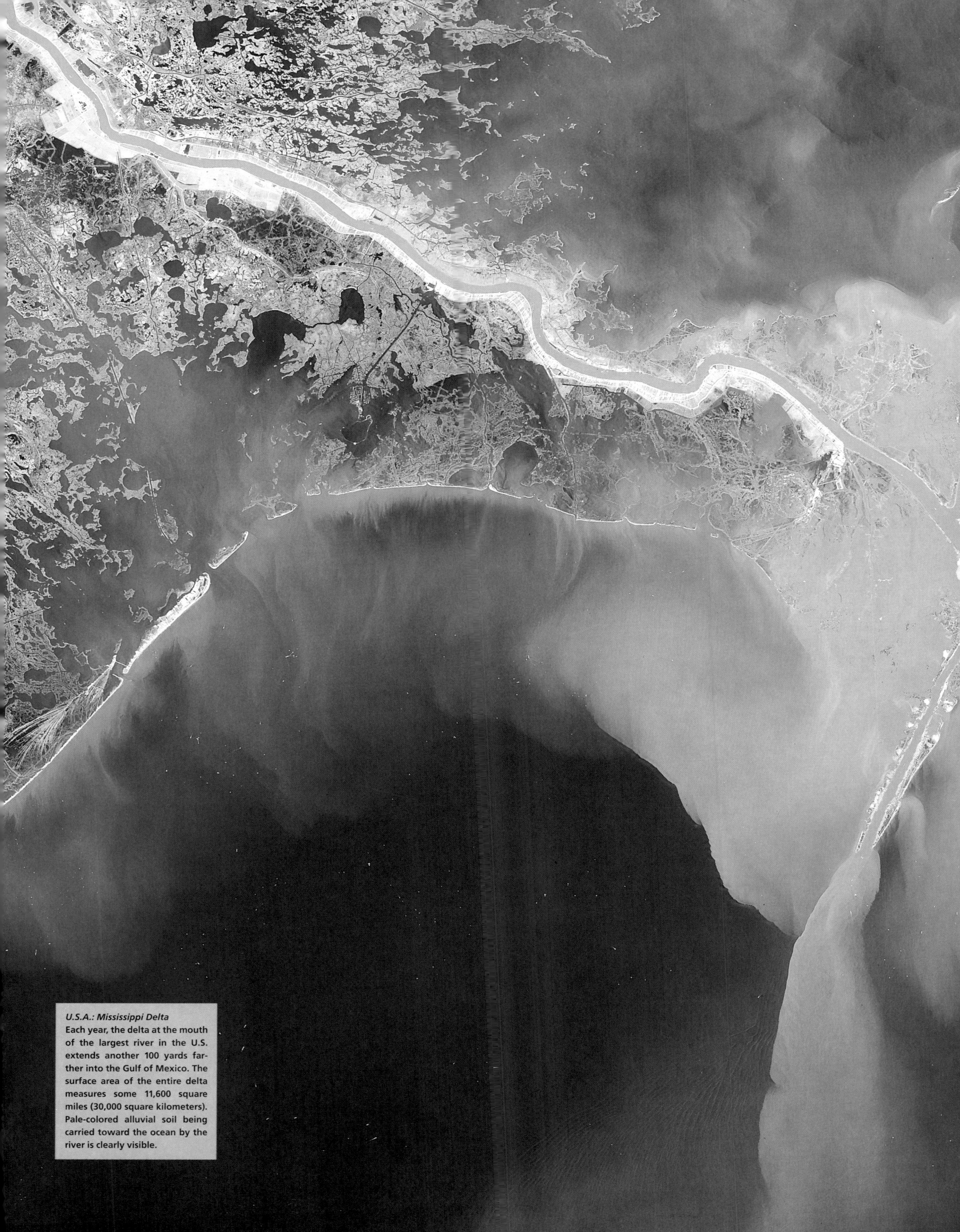

U.S.A.: Mississippi Delta
Each year, the delta at the mouth of the largest river in the U.S. extends another 100 yards farther into the Gulf of Mexico. The surface area of the entire delta measures some 11,600 square miles (30,000 square kilometers). Pale-colored alluvial soil being carried toward the ocean by the river is clearly visible.

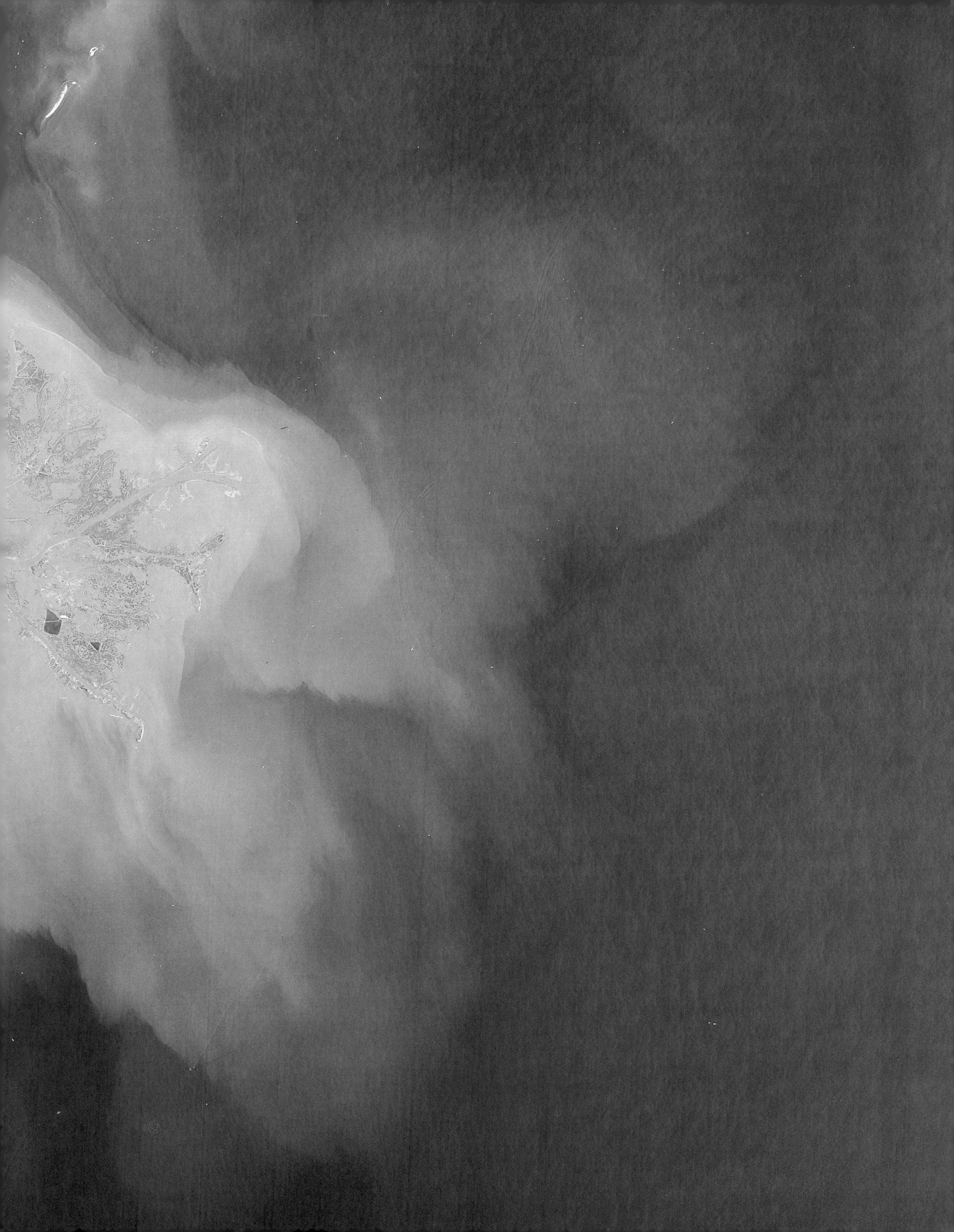

Brazil: Amazon River
To the east of the city of Manaus, the dark waters of the Rio Negro meet the coffee-colored waters of the Amazon. The gradual mixing of water from the two rivers is clearly visible at the photograph's upper right corner. The region's chief characteristic is the tropical rain forest, an endangered ecosystem.

Switzerland: Upper Rhône Valley
The valley of the Upper Rhône crosses the depicted region from the northeast to the southwest. Sickle-shaped Aletsch Glacier, the Alps' largest river of ice, can be seen at the center. Together with its branches, the glacier measures 15 miles (24 km) long with an area of 46 square miles (120 sq. km). Lake Brienz and Lake Thun at the upper left occupy valleys that have been deepened by glacial erosion.

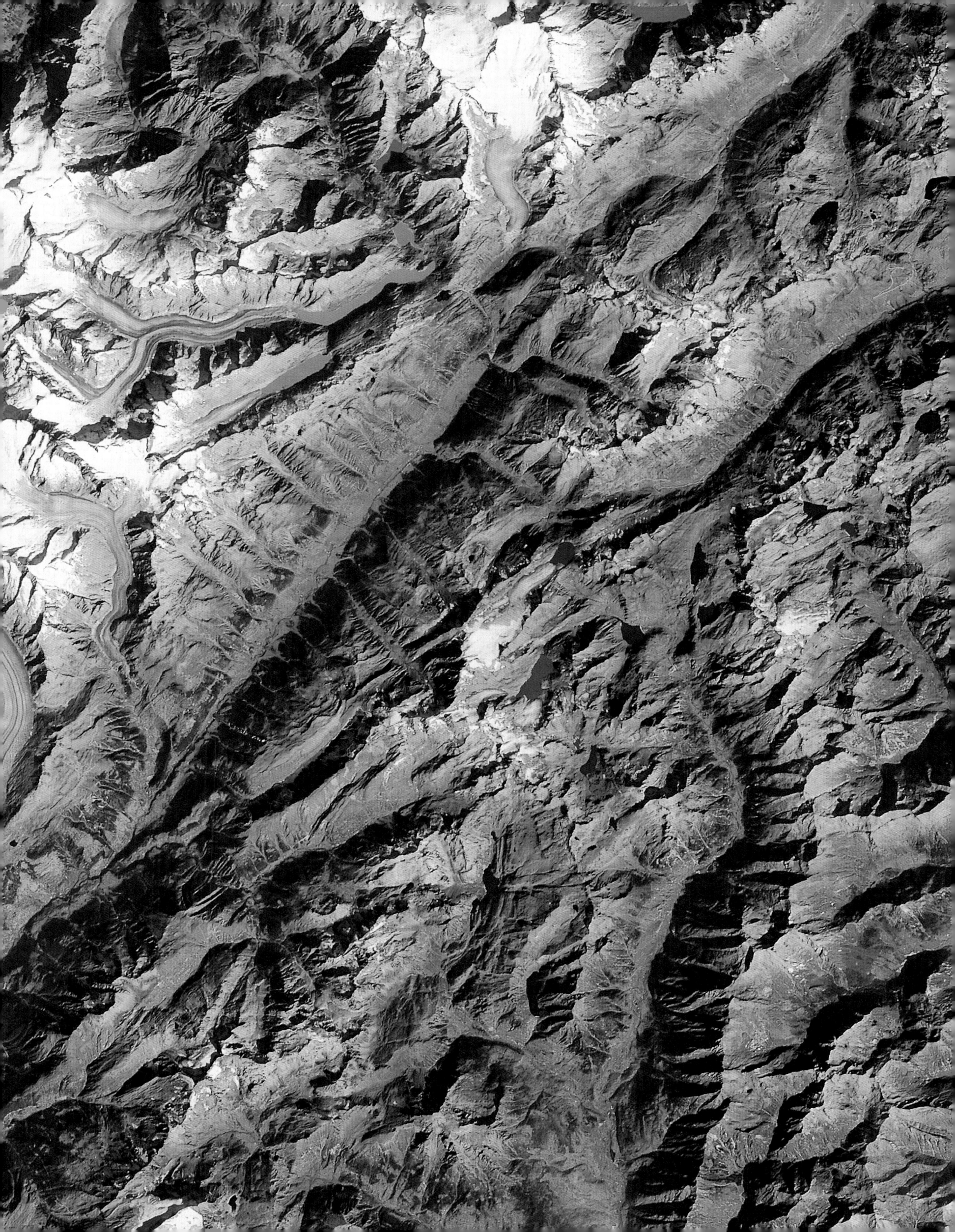

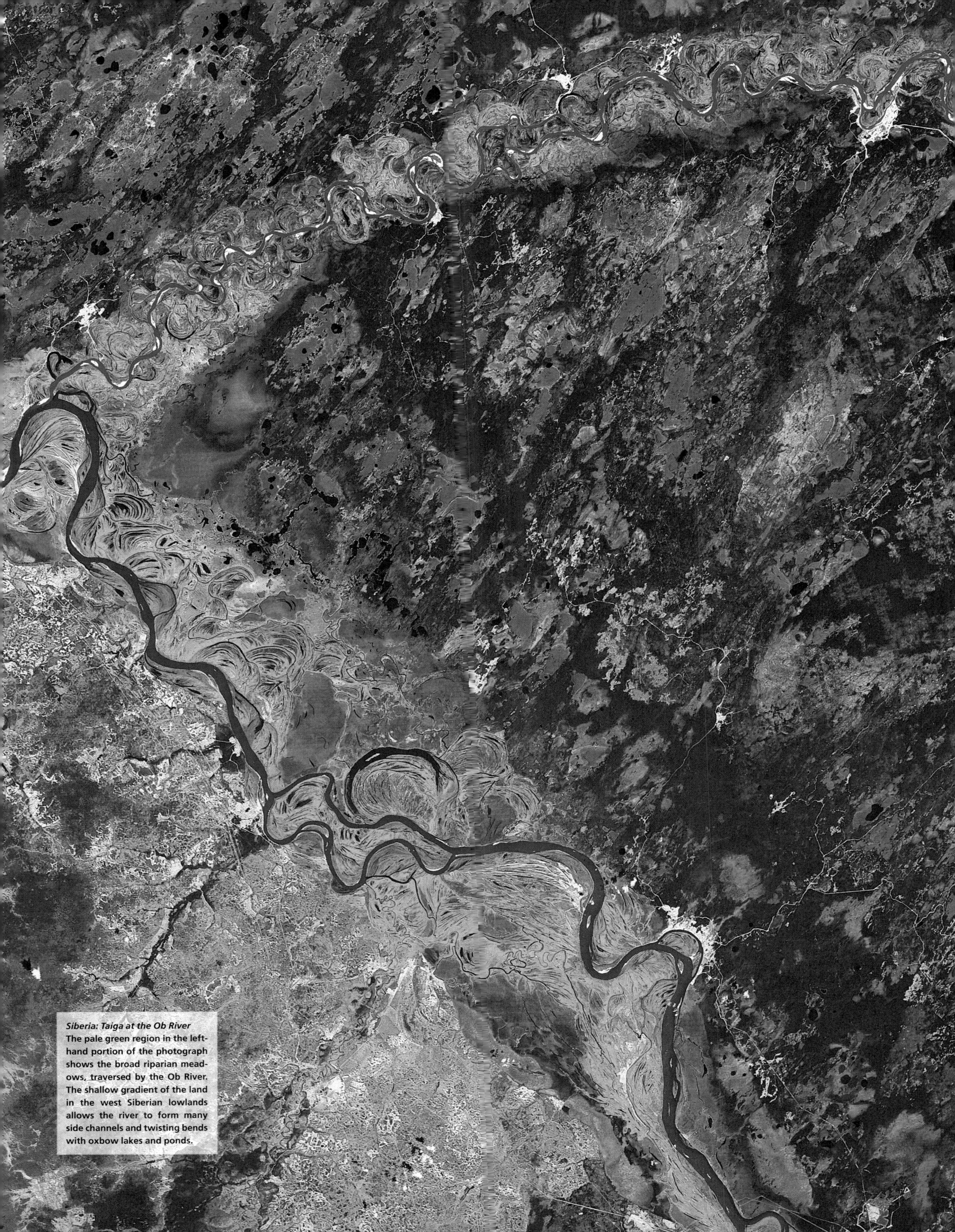

Siberia: Taiga at the Ob River
The pale green region in the left-hand portion of the photograph shows the broad riparian meadows, traversed by the Ob River. The shallow gradient of the land in the west Siberian lowlands allows the river to form many side channels and twisting bends with oxbow lakes and ponds.

A 96° B 94° C 92° 31 D 90° E 88° -6h Gr. Time -5h Gr. Time 84° H 82° J 25 80° K 78° L 76° M 74°

2

Half Way
Hills 183
Baker Lake
64°
122
Bowell
Is.

N
o
r
t
h

123

354

206

91

White
I.
Opposite I.
137
C. Dominion
Vansittart
I.
C. Welsford
298
C. Comfort
C. Dobbs
116
564
472
Porsild 625
Mts.
Foxe
C. Dorchester
Nabukjuak B.
C. Ketoria

Foxe Peninsula
Channel
Kingha: Range 293 137 Alareak
King Charles C. Cape Dorset Diamond I.
152 Dorset I.
Okolli I.
Chamberlain
Mill I.
390

Salisbury
305

Nottingham
I. 244

Digges Is. C. Wolstenholme 385
Charles I. 152
Ivujivik C. de Nouvelle-

3

154 139

Hanbury
I.
Cap Silumiut
Rockhouse I.
381
Chesterfield Inlet

w
e
s
t

Caribou
Coral Harbour
Southampton
Island
159
South
Bay
Bell Peninsula
226
Seahorse Pt. 312

C. Kendall
63

Ruin Pt. Native
Pt.

Rankin Inlet

Pangnirtat Pen.
114
Corbett Inlet
Park Pen.
Marble I.
Cape
Jones 18

T
e
r

H
u
d

447

60°

Salluit
Déception

62°

Whale Cove
Term Pt.

of Gods Mercy
Manico Pt.
Native
Bay
Bear Cove Pt. 108
Leyson Pt.

Evans Strait

Deception

681

4

Bibby I.
Angusko Pt.
16

C. Low

Fisher Strait
Calanus
Bay
152 C. Pembroke
Coals
Santianna Island
Pt.
C.
Southampton
Shean Bay
92

Mansel
Island

Monts de Povungnituk 552
Cratère
Nouveau-C.

Austin I.
Maguse Pt.
Maguse River
Eskimo Point

124

227

231

C. Acadia

429

P
é
n
i
n

31

98

162

187

233

171

163 Smith I. 308
C. Smith
Mosquito Bay
Pte. Demers
Pte. Cusson

D'

u
n

60°

119

187

5

257

144

Pte.
Dufrost
Povungnituk
162
40

58°

H
u
d
s
o
n

42

133

Gilmour I.
Perley I.
Ottawa Islands
Pte. aux Écueils

Kogaluc

102

49

156

192

Two Brothers
Elsie I.
Cox I.
Pte. Bonnissant

Farmer I.
Inukjuak
(Port Harrison) 164

Hopewell Islands

C
A

N

L

Q

6

C. Tatnam

M a n i t o b a

Kettle R.

Black Duck

197

133

Fort Severn
Partridge I.

Sleeper Is. 91
Kidney I.

King George
Islands
Broughton I. 472
Davieau I.

N a s t a p o k a I s.

56°

7

Sachigo R.

Winisk

Polar

Wood

18
Wabuk Pt.

Bear

Split I.
North
Belcher Is.
Johnson I.
Bakers
Dozen Is.
Belcher Lillico Pt.
Kugong
Gushie
Pt. C. Bartlett
Islands
Tukarak I.
Belcher Islands
McLeary Pt.
Flaherty Island
Innetalling I.

Gillies I.

Anderson I.
Belanger I.
Cairn

35

35

Peawanuck

C. Lo ut

Freakly
Pt.
Snape I. Sainsbury Pt.

Castle I.

Merry I.

54°

O n t a r i o

Provincial

Park

C. Henrietta Maria
49

Hook Pt.

Poste-de-la-Baleine

Long I.

8

Big Trout Lake
Big Trout Lake
Ind. Res.

Kasabonika

Indian
Reserve

James

Bay

Bear I.

C. Iones

Pte. Kakachischuan

90° E 35 88° F 86° G 84° H 82° J 80° K 78° L 76° 38 M 74°

Scale 1 : 4,500,000
0 40 80 120 160 200 Kilometers
0 40 80 120 160 Statute Miles

Scale 1 : 4,500,000

| 0 | 40 | 80 | 120 | 160 | 200 Kilometers |

| 0 | 40 | 80 | 120 |

Statute Miles

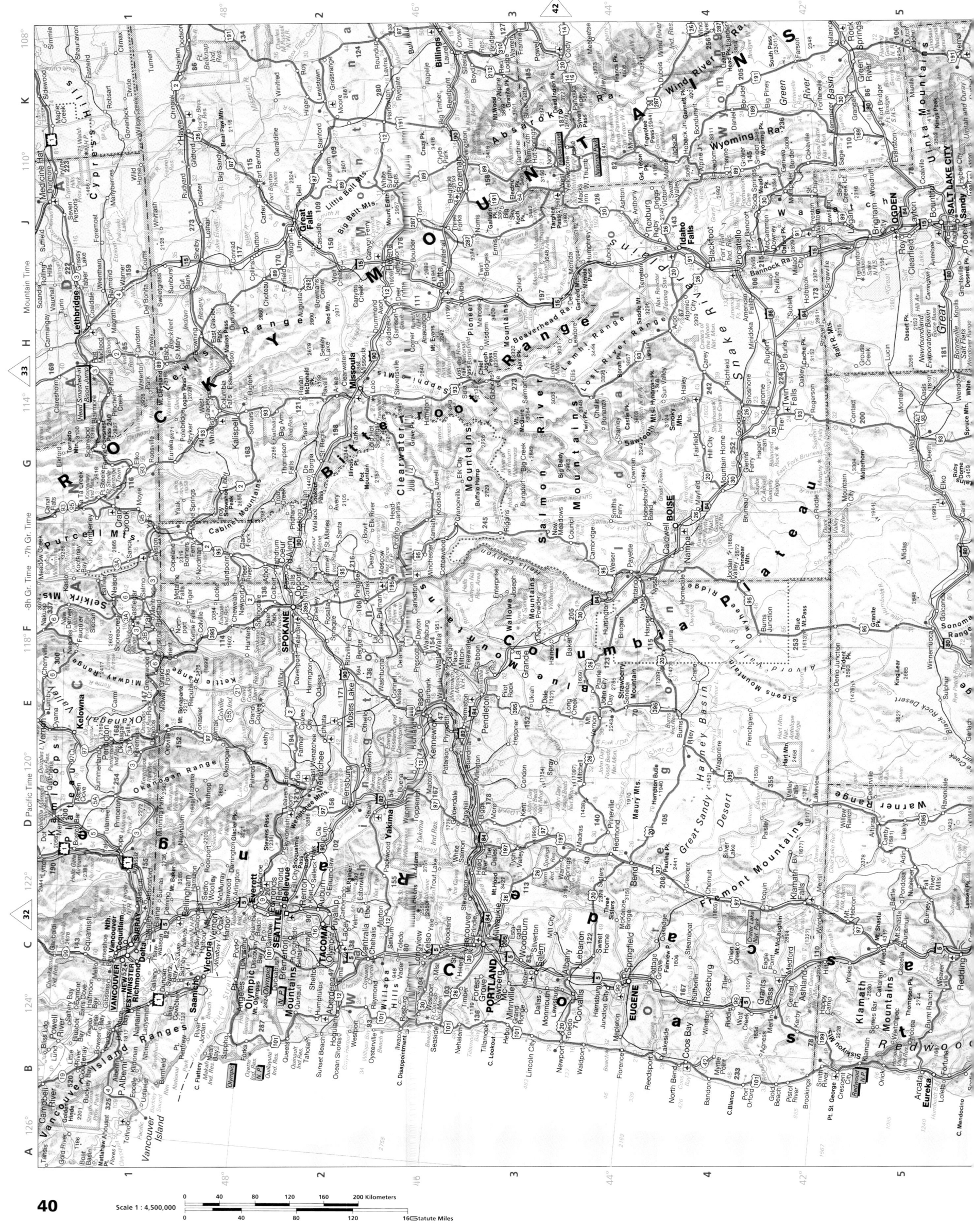

Scale 1 : 4,500,000

0   40   80   120   160   200 Kilometers

0   40   80   120   16 Statute Miles

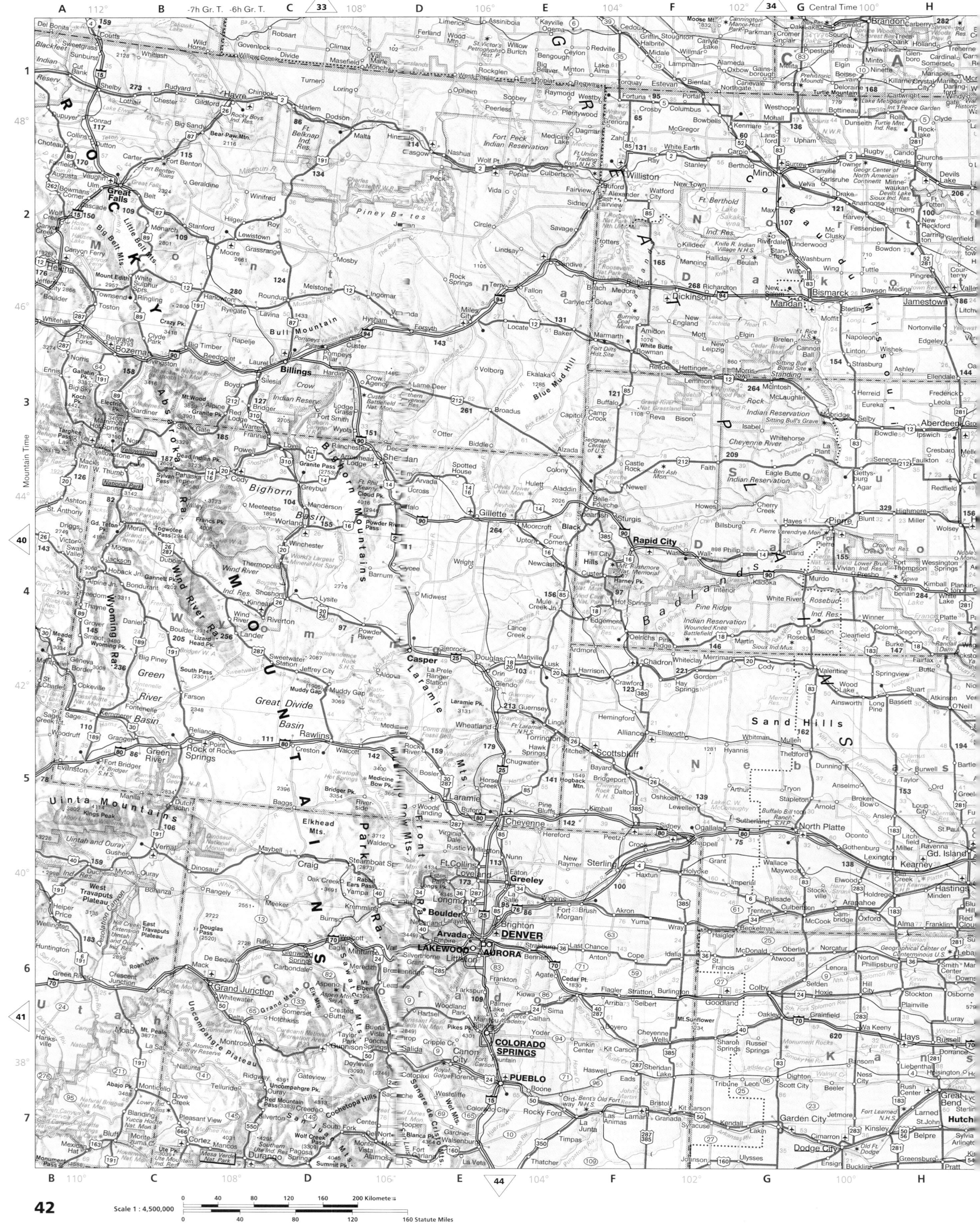

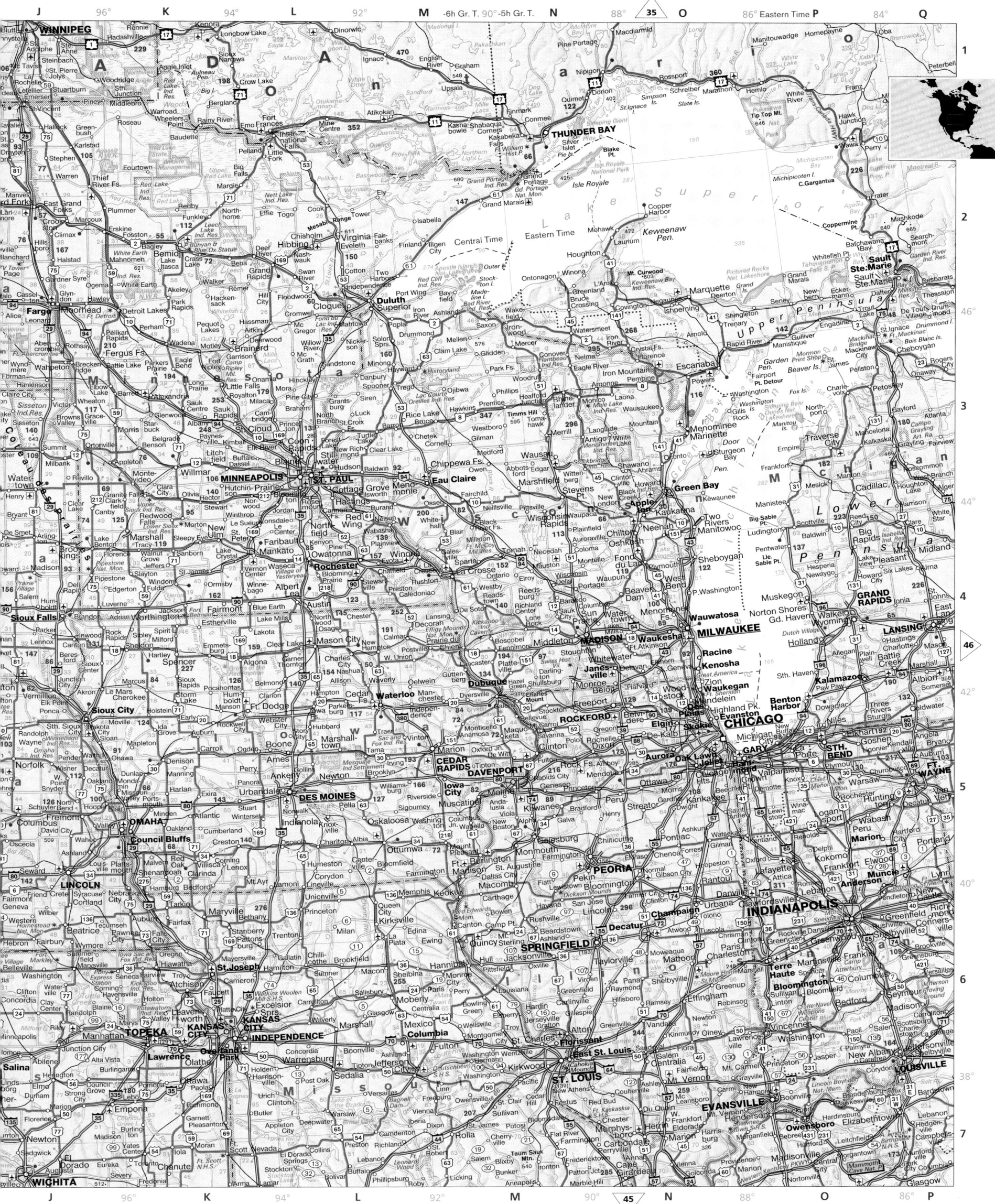

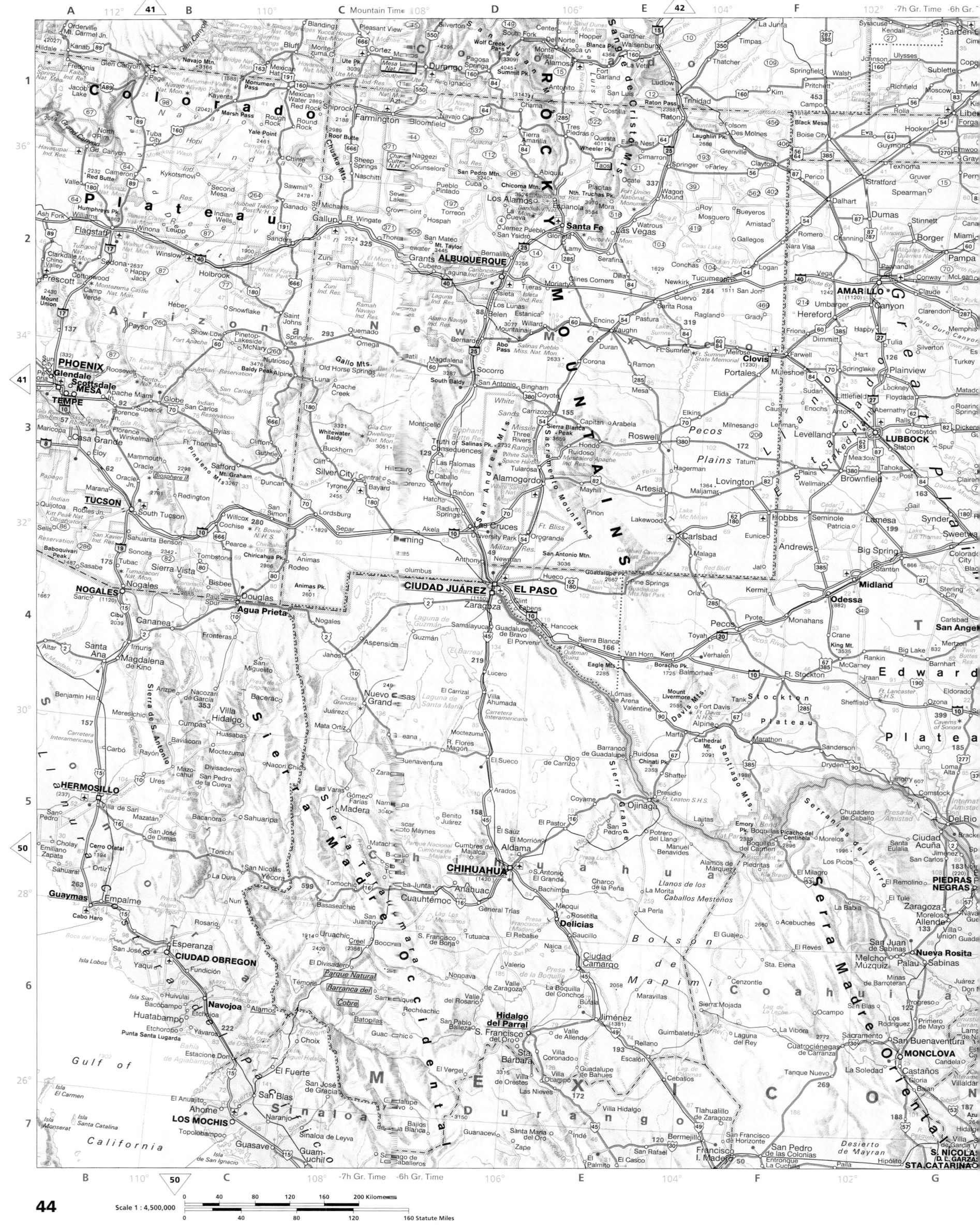

Scale 1 : 4,500,000

0   40   80   120   160   200 Kilome

0   40   80   120

160 Statute Miles

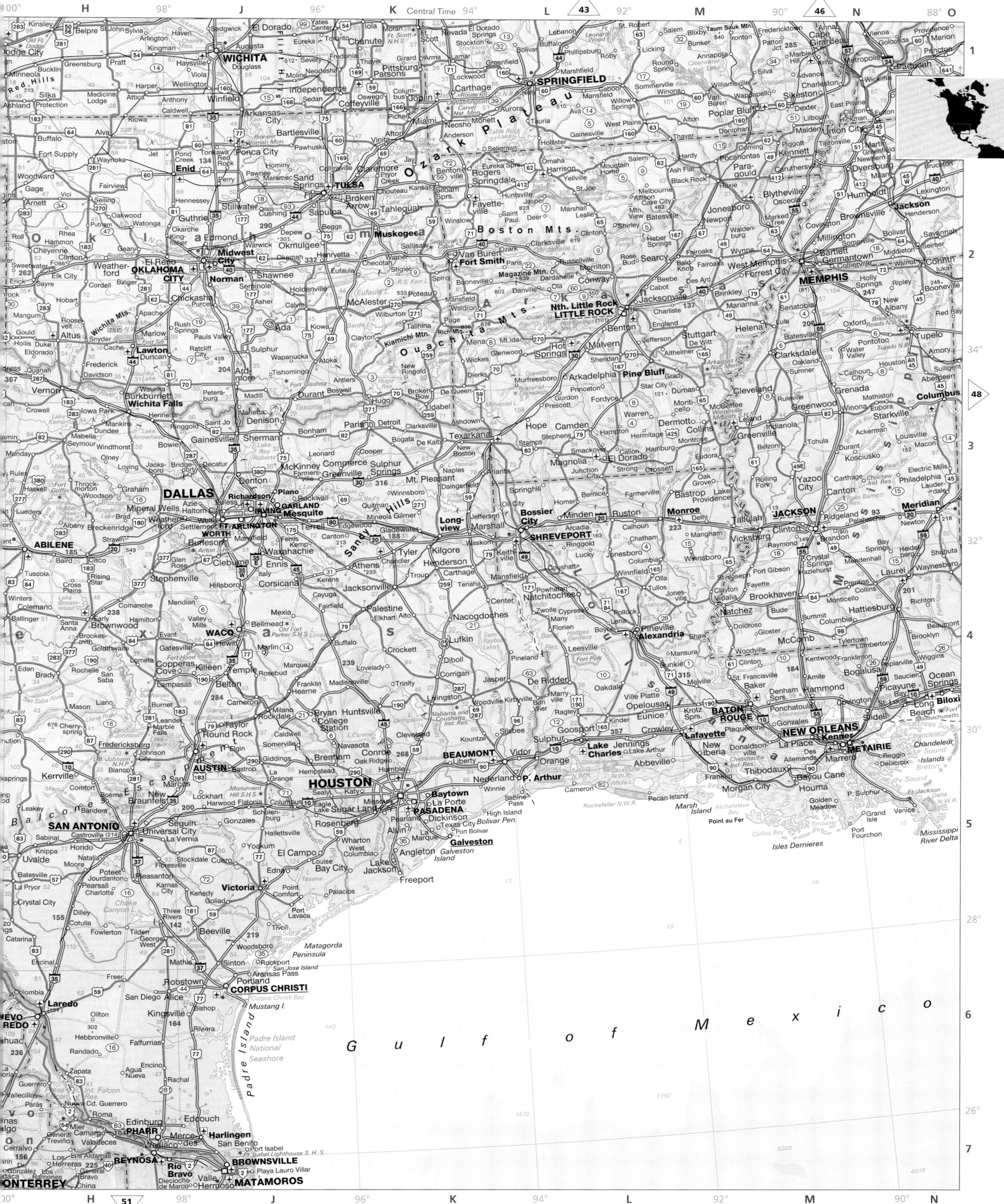

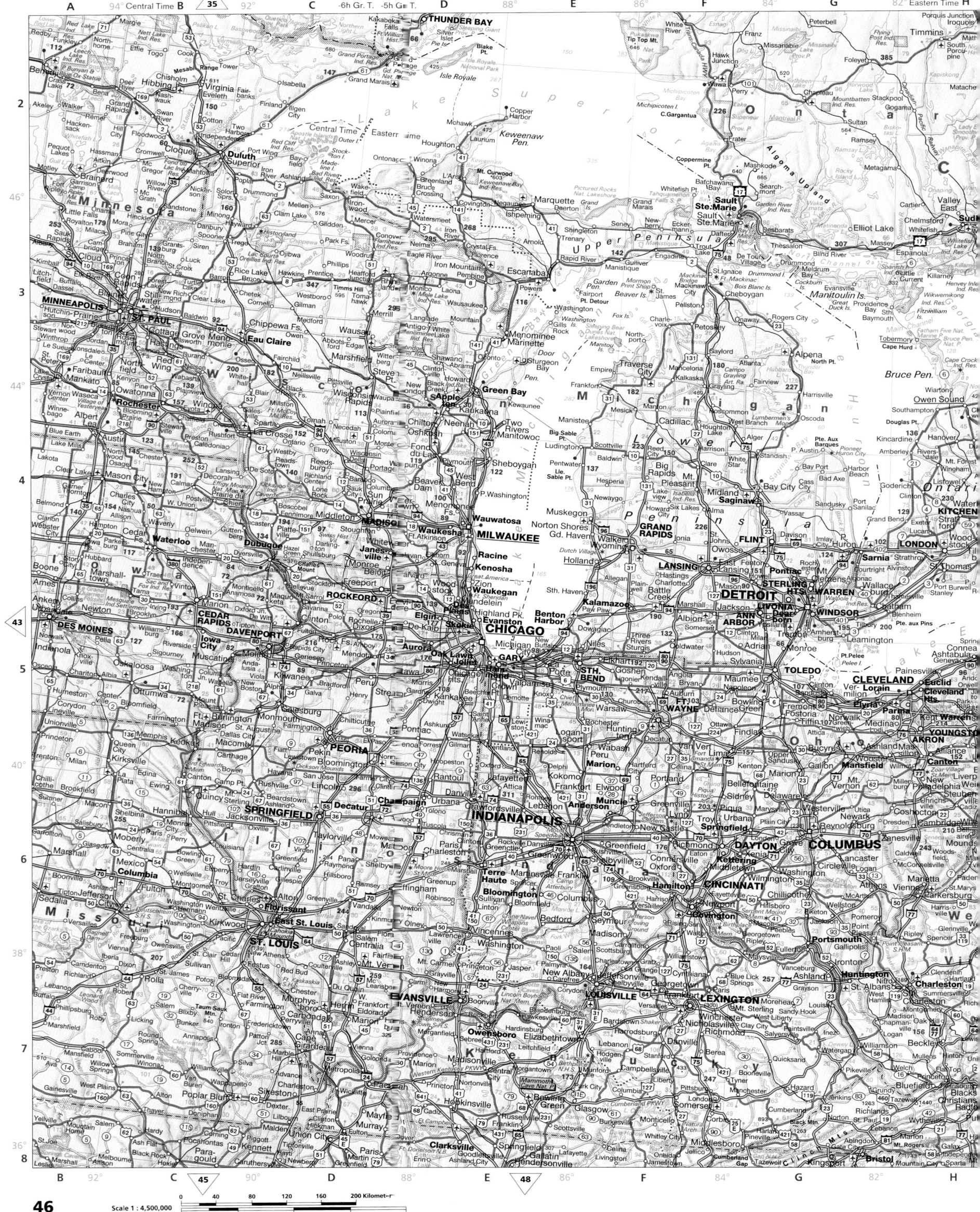

Scale 1 : 4,500,000

0 40 80 120 160 200 Kilometers

0 40 80 120 Statute Miles

Revilla Gigedo Islands

Scale 1 : 4,500,000

| 0 | 40 | 80 | 120 | 160 | 200 Kilometers |

| 0 | 40 | 80 | 120 |

50 Statute Miles

A

88° **86°** **84°** **82°** **80°**

1

Venice
Port Charlotte
Palmdale
La Belle · Brighton
Seminole Ind. Res.
Pahokee
Belle
Glade
West Palm Beach
Cape Coral · Fort Myers
Immokalee Seminole
Ind. Res.
Lake Worth
Delray Beach
Boca Raton
Deerfield Beach
Pompano Beach
FT. LAUDERDALE
HOLLYWOOD
Hallandale

**UNITED
STATES**

Naples
Golden
Gate
Miles City
Marco
Ochopee
Carol City
HIALEAH
MIAMI
Miami Beach

Florida

C. Romano
Everglades
City
Kendall
Perrine
Homestead
C. Florida

2

Gulf   of   Mexico

C. Sable
Flamingo
Everglades
National
Park
Florida Bay
Islamorada
Key Largo
Elliot Key

Dry Tortugas
Fort Jefferson
Nat. Mem.
Marquesas
Keys
Pine Islands
Marathon
Big Pine
158
Florida Keys

Key West

3   Tropic of Cancer

4

5

◁ **53**

6

7

54
Scale 1 : 4,500,000

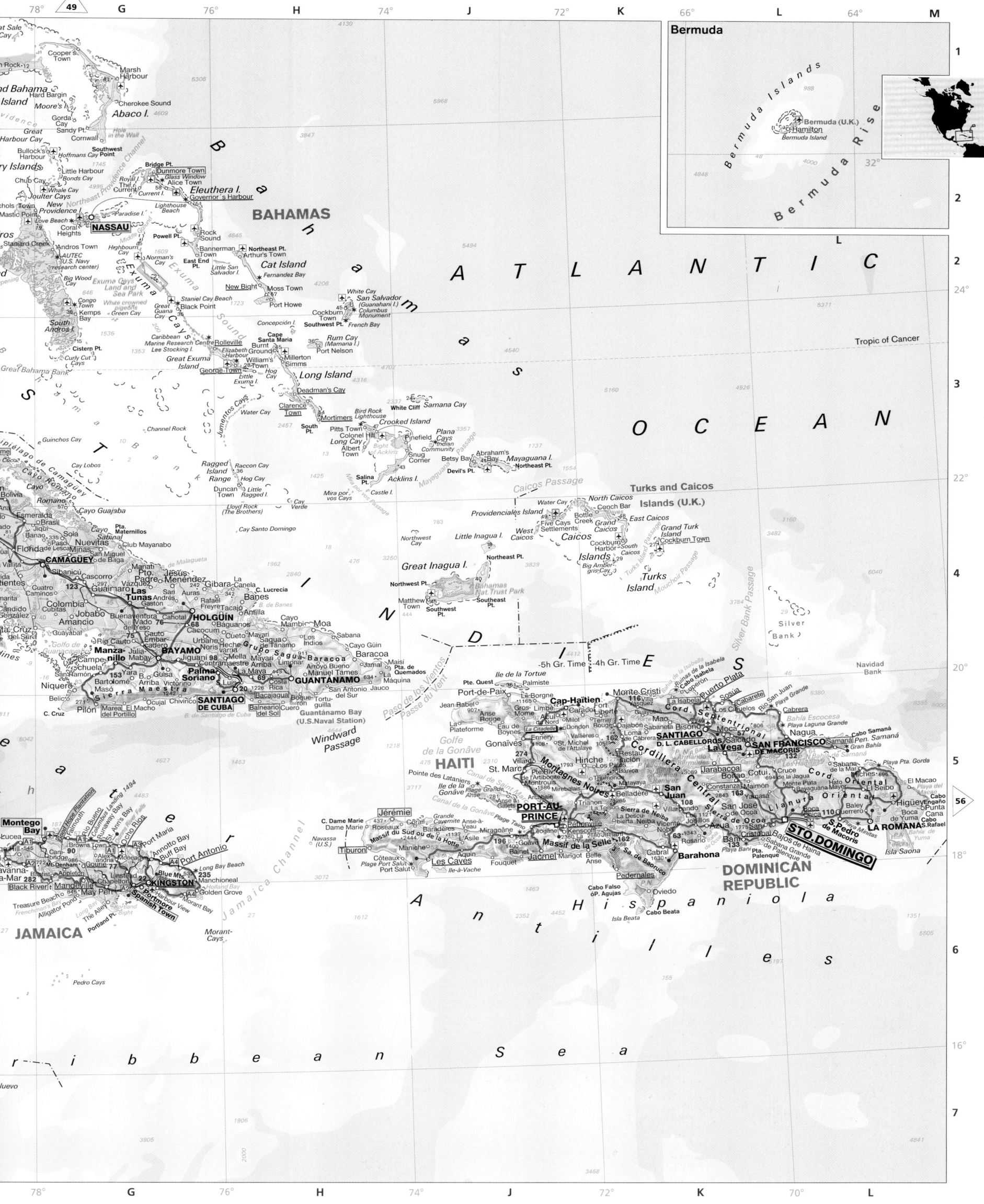

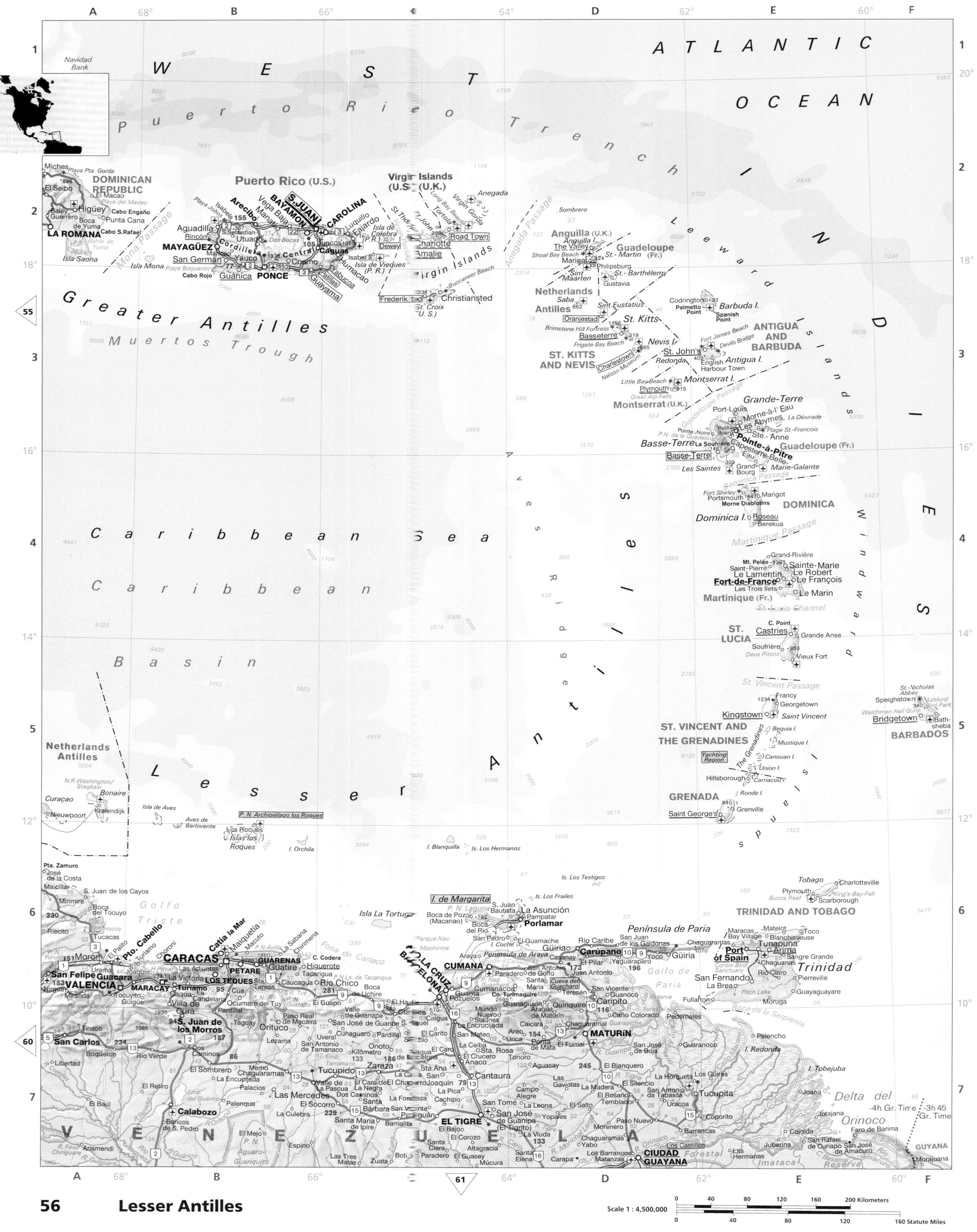

Scale 1 : 4,500,000

0 40 80 120 160 200 Kilometers

0 40 80 120 160 Statute Miles

South America – continent of natural highlights

Since most of South America's 6,872,580 square miles (17.8 million sq. km) are located in the Southern Hemisphere, it is considered a southern continent, like Africa. The continent is even connected with the Antarctic via the Southern Antilles and submarine rises. With the exception of the polar ice region, all climatic and vegetation zones are represented on the continent; the tropical climate is predominant, however. The western part of the continent is characterized by the volcano-studded mountain range of the Cordilleras de Los Andes, which is close to 4,660 miles (7,500 km) long and reaches a height of almost 23,000 feet (7,000 m). Parallel to them runs a continuous deep-sea trench in the Pacific Ocean. Over half of the

An early documentation of intercultural encounter: Zacharias Wagner created this depiction of an Indian dance during his sojourn in Brazil (1634–37) and subsequently published it in his "Bestiary."

continent's land mass is taken up by the giant lowlands of the Orinoco, the Amazon and the Paraná. Adjacent to the southeastern coast is a broad continental shelf cresting in the Falkland Islands (called Islas Malvinas by Argentina). More animal and plant species are found in South America than anywhere else in the world: More than 250 of the 350 known flowering plant families originate there; it is home to one-third of all bird species, and the number of insect species is beyond estimation. The Amazon Basin not only is the largest river region on Earth but also contains the greatest area of tropical forest.

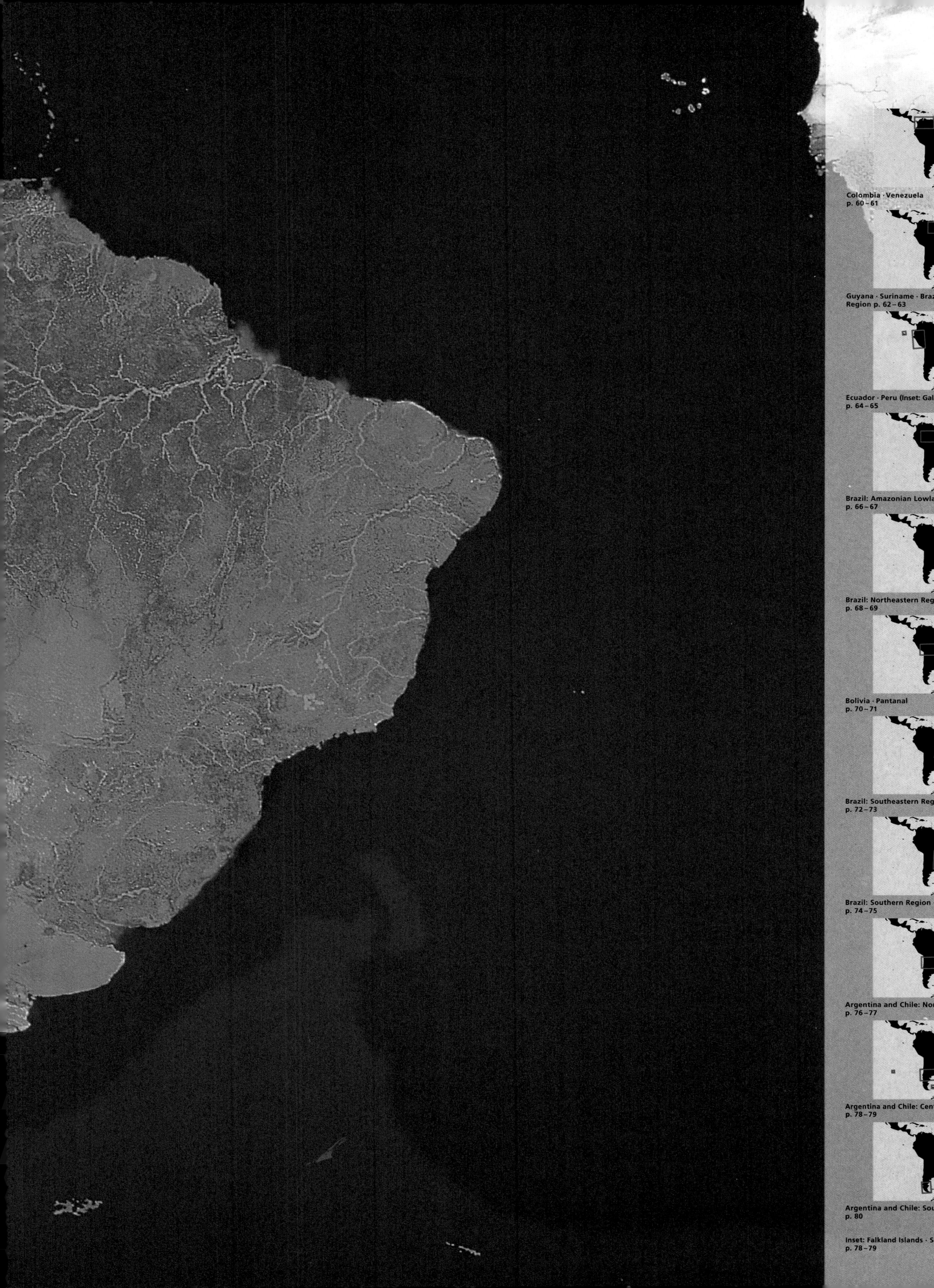

Caribbean Sea

PACIFIC

OCEAN

PANAMA

PANAMÁ

Portobelo
Colón
Chepo

Golfo de Panamá

Golfo del Darién

CARTAGENA

BARRANQUILLA
SOLEDAD
Ciénaga

SANTA MARTA

Sierra Nevada de
Santa Marta

VALLEDUPAR

MARACAIBO

CABIMAS
Ciudad Ojeda

Lago de
Maracaibo

MÉRIDA

Riohacha
Maicao

Península
de la
Guajira

Golfo de
Venezuela

SINCELEJO Magangué

MONTERÍA

Turbo

Quibdó

Buenaventura

MEDELLÍN **BELLO**
ITAGÜÍ
Envigado

BUCARAMANGA
Floridablanca

BARRANCABERMEJA

CÚCUTA
SAN CRISTÓBAL

Ocaña

Pamplona

MANIZALES

PEREIRA
Cartago
ARMENIA
IBAGUÉ
Girardot

Cordillera Central

Cordillera Oriental

BOGOTÁ

Soacha

TUNJA

Duitama
Sogamoso

VILLAVICENCIO

LLANOS

CALI
PALMIRA

Buga
TULUÁ

NEIVA

Florencia

POPAYÁN

Cordillera Occidental

PASTO
Tumaco

COLOMBIA

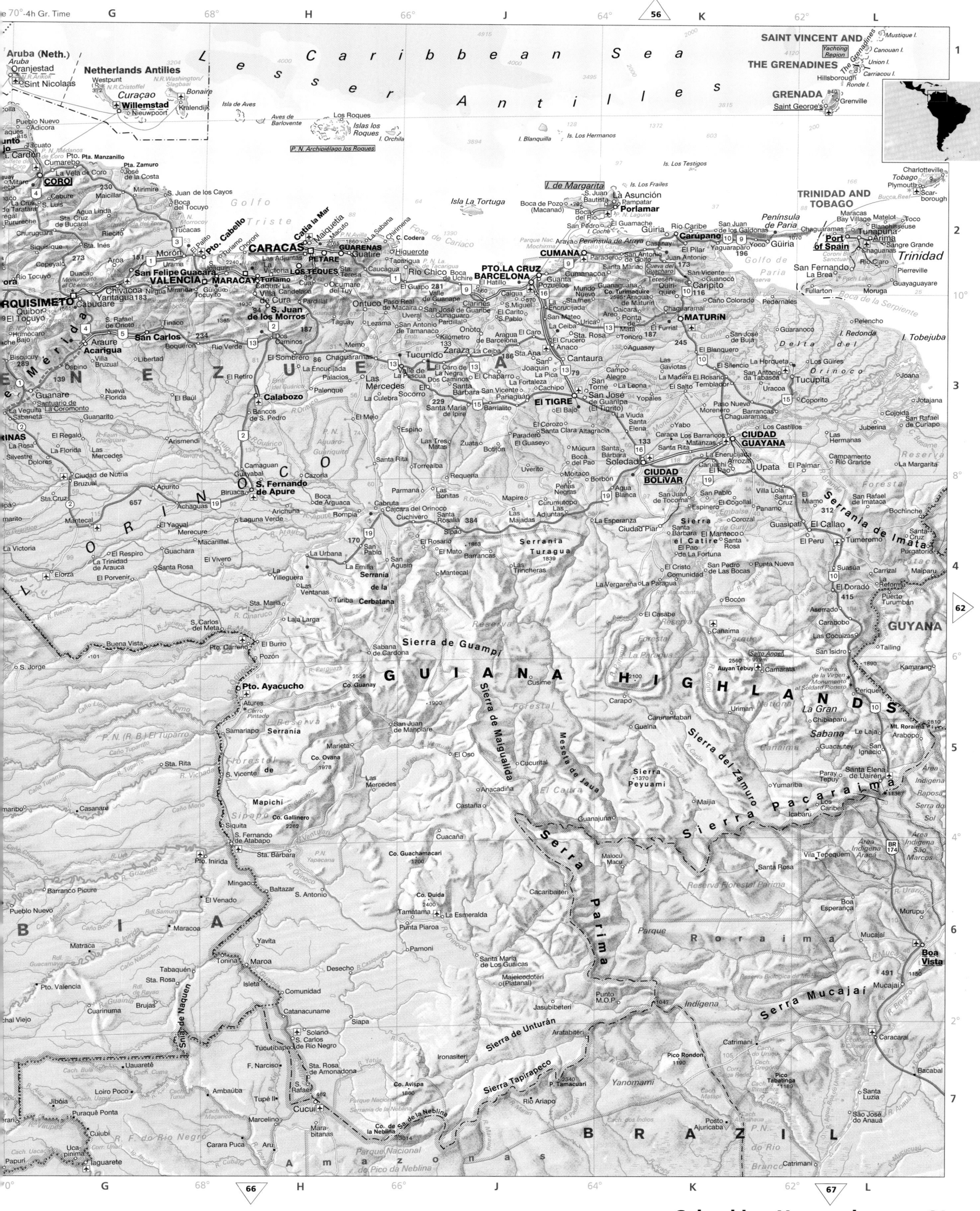

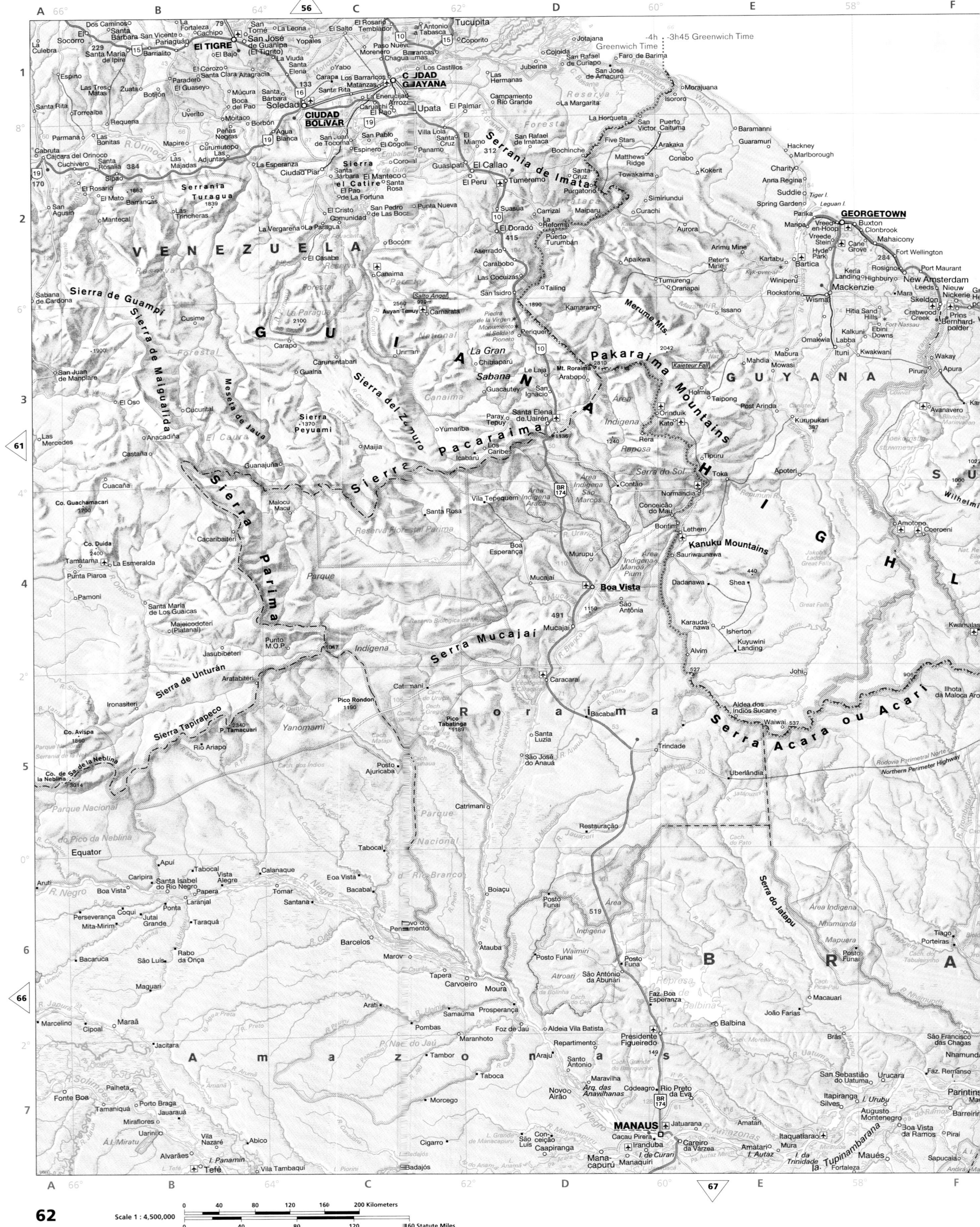

A 66°   B   56   C   62°   D   60°   E   58°   F

1

-4h -3h45 Greenwich Time
Greenwich Time

VENEZUELA

G U I A N A

Sierra de Guampi
Sierra de Maigualida

Sierra del Zapuro
Sierra Pacaraima

Sierra Parima

Serrania de Imataca
Serrania de Imataca

Pakaraima Mountains

Merume Mts.

GUYANA

GEORGETOWN

H I G H L A N D S

Sierra de Unturán

Sierra Tapirapeco

Serra Mucajaí

Roraima

Kanuku Mountains

Serra Acara ou Acari

Serra do Sol

2

61

3

4

5

Equator

B R A

A m a z o n a s

MANAUS

Northern Perimeter Highway

6

66

7

A 66°   B   C   62°   D   60°   67   E   58°   F

62

Scale 1 : 4,500,000

0   40   80   120   160   200 Kilometers

0   40   80   120   160 Statute Miles

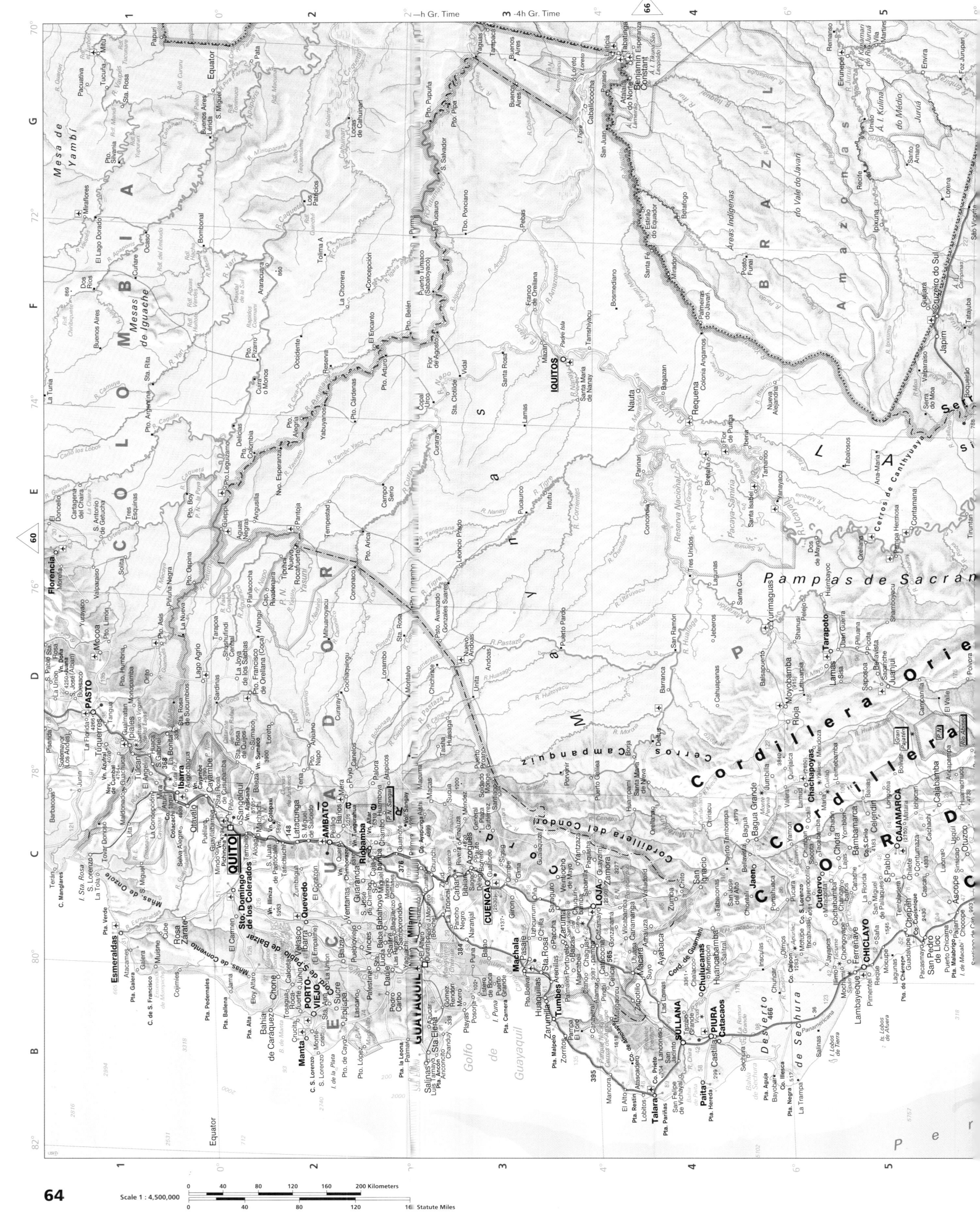

Scale 1 : 4,500,000

0   40   80   120   160   200 Kilometers

0   40   80   120

Statute Miles

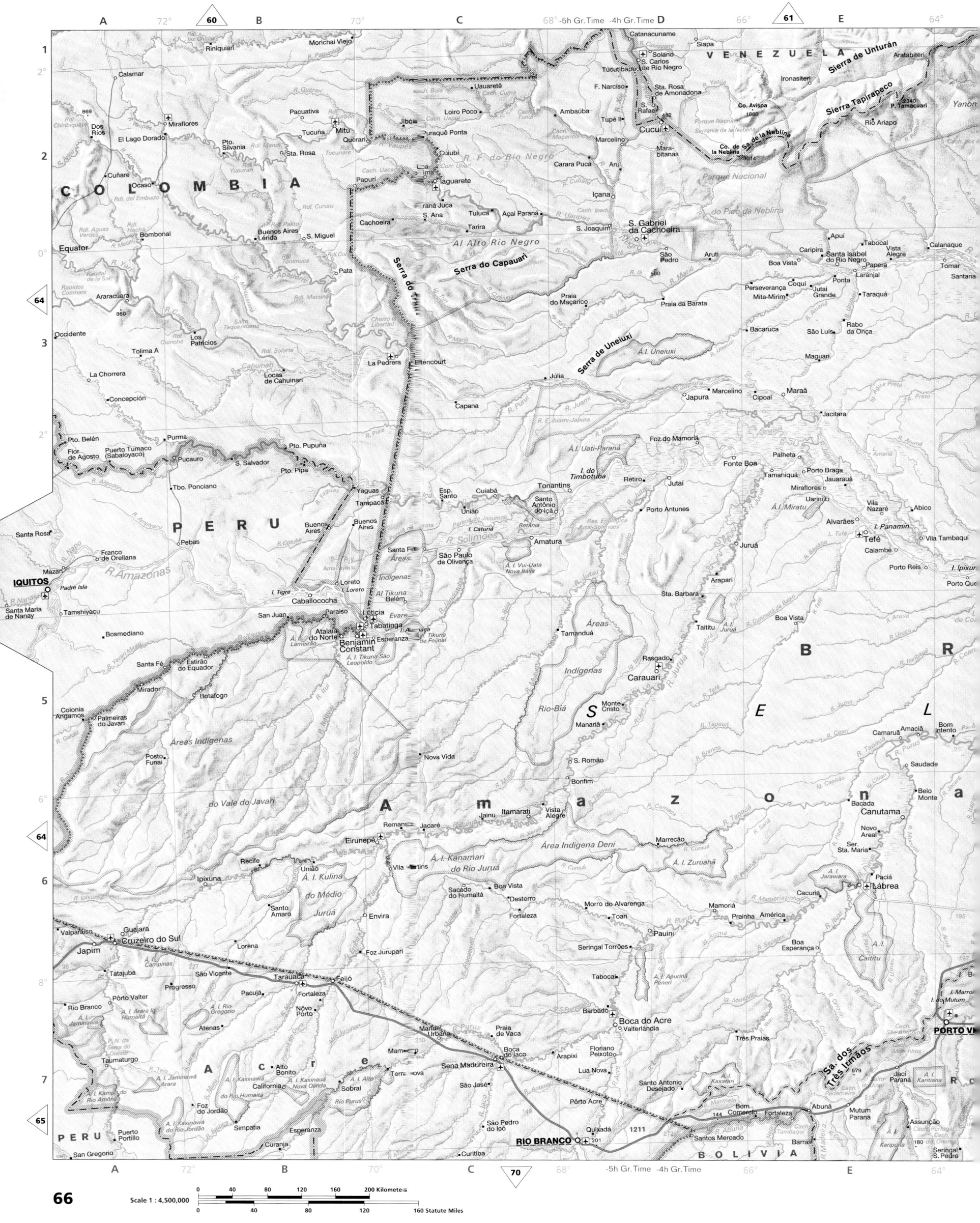

A · 72° · B · 70° · C · 68° -5h Gr. Time · -4h Gr. Time · D · 66° · E · 64°

VENEZUELA

Sierra de Unturán

Catanacuname · Siapa · Aratabiteri

Morichal Viejo · Solano · Ironasiten · Sierra Tapirapeco · P. Tamacuari 2340

Riniquiari · R. Papunáa · Casiquiare · S. Carlos de Rio Negro · Co. Avispa 1800 · Yanon

Calamar · Miraflores · Tucuña · Mitú · Jibó · Uauaretê · Loiro Poco · Cach. Cuma · Tucutibapó · Sta. Rosa de Amonadona · Parque Nacion · Serrania de la Neblina · Rio Ariapo

Dos Rios 869 · El Lago Dorado · Pacuativa · Turbín · Quérari · Puraqué Ponta · Ambaúba · Tupé II · S. Rafael 892 · Co. de Sa. de la Neblina 3014

C O L O M B I A

Ocaso · Pto. Silvania · Sta. Rosa · Culubi · R. F. do Rio Negro · Marcelino · Mara- · bitanas · Parque Nacional do Pico da Neblina

Cuñare · Papuri · ra · ima · Iaguarete · Carara Puca · Aru · Içana

Equator · S. Ana · Tuluca · Açai Paraná · S. Joaquim · S. Gabriel · Apuí · Tabocal

Buenos Aires · Cachoeira · Tarira · S. Pedro · Aruti · Caripira · Santa Isabel · Vista

Bombonal · Lérida · S. Miguel · **Al Alto Rio Negro** · **Serra do Capauari** · São · Pedro · Boa Vista · do Rio Negro · Papera · Alegre · Tomar

64° · Araracuara · Pata · Praia · do Maçarico · Praia da Barata · Perseverança · Coqui · Larânjal · Santana

Occidente · Los Patricios · Serra do · Chorro de Libertad · Praia da Barata · Mita-Mirim · Jutaí Grande · Taraquá · Rabo

Tolima A · La Pedrera · Etencourt · **Serra de Uneiuxi** · Á. I. Uneiuxi · Bacaruca · São Luis · da Onça

La Chorrera · Locas de Cahuinari · Júlia · Japura · Marcelino · Cipoal · Maguari

Concepción · Capana · R. Purui · R. E. Juami-Jabura · Maraã · Jacitara

2° · Pto. Belén · Purma · Pto. Pupuña · R. Puré · Foz do Mamoriá · Paiheta · Porto Braga · Amaná

Flor de Agosto · Puerto Tumaco (Sabaloyaco) · Pucauro · S. Salvador · Pto. Pipa · Á. I. Uati-Paraná · Fonte Boa · Tamaniquá · Jauarauá

Pucruz · Tbo. Ponciano · Yaguas · Tarapacá · Esp. Santo · Cuiabá · Tonantins · Retiro · Jutaí · Miraflores · Uarini · Vila

Buenos Aires · Buenos Aires · União · Santo Antônio do Içá · Porto Antunes · Á. I. Miratu · Nazaré · Abico

Santa Rosa · Pebas · Santa Fé · Áreas · São Paulo · Á. I. Caturiá · Betânia · Res. Ecológica · Jutaí-Solimões · Porto Reis · I. Panamin

Franco de Orellana · Indigenas · de Olivença · Amatura · Juruá · Caiambé · Tefé · Vila Tambaqui

IQUITOS · Mazan · Padre Isla · **R. Amazonas** · Al Tikuna · Loreto · Á. I. Vui-Uata · Nova Itália · Araparí · I. Ipixur

Santa Maria de Nanay · Tamshiyacu · I. Tigre · Loreto · Belém · Sta. Barbara · Porto Que

San Juan · Caballococha · Paraiso · **Leticia** · Evare · Taititu · Á. I. · Juruá · Boa Vista

Bosmediano · Atalaia · **Tabatinga** · Tamanduá · Áreas · R. Jutaí

do Norte · **Benjamin** · Esperanza · Tikuna · de Feijoal · Rasgado

Santa Fé · Estirão · **Constant** · Á. I. Tikuna São · Indígenas · **Carauari** · B · R

do Equador · Leopoldo · Rio-Biá · Monte · Cristo

Mirador · Botafogo · Manariã · Camaruã · Amaciã · Bom · Intento

5° · Colonia · Palmeiras · Nova Vida · S. Romão · Saudade

Angamos · do Javari · **Áreas Indígenas** · Bonfim · E · L

Posto · Funai · Belo · Monte

do Vale do Javari · A · m · a · Bacada · z · Canutama · o · n · a

6° · Jainu · Itamarati · Vista · R. Carreiro · Novo · Areal

64° · Remans · Jacaré · Alegre · Marrecão · Ser. Sta. Maria

Eirunepé · **Área Indígena Deni** · Á. I. Zuruahã · Á. I. · Jawawara · Paciá

Recife · Vila · rtins · Á. I. Kanamari · **Lábrea**

Ipixuna · União · **do Rio Juruá** · Cacuria

6° · Á. I. Kulina · Sacado · Boa Vista · Morro do Alvarenga · Mamoriá · Prainha · América

Santo · **do Médio** · do Humaitá · Desterro · Toari · Boa

Amaro · **Juruá** · Envira · Fortaleza · Pauini · Esperança · Á. I.

Valparaíso · Guajara · Lorena · Seringal Torrões · Á. I.

Cruzeiro do Sul · Foz Jurupari · Caititu

Japim · Á. I. · Campinas · Tabocal · Á. I. Apurinã · Pêneri · **PORTO VE**

8° · Tatajuba · São Vicente · **Tarauacá** · Feijó · Barbado · I. Marroi

Pôrto Valter · Progresso · Pacujá · Fortaleza · Manuel · **Boca do Acre** · I. do Mutum

Rio Branco · Á. I. Arara Ig. · Nôvo · Urbano · Valterlândia · Três Praias

Atenas · Á. I. Rio · Pôrto · Mam · Boca · Arapixi · S. dos

P. N. da · Gregorio · Alto · do Ioco · Floriano · Três Irmãos · 579

Taumaturgo · Á. I. Jaminawá · Bonito · Terra · ova · Sena Madureira · Peixoto · Jaci · R

Arara · Á. I. Alto · California · do Rio Humaitá · São José · Lua Nova · Paraná

65° · Á. I. Kaxinawá · Nova Olinda · Sobral · São Antonio · Abunã · Mutum

PERU · Á. I. Kaxinawá · Foz · do Jordão · Simpatia · Esperanza · São Pedro · Desejado · Pôrto Acre · Bom · Paraná · Assunção

Puerto · Portillo · do Rio Jordão · Curanja · do Ioó · **RIO BRANCO** · Quixadá · 1211 · Santos Mercado · Fortaleza · Barras

San Gregorio · Curitiba · **BOLIVIA** · Seringal · S. Pedro

A · 72° · B · 70° · C · 68° · -5h Gr. Time · -4h Gr. Time · 66° · E

Scale 1 : 4,500,000

0 · 40 · 80 · 120 · 160 · 200 Kilometes

0 · 40 · 80 · 120 · 160 Statute Miles

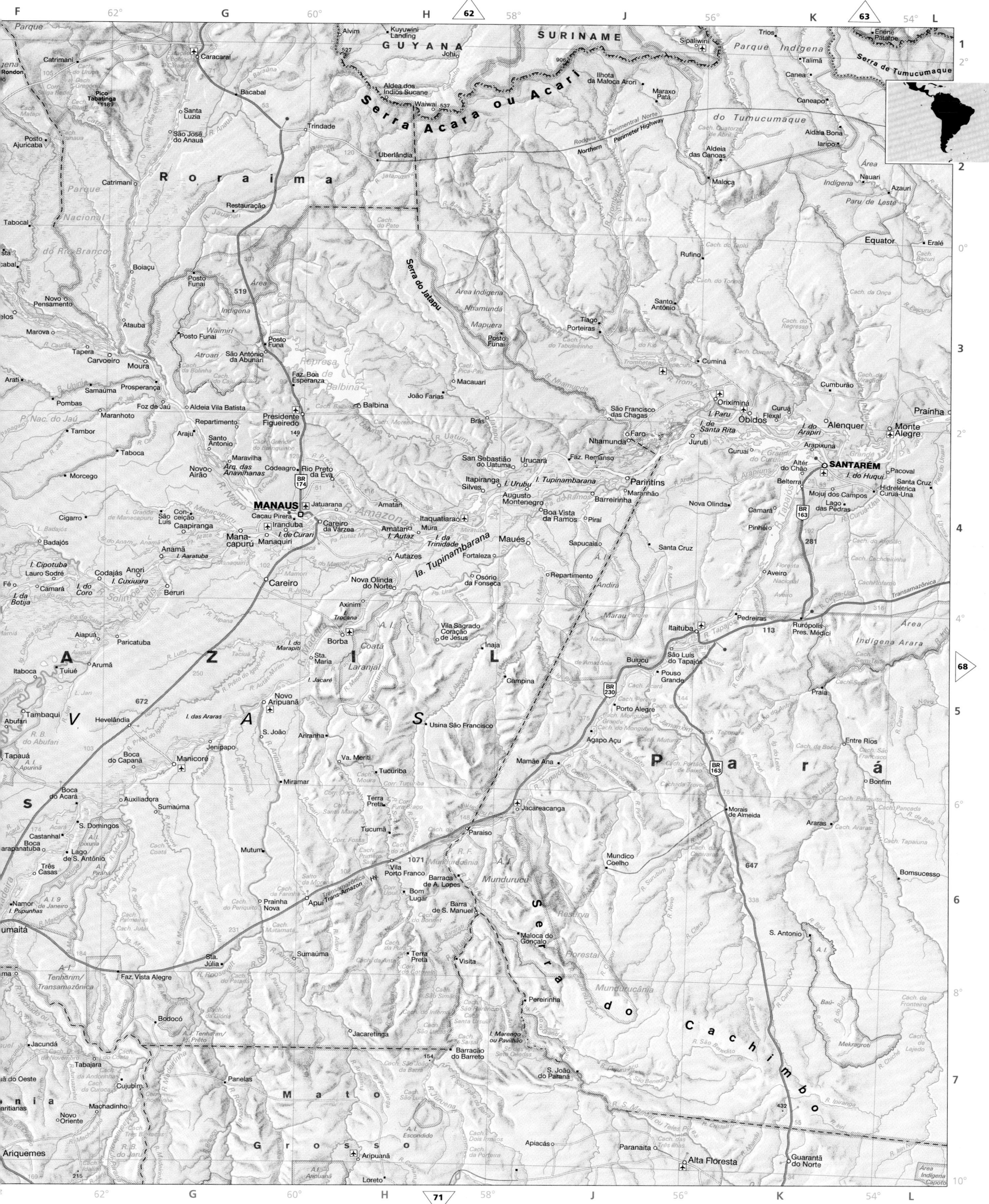

Santa Clara · São Tomé · Santa Cruz do Arari · Cajuina · Pta. Curuçá · Cajutuba · Pta. de Atalaia · Marudá · Salinópolis
Born Jardim · S. Cosme · Maria de · San Marcos · Ilha de Marajó · Punto da Barca · São Caetano de Odivelas · Salvaterra · São Caetano · Perseverança · Japerica · Marapanim · Marapanim · Pta. de Quatipuru · Pta. de Mariau
Barraca da Boca · Cach. Maracanai · Cach. de S. Antônio · Beiradão · Santana · Pagas Divisas · Boca do Jari · I. Grande · I. Urutaí · Punto da Barca · Boa Vista · Cachoeira do Arari · Mosqueiro · Colares · Terra... · Marudá · Maracanã · Santarém Novo · Primavera · Caratateua · Carataua · I. Apeú · I.S. Jorge
Monte Dourado · Serra do Almeirim · Ramos · Boca do Jari · I. dos Macacos · S. Miguel · Macacos · Viana · Ponta de Pedras · BELÉM · Benevides · Barcarena · Bujaru · Sta. Maria do Pará · Bonito · Ourém · Capanema · Bragança · Vizeu

Serra Paranaquara · Almeirim · Gurupá · I. da Laguna · São Sebastião da Boa Vista · Curralinho · Abaetetuba · S. Domingos do Capim · S. Miguel do Guama · Irituia · Colônia Osório
Prainha · I. do Aquiqui · Porto do Moz · Melgaço · São João · Portel · Bagre · Limoeiro de Ajuru · Maiauatá · Acará · Concordia do Pará · Vicente Franco · Boa Nova
Monte Alegre · Rio Amazonas · Baía do Florestal de Caxiuanã · Boa Vista · Caxiuaná · Marcelo · Aru · Igarapé Mirim · Santana · Curupaiti · Vila Aurora · Maracaçumé
Hidrelétrica Curuá-Una · Santa Cruz · Pacoval · São Pedro · Acamaitá · Joana Coeli · Cametá · Carapajó · Cairari · Tomé-Açu · S. Francisco · Vila Ipixuna

Pará

Aricaria · Senador José Porfírio · Parada · Prenha · São José · Mocajuba · Baião · I. do Bacuri · S. Bento · Paragominas · Serra do Tiracambu
Vitoria · Belo Monte do Pontal · Cach. Vira-e-Volta · Bailique · Cach. Uruaru
Altamira · Paquiçama · Pedra · Novo Acordo · Transamazon Highway · Caima · Trans-Amazon Highway · BR 230 · 935 · Goianésia do Pará · PA 150 · Tucuruí · Represa de Tucuruí

67

Área Indígena Arara · Á. I. Kararaô · R. Xingu · Á. I. · Área Guariba · Indígena Jatobá · Araweté · Indígena Bacajá · Represa de Tucuruí · MARABÁ · Araparí · S. João do Araguaia · Apinajés · Araguatins · IMPERATRIZ · Amarante do Maranhão

Bonfim · Cach. São Francisco · Trav. da Onça · José Rodrigues · Eldorado · Curionópolis · Paranapebas · Carajas · Sta. Isabel do Araguaia · S. Geraldo do Araguaia · Tocantinópolis · Estreito · Grajaú

Bomsucesso · São Felix do Xingu · Ourilândia · Xinguara · Garimpinho · Muricilândia · Babaçulândia · Carolina · Riachão · Balsas

Posto Cocraimore · Gradaús · Faz. Cumaru · Redenção · Jenipapo · Campo Alegre · ARAGUAÍNA · Filadélfia · Goiatins

Kayapó · Faz. Rio Dourado · Roça Tapirapé · Conceição do Araguaia · Colinas · Tupiratins · Itacaja

Jarina · S. José do Xingu · Porto Alegre do Norte · Ilha do Bananal · Goianorte · Colméia · Guaraí · Pedro Alonso · Palmeirante

Santa Terezin · Santa Terezinha · S. Felix do Araguaia · Parque Bananal · Paraíso do Tocantins · Palmas · Porto Nacional

Mato Grosso · do Xingu · Consul · Alô Brasil · S. Miguel · Fazenda Foz do Christalino · Barreira do Peixi · Gurupi · Peixe · Almas · Dianópolis

Tocantins

Scale 1 : 4,500,000

0 40 80 120 160 200 Kilometer
0 40 80 120 160 Statute Miles

68

PACIFIC

OCEAN

Peru Chile Trench

(Atacama Chile Trench)

LA MONTAÑA

P E R U

Cord. Vilcabamba

Cord. de Carabaya

Cord. de Vilcanota

Cord. de Huanzo

Cord. de Chilca

Cord. de Ampato

Parque Nacional Manú

Machu Picchu (2280)

CUZCO (3310)

Abancay

Sicuani (3690)

AREQUIPA

Mollendo

Moquegua

Ilo

TACNA

Arica

IQUIQUE

Pozo Almonte

C H I L E

Cord. de Lipez

-5h Greenwich Time

-4h Greenwich Time

JULIACA (3825)

PUNO (3855)

L. Titicaca

Copacabana

LA PAZ (3636)

Nev. del Illimani 6882

A L T I P L A N O

Nev. Huayna Potosi 6200

Nev. de Sajama 6520

ORURO (3704)

Salar de Coipasa

Salar de Uyuni

Gran Pampa Salada

Cord. Real de Sicasica

Cord. Oriental

COCHABAMBA (2570)

SUCRE (2790)

POTOSI (4070)

B O L I V I A

Llanos de Mojos

Y P N Isiboro Sécure

RIO BRANCO

Guayaramerin

Guajará-Mirim

Riberalta

Serra do

TRINIDAD

Cerros de Bala

Caupolican

70

Scale 1 : 4,500,000

0   40   80   120   160   200 Kilometers

0   40   80   120

50 Statute Miles

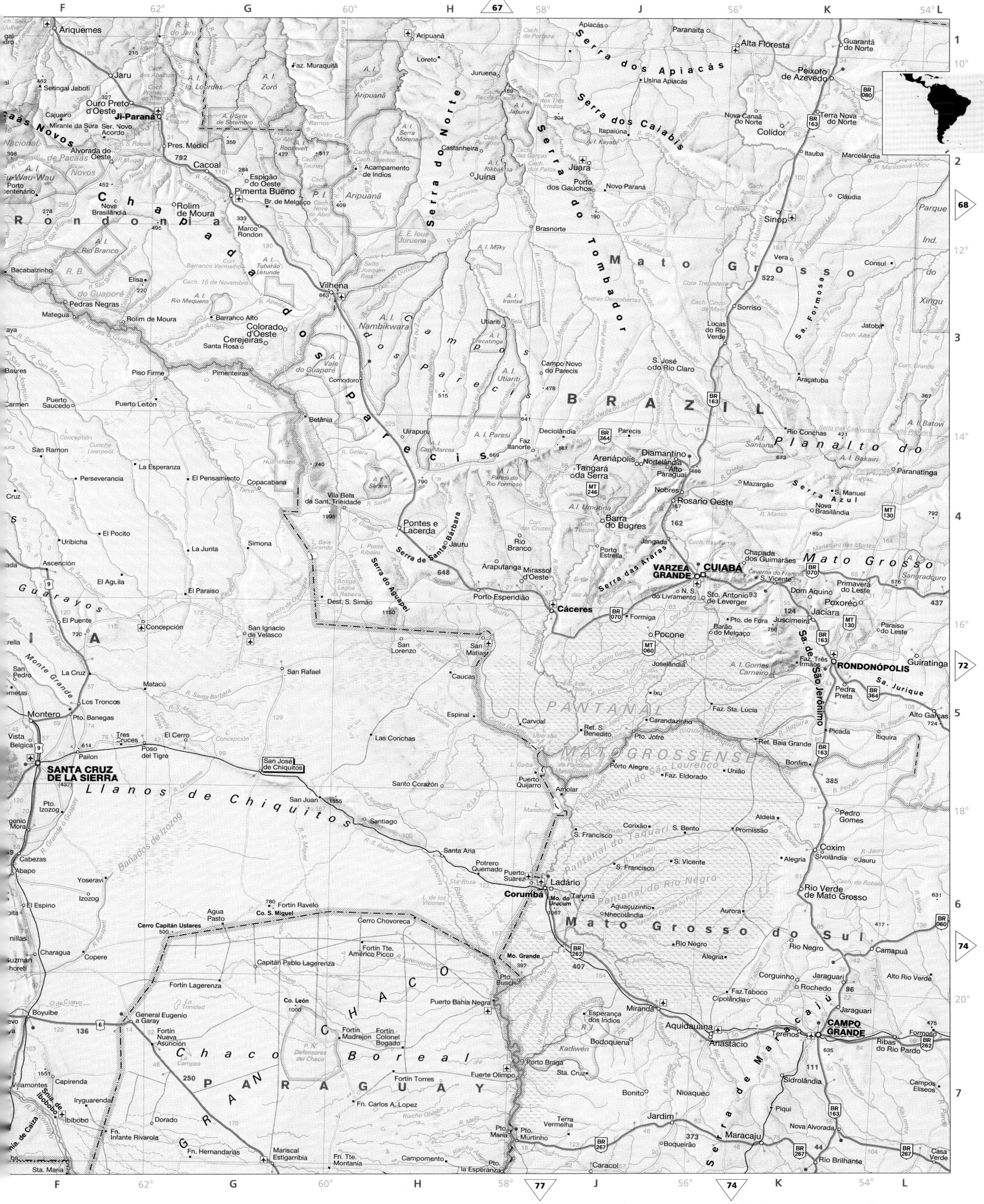

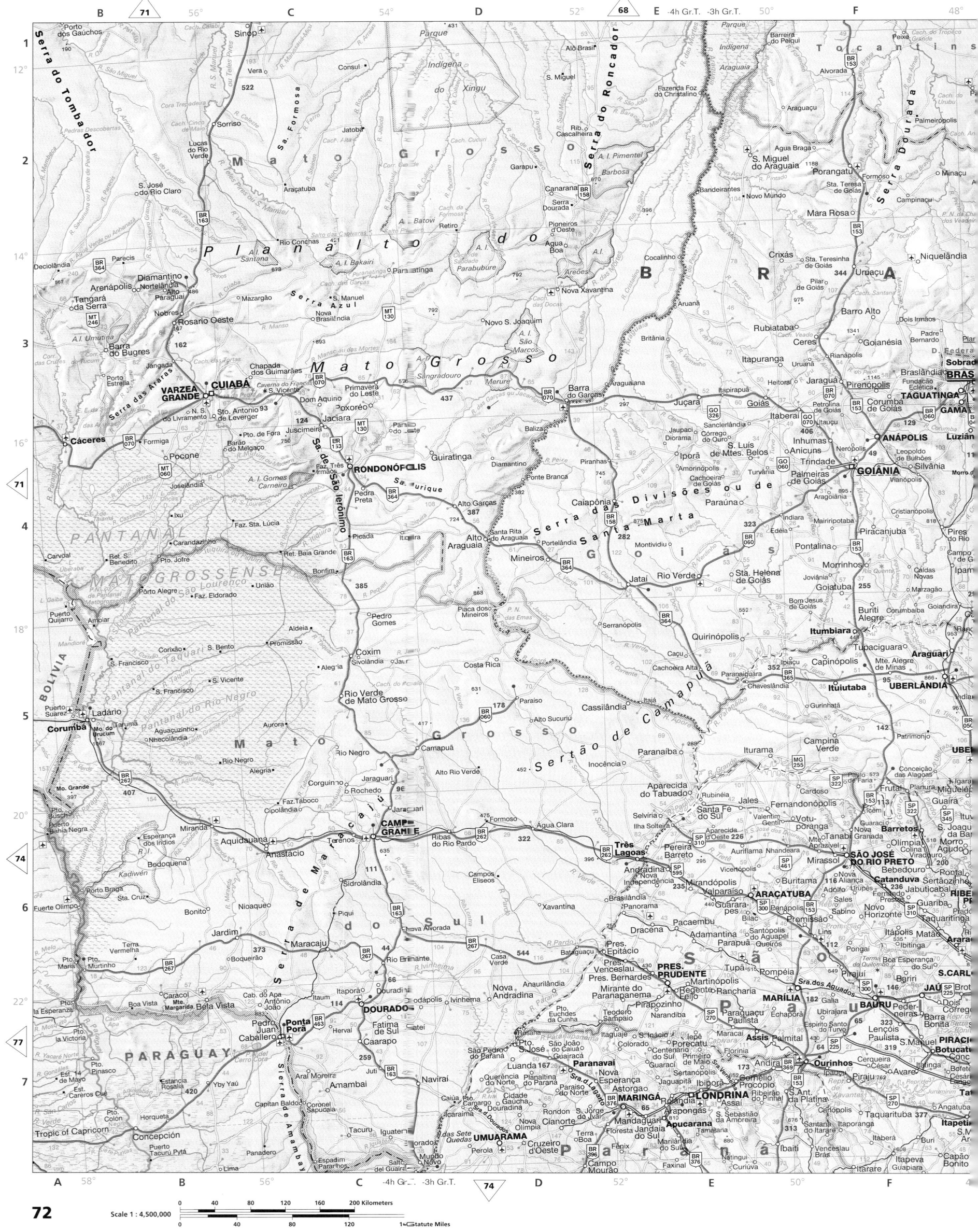

Scale 1 : 4,500,000

0   40   80   120   160   200 Kilometers

0   40   80   120

1 = Statute Miles

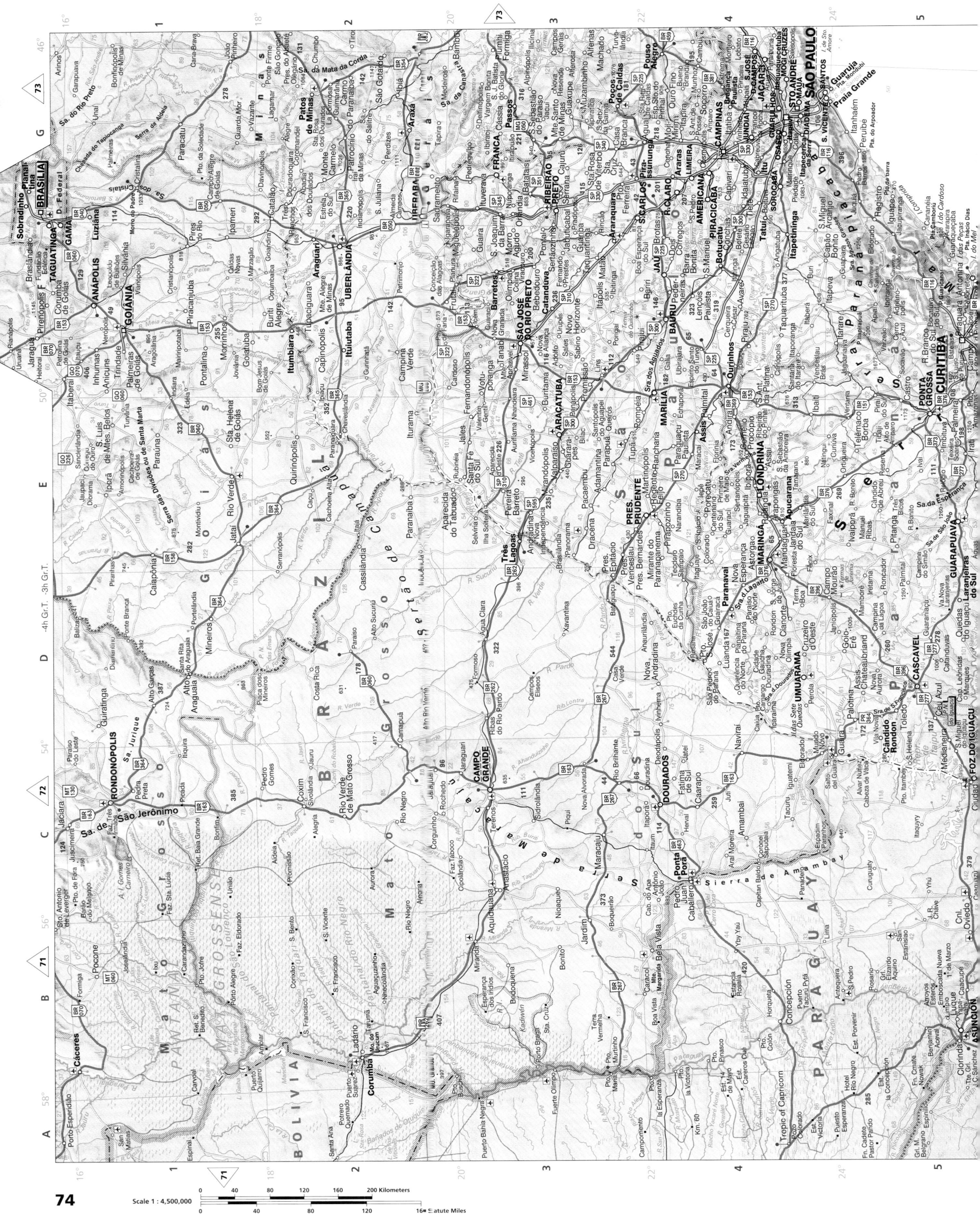

Scale 1 : 4,500,000

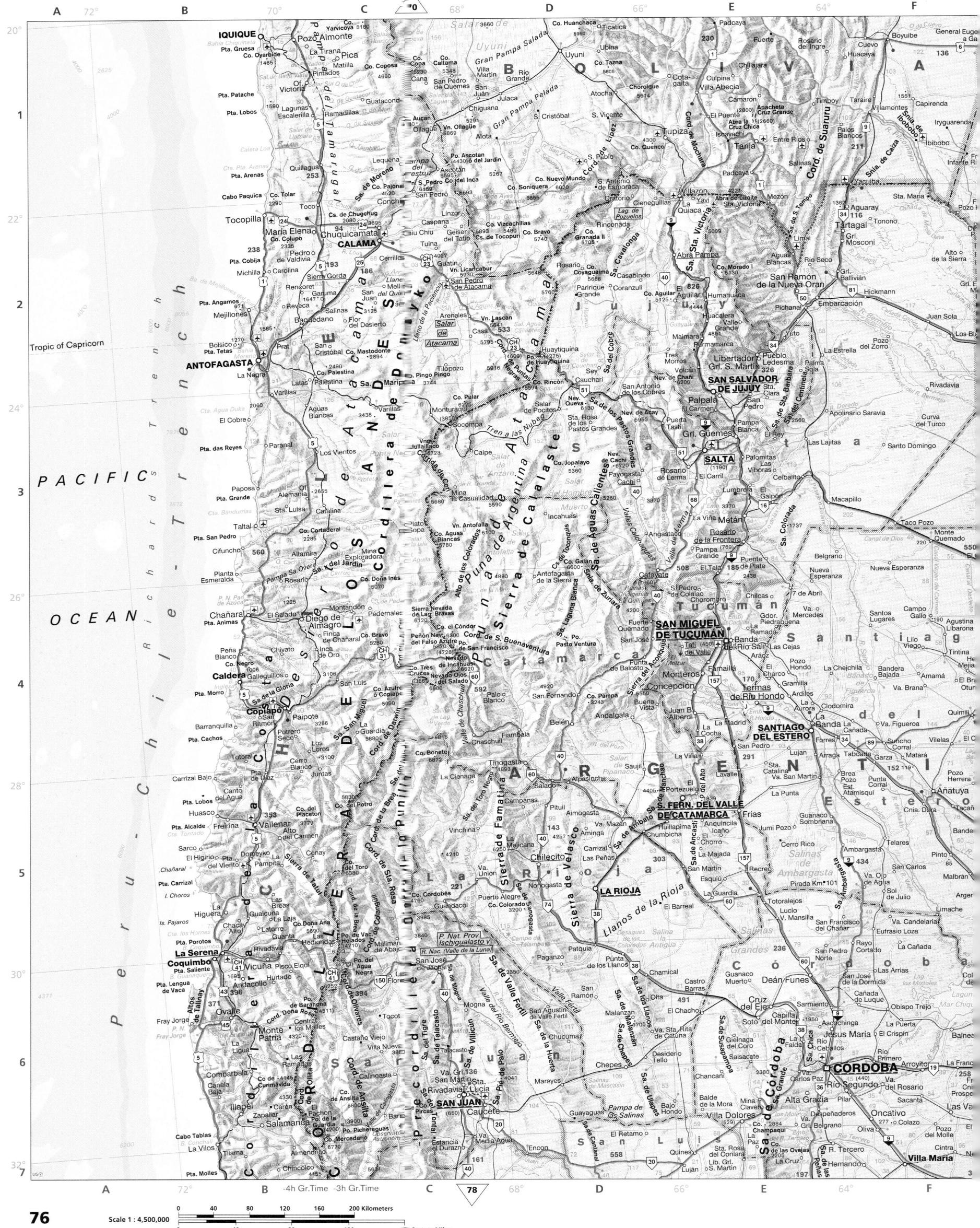

Scale 1 : 4,500,000

| 0 | 40 | 80 | 120 | 160 | 200 Kilometers |

| 0 | 40 | 80 | 120 | Statute Miles |

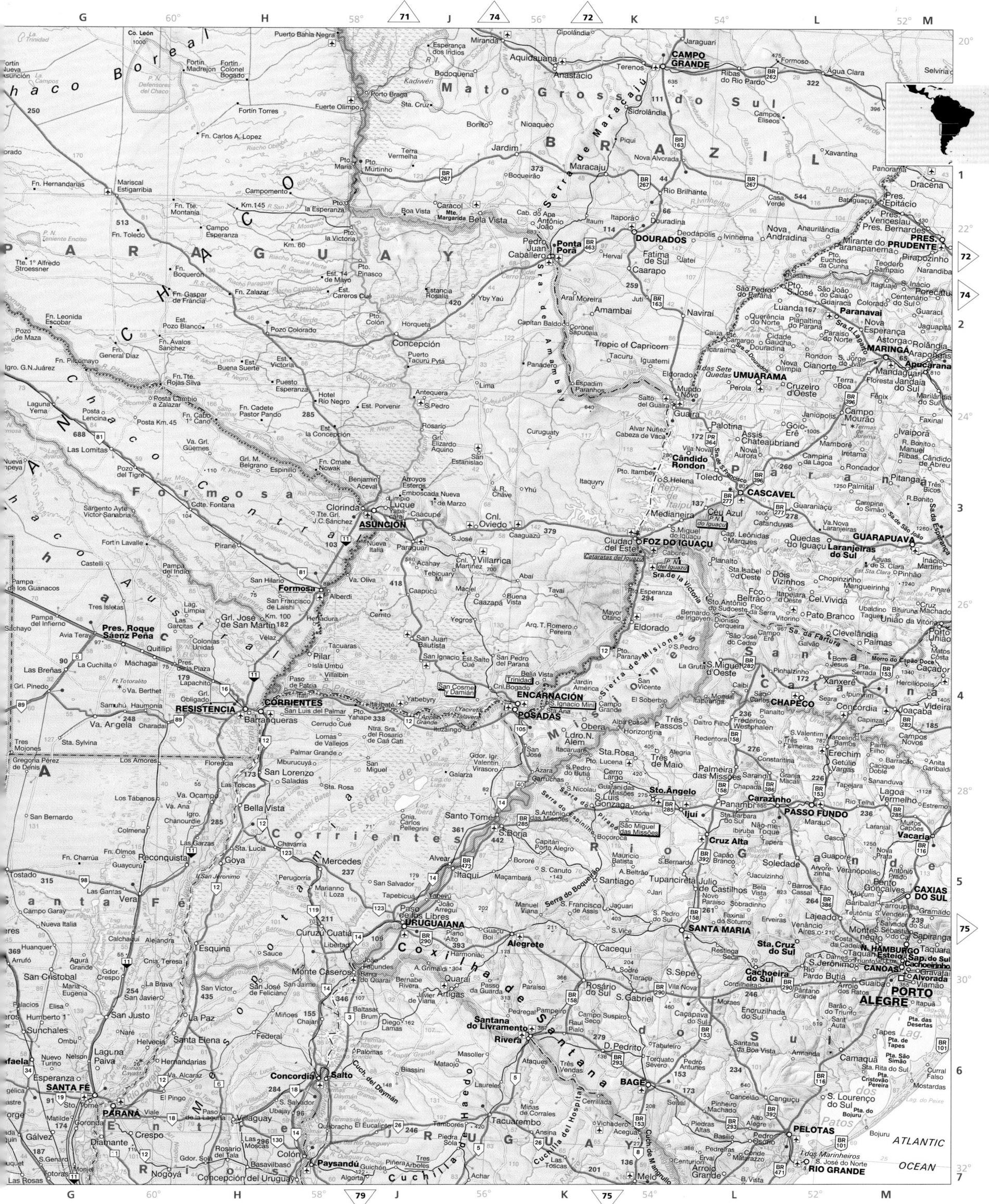

B 80° C 72° D -4h Gr.T. -3h Gr.T. 70° E 68° F 66° G

Juan Fernández Islands

PACIFIC OCEAN

Isla Alejandro Selkirk Islas Juan Fernández (Chile) S. Juan Bautista
Isla Santa Clara Isla Más a Tierra

Easter Island

PACIFIC OCEAN

Isla de Pascua (Rapa Nui) (Chile)
Hanga Roa Moai

PACIFIC OCEAN

CHILE

MENDOZA GODOY CRUZ
SANTIAGO
VIÑA DEL MAR
VALPARAÍSO
Quilpé
PUENTE ALTO
San Antonio SAN BERNARDO
Peñaflor
RANCAGUA
San Luis
Mercedes
RÍO CUARTO

San Rafael
CURICÓ
TALCA

CHILLÁN
TALCAHUANO
CONCEPCIÓN
Coronel
Los Angeles

La Pampa
Neuquén NEUQUÉN
Grl. Roca
Cipolletti
Villa Regina
Choele Choel

TEMUCO
VALDIVIA
OSORNO
San Carlos de Bariloche
PTO. MONTT

Río Negro
Patagonia
Chubut

Ancud
Castro
Chiloé
Esquel
Trevelin
Trelew
Rawson

Scale 1 : 4,500,000
0 40 80 120 160 200 Kilometers
0 40 80 120 160 Statute Miles

78

Falkland Islands

South Georgia

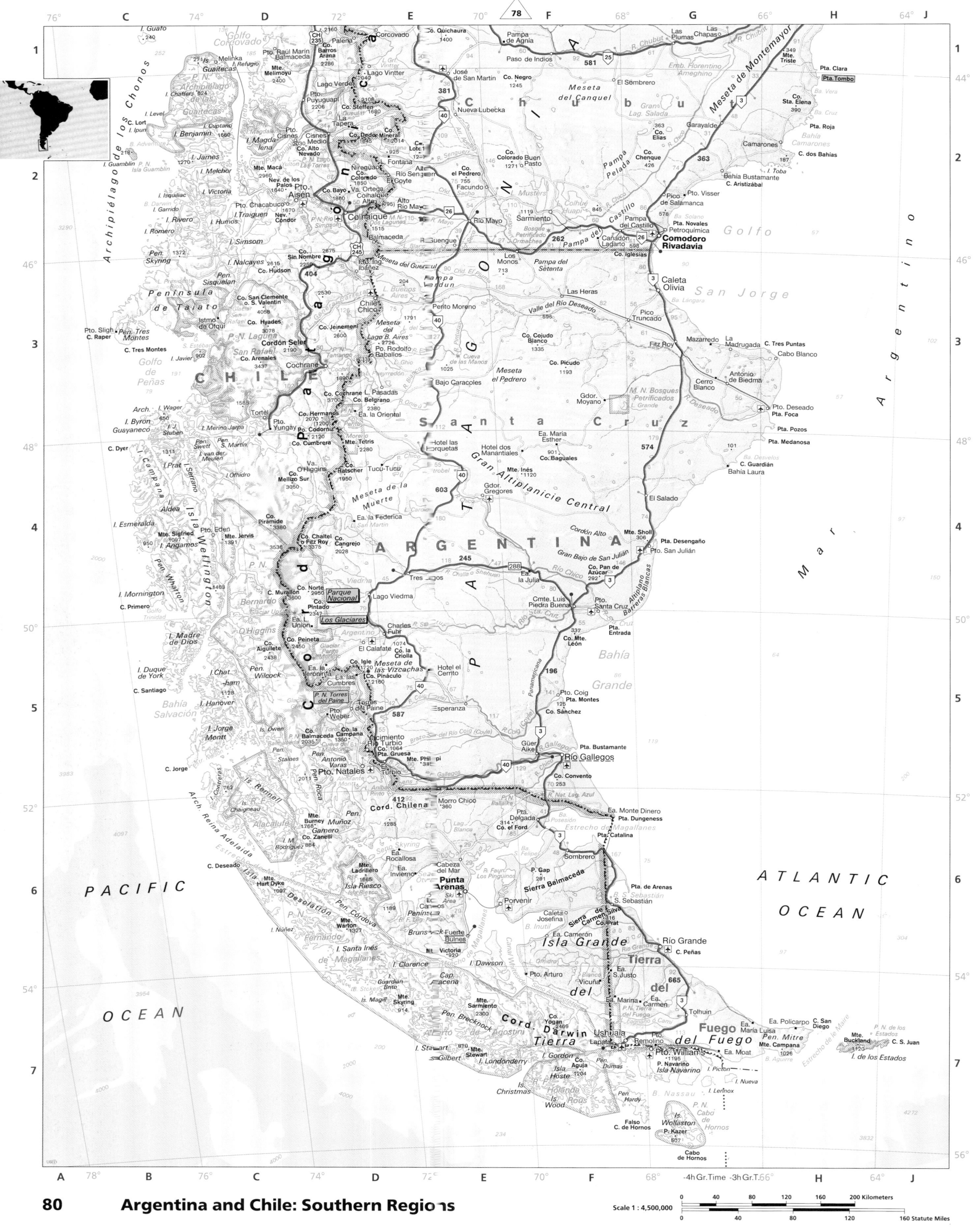

Scale 1 : 4,500,000

PACIFIC OCEAN

ATLANTIC OCEAN

Europe – a continent with border troubles

With an area of 4,054,050 sq. miles (10.5 million sq. km), Europe is the fourth largest continent. From the point of view of physical geography it merely represents a peninsula of Eurasia, jutting out to the west. Europe and Asia have the least well defined delimitation among all continents. The traditional borderline runs along the Ural Mountains the Ural River, the Caspian Sea, the northern edge of the Caucasus, the Black Sea, the Bosporus and the Aegean Sea. In Russia, which is part European and part Asian, this demarcation line is meaningless. A belt of high mountains in which the Alps are the highest range separates the South from the remainder of the continent. Adjacent to the North is the European

An aid to international trade: "New Map of Europe" including "the most noteworthy products and the foremost trading sites." J. Adams made this copperplate engraving in 1787.

medium-height mountainscape followed by a strip of lowlands that widens to the East. The British Isles are, geologically speaking, also part of the northern mountain areas. Its many islands and peninsulas interlace the continent with the Atlantic Ocean and the European Mediterranean Sea. Europe determined the destiny of the world some years into the twentieth century: The scientific research of the planet, the industrial revolution, great inventions and discoveries, but also colonization and thus the transmission of European influences to other parts of the world had their origins here.

Svalbard · Novaya Zemlya
p. 84 – 85

Scandinavia (Inset: Iceland)
p. 86 – 87

Finland · Northern Ural Mountains
p. 88 – 89

Western Europe
p. 90 – 91

Central Europe
p. 92 – 93

Eastern Europe
p. 94 – 95

Ural Mountains
p. 96 – 97

Southwestern Europe
p. 98 – 99

Southern Europe
p. 100 – 101

Southeastern Europe
p. 102 – 103

Caucasus
p. 104

Top coordinate/column markers:
A 0° B 2° C 4° D 6° E 8° F 10° G 2° H 14° J 16° K 18° L 20° M 22° N 24° O 26° P 28° Q 30° R 32° S 34° T 36° U 38° V 40° W 42°

Left latitude markers: 78° 76° 74° 72° 70° 68°

ARCTIC

Greenwich Time · 1h Greenwich Time

+1h Greenwich Time   +3h Gr. Time   +4h Greenwich Time

Greenland Sea

Danskøya
Sjubre-banken
Verlegen-huken
Fuglehuken
Grampianfjella
Prins Karls-land
Ny Ålesund
Forland
Daudmannsodden
Isfjord Radio
Barentsburg
Lågneset
Bellsund
Wedel
Jarlsberg land
Homsundtind
Sørkapp land
Øyrlandsodden
Sørkappøya

Nordkapp
Snøtoppen
Storsteen-halvøya
Kapp Platen
Gustav V land
Nordaust-Svalbard nat-res
Gustav Adolf land
Kapp Laura
Storøya
Kvitøya (Nor.)

o. Viktorija (Rus.)

Newtontoppen 1717
Dickson land
Svea

Spitsbergen

Svalbard (Norway)

Olgastretet
Erik Eriksenstretet
Svenskøya
Kongsøya
Abeløya

Kong Karls land

Haasfberget
Barentsøya
Edgøya
Stonepynten
Tjuvfjorden
Tusen-øyane
Halvmåneøya

Storfjordrena
Storfjordbanken

Hopen
Hopen Radio
370
Hopen-banken

Bjørnøya Bank

Bjørnøy Radio
Bjørnøya (Nor.) · Tunheim
Perleporten

Norwegian

B a r e n t s

Sea

Fugløy Bank
London
Lopphavet
Fugløy Bank

Kr. skjelodden
Magerøya
Nordkapp
Skarsvåg
Havøysund
Måsøy
Honningsvåg
Nordkinn-halvøya
Gamvik
Mehamn
Berlevåg
Båtsfjord

Sørøya
Hammerfest
Brevikbotn
Hasvik
Seiland
Kvalsund
Kåfjord
Porsanger-
Langnes
Rustefjelbma
Varanger-halvøya
Vadsø
Vardø

Arnøya
Skjervøy
Øksfjord
Oldfjord
Øksfjordjøkelen
Kvalsund
Ifjord

Tromsø
Kvaløya
Nord-
reisa
Sørstraumen
Alta
Cuokkarassa
Lakselv
Tana
bru
Nesseby
Hurtigrute

Balsfjord
Finnsnes
Rieppe
396
Alta
138
Rastigaissa
Jakobselv

Andenes
Harstad
Grytøya
Kvæfjord
Andselv
Setermoen
Øvergård
Masi
Karasjok
Karigasniemi
Utsjoki
Grense Jakobselv
Kirkenes
Neiden

NORWAY

Finnmarks-vidda

Kautokeino
Bidjovagge

Narvik
Ballangen
Abisko
Kaaresuvanto
Enontekiö
Kaamanen
Inari
Menesjø
Nautsi
Nellim
Nyrud

p-ov. Rybačij
mys Cypnavolok
d'Ejna
Linahamari
Pečenga
Nikel
Zapoljarnyj
Urgguba
Prirečnyj
o. Kil'din
Poljarnyj
Murmansk

SWEDEN

Kebnekaise
Nikkaluokta

FINLAND

RUSSIA

Murmanskoye Rise
North Kani Bank

Kiruna

+1h Gr. Time   86   +2h Gr. Time   +3h Gr. Time   +3h Gr. Time   +5h Gr

K 18° L 20° M N 24° O P 28° Q +3h Gr. Time R 32° S 34° T 36° U 38° V 40°

84

Scale 1 : 4,500,000

0 40 80 120 160 200 Kilometers
0 40 80 120 160 Statute Miles

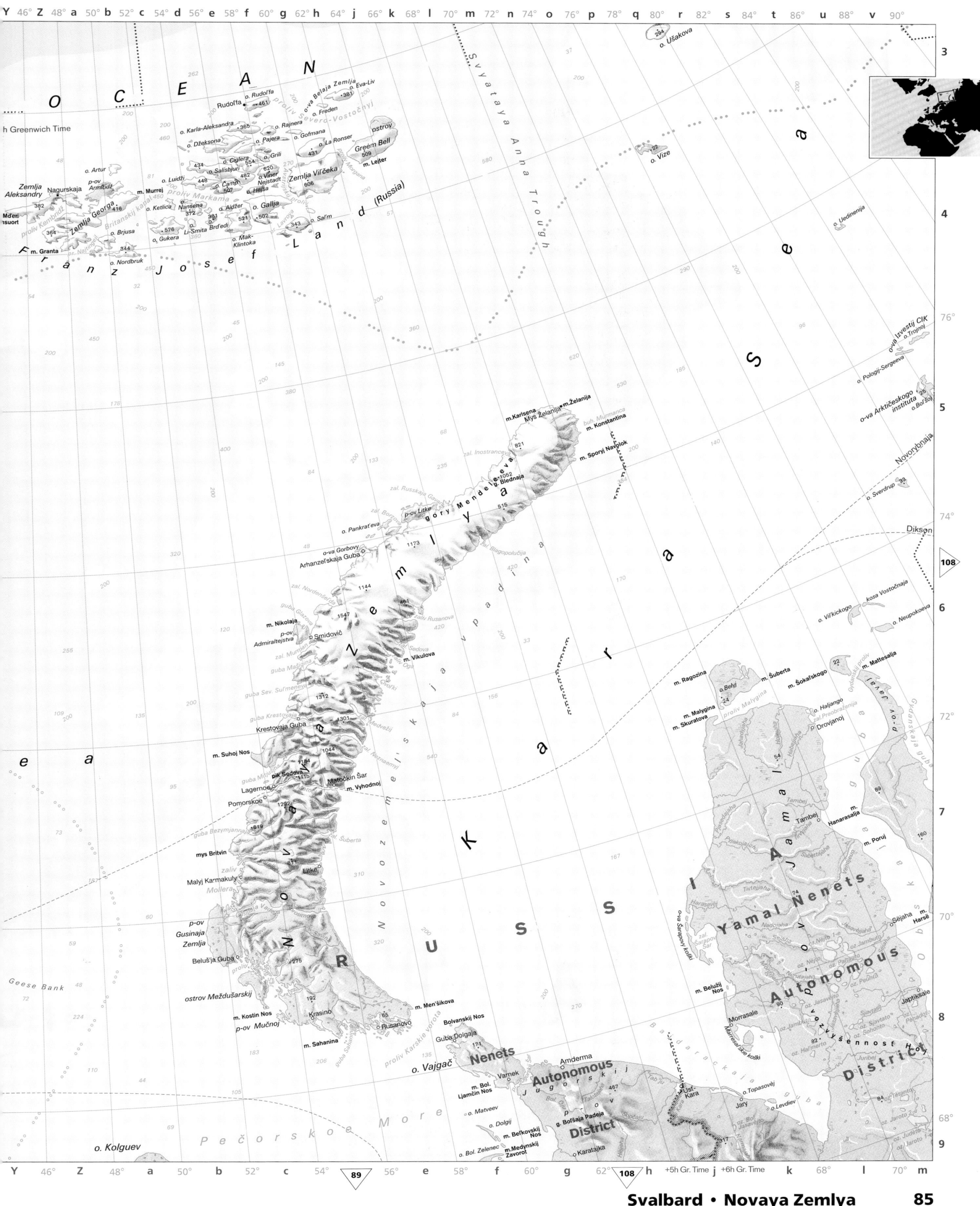

O C E A N

h Greenwich Time

o. Rudolfa
Rudolfa · 461
Eva-Liv
o. Karla-Aleksandra · 365 · 381
o. Džeksona
o. Pajera
o. Rajnera
Gofmana
o. La Ronser
Green Bell
ostrov
509
m. Lejter
o. Ciglera · 554 · Grili
o. Salisbjun
o. Luidži · 448 · 482 · Viner Nejstadt
Zemlja Vil'čeka
606
o. Artur
p-ov Armitidž
m. Murrej
proliv Markama
· Camp · 372
Nansena
Zemlja
Aleksandry
Nagurskaja
Zemlja Georga
416
o. Ketlica
o. Aidžer
o. Gallja
Mdeři
nsuort
364
382
o. Brjusa
o. Gukera · 576
Li-Smita Brd'edi
521 · 502 · Sal'm
m. Franta
344
o. Nordbruk
343 · Mak-Klintoka

F r a n z   J o s e f   L a n d   (Russia)

S v a t a y a   A n n a   T r o u g h

o. Ušakova

o. Vize

o. Uedinenija

o-va Izvestij CIK
o. Trojnoj

Novorybnaja

Dikson

m.Karlsena
Mys Želanija m.Želanija
m. Konstantina
821
g. Bednaja
gory Mendeleeva
515
o-va Gorbovy
Arhangel'skaja Guba
1173
1144
1547
m. Nikolaja
p-ov Admiraltejstva
o. Smidovič
m. Vikulova
1512
4301
Krestovaja Guba
m. Suhoj Nos
1044
pik Sedova
Matočkin Šar
Lagernoe
m. Vyhodnoj
Pomorskoe
1292
mys Britvin
Malyj Karmakuly
Litke
Mollera
p-ov Gusinaja Zemlja
Beluš'ja Guba
275
ostrov Meždušarskij
m. Kostin Nos
p-ov Mučnoj
Krasino
m. Sahanina
o. Vajgač
m. Men'šikova
Rusanovo
Bolvanskij Nos
Guba Dolgaja

m. Sporyj Navolok

o. Sverdrup

o. Vil'kickogo
kosa Vostočnaja
o. Neupokoeva

m. Mattesalja
m. Ragozina
o. Belyj
m. Šuberta
m. Šokal'skogo
m. Malygina
zal. Preobraženija
o. Haljango
m. Skuratova
o. Drovjanoj

Y A M A L
Yamal Nenets

Autonomous

District

R   U   S   S   I   A

Nenets
Autonomous
Amderma
p-ov Jugorskij
Ust'-Kara
District
Jary

Varnek
m. Bol. Ljamčin Nos
o. Matveev
o. Dolgij
m. Bel'kovskij Nos
g. Bol'šaja Padeja
o. Bol. Zelenec
m. Medynskij Zavorot
Karatajka

o. Kolguev

Geese Bank

Pečorskoe More

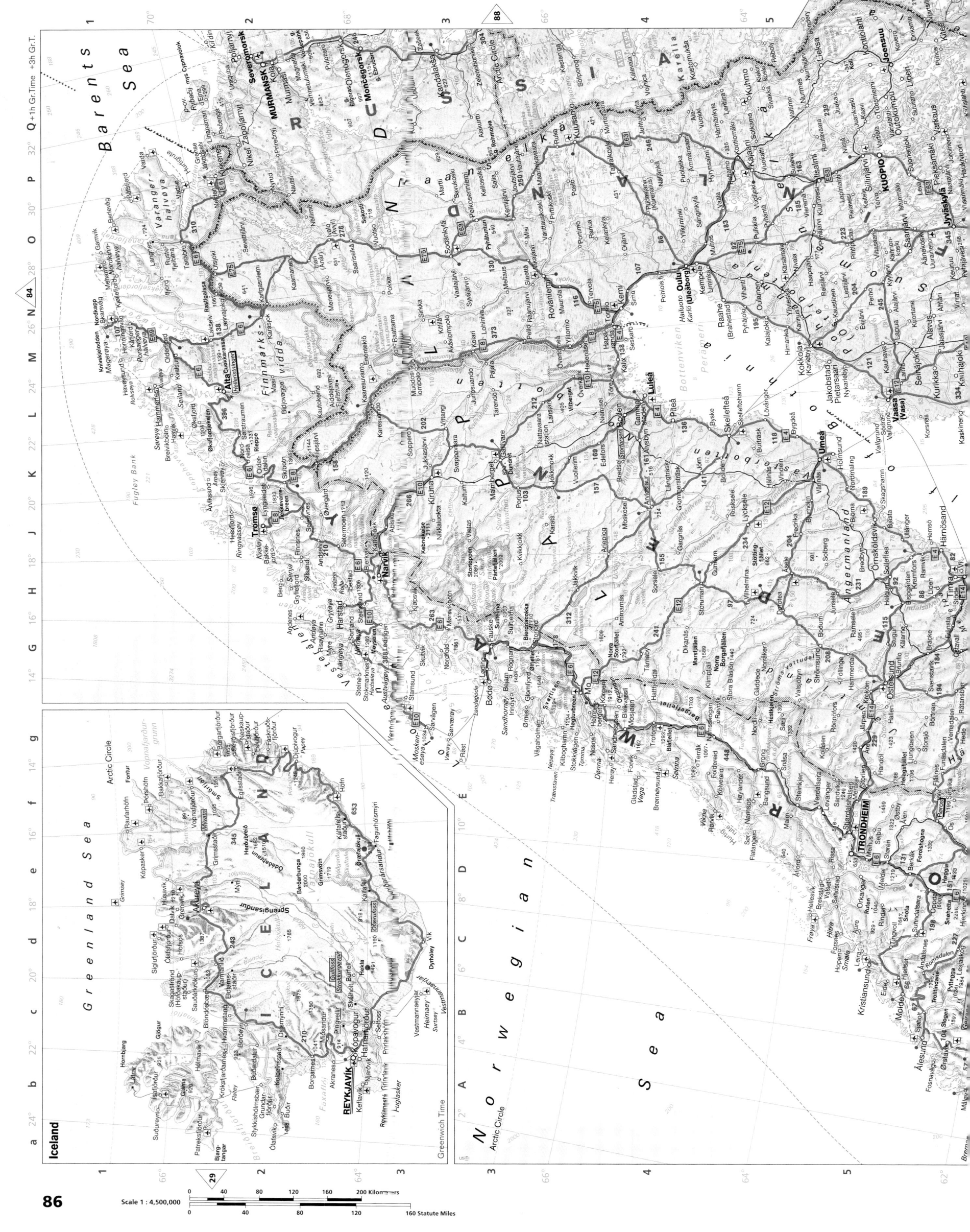

Iceland

Scale 1 : 4,500,000

0 40 80 120 160 200 Kilometers
0 40 80 120 160 Statute Miles

Norwegian Sea

B a r e

Murmanskoye Rise

N O R W A Y

S W E D E N

L A P P L A N D

F I N L A N D

K a r e l i a

Kola Peninsula

Tromsø
Narvik
Bodø
Mo i Rana
Harstad
Alta
Hammerfest
Nordkapp
Kirkenes
Nikel
MURMANSK
Severomorsk
Poljarnyj
Olenegorsk
Mončegorsk
Apatity
Kirovsk
Kandalakša
Kiruna
Gällivare
Rovaniemi
Kemijärvi
Kuusamo
Oulu (Uleåborg)
Raahe (Brahestad)
Luleå
Piteå
Skellefteå
Umeå
Örnsköldsvik
Härnösand
Sundsvall
Vaasa (Vasa)
Kokkola (Karleby)
Kajaani
Kuhmo
Belomorsk
Kem'
Kuopio
Jyväskylä
Joensuu
Tampere
Pori
Rauma
Hämeenlinna
Lahti
Mikkeli
Lappeenranta
Imatra
Savonlinna
Sortavala
PETROZAVODSK
Kondopoga
Turku / Åbo
Naantali
Salo
Lohja
ESPOO / ESBO
VANTAA
HELSINKI / HELSINGFORS
Kotka
Hamina
Vyborg
Svetogorsk
Priozersk
Kamennogorsk
Ladožskoe ozero
Onežskoe ozero
(ST. PETERSBURG) S.-PETERBURG
Kronstadt
Sosnovyj Bor
Petrodvorec
Puškin
Pavlovsk
KOLPINO
Gatčina
Slisselburg
Vsevoložsk
Lodejnoe Pole
Olonec
Vytegra
Pudož
Tihvin
Narva
Ivangorod
Kingisepp
Kohtla-Järve
Sillamäe
TALLINN
ESTONIA
Maardu
Haapsalu
Hiiumaa s.
Åland (Ahvenanmaa)
Mariehamn (Maarianhamina)
Gulf of Finland
Baltic Sea
Bottenhavet
Bottenviken
Perämeri
Selkämeri
G u l f   o f   B o t h n i a
Arctic Circle
Varanger-halvøya
Finnmarksvidda
Vesterålen

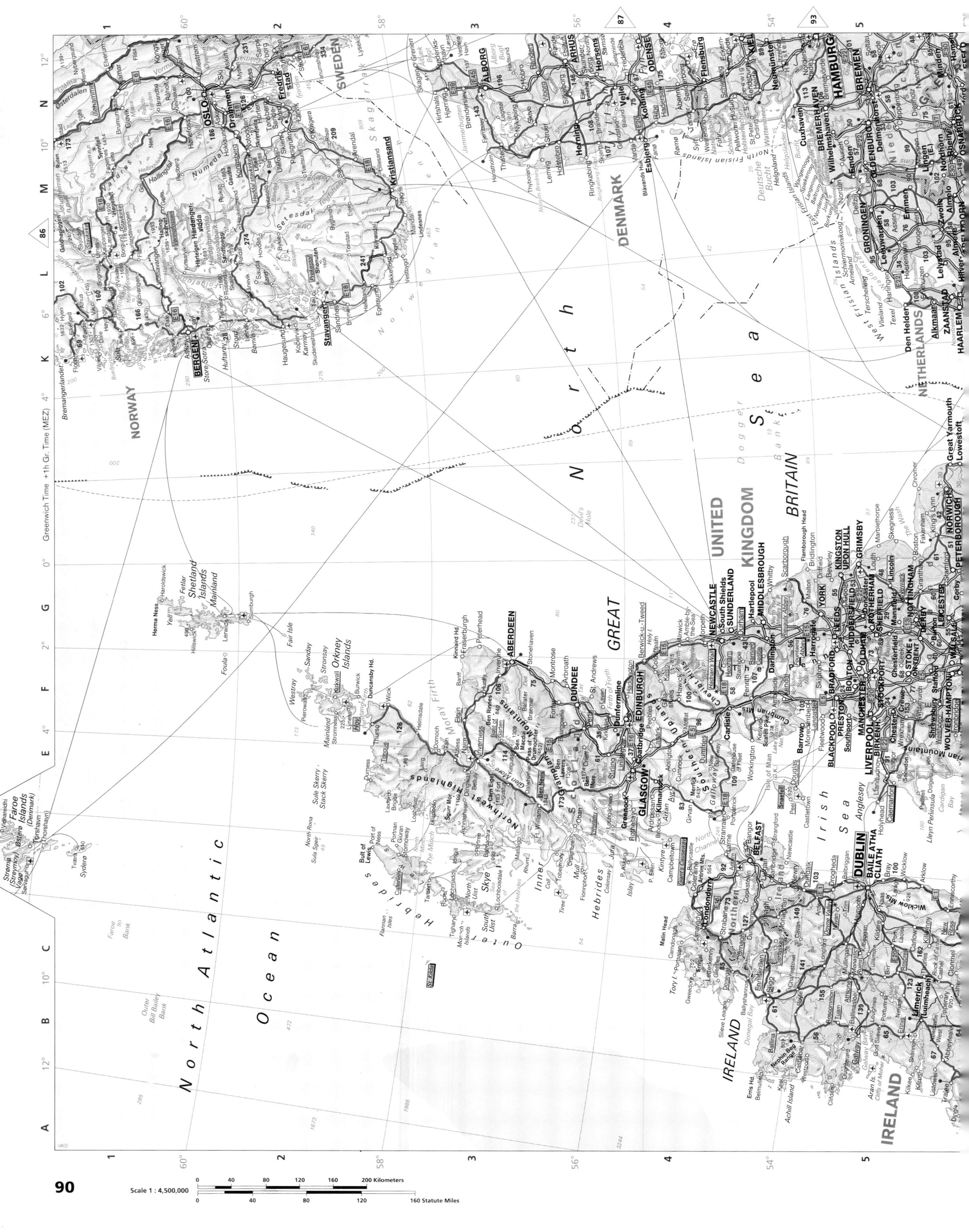

Scale 1 : 4,500,000

0   40   80   120   160   200 Kilometers

0   40   80   120   160 Statute Miles

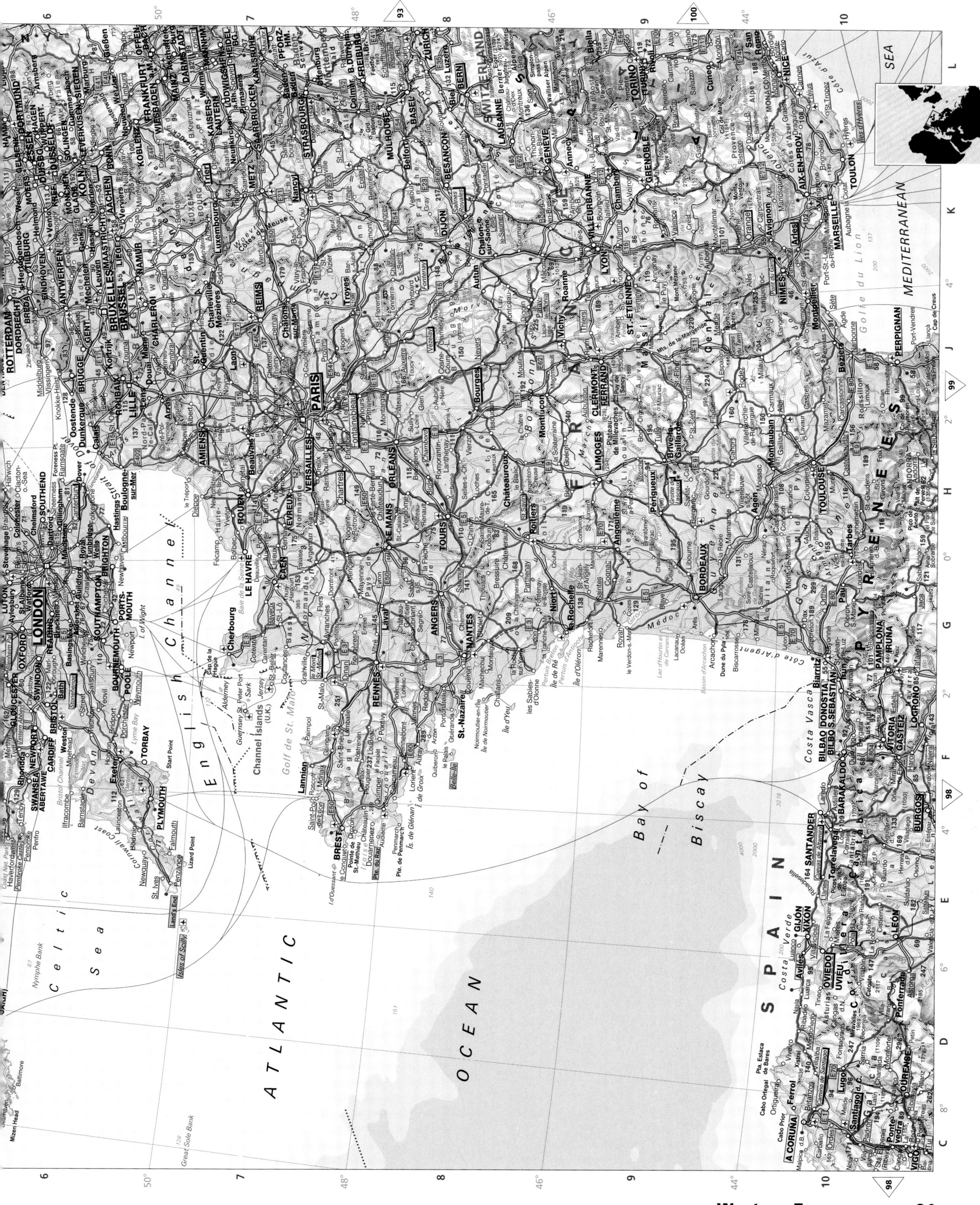

Scale 1 : 4,500,000

0   40   80   120   160   200 Kilometers

0   40   80   120   160 Statute Miles

+6h Gr. Time   +5h Gr. Time

Scale 1 : 4,500,000

0   40   80   120   160   200 Kilometers

0   40   80   120

50 Statute Miles

Scale 1 : 4,500,000

Scale 1 : 4,500,000

0   40   80   120   160   200 Kilome

0   40   80   120   160 Statute Miles

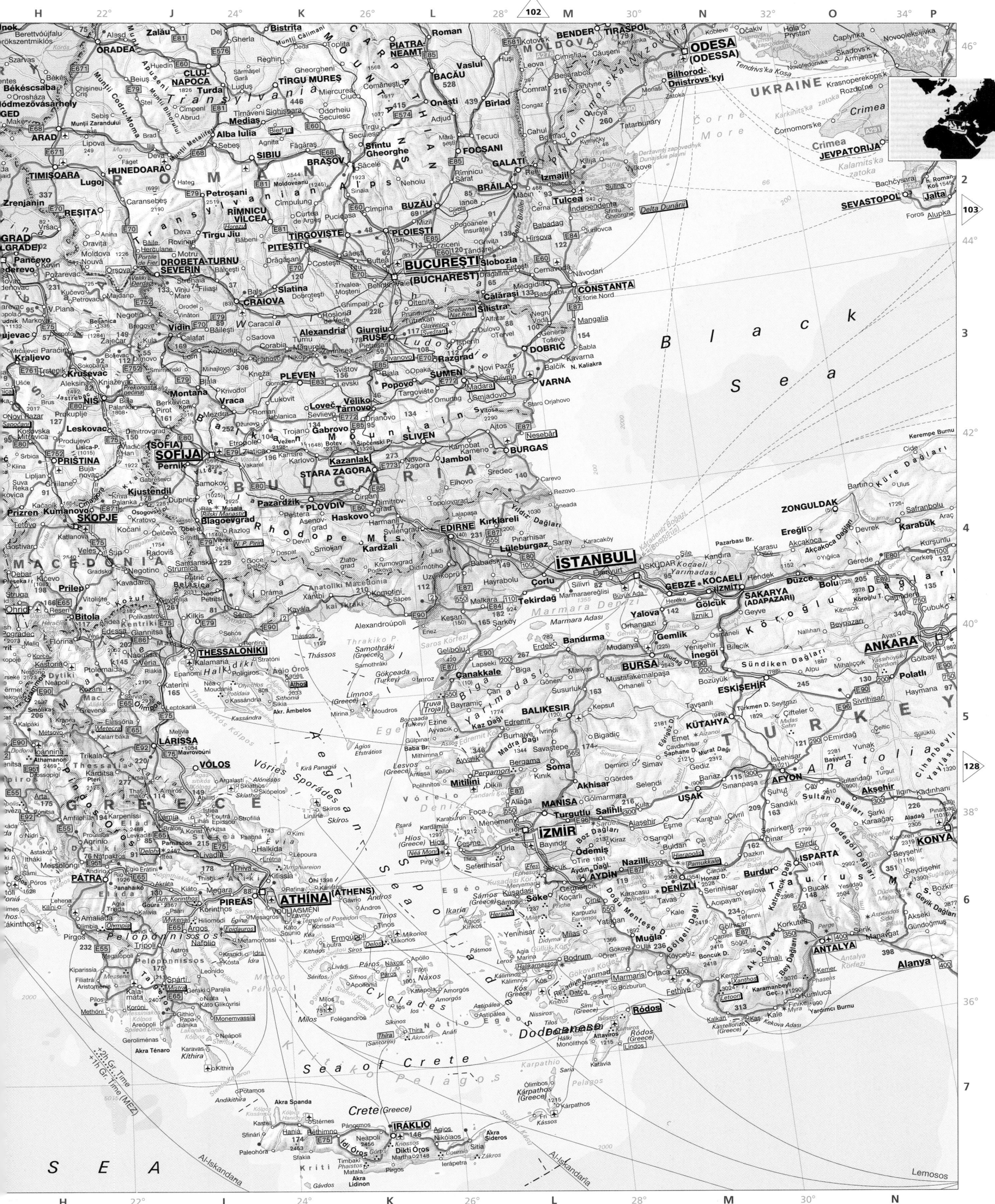

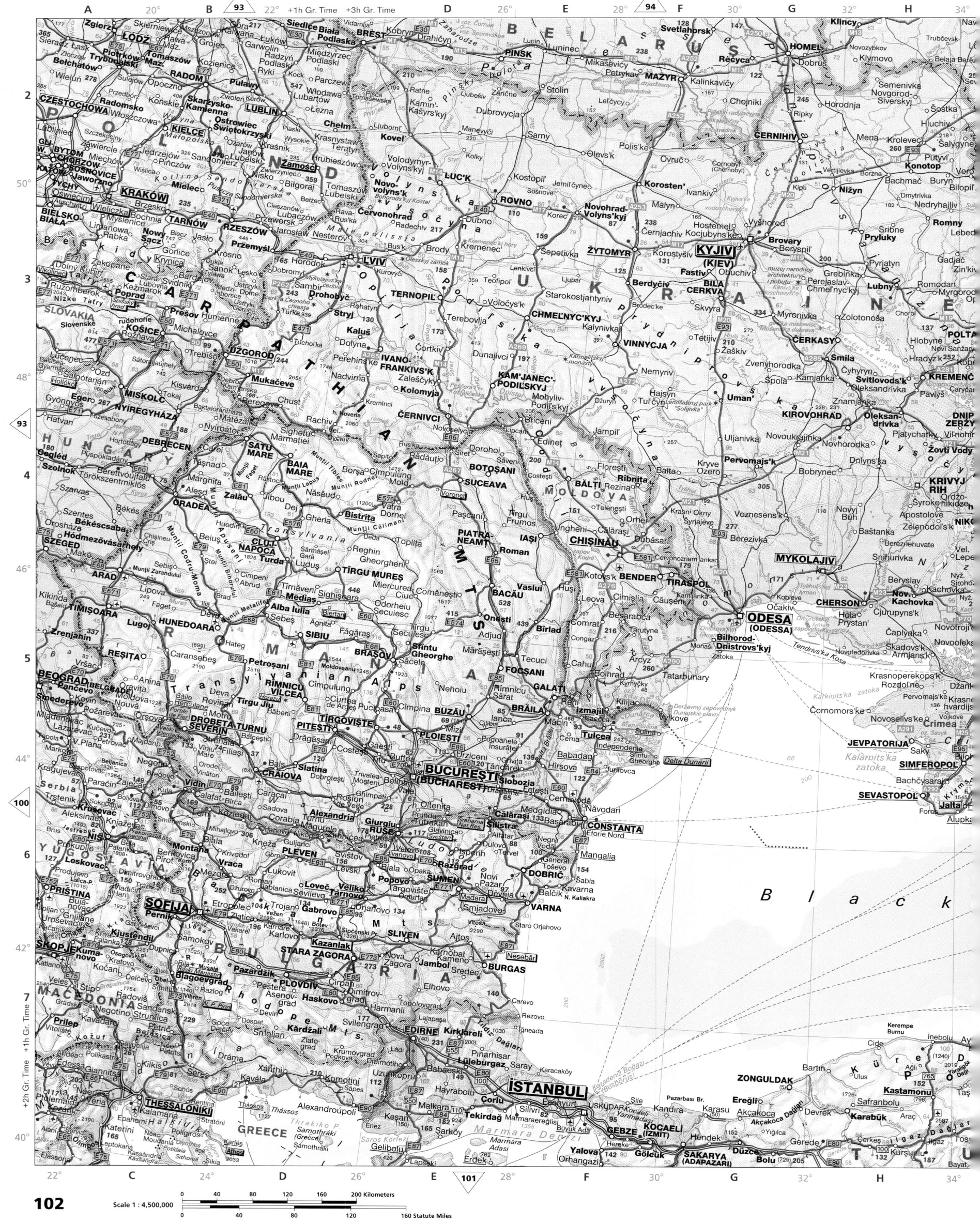

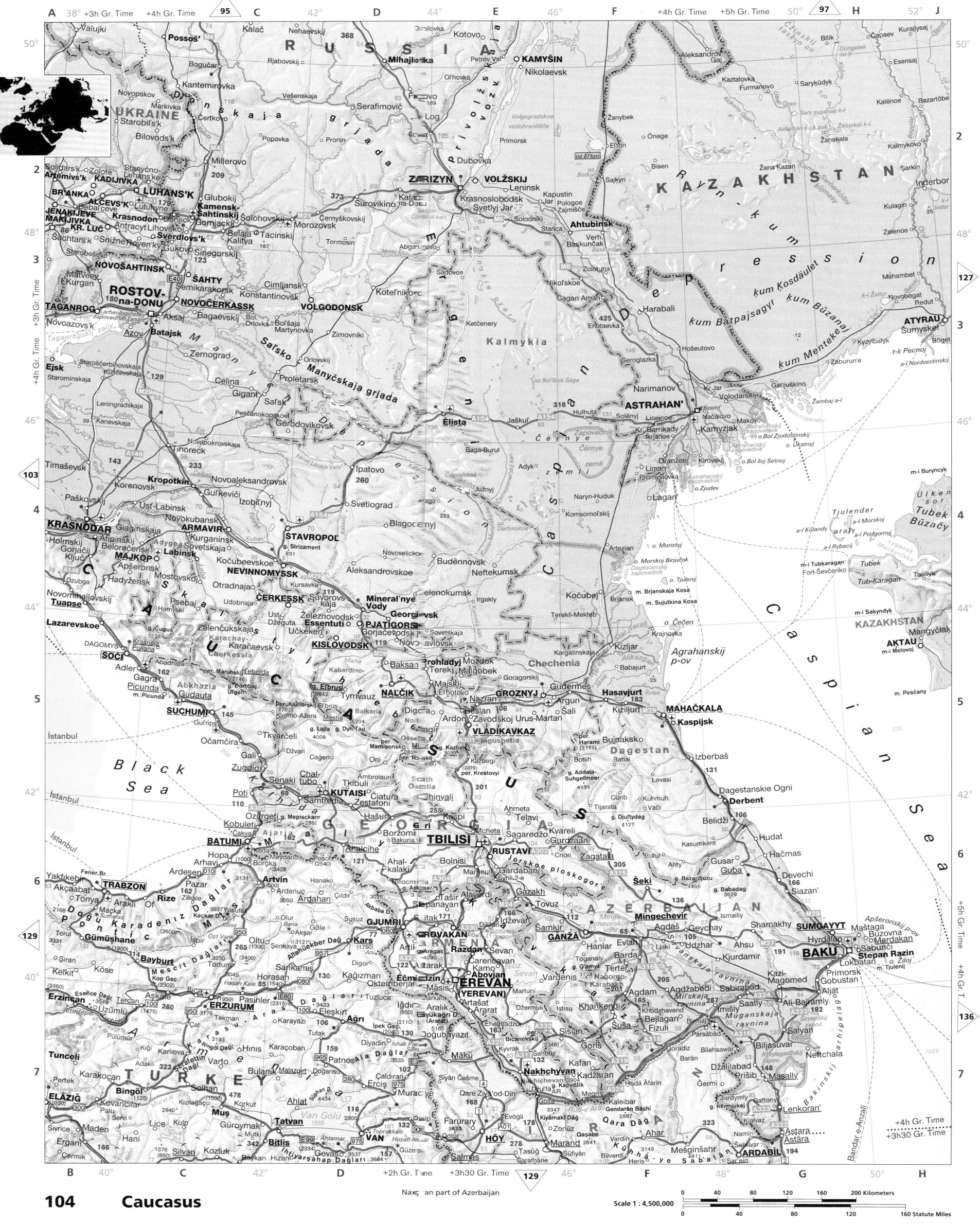

Nax... an part of Azerbaijan

Scale 1 : 4,500,000

0   40   80   120   160   200 Kilometers

0   40   80   120   160 Statute Miles

Asia – continent of contrasts

This 17,142,840 square mile (4.4 million sq. km) continent, the largest in the world, incorporates all climatic and vegetation zones from the polar to the tropical region. The major landscapes of Europe continue in Asia to the East: in the North, the western Siberian lowlands, joined by the central Siberian ranges and the eastern Siberian mountains; farther South, the mountain chains converging on the node of Ararat, at the Hindu Kush and in Indochina, encircling several plateaus, including the Tibetan highlands, the highest such feature on Earth at 14,764 feet (4,500 m). South of the mountain chains lie the plateaus of Arabia and the Indian subcontinent. Toward the Pacific the continent is delimited by garlands of islands and by sea trenches.

Asia in a copperplate engraving: This detailed map with boundaries and relief features in color was drawn by imperial cartographer Johann Baptist Homann in Nuremberg (circa 1700).

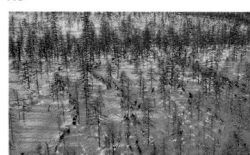

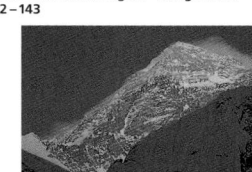

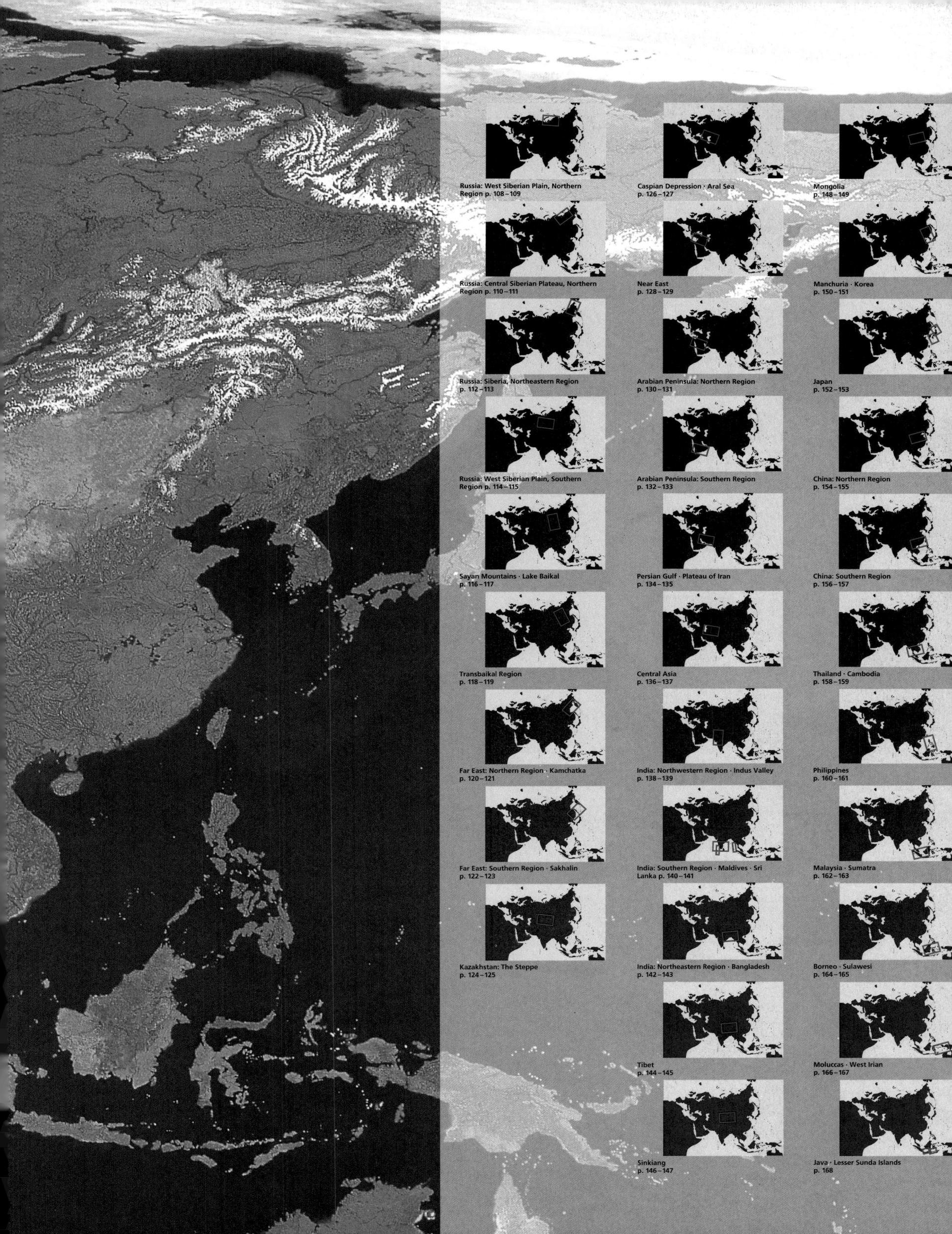

Russia: West Siberian Plain, Northern
Region p. 108–109

Caspian Depression · Aral Sea
p. 126–127

Mongolia
p. 148–149

Russia: Central Siberian Plateau, Northern
Region p. 110–111

Near East
p. 128–129

Manchuria · Korea
p. 150–151

Russia: Siberia, Northeastern Region
p. 112–113

Arabian Peninsula: Northern Region
p. 130–131

Japan
p. 152–153

Russia: West Siberian Plain, Southern
Region p. 114–115

Arabian Peninsula: Southern Region
p. 132–133

China: Northern Region
p. 154–155

Sayan Mountains · Lake Baikal
p. 116–117

Persian Gulf · Plateau of Iran
p. 134–135

China: Southern Region
p. 156–157

Transbaikal Region
p. 118–119

Central Asia
p. 136–137

Thailand · Cambodia
p. 158–159

Far East: Northern Region · Kamchatka
p. 120–121

India: Northwestern Region · Indus Valley
p. 138–139

Philippines
p. 160–161

Far East: Southern Region · Sakhalin
p. 122–123

India: Southern Region · Maldives · Sri
Lanka p. 140–141

Malaysia · Sumatra
p. 162–163

Kazakhstan: The Steppe
p. 124–125

India: Northeastern Region · Bangladesh
p. 142–143

Borneo · Sulawesi
p. 164–165

Tibet
p. 144–145

Moluccas · West Irian
p. 166–167

Sinkiang
p. 146–147

Java · Lesser Sunda Islands
p. 168

Inset map (top left) — Severnaya Zemlya

Z a b m. Arktičeskij
94° a b c 100° d 102° e 104° f 106° g

Y

Laptev Sea

m. Kujbyševa
m. Litvinova
m. Frunze

lednik Akademii Nauk
781
o. Komsomolec

m. Rozy Ljuksemburg

382
o. Pioner
Krupskoj
Arhipelag Sedov

781
lednik Rusanova
m. Berga

m. Peščanyj

Severnaya Zemlya

lednik Vavilova
o. Oktjabr'skoj Revoljucii
lednik Universitetskij
800
725
935
m. Cingera
mys Morozova

m. Ðlinnyj
m. Mednyj

m. Sverdlova
o-va Krasnoflotskie
o. Boľ ševik

Kara Sea

o. Voronina
m. Obryvistyj
258
m. Vajgač

m. Tajmyra

+8h Gr. Time

Main map

A 46° B 48° C 50° D 52° E
E 54° F 56° G 58° H 60° J 62° K 64° L 66° M 68° N 70° O 72° P 74° Q 76° R

Barents Sea

Murmansk

m. Suhoj Nos
Krestovaja Guba
1312
1301
guba Mitjušiha
1184
pik Sedova 1044
Lagernoe 1115
Pomorskoe 1292
mys Britvin 1619
Malyj Karmakuly
811
Litke

Belušja Guba
ostrov Meždušarskij
+275
m. Kostin Nos
p-ov Mučnoj
192
Krasino
183
m. Sahanina
65
Rusanovo
m. Menšikova

m. Karlsena
Mys Želanija   m. Želanija
821
o. Pankrateva
Arhanzeľskaja Guba
gory Mendeleeva
1052
g. Blednaja
m. Konstantina
m. Sporyj Navolok
1173
515
1547
Nikolaja p-ov Admiraltejstva
Smidovič
1144
461
m. Vikulova

Novaya Zemlya

Novozemeľskaja vpadina

Kara Sea

m. Ragozina
o. Belyj
o. Viľkickogo kosa Vostočnaja
m. Malygina 24
m. Skuratova m. Šuberta
proliv Malygina
m. Šokaľskogo 22
o. Neupokoeva
o. Sibir
m. Mattesalja
o. Olenij 16
o. Olenij

Arhangeľsk

Pečorskoe More

p-ov Russkij Zavorot
o-va Guljaevskie Koški
Timanskij bereg
o. Dolgij
Tobseda
o. Tenja Sedu
Malozemeľskaja tundra
Pečorskaja guba
Jušino
Čornaja

Boľvanskij Nos
Gubna Dolgaja
121
m. Bol. Ljamčin Nos Varnek
o. Matveev
o. Bol. Zelenec
Pesjakovo Varandej
m. Beľkovskij Nos
m. Medynskij Zavorot
o. Vajgač

Jugorskij
g. Borš ja Padeja 467
Amderma
Ust-Kara
Karamijka

m. Beluži Nos
Morrasale

Jamal p-ov

Tambej
Hanarasalja
Sejaha
m. Poruj
m. Harse
m. Trehbugornyj
Mys-Kamennyj kosa Kamennaja
m. Čugor
Antipajuta
Japtiksale
Tadebjajaha
Juribejskaja grjada
Gydan p-ov
Gydansk

Jary
Topasovej
o. Levdiev
Levkiev

Nenets Autonomous District

Narjan-Mar
Boľšezemeľskaja tundra
242
176
Horej-Ver
Arctic Circle
Mutnyj Materik
Kipievo
Ščeľjabož Novikbož
Usinsk
Ust-Lyža
Kožva
Pečora
Kadžerom
Konecbor
Kožym
Synja
Inta
Abaz
191
Sivomaskinskij
Elecki
hr. Obeiz
hr. Zap. Saledy
1435 Vojkar-Syninskij massiv
1137
549

Vorgašor Severnyj
Komsomoľskij
VORKUTA
1317
g. Očenyrd 1363 1345

Salehard
Labyntangi
Aksarka
Salemal
Jar-Sale
Novyj Port
Nahodka
o. Nareči
Kutopjugan
Nyda
Tazovskij

Yamal Nenets Autonomous District

Western Siberia

Scale 1 : 4,500,000

0 40 80 120 160 200 Kilometers
0 40 80 120 160 Statute Miles

108

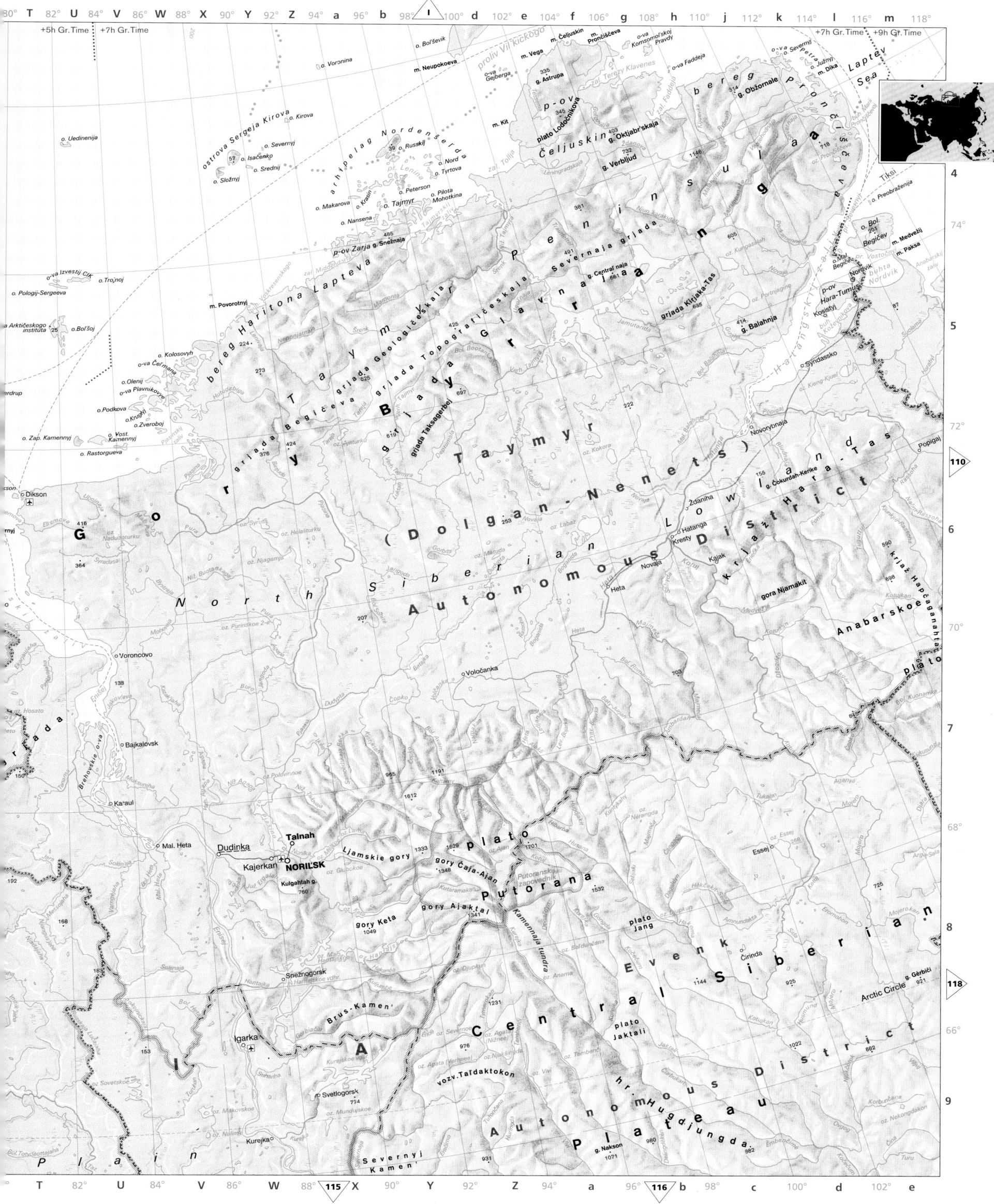

74°

+7h Gr. Time +9h Gr. Time +9h Gr. T

m. Dika

Dikson

L a p t e v   S e a

Severnaja grjada

g. Central naja

681

697

grjada Kirjaka-Tas

635

595

718

Pronščičeva

buh Marii Pronščičevoj

o. Preobraženija

T a y m y r

222

414

g. Balahnja

oz. Portnjagino

Bol. Balahna

Bol. Begičev

o-ov

p-ov

201

Hara-Tumus

Mal.
Begičev

Nordvik

m. Medvežij

m. Paksa

buh.
Nordvik

3

(D o l g a n - N e e n e t s)

N o r t h   S i b e r i a n

A u t o n o m o u s   D i s t r i c t

Syndassko

Kosistý

87

Anabarskij zaliv

krjaž Pron. čiščeva

315

p-ov Terpjaj-Tumsa

o-va Aéros"emki

o. Samoleta

Novorybnaja

o. Salkaj

o-va Dynaj

109

Ždaniha

Heta

Kresty

Novaja

Hatanga

krjaž   Hara - Tas

156

g. Čokurdah-Kerike

Ust-Olenëk

o. Džargylah

o. Kuba-Aryta

m. Doktorskij

o. Amerika-
Kuba-Aryta

Ust-Lenskij
zapovednik
(učastok Deftovyj)

o. Arga-
Muora-Sise

22

L e n a
R i v e r
D e l t a

Sagastyr

4

Kajak

krjaž

gora Njamakit

590

709

Popigaj

403

Dorucha

Saskylah

krjaž Sjurjah-Džangy

Olenëkskij   zaliv

Ystannah-Hočo

Tajmylyr

529

krjaž Čekanovskogo

132

Sobo-Sise

Ust-Lenskij
zapovednik

A n a b a r s k o e

p l a t o

698

Ébeljah

Amakinskij

227

Žilinda

251

Sklad

p l a t o

Tit-Ary

Bykovskij

245

Bykovskij

m. Muo

70°

C e n t r a l   S i b e r i a n

Evenk

Autonomous

District

725

496

Kirbéj

Haryjalah

Olenëk

377

443

K y s t y k

375

gora Čúrbuka

403

990

Tuora-Sis

489

m. Ork
Kam

Y a

k

u

Kjusjur

Siktjah

1378

Hara ulahskij hrebet

5

953

P l a t e a u

Arctic Circle

520

288

Džardžan

444

S

2281

Verhojanskij

6

Alakit

Poljarnyj

Udačnyj

Menkerja

hrebet Orulgan

19

66°

Ajhal

756

566

438

133

Kystatyam

Batagaj-Al

2032

Ho

Džarg

7

R

U

257 Kuonara

Žigar sk

Bahynaj

S

1975

Ečijskij
massiv

2081

2095

64°

189

Bestjah

1056

Sebjan-Kju

C e n t r a l n o j a k u t s k a j a

Kjulekjan

Kirovo

hre

2084

8

+8h Gr.
Time

476

577

223 Bagadja

Kjubjainde

Botulu

Sajlyk

Terbjas

Satagaj

Balagačëy

r a v n i n a

Scale 1 : 4,500,000

0 40 80 120 160 200 Kilometer

0 40 80 120 160 Statute Miles

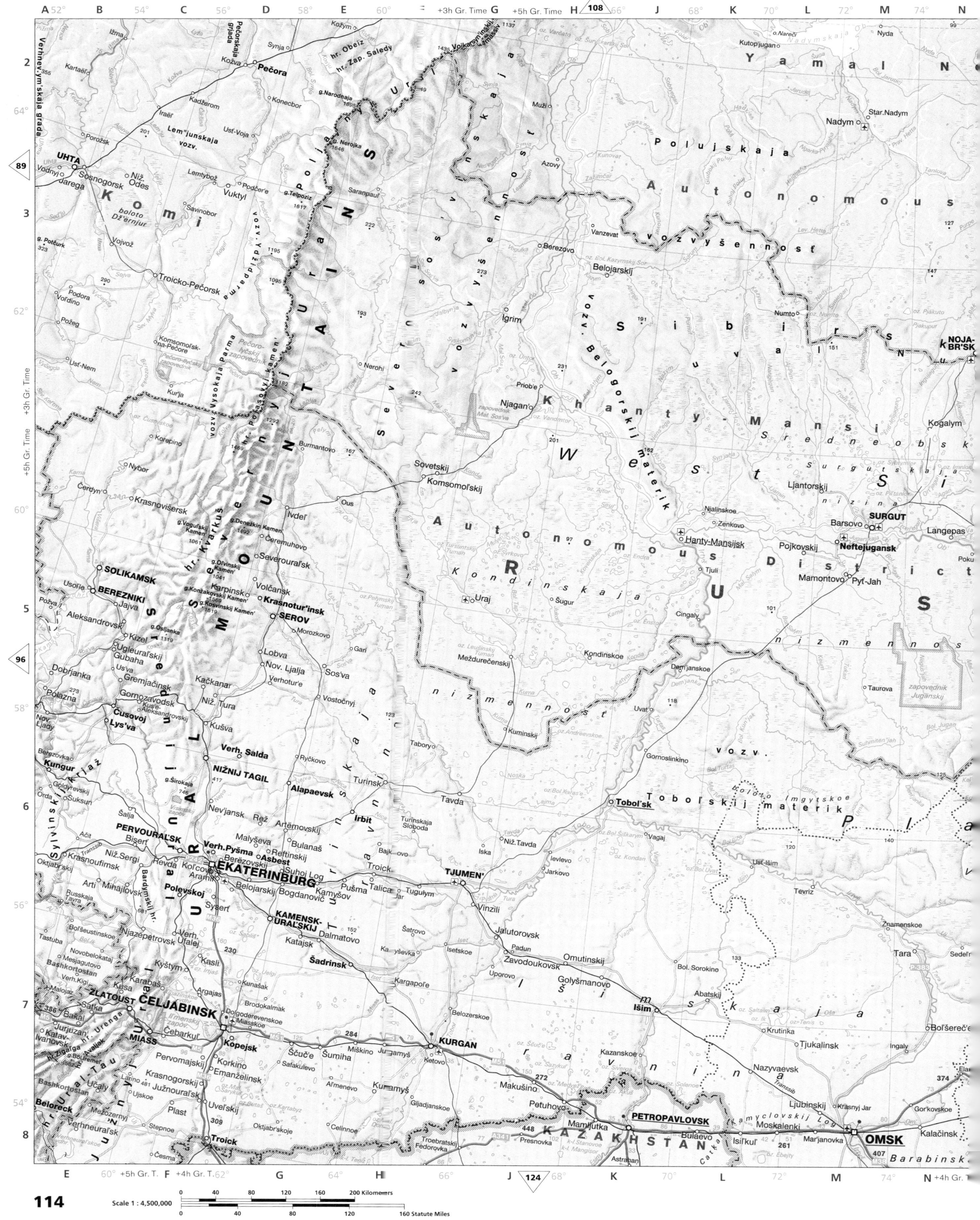

Verhnev'ym'skaja grada

Izma
Kartaёl'j 355

Pečorskaja grada

hr. Obeiz
hr. Zap. Saledy

Vojkarsynskij massiv 1137

Ob

Kožym
Synja

Varčata

Ob

Nyda

Nareči

Nadymskaja

Kadžerom
Iraёl'
Porožsk
201

Kožva
Pečora

g. Narodnaja 1895
Muži

Kutopjugan

Nyda
99

Y a m a l N

Savinobor
Lem"junskaja vozv.
Lemtybož
Podčer'e
Vuktyl

g. Telpoziz
1617

Saranpaul'

222

Azovy

Star.Nadym
Nadym

UHTA
Vodnyj
Sosnogorsk
Niž. Odes
darega

Kartaёl'j

Komi

boloto Dž'ernjur
Vojvož
Požeg

g. Potčurk
323

1195

Troicko-Pečorsk

Vanzevat

Berezovo

Polujskaja

Autonomous

vozvyšennosť

127

Podora
Vol'dino
Sojva
1095

Savinobor

1617

Belojarskij
Bol. Kazymskij Sor

147

Usť-Nem
Vižaiju
V'ёgga

Kurja

1182

1293

Igrim

193

Numto

Njagan'

Khanty-

S i b i r s

Nybor
Cerdyn'

Krasnovišersk

Ivdel'

Nerohi

Priob'e
242

231

191

oz. Pjakuto

NOJA-
BR'SK

151

SOLIKAMSK
BEREZNIKI
Usolje
Jajva

g. Denežkin Kamen' 1492
Čeremuhovo
Severoural'sk

Burmantovo 167

Sovetskij

Komsomol'skij

Mansi
Srednerobsk

Surgutskaja

Kogalym

Krasnovišersk

Aleksandrovsk
Kizel
Uglorab'skij
Gubaha

g. Ol'vinskij Kamen'
1041
Karpinsk
g. Konžakovskij Kamen' 1569
g. Kosvinskij Kamen' 1519

Volčansk

Morozkovo

Njalinskoe
Zenkovo

Hanty-Mansijsk
97

Autonomous

nizina

S i

Barsovo SURGUT

Neftejugansk

Langepas

Poku

Dobrjanka
Polazna

Us'va
Gremjačinsk

Lobva
Nov. Ljalja
Sos'va

Gari

Kondinskoe Konda

Mežduečenskij

Kondinskaja

Šugur

Tjuli

Uraj

Cingaly

Demjanka

Pyť-Jah
Mamontovo

101

R

Kačkanar

Verhotur'e
123

Kuminskij

118

Uvat

U

Nov.
Ljady
Čusovoj
Lys'va

g. Širokaja 749

Niž. Tura
Kušva

Vostočnyj

nizmennost

Taurova

zapovednik
Juganskij

S

Kungur
g. Širokaja

Verh. Salda
Ryčkovo

Tabory

Bol. Jugan

nizmennost

Berezovka
Goldyrevskij
Orda
Suksun

NIŽNIJ TAGIL
417

Turinsk

Gornoslinkino

Bol.Šiškarym

vozv.

125

PERVOURAL'SK
Bišert

Nev'jansk
Rež
Artёmovskij

Alapaevsk

Tavda

Tobol'sk

Tobol'skij materik

140

Irbit
Turinskaja Sloboda

Tavda

oz. Kondan

P l a

Šalja
Ačit
Niž. Sergi

Verh. Pyšma
Asbest
Reftinskij

Bajk ovo

Ievlevo

120

Ust-Išim

Oktjabr'skij
Krasnoufimsk

EKATERINBURG
Berёzovskij
Suhoj Log

Iska

Jarkovo

Tevriz

Irtyš

Arti
Mihajlovsk

Polevskoj
Belojarskij
Bogdanovič
Kamyšov
Pušma
Talica
Tugulym

TJUMEN'

Russkaja Tavra

Kol'covo
Aramil'
Sysert'

Vinzili

Bol'šeustinskoe
Njazepetrovsk
Utalej

Verh.
Sёrgi

KAMENSK-
URAL'SKIJ
152
Dalmatovo
Katajsk

Šatrovo

Jalutorovsk

Padun
Isetskoe

Omutinskij

Zavodoukovsk

Bol. Sorokino

133

Tara

Sedel

Kasli
230

Kyštym
Karabaš

Kunašak

Kargapol'e

Uporovo
Golyšmanovo

Abatskij

Znamenskoe

ZLATOUST
ČELJABINSK
386

Argajas

Brodokalmak

Belozerskoe

Išim

Nazyvaevsk

Tjukalinsk

Ingaly

Bakal
Jurjuzan'
Katav-
Ivanovsk

Miasskoe

Dolgoderevenskoe

284

KURGAN

Krutinka

Bol'šereč'e

374

MIASS
Čebarkul'
Kopejsk
Korkino

Ščuč'e
Šumiha

Ketovo

Kazanskoe

PETROPAVLOVSK

OMSK

407

Pervomajskij
Emanželinsk

Miškino
Jugamyš

Kuamyš

272

Makušino

Petuhovo

Moskalenki
Mar'janovka

Kalačinsk

Beloreck
Verhneural'sk
Plast
Uvel'skij
309

Celinnoe

Gljadjanskoe

448

Mamljutka

261

Isil'kul'

B a r a b i n s k

KAZAKHSTAN

Scale 1 : 4,500,000

0 40 80 120 160 200 Kilometers

0 40 80 120 160 Statute Miles

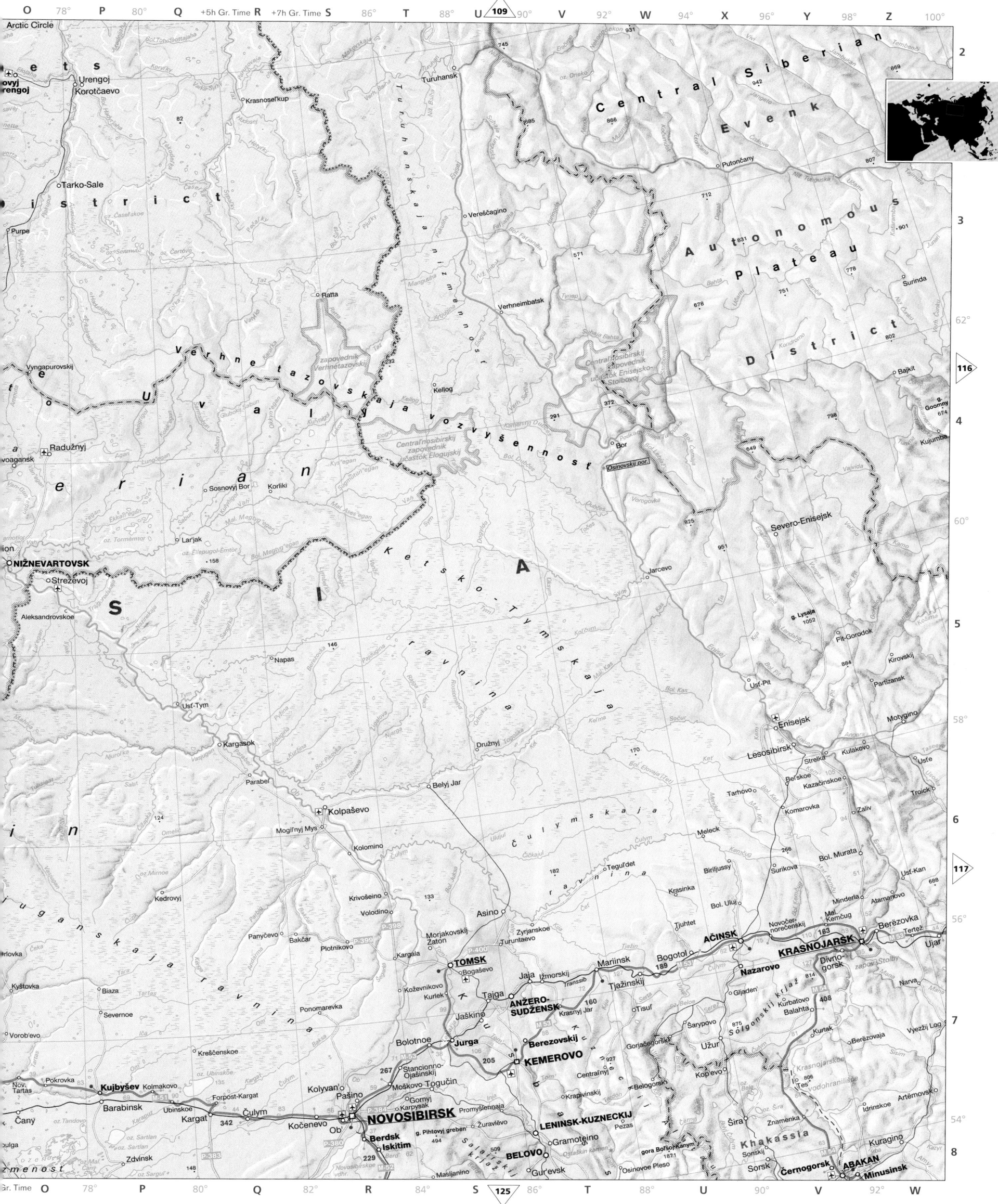

Scale 1 : 4,500,000

Scale 1 : 4,500,000

0   40   80   120   160   200 Kilometers

0   40   80   120   160 Statute Miles

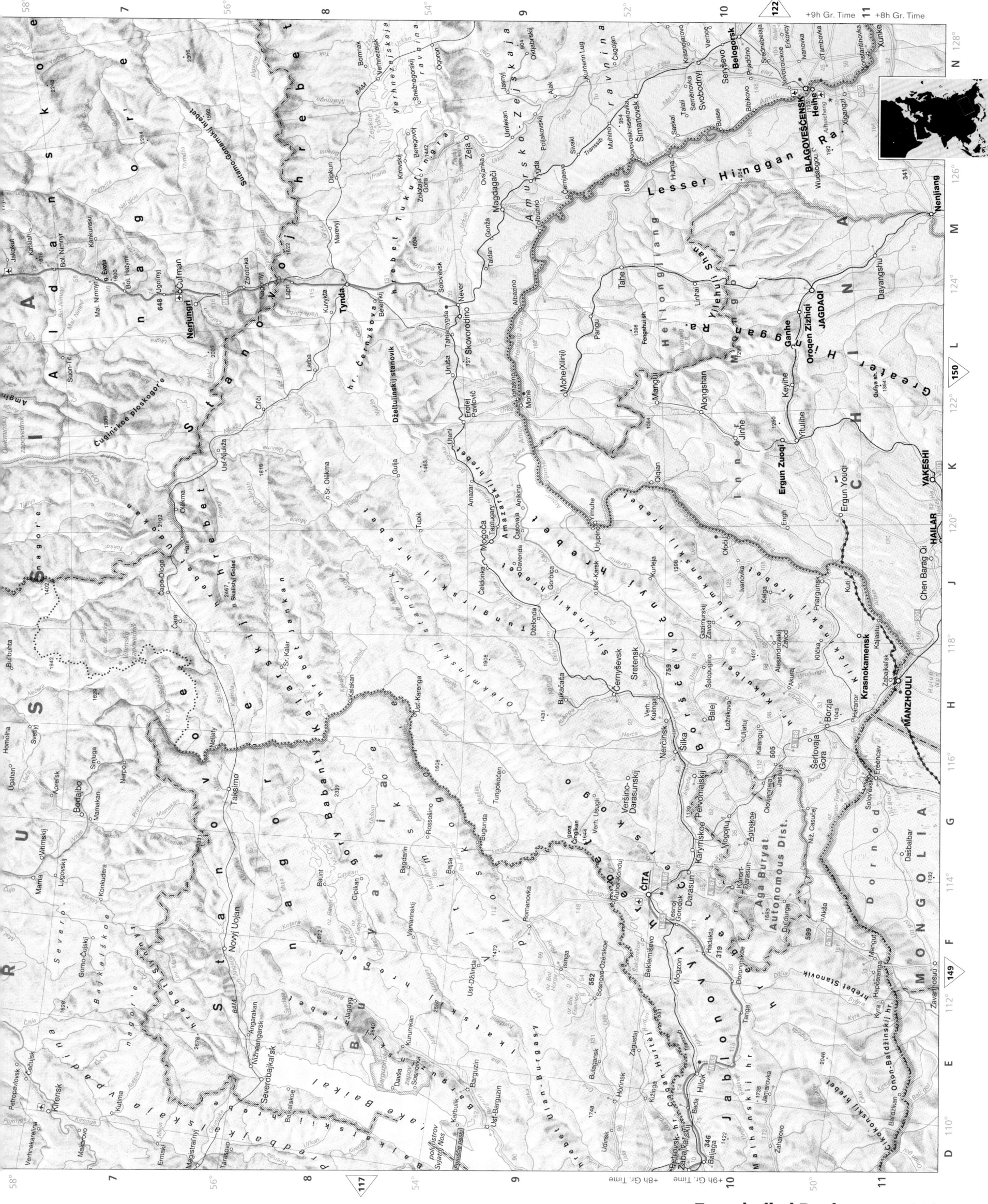

Commander Islands

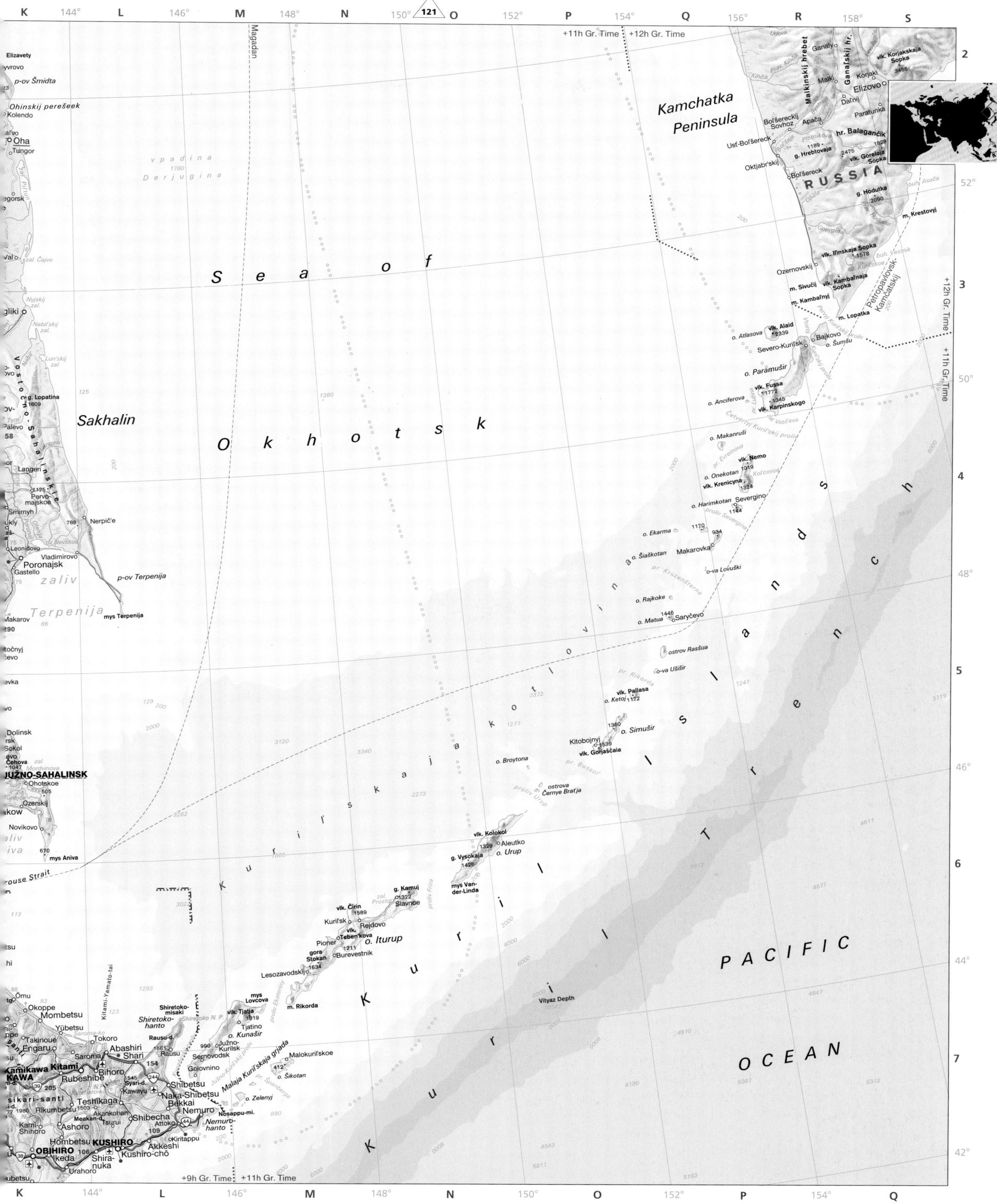

K 144° L 146° M 148° N 150° △121 O 152° P 154° Q 156° R 158° S

2

Kamchatka
Peninsula

Elizavety
·yvrovo
p-ov Šmidta
Ohinskij perešeek
Kolendo
·ło
Oha
Tungor

vpadina
Derjugina
1780

Ganaľskij hr.
vlk. Korjakskaja
Sopka
3456

Malkinskij hrebet
Ganaly
Korjaki
Elizovo

Prav. Kihčik
Kihčik
Malk
Apača

Boľšereckij
Sovhoz
Ust-Boľšereck
Boľšereck
Oktjabr'skij
Dalnij
Paratunka

hr. Balagančik
1189· 1828
g. Hrebtovaja 2475
vlk. Gorelaja
Sopka

RUSSIA

52°

·gorsk

g. Hodutka
2090

buh. Asača

·gliki
Nyjskij
zal.

S e a   o f

m. Krestovyj

3

·58
Sakhalin

O k h o t s k

vlk. Iľinskaja Šopka
·1578

buh. Vestnik

·Nabiľskij
zal.

Ozernovskij

m. Sivučij
vlk. Kambaľnaja
Sopka

Petropavlovsk-
Kamčatskij

·vo
g. Lopatina
1609

vpadina

m. Kambaľnyj

m. Lopatka

+12h Gr. Time

Palevo

o. Atlasova
vlk. Alaid
·2339

pov Kur. Voz.

Severo-Kuriľsk
Bajkovo
o. Šumšu

+11h Gr. Time

50°

·ukly
·Leonidovo
Vladimirovo

788
Nerpič'e

1125

o. Paramušir

vlk. Fussa
1772
·1345
vlk. Karpinskogo

Četvertyj Kuriľskij proliv

Pervo-
majskoe
Smirnyh

o. Anciferova

o. Vasiľ eva

Poronajsk
Gastello

Vladimirovo

o. Makanruši

Severno

4

zaliv
p-ov Terpenija

vlk. Nemo
1019

o. Onekotan
vlk. Krenicyna
1324

Koľcovog

·Makarov
66
mys Terpenija

o. Harimkotan
·1144

proliv Severgina

Severgino

Ušišir

T e r p e n i j a

o. Ekarma
1170
934

·čevo
·točnyj

o. Šiaškotan
Makarovka

o-va Lovuški

48°

·evka

o. Rajkoke

5

·Dolinsk
·rsk
·Sokol

129 200

3372

o. Matua
1446
Saryčevo

ostrov Rassua

o-va Ušišir

Pr. Rikorda
1247

·Cehova
1047
Mordvinova
505

JUŽNO-SAHALINSK
Ohotskoe
Ozerskij

vlk. Pallasa
o. Ketoj 1172

o. Simušir
1360

·kow

2000

1277

Kitobojnyj
·3536
vlk. Gorjaščaia

·Novikovo
670
mys Aniva

3120

3340

o. Broytona

pr. Bussoľ

46°

·liv
·iva

3282

2273

ostrova
Černye Braťja

proliv Urup

rouse Strait

vlk. Kolokol
1329
Aleutko
g. Vysokaja
1426
o. Urup

6

·113

1585

g. Kamuj
1322
Slavnoe

mys Van-
der-Linda

3022

zal.
Prostor

vlk. Čirin
1589
Kuriľsk
Rejdovo
vlk.
Teben'kova
1211
o. Iturup

4611

·tsu
·hi

Pioner
gora
Stokan
1634
Burevestnik

Lesozavodskij

Vityaz Depth

P A C I F I C

44°

·Ōmu
Okoppe
Mombetsu

1293

mys
Lovcova
vlk. Tjatja
1819
m. Rikorda

Shiretoko-
misaki
Shiretoko-
hanto
Rausu-d.

Tjatino
o. Kunašir

7

Yūbetsu
Takinoue
Engaru

Abashiri
Rausu

990
Južno-
Kuriľsk
Segnovodsk
Golovnino

O C E A N

Kamikawa Kitami
KAWA
Rubeshibe

1661
1503·

154

Malokuriľskoe
412·
o. Šikotan

sikari-santi
·77 1986

Teshikaga
Bihoro

1545
Syari-d.
244

Shibetsu
Naka-Shibetsu
Kawayu

Malaja Kuriľskaja grjada

o. Zelenyj

·Kami-
·Shihoro

Meakan-d.
Tsuyu

Shibecha
Akankohan

Bekkai
Nemuro

Nosappu-mi.

42°

·Hombetsu KUSHIRO
OBIHIRO
·eda Ikeda

Ashoro

Attoko
nuka

o. Kiritappu

880

K 144° L 146° M 148° N 150° O 152° P 154° Q
+9h Gr. Time +11h Gr. Time

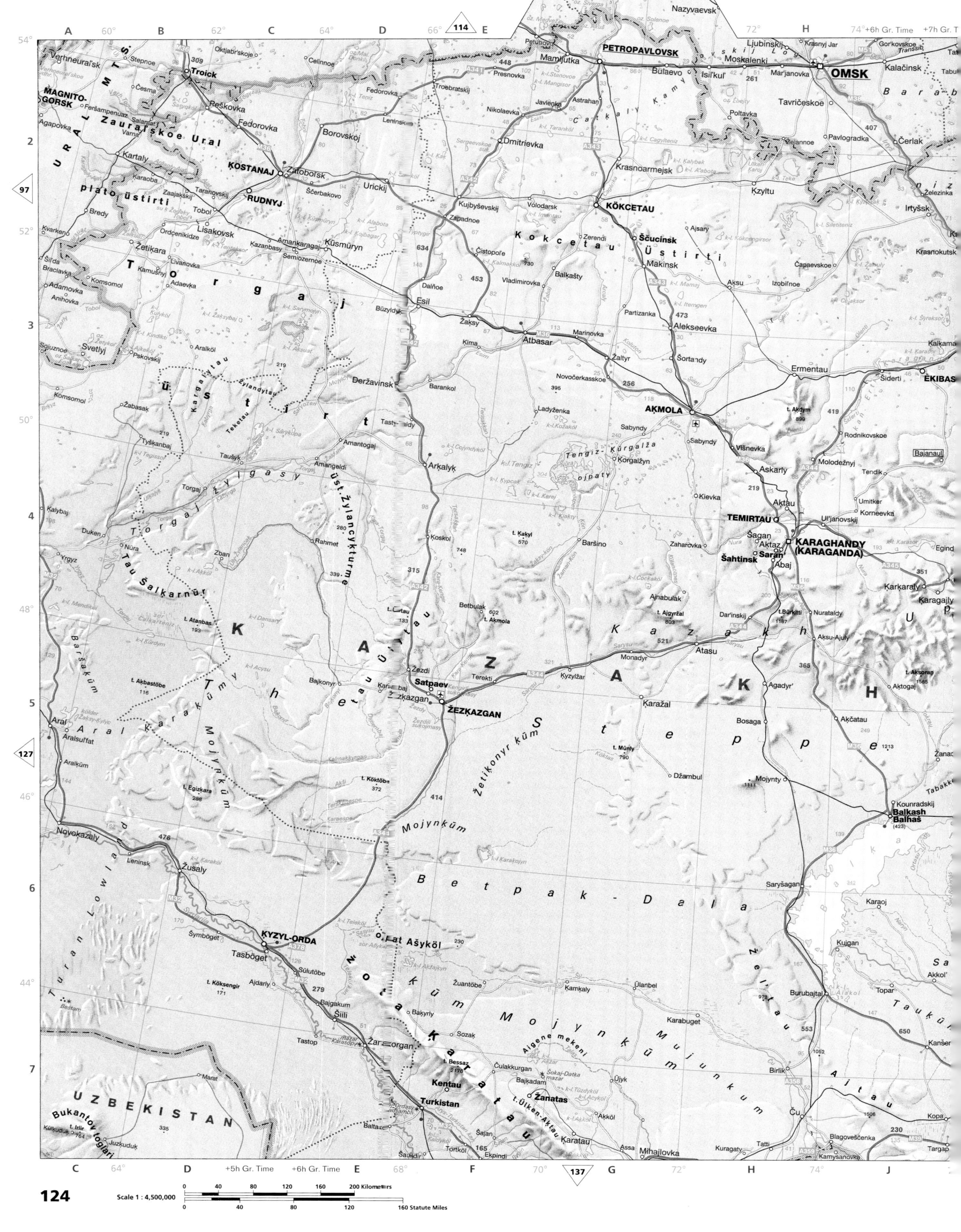

NOVOSIBIRSK

Kargat 342 · Čulym · Kočeněvo · Ob' · Promyšlennaja

Berdsk · Iskitim · g. Pihtovyj greben · **LENINSK-KUZNECKIJ**
Zdvinsk · 494 · Gramoteino

Kupino · Karasuk · Ordynskoe · **BELOVO**
Čerepanovo · Gur'evsk · Artyšta

Suzun · **KISELEVSK**
Kamen-na-Obi · **PROKOP'EVSK** · **NOVOKUZNECK**
Beregovoe · Myski · Meždurečensk

BARNAUL · Osinniki
Novoaltajsk · Malinovka · Kuzedeevo

Slavgorod · Jarovoe · **RUSSIA**
Blagoveščenka · Mamontovo · Taštagol

Western Sayan Mts.

Kulunda · **BIJSK** · Gorno-Altajsk

RUBCOVSK · Belokuriha · **ALTAJ**

Gorno-Altaj

SEMEY (SEMIPALATINSK) · Leninogorsk

ÖSKEMEN (UST'-KAMENOGORSK) · Zyrjanovsk · **MONGOLIA**

Serebrjansk · Ölgij

Georgievka · Katon-Karagaj

PAVLODAR · Kŭlyndy

Karaungir

Karakŭm

Xinjiang (Sinkiang)

KARAMAY · Junggar Pendi · Dzungarian Basin

Gurbantünggüt Shamo

TALDYKORGAN · žota Dzungarskij Alatau · **CHINA**

Kuytun · **SHIHEZI** · **CHANGJI**

Borohoro Shan · **ÜRÜMQI** · Bogda Shan

YINING · **TIAN SHAN** · **Turpan**

ALMATY

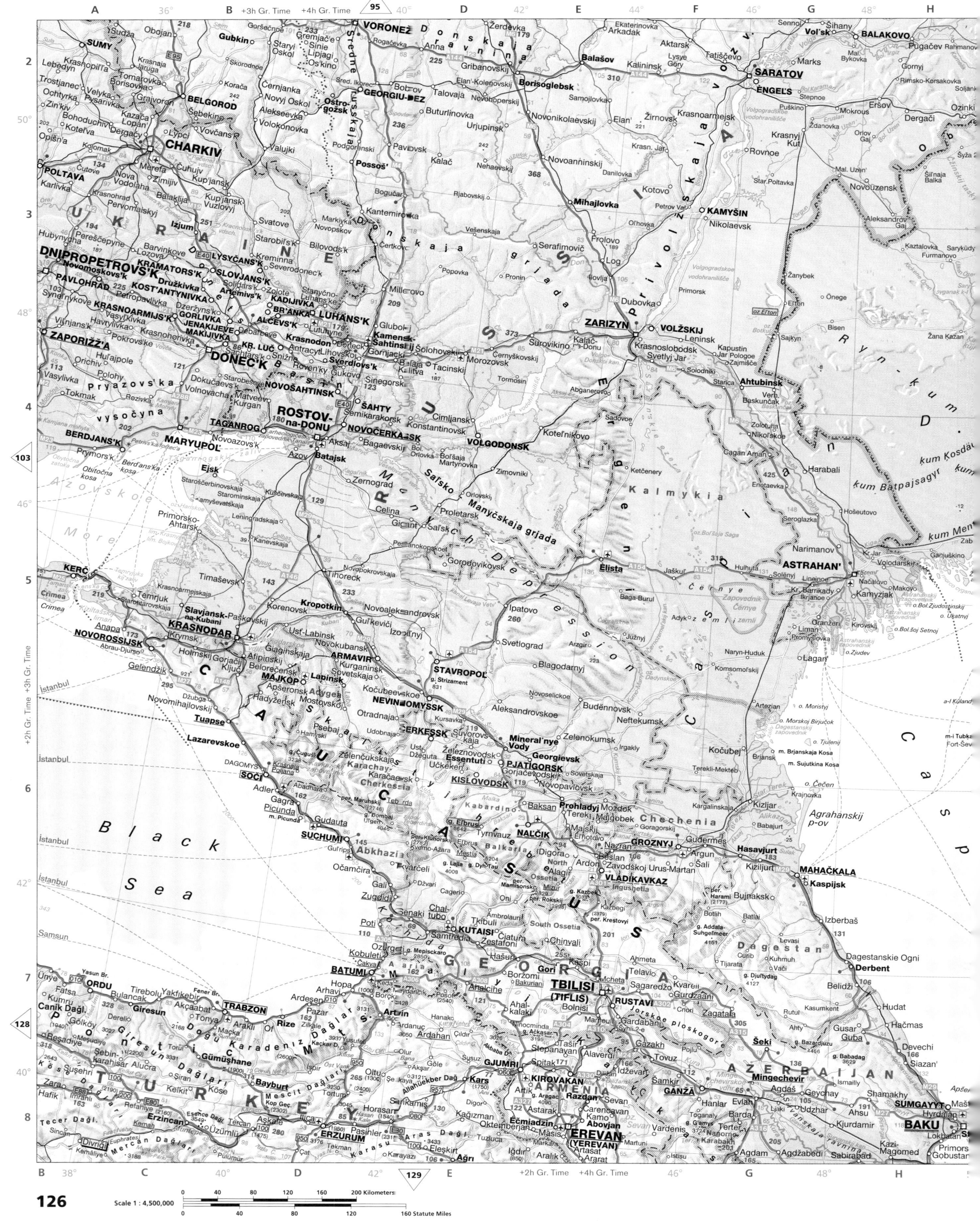

-4h Gr. Time +5h Gr. Time

K 54° L 56° M 58° N 97 60° O 62° P 64° Q 124 66° R

2

Bol.
Černigovka
Kurlin 297 Novosergievka
257 Pervomajskij Tašla Kargala **ORENBURG** Zilairskoe
Perevolockij Saraktaš plato Inklinskoe
Rannee Ilek Uranbaš Ak'jar Silfa Komsomol
ovosovetsk Fedorovka Aksaj Perevolockij Kuvandyk Braclavka Adamovka
rmetovsk Amankeldi Šyngyrlau Krasnoholm Krjučkovka Mednogorsk Novoorsk Anihovka
ORAL Budarino Algabas Šyngyrlau Büranoe Donskoe **NOVOTROICK** **ORSK** Svetlyj
Pugačev Kurajlysaj Žambejti Aksu Akbulak Beljaevka Bol. Kumak Jasnyj Sjujunduk
muzej-u Žambejti 129 Martok Studenčeskoe Kyzylžar Komsomol
ynovo Capaev Kurajlysaj 221 Novonadeždinka Petropavlovka Dombarovskij Žabask
153 Döngelek Büldyrty Leninskoe Batamšy Komsomol Tyškanbaj
henka Šagan Kalmykovo M32 Akrab **AKTÖBE** Hromtau Bogetsaj 619 Karabutak Taušyk
Esensaj 474 114 Novorossijskoe Opyrkara Dongelekor Karabutak Rahmet
Kalënoe Bazartöbe Karatöbe Alga 462 Düken Nūra
Karakamys Oktjabr'sk Kümsaj Kalybaj Tau Šalkarnūr
Kalmykovo Bestamak Pokrovka Žüryn Bala-Taldyk Kalybaj 124
Inderbor Mijaly Šubarküdyk Kalybaj Žylan L. Atanbas 193
Kulagin Karabau Altykarasu Embi Bercogyr 657 Žabysty k-l Mendiköl k-l Kärdym
Zelenoe 25 Karaköl Bajganin Šubarsy 70 t. Akbastöbe 116
Šarkin Sagyz Žarkamys 408 Saksauyl Aral Aralsul'fat
Makat Karabau Ženterek Aktolagaj tizbegi k-l Tebez O. Barsaküm Karaköl
Māhambet Dossor Bekbeket Ojmauyt 215 Ak'tümsyk 345 Aral Aralkum Egizkara 298
Novobogat Redut Kockar Karaoba Južnyj Saksauyl 476
ATYRAU Komsomol Želtau Kosbulak sor Syrdarja Novokazaly Žusaly
Sumysker Bajčunas 149 56 Mynsualmas sor Astantaj-Mataj Barsakelmes Leninsk M32
Böget Karaton Opornyj Mynsualmas Goszapovednik 102 Bozköl Karaköl 170
Kyzylbalyk Sarykamys Prorva Külandy tub. Barsakelmes Karaköl
Karaton Opornyj Küland zapov. Kontübek 1970 shoreline
m-i Burynčyk a-l Durnev Bejneu kum Sam Aral Vozroždenija otasi 1995 shoreline
Ülken sor 149 153 XVI-XX g.g Sea Ujaly
Tubek 153 arhitektura 53 t. Sulukaska
Būzačy kompleksy tau Köksengir 126 Bestam
Karatau tau Žamanajrykty Ujaly Karatulej Ustjurtdagi Komsomol'sk
taulary Mangystau Karatau 229 Saj-Utjes Ušsaj Mujnak Kiziolkum
Šetre tau Bescoky 556 Mujnak Kažak darė tepalik Beltov 146 Bukantov toglari
Mangyšlak tau Kölba 321 Sudač'e 101 Tahtaküpir kumlik Taškuduk k-l Irir 764
m-i Melovoj **AKTAU** Žetybaj Özen 340 Barsakel mes Kümdik Oltinkül Čimboj kumlik Taškuduk Mingbulak Učkuduk
Bostankum Novyj Uzen' Karabaur pastligi Kün̄girod 133 Kegajli Mingbulok čukurligi
m. Pesčany Kuryk Mangyšlak Karabaur pastligi 321 Sumanaj Mangit Mingbulok
vpadina Kaundy Bokter Müzbel Kizy Baudak **NUKUS** S. Accitov 473
m. Rakušečnyj 57 Fetisovo Karynžaryk Tahtatoš Sultan Ubajs Urgenč
Kazahskij Kendyrli kudus Deu skenkala Lenin Mangit Gurlan 70
zaliv Kajasanskoe plato 770 Sarto Sirvankaja Köne- ürgenč Birtkikala
pl6at 30 pl6at Ilijali **DAŽHOWUZ** Berüni Türkül 100
Bekdaš g. Bekmurat Denkola 81 Tahta **URGANČ** Omizatov
Kulandag 364 zapovednik Sahsenem Heval toglari
zaliv Kimalтag plato Kaplankyr vpad. Akdžakalaja Hazorasp Gazačak 556
Karabogazgöl Kunguzskie Zigerbent Dargan-Ata 180
m Čagyl Akkyr Zaunguzskie Gērel'd 137
S Karabogazköl Koimatdag Karakumy Kabaklyoba 210
e Kuuli Majak Krasnovodskoe Košoba **TURKMENISTAN** Darvaza Erdzik
a plato Čirmamedkum 483 Kabaklyoba 244
Žiloj **Krasnovodsk** Džanga 350 Čirmamedkum Unguz Uzboj
enij 200 M37 136

48°
124
+6h Gr. Time
+5h Gr. Time
44°
42°
40°

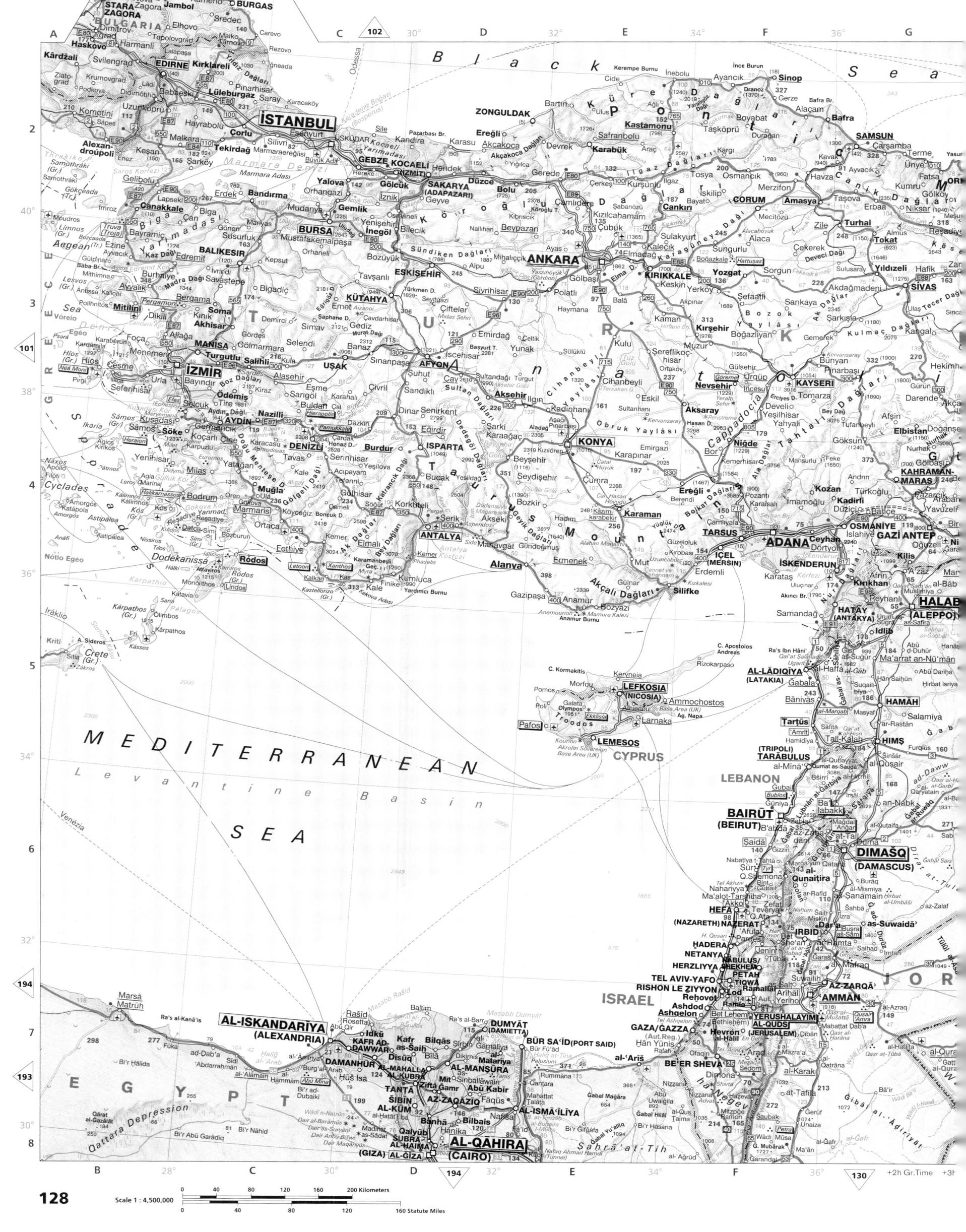

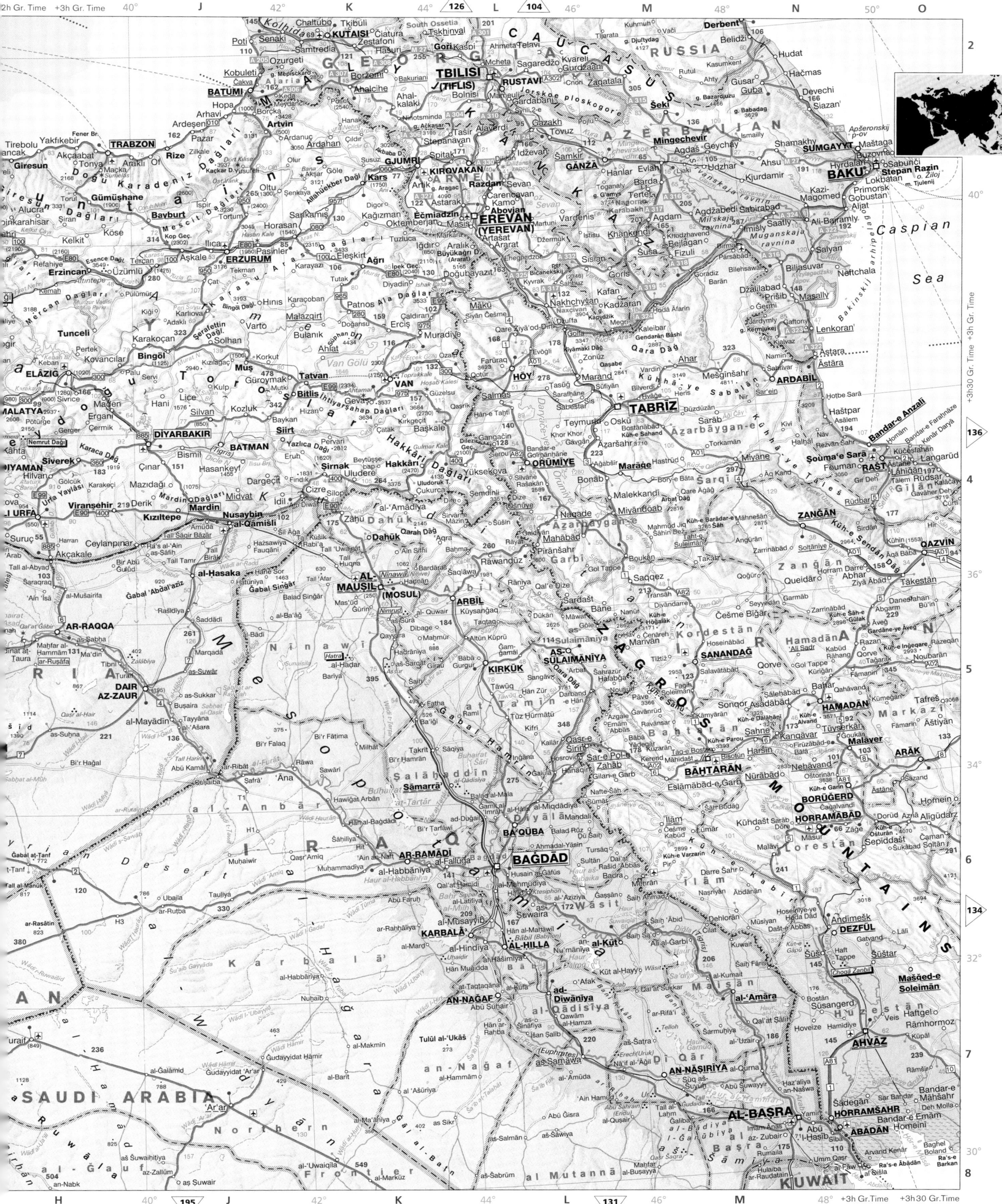

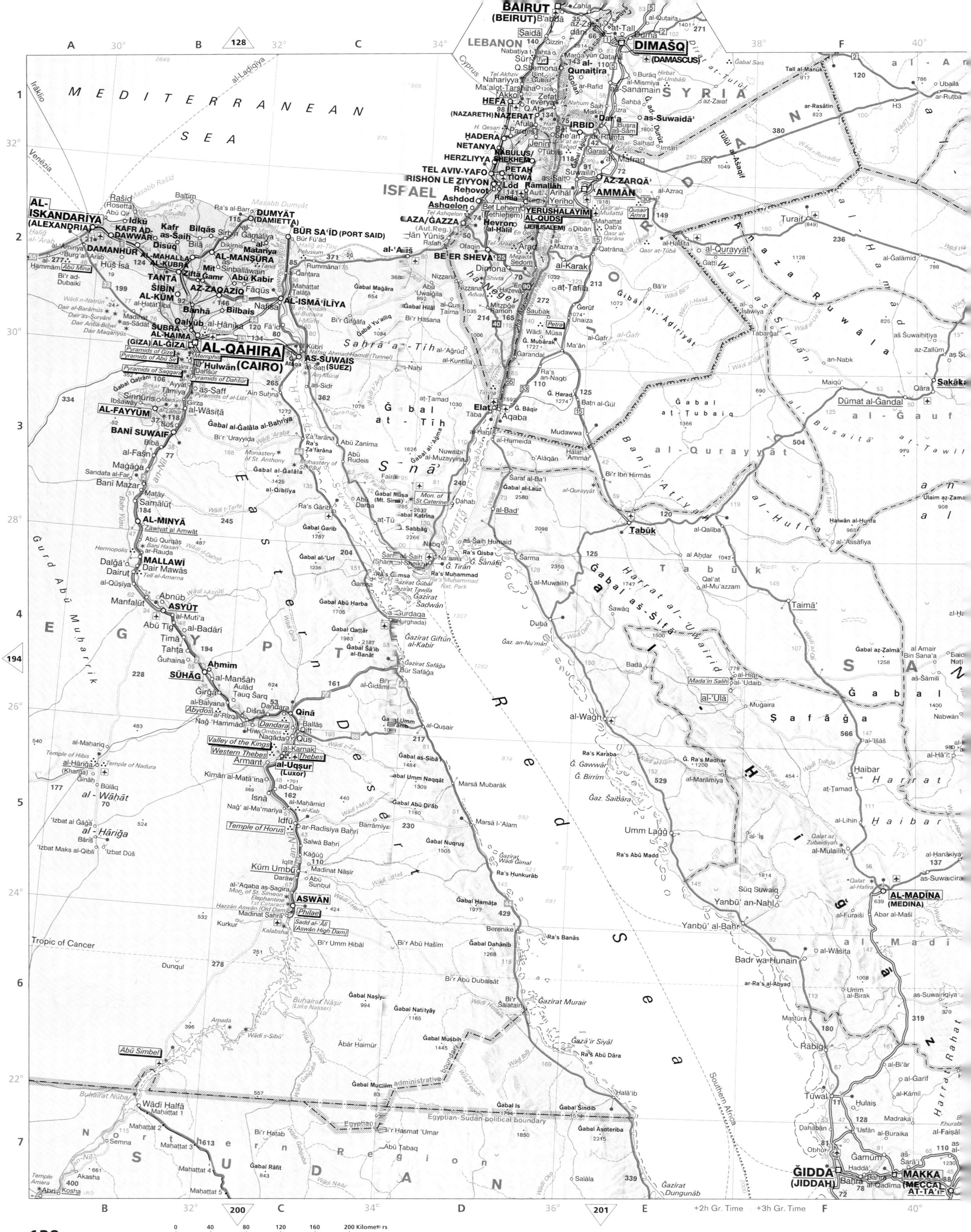

MEDITERRANEAN SEA

LEBANON

BAIRUT (BEIRUT)

DIMAŠQ (DAMASCUS)

SYRIA

ISRAEL

HEFA (NAZARETH) NAZERAT

IRBID

as-Suwaidā'

HADERA
NETANYA
HERZLIYYA
TEL AVIV-YAFO
RISHON LE ZIYYON
Ashdod
Ashgelon
GAZA/GAZZA (Aut.Reg.)

NABULUS/ SHEKHEM
PETAH TIQWA
Lod Ramallah
Rehovot
YERUSHALAYIM (JERUSALEM)
AL-QUDS

AMMAN
AZ-ZARQĀ'

BE'ER SHEVA

JORDAN

al-Karak

at-Tafila

Turaif

AL-ISKANDARIYA (ALEXANDRIA)
KAFR AD-DAWWAR
DAMANHŪR
AL-MAHALLA AL-KUBRA
AL-MANSŪRA
DUMYĀT (DAMIETTA)
BŪR SAʿĪD (PORT SAID)
TANTĀ
AZ-ZAQĀZIQ
AL-ISMĀʿĪLĪYA
SUBRĀ AL-HAIMA
(GIZA) AL-GĪZA
AL-QAHIRA (CAIRO)
AS-SUWAIS (SUEZ)
Hulwān

AL-FAYYŪM
BANĪ SUWAIF

EGYPT

AL-MINYĀ
MALLAWĪ

ASYŪT

SŪHĀG

Sinai (Sīnāʾ)

Elat
Aqaba

Tabūk

SAUDI ARABIA

Taimāʾ

QINĀ
AL-UQSUR (Luxor)
Karnak
Thebes
Valley of the Kings
Western Thebes

Red Sea

al-Wagh

Madāʾin Sālih
al-ʿUlā

Idfū
Kūm Umbū
ASWĀN
Philae
Aswān High Dam
Abū Simbel

Tropic of Cancer

Buhairat Nāsir (Lake Nasser)

Wādī Halfā

SUDAN
Northern Region

Egyptian-Sudan political boundary

AL-MADĪNA (MEDINA)

Yanbūʿ an-Nahl
Yanbūʿ al-Bahr

Badr wa-Hunain

Rābigh

ĞIDDA (JIDDAH)
MAKKA (MECCA)
AT-TĀ'IF

+2h Gr. Time   +3h Gr. Time

Scale 1 : 4,500,000

0   40   80   120   160   200 Kilometers

0   40   80   120   160 Statute Miles

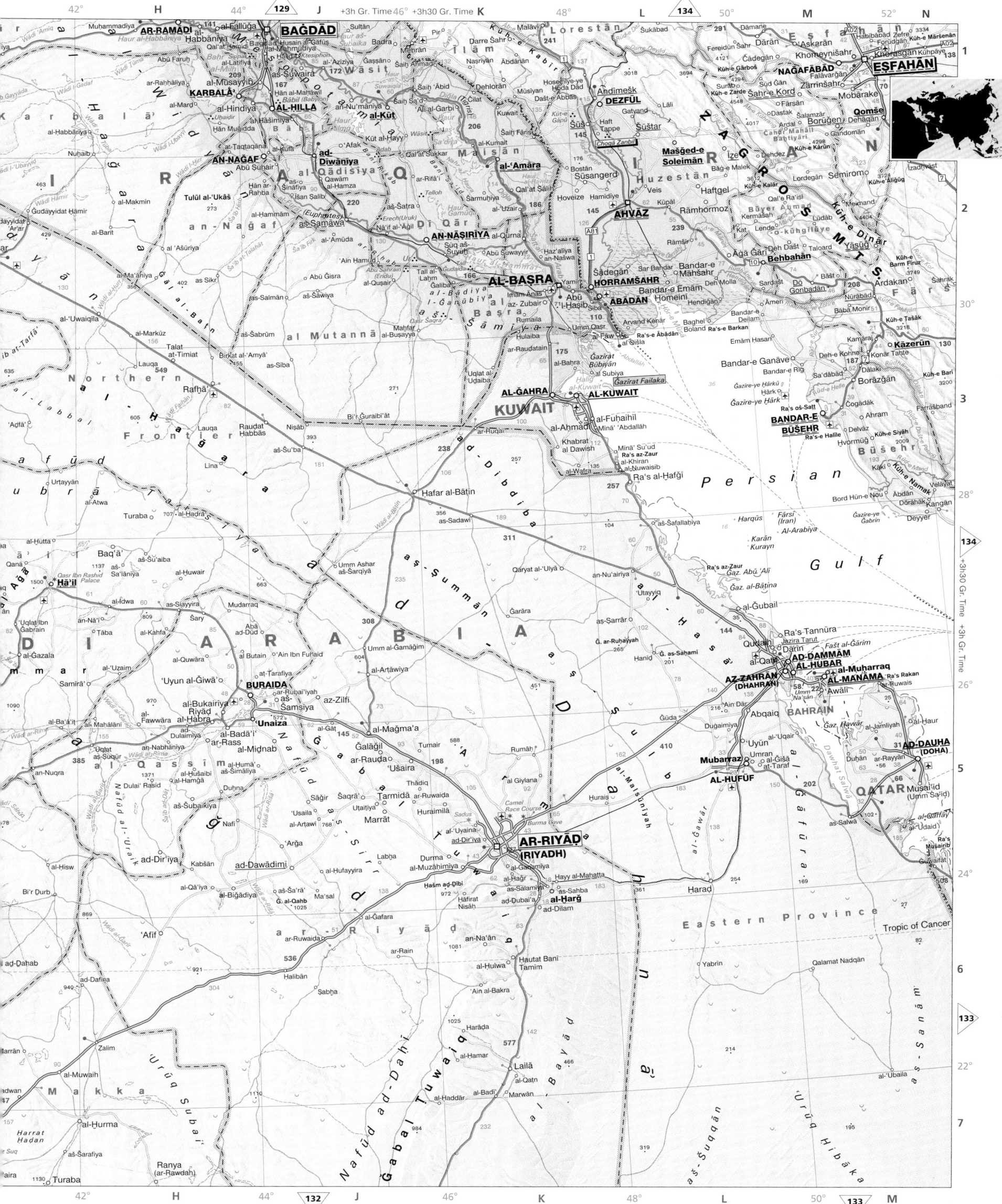

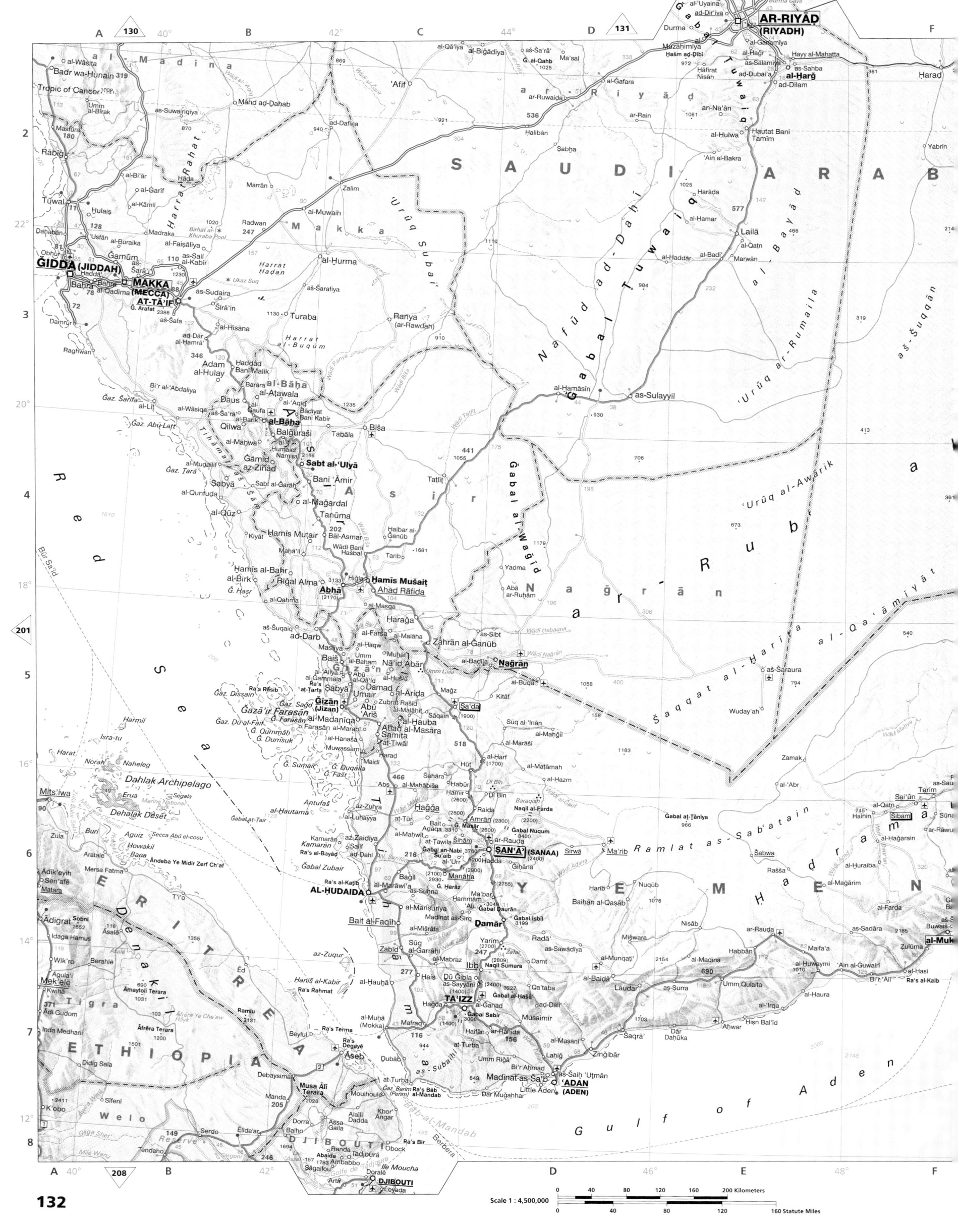

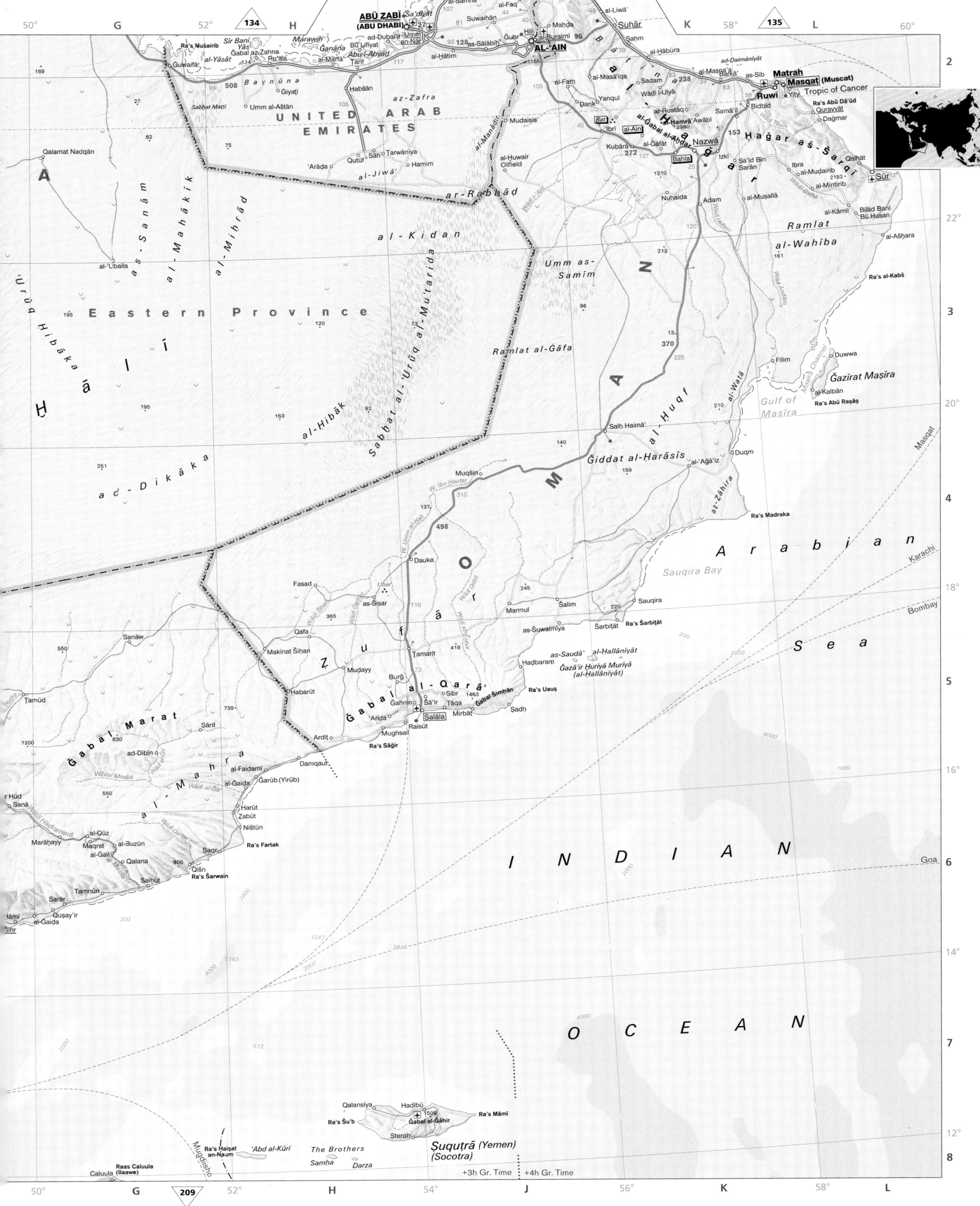

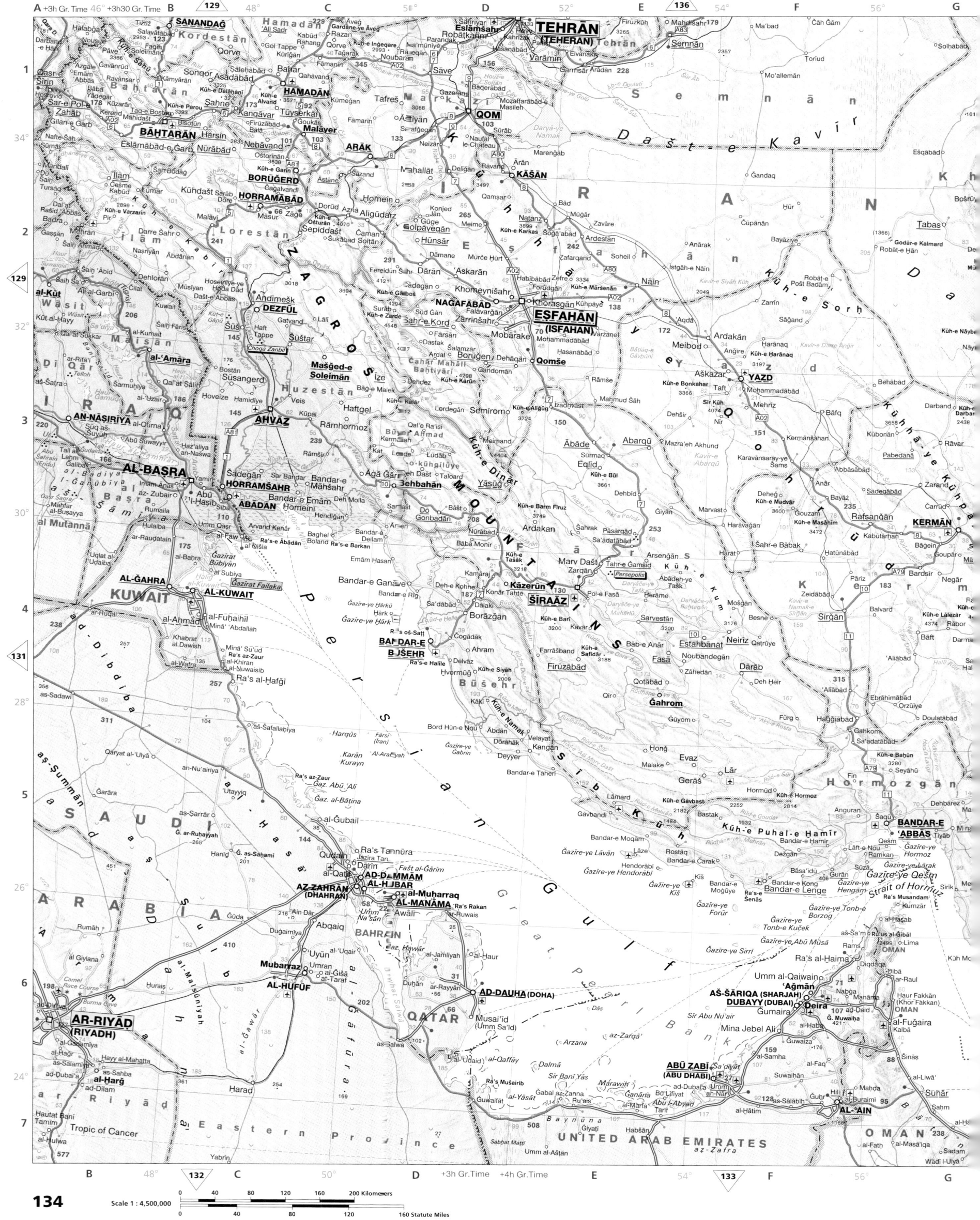

Scale 1 : 4,500,000

0   40   80   120   160   200 Kilometers

0   40   80   120   160 Statute Miles

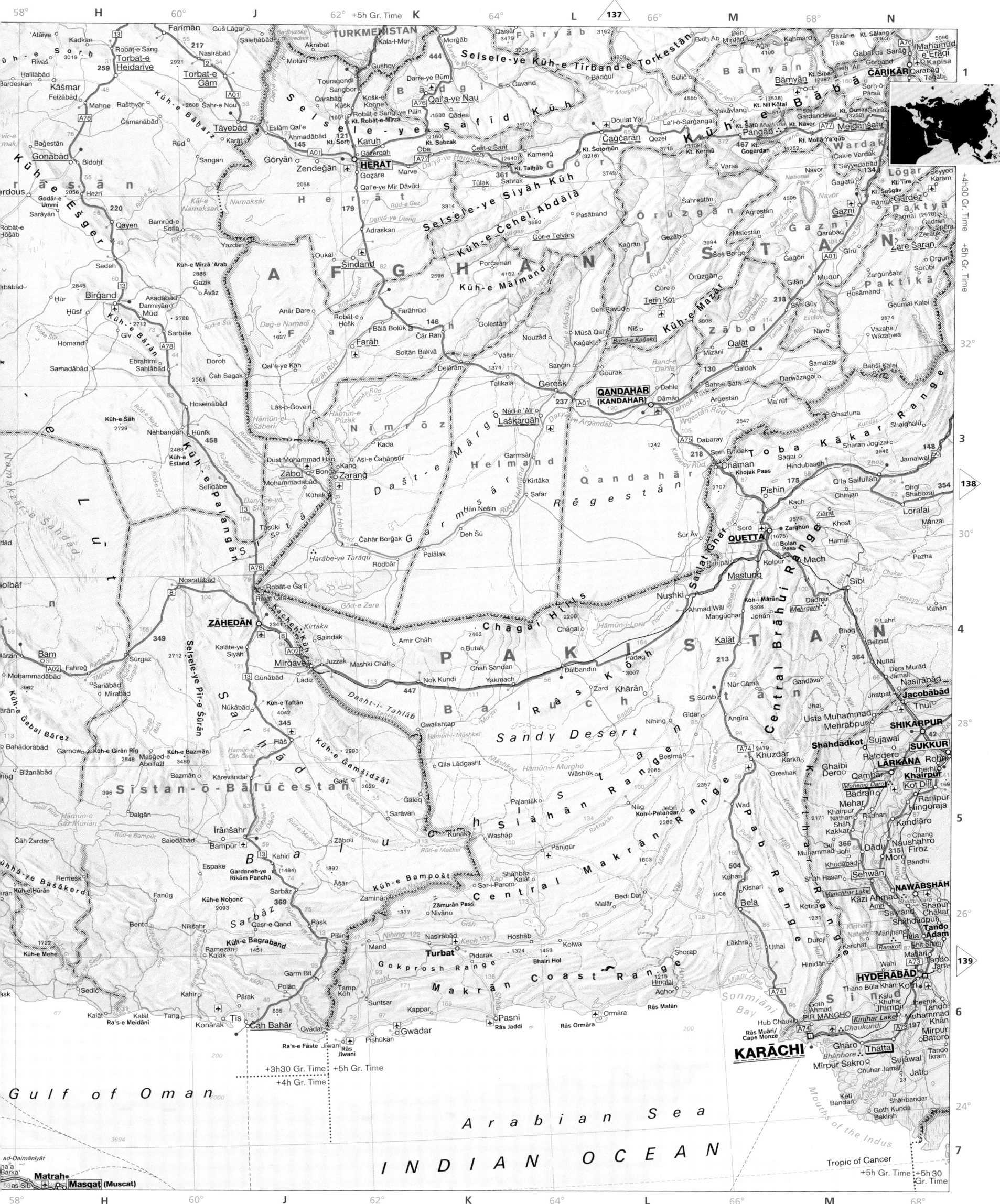

RUSSIA

Karakūm

A B 50° C 52° D 54° E 56° F 58° G 60°

KAZAKHSTAN

AKTAU

AZERBAIJAN

SUMGAYYT
BAKU
Stepan Razin

Krasnovodsk

Nebitdag

TURKMENISTAN

AŞGABAT (Ašhabad)

RAŠT
QAZVĪN
KARAĞ
Eslāmšahr
TEHRĀN
(TEHERAN)

SĀRĪ
GORGĀN
Gonbad-e Qabūs

SABZEVĀR
Nēšāpūr
MAŠHAD

QOM

KĀSĀN

IRAN

Dašt-e Kavīr

Eşfahān

Khorāsān

B 134 52° C 54° D 56° E 58° F +3h30 Gr. Time +4h30 Gr. Time

136

Scale 1 : 4,500,000

0 40 80 120 160 200 Kilometers
0 40 80 120 160 Statute Miles

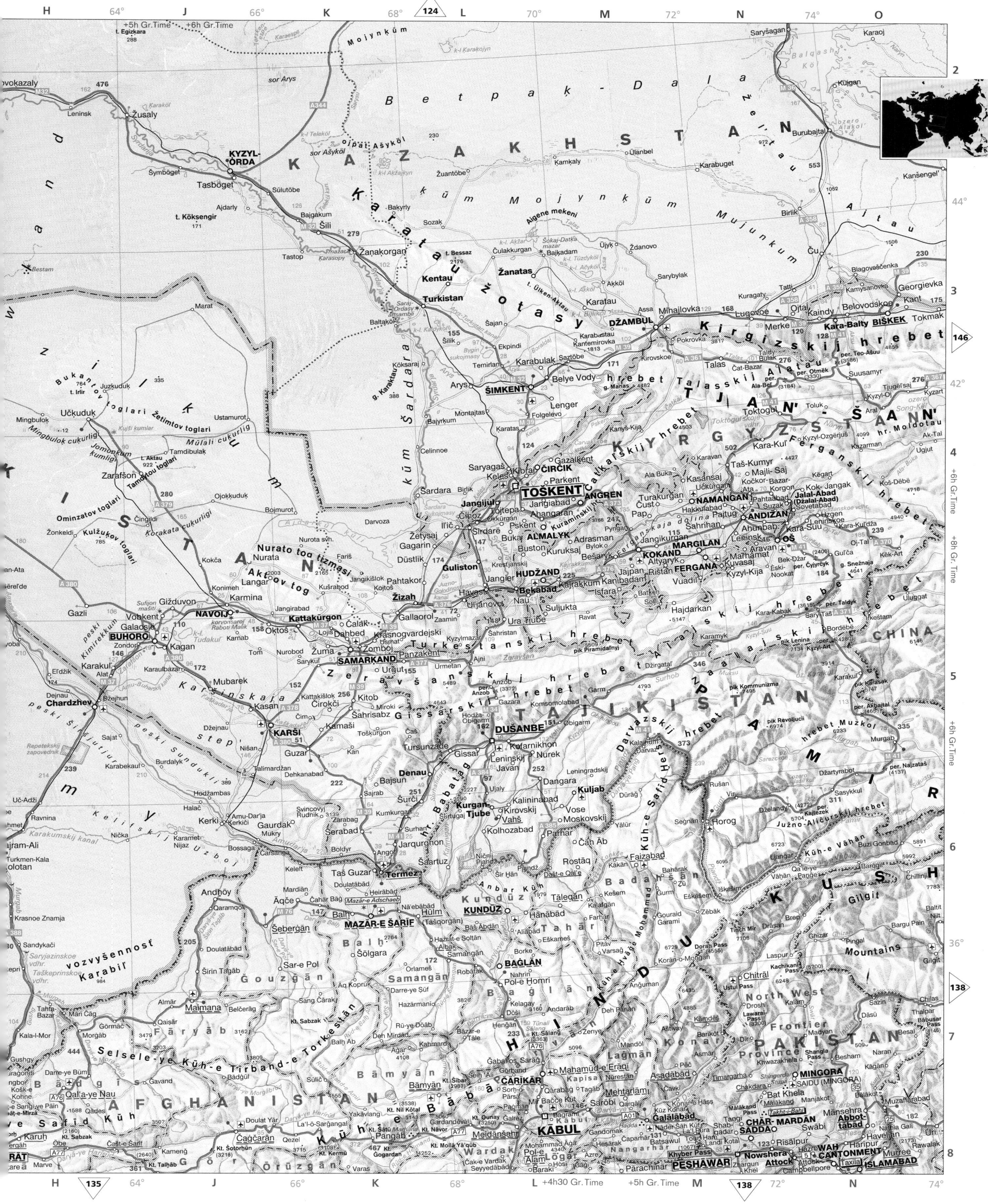

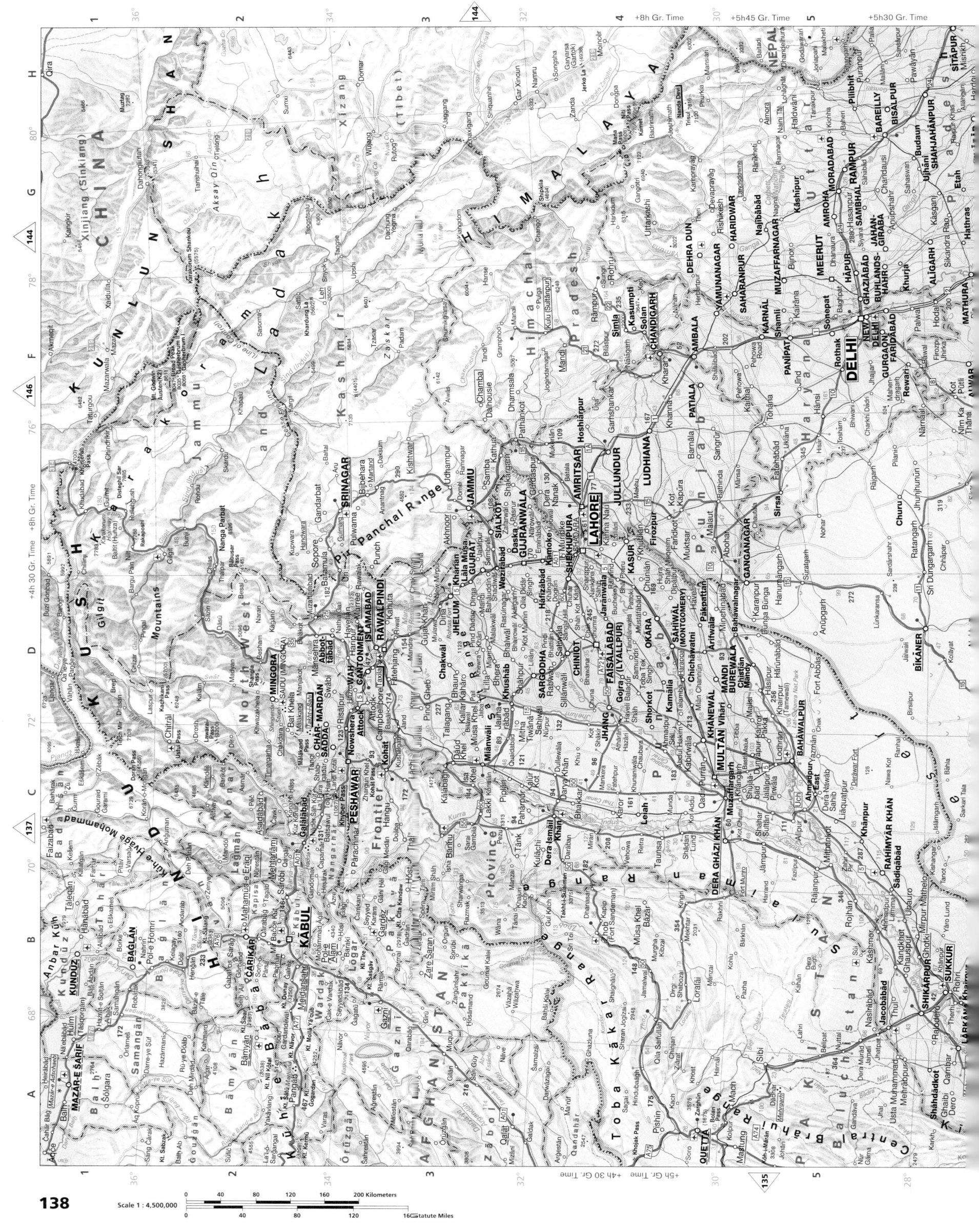

Scale 1 : 4,500,000

0   40   80   120   160   200 Kilometers

0   40   80   120

16 Statute Miles

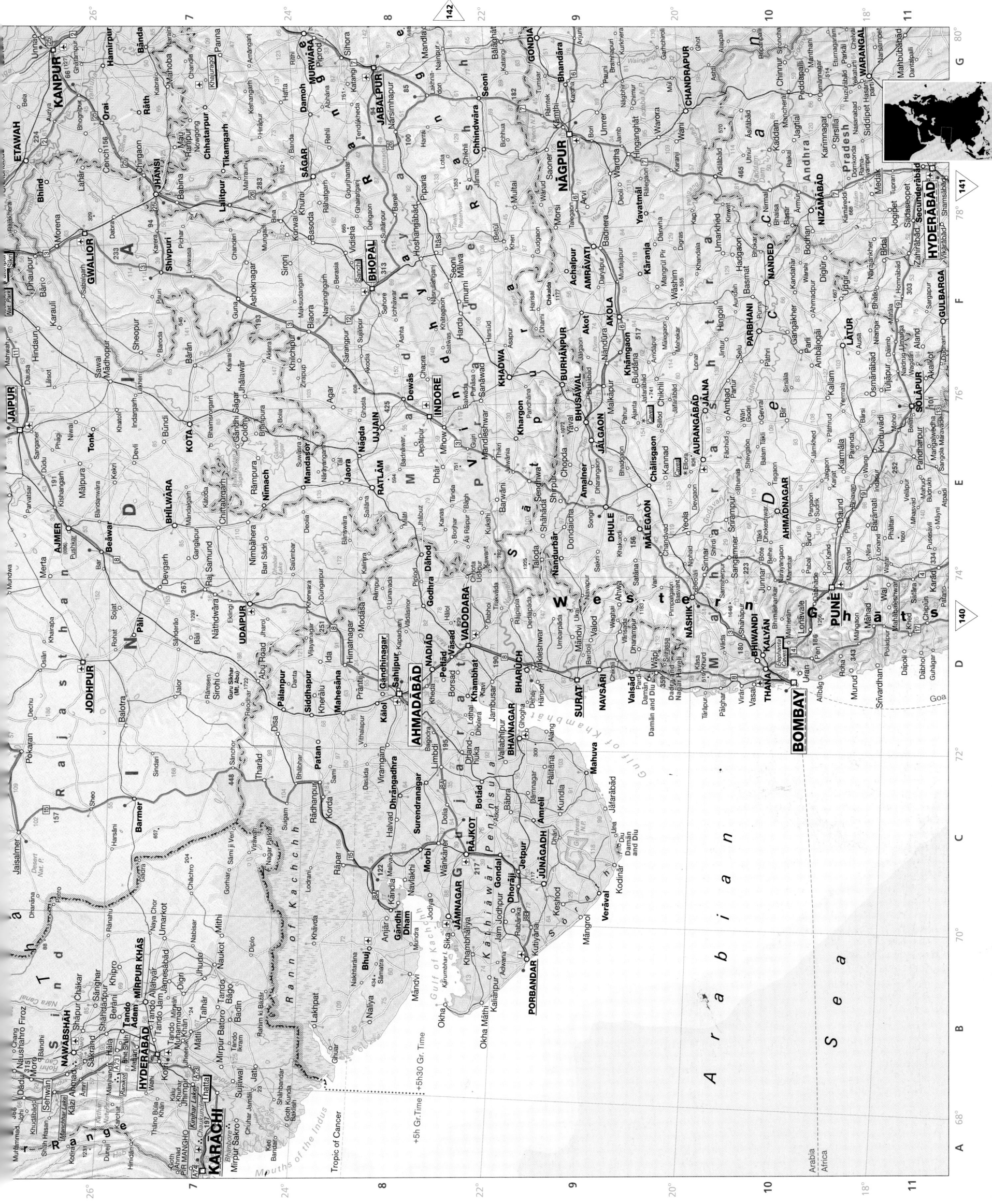

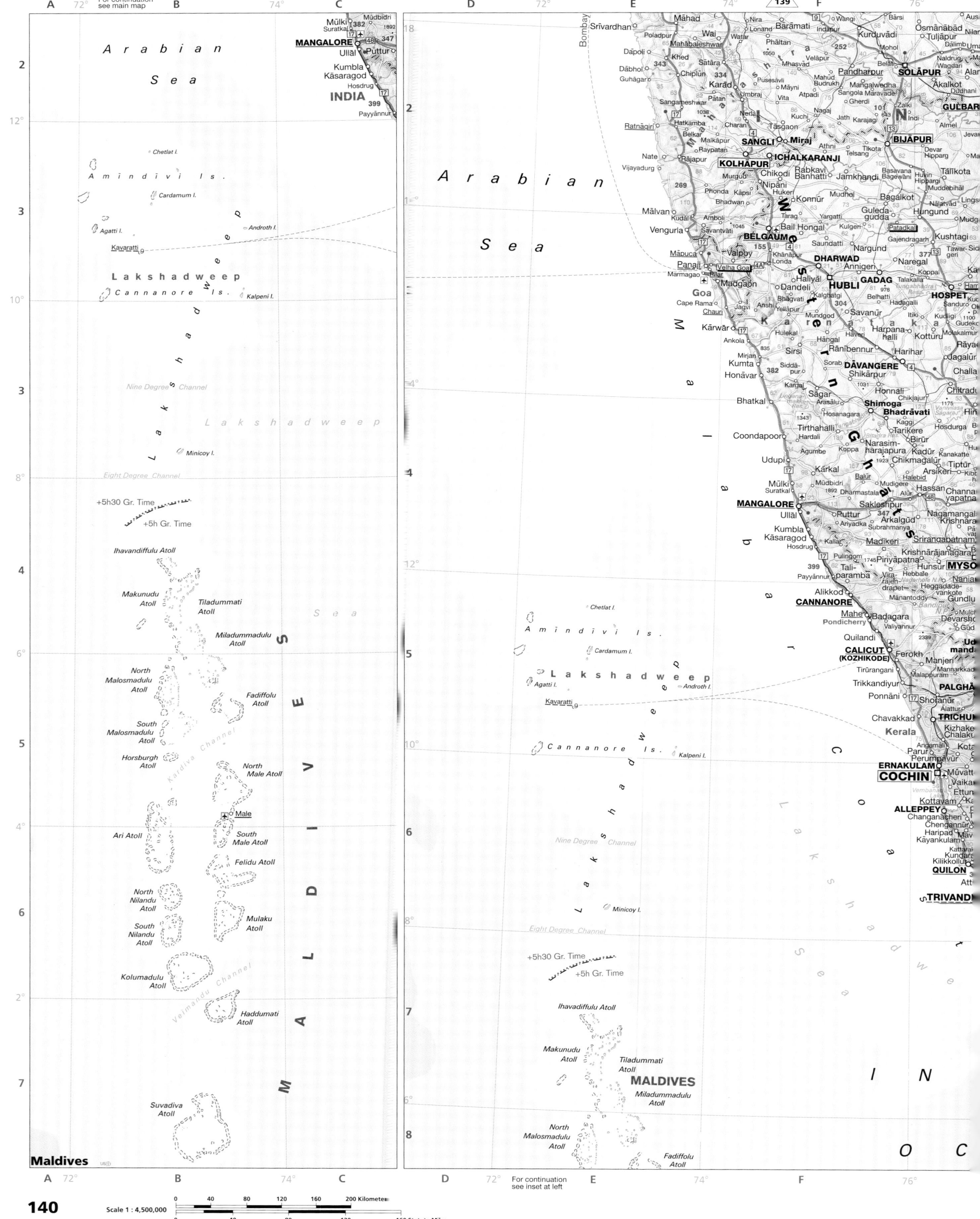

Scale 1 : 4,500,000

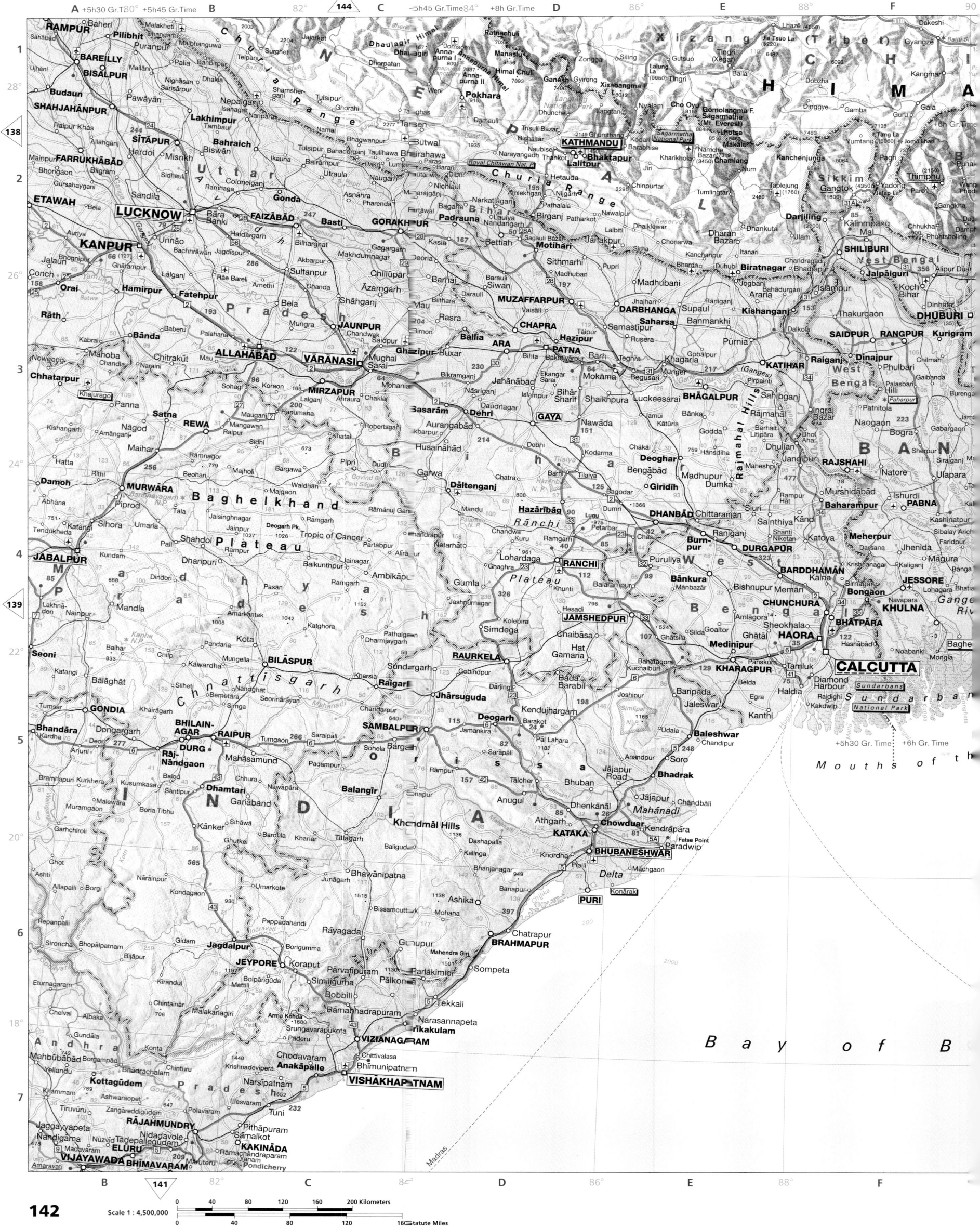

Scale 1 : 4,500,000

0   40   80   120   160   200 Kilometers

0   40   80   120   16⊂Statute Miles

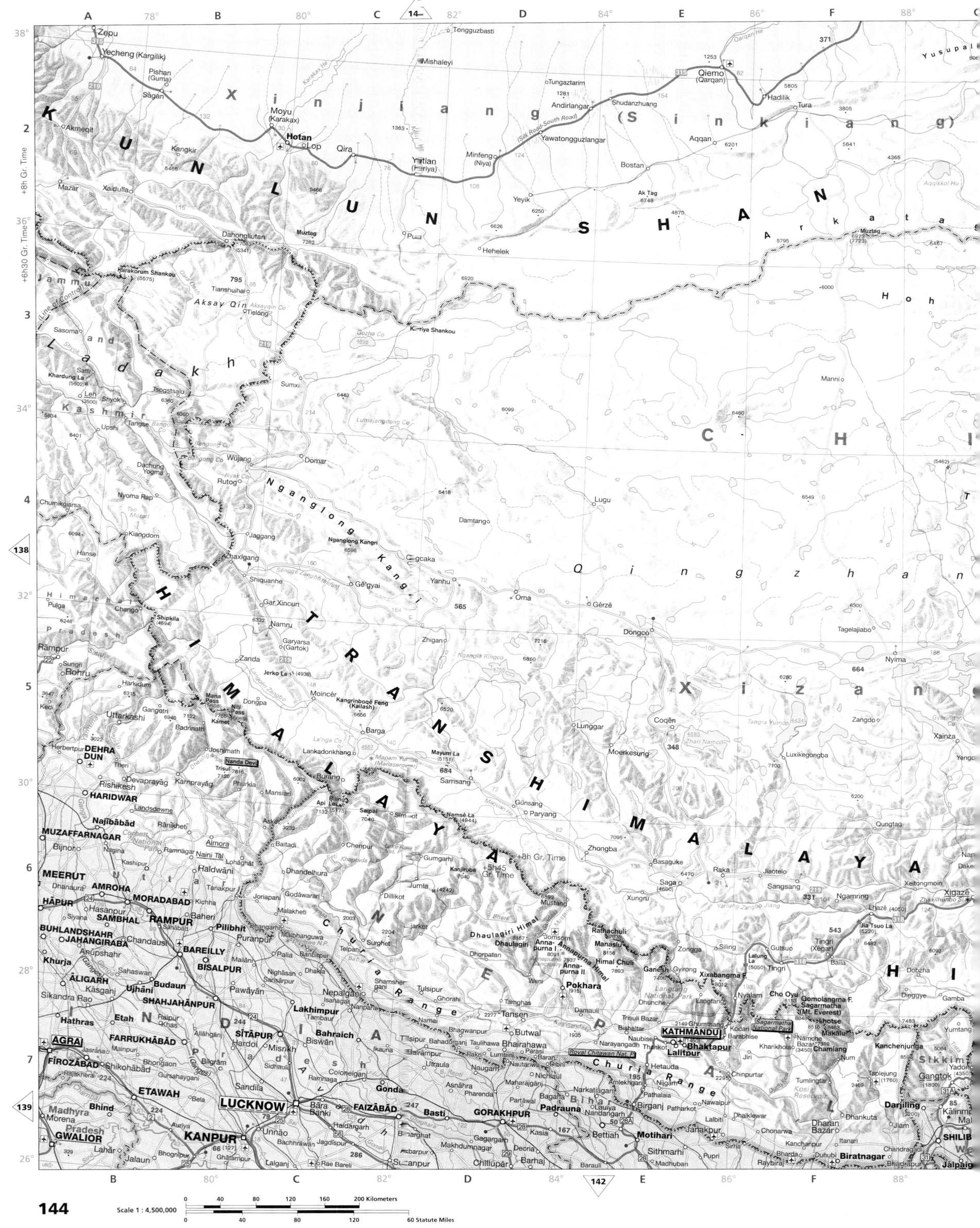

A 78° B 80° C 82° D 84° E 86° F 88° G

K U N L U N

Zepu
Yecheng (Kargilik)
Pishan (Guma)
Sāgān
Akmeqit
Kangkir
Mazar
Xaidulla
Moyu (Karakax)
Hotan
Lop
Qira
Yütian (Keriya)
Minfeng (Niya)
Tongguzbasti
Mishaleyi
Tungaztarim
Andirlangar
Shudanzhuang
Yawatongguzlangar
Aqqan
Qiemo (Qarqan)
Hadilik
Tura
Bostan
Ak Tag
6748
Yeyik
Hehelek

X i n j i a n g (S i n k i a n g)

Yusupal

371

K U N L U N S H A N

H o h

Dahongliutan
Karakorum Shankou (5575)
Tianshuihai
Aksay Qin
Tielong
Gozha Co
K riya Shankou
Sumxi
Muztag
Pu

Karakata

Muztag 6973 (7723)

+8h Gr. Time
+6h30 Gr. Time

J a m m u

L a d a k h
Khardung La (5602)
Leh (3500)
Shyok
Tsogstsalu
Upshi
Tangtse
Bangong Co
Pangong Co
Dachung Yogma
Nyak Co
Rutog
Nyoma Rap
Tso Morari
Chumikgiarsa
Kiangdom
Hanse
Zhaxigang
Shiquanhe
Gar Xincun
Gê'gyai
Domar
Wujang

K a s h m i r
Sasoma

C H I

Manni

Nganglong Kangri

Q i n g z h a n

Lumajangdong Co
Damtango
Lugu
Ngangla Ringco
Gêrzê
Dongco
Nyima
Tagelajiabo

Xainza
Yengc

T
Xianza

Pulga
Chango
Shipki La (4694)
Rampur
Rohru
Namru
Garyarsa (Gartok)
Zanda
Jerko La (4938)
Moincêr
Zhigano
Günsang
Paryang

H i m a c h a l

P r a d e s h

H I M A L A Y A

T R A N S H I M A L A Y A

X I Z A N

Coqên
Moerkesung
348
Lunggar
Zhari Namco (4685)
Tangra Yumco
Zangdo
Gyaring Co
Luxikegongba

664

Kedi
Uttarkashi
Gangotri
Badrinath
Kamet
Mana Pass (5608)
Niti Pass (5068)
Dongpa
Kangrinboqê Feng (Kailash)
Barga
Mayum La (5151)
Samsang
Zhongba
Raka
Jiaotelo
Saga (4600)
Sangsang
Ngamring
Xeitongmoin
Lhazê (4050)
Xigazê
Zhaxilhünbo Si

DEHRA DUN
Herbertpur
Theri
Joshimath
Nanda Devi
Trisul 7816
Lankadonkhang
Mapam Yumco (Manasarovar)
684
Burang
Api 7132 (5179)
Saipal
684

RISHIKESH
HARIDWAR
Devaprayag
Kamprayag
Phurkia
Mansiari
Namsê La (4944)
Günsang
Basaguke
Xungru
Qungtag

7095

Nar
Dake

Ngamring
331

Xigazê
543
Jia Tsuo La (5220)
Tingri
Baila

NAJIBABAD
Landsdowne
Aimora
Baitadi
Askot
Chenpur
Jumla
Gumgarhi
Kanjiroba 7040

MUZAFFARNAGAR
Bijnor
Nagina
Ramnagar
Naini Tal
Lohaghat
Dhandelhura
Dillikot

+8h Gr. Time
+5h45 Gr. Time

Mustang
Zongga
Siling
Gyirong
Gutsuo
Lalung La (5050)
Tingri
Xixabangma F.
8012
Nyalam
Cho Oyu 8153
Qomolangma F. Sagarmatha (Mt. Everest) 8848
Shishapangma

Gangtok
Darjiling

MEERUT
AMROHA
HAPUR
MORADABAD
RAMPUR
SAMBHAL
Hasanpur
Siyana
Baheri
Pilibhit
Puranpur
Maibhanguwa
Surghet
Telpani
Dhorpatan
Dhaulagiri Himal
Dhaulagiri 8167
Annapurna I 8091
Manaslu 8156
Himal Chuli 7893
Annapurna II
Ganesh
Langtang
Langtang National Park
Dhunche
Rathachuli
Rasuwa
Trisuli Bazar
Bishaltar
Barabhise
Kodari
Jiri
Kharikhola
Makalu 8475
Chamlang
Num
Kanchenjunga 8598
Sikkim
Yadong

BUHLANDSHAHR
JAHANGIRABA
BAREILLY
BISALPUR
Chandausi
Mailani
Palia
Banbirpur
Shamsher ganj
Tulsipur
Ghorahi
Tansen
Damauli
Pokhara (915)
Hetauda
Narayangadh
Thankot
Nuwakot
KATHMANDU
Bhaktapur
Lalitpur
Sagarmatha National Park
Tumlingtar
Taplejung (1760)
Dhankuta

Khurja
ALIGARH
Kasganj
Ujhani
Budaun
SHAHJAHANPUR
Pawayan
Nighasan
Dhaka
Nepalganj
Nanpara
Namai
Bhagwanpur
Butwal
Tamghas
Weni
Bhairahawa
Parasi
Baran
Nijgarh
Hetauda
Bhimphedi
Chamlang
Jiri
Chipurtar
Dharan Bazar

Sikandra Rao
Hathras
Etah
FARRUKHABAD
Kasganj
Raipur
Khas
Kichha
Bahraich
Biswan
Mahasarpur
Sansarpur
Bahadurganj
Tauliawa
Lumbini
Nautanwa
Nichiaul
Maharajganj
Pathlaia
Narkatiaganj
Amlekhganj
Birganj
Nawalpur
Dhalkewar
Lalbiti
Janakpur
Sirha
Pupri
Chandragadhi
Jalpai

AGRA
FIROZABAD
Jasrana
Mainpuri
Bhongaon
Shikohabad
Rajakhera
Madhya Pradesh
Morena
GWALIOR
Bhind
ETAWAH
Sandila
Bela
Ramnagar
Colonelganj
GONDA
FAIZABAD
BASTI
GORAKHPUR
Padrauna
Motihari
Sithmarhi
Bettiah
Bagaha
Raxaul
Birganj
Bharda
Duhabi
BIRATNAGAR
Jogbani
SHILIB
Jalpaiguri

LUCKNOW
Bara Banki
Haidargarh
Jagdispur
Barhaj
Deoria
Kasia
Barauli
Madhuban
Raybirai

KANPUR
Unnao
Bachhrawan
Rae Bareli
Sultanpur
Chillupar
Barhaj
Bharauli

Scale 1 : 4,500,000

0 40 80 120 160 200 Kilometers
0 40 80 120 60 Statute Miles

B 80° C 82° D 84° E 86° F 88°

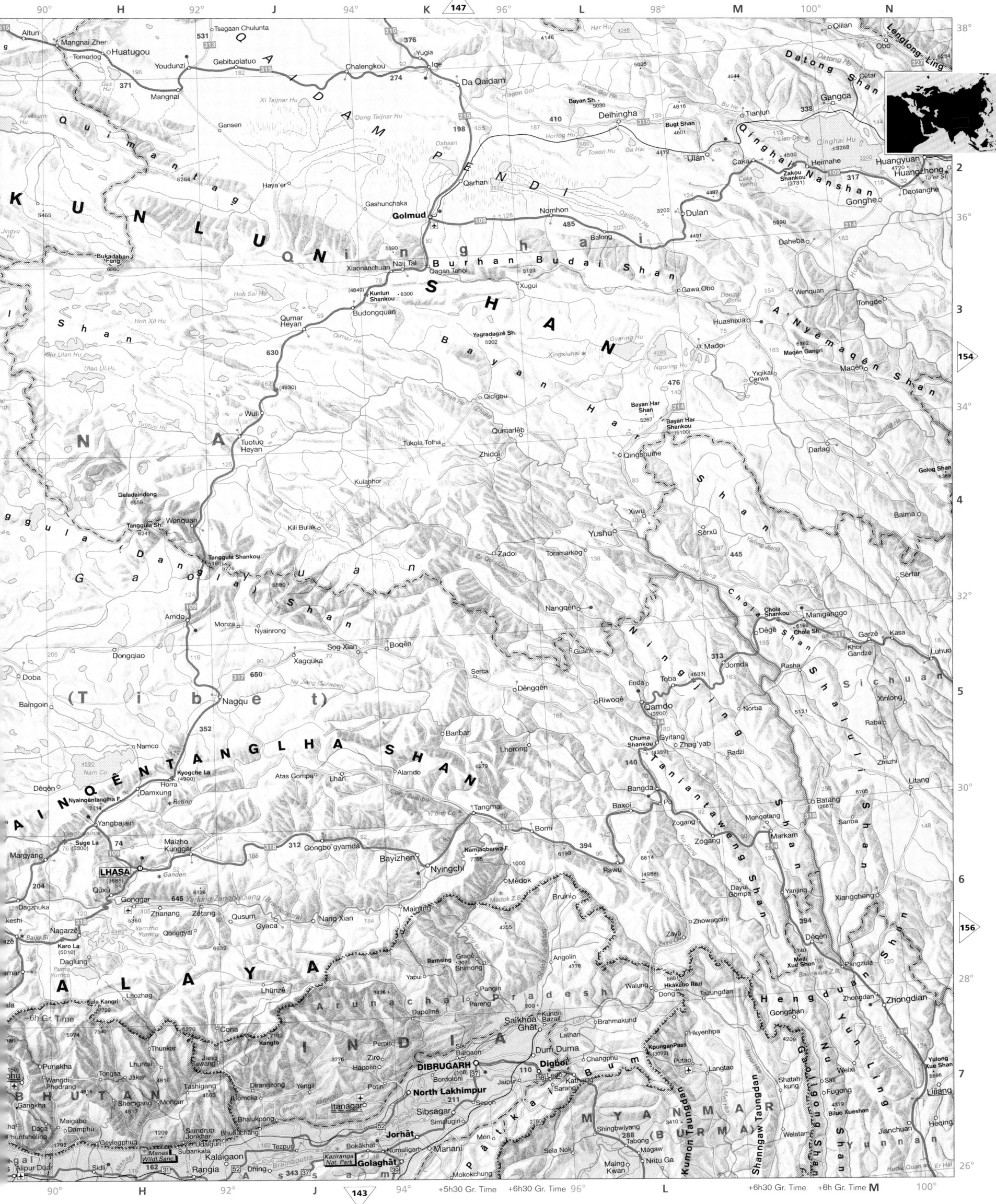

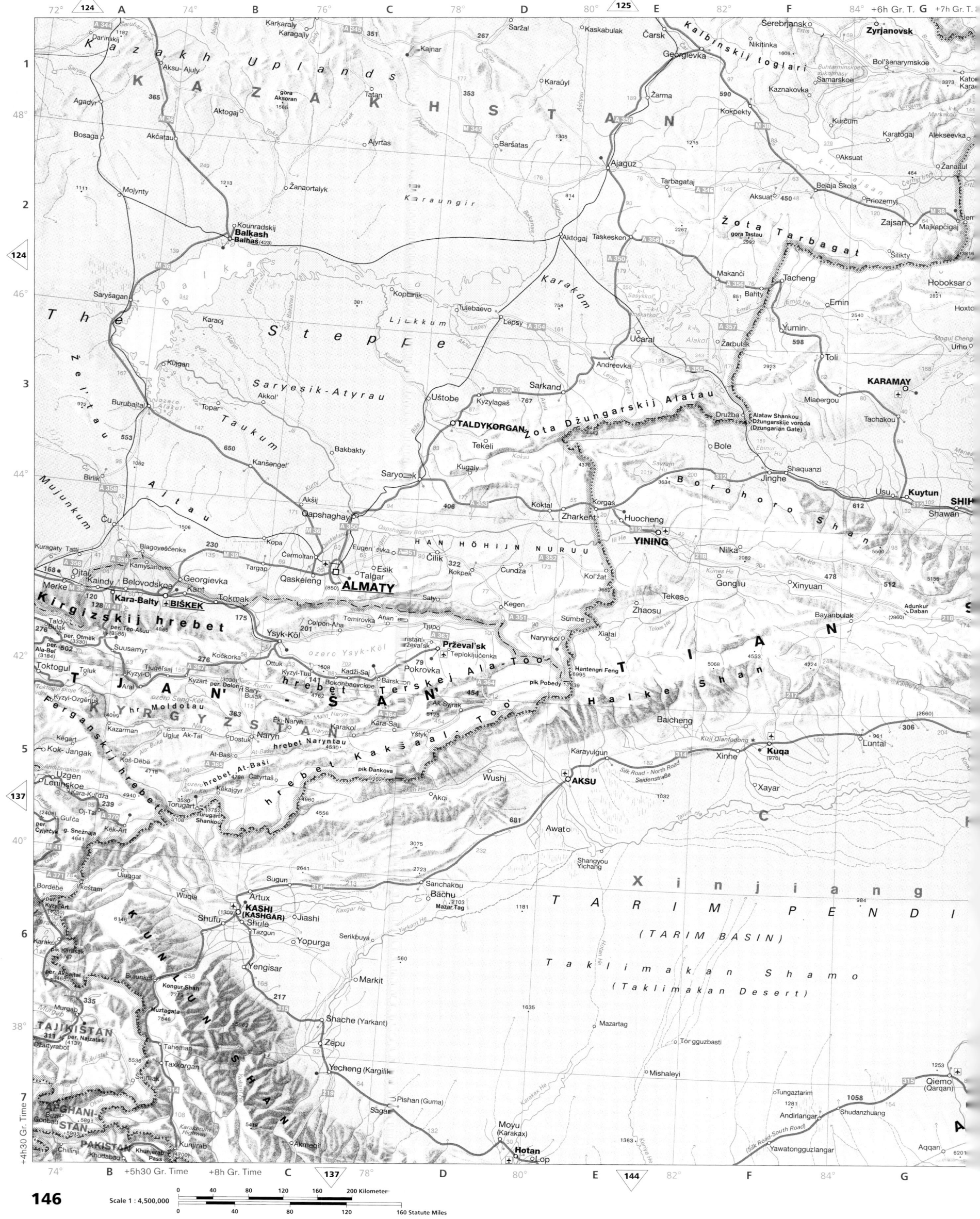

Zyrjanovsk

Kazakh Uplands
KAZAKHSTAN

Karkaraly
Karagajly
Saržal
Kaskabulak
Čarsk
Kalbinskij toglari
Serebrjansk
Nikitinka

gora
Aksoran
1566
Tatan
Kajnar
267
Georglevka
Bol'šenarymskoe
Samarskoe

Agadyr
365
Aktogaj
Alyrtas
353
Žarma
590
Kokpekty
Kurčum
Karatogaj
Alekseevka

Bosaga
Akčatau
Baršatas
1305
Ajaguz
Tarbagataj
Aksuat
450
Belaja Škola
Žanaaul

Mojynty
1111
Zanaortalyk
Karaungir
Tarbagataj
Aksuat
Zajsan
Majkapčigaj

Kounradskij
Balkash
Balhaš
Kol
Aktogaj
Taskesken
Makanči
Tacheng
Hoboksar

Sarýšagan
Kol
Koplik
Tulebaevo
Ljukkum
Lepsy
Učaral
Žarbulak
Emin
Hoxto

The Steppe
Saryesik-Atyrau
Sarkand
Andreevka
Yumin
598
Toli

Kujgan
Topar
Uštobe
Kyzylagaš
767
Zota Džungarskij Alatau
Miaoergou
KARAMAY

Birlik
Taukum
TALDYKORGAN
Tekeli
Kugaly
Druzba
Tachakou

Burubajtal
Kanšengel
Bakbakty
Saryozek
Kugaly
Borohoro Shan
Jinghe
Kuytun
SHIH

Čilik
Kokpek
Korgas
Huocheng
YINING
Nilka
Usu
Shawan

Almaty
Talgar
Esik
Čilik
Kol'žat
Tekes
Gongliu
Xinyuan

BIŠKEK
Kant
Tokmak
Narynkol
Zhaosu
Bayanbulak
TIAN SHAN

Pokrovka
Terskej Ala-Too
pik Pobedy
Halke Shan
Baicheng
Kuqa

AKSU
Xinhe
Luntai

Kashi
(KASHGAR)
Xinjiang
TARIM PENDI
(TARIM BASIN)

Taklimakan Shamo
(Taklimakan Desert)

Hotan

Scale 1 : 4,500,000

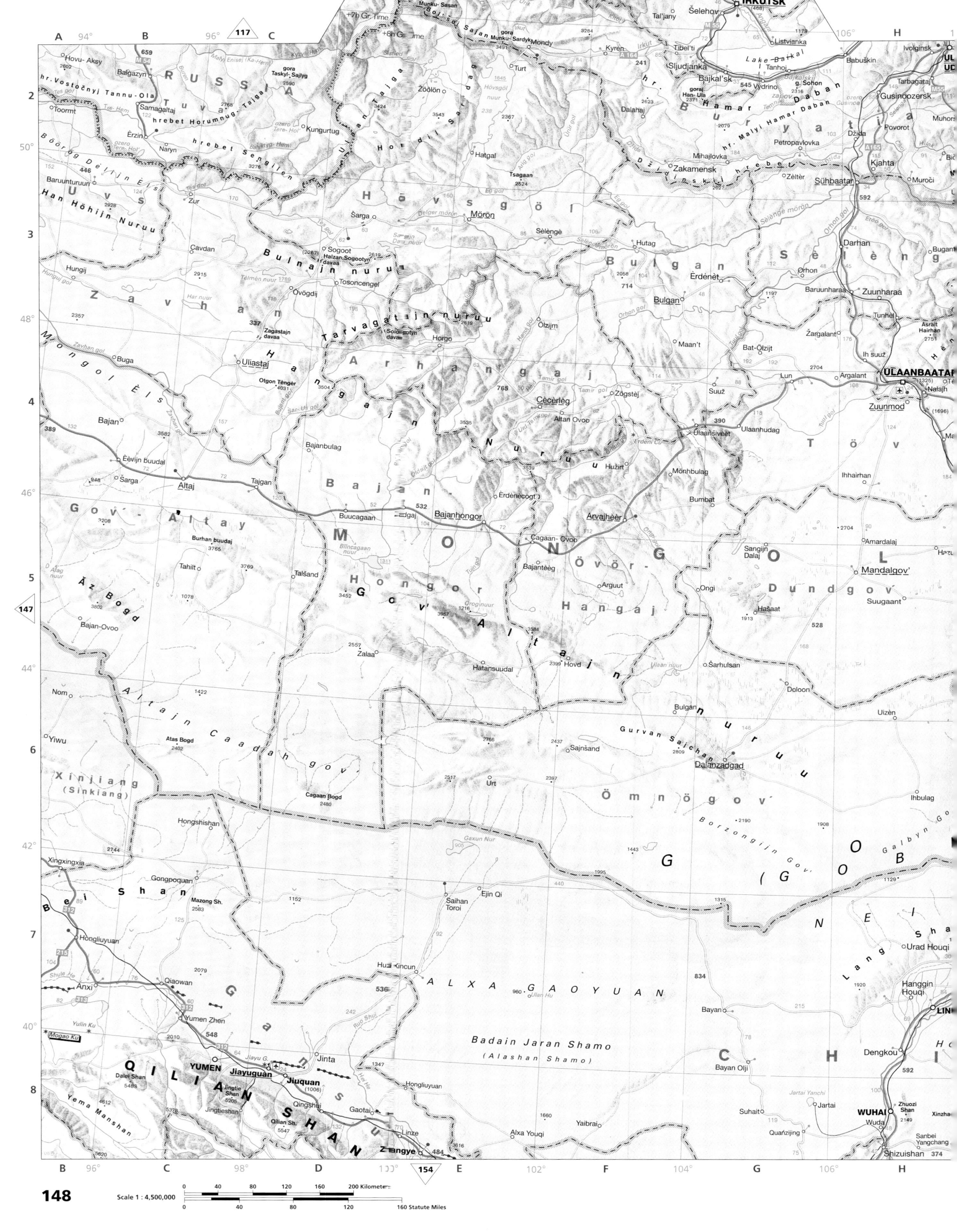

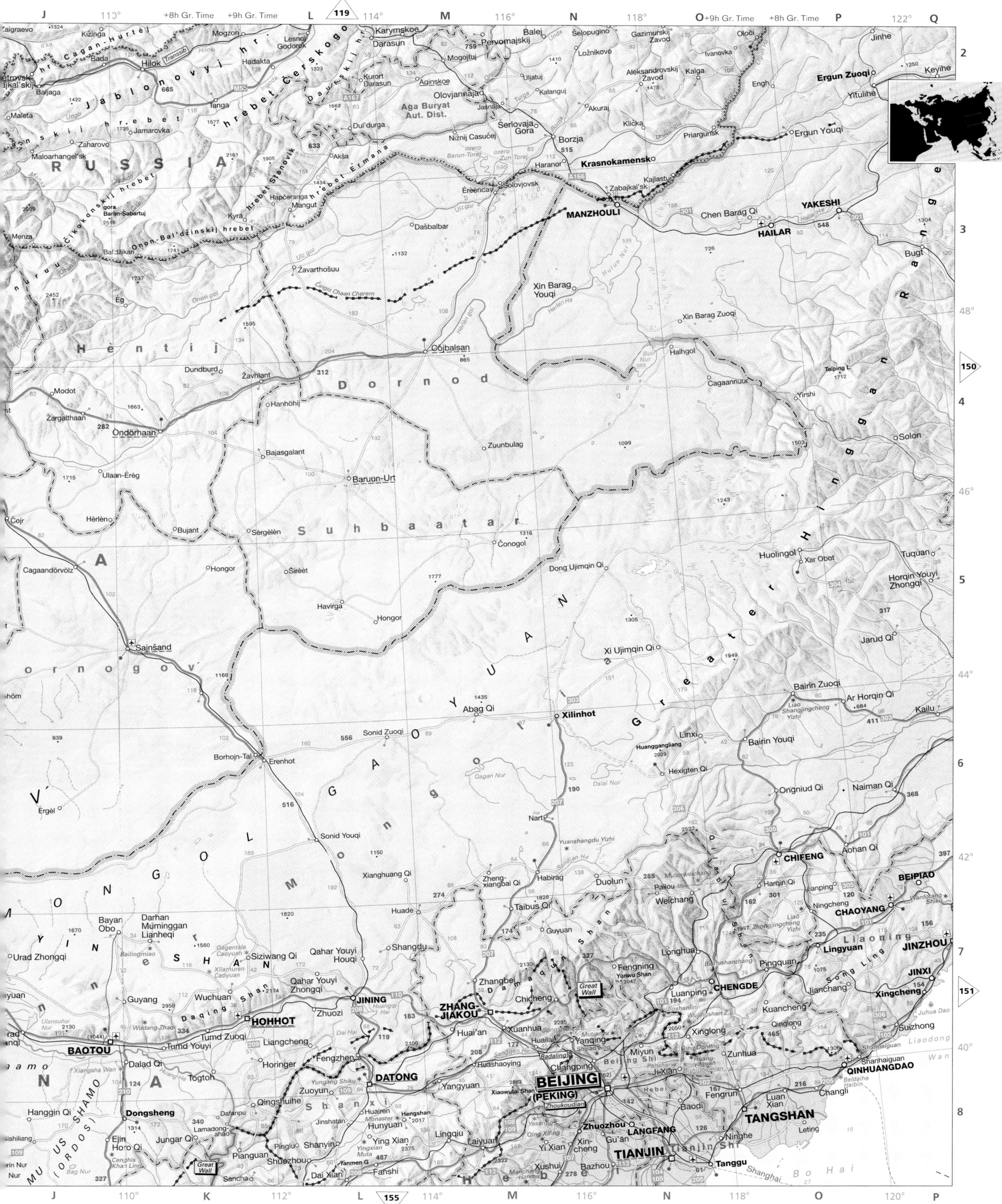

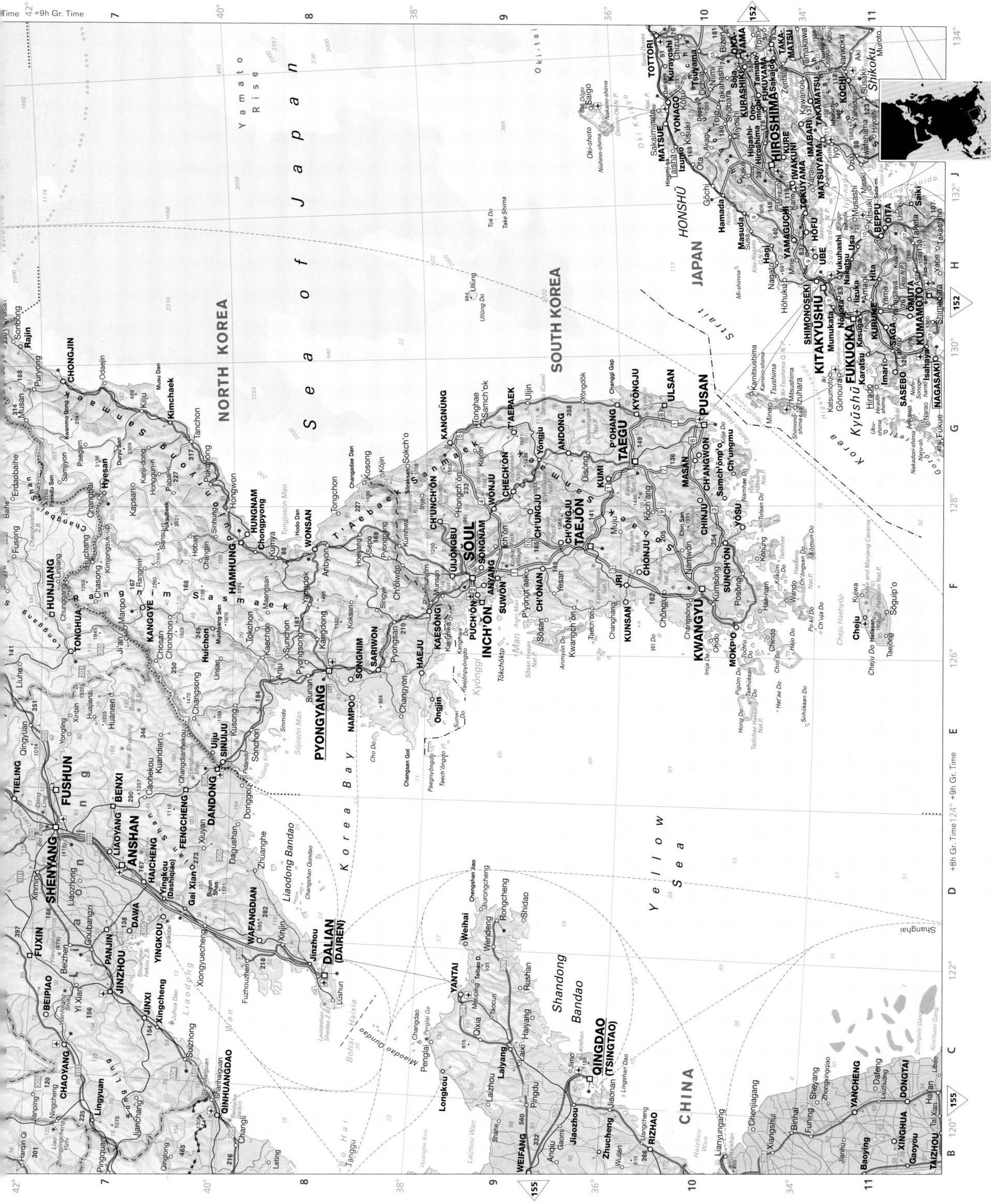

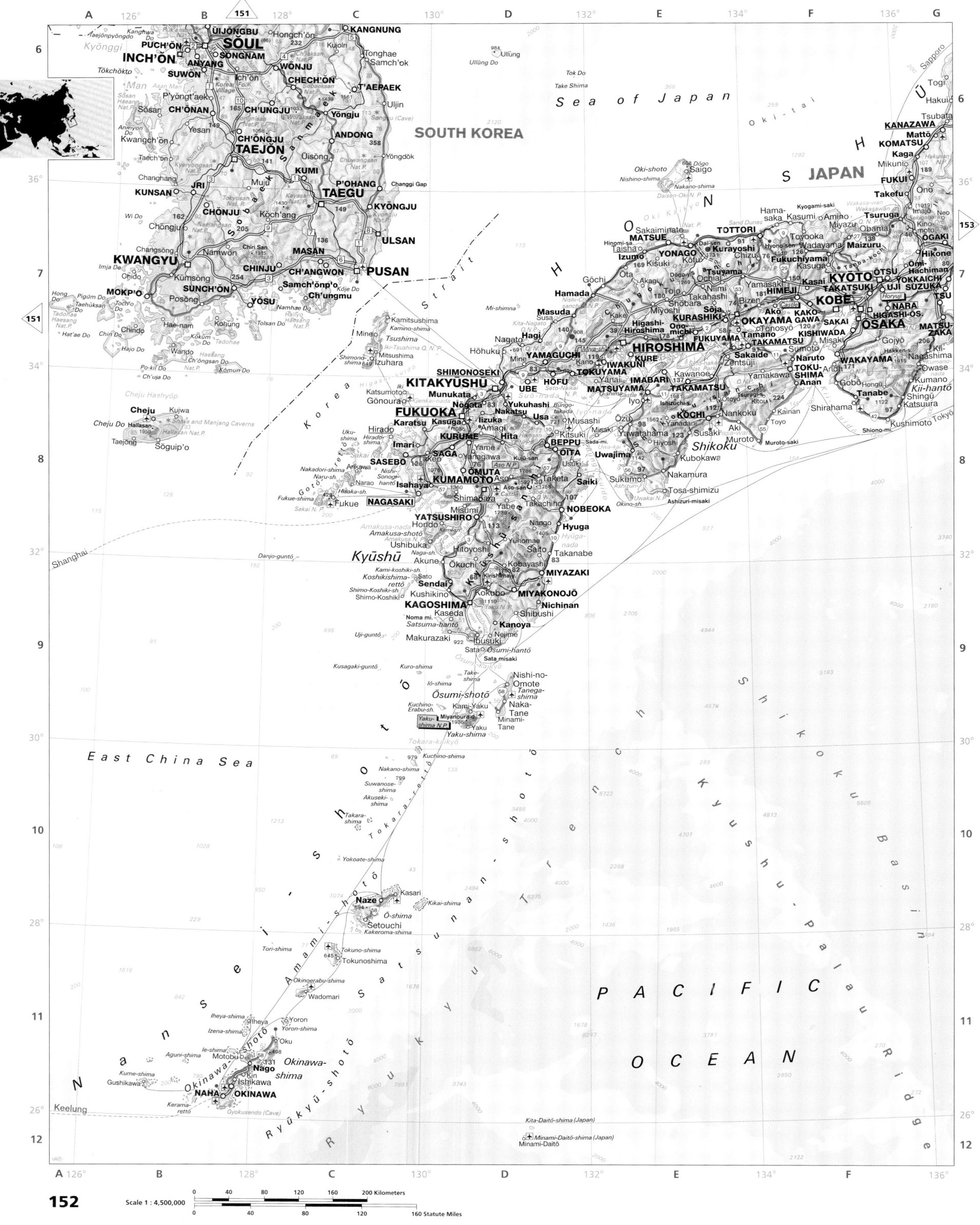

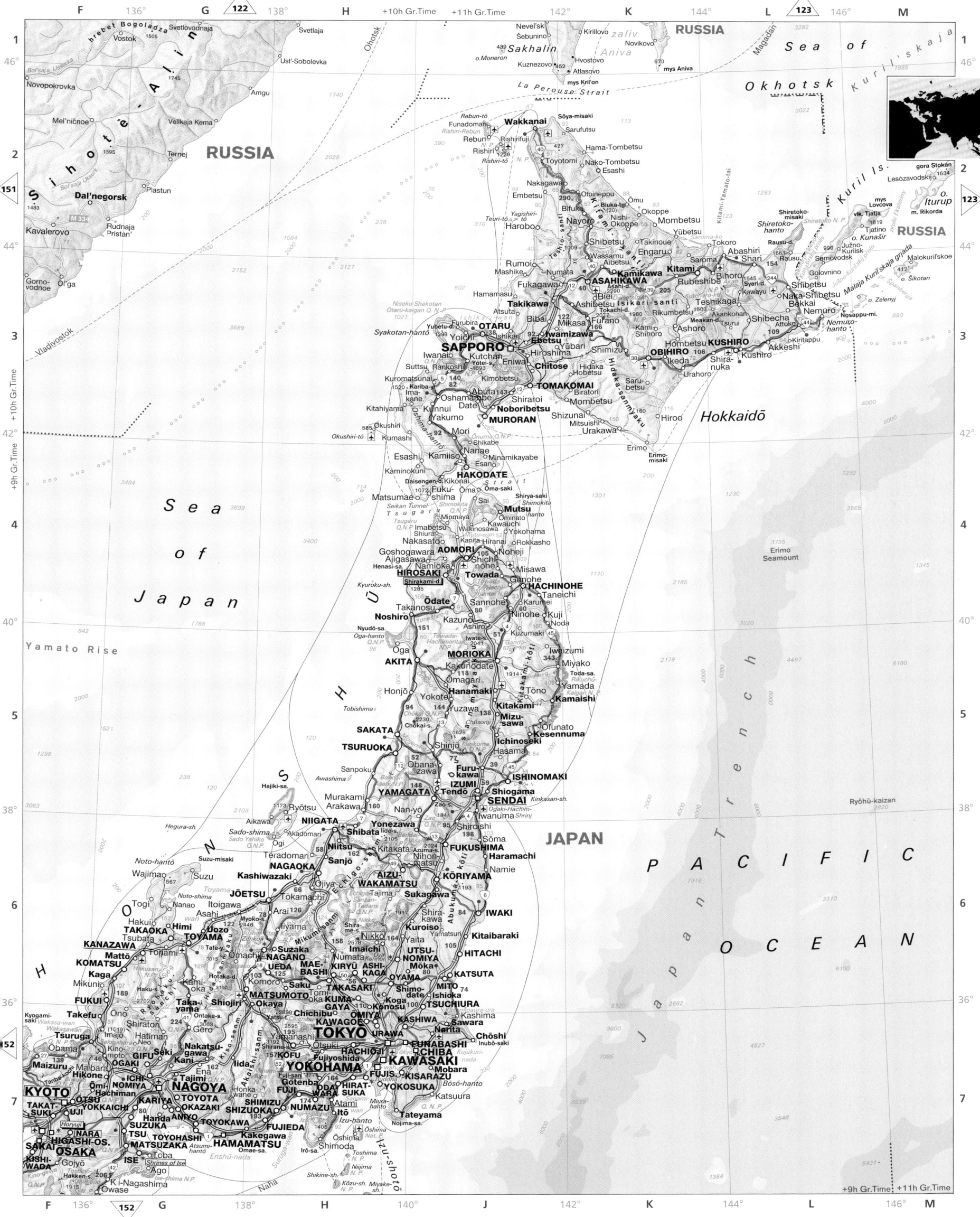

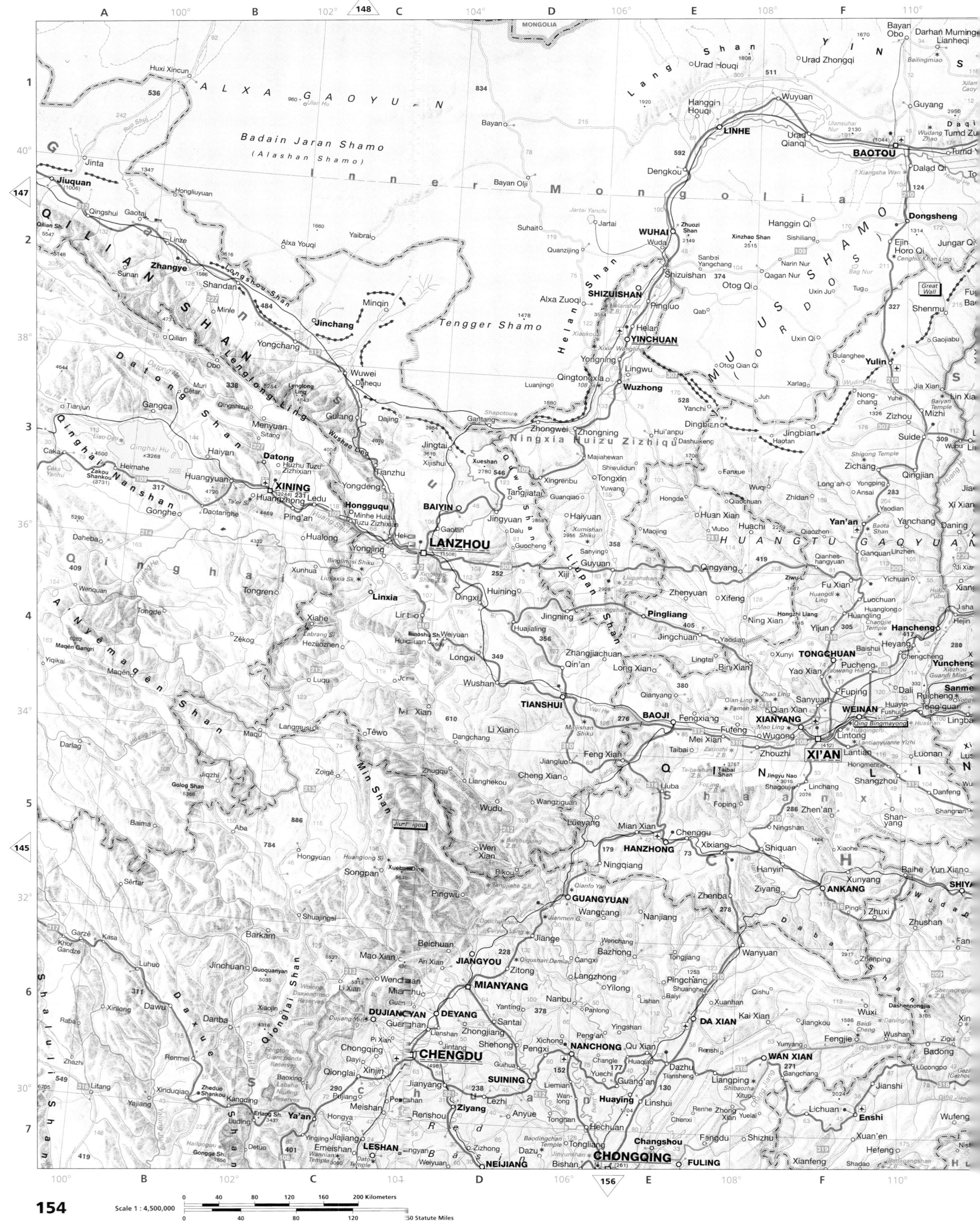

CHENGDU
SUINING
Chongqing
Jianyang
Xinjin
Guihua
Jintang
Dayi
Qionglai
Jiajiang
Lezhi
Liemian
Guang'an
Wan-long
Linshui
Jianshi
Huaying
Zhong Xian
Yuelai
Lichuan
Wufeng
Enshi
Ya'an
Meishan
Pengshan
Anyue
Tongnan
Hechuan
130
Chenxi
Fengdu
Shizhu
Xuan'en
Hefeng
Emeishan
LESHAN
Jingyan
Fong
Renshou
Dazu
Tongliang
Jiangbei
Nantong
NEIJIANG
Rongchang
Bishan
CHONGQING
FULING
Qianjiang
Xianfeng
Longshan
Dayong
Hanyuan
Ebian
Qianwei
ZIGONG
Long-chang
Yongchuan
Lishi
Jiangjin
JIULONGPO
Nanchuan
Wulong
Pengshui
Youyang
Laifeng
Ganxi
Shimian
Muchuan
Daguan
LUZHOU
Qijiang
Jinfo Sh.
Daozhen
Wuchuan
Yanhe
Lianghe
Yongshun
YIBIN
Suijiang
Changning
Huguo
Hejiang
Chishui
Zheng'an
Yanhe
Huayuan
Xide
Gong Xian
Xingwen
Xuyong
Xishui
Wenshu
ZUNYI
Xiazi
Meitan
Sinan
Jiangkou
JISHOU
Luxi
ZHAOJUE
XICHANG
Butuo
Yanjin
Daguan
Yiliang
Weixin
Changyang
Renhuai
Suiyang
Fenggang
Yinjiang
Tongren
Fenghuang
Chenxi
Mayang
Xupu
Dechang
Puge
Wuyi
ZHAOTONG
Yuhe
Tongzi
Qingkou
Yuping
Tianzhu
Hongjiang
Dongkou
Yulong Xue Shan
Guangmao Shan
Liangping
Yongsheng
Huaping
Miyi
Ningan
Qiaojia
Ludian
Hezhang
Magu
Wining
Jinsha
Xifeng
Qianxi
Kaiyang
Shibing
Zhenyuan
Weng'an
Sansui
Jinping
HUAIHUA
Liliang
Huidong
Zhehai
Bijie
Dafang
Jichang
Zhijin
Qianxi
GUIYANG
Guiding
Majiang
Leigong Sh.
Liping
Tongdao
PANZHIHUA
Yongren
Caiyuan
Wozhang Shan
Huize
Xuanwe
LIUPANSHUI
Liuzhi
Dashan
Pingba
Huaxi
KAILI
Jiannhe
Nanzhai
Chengbu
DALI
Dayao
Yuanmou
DONGCHUAN
Pan Xian
Guanling
Changshun
Huishui
DUYUN
Danzhai
Pingjiang
Maogong
Rongjiang
Sanjiang
Longsheng
Midu
Nanhua
Wuding
Songming
Maguohe
Fuyuan
QUJING
Yingshang
Pu'an
Niuchang
Duanshan
Pingtang
Dushan
Rongjiang
Congjiang
Guilin
Nanjian
Lufeng
Anning
KUNMING
Yiliang
Luliang
Luoping
Xingren
Zengfeng
Anlong
Wangmo
Dating
Luzhai
Tian'e
Nandan
Yangshuo
Pingle
Chuxiong
Yimen
Jinning
Lunan
Shizong
554
Bajie
Longlin
Jiuzhou
Qinwanglao Shan
Donglan
Jiuxu
Hechi
Yishan
Lipu
Yuxi
Huaning
Xinhao
212
Luxi
Xilin
Ding'an
Lucheng
Fengshan
Bama
Maonanzu
Tunqiu
Yongfu
Gongc
Zhenyuan
Echan
Tonghai
Qiubei
Tianlin
LIUZHOU
Jinggu
Kaiyuan
Jianshui
Pinguanjie
Majie
Babao
Funing
Bose
Tianyang
Du'an
Heshan
Laibin
Wuxuan
Pingnan
Taiping
YUANJIANG
GEJIU
Jije
Yanshan
Mengzi
Wenshan
zhou
Mugang
Tiandong
Linpeng
Shanglin
Mashan
Simao
Mirong
Luchun
Dougmuge
Wantang
Maguan
Napo
Debao
82
Pingguo
Wuming
Silong
Litang
Guiping
Teng Xian
Cenxi
Pu'er
Yuanyang
Jinping
Maijmo
Thao Phi Tung
Bao Lac
Trung Khanh
Daxin
Pingxiang
NANNING
Fusui
Wuxu
Heng Xian
Rong Xian
YULIN
Lingshan
Luchuan
Bobai
Pubei
Baoxu
QINZHOU
Xishuangbanna
Jinghong
Xinxu
Jingxi
Shangying
Taiping
Ningming
Siyang
Bangun
QINZHOU
MAOM
Fangcheng
Dongxing
Huazhou
Qingping
Lianjiang
Suixi
ZHANJIANG
BEIHAI
Xuwen
LAOS
VIETNAM
HÀ NỘI
HẢI PHÒNG
CẨM PHẢ
HỒNG GAI
THÁI NGUYÊN
BẮC NINH
NAM ĐỊNH
NINH BÌNH
THANH HÓA
VINH
Gulf of Tonkin
HAINAN DAO
HAIKOU
SANYA
HAINAN SEZ
Louangphrabang
VIANGCHAN (VIENTIANE)
CAMBODIA
THAILAND
MYANMAR
Leizhou Bandao

Scale 1 : 4,500,000

0 40 80 120 160 200 Kilometers
0 40 80 120 Statute Miles

China: Southern Region   **157**

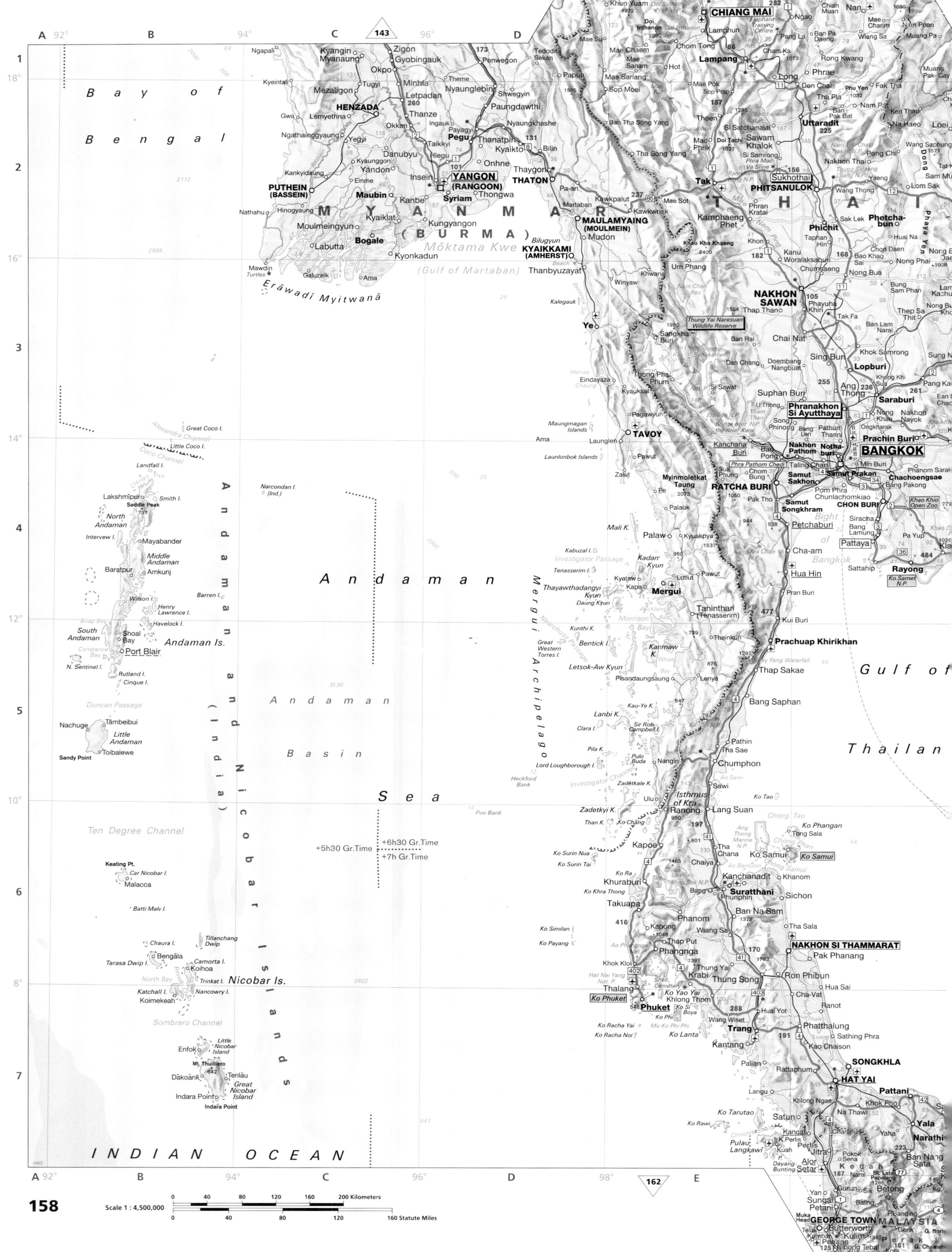

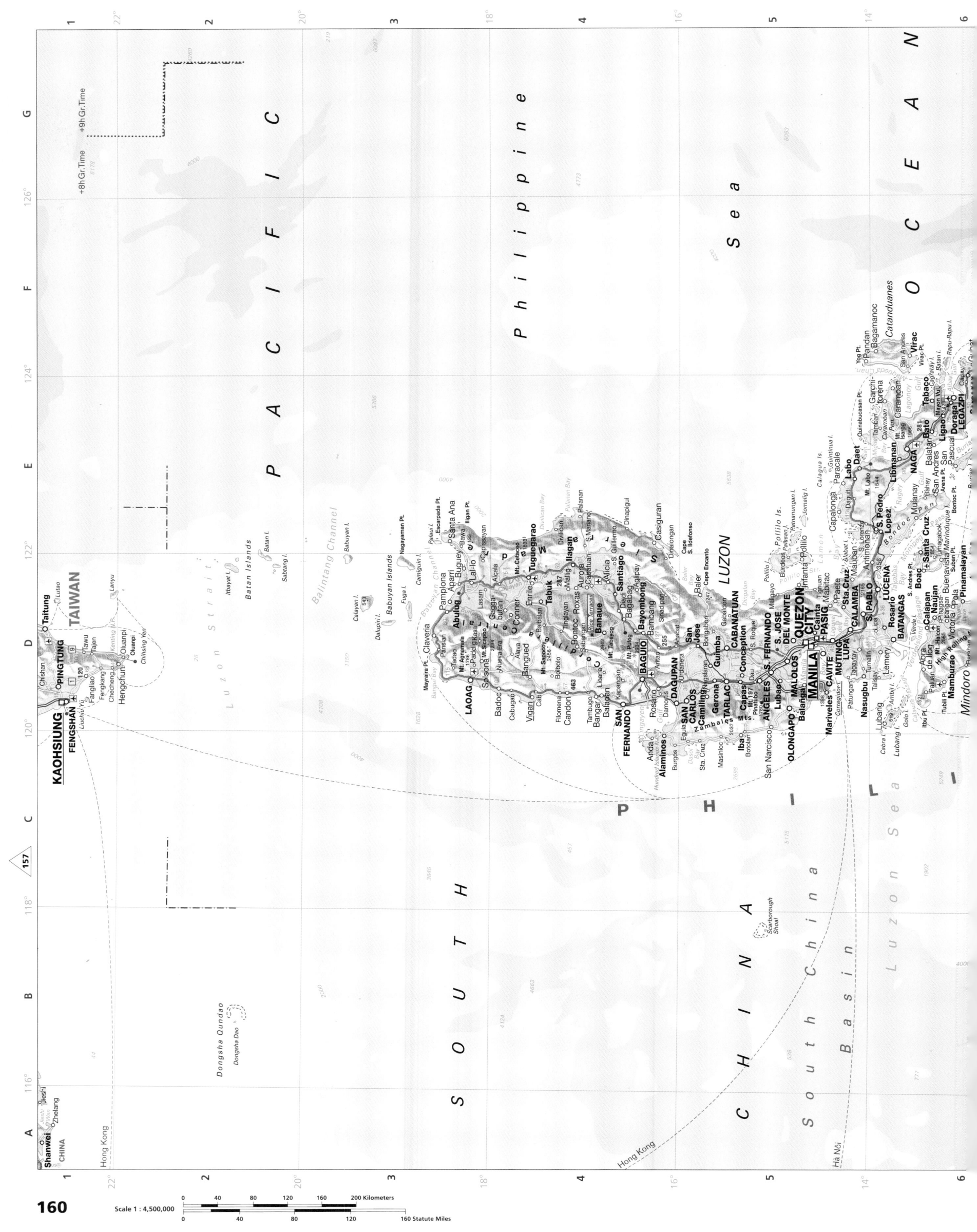

Scale 1 : 4,500,000

0   40   80   120   160   200 Kilometers

0   40   80   120   160 Statute Miles

△ **157**

KAOHSIUNG
TAIWAN
FENGSHAN
OPINGTUNG
Taitung

CHINA
Shanwei
Zhelang
Hong Kong

Dongsha Qundao
Dongsha Dao

P A C I F I C

O C E A N

Philippine

S e a

S O U T H

C H I N A

South China

Basin

L u z o n   S e a

Batan Islands

Babuyan Islands

Luzon Strait

Balintang Channel

Babuyan Channel

LUZON

MANILA
QUEZON CITY

LAOAG

BAGUIO

TARLAC

ANGELES

OLONGAPO

BATANGAS

LUCENA

LEGAZPI

NAGA

SAN FERNANDO

SAN CARLOS

DAGUPAN

Mindoro

P   H   I   L   I

Hong Kong

Hà Nôi

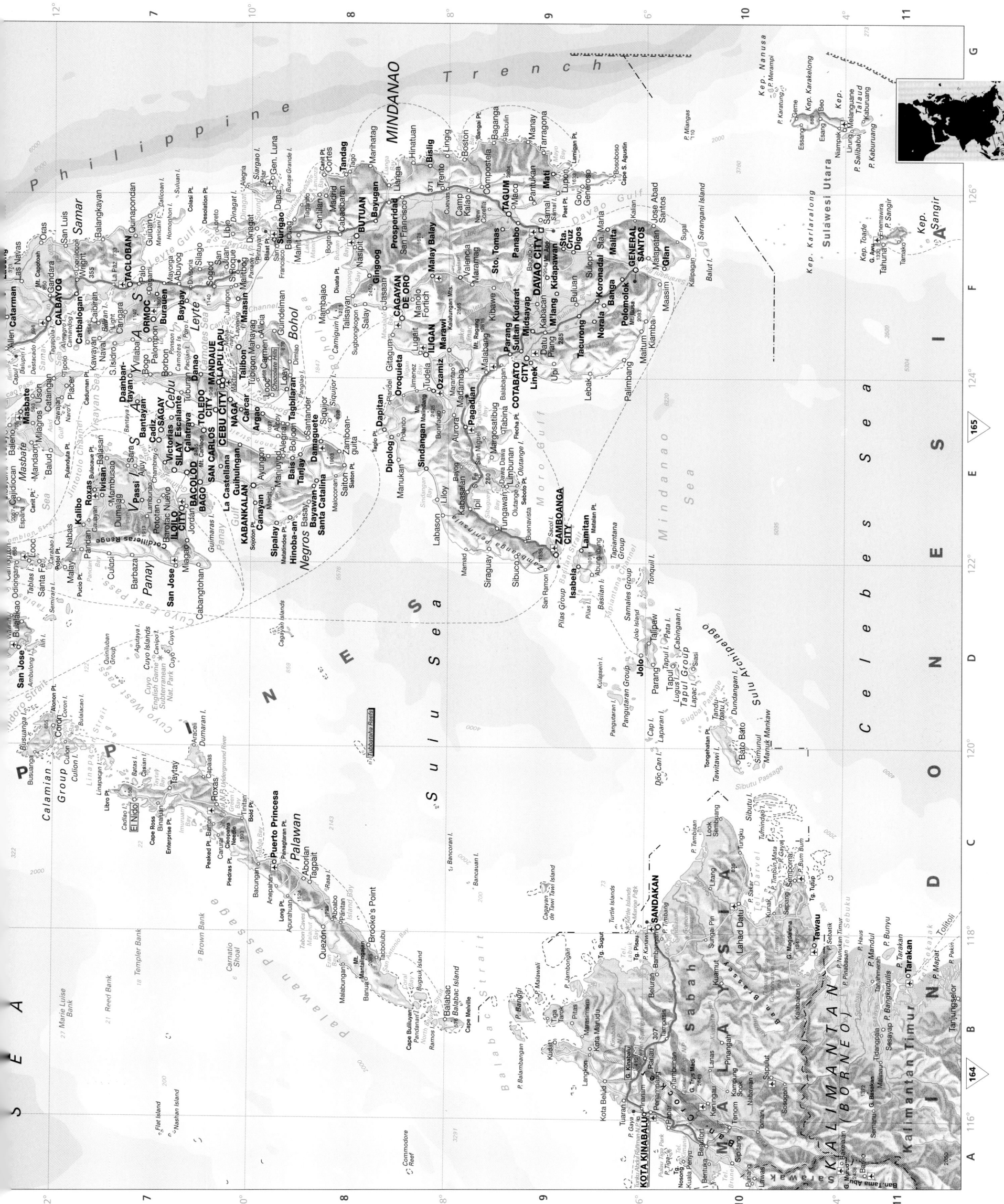

THAILAND
Ko Tarutao · Na Thawi · Khok Pho · 42 · Sai Buri
Ko Rawi · Satun · Kangat · Yala
Pulau Langkawi · Ko Lipe · Perlis · Ban Nang Sata · Narathiwat
Dayang Bunting · Kuah · Jitra · Alor Setar · Betong · Pengkalan Kubor
KOTA BHARU · Peringat · P. Perhentian Besar
Kedah · Pokok Sena · Bt. Lada · Papalang · 77 · Pasir Puteh · Jerteh · P. Redang
Gurun · Yan · Sik · Nami · 187 · Machang · Kuala Krai · 140 · Kg. Merang · Batu Rakit
Sungai Petani · Muka Head · Baling · Genk · Kg. Noring · Kuala · Ayer Deras · KUALA TERENGGANU
Pulau Penang · Butterworth · Kulim · G. Chamah · Kubu · Marang · Wakaf Tapai
GEORGE TOWN · Teluk Kumbar · Perak · Selama · Kota · Tembeling · Kg. Jorangau · Bongkok
Penang · Nibong Tebal · Tanjung Piandang · Taiping Siput · G. Korbu · Gua Musang · 220 · Kuala Dungun
Changkot Jering · 125 · K. Kangsar · Kg. Gajah · Meropoh · Kemasik
IPOH · Tanah · Gopeng · Kuala Lipis · Chukai
Ayer Tawar · Pantai Remis · Parit · Gajah · Kampar · Kg. Cherating
Damar Laut · P. Pangkor · Teluk Intan · Benta · Jerantut · Kuantan
Kampung Koh · Bidor · Raub · G. Benum · Maran
P. Sembilan · Bagan Datuk · Slim River · Bentong · Temerloh · Pekan
Kg. Sekinchan · Selangor · Kubu Baharu · Triang · Nenasi
Tanjung Karang · Sungai Buloh · Rawang · KUALA LUMPUR · PETALING JAYA · Nenasi
KLANG · Shah Alam · Kajang · Bahau · Gambang
SERAMBAN · Port Dickson · K. Pilah · Negeri Sembilan · Segamat · Mersing
Pasir Panjang · Tampin · Gemas · Labis · P. Tioman
Bagansiapiapi · Tg. Medang · Melaka · Muar · Chaah · Kluang · P. Pemanggil
Dumai · P. Rupat · Batupanjang · Batu Pahat · Ayer Hitam · P. Sibu
Bengkalis · Pontian Kecil · Kukup · Kulai · Kota Tinggi
P. Bengkalis · Duri · Sungaipakning · JOHOR BAHRU · Desaru
Selatpanjang · Minas · SINGAPORE · SINGAPORE · Pulau Bintan
PEKANBARU · Buatan · P. Batam · Tanjungpinang
Bangkinang · Parit · Riau · Tembilahan · P. Kundur · P. Combol
Langgam · Rengat · P. Basu · P. Singkep · Selat Berhala
Taluk · Banjarkasang · Dusunmudo · Simpang

Banda Aceh (Baiturahman) · Tanjung Ba'u · P. Weh · P. Breueh · Lambaro · Arigan
Seulimeum · Sigli · U. Pidie · Tg. Bateeputih · Lampanaih
Jantho · 218 · Lammeulo · Meureudu · Keudemane
Lamno · Bireuen · Glumpangdua · Lhokseumawe · Kutabagok · Tg. Jambuair
Lageuen · Takengon · Oreng · Bayu · Lhoksukon · Idi · Langkahan · Tg. Peureulak
Calang · Rumahbaru · Pameug · Pendeng · Peureulak
Keudeuteunom · Tangse · Kualalangsa · Langsa
Meulaboh · Terujak · Pantekra · Kualasimpang · U. Tamiang
Blangkejeren · Kutanibong · Koneng · Tanjungmarcang
Langka · Lamainong · Pangkalansusu
Blangpidie · G. Leuser · Tanjungpura · Pangkalanbrandan
Labuhanhaji · Kutacane · Hampenanperak · Belawan
Tapaktuan · Genting · Binjai · MEDAN · Delitua · Bungan · Sungaibamban
Tg. Dewa · Geloketapang · Bangunpurba · Lubuk Pakan · Kualatanjung
Sibigo · Kandang · TEBINGTINGGI · Indrapura
P. Simeulue · Bakungan · Seribudolok · PEMATANG SIANTAR · Labuhanruku
Kutaining · Ivabah · Sinabang · Sidikalang · Simanindo · Kisaran · Tanjungbalai
Ballasetas · Pulaksama · Pangururan · Ambarita · Teluknibung · Simpangkawat
Alaban · Barus · Porsea · Danau Toba · Tomok · Pulau Samosir · Bandarpasirmandogai
P. Babi · Bangkaru · P. Tuangku · Singkilbaru · Onanganjang · Baligg · Parsoburan · Tanjung Bangsi
Sorkam · Tarutung · Siborongborong · G. Sihabubu · Beremban · Negiralama
Kep. Banyak · Sibolga · Sibalanga · Rantauprapat · Labuhanbilik
Sifahandra · Sipiok · Gunungtua · Onanhasang · Sipiongot · Kotapinang
Lahewa · Padang Sidimpuan · Pintupadang · Binanga · Baganinsembah · Bagansiapiapi
Gunungsitoli · Sirombu · Pasarsibuhuan · Daludalu · Duri
P. Nias · Siabu · G. Malea · Pasirpengarayan · Titigading
Hilismaetano · Lagudri · Muarasoma · Kotanopan · Ujungbatu · Aliantan
Telukdalam · Natal · Rao · Rokan · Bangkinang
Hutanopan · Panti · Muaro Takus Ruins · Rantauparangin
Kep. Batu · Airbangis · Talu · Candi Muaratakus
Pulau Pini · Bonjol · G. Ophir · Suliki · Kotabaru · Reninjuan
P. Simuk · Mandiangin · Lubuksikaping · Tigapulan · Dusunmudo
Bawo · Ofuloa · Pulau Tanahmasa · Bukittinggi · Payakumbuh · Airmolek · Rengat
Pulau Tanahbala · Maninjau · G. Merapi · Batusangkar · Sungaidareh
Tiku · Padangpanjang · Talawi · Taluk
Kagologolo · Pariaman · Singkarak · Sawahlunto · Banjarkasang
Lubukalung · Solok · Muara · Tanjungiolo · Seberida
Pulau Siberut · PADANG · Telukbayur · Lubukbargalung · Batuampar · Kualatungkal
Muarasimatulu · G. Batumandi · Alahanpanjang · Kotabaru · Dusunpasirmajang
Muarasiberut · Tarusan · Painan · Muarabungo · Sungaibengkal
Sumatera Barat · U. Teluklembu · G. Kerinci · Muara tebo · 212 · JAMBI (TELANAIPURA)
Taibelee · Kambang · Muaratembesi · Muarabulian · Rantaupanjang
Sumatera · Balaiselasa · Sungai Penuh · Bangko · Bayunglincir
Sigoisooinan · Siulakderas · Pondung · Pauh · Dabuk · Sumatera Selatan
Pulau Sipura · Siberimanua · Tapan · Lamagagang · Sarolangun · Bingintelok
Sabeugukgunig · Simakalo · Mukomuko · Pasarbantal · Surulangun · Babat · Talangb
P. Pagai Selatan · Taitaitanopo · Pulau · Lebongtandai · Sukamenang · PALEMBANG
Tiop · G. Seblat · Trawas · Semeteh · Gelumbang
Muaraaman · Tabingbulang · Lubuklinggau · Muarabeliti · Pendopo
Lais · Curup · Kepahiang · Tebingtinggi · Bungamas · Muaraenim · Perabumulih
Ketahun · Angading · Lubuklinggau · Lahat · Tanjungenim · Pagerdewa
Bengkulu · Pasarbembah · Sugihwaras · 497 · Pagaralam · Baturaja
Tanjung Kerbau · Tais · G. Dempo · Manna · Sugihwaras · Martapura
Bengkulu · Padangangat · Padangguci · Muaradua · Bintuan
Pulau Enggano · Kayaapu · Ngaras · Belimbing
Krui · Tanjung · Bengkunat

Sumatera Utara · Aceh · Istimewa · Daerah · Daerah Istimewa Aceh
Riau · Jambi · Bengkulu · Sumatera Barat · Sumatera Selatan

Strait of Malacca
Malay Peninsula
INDIAN OCEAN
Java Trench
Mentawai Strait
Selat Siberut · Selat Bungalaut · Selat Sikakap · Selat Sanding · Selat Bang · Selat Berhala
Kep. Mentawai
Sumatera
Equator

Scale 1 : 4,500,000
0 40 80 120 160 200 Kilometers
0 40 80 120 160 Statute Miles

SOUTH CHINA SEA

8 Friendship Shoal

4 North Luconia
Shoals

3 Seahorse Shoal

5 South Luconia
Shoals

L   A   Y   S   I   A

Kota Kinabalu

Kuala
Belait
Lumut
Seria
BRUNEI
Lutong
Miri
Labi
Batu Danau
Batu Baram
Kuala Baram

P. Laut

Marudi
Bekenu
Batu Satu
R. Sare
G. Mulu
Long Lama

P. Salor
Telukbutun
P.Natuna Besar
Ranai
P. Batu
Pestilyon
Panarik
P. Lagong

Beluru
R. Entebang
Niah
Niah N.P.
Niah Caves
G. Mulu N.P.
Long Palai

Tg. Payong
Suai
530

Kep. Anambas
P. Matak
Tarempa
Kepulauan   Natuna

Djems Bank

Bintulu
Kuala Tatau
Tubau
Sebauh

P. Midai

Mukah
Oya
Balingian
Tatau

P. Jemaja
P. Raibu

P. Subi
P. Subi Besar
P. Panjang
P. Seraya
P. Serasan
441

Belaga
Kejaman
Merit
Bk. Batu
2012
Tungku
Rumah Kulit
Longnawan
G. Tibau
1555

Laut   Natuna

Sel.   Serasan

Sirik
Pulau Bruit
Daro
Matu
Dalat
Nanga
Tamin

S   a   r   a   w   a   k

Tg. Datu
Tel. Datu
Tg. Api
Sematan
Tg. Sipang
Bako N.P.
Santubong
Paloh
Kundu
Sampadi
KUCHING
Semera

Rajang
Sarikei
SIBU
Bitangor
Kanowit
Song
Kapit
Peg.
Hose

Roban
Saratok
Budu
Pakan
261
163
Beton
Engkilili

Kapuas   Hulu

G. Lawit

Kep. Tambelan
P.Uwi
P. Tambelan
Besar
P. Benua

Sambas
Siluas
Siburan
Padawan
Bau
G. Niut
1701
Serian
Tebedu
Pantu

Pusa
Sebuyau
Debak
Lingga
Simunjan
Bandar Sri Aman
(Simanggang)

Kuda
G. Lawit
Putusibau
Kualakenau
G. Liangpran
2240

SINGKAWANG
P. Lemukutan
Benkayang
Balaikarangan
190

Lubok Antu
Semitau
1744

Peg.   Muller

G. Pancungapang
1736

Kep. Badas

Sungairaya
Pinang
Mempawah
Tg. Bangkai
Ngabang
Sosok
Mandor
Sanggau
Sintang

Kalimantan

Longkay

164

P. Pejantan

PONTIANAK
P. Tanjungsaleh
Tayan

Nanga Pinoh

Sanpei
Purukcahu
Equator

Tg. Putus
Kertamulia

Balaiberkuak

Barat
G. Saran

G. Raya
2278
Schwaner
Tumbanglahung
302
1728
Olongliko

Tg. Padangtikar

Jawi

Nangak Sokan
(BORNEO)
Tewah

K   a   r   i   m   a   t   a

O

N

E

S

I

A

Kalimantan

Buntok

P. Penebangan
R. Maya
Tg. Pasir
Tel.
Sukadana
Sukadana
Teratak
Nanga Tayap
G. Sebuyau
1377
Peg.
Schwaner
509
Mendawai
Tumbangsamba

Mengkatip

P. P. Pelapis
P. Buan
P. Karimata
Kep. Karimata
P. Serutu

Tg. Bawang
Ketapang

Marau
Tanjungwaringin
Rantaupulut
Belangan
Pandehang

Tengah

Palangkaraya
Pilang

Sukaraja
Sadau
Pangkalanbuun
Kumai
Sampit
Pulangpisau

Kendawangan

D. Sembulu

Kualakapus
Marabahan

Tg. Samuk
Belinyu
Tg. Tiung
Matras Beach
P. Bawal
P. Gelam
Kualapembuang
Telagapulang
Senuda
Bahaur
Samsudin
Noor

Kelapa
Sungaiselan
Sungailiat
Tg. Raya
Tel.
Airhitam
Tg. Keluang
Kotawaringin
Tel.
Kumai
Pegatan
Tel.
Sebangau
BANJARMASIN
MARTAPURA

PANGKALPINANG
Koba
Pulau Belitung
Buding
Manggar
Tg. Puting
Kualapembuang
Tg. Malacu
Batibati

Payung
Sungaiselan
Tg. Berikat
P. Liat
Badau
Dendang
Pelaihari

P. Bangka
Toboali
Tg. Saranglayang
Tg. Baginda
P. Lepar
Membalong
13
Batakan
Tg. South

Tg. Koyan
Tanjung Kait
P. Selui

G   R   E   A   T   E   R   S   U   N   D   A

Tg. Lumut
Tanjung Lumut
55

+8h Gr. Time

I   S   L   A   N   D   S

P. Karamian
+7h Gr. Time

Menggala
Gayohpecoh
Surabaya

J   a   v   a   S   e   a
54
60

P. Masalembo-
besar

Dintiteladas

BANDAR LAMPUNG
Panjang
Natar
Labuhanmeringgai

J   A   V   A

Kep. Seribu
Kep. Karimunjawa
P. Bawean
Bitian Bank

Tg. Krawang
Semarang
Surabaya

Merak
P. Panjang
JAKARTA
Java
Barat
P. Rakit

Kandang-
haur
Indramayu
Karangampel

SERANG
BEKASI
KARA-
WANG
Pamanukan
Cilamaya
Tg. Cimanuk
Subang
Jatibarang
CIREBON

Tang-
rang
Rangkas-
pitung
BOGOR
(BUITENZORG)
Plered
PURWA-
KARTA
Sumedang
Jatiwangi

Ujung Kulon
Nat. Park
CIANJUR
CIMAHI
SUKABUMI
BANDUNG

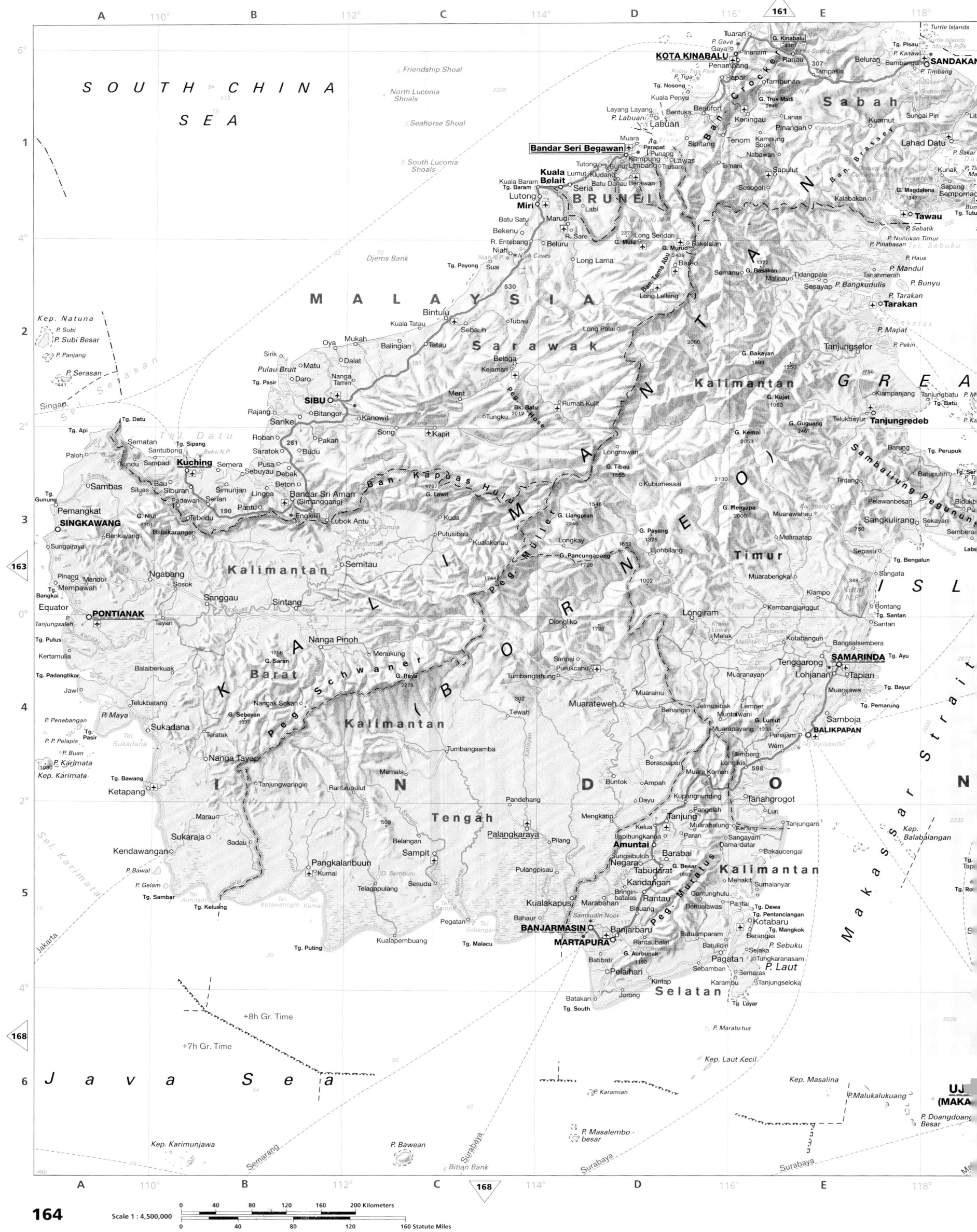

SOUTH CHINA SEA

Friendship Shoal

North Luconia Shoals

Seahorse Shoal

South Luconia Shoals

Djems Bank

Kep. Natuna
P. Subi
P. Subi Besar
P. Panjang
P. Serasan

MALAYSIA

BRUNEI
Bandar Seri Begawan
Kuala Belait
Miri

KOTA KINABALU
Sabah
SANDAKAN

G. Kinabalu
Labuan

Tawau

Sarawak

SIBU
Kuching

SINGKAWANG

PONTIANAK

Kalimantan
Barat

Kalimantan
Tengah

Kalimantan
Timur

SAMARINDA
BALIKPAPAN

Kalimantan
Selatan

BANJARMASIN
MARTAPURA

Tanjungredeb

Tarakan

B O R N E O

K A L I M A N T A N

Peg. Schwaner
Peg. Muller
Ban. Kapuas Hulu

Makassar Strait

J a v a   S e a

Equator

+8h Gr. Time
+7h Gr. Time

Kep. Karimunjawa
P. Bawean
Bitjan Bank

Scale 1 : 4,500,000

0   40   80   120   160   200 Kilometers
0   40   80   120   160 Statute Miles

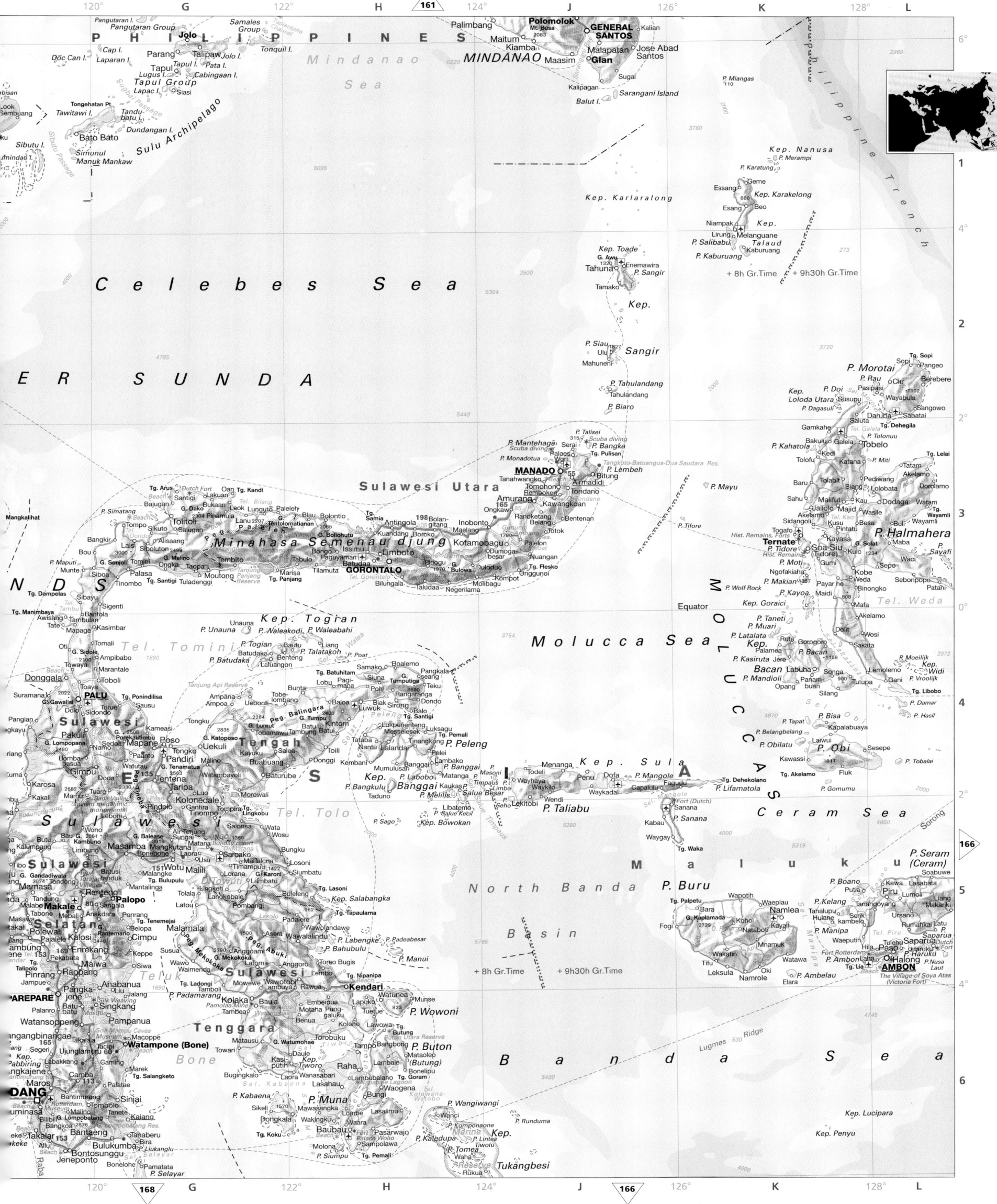

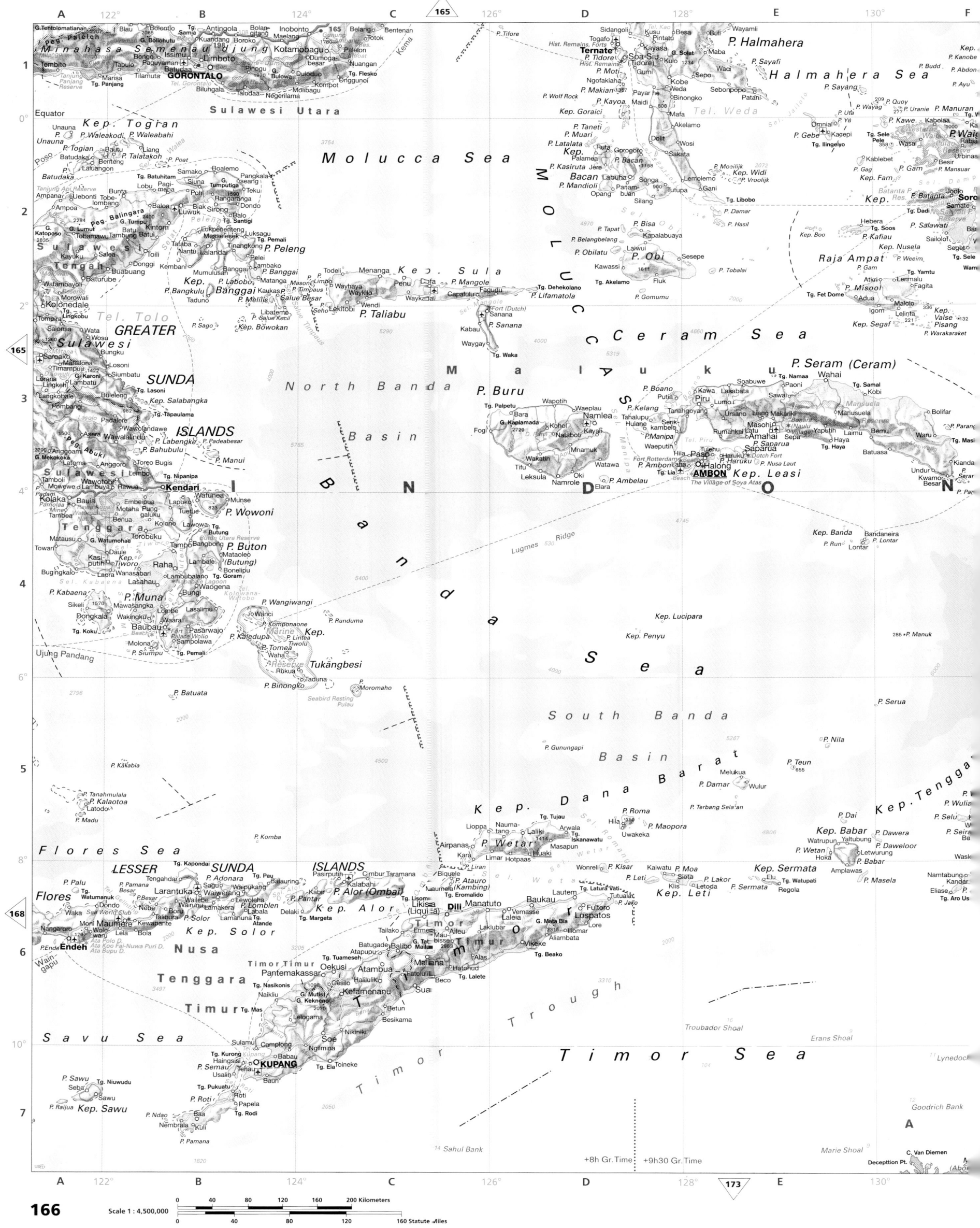

Scale 1 : 4,500,000

0 40 80 120 160 200 Kilometers

0 40 80 120 160 Statute Miles

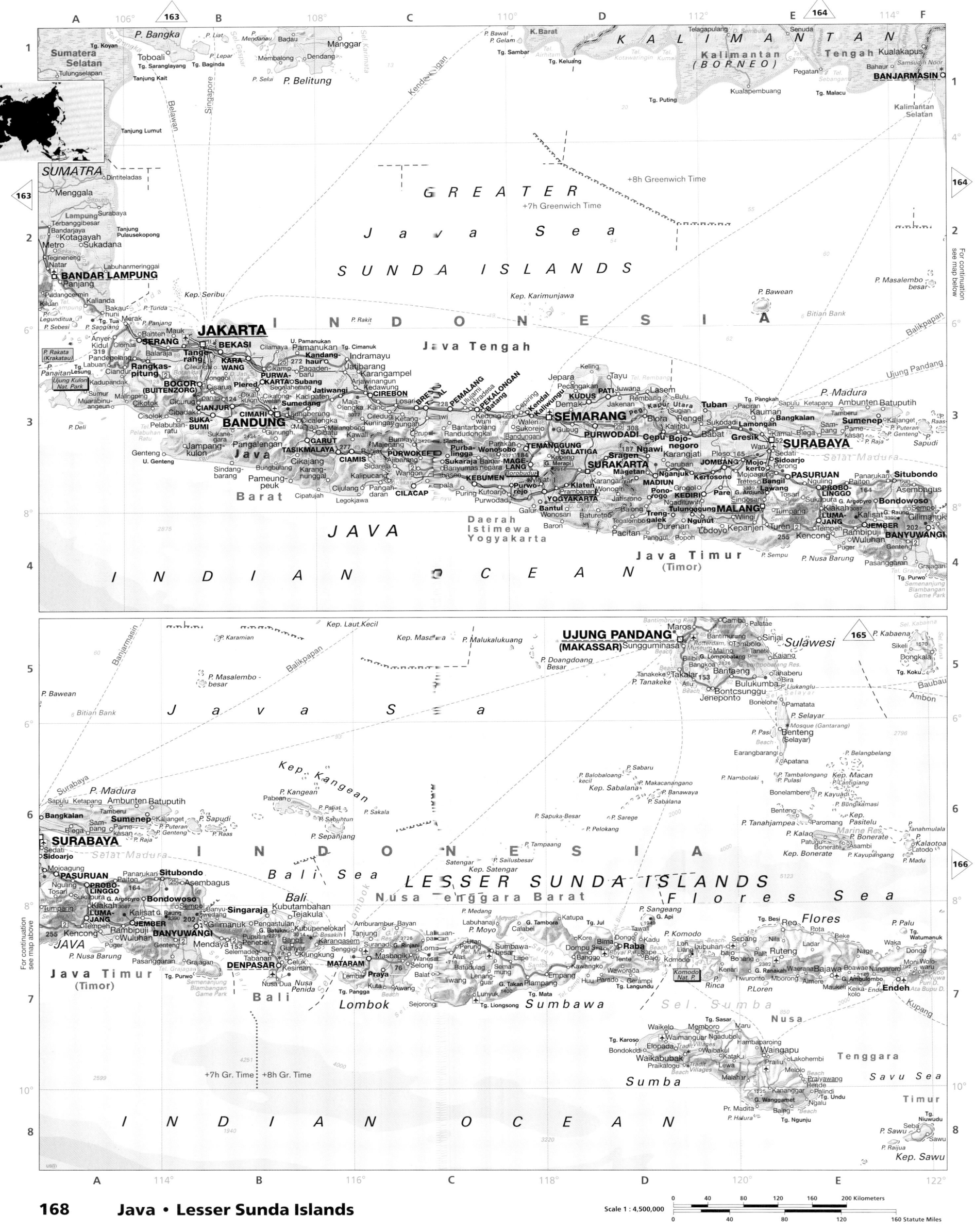

Scale 1 : 4,500,000

0 40 80 120 160 200 Kilometers

0 40 80 120 160 Statute Miles

Australia and Oceania – a new world in the Pacific

The smallest continent (2,972,970 square miles/7.7 million sq. km) is also the one farthest from all the others. Australia's distance from Europe and the inaccessibility of its shores, due among other things to the coral reefs that extend north and east, were among the causes for its late exploration. Distinctive features are the western plateau with average heights of between 656 and 1,640 feet (200 – 500 m), the central lowlands with the internal drainage basin of Lake Eyre and the mountain areas in the East including the island of Tasmania. The archipelagos north and east of Australia, including the world's second largest island, New Guinea, and the two-island

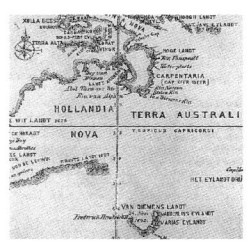

Australia as it was charted in 1644 by the Dutch Abel Tasman. It was not until 1770 that the eastern coast was explored by James Cook.

nation of New Zealand, are sometimes called Oceania, and comprise some 7,500 islands with an area of 501,930 square miles (1.3 million sq. km) dispersed over a sea area of 27,027,000 square miles (70 million sq. km). Melanesia and New Zealand constitute the outer arc of islands, Micronesia and Polynesia the inner. The islands sit partially on old mountains of volcanic origin beneath the sea and partially on elevated coral reefs. The 180th meridian, the dateline, runs through the middle of the region.

Australia: Northwestern Region
p. 172 – 173

Australia: Northeastern Region
p. 174 – 175

Australia: Southwestern Region
p. 176 – 177

Australia: Eastern Region
p. 178 – 179

Australia: Southeastern Region, Tasmania
p. 180 – 181

New Zealand
p. 182

Papua New Guinea
p. 183

Solomon Islands · Vanuatu · Fiji · Samoa · Tonga p. 184

B   116°   C   118°   D   120°   E   122°   F

1

J a v a   T r e n c h
6000
5620

INDIAN

12°

2
5815

North   Australian
5733

Basin

OCEAN

14°

3

6218

4

6039
5523

Exmouth

16°

Hibernia Reef
Sahu
Ashmore Reef
Car
Isle

Seringapatam Reef

Scott Reef   Brow

Beagle Reef

Lynher Reef   Churchill Reef
Adele'I.
Mavis Re

Buccaneer Archip.
Mining Area
Yampi Sound
Collier Bay
C. Leveque   19
Lombadina   Pender
Emeriau Pt.   Bay
Lacepede Is.   Beagle Bay
Beagle Bay   Dampier
Rowley Shoals   C. Baskerville   Beagle Bay   Abor. Land   Land
Mermaid Reef   Coulomb Pt.   Pt.
Clerke Reef   Derby   Torment
Imperieuse Reef   Broome   Roebuck   Mowanjum
Gantheaume Pt.   Roadhouse   Manguel
Rowley Shelf   Thangoo   Creek

Willare Bridge
Roadhouse
Kilto
145

C. Bartholet
Wildlife Sanct.

5   La Grange   Dampier Downs   247
18°   C. Latouche Treville   Bay   Babrongar
La Grange   Tower
C. Bossut   La Grange   Ras.
Edgar
Nita Downs
Anna Plains   W e s t

Exmouth   Mendora   561
Plateau   Wallal Downs   Sandfire Flat   Great   Sand
820   Roadhouse
Poissonnier
5   Point   C. Keraudren
Larrey Pt.   Pardoo
Spit Pt.   Roadhouse   Eighty Mile Beach   546
20°   C. Thouin   Port Hedland   Great Northern Hwy   64
Legendre I.   Strelley   Goldsworthy
Montebello Is.   Sloping   191 Mount   Shay Gap   A u s t
34   Pt.   C. Lambert   Goldsworthy   87
Dampier   Wickham   138   Carlindi   170   Callawa
Archipelago   Karratha   Roebourne   Mundabul-   Muccan   Yarrie
C. Dupuy   Dampier   [Hist. Town]   langana   1391   Warrawagine
Barrow I.   C. Preston   Wallareenya   Eginbah   346   Bamboo
Barrow I.   Wapet Camp   Karratha   Whim   Mallina   Lalla Rookh   345 371   Creek
Oil Field   Roadhouse   Creek   Gilliam   Marble Bar   371   Mt. Edgar
South End   Mardie I.   306   Yandeearra   880   Mount
Pasco Island   Mardie   Yandeearra   440   Abydos   Edgar
6   223   Fortescue Riv.   Mt. Richthofen   Hillside
Barrow I.   Roadhouse   356   Mt.   Mt.   Woodi Woodi
Shoals   718 Pannawonica   Mount   Gratwick   Mining Centre   Telfer
Thevenard I.   Mary Anne   Millstream   Florance   Abor. Land   Bonney   Mt. Cooke   L. Waukarlycarly   Paterson Rv.
Group   Mt. Enid   Mill-   Tambrey   842   Nullagine   Downs   Isabelle
Beadon Pt.   Yarraloola   Mining Area   stream   Mt. Margaret   550   Mt. McKay   Gregory Rv.
North West C.   Mt. Elvire   Pk. Hester   Wittenoom   138   Mount Divide   L. Dora   L. Au
Muiron Is.   Onslow   Hamersley   Chichester Ra.   Rudall River   Eva Broadhurst L.
U.S.Navy's   82   Red Hill   Ra.   1031   Bonney   Roy Hill   457   National Park
SRC Base   Peedamulla   Pilbara   826   Downs   Roy Hill   Hanging Rock   Mt. Connaughton   L. Blanche
Exmouth   Cane River   Mount   932   Mt. George   146   536
Mt. Hollister   Brockman   1176   Mt. Marsh   Balfour Downs   L. Winifre
C. Range   315   Learmonth   Koordarrie   Mt.   1235 Mt. Bruce   Roy Hill   Harbutt Rv.
Mt.   1132   Mining Area   Ethel Creek   McKay Rv.   No. 24 Well
Stuart   Hamersley   [Iron Ore]   Talawana   Runton Rv.
Nanutarra   Ashburton Riv   Tom   Hamersley   1083   Juna
Roadhouse   957   Price   [Range]   Downs   1251   Walgun   Robertson Ra.   L. Disappointment
Giralia   Wyloo   Mt. Wall   1064   Jiggalong
Yanrey   136   Tom Price   Mt. Bennett   Mt. Meharry   1157   Newman   Jiggalong
Uaroo   Rocklea   [Nat.P.]   Ophthalmia Ra.   Jiggalong   Abor. Land
Ningaloo   Kooline   Mt.Whaleback   Prairie
Bullara   228   Paraburdoo   Parraburdu   Mining Area   Downs
Towera   Mt. Palgrave   Mining Area   [Iron Ore]   Savory Rv.
228   700   Ashburton   [Iron Ore]
Coral Bay   Winning   Downs

A   114°   B   116°   C   118°   D   120°   E   122°   F

Scale 1 : 4,500,000

0   40   80   120   160   200 Kilometers
0   40   80   120   160 Statute Miles

176

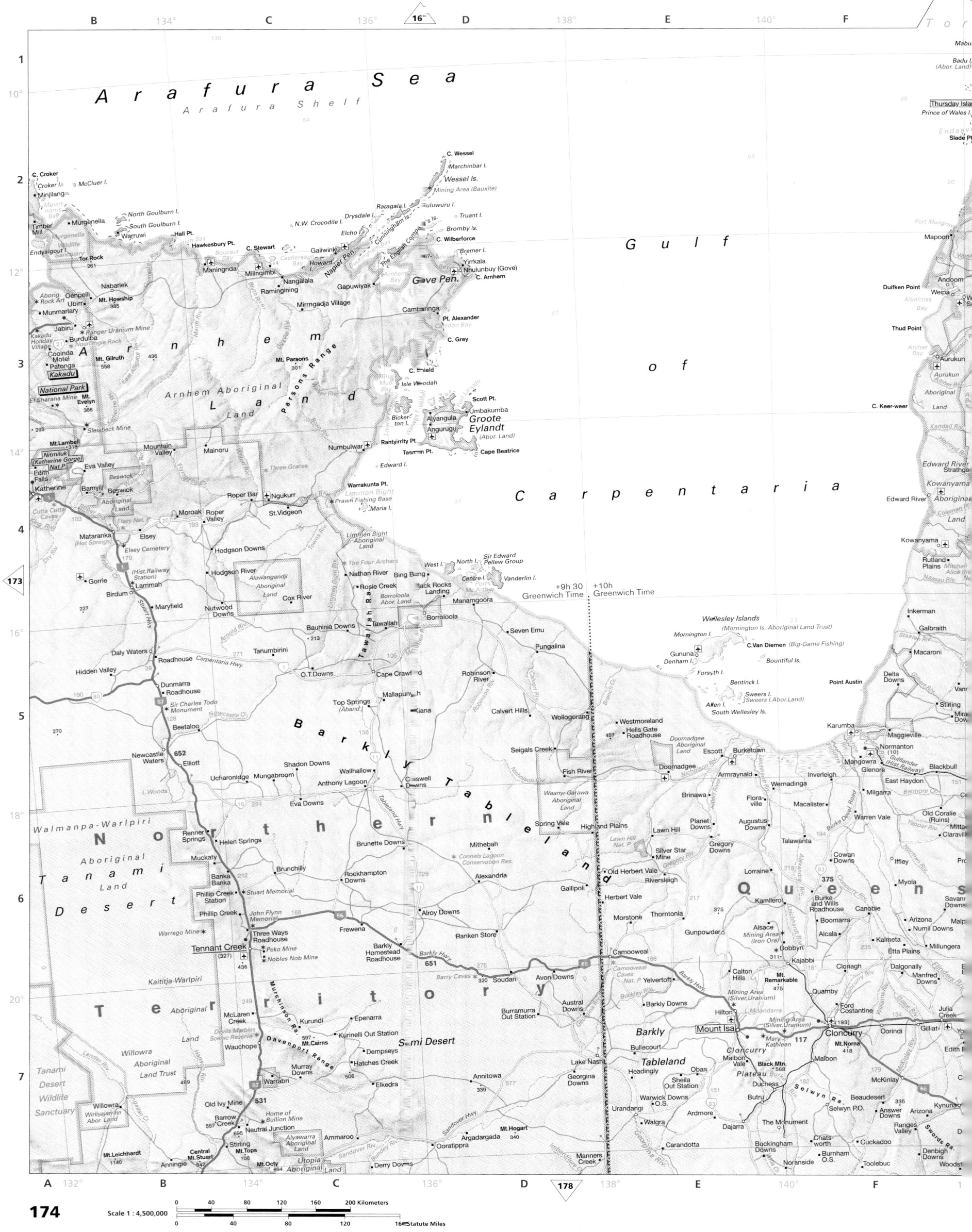

Arafura Sea
Arafura Shelf

C. Croker
Croker I. McCluer I.
Minjilang
Mount horns Bay
Timber Mill
Murgenella
Murgenella
Warruwi North Goulburn I.
South Goulburn I.
Hall Pt.
Endyalgout I.
Wildlife
Sanctuary
Tor Rock 261
Hawkesbury Pt. Boucaut Bay

C. Wessel
Marchinbar I.
Wessel Is.
Mining Area (Bauxite)
Raragala I. Guluwuru I.
Drysdale I.
N.W. Crocodile I. Cunningham Is. 's I. Truant I.
Elcho I. Bromby Is.
C. Wilberforce
C. Stewart Galiwinku The English Compa
Maningrida Milingimbi Howard Napier Pen. Bremer I.
Nangalala Yirrkala
Ramingining Gapuwiyak Nhulunbuy (Gove)
Gove Pen. C. Arnhem
Mirrngadja Village
Camuranga

Aborig.
Rock Art
Ubirr
Nabarlek
Oenpelli
Munmarlary Mt. Howship
385
Jabiru
Burdulba
Ranger Uranium Mine
Kakadu
Holiday
Village
Cooinda
Motel
Patonga
Kakadu
National Park
El Sharana Mine Mt.
Evelyn
366
295
Mt.Lambell
318
Nitmiluk
(Katherine Gorge)
Nat.P.
Edith
Falls
Katherine
Cutta Cutta
Caves
103

Mt. Gilruth
558 436

Arnhem
Aboriginal
Land

Mt. Parsons
301
C. Shield
Blue
Mud Isle Woodah
Bay
Bickerton I.
Alyangula
Angurugu Groote
Eylandt
(Abor. Land)
Scott Pt.
Umbakumba

Pt. Alexander
Caledon Bay
C. Grey

Parsons Range

A r n h e m

Land

Mountain
Valley Mainoru
Eva Valley
Beswick
Bamyili Beswick
Aboriginal
Land
Matranka
(Hot Springs)
Elsey
Elsey Cemetery
Gorrie (Hist.Railway
Station)
Birdum Larrimah
Maryfield
Daly Waters
Hidden Valley Roadhouse Carpentaria Hwy.
Dunmarra
Roadhouse
Sir Charles Todo
Monument
128
Beetaloo
270
Newcastle
Waters 652
Elliott
L.Woods

Roper Bar Ngukurr
Moroak Roper
Valley St.Vidgeon
193
Hodgson Downs
Hodgson River
Nutwood
Downs
Alawangandji
Aboriginal
Land
Cox River
271
Tanumbirini
1
O.T.Downs
156

Numbulwar Rantyirrity Pt.
Tasm Pt.
Cape Beatrice
Edward I.
Three Graces
Warrakunta Pt.
Limmen Bight
Prawn Fishing Base
Maria I.
Limmen Bight
Aboriginal
Land
The Four Archers
Nathan River West I. North I. Sir Edward
Rosie Creek Bing Bong Pellew Group
Black Rocks Centre I. Vanderlin I.
Landing
Manamgoora
Borroloola
Abor. Land
Bauhinia Downs 213
Tawallah
Borroloola

Seven Emu

Pungalina

+9h 30 +10h
Greenwich Time Greenwich Time

Wellesley Islands
(Mornington Is. Aboriginal Land Trust)
Mornington I.
Gununa C.Van Diemen (Big-Game Fishing)
Denham I.
Forsyth I. Bountiful Is.

Cape Crawf Robinson
River
Top Springs
(Aband.)
Mallapum h
Kiana

Calvert Hills

Wollogorang

Westmoreland
Hells Gate
457 Roadhouse

Bentinck I.
Sweers I.
Allen I. (Sweers I.Abor.Land)
South Wellesley Is.

Point Austin

B a r k l y

N o r t h e r n

Walmanpa-Warlpiri

Aboriginal
Tanami
Land
Desert

Renner
Springs
Helen Springs
Muckaty
Banka
Banka
212
Phillip Creek
Station
John Flynn
Phillip Creek Memorial 188
Warrego Mine
Tennant Creek
(327)
436
Peko Mine
Nobles Nob Mine

Kaititja-Warlpiri

Aboriginal

Land

Devils Marbles
Scenic Reserve
Wauchope
Willowra
Aboriginal
Land Trust

Tanami
Desert
Wildlife
Sanctuary
Willowra
Wirliyajarrayi
Abor. Land

Mt.Leichhardt
1140

Central
Mt.Stuart

Anningie

Shadon Downs
Mungabroom Wallhallow
Anthony Lagoon
224
Eva Downs

Brunette Downs

Brunchilly

Three Ways
Roadhouse

McLaren
Creek
Kurundi
597 Mt.Cairns
Murray
Downs
Warrabri
531
Barrow
557 Creek
895 Neutral Junction
Alyawarra
Aboriginal
Land
Ammaroo

T e r r i t o r y

Kaitrelli Out Station
Dempseys Hatches Creek
506
Elkedra

Oorippra

Kurinelli Out Station

Caswell
Downs

Alexandria

Alroy Downs

Frewena Ranken Store

Barkly
Homestead
Roadhouse 651
Barry Caves 320 Soudan
249
Epenarra

Mithebah
Connels Lagoon
Conservation Res.
226
Gallipoli

Avon Downs
Burramurra
Out Station
Austral
Downs

Lake Nash

Annitowa
339
577
Georgina
Downs

Argadargada
Mt.Hogart
340

Manners
Creek

T a b l e l a n d

Seigals Creek
Fish River
Doomadgee
Spring Vale
Highland Plains

Doomadgee
Aboriginal
Land
Waanyi-Garawa
Aboriginal
Land

Escott Burketown

Brinawa
Planet
Downs
Lawn Hill
Nat. P. Silver Star
Mine
Herbert Vale
Old Herbert Vale
Riversleigh
217
Gunpowder

Morstone
Thorntonia

Camooweal

Camooweal
Caves
Nat. P. Yelvertoft
Buckley Riv.
Barkly Downs

Hilton
Barkly

Mount Isa
Bullecourt
Cloncurry
Barkly
Tableland
Headingly
Urandangi
Warwick Downs
O.S.
Ardmore
Carandotta

Floravile
Augustus-
Downs
Lorraine

Kamileroi

Alsace
Mining Area
(Iron Ore)
Alcala
Dobbyn
311
Kajabbi
Mary
Kathleen
117
Malbon
Vale
Mt.Norna
418
Black Mtn.
Oban
Sheila
Out Station
Duchess
151
Butru
The Monument
Dajarra

G u l f

Duifken Point
Andoom
Weipa

Thud Point
Aurukun

C. Keer-weer

Edward River
Strathgo
Kowanyama
Edward River

C a r p e n t a r i a

Inkerman
Galbraith

Karumba
Normanton
(10)
Mangowra
Glenore
Delta
Downs
Stirling

Maggieville

Gulflander
(Hist.Railway) Blackbull
East Haydon
151
Armraynald
Wernadinga
Inverleigh
Milgarra
Macalister Warren Vale
Old Coralie
(Ruins)
Gregory
Downs
Talawanta
194
Cowan
Downs
Iffley

Burke
and Wills
Roadhouse
Boomarra
Canobie
Arizona
Numil Downs
Clonagh
Kalmeta
Etta Plains
Millungera

Q u e e n s

375

Myola

Dalgonally
Manfred
Downs
Quamby
Ford
Costantine
134
Cloncurry
Oorindi
Julia
Creek
Edith P.
Gilliat

Malbon
McKinlay
Beaudesert
Answer
Downs
Ranges
Valley

Chatsworth
Cuckadoo
Denbigh
Downs
Toolebuc
Woodst

Sel wyn Ra.

S e m i Desert

Scale 1 : 4,500,000

0 40 80 120 160 200 Kilometers

0 40 80 120 16 Statute Miles

Scale 1 : 4,500,000

| 0 | 40 | 80 | 120 | 160 | 200 Kilometers |

| 0 | 40 | 80 | 120 | 160 Statute Miles |

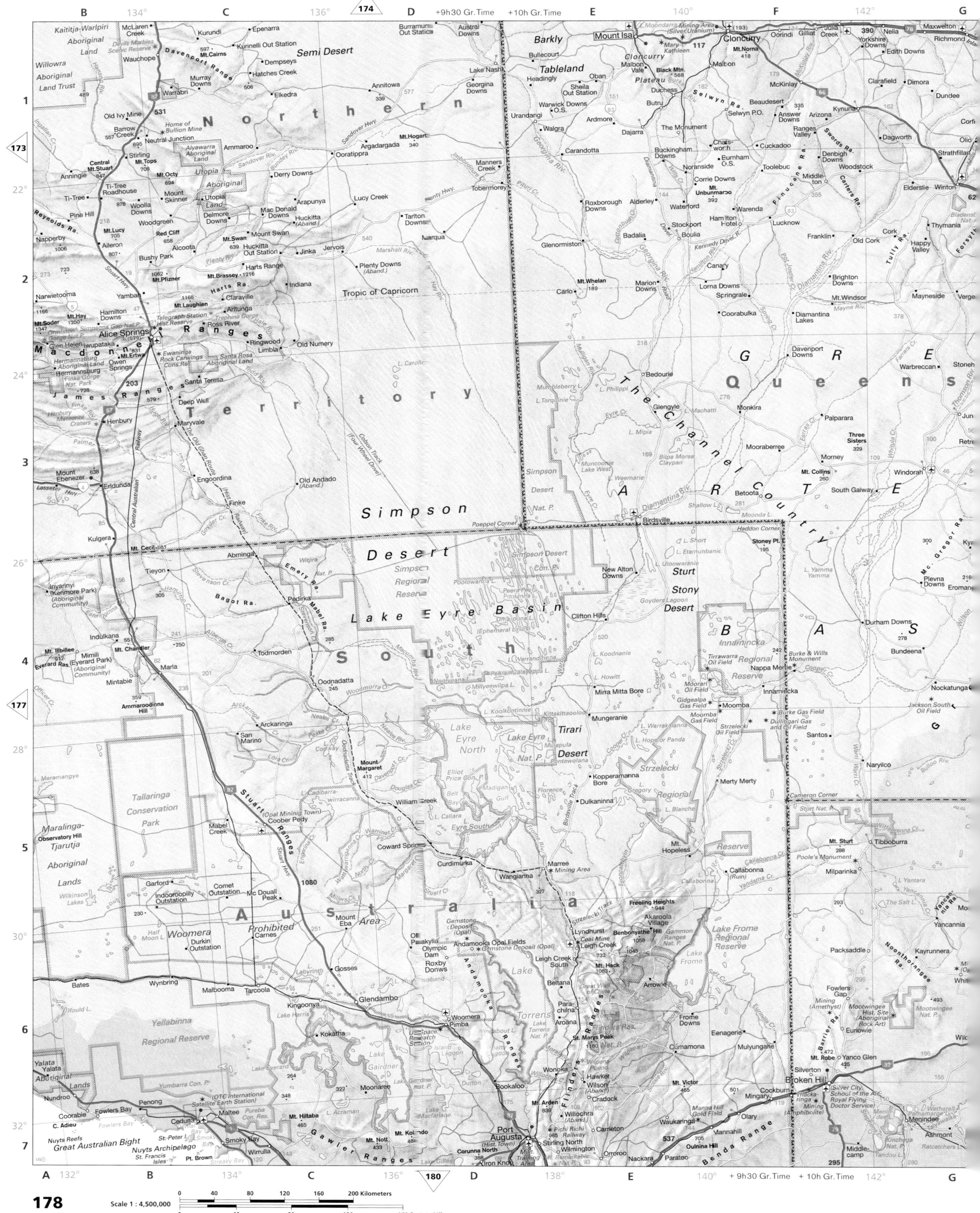

+9h30 Gr. Time   +10h Gr. Time

B   134°   C   136°   174   D   +9h30 Gr. Time   +10h Gr. Time   E   140°   F   142°   G

1

Scale 1 : 4,500,000

0   40   80   120   160   200 Kilometers

0   40   80   120   160 Statute Miles

A   132°   B   134°   C   136°   180   D   138°   E   140°   + 9h30 Gr. Time   + 10h Gr. Time   142°   G

Great
Australian
Bight

177

Eyre

Peninsula

South

Aus   t   r   a   l   i   a

Murray River

B a s i n
Sunset
Country

Big
Desert

Little
Desert
Wimmera

The
Grampians

ADELAIDE

Spencer
Gulf

Yorke
Peninsula

Gulf

S o u t h   A u s t r a l i a

B a s i n

I N D I A N   O C E A N

+9h 30 Greenwich Time   +10h Greenwich Time

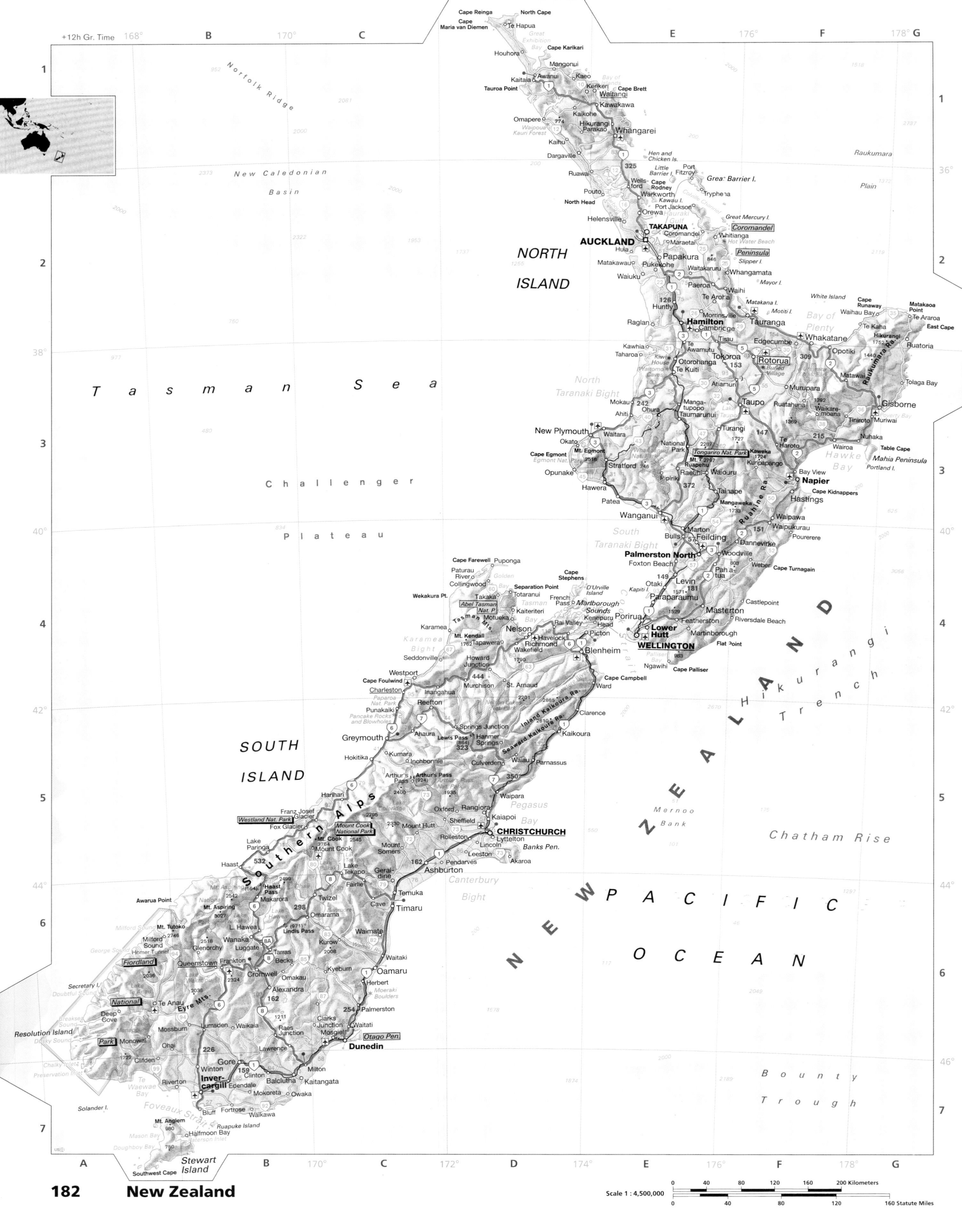

182   **New Zealand**

Scale 1 : 4,500,000

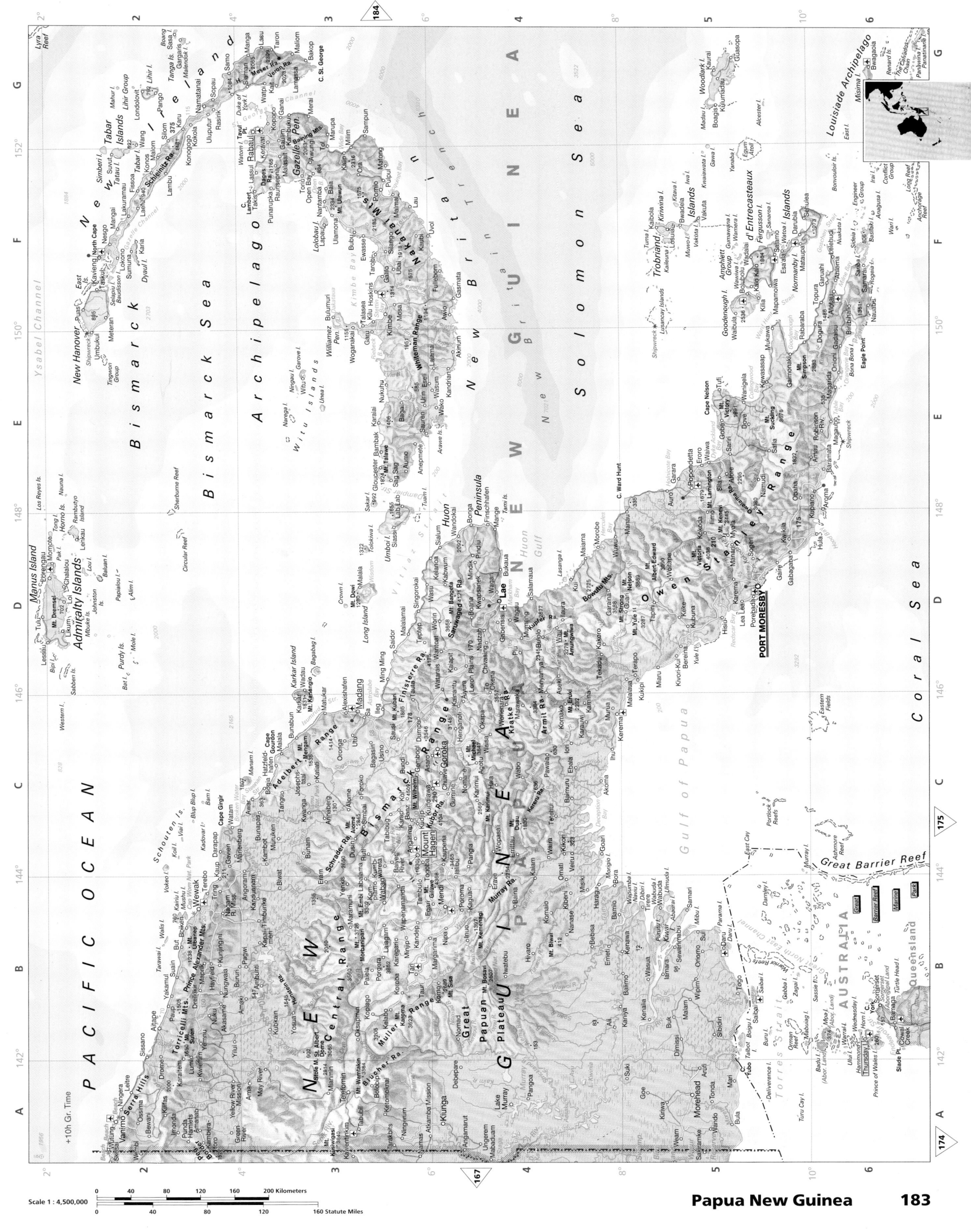

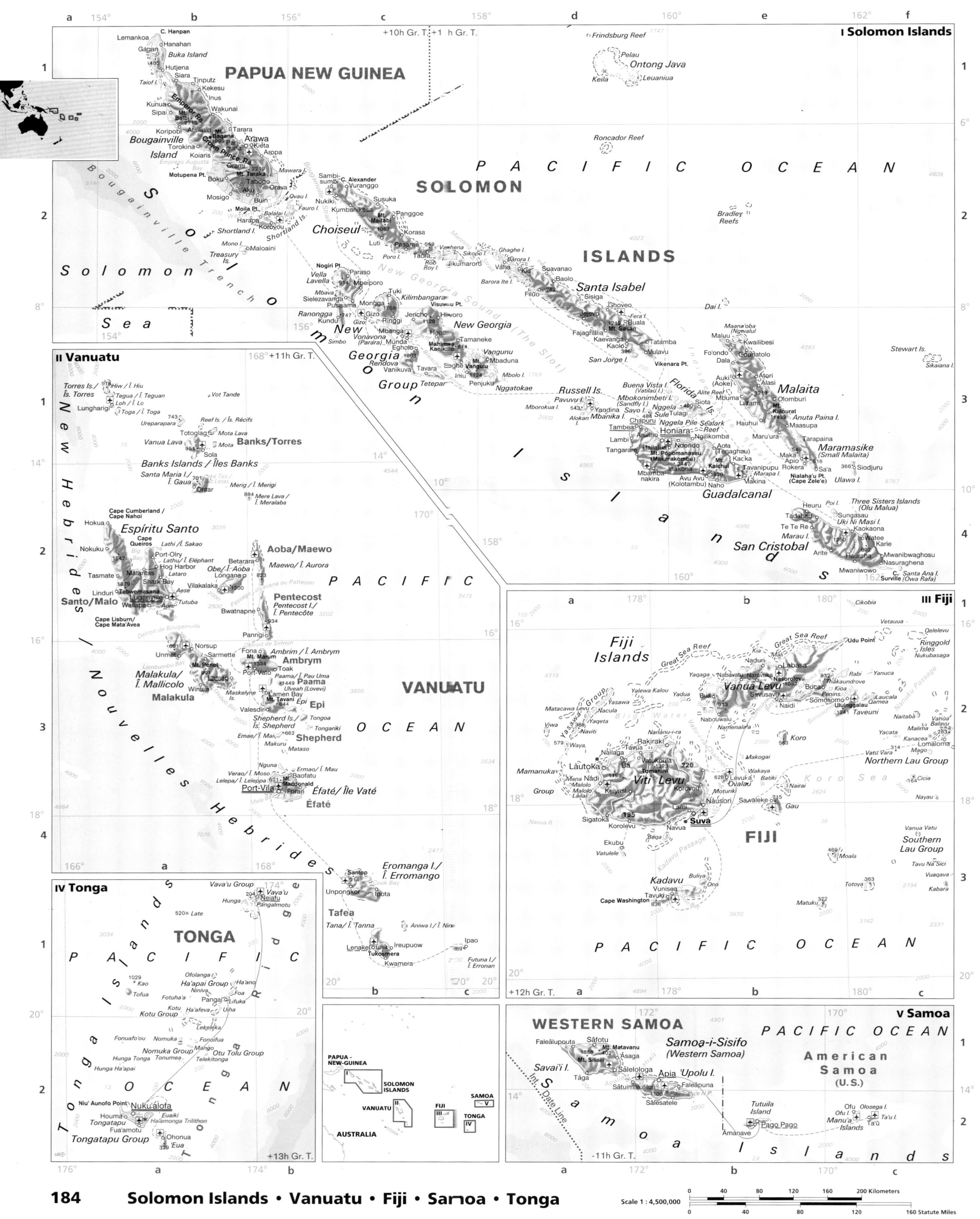

+10h Gr. T. +11 h Gr. T.

PAPUA NEW GUINEA

Frindsburg Reef

C. Hanpan
Lemankoa
Hanahan
Gagan
Buka Island
Siara
Hutjena
Taiof I.
Tinputz
Kekesu
Inus
Kunuwai
Wakunai
Sipai
Koripobi
Atsunui
Tarara
MT. BALBI
Bougainville
Island
Torokina
Kieta
Koiari
Arawa
Motupena Pt.
Orami
Aropa
Boku
Buin
MT. TARAKA
Taboco
Aku
Ovau I.
Orava
Mosigo
Balalai
Buin

Pelau
Ontong Java
Keila
Leuaniua

PACIFIC OCEAN

SOLOMON

Roncador Reef

Bradley Reefs

ISLANDS

C. Alexander
Sambi-sumbi
C. Vuranggo
Nukiki
Susuka
Kumanikassa
Panggoe
Fauro I.
Mt. Maitabi
Korasa
Shortland I.
Korovou
Luti
Pasara
Vanehena
Ghaghe I.
Sikopo I.
Mono I.
Maloaini
Taora
Rob Roy I.
Jikumaroro
Vaha
Suavanao
Baolo
Santa Isabel

Choiseul

Stewart Is.

Dai I.
Maana'oba (Ngwalul)
Maluu
Kwaiibesi
Fo'ondo
Dala
Auki (Aoke)
Atori
Alasi
Olomburi
Mt. Kolourat
Anuta Paina I.
Masupa

Malaita

New Georgia
Group

Russell Is.

Florida

Honiara

Guadalcanal

San Cristobal

168° +11h Gr. T.

Torres Is. / Îs. Torres
Hiw / Î. Hiu
Tegua / Î. Teguan
Lunghariggi
Loh / Î. Lo
Toga / Î. Toga
Vot Tande
Reef Is. / Îs. Récifs
Ureparapara
Totoglag
Mota Lava
Vanua Lava
Sola
Mota
Banks/Torres
Banks Islands / Îles Banks
Santa Maria / Î. Gaua
Merig / Î. Merigi
Mere Lava / Î. Meralaba

Cape Cumberland / Cape Nahoi
Hokua
Espíritu Santo
Nokuku
Cape Queiros
Lathi / Î. Sakao
Lathu / Î. Éléphant
Port-Olry
Aoba/Maewo
Maewo / Î. Aurora
Betarara
Obe / Î. Aoba
Tasmate
Mataritas
Hog Harbor
Longana
Shark Bay
Lataro
Vilakalaka
Linduri
Tabwemasana
Luganville
Aese
Santo/Malo
Wailapa
Tutuba
Cape Lisburn / Cape Mata'Avea
Pentecost
Pentecost I. / Î. Pentecôte
Bwatnapne
Panngi

Unmet
Norsup
Sarmette
Ambrym
Mt. Penot
Fona
Mt. Marum
Toak
Malakula/ Î. Mallicolo
Lamap
Paama
Port-Vato
Paama / Î. Pau Uma
Wintua
Uleva'n (Lovevi)
Malakula
Maskelyne Is.
Lamen Bay
Mt. Tavani
Epi
Valesdir
Shepherd Is. / Îs. Shepherd
Tongoa
Tongariki
Emae / Î. Mai
Shepherd
Makura
Matoso
Nguna
Ermao / Î. Mau
Verao / Î. Moso
Baofatu
Lelepa / Î. Leleppa
Macdonald
Foran
Port-Vila
Éfaté / Île Vaté
Éfaté

VANUATU

PACIFIC

OCEAN

Santop
Eromanga I. / Î. Erromango
Unpongkor
Ipota
Tafea
Tana / Î. Tanna
Aniwa I. / Î. Niwa
Ipao
Lenakel
Ireupuow
Tukosmera
Futuna I. / Î. Erronan
Kwamera

Cikobia
Vetauua

Fiji Islands
Great Sea Reef
Udu Point
Qelelevu
Ringgold Isles
Nukubasaga
Kia
Mali
Labasa
Yaqaga
Nabouwalu
Naduri
Naviti
Nasorolevu
Vanua Levu
Savusavu
Rabi
Yanuca
Bucao
Koro Peninsula
Laucala
Qamea
Taveuni
Naitaba
Malima
Avea
Mago
Yasawa Group
Naviti
Yaqeta
Rakiraki
Koro
Nananu-i-ra
Makogai
Nal/laga
Ba
Vatukoula
Tavua
Vaileka
Wakaya
Viti Levu
Lautoka
Nadi
Mana
Keiyasi
Levuka
Ovalau
Batiki
Korovou
Moturiki
Nausori
Sawaleke
Nairai
Gau
Northern Lau Group
Cicia
Sigatoka
Lami
SUVA
Korolevu
Navua
FIJI
Nayau
Ekubu
Beqa
Vanua Vatu
Vatulele
Southern Lau Group
Kadavu
Moala
Vunisea
Tavuki
Buliya
Ono
Matuku
Cape Washington
Totoya
Vuaqava
Kabara

PACIFIC OCEAN

Vava'u Group
Neiafu
Vava'u
Hunga
Pangaimotu
Late

TONGA

PACIFIC

Ofolanga
Kao
Ha'apai Group
Niniva
Tofua
Fotuha'a
Foa
Pangai
Lifuka
Ha'afeva
Kotu Group
Lekeleka

Tonga Islands

Fonuafo'ou
Nomuka
Fonofua
Nomuka Group
Mango
Otu Tolu Group
Hunga Tonga
Telekitonga
Hunga Ha'apai

OCEAN

Niu' Aunofo Point
Nuku'alofa
Euaiki
Houma
Tongatapu
Ohonua
'Eua
Tongatapu Group

+13h Gr. T.

PAPUA - NEW-GUINEA
SOLOMON ISLANDS
VANUATU — II
FIJI — III
SAMOA — V
TONGA — IV
AUSTRALIA

+12h Gr. T.

WESTERN SAMOA

Samoa-i-Sisifo (Western Samoa)

PACIFIC OCEAN

Faleālupouta
Sāfotu
Mt. Matavanu
Āsaga
Savai'i I.
Mt. Silisili
Sālelologa
Apia
'Upolu I.
Tāga
Sātaimaleulu
Faleāpuna
Sālesatele

American Samoa (U.S.)

Pago Pago
Tutuila Island
Ofu
Olosega I.
Manu'a Islands
Ta'u
Amanave

Int'l Date Line

-11h Gr. T.

Scale 1 : 4,500,000

0 40 80 120 160 200 Kilometers
0 40 80 120 160 Statute Miles

Africa – a continent of many faces

Africa, the second largest continent on Earth, takes up one-fifth of the total land mass on the planet. It is characterized by a coastline that contains few gulfs and peninsulas, the triangular southern cone with the northern trapeze on top and the division into Upper Africa in the southeast and Lower Africa in the northwest. The highlands with basins and rises as well as an extended rift valley system shape its surface. Africa contains all tropical landscape and climatic areas of the world, distributed primarily along the latitude lines on both sides of the Equator. One-third of Africa is occupied by the largest desert on Earth,

Johann Baptist Homann made this copperplate engraving of Africa around the year 1690, approximately 150 before Europeans first began to explore the continent's interior.

the Sahara. This environment, hostile to life, separates white Africa, mostly settled by Islamic Arab peoples, from black Africa, characterized by the Sudanese and Bantu peoples. Ethiopia has unique population and culture. Contrary to the imaginary picture of the "dark continent," Africa has a vibrant culture and history. This is where, over three million years ago, our early ancestors learned to walk upright, and nowadays its melange of peoples, races, languages and traditions is only beginning to be appreciated.

Morocco · Canary Islands
p. 188–189

Algeria · Tunisia
p. 190–191

Libya
p. 192–193

Egypt
p. 194–195

Mauritania · Mali: Northern Region
p. 196–197

Niger · Chad
p. 198–199

Sudan: Northern Region · Eritrea
p. 200–201

Upper Guinea
p. 202–203

Ghana · Togo · Benin · Nigeria · Cameroon
p. 204–205

Central African Republic · Sudan:
Southern Region p. 206–207

Ethiopia · Somali Peninsula
p. 208–209

Lower Guinea
p. 210–211

East Africa: Northern Region
p. 212–213

East Africa: Southern Region
p. 214–215

Angola · Namibia: Northern Region
p. 216–217

Zambia · Zimbabwe · Mozambique
p. 218–219

South Africa
220–221

Madagascar · Comoros
p. 222–223

Seychelles · Réunion · Mauritius
p. 224

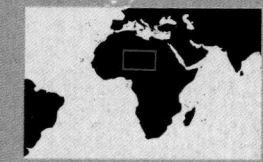

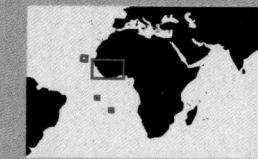

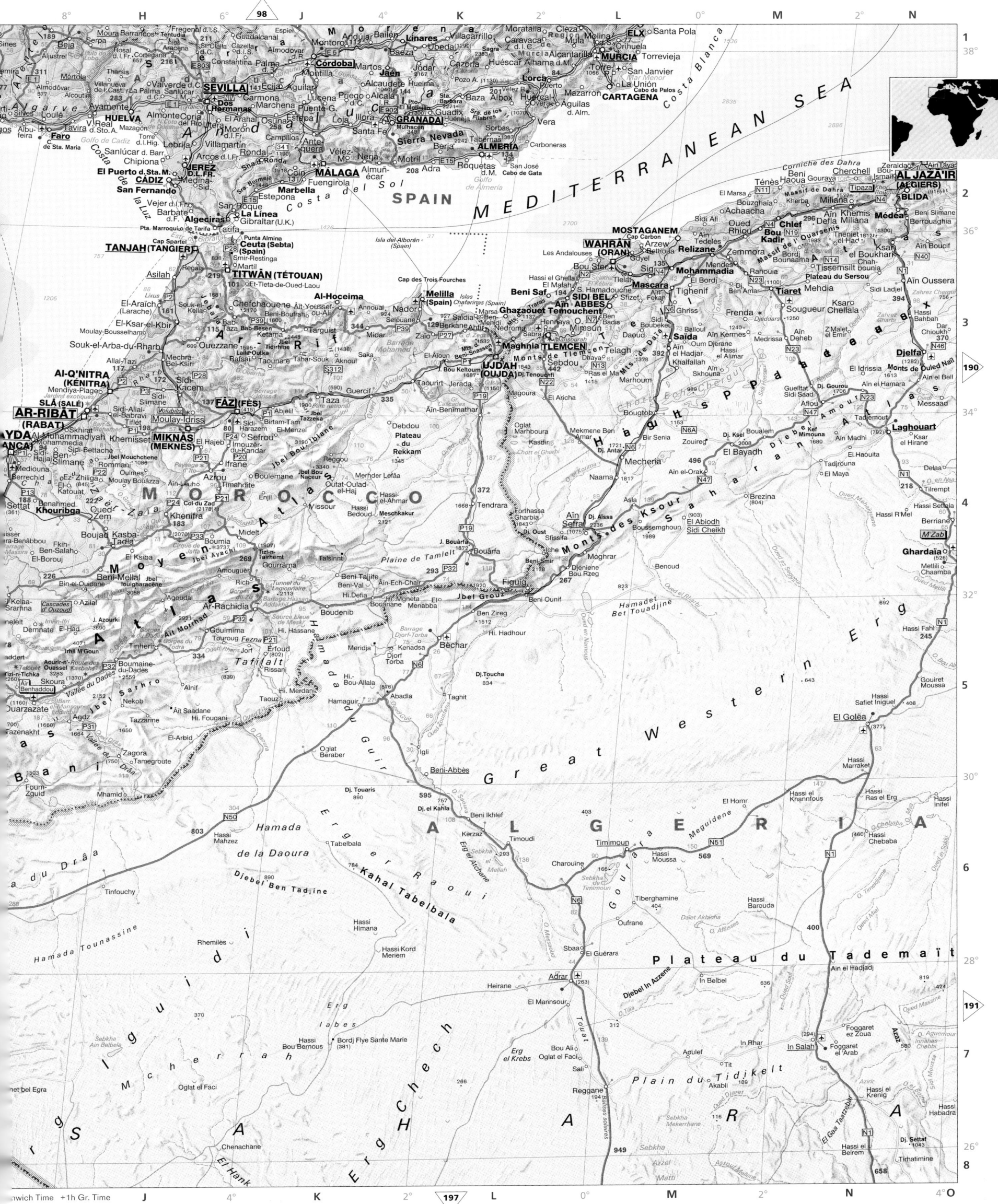

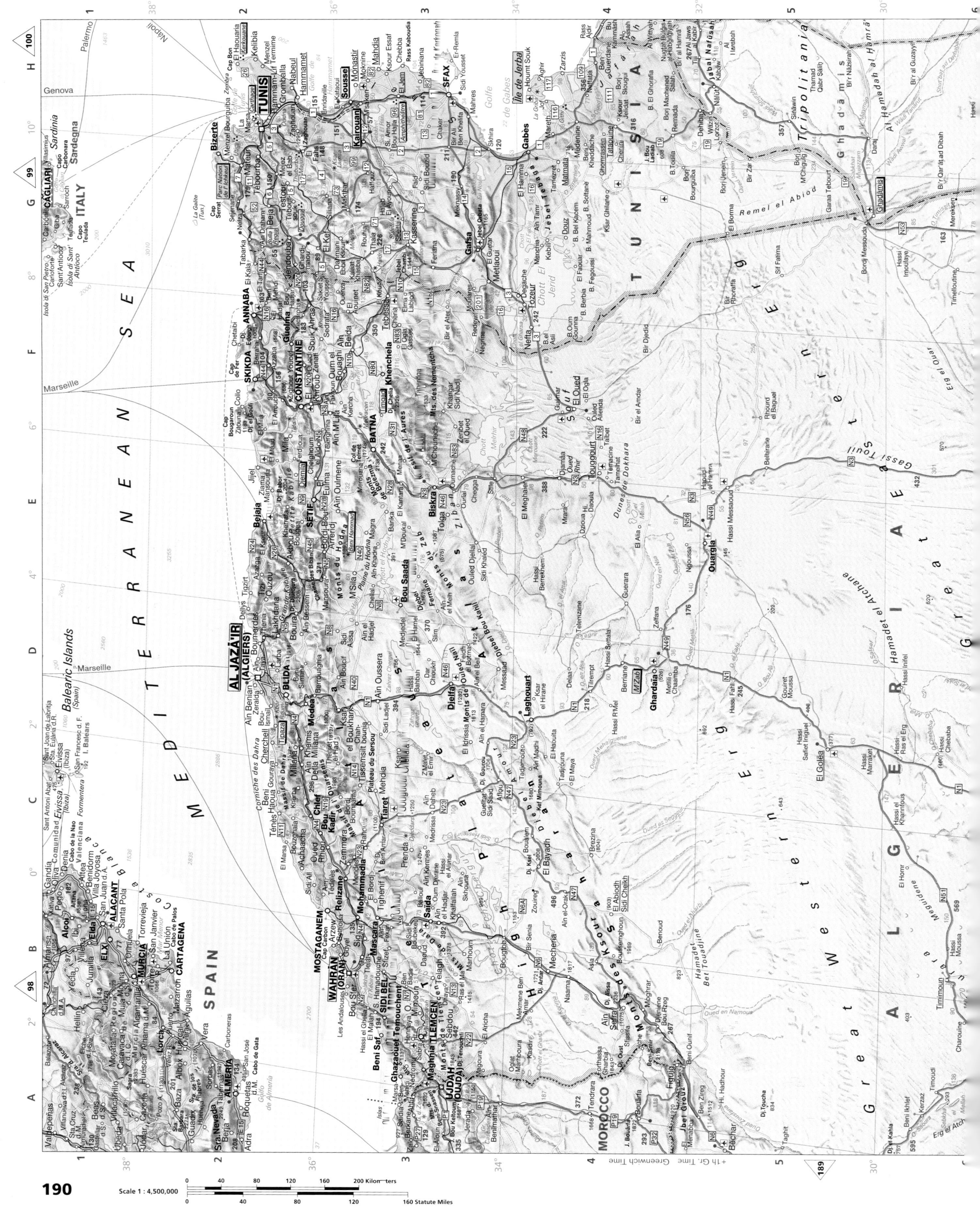

190

Scale 1 : 4,500,000

0 40 80 120 160 200 Kilometers

0 40 80 120 160 Statute Miles

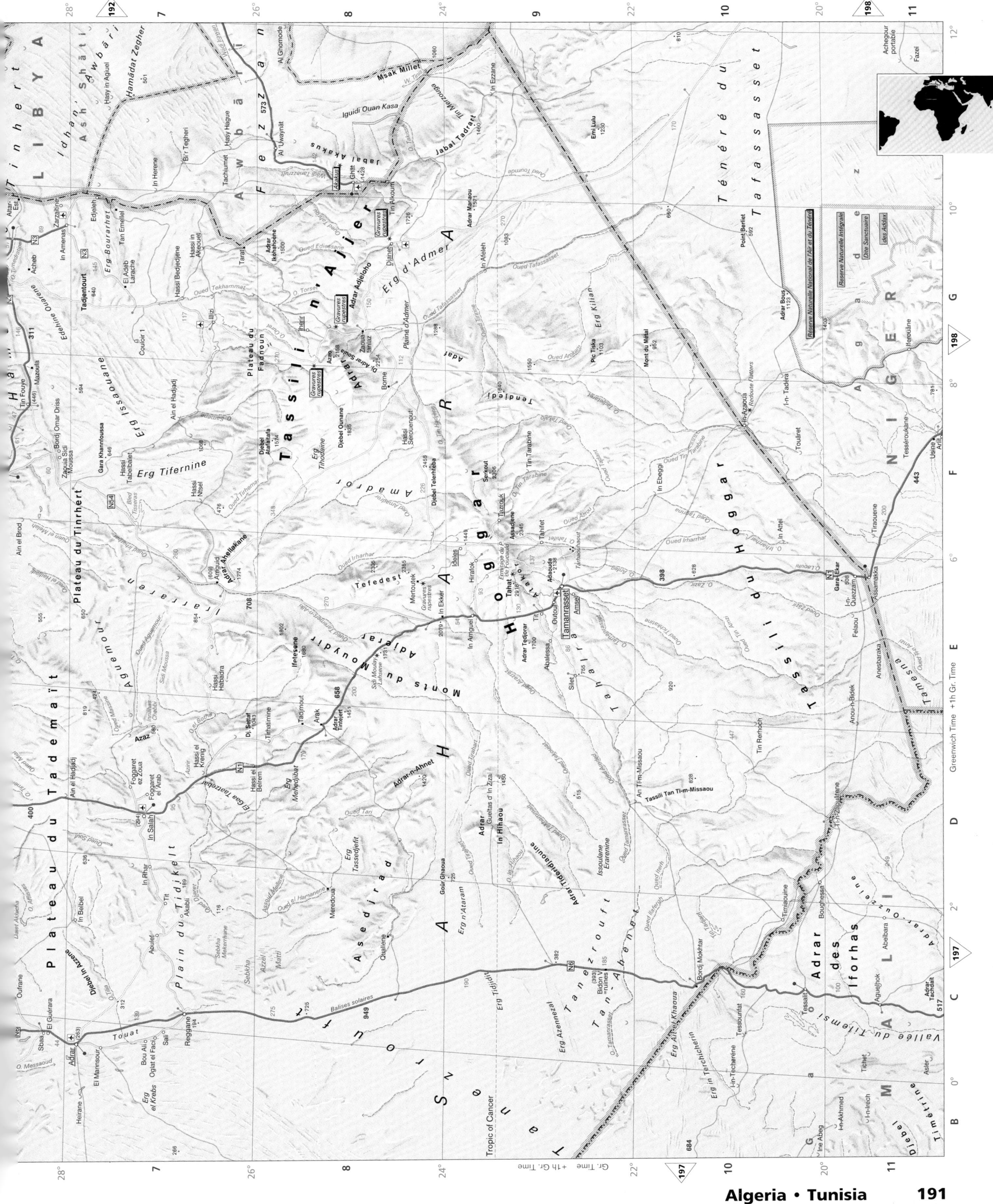

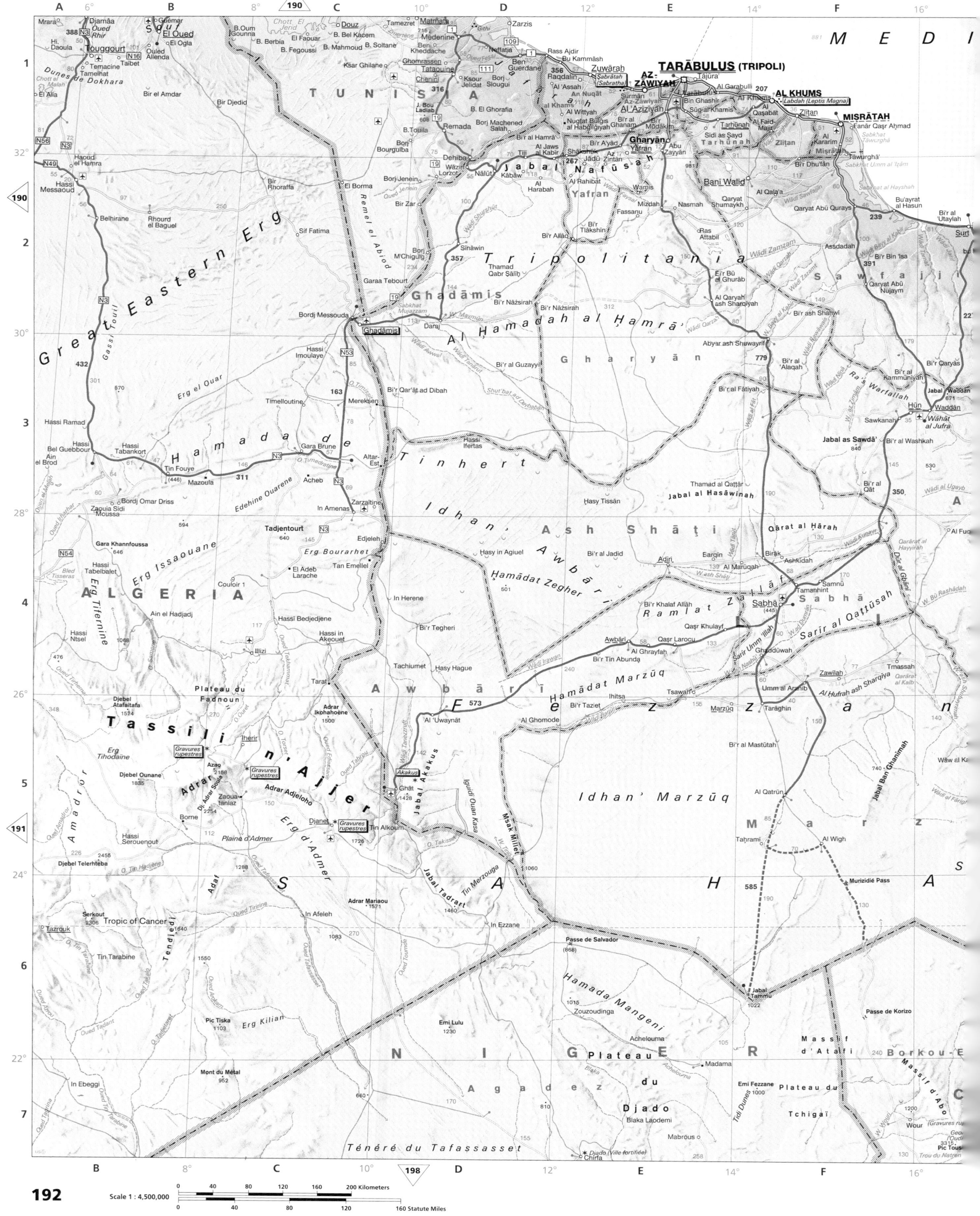

Scale 1 : 4,500,000

0   40   80   120   160   200 Kilometers
0   40   80   120   160 Statute Miles

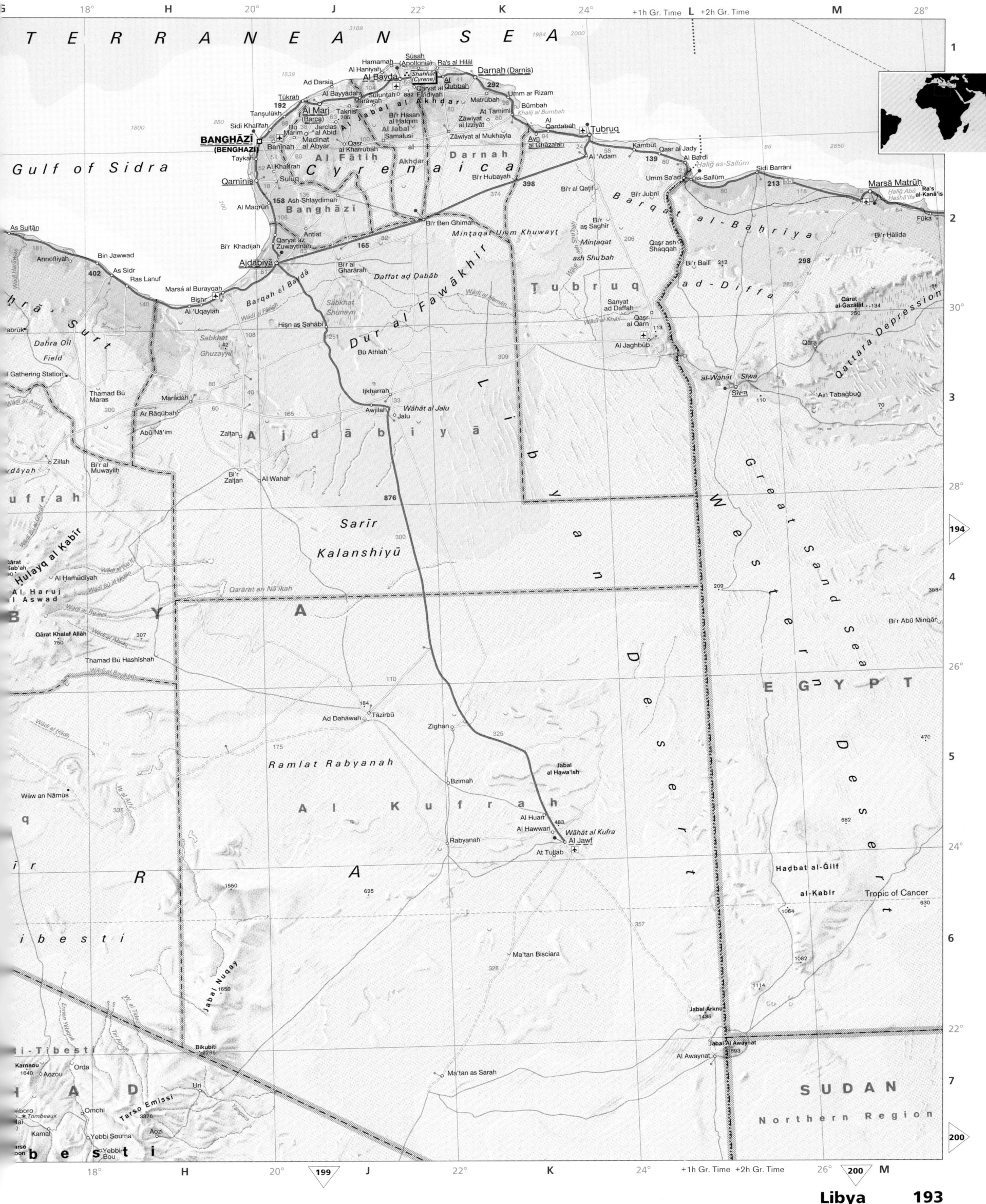

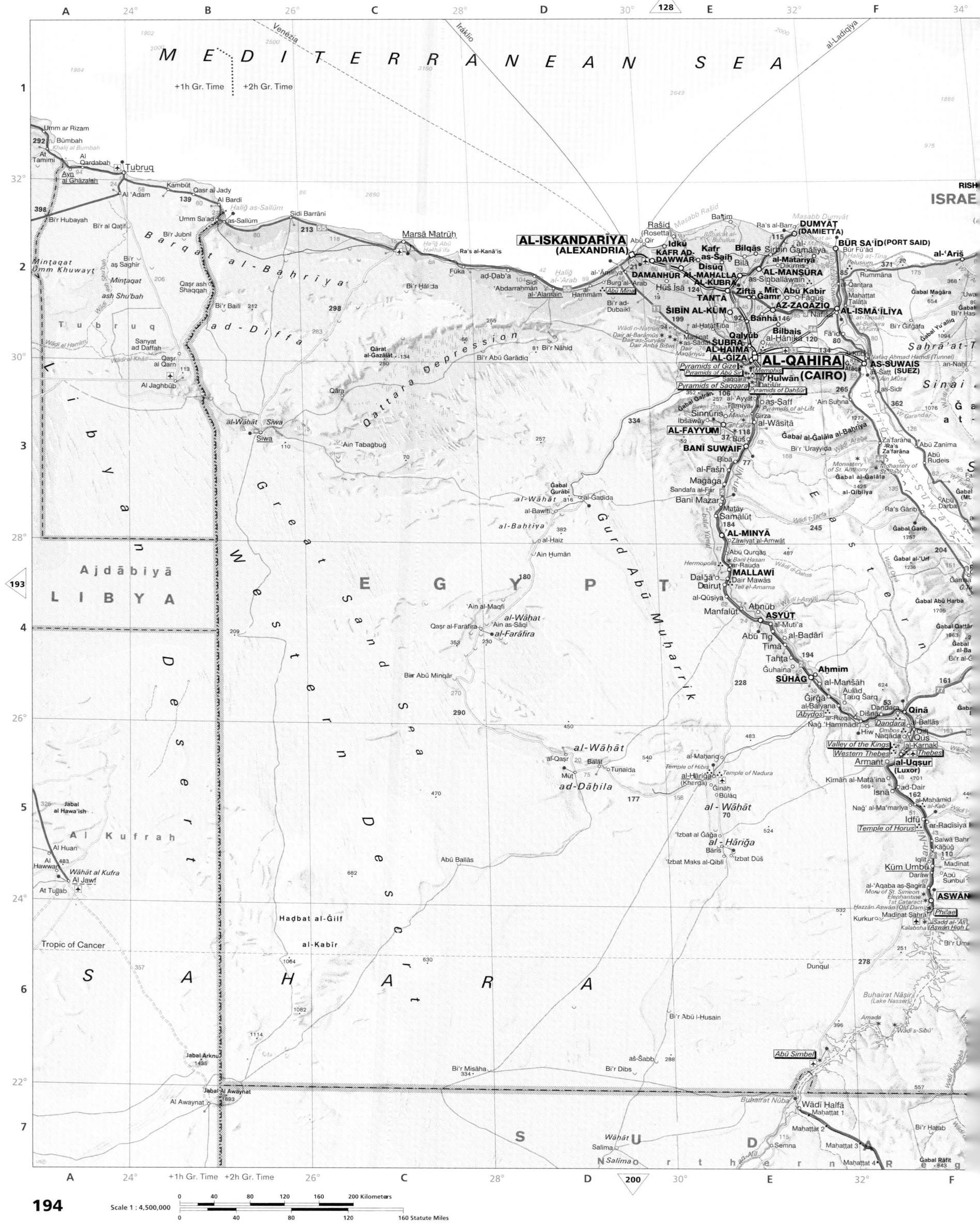

MEDITERRANEAN SEA

+1h Gr. Time   +2h Gr. Time

Venezia

Iraklio

al-Ladiqiya

RISH
ISRAE

AL-ISKANDARĪYA (ALEXANDRIA)

Rašid (Rosetta)
Abū Qīr
Idkū
KAFR AD-DAWWĀR
Kafr as-Saib
Disūq
Bilā
Bilqās
Sirbīn Gamāliya
AL-MANSŪRA
al-Matarīya
Dikirnis
DUMYĀT (DAMIETTA)
Bur Fū'ad
BŪR SA'ĪD (PORT SAID)
Rummāna
al-'Arīš

DAMANHŪR AL-MAHALLA AL-KUBRA
Hūs Īsa
TANTĀ
SUBRA
AL-HAIMA
ŠIBĪN AL-KUM
Burg al-'Arab
Abū Mina
al-'Alamain
Hammām
'Abdarrahmān
Sidi 'Abdarrahmān
ad-Dab'a
Fūka
Ra's al-Kanā'is
Marsā Matrūh
Sidi Barrāni
Halīg as-Sallūm
Ras-Sallūm
Umm Sa'ad
Qasr al Jady
Al Bardī
Kambūt
Al Qardabah
Al 'Adam
Tubruq
Ayn al-Ghazālah
At Tamīmi
Al Qatīf
Bī'r Hubayah

AL-QAHIRA (CAIRO)
Pyramids of Gize
Pyramids of Abū Sir
Memphis
Pyramids of Saqqara
Saqqara
Hulwān
Pyramids of Dahsūr
AL-GIZA
AS-SUWAIS (SUEZ)
Qalyūb
Bilbais
Fā'id
Bāhā
AZ-ZAQĀZĪQ
AL-ISMĀ'ĪLĪYA
Sinai

AL-FAYYŪM
as-Saff
BANĪ SUWAIF
Bibā
al-Fašn
Magāga
Bani Mazar
Matāy
Samālūt
AL-MINYĀ
Abū Qurqas
Mallawī
Dalga
Dair Mawās
Tell el-Amarna
Dairut
al-Qūsiya
Manfalūt
Abnūb
ASYŪT
al-Muti'a
Abū Tig
al-Badāri
Tahta
Timā
Guhaina
SŪHĀG
Ahmim
al-Manšāh
Girgā
Aulād
Tauq Sarq
al-Balyana
Abydos
Dišna
Qinā
Dandara
Naqāda
Qift
Qus
Valley of the Kings
al-Karnak
Western Thebes
Thebes
Armant
al-Uqsur (Luxor)
Isnā
al-Mahāmid
Idfū
ar-Radīsiya
Kūm Umbū
Darāw
ASWĀN
Philae
Sadd al-'Ali Aswān High
Dunqul
Abū Simbel
Buhairat Nāsir (Lake Nasser)
Wādī Halfā
Mahattat 1
Mahattat 2
Mahattat 3

LIBYA
Ajdābiyā

Barqat al-Bahrīya
ad-Diffa
Minṭaqat Umm Khuwayt
Mintaqat ash Shu'bah
Qasr ash Shaqqah
Bī'r as Saghir
Bī'r Baili
Bī'r Hal da

Qattara Depression
Qārat al-Gazālat
Qāra
al-Wāhāt Siwa
Siwa
'Ain Tabagbug

Great Sand Sea

Western Desert

EGYPT

Ğabal Gurābi
al-Wāhāt
al-Gadida
al-Bawiti
al-Bahrīya
al-Haiz
'Ain Human

al-Wāhāt
al-Qasr
Balāt
Mūt
Tūnaida
ad-Dāhila

Qasr al-Farāfira
al-Wāhat
'Ain as-Sāqi
al-Farāfira

Bir Abū Minqār

Bir Abū I-Husain

al-Wāhāt
al-Maharig
al-Hariga (Kharga)
Temple of Hibis
Temple of Nadura
Ginah
Būlāq
al-Wāhāt
al-Hāriga
Bāris
'Izbat Maks al-Qibli
'Izbat Dūš

Abū Ballās

Haḍbat al-Ğilf
al-Kabīr

Tropic of Cancer

S A H A R A

Jabal al Hawa'ish
Al Huan
Al Hawwari
Al Jawf
At Tujlab
Al Kufrah
Wāhāt al Kufra

Jabal Arknu

Jabal al Awaynat
Al Awaynat

Bī'r Misāha
aš-Šabb
Bī'r Dibs

SUDAN
Wāhāt Salima
Salima
Semna
Bī'r Hatab
Northern

+1h Gr. Time   +2h Gr. Time

200
193
292

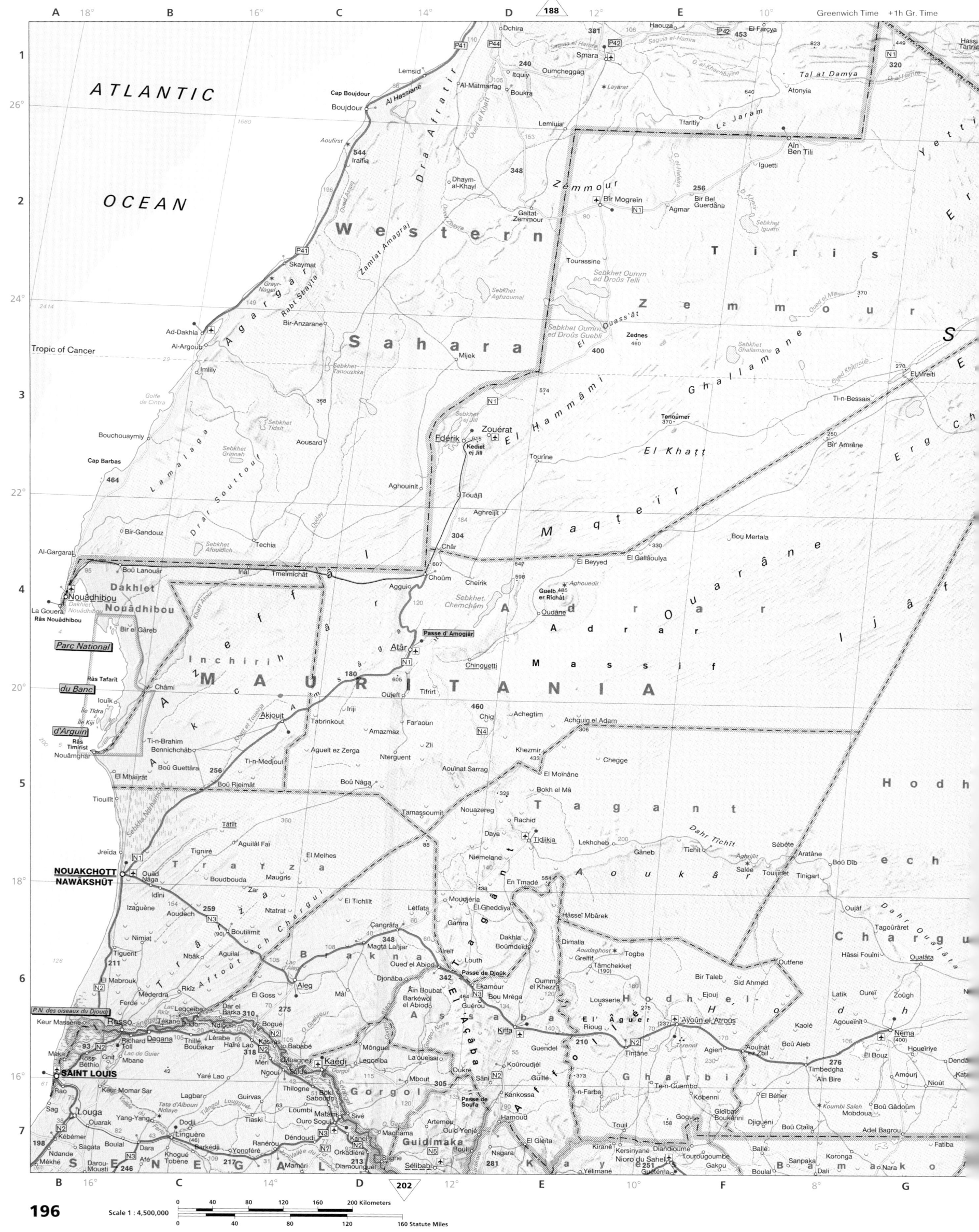

Greenwich Time   +1h Gr. Time

ATLANTIC

OCEAN

Tropic of Cancer

Western   Sahara

Zemmour

Tiris

Zemmour

El Hammâmi

Ghallamane

El Khatt

Maqteïr

Adrar   Ouarâne

Adrar   Adrar Ijâf

Massif

MAURITANIA

Inchirih

Parc National

du Banc

d'Arguin

Dakhlet
Nouâdhibou

Trarza

Tagant

Hodh

ech

Brakna

Aoukâr

Assaba

Hodh

el Gharbi

Gorgol

Guidimaka

Kayes

SENEGAL

NOUAKCHOTT
NAWĀKSHŪT

SAINT LOUIS

Scale 1 : 4,500,000

0   40   80   120   160   200 Kilometers

0   40   80   120

160 Statute Miles

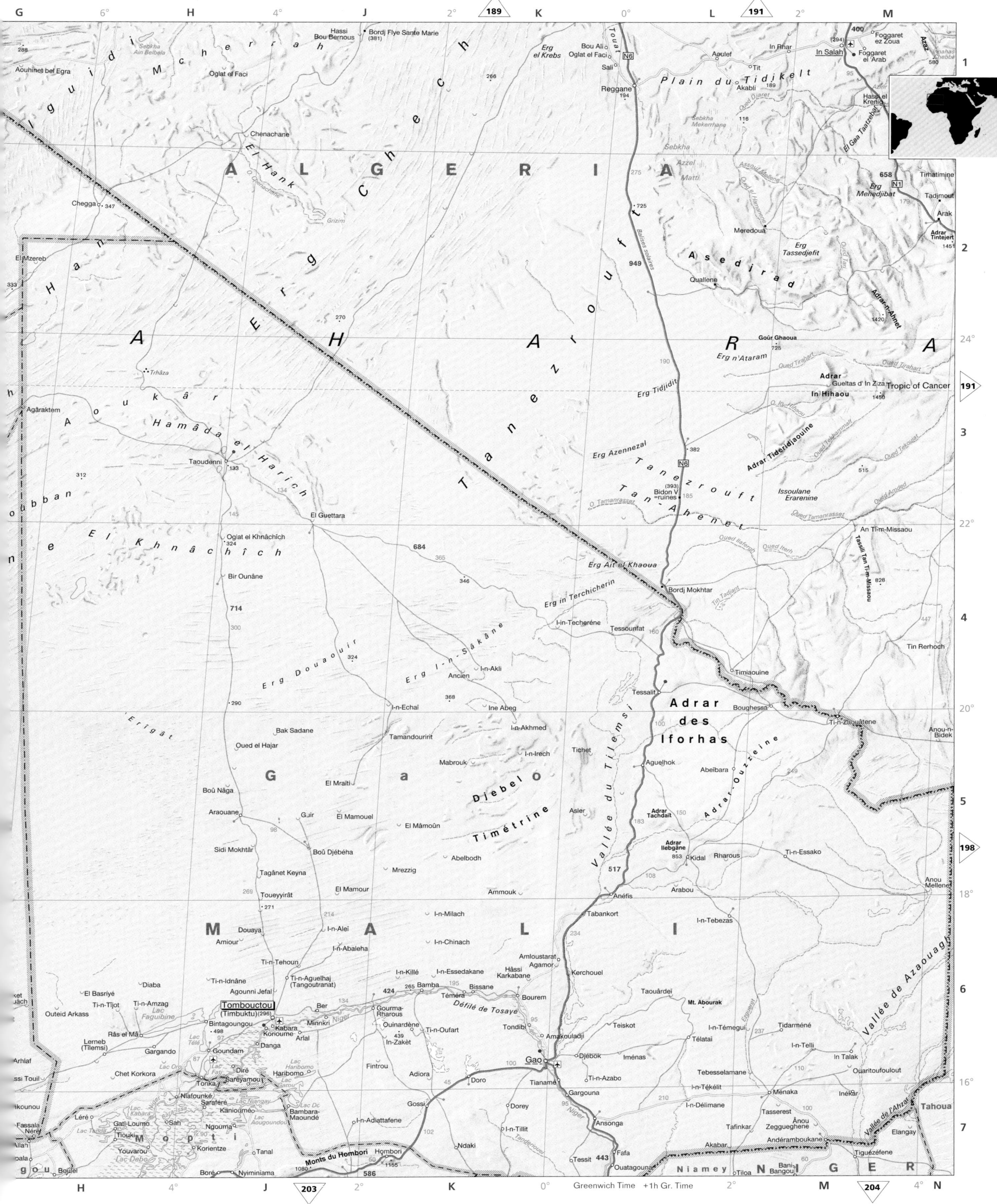

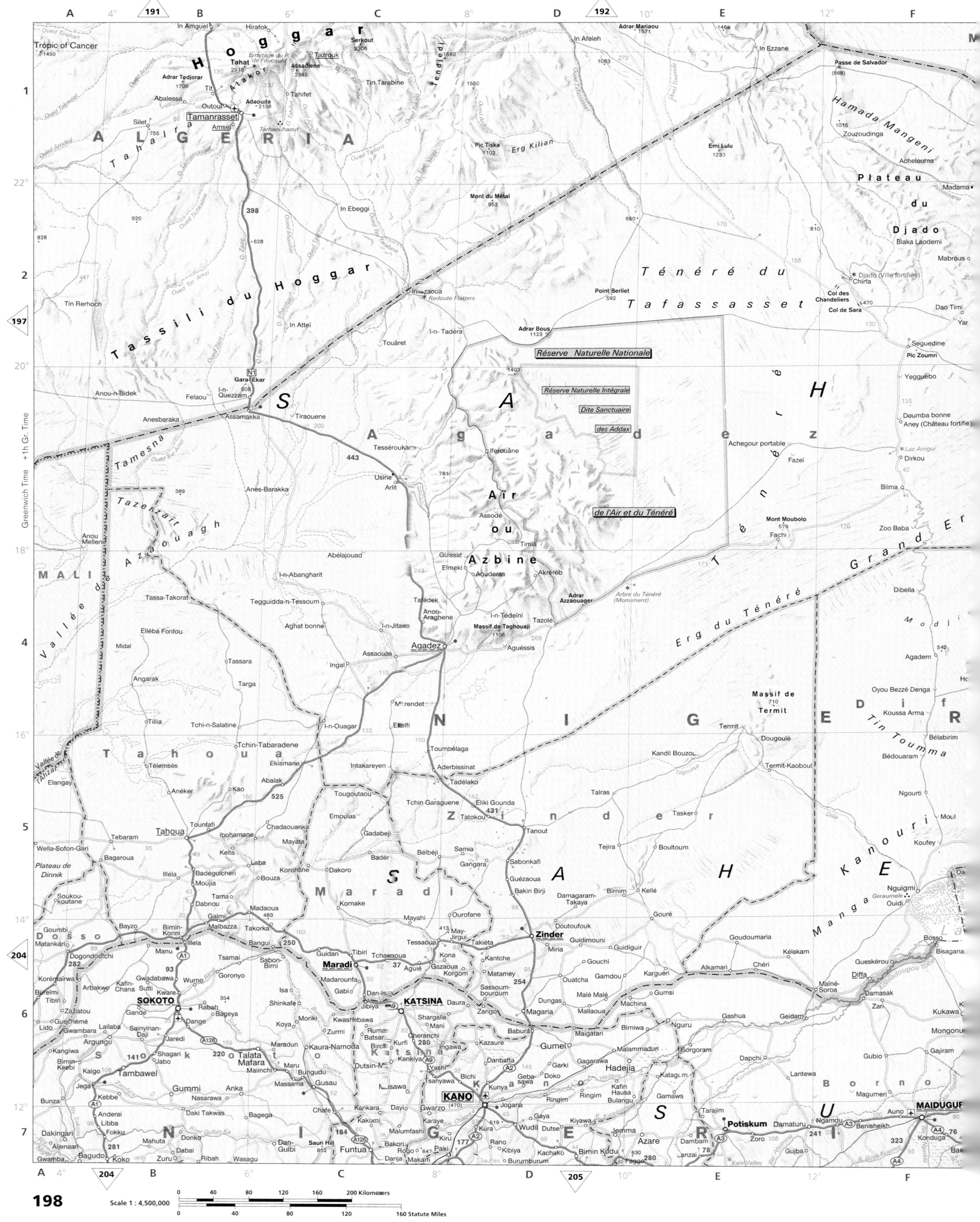

Tropic of Cancer

H o g g a r

ALGERIA

Tahat
2918

Tamanrasset

Assadjene
2345

In Amguel

Hirafok

Serkout
2306

Tazrouk

In Afeleh

Adrar Mariaou
1571

In Ezzane

Passe de Salvador
(868)

Hamada Mangeni

Adrar Tedjorar
1700

Abalessa

Outoul

Adaouda
2138

Tahifet

Tin Tarabine

1550

Zouzoudinga
1015

Acheloûma

P l a t e a u

Silet
755

Amsel

Tit

Pic Tiska
1103

Erg Kilian

Emi Lulu
1230

810

Madama

d u

D j a d o

Mont du Métal
952

660

Blaka Laodemi

Mabrous

T é n é r é   d u

Djado (Ville fortifiée)
Chirfa

In Ebeggi

398

In Atteï

In-zaoua
Redoute Flatters

Point Berliet
592

T a f a s s a s s e t

Col des
Chandeliers

Col de Sara

130

Dao Timi

Yar

Tassili du Hoggar

Touâret

I-n- Tadéra

Adrar Bous
1123

Réserve   Naturelle   Nationale

1403

Seguedine

Pic Zoumri

Yegguébo

N1
Gara-Ekar

508
I-n-
Quezzam

Réserve Naturelle Intégrale

155

135

Anou-n-Bidek

Felaou

S

Assamakka

Tiraouene

Tesséroukar

200

Réserve Naturelle Intégrale
Dite Sanctuaire
des Addax

A

z

Doumba bonne
Aney (Château fortifié)

Achegour portable

Anesbaraka

Tamesna

443

Iferouâne

781

A

i

r

d

e

de l'Air et du Ténéré

Lac Arrigui

Dirkou

Fazeï

Bilma

40

Anes-Barakka

389

Usine
Arlit

Assodé

o u

Timia

Mont Moubolo
579

Fachi

Zoo Baba

170

Anou
Mellen

Abélajouad

Guissat

Elmeki

A z b i n e

Aouderas

Akréréb

243

G

r

a

n

d

E

r

Dibella

Tassa-Takorat

I-n-Abangharit

Teggidda-n-Tessoum

Tarédek

Adrar
Azzaouager

Arbre du Ténéré
(Monument)

121

M

o

d

j

Midal

Elléba Fonfou

Aghat bonne

Anou-
Araghene

I-n-Jita

I-n-Tédeïni

Tazolé

Massif de Taghouaji
1106

269

542

Agadem

Angarak

Tassara

Targa

Assaouas

Agadez

Aguéssis

E r g   d u   T é n é r é

Oyou Bezzé Denga

Tillia

Ingal

110

N

Koussa Arma

Tin Toumma

Tchi-n-Salatine

I-n-Ouagar

M'rendet

133

Elolfi

I

G

Massif de
Termit

710

E

D

i

f

Bélabirim

Tchin-Tabaradene

150

Toumbélaga

Termit

Dougoulé

Bédouaram

Telemsès

T a h o u a

Ekismane

Aderbissinat

Kandil Bouzol

Termit-Kaoboul

Ngourti

Elangay

Anéker

Kao

160

525

Abalak

Tougoutaou

Tadélako

142

Talras

Tasker

Moul

Tebaram

Tountafi

Chadaouanka

Mayata

Emoulas

Tchin Garaguene

Tatokou

431

Z i n d e r

Koufey

Tahoua

Ibohamane

Gadabeji

Tanout

Tejira

Boultoum

Wella-Sofon-Gari

Bagaroua

Keita

Laba

Bader

Bélbéji

Samia

Gangara

Sabonkafi

Guézaoua

K

a

n

o

u

r

i

Nguigmi

Plateau de
Dinnik

Illéla

Badéguicheri

Moujia

Bouza

Korohône

Dakoro

S

Kornake

Mayahi

Ourofane

Bakin Birji

Damagaram-
Takaya

Birnim

Kellé

Gouré

Geraumele
Ouidi

Soukou-
koutane

Tama

Dabnou

Galmi

483

Madaoua

M a r a d i

413

May-
Jirgui

Takiéta

52

Doutoufouk

Zinder

Guidimouni

Goudoumaria

Goumbi

Bayzo

Birnin-
Konni

Takorka

160

Bangui

250

Guidan

Tibiri

Tchadoua

Tessaoua

31

Kona

Kantche

95

Guidiguir

Miria

Gouchi

Gamdou

Kélakam

Bisagana

Bosso

Dosso

Matankari

Manu

Tsamai

Sabon-
Birni

Maradi

Madarounfa

92

Aguié

37

Gazaoua

Korgom

Matamey

Zango

Magaria

Ouatcha

Malé Malé

Machina

Alkamari

Chéri

Karguéri

Gueskérou

Diffa

Damasak

Dogondoutchi
282

93

Koré-
mairwa

Kafin-
Chana

Gwadabawa

Sutti

Goronyo

Isa

Gabi

Dan-Is

Sassoum-
bouroum

254

Dungas

Malé

Gamdou

Gumsi

Mainé-
Soroa

Zari

Kukawa

Bureimi

Tibiri

Zäziatou

Kware

Wurno

354

Koya

Moriki

Zurmi

Shinkafe

KATSINA

Daura

Babura

Magaria

Maigatari

Birniwa

Nguru

Malammaduri

Gagarawa

Dapchi

Lantewa

Gubio

Mongonu

Lido

Guéchémé

Lailaba

Sainyinan-
Daji

SOKOTO

Rabah

Dange

Bageya

Jibiya

Kwashebawa

Mani

Shargalle

Zango

Kazaure

Gumel

Garki

Birniwa

Gagarawa

Garin

Gashua

Geidam

Gajiram

B o r n o

Kangiwa

Argungu

Birnin-
Kebbi

Jaredi

A126

159

Maradun

Kaura-Namoda

Birci

Kurfi

Danbatta

280

Ingawa

Kankiya

A9

Yashi

Doko

Ringim

Kafin
Hausa

Bulangu

Gamawa

Katagum

Ringim

Magumeri

S

1410

Shagari

Jabo

220

Talata
Mafara

Maru

Maïinchi

Bungudu

Gusau

Isawa

Bichi

Kunya

Tsanyawa

a

n

Gaya

Kiyawa

Tarajim

Damaturu

Ngamdu

Benisheikh

Auno

MAIDUGURI

Kalgo

106

Tambawel

Gummi

Anka

Massama

52

KANO
(470)

Jogana

Dutse

Ringim

Jemma

Azare

Potiskum

Zoro

108

241

323

Bunza

Jega

A1

Kebbe

Daki Takwas

Nasarawa

Chafe

Kankara

Dayi

Gwarzo

Kura

Wudil

Rano

Gaya

Dutse

69

Dambam

78

Birnin Kudu

Fagge

280

Lanzai

A4

Konduga

Dakingari

Anderai

Libba

Fokku

Donko

184

Sauri Hill
852

Kakumi

Karaye

Kiru

Kura

Paki

Kachako

A3

76

Gwamba

Koko

Zuru

Ribah

Wasagu

Dan-
Gulbi

Funtua

Bakori

Danja

Makairi

Burumburum

Gujba

A4

Scale 1 : 4,500,000

0   40   80   120   160   200 Kilometers

0   40   80   120   160 Statute Miles

Greenwich Time   +1h Gr. Time

MALI

NIGER

S A H A R A

S A H E L

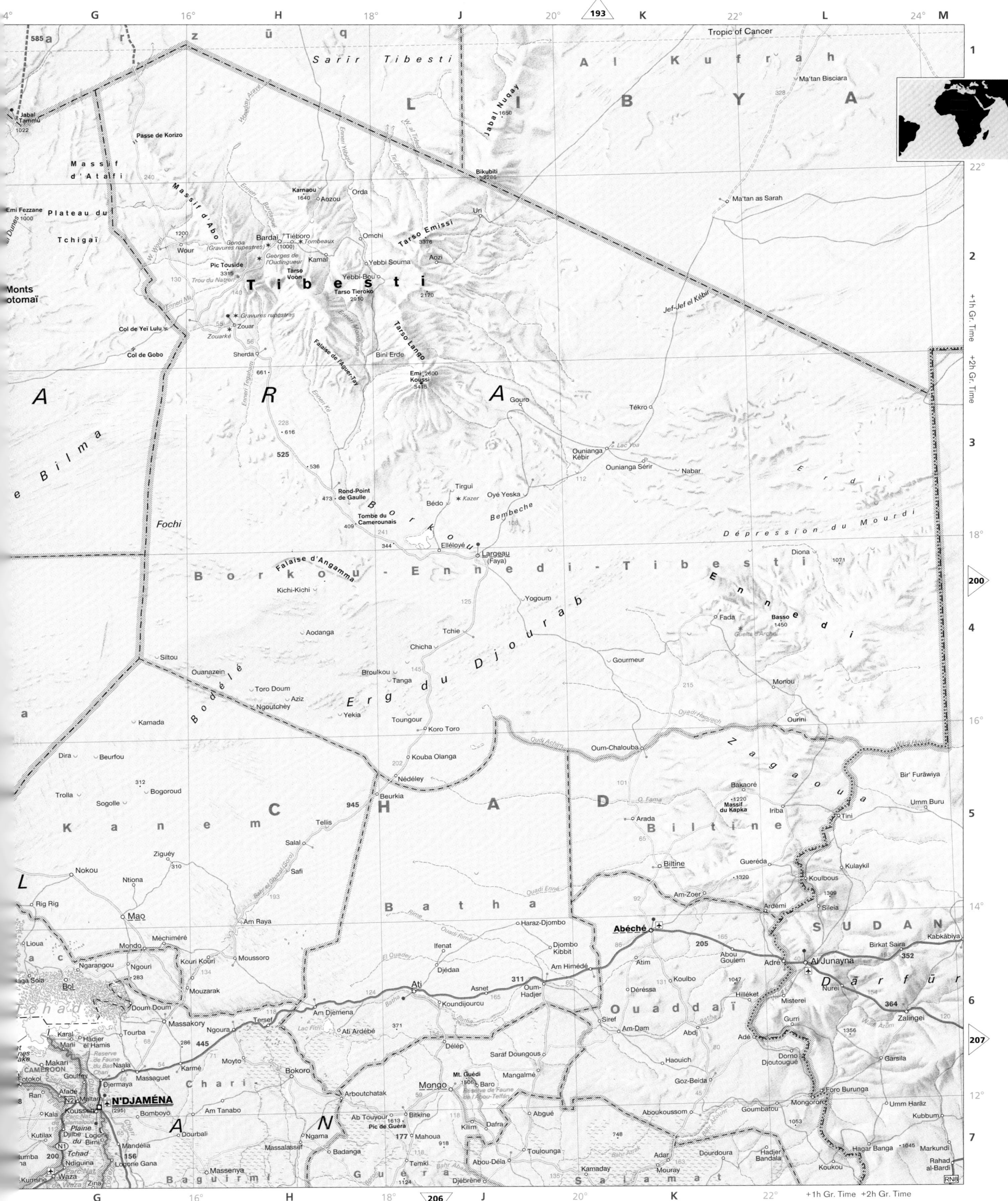

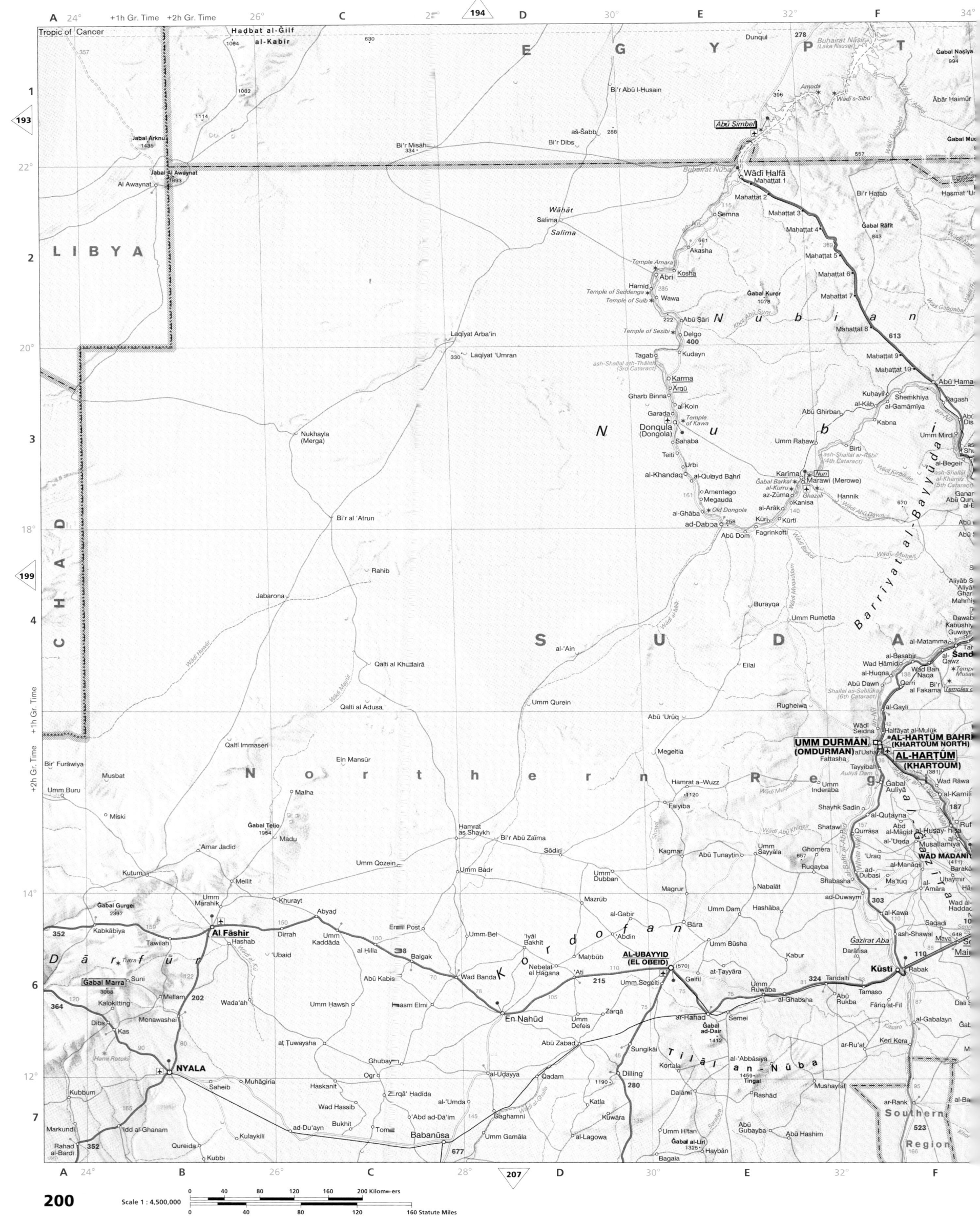

Tropic of Cancer
Haḍbat al-Ǧilf
al-Kabīr

E G Y P T

LIBYA

CHAD

SUDAN

Northern Region

Dār fūr

Kordofan

Tilāl an-Nūba

Wādī Halfā

Donqula
(Dongola)

Karima

AL-HARTŪM BAHRĪ
(KHARTOUM NORTH)
UMM DURMĀN
(OMDURMAN)
AL-HARTŪM
(KHARTOUM)

Al Fāshir

AL-UBAYYID
(EL OBEID)

Kūsti

WAD MADANĪ

En Nahūd

NYALA

Gabal Marra

Babanūsa

Scale 1 : 4,500,000

0   40   80   120   160   200 Kilometers
0   40   80   120   160 Statute Miles

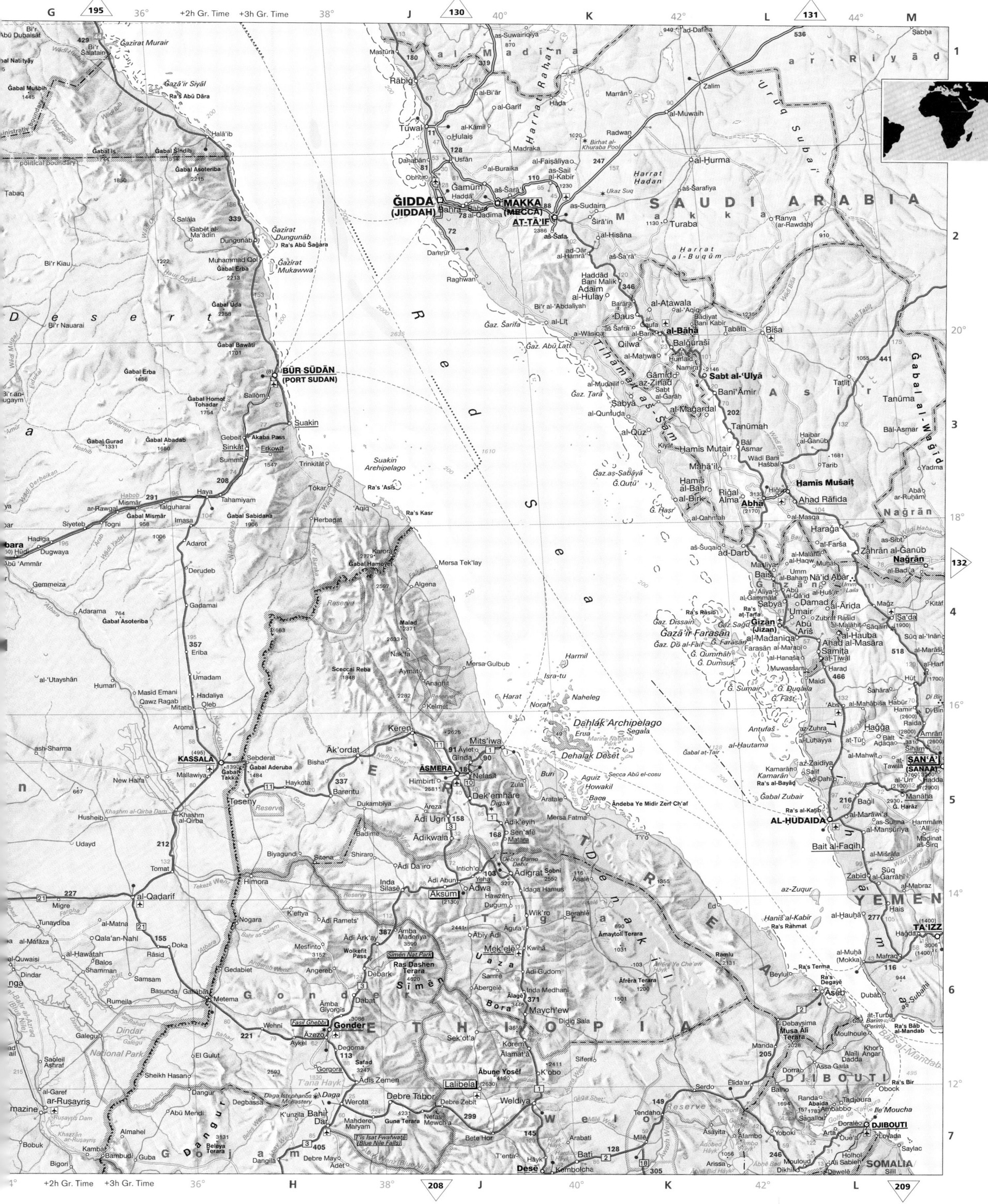

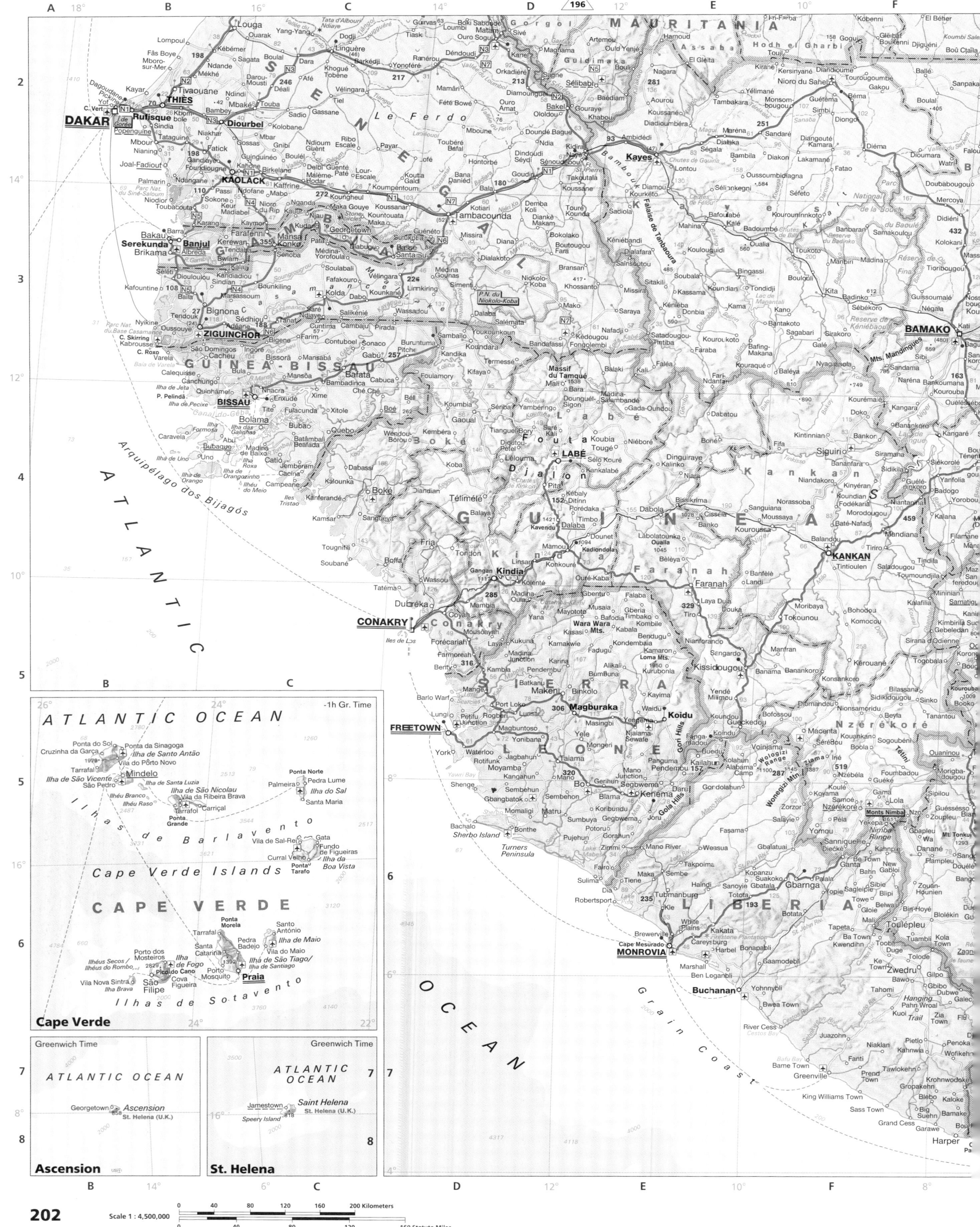

Map labels

A 18° B 16° C 14° D 12° E 10° F

MAURITANIA

In-Farba · Kobenni · El Béïer

Gogui · 158 · Djiguéni · Koumbi Saleh

Gorgol · Hamoud · Assaba · Hodh el Gharbi · Touil · Boû Ctaïla

Ould Yenjé · Maghama · Guidimaka · El Gleïta · Kirane · Kersinyané · Diandioume · Ballé

Nagara · 281 · 236 · Nioro du Sahel · Touroùgoumbé · Gakou · Sanpaka

Bakel · Gouraye · Khabou · Diadioumbéra · Baédiam · Diangounté · Simbi · Diongo · Diéma · Boulal · 405

SENEGAL

Louga · Lompoul · Fâs Boye · Mboro-sur-Mer · Kayar · C. Vert · DAKAR · Rufisque · Thiès · Tivaouane · Mbour · Nianing · Joal-Fadiout

KAOLACK · Diourbel · Touba

ZIGUINCHOR · GUINEA-BISSAU · BISSAU · Bolama

Serekunda · Banjul · Brikama

BAMAKO

MALI · Kati · 163 · Bagu · Mts. Mandingues · 480

Kayes · 251 · Bafoulabé · Kita · Badinko · 612

GUINEA

LABÉ · Fouta Djalon · KANKAN · Siguiri · 459

Kindia · CONAKRY · Faranah · Kissidougou · Nzérékoré

Monts Nimba · 519

SIERRA LEONE · FREETOWN · Makeni · Magburaka · Koidu · Kenema · Bo

LIBERIA · MONROVIA · Buchanan · Gbarnga · Greenville · Harper

ATLANTIC OCEAN

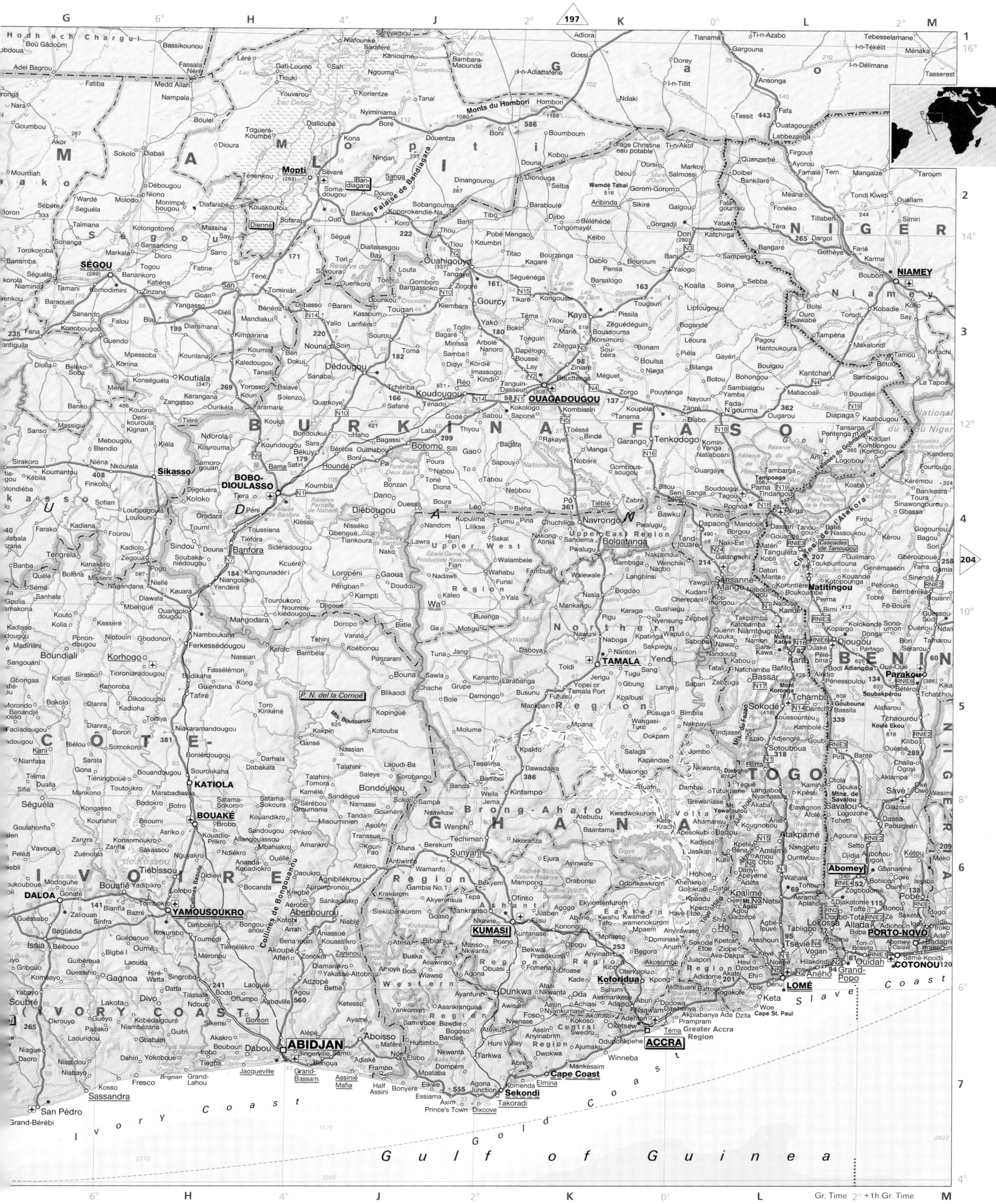

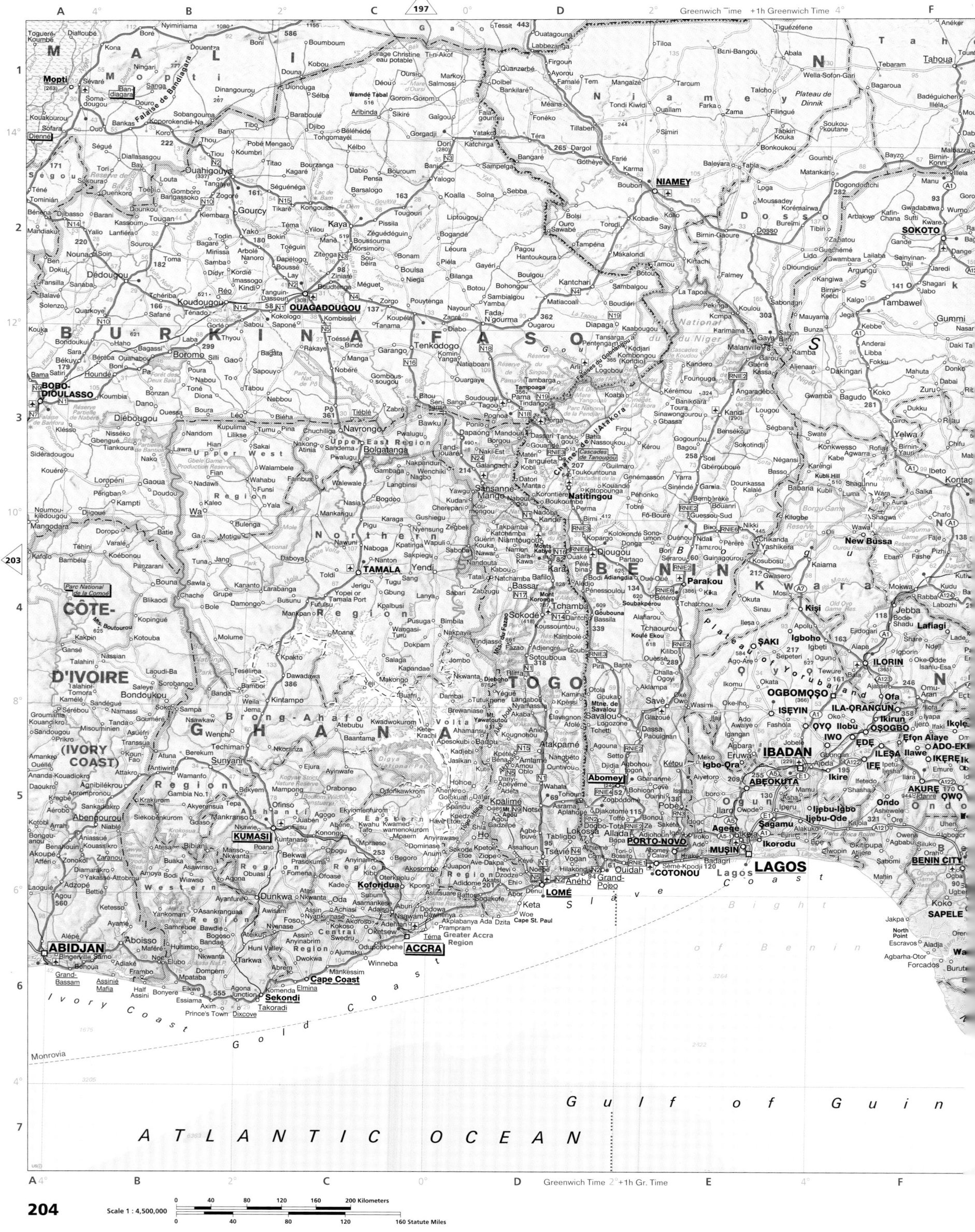

Scale 1 : 4,500,000

0   40   80   120   160   200 Kilometers

0   40   80   120   160 Statute Miles

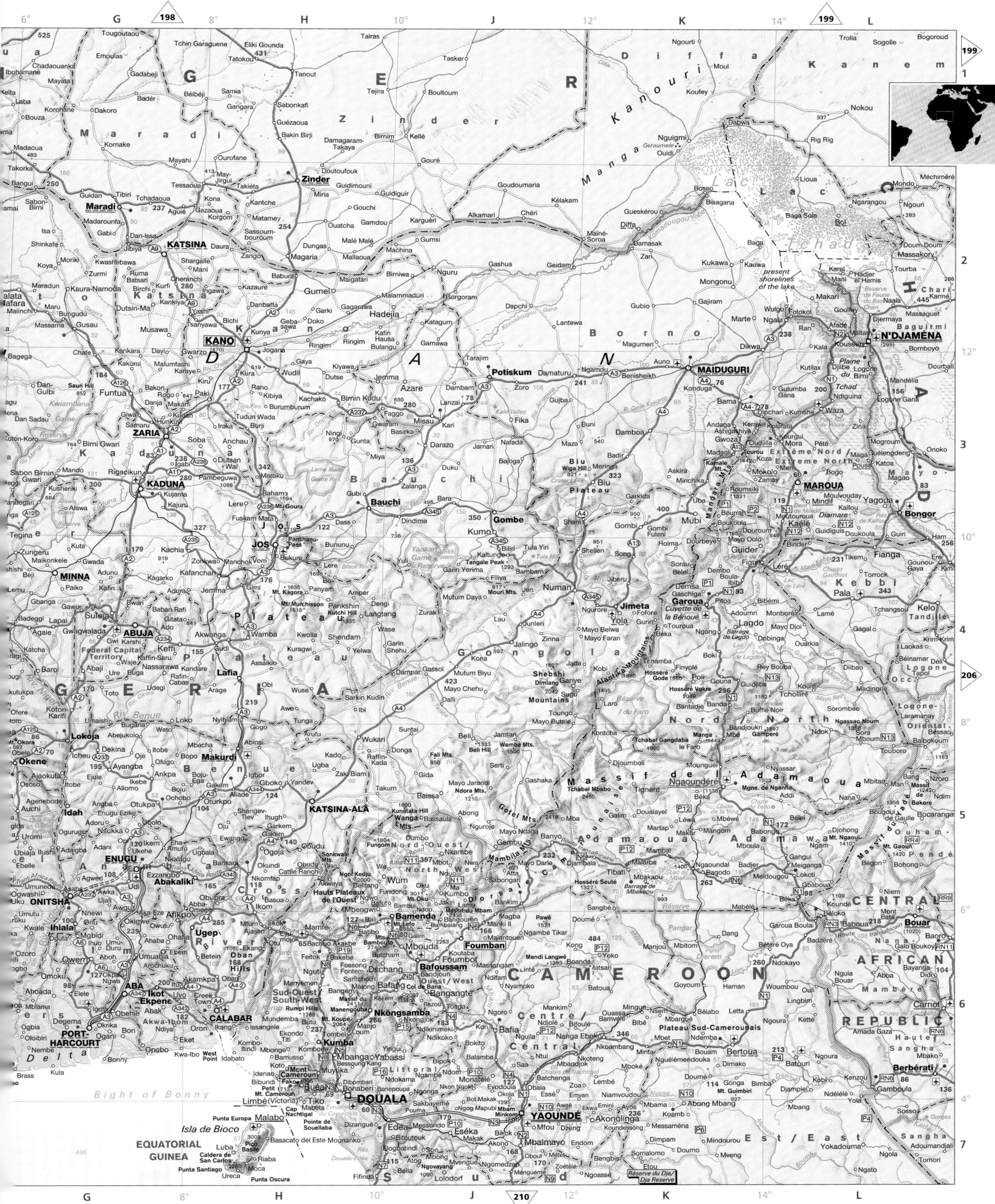

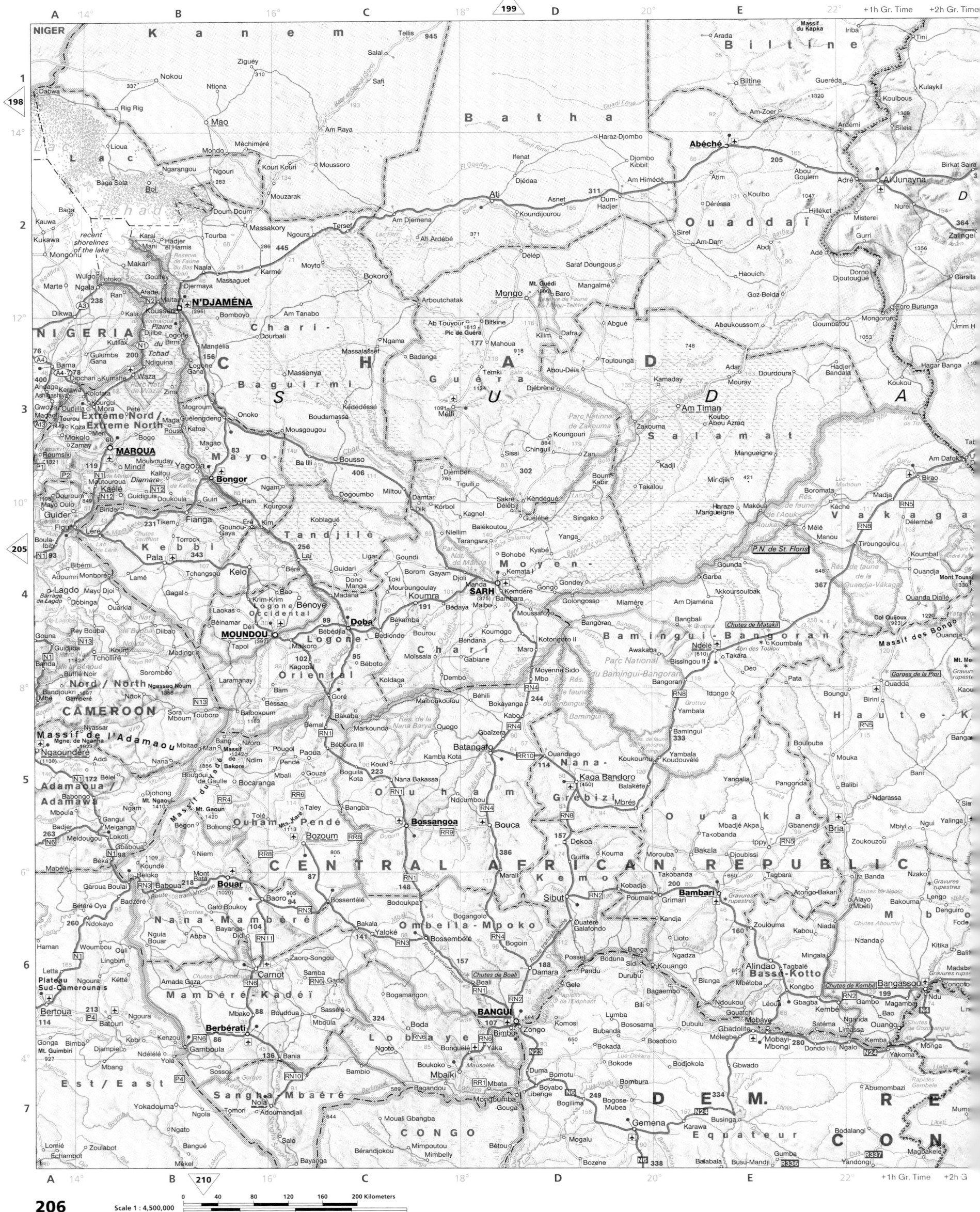

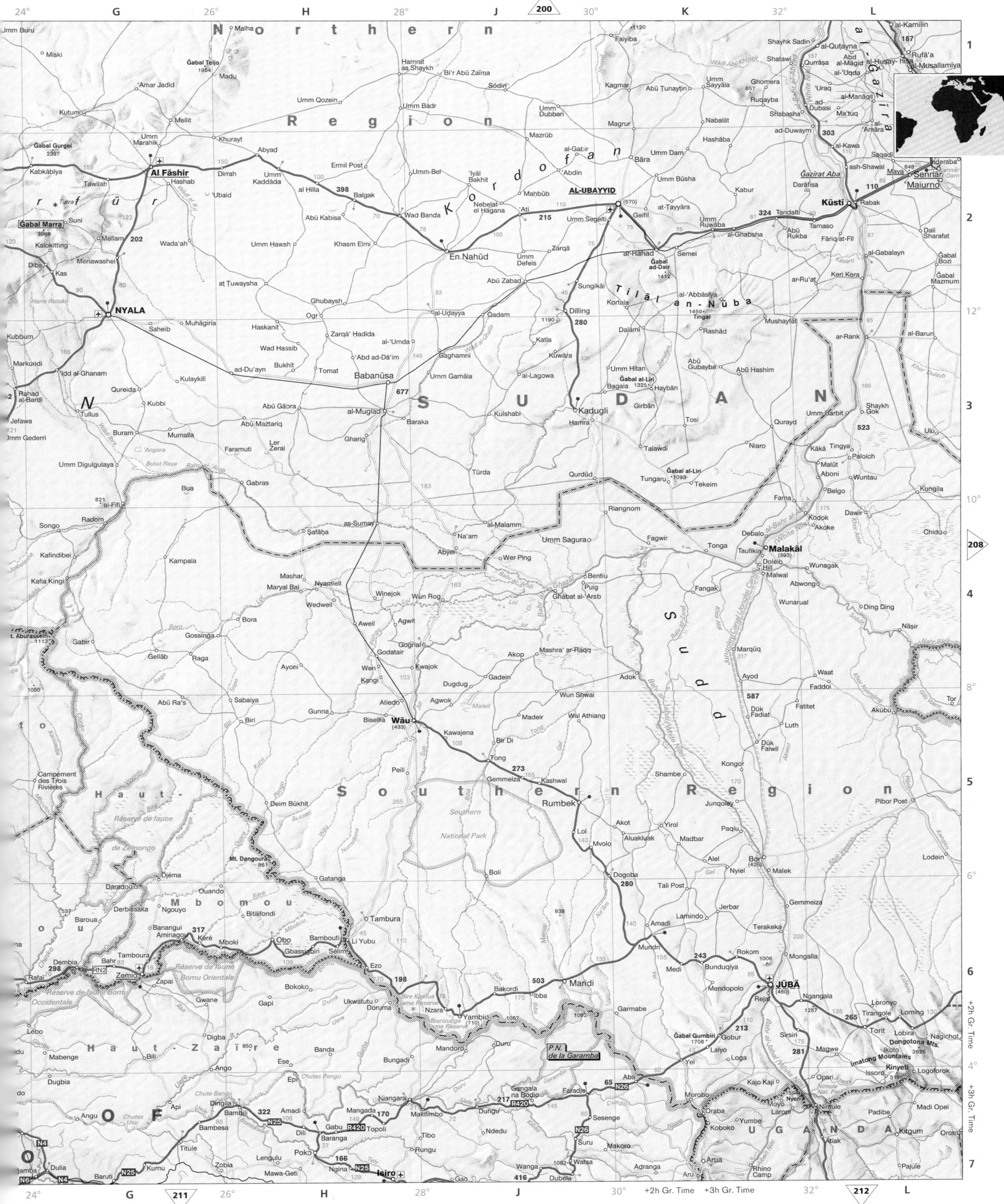

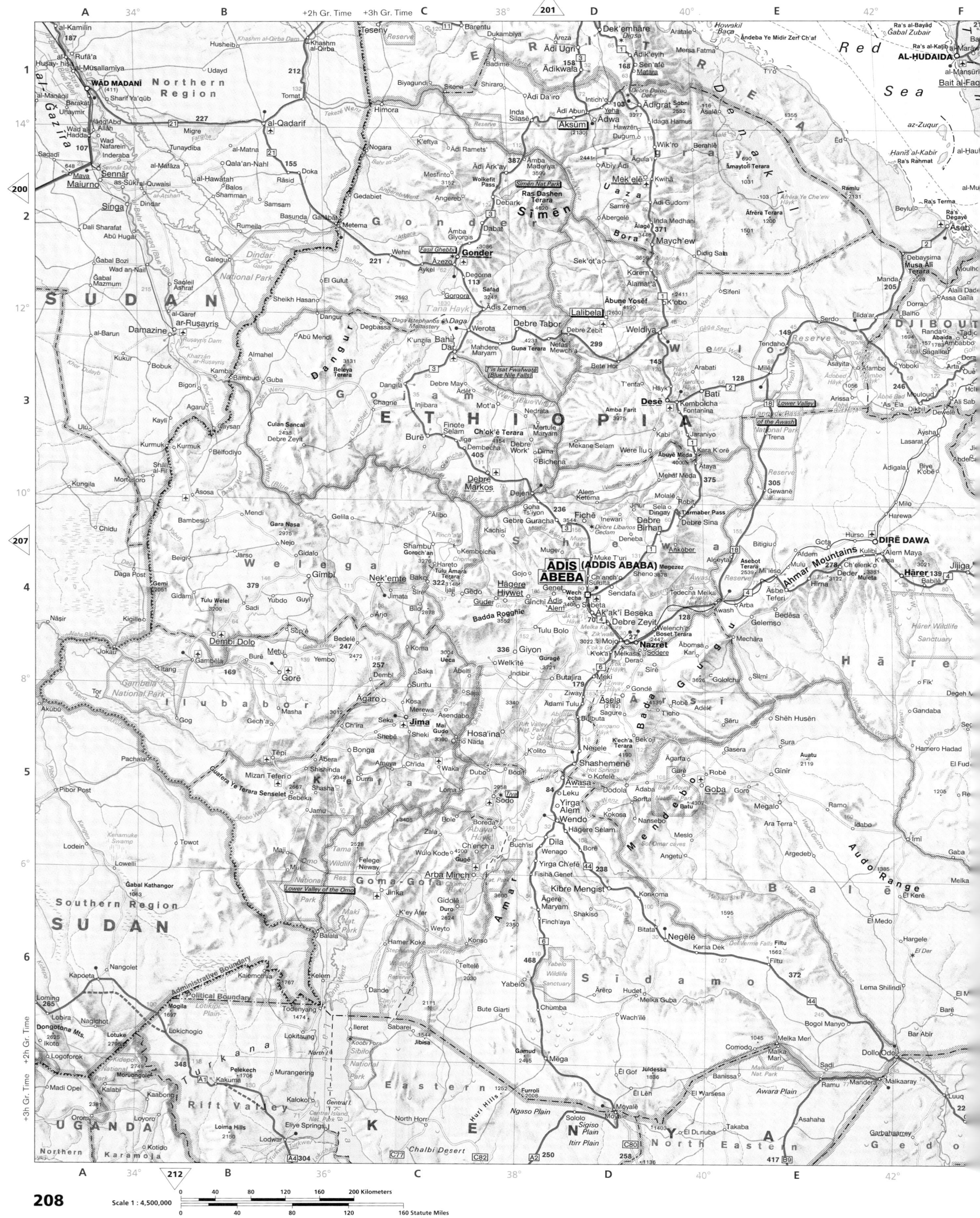

Ethiopia · Somali Peninsula   **209**

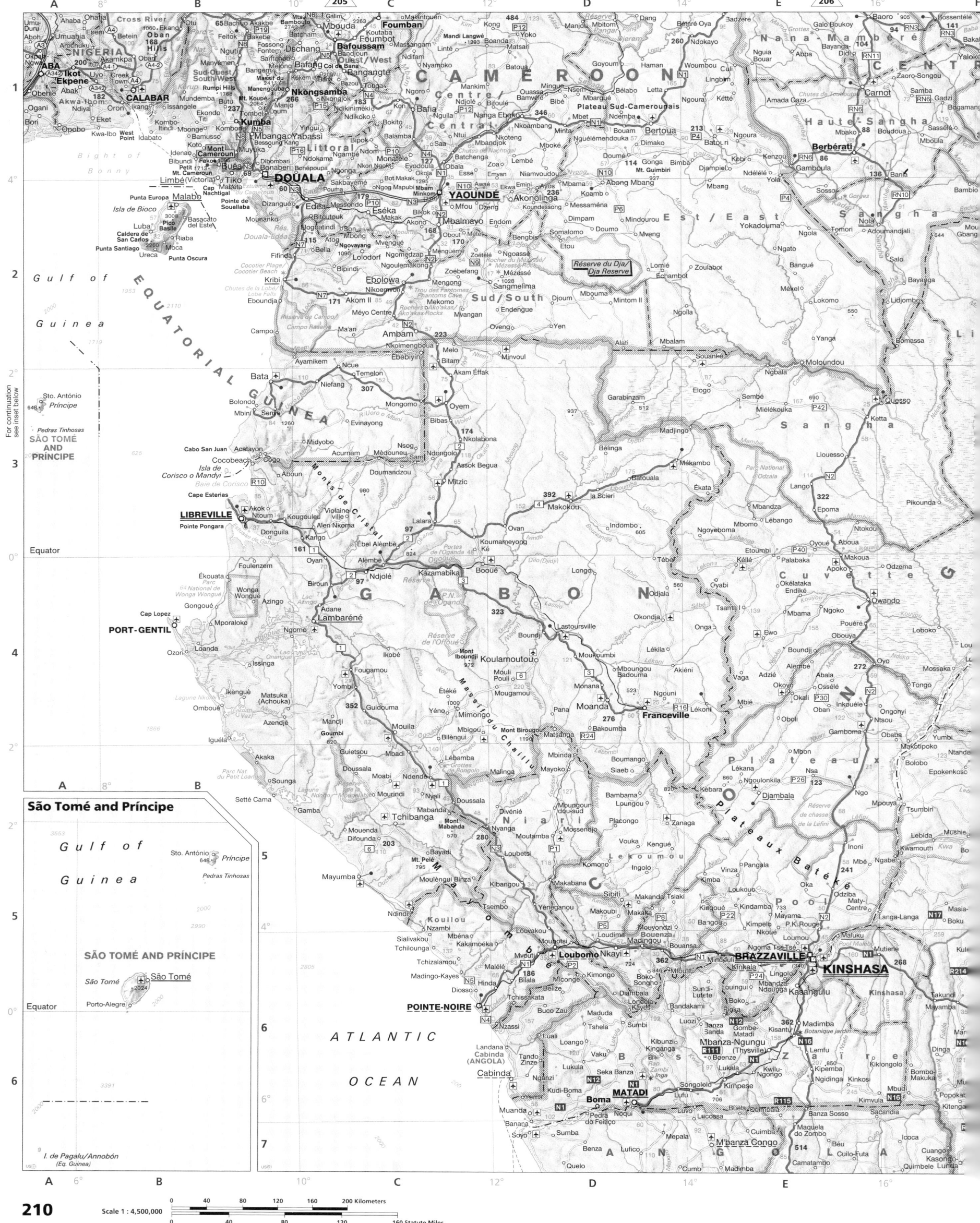

Scale 1 : 4,500,000

0 40 80 120 160 200 Kilometers

0 40 80 120 160 Statute Miles

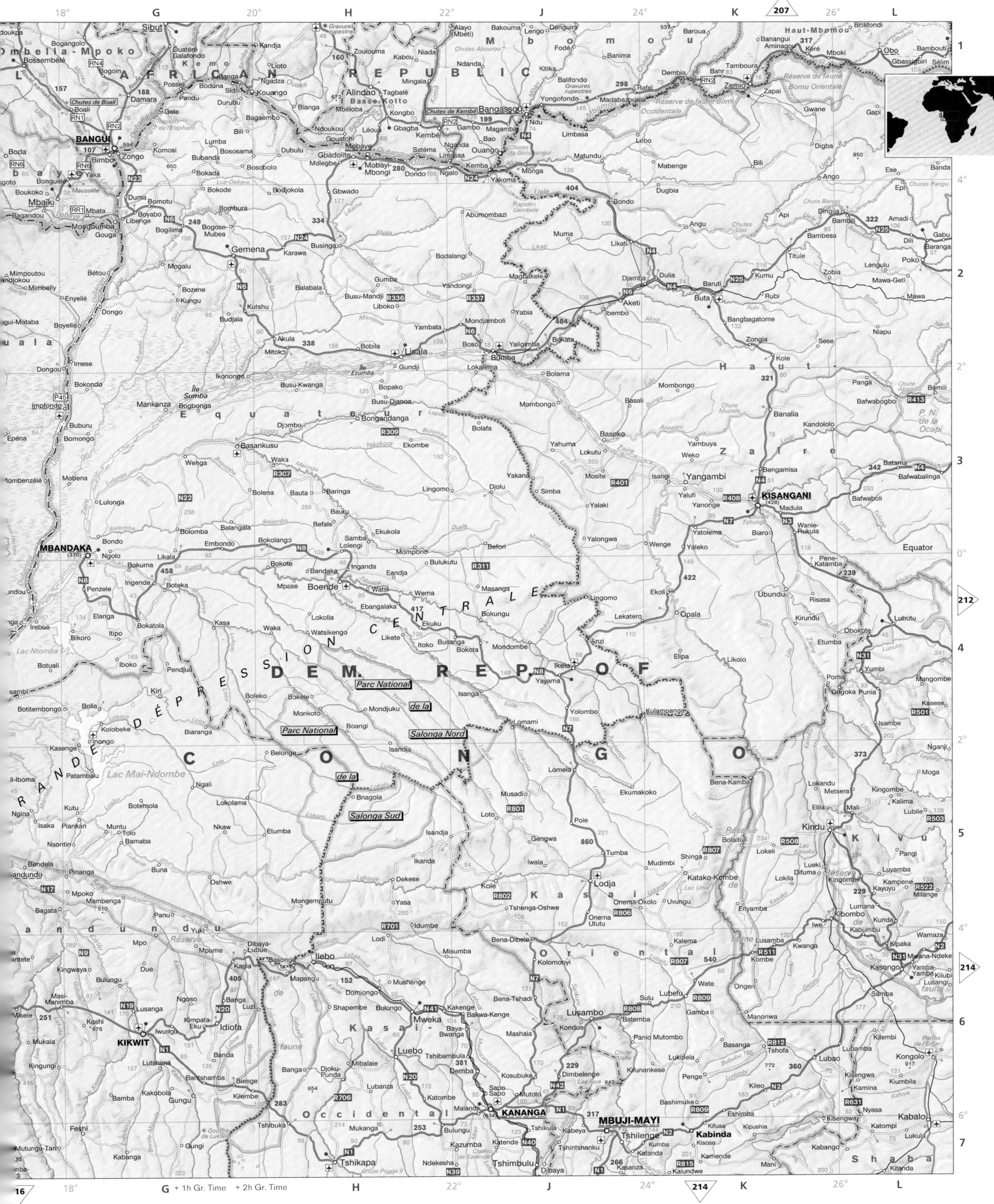

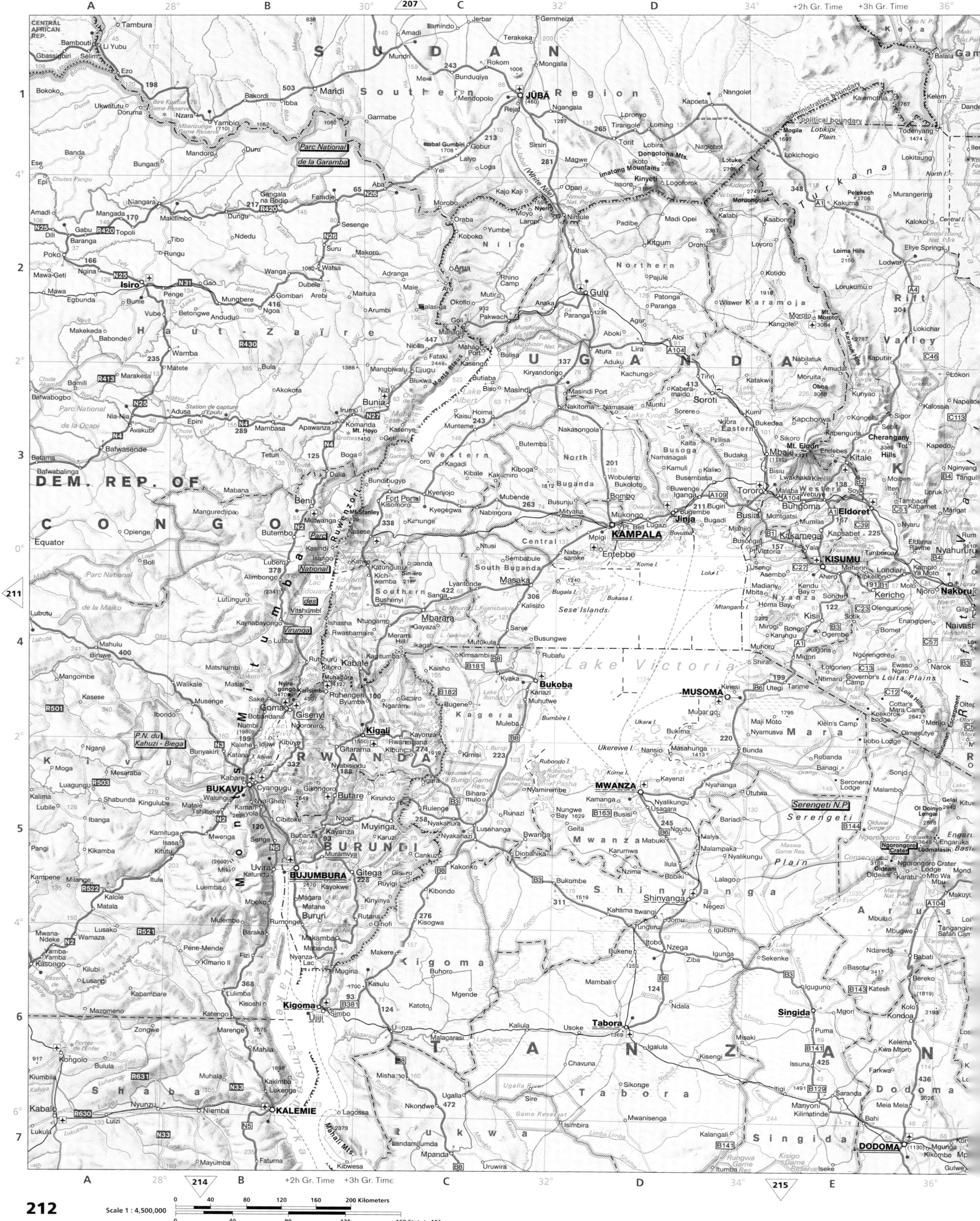

Scale 1 : 4,500,000

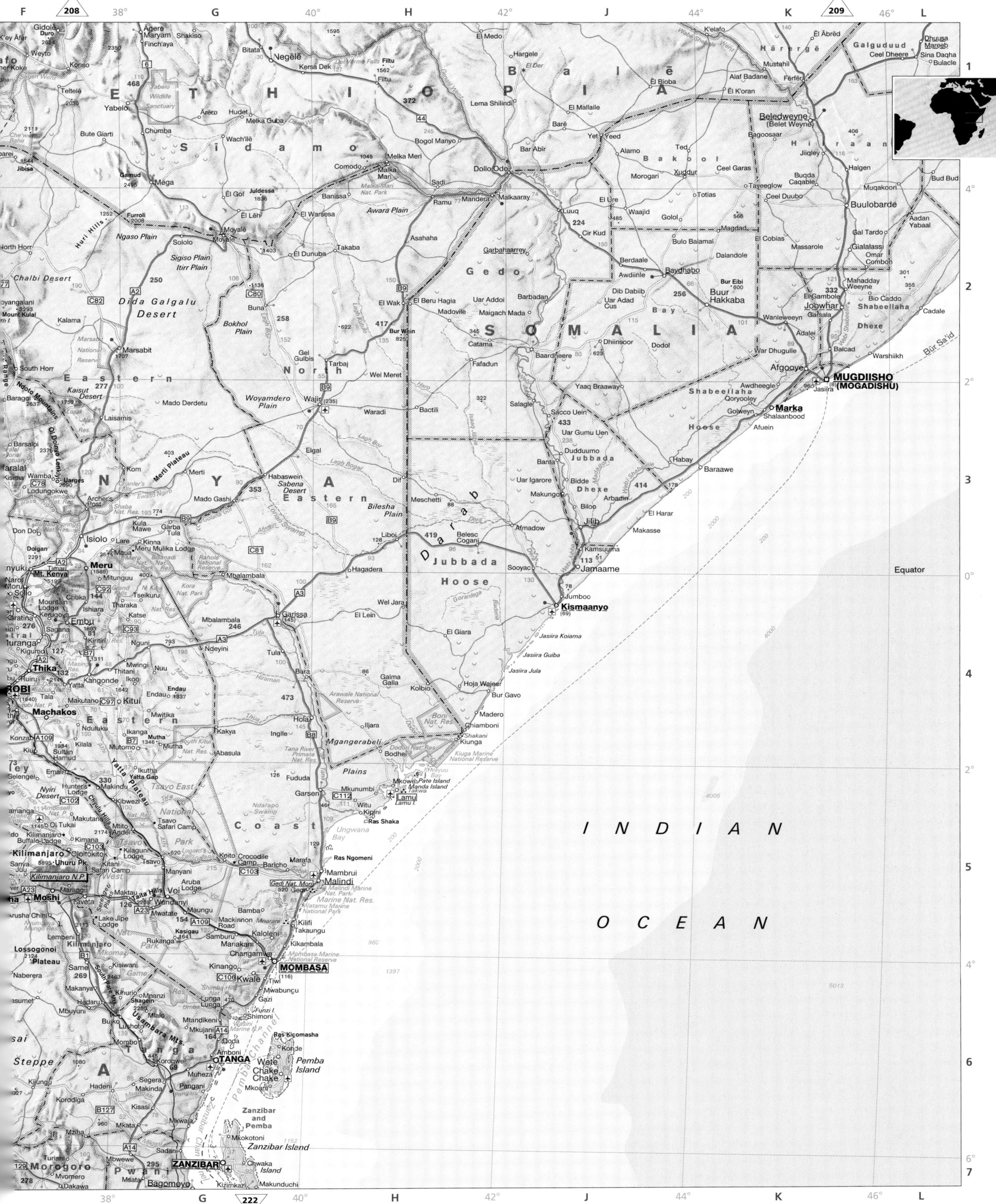

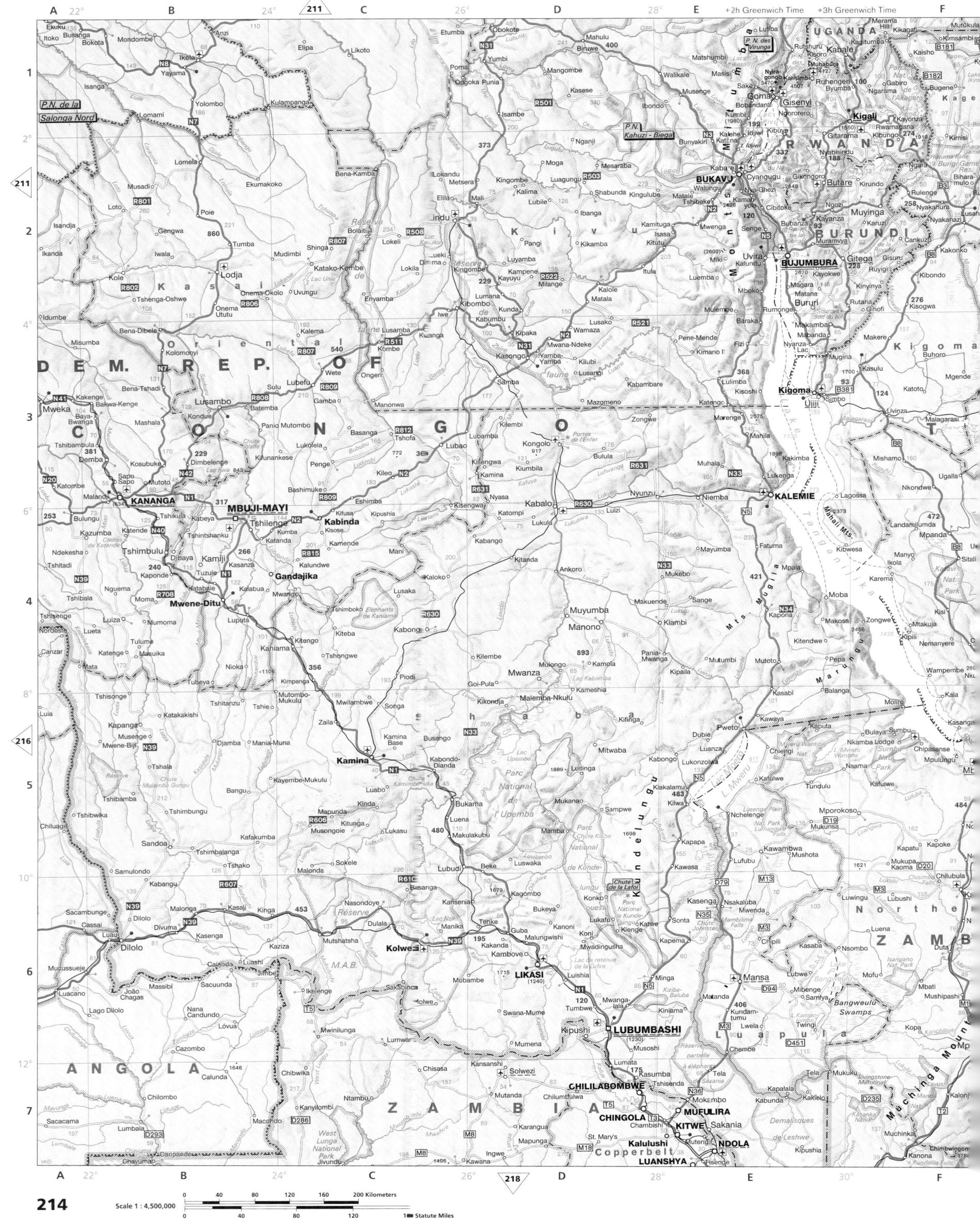

Scale 1 : 4,500,000

0   40   80   120   160   200 Kilometers

0   40   80   120

1 ▬▬ Statute Miles

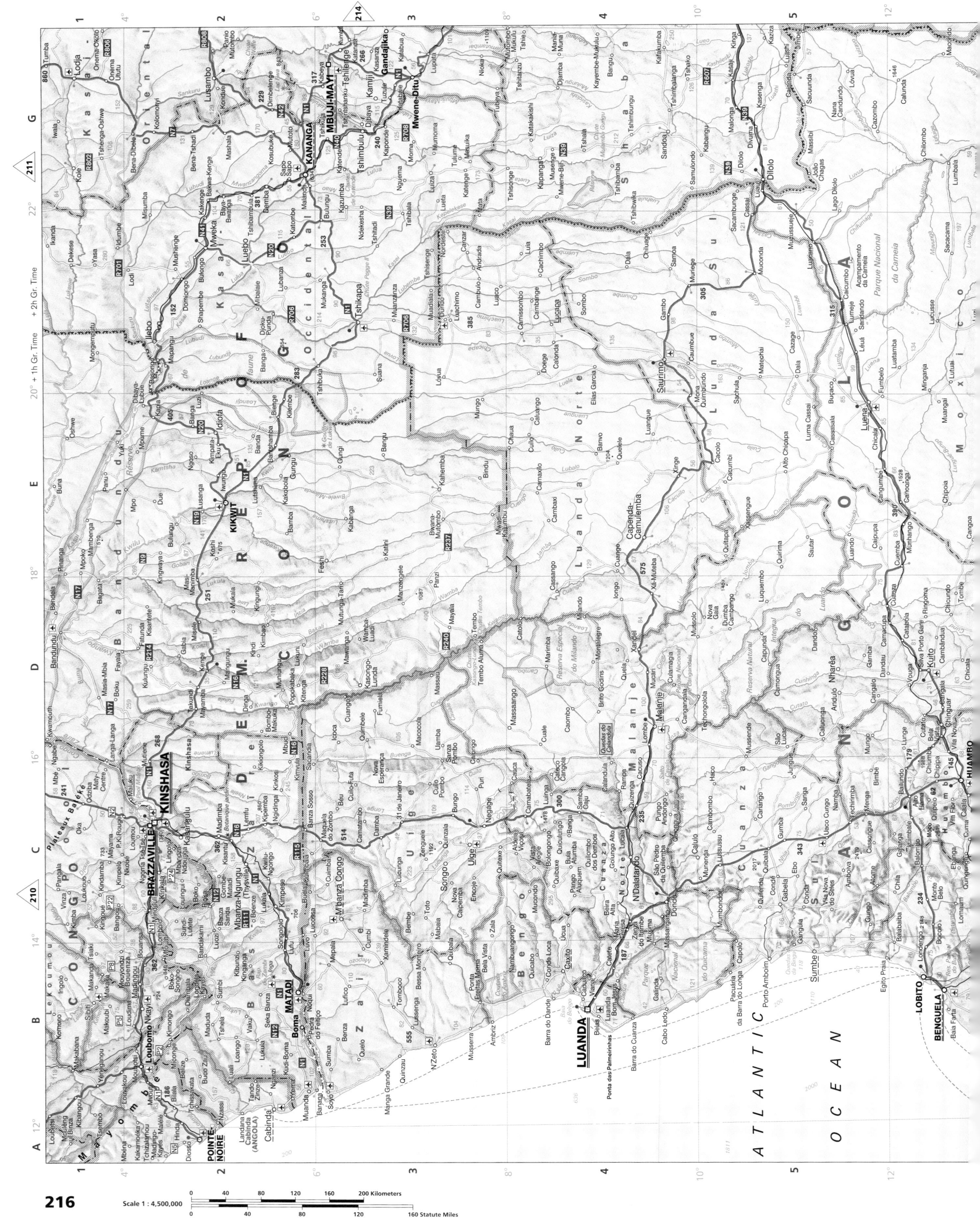

Scale 1 : 4,500,000

0   40   80   120   160   200 Kilometers

0   40   80   120   160 Statute Miles

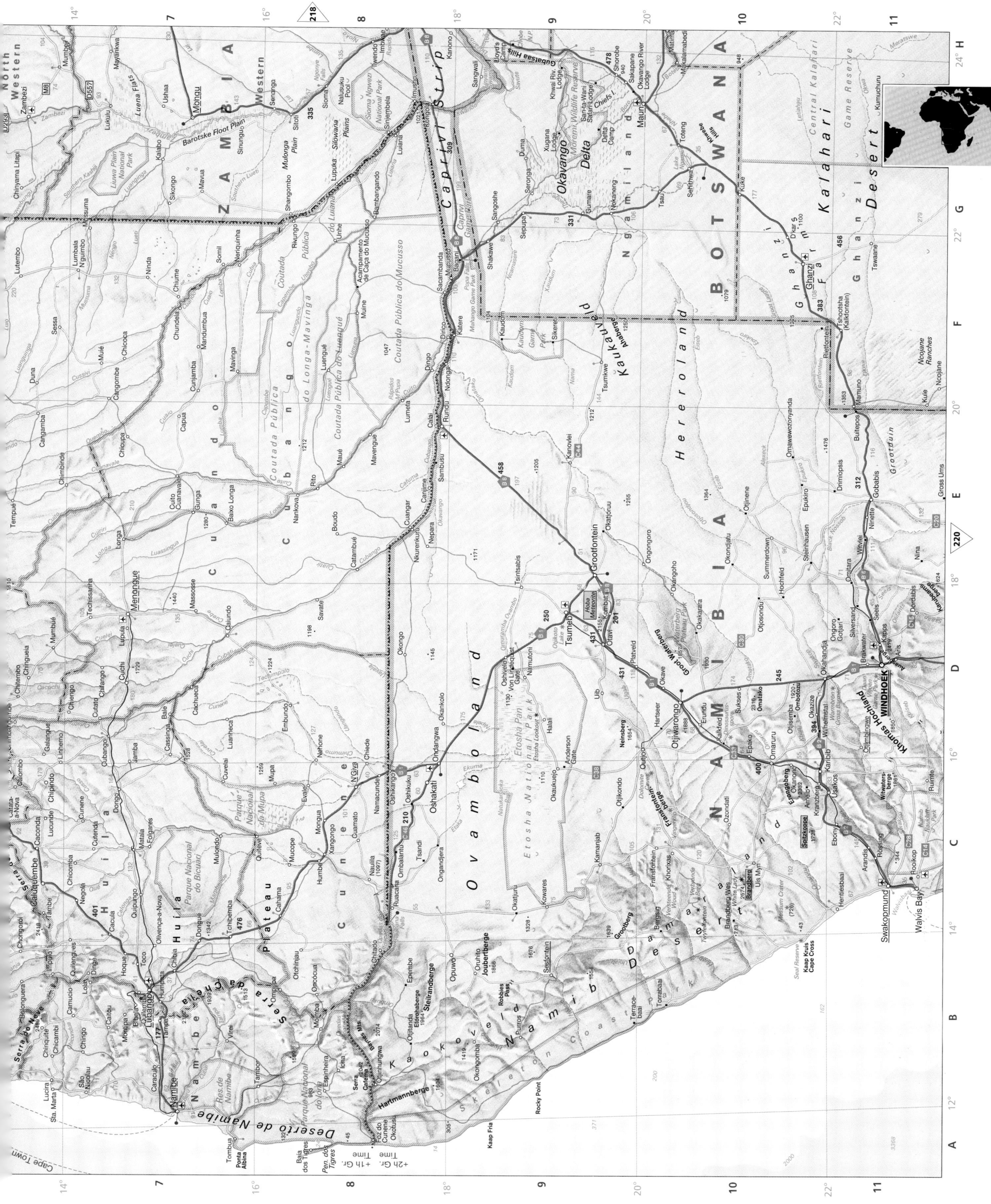

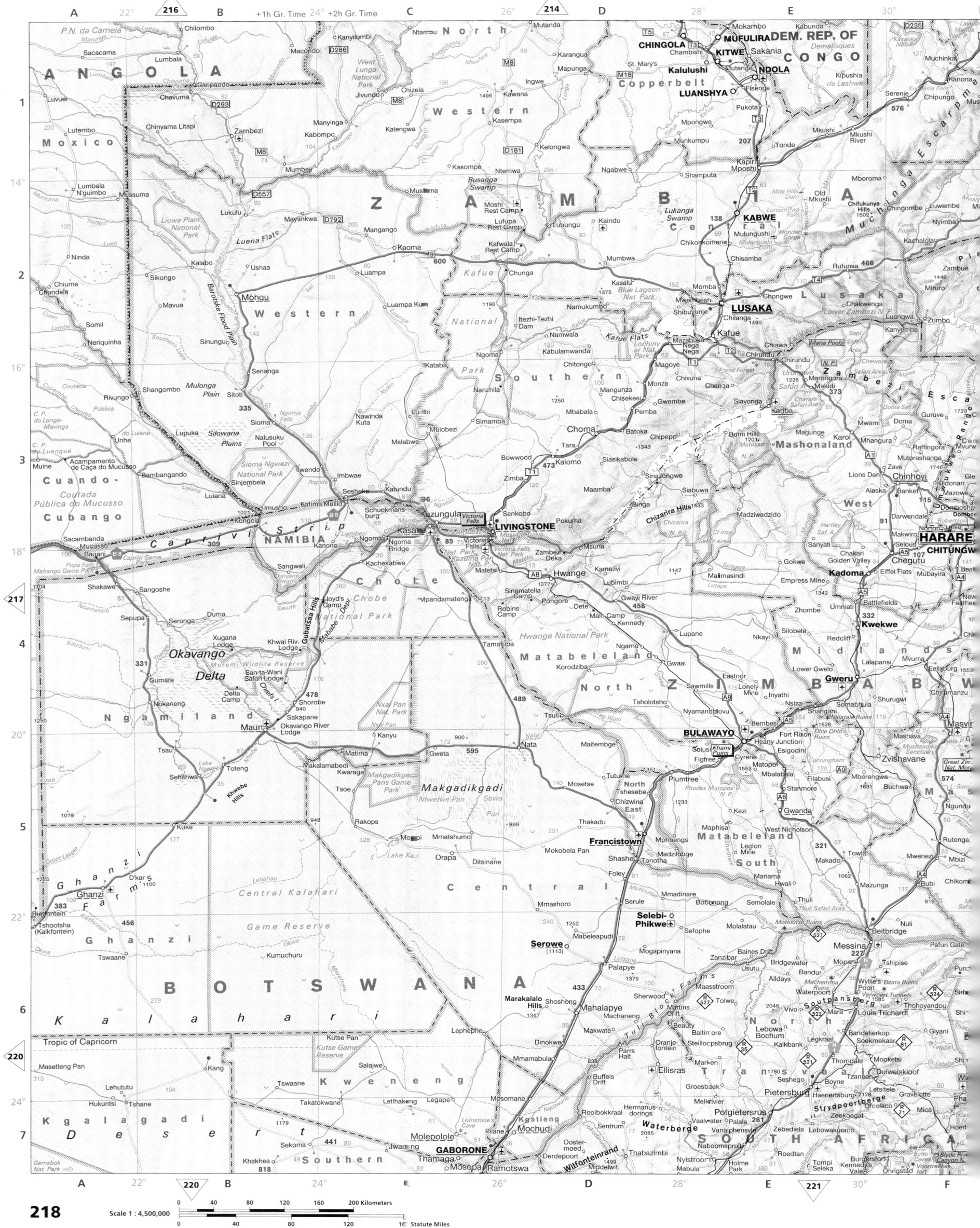

Scale 1 : 4,500,000

0   40   80   120   160   200 Kilometers

0   40   80   120

Statute Miles

Scale 1 : 4,500,000

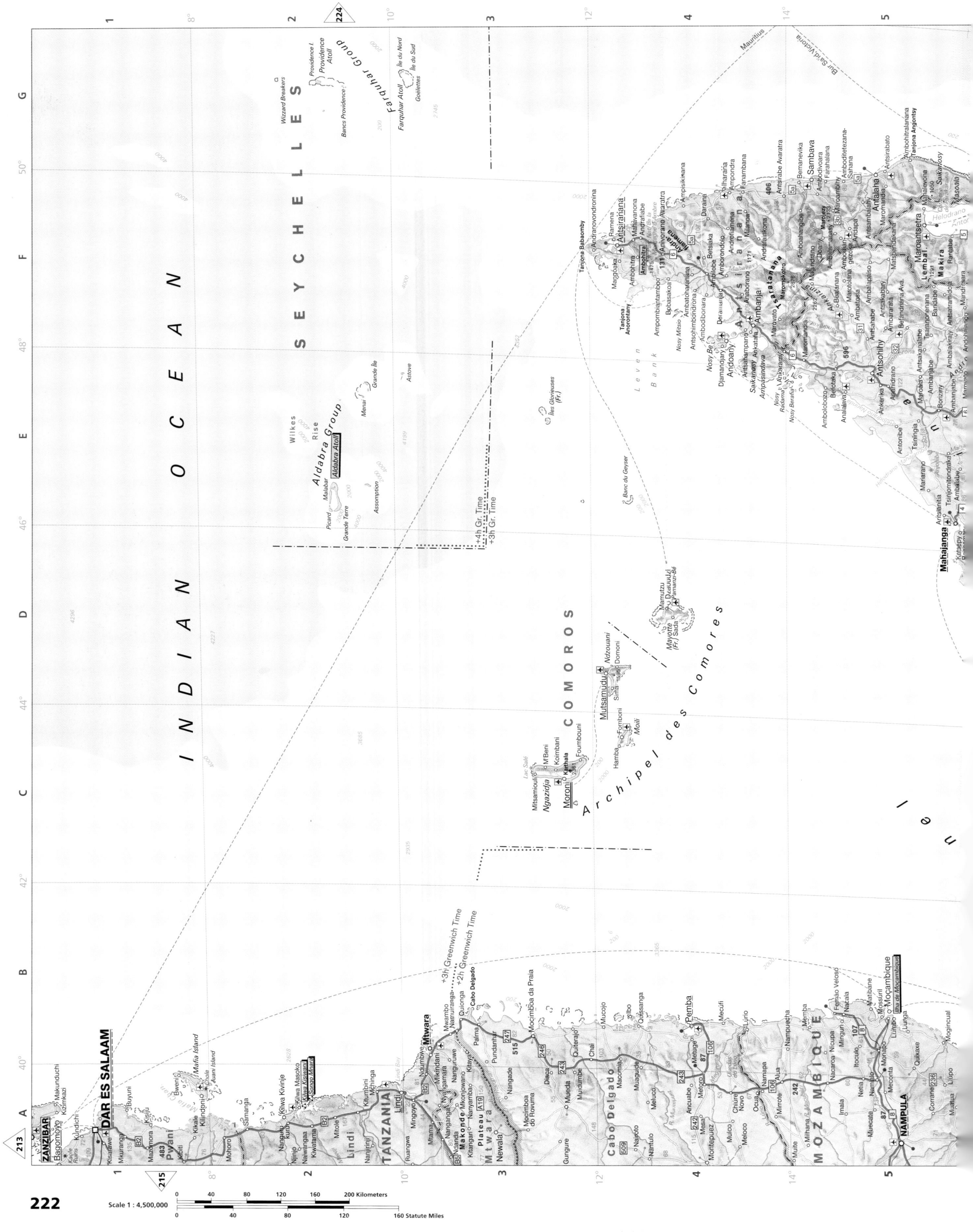

INDIAN OCEAN

SEYCHELLES

Wizard Breakers

Providence I.
Providence
Atoll

Farquhar Atoll
Bancs Providence

Île du Nord
Île du Sud
Goélettes

Wilkes Rise

Aldabra Group

Malabar
Picard
Grande Terre
Assomption

Menai
Grande Île
Astove

Îles Glorieuses
(Fr.)

Banc du Geyser

+4h Gr. Time
+3h Gr. Time

COMOROS

Archipel des Comores

Mitsamiouli
Ngazidja
M'Beni
Koimbani
Moroni
Foumbouni
Lac Salé

Mutsamudu
Ndzouani
Domoni
Sima
Hamba
Fomboni
Moili

Mamutzu
Dzaoudzi
Pamanzi-Bé
Mayotte
(Fr.) Sada

Leven Bank

Mahajanga
Katsepy
Antalalitia
Tsinjomitondraka
Marierano
Antonibe
Tsiningia

MADAGASCAR (region labels)
Antsiranana
Antsirabe Avaratra
Bemanevika
Sambava
Ambodivoara
Antsiratato
Tanjona Angontsy

Ampahana
Andrahanjo
Vohémar
Daraina

Ambanja
Nosy Be
Andoany
Ambilobe
Antsohihy
Befandriana Ava.
Mandritsara

INDIAN OCEAN

TANZANIA

DAR ES SALAAM
ZANZIBAR
Bagamoyo
Makunduchi
Kizimkazi
Mkuranga
Buyuni
Kisiju
Mafia Island
Juani Island
Pwani
Kilindoni
Mohoro
Kisarawe
Bwenje
Kivinje
Kilwa Masoko
Kilwa Kivinje
Songo Mnara
Samanga
Njinjo
Kitumbini
Nangurukuru
Njingwa
Lindi
Kitangari
Mtwara
Newala
Makonde Plateau
Mtwara
Masasi
Nangade
Diaca

MOZAMBIQUE

Cabo Delgado
Mocímboa da Praia
Cabo Delgado
Palma
Mucojo
Quissanga
Pemba
Mecúfi
Metuge
Ancuabe
Chiúre
Quiterajo
Nampula
Monapo
Mossuril
Namialo
Mecúburi
Moçambique
Ilha de Moçambique
Nacala
Fernão Veloso
Mossuril

Scale 1 : 4,500,000

0   40   80   120   160   200 Kilometers

0   40   80   120   160 Statute Miles

222

+3h Greenwich Time
+2h Greenwich Time

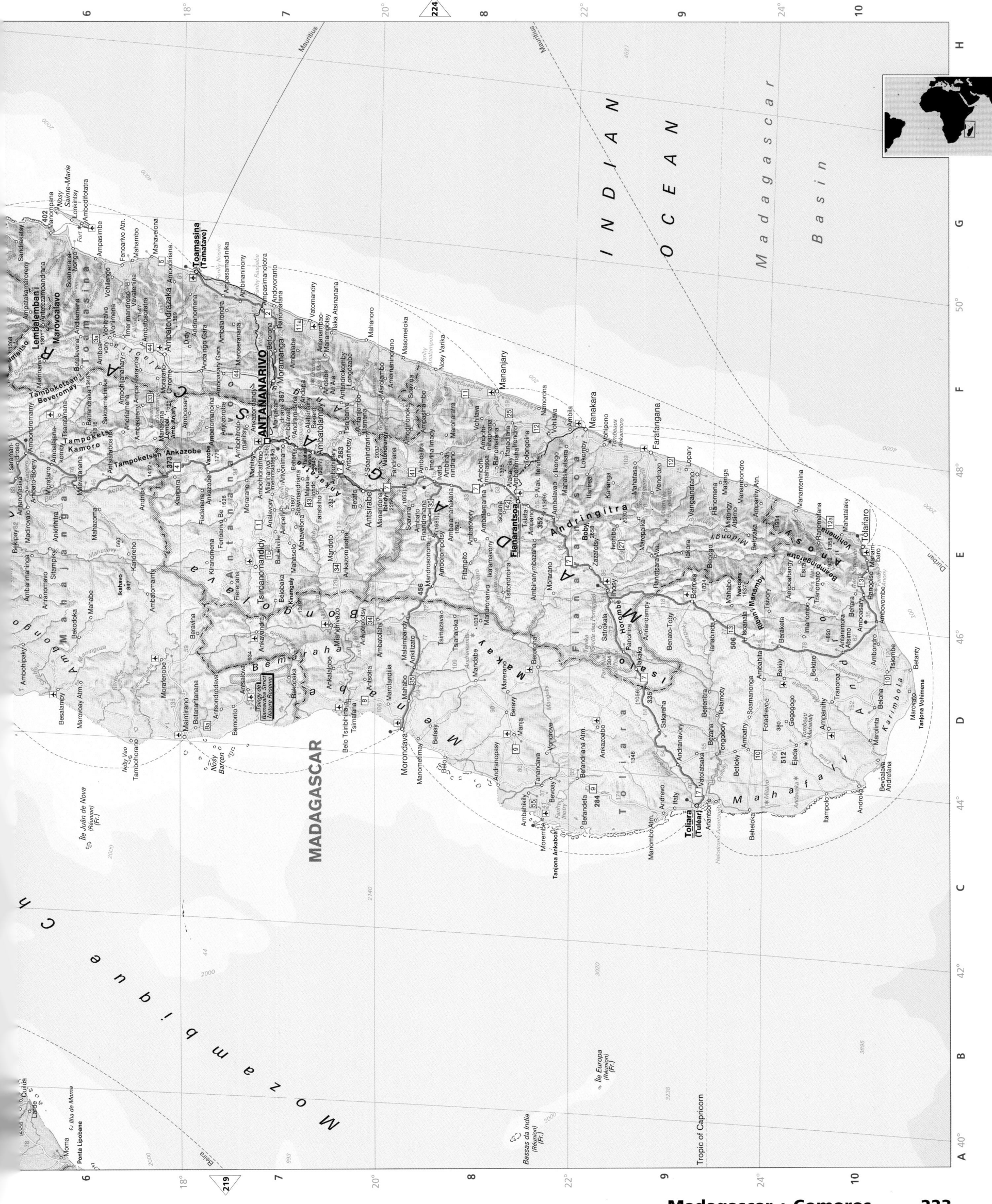

MADAGASCAR

INDIAN OCEAN

Madagascar • Comoros 223

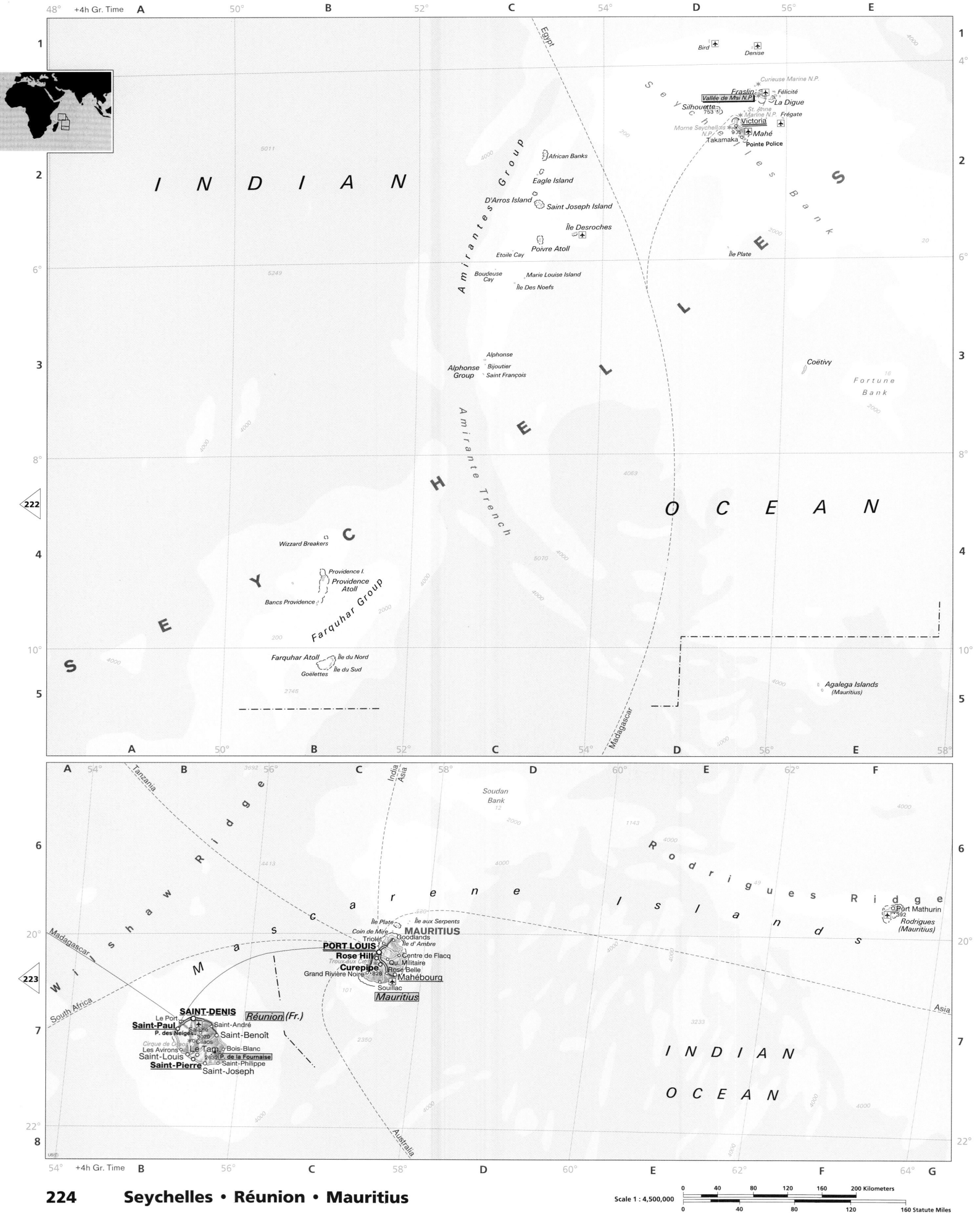

Egypt

Bird ✈
Denise ✈

Curieuse Marine N.P.

S e y c h e l l e s
Fraslin ✈ • Félicité
Vallée de Mai N.P. La Digue
Silhouette 753 St. Ahne Frégate
Marine N.P.
Morne Seychelles 905 Victoria ✈
N.P. Mahé
Takamaka Pointe Police

200

I N D I A N

African Banks

Eagle Island

D'Arros Island
Saint Joseph Island

Île Desroches

Etoile Cay
Poivre Atoll

Boudeuse
Cay
Marie Louise Island
Île Des Noefs

Île Plate

20

2000

Alphonse
Alphonse Bijoutier
Group Saint François

Coëtivy

Fortune
Bank

16

2000

4069

O C E A N

S E Y C
Wizzard Breakers

Providence I.
Providence
Atoll
Bancs Providence

Farquhar Group

2000

200

Farquhar Atoll Île du Nord
Goélettes Île du Sud

2746

Agalega Islands
(Mauritius)

4000

Madagascar

Tanzania

India
Asia

Soudan
Bank

12

2000

1143

4000

R o d r i g u e s
R i d g e

W
i
s
h
a
w

R
i
d
g
e

M
a
s
c
a
r
e
n
e

I s l a n d s

Port Mathurin ✈
Rodrigues
(Mauritius)

Madagascar

Île Plate
Île aux Serpents
Coin de Mire MAURITIUS
Triolet Goodlands
PORT LOUIS Île d'Ambre
Rose Hill Centre de Flacq
Curepipe Qu. Militaire
Grand Rivière Noire Rosé Belle
Souillac Mahébourg
Mauritius

South Africa

SAINT-DENIS Réunion (Fr.)
Le Port Saint-André
Saint-Paul
P. des Neiges Saint-Benoît
Cirque de Cilaos Bois-Blanc
Les Avirons Le Tam P. de la Fournaise
Saint-Louis Saint-Philippe
Saint-Pierre Saint-Joseph

I N D I A N

O C E A N

Asia

Australia

Scale 1 : 4,500,000

0 40 80 120 160 200 Kilometers

0 40 80 120 160 Statute Miles

Abbreviations

A

A.	Alm (Ger.) mountain meadow
Abb.	Abbaye (Fr.) abbey
Abor.	(Engl.) aboriginal
Aç.	Açude (Port.) small reservoir
Ad.	Adası (Turk.) island
A.F.B.	(Engl.) Air Force Base
Ag.	Agios (Gr.) saint
Á.I.	Área Indígena (Port.) Indian reservation
Ald.	Aldeia (Port.) village, hamlet
Arch.	(Engl.) archipelago
Arch.	Archipiélago (Span.) archipelago
Arh.	Arhipelag (Rus.) archipelago
Arq.	Arquipélago (Port.) archipelago
Arr.	Arroyo (Span.) brook
Art.Ra.	(Engl.) artillery range
Aut.	(Engl.) autonomous
Aut.Dist.	(Engl.) autonomous district
Aut.Reg.	(Engl.) autonomous region

B

B.	Baie (Fr.) bay
B.	Biológica, -o (Span.) biological
Ba.	Bahía (Span.) bay
Bal.	Balka (Rus.) gorge
Ban.	Banjaran (Mal.) mountains
Bel.	Belo, -yj, -aja, -oe (Rus.) white
Bk.	Bukit (Mal.) mountain, hill
Bol.	Boloto (Rus.) swamp
Bol.	Bolšoj, -aja, -oe (Rus.) big
Bot.	(Engl.) botanical
B.P.	(Engl.) battlefield park
Brj.	Baraj (Turk.) dam
Buch.	Buchta (Ukr.) bay
Buh.	Buhta (Rus.) bay

C

C.	Cap (Fr.) cape, point
C.	Cabo (Port., Span.) cape, point
Cab.	Cabeça (Port.) heights, summit
Cach.	Cachoeira (Port.) rapids
Cal.	Caleta (Span.) bay
Can.	Canalul (Rom.) canal
Can.	Canal (Span.) canal
Cast.	Castello (Ital.) castle, palace
Cd.	Ciudad (Span.) city
Cga.	Ciénaga (Span.) swamp, moor
Ch.	Chenal (Fr.) canal
Chr.	Chrebet (Ukr.) mountains
Co.	Cerro (Span.) mountain, hill
Col.	Colonia (Span.) colony
Conv.	Convento (Span.) monastery
Cord.	Cordillera (Span.) mountain chain
Corr.	Corredeira (Port.) rapids
Cpo.	Campo (Port.) field
Cr.	(Engl.) creek
Cs.	Cerros (Span.) mountain, hill

D

D.	Dake (Jap.) mountain
Dağl.	Dağlar (Turk.) mountains
Dist.	(Engl.) district
Df.	Dorf (Ger.) village
Dl.	Deal (Rom.) heights, hill

E

Ea.	Estancia (Span.) ranch
Ej.	Ejido (Span.) common
Emb.	Embalse (Span.) reservoir
Ens.	Enseada (Port.) small bay
Erm.	Ermita (Span.) hermitage
Ero.	Estero (Span.) estuary
Esp.	España (Span.) Spain
Est.	Estación (Span.) railroad terminal
Estr.	Estrecho (Span.) straight, sound
Ez.	Ezero (Bulg.) lake

F

Faz.	Fazenda (Port.) ranch
Fk.	(Engl.) fork
Fn.	Fortín (Span.) fort
Fr.	(Engl.) France
Fs.	(Engl.) falls, waterfall
Ft.	(Engl.) fort

G

Ǧ.	Ǧabal (Arab.) mountain
G.	Gawa (Jap.) lagoon
G.	Gîtul (Rom.) pass
G.	Golfo (Span.) bay, gulf
G.	Gora (Rus.) mountain
Gde.	Grande (Span.) big

Gds. Grandes (Span.) big

Gds.	Grandes (Span.) big
Glac.	Glacier (Fr.) glacier
Gos.	Gosudarstvennyj, -aja (Rus.) national
Gr.	(Engl.) Greece
Gr.Br.	(Engl.) Great Britain
Grd.	Grand (Fr.) big
Grl.	General (Span.) general

H

H.	Hora (Ukr.) mountain
H.	Hütte (Ger.) mountain hut
Harb.	(Engl.) harbor
Hist.	(Engl.) historic
Hm.	Heim (Ger.) home
Hr.	Hrebet (Rus.) mountains
Hte.	Haute (Fr.) high
Hwy.	(Engl.) highway

I

I.	(Engl.) island
Î.	Île (Fr.) island
I.	Ilha (Port.) island
I.	Isla (Span.) island
Igl.	Iglesia (Span.) church
In.	Insulă (Rom.) island
Ind.	(Engl.) Indian
Ind.Res.	(Engl.) Indian reservation
Int.	(Engl.) international
Is.	(Engl.) islands
Is.	Islas (Span.) islands

J

Jaz.	Jazovir (Bulg.) reservoir
Jct.	(Engl.) junction
Jez.	Jezero (Slovenian) lake
Juž.	Južnyj, -aja (Rus.) southern

K

Kan.	Kanal (Ger.) canal
Kep.	Kepulauan (Indon.) archipelago
Kg.	Kampong (Indon.) village
K-l.	Köli (Kazakh.) lake
K-l.	Küli (Uzbek.) lake
Kör.	Körfez (Turk.) gulf, bay
Kp.	Kólpos (Gr.) gulf, bay
Kr.	Krasno, -yj, -aja, -oe (Rus.) red

L

L.	(Engl.) lake
L.	Lac (Fr.) lake
L.	Lacul (Rom.) lake
L.	Lago (Span.) lake
Lag.	Laguna (Rus.) lagoon
Lev.	Levyj, -aja (Rus.) left
Lim.	Liman (Rus.) lagoon
Lim.	Limni (Gr.) lake
Lte.	(Engl.) little

M

M.	Munte (Rom.) mountain
M.	Mys (Rus.) cape, point
Mal.	(Engl.) Malaysia
Mal.	Malo, -yj, -aja, -oe (Rus.) little
Man.	Manastir (Bulg.) monastery
Man.	Manastır (Turk.) monastery
Măn.	Mănăstire (Rom.) monastery
Mem.	(Engl.) memorial
Mgne.	Montagne (Fr.) mountain, mountains
Mi.	Misaki (Jap.) cape, point
Mil.Res.	(Engl.) military reservation
Milli P.	Milli Park (Turk.) national park
Min.	(Engl.) mineral
Mñas.	Montañas (Span.) mountains
Moh.	Mohyla (Ukr.) tomb
Mon.	Monasterio (Span.) monastery
M.P.	(Engl.) military park
Mt.	(Engl.) mount
Mte.	Monte (Span.) mountain
Mti.	Monti (Ital.) mountains
Mtn.	(Engl.) mountain
Mtns.	(Engl.) mountains
Mtn.S.P.	(Engl.) mountain state park
Mts.	(Engl.) mountains
Mts.	Montes (Span.) mountains
Munț.	Munții (Rom.) mountains
Mus.	(Engl.) museum

N

N.	Nehir/ Nehri (Turk.) river, stream
N.	Nudo (Span.) peak
Nač.	Nacional (Span.) national

Nac. Nacional'nyj, -aja, -oe (Rus.) national

Nac.	Nacional'nyj, -aja, -oe (Rus.) national
Nat.	(Engl.) national
Nat.Mon.	(Engl.) national monument
Nat.P.	(Engl.) national park
Nat.Seas.	(Engl.) national seashore
Naz.	Nazionale (Ital.) national
N.B.P.	(Engl.) national battlefield park
N.B.S.	(Engl.) national battlefield site
Ned.	Nederland (Neth.) Netherlands
Nev.	Nevado (Span.) snow-capped mountain
N.H.P.	(Engl.) national historic park
N.H.S.	(Engl.) national historic site
Niž.	Niže, -nij, -naja, -neje (Rus.) lower
Nizm.	Nizmennost' (Rus.) lowlands
N.M.P.	(Engl.) national military park
Nördl.	Nördlich (Ger.) northern
Nov.	Novo, -yj, -aja, -oe (Rus.) new
N.P.	(Engl.) national park
N.R.A.	(Engl.) national recreation area
Nsa.Sra.	Nossa Senhora (Port.) Our Lady
Nth.	(Engl.) north
Ntra.Sra.	Nuestra Señora (Span.) Our Lady
Nva.	Nueva (Span.) new
Nvo.	Nuevo (Span.) new
N.W.R.	(Engl.) national wildlife refuge

O

O.	Ostrov (Rus.) island
Obl.	Oblast (Rus.) district
Ö.	Östra (Swed.) eastern
Öv.	Övre (Swed.) upper
Of.	Oficina (Span.) office
Ostr.	Ostrov (Rom.) island
O-va.	Ostrova (Rus.) islands
Oz.	Ozero (Rus.) lake

P

P.	(Engl.) port
P.	Passe (Fr.) pass
P.	Pico (Span.) peak
P.	Pulau (Indon.) island
Peg.	Pegunungan (Indon.) mountains
Pen.	(Engl.) peninsula
Pen.	Península (Span.) peninsula
Per.	Pereval (Rus.) pass
Picc.	Piccolo (Ital.) little
P-iv.	Pivostriv (Ukr.) peninsula
Pk.	(Engl.) peak
Pkwy.	(Engl.) parkway
Pl.	Planina (Bulg.) mountain, mountains
P.N.	Parque Nacional (Span.) national park
Po.	Paso (Span.) pass
Por.	Porog (Rus.) rapids
P-ov.	Poluostrov (Rus.) peninsula
Pr.	Proliv (Rus.) strait, sound
Pr.	Prohod (Bulg.) pass
Presq.	Presqu'île (Fr.) peninsula
Prov.	(Engl.) provincial
Prov.P.	(Engl.) provincial park
Pso.	Passo (Ital.) pass
Psto.	Puesto (Span.) outpost
Pt.	(Engl.) point
Pta.	Ponta (Port.) point
Pta.	Punta (Span.) point
Pte.	Pointe (Fr.) point
Pto.	Pôrto (Port.) port
Pto.	Puerto (Span.) port, pass
Pzo.	Pizzo (Ital.) point

Q

Q.N.P.	(Jap.) quasi national park

R

R.	Reka (Bulg.) river
R.	Reserva (Span.) reservation
R.	Rio (Port.) river
R.	Río (Span.) river
Ra.	(Engl.) range
Rch.	Riachão (Port.) small river
Rch.	Riacho (Span.) small river
Rdl.	Raudal (Span.) stream
Rep.	(Engl.) republic
Repr.	Represa (Port.) dam
Rère.	Rivière (Fr.) river
Res.	(Engl.) reservoir
Res.	Reserva (Port.) reservation
Resp.	Respublika (Rus.) republic
Rib.	Ribeira (Port.) shore
Rib.	Ribeiro (Port.) small river
Rif.	Rifugio (Ital.) mountain hut
Riv.	(Engl.) river

Rom.	(Engl.) Romania
Rom.	Romano, -na (Span.) Roman
Rus.	(Engl.) Russia

S

S.	San (Jap.) mountain, mountains
S.	San (Span.) saint
S.	São (Port.) saint
Sa.	Saki (Jap.) cape
Sa.	Serra (Port.) mountains
Sal.	Salar (Span.) salt desert, salt lagoon
Sanm.	Sanmyaku (Jap.) mountains
Sd.	(Engl.) sound
Sel.	Selat (Indon.) road
Sev.	Sever, -nyj, -naja, -noe (Rus.) north
Sf.	Sfintu (Rom.) holy
Sh.	Shima (Jap.) island
S.H.P.	(Engl.) state historic park
S.H.S.	(Engl.) state historic site
S.M.	(Engl.) state monument
Sna.	Salina (Span.) salt flat
Snas.	Salinas (Span.) salt flats
Snía.	Serranía (Span.) ridge
S.P.	(Engl.) state park
Sr.	Srednе, -ij, -aja, -ee (Rus.) middle, central
Sra.	Sierra (Span.) mountains
St.	(Engl.) saint
St.	Saint (Fr., Span.) saint
Sta.	Santa (Span.) saint
Sta.	Staro, -ij, -aja, -oe (Rus.) old
Ste.	Sainte (Fr.) saint
Sth.	(Engl.) south
St.Mem.	(Engl.) state memorial
Sto.	Santo (Port.) saint
Str.	(Engl.) strait
Suh.	Suho, -aja (Rus.) dry
Sv.	Svet, -a, -o (Bulg.) saint
Sv.	Sveti (Croatian) saint

T

T.	Take (Jap.) peak, heights
Tel.	Teluk (Indon.) bay
Tg.	Tanjung (Indon.) cape
Tg.	Tōge (Jap.) pass
Tte.	Teniente (Span.) lieutenant

U

Ülk.	Ülken (Kazakh.) big
U.K.	(Engl.) United Kingdom
U.S.	(Engl.) United States

V

V.	Vallée (Fr.) valley
Va.	Villa (Span.) market town
Vda.	Vereda (Port.) path
Vdhr.	Vodohranilišče (Rus.) reservoir
Vdp.	Vodospad (Ukr.) waterfall
Vel.	Veliko, -ij, -aja, -oe (Rus.) big
Verh.	Verhnie, -yj, aja, -ee (Rus.) upper
Vf.	Virf (Rom.) peak, heights
Vill.	(Engl.) village
Vis.	Visočina (Bulg.) heights
Vjal.	Vjalikie (Belarus.) big
Vlk.	Vulkan (Ger.) volcano
Vn.	Volcán (Span.) volcano
Vod.	Vodopad (Rus.) waterfall
Vol.	Volcán (Span.) volcano
Vul.	Vulcano (Philip.) volcano

W

W.A.	(Engl.) wilderness area

Y

Y.	Yama (Jap.) mountain, mountains

Z

Zal.	Zaliv (Rus.) gulf, bay
Zap.	Zapadne, -ij, -aja, -noe (Rus.) west
Zapov.	Zapovednik (Rus.) protected area

Selected References

Index of Map Names

The index contains all names found on the maps in this atlas. The index's alphabetical listing corresponds to the sequence of letters in the Roman alphabet. Diacritical marks and special letters have been ignored in alphebetizing, e.g.:

A ....Á, À, Â, Ă, Å, Ą, Ā, Ã, Ä, Æ

The ligatures æ, œ are treated as ae and oe in the alphabetical listing.

Names that have been abbreviated on the maps are generally written in full in the index.

Generic concepts follow geographic names, e.g. Mexico, Gulf of; Ventoux, Mont. Exception: colors (e.g. Mount Blanc) and adjectives (e.g. Big, Little) come first. Official additions (e.g. Rothenburg ob der Tauber) are included in the alphabetizing.

To a certain degree, the index also includes official alternate forms, linguistic variants, renamings and other secondary denominations. In such cases, the index refers to names as they appear on the maps, e.g. Meran = Merano, Leningrad = Sankt-Peterburg.

Abbreviations in parentheses help distinguish between places bearing the same names. Abbreviations as used on international motor-vehicle license plates have been given priority; where this is insufficient, administrative information like federal lands, provinces, regions, etc. are indicated.

Icons, which immediately follow the names, are used to indicate fundamental geographic concepts.

New York	o ••	**USA**	(NY)	46-47	M 5
① Search concept	② Icon	③ Nation	④ Administrative unit	⑤ Page	⑥ Search grid designation

② **Icons:**

■ ....Sovereign nation
◘ ....Administrative unit
★ ....Capital city (national capital)
☆ ....State (provincial) capital
o ....Place
⩡ ....Landscape
∩ ....Island
◡ ....Depression
▲▲ ....Mountains
▲ ....Mountain
▲ ....Active volcano
≈ ....Ocean, part of an ocean
○ ....Lake, salt lake
~ ....River, waterfall
⊂ ....glacier
< ....dam
≃ ....Undersea topography
⊥ ....National park
Ⱥ ....Reservation
xx ....Military installation
II ....Transportation construction
✈ ....Airport
∴ ....Ruins, ruined city
••• ....World cultural or natural heritage site
•• ....Point of major interest
• ....Point of interest

③ **Souvereign States and Territories (Abbrevations in *italics:* Abbrevation not official)**

A ....Austria
AFG ....Afghanistan
AG ....Antigua and Barbuda
AL ....Albania
AND ....Andorra
ANG ....Angola
AR ....Armenia
ARK ....Antarctica
ARU ....Aruba
AUS ....Australia
AUT ....Autonomous region
AZ ....Azerbaijan
B ....Belgium
BD ....Bangladesh
BDS ....Barbados
BF ....Burkina Faso
BG ....Bulgaria
BH ....Belize
BHT ....Bhutan
BIH ....Bosnia and Herzegovina
BOL ....Bolivia
BR ....Brazil
BRN ....Bahrain
BRU ....Brunei
BS ....Bahamas
BU ....Burundi
BY ....Belarus
C ....Cuba
CAM ....Cameroon
CDN ....Canada
CH ....Switzerland
CI ....Côte d'Ivoire (Ivory Coast)
CL ....Sri Lanka
CO ....Colombia
COM ....Comoros
CR ....Costa Rica
CV ....Cape Verde
CY ....Cyprus
CZ ....Czech Republic
D ....Germany
DJI ....Djibouti
DK ....Denmark
DOM ....Dominican Republic
DVR ....North Korea
DY ....Benin
DZ ....Algeria
E ....Spain
EAK ....Kenya
EAT ....Tanzania
EAU ....Uganda
EC ....Ecuador
ER ....Eritrea
ES ....El Salvador
EST ....Estonia
ET ....Egypt
ETH ....Ethiopia
F ....France
FIN ....Finland
FJI ....Fiji
FL ....Liechtenstein
FR ....Faroe Islands
FSM ....Micronesia
G ....Gabon
GB ....United Kingdom
GBA ....Alderney
GBG ....Guernsey
GBJ ....Jersey
GBM ....Isle of Man
GBZ ....Gibraltar
GCA ....Guatemala
GE ....Georgia
GH ....Ghana
GNB ....Guinea-Bissau
GQ ....Equatorial Guinea
GR ....Greece
GRØ ....Greenland
GUY ....Guyana
H ....Hungary
HN ....Honduras
HR ....Croatia
I ....Italy
IL ....Israel
IND ....India
IR ....Iran
IRL ....Ireland
IRQ ....Iraq
IS ....Iceland
J ....Japan
JA ....Jamaika
JOR ....Jordan
K ....Cambodia
KA ....Kazakhstan
KAN ....Saint Kitts and Nevis
KIB ....Kiribati
KS ....Kyrgyzstan
KSA ....Saudi Arabia
KWT ....Kuwait
L ....Luxembourg
LAO ....Laos
LAR ....Libya
LB ....Liberia
LS ....Lesotho
LT ....Lithuania
LV ....Latvia
M ....Malta
MA ....Morocco
MAI ....Marshall Islands
MAL ....Malaysia
MAU ....Mongolia
MC ....Monaco
MD ....Moldova
MEX ....Mexico
MK ....Macedonia
MOC ....Mozambique
MS ....Mauritius
MV ....Maldives
MW ....Malawi
MYA ....Myanmar (Burma)
N ....Norway
NA ....Netherlands Antilles
NAM ....Namibia
NAU ....Nauru
NEP ....Nepal
NIC ....Nicaragua
NL ....Netherlands
NZ ....New Zealand
OM ....Oman
P ....Portugal
PA ....Panama
PAL ....Palau
PE ....Peru
PK ....Pakistan
PL ....Poland
PNG ....Papua New Guinea
PY ....Paraguay
Q ....Qatar
RA ....Argentina
RB ....Botswana
RC ....Taiwan
RCA ....Central African Republic
RCB ....Congo
RCH ....Chile
RG ....Guinea
RH ....Haiti
RI ....Indonesia
RIM ....Mauritania
RL ....Lebanon
RM ....Madagaskar
RMM ....Mali
RN ....Niger
RO ....Romania
ROK ....South Korea
ROU ....Uruguay
RP ....Philippines
RSM ....San Marino
RT ....Togo
RUS ....Russia
RWA ....Rwanda
S ....Sweden
SCV ....Vatican City
SD ....Swaziland
SGP ....Singapore
SK ....Slovakia
SLO ....Slovenia
SME ....Suriname
SN ....Senegal
SOL ....Solomon Islands
SP ....Somalia
STP ....São Tomé and Príncipe
SUD ....Sudan
SY ....Seychelles
SYR ....Syria
TCH ....Chad
THA ....Thailand
TJ ....Tajikistan
TM ....Turkmenistan
TN ....Tunisia
TON ....Tonga
TR ....Turkey
TT ....Trinidad and Tobago
TUV ....Tuvalu
UA ....Ukraine
UAE ....United Arab Emirates
US ....Uzbekistan
USA ....United States
VAN ....Vanuatu
VN ....Vietnam
VRC ....China
WAG ....Gambia
WAL ....Sierra Leone
WAN ....Nigeria
WB ....West Bank
WD ....Dominica
WG ....Grenada
WL ....Saint Lucia
WS ....Western Samoa
WSA ....Western Sahara
WV ....Saint Vincent and the Grenadines
Y ....Yemen
YU ....Yugoslavia
YV ....Venezuela
Z ....Zambia
ZA ....South Africa
ZRE ....Democratic Republic of Congo
ZW ....Zimbabwe

A

Al 'Azīzīyah ☆ LAR 192-193 E 1
Alba o I 100-101 B 2
Albacete o E 98-99 F 4
Albacutya, Lake ≈ AUS 180-181 G 6
al-Badâri ☆ ET 194-195 E 4
Âlbæk Bugt ≈ DK 86-87 E 8
al-Bahr al-Azraq ~ SUD 200-201 G 6
al-Bahriya, Barqat ± ET 192-193 L 2
Alba Iulia ☆· RO 102-103 H 4
Albâka o IND 142-143 B 6
al-Balîh, Nahr ~ SYR 128-129 H 4
al-Ballâs o ET 194-195 F 4
al-Balyana o ET 194-195 F 4
Alban o CDN 38-39 D 5
Alban o CO 60-61 D 5
Alban = San José o CO 64-65 D 1
Albanel, Lac o CDN 38-39 H 3
Albania = Shqipëri ▪ AL 100-101 G 4
Albany o AUS 176-177 D 7
Albany o USA (GA) 48-49 F 4
Albany o USA (MO) 42-43 K 3
Albany o USA (OR) 40-41 C 4
Albany o USA (TX) 44-45 H 3
Albany ☆ USA (NY) 46-47 M 4
Albany Downs o AUS 178-179 J 4
Albany Highway ‖ AUS 176-177 D 6
Albany Island ☆ CDN 34-35 Q 4
Albany River ~ CDN 34-35 P 4
Alba Posse o RA 76-77 K 4
al-Barâmús, Dair ∴· ET 194-195 E 2
Al Bardi o LAR 192-193 L 2
Albarracín o· E 98-99 F 4
al-Barun o SUD 208-209 A 3
al-Basabir o SUD 200-201 F 3
al-Bâtina, Ğazírat ~ KSA 130-131 L 4
Albatros Bank ≈ 22-23 U 4
Albatross Bay ≈ 174-175 F 3
al-Bauga o SUD 200-201 F 3
al-Bawiti o ET 194-195 D 3
Al Bayâdah, Wâdi ~ LAR 192-193 H 4
Al Bayda o LAR 192-193 J 1
Al Bayda ☆ LAR 192-193 J 1
Al Bayda, Barqah ± LAR 192-193 H 2
Albay Gulf ≈ 160-161 E 6
al Bayyâdah o LAR 192-193 K 2
Albazino o RUS 118-119 M 9
al-Begeir o SUD 200-201 F 3
Albemarle o USA 48-49 H 2
Albemarle Sound ≈ 48-49 K 1
Albenga o I 100-101 B 2
Alberca, La o· E 98-99 D 4
Alberdi o PY 76-77 H 4
Alberfoyle o AUS 178-179 H 1
Alberga Creek ~ AUS 178-179 C 4
Albergaria-a-Velha o P 98-99 C 4
Alberni o RA 78-79 J 3
Alberobello o· I 100-101 F 4
Albert o P 90-91 J 6
Albert, Cape ▲ CDN 26-27 N 4
Albert, Lake o AUS 180-181 E 3
Albert, Lake o USA 40-41 D 4
Albert, Lake = Lac Mobutu-Sese-Seko o EAU 212-213 D 3
Albert, Port o AUS 180-181 J 5
Alberta o CDN 32-33 L 4
Alberta o USA 46-47 K 7
Albert Edward, Mount ▲ PNG 183 D 5
Albert Edward Bay ≈ 24-25 U 6
Alberti o RA 78-79 J 3
Albert I Land ∴ N 84-85 G 3
Albertinia o ZA 220-221 E 7
Albert Law, Mont ▲ CDN 36-37 N 4
Albert Lea o USA 42-43 L 4
Albert Markham, Mount ▲ ARK 16 E 0
Albert Nile ~ EAU 212-213 C 2
Alberto de Agostini, Parque Nacional ⊥ RCH 80 E 7
Albert River ~ AUS 174-175 E 6
Albert Town o BS 54-55 H 3
Albert Town o JA 54-55 G 5
Albertville o USA 48-49 E 4
Albi ☆· F 90-91 J 9
Albia o USA 42-43 L 5
Albina o SME 62-63 G 3
Albina, Ponta ▲ ANG 216-217 A 7
Albion o USA 46-47 E 4
Albion o USA (NE) 42-43 J 5
Alborán, Isla del ~ E 98-99 F 7
Âlborg o DK 86-87 D 8
Âlborg Bugt ≈ 86-87 E 8
Albox o E 98-99 F 6
Albreda o WAG 202-203 B 3
Albro o AUS 178-179 J 2
Albufeira o P 98-99 C 6
Albuquerque o· E 98-99 D 4
Albuquerque ☆ USA 44-45 D 2
Albuquerque, Cayos de ~ CO 52-53 D 5
al-Burullus, Buhairat o ET 194-195 E 2
Albury-Wodonga o AUS 180-181 J 4
Alcácer do Sal o P 98-99 C 5
Alcáçovas o P 98-99 C 5
Alcala o AUS 174-175 D 4
Alcala o RP 160-161 D 4
Alcalá de Chivert = Alcalà de Xivert o E 98-99 H 4
Alcalá del Júcar o E 98-99 F 5
Alcalà de Xivert o E 98-99 H 4
Alcalá la Real o E 98-99 E 6
Alcalde, Punta ▲ RCH 76-77 B 5
Álcamo o I 100-101 D 6
Alcañices o· E 98-99 D 4
Alcañiz o· E 98-99 G 4
Alcântara o BR 68-69 G 3
Alcantara Lake o CDN 30-31 P 5
Alcantarilla o· E 98-99 G 6
Alcaracejos o E 98-99 E 5
Alcaraz o E 98-99 F 5
Alcatrazes, Ilha do ~ BR 72-73 H 8
Alcaudete o· E 98-99 E 6
Alcázar o· E 98-99 G 6
Alcázar de San Juan o E 98-99 F 5
Alcedo, Volcán ▲ EC 64-65 B 10

Alcester Island ~ PNG 183 G 5
Alčevs'k o UA 102-103 L 3
Alcira o RA 78-79 G 2
Alcobaça o ··· P 98-99 C 5
Alcoi o E 98-99 G 5
Alcolea del Pinar o E 98-99 F 4
Alcorcón o E 98-99 F 4
Alcorta o RA 78-79 J 2
Alcoutim o P 98-99 D 6
Alcova o USA 42-43 D 4
Alcoy o RP 160-161 E 8
Alcúdia o E 98-99 J 4
Alcúdia, l' o E 98-99 G 5
Alcurve o CDN 32-33 P 5
Aldabra Atoll ∴···· SY 222-223 E 2
Aldabra Group ~ SY 222-223 E 2
Aldaia Bona o BR 62-63 G 5
Aldama o MEX (CHA) 50-51 J 3
Aldama o MEX (TAM) 50-51 K 6
Aldamas, Los o MEX 50-51 K 4
Aldan ☆ RUS (SAH) 118-119 M 6
Aldan ~ RUS 118-119 N 6
Aldan ~ RUS 118-119 L 7
Aldan ~ RUS 118-119 P 4
Aldan ~ RUS 120-121 F 2
Aldanskoe nagor'e ▲ RUS 118-119 L 6
Aldea, Isla ~ RCH 80 C 4
Aldea dos Indios Sucane o GUY 62-63 G 5
Aldehuela Gallinal o ROU 78-79 M 2
Aldeia o BR (BA) 68-69 E 7
Aldeia o BR (GSU) 70-71 K 6
Aldeia o BR (MAR) 68-69 E 5
Aldeia, Serra de ▲ BR 72-73 G 4
Aldeia Beltrão o BR 76-77 K 5
Aldeia das Canoas o BR 62-63 G 5
Aldeia Grimaldi o BR 76-77 J 4
Aldeia Manuel Antonio o BR 68-69 E 3
Aldeia Velha o BR 68-69 F 4
Aldeia Viçoşa o ANG 216-217 C 4
Aldeia Vila Batista o BR 62-63 D 6
Alder Creek o CDN 46-47 L 4
Alder Flats o CDN 32-33 N 5
Alderley o AUS 178-179 E 2
Alderley o ZA 220-221 H 6
Alderney o GB 90-91 F 7
Alder Peak ▲ USA 40-41 C 4
Alder Point ▲ USA 40-41 B 3
Aldoma o RUS 120-121 H 5
Aldoma o RUS 120-121 G 5
Aldrich, Cape ▲ CDN 26-27 Q 2
Aldžer, ostrov ~ RUS 84-85 e 2
Alédjo, Faillé-d' ▲· RT 202-203 L 5
Aleg ~ RIM 196-197 D 6
Alegre o BR (ESP) 72-73 K 6
Alegre o BR (MIN) 72-73 G 5
Alegre, Riacho ~ PY 76-77 H 1
Alegre, Rio ~ BR 70-71 H 4
Alegre o BR 76-77 K 5
Alegria o BR (GSU) 70-71 K 6
Alegria o BR (RSU) 76-77 K 4
Alegria o RP 160-161 E 8
Aléhovščina o RUS 94-95 N 1
Alei, Inl o RMM 196-197 J 6
Aleiandia o CO 60-61 D 3
Alej ~ RUS 124-125 N 2
Alejandra o RA 76-77 H 5
Alejandria o BOL 70-71 E 3
Alejandro Selkirk, Isla ~ RCH 78-79 B 1
Alejsk o RUS 124-125 N 2
Aleknagik o USA 22-23 R 3
Aleknagik, Lake o USA 22-23 R 3
Aleko-Kjuёf o RUS 110-111 d 5
Aleksandrovskij, zaliv o RUS 122-123 J 3
Aleksandra, mys ▲ RUS 120-121 H 6
Aleksandra, l. zeml'a ~ ARK 16 G 29
Aleksandrija = Oleksandrivka o UA 102-103 H 3
Aleksandrov o· RUS 94-95 Q 3
Aleksandrovka o RUS 96-97 J 7
Aleksandrovskij, Kus'e- o RUS 96-97 L 4
Aleksandrovskoe o RUS (STA) 126-127 E 5
Aleksandrovskoe o RUS (TOM) 114-115 O 4
Aleksandrovsk-Sahalinsij ☆· RUS 122-123 J 3
Aleksandry, ostrov ~ RUS 120-121 H 6
Aleksandry, Zemlja ~ RUS 84-85 J 2
Alekseevaka o RUS 102-103 L 2
Aleksa River ~ CDN 30-31 M 2
Alekseevka o KA 124-125 O 4
Alekseevka ☆ KA 124-125 G 2
Alekseevka o RUS 118-119 M 5
Aleksee River ~ RUS (SAM) 96-97 G 7
Alekseevskoe o RUS 96-97 G 6
Aleksin o· RUS 94-95 P 4
Aleksinac o· YU 100-101 H 3
Alel o SUD 206-207 K 5
Âlem o S 86-87 H 8
Alemania o EC 64-65 B 10
Alèmbé o G 210-211 C 4
Alembé o RCB 210-211 E 4
'Alem Ketema o ETH 208-209 D 3
'Alem Maya o ETH 208-209 E 4
Além-Paraíba o BR 72-73 J 6
Âlen ~ N 86-87 E 5
Alençon ☆· F 90-91 H 7
Alen Nkoma o G 210-211 D 3
Alençar o BR 62-63 G 6
Alentejo ± P 98-99 C 6
Alenuihaha Channel ≈ 48-49 D 7
Alépé o CI 202-203 J 7
Aleppo = Halab ☆ SYR 128-129 G 4
Alerces, Parque Nacional los ⊥ RA 78-79 D 7
Aleria o F 98-99 M 3
Alert o CDN 26-27 T 2
Alerta o PE 70-71 F 5

Alert Bay o CDN 32-33 G 6
Alert Point ▲ CDN 26-27 G 2
Alès o P 90-91 K 9
Alesandrovskij Zavod o RUS 118-119 H 10
Alessándria o· I 100-101 B 2
Âlesund o N 86-87 C 5
Aleutian Basin ≈ 22-23 C 4
Aleutian Islands ~ USA 22-23 H 6
Aleutian Range ▲ USA 22-23 R 4
Aleutian Trench ≈ 22-23 K 7
Aleutko o RUS 38-39 Q 2
Alexander o USA (AK) 20-21 P 6
Alexander o USA (ND) 42-43 F 2
Alexander, Cape ▲ SOL 184 I c 2
Alexander, Kap ▲ GRØ 26-27 O 4
Alexander, Point ▲ AUS 174-175 D 3
Alexander Archipelago ~ USA 32-33 J 7
Alexanderbaai = Alexander Bay o ZA 220-221 C 4
Alexander Bay = Alexanderbaai o ZA 220-221 C 4
Alexander City o USA 48-49 F 3
Alexander Graham Bell National Historic Park ⊥ CDN 38-39 O 5
Alexander Island ~ CDN 24-25 U 3
Alexandra o AUS 180-181 H 4
Alexandra o NZ 182 B 6
Alexandra, Cape ▲ GB 78-79 O 7
Alexandra Bay o 174-175 H 5
Alexandra Channel ≈ 140-141 L 2
Alexandra Falls o CDN 30-31 L 5
Alexandra Fiord o CDN 26-27 N 4
Alexandra River ~ AUS 174-175 F 3
Alexandria o AUS 174-175 D 3
Alexandria o BR 68-69 J 5
Alexandria o CDN 38-39 G 6
Alexandria o GR 100-101 J 4
Alexandria o JA 54-55 G 5
Alexandria ☆· RO 102-103 D 6
Alexandria o USA (LA) 44-45 L 4
Alexandria o USA (MN) 42-43 K 3
Alexandria o USA (VA) 46-47 K 6
Alexandria, Lake o AUS 180-181 E 3
Alexandroúpoli ☆· GR 100-101 K 4
Alexeck o NAM 216-217 E 10
Alexis Creek o CDN 32-33 J 5
Alexishafen o PNG 183 C 3
Alexis River ~ CDN 38-39 Q 2
Alex Morrison National Park ⊥ AUS 176-177 E 4
Al Faid-Majir o LAR 192-193 F 1
Alfarez de Navio Sobral o ARK 16 C 31
Alfa River o CDN 24-25 I 4
Alfarrás o E 98-99 H 4
al Fâshir o· SUD 200-201 B 6
al-Fâshir o SUD 200-201 B 6
al-Fašn o ET 194-195 E 3
Al Fât, Wâdi ~ LAR 192-193 F 3
al Fâtih o LAR 192-193 J 1
al-Fâtiyah, Bi'r < LAR 192-193 H 2
al-Fayyûm ☆· ET 194-195 E 3
Alfenas o BR 72-73 H 6
al-Fifi o SUD 206-207 J 3
Âlfötbreen ≈ N 86-87 B 6
Alfred, Cape ▲ CDN 24-25 V 6
Alfred and Marie Range ▲ AUS 176-177 H 2
Alfredo Chaves o BR 72-73 K 6
Alfredo M. Terrazas o MEX 50-51 K 7
Alfredo Wagner o BR 74-75 F 4
Alfta o S 86-87 G 6
al-Fuqâhâ' o LAR 192-193 G 4
Alga o KA 126-127 M 3
al-Galabaiun o SUD 200-201 F 6
Algabas o KA 96-97 H 8
al-Gabir o SUD 200-201 F 5
al-Ğâhir, Ğabal ▲ Y 132-133 J 7
al-Ğalala al-Bahriya, Ğabal ▲ ET 194-195 E 3
al-Ğalala al-Qibliya, Ğabal ▲ ET 194-195 F 3
Algama ~ RUS 118-119 O 8
Algama ~ RUS 120-121 D 5
al-Ğamâliya o ET 194-195 E 2
al-Ğamâmiyah o SUD 200-201 F 5
Algan ~ RUS 112-113 Q 4
Algansk krjaž ▲ RUS 112-113 Q 4
Al Garabulli o LAR 192-193 G 1
al-Garef o SUD 200-201 G 3
al-Gargarat o MA 196-197 B 4
Algarrobal, Quebrada ~ RCH 76-77 B 5
Algarrobo o RCH 78-79 D 4
Algarrobo del Aguila o RA 78-79 F 4
Algarve ± P 98-99 C 6
al-Gauf ± KSA 132-133 F 2
al-Gayli o SUD 200-201 F 5
al-Gazālāt, Qârat ▲ ET 194-195 C 2
al-Gazira ± SUD 200-201 F 5
Algeciras o· E 98-99 E 6
Algena o ER 200-201 J 4
Alger o USA 46-47 F 2
Algeria = Al Jazā'ir ▪ DZ 190-191 B 6
Algerian Provencaal Basin ≈ 98-99 K 4
al-Ghâbah o SUD 200-201 E 3
al-Ghabshah o SUD 200-201 D 6
al-Ghalla, Wâdi ~ SUD 206-207 J 3
al Ghararân, Bi'r < LAR 192-193 J 2
al-Ghazâl, Nahr ~ SUD 206-207 K 5
Alghero o· I 100-101 B 4
Al Ghirâf, Wâdi Bü ~ LAR 192-193 G 4
Al Ghomode o LAR 192-193 J 5
al Ghrayfah o LAR 192-193 E 4
al-Ğidâmi, Bi'r < ET 194-195 F 2

Algiers = Al Jazâ'ir ★ ··· DZ 190-191 B 6
al-Gilf al-Kabir, Haqbat ▲ ET 192-193 L 4
al-Ğiza o ☆· ET 194-195 E 2
al-Ğizi, Wâdi ~ OM 132-133 K 1
Algoa Bay ≈ 220-221 G 6
Algodón, Rio ~ PE 64-65 F 3
Algona o USA 42-43 K 4
Algonac o CDN 38-39 C 7
Algonquin Park o CDN 38-39 E 6
Algonquin Provincial Park ⊥ CDN 38-39 E 6
Algonquin Upland ▲ CDN 38-39 E 5
Algorta o ROU 78-79 L 2
al-Gurdaqa o· ET 194-195 F 4
Al Guzayyil, Bi'r < LAR 192-193 H 2
al Hâdh, Wâdi ~ LAR 192-193 G 5
al-Haiz o ET 194-195 D 3
Alhama de Murcia o E 98-99 G 6
Alhambra · E 98-99 F 6
Al Hamim, Wâdi ~ LAR 192-193 K 2
al-Hamsa, Bi'r < ET 192-193 L 2
Al Hamûdiyah < LAR 192-193 G 4
alhanćurtiksij kanal < RUS 126-127 F 6
al-Hârah, Qârat ▲ LAR 192-193 F 4
al-Ħârija ~· ET 194-195 E 3
al-Ħârija, al-Wâhât ± ET 194-195 E 5
al-Hârtûm ★·· SUD 200-201 F 5
al-Hartûm Bahri o SUD 200-201 F 5
Al Haruj al Aswad ▲ LAR 192-193 G 4
Al Hasâwinah, Jabal ▲ LAR 192-193 E 3
Al Hassiane ~ MA 188-189 D 7
al-Ħatâtiba o ET 194-195 E 2
al-Hawad, Wâdi ~ SUD 200-201 F 5
al-Hawa'ish, Jabal ▲ LAR 192-193 K 5
al-Ħawâtah o SUD 200-201 G 6
al-Hawwari o LAR 192-193 K 2
Al Hayshah, Sabkhat o LAR 192-193 E 3
Al Hayyirah, Qarârat ~ LAR 192-193 F 4
Alheit o ZA 220-221 D 4
al-Ħilla o SUD 206-207 J 3
Al Hoceima ☆· MA 188-189 K 3
Al Huan o LAR 192-193 K 5
Al Hufrah ash Sharqiyah ± LAR 192-193 H 4
Al Hulayq al Kabir ▲ LAR 192-193 G 4
al-Huqnah o SUD 200-201 F 4
Âlhus o N 86-87 B 6
al-Husayhisah o SUD 200-201 F 5
al-Ħuwair Oilfield o OM 132-133 J 2
Ali o PNG 183 B 4
'Ali, Bi'r < Y 132-133 F 6
'Aliâbâd o AFG 136-137 L 6
'Aliâbâd o IR 134-135 F 4
'Aliâbâd o IR 136-137 D 6
Aliade o WAN 204-205 H 5
Aliaga o E 98-99 G 4
Aliağa ☆ TR 128-129 B 3
Aliákomon ~ GR 100-101 J 4
'Ali al-Garbi o IRQ 128-129 M 6
Aliambata o RI 166-167 D 6
Aliantan o RI 162-163 F 4
Alianza, La o CO 60-61 C 6
Alibâg o IND 140-141 G 7
Ali-Bajramly = Äli Bayramli o AZ 128-129 N 3
Alibates Flint Quarries National Monument · USA 44-45 G 2
Alibori ~ DY 204-205 E 3
Aliboy Knob ▲ AUS 172-173 J 4
Alicante = Alacant o E 98-99 G 5
Alice o AUS 178-179 M 3
Alice o USA (ND) 42-43 J 3
Alice o USA (TX) 44-45 H 6
Alice, Punta ▲ I 100-101 F 5
Alice Arm o CDN 32-33 F 4
Alice River ~ AUS 174-175 F 4
Alice Springs ☆· AUS 176-177 B 2
Alice Town o BS 54-55 G 2
Alice Town o BS 54-55 F 2
Aliceville o USA 48-49 D 3
Alicia o RP 160-161 D 4
Alicudi, Ísola di ~ I 100-101 E 5
Aligarh o IND 138-139 G 6
Aligúdarz o IR 134-135 D 3
'Aligüq, Küh-e ▲ IR 134-135 D 3
Alikali o WAL 202-203 E 5
Alikazgan ~ RUS 126-127 G 6
Alikkod o IND 140-141 F 5
Alima ~ RCB 210-211 E 4
Alimbet o KA 126-127 G 6
Alimbongo o ZRE 212-213 B 4
Alim Island ~ PNG 183 D 2
Alingâr, Darre-ye ~ AFG 136-137 M 7
Alingly o CDN 34-35 Q 4
Alingsås ☆ S 86-87 F 8
Alinshan ▲ VRC 144-145 C 4
Alipur o PK 138-139 C 5
Alipur Duâr o IND 142-143 H 4
Allomo o WAN 204-205 G 4
Aliquisanda o MOC 214-215 H 7
Aliraipur o IND 138-139 F 6
Aliseang-rì ▲ RI 164-165 G 3
'Ali Sadr o IR 128-129 N 5
Alisma o· RC 156-157 M 5
al-Iskandariya = Alexandria o ☆· ET 194-195 D 2
Aliskerovo o RUS 112-113 O 3
al-Ismâ'ïliya ☆ ET 194-195 F 2

Aitak, Cape ▲ USA 22-23 T 4
Aitak Bay ≈ 22-23 T 4
Aliite Reef ≈ SOL 184 I 4 1
Aliulik Peninsula ~ USA 22-23 U 4
Aliwal-Noord = Aliwal North o ZA 220-221 H 5
Aliwal North = Aliwal-Noord o ZA 220-221 H 5
al-Mahalla al-Kubra o ET 194-195 E 2
al-Mahâmid o ET 194-195 F 4
al-Maharīq o ET 194-195 E 4
'Aliyâb Gharb o SUD 200-201 F 4
'Aliyâb Sharq o SUD 200-201 F 4
Aliyaq, Godâr-e o IR 136-137 E 6
al-Jabal al Akhdar ▲ LAR 192-193 J 1
Al Jabal al Akhdar ▲ LAR 192-193 J 1
al-Jabal, Bahr ~ SUD 206-207 K 5
al Jadid, Bi'r < LAR 192-193 L 4
al-Jaghbûb o LAR 192-193 L 3
al Jalu, Wâhât ± LAR 192-193 J 3
Aljat o AZ 128-129 N 3
al Jawf o LAR 192-193 J 3
Al Jaws al Kabir o LAR 192-193 D 2
al Jufrah ± LAR 192-193 G 3
al Kâb o· ET 194-195 F 5
al-Kâb o SUD 200-201 F 3
Al Kalb, Qarârat ~ LAR 192-193 G 4
Alkamari o RN 198-199 G 6
al Kammûniyah, Bi'r < LAR 192-193 H 2
al-Kanâ'is, Ra's ▲ ET 194-195 C 2
Al Karârim o LAR 192-193 F 1
al-Karnak o· ET 194-195 F 4
Al-Kawa o SUD 200-201 F 6
al-K'rachbiyine, Oued ~ MA 188-189 F 2
Al Khadrah o LAR 192-193 H 3
Al Khâlí, Wâdi ~ LAR 192-193 K 2
al-Khârim, ash-Shallâl = 5th Cataract ~ SUD 200-201 F 3
al-Khandaq o SUD 200-201 E 3
Al Kh'ums o LAR 192-193 E 1
Al Kh'ums ☆ LAR (Akm) 192-193 F 1
Alkmaar o· NL 92-93 H 2
al-Koin o SUD 200-201 E 3
al-Kû, Wâdi ~ SUD 200-201 E 6
al-Kûbri o ET 194-195 F 2
Al Kufayfiyah o KSA 130-131 J 5
al Kufra, Wâhât ± LAR 192-193 K 5
Al Kufrah o LAR 192-193 K 5
al-Kuntilla o ET 194-195 G 3
al-Kurru o SUD 200-201 F 3
Allada o DY 204-205 E 3
Allagash o USA 46-47 O 2
Allagash River ~ USA 46-47 O 2
Al-Lagowa o SUD 206-207 J 3
Allagudda o IND 140-141 G 4
Allahâbâd o· IND 142-143 B 3
Alláhânganj o IND 138-139 G 6
Allah-Jun' o RUS 120-121 H 3
Allah-Jun' ~ RUS 120-121 H 3
Allahüekber Dağları ▲ TR 128-129 K 2
al-Lâhūn ∴· ET 194-195 E 3
Allaiha ~ RUS 110-111 Z 5
Allakaket o USA 20-21 O 3
Allal-bou-Fenzi o MA 188-189 H 5
Allal-Tazi o MA 188-189 H 3
Allangouassou o CI 202-203 H 6
Allanridge o ZA 220-221 H 4
Allapalli o IND 142-143 B 6
Allardville o CDN 38-39 M 5
Allariz o E 98-99 C 3
Alldays o ZA 218-219 C 6
Âlleberg ▲ S 86-87 F 7
Allegan o USA 46-47 F 4
Allegany State Park ⊥ USA 46-47 J 4
Allegheny River Reservoir < USA 46-47 J 3
Allemand, Lac o CDN 36-37 M 4
Allemands, Des o USA 44-45 M 5
Allemanskraaldam < ZA 220-221 H 4
Allen o RP 160-161 F 6
Allendale o USA 48-49 H 3
Allende o MEX (COA) 50-51 J 3
Allende o MEX (NL) 50-51 J 5
Allen Island ~ AUS 174-175 E 5
Allentown o USA 46-47 L 4
Allen Young Point ▲ CDN 24-25 V 4
Alleppey o IND 140-141 G 6
Allgäu ± D 92-93 L 5
Alliance o CDN 32-33 P 5
Alliance o USA (NE) 42-43 F 4
Alliance o USA (OH) 46-47 H 5
Allier ~ F 90-91 J 8
Alliford Bay o CDN 32-33 E 5
Alligator Pond o JA 54-55 G 5
Allingaram o IND 140-141 G 5
Allington, Cape ▲ CDN 24-25 a 5
Allipen, Rio ~ RCH 78-79 D 5
al-Liri, Ğabal ▲ SUD 206-207 K 3
Allison o USA (AR) 44-45 L 2
Alloa o GB 90-91 E 3
Allomo o WAN 204-205 G 4
Allu o RI 164-165 F 6
Allumettes, Île des ~ CDN 38-39 F 6
Âllūr o IND 140-141 H 4
Alluttoq o GRØ 28-29 P 2
Alluviag, Fiord ≈ 36-37 R 5
Alluviag, Rivière ~ CDN 36-37 R 5
Alma ~ UA 102-103 H 3
Alma o USA (GA) 48-49 G 4
Alma o USA (MI) 46-47 G 4
Alma o USA (NE) 42-43 H 5

Alma, Mount ▲ AUS 178-179 L 2
Alma-Ata = Almaty ★ KA 146-147 C 4
Almaden o AUS 174-175 H 5
Almadén o E 98-99 E 5
al-Mafâza o SUD 200-201 G 6
Almagro Island ~ RP 160-161 F 7
al-Mahalla al-Kubra o ET 194-195 E 2
Almahel o ETH 208-209 B 3
Al Majnínín, Wâdi ~ LAR 192-193 F 2
al-Malamm o SUD 206-207 J 4
al-Manâqil o SUD 200-201 F 5
Almanor, Lake o USA 40-41 D 5
Almansa o E 98-99 G 5
Almansa, Puerto de ▲ E 98-99 G 5
al-Mansûra o ET 194-195 E 2
al-Manzila, Buhairat o ET 194-195 E 2
Almanzor ▲ E 98-99 E 4
Alma Peak ▲ CDN 32-33 G 3
al-Maqrûn o LAR 192-193 J 2
Almâr o AFG 138-139 B 3
Almara o AFG 138-139 B 3
Almarcha, La o E 98-99 F 5
Al Marj o ··· LAR 192-193 J 1
al Marûqah o LAR 192-193 H 3
Almas o BR 68-69 E 7
Almas, Rio das ~ BR 72-73 F 3
Almas, Rio das ~ BR 72-73 F 2
Al-Massira, Barrage < MA 188-189 H 4
Al Mastûtah, Bi'r < LAR 192-193 K 4
al-Matamma o SUD 200-201 F 4
al-Matariya o ET 194-195 F 2
al-Matmarfaq o MA 188-189 E 7
al-Matna o SUD 200-201 G 6
al-Mausil ☆ IRQ 128-129 K 4
Almazán o· E 98-99 F 4
Almaznyj o RUS 118-119 G 4
Almeida o P 98-99 D 4
Almeida Campos o BR 72-73 G 5
Almeirim o BR 62-63 H 4
Almeirim o P 98-99 C 5
Almeirim, Serra do ▲ BR 62-63 H 4
Almel o IND 140-141 G 2
Almelo o· NL 92-93 J 2
Almenara o BR 72-73 K 4
Almenar de Soria o E 98-99 F 4
Almendralejo o· E 98-99 D 5
Almendrillo o RCH 78-79 D 5
Al'menevo o RUS 114-115 G 7
Almere o NL 92-93 H 2
Almería o· E 98-99 F 6
Almería, Golfo de ≈ 98-99 F 6
Al'met'evsk = Älmät'evsk o RUS 96-97 H 6
Al'met'evsk = Al'met'evsk o RUS 96-97 H 6
Âlmhult o S 86-87 G 8
al-Milk, Wâdi ~ SUD 200-201 E 4
al-Minya ☆ ET 194-195 E 3
Almina, Punta ▲ E 98-99 E 6
Almirós o GR 100-101 J 5
Almodôvar o P 98-99 C 6
Almodóvar del Río o E 98-99 E 6
Almonte o CDN 38-39 F 6
Almonte o E 98-99 D 6
Almonte, Rio ~ E 98-99 D 5
Almora o· IND 138-139 G 5
al-Muglad o SUD 206-207 J 3
al-Mûh, Sabhat o SYR 128-129 H 5
al-Muhammadiyah = Mohammedia o MA 188-189 H 4
al-Mukallá o· Y 132-133 F 6
Almuñécar o· E 98-99 F 6
Almunia de Doña Godina, La o E 98-99 G 4
Almus o TR 128-129 F 2
Al Muwaylih, Bi'r < LAR 192-193 H 3
Alnašî o RUS 96-97 J 5
Alness o GB 90-91 E 3
Alnif o MA 188-189 J 5
Alnwick o GB 90-91 F 5
Alóag o EC 64-65 C 2
Alô Brasil o BR 72-73 E 2
Aloi o EAU 212-213 D 2
Aloja o LV 94-95 J 3
Aloma, River o WAN 204-205 H 5
Alongshan o VRC 150-151 D 2
Alónissos ~ GR 100-101 J 5
Alonon Point ▲ RP 160-161 D 6
Alor, Kepulauan ~ RI 166-167 C 6
Alor, Pulau ~ RI 166-167 C 6
Aloro, Rio ~ BOL 76-77 D 1
Alor Setar ☆ MAL 162-163 D 2
Alos o RI 164-165 F 6
Alota o BOL 76-77 D 1
Alotau o PNG 183 F 6
Alpachiri o RA 78-79 H 4
Alpamayo ▲ PE 64-65 D 6
Alpasinche o RA 76-77 D 5
Alpena o USA 46-47 G 3
Alpercata, Rio ~ BR 72-73 H 4
Alpercatas, Serra das ▲ BR 68-69 F 5
Alpha o AUS 178-179 J 2
Alpha o USA 46-47 O 5
Alpha Creek ~ AUS 178-179 J 2
Alphonse Group ~ SY 224 C 3
Alphonse Island ~ SY 224 C 3
Alpine o USA (AZ) 44-45 C 3
Alpine o USA (TX) 44-45 F 4
Alpine Junction o USA 40-41 J 4
Alpine Lakes Wilderness ⊥ USA 40-41 D 2
Alpine National Park ⊥ AUS 180-181 J 4
Alpinópolis o BR 72-73 G 6
Alpouro ~ WAN 204-205 E 4

Alps = Alpen ▲ 92-93 J 6
Alps, The ▲ AUS 178-179 K 2
Alpu o TR 128-129 D 3
al-Qâhira ★·· ET 194-195 E 2
Al Qala'a o LAR 192-193 F 2
al-Qantara o ET 194-195 F 2
Al Qardabah o LAR 192-193 K 1
Al Qasabât o LAR 192-193 F 2
al-Qâsh, Nahr ~ SUD 200-201 H 5
al-Qasr o LAR 192-193 F 2
Al Qât, Bi'r < LAR 192-193 F 3
Al Qatif, Bi'r < LAR 192-193 F 3
Al Qatrún o LAR 192-193 F 5
Al Qawz o SUD 200-201 G 6
al-Qirbah Dam, Khashm < SUD 200-201 G 5
Al-Q'nitra o MA 188-189 H 3
Al Qubbah o LAR 192-193 K 1
Alqueva, Barragem do < P 98-99 D 5
Alquízar o C 54-55 D 3
al-Qulayd Bahri o SUD 200-201 E 3
al-Qurayyât o KSA 130-131 E 3
al-Qusair o ET 194-195 G 4
al-Qûsiya o ET 194-195 E 3
al-Qus Taima o ET 194-195 G 2
al-Qutaynah o SUD 200-201 F 5
al-Quwaisi o SUD 200-201 G 6
Al Rahibat o LAR 192-193 E 2
Alroy Downs o AUS 174-175 D 6
Alsace o USA 178-179 L 6
Alsace ± F 90-91 L 8
Alsask o CDN 32-33 Q 5
Alsasu o E 98-99 F 3
Alsek River ~ CDN 20-21 W 6
Alshi o EC 64-65 N 5
Alsike o CDN 32-33 N 5
Alta ~ N 86-87 L 2
Alta, Cachoeira ~ BR 70-71 K 3
Alta, Pampa ~ RA 78-79 G 4
Alta, Punta ▲ EC 64-65 B 2
Altaelva ~ N 86-87 L 2
Alta Floresta o BR 66-67 K 7
Alta Gracía o RA 76-77 E 6
Altagracia o YV 60-61 F 2
Altagracia o YV (ZUL) 60-61 F 2
Altaj ▲ MAU 148-149 C 4
Altaj = Bor-Uzuur o MAU 146-147 L 3
Altajn Caadah Gov' ± MAU 146-147 M 4
Altajsk, Gorno o RUS 124-125 O 3
Altajskij zapovednik ⊥ RUS 124-125 Q 3
Altamachi, Rio ~ BOL 70-71 D 5
Altamaha River ~ USA 48-49 G 4
Altamira o BR 68-69 B 3
Altamira o CO 60-61 C 5
Altamira o MEX 50-51 L 6
Altamira o RCH 76-77 C 3
Altamira o YV 60-61 F 7
Altamira, Cuevas de ··· E 98-99 E 3
Altamira do Maranhão o BR 68-69 F 4
Altamirano o MEX 52-53 H 3
Altamonte Springs o USA 48-49 H 5
Altamura o· I 100-101 F 4
Altan Ovoo o MAU 148-149 E 4
Altan ovoo ▲ MAU 146-147 K 3
Altar o MEX 50-51 D 2
Altar, Desierto de ± MEX 50-51 B 1
Altar, Rio ~ MEX 50-51 D 2
Altar, Volcán ▲ EC 64-65 C 2
Altar de Sacrificios ··· GCA 52-53 J 3
Altar-Est o DZ 190-191 G 4
Altata o MEX 50-51 F 5
Alta Vista o USA 42-43 J 6
Altavista o USA 46-47 J 7
Altay o VRC 146-147 J 2
Altay Mountains = Altaj ▲ KA 124-125 N 3
Altay Shan ▲ VRC 146-147 H 1
Altdorf ☆· CH 92-93 K 5
Altea o E 98-99 G 5
Altenburg o· D 92-93 M 3
Altér do Chão o BR (PIA) 68-69 H 4
Alter do Chão o P 98-99 D 5
Alterosa o BR 72-73 G 6
Altevatnet o N 86-87 H 2
Altheimer o USA 44-45 M 2
Al Tidedi, Wâdi ~ LAR 192-193 G 8
Aí Tikuna Evare, Áreas Indigena ✕ BR 66-67 C 4
Altntenpe ∴· TR 128-129 H 3
Altiplanicie del Payún ▲ RA 78-79 E 4
Altmühl ~ D 92-93 L 4
Alto o USA 44-45 K 4
Alto, El o PE 64-65 B 4
Alto, Cerro ▲ RA 78-79 D 6
Alto, Raudal ~ YV 60-61 J 4
Alto Alegre o BR (PIA) 68-69 H 4
Alto Alegre o BR (RSU) 74-75 D 8
Alto Anapu, Rio ~ BR 68-69 C 3
Alto Araguaia o BR 72-73 E 4
Alto Bonito o BR 66-67 B 2
Alto Chandless, Rio ~ PE 70-71 B 2
Alto Chicapa o ANG 216-217 E 5
Alto de Amparo o BR 74-75 E 5
Alto de Carrizal ▲ CO 60-61 C 4
Alto de la Sierra o RA 76-77 F 2
Alto del Carmen o RCH 76-77 B 5
Alto de los Colorados ▲ RA 76-77 C 4
Alto Garças o BR 72-73 D 4
Alto Hama o ANG 216-217 C 6
Alto Jurupari o BR 66-67 B 7
Alto Ligonha o MOC 218-219 K 2
Alto Longá o BR 68-69 G 4
Alto Madre de Dios, Rio ~ PE 70-71 F 3
Alto Molócuè o MOC 218-219 J 2
Alton o USA (IL) 44-45 M 1
Alton o USA (MO) 44-45 M 1
Altoona o USA 46-47 J 5
Alto Pacajaí, Rio ~ BR 68-69 C 3
Alto Paraguai o BR 70-71 J 4
Alto Paraíso de Goiás o BR 72-73 G 3
Alto Parnaíba o BR 68-69 F 6

Alto Pencoso ○ **RA** 78-79 F 2
Alto Purus, Río ~ **PE** 70-71 B 2
Alto Quiel ○ **PA** 52-53 C 7
Alto Quimari ▲ **CO** 60-61 C 3
Alto Rabagão, Barragem do ◁ **P** 98-99 D 4
Alto Rio Guama, Área Indígena ⅄ **BR** 68-69 E 3
Alto Rio Mayo ○ **RA** 80 E 2
Alto Rio Negro, Área Indígena ⅄ **BR** 66-67 C 3
Alto Rio Novo ○ **BR** 72-73 K 5
Alto Rio Purus, Área Indígena ⅄ **BR** 66-67 B 7
Alto Rio Senguerr ○ **RA** 80 E 2
Alto Rio Verde ○ **BR** 72-73 D 5
Altos ○ **BR** 68-69 G 4
Altos de Talinay ▲ **RCH** 76-77 B 6
Altotonga ○ **MEX** 52-53 F 2
Alto Turiaçú, Área Indígena ⅄ **BR** 68-69 E 3
Altsohl = Zvolen ○ **SK** 92-93 P 4
Altstadt = Staré Mésto ○ **CZ** 92-93 O 4
Altun ○ **VRC** 146-147 J 6
Altun Ha ∴ **BH** 52-53 K 3
Altún Küprü ○ **IRQ** 128-129 L 5
Altun Shan ▲ **VRC** 146-147 G 6
Alturas ○ **USA** 40-41 D 5
Altus ○ **USA** 44-45 H 4
Altvater = Pradèd ▲ **CZ** 92-93 O 3
Altyaryk ○ **US** 136-137 M 4
Altyb ~ **RUS** 116-117 M 5
Altykarasu ○ **KA** 126-127 L 3
Alua ○ **MOC** 218-219 K 1
Aluakluak ○ **SUD** 206-207 K 5
al-Ubayyid = El Obeid ☆ **SUD** 200-201 E 6
Alučin ~ **RUS** 112-113 N 3
Alucra ☆ **TR** 128-129 H 2
al-Udayya ○ **SUD** 200-201 D 6
Al Ugayb, Wádi ◁ **LAR** 192-193 H 4
Aluize, Rio ~ **MOC** 218-219 G 6
Alüksne ○ **LV** 94-95 K 3
al-'Umda ○ **SUD** 206-207 J 3
Aluminé ○ **RA** 78-79 D 5
Aluminé, Rio ~ **RA** 78-79 D 5
A Lú'ú' ☆ **VN** 158-159 J 2
Al 'Uqaylah = Al 'Uqayla ○ **LAR** 192-193 H 2
al-'Uqdah ○ **SUD** 200-201 F 5
al-Uqsur ○ **ET** 194-195 F 5
Alür ○ **IND** 140-141 F 4
Älür ○ **IND** 140-141 G 3
al-Urdunn, Nahr ~ **JOR** 130-131 D 2
al-'Urf, Ġabal ▲ **ET** 194-195 F 4
Al 'Ushara ○ **SUD** 200-201 F 5
Alušta ○ **UA** 102-103 J 5
Al 'Utaylah, Bi'r ◁ **LAR** 192-193 G 2
al-'Utayshán ○ **SUD** 200-201 G 4
Alut Oya ○ **CL** 140-141 J 6
Al 'Uwaynát = Uwaynat ○ **LAR** 190-191 H 8
al-'Uzaym, Nahr ~ **IRQ** 128-129 L 5
Alva ○ **USA** 44-45 H 1
Alvand, Küh-e ▲ **IR** 134-135 C 1
Alvarado ○ **CO** 60-61 D 5
Alvarado ○ **MEX** 52-53 G 2
Alvarães ○ **BR** 66-67 E 4
Alvarenga ○ **BR** 72-73 K 5
Alvar Nuñez Cabeza de Vaca ○ **PY** 76-77 K 3
Álvaro Obregón, Presa ◁ **MEX** 50-51 E 4
Álvaro Obregón, Presa ◁ **MEX** 50-51 E 3
Alvdal ☆ **N** 86-87 E 5
Älvdalen ○ **S** 86-87 F 6
Alvear ○ **RA** 76-77 J 5
Alves ○ **BR** 72-73 L 2
Alvesta ☆ **S** 86-87 G 8
Alvim ○ **GUY** 62-63 E 4
Alvin ○ **USA** 44-45 K 5
Alvinston ○ **CDN** 38-39 D 7
Alvito ○ **P** 98-99 D 5
Älvkarleby ☆ **S** 86-87 H 6
Alvorada ○ **BR (RSU)** 74-75 E 8
Alvorada ○ **BR (TOC)** 72-73 G 3
Alvorada do Norte ○ **BR** 72-73 G 3
Alvord Lake ○ **USA** 40-41 E 4
Alvord Valley ◡ **USA** 40-41 E 4
Älvsbyn ○ **S** 86-87 K 4
Al Wahah ○ **LAR** 192-193 J 3
al-Wáhát al-Bahriya ⌄ **ET** 194-195 D 3
Al Wa'ir, Wádi ~ **LAR** 192-193 H 4
Awar Hills ▲ **IND** 138-139 F 6
Awás ○ **IND** 138-139 F 3
Al Washkah, Bi'r ◁ **LAR** 192-193 F 3
al-Wásitá ○ **ET** 194-195 E 3
Alwero Wenz ~ **ETH** 208-209 B 4
Al Wigh ○ **LAR** 192-193 H 5
Al Wáytah ○ **LAR** 192-193 G 5
Alxa Gaoyuan ⌄ **VRC** 148-149 E 7
Alxa Youqi ○ **VRC** 154-155 B 2
Alxa Zuoqi ○ **VRC** 154-155 D 2
Al Yaman ▼ **Y** 132-133 E 6
Alyangula ○ **AUS** 174-175 D 3
Alyawarra Aboriginal Land ⅄ **AUS** 178-179 C 1
Alyeska Resort & Ski Area · **USA** 20-21 Q 6
Aly-Jurjah ~ **RUS** 112-113 H 4
Alymdža ~ **RUS** 118-119 L 4
Alyta, Batagaj ~ **RUS** 110-111 S 6
Alytus ☆ **LT** 94-95 J 4
Alzada ○ **USA** 42-43 E 3
Alzamaj ○ **RUS** 116-117 J 8
Alzira ○ **E** 98-99 G 5
Ama ○ **PNG** 183 A 3
Amaam, laguna ≈ **RUS** 112-113 U 5
Amacayacu, Parque Nacional ⊥ **CO** 66-67 B 4
Amaciá ○ **BR** 66-67 E 5
Amacuzac, Rio ~ **MEX** 52-53 E 2
Amada ∴ **ET** 194-195 F 6
Amada Gaza ○ **RCA** 206-207 B 6
Amadeus, Lake ○ **AUS** 176-177 L 2
Amadi ○ **SUD** 206-207 K 6
Amadi ○ **ZRE** 210-211 L 2

'Amádiya, ai- ☆ **IRQ** 128-129 K 4
Amadjuak Bay ≈ **CDN** 36-37 N 3
Amadjuak Lake ○ **CDN** 36-37 O 2
Amadjuak River ~ **CDN** 36-37 O 2
Amadora ○ **P** 98-99 C 5
Amador, Oued ~ **DZ** 190-191 F 8
Amadror, Oued ~ **DZ** 190-191 F 8
Amaga ○ **CO** 60-61 D 4
Amagi ○ **J** 152-153 D 8
Amahai ○ **RI** 166-167 E 3
Amahtonskij, zaliv ≈ **RUS** 120-121 N 4
Amair Bin Sana'a, al- ○ **KSA** 130-131 G 4
Amajac, Rio ~ **MEX** 52-53 E 1
Amaki ○ **PNG** 183 B 3
Amakinskij ○ **RUS** 110-111 K 4
Amakouladji ○ **RMM** 196-197 K 6
Amakusa-nada ≈ **J** 152-153 C 8
Amakusa-shotō ⌒ **J** 152-153 D 8
'Amál ☆ **S** 86-87 F 7
Amala ~ **EAK** 212-213 E 4
Amalapuram ○ **IND** 140-141 K 2
Amalat ~ **RUS** 118-119 G 8
Amalfi ○ **I** 100-101 E 4
Amalia ○ **ZA** 220-221 G 3
Amaliáda ○ **GR** 100-101 H 6
Amalner ○ **IND** 138-139 E 9
Amaluza ○ **EC (CAN)** 64-65 C 3
Amaluza ○ **EC (LOJ)** 64-65 C 3
Amaluza, Embalse ◁ **EC** 64-65 C 3
Amamá ○ **RA** 76-77 F 4
Amamapare ○ **RI** 166-167 J 4
Amamba ○ **MOC** 218-219 G 5
Amambai ○ **BR** 76-77 K 2
Amambai, Rio ~ **BR** 76-77 K 2
Amambay, Sierra de ▲ **PY** 76-77 K 2
Amami-shotō ⌒ **J** 152-153 C 11
Amaná, Lago ○ **BR** 66-67 E 4
Amaná, Rio ~ **BR** 66-67 F 5
Amana, Río ~ **YV** 60-61 K 3
Amanab ○ **PNG** 183 A 2
Åmanave ○ **USA** 184 V b 2
Amancio ○ **C** 54-55 G 4
Amaneye, Área Indígena ⅄ **BR** 68-69 D 3
Amangeldi ○ **KA** 124-125 D 3
Amaniú ○ **BR** 68-69 H 7
Amankaragaj ○ **KA** 124-125 D 2
Amankeldi ○ **KA** 96-97 H 8
Amankro ○ **CI** 202-203 J 6
Amanótkef ○ **KA** 126-127 O 4
Amantani, Isla ⌒ **PE** 70-71 C 4
Amantea ○ **I** 100-101 F 5
Amantenango del Valle ○ **MEX** 52-53 H 3
Amantogaj ○ **KA** 124-125 D 3
Amaranmynama ○ **ZW** 218-219 D 4
Amanzimtoti ○ **ZA** 220-221 K 5
Amapá ○ **BR** 62-63 J 4
Amapá ○ **BR** 70-71 C 2
Amapá Grande, Rio ~ **BR** 62-63 J 4
Amapari, Rio ~ **BR** 62-63 H 5
Amar ▲ **ETH** 208-209 C 6
Amar ○ **RI** 166-167 G 3
'Amára, al- ★ **IRQ** 128-129 M 7
Amara, Temple · **SUD** 200-201 E 2
Amarac National Wildlife Refuge ⊥ **USA** 42-43 K 2
Amaraji ○ **BR** 68-69 L 6
Amaramba, Lago ○ **MOC** 218-219 H 2
Amarante ○ **BR** 68-69 G 5
Amarante do Maranhão ○ **BR** 68-69 E 4
Amaranth ○ **CDN** 34-35 G 5
Amarapura ○ **MYA** 142-143 K 5
Amarapuram ○ **IND** 140-141 G 3
Amaravati ○ **IND** 140-141 G 3
Amaravati ○ **IND** 140-141 J 2
Amardalaj ○ **MAU** 148-149 H 4
Amarga, Bañados de la ○ **RA** 78-79 G 3
Amarga, Laguna la ○ **RA** 78-79 F 5
Amargosa Range ▲ **USA** 40-41 F 7
Amargosa River ~ **USA** 40-41 F 7
Amarillo ○ **USA** 44-45 G 4
Amarinthos ○ **GR** 100-101 J 5
'Amar Jadid ○ **SUD** 200-201 B 5
Amarkantak ○ **IND** 142-143 B 4
Amarortalik ⌒ **GRØ** 26-27 Y 7
Amaru, Danau ○ **RI** 166-167 E 3
Amasu ~ **KA** 124-125 G 5
Amasya ☆ · **TR** 128-129 F 2
Amata ⅄ **AUS** 176-177 L 3
Amatari ○ **BR** 66-67 H 4
Amates, Los ○ **GCA** 52-53 K 4
Amatignak Island ⌒ **USA** 22-23 G 7
Amatique, Bahía de ≈ **GCA** 52-53 K 4
Amatitlán ○ **GCA** 52-53 J 4
Amatlán de Cañas ○ **MEX** 52-53 B 1
Amatura ○ **BR** 66-67 C 4
Amau ○ **PNG** 183 E 6
Àmáytoli Terara ▲ **ETH** 200-201 K 6
Amazar ○ **RUS** 118-119 J 8
Amazar ~ **RUS** 118-119 K 9
Amazarskij hrebet ▲ **RUS** 118-119 K 9
Amazmaz ~ **RIM** 196-197 E 6
Amazonas ○ **BR** 66-67 C 6
Amazon Canyon ≃ 62-63 K 5
Amazon Fan ≃ 62-63 K 4
Amazônia, Parque Nacional de ⊥ **BR** 66-67 J 3
Amazon Shelf ≃ 62-63 K 4
Ambabbo ○ **DJI** 208-209 D 3
Ambad ○ **IND** 138-139 E 10
Amba Farit ▲ **ETH** 208-209 D 3
Ámba Giyorgis ○ **ETH** 200-201 H 6
Ambahikily ○ **RM** 222-223 C 8
Ambahivahibe ○ **RM** 222-223 E 9
Ambajögöäi ○ **IND** 138-139 F 10
Ambakireny ○ **RM** 222-223 E 7
Ambala ○ **IND** 138-139 F 4
Ambalabe ○ **RM** 222-223 E 6
Ambalajanakomby ○ **RM** 222-223 E 7
Ambalakirajy ○ **RM** 222-223 F 5
Ambalamanaka ○ **RM** 222-223 E 5
Ambalamarina ○ **RM** 222-223 E 8
Ambalapaiso ○ **RM** 222-223 F 5

Ambalarondra ○ **RM** 222-223 F 7
Ambalavao ○ **RM** 222-223 E 8
Ambam ○ **CAM** 210-211 C 2
Ámba Maderiya ○ **ETH** 200-201 J 6
Ambang Reserve, Gunung ⊥ · **RI** 164-165 J 3
Ambanja ○ **RM** 222-223 E 6
Ambanjabe ○ **RM** 222-223 E 5
Ambar ○ **PE** 64-65 D 7
Ambar ○ **RM** 222-223 E 5
Ambararata ○ **RM** 222-223 E 5
Ambarčik ○ **RUS (KRN)** 116-117 G 8
Ambarčik ○ **RUS (SAH)** 112-113 M 2
Ambardah ~ **RUS** 108-109 J 0
Ambargasta ○ **RA** 76-77 F 4
Ambargasta, Salinas de ○ **RA** 76-77 F 4
Ambargasta, Sierra ▲ **RA** 76-77 F 5
Ambarimaninga ○ **RM** 222-223 E 6
Ambarita · **RI** 164-165 J 3
Ambarnyj ○ **RUS** 88-89 M 4
Ambato ○ **EC** 64-65 C 2
Ambato, Sierra de ▲ **RA** 76-77 D 5
Ambatoboeny ○ **RM** 222-223 E 6
Ambato Finandrahana ○ **RM** 222-223 E 8
Ambatoharanana ○ **RM** 222-223 F 4
Ambatolahy ○ **RM** 222-223 D 8
Ambatolampy ○ **RM** 222-223 E 7
Ambatomainty ○ **RM** 222-223 D 6
Ambatomanoina ○ **RM** 222-223 E 7
Ambatondrazaka ○ **RM** 222-223 F 6
Ambatosia ○ **RM** 222-223 E 6
Ambatosoratra ○ **RM** 222-223 E 8
Ambatovory ○ **RM** 222-223 E 8
Ambatry ○ **RM** 222-223 D 9
Ambaúba ○ **BR** 66-67 D 2
Ambazac ○ **F** 90-91 H 9
Ambe ~ **ZRE** 210-211 K 5
Ambelau, Pulau ⌒ **RI** 166-167 D 3
Amberg ○ **D** 92-93 L 4
Ambergris Cay ⌒ **BH** 52-53 L 3
Ambérieu-en-Bugey ○ **F** 90-91 K 9
Amberley ○ **NZ** 182 Q 7
Ambert ○ **F** 90-91 J 9
Ambidédi ○ **RMM** 202-203 E 2
Ambikapur ○ **IND** 142-143 C 4
Ambila ○ **RM** 222-223 E 8
Ambil Island ⌒ **RP** 160-161 D 6
Ambilobe ○ **RM** 222-223 E 6
Ambinanindrano ○ **RM** 222-223 F 8
Ambinanindrano ○ **RM** 222-223 F 7
Ambinanironry ○ **RM** 222-223 F 7
Ambinanymbazaha ○ **RM** 222-223 E 6
Ambition Mountain ▲ **CDN** 32-33 E 3
Ambitle Island ⌒ **PNG** 183 G 3
Amble-by-the-Sea ○ **GB** 90-91 G 4
Ambler ○ **USA** 20-21 M 3
Ambler River ~ **USA** 20-21 M 3
Ambleside ○ **GB** 90-91 F 4
Ambo ○ **PE** 64-65 D 7
Amboahangibe ○ **RM** 222-223 F 5
Amboahangy ○ **RM** 222-223 E 10
Amboasary ○ **RM** 222-223 E 10
Amboasary Gara ○ **RM** 222-223 F 7
Amboavory ○ **RM** 222-223 F 6
Ambodiangezoka ○ **RM** 222-223 F 5
Ambodibonara ○ **RM** 222-223 F 8
Ambodifotatra ○ **RM** 222-223 F 6
Ambodiriana ○ **RM** 222-223 F 7
Ambodibelazana-Sahana ○ **RM** 222-223 F 5
Ambodivoara ○ **RM** 222-223 G 5
Ambohibada ○ **RM** 222-223 F 5
Ambohibary ○ **RM** 222-223 E 7
Ambohidratrimo ○ **RM** 222-223 E 7
Ambohijanahary ○ **RM** 222-223 F 6
Ambohimahasoa ○ **RM** 222-223 E 8
Ambohimanga ○ **RM** 222-223 E 8
Ambohinihaonana ○ **RM** 222-223 E 8
Ambohipaky ○ **RM** 222-223 D 6
Ambohitra ○ **RM (ASA)** 222-223 F 4
Ambohitra ▲ · **RM (ASA)** 222-223 F 4
Ambohitralanana ○ **RM** 222-223 G 5
Ambohitrolomahitsy ○ **RM** 222-223 E 7
Amboi, Kepulauan ⌒ **RI** 166-167 J 2
Amboise ○ **F** 90-91 H 8
Ambol ○ **IND** 140-141 E 3
Ambolobozo ○ **RM** 222-223 E 6
Ambolomoty ○ **RM** 222-223 E 6
Ambolten ~ **GRØ** 26-27 q 4
Ambon ○ **RI** 166-167 E 3
Ambon, Pulau ⌒ **RI** 166-167 D 3
Ambondro ○ **RM** 222-223 D 10
Ambondromamy ○ **RM** 222-223 E 6
Ambongo ⌄ **RM** 222-223 D 6
Amboni ○ **EAT** 212-213 G 4
Amboriala ○ **RM** 222-223 F 6
Amborompotsy ○ **RM** 222-223 E 8
Amborondolo ○ **RM** 222-223 F 4
Amboseli, Lake ○ **EAK** 212-213 F 5
Amboseli National Park ⊥ **EAK** 212-213 F 5
Ambositra ○ **RM** 222-223 E 8
Ambovombe ○ **RM** 222-223 E 10
Amboy ○ **USA (CA)** 40-41 G 8
Amboy ○ **USA (IL)** 46-47 D 5
Ambre, Cap d' = Tanjona Babaomby ▲ **RM** 222-223 E 5
Ambre, Île d' ⌒ **MS** 224 C 7
Ambrim = Île Ambrym ⌒ **VAN** 184 II b 3
Ambriz ○ **ANG** 216-217 B 3
Ambriz, Coutada do ⊥ **ANG** 216-217 B 3
Ambrolauri ○ **GE** 126-127 E 6
Ambrosio ○ **BR** 68-69 F 5
Ambrym = Île Ambrym ⌒ **VAN** 184 II b 3
Ambrym, Île = Ambrim ⌒ **VAN** 184 II b 3
Ambuaki ○ **RI** 166-167 G 4
Ambulombo, al- ○ **RI** 168 E 7
Ambulong Island ⌒ **RP** 160-161 D 6
Ambunten ○ **RI** 168 E 7
Ambunti ○ **PNG** 183 B 3
Ambur ○ **IND** 140-141 H 4

Amchitka Pass ≈ 22-23 G 7
Am Dafok ○ **RCA** 206-207 F 3
am-Dam ○ **TCH** 198-199 K 6
Amdápur ○ **IND** 138-139 F 9
Amdassa ○ **RI** 166-167 F 5
Amded, Oued ~ **DZ** 190-191 D 9
Amderma ○ **RUS** 108-109 J 7
Am Djamena ○ **RCA** 206-207 E 4
Amdo ○ **VRC** 144-145 H 4
Am Djemena ○ **TCH** 198-199 H 6
Amdrup Højland ▲ **GRØ** 26-27 m 3
Amealco ○ **MEX** 52-53 D 1
Ameca ○ **MEX** 52-53 C 1
Ameca, Río ~ **MEX** 52-53 B 1
Amediči ~ **RUS** 118-119 L 7
Ameib ○ **NAM** 216-217 C 10
Ameland ⌒ **NL** 92-93 H 2
Amellougui ○ **MA** 188-189 H 5
Amenia ○ **USA** 46-47 M 5
Amentego ○ **SUD** 200-201 D 3
Amerálik ≈ 28-29 P 4
América ○ **BR** 68-69 H 7
America-Antarctic Ridge ≃ 6-7 H 14
América Dourada ○ **BR** 68-69 H 7
Americana ○ **BR** 72-73 G 7
American Falls ○ **USA** 40-41 H 4
American Falls Reservoir ◁ **USA** 40-41 H 4
American Fork ○ **USA** 40-41 J 5
American Highland ▲ **ARK** 16 F 8
American Samoa ▽ **USA** 184 V c 1
Americus ○ **USA** 48-49 F 3
Amerika-Kuba-Aryta, ostrov ⌒ **RUS** 110-111 R 3
Amersfoort ○ **NL** 92-93 H 2
Amersfoort ○ **ZA** 220-221 J 4
Amersham ○ **GB** 90-91 G 6
Amery Ice Shelf ⌾ **ARK** 16 F 8
Ames ○ **USA** 42-43 L 4
Amesbury ○ **USA** 46-47 N 4
Amesdale ○ **CDN** 34-35 K 5
Amethi ○ **IND** 142-143 B 2
Ameya ○ **ETH** 208-209 C 5
Amfilohia ○ **GR** 100-101 H 5
Amga ○ **RUS** 120-121 X 4
Amga ~ **RUS** 118-119 L 6
Amga ~ **RUS** 120-121 X 4
Amginskij hrebet ▲ **RUS** 118-119 L 6
Amgotro ○ **RI** 166-167 L 3
Amgu ○ **RUS** 122-123 G 6
Amguèma ~ **RUS** 112-113 V 3
Amguèma, laguna ≈ **RUS** 112-113 W 2
Amguemskaja vpadina ⌄ **RUS** 112-113 V 3
Amguid ○ **DZ** 190-191 E 7
Amgun' ~ **RUS** 122-123 F 3
Amgun ~ **RUS** 122-123 G 3
Amsel ○ **DZ** 190-191 E 9
Amherst ○ **CDN** 38-39 L 6
Amherst ○ **USA (MA)** 46-47 M 4
Amherst ○ **USA (VA)** 46-47 J 7
Amherst = Kyaikkami ○ **MYA** 158-159 J 2
Amherstburg ○ **CDN** 38-39 C 7
Amherst Island ⌒ **CDN (NWT)** 24-25 e 6
Amherst Island ⌒ **CDN (ONT)** 38-39 H 6
Am Timan ☆ **TCH** 198-199 H 6
Ami ~ **IND** 142-143 C 2
Amiata, Monte ▲ **I** 100-101 C 3
Amidon ○ **USA** 42-43 F 2
Amiens ○ ☆ **F** 90-91 J 7
Aminag ○ **RCA** 206-207 D 6
Amindivi Islands ⌒ **IND** 140-141 E 5
Aminga ○ **RA** 76-77 D 4
Aminuis ○ **NAM** 216-217 E 8
Amino ○ **J** 152-153 F 7
Amiour ○ **RMM** 196-197 J 6
'Amiq, Qasr ○ **IRQ** 128-129 J 6
'Amiq, Wádi ~ **IRQ** 128-129 J 6
Amirábád ○ **IR** 134-135 D 2
Amirantes Group ⌒ **SY** 224 C 3
Amirante Trench ≃ 224-225 J 5
Amir Cháh ○ **PK** 134-135 K 4
Amisk Lake ○ **CDN** 34-35 G 3
Amistad ○ **USA** 44-45 F 2
Amistad, Parque Internacional La ⊥ ··· **CR** 52-53 C 7
Amistad, Presa la ◁ **MEX** 50-51 J 3
Amite ○ **USA** 44-45 M 4
Amitioke Peninsula ⌄ **CDN** 24-25 f 6
Amiuté, Ribeiro do ~ **BR** 62-63 J 5
Amizmiz ○ **MA** 188-189 G 5
'Ammán ★ **JOR** 130-131 D 2
Ämmänsaari ○ **FIN** 88-89 K 4
Ammapettai ○ **IND** 140-141 G 5
Ammapettai ○ **IND** 140-141 H 5
Ammarnäs ○ **S** 86-87 H 4
Ammaroo ○ **AUS** 178-179 C 1
Ammaroodinna Hill ▲ **AUS** 176-177 M 3
Ammassalik ☆ **GRØ** 28-29 W 4
Ammassivik = Sletten ○ **GRØ** 28-29 S 6
Ammer ~ **D** 92-93 L 4
Ammersee ○ **D** 92-93 L 5
Ammochostos ☆ **TR** 128-129 E 5
Amnouk ○ **RMM** 196-197 K 5
Amnat Charoen ○ **THA** 158-159 H 3
Amnija ~ **RUS** 114-115 J 3
Amnok Gang ~ **DVR** 150-151 F 7
Amnundaka ~ **RUS** 116-117 K 2
Amnura ○ **BD** 142-143 S 4
Amodinonka ○ **RM** 222-223 E 8
Amogjár, Passe d' ▲ **RIM** 196-197 D 4
Åmol ○ **IR** 136-137 O 6
Amoltepec ○ **MEX** 52-53 F 3
Amon ○ **MA** 188-189 F 6

Amontada ○ **BR** 68-69 J 3
Amores, Arroyo ~ **RA** 76-77 H 5
Amores, Los ○ **RA** 76-77 H 5
Amorgós ○ **GR** 100-101 K 6
Amorgós ⌒ **GR** 100-101 K 6
Amorinópolis ○ **BR** 72-73 E 4
Amory ○ **USA** 48-49 E 3
Amos ○ **CDN** 38-39 E 4
Amotape, Cerros de ▲ **PE** 64-65 B 4
Amotopo ○ **SME** 62-63 F 4
Amou ○ **RT** 202-203 L 6
Amougëur ▲ **RIM** 196-197 J 4
Amou Oblo ○ **RT** 202-203 L 6
Amour, Djebel ▲ **DZ** 190-191 C 4
Amoya ○ **GH** 202-203 J 6
Amozoc ○ **MEX** 52-53 G 2
Ampah ○ **RI** 164-165 G 4
Ampana ○ **RI** 164-165 G 4
Ampang ○ **RI** 168 C 7
Ampanavoana ○ **RM** 222-223 G 6
Ampanga, Lakandrano ◁ **RM** 222-223 F 6
Ampanihy ○ **RM** 222-223 D 10
Amparafaravola ○ **RM** 222-223 F 6
Amparai ○ **CL** 140-141 J 7
Amparihy Atsinanana ○ **RM** 222-223 F 6
Amparo ○ **BR** 72-73 G 7
Amparo, El ○ **YV** 60-61 F 4
Ampasamadinika ○ **RM** 222-223 F 7
Ampasimandrotra ○ **RM** 222-223 F 7
Ampasimbe ○ **RM** 222-223 F 6
Ampasinambo ○ **RM** 222-223 F 8
Ampatakamaroreny ○ **RM** 222-223 F 6
Ampato, Cordillera de ▲ **PE** 64-65 F 9
Ampefy ○ **RM** 222-223 E 7
Amper ○ **WAN** 204-205 H 3
Ampère Seamount ≃ 188-189 E 3
Ampibako ○ **RI** 164-165 G 4
Ampisikinana ○ **RM** 222-223 F 4
Ampiyacu, Río ~ **PE** 64-65 E 5
Amplawas ○ **RI** 166-167 E 6
Ampoa ○ **RI** 164-165 G 4
Ampombiantambo ○ **RM** 222-223 F 4
Ampondra ○ **RM** 222-223 F 5
Amputa ~ **RUS** 114-115 O 3
Amqui ○ **CDN** 38-39 L 4
'Amrán ○ **Y** 132-133 C 6
Amráne, Bîr' ◁ **RIM** 196-197 F 3
Amrávati ○ **IND** 138-139 F 9
Amreli ○ **IND** 138-139 C 9
Amri ○ **PK** 138-139 B 6
'Amrit ○ **SYR** 128-129 G 5
Amritsar ○ **IND** 138-139 E 4
Amroha ○ **IND** 138-139 G 5
Amság ~ **RIM** 196-197 C 4
Amsel ○ **DZ** 190-191 E 9
Amsterdam ○ **CDN** 34-35 E 5
Amsterdam ★ ·· **NL** 92-93 H 2
Amsterdam ○ **USA** 46-47 L 4
Amsterdam ○ **ZA** 220-221 K 4
Amsterdam, Fort ·· **NA** 56 D 2
Amsterdam, Île ⌒ **F** 12 F 8
Amstetten ○ **A** 92-93 N 4
Am Tanabo ○ **TCH** 198-199 H 6
Amu-Buharskij kanal ◁ **US** 136-137 H 3
'Ámúdá ○ **SYR** 128-129 J 4
'Amúda, al- ○ **IRQ** 128-129 L 7
Amu-Darjä ○ **TM** 136-137 J 4
Amudar'ja ~ **US** 136-137 H 4
Amudat ○ **EAU** 212-213 E 3
Amukta Island ⌒ **USA** 22-23 L 6
Amukta Pass ≈ 22-23 L 6
Amund Ringnes Island ⌒ **CDN** 24-25 X 1
Amundsen, Mount ▲ **ARK** 16 G 11
Amundsen Bay ≈ 16 G 5
Amundsen Glacier ⌾ **ARK** 16 E 0
Amundsen Gulf ≈ 24-25 J 5
Amundsen havet ≈ 16 G 26
Amundsen-Scott ○ **ARK** 16 E 0
Amungwiwa, Mount ▲ **PNG** 183 D 4
Amur ~ **RUS** 118-119 K 9
Amur ~ **RUS** 122-123 J 2
Amur ~ **RUS** 122-123 E 4
'Amúr, Wádi ~ **SUD** 200-201 G 3
Amurang ○ **RI** 164-165 J 3
Amursk ○ **RUS** 122-123 G 3
Amurskaja oblast' ▽ **RUS** 118-119 M 9
Amurskij liman ≈ **RUS** 122-123 J 2
Amursko-Zejskaja ravnina ⌄ **RUS** 118-119 M 9
Amutu-Besar, Pulau ⌒ **RI** 166-167 G 3
Amyderya ○ **TM** 136-137 H 4
Amyl ~ **RUS** 116-117 F 9
Amzi, Oued Tin ~ **DZ** 198-199 B 2
Amzi, Oued Tin ~ **RN** 198-199 B 3
Am-Zoer ○ **TCH** 198-199 K 5
'Äna ○ **IRQ** 128-129 K 5
Ana, Cachoeira ~ **BR** 62-63 F 6
Anabanua ○ **RI** 164-165 G 5
Anabar ~ **RUS** 110-111 J 4
Anabarskij zaliv ≈ **RUS** 110-111 J 3
Anabarskoe plato ▲ **RUS** 110-111 F 4
Anabat ○ **RP** 160-161 D 4
Anaborano ○ **RM** 222-223 E 6
Anacadiña ○ **YV** 60-61 J 5
Anaco ○ **YV** 60-61 J 3
Anaconda ○ **USA** 40-41 H 2
Anaconda-Pintler Wilderness ⊥ **USA** 40-41 H 2
Anacortes ○ **USA** 40-41 C 1
Anacollo ○ **RCH** 78-79 C 6
Anacuao, Mount ▲ **RP** 160-161 E 4
Anda ○ **RP** 160-161 C 4
Anda ○ **VRC** 150-151 E 4
Andacollo ○ **RCH** 78-79 D 5
Andacollo ○ **RA** 78-79 D 5
Andacuaylas ○ **PE** 64-65 F 8
Andaí, Rio ~ **BR** 72-73 J 5
Andaingo Gara ○ **RM** 222-223 F 7
Andalaka ~ **RA** 222-223 E 5
Andalamanka ○ **RA** 76-77 D 4

Anadyrskoye Ploskogor'ye = Anadyrskoe ploskogor'e ▲ **RUS** 112-113 P 3
Anáfi ○ **GR** 100-101 K 6
Anaghit ○ · **ER** 200-201 J 4
Anagni ○ · **I** 100-101 D 4
Anagusta Island ⌒ **PNG** 183 F 6
Anaharávi ○ **GR** 100-101 G 5
Anahidrano ○ **RM** 222-223 E 5
Anahim Lake ○ **CDN** 32-33 H 5
Anáhuac ○ **MEX (CHA)** 50-51 F 4
Anáhuac ○ **MEX (NL)** 50-51 E 3
Anaimalai ○ **IND** 140-141 G 5
Anai ○ **RM** 222-223 E 6
Anaj ~ **RUS** 116-117 N 9
Anajás ○ **BR** 62-63 K 6
Anajatuba ○ **BR** 68-69 F 3
Anajé ○ **BR** 72-73 K 4
Anaka ○ **EAU** 212-213 C 2
Anakalang ○ **RI** 168 C 7
Anakápalle ○ **IND** 142-143 C 7
Anakao ○ **MA** 188-189 E 7
Anakdara ○ **RI** 164-165 G 5
Anakie ○ **AUS** 178-179 J 2
Anaktuak Pass ○ **USA** 20-21 P 2
Anaktuvuk River ~ **USA** 20-21 P 2
Anamã ○ **BR** 66-67 G 4
Anamã, Igarapé do ~ **BR** 66-67 G 4
Anamã, Lago ○ **BR** 66-67 G 4
Anama, ozero ○ **RUS** 116-117 G 2
Anama Bay ○ **CDN** 34-35 G 5
Ana Maria ○ **PE** 64-65 G 5
Ana María, Golfo de ≈ **C** 54-55 F 4
Anambas, Kepulauan ⌒ **RI** 162-163 G 5
Anambra ▽ **WAN** 204-205 G 5
Anamoose ○ **USA** 42-43 G 2
Anamosa ○ **USA** 46-47 C 4
Anamu, Rio ~ **BR** 62-63 F 5
Anamur ☆ **TR** 128-129 E 4
Anamur Burnu ▲ **TR** 128-129 E 4
Anan ○ **J** 152-153 F 8
Ananás ○ **BR** 68-69 D 5
Ananás, Cachoeira ~ **BR** 68-69 B 5
Ananda-Kouadiokro ○ **CI** 202-203 H 6
Anandpur ○ **IND** 142-143 E 5
Anan'evo ○ **KS** 146-147 O 4
Añangu ○ **EC** 64-65 D 2
Ananta, Lago ○ **PE** 70-71 B 4
Anantapur ○ **IND** 140-141 G 3
Anantnag ○ **IND** 138-139 E 3
Anantsono ○ **RM** 222-223 C 9
Anapka, zaliv ≈ **RUS** 120-121 V 3
Anápolis ○ **BR** 72-73 F 4
Anapu, Rio ~ **BR** 68-69 D 3
Anár ○ **IR** 134-135 G 3
Anárak ○ **IR** 134-135 E 2
Anárbár, Rüd-e ~ **IR** 134-135 D 2
Anár Dare ○ **AFG** 134-135 J 2
Änarjohka ~ **FIN** 88-89 J 2
Anárjohka ○ **FIN** 88-89 J 2
Anarnitscq ○ **GRØ** 28-29 Q 6
Anastasia ○ **BR** 70-71 K 7
Anastácio, Rio ~ **BR** 72-73 H 5
Anastasii, buhta ≈ **RUS** 112-113 R 6
Anatolia = Anatolia ⌄ 128-129 D 3
Anatolia ○ **TR** 128-129 D 3
Anatoliki Macedonia Kai Thráki ▽ **GR** 100-101 K 4
Anatone ○ **USA** 40-41 F 2
Anatuya ○ **RA** 76-77 F 5
Anauá, Fio ~ **BR** 62-63 E 5
Anauerutat Lake ○ **CDN** 30-31 R 5
Anauriländia ○ **BR** 72-73 E 7
Anavgaj ○ **RUS** 120-121 V 4
Anavilhanas, Arquipélago das ⌒ **BR** 66-67 G 4
'Anaza Ruwálla ▲ **KSA** 130-131 E 2
Anbá Biswi, Dayr · **ET** 194-195 E 2
Anbár, al- ○ **IRQ** 128-129 K 6
Anbar Küh ▲ **AFG** 136-137 L 4
Anbyon ○ **DVR** 150-151 F 8
Anča ~ **RUS** 120-121 H 3
An Cabhán = Cavan ☆ **IRL** 90-91 D 5
An Caiseán Nua = Newcastle West ○ **IRL** 90-91 C 5
An Caol = Keel ○ **IRL** 90-91 B 5
Ancash ▽ **PE** 64-65 D 7
Ancasti del Alto, Sierra de ▲ **RA** 76-77 E 5
Ancenis ○ **F** 90-91 G 8
An Chathair = Caher ○ **IRL** 90-91 D 5
Anchau ○ **WAN** 204-205 H 3
Ancho, Canal ≈ 80 C 5
Anchorage ○ **USA** 20-21 Q 6
Anchorena ○ **RA** 78-79 G 3
Ancien ○ **RMM** 196-197 K 4
Anciferova, ostrov ⌒ **RUS** 122-123 Q 3
Ancilitas, Cayos ⌒ **C** 54-55 F 4
An Clochán = Clifden ○ **IRL** 90-91 B 5
An Clochán = Cobh ○ **IRL** 90-91 C 6
An Coireán = Waterville ○ **IRL** 90-9′ B 6
Ancon ○ **PE** 64-65 D 7
Ancon, Punta ▲ **EC** 64-65 B 3
Ancona ○ ☆ · **I** 100-101 D 3
Ancón de Sardinas, Bahía de ≈ 64-65 C 1
Ancuabe ○ **MOC** 218-219 H 3
Ancud ○ **RCH** 78-79 C 6
Ancud, Golfo de ≈ 78-79 C 6
Anda ○ **RP** 160-161 C 4
Anda ○ **VRC** 150-151 E 4
Åndalsnes ○ **N** 86-87 C 5
Andalucía ▽ **E** 98-99 D 6
Andalusia ○ **USA (AL)** 48-49 E 4
Andalusia ○ **USA (IL)** 46-47 C 5
Andám, Wádi ~ **OM** 132-133 L 3
Andaman and Nicobar Islands ▽ **IND** 140-141 L 4
Andaman Basin ≃ 158-159 C 5
Andaman Islands ⌒ **IND** 140-141 L 3
Andaman Sea ≈ 158-159 C 4
Andamarca ○ **BOL** 70-71 D 6
Andamooka Opal Fields ○ **AUS** 178-179 D 3
Andamooka Ranges ▲ **AUS** 178-179 D 3
Andapa ○ **RM** 222-223 E 7
Andaráb ○ **AFG** 136-137 L 7
Andaraí ○ **BR** 72-73 K 2
Andarma ~ **RUS** 114-115 Q 6
Andavaka · ○ **RM** 222-223 F 4
Andeba Ye Midir Zerf Ch'af ▲ **ER** 200-201 K 5
Andelys, les ○ **F** 90-91 H 7
Andenes ○ **N** 86-87 H 2
Anderai ~ **WAN** 204-205 N 3
Andérambokane ○ **RMM** 196-197 M 7
Änderdalen nasjonalpark ⊥ **N** 86-87 H 2
Andermatt ○ **CH** 92-93 K 5
Andersen, Salto ~ **RA** 78-79 G 5
Anderson ○ **USA (IN)** 46-47 F 5
Anderson ○ **USA (MO)** 44-45 K 1
Anderson ○ **USA (SC)** 48-49 G 2
Anderson Channel ≈ 36-37 R 3
Anderson Gate ⌄ **NAM** 216-217 C 9
Anderson Island ⌒ **CDN** 36-37 L 6
Anderson River ~ **CDN** 20-21 a 2
Andersonville National Historic Site ·. **USA** 48-49 F 3
Andes ○ **CO** 60-61 D 5
Andes = Andes, Cordillera de los ▲ 5 D 8
Andes, Los ○ **RCH** 78-79 D 2
Andes, Los = Sotomayor ○ **CO** 64-65 D 1
Andfjorden ≈ 86-87 H 2
Andhöy ○ **AFG** 136-137 J 8
Andhra Pradesh ▽ **IND** 140-141 H 2
Andijskoe Kojsu ~ **RUS** 126-127 F 6
Andikíthira ⌒ **GR** 100-101 J 7
Andilamena ○ **RM** 222-223 F 6
Andimeśk ○ **IR** 134-135 C 2
Andino, Parque Nacional ⊥ **RCH** 78-79 C 6
Andiparos ⌒ **GR** 100-101 K 6
Andira ○ **BR** 72-73 E 7
Andirá, Rio ~ **BR** 66-67 D 5
Andirá, Rio ~ **BR** 66-67 J 4
Andirá-Marau, Área Indígena ⅄ **BR** 66-67 J 4
Andirin ☆ **TR** 128-129 G 3
Andirio ○ **GR** 100-101 H 5
Andirlangar ○ **VRC** 144-145 D 2
Andižan ☆ **US** 136-137 M 4
Andižanskaja oblast' ▽ **US** 136-137 M 4
Andižanskoe vodohranilišče ◁ **KS** 136-137 N 4
Andoain ○ **E** 98-99 F 3
Andoany ○ **RM** 222-223 F 4
Andoas ○ **PE** 64-65 D 3
Andohajango ○ **RM** 222-223 F 5
Andoi ○ **RI** 166-167 G 4
Andong ○ **ROK** 150-151 G 9
Andoom ○ **AUS** 174-175 F 3
Andorinha ○ **BR** 68-69 J 7
Andorinha, Cachoeira da ~ **BR** 66-67 G 7
Anderja ⌒ **N** 86-87 H 2
Andorra ■ **AND** 98-99 H 3
Andorra La Vella = ★ **AND** 98-99 H 3
Andorskaja grjada ▲ **RUS** 94-95 P 2
Andover ○ **USA (OH)** 46-47 H 5
Andover ○ **USA (SD)** 42-43 J 3
Andovoranto ○ **RM** 222-223 F 7
Andøya ⌒ **N** 86-87 G 2
Andrada ○ **ANG** 216-217 F 3
Andradina ○ **BR** 72-73 E 7
Andrafainikona ○ **RM** 222-223 F 4
Andrafiabe ○ **RM** 222-223 F 4
Andramasina ▲ **RM** 222-223 E 7
Andranovory ○ **RM** 222-223 D 9
Andranomena ○ **RM** 222-223 C 8
Andranomita · **RM** 222-223 D 8
Andranopasy ○ **RM** 222-223 C 8
Andranovondronina ○ **RM** 222-223 F 4
Andranovory ○ **RM** 222-223 D 9
Andreafsky River ~ **USA** 20-21 J 5
Andrecyk Lake ○ **CDN** 30-31 R 5
Andrée Land = **GRØ** 26-27 Y 7
Andrée land ◁ 16 G 24
Andreevka ○ **KA** 124-125 M 6
Andreevka ~ **RUS** 96-97 G 7
Andreevskoe, ozero ○ **RUS** 114-115 J 5
André Felix, Parc National ⊥ **RCA** 206-207 F 4
Andre Lake ○ **CDN** 36-37 R 7
Andrelândia ○ **BR** 72-73 H 6
Andrequicé ○ **BR** 72-73 H 5
Andrevo ○ **RM** 222-223 C 9
Andrew Gordon Bay ≈ 36-37 M 2
Andrew Lake ○ **CDN** 34-35 E 1
Andrew River ~ **CDN** 20-21 a 2
Andrews ○ **USA** 44-45 F 3
Àndria ○ **I** 100-101 F 4
Andriamena, Lavarie d' · **RM** 222-223 E 6
Andrieskraal ○ **ZA** 220-221 G 6
Andrijevica ○ · **YU** 100-101 G 3
Andringitra ▲ **RM** 222-223 E 8
Andrjuškino ○ **RUS** 112-113 H 2
Androhibe ○ **RM** 222-223 E 5

Androka o RM 222-223 D 10
Androna ± RM 222-223 E 5
Andronica Island ▲ USA 22-23 R 5
Andropov = Rybinsk ☆ RUS 94-95 Q 2
Androranga ~ RM 222-223 F 5
Androscoggin River ~ USA 46-47 N 3
Ándros ∩ GR 100-101 K 6
Andros Island ∩ BS 54-55 F 2
Andros Town o BS 54-55 G 2
Androth Island ∩ IND 140-141 E 5
Androy o RT 202-203 L 6
Andru River ~ PNG 183 E 4
Andselv ~ N 86-87 J 2
Andudu o ZRE 212-213 B 2
Andújar ☆ E 98-99 E 5
Andulo o RM 216-217 D 5
Andyilvan ~ RUS 112-113 M 4
Anec, Lake ▲ AUS 176-177 K 1
Anecón Chico, Cerro ▲ RA 78-79 K 4
Anecón Grande, Cerro ▲ RA 78-79 D 6
Anéfis o RMM 196-197 L 5
Anegada □ GB 56 C 2
Anegada, Bahía ≈ 78-79 H 6
Anegada, Punta ▲ PA 52-53 D 8
Anegada Passage ≈ 56 D 2
Aného o RT 202-203 L 6
Anekal o IND 140-141 G 4
Anéker o RN 198-199 B 5
Añelo o RA 78-79 E 5
Anemounon ∴ TR 128-129 E 4
Anepahan o RP 160-161 C 8
Anepmete o PNG 183 E 3
Anesbaraka ⊂ DZ 198-199 B 3
Anes-Barakka ∣ RN 198-199 C 3
Aneto, Pico de ▲ E 98-99 H 3
Anette Island ∩ USA 32-33 E 4
Anette Island Indian Reservation ⋏ USA 32-33 E 4
Aney o RN 198-199 F 3
Anfeg, Oued ~ DZ 190-191 E 9
Anfu o VRC 156-157 J 3
Anga, Bol'šaja ~ RUS 116-117 N 8
Angading o RI 162-163 G 6
Angajurjualuk Lake o CDN 24-25 g 5
Angalimp o PNG 183 C 3
Angamáli o IND 140-141 G 5
Angamarut o PNG 183 A 4
Angamma, Falaise d' ▲ TCH 198-199 H 4
Angamos, Isla ∩ RCH 80 C 4
Angamos, Punta ▲ RCH 76-77 B 2
Angangueo o MEX 52-53 D 2
Ang'ang Xi ∴ VRC 150-151 D 4
Angara ~ RUS 116-117 L 9
Angara o RUS 116-117 P 6
Angara ~ RUS 116-117 N 6
'Angara o SUD 206-207 G 3
Angaradébou o DY 204-205 E 3
Angarakan o RUS 118-119 G 8
Angarka o RUS 112-113 N 3
Angarka ~ RUS 112-113 N 3
Angarsk o RUS 116-117 L 9
Angarskij krjaž ▲ RUS 116-117 K 8
Angastaco o RA 76-77 D 3
Angaston o AUS 180-181 E 3
Angatuba o BR 72-73 F 7
Angavo ± RM 222-223 E 7
Angba o WAN 204-205 G 5
Angel, El o EC 64-65 D 1
Ángel, Salto ~ YV 60-61 K 5
Ángel de la Guarda, Isla ∩ MEX 50-51 C 3
Angeles o RP 160-161 D 5
Angeles, Los o RCH 78-79 C 4
Ängelholm o S 86-87 F 8
Angélica o RA 76-77 G 6
Angelim o BR 68-69 K 6
Angelina River ~ USA 44-45 K 4
Angelin Bjerg ▲ GRØ 26-27 n 7
Angellala Creek ~ AUS 178-179 J 4
Angelo River ~ AUS 176-177 D 1
Ängelsberg o ~ S 86-87 H 7
Angels Camp o USA 40-41 D 6
Angemuk, Gunung ▲ RI 166-167 K 5
Angerburg = Węgorzewo o · PL 92-93 Q 1
Angereb ~ ETH 200-201 H 6
Angereb Wenz ~ ETH 200-201 H 6
Ångermanälven ~ S 86-87 H 5
Ångermanland ± S 86-87 H 5
Angermünde o · D 92-93 N 2
Angers o F 90-91 G 8
Ängesån ~ S 86-87 L 3
Angetu o ETH 208-209 D 5
Anggoami o RI 164-165 G 5
Anggoro o RI 164-165 G 5
Angical o BR 68-69 K 4
Angijak Island ∩ CDN 36-37 T 2
Angikuni Lake o CDN 30-31 U 4
Angira o PK 134-135 M 4
Angïre o IR 134-135 F 2
Angisoq = Loransation o GRØ 28-29 S 7
Angkor Wat ··· KH 158-159 H 4
Ångk Sniion o K 158-159 H 4
Angle Inlet o CDN 34-35 J 6
Anglem, Mount ▲ NZ 182 A 7
Anglesea o AUS 180-181 H 5
Anglesey ∩ GB 90-91 G 5
Angleton o USA 44-45 K 5
Angmagssalik Fjord ≈ 28-29 W 4
Ango o ZRE 206-207 G 6
Angochagua o EC 64-65 C 1
Angoche o MOC 218-219 K 3
Angohrän o IR 134-135 G 5
Angol o RCH 78-79 C 4
Angola ■ ANG 216-217 C 5
Angola o USA 46-47 F 5
Angola Abyssal Plain = Namibia Abyssal Plain ≃ 6-7 K 11
Angola Basin ≃ 6-7 K 10
Angolin o IND 142-143 J 1
Angonia, Planalto de ▲ MOC 218-219 G 2
Angontsy, Tanjona ▲ RM 222-223 G 5
Angoon o USA 32-33 C 4
Angor o US 136-137 K 6

Angoram o PNG 183 C 3
An Gort = Gort o IRL 90-91 C 5
Angostura, Presa de la < MEX (CHI) 52-53 H 3
Angostura, Presa de la < MEX (SON) 50-51 E 2
Angostura Reservoir < USA 42-43 F 4
Angoulême ☆ · F 90-91 H 9
Angpawing Bum ▲ MYA 142-143 J 3
Angra dos Reis o · BR 72-73 H 7
Agramios, Pulau ∩ RI 166-167 H 3
Angren o US 136-137 M 4
Ang Thong Marine National Park ⊥ THA 158-159 E 6
Angu o ZRE 210-211 K 2
Anguilla □ GB 56 D 2
Anguilla Cays ∩ BS 54-55 F 3
Anguilla Island ∩ GB 56 D 2
Anguille, Cape ▲ CDN 38-39 P 5
Anguille Mountains ▲ CDN 38-39 P 5
Anğuman o AFG 136-137 M 7
Anguo o VRC 154-155 J 2
Angürän o IR 128-129 M 4
Anguran o IR 134-135 F 5
Angurugu ⋏ AUS 174-175 D 3
Anguilla o PE 64-65 E 2
Angusko Point ▲ CDN 30-31 X 5
Angwa ~ ZW 218-219 F 3
An Häi ~ VN 156-157 E 6
Anhanduí-Guaçu, Rio ~ BR 76-77 K 1
Anholt ∩ DK 86-87 E 8
Anhua o VRC 156-157 G 2
Anhui □ VRC 154-155 K 5
Ani · TR 128-129 K 2
Aniak o USA 20-21 L 6
Aniak River ~ USA 20-21 L 6
Aniakchak Crater · USA 22-23 R 4
Aniakchak National Monument and Preserve ⊥ USA 22-23 S 4
Aniak Bay ≈ 22-23 S 4
Aniassue o CI 202-203 J 6
Anibal Pinto, Lago o RCH 80 D 5
Anicuns o BR 72-73 F 4
Anié o RT (DPL) 202-203 L 6
Anié, Pic d' ▲ F 90-91 G 10
Anihovka o RUS 124-125 B 3
Anikino o RUS 118-119 K 9
Anil o BR 68-69 F 3
Anil, Igarapé do ~ BR 66-67 J 7
Animas o USA 44-45 C 4
Animas, Las o MN 52-53 L 4
Animas, Punta ▲ RCH 76-77 B 4
Animas, Quebrada de las ~ RCH 76-77 B 4
Animas Peak ▲ USA 44-45 C 4
Animas River ~ USA 44-45 D 1
Anina o RO 102-103 B 5
Aninuas Pass ≈ ZA 220-221 C 4
Anisij, mys ▲ RUS 110-111 W 1
Anita Garibaldi o BR 74-75 E 6
Aniva o RUS 122-123 K 5
Aniva, mys ▲ RUS 122-123 K 5
Aniva, zaliv ≈ RUS 122-123 K 5
Anivorano Avaratra o RM 222-223 F 4
Aniwa Island = Île Nina ∩ VAN 184 II b 4
Anijo o J 152-153 G 7
Anjafy, Lembalemba Ambonin ▲ RM 222-223 E 6
Anjär o IND 138-139 C 8
Anji o VRC 154-155 L 6
Anjohibe · RM 222-223 E 5
Anjombony ~ RM 222-223 F 5
Anjou ± F 90-91 G 8
Anjozorobe o RM 222-223 E 7
Anju o DVR 150-151 E 8
Anju o RUS 122-123 G 4
Anjuj, Bol'šoj ~ RUS 112-113 M 3
Anjuj, Malyj ~ RUS 112-113 O 3
Anjujsk o RUS 112-113 L 2
Anjujskij hrebet ▲ RUS 112-113 M 3
Anka o WAN 198-199 B 6
Ankaboa, Tanjona ▲ RM 222-223 C 8
Ankaimoro, Tombeaux · RM 222-223 F 7
Ankaizina ± RM 222-223 F 5
Ankalobe o RM 222-223 D 7
Ankang o VRC 154-155 F 5
Ankara ★ · TR 128-129 E 3
Ankaramy o RM 222-223 E 5
Ankaratra ▲ RM 222-223 E 7
Ankasa National Park ⊥ GH 202-203 J 7
Ankatafa o RM 222-223 F 4
Ankavanana ~ RM 222-223 F 6
Ankavandra o RM 222-223 D 7
Ankazoabo o RM 222-223 D 8
Ankazobe o RM 222-223 E 7
Ankazobe, Tampoketsan' ▲ RM 222-223 E 7
Ankazomiriotra o RM 222-223 E 7
Ankazondandy o RM 222-223 E 7
Ankeny o USA 42-43 L 5
Ankerika o RM 222-223 E 6
An Khê o VN 158-159 K 4
Ankihalli o IND 140-141 F 4
Ankilizato o RM 222-223 D 8
Ankirihitra o RM 222-223 E 6
Anklam o D 92-93 M 2
Ankleshwar o IND 138-139 D 9
Ankli o IND 140-141 F 2
Ankober o ETH 208-209 D 4
Ankobra ~ GH 202-203 J 7
Ankola o IND 140-141 F 3
Ankotrofotsy o RM 222-223 D 7
Ankpa o WAN 204-205 G 5
An Láithreach = Laragh o · IRL 90-91 D 5
Anliu o VRC 156-157 J 5
Anlóns, Rio o GB 38-39 M 4
Anlong o VRC 156-157 D 4
An Longfort = Longford ☆ · IRL 90-91 D 5
Antigo o USA 46-47 D 3

Anlu o VRC 154-155 H 6
An Muileann-gCearr = Mullingar · IRL 90-91 D 5
Anmyön Do o ROK 150-151 F 9
Ann, Cape ▲ USA 46-47 N 4
Anna o RUS 102-103 M 2
Anna, Lake o USA 46-47 D 7
Anna, Lake o USA 46-47 K 6
Annaba o · DZ 190-191 F 2
Annaberg o PNG 183 C 3
Anna Bistrup, Kap ▲ GRØ 26-27 q 4
an-Nabk o SYR 128-129 G 5
an-Naḥl, Qarärat o LAR 192-193 J 5
An Námús, Wäw o LAR 192-193 G 5
Anna Plains o AUS 172-173 E 5
Annapolis o USA (MO) 46-47 C 7
Annapolis ☆ USA (MD) 46-47 K 6
Annapolis Royal o CDN 38-39 N 6
Annapurna Himal ▲ NEP 144-145 D 6
Annapurna I ▲ NEP 144-145 D 6
Annapurna II ▲ NEP 144-145 E 6
Annapurna Sanctuary ⊥ · NEP 144-145 D 6
Ann Arbor o USA 46-47 G 5
Anna Regina o GUY 62-63 E 2
An Nás = Naas ☆ IRL 90-91 D 5
Annaville o USA 38-39 H 5
Anne, Mount ▲ AUS 180-181 J 7
Annean, Lake o AUS 176-177 E 3
Annecy o F 90-91 L 9
Annenkov Island ∩ GB 78-79 O 7
Annigeri o IND 140-141 F 3
an-Nil ~ ET 194-195 E 3
Anning o VRC 156-157 C 4
Anningie o AUS 178-179 B 1
Anniston o USA 48-49 F 3
Annitowa o AUS 178-179 D 1
Annofliyah o LAR 192-193 G 2
Annonay o F 90-91 K 9
Annotto Bay o JA 54-55 G 5
Annual o MA 188-189 G 3
an-Nugaym, Bi'r < SUD 200-201 G 3
An Nuqät al Khams o LAR 192-193 D 1
Anola o CDN 34-35 H 6
An Ómaigh = Omagh ☆ · GB 90-91 D 4
Año Nuevo, Seno ≈ SO 80 F 7
Año Nuevo Point ▲ USA 40-41 C 7
Anony, Farihy o RM 222-223 E 10
Anori o BR 66-67 G 4
Anorotong o BR 28-29 T 6
Anorontany, Tanjona ▲ RM 222-223 F 4
Anosibe An'ala o RM 222-223 F 7
Anosy ± RM 222-223 E 10
Anpo Gang ~ VRC 156-157 F 6
Anqing o VRC 154-155 K 6
Anqiu o VRC 154-155 L 3
Anquincila o RA 76-77 D 5
Anronofasika o RM 222-223 E 6
Anranomavo o RM 222-223 D 6
Anriandampy o RM 222-223 D 9
Ansai o VRC 154-155 F 3
Ansan o RI 166-167 H 2
Ansbach o · D 92-93 L 4
Anse-à-Galets o RH 54-55 J 5
Anse-à-Veau o RH 54-55 J 5
Ânsebe Shet' ~ ER 200-201 J 4
Anselmo o USA 42-43 H 5
Anserma o CO 60-61 D 5
Anse Rouge o RH 54-55 J 5
Anshan o VRC 150-151 D 7
Anshun o VRC 156-157 D 3
Ansilta, Cerro de ▲ RA 76-77 C 6
Ansilta, Cordillera de ▲ RA 76-77 C 6
Ansina o ROU 76-77 K 6
Ansley o USA 42-43 H 5
Anson o USA 44-45 H 3
Anson Bay ≈ 172-173 J 2
Ansongo o RMM 202-203 L 2
Answer Downs o AUS 178-179 F 4
Anta o PE 64-65 F 8
Anta, Cachoeira da ~ BR 66-67 H 6
Antabamba o PE 64-65 F 9
Antakya = Hatay ☆ TR 128-129 G 4
Antalaha o RM 222-223 G 5
Antalya ☆ TR 128-129 D 4
Antalya Körfezi ≈ 128-129 D 4
Antananarivo ★ RM 222-223 F 6
Antananarivo □ RM (ATN) 222-223 E 7
Antandrokomby o RM 222-223 F 7
Antanifotsy o RM 222-223 E 7
Antanimora Atsimo o RM 222-223 D 10
Antanjombolamena o RM 222-223 E 7
An tAonach = Nenagh o · IRL 90-91 C 5
Antar, Djebel ▲ DZ 188-189 L 4
Antarctica ⊥ ARK 16 F 28
Antarctic Bugt ≈ 26-27 s 3
Antarctic Circle ARK 16 V 6
Antarctic Peninsula ⊔ ARK 16 G 30
Antarctic Sound ≈ 16 G 31
Antares, Gunung ▲ RI 166-167 L 4
Antas o BR 68-69 J 7
Antécume Pata o F 62-63 G 4
Antelope o CDN 32-33 Q 6
Antelope Island ∩ USA 40-41 H 5
Antelope Mine o ZW 218-219 E 5
Antenor Navarro o BR 68-69 J 5
Antequera o E 98-99 E 6
Antequera o PY 76-77 J 3
Antetezampandrana o RM 222-223 F 6
An Thới, Quân Đảo ∩ VN 158-159 H 6
Anthony o USA (KS) 44-45 H 1
Anthony o USA (NM) 44-45 D 3
Anthony Island ··· CDN 32-33 D 4
Anthony Lagoon o AUS 174-175 C 5
Anthropological Museum ·· RI 166-167 L 3
Anti Atlas ▲ MA 188-189 G 6
Anticosti, Île d' ∩ CDN 38-39 M 4
Antiga Lagoa da Rabeca o BR 70-71 H 4
Antigo o BR 72-73 J 7
Antigo o USA 46-47 D 3

Antigonish o CDN 38-39 N 6
Antigua o · MEX 52-53 F 2
Antigua, Salina la o RA 76-77 E 5
Antigua and Barbuda ■ AG 56 E 3
Antigua Guatemala ☆ · · GCA 52-53 J 4
Antiguo Morelos o MEX 50-51 K 6
Antiguo Cauce del Río Bermejo ~ RA 76-77 F 2
Antilla o C 54-55 H 4
Antimari, Rio ~ BR 66-67 D 6
An Ti-m-Missaou ∴ DZ 196-197 M 4
Antimonan o RP 160-161 D 6
Antimony o USA 40-41 J 6
Antinaëtajaha ~ RUS 108-109 R 7
Antingola o RI 164-165 H 3
Antioquia o CO 60-61 D 4
Antipajuta o RUS 108-109 R 7
Antipodes Islands ∩ NZ 13 J 7
Antisana, Volcán ▲ EC 64-65 C 2
Ántissa o GR 100-101 K 5
An tlúr = Newry o · GB 90-91 D 4
Antiwolfifiyah o LAR 192-193 J 2
Antlat o LAR 192-193 J 2
Antlers o USA 44-45 K 2
Antofagasta o RA 76-77 B 3
Antofagasta de la Sierra o RA 76-77 D 4
Antofalla, Salar de o RA 76-77 D 4
Antofalla, Volcán ▲ RA 76-77 D 3
Antoinette Bay ≈ 26-27 L 3
Anton o USA (CO) 42-43 F 4
Anton o USA (TX) 44-45 F 2
Antongil, Helodrano ≈ RM 222-223 F 5
Antongomena-Bevary o RM 222-223 E 5
Antonibe o RM 222-223 E 5
Antonina o BR (CEA) 68-69 J 5
Antonina o BR (PAR) 74-75 F 5
Apača o RUS 122-123 R 2
Antônio Dias o BR 72-73 J 5
Antônio Gonçalves o BR 68-69 H 7
Antônio João o BR 76-77 K 2
Antônio Martins o BR 68-69 K 5
Antônio Prado o BR 74-75 E 7
Antonio Varas, Península ∩ RCH 80 D 5
Antonito o USA 44-45 D 1
Antón Lizardo o MEX 52-53 F 2
Antracyt o UA 102-103 L 3
Antrim o GB 90-91 D 4
Antrim Mountains ▲ GB 90-91 D 4
Antsahabe o RM 222-223 F 5
Antsalova o RM 222-223 D 7
Antsampano o RM 222-223 F 4
Antsakabary o RM 222-223 F 5
Antsakanalabe o RM 222-223 F 5
Antsalova o RM 222-223 D 7
Antsambalahy o RM 222-223 F 5
Antsaravibe o RM 222-223 F 5
Antsatramidola o RM 222-223 F 5
Antsiafabositra o RM 222-223 E 6
Antsianitia o RM 222-223 E 6
Antsirabato o RM 222-223 G 5
Antsirabe o RM 222-223 E 7
Antsirabe Afovoany o RM 222-223 F 4
Antsirabe Avaratra o RM 222-223 F 4
Antsiranana o RM 222-223 F 4
Antsiranana □ RM 222-223 F 4
Antsla o EST 94-95 K 3
Antsoha o RM 222-223 D 7
Antsohihy o RM 222-223 E 5
Antsohimbondrona o RM 222-223 F 4
Antsondrodava o RM 222-223 D 7
Antu o VRC 150-151 G 6
Antuco o RCH 78-79 D 4
Antuco, Volcán ▲ RCH 78-79 D 4
Antufaš ∩ Y 132-133 C 6
Antwerpen ☆ · B 92-93 H 3
Antykan o RUS 120-121 F 6
An Xian o VRC 156-157 J 3
Anxi o VRC (JXI) 156-157 J 2
Anxious Bay ≈ 180-181 C 2
Anyang o ROK 150-151 F 9
Anyang o VRC 154-155 J 3
A'nyêmaqên Shan ▲ VRC 144-145 M 3
Anyer-Kidul o RI 168 A 3
Aniynam o GH 202-203 K 6
Anyirawase o GH 202-203 K 6
Anyk'ščiai ☆ · LT 94-95 J 4
Anyuan o VRC 154-155 D 6
Anyue o VRC 154-155 D 6
Anza-Borrego Desert State Park ⊥ USA 40-41 F 9
Anza o CDN 32-33 P 3
Anze o VRC 154-155 H 3
Anzali, Bandar-e o IR 128-129 N 4
Anže o VRC 154-155 H 3
Anžero-Sudžensk o RUS 114-115 T 6
Anzerskij, ostrov ∩ RUS 88-89 O 4
Anzhero Sudzhensk = Anžero-Sudžensk o RUS 114-115 T 6
Anzi o ZRE 210-211 J 4
Ánzio o I 100-101 D 4
Anzoategui o CO 60-61 D 5
Anzob, pereval ∴ TJ 136-137 L 5
Anžu, ostrova ∩ RUS 110-111 U 1
Aoba, Île o VAN 184 II b 3
Aoba/Maewo ∩ VAN 184 II b 2
Ao Ban Don ≈ 158-159 E 6

Aodanga ~ TCH 198-199 H 4
Aohan Qi o VRC 148-149 O 6
Aoiz ☆ E 98-99 G 3
Aoke = Auki ☆ SOL 184 I e 3
Aola = Tenaghau o SOL 184 I e 3
Aomen = Macao o P 156-157 H 5
Aomori ☆ J 152-153 J 4
Ao Phangnga National Park ⊥ THA 158-159 E 6
Aore ∩ VAN 184 II a 2
Aora o RI 166-167 D 3
Ao Sawi ≈ 158-159 E 6
Aosta = Aoste ☆ I 100-101 A 2
Aosta, Valle d' = Vallé d'Aoste □ I 100-101 A 2
Aoste, Vallée d' = Valle d'Aosta □ I 100-101 A 2
Ao Trat ≈ 158-159 G 4
Aouara o F 62-63 H 3
Aoudaghost ∴ · RIM 196-197 C 6
Aouderas o RN 198-199 B 5
Aoufirst ~ MA 196-197 C 2
Aouçoundou, Lac o RMM 202-203 J 2
Aouhinet bel Egra < DZ 188-189 H 7
Aouïnat Sarrag < RIM 196-197 D 5
Aouk, Bahr ~ TCH 206-207 D 4
Aoukalé ~ TCH 206-207 E 4
Aouk-Aoukale, Réserve de faune de l' ⊥ RCA 206-207 E 4
Aoukâr ± RMM 196-197 E 5
Aoukâr ∴ RMM 196-197 H 3
Aoulef o DZ 196-197 H 3
Aoulime, Ibel ▲ MA 188-189 G 5
Aoulou o MA 188-189 G 5
Aourir n' Ouassel ▲ MA 188-189 H 5
Aourou o RMM 202-203 E 2
Aousard o MA 196-197 C 3
Aozi o TCH 198-199 J 2
Aozou o TCH 198-199 H 2
Apača o RUS 122-123 R 2
Apache o USA 44-45 H 2
Apache Creek o USA 44-45 C 3
Apache Junction o USA 40-41 J 9
Apacheta Cruz Grande ▲ BOL 76-77 E 1
Apaikwa o GUY 62-63 E 2
Apakapur ~ RUS 114-115 O 3
Apalachee Bay ≈ 48-49 F 5
Apalachicola o USA 48-49 F 5
Apalachicola River ~ USA 48-49 F 4
Apan o MEX 52-53 E 2
Apapegino o RUS 112-113 Q 2
Apaporis, Rio ~ CO 66-67 B 3
Aq Kand o IR 128-129 N 4
Aq Qal'e o IR 134-135 G 2
Aqqan o VRC 144-145 E 2
Aparados da Serra o BR 72-73 E 8
Aparados da Serra, Parque Nacional ⊥ · BR 74-75 E 7
Aparecida de Goiânia o BR 72-73 E 4
Aparecida do Tabuado o BR 72-73 E 5
Aparri o RP 160-161 D 5
Apastovo o RUS 96-97 F 6
Apatana o RI 168 E 4
Apatity o RUS 88-89 M 3
Apatou o F 62-63 G 3
Apatzingán de la Constitución o MEX 52-53 C 2
Apauwar o RI 166-167 K 3
Apauwar ~ RI 166-167 K 3
Apawanza o ZRE 212-213 B 3
Apaxtla de Castrejón o MEX 52-53 E 2
Ape o LV 94-95 K 3
Apedià, Rio ~ BR 70-71 G 3
Apeldoorn o · NL 92-93 H 2
Apeleg, Arroyo ~ RA 80 E 2
Apennines = Appennini ▲ · I 100-101 D 3
Apere, Rio ~ BOL 70-71 F 4
Apesokubi o GH 202-203 L 6
Apetina = Puleowine o SME 62-63 G 4
Apeú, Ilha ∩ BR 68-69 E 2
Apex Mountain ▲ CDN 20-21 V 5
Aphrodisias ·· TR 128-129 C 4
Api ▲ NEP 144-145 C 5
Api o ZRE 210-211 K 2
Api, Gunung ▲ RI 168 D 7
Apia o CO 60-61 D 5
Ãpia ★ WS 184 V b 1
Apiacás o BR 66-67 J 7
Apiaí o BR 74-75 F 5
Apinaco, Cachoeira ~ BR 70-71 K 2
Apiñacocha, Lago o PE 64-65 F 9
Apinajes o BR 68-69 D 8
Apio o SOL 184 I e 3
Apishapa River ~ USA 42-43 F 7
Apitpac o MEX 52-53 H 3
Aplahoué o DY 202-203 L 6
Aplao o PE 70-71 A 5
Apo, Mount ▲ RP 160-161 F 9
Apodaca o MEX 50-51 J 5
Apodi o BR 68-69 K 4
Apodi, Chapada do ▲ BR 68-69 J 4
Apodi, Rio ~ BR 68-69 J 4
Apo East Pass ≈ 160-161 D 6
Apoko o RCB 210-211 E 4
Apolima Strait ≈ 184 V a 1
Apolinario Saravia o RA 76-77 F 3
Apollo Bay o AUS 180-181 H 5
Apollonia = Süsah o · LAR 192-193 J 1
Apolo o BOL 70-71 C 4
Apolu o WAN 204-205 F 4
Apopa o ES 52-53 K 5
Apopka o USA 48-49 H 5
Apoquitaua, Rio ~ BR 66-67 J 5
Aporá o BR 68-69 J 7
Aporé, Rio ~ BR 72-73 E 4
Apo Reef National Park ⊥ RP 160-161 D 6
Aporema o BR 62-63 J 5
Aporoma o BR 62-63 J 5

Appat ∩ GRØ 26-27 Z 8
Appé Grande, Ilha ∩ RA 76-77 J 4
Appennino Abruzzese ▲ I 100-101 D 3
Appleton o JA 54-55 G 5
Appleton o USA (MN) 42-43 J 3
Appleton o USA (WI) 46-47 D 3
Appleton City o USA 42-43 L 6
Appomattox o USA 46-47 J 7
Appomattox Court House National Historic Park · USA 46-47 J 7
Approuague ~ F 62-63 H 4
Apraksin Bor o RUS 94-95 M 2
Aprefsk o RUS 118-119 G 6
Apricena o I 100-101 E 4
Aprilia o I 100-101 D 4
April River ~ PNG 183 C 3
Aprompronou o CI 202-203 J 6
Apšeronsk o RUS 126-127 C 5
Apšeronskij poluostrov ∩ AZ 128-129 O 3
Apsley o CDN 38-39 E 6
Apsley River ~ AUS 178-179 L 6
Apt o F 90-91 K 10
Apu o RI 166-167 D 3
Apucarana o BR 72-73 E 7
Apuf o BR (AMA) 66-67 E 3
Apuí o BR (AMA) 66-67 H 6
Apuka o RUS 112-113 Q 6
Apukskij hrebet ▲ RUS 112-113 Q 6
Apura o SME 62-63 F 3
Apurahuan o RP 160-161 C 8
Apure □ YV 60-61 H 4
Apure, Río ~ YV 60-61 J 4
Apurímac □ PE 64-65 F 8
Apurímac, Río ~ PE 64-65 F 8
Apurina, Área Indígena ⋏ BR 66-67 D 7
Apurina Peneri, Área Indígena ⋏ BR 66-67 D 7
Apurito o YV 60-61 H 4
Apurlec ∴ PE 64-65 C 5
Aputi o RI 166-167 D 3
Aqaba = Al 'Aqabah ☆ JOR 130-131 D 3
'Aqaba, Gulf of = 'Aqaba, Ḥaliǧ al- ≈ ET 130-131 D 3
'Aqaba, Gulf von = 'Aqaba, Ḥaliǧ al- ≈ ET 130-131 D 3
'Aqaba, Ḥaliǧ al- ≈ ET 130-131 D 3
Âqā Bābā o IR 128-129 N 4
Âçce o AFG 136-137 K 6
'Aqdā o IR 134-135 F 3
'Aqiq, al- o KSA 132-133 B 3
'Aqiq, Wädi al- ~ KSA 130-131 G 5
Aqissersarp o GRØ 28-29 R 3
Aqitag ▲ VRC 146-147 K 5
Aq Kand o IR 128-129 N 4
Aq Qal'e o IR 134-135 G 2
'Aqra o IRQ 128-129 K 4
Âq Sü o IR 134-135 G 2
Aqtaū = Aktau ☆ KA 126-127 J 6
Aqtöbe = Aktöbe ☆ KA 126-127 M 2
'Agra o IRQ 128-129 K 4
Aquacanta, Raudal ~ YV 60-61 K 4
Aquidabán, Rio ~ PY 76-77 J 2
Aquidauana, Rio ~ BR 70-71 K 7
Aquijes, Los o PE 64-65 E 9
Aquila o MEX 52-53 C 2
Aquin o RH 54-55 J 5
Aquiqui, Ilhas do ~ BR 62-63 J 6
Aquitaine □ F 90-91 G 10
Ara o IND 144-145 F 3
'Arab ~ SUD 200-201 G 4
Arab o USA 48-49 E 2
'Arab, 'Ain al- o SYR 128-129 H 4
'Araba, Wädi l- ~ ET 194-195 F 3
'Arabābād o IR 134-135 G 2
Araban ☆ TR 128-129 G 4
Arabati o ETH 208-209 D 3
Arabats'ka zatoka ≈ 102-103 J 3
Arabela o USA 44-45 E 3
Arabian Basin ≃ 12 E 3
Arabian Oryx Sanctuary ⊥ · · OM 132-133 K 4
Arabian Peninsula ☆ KSA 10-11 C 6
Arabian Sea ≈ 12 E 3
Arabiya, al- o KSA 134-135 D 5
Araboporó o YV 62-63 D 3
Arabos, Los o C 54-55 E 3
Arabou < RMM 196-197 L 5
Araç o TR 128-129 E 2
Araca o BOL 70-71 D 5
Aracá, Área Indígena ⋏ BR 62-63 D 4
Araçá, Rio ~ BR 62-63 D 4
Aracaí, Cachoeira do ~ BR 68-69 D 3
Aracaju ☆ · BR 68-69 K 7
Aracati o BR 68-69 K 4
Aracatu o BR 72-73 K 3
Araçatuba o BR (BAH) 70-71 K 3
Araçatuba o BR (PAU) 72-73 E 6
Aracebí o RP 160-161 F 6
Aracena o E 98-99 D 6
Araci o BR 68-69 J 7
Araçu, Rio ~ BR 66-67 G 5
Araçuaí o BR 72-73 J 4
Araçuaí, Rio ~ BR 72-73 J 4
Arad o RO 102-103 B 5
Arad, Tel ··· IL 130-131 D 2
Árada o TCH 198-199 K 5
'Aráda o UAE 132-133 H 4
Aradan o IR 134-135 F 2
Aradu o RUS 116-117 F 9
Arafura Sea ≈ 166-167 G 8
Arag, gora ▲ AR 128-129 L 3
Arage o WAN 204-205 H 4
Araghene, Anou- o RN 198-199 C 4
Aragôiânia o BR 72-73 F 4
Aragón □ E 98-99 G 4
Aragón, Río ~ E 98-99 G 3
Araguacema o BR 68-69 D 6
Araguaçu o BR 72-73 F 2

Araguaçu o BR 68-69 D 6
Aragua de Barcelona o YV 60-61 J 3
Aragua de Maturín o YV 60-61 K 3
Araguaia, Parque Indígena ⋏ BR 68-69 C 7
Araguaia, Parque Nacional do ⊥ BR 68-69 C 7
Araguaia, Rio ~ BR 68-69 D 5
Araguaiana o BR 72-73 E 3
Araguaína o BR 68-69 D 5
Araguanã o BR 68-69 D 5
Araguari o BR 72-73 F 5
Araguari, Rio ~ BR 62-63 J 5
Araguari, Rio ~ BR 72-73 F 5
Araguatins o BR 68-69 D 4
Arahal o E 98-99 E 6
Arai o BR 72-73 G 2
Arai o J 152-153 J 5
Araias do Araguaia, Rio das ~ BR 68-69 C 6
Arail Khan ~ BD 142-143 G 4
Araioses o BR 68-69 H 3
Araju o BR 66-67 G 4
Arak o DZ 190-191 D 8
Aräk ★ · IR 134-135 C 1
Arakaka o GUY 62-63 D 2
Arakamčečen, ostrov ∩ RUS 112-113 Y 4
Arakan Yoma = Ragaing Yôma ▲ MYA 142-143 H 6
Arakawa o J 152-153 H 5
Arakawa-gawa ~ J 152-153 H 5
Araklı ☆ TR 128-129 J 2
Arak's = AR 128-129 L 2
Aral ~ KA 126-127 O 4
Aral o KS 146-147 B 5
Aralık ☆ TR 128-129 L 3
Aral karakümy ⊥ KA 126-127 P 4
Aralköl o KA 124-125 C 3
Aralküm o KA 126-127 N 4
Aral Moreira o BR 76-77 K 2
Aral Sea ≈ 126-127 N 5
Arafsk ☆ KA 126-127 O 4
Aralsor, köl o KA (ZPK) 96-97 F 9
Aralsor, köl o KA (ZPK) 96-97 H 9
Aralsultat o KA 126-127 O 4
Araltöbe o KA 96-97 H 8
Aramac o AUS 178-179 H 2
Aramaca, Ilha ∩ BR 66-67 C 5
Arame o BR 68-69 E 4
Aramia River ~ PNG 183 B 4
Aramil o RUS 96-97 M 5
Äran o IR 134-135 D 1
Arancay o PE 64-65 D 6
Aranda de Duero o E 98-99 F 4
Arandai o RI 166-167 H 4
Arandas o MEX 52-53 C 1
Arandis o NAM 216-217 C 11
Arani o BOL 70-71 E 5
Árani o IND 140-141 H 4
Aran Islands ∩ IRL 90-91 C 5
Aranjuez o · E 98-99 F 4
Aranos o NAM 220-221 D 2
Aransas Pass o USA 44-45 J 6
Arantangi o IND 140-141 H 5
Arantes, Ribeiro ~ BR 72-73 E 5
Aranyaprathet o THA 158-159 G 4
Araouane o RMM 196-197 J 5
Aráoz o RA 76-77 E 4
Arapa o PE 70-71 B 4
Arapa, Lago de o PE 70-71 B 4
Arapahoe o USA 42-43 H 5
Arapari o BR (AMA) 66-67 D 4
Arapari o BR (P) 68-69 D 4
Arapey Grande, Rio ~ ROU 76-77 J 6
Arapicos o EC 64-65 C 6
Arapiraca o BR 68-69 K 6
Arapiri, Ilha do ~ BR 66-67 K 4
Arapiuns, Rio ~ BR 66-67 K 4
Arapixó o BR 66-67 C 7
Araporã o BR 72-73 E 5
Arapunya o AUS 178-179 C 2
Araputanga o BR 70-71 H 4
Arara, Área Indígena ⋏ BR 66-67 K 5
Arara, Paraná ~ BR 68-69 B 4
Araraçuara o CO 64-65 F 2
Arara Igarapé Humaitá, Área Indígena ⋏ BR 64-65 F 6
Araranguá o BR 74-75 F 7
Ararapira o BR 74-75 F 6
Araraquara o BR 72-73 F 6
Araras o BR (P) 66-67 K 6
Araras o BR (PAU) 72-73 G 7
Araras, Cachoeira ~ BR 66-67 G 5
Araras, Ilha das ∩ BR 66-67 C 6
Araras, Serra das ▲ BR 70-71 J 4
Ararat ▲ AR 128-129 L 3
Ararat o AUS 180-181 G 4
Araraú o BR 68-69 H 3
Ararenda o BR 68-69 H 4
Arari o BR 68-69 H 3
Araria o IND 144-145 G 3
Araribóia, Área Indígena ⋏ BR 68-69 E 4
Araripe o BR 68-69 H 5
Araripina o BR 68-69 H 5
Araruama o BR 72-73 J 7
Araruama, Lagoa de ≈ BR 72-73 J 7
Aras, Rüd-e ~ IR 128-129 M 3
Arasalu o IND 140-141 F 4
Aras Nehri ~ TR 128-129 K 2
Aras Nehri ~ TR 128-129 J 3
Aratane · RIM 196-197 F 5
Ara Terra o ETH 208-209 E 5
Arati o BR 68-69 D 7
Araticu, Rio ~ BR 68-69 D 3
Araua, Rio ~ BR 66-67 E 6
Arauá, Rio ~ BR 66-67 G 5
Arauca ☆ CO 60-61 G 4

Arauca, Río ○ **YV** 60-61 H 4
Araucária ○ **BR** 74-75 F 5
Arauco ○ **RCH** 78-79 C 4
Arauco, Golfo de ≈ 78-79 C 4
Araure ○ **YV** 60-61 G 3
'Arava, ha ∴ **IL** 130-131 D 2
Arávalli Range ▲ **IND** 138-139 D 7
Aravan ○ **KS** 136-137 N 4
Aravete ○ **EST** 94-95 J 2
Arawa ☆ **PNG** 184 I b 2
Arawale National Reserve ⊥ **EAK** 212-213 H 4
Arawe Islands ∩ **PNG** 183 E 4
Araweté Igarapé Ipixuna, Área Indígena ✕ **BR** 68-69 B 4
Araxá ○ **BR** 72-73 G 5
Araya, Península de ∪ **YV** 60-61 J 2
Arayé, Wâdi ∼ **TCH** 192-193 G 6
Araz ∼ **AZ** 128-129 N 3
Arazraz, Oued ∼ **DZ** 190-191 E 9
Arbadin ☆ **SP** 212-213 J 3
Arbakwe ○ **WAN** 198-199 B 6
Arba Minch ○ **ETH** 208-209 C 6
'Arbat ∴ **IRQ** 128-129 L 5
Árbatax ○ **I** 100-101 B 5
Arbat Dâg ▲ **IR** 128-129 M 4
Arbau ○ **RI** 166-167 F 4
Arbi ∼ **RUS** 118-119 N 9
Arbîl ▣ **IRQ** 128-129 K 4
Arbîl ☆ **IRQ** (ARB) 128-129 L 4
Arboga ○ **S** 86-87 G 7
Arbolé ○ **BF** 202-203 J 3
Arboledas ○ **CO** 60-61 E 4
Arboledas ○ **RA** 78-79 J 4
Arboletes ○ **CO** 60-61 C 3
Arbor ○ **ZA** 220-221 J 3
Arborg ○ **CDN** 34-35 H 5
Arboutchatak ○ **TCH** 198-199 H 6
Arbre du Ténéré ∗ **RN** 198-199 G 4
Arbroath ○ **GB** 90-91 F 3
Arbutla ∼ **RUS** 120-121 Q 3
Arcabuco ○ **CO** 60-61 E 5
Arcachon ○ **F** 90-91 G 9
Arcadia ○ **USA** (FL) 48-49 H 6
Arcadia ○ **USA** (LA) 44-45 L 3
Arcahaie ○ **RH** 54-55 J 5
Arcaly ∼ **KA** 124-125 F 2
Arcángelo, Monte ▲ **I** 100-101 E 4
Arcas, Quebradas de ∼ **RCH** 76-77 C 1
Arcata ○ **USA** 40-41 B 5
Arcelia ○ **MEX** 52-53 D 2
Arc-et-Senans ○••• **F** 90-91 K 8
Archeï, Guelta d' ∗ **TCH** 198-199 K 4
Archer Bay ≈ 174-175 D 3
Archer Bend National Park ⊥ **AUS** 174-175 D 3
Archer Fiord ≈ 26-27 Q 3
Archer's Post ○ **EAK** 212-213 H 3
Archerwill ○ **CDN** 34-35 E 4
Arches National Park ⊥ **USA** 42-43 C 6
Archipelago of the Recherche ∩ **AUS** 176-177 D 7
Archipiélago de las Guaitecas, Parque Nacional ⊥ **RCH** 80 C 2
Archipiélago los Roques, Parque Nacional ⊥••• **YV** 60-61 H 2
Arckaringa ○ **AUS** 178-179 C 4
Arckaringa Creek ∼ **AUS** 178-179 C 4
Arčman ○ **TM** 136-137 E 5
Arco ○ **USA** 40-41 H 4
Arco, El ○ **MEX** 50-51 C 3
Arco, Paso del ▲ **RA** 78-79 D 5
Arcos ○ **BR** 72-73 H 6
Arcos de la Frontera ○ **E** 98-99 E 6
Arcoverde ○ **BR** 68-69 K 6
Arctic Bay ○ **CDN** 24-25 d 4
Arctic Circle 16 C 4
Arctic Circle Hot Springs • **USA** 20-21 S 4
Arctic Harbour ≈ 28-29 G 2
Arctic Institute Range ▲ **ARK** 16 F 16
Arctic Ocean ≈ 16 B 33
Arctic Red River ∼ **CDN** 20-21 Z 4
Arcturus ○ **ZW** 218-219 F 3
Arcyz ☆ **UA** 102-103 F 5
Ardabil ○• **IR** 128-129 N 3
Ardahan ○ **TR** 128-129 K 2
Ardakān ○ **IR** 134-135 G 2
Ardakan ○ **IR** 134-135 D 3
Ardal ○ **IR** 134-135 D 3
Ardanuç ○ **TR** 128-129 K 2
Ardatov ○ **RUS** 94-95 S 4
Ardavidu ○ **IND** 140-141 H 3
Ardébé, Ati ○ **TCH** 198-199 H 6
Ard = Baile Átha Fhirdhia ○ **IRL** 90-91 D 5
Ardémi ○ **TCH** 198-199 L 5
Arden, Mount ▲ **AUS** 180-181 D 2
Ardencaple Fjord ≈ 26-27 p 6
Ardennes ▲ 92-93 H 4
Ardegen ○ **TR** 128-129 J 2
Ardestán ○ **IR** 134-135 E 2
Ardila, Ribeira de ∼ **P** 98-99 D 5
Ardila, Río ∼ **E** 98-99 D 5
Ardiles ○ **RA** 76-77 E 4
Ardilla, Cerro La ▲ **MEX** 50-51 H 6
Ardit ○ **OM** 132-133 H 5
Ardlethan ○ **AUS** 180-181 J 3
Ard Mhacha = Armagh ☆ • **GB** 90-91 D 4
Ardmore ○ **AUS** 178-179 E 1
Ardmore ○ **USA** (OK) 44-45 J 2
Ardmore ○ **USA** (SD) 42-43 F 4
Ardon ○ **RUS** 126-127 F 6
Ardon ∼ **RUS** 126-127 F 6
Ardrossan ○ **AUS** 180-181 D 3
Áre ○ **S** 86-87 F 5
Arebi ○ **ZRE** 212-213 B 2
Areco, Río ∼ **RA** 78-79 J 4
Aredo ○ **RI** 166-167 G 3
Aregičinski, mys ▲ **RUS** 120-121 Q 3
Areia, Cachoeira ∼ **BR** 68-69 D 7
Areia, Ribeira da ∼ **BR** 72-73 H 3
Areia Branca ○ **BR** 68-69 K 4
Areias, Rio ∼ **BR** 68-69 D 7

Areka ○ **ETH** 208-209 C 5
Arena, Isla ∼ **MEX** 50-51 C 4
Arena, La ○ **RCH** 78-79 C 4
Arena, Point ▲ **USA** 40-41 C 6
Arenal, Volcán ▲ **CR** 52-53 B 6
Arenales ○ **RCH** 76-77 D 2
Arenales, Cerro ▲ **RCH** 80 D 3
Arena Point ▲ **RP** 160-161 E 6
Arenápolis ○ **BR** 70-71 J 4
Arenas ○ **PA** 52-53 D 8
Arenas, Punta ▲ **RCH** 78-79 B 1
Arenas, Punta de ▲ **RA** 80 F 6
Arendal ○ **N** 86-87 D 7
Arenillas ○ **EC** 64-65 B 3
Arenosa ○ **PA** 52-53 E 7
Areópoli ○ **GR** 100-101 J 6
Areõs, Área Indígena ✕ **BR** 72-73 D 3
Arequipa • **PE** 70-71 B 5
Arêro ○ **ETH** 208-209 D 6
Arerungua, Arroyo ∼ **ROU** 76-77 J 6
Arestruz, Pampa del ⊥ **RCH** 76-77 C 1
Arévalo ○ **E** 98-99 E 4
Áreza ○ **ER** 200-201 J 5
Arezzo ○ **I** 100-101 C 3
Arfersiorfik ≈ 28-29 O 2
'Arga ○ **KSA** 130-131 J 5
Argada ○ **RUS** 118-119 E 8
Argadargada ○ **AUS** 178-179 D 1
Argahtah ○ **RUS** 110-111 d 5
Argajas ○ **RUS** 96-97 M 6
Arga-Jurjah ∼ **RUS** 110-111 S 5
Arga Jurjah ∼ **RUS** 110-111 N 2
Argalant ○ **MAU** 148-149 G 4
Argalastí ○ **GR** 100-101 J 5
Arga-Muora-Sise, ostrov ∩ **RUS** 110-111 P 3
Argan ○ **VRC** 146-147 J 5
Arganda ○ **E** 98-99 F 4
Argandáb, Daryā-ye ∼ **AFG** 134-135 M 2
Argao ○ **RP** 160-161 E 8
Argas ○ **RUS** 118-119 H 4
Arga Sala ∼ **RUS** 110-111 H 5
Arga-Sala ∼ **RUS** 116-117 M 2
Arga-Tjung ∼ **RUS** 110-111 K 6
Argazi vodohranilišče < **RUS** 96-97 M 6
Argedeb ○ **ETH** 208-209 E 5
Argelia ○ **CO** 60-61 C 6
Argent, Côte d' ∪ **F** 90-91 G 10
Argenta ○ **I** 100-101 C 2
Argentan ○ **F** 90-91 H 7
Argentia ○ **CDN** 38-39 I S 5
Argentina ○ **RA** 76-77 D 4
Argentina ■ **RA** 78-79 E 4
Argentina, La ○ **RA** 60-61 C 6
Argentina, Laguna la ○ **RA** 78-79 L 4
Argentina Rise ≃ 6-7 D 13
Argentine Abyssal Plain ≃ 6-7 D 13
Argentine Basin ≃ 6-7 D 13
Argentine Islands ○ **ARK** 16 G 30
Argentino, Lago ○ **RA** 80 D 5
Argentino, Mar ≈ 80 H 5
Argenton-sur-Creuse ○ **F** 90-91 H 8
Argeş ∼ **RO** 102-103 E 5
Argestán ○ **AFG** 134-135 M 3
Argestán Rûd ∼ **AFG** 134-135 M 3
Argi ∼ **RUS** 120-121 C 6
Argoim ○ **BR** 72-73 L 2
Argolão, Cachoeira do ∼ **BR** 66-67 K 4
Argolikos Kólpos ≈ 100-101 J 6
Argonne ▲ 90-91 K 7
Argopyro, Gunung ▲ **RI** 168 E 3
Árgos ○ **GR** 100-101 J 6
Árgos Orestikó ○ **GR** 100-101 H 4
Argostóli ○ **GR** 100-101 H 5
Arguello, Point ▲ **USA** 40-41 D 8
Argun' ∼ **RUS** (CEC) 126-127 F 6
Argun ∼ **RUS** 118-119 K 10
Argun ∼ **RUS** 118-119 J 11
Argun ∼ **RUS** 126-127 F 6
Argungu ○ **WAN** 198-199 B 6
Arguut ○ **MAU** 148-149 F 5
Arguvan ○ **TR** 128-129 H 3
Argyle, Lake ○ **AUS** 172-173 J 4
Arhangaj ▣ **MAU** 148-149 G 4
Arhangelsk ☆ **RUS** 88-89 Q 4
Arhangelskoe ☆ **RUS** 96-97 K 6
Arhanzelskaja Guba ○ **RUS** 108-109 H 4
Arhara ○ **RUS** 122-123 D 4
Arhara ∼ **RUS** 122-123 D 4
Arhavi ○ **TR** 128-129 J 2
arheologičeskij zapovednik Tanais • **RUS** 102-103 L 4
Arhipelag Sedova ∩ **RUS** 108-109 Y 2
Arhipovka ○ **RUS** 94-95 M 4
Ar Horqin Qi ○ **VRC** 150-151 C 6
Århus ○ **DK** 86-87 E 8
Ariadnoe ○ **RUS** 122-123 F 6
Ariake-kai ≈ 152-153 D 8
Ariamsvlei ○ **NAM** 220-221 D 4
Ariano Irpino ○ **I** 100-101 E 4
Ariari, Río ∼ **CO** 60-61 E 6
Aria River ∼ **PNG** 183 E 3
Arias ○ **RA** 78-79 H 2
Ari Atoll ∩ **MV** 140-141 B 6
Aribinda ○ **BF** 202-203 K 2
Arica ○ **RCH** 70-71 B 6
Aricapampa ○ **PE** 64-65 D 5
Aricaria ○ **BR** 68-69 B 3
Arichat ○ **CDN** 38-39 O 6
Arichuna ○ **YV** 60-61 G 5
Aricota, Lago ○ **PE** 70-71 B 5
Arid, Cape ▲ **AUS** 176-177 G 7
Árida, al- ○ **KSA** 132-133 D 5
Ariège ∼ **F** 90-91 H 10
Ariel ○ **RA** 78-79 K 4
Árifwâla ○ **PK** 138-139 D 4
Arig gol ∼ **MAU** 148-149 G 4

Arihāl ☆ • **AUT** 130-131 D 2
Arihanha, Rio ∼ **BR** 72-73 D 4
Arikaree River ∼ **USA** 42-43 F 6
Arikawa ○ **J** 152-153 C 8
Arikok, National Reservaat ⊥ **ARU** 60-61 G 1
Arima ○ **TT** 60-61 L 2
Arimu Mine ○ **GUY** 62-63 E 2
Arinos ○ **BR** 72-73 G 3
Arinos, Rio ∼ **BR** 70-71 J 3
Ariogala ○ **LT** 94-95 H 4
Aripuanā ○ **BR** 70-71 G 5
Aripuanā, Área Indígena ✕ **BR** 70-71 H 2
Aripuanā, Parque Indígena ✕ **BR** 70-71 G 2
Aripuanā, Rio ∼ **BR** 66-67 G 6
Ariquemes ○ **BR** 66-67 F 7
Airanha ○ **BR** 66-67 H 5
Arish, El ∼ **AUS** 174-175 J 5
Arismendi ○ **YV** 60-61 G 3
Arissa ○ **ETH** 208-209 E 3
Aristazabal Island ∩ **CDN** 32-33 F 5
Aristizábal, Cabo ▲ **RA** 80 G 2
Aristoménis ○ **GR** 100-101 H 6
Aritao ○ **RP** 160-161 D 4
Arite ○ **SOL** 184 I e 4
Arivonimamo ○ **RM** 222-223 E 7
Ariyadka ○ **IND** 140-141 G 4
Ariyalur ○ **IND** 140-141 H 5
Ariza ○ **E** 98-99 F 4
Arizaro, Salar de ○ **RA** 76-77 D 3
Arizona ○ **RA** 78-79 G 4
Arizona ▣ **USA** (QLD) 174-175 F 6
Arizona ▣ **USA** (QLD) 178-179 F 1
Arizona ▣ **USA** 40-41 H 8
Arizpe ○ **MEX** 50-51 D 2
Årjäng ☆ **S** 86-87 F 7
Arjawinangun ○ **RI** 168 C 3
Arjeplog ○ **S** 86-87 H 3
Árjo ○ **ETH** 208-209 C 4
Arjona ○ **CO** 60-61 D 2
Arjuna, Gunung ▲ **RI** 168 E 3
Arjuni ○ **IND** 142-143 B 5
Arka ∼ **RUS** 120-121 K 3
Arka ∼ **RUS** 120-121 J 3
Arkadak ○ **RUS** 102-103 N 2
Arkadelphia ○ **USA** 44-45 L 2
Arkagala ○ **IND** 140-141 G 4
Arkalyk ☆ **KA** 124-125 E 3
Arkansas ▣ **USA** 44-45 L 2
Arkansas City ○ **USA** 44-45 J 1
Arkansas Post National Memorial ∴ **USA** 44-45 M 2
Arkansas River ∼ **USA** 42-43 D 6
Arkansas River ∼ **USA** 44-45 M 2
Arka-Pojlovajaha ∼ **RUS** 108-109 Q 8
Arkaroola Village ○ **AUS** 178-179 D 5
Arka-Tab°jaha ∼ **RUS** 108-109 Q 8
Arkatag ▲ **VRC** 146-147 F 2
Arkell, Mount ▲ **CDN** 20-21 X 6
Arkhangelsk = Arhangelsk ☆ **RUS** 88-89 Q 4
Arklow = An tInbhear Mór ○ **IRL** 90-91 D 5
Arknu, Jabal ▲ **LAR** 192-193 L 6
Arkona, Kap ▲ • **D** 92-93 M 1
Arkonam ○ **IND** 140-141 H 4
Arktičeskij, mys ▲ **RUS** 108-109 b 1
Arktičeskogo instituta, ostrova ∩ **RUS** 108-109 T 4
Arktik Hoyland ⊥ **GRØ** 26-27 R 5
Arlal ○ **RMM** 196-197 J 5
Arlan, gora ▲ **TM** 136-137 D 5
Arlanza, Río ∼ **E** 98-99 F 3
Arlanzón ○ **E** 98-99 F 3
Arlanzón, Río ∼ **E** 98-99 E 3
Arlee ○ **USA** 40-41 G 2
Arles ○••• **F** 90-91 K 10
Arló ○ **BF** 202-203 L 4
Arli, Parc National de l' ⊥ **BF** 202-203 L 4
Arli, Réserve de l' ⊥ **BF** 202-203 L 4
Arlington ○ **USA** (GA) 48-49 G 4
Arlington ○ **USA** (KS) 44-45 H 1
Arlington ○ **USA** (OR) 40-41 D 3
Arlington ○ **USA** (SD) 42-43 J 3
Arlington ○ **USA** (TX) 44-45 J 2
Arlington ○ **USA** (VA) 46-47 K 6
Arlington ○ **USA** (WA) 40-41 C 1
Arlington ○ **ZA** 220-221 H 4
Arlit ○ **RN** 198-199 C 3
Arlon ☆ **B** 92-93 H 4
Arltunga ○ **AUS** 178-179 C 2
Arma ○ **USA** 44-45 K 1
Armação dos Búzios ○ **BR** 72-73 K 7
Armagh ☆ **GB** 90-91 D 4
Armagnac ⊥ **F** 90-91 H 10
Arma Konda ▲ **IND** 142-143 C 6
Arman° ○ **RUS** 120-121 O 4
Arman° ∼ **RUS** 120-121 O 4
Armando ○ **BR** 74-75 D 8
Armando Bermúdes, Parque Nacional ⊥ **DOM** 54-55 K 5
Armant ○ **ET** 194-195 F 5
Armark Lake ○ **CDN** 30-31 T 2
Armark River ∼ **CDN** 30-31 T 2
Armas, Las ○ **RA** 78-79 L 4
Armavir ○ **RUS** (STV) 102-103 M 5
Armenia = Armenija ⊥ 128-129 J 3
Armenia = Armenija ■ **AR** 128-129 L 2
Armeria ○ **MEX** 52-53 C 2
Armeria, Río de ∼ **MEX** 52-53 C 2
Armidale ○ **AUS** 178-179 L 6
Armil Lake ○ **CDN** 30-31 T 3
Arminavallen ∼ **SME** 62-63 G 3
Armit ○ **CDN** 34-35 F 4
Armitdž, poluostrov ∪ **RUS** 84-85 a 2
Armit Range ▲ **PNG** (HAM) 134-5 J 4
Armjan's'k ○ **UA** 102-103 H 4
Armley ○ **CDN** 34-35 D 4
Armour ○ **USA** 42-43 H 4
Arñan ○ **RUS** 116-117 J 9
Armraynald ○ **AUS** 174-175 E 5

Arm River ∼ **CDN** 34-35 D 5
Armstrong ○ **CDN** (BC) 32-33 L 6
Armstrong ○ **CDN** (ONT) 34-35 M 5
Armstrong River ∼ **AUS** 172-173 K 4
Ārmūr ○ **IND** 138-139 G 10
Árnafjall ▲ **Ù 88-69 H 5
Arnauld (Payne), Rivière ∼ **CDN** 36-37 O 4
Arnedo ○ **E** 98-99 F 3
Arneiroz ○ **BR** 68-69 H 5
Arnett ○ **USA** 44-45 H 1
Arnhem ∘ **NL** 92-93 H 2
Arnhem, Cape ▲ **AUS** 174-175 D 3
Arnhem Aboriginal Land ⊥ **AUS** 174-175 B 3
Arnhem Bay ≈ 174-175 D 3
Arnhem Highway II **AUS** 172-173 K 2
Arnhem Land ⊥ **AUS** 174-175 B 3
Arno ∼ **I** 100-101 C 3
Arno Bay ○ **AUS** 180-181 D 2
Arnold ○ **USA** (NE) 42-43 G 5
Arnold River ∼ **AUS** 174-175 C 5
Arnott Strait ≈ 24-25 U 2
Arnøy ∩ **N** 86-87 K 1
Arnprior ○ **CDN** 38-39 F 6
Arnsberg ○ • **D** 92-93 K 3
Arnstadt ○ • **D** 92-93 L 3
Aro, Río ∼ **YV** 60-61 J 4
Aroab ○ **NAM** 220-221 D 3
Arochuku ○ **WAN** 204-205 G 6
Aroeiras ○ **BR** 68-69 L 5
Arokam, Oued ∼ **DZ** 190-191 G 9
Aroland ○ **CDN** 34-35 N 5
Arolik River ∼ **USA** 22-23 Q 3
Aroma ○ **PNG** 183 C 4
Aroma ∼ **RCH** 70-71 C 6
Aroma ○ **SUD** 200-201 H 5
Aroma, Quebrada de ∼ **RCH** 70-71 C 6
Aroona ○ **AUS** 178-179 E 6
Aroostock River ∼ **USA** 46-47 O 2
Aropa ○ **PNG** 184 I b 2
Arorae ∩ **KIB** 13 J 3
Aroroy ○ **RP** 160-161 E 6
Aro Usu, Tanjung ▲ **RI** 166-167 F 6
Arpa Çayı ∼ **TR** 128-129 K 2
Arpajon ○ **F** 90-91 J 7
Arpangasia ∼ **BD** 142-143 F 4
Arpoador, Ponta do ▲ **BR** 74-75 G 5
Arq. T. Romero Pereira ○ **PY** 76-77 K 4
Arqū ○ **SUD** 200-201 F 5
Arque, Río ∼ **BOL** 70-71 D 5
Arquata del Tronto ○ **I** 100-101 D 3
Arra ∼ **PK** 134-135 L 5
ar-Râbi', ash-Shallâl = 4th Cataract ∼ **SUD** 200-201 F 5
Ar-Rachidia ☆ **MA** 188-189 J 3
ar-Radd, Wâdi ∼ **SYR** 128-129 J 4
ar-Radisiya Bahri ○ **ET** 194-195 F 5
ar-Rafid ○ **SYR** 128-129 F 6
ar-Rahad ○ **SUD** 200-201 G 6
ar-Rahad ∼ **SUD** 200-201 G 6
Arraial do Cabo ○ **BR** 72-73 J 7
Arraias ○ **BR** 68-69 E 4
Arraias, Rio ∼ **BR** 68-69 A 7
Arraida ○ **OM** 132-133 J 5
Arran ∩ **GB** 90-91 E 4
Arrandale ○ **CDN** 32-33 F 4
Ar-Rank ○ **SUD** 200-201 G 6
Ar Râqûbah ○ **LAR** 192-193 H 3
Arras ○ **CDN** 32-33 K 4
Arras ☆ • **F** 90-91 J 6
Ar Rashidiyah = Ar Rachidia ☆ **MA** 188-189 J 3
ar-Rauda ○ **ET** 194-195 E 4
ar-Rawdah = Ranya ○ **KSA** 132-133 C 3
ar-Rawdah, Sabhat ○ **SYR** 128-129 J 5
ar-Rawgal ○ **SUD** 200-201 G 3
ar-Rawgal ∼ **SUD** 200-201 G 3
ar-Rizqa ○ **ET** 194-195 F 4
Arroio dos Ratos ○ **BR** 74-75 E 8
Arrojado, Rio ∼ **BR** 72-73 H 2
Arrojolândia ○ **BR** 72-73 H 4
Arroio da Ventana ○ **RA** 78-79 F 6
Arroyo de los Huesos ○ **RA** 78-79 K 4
Arroyo Grande ○ **USA** 40-41 D 8
Arroyos de Mantua ○ **C** 54-55 C 3
Arroyos Esteros ○ **PY** 76-77 K 4
Arrozal ○ **YV** 60-61 K 5
Árs ○ **B** 92-93 H 3
Āša ∼ **RUS** 96-97 M 6
Asa ○ **NAM** 220-221 C 2
Asaba ○ **WAN** 204-205 G 5
Asadābād ☆ • **AFG** 138-139 C 1
Asadābād ○ **IR** (HOR) 134-135 C 1
Asadābād ○ **IR** (HAM) 134-135 C 1
Asahan ∼ **RI** 166-167 A 3
Asadbuharat al- < **SYR** 126-129 H 4
Asaga ○ **WS** 184 V a 1

ash-Shurayk ○ **SUD** 200-201 F 3
Ashta ○ **IND** 138-139 F 8
Ashtabula ○ **USA** 46-47 H 5
Ashtabula, Lake ○ **USA** 42-43 H 2
Ashton ○ **USA** 40-41 J 3
Ashton ○ **ZA** 220-221 D 6
Ashuanipi Lake ○ **CDN** 38-39 L 2
Ashuapmushuan, Réserve Faunique d' ⊥ **CDN** 38-39 H 4
Ashuapmushuan, Rivière ∼ **CDN** 38-39 H 4
Ashville ○ **CDN** 34-35 F 5
Ashwaraopet ○ **IND** 142-143 B 7
Asia ○ **PE** 70-71 B 4
Asia, Estrecho ≈ 80 C 5
Asiak River ∼ **CDN** 30-31 N 2
Asientos, Los ○ **PA** 52-53 D 8
Asif Melloul ∼ **MA** 188-189 H 4
Asilah ○ **MA** 188-189 H 3
Asile, L' ○ **RH** 54-55 J 5
Asillo ○ **PE** 70-71 B 4
Asinara, Golfo dell' ≈ 100-101 B 4
Asinara, Ísola ∩ **I** 100-101 B 4
Asindonhopo ○ **SME** 62-63 G 4
Asi Nehri ∼ **TR** 128-129 G 4
Asino ○ **RUS** 114-115 T 6
Asir ○ **KSA** 132-133 C 4
'Asis, Ra's ▲ **SUD** 200-201 J 3
Aşkale ☆ **TR** 128-129 J 3
'Askarān ○ **IR** 134-135 D 2
Askarly ∼ **KA** 124-125 H 3
Askarovo ○ **RUS** 96-97 L 7
Aškazar ○ **IR** 134-135 F 3
Askeaton ○ **ZA** 220-221 H 5
Asker ○ **N** 86-87 E 7
Askersund ○ • **S** 86-87 G 7
Askim ○ **N** 86-87 E 7
Askino ○ **RUS** 96-97 L 6
Askinuk Mountains ▲ **USA** 20-21 H 6
Askira ○ **WAN** 204-205 K 3
Askiz ○ **RUS** 116-117 T 9
Askøping ○ **S** 86-87 H 7
Askot ○ **IND** 144-145 C 6
Askay ○ **N** 86-87 B 6
Asla ○ **DZ** 188-189 L 4
Asl-e Čahānsūr ○ **AFG** 134-135 K 3
Asler < **RMM** 196-197 L 5
Asmār ○ **AFG** 138-139 M 7
Åsmara ★ **ER** 200-201 J 5
Asmara, Wâdi ∼ **KSA** 130-131 G 4
Asmat Woodcarvings ○ • **RI** 166-167 K 6
Åsmera = Åsmara ★ **ER** 200-201 J 5
Ašmjany ☆ **BY** 94-95 K 4
Asnâhra ○ **IND** 142-143 C 2
Asnet ○ **TCH** 198-199 J 6
Åsnö ○ **MA** 188-189 H 5
Aso ○ **J** 152-153 D 8
Aso National Park ⊥•• **J** 152-153 D 8
Asori ○ **RI** 166-167 J 3
Ásosa ○ **ETH** 208-209 B 3
Aso-san ▲ **J** 152-153 D 8
Asoteriba, Gabal ▲ **SUD** 200-201 J 3
Aspen ○ **USA** 42-43 D 6
Aspen Cove ○ **CDN** 32-33 K 7
Aspendos ○ • **TR** 128-129 D 4
Aspen Mountain Ski Area • **USA** 42-43 D 6
Aspermont ○ **USA** 44-45 G 3
Aspiring, Mount ▲ **NZ** 182 B 6
Aspy Bay ≈ 38-39 O 5
Asrama ○ **RT** 202-203 L 6
Asriko ○ **CI** 202-203 H 6
Assa ○ **KA** 136-137 M 3
Assa ∼ **KA** 136-137 M 3
Assa ∼ **WAN** 198-199 B 3
As Sab'ah, Qârat ▲ **LAR** 192-193 G 4
as-Sablúkah, Shallâl = 6th Cataract ∼ **SUD** 200-201 F 4
Assadjene ▲ **DZ** 190-191 F 9
as-Saff ○ **ET** 194-195 E 3
'Assáfiya, al- ○ **KSA** 130-131 F 3
As Saghîr, Bi'r < **LAR** 192-193 J 3
as-Sáhiliya, Gabal ▲ **SYR** 128-129 G 5
Assahoun ○ **RT** 202-203 L 6
Assaï ○ **BR** 72-73 E 7
Assaikio ○ **WAN** 204-205 H 4
Assaka ○ **MA** 188-189 G 6
Assal, Lac ○ **DJI** 208-209 F 3
as-Sallúm ○ **ET** 192-193 L 2
as-Sallum, Halíg ≈ 192-193 L 2
Assam ▣ **IND** 142-143 H 2
Assamakka ○ **RN** 198-199 B 3
Assaouas ○ **RN** 198-199 C 3
Assaq, Oued ∼ **MA** 196-197 C 2
Assaré ○ **BR** 68-69 J 5
Assateague Island ∩ **USA** 46-47 L 6
Assateague Islands National Seashore ⊥ **USA** 46-47 L 6
as-Šatt ○ **ET** 194-195 F 3
As Sawdá', Jabal ▲ **LAR** 192-193 J 3
As Sawdáyah ∼ **LAR** 192-193 J 3
as-Sawirah ☆ **MA** 188-189 G 5
Assdadah ○ **LAR** 192-193 J 2
Asse, River ∼ **WAN** 204-205 G 6
Assegai ∼ **SD** 220-221 K 3
Assegaon ○ **IND** 138-139 F 9
Assen ○ **NL** 92-93 J 2
Assen ○ **ZA** 220-221 F 5
as-Sibā'i, Gabal ▲ **ET** 194-195 G 5
As Siba'h ○ **KSA** 130-131 J 4
As Sidr ○ **LAR** 192-193 H 2
As Sila'ah ○ **UAE** 130-131 J 4
Assina River ∼ **PNG** 183 B 2
as-Sinballáwain ○ **ET** 194-195 L 6
Assiniboia ○ **CDN** 34-35 D 6
Assiniboine, Fort ○ **CDN** 32-33 N 4
Assiniboine River ∼ **CDN** 34-35 E 4
Assinica, Lac ○ **CDN** 38-39 G 3
Assinica, Réserve Faunique ⊥ **CDN** 38-39 G 3

Assinié Mafia ○ • CI 202-203 J 7
Assin Nyankumase ○ GH 202-203 K 7
Assis ○ BR 72-73 E 7
Assis Brasil ○ BR 70-71 C 4
Assis Chateaubriand ○ BR 74-75 D 5
Assisi ∴ I 100-101 D 3
Assodé ⊀ RN 198-199 D 3
Assok Begua ○ G 210-211 C 3
Assomption Sar ⊻ SY 222-223 E 2
Assos ∴∴ TR 128-129 B 3
Assu ○ BR 68-69 K 4
Assu, Rio ∼ BR 68-69 K 4
as-Süki ○ SUD 200-201 F 6
as-Sulayyil ○ KSA 132-133 D 5
As Sulṭān ○ LAR 192-193 G 2
as-Sumay ○ SUD 206-207 H 4
Assunção ○ BR 66-67 E 7
Assur ∴∴ IRQ 128-129 K 5
as-Suryāni, Dair ∴∴ ET 194-195 E 2
as-Süs ∴ MA 188-189 G 3
as-Suwais, Ḫalīğ ⌣ ET 194-195 F 3
as-Suwais, Qanāt ⌣ ET 194-195 F 2
Assyni ∼ RUS 122-123 F 2
Aštān, Umm al ○ UAE 132-133 H 2
Āstāne ○ IR 128-129 N 4
Āstāne ○ IR 134-135 C 2
Astantaj-Mataj, sor ∼ KA 126-127 M 5
Astara ○ AZ 128-129 N 3
Āstārā ○ IR 128-129 L 2
Asti ○ • I 100-101 B 2
Astillero,El ○ E 98-99 F 3
Astipálea ○ GR 100-101 L 6
Astipálea ∼ GR 100-101 L 6
Āštivay ○ AFG 134-135 M 1
Aštiyān ○ IR 134-135 C 1
Astorga ○ BR 72-73 E 7
Astorga ○ E 98-99 D 3
Astoria ○ USA 40-41 C 2
Astove Island ∼ SY 222-223 E 3
Astrachan ○ KA 124-125 F 1
Astrahan' ☆ RUS 96-97 E 10
Astrahanskij zapovednik ⊥ RUS 126-127 Q 5
Astrahanskij zapovednik ⊥ RUS (AST) 96-97 F 10
Astrakhan' = Astrahan' ☆ RUS 126-127 H 4
Astray ○ CDN 36-37 Q 7
Astrolabe Bay ⌣ 183 C 3
Astronomical Society Islands ∼ CDN 24-25 a 6
Ástros ○ GR 100-101 J 6
Astrovna ○ BY 94-95 L 4
Astura, gora ▲ RUS 108-109 e 3
Asturias ◆ E 98-99 D 3
Asuéfri ○ CI 202-203 J 6
Asunción ○ CR 52-53 C 7
Asunción • ∗ PY 76-77 J 3
Asunción, La ☆ YV 60-61 K 2
Asuncion, Río de la ∼ MEX 50-51 C 2
Asunción Nochixtlán ○ MEX 52-53 F 3
Asundi ○ IND 140-141 F 3
'Ašŭriya, al- ○ IRQ 128-129 K 7
Asustado, Arroyo el ∼ MEX 50-51 D 1
Asutsuare ○ GH 202-203 L 6
Aswa ∼ EAU 212-213 D 2
Aswān ☆∗ ET 194-195 F 4
Aswān High Dam = Sadd al-'Âli ⊀•∗ ET 194-195 F 4
Ašykŏl, sor ∼ KA 124-125 J 4
Ašykŏl ojpat ∼ KA 124-125 E 6
Asyma ○ RUS 118-119 N 4
Asyŭt ★∗ ET 194-195 F 4
Asyŭtī, Wādī ⌣ ∼ ET 194-195 E 4
Ata, Qiryat ○ IL 130-131 D 1
Ataa ○ GRØ 28-29 P 2
Ata Bupu Danau • RI 168 C 7
Atacama, Desierto de ∴ RCH 76-77 B 4
Atacama, Puna de ∴ RA 76-77 C 4
Atacama, Salar de ∼ RCH 76-77 C 2
Atacama Trench ≃ 70-71 A 5
Atacames ○ EC 64-65 C 1
Atafaitafa, Djebel ▲ DZ 190-191 F 8
Atafu, Massif d' ▲ RN 192-193 H 4
'Atâiye ○ IR 136-137 F 7
Atajaña, Cerro ▲ RCH 70-71 B 6
Ata Koo Fai-Nuwa Puri Danau • RI 168 C 7
Atakor ▲ DZ 190-191 F 8
Atakora, Chaîne de l' ▲ DY 202-203 L 4
Atakora, Zone Cynégétique de l' ⊥ DY 202-203 L 4
Atakpamé ○ RT 202-203 L 6
Atalaia ○ BR 68-69 K 6
Atalaia, Ponta da ▲ BR 68-69 E 2
Atalaia do Norte ○ BR 66-67 B 5
Atalaya ○ PE 64-65 F 7
Atalaya, Cerro ▲ PE 70-71 B 3
Ataléia ○ BR 72-73 K 5
Atamanovo ○ RUS 116-117 F 7
Atambua ○ RI 166-167 C 6
Atami ○ • J 152-153 M 7
Atammik ○ GRØ 28-29 O 4
Atanbas, tau ▲ KA 126-127 P 3
Atande, Tanjung ▲ RI 166-167 B 6
Atanik ○ USA 20-21 L 1
Atapange ○ RI 164-165 G 6
Ata Polo Danau • RI 168 C 7
Atapupu ○ RI 166-167 C 6
'Atâqa, Ǧabal ▲ ET 194-195 F 3
Ataques ○ ROU 76-77 H 5
Atâr ☆ RIM 196-197 D 4
Atar, Khor ∼ SUD 206-207 K 4
Atas Bogd ▲ MAU 148-149 C 6
Atascadero ○ PE 64-65 B 4
Atascadero ○ USA 40-41 D 4
Atasi Nkwanta ○ GH 202-203 K 7
Atasu ○ MEX 52-53 H 2
Atasu ○ KA 124-125 G 4
Atatürk Baraji ⌣ TR 128-129 H 4
Atauba ○ BR 62-63 D 6
Atauro, Pulau (Kambing) ∼ RI 166-167 C 6

Ataŵala, al- ○ KSA 132-133 B 3
Ataya ○ ETH 208-209 D 3
'Atbara ○ SUD 200-201 H 6
'Atbara ∼ SUD 200-201 G 6
'Atbara ∼ SUD 200-201 G 6
Atbasar ○ KA 124-125 F 3
At-Baši ○ KS 146-147 B 5
At-Baši, hrebet ▲ KS 146-147 B 5
Atchafalaya Bay ⌣ USA 44-45 M 5
Atchane, Erg el ∼ DZ 188-189 L 6
Atchane, Hamadet el ∴ DZ 190-191 E 6
Atchison ○ USA 42-43 K 6
Atchuelinguk River ∼ USA 20-21 K 5
Atebubu ○ GH 202-203 K 6
Ateiku ○ GH 202-203 K 7
Aten, Río ∼ BOL 70-71 C 4
Atenango del Río ○ MEX 52-53 F 3
Atenas ○ BR 66-67 B 7
Atencingo ○ MEX 52-53 E 2
Atequiza ○ MEX 52-53 C 1
Aterau ☆ KA 96-97 H 10
Ateraü = Aterau ☆ KA 126-127 H 4
Atesa ○ GH 202-203 J 6
Athabasca ○ CDN 32-33 O 4
Athabasca, Lake ○ CDN 30-31 P 6
Athabasca River ∼ CDN 32-33 P 2
Athamánon ▲ GR 100-101 H 5
Athamar • TR 128-129 K 3
Athapap ○ CDN 34-35 F 3
Athapapuskow Lake ○ CDN 34-35 F 3
Athārān Hazāri ○ PK 138-139 D 4
Athenia ▲ CDN 30-31 O 4
Athens ○ USA (AL) 48-49 E 2
Athens ○ USA (GA) 48-49 G 3
Athens ○ USA (OH) 46-47 G 6
Athens ○ USA (TN) 48-49 F 2
Athens ○ USA (TX) 44-45 K 4
Athens = Athína ★∗ GR 100-101 J 5
Atherton ○ AUS 174-175 H 5
Atherton Tableland ▲ AUS 174-175 H 5
Athgarh ○ IND 142-143 D 5
Athi ∼ EAK 212-213 F 4
Athiémè ○ DY 202-203 L 6
Athienou ○ CY 128-129 F 5
Athi River ∼ EAK 212-213 F 4
Athl, Wādi al ∼ LAR 192-193 H 5
Athlone = Baile Átha Luain ○ IRL 90-91 D 5
Athni ○ IND 140-141 F 2
Athol ○ USA 40-41 F 2
Atholl, Kap ▲ GRØ 26-27 P 5
Áthos ▲∗∗ GR 100-101 K 4
'Ati ○ SUD 200-201 D 6
Ati ○ TCH 198-199 J 6
Atiak ○ EAU 212-213 D 2
Atiamuri ○ NZ 182 F 3
Atibaia ○ BR 72-73 G 7
Atico ○ PE 70-71 A 5
Atiedo ○ SUD 206-207 H 5
Atienza ○ E 98-99 F 4
Atijere ○ WAN 204-205 F 5
Atikaki Provincial Wilderness Park ⊥ CDN 34-35 J 5
Atikameg Lake ○ CDN 30-31 S 5
Atikameg River ∼ CDN 34-35 P 4
Atiki ⊡ GR 100-101 J 5
Atik Lake ○ CDN 34-35 H 3
Atikokan ○ CDN 34-35 L 6
Atim ○ CDN 38-39 M 2
Atinia, Nakong- ○ GH 202-203 K 5
Atitlán, Lago de ○ GCA 52-53 J 4
Atitlán, Volcán ▲ GCA 52-53 J 4
Atka ○ RUS 120-121 Q 3
Atka Island ∼ USA 22-23 J 6
Atka ○ USA 22-23 J 6
Atkamba Mission ○ PNG 183 A 3
Atka Pass ≃ 22-23 J 6
Atkinson ○ USA 42-43 H 4
Atkinson Lake ○ CDN 30-31 R 5
Atkinson Point ▲ CDN 20-21 Z 2
Atkŏt ○ IND 138-139 C 8
Atkri ○ RI 166-167 G 5
Atlacomulco ○ MEX 52-53 E 2
Atlanta ○ USA (MI) 46-47 F 4
Atlanta ○ USA (KS) 44-45 K 3
Atlanta ★ USA (GA) 48-49 F 3
Atlantic ○ USA (IA) 42-43 K 4
Atlantic ○ USA (NC) 48-49 K 2
Atlantic City ○ USA 46-47 L 6
Atlantic Ocean ≈ 6-7 D 6
Atlantida ○ ROU 78-79 K 4
Atlantis Fracture Zone ≃ 6-7 D 5
Atlasova, ostrov ∼ RUS 122-123 Q 3
Atlasovo ○ RUS (KMC) 120-121 S 6
Atlasovo ○ RUS (SHL) 122-123 N 6
Atlee Creek ∼ USA 172-173 K 6
Atlin ○ CDN 20-21 Y 7
Atlin Lake ○ CDN 20-21 Y 7
Atlin Provincial Park ⊥ CDN 32-33 G 4
Atlixco ○ MEX 52-53 E 2
Ātmakŭr ○ IND 140-141 H 3
Ātmakŭr ○ IND (ANP) 140-141 G 2
Ātmakŭr ○ IND (ANP) 140-141 H 3
Atmis ∼ RUS 108-109 G 5
Atmore ○ CDN 32-33 O 4
Atmore ○ USA 48-49 E 4
Atna Peak ▲ CDN 32-33 G 4
Atna Range ▲ CDN 32-33 G 3
Atnbrua ○ N 86-87 H 7
Atocha ○ BOL 70-71 D 7
Atog ○ CAM 210-211 C 2
Atoka ○ USA 44-45 J 2
Atome ○ ANG 216-217 C 6
Atongo-Bakari ○ RCA 206-207 E 6
Atonyia ∼ MA 188-189 J 7
Atori ○ SOL 184 I a 3
Atotonilco ○ MEX 52-53 E 2
Atotonilco el Alto ○ MEX 52-53 C 1
Atotonilco El Grande ○ MEX 52-53 E 1
Atouat, Mount ▲ LAO 158-159 J 3
Atoyac ∼ MEX 52-53 F 3
Atoyac, Río ∼ MEX 52-53 F 3
Atoyac de Álvarez ○ MEX 52-53 E 3
Atoyatempan ○ MEX 52-53 F 2
Atpadi ○ IND 140-141 F 2
Atqasuk ○ USA 20-21 M 1

Atrak, Rŭd-e ∼ IR 136-137 E 6
Atran ∼ S 86-87 F 8
Atrato, Río ∼ CO 60-61 C 4
Atrek ∼ TM 136-137 D 6
Atsumi-hantō ◢ J 152-153 G 7
Atsuta ○ J 152-153 J 3
Atsy ○ RI 166-167 K 5
Atta ○ CAM 204-205 J 5
Attalla ○ USA 48-49 E 2
at-Tamad ○ ET 194-195 F 3
At Tamimi ○ LAR 192-193 K 1
at-Tant, Ǧabal ▲ SYR 128-129 H 6
Attāni ○ IND 140-141 G 5
Attapu ○ LAO 158-159 J 3
Attar, Oued el ∼ DZ 190-191 E 4
at-Tayyārah ○ SUD 200-201 F 6
Attel, In ⊡ DZ 198-199 C 2
Attendorn ○ D 92-93 J 2
Attica ○ USA (IN) 46-47 E 5
Attica ○ USA (KS) 44-45 H 1
Attica ○ USA (OH) 46-47 G 5
at-Tih, Ǧabal ▲ ET 194-195 F 3
at-Tih, Sahrā' ∼ ET 194-195 F 2
Attikamagen Lake ○ CDN 36-37 Q 7
Attila, al- ○ IRQ 128-129 J 6
at-Tina, Ḫaliǧ ⌣ 194-195 F 2
Attingal ○ IND 140-141 G 6
Attipára ○ IND 140-141 G 6
Attobrou, Yakass- ○ CI 202-203 J 6
Attock ○ PK 138-139 D 3
Attock-Campbellpore ○ PK 138-139 D 3
Attoko ○ J 152-153 J 1
Attu ○ GRØ 28-29 O 3
Attu ○ USA 22-23 C 6
Attu Island ∼ USA 22-23 C 6
At Tullab ○ ET 192-193 K 5
at-Tŭr ★ ET 194-195 F 3
Attur ○ IND 140-141 G 5
at-Tuwaysham ○ SUD 200-201 C 6
Atuel, Río ∼ RA 78-79 E 3
Atuka ○ RI 166-167 J 4
Atuna ○ GRØ 28-29 Q 3
Atuntaqui ○ EC 64-65 C 1
Atura ○ EAU 212-213 D 2
Atures ∼ YV 60-61 H 5
Atutia, Río ∼ MEX 52-53 C 6
Åtvidaberg ○ S 86-87 H 7
Atwa, al- ○ KSA 130-131 H 3
Atwater ○ USA 40-41 D 7
Atwood ○ USA (IL) 46-47 E 6
Atwood ○ USA (KS) 42-43 G 6
Atwood Cay = Samana Cays ∼ BS 54-55 J 3
Atykan, ostrov ∼ RUS 120-121 Q 4
Atzinging Lake ○ CDN 30-31 S 5
Aŭ, Chutes de l' ∼ ZRE 212-213 C 3
Aua River ∼ CDN 24-25 e 7
Auasberge ▲ NAM 216-217 D 11
Auasbila ○ HN 52-53 B 4
Auati-Paraná ∼ BR 66-67 F 2
Auatu ▲ CDN 38-39 M 2
Aubagne ○ F 90-91 K 10
Aube ∼ F 90-91 K 8
Aubenas ○ F 90-91 K 9
Aubigny-sur-Nère ○ F 90-91 J 8
Aubry Lake ○ CDN 30-31 Q 2
Auburn ○ AUS (QLD) 178-179 L 3
Auburn ○ USA (AL) 48-49 F 3
Auburn ○ USA (IL) 46-47 D 6
Auburn ○ USA (IN) 46-47 F 5
Auburn ○ USA (IA) 42-43 K 4
Auburn ○ USA (ME) 46-47 N 3
Auburn ○ USA (NE) 42-43 J 5
Auburn ○ USA (NY) 46-47 K 4
Auburn ○ USA (WA) 41-41 C 2
Auburn Range ▲ AUS 178-179 L 3
Aubusson ○ F 90-91 J 9
Auca Mahuida, Sierra de ▲ RA 78-79 E 4
Auçan, Cerro ▲ RCH 76-77 C 1
Aucara ○ PE 64-65 D 9
Aucayacu ○ PE 64-65 D 6
Auch ○ F 90-91 H 10
Auchi ○ WAN 204-205 G 5
Auckland ★ NZ 182 E 2
Auckland Bay ⌣ 158-159 E 4
Auckland Island ∼ NZ 13 H 8
Aude ∼ F 90-91 J 10
Aude ○ F 90-91 J 10
Audhili Bay ⌣ 26-27 E 3
Audierne ○ F 90-91 F 8
Audo Range ▲ ETH 208-209 E 5
Audru ○ EST 94-95 J 2
Aue ○ D 92-93 M 3
Augathella ○ AUS 178-179 J 3
Augrabies ○ ZA 220-221 E 4
Augrabies Falls ○ •∗ ZA 220-221 E 4
Augrabies Falls National Park ⊥ ZA 220-221 E 4
Augsburg ○ • D 92-93 L 4
Aug Thong ○ THA 158-159 F 3
Augusta ○ AUS 176-177 C 7
Augusta ⊡ I 100-101 E 6
Augusta ○ USA (AR) 44-45 M 2
Augusta ○ USA (KS) 42-43 J 7
Augusta ★ USA (ME) 46-47 N 3
Augusta, Cabo ▲ CO 60-61 D 2
Augusta, Mount ▲ USA 20-21 U 6
Augustina Libarona ○ RA 76-77 H 5
Agustin Codazzi ○ CO 60-61 E 2
Augusto Severo ○ BR 68-69 K 4
Augustów ○ PL 92-93 S 2
Augusto Montenegro ○ BR 66-67 J 4
Augustus, Mount ▲ AUS 176-177 C 4
Augustus Downs ○ AUS 174-175 G 4
Augustus Island ∼ AUS 172-173 G 3

Augustus Island ∼ CDN 36-37 Q 3
Auitia, Rio ∼ BR 72-73 D 2
Auke Bay ○ USA 20-21 Z 3
Auki ∼ Aoke ☆ SOL 184 I e 3
Aukpar River ∼ CDN 28-29 N 5
Aulād Tauq Šarq ○ ET 194-195 F 4
Auld, Lake ○ AUS 172-173 F 7
Auliräipāra ○ BR 66-67 K 4
Aulitivik Island ∼ CDN 28-29 G 2
Auliyā Dam ⌣ SUD 200-201 F 5
Aulneau Peninsula ◢ CDN 34-35 K 6
Aul Sarykobda ○ KA 126-127 M 3
Aumo ○ PNG 183 D 3
Auna ○ WAN 204-205 F 3
Aundah ○ IND 138-139 F 10
Auno ○ WAN 204-205 K 3
Auob ∼ NAM 220-221 D 2
Aupwel ○ PNG 183 B 3
Aur, Pulau ∼ MAL (KED) 162-163 F 3
Aura ○ C 54-55 G 4
Auray ○ F 90-91 F 8
Aurbunak, Gunung ▲ RI 164-165 D 5
Auram ∼ NAM 220-221 C 3
Aurangābād ○ IND 142-143 D 3
Aurangābād ○ • IND 138-139 E 10
Auras ∼ C 54-55 G 4
Aure ∼ N 86-87 D 5
Aure River ∼ PNG 183 C 4
Aures, Massif de l' ▲ DZ 190-191 F 3
Aure Scarp ≃ PNG 183 C 4
Auri, utes ∼ RUS 122-153 H 1
Aurich (Ostfriesland) ○ D 92-93 J 2
Aurilac ☆ F 90-91 J 9
Aurinkó ○ IND 138-139 G 6
Aurlandsvangen ○ N 86-87 C 6
Auro ○ PNG 183 E 5
Aurora ○ BR (CEA) 68-69 J 5
Avor Downs ○ AUS (QLD) 178-179 J 1
Avor River ∼ AUS 176-177 D 6
Avontuur ○ ZA 220-221 F 6
Avranches ○ F 90-91 G 7
Avstrijskij proliv ≈ 84-85 f 2
Avu Avu = Kolotambu ○ SOL 184 I e 3
Avuavu ○ SOL 184 I e 3
Awaʼ Island ○ 132-133 V 7
Awad, al- ○ IRQ 128-129 L 6
Awad, al- ○ SUD 200-201 G 7
Awaji-shima ∼ J 152-153 F 7
Awakaba ○ RCA 206-207 E 4
'Awāli ○ BRN 134-135 D 5
Awang ○ RI 166-167 J 4
Awanui ○ NZ 182 D 1
Awar ○ PNG 183 C 3
Awara Plain ∼ EAK 212-213 H 4
Awara soela ∼ SME 62-63 G 4
Awarē ○ ETH 208-209 D 5
Awarua Point ▲ NZ 182 B 6
Awarua River ∼ NZ 182 D 4
Awasa ☆ ETH 208-209 D 5
'Awāsim ∼ GH 202-203 K 7
Awash ○ ETH 208-209 D 4
Awash National Park ⊥ ETH 208-209 D 4
Awash Reserve ⊥ ETH 208-209 D 4
Awash Wenz ∼ ETH 208-209 D 4
Awat ○ VRC 146-147 E 5
Awaẗa Shetʼ ∼ ETH 208-209 D 5
Awatere River ∼ NZ 182 D 4
Awbāri ○ LAR 190-191 H 7
Awbāri ∼ LAR 192-193 H 7
Awe ○ WAN 204-205 H 4
Aweil ○ SUD 206-207 H 5
Awgu ○ WAN 204-205 G 5
Awio ○ PNG 183 F 4
Awiwo River ∼ PNG 183 F 4
Awisam ○ GH 202-203 K 7
Awisang ○ RI 164-165 F 4
Awjilah ○ LAR 192-193 J 3
Awka ○ WAN 204-205 G 5
Awrā, Wādī al ∼ LAR 192-193 G 3
Awu, Gunung ▲ RI 164-165 J 2
Awun, River ∼ WAN 204-205 F 4
Awuna River ∼ USA 20-21 M 2
Awungi ○ PNG 183 F 3
Awura, Tanjung ▲ RI 166-167 F 4
Awwal, Wādī ∼ LAR 190-191 H 6
Axe Hill ○ AUS 176-177 J 3
Axel Heiberg Island ∼ CDN 26-27 C 3
Axim ○ BR 66-67 H 5
Aximim ○ BR 66-67 H 5
Axui ○ BR 68-69 G 3
Auverrgne ○ AUS 172-173 J 6
Auvergne ◆ F 90-91 J 9
Aux Barques, Pointe ▲ USA 46-47 G 4
Auxerre ○ F 90-91 J 8
Auxiliadora ○ BR 66-67 G 6
Auyan Tebuy ▲ YV 60-61 K 5
Auyuittuq National Park ⊥ CDN 28-29 O 3
Ava ○ MYA 142-143 J 5
Ava ○ USA 44-45 L 1
Avaič ∼ RUS 120-121 S 7
Avačinskaja, guba ⌣ RUS 120-121 S 7
Avačinskij zaliv ⌣ 120-121 S 7
Avadh ∼ IND 138-139 H 6
Avadi ○ IND 140-141 J 4
Avakubi ○ ZRE 210-211 L 3
Avaljak hrebet ▲ RUS 96-97 H 6
Avallon ○ F 90-91 J 8
Avalos, Arroyo ∼ RA 76-77 H 5
Avalos, Cabo ▲ CO 60-61 D 2
Avalon Peninsula ◢ CDN 38-39 I S 5
Avalos, Arroyo ∼ RA 76-77 H 5
Avannaarsua = Nordgrønland ◆ GRØ 26-27 V 4
Avare ○ BR 72-73 F 7
Avaré ○ BR 72-73 F 7
Avarskoe Kojsu ∼ RUS 126-127 G 6
Avatanak Island ∼ USA 22-23 O 5
Avatanak Strait ≈ 22-23 O 5
Ávaz ○ IR 134-135 J 2

Ave, Rio ∼ P 98-99 C 4
Ave-Dakpa ○ GH 202-203 L 6
Āweǧ ○ IR 128-129 N 5
Ǎveg, Gardāne-ye ⌣ IR 128-129 N 5
Aveiro ○ BR 66-67 K 4
Aveiro ○ • P 98-99 C 4
Avekova ∼ RUS 112-113 L 5
Avelino Lopes ○ BR 68-69 G 6
Avellaneda ○ RA 78-79 K 3
Avellino ○ • I 100-101 E 4
Avenne of the Giants • USA 40-41 C 5
Avery ○ USA 40-41 H 2
Aves, Isla de ∼ YV 56 D 4
Aves, Islas de ∼ YV 60-61 H 1
Aves de Barlovente ∼ YV 60-61 H 2
Aves Ridge ≃ 56 D 5
Avezzano ○ I 100-101 D 3
Avia Teray ○ RA 76-77 G 4
Avignon ○ • F 90-91 K 10
Avila de los Caballeros ○∗∗ E 98-99 E 4
Avilés ○ E 98-99 E 3
Avilla, Parque Nacional ⊥ YV 60-61 H 2
Avinurme ○ EST 94-95 K 2
Avirons, Les ○ F 224 B 7
Avis ○ P 98-99 C 5
Avispa, Cerro ▲ YV 66-67 E 2
Avissawella ○ CL 140-141 J 7
Avlandja, Bolšaja ∼ RUS 112-113 L 5
Avoca ○ AUS (TAS) 180-181 J 6
Avoca ○ AUS (VIC) 180-181 G 4
Avoca River ∼ AUS 180-181 G 4
Avola ○ CDN 32-33 L 6
Avon ○ USA 40-41 H 2
Avon, Lake ○ AUS 180-181 L 3
Avondale ○ USA 40-41 H 9
Avor do Tocantins ○ BR 72-73 G 2
Avor Downs ○ AUS (QLD) 178-179 J 1
Avor River ∼ AUS 176-177 D 6
Avon Park ○ USA 48-49 H 6
Avontuur ○ ZA 220-221 F 6
Avranches ○ F 90-91 G 7
Avstrijskij proliv ≈ 84-85 f 2
Avu Avu = Kolotambu ○ SOL 184 I e 3
Avuavu ○ SOL 184 I e 3
Ava, Rio ∼ BOL 70-71 F 6
Azamgarh ○ IND 142-143 C 2
Azanaques, Cerro ▲ BOL 70-71 D 6
Azanaques, Cordillera de ▲ BOL 70-71 D 6
Azangaro ○ PE 70-71 A 4
Azao ▲ DZ 190-191 G 8
Azaouak, Vallée de l' ▲ RMM 196-197 H 4
Azara ○ RA 76-77 K 5
Azᵃrbāyĵān-e Ǧarbi ◆ IR 128-129 L 3
Azᵃrbāyĵān-e Šarqi ◆ IR 128-129 M 4
Azare ○ WAN 204-205 J 3
Azᵃršahr ○ IR 128-129 L 3
Azas ∼ RUS 116-117 H 9
Azas, cero = Todža, ozero ∼ RUS 116-117 H 9
Azauri ○ BR 62-63 G 5
Azbine, Aïr ou ∼ RN 198-199 D 3
Až Bogd ▲ MAU 148-149 C 6
Azeffāl ∼ RIM 196-197 C 5
Azemmour ○ MA 188-189 G 4
Azendjé ○ G 210-211 B 4
Azennezal, Erg ∼ DZ 190-191 G 9
Azerbaijan = Azerbajdžan ⊡ AZ 128-129 M 2
Azero, Río ∼ BOL 70-71 F 6
Azevedo Sodré ○ BR 76-77 K 6
Ǎzezo ○ ETH 200-201 H 6
Azgale ○ IR 134-135 A 1
Azilal • MA 188-189 H 5
Azingo, Lac ○ G 210-211 B 4
Azirir ○ DZ 190-191 F 6
Aziz ⊀ TM 198-199 H 4
'Azīziyah, al- ○ IRQ 128-129 L 6
'Aziziyah, Al ∼ LAR 192-193 E 1
'Aziziyah, Al ☆ LAR 192-193 E 1
Azlam, Wādī ∼ KSA 130-131 E 4
Azle ○ USA 44-45 J 3
Aznā ○ IR 134-135 C 2
Aznakaevo ○ RUS 96-97 H 6
Azogues ○ EC 64-65 C 3
Azoren ⊡ P 6-7 E 9
Azores = Açores, Arquipélago dos ∼ P 188-189 C 4
Azores-Biscaya Rise ≃ 6-7 G 4
Azores-Cape Saint Vincent Ridge ≃ 188-189 D 2
Azoum, Bahr ∼ TCH 206-207 E 3
Azourki, Ibel ▲ MA 188-189 H 5
Azov ∼ RUS 102-103 L 4
Azov, Sea of = Azovskoe more ≈ RUS 102-103 J 4
Azovskoe More ≈ 102-103 J 4
Azovy ○ RUS 114-115 H 2
Azpeitia ○ E 98-99 F 3
Azrak, Bahr ∼ ETH 208-209 C 3
Azraq, al- ○ JOR 130-131 E 2
Ǎzre ○ AFG 138-139 B 2
Azrou ○ MA 188-189 J 4
Azrou, Oued ∼ DZ 190-191 F 3
Aztec ○ USA (AZ) 40-41 H 9
Aztec ○ USA (NM) 40-41 D 6
Aztec Ruins National Monument ∴∴ USA 40-41 D 6
Aztecas, Los ○ MEX 50-51 G 6
Azua ○ DOM 54-55 K 5
Azuaga ○ E 98-99 E 5
Azúcar ○ EC 64-65 B 3
Azuer ∼ E 98-99 F 5
Azuero, Península de ◢ PA 52-53 D 8
Azufral, Volcán ▲ CO 60-61 D 1
Azufre, Paso del ⌣ RA 76-77 C 4
Azufre ó Copiapó, Cerro ▲ RCH 76-77 C 4
Azul ∼ MEX 50-51 J 4
Azul ○ RA 78-79 K 4
Azul ○ TR 128-129 B 4
Azul, Cerro ▲ CR 52-53 B 7
Azul, Cerro ∼ EC 64-65 B 10
Azul, Cerro ▲ PE 64-65 B 9
Azul, Río ∼ BR 64-65 J 6
Azul, Rio ∼ MEX 52-53 K 3

Azuma-san ▲ J 152-153 J 6
Azurduy ○ BOL 70-71 E 6
Azzaba ○ DZ 190-191 F 2
az-Zāb aṣ-Ṣaġir, Nahr ∼ IRQ 128-129 K 5
az-Zāb al-Kabir, Nahr ∼ IRQ 128-129 L 5
az-Zahrān ○ KSA 134-135 D 5
az-Zaqāziq ★ ET 194-195 E 2
az-Zaraf, Bahr ∼ SUD 206-207 K 4
az-Zarqā' ∼ UAE 128-129 N 5
az-Zāwiyah ○ LAR 192-193 E 1
az-Zāwiyah ∼ LAR 192-193 E 1
Azzel Matti, Sebkha ∼ DZ 190-191 C 7
Az Zintān ○ LAR 192-193 J 2
az-Zūmah ○ SUD 200-201 E 3

B

Ba ○ FJI 184 III a 2
Baa ○ RI 166-167 B 7
Ba'āğ, al- ○ IRQ 128-129 J 4
Ba'ā'it, al- ○ KSA 130-131 G 4
Baantama ○ GH 202-203 K 6
Baardheere ○ SP 212-213 J 2
Bāb, al- ★ SYR 128-129 G 4
Baba ○ EC 64-65 C 2
Baba ∼ RCA 206-207 E 6
Bābā, Kūh-e ▲ AFG 134-135 M 1
Bababé ○ RIM 196-197 D 6
Baba Burnu ▲ TR 128-129 B 3
Babacu ○ BR 68-69 F 5
Babaçulândia ○ BR 68-69 E 5
Babadag ○ RO 102-103 F 5
Babadag, gora ▲ AZ 128-129 N 2
Babadayhan ○ TM 136-137 G 6
Babaera ○ ANG 216-217 C 6
Babaeski ○ TR 128-129 B 2
Babaevo ○ RUS 94-95 O 2
Bābā Gurgur ○ IRQ 128-129 L 5
Babahoyo ○ EC 64-65 C 2
Babai ∼ NEP 144-145 C 6
Babajurt ○ RUS 126-127 G 6
Babalegi ○ ZA 220-221 J 2
Bāb al-Mandab ≈ 132-133 C 7
Bāb al-Mandab, Ra's ▲ Y 132-133 C 7
Bābā Monir ○ IR 134-135 D 3
Babana ○ RI 164-165 F 5
Babana ○ WAN 204-205 E 3
Baban Rafi ∼ WAN 204-205 G 4
Babanty, gory ▲ RIB 118-119 F 8
Babanúsa ○ SUD 206-207 H 4
Babao ○ VRC 156-157 D 5
Babar, Kepulauan ∼ RI 166-167 E 5
Babar, Pulau ∼ RI 166-167 E 5
Babasa Island ∼ PNG 183 G 3
Babat ○ RI (JTI) 168 C 7
Babat ○ RI (SUS) 162-163 E 6
Babat ○ RI (SUS) 162-163 F 6
Babatag, hrebet ▲ US 136-137 K 6
Babati ○ EAT 212-213 F 6
Babau ○ RI 166-167 B 7
Bābā Yādegār ○ IR 128-129 L 4
Babb ○ USA 40-41 H 1
Babbage River ∼ CDN 20-21 V 2
Bab-Besen ○ MA 188-189 J 4
B'abdâ ☆ RL 128-129 F 6
Bāb-e Anār ○ IR 134-135 F 3
Babel, Mont de ▲ CDN 38-39 K 3
Bābeni ○ RO 102-103 D 5
Babenu ○ IND 142-143 B 3
Babetville ○ RM 222-223 E 7
Babi, Pulau ∼ RI 162-163 B 3
Babia, La ○ MEX 50-51 H 3
Bābil ○ IRQ 128-129 L 6
Bābil (Babylon) ∴∗ IRQ 128-129 L 6
Babilé ○ ETH 208-209 F 4
Babina ○ IND 138-139 G 6
Babinda ○ AUS 174-175 H 5
Babine Lake ○ CDN 32-33 H 4
Babine Range ▲ CDN 32-33 G 4
Babine River ∼ CDN 32-33 G 4
Babo ○ RI 166-167 G 3
Bābol ○ IR 136-137 C 6
Babonde ○ ZRE 212-213 A 2
Babongo ○ CAM 206-207 B 6
Baboquivari Peak ▲ USA 40-41 J 10
Babor, Djebel ▲ DZ 190-191 F 2
Baboua ○ RCA 206-207 B 6
Bābra ○ IND 138-139 C 9
Babrongan Tower ▲ AUS 172-173 F 5
Babtai ○ LT 94-95 H 4
Babura ○ WAN 198-199 F 6
Bābusar Pass ⌣ PK 138-139 E 2
Babuškina, mys ▲ RUS 120-121 Q 4
Babuškina, zaliv ⌣ RUS 120-121 P 4
Babuyan Channel ≈ 160-161 D 3
Babuyan Island ∼ RP 160-161 D 3
Babuyan Islands ∼ RP 160-161 D 3
Baca ○ ER 200-201 K 5
Bacaadweyn ○ SP 208-209 H 5
Bacabal ○ BR (AMA) 66-67 F 7
Bacabal ○ BR (MAR) 68-69 F 3
Bacabal ○ BR (ROR) 62-63 D 5
Bacabalzinho ○ BR 70-71 F 3
Bacaja, Área Indígena ⤳ BR 68-69 C 4
Bacajá ∼ BR 68-69 C 4
Bacajagua ○ C 54-55 H 5
Bacan, Kepulauan ∼ RI 164-165 J 4
Bacan, Pulau ∼ RI 164-165 J 4
Bacanora ○ MEX 50-51 D 3
Bacanão ○ BR 66-67 E 3
Bacaitero ○ BR 68-69 D 8
Bắc Bình ○ VN 158-159 K 5

Bacchus Marsh ○ **AUS** 180-181 H 4
Bacerac ○ **MEX** 50-51 E 2
Bắc Giang ★ **VN** 156-157 E 6
Bắc Hà ○ **VN** 156-157 D 5
Bachalo ○ **WAL** 202-203 D 6
Bachaquero ○ **YV** 60-61 F 3
Bachbone, Mount ▲ **USA** 46-47 J 6
Bachčysaraj ○ **UA** 102-103 H 5
Bache Peninsula ᴗ **CDN** 26-27 M 4
Bachhräwän ○ **IND** 142-143 D 4
Bachimba ○ **MEX** 50-51 G 3
Báchiniva ○ **MEX** 50-51 F 3
Bachmač ○ **UA** 102-103 H 2
Bạch Thông ○ **VN** 156-157 D 5
Bachu ○ **VRC** 146-147 D 6
Bachuo Akakbe ○ **CAM** 204-205 H 6
Bačka Palanka ○ **YU** 100-101 G 2
Bačka Topola ○ **YU** 100-101 G 2
Backbone Ranges ▲ **CDN** 30-31 E 4
Bäckefors ○ **S** 86-87 F 7
Bäckhammar ○ **S** 86-87 G 7
Back River ~ **CDN** 30-31 S 3
Backstairs Passage ≈ 180-181 D 4
Bắc Lạc ○ **VN** 156-157 D 6
Bắc Mê ○ **VN** 156-157 D 5
Bắc Ninh ★ **VN** 156-157 D 5
Baco, Mount ▲ **RP** 160-161 D 6
Bacobampo ○ **MEX** 50-51 E 2
Bacolod ○ **RP** 160-161 E 7
Bắc Quang ○ **VN** 156-157 D 5
Bacqueville, Lac ○ **CDN** 36-37 M 5
Bactli ○ **RP** 212-213 H 3
Bacuag ○ **RP** 160-161 F 8
Bacungan ○ **RP** 160-161 C 8
Bacuri ○ **BR** 68-69 F 2
Bacuri, Cachoeira ~ **BR** 62-63 H 6
Bacuri, Ilha do ~ **BR** 68-69 D 3
Bacuri, Lago de ○ **BR** 68-69 G 5
Bād ○ **IR** 134-135 D 2
Bad', al- ○ **KSA** 130-131 D 3
Bada ▲ **ETH** 208-209 D 3
Bada ○ **KSA** 130-131 E 4
Bada ○ **RUS** 118-119 D 10
Bada Barabil ○ **IND** 142-143 D 4
Badagangshan Z.B. ⊥ · **VRC** 156-157 J 2
Badagara ○ **IND** 140-141 F 5
Badago ○ **RMM** 202-203 F 4
Badagri ○ **WAN** 204-205 D 5
Badahšán ○ **AFG** 136-137 M 6
Bada'ï', al- ○ **KSA** 130-131 H 4
Bacain Jaran Shamo ⊥ **VRC** 148-149 J 4
Badajós ○ **BR** 66-67 F 4
Badajós, Lago ○ **BR** 66-67 F 4
Badajoz ○ **E** 98-99 D 5
Badajoz ★ **E** 98-99 D 5
Badalia ○ **AUS** 178-179 E 2
Badaling ○ **VRC** 154-155 J 1
Badam ~ **KA** 136-137 L 3
Badanga ○ **TCH** 206-207 C 3
Badas, Kepulauan ~ **RI** 162-163 G 4
Badau ○ **RI** 162-163 G 6
Bada Valley ∴ **RI** 164-165 G 4
Bad Axe ○ **USA** 46-47 G 4
Badda Rogghie ▲ **ETH** 208-209 C 4
Baddeck ○ **CDN** 38-39 O 5
Baddo ○ **PK** 134-135 J 4
Bad Dürrheim ○ **D** 92-93 K 4
Badeggi ○ **WAN** 204-205 D 4
Badéguicheri ○ **RN** 198-199 B 5
Baden ○ **A** 92-93 O 5
Baden ○ **CH** 92-93 K 5
Badena ○ **SP** 212-213 H 4
Baden-Baden ○ **D** 92-93 K 4
Baden-Württemberg ▣ **D** 92-93 K 4
Bädepalli ○ **IND** 140-141 F 7
Badér ○ **RN** 198-199 C 5
Badgastein ○ · **A** 92-93 M 5
Badger ○ **CDN** 38-39 I Q 4
Badgingarra ○ **AUS** 176-177 C 5
Badgingarra National Park ⊥ **AUS** 176-177 C 5
Bädgîs ▣ **AFG** 136-137 H 7
Bädgûl ○ **AFG** 136-137 J 7
Bad Hersfeld ○ **D** 92-93 K 3
Badhyzskij zapovednik ⊥ **TM** 136-137 G 7
Bädi, al- ○ **IRQ** 128-129 J 5
Bädi', al- ○ **KSA** 130-131 K 6
Badï'a, al- ○ **KSA** 132-133 D 5
Badiara ~ **SN** 202-203 D 2
Badikaha ○ **CI** 202-203 H 5
Badime ○ **ETH** 200-201 H 5
Badin ○ **PK** 138-139 B 7
Badinko ○ **RMM** 202-203 F 3
Badinko, Reserve du ⊥ **RMM** 202-203 F 3
Badinn-Ko ~ **RMM** 202-203 F 3
Bad Ischl ○ · **A** 92-93 M 5
Bädïyat Bani Kabir ○ **KSA** 132-133 B 3
Badjariha ○ **RUS** 110-111 Z 6
Badjer ○ **CAM** 204-205 G 4
Bad Kissingen ○ **D** 92-93 L 3
Bad Kreuznach ○ **D** 92-93 J 4
Badlands ∴ **USA** 42-43 F 4
Badlands National Park ⊥ **USA** 42-43 F 4
Badnäwar ○ **IND** 138-139 F 9
Badnera ○ **IND** 138-139 F 9
Bad Neuenahr-Ahrweiler ○ · **D** 92-93 J 4
Bado ○ **RI** 166-167 K 5
Badoc ○ **RP** 160-161 D 4
Ba Đồng ○ **VN** 158-159 J 6
Badong ○ **VRC** 154-155 G 6
Badou ○ **RT** 202-203 L 6
Badoumbé ○ **RMM** 202-203 F 3
Badplaas ○ **ZA** 220-221 K 2
Badra ~ **IND** 142-143 E 5
Bädra ~ **PK** 134-135 M 4
Bad Radkersburg ○ **A** 92-93 N 5
Bädrah ○ **PK** 138-139 B 6
Bad Rapids ~ **CDN** 32-33 N 3
Bad Reichenhall ○ **D** 92-93 M 5
Badrinath ○ **IND** 138-139 G 4
Bad River ~ **USA** 42-43 F 4

Bad River Indian Reservation ✕ **USA** 46-47 C 2
Badr wa-Hunain ○ **KSA** 130-131 F 6
Bad Segeberg ○ **D** 92-93 L 2
Bad Tölz ○ **D** 92-93 L 5
Badu ○ **VRC** 156-157 J 3
Badu Island ~ **AUS** 174-175 G 4
Badulla ○ **CL** 140-141 J 7
Badvel ○ **IND** 140-141 H 3
Badwater River ~ **CDN** 30-31 R 6
Badžal ~ **RUS** 122-123 J 4
Badžal'skij hrebet ▲ **RUS** 122-123 E 3
Badzéré ○ **CAM** 206-207 B 6
Baediam ○ **RIM** 202-203 E 2
Baer ○ **VRC** 144-145 B 4
Baerskin Lake ○ **CDN** 34-35 L 4
Baeza ○ **E** 98-99 F 6
Baeza ○ **EC** 64-65 D 2
Baezaeko River ~ **CDN** 32-33 H 5
Bafang ○ **CAM** 204-205 H 6
Bafata ★ **GNB** 202-203 C 3
Baffin Basin ≃ 26-27 R 7
Baffin Bay ≈ 26-27 P 7
Baffin Bay ≈ 44-45 J 6
Baffin-Greenland Rise ≃ 28-29 L 3
Baffin Island ~ **CDN** 24-25 e 5
Bafia ○ **CAM** 204-205 J 6
Bafilo ○ **RT** 202-203 L 5
Bafing ~ **RMM** 202-203 E 3
Bafing-Makana ○ **RMM** 202-203 E 3
Bafodia ○ **WAL** 202-203 E 5
Bafoulabé ○ **RMM** 202-203 E 3
Bafoussam ★ **CAM** 204-205 J 6
Bäfq ○ **IR** 134-135 F 3
Bafra ★ **TR** 128-129 F 2
Bafra Burnu ▲ **TR** 128-129 F 2
Bäft ○ **IR** 134-135 G 4
Bafut ○ **CAM** 204-205 J 5
Bafwabalinga ○ **ZRE** 212-213 A 3
Bafwabogbo ○ **ZRE** 210-211 L 3
Bafwaboli ○ **ZRE** 210-211 L 3
Bafwasende ○ **ZRE** 212-213 A 3
Baga ○ **WAN** 198-199 H 5
Bagabag ○ **RP** 160-161 D 4
Bagabag Island ~ **PNG** 183 C 3
Bagaces ○ **CR** 52-53 B 6
Bagadja ○ **RUS** 118-119 J 3
Bagaembo ○ **ZRE** 206-207 F 6
Bagaevskij = stanica Bagaevskaja ○ **RUS** 102-103 M 4
Bagagem, Rio ~ **BR** 68-69 D 7
Bagai ○ **PNG** 183 E 3
Bagalkot ○ **IND** 140-141 F 2
Bägälür ○ **IND** 140-141 G 4
Bagamanoc ○ **RP** 160-161 F 6
Bagan Datuk ○ **MAL** 162-163 D 2
Bagandou ○ **RCA** 210-211 F 2
Bagani ○ **NAM** 216-217 E 5
Bagansiapiapi ○ **RI** 162-163 D 3
Bagansinembah ○ **RI** 162-163 D 4
Baganuur = Nuurst ○ **MAU** 148-149 J 4
Bagaré ○ **BF** 202-203 J 3
Bagaroua ○ **RN** 198-199 B 5
Bagasin ○ **PNG** 183 C 3
Baga Sola ○ **TCH** 198-199 G 6
Bagassi ○ **BF** 202-203 J 4
Bagata ○ **BF** 202-203 J 4
Bagata ○ **ZRE** 210-211 F 5
Bagazan ○ **PE** 64-65 F 4
Bagbe ~ **WAL** 202-203 E 5
Bagdād □ **IRQ** 128-129 L 6
Bagdad ★ **IRQ** 128-129 L 6
Bagdad ○ **USA** 40-41 H 8
Bagdarin ○ **RUS** 118-119 F 8
Bagé ○ **BR** 76-77 K 6
Bagega ○ **WAN** 204-205 F 3
Bägein ○ **IR** 134-135 G 3
Bäg-e Malek ○ **IR** 134-135 C 3
Bägepalli ○ **IND** 140-141 G 4
Bägestän ○ **IR** 134-135 H 1
Bageya ○ **WAN** 198-199 G 6
Bäggïrân ○ **IR** 136-137 F 6
Baggs ○ **USA** 42-43 D 5
Bagley ○ **USA** 42-43 K 2
Bagley Icefield ⊂ **USA** 20-21 T 6
Bagnell Dam ∴ **USA** 42-43 L 6
Bagnères-de-Bigorre ○ **F** 90-91 H 10
Bago ○ **RP** 160-161 E 7
Bago, Pulau ~ **RI** 162-163 B 3
Bagodar ○ **IND** 142-143 D 4
Bagodo ○ **CAM** 204-205 K 5
Bagodra ○ **IND** 138-139 D 8
Bagoé ~ **RMM** 202-203 G 3
Bagomoyo ○ **EAT** 214-215 K 4
Bagoosaar ○ **SP** 208-209 G 4
Bagot Range ▲ **AUS** 178-179 C 4
Bagou ○ **DY** 204-205 F 3
Bagraband, Kühe ▲ **IR** 134-135 J 5
Bagrämi ○ **AFG** 138-139 B 4
Bagrationovsk ○ · **RUS** 94-95 G 4
Bagre ○ **BF** 62-63 J 6
Bag Tug ~ **VRC** 154-155 F 2
Bagua ○ **PE** 64-65 C 4
Bagua Grande ○ **PE** 64-65 C 4
Báguales, Cerro ▲ **RA** 80 F 4
Báguanos ○ **C** 54-55 G 4
Bagudo ○ **WAN** 204-205 F 3
Baguinéda ○ **RMM** 202-203 G 3
Baguio ○ **RP** (DAO) 160-161 F 9
Baguio ★ · **RP** (BEN) 160-161 D 4
Bagyrlaj ~ **KA** 96-97 G 9
Bäha, al- ○ **KSA** 132-133 B 3
Bahádórabad ○ **IR** 134-135 G 4

Bahadurabad Ghat ○ **BD** 142-143 F 3
Bähädurganj ○ **IND** 142-143 E 2
Baham, Umm al- ○ **KSA** 130-131 C 5
Bahamas = Bahamas, The ■ **BS** 54-55 J 4
Bahamas National Trust Park ⊥ **BS** 54-55 J 4
Bahapča ~ **RUS** 120-121 O 3
Bahär ○ **IR** 134-135 B 1
Bähäragora ○ **IND** 142-143 E 4
Bahärak ○ **AFG** 136-137 M 6
Baharampur ○ **IND** 142-143 F 3
Bahardok ○ **TM** 136-137 F 6
Bahariya Oasis = Bahriya, al-Wähät al-··· **ET** 194-195 D 3
Bähär, Küh-e ▲ **IR** 136-137 F 7
Bahau ○ **MAL** 162-163 E 3
Bahaur ○ **RI** 164-165 D 5
Bahäwalnagar ○ **PK** 138-139 D 5
Bahäwalpur ○ **PK** 138-139 D 5
Bahay ○ **RP** 160-161 F 6
Bahçe ★ **TR** 128-129 G 4
Baheri ○ **IND** 138-139 G 5
Bahi ○ **BR** 68-69 H 7
Bahi ○ **BR** 72-73 H 2
Bahía, Islas de la ~ **HN** 52-53 L 3
Bahia, Tanjung ▲ **RI** 166-167 H 4
Bahia Asunción ○ **MEX** 50-51 B 4
Bahía Blanca ○ **RA** 78-79 H 5
Bahía Bustamante ○ **RA** 80 G 2
Bahía Creek ○ **RA** 78-79 H 6
Bahía de Caráquez ○ **EC** 64-65 B 2
Bahía de Los Angeles ○ **MEX** 50-51 C 3
Bahía Honda ○ **C** 54-55 D 3
Bahía Kino ○ **MEX** 50-51 D 3
Bahía Laura ○ **RA** 80 G 4
Bahía Mansa ○ **RCH** 78-79 C 6
Bahlas, Cabo dos ▲ **RA** 80 H 2
Bahía Solano ○ **CO** 60-61 C 4
Bahir, Che'w ~ **ETH** 208-209 C 6
Bahir Dar ★ **ETH** 208-209 C 3
Bähla ○ **IR** 138-139 O 6
Bahma ~ **IRQ** 128-129 L 4
Bahn ○ **LB** 202-203 F 6
Bahr ○ **RCA** 206-207 G 6
Bahra, al- ○ **KWT** 130-131 K 3
Bahra'in = Bahrain, al- ■ **BRN** 134-135 D 6
Bahr al-Milh ○ **IRQ** 128-129 K 6
Bahret Lut = Yam Hamelah ○ **JOR** 130-131 D 2
Bähtî Kalai ○ **AFG** 138-139 B 4
Bahta ~ **RUS** 114-115 U 3
Bähta ~ **RUS** 114-115 V 4
Bähtärän □ **IR** (BAH) 134-135 B 1
Bähtärän ○ · **IR** (BAH) 134-135 B 1
Bähtegân, Daryä-ce ○ **IR** 134-135 E 3
Bahtemir ○ **RUS** 126-127 G 5
Bahty ○ **KA** 124-125 N 5
Bahubulu, Pulau ~ **RI** 164-165 H 5
Bähü Kalät, Rüdhäne-ye ~ **IR** 134-135 J 6
Bahusnai ○ **RI** 164-165 G 5
Bahynaj ○ **RUS** 110-111 O 6
Baia ○ **PNG** 183 F 3
Baía, Rio da ~ **BR** 68-69 B 5
Baía dos Tigres ○ **ANG** 216-217 A 8
Baía Farta ○ **ANG** 216-217 D 7
Baía Formosa ○ **BR** 68-69 H 7
Baía Grande, Lago ○ **BR** 70-71 G 4
Baia Mare ★ · **RO** 102-103 C 4
Baianópolis ○ **BR** 72-73 H 2
Baião ○ **BR** 68-69 D 3
Baia River ~ **PNG** 183 B 4
Baibokoum ○ **TCH** 206-207 B 4
Baicheng ○ **VRC** (JIL) 150-151 D 5
Baicheng ○ **VRC** (XUZ) 146-147 E 5
Baïcoi ○ **RO** 102-103 D 5
Baïda', al- ○ **Y** 132-133 D 7
Baïdä' Natíl ○ **KSA** 130-131 G 4
Baidi Cheng · **VRC** 154-155 F 6
Baïdou ~ **RCA** 206-207 E 6
Baie, La ○ **CDN** 38-39 J 4
Baie-à-la-Loutre ○ **CDN** 38-39 N 4
Baie-Comeau ○ **CDN** 38-39 K 4
Baie-des-Sables ○ **CDN** 38-39 L 4
Baie-du-Poste ○ **CDN** 38-39 H 3
Baie Johan-Beetz ○ **CDN** 38-39 N 3
Baie-Sainte-Claire ○ **CDN** 38-39 M 4
Baie-Saint-Paul ○ **CDN** 38-39 J 5
Ba'ïgï ○ **IRQ** 128-129 K 5
Baïhán al-Qasáb ○ **Y** 132-133 D 6
Baihe ○ **VRC** (JIL) 150-151 G 6
Baihe ○ **VRC** (SXI) 154-155 G 5
Baija ○ **N** 92-93 P 5
Baikal = Bajkal, ozero ○ **RUS** 116-117 N 9
Baikal-Amur-Magistrale = BAM II **RUS** 118-119 E 7
Baikoré, Bahr ~ **TCH** 206-207 C 3
Baikunthpur ○ **IND** 142-143 C 4
Baïla ○ **SN** 202-203 D 2
Baila ○ **VRC** 144-145 F 6
Bailang ○ **VRC** 156-157 G 6
Baile Átha Cliath = Dublin ★ ·· **IRL** 90-91 D 5
Baile Átha Fhirdhia = Ardee ○ **IRL** 90-91 D 5
Baile Átha Luain = Athlone ○ **IRL** 90-91 C 5
Baile Átha Troim = Trim ★ · **IRL** 90-91 D 5
Baile Brigín = Balbriggan ○ **IRL** 90-91 D 5
Baile Chathail = Charlestown ○ **IRL** 90-91 C 5
Baile Shleáin-Bhéarra = Castletown Bearhaven ○ **IRL** 90-91 B 6
Baile Locha Riach = Loughrea ○ **IRL** 90-91 C 5

Baile Mhistéala = Mitchelstown ○ **IRL** 90-91 C 5
Bailén ○ **E** 98-99 F 5
Bäileşti ○ **RO** 102-103 C 5
Bailey ○ **ZA** 220-221 H 6
Bailey Point ▲ **CDN** 24-25 O 3
Bailey Range ▲ **AUS** 178-179 G 4
Bail Hongal ○ **IND** 140-141 F 3
Baili, Bi'r ○ **ET** 192-193 L 7
Bailidujuan · **VRC** 156-157 E 2
Bailin ○ **VRC** 156-157 H 3
Bailingmiao · **VRC** 148-149 K 7
Bailique ○ **BR** (APA) 62-63 J 5
Bailique ○ **BR** (P) 68-69 D 5
Bailique, Ilha ~ **BR** 62-63 K 5
Bailleul ○ **F** 90-91 J 3
Ba Illi ○ **TCH** 206-207 C 3
Ba Illi ~ **TCH** 206-207 C 3
Baillie Hamilton Island ~ **CDN** 24-25 Z 3
Baillie Islands ~ **CDN** 24-25 G 5
Baillie River ~ **CDN** 30-31 N 3
Bailong Jiang ~ **VRC** 154-155 D 5
Bailundo ○ **ANG** 216-217 D 6
Baima ○ **VRC** (SIC) 154-155 D 5
Baima ○ **VRC** (SIC) 156-157 E 2
Baimaxue Shan Z.B. ⊥ · **VRC** 144-145 M 6
Baimka ○ **RUS** 112-113 N 3
Baimun ○ **RI** 166-167 H 4
Baimuru ○ **PNG** 183 B 4
Baina ○ **PNG** 183 B 4
Bainbridge ○ **USA** 48-49 F 4
Baines Drift ○ **RB** 218-219 E 6
Bainet ○ **RH** 54-55 J 5
Baing ○ **RI** 168 E 8
Baining Mountains ▲ **PNG** 183 G 3
Baiona ○ **E** 98-99 C 3
Baiquan ○ **VRC** 150-151 F 4
Ba'ir ○ **JOR** 130-131 E 2
Ba'ir, Wädï ~ **JOR** 130-131 E 2
Baird ○ **USA** 44-45 H 5
Baird, Cape ▲ **CDN** 26-27 R 3
Baird Inlet ≈ 20-21 H 4
Baird Mountains ▲ **USA** 20-21 K 3
Baird Peninsula ᴗ **CDN** 24-25 h 6
Bairds Table Mountain ▲ **AUS** 174-175 G 4
Baire ○ **C** 54-55 G 4
Bairiki ★ **KIB** 13 J 2
Bairin Youqi ○ **VRC** 148-149 O 6
Bairin Zuoqi ○ **VRC** 148-149 O 5
Bairnsdale ○ **AUS** 180-181 J 7
Baïrüt ★ **RL** 128-129 F 6
Baïs ○ **RP** 160-161 E 8
Baïs ○ **RP** 160-161 C 5
Baïse ~ **F** 90-91 H 10
Baïsha ○ **VRC** (HAI) 156-157 F 7
Baïsha ○ **VRC** (SIC) 156-157 E 2
Baishan ○ **VRC** 150-151 F 6
Ba Shan ▲ **VRC** 146-147 L 5
Baishanzu ▲ **VRC** 156-157 L 3
Baishilazi Z.B. ⊥ · **VRC** 150-151 E 7
Baishiling · **VRC** 156-157 G 7
Baishui ○ **VRC** 154-155 F 5
Baishuijiang Z.B. ⊥ · **VRC** 154-155 D 5
Baisogala ○ · **LT** 94-95 H 4
Baïssa ○ **WAN** 204-205 J 5
Bait Adäqa ○ **Y** 132-133 C 6
Baïtadi ○ **NEP** 144-145 C 6
Bait al-Faqïh ○ **Y** 132-133 C 6
Bait Lahm = Bet Lehem ○ · · **WB** 130-131 D 2
Bait Range ▲ **CDN** 32-33 G 4
Baixa do Tubará, Rio ~ **BR** 68-69 J 7
Baixa Grande ○ **BR** 68-69 H 7
Baixão ○ **BR** 72-73 K 2
Baixo Guandu ○ **BR** 72-73 K 5
Baixo Longa ○ **ANG** 216-217 E 7
Baiyang Gou · **VRC** 146-147 H 3
Baiyan Temple · **VRC** 154-155 H 4
Baiyer River ○ **PNG** 183 C 3
Baiyer River National Park ⊥ **PNG** 183 C 3
Baiyin ○ **VRC** 154-155 E 6
Baiyin → **VRC** 154-155 E 6
Baizeklik Qianfodong · **VRC** 146-147 J 3
Baja ○ **H** 92-93 P 5
Baja, Punta ▲ **MEX** (BCN) 50-51 B 3
Baja, Punta ▲ **MEX** (SON) 50-51 D 3
Baja California □ **MEX** 50-51 B 2
Baja California Norte □ **MEX** 50-51 B 2
Baja California Sur □ **MEX** 50-51 C 4
Bajada, Gr. ○ **C** 54-55 C 4
Bajada del Agrio ○ **RA** 78-79 D 5
Bajaga ~ **RUS** 120-121 E 2
Baján ○ **MAU** 146-147 M 2
Baján ○ **MEX** 50-51 J 4
Bajanaul ★ **KA** 124-125 M 3
Bajanbulag ○ **MAU** 148-149 D 4
Bajančandman = Ih suuž ○ **MAU** 148-149 F 4
Bajandėlgėr = Širėėt ○ **MAU** 148-149 J 5
Bajangol=Baruunharaa ○ **MAU** 148-149 H 3
Bajan-Hongor □ **MAU** 148-149 D 4
Bajanhongor ★ **MAU** 148-149 E 4
Bajanlig = Hatansuudal ○ **MAU** 146-147 K 1
Bajanmönh = Ulaan-Èrėg ○ **MAU** 148-149 J 4
Bajan-Ölgij □ **MAU** 146-147 J 1
Bajan-Öndör = Bumbat ○ **MAU** 148-149 E 4
Bajan-Önzuul = Ihhairhan ○ **MAU** 148-149 F 4
Bajan-Ovoo = Žavhlant ○ **MAU** 148-149 J 4
Bajan-Ovoo = Žavhlant ○ **MAU** 148-149 J 4
Bajantėg ○ **MAU** 148-149 E 5
Bajan Uul = Bajan ○ **MAU** 146-147 M 2
Bajan-Uul = Žavarthošuu ○ **MAU** 148-149 L 3
Bajasgalant = Hajirhan ○ **MAU** 148-149 L 4
Bajawa ○ **RI** 168 E 8

Bajdarackaja guba ≈ 108-109 L 7
Bajdarata ~ **RUS** 108-109 M 8
Bajdrag gol ~ **MAU** 148-149 D 4
Baiganin ○ **KA** 126-127 M 3
Bajie ○ **VRC** 156-157 F 4
Bajimba, Mount ▲ **AUS** 178-179 M 5
Bajina Bašta ○ **YU** 100-101 G 3
Bajjio de Ahuichila ○ **MEX** 50-51 H 5
Bajkadam ○ **KA** 136-137 L 3
Bajkadam ~ **KA** 136-137 L 3
Bajkal ○ **RUS** 116-117 M 10
Bajkal, zaliv ≈ **RUS** 122-123 J 3
Bajkalovo ○ **RUS** 114-115 J 6
Bajkalsk ○ **RUS** 118-119 U 6
Bajkalsk ○ **RUS** 116-117 L 10
Bajkal'skij hrebet ▲ **RUS** 116-117 O 8
Bajkal'skij zapovednij ⊥ **RUS** 116-117 M 10
Bajkal'skoe ○ **RUS** 118-119 D 8
Bajki ○ **RUS** 96-97 K 6
Bajkit ○ **RUS** 116-117 H 5
Bajkonyr ○ **KA** 124-125 L 3
Bajkonyr ~ **KA** 124-125 D 5
Bajkovo ○ **RUS** 122-123 R 3
Bajmak ○ **RUS** 96-97 L 7
Bajo ○ **RI** 168 D 7
Bajo, El ○ **YV** 60-61 J 3
Bajo Caracoles ○ **RA** 80 E 3
Bajoga ○ **WAN** 204-205 J 3
Bajo Hondo ○ **RA** 76-77 D 6
Bajo Nuevo ○ **AUS** 178-179 L 2
Bajool ○ **AUS** 178-179 L 2
Bajos de Haina ○ **DOM** 54-55 K 5
Bajram-Ali ○ **TM** 136-137 H 6
Bajsa ~ **RUS** 118-119 F 8
Bajsun ○ **US** 136-137 K 5
Bajugan ○ **RI** 164-165 G 3
Bajrykūm ○ **KA** 136-137 L 3
Baká ○ **NIC** 52-53 B 5
Bakaba ~ **TCH** 206-207 C 5
Bakari, Área Indígena ✕ **BR** 70-71 K 4
Bakal ○ **RUS** 96-97 L 6
Bakala ○ **RCA** (OMB) 206-207 C 5
Bakala ○ **RCA** (Oua) 206-207 C 5
Bakali ~ **ZRE** 210-211 F 6
Bakaly ○ **RUS** 96-97 J 6
Bakanas ~ **KA** 124-125 L 4
Bakaoré ~ **TCH** 198-199 K 5
Bakau ○ **WAG** 202-203 B 3
Bakebe ○ **CAM** 204-205 H 6
Bakel ○ **SN** 202-203 D 2
Bakelalan ○ **MAL** 162-163 G 3
Bala-Talcyk ~ **RUS** 96-97 K 6
Bakan ○ **RP** 160-161 E 6
Bakau ○ **KA** 124-125 K 6
Bakčar ○ **RUS** 114-115 R 6
Bakčar ~ **RUS** 114-115 R 6
Baker ○ **USA** (CA) 40-41 F 8
Baker ○ **USA** (LA) 44-45 M 4
Baker ○ **USA** (MT) 42-43 E 2
Baker ○ **USA** (OR) 40-41 F 3
Baker ○ **USA** (WV) 46-47 H 5
Baker, Canal ≈ 80 C 3
Baker, Mount ▲ **USA** 40-41 D 1
Baker Creek ○ **CDN** 32-33 J 3
Baker Island ~ **USA** 13 K 2
Baker Island ~ **USA** 32-33 D 4
Baker Lake ○ **CDN** (NWT) 30-31 V 3
Baker Lake ○ **CDN** (NWT) 30-31 V 3
Baker Range ▲ **AUS** 176-177 H 2
Bakers Dozen Islands ~ **CDN** 36-37 K 6
Bakersfield ○ **USA** 40-41 E 8
Bakerville ○ **ZA** 220-221 H 3
Ba Khe ○ **VN** 156-157 D 6
Bakhtiyárpur ○ **IND** 142-143 D 3
Bakı ★ **AZ** 128-129 N 2
Bakin Birji ○ **RN** 198-199 D 5
Bakinskij arhipelago ~ **AZ** 128-129 N 3
Bakırçay ~ **TR** 128-129 B 3
Bakkaflördur ○ **IS** 86-87 f 1
Bakkejord ○ **N** 86-87 H 2
Baknars Tâl ○ **IND** 142-143 C 2
Bako ○ **CI** 202-203 G 4
Bako ○ **ETH** 208-209 C 4
Bako National Park ⊥ **MAL** 162-163 F 4
Bakong, Pulau ~ **RI** 162-163 F 4
Bakongan ○ **RI** 162-163 B 3
Bakool □ **SP** 208-209 F 6
Bakordi ○ **SUD** 206-207 J 6
Bakore, Massif de ▲ **RCA** 206-207 B 5
Bakori ○ **WAN** 204-205 G 3
Bakouma ○ **RCA** 206-207 E 6
Bakoye ~ **RMM** 202-203 F 3
Baksa ~ **RUS** 114-115 R 7
Bak Sadane ~ **RMM** 196-197 J 5
Baksaj ~ **KA** 96-97 G 9
Baksan ○ **RUS** 126-127 F 5
Baksan ~ **RUS** 126-127 F 5
Baktalórántháza ○ **H** 92-93 R 5
Baku = Bakı ★ **AZ** 128-129 N 2
Bakuto ○ **RI** 164-165 K 3
Bakung, Pulau ~ **RI** 162-163 F 4
Bakuriani ○ **GE** 126-127 E 7
Bakwa-Kenge ○ **ZRE** 210-211 J 5
Baky ~ **RUS** 110-111 V 5
Bakyrly ○ **KA** 124-125 E 6
Bala ○ **CDN** 38-39 F 6
Bala ○ **RUS** 110-111 T 6
Bala ★ **TR** 128-129 E 3
Bala ○ **WAN** 204-205 D 2
Bala, Cerros de ▲ **BOL** 70-71 C 3
Balabac Island ~ **RP** 160-161 B 9
Balabac Strait ≈ 160-161 B 9
Balabagan ○ **RP** 160-161 F 8
Balabaiba ○ **ANG** 216-217 B 6
Balac ○ **RP** 160-161 D 5
Baler ○ **RP** 160-161 D 5
Baler Bay ≈ 160-161 D 5

Balabalangar, Kepulauan ~ **RI** 164-165 L 5
Bäla Bolük ○ **AFG** 134-135 K 2
Balad al-Mala ○ **IRQ** 128-129 L 5
Balade ○ **IR** 134-135 C 1
Baladjie Lake ○ **AUS** 176-177 E 5
Balad Rüz ○ **IRQ** 128-129 L 6
Balad Singâr ○ **IRQ** 128-129 J 5
Balagaččy ○ **RUS** 118-119 L 3
Balaganah ○ **RUS** 118-119 H 6
Balagannoe ○ **RUS** 120-121 N 4
Balagansk ○ **RUS** 116-117 L 9
Balagan-Taas ~ **RUS** 110-111 Z 6
Balaguer ○ **E** 98-99 H 4
Balahna ○ **RUS** 94-95 S 3
Balahninskij hrebet ▲ **RUS** 110-111 f 5
Balahonovskoe ○ **RUS** 126-127 E 5
Balahta ○ **RUS** 116-117 E 8
Ba Lai, Sông ~ **VN** 158-159 J 5
Balaipungut ○ **RI** 162-163 J 4
Balaikarangan ○ **RI** 162-163 J 4
Balaipungut ○ **RI** 162-163 D 4
Balaiselasa ○ **RI** 162-163 C 5
Balaka ○ **MW** 218-219 H 2
Balakbal ∴ · **MEX** 52-53 K 3
Balakėte ○ **RCA** 206-207 E 3
Balaki ○ **RG** 202-203 E 3
Balaklava ○ **AUS** 180-181 E 3
Balaklija ○ **UA** 102-103 K 3
Bälälėot ○ **PK** 138-139 D 2
Balakovo ○ **RUS** 96-97 G 7
Balala ○ **ETH** 208-209 D 5
Balama ○ **MOC** 218-219 K 1
Balambangan, Pulau ~ **MAL** 160-161 B 9
Balam Täkli ○ **IND** 138-139 E 10
Balancán de Domínguez ○ **MEX** 52-53 J 3
Balanced Rock · **USA** 40-41 G 4
Balandou ○ **RG** 202-203 F 4
Balaôa ○ **RP** 160-161 D 5
Balanga ○ **ZRE** 214-215 E 5
Balangala ○ **ZRE** 210-211 G 3
Ba Lang An, Müi ▲ **VN** 158-159 K 3
Balängïr ○ **IND** 142-143 C 5
Balangkavan ○ **RP** 160-161 F 7
Balangoda ○ **CL** 140-141 J 7
Balao ○ **EC** 64-65 C 3
Balaoan ○ **RP** 160-161 D 5
Balapitiya ○ **CL** 140-141 J 7
Balaraja ○ **RI** 168 B 3
Balarámpur ○ **IND** 142-143 E 4
Balasan ○ **RP** 160-161 F 7
Balašiha ○ **RUS** 94-95 P 4
Bäi-Salavat ○ **KA** 132-133 C 4
Balašov ○ **RUS** 102-103 N 2
Balassagyarmat ○ **H** 92-93 P 4
Balät ○ **ET** 194-195 D 3
Balat (Labuhanbalat) ○ **RI** 168 C 7
Balatan ○ **RP** 160-161 E 6
Balaton ○ **H** 92-93 O 5
Balatonfüred ○ **H** 92-93 O 5
Balauring ○ **RI** 166-167 B 6
Balava ○ **RG** 202-203 H 3
Balazote ○ **E** 98-99 F 5
Balbalan ○ **RP** 160-161 D 4
Balbalasang ○ **RP** 160-161 D 4
Balbao ○ **PA** 52-53 E 7
Balbi, Mount ▲ **PNG** 184 I b 1
Balbina ○ **BR** 62-63 E 6
Balbina, Cachoeira ~ **BR** 62-63 E 6
Balbina, Represa de ◁ **BR** 62-63 E 6
Balboa ○ **CO** 60-61 D 5
Balbriggan = Baile Brigín ○ **IRL** 90-91 D 5
Balcad ○ **SP** 212-213 G 2
Balcarce ○ **RA** 78-79 K 4
Balcarres ○ **CDN** 34-35 D 5
Bälceşti ○ **RO** 102-103 D 5
Balchaš, ozero = Balqash Köl ○ **KA** 124-125 H 6
Balčik ○ **BG** 102-103 F 6
Balcutha ○ **NZ** 182 B 7
Balcones Escarpment ᴗ **USA** 44-45 H 5
Balde de la Mora ○ **RA** 76-77 D 6
Baldenourg = Biały Bór ○ **PL** 92-93 O 2
Bald Head ▲ **AUS** 176-177 D 6
Bald Hill ▲ **CDN** 20-21 Z 4
Bald Hill No. 2 ▲ **AUS** 178-179 L 4
Bald Knob ○ **USA** 44-45 M 2
Baldock Lake ○ **CDN** 34-35 H 4
Baldwin ○ **USA** (MI) 46-47 F 4
Baldwin ○ **USA** (WI) 42-43 L 3
Baldwin Bank ~ **AUS** 172-173 H 2
Baldwin Peninsula ᴗ **USA** 20-21 J 3
Baldy Mountain ▲ **CDN** 34-35 F 5
Baldy Peak ▲ **USA** 44-45 D 4
Bafdžikan ○ **RUS** 118-119 E 11
Bale ○ **ANG** 216-217 D 7
Bale ○ **ETH** 208-209 D 5
Balé ~ **RG** 202-203 E 4
Bale ~ **RMM** 202-203 F 4
Bâle = Basel ○ · **CH** 92-93 J 5
Baleares, Islas = Balears, Illes ▲ **E** 98-99 H 5
Balearic Islands = Balears, Illes ▲ **E** 98-99 J 5
Balease ○ **RI** 164-165 G 5
Balease, Gunung ▲ **RI** 164-165 G 5
Baleh ~ **MAL** 162-163 K 3
Baleia, Ponta da ▲ **BR** 72-73 L 4
Baleine, Rivière à la ~ **CDN** 36-37 O 5
Balej ★ **RUS** 118-119 H 10
Balékoutou ○ **TCH** 206-207 B 3
Baléla ○ **MAU** 202-203 F 3
Balelesberg ▲ **ZA** 220-221 K 4
Bálên ~ **RUS** 118-119 F 8
Baler ○ **RP** 160-161 D 5

Baleshwar ○ **IND** 142-143 E 5
Balestrand ○ · **N** 86-87 C 6
Baléya ○ **RMM** 202-203 E 3
Baleyara ○ **RN** 204-205 E 2
Baley Guerrero ○ **DOM** 54-55 L 5
Balezino ★ **RUS** 96-97 H 5
Balfour ○ **CDN** 32-33 M 7
Balfour ○ **ZA** (CAP) 220-221 H 6
Balfour ○ **ZA** (TRA) 220-221 J 3
Balfour Downs ○ **AUS** 172-173 E 7
Balgak ○ **SUD** 200-201 C 6
Balguntay ○ **VRC** 146-147 H 4
Balǧuraši ○ **KSA** 132-133 B 4
Balḩ ○ **AFG** 136-137 K 6
Balḩ ~ **AFG** 136-137 K 6
Balḩ, Daryā-ye ~ **AFG** 136-137 K 6
Balḩ Ab, Rūd-e ~ **AFG** 136-137 K 7
Balhaš = Balkash ○ **KA** 124-125 J 5
Balhaš = Balkash köl ○ **KA** 124-125 J 5
Balho ○ **DJI** 200-201 L 6
Bali ○ **CAM** 204-205 J 5
Bali ○ **IND** 142-143 F 4
Bali ○ **RI** 168 B 6
Bali, Laut ≈ 168 B 6
Bali, Pulau ~ **RI** 168 B 7
Bali, Selat ≈ 168 B 7
Balibi ○ **RCA** 206-207 E 5
Balibo ○ **RI** 166-167 C 6
Baliem ~ **RI** 166-167 K 4
Baliem Valley ᴗ **RI** 166-167 K 3
Balifondo ○ **RCA** 206-207 F 6
Balige ○ **RI** 162-163 C 3
Balikesir ★ **TR** 128-129 B 3
Balikpapan ○ **RI** 164-165 E 4
Balikpapary, Teluk ≈ 164-165 E 4
Balimela Reservoir ◁ **IND** 142-143 C 6
Balimo ○ **PNG** 183 B 5
Baling ○ **MAL** 162-163 D 2
Balingara, Pegunungan ▲ **RI** 164-165 G 4
Balingian ○ **MAL** 162-163 K 3
Balinn ~ **RMM** 202-203 E 3
Balintang Channel ≈ 160-161 D 3
Balíza ○ **BR** 72-73 D 4
Baljaga ~ **RUS** 116-117 O 10
Balkaš ○ **KA** 124-125 J 5
Balkašty ○ **KA** 124-125 F 2
Balkon-Myľk, gora ▲ **RUS** 88-89 O 2
Ball, Mount ▲ **AUS** 172-173 H 5
Balladonia Motel ○ **AUS** 176-177 G 6
Ballangen ○ **N** 86-87 H 2
Ballantyne, Lac ○ **CDN** 36-37 P 5
Ballarat ○ **AUS** 180-181 G 4
Ballard, Lake ○ **AUS** 176-177 F 4
Ballaroco ○ **AUS** 178-179 F 4
Ballasetas ○ **RI** 162-163 B 3
Ballater ○ **GB** 90-91 F 3
Ballé ○ **RMM** 202-203 F 2
Ballena, Punta ▲ **EC** 64-65 B 3
Ballenas, Canal de ≈ 50-51 C 3
Ballenero, Canal ≈ 80 E 7
Ballia ○ **IND** 142-143 D 3
Ballidu ○ **AUS** 176-177 C 5
Ballina ○ **AUS** 178-179 M 5
Ballina = Béal an Átha ○ **IRL** 90-91 C 4
Ballinasloe = Béal Átha na Sluaighe ○ **IRL** 90-91 C 5
Ballinger ○ **USA** 44-45 H 4
Ball Lake ○ **CDN** 34-35 K 5
Ballone Highway II **AUS** 178-179 J 4
Ballou ○ **DZ** 190-191 C 3
Ball's Pyramid ~ **AUS** 180-181 N 7
Ballycastle ○ **GB** 90-91 D 4
Ballyshannon ○ **IRL** 90-91 C 4
Balmacara ○ **GB** 90-91 D 3
Balmaceda ○ **RCH** 80 E 2
Balmaceda, Cerro ▲ **RCH** 80 D 5
Balmaceda, Parque Nacional ⊥ **RCH** 80 D 5
Balmaceda, Sierra ▲ **RCH** 80 F 6
Balmoral ○ **AUS** 180-181 F 4
Balmoral ○ **ZA** 220-221 J 2
Balmorhea ○ **USA** 44-45 F 4
Balneária ○ **RA** 76-77 F 6
Balneário Camboriú ○ **BR** 74-75 F 6
Balneario del Sol ○ **C** 54-55 H 5
Balneario las Grutas ○ **RA** 78-79 F 6
Balneario Massini ○ **RA** 78-79 H 6
Balo ○ **RI** 164-165 H 4
Baloa ○ **RI** 164-165 H 4
Balobalong-Kecil, Pulau ~ **RI** 168 D 6
Balod ○ **IND** 142-143 B 5
Balohan, Teluk ≈ 162-163 A 2
Balok, Kampung ○ **MAL** 162-163 E 3
Balombo ○ **ANG** 216-217 C 6
Balong ○ **RI** 168 D 7
Balong ○ **VRC** 144-145 L 2
Balonne River ~ **AUS** 178-179 K 5
Balqash Köl = Balkaš köl ○ **KA** 124-125 H 6
Balrāmpur ○ **IND** 142-143 C 2
Balranald ○ **AUS** 180-181 G 3
Balş ○ **RO** 102-103 D 5
Balsa Nova ○ **BR** 74-75 F 5
Balsapuerto ○ **PE** 64-65 D 4
Balsas ○ **BR** 68-69 E 6
Balsas ○ **MEX** 52-53 E 3
Balsas, Rio das ~ **BR** 68-69 E 7
Balsas, Rio das ~ **BR** 68-69 D 7
Balsinhas, Ribeiro ~ **BR** 68-69 D 7
Balta ○ · **UA** 102-103 F 4
Balta Brăilei ⊥ **RO** 102-103 E 5
Baltakoľ ○ **KA** 136-137 K 3
Baltakoľ ~ **KA** 136-137 K 3

Baltal ○ **IND** 138-139 E 2
Baltasar Brum ○ **ROU** 76-77 J 6
Baltasi ~ **RUS** 96-97 H 5
Baltazar ○ **YV** 60-61 H 6
Bălți ☆ **MD** 102-103 E 4
Baltic Sea ≈ 86-87 H 9
Baltijsk ○ **RUS** 94-95 F 4
Baltim ○ **ET** 194-195 E 2
Baltimore ○ **USA** 46-47 K 6
Baltimore ○ **ZA** 218-219 E 6
Baltimore = Dún na Séad ○ **IRL**
  90-91 C 6
Baltit ○ **PK** 138-139 E 1
Baltiysk = Baltijsk ○ **RUS** 94-95 F 4
Baltra, Isla ∧ **EC** 64-65 B 10
Baltrum ○ **D** 92-93 J 2
Ba Lụa, Quần Đảo ∧ **VN** 158-159 H 5
Baluan Island ∧ **PNG** 183 D 2
Bālūčestán, Sístán -ó- ⊥ **IR** 134-135 H 5
Baluchistán ○ **PK** 134-135 K 4
Baluchistan = Bālūčestan ⊥ **IR**
  134-135 K 4
Balud ~ **MAL** 164-165 D 2
Balui ~ **MAL** 164-165 D 2
Balūr ○ **IND** 140-141 F 4
Baluran Game Park ⊥ **RI** 168 B 6
Balut Island ∧ **RP** 160-161 F 10
Balvard ○ **IR** 134-135 G 4
Balvi ☆⋆ **LV** 94-95 K 3
Balwāda ○ **IND** 138-139 E 8
Balwina Aboriginal Land ⅄ **AUS**
  172-173 J 6
Balygyčan ○ **RUS** 112-113 H 5
Balygyčan ~ **RUS** 112-113 H 5
Balygyčan, Verhnij ○ **RUS** 112-113 H 5
Balyhta ○ **RUS** 116-117 M 8
Balykča ○ **RUS** 124-125 P 3
Balyktah ~ **RUS** 110-111 W 2
Balyktyg-Hem ~ **RUS** 116-117 H 10
Balzar ○ **EC** 64-65 C 2
Balzas ○ **RG** 202-203 J 7
Balž gol ~ **MAU** 148-149 K 3
Bam ○ **IR** 134-135 H 5
Bam ○ **TCH** 206-207 C 4
BAM = Baikal-Amur-Magistrale II **RUS**
  118-119 J 7
Bam, Lac de ○ **BF** 202-203 K 3
Bama ○ **BF** 202-203 H 4
Bama ○ **VRC** 156-157 E 4
Bama ○ **WAN** 204-205 K 3
Bamaba ○ **ZRE** 210-211 G 5
Bamaga △ **AUS** 174-175 G 2
Bamaji Lake ○ **CDN** 34-35 L 5
Bamake ○ **LB** 202-203 G 7
Bamako ● **RMM** 202-203 F 2
Bamako ● **RMM** (BAM) 202-203 F 3
Bamba ○ **EAK** 212-213 G 5
Bamba ~ **RCA** 206-207 D 6
Bamba ○ **RMM** 196-197 H 6
Bamba ○ **ZRE** 210-211 G 6
Bambadinca ○ **GNB** 202-203 C 3
Bambak ○ **PNG** 183 E 3
Bambalang ○ **CAM** 204-205 J 6
Bambam ○ **WAN** 204-205 J 4
Bambama ○ **RCB** 210-211 D 5
Bambamarca ○ **PE** 64-65 C 5
Bambana, Río ~ **NIC** 52-53 B 5
Bambang ○ **RI** 162-163 E 7
Bambang ○ **RP** 160-161 D 4
Bambangan ○ **MAL** 160-161 B 10
Bambangando ○ **ANG** 218-219 B 3
Bambara ○ **TCH** 206-207 D 4
Bambara-Maoundé ○ **RMM**
  202-203 H 4
Bambari ○ **RCA** 206-207 E 6
Bambaroo ○ **AUS** 174-175 H 4
Bambéla ○ **CI** 202-203 H 5
Bamberg ○ **D** 92-93 L 4
Bamberg ○ **USA** 48-49 H 3
Bambesa ○ **ZRE** 210-211 K 2
Bambesi ○ **ETH** 208-209 B 4
Bambey ○ **SN** 202-203 B 2
Bambila ○ **RMM** 202-203 E 2
Bambili ○ **ZRE** 210-211 L 2
Bambio ○ **RCA** 210-211 F 2
Bamboesberg ⅄ **ZA** 220-221 G 5
Bamboi ○ **GH** 202-203 J 5
Bamboo Creek ○ **AUS** 172-173 E 6
Bambou ~ **RMM** 202-203 E 2
Bambouti ○ **RCA** 206-207 H 6
Bambouto, Monts ▲ **CAM** 204-205 J 6
Bambudi ○ **ETH** 208-209 B 3
Bambui ○ **BR** 72-73 H 6
Bambui ○ **CAM** 204-205 J 6
Bambujka ~ **RUS** 118-119 G 8
Bamenda ☆ **CAM** 204-205 J 6
Bamendjing, Lac de ○ **CAM** 204-205 J 6
Bamne Town ○ **LB** 202-203 F 7
Bamfield ○ **CDN** 32-33 H 7
Bami ○ **TM** 136-137 G 4
Bamingui ○ **RCA** 206-207 D 4
Bamingui ~ **RCA** 206-207 D 4
Bamingui-Bangoran ⊓ **RCA** 206-207 D 4
Bamingui-Bangoran, Parc National du ⊥
  RCA 206-207 D 4
Bamio ○ **PNG** 183 B 4
Bam Island ∧ **PNG** 183 C 2
Bamkeri ○ **RI** 166-167 F 2
Bampoôt, Kûh-e ▲ **IR** 134-135 K 5
Bampūr ○ **IR** 134-135 J 5
Bampūr, Rūd-e ~ **IR** 134-135 J 5
Bamra Hills ⅄ **IND** 142-143 D 5
Bamrúd-e Soflá ○ **IR** 134-135 J 2
Bamu River ~ **PNG** 183 B 4
Bamusso ○ **CAM** 204-205 H 6
Bāmyán ⊓ **AFG** 136-137 K 5
Bāmyán ☆ **AFG** (BM) 134-135 M 1
Bámyán ○ **AFG** 136-137 K 7
Bamyili ⅄ **AUS** 172-173 J 4
Ban ○ **BF** 202-203 J 4
Bana ○ **CAM** 204-205 J 6
Bana -.- ~ **TR** 128-129 K 2
Bana, Col de ▲ **CAM** 204-205 J 6
Banā, Wádi ~ **Y** 132-133 D 7
Banaadir ○ **SP** 212-213 K 2
Banabuiu, Açude ○ **BR** 68-69 J 4
Banabuiú, Rio ~ **BR** 68-69 J 4
Bana Daniéd ○ **SN** 202-203 D 2

Banagi ○ **EAT** 212-213 E 5
Banaigarh ○ **IND** 142-143 D 5
Banalia ○ **ZRE** 210-211 K 3
Banama ○ **RG** 202-203 F 5
Banamba ○ **RMM** 202-203 G 3
Banana ○ **AUS** 178-179 L 3
Banana ~ **BR** 68-69 L 4
Banana, Ilha do ∧ **BR** 68-69 C 7
Bananal, Rio ~ **BR** 68-69 D 6
Banana Range ⅄ **AUS** 178-179 L 3
Banandjé ○ **CI** 202-203 G 5
Bananeiras ○ **BR** 68-69 L 5
Bananfara ○ **RG** 202-203 F 5
Banangui ○ **RCA** 206-207 G 6
Banankoro ○ **RG** 202-203 F 5
Banankoro ○ **RMM** (SÉ) 202-203 G 3
Banankoro ○ **RMM** (SIK) 202-203 F 4
Banao ○ **C** (CG) 54-55 G 4
Banao ○ **C** (SS) 54-55 F 4
Banapur ○ **IND** 142-143 D 6
Banas ○ **IND** 138-139 D 7
Banās ○ **IND** 138-139 D 7
Banas ○ **IND** 142-143 B 3
Banās, Ra's ▲ **ET** 194-195 G 6
Banaue ○ **RP** 160-161 D 4
Banaz ☆ **TR** 128-129 C 3
Banaz Çayı ~ **TR** 128-129 C 3
Banba ○ **RMM** 202-203 J 3
Ban Bakha ○ **LAO** 156-157 D 7
Ban Ban ○ **AUS** 178-179 G 3
Ban Ban ○ **LAO** 156-157 C 7
Ban Ban ○ **VN** 156-157 D 7
Banbar ○ **VRC** 144-145 K 5
Banbaran ○ **RMM** 202-203 F 3
Banbirpur ○ **IND** 144-145 C 6
Ban Boun Tai ○ **LAO** 156-157 B 6
Banbridge ○ **GB** 90-91 D 4
Banbury ○ **GB** 90-91 G 5
Bancauan Island ∧ **RP** 160-161 C 9
Banc d'Arguin, Parc National du ⊥ •••• **RIM**
  196-197 B 4
Ban Chamrung ○ **THA** 158-159 G 4
Ban Chiang ⟡⟡⟡ **THA** 158-159 G 2
Banco, El ○ **CO** 60-61 E 3
Bancoran Island ∧ **RP** 160-161 C 9
Bancos de San Pedro ∧ **YV** 60-61 H 3
Bancroft ○ **CDN** 38-39 F 6
Bancroft ○ **USA** 40-41 J 4
Bancs Providence ∧ **SY** 224 B 4
Banda ○ **CAM** 204-205 J 6
Banda ○ **GH** 202-203 J 5
Banda ○ **IND** 138-139 G 8
Bānda ○ **IND** 142-143 B 3
Banda ○ **ZRE** (BAN) 210-211 G 6
Banda ○ **ZRE** (Hau) 206-207 H 6
Banda, Kepulauan (Nutmeg Kepulauan)
  ∧•••• **RI** 166-167 J 4
Banda, La ○ **RA** 76-77 E 5
Banda Aceh = Baiturahman ☆ **RI**
  162-163 A 2
Banda Banda, Mount ▲ **AUS**
  178-179 M 6
Bandabe ○ **RMM** 222-223 F 5
Banda del Río Salí ○ **RA** 76-77 E 4
Bandae ○ **GH** 202-203 J 7
Banda Elat ○ **RI** 166-167 G 4
Bandafassi ○ **SN** 202-203 D 3
Bandai-Asahi National Park ⊥ **J** (NII)
  152-153 N 4
Bandai-Asahi National Park ⊥ **J** (YAM)
  152-153 N 5
Bandak ○ **N** 86-87 D 7
Bandaka ○ **ZRE** 210-211 H 4
Bandakami ○ **ZRE** 210-211 D 6
Ban Dakchoun ○ **LAO** 158-159 J 3
Bandama ○ **CI** 202-203 H 6
Bandama Blanc ~ **CI** 202-203 J 5
Bandama Rouge ~ **CI** 202-203 G 5
Bandanaira ○••• **RI** 166-167 K 4
Bāndanwāra ○ **IND** 138-139 E 6
Bandar ○ **RI** 168 C 3
Bandaragama ○ **CL** 140-141 H 7
Bandarban ○ **BD** 142-143 G 4
Bandarbeyla ○ **SP** 208-209 K 4
Bandar-e 'Abbās ☆⋆ **IR** 134-135 G 5
Bandar-e Anzali ○ **IR** 128-129 N 4
Bandar-e Büšehr ☆⋆ **IR** 134-135 F 5
Bandar-e Čarak ○ **IR** 134-135 F 5
Bandar-e Deilam ○ **IR** 134-135 D 3
Bandar-e Emām Homeini ○ **IR**
  134-135 C 3
Bandar-e Ganāve ○ **IR** 134-135 D 4
Bandar-e Gaz ○ **IR** 134-135 F 1
Bandar-e Golmânhâne ○ **IR** 128-129 L 4
Bandar-e Hamir ○ **IR** 134-135 F 5
Bandar-e Kong ○ **IR** 134-135 F 5
Bandar-e Lenge ○ **IR** 134-135 F 5
Bandar-e Mâhšahr ○ **IR** 134-135 C 3
Bandar-e Moqām ○ **IR** 134-135 F 5
Bandar-e Rig ○ **IR** 134-135 D 4
Bandarban Balagra ○ **IND** 138-139 D 3
Bandarjaya ○ **RI** 162-163 F 7
Bandar Lampung ☆ **RI** 162-163 F 7
Bandar Murcaayo ○ **SP** 208-209 K 3
Bandarpasirmandogai ○ **RI** 162-163 C 3
Bandar Seri Begawan ★•• **BRU**
  164-165 D 1
Bandar Sri Aman (Simanggang) ○ **MAL**
  162-163 J 4
Bandar Wanaag ○ **SP** 208-209 G 4
Banda Sea = Banda, Laut ≈
  166-167 G 3
Band-e Amir, Rūd-e ~ **AFG**
  136-137 K 7
Bandeira ○ **BR** 72-73 K 3
Bandeira, Pico da ▲ **BR** 72-73 J 6
Bandeirante, Rio ~ **BR** 72-73 E 7
Bandeirantes ○ **BR** (GOI) 72-73 G 4
Bandeirantes ○ **BR** (MAT) 70-71 J 2
Banduwer Barat Parit ~ **RI** 160-161 B 9
Bandei ○ **RCA** 206-207 E 6
Bandelierkop ○ **ZA** 218-219 F 2
Bandelier National Monument • **USA**
  44-45 D 2
Bandera ○ **RA** 76-77 F 5
Bandera ○ **USA** 44-45 H 5
Bandera Bajada ○ **RA** 76-77 F 4
Banderas, Ilha dos ∧ **BR** 72-73 D 7
Banderantes ○ **RI** 162-163 C 3

Banderas, Bahía de ≈ 52-53 B 1
Banderilla ○ **MEX** 52-53 F 2
Bandhavagarh National Park ⊥ **IND**
  142-143 B 4
Bāndhi ○ **PK** 134-135 K 4
Bandia ~ **IND** 142-143 B 6
Bandiagara ○••• **RMM** 202-203 J 2
Bandiagara, Falaise de ⅄ **RMM**
  202-203 J 2
Bandirma ☆ **TR** 128-129 B 2
Bandipur National Park ⊥ • **IND**
  140-141 G 5
Banding ○ **RI** 162-163 F 7
Bandjoukri ○ **CAM** 204-205 K 4
Bandjoun ○ **CAM** 204-205 J 6
Bandon ○ **USA** 40-41 B 4
Bandon = Droichead na Bandan ○ **IRL**
  90-91 C 6
Bandua ○ **MOC** 218-219 H 4
Bandula ○ **MOC** 218-219 G 4
Bandundu ○ **ZRE** 210-211 G 4
Bandundu ☆ **ZRE** (Ban) 210-211 F 5
Bandung ○ **RI** 168 B 3
Ban Dung ○ **THA** 158-159 G 2
Bandungan ○•• **RI** 168 D 3
Bandur ○ **ZA** 218-219 F 6
Bandurrias, Caleta ≈ 76-77 B 3
Bandya ○ **AUS** 176-177 G 3
Bâne ○ **IR** 128-129 L 2
Băneasa ○ **RO** 102-103 E 5
Banes ○ **C** 54-55 H 4
Banes, Bahía de ≈ 54-55 H 4
Banfèle ○ **RG** 202-203 E 4
Banff ○ **CDN** 32-33 N 6
Banff ☆⋆ **GB** 90-91 G 4
Banff National Park ⊥ **CDN** 32-33 N 6
Banfora, Falaise de ⅄ **BF** 202-203 H 6
Bang ○ **RCA** 206-207 B 5
Banga ○ **ANG** 216-217 C 4
Banga ○ **BD** 142-143 G 4
Banga ○ **RCA** (Kem) 206-207 D 6
Banga ○ **RCA** (Bam) 206-207 C 5
Banga ○ **RP** 160-161 F 9
Banga ○ **ZRE** (KOC) 210-211 H 6
Bangabong ○ **RP** 160-161 D 6
Bangala, Lake ○ **ZW** 218-219 F 5
Bangalore ☆⋆ **IND** 140-141 G 4
Banga Melo ○ **ZRE** 210-211 H 2
Bangana ○ **RCA** 206-207 F 6
Banganapalle ○ **IND** 140-141 G 4
Bangangté ○ **CAM** 204-205 J 6
Bangar ○ **RP** 160-161 D 4
Bangaré ○ **RN** 202-203 J 3
Bangarpet ○ **IND** 140-141 H 4
Bangassoko ○ **BF** 202-203 J 3
Bangassou ○ **RCA** 206-207 G 6
Bangba ○ **RCA** 206-207 C 5
Bangbagatome ○ **ZRE** 210-211 K 2
Bangbali ○ **RCA** 206-207 E 4
Bangbong ○ **RI** 164-165 H 6
Bangda ○ **VRC** 144-145 L 5
Bangem ○ **CAM** 204-205 H 6
Banggai ○ **RI** 164-165 H 4
Banggai, Kepulauan ∧ **RI** 164-165 H 4
Banggai, Pulau ∧ **RI** 164-165 H 4
Banggi, Pulau ∧ **MAL** 160-161 B 9
Banggo ○ **RI** 168 D 7
Ban Ghanimah, Jabal ⅄ **LAR**
  192-193 F 5
Banghāzi ⊓ **LAR** 192-193 J 2
Banghāzi ☆ **LAR** 192-193 J 1
Banghiang ~ **LAO** 158-159 J 2
Bangil ○ **RI** 168 E 3
Bangka, Pulau ∧ **RI** (SLU) 164-165 J 3
Bangka, Pulau ∧ **RI** (SUS) 162-163 F 6
Bangka, Selat ≈ 162-163 F 6
Bangkai, Tanjung ▲ **RI** 162-163 H 4
Bangkalan ○ **RI** 168 E 3
Bangkaru, Pulau ∧ **RI** 162-163 B 3
Bangkdulis, Pulau ∧ **RI** 164-165 E 2
Bangkinang ○ **RI** 162-163 D 4
Bangkir ○ **RI** 164-165 G 3
Bangko ○ **RI** 162-163 F 6
Bangkoa ○ **RI** 164-165 F 6
Bangkok ☆⋆ **THA** 158-159 F 4
Bangkok, Bight of ≈ 158-159 F 4
Bangkulu, Pulau ∧ **RI** 164-165 H 4
Bangli ○ **RI** 168 B 7
Bangli Ô ○ **THA** 158-159 E 6
Bangli ○ **RI** 168 B 7
Bango ○ **CI** 202-203 H 6
Bangong Co ○ **IND** 138-139 G 3
Bangong Co ~ **VRC** (XIZ) 144-145 B 4
Bangong Co ~ **VRC** (XIZ) 144-145 B 4
Bangor ○ **GB** (NIR) 90-91 E 4
Bangor ○ **GB** (WAL) 90-91 F 5
Bangor ○ **USA** 46-47 O 3
Bangoran ○ **RCA** 206-207 D 4
Bangoran ~ **RCA** (Bam) 206-207 C 4
Bangou ○ **RCB** 210-211 D 5
Bangoulap ○ **CAM** 204-205 J 6
Bang Pakong ~ **THA** 158-159 F 4
Bangsalsembera ○ **RI** 164-165 G 4
Bang Saphan ○ **THA** 158-159 E 5
Bangsund ○ **N** 86-87 E 4
Bangu ○ **ZRE** (BAN) 216-217 E 3
Bangu ○ **ZRE** (SHA) 214-215 B 5
Bangu, Chute ~ **ZRE** 210-211 L 2
Bangued ○ **RP** 160-161 D 4
Banguey Barat Parit ~ **RI** 160-161 B 9
Bangui ★ **RCA** 206-207 C 6
Bangui ○ **RN** 199-199 C 6
Bangui Bay ≈ 160-161 D 3
Bangui Kété ~ **RCA** 206-207 E 6
Bangui-Motaba ~ **RCB** 210-211 F 2
Bangula ○ **MW** 218-219 H 3
Bangunan ○ **VRC** 156-157 E 5
Bangunpurba ○ **RI** 162-163 C 3

Bangweulu, Lake ○ **Z** 214-215 E 6
Bangweulu Swamps ≈ **Z** 214-215 E 6
Banhā ☆ **ET** 194-195 E 2
Ban Tabôk ○ **LAO** 156-157 C 7
Ban Haew Ta Bua ○ **THA** 158-159 H 2
Ban Hat Lek ○ **THA** 158-159 G 5
Banhine, Parque Nacional de ⊥ **MOC**
  218-219 G 6
Ban Hinkhan ○ **LAO** 158-159 H 2
Ban Houayxay ○ **LAO** 156-157 B 6
Bani ○ **BF** 202-203 K 3
Bani ○ **DOM** 54-55 K 5
Bani ~ **RMM** 202-203 H 3
Bani, Ibel ⅄ **MA** 188-189 G 6
Ban Tha Rae ○ **THA** 158-159 H 2
Ban Tha Song Yang ○ **THA**
  158-159 D 3
Bani 'Âmir ○ **LAO** 156-157 C 7
Bani 'Atiya ⊥ **KSA** 130-131 C 4
Bani-Bangou ○ **RN** 204-205 E 1
Bánica ○ **DOM** 54-55 K 5
Baniff ○ **RMM** 202-203 G 4
Banifing ~ **RMM** 202-203 H 3
Bani Hasan .⚬. **ET** 194-195 E 3
Bani Hašbal, Wādi ~ **KSA** 132-133 D 5
Bani Mazar ○ **ET** 194-195 E 3
Baninah ☆ **LAR** 192-193 J 1
Bani Rikāb ⊥ **IRQ** 128-129 L 7
Banir Rivev ~ **PNG** 183 D 4
Bani Sa'id ○ **IRQ** 128-129 M 7
Banissa ○ **EAK** 212-213 H 2
Bani Suwaif ⊓ **ET** 194-195 E 3
Bani Walid ☆ **LAR** 192-193 E 2
Bâniyâs ○ **IRQ** 128-129 K 6
Banja Luka ☆ **BIH** 100-101 F 2
Banz ○ **PNG** 183 C 3
Banzana ○ **RMM** 202-203 G 4
Banzare Land ⊥ **ARK** 16 S 13
Banze Sanda ○ **ZRE** 210-211 G 6
Banza Sosso ○ **ANG** 216-217 C 2
Banzi ○ **CI** 202-203 G 5
Bao ○ **TCH** 206-207 C 4
Bao, Río ~ **DOM** 54-55 K 5
Baode ○ **VRC** 154-155 H 2
Baodi ○ **VRC** 154-155 K 2
Baoding ○ **VRC** 156-157 F 2
Baojiqu ○ **VRC** 155-155 D 3
Baokang ○ **VRC** 154-155 G 6
Bao Khao Sai ○ **THA** 158-159 F 2
Baolo ○ **SOL** 184 I d 2
Baoqing ○ **VRC** 150-151 J 4
Baoqing ○ **VRC** 154-155 L 5
Báp ○ **IND** 138-139 D 6
Bápatla ○ **IND** 140-141 J 3
Bappagaj ~ **RUS** 118-119 M 4
Bapsfontein ○ **ZA** 220-221 J 2
Banli ○ **VRC** 156-157 E 5
Banmankhi ○ **IND** 142-143 E 3
Banmauk ○ **MYA** 142-143 G 3
Ban Mouang ○ **LAO** 156-157 B 7
Ban Na Inh Noi ○ **LAO** 158-159 J 2
Bannaja ~ **RUS** 112-113 L 3
Ban Nakala ○ **LAO** 156-157 D 7
Ban Na Mang ○ **LAO** 156-157 D 6
Ban Nambak ○ **LAO** 156-157 C 6
Ban Nang Sata ○ **THA** 158-159 F 7
Ban Napè ○ **LAO** 156-157 D 7
Ban Na Phao ○ **LAO** 158-159 H 2
Ban Na Sang ○ **THA** 158-159 E 5
Bannerman Town ○ **BS** 54-55 G 2
Banner Reef ∧ **JA** 54-55 F 6
Banning ○ **USA** 40-41 D 5
Bannockburn ○ **CDN** 38-39 G 6
Bannu ○ **PK** 138-139 C 2
Bano Nong Chaeng ○ **THA** 158-159 F 3
Ban Nong Phu ○ **THA** 158-159 H 3
Ban Nongsim ○ **LAO** 158-159 H 3
Bannu ○ **PK** 138-139 C 2
Bannur ○ **IND** 140-141 G 4
Baños ○ **EC** 64-65 C 2
Banos ○ **PE** 64-65 D 7
Baños, Los ○ **EC** 64-65 C 2
Banos, Los ○ **USA** 40-41 C 4
Ban Pa Daeng ○ **THA** 142-143 M 6
Ban Pak Bat ○ **THA** 158-159 G 2
Ban Pakbông ○ **LAO** 158-159 J 3
Ban Phai ○ **THA** 158-159 G 2
Ban Pho ○ **THA** 158-159 G 4
Ban Phu ○ **THA** 158-159 G 2
Ban Pong ○ **THA** 158-159 E 4
Ban Rai ○ **THA** 158-159 E 3
Ban San Chao Po ○ **THA** 158-159 F 3
Ban Sênkhan ○ **LAO** 156-157 C 6
Banská Bystrica ○ **SK** 92-93 P 4
Banská Štiavnica ... **SK** 92-93 P 4
Bânswāra ○ **IND** 138-139 E 8

Banta ○ **SP** 212-213 J 3
Banta, Pulau ∧ **RI** 168 D 7
Bantaeng ○ **RI** 164-165 F 6
Bantadjé ○ **CAM** 204-205 K 4
Bantakoto ○ **RMM** 202-203 D 3
Bantala ~ **RG** 202-203 E 5
Bantarbolang ○ **RI** 168 C 3
Bantarkawung ○ **RI** 168 C 3
Bantayan ○ **RP** 160-161 E 7
Bantayan Island ∧ **RP** 160-161 E 7
Bantè ○ **DY** 202-203 L 5
Banten ○ **RI** 168 B 3
Ban Thieng ○ **LAO** 156-157 C 7
Bantimurung ○ **RI** 164-165 F 6
Bantimurung Reserve ⊥ • **RI**
  164-165 F 6
Bânton ○ **IR** 128-129 M 3
Banton Island ∧ **RP** 160-161 E 6
Bantul ○ **RI** 168 D 3
Ban Tung ○ **LAO** 158-159 H 2
Banua ○ **RP** 160-161 F 6
Banvo ○ **CAM** 204-205 J 5
Ban Xang ○ **VN** 156-157 D 7
Ban Xésavang ○ **LAO** 158-159 H 2
Banyak, Kepulauan ∧ **RI** 162-163 B 4
Banynasin ~ **RI** 162-163 F 6
Banyo ○ **CAM** 204-205 J 5
Banyoles ○ **E** 98-99 J 3
Banyumas ○ **RI** 168 C 3
Banyuwangi ○ **RI** 168 B 7
Banyuwedang ○ **RI** 168 B 7
Banz ○ **PNG** 183 C 3
Banjanzana ○ **RMM** 202-203 G 4
Banjar ○ **RI** 168 C 3
BanjanjBintang ⅄ **MAL** 162-163 C 3
Banjar Brassey ⅄ **MAL**
  160-161 B 10
Banjar Sanda ○ **ZRE** 210-211 G 6
Banjarmasin ☆ **RI** 164-165 D 5
Banjaran Timur ⅄ **MAL** 162-163 K 3
Banjaran Titiwangsa ⅄ **MAL**
  162-163 D 3
Banjarbaru ○ **RI** 164-165 D 5
Banjarkasang ○ **RI** 162-163 K 2
Banjarmasin ☆ **RI** 164-165 D 5
Banjarnegara ○ **RI** 168 C 3
Banjul ★ **WAG** 202-203 B 3
Bank ○ **AZ** 128-129 N 3
Bānka ○ **IND** 142-143 E 3
Banka Banka ○ **AUS** 174-175 C 6
Bankapur ○ **IND** 140-141 F 3
Bankas ○ **RMM** 202-203 J 3
Bankberg ⅄ **ZA** 220-221 G 6
Banket ○ **ZW** 218-219 F 3
Bankiláré ○ **RN** 202-203 L 2
Bankim ○ **CAM** 204-205 J 5
Banko ○ **RG** 202-203 E 4
Banko ○ **RMM** 202-203 G 3
Bankon ○ **RG** 202-203 F 4
Bankoumana ○ **RMM** 202-203 F 3
Banks, Cape ▲ **AUS** 180-181 M 6
Banks, Îles = Banks Island ∧ **VAN**
  184 II a 2
Banks, Point ▲ **USA** 22-23 U 3
Banks/Torres ⊓ **VAN** 184 II b 1
Banks Island ∧ **CDN** (BC) 32-33 E 5
Banks Island ∧ **CDN** (NWT) 24-25 L 4
Banks Islands = Îles Banks ∧ **VAN**
  184 II a 2
Banks Lake ○ **CDN** 30-31 W 4
Banks Lake ○ **USA** 40-41 D 2
Banks Peninsula ⊔ **CDN** 30-31 P 2
Banks Strait ≈ 180-181 J 6
Bánli ○ **VRC** 156-157 E 5
Ban Lam Narai ○ **THA** 158-159 F 3
Ban La Pha ○ **LAO** 158-159 H 2
Banli ○ **VRC** 156-157 E 5
Banmankhi ○ **IND** 142-143 E 3
Banmauk ○ **MYA** 142-143 G 3
Ban Mouang ○ **LAO** 156-157 B 7
Ban Na Inh Noi ○ **LAO** 158-159 J 2
Bannaja ~ **RUS** 112-113 L 3
Ban Nakala ○ **LAO** 156-157 D 7
Ban Na Mang ○ **LAO** 156-157 D 6
Ban Nambak ○ **LAO** 156-157 C 6
Ban Nang Sata ○ **THA** 158-159 F 7
Ban Napè ○ **LAO** 156-157 D 7
Ban Na Phao ○ **LAO** 158-159 H 2
Ban Na Sang ○ **THA** 158-159 E 5

Bara-Issa ~ **RMM** 202-203 H 2
Barajý ~ **RUS** 120-121 E 2
Baraka ~ **ER** 200-201 H 5
Baraka ○ **ZRE** 212-213 B 6
Baraka, Khor ~ **SUD** 200-201 H 4
Barakan ○ **RI** 166-167 H 5
Barakat Sharif Ya'qūb ○ **SUD**
  200-201 F 5
Baraki ○ **AFG** 138-139 B 3
Baral ~ **BD** 142-143 F 3
Baralzon Lake ○ **CDN** 30-31 V 5
Baram ~ **MAL** 164-165 D 1
Baram, Tanjung ▲ **MAL** 162-163 K 2
Baramani ○ **GUY** 62-63 E 2
Baramata ○ **PNG** 183 C 3
Bārān ○ **IND** 138-139 F 7
Bārān, Kūh-e ⅄ **IR** 134-135 H 2
Baranainha ○ **RUS** 112-113 P 2
Baranicol ○ **KA** 124-125 E 3
Baranoa ○ **CO** 60-61 D 2
Baranof ○ **USA** 32-33 C 3
Baranof Island ∧ **USA** 32-33 C 3
Baranoviči = Baranavičy ☆ **BY**
  94-95 K 5
Barão de Grajau ○ **BR** 68-69 G 5
Barão de Melgaço ○ **BR** 70-71 G 2
Barão do Melgaço ○ **BR** 70-71 K 5
Barão do Triunfo ○ **BR** 74-75 E 8
Baraouéli ○ **RMM** 202-203 G 3
Baraqish .⚬. • **Y** 132-133 D 6
Barāra ○ **KSA** 132-133 B 3
Bararati, Rio ~ **BR** 66-67 H 6
Bararis, togga ~ **SP** 208-209 G 3
Baratang Bay ≈ 148-49 D 5
Barauli ○ **IND** 142-143 D 2
Baraúna, Rio ~ **BR** 62-63 D 5
Baraya ○ **CO** 60-61 D 6
Barbacena ○ **BR** 72-73 J 6
Barbacoas ○ **CO** 64-65 C 1
Barbadon ○ **BR** 66-67 D 7
Barbado, Rio ~ **BR** 70-71 H 4
Barbados ○ **BDS** 56 F 5
Barbágia Belvi ⊥ **I** 100-101 B 5
Barbalha ○ **BR** 68-69 J 5
Barbar ○ **SUD** 200-201 G 3
Barbastro ○ **E** 98-99 H 3
Barbate de Franco ○ **E** 98-99 E 6
Barbaza ○ **RP** 160-161 E 7
Bárbele ○ **LV** 94-95 K 3
Barberton ○ **ZA** 220-221 K 2
Barbes, Cap ▲ **MA** 196-197 B 3
Barbiritsa ~ **RUS** 116-117 J 9
Barbosa ○ **CO** 60-61 E 5
Barbour Bay ≈ 30-31 X 4
Barbuda Island ∧ **AG** 56 E 3
Barbwire Range ⅄ **AUS** 172-173 G 5
Barca = Al Marj ○ **LAR** 192-193 J 1
Barca, La ○ **MEX** 52-53 C 1
Barcaldine ○ **AUS** 178-179 J 6
Barcarena ○ **BR** 62-63 K 6
Barcarrota ○ **E** 98-99 E 5
Barcelona ○ **BR** 68-69 L 4
Barcelona ☆⋆ **E** 98-99 J 4
Barcelona ○ **YV** 60-61 J 2
Barcelonnette ○ **F** 90-91 L 6
Barcelos ○ **BR** 66-67 F 5
Barcelos ○ **PL** 92-93 Q 1
Barciany ○ **PL** 92-93 Q 1
Barclay, Kap ∧ **GRØ** 28-29 J 2
Barclay Bugt ≈ 28-29 c 2
Barcoo River ~ **AUS** 178-179 G 3
Barcs ○ **H** 92-93 O 6
Barçyn ☆ **KA** 124-125 F 4
Barda ○ **AZ** 128-129 M 2
Barda, Arroyo de la ~ **RA** 78-79 F 4
Barda = Barda ○ **AZ** 128-129 M 2
Bardaale ○ **SP** 208-209 H 4
Barda del Medio ○ **RA** 78-79 D 5
Bardagué ~ **TCH** 198-199 H 2
Bardaï ○ **TCH** 198-199 H 2
Bardárbunga ⅄ **IS** 86-87 d 2
Bardas Blancas ○ **RA** 78-79 D 4
Barddhamán ○ **IND** 142-143 E 4
Bardejov ○ **SK** 92-93 Q 4
Bardeskan ○ **IR** 136-137 G 7
Bardoli ○ **IND** 138-139 D 8
Bardsir ○ **IR** 134-135 G 4
Bardstown ○ **USA** 46-47 F 7
Barduela ~ **N** 86-87 J 2
Bardula ○ **IND** 142-143 C 5
Bardymskij hrebet ⅄ **RUS** 96-97 L 5
Barê ○ **ETH** 208-209 F 6
Bareh ○ **IND** 140-141 F 3
Bareilly ○ **IND** 138-139 G 5
Bareli ○ **IND** 138-139 G 8
Barentsburg ○ **N** 84-85 J 3
Barentsøya ∧ **N** 84-85 O 3
Barentu ○ **ER** 200-201 H 5
Bareo ○ **MAL** 164-165 D 2
Barfolomeevsk ○ **RUS** 122-123 E 6
Bârgâ ○ **IR** 134-135 G 5
Bargaal ○ **SP** 208-209 K 3
Bargarh ○ **IND** 142-143 D 5
Barğavín, Kûh-e ▲ **IR** 136-137 F 6
Barguzin ~ **RUS** 118-119 F 8
Barguzin ○ **RUS** 116-117 O 9
Barguzinskij, zapovednik ⊥ **RUS**
  118-119 D 8
Barguzinskij hrebet ⅄ **RUS**
  118-119 D 9

Bärh ○ **IND** 142-143 D 3
Bar Harbor ○ **USA** 46-47 O 3
Barhi ○ **IND** 138-139 F 4
Bari ○ **I** 100-101 F 4
Bāri ○ **IND** 138-139 F 6
Bari ○ **SP** 208-209 K 3
Bari ○ **WAN** 204-205 F 2
Bariadi ○ **EAT** 212-213 D 5
Baricho ○ **EAK** 212-213 G 5
Barik, al- ○ **KSA** 132-133 B 3
Barika ○ **DZ** 190-191 J 2
Barika ~ **DZ** 190-191 J 3
Barikôt ○ **AFG** 136-137 M 7
Barillas ○ **GCA** 52-53 J 4
Barim, Ğazirat ∧ **Y** 132-133 C 7
Barinas ☆ **YV** 60-61 F 3
Baring, Cape ▲ **CDN** 24-25 N 5
Baringa ○ **ZRE** 210-211 H 3
Baring Channel ≈ 24-25 W 4
Baringo, Lake ○ **EAK** 212-213 F 3
Baripāda ○ **IND** 142-143 E 5
Bariri ○ **BR** 72-73 F 7
Bariri, Represa < **BR** 72-73 F 7
Bāris ○ **ET** 194-195 E 5
Bari Sādri ○ **IND** 138-139 E 7
Barisal ☆ **BD** 142-143 G 4
Barisan, Pegunungan ⅄ **RI** 162-163 D 5
Barit, al- ○ **IR** 128-129 K 7
Barito ~ **RI** 164-165 D 4
Baritu, Parque Nacional ⊥ **RA** 76-77 E 2
Bariya ○ **IRQ** 128-129 L 5
Barjūj, Wádi ~ **LAR** 192-193 E 5
Barká ○ **OM** 132-133 K 2
Barkal, Ğabal • **SUD** 200-201 E 3
Barkam ○ **VRC** 154-155 C 6
Barkan, Ra's-e ▲ **IR** 134-135 C 4
Barkava ○ **LV** 94-95 K 3
Barkédji ○ **SN** 202-203 C 2
Barkerville ○ **CDN** 32-33 K 5
Barkéwol Abioð ○ **RIM** 196-197 D 6
Bärkhân ○ **PK** 138-139 C 3
Barkley, Lake ○ **USA** 46-47 F 7
Barkley Downs ○ **AUS** 174-175 E 7
Barkly East ○ **ZA** 220-221 H 5
Barkly Highway II **AUS** 174-175 D 6
Barkly Homestead Roadhouse ○ **AUS**
  174-175 C 6
Barkly Pass ○ **ZA** 220-221 H 5
Barkly Tableland ⅄ **AUS** 174-175 C 5
Barkly West ○ **ZA** 220-221 F 4
Barkol ○ **VRC** 146-147 L 4
Barkol, Wádi ~ **SUD** 200-201 E 4
Barkol Hu ○ **VRC** 146-147 L 4
Barlavento, Ilhas de ∧ **CV** 202-203 B 5
Bar-le-Duc ☆⋆ **F** 90-91 K 4
Barlee, Lake ○ **AUS** 176-177 E 4
Barlee Range ⅄ **AUS** 176-177 D 1
Barletta ○ **I** 100-101 F 4
Barlo Warf ○ **WAL** 202-203 D 5
Barloweerie, Mount ▲ **AUS** 176-177 D 3
Barlyk ⅄ **RUS** 116-117 H 10
Barma ○ **RI** 166-167 G 2
Barmedman ○ **AUS** 180-181 J 3
Barmer ○ **IND** 138-139 C 7
Barmera ○ **AUS** 180-181 F 3
Barm Firuz, Kûh-e ▲ **IR** 134-135 D 3
Barnala ○ **IND** 138-139 E 4
Barnard Castle ○• **GB** 90-91 G 4
Barnard Point ▲ **CDN** 24-25 P 4
Barnard River ~ **AUS** 178-179 L 6
Barnato ○ **AUS** 178-179 H 3
Barnaul ☆ **RUS** 124-125 N 2
Barnaulka ~ **RUS** 124-125 N 2
Barne Glacier ∧ **ARK** 16 E 0
Barnes Ice Cap ○ **CDN** 26-27 O 8
Barneys Brook ~ **CDN** 38-39 Q 4
Barneys Lake ○ **AUS** 180-181 H 2
Barnhart ○ **USA** 44-45 G 4
Barnstable ○ **USA** 46-47 N 5
Barnstaple ○• **GB** 90-91 F 5
Barnum ○ **USA** 42-43 D 4
Barnwell ○ **USA** 48-49 H 3
Baro ○ **TCH** 198-199 J 3
Baro ○ **WAN** 204-205 F 2
Baroe ○ **ZA** 220-221 G 6
Barógil ○ **RG** 136-137 N 6
Baron ○ **RI** (JTI) 168 D 3
Baron ○ **RI** (YOG) 168 D 3
Barora Island ∧ **SOL** 184 I d 2
Barora Ite Island ∧ **SOL** 184 I d 2
Barossa Valley ⊔ **AUS** 180-181 E 3
Barotac Nuevo ○ **RP** 160-161 E 7
Barotse Floot Plain = **Z** 218-219 D 2
Baroua ○ **RCA** 206-207 D 3
Barouda, Hassi < **DZ** 190-191 C 6
Baro Wenz ~ **ETH** 208-209 B 4
Barpeta ○ **IND** 142-143 G 2
Barqah ⊥ **LAR** 192-193 J 2
Barquisimeto ☆ **YV** 60-61 G 2
Barra ○ **BR** (BAH) 68-69 G 7
Barra ○ **BR** (CAT) 74-75 F 7
Barra ~ **WAG** 202-203 B 3
Barra, Ponta da ▲ **BR** 74-75 D 7
Barraba ○ **AUS** 178-179 L 6
Barra Bonita ○ **BR** 72-73 F 7
Barra Bonita, Represa de < **BR**
  72-73 F 7
Barraca da Boca ○ **BR** 62-63 H 6
Barraca de A. Lopes ○ **BR** 66-67 H 6
Barração do Barreto ○ **BR** 66-67 H 7
Barracas ○ **E** 98-99 G 4
Barracouta Shoal ∧ **AUS** 172-173 G 2
Barra da Estiva ○ **BR** 72-73 K 2
Barradale Roadhouse ○ **AUS**
  172-173 B 2
Barra de Mamanguape ○ **BR** 68-69 L 5
Barra de Santa Rosa ○ **BR** 68-69 L 5
Barra de São Francisco ○ **BR** 72-73 K 5
Barra de São Manuel ○ **BR** 66-67 H 6
Barra de São Miguel ○ **BR** (ALA)
  68-69 L 6

Barra de São Miguel ○ BR (PA) 68-69 K 5
Barra de Tuxpan ○ MEX 52-53 F 1
Barra do Bugres ○ BR 70-71 J 4
Barra do Corda ○ BR 68-69 F 4
Barra do Cuanza ○ ANG 216-217 B 4
Barra do Dande ○ ANG 216-217 B 4
Barra do Garças ○ BR 72-73 D 3
Barra do Mendes ○ BR 68-69 G 7
Barra do Ouro ○ BR 74-75 E 7
Barra do Pirai ○ BR 72-73 J 7
Barra do Quaraí ○ BR 76-77 D 4
Barrage Mercier ∴ CDN 38-39 G 5
Barra Longa ○ BR 72-73 J 6
Barra Mansa ○ BR 72-73 H 7
Barrâmiya ○ ET 194-195 F 5
Barranca ○ PE (LIM) 64-65 D 7
Barranca ○ PE (LOR) 64-65 D 4
Barrancabermeja ○ CO 60-61 E 4
Barranca del Cobre, Parque Natural ⊥ MEX 50-51 E 3
Barranca de Upía = Cumaral ○ CO 60-61 F 3
Barrancas ○ YV (BOL) 60-61 J 4
Barrancas ○ YV (MON) 60-61 K 3
Barrancas, Arroyo ~ RA 78-79 J 2
Barrancas, Rio ~ RA 78-79 D 4
Barranco Alto ○ BR 70-71 G 3
Barranco de Guadalupe ○ MEX 50-51 G 2
Barranco de Loba ○ CO 60-61 D 3
Barranco Picure ○ CO 60-61 G 6
Barrancos ○ P 98-99 D 5
Barrancos, Los ○ YV 60-61 K 3
Barranqueras ○ RA 76-77 H 4
Barranquilla ○ CO 60-61 D 2
Barranquilla ○ RCH 76-77 B 4
Barranquitas ○ YV 60-61 E 2
Barras ○ BR 66-67 E 7
Barra Seca ○ BR 72-73 K 6
Barraute ○ CDN 38-39 F 4
Barre ○ USA 46-47 M 3
Barreal, El ○ MEX 50-51 F 2
Barreal, El ○ RA 76-77 D 5
Barreira Branca ○ BR 68-69 C 6
Barreira da Cruz ○ BR 68-69 D 7
Barreira do Peiqui ○ BR 72-73 F 2
Barreiras ○ BR 72-73 H 2
Barreiras, Rio das ~ BR 68-69 D 6
Barreirinha ○ BR 66-67 J 4
Barreirinhas ○ BR 68-69 G 3
Barreiro ○ P 98-99 C 5
Barreiros ○ BR 68-69 L 6
Barrême ○ F 90-91 L 10
Barren, Nosy ~ RM 222-223 C 7
Barren Grounds ⊥ CDN 30-31 O 2
Barren Island ~ IND 140-141 L 3
Barren Island, Cape ▲ AUS 180-181 K 6
Barren Islands ~ USA 22-23 U 3
Barren River Lake ○ USA 46-47 E 7
Barreras Blancas, Antiplano ⊥ RA 80 F 5
Barretal, El ○ MEX 50-51 K 5
Barretos ○ BR 72-73 F 6
Barrett ○ USA 42-43 K 3
Barrhead ○ CDN 32-33 N 4
Barrialito ○ YV 60-61 J 3
Barrie ○ CDN 38-39 E 6
Barrie Island ~ CDN 38-39 C 6
Barrière ○ CDN 32-33 K 6
Barrier Highway || AUS 178-179 G 6
Barrier Inlet ≈ 36-37 P 3
Barrier Range ▲▲ AUS 178-179 F 6
Barrier River ~ CDN 34-35 D 4
Barril, El ○ MEX 50-51 H 5
Barrilles, Los ○ MEX 50-51 F 5
Barrington ○ CDN 38-39 M 7
Barrington, Mount ▲ AUS 180-181 L 2
Barrington Lake ○ CDN 34-35 F 2
Barrington Tops National Park ⊥ AUS 178-179 L 6
Barriyal al-Bayyûda ⊥ SUD 200-201 F 4
Barro Alto ○ BR 72-73 F 3
Barro Duro ○ BR 68-69 G 4
Barron ○ USA 46-47 C 3
Barros ○ BR 68-69 G 4
Barros, Lagoa dos ○ BR 74-75 E 7
Barros, Los ○ RCH 78-79 D 4
Barros Arana, Cerro ▲ RCH 78-79 C 7
Barros Cassal ○ BR 74-75 D 7
Barrow ~ IRL 90-91 D 5
Barrow ○ USA 20-21 M 1
Barrow, Point ▲ USA 20-21 M 1
Barrow Creek ○ AUS 178-179 B 1
Barrow-in-Furness ○ GB 90-91 F 4
Barrow Island ▲ AUS 172-173 B 6
Barrow Island Oil Field • AUS 172-173 B 6
Barrow Island Shoals ~ AUS 172-173 B 6
Barrow Peninsula ◡ CDN 36-37 Q 3
Barrow River ~ CDN 24-25 e 7
Barrows ○ CDN 34-35 F 4
Barrow Strait ≈ 24-25 Y 3
Barru ○ RI 164-165 F 6
Barry Caves ∴ USA 174-175 D 7
Barryville ○ ZA 220-221 G 6
Barry Islands ○ CDN 30-31 P 2
Barry's Bay ○ CDN 38-39 F 6
Barsa ○ SYR 128-129 H 4
Barsakelmes, ostrov ~ KA 126-127 O 5
Barsakel mes, Sor ○ US 136-137 E 3
Barsakelmes zapovednik ⊥ KA 126-127 N 3
Baršatau ⊥ KA 126-127 O 4
Barsalogo ○ BF 202-203 K 4
Barsaloi ○ EAK 212-213 F 3
Bärsatas ○ RA 124-125 L 4
Baršino ○ KS 146-147 C 4
Barskoon ○ KS 146-147 C 4
Barsoi ○ IND 138-139 E 10
Barsono ○ RUS 114-115 M 4

Barstow ○ USA 40-41 F 8
Bar-sur-Aube ○ F 90-91 K 7
Bartang ~ TJ 136-137 M 5
Barten = Barciany ○ PL 92-93 Q 1
Barter Island ▲ USA 20-21 T 1
Bartica ○ GUY 62-63 E 2
Bartin ★ TR 128-129 E 2
Bartle ○ USA 40-41 D 5
Bartle Frere ▲ AUS 174-175 H 5
Bartlesville ○ USA 44-45 K 1
Bartlett ○ USA 44-45 H 5
Bartlett ○ USA (TN) 48-49 D 2
Bartlett, Cape ▲ CDN 36-37 K 6
Bartlett Lake ○ CDN 30-31 K 4
Bartok Lake, De ○ CDN 30-31 U 5
Bartolomé Masó ○ C 54-55 G 4
Barton ○ RP 160-161 C 7
Bartoszyce ○ PL 92-93 Q 1
Bartow ○ USA 48-49 H 6
Bartylaakty, köl ○ KA 96-97 H 10
Baru ○ CO 60-61 D 2
Baru ○ RI (IRJ) 166-167 G 2
Bárú, Nahr ~ SUD 208-209 A 4
Baru ○ RI (MAL) 164-165 K 3
Baru, Punta ▲ CO 60-61 D 2
Barukova, mys ▲ RUS 112-113 U 5
Barumun ~ RI 162-163 C 3
Barun-Torej, ozero ≈ RUS 118-119 G 10
Barus ○ RI 162-163 C 3
Barusiahe ○ RI 162-163 C 3
Baruti ○ ZRE 210-211 K 2
Baruunharaa ○ MAU 148-149 H 3
Baruuntuuruul ○ MAU 116-117 G 11
Baruun-Urt ★ MAU 148-149 L 4
Barva, Volcán ▲ CR 52-53 B 9
Barvinkove ○ UA 102-103 K 3
Barwäni ○ IND 138-139 E 8
Barwidgi ○ AUS 174-175 H 5
Barwon River ~ AUS 178-179 J 5
Barycz ~ PL 92-93 O 3
Barylas ○ RUS 110-111 T 7
Baryš ○ RUS 96-97 J 7
Barysaw ★ BY 94-95 L 4
Barysaw = Barysaw ★ BY 94-95 L 4
Bâš Âbdân ○ AFG 136-137 L 6
Basacato del Este ○ GQ 210-211 B 2
Basaguke ○ VRC 144-145 E 6
Bāsa'idü ○ IR 134-135 F 5
Basák ~ K 158-159 H 5
Basakan, Gunung ▲ RI 164-165 E 2
Baškkerd, Kühhä-ye ▲ IR 134-135 G 5
Basál ○ PK 138-139 D 2
Bâš-Alatau hrebet ▲▲ RUS 96-97 K 7
Basali ○ ZRE 210-211 J 3
Basame, Caño ~ YV 60-61 J 5
Basanga ○ ZRE 210-211 K 6
Basankusu ○ ZRE 210-211 J 3
Basarabi ○ RO 102-103 F 5
Basaseachi ○ MEX 50-51 E 3
Basaseachic Falls ∴ MEX 50-51 E 3
Basavana Bägevädi ○ IND 140-141 F 2
Basavilbaso ○ RA 78-79 K 2
Basay ○ RP 160-161 C 7
Bascán, Río ~ MEX 52-53 H 3
Bäšcelakskij hrebet ▲ RUS 124-125 N 3
Bas Chari, Reserve de faune du ⊥ TCH 198-199 G 6
Bascombe Well Conservation Park ⊥ AUS 180-181 C 2
Base Casamance, Parc National du ⊥ SN 202-203 B 3
Basel ★ CH 92-93 J 5
Basettihalli ○ IND 140-141 G 4
Bashaw ○ CDN 32-33 O 5
Bashee Bridge ○ ZA 220-221 H 5
Basheeriver ~ ZA 220-221 H 5
Bashi Haixia ≈ 156-157 M 6
Bashimuke ○ ZRE 210-211 K 6
Bashkortostan = Respublika Baškortostan □ RUS 96-97 J 6
Basi ○ IND 138-139 F 4
Basiano ○ RI 164-165 H 4
Basilaki Island ~ PNG 183 F 6
Basilan Island ~ RP (BTN) 160-161 D 9
Basilan Strait ≈ 160-161 D 9
Basile, Pico ▲ GQ 210-211 B 2
Basilicata □ I 100-101 K 4
Basilio ○ BR 74-75 D 8
Basingstoke ○ GB 90-91 G 6
Basin Lake ○ CDN 34-35 D 4
Basiri, al- ○ SYR 128-129 G 5
Basirka ○ WAN 204-205 J 3
Baška ○ HR 100-101 E 2
Başkale ○ TR 128-129 K 3
Baskan ~ KA 124-125 L 6
Baskatong, Réservoir ○ CDN 38-39 G 5
Baškaus ~ RUS 124-125 Q 3
Baskerville, Cape ▲ AUS 172-173 F 4
Baskineig Falls ~ CDN 34-35 N 4
Baškirskij zapovednik ⊥ RUS 96-97 K 7
Baskunčak, ozero ≈ RUS 126-127 G 4
Basler Lake ○ CDN 30-31 M 4
Basmat ○ IND 138-139 F 10
Bašnja Šamilja • RUS 102-103 J 2
Bāsoda ○ IND 138-139 F 8
Basoko ○ ZRE 210-211 J 3
Basongo ○ ZRE 210-211 H 6
Basoti ○ EAT 212-213 E 6
Basova, mys ▲ RUS 112-113 J 3
Başra, al- ○ IRQ 130-131 K 2
Basra, al- = Başra, al- ○ IRQ 130-131 K 2
Bassano ○ CDN 32-33 O 6
Bassano del Grappa ○ I 100-101 C 2
Bassar ○ RT 202-203 L 4
Bassas da India ~ F 218-219 G 6
Bassaula ○ WAN 204-205 J 5
Bassein ~ MYA 158-159 T 2
Bassein = Puthein ○ MYA 158-159 C 2
Basse-Kotto □ RCA 206-207 E 6
Basse-Normandie □ F 90-91 G 7
Basse-Santa Su ★ WAG 202-203 C 3
Basse-Terre ★ F 56 E 3
Basse-Terre ~ F 56 E 3
Basseterre ★ KAN 56 D 3
Basset ○ USA 42-43 K 3

Bass Highway || AUS 180-181 H 6
Bassikounou ○ RIM 196-197 H 7
Bassila ○ DY 202-203 L 5
Basso ○ DY 204-205 E 3
Basso ▲ TCH 198-199 L 4
Bassoues ○ F 98-99 H 3
Bass River ○ CDN 38-39 M 5
Basswood Lake ○ USA 46-47 C 1
Bastak ○ IR 134-135 F 5
Bastar ○ IND 142-143 B 6
Baştau hrebet ▲ RUS 96-97 K 7
Bastenaken = Bastogne ○ B 92-93 H 3
Bastia ★ F 98-99 M 3
Basti Maluk ○ PK 138-139 C 5
Bastogne ○ B 92-93 H 3
Bastrop ○ USA (LA) 44-45 M 3
Bastrop ○ USA (TX) 44-45 J 4
Basu, Pulau ~ RI 162-163 E 5
Basu, Tanjung ▲ RI 162-163 E 5
Basua ○ WAN 204-205 H 5
Basunda ○ SUD 200-201 G 6
Başur Tepe ▲ TR 128-129 H 3
Bat ••• OM 132-133 K 2
Bata ○ GQ 210-211 B 3
Batabanó ○ C 54-55 D 3
Batabanó, Golfo de ≈ 54-55 D 3
Batabi ○ WAN 204-205 F 4
Bataf ○ RI 166-167 K 3
Batagaj ○ RUS 110-111 U 6
Batagaj-Alyta ○ RUS 110-111 S 6
Batag Island ~ RP 160-161 F 6
Bataguaçu ○ BR 72-73 D 6
Batajka ~ RUS 108-109 Z 6
Batajsk ○ RUS 102-103 L 4
Batakan ○ RI 164-165 D 6
Bataker Palace • RI 162-163 C 3
Batak Houses • RI 162-163 C 3
Batala ○ IND 138-139 E 4
Batalha ○ BR (ALA) 68-69 K 6
Batalha ○ BR (PIA) 68-69 G 4
Batalha, Mosteiro de •• P 98-99 C 5
Batam, Pulau ~ RI 162-163 E 4
Batama ○ ZRE 210-211 K 3
Batamaj ○ RUS 118-119 O 4
Batâmbali Beafada ○ GNB 202-203 C 4
Batamšy ~ KA 126-127 N 2
Batan ○ VRC 154-155 B 4
Batang ○ RI 162-163 E 5
Batang ○ VRC 144-145 M 6
Batangafo ○ RCA 206-207 D 5
Batangas ○ RP 160-161 D 6
Batan Island ~ RP (ALB) 160-161 F 6
Batan Island ~ RP (BTN) 160-161 E 4
Batan Islands ~ RP 160-161 E 4
Batanta, Pulau ~ RI 166-167 F 2
Batanta Pulau Reserve ⊥ RI 166-167 F 2
Batas Island ~ RP 160-161 C 7
Batatais ○ BR 72-73 G 6
Batavia ○ USA 46-47 J 4
Batavia = Jakarta ★ RI 168 B 3
Batavia Downs ○ AUS 174-175 G 3
Batchawana Bay ○ CDN 34-35 O 7
Batchelor ○ AUS 172-173 K 2
Batchenga ○ CAM 204-205 J 6
Bâtdâmbâng ○ K 158-159 G 4
Bateckij ○ RUS 94-95 M 2
Bateeputih, Tanjung ▲ RI 162-163 A 2
Bateias ○ BR 74-75 F 5
Batéké, Plateaux ▲▲ RCB 210-211 E 5
Batel, Esteros del ≈ RA 76-77 H 5
Batelito, Arroyo ~ RA 76-77 H 5
Batemans Bay ○ AUS 180-181 L 3
Batemba ○ ZRE 210-211 J 4
Baté-Nafadj ○ RG 202-203 F 4
Bates, Cerro de la • RA 78-79 D 4
Bates ○ USA 176-177 M 5
Batesburg ○ USA 48-49 H 3
Batesland ○ USA 42-43 G 4
Batesville ○ USA (AR) 44-45 M 2
Batesville ○ USA (MS) 48-49 D 2
Batesville ○ USA (TX) 44-45 H 5
Bath ○ ••• GB 90-91 F 6
Bath ○ JA 54-55 G 6
Bath ○ USA 38-39 G 7
Batha ~ TCH 198-199 J 6
Batha ~ TCH 198-199 J 6
Bathã, Wādil- ~ OM 132-133 L 2
Batha de Laïri ~ TCH 206-207 C 3
Batheaston ○ AUS 178-179 K 2
Bathinda ○ IND 138-139 E 4
Baths, The ~ GB 56 C 2
Bathsheba ○ BDS 56 F 5
Bathurst ○ AUS 180-181 K 2
Bat.Thu'óc ~ VN 156-157 D 8
Bathurst ○ AUS 180-181 K 2
Bathurst ○ CDN 38-39 M 5
Bathurst ○ ZA 220-221 H 6
Bathurst = Banjul ★ • WAG 202-203 B 3
Bathurst, Cape ▲ CDN 24-25 H 5
Bathurst Inlet ≈ CDN 30-31 O 3
Bathurst Inlet ○ CDN 30-31 P 3
Bathurst Island ~ AUS 172-173 K 1
Bathurst Island ~ CDN 24-25 V 3
Bati ○ ETH 208-209 E 3
Batia ○ DY 202-203 L 4
Batibati ○ RI 164-165 D 6
Batibo ○ CAM 204-205 H 6
Batié ○ BF 202-203 J 5
Batiki ~ FJI 184 III b 2
Bāū-Mekragroti, Área Indígena ✗ BR 66-67 K 6
Bātin, Wādi al- ~ KSA 130-131 J 3
Bāṭina ⊥ OM 132-133 K 1
Batinga ○ BR 72-73 K 4
Batiscan, Rivière ~ CDN 38-39 H 5
Bat Island ~ PNG 183 B 2
Batkanu ○ WAL 202-203 D 5
Batken ○ KS 136-137 M 4
Bat Khela ○ PK 138-139 C 2
Batlai ○ RUS 108-109 L 4
Bātlāq-e Gävhūni ≈ IR 134-135 E 2
Batlow ○ AUS 180-181 K 3

Batman ★ TR 128-129 J 4
Batn, Ğal al- ▲ IRQ 130-131 H 2
Batnorov = Dundburd ○ MAU 148-149 K 4
Ba To' ○ VN 158-159 K 3
Bato Bato ○ RP 160-161 C 10
Batoka ○ Z 218-219 D 3
Bat-Ölzijt ○ MAU 148-149 G 5
Batomga ○ RUS 120-121 G 5
Batomga ~ RUS 120-121 G 5
Baton Rouge ★ USA 44-45 M 4
Batopilas ○ MEX 50-51 E 4
Batou ○ MEX 50-51 F 4
Batouala ○ G 210-211 D 3
Batouri ○ CAM 206-207 D 6
Batovi, Área Indígena ✗ BR 72-73 D 2
Batovil, Rio ~ BR 72-73 D 2
Batpajsagyr, kum ~ KA 96-97 F 10
Ba Tri ○ VN 158-159 J 5
Batsari ○ WAN 198-199 C 6
Batsawul ○ AFG 138-139 C 2
Bâtsfjord ○ N 86-87 O 1
Batterbee Range ▲ ARK 16 F 30
Batticaloa ○ CL 140-141 J 7
Batti Malv Island ~ IND 140-141 L 5
Battir ••• IL 130-131 D 3
Battle Camp ○ AUS 174-175 H 4
Battle Creek ~ CDN 32-33 Q 7
Battle Creek ○ USA 46-47 F 4
Battlefields ○ ZW 218-219 E 4
Battleford ○ CDN 32-33 R 5
Battle Ground ○ USA 40-41 C 3
Battle Harbour ○ CDN 36-37 S 4
Battle Lake ○ USA 42-43 K 2
Battle Mountain ○ USA 40-41 F 5
Battle River ~ CDN 32-33 P 5
Battor ○ GH 202-203 L 6
Batu ▲ ETH 208-209 D 5
Batu, Bukit ▲ MAL 162-163 A 5
Batu, Kepulauan ~ RI 162-163 C 4
Batu, Tanjung ▲ RI (KTI) 164-165 F 3
Batu, Tanjung ▲ RI (SUB) 162-163 D 6
Batuaga ○ RI 164-165 H 6
Batuampar ○ RI 162-163 D 5
Batuamparan ○ RI 164-165 D 5
Batuasa ○ RI 166-167 F 3
Batuata, Pulau ~ RI 166-167 B 5
Batubatu ○ RI 164-165 G 4
Batuberagam, Tanjung ▲ RI 162-163 D 5
Batudaka ○ RI 164-165 G 4
Batudaka, Pulau ~ RI 164-165 G 4
Batu Danau ○ RI 166-167 F 2
Batudulag ○ RI 168 C 7
Batugade ○ RI 166-167 C 6
Batuhitam, Tanjung ▲ RI 164-165 H 4
Batui ○ RI 164-165 H 4
Batukangkung ○ RI 162-163 D 5
Batukau, Gunung ▲ RI 168 B 7
Batulicin ○ RI 164-165 D 6
Batumandi, Tanjung ▲ RI 162-163 D 5
Batumi ★ GE 126-127 D 7
Batu Pahat ○ MAL 162-163 E 5
Batupanjang ○ RI 162-163 D 4
Batuputih, Gunung ▲ MAL 162-163 D 4
Baty-Jurjah ~ RUS 108-109 c 6
Batyr ~ RUS 118-119 E 4
Batyrevo ○ RUS 96-97 E 6
Bau ○ MAL 162-163 J 4
Baú, Rio ~ BR 66-67 K 6
Baú, Rio ~ BR 66-67 K 7
Bau'u, Tanjung ▲ RI 162-163 A 2
Bauana, Rio ~ BR 66-67 E 4
Baubau ○ RI 164-165 H 6
Bauchi ★ WAN (BAU) 204-205 H 3
Baudette ○ USA 42-43 K 1
Baudisson Island ~ PNG 183 F 2
Baudó, Serranía de ▲▲ CO 60-61 C 4
Bauer Basin ≈ 14 H 5
Baugé ○ F 62-63 H 3
Bauhinia Downs ○ AUS (NT) 174-175 C 5
Bauhinia Downs ○ AUS (QLD) 178-179 K 3
Bauia ○ RI 164-165 G 6
Baukau ○ RI 166-167 D 6
Baúl, El ○ YV 60-61 G 3
Baúl, El ○ YV 60-61 G 3
Bauld, Cape ▲ CDN 36-37 S 4
Baule-Escoublac, la ○ • F 90-91 F 8
Baumann Fiord ≈ 24-25 d 2
Baunei ○ I 100-101 C 5
Baunagar ○ RP 160-161 F 8
Baunt ○ IND 142-143 H 4
Baunt, ozero ≈ RUS 118-119 F 8
Bauru ○ BR 72-73 F 7
Bauru ○ ZRE 210-211 J 4
Bauska ○ LV 94-95 J 3
Bauta ○ C 54-55 D 3

Bauta ○ ZRE 210-211 H 3
Batn al-Ğûl ○ JOR 130-131 D 3
Bautzen ○ D 92-93 N 3
Bauvispe, Rio ~ MEX 50-51 E 2
Bavly ~ RUS 96-97 H 6
Bavon ○ USA 46-47 K 7
Bawa ○ RP 160-161 C 10
Bawal ○ IND 138-139 F 5
Bawanbir ○ IND 138-139 F 9
Bawang, Tanjung ▲ RI 162-163 H 5
Bawangling Z.B. ⊥ VRC 156-157 F 7
Bawâti, Ğabal ▲ SUD 200-201 H 3
Baw Baw National Park ⊥ AUS 180-181 J 4
Bawdie ○ GH 202-203 J 7
Bawe ○ RI (IRJ) 166-167 H 2
Bawe ○ RI 166-167 F 3
Bawean, Pulau ~ RI 168 E 2
Bawen ○ RI 168 D 3
Bawku ○ GH 202-203 K 4
Bawlake ○ MYA 142-143 K 4
Bawo ○ LB 202-203 F 7
Bawo Ofuloa ○ RI 162-163 C 5
Ba Xay ○ LAO 156-157 C 6
Baxkorgan ○ VRC 146-147 K 6
Baxley ○ USA 48-49 H 4
Baxoi ○ VRC 144-145 L 5
Baxter ○ USA 42-43 K 2
Baxter Cliffs ▲ AUS 176-177 H 6
Bay ○ RMM 202-203 J 3
Bay ☆ SP 212-213 J 2
Bay, Reserve de ⊥ RMM 202-203 J 3
Baya-Bwanga ○ ZRE 210-211 J 6
Bayād, al- ▲ KSA 132-133 G 4
Bayād, Ra's al- ▲ Y 132-133 G 5
Bayadi ○ G 210-211 C 5
Bayaguana ○ DOM 54-55 L 5
Bayamo ☆ C 54-55 H 4
Bayan ○ VRC 150-151 F 4
Bayanbulak ○ VRC 146-147 G 4
Bayanga ○ RCA 206-207 C 6
Bayanga-Didi ○ RCA 206-207 B 6
Bayan Har Shan ▲▲ VRC 144-145 K 3
Bayan Har Shankou ▲ VRC 144-145 L 3
Bayan Obo ○ VRC 148-149 J 7
Bayan Olji ○ VRC 154-155 D 1
Bayan Shan ▲ VRC 144-145 L 2
Bayard ○ USA (NE) 42-43 F 5
Bayard ○ USA (NM) 44-45 C 3
Bayat ☆ TR 128-129 E 3
Bayawan ○ RP 160-161 E 8
Bayâ' ○ IR 134-135 F 3
Bayâz̄iye ○ IR 134-135 F 3
Baybay ○ RP 160-161 F 7
Bay Bulls ○ CDN 38-39 I 5
Bayburt ★ TR 128-129 J 2
Bay City ○ USA (MI) 46-47 G 4
Bay City ○ USA (TX) 44-45 K 5
Baydhabo ☆ SP 212-213 J 2
Bayerischer Wald ▲ D 92-93 M 4
Bayern □ D 92-93 L 4
Bayeux ○ BR 68-69 L 5
Bayeux • F 90-91 G 7
Bayfield ○ USA 46-47 C 2
Bay Fiord ≈ 26-27 J 4
Bây Háp, Cú'a Sông ≈ 158-159 H 6
Bayındır ★ TR 128-129 B 3
Bâyir ○ JOR 130-131 D 3
Bäyir Ğovein, Küh-e ▲ IR 136-137 E 6
Bayizhen ○ VRC 144-145 K 5
Baykan ★ TR 128-129 J 3
Baykonur = Bajkonyr ☆ KA 124-125 G 3
Bay Mills Indian Reservation ✗ • USA 46-47 F 2
Bay Minette ○ USA 48-49 E 4
Baynes Mountains ▲ NAM 216-217 B 8
Baynūna ⊥ UAE 132-133 H 2
Bayo, Cerro ▲ RCH 80 D 2
Bayobar ○ PE 64-65 B 4
Bay of Whales ≈ 16 F 20
Bayog ○ RP 160-161 E 9
Bayo Mesa, Cerro ▲ RA 78-79 E 5
Bayon Macon ○ USA 44-45 M 4
Bayonne • F 90-91 G 10
Bayou Bartholomew River ~ USA 44-45 M 4
Bayou Cane ○ USA 44-45 M 5
Bay Port ○ USA 46-47 G 4
Bayramiç ★ TR 128-129 B 3
Bayreuth ○ D 92-93 L 4
Bays, Lake of ≈ CDN 38-39 E 6
Bay Saint Louis ○ USA 48-49 D 4
Bay Shore ○ USA 46-47 M 5
Bay Springs ○ USA 48-49 D 3
Baytik Shan ▲▲ VRC 146-147 K 3
Baytown ○ USA 44-45 K 5
Bay Tree ○ CDN 32-33 L 4
Bayu ○ RI (ACE) 162-163 B 3
Bayu ○ RI (STG) 164-165 H 5
Bayugan ○ RP 160-161 F 8
Bayunglincir ○ RI 162-163 E 6
Bayun Gol He ~ VRC 144-145 L 2
Bayur, Tanjung ▲ RI 164-165 E 4
Bayur, Teluk ≈ 162-163 D 5
Bay View ○ NZ 182 F 3
Bayy al Kabir ~ LAR 192-193 F 2
Bayy al Kabir, Wādi ~ LAR 192-193 F 2
Bayzo ○ RN 198-199 B 6
Baza ○ E 98-99 F 6
Bazardjuzu, gora ▲ RUS 126-127 G 7
Bāzār-e Tāle ○ AFG 136-137 L 7
Bāžārgān ○ IR 128-129 L 3
Bazarny Mataki ☆ RUS 96-97 F 6
Bazaruto, Ilhas do ~ MOC 218-219 H 5
Bazaruto, Parque Nacional do ⊥ MOC 218-219 H 5
Bazavluk ~ UA 102-103 J 4
Baženovo ○ RUS 96-97 J 6
Bazhong ○ VRC 154-155 B 4
Bazhou ○ VRC 154-155 K 2
Bazmán ○ IR 134-135 J 5

Bazmán, Küh-e ▲ IR 134-135 H 4
Bazou ○ CAM 204-205 J 6
Bazré ○ TCH 206-207 C 4
Be, Nosy ~ RM 222-223 F 4
Beach ○ USA 42-43 F 2
Beach Point ▲ CDN 24-25 d 7
Beachport ○ AUS 180-181 E 4
Beacon ○ AUS 176-177 D 5
Beacon ○ USA 46-47 M 5
Beacon Bay ○ ZA 220-221 H 6
Beadell, Mount ▲ AUS 176-177 F 4
Beadon Point ▲ AUS 172-173 B 6
Beafada, Batâmbali ○ GNB 202-203 C 4
Beagle, Canal ≈ 80 F 7
Beagle Bay ≈ AUS 172-173 F 4
Beagle Bay X AUS 172-173 F 4
Beagle Bay Aboriginal Land X AUS 172-173 F 4
Beagle Gulf ≈ 172-173 J 2
Beagle Island ~ AUS 176-177 C 4
Beagle Reef ~ AUS 172-173 F 3
Beako, Tanjung ▲ RI 166-167 D 6
Bealanana ○ RM 222-223 F 4
Béal an Atha = Ballina ○ IRL 90-91 C 4
Béal an Mhuirthead = Belmullet ○ IRL 90-91 C 5
Béal Átha na Sluaighe = Ballinasloe ○ IRL 90-91 C 5
Beale Air Force Base ✗✗ USA 40-41 D 6
Beals Creek ~ USA 44-45 G 3
Beampingaratra ▲ RM 222-223 E 10
Beanntraí = Bantry ○ IRL 90-91 B 6
Bear, Mount ▲ USA 20-21 U 6
Bear Bay ≈ 24-25 c 3
Bear Cove ○ CDN (BC) 32-33 G 6
Bear Cove ○ CDN (NWT) 36-37 G 3
Bear Cove Point ▲ CDN 36-37 H 3
Beardmore ○ CDN 34-35 N 6
Beardmore Glacier ▲ ARK 16 E 0
Beardmore Reservoir < AUS 178-179 K 4
Beardstown ○ USA 46-47 C 5
Beardy River ~ AUS 178-179 L 5
Bearhead Creek ~ CDN 32-33 M 4
Bear Island ☆ ARK 16 F 26
Bear Island ~ CDN 34-35 O 5
Bear Islands = Medveži ostrova ~ RUS 112-113 L 1
Bear Lake ○ CDN 34-35 H 4
Bear Lake ○ USA 40-41 J 5
Bear Mount ▲ USA 20-21 T 2
Bearpaw Mount ▲ USA 42-43 C 1
Bear Paw Mountain ▲ USA 42-43 C 1
Bear River ~ CDN 34-35 D 4
Bear River ~ USA 40-41 J 5
Bearskin Lake ○ CDN 34-35 L 4
Beatrice ○ USA 42-43 J 5
Beatrice, Cape ▲ AUS 174-175 D 3
Beatton Fiver ~ CDN (BC) 32-33 K 3
Beatton Fiver ~ CDN 32-33 K 3
Beatty ○ CDN 34-35 D 5
Beatty ○ USA 40-41 F 7
Beattyville ○ CDN 38-39 F 4
Beauceville ○ CDN 38-39 J 5
Beaudesert ○ AUS (QLD) 178-179 L 4
Beaudesert ○ AUS (QLD) 178-179 F 1
Beaufort ○ MAL 160-161 A 10
Beaufort ○ USA (NC) 48-49 K 2
Beaufort ○ USA (SC) 48-49 H 3
Beaufort Sea ≈ 20-21 U 2
Beaufort-Wes = Beaufort West ○ ZA 220-221 F 6
Beaufort West = Beaufort-Wes ○ ZA 220-221 F 6
Beaugency ○ F 90-91 H 8
Beaulieu River ~ CDN 30-31 N 4
Beauly • GB 90-91 E 3
Beaumont ○ USA (MS) 48-49 D 4
Beaumont ○ USA (TX) 44-45 K 4
Beaumont-de-Lomagne ○ F 90-91 H 10
Beaumont-sur-Oise = F 90-91 J 7
Beaune ○ F 90-91 K 8
Beaupré, Kap ▲ GRØ 28-29 c 2
Beauregard ○ USA 48-49 F 3
Beauséjour ○ CDN 34-35 H 5
Beauséjour National Historical Park, Fort ∴· CDN 38-39 M 6
Beauty ○ ZA 218-219 D 6
Beauvais ★ • F 90-91 J 7
Beauvais Lake ○ CDN 30-31 R 5
Beauveau, Lac ○ CDN 38-39 G 2
Beaver ○ USA (AK) 20-21 R 3
Beaver ○ USA (UT) 40-41 H 6
Beaver Creek ~ USA 20-21 R 4
Beaver Creek ~ USA 42-43 G 6
Beaver Creek ~ USA 42-43 G 2
Beaver Creek ~ USA 42-43 F 7
Beaverbodge Lake ○ CDN (NWT) 30-31 R 3
Beaverbodge Lake ○ CDN (SAS)
Beaver Dam ○ USA 46-47 D 4
Beaver Hill Lake ○ CDN 34-35 J 3
Beaverhill Lake ○ CDN (NWT) 30-31 R 4
Beaver Island ~ USA 46-47 F 3
Beaver Lake ○ USA 44-45 K 1
Beaver Lodge ○ CDN 32-33 L 4
Beaver Mountain ▲ CDN 30-31 U 5
Beavermouth ○ CDN 32-33 M 6
Beaver River ~ CDN 32-33 Q 5
Beaver River ~ USA 44-45 G 1

Beaver River = Ruisseau du Castor ~ CDN 38-39 E 2
Beaverstone River ~ CDN 34-35 L 3
Beaverton ○ USA 38-39 E 6
Beâwar ○ IND 138-139 E 6
Beazley ○ RA 78-79 F 2
Bebarama ○ CO 60-61 C 4
Bébédjia ○ TCH 206-207 C 4
Bebeka ○ ETH 208-209 B 5
Bebenoro ○ RM 222-223 F 6
Bebika ○ PNG 183 B 4
Béboto ○ TCH 206-207 C 4
Béboura III ○ RCA 206-207 C 5
Bebra ○ D 92-93 K 3
Becal ·:· MEX 52-53 J 1
Becan ∴ MEX 52-53 K 2
Becanchén ○ MEX 52-53 K 2
Bécard, Lac ○ CDN 36-37 N 4
Bečenča ○ RUS 118-119 G 5
Becerréa ○ E 98-99 D 3
Becerro, Cayos ~ HN 54-55 D 7
Béchar ○ DZ 188-189 K 5
Becharof Lake ○ USA 22-23 S 4
Becher, Cape ▲ CDN 24-25 Y 2
Bechevin Bay ≈ 22-23 P 5
Becilla de Valderaduey ○ E 98-99 E 3
Beckley ○ USA 46-47 H 7
Becks ○ NZ 182 B 6
Beco ○ RI 166-167 C 6
Bedarra Island ~ AUS 174-175 J 6
Bédaya ○ TCH 206-207 C 4
Beddouza, Cap ▲ MA 188-189 G 4
Bedelé ○ ETH 208-209 C 5
Bedesa ○ ETH 208-209 E 4
Bedford ○ CDN 38-39 H 6
Bedford ○ GB 90-91 G 5
Bedford ○ USA (IN) 46-47 F 6
Bedford ○ USA (PA) 46-47 J 5
Bedford ○ USA (VA) 46-47 J 7
Bedford ○ ZA 220-221 H 6
Bedford, Cape ▲ AUS 174-175 H 4
Bedford, Lake ○ AUS 176-177 G 3
Bedford, Mount ▲ AUS 172-173 H 4
Bedford Downs ○ AUS 172-173 H 4
Bediako ○ GH 202-203 J 6
Bediani ○ GE 126-127 F 7
Bedi Dat ○ PK 134-135 J 5
Bediondo ○ TCH 206-207 C 4
Bedjerdjene, Hassi < DZ 190-191 G 7
Bednesti ○ CDN 32-33 J 5
Bednodem'janovsk ○ RUS 94-95 S 5
Bédo ○ TCH 198-199 J 3
Bedoba ○ RUS 116-117 H 6
Bédouaram < RN 198-199 F 5
Bedoud, Hassi < MA 188-189 K 4
Beebe ○ USA 44-45 M 2
Beechal River ~ AUS 178-179 H 4
Beecher ○ USA 46-47 E 5
Beechey Lake ○ CDN 30-31 Q 3
Beechey Point ○ USA 20-21 P 1
Beechworth ○ AUS 180-181 J 4
Beechy ○ CDN 34-35 C 5
Beekman Peninsula ◡ CDN 36-37 R 3
Beeler ○ USA 42-43 G 6
Beencïme ~ RUS 110-111 N 4
Beenleigh ○ AUS 178-179 M 4
Be'er Sheva' ☆ IL 130-131 D 3
Beerwah ○ AUS 178-179 N 2
Beeskow ○ D 92-93 N 2
Beestekraal ○ ZA 220-221 G 4
Beetaloo ○ AUS 174-175 B 5
Beeville ○ USA 44-45 J 5
Befale ○ ZRE 210-211 J 3
Befandefa ○ RM 222-223 C 9
Befandriana Atsimo ○ RM 222-223 C 9
Befandriana Avaratra ○ RM 222-223 F 5
Befasy ○ RM 222-223 B 8
Beffa ○ DY 204-205 E 4
Befori ○ ZRE 210-211 J 3
Beforona ○ RM 222-223 F 7
Befotaka ○ RM 222-223 E 9
Bega ○ AUS 180-181 K 4
Begičeva, grjada ▲▲ RUS 108-109 X 5
Begidžian ~ RUS 110-111 P 6
Begna ~ N 86-87 D 6
Begogo ○ RM 222-223 D 9
Bégon ○ RCA 206-207 B 5
Begoro ○ GH 202-203 K 6
Begunicy ○ RUS 94-95 L 2
Begusarai ○ IND 142-143 E 3
Beh ~ RI 168 C 7
Behâbâd ○ IR 134-135 G 3
Béhague, Pointe ▲ F 62-63 J 3
Behara ○ RM 222-223 E 10
Behbahān ○ • IR 134-135 F 3
Beheloka ○ RM 222-223 C 9
Behenjy ○ RM 222-223 F 6
Béhili ○ RCA 206-207 D 5
Behm Canal ≈ 32-33 E 4
Behring Point ○ BS 54-55 G 2
Behšahr ○ • IR 136-137 C 6
Bei'an ○ VRC 150-151 F 3
Béibouo ○ CI 202-203 G 6
Beibu Wan ≈ 156-157 F 6
Beichuan ○ VRC 154-155 B 4
Beida = Goz ~ TCH 198-199 K 6
Beidaihe Haibin • VRC 154-155 L 2
Beidanelkechuke ○ VRC 144-145 F 5
Beidou ○ VRC 156-157 N 6
Beigi ○ ETH 208-209 B 4
Beihai ○ VRC 156-157 F 6
Bei Jiang ~ VRC 156-157 H 5
Bei Jiao ~ VRC 158-159 L 2
Beijing ★ ••• VRC 154-155 K 2
Beijing Shi □ VRC 154-155 K 2
Bei Ling ••• VRC 150-151 D 7
Beiliu ○ VRC 156-157 G 5
Béinamar ○ TCH 206-207 B 4
Beipan Jiang ~ VRC 156-157 D 4
Beipiao ○ VRC 150-151 D 7
Beira ○ MOC 218-219 G 4
Beira Alta ○ ANG 216-217 C 4
Beiradão ○ BR 62-63 H 6

Beirut = Bairūt ★ **RL** 128-129 F 6
Beiseker o **CDN** 32-33 O 6
Bei Shan ▲▲ **VRC** 146-147 M 5
Beishan • **VRC** (JIL) 150-151 E 6
Beishan • **VRC** (ZHE) 156-157 L 2
Beitan o **VRC** 156-157 F 6
Beitau o **VRC** 156-157 F 6
Beitbridge o **ZW** 218-219 F 6
Beitstadfjorden ≈ 86-87 E 5
Beitun o **VRC** 146-147 H 2
Beizhangdian o **VRC** 154-155 H 3
Beizhen o **VRC** 150-151 C 7
Beja o•• **P** 98-99 D 5
Beja ☆ **TN** 190-191 G 2
Bejaja ☆• **DZ** 190-191 E 2
Béjar o• **E** 98-99 E 4
Bejarn o **N** 86-87 G 3
Beji ~ **PK** 138-139 B 5
Beji o **WAN** 204-205 G 4
Bejlagan = Beylagan o **AZ** 128-129 M 3
Bejneu ☆ **KA** 126-127 L 5
Bejsug ~ **RUS** 102-103 L 5
Bejsugskij liman ≈ 102-103 L 4
Bejucal o **C** 54-55 D 3
Bek ~ **CAM** 210-211 E 2
Béka o **CAM** (ADA) 204-205 K 5
Béka o **CAM** (ADA) 206-207 B 5
Béka o **CAM** (NOR) 204-205 K 4
Bekabad o **US** 136-137 L 4
Békamba o **TCH** 206-207 C 4
Bekasi o **RI** 168 B 3
Bekati o **US** 136-137 K 4
Bekbeket o **KA** 96-97 H 10
Bekdaš o **TM** 136-137 C 4
Bek-Džar o **KS** 136-137 N 4
Beke o **RI** 168 E 7
Bèkè ~ **RUS** 110-111 K 6
Beke o **ZRE** 214-215 D 5
Bekenu o **MAL** 162-163 K 2
Békés o **H** 92-93 Q 5
Békéscsaba o **H** 92-93 Q 5
Bekily o **RM** (TLA) 222-223 D 10
Bekipay o **RM** 222-223 E 6
Bekitro o **RM** 222-223 D 10
Bekkai o **J** 152-153 L 3
Bekmurat, gora ▲ **TM** 136-137 D 4
Bekodoka o **RM** 222-223 D 6
Bek'oji o **ETH** 208-209 D 5
Bekopaka o **RM** 222-223 D 7
Békuy o **BF** 202-203 J 4
Bekwai o **GH** 202-203 K 6
Bekyem o **GH** 202-203 J 6
Bela ~ **BR** 70-71 H 3
Bela o **IND** 142-143 C 3
Bela o **PK** 134-135 M 5
Bélabirim < **RN** 198-199 F 5
Bélabo o **CAM** 204-205 K 6
Bela Estrela o **BR** 68-69 E 4
Belaga o **MAL** 162-163 K 3
Bel Air o **USA** 46-47 K 6
Belaja ~ **RUS** 96-97 L 6
Belaja ~ **RUS** 112-113 R 4
Belaja ~ **RUS** 112-113 O 5
Belaja ~ **RUS** 116-117 L 9
Belaja ~ **RUS** 122-123 C 3
Belaja ~ **RUS** 126-127 D 5
Belaja, gora ▲ **RUS** 112-113 S 4
Belaja, Ust'- o **RUS** 112-113 R 4
Belaja Berëzka o **RUS** 94-95 N 5
Belaja Cerkov' = Bila Cerkva ☆ **UA** 102-103 G 3
Belaja Gora o **RUS** 110-111 a 5
Belaja Holunica ☆ **RUS** 96-97 G 4
Belaja Kalitva o **RUS** 102-103 M 3
Belaja Škola o **KA** 124-125 N 5
Belajau, Danau ⬭ **RI** 162-163 K 6
Belaja Zemlja, ostrova ∩ **RUS** 84-85 g 2
Belalcázar o **E** 98-99 E 5
Bela Lorena o **BR** 72-73 G 3
Belamoty o **RM** 222-223 D 9
Belang o **RI** 164-165 J 3
Belangan o **RI** 162-163 K 6
Belangbelang, Pulau ∩ **RI** (MAL) 164-165 K 4
Belangbelang, Pulau ∩ **RI** (SSE) 168 E 6
Belanger Island ∩ **CDN** 36-37 L 6
Belanger River ~ **CDN** 34-35 H 4
Bela Palanka o• **YU** 100-101 J 3
Belarus = Belarus' ■ **BY** 94-95 K 5
Belas o **ANG** 216-217 B 4
Belāti o **IND** 140-141 F 2
Bela Vista o **ANG** (BGO) 216-217 B 3
Bela Vista o **ANG** (HBO) 216-217 D 6
Bela Vista o **BR** (APA) 62-63 J 4
Bela Vista o **BR** (GSU) 76-77 J 2
Bela Vista o **BR** (RSU) 74-75 D 7
Bela Vista o **MOC** 220-221 L 3
Bela Vista, Cachoeira ~ **BR** 68-69 C 3
Belawan o **RI** 162-163 C 3
Belayan ~ **RI** 164-165 E 3
Bélbéji o **RN** 198-199 C 5
Belbela, Sebkha Aïn ⬭ **DZ** 188-189 J 7
Bèl'c' = Bălţi ☆ **MD** 102-103 E 4
Belčerāg o **AFG** 136-137 J 7
Bełchatów o **PL** 92-93 P 3
Belcher Channel ≈ 24-25 X 2
Belcher Islands o **CDN** (NWT) 36-37 K 6
Belcher Islands ∩ **CDN** 34-35 R 2
Belcher Islands ∩ **CDN** (NWT) 36-37 J 6
Belcher Point ▲ **CDN** 24-25 g 3
Belchite o **E** 98-99 G 4
Bel'cy = Bălţi ☆ **MD** 102-103 E 4
Belda o **IND** 142-143 E 4
Belden o **USA** 40-41 D 5
Bel'dir, Uš o **RUS** 116-117 J 10
Bel'dunčana, ozero ⬭ **RUS** 116-117 G 2
Bele, ozero ⬭ **RUS** 116-117 E 8
Belebej ☆ **RUS** 96-97 J 6
Belebelka o **RUS** 94-95 M 3
Beledweyne ☆ **SP** 208-209 G 6
Béléhédé o **BF** 202-203 K 2
Beléko-Soba o **RMM** 202-203 G 3
Bélel o **CAM** 206-207 B 5
Belel o **WAN** 204-205 K 4
Belele o **AUS** 176-177 D 3
Belém o **BR** (AMA) 66-67 C 5
Belém o **BR** (PA) 68-69 L 5
Belém ☆• **BR** (P) 62-63 K 6
Belem o **PE** 70-71 C 4
Belem de São Francisco o **BR** 68-69 J 6
Belen o **CO** 60-61 E 4
Belen ~ **PA** 52-53 D 7
Belén o **RA** 76-77 D 4
Belén o **RCH** 70-71 C 6
Belen o **USA** 44-45 D 2
Belén, Río ~ **RA** 76-77 D 4
Belen'kij o **RUS** 118-119 M 8
Belesc Cogani o **SP** 212-213 H 3
Beles Wenz ~ **ETH** 208-209 C 3
Belet Weyne = Beledweyne ☆ **SP** 208-209 G 6
Beleuli ∴• **US** 136-137 E 2
Belev ☆ **RUS** 94-95 P 5
Bèlèya o **RG** 202-203 E 4
Beleya Terara ▲ **ETH** 208-209 C 3
Beleza, Ribeiro ~ **BR** 68-69 C 6
Belezma, Monts de ▲▲ **DZ** 190-191 E 3
Belfast ☆• **GB** 90-91 E 4
Belfast o **USA** 46-47 O 3
Belfast o **ZA** 220-221 K 2
Belfield o **USA** 42-43 F 2
Bëlfodiyo o **ETH** 208-209 B 3
Belfort ☆• **F** 90-91 L 8
Belgaum o• **IND** 140-141 F 3
Belgica, La o **BOL** 70-71 F 5
Belgica Bank ≃ 26-27 s 4
Belgica Mountains ▲▲ **ARK** 16 F 3
Belgium = België = Belgique ■ **B** 92-93 G 3
Bel'go o **RUS** 122-123 G 3
Belgo o **SUD** 206-207 L 3
Belgorod o **RUS** 102-103 K 2
Belgorod-Dnestrovskij ☆ **UA** 102-103 G 4
Belgrade o **USA** (MN) 42-43 K 3
Belgrade o **USA** (MT) 40-41 J 3
Belgrade = Beograd ★•• **YU** 100-101 H 2
Belgrano o **RA** 76-77 F 3
Belgrano, Cerro ▲ **RA** 80 E 3
Bel Guerdâne, Bir < **RIM** 196-197 E 2
Belhatti o **IND** 140-141 F 3
Belhaven o **USA** 48-49 K 2
Belhe o **IND** 138-139 E 10
Belhirane o **DZ** 190-191 F 5
Béli ~ **BF** 202-203 K 2
Béli o **GNB** 202-203 D 4
Beli o **WAN** 204-205 J 5
Belic o **C** 54-55 G 5
Bélice ~ **I** 100-101 D 6
Beličij, ostrov ∩ **RUS** 120-121 G 6
Belidži o **RUS** 126-127 H 7
Belifang o **CAM** 204-205 J 5
Beli Hill ▲ **WAN** 204-205 J 5
Belimbing o **RI** (LAM) 162-163 F 7
Belimbing o **RI** (SUS) 162-163 F 6
Belimbing, Tanjung ▲ **RI** 162-163 F 7
Belimbing, Teluk ≈ 162-163 F 7
Bélinga o **G** 210-211 D 3
Belinskij o **RUS** 94-95 R 5
Belinskoe o **RUS** 122-123 K 4
Belinyu o **RI** 162-163 F 5
Belitung, Pulau ∩ **RI** 162-163 H 6
Belize o **ANG** 210-211 D 6
Belize ■ **BH** 52-53 K 3
Belize City o **BH** 52-53 K 3
Belize River ~ **BH** 52-53 K 3
Bélizon o **F** 62-63 H 3
Beljaevka ☆ **RUS** 96-97 K 8
Beljaka, kosa ⌣ **RUS** 112-113 X 3
Beljanica ▲ **YU** 100-101 H 2
Beljanka ~ **RUS** 118-119 O 4
Bel Kacem, Bir < **TN** 190-191 G 4
Bel'kači o **RUS** 120-121 D 4
Bel'kači ~ **RUS** 120-121 D 4
Belkar o **IND** 140-141 E 2
Bel'kovskij, ostrov ∩ **RUS** 110-111 U 2
Bel'kovskij Nos, mys ▲ **RUS** 108-109 J 7
Bell o **ZA** 220-221 H 6
Bell, Rivière ~ **CDN** 38-39 F 4
Bella o **CAM** 210-211 C 2
Bella, Laguna la ⬭ **RA** 76-77 G 3
Bella Bella o **CDN** 32-33 F 5
Bellac o **F** 90-91 H 8
Bella Coola o **CDN** 32-33 G 5
Bella Coola River ~ **CDN** 32-33 G 5
Belladère o **RH** 54-55 J 5
Bella Flor o **BOL** 70-71 D 2
Bellaire o **USA** 46-47 H 6
Bellary o **IND** 140-141 G 3
Bellata o **AUS** 178-179 K 5
Bellavista o **EC** 64-65 B 10
Bellavista o **PE** (CAJ) 64-65 C 4
Bellavista o **PE** (MAR) 64-65 D 5
Bella Vista o **PY** 76-77 K 4
Bella Vista o **RA** 76-77 H 5
Bella Vista, Salar de ⬭ **RCH** 70-71 C 7
Bell Bay ≈ 24-25 e 5
Bellburns o **CDN** 38-39 Q 3
Belle, La o **USA** 48-49 H 6
Belle Anse o **RH** 54-55 J 5
Belle Bay ≈ 38-39 I R 5
Bellefontaine o **USA** 46-47 G 5
Bellefonte o **USA** 46-47 K 5
Belle Fourche o **USA** 42-43 F 3
Belle Fourche Reservoir < **USA** 42-43 F 3
Belle Fourche River ~ **USA** 42-43 E 4
Belle Glade o **USA** 48-49 H 6
Belle-Île ∩ **F** 90-91 F 8
Belle Isle ∩ **CDN** 38-39 R 3
Belle Isle, Strait of ≈ 38-39 Q 3
Bellenden Ker o **AUS** 174-175 H 5
Bellenden Ker National Park ⊥ **AUS** 174-175 H 5
Belleoram o **CDN** 38-39 I R 5
Belleterre o **CDN** 38-39 E 5
Belleville o **CDN** 38-39 F 6
Belleville o **USA** 42-43 J 6
Bellevue o **AUS** 174-175 H 5
Bellevue o **USA** (IA) 46-47 C 4
Bellevue o **USA** (WA) 40-41 C 2
Bellevue de–Inini, Mont ▲ **F** 62-63 H 4
Bellingen o **AUS** 178-179 M 6
Bellinger, Lac ⬭ **CDN** 38-39 G 3
Bellingham o **USA** 40-41 C 1
Bellingshausen Abyssal Plain ≈ **ARK** 16 G 27
Bellingshausen Sea ≈ **ARK** 16 G 28
Bellinzona ☆• **CH** 92-93 K 5
Bell-Irving River ~ **CDN** 32-33 F 3
Bell Island ∩ **CDN** (NFL) 38-39 R 3
Bell Island ∩ **CDN** (NFL) 38-39 I S 5
Bell Island Hot Springs o **USA** 32-33 E 4
Bellmead o **USA** 44-45 J 4
Bell National Historic Park, Alexander Graham ∴ **CDN** 38-39 O 5
Bello o **CO** 60-61 D 4
Bellocq o **RA** 78-79 J 3
Bellona Island ∩ **SOL** 184 I d 4
Bellows Falls o **USA** 46-47 M 4
Bellpat o **PK** 138-139 B 5
Bell Peninsula ⌣ **CDN** 36-37 H 3
Bell River ~ **AUS** 180-181 K 2
Bell River ~ **CDN** 20-21 W 3
Bellsund ≈ **N** (SVA) 84-85 H 4
Belluno ☆ **I** 100-101 D 1
Bell Ville o **RA** 78-79 H 2
Bellville o **ZA** 220-221 D 6
Belly River ~ **CDN** 32-33 O 7
Belmond o **USA** 42-43 L 4
Belmont o **AUS** 180-181 L 2
Belmont o **ZA** 220-221 G 4
Belmont, Fort ∴ **USA** 46-47 C 4
Belmonte o **BR** 72-73 L 3
Belmopan ★ **BH** 52-53 K 3
Belmore Creek ~ **AUS** 174-175 F 6
Belmullet = Béal an Mhuirthead o **IRL** 90-91 C 4
Belo o **RM** 222-223 D 8
Belobaka o **RM** 222-223 D 7
Belobrova, proliv ≈ 108-109 Z 1
Belo Campo o **BR** 72-73 K 3
Beloe, ozero ⬭ **RUS** 94-95 P 1
Beloe, ozero ⬭ **RUS** 114-115 U 7
Belogolovaja ~ **RUS** 120-121 R 5
Belogorsk o **RUS** (AMR) 122-123 C 3
Belogorsk o **RUS** (KMR) 114-115 U 7
Belogorskij materik ≐ **RUS** 114-115 J 3
Belogorskij materik, vozvšennost' ▲▲ **RUS** 114-115 J 3
Beloha o **RM** 222-223 D 10
Belo Horizonte ☆ **BR** 72-73 J 5
Beloit o **USA** (KS) 42-43 H 6
Beloit o **USA** (WI) 46-47 D 4
Belo Jardim o **BR** 68-69 K 6
Belojarovo o **RUS** 122-123 C 3
Belojarskij o **RUS** 114-115 J 3
Belojarskij ☆ **RUS** (SVR) 96-97 M 5
Béloko o **RCA** 206-207 B 6
Belokuriha o **RUS** 124-125 O 3
Belo Monte o **BR** (ALA) 68-69 K 6
Belo Monte o **BR** (AMA) 66-67 E 6
Belo Monte do Pontal o **BR** 68-69 C 3
Belomorsk o **RUS** 88-89 N 4
Belomorsko-Baltijskij kanal < **RUS** 88-89 N 4
Belomorsko-Kulojskoje-plato ▲▲ **RUS** 88-89 Q 4
Belonge o **ZRE** 210-211 H 5
Belopa o **RI** 164-165 G 5
Beloreċensk o **RUS** 126-127 C 5
Beloreck ☆ **RUS** 96-97 L 7
Belot, Lac ⬭ **CDN** 30-31 G 2
Belo Tsiribihina o **RM** 222-223 D 7
Belousovka o **KA** 124-125 N 3
Belovo ☆ **RUS** 114-115 T 7
Belovodskoe o **KS** 146-147 B 4
Beloye Ozero = Beloe, ozero ⬭ **RUS** 94-95 P 1
Belozersk o **RUS** 94-95 P 1
Belozerskoe ☆ **RUS** 114-115 H 7
Belozersko-Kirillovskie grjady ▲▲ **RUS** 94-95 P 1
Belpre o **USA** 42-43 H 7
Belrem, Hassi el < **DZ** 190-191 D 7
Bel'skaja vozvyšennost' ▲▲ **RUS** 94-95 N 4
Bel'skie, Ust'-gory ▲▲ **RUS** 112-113 R 4
Bel'skoe o **RUS** 116-117 F 7
Belt o **USA** 40-41 J 2
Belt Bay ⬭ **AUS** 178-179 D 5
Belterra o **BR** 66-67 K 4
Belton o **USA** (SC) 48-49 G 2
Belton o **USA** (TX) 44-45 J 4
Belton Lake ⬭ **USA** 44-45 J 4
Beltov tepalik ≐ **US** 136-137 G 3
Belubula River ~ **AUS** 180-181 K 2
Beluga Lake ⬭ **USA** 20-21 P 6
Beluha, gora ▲ **KA** 124-125 P 4
Beluran o **MAL** 160-161 B 10
Beluru o **MAL** 164-165 D 2
Beluš'e o **RUS** 88-89 T 3
Belušja Guba o **RUS** 108-109 E 6
Beluzij Nos, mys ▲ **RUS** 108-109 M 6
Belvedere Maríttimo o **I** 100-101 E 5
Belvidere o **USA** 46-47 D 4
Belwa, River ~ **WAN** 204-205 J 4
Belwali o **LB** 202-203 F 6
Belyando River ~ **AUS** 178-179 J 2
Belye Vody ☆ **KA** 136-137 L 3
Belyj ☆ **RUS** 94-95 N 4
Belyj, ostrov ∩ **RUS** 108-109 O 5
Belyj Čulym ~ **RUS** 114-115 U 7
Belyj Jar ☆ **RUS** 114-115 S 5
Belyj Urjum ~ **RUS** 118-119 H 9
Belyy, Ostrov = Belyj, ostrov ∩ **RUS** 108-109 O 5
Bełżec o **PL** 92-93 R 3
Belzoni o **USA** 44-45 M 3
Béma o **RMM** 202-203 F 2
Bémal o **RCA** 206-207 C 5
Bemanevika o **RM** 222-223 G 5
Bemaraha ≐ **RM** 222-223 D 7
Bemarivo ~ **RM** 222-223 E 6
Bembe o **ANG** 216-217 C 3
Bembeche ≐ **TCH** 198-199 J 3
Bembèrèkè o **DY** 204-205 E 3
Bembesi o **ZW** 218-219 E 4
Bemetāra o **IND** 142-143 B 5
Bemidji o **USA** 42-43 K 2
Bemonto o **RM** 222-223 D 7
Bemu o **RI** 166-167 E 3
Ben o **BF** 202-203 H 3
Bena o **USA** 42-43 K 2
Bena o **WAN** 204-205 F 3
Benabarre o• **E** 98-99 H 3
Benada o **IND** 138-139 G 9
Bena-Dibele o **ZRE** 210-211 J 6
Benagerie o **AUS** 178-179 F 6
Benahmed o **MA** 188-189 H 4
Benahouin o **CI** 202-203 J 6
Benain ~ **RI** 166-167 C 6
Bena-Kamba o **ZRE** 210-211 K 5
Benalla o **AUS** 180-181 H 4
Ben Ash Monument ∴ **USA** 42-43 F 3
Benato-Toby o **RM** 222-223 D 9
Bena-Tshadi o **ZRE** 210-211 J 6
Benaule o **PNG** 183 F 3
Benavente o **E** 98-99 E 3
Benbonyathe Hill ▲ **AUS** 178-179 E 6
Ben Boyd National Park ⊥ **AUS** 180-181 K 4
Bencubbin o **AUS** 176-177 D 5
Bend o **USA** 40-41 D 3
Bèndana o **TCH** 206-207 D 4
Benda Range ▲▲ **AUS** 180-181 E 2
Bendel □ **WAN** 204-205 F 5
Bendela o **ZRE** 210-211 F 5
Bendeleben Mountains ▲▲ **USA** 20-21 H 4
Bendemeer o **AUS** 178-179 L 6
Bender = Tighina o **MD** 102-103 F 4
Bender Cassim = Boosaaso = Bender Qaasim ☆ **SP** 208-209 J 3
Bender Qaasim = Boosaaso ☆ **SP** 208-209 J 3
Bendery = Tighina o **MD** 102-103 F 4
Bendieuta Creek ~ **AUS** 178-179 E 6
Bendigo o• **AUS** 180-181 H 4
Bend of the Boyne ••• **IRL** 90-91 D 5
Bendugu o **WAL** 202-203 E 5
Bene o **MOC** 218-219 G 2
Benedict, Mount ▲ **CDN** 36-37 U 7
Benedict Fjord ≈ 26-27 f 2
Benedictine Monastery • **AUS** 176-177 D 5
Benedito Leite o **BR** 68-69 F 5
Bénéna o **RMM** 202-203 H 3
Benenitra o **RM** 222-223 D 9
Benešov o **CZ** 92-93 N 4
Benevento ☆• **I** 100-101 E 4
Benevides o **BR** 62-63 K 6
Benfica o **BR** 72-73 J 6
Benga o **MOC** 218-219 G 3
Benga o **MW** 218-219 H 1
Bengābād o **IND** 142-143 E 3
Bengal, Bay of ≈ 12 G 3
Bengala o **CO** 60-61 E 5
Bengāla o **IND** 140-141 L 5
Bengalun, Tanjung ▲ **RI** 164-165 E 3
Bengamisa o **ZRE** 210-211 K 3
Bengawan ~ **RI** 168 E 3
Bengbis o **CAM** 210-211 D 2
Bengbu o **VRC** 154-155 K 5
Benge o **USA** 40-41 E 2
Benghazi = Banghāzī ☆ **LAR** 192-193 J 1
Bengkalis o **RI** 162-163 E 4
Bengkalis, Pulau ∩ **RI** 162-163 E 4
Bengkayang o **RI** 162-163 H 4
Bengkulu □ **RI** 162-163 E 7
Bengkulu ☆ **RI** 162-163 E 6
Bengkunat, Teluk ≈ 162-163 F 7
Bengo □ **ANG** 216-217 B 4
Bengo ~ **ANG** 216-217 B 4
Bengo, Baia do ≈ 216-217 B 4
Bengough o **CDN** 34-35 D 6
Benguela □ **ANG** 216-217 B 6
Benguela ☆ **ANG** (BGU) 216-217 B 6
Ben Guerdane o **TN** 190-191 H 4
Benguerir o **MA** 188-189 H 4
Beni o **ZRE** 212-213 B 3
Beni, Río ~ **BOL** 70-71 D 3
Beni-Abbès o• **DZ** 188-189 K 5
Beniah Lake ⬭ **CDN** 30-31 N 4
Beni-Boufrah o **MA** 188-189 J 3
Benicarló o **E** 98-99 H 4
Benicasim = Benicàssim o **E** 98-99 H 4
Benicito, Río ~ **BOL** 70-71 E 2
Benidorm o **E** 98-99 G 5
Beni Hammad ••• **DZ** 190-191 E 3
Beni Haoua o **DZ** 190-191 C 2
Beni Ikhlef o **DZ** 188-189 L 6
Beni Kheddache o **TN** 190-191 H 4
Beni-Mellal ☆ **MA** 188-189 H 4
Benin ■ **DY** 204-205 D 4
Benin, Bight of ≈ 204-205 E 6
Benin, River ~ **WAN** 204-205 F 6
Benin City ☆• **WAN** 204-205 F 5
Beni Ounif o **DZ** 188-189 L 4
Beni Saf o **DZ** 188-189 L 3
Benisheikh o **WAN** 204-205 K 3
Beni Slimane o **DZ** 190-191 D 2
Beni-Smir ▲ **DZ** 188-189 L 4
Beni-Snassen, Monts des ▲▲ **MA** 188-189 K 3
Beni Tajjite o **MA** 188-189 K 4
Benito o **CDN** 34-35 F 5
Benito Juárez o **MEX** 50-51 F 3
Benito Juárez o **RA** 78-79 K 4
Benito Juárez, Parque Nacional ⊥ **MEX** 52-53 F 3
Benito Juárez, Presa < **MEX** 52-53 G 3
Beni-Val < **MA** 188-189 K 4
Benjamin o **USA** 44-45 H 3
Benjamin, Isla ∩ **RCH** 80 C 2
Benjamin Aceval o **PY** 76-77 J 3
Benjamin Constant o **BR** 66-67 B 5
Benjamin Hill o **MEX** 50-51 D 2
Benjina o **RI** 166-167 H 5
Benkelman o **USA** 42-43 G 5
Ben Lawers ▲ **GB** 90-91 E 3
Ben Loganbli o **LB** 202-203 E 6
Ben Lomond ▲ **AUS** 180-181 J 6
Ben Macdui ▲ **GB** 90-91 F 3
Ben Mehidi o **DZ** 190-191 F 2
Ben More ▲ **GB** 90-91 E 3
Benmore, Lake ⬭ **NZ** 182 C 6
Bennett o **USA** 42-43 E 6
Bennett, Lake ⬭ **AUS** 172-173 K 7
Bennett, Mount ▲ **AUS** 172-173 C 7
Bennetta, ostrov ∩ **RUS** 110-111 b 1
Bennett Lake ⬭ **CDN** 20-21 X 6
Bennettsville o **USA** 48-49 J 2
Ben Nevis ▲•• **GB** 90-91 E 3
Bennichâb o **RIM** 196-197 C 5
Bennington o **USA** 46-47 M 4
Benoni o **ZA** 220-221 J 3
Benoud < **DZ** 190-191 C 4
Bénoué ~ **CAM** 204-205 K 5
Bénoué, Cuvette de la ≐ **CAM** 204-205 K 4
Bénoué, Parc National de la ⊥ **CAM** 204-205 K 4
Bénoye o **TCH** 206-207 C 4
Ben Quang o **VN** 158-159 J 2
Bễn Quang o **VN** 158-159 J 2
Ben Rinnes ▲ **GB** 90-91 F 3
Bensbach River ~ **PNG** 183 A 5
Bensékou o **DY** 204-205 E 3
Ben-Slimane ☆ **MA** 188-189 H 4
Benson o **USA** (AZ) 44-45 B 4
Benson o **USA** (MN) 42-43 K 3
Ben S'Rour o **DZ** 190-191 E 3
Bent o **IR** 134-135 H 5
Bent, Rūdḫāne-ye ~ **IR** 134-135 H 5
Ben Tadjine, Djebel ▲▲ **DZ** 188-189 K 6
Benta Seberang o **MAL** 162-163 D 2
Bentenan o **RI** 164-165 J 3
Benteng o **RI** (SLT) 164-165 G 4
Benteng o **RI** (SSE) 168 E 6
Benteng Tanahjampea o **RI** 168 E 6
Bentiaba ~ **ANG** 216-217 B 7
Bentick Island ∩ **MYA** 158-159 E 5
Bentinck Island ∩ **AUS** 174-175 E 5
Bentinck Sound ≈ 158-159 D 3
Bentiu o **SUD** 206-207 J 4
Bentley o **CDN** 32-33 N 5
Bento Gomes, Rio ~ **BR** 70-71 J 5
Bento Gonçalves o **BR** 74-75 E 7
Benton o **USA** (AL) 48-49 E 3
Benton o **USA** (AR) 44-45 L 2
Benton o **USA** (CA) 40-41 E 7
Bentong o **MAL** 162-163 D 3
Benton Harbor o **USA** 46-47 E 4
Bentonville o **USA** 44-45 K 1
Bentota o **CL** 140-141 H 7
Bến Tre ☆ **VN** 158-159 J 5
Bent's Old Fort National Historic Site ∴ **USA** 42-43 F 6
Bentuka o **MAL** 160-161 A 10
Benty o **RG** 202-203 D 5
Benua o **RI** 164-165 H 6
Benua, Pulau ∩ **RI** 162-163 G 4
Benualawas o **RI** 164-165 D 5
Benue □ **WAN** 204-205 G 5
Benue, River ~ **WAN** 204-205 G 4
Benum, Gunung ▲ **MAL** 162-163 E 3
Benum,Gunung ▲ **MAL** 162-163 E 3
Benut o **MAL** 162-163 E 4
Benxi o **VRC** 150-151 D 7
Benxi Shuidong • **VRC** 150-151 E 7
Benye o **ZRE** 210-211 F 4
Ben Zireg o **DZ** 188-189 L 5
Beo o **RI** 164-165 K 1
Beoga o **RI** 166-167 J 3
Beograd ★•• **YU** 100-101 H 2
Beoumi o **CI** 202-203 H 6
Bepondi, Pulau ∩ **RI** 166-167 H 2
Beppu o• **J** 152-153 D 8
Beqa ∩ **FJI** 184 III b 3
Beque, De o **USA** 42-43 C 6
Bequia Island ∩ **WV** 56 E 5
Bequimão o **BR** 68-69 F 3
Ber o **RMM** 196-197 J 6
Berabevú o **RA** 78-79 J 2
Berafia, Nosy ∩ **RM** 222-223 E 4
Berahlē o **ETH** 200-201 K 6
Beraketa o **RM** 222-223 D 10
Beramanja o **RM** 222-223 F 4
Bérandjokou o **RCB** 210-211 F 2
Berangas o **RI** 164-165 E 5
Berāni o **PK** 138-139 B 7
Berat ☆•• **AL** 100-101 G 4
Berau ~ **RI** 164-165 E 2
Berau, Teluk ≈ 166-167 G 3
Beraun = Beroun o **CZ** 92-93 N 4
Beravina o **RM** 222-223 D 7
Beravy o **RM** 222-223 D 8
Berazino ☆ **BY** 94-95 L 5
Berbera o **SP** 208-209 G 3
Berbérati ☆ **RCA** 206-207 B 6
Berbia, Bir < **TN** 190-191 G 4
Berbice ~ **GUY** 62-63 E 4
Berchtesgaden o **D** 92-93 M 5
Bercogyi o **KA** 126-127 N 3
Berd' ~ **RUS** 114-115 S 7
Berd' ~ **RUS** 124-125 N 1
Berdaale o **SP** 212-213 J 2
Berd'ans'ka kosa ⌣ **UA** 102-103 K 4
Berdensar, köl ⬭ **KA** 126-127 N 4
Berdičev = Berdyčiv ☆ **UA** 102-103 F 3
Berdigestjah ☆ **RUS** 118-119 N 4
Berdjans'k o **UA** 102-103 K 4
Berdsk o **RUS** 124-125 N 1
Berdyans'k = Berdjans'k o **UA** 102-103 K 4
Berdyčiv ☆ **UA** 102-103 F 3
Béré o **TCH** 206-207 C 4
Berea o **USA** 46-47 F 7
Béréba o **BF** 202-203 J 4
Berebere o **RI** 164-165 L 2
Bereeda o **SP** 208-209 K 3
Bereg Djogos Jar ⌣ **RUS** 110-111 X 3
Bereg Haritona Lapteva ⌣ **RUS** 108-109 W 4
Beregovoe o **RUS** 124-125 M 2
Beregovoj o **RUS** 118-119 N 8
Bereg Prončiščeva ⌣ **RUS** 108-109 h 3
Berehove ☆ **UA** 102-103 C 3
Bereina o **PNG** 183 D 5
Bereja ~ **RUS** 122-123 B 3
Bereku o **EAT** (DOD) 212-213 E 6
Berekua o **WD** 56 E 4
Berekum o **GH** 202-203 J 6
Bërëlëh ~ **RUS** 110-111 b 4
Bërëlëh ~ **RUS** 120-121 M 2
Berembang o **RI** 162-163 D 3
Berenda o **USA** 40-41 D 7
Berendi o **TR** 128-129 F 4
Berenike o **ET** 194-195 G 6
Berens Island ∩ **CDN** 34-35 H 4
Berens Islands ∩ **CDN** 30-31 N 2
Berens River o **CDN** (MAN) 34-35 H 4
Berens River ~ **CDN** 34-35 H 4
Bereš ~ **RUS** 114-115 U 7
Beresford o **USA** 42-43 J 4
Berettyóújfalu o **H** 92-93 Q 5
Berezivka o **UA** 102-103 G 4
Berežnaja o **RUS** 88-89 R 6
Bereznehuvate o **UA** 102-103 H 4
Bereznik o **RUS** 88-89 R 5
Berezniki o **RUS** 114-115 D 5
Berežnyh, mys ▲ **RUS** 110-111 X 1
Berezova o **RUS** 88-89 M 4
Berëzovaja o **RUS** 116-117 F 8
Berezovaja ~ **RUS** 112-113 R 5
Berëzovka ☆ **RUS** (KRN) 116-117 F 7
Berezovka ☆ **RUS** (PRM) 96-97 K 5
Berezovka ~ **RUS** 112-113 J 3
Berëzovka ~ **RUS** 112-113 H 3
Berezovka ~ **RUS** 114-115 D 4
Berezovka ~ **RUS** 114-115 R 5
Berezovo ☆ **RUS** 114-115 H 3
Berezovskij o **RUS** 114-115 T 7
Berëzovskij ☆ **RUS** 96-97 M 5
Berg o **N** 86-87 H 2
Berga o **E** 98-99 H 3
Berga, mys ▲ **RUS** 108-109 c 1
Bergama ☆• **TR** 128-129 B 3
Bérgamo ☆• **I** 100-101 B 2
Bergara o **E** 98-99 F 3
Bergen ☆••• **N** 86-87 B 6
Bergen o• **NL** 92-93 H 2
Bergen (Rügen) o **D** 92-93 M 1
Berg en Dal o **SME** 62-63 G 3
Bergerac o **F** 90-91 H 9
Bergland o **CDN** 34-35 J 6
Bergsig o **NAM** 216-217 C 10
Bergville o **ZA** 220-221 J 4
Berhait o **IND** 142-143 E 3
Berhala, Selat ≈ 162-163 F 5
Berhampur = Brahmapur o **IND** 142-143 D 6
Berikat, Tanjung ▲ **RI** 162-163 G 6
Berilo o **BR** 72-73 J 4
Beringa, mogila • **RUS** 120-121 V 6
Beringa, mys ▲ **RUS** 112-113 X 4
Beringa, ostrov ∩ **RUS** 120-121 W 6
Beringarra o **AUS** 176-177 D 3
Bering Glacier ⊂ **USA** 20-21 T 6
Bering Land Bridge Nature Reserve ⊥ **USA** 20-21 G 4
Bering Sea = Beringovo more ≈ 22-23 D 3
Bering Strait = Beringov proliv ≈ 112-113 a 4
Beripeta o **IND** 140-141 J 4
Beris ~ **RUS** 110-111 Q 4
Berisso o **RA** 78-79 L 3
Beriza o **BR** 72-73 K 3
Berja o **E** 98-99 F 6
Berkåk ☆ **N** 86-87 E 5
Berkane o **MA** 188-189 K 3
Berkeley o **USA** 40-41 C 7
Berkeley, Cape ▲ **CDN** 24-25 V 4
Berkeley Point ▲ **CDN** 24-25 M 5
Berkeley River ~ **AUS** 172-173 H 3
Berkeley Sound ≈ 78-79 M 6
Berkley Group ∩ **CDN** 24-25 V 2
Berkner Island ∩ **ARK** 16 F 30
Berkovica o **BG** 102-103 C 6
Berland River ~ **CDN** 32-33 M 5
Berlengas, Rio ~ **BR** 68-69 G 5
Berlevåg o **N** 86-87 O 1
Berliet, Point ▲ **RN** 198-199 D 2
Berlin ★••• **D** 92-93 M 2
Berlin o **USA** (MD) 46-47 L 6
Berlin o **USA** (NH) 46-47 N 3
Berlin, Mount ▲ **ARK** 16 F 23
Berlinguet Inlet ≈ 24-25 d 5
Bermagui o **AUS** 180-181 L 4
Bermego, Río ~ **RA** 76-77 C 5
Bermeja, Sierra ▲▲ **E** 98-99 E 6
Bermejillo o **MEX** 50-51 H 5
Bermejo, Isla ∩ **RA** 78-79 J 5
Bermejo, Río ~ **RA** 76-77 F 2
Bermejo, Río ~ **RA** 76-77 D 6
Bermuda Island ∩ **GB** 54-55 L 1
Bermuda Islands ∩ **GB** 54-55 L 2
Bermuda Rise ≃ 6-7 C 5
Bern ★••• **CH** 90-91 J 5
Bernabe Rivera o **ROU** 76-77 J 6
Bernalillo o **USA** 44-45 D 2
Bernam ~ **MAL** 162-163 D 3
Bernard Island ∩ **CDN** 24-25 J 4
Bernardo o **USA** 44-45 D 2
Bernardo de Irigoyen o **RA** 74-75 D 6
Bernardo O'Higgins, Parque Nacional ⊥ **RCH** 80 C 5
Bernardo Sacuita, Ponta do ▲ **BR** 68-69 F 2
Bernard River ~ **CDN** 24-25 K 4
Bernay o **F** 90-91 H 7
Bernburg (Saale) o• **D** 92-93 L 3
Berner Alpen ▲▲ **CH** 92-93 J 5
Bernice o **USA** 44-45 L 3
Bernier, Cape ▲ **AUS** 172-173 H 3
Bernier Bay ≈ 24-25 b 5
Bernier Island ∩ **AUS** 176-177 B 2
Bernina, Piz ▲ **CH** 92-93 K 5
Berninapass ▲ **CH** 92-93 L 5
Bernstorffs Isfjord ≈ 28-29 U 5
Bero ~ **ANG** 216-217 B 7
Beroroha o **RM** 222-223 D 8
Beroun o **CZ** 92-93 N 4
Berounka ~ **CZ** 92-93 M 4
Berrahal o **DZ** 190-191 F 2
Berrechid o **MA** 188-189 H 4
Berrekhem, Hassi < **DZ** 190-191 E 4
Berri o **AUS** 180-181 F 3
Berriane o **DZ** 190-191 D 4
Berridale o **AUS** 180-181 K 4
Berrigan o **AUS** 180-181 H 3
Berriwillock o **AUS** 180-181 G 3
Berrouaghia o **DZ** 190-191 D 2
Berrugas o **CO** 60-61 D 3
Berry ▲ **F** 90-91 H 8
Berryessa, Lake ⬭ **USA** 40-41 C 6
Berry Islands ∩ **BS** 54-55 F 2
Berseba o **NAM** 220-221 C 3
Berté, Lac ⬭ **CDN** 38-39 K 3
Berthierville o **CDN** 38-39 H 5
Berthold o **USA** 42-43 G 1
Bertiehaugh o **AUS** 174-175 G 3
Bertinho o **BR** 68-69 C 3
Bertolínia o **BR** 68-69 G 5
Bertoua ☆ **CAM** 204-205 K 6
Bertram o **CDN** 34-35 O 6
Bertrand o **CDN** 38-39 M 5
Bertwell o **CDN** 34-35 E 4
Berunij ☆ **US** 136-137 G 4
Beruri o **BR** 66-67 G 4
Beruwala o **CL** 140-141 H 7
Berwick o **CDN** 38-39 M 6
Berwick-upon-Tweed o• **GB** 90-91 F 4
Beryl Junction o **USA** 40-41 H 7
Beryslav o **UA** 102-103 H 4
Besa o **RI** 164-165 K 3
Besal o **PK** 138-139 D 2
Besalampy o **RM** 222-223 D 6
Besançon ☆•• **F** 90-91 L 8
Bešankovičy ☆ **BY** 94-95 L 4
Besar, Gunung ▲ **MAL** 162-163 E 3
Besar, Gunung ▲ **RI** 164-165 D 5
Besar, Pulau ∩ **RI** 166-167 B 6
Besarabca o **MD** 102-103 F 4
Besarabjaska = Besarabca o **MD** 102-103 F 4
Besar Hantu, Gunung ▲ **MAL** (SEL) 162-163 D 3
Besa River ~ **CDN** 32-33 J 3
Bešaryk o **US** 136-137 M 4
Besbes, Oued ~ **DZ** 190-191 E 3
Besboro Island ∩ **USA** 20-21 K 4
Bescoky, tau ▲ **KA** 126-127 K 5
Besedz' ~ **BY** 94-95 M 5
Besham o **PK** 138-139 D 2
Beshlo ~ **ETH** 208-209 D 3
Besi, Tanjung ▲ **RI** 168 E 7
Besikama o **RI** 166-167 C 6
Besima o **PK** 134-135 L 5
Besir o **RI** 166-167 F 2
Bësjuke ~ **RUS** 110-111 Q 4
Beskid Mountains = Beskidy ▲▲ **PL** 92-93 P 4
Beskidy Zachodnie ▲▲ **PL** 92-93 P 4
Beslan o **RUS** 126-127 F 6
Besnard Lake ⬭ **CDN** 34-35 D 3
Besne o **IR** 134-135 F 4
Besni ☆ **TR** 128-129 G 4
Bessa Monteiro o **ANG** 216-217 B 3
Béssao o **TCH** 206-207 B 5
Bessarabia = Bessarabija ≐ **MD** 102-103 E 3
Bessarabka = Aul Sarykobda o **KA** 126-127 M 3
Bessarabka = Besarabca o **MD** 102-103 F 4
Bessaz, gora ▲ **KA** 136-137 L 3
Bessaz, togi ▲ **KA** 136-137 L 3
Besselfjord ≈ 26-27 p 6
Bessemer o **USA** 48-49 E 3
Bessoung Kang o **CAM** 204-205 H 6
Bestām o• **IR** 136-137 D 6
Bestam ∴• **KA** 136-137 H 3
Bestamak o **KA** 126-127 L 3
Bestjah o **RUS** (SAH) 110-111 P 7
Bestjah o **RUS** (SAH) 118-119 O 5
Beswick o **AUS** 174-175 B 4
Beswick Aboriginal Land X **AUS** 172-173 L 3
Betafo o **RM** 222-223 E 7
Betalevana o **RM** 222-223 F 6
Betanantanana o **RM** 222-223 D 7
Betânia o **BR** (MAT) 70-71 G 4
Betânia o **BR** (PER) 68-69 J 6
Betânia, Área Indígena X **BR** 66-67 C 4
Betanty o **RM** 222-223 D 10
Betanzos o **BOL** 70-71 E 6
Betanzos o **E** 98-99 C 3
Betarara o **VAN** 184 II b 2
Bétaré Oya o **CAM** 206-207 B 6
Betbakdala ≐ **KA** 124-125 E 6
Betbulak o **KA** 124-125 F 4
Bete Hor o **ETH** 208-209 D 3
Betein o **WAN** 204-205 H 6
Betenkës o **RUS** 110-111 U 6
Bétérou o **DY** 204-205 E 4
Bethal o **ZA** 220-221 J 3
Bethanie ☆ **NAM** 220-221 C 3
Bethany o **USA** 42-43 K 5
Bethel o **USA** (AK) 20-21 K 6
Bethel o **USA** (ME) 46-47 N 3
Bethel o **USA** (NC) 48-49 K 2
Bethel o **USA** (VT) 46-47 M 4
Bethesdaweg o **ZA** 220-221 G 5
Bethlehem o **SME** 62-63 G 3
Bethlehem o **USA** 46-47 L 5
Bethlehem o **ZA** 220-221 J 4
Bethlehem = Bet Leḥem ☆•• **IL** 130-131 D 2
Bethulie o **ZA** 220-221 G 5
Betinče ~ **RUS** 118-119 G 5
Betioky o **RM** 222-223 D 9
Bet Leḥem ☆•• **WB** 130-131 D 2
Beton o **MAL** 162-163 J 4
Betong o **THA** 158-159 F 8
Betongwe o **ZRE** 212-213 B 2
Betoota o **AUS** 178-179 F 3
Bétou o **RCB** 210-211 G 2
Be Town o **LB** 202-203 F 6
Betpak Dala = Betbakdala ≐ **KA** 124-125 E 6
Betrandraka o **RM** 222-223 E 6
Betroka o **RM** 222-223 E 9
Bet She'an o **IL** 130-131 D 1
Betsiaka o **RM** 222-223 F 4
Betsiamites X **CDN** 38-39 K 4
Betsiamites, Rivière ~ **CDN** 38-39 J 3

Beirut — Betsiamites, Rivière 239

Betsiamites, Rivière ~ **CDN** 38-39 K 4
Betsiboka ~ **RM** 222-223 E 6
Betsjoeanaland ⊥ **ZA** 220-221 E 3
Betsy Bay ○ **BS** 54-55 J 3
Bettiah ○ **IND** 142-143 D 2
Bettié ○ **CI** 202-203 J 6
Bettiesdam ○ **ZA** 220-221 J 3
Bettioua ○ **DZ** 188-189 L 3
Bettles ○ **USA** 20-21 P 3
Bet Touadjine, Hamadet ⊥ **DZ** 190-191 G 2
Betty, Lake ○ **AUS** 172-173 H 5
Betül ○ **IND** 138-139 F 9
Betulia ○ **CO** (ANT) 60-61 D 4
Betulia ○ **CO** (SAN) 60-61 E 4
Betun ○ **RI** 166-167 C 6
Betuwe ≈ **RI** 164-165 F 5
Betwa ~ **IND** 138-139 G 7
Betwa ~ **IND** 142-143 D 3
Béu ○ **ANG** 216-217 C 3
Beu, Serranía del ▲ **BOL** 70-71 C 4
Beulah ○ **AUS** 180-181 G 3
Beulah ○ **USA** 42-43 G 2
Beurfou ○ **TCH** 198-199 G 5
Beurkia ○ **TCH** 198-199 H 5
B. Everett Jordan Lake < **USA** 48-49 J 2
Bever Lake Indian Reserve ⊀ **CDN** 32-33 P 4
Beverley ○ **AUS** 176-177 D 6
Beverley ○ **CDN** 34-35 M 3
Beverley ○ **GB** 90-91 G 5
Beverley, Lake ○ **USA** 22-23 R 3
Beverley Springs ○ **AUS** 172-173 G 4
Beverly ○ **USA** 40-41 E 2
Beverly Lake ○ **CDN** 30-31 T 3
Beveromay ▲ **RM** 222-223 E 6
Beveromay, Tampoketsan'i ▲ **RM** 222-223 E 6
Bevolaava Andrefana ○ **RM** 222-223 D 6
Bevoay ○ **RM** 222-223 C 8
Bewani ○ **PNG** 183 A 2
Bewar ○ **IND** 138-139 G 6
Bewick Lake ○ **CDN** 30-31 R 4
Bey Dağ ▲ **TR** 128-129 G 3
Bey Dağları ▲ **TR** 128-129 D 4
Beyla ○ **RG** 202-203 F 5
Beylul ○ **ER** 200-201 L 6
Beylul Bahire Sekat'e ≈ 200-201 L 6
Beypazan ○ **TR** 128-129 D 2
Beyra ○ **SP** 208-209 H 5
Beyşehir ○ **TR** 128-129 D 4
Beyşehir Gölü ○ **TR** 128-129 D 4
Beytüşşebap ○ **TR** 128-129 K 4
Bezaha ○ **RM** 222-223 D 9
Bežanica ○ **RUS** 94-95 L 3
Bežanicy ○ **RUS** 94-95 J 6
Bežeck ★ **RUS** 94-95 N 3
Bežeckij verh ▲ **RUS** 94-95 P 3
Bezenčuk ○ **RUS** 96-97 F 7
Bezergon ○ **US** 136-137 G 4
Bezerra ou Montes Claros, Rio ~ **BR** 72-73 G 2
Béziers ○ **F** 90-91 J 10
Bezmein ○ **TM** 136-137 F 5
Bezymjannaja, guba ≈ **RUS** 108-109 E 5
Bhābhar ○ **IND** 138-139 C 7
Bhadgaon ○ **IND** 138-139 E 9
Bhador ○ **IND** 138-139 C 9
Bhadrāchalam ○ **IND** 142-143 B 7
Bhadrak ○ **IND** 142-143 E 5
Bhadra Reservoir < **IND** 140-141 F 4
Bhadwan ○ **IND** 140-141 F 4
Bhāg ○ **PK** 134-135 M 4
Bhāgalpur ○ **IND** 142-143 E 3
Bhāgirathi ~ **IND** 138-139 G 4
Bhāgirathi ~ **IND** 142-143 G 4
Bhāgirathi ~ **VRC** 144-145 B 5
Bhāgvati ○ **IND** 140-141 F 3
Bhagwanpur ○ **NEP** 144-145 D 7
Bhagyakul ○ **BD** 142-143 G 4
Bhainsrorgarh ○ **IND** 138-139 E 7
Bhāi Pheru ○ **PK** 138-139 D 2
Bhairab Bazar ○ **BD** 142-143 G 3
Bhairahawa ○ **NEP** 144-145 D 7
Bhairi Hol ▲ **PK** 134-135 L 6
Bhairowāl ○ **PK** 138-139 E 1
Bhaisa ○ **IND** 138-139 F 10
Bhakkar ○ **PK** 138-139 C 1
Bhaktapur ○ **NEP** 144-145 E 7
Bhāki ○ **IND** 138-139 H 6
Bhaluka ○ **BD** 142-143 G 3
Bhalukpong ○ **IND** 142-143 H 2
Bhalwāl ○ **PK** 138-139 D 3
Bhamo ○ **MYA** 142-143 K 3
Bhanas ○ **IND** 138-139 E 10
Bhanbore ∴ **IND** 134-135 M 6
Bhandāra ○ **IND** 138-139 G 9
Bhanjanagar ○ **IND** 142-143 D 6
Bhānpura ○ **IND** 138-139 E 7
Bharatpur ○ **IND** 140-141 J 3
Bharatpur ○ **IND** 138-139 F 6
Bhareli ~ **IND** 142-143 H 2
Bharūch ○ **IND** 138-139 D 9
Bhasa ○ **NEP** 144-145 E 7
Bhatiapara ○ **BD** 142-143 F 4
Bhatkal ○ **IND** 140-141 F 3
Bhātpāra ○ **IND** 142-143 F 4
Bhaun ○ **PK** 138-139 D 3
Bhavāni ○ **IND** 140-141 G 5
Bhavnagar ○ **IND** 138-139 D 9
Bhawāna ○ **PK** 138-139 D 4
Bhawānipatna ○ **IND** 142-143 C 6
Bhera ○ **PK** 138-139 D 3
Bheri ~ **NEP** 144-145 C 6
Bhiavan ○ **IND** 138-139 F 10
Bhilainagar ○ **IND** 142-143 B 5
Bhilwāra ○ **IND** 138-139 E 6
Bhima ~ **IND** 138-139 D 10
Bhima ~ **IND** 140-141 F 2
Bhimashankar ○ **IND** 138-139 D 10
Bhimavaram ○ **IND** 142-143 C 7
Bhind ○ **IND** 138-139 G 6
Bhinmal ○ **IND** 138-139 D 7
Bhit Shāh ○ **PK** 138-139 B 7

Bhiwandi ○ **IND** 138-139 D 10
Bhognipur ○ **IND** 138-139 G 6
Bhokar ○ **IND** 138-139 F 10
Bhongaon ○ **IND** 138-139 G 6
Bhongir ○ **IND** 140-141 H 2
Bhopāl ○ **IND** 138-139 F 8
Bhowāli ○ **IND** 138-139 G 5
Bhuban ○ **IND** 142-143 D 5
Bhubaneshwar ○ ∙∙ **IND** 142-143 D 5
Bhuj ○ **IND** 138-139 B 8
Bhusāwal ○ **IND** 138-139 E 9
Bhutan ■ **BHT** 142-143 F 3
Biá, Rio ~ **BR** 66-67 D 5
Biafra ~ **WAN** 204-205 J 7
Biak ○ **RI** (IRJ) 166-167 J 2
Biak ○ **RI** (SLT) 164-165 H 4
Biak, Pulau ▲ **RI** 166-167 J 2
Biała, Bielsko- ★ **PL** 92-93 P 4
Biała Podlaska ○ **PL** 92-93 R 2
Bialogard ○ **PL** 92-93 N 1
Białowieski Park Narodowy ⊥ ∙∙ **PL** 92-93 R 2
Biały Bór ○ **PL** 92-93 O 2
Białystok ★ **PL** 92-93 R 2
Bian ~ **RI** 166-167 L 5
Biang ○ **RI** 164-165 K 3
Bianga ○ **RCA** 206-207 G 4
Biankouma ○ **CI** 202-203 G 6
Biaora ○ **IND** 138-139 F 8
Biar ○ **PK** 138-139 D 2
Bi'ār, al- ○ **KSA** 130-131 F 6
Biaranga ○ **ZRE** 210-211 G 4
Biārğmand ○ **IR** 136-137 D 6
Biaro ○ **ZRE** 210-211 K 3
Biaro, Pulau ▲ **RI** 164-165 J 2
Biarritz ○ **F** 90-91 G 10
Bias Fortes ○ **BR** 72-73 J 6
Biasi ~ **ZRE** 212-213 A 4
Biassini ○ **ROU** 76-77 J 6
Biata, Rio ~ **BOL** 70-71 D 2
Biau ~ **RI** 166-167 K 6
Biaza ○ **RUS** 114-115 P 6
Bibā ○ **ET** 194-195 E 2
Bibai ○ **J** 152-153 J 3
Bibala ○ **ANG** 216-217 B 7
Biban, Chaîne de ▲ **DZ** 190-191 E 2
Bibas ○ **G** 210-211 C 3
Bibbiena ○ **I** 100-101 E 3
Bibby Island ∧ **CDN** 30-31 X 5
Bibé ○ **CAM** 204-205 K 6
Bibémi ○ **CAM** 204-205 K 4
Biberach an der Riß ○ **D** 92-93 K 4
Bibiani ○ **GH** 202-203 J 6
Bibikovo ○ **RUS** 122-123 B 3
Bibirevo ○ **RUS** 94-95 N 3
Biblian ○ **EC** 64-65 C 3
Biboohra ○ **AUS** 174-175 H 5
Bibundi ○ **CAM** 204-205 H 6
Bičaneckaij, pereval ▲ **ZRE** 128-129 L 3
Bicas ○ **BR** 72-73 J 6
Bičevaja ○ **RUS** 122-123 F 5
Biche, Lac la ○ **CDN** 32-33 O 4
Bichena ○ **ETH** 208-209 D 3
Bicheno ○ **AUS** 180-181 K 5
Biche Range, La ▲ **CDN** 30-31 G 5
Biche River, La ~ **CDN** 30-31 G 5
Bichhua ○ **IND** 138-139 G 9
Bichi ○ **WAN** 198-199 D 9
Biči ~ **RUS** 122-123 G 3
Bickerton Island ∧ **AUS** 174-175 D 3
Bicuari, Parque Nacional do ⊥ **ANG** 216-217 C 7
Bičura ○ **RUS** 116-117 N 10
Bida ○ **WAN** 204-205 G 4
Bidadari, Tanjung ▲ **MAL** 160-161 C 10
Bidal ~ **IND** 166-167 J 4
Bidbid ○ **OM** 132-133 L 2
Bidde ○ **SP** 212-213 J 3
Biddeford ○ **USA** 46-47 N 4
Biddle ○ **USA** 42-43 J 3
Bideford ○ ∙ **GB** 90-91 E 6
Bidek, Anou-n- ⊏ **DZ** 198-199 B 3
Bidjovagge ○ **N** 86-87 L 2
Bidoht ○ **IR** 134-135 H 1
Bidon V ○ **DZ** 190-191 C 9
Bidor ○ **MAL** 162-163 D 2
Bidukbiduk ○ **RI** 164-165 F 3
Bidžan ○ **RUS** 122-123 D 5
Bié ○ **ANG** 216-217 D 6
Biéha ○ **BF** 202-203 K 4
Biei ○ **J** 152-153 K 3
Biel ○ **CH** 92-93 J 5
Bielefeld ○ **D** 92-93 K 2
Bieler Lake ○ **CDN** 26-27 O 8
Biella ★ ∙ **I** 100-101 F 3
Biélou ○ **CI** 202-203 G 5
Bielsa ○ **E** 98-99 H 3
Bielsko-Biala ★ **PL** 92-93 P 4
Bielsk Podlaski ○ **PL** 92-93 R 2
Biharamulo Game Reserval ⊥ **EAT** 212-213 C 5
Biên Đông ○ **158-159** J 7
Bien ○ **RCA** 206-207 F 3
Bienfait ○ **CDN** 34-35 S 6
Bienge ○ **ZRE** 210-211 G 6
Biên Hòa ★ ∙ **VN** 158-159 J 5
Bienne = Biel ○ **CH** 92-93 J 5
Bienville, Lac ○ **CDN** 36-37 N 7
Bierdnačoŏka ▲ **N** 86-87 P 4
Biertan ○ ∙∙ **RO** 102-103 D 4
Biesiesvlei ○ **ZA** 220-221 G 3
Bieszczadzki Park Narodowy ⊥ **PL** 92-93 R 4
Bifoulé ○ **CAM** 204-205 K 6
Bifuka ○ **J** 152-153 K 2
Biga ☆ **TR** 128-129 B 2
Biğadiç ○ **TR** 128-129 C 3
Biğadiya, al- ○ **KSA** 130-131 H 5
Big Ambergris Cay ∧ **GB** 54-55 K 4
Bigand ○ **RA** 78-79 J 2
Big Arm ○ **USA** 40-41 G 2
Biga Yanmadaşı ~ **TR** 128-129 B 3
Bigāner ○ **RUS** 124-125 P 2
Big Bay ≈ 36-37 T 7
Big Bay ○ **184** II a 2
Big Beaver ○ **CDN** 34-35 D 6
Bigbé ○ **CI** 202-203 H 6

Big Bell ○ **AUS** 176-177 D 3
Big Belt Mountains ▲ **USA** 40-41 J 2
Big Bend ○ **SD** 220-221 K 3
Big Bend National Park ⊥ **USA** 44-45 F 5
Big Black River ~ **USA** 48-49 D 3
Big Blue River ~ **USA** 42-43 J 5
Big Creek ○ **USA** 40-41 G 3
Big Cypress Seminole Indian Reservation ⊀ **USA** 48-49 H 6
Big Cypress Swamp ○ **USA** 48-49 H 6
Big Desert ⊥ **ZA** 220-221 H 4
Big Desert Wilderness ⊥ **AUS** 180-181 F 3
Big Dry Creek, The ~ **USA** 42-43 C 3
Bigene ○ **GNB** 202-203 C 3
Big Falls ○ **USA** 42-43 L 1
Bigfork ○ **USA** 40-41 G 1
Biggar ○ **CDN** 34-35 Q 4
Bigge Island ∧ **AUS** 172-173 G 3
Biggenden ○ **AUS** 178-179 M 3
Biggs ○ **USA** 40-41 D 3
Big Hips Island ∧ **CDN** 30-31 W 3
Big Hole ∙ **ZA** 220-221 G 4
Big Hole National Battlefield ∴ **USA** 40-41 H 3
Big Hole River ~ **USA** 40-41 H 3
Big Hole Tract Indian Reserve ⊀ **CDN** 38-39 M 5
Bighorn Basin ⊥ **USA** 42-43 C 3
Bighorn Canyon National Recreation Area ⊥ **USA** 42-43 C 3
Bighorn Lake ○ **USA** 42-43 C 3
Bighorn Mountains ▲ **USA** 42-43 D 3
Bighorn River ~ **USA** 42-43 C 3
Bight, The ○ **BS** 54-55 H 2
Big Island ∧ **CDN** (ALB) 30-31 N 4
Big Island ∧ **CDN** (NFL) 36-37 S 5
Big Island ∧ **CDN** (NWT) 30-31 M 5
Big Island ∧ **CDN** (NWT) 30-31 L 5
Big Island ∧ **CDN** (NWT) 36-37 J 6
Big Island ∧ **CDN** (ONT) 34-35 J 4
Big Island ∧ **CDN** (QUE) 36-37 J 5
Big John Creek ~ **AUS** 178-179 C 6
Big Kalzas Lake ○ **CDN** 20-21 X 5
Big Koniuji Island ∧ **USA** 22-23 R 5
Big Lake ○ **CDN** 30-31 N 3
Big Lake ○ **USA** 44-45 G 4
Big Lake Ranch ○ **CDN** 32-33 K 5
Big Lost River ~ **USA** 40-41 H 4
Big Mossy Point ▲ **CDN** 34-35 G 4
Big Muddy Creek ~ **USA** 42-43 E 1
Bignona ○ **SN** 202-203 B 3
Bigoray River ~ **CDN** 32-33 N 5
Bigori ○ **SUD** 208-209 B 3
Big Pine ○ **USA** (CA) 40-41 E 7
Big Pine ○ **USA** (FL) 48-49 H 7
Big Piney ○ **USA** 40-41 J 4
Big Piney River ~ **USA** 44-45 L 1
Big Piskwanish Point ▲ **CDN** 34-35 Q 5
Big Pond ○ **CDN** 38-39 O 6
Big Rapids ○ **USA** 46-47 F 4
Big River ~ **CDN** (SAS) 34-35 Q 4
Big River ~ **CDN** 34-35 K 4
Big River ~ **CDN** 34-35 G 4
Big River ~ **USA** 36-37 U 7
Big River Indian Reserve ⊀ **CDN** 34-35 Q 4
Big Sable Point ▲ **USA** 46-47 E 3
Big Salmon Range ▲ **CDN** 20-21 Y 6
Big Salmon River ~ **CDN** 20-21 X 6
Big Sand Lake ○ **CDN** 34-35 G 2
Big Sandy ○ **USA** 40-41 J 1
Big Sandy Creek ~ **USA** 42-43 F 6
Big Sandy Lake ○ **CDN** 34-35 R 3
Big Sandy River ~ **USA** 40-41 H 8
Big Sandy River ~ **USA** 42-43 C 5
Big Sky ○ **USA** 40-41 J 3
Big Smoky Valley ~ **USA** 40-41 F 7
Big South Fork National River ⊥ **USA** 48-49 F 1
Big Spring ○ **USA** 44-45 G 3
Bigstone Lake ○ **CDN** 34-35 H 4
Big Stone Lake ○ **USA** 42-43 J 3
Bigstone River ~ **CDN** 34-35 J 3
Big Suehn ○ **LB** 202-203 F 7
Big Sur ○ **USA** 40-41 D 7
Big Timber ○ **USA** 42-43 C 3
Big Trout Lake ○ **CDN** (ONT) 34-35 M 4
Big Trout Lake ○ **CDN** (ONT) 36-37 J 5
Big Trout Lake Indian Reservation ⊀ **CDN** 34-35 M 4
Big Warrambool River ~ **AUS** 178-179 K 5
Big Water ○ **USA** 40-41 J 7
Big White River ~ **USA** 42-43 F 4
Big Willow River ~ **CDN** 34-35 P 4
Big Wood Cay ∧ **BS** 54-55 G 2
Big Wood River ~ **USA** 40-41 G 4
Bihać ○ **BIH** 100-101 F 3
Bihar ○ **IND** 142-143 D 3
Biharamulo ○ **EAT** 212-213 C 5
Bihār Sharif ○ **IND** 142-143 D 3
Bihoro ○ **J** 152-153 L 3
Bihorului, Muntii ▲ **RO** 102-103 C 4
Bihta ○ **IND** 142-143 D 3
Bijā ~ **RUS** 124-125 P 3
Bija ~ **RUS** 124-125 O 2
Bijagos, Arquipélago dos ∧ **GNB** 202-203 B 4
Bijāpur ○ ∙∙ **IND** 140-141 F 2
Bijbehara ○ **IND** 138-139 E 3
Bijelo Polje ○ **YU** 100-101 G 3
Bijie ○ **VRC** 156-157 D 3
Bijilkof, ozero ○ **KA** 136-137 M 3
Bijnor ○ **IND** 138-139 G 5
Bijou Creek ~ **USA** 42-43 E 6
Bijoutier Island ∧ **SY** 224 C 3
Bijsk ★ **RUS** 124-125 O 2
Bijskaja Griva, hrebet ▲ **RUS** 124-125 P 2
Bikaner ○ **IND** 138-139 D 5
Bikin ~ **RUS** 122-123 F 5
Bikita ○ **ZW** 218-219 F 5
Bikok ○ **CAM** 210-211 C 2

Bikoro ○ **ZRE** 210-211 G 4
Bikou ○ **VRC** 154-155 D 5
Bikramganj ○ **IND** 142-143 D 3
Bikubiti ○ **LAR** 198-199 G 5
Bilâ ○ **ET** 194-195 E 2
Bila ~ **RI** 162-163 F 5
Bilaat Point ∧ **RP** 160-161 F 8
Bilac ○ **BR** 72-73 E 6
Bila Cerkva = Bila Cerkva ☆ **UA** 102-103 G 3
Bilala ○ **RCB** 210-211 D 6
Bilang, Teluk ≈ **164-165** G 3
Bilanga ○ **BF** 202-203 K 3
Bilap Bay ≈ 140-141 L 4
Bilāspura ○ **IND** 142-143 G 2
Bilāspur ○ **IND** (MAP) 142-143 C 4
Bilāspur ○ **IND** (UTP) 138-139 G 5
Bilassana ○ **RG** 202-203 E 3
Bilaté Shet' ~ **ETH** 208-209 D 5
Bilati ~ **ZRE** 212-213 A 4
Bila Tserkva = Bila Cerkva ☆ **UA** 102-103 G 3
Bilauri ○ **NEP** 144-145 C 6
Bilāwal ○ **PK** 138-139 C 3
Bilbais ○ **ET** 194-195 E 2
Bilbao = Bilbao ○ **E** 98-99 F 3
Bilberatha Hill ▲ **AUS** 176-177 D 4
Bilbo = Bilbao ○ **E** 98-99 F 3
Bilecik ○ **TR** 128-129 C 2
Bilehsawār ○ **IR** 128-129 N 3
Bilēngui ○ **G** 210-211 C 4
Bilesha Plain ≈ **EAK** 212-213 H 3
Bilgoraj ○ **PL** 92-93 R 3
Bilgrâm ○ **IND** 142-143 B 2
Bilhorod-Dnistrovs'kyj ☆ **UA** 102-103 G 4
Bili ○ **ZRE** 206-207 G 6
Bili ~ **ZRE** (Hau) 206-207 G 6
Bili ~ **ZRE** 206-207 F 6
Bilibili ○ **RI** 164-165 F 6
Bilibino ○ **RUS** 112-113 O 2
Bilikköl ○ **KA** 136-137 M 3
Bilimora ○ **IND** 138-139 D 9
Bilin ○ **MYA** 158-159 D 2
Biling La ▲ **NEP** 144-145 C 5
Biliran Island ∧ **RP** 160-161 F 7
Biliri ○ **WAN** 204-205 J 4
Biljasuvar = Bilasuvar ○ **AZ** 128-129 N 3
Billabong Creek ~ **AUS** 180-181 J 3
Billefjorden ≈ 84-85 K 3
Billenbach ○ **AUS** 178-179 K 4
Billete, Cerro El ▲ **MEX** 52-53 D 2
Billiat Conservation Park ⊥ **AUS** 180-181 F 3
Billiluna ○ **AUS** 172-173 H 5
Billings ○ **RUS** 112-113 S 2
Billings ○ **USA** 42-43 C 3
Billingsa, mys ▲ **RUS** 112-113 T 2
Billjah ~ **RUS** 110-111 S 6
Billsburg ○ **USA** 42-43 G 3
Billund ○ **DK** 86-87 C 4
Bill Williams River ~ **USA** 40-41 H 8
Billy, Chutes de ~ **RMM** 202-203 F 3
Bilma ○ **RN** 198-199 F 3
Bilma, Grand Erg de ≈ **RN** 198-199 F 4
Biloela ○ **AUS** 178-179 L 3
Bilohorsk ☆ **UA** 102-103 J 5
Biloku ○ **SP** 212-213 J 3
Bilopill'a ☆ **UA** 102-103 J 3
Bilou ○ **CI** 202-203 G 5
Bilovods'k ○ **UA** 102-103 L 3
Biloxi ○ **USA** 48-49 D 4
Bilpa Morea Claypan ○ **AUS** 178-179 E 3
Bilqâs ○ **ET** 194-195 E 2
Bilthara ○ **IND** 142-143 C 2
Biltine ☆ **TCH** 198-199 K 5
Biltine ○ **TCH** 198-199 K 5
Bilugyun ~ **MYA** 158-159 D 2
Bilungala ○ **RI** 164-165 H 5
Biluo Xueshan ▲ **VRC** 142-143 L 2
Bilverdi ○ **IR** 128-129 M 3
Bilyj Čeremoš ~ **UA** 102-103 D 4
Bima ○ **RI** 168 D 7
Bima ≈ **ZRE** 210-211 G 7
Bimba ○ **CAM** 206-207 B 6
Bimban ○ **ET** 194-195 E 3
Bimberi Peak ▲ **AUS** 180-181 K 3
Bimbijiy ○ **AUS** 176-177 E 4
Bimbila ○ **GH** 202-203 L 5
Bimbo ○ **RCA** 206-207 D 6
Bimi, Sabon- ○ **WAN** 198-199 C 6
Bimini Islands ∧ **BS** 54-55 F 2
Bina ○ **IND** 138-139 F 7
Binalud Kūh ▲ **IR** 160-161 C 7
Biname Lake ○ **CDN** 24-25 K 6
Binanga ○ **RI** 162-163 C 4
Binbee ○ **AUS** 174-175 J 7
Bindé ○ **BF** 202-203 K 4
Bindegolly, Lake ○ **AUS** 178-179 H 5
Binder ○ **TCH** 206-207 B 4
Bindi Bindi ○ **AUS** 176-177 D 5
Bindu ○ **ZRE** 216-217 E 3
Bindura ☆ **ZW** 218-219 F 4
Bin-el-Ouidane ○ **MA** 188-189 H 4
Binga ○ **AUS** 178-179 C 5
Binga, Monte ▲ **MOC** 218-219 G 4
Binga, Quedas de Agua ~ **ANG** 216-217 C 5
Bingara ○ **AUS** 178-179 L 5
Bingassi ○ **RMM** 202-203 E 3
Bing Bong ○ **AUS** 174-175 D 4
Binger ○ **USA** 44-45 H 2
Bingerville ○ **CI** 202-203 J 7
Bingham ○ **USA** (ME) 46-47 O 3
Bingham ○ **USA** (NM) 44-45 D 3
Binghamton ○ **USA** 46-47 K 3
Bin Ghashir ○ **LAR** 192-193 E 1
Bingintelok ○ **RI** 162-163 D 6
Binglingsi Shankou ▲ **VRC** 154-155 C 4
Bingöl ☆ **TR** 128-129 J 3
Bingöl Dağları ▲ **TR** 128-129 J 3
Binh Chánh ○ **VN** 158-159 J 5
Binh Châu ○ **VN** 158-159 J 5
Binh Đinh ○ **VN** 158-159 K 4
Binh Giã ○ **VN** 158-159 J 5

Binh Gia ○ **VN** 156-157 E 6
Binh Lâm ○ **VN** 158-159 K 3
Binh Long ○ **VN** 158-159 J 5
Bin-Hoyé ○ **CI** 202-203 F 6
Binibihali ○ **PNG** 183 F 6
Bini Drosso ○ **TCH** 198-199 J 5
Bini Erde < **TCH** 198-199 J 2
Binjai ○ **RI** 162-163 C 3
Binjua ~ **IND** 142-143 F 4
Binjuda ~ **RUS** 108-109 X 5
Binkolo ○ **WAL** 202-203 E 5
Binnaway ○ **AUS** 178-179 K 6
Binongko ~ **RI** 164-165 H 6
Binongko, Pulau ~ **RI** 164-165 H 6
Binsak ○ **CDN** 34-35 T 5
Binscarth ○ **CDN** 34-35 S 5
Bintagoungou ○ **RMM** 196-197 J 6
Bintan, Pulau ~ **RI** 162-163 F 4
Bintang, Banjaran ▲ **MAL** 162-163 D 2
Bintuan ○ **RI** 162-163 E 7
Bintuhan ○ **RI** 162-163 D 6
Bintuni ○ **RI** 166-167 J 3
Bintuni, Teluk ≈ **166-167** G 3
Binuang ○ **RI** 164-165 C 5
Bin Xian ○ **VRC** 150-151 F 5
Binyang ○ **VRC** 156-157 F 5
Binz, Ostseebad ○ **D** 92-93 M 1
Binzhou ○ **VRC** 154-155 K 3
Bioblo, Río ~ **RCH** 78-79 C 4
Bioco, Isla de ▲ **GQ** 210-211 D 3
Biograd na Moru ○ **HR** 100-101 E 3
Biokovo ▲ **HR** 100-101 F 3
Biorra = Birr ○ **IRL** 90-91 D 5
Biosphere II ∙∙ **USA** 44-45 B 3
Biougra ○ **MA** 188-189 G 5
Bipi Island ~ **PNG** 183 D 2
Bipindi ○ **CAM** 204-205 J 6
Biquele ○ **RI** 166-167 C 6
Bir ○ **IND** 138-139 E 10
Bir, Ras ▲ **DJI** 200-201 L 6
Bira ~ **RI** 164-165 G 6
Bira ○ **RUS** 122-123 E 4
Bi'r Abū Ğulud ○ **SYR** 128-129 H 4
Birāk ○ **LAR** 192-193 F 4
Birāk, Tall al ∙∙ **SYR** 128-129 J 4
Birak, Umm al- ○ **KSA** 130-131 F 6
Bir al Ghanam ○ **LAR** 192-193 E 1
Bir Ali Ben Khelifa ○ **TN** 190-191 H 3
Bi'r Allâq ○ **LAR** 192-193 E 1
Bi'r Anzarane ○ **MA** 196-197 C 3
Birao ○ **RCA** 206-207 E 3
Biratnagar ○ **NEP** 144-145 E 7
Biratori ○ **J** 152-153 K 3
Bi'r A'yad ○ **LAR** 192-193 E 1
Bi'r Ben Ghimah ○ **LAR** 192-193 J 2
Birca ○ **RO** 102-103 C 6
Birch Bay ○ **CDN** 20-21 S 3
Birch Creek ○ **USA** 20-21 S 3
Birch Creek ~ **USA** 20-21 S 3
Birch Creek ~ **USA** 20-21 P 5
Birch Creek ~ **USA** 40-41 H 3
Birch Island ∧ **CDN** 34-35 G 4
Birch Lake ○ **CDN** (SAS) 32-33 P 5
Birch Lake ○ **CDN** (NWT) 30-31 L 4
Birch Lake ○ **CDN** (ONT) 34-35 L 3
Birch Mountains ▲ **CDN** 32-33 N 3
Birch River ~ **CDN** (MAN) 34-35 F 4
Birch River ~ **CDN** 32-33 O 3
Bircot ○ **ETH** 208-209 F 5
Bird Cape ▲ **USA** 22-23 V 4
Bird Island ~ **GB** 78-79 N 7
Bird Island ~ **SY** 224 D 1
Bird Island ~ **AUS** 22-23 R 5
Bird Rock Lighthouse ∙ **BS** 54-55 H 3
Birdsville ○ **AUS** 178-179 E 3
Birdsville Track ~ **AUS** 178-179 E 5
Birdum ○ **AUS** 174-175 B 4
Birdum Creek ~ **AUS** 172-173 L 5
Bi'r Durb ○ **KSA** 130-131 G 4
Birecik ○ **TR** 128-129 G 4
Bireik ○ **RCA** 206-207 D 6
Bi'r Faig' 'Amya' ○ **KSA** 130-131 G 4
Birganj ○ **NEP** 144-145 D 7
Bi'r Ğuraibi'āt ○ **IRQ** 130-131 J 3
Bi'r Hağal < **SYR** 128-129 H 5
Bi'r Hamrān < **IRQ** 128-129 K 5
Bi'r Hasana ○ **ET** 194-195 F 2
Birhat al-Khurada Pool ∙ **KSA** 130-131 G 6
Biri ○ **SUD** (SR) 206-207 H 5
Biri ~ **SUD** 206-207 G 5
Biridi ○ **WAN** 198-199 D 6
Biriinujussy ○ **RUS** 116-117 F 7
Birini ○ **RCA** 206-207 E 4
Biritinga ○ **BR** 68-69 J 7
Birjuk ~ **RUS** 118-119 J 5
Birjusa ~ **RUS** 116-117 H 7
Birjusa = Ona ~ **RUS** 116-117 G 7
Birjusinsk ○ **RUS** 116-117 G 7
Birjusinskoe plato ▲ **RUS** 116-117 J 7
Birka ∙∙∙ **S** 86-87 J 7
Birkat al-'Amyā' ○ **IRQ** 130-131 H 3
Birkat Saira ○ **SUD** 198-199 L 6
Birkeland ○ **N** 86-87 C 4
Birkenhead ○ **GB** 90-91 F 6
Birkenhead ○ **AUS** 178-179 J 3
Bi'r Khadijah ○ **LAR** 192-193 J 2
Birmal ○ **AFG** 138-139 B 3
Birni, Gazirat ∧ **KSA** 130-131 G 6
Birri ○ **TM** 190-191 G 2
Birrimdu ○ **AUS** 172-173 J 5
Birsilpur ○ **IND** 138-139 D 5
Birsk ☆ **RUS** 96-97 J 6
Birsuat ~ **RUS** 124-125 B 2
Birtam-Tam ○ **CAM** 188-189 J 4
Birtle ○ **CDN** 34-35 P 5
Biruaca ○ **YV** 60-61 H 4
Birufu ○ **RI** 166-167 K 4
Birūr ○ **IND** 140-141 F 4
Birzai ★ ∙ **LT** 94-95 J 3
Bir Zar ○ **TN** 190-191 H 3
Biša ○ **KSA** 132-133 C 3
Biša, Wādi ~ **KSA** 132-133 C 3
Bisagana ○ **WAN** 198-199 F 6
Bisalpur ○ **IND** 138-139 G 5
Bisanadi National Reserve ⊥ **EAK** 212-213 G 3
Bisbee ○ **USA** 44-45 C 4
Biscarrosse ○ **F** 90-91 G 9
Biscay, Bay of ≈ 90-91 F 8
Biscay Abyssal Plain ≃ 6-7 J 4
Biscayne Bay ≈ 48-49 H 7
Biscayne National Park ⊥ **USA** 48-49 H 7
Bischofshofen ○ **A** 92-93 M 5
Biscoe Islands ~ **ARK** 16 G 30
Biscucuy ○ **YV** 60-61 G 3
Bisellia ○ **SUD** 206-207 H 5
Bisen ○ **RA** 96-97 F 8
Bisert' ○ **RUS** 96-97 L 5
Bisha ○ **ER** 200-201 H 5
Bishan ○ **VRC** 156-157 F 2
Bishinujussy ○ **VRC** 148-149 N 7
Bisina, Lake ○ **EAU** 212-213 E 3
Bisiu ○ **EAU** 212-213 C 5
Bišker ★ **KS** 146-147 B 4
Bishnah ○ **BD** 142-143 G 4
Bishnupur ○ **IND** 142-143 E 4
Bisho ○ **ZA** 220-221 H 6
Bishop ○ **USA** (CA) 40-41 E 7
Bishop Range ▲ **AUS** 172-173 H 6
Bishop's Falls ○ **CDN** 38-39 I R 4
Bishopville ○ **USA** 48-49 H 3
Bishri ○ **LAR** 192-193 H 2
Bishushanzhang ○ **VRC** 148-149 N 7
Bisina, Lake ○ **EAU** 212-213 E 3
Bisiu ○ **EAU** 212-213 C 5
Biskotasi Lake ○ **CDN** 38-39 D 5
Biskra ☆ **DZ** 190-191 E 3
Biskupiec ○ **PL** 92-93 Q 2
Bismarck ▲ **USA** 42-43 G 2
Bismarck (TX) ○ **USA** 44-45 J 6
Bismarck Archipelago ∧ **PNG** 183 E 2
Bismarck Range ▲ **PNG** 183 C 3
Bismarck Sea ≈ 183 C 3
Bismarckstraße ≈ 16 G 30
Bismil ○ **TR** 128-129 J 4
Biso ○ **EAU** 212-213 D 4
Bison ○ **USA** 42-43 F 3
Bisonó ○ **DOM** 54-55 K 5
Bisotun ○ **IR** 134-135 B 1
Bispgården ○ **S** 86-87 H 5
Bissaune ○ **RMM** 196-197 K 6
Bisset Lake ○ **CDN** 38-39 D 5
Bissikrima ○ **RG** 202-203 E 4
Bissora ○ **GNB** 202-203 C 4
Bistcho Lake ○ **CDN** 30-31 K 6
Bistineau, Lake ○ **USA** 44-45 L 3
Bistrita ☆ **RO** 102-103 D 4
Biswān ○ **IND** 142-143 B 2
Bita ~ **RCA** 206-207 D 5
Bita, Río ~ **CO** 60-61 G 4
Bitam ○ **G** 210-211 C 2
Bitangor ○ **MAL** 162-163 J 3
Bitata ○ **ETH** 208-209 D 6
Bitencourt ○ **BR** 66-67 C 3
Bitian Bank ≃ **168** C 2
Bitigiu ○ **ETH** 208-209 E 4
Bitik ○ **KA** 96-97 G 8
Bitilifondi ○ **RCA** 206-207 F 6
Bitjug ~ **RUS** 94-95 R 5
Bitjug ~ **RUS** 102-103 M 2
Bitlis ☆ **TR** 128-129 K 3
Bitola ○ **MK** 100-101 H 4
Bitou ○ **BF** 202-203 K 4
Bitter Creek ~ **USA** 42-43 C 5
Bitterfeld ○ **D** 92-93 M 2
Bitterfontein ○ **ZA** 220-221 D 5
Bitterroot Range ▲ **USA** 40-41 G 2
Bitterroot River ~ **USA** 40-41 G 2
Bittou ○ **PNG** 183 B 5

Birlad ~ **RO** 102-103 E 4
Bitung ○ **RI** 164-165 J 3
Bituruna ○ **BR** 74-75 E 6
Bitzhtini Mount ▲ **USA** 20-21 P 4
Biu ○ **WAN** 204-205 K 3
Biuka-töge ▲ **J** 152-153 K 2
Biu Plateau ▲ **WAN** 204-205 K 3
Biwai, Mount ▲ **PNG** 183 B 4
Biwa-ko ○ **J** 152-153 K 5
Biwako Quasi National Park ⊥ **J** 152-153 F 7
Biwat ○ **PNG** 183 B 3
Biyagundi ○ **PNG** 183 B 3
Biyang ○ **VRC** 154-155 H 5
Biye K'obé ○ **ETH** 208-209 F 3
Bizana ○ **ZA** 220-221 J 5
Bizana ○ **ZA** 220-221 J 5
Bižanābād ○ **IR** 134-135 H 5
Bižbuljak ▲ **RUS** 96-97 J 7
Bize ~ **KA** 124-125 K 6
Bizen ○ **J** 152-153 F 7
Bizerte = ∙ **TN** 190-191 G 2
Bizigui ~ **BF** 202-203 K 3
Bjahoml' ○ **BY** 94-95 L 4
Bjala ○ **BG** 102-103 D 6
Bjala Slatina ○ **BG** 102-103 C 6
Bjarëzina ~ **BY** 94-95 L 5
Bjareziński zapavednik ⊥ **BY** 94-95 L 4
Bjargtangar ▲ **IS** 86-87 a 2
Bjaroza ○ **BY** 94-95 J 5
Bjas'-Kjuёr ~ **RUS** (SAH) 118-119 N 4
Bjas'-Kjuёr ~ **RUS** (SAH) 118-119 J 6
Bjästa ○ **S** 86-87 J 5
Bjelašnica ▲ **BIH** 100-101 G 3
Bjelovar ○ **HR** 100-101 F 2
Bjerkvik ○ **N** 86-87 H 2
Bjôrna ○ **S** 86-87 J 5
Bjørnafjorden ≈ 86-87 B 6
Bjørne Øer ∧ **GRØ** 26-27 n 8
Bjorne Peninsula ∧ **CDN** 24-25 c 2
Bjørnesk Ø ∧ **GRØ** 26-27 q 5
Bjørnøya ∧ **N** 84-85 L 5
Bjørnøya Radio ○ **N** 84-85 L 5
Bjurholm ○ **S** 86-87 J 5
Bjutejdjah ~ **RUS** 120-121 D 3
Bla ○ **RMM** 202-203 H 3
Black ○ **USA** 20-21 H 5
Blackall ○ **AUS** 178-179 H 3
Black Bay ○ **CDN** 34-35 M 6
Black Bear River ~ **CDN** 34-35 L 3
Blackbear River ~ **CDN** 34-35 M 5
Black Bear River ~ **CDN** 38-39 Q 2
Black Birch Lake ○ **CDN** 34-35 Q 2
Black Braes ○ **AUS** 174-175 H 6
Blackbull ○ **AUS** 174-175 F 5
Blackburn, Mount ▲ **USA** 20-21 T 6
Black Canyon of the Gunnison National Monument ∙ **USA** 42-43 D 6
Black Cape ▲ **USA** 22-23 U 3
Black Creek ○ **CDN** 46-47 D 3
Black Diamond ○ **CDN** 33-33 N 6
Blackdown ○ **AUS** 174-175 H 6
Blackdown Tableland National Park ⊥ **AUS** 178-179 K 2
Black Duck River ~ **CDN** 34-35 M 2
Blackfeet Indian Reservation ⊀ **USA** 40-41 H 1
Blackfoot ○ **CDN** 32-33 P 5
Blackfoot ○ **USA** 40-41 H 4
Blackfoot Indian Reserve ⊀ **CDN** 32-33 N 6
Blackfoot River ~ **USA** 40-41 H 2
Black Forest = Schwarzwald ▲ **D** 92-93 K 4
Black Hills ▲ **USA** 42-43 E 3
Blackie ○ **CDN** 32-33 O 6
Black Lake ○ **CDN** (QUE) 38-39 J 5
Black Lake ○ **CDN** (SAS) 30-31 R 6
Black Lake ○ **USA** 22-23 R 4
Black Lake Bayou ~ **USA** 44-45 L 3
Black Mesa ▲ **USA** 44-45 F 1
Black Mountain ▲ **AUS** 178-179 E 1
Black Mountain ▲ **CDN** 26-27 G 3
Black Mountain ▲ **AUS** 46-47 G 7
Black Mountains ▲ **USA** 40-41 H 7
Black Nossob ~ **NAM** 216-217 E 10
Black Point ∧ **BS** 54-55 G 2
Black Point ▲ **AUS** 22-23 U 4
Blackpool ○ **GB** 90-91 F 5
Black River ~ **USA** 20-21 Z 6
Black River ~ **USA** 48-49 J 4
Black River ○ ∙∙ **JA** 54-55 G 5
Black River ~ **USA** 22-23 T 5
Black River ~ **USA** 44-45 M 2
Black River ~ **USA** 44-45 M 3
Black River ~ **USA** 44-45 C 3
Black River ~ **USA** 46-47 G 3
Black River ~ **USA** 46-47 C 3
Black River ~ **USA** 46-47 L 4
Black River Falls ○ **USA** 46-47 C 3
Black Rock ○ **USA** 44-45 M 1
Black Rock Desert ~ **USA** 40-41 F 5
Black Rock Point ▲ **CDN** 36-37 R 4
Black Rocks ▲ **WAN** 204-205 H 4
Black Rocks Landing ∧ **USA** 174-175 D 4
Blacksburg ○ **USA** 46-47 H 7
Black Sea ≈ 102-103 G 6
Blacks Fork ~ **USA** 40-41 J 5
Blacks Harbour ○ **CDN** 38-39 L 6
Blackstone ○ **USA** 46-47 J 7
Blackstone River ~ **CDN** 20-21 V 4
Blackstone River ~ **CDN** 30-31 H 5
Blackstone River ~ **CDN** 32-33 M 5
Blackville ○ **AUS** 178-179 L 6
Black Volta ~ **GH** 202-203 J 5
Blackwater Creek ~ **AUS** 178-179 H 3
Blackwater Lake ○ **CDN** 180-181 L 2
Blackwater Lake ○ **CDN** 30-31 H 4
Blackwell ○ **USA** 44-45 J 1
Blackwater River ~ **AUS** 176-177 D 6
Bladensburg National Park ⊥ **AUS** 178-179 G 2
Bladgrond ○ **ZA** 220-221 D 4

Blåfjellet ▲ N 86-87 F 4
Blagodarnyj o RUS 102-103 N 5
Blagoevgrad o BG 102-103 C 6
Blagoevo o RUS 88-89 T 5
Blagopolučija, zaliv ≈ RUS 108-109 K 4
Blagoveščenka o KA 146-147 B 4
Blagoveščensk o• RUS 122-123 B 3
Blagoveščensk o RUS 124-125 L 2
Blagoveščensk (BAS) o RUS 96-97 J 6
Blagoveščenskij proliv ≈ 110-111 Z 2
Blagoveščensk = Blagoveščensk ☆ RUS 118-119 N 10
Blaine o USA (KS) 42-43 J 6
Blaine o USA (MN) 42-43 L 3
Blaine o USA (WA) 40-41 C 1
Blaine Lake o CDN 34-35 C 4
Blair o USA (NE) 42-43 J 5
Blair o USA (WI) 46-47 C 3
Blair Athol o AUS 178-179 J 2
Blairbeth o ZA 220-221 H 2
Blairgowrie o GB 90-91 F 3
Blairmore o CDN 32-33 N 7
Blairsdile o USA 40-41 D 6
Blairsville o USA (GA) 48-49 G 2
Blairsville o USA (PA) 46-47 J 5
Blaka ~ RN 198-199 F 2
Blake Bay ≈ 24-25 e 7
Blakely o USA 48-49 F 4
Blake Plateau ≃ 48-49 J 4
Blake Point ▲ USA 46-47 D 1
Blama o WAL 202-203 E 6
Blanc, le o F 90-91 H 8
Blanca, Bahía ≈ 78-79 H 5
Blanca, Cordillera ▲ PE 64-65 D 6
Blanca, Lago o RCH 70-71 C 5
Blanca, Laguna o RA 78-79 H 8
Blanca, Punta ▲ MEX 50-51 B 3
Blanca, Río ~ BOL 70-71 D 7
Blanca Grande, Laguna la o RA 78-79 H 5
Blanca Peak ▲ USA 42-43 E 7
Blancas, Sierras ▲ RA 78-79 F 6
Blanchard o USA 42-43 J 2
Blanchard Springs Caverns • USA 44-45 L 2
Blanche, Lake o AUS (SA) 178-179 E 5
Blanche, Lake o AUS (WA) 172-173 F 7
Blanche Channel ≈ 184 I c 3
Blanche-Marievallen o SME 62-63 F 3
Blanchet Island o CDN 30-31 N 4
Blanchetown o AUS 180-181 E 3
Blanchisseuse o TT 60-61 L 2
Blanco o USA 44-45 H 4
Blanco, Cabo ▲ CR 52-53 D 7
Blanco, Cerro ▲ RA 78-79 D 6
Blanco, Lago ~ RA 80 F 7
Blanco, Río ~ BOL 70-71 E 5
Blanco, Río ~ PE 64-65 F 4
Blanco, Río ~ RA 76-77 C 6
Blanco, Río ~ RA 76-77 C 5
Blanco, Río ~ RA 76-77 B 6
Blanco, Río ~ RA 78-79 D 2
Blanco, Río ~ RA 80 E 3
Blancos, Los o RA 76-77 F 2
Blancos del Sur, Cayos ∴ C 54-55 E 3
Blanc-Sablon o CDN 38-39 Q 3
Blandá o IS 86-87 d 2
Bland Creek ~ AUS 178-179 J 3
Blanding o USA 42-43 C 7
Blanes o E 98-99 J 4
Blanfla o CI 202-203 H 6
Blangkejeren o RI 162-163 B 2
Blangpidie o RI 162-163 B 3
Blanquero, El o YV 60-61 K 3
Blanquilla, Isla ∴ YV 60-61 L 2
Blanquillo o ROU 78-79 M 2
Blantyre ☆ MW 218-219 H 3
Blåsjøen o N 86-87 C 7
Blau o RI 164-165 H 3
Blaye o F 90-91 G 7
Blayney o AUS 180-181 K 2
Bleaker Island ∴ GB 78-79 L 7
Blebo o LB 202-203 G 7
Blednaja, gory ▲ RUS 108-109 L 3
Bled Tisseras o DZ 190-191 E 7
Blega o RI 168 E 3
Bleikvassli o N 86-87 F 4
Blendio o RMM 202-203 G 4
Blenheim o CDN 38-39 D 7
Blenheim o NZ 182 D 4
Blenheim Palace ••• GB 90-91 G 6
Blesmanspos o ZA 220-221 G 3
Bleus, Monts ▲ ZRE 212-213 C 3
Blicade o F 62-63 H 4
Blida o DZ 190-191 D 2
Bligh Island ∴ USA 20-21 R 6
Bligh Water ≈ 184 III a 2
Blikandi o CI 202-203 J 5
Blina o AUS 172-173 G 4
Blina Oil Field • AUS 172-173 G 4
Blind Channel o CDN 32-33 H 6
Blind River o CDN 38-39 C 5
Blinisht o AL 100-101 G 4
Blipi o LB 202-203 H 6
Bliss Bugt ≈ 26-27 I 2
Bliss Landing o CDN 32-33 H 6
Blitchton o USA 48-49 H 3
Blitta o RT 202-203 L 5
Blixby o USA 42-43 M 7
Block Island ∴ USA 46-47 N 5
Bloemfontein ☆ ZA 220-221 H 4
Bloemhof o ZA 220-221 H 3
Bloemhof Dam < ZA 220-221 G 3
Blois o F 90-91 H 8
Blolékin o CI 202-203 G 6
Blommesteinmeer, W.J. van ◁ SME 62-63 G 3
Blönduós ☆ IS 86-87 c 2
Blood Indian Reserve ⋏ CDN 32-33 O 7
Blood River Monument • ZA 220-221 K 4
Bloodvein River ~ CDN 34-35 H 5

Bloody Falls ~ CDN 30-31 M 2
Bloomfield o USA (IA) 42-43 L 5
Bloomfield o USA (IN) 46-47 E 6
Bloomfield o USA (NM) 44-45 D 1
Bloomfield River ~ AUS 174-175 H 4
Blooming Prairie o USA 42-43 L 4
Bloomington o USA (IL) 46-47 D 5
Bloomington o USA (IN) 46-47 E 6
Bloomington o USA (MN) 42-43 L 3
Bloomsburg o USA 46-47 K 5
Bloomsbury o AUS 178-179 K 7
Bloomsdale o USA 46-47 C 6
Blora o RI 168 D 3
Blosseville Kyst ◁ GRØ 28-29 a 2
Blossom, mys ▲ RUS 112-113 U 1
Bloukranspas ≈ ZA 220-221 D 5
Blowering Reservoir < AUS 180-181 K 3
Blow River ~ CDN 20-21 W 2
Bloxsome Bay ≈ 24-25 K 2
Blubber Bay o CDN 32-33 H 7
Blucher Range ▲ PNG 183 A 3
Bludnaja ~ RUS 110-111 F 3
Bludnaja ~ RUS 118-119 E 10
Blueberry River ~ CDN 32-33 K 3
Blue Earth o USA 42-43 K 4
Bluefield o USA 46-47 H 7
Bluefields ∴ NIC 52-53 C 5
Bluefields, Bahía de ≈ 52-53 C 6
Bluefish River ~ CDN 30-31 F 2
Bluegrass Prairie ⊥ CDN 36-37 N 2
Bluegoose River ~ CDN 36-37 N 2
Blue Hill o USA 42-43 H 5
Blue Hills ▲ CDN 24-25 O 3
Blue Hills of Couteau ▲ CDN 38-39 O 5
Blue Hole National Park ⊥ BH 52-53 K 3
Blue Knob ▲ AUS 178-179 M 6
Blue Lagoon National Park ⊥ Z 218-219 D 2
Blue Lick Spring o USA 46-47 F 6
Blue Mesa Reservoir < USA 42-43 D 6
Blue Mountain o IND 142-143 H 4
Blue Mountain ▲ AUS 46-47 N 3
Blue Mountain Lake o USA 46-47 L 4
Blue Mountains ▲ JA 54-55 G 5
Blue Mountains ▲ USA 40-41 E 3
Blue Mountains ▲ USA 40-41 E 3
Blue Mountains National Park ⊥•• AUS 180-181 L 2
Blue Mount Pass ▲ USA 40-41 F 4
Blue Mud Bay ≈ 174-175 C 3
Blue Mud Hills ▲ USA 42-43 H 5
Blue Nile = Abay Wenz ~ ETH 208-209 C 3
Blue Nile Falls = T'is Isat Fwafwatē ~•• ETH 208-209 C 3
Bluenose Lake o CDN 24-25 M 6
Blue Ridge o USA 48-49 F 2
Blue Ridge ▲ USA 46-47 J 7
Blue River o CDN 32-33 L 5
Blue Robin Hill o AUS 176-177 H 4
Blue Springs o USA 48-49 F 4
Blue Springs Caverns • USA 46-47 E 6
Bluewater o AUS 174-175 J 6
Bluewater o USA 44-45 D 2
Bluff o AUS 178-179 K 2
Bluff o NZ 182 B 7
Bluff o USA (AK) 20-21 J 4
Bluff o USA (UT) 42-43 C 7
Bluff, Cape o CDN 38-39 R 2
Bluff, The o BS 54-55 G 2
Bluff Face Range ▲ AUS 172-173 H 4
Bluff Point o AUS 172-173 C 6
Bluff Point ▲ NZ 98-99 J 4
Blukwa o ZRE 212-213 C 3
Blumenau o• BR 74-75 F 6
Blunt o USA 42-43 H 3
Blunt Peninsula ∪ CDN 36-37 R 3
Blup Blup Island ∴ PNG 183 C 2
Bly o USA 40-41 D 4
Blyde River Canyon Nature Reserve ⊥ ZA 220-221 K 2
Blythe o USA 40-41 G 9
Blytheville o USA 48-49 D 2
Blyth Lagoon o AUS 176-177 H 2
Blyth River ~ AUS 174-175 C 3
Bragola o ZRE 210-211 H 5
B'Nom So'Ro'Long ▲ VN 158-159 J 5
Bø o N 86-87 D 7
Bo ☆ WAL 202-203 F 6
Boa o CI 202-203 G 5
Boac o RP 160-161 D 6
Boaco o NIC 52-53 B 5
Boa Esperança o BR (AMA) 66-67 G 4
Boa Esperança o BR (MIN) 66-67 J 5
Boa Esperança o BR (ROR) 62-63 D 4
Boa Esperança do Sul o BR 72-73 G 6
Boa Fé o BR 66-67 F 4
Boagis o PNG 183 B 5
Boalemo o RI 164-165 H 4
Boali o RCA 206-207 D 6
Boali, Chutes de ~ RCA 206-207 D 6
Boanamary o RM 222-223 E 5
Boanda o CAM 204-205 K 6
Boane o MOC 220-221 L 3
Boangi o DRE 210-211 H 4
Boang Island ∴ PNG 183 E 3
Boano, Pulau ∴ RI 164-165 H 5
Boano, Selat ≈ 166-167 D 3
Boa Nova o BR (P) 68-69 G 2
Boa Nova o BR (RON) 66-67 F 7
Boardman o USA 40-41 E 3
Boas River ~ CDN 36-37 M 3
Boatman o AUS 178-179 J 5
Boat of Garten o GB 90-91 F 3
Boatswain, Baie ≈ 38-39 R 3
Boa Viagem o BR 68-69 J 4
Boa Vista o BR (AMA) 66-67 D 3
Boa Vista o BR (AMA) 66-67 E 4
Boa Vista o BR (AMA) 66-67 F 4
Boa Vista o BR (AMA) 66-67 F 4
Boa Vista o BR (GSU) 76-77 J 2
Boa Vista o BR (P) 62-63 H 6
Boa Vista o BR (RSU) 74-75 D 9
Boa Vista o BR (ROR) 62-63 D 4

Boa Vista, Ilha de ∴ CV 202-203 C 5
Boa Vista da Ramos o BR 66-67 F 4
Boa Vista das Palmas o BR 72-73 K 2
Boa Vista do Tupim o BR 72-73 K 2
Boawae o RI 168 E 7
Bobadah o AUS 180-181 J 2
Bobai o VRC 156-157 F 5
Bobandana o BR 212-213 A 6
Bobasakoa o RM 222-223 E 4
Bobbie Burns Creek ~ CDN 32-33 M 6
Bobbili o IND 142-143 G 6
Bobila o ZRE 210-211 H 2
Bobo o RCA 206-207 C 5
Bobo-Dioulasso ☆ BF 202-203 H 4
Bobolice o PL 92-93 O 2
Bobonaza, Río ~ EC 64-65 D 2
Bobonong o RB 218-219 E 5
Bobopayo o RI 164-165 K 3
Bobr ~ BY 94-95 L 4
Bóbr ~ PL 92-93 N 3
Bobrof Island ∴ USA 22-23 H 7
Bobrov o RUS 102-103 L 2
Bobrujsk = Babrujsk ☆ BY 94-95 L 5
Bobrynec' o UA 102-103 H 3
Bobuk o SUD 208-209 D 4
Bobures o YV 60-61 F 3
Boby ▲ RM 222-223 E 9
Boca, Cachoeira da ~ BR 66-67 K 5
Boca, La o BOL 70-71 E 4
Boca Arenal o CR 52-53 B 6
Boca Candelaria o CO 60-61 C 5
Boca Caragual o CO 60-61 L 5
Boca Chica ∴ DOM 54-55 L 5
Boca de Anaro o YV 60-61 G 4
Boca de Arguaca o YV 60-61 H 4
Boca de la Serpiente ≈ 60-61 L 3
Boca del Pao o YV 60-61 J 3
Boca del Río o YV 60-61 J 2
Boca del Río o MEX 52-53 F 2
Boca del Río o YV 60-61 G 2
Boca del Río Indio o PA 52-53 D 7
Boca del Tocuyo o YV 60-61 G 2
Boca de Uchire o YV 60-61 J 2
Boca de Yuma o DOM 54-55 L 5
Boca do Acará o BR 66-67 F 6
Boca do Acre o BR 66-67 D 7
Boca do Capanã o BR 66-67 G 5
Boca do Carapanatuba o BR 66-67 F 6
Boca do Jari o BR 62-63 J 6
Bocaina de Minas o BR 72-73 H 7
Bocaína do Sul o BR 74-75 F 6
Bocana, La o MEX 50-51 B 3
Bocanda o CI 202-203 H 6
Bocaranga o RCA 206-207 B 5
Boca Raton o USA 48-49 H 6
Bocas del Toro o PA 52-53 C 7
Bocas del Toro, Archipiélago de ∴ PA 52-53 C 7
Bocay, Río ~ NIC 52-53 B 5
Bochart o CDN 38-39 H 4
Bochinche o YV 62-63 D 2
Bocholt o D 92-93 H 3
Bocoio o ANG 216-217 C 6
Bocón o YV 60-61 K 4
Bocon, Caño ~ CO 60-61 G 6
Bocono o YV 60-61 H 4
Boçoroca o BR 76-77 K 5
Bocoyna o MEX 50-51 F 4
Boda o RCA 206-207 C 6
Böda o S 86-87 H 8
Bodajbo o RUS 118-119 G 7
Bodalangi o ZRE 210-211 J 2
Bodalla o AUS 180-181 L 3
Bodallin o AUS 176-177 E 5
Bodangora, Mount ▲ AUS 180-181 K 2
Boddington o AUS 176-177 D 6
Bodélé ≃ TCH 198-199 H 4
Boden o CH 92-93 H 5
Bodensee o CH 92-93 H 5
Bode-Shadu o WAN 204-205 F 4
Bodhan o IND (ANP) 138-139 F 10
Bodhan o IND (KAR) 140-141 G 2
Bodhei o EAK 212-213 H 4
Bodh Gaya o IND 142-143 D 3
Bodi o DY 202-203 L 5
Bodi o BR 202-203 J 6
Bodinga o RCA 210-211 F 2
Boditi o ETH 208-209 C 5
Bod'ja, Jaškur- o RUS 96-97 H 5
Bodjokola o ZRE 210-211 H 2
Bodmin o CDN 34-35 C 4
Bodmin o GB 90-91 E 6
Bodo o CI 202-203 H 7
Bodø o N 86-87 G 3
Bodoco o BR 66-67 G 7
Bodocó o BR 68-69 J 5
Bodokro o CI 202-203 H 6
Bodoquena o BR 70-71 J 7
Bodoukpa o RCA 206-207 D 6
Bodrum ☆ TR 128-129 B 4
Boduna o RCA 206-207 D 6
Boé o• GNB 202-203 E 4
Boêkovo o RUS 112-113 L 2
Boende o ZRE 210-211 H 4
Boenze o ZRE 210-211 E 6
Boerne o USA 44-45 H 5
Boesmansrivier ~ ZA 220-221 H 6
Boesmansriviermond o ZA 220-221 H 6
Boevaja gora ~ RUS 96-97 J 8
Bofete o BR 72-73 F 7
Boffa o RG 202-203 F 5
Bofossou o RG 202-203 G 6
Boki, Lagh ~ EAK 212-213 H 3
Bogale o MYA 158-159 C 2
Bogalusa o USA 48-49 D 4
Bogande o BF 202-203 K 4
Bogan River ~ AUS 180-181 J 2
Bogangolo o RCA 206-207 D 6
Boganida ~ RUS 108-109 c 5
Bogantungan o AUS 178-179 J 2

Bogaševo o RUS 114-115 S 6
Bogondo o ZRE 210-211 G 3
Bogoro o TCH 198-199 H 6
Bogatyé Saby ☆ RUS 96-97 G 6
Boko-Songho o RCB 210-211 D 6
Bogcang Zangpo ~ VRC 144-145 F 5
Bogd = Hovd ~ MAU 148-149 F 5
Bogda Feng ▲ VRC 146-147 J 4
Bogdanovič o RUS 114-115 G 6
Bogdanovka o RUS 96-97 G 7
Bogda Shan ▲ VRC 146-147 J 4
Bogdoo o GH 202-203 K 4
Böget ▲ KA 146-147 D 4
Bogetsaj o KA 126-127 N 2
Boggabilla o AUS 178-179 L 5
Boggabri o AUS 178-179 L 6
Boggola, Mount ▲ AUS 176-177 D 1
Bogia o PNG 183 C 3
Bogilima o ZRE 210-211 G 2
Bognuro o IR 136-137 E 6
Bogo o CAM 206-207 B 3
Bogo o RP 160-161 F 7
Bogoin o RCA 206-207 D 6
Bogoladza, hrebet ▲ RUS 122-123 F 5
Bogol Manyo o ETH 208-209 E 6
Bogong, Mount ▲ AUS 180-181 J 4
Bogong National Park ⊥ AUS 180-181 J 4
Bogor (Buitenzorg) o RI 168 B 3
Bogoria, Lake o• EAK 212-213 F 3
Bogorodick o RUS 94-95 O 5
Bogorodsk o RUS 94-95 S 3
Bogorodsk o RUS (PRM) 96-97 K 5
Bogorodskoe ☆ RUS (KIR) 96-97 G 5
Bogorodskoe o RUS 122-123 J 2
Bogoroud o TCH 198-199 G 5
Bogose-Mubea o ZRE 210-211 G 2
Bogoslof Island ∴ USA 22-23 N 6
Bogoso o RB 202-203 J 7
Bogotá ★ CO 60-61 D 5
Bogotol o RUS 114-115 U 6
Bogra o BD 142-143 F 3
Bogučany o RUS 114-115 U 6
Boguçar o RUS 102-103 M 3
Bogué o RIM 196-197 C 6
Bogue Chitto River ~ USA 44-45 M 4
Boguédia o CI 202-203 G 6
Boguila Kota o RCA 206-207 C 5
Bogunda o AUS 178-179 H 1
Bo Hai ≈ 154-155 L 2
Bohai Haixia ≈ 150-151 C 8
Bohai Wan ≈ 154-155 K 2
Bohemia Downs o AUS 172-173 H 5
Bohena Creek ~ AUS 178-179 K 6
Bohicon o DY 204-205 E 4
Böhmisch-Trübau = Česká Třebová o• CZ 92-93 O 4
Bohobé o TCH 206-207 D 4
Bohodou o RG 202-203 G 6
Bohoduchiv o UA 102-103 J 2
Bohol ∴ RP 160-161 F 8
Bohol Sea ≈ 160-161 F 8
Bohol Strait ≈ 160-161 E 8
Bohong o RCA 206-207 C 5
Bohongou o BF 202-203 L 3
Böhönye o H 92-93 O 5
Bohorods'kyj Kostel • UA 102-103 D 2
Böhöt o MAU 148-149 J 5
Boi o WAN 204-205 H 4
Boi, Ponta de ▲ BR 72-73 H 7
Bóia, Rio ~ BR 66-67 D 5
Boiaçu o BR 62-63 D 6
Boiboido o BR 202-203 F 6
Boiekevie Hill ▲ AUS 180-181 J 2
Boigu Island ∴ AUS 183 B 5
Boiken o PNG 183 C 3
Boila o MOC 218-219 K 3
Boina ∴ RM 222-223 E 6
Boipárigüia o IND 142-143 E 4
Boipeba, Ilha de ∴ BR 72-73 L 2
Bois, Lac des o CDN 30-31 J 2
Bois, Rio dos ~ BR 68-69 D 6
Bois, Rio dos ~ BR 72-73 F 4
Bois, Rio dos ~ BR 72-73 F 4
Bois-Blanc o F 224 B 7
Bois Blanc Island ∴ USA 46-47 F 3
Boise ★ USA 40-41 F 4
Boise City o USA 44-45 F 1
Boissevain o CDN 34-35 F 6
Boituva o BR 72-73 G 7
Boja o RI 168 C 3
Bojano o I 100-101 E 4
Bojarka o RUS 108-109 b 6
Bojarsk o RUS 116-117 N 7
Bojčinovci o BG 102-103 C 6
Bojkov, liman ≈ 102-103 K 5
Bojnegoro o RI 168 D 3
Boju o WAN 204-205 G 5
Boju-Ega o WAN 204-205 G 4
Bojuru o BR 74-75 E 8
Bojuru, Ponta do ▲ BR 74-75 E 8
Bokada o BR 206-207 D 6
Bokákbát o IND 142-143 H 2
Boka Kotorska ≈ 100-101 G 3
Bokala o ZRE 210-211 F 5
Bokata o ZRE 210-211 J 4
Bokatola o ZRE 210-211 G 4
Bokayanga o RCA 206-207 D 5
Boké o RG 202-203 C 4
Boké o BR 202-203 C 4
Bokhara River ~ AUS 178-179 J 5
Bokh el Abd ~ EAK 212-213 G 4
Bokhol Plain ⊥ EAK 212-213 H 2
Bokin o BF 202-203 J 4
Boki Saboudo o RIM 196-197 K 3
Bokkeveldberge ▲ ZA 220-221 D 5
Boknafjorden ≈ 86-87 B 7
Boko o RCB 210-211 E 6
Bokoko o ZRE 210-211 H 3
Bokolango o SN 202-203 D 3
Bokolango o ZRE 210-211 H 3
Bokolo o CI 202-203 G 5

Bokonbaevckoe o KS 146-147 C 4
Bokondo o ZRE 210-211 G 3
Bokoro o TCH 198-199 H 6
Bokote o ZRE 210-211 J 4
Boksburg o ZA 220-221 J 3
Bol ☆ RI 166-167 B 6
Bola, Bahr ~ TCH 206-207 D 3
Bolaiti o ZRE 210-211 K 5
Bolama o ZRE 210-211 J 3
Bolama o ZRE 210-211 J 3
Bolangitang o RI 164-165 H 3
Bolaños, Río ~ MEX 50-51 H 7
Bolan Pass ≈ PK 134-135 M 4
Bolbec o F 90-91 H 7
Bolbolo o RP 160-161 D 4
Bolčiha o RUS 124-125 M 2
Bold Point ▲ CDN 160-161 C 7
Boldyr o US 136-137 K 6
Bole o GH 202-203 J 5
Bole o VRC 146-147 F 3
Bolek o ZRE 210-211 G 4
Bolena o ZRE 210-211 G 3
Bolgar o RUS 176-177 D 5
Bolgatanga o• GH 202-203 K 4
Bolhov o RUS 94-95 O 5
Bolhrad o UA 102-103 F 5
Boli o VRC 150-151 H 5
Bolia o ZRE 210-211 G 4
Bolia o ZRE 210-211 G 4
Boliche = Pedro J. Montero o EC 64-65 C 3
Boliden o S 86-87 K 4
Bolifar o RI 166-167 F 3
Bolinha, Cachoeira da ~ BR 62-63 D 6
Bolintin-Vale o RO 102-103 D 5
Boliohutu, Gunung ▲ RI 164-165 H 3
Bolívar (COC) o 70-71 D 5
Bolívar (PAN) o 70-71 D 3
Bolívar o CO 60-61 C 7
Bolívar o PE 64-65 D 5
Bolívar (MO) o 44-45 L 1
Bolívar (TN) o 48-49 D 2
Bolívar, Pico ▲•• YV 60-61 F 3
Bolívar Peninsula ∪ USA 44-45 K 5
Bolivia ■ BOL 70-71 D 5
Bolivia o C 54-55 F 3
Boljevac o YU 100-101 H 3
Boljoan o RP 160-161 E 8
Bolkar Dağları ▲ TR 128-129 F 4
Bollène o F 90-91 K 9
Bollnäs o S 86-87 H 6
Bollock, Mount ▲ CDN 24-25 W 3
Bollon o AUS 178-179 J 4
Bollons Seamount ≃ 14-15 L 13
Bolmen o S 86-87 F 8
Bolobo o ZRE 210-211 F 5
Boločaevka-2-ja o RUS 122-123 F 4
Bolodek o RUS 122-123 E 2
Bologna ☆• I 100-101 C 2
Bologoesi o PE 64-65 D 7
Bologoe o RUS 94-95 O 3
Bololedi o EAT 212-213 E 5
Bolomba o ZRE 210-211 G 3
Bolombo o ZRE 210-211 H 3
Bolon', ozero o RUS 122-123 G 4
Bolora o BF 202-203 K 4
Bolonchén o• MEX 52-53 J 3
Bolonchén de Rejón o MEX 52-53 K 1
Bolondo o GQ 210-211 D 4
Bolongongo o ANG 216-217 C 4
Bolonguera o ANG 216-217 B 6
Bolontio o RI 164-165 H 3
Bolotnoe o RUS 114-115 S 7
Bolovens, Plateau des ▲ LAO 158-159 J 3
Bol'šaja ~ RUS 110-111 a 2
Bol'šaja ~ RUS 122-123 R 2
Bol'šaja ~ RUS 116-117 N 7
Bol'šaja Belaja ~ RUS 116-117 K 9
Bol'šaja Bi'ca ~ RUS 114-115 L 4
Bol'šaja Birjusa ~ RUS 116-117 H 8
Bol'šaja Bootankaga ~ RUS 108-109 a 4
Bol'šaja Čeremšan ~ RUS 96-97 G 6
Bol'šaja Čërmigovka ~ RUS 96-97 G 7
Bol'šaja Erëma ~ RUS 116-117 N 5
Bol'šaja Glušica ~ RUS 96-97 G 7
Bol'šaja Horga, ozero o RUS 118-119 E 9
Bol'šaja Ket' ~ RUS 114-115 R 5
Bol'šaja Kuropatočja ~ RUS 112-113 J 1
Bol'šaja Lebjaž'ja ~ RUS 116-117 E 5
Bol'šaja Martynovka = Sloboda Bol'šaja Martynovka o RUS 102-103 M 4
Bol'šaja Murata ☆ RUS 116-117 F 7
Bol'šaja Nisogora o RUS 88-89 S 4
Bol'šaja Pula ~ RUS 88-89 V 3
Bol'šaja Rečka o RUS 96-97 N 5
Bol'šaja Saga, ozero o RUS 96-97 D 10

Bol'šaja Sosnovka ☆ RUS 96-97 J 5
Bol'šaja Tira ~ RUS 116-117 M 7
Bol'šaja Usa ~ RUS 96-97 J 5
Bol'šaja Ussurka ~ RUS 122-123 F 6
Bol'šaja Uzen' ~ RUS 96-97 F 8
Bol'šakovo o RUS 124-125 L 3
Bol'šanaromskoe o KA 124-125 L 3
Bol'šereč'e ~ RUS 114-115 N 6
Bol'šereck o RUS 120-121 U 6
Bol'šerek, Ust'- ☆ RUS 122-123 R 2
Bol'šereckij Sovhoz o RUS 122-123 P 2
Bol'šeustinskoe ☆ RUS 96-97 L 6
Bol'ševik, ostrov ∴ RUS 108-109 d 2
Bol'šezemel'skaja tundra ⊥ RUS 88-89 W 3
Bol'šoe ▲ CO 64-65 F 1
Bol'šoj o TCH 198-199 G 6
Bol'šoe Eravnoe, ozero o RUS 118-119 E 9
Bol'šoe Jarovoe ozero o RUS 124-125 L 2
Bol'šoe Jasavejto, ozero o RUS 108-109 M 7
Bol'šoe Kizi, ozero o RUS 122-123 J 3
Bol'šoe Morskoe, ozero o RUS 112-113 K 1
Bol'šoj o US 136-137 K 6
Bol'šoj Aim ~ RUS 120-121 E 5
Bol'šoj Akzar o KA 124-125 L 3
Bol'šoj Amalat ~ RUS 118-119 E 8
Bol'šoj Anjuj ~ RUS 112-113 L 2
Bol'šoj Atlym ~ RUS 114-115 J 3
Bol'šoj Balhan, hrebet ▲ TM 136-137 D 5
Bol'šoj Baranov, mys ▲ RUS 112-113 M 2
Bol'šoj Begičev, ostrov ∴ RUS 110-111 X 2
Bol'šoj Čerëmšan ~ RUS 96-97 G 6
Bol'šoj Čurki ~ RUS 88-89 T 5
Bol'šoj Dubčes ~ RUS 114-115 T 4
Bol'šoj Enisej ~ RUS 116-117 G 10
Bol'šoj Homus Jurjah ~ RUS 110-111 d 4
Bol'šoj Ik ~ RUS 96-97 K 7
Bol'šoj Ik ~ RUS 96-97 L 6
Bol'šoj Irgiz ~ RUS 120-121 C 6
Bol'šoj Iremjet, gora ▲ RUS 96-97 K 6
Bol'šoj Jarhodon ~ RUS 112-113 H 8
Bol'šoj Jaruodej ~ RUS 108-109 L 8
Bol'šoj Jugan ~ RUS 114-115 M 4
Bol'šoj Kamen' o RUS 122-123 E 7
Bol'šoj Karaman ~ RUS 96-97 F 8
Bol'šoj Kas ~ RUS 116-117 E 6
Bol'šoj Kazymskij Sor, ozero o RUS 114-115 J 3
Bol'šoj Ljapin ~ RUS 88-89 U 5
Bol'šoj Loptjuga ~ RUS 108-109 U 4
Bol'šoj Megtyg'egan ~ RUS 114-115 R 4
Bol'šoj Nimnyr o RUS 118-119 M 6
Bol'šoj Nimnyr ~ RUS 118-119 M 6
Bol'šoj Ofdoj ~ RUS 118-119 L 8
Bol'šoj On ~ RUS 124-125 Q 3
Bol'šoj Ona ~ RUS 124-125 Q 3
Bol'šoj Oju ~ RUS 108-109 J 7
Bol'šoj Patom ~ RUS 118-119 J 6
Bol'šoj Peledon ~ RUS 112-113 O 3
Bol'šoj Pit ~ RUS 116-117 F 7
Bol'šoj Pyrkavaam ~ RUS 112-113 S 3
Bol'šoj Rautan, ostrov ∴ RUS 112-113 Q 2
Bol'šoj Sajan ▲ RUS 116-117 J 9
Bol'šoj Santar ~ RUS 114-115 L 4
Bol'šoj Šantar, ostrov ∴ RUS 120-121 G 6
Bol'šoj Selerikan ~ RUS 110-111 X 7
Bol'šoj Šantar, ostrov ∴ RUS 126-127 H 5
Bol'šoj Šiskarym ozero o RUS 114-115 K 6
Bol'šoj Tap ~ RUS 114-115 H 4
Bol'šoj Turtas ~ RUS 114-115 L 5
Bol'šoj Tyrkan ~ RUS 120-121 E 5
Bol'šoj Uluj ☆ RUS 116-117 F 7
Bol'šoj Urkan ~ RUS 118-119 M 8
Bol'šoj Uvat ozero o RUS 114-115 L 6
Bol'šoj Uzen' ~ RUS 96-97 F 8
Bol'šoj Zelenzuk ~ RUS 118-119 N 6
Bol'šoj Zelenec, ostrov ∴ RUS 108-109 H 7
Bol'šoj Žužmuj, ostrov ∴ RUS 88-89 N 4
Bol'šoj Železnec ☆ RUS 126-127 J 5
Bolson de Mapimi ⊥ MEX 50-51 G 5
Boltodden ▲ N 84-85 L 4
Bolton o GB 90-91 F 5
Bolton o USA 48-49 J 2
Bolu o TR 128-129 D 2

Bolubolu o PNG 183 F 5
Bolvaninka o RUS 116-117 H 6
Bolvanskij Nos ▲ RUS 108-109 H 6
Bolzano = Bozen o• I 100-101 C 1
Boma o ZRE 210-211 D 6
Bomaderry, Nowra- o• AUS 180-181 L 3
Bomadi o WAN 204-205 F 6
Bomassa o RCB 210-211 F 2
Bombabasua o RI 164-165 F 4
Bombala o AUS 180-181 K 4
Bombay o• IND 138-139 D 10
Bomberai ∴ RI 166-167 G 3
Bomberai Peninsula ∪ RI 166-167 G 3
Bombo o EAU 212-213 D 3
Bombo o RI 166-167 B 6
Bömbögör = Zadgaj o MAU 148-149 D 4
Bombo-Makuba o ZRE 210-211 F 6
Bombonal o CO 64-65 F 1
Bomboya o TCH 198-199 G 6
Bombura o ZRE 210-211 G 2
Bom Comercio o BR 66-67 E 7
Bom Conselho o BR 68-69 K 6
Bom Despacho o BR 72-73 H 5
Bomdila o IND 142-143 H 2
Bomi o EAK 212-213 J 4
Bomi o VRC 144-145 K 5
Bomili o ZRE 212-213 A 6
Bom Intento o BR 66-67 K 5
Bom Jardim o BR (MAR) 68-69 F 3
Bom Jardim o BR (P) 62-63 J 7
Bom Jardim o BR (RIO) 72-73 J 7
Bom Jardim de Minas o BR 72-73 H 6
Bom Jardim ou Bacabal, Igarapé ~ BR 66-67 J 5
Bom Jesus o ANG 216-217 B 4
Bom Jesus o BR (CAT) 74-75 D 5
Bom Jesus o BR (PB) 68-69 F 6
Bom Jesus o BR (RSU) 74-75 D 7
Bom Jesus, Rio ~ BR 68-69 F 5
Bom Jesus da Gurguéira, Serra ▲ BR 68-69 G 6
Bom Jesus da Lapa o BR 72-73 J 2
Bom Jesus da Penha o BR 72-73 G 6
Bom Jesus de Goiás o BR 72-73 F 5
Bom Jesus do Amparo o BR 72-73 J 5
Bom Jesus do Galho o BR 72-73 J 5
Bom Jesus do Itabapoana o BR 72-73 K 6
Bømlo ∴ N 86-87 B 7
Bom Lugar o BR 66-67 H 6
Bomnak o RUS 118-119 O 8
Bomokandi ~ ZRE 210-211 G 2
Bomongo o ZRE 210-211 G 3
Bomotu o ZRE 210-211 G 2
Bom Princípio o BR 68-69 E 6
Bomsucesso o BR 68-69 F 3
Bom Sucesso o BR (MIN) 72-73 H 6
Bom Sucesso o BR (PA) 68-69 K 5
Bomu ~ ZRE 206-207 D 4
Bomu Occidental, Réserve de faune ⊥ ZRE 206-207 B 4
Bomu Orientale, Réserve de faune ⊥ ZRE 206-207 D 4
Bon, Cap ▲ TN 190-191 J 2
Bona, Mount ▲ USA 20-21 U 6
Bonab o IR 128-129 M 4
Bonaberi o CAM 204-205 H 6
Bona Bona Island ∴ PNG 183 E 6
Bonaire ∴ NL 60-61 G 1
Bonam o BF 202-203 K 3
Bonampak ∴•• MEX 52-53 J 3
Bonang o AUS 180-181 K 4
Bonang o RI 168 E 7
Bonanza o NIC 52-53 B 4
Bonanza o USA (ID) 40-41 G 3
Bonanza o USA (UT) 42-43 D 5
Bonao o DOM 54-55 K 5
Bonapabli o LB 202-203 F 6
Bonaparte, Mount ▲ USA 40-41 E 1
Bonaparte Archipelago ∴ AUS 172-173 G 3
Bonaparte River ~ CDN 32-33 K 6
Boñar o E 98-99 E 3
Bonara (Naulu Village) ⊥•• RI 166-167 E 3
Bonaventure o CDN 38-39 M 4
Bonavista, Cape ▲•• CDN 38-39 S 4
Bonavista Bay ≈ 38-39 S 4
Bonavista Peninsula ∪ CDN 38-39 S 4
Boncuk Dağı ▲ TR 128-129 C 4
Bondari o RUS 94-95 S 5
Bondo o ZRE (EQU) 210-211 G 3
Bondo o ZRE (Hau) 210-211 J 2
Bondoc Peninsula ∪ RP 160-161 E 6
Bondokodi o RI 168 D 7
Bondoukou o CI 202-203 J 5
Bondoukui o BF 202-203 J 4
Bondowoso o RI 168 E 3
Bonds Cay ∴ BS 54-55 G 2
Bondurant o USA 40-41 J 4
Boné o RG 202-203 E 4
Bone o RI 164-165 H 3
Bone = Watampone o RI 164-165 G 6
Bonebone o• RI 164-165 G 5
Bone-Dumoga National Park ⊥•• RI 164-165 H 3
Bonelambere o RI 168 E 6
Bonelipu o RI 164-165 H 6
Bonelohe o RI 164-165 G 5
Bonépoupa o CAM 204-205 J 6
Bonerate o RI 168 E 6
Bonerate, Kepulauan ∴ RI 168 E 6
Bonerate, Pulau ∴ RI 168 E 6
Bonete, Cerro ▲ RA 76-77 C 4
Bonete, Río ~ RA 76-77 C 5
Bone Teluk ≈ 164-165 G 5
Bonfim o BR (MAT) 70-71 K 5
Bonfim o BR (P) 66-67 K 5
Bonfim o BR (ROR) 62-63 E 4
Bonfinópolis de Minas o BR 72-73 H 4
Bonga o ETH 208-209 C 5
Bonga o PNG 183 D 4

Bongabon o **RP** 160-161 D 5
Bongandanga o **ZRE** 210-211 H 3
Bongaon o **IND** 142-143 F 4
Bongâr o **IR** 134-135 J 3
Bông Hu'ng o **VN** 156-157 E 6
Bongka o **RI** 164-165 G 4
Bongo o **RI** 164-165 H 3
Bongo, Massif des ▲ **RCA** 206-207 F 4
Bongolava ⊥ **RM** 222-223 H 7
Bongolo, Grottes de • **G** 210-211 C 5
Bongor o **TCH** 206-207 B 3
Bongouanou o **CI** 202-203 H 6
Bongouanou, Collines de ▲ **CI** 202-203 H 6
Bonham o **USA** 44-45 J 3
Boni o **BF** 202-203 J 4
Boni o **RMM** 202-203 J 2
Boniérdougou o **CI** 202-203 H 5
Bonifacio o • **F** 98-99 M 4
Bonifacio o **RP** 160-161 D 4
Bonifacio, Bocche di ≈ **I** 100-101 B 4
Bonifacio, Bouches de ≈ 98-99 M 4
Bonifay o **USA** 48-49 F 4
Boninal o **BR** 72-73 K 2
Boni National Reserve ⊥ **EAK** 212-213 H 4
Bonin National Park ⊥ **GH** 202-203 J 7
Bonin Trench ≈ 14-15 G 4
Bonitas, Ias o **YV** 60-61 J 4
Bonito o **BR** (BAH) 68-69 H 7
Bonito o **BR** (GSU) 76-77 J 1
Bonito o **BR** (MIN) 72-73 H 3
Bonito o **BR** (PER) 68-69 E 2
Bonito o **BR** (PER) 68-69 L 6
Bonito, Pico ▲ **HN** 52-53 L 4
Bonito, Rio ~ **BR** 72-73 E 4
Bonito Pico, Parque Nacional ⊥ **HN** 52-53 L 4
Bonjol o **RI** 162-163 D 4
Bonkahar, Küh-e ▲ **IR** 134-135 E 3
Bonkoukou o **RN** 204-205 E 1
Bonn o • **D** 92-93 J 3
Bonne Bay ≈ 38-39 P 4
Bonnechere Caves • **CDN** 38-39 F 6
Bonners Ferry o **USA** 40-41 F 1
Bonnet, Cachoeira do ~ **BR** 66-67 H 6
Bonneville Salt Flats ⊥ **USA** 40-41 H 5
Bonney, Lake o **AUS** 180-181 F 4
Bonney Downs o **AUS** 172-173 D 7
Bonnie Rock o **AUS** 176-177 E 5
Bonnissant, Pointe ▲ 36-37 K 5
Bonny o **WAN** 204-205 G 6
Bonny, Bight of ≈ 204-205 G 6
Bonnyville o **CDN** 32-33 P 4
Bonoi o **RI** 166-167 J 2
Bonou o **DY** 204-205 E 5
Bonshaw o **AUS** 178-179 L 5
Bonsoaga ~ **BF** 202-203 L 3
Bontang o **RI** 164-165 E 3
Bontekoe Ø ▲ **GRØ** 26-27 p 7
Bonthe o **WAL** 202-203 D 6
Bontoc o **RP** 160-161 D 4
Bontoc Point ▲ **RP** 160-161 F 6
Bontosunggu o **RI** 164-165 F 6
Bontosunggu-Jenepanto o **RI** 164-165 F 6
Bonvouloir Islands ∾ **PNG** 183 F 6
Bon Wier o **USA** 44-45 L 4
Bonyere o **GH** 202-203 J 7
Bonyhád o **H** 92-93 P 5
Bonzan o **BF** 202-203 J 4
Boo, Kepulauan ∾ **RI** 166-167 E 2
Boobare o **AUS** 178-179 H 4
Boodi Boodi Range ▲ **AUS** 176-177 G 2
Bookaloo o **AUS** 178-179 D 4
Booko o **CI** 202-203 G 5
Boola o **RG** 202-203 F 5
Boolardy o **AUS** 176-177 D 3
Boolba o **AUS** 178-179 K 4
Booligal o **AUS** 180-181 H 4
Boolthardu Hill ▲ **AUS** 178-179 F 6
Boomarra o **AUS** 174-175 F 6
Boomi River ~ **AUS** 178-179 K 5
Boonah o **AUS** 178-179 M 5
Bööncagaan nuur o **MAU** 148-149 D 5
Boondooma Reservoir o **AUS** 178-179 L 4
Boone o **USA** (CO) 42-43 E 6
Boone o **USA** (IA) 42-43 L 4
Boone o **USA** (NC) 48-49 H 1
Booneville o **USA** (AR) 44-45 L 2
Booneville o **USA** (KY) 46-47 G 7
Booneville o **USA** (MS) 48-49 D 2
Boongaree Island ∾ **AUS** 172-173 G 3
Boonville o **USA** (IN) 46-47 D 6
Boonville o **USA** (MO) 42-43 L 6
Boorabbin o **AUS** 176-177 F 5
Boorabbin National Park ⊥ **AUS** 176-177 F 5
Boorama o **SP** 208-209 F 4
Böörög Delijn Els ⊥ **MAU** 116-117 F 10
Booroondara, Mount ▲ **AUS** 178-179 H 4
Boorowa o **AUS** 180-181 K 3
Boort o **AUS** 180-181 G 4
Boosaaso = Bender Qaasim ★ **SP** 208-209 J 4
Boothbay Harbor o **USA** 46-47 O 4
Boothby, Cape ▲ **ARK** 16 G 11
Boothby, Mount ▲ **AUS** 180-181 E 3
Boothia, Gulf of ≈ 24-25 3 4
Boothia Isthmus ∪ **CDN** 24-25 D 6
Boothia Peninsula ∪ **CDN** 24-25 Y 5
Booth Islands ∾ **CDN** 24-25 C 4
Booth's River ~ **BH** 52-53 K 3
Boothulla o **AUS** 178-179 H 4
Booti Booti National Park ⊥ **AUS** 180-181 M 2
Booué o **G** 210-211 C 4
Booylgoo Spring o **AUS** 176-177 E 3
Bopako o **ZRE** 210-211 H 3
Bopo o **DY** 202-203 L 6
Borno o **WAN** 198-199 E 6

Bophuthatswana (former Homel., now part of North-West) □ **ZA** 220-221 F 3
Bopo o **WAN** 204-205 G 5
Boqên o **VRC** 144-145 K 5
Boqueirão o **BR** (BAH) 68-69 G 7
Boqueirão o **BR** (PA) 68-69 K 5
Boqueirão, Serra do ▲ **BR** 68-69 G 7
Boqueirão, Serra do ▲ **BR** 72-73 H 2
Boqueirão, Serra do ▲ **BR** 76-77 K 5
Boquerón o **C** 54-55 H 5
Boqueron o **YV** 60-61 G 3
Boquete, Cerro ▲ **RA** 78-79 E 7
Boquilla, Presa de la < **MEX** 50-51 G 4
Boquilla del Conchos, La o **MEX** 50-51 G 4
Boquillas o **USA** 44-45 F 5
Boquillas del Carmen o **MEX** 50-51 H 3
Boquira o **BR** 72-73 J 2
Bor o **RUS** 116-117 F 5
Bor o **SUD** 206-207 E 4
Bor o **TR** 128-129 F 4
Bor, Lagh ~ **EAK** 212-213 G 2
Bora ▲ **ETH** 200-201 J 6
Bora o **PNG** 183 B 4
Bora o **SUD** 206-207 H 4
Borabu o **THA** 158-159 G 2
Borabu Part ▲ **THA** 158-159 G 2
Boracho Peak ▲ **USA** 44-45 E 4
Borah Peak ▲ **USA** 40-41 H 3
Boraldaj o **KA** 136-137 J 4
Boraldaj, žota ▲ **KA** 136-137 J 4
Borang, Tanjung ▲ **RI** 166-167 G 4
Borås o **S** 86-87 F 8
Borãzgãn o **IR** 134-135 D 4
Borba ▲ **BR** 66-67 H 5
Borbon o **RP** 160-161 F 7
Borborema, Planalto da ⊥ **BR** 68-69 K 5
Borçka o **TR** 128-129 J 2
Borde Alto del Payún ▲ **RA** 78-79 E 4
Bordeaux ★ • **F** 90-91 G 9
Bordebê o **KS** 136-137 N 5
Borden o **AUS** 176-177 E 7
Borden o **CDN** 30-31 H 4
Borden Island ∾ **CDN** 24-25 Q 1
Borden Peninsula ∪ **CDN** 24-25 e 4
Borden River ~ **CDN** 30-31 Z 3
Bordertown o **AUS** 40-41 J 4
Border, Pegunungan ▲ **RI** 166-167 L 3
Border City Lodge o **USA** 20-21 U 5
Bordertown o **AUS** 180-181 F 4
Bordeyri o **IS** 86-87 c 2
Bord Hün-e Nou o **IR** 134-135 D 4
Bordighera o **I** 100-101 B 3
Bordj Bou Arreridj o **DZ** 190-191 E 2
Bordj Bounaama o **DZ** 190-191 C 3
Bordj Flye Sante Marie o **DZ** 188-189 K 7
Bordj Messouda o **DZ** 190-191 G 3
Bordj Mokhtar o **DZ** 196-197 L 4
Bordj Omar Driss o **DZ** 190-191 G 4
Bordo, El = Patia o **CO** 60-61 C 4
Bordoloni o **IND** 142-143 J 2
Borê o **ETH** 208-209 D 5
Boré o **RMM** 202-203 J 2
Boreda o **ETH** 208-209 C 5
Borensberg o **S** 86-87 G 7
Boren Xuanguan ∴ **VRC** 156-157 D 2
Borgä = Porvoo o **FIN** 88-89 H 6
Borgampäd o **IND** 142-143 B 7
Borgarfjörður o **IS** 86-87 g 2
Borgarnes o **IS** 86-87 c 2
Børgefjellet ▲ **N** 86-87 F 4
Børgefjell nasjonalpark ⊥ **N** 86-87 F 4
Bergen, Kap ▲ **GRØ** 26-27 q 6
Borger o **USA** 44-45 G 2
Borgholm ★ • **S** 86-87 H 8
Borgi o **IND** 142-143 B 6
Borgia, De o **USA** 40-41 G 2
Børg Jøkel Bræ ⊂ **GRØ** 26-27 n 5
Borg Massif = Borgmassivet ▲ **ARK** 16 F 36
Borgne, Lake o **USA** 48-49 D 4
Borgne, Le o **RH** 54-55 J 5
Borgomanero o **I** 100-101 B 2
Borgo San Lorenzo o **I** 100-101 C 3
Borgu o **RT** 202-203 L 4
Borgu Game Reserve ⊥ **WAN** 204-205 E 3
Borgund o **N** 86-87 C 6
Borgund stavkirke • **N** 86-87 C 6
Borhojn-Tal o **MAU** 148-149 K 6
Bori o **DY** 204-205 E 4
Bori o **IND** 138-139 G 9
Bori o **WAN** 204-205 G 6
Boria Tibhu o **IND** 142-143 B 5
Borigumma o **IND** 142-143 C 6
Börili o **KA** 96-97 H 8
Borivice o **VRC** 144-145 E 2
Borisoglebsk o **RUS** 102-103 N 2
Borisov = Barysaw ★ **BY** 94-95 L 4
Borisova, mys ▲ **RUS** 120-121 G 6
Borisovka o **RUS** 102-103 H 4
Borisovo-Sudskoe o **RUS** 94-95 P 2
Borizjny o **RM** 222-223 E 5
Borja o **PE** 64-65 D 4
Borj Bourguiba o **TN** 190-191 G 4
Borjhar o **IND** 138-139 G 4
Borj Jenein o **TN** 190-191 H 5
Borj M'Chiguig o **TN** 190-191 H 4
Borj Slougui o **TN** 190-191 H 4
Borko o **AFG** 136-137 L 4
Borkou ⊥ **TCH** 198-199 H 3
Borkou-Ennedi-Tibesti □ **TCH** 198-199 H 4
Borkum ∾ **D** 92-93 J 2
Borlänge o **S** 86-87 G 6
Borne o **DZ** 190-191 F 8
Borneo = Kalimantan ∾ 164-165 B 4
Bornholm ∾ **DK** 86-87 G 9
Bornholmsgattet ≈ 86-87 G 9
Borno □ **WAN** 198-199 E 6

Botija, Ilha da ∾ **BR** 66-67 F 4
Botijón o **YV** 60-61 J 3
Botin, El o **YV** 60-61 F 4
Botitembongo o **ZRE** 210-211 G 4
Botkul, ozero o **RUS** 126-127 G 6
Botlih o **RUS** 126-127 G 6
Bot Makak o **CAM** 210-211 C 2
Botolan o **RP** 160-161 D 5
Botomoju o **RI** 164-165 H 3
Botopasi o **SME** 62-63 G 3
Botoşani ★ **RO** 102-103 E 4
Botou o **BF** (EST) 202-203 L 3
Botou o **BF** (EST) 204-205 E 2
Botou o **VRC** 154-155 K 2
Botro o **CI** 202-203 H 6
Botswana ■ **RB** 218-219 D 5
Bottenhavet ≈ 86-87 J 6
Botterkloof o **ZA** 220-221 D 5
Bottineau o **USA** 42-43 G 1
Bottle Creek o **GB** 54-55 K 4
Botua o **CI** 202-203 H 6
Botuali o **ZRE** 210-211 F 4
Botucatu o **BR** 72-73 F 7
Botulu o • **RUS** 118-119 J 3
Botumirim o **BR** 72-73 J 4
Botuobuja, Ulahan ~ **RUS** 118-119 E 5
Botwood o **CDN** 38-39 I R 4
Bou ~ **CI** 202-203 H 5
Bou Akba o **DZ** 188-189 H 6
Bouaflé o **CI** 202-203 H 6
Bou Akba o **DZ** 188-189 H 6
Bouaké • **CI** 202-203 H 6
Bou Alam o **DZ** 190-191 C 4
Boū Naïreh o **RMM** 196-197 J 5
Bou Ali o **DZ** 188-189 K 5
Bou Ali, Oued o **DZ** 190-191 D 5
Bou-Allala, Hassi < **DZ** 188-189 K 5
Bouam o **CAM** 204-205 K 6
Bouânane o **MA** 188-189 K 4
Bouandougou o **CI** 202-203 H 5
Bouanri o **DY** 204-205 E 3
Bouansa o **RCB** 210-211 E 4
Bouar ★ **RCA** 206-207 B 6
Buârfa o **MA** 188-189 L 4
Boū Aïssaa, Hassi < **DZ** 188-189 K 7
Boualem o **DZ** 190-191 C 4
Bouba Ndjida, Parc National de ⊥ **CAM** 206-207 B 4
Boubela o **CI** 202-203 G 7
Bou Bernous, Hassi < **DZ** 188-189 K 7
Boubon o **RN** 202-203 L 3
Boubouri o **RN** 202-203 H 7
Bouca o **RCA** 206-207 D 5
Boucaut Bay ≈ 174-175 C 2
Bouchard o **RA** 78-79 H 3
Bouchette, Lac- o **CDN** 38-39 H 4
Bouckaville o **DZ** 190-191 E 1
Boucle du Baoulé, Parc National de la ⊥ **RMM** 202-203 F 2
Boudamasa o **TCH** 206-207 B 4
Boudbouda ~ **RIM** 196-197 C 5
Boudenib o **MA** 188-189 K 5
Boudeuse Cay ∾ **SY** 224 C 3
Boū Dîb o **RMM** 196-197 J 5
Boudjour o **MA** 188-189 D 7
Bou Kadir o **DZ** 190-191 C 2
Boudoua o **RCA** 206-207 D 6
Boudtenga o **BF** 202-203 K 3
Bouénguidi ~ **G** 210-211 D 4
Bouenza o **RCB** 210-211 D 4
Bouenza □ **RCB** 210-211 D 5
Bougaa o **DZ** 190-191 C 2
Boū Gâdoûm o **RIM** (HCH) 196-197 F 6
Boū Gâdoûm o **RIM** (HCH) 202-203 G 2
Bougainville, Cape ▲ **AUS** 172-173 H 2
Bougainville, Cape ▲ **GB** 78-79 L 6
Bougainville Island ∾ **PNG** 184 I b 2
Bougainville Reef ∾ **AUS** 174-175 J 4
Bougainville Strait ≈ 184 I c 2
Bougainville Trench ≈ 183 G 3
Bougaroun, Cap ▲ **DZ** 190-191 F 1
Boughessa ~ **RMM** 196-197 M 4
Bougouni o **RCA** 206-207 E 5
Bougouni o **RMM** 202-203 G 4
Bougourba ~ **BF** 202-203 K 4
Bougouso o **CI** 202-203 G 5
Bougtob o **DZ** 190-191 C 3
Bouguer, Cape ▲ **AUS** 180-181 D 4
Boū Guettâra < **RIM** 196-197 C 5
Bou Hadjar o **DZ** 190-191 C 2
Bou Iblane, Jbel ▲ **MA** 188-189 J 4
Bou-Izakarn o **MA** 188-189 G 4
Boujad o **MA** 188-189 H 4
Boujdour, Cap ▲ **MA** 188-189 D 7
Bou Kadir o **DZ** 190-191 C 2
Bou Kahil, Djebel ▲ **DZ** 190-191 D 3
Boukan o **IR** 128-129 M 4
Bou Keltoum, Jbel ▲ **MA** 188-189 K 3
Boukoko o **RCA** 206-207 D 6
Boukoula o **CAM** 204-205 K 3
Boukoumbé o **DY** 202-203 L 4
Boukra o **MA** 188-189 D 7
Boula Ibib o **CAM** 204-205 K 4
Boulal o **RMM** 202-203 F 2
Boulal o **SN** 202-203 C 2
Boū Lanouâr o **RIM** 196-197 B 4
Boulaouane • **MA** 188-189 G 4
Boulay ~ **MA** 188-189 H 4
Boulé o **SN** 202-203 C 2
Boulemane o **MA** 188-189 J 4
Boulgou o **BF** 202-203 L 3
Bouli ~ **RMM** 196-197 K 3
Bouli o **RIM** 196-197 E 7
Boulia o **AUS** 174-175 E 7
Boulogne-sur-Mer ★ **F** 90-91 H 6
Boulouli o **RMM** 202-203 G 2
Boulsa o **BF** 202-203 K 3

Boulsmail o **DZ** 190-191 D 2
Boultoum o **RN** 198-199 E 5
Boumaine-du-Dades o **MA** 188-189 J 5
Boumango o **G** 210-211 D 4
Boumba ~ **CAM** 210-211 D 2
Boumbé I ~ **RCA** 206-207 B 6
Boumbé II ~ **RCA** 206-207 B 6
Boumbia o **CI** 202-203 G 7
Boumboum o **RMM** 202-203 K 2
Boumda National Park ⊥ **AUS** 180-181 K 4
Boûmdeïd o **RIM** 196-197 E 6
Boumerdes o **DZ** 190-191 D 2
Boum Kabir o **TCH** 206-207 C 3
Boumia o **MA** 188-189 J 4
Boum Mréga ~ **RIM** 196-197 F 4
Bouna o **CI** 202-203 J 5
Bou Naceur, Ibel ▲ **MA** 188-189 K 4
Boū Nâga o **RIM** 196-197 D 5
Boū Nâga < **RMM** 196-197 D 5
Bozkir o **TR** 128-129 E 4
Boundary o **USA** 40-41 F 1
Boundary Mountains ▲ **USA** 46-47 N 3
Boundary Peak ▲ **USA** 40-41 E 6
Boundary Ranges ▲ **CDN** 32-33 J 3
Boundiali o **CI** 202-203 G 5
Boundji o **RCB** 210-211 E 4
Boungo ~ **RCA** 206-207 D 4
Boungou o **RCA** 206-207 C 5
Bouniandjé ~ **G** 210-211 D 3
Bounkiling o **SN** 202-203 C 3
Bounoum ~ **SN** 202-203 C 2
Bountiful o **USA** 40-41 J 5
Bountiful Islands ∾ **AUS** 174-175 D 5
Bounty Islands ∾ **NZ** 13 J 7
Bounty Plateau ≈ 13 J 7
Bounty Trough ≈ 13 J 7
Bouquet o **RA** 78-79 J 2
Bourarhet, Erg ⊥ **DZ** 190-191 G 7
Bourbonnais ~ **F** 90-91 J 8
Bourdel, Lac o **CDN** 36-37 M 6
Bourem o **RMM** 196-197 K 6
Bourg-en-Bresse o • **F** 90-91 K 8
Bourges ★ • **F** 90-91 J 8
Bourgogne ~ **F** 90-91 K 8
Bourgogne ∴ **F** 90-91 K 8
Bourgoin-Jallieu o **F** 90-91 K 9
Bourg-Saint-Maurice o **F** 90-91 L 9
Bouria o **DZ** 190-191 D 2
Bourke o **AUS** 178-179 H 6
Bournemouth o **GB** 90-91 G 6
Bourrah o **CAM** 204-205 K 3
Bourza o **TCH** 206-207 B 3
Bourzanga o **BF** 202-203 K 3
Bous, Adrar ▲ **RN** 198-199 D 2
Boussaada o • **DZ** 190-191 E 2
Bousse o **BF** 202-203 K 3
Boussemghoun o **DZ** 190-191 C 4
Bousso o **TCH** 206-207 C 3
Bousso River o **CDN** 30-31 M 4
Boussouma o **BF** 202-203 K 3
Boutilimit o **RIM** 196-197 C 6
Boutougou Fara o **SN** 202-203 D 3
Boutourou, Monts ▲ **CI** 202-203 J 5
Bouza o **RN** 198-199 C 5
Bouzghaïa o **DZ** 190-191 C 2
Bovill o **USA** 40-41 F 2
Bowbells o **USA** 42-43 F 1
Bowdle o **USA** 42-43 H 3
Bowdon o **USA** 42-43 H 2
Bowell Islands ∾ **CDN** 30-31 W 3
Bowen o **RA** 78-79 F 3
Bowen o **USA** 46-47 C 5
Bowen, Cape ▲ **AUS** 174-175 H 4
Bowenville o **AUS** 178-179 L 4
Bowers Basin ≈ 22-23 E 5
Bowers Ridge ≈ 22-23 E 5
Bowie o **USA** 44-45 J 3
Bowie National Historic Site, Fort ∴ **USA** 44-45 D 4
Bowling Green o **USA** (KY) 46-47 E 7
Bowling Green o **USA** (MO) 42-43 L 6
Bowling Green o **USA** (OH) 46-47 F 5
Bowling Green o **USA** (VA) 46-47 K 6
Bowling Green Bay National Park ⊥ **AUS** 174-175 J 6
Bowman o **USA** 42-43 F 2
Bowman Bay ≈ 36-37 N 2
Bowman Island ∾ **ARK** 16 G 11
Bowmans Corner o **USA** 40-41 H 2
Bowokan, Kepulauan ∾ **RI** 164-165 H 5
Bowral o **AUS** 180-181 L 3
Bow River ~ **AUS** 172-173 H 3
Bow River ~ **CDN** 32-33 O 6
Bowron Lake Provincial Park ⊥ **CDN** 32-33 N 5
Bowser o **CDN** 32-33 H 7
Bowutu Mountains ▲ **PNG** 183 D 4
Bowwood o **Z** 218-219 D 4
Box Elder Creek ~ **USA** 42-43 C 2
Box Elder Creek ~ **USA** 42-43 G 2
Box Lake o **CDN** 30-31 Q 6
Boxwood Hill o **AUS** 176-177 E 7
Boyabat o **TR** 128-129 F 2
Boyacá o **CO** (BOL) 60-61 D 5
Boyacá o **CO** (BOY) 60-61 E 5
Boyang o **VRC** 156-157 K 4
Boyce o **USA** 44-45 L 4
Boyd o **CDN** 34-35 H 3
Boyd, Lac o **CDN** 38-39 E 4
Boyd River ~ **AUS** 178-179 M 5
Boyelé o **RCB** 210-211 G 5
Boyeros o **C** 54-55 G 4
Boyle o **USA** 42-43 F 6
Boyer River ~ **CDN** 30-31 L 2
Brasília o **BR** 72-73 G 3

Boyer River ~ **USA** 42-43 K 5
Boyle o **CDN** 32-33 O 4
Boyle = Mainistir na Búille o **IRL** 90-91 C 5
Boylston o **USA** 38-39 O 6
Boyne o **ZA** 218-219 E 6
Boyne Valley ~ **IRL** 90-91 D 5
Boyolali o **RI** 168 D 3
Boysen Reservoir < **USA** 42-43 C 4
Boyte o **CDN** 32-33 O 4
Boyuibe o **BOL** 70-71 F 7
Boyup Brook o **AUS** 176-177 D 6
Bozburun o **TR** 128-129 C 4
Bozcaada ∾ **TR** 128-129 B 3
Bozdağlar ▲ **TR** 128-129 B 3
Bozdoğan o **TR** 128-129 C 4
Boždomova, mys ▲ **RUS** 120-121 T 3
Bozeman o **USA** 40-41 J 3
Bozen = Bolzano o • **I** 100-101 C 1
Bozhou o **VRC** 154-155 J 5
Bozkir o **TR** 128-129 E 4
Bozkol o **KA** 126-127 O 5
Bozok Yaylâsı ▲ **TR** 128-129 F 3
Bozoum o **RCA** 206-207 C 5
Bozova o **TR** 128-129 H 4
Boztüyük o **TR** 128-129 D 3
Boøzyazı o **TR** 128-129 F 4
Brabant, Île ∾ **ARK** 16 G 30
Bračٍ ∾ **HR** 100-101 F 3
Bracciano, Lago di o **I** 100-101 D 3
Bräcke o **S** 86-87 G 5
Brackett Lake o **CDN** 30-31 G 3
Brackettville o **USA** 44-45 G 5
Bracknell o **GB** 90-91 G 6
Braclavka o **RUS** 124-125 B 3
Braço do Lontra ~ **BR** 68-69 F 7
Braço do Norte o **BR** 74-75 F 7
Braço Menor do Araguaia ou Jauaés ~ **BR** 68-69 D 7
Brad o **RO** 102-103 C 4
Brad o **USA** 44-45 H 3
Brádano ~ **I** 100-101 E 4
Bradenton o **USA** 48-49 G 6
Bradford o **GB** 90-91 G 5
Bradford o **USA** (IL) 46-47 D 5
Bradford o **USA** (PA) 46-47 J 5
Bradley o **USA** 40-41 D 8
Bradore, Baie de ≈ 38-39 Q 3
Bradwell o **CDN** 34-35 C 5
Brady o **USA** 44-45 H 4
Brady Glacier ⊂ **USA** 32-33 R 2
Braemar o **GB** 90-91 F 3
Braemar o **USA** 180-181 E 2
Braga o • **P** 98-99 C 5
Bragado o **RA** 78-79 J 3
Bragança o **BR** 68-69 E 2
Bragança ∴ **P** 98-99 D 4
Bragança o **BR** 68-69 E 2
Bragança Paulista o **BR** 72-73 G 7
Bragg, For: o **USA** 40-41 C 5
Bragg Creek o **CDN** 32-33 N 6
Braham o **USA** 42-43 L 3
Brahestad = **FIN** 88-89 H 4
Brahim, Hassi < **MA** 188-189 G 6
Brahmani ~ **IND** 142-143 E 5
Brahmapur o **IND** 142-143 D 6
Brahmaputra ~ 142-143 H 2
Braidwood o **AUS** 180-181 K 3
Brainerd o **CDN** 32-33 L 4
Brainerd o **USA** 42-43 K 2
Braintree o **GB** 90-91 H 6
Brajarajnagar o **IND** 142-143 C 5
Brakna □ **RIM** 196-197 D 6
Brakpan o **ZA** 220-221 J 3
Braksprutit o **ZA** 220-221 H 4
Brakwater o **NAM** 216-217 D 11
Brålos o **GR** 100-101 J 5
Bramhapuri o **IND** 138-139 G 9
Brampton o **CDN** 38-39 E 7
Brampton Islands ∾ **AUS** 174-175 K 7
Bramwell o **AUS** 174-175 G 4
Branca, Serra ▲ **BR** 68-69 F 5
Branch o **CDN** 38-39 I S 5
Branch Creek ~ **AUS** 174-175 E 5
Branchville o **USA** 48-49 H 3
Branco, Ilhéu ∾ **CV** 202-203 B 5
Branco, Rio ~ **BR** 62-63 D 4
Branco, Rio ~ **BR** 66-67 G 7
Branco, Rio ~ **BR** 66-67 H 4
Branco, Rio ~ **BR** 70-71 E 3
Branco, Rio ~ **BR** 70-71 H 3
Branco, Rio ~ **BR** 70-71 G 2
Branco ou Cabixi, Rio ~ **BR** 70-71 G 3
Brandberg ~ **NAM** 216-217 C 10
Brandbu o **N** 92-93 M 3
Brandenburg o • **D** 92-93 M 3
Brandenburg □ **D** 92-93 M 2
Brandenburg an der Havel o • **D** 92-93 M 2
Brandfort o **ZA** 220-221 H 4
Brandon o **CDN** 34-35 G 6
Brandon o **USA** (FL) 48-49 G 6
Brandon o **USA** (MS) 48-49 D 3
Brandon o **USA** (SD) 42-43 J 4
Brandsen o **RA** 78-79 K 3
Brandvlei o **ZA** 220-221 E 5
Brandýs nad Labem-Stará Boleslav o **CZ** 92-93 N 3
Branford o **USA** 48-49 G 5
Brang, Kuala o **MAL** 162-163 E 2
Braniewo o **PL** 92-93 P 1
Bran'ka o **UA** 102-103 L 3
Branqueada do Salto o **BR** 74-75 D 9
Bransan o **SN** 202-203 D 3
Bransfield Strait ≈ 16 G 30
Brantford o **CDN** 38-39 D 7
Brantôme o **F** 90-91 H 9
Brás o **BR** 66-67 H 4
Brasil = Brazil ■ **BR** 72-73 G 3
Brasília o **BR** 72-73 G 3
Brasiléia o **BR** 70-71 C 2

Brasiléia o **BR** 70-71 C 2
Brasília ★••• **BR** 72-73 G 3
Brasília, Lago de ~ **BR** 72-73 G 3
Brasília de Minas o **BR** 72-73 H 4
Braslândia o **BR** 72-73 F 3
Braslav o **BY** 94-95 K 4
Brasnorte o **BR** 70-71 H 2
Brass o **WAN** 204-205 G 6
Brasschaat o **B** 92-93 H 3
Brassey, Banjaran ▲ **MAL** 160-161 B 10
Brassey, Mount ▲ **AUS** 178-179 C 2
Brassey Range ▲ **AUS** 176-177 G 3
Brasstown Bald ▲ **USA** 48-49 G 2
Bratagi o **RI** 162-163 C 3
Bratislava ★••• **SK** 92-93 O 4
Bratovoeşti o **RO** 102-103 C 5
Bratsk ★ **RUS** 116-117 K 7
Bratskoe vodohranilišče < **RUS** 116-117 J 8
Bratskoye Vodohranilishche = Bratskoe vodohranilišče < **RUS** 116-117 K 8
Brattleboro o **USA** 46-47 M 4
Braulio Carrillo, Parque Nacional ⊥ **CR** 52-53 C 6
Braúnas o **BR** 72-73 J 5
Braunau am Inn o **A** 92-93 M 4
Braunlage o **D** 92-93 L 3
Braunschweig o • **D** 92-93 L 2
Brava, Ilha ∾ **CV** 202-203 B 6
Brava, La o **RA** 76-77 G 6
Brava, Laguna la o **RA** 78-79 H 2
Bravo, Cerro ▲ **BOL** (COC) 70-71 C 6
Bravo, Cerro ▲ **BOL** (POT) 76-77 D 2
Bravo, Cerro ▲ **RCH** 76-77 D 2
Bravo, El o **RA** 76-77 C 5
Bravo del Norte, Rio ~ **MEX** 50-51 J 3
Bravo River ~ **BR** 52-53 K 3
Brawley o **USA** 40-41 G 9
Bray o **ZA** 220-221 F 2
Bray = Bré o **IRL** 90-91 D 5
Bray Island ∾ **CDN** 24-25 h 6
Bray-sur-Seine o **F** 90-91 J 7
Brazeau, Mount ▲ **CDN** 32-33 M 5
Brazeau River ~ **CDN** 32-33 M 5
Brazil = Brasil ■ **BR** 74-75 C 2
Brazil Basin ≈ 6-7 G 10
Brazilian Highlands = Brasileiro, Planalto ⊥ **BR** 72-73 G 3
Brazo Aná Cuá ~ **PY** 76-77 J 4
Brazo de Loma ~ **CO** 60-61 D 3
Brazos River ~ **USA** 44-45 H 3
Brazo Sur del Rio Coig ~ **RA** 80 E 5
Brazzaville ★ **RCB** 210-211 D 5
Brčko o **BIH** 100-101 G 2
Brdy ▲ **CZ** 92-93 M 4
Bré = Bray o **IRL** 90-91 D 5
Brea, Cordillera de la ▲ **RA** 76-77 C 5
Brea, La o **TT** 60-61 L 2
Breaden, Lake o **AUS** 176-177 H 2
Breaksea Sound ≈ 182 A 6
Brea Pozo o **RA** 76-77 F 5
Breas, Las o **RCH** 76-77 B 5
Brebes o **RI** 168 C 3
Breckenridge o **USA** (CO) 42-43 D 5
Breckenridge o **USA** (MN) 42-43 J 2
Breckenridge o **USA** (TX) 44-45 H 3
Brecknock, Peninsula ∪ **RCH** 80 E 7
Brecon o **GB** 90-91 F 6
Brecon Beacons National Park ⊥ **GB** 90-91 F 6
Breda o • **NL** 92-93 H 3
Bredasdorp o **ZA** 220-221 E 7
Bredbo o **AUS** 180-181 K 3
Bredbyn o **S** 86-87 H 5
Brèdi, ostrov ∾ **RUS** 84-85 d 2
Bredsel o **S** 86-87 K 4
Bredy o **RUS** 124-125 C 3
Breede ~ **ZA** 220-221 E 7
Breeza Plains Out Station o **AUS** 174-175 H 4
Bregalnica ~ **MK** 100-101 J 4
Bregenz o **A** 92-93 K 5
Bregovo o **BG** 102-103 C 5
Bréhal o **F** 90-91 G 7
Brehovskie ostrova ∾ **RUS** 108-109 U 6
Breidafjörður ≈ 86-87 b 2
Breivikbotn o **N** 86-87 L 1
Brejão da Caatinga o **BR** 68-69 H 7
Brejinho o **BR** 68-69 G 3
Brejo, Riachão do ~ **BR** 68-69 J 5
Brejo da Madre de Deus o **BR** 68-69 K 6
Brejo de São Félix o **BR** 68-69 G 4
Brejo do Cruz o **BR** 68-69 K 5
Brejo do Serra ~ **BR** 68-69 G 7
Brejo Grande o **BR** (CEA) 68-69 J 5
Brejo Grande o **BR** (SER) 68-69 K 7
Brejolândia o **BR** 72-73 J 2
Brejo Velho, Riachão ~ **BR** 72-73 J 2
Brekken o **N** 86-87 E 5
Brekstad o **N** 86-87 D 5
Brelen o **USA** 42-43 G 2
Bremangerland ∾ **N** 86-87 B 6
Bremen o • **D** 92-93 K 2
Bremen o **USA** 48-49 F 3
Bremer Bay ≈ 176-177 E 7
Bremer Bay o **USA** 176-177 E 7
Bremerhaven o **D** 92-93 K 2
Bremer Island ∾ **AUS** 174-175 D 3
Bremer Range ▲ **AUS** 176-177 F 6
Bremerton o **USA** 40-41 C 2
Bremervörde o **D** 92-93 K 2
Brenãs, Las o **RA** 76-77 G 4
Brenham o **USA** 44-45 J 4
Brennerpaß = Passo del Brennero ▲ **A** 92-93 L 5
Brennevinsfjorden ≈ 84-85 L 2
Brenta ~ **I** 100-101 C 2
Brentford Bay ≈ 24-25 Z 5
Brenzia o **DZ** 190-191 C 4
Brep o **PK** 138-139 D 1
Bresaylor o **CDN** 32-33 C 1
Bréscia o • **I** 100-101 C 2
Bresnahan, Mount ▲ **AUS** 176-177 D 1
Bressanone = Brixen o **I** 100-101 C 1
Bressuire o **F** 90-91 G 8

Burhan Budai Shan ▲ VRC 144-145 K 3
Burhan buudai ▲ MAU 148-149 C 5
Burhaniye ○ TR 128-129 B 3
Burhânpur ○ IND 138-139 F 9
Burhi Rapti ~ IND 142-143 D 2
Buri ○ BR 72-73 F 7
Buri ○ ER 200-201 J 5
Burias Island ~ RP 160-161 E 6
Burias Pass ≈ 160-161 E 6
Burica, Punta ▲ PA 52-53 C 7
Buried Village ∴ NZ 182 F 3
Burigi, Lake ○ EAT 212-213 C 5
Burigi Game Reservat ⊥ EAT 212-213 C 5
Burin ○ CDN 38-39 I R 5
Burin Peninsula ⋃ CDN 38-39 I R 5
Buri Ram ○ THA 158-159 G 3
Buritama ○ BR 72-73 E 6
Buriti, Ribeiro ~ BR 70-71 K 7
Buriti, Rio ~ BR 68-69 G 3
Buriti, Rio ~ BR 70-71 H 3
Buriti Alegre ○ BR 72-73 F 5
Buriti Bravo ○ BR 68-69 G 4
Buriticupu, Rio ~ BR 68-69 F 4
Buriti dos Lopes ○ BR 68-69 H 3
Buritirama ○ BR 68-69 G 7
Buritis ○ BR 72-73 G 3
Burjassot ○ E 98-99 G 5
Burji ○ WAN 204-205 H 3
Burkand'ja ○ RUS 120-121 M 2
Burkanoko, Lake ○ AUS 178-179 H 5
Burkburnett ○ USA 44-45 H 2
Burke ○ USA 42-43 H 4
Burke and Wills Roadhouse ○ AUS 174-175 F 6
Burke Channel ≈ 32-33 G 6
Burke Development Road ‖ AUS 174-175 F 6
Burke River ~ AUS 178-179 E 1
Burke's Pass ⋗ ZA 220-221 C 4
Burkesville ○ USA 46-47 F 7
Burketown ○ AUS 174-175 E 6
Burkeville ○ USA 46-47 J 7
Burke & Wills Monument • AUS 178-179 E 6
Burkina Faso ■ BF 202-203 H 4
Burkitkala ∴ US 136-137 G 4
Bürkitti, tau ▲ KA 124-125 H 4
Burkot ○ RUS 120-121 P 3
Burk's Falls ○ CDN 38-39 E 6
Burla ○ RUS 124-125 M 2
Burleigh ○ AUS 174-175 G 7
Burleson ○ USA 44-45 J 3
Burley ○ USA 40-41 H 4
Burlingame ○ USA 42-43 K 6
Burlington ○ CDN (NFL) 38-39 Q 4
Burlington ○ CDN (ONT) 38-39 E 7
Burlington ○ USA (CO) 42-43 F 6
Burlington ○ USA (IA) 46-47 C 5
Burlington ○ USA (KS) 42-43 J 6
Burlington ○ USA (NC) 48-49 J 1
Burlington ○ USA (VT) 46-47 M 3
Burney ○ USA 40-41 D 5
Burney, Monte ▲ RCH 80 D 6
Burnham Out Station ○ AUS 178-179 F 2
Burnie-Somerset ○ AUS 180-181 H 6
Burni Gandak ~ IND 142-143 D 2
Burning Coal Mines ∴ USA 42-43 F 2
Burnley ○ GB 90-91 F 5
Burnpur ○ IND 142-143 E 4
Burns ○ USA (CO) 42-43 D 6
Burns ○ USA (OR) 40-41 E 4
Burnside ○ CDN 38-39 I 4
Burnside, Lake ○ AUS 176-177 G 2
Burnside River ~ CDN 30-31 O 7
Burns Indian Reservation ⋊ USA 40-41 K 4
Burns Junction ○ USA 40-41 F 4
Burns Lake ○ CDN 32-33 H 4
Bumtbush River ~ CDN 38-39 E 4
Burnt Creek ○ CDN 38-39 Q 7
Burnt Ground ○ BS 54-55 H 3
Burnt Lake = Lac Brûlé ○ CDN 38-39 N 2
Burnt Ranch ○ USA 40-41 C 5
Burntwood Lake ○ CDN 34-35 G 4
Burntwood River ~ CDN 34-35 G 3
Buro ~ RUS 108-109 W 6
Burpee, Cape ▲ CDN 24-25 i 6
Burqin ○ VRC 146-147 H 2
Burra ○ AUS 180-181 E 2
Burracoppin ○ AUS 176-177 E 5
Burramurra Out Station ○ AUS 174-175 D 7
Burras, Rio de las ~ RA 76-77 D 2
Burrel ○ AL 100-101 H 4
Burrendong Reservoir < AUS 180-181 K 2
Burren Junction ○ AUS 178-179 K 6
Burrgum Hill ▲ AUS 178-179 M 3
Burrinjuck Reservoir < AUS 180-181 K 3
Burro, El ○ YV 60-61 H 4
Burro, Serranías del ▲ MEX 50-51 H 3
Burr Point ▲ USA 22-23 U 3
Burrton ○ USA 42-43 J 6
Burrumbeet, Lake ○ AUS 180-181 G 4
Burrum Heads ○ AUS 178-179 M 3
Bursa ○ TR 128-129 C 2
Bür Safâğa ○ ET 194-195 F 4
Bür Sa'id ★ ET 194-195 F 2
Bursting Brook ~ CDN 38-39 R 4
Bür Südân ★ SUD 200-201 H 3
Bür Taufîq ○ ET 194-195 F 2
Bür Tinle ○ SP 208-209 H 5
Burton, Baie de ○ ZRE 212-213 B 6

Burton, Lac ○ CDN 36-37 K 7
Burton upon Trent ○ GB 90-91 G 5
Burträsk ○ S 86-87 K 4
Buru, Pulau ~ RI 166-167 D 3
Burubajtal ○ KA 124-125 G 6
Buru Island ~ AUS 183 B 5
Burukan ○ RUS 122-123 P 2
Burumburum ~ WAN 204-205 H 3
Burunda ~ RUS 118-119 N 3
Buruntuma ○ RUS 118-119 N 3
Buruolah ~ RUS 118-119 N 3
Bururi ○ BU 212-213 B 5
Bururu ~ PNG 183 B 2
Burutu ○ WAN 204-205 F 6
Burwash Bay ≈ 36-37 O 2
Burwell ○ USA 42-43 H 5
Burwick ○ GB 90-91 F 2
Buryatia = Respublika Burjatija □ RUS 116-117 K 9
Buryn' ○ UA 102-103 H 3
Buryncyk mujisi ▲ KA 126-127 J 5
Burynšik, mys ▲ KA 126-127 J 5
Bury Saint Edmunds ○ • GB 90-91 H 5
Buš ○ ET 194-195 E 3
Busaira ○ SYR 128-129 J 5
Busaità', al- ⋊ KSA 130-131 F 3
Busang ~ RI 162-163 K 4
Busanga ○ ZRE (EQU) 210-211 J 4
Busanga ○ ZRE (SHA) 214-215 C 6
Busanga Swamp ⋗ Z 218-219 C 2
Busango ○ ZRE 214-215 C 5
Busayya, Mahfar al- ○ IRQ 130-131 K 2
Busby ○ CDN 32-33 O 5
Büsehr ○ IR 134-135 D 4
Büšehr, Bandar-e ☆ • IR 134-135 D 4
Busembatia ○ EAU 212-213 D 3
Bushat ○ AL 100-101 G 4
Bushell ○ CDN 30-31 P 6
Bushenyi ○ EAU 212-213 C 4
Bushe River Indian Reserve ⋊ CDN 30-31 L 6
Bushman Drawings ∴ ZA 220-221 F 5
Bushman Paintings ∴ SD 220-221 K 3
Bushman Paintings ∴ Z 218-219 F 3
Bushy Park ○ AUS 178-179 B 2
Busia ○ EAU 212-213 D 3
Businga ○ ZRE 210-211 H 2
Busira ~ ZRE 210-211 G 4
Busisi ○ EAT 212-213 D 5
Bus'k ⋗ UA 102-103 D 3
Busoga □ EAK 212-213 E 3
Busonga ~ EAK 212-213 E 3
Buşra aš-sám ○•• SYR 128-129 G 6
Busse ~ RUS 122-123 B 3
Busselton ○ AUS 176-177 C 6
Busser ~ SUD 206-207 H 5
Bussol', proliv ≈ RUS 122-123 Q 5
Bustah, ozero ○ RUS 110-111 Y 3
Bustamante ○ MEX 50-51 K 6
Bustamante, Punta ▲ RA 80 F 5
Bustamante, Punta ▲ RA 80 F 5
Buston ○ TJ 136-137 L 4
Busu ~ RI 164-165 L 4
Busuanga ○ RP 160-161 C 6
Busuanga Island ~ RP 160-161 D 6
Busu-Djanoa ○ ZRE 210-211 H 3
Busu-Kwanga ○ ZRE 210-211 H 3
Busu-Mandji ○ ZRE 210-211 H 3
Busungwe ~ EAU 174-175 F 5
Busunju ○ EAU 212-213 D 3
Busunu ○ GH 202-203 K 5
But ○ PNG 183 B 2
Buta ○ ZRE 210-211 K 2
Butahuao, Cerro ▲ RA 78-79 D 5
Butain, al ○ KSA 130-131 H 4
Butajira ○ ETH 208-209 D 4
Butak ○ PK 134-135 K 4
Buta Mallin, Paso de ▲ RA 78-79 D 4
Buta Ranquil ○ RA 78-79 E 4
Butare ○•• RWA 212-213 B 5
Butaritari Island ⋊ KIB 13 J 2
Butaš, ozero ○ RUS 114-115 G 7
Butat Raya ⋊ SUD 206-207 G 4
Bute ○ AUS 180-181 D 2
Butedale ○ CDN 32-33 F 4
Bute Giarti ○ ETH 208-209 C 6
Bute Inlet ≈ 32-33 H 6
Butemba ○ EAU 212-213 C 3
Butembo ○ ZRE 212-213 B 3
Butha-Buthe ○ LS 220-221 J 4
Buthidaung ○ MYA 142-143 H 5
Buthurst Inlet ≈ 30-31 Q 7
Butiá ○ BR 74-75 E 6
Butiaba ○ EAU 212-213 C 3
Butler ○ USA (AL) 48-49 D 3
Butler ○ USA (GA) 48-49 F 3
Butler ○ USA (MO) 42-43 K 6
Butler ○ USA (PA) 46-47 J 5
Butler Creek ~ CDN 34-35 Q 5
Butolo, al ○ BR 68-69 G 6
Buton, Pulau ~ RI 164-165 H 6
Buton, Selat ≈ 164-165 H 6
Buton Utara Reserve ⋊ RI 164-165 H 6
Buto River ~ CDN 32-33 F 5
Butrint ∴•• AL 100-101 H 5
Butru ○ AUS 178-179 E 1
Butte ○ USA (MT) 40-41 H 3
Butte ○ USA (NE) 42-43 H 4
Butte, The ▲ AUS 20-21 S 4
Butterpot Provincial Park ⊥ CDN 38-39 I R 5
Butterworth ○ MAL 162-163 D 2
Butterworth ○ ZA 220-221 J 6
Butt of Lewis ▲ GB 90-91 D 2
Button Islands ~ CDN 36-37 R 4
Butu ○ CAM 204-205 H 8
Butuan ☆ RP 160-161 F 8
Butuan Bay ≈ 160-161 F 8
Butuí, Rio ~ BR 76-77 J 5
Butung = Pulau Buton ~ RI 164-165 H 6
Butung, Tanjung ▲ RI 164-165 H 6
Butuo ○ VRC 156-157 C 3
Buturlinovka ○ RUS 102-103 M 2
Butwal ○ NEP 144-145 D 7
Buucagaan ○ MAU 148-149 D 4

Buulobarde ○ SP 212-213 K 2
Buur Hakkaba ○ SP 212-213 K 2
Buuva Island ~ EAU 212-213 D 3
Buwaiš ~ Y 132-133 F 6
Buwenge ○ EAU 212-213 D 3
Buxar ○ IND 142-143 D 3
Buxton ○ GUY 62-63 E 2
Büyer Ahmad-o-Kühgilüye □ IR 134-135 D 3
Buyo ○ CI 202-203 G 6
Buyo, Lac de ○ CI 202-203 G 6
Buyspoort ○ ZA 220-221 F 6
Büyük Ada ○ TR 128-129 C 2
Büyükağrı Dağı (Ararat) ▲•• TR 128-129 J 3
Büyük-menderes N. ~ TR 128-129 B 3
Büyük Menderes Nehri ~ TR 128-129 B 3
Buyuni ○ EAT 214-215 K 4
Buyun Shan ▲ VRC 150-151 D 7
Buzan ○ RUS 96-97 F 10
Buzanaj, kum ⋊ KA 96-97 F 10
Buzău ⋗ RO 102-103 E 5
Buzău, Rio ~ RUS 96-97 J 6
Buzdjak ⋗ RUS 96-97 J 6
Buzi ○ MOC 218-219 H 4
Buzi Gonbad ○ AFG 146-147 M 2
Búzios ○ BR 68-69 L 5
Búzios, Cabo dos ▲ BR 72-73 K 7
Búzios, Ilha de ~ BR 68-69 L 5
Buzovna ○ AZ 128-129 J 7
Buzuluk ○ RUS 96-97 H 7
Buzuluk ~ RUS 102-103 N 2
Buzún, al- ○ Y 132-133 G 6
Büzyldyk ⋊ KA 124-125 E 3
Bwadela ○ PNG 183 E 2
Bwana-Mutombo ○ ZRE 216-217 E 3
Bwanga ○ EAT 212-213 C 5
Bwari ○ WAN 204-205 H 5
Bwatnapne ○ VAN 184 II b 2
Bwea Town ○ LB 202-203 F 7
Bwele-Milonda ~ ZRE 216-217 E 3
Bweni ○ EAT 214-215 K 4
Bwiam ○ WAG 202-203 B 6
Byadgi ○ IND 140-141 F 3
Byam Channel ≈ 24-25 T 3
Byam Martin Channel ≈ 24-25 S 2
Byam Martin Island ~ CDN 24-25 T 3
Bydgoszcz ☆ • PL 92-93 P 2
Byfield ○ AUS 178-179 L 2
Byfield National Park ⊥ AUS 178-179 L 2
Byford ○ AUS 176-177 D 6
Bygdeå ○ S 86-87 K 4
Bygin ~ KA 136-137 L 3
Bygin sukqimasy ⋊ KA 136-137 L 3
Bygland ~ N 86-87 C 7
Bykle ○ N 86-87 D 7
Bylas ○ USA 44-45 B 3
Bylok ○ TJ 136-137 M 4
Bylong ○ AUS 180-181 L 2
Bylot Island ~ CDN 24-25 g 4
Bynoe River ~ AUS 174-175 F 5
Byohori ○ IND 142-143 B 3
Byrakan ~ RUS 118-119 K 4
Byrd ○ ARK 16 F 25
Byrd Land ⋊ ARK 16 E 0
Byrock ○ AUS 178-179 J 6
Byron, Cape ▲ AUS 178-179 M 5
Byron, Isla ~ RCH 80 C 3
Byron Bay ○ 36-37 V 7
Byron Bay ≈ 178-179 M 5
Byron Sound ≈ 78-79 K 6
Byrranga, Gory ▲ RUS 108-109 U 5
Byske ○ S 86-87 K 4
Byskeälven ~ S 86-87 K 4
Byssa ~ RUS 122-123 D 2
Bystraja ~ RUS 108-109 V 5
Bystraja ~ RUS 120-121 S 6
Bystranka ○ RUS 124-125 N 2
Bystrjanka ~ RUS 124-125 N 2
Bystryj Istok ⋗ RUS 124-125 N 2
Bystryj Tanyp ~ RUS 96-97 J 6
Bystrzyca ~ PL 92-93 O 3
Bysyttah ○ RUS 118-119 N 3
Bytantaj ~ RUS 110-111 T 5
Bytom ○ PL 92-93 P 3
Bytów ○ PL 92-93 O 1
Byumba ○ RWA 212-213 C 4
Byxelkrok ○ S 86-87 H 8
Byzanz = Istanbul ★•• TR 128-129 C 2
Bzimah ○ LAR 192-193 K 4
Bzyb' ~ GE 126-127 D 6

C

Caača ○ TM 136-137 Q 6
Caacupé ○ PY 76-77 J 3
Caaguazú ○ PY 76-77 J 3
Caala ○ ANG 216-217 C 6
Caamaño Sound ≈ 32-33 F 5
Caapiranga ○ BR 66-67 G 4
Caapucu ○ PY 76-77 J 4
Caarapo ○ BR 76-77 J 2
Caatiba ○ BR 72-73 K 3
Caatingas ⋗ BR 68-69 G 7
Caazapá ⋗ PY 76-77 J 4
Cab ○ RP 160-161 F 8
Cabaad, Raas ⋊ SP 208-209 J 5
Cabacal, Rio ~ BR 70-71 H 4
Cabaceiras ○ BR 68-69 K 5
Cabadbaran ○ RP 160-161 F 8
Cabaiguán ○ C 54-55 F 3
Caballo ○ USA 44-45 D 3
Caballococha ○ PE 66-67 E 4
Caballones, Cayo ~ C 54-55 F 3
Caballo Reservoir < USA 44-45 D 3
Caballos, Bahía de ≈ 64-65 E 9

Caballos Mesteños, Llanos de los ⊥ MEX 50-51 G 3
Cabañas ○ C 54-55 D 3
Cabanatuan ○ RP 160-161 D 5
Cabangtohan ○ RP 160-161 F 7
Cabano ○ CDN 38-39 K 5
Cabarete, Punta ▲ DOM 54-55 K 5
Cabeça do Salsa, Igarapé ~ BR 66-67 F 5
Cabeceiras ○ BR (GOI) 72-73 G 3
Cabeceiras ○ BR (PIA) 68-69 G 4
Cabeceiras de Basto ○ P 98-99 D 4
Cabeço do Apa ~ BR 76-77 K 2
Cabedelo ○ BR 68-69 L 5
Cabelelo da Velha, Baía ≈ 68-69 F 2
Cabeza del Este, Cayo ~ C 54-55 F 4
Cabeza Mechuda, Punta ▲ MEX 50-51 D 5
Cabezas ○ BOL 70-71 F 6
Cabildo ○ RCH 78-79 D 2
Cabimas ○ YV 60-61 F 2
Cabinda □ ANG 210-211 C 6
Cabinda ☆ ANG (Cab) 210-211 D 6
Cabinet Mountains ▲ USA 40-41 H 1
Cabingaan Island ~ RP 160-161 D 10
Cabitutu, Rio ~ BR 72-73 L 4
Cable Beach ⊥ AUS 172-173 F 5
Cabo ○ BR 68-69 L 6
Cabo Blanco ○ RA 80 G 7
Cabo de Hornos, Parque Nacional ⊥ RCH 80 G 7
Cabo Delgado □ MOC 214-215 K 7
Cabo Frio, Ilha do ~ BR 72-73 K 7
Câboksar ○ IR 136-137 B 6
Cabo Ledo ○ ANG 216-217 B 4
Cabonga, Réservoir < CDN 38-39 F 5
Cabo Orange, Parque Nacional do ⊥ BR 62-63 J 3
Cabo Polonio, Parque Forestal de ⊥ ROU 74-75 D 10
Cabora Bassa, Lago de < MOC 218-219 F 2
Caborca ⋗ MEX 50-51 C 2
Cabo San Lucas ○ MEX 50-51 E 6
Cabot ○ USA 44-45 L 2
Cabot Strait ≈ 38-39 Q 5
Cabra Corral, Embalse < RA 76-77 D 3
Cabra Island ~ RP 160-161 D 6
Cabral ○ DOM 54-55 K 5
Cabral, Serra do ▲ BR 72-73 H 3
Cabramurra ○ AUS 180-181 K 3
Cabrera ○ CO 60-61 D 6
Cabrera ○ DOM 54-55 L 5
Cabreras, Las ⋃ C 54-55 G 4
Cabrero ○ RCH 78-79 C 4
Cabreúva ○ BR 72-73 G 7
Cabrillo National Monument • USA 40-41 F 4
Cabrobó ○ BR 68-69 J 6
Cabruta ○ YV 60-61 H 4
Cabuca ○ BR 70-71 H 4
Cabudare ○ YV 60-61 G 2
Cabugao ○ RP 160-161 D 4
Cabure ○ YV 60-61 G 2
Cabure, El ○ RA 76-77 K 3
Caburgua, Lago ○ RCH 78-79 D 5
Cabuyaro ○ CO 60-61 E 5
Čača ~ RUS 118-119 J 9
Caça do Mucossuo, Acampamento de ○ ANG 216-217 F 8
Caçador ○ BR 74-75 E 6
Čačak • YU 100-101 H 3
Cacao ○ F 62-63 H 3
Caçapava do Sul ○ BR 74-75 D 8
Cacaribaiteri ○ YV 66-67 G 2
Cacau Pirera ○ BR 66-67 G 4
Cachachi ○ PE 64-65 C 5
Cachapoal, Rio ~ RCH 78-79 D 3
Cacharí ○ RA 78-79 K 4
Cache ○ USA 44-45 H 2
Cache Creek ○ CDN 32-33 K 6
Cachendo ○ PE 70-71 E 8
Cache Peak ▲ USA 40-41 H 4
Cacheu ☆ GNB 202-203 B 3
Cacheu, Rio ~ GNB 202-203 C 3
Cachimbo, Serra do ▲ BR 66-67 J 6
Cachipo ○ YV 60-61 J 3
Cachira ○ CO 60-61 E 4
Cachoeira ○ BR (AMA) 66-67 C 2
Cachoeira ○ BR (BAH) 72-73 L 2
Cachoeira Alta ○ BR 72-73 E 5
Cachoeira de Goiás ○ BR 72-73 E 4
Cachoeira do Arari ○ BR 62-63 K 6
Cachoeira do Sul ○ BR 74-75 D 8
Cachoeiras de Macacu ○ BR 72-73 J 7
Cachoeirinha ○ BR 66-67 J 6
Cachoeirinha, Cachoeira ~ BR 66-67 J 6
Cachoeirinha, Corredeira ~ BR 66-67 J 6
Cachoeiro ○ BR 74-75 E 7
Cachoeiro de Itapemirim ○ BR 72-73 K 6
Cachos, Punta ▲ RCH 76-77 B 4
Cachueca ○ ANG 216-217 D 7
Cachuela Esperanza ○ BOL 70-71 F 2
Cacimba de Dentro ○ BR 68-69 L 5
Cacina ○ GNB 202-203 B 4
Caciporé, Rio ~ BR 62-63 J 4
Caciporé, Rio ~ BR 62-63 J 4
Cacique Doble ○ BR 74-75 D 6

Cacoal ○ BR 70-71 G 2
Cacocum ○ C 54-55 G 4
Cacolo ○ ANG 216-217 E 5
Caconda ○ ANG 216-217 C 6
Caçu ○ BR 72-73 E 5
Cacuaco ○ ANG 216-217 B 4
Cacuchi ~ ANG 216-217 D 6
Caico ○ BR 68-69 K 5
Cacula ○ ANG 216-217 B 6
Caicumba, Ilha ~ BR 72-73 L 4
Caculé ○ BR 72-73 J 3
Cacumbi ○ ANG 216-217 E 5
Cacuria ○ BR 66-67 E 6
Cacuso ○ ANG 216-217 C 4
Cada, Rio ~ CO 60-61 F 6
Cadadado ○ SP 208-209 H 5
Cadale ○ SP 212-213 L 2
Cadan ⋊ RUS 116-117 L 10
Cadarri, Rio ~ BR 66-67 J 6
Caddo Lake ○ USA 44-45 K 3
Čadegän ○ IR 134-135 D 2
Cadena, Arroyo de la ~ MEX 50-51 J 4
Cadereyta ○ MEX 50-51 J 5
Cadibarrawirracanna, Lake ○ AUS 178-179 C 5
Cadillac ○ CDN 34-35 C 6
Cadillac ○ USA 46-47 F 3
Cadill, Embalse el < RA 76-77 E 4
Cádiz ○ E 98-99 D 6
Cadiz ○ USA (KY) 46-47 E 7
Cadiz ○ USA (OH) 46-47 H 5
Cádiz, Golfo de ≈ 98-99 C 6
Cadlao Island ~ RP 160-161 C 7
Cadman = Urd gol ○ MAU 146-147 L 2
Čadobec ~ RUS 116-117 J 6
Cadogan Glacier ○ CDN 26-27 L 4
Cadogan Inlet ≈ 26-27 M 4
Cadomin ○ CDN 32-33 M 5
Cadotte Lake ○ CDN 32-33 N 4
Cadotte River ~ CDN 32-33 M 3
Cadoux ○ AUS 176-177 C 5
Caduman Point ⋊ RP 160-161 F 7
Caek ⋊ KS 146-147 B 5
Caen ☆ • F 90-91 G 7
Caerdydd = Cardiff ☆ GB 90-91 F 6
Caerfyrddin = Carmarthen ○ GB 90-91 E 6
Caernarfon ○••• GB 90-91 E 5
Caerphilly Castle •• GB 90-91 F 6
Caesaera Scugog, Lake ○ CDN 38-39 E 6
Cáetas ○ BR 210-211 C 6
Caeté ○ BR 72-73 J 5
Caeté, Baía do ≈ BR 68-69 E 2
Caeté, Rio ~ BR 66-67 C 7
Caetité ○ BR 72-73 J 3
Čaevo ○ RUS 94-95 P 2
Cafarnaum ○ BR 68-69 H 7
Cafayate ○ RA 76-77 E 4
Cafema, Serra ▲ ANG 216-217 B 8
Cafuma ~ ANG 216-217 E 8
Cagan Bogd ▲ MAU 148-149 D 6
Cagaandörvölž ○ MAU 148-149 J 5
Cagaannuur ○ MAU 146-147 J 1
Cagaan-Ovoo ○ MAU 148-149 J 4
Cagaan-Uul = Šarga ○ MAU 148-149 D 3
Čağalvandi ○ IR 134-135 C 2
Cagan ⋊ KA 124-125 L 3
Čagan ~ RUS 96-97 H 8
Cagan Aman ☆ RUS 96-97 E 10
Cagayan de Oro ☆ RP 160-161 F 8
Cagayan de Tawi Tawi Island ~ RP 160-161 C 9
Cagayan Islands ~ RP 160-161 D 8
Čağčarän ○ AFG 134-135 L 1
Čagda ○ RUS (SAH) 118-119 M 4
Čagda ~ RUS (SAH) 120-121 O 4
Cageri ○ GE 126-127 E 6
Čagliari ○ I 100-101 C 5
Čağlianka ~ KA 124-125 N 2
Cagliari, Golfo di ≈ 100-101 C 5
Cáceres ○ BR 70-71 H 5
Cáceres ○•• E 98-99 D 5
Čačević'y ⋗ BY 94-95 L 5
Cachachi ○ PE 64-65 C 5
Cachari ○ RA 78-79 K 4
Cache Creek ~ USA 40-41 C 5
Cagnano Varano ○ I 100-101 E 4
Cagojan ⋗ RUS 122-123 O 2
Čagra ~ RUS 96-97 G 7
Cagraray Island ~ RP 160-161 E 6
Caguán, Río ~ CO 64-65 E 1
Čagyl ⋗ TM 136-137 D 4
Čagylteniz, köli ○ KA 124-125 F 1
Čäh Āb ⋊ AFG 136-137 L 3
Cahabón, Río ~ GCA 52-53 K 4
Cahama ○ ANG 216-217 C 8
Čähär Bāğ ○ AFG 136-137 K 6
Čähär Māhāll-o-Bahtiyārī □ IR 134-135 D 3
Čäh Bahār, Bandar-e ≈ 134-135 J 6
Čäh Bahār, Ra's-e ⋊ 134-135 J 6
Caher = An Chathair ○ IRL 90-91 D 5
Čäh Ğäm ○ IR 136-137 D 7
Cahkwaktolik ⋗ USA 20-21 J 6
Cahobas, Las ○ RH 54-55 K 5
Cahokia Mounds ∴••• USA 46-47 C 6
Cahors ☆ • F 90-91 H 9
Cahotal ○ C 54-55 E 3
Cahuacho ○ PE 64-65 F 9
Cahuapanas ○ PE 64-65 D 5
Cahuinari, Río ~ CO 66-67 B 3
Cahul ⋗ MD 102-103 F 5
Cái, Cachoeira do ~ BR 66-67 F 7
Caia ○ MOC 218-219 H 3
Caiabi, Cachoeira ~ BR 70-71 K 2
Caiabis, Serra dos ▲ BR 70-71 J 2
Caianda ○ ANG 214-215 D 7
Caiapô, Rio ~ BR 68-69 D 6
Caiapó, Rio ~ BR 72-73 E 4
Caiapônia ○ BR 72-73 E 4
Caibarién ○ C 54-55 F 3
Caibi ○ BR 74-75 D 6

Caibiran ○ RP 160-161 F 7
Caicara ○ YV 60-61 K 3
Caiçara do Rio do Vento ○ BR 68-69 K 4
Caicedo ○ CO 60-61 D 4
Caicedonia ○ CO 60-61 D 5
Caico ○ BR 68-69 K 5
Caicos Islands ~ GB 54-55 J 4
Caicos Passage ≈ 54-55 J 3
Caicumbo ○ ANG 216-217 E 5
Cái Đầu ○ VN 158-159 H 5
Caigua ○ YV 60-61 J 3
Cai Hu ~ VRC 154-155 H 6
Cái Lậy ○ VN 158-159 J 5
Caillou Bay ≈ 44-45 M 5
Caima ○ BR 68-69 B 3
Caimanero ○ MEX 50-51 F 6
Caimanero, Laguna del ○ MEX 50-51 F 6
Caimbambo ○ ANG (BGU) 216-217 C 6
Caimbambo ○ ANG 216-217 B 6
Caimito ○ CO 60-61 D 3
Caimito River ~ USA 44-45 L 4
Caine, Rio ~ BOL 70-71 F 6
Cainta ○ RP 160-161 D 5
Caiongo ○ ANG 216-217 C 3
Caipe ○ RA 76-77 D 3
Caipupa ○ ANG 216-217 E 5
Cairari ○ BR 68-69 E 2
Cairn, Ile ~ CDN 36-37 L 6
Cairn Mountain ▲ USA 20-21 N 6
Cairns ○•• AUS 174-175 H 5
Cairns Lake ○ CDN 34-35 J 5
Cairns Section ⊥ AUS 174-175 J 4
Cairo ○ USA (GA) 48-49 F 4
Cairo ○ USA (IL) 44-45 M 1
Cairo = al-Qâhira ★•• ET 194-195 E 2
Cairo, Cape ▲ CDN 24-25 V 1
Cairu ○ BR 72-73 L 2
Caiseal = Cashel ○ IRL 90-91 D 5
Caisleán an Bharraigh = Castlebar ⋊ IRL 90-91 C 5
Çaldıran ☆ TR 128-129 K 3
Caititu, Área indígena ⋊ BR 66-67 F 6
Caitou ○ ANG 216-217 B 6
Caiúá ○ BR 72-73 D 7
Caiundo ○ ANG 216-217 D 7
Caixa, Rio de ~ BR 72-73 J 2
Caiyuan ○ VRC 156-157 C 3
Caiza, Serranía de ▲ BOL 76-77 F 1
Čaja ~ RUS 114-115 P 5
Čaja ~ RUS 118-119 D 6
Čaja-Ajan, gory ▲ RUS 108-109 Z 7
Cajabamba ○ EC 64-65 D 3
Cajabamba ○ PE 64-65 C 5
Cajacay ○ PE 64-65 D 7
Cajamarca ☆ • PE 64-65 C 5
Cajamarquilla ∴ PE 64-65 D 7
Čajan ⋗ KA 124-125 L 3
Cajanda ~ RUS 118-119 F 5
Cajatambo ○ PE 64-65 D 6
Cajazeiras ○ BR 68-69 J 5
Cajazeiras, Rio ~ BR 68-69 J 5
Čajbuha ○ RUS 120-121 T 3
Cajdam ~ RUS 118-119 F 5
Cajeira ○ BR (MIN) 72-73 H 3
Cajueiro ○ BR (MAR) 68-69 F 3
Cajuru ○ BR 72-73 G 6
Cajuti, Cachoeira ~ BR 62-63 G 6
Cajuruna ○ BR 62-63 K 6
Čajvo, zaliv ≈ RUS 122-123 R 2
Caka ○ VRC 144-145 H 2
Caka Yanhu ○ VRC 144-145 M 2
Čak-e Vardak ○ AFG 138-139 B 2
Čakne'ey Päin ○ IR 136-137 N 5
Cakranegara ○ RI 168 C 7
Čaku ○ GE 126-127 D 7
Čäkyja ~ RUS 118-119 O 4
Čäl ○ AFG 136-137 L 4
Çal ⋗ TR 128-129 C 3
Cal, Rio La ~ BOL 70-71 F 5
Čala ~ CY 128-129 K 5
Calabar ☆ WAN 204-205 H 6
Calabazar de Sagua ○ C 54-55 F 3
Calabei ○ RI 168 C 7
Calabozo ○ YV 60-61 H 3
Calabria □ I 100-101 F 5
Calabria, Parco Nazionale della ⊥ I 100-101 F 5
Calacoa ○ PE 70-71 B 5
Calacoto ○ BOL 70-71 D 6
Calafat ○ RO 102-103 C 5
Calafate, El ○ RA 80 D 6
Calafquen, Lago ○ RCH 78-79 C 5
Calagua Islands ~ RP 160-161 E 5
Calahorra ○ E 98-99 G 3
Calais ○ • F 90-91 H 6
Calais ○ USA 46-47 P 3
Čalak ⋊ US 136-137 K 5
Calalaste, Sierra de ▲ RA 76-77 D 4
Calalzo di Cadore ○ I 100-101 D 1
Calama ○ BR 66-67 F 7
Calamar ○ CO (ATL) 60-61 D 2
Calamar ○ CO (VAU) 60-61 E 6
Calamarca ○ BOL 70-71 D 5
Calamian Group ~ RP 160-161 C 6
Calamocha ○ E 98-99 G 4
Calamuya ∴• HN 52-53 L 4
Calanaque ○ BR 66-67 E 5
Calandula ○ ANG 216-217 C 4

Calandula, Quedas do ~•• ANG 216-217 C 4
Calang ○ RI 162-163 A 2
Calanga ○ PE 64-65 D 8
Calanus Bay ≈ 36-37 H 3
Calapan ○ RP 160-161 D 6
Cala Rajada ○ E 98-99 J 5
Călărasi ⋗ MD 102-103 F 4
Călărasi ☆ RO 102-103 E 5
Calarca ○ CO 60-61 D 5
Calatambo ○ BR 70-71 C 6
Calatayud ○ E 98-99 G 4
Calatrava ○ RP 160-161 E 7
Calavite Passage ≈ 160-161 D 6
Calayan Island ~ RP 160-161 D 3
Calbayog ○ RP 160-161 F 6
Calbore ○ PA 52-53 D 7
Calbuco ○ RCH 78-79 C 6
Calbuco, Volcán ▲ RCH 78-79 C 6
Calca ○ PE 70-71 B 3
Calcasieu Lake ○ USA 44-45 L 5
Calcasieu River ~ USA 44-45 L 4
Calceta ○ EC 64-65 B 2
Calchaquí ○ RA 76-77 G 5
Calchaquí, Río ~ RA 76-77 D 4
Calchaquí, Río ~ RA 76-77 D 4
Calchaquí las Aves, Laguna ○ RA 76-77 G 5
Calçoene ○ BR 62-63 J 4
Calçoene, Rio ~ BR 62-63 J 4
Calcutta ☆ • IND 142-143 E 4
Caldas ○ CO 60-61 D 4
Caldas Novas ○ BR 72-73 F 4
Caldeiras ○ BR 72-73 J 2
Caldera ○ CR 52-53 B 7
Caldera ○ RCH 76-77 B 4
Caldera de Taburiente, Parque Nacional de la ⊥ E 188-189 C 6
Calderon, Cerro ▲ RA 78-79 E 6
Calder River ~ CDN 30-31 M 3
Çaldıran ☆ TR 128-129 K 3
Caldwell ○ USA (ID) 40-41 F 4
Caldwell ○ USA (KS) 44-45 J 1
Caldwell ○ USA (OH) 46-47 H 6
Caldwell ○ USA (TX) 44-45 J 4
Caledon ○ ZA 220-221 D 7
Caledon Bay ≈ 174-175 D 3
Caledonia ○ CDN 38-39 E 7
Caledonia ○ USA 46-47 C 4
Caledonia Hills ▲ 38-39 M 6
Caledonrivier ~ ZA 220-221 H 4
Calen ○ AUS 174-175 H 7
Calequisse ○ GNB 202-203 B 3
Calera, La ○ RCH 78-79 D 2
Caleta Josefina ○ RCH 80 F 6
Caleta Olivia ○ RA 80 G 5
Caleta Vitor ○ RCH 70-71 B 6
Caleufú ○ RA 78-79 G 3
Caleufú, Rio ~ RA 78-79 D 6
Caléxico ○ USA 40-41 G 9
Calgary ○ CDN 32-33 N 6
Calhan ○ USA 42-43 F 6
Calhoun ○ USA (GA) 48-49 F 2
Calhoun ○ USA (LA) 44-45 L 3
Calhoun City ○ USA 48-49 D 2
Calhoun Falls ○ USA 48-49 G 2
Calhua ○ PE 64-65 F 9
Cali ○ CO 60-61 D 5
Calicoan Island ▲ RP 160-161 F 7
Calico Ghost Town ∴• USA 40-41 F 8
Calicut = Kozhikode • IND 140-141 F 5
Caliente ○ USA (CA) 40-41 E 8
Caliente ○ USA (NV) 40-41 G 7
California ○ BR 66-67 F 6
California ○ USA 40-41 D 5
California, Gulf of = California, Golfo de ≈ MEX 50-51 B 2
California Aqueduct < USA 40-41 D 7
Calik ~ RI 162-163 F 6
Calilegua, Parque Nacional ⊥ RA 76-77 E 2
Calima = Darien ○ CO 60-61 C 6
Călimani, Munţii ▲ RO 102-103 D 4
Calingasta ○ RA 76-77 C 6
Calingasta, Valle de ~ RA 76-77 C 6
Calingiri ○ AUS 176-177 D 5
Calintaan ○ RP 160-161 D 6
Calion ○ USA 44-45 L 3
Calipatria ○ USA 40-41 G 9
Calipuy, Reserva Nacional ⊥ PE 64-65 C 6
Calistoga ○ USA 40-41 C 6
Calitzdorp ○ ZA 220-221 E 7
Calkar köl ○ KA 96-97 G 8
Calkarteniz, sor ○ KA 126-127 P 3
Calkini ○ MEX 52-53 J 1
Callabonna ○ AUS 178-179 F 5
Callabonna, Lake ○ AUS 178-179 F 5
Callabonna Creek ~ AUS 178-179 F 5
Callagiddy ○ AUS 176-177 C 2
Callahan ○ USA (CA) 40-41 C 5
Callahan ○ USA (FL) 48-49 H 4
Callahan, Mount ▲ USA 42-43 E 6
Callama ó Quirce, Rio ~ BOL 70-71 D 7
Callana, Rio ~ PE 64-65 C 5
Callander ○ CDN 38-39 E 5
Callanish ○ GB 90-91 D 2
Callao ○ PE 64-65 D 8
Callao, El ○ YV 62-63 D 2
Callao, El ○ YV 62-63 D 2
Callaqui, Volcán ▲ RCH 78-79 D 4
Callara, Lake ○ AUS 178-179 D 5
Callatharra Springs ○ AUS 176-177 C 2
Callawa ○ AUS 172-173 H 4
Callaway ○ USA 48-49 F 4
Calle Calle, Rio ~ RCH 78-79 C 5
Calles ○ MEX 50-51 K 5
Calling Lake ○ CDN (ALB) 32-33 O 4
Calling Lake ○ CDN (ALB) 32-33 O 4
Calling River ~ CDN 32-33 O 4
Calliope ○ AUS 174-175 L 8
Cal Madow, Buuraha ▲ SP 208-209 J 3
Calmar ○ CDN 32-33 O 5
Calmar ○ USA 46-47 C 4
Cal Miskaat, Buuraha ▲ SP 208-209 J 3
Calm Point ▲ USA 22-23 Q 3

Čalna o RUS 88-89 N 6
Calombo o ANG 216-217 C 6
Calonda o ANG 216-217 F 4
Calonga ~ ANG 216-217 C 7
Caloosahatchee River ~ USA 48-49 H 6
Caloto o CO 60-61 C 6
Caloundra o AUS 178-179 M 4
Calpon, Cerro ▲ PE 64-65 C 6
Calpulalpan o MEX 52-53 E 1
Calstock o CDN 34-35 O 6
Caltagirone o I 100-101 E 6
Caltama, Monte ▲ BOL 70-71 D 4
Caltanissetta o I 100-101 E 6
Calton Hills o AUS 174-175 E 7
Ca Lu o VN 158-159 J 2
Caluango o ANG 216-217 E 4
Calucinga ~ ANG 216-217 D 5
Calulo o ANG 214-215 B 7
Caluquembe o ANG 216-217 C 6
Čalūs o IR 136-137 B 6
Caluula o SP 208-209 K 3
Calvert Hills o AUS 174-175 D 5
Calvert Island ∧ CDN 32-33 F 6
Calvi o ∘ F 98-99 M 3
Calvillo o MEX 50-51 H 7
Calvin o USA 44-45 J 2
Calvinia o ZA 220-221 D 5
Calzada de Calatrava o E 98-99 F 5
Camabatela o ANG 216-217 C 4
Camacã o BR 72-73 L 3
Camaçari o BR 68-69 K 7
Camacupa o ANG 216-217 D 6
Camaguan o YV 60-61 H 3
Camagüey ✰ o C 54-55 G 4
Camagüey, Archipiélago de ∧ C 54-55 F 3
Camaipi o BR 62-63 J 5
Camaiú, Rio ~ BR 66-67 H 5
Camalote o C 54-55 G 4
Camamu o BR 72-73 L 2
Camana o PE 70-71 A 5
Čamanbād o IR 134-135 H 1
Camanaú, Rio ~ BR 62-63 D 6
Čaman Bid o IR 136-137 E 6
Camandó Island ∧ RP 160-161 F 7
Čaman Soltān o IR 134-135 C 2
Camapuã o BR 70-71 K 6
Camaquã o BR 74-75 E 8
Camará o BR (AMA) 66-67 F 4
Camará o BR (P) 66-67 K 4
Camaragibe o BR 68-69 L 6
Camaraipi, Rio ~ BR 68-69 C 3
Camararé, Rio ~ BR 70-71 H 3
Camarata o YV 60-61 K 5
Camargo o MEX 50-51 K 4
Camaron o BOL 76-77 E 1
Camarón, Cabo ▲ HN 54-55 C 7
Camarones o RA 80 H 2
Camarones, Bahía ≈ 80 H 2
Camarones, Rio ~ RCH 70-71 C 6
Camaruã o BR 66-67 E 5
Camarvik Creek ~ CDN 30-31 Z 3
Camata, Río ~ BOL 70-71 D 4
Camatambo o ANG 216-217 C 3
Cà Mau o VN 158-159 H 6
Camaxilo o ANG 216-217 D 4
Camba o RI 164-165 F 6
Čamba ~ RUS 116-117 L 5
Cambaju o GNB 202-203 C 3
Cambalin o ANG 172-173 G 4
Cambândua o ANG 216-217 D 6
Cambange o ANG 216-217 F 4
Cambao o CO 60-61 D 5
Cambará do Sul o BR 74-75 E 7
Cambaxi o ANG 216-217 C 4
Cambellford o CDN 38-39 F 6
Cambo ~ ANG 216-217 D 4
Cambodia = Kâmpŭchéa ■ K 158-159 G 4
Camboeiro, Riachão do ~ BR 68-69 F 7
Cambombo o ANG 216-217 D 4
Camboon P.O. o AUS 178-179 L 3
Camboriú, Ponta ▲ BR 74-75 G 5
Cambrai o F 90-91 J 6
Cambrian Mountains ▲ GB 90-91 F 5
Cambridge o CDN 38-39 D 7
Cambridge o ∘∘ GB 90-91 H 5
Cambridge o JA 54-55 G 5
Cambridge o NZ 182 E 2
Cambridge o USA (ID) 40-41 F 3
Cambridge o USA (MA) 46-47 N 4
Cambridge o USA (MD) 46-47 K 6
Cambridge o USA (MN) 42-43 L 3
Cambridge o USA (NE) 42-43 G 5
Cambridge o USA (OH) 46-47 H 5
Cambridge Bay ≈ 24-25 T 6
Cambridge Bay o CDN 24-25 U 6
Cambridge Gulf ≈ 172-173 G 3
Cambridge Point ▲ CDN 24-25 g 3
Cambrils o E 98-99 H 4
Cambu, Rio ~ BR 62-63 K 6
Cambuí o BR 72-73 G 7
Cambulo o ANG 216-217 F 3
Camburinga ✕ AUS 174-175 D 3
Cambutal o PA 52-53 D 8
Camden o USA (AL) 48-49 E 4
Camden o USA (AR) 44-45 L 3
Camden o USA (NY) 46-47 L 4
Camden o USA (SC) 48-49 H 2
Camden Bay ≈ 20-21 S 1
Camdenton o USA 42-43 L 6
Cameia, Parque Nacional da ⊥ ANG 216-217 F 5
Camel Creek o AUS 174-175 H 6
Çameli o TR 128-129 C 4
Camel Race Course ✕ KSA 130-131 K 5
Cameron o USA (AZ) 40-41 J 8
Cameron o USA (LA) 44-45 L 5
Cameron o USA (MO) 42-43 K 6
Cameron o USA (TX) 44-45 J 4
Cameron Corner ✕ AUS 178-179 F 5
Cameron Island ∧ CDN 24-25 U 2
Cameron River ~ CDN 30-31 N 4
Cameroon = Cameroun ■ CAM 204-205 J 6

Cameroon, Mount = Mont Cameroun ▲• CAM 204-205 H 6
Cameroun, Estuaire du ≈ 210-211 B 2
Cameroun, Mont = Mount Cameroun ▲• CAM 204-205 H 6
Cametá o BR 68-69 D 3
Camfield o AUS 172-173 K 4
Camiaco o BOL 70-71 E 4
Camiguin Island ∧ RP (CAG) 160-161 D 3
Camiguin Island ∧ RP (MSO) 160-161 F 8
Camiling o RP 160-161 D 5
Camilla o USA 48-49 F 4
Camiña o RCH 70-71 C 6
Caming o RI 164-165 G 6
Caminha o P 98-99 C 4
Camino de Santiago ••• E 98-99 D 3
Caminos, Dos o YV 60-61 J 3
Camisea o PE 70-71 C 6
Camissombo o ANG 216-217 F 4
Čamkani o AFG 138-139 B 3
Çamlıdere o TR 128-129 D 2
Cammarata, Monte ▲ I 100-101 D 6
Camocim o BR 68-69 H 3
Camocim de São Felix o BR 68-69 L 6
Camogton o RP 160-161 E 6
Camongua o ANG 216-217 D 5
Camooweal o AUS 174-175 E 6
Camooweal Caves National Park ⊥ AUS 174-175 E 6
Camopi o F 62-63 H 4
Camopi ~ F 62-63 H 4
Camorta Island ∧ IND 140-141 L 5
Camotes Islands ∧ RP 160-161 F 7
Camotes Sea ≈ 160-161 F 7
Čamp, ostrov ∧ RUS 84-85 e 2
Campamento o HN 52-53 L 4
Campamento Río Grande o YV 60-61 L 3
Campana, Cerro ▲ RCH 80 D 5
Campana, Isla ∧ RCH 80 C 4
Campana, Monte ▲ RA 80 H 7
Campana, Parque Nacional la ⊥ RCH 78-79 D 2
Campanario o BR 72-73 K 5
Campanario, Cerro ▲ RA 78-79 D 3
Campanas o BR 76-77 D 5
Campania o I 100-101 E 4
Campanilla o PE 64-65 D 5
Campanquiz, Cerros ▲ PE 64-65 D 4
Campaspe o AUS 174-175 J 7
Camp Atterbury ✕✕ USA 46-47 E 6
Campbell o ZA 220-221 F 4
Campbell, Cape ▲ NZ 182 E 4
Campbell ~ USA 46-47 E 7
Campbell Bay ≈ 24-25 G 6
Campbell Lake o CDN (NWT) 20-21 Y 2
Campbell Lake o CDN (NWT) 30-31 Q 4
Campbell Military Reservation, Fort ✕✕ USA 46-47 E 7
Campbell Plateau ≃ 13 H 7
Campbell River o CDN 32-33 H 6
Campbell's Bay o CDN 38-39 F 6
Campbellsville o USA 46-47 F 7
Campbellton o CDN 38-39 S 5
Campbell Town o AUS 180-181 J 6
Campbelltown o AUS 180-181 K 5
Camp Century o GRØ 26-27 U 5
Camp Crook o USA 42-43 F 3
Campeana o GNB 202-203 C 4
Campeche ∎ MEX 52-53 J 2
Campeche ✰ o MEX 52-53 J 2
Campeche, Bahía de ≈ 52-53 G 2
Campechuela o C 54-55 G 4
Camperdown o AUS 180-181 G 5
Camperdown o ZA 220-221 K 4
Camperville o CDN 34-35 F 5
Cẩm Phả o VN 156-157 F 6
Campidano ⌓ I 100-101 B 5
Campillos o E 98-99 E 6
Campín, El o CO 60-61 F 5
Campina, Rio o BR 66-67 J 5
Campina da Lagoa o BR 74-75 D 5
Campina do Simão o BR 74-75 D 5
Campina Grande o BR 68-69 L 5
Campinas o BR (BAH) 72-73 J 2
Campinas o BR (PAU) 72-73 G 7
Campinas, Área Indígena ✕ BR 64-65 F 5
Campina Verde o BR 72-73 F 5
Camping Island o CDN 24-25 P 2
Campinho o BR (BAH) 72-73 L 2
Campinho o BR (PAU) 72-73 L 2
Camp Lloyd o GRØ 28-29 P 3
Camplong o RI 166-167 B 7
Campo o ∘ CAM 210-211 B 2
Campo o MOC 218-219 J 3
Campo o USA 44-45 F 1
Campo, Réserve de = Campo Reserve ⊥ CAM 210-211 B 2
Campo Alegre o BR (ALA) 68-69 K 6
Campo Alegre o BR (PIA) 68-69 H E
Campo Alegre o BR (TOC) 68-69 D 7
Campoalegre o CO 60-61 D 6
Campo Alegre o YV 60-61 K 3
Campo Alegre de Goiás o BR 72-73 G 4
Campo Alegre de Lourdes o BR 68-69 G 6
Campobasso o ✰ I 100-101 E 4
Campo Belo o BR 72-73 H 6
Campo Bernal o YV 60-61 E 3
Campo Camalajue o MEX 50-51 B 3
Campo de Carabobo, Parque • YV 60-61 G 2
Campo de Talampaya • RA 76-77 D 3
Campo del Padre, Morro ▲ BR 74-75 F 2
Campo Erê o BR 74-75 D 6
Campo Esperanza o PY 76-77 H 2
Campo Gallo o RA 76-77 G 5
Campo Garay o RA 76-77 G 5
Campo Grande ∎ BR 70-71 K 7

Campo Grande o RA 76-77 K 4
Campo Grande, Cachoeira ~ BR 70-71 F 2
Campo Grayling Artillery Range ✕✕ USA 46-47 F 3
Campo Largo o BR 74-75 F 5
Campo Maior o BR 68-69 G 4
Campo Maior o P 98-99 D 5
Campomento o PY 76-77 H 1
Campo Mourão o BR 74-75 D 5
Campo Novo do Parecis o BR 70-71 H 2
Campo Nuevo o MEX 50-51 B 3
Campo Reserve = Réserve de Campo ⊥ CAM 210-211 B 2
Campos o BR 72-73 K 6
Campos ⊥ BR 68-69 G 7
Campos, Laguna o PY 70-71 G 7
Campos, Tierra de ▲ E 98-99 E 4
Campos Belos o BR 72-73 G 2
Campos do Jordão o BR 72-73 H 7
Campos dos Parecis ⊥ BR 70-71 H 3
Campo Seco o BR 76-77 K 6
Campos Eliseos o BR 72-73 D 6
Campo Serio o PE 64-65 E 2
Campos Gerais o BR 72-73 H 6
Campos Novos o BR 74-75 E 6
Campos Sales o BR 68-69 G 5
Camp Pendleton Marine Corps Base ✕✕ USA 40-41 H 9
Camp Point o USA 46-47 C 5
Camp Ripley Military Reservation ✕✕ USA 42-43 K 2
Camp Verde o USA 40-41 J 8
Camp Wood o USA 44-45 G 5
Cam Ranh o VN 158-159 K 5
Camrose o CDN 32-33 O 5
Camsell Bay o CDN 28-29 F 3
Camsell Lake o CDN 30-31 O 4
Camú, Rio ~ DOM 54-55 K 5
Camucuo o ANG 216-217 E 7
Camulemba, Capenda- ~ ANG 216-217 E 4
Camuya, Río ~ CO 64-65 F 1
Čamzinka o RUS 96-97 D 6
Čamzinka ~ RUS 96-97 D 6
Çan ✰ TR 128-129 B 2
Cana o BOL 70-71 C 7
Caña, La o CO 60-61 C 3
Canaã o BR 68-69 F 5
Canaã, Rio ~ BR 70-71 F 2
Canabal o E 98-99 D 3
Cana-Brava o BR 72-73 H 4
Cana Brava, Rio ~ BR 72-73 H 3
Cana-Brava, Serra ▲ BR 72-73 K 4
Canadá o BR 68-69 F 2
Canada ▮ CDN 38-39 D 3
Cañada, La o RA (COD) 76-77 F 4
Cañada, La o RA (SAE) 76-77 F 4
Canada Basin ≃ 16 B 33
Canada Bay ≈ 38-39 Q 3
Cañada de Gómez o RA 78-79 J 2
Cañada de Luque o RA 78-79 G 1
Cañada Rosquín o RA 78-79 J 2
Cañada Seca o RA 78-79 H 3
Canadian o USA 44-45 G 2
Canadian-Pacific-Railway ■ CDN 32-33 Q 5
Canadian River ~ USA 44-45 G 2
Cañadón El Pluma o RA 80 E 3
Cañadón Lagarto o RA 80 F 2
Cañadón Sacho o RA 80 E 4
Cañadón Seco o RA 80 E 2
Canagu, Rio ~ YV 60-61 H 4
Canaima o YV 60-61 K 4
Canaima, Parque Nacional ⊥ YV 60-61 K 5
Çanakkale ✰ TR 128-129 B 2
Çanakkale Boğazı ≈ 128-129 B 2
Canal de Túnis ≈ 100-101 C 6
Canale di Sicilia ≈ 100-101 C 6
Canal Flats o CDN 32-33 N 6
Canalí o MEX 52-53 E 1
Canal P.O. o AUS 178-179 K 3
Canals o RA 78-79 H 2
Canamã, Rio ~ BR 70-71 H 2
Cananari, Rio ~ CO 66-67 B 2
Canandaigua o USA 46-47 K 4
Cananea o MEX 50-51 C 2
Cananéia o BR 74-75 G 5
Canar o EC 64-65 C 3
Canarana o BR (BAH) 68-69 H 7
Canarana o BR (MAT) 72-73 D 2
Canárias, Ilha das ∧ BR 68-69 H 3
Canarreos, Archipiélago de los ∧ C 54-55 E 4
Canary o AUS 178-179 F 2
Canary Islands = Canarias, Islas ∧ E 188-189 C 6
Cañas o MEX 52-53 D 2
Cañas, Bahía las ≈ 78-79 C 3
Cañas, Las o CR 52-53 B 6
Cañas, Playa las o CR 54-55 D 3
Cañas, Rio ~ RA 76-77 E 4
Cañasgordas o CO 60-61 C 4
Canastra, Rio ~ BR 68-69 D 7
Canastra, Serra da ▲ BR 68-69 J 7
Canastra, Serra da ▲ BR 72-73 G 6
Canatián o MEX 50-51 G 5
Canatiba o BR 72-73 J 2
Canaveral o EC 64-65 B 3
Canaveral, Cape ▲ USA 48-49 H 5
Cañaveras o E 98-99 F 4
Canaveieiras o BR 72-73 L 3
Canayan o RP 160-161 E 8
Cañazas o PA (Pan) 52-53 E 7
Cañazas o PA (Ver) 52-53 D 7
Canberra ✰ AUS 180-181 K 3
Canberra Space Centre • AUS 180-181 K 3

Cancuc o MEX 52-53 H 3
Cancuén ∴∴ GCA 52-53 J 3
Cancún, Isla ∧ MEX 52-53 L 1
Cancún o MEX 52-53 L 1
Candarave o PE 70-71 B 5
Çandarlı Körfezi ≈ 128-129 B 3
Candeado o MOC 218-219 G 4
Candeias o BR 72-73 L 2
Candeias, Rio ~ BR 66-67 F 7
Candela o MEX 50-51 J 4
Candelaria o BR 74-75 E 5
Candelaria, La o CO 60-61 F 5
Candelaria, La o YV 60-61 H 1
Candelaria, Río ~ MEX 52-53 J 2
Candelda o E 98-99 E 4
Candi o RI (LAM) 162-163 C 1
Candi o RI (RIA) 162-163 D 1
Candi Besakih • RI 168 B 7
Cândido de Abreu o BR 74-75 E 5
Cándido González o C 54-55 F 4
Cândido Mendes o BR 68-69 F 2
Cândido Rondon o BR 76-77 K 3
Cândido Sales o BR 72-73 K 3
Candi Mendut • RI 168 D 3
Candi Pura • RI 168 D 3
Candi Sukuh • RI 168 D 3
Candle o USA 20-21 K 4
Candle Lake o CDN (SAS) 34-35 D 4
Candle Lake ≈ CDN (SAS) 34-35 D 4
Cando o CDN 32-33 Q 5
Cando o USA 42-43 H 1
Candon o RP 160-161 D 4
Candover o ZA 220-221 K 3
Candulo o MOC 214-215 J 6
Cãn Dương o VN 158-159 J 3
Cãn Đước o VN 158-159 J 5
Canea o BR 62-63 G 5
Caneapo o BR 62-63 G 5
Canegrass o AUS 180-181 F 2
Cane Grove o GUY 62-63 F 2
Canela, La o CO 60-61 D 2
Canela Baja o RCH 76-77 B 6
Canelones o RA 78-79 L 3
Canelos o EC 64-65 D 2
Canelos, Los o RCH 80 E 6
Cane River ~ AUS 172-173 B 7
Cane River ~ AUS 172-173 B 7
Cañete o E 98-99 G 4
Cañete o USA (GA) 48-49 F 2
Cañete o USA (MO) 46-47 C 5
Cañete, Rio de ~ PE 64-65 D 8
Cangada ~ RUS 108-109 c 7
Cangaíme, Río ~ EC 64-65 D 3
Cangala o ANG 216-217 D 6
Cangalo o PE 64-65 E 8
Cangandala o ANG 216-217 D 4
Cangandala, Parque Nacional de ⊥ ANG 216-217 D 4
Cangas o E 98-99 C 3
Cangas del Narcea o E 98-99 D 3
Cangas de Luque o RA 78-79 K 2
Cangjie Temple • VRC 154-155 F 4
Cangoa o ANG 216-217 D 7
Cangombe o ANG 216-217 F 7
Cangrejo, Cerro ▲ RA 80 D 4
Cangshan o VRC 154-155 L 4
Canguaretama o BR 68-69 L 5
Cangucu o BR 74-75 E 8
Čangüle, Rüdhane-ye ~ IRQ 128-129 M 6
Cangumbe o ANG 216-217 E 5
Cangxi o VRC 154-155 E 3
Cangyanshan • VRC 154-155 J 3
Cangyuan o VRC 142-143 L 4
Cangzhou o VRC 154-155 K 2
Can Hasan Höyüğü •∴• TR 128-129 E 4
Canhotinho o BR 68-69 L 6
Caniapiscau, Lac o CDN 36-37 P 7
Caniapiscau, Réservoir de < CDN 36-37 P 7
Caniapiscau, Rivière ~ CDN 36-37 P 7
Canicatti o I 100-101 D 6
Canigao Channel ≈ 160-161 F 7
Canik Dağları ▲ TR 128-129 G 2
Canim Lake o CDN (BC) 32-33 K 6
Canim Lake o CDN (BC) 32-33 K 6
Canindé o BR 68-69 J 4
Canindé, Rio ~ BR 68-69 G 5
Caninde de São Francisco o BR 68-69 K 6
Canipo Island ∧ RP 160-161 D 7
Canister Fall ~ GUY 62-63 E 3
Canit Point ▲ RP 160-161 K 6
Canjime o ANG 216-217 D 6
Çankiri ✰ TR 128-129 E 2
Cankuzo o BU 212-213 C 5
Canlaon, Mount ▲ RP 160-161 E 7
Canmang o VRC 156-157 G 2
Canmore o CDN 32-33 N 6
Cann, Mount ▲ AUS 180-181 K 4
Cannac Island ∧ PNG 183 B 5
Cannanore o IND 140-141 F 5
Cannanore Islands ∧ IND 140-141 E 5
Cannes o ∘ F 90-91 L 10
Canning Hill ▲ AUS 176-177 D 4
Canning River ~ USA 20-21 R 2
Canning Stock Route ■ AUS 172-173 G 4
Cannington Manor Historic Park ∴∴ CDN 34-35 E 4
Cannon Ball o USA 42-43 G 2
Cannonball River ~ USA 42-43 G 2
Cannondale Mount ▲ AUS 178-179 K 3
Cannon Falls o USA 42-43 L 3
Cannonville o USA 40-41 J 7
Cann River o AUS (VIC) 180-181 K 4
Cann River ~ AUS 180-181 K 4
Caño, El o PA 52-53 D 7
Caño, Isla de ∧ CR 52-53 B 7
Cano, Pico do ▲ CV 202-203 B 6
Canoa o HN 52-53 K 4
Canoas o BR 74-75 E 7
Canoas ~ MEX 50-51 K 6
Canoas, Punta ▲ MEX 50-51 B 3
Canobie o AUS 174-175 F 6

Canobolas, Mount ▲ AUS 180-181 K 2
Canoe Creek Indian Reserve ✕ CDN 32-33 J 6
Canoe Lake o CDN 32-33 Q 4
Canoe Reach o CDN 32-33 L 5
Caño Hondo, Cuevas de ∴∴• DOM 54-55 L 5
Canoinhas o BR 74-75 E 6
Canon o ∘ DZ 190-191 F 3
Canonaco, Rio ~ EC 64-65 D 2
Canonba o AUS 180-181 D 3
Cañoncito Indian Reservation ✕ USA 44-45 D 2
Canon City o USA 42-43 E 6
Cañon del Sumidero, Parque Nacional ⊥ MEX 52-53 H 3
Cañon de Río Blanco, Parque Nacional ⊥ MEX 52-53 F 2
Cañon Fiord ≈ 26-27 J 3
Canora o CDN 34-35 E 4
Canosa di Púglia o I 100-101 F 4
Canouan Island ∧ WV 56 J 6
Canowindra o AUS 180-181 K 2
Canquel, Meseta del ▲ RA 80 F 2
Canrobert Hills ▲ CDN 24-25 N 2
Canso o PE 64-65 D 7
Canso, Strait of ≈ 38-39 O 6
Canso Channel ≈ 28-29 J 3
Canta o PE 64-65 D 7
Cantabria ▲ E 98-99 E 3
Cantábrica, Cordillera ▲ E 98-99 D 3
Cantador, Cerro el ▲ MEX 52-53 C 2
Cantagalo, Ponta ▲ BR 74-75 F 6
Cantalejo o E 98-99 F 4
Cantalpino o E 98-99 E 4
Cantamar o MEX 50-51 A 1
Cantanal, Sierra de ▲ RA 76-77 D 6
Cantário, Rio ▲ BR 70-71 F 2
Cantaura o YV 60-61 J 2
Canterbury o∘∘ GB 90-91 H 6
Canterbury Bight ≈ 182 D 5
Cân Thơ ✰ VN 158-159 H 5
Canthyuaya, Cerros de ▲ PE 64-65 E 5
Cantil o USA 40-41 F 8
Cantilan o RP 160-161 F 8
Cantiles, Cayo ∧ C 54-55 D 4
Canto del Agua o RCH 76-77 B 5
Canto do Buriti o BR 68-69 G 6
Canton o USA (GA) 48-49 F 2
Canton o USA (MO) 46-47 C 5
Canton o USA (MS) 44-45 M 3
Canton o USA (NY) 46-47 L 3
Canton o USA (OH) 46-47 H 4
Canton o USA (PA) 46-47 K 5
Canton o USA (SD) 42-43 J 4
Canton o USA (TX) 44-45 K 3
Canton, El o YV 60-61 F 3
Canton = Guangzhou ✰• VRC 156-157 H 5
Cantwell o USA 20-21 Q 5
Canudos o BR 68-69 J 6
Cañuelas o RA 78-79 K 3
Canumã, Rio ~ BR 66-67 H 5
Canunda National Park ⊥ AUS 180-181 F 4
Canutama o BR 66-67 E 6
Canxixe o MOC 218-219 H 3
Canyon o USA 44-45 F 2
Canyon City o USA 40-41 D 3
Canyon Chelly National Monument • USA 44-45 C 1
Canyon Creek o USA 40-41 H 2
Canyon Ferry o USA 40-41 J 2
Canyon Ferry Lake o USA 40-41 J 2
Canyonlands National Park ⊥ USA 42-43 C 6
Canyon Ranges ▲ CDN 30-31 G 4
Canyon River ~ CDN 36-37 G 2
Canzar o ANG 216-217 F 3
Cao Bằng ✰• VN 156-157 E 5
Caohekou o VRC 150-151 D 7
Caojian o VRC 142-143 L 3
Cao Lãnh o VN 158-159 H 5
Cao Xian o VRC 154-155 J 4
Čapa ✰ RUS 114-115 O 7
Čapaev = Čapaevo o KA 96-97 G 8
Čapaevka ~ RUS 96-97 G 7
Čapaevo o KA 96-97 G 8
Čapaevo = Čapaev o KA 96-97 G 8
Čapaevsk o RUS 96-97 G 7
Capachica o PE 70-71 C 4
Capacho o YV 60-61 E 3
Capachú, Rio ~ BR 70-71 F 2
Capaia o ANG 216-217 F 4
Capaies o RP 160-161 C 7
Capalonga o RP 160-161 E 6
Capalulu o RI 164-165 J 4
Capana, Punta ▲ YV 60-61 F 2
Capanaparo, Rio ~ YV 60-61 G 3
Capanema o BR 74-75 E 6

Cape Bertholet Wildlife Sanctuary ⊥ AUS 172-173 F 4
Cape Borda o AUS 180-181 D 3
Cape Breton Highlands National Park ⊥ CDN 38-39 S 5
Cape Breton Island ∧ CDN 38-39 S 5
Cape Byrd ▲ ARK 16 G 8
Cape Canaveral o USA 48-49 H 5
Cape Canaveral Air Force Station ✕✕ USA 48-49 H 5
Cape Charles Lighthouse • USA 46-47 L 7
Cape Chidley Islands ∧ CDN 36-37 R 4
Cape Coast ✰ GH 202-203 K 7
Cape Cod Bay ≈ 46-47 N 5
Cape Cod National Seashore ⊥ USA 46-47 O 4
Cape Cod Peninsula ∪ USA 46-47 O 5
Cape Colbeck ▲ ARK 16 F 21
Cape Coral o USA 48-49 G 6
Cape Crawford o AUS 174-175 C 5
Cape Croker Indian Reserve ✕ CDN 38-39 D 6
Cape Dart ▲ ARK 16 F 24
Cape Dorset o CDN 36-37 L 2
Cape Fear River ~ USA 48-49 J 2
Cape Flying Fish ▲ ARK 16 F 26
Cape Freshfield ▲ ARK 16 G 16
Cape Gantheaume Conservation Park ⊥ AUS 180-181 D 4
Cape Girardeau o USA 46-47 D 7
Cape Girgir ▲ PNG 183 C 2
Cape Hatteras National Seashore ⊥ USA 48-49 L 2
Cape Hope Islands ∧ CDN 38-39 E 2
Cape Horn = Hornos, Cabo de ▲ RCH 80 G 8
Cape Jervis o AUS 180-181 E 3
Cape Krusenstern National Monument ⊥ USA 20-21 H 3
Capel o AUS 176-177 C 6
Capel, Cape ▲ CDN 24-25 X 3
Capela do Mato Verde o BR 72-73 H 4
Cape Le Grand National Park ⊥ AUS 176-177 G 6
Capelinha o BR 72-73 J 4
Capeľka o RUS 94-95 L 2
Capella o AUS 178-179 K 2
Capelle, la o F 90-91 J 7
Cape Lookout National Seashore ⊥ USA 48-49 K 2
Cape May o USA 46-47 L 6
Capembe ~ ANG 216-217 D 6
Cape Melville National Park ⊥ AUS 174-175 H 4
Cape Monze = Rãs Muari ▲ PK 134-135 M 6
Cape Moore ▲ ARK 16 F 17
Capenda-Camulemba o ANG 216-217 E 4
Cape of Good Hope ▲• ZA 220-221 D 7
Cape of Good Hope = Kaap die Goeie Hoop ▲• ZA 220-221 D 7
Cape Palmer ▲ ARK 16 F 7
Cape Parry o CDN 24-25 K 5
Cape Peninsula ∪ ZA 220-221 D 7
Cape Pole o USA 32-33 D 3
Cape Race o CDN 38-39 I 5 5
Cape Rama o IND 140-141 E 4
Cape Range ▲▲ AUS 172-173 A 7
Cape Range National Park ⊥ AUS 172-173 A 7
Cape River ~ AUS 174-175 H 7
Cape Sable Island ∧ CDN 38-39 M 7
Cape Saint Francis o ZA 220-221 G 7
Čapešlú o IR 136-137 H 7
Cape Smiley ▲ ARK 16 F 29
Capesterre-Belle-Eau o F 56 E 3
Cape Surville ▲ SOL 184 I 14
Cape Tormentine o CDN 38-39 N 5
Cape Town o USA 24-25 P 2
Cape Town = Cape Town = Kaapstad ✰• ZA 220-221 D 7
Cape Tribulation National Park ⊥ AUS 174-175 H 4
Cape Upstart National Park ⊥ AUS 174-175 J 6
Cape Verde = Cabo Verde ∎ CV 202-203 B 6
Cape Verde Islands = Cabo Verde, Arquipélago de ∧ CV 202-203 B 6
Cape Verde Plateau ≃ 6-7 G 5
Cape Vincent o USA 46-47 K 3
Cape Washington ▲ FJI 184 III a 3
Cape York Peninsula ∪ AUS 174-175 G 3
Cape Young o CDN 24-25 O 6
Cape Zele'e = Nialaha'u Point ▲ SOL 184 I 4 7
Cap-Haïtien ✰ RH 54-55 J 5
Capiá, Rio o BR 68-69 K 6
Capibaribe, Rio ~ BR 68-69 L 5
Capilla del Monte o RA 76-77 E 6
Capim o RI 164-165 J 4
Capim, Rio ~ BR 62-63 K 6
Capim Grosso o BR 68-69 H 7
Capinópolis o BR 72-73 F 5
Capinzal o BR 74-75 E 6
Capirenda o BOL 76-77 F 1
Cap Island o RP 160-161 D 10
Capissayan o RP 160-161 E 3
Capistrano o BR 68-69 J 4
Capitan o USA 44-45 E 3
Capitán Aracena, Isla ∧ RCH 80 E 7
Capitán Baldo o PY 76-77 H 3
Capitán Pablo Lagerenza ✰ PY 70-71 G 7
Capitán Porto Alegre o BR 76-77 K 5
Capitán Sarmiento o RA 78-79 K 3
Capitán Ustáres, Cerro ▲ BOL 70-71 G 6
Capitão, Igarapé ~ BR 66-67 E 6
Capitão Cardoso, Rio ~ BR 70-71 G 2
Capitão Enéas o BR 72-73 J 4
Capitão Leônidas Marques o BR 74-75 D 5
Capitão Poço o BR 68-69 E 2

Capitão Rivadenaira o EC 64-65 D 2
Capitol o USA 42-43 E 3
Capitol Reef National Park ⊥ USA 40-41 J 6
Capivara, Represa < BR 72-73 F 4
Capivara, Rio o BR 68-69 D 6
Capivaras, Cachoeira das ~ BR 66-67 K 6
Capivari o BR 72-73 G 7
Capivari, Rio ~ BR 70-71 J 6
Capixaba o BR 68-69 G 7
Čaplanovo o RUS 122-123 K 5
Čaplino o RUS 112-113 Y 4
Čaplino, Novoe o RUS 112-113 Y 4
Čapljina o BIH 100-101 F 3
Čaplygin o RUS 94-95 Q 5
Čaplynka o UA 102-103 H 4
Cap Marcos, Área Indígena ✕ BR 70-71 H 4
Capoche ~ MOC 218-219 G 2
Capoeira do Rei o BR 62-63 J 5
Capolo o ANG 216-217 B 5
Capoma ~ RUS 88-89 P 3
Caponda o MOC 218-219 F 2
Čapo-Ologo ~ RUS 118-119 J 7
Capo Rizzuto o I 100-101 F 5
Capot Blanc, Lac o CDN 30-31 O 4
Capoto, Área Indígena ✕ BR 68-69 B 6
Capotoah, Mount ▲ RP 160-161 F 6
Cappadocia = Capadocia ∴ TR 128-129 F 3
Capps o USA 48-49 G 4
Capráia, Ísola di ∧ I 100-101 B 3
Capri, Ísola di ∧∼• I 100-101 E 4
Capricorn, Cape ▲ AUS 178-179 L 2
Capricorn Group ∧ AUS 178-179 L 2
Capricorn Highway II AUS 178-179 K 2
Capricorn Section ⊥ AUS 178-179 M 2
Caprivi Game Park ⊥ NAM 218-219 E 3
Caprivi Strip = Caprivistrook ⊥ NAM 218-219 D 3
Cap-Seize o CDN 38-39 J 4
Captain Cook o USA 48-49 E 8
Captains Flat o AUS 180-181 K 3
Capua o ANG 216-217 F 7
Capucapu, Rio ~ BR 62-63 D 6
Capulin Mountain National Monument • USA 44-45 F 1
Capul Island ∧ RP 160-161 F 6
Capunda o ANG 216-217 D 5
Cap Worn National Park ⊥ PNG 183 B 2
Čaqläve, Čam-e ~ IRQ 128-129 L 5
Caqua o YV 60-61 J 2
Caquena o RCH 70-71 C 6
Caquetá, Rio ~ CO 66-67 C 2
Caqueza o CO 60-61 D 5
Car ~ KA 124-125 M 4
Čara ✰ RUS (CTN) 118-119 J 7
Čara ~ RUS 118-119 J 6
Čara ~ RUS 118-119 K 5
Čara ~ RUS 118-119 K 5
Čara ~ RUS 118-119 H 6
Carabao Island ∧ RP 160-161 D 6
Carabaya, Cordillera de ▲ PE 70-71 B 3
Carabaya, Rio ~ PE 70-71 C 4
Carabayllo o PE 64-65 D 7
Carabinani, Rio ~ BR 66-67 G 4
Carabobo o YV 60-61 G 2
Caracal o RO 102-103 D 5
Caracal, Rio ~ BR 68-69 E 6
Caracara, Estação Ecológica ⊥ BR 62-63 D 5
Caracaraí o BR 62-63 D 5
Caracas ✰• YV 60-61 H 2
Caracol ∴∴• BZ 52-53 J 3
Caracol o BR 68-69 G 6
Caracol o BR 76-77 J 2
Caracol ~ MEX 50-51 D 5
Caracol o CO 60-61 E 2
Caracoles ∴∴ BR 68-69 H 6
Caracollo o BOL 70-71 E 5
Caracuja Falls ~ CDN 30-31 F 3
Caracuto o ANG 216-217 D 7
Carad o RH 54-55 J 5
Caraguatá, Arroyo ~ ROU 78-79 M 2
Carai o BR 72-73 K 4
Caraiari, Rio ~ BR 68-69 B 4
Caraíva o BR 72-73 L 4
Carajas o BR 68-69 C 5
Carajás, Serra dos ▲ BR 68-69 C 5
Čarak, Bandar-e o IR 134-135 F 5
Caramat o CDN 34-35 N 6
Caramelo o CO 60-61 D 3
Caramoan o RP 160-161 E 6
Caramoan Peninsula ∪ RP 160-161 E 6
Caraná, Rio ~ BR 70-71 H 3
Caranavi o BOL 70-71 D 4
Carandaí o BR 72-73 J 6
Carandazinho o BR 70-71 J 5
Carandotta o AUS 178-179 E 1
Carangola o BR 72-73 J 6
Caransebeş o RO 102-103 C 5
Carapa o YV 60-61 K 3
Carapajó o BR 68-69 D 2
Carapán o MEX 52-53 C 2
Cara-Paraná, Rio ~ CO 64-65 F 2
Carapé, Sierra de ▲ ROU 78-79 M 3
Carapebus o BR 72-73 K 7
Carapo o YV 60-61 K 5
Caraquet o CDN 38-39 M 5
Carara Puca o BR 66-67 D 2
Carat, Tanjung ▲ RI 162-163 F 6
Caratasca, Cayo ∧ HN 54-55 D 6
Caratasca, Laguna de ≈ 54-55 C 7
Caratateua o BR 68-69 E 3
Caratinga o BR 72-73 J 5
Carauari o BR 66-67 D 5
Caraúbas o BR 68-69 K 4
Caravaca de la Cruz o E 98-99 G 5
Caravela o GNB 202-203 B 3
Caravelas o BR 72-73 L 4
Caraveli o PE 64-65 F 9
Caraz o PE 64-65 D 6
Carazinho o BR (CAT) 74-75 E 7
Carazinho o BR (RSU) 74-75 D 7
Carballino, O o E 98-99 C 3

Chena Hot Springs ○ **USA** 20-21 R 4
Chena River ~ **USA** 20-21 R 4
Chen Barag Qi ○ **VRC** 150-151 B 3
Ch'ench'a ○ **ETH** 208-209 C 5
Chencoyi ○ **MEX** 52-53 J 2
Chenereh, Kampung ○ **MAL** 162-163 E 2
Cheney ○ **USA** 40-41 F 2
Cheney Reservoir < **USA** 42-43 J 7
Chengalpattu ○ **IND** 140-141 H 4
Chengam ○ **IND** 140-141 H 4
Chengannūr ○ **IND** 140-141 G 6
Chengbu ○ **VRC** 156-157 F 3
Chengcheng ○ **VRC** 154-155 K 1
Chengde ☆ **VRC** 154-155 K 1
Chengdu ☆ **VRC** 154-155 D 6
Chenggu ○ **VRC** 154-155 E 5
Chenghai ○ **VRC** 156-157 K 5
Cheng Hai ○ **VRC** 142-143 M 2
Chengkung ○ **RC** 156-157 M 5
Chengmai ○ **VRC** 156-157 G 7
Chengqian ○ **VRC** 154-155 J 4
Chengshan Jiao ▲ **VRC** 154-155 N 3
Chengwu ○ **VRC** 154-155 J 4
Cheng Xian ○ **VRC** 154-155 D 5
Chenik ○ **USA** 22-23 T 3
Chenini ○ **TN** 190-191 H 4
Chenjiagang ○ **VRC** 154-155 L 4
Chenoa ○ **USA** 46-47 D 5
Chenpur ○ **NEP** 144-145 C 6
Chenque, Cerro ▲ **RA** 80 G 2
Chenxi ○ **VRC** (HUN) 156-157 G 2
Chenxi ○ **VRC** (SIC) 156-157 G 2
Chenzhou ○ **VRC** 156-157 H 4
Cheo Reo ○ **VN** 158-159 K 4
Chepen ○ **PE** 64-65 C 5
Chepes ○ **RA** 76-77 D 6
Chepes, Sierra de ▲ **RA** 76-77 D 6
Chepo ○ **PA** 52-53 E 7
Chepstow ○ **GB** 90-91 F 6
Chequamegon Bay ≈ **USA** 46-47 C 2
Cheran ○ **MEX** 52-53 D 2
Cheranchi ○ **WAN** 198-199 C 6
Cherangany Hills ▲ **EAK** 212-213 E 3
Cheraw ○ **USA** 48-49 J 2
Cherbourg ○ **F** 90-91 G 7
Cherchell ○ **DZ** 190-191 F 3
Cherepani ○ **IND** 140-141 H 2
Cherepovets ○ Čerepovec ☆ **RUS** 94-95 P 2
Cherful, Cape ▲ **USA** 22-23 N 5
Chergui, Khrebet ▲ **RIM** 196-197 C 6
Chergui, Zahrez ○ **DZ** 190-191 D 3
Cherhill ○ **CDN** 32-33 N 5
Chéri ○ **RN** 198-199 G 4
Cheria ○ **DZ** 190-191 F 3
Cheriāl ○ **IND** 140-141 H 2
Cherkasy ○ Čerkasy ☆ **UA** 102-103 H 3
Chernabura Island ∩ **USA** 22-23 R 5
Cherni Island ∩ **USA** 22-23 P 5
Chernivtsi ○ Černivci ☆ **UA** 102-103 D 3
Chernobyl ○ Čornobyl' ○ **UA** 102-103 G 2
Chernyakhovsk ○ Černjahovsk ○ **RUS** 94-95 G 4
Cherokee ○ **BS** 54-55 G 1
Cherokee ○ **USA** 42-43 K 4
Cherokee Indian Reservation ☒ **USA** 48-49 G 2
Cherokee Lake ○ **USA** 48-49 G 1
Cherokee Sound ○ **BS** 54-55 G 1
Cherrabun ○ **AUS** 172-173 G 5
Chérrepe, Punta de ▲ **PE** 64-65 C 5
Cherry Creek ○ **USA** 44-45 H 4
Cherryspring ○ **USA** 44-45 H 4
Cherryville ○ **CDN** 32-33 L 6
Cherryville ○ **USA** 42-43 M 7
Cherskogo, Khrebet ○ Čerskogo, hrebet ▲ **RUS** 110-111 W 5
Cherson ○ **UA** 102-103 H 4
Chesapeake ○ **USA** 46-47 K 7
Chesapeake Bay ≈ **USA** 46-47 K 6
Chesapeake Bay Bridge Tunnel II **USA** 46-47 L 7
Chesea, Río ~ **PE** 64-65 F 6
Chéshskaya Guba ○ Češskaja guba ≈ **RUS** 88-89 S 3
Chester ○ **CDN** 38-39 M 6
Chester ○ •• **GB** 90-91 F 5
Chester ○ **USA** (IA) 42-43 L 4
Chester ○ **USA** (IL) 46-47 D 7
Chester ○ **USA** (MT) 40-41 J 1
Chester ○ **USA** (PA) 46-47 L 6
Chester ○ **USA** (SC) 48-49 H 2
Chesterfield ○ **GB** 90-91 F 5
Chesterfield Inlet ○ **CDN** 30-31 X 4
Chesterfield Inlet ≈ **CDN** 30-31 Y 4
Chesterton Range ▲ **AUS** 178-179 J 3
Chestertown ○ **USA** 46-47 K 6
Chesuncook Lake ○ **USA** 46-47 O 3
Chétaibi ○ **DZ** 190-191 F 2
Chetek ○ **USA** 46-47 C 3
Chéticamp ○ **CDN** 38-39 O 5
Chetlat Island ∩ **IND** 140-141 E 5
Chetumal ☆ **MEX** 52-53 K 2
Chetumal, Bahía de ≈ **MEX** 52-53 K 2
Chetwynd ○ **CDN** 32-33 K 4
Chevak ○ **USA** 20-21 H 6
Chevejecure, Río ~ **BOL** 70-71 D 4
Cheviot Hills, The ▲ **GB** 90-91 F 4
Cheviot Range ▲ **AUS** 178-179 G 3
Chewack River ~ **USA** 40-41 D 1
Chewelah ○ **USA** 40-41 F 1
Chewore Safari Area ⊥ **ZW** 218-219 G 4
Cheyenne ○ **USA** (OK) 44-45 H 2
Cheyenne ☆ **USA** (WY) 42-43 E 5
Cheyenne River ~ **USA** 42-43 E 4
Cheyenne River Indian Reservation ☒ **USA** 42-43 G 3
Cheyenne Wells ○ **USA** 42-43 F 6
Cheyūr ○ **IND** 140-141 J 4
Chhāpar ○ **IND** 138-139 E 6
Chhatak ○ **BD** 142-143 G 3
Chhatarpur ○ **IND** 138-139 G 7

Chhattisgarh ⊥ **IND** 142-143 B 5
Chhaygaon ○ **IND** 142-143 G 2
Chheharta ○ **IND** 138-139 G 4
Chhindwāra ○ **IND** 138-139 G 8
Chhota Udepur ○ **IND** 138-139 E 8
Chhukha ○ **BHT** 142-143 F 2
Chhura ○ **IND** 142-143 A 4
Chiachi Island ∩ **USA** 22-23 R 5
Chiambon ○ **SP** 212-213 H 4
Chiangchūn ○ **RC** 156-157 M 5
Chiang Dao ○ **THA** 142-143 L 6
Chiang Kan ○ **THA** 158-159 F 6
Chiang Kham ○ **THA** 142-143 M 6
Chiang Khong ○ **THA** 142-143 M 5
Chiang Mai ☆ **THA** 142-143 L 6
Chiang Rai ○ **THA** 142-143 L 6
Chian Muan ○ **THA** 142-143 M 6
Chiapa ○ **MEX** 52-53 H 3
Chiapa de Corzo ○ **MEX** 52-53 H 3
Chiapas ⊟ **MEX** 52-53 H 3
Chiari ○ **I** 100-101 B 2
Chiasien ○ **RC** 156-157 M 5
Chiautla ○ **MEX** 52-53 E 2
Chiávari ○ **I** 100-101 B 2
Chiavenna ○ **I** 100-101 B 1
Chiawa ○ **Z** 218-219 E 2
Chiayi ○ **RC** 156-157 M 5
Chiba ☆ **J** 152-153 J 7
Chibabava ○ **MOC** 218-219 G 5
Chibembe ○ **Z** 218-219 G 1
Chibia ○ **ANG** 216-217 B 6
Chibiapani ○ **YV** 62-63 D 3
Chibi Moya ○ **VRC** 156-157 H 2
Chikodi ○ **IND** 140-141 F 2
Chibombo ○ **Z** 218-219 D 2
Chibougamau ○ **CDN** 38-39 G 4
Chibougamau, Lac ○ **CDN** 38-39 G 4
Chibougamau, Rivière ~ **CDN** 38-39 G 4
Chibuto ○ **MOC** 220-221 L 2
Chibuzhanghu ○ **VRC** 144-145 H 4
Chibwika ○ **Z** 214-215 C 7
Chica, Sierra ▲ **RA** 76-77 E 4
Chicago ○ •▲ **USA** 46-47 E 5
Chicago Heights ○ **USA** 46-47 E 5
Chicala ○ **ANG** (BIE) 216-217 D 6
Chicala ○ **ANG** (MOX) 216-217 D 6
Chicamba ○ **MOC** 218-219 G 4
Chicamba Real, Barragem de < **MOC** 218-219 G 4
Chicamba ○ **ANG** 216-217 D 6
Chicana ○ •.•• **MEX** 52-53 K 2
Chicapa ○ **ANG** 216-217 F 3
Chicas, Salinas ○ **RA** 78-79 H 5
Chicbul ○ **MEX** 52-53 J 1
Chicala ○ **ANG** 216-217 D 6
Chicha < **TCH** 198-199 J 4
Chichagof ○ **USA** 32-33 B 3
Chichagof Island ∩ **USA** 32-33 B 3
Chichancanab, Laguna ○ **MEX** 52-53 K 2
Chichaoua ○ **MA** 188-189 G 5
Chicharrona, La ○ **MEX** 50-51 H 6
Chicháwatni ○ **PK** 138-139 D 4
Chiché, Río ~ **BR** 68-69 B 6
Chicheng ○ **VRC** 154-155 J 1
Chichén Itzá •.•• **MEX** 52-53 K 1
Chichester Range ▲ **AUS** 172-173 D 7
Chichibu ○ **J** 152-153 H 7
Chichibu-Tama National Park ⊥ **J** 152-153 H 7
Chichigalpa ○ **NIC** 52-53 L 5
Chichirate ○ **EC** 64-65 D 3
Chichón, Volcan ▲ **MEX** 52-53 H 3
Chickaloon ○ **USA** 20-21 Q 6
Chickamauga Lake < **USA** 48-49 F 2
Chickasha ○ **USA** 44-45 J 2
Chic Kata ○ **RH** 54-55 J 5
Chicken ○ **USA** 20-21 U 4
Chiclayo ☆ **PE** 64-65 C 5
Chico ○ **MOC** 218-219 G 5
Chico ○ **USA** 40-41 D 6
Chico, Arroyo ~ **RA** 78-79 L 4
Chico, Río ~ **RA** 76-77 E 4
Chico, Río ~ **RA** 78-79 D 7
Chico, Río ~ **RA** 80 G 2
Chico, Río ~ **RA** 80 F 4
Chico, Río ~ **RA** 80 F 4
Chicoa ○ **MOC** 218-219 G 2
Chicoasén ○ **MEX** 52-53 H 3
Chicoasén, Presa < **MEX** 52-53 H 3
Chicoca ○ **ANG** 216-217 F 7
Chicoma Mountain ▲ **USA** 44-45 D 1
Chicomba ○ **ANG** 216-217 D 6
Chicomo ○ **MOC** 220-221 M 2
Chicomoztoc ∴ **MEX** 50-51 H 6
Chicomuselo ○ **MEX** 52-53 H 3
Chiconcua ○ **ANG** 216-217 B 7
Chicontepec de Tejeda ○ **MEX** 52-53 E 1
Chicopee ○ **USA** 46-47 M 4
Chicoral ○ **CO** 60-61 D 4
Chicoutimi ○ **CDN** 38-39 J 4
Chicualacuala ○ **MOC** 218-219 F 6
Chicuma ○ **ANG** 216-217 C 6
Chicundo ○ **ANG** 216-217 D 6
Chicupa ○ **ANG** 216-217 F 4
Ch'ida ○ **ETH** 208-209 C 5
Chidambaram ○ •• **IND** 140-141 H 5
Chidenguele ○ **MOC** 220-221 M 2
Chido ○ **ROK** 150-151 F 10
Chiede ○ **ANG** 216-217 C 8
Chief Joseph Pass ▲ **USA** 40-41 H 3
Chiefland ○ **USA** 48-49 H 5
Chief Menominee Monument • **USA** 46-47 F 5
Chiefs Island ∩ **RB** 218-219 B 4
Chiemsee ○ **D** 92-93 M 5
Chiengi ○ **Z** 214-215 F 5
Chiềng Khư'o'ng ○ **VN** 156-157 C 6
Chiengo ○ **ANG** 216-217 D 6
Chieo Lan Reservoir < **THA** 158-159 E 6
Chiese ~ **I** 100-101 C 2
Chieti ☆ **I** 100-101 E 3
Chifeng ○ **VRC** 148-149 O 6

Chifre, Serra do ▲ **BR** 72-73 K 4
Chifu ○ **WAN** 204-205 J 4
Chifukunya Hills ▲ **Z** 218-219 E 2
Chifumage ○ **ANG** 216-217 F 5
Chifunda ○ **Z** 214-215 G 6
Chifunde ○ **MOC** 218-219 G 2
Chig < **RIM** 196-197 D 5
Chigamane ○ **MOC** 218-219 G 5
Chiginagak, Mount ▲ **USA** 22-23 S 4
Chiginagak Bay ≈ **USA** 22-23 S 4
Chigmit Mountains ▲ **USA** 22-23 U 3
Chignecto, Cape ▲ **CDN** 38-39 M 6
Chignecto Bay ≈ **USA** 38-39 M 6
Chignik ○ **USA** 22-23 R 4
Chignik Bay ≈ **USA** 22-23 R 4
Chigombe, Rio ~ **MOC** 218-219 G 6
Chigorodo ○ **CO** 60-61 C 4
Chiguana ○ **BOL** 70-71 D 7
Chigubo ○ **MOC** 218-219 G 5
Chihli, Gulf of = Bo Hai ≈ **VRC** 154-155 L 2
Chijmuni ○ **BOL** 70-71 D 7
Chikanda ○ **WAN** 204-205 E 4
Chik Ballāpur ○ **IND** 140-141 G 4
Chikhli ○ **IND** (GUJ) 138-139 D 9
Chikhli ○ **IND** (MAH) 138-139 F 8
Chikhli ○ **IND** (MAP) 138-139 G 8
Chikjajur ○ **IND** 140-141 G 3
Chikmagalūr ○ **IND** 140-141 F 4
Chiknāyakanhalli ○ **IND** 140-141 G 4
Chikodi ○ **IND** 140-141 F 2
Chikombedzi ○ **ZW** 218-219 F 5
Chikonkomene ○ **Z** 218-219 E 2
Chikuma-gawa ~ **J** 152-153 H 6
Chikuminuk Lake ○ **USA** 20-21 L 6
Chikwa ○ **Z** 214-215 G 6
Chikwawa ○ **MW** 218-219 H 3
Chikwina ○ **MW** 214-215 H 6
Chikyu-misaki ▲ **J** 152-153 J 3
Chila ○ **ANG** 216-217 C 6
Chila, Laguna ○ **MEX** 50-51 K 6
Chilakalūrupet ○ **IND** 140-141 J 2
Chilako River ~ **CDN** 32-33 J 5
Chilan ○ **RC** 156-157 M 4
Chilanga ○ **Z** 218-219 E 2
Chilanko River ~ **CDN** 32-33 H 5
Chilapa ○ **MEX** 52-53 E 3
Chilapa de Díaz ○ **MEX** 52-53 F 3
Chilas ○ **IND** 138-139 D 2
Chilaw ○ **CL** 140-141 H 7
Chilca ○ **PE** 64-65 D 8
Chilca, Punta ▲ **PE** 64-65 D 8
Chilcas ○ **RA** 76-77 E 4
Chilcaya ○ **RCH** 70-71 C 6
Chilcoot ○ **USA** 40-41 D 6
Chilcotin Point ▲ **USA** 22-23 J 6
Chilcott Island ∩ **AUS** 178-179 K 3
Childers ○ **AUS** 178-179 M 3
Childersburg ○ **USA** 48-49 E 3
Childress ○ **USA** 44-45 G 2
Chile ■ **RCH** 78-79 C 5
Chile Chico ○ **RCH** 80 E 3
Chilecito ○ **RA** 76-77 D 5
Chileka ○ **MW** 218-219 H 3
Chilembwe ○ **Z** 218-219 F 1
Chilena, Cordillera ▲ **RCH** 80 D 6
Chilengue, Serra do ▲ **ANG** 216-217 C 6
Chile Rise ≈ **S** 5 B 8
Chiles, Los ○ **CR** 52-53 B 6
Chilete ○ **PE** 64-65 C 5
Chili, Gulf of = Bo Hai ≈ **VRC** 154-155 L 2
Chilikadrotna River ~ **USA** 20-21 N 6
Chililabombwe ○ **Z** 214-215 F 7
Chilkat ○ **USA** 20-21 W 7
Chilkat Bald Eagle Preserve ⊥ **USA** 20-21 W 7
Chilkat Inlet ≈ 20-21 X 7
Chilko Lake ○ **CDN** 32-33 H 6
Chilkoot Pass ▲ **USA** 20-21 X 7
Chilko River ~ **CDN** 32-33 H 6
Chilla ○ **EC** 64-65 C 3
Chillagoe ○ **AUS** 174-175 H 5
Chillajara ○ **BOL** 70-71 E 7
Chillán ○ **RCH** 78-79 C 4
Chillán, Río ~ **RCH** 78-79 D 4
Chillán, Volcán ▲ **RCH** 78-79 D 4
Chillar ○ **RA** 78-79 J 4
Chilla Well ○ **AUS** 172-173 K 6
Chillicothe ○ **USA** (IL) 46-47 D 5
Chillicothe ○ **USA** (MO) 42-43 L 6
Chillicothe ○ **USA** (OH) 46-47 H 6
Chillinji ○ **IND** 138-139 E 1
Chillúa Tāl ○ **IND** 142-143 C 2
Chillúpar ○ **IND** 142-143 C 2
Chilmari ○ **BD** 142-143 F 2
Chiloango ~ **ANG** 210-211 D 6
Chilobwe ○ **MW** 218-219 H 3
Chiloé, Isla de ∩ **RCH** 78-79 C 6
Chiloé, Parque Nacional ⊥ **RCH** 78-79 B 7
Chilolombo ○ **ANG** 214-215 B 7
Chilongozi ○ **Z** 218-219 F 1
Chiloquin ○ **USA** 40-41 D 4
Chilpancingo de los Bravos ☆ **MEX** 52-53 E 3
Chilpi ○ **IND** 142-143 B 4
Chiltepec ○ **MEX** 52-53 H 2
Chilton ○ **USA** 46-47 D 3
Chiluage ○ **ANG** 216-217 F 4
Chilubula ○ **Z** 214-215 F 6
Chilumba ○ **MW** 214-215 H 6
Chilumbulwa ○ **Z** 214-215 E 7
Chilwa, Lake ○ **MW** 218-219 H 2
Chimala ○ **EAT** 214-215 H 5
Chimalapa, Bahía ≈ **PE** 64-65 B 7
Chimaltenango ○ **GCA** 52-53 J 4
Chimán ○ **PA** 52-53 E 7
Chimanimani •• **ZW** 218-219 G 4

Chimanimani National Park ⊥ **ZW** 218-219 G 4
Chimasula ○ **Z** 218-219 F 2
Chimban ○ **PE** 64-65 C 5
Chimbangombe ○ **ANG** 216-217 D 6
Chimbinde ○ **ANG** 216-217 E 6
Chimbo, Río ~ **EC** 64-65 C 3
Chimborazo, Volcán ▲ **EC** 64-65 C 2
Chimbote ○ **PE** 64-65 C 6
Chimbwingombi ○ **Z** 218-219 F 1
Chiméal ○ **K** 158-159 J 5
Chimimanimani ○ **MOC** 218-219 G 4
Chimimuro ○ **ANG** 218-219 E 2
Chimina ○ **YV** 60-61 H 2
Chimney Rock National Historic Site ∴ **USA** 42-43 F 5
Chimoio ☆ **MOC** 218-219 G 4
Chimumo ○ **MOC** 218-219 H 3
Chimna ○ **MEX** 50-51 K 5
Chimna = Zhongguo ■ **VRC** 144-145 G 6
Chimnach, I~n~ < **RMM** 196-197 K 6
Chinacota ○ **CO** 60-61 F 3
Chinake ○ **IND** 140-141 F 2
Chinampas ○ **MEX** 50-51 J 3
Chinati Peak ▲ **USA** 44-45 E 5
Chincha, Islas de ∩ **PE** 64-65 D 8
Chincha Alta ○ **PE** 64-65 D 8
Chinchaga River ~ **CDN** 30-31 K 6
Chinchilla ○ **AUS** 178-179 L 4
Chinchilla de Monte Aragón ○ **E** 98-99 G 5
Chinchina ○ **CO** 60-61 D 5
Chinchorro, Banco ~ **MEX** 52-53 L 2
Chincoteague Bay ≈ **USA** 46-47 L 6
Chincua, Bahía ≈ **PE** 64-65 C 7
Chincultic ∴ **MEX** 52-53 H 3
Chinde ○ **MOC** 218-219 H 3
Chindo ○ **ROK** 150-151 F 10
Chin Do ○ **ROK** 150-151 F 10
Chindwin Myit ~ **MYA** 142-143 J 3
Chinese ○ **Z** 214-215 F 6
Chingando ○ **ANG** 216-217 D 6
Chingaza, Parque Nacional ⊥ **CO** 60-61 E 5
Chingo ○ **ANG** 216-217 B 7
Chingola ○ **Z** 214-215 D 7
Chingombe ○ **Z** 218-219 E 2
Chinguar ○ **ANG** 216-217 D 6
Chingueia ○ **ANG** 216-217 D 6
Chinguetti ○ **RIM** 196-197 D 4
Chingwin Bum ▲ **MYA** 142-143 L 3
Chinhama ○ **ANG** 216-217 D 6
Chinhanda ○ **MOC** 218-219 G 2
Chinhanguanine ○ **MOC** 220-221 L 2
Chin Hills ▲ **MYA** 142-143 H 4
Chinhoyi ○ **ZW** 218-219 F 3
Chinhsien ○ **CO** 60-61 C 4
Chiniak, Cape ▲ **USA** 22-23 U 4
Chiniak Bay ≈ 22-23 U 4
Chiniot ○ **PK** 138-139 D 4
Chinipas ○ **MEX** 50-51 F 4
Chinju ○ **ROK** 150-151 G 10
Chinko ~ **RCA** 206-207 G 6
Chinle ○ **USA** 44-45 D 1
Chinmen ○ **RC** 156-157 L 4
Chinmen Tao ∩ **RC** 156-157 L 4
Chinnūr ○ **IND** 138-139 G 10
Chino ○ **USA** 44-45 C 1
Chinon ○ **F** 90-91 H 8
Chinook ○ **USA** 42-43 L 1
Chinook Trough ≈ 14-15 L 3
Chinook Valley ○ **CDN** 32-33 M 3
Chino Valley ○ **USA** 44-45 D 2
Chinpurtar ○ **NEP** 144-145 E 7
Chinquite ○ **ANG** 216-217 B 6
Chinsali ○ **Z** 214-215 G 6
Chintāmani ○ **IND** 140-141 H 4
Chinteche ○ **MW** 214-215 H 6
Chinturu ○ **IND** 142-143 B 7
Chinvali ○ **GE** 126-127 F 6
Chinyama Litapi ○ **Z** 218-219 B 1
Chioa, Lago ~ **PE** 64-65 G 6
Chioco ○ **MOC** 218-219 G 2
Chióggia ○ **I** 100-101 D 2
Chipai Lake ○ **CDN** 34-35 N 4
Chipanga ○ **MOC** 218-219 G 3
Chipasanse ○ **Z** 214-215 F 6
Chipata ☆ **Z** 218-219 G 1
Chipepo ○ **Z** 218-219 D 2
Chiperone, Monte ▲ **MOC** 218-219 H 3
Chipewyan Indian Reserve ☒ **CDN** 30-31 O 4
Chipewyan River ~ **CDN** 32-33 O 3
Chipili ○ **Z** 214-215 F 6
Chipinda Pools ○ **ZW** 218-219 F 5
Chipindo ○ **ANG** 216-217 D 6
Chipinga ○ **ZW** 218-219 G 5
Chipinga Safari Area ⊥ **ZW** 218-219 G 5
Chipinge ○ **ZW** 218-219 G 5
Chipiona ○ **E** 98-99 D 6
Chipipa ○ **ANG** 216-217 C 6
Chipiriri, Río ~ **BOL** 70-71 E 5
Chip Lake ○ **CDN** 32-33 N 5
Chipman Lake ○ **CDN** 34-35 N 4
Chipman River ~ **CDN** 34-35 N 6
Chipogolo ○ **EAT** 214-215 H 5
Chipoka ○ **MW** 218-219 H 1
Chipolopole ○ **Z** 214-215 F 6
Chippenham ○ **GB** 90-91 F 6
Chippewa, Lake ○ **USA** 46-47 C 3
Chippewa Falls ○ **USA** 46-47 C 3
Chipungo ○ **Z** 218-219 G 1
Chiputneticook Lakes ~ **USA** 46-47 P 3
Chiputo ○ **MOC** 218-219 G 2
Chiquián ○ **PE** 64-65 D 6
Chiquilá ○ **MEX** 52-53 L 1
Chiquimula ○ **GCA** 52-53 J 4
Chiquimulilla ○ **GCA** 52-53 J 4
Chiquinata, Bahía ≈ **RCH** 70-71 C 7
Chiquinquirá ○ **CO** 60-61 E 5
Chiquitos, Llanos de ∴ **BOL** 70-71 G 6

Ch'ira ○ **ETH** 208-209 C 5
Chira, Río ~ **PE** 64-65 B 4
Chirala ○ **IND** 140-141 J 3
Chiramba ○ **MOC** 218-219 H 3
Chiredzi ○ **ZW** 218-219 F 5
Chirfa ○ **RN** 198-199 J 2
Chiriaco ○ **PE** 64-65 C 5
Chiribiquete, Raudal ≈ **CO** 64-65 F 1
Chiricahua Peak ▲ **USA** 44-45 E 5
Chiriguare, Reserva Faunística ⊥ **YV** 60-61 G 3
Chirimena ○ **YV** 60-61 H 2
Chiriqui, Golfo de ≈ **PA** 52-53 C 7
Chiriqui, Laguna de ≈ **PA** 52-53 C 7
Chiriqui Grande ○ **PA** 52-53 C 7
Chiris, Río ~ **PE** 64-65 E 8
Chiri San ▲ **ROK** 150-151 F 10
Chirisan National Park ⊥ **ROK** 150-151 F 10
Chirma Safari Area ⊥ **ZW** 218-219 E 3
Chirmiri ○ **IND** 142-143 B 4
Chirombo ○ **MW** 214-215 H 6
Chiromo ○ **MW** 218-219 H 3
Chirpan ○ **BG** 102-103 L 7
Chirripó, Río ~ **CR** 52-53 C 7
Chirripó del Atlántico, Río ~ **CR** 52-53 C 7
Chirripó Grande, Cerro ▲ **CR** 52-53 C 7
Chirumanzu ○ **ZW** 218-219 F 4
Chirundu ○ **Z** 218-219 E 3
Chirundu ○ **ZW** 218-219 E 3
Chisamba ○ **Z** 218-219 E 2
Chisana ○ **USA** 20-21 U 5
Chisana River ~ **USA** 20-21 U 5
Chisasa ○ **Z** 214-215 C 7
Chisasibi ○ **CDN** 38-39 E 2
Chisec ○ **GCA** 52-53 J 4
Chisekesi ○ **Z** 218-219 D 3
Chisenga ○ **MW** 214-215 H 5
Chishan ○ **RC** 156-157 M 5
Chishang ○ **RC** 156-157 M 5
Chisholm ○ **USA** 42-43 L 2
Chishtian Mandy ○ **PK** 138-139 D 5
Chishui ○ **VRC** 156-157 D 2
Chishuihe ○ **VRC** 156-157 D 2
Chishui He ~ **VRC** 156-157 D 2
Chisik Island ∩ **USA** 20-21 O 6
Chisimba Falls ≈ **Z** 214-215 F 6
Chişinău ★ **MD** 102-103 E 4
Chissano ○ **MOC** 220-221 L 2
Chissibuca ○ **MOC** 220-221 M 2
Chissinguane ○ **MOC** 218-219 H 2
Chistián Mandy ○ **PK** 138-139 D 5
Chisumbanje ○ **ZW** 218-219 G 5
Chita ○ **BOL** 70-71 D 4
Chita ○ **EAT** 214-215 H 4
Chita = Čita ☆ **RUS** 118-119 F 9
Chitado ○ **ANG** 216-217 B 8
Chitaga ○ **CO** 60-61 F 4
Chitāpur ○ **IND** 140-141 G 2
Chitek ○ **CDN** 34-35 H 5
Chitek Lake ○ **CDN** 34-35 K 5
Chitembo ○ **ANG** 216-217 D 6
Chí Thanh ○ **VN** 158-159 K 4
Chitina ○ **USA** 20-21 T 6
Chitina River ~ **USA** 20-21 T 6
Chitipa ○ **MW** 214-215 G 5
Chitkanook ○ **AUS** 180-181 G 3
Chitobe ○ **MOC** 218-219 G 4
Chitongo ○ **Z** 218-219 D 3
Chitose ○ **J** 152-153 K 3
Chitowe ○ **EAT** 214-215 K 6
Chitradurga ○ **IND** 140-141 G 3
Chitrakūt ○ **IND** 142-143 B 3
Chitré ○ **PA** 52-53 D 8
Chittagong ○ **BD** 142-143 G 4
Chittaurgarh ○ **IND** 138-139 E 7
Chittivalasa ○ **IND** 142-143 C 7
Chittoor ○ **IND** 140-141 H 4
Chitungwiza ○ **ZW** 218-219 F 3
Chityal ○ **IND** 140-141 H 2
Chiu Chiu ○ **RCH** 70-71 D 7
Chiulezi, Rio ~ **MOC** 214-215 J 6
Chiumbe ~ **ANG** 216-217 F 4
Chiumbo ○ **ANG** 216-217 D 6
Chiume ○ **ANG** 216-217 F 7
Chiúre Novo ○ **MOC** 218-219 K 1
Chivacoa ○ **YV** 60-61 G 2
Chivasing ○ **PNG** 183 D 4
Chivasso ○ **I** 100-101 A 2
Chivato ○ **RCH** 76-77 B 4
Chivay ○ **PE** 70-71 B 4
Chivé ○ **BOL** 70-71 D 3
Chiviru ○ **ZW** 218-219 F 4
Chivilcoy ○ **RA** 78-79 K 3
Chivirico ○ **C** 54-55 G 5
Chiviringa Falls ≈ **ZW** 218-219 D 3
Chivuna ○ **Z** 218-219 D 3
Chiweta ○ **MW** 214-215 H 6
Chixoy o Negro, Río ~ **GCA** 52-53 J 4
Chizarira Hills ▲ **ZW** 218-219 D 3
Chizarira National Park ⊥ **ZW** 218-219 D 3
Chizela ○ **Z** 218-219 C 1
Chizu ○ **J** 152-153 F 7
Chizwina ○ **RB** 218-219 C 3
Chlef ☆ **DZ** 190-191 C 2
Chmel'nyc'kyj ○ **UA** 102-103 D 3
Chmel'nyc'kyj, Perejaslav- ○ **UA** 102-103 G 2
Chnattisgarh ⊥ **IND** 142-143 B 5
Chôâm Khsant ○ **K** 158-159 H 3
Choapa, Río ~ **RCH** 76-77 B 6
Choapas, Las ○ **MEX** 52-53 G 3
Chobe □ **RB** 218-219 C 3
Chobe, Rio ~ **Z** 218-219 C 4
Chobe National Park ⊥ **RB** 218-219 C 4
Chocaca, Cerro ▲ **PE** 64-65 E 9
Chochola ○ **MEX** 52-53 J 1
Choconta ○ **CO** 60-61 E 5

Christina River ~ **CDN** 32-33 P 3
Christino Castro ○ **BR** 68-69 F 6
Christmas, Islas ∩ **MOC** 8 D 7
Christmas Creek ○ **AUS** 172-173 G 5
Christmas Creek ~ **AUS** 172-173 H 5
Christmas Island ∩ **AUS** 13 B 4
Christopher Lake ○ **CDN** 34-35 J 5
Chromer ○ **GB** 90-91 H 5
Chuali, Lagoa ○ **MOC** 220-221 L 2
Chuave ○ **PNG** 183 C 4
Chub Cay ∩ **BS** 54-55 G 2
Chubu-Sangaku National Park ⊥ **J** 152-153 G 6
Chubut □ **RA** 78-79 D 7
Chubut, Río ~ **RA** 78-79 E 7
Chuchi Lake ○ **CDN** 32-33 H 4
Chucuma ○ **RA** 76-77 D 6
Chucunaque ~ **PA** 52-53 E 7
Chu Dang Sin ▲ **VN** 158-159 K 4
Chudleigh ○ **AUS** 38-39 D 5
Chudskoye Ozero = Čudskoe ozero ○ **RUS** 94-95 K 2
Chugach Islands ∩ **USA** 22-23 V 4
Chugach Mountains ▲ **USA** 20-21 R 6
Chugchug, Cerros de ▲ **RCH** 76-77 C 2
Chugchug, Quebrada ~ **RCH** 76-77 C 2
Chugiak ○ **USA** 20-21 Q 6
Chuginadak Island ∩ **USA** 22-23 L 6
Chugoku-sanchi ▲ **J** 152-153 E 7
Chugul Island ∩ **USA** 22-23 J 7
Chugwater ○ **USA** 42-43 E 5
Chuhar Jamāli ○ **PK** 134-135 M 6
Chuhar Kāna ○ **PK** 138-139 D 4
Ch'uja Do ∩ **ROK** 150-151 F 11
Chuka ○ **EAK** 212-213 F 4
Chukai ○ **MAL** 162-163 E 2
Chukchi Autonomous District = Čukotskij avtonomnyj okrug ▫ **RUS** 112-113 N 3
Chukchi Plateau ≈ 16 B 35
Chukchi Sea ≈ 112-113 X 1
Chukotat, Rivière ~ **CDN** 36-37 L 4
Chukotskiy Poluostrov = Čukotskij poluostrov ∩ **RUS** 112-113 W 3
Chulas, Raudal las ≈ **CO** 60-61 F 6
Chulitna River ~ **USA** 20-21 Q 6
Chulucanas ○ **PE** 64-65 B 4
Chuma ○ **BOL** 70-71 D 4
Chuma Shankou ▲ **VRC** 144-145 L 5
Chumba ○ **ETH** 208-209 D 6
Chumbicha ○ **RA** 76-77 D 5
Chumbo ○ **BR** 72-73 G 5
Chumikgiarsa ○ **IND** 138-139 F 3
Chumphae ○ **THA** 158-159 G 2
Chumphon ○ **THA** 158-159 E 5
Chumpi ○ **PE** 64-65 F 9
Chumpón ○ **MEX** 52-53 L 2
Chumsaeng ○ **THA** 158-159 F 3
Chumul ∴ **MEX** (YUC) 52-53 K 2
Chumul ∴ **MEX** (YUC) 52-53 K 1
Chun ○ **THA** 142-143 M 6
Chunán ○ **VRC** 156-157 L 2
Chunán ○ **VRC** 156-157 B 4
Chuncar ○ **PE** 64-65 C 9
Chunchanga, Pampa de ∴ **PE** 64-65 E 9
Chunchi ○ **EC** 64-65 C 3
Ch'unch'ŏn ○ **ROK** 150-151 F 9
Chunchura ○ **IND** 142-143 F 4
Chunga ○ **Z** 218-219 F 7
Chungara, Lago ○ **RCH** 70-71 C 6
Chunggang ○ **DVR** 150-151 F 7
Ch'ungju ○ **ROK** 150-151 F 9
Chungu ○ **Z** 214-215 F 6
Chungui ○ **PE** 64-65 F 8
Chungyang Shanmo ▲ **RC** 156-157 M 5
Chúnian ○ **PK** 138-139 D 4
Chuniespoort ○ **ZA** 220-221 J 2
Chunshui ○ **VRC** 154-155 H 5
Chunu, Cape ▲ **USA** 22-23 H 7
Chunya ○ **EAT** 214-215 G 5
Chuŏr Phnum Dângrek ▲ **K** 158-159 G 3
Chupabe, Caño ~ **CO** 60-61 G 6
Chupadero de Caballo ○ **MEX** 50-51 J 3
Chu' Pha ○ **VN** 158-159 J 4
Chuquibamba ○ **PE** 64-65 F 9
Chuquicamata ○ **RCH** 76-77 C 2
Chuquicara ○ **PE** 64-65 C 6
Chuquiribamba ○ **EC** 64-65 C 3
Chuquis ○ **PE** 64-65 D 7
Churachándpur ○ **IND** 142-143 H 3
Churcampa ○ **PE** 64-65 E 8
Churchbridge ○ **CDN** 34-35 F 5
Churchill ○ **CDN** 30-31 W 6
Churchill, Cap ▲ **CDN** 30-31 X 6
Churchill Falls ○ **CDN** 38-39 M 2
Churchill Lake ○ **CDN** 30-31 P 6
Churchill Reef ∩ **AUS** 172-173 F 3
Churchill Sound ○ 36-37 J 7
Churchs Ferry ○ **USA** 42-43 H 1
Chureo o Deshecho, Paso ▲ **RA** 78-79 D 4
Churia Range ▲ **NEP** 144-145 E 7
Churin ○ **PE** 64-65 D 7
Churubusco ○ **USA** 46-47 F 5
Churu ○ **IND** 138-139 E 6
Churuguara ○ **YV** 60-61 G 2
Chuska Mountains ▲ **USA** 44-45 C 1
Chusmisa ○ **RCH** 70-71 C 6
Chūsonji ○ **J** 152-153 J 5
Chust ○ **UA** 102-103 C 3
Chute-des-Passes ○ **CDN** 38-39 J 4
Chutine Landing ○ **CDN** 32-33 E 3
Chuvashia = Čavaš respubliki ▫ **RUS** 96-97 E 6

Chuwangsan National Park ⊥ • ROK 150-151 G 9
Chuxiong ○ VRC 156-157 B 4
Chuy ○ ROU 74-75 D 9
Chuzhou ○ VRC 154-155 L 5
Chwaka ○ EAT 214-215 K 4
Chyulu Hills ▲ EAK 212-213 F 5
Ciágola, Monte ▲ I 100-101 E 5
Ciamis ○ RI 168 C 3
Ciandur ○ RI 168 A 3
Cianjur ○ RI 168 B 3
Ciano ○ EC 64-65 C 3
Cianorte ○ BR 72-73 D 7
Čiatura ○ GE 126-127 E 6
Cibadak ○ RI 168 B 3
Čibagalah ~ RUS 110-111 Y 6
Čibagalahskij hrebet ▲ RUS 110-111 W 6
Cibatu ○ RI 168 B 3
Čibit ○ RUS 124-125 P 3
Cibit ○ RUS 124-125 P 3
Cibitoke ○ BU 212-213 B 5
Cibu ▲ MEX 50-51 D 2
Cicalengka ○ RI 168 B 3
Čičatka, Bol'šaja ~ RUS 118-119 K 8
Cícero Dantas ○ BR 68-69 J 7
Cicia ⌒ FJI 184 III c 2
Čičkajul ~ RUS 114-115 T 6
Cicurug ○ RI 168 B 3
Cidade Gaúcha ○ BR 72-73 D 7
Cide ☆ TR 128-129 E 2
Ciechanów ☆ • PL 92-93 Q 2
Ciego, El ○ C 54-55 G 4
Ciego de Ávila ☆ C 54-55 F 4
Ciempozuelos ○ E 98-99 F 4
Ciénaga ○ CO 60-61 D 2
Cienaga, La ○ RA 76-77 C 5
Ciénaga Grande de Santa Marta ≈ 60-61 D 2
Cieneguillas ○ RA 76-77 E 2
Cienfuegos ☆ C 54-55 E 3
Cieszanów ○ PL 92-93 R 3
Cieza ○ E 98-99 G 5
Çifteler ☆ TR 128-129 D 3
Cifuentes ○ C 54-55 E 3
Cifuentes ○ E 98-99 F 4
Cifuncho ○ RCH 76-77 B 3
Cigarette Springs Cave • USA 42-43 C 7
Cigarro ○ BR 66-67 F 4
Ciglera, ostrov ⌒ RUS 84-85 e 2
Cihanbeyli ☆ TR 128-129 E 3
Cihanbeyli Yaylası ▲ TR 128-129 E 3
Cihuatlán ○ MEX 52-53 B 2
Čiili ○ KA 124-125 E 6
Cíjara, Reserva Nacional de ⊥ E 98-99 E 5
Cijulang ○ RI 168 C 3
Cikajang ○ RI 168 B 3
Cikalongkulon ○ RI 168 B 3
Cikalongwetan ○ RI 168 B 3
Cikampek ○ RI 168 B 3
Čikoj ○ RUS 116-117 N 10
Čikoj ~ RUS 116-117 N 10
Čikoj ~ RUS 116-117 O 10
Čikoj ~ RUS 118-119 E 10
Čikoj ~ RUS 118-119 E 11
Čikokon ~ RUS 118-119 E 10
Čikokonskij, hrebet ▲ RUS 118-119 D 11
Cikotok ○ • RI 168 B 3
Čikšina ~ RUS 88-89 Y 4
Čikšina ~ RUS 114-115 D 2
Cilacap ○ RI 168 C 3
Cilamaya ○ RI 168 B 3
Cilaos ○ F 224 B 7
Cilaos, Cirque de • F 224 B 7
Čilat ○ IRQ 128-129 M 6
Čil'či ○ RUS 118-119 L 7
Çıldır ○ TR 128-129 K 2
Çıldır Gölü ○ TR 128-129 K 2
Ciledug ○ RI 168 C 3
Cileungsi ○ RI 168 B 3
Cili ○ VRC 156-157 G 2
Cilibia ○ RO 102-103 E 5
Čilik ○ KA 146-147 D 4
Čilik ~ KA 146-147 C 4
Čilipi ○ HR 100-101 G 3
Cill Airne = Killarney ○ • IRL 90-91 C 5
Cill Bheagáin = Kilbeggan ○ IRL 90-91 D 5
Cill Chainnigh = Kilkenny ☆ • IRL 90-91 D 5
Cill Chaoi = Kilkee ○ IRL 90-91 C 5
Cill Dara = Kildare ○ IRL 90-91 D 5
Čilli ~ RUS 118-119 J 3
Cill Mhantáin = Wicklow ☆ IRL 90-91 D 5
Cill Orglan = Killorglin ○ IRL 90-91 C 5
Cill Rois = Kilrush ○ IRL 90-91 C 5
Čil'ma ~ RUS 88-89 U 4
Čil'ma ~ RUS 88-89 V 4
Čil'mamedkum ∸ TM 136-137 D 4
Cimahi ○ RI 168 B 3
Cimanggu ○ RI 168 A 3
Cimanuk, Tanjung ▲ RI 168 C 3
Cimarron ○ USA (KS) 42-43 G 7
Cimarron ○ USA (NM) 44-45 E 1
Cimarron ~ USA 44-45 H 1
Cimarron National Grassland ⊥ USA 44-45 G 1
Cimarron River ~ USA 44-45 F 1
Čimbaj ○ US 136-137 F 3
Čimboj ☆ US 136-137 F 3
Cimbur ○ RI 166-167 C 6
Čimčememel' ~ RUS 112-113 O 3
Čimidikjan ~ RUS 110-111 M 6
Cimişlia ☆ MD 102-103 F 4
Cimitarra ○ CO 60-61 E 4
Čimljansk ○ RUS 102-103 N 4
Cimljanskoe vodohranilišče < RUS 102-103 N 4
Cimmermanovka ○ RUS 122-123 H 3
Cîmpeni ○ RO 102-103 C 4
Cîmpina ○ • RO 102-103 D 5
Cimpu ○ RI 164-165 G 5
Cîmpulung ○ • RO 102-103 D 5
Cîmpulung Moldovenesc ○ • RO 102-103 D 4
Čina ~ RUS 116-117 L 3
Čina ~ RUS 118-119 F 8
Cina, Tanjung ▲ RI 162-163 F 7
Çınar ☆ TR 128-129 J 4
Cinaruco, Río ~ YV 60-61 H 4
Cincel, Río ~ RA 76-77 D 2
Cincinnati ○ USA 46-47 F 6
Cinco Balas, Cayos ⌒ C 54-55 F 4
Cinco de Maio, Cachoeira ~ BR 70-71 K 3
Çine ☆ • TR 128-129 C 4
Činejveem ~ RUS 112-113 Q 3
Cingaly ○ RUS 114-115 K 4
Čingandža, gora ▲ RUS 112-113 H 4
Cingera, mys ▲ RUS 108-109 f 2
Čingildi ○ US 136-137 J 4
Cingirlau ○ KA 96-97 H 8
Čingis Chaan Cherem ∴ • MAU 148-149 L 3
Cinnabar Mountain ▲ USA 40-41 F 4
Činoz ☆ US 136-137 L 4
Činozero, ozero ○ RUS 88-89 M 5
Cinque Island ⌒ IND 140-141 L 4
Cinta, Serra da ▲ BR 68-69 E 5
Cintalapa de Figueroa ○ MEX 52-53 H 3
Cinto, Monte ▲ F 98-99 M 3
Cintra ○ RA 78-79 H 2
Cintra, Golfe de ≈ 196-197 B 3
Cinuelos, Los ○ DOM 54-55 K 5
Cinzas, Rio das ~ BR 72-73 E 7
Ciotat, la ○ F 90-91 K 10
Čipa ~ RUS 118-119 G 8
Cipanda ○ RUS 120-121 F 4
Cipatujah ○ RI 168 C 3
Čipikan ○ RUS 118-119 F 8
Čipikan ~ RUS 118-119 E 8
Cipo, Rio ~ BR 72-73 J 5
Cipoal ○ BR 66-67 E 3
Cipolândia ○ BR 70-71 K 7
Cipolletti ○ RA 78-79 F 5
Cipotuba, Ilha ⌒ BR 66-67 F 4
Čir ~ RUS 102-103 N 3
Circa ○ PE 64-65 F 8
Čirčik ○ US 136-137 L 4
Čirčik ~ US 136-137 L 4
Circle ○ USA (AK) 20-21 S 4
Circle ○ USA (MT) 42-43 E 2
Circleville ○ USA 46-47 G 6
Circular Head ▲ AUS 180-181 H 6
Circular Reef ⌒ PNG 183 D 2
Cirebon ○ • RI 168 C 3
Čirikovo ○ RUS 94-95 P 4
Čirin, vulkan ▲ RUS 122-123 M 6
Čirinda ○ RUS 116-117 K 2
Ciriquiri, Rio ~ BR 66-67 E 7
Čirka Kem' ~ RUS 88-89 M 5
Cir Kud ○ SP 212-213 J 2
Čirkuo ~ RUS 118-119 D 4
Cirò ○ I 100-101 F 5
Čirokči ○ US 136-137 K 5
Čirpan ○ BG 102-103 D 6
Cirque, Cerro ▲ BOL 70-71 C 5
Cirque Mountain ▲ CDN 36-37 S 5
Ciruelo, El ○ MEX 50-51 D 5
Cisarua ○ RI 168 B 3
Cisco ○ USA (TX) 44-45 H 3
Cisco ○ USA (UT) 42-43 C 6
Ciskei (former Homeland, now part of East-Cape) ◻ ZA 220-221 H 5
Čiskova ~ RUS 116-117 G 3
Čišmy ☆ RUS 96-97 J 6
Cisne, Islas del = Islas Santanilla ⌒ HN 54-55 D 6
Cisne, Laguna del ○ RA 76-77 F 5
Cisne, Santuario del • EC 64-65 C 3
Cisnes, Río ~ RCH 80 E 2
Cisnes Medio ○ RCH 80 D 2
Cisolok ○ RI 168 B 3
Cisséla ○ RG 202-203 E 4
Cistern Point ▲ BS 54-55 G 3
Cistierna ○ E 98-99 E 3
Čistoe, ozero ○ RUS 120-121 O 4
Čistopol' ☆ RUS 96-97 G 6
Čistopol'e ☆ KA 124-125 E 2
Čita ☆ • RUS 118-119 F 9
Čita ~ RUS 118-119 F 9
Citadelle, La ∴ ••• RH 54-55 J 5
Cita Kandaw, Kōtal-e ▲ AFG 138-139 B 3
Citaré, Rio ~ BR 62-63 G 5
Citiari, Igarapé ~ BR 66-67 E 6
Citronelle ○ USA 48-49 D 4
Citrusdal ○ ZA 220-221 D 6
Citrus Heights ○ USA 40-41 D 6
Città del Vaticano ★ ••• SCV 100-101 D 4
Cittanova ○ I 100-101 F 5
Ciu ○ RI 164-165 L 2
Ciudad ○ MEX 50-51 G 6
Ciudad Acuña ○ MEX 50-51 J 3
Ciudad Altamirano ○ MEX 52-53 D 2
Ciudad Bolívar ☆ • YV 60-61 K 3
Ciudad Camargo ○ • MEX 50-51 G 4
Ciudad Colon ○ CR 52-53 B 7
Ciudad Constitución ○ • MEX 50-51 D 5
Ciudad Cortes ○ CR 52-53 C 7
Ciudad Cuauhtémoc ○ MEX 52-53 J 4
Ciudad Darío ○ • NIC 52-53 L 5
Ciudad de Guatemala = Guatemala ★ •• GCA 52-53 J 4
Ciudad del Carmen ○ • MEX 52-53 J 2
Ciudad del Este ☆ PY 76-77 K 3
Ciudad del Maíz ○ MEX 50-51 K 6
Ciudad de México = México ★ ••• MEX 52-53 E 2
Ciudad de Nutria ○ YV 60-61 G 3
Ciudad Guayana ○ • YV 60-61 K 3
Ciudad Guzman ○ • MEX 52-53 C 2
Ciudad Hidalgo ○ MEX 52-53 D 2
Ciudad Ixtepec ○ MEX 52-53 G 3
Ciudad Juárez ○ • MEX 50-51 F 2
Ciudad Lerdo ○ MEX 50-51 H 5
Ciudad López Mateos ○ MEX 52-53 E 2
Ciudad Madero ○ MEX 50-51 L 6
Ciudad Mante ○ MEX 50-51 K 6
Ciudad Melchor de Mentos ○ GCA 52-53 K 3
Ciudad Mutis = Bahía Solano ○ CO 60-61 C 4
Ciudad Neily ○ CR 52-53 C 7
Ciudad Nezahualcóyotl ○ MEX 52-53 E 2
Ciudad Obregón ○ MEX 50-51 E 4
Ciudad Ojeda ○ YV 60-61 F 2
Ciudad Pemex ○ MEX 52-53 H 3
Ciudad Piar ○ YV 60-61 K 4
Ciudad Quesada ○ CR 52-53 B 6
Ciudad Real ○ • E 98-99 F 5
Ciudad-Rodrigo ○ •• E 98-99 D 4
Ciudad Sahagún ○ MEX 52-53 E 2
Ciudad Serdán ○ MEX 52-53 F 2
Ciudad Valles ○ MEX 50-51 K 7
Ciudad Victoria ☆ • MEX 50-51 K 6
Ciutadella ○ E 98-99 J 5
Civil'sk ○ RUS 96-97 E 6
Civita Castellana ○ • I 100-101 D 3
Civitanova Marche ○ I 100-101 D 3
Civitavécchia ○ I 100-101 C 3
Civol'ki, zaliv ○ RUS 108-109 H 4
Çivril ☆ TR 128-129 C 3
Ciwidey ○ RI 168 B 3
Cixi ○ VRC 154-155 M 6
Čiža ○ RUS 88-89 S 3
Čižapka ~ RUS 114-115 P 5
Čižinskij taskyn cu ○ KA 96-97 F 8
Cizre ☆ TR 128-129 K 4
Cjurupyns'k ○ UA 102-103 H 4
Čkalov ○ RUS 110-111 Z 4
Čkalovsk ○ RUS 94-95 S 3
Clacton-on-Sea ○ GB 90-91 H 6
Clain ~ F 90-91 H 8
Claire, Lake ○ CDN 30-31 N 6
Claire City ○ USA 42-43 J 3
Clairemont ○ USA 44-45 G 3
Clair Engle Lake ○ USA 40-41 C 5
Clair Falls ~ CDN 30-31 X 3
Clairview ○ AUS 178-179 K 2
Clamecy ○ F 90-91 J 8
Clam Lake ○ USA 46-47 C 2
Clanton ○ USA 48-49 E 3
Clanville ○ ZA 220-221 H 5
Clanwilliam ○ ZA 220-221 D 6
Claquato Church ∴ USA 40-41 C 2
Clara, Punta ▲ RA 78-79 G 7
Clara City ○ USA 42-43 K 3
Clarafield ○ AUS 178-179 G 1
Clara Island ⌒ MYA 158-159 D 5
Claravale ○ AUS 172-173 K 3
Claraville ○ AUS (NT) 178-179 C 2
Claraville ○ AUS (QLD) 174-175 F 6
Clare ○ AUS (QLD) 174-175 J 6
Clare ○ AUS (QLD) 178-179 H 2
Clare ○ AUS (SA) 180-181 E 2
Clare ○ USA 46-47 F 4
Claremont ○ USA 46-47 M 4
Claremore ○ USA 44-45 K 1
Clarence ○ NZ 182 D 5
Clarence, Cape ▲ CDN 24-25 b 4
Clarence, Isla ⌒ RCH 80 E 6
Clarence, Port ≈ 20-21 G 4
Clarence Island ⌒ ARK 16 G 31
Clarence River ~ AUS 178-179 M 5
Clarence Strait ≈ 32-33 D 3
Clarence Strait ≈ 172-173 K 2
Clarence Town ○ • BS 54-55 H 3
Clarendon ○ USA 44-45 G 2
Clarens ○ ZA 220-221 J 4
Clarenville ○ CDN 38-39 R 4
Claresholm ○ CDN 32-33 O 6
Clarie, Terre ∸ ARK 16 G 14
Clarinda ○ USA 42-43 K 5
Clarines ○ • YV 60-61 J 3
Clarion ○ USA (IA) 42-43 L 4
Clarion ○ USA (PA) 46-47 J 5
Clarión, Isla ⌒ MEX 50-51 A 7
Clarion Fracture Zone ≃ 14-15 O 6
Clarion River ~ USA 46-47 J 5
Clark ○ USA 42-43 J 3
Clark, Lake ○ USA 20-21 N 6
Clark Canyon Reservoir < USA 40-41 H 3
Clarkdale ○ USA 40-41 H 8
Clarke, Cape ▲ CDN 24-25 d 7
Clarke City ○ CDN 38-39 L 3
Clarke Island ⌒ AUS 180-181 K 6
Clarke Lake ○ CDN 34-35 C 3
Clarke Range ▲ AUS 174-175 J 7
Clarke River ~ AUS 174-175 H 6
Clarke River ~ CDN 30-31 S 4
Clarke River P.O. ○ AUS 174-175 H 6
Clarkfield ○ USA 42-43 K 3
Clark Fork ○ USA 40-41 F 1
Clark Fork River ~ USA 40-41 G 2
Clarkleigh ○ CDN 34-35 G 5
Clark Mountain ▲ USA 40-41 G 8
Clarks ○ USA 42-43 J 5
Clarksburg ○ USA 46-47 H 6
Clarksdale ○ USA 44-45 M 2
Clarks Fork River ~ USA 42-43 C 3
Clarks Hill Lake ○ USA 48-49 G 3
Clarks Junction ○ NZ 182 C 6
Clarkson ○ ZA 220-221 G 6
Clarks Point ○ USA 22-23 R 3
Clarkston ○ USA 40-41 F 2
Clarksville ○ USA (AR) 44-45 L 2
Clarksville ○ USA (TN) 48-49 E 1
Clarksville ○ USA (TX) 44-45 K 3
Clarksville ○ USA (VA) 46-47 J 7
Claro, Rio ~ BR 66-67 K 6
Claro, Rio ~ BR 72-73 D 4
Claro, Rio ~ BR 72-73 E 4
Claromecó ○ RA 78-79 J 5
Claros, Los ○ YV 60-61 F 2
Clatsop National Memorial, Fort ∴ USA 40-41 C 2
Claude ○ USA 44-45 G 2
Cláudia ○ BR 70-71 K 2
Claudio Gay, Cordillera ▲ RCH 76-77 C 4
Claushavn = Ilimanaq ○ GRØ 28-29 P 2
Claveria ○ RP (CAG) 160-161 D 3
Claveria ○ RP (MAS) 160-161 E 6
Claxton ○ USA 48-49 H 3
Claybank ○ CDN 34-35 D 5
Clay Belt ∸ CDN 34-35 Q 5
Clay Center ○ USA (KS) 42-43 J 6
Clay Center ○ USA (NE) 42-43 H 5
Clay City ○ USA 46-47 G 7
Clayoquot Sound ≈ 32-33 G 7
Clay River ~ PNG 183 C 3
Clayton ○ USA (AL) 48-49 F 4
Clayton ○ USA (GA) 48-49 G 2
Clayton ○ USA (LA) 44-45 M 4
Clayton ○ USA (NM) 44-45 F 1
Clayton ○ USA (OK) 44-45 K 2
Clear Creek ~ USA 20-21 R 4
Cleardale ○ CDN 32-33 L 3
Cleare, Cape ▲ USA 20-21 R 7
Clearfield ○ USA (PA) 46-47 J 5
Clearfield ○ USA (SD) 42-43 G 4
Clearfield ○ USA (UT) 40-41 H 5
Clear Fork Brazos ~ USA 44-45 H 3
Clear Hills ▲ CDN 32-33 L 3
Clear Lake ○ USA (IA) 42-43 L 4
Clear Lake ○ USA (SD) 42-43 J 3
Clear Lake ○ USA (WI) 42-43 L 3
Clear Lake ○ USA (CA) 40-41 C 6
Clear Lake Reservoir ○ USA 40-41 D 5
Clear Prairie ○ CDN 32-33 L 3
Clearwater ○ CDN 32-33 K 6
Clearwater ○ USA (FL) 48-49 G 6
Clearwater ○ USA (MT) 40-41 H 2
Clearwater Creek ~ CDN 30-31 F 4
Clearwater Lake ○ CDN 34-35 F 3
Clearwater Lake ○ USA 46-47 C 7
Clearwater Mountains ▲ USA 40-41 G 2
Clearwater Provincial Park ⊥ CDN 34-35 F 3
Clearwater River ~ CDN 32-33 N 6
Clearwater River ~ CDN 32-33 P 3
Clearwater River ~ USA 40-41 F 2
Cleburne ○ USA 44-45 J 3
Cle Elum ○ USA 40-41 D 2
Clematis Creek ~ AUS 178-179 K 3
Clements Markham Inlet ≈ 26-27 R 2
Clemesi, Pampa de la ∸ PE 70-71 B 5
Clemson ○ USA 48-49 G 2
Clendenin ○ USA 46-47 H 6
Cleopatra Needle ▲ RP 160-161 C 7
Clephane Bay ≈ 28-29 J 3
Clerke Reef ⌒ AUS 172-173 D 4
Clerke Rocks ⌒ GB 78-79 P 7
Clermont ○ AUS 178-179 J 2
Clermont ○ F 90-91 J 7
Clermont ○ USA 48-49 H 5
Clermont-Ferrand ☆ • F 90-91 J 9
Clermont-l'Hérault ○ F 90-91 J 10
Cleugh Passage ≈ 140-141 L 3
Cleve ○ AUS 180-181 D 2
Cleveland ○ USA (GA) 48-49 G 2
Cleveland ○ USA (MS) 44-45 M 3
Cleveland ○ USA (TN) 48-49 F 2
Cleveland ○ USA (TX) 44-45 K 4
Cleveland ○ • USA (OH) 46-47 H 5
Cleveland, Kap ▲ GRØ 26-27 P 5
Cleveland, Mount ▲ USA (AK) 22-23 M 6
Cleveland, Mount ▲ USA (MT) 40-41 H 1
Cleveland Heights ○ USA 46-47 H 5
Clevelândia ○ BR 74-75 D 6
Cleveland Peninsula ⌣ USA 32-33 D 4
Cleveland River ~ CDN 36-37 G 2
Clewiston ○ USA 48-49 H 6
Clifden ○ NZ 182 A 7
Clifden = An Clochán ○ • IRL 90-91 B 5
Cliff ○ USA 44-45 C 3
Cliffs of Moher •• IRL 90-91 C 5
Clifton ○ USA (AZ) 44-45 C 3
Clifton ○ USA (KS) 42-43 J 6
Clifton Forge ○ USA 46-47 J 7
Clifton Hills ○ AUS 178-179 E 4
Clifton Point ▲ CDN 24-25 N 6
Cli Lake ○ CDN 30-31 H 4
Climax ○ CDN 32-33 Q 7
Climax ○ USA (GA) 48-49 F 4
Climax ○ USA (MN) 42-43 J 2
Clinch Mountains ▲ USA 48-49 G 1
Cline ○ USA 44-45 G 5
Clines Corners ○ USA 44-45 E 2
Clingmans Dome ▲ USA 48-49 G 2
Clint ○ USA 44-45 D 4
Clinton ○ CDN (BC) 32-33 K 6
Clinton ○ CDN (ONT) 38-39 D 7
Clinton ○ NZ 182 B 7
Clinton ○ USA (AR) 44-45 L 2
Clinton ○ USA (IA) 46-47 C 5
Clinton ○ USA (IL) 46-47 D 5
Clinton ○ USA (IN) 46-47 E 6
Clinton ○ USA (KY) 46-47 D 7
Clinton ○ USA (LA) 44-45 M 4
Clinton ○ USA (MI) 46-47 G 4
Clinton ○ USA (MO) 42-43 L 6
Clinton ○ USA (MS) 44-45 M 3
Clinton ○ USA (NC) 48-49 J 2
Clinton ○ USA (OK) 44-45 H 2
Clinton ○ USA (SC) 48-49 H 2
Clinton, Cape ▲ AUS 178-179 L 2
Clinton, Port ≈ 178-179 L 2
Clinton-Colden Lake ○ CDN 30-31 Q 3
Clinton Point ○ CDN 24-25 M 6
Clintonville ○ USA 46-47 D 3
Clio ○ USA 48-49 F 4
Cliong Karik Tagh ▲ VRC 144-145 H 2
Clipperton Fracture Zone ≃ 14-15 O 7
Clive Lake ○ CDN 30-31 K 4
Člja ○ RUS 122-123 J 2
Člja, ozero ○ RUS 122-123 J 2
Clocolan ○ ZA 220-221 H 4
Clodomira ○ RA 76-77 E 4
Clonagh ○ AUS 174-175 F 7
Clonbrook ○ GUY 62-63 F 2
Cloncurry ○ AUS 174-175 F 7
Cloncurry Plateau ∸ AUS 178-179 E 1
Cloncurry River ~ AUS 174-175 F 6
Clonmacnoise ○ •• IRL 90-91 D 5
Clonmel = Cluain Meala ○ IRL 90-91 D 5
Cloppenburg ○ D 92-93 K 2
Cloquet ○ USA 42-43 L 2
Cloquet River ~ USA 42-43 L 2
Cloridorme ○ CDN 38-39 M 4
Clorinda ○ RA 76-77 J 3
Cloud Peak ▲ USA 42-43 D 3
Cloud River ~ CDN 38-39 Q 3
Clouds Creek ○ AUS 178-179 M 6
Cloudy Mountain ▲ USA 20-21 M 5
Cloverdale ○ USA 40-41 C 6
Clovis ○ USA (CA) 40-41 E 7
Clovis ○ USA (NM) 44-45 F 2
Cloyne ○ CDN 38-39 F 6
Cluain Meala = Clonmel ○ IRL 90-91 D 5
Club Mayanabo ○ C 54-55 G 4
Cluj-Napoca ☆ • RO 102-103 C 4
Clyde ○ CDN (ALB) 32-33 O 4
Clyde ○ CDN (NWT) 26-27 Q 8
Clyde ~ GB 90-91 F 4
Clyde ○ USA 42-43 H 1
Clyde Inlet ≈ 26-27 Q 8
Clyde Park ○ USA 40-41 J 3
Clyde River ○ CDN 38-39 M 7
Cna ~ RUS 94-95 R 5
Cnori ○ GE 126-127 F 7
Coachella ○ USA 40-41 F 9
Coachella Canal < USA 40-41 G 9
Coahuayana ○ MEX 52-53 C 2
Coahuayutla ○ MEX 52-53 D 2
Coahuila ◻ MEX 50-51 H 4
Coalcomán, Río ~ MEX 52-53 C 2
Coalcomán de Matamoros ○ MEX 52-53 C 2
Coal Creek ○ USA 20-21 T 4
Coaldale ○ CDN 32-33 O 7
Coaldale ○ USA 40-41 F 6
Coalinga ○ USA 40-41 D 7
Coal Mine • AUS 178-179 E 6
Coal River ○ CDN (BC) 30-31 F 6
Coal River ~ CDN 30-31 F 5
Coalspur ○ CDN 32-33 M 5
Coalville ○ USA 40-41 J 5
Coaraci ○ BR 72-73 L 3
Coari ○ BR 66-67 F 5
Coari, Lago de ○ BR 66-67 F 5
Coari, Rio ~ BR 66-67 F 5
Coasa ○ PE 70-71 B 4
Coast ◻ EAK 212-213 G 5
Coastal Plains Research Station ○ AUS 172-173 K 2
Coast Mountains ▲ CDN 32-33 D 2
Coast of Labrador ∸ CDN 36-37 R 5
Coast Range ▲ AUS 178-179 L 2
Coast Range ▲ AUS 178-179 L 3
Coast Range ▲ USA 40-41 C 3
Coata ○ PE 70-71 C 4
Coatá, Cachoeira ~ BR 66-67 G 6
Coatá, Cachoeira do ~ BR 66-67 F 7
Coatá Laranjal, Área Indígena X BR 66-67 H 5
Coatbridge ○ GB 90-91 E 4
Coatepec ○ MEX 52-53 F 2
Coatepeque ○ GCA 52-53 J 4
Coatesville ○ USA 46-47 L 6
Coaticook ○ CDN 38-39 J 6
Coats Bay ≈ 36-37 K 6
Coats Island ⌒ CDN 36-37 H 3
Coats Land ∸ ARK 16 F 34
Coatzacoalcos ○ • MEX 52-53 G 2
Coatzacoalcos, Río ~ MEX 52-53 G 3
Coba ∴ • MEX 52-53 L 1
Cobadin ○ RO 102-103 F 5
Cobán ☆ GCA 52-53 J 4
Cobar ○ AUS 178-179 H 6
Cobargo ○ AUS 180-181 K 4
Cobb, Lake ○ AUS 176-177 J 2
Cobberas, Mount ▲ AUS 180-181 K 4
Cobb Highway II AUS 180-181 G 2
Cobden ○ AUS 180-181 G 5
Cobequid Mountains ▲ CDN 38-39 M 6
Cobh = An Cóbh ○ IRL 90-91 C 6
Cobham River ~ CDN 34-35 J 4
Cobija ☆ BOL 70-71 C 2
Cobija, Punta ▲ RCH 76-77 B 2
Cobleskill ○ USA 46-47 L 4
Coboconk ○ CDN 38-39 E 6
Cobourg ○ CDN 38-39 E 7
Cobourg Peninsula ⌣ AUS 172-173 K 1
Cobquecura ○ RCH 78-79 C 4
Cobra ○ AUS 176-177 D 2
Cobre, El ○ RCH 76-77 B 3
Cobre, Sierra del ▲ RA 76-77 D 2
Cobué ○ MOC 214-215 H 7
Coburg ○ • D 92-93 L 3
Coburg Island ⌒ CDN 24-25 h 2
Coburg Marine Park ⊥ AUS 172-173 K 1
Coburn ○ AUS 176-177 C 3
Coburn Mount ▲ USA 46-47 N 3
Coca = Puerto Francisco de Orellana ○ EC 64-65 D 2
Coca, Rio ~ EC 64-65 D 2
Cocachacra ○ PE 64-65 D 7
Cocal ○ BR 68-69 H 3
Cocalinho ○ BR (MAR) 68-69 F 3
Cocalinho ○ BR (MAT) 72-73 E 3
Cocha, La ○ RA 76-77 E 4
Cochabamba ☆ BOL 70-71 D 5
Cochabamba ○ PE 64-65 C 5
Cochagne ○ CDN 38-39 M 5
Cochagón, Cerro ▲ NIC 52-53 B 5
Cochamarca ○ PE 64-65 D 7
Cochamó ○ RCH 78-79 C 6
Cochaquingu ○ EC 64-65 D 2
Coche, Isla ⌒ YV 60-61 K 2
Cochem ○ • D 92-93 J 3
Cochenour ○ CDN 34-35 K 5
Cochetopa Hills ▲ USA 42-43 D 7
Cochico, Sierra de ▲ RA 78-79 D 4
Cochiguas, Río ~ RCH 76-77 B 6
Cochin ○ •• IND 140-141 G 6
Cochinos, Bahía de ≈ 54-55 E 3
Cochise ○ USA 44-45 C 3
Cochran ○ USA 48-49 G 3
Cochrane ○ CDN (ALB) 32-33 N 6
Cochrane ○ CDN (ONT) 34-35 Q 6
Cochrane ○ RCH 80 D 3
Cochrane, Cerro ▲ RCH 80 D 3
Cochrane, Lago ≈ 80 D 3
Cockaköl ○ KA 124-125 G 4
Cockaköl kyrkasy ▲ KA 126-127 N 4
Cockburn ○ AUS 180-181 F 2
Cockburn, Canal ≈ 80 E 7
Cockburn, Cape ▲ CDN 24-25 V 3
Cockburn, Mount ▲ AUS (NT) 172-173 K 7
Cockburn, Mount ▲ AUS (NT) 176-177 K 2
Cockburn Harbor ○ GB 54-55 K 4
Cockburn Island ⌒ CDN 38-39 C 6
Cockburn Islands ⌒ CDN 24-25 R 6
Cockburn North, Mount ▲ AUS 172-173 J 3
Cockburn Town ○ BS 54-55 H 2
Cockburn Town ☆ GB 54-55 K 4
Cocklebiddy Cave • AUS 176-177 H 5
Cocklebiddy Motel ○ AUS 176-177 J 6
Cockram Strait ≈ 28-29 C 3
Coco, Cayo ⌒ C 54-55 F 3
Coco, El ○ CR 52-53 B 6
Coco, Punta ▲ CO 60-61 C 6
Coco, Río ~ NIC 52-53 L 5
Côco, Rio do ~ BR 68-69 D 6
Cocoa ○ USA 48-49 H 5
Cocobeach ○ G 210-211 B 3
Coco Channel ≈ 140-141 L 3
Cococi ○ BR 68-69 H 5
Coconho, Ponta ▲ BR 68-69 L 4
Coco o Segovia = Río Wangkí ~ HN 52-53 B 4
Cocoparra National Park ⊥ AUS 180-181 J 3
Cocorna ○ CO 60-61 D 4
Cocorocuma, Cayos ⌒ NIC 54-55 D 7
Côcos ○ BR 72-73 H 2
Cocos ○ BR (BAH) 72-73 H 3
Cocos ○ BR (MAR) 68-69 G 4
Cocos Basin ≃ 12 H 4
Cocos Island ⌒ AUS 12 H 6
Cocos Ridge ≃ 5 C 4
Cocotier Beach = Cocotier Plage ∸ • CAM 210-211 B 2
Cocotier Plage = Cocotier Beach ∸ • CAM 210-211 B 2
Cocuí, Parque Nacional el ⊥ CO 60-61 E 4
Cocuizas, Las ○ YV 62-63 D 2
Cocula ○ MEX 52-53 C 1
Cod, Cape ▲ USA 46-47 N 4
Codajás ○ BR 66-67 F 4
Codeagro ○ BR 66-67 G 4
Codera, Cabo ▲ YV 60-61 H 2
Cod Island ⌒ CDN 36-37 T 6
Codó ○ BR 68-69 G 4
Codo de Pozuzo ○ PE 64-65 E 6
Codorníz, Paso ▲ RCH 80 D 3
Codozinho ○ BR 68-69 F 4
Codpa ○ RCH 70-71 C 6
Codrii ▲ MD 102-103 E 3
Codrington ○ AG 56 E 3
Codru-Moma, Munții ▲ RO 102-103 C 4
Cody ○ USA (NE) 42-43 G 4
Cody ○ USA (WY) 42-43 C 3
Coelemu ○ RCH 78-79 C 4
Coelho Neto ○ BR 68-69 G 4
Coen ○ AUS 174-175 G 3
Coerney ○ ZA 220-221 G 6
Coeroeni ○ SME 62-63 F 4
Coesfeld ○ • D 92-93 J 3
Coëtivy Island ⌒ SY 224 E 3
Coeur d'Alene ○ USA 40-41 F 2
Coeur d'Alene Indian Reservation X USA 40-41 F 2
Coeur d'Alene Lake ○ USA 40-41 F 2
Coeur d'Alene River ~ USA 40-41 F 2
Coevorden ○ NL 92-93 J 2
Coffee Bay ○ ZA 220-221 J 5
Coffee Creek ○ CDN 20-21 V 5
Coffeeville ○ USA 48-49 D 4
Coffeyville ○ USA 44-45 K 1
Coffin Bay ≈ 180-181 C 3
Coffin Bay National Park ⊥ AUS 180-181 C 3
Coffs Harbour ○ AUS 178-179 M 6
Cofimvaba ○ ZA 220-221 H 6
Čogādāk ○ IR 134-135 D 4
Čogar ~ RUS 120-121 E 6
Cogatí, Embalse < RCH 76-77 B 6
Coghlan ○ ZA 220-221 J 5
Cognac ○ • F 90-91 G 9
Cogo ○ GQ 210-211 B 3
Cogollal, El ○ YV 60-61 K 4
Cogotí, Río ~ RCH 76-77 B 6
Čograjskoe vodohranilišče ○ RUS 126-127 F 5
Cogt = Tahilt ○ MAU 148-149 C 5
Cogt-Ovoo = Doloon ○ MAU 148-149 G 5
Coguno ○ MOC 220-221 M 2
Cohade, Rivière ~ CDN 36-37 N 5
Cohoes ○ USA 46-47 M 4
Coiba, Isla de ⌒ PA 52-53 D 8
Coig, Río ~ RA 80 E 5
Coihaique ☆ RCH 80 D 2
Coihaique Alto ○ RCH 80 E 2
Coihué ○ RCH 78-79 C 4
Coihueco ○ RCH 78-79 D 4
Coimbatore ○ IND 140-141 G 5
Coimbra ○ BR 72-73 J 6
Coimbra ☆ • P 98-99 C 4
Coín ○ E 98-99 E 6
Coin de Mire ⌒ MS 224 C 6
Coipasa, Cerro ▲ BOL 70-71 C 6
Coipasa, Salar de ○ BOL 70-71 C 6
Coipasa, Lago de ○ BOL 70-71 C 6
Čojbalsan ☆ MAU 148-149 M 3
Cojedes, Río ~ YV 60-61 G 3
Cojimíes ○ EC 64-65 B 1
Cojoida ○ YV 60-61 L 3
Čojr ○ MAU 148-149 J 4
Cojúa ○ YV 60-61 F 2
Cojudo Blanco, Cerro ▲ RA 80 F 3
Cojutepeque ☆ ES 52-53 K 5
Cojyndykǒl ○ KA 124-125 E 3
Cokeville ○ USA 40-41 J 4
Čokrakbejik, Gora ▲ TM 136-137 F 5
Čokurdah-Kerike, gora ▲ RUS 110-111 F 3
Colac ○ AUS 180-181 G 5
Colaksor, kōli ○ KA 124-125 J 2
Colan, Cape ▲ CDN 26-27 R 2
Colán Conhué ○ RA 78-79 E 7
Colangüil, Cordillera de ▲ RA 76-77 C 5
Colares ○ BR 62-63 K 6
Colasi Point ▲ RP 160-161 F 7
Colatina ○ BR 72-73 K 5
Colazo ○ RA 76-77 F 6
Colbert ○ USA 40-41 F 2
Čolbon ○ RUS 110-111 U 6
Colborne, Port ○ CDN 38-39 E 7
Colby ○ USA 42-43 G 6
Colca, Río ~ PE 64-65 F 9
Colcabamba ○ PE 64-65 F 9
Colchester ○ • GB 90-91 H 6
Colchester ○ USA 46-47 M 3
Colchester ○ ZA 220-221 G 6
Cold Bay ○ USA 22-23 P 5
Cold Lake ○ CDN 32-33 Q 4
Coldspring Mountain ▲ CDN 20-21 W 5
Coldstream ○ GB 90-91 F 4
Coldwater ○ USA 46-47 F 5
Coleambally ○ AUS 180-181 H 3
Coleambally Creek ~ AUS 180-181 H 3
Cole Bay ○ CDN 32-33 Q 4
Colebrook ○ USA 46-47 N 3
Coleen River ~ USA 20-21 T 3
Colekeplaas ○ ZA 220-221 G 6
Coleman ○ USA 44-45 H 4
Coleman River ~ AUS 174-175 F 4
Colenso ○ ZA 220-221 J 4
Coleraine ○ AUS 180-181 F 4
Coleraine ○ GB 90-91 D 4
Coleridge, Lake ○ NZ 182 C 5
Coleroon ~ IND 140-141 H 5
Coles, Punta ▲ PE 70-71 B 5
Colesberg ○ ZA 220-221 G 5
Coles Island ○ CDN 38-39 M 6
Colfax ○ USA (CA) 40-41 D 6
Colfax ○ USA (WA) 40-41 F 2
Colga Downs ○ AUS 176-177 E 3
Colguula ○ SP 208-209 H 5
Colhué Huapi, Lago ○ RA 80 F 2
Colidor ○ BR 70-71 K 2
Colignan ○ AUS 180-181 G 3
Coligny ○ ZA 220-221 H 3
Colima ◻ MEX 52-53 B 2
Colima ☆ • MEX (COL) 52-53 C 2
Colina ○ BR 72-73 F 6
Colin Archer Peninsula ⌣ CDN 24-25 a 2
Colinas ○ BR 68-69 F 5
Colinas do Tocantins ○ BR 68-69 D 6
Colindina, Mount ▲ AUS 176-177 G 4
Colinet ○ CDN 38-39 S 5
Coliseo ○ C 54-55 E 3
Coll ⌒ GB 90-91 D 3
Collacagua ○ RCH 70-71 C 7
Colladere ○ RH 54-55 J 5
Collado-Villalba ○ E 98-99 F 4
Collarenebri ○ AUS 178-179 K 5
Collaroy ○ AUS 178-179 K 2
Collector ○ AUS 180-181 K 3
College Park ○ USA 48-49 F 3
College Place ○ USA 40-41 E 2
College Station ○ USA 44-45 J 4
Collerina ○ AUS 178-179 J 5
Collie ○ AUS 176-177 D 6
Collier Bay ≈ 172-173 G 4
Collier Bay Aboriginal Land X AUS 172-173 F 4
Collier Range ▲ AUS 176-177 E 2
Collier Range National Park ⊥ AUS 176-177 E 2
Collierville ○ USA 48-49 D 2
Collingwood ○ CDN 38-39 D 6
Collingwood ○ NZ 182 D 4
Collingwood Bay ≈ 183 E 5
Collins ○ CDN 34-35 M 5
Collins ○ USA (AR) 44-45 M 3
Collins ○ USA (IA) 42-43 L 5
Collins ○ USA (MO) 42-43 L 7
Collins ○ USA (MS) 48-49 D 4
Collins ○ USA (MT) 40-41 J 2
Collins, Mount ▲ AUS 178-179 F 3
Collinson, Cape ▲ CDN 26-27 P 3
Collinson Peninsula ⌣ CDN 24-25 V 5
Collinsville ○ AUS 174-175 J 7
Collinsville ○ USA (AL) 48-49 F 2
Collinsville ○ USA (OK) 44-45 K 1
Collipulli ○ RCH 78-79 C 4
Collo ○ DZ 190-191 F 2
Collón Curá, Río ~ RA 78-79 D 6
Colmar ☆ • F 90-91 L 7
Colméia ○ BR 68-69 D 6
Colmena ○ RA 76-77 G 5
Colmenar Viejo ○ E 98-99 F 4
Colnett ○ MEX 50-51 A 2
Colnett, Cabo ▲ MEX 50-51 A 2
Cologne = Köln ○ • D 92-93 J 3
Cololo, Arroyo ~ ROU 78-79 L 2
Coloma ○ USA 46-47 D 3
Colombia ○ C 54-55 G 4
Colombia ○ CO 60-61 D 6
Colombia ■ CO 60-61 D 6
Colombia ○ MEX 50-51 K 4
Colombia Basin ≃ 5 D 3
Colombier ○ CDN 38-39 K 4
Colombo ○ BR 68-69 F 3
Colombo ☆ • CL 140-141 H 7
Colome ○ USA 42-43 H 4
Colomiers ○ F 90-91 H 10
Colón ○ C 54-55 E 3
Colón ☆ PA 52-53 E 7
Colón ○ RA (BUA) 78-79 J 2
Colón ○ RA (ERI) 78-79 K 2
Colón, Archipiélago de = Islas Galápagos ⌒ EC 64-65 B 9
Colonelganj ○ IND 142-143 B 2
Colonel Hill ○ BS 54-55 H 3
Colonia 10 de Julio ○ RA 76-77 F 6
Colonia Angamos ○ PE 64-65 F 4
Colonia Carlos Pellegrini ○ RA 76-77 J 5
Colonia del Sacramento ☆ • ROU 78-79 L 3
Colonia Dora ○ RA 76-77 F 5
Colônia Leopoldina ○ BR 68-69 L 6
Colonial Heights ○ USA 46-47 K 7

Chuwangsan National Park — Colonial Heights 249

Coulta ○ AUS 180-181 C 3
Coulterville ○ USA 46-47 D 6
Council ○ USA (AK) 20-21 J 4
Council ○ USA (ID) 40-41 F 3
Council Bluffs ○ USA 42-43 K 5
Council Grove ○ USA 42-43 J 6
Council Grove Lake ⊖ USA 42-43 J 6
Counselors ○ USA 44-45 D 1
Country Force Base Suffield ✕✕ CDN 32-33 P 6
Courageous Lake ⊖ CDN 30-31 O 3
Courantyne ~ GUY 62-63 F 4
Courmayeur ○ I 100-101 A 2
Cours, Cours-sur-Loire- ○ F 90-91 J 8
Courtenay ○ CDN 32-33 H 7
Courtenay ○ USA 42-43 H 2
Courtis River ~ CDN 24-25 c 7
Courtright ○ CDN 38-39 C 7
Coushatta ○ USA 44-45 L 3
Coutances ○ F 90-91 G 7
Couto de Magalhães, Rio ~ BR 72-73 D 2
Couto de Magelhães de Minas ○ BR 72-73 J 5
Coutras ○ F 90-91 G 9
Coutts ○ CDN 32-33 P 7
Couture, Lac ⊖ CDN 36-37 M 4
Cova Figueira ○ CV 202-203 B 6
Covè ○ DY 204-205 E 5
Cove Fort ○ USA 40-41 H 6
Coventry ○ GB 90-91 G 5
Coventry Lake ⊖ CDN 30-31 R 5
Cove Palisades State Park, The ⊥ • USA 40-41 D 3
Covilhã ○ P 98-99 D 4
Covington ○ USA (GA) 48-49 G 3
Covington ○ USA (KY) 46-47 F 6
Covington ○ USA (LA) 44-45 M 4
Covington ○ USA (MI) 46-47 D 2
Covington ○ USA (TN) 48-49 D 2
Covington ○ USA (VA) 46-47 H 7
Covunco, Arroyo ~ RA 78-79 E 5
Cowal, Lake ⊖ AUS 180-181 J 2
Cowal Creek ✕ AUS 174-175 G 2
Cowan ○ CDN 34-35 F 4
Cowan, Cerro ▲ EC 64-65 B 10
Cowan, Lake ⊖ AUS 176-177 G 5
Cowan Downs ○ AUS 174-175 F 6
Cowan Hill ▲ AUS 176-177 F 5
Cowansville ○ CDN 38-39 H 6
Coward Springs ○ AUS 178-179 D 5
Cowcowing Lakes ⊖ AUS 176-177 D 5
Cow Creek ~ USA 40-41 E 2
Cowell ○ AUS 180-181 D 2
Cowichan Lake ⊖ CDN 32-33 H 7
Cowie Point ▲ CDN 24-25 c 7
Cowlitz River ~ USA 40-41 C 2
Cowra ○ AUS 180-181 K 2
Cowval ~ GUY 62-63 F 3
Coxilha de Santana ▲▲ BR 76-77 J 5
Coxim ○ BR 70-71 K 6
Cox Island ⌒ CDN 36-37 K 5
Cox River ~ AUS 174-175 C 4
Cox's Bazar ○ • BD 142-143 H 5
Cox's Cove ○ CDN 38-39 P 4
Coxs Creek ~ AUS 178-179 K 6
Coyaguaima, Cerro ▲ RA 76-77 D 2
Coyah ○ RG 202-203 D 5
Coyaima ○ CO 60-61 D 6
Coyame ○ MEX 50-51 G 3
Coyoacan ○ MEX 52-53 E 2
Coyolate, Río ~ GCA 52-53 J 4
Coyolito ○ HN 52-53 L 5
Coyote ○ USA 44-45 E 3
Coyote, Bahía ≈ 50-51 D 5
Coyote, Río ~ MEX 50-51 C 2
Coyotitán ○ MEX 50-51 F 6
Coyte, El ○ RA 80 E 2
Coyuca de Benítez ○ MEX 52-53 D 3
Cozes ○ F 90-91 G 9
Cozumel ○ • MEX 52-53 L 1
Cozumel, Isla del ⌒ •• MEX 52-53 L 1
Crabwood Creek ○ GUY 62-63 F 3
Cracow ○ AUS 178-179 L 3
Cradle Mountain Lake St. Clair National Park ⊥ AUS 180-181 H 6
Cradle Valley ○ AUS 180-181 H 6
Cradock ○ AUS 180-181 E 2
Cradock ○ ZA 220-221 G 6
Craig ○ USA (AK) 32-33 D 4
Craig ○ USA (CO) 42-43 D 5
Craigend ○ CDN 32-33 P 4
Craig Harbour ○ CDN 24-25 f 3
Craigie ○ AUS 174-175 H 6
Craigieburn ○ AUS 180-181 H 4
Craigmore ○ CDN 38-39 O 6
Craignure ○ GB 90-91 E 3
Craik ○ CDN 34-35 D 5
Craiova ☆ • RO 102-103 C 5
Cramond ○ ZA 220-221 E 3
Cranberry Junction ○ CDN 32-33 F 4
Cranberry Portage ○ CDN 34-35 F 3
Cranbourne ○ AUS 180-181 H 5
Cranbrook ○ AUS 176-177 D 7
Cranbrook ○ CDN 32-33 N 7
Crane ○ USA (OR) 40-41 E 4
Crane ○ USA (TX) 44-45 F 4
Crane Lake ⊖ CDN 32-33 Q 6
Cranston ○ USA 46-47 N 5
Cranstown, Kap ▲ GRØ 26-27 X 8
Cranswick River ~ CDN 20-21 Y 4
Crary Mountains ▲▲ ARK 16 F 25
Crasna ~ RO 102-103 C 4
Crater Lake ⊖ USA 40-41 C 4
Crater Lake ⩲ • WAN 204-205 K 3
Crater Lake National Park ⊥ •• USA 40-41 C 4
Crater Mountain ▲ USA 20-21 M 5
Crater of Diamonds State Park • USA 44-45 L 3
Craters of the Moon National Monument • USA 40-41 H 4
Cratéus ○ BR 68-69 H 4
Crati ~ I 100-101 F 5
Crato ○ BR 68-69 J 5
Crauford, Cape ▲ CDN 24-25 e 4
Cravari ou Curucuinazá, Rio ~ BR 70-71 J 3
Craven ○ CDN 34-35 D 5
Cravo Norte ○ CO 60-61 F 4
Crawford ○ USA (GA) 48-49 G 3
Crawford ○ USA (NE) 42-43 F 4
Crawfordsville ○ USA 46-47 E 5
Crazy Peak ▲ USA 40-41 J 2
Creede ○ USA 42-43 D 7
Creek Town ○ WAN 204-205 H 6
Creel ○ • MEX 50-51 F 4
Cree Lake ⊖ CDN 34-35 C 2
Creen Lake ⊖ CDN 34-35 C 3
Creil ○ F 90-91 J 7
Cremona ○ CDN 32-33 N 6
Cremona ☆ I 100-101 C 2
Crepori, Rio ~ BR 66-67 J 6
Cres ○ HR 100-101 E 2
Cres ⩲ HR 100-101 E 2
Cresbard ○ USA 42-43 H 3
Crescent ○ USA 40-41 D 4
Crescent, La ○ USA 46-47 C 4
Crescent City ○ USA (CA) 40-41 B 5
Crescent City ○ USA (FL) 48-49 H 5
Crescent Group = Yongle Qundao ⌒ VRC 158-159 L 2
Crescent Head ○ AUS 178-179 M 6
Crescent Junction ○ USA 42-43 C 6
Crespo ○ RA 78-79 J 2
Crest ○ F 90-91 K 9
Crested Butte ○ USA 42-43 D 6
Creston ○ CDN 32-33 M 7
Creston ○ USA (IA) 42-43 K 5
Creston ○ USA (WY) 42-43 D 5
Crestón, Cerro ▲ RA 76-77 E 3
Crestview ○ USA 48-49 E 4
Creswell Bay ≈ 24-25 Z 4
Creswell Downs ○ AUS 174-175 C 5
Crete ○ USA 42-43 J 5
Crete = Kriti ⌒ GR 100-101 K 7
Crete, Sea of = Kritiko Pélagos ≈ GR 100-101 J 6
Creus, Cap de ▲ E 98-99 J 3
Creuse ~ F 90-91 J 8
Crewe ○ GB 90-91 F 5
Criaba, Rio ~ BR 70-71 J 4
Criciúma ○ BR 74-75 F 7
Crieff ○ GB 90-91 F 3
Crikvenica ○ HR 100-101 E 2
Crimea = Krym, Respublika □ UA 102-103 H 5
Crimea = Kryms'kyj pivostriv ᴗ UA 102-103 H 5
Criminosa, Cachoeira ~ BR 62-63 D 6
Criminosa, Cachoeira ~ BR 70-71 E 2
Crimson Cliffs ▲▲ GRØ 26-27 R 5
Criolla, Cerro la ▲ RA 80 E 5
Cripple ○ USA 20-21 M 5
Cripple Creek ○ USA 42-43 E 6
Criş, Chişineu- ○ RO 102-103 B 4
Crisfield ○ USA 46-47 L 7
Crisostomo, Ribeiro ~ BR 68-69 C 7
Crispín, El ○ RA 76-77 F 6
Cristais, Serra dos ▲▲ BR 72-73 G 4
Cristal, Monts de ▲▲ G 210-211 C 3
Cristalândia ○ BR 68-69 D 7
Cristalina ○ BR 72-73 G 4
Cristalino, Rio ~ BR 66-67 K 7
Cristalino, Rio ~ BR 72-73 E 2
Cristiano Muerto, Arroyo ~ RA 78-79 K 5
Cristianópolis ○ BR 72-73 F 4
Cristianos, Los ○ E 188-189 C 6
Cristo, El ○ YV 60-61 K 4
Cristobal, Punta ▲ EC 64-65 B 10
Cristóbal Cólon, Pico ▲ •• CO 60-61 E 2
Cristoffel, National Reservaat ⊥ NL 60-61 G 1
Cristópolis ○ BR 72-73 H 2
Cristovão Pereira, Ponta ▲ BR 74-75 E 8
Criterion, Cerro ▲ PE 64-65 E 9
Crixás ○ BR 72-73 F 3
Crixás, Rio ~ BR 68-69 D 7
Crixás Açu, Rio ~ BR 72-73 E 2
Crixas Mirim, Rio ~ BR 72-73 E 2
Crna gora ▲▲ MK 100-101 H 3
Crni vrh ▲ BIH 100-101 F 2
Croajingolong National Park ⊥ AUS 180-181 K 4
Croatá ○ BR 68-69 H 4
Croatia = Hrvatska ■ HR 100-101 E 2
Crocker, Banjaran ▲▲ MAL 160-161 A 10
Crocker Range National Park ⊥ MAL 160-161 B 10
Crockett ○ USA 44-45 K 4
Crocodile Camp ○ EAK 212-213 G 5
Crocodile Farm • AUS 172-173 K 2
Crocodiles • BF 202-203 J 3
Crofton ○ USA 42-43 J 4
Croher River ~ CDN 24-25 M 6
Croix, Lac à la ⊖ CDN 38-39 J 3
Croix des Bouquets ○ RH 54-55 J 5
Croix-de-Vie, Saint-Gilles- ○ F 90-91 G 8
Croker, Cape ▲ AUS 172-173 L 1
Croker Bay ≈ 24-25 e 3
Croker Island ⌒ AUS 172-173 L 1
Cromer ○ CDN 34-35 F 6
Cromwell ○ NZ 182 B 6
Cromwell ○ USA 42-43 L 2
Crông Kno ~ VN 158-159 K 4
Crook ○ USA 42-43 F 5
Crooked Creek ○ USA 20-21 L 6
Crooked Island ⌒ BS 54-55 H 3
Crooked Island ⌒ USA 22-23 Q 3
Crooked Island Passage ≈ 54-55 H 3
Crooked Lake ⊖ CDN 24-25 X 4
Crooked River ○ CDN (SAS) 34-35 E 4
Crooked River ~ CDN 32-33 J 4
Crooked River ~ USA 40-41 D 3
Crooks Inlet ≈ 36-37 O 3
Crookston ○ USA 42-43 J 2
Crookwell ○ AUS 180-181 K 3
Croppa Creek ~ AUS 178-179 L 5
Crosby ○ CDN 38-39 H 6
Crosby ○ USA 42-43 F 1
Crosbyton ○ USA 44-45 G 3
Cross, Cape = Kaap Kruis ▲ NAM 216-217 B 10
Cross City ○ USA 48-49 G 5
Crosse, La ○ USA 40-41 F 2
Crossett ○ USA 44-45 M 3
Crossfield ○ CDN 32-33 N 6
Cross Lake ○ CDN (MAN) 34-35 H 3
Cross Lake ⊖ CDN (MAN) 34-35 H 3
Crossley Lakes ⊖ CDN 20-21 a 2
Cross Plains ○ USA 44-45 H 3
Cross River □ WAN 204-205 H 5
Cross River ~ WAN 204-205 H 6
Cross Sound ≈ 32-33 B 2
Crossville ○ USA 48-49 F 2
Crosswind Lake ⊖ USA 20-21 S 5
Crotone ○ I 100-101 F 5
Crow Agency ○ USA 42-43 D 3
Crow Creek ~ USA 42-43 E 5
Crow Creek Indian Reservation ✕ USA 42-43 H 3
Crowdy Bay National Park ⊥ AUS 178-179 M 6
Crowell ○ USA 44-45 H 3
Crow Indian Reservation ✕ USA 42-43 C 3
Crow Lake ○ CDN 34-35 K 6
Crowl Creek ~ AUS 180-181 H 2
Crowley ○ USA 44-45 L 4
Crowley, Lake ⊖ USA 40-41 E 7
Crown Island ⌒ PNG 183 D 3
Crownpoint ○ USA 44-45 C 2
Crown Point ○ USA 46-47 E 5
Crown Prince Christian Land = Kronprins Christian Land ⩲ GRØ 26-27 q 3
Crown Prince Frederik Island ⌒ CDN 24-25 c 6
Crown Prince Range ▲▲ PNG 184 I b 2
Crow River ~ CDN 30-31 G 6
Crows Nest ○ AUS 178-179 M 4
Crowsnest Pass ▲ CDN 32-33 N 7
Croydon ○ AUS 174-175 G 6
Croydon ○ SD 220-221 K 3
Crozet, Îles ⌒ F 9 J 10
Crozier Channel ≈ 24-25 M 3
Crozon ○ F 90-91 E 7
Cruce, El ○ GCA 52-53 K 3
Cruce de la Jagua ○ DOM 54-55 L 5
Crucero ○ PE 70-71 B 4
Crucero, El ○ MEX 50-51 B 3
Crucero, El ○ YV 60-61 J 3
Cruces ○ C 54-55 E 3
Cruces, Las ○ MEX 52-53 H 3
Cruces, Las ○ USA 44-45 D 3
Cruces, Punta ▲ CO 60-61 C 4
Crucetillas, Puerto de las ▲ E 98-99 F 5
Crucita ○ EC 64-65 B 2
Cruilas ○ MEX 50-51 K 5
Cruz, Bahía ≈ 80 H 2
Cruz, Cabo ▲ C 54-55 G 5
Cruz, Ilha ⌒ BR 72-73 L 3
Cruz, La ○ BOL (SAC) 70-71 F 5
Cruz, La ○ BOL (SAC) 70-71 F 4
Cruz, La ○ CR 52-53 B 6
Cruz, La ○ MEX (SIN) 50-51 F 6
Cruz, La ○ MEX (TAM) 50-51 L 6
Cruz, La ○ RA 78-79 G 2
Cruz, La ○ RA 78-79 J 6
Cruz Alta ○ BR 74-75 D 7
Cruz de Elorza ○ MEX 50-51 J 6
Cruz del Eje ○ RA 76-77 E 6
Cruz de Loreto, La ○ MEX 52-53 B 2
Cruz de Taratara, La ○ YV 60-61 G 2
Cruzeiro ○ BR 72-73 H 7
Cruzeiro ○ MOC 218-219 H 5
Cruzeiro d'Oeste ○ BR 72-73 D 7
Cruzeiro do Nordeste ○ BR 68-69 K 6
Cruzeiro do Sul ○ BR 64-65 F 5
Cruzen Island ⌒ ARK 16 F 23
Cruzes, Corredeira das ~ BR 70-71 J 4
Cruz Grande ○ MEX 52-53 E 3
Cruzinha da Garca ○ CV 202-203 B 5
Cruz Machado ○ BR 74-75 E 6
Crysdale, Mount ▲ CDN 32-33 J 4
Crystal Bay ≈ 48-49 G 5
Crystal Brook ○ AUS 180-181 E 2
Crystal Cave • USA 42-43 L 3
Crystal City ○ CDN 34-35 G 6
Crystal City ○ USA 44-45 H 5
Crystal Creek National Park ⊥ AUS 174-175 J 6
Crystal Falls ○ USA 46-47 D 2
Crystal Lake Cave • USA 46-47 C 4
Crystal River ○ USA 48-49 G 5
Crystal River State Archaeological Site ∴ • USA 48-49 G 5
Crystal Springs ○ CDN 34-35 D 4
Crystal Springs ○ USA 44-45 M 4
Csenger ⩲ H 92-93 P 5
C. Silverberge Ø ⌒ GRØ 26-27 p 5
Csorna ○ H 92-93 O 5
Cu ~ KA 124-125 H 6
Ču ~ KS 146-147 B 4
Cúa ○ YV 60-61 H 2
Cù'a Bày Hôp ≈ 158-159 H 6
Cuacuala ○ YV 60-61 J 5
Cuácua, Rio ~ MOC 218-219 J 3
Cù'a Cung Hâu ≈ 158-159 J 6
Cuaio ~ ANG 216-217 F 7
Cuajinicuilapa ○ MEX 52-53 E 3
Cuale ○ ANG 216-217 D 4
Cuamato ○ ANG 216-217 C 8
Cuamba ○ MOC 218-219 J 2
Cuanavale ~ ANG 216-217 E 7
Cuando ~ ANG 216-217 F 7
Cuando-Cubango □ ANG 216-217 E 7
Cuangar ○ ANG 216-217 E 8
Cuango ○ ANG 216-217 D 3
Cuango ○ ANG (LUN) 216-217 E 4
Cuango ~ ANG 216-217 D 4
Cuanza ○ ANG (BIE) 216-217 D 5
Cuanza ~ ANG 216-217 D 4
Cuanza Norte □ ANG 216-217 C 4
Cuanza Sul □ ANG 216-217 C 5
Cuao, Río ~ YV 60-61 H 5
Cuareim, Rio ~ ROU 76-77 J 6
Cuarinuma ○ CO 60-61 G 6
Cuaró Grande, Arroyo ~ ROU 76-77 J 6
Cuarto, Río ~ RA 78-79 G 2
Cù'a Soi Rap ≈ 158-159 J 5
Cuatir ~ ANG 216-217 E 8
Cuatro Bocas, Las ○ YV 60-61 F 2
Cuatro Caminos ○ C 54-55 G 4
Cuatrocienegas de Carranza ○ MEX 50-51 H 4
Cuauhtémoc ○ MEX (CHA) 50-51 F 3
Cuauhtémoc ○ MEX (TAM) 50-51 K 6
Cuautitlán ○ MEX 52-53 E 2
Cuautla ○ MEX 52-53 B 1
Cuautla de Morelos ○ MEX 52-53 E 2
Cuba ■ C 54-55 E 4
Cuba ⌒ C 5 C 2
Cuba ○ USA 44-45 D 1
Cù Bai ○ VN 158-159 J 2
Cubal ○ ANG (BGU) 216-217 C 6
Cubal ~ ANG 216-217 C 5
Cubal ~ ANG 216-217 B 7
Cubango ○ ANG 216-217 D 7
Cubango ~ ANG 216-217 E 8
Cubaté, Rio ~ BR 66-67 D 2
Cubati ~ ANG 216-217 D 7
Cube ○ EC 64-65 C 1
Cubero ○ USA 44-45 D 2
Cubia ~ ANG 216-217 F 7
Cubitas ○ C 54-55 G 4
Čublas ○ RUS 88-89 S 4
Čubuk ☆ TR 128-129 E 2
Čubuka-Tala, gora ▲ RUS 110-111 a 7
Čubukulah, gora ▲ RUS 110-111 d 6
Čubukulah, krjaž ▲▲ RUS 110-111 d 7
Cubulco ○ GCA 52-53 J 4
Cuchi ○ ANG (CUA) 216-217 D 7
Cuchi ~ ANG 216-217 D 6
Cuchilla, La ○ RA 76-77 G 4
Cuchillo-Co ○ RA 78-79 G 5
Cuchivero ○ YV 60-61 J 4
Cuchivero, Río ~ YV 60-61 J 4
Cucho Ingenio ○ BOL 70-71 E 6
Cuchumatanas, Parque Nacional Los ⊥ • GCA 52-53 J 4
Cuchumatanes, Sierra de los ▲▲ GCA 52-53 J 4
Cuckadoo ○ AUS 178-179 F 1
Cucuí ○ BR 66-67 D 2
Cucumbi ~ ANG 216-217 E 4
Cucurí, Cachoeira ~ BR 72-73 D 2
Cucurital ○ YV 60-61 J 5
Cucuta ☆ CO 60-61 E 4
Cuddalore ○ IND 140-141 H 5
Cuddapah ○ IND 140-141 H 3
Čudovo ☆ RUS 94-95 M 2
Čudskoe ozero ⊖ RUS 94-95 K 2
Čudzjavr, ozero ⊖ RUS 88-89 N 2
Cue ○ AUS 176-177 D 3
Cuebe ~ ANG 216-217 D 7
Cueio ~ ANG 216-217 D 7
Cueiras, Rio ~ BR 66-67 G 4
Cuélab • PE 64-65 D 5
Cuelei ~ ANG 216-217 D 7
Cuéllar ○ E 98-99 E 4
Cuemba ○ ANG 216-217 E 6
Cuenca ○ E 98-99 F 4
Cuenca ☆ •• EC 64-65 C 3
Cuenca, Serranía de ▲▲ E 98-99 F 4
Cuenca del Añelo ⩲ RA 78-79 E 5
Cuencamé ○ MEX 50-51 H 5
Cuengo ~ ANG 216-217 E 4
Cueramaro ○ MEX 52-53 D 1
Cuernavaca ☆ • MEX 52-53 E 2
Cuero ○ C 54-55 H 5
Cuero ○ USA 44-45 J 5
Cuervo ○ USA 44-45 E 2
Cueto ○ C 54-55 H 4
Cuetzalń ○ • MEX 52-53 F 1
Cueva de la Quebrada del Toro, Parque Nacional ⊥ YV 60-61 G 2
Cuevas, Las ○ RA 78-79 D 2
Cuevas o de las Cañas, Río ~ RA 76-77 E 3
Cuevo ○ BOL 70-71 F 7
Cuevo, Quebrada de ~ BOL 70-71 F 7
Čuga ~ RUS 118-119 L 7
Čuginskoe ploskogor'e ▲▲ RUS 118-119 K 7
Cugo ~ ANG 216-217 D 3
Čugor', mys ▲ RUS 108-109 Q 7
Čugor'jaha ~ RUS 108-109 Q 7
Čuguš, gora ▲ RUS 126-127 D 6
Čuhloma ○ RUS 94-95 S 2
Čuhujiv ○ UA 102-103 K 3
Cuiabá ○ BR (AMA) 66-67 C 4
Cuiabá ☆ BR (MAT) 70-71 J 4
Cuiabá, Rio ~ BR 70-71 J 5
Cuije ~ ANG 216-217 D 4
Cuilapa ☆ GCA 52-53 J 4
Cuilo ○ ANG 216-217 E 4
Cuilo ~ ANG 216-217 E 4
Cuilo ~ ANG 216-217 E 5
Cuilo ~ ANG 216-217 C 3
Cuilo-Futa ○ ANG 216-217 C 3
Cuilo Pombo ○ ANG 216-217 C 3
Cuima ○ ANG 216-217 C 6
Cuimba ○ ANG 216-217 C 3
Cuio ○ ANG 216-217 B 6
Cuira o Monos ○ CO 64-65 F 2
Cuiriri ~ ANG 216-217 E 7
Cuito ~ ANG 216-217 E 8
Cuito Cuanavale ○ ANG 216-217 E 7
Cuiubi ○ BR 66-67 C 2
Cuiuni, Rio ~ BR 66-67 F 3
Cuiyun Lang • VRC 154-155 D 5
Čuja ~ RUS 118-119 F 6
Čuja ~ RUS 124-125 Q 3
Čuja ~ RUS 124-125 P 3
Čuja, Bol'šaja ~ RUS 118-119 E 7
Cujar, Río ~ PE 64-65 F 7
Čujskij, Gorno ○ RUS 118-119 E 7
Cujubim ○ BR 66-67 G 7
Čukar ○ RUS 118-119 H 4
Cukas, Pulau ⌒ RI 162-163 F 5
Čukča ~ RUS 110-111 Z 6
Čukčagirskoe, ozero ⊖ RUS 122-123 G 3
Čukoč'e, ozero ⊖ RUS 112-113 L 2
Čukoč'ja, Bol'šaja ~ RUS 112-113 K 2
Čukotskij, mys ▲ RUS 112-113 Y 4
Čukotskij poluostrov ᴗ RUS 112-113 W 3
Čukotskoe more ≈ 112-113 V 1
Čukša ~ RUS 116-117 J 7
Çukurca ☆ TR 128-129 K 4
Cula ~ MD 102-103 F 4
Čulakan ~ RUS 116-117 M 6
Čulakkurgan ○ KA 136-137 L 3
Culamagia ○ ANG 216-217 D 4
Cu Lao Thu ⌒ VN 158-159 K 5
Cù Lao Thu = Phù Qúy ⌒ VN 158-159 K 5
Čulas ~ RUS 88-89 T 4
Čulasa ○ RUS 88-89 T 4
Culasi ○ RP 160-161 E 7
Culbertson ○ USA (MT) 42-43 E 1
Culbertson ○ USA (NE) 42-43 G 5
Culebra, La ○ YV 60-61 H 3
Culebras ○ PE 64-65 C 6
Culebras, Punta ▲ PE 64-65 C 6
Culgoa River ~ AUS 178-179 J 5
Culiacán Rosales ☆ MEX 50-51 F 5
Culion ○ RP 160-161 D 7
Culion Island ⌒ RP 160-161 C 7
Culiseu, Rio ~ BR 72-73 D 2
Cullera ○ E 98-99 G 5
Cullinan ○ ZA 220-221 J 2
Cullmann ○ USA 48-49 E 2
Cullulleraine ○ AUS 180-181 F 3
Čul'man ○ RUS 118-119 M 7
Čul'man ~ RUS 118-119 M 7
Culpeper ○ USA 46-47 K 6
Culpina ○ BOL 70-71 E 7
Culross Island ⌒ USA 20-21 R 6
Culuene, Rio ~ BR 72-73 D 2
Čuluunhoroom = Érèèncav ○ MAU 148-149 M 3
Čuluut gol ~ MAU 148-149 E 3
Culver, Point ▲ AUS 176-177 H 6
Culverden ○ NZ 182 D 5
Čulym ☆ RUS (NVS) 114-115 Q 7
Čulym ~ RUS 114-115 U 6
Čulym ~ RUS 116-117 E 8
Čulym ~ RUS 124-125 L 1
Čulymskaja, ravnina ᴗ RUS 114-115 T 6
Čulyšman ~ RUS 124-125 P 3
Čulyšman ~ RUS 124-125 Q 3
Čulyšmanskoe, nagor'e ⩲ •• RUS 124-125 Q 3
Čulyšmanskoe nagorie ▲▲ RUS 124-125 P 3
Cuma ○ ANG 216-217 C 6
Cumã, Baía do ≈ 68-69 F 3
Cuma, Cachoeira ~ BR 66-67 C 2
Cumana ☆ • YV 60-61 J 2
Cumanacoa ○ YV 60-61 K 2
Cumanayagua ○ C 54-55 E 3
Cumanda ○ EC 64-65 C 3
Cumaral ○ CO 60-61 E 5
Cumaral = Barranca de Upía ○ CO 60-61 E 5
Cumaral, Raudal ~ CO 60-61 F 6
Cumaribo ○ CO 60-61 G 5
Cumaru, Cachoeira ~ BR 62-63 G 6
Cumbe ○ EC 64-65 C 3
Cumberland ○ USA (IA) 42-43 K 5
Cumberland ○ USA (KY) 46-47 G 7
Cumberland ○ USA (VA) 46-47 J 7
Cumberland, Cape = Cape Nahoi ▲ VAN 184 II a 2
Cumberland, Lake ⊖ USA 46-47 F 7
Cumberland Bay ≈ 78-79 O 7
Cumberland Downs ○ AUS 178-179 J 2
Cumberland Gap ▲ USA 48-49 G 1
Cumberland Gap National Historic Park ∴ USA 46-47 G 7
Cumberland House ○ CDN 34-35 E 4
Cumberland Island ⌒ USA 48-49 H 4
Cumberland Island National Seashore ⊥ USA 48-49 H 4
Cumberland Islands ⌒ AUS 174-175 K 7
Cumberland Lake ⊖ CDN 34-35 E 3
Cumberland Parkway II USA 46-47 F 7
Cumberland Peninsula ᴗ CDN 28-29 G 3
Cumberland Plateau ▲▲ USA 48-49 E 2
Cumberland River ~ USA 48-49 F 1
Cumberland Sound ≈ 36-37 R 2
Cumbi ○ ANG 216-217 B 3
Cumborah ○ AUS 178-179 J 5
Cumbre, Paso de la ▲ RA 78-79 E 2
Cumbre, Volcán La ▲ EC 64-65 B 10
Cumbrera, Cerro ▲ RCH 80 D 4
Cumbres de Majalca ○ MEX 50-51 F 3
Cumbres de Majalca, Parque Nacional ⊥ MEX 50-51 F 3
Cumbrian Mountains ▲▲ GB 90-91 F 4
Cumbum ○ IND 140-141 H 3
Cumburão ○ BR 62-63 G 6
Čumikan ☆ RUS 120-121 F 6
Čumikan ~ RUS 120-121 F 5
Cuminá ○ BR 62-63 F 6
Cuminá, Rio ~ BR 62-63 F 5
Cuminapanema, Rio ~ BR 62-63 G 6
Cummings ○ USA 40-41 C 6
Cummins ○ AUS 180-181 C 3
Cummins Range ▲▲ AUS 172-173 H 5
Cumnock ○ GB 90-91 E 4
Čumpu-Kytyl ○ RUS 110-111 Y 7
Çumra ☆ TR 128-129 E 4
Cumuetė, Rio ~ BR 68-69 C 6
Čumyš ~ RUS 124-125 N 2
Čumyš ~ RUS 124-125 P 2
Čuna ~ RUS 116-117 H 7
Cunaguaro ○ YV 60-61 J 3
Cunani ○ BR 62-63 J 4
Cuñare ○ CO 64-65 F 1
Cunamo ○ RCH 78-79 C 6
Cunauaru, Rio ~ BR 66-67 F 4
Cund ~ ANG 216-217 D 6
Cunday ○ CO 60-61 D 5
Cundeelee ✕ AUS 176-177 G 5
Cundeelee Aboriginal Land ✕ AUS 176-177 G 5
Cunderdin ○ AUS 176-177 D 5
Cunduacán ○ MEX 52-53 H 2
Cundza ○ KA 146-147 D 4
Cunene ○ ANG 216-217 C 7
Cunene □ ANG 216-217 C 8
Cunene ~ ANG 216-217 C 8
Cunene ~ ANG 216-217 D 7
Cúneo ☆ I 100-101 A 2
Cung Hâu, Cù'a ≈ 158-159 J 6
Cunha ○ BR 72-73 H 7
Cunhãs, Rio das ~ BR 68-69 D 5
Cunhinga ~ ANG 216-217 D 5
Cunia, Estação Ecológica ⊥ BR 66-67 F 7
Cuniuá, Rio ~ BR 66-67 D 6
Čunja ~ RUS 116-117 K 5
Čunja, Strelka ○ RUS 116-117 L 5
Cunjamba ○ ANG 216-217 F 7
Cunnamulla ○ • AUS 178-179 H 5
Cunningham, Lake ⊖ ZW 218-219 E 5
Cunningham Islands ⌒ AUS 174-175 D 2
Čunskij ○ RUS 116-117 H 7
Čun'skij ☆ RUS 116-117 J 7
Cuntima ○ GNB 202-203 C 3
Čuokkarašša ▲ N 86-87 M 2
Čupa ○ RUS 88-89 M 3
Čūpānān ○ IR 134-135 F 2
Cupari, Rio ~ BR 66-67 K 4
Cupica ○ CO 60-61 C 4
Cupica, Golfo de ≈ 60-61 C 4
Cupisnique, Cerro ▲ PE 64-65 C 5
Cupixi ○ BR 62-63 J 5
Čuprovo ○ RUS 88-89 T 4
Cuptano, Isla ⌒ RCH 80 D 2
Curaça ○ BR 68-69 J 6
Curaça, Rio ~ BR 68-69 J 6
Curaçao ⌒ NL 60-61 G 1
Curacautín ○ RCH 78-79 D 5
Curacaví ○ RCH 78-79 D 2
Curachi ○ GUY 62-63 D 2
Curácuaro de Morelos ○ MEX 52-53 D 2
Curahuara de Carangas ○ BOL 70-71 C 5
Curale ○ ETH 208-209 G 5
Cura Malal, Sierra de ▲▲ RA 78-79 H 4
Curanilahué ○ RCH 78-79 C 4
Curanja ○ BR 66-67 B 7
Curanja, Río ~ PE 70-71 B 2
Čurapča ☆ • RUS 120-121 E 3
Curaray ○ EC 64-65 D 2
Curaray ○ PE 64-65 E 3
Curaray, Río ~ PE 64-65 E 3
Curari, Ilha de ⌒ BR 66-67 G 4
Curaru ○ RA 78-79 H 3
Curauaí, Rio ~ BR 66-67 H 5
Čurbuka, gora ▲ RUS 110-111 Q 4
Čurbukan ~ RUS 116-117 H 2
Curdimurka ○ AUS 178-179 D 5
Čūre ○ AFG 134-135 M 2
Curecanti National Recreation Area ⊥ • USA 42-43 D 6
Curepipe ○ MS 224 C 7
Curepto ○ RCH 78-79 C 3
Curib ○ RUS 126-127 G 6
Curibaya ○ PE 70-71 B 5
Curiche Liverpool ⊖ BOL 70-71 F 4
Curichi de Oquiriquia ~ BOL 70-71 G 5
Curichi Tunas ~ BOL 70-71 G 5
Curico ○ RCH 78-79 D 3
Curicuriari, Rio ~ BR 66-67 C 3
Curieuse Marine National Park ⊥ SY 224 D 2
Curi Leuvú, Arroyo ~ RA 78-79 D 4
Curimatá ○ BR 68-69 F 7
Curimatá, Rio ~ BR 68-69 F 6
Curimatá de Baixo, Rio ~ BR 66-67 E 5
Curimávida, Cerro de ▲ RCH 76-77 B 6
Curionópolis ○ BR 68-69 D 5
Curitiba ○ BR (ACR) 70-71 C 2
Curitiba ☆ • BR (PAR) 74-75 F 5
Curitibanos ○ BR 74-75 E 6
Curiúva ○ BR 74-75 E 5
Čurkin, mys ▲ RUS 110-111 W 3
Curly Cut Cays ⌒ BS 54-55 G 3
Curnamona ○ AUS 178-179 E 6
Čuro ~ RUS 118-119 F 7
Curoca ~ ANG 216-217 B 8
Curoca, Cachoeira da ~ BR 66-67 G 7
Currais Novos ○ BR 68-69 K 5
Curral Alto ○ BR 74-75 D 9
Curral Falso ○ BR 74-75 E 8
Curralinho ○ BR 62-63 K 6
Curral Novo ○ BR 68-69 H 6
Curral Velho ○ BR 72-73 H 2
Curral Velho ○ CV 202-203 C 5
Currant ○ USA 40-41 G 6
Currarehue ○ RCH 78-79 D 5
Currawinya ○ AUS 178-179 H 5
Currawinya National Park ⊥ AUS 178-179 H 5
Current Island ⌒ BS 54-55 G 2
Currie ○ AUS 180-181 G 5
Currie ○ USA 40-41 G 5
Currie Indian Reserve, Mount ✕ CDN 32-33 J 6
Currituck Sound ≈ 48-49 M 4
Curtea de Argeş ○ • RO 102-103 D 5
Čurti ○ IR 136-137 B 6
Curtin ○ AUS 176-177 G 5
Curtin Springs ○ AUS 176-177 L 2
Curtis Island ⌒ AUS 178-179 L 2
Curtis Lake ⊖ CDN 30-31 Z 2
Curtis River ~ CDN 30-31 Z 2
Curu, Rio ~ BR 68-69 J 3
Curuá ○ BR 62-63 G 6
Curuá, Ilha do ⌒ BR 62-63 J 5
Curuá, Rio ~ BR 62-63 G 6
Curuá, Rio ~ BR 66-67 K 7
Curuaés, Rio ~ BR 66-67 K 7
Curuai ○ BR 66-67 K 4
Curuá ou Cururu, Rio ~ BR 72-73 D 3
Curuá-Una, Rio ~ BR 66-67 K 4
Curuá-Una, Rio ~ BR 66-67 K 4
Curuça ○ BR 68-69 E 2
Curuçá, Ponta ▲ BR 68-69 E 2
Curuça, Rio ~ BR 64-65 F 4
Curuduri, Rio ~ BR 66-67 F 2
Curuguaty ○ PY 76-77 K 3
Curuma la Grande, Cerro ▲ RA 78-79 H 4
Curumutopo ○ YV 60-61 J 4
Curup ○ RI 162-163 E 6
Curupá ○ BR 68-69 F 6
Curupaiti ○ BR 68-69 E 3
Curupira ○ BR 68-69 J 4
Curuquetê, Rio ~ BR 66-67 E 7
Cururu, Raudal ~ CO 66-67 B 2
Cururu-Açu, Rio ~ BR 66-67 J 7
Cururu ou Cururuí, Rio ~ BR 66-67 J 7
Cururupu ○ BR 68-69 F 2
Curuzú Cuatiá ○ RA 76-77 H 5
Curva del Turco ○ RA 76-77 F 3
Curva Grande ○ BR 68-69 F 3
Curvelo ○ BR 72-73 H 5
Curwood, Mount ▲ USA 46-47 D 2
Cushabatay, Río ~ PE 64-65 E 5
Cushamen ○ RA 78-79 D 7
Cushing ○ USA 44-45 J 2
Cusime ○ YV 60-61 J 5
Cusipata ○ PE 70-71 B 3
Cusis, Río ~ BOL 70-71 H 5
Čusovaja ~ RUS 96-97 L 5
Čusovoj ☆ RUS 96-97 K 4
Čusovskoe, ozero ⊖ RUS 114-115 D 4
Cusseta ○ USA 48-49 F 3
Cussivi ~ ANG 216-217 F 7
Cusso ~ ANG 216-217 C 7
Cusson, Pointe ▲ CDN 36-37 K 4
Čust ○ US 136-137 M 4
Custer ○ USA (MT) 42-43 D 2
Custer ○ USA (SD) 42-43 F 4
Custer Battlefield National Monument ∴ • USA 42-43 D 3
Custer State Park ⊥ USA 42-43 F 4
Custódia ○ BR 68-69 K 6
Cusuco, Parque Nacional ⊥ HN 52-53 K 4
Cutato ○ ANG (BIE) 216-217 D 6
Cutato ○ ANG (CUA) 216-217 D 7
Cutato ~ ANG 216-217 D 7
Cutato ~ ANG 216-217 D 5
Cut Bank ○ USA 40-41 H 1
Cutbank River ~ CDN 32-33 L 4
Cutenda ○ ANG 216-217 C 7
Cutervo ○ PE 64-65 C 5
Cutervo, Parque Nacional de ⊥ PE 64-65 C 5
Cuthbert ○ USA 48-49 F 4
Čutove ○ UA 102-103 J 3
Cuttaburra Creek ~ AUS 178-179 H 5
Cutta Cutta Caves • AUS 172-173 L 3
Cuttak=Kataka ○ IND 142-143 D 5
Cutzamala de Pinzón ○ MEX 52-53 D 2
Cù'u Long, Cù'a Sông ⩲ VN 158-159 J 6
Čuvanajskie gory ▲▲ RUS 112-113 O 3
Čuvanskij hrebet ▲▲ RUS 112-113 O 4
Čuvanskoe ○ RUS 112-113 O 4
Cuvelai ○ ANG 216-217 C 7
Cuvelai ~ ANG 216-217 D 7
Cuvette □ RCB 210-211 E 4
Cuvo ~ ANG 216-217 C 5
Cuxhaven ○ D 92-93 K 2
Cuxiuara, Ilha ⌒ BR 66-67 G 4
Cuy, El ○ RA 78-79 E 5
Cuyabeno, Reserva Faunística ⊥ EC 64-65 E 2
Cuyahoya Valley National Recreation Area ⊥ USA 46-47 H 5
Cuyo, El ○ MEX 52-53 L 1
Cuyo East Pass ≈ 160-161 D 7
Cuyo 'English Game' Subterranean National Park ⊥ RP 160-161 D 7
Cuyo Island ⌒ RP 160-161 D 7
Cuyo Islands ⌒ RP 160-161 D 7
Cuyo West Pass ≈ 160-161 D 7
Cuyuni, Río ~ YV 62-63 D 2
Cuzco ☆ ••• PE 70-71 B 3
Čuzik ~ RUS 114-115 P 6
Čvrisnica ▲ BIH 100-101 F 3
Cyangugu ○ RWA 212-213 B 5
Čyappara ○ RUS 118-119 P 4
Čyb ~ RUS 88-89 V 5
Čybyda ~ RUS 118-119 K 4
Cyclades = Kiklàdes ⌒ GR 100-101 K 6
Cycloop, Pegunungan ▲▲ RI 166-167 L 3
Cyclop Mountains Reserve ⊥ • RI 166-167 L 3
Čyhyryn ○ UA 102-103 H 3
Čyjyrčyk, pereval ▲ KS 136-137 N 4
Čym ○ RUS 108-109 K 8
Čyna ~ RUS 118-119 M 5
Cynthia ○ AUS 178-179 L 3
Cynthiana ○ USA 46-47 F 6
Cyohoha Sud, Lac ⊖ BU 212-213 C 5
Cypnavolok, mys ▲ RUS 88-89 M 2
Cypress ○ USA 44-45 L 4
Cypress Gardens ∴ • USA 48-49 H 6
Cypress Hills ▲▲ CDN 32-33 P 7
Cypress Hills Provincial Park ⊥ CDN 32-33 P 7
Cyprus = Kypros ■ CY 128-129 E 5
Čyra ~ RUS 118-119 M 5
Cyrene ○ ZW 218-219 E 5
Cyrene = Shahhāt ∴ ••• LAR 192-193 J 1
Cyrus Field Bay ≈ 36-37 R 3
Čyrvonae, vozero ⊖ BY 94-95 L 5
Cytherea ○ AUS 178-179 J 4
Czaplinek ○ • PL 92-93 O 2
Czar ○ CDN 32-33 P 5
Czarnków ○ PL 92-93 O 2
Czech Republic = Česká Republika ■ CZ 92-93 M 4
Czersk ○ PL 92-93 O 2
Częstochowa ☆ •• PL 92-93 P 3
Człuchów ○ • 92-93 O 2

D

Da'an ○ VRC 150-151 E 5
Daanbantayan ○ RP 160-161 F 7
Daan Viljoen Game Park ⊥ NAM 216-217 D 11
Daaquam ○ CDN 38-39 J 5
Ḑab'a, Maḥaṭṭat ○ JOR 130-131 E 2
Dabadougou ○ CI 202-203 G 5
Dabaga ○ EAT 214-215 H 5
Dabai ○ WAN 204-205 F 3

Coulta — Dabai **251**

Debre Tabor ○ **ETH** 208-209 D 3
Debre Work' ○ **ETH** 208-209 D 3
Debre Zebit ○ **ETH** 208-209 D 3
Debre Zeyit ○ **ETH** 138-139 D 3
Debre Zeyit ○ **ETH** (Goj) 208-209 B 3
Debre Zeyit ○ **ETH** (She) 208-209 D 4
Decatur ○ **USA** (AL) 48-49 E 2
Decatur ○ **USA** (GA) 48-49 F 3
Decatur ○ **USA** (IL) 46-47 D 6
Decatur ○ **USA** (IN) 46-47 F 5
Decatur ○ **USA** (NE) 42-43 J 5
Decatur ○ **USA** (TX) 44-45 J 3
Decazeville ○ **F** 90-91 J 9
Deccan ⊥ **IND** 10-11 G 7
Decelles, Réservoir ⬭ **CDN** 38-39 F 5
Decepcion ○ **CDN** 36-37 M 3
Déception ○ **CDN** 36-37 M 3
Déception, Rivière ∿ **CDN** 36-37 M 3
Déception Bay ≈ **CDN** 36-37 M 3
Déception Bay ≈ **183** C 4
Deception Lake ⬭ **CDN** 34-35 D 2
Deception Point ▲ **AUS** 172-173 K 1
Dechang ○ **VRC** 156-157 C 3
Dechu ○ **IND** 138-139 D 6
Děčín ○ **CZ** 92-93 N 3
Decize ○ **F** 90-91 J 8
Decker ○ **USA** 42-43 D 3
Decker Field ○ **USA** 176-177 H 2
Decorah ○ **USA** 46-47 C 4
Dedegöl Dağları ▲ **TR** 128-129 D 4
Deder ○ **ETH** 208-209 E 4
Dédiápada ○ **IND** 138-139 D 9
Dedo, Cerro ▲ **RA** 80 E 2
Dédougou ○ **BF** 202-203 J 3
Dedoviči ⊙ **RUS** 94-95 L 3
Dedza ○ **MW** 218-219 H 2
Dee ∿ **GB** 90-91 F 5
Dee ∿ **GB** 90-91 H 3
Deep Bay ≈ **CDN** 30-31 L 5
Deep Cove ○ **NZ** 182 A 6
Deep River ○ **CDN** 38-39 F 5
Deep River ○ **USA** 48-49 J 2
Deep Rose Lake ⬭ **CDN** 30-31 U 3
Deepwater ○ **AUS** 178-179 L 5
Deepwater ○ **USA** 42-43 L 6
Deep Well ○ **AUS** 178-179 C 3
Deer ○ **USA** 44-45 L 2
Deer Bay ≈ 24-25 T 1
Deerfield Beach ○ **USA** 48-49 H 6
Deering ○ **USA** 20-21 J 3
Deering, Mount ▲ **AUS** 176-177 K 2
Deer Island ∩ **CDN** 34-35 H 5
Deer Island ∩ **USA** 22-23 P 5
Deer Lake ○ **CDN** (NFL) 38-39 Q 4
Deer Lake ○ **CDN** (ONT) 34-35 J 4
Deer Lake ⬭ **CDN** (NFL) 38-39 Q 4
Deer Lodge ○ **USA** 40-41 H 2
Deer Park ○ **USA** 40-41 F 2
Deerpass Bay ≈ **CDN** 30-31 J 3
Deer Pond ○ **CDN** 38-39 I R 4
Deer River ○ **CDN** 34-35 J 2
Deer River ○ **USA** 42-43 L 2
Deerton ○ **USA** 46-47 E 2
Deerwood ○ **USA** 42-43 L 2
Deeth ○ **USA** 40-41 G 5
Defensores del Chaco, Parque Nacional ⊥ **PY** 70-71 G 7
Defferrari ○ **RA** 78-79 K 5
Defia, Hassi √ **MA** 188-189 K 4
Defiance ○ **USA** 46-47 F 5
Défilé de Tosaye ⊥ **RMM** 196-197 K 6
Degache ○ **TN** 190-191 G 4
Degali ∿ **RUS** 116-117 F 4
Degayè, Ra's ▲ **ER** 200-201 L 6
Dêgê ○ **VRC** 144-145 M 5
Degeh Bur ○ **ETH** 208-209 F 4
Degeh Medo ○ **ETH** 208-209 F 5
Dégelis ○ **CDN** 38-39 K 5
Degema ○ **WAN** 204-205 G 6
Deggendorf ○ **D** 92-93 M 4
Degollado ○ **MEX** 52-53 C 1
Degoma ○ **ETH** 200-201 H 4
Dégrad Claude ⬭ **F** 62-63 H 4
Dégrad des Emerillon = Dégrad Claude ⬭ **F** 62-63 H 4
Dégrad Saint-Léon ⬭ **F** 62-63 H 4
Dégrad Vitalo ⬭ **F** 62-63 H 4
De Grey River ∿ **AUS** 172-173 D 6
Dehalak Desèt ∩ **ER** 200-201 K 5
Dehägän ○ **IR** 134-135 D 3
Dehbärez ○ **IR** 134-135 G 5
Dehbid ○ **IR** 134-135 E 3
Deh Dašt ○ **IR** 134-135 D 3
Dehdez ○ **IR** 134-135 D 3
Dehej ○ **IR** 134-135 F 5
Dehej ○ **IND** 138-139 D 9
Deh-e Kohne ○ **IR** 134-135 D 4
Dehekolano, Tanjung ▲ **RI** 164-165 K 4
Dehepodo ○ **RI** 164-165 K 3
Deh Heir ○ **IR** 134-135 C 4
Dehibat ○ **TN** 190-191 H 4
Dehkanabad ○ **UB** 136-137 K 5
Dehlorän ○ **IR** 134-135 B 1
Deh Mirdäd ○ **AFG** 136-137 K 7
Deh Molla ○ **IR** 134-135 C 3
Dehra Dun ○ **IND** 138-139 G 4
Deh Rävüd ○ **AFG** 134-135 L 2
Dehri ○ **IND** 142-143 D 3
Dehšür ○ **IR** 134-135 K 3
Deh Šu ○ **AFG** 134-135 K 3
Dehua ○ **VRC** 156-157 L 4
Dehui ○ **VRC** 150-151 L 5
Deilam, Bandar-e ○ **IR** 134-135 D 3
Deim Bükhit ○ **SUD** 206-207 H 5
Deira ○ **UAE** 134-135 F 6
Dej ○ **RO** 102-103 C 4
Dejen ○ **ETH** 208-209 D 3
Dejjian ○ **VRC** 154-155 E 3
Dejnau ○ **TM** 136-137 H 2
De Jongs, Tanjung ▲ **RI** 166-167 K 5
De-Kastri ○ **RUS** 122-123 J 3
Dek'emhäre ○ **ER** 200-201 J 5
Dekese ○ **ZRE** 210-211 H 5
Dekina ○ **WAN** 204-205 G 5
Dekoa ○ **RCA** 206-207 D 5
Delaa ○ **DZ** 190-191 D 4

Delacroix ○ **USA** 48-49 D 5
Delaki ○ **RI** 166-167 C 6
Delaney ○ **USA** 40-41 F 2
Delanggu ○ **RI** 168 D 3
Delano ○ **USA** 40-41 E 8
Delärám ○ **AFG** 134-135 K 2
Delareyville ○ **ZA** 220-221 G 3
Delarof Islands ∩ **USA** 22-23 G 7
Delaronde Lake ⬭ **CDN** 34-35 C 3
Delavan ○ **USA** 46-47 D 4
Delaware ○ **USA** 46-47 F 5
Delaware □ **USA** 46-47 L 6
Delaware Bay ≈ **USA** 46-47 L 6
Delaware Lake ⬭ **USA** 46-47 G 5
Delaware River ∿ **USA** 46-47 L 5
Delbi ○ **SN** 202-203 C 3
Del Bonita ○ **CDN** 32-33 O 7
Delburne ○ **CDN** 32-33 O 5
Del Cano Rise ≃ 9 H 10
Delčevo ○ **MK** 100-101 J 4
Deleau ○ **CDN** 34-35 F 6
Deleg ○ **EC** 64-65 C 2
Delegate River ∿ **AUS** 180-181 K 4
Délémbé ○ **RCA** 206-207 F 4
Délep ○ **TCH** 198-199 J 6
Delfino ○ **BR** 68-69 H 7
Delfinópolis ○ **BR** 72-73 G 6
Delft ○ **NL** 92-93 H 2
Delfus ○ **PE** 64-65 D 4
Delfzijl ○ **NL** 92-93 J 2
Dèlger = Tajgan ○ **MAU** 148-149 C 4
Dèlgerèh = Hongor ○ **MAU** 148-149 K 5
Dèlgèrhangaj = Hašaat ○ **MAU** 148-149 G 5
Dèlger mörön ∿ **MAU** 148-149 D 3
Delgo ○ **SUD** 200-201 G 2
Delhi ∴ **IND** 138-139 F 5
Delhi ○ **USA** (LA) 44-45 M 3
Delhi ○ **USA** (NY) 46-47 L 4
Déli ○ **TCH** 206-207 B 4
Delia ○ **CDN** 32-33 J 7
Delicias ○ **CO** 64-65 E 2
Delicias ○ **MEX** 50-51 G 3
Delicias, Las ○ **CO** 60-61 F 5
Deliğän ○ **IR** 134-135 D 1
Délimene, I-n- < **RMM** 202-203 L 2
Delingdé ∿ **RUS** 110-111 O 7
Delingdèkèn ∿ **RUS** 116-117 H 3
Delingha ○ **VRC** 144-145 L 2
Delin'ja ∿ **RUS** 110-111 V 7
Delisle ○ **CDN** (QUE) 38-39 J 4
Delisle ○ **CDN** (SAS) 34-35 C 5
Delissaville X **AUS** 172-173 K 2
Delitua ○ **RI** 162-163 C 3
Deliverance Island ∩ **AUS** 183 A 5
Deljankir ∿ **RUS** 110-111 a 7
Defkju-Ohotskaja ∿ **RUS** 120-121 J 3
Dëfku ∿ **RUS** 110-111 a 6
Dell ○ **USA** 40-41 H 3
Dell Rapids ○ **USA** 42-43 J 4
Dellys ○ **DZ** 190-191 D 2
Delmas ○ **ZA** 220-221 J 3
Delmenhorst ○ **D** 92-93 K 2
Delmore Downs ○ **AUS** 178-179 C 2
Del Norte ○ **USA** 42-43 D 7
De-Longa, ostrova ∩ **RUS** 110-111 b 1
Deloraine ○ **AUS** 180-181 J 6
Deloraine ○ **CDN** 34-35 F 6
Delos ••• **GR** 100-101 K 6
Delphi ••• **GR** 100-101 J 5
Delphi ○ **USA** 46-47 E 5
Delportshoop ○ **ZA** 220-221 G 2
Delray Beach ○ **USA** 48-49 H 6
Del Rio ○ **USA** 44-45 G 5
Delsbo ○ **S** 86-87 H 6
Delta ○ **CDN** (BC) 32-33 J 7
Delta ○ **CDN** (MAN) 34-35 G 5
Delta ○ **USA** (CO) 42-43 C 6
Delta ○ **USA** (UT) 40-41 H 6
Delta ○ **IND** 138-139 G 9
Deolia ○ **IND** 138-139 E 7
Delta del Tigre ○ **ROU** 78-79 L 3
Delta Downs ○ **AUS** 174-175 F 5
Delta Dunării ∿ **RO** 102-103 F 5
Delta Junction ○ **USA** 20-21 S 4
Delta, River ∿ **WAN** 204-205 H 4
Delta Mendota Canal ⊂ **USA** 40-41 D 7
Delta National Wildlife Refuge ⊥ **USA** 48-49 D 5
Delthore Mountain ▲ **CDN** 30-31 F 4
Deftula ∿ **RUS** 116-117 E 3
Delungra ○ **AUS** 178-179 L 5
Dèluun = Rašaant ○ **MAU** 146-147 K 2
Del Verme Falls ∿ **ETH** 208-209 E 6
Deptumala ∿ **RUS** 108-109 a 5
Deputatskij ☆ **RUS** 110-111 W 5
Dêqên ○ **VRC** (XIZ) 144-145 L 6
Dêqên ○ **VRC** (YUN) 144-145 M 6
Deqing ○ **VRC** 156-157 G 5
Dera ○ **ETH** 208-209 D 4
Dera ∿ **SP** 212-213 J 4
Dera Bugti ○ **PK** 138-139 B 5
Dera Ghäzi Khän ○ **PK** 138-139 C 4
Dera Ismäil Khän ○ **PK** 138-139 C 4
Derale ▲ **AUS** 180-181 K 2
Dera Muräd Jamali ○ **PK** 138-139 B 5
Dera Nänak ○ **IND** 138-139 E 3
Deravica ▲∿ **YU** 100-101 H 3
Deräwar Fort ○ **PK** 138-139 C 5
Derbeikan, Wädi ∿ **SUD** 200-201 G 3
Derbeke ∿ **RUS** 110-111 U 7
Derbekinskaja vpadina ⌣ **RUS** 110-111 U 7
Derbent ○ **RUS** 126-127 H 6
Derbissaka ○ **RCA** 206-207 G 6
Derby ○ **AUS** (TAS) 180-181 J 6
Derby ○ **AUS** (WA) 172-173 F 4
Derby ○ **USA** 44-45 J 2
Derby ○ **ZA** 220-221 H 2
Derby Lake ⬭ **CDN** 30-31 X 2
Derdepoort ○ **ZA** 220-221 H 2
Dereli ○ **TR** 128-129 H 2
Deren, Adrar-n- ▲ **MA** 188-189 G 5
Déréssa ○ **TCH** 198-199 K 6
Derg, Lough ⬭ **IRL** 90-91 C 5
Dergači ○ **UA** 102-103 K 2

Dempster Highway II **CDN** 20-21 V 4
Dempta ○ **RI** 166-167 L 3
Dêmqog ○ **IND** 138-139 G 3
Demsa ○ **CAM** 204-205 K 4
Denakil ⊥ **ETH** 200-201 K 5
Denali Highway II **USA** 20-21 Q 5
Denali National Park ⊥ **USA** 20-21 P 5
Denali National Park and Preserve ⊥ **USA** 20-21 P 5
Denan ○ **ETH** 208-209 F 5
Denau ○ **US** 136-137 K 5
Denbigh ○ **CDN** 38-39 F 6
Denbigh, Cape ▲ **USA** 20-21 N 4
Denbigh Downs ○ **AUS** 178-179 F 2
Den Chai ○ **THA** 158-159 F 2
Dendang ○ **RI** 162-163 G 6
Dendâra ○ **RIM** 196-197 G 6
Déndoudi ○ **SN** 202-203 B 2
Deneba ○ **ETH** 208-209 D 4
Denežkin Kamen', gora ▲ **RUS** 114-115 J 4
Dengfeng ○ **VRC** 154-155 H 4
Dengi ○ **WAN** 204-205 H 4
Dengkou ○ **VRC** 154-155 E 1
Dengên ○ **VRC** 144-145 K 5
Denguiro ○ **RCA** 206-207 D 5
Dengyuan ○ **VRC** 156-157 D 2
Dengzhou ○ **VRC** 154-155 H 5
Den Haag = 's-Gravenhage ☆ ••• **NL** 92-93 H 2
Denham ○ **AUS** 176-177 B 2
Denham, Mount ▲ **JA** 54-55 G 5
Denham Island ∩ **AUS** 174-175 E 5
Denham Range ▲ **AUS** 178-179 J 2
Denham Sound ≈ **AUS** 176-177 B 2
Denham Springs ○ **USA** 44-45 M 4
Den Helder ○ **NL** 92-93 H 2
Denholm ○ **CDN** 34-35 C 4
Deni, Pulau ∩ **RI** 168 A 3
Denial Bay ≈ **AUS** 176-177 M 6
Denikouroula ○ **RMM** 202-203 H 4
Deniliquin ○ **AUS** 180-181 H 3
Denio Junction ○ **USA** 40-41 F 5
Denise Island ∩ **SY** 224 D 1
Denison ○ **USA** (IA) 42-43 K 4
Denison ○ **USA** (TX) 44-45 J 3
Denison Range ▲ **AUS** 172-173 J 5
Denizli ☆ **TR** 128-129 C 4
Denkanikota ○ **IND** 140-141 G 4
Denkola ∴• **TM** 136-137 E 4
Denman ○ **AUS** 180-181 L 2
Denman Glacier 〜 **ARK** 16 G 10
Denmark ○ **AUS** 176-177 D 7
Denmark ○ **USA** 48-49 H 3
Denmark = Danmark ■ **DK** 86-87 C 9
Denmark Strait ≈ 6-7 G 2
Denmark Strait ≈ 6-7 F 2
Dennis, Lake ⬭ **AUS** 172-173 J 3
Den Oever ○ **NL** 92-93 H 2
Denpasar ○ **RI** 168 B 7
Dent, La ▲ **CI** 202-203 J 6
Denton ○ **USA** (MD) 46-47 L 6
Denton ○ **USA** (TX) 44-45 J 3
D'Entrecasteaux, Point ▲ **AUS** 176-177 B 7
D'Entrecasteaux Islands ∩ **PNG** 183 F 5
D'Entrecasteaux National Park ⊥ **AUS** 176-177 C 7
Denu ○ **GH** 202-203 L 6
Denver ☆ **USA** 42-43 E 6
Déo, Mayo ∿ **CAM** 204-205 K 5
Deoband ○ **IND** 138-139 F 5
Deodápolis ○ **BR** 78-79 J 2
Deogarh ○ **IND** 142-143 D 5
Deogarh Peak ▲ **IND** 142-143 C 4
Deoghar ○ **IND** 142-143 E 3
Deoläli ○ **IND** 138-139 D 10
Deoli ○ **IND** 138-139 G 9
Deolia ○ **IND** 138-139 E 7
Deori ○ **IND** 142-143 B 5
Déou ○ **BF** 202-203 K 2
Des Plaines ∿ **USA** 46-47 E 4
Dep ∿ **RUS** 118-119 N 9
Dep ∿ **RUS** 122-123 C 2
Dep, River ∿ **WAN** 204-205 H 4
Depälpur ○ **IND** 138-139 E 8
De Panne ○ **B** 92-93 G 3
Depapre ○ **RI** 166-167 L 3
Departure Bay ≈ **CDN** 32-33 J 7
Depew ○ **USA** 44-45 J 2
Dépôt-de-la-Lièvre ○ **CDN** 38-39 H 4
Dépôt Lézard Rnes ○ **F** 62-63 H 3
Deptumala ∿ **RUS** 108-109 a 5
Détour, Point ▲ **USA** 46-47 E 3
Detpa ○ **AUS** 180-181 F 4
Detrin ∿ **RUS** 120-121 N 3
Detroit ○ **USA** (TX) 44-45 K 3
Detroit ○ **USA** (MI) 46-47 G 4
Detroit, Fort ∴ **USA** 42-43 K 2
Detroit de Bougainville ≈ **184** II a 2
Detroit Lakes ○ **USA** 40-41 C 3
Detroit Lakes ○ **USA** 42-43 K 2
Dettifoss ∿ **IS** 86-87 F 1
Det Udom ○ **THA** 158-159 H 3
Detuno ○ **VRC** 156-157 C 2
Deua National Park ⊥ **AUS** 180-181 K 3
Deukeskenkala ∴• **TM** 136-137 F 4
Deustua ○ **PE** 70-71 F 4
Deutsch Brod = Havlíčkův Brod ○• **CZ** 92-93 N 4
Deutsche Bucht ≈ **D** 92-93 J 1
Deutschland State Historic Site ∴ **USA** 46-47 C 6
Deux Balé, Forêt des ⊥ **BF** 202-203 J 4
Deux Bassins, Col de ▲ **DZ** 190-191 J 2
Deux Pietons • **WL** 56 E 5
Deva ☆ **RO** 102-103 C 5
Devadurg ○ **IND** 140-141 G 2
Devakottai ○ **IND** 140-141 H 6
Devanhalli ○ **IND** 140-141 G 4
Devar Hippargi ○ **IND** 140-141 G 2
Devarkonda ○ **IND** 140-141 H 3
Devarshola ○ **IND** 140-141 G 5
Devechi = Dävaçi ○ **AZ** 128-129 N 2
Deveci Dağı ▲ **TR** 128-129 F 2

Derickson Seamount ≃ 22-23 Q 6
Derik ○ **TR** 128-129 J 4
Derjugina, vpadina ≃ 122-123 L 2
Derkül ∿ **KA** 96-97 G 8
Derm ∿ **NAM** 220-221 D 1
Dermott ○ **USA** 44-45 M 3
Dernieres, Isles ∩ **USA** 44-45 M 5
Derramadero ⬭ **C** 54-55 F 4
Derre ○ **MOC** 218-219 J 3
Derri ○ **SP** 208-209 H 6
Derry ○ **USA** 44-45 L 4
Derry Doire = Londonderry ☆ • **GB** 90-91 D 4
Derry Downs ○ **AUS** 178-179 C 2
Derudeb ○ **SUD** 200-201 H 4
Derval ○ **F** 90-91 G 8
Derville, Rivière ∿ **CDN** 36-37 L 3
Derwent ○ **AUS** 176-177 M 1
Derwent, River ∿ **AUS** 180-181 J 7
Derwent ∿ **CDN** 32-33 P 5
Derženka, buhta ≈ **RUS** 112-113 N 2
Dežneva, mys ▲ **RUS** 112-113 a 3
Dezong ○ **VRC** 144-145 H 4
Desaguadero, Río ∿ **BOL** 70-71 D 5
Desaguadero, Río ∿ **RA** 78-79 D 4
Desagües de los Colorados ○ **RA** 76-77 D 5
Des Arc ○ **USA** 44-45 M 2
Desaru ○ **MAL** 162-163 E 4
Desbarats ○ **CDN** 38-39 C 5
Desbarats Strait ≈ 24-25 T 2
Descabezado Grande, Volcán ▲ **RCH** 78-79 D 3
Descanso ○ **USA** 40-41 F 9
Descanso, El ○ **PE** 70-71 B 4
Deschaillons ○ **CDN** 38-39 H 5
Deschambault Lake ⬭ **CDN** 34-35 D 3
Descharme River ∿ **CDN** 32-33 Q 3
Deschutes River ∿ **USA** 40-41 D 3
Descoberto ○ **BR** 72-73 H 7
Descubierta, La ○ **DOM** 54-55 K 5
Desè ☆ **ETH** 208-209 D 3
Deseado, Cabo ▲ **RCH** 80 C 6
Deseado, Río ∿ **RA** 80 G 3
Desecho ○ **YV** 66-67 H 5
Desemboque, El ○ **MEX** 50-51 C 2
Desengaño, Punta ▲ **RA** 80 H 4
Desenzano del Garda ○ **I** 100-101 C 4
Deseret Peak ▲ **USA** 40-41 H 5
Desert Center ○ **USA** 40-41 G 9
Desert Hot Springs ○ **USA** 40-41 F 9
Desert National Park ⊥ **IND** 138-139 C 6
Desert National Wildlife Range ⊥ **USA** 40-41 G 7
Desert Peak ▲ **USA** 40-41 H 6
Desert Range ×× **USA** 40-41 H 6
Desert Test Center ×× **USA** 40-41 H 5
Desiderio Tello ○ **RA** 76-77 D 4
Desierto, Canal el ≈ **RCH** 76-77 F 4
Desierto Central de Baja California, Parque Nacional del ⊥ **MEX** 50-51 B 3
Desirade, La ∩ **F** 56 E 3
Desmarais Lake ⬭ **CDN** 30-31 R 5
Des Moines ☆ **USA** (IA) 42-43 L 5
Des Moines ☆ **USA** (IA) 42-43 L 5
Des Moines River ∿ **USA** 42-43 K 4
Dhaka ★ •• **BD** 142-143 F 4
Dhakia ○ **IND** 142-143 C 6
Dhaleswari ∿ **BD** 142-143 F 3
Dhanána ○ **IND** 138-139 B 4
Dhanasar ○ **PK** 138-139 B 4
Dhanaura ○ **IND** 138-139 G 5
Dhanbäd ○ **IND** 142-143 E 4
Dhandelhura ○ **NEP** 144-145 C 6
Dhandhuka ○ **IND** 138-139 C 8
Dhangarhi ○ **NEP** 144-145 C 6
Dhankuta ○ **NEP** 144-145 F 4
Dhanpuri ○ **IND** 142-143 B 4
Dhanushkodi ○ **IND** 140-141 H 6
Dhär ○ **IND** 138-139 E 8
Dharampur ○ **IND** 140-141 G 4
Dharamsala ○ **IND** 140-141 G 4
Dharamsala ○ **IND** 138-139 F 3
Dhárni ○ **IND** 138-139 F 9
Dharwad ○ **IND** 140-141 F 2
Dhasän ∿ **IND** 138-139 G 7
Dhaulagarī ∿ **IND** 138-139 G 8
Dhaulagiri Himäl ▲ **NEP** 144-145 D 6
Dhauliganga ∿ **IND** 138-139 G 4
Dhaulpur ○ **IND** 138-139 F 6
Dhaya ○ **DZ** 188-189 L 3
Dhaym-al-Khayl ∿ **MA** 196-197 D 2
Dhebar Lake ⬭ **IND** 138-139 D 7
Dhekelia Sovereign Base Area (GB) ×× **CY** 128-129 C 6
Dhenkänäl ○ **IND** 142-143 D 5
Dhiinsoor ○ **SP** 212-213 J 2
Dhing ○ **IND** 142-143 G 2
Dhlo Dhlo Ruins ∴• **ZW** 218-219 E 4
Dholera ○ **IND** 138-139 D 8
Dhone ○ **IND** 140-141 G 3
Dhoodi, Bannaanka ⊥ **SP** 208-209 H 4
Dhorpatan ○ **NEP** 144-145 D 6
Dhrängadhra ○ **IND** 138-139 C 8
Dhubbato ○ **SP** 208-209 G 4
Dhuburi ○ **IND** 142-143 F 2
Dhud, togga ∿ **SP** 208-209 J 3
Dhule ○ **IND** 138-139 E 9
Dhulian ○ **IND** 142-143 F 3
Die Bos ○ **ZA** 220-221 D 2
Dhunat ○ **BD** 142-143 F 3
Dhunche ○ **NEP** 144-145 E 6
Dhündär ○ **IND** 138-139 F 6
Dhurbo ○ **SP** 208-209 K 3
Dhuudo, togga ∿ **SP** 208-209 J 3
Dhuusa Mareeb ☆ **SP** 208-209 H 6
Di ○ **LB** 202-203 E 6
Dia ∩ **GR** 100-101 K 7

Develi ☆ **TR** 128-129 F 3
Deverill ○ **AUS** 178-179 K 2
Devgarh ○ **IND** 138-139 D 7
Deviation Peak ▲ **USA** 20-21 K 3
Devica ∿ **RUS** 102-103 L 2
Devil Mountain ▲ **USA** 20-21 H 3
Devil Mountain Lake ⬭ **USA** 20-21 H 3
Devil Mountain Lake ⬭ **USA** 44-45 E 6
Devil's Bridge ⊥ **AG** 56 E 3
Devil's Gate ▲ **USA** 40-41 E 6
Devil's Hole ≃ 90-91 H 3
Devil's Hole National Monument • **USA** 40-41 F 7
Devil's Island = Diable, Île du ∩ **F** 62-63 H 3
Devils Lake ○ **USA** (ND) 42-43 H 1
Devils Lake ○ **USA** 42-43 H 1
Devils Lake Sioux Indian Reservation X **USA** 42-43 H 1
Devils Marbles Scenic Reserve • **AUS** 174-175 C 7
Devil's Point ○ **BS** 54-55 J 3
Devils Postpile National Monument • **USA** 40-41 E 7
Devls River ∿ **USA** 44-45 G 4
Devils Tower National Monument • **USA** 42-43 E 3
Devin ○ **BG** 102-103 D 7
Devipattinam ○ **IND** 140-141 H 6
Devli ○ **IND** 138-139 E 7
Devnja ○ **BG** 102-103 E 6
Devoll ∿ **AL** 100-101 H 4
Devon ∿ **GB** 90-91 E 6
Devon ○ **ZA** 220-221 J 3
Devon 30 Indian Reserve X **CDN** 38-39 L 5
Devon Island ∩ **CDN** 24-25 b 3
Devonport ○ **AUS** 180-181 H 6
Devonshire ○ **AUS** 178-179 H 2
Devrek ☆ **TR** 128-129 D 2
Devure ∿ **ZW** 218-219 F 4
Dewa, Tanjung ▲ **RI** (ACE) 162-163 A 3
Dewa, Tanjung ▲ **RI** (KSE) 164-165 C 5
Dewäs ○ **IND** 138-139 F 8
Dewelé ○ **ETH** 208-209 F 3
Dewetsdorp ○ **ZA** 220-221 H 4
Dewey Lake ⬭ **USA** 46-47 G 7
Dexing ○ **VRC** 156-157 K 2
Dexter ○ **USA** 44-45 D 7
Dexter, USA 40-41 E 6
Deyang ○ **VRC** 154-155 D 6
Dey-Dey, Lake ⬭ **AUS** 176-177 L 4
Deyhük ○ **IR** 134-135 G 3
Deyyer ○ **IR** 134-135 D 5
Dez, Rüd-e ∿ **IR** 134-135 C 2
Dezadeash ○ **CDN** 20-21 W 6
Dezadeash Lake ⬭ **CDN** 20-21 W 6
Dezful ○ **IR** 134-135 C 2
Dezhou ○ **VRC** 154-155 J 3
Dežneva, Mys = Dežneva, mys ▲ **RUS** 112-113 a 3
Dezhou ○ **VRC** 154-155 K 3
Dežneva, buhta ≈ **RUS** 112-113 N 2
Dežneva, mys ▲ **RUS** 112-113 a 3
Dhahran = az-Zahrán ○ **KSA** 134-135 D 5
Dhahran = Zahrän, az- ○ **KSA** 134-135 D 5

Diaba < **RMM** 196-197 H 6
Diabakania ○ **RG** 202-203 E 4
Diabali ○ **RMM** 202-203 H 3
Diable, Île du ∩ **F** 62-63 H 3
Diablo, Punta del ○ **ROU** 74-75 D 10
Diablo Range ▲ **USA** 40-41 D 7
Diablotins, Morne ▲ **WD** 56 E 4
Điện Biên ○ **VN** 156-157 C 6
Điện Châu ○ **VN** 156-157 D 7
Dieng Plateau • **RI** 168 D 3
Điện Khánh ○ **VN** 158-159 K 4
Dienné ○ **RMM** 202-203 H 3
Diepholz ○ **D** 92-93 K 2
Dieppe ○ **F** 90-91 H 7
Dierks ○ **USA** 44-45 K 2
Die Venster ∿ **ZA** 220-221 D 5
Dif ○ **EAK** 212-213 H 3
Diffa □ **RN** 198-199 F 6
Diffa ○ **RN** (DIF) 198-199 F 6
Difounda ○ **RG** 210-211 K 5
Difuma ○ **ZRE** 210-211 K 5
Dig ○ **IND** 138-139 F 6
Digba ○ **ZRE** 206-207 G 6
Digboi ○ **IND** 142-143 J 2
Digby ○ **CDN** 38-39 M 6
Digges ○ **CDN** 30-31 W 6
Digges Islands ∩ **CDN** 36-37 K 3
Digges Sound ≈ **CDN** 36-37 K 3
Dighanchi ○ **IND** 140-141 F 2
Dighton ○ **USA** 42-43 F 6
Diğla ∿ **IRQ** 128-129 M 6
Diğlür ○ **IND** 138-139 F 10
Digne-les-Bains ○ **F** 90-91 L 9
Digoin ○ **F** 90-91 K 8
Digor ☆ **TR** 128-129 K 2
Digora ○ **RUS** 126-127 F 6
Digos ○ **RP** 160-161 J 5
Digri ○ **PK** 138-139 B 6
Digsa ○ **ER** 200-201 J 5
Digua ○ **RCH** 78-79 C 4
Digue Island, La ∩ **SY** 224 D 1
Diguillin, Río ∿ **RCH** 78-79 D 4
Diguilu ○ **IND** 166-167 L 5
Digya National Park ⊥ **GH** 202-203 K 6
Dihang or Siang ∿ **IND** 142-143 J 1
Diibao ○ **CAM** 206-207 B 4
Dijar ○ **KA** 126-127 P 4
Dijmphna Sund ≈ 26-27 p 4
Dijon ☆ • **F** 90-91 K 8
Dijur ○ **RUS** 88-89 W 4
Dik ○ **TCH** 206-207 C 4
Dika, mys ▲ **RUS** 108-109 k 3
Dikáka, ad- ⊥ **KSA** 132-133 G 4
Dikanäs ○ **S** 86-87 G 4
Dikhil ○ **DJI** 208-209 F 3
Dikhu ∿ **IND** 142-143 J 2
Dikili ☆ **TR** 128-129 B 3
Dikimis ○ **ET** 194-195 E 2
Dikodougou ○ **CI** 202-203 H 5
Dikson ○ **RUS** 108-109 T 5
Dikson, ostrov ∩ **RUS** 108-109 T 5
Dikulwe ∿ **ZRE** 214-215 D 6
Dikwa ○ **WAN** 198-199 F 6
Qila ○ **AFG** 138-139 A 3
Dila ○ **ETH** 208-209 D 5
Dilam, ad- ○ **KSA** 132-133 E 4
Dilezi Geçidi ▲ **TR** 128-129 L 4
Dili ○ **RI** 166-167 C 6
Dili ∿ **ZRE** 210-211 L 2
Dilia ∿ **RN** 198-199 F 5
Dilia ○ **USA** 44-45 G 3
Di Linh ○ **VN** 158-159 K 5
Diližan ○ **AR** 128-129 L 2
Dilžanskij zapovednik ⊥ **AR** 128-129 L 2
Dilj ▲ **HR** 100-101 F 3
Dilke ○ **CDN** 34-35 D 5
Dilley ○ **USA** 44-45 H 5
Dilli ○ **RMM** 202-203 H 3
Dilling ○ **SUD** 200-201 F 6
Dillingham ○ **USA** 22-23 R 3
Dillon ○ **USA** (MT) 40-41 H 3
Dillon ○ **USA** (SC) 48-49 J 2
Dillon River ∿ **CDN** 32-33 P 4
Dilolo ○ **ZRE** 210-211 D 4
Dilts Historic Site, Fort ∴ **USA** 42-43 F 2
Dima ○ **ETH** 208-209 D 3
Dimako ○ **CAM** 204-205 K 6
Dimalla ○ **RIM** 196-197 F 5
Dimäpur ○ **IND** 142-143 H 3
Dimaş ★ ••• **SYR** 128-129 F 6
Dimbaza ○ **ZA** 220-221 H 6
Dimbelenge ○ **ZRE** 210-211 J 6
Dimbokro ☆ **CI** 202-203 H 6
Dimboola ○ **AUS** 180-181 G 4
Dimbulah ○ **AUS** 174-175 H 5
Dimissi ○ **PNG** 183 B 3
Dimitrievka ○ **RUS** 94-95 R 5
Dimitrovgrad ○ **BG** 102-103 D 6
Dimitrovgrad ○ **RUS** 96-97 K 6
Dimitrovgrad ○ **YU** 102-103 K 3
Dimlang ▲ **WAN** 204-205 J 4
Dimlo ○ **RP** 160-161 F 8
Dimlik ∿ **TCH** 206-207 C 4
Dimma Lake ⬭ **CDN** 30-31 T 5
Dimmitt ○ **USA** 44-45 F 2
Dimona ☆ **IL** 130-131 D 2
Dimora ○ **AUS** 178-179 G 1
Dimovo ○ **BG** 102-103 H 2
Dimpam ○ **CAM** 210-211 D 2
Dina ○ **PK** 138-139 D 3
Dinagat ○ **RP** 160-161 F 8
Dinagat Island ∩ **RP** 160-161 F 7
Dinajpur ○ **BD** 142-143 F 3
Dinalongan ○ **RP** 160-161 D 7
Dinan ○• **F** 90-91 G 7
Dinangourou ○ **RMM** 202-203 J 2
Dinant ○ **B** 92-93 H 3
Dinapigul ○ **RP** 160-161 E 4
Dinar ☆ **TR** 128-129 D 3
Dinar, Küh-e ▲ **IR** 134-135 D 3
Dinara ▲ **YU** 100-101 E 4
Dinchiya Shet' ∿ **ETH** 208-209 D 4
Dindar ○ **SUD** 200-201 F 6

Dindar National Park ⊥ SUD 200-201 G 6
Dinder Wenz ~ ETH 208-209 B 3
Dindi o ZW 218-219 G 3
Dindigul o IND 140-141 G 5
Dindima o WAN 204-205 J 3
Dindori o IND 142-143 B 4
Dindoudi Séydi o SN 202-203 D 2
Dinga o PK 138-139 D 3
Dinga o ZRE 210-211 F 6
Ding'an o VRC 160-161 D 5
Dingbian o VRC 154-155 E 3
Ding Ding o SUD 206-207 L 4
Dinge o ANG 216-217 B 7
Dinggye o VRC 144-145 G 6
Dinghushan • VRC 156-157 H 5
Dinghushan Z.B. ⊥ • VRC 156-157 H 5
Dingila o ZRE 210-211 L 2
Dingjie o VRC 144-145 G 6
Dingle = An Daingean o IRL 90-91 B 5
Dingle Bay ≈ IRL 90-91 B 5
Dingley Dell Cons. P. • AUS 180-181 F 5
Dingnan o VRC 156-157 H 5
Dingo o ANG 216-217 F 8
Dingo o AUS 178-179 K 2
Dingtao o VRC 154-155 F 4
Dinguirayé o RG 202-203 E 4
Dingwall o GB 90-91 E 3
Dingxi o VRC 154-155 D 4
Dingxiang o VRC 154-155 H 2
Dingyuan o VRC 154-155 K 5
Dingzhou o VRC 154-155 J 2
Dingzikou o VRC 146-147 L 6
Dinhata o IND 142-143 F 2
Đinh Lạp ☆ VN 156-157 E 6
Dinnik, Plateau de ▲ RN 204-205 L 1
Dinokwe o RB 218-219 D 6
Dinorwic o CDN 34-35 K 6
Dinosaur o USA 42-43 C 5
Dinosaur National Monument • USA 42-43 C 5
Dinosaur Provincial Park ⊥ ••• CDN 32-33 P 6
Dinosaurusspore • NAM 216-217 D 10
Dinsmore o CDN 34-35 C 5
Dintiteladas o RI 162-163 F 7
Dinuba o USA 40-41 E 7
d'In Ziza, Gueltas ▲ DZ 190-191 D 9
Dioila o RMM 202-203 G 3
Diokana o TCH 198-199 H 6
Diomandou o RG 202-203 F 5
Diona o BF 202-203 J 4
Diona o TCH 198-199 L 4
Dionisio o BR 72-73 J 5
Dionisio Cerqueira o BR 74-75 D 6
Dionouga o BF 202-203 K 2
Diorama o BR 72-73 E 4
Dios, Canal de ≈ RCH 76-77 F 3
Diosso o RCB 210-211 C 6
Diou o F 90-91 J 8
Dioulatiédougou o CI 202-203 G 5
Diouloulou o SN 202-203 B 3
Dioumara o RMM 202-203 F 2
Dioundiou o RN 204-205 L 2
Dioura o RMM 202-203 H 2
Diourou o RMM 202-203 H 3
Dipalpur o PK 138-139 E 3
Dipchari o WAN 204-205 K 3
Diphu o IND 142-143 H 3
Dipkun o RUS 118-119 N 8
Diplo o PK 138-139 B 7
Dipolog o RP 160-161 E 8
Dippa ~ RUS 118-119 K 3
Dipper Lake o CDN 34-35 C 3
Dipperu National Park ⊥ AUS 178-179 K 1
Đi Qär o IRQ 128-129 M 7
Diqdãqa o UAE 134-135 F 6
Dira ⟨ TCH 198-199 G 5
Dirat at-Tulül o SYR 128-129 G 6
Dire o IRQ 128-129 L 4
Diré o RMM 196-197 J 6
Direction, Cape ▲ AUS 174-175 G 3
Diré Dawa o • ETH 208-209 E 4
Dirgi Shabazai o PK 138-139 B 4
Diriamba o NIC 52-53 L 4
Dirico o ANG 216-217 F 8
Dir'iya, ad- o KSA (QAS) 130-131 H 5
Dir'iya, ad- o • KSA (RIY) 130-131 K 5
Dirk Hartog Island ~ AUS 176-177 B 2
Dirkou o RN 198-199 J 3
Dirrah o SUD 200-201 C 6
Dirranbandi o AUS 178-179 K 5
Dirty Devil River ~ USA 40-41 J 6
Disa o IND 138-139 D 7
Disang ~ IND 142-143 J 2
Disappointment, Cape ▲ GB 78-79 O 7
Disappointment, Cape ▲ USA 40-41 B 2
Disappointment, Lake o AUS 176-177 G 1
Discovery, Cape ▲ CDN 26-27 M 2
Discovery Bay ≈ 180-181 F 5
Discovery Bay o USA 40-41 C 2
Discovery Reef = Huaguang Jiao ~ VRC 158-159 J 2
Discovery Seamounts ≃ 6-7 K 13
Dishkakat o USA 20-21 M 5
Dishna River ~ USA 20-21 M 5
Disko Banke ≃ 28-29 M 2
Disko Bugt ≈ 28-29 N 2
Disko Fjord ≈ 28-29 N 2
Diskofjord = Kangerluk o GRØ 28-29 N 2
Disko Ø ~ GRØ 28-29 N 2
Dismal Lakes o CDN 30-31 L 2
Dismal Swamp • USA 48-49 K 1
Dišnā o ET 194-195 F 4
Disney o AUS 178-179 J 1
Disneyland • USA 40-41 F 9
Dispur ☆ IND 142-143 G 2
Disputada, El o RCH 76-77 B 6
Disraeli Fiord ≈ 26-27 O 2
Diss o GB 90-91 G 5
Dissain, Ġazīrat ~ KSA 132-133 B 5
Disteghil Sar ▲ IND 138-139 E 1

Distrito Federal □ BR 72-73 F 3
Distrito Federal □ MEX 52-53 E 2
Disûq o ET 194-195 E 2
Ditang o VRC 156-157 F 2
Ditinn o RG 202-203 D 4
Ditsinane ⟨ RB 218-219 C 5
Ditu, Mwene- o ZRE 214-215 B 4
Diu o IND 138-139 C 9
Divândarre o IR 128-129 M 5
Divénié o RCB 210-211 C 5
Divide o CDN 32-33 Q 7
Divide o USA 40-41 H 3
Divilican o RP 160-161 E 4
Divilican Bay ≈ 160-161 E 4
Divinhe o MOC 218-219 H 5
Divinolândia de Minas o BR 72-73 J 5
Divisa o PA 52-53 D 7
Divisadero, El o MEX 50-51 F 4
Divisaderos o MEX 50-51 E 2
Divisões ou de Santa Marta, Serra das ▲ BR 72-73 D 4
Divisópolis o BR 72-73 K 3
Divisor, Serra de ▲ BR 64-65 F 5
Divisoria o RP 160-161 F 7
Divisorio, El o RA 78-79 J 5
Divnogorsk o RUS 116-117 F 8
Divo o CI 202-203 H 7
Divor, Ribeira do ~ P 98-99 C 5
Divriği ☆ TR 128-129 H 3
Divuma o ZRE 214-215 B 6
Diwaniya, ad- o IRQ 128-129 L 7
Diwopu J. II ▲ VRC 146-147 H 4
Diwoumé, Mare ~ DY 202-203 L 4
Dixcove o GH 202-203 K 7
Dixiasenlin ▲ VRC 150-151 G 5
Dixon o USA (IL) 46-47 D 5
Dixon Entrance ≈ 32-33 D 4
Dixonville o CDN 32-33 M 3
Dixonville o RA 78-79 G 3
Diyadin ☆ TR 128-129 K 3
Diyālā ~ IRQ 128-129 L 6
Diyarbakir ☆ TR 128-129 J 4
Dizangué o CAM 210-211 D 2
Dize o NR 198-199 L 5
Dizhipoumian ⊥ • VRC 154-155 K 1
Dja ~ CAM 210-211 D 2
Dja, Réserve du = Dja Reserve ⊥ ••• CAM 210-211 D 2
Djado ∴ RN 198-199 J 2
Djado, Plateau du ▲ RN 198-199 F 1
Djakarta = Jakarta ☆ RI 168 B 3
Djakotomè o DY 202-203 L 6
Djalasiga o ZRE 212-213 C 2
Djale ~ ZRE 210-211 J 5
Djalon, Fouta ▲ RG 202-203 D 4
Djaluwon Creek ~ AUS 172-173 H 6
Djamãa o DZ 190-191 J 4
Djamandjary o RM 222-223 F 4
Djamba o ZRE (HAU) 210-211 K 2
Djamba o ZRE (SHA) 214-215 B 5
Djambala o CAM 204-205 K 5
Djambala o RCB 210-211 C 5
Djampiel o CAM 206-207 B 6
Djanet ☆ DZ 190-191 G 8
Djangylah, ostrov ~ RUS 110-111 N 3
Djanyska ~ RUS 110-111 O 7
Djara ~ RUS 110-111 F 5
Dja Reserve = Réserve du Dja ⊥ ••• CAM 210-211 D 2
Djaret, Oued ~ DZ 190-191 D 7
Djarua ~ RI 166-167 G 3
Djat'kovo o RUS 94-95 O 5
Djeboho ▲ GH 202-203 L 5
Djebok o RMM 196-197 L 6
Djébrène o TCH 206-207 D 3
Djédaa o TCH 198-199 J 6
Djeddars • DZ 190-191 C 3
Djedi, Oued ~ DZ 190-191 E 3
Djedid, Bir ⟨ DZ 190-191 F 4
Djelfa ☆ DZ 190-191 D 3
Djéma o RCA 206-207 G 5
Djemadja, Pulau ~ RI 162-163 F 3
Djèmber o TCH 206-207 C 3
Djemila ∴ • DZ 190-191 E 2
Djems Bank ≃ 162-163 K 2
Djerem ~ CAM 204-205 K 6
Djérem ~ CAM 204-205 K 5
Djerma o TCH 198-199 G 6
Djibasso o BF 202-203 H 3
Djibo o BF 202-203 K 2
Djiborosso o CI 202-203 G 5
Djibouti ■ DJI 208-209 F 3
Djibouti ☆ DJI 208-209 F 3
Djidja o DY 202-203 L 6
Djigouo o BF 202-203 J 4
Djiguéra o BF 202-203 H 4
Djiguéni o RIM 196-197 F 7
Djiroutou o CI 202-203 G 7
Djohong o CAM 206-207 B 5
Djoku-Punda o ZRE 210-211 H 6
Djoli o TCH 206-207 D 4
Djolu o ZRE 210-211 H 3
Djombo o ZRE 210-211 H 3
Djombo = Haraz o TCH 198-199 J 6
Djombo Kibbit o TCH 198-199 J 6
Djona, Zone Cynégétique de ⊥ DY 204-205 J 3
Djonâba o RIM 196-197 D 6
Djorf Torba o DZ 188-189 K 5
Djorf-Torba, Barrage ⟨ DZ 188-189 K 5
Djoua ~ G 210-211 D 3
Djoubissi o RCA 206-207 E 5
Djoudj, Parc National des oiseaux du ⊥ ••• SN 196-197 B 6
Djoué o RCB 210-211 C 5
Djougou o DY 202-203 L 5
Djoúk, Passe de ▲ RIM 196-197 D 6
Djoum o CAM 210-211 D 2
Djoumboli o CAM 204-205 L 6
Djourab, Erg du ⊥ TCH 198-199 H 4
Djoutou-Pétel o RG 202-203 D 4
Djugadjak ~ RUS 112-113 K 4
Djugu o ZRE 212-213 C 3

Djulljuku o RUS 118-119 K 4
Djuʹtydag, gora ▲ RUS 126-127 G 7
Djúpivogur o IS 86-87 F 2
Djupkun, ozero o RUS (EVN) 108-109 c 7
Djupkun, ozero o RUS (EVN) 116-117 F 2
Djura, Kytyl- o RUS 118-119 M 5
Djurdjura, Djebel ▲ DZ 190-191 E 2
Djurtjuli ☆ RUS 96-97 J 6
D'kar o BR 216-217 F 10
Dla ~ RMM 202-203 F 3
Dlinnyj, ostrov ~ RUS 108-109 Y 2
Dlowana o ZA 220-221 K 4
Dmitrievka o KA 124-125 E 2
Dmitriev-L'govskij o RUS 94-95 O 5
Dmitrija Lapteva, proliv ≈ 110-111 W 3
Dmitrov ☆ RUS 94-95 P 3
Dmytrivka o UA 102-103 H 2
Dnepr ~ RUS 94-95 M 4
Dneprodzeržinsk = Dniprodzeržyns'k o UA 102-103 J 3
Dnepropetrovsk = Dnipropetrovs'k ☆ UA 102-103 J 3
Dnestr = Dnister ~ UA 102-103 E 3
Dnestr = Nistru ~ MD 102-103 F 4
Dnipro ~ UA 102-103 J 3
Dnipro ~ UA 102-103 J 3
Dniprodzeržyns'k o UA 102-103 J 3
Dniprodzerzhyns'k = Dneprodzeržinsk o UA 102-103 J 3
Dnipropetrovs'k ☆ UA 102-103 J 3
Dniprorudne o UA 102-103 J 3
Dniprovs'kyj lyman ≈ 102-103 G 4
Dniprovs'kyj lyman ≈ 102-103 H 4
Dnister ~ UA 102-103 E 3
Dnistrovs'kyj lyman ≈ 102-103 G 4
Dnjapro ~ BY 94-95 M 5
Dnjaprovska-Buhski, Kanal ⟨ BY 94-95 J 5
Dno ~ RUS 94-95 L 3
Do, Lac ~ RMM 202-203 J 2
Doa o MOC 218-219 H 3
Doaba o PK 138-139 C 3
Doaktown o CDN 36-37 L 5
Doangdoangan Besar, Pulau ~ RI 164-165 E 6
Doba ☆ TCH 206-207 C 4
Doba o VRC 144-145 G 6
Dobbiaco = Toblach o I 100-101 D 1
Dobbin Bay ≈ 26-27 N 4
Dobbs, Cape ▲ CDN 36-37 F 2
Dobbspet o IND 140-141 G 4
Dobbyn o AUS 174-175 F 6
Doberai Peninsula ∪ RI 166-167 F 2
Dobie River ~ CDN 34-35 L 5
Dobinga o CAM 204-205 K 4
Doblas o RA 78-79 H 4
Dobo o RI 166-167 H 4
Doboj ☆ BIH 100-101 G 2
Dobre Miasto o • PL 92-93 Q 2
Dobrič o BG 102-103 G 6
Dobrich = Dobrič o BG 102-103 E 6
Dobrinka o RUS 94-95 R 5
Dobrjanka o RUS 96-97 K 4
Dobromyl' o UA 102-103 C 3
Dobron' o UA 102-103 B 3
Dobropillya o UA 102-103 K 3
Dobrotești o RO 102-103 D 5
Dobruči o RUS 94-95 K 2
Dobruš o BY 94-95 M 5
Dobrzańskogo, ostrov ~ RUS 112-113 M 5
Dobzha o VRC 144-145 G 6
Docas, Cachoeira das ~ BR 72-73 D 3
Doc Can Island ~ RP 160-161 C 10
Doce, Rio ~ BR 72-73 K 5
Doce, Rio ~ BR 72-73 E 4
Dochigam National Park ⊥ IND 138-139 E 2
Docker River o AUS (NT) 176-177 K 2
Docker River ~ AUS 176-177 K 2
Docking o GB 90-91 H 5
Dockrell, Mount ▲ AUS 172-173 H 5
Dockyard, The ⟨ AG 56 E 3
Doctor Arroyo o MEX 50-51 L 6
Doctor González o MEX 50-51 K 5
Doctor Pedro P. Peña o PY 76-77 F 2
Doda o EAT 212-213 G 6
Doda ~ IND 164-165 L 3
Dod Ballapur o IND 140-141 G 4
Dodecanese = Dodekanissa ~ GR 100-101 L 4
Dødes Fjord, De ≈ 26-27 R 5
Dodge City o USA 42-43 G 7
Dodge Lake o CDN 30-31 R 6
Dodge River ~ CDN 36-37 P 3
Dodinga o RI 164-165 K 3
Dodji o SN 202-203 C 2
Dodol ⟨ SP 212-213 J 2
Dodola o ETH 208-209 D 4
Dodoma o EAT 212-213 E 6
Dodoma • EAT (DOD) 214-215 H 4
Dodori ~ EAK 212-213 H 4
Dodori National Reserve ⊥ EAK 212-213 H 4
Dodowa o GH 202-203 K 7
Dodson o USA 42-43 C 1
Dodson Peninsula ∪ ARK 16 F 30
Doege o ANG 216-217 F 4
Doembang Nangbuat o THA 158-159 F 3
Dofa o RI 164-165 J 4
Dôgai Coring o VRC 144-145 G 3
Dogaʹdyn ~ RUS 108-109 a 7
Doğanşehir o TR 128-129 G 3
Dogbo-Tota o DY 202-203 L 6
Dogdo ~ RUS 110-111 V 6
Dog Island ~ RI 162-163 J 6
Dog Island ~ USA 48-49 F 5
Dog Lake o CDN (MAN) 34-35 G 5

Dog Lake o CDN (ONT) 34-35 M 6
Dog Lake o CDN (ONT) 34-35 O 6
Dōgo ~ J 152-153 F 5
Dogo o RMM 202-203 G 4
Dogoba o SUD 206-207 J 5
Dogondoutchi o RN 204-205 L 2
Dogoutchi o RN 198-199 B 6
Dôgo-yama ▲ J 152-153 E 7
Dogpound Creek ~ CDN 32-33 N 6
Dog Salmon River ~ USA 22-23 S 4
Doğubayazıt ☆ TR 128-129 L 3
Doğu Karadeniz Dağları ▲ TR (61) 128-129 H 2
Doğu Menteşe Dağları ▲ TR 128-129 C 4
Dogura o PNG 183 F 6
Dogwall o GB 90-91 F 3
Dogwood Creek ~ AUS 178-179 K 4
Doi, Pulau ~ RI 164-165 K 3
Doigan ~ EAK 212-213 F 3
Doig River ~ CDN 32-33 K 3
Doi Inthanon ▲ THA 142-143 L 6
Doi Inthanon National Park ⊥ THA 142-143 L 6
Dois Corregos o BR 72-73 F 7
Dois de Novembro, Cachoeira ~ BR 66-67 F 7
Dois Irmãos o BR 72-73 F 3
Dois Irmãos, Cachoeira ~ BR 66-67 H 7
Dois Riachos, Rio ~ BR 68-69 K 6
Doi Suthep-Poi National Park ⊥ THA 142-143 L 6
Dois Vizinhos o BR 74-75 D 5
Doi Tachi ▲ THA 158-159 E 2
Doka o RI 166-167 H 4
Doka ~ SUD 200-201 F 5
Dokhara, Dunes de ∴ DZ 190-191 K 4
Dokis Indian Reserve X CDN 38-39 E 5
Doko o RG 202-203 E 4
Doko o WAN 198-199 D 6
Dokpam o GH 202-203 K 5
Doktorskij, mys ▲ RUS 108-109 H 7
Dokučaevs'k o UA 102-103 K 4
Dokui o BF 202-203 J 3
Dolak, Pulau ~ RI 166-167 K 5
Dolak Pulau Reserve ⊥ • RI 166-167 J 5
Doland o USA 42-43 H 3
Dolavon o RA 78-79 G 7
Dolbeau o CDN 38-39 H 4
Dolbel o RN 202-203 L 2
Dolby Lake o CDN 30-31 R 5
Dole o F 90-91 K 8
Doleib Hill o SUD 206-207 K 5
Dolenci o MK 100-101 H 4
Dolgellau o GB 90-91 F 5
Dolgij, ostrov ~ RUS 108-109 H 7
Dolgij, ostrov ~ RUS (NAO) 88-89 X 2
Dolgij Most o RUS 116-117 H 7
Dolgoderevenskoe ☆ RUS 96-97 M 6
Dolgoi Island ~ USA 22-23 U 5
Dolia o IND 138-139 C 8
Dolina gejzerov ~ RUS 120-121 S 6
Dolinovka o RUS 120-121 S 6
Dolinsk o RUS 122-123 K 5
Dolit o RI 164-165 K 4
Dolleman Island ~ ARK 16 F 30
Dollo Odo o ETH 208-209 F 5
Dolni Lom o BG 102-103 C 6
Dolný Kubín o SK 92-93 P 4
Dolo o RI 164-165 F 4
Dolokmerawan o RI 162-163 C 3
Dolok Pinapan o RI 162-163 C 3
Dolomiti = Dolomiten ▲ I 100-101 C 1
Dolon, pereval ▲ KS 146-147 B 5
Dolong o RI 164-165 H 4
Doloon o MAU 148-149 G 5
Dolores o CO 60-61 D 4
Dolores o GCA 52-53 K 3
Dolores o RA 78-79 L 4
Dolores o ROU 78-79 K 3
Dolores o RP 160-161 F 6
Dolores o YV 60-61 G 3
Dolores Hidalgo o • MEX 50-51 J 7
Doloroso o USA 44-45 M 4
Dolphin, Cape ▲ GB 78-79 M 8
Dolphin and Union Strait ≈ 24-25 O 6
Đô Lương ∻ VN 156-157 D 7
Dolyna o UA 102-103 D 3
Dolyns'ka o UA 102-103 H 3
Dom, Gunung ▲ RI 166-167 J 3
Domar o VRC 144-145 C 4
Doma Safari Area ⊥ ZW 218-219 F 3
Domažlice o CZ 92-93 M 4
Dombaj o RUS 126-127 G 7
Dombarovskij ☆ RUS 126-127 N 2
Dông Phạya Yen ▲ THA 158-159 F 2
Dombe Grande o ANG 216-217 B 6
Dombey, Cape ▲ AUS 180-181 E 4
Dombo o RI 166-167 J 2
Domboshawa o ZW (Mle) 218-219 F 4
Domboshawa ▲ ZW (Mle) 218-219 F 4
Dombóvár o H 92-93 P 5
Dom Cavat o BR 72-73 J 5
Dome o IND 138-139 E 5
Dome Bay ≈ 24-25 U 1
Domett o NZ 182 F 5
Domeyko o RCH 76-77 B 5
Domeyko, Cordillera de ▲ RCH 76-77 C 4
Domfront o F 90-91 G 7
Dominase o GH 202-203 K 6
Domingos Martins o BR 72-73 K 6
Domingo Mourão o BR 68-69 H 4
Dominica ■ WD 56 E 4
Dominica Island ~ WD 56 E 4
Dominical o CR 52-53 C 7

Dominican Republic = Republica Dominicana ■ DOM 54-55 K 6
Dominica Passage ≈ 56 E 4
Dominion Range ▲ ARK 16 C 3
Domingo o ZRE 210-211 H 6
Domkonda o IND 138-139 G 10
Domo o ETH 208-209 H 5
Domodedovo ☆ RUS 94-95 P 4
Domodóssola o I 100-101 B 1
Domoni o COM 222-223 D 4
Dom Pedrito o BR 76-77 K 6
Dom Pedro o BR 68-69 F 4
Dompem o BR 202-203 J 7
Dompu o RI 168 D 7
Domrémy o CDN 34-35 D 4
Dom Silvério o BR 72-73 J 5
Domuyo, Volcán ▲ RA 78-79 D 4
Domuzla o RUS 96-97 K 8
Domville, Mount ▲ AUS 178-179 L 5
Don ~ RUS 94-95 Q 5
Don ~ RUS 94-95 Q 5
Don Juan o DOM 54-55 L 5
Don Martin o MEX 50-51 J 4
Donald o AUS 180-181 G 4
Donald Landing o CDN 32-33 H 4
Donaldsonville o USA 44-45 M 4
Doña Rosa, Cordillera ▲ RCH 76-77 B 6
Donau ~ 8 4
Donau ~ D 92-93 L 4
Donauwörth o • D 92-93 L 4
Don Benito o E 98-99 E 5
Doncaster o AUS 174-175 G 7
Doncaster o GB 90-91 F 5
Doncaster, Réserve Indienne de X CDN 38-39 G 5
Doncello, El o CO 64-65 E 1
Dondaicha o IND 138-139 E 5
Donderkamp o SME 62-63 F 3
Dondo o ANG 216-217 C 4
Dondo o MOC 218-219 H 4
Dondo o RI (NTI) 168 F 7
Dondo o RI (SLT) 164-165 H 4
Dondo o ZRE 210-211 H 4
Dondon o RH 54-55 J 5
Dongeleksor o KA 126-127 O 3
Döngelek su kojmasy ⟨ KA 96-97 G 3
Đông Đăng o VN 156-157 E 6
Dongara o AUS 176-177 C 4
Dongargarh o IND 142-143 B 5
Dongchuan o VRC 156-157 C 3
Dongco o VRC 144-145 E 4
Dongela o VRC 144-145 G 6
Dongfang o VRC (HAI) 156-157 F 7
Dongfang o VRC (HUN) 156-157 F 2
Dongfanghong o VRC 150-151 J 4
Dongfeng o VRC 150-151 E 8
Donggala o RI 164-165 F 4
Donggi o RI 164-165 H 4
Donggi Cona o VRC 144-145 M 3
Dongguan o VRC 150-151 E 8
Dongguan o VRC 156-157 B 5
Dongguang o VRC (GDG) 156-157 J 2
Đông Hà o VN 158-159 J 2
Dong Hai o VRC 156-157 G 6
Donghai o VRC 154-155 L 4
Donghai Dao ~ VRC 156-157 G 6
Đông Hới o VN 158-159 J 2
Dong Jiang ~ VRC 156-157 M 2
Dongjingcheng o VRC 150-151 F 7
Dongkait, Tanjung ▲ RI 164-165 F 5
Dongkalang o RI 164-165 H 4
Dongkeng o VRC 156-157 L 3
Donglan o VRC 156-157 E 4
Dongliang o VRC 154-155 H 2
Dong Ling • VRC 150-151 D 7
Dongmen o VRC 156-157 E 5
Dongning o VRC 150-151 H 5
Dongo o ANG 216-217 C 7
Dongo o ZRE 210-211 G 3
Dongola = Dunqula o SUD 200-201 E 3
Dongou o RCB 210-211 G 2
Dong Phaya Yen ▲ THA 158-159 F 2
Dongqiao o VRC 144-145 G 3
Dongshan Wan ≈ VRC 156-157 K 5
Dongshanling • VRC 156-157 G 7
Dongsheng o VRC 154-155 F 2
Dongtai o VRC 154-155 M 5
Dongtaijnar Hu o VRC 144-145 K 2
Dongting Hu o VRC 156-157 H 2
Đông Triều o VN 156-157 H 2
Dos Lagunas o GCA 52-53 K 3
Dô Sơn o VN 156-157 E 6

Dongzhai o VRC 154-155 H 2
Dongzhaigang Z.B. ⊥ • VRC 156-157 G 7
Dongzhi o VRC 154-155 K 6
Doniphan o USA 46-47 C 7
Donji Vakuf o BIH 100-101 F 2
Donkar o BHT 142-143 G 2
Donkerpoort o ZA 220-221 G 5
Donko o WAN 204-205 F 3
Donmatia o IND 142-143 G 3
Donna ~ N 86-87 F 3
Donnacona o CDN 38-39 J 4
Donnelly o CDN 32-33 M 4
Donnybrook o AUS 176-177 C 6
Donnybrook o ZA 220-221 J 4
Dono Mangá o TCH 206-207 C 3
Donon ▲ F 90-91 L 8
Donostia-San Sebastián o •• E 98-99 G 3
Doña Ana, Cerro ▲ RCH 76-77 B 5
Doña Inés, Cerro ▲ RCH 76-77 B 5
Doña Juana, Volcán ▲ CO 64-65 D 1
Đon Quê o VN 158-159 J 2
Donqula o SUD 200-201 E 3
Don River o AUS 174-175 J 7
Donskaja grada ▲ RUS 100-101 G 6
Donskaja ravnina ▲ RUS 94-95 R 5
Donskoe o RUS 96-97 K 8
Donskoj ☆ RUS 94-95 Q 5
Donyztau ▲ KA 126-127 M 4
Doolgunna o AUS 176-177 E 2
Doolnavauna o AUS 172-173 J 6
Doomik = Tournai o • B 92-93 G 3
Doomadgee X AUS 174-175 E 5
Doomadgee Aboriginal Land X AUS 174-175 E 5
Doonerak, Mount ▲ USA 20-21 P 3
Doongmabulla o AUS 178-179 J 2
Doomik = "ournai o • B 92-93 G 3
Doorns, De o ZA 220-221 D 6
Door Peninsula ∪ USA 46-47 E 3
Dora, Lake o AUS 172-173 F 7
Dora, Mount ▲ USA 42-43 E 7
Dorada, La o CO 60-61 D 5
Dorado o PY 76-77 G 1
Dorado, El o CO 64-65 E 1
Dorado, El o YV 62-63 D 2
Dorado, Río ~ RA 76-77 F 3
Doraga o RP 160-161 E 6
Dörähäk o IR 134-135 D 5
Doralé o DJI 208-209 F 3
Dorânâla o IND 140-141 H 3
Doran Lake o CDN 30-31 Q 5
Dorbod o VRC 150-151 E 6
Dorchester ☆ GB 90-91 F 6
Dorchester, Cape ▲ CDN 36-37 J 2
Dordabis o NAM 216-217 D 11
Dordogne ~ F 90-91 H 9
Dordrecht o • NL 92-93 H 3
Dordrecht o ZA 220-221 H 5
Doreen, Mount ▲ AUS 172-173 K 7
Doré Lake o CDN (SAS) 34-35 C 3
Doré Lake o CDN (SAS) 34-35 C 3
Dores do Rio Preto o BR 72-73 K 6
Dores Turvo o BR 72-73 J 6
Dorey o RMM 202-203 K 2
Dörgön = Seer o MAU 146-147 L 1
Dori ☆ BF 202-203 K 2
Doringbaai o ZA 220-221 D 5
Doringrivier ~ ZA 220-221 D 6
Dorintosh o CDN 32-33 Q 4
Dorion o CDN 34-35 M 6
Dorion o CDN (QUE) 38-39 H 5
Dorisvale o AUS 172-173 K 3
Dorlin o F 62-63 H 4
Dormentes o BR 68-69 H 6
Dornakal o IND 142-143 B 6
Dornoch o GB 90-91 F 3
Dornod □ MAU 148-149 L 4
Dornogovĭ □ MAU 148-149 J 5
Dornod'v ☆ MAU 146-147 D 4
Doro o RMM 196-197 K 6
Dorogobuž o RUS 94-95 N 4
Doroh o IR 134-135 J 2
Dorohoi o RO 102-103 E 4
Dorohovo o RUS 94-95 P 4
Dorolo'o o CI 202-203 G 6
Doroninskoe o RUS 118-119 F 10
Döröö muur o MAU 146-147 L 2
Doropo o CI 202-203 G 5
Dorotea o S 86-87 H 4
Dorothy o CDN 32-33 O 6
Dorowa o ZW 218-219 F 4
Dorožnyj o RUS 118-119 G 5
Dorre Island ~ AUS 176-177 B 2
Dorrigo o AUS 178-179 M 6
Dorrigo National Park ⊥ AUS 178-179 M 6
Dorsale Camerounaise ▲ CAM 204-205 D 2
Dorset ■ GB 90-91 F 6
Dört Krise ∴ TR 128-129 J 2
Dörtyol o TR 128-129 G 4
Dorūcha o RUS 110-111 J 3
Doruma o ZRE 206-207 H 6
Doruvu o BR 72-73 J 6 (?)
Dörvöljin = Buga o MAU 146-147 M 2
Dôsi o AFG 136-137 L 7
Dos, El ~ MEX 52-53 L 1
Dos Caminos o C 54-55 H 4
Dos Caminos o YV 60-61 H 3
Dos de Mayo o PE 64-65 D 5
Doseo Bahr ⟨ TCH 206-207 D 4
Dos Hermanas o E 98-99 E 6
Dôsi o AFG 136-137 L 7
Dospet o BG 102-103 D 7
Dos Filos o CO 64-65 F 1
Dossa o RN (DOS) 204-205 E 2
Dossor o KS 146-147 B 5
Dostuk o KS 146-147 B 5
Doswell o USA 46-47 K 7

Dot o CDN 32-33 K 6
Dothan o USA 48-49 F 4
Dotswood o AUS 174-175 J 2
Douai o F 90-91 J 6
Douala ☆ CAM 204-205 K 5
Douala-Edéa, Réserve ⊥ CAM 210-211 C 2
Doualayel o CAM 204-205 K 5
Douaouir, Erg ▲ RMM 196-197 J 6
Douarnenez o F 90-91 E 7
Douaya ☆ RMM 196-197 J 6
Doubabougou o RMM 202-203 G 2
Double Island Point ▲ AUS 178-179 M 3
Double Mer ≈ 36-37 U 7
Double Mountain ▲ AUS 178-179 L 2
Double Mountain Fork Brazos River ~ USA 44-45 G 3
Doubob o BF 202-203 L 4
Doubs ~ F 90-91 L 8
Doubtful Bay ≈ 172-173 G 4
Doubtful Island Bay ≈ 176-177 F 7
Doubtful Sound ≈ 182 A 6
Douchuishan • VRC 154-155 D 5
Doudou o BF 202-203 J 4
Doué ~ SN 196-197 C 6
Douélé o CI 202-203 G 6
Douentza ■ RMM 202-203 J 2
Dougga ∴ • TN 190-191 G 2
Doughboy Bay ≈ 182 A 7
Douglas o GB 78-79 L 6
Douglas ☆ • GBM 90-91 E 4
Douglas o AUS 172-173 K 2
Douglas o USA (AK) 32-33 C 2
Douglas o USA (GA) 48-49 G 4
Douglas o USA (WY) 42-43 E 4
Douglas o ZA 220-221 F 4
Douglas, Cape ▲ USA 22-23 U 3
Douglas, Mount ▲ USA 22-23 U 3
Douglas Channel ≈ 32-33 F 5
Douglas Creek ~ AUS 178-179 D 5
Douglas Lake o CDN 30-31 Q 4
Douglas Lake o USA 48-49 G 2
Douglas Lake Indian Reserve X CDN 32-33 K 6
Douglas Pass ▲ USA 42-43 C 6
Douglas Peninsula ∪ CDN 30-31 P 4
Douglas Point ▲ CDN 38-39 D 4
Douglas Ponds Creek ~ AUS 178-179 D 5
Douglas Range ▲ ARK 16 G 29
Douglass o USA 44-45 J 1
Dougmogue ▲ VRC 156-157 D 4
Douhongpo o VRC 156-157 D 4
Douka o Bahr Keita ou ~ TCH 206-207 C 4
Doukhobor Village ∴ CDN 32-33 M 7
Doukoula o CAM 206-207 B 3
Doulatâbâd o AFG (BAL) 136-137 K 6
Doulatâbâd o AFG (FÁ) 136-137 J 4
Doulati, Ab-e ~ IR 134-135 L 1
Doulat Yár o AFG 134-135 L 1
Doullens o F 90-91 J 6
Doumandzou o G 210-211 C 3
Doumba bonne ⟨ RN 198-199 F 3
Doumé o CAM 206-207 B 6
Doumen ⟨ VRC 156-157 D 4
Doumo o CAM 210-211 D 2
Douna o BF 202-203 H 4
Douna ~ RMM 202-203 K 2
Doundé Bagué o SN 202-203 D 2
Dounet o RG 202-203 E 4
Doungél-Sigon o RG 202-203 D 4
Dounkassa o DY 204-205 L 3
Dounkou o BF 202-203 J 3
Douqing o VRC 156-157 D 3
Dourada, Serra ▲ BR 72-73 F 3
Douradina o BR (BSU) 76-77 K 2
Douradina o BR (PAR) 72-73 D 7
Douradoquara o BR 72-73 G 5
Dourados o BR 76-77 K 2
Dourados, Rio ~ BR 76-77 K 2
Dourados, Serra dos ▲ BR 72-73 D 7
Dour Bábá o AFG 138-139 C 2
Dourbie ~ F 90-91 J 9
Dourbiga o ZW 218-219 F 4
Dourdoura o TCH 206-207 E 3
Douro ~ RMM 202-203 J 2
Douro, Rio ~ P 98-99 D 4
Douroum o CAM 204-205 K 3
Doussala o G 210-211 C 3
Doutoulou o RN 198-199 D 6
Douz o TN 190-191 G 2
Dove ~ PNG 183 B 6
Dove Bugt ≈ 26-27 q 5
Dove Creek o USA 42-43 C 7
Dover o AUS 180-181 J 7
Dover o GB 90-91 H 6
Dover o USA (NH) 46-47 N 4
Dover o USA (TN) 48-49 E 1
Dover ☆ USA (DE) 46-47 L 5
Dover, Strait of ≈ 90-91 H 6
Dover-Foxcroft o USA 46-47 O 3
Dover River ~ CDN 32-33 H 3
Dovrefjell ▲ N 84-85 H 3
Dovsk o BY 94-95 M 5
Dowa o MW 218-219 G 1
Dowagiac o USA 46-47 E 5
Dowerin o AUS 176-177 D 5
Dowi, Mount ▲ PNG 183 D 4
Downey o USA 40-41 H 4
Downton, Mount ▲ CDN 32-33 H 5
Doyle o USA 40-41 D 5
Doylesville o USA 42-43 D 6
Doze de Outubro, Rio ~ BR 70-71 H 3
Dozgah, Rūdhāne-ye ~ IR 134-135 L 4
Dozois, Réservoir ⟨ CDN 38-39 F 5
Drâa, Cap ▲ MA 188-189 F 6

Ede ○ WAN 204-205 F 5
Edéa ○ CAM 210-211 C 2
Edefors ○ S 86-87 K 3
Edehine Ouarene ± DZ 190-191 G 6
Edehon Lake ○ CDN 30-31 V 5
Edéia ○ BR 72-73 F 4
Eden ○ AUS 180-181 K 4
Eden ○ USA (NC) 48-49 J 1
Eden ○ USA (TX) 44-45 H 4
Edenburg ○ ZA 220-221 G 4
Edendale ○ NZ 182 B 7
Edendale ○ ZA 220-221 K 4
Edenhope ○ AUS 180-181 F 4
Edenton ○ USA 48-49 K 1
Edenville ○ ZA 220-221 H 3
Edenwold ○ CDN 34-35 K 3
Ede Point ▲ CDN 24-25 V 4
Édessa ○•▶ GR 100-101 J 4
Edgar ○ USA 46-47 D 3
Edgar, Mount ▲ AUS 172-173 E 6
Edgar Ranges ▲ AUS 172-173 F 5
Edgartown ○ USA 46-47 N 5
Edgecumbe ○ NZ 182 F 4
Edgeley ○ USA 42-43 J 4
Edgell Island ∩ CDN 36-37 R 4
Edgemont ○ USA 42-43 F 4
Edgeøya ∩ N 84-85 M 4
Edgeøyjøkulen ⊂ N 84-85 N 4
Edgerton ○ USA 42-43 J 4
Edgewater ○ CDN 32-33 M 6
Edgewood ○ USA 44-45 K 3
Ediessane, Oued ∼ DZ 190-191 G 8
Edillile ○ AUS 180-181 C 3
Edina ○ USA 42-43 L 5
Edinburg ○ USA 44-45 H 6
Edinburgh ☆•▶ GB 90-91 F 4
Edincy ○ = Edineţ ☆ MD 102-103 E 3
Edinec ○ = Edineţ ☆ MD 102-103 E 3
Edineţ ☆ MD 102-103 E 3
Edingeni ○ MW 214-215 G 7
Edirne ○•▶ TR 128-129 B 2
Edisto River ∼ USA 48-49 H 3
Edith, Mount ▲ USA 40-41 J 2
Edith Downs ○ AUS 174-175 G 7
Edith Falls ○ AUS 172-173 L 3
Edithvale ○ AUS 172-173 J 4
Edjeleh ○ DZ 190-191 G 7
Edkins Range ▲ AUS 172-173 G 4
Edmond ○ USA 44-45 J 2
Edmonds ○ USA 40-41 C 2
Edmond Walker Island ∩ CDN 24-25 U 2
Edmonton ☆ CDN 32-33 O 5
Edmund Lake ○ CDN 34-35 K 3
Edmundston ○ CDN 38-39 K 5
Edna ○ USA 44-45 J 5
Èdolo ○ I 100-101 C 1
Edouard, Lac ○ = Lake Edward ○ ZRE 212-213 B 4
Edough, Djebel ▲ DZ 190-191 F 2
Edremit ○ TR 128-129 K 3
Edremit ○ TR 128-129 B 3
Edremit Körfezi ≈ TR 128-129 B 3
Edremo ○ ETH 208-209 B 5
Edsbyn ○ S 86-87 G 6
Edsel Ford Range ▲ ARK 16 F 23
Edson ○ CDN 32-33 M 5
Edson River ∼ CDN 32-33 M 5
Eduard Holm, Kap ▲ GRØ 28-29 Y 3
Eduni, Mount ▲ CDN 30-31 S 3
Edvard Ø ∩ GRØ 26-27 p 5
Edward, Lake ○ = Lac Edouard ○ ZRE 212-213 B 4
Edward Island ∩ CDN 174-175 C 4
Edward River ∼ AUS 180-181 G 3
Edward River ∼ AUS 174-175 F 4
Edward River Kowanyama Aboriginal Land X AUS 174-175 F 4
Edwards ○ USA 40-41 F 8
Edwards Air Force Base xx USA 40-41 F 8
Edwards Plateau ▲ USA 44-45 G 4
Edwards State Memorial, Fort ∴ USA 46-47 C 5
Edward VIIth Peninsula ∩ ARK 16 F 22
Edwin ○ CDN 34-35 G 6
Edziza Peak ▲ CDN 32-33 H 3
Edzna ∴ ∼ MEX 52-53 J 2
Edzo ○ CDN 30-31 M 4
Eek ○ USA 20-21 J 6
Eekit ∼ RUS 110-111 P 4
Eeklo ○ B 92-93 G 3
Eek River ∼ USA 20-21 J 6
Eel River ∼ USA 40-41 C 5
Eel River ∼ USA 46-47 F 5
Eendekuil ○ ZA 220-221 D 6
Èèvijn buudal ∼ MAU 146-147 M 2
Efatè ○ = Île Vatè ∩ VAN 184 II b 3
Efatè ∩ = Île Vaté ∩ VAN 184 II b 3
Efes ∴ ∼ TR 128-129 B 3
Effie ○ USA 42-43 L 2
Effigy Mounds National Monument ∴ USA 46-47 C 4
Effingham ○ USA 46-47 D 6
Efimovski ○ RUS 94-95 O 2
Efon Alaye ○ WAN 204-205 F 5
Eforie Nord ○•▶ RO 102-103 F 5
Efremov ○ RUS 94-95 Q 5
Efremova, buhta ≈ RUS 108-109 T 5
Efremova, bubta ∼ RUS 108-109 T 5
Eg ○ MAU 148-149 K 3
Ègadi, Ìsole ∩ I 100-101 D 6
Eganville ○ CDN 38-39 F 6
Egari ○ PNG 183 B 4
Egayit ○ MYA 142-143 J 6
Egbe ○ WAN 204-205 F 4
Egbunda ○ ZRE 210-211 L 2
Ege Denizi ≈ 128-129 A 3
Egedesminde ○ = Aasiaat ○ GRØ 28-29 O 2
Egenolf Lake ○ CDN 30-31 U 6
Egeo Pelagos ≈ 100-101 K 5
Eger ○ H 92-93 Q 5
Eger = Cheb ○ CZ 92-93 M 3
Eger = Ohře ∼ CZ 92-93 M 3
Egersund ☆ N 86-87 C 7

Egerton, Cape ∩ CDN 26-27 K 2
Egerton, Mount ▲ AUS 176-177 D 2
Eggenfelden ○ D 92-93 M 4
Egg Lake ○ CDN 34-35 D 3
Èg gol ∼ MAU 148-149 K 3
Egholo ○ SOL 184 I c 3
Ègilsstaðir ○ IS 86-87 f 2
Egina ○ GR 100-101 J 6
Ègina ∩ GR 100-101 J 6
Eginbah ○ AUS 172-173 D 6
Egindybulak ○ KA 124-125 K 4
Ègio ○ GR 100-101 J 5
Egito Praia ○ ANG 216-217 B 5
Egizkara, tau ▲ KA 124-125 G 6
Eglin Air Force Base xx USA 48-49 J 4
Eglington Island ∩ CDN 24-25 M 3
Egmont ○ CDN 32-33 J 7
Egmont, Cape ▲ NZ 182 D 4
Egmont, Mount ▲ NZ 182 E 3
Egmont Bay ≈ 38-39 M 5
Egmont National Park ⊥ NZ 182 E 3
Egol'jah ∼ RUS 114-115 M 4
Egor'evsk ○ RUS 94-95 Q 4
Egorlyk ∼ RUS 102-103 N 5
Egošinskaja guba ≈ RUS 96-97 F 3
Egra ○ IND 142-143 E 5
Ègrigöz Daği ▲ TR 128-129 C 3
Eguia ○ RP 160-161 C 5
Èguja, gora ▲ RUS 120-121 P 4
Egum Atoll ∩ PNG 183 F 5
Ègvekinot ∼ RUS 112-113 V 3
Egypt = al-Misr ■ ET 194-195 F 4
Eha-Amufu ○ WAN 204-205 G 5
Ehegnadzor ○ AR 128-129 L 3
Eh-Eh, Riacho ∼ RA 76-77 J 3
Ehi ○ GH 202-203 L 6
Ehodak ○ N 86-87 L 2
Eibi, Bur ▲ SP 212-213 K 2
Eichstätt ○ D 92-93 L 4
Eide ○ N 86-87 C 5
Eider Island ∩ CDN 36-37 P 4
Eidsbotn West Fiord ≈ CDN 26-25 b 2
Eidsemub ○ NAM 220-221 C 2
Eidsvold ○ AUS 178-179 L 3
Eidukal ∼ SUD 200-201 G 3
Eielson ○ USA 20-21 R 4
Eifel ▲ D 92-93 J 3
Eiffel Flats ○ ZW 218-219 E 4
Eiger ▲ CH 92-93 K 4
Eight Degree Channel ≈ 140-141 E 6
Eights Coast ∼ ARK 16 F 27
Eighty Mile Beach ≈ AUS 172-173 E 5
Eikefjord ○ N 86-87 B 6
Eikwe ○ GH 202-203 J 7
Eilai ○ SUD 200-201 E 4
Eildon ○ AUS 180-181 H 4
Eildon, Lake ○ AUS 180-181 H 4
Eileen Lake ○ CDN 30-31 U 4
Eilerts de Haan, National Reservaat ⊥ SME 62-63 F 4
Eilerts de Haan Gebergte ▲ SME 62-63 F 4
Einasleigh ○ AUS 174-175 H 6
Einasleigh River ∼ AUS 174-175 G 5
Eindayaza ○ MYA 158-159 E 3
Eindhoven ○ NL 92-93 H 3
Einme ○ MYA 158-159 C 2
Eirik Ridge ≃ 6-7 E 3
Èiriksjökull ⊂ IS 86-87 c 2
Eirunepé ○ BR 66-67 E 6
Eiseb ∼ NAM 216-217 F 10
Eisenach ○•▶ D 92-93 L 3
Eisenerz ○ A 92-93 N 5
Eisenhower, Mount ▲ CDN 32-33 N 6
Eisenstadt ☆ A 92-93 O 5
Eišiškes ○ LT 94-95 J 4
Eivanaki ○ IR 136-137 C 7
Eivissa ○•▶ E (BAL) 98-99 H 5
Eivissa ∩ E (BAL) 98-99 H 5
Eja ∼ RUS 102-103 L 4
Èjea de los Caballeros ○ E 98-99 G 3
Ejeda ○ RM 222-223 D 10
Ejer Bavnehøj ▲ DK 86-87 D 9
Èjido ○ YV 60-61 F 3
Ejidogari ○ WAN 204-205 F 4
Ejido Pancho Villa ○ MEX 50-51 C 5
Èjim ∼ RUS 118-119 L 4
Ejin Horo Qi ○ VRC 154-155 F 2
Ejin Qi ○ VRC 148-149 E 7
Ejirin ○ WAN 204-205 F 5
Ejisu ○ GH 202-203 K 6
ej-Jemâa ○ MA 188-189 G 5
Èj Jill, Kediet ▲ RIM 196-197 E 3
Èj Jill, Sebkhet ○ RIM 196-197 D 3
Ejka ∼ RUS 116-117 M 4
Èjna ○ RUS 88-89 M 2
Ejouj ○ RIM 196-197 F 6
Ejrinejskaja guba ≈ RUS 120-121 L 4
Ejsk ○ RUS 102-103 L 4
Èjt'ja ∼ RUS 114-115 L 4
Ejule ○ WAN 204-205 G 5
Ejura ○ GH 202-203 K 6
Ejutla ○ MEX 52-53 G 3
Èkalaka ○ USA 42-43 G 3
Ekalluk River ∼ CDN 24-25 T 5
Ekalugad Fiord ≈ 28-29 F 2
Ekamour ○ RIM 196-197 F 6
Ekang ○ WAN 204-205 G 5
Ekar, Gara ▲ DZ 198-199 B 3
Ekarjaujaha ∼ RUS 108-109 T 6
Èkarma, ostrov ∩ RUS 122-123 P 4
Èkata ○ ZRE 210-211 G 5
Ekaterinburg ☆ RUS 96-97 N 6
Ekaterinoslavka ○ RUS 122-123 C 3
Ekateriny, proliv ≈ RUS 122-123 M 6
Ekbalám ∴ MEX 52-53 K 1
Ekbław Glacier ⊂ CDN 26-27 M 4
Èkéfi ○ WAN 204-205 G 5
Ekenäs ○•▶ FIN 88-89 G 7
Ekibastúz ☆ KA 124-125 J 3
Ekibastuz = Ekibastúz ☆ KA 124-125 J 3
Èkimčan ○ RUS 122-123 E 2

Ekismane ∼ RN 198-199 C 5
Èkityki ∼ RUS 112-113 V 3
Èkityki, ozero ○ RUS 112-113 U 3
Èkjuččju ∼ RUS 110-111 S 6
Ekka Islands ∩ CDN 30-31 J 2
Èkkan'egan ∼ RUS 114-115 P 4
Ekker, In ○ DZ 190-191 E 8
Eklindli ○ IND 138-139 D 7
Ekok ○ CAM 204-205 H 6
Ekoli ○ ZRE 210-211 K 4
Ekom, Chutes, d' ∼ CAM 204-205 J 6
Ekombe ○ ZRE 210-211 J 5
Ekondo Titi ○ CAM 204-205 H 6
Ekor ○ RI 164-165 K 3
Ekpe ○ WAN 204-205 G 5
Ekpindi ∼ KA 136-137 L 3
Èkshárad ○ S 86-87 E 6
Eksjö ☆•▶ S 86-87 G 8
Ektrema ○ BR 72-73 G 7
Eku ○ WAN 204-205 F 5
Eku, River ∼ WAN 204-205 F 4
Ekubu ○ FJI 184 III a 3
Èkugvaam ∼ RUS 112-113 W 3
Ekukola ○ ZRE 210-211 H 3
Ekuku ○ ZRE 210-211 J 4
Ekuma ∼ NAM 216-217 C 9
Ekumakoko ○ ZRE 210-211 J 5
Èkvyvatapskij hrebet ▲ RUS 112-113 S 2
Èkvyvatop ∼ RUS 112-113 T 2
Ekwa ○ CAM 210-211 D 2
Ekwan Point ▲ CDN 34-35 P 4
Ekwan River ∼ CDN 34-35 P 4
Ekyiomenfurom ○ GH 202-203 K 6
Ela, Tanjung ▲ RI 166-167 C 7
Èl Àbrèd ○ ETH 208-209 G 6
Elabuga ○ RUS 96-97 H 6
El 'Açâba ▲ RIM 196-197 D 6
Elada ○ GR 100-101 H 5
Elâda Steiréa ○ GR 100-101 H 5
El Adeb Larache ○ DZ 190-191 G 7
Elahera ○ CL 140-141 J 7
el-Ahmar, Hassi ▲ MA 188-189 K 4
el-Àioun ○ MA 188-189 K 3
Elalia ○ DZ 190-191 E 4
el-Alimar, Hassi ▲ DZ 190-191 C 3
el-Amrana, Bir ▲ ET 194-195 C 4
el-Amdar, Bir ▲ DZ 190-191 F 4
Elan Bank ≃ = Elan Bank ≃ 12 F 10
Elandsbaai ○ ZA 220-221 D 6
Elands Height ▲ ZA 220-221 J 5
Elandslaagte ○ ZA 220-221 J 4
Elandsrivier ∼ ZA 220-221 J 4
Elanga ○ ZRE 210-211 J 5
Elangay ○ RIM 196-197 M 7
Elanka ○ RUS 114-115 N 7
Elan'-Kolenovskij ○ RUS 102-103 M 2
El Arab, Oued ∼ DZ 190-191 F 3
El Araïch ○ MA 188-189 H 3
el-Arbid ○ MA 188-189 J 5
El Arhlaf ∼ RIM 196-197 H 6
El Aricha ○ DZ 188-189 L 3
El Arrouch ○ DZ 190-191 F 2
El Asli, Bir ▲ TN 190-191 F 4
Elassóna ○ GR 100-101 J 5
Elat ○ IL 130-131 D 3
Èlavagny ∼ RT 202-203 L 6
Èlâžiğ ○•▶ TR 128-129 H 3
Elba, Ìsola d' ∩ I 100-101 C 3
Èlban ○ RUS 122-123 G 3
Elbasan ○•▶ AL 100-101 H 4
El Basriyé ○ RMM 196-197 G 5
El Bayadh ○ DZ 190-191 E 3
Elbe ○ D 92-93 L 2
Elbe = Labe ∼ CZ 92-93 N 3
Èl Bèher ○ RIM 196-197 D 6
El Beid ∼ WAN 198-199 G 6
Elbert, Mount ▲ USA 42-43 D 6
Elberton ○ USA 48-49 G 2
El Beru Hagia ○ SP 212-213 H 2
Elbeuf ○ F 90-91 H 7
El Beyyed ○ RIM 196-197 H 6
El Bioba ○ ETH 208-209 F 6
Elbistan ☆ TR 128-129 G 3
Elbjug, Kulun ∼ RUS 110-111 Y 6
Èblag ○•▶ PL 92-93 P 1
El Bordj ○ DZ 190-191 G 3
El Borma ○ TN 190-191 G 5
el-Borouj ○ MA 188-189 H 4
El Botha, Oued ∼ DZ 190-191 D 7
El Bouz ○ RMM 196-197 H 4
Elbow ○ CDN 34-35 C 5
Elbow Lake ○ USA 42-43 K 3
Èl'brus ○ RUS 126-127 E 6
Èl'brus, gora ▲••▶ RUS 126-127 E 6
El Caura, Reserva Forestal ⊥ YV 60-61 J 4
El Chaco, Parque Nacional ⊥ RA 76-77 H 4
Elche = Elx ○ E 98-99 F 5
Elche de la Sierra ○ E 98-99 F 5
Elcho Island ∩ AUS 174-175 C 2
El Cobias ○ SP 212-213 K 2
Elçy ○ RUS 94-95 N 3
Elda ○ E 98-99 G 5
El Der ○ ETH 208-209 F 6
El Dere ○ SP 208-209 H 7
Elderslie ○ AUS 178-179 G 2
Èldikan ○ RUS 110-111 V 6
Eldjarnsstaðir ○ IS 86-87 d 2
Eldorado ○ BR (GSU) 76-77 K 2
Eldorado ○ BR (PA) 68-69 D H
Eldorado ○ BR (PAU) 74-75 F 5
Eldorado ○ HN 52-53 H 5
Eldorado ○ USA (AR) 44-45 L 4
El Dorado ○ USA (IL) 46-47 D 6
El Dorado ○ USA (KS) 42-43 J 7
Eldorado ○ USA (OK) 44-45 H 2

Eldorado ○ USA (TX) 44-45 G 4
El Dorado Springs ○ USA 42-43 L 7
El Dunaba ○ EAK 212-213 G 3
El Dzibk ○ TM 136-137 H 5
Elec ○ RUS 94-95 Q 5
Elečej ○ RUS 120-121 S 3
Eleciej ○ RUS 108-109 L 8
Electric Mills ○ USA 48-49 G 1
Electric Peak ▲ USA 40-41 J 3
Elefantes ○ RI 80 C 3
Elefantes, Rios dos ∼ MOC 218-219 J 6
Eleja ∼ LV 94-95 H 4
Elektrėnai ○ LT 94-95 J 4
Elektrostal' ○ RUS 94-95 Q 4
Elektrostal' = Èlektrostal ○ RUS 94-95 Q 4
Eleku ∼ ZRE 210-211 K 5
Elele ○ WAN 204-205 G 5
Èléphant, Île = ∼ VAN 184 II a 2
Elephanta Caves ··· IND 138-139 D 10
Elephantine ∴•▶ ET 194-195 F 5
Elephant Island ∩ ARK 16 G 31
Elephant Point ▲ BD 142-143 H 5
Elephant Point ▲ USA 20-21 K 5
Éléphants de Kaniama, Réserve ⊥ ZRE 214-215 J 4
Elesbão Veloso ○ BR 68-69 G 5
Eleşkirt ○ TR 128-129 K 3
El Eulma ○ DZ 190-191 F 2
Eleuthera Island ∩ BS 54-55 G 2
El Fahl, Oued ∼ DZ 190-191 D 5
El Fahs ○ TN 190-191 G 2
El Faouar ○ TN 190-191 G 4
El Farcya ○ MA 188-189 G 7
El Fedjaj, Chott ○ TN 190-191 G 4
Elfin Cove ○ USA 32-33 B 2
El Fouz ∼ RIM 196-197 D 6
Elfros ○ CDN 34-35 E 5
El Fud ○ ETH 208-209 F 6
El Fuerte ○ MEX 50-51 D 4
El Gaa Taatzebar ∼ DZ 190-191 D 7
Elgal ○ EAK 212-213 G 2
El Gallâoulya ○ RIM 196-197 E 4
El Gambole ○ SP 212-213 K 2
El Gareb, Bir ▲ RMM 196-197 B 4
El Gârsa, Chott ○ TN 190-191 G 4
El Ghazal, Bahr ∼ TCH 198-199 H 5
El Ghazal, Bahr ∼ TCH 198-199 H 5
El Gheddiya ○ RIM 196-197 D 5
El Ghorafia, Bir ▲ TN 192-193 D 1
Èlgi ∼ RUS 110-111 X 7
El Giara ○ SP 212-213 H 4
Elgin ○ CDN 34-35 D 5
Elgin •▶ GB 90-91 F 3
Elgin ○ USA (IL) 46-47 D 4
Elgin ○ USA (ND) 42-43 G 2
Elgin ○ USA (NV) 40-41 G 7
Elgin ○ USA (TN) 48-49 F 1
Elgin ○ USA (TX) 44-45 H 5
Elgin, Mount ▲ EAU 212-213 E 3
Elgoras, gora ▲ RUS 88-89 L 2
El Goss ∼ RIM 196-197 B 4
El Goûfi, Djebel ▲ DZ 190-191 F 2
El Guérara ○ DZ 188-189 L 6
El Guetar ○ TN 190-191 G 3
El Guettara ○ RMM 196-197 J 3
Èlgygytgyn, ozero ○ RUS 112-113 U 3
Èlgykakym ∼ RUS 112-113 V 3
el-Had ○ MA 188-189 H 5
El Hadjar ○ DZ 190-191 F 2
el-Hafeira, Oued ∼ RIM 196-197 E 2
El Haggounia ○ MA 188-189 E 7
El Hajeb ○ MA 188-189 J 4
El Hallaïl, Oued ∼ DZ 190-191 D 3
El Ham, Oued ∼ DZ 190-191 D 3
El Hamanene, Oued ∼ DZ 190-191 C 8
El Hamel ○ DZ 190-191 E 3
El Hamma ○ TN 190-191 G 4
El Hammâmi ▲ RIM 196-197 D 3
el-Hamra, Oued ∼ RIM 188-189 G 7
El Hamurre ○ SP 208-209 J 6
El Han ∼ DZ 196-197 G 2
El Hank ± DZ 196-197 H 2
El Haouaria ○ TN 190-191 H 2
El Haouita ○ DZ 190-191 E 4
El Harar ○ SP 212-213 J 3
El Harich, Hamâda ± RIM 196-197 H 3
El Haricha, Hamâda ± RMM 196-197 H 3
El Harrach, Oued ∼ DZ 190-191 D 2
El Homr ○ DZ 190-191 E 6
Elias, Cerro ▲ RA 80 C 2
Eliase ○ RI 166-167 F 6
Elias Garcia ○ ANG 216-217 F 4
Elida ○ USA 44-45 F 3
El Idrissia ○ DZ 190-191 E 3
Elie ○ CDN 34-35 H 6
Elif ∴ ∼ TR 128-129 H 4
Eliki Gounda ○ RN 198-199 D 5
Elila ○ ZRE 210-211 K 5
Elila ∼ ZRE 210-211 K 5
Elim ○ USA 20-21 J 4
Eliot, Mount ▲ CDN 36-37 S 5
Elipa ○ ZRE 210-211 K 4
Elisa ○ BR 70-71 F 3
Eliseu Martins ○ BR 68-69 G 6
Elista ☆ RUS 126-127 G 5
Eliista ∼ RUS 120-121 U 3
Eliye Springs ○ EAK 212-213 F 2
Eliza, Lake ○ AUS 180-181 D 4

Elizabeth ○ USA 46-47 L 5
Elizabeth, Lac ○ CDN 36-37 M 7
Elizabeth, Point ▲ USA 20-21 e 7
Elizabeth City ○ USA 48-49 K 1
Elizabeth Downs ○ AUS 172-173 K 2
Elizabeth Harbour ≈ BS 54-55 H 3
Elizabeth Reef ∩ 13 G 5
Elizabethton ○ USA 48-49 G 1
Elizabethtown ○ USA (KY) 46-47 F 7
Elizabethtown ○ USA (NC) 48-49 J 2
Elizavety, mys ▲ RUS 120-121 K 6
Elizovo ○ RUS 122-123 S 7
el-Jadida ○ MA 188-189 G 4
El Jem ∼ TN 190-191 H 3
El Jerid, Chott ○ TN 190-191 G 4
Elk ○ PL 92-93 R 2
El Kahla, Djebel ▲ DZ 188-189 L 6
El Kala ○ DZ 190-191 G 2
El Kantara ○ DZ 190-191 F 3
El Kantour, Col d' ▲ DZ 190-191 F 2
El Kataoui ○ TN 190-191 H 4
El Kef ☆ TN 190-191 G 2
el-Kelaa-des-Srarhna ○ MA 188-189 H 4
Èl Kerè ○ ETH 208-209 F 6
El Kerma, Hassi ▲ MA 188-189 G 6
Elkford ○ CDN 32-33 N 6
El Khannfous, Hassi ▲ DZ 190-191 D 6
el-Khaoula ○ MA 188-189 H 4
Elkhart ○ USA (IN) 46-47 F 5
Elkhart ○ USA (TX) 44-45 K 4
El Khatt ○ RIM 196-197 E 3
El Khatt, Oued ∼ MA 196-197 D 2
Elkhead Mounts ▲ USA 42-43 D 5
Elkhorn ○ CDN 34-35 F 6
Elkhorn ○ USA 46-47 D 4
Elkhorn River ∼ USA 42-43 H 4
El Khroub ○ DZ 190-191 F 2
Elkin ○ USA 48-49 H 1
Elkins ○ USA (NM) 44-45 E 3
Elkins ○ USA (WV) 46-47 J 6
Elk Island ∩ CDN 34-35 H 5
Elk Island National Park ⊥ CDN 32-33 O 5
Elk Lake ○ CDN 38-39 D 5
Elk Mountains ▲ USA 42-43 D 6
Elko ○ CDN 32-33 N 7
Elko ○ USA 40-41 G 5
Èl'konka ○ RUS 118-119 N 6
Èl K'oran ○ ETH 208-209 D 7
Elk Point ○ CDN 32-33 O 5
Elk Point ○ USA 42-43 J 4
El Krebs, Erg ∼ DZ 188-189 L 7
El Krenig, Hassi ▲ DZ 190-191 D 7
Elk River ∼ USA (ID) 40-41 F 2
Elk River ∼ USA (MN) 42-43 L 3
Elk River ∼ USA 46-47 H 6
El Ksar el Kbir ○ MA 188-189 J 3
El Kseur ○ DZ 190-191 E 2
El Ksiba ○ MA 188-189 J 4
Ella Ø ∩ GRØ 26-27 n 7
El Bay ≈ 36-37 F 2
Elléba Fonfou ○ RN 198-199 B 4
Ellef Ringnes Island ∩ CDN 24-25 U 1
Èl Lëh ○ ETH 208-209 D 7
El Lein ○ EAK 212-213 H 4
Ellélóyé ○ TCH 198-199 J 4
Ellen, Mount ▲ USA 40-41 J 7
Ellendale ○ USA 42-43 H 2
Ellensburg ○ USA 40-41 D 2
Ellery, Mount ▲ AUS 180-181 K 4
Ellesmere Island ∩ CDN 24-25 e 2
Ellice Islands ∼ TUV 13 J 3
Ellice River ∼ CDN 30-31 V 3
Elliot ○ ZA 220-221 H 5
Elliot, Mount ▲ AUS 174-175 J 6
Elliot Lake ○ CDN 38-39 D 5
Elliot Price Conservation Park ⊥ AUS 178-179 D 5
Elliott ○ AUS 174-175 B 4
Elliott, Mount ▲ AUS 172-173 H 6
Elliott Key ∩ USA 48-49 H 7
Ellis ○ USA 42-43 H 6
Ellisras ○ ZA 218-219 D 6
Elliston ○ AUS 180-181 C 2
Ellora ○•▶ IND 138-139 E 9
Ellora Caves ··· IND 138-139 E 9
Ellsworth ○ USA (KS) 42-43 H 6
Ellsworth ○ USA (ME) 46-47 O 3
Ellsworth ○ USA (WI) 42-43 L 3
Ellsworth Highland ▲ ARK 16 F 28
Ellwell, Lake ○ USA 40-41 J 1
Elwood ○ USA (IN) 46-47 F 5
Elwood ○ USA (NE) 42-43 H 5
Elma ○ CDN 34-35 J 4
Elma ○ USA 40-41 C 2
El Ma, Oued ∼ RIM 196-197 F 2
El Mabrouk ○ RIM 196-197 F 2
El Maad ○ DZ 190-191 G 4
Elmadağ ○•▶ TR 128-129 E 3
El Mahbas ○ MA 188-189 G 7
Elma Daği ▲ TR 128-129 E 3
El Malah ○ DZ 188-189 L 3
El Mallalie ○ ETH 208-209 D 6
El Mamouel ∼ RMM 196-197 J 5
El Mamour < RMM 196-197 J 5
El Mamsour ○ DZ 190-191 E 5
El Mannsour ○ DZ 190-191 E 5
el-Mansour-Eddahbi, Barrage < MA 188-189 H 5
El Marsa ○ DZ 190-191 C 2
El Maya ○ DZ 190-191 D 4
El Medo ○ ETH 208-209 E 6
El Meghaier ○ DZ 190-191 F 4

Elmeki ∼ RN 198-199 D 4
El Melah, Ouen ∼ DZ 190-191 D 5
El Melhes ○ RIM 196-197 D 5
El Menabba ○ DZ 188-189 K 5
el-Menzel ○ MA 188-189 J 4
Elmer ○ USA 46-47 L 6
Elm Fork Red River ∼ USA 44-45 G 2
El Milia ○ DZ 190-191 F 2
Elmina ○•▶ GH 202-203 K 7
Elmira ○ CDN 38-39 N 5
Elmira ○ USA 46-47 K 5
Elmo ○ USA 42-43 J 6
El Moináne ▲ RIM 196-197 E 5
Elmore ○ AUS 180-181 H 4
El Morro National Monument ∴ USA 44-45 C 2
El Mounir, Hassi ▲ DZ 188-189 H 6
El Mraïti ▲ RMM 196-197 J 3
El Mreïti ∼ RIM 196-197 G 3
Elmwood ○ USA 44-45 G 1
El Nido ○•▶ RP 160-161 C 7
Éfnja ○ RUS 88-89 Q 4
El Obeid = al-Ubayyid ☆•▶ SUD 200-201 E 6
El Obeid = Ubayyid, al- ☆•▶ SUD 200-201 E 6
Elogbatindi ○ CAM 210-211 D 2
El Ogla ○ DZ 190-191 F 3
El Ogla Gasses ○ DZ 190-191 F 3
Elogo ○ RCB 210-211 E 3
Eloguj ∼ RUS 114-115 S 3
Elogujskij, učastok ⊥ RUS 114-115 S 4
Elojaha ∼ RUS 108-109 R 8
Elopada ○ RI 168 D 7
Elorza ○ YV 60-61 H 4
Elota ∼ MEX 50-51 F 6
El Ouadey ○ TCH 198-199 J 3
el-Oualidia ○ MA 188-189 G 4
El Ouar, Erg ∼ DZ 190-191 F 6
El Ouass'â: ± RIM 196-197 F 3
El Oued ○•▶ DZ 190-191 G 3
Elovaja, Bol'šaja (Tet) ∼ RUS 114-115 U 5
Elovka ∼ RUS 120-121 T 5
Elovo ○ RUS 96-97 J 5
Eloy ○ USA 40-41 J 9
Eloy Alfaro ○ EC (GUA) 64-65 C 3
Eloy Alfaro ○ EC (MAN) 64-65 B 2
El Paso ○ USA 44-45 D 4
Elphant, Rapides de l' ∼ ZRE 206-207 J 4
Elphinstone ○ AUS 178-179 K 1
Elphinstone ○ CDN 34-35 F 5
Elpitiya ○ CL 140-141 J 7
El Portal ○ USA 40-41 E 7
Elqui, Río ∼ RCH 76-77 B 6
El Rharbi, Oued ∼ DZ 190-191 C 4
Elrose ○ CDN 32-33 Q 6
Elroy ○ USA 46-47 C 4
El Salvador ■ ES 52-53 K 5
Elsa ○ CDN 32-33 J 3
Elsberry ○ USA 46-47 C 6
Elsey ○ AUS 174-175 B 4
Elsey Cemetery ○ AUS 174-175 B 4
El Sharana Mine • AUS 172-173 L 2
Elsie Hills ▲ USA 178-179 J 3
Elsie Island ∩ CDN 36-37 K 5
Elstad ○ N 86-87 E 6
Elstow ○ CDN 34-35 D 5
Eltanin Fracture Zone System ≃ 14-15 O 13
El Tarf ○ TN 190-191 G 2
Eltice Island ○ CDN 20-21 X 2
El Tichlilt ∼ RIM 196-197 D 5
Elton ○ RUS 96-97 E 9
Elton, ozero ○ RUS 96-97 E 9
El Tuparro, Parque Nacional ⊥ CO 60-61 G 5
Eltyreva ∼ RUS 114-115 R 5
Elu ○ RI 166-167 E 6
Elu Inlet ≈ 24-25 T 6
El Ure ○ SP 212-213 J 2
Èlüru ○ IND 140-141 J 2
Elva ∼ EST 94-95 K 2
Èlva ∼ RUS 88-89 V 5
Elvas ○•▶ P 98-99 D 5
Elverum ☆ N 86-87 E 6
Elvira ∼ RA 78-79 K 3
Elvira, Cape ▲ CDN 24-25 S 4
Elvira Island ∩ CDN 24-25 S 4
Elvire, Mount ▲ AUS 172-173 C 6
Elvire River ∼ AUS 172-173 J 5
Elvita, Río ∼ CO 60-61 F 4
El Wak ○ EAK 212-213 H 2
El Warsesa ∼ EAK 212-213 G 2
Elwell, Lake ○ USA 40-41 J 1
Elwood ○ USA (IN) 46-47 F 5
Elwood ○ USA (NE) 42-43 H 5
Elx ○ E 98-99 G 5
Ely •▶ GB 90-91 H 5
Ely ○ USA (MN) 46-47 C 2
Ely ○ USA (NV) 40-41 G 6
Elyria ○ USA 46-47 G 5
Emae = Île Mai ∩ VAN 184 II b 3
Email ○ EAK 212-213 F 1
Emám 'Abbâs ○ IR 134-135 A 1
Emám Hasan ○ IR 134-135 D 4
Emám Homeini, Bandar-e ○ IR 134-135 C 3
Emám Tâqi ○ IR 136-137 F 7
Emán ∼ S 86-87 G 8
Èmanda, ozero ○ RUS 110-111 U 7
Emas, Parque Nacional das ⊥ BR 72-73 D 5
Embarcación ○ RA 76-77 E 2
Embarrass River ∼ USA 46-47 E 6
Èmbenčime ∼ RUS 116-117 J 3
Embetsu ○ J 152-153 J 2
Embi ∼ KA 126-127 N 3
Embi ○ KA 156-157 L 6
Embí ∼ RUS 96-97 H 10
Èmbí, Mount ▲ PNG 183 B 3

Embilipitiya ○ CL 140-141 J 7
Embira ○ BR 68-69 F 5
Embira, Rio ∼ BR 66-67 B 6
Embocada ○ BOL 70-71 F 4
Embondo ○ ZRE 210-211 G 5
Emboraçação, Represa ∼ BR 72-73 G 5
Emboraí, Baía do ≈ BR 68-69 E 2
Emboscada ○ BOL 70-71 F 4
Emboscada ○ BOL 70-71 E 2
Emboscada Nueva ○ PY 76-77 J 3
Embu ☆ EAK 212-213 F 4
Embudo, Raudal del ∼ CO 64-65 F 1
Embudo ∼ ANG 216-217 D 8
Emca ∼ RUS 88-89 Q 5
Emca ∼ RUS 88-89 Q 5
Emcisweni ○ MW 214-215 G 6
Emden ○•▶ D 92-93 J 2
Emeck ○ RUS 88-89 Q 5
Emeishan ○ VRC (SIC) 156-157 C 2
Emeishan ∼ VRC (SIC) 156-157 C 2
Émef ∼ KA 124-125 N 5
Emeïjanovskaja ○ RUS 88-89 Q 4
Emerald ○ AUS 178-179 K 2
Emerald Bank ≃ 38-39 N 7
Emerald Isle ∩ CDN 24-25 P 2
Emeriau Point ▲ AUS 172-173 F 4
Emerillon ○ F 62-63 H 4
Emerson ○ CDN 34-35 H 6
Emery Range ▲ AUS 178-179 C 4
Emet ☆ TR 128-129 C 3
Emeti ○ PNG 183 B 4
Emigrant Gap ○ USA 40-41 D 6
Emilia, La ○ YV 60-61 H 4
Emiliano Zapata ○ MEX (CHI) 52-53 J 3
Emiliano Zapata ○ MEX (COA) 50-51 H 5
Emiliano Zapata ○ MEX (SON) 50-51 H 5
Emilia-Romagna □ I 100-101 B 2
Emin ○ VRC 146-147 F 2
Eminâbâd ○ PK 138-139 E 3
Eminee ○ RI 166-167 K 5
Emin He ∼ VRC 146-147 F 2
Emini ○ CAM 210-211 D 2
Emin Pasha Gulf ≈ EAT 212-213 C 5
Emirdağ ○ TR 128-129 D 3
Emirgazi ○ TR 128-129 E 4
Emlinskaja, buhta ≈ RUS 120-121 Q 3
Emma, Mount ▲ CDN 24-25 g 4
Emmaboda ○ S 86-87 G 8
Emma Fiord ≈ 26-27 K 2
Emmen ○ NL 92-93 J 2
Emmet ○ AUS 178-179 H 3
Emmetsburg ○ USA 42-43 K 4
Emmiganuru ○ IND 140-141 G 3
Emmonak ○ USA 20-21 H 5
Èmmy, mys ▲ RUS 110-111 a 1
Emo ○ CDN 34-35 K 6
Emory Peak ▲ USA 44-45 F 5
Emoulas ○ RN 198-199 C 5
Empalme ○ MEX 50-51 D 4
Empalme, El = Velasco Ibarra ○ EC 64-65 C 2
Empangeni ○ ZA 220-221 K 4
Empedrado ○ RCH 78-79 C 3
Emperado, El ○ YV 60-61 F 3
Emperor Range ▲ PNG 184 I b 1
Emperor Seamount Chain ≃ 14-15 K 3
Emperor Trough ≃ 14-15 K 3
Empexca, Salar de ○ BOL 70-71 C 7
Empire ○ USA (CO) 42-43 E 6
Empire ○ USA (MI) 46-47 E 3
Emporia ○ USA (KS) 42-43 J 6
Emporia ○ USA (VA) 46-47 K 7
Empress Augusta Bay ≈ 184 I b 2
Empress Mine ○ ZW 218-219 E 4
Ems ○ D 92-93 J 2
Emu Park ○ AUS 178-179 L 2
Emure ○ WAN 204-205 F 5
Emva ○ RUS 88-89 V 5
Emvan ○ CAM 204-205 K 6
Ena ○ J 152-153 G 7
Enakievo = Jenakijeve ○ UA 102-103 L 3
Enangiperi ○ EAK 212-213 E 4
Enarotali ○ RI 166-167 K 4
Enašimo ∼ RUS 116-117 F 5
Encantado, Valle ∼ RA 78-79 D 6
Encanto, Cape ▲ RP 160-161 D 5
Encanto, El ○ CO 64-65 F 2
Encarnación ○•▶ PY 76-77 K 4
Encarnacion de Díaz ○ MEX 50-51 J 6
Encinal ○ USA 44-45 H 5
Encinal, El ○ MEX 50-51 K 5
Encinitas ○ USA 40-41 F 9
Encino ○ CO 60-61 E 4
Encino ○ USA (NM) 44-45 E 3
Encino ○ USA (TX) 44-45 H 6
Encoje ○ ANG 216-217 C 3
Encon ○ RA 78-79 F 2
Encontrados ○ YV 60-61 E 3
Encounter Bay ≈ AUS 180-181 E 4
Encrucijada, La ○ YV 60-61 H 3
Encruzilhada ○ BR 74-75 D 8
Encruzilhada do Sul ○ BR 74-75 D 8
Encucijada, La ○ YV 60-61 H 3
Enda ○ VRC 144-145 L 1
Endako ○ CDN 32-33 H 4
Endau ∼ EAK (EAS) 212-213 G 4
Endau ∼ EAK (EAS) 212-213 G 4
Èndè ∼ RUS 116-117 J 2
Ende, Pulau ∩ RI 168 E 7
Endeavor ○ CDN 34-35 E 4
Endebess ○ EAK 212-213 F 4
Endeh ○ RI 168 E 7
Endeavour Strait ≈ 174-175 G 2
Endicott Arm ≈ 32-33 C 2
Endicott Mountains ▲ USA 20-21 N 3
Endicott Mountains Range ▲ USA 20-21 N 3
Endiké ○ RCB 210-211 E 4

Endimari, Rio ∼ BR 66-67 D 7
Endom o CAM 210-211 D 2
Endra, ozero ∼ RUS 114-115 J 4
Endyalgout Island ∼ AUS 172-173 L 1
Ene, Rio ∼ PE 64-65 E 7
Eneabba o AUS 176-177 C 4
Enemawira o RI 164-165 J 2
Enéné Patatpe o F 62-63 G 4
Energía o RA 78-79 K 5
Enerucijada, La o YV 60-61 H 3
Enez ✩ TR 128-129 B 2
Enfer, Portes de l' ∿∼ ZRE 212-213 A 6
Enfield o CDN 38-39 N 6
Enfield o USA (CT) 46-47 M 5
Enfield o USA (NC) 48-49 K 1
Enfok o IND 140-141 L 6
Engadin ⊥ CH 92-93 B 5
Engadine o USA 46-47 F 2
Engaño, Cabo ▲ DOM 54-55 L 5
Engaru o J 152-153 K 2
Engaruka o EAT (ARV) 212-213 E 5
Engaruka ∴∴ EAT (MA) 212-213 E 5
Engaruka Basin ⊥ EAT 212-213 F 5
Engcobo o ZA 220-221 H 5
En Gedi ⊾ IL 130-131 D 2
Engelhard o USA 48-49 L 2
Ėngel's o RUS 96-97 E 8
Ėngel's = Ėngel's o RUS 96-97 E 8
Engelsbergs bruk ••• S 86-87 H 7
Engenheiro Navarro o BR 72-73 J 4
Engenio, El o PE 64-65 E 9
Engerina Creek ∼ AUS 178-179 H 5
Enggano, Pulau ∼ RI 162-163 E 7
Engh o VRC 150-151 B 2
Engida o RUS 116-117 G 5
Engineer o CDN 20-21 X 7
Engineer Group ∼ PNG 183 F 6
Engkilili o MAL 162-163 J 4
England o GB 90-91 F 5
England o USA 44-45 M 4
Englee o CDN 38-39 Q 3
Englefield, Cape ▲ CDN 24-25 d 6
Englehart o CDN 38-39 E 5
English Channel = English Channel = La Manche ≈ GB 90-91 G 6
English Coast ∿ ARK 16 F 29
English Company's Islands, The ∼ AUS 174-175 J 2
English Harbour East o CDN 38-39 I R 5
English Harbour Town o AG 56 E 3
English Harbour West o CDN 38-39 I R 5
English River o CDN 34-35 L 6
Engordina o AUS 178-179 C 3
Engozero o RUS 88-89 M 4
Engure o LV 94-95 H 3
Enid o USA 44-45 J 1
Enid Mining Area, Mount ∼ AUS 172-173 C 6
Enisej ∼ 10-11 H 2
Enisej ∼ RUS 10-11 H 2
Enisejsk ✩ RUS 116-117 F 6
Enisejskij zaliv ≈ 108-109 S 5
Enisejsko-Stolbovoj, učastok ⊥ RUS 114-115 U 3
Eniwa o J 152-153 J 3
Enjil o MA 188-189 J 4
Enjukovo o RUS 94-95 P 2
Ênkên, mys ▲ RUS 120-121 J 5
Enkhuizen o NL 92-93 H 2
Enköping o S 86-87 H 7
Enmelen o RUS 112-113 X 4
Ênmelen o RUS 112-113 T 4
Ênmyvaam ∼ RUS 112-113 R 3
Enna o I 100-101 E 6
Ennadai o CDN 30-31 T 5
Ennadai Lake o CDN 30-31 T 5
En Naga, Oued ∼ DZ 188-189 H 6
En Nahûd o SUD 200-201 D 6
Enné, Ouadi ∼ TCH 198-199 J 5
Ennedi ▲ TCH 198-199 K 4
Ennery o RH 54-55 J 5
Enngonia o AUS 178-179 H 5
Ennis o USA (MT) 40-41 J 3
Ennis o USA (TX) 44-45 J 3
Ennis = Inis ★ IRL 90-91 C 5
Enniscorthy = Inis Córthaidh o IRL 90-91 D 5
Enniskillen ✩ GB 90-91 D 4
En Noual, Sebkhet ∼ TN 190-191 G 3
Enns ∼ A 92-93 N 5
En Nsa, Oued ∼ DZ 190-191 E 4
Enochs o USA 44-45 F 3
Enontekiö o FIN 88-89 G 2
Enotaevka ✩ RUS 96-97 E 10
Enozero o RUS 88-89 O 2
Enping o VRC 156-157 H 5
Enrekang o RI 164-165 F 5
Enriadville o TN 190-191 H 2
Enrile o RP 160-161 J 2
Enriquillo, Lago o DOM 54-55 K 5
Enschede o NL 92-93 J 2
Ensenada o MEX 50-51 A 2
Ensenada o RCH 78-79 C 6
Enshi o VRC 154-155 F 6
Enshū-nada ≈ 152-153 G 7
Ensign o USA 44-45 G 1
Ênstor, ozero o RUS 114-115 K 4
Entebang, Rumah o MAL 162-163 K 3
Entebbe o EAU 212-213 D 3
Enterprise o CDN 30-31 L 5
Enterprise o USA (AL) 48-49 F 4
Enterprise o USA (OR) 40-41 F 3
Enterprise Point ▲ RP 160-161 C 7
Entiako River ∼ CDN 32-33 H 5
Entiat o USA 40-41 D 2
Êntf-Imijagun ∼ RUS 114-115 M 3
En Tmadé < RIM 196-197 E 3
Entrada, Punta o RA 80 F 5
Entrance o CDN 32-33 M 5
Entre Lagos o RCH 78-79 C 6
Entre Rios o BOL 76-77 E 1
Entre Rios o BR 68-69 J 7
Entre Rios o RA 76-77 H 6
Entre Rios, Cordillera ▲ HN 52-53 B 4

Entrocamento o BR 68-69 F 5
Entroncamento o BR 68-69 E 4
Entronque La Cuchilla o MEX 50-51 H 5
Entrop o RI 166-167 L 3
Entumeni o ZA 220-221 K 4
Ëntuziastov o RUS 110-111 U 4
Entwistle o CDN 32-33 N 5
Enu, Pulau ∼ RI 166-167 L 6
Enugu ★ WAN 204-205 G 5
Enugu Ezike o WAN 204-205 G 5
Enumclaw o USA 40-41 D 2
Ênurnino o RUS 112-113 Z 3
Envigado o CO 60-61 D 4
Envira o BR 66-67 B 6
Enxudé o GNB 202-203 C 4
Enyamba o ZRE 210-211 K 5
Enyčavajam ∼ RUS 112-113 O 6
Enyelé o RCB 210-211 G 2
Ênyngvajam ∼ RUS 120-121 V 3
Eo, Rio ∼ E 98-99 D 3
Eochaill = Youghal o IRL 90-91 D 6
Éolie o Lípari, Isole ∼ I 100-101 E 5
Epako o NAM 216-217 D 10
Epanomí o GR 100-101 J 4
Epatlán o MEX 52-53 K 2
Epe o WAN 204-205 F 5
Epecuén, Laguna o RA 78-79 H 4
Epembe o NAM 216-217 B 8
Epéna o RCB 210-211 F 3
Epenarra o AUS 174-175 C 7
Epernay o F 90-91 J 7
Ephesus = Efes ∴∴ TR 128-129 B 3
Ephraim o USA 44-45 H 1
Ephrata o USA (WA) 40-41 E 2
Ephrata o USA (PA) 46-47 K 5
Epi o VAN 184 II b 3
Epi = VAN (EPI) 184 II b 3
Epi o ZRE 210-211 L 2
Epidauros ••• GR 100-101 J 6
Epini o ZRE 212-213 B 3
Epizana o BOL 70-71 E 5
Epokenkoso o ZRE 210-211 F 5
Epoma o RCB 210-211 E 3
Epping Forest o AUS 178-179 J 2
Epping Forest National Park ⊥ AUS 178-179 J 2
Epsom o AUS 178-179 K 1
Epu, River ∼ WAN 204-205 G 4
Epukiro o NAM 216-217 E 10
Epukiro ∼ NAM 216-217 E 10
Epulu ∼ ZRE 212-213 B 3
Epulu, Station de capture d' • ZRE 212-213 B 3
Epupa Falls ∼ NAM 216-217 B 8
Epuyén o RA 78-79 D 7
Eqlid o IR 134-135 E 3
Equateur ∼ ZRE 210-211 G 3
Equator 14-15 Q 7
Equatorial Guinea = Guinea Ecuatorial ■ GQ 210-211 B 2
Equinox Mountain ▲ USA 46-47 M 4
Eračimo ∼ RUS 116-117 E 3
Erahtur o RUS 94-95 N 4
Eralé o BR 62-63 H 5
Eram o PNG 183 B 3
Eran Bay ≈ 160-161 B 8
Erave o PNG 183 C 4
Erave River ∼ PNG 183 B 4
Eravur o CL 140-141 J 7
Erãwadi Myit ∼ MYA 142-143 J 5
Erãwadi Myitwanyã ∼ MYA 158-159 C 3
Erawan National Park ⊥ THA 158-159 C 3
Erba, Ǧabal ▲ SUD (Ahm) 200-201 H 2
Erba, Ǧabal ▲ SUD (Ahm) 200-201 H 2
Erbaa ★ TR 128-129 G 2
Erbogačen ★ RUS 116-117 N 5
Ërča, Bol'šaja ∼ RUS 110-111 b 5
Erçek Gölü o TR 128-129 K 3
Erçiş ★ TR 128-129 K 3
Erciyes Dağı ▲ TR 128-129 F 3
Erdaobaihe o VRC 150-151 G 4
Erdek ★ TR 128-129 B 2
Erdemli ★ TR 128-129 F 4
Ërdènècagaan = Čonogol o MAU 148-149 M 5
Ërdènècogt o MAU 148-149 E 4
Ërdènèdalaj = Sangijn Dalaj o MAU 148-149 J 4
Ërdènèmandal = Ölzijm o MAU 148-149 E 3
Ërdènèsant = Ulaanhudag o MAU 148-149 K 4
Ërdènèt o MAU 148-149 G 3
Ërdèni Uu o MAU 148-149 F 4
Erdi ⊥ TCH 198-199 L 3
Eré o TCH 206-207 B 4
Erebus, Mount ▲ ARK 16 F 17
Erebus and Terror Gulf ≈ 16 G 31
Erebus Bay ≈ 24-25 W 6
Erech ∴∴ IRQ 128-129 L 7
Erechim o BR 74-75 D 6
Érèbncav o MAU 148-149 M 3
Ereğli ★ TR 128-129 F 4
Ereğli ★ TR 128-129 D 2
Eréké o RCA 206-207 E 5
Erêma o RUS 116-117 N 5
Erëma, Bol'šaja ∼ RUS 116-117 M 5
Erenhot o VRC 148-149 K 6
Erepecuru, Lago de o BR 62-63 F 6
Ereré o BR 68-69 J 5
Ërer Wenz ∼ ETH 208-209 F 5
Erevan ★ AR 128-129 J 2
Erfenisdam ⊂ ZA 220-221 H 4
Erfoud o MA 188-189 J 4
Ergani ★ TR 128-129 H 3
Ërgèl o MAU 148-149 J 6
Ergèlèh o RUS 118-119 O 4
Ergene Çayı ∼ TR 128-129 B 2
Ergene Nehri ∼ TR 128-129 B 2
Ergeni ▲ RUS 96-97 D 9
Ërgi o LV 94-95 J 3
Erguig, Bahr ∼ TCH 206-207 C 3

Ergun He ∼ VRC 150-151 C 1
Ergun Youqi o VRC 150-151 C 2
Ergun Zuoqi o VRC 150-151 C 2
Ërguvaam ∼ RUS 112-113 X 4
Er Hai ∼ VRC 142-143 M 3
Eria, Rio ∼ E 98-99 D 3
Eri, River ∼ WAN 204-205 H 4
Eriba o SUD 200-201 H 4
Eric o CDN 38-39 M 3
Erica o AUS 180-181 J 5
Erichsen Lake o CDN 24-25 f 5
Erick o USA 44-45 H 2
Erickson o CDN 34-35 D 5
Eridu = Abū Šahrain ∴∴ IRQ 130-131 J 2
Erie o USA 46-47 H 4
Erie, Lake o 46-47 H 4
Erie Canal ∼ USA 46-47 L 4
Eriečka ∼ RUS 108-109 e 6
'Erïgât ⊥ RMM 196-197 H 5
Eriksdale o CDN 34-35 D 5
Eríksmála o S 86-87 G 8
Erimo o J 152-153 K 4
Erimo-misaki ▲ J 152-153 K 4
Erimo Seamount ≃ 152-153 L 4
Erin o USA 48-49 E 1
Erith River ∼ CDN 32-33 M 5
Eritrea ■ ER 200-201 H 5
Erkalnadejpur ∼ RUS 114-115 P 3
Erkovcy o RUS 122-123 C 3
Erkowit o SUD 200-201 H 4
Erlangen o D 92-93 L 4
Erlang Shan ▲ VRC 156-157 C 2
Erldunda o AUS 176-177 M 2
Erlistoun Creek ∼ AUS 176-177 F 3
Erlongshan • VRC 150-151 G 4
Ermaki o RUS 116-117 N 7
Ermaо = Ȋle Mau ∼ VAN 184 II b 3
Ermelo o ZA 220-221 J 3
Ermeneevo o RUS 96-97 H 6
Ermenek ★ TR 128-129 E 4
Ermentau o KA 124-125 H 3
Ermera o RI 166-167 G 6
Ermil Post o SUD 200-201 C 6
Ermoúpoli = ∼ RUS 100-101 K 6
Ernakulam o IND 140-141 G 6
Emée o F 90-91 G 7
Ernest Giles Range ▲ AUS 176-177 G 3
Ernest Sound ≈ 32-33 D 4
Erode o IND 140-141 G 5
Erofej Pavlovič o RUS 118-119 L 8
Eromanga, Tanjung ▲ RI 166-167 C 6
Eromanga o AUS 178-179 G 4
Eromanga Island = Ȋle Erromango ∼ VAN 184 II b 4
Eromohon o RUS 116-117 L 2
Erong Springs o AUS 176-177 D 2
Erŏö = Bugant o MAU 148-149 H 3
Erŏö gol ∼ MAU 148-149 H 3
Eropol ∼ RUS 112-113 O 4
Eroro o PNG 183 E 5
Errabiddy o AUS 176-177 D 2
Erragondapalem o IND 140-141 H 2
Er Raoui, Erg ⊥ DZ 188-189 K 6
Errego o MOC 218-219 J 3
er-Remla o TN 190-191 H 3
Er Richart, Guelb ▲ RIM 196-197 E 4
Errigal Mountain ▲ IRL 90-91 C 4
Erris Head ▲ IRL 90-91 B 4
Errittau o PNG 183 C 4
Errol o USA 46-47 N 3
Erromango, Ȋle = Eromanga Island ∼ VAN 184 II b 4
Erronan, Ȋle = Futuna Island ∼ VAN 184 II c 4
Ersa ∼ RUS 88-89 W 3
Ersekë + AL 100-101 H 4
Erši o RUS 94-95 O 4
Erskine o USA 42-43 J 2
Erskine Inlet ≈ 24-25 V 2
Erŝova ▲ RUS 96-97 F 8
Erŝova o RUS 116-117 L 7
Ert o RUS 118-119 M 4
Ertai o VRC 146-147 K 2
Ertil' o RUS 102-103 M 2
Ertis ∼ KA 124-125 L 3
Ertis-Karaganda kanal ∼ KA 124-125 H 3
Ertix He ∼ VRC 146-147 G 2
Ërtom ∼ RUS 88-89 T 5
Ërtoma o RUS 88-89 T 5
Ertwa, Mount ▲ AUS 176-177 M 1
Erua o PNG 183 B 4
Erufa o USA 44-45 F 4
Eruh ★ TR 128-129 K 4
Eruki, Mount ▲ PNG 183 C 4
Erundu o NAM 216-217 D 10
Eruslan ∼ RUS 96-97 F 8
Eruwa o WAN 204-205 E 5
Erval o BR 74-75 D 9
Erveiras o BR 74-75 D 7
Ervent o TM 136-137 F 5
Erzgebirge ▲ D 92-93 M 3
Êrzin ★ RUS 116-117 G 10
Êrzin ∼ RUS 116-117 G 10
Erzincan ★ TR 128-129 H 3
Erzurum ★ TR 128-129 J 3
Eržvilkas o LT 94-95 H 4
Esa, Iushan o WAN 204-205 F 4
Esa'ala o PNG 183 F 5
Esan o J 152-153 J 4
Esang o RI 164-165 K 1
Esashi o J (HOK) 152-153 J 4
Esashi o J (HOK) 152-153 K 2
Esayoo Bay ≈ 24-25 e 2
Esbjerg o DK 86-87 D 9
Esbo = Espoo o FIN 88-89 H 6
Escada o BR 68-69 L 6
Escala, La o BOL 70-71 F 6
Escalante o USA 44-45 H 1
Escalante River ∼ USA 40-41 J 7
Escalerita o RCH 76-77 C 1

Escalón o MEX 50-51 G 4
Escambia River ∼ USA 48-49 E 4
Escanaba o USA 46-47 E 3
Escanaba River ∼ USA 46-47 E 2
Escara o BOL 70-71 E 5
Escárcega o MEX 52-53 J 2
Escarpada Point ▲ RP 160-161 E 3
Eschscholtz Bay ≈ 20-21 M 3
Eschwege o D 92-93 L 3
Escocesa, Bahía ≈ 54-55 L 5
Escola o BOL 70-71 F 7
Escondida, La o MEX 50-51 K 5
Escondida, Punta ▲ MEX 52-53 F 4
Escondido o MEX 40-41 F 9
Escondido, Área Indígena ✕ BR 66-67 H 7
Escondido, Río ∼ MEX 52-53 K 2
Escondido, Río ∼ NIC 52-53 B 5
Escoporanga o BR 72-73 K 5
Escorial, El ··· MEX 52-53 K 1
Escott o AUS 174-175 E 5
Escoumins, Les o CDN 38-39 K 4
Escravos o WAN 204-205 F 5
Escuinapa de Hidalgo o MEX 50-51 G 5
Escuintla o GCA 52-53 J 4
Escuminac o CDN 38-39 M 5
Escuminac, Point ▲ CDN 38-39 M 5
Ese o ZRE 206-207 H 6
Esè-Hajja o RUS 110-111 U 6
Eséka o CAM 210-211 C 2
Eseli o PNG 183 E 4
Esenanhaty o KA 96-97 H 8
Eşen Çayı ∼ TR 128-129 C 4
Esence Dağları ▲ TR 128-129 H 3
Esenguli o TM 136-137 C 4
Esensaji o KA 96-97 H 8
Esenyurt o TR 128-129 G 3
Eşfahan ⊾ IR 134-135 D 2
Eşfahan = IR (ESF) 134-135 D 2
Esfarāyen o IR 136-137 E 6
Esfolado, Rio o BR 68-69 G 5
Ěsger, Kûh-e ▲ IR 134-135 H 1
Eshan o VRC 156-157 C 4
Eshimba o ZRE 210-211 K 6
Eshowe o ZA 220-221 K 4
Esiama o GH 202-203 J 7
Esigodini o ZW 218-219 E 5
Esik o KA 146-147 C 4
Esil ✩ KA 124-125 F 3
Esil ∼ KA 124-125 E 3
Esim ∼ KA 124-125 F 1
Esinskaja o RUS 94-95 R 1
Espino o YV 60-61 H 3
Espino, El o BOL 70-71 F 6
Espino, El o PA 52-53 E 7
Espinosa o BR 72-73 J 3
Espírito Santo o BR 66-67 C 4
Espírito Santo ∼ BR 72-73 K 5
Espírito Santo do Turvo o BR 72-73 F 7
Espíritu Santo o MEX 50-51 J 5
Espíritu Santo ∼ VAN 184 II a 2
Espírito Santo, Bahía del ≈ MEX 52-53 L 2
Espíritu Santo, Isla ∼ MEX 50-51 D 5
Espírito Santo do Pinhal o BR 72-73 G 7
Espita o MEX 52-53 K 1
Esplanada o BR 68-69 K 7
Espoo o FIN 88-89 H 6
Espungabera o MOC 218-219 G 5
Ėşŝābād o IR 134-135 G 1
Esquel o RA 78-79 D 7
Esquibel, Gulf of ≈ 32-33 D 4
Esquina o RA 76-77 H 6
Esquina o RCH 70-71 C 6
Esquió o RA 76-77 E 5
Ěss ∼ RUS 114-115 G 4
Essaouira = as-Sawirah ✩ MA 188-189 G 3
Essaouira = As-Sawirah ✩ MA 188-189 G 3
Essé o CAM 204-205 J 6
Es-Sed, Oued ∼ TN 190-191 G 3
Es Seggeur, Oued ∼ DZ 190-191 C 4
Essej o RUS 108-109 e 7
Essej, ozero o RUS 108-109 e 7
Essen o D 92-93 H 3
Essen • D 92-93 J 3
Essendon, Mount ▲ AUS 176-177 F 2
Essentuki o RUS 126-127 E 5
Essequibo ✩ GUY 62-63 E 2
Essequibo River ∼ GUY 62-63 E 2
Essex o USA (CA) 40-41 G 8
Essex o USA (MT) 40-41 H 1
Essex Junction o USA 46-47 M 3
Essington, Port o 172-173 K 1
Essiama o GH 202-203 J 7
Esslingen am Neckar o D 92-93 K 4
Est = East, Pointe de l' ▲ CDN 38-39 O 4
Estabrook Lake o CDN 24-25 K 6
Estacada o USA 40-41 C 3
Estaca de Bares, Punta de ▲ E 98-99 D 3
Estação Catur o MOC 218-219 H 1
Estacia Camacho o MEX 50-51 K 4
Estación 14 de Mayo o PY 76-77 K 2
Estación Atamisqui o RA 76-77 F 5
Estacion biologica • EC 64-65 B 10
Estación Buena Suerte o PY 76-77 H 2
Estación Candela o MEX 50-51 J 4
Estación Careros Cué o PY 76-77 H 2
Estacincne Don o MEX 50-51 E 4
Estación Km. 329 o ROU 78-79 F 7
Estación la Concepción o PY 76-77 H 1
Estación Pozo Blanco o PY 76-77 H 2
Estación Salto Cué o PY 76-77 J 4
Estación Simón o MEX 50-51 H 5
Estación Vanegas o MEX 50-51 J 4
Estación Victoria o PY 76-77 H 2
Estado Cañitas de Felipe Pescador o MEX 50-51 H 6
Estado la Calle o MEX 52-53 D 1
Estado Las Tablas o MEX 52-53 D 1
Estado Pabellones o MEX 50-51 H 6
Estados, Isla de los ∼ RA 80 H 9
Estados, Parque Nacional de los ⊥ RA 80 H 7
Eştahbānāt o IR 134-135 F 4
Estambul o BOL 70-71 D 4
Estância o BR 68-69 K 7
Estância Camerón o RCH 80 E 7
Estancia el Durazno o RA 76-77 C 6
Estancia la Federica o RA 80 D 5
Estancia Invierno o RCH 80 D 5
Estancia Laguna Union o RA 80 D 5
Estancia la Jerónima o RA 80 F 7
Estancia la Julia o RA 80 F 4
Estancia la Oriental o RA 80 D 3
Estancia las Cumbres o RCH 80 D 5
Estancia María Esther o RA 80 F 4
Estancia María Luisa o RA 80 F 7
Estancia Marina o RA 80 F 7
Estancia Monte Dinero o RA 80 F 6
Estancia Policarpo o RA 80 H 7
Estancia Rocollosa o RCH 80 E 6
Estancia San Justo o RA 80 F 7
Estand, Kûh-e ▲ IR 134-135 J 3
Estandarte o BR 68-69 F 2
Estanica o USA 44-45 D 2
Estanques o YV 60-61 F 3
Estarca, Rio ∼ BOL 76-77 D 1
Estcourt o ZA 220-221 J 4
Este, Laguna del ≈ 52-53 J 2
Este, Parque nacional del ⊥ DOM 54-55 L 5
Este, Punta del ▲ ROU 78-79 M 3
Esteban, Canal ≈ 80 C 5
Eştehārd o IR 136-137 B 7
Esteio o BR 74-75 E 7
Esteli o NIC 52-53 L 5
Estella o E 98-99 F 3
Estelline o USA 44-45 G 2
Estépar o E 98-99 E 3
Estepona o E 98-99 E 6
Ester o USA 20-21 R 4
Esteras o RA 76-77 J 1
Esterhazy o CDN 34-35 E 5
Esteriktjah-Tas, hrebet ▲ RUS 110-111 X 5
Estero o USA 48-49 H 6
Estero Bay ≈ 40-41 D 8
Estero Blanco ∼ RCH 76-77 B 5

Estero de Boca o EC 64-65 B 3
Estes Park o USA 42-43 E 5
Estevan o CDN 34-35 E 5
Estevan Group ∼ CDN 32-33 E 5
Esther Island o CDN 20-21 R 6
Estherville o USA 42-43 K 4
Estill o USA 48-49 H 3
Estima o MOC 218-219 G 2
Estique o PE 70-71 B 5
Estirão do Equador o BR 66-67 B 5
Estiva o BR 68-69 F 2
Estiva, Riachão da ∼ BR 68-69 F 5
Estlin o CDN 34-35 D 5
Eston o CDN 32-33 G 6
Estonia = Eesti ■ EST 94-95 J 2
Estor, El o GCA 52-53 K 4
Estrecho, El o CO 60-61 C 7
Estreito o BR 68-69 H 6
Estrela, Serra da ▲ P 98-99 D 5
Estrela do Sul o BR 72-73 G 5
Estrella, La o BOL 70-71 F 7
Estrella, La o BR 76-77 K 1
Estrella, La o RCH 76-77 C 1
Estrella, Punta ▲ MEX 50-51 C 2
Estrelito, Serra do ▲ BR 68-69 G 7
Estremadura ⊥ P 98-99 C 5
Estremo o BR 74-75 E 7
Estremoz o P 98-99 D 5
Estrondo, Serra do ▲ BR 68-69 D 6
Esumba, Ile o ZRE 210-211 H 3
Etacho Point ▲ CDN 24-25 L 3
Etah o GRØ 26-27 O 4
Etah o IND 138-139 G 6
Etaka ▲ NAM 216-217 C 9
Étampes o F 90-91 J 7
Etamunbanie, Lake o AUS 178-179 G 4
Etawah o IND 138-139 G 6
Etchojoa o MEX 50-51 E 4
Etchoropo o MEX 50-51 E 4
Étéké o G 210-211 C 4
Ěterikan, proliv ≈ 110-111 X 3
Ethelbert o CDN 34-35 D 5
Ethel Creek o AUS 172-173 E 7
Etheldale o AUS 174-175 G 6
Ethel Lake o CDN 20-21 W 5
Ethel River o AUS 176-177 E 2
Ethiopia = Ȋtyopya ■ ETH 208-209 C 3
Etivluk River ∼ USA 20-21 N 2
Etler Rasmussen, Kap ▲ GRØ 26-27 p 2
Etna, Monte ▲ I 100-101 E 6
Etna Lake o CDN 30-31 K 3
Etoile Cay ∼ SY 224 C 2
Etolin, Cape ▲ USA 20-21 G 6
Etolin Island ∼ USA 32-33 D 4
Etolin Point ▲ USA 22-23 R 3
Etolin Strait ≈ 20-21 H 6
Eton o USA 178-179 K 1
Etorohaberge ▲ NAM 216-217 B 8
Etosha Lookout ∼ NAM 216-217 D 9
Etosha National Park ⊥ NAM 216-217 C 9
Etosha Pan o NAM 216-217 D 9
Etou o CAM 210-211 D 2
Etoumbi o RCB 210-211 E 3
Etowah o USA 48-49 F 2
Etowah Mounds State Historic Site ∴∴ USA 48-49 F 2
Etowah River ∼ USA 48-49 F 2
Etropole o BG 102-103 D 6
Ettaiyāpuram o IND 140-141 G 6
Etta Plains o AUS 174-175 F 6
Et Tarf, Garaet o DZ 190-191 F 3
Etthen Island o CDN 30-31 O 4
Ettington o CDN 34-35 O 6
Etturnanur o IND 140-141 G 6
Etumba o ZRE (Ban) 210-211 H 5
Etumba o ZRE (HAU) 210-211 K 4
Ěturerveem ∼ RUS 112-113 X 3
Eturnagaram o IND 142-143 D 6
Ětyrkěn o RUS 122-123 D 3
Etzatlan o MEX 52-53 B 1
Etzikom Coulee ∼ CDN 32-33 O 7
'Eua ∼ TON 184 IV a 2
Euabalong o AUS 180-181 J 2
Euaiki ∼ TON 184 IV a 2
Euca o BR 66-67 G 4
Eucalypt, El o ROU 78-79 M 3
Eucla Motels o AUS 176-177 H 5
Euclid o USA 46-47 H 5
Euclides da Cunha o BR 68-69 J 7
Eucumbene, Lake o AUS 180-181 K 4
Eudistes, Lac des o CDN 38-39 M 3
Eudora o USA 44-45 M 3
Eudunda o AUS 180-181 F 3
Eufaula o USA (AL) 48-49 F 4
Eufaula o USA (OK) 44-45 K 2
Eufaula Lake o USA 44-45 K 2
Eufrasio Loza o RA 76-77 F 6
Eugene o USA 40-41 C 4
Eugene McDermott Shoal ∼ AUS 172-173 G 2
Eugênia, Rio da ∼ BR 70-71 H 2
Eugowra o AUS 180-181 K 2
Euless o USA 44-45 J 3
Eulo o AUS 178-179 H 4
Eumara Springs o AUS 174-175 H 6
Eunápolis o BR 72-73 L 4
Eungella o AUS 178-179 K 1
Eungella National Park ⊥ AUS 174-175 K 5
Eunice o USA (LA) 44-45 L 4
Eunice o USA (NM) 44-45 F 3
Eupen o B 92-93 J 3
Euphrat ∼ 128-129 L 7
Euphrates = Furāt, al- ∼ SYR 128-129 J 7
Eupora o USA 48-49 D 3
Eura o FIN 88-89 G 6
Eurasburg ∼ D 92-93 J 3
Eure ∼ F 90-91 H 7

Eureka o USA (CA) 40-41 B 5
Eureka Sound ≈ 26-27 V 3
Eureka Springs o USA 44-45 L 1
Eurimbula National Park ⊥ AUS 178-179 L 3
Eurinilla Creek ∼ AUS 178-179 F 6
Euriowie o AUS 178-179 F 6
Euroa o AUS 180-181 H 4
Euromos • TR 128-129 B 4
Europa, Ȋle ∼ F 218-219 L 6
Europa, Picos de ▲ E 98-99 E 3
Europa, Punta ▲ GQ 210-211 B 2
Europoort ∼ NL 92-93 H 3
Eurotunnel II • 92-93 H 3
Euskadi o E 98-99 F 3
Euskadi Pis.-Vasco ∼ E 98-99 F 3
Eustis o USA 48-49 H 5
Eutaw o USA 48-49 E 3
Euthini o MW 214-215 G 6
Eutin o D 92-93 L 1
Eutsuk Lake o CDN 32-33 G 5
Eva o USA 44-45 G 1
Eva Broadhurst Lake o AUS 172-173 F 7
Eva Downs o AUS 174-175 C 6
Evale o ANG 216-217 C 8
Eva-Liv, ostrov ∼ RUS 84-85 h 2
Evandale o CDN 38-39 L 6
Evander o ZA 220-221 J 3
Evans, Lac o CDN 38-39 F 3
Evans, Mount ▲ USA 40-41 J 5
Evans Island ∼ USA 20-21 Q 7
Evans Shoal ≃ 166-167 E 6
Evans Strait ≈ 36-37 H 3
Evanston o USA (IL) 46-47 E 4
Evanston o USA (WY) 40-41 J 5
Evansville o CDN 38-39 D 6
Evansville o USA 46-47 E 7
Evant o USA 44-45 H 4
Evaton o ZA 220-221 H 3
Eva Valley o AUS 172-173 L 3
Evaz o IR 134-135 G 5
Eveleth o USA 42-43 L 2
Evelyn, Mount ▲ 172-173 L 2
Evenk Autonomous District = Ėvenkijskij avtonomnyj okrug o RUS 116-117 G 2
Ėvensk o RUS 120-121 S 3
Everard, Lake o AUS 178-179 C 6
Everard Junction o AUS 176-177 H 2
Everard Ranges ▲ 176-177 M 3
Everest, Mount ▲ NEP 144-145 F 7
Everett o USA (GA) 48-49 H 4
Everett o USA (WA) 40-41 D 2
Everett, Mount ▲ USA 46-47 M 4
Everett Mountains ▲ CDN 36-37 Q 3
Evergreen o USA 48-49 E 4
Evesham o AUS 178-179 G 2
Evgen'evka o KA 146-147 C 4
Évia ∼ GR 100-101 J 5
Evijärvi o FIN 88-89 H 5
Evinayong o GQ 210-211 C 3
Evje o N 86-87 C 7
Evlah = Yevlax o AZ 128-129 M 2
Evodoula o CAM 204-205 J 6
Evöğli o IR 128-129 L 3
Évora o P 98-99 D 5
Evoron, ozero o RUS 122-123 G 3
Evota, gora ▲ RUS 118-119 M 7
Evpatorija = Jevpatorija ✩ UA 102-103 H 5
Evreinova, mys ▲ RUS 120-121 P 4
Evreinova, proliv ≈ RUS 122-123 J 4
Évreux o F 90-91 H 7
Evron o F 90-91 G 7
Ěvur ∼ RUS 122-123 G 3
Ěwa ∼ RUS 88-89 U 5
Ewan o USA 40-41 F 2
Ewango o WAN 204-205 H 5
Ewarton o JA 54-55 G 5
Ewaso Ngiro ∼ EAK (RIF) 212-213 E 4
Ewaso Ngiro ∼ EAK 212-213 F 3
Ewasse o PNG 183 F 3
Ewing o USA (MO) 46-47 C 5
Ewing o USA (NE) 42-43 H 4
Ewo o RCB 210-211 E 3
Exaltación de Boli (BEN) 70-71 E 3
Exaltación o BOL (PAN) 70-71 D 2
Excelsior o ZA 220-221 H 4
Excelsior Springs o USA 42-43 K 6
Executive Committee Range ▲ ARK 16 F 24
Exeter o CDN 38-39 D 7
Exeter o GB 90-91 F 6
Exeter o USA (CA) 40-41 E 7
Exeter o USA (NH) 46-47 N 4
Exeter Bay ≈ 28-29 K 3
Exeter Lake o CDN 30-31 O 3
Exeter Sound ≈ 28-29 K 3
Exira o USA 42-43 K 5
Exmoor National Park ⊥ GB 90-91 F 6
Exmore o USA 46-47 L 6
Exmouth o AUS 172-173 B 7
Exmouth Gulf ≈ 172-173 B 7
Exmouth Lake o CDN 30-31 M 3
Exmouth Plateau ≃ 13 C 4
Expedition National Park ⊥ AUS 178-179 K 3
Expedition Range ▲ AUS 178-179 K 3
Expedito Lopes Francisco Santos, D. o BR 68-69 H 5
Exploits, Bay of ≈ 38-39 I R 4
Exploits Islands o CDN 38-39 I R 4
Exploits River ∼ CDN 38-39 I Q 4
Explorer Mountain ▲ USA 22-23 Q 3
Exstew o CDN 32-33 F 4
Extremadura ⊥ P 98-99 D 5
Extreme Nord = Extreme North ⊡ CAM 206-207 B 2
Extreme North = Extrême Nord ⊡ CAM 206-207 B 2
Exu o BR 68-69 J 5
Exuma Cays ∼ BS 54-55 G 2

Freycinet National Park ⊥ AUS 180-181 K 7
Freycinet Peninsula ∼ AUS 180-181 J 7
Fria ○ RG 202-203 D 4
Fria, Kaap ▲ NAM 216-217 A 9
Fria, La ○ YV 60-61 E 3
Frías ○ RA 76-77 E 5
Friday Harbour ○ USA 40-41 C 1
Friedberg (Hessen) ○ D 92-93 K 3
Friedrichshafen ○ D 92-93 K 5
Friend ∼ 42-43 J 7
Friendship Hill National Historic Site ∴ USA 46-47 J 6
Friendship Shoal ≈ 162-163 K 2
Frigate Bay Beach ∴ KAN 56 D 3
Friggesund ○ S 86-87 H 6
Frindsburg Reef ∼ SOL 184 I d 1
Frio, Cabo ▲ BR 72-73 J 4
Friona ○ USA 44-45 F 2
Fritz Hugh Sound ≈ 32-33 G 6
Friuli-Venézia Giúlia ▫ I 100-101 D 1
Friza, proliv ≈ RUS 122-123 N 6
Frobisher Bay ≈ 36-37 Q 3
Frobisher Bay ○ CDN 36-37 P 3
Frobisher Lake ○ CDN 32-33 Q 3
Frog Lake ○ CDN 32-33 P 5
Frog River ∼ CDN 32-33 G 3
Frog River ∼ CDN 34-35 M 3
Frohavet ≈ 86-87 D 5
Frolovo ○ RUS 116-117 L 6
Frolovo ○ RUS (VLG) 102-103 N 3
Frome, Lake ○ AUS 178-179 E 6
Frome Downs ○ AUS 178-179 E 6
Fronteira ○ E 188-189 C 7
Frontera ○ MEX 52-53 H 2
Frontera, Punta ▲ MEX 52-53 H 2
Frontera Comalapa ○ MEX 52-53 H 4
Fronteras ○ MEX 50-51 E 2
Front Range ▲ USA 42-43 E 5
Front Royal ○ USA 46-47 J 6
Frosinone ○ I 100-101 D 4
Frøya ∼ N 86-87 D 5
Frozen Strait ≈ 24-25 d 7
Frunze = Biškek ★ KS 146-147 B 4
Frunze, mys ▲ RUS 108-109 Y 1
Fruta de Leite ○ BR 72-73 J 4
Frutal ○ BR 72-73 F 6
Frutillar ○ RCH 78-79 C 6
Fua'amotu ○ TON 184 IV a 2
Fucheng ○ VRC 154-155 K 3
Fuding ○ VRC 156-157 M 3
Fududa ◁ EAK 212-213 G 5
Fuego, Tierra del ∴ RCH 80 E 7
Fuencaliente ○ E 188-189 C 6
Fuencaliente de la Palma ○ E 188-189 C 2
Fuengirola ○ E 98-99 E 6
Fuente de Cantos ○ E 98-99 D 5
Fuente del Fresno ○ E 98-99 F 5
Fuente de San Esteban, La ○ E 98-99 D 4
Fuente Obejuna ○ E 98-99 E 5
Fuentesaúco ○ E 98-99 E 4
Fuerte ○ BOL 70-71 E 7
Fuerte, El ○ MEX 50-51 E 4
Fuerte, Río ∼ MEX 50-51 E 4
Fuerte Bulnes ○ RCH 80 E 6
Fuerte Olimpo ○ PY 76-77 J 1
Fuerte Quemado ○ RA 76-77 D 4
Fuerte San Lorenzo ∴··· PA 52-53 L 7
Fuerte San Rafael · RA 78-79 E 3
Fuerteventura ∼ E 188-189 D 6
Fufeng ○ VRC 154-155 D 4
Fufulso ○ GH 202-203 K 5
Fuğaira, al- ○ UAE 134-135 G 6
Fuga Island ∼ RP 160-161 D 3
Fuglasker ∼ IS 86-87 b 3
Fuglehuken ▲ N 84-85 G 3
Fugløy Bank ≃ 86-87 J 1
Fugma ○ Y 132-133 F 5
Fugong ○ VRC 142-143 L 2
Fugou ○ VRC 154-155 J 4
Fuhai ○ VRC 146-147 H 2
Fuhaihil, al- ○ KWT 130-131 L 3
Fujian ○ VRC 156-157 L 3
Fu Jiang ∼ VRC 154-155 D 6
Fujieda ○ J 152-153 M 5
Fuji-gawa ∼ J 152-153 H 7
Fuji-Hakone-Izu National Park ⊥ J 152-153 H 7
Fujin ○ VRC 150-151 J 4
Fuji-san ▲·· J 152-153 H 7
Fujisawa ○ J 152-153 H 7
Fujiyoshida ○ J 152-153 H 7
Fúka ○ ET 194-195 C 2
Fukagawa ○ J 152-153 K 3
Fukang ○ VRC 146-147 H 3
Fukuchiyama ○ J 152-153 F 7
Fukue ○ J 152-153 C 8
Fukuei Chiao ▲ RC 156-157 M 4
Fukue-shima ∼ J 152-153 C 8
Fukui ★ J 152-153 H 7
Fukuoka ☆ · J 152-153 D 8
Fukushima ○ J (HOK) 152-153 J 4
Fukushima ★ J (FUK) 152-153 J 6
Fukuyama ○ J 152-153 F 7
Fulacunda ○ GNB 202-203 C 4
Fulda ∼ D (HES) 92-93 K 3
Fulda ∼ D 92-93 K 3
Fuli ○ RC 156-157 M 5
Fuling ○ VRC 156-157 E 2
Fullarton ○ TT 60-61 L 2
Fulleborn ○ PNG 183 F 4
Fullerton ○ USA 42-43 C 5
Fulton ○ USA (IL) 46-47 C 5
Fulton ○ USA (KY) 46-47 D 7
Fulton ○ USA (MO) 46-47 D 7
Fulton ○ USA (NY) 46-47 D 6
Fultorp ○ RI 166-167 D 6
Fulula ○ ZRE 210-211 F 6
Fulunäs ○ S 86-87 F 6
Fumbelo ○ ANG 216-217 E 5
Fumel ○ F 90-91 H 9

Fumiela ○ ANG 216-217 D 3
Funabashi ○ J 152-153 H 7
Funadomari ○ J 152-153 J 2
Funafuti Atoll ∼ TUV 13 J 3
Funan ○ VRC 154-155 J 5
Funäsdalen ○ S 86-87 F 5
Funchal ○ P 188-189 C 4
Fundação ○ CO 60-61 D 2
Fundação Eclética ○ BR 72-73 F 3
Fundão ○ BR 72-73 K 5
Fundão ○ P 98-99 D 4
Fundición ○ MEX 50-51 E 4
Fundo, Rio ∼ BR 68-69 G 6
Fundo das Figueiras ○ CV 202-203 C 5
Fundong ○ CAM 204-205 J 5
Fundy, Bay of ≈ 38-39 L 6
Fundy National Park ⊥ CDN 38-39 M 6
Fungom ▲ CAM 204-205 J 5
Funhalouro ○ MOC 218-219 H 6
Funiak Springs, De ○ USA 48-49 L 4
Funing ○ VRC (JIA) 154-155 L 5
Funing ○ VRC (YUN) 156-157 D 5
Funkley ○ USA 42-43 H 2
Funsi ○ GH 202-203 K 4
Funtua ○ WAN 204-205 H 3
Funzi Island ∼ EAK 212-213 G 6
Fuping ○ VRC (HEB) 154-155 J 2
Fuping ○ VRC (SXI) 154-155 F 4
Fuqing ○ VRC 156-157 L 4
Fuquan ○ VRC 156-157 E 3
Fura Braço, Corredeira ∼ BR 66-67 H 6
Furaiši, al- ○ KSA 130-131 F 5
Furancungo ○ MOC 218-219 G 2
Furano ○ J 152-153 K 3
Furano, Kami- ○ J 152-153 K 3
Furāwiya, Bi'r ⊂ SUD 198-199 L 5
Fürg ○ IR 134-135 F 4
Furkwa ○ EAT (DOD) 212-213 E 6
Furnas, Represa de ⊂ BR 72-73 G 6
Furneaux Group ∼ AUS 180-181 K 6
Furo Carandazinho ∼ BR 68-69 B 3
Furo do Jurupari ∼ BR 68-69 B 3
Furo do Tajapuru ∼ BR 62-63 J 6
Furglüjs ○ SYR 128-129 G 5
Furrial, El ○ YV 60-61 K 2
Furroli ▲ ETH 208-209 D 7
Fürstenfeld ○ A 92-93 O 5
Fürstenwalde (Spree) ○ · D 92-93 N 2
Fürth ○ D 92-93 L 4
Furukawa ○ J 152-153 J 5
Fusagasuga ○ CO 60-61 D 5
Fushui ○ VRC 154-155 F 4
Fushun ○ VRC 150-151 D 7
Fusilier ○ CDN 32-33 Q 6
Fuskam Mata ○ WAN 204-205 H 3
Fusong ○ VRC 150-151 F 6
Fussa, vulkan ▲ RUS 122-123 Q 3
Füssen ○ · D 92-93 L 5
Fusui ○ VRC 156-157 E 5
Futa, Cuilo- ○ ANG 216-217 C 3
Futaloufquen, Lago ⊂ RA 78-79 D 7
Futaleufú ○ RCH 78-79 D 7
Futaleufú, Río ∼ RCH 78-79 D 7
Futrono ○ RCH 78-79 C 6
Futuna Island = Île Erronan ∼ VAN 184 II c 4
Fu Xian ○ VRC 154-155 F 4
Fuxian Hu ⊂ VRC 156-157 C 4
Fuxin ○ VRC 150-151 C 6
Fuxing ○ VRC 156-157 J 2
Fuyang ○ VRC 154-155 J 5
Fuyu ○ VRC (HEI) 150-151 E 5
Fuyu ○ VRC (JIL) 150-151 E 6
Fuyuan ○ VRC (HEI) 150-151 H 4
Fuyuan ○ VRC (YUN) 156-157 D 4
Fuyun ○ VRC 146-147 J 2
Fuzhou · VRC 156-157 L 3
Fuzhouzhen ○ VRC 150-151 C 8
Fwa, Lac ⊂ ZRE 210-211 F 6
Fyllas Banke ≃ 28-29 O 5
Fyn ∼ DK 86-87 E 9
Fyresvatn ⊂ N 86-87 D 7

G

Ga ○ GH 202-203 J 5
Gaalkacyo ☆ SP 208-209 H 5
Gaamodebli ⊂ LB 202-203 F 6
Gaasefjord ≈ 26-27 m 8
Gaaseland ∴ GRØ 26-27 m 8
Gaase Pynt ▲ GRØ 26-27 m 8
Gåb, al- ∴ SYR 128-129 G 5
Gaba ○ ETH 208-209 F 5
Gabagaba ○ PNG 183 E 5
Gabal, al-Aḥdar ▲ OM 132-133 K 2
Gabala ○ · SYR 128-129 J 4
Gabal 'Abdal'aziz ▲ SYR 128-129 J 4
Gabalantual ○ LB 202-203 F 6
Gabaldon ○ RP 160-161 D 5
Gabal Auliyâ ○ SUD 200-201 F 5
Gabal Bozi ○ SUD 200-201 F 6
Gabal ou Sarâğ ▲ AFG 136-137 L 7
Gabargaon ○ BD 142-143 F 3
Gabarus ○ CDN 38-39 O 6
Gabbac, Raas ▲ SP 208-209 K 4
Gabba Island ∼ AUS 183 B 5
Gabbro Lake ⊂ CDN 38-39 M 2
Gabbs ○ USA 40-41 F 6
Gåbbúil, Sabhat al- ○ SYR 128-129 G 4
Gabela ○ ANG 216-217 B 5
Gabensis ○ PNG 183 D 4
Gabes ☆ TN 190-191 H 4
Gabes = Gabès ☆ TN 190-191 H 4
Gabès, Golfe de ≈ TN 190-191 H 4
Gabès, Gulf of = Gabès, Golfe de ≈ TN 190-191 H 4
Gabalachipa ○ BD 142-143 G 4
Gabèt al-Ma'âdin ○ SUD 200-201 H 4
Gabgaba, Wâdi ∼ SUD 200-201 G 6
Gabi ○ RN 198-199 C 6

Gabia ○ ZRE 210-211 F 6
Gabiane ○ TCH 206-207 D 4
Gåbir ○ SUD 200-201 D 6
Gabiro ○ RWA 212-213 C 4
Gabo Island ∼ AUS 180-181 K 4
Gabon, Estuaire de ≈ 210-211 B 3
Gabon ■ 210-211 C 4
Gaborone ★ RB 220-221 F 5
Gabras ○ SUD 206-207 H 3
Gabriel, Lac ⊂ CDN 36-37 L 4
Gabriel Strait ≈ 36-37 R 4
Gabriel Vera ○ BOL 70-71 E 6
Gabriel Zamora ○ MEX 52-53 C 2
Gåbrin, Rüd-e ∼ IR 134-135 G 4
Gabrin, Zarde-ye ○ IR 134-135 D 5
Gabrovo ○ BG 102-103 D 6
Gabú ☆ GNB 202-203 C 3
Gabu ○ ZRE 212-213 A 2
Gacheta ○ CO 60-61 D 5
Gacko ○ BIH 100-101 G 3
Gačsar ○ IR 134-135 E 2
Gadabeji ○ RN 198-199 C 5
Gadaf, Wâdi l- ∼ JOR 130-131 E 2
Gadag ○ IND 140-141 F 3
Gadaisu ○ PNG 183 F 5
Gadamai ○ SUD 200-201 H 4
Gada-Oundou ○ RG 202-203 D 4
Gåddede ○ S 86-87 G 4
Gadein ○ SUD 206-207 J 4
Gado Bravo, Serra do ▲ BR 68-69 G 4
Gádra ○ PK 138-139 C 7
Gadsden ○ USA 48-49 K 4
Gadūn, Wâdi ∼ OM 132-133 H 4
Gadwal ○ IND 140-141 G 2
Gadzi ○ RCA 206-207 C 6
Gael Hamke Bugt ≈ 26-27 p 6
Gäești ○ RO 102-103 D 5
Gaeta, Golfo di ≈ 100-101 D 4
Gafara, al- ∴ KSA 130-131 J 4
Ğa'farâbad = Abgarm ○ IR 128-129 N 5
Gafat, al- ○ OM 132-133 K 2
Gaffney ○ USA 48-49 H 2
Gafour ○ · JOR 130-131 D 2
Ğafr, al- ∴ JOR (MAA) 130-131 E 2
Ğafr, al- ∼ JOR (MAA) 130-131 E 2
Gafsa ☆ · TN 190-191 G 3
Gaftony ○ USA 48-49 H 2
Gåfūra, al- ∴ KSA 134-135 D 6
Gag, Pulau ∼ RI 166-167 E 2
Gagal ○ TCH 206-207 B 4
Gagan ○ PNG 184 I b 1
Gagarawa ○ WAN 198-199 D 6
Gagargarh ○ IND 142-143 C 2
Gagarin ★ RUS 94-95 O 4
Ğağarm ○ IR 136-137 B 4
Ğağarm, Käl-e Šür ∼ IR 136-137 E 6
Gagatú ○ AFG 138-139 B 3
Gagau, Gunung ▲ MAL (PAH) 162-163 J 2
Gage ○ USA 44-45 H 1
Gagere ∼ WAN 198-199 C 6
Gaggabutan ○ RP 160-161 D 4
Ğağğağa, Nahr ∼ SYR 128-129 J 4
Gaghamni ○ SUD 206-207 J 3
Ğâği ○ AFG 138-139 B 3
Ğâği Meidân ○ AFG 138-139 C 3
Gagnoa ○ CI 202-203 H 6
Gagnon ○ CDN 38-39 K 3
Ğâgöri ○ AFG 134-135 M 2
Gagra ○ GE 126-127 D 6
Ğağrüd, Rüdhâne-ye ∼ IR 136-137 B 7
Ga Hai ∼ VRC 144-145 L 2
Gahkom ○ IR 134-135 F 4
Gahnin ○ OM 132-133 J 4
Ğahra, al- ∴ KWT 130-131 K 3
Ğahrom ∼ IR 134-135 F 4
Gaïba, Lago ⊂ BOL 70-71 H 7
Gaibanda ○ BD 142-143 F 3
Gaida, al- ○ Y 132-133 H 5
Gaida, al- ○ Y 132-133 G 6
Gaïgou ○ BF 202-203 K 2
Gail ∼ A 92-93 M 5
Gail, al- ○ Y 132-133 G 6
Gail Bäwazir ∼ Y 132-133 F 6
Gaillac ○ F 90-91 H 10
Gaillimh = Galway ★ · IRL 90-91 C 5
Gaiman ○ RA 78-79 G 7
Gaimonaki ○ PNG (MO) 42-43 L 6
Gainesville ○ USA (FL) 48-49 G 5
Gainesville ○ USA (GA) 48-49 G 4
Gainesville ○ USA (MO) 44-45 J 1
Gainesville ○ USA (TX) 44-45 J 3
Gainsborough ○ CDN 34-35 D 6
Gairdner, Lake ⊂ AUS 178-179 C 6
Gairdner River ∼ AUS 176-177 E 6
Gaire ○ PNG 183 D 5
Gairezi ∼ ZW 218-219 G 3
Gairo ○ EAT (MOR) 214-215 J 4
Gaital, Cerro ▲ PA 52-53 D 7
Gaivota ○ BR 62-63 J 5
Gai Xian ○ VRC 150-151 D 7
Gaj ○ RUS 96-97 J 3
Gaja, Pulau ∼ MAL 160-161 C 10
Gajah, Kampung ○ MAL 162-163 D 2
Gajahmungkur, Danau ⊂ RI 168 D 3
Gajicavem ∼ RUS 112-113 O 5
Gajendragarh ○ IND 140-141 F 3
Gaji, River ∼ WAN 204-205 J 3
Gajiram ○ WAN 198-199 F 6
Gajny ☆ RUS 96-97 J 3
Gajwel ○ IND 140-141 H 2
Gakarosa ▲ ZA 220-221 F 3
Gakona ○ WAN 204-205 H 5
Gakona ○ USA 20-21 S 5
Gakona River ∼ USA 20-21 S 5
Gakou ○ RMM 202-203 G 2
Gakuch ○ PK 138-139 L 6
Gala ○ VRC 144-145 G 6
Galachipa ∼ BD 142-143 G 4
Gal Adhale ○ SP 208-209 H 5
Galadi ○ ETH 208-209 H 6
Galaï, al- ∼ SUD 200-201 H 4
Galal, togga ∼ SP 208-209 K 3

Galâlâbâd ☆ AFG 138-139 C 2
Galam ∼ RUS 122-123 E 2
Galam, Selat ≈ 162-163 E 4
Galâmid, al- ∴ KSA 130-131 G 2
Galán ○ CO 60-61 E 4
Galán, Cerro ▲ RA 76-77 D 3
Galana ∼ EAK 212-213 G 5
Galandùk ○ IR 136-137 B 7
Galanga ○ ANG 216-217 C 6
Galangachi ○ RT 202-203 L 4
Galangue ○ ANG 216-217 D 6
Galaosié ○ US 136-137 G 6
Galápagos, Islas = Archipiélago de Colón ∼ EC 64-65 B 9
Galápagos, Parque Nacional de ⊥ ··· EC 64-65 B 9
Galápagos Fracture Zone = Galapagos Fracture Zone ≃ 14-15 P 8
Galápagos Islands = Islas Galápagos ∼ EC 64-65 B 9
Galapagos Rise = Galápagos Rise ≃ 5 B 4
Galarza ○ RA 76-77 J 5
Galarza, Laguna ⊂ RA 76-77 J 5
Galas ∼ MAL 162-163 D 2
Galashiels ○ GB 90-91 F 4
Galata ○ CY 128-129 E 5
Galați ☆ RO 102-103 E 5
Galax ○ USA 46-47 H 7
Galbraith ○ AUS 174-175 F 5
Galbraith ○ CDN 20-21 Y 7
Galbyn Gov' ∴ MAU 148-149 H 6
Ğaldak ○ AFG 134-135 M 3
Gáldar ○ E 188-189 D 6
Galdhøpiggen ▲·· N 86-87 D 6
Ğaldiyan ○ IR 128-129 L 4
Galé ○ RMM 202-203 F 3
Galeana ○ MEX (CHA) 50-51 F 2
Galeana ○ MEX (NL) 50-51 F 3
Galena ○ USA (AK) 20-21 M 4
Galena ○ USA (IL) 46-47 C 5
Galena Bay ○ CDN 32-33 M 6
Galenbindunuwewa ○ CL 140-141 H 6
Galeo ○ LB 202-203 F 7
Ğâleq ○ IR 134-135 J 3
Galera ○ EC 64-65 B 1
Galera, Punta ▲ EC 64-65 B 1
Galera, Rio ∼ BR 70-71 H 4
Galesburg ○ USA 46-47 C 5
Galesong ○ RI 164-165 F 6
Galesville ○ USA 46-47 C 3
Galéti Shet' ∼ ETH 208-209 E 4
Galeton ○ USA 46-47 K 5
Galgamuwa ○ CL 140-141 J 7
Galgaduud ⊡ SP 208-209 H 6
Galheirão, Rio ∼ BR 72-73 H 2
Galheiro, Rio ∼ BR 72-73 H 2
Gali ○ GE 126-127 D 6
Galia ○ BR 72-73 F 7
Galiano ○ CDN 32-33 J 7
Ğaliba ○ SME 62-63 J 5
Galibi ○ SME 62-63 J 5
Galibi, National Reservaat ⊥ SME 62-63 J 5
Galič ○ RUS 94-95 S 2
Galicia ⊡ E 98-99 C 3
Galička vozvyšennost' ▲ RUS 94-95 R 3
Galilee ○ CDN 34-35 D 6
Galilee, Lake ⊂ AUS 178-179 H 2
Galiléia ○ BR 72-73 K 5
Galilo ○ PNG 183 B 4
Galim ○ CAM (ADA) 204-205 K 5
Galim ○ CAM (OUE) 204-205 J 6
Galimovskij hrebet ▲ RUS 112-113 H 4
Galimyj ○ RUS 112-113 H 5
Galina · JA 54-55 G 5
Galinda ○ ANG 216-217 B 4
Galinhas, Ilha das ∼ GNB 202-203 C 4
Galion ○ USA 46-47 G 5
Galite, La ∼ TN 190-191 G 2
Galivedu ○ IND 140-141 G 3
Galiwinku ◁ AUS 174-175 C 3
Gallâbât ○ SUD 200-201 H 5
Gallaorol ○ US 136-137 K 5
Gallatin ○ USA (MO) 42-43 H 6
Gallatin ○ USA (TN) 48-49 E 1
Gallatin Peak ▲ USA 40-41 J 3
Gallatin River ∼ USA 40-41 J 3
Galle ○ · CL 140-141 J 7
Gállego, Rio ∼ E 98-99 G 3
Gallego Rise ≃ 14-15 R 8
Gallegos ○ USA 44-45 F 2
Gallegos, Rio ∼ RA 80 D 6
Galleguillos ○ RCH 76-77 B 4
Gallinas, Punta ▲ CO 60-61 F 1
Gallinero, Cerro ▲ YV 60-61 H 5
Gallipoli ○ AUS 174-175 D 6
Gallipolis ○ USA 46-47 G 6
Gällivare ○ · S 86-87 K 3
Gallja, ostrov ∼ RUS 84-85 a 3
Gallo Mountains ▲ USA 44-45 C 2
Galloway ∴ GB 90-91 E 4
Gallup ○ USA 44-45 C 2
Galma, River ∼ WAN 204-205 H 3
Galma Galla ∼ EAK 212-213 H 4
Galmi ○ RN 198-199 B 6
Galo Boukoy ○ RCA 206-207 B 6
Gal Oya National Park ⊥ CL 140-141 J 7
Galpón, El ○ RA 76-77 E 3
Gálréz ○ AFG 138-139 B 2
Gangala na Bodio ○ ZRE 212-213 B 2
Gal Tardo ○ SP 212-213 K 1
Gan Gan ○ RA 78-79 F 7
Ğalugâh ○ IR 136-137 C 6
Ğalûlâ'i ○ IRQ 128-129 L 5
Galung ○ IR 164-165 F 5
Galur ○ RI 168 D 3

Galva ○ USA 46-47 C 5
Galvão ○ BR 74-75 D 6
Gálves ○ RA 78-79 J 2
Galveston ○ USA 44-45 K 5
Galveston Bay ≈ 44-45 K 5
Galvez, Río ∼ PE 64-65 F 4
Galway ☆ · IRL 90-91 C 5
Galway = Gaillimh ★ · IRL 90-91 C 5
Galway's Soufrière ▲ GB 56 D 3
Gam, Pulau ∼ RI 166-167 F 2
Gama ○ BR 72-73 F 3
Gama, Isla ∼ RA 78-79 H 6
Gâmâgîm, Umm al- ○ KSA 130-131 J 4
Gamana, River ∼ WAN 204-205 H 3
Gama River ∼ PNG 183 B 4
Gamawa ○ WAN 198-199 E 6
Gamba ○ G 210-211 C 5
Gamba ○ VRC 144-145 G 6
Gamba ○ ZRE 210-211 K 6
Gambaga ○ GH 202-203 K 4
Gambang ∼ MAL 162-163 E 2
Gambara ○ MEX 52-53 C 2
Gambela National Park ⊥ ETH 208-209 A 5
Gambell ○ USA 20-21 K 4
Gambia ■ WAG 202-203 C 3
Gambia, River ∼ WAG 202-203 B 3
Gambia No.1 ○ GH 202-203 J 6
Gambier Islands ∼ AUS 180-181 D 3
Gambo ○ ANG 216-217 C 4
Gambo ○ CDN 38-39 R 4
Gambo ○ RCA 206-207 C 6
Gamboa ○ PA 52-53 E 7
Gamboma ○ RCB 210-211 E 5
Gamboula ○ RCA 206-207 B 6
Gamčen, hrebet ▲ RUS 120-121 T 6
Gamčen, vulkan ▲ RUS 120-121 T 6
Gamdou ○ RN 198-199 D 6
Gamela ○ RI 164-165 K 3
Gamela, Teluk ≈ 164-165 K 3
Gamena ∼ USA 20-21 S 5
Gamëroma, al- ∴ KSA 130-131 J 4
Gamès ○ NAM 220-221 C 4
Gami ∼ KSA 132-133 C 5
Gammelstaden ○ · S 86-87 L 4
Gammouda = Sidi Bouzid ☆ TN 190-191 G 3
Gamoep ○ ZA 220-221 D 4
Gamo-Gofa ⊡ ETH 208-209 C 6
Gamova, mys ▲ RUS 122-123 D 7
Gamperé ▲ CAM 206-207 B 5
Gamping ○ RI 168 D 3
Gamra ○ ET 194-195 F 4
Ğamsa ○ ET 194-195 F 4
Ğamsa, Ra's ▲ ET 194-195 F 4
Gamsberg ▲ NAM 220-221 C 1
Ğamšidzâi, Küh-e ▲ IR 134-135 J 4
Gamūd ▲ ETH 208-209 D 6
Ğamûm ○ KSA 132-133 A 3
Gamvik ○ N 86-87 N 1
Ğ'amys, gora ▲ AZ 128-129 M 2
Gana, Komadougou ∼ WAN 198-199 F 6
Ğanad, al- ○ Y 132-133 B 4
Ganado ○ USA 44-45 B 2
Ganal'skij hrebet ▲ RUS 120-121 P 6
Ganaly ○ RUS 120-121 P 6
Ğanamiya, al- ○ KSA 130-131 K 5
Ğanâna ○ UAE 134-135 F 6
Ganané ○ CDN 38-39 J 4
Ğanâva, Bandar-e ○ IR 134-135 D 4
Gancheng ○ VRC 156-157 F 7
Gand = Gent ☆ · B 92-93 G 3
Ganda ○ ANG 216-217 C 6
Gandaba ○ ETH 208-209 F 5
Gandadiwata, Gunung ▲ RI 164-165 F 5
Gandajika ○ ZRE 214-215 D 3
Gandak ∼ IND 142-143 D 2
Ğandaq ○ IR 134-135 F 1
Gandâva ○ PK 134-135 M 4
Gande ○ WAN 144-145 H 6
Gander ○ CDN 38-39 I R 4
Gander Bay ○ CDN 38-39 R 4
Gander Lake ⊂ CDN 38-39 I R 4
Gander River ∼ CDN 38-39 I R 4
Gândhi Dhâm ○ IND 138-139 D 8
Gândhinagar ★ IND 138-139 D 8
Gândhi Sâgar ⊂ IND 138-139 E 7
Gandía ○ E 98-99 G 5
Gandiaye ○ SN 202-203 B 3
Gandó-ko < J 152-153 J 5
Gandomán ○ IR 134-135 O 2
Gandu ○ BR 72-73 L 2
Gâneb ∼ RIM 196-197 E 5
Ganespur ○ IND 142-143 B 2
Ganga, Mouths of the ≈ 142-143 F 5
Gangâčin ○ IR 128-129 L 4
Gângakher ∼ IND 138-139 F 10
Gangala na Bodio ○ ZRE 212-213 B 2
Gangan ▲ RG 202-203 D 4
Ganganagar ○ IND 138-139 E 5
Gângâpur ○ IND (RAJ) 138-139 F 6
Gângâpur ○ IND (RAJ) 138-139 E 7
Gangara ○ RN 198-199 D 5

Gangaw ○ MYA 142-143 J 4
Gangca ○ VRC 154-155 B 3
Gangchang ○ VRC 154-155 F 6
Ganges ○ F 90-91 J 10
Ganges ∼ IND 10-11 H 6
Ganges = Ganga ∼ IND 10-11 H 6
Ganges, Mouths of the ≈ 142-143 F 5
Ganges Fan = Bengal Fan ≃ 12 G 3
Ganges River Delta = Ganga Delta ∼ IND 142-143 F 4
Gangir, Rüdhâne-ye ∼ IR 134-135 A 2
Gangkha ○ BHT 142-143 F 2
Gango ∼ ANG 216-217 C 5
Gangos ∼ BR 72-73 F 3
Gangtok ☆ · IND 142-143 F 2
Gangu ○ VRC 154-155 D 4
Gangui ○ CAM 206-207 C 6
Gangula ○ ANG 216-217 B 5
Ganhe ○ VRC 150-151 D 2
Gani ○ RI 164-165 J 2
Gâni Hêl ○ AFG 138-139 B 3
Gan Jiang ∼ VRC 156-157 J 3
Ganjuškino ★ KA 96-97 F 10
Ganluo ○ VRC 156-157 C 2
Gannan ○ VRC 150-151 C 4
Gannat ○ F 90-91 J 8
Gannett Peak ▲ USA 42-43 C 4
Ganquan ○ VRC 154-155 F 3
Gansbaai ○ ZA 220-221 D 7
Gansé ○ CI 202-203 J 5
Gansu ○ VRC 148-149 D 7
Ganta ○ LB 202-203 F 6
Gantang ○ VRC 154-155 D 3
Gantas, Las ○ RA 76-77 J 5
Gantheaume, Cape ▲ AUS 180-181 D 4
Gantheaume Bay ≈ 176-177 C 3
Gantheaume Point ▲ AUS 172-173 F 4
Ganti ○ RI 168 C 7
Gantira ○ RI 164-165 G 5
Gantisan ○ MAL 160-161 B 9
Ğanúbiya, al-Bâdiya l- ∴ IRQ 130-131 < 2
Ganxi ○ VRC 156-157 F 2
Ganye ○ WAN 204-205 K 4 .
Ganyesa ○ ZA 220-221 G 3
Ganyu ○ VRC 154-155 L 4
Ganza ○ AZ 128-129 M 2
Ganzé ∼ ZRE 210-211 K 6
Ganzhou ○ VRC 156-157 J 2
Gao ○ BF 202-203 J 7
Gao ○ · RMM (GAO) 196-197 K 6
Gao ☆ ZRE 212-213 B 2
Gao'an ○ VRC 156-157 J 2
Gaochun ○ VRC 154-155 L 6
Gaofengtao ○ VRC 154-155 L 4
Gaogou ○ VRC 154-155 L 4
Gaohezhen ○ VRC 154-155 L 4
Gaojiabu ○ VRC 154-155 G 3
Gaolan ○ VRC (GAN) 154-155 C 3
Gaolan · VRC (HUB) 154-155 G 5
Gaoligong Shan ▲ VRC 142-143 L 2
Gaomi ○ VRC 154-155 L 3
Gaoping ○ VRC 154-155 H 4
Gaotai ○ VRC 154-155 C 3
Gaotang ○ VRC 154-155 K 3
Gaotou ○ VRC 154-155 A 2
Gaoua ☆ BF 202-203 J 4
Gaoual ○ RG 202-203 D 4
Gaoun, Mont ▲ RCA 206-207 D 5
Gao Xian ○ VRC 156-157 D 2
Gaoyi ○ VRC 154-155 J 3
Gaozhou ○ VRC 156-157 G 5
Gap ○ F 90-91 L 9
Gap, Pico ▲ RCH 80 E 7
Gapi ○ ZRE 206-207 H 6
Gapuwiyak ◁ AUS 174-175 C 3
Gar' ∼ RUS 122-123 C 2
Garaa Tebourt ⊂ TN 190-191 H 5
Garabinzam ○ RCB 210-211 D 3
Ğârâblus ○ SYR 128-129 H 4
Garabogazköl ∼ VRC (KRS) 136-137 C 4
Gara Brune ∼ DZ 190-191 G 6
Garacad ○ SP 208-209 J 5
Garachico ○ E 188-189 C 6
Garada ○ SUD 200-201 E 3
Garadag ○ SP 208-209 H 4
Gara Dragoman ○ BG 102-103 C 6
Ğarâğîr, Wâdi al- ∼ KSA 130-131 G 2
Garagoa ○ CO 60-61 E 4
Garaguene, Tichit ∼ RN 198-199 D 5
Garagum = Tm 136-137 H 5
Garaïna ○ PNG 183 D 4
Garajonay, Parque Nacional de ⊥ ··· E 188-189 C 6
Garalo ○ RMM 202-203 G 4
Garamba ○ ZRE 212-213 B 2
Garamba, Parc National de la ⊥ ··· ZRE 206-207 H 6
Garampani ○ IND 142-143 H 2
Garandal ○ JOR 130-131 D 2
Garandal, Wâdi ∼ ET 194-195 F 3
Garango ○ BF 202-203 K 4
Garanhune ∼ BR 68-69 K 6
Ga-Rankuwa ○ ZA 220-221 G 3
Garapa, Serra do ▲ BR 72-73 J 4
Garapu ○ BR 72-73 D 2
Garapuava ○ BR 72-73 G 4
Ğarârâ ○ KSA 130-131 K 4
Garara ○ PNG 183 E 5
Garawa ∼ JOR 130-131 D 2
Garawe ○ LB 202-203 G 7
Garayalde ○ RA 78-79 G 7
Garba ○ RCA 206-207 E 4
Garbahaarrey ○ SP 212-213 K 1
Garba Tula ○ EAK 212-213 G 3
Garberville ○ USA 40-41 C 5
Garbi, 'Ali al- ○ IRQ 128-129 M 6
Gârbôš, Küh-e ▲ IR 134-135 D 2
Garça ○ BR 72-73 G 7
Garças, Las ○ RA 76-77 J 5
Garças, Rio das ∼ BR 72-73 E 3
Garce ○ VRC 144-145 M 5
Garda ○ RA 76-77 H 5
Garden ○ CO 60-61 D 6
Garças, Cachoeira das ∼ BR 70-71 H 2
Gasan Kuli ○ TM 136-137 C 6

Garças ou Jacarégueau, Rio das ∼ BR 72-73 E 3
Garchitorena ○ RP 160-161 E 6
Garcitas, Las ○ RA 76-77 H 4
Garco ○ VRC 144-145 G 4
Gardabani ○ GE 126-127 F 7
Gardandéval ○ AFG 138-139 B 2
Garde Lake ⊂ CDN 30-31 Q 4
Garde Lake ⊂ CDN 30-31 Q 4
Gardelegen ○ · D 92-93 L 2
Garden City ○ USA (AL) 48-49 E 2
Garden City ○ USA (KS) 42-43 G 7
Gardenia Lake ⊂ CDN 30-31 R 4
Garden Peninsula ∴ USA 46-47 E 3
Garden River Indian Reserve ⅄ CDN 34-35 O 7
Gardēz ☆ AFG 138-139 B 3
Gardiner ○ CDN 34-35 D 6
Gardiner ○ USA (ME) 46-47 O 3
Gardiner ○ USA (MT) 40-41 J 3
Gardiner, Mount ▲ AUS 178-179 K 2
Gardner ∼ KIB 13 K 3
Gardner ○ USA (CO) 42-43 F 7
Gardner ○ USA (IL) 46-47 D 5
Gardner ○ USA (ND) 42-43 J 2
Gardner Pinnacles ∼ USA 14-15 M 5
Gardner Plateau ≃ AUS 172-173 J 5
Gardner Range ▲ AUS 172-173 J 5
Gardnerville ○ USA 40-41 E 6
Gardunha, Serra da ▲ P 98-99 D 4
Garei ∼ BD 142-143 F 4
Gareloi Island ∼ USA 22-23 O 7
Gare Tigre ○ F 62-63 H 3
Garfa, Oued ∼ RIM 196-197 D 7
Garfield ○ AUS 178-179 H 2
Garfield Mountain ▲ USA 40-41 H 3
Garford ○ USA 176-177 M 4
Gargando ∼ RMM 196-197 H 6
Gargano, Promontorio del ▲ I 100-101 E 4
Gargantua, Cape ▲ CDN 34-35 O 7
Gargaris ○ PNG 183 G 3
Gargnäs ○ S 86-87 H 4
Gargouna ○ RMM 202-203 L 2
Gargždai ∼ LT 94-95 G 4
Garhjät Hills ▲ IND 142-143 E 4
Garhshankar ○ IND 138-139 F 4
Gari ○ RUS 114-115 G 5
Gariau ○ RI 166-167 H 3
Gârib, Ra's ○ ET 194-195 F 3
Garibaldi ○ BR 74-75 E 7
Garibaldi ○ CDN 32-33 J 7
Garibaldi Provincial Park ⊥ CDN 32-33 J 7
Garies ○ ZA 220-221 D 5
Garif, al- ○ KSA 130-131 F 6
Gariganus ∼ NAM 220-221 D 3
Garimpinho ○ BR 68-69 D 5
Garin, Küh-e ▲ IR 134-135 C 2
Garin Shehu ○ WAN 204-205 J 4
Garin Yerima ○ WAN 204-205 J 4
Ğarir, Wâdi ∼ KSA 130-131 H 5
Garissa ☆ EAK 212-213 G 4
Garkem ○ WAN 204-205 J 4
Garki ○ WAN 198-199 D 6
Garkida ○ WAN 204-205 K 3
Garladinne ○ IND 140-141 G 3
Garland ○ CDN 34-35 F 5
Garland ○ USA 44-45 J 3
Garm ○ TJ 136-137 M 5
Gârmâb ○ IR 128-129 N 5
Garmabe ○ SUD 206-207 K 6
Garmanda ○ RUS 112-113 K 5
Garmanda, Bol'šaja ∼ RUS 112-113 K 5
Garm Bît ○ IR 134-135 J 6
Garme ○ IR 136-137 E 6
Garmisch-Partenkirchen ○ · D 92-93 L 5
Garmsâr ○ IR 134-135 L 3
Garmsâr ▲ AFG 134-135 K 3
Garmsâr ○ IR 136-137 D 7
Garner ○ USA 42-43 J 4
Garnet Bank ≃ 74-75 F 9
Garnet Bay ≈ 36-37 M 2
Garnett ○ USA 42-43 K 6
Garoowe ☆ SP 208-209 J 4
Garou ∼ DY 204-205 J 4
Garou, our ∼ RMM 196-197 J 6
Garoua ☆ CAM 204-205 K 4
Garoua Boulaï ○ CAM 206-207 B 6
Garove Island ∼ PNG 183 E 3
Garré ○ RA 78-79 H 4
Garrett Fracture Zone ≃ 14-15 R 9
Garrido, Isla ∼ RCH 80 C 7
Garrison ○ USA (MO) 42-43 L 2
Garrison ○ USA (MT) 40-41 H 2
Garro ○ MEX 52-53 K 4
Garrobo, El ○ NIC 52-53 B 5
Garruchas ○ BR 76-77 K 5
Garry, Cape ▲ CDN 24-25 Z 4
Garry Bay ≈ 24-25 d 6
Garry Lake ⊂ CDN 30-31 T 3
Garsala ○ SP 212-213 L 2
Garsen ○ EAK 212-213 H 5
Garson Lake ⊂ CDN 32-33 Q 3
Gartempe ∼ F 90-91 H 8
Gartok = Garyarsa ○ VRC 144-145 C 5
Garu ○ PNG 183 F 3
Garuahi ○ PNG 183 F 5
Garub ○ NAM 220-221 C 3
Ğârûb ○ Y 132-133 D 6
Garuma ○ RCH 76-77 C 2
Garupá, Rio ∼ BR 76-77 J 6
Garut ○ RI 168 D 3
Garvão ○ BR 72-73 H 2
Garwa ○ IND 142-143 C 3
Garwolin ○ PL 92-93 Q 3
Gary ○ USA 46-47 E 5
Garyarsa ○ VRC 144-145 C 5
Garzê ○ VRC 144-145 M 5
Garzón ○ CO 60-61 D 6
Garças, Cachoeira das ∼ BR 70-71 H 2
Gasan Kuli ○ TM 136-137 C 6

Glen o **AUS** 176-177 D 3
Glen o **USA** 46-47 N 3
Glen o **ZA** 220-221 H 4
Glénan, Îles de ∴ **F** 90-91 F 8
Glenayle o **AUS** 176-177 G 2
Glenboro o **CDN** 34-35 G 6
Glenburgh o **AUS** 176-177 D 2
Glen Canyon ∪ **USA** 40-41 J 7
Glen Canyon National Recreation Area ⊥ **USA** 40-41 J 7
Glencoe o **ZA** 220-221 K 4
Glendale o **USA** (AZ) 40-41 H 9
Glendale o **USA** (CA) 40-41 E 8
Glendale o **ZW** 218-219 F 3
Glendambo o **AUS** 178-179 C 6
Glenden o **AUS** 178-179 K 1
Glendive o **USA** 42-43 H 2
Glendo o **USA** 42-43 E 4
Glendo Reservoir ∪ **USA** 42-43 E 4
Glenelg River ∼ **AUS** 180-181 F 4
Glenfield o **USA** 42-43 H 2
Glengyle o **AUS** 178-179 E 3
Glen Helen o **AUS** 176-177 M 1
Glenholme o **CDN** 38-39 N 6
Glen Innes o **AUS** 178-179 L 5
Glen Kerr o **CDN** 34-35 C 5
Glenlivet < **ZW** 218-219 F 5
Glenlyon Dam < **AUS** 178-179 L 5
Glenmire o **AUS** 178-179 H 3
Glen Mor ∪ **GB** 90-91 E 3
Glen More ∪ **GB** 90-91 E 3
Glenmorgan o **AUS** 178-179 K 4
Glennallen o **USA** 20-21 S 5
Glenn Highway II **USA** 20-21 R 6
Glenns o **USA** 46-47 K 7
Glenns Ferry o **USA** 40-41 G 4
Glennville o **USA** 40-41 E 8
Glenora o **USA** 174-175 G 6
Glenorchy o **AUS** 180-181 J 7
Glenorchy o **NZ** 182 B 6
Glenore o **AUS** 174-175 F 5
Glenormiston o **AUS** 178-179 E 2
Glenrock o **USA** 42-43 E 4
Glen Rose o **USA** 44-45 J 3
Glens Falls o **USA** 46-47 M 4
Glenties o **IRL** 90-91 C 4
Glenville o **USA** 46-47 H 6
Glenwood o **USA** (AR) 44-45 L 2
Glenwood o **USA** (MN) 42-43 K 3
Glenwood Springs o · **USA** 42-43 D 6
Glidden o **CDN** 32-33 G 6
Glidden o **USA** 46-47 C 2
Glina o **HR** 100-101 F 2
Glittertinden ▲ **N** 86-87 D 6
Gliwice o · **PL** 92-93 P 3
Gijaden' o **RUS** 116-117 B 8
Gijadjanskoe ☆ **RUS** 114-115 H 7
Globe o · **USA** 44-45 B 3
Głogów o · **PL** 92-93 O 3
Gloie o **LB** 202-203 F 6
Glomfjord o **N** 86-87 F 3
Glommersträsk o **S** 86-87 J 4
Gloria o **MEX** 50-51 J 4
Gloria, Bahía de la ≈ **RCH** 54-55 G 4
Glória, Cachoeira da ∼ **BR** 66-67 G 7
Gloria, La o **CO** 60-61 E 3
Gloria, La o **MEX** 50-51 K 4
Gloria, Sierra de la ▲ **RCH** 76-77 B 4
Glorias, Las o **MEX** 50-51 G 5
Glorieta o **USA** 44-45 G 2
Glorieuses, Îles · **F** 222-223 E 3
Gloster o **USA** 44-45 L 4
Gloucester o **AUS** 180-181 L 2
Gloucester o **GB** 90-91 F 6
Gloucester o **PNG** 183 E 3
Gloucester o **USA** (MA) 46-47 N 4
Gloucester o **USA** (VA) 46-47 L 6
Gloucester Island o **AUS** 174-175 K 7
Glover Island ∩ **CDN** 38-39 I Q 4
Gloversville o **USA** 46-47 L 4
Glovertown o **CDN** 38-39 I R 4
Glubczyce o · **PL** 92-93 O 3
Glubokaja, buhta o **RUS** 112-113 R 6
Glubokaja, laguna o **RUS** 112-113 U 5
Glubokij **RUS** 102-103 M 3
Glubokij Poluj ∼ **RUS** 114-115 K 2
Glubokij Sabun ∼ **RUS** 114-115 Q 3
Glubokoe, ozero o **RUS** 108-109 Y 7
Gluharinyj o **RUS** 110-111 O 7
Glumpangdua o **RI** 162-163 B 2
Glymur ∼ **IS** 86-87 c 2
Glyndon o **USA** 42-43 J 2
Gmünd o · **A** 92-93 N 4
Gmunden o · **A** 92-93 M 5
Gnaraloo o **AUS** 176-177 B 1
Gnarp o **S** 86-87 H 5
Gnibi o · **SN** 202-203 C 2
Gniezno o · **PL** 92-93 O 2
Gnit o **SN** 196-197 C 6
Gnjilane o **YU** 100-101 H 3
Gnowangerup o **AUS** 176-177 D 6
Gnows Nest Range ▲ **AUS** 176-177 D 4
Goa o **IND** 140-141 E 3
Goageb o **NAM** 220-221 C 3
Goälpärä o **IND** 142-143 F 4
Goaltor o **IND** 142-143 E 4
Goa Mampu Caves · **RI** 164-165 G 6
Goan o **RMM** 202-203 G 2
Goari o **PNG** 183 C 4
Goaso o **GH** 202-203 J 6
Goat Rocks Wilderness ⊥ **USA** 40-41 D 2
Goba ☆ **ETH** 208-209 D 5
Goba o **MOC** 220-221 M 4
Gobabeb o **NAM** 220-221 C 3
Gobabis o **NAM** 216-217 E 11
Goba Fronteira o **MOC** 220-221 L 3
Gobatläng o **IND** 142-143 E 3
Gobari ∼ **ZRE** 210-211 G 6
Gobe o **PNG** 183 C 4
Gobèlé Wenz ∼ **ETH** 208-209 E 4
Gobernador Crespo o **RA** 76-77 G 6
Gobernador Gregores o **RA** 80 E 4

Gobernador Ingeniero Valentín Virasoro o **RA** 76-77 J 5
Gobernador Moyano o **RA** 80 F 3
Gobernador Piedrabuena o **RA** 76-77 J
Gobernador Solá o **RA** 78-79 K 2
Gobi = Gov' ⊥ **MAU** 148-149 F 6
Gobnangou, Falaises du ▲ ·· **BF** 202-203 L 4
Gobó o **J** 152-153 F 8
Gobo, Col de ▲ **RN** 198-199 G 3
Goboumo o **RA** 76-77 J 5
Gobur o **SUD** 206-207 D 4
Gobustan o **AZ** 128-129 N 2
Gobustan o **AZ** 128-129 N 2
Goce Delčev o **BG** 102-103 C 7
Gochas o **NAM** 220-221 D 3
Göchi o **J** 152-153 E 7
Gò Công Đông o **VN** 158-159 J 5
Godáfoss o **IS** 86-87 e 2
Godair o **SUD** 206-207 H 4
Godávari ∼ **IND** 138-139 E 10
Godávari ∼ **IND** 142-143 B 7
Godbout o **CDN** 38-39 D 5
Godda o **IND** 142-143 E 3
Godé o **ETH** 208-209 F 4
Gode, Hosséré ▲ **CAM** 204-205 K 4
Godegode o **EAT** 214-215 H 5
Goderich o **CDN** 38-39 D 7
Godfreys Tank < **AUS** 172-173 H 6
Godfried Hansen o ▲ **GRØ** 26-27 p 5
Godhavn = Qeqertarsuaq ☆ **GRØ** 28-29 O 2
Godhra o **IND** 138-139 D 8
Godhyogol o **SP** 208-209 F 4
Godi, Mayo ∼ **CAM** 206-207 B 4
Godinlabe o **SP** 208-209 H 6
Godofredo Viana o **BR** 68-69 F 2
Godong o **RI** 168 D 3
Godong Kangri ▲ **VRC** 144-145 D 5
Godoy Cruz o **RA** 78-79 F 2
Gods Lake o **CDN** 34-35 J 3
Gods Lake Indian Reserve ⋏ **CDN** 34-35 J 3
Gods Lake Narrows o **CDN** 34-35 J 3
Gods Mercy, Bay of o 36-37 F 3
Gods River ∼ **CDN** 34-35 J 3
Godthåb = Nuuk ☆ **GRØ** 28-29 P 4
Godwin Austen, Mount = K2 ▲ **PK** 138-139 F 2
Goe o **PNG** 183 A 5
Goeie Hoop, Kaap die = Cape of Good Hope ▲ **ZA** 220-221 D 7
Goejegebergte, De ▲ **SME** 62-63 G 4
Goéland, Lac o **CDN** 38-39 F 4
Goëlettes ∩ **SY** 224 B 5
Goeree o **NL** 92-93 G 3
Goes o **NL** 92-93 G 3
Goeygina o **RUS** 122-123 R 3
Gofar Fracture Zone ≃ 14-15 S 8
Gofmana, ostrov ∩ **RUS** 84-85 g 2
Goft'ima Sebeka o **ETH** 208-209 C 3
Gog o **ETH** 208-209 B 5
Gogama o **CDN** 38-39 D 5
Gogango o **AUS** 178-179 L 2
Gogardan, Kötal-e ▲ **AFG** 134-135 M 1
Gò-gawa ∼ **J** 152-153 F 7
Gogebic, Lake o **USA** 46-47 D 2
Gogland, ostrov ∩ **RUS** 94-95 K 1
Gogo o **AUS** 172-173 G 5
Gogo o **WAN** 204-205 D 4
Gogogogo o **RM** 222-223 D 10
Gogói o **MOC** 218-219 G 5
Gogorrón, Parque Natural ⊥ **MEX** 50-51 J 7
Gogounou o **DY** 204-205 E 3
Gogrial o **SUD** 206-207 J 4
Gogui o **RMM** 196-197 F 7
Goh o **IND** 142-143 D 4
Goha Ts'Íyon o **ETH** 208-209 D 3
Goiana o **BR** 68-69 L 5
Goiandira o **BR** 72-73 F 5
Goiânia ☆ · **BR** 72-73 F 3
Goianésia do Pará o **BR** 68-69 D 3
Goiânia o **BR** 72-73 F 4
Goianinha o **BR** 68-69 L 5
Goianorte o **BR** 68-69 D 6
Goiás o · **BR** 72-73 D 4
Goiatins o **BR** 68-69 E 5
Goiatuba o **BR** 72-73 F 5
Goio, Rio ∼ **BR** 72-73 D 7
Goio-Erê o **BR** 74-75 D 5
Goi-Pula o **ZRE** 214-215 D 4
Gojeb Wenz ∼ **ETH** 208-209 C 5
Gojo o **ETH** 208-209 D 4
Gojra o **PK** 138-139 D 4
Goiyo o **J** 152-153 F 7
Gökçeada ∩ **TR** 128-129 A 2
Gökırmak ∼ **TR** 128-129 F 2
Gökova o **TR** 128-129 C 4
Gökova Körfezi ≈ 128-129 B 4
Gokprosh Range ▲ **PK** 134-135 K 5
Göksu Çayı ∼ **TR** 128-129 G 3
Göksun o **TR** 128-129 G 3
Göksu Nehri ∼ **TR** 128-129 E 4
Gokteik Viaduct · **MYA** 142-143 K 4
Gokwe o **ZW** 218-219 E 4
Gol o **N** 86-87 D 6
Golaghát o **IND** 142-143 H 2
Gola Hills o **WAL** 202-203 E 6
Golaja, gora ▲ **RUS** 112-113 K 4
Golan ▲ **SYR** 128-129 F 2
Golana Gof o **EAK** 212-213 G 2
Golbaf o **IR** 134-135 G 4
Gölbaşı o **TR** 128-129 G 3
Gölbağı ★ **TR** 128-129 D 4
Gökova o **TR** 128-129 H 4
Gölcük ★ **TR** 128-129 C 2
Goldap o **PL** 92-93 R 1
Gold Bar o **CDN** 32-33 J 3
Gold Beach o **USA** 40-41 C 3

Gold Bridge o **CDN** 32-33 J 6
Gold Coast ∪ **AUS** 178-179 N 4
Gold Coast ∪ **GH** 202-203 K 7
Golden o **CDN** 32-33 M 6
Golden Bay ≈ 182 D 4
Goldendale o **USA** 40-41 D 3
Golden Ears Provincial Park ⊥ **CDN** 32-33 J 7
Golden Gate o **USA** 48-49 H 6
Golden Gate Bridge ·· **USA** 40-41 C 7
Golden Grove o **JA** 54-55 G 6
Golden Hinde ▲ **CDN** 32-33 H 7
Golden Meadow o **USA** 44-45 M 5
Golden Spike National Historic Site ∴ **USA** 40-41 H 5
Golden Valley o **ZW** 218-219 E 4
Goldeck ▲ **USA** 40-41 H 2
Goldfield o **USA** 40-41 F 7
Goldoika o **RUS** 116-117 R 4
Gold River o **CDN** 32-33 G 7
Goldsand Lake o **CDN** 34-35 F 2
Goldsboro o **USA** 48-49 K 2
Goldsmith Channel ≈ 24-25 T 4
Goldstream River ∼ **CDN** 32-33 L 6
Goldsworthy o **AUS** 172-173 D 6
Goldsworthy, Mount ▲ **AUS** 172-173 D 6
Goldthwaite o **USA** 44-45 H 4
Goldyrevskij o **RUS** 96-97 K 5
Göle o **TR** 128-129 L 2
Göle ★ **TR** 128-129 L 2
Goleniów o **PL** 92-93 N 2
Goleniščeva, mys ▲ **RUS** 120-121 V 4
Golestán o **AFG** 134-135 K 2
Golfa o **IR** 128-129 L 2
Golfete, El o **GCA** 52-53 K 4
Golfito o · **CR** 52-53 C 7
Golfo Aranci o **I** 100-101 D 4
Golfo de Santa Clara, El o **MEX** 50-51 B 2
Golfo Nuevo ≈ 78-79 G 7
Gölgeli Dağları ▲ **TR** 128-129 C 4
Gol Gol o **AUS** 180-181 G 2
Gölhisar o **TR** 128-129 C 4
Goli o **EAU** 212-213 C 4
Goliad o **USA** 44-45 J 5
Golija ▲ · **YU** 100-101 H 3
Goliševa o **LV** 94-95 K 3
Gölköy ★ **TR** 128-129 G 4
Golmánhäne, Bandar-e o **IR** 128-129 L 4
Gölmarmara o **TR** 128-129 B 3
Golmud o **VRC** 144-145 K 2
Golodnaja Guba, ozero o **RUS** 88-89 W 3
Golog Shan ▲ **VRC** 154-155 B 5
Golo Island ∩ **RP** 160-161 D 6
Golokuati o **GH** 202-203 L 6
Golol o **SP** 212-213 J 2
Gololcha o **ETH** 208-209 E 4
Golomoti o **MW** 218-219 H 2
Golongosso o **RCA** 206-207 D 4
Goloustnaja ∼ **RUS** 116-117 M 9
Golovin o **USA** 20-21 J 4
Golovin Bay ≈ 20-21 J 4
Golovin Mission o **USA** 20-21 J 4
Golovino o **RUS** 122-123 E 4
Golovnino o **RUS** 122-123 L 7
Golpâyegân o **IR** 134-135 D 2
Gölpazarı o **TR** 128-129 D 2
Golto o **RUS** 122-123 J 7
Golumbita o **RUS** 116-117 J 6
Golungo o **ANG** 216-217 C 4
Golva o **USA** 42-43 G 2
Golweyn o **SP** 212-213 K 3
Golýšmanovo ★ **RUS** 114-115 K 6
Goma o **ZRE** 212-213 D 2
Goma-Gofa o **ETH** 208-209 E 4
Gomati ∼ **IND** 142-143 C 3
Gomati ∼ **IND** 144-145 C 3
Gombari o **ZRE** 212-213 B 2
Gombe o **WAN** 204-205 K 3
Gombe-Matadi o **ZRE** 210-211 F 5
Gombi o **WAN** 204-205 K 3
Gombo Fulani o **WAN** 204-205 K 3
Gombo o **RG** 202-203 J 3
Gomboro o **BF** 202-203 J 3
Gombussougou o **BF** 202-203 K 4
Gomel' = Homel' o **BY** 94-95 M 5
Gomera, La ∩ · **E** 188-189 C 6
Gomes Carneiro, Área Indígena ⋏ **BR** 70-71 K 5
Gómez, Laguna de o **RA** 78-79 J 3
Gómez Farías o **MEX** (CHA) 50-51 F 3
Gómez Farías o **MEX** (TAM) 50-51 K 6
Gómez Palacio o **MEX** 50-51 H 5
Gómez Rendón o **EC** 64-65 B 3
Gomišan o **IR** 136-137 N 4
Gomon o · **CI** 202-203 H 7
Gomontang Caves · **MAL** 160-161 C 10
Gomorovići o **RUS** 94-95 O 1
Gomumu, Pulau ∩ **RI** 164-165 K 4
Gona o **CI** 202-203 J 5
Gonäbäd o · **IR** 134-135 H 1
Gonaïves ★ **RH** 54-55 J 5
Gonam o **RUS** 120-121 D 5
Gonamskij, Sutamo-hrebet ▲ **RUS** 118-119 N 7
Gonarezhou National Park ⊥ **ZW** 218-219 F 5
Gonaté o **CI** 202-203 G 6
Gonâve, Canal de la ≈ 54-55 J 5
Gonâve, Golfe de la ≈ 54-55 J 5
Gonâve, Île de la ∩ **RH** 54-55 J 5
Gonbad-e Kabüd o **IR** 136-137 F 6
Gonçalo, Canal de ∼ **BR** 74-75 D 9
Gonçalves Dias o **BR** 68-69 F 4
Gonda o **IND** 142-143 C 3
Gondal o **IND** 138-139 C 9
Gonder o **ETH** 200-201 H 6
Gondey o **TCH** 206-207 D 4
Gondia o **IND** 142-143 B 5
Gondola o **MOC** 218-219 G 4

Gondolahun o **LB** 202-203 E 6
Gondomar o **P** 98-99 C 4
Gönen o **TR** 128-129 B 2
Gonga o **CAM** 204-205 K 6
Gongchen o **VRC** 154-155 H 6
Gongda ∼ **RUS** 108-109 P 7
Gonggar o **VRC** 144-145 H 6
Gongga Shan ▲ **VRC** 156-157 D 3
Gongguan o **VRC** 156-157 B 3
Gongliu o **VRC** 146-147 F 4
Gongola ∼ **WAN** 204-205 K 4
Gongola, River ∼ **WAN** 204-205 K 4
Gongojon o **AUS** 178-179 J 4
Gongoué o **G** 210-211 B 4
Gongpoquan o **VRC** 148-149 C 7
Gongshan o **VRC** 142-143 L 2
Gong Xian o **VRC** (HEN) 154-155 H 4
Gong Xian o **VRC** (SIC) 156-157 D 2
Gongzhuling o **VRC** 150-151 E 6
Gonikoppla o **IND** 140-141 F 4
Gono, togga ∼ **SP** 208-209 H 5
Gonohe o **J** 152-153 J 4
Gonoruwa o **CL** 140-141 J 7
Gönoura o **J** 152-153 D 7
Gonža o **RUS** 118-119 M 9
Gonzales o **USA** (LA) 44-45 M 4
Gonzales o **USA** (TX) 44-45 J 5
Gonzáles, Río o **PY** 76-77 H 2
Gonzales Moreno o **RA** 78-79 H 3
Gonzáles Suares o **PE** 64-65 E 3
González o **MEX** 50-51 K 6
Gonzanamá o **EC** 64-65 C 4
Goobang Creek ∼ **AUS** 180-181 J 2
Gooch Range ▲ **AUS** 176-177 C 1
Goode, Mount ▲ **ARK** 16 G 13
Goodenough, Cape ▲ **ARK** 16 G 13
Goodenough Bay ≈ 183 F 5
Goodenough Island ∩ **PNG** 183 F 5
Goodenough Land ∩ **GRØ** 26-27 I 7
Goodeve o **CDN** 34-35 G 5
Good Hope Plantation o · **JA** 54-55 G 5
Goodhouse o **ZA** 220-221 D 4
Gooding o **USA** 40-41 G 4
Goodland o **USA** 42-43 G 6
Goodlands o **MS** 224 C 7
Goodlettsville o **USA** 48-49 E 1
Goodnews Mining Camp o **USA** 22-23 J 3
Goodooga o **AUS** 178-179 J 5
Goodparla o **AUS** 172-173 L 2
Goodpaster River ∼ **USA** 20-21 S 4
Goodrich Bank ≃ 166-167 F 7
Goodsoil o **CDN** 32-33 Q 4
Good Spirit Lake o **CDN** 34-35 S 5
Goodwin o **CDN** 32-33 L 4
Goold Island ∩ **AUS** 174-175 J 6
Goole o **GB** 90-91 F 5
Googlowi o **AUS** 180-181 H 2
Goolwa o **AUS** 180-181 E 3
Goomadeer River ∼ **AUS** 174-175 B 3
Goomalling o **AUS** 176-177 D 5
Goomeri o **AUS** 178-179 M 4
Goondiwindi o **AUS** 178-179 L 5
Goongarrie, National Park ⊥ **AUS** 176-177 F 4
Goonyella Mine o **AUS** 178-179 K 1
Goorly, Lake o **AUS** 176-177 D 5
Goornong o **AUS** 180-181 H 4
Goose Bay o **CDN** (BC) 32-33 G 6
Goose Bay o **CDN** (NFL) 38-39 O 2
Gooseberry River ∼ **USA** 42-43 C 3
Goose Creek o **CDN** 34-35 J 3
Goose Creek o **USA** (SC) 48-49 H 3
Goose Lake o **CDN** 34-35 G 5
Goose Lake o **USA** 40-41 D 5
Goose River ∼ **CDN** 32-33 M 4
Goosport o **USA** 44-45 L 4
Gooty o **IND** 140-141 G 3
Gopalganj o **IND** 142-143 D 3
Gopichettipalaiyam o **IND** 140-141 G 5
Goplo, Jezioro o **PL** 92-93 P 2
Goppe Bazar o **MYA** 142-143 H 5
Gô Quao o **VN** 158-159 H 6
Gör o **AFG** 134-135 K 1
Goradiz o **AZ** 128-129 M 3
Goragorskij o **RUS** 126-127 F 6
Gorahun o **WAL** 202-203 E 6
Goraici, Kepulauan ∩ **RI** 164-165 K 4
Goja Kalwaria o **PL** 92-93 Q 3
Goram, Tanjung ▲ **RI** 164-165 H 4
Goran, Île de la ∩ **AUS** 178-179 L 6
Goranlega o **SP** 212-213 H 4
Gorantla o **IND** 140-141 G 4
Goräzde o **BIH** 100-101 G 3
Gorbea o **RCH** 78-79 C 5
Gorbi ∼ **RUS** 120-121 G 4
Gorbiačin o **RUS** 108-109 X 8
Gorbica o **RUS** 118-119 J 9
Gorbilok ∼ **RUS** 116-117 G 6
Gorbita ∼ **RUS** 108-109 o 5
Gorbovy, ostrova ∩ **RUS** 108-109 H 4
Gorbyl' ∼ **RUS** 122-123 G 6
Gorda, Punta ▲ **NIC** 52-53 C 4
Gorda, Punta ▲ **RCH** 70-71 B 6
Gorda Cay ∩ **BS** 54-55 G 1
Gördes ★ **TR** 128-129 B 3
Gore o **USA** (AK) 20-21 U 2
Gore o **USA** (NE) 42-43 F 4
Gore, Isla ∩ **RCH** 80 F 7
Gordon, Lake o **AUS** 180-181 J 7
Gordon Downs o **AUS** 172-173 H 4
Gordon Lake o **CDN** (ALB) 32-33 P 3
Gordon Lake o **CDN** (NWT) 30-31 N 4

Gordon River ∼ **CDN** 30-31 Z 3
Gordon's Bay o **ZA** 220-221 D 7
Gordonsville o **USA** 46-47 J 6
Gordonvale o **USA** 174-175 H 5
Gorè o **ETH** 208-209 B 4
Goré o **TCH** 206-207 C 5
Gore Bay o 24-25 d 7
Gorée, Île o ∼··· **SN** 202-203 B 2
Gorelaja Sopka, vulkan ▲ **RUS** 120-121 S 7
Göreme o ··· **TR** 128-129 F 3
Gori o **GE** 126-127 F 7
Goricy o **RUS** 94-95 P 3
Gori Hills ▲ **WAL** 202-203 E 6
Gorinchem o **NL** 92-93 H 3
Goris o **AR** 128-129 M 3
Gorizia o **I** 100-101 E 2
Gorjačegorsk o **RUS** 114-115 U 7
Čoukár o **IR** 134-135 C 1
Gorjačevodskij o **RUS** 126-127 E 5
Gorjačij Ključ o **RUS** 126-127 C 5
Gorjaščaia, vulkan ▲ **RUS** 122-123 R 5
Gorjun ∼ **RUS** 122-123 G 3
Gorka, mys ▲ **RUS** 120-121 R 3
Gor'kaja Balka < **RUS** 126-127 F 5
Gorkij = Nižnij Novgorod ☆ **RUS** 94-95 S 3
Gor'kij = Nižnij Novgorod ☆ ·· **RUS** 94-95 S 3
Gor'koe, ozero o **RUS** 124-125 M 2
Gor'ko-Pereščečnoe, ozero o **RUS** 124-125 M 3
Gor'kovskoe o **RUS** 114-115 N 7
Gorkovskoe Vodohranilišče ∼ Gor'kovskoe vodohranilišče < **RUS** 94-95 S 3
Gorlice o · **PL** 92-93 Q 4
Görlitz o · **D** 92-93 N 3
Gorlovka = Horlivka o **UA** 102-103 L 3
Gôrmać o **AFG** 136-137 H 7
Gorman o **USA** 40-41 E 8
Gornaja Ob' ∼ **RUS** 114-115 N 2
Goma Mitropolia o **BG** 102-103 D 6
Gornjackij o **RUS** 102-103 M 3
Gornjak o **RUS** 124-125 N 2
Gorno-Altajsk ☆ **RUS** 124-125 O 3
Gorno-Altaj = Gornyj Altaj, Respublika □ **RUS** 124-125 P 3
Gornostaj o **RUS** 122-123 G 5
Gornoslinkino o **RUS** 114-115 K 5
Gornovodnoe o **RUS** 122-123 J 5
Gornozavodsk o **RUS** (PRM) 96-97 L 4
Gornozavodsk o **RUS** 122-123 K 5
Gornyj Altaj, Respublika ■ **RUS** 124-125 P 3
Gornyj o **RUS** (HBR) 122-123 G 3
Gornyj o **RUS** (NVS) 114-115 R 7
Gornyj ☆ **RUS** (SAR) 96-97 F 8
Goro o **ETH** 208-209 E 5
Goroch'an ▲ **ETH** 208-209 C 4
Gorodec o **RUS** 94-95 S 3
Gorodeck o **RUS** 88-89 S 5
Gorodišče o **RUS** 96-97 D 7
Gorodok, Lesnoj = Nižnij-Čir 118-119 F 10
Gorodovikovsk o **RUS** 102-103 M 4
Gorogoro o **RI** 164-165 K 4
Goroh, Tanjung ▲ **RI** 162-163 F 5
Gorohovec o **RUS** 94-95 S 3
Goroka ☆ **PNG** 183 C 3
Gorom o **AUS** 180-181 F 4
Gorom-Gorom o **BF** 202-203 K 2
Gorona, Isla ∩ **CO** 60-61 D 3
Gorong, Kepulauan ∩ **RI** 166-167 F 4
Gorong, Pulau ∩ **RI** 166-167 F 3
Gorongosa ▲ **MOC** (Sof) 218-219 H 4
Gorongosa ▲ **MOC** (Sof) 218-219 H 4
Gorongosa, Parque Nacional de ⊥ **MOC** 218-219 H 4
Gorongosa, Rio ∼ **MOC** 218-219 H 5
Gorontalo o **RI** 164-165 H 3
Gorontalo, Teluk ≈ 164-165 H 3
Goronyo o **WAN** 198-199 B 6
Goro ☆ **ETH** 208-209 E 5
Gorou, Djebel ▲ **DZ** 190-191 O 4
Goroumbou o **RMM** 202-203 K 2
Gorovatka o **RUS** 122-123 J 5
Gorra, Tanjung ▲ **RI** 164-165 H 3
Görsečnoe o **RUS** 102-103 L 2
Gort = An Gort o **IRL** 90-91 C 5
Göryân o **AFG** 134-135 J 2
Gorzów Wielkopolski ★ · **PL** 92-93 N 2
Goschen Strait ≈ 183 F 6
Gosford-Woy Woy o · **AUS** 180-181 L 2
Goshen o **USA** 46-47 F 5
Goshogawara o **J** 152-153 J 4
Goshute Indian Reservation ⋏ **USA** 40-41 G 6
Goslar o · **D** 92-93 L 3
Gospić o **HR** 100-101 E 2
Gossas o **SN** 202-203 B 2
Gosselies o **USA** 184 I a 1
Gossi o **RMM** 202-203 K 2
Gossinga o **SUD** 206-207 G 4
Gostivar o **MK** 100-101 H 4
Gostynin o **PL** 92-93 P 2
Goszapovednik o **KA** 126-127 N 5
Gozare o **AFG** 134-135 K 1
Goz-Beida o **TCH** 198-199 K 6
Gozha Co o **VRC** 144-145 G 5
Gota o **ETH** 208-209 E 4
Göta älv ∼ **S** 86-87 F 8
Götaland o **S** 86-87 F 8
Göteborg o · **S** 86-87 E 8
Gotel Mountains ▲ **WAN** 204-205 J 5
Gotenba o **J** 152-153 N 7
Gotera = San Francisco ★ **ES** 52-53 K 5
Gotha o · **D** 92-93 L 3
Goth Ahmad o **PK** 134-135 M 6

Grabouw o **ZA** 220-221 D 7
Grace (South), Lake o **AUS** 176-177 E 6
Gracefield o **CDN** 38-39 F 5
Graceville o **USA** 42-43 J 3
Gračevka ☆ **RUS** 96-97 H 7
Gracho Cardoso o **BR** 68-69 K 7
Gracias ☆ **HN** 52-53 K 4
Gracias a Dios, Cabo de ▲ **HN** 54-55 D 7
Gradaús o **BR** 68-69 C 5
Gradaus, Serra dos ▲ **BR** 68-69 C 6
Grado, Embalse de El < **E** 98-99 H 3
Gradsko o **MK** 100-101 H 4
Grady o **USA** (AR) 44-45 M 2
Grady o **USA** (NM) 44-45 F 2
Grady Harbour o **CDN** 38-39 Q 2
Grady Island o **CDN** 38-39 Q 2
Gradedefjorden ≈ **GRØ** 28-29 P 5
Grafton o **AUS** 178-179 N 5
Grafton o **USA** (IL) 46-47 C 6
Grafton o **USA** (ND) 42-43 J 1
Grafton o **USA** (NH) 46-47 N 4
Grafton o **USA** (WV) 46-47 H 6
Gragnon Lake o **CDN** 30-31 O 5
Graham o **CDN** 34-35 L 6
Graham, Mount ▲ **USA** 44-45 C 3
Graham Creek ∼ **USA** 48-49 F 1
Graham Island o **CDN** (BC) 32-33 D 5
Graham Island o **CDN** (NWT) 24-25 a 2
Graham Lake o **CDN** 32-33 N 9
Graham Moore, Cape ▲ **CDN** 24-25 J 4
Graham Moore Bay ≈ 24-25 V 3
Grahamstad = Grahamstown o **ZA** 220-221 H 6
Grahamstown = Grahamstad o **ZA** 220-221 H 6
Grahovo ☆ **RUS** 96-97 H 5
Gråns ∼ **GRØ** 28-29 V 4
Grain Coast ∪ **LB** 202-203 E 7
Graines, Rivière-aux- o **CDN** 38-39 M 3
Grainfield o **USA** 42-43 G 6
Grajagan o **RI** 168 B 7
Grajagan, Teluk ≈ 168 B 7
Grajaú o **BR** 68-69 E 4
Grajaú, Rio ∼ **BR** 68-69 F 3
Grajewo o **PL** 92-93 R 2
Grajvoron o **RUS** 102-103 J 2
Gramado · **BR** 74-75 E 7
Gramilla o **RA** 76-77 E 4
Grammos ▲ **GR** 100-101 H 4
Gramoteino o **RUS** 114-115 T 7
Gramphoo o **IND** 138-139 F 3
Grampianfjella ▲ **N** 84-85 G 3
Grampian Mountains ▲ **GB** 90-91 E 3
Grampians National Park ⊥ **AUS** 180-181 G 4
Gramsh ☆ **AL** 100-101 H 4
Granaatboskolk o **ZA** 220-221 D 5
Granada o **CO** (ANT) 60-61 D 4
Granada o **CO** (MET) 60-61 E 6
Granada o ···· **E** 98-99 F 6
Granada ☆ ·· **NIC** 52-53 B 6
Granada o **USA** 42-43 F 6
Granada II, Cerro ▲ **RA** 76-77 D 2
Gran Altiplanicie Central ∪ **RA** 80 E 4
Gran Bahía ∼ **DOM** 54-55 L 5
Gran Bajo del Gualicho ∪ **RA** 78-79 G 6
Gran Bajo de San Julián ∪ **RA** 80 F 4
Granby o **CDN** 38-39 H 4
Granby o **USA** 42-43 D 5
Gran Canaria ∩ · **E** 188-189 D 7
Gran Chaco ⊥ **RA** 76-77 F 3
Grand Bahama Island ∩ **BS** 54-55 F 1
Grand Ballon, le ▲ **F** 90-91 L 8
Grand Banks of Newfoundland ≃ 6-7 J 4
Grand-Bassam o **CI** 202-203 J 7
Grand Bend o **CDN** 38-39 D 7
Grand Bérébi o **CI** 202-203 G 7
Grand-Bérébi o **CI** 202-203 G 7
Grand-Bourg o **F** 56 E 4
Grand Bruit o **CDN** 38-39 P 5
Grandby, Lake o **USA** 42-43 D 5
Grand Caicos ∩ **GB** 54-55 K 4
Grand Canal ∼ **IRL** 90-91 D 5
Grand Canyon o **USA** (AZ) 40-41 H 7
Grand Canyon ∪ **USA** 40-41 H 7
Grand Canyon Caverns · **USA** 40-41 H 8
Grand Canyon National Park ⊥ ···· **USA** 40-41 H 7
Grand Canyon of the Liard ∪ **CDN** 30-31 G 6
Grand Cayman ∩ **GB** 54-55 C 5
Grand Centre o **CDN** 32-33 P 4
Grand Cess o **LB** 202-203 F 7
Grand-Combe, la o **F** 90-91 K 9
Grand Coulee o **USA** 40-41 E 2
Grand Coulee Dam < **USA** 40-41 E 2
Grande, Arroyo ∼ **RA** 78-79 K 4
Grande, Arroyo ∼ **ROU** 78-79 J 2
Grande, Bahía ≈ 80 F 5
Grande, Cayo ∩ **C** 54-55 F 4
Grande, Ciénaga o **CO** 60-61 D 3
Grande, Corredeira ∼ **BR** 66-67 K 2
Grande, Cuchilla ▲ **ROU** 78-79 K 2
Grande, Ilha ∼ **BR** 72-73 H 7
Grande, La o **USA** 40-41 E 3
Grande, Lago o **BR** 66-67 G 4
Grande, Lago o **RA** 80 D 3
Grande, Monte ▲ **BR** 70-71 J 6
Grande, Playa ∼ **DOM** 54-55 L 5
Grande, Ponta ▲ **CV** 222-203 B 9
Grande, Ponta ▲ **BR** 64-65 D 9
Grande, Río ∼ **BOL** 70-71 G 4
Grande, Río ∼ **BR** 68-69 G 7
Grande, Río ∼ **BR** 72-73 H 2
Grande, Río ∼ **BR** 72-73 F 6
Grande, Río ∼ **BR** 72-73 F 6
Grande, Río ∼ **BR** 72-73 F 6
Grande, Río ∼ **GCA** 52-53 K 4
Grande, Río ∼ **PE** 64-65 E 9
Grande, Río ∼ **RA** 76-77 D 4
Grande, Río ∼ **RA** 76-77 D 4
Grande, Río ∼ **RA** 78-79 D 4
Grande, Río ∼ **RA** 80 F 6

Halkanskij hrebet ▲ RUS 120-121 L 3
Halke Shan ∩ VRC 146-147 E 4
Halkett, Cape ▲ USA 20-21 O 1
Hálki ∩ GR 100-101 L 6
Halkida o GR 100-101 L 5
Halkidiki ⊥ GR 100-101 J 4
Halkirk o CDN 32-33 O 5
Halland ∩ S 86-87 F 8
Hallandale o USA 48-49 H 7
Halláníyät, al- ∩ Y 132-133 K 5
Hallasan o ▲ ROK 150-151 F 11
Hallasan National Park ⊥ · ROK 150-151 F 11
Hall Bassin ≈ 26-27 T 3
Hall Beach o CDN 24-25 f 6
Hall Bredning ≈ 26-27 n 8
Halle (Saale) o · D 92-93 L 3
Hallein o A 92-93 M 5
Hallen o S 86-87 G 5
Hallersville o USA 22-23 S 3
Hallett o AUS 180-181 E 2
Halliday o USA 42-43 J 2
Halliday Lake o CDN 30-31 P 5
Hall Indian Reservation, Fort ⋊ USA 40-41 H 4
Hallingdal ∪ N 86-87 D 6
Hallingdalselvi ∩ N 86-87 D 6
Hallingskarvet ▲ N 86-87 C 6
Hall in Tirol o A 92-93 L 5
Hall Island ∩ FSM 13 G 2
Hall Island ∩ USA 112-113 Y 6
Hall Lake o CDN 24-25 f 6
Hall Land □ GRØ 26-27 U 3
Hällnäs o S 86-87 J 4
Hallock o USA 42-43 J 1
Hall Peninsula ∪ CDN 36-37 Q 3
Hall Point ▲ AUS 174-175 E 2
Halls Creek o AUS 180-181 G 4
Halls Gap o AUS 180-181 G 4
Hallson o USA 42-43 J 1
Hallyŏ Haesang National Park ⊥ · ROK 150-151 G 10
Halmahera, Pulau ∩ RI 164-165 L 4
Halmahera Sea = Halmahera, Laut ≈ RI 166-167 E 1
Halmerto, ozero ⊂ RUS 108-109 N 7
Halmstad o S 86-87 F 8
Hálol o IND 138-139 D 8
Halong o RI 166-167 E 3
Halšany o BY 94-95 K 4
Halstad o USA 42-43 J 2
Haltom City o USA 44-45 J 3
Halturin o RUS 96-97 F 4
Halura, Pulau ∩ RI 168 E 8
Halvad o IND 138-139 C 8
Halverson Ridge ▲ CDN 32-33 L 3
Halvmåneøya ∩ N 84-85 N 4
Halwán al-∩ RUS 120-121 H 2
Halza Sogootyn davaa ▲ MAU 148-149 D 3
Ham ∼ NAM 220-221 D 4
Ham o TCH 206-207 B 3
Hamab o NAM 220-221 D 4
Hamâd, al- ⊥ KSA 130-131 F 2
Hamada o J 152-153 E 7
Hamadán o IR 134-135 C 1
Hamadán ⊞ IR 134-135 C 1
Hamaguir o DZ 188-189 K 5
Hamäh ∗ SYR 128-129 G 5
Hamamah o LAR 192-193 J 1
Hamamatsu o J 152-153 J 3
Hamamatsu o J 152-153 G 7
Haman o CAM 204-205 K 6
Hamar ∗ N 86-87 E 6
Hamar, al- o KSA 130-131 K 6
Hamar-Daban, hrebet ▲ RUS 116-117 L 10
Hamasaka o J 152-153 F 7
Hamâsin, al- o KSA 132-133 D 3
Hamáta, Ğabal ▲ ET 194-195 G 5
Hamba o COM 222-223 C 4
Hambantota o CL 140-141 J 7
Hambaparoing o RI 168 E 7
Hamberg o USA 42-43 H 2
Hambidge Conservation Park ⊥ AUS 180-181 D 2
Hamborgerland ∩ GRØ 28-29 O 4
Hamburg ∩ · D 92-93 L 2
Hamburg o SME 62-63 G 3
Hamburg o USA (AR) 44-45 M 3
Hamburg o USA (IA) 42-43 K 5
Hamburg o USA (NY) 46-47 J 4
Hamburg o ZA 220-221 H 6
Hamchang o VRC 144-145 B 4
Hamd, Wâdi al- ∩ KSA 130-131 E 5
Hämeenlinna o FIN 88-89 H 6
Hamelin o AUS 176-177 C 3
Hamelin, Mount ▲ CDN 24-25 P 3
Hamelin Pool ≈ 176-177 B 3
Hameln o · D 92-93 K 2
Hamen Wan ≈ VRC 156-157 K 5
Hamer Koke o ETH 208-209 F 5
Hamero Hadad o ETH 208-209 F 5
Hamersley o AUS 172-173 C 6
Hamersley Lakes o AUS 176-177 E 5
Hamersley Range ▲ AUS 172-173 C 6
Hamersley Range National Park ⊥ ·· AUS 172-173 C 6
Hamğã, al- o KSA 130-131 H 5
Hamhung o DVR 150-151 F 8
Hami o VRC 146-147 L 4
Hämi, al- o Y 132-133 F 6
Hamid o SUD 200-201 E 2
Hamid, Qal'at o IRQ 128-129 L 6
Hamidiye o SYR 128-129 F 5
Hamidiye o IR 134-135 C 3
Hamilton o AUS (TAS) 180-181 H 7
Hamilton o AUS (VIC) 180-181 G 4
Hamilton o CDN 38-39 D 7
Hamilton o GB 54-55 L 1
Hamilton o NZ 182 E 2
Hamilton o USA (AK) 20-21 J 5
Hamilton ○ USA (AL) 48-49 E 2

Hamilton o USA (MO) 42-43 K 6
Hamilton o USA (MT) 40-41 G 2
Hamilton o USA (TX) 44-45 H 4
Hamilton o USA (WA) 40-41 D 1
Hamilton Bank ≈ 6-7 D 3
Hamilton Creek ∩ AUS 176-177 M 3
Hamilton Downs o AUS 176-177 M 1
Hamilton Hotel o AUS 178-179 F 2
Hamilton Island ∩ AUS 174-175 K 7
Hamilton River ∼ AUS 178-179 F 2
Hamilton Sound ≈ 38-39 I R 4
Hamim o UAE 132-133 J 2
Hamina o FIN 88-89 J 6
Hamiota o CDN 34-35 F 5
Hami Pendi ⊥ VRC 146-147 L 4
Hâmir o Y 132-133 F 6
Hâmir, Wâdi ∼ IRQ 128-129 J 7
Hâmir, Wâdi ∼ KSA 130-131 G 2
Hamir o Y 132-133 F 6
Hami Rotoki ∼ SUD 200-201 B 6
Hamirpur o IND 142-143 B 3
Hamis al-Bahr o KSA 132-133 B 4
Hamis Mušait o KSA 132-133 C 4
Hamis Mutair o KSA 132-133 C 4
Hamlen Bay ≈ 36-37 Q 3
Hamlet, Mount ▲ USA 20-21 H 2
Hankey o ZA 220-221 G 6
Hamlin o USA 44-45 G 3
Hâm Luông ∼ VN 158-159 J 5
Hamm o · D 92-93 J 3
Hammâm, al- o IRQ 128-129 L 7
Hammâm 'Alï o Y 132-133 D 6
Hammamet o TN 190-191 H 2
Hammamet, Golfe de ≈ 190-191 H 2
Hammâm-Lif ∗ TN 190-191 H 2
Hamman, Oued ∼ DZ 190-191 C 3
Hammer, Kap ▲ GRØ 28-29 Z 2
Hammerdal o S 86-87 G 5
Hammerfest o ∗ N 86-87 L 1
Hammern ∼ GRØ 26-27 g 4
Hammock, Kap ▲ GRØ 26-27 d 2
Hammond o USA (IN) 46-47 E 5
Hammond o USA (LA) 44-45 M 4
Hammond Island ∩ AUS 183 B 6
Hammonton o USA 46-47 L 6
Hamnöya o RUS 84-85 U 3
Hampden o CDN 38-39 Q 4
Hampenanperak o RI 162-163 C 3
Hampi o IND 140-141 G 3
Hampton o CDN 38-39 M 6
Hampton o USA (AR) 44-45 L 3
Hampton o USA (IA) 42-43 L 4
Hampton o USA (NH) 46-47 N 4
Hampton o USA (SC) 48-49 H 3
Hampton o USA (VA) 48-49 K 2
Hampton Butte ▲ USA 40-41 D 4
Hamra ∼ RUS 118-119 J 7
Hamra o SUD 206-207 J 3
Hamrâ', al- o OM 132-133 K 2
Hamran, Bi'r o IRQ 128-129 K 5
Hamrânge o S 86-87 H 6
Hamrat al-Wuzz o SUD 200-201 E 5
Hamrat as-Shaykh o SUD 200-201 C 5
Hamrin, Ğabal ▲ IRQ 128-129 L 5
Hamsara ∼ RUS 116-117 H 9
Hams Fork ∼ USA 40-41 J 5
Hàm Thuan o VN 158-159 K 5
Hamúd, 'Ain o IRQ 128-129 J 2
Hamuku o RI 166-167 H 3
Hâmún-e Ğaz Mûrïân o IR 134-135 H 5
Hâmún-i-Lora o PK 134-135 L 4
Hamyski o RUS 126-127 D 5
Hana o USA 48-49 D 7
Hänäbäd o AFG 134-135 L 6
Hanabanilla, Presa del < · C 54-55 G 3
Hanahan o PNG 184 I b 1
Hanak o TR 128-129 J 2
Hanâkiya, al- o KSA 130-131 G 5
Hanâkiya, Wâdi al- ∼ KSA 130-131 G 5
Hän al-Bağdâdï o IRQ 128-129 K 6
Hanalei o USA 48-49 C 6
Hän al-Mahâwïl o IRQ 128-129 L 6
Hà Nam o VN 156-157 D 6
Hanamaki o J 152-153 J 5
Hanapepe o USA 48-49 C 7
Hänaqin ∗ IRQ 128-129 L 5
Hanarasalja, mys ▲ RUS 108-109 P 6
Hänäqir o RUS 108-109 P 6
Hänäşir o KSA 132-133 C 5
Hänäşir o SYR 128-129 G 5
Hän Bełen o IR 134-135 D 6
Hanbogd = Ihbulag o MAU 148-149 G 6
Hapčeranga o RUS 118-119 F 11
Hapica, Bol'šaja ∼ RUS 120-121 T 6
Hapo o RI 164-165 L 2
Hapolio o USA 142-143 H 2
Happy o USA 44-45 G 2
Happy Camp o USA 40-41 C 5
Happy Jack o USA 40-41 J 8
Happy Valley o AUS 178-179 G 4
Happy-Valley-Goose Bay o CDN 38-39 O 2
Hapsal = Haapsalu ∗ EST 94-95 H 2
Haptagaj o RUS 116-117 N 8
Hâpur o IND 138-139 O 5
Haql, al- o KSA 130-131 D 3
Harabali o RUS 96-97 E 10
Harâbe-ye Tarâqú ∴· AFG 134-135 J 3
Harabyl ∼ RUS 110-111 H 3
Harad o KSA 132-133 L 5
Hârâda o KSA 130-131 K 6
Haradok o BY 94-95 L 4
Haraga o KSA 132-133 C 5
Haragei o PNG 183 B 4
Harajaha ∼ RUS 88-89 Y 3
Harald Moltke, Kap ▲ GRØ 28-29 N 2
Haramachi o J 152-153 J 6
Harami, pereval ⌃ RUS 126-127 G 6
Harampur ∼ RUS 114-115 P 2

Hanga Roa o RCH 78-79 B 2
Hanger Wenz ∼ ETH 208-209 C 4
Hanggin Houqi o VRC 154-155 E 1
Hanggin Qi o VRC 154-155 F 2
Hangingstone River ∼ CDN 32-33 P 3
Hanglong o VRC 156-157 E 4
Hangö o ∗∗ FIN 88-89 G 7
Hangu o PK 138-139 C 3
Hangzhou o VRC 156-157 K 4
Hangzhou Wan ≈ 154-155 M 6
Hanhöhij o MAU 148-149 L 4
Hanhöhij Nuruu ▲ MAU 116-117 F 11
Hani o RUS 118-119 J 7
Hani o RUS 118-119 K 7
Hani ∗ TR 128-129 H 4
Haniá o GR 100-101 K 7
Hanid o KSA 130-131 F 1
Hanišal al-Kabir ∼ Y 132-133 C 7
Hanja o ANG 212-213 E 7
Han Jiang ∼ VRC 156-157 K 5
Hanka ∗ US 136-137 G 4
Hanka, ozero o RUS 122-123 E 6
Hankendi = Khankendi ∗ AZ 128-129 M 3
Hankinson o USA 42-43 J 2
Hanko = Hangö o ∗∗ FIN 88-89 G 7
Hanksville o USA 40-41 J 6
Hanlar = Xanlar o AZ 128-129 M 2
Hanley o CDN 34-35 C 5
Hanmer Springs o NZ 182 D 5
Hän Muğidda o IRQ 128-129 K 6
Hann, Mount ▲ AUS 172-173 E 3
Hanna o CDN 32-33 P 6
Hannah Bay ≈ 38-39 C 3
Hannibal o USA 46-47 C 6
Hannik < SUD 200-201 F 3
Hannja ∼ RUS 110-111 L 7
Hann Münden o · D 92-93 K 3
Hannover ∗ · D 92-93 K 2
Hann River ∼ AUS 172-173 H 4
Hann River ∼ AUS 174-175 G 4
Hanöbukten ≈ 86-87 G 9
Hà Nội ∗ VN 156-157 D 6
Hanoi = Hà Nội ∗ ·· VN 156-157 D 6
Hanover o DR 38-39 D 6
Hanover o ZA 220-221 G 5
Hanover = Hannover ∗ · D 92-93 K 2
Hanover, Isla ∩ RCH 80 C 5
Hanover Road ∼ ZA 220-221 G 5
Hän Šaihún o SYR 128-129 G 5
Hänsdína o IND 142-143 E 3
Hanse o IND 138-139 N 3
Hansenfjella ▲ ARK 16 G 6
Hanshou o VRC 156-157 G 2
Han Shui ∼ VRC 154-155 H 6
Hänsi o IND 138-139 E 5
Hansine Lake o CDN 36-37 G 2
Hanskoe, ozero o RUS 102-103 L 4
Hans Meyer Range ▲ PNG 183 G 3
Hanson, Lake o AUS 178-179 D 3
Hanson River ∼ AUS 174-175 B 7
Hänsot o IND 138-139 D 9
Hantas Tavsens Iskappe ⊂ GRØ 26-27 f 2
Hanstholm o DK 86-87 D 8
Hantai o VRC 156-157 G 2
Hantajka ∼ RUS 108-109 W 7
Hantajskoe vodohranilišče o RUS 108-109 X 7
Hantamsberg ▲ ZA 220-221 D 5
Hantengri Feng ▲ KA 146-147 E 4
Hantoukoura o BF 202-203 L 3
Hanty-Mansijsk ∗ RUS 114-115 K 4
Hantzsch River ∼ CDN 28-29 F 2
Hanuj gol ∼ MAU 148-149 E 3
Hanumana o IND 142-143 C 3
Hanumängarh o IND 138-139 E 5
Hanyin o VRC 154-155 F 5
Hanyuan o VRC 156-157 E 2
Hanzhong o VRC 154-155 E 5
Hän Yûnis o AUT 130-131 C 2
Hän Zür o IRQ 128-129 L 5
Haora o IND 142-143 F 4
Haotan o VRC 154-155 F 4
Haouach, Ouadi ∼ TCH 198-199 K 4
Haoud El Hamra o DZ 190-191 E 5
Haouich o TCH 198-199 K 6
Haouza o MA 188-189 F 7
Hapai o SOL 184 I c 3
Hapakant o MYA 142-143 K 3
Haparanda o S 86-87 M 4
Hapčaganahta, krjaž ▲ RUS 110-111 H 2

Hârânaq o IR 134-135 F 2
Hârânaq, Kûh-e ▲ IR 134-135 F 2
Haranor o RUS 118-119 H 10
Harapa o SOL 184 I b 2
Harappa o · PK 138-139 D 4
Harare ∗ · ZW 218-219 F 3
Harasavèj ∼ RUS 108-109 M 6
Harat ∩ ER 200-201 J 4
Harât o IR 134-135 F 3
Harau Canyon · RI 162-163 D 5
Hara-Tas, krjaž ▲ RUS 108-109 e 6
Hara-Tumus, poluostrov ∪ RUS 110-111 H 3
Harau View o JA 54-55 G 6
Harbutt Range ▲ AUS 172-173 C 7
Harcourt o AUS 180-181 H 4
Harcourt o CDN 38-39 M 5
Harda o IND 138-139 F 8
Hardali o IND 140-141 G 4
Hardangerfjorden ≈ 86-87 C 6
Hardangerjøkulen ⊂ N 86-87 C 6
Hardangervidda ▲ N 86-87 C 6
Hardangervidda nasjonalpark ⊥ N 86-87 C 6
Hard Bargin o BS 54-55 G 1
Hardeeville o USA 48-49 H 3
Harderwijk o NL 92-93 H 2
Hardey River ∼ AUS 172-173 C 7
Hardin o USA (IL) 46-47 C 6
Hardin o USA (MT) 42-43 D 3
Harding o ZA 220-221 J 5
Hardinge Bay ≈ 24-25 K 2
Harding River ∼ AUS 172-173 C 6
Hardinsburg o USA 46-47 F 6
Hardisty o CDN 32-33 P 5
Hardisty Lake o CDN 30-31 K 3
Hardoi o IND 142-143 B 3
Hardwick o USA (GA) 48-49 G 3
Hardwick o USA (VT) 46-47 M 3
Hardwicke Bay ≈ 180-181 D 3
Hardy o AUS 44-45 M 1
Hardy, Península ∪ RCH 80 F 7
Hardy Bay ≈ 24-25 O 3
Hardy Lake o CDN 30-31 P 3
Hare Bay ≈ 38-39 Q 3
Hare Fiord ≈ 26-27 G 3
Hare Indian River ∼ CDN 30-31 F 2
Hare ∩ · GRØ 28-29 N 1
Härer ∗ ETH 208-209 F 4
Härergë ∩ ETH 208-209 E 4
Härer Wildlife Sanctuary ⊥ ETH 208-209 F 4
Häresäbäd o IR 136-137 C 6
Hareto o ETH 208-209 C 4
Harfa, al- o Y 132-133 D 5
Harğ, al- o KSA 132-133 K 5
Hargele o ETH 208-209 F 4
Hargeysa ∗ SP 208-209 G 4
Hargrave River ∼ CDN 34-35 G 3
Har Hu o VRC 146-147 N 6
Hari ∼ RU 162-163 F 6
Harïa o E 188-189 E 6
Harib o Y 132-133 D 6
Haribomo o RMM 196-197 J 6
Haribongo, Lac o RMM 196-197 J 6
Haridwar o· IND 138-139 G 5
Harihar o IND 140-141 F 3
Harihari o NZ 182 C 5
Hä Rikät o OM 132-133 J 4
Harilek ∼ RI 162-163 F 6
Härim ∗ SYR 128-129 G 5
Harima-nada ≈ 152-153 F 7
Harimkotan, ostrov ∩ RUS 122-123 Q 4
Haringhata ∼ BD 142-143 F 4
Haripad o IND 140-141 G 6
Haripur o PK 138-139 D 2
Hariri, Tall ∗ SYR 128-129 J 5
Harïrüd, Daryâ-ye ∼ AFG 134-135 K 1
Harïrüd, Daryâ-ye ∼ AFG 136-137 G 7
Harisal o IND 138-139 F 9
Härjedalen ⊥ S 86-87 F 5
Härk, Ğazïre-ye ∩ IR 134-135 D 4
Härkány o H 92-93 P 6
Harkidum o IND 138-139 G 4
Harkin Bay ≈ 36-37 K 2
Har'kov = Harkiv ∗ UA 102-103 K 3
Härkü, Ğazïre-ye ∩ IR 134-135 D 4
Harlan o USA (IA) 42-43 K 5
Harlan o USA (KY) 46-47 G 7
Harlan County Lake o USA 42-43 H 5
Harlem o USA 42-43 C 1
Harlin o AUS 178-179 M 4
Harlingen o· NL 92-93 H 2
Harlingen o USA 44-45 J 6
Harlovka o RUS (MUR) 88-89 O 2
Harlovka ∼ RUS 88-89 O 2
Harmanli o BG 102-103 D 7
Harmil ∩ ER 200-201 K 4
Harmonia o BR 76-77 J 6
Harmony o USA 46-47 O 3
Harnai o PK 138-139 B 4
Harney Basin · USA 40-41 E 4
Harney Lake o USA 40-41 E 4
Harney Peak ▲ USA 42-43 F 4
Härnösand ∗ S 86-87 H 5
Har nuur o MAU (HOV) 146-147 L 1
Har nuur o MAU (ZAV) 148-149 C 3
Haro o E 98-99 F 3
Haro ∼ PK 138-139 D 3
Haro o SP 212-213 H 3

Haro, Cabo ▲ MEX 50-51 D 4
Harobo o J 152-153 J 2
Harold Byrd Range ▲ ARK 16 E 0
Haroldswick o GB 90-91 G 1
Harovsk o RUS 94-95 R 2
Harovskaja grjada ▲ RUS 94-95 R 2
Harpanahalli o IND 140-141 F 3
Harper ∗ LB 202-203 G 7
Harper o USA (KS) 44-45 H 1
Harper o USA (OR) 40-41 F 4
Harper, Mount ▲ USA 20-21 T 4
Harper Creek ∼ CDN 30-31 M 6
Harpers Ferry National Historic Park ∴· USA 46-47 K 6
Harpin ∼ RUS 122-123 G 3
Harqin Qi o VRC 148-149 O 7
Harğûs ∩ KSA 130-131 L 4
Harrai o IND 138-139 G 8
Harran ∗ TR 128-129 H 4
Harraz-Djombo o TCH 198-199 G 6
Harbalah ∼ RUS 120-121 F 2
Harbel o LB 202-203 E 6
Harbin ∗ VRC 150-151 F 5
Harbor Beach o USA 46-47 G 4
Harbor Breton o CDN 38-39 I R 5
Harbour Deep o CDN 38-39 Q 3
Harbour View o JA 54-55 G 6
Harbutt Range ▲ AUS 172-173 C 7
Harricana, Rivière ∼ CDN 38-39 E 3
Harrigan, Cape ▲ CDN 36-37 T 7
Harriman o USA 48-49 F 2
Harrington o USA (DE) 46-47 L 6
Harrington o USA (WA) 40-41 E 2
Harrington Harbour o CDN 38-39 P 3
Harris o CDN 34-35 C 5
Harris, Lake o USA 48-49 H 6
Harris, Mount ▲ AUS 176-177 K 2
Harrisburg o USA (IL) 46-47 D 7
Harrisburg o USA (OR) 40-41 C 3
Harrisburg o USA (PA) 46-47 K 5
Harris Lake o AUS 176-177 G 5
Harrismith o ZA 220-221 J 4
Harrison o USA (AR) 44-45 L 1
Harrison o USA (MI) 46-47 F 3
Harrison o USA (NE) 42-43 F 4
Harrison o USA (OH) 46-47 F 6
Harrison, Cape ▲ CDN 36-37 V 7
Harrison Bay ≈ 20-21 O 1
Harrison Islands ∩ CDN 24-25 b 6
Harrison Lake o CDN 32-33 K 7
Harrisonville o USA 42-43 K 6
Harrisville o USA (MI) 46-47 G 4
Harrisville o USA (WV) 46-47 H 6
Harrodsburg o USA 46-47 F 6
Harrogate o CDN 32-33 M 6
Harrogate o· GB 90-91 G 4
Harrow o AUS 180-181 F 4
Harrowby Bay ≈ 24-25 H 5
Har Rüd ∼ IR 134-135 N 5
Harry Strunk Lake o USA 42-43 G 5
Harsâni o IND 138-139 C 7
Harse, mys ▲ RUS 108-109 P 6
Harsin o· IR 134-135 B 1
Harşıt Çayı ∼ TR 128-129 H 2
Harstad o N 86-87 H 2
Harsüd o IND 138-139 F 8
Harşûri o NE 128-129 L 7
Hart o USA 44-45 F 2
Hart, Cape ▲ AUS 180-181 D 3
Hart, Lake o AUS 176-177 D 6
Hart, Mount ▲ CDN 20-21 W 5
Har Tavor ∼ IL 130-131 D 1
Hartbeesfontein o ZA 220-221 H 3
Hart Dyke, Monte ▲ RCH 80 C 6
Hartbeestrivier ∼ ZA 220-221 E 4
Härteigen ▲ N 86-87 C 6
Hartford o USA (AL) 48-49 F 4
Hartford o USA (KY) 46-47 E 6
Hartford o USA (CT) 46-47 M 5
Hartford City o USA 46-47 F 6
Hartland o USA 46-47 H 6
Hartlepool o· GB 90-91 G 4
Hartley o USA 42-43 H 2
Hartley Safari Area ⊥ ZW 218-219 E 3
Hartmannberge ▲ NAM 216-217 B 8
Hart Mount o USA 34-35 T 4
Hart Mountain ▲ USA 40-41 E 4
Hart Mountain National Antelope Refuge · USA 40-41 E 4
Hartola o FIN 88-89 J 6
Harts ∼ CDN 20-21 W 4
Hartseer o NAM 216-217 D 10
Hartsel o USA 42-43 E 6
Hartselle o USA 48-49 E 2
Hartsville o USA 48-49 H 3
Hartsrivier ∼ ZA 220-221 G 3
Hartum, al- ∗ · · SUD 200-201 F 5
Hartwell o USA 48-49 G 2
Hartwell Lake < USA 48-49 G 2
Harty o CDN 34-35 D 6
Hartz Mountains ▲ CDN 24-25 e 4
Hatuhud o RI 166-167 C 6
Haruku, Pulau ∩ RI 166-167 E 3
Härûnâbâd o PK 138-139 D 4
Harur o IND 140-141 H 4
Har-Us ∼ MAU 146-147 L 1
Har Us nuur o MAU 146-147 L 1
Harut ∼ Y 132-133 H 5
Hârüt Rûd ∼ AFG 134-135 J 2
Harvest Home o AUS 174-175 J 7
Harvey o USA 46-47 D 4
Harvey o AUS 176-177 C 6
Harvey, Lake o USA 176-177 D 5
Harvey Junction o CDN 38-39 H 5
Harward Øer ∩ GRØ 26-27 R 5
Harwich o· GB 90-91 H 5
Harwood o USA 44-45 J 5
Harwood o· GB 90-91 H 6
Haryalah ∼ RUS 110-111 J 5
Haryn' ∼ BY 94-95 K 5
Harz ∩ · D 92-93 L 3
Hāš ⊗ IR 134-135 J 4
Hasâ' al- ⊥ KSA 130-131 K 4
Hasâ, Wâdi ∼ JOR 130-131 D 2
Hašaat o MAU 148-149 F 6
Haşäh o OM 132-133 K 4
Hasaka, al- ∗ SYR 128-129 J 4

Hasama o J 152-153 J 5
Hasan o RUS 122-123 D 7
Hasanäbäd o IR 134-135 E 3
Hasanäbäd o IR (ESF) 134-135 E 2
Hasanäbäd o IR (TEH) 136-137 B 7
Hasan al Halqim, Bi'r · LAR 192-193 J 1
Hasan Dağı ▲ TR 128-129 F 3
Hasankeyf o TR 128-129 J 2
Hasanparti o IND 138-139 G 10
Hasanpur o IND 138-139 G 5
Hasavjurt o RUS 126-127 G 6
Hasaweb ∼ NAM 220-221 C 2
Hasawïya Fauqäni o SYR 128-129 J 4
Hasenpoth = Aizpute o· · LV 94-95 G 3
Hashab o SUD 200-201 B 6
Hasi, al- o Y 132-133 F 6
Hașib, Abú I- ∗ IRQ 130-131 K 2
Hasil, Pulau ∩ RI 164-165 L 4
Häsilpur o PK 138-139 D 4
Häšimiya, al- ∗ IRQ 128-129 L 6
Haskanit o SUD 206-207 H 3
Haskell o USA 44-45 H 3
Haskovo o BG 102-103 D 7
Hašm ad-Qibi ⊥ KSA 130-131 K 5
Hasmat 'Umar, Bi'r < SUD 200-201 G 2
Hasnäbäd o IND 142-143 F 4
Haşr, Ğazirat ∩ KSA 132-133 B 4
Hassa ∗ TR 128-129 G 5
Hassan o IND 140-141 G 4
Hassan-Addakhil, Barrage < MA 188-189 J 5
Hassane, Hassi < MA 188-189 K 5
Hassayampa River ∼ USA 40-41 H 9
Hassela o S 86-87 H 5
Hassel Highway II AUS 176-177 E 6
Hassel National Park ⊥ AUS 176-177 E 7
Hassel Sound ≈ 24-25 W 1
Hasselt ∗ B 92-93 H 3
Hassi Bahbah o DZ 190-191 D 3
Hassi Bel Guebbour o DZ 190-191 F 6
Hassi el Ghella o DZ 188-189 L 3
Hassi Messaoud o DZ 190-191 E 5
Hassi-Onuz o MA 188-189 F 6
Hassi R'Mel o DZ 190-191 D 4
Hässleholm o S 86-87 F 8
Hassman o USA 42-43 K 3
Hastah ∼ RUS 110-111 X 6
Hastah ∼ RUS 110-111 X 3
Hastings o AUS 180-181 H 5
Hastings o GB 90-91 H 6
Hastings o NZ 182 F 3
Hastings o USA (MI) 46-47 F 4
Hastings o USA (MN) 42-43 L 3
Hastings o USA (NE) 42-43 H 5
Hastings, Port o CDN 38-39 O 6
Hastings River ∼ AUS 178-179 M 6
Haştpar o IR 128-129 N 3
Hastrüd o IR 128-129 M 4
Haşüri o GE 128-129 E 7
Hasvik o N 86-87 L 1
Haswell o USA 42-43 F 6
Hasyn ∼ RUS 120-121 O 3
Haţab, Bi'r < SUD 200-201 F 4
Hat'ae Do ∩ ROK 150-151 E 10
Hatanbulag = Ergel o MAU 148-149 J 6
Hatanga o RUS 108-109 a 6
Hatanga ∼ RUS 108-109 f 5
Hatangskij zaliv ≈ 110-111 F 3
Hatansuud o MAU 148-149 E 5
Hatay (Antakya) ∗ TR 128-129 G 4
Hatch o USA (NM) 44-45 D 3
Hatch o USA (UT) 40-41 H 7
Hatches Creek o AUS 174-175 C 7
Hatchet Lake o CDN 30-31 S 6
Hatchie River ∼ USA 48-49 D 2
Hat Nai Yang National Park ⊥ THA 158-159 D 6
Hato Corozal o CO 60-61 F 4
Hatohud o RI 166-167 C 6
Hatra ∗ · IRQ 128-129 K 5
Hatscher, Cerro ▲ RA 80 D 4
Hatta o IND 138-139 G 7
Hattah o AUS 180-181 G 3
Hattah-Kulkyne National Park ⊥ AUS 180-181 G 3
Hatteras o USA 48-49 L 2
Hatteras, Cape ▲ USA 48-49 L 2
Hatteras Abyssal Plain ≃ 6-7 B 5
Hatteras Island ∩ USA 48-49 L 2
Hattfjelldal o N 86-87 F 4
Hattiesburg o USA 48-49 D 4
Hattieville o BH 52-53 K 3
Hatton-Dikoya o CL 140-141 J 7
Hattuşaş ∗∗ TR 128-129 F 2
Haţünäbäd o IR 134-135 G 3
Hâtüniya o SYR 128-129 J 4
Hatvan o H 92-93 P 5
Haty o RUS 118-119 H 4
Hat Yai ∗ THA 158-159 F 7
Hatygyn-Ûëlete ∼ RUS 110-111 J 3
Hatymy ∼ RUS 118-119 H 4
Hatyngnah o RUS (MAG) 120-121 Q 3
Hatyngnah o RUS (SAH) 110-111 d 6
Hatyngnah o RUS (SAH) 110-111 Y 5
Hatynnah ∼ RUS 110-111 Y 5
Hatyrka o RUS 112-113 S 5

Hatyrka ∼ RUS 112-113 R 5
Hatystyr o RUS 118-119 M 6
Hatzfeldhafen o PNG 183 C 3
Hauba, al- o Y 132-133 C 5
Haud ⊥ ETH 208-209 G 4
Hau Giang ∼ VN 158-159 J 5
Haugesund ∗ N 86-87 B 7
Hauhã, al- o Y 132-133 C 7
Hauhui o SOL 184 I e 3
Haukeligrend o N 86-87 C 7
Haukivesi o FIN 88-89 K 5
Haukivuon o FIN 88-89 J 6
Haultain River ∼ CDN 34-35 C 2
Haumonia o RA 76-77 G 4
Haura, al- o Y 132-133 D 6
Haura, al- o Y 132-133 G 6
Hauraha o SOL 184 I e 4
Hauraki Gulf ≈ 182 E 2
Haur al-Habbäniya < IRQ 128-129 K 6
Haur al-Hammâr o IRQ 130-131 K 2
Haur al-Hawiza o IRQ 128-129 L 6
Haurän, Wâdi ∼ IRQ 128-129 K 6
Haur as-Sa'diya o IRQ 128-129 M 6
Haur aš-Šubaika o IRQ 128-129 L 6
Haur Dayät ∼ SUD 200-201 J 5
Haur Fakkän o UAE 134-135 G 6
Haur Ğamûqa o IRQ 128-129 M 7
Hauser Lake o USA 40-41 J 2
Haut, Isle au ∩ USA 46-47 O 3
Hautajärvi o FIN 88-89 K 4
Hautat Bani Tamim o KSA 130-131 K 6
Hautavaara o RUS 88-89 M 5
Haute-Kotto □ RCA 206-207 E 5
Haute-Normandie □ F 90-91 H 7
Hauterive o CDN 38-39 K 4
Haut-Mbomou □ RCA 206-207 G 5
Hauts Plateaux de l'Ouest ▲ CAM 204-205 H 5
Haut-Zaïre □ ZRE 210-211 K 2
Hauz-Han □ TM 136-137 G 9
Hauz-Hanskoe vodohranilišče < TM 136-137 G 9
Häv o IR 128-129 M 5
Havana o USA 46-47 C 5
Havana = La Habana ∗ · · C 54-55 D 3
Havast o US 136-137 L 4
Havasu Lake o USA 40-41 G 8
Havasupai Indian Reservation ⋊ USA 40-41 H 7
Havchinäl o IND 140-141 F 3
Have Etoe o GH 202-203 L 6
Havel ∼ D 92-93 M 2
Haveli o PK 138-139 D 4
Havelián o PK 138-139 D 3
Haveli Baladur Shäh o PK 138-139 D 4
Havelock o CDN 38-39 H 6
Havelock o NZ 182 D 4
Havelock o USA 48-49 K 2
Havelock Island ∩ IND 140-141 L 4
Haven o USA 42-43 J 7
Haven, Cape ▲ CDN 36-37 R 3
Havensville o USA 42-43 J 6
Haverfordwest o GB 90-91 E 6
Haverhill o USA 46-47 N 4
Häveri o IND 140-141 F 3
Havirga o MAU 148-149 J 5
Havre o USA 42-43 C 1
Havre, Le o F 90-91 H 7
Havre-Aubert o CDN 38-39 O 5
Havre-Saint-Pierre o CDN 38-39 N 3
Havrylivka o UA 102-103 K 3
Havza ∗ TR 128-129 F 2
Hawaii □ USA (HI) 48-49 E 8
Hawaiian Islands ∩ USA 48-49 B 6
Hawaiian Ridge ≃ 48-49 B 6
Hawaii Volcanoes National Park ⊥ · · · USA 48-49 E 8
Hawal, River ∼ WAN 204-205 K 3
Hawär, Ğazirat ∩ BRN 134-135 D 6
Hawea, Lake o NZ 182 B 6
Hawera o NZ 182 E 3
Hawesville o USA 46-47 E 6
Hawi o USA 48-49 E 7
Hawick o GB 90-91 F 4
Hawiğat Arbän o IRQ 128-129 K 5
Hawke, Cape ▲ AUS 180-181 M 2
Hawke Bay ≈ 182 F 3
Hawke Island ∩ CDN 38-39 Q 2
Hawke River ∼ CDN 38-39 Q 2
Hawkes, Mount ▲ ARK 16 E 0
Hawke's Bay □ NZ 182 F 3
Hawkesbury o CDN 38-39 H 5
Hawkesbury Island ∩ CDN 32-33 F 5
Hawkesbury Point ▲ AUS 174-175 C 2
Hawk Hill Lake o CDN 30-31 U 5
Hawk Inlet o USA 32-33 C 3
Hawkins o USA 46-47 C 3
Hawkins Island ∩ USA 20-21 R 6
Hawk Junction o CDN 34-35 O 6
Hawks Cape ▲ CDN 26-27 O 4
Hawk Springs o USA 42-43 E 5
Hawley o USA 42-43 J 2
Hawston o ZA 220-221 D 7
Hawthorne o USA (FL) 48-49 G 5
Hawthorne o USA (NV) 40-41 E 6
Haxtun o USA 42-43 F 5
Hay o USA 180-181 H 3
Hay, Cape ▲ CDN 24-25 g 4
Hay, Mount o AUS 176-177 M 1
Hay, Mount ▲ CDN 20-21 W 7
Haya o RI 166-167 E 3
Haya, Tanjung ▲ RI 166-167 E 3
Haya'er o VRC 144-145 J 4
Hayabän o SUD 206-207 K 3
Hayes o USA 42-43 G 3
Hayes, Mount ▲ USA 20-21 R 5
Hayes Creek o AUS 172-173 K 2
Hayes Fiord ≈ 26-27 M 4

Hayes Halvø ⌣ **GRØ** 26-27 Q 4
Hayes River ∼ **CDN** 30-31 W 2
Hayes River ∼ **CDN** 34-35 K 2
Hayfield o **PNG** 183 B 2
Häyk' o **ETH** 208-209 D 3
Häyk' Häyk' o **ETH** 208-209 D 3
Haykota o **ER** 200-201 H 5
Hayla, Wâdi ∼ **OM** 132-133 H 5
Hay Lake Indian Reserve ⋆ **CDN** 30-31 K 6
Hay Lakes o **CDN** 32-33 O 5
Haymana ☆ **TR** 128-129 E 3
Hayman Island ∼ **AUS** 174-175 K 7
Hayrabolu ☆ **TR** 128-129 B 2
Hay River o∼ **AUS** 178-179 D 2
Hay River o∙ **CDN** 30-31 M 5
Hay River ∼ **CDN** 30-31 K 6
Hays o **USA** 42-43 H 6
Haysardah ∼ **RUS** 110-111 U 6
Hay Springs o **USA** 42-43 F 4
Haystack Mount ▲ **USA** 20-21 O 4
Haystack Peak ▲ **USA** 44-45 J 1
Haysville o **USA** 44-45 J 1
Hayward o **USA** (CA) 40-41 C 7
Hayward o **USA** (WI) 46-47 C 2
Haywood Channel ≈ 142-143 H 4
Hayy al-Mahaţţa ○ **KSA** 130-131 K 5
Hazar, 'En o **IL** 130-131 D 2
Hazārābād o **IR** 136-137 L 6
Hazard o **USA** 46-47 E 2
Hāzāribāg o∙ **IND** 142-143 D 4
Hazaribag National Park ⊥ **IND** 142-143 J 3
Hāzāribāg Plateau ▲ **IND** 142-143 D 4
Hazărmani o **AFG** 136-137 K 7
Hazel Green o **USA** 46-47 C 4
Hazelton o **CDN** 32-33 G 4
Hazelton Mountains ▲ **CDN** 32-33 F 4
Hazen, Lake o **CDN** 26-27 P 3
Hazen Bay ≈ 20-21 H 6
Hazen Land ⊥ **GRØ** 26-27 e 2
Hazen Strait ≊ 24-25 Q 2
Hazeva, 'En o **IL** 130-131 D 2
Hazipur o **IND** 142-143 D 4
Hazlehurst o **USA** (GA) 48-49 G 4
Hazlehurst o **USA** (MS) 44-45 M 4
Hazlet o **CDN** 32-33 Q 6
Hazleton o **USA** 46-47 L 5
Hazlett, Lake o **AUS** 172-173 J 6
Hazm, al- o **Y** 132-133 D 5
Hazorasp ☆ **US** 136-137 G 4
Hazrat-e Soltān o **AFG** 136-137 K 6
Hazro o **PK** 138-139 D 3
Hažuu-Us o **MAU** 148-149 H 5
Ḩazzān Aswān o∙ **ET** 194-195 F 5
Headingly o **AUS** 178-179 E 1
Headlands o **ZW** 218-219 G 4
Head of Bight ≈ 176-177 L 5
Headquarters o **USA** 40-41 G 2
Head Smashed-In Bison Jump ∙∙∙ **CDN** 32-33 O 7
Heafford Junction o **USA** 46-47 C 2
Healesville o **AUS** 180-181 H 4
Healey Lake o **CDN** 30-31 Q 3
Healy o **USA** 20-21 O 5
Heany Junction o **ZW** 218-219 E 5
Heard Island ∼ **AUS** 12 F 10
Hearne o **USA** 44-45 J 4
Hearst o **CDN** 34-35 P 6
Hearst Island ∼ **ARK** 16 G 30
Heart River ∼ **USA** 42-43 G 2
Heart's Content o **CDN** 38-39 I S 5
Heath, Rio ∼ **BOL** 70-71 G 3
Heathcote o **AUS** 180-181 H 4
Hebbale o **IND** 140-141 F 4
Hebbronville o **USA** 44-45 H 6
Hebburli o **IND** 140-141 F 4
Hebei □ **VRC** 154-155 J 2
Hebel o **AUS** 178-179 J 5
Hebera o **RI** 166-167 E 2
Heber o **USA** 44-45 J 2
Heber City o **USA** 40-41 J 5
Heber Springs o **USA** 44-45 M 2
Hébertville o **CDN** 38-39 J 4
Hebgen Lake o **USA** 40-41 I 4
Hebi o **VRC** 154-155 J 4
Hebo o **USA** 40-41 C 3
Hebri o **IND** 140-141 F 4
Hebrides, Sea of the ≈ 90-91 D 3
Hebron o **CDN** 36-37 S 5
Hebron o **USA** 42-43 J 3
Hebron = Hevron ☆ **IL** 130-131 D 2
Hebron, Mount ▲ **USA** 40-41 C 5
Hebron Fiord ≈ 36-37 S 5
Heby o **S** 86-87 H 7
Hecate Strait ≈ 32-33 E 5
Hecelchakán o∙ **MEX** 52-53 J 1
Heceta Island ∼ **USA** 32-33 D 4
Hechevarría o **C** 54-55 H 4
Hechi o **VRC** 156-157 F 4
Hechun o **VRC** 156-157 G 6
Heckford Bank ∼ 158-159 D 5
Hecla o **CDN** 34-35 H 5
Hecla and Griper Bay ≈ 24-25 P 2
Hecla Island ∼ **CDN** 34-35 H 5
Hecla Provincial Park ⊥ **CDN** 34-35 H 5
Hector o **USA** 42-43 K 3
Hectorsprunt o **ZA** 220-221 K 2
Hector Tejada o **PE** 70-71 B 4
Hedaru o **EAT** 212-213 F 6
Heddal stavkirke ∙∙ **N** 86-87 D 7
Hede o **S** 86-87 F 5
Hediondas, Las o **RCH** 76-77 C 5
Hedi SK ∼ **VRC** 156-157 G 6
Heerenveen o **NL** 92-93 H 2
Heer Land ⊥ 84-85 K 4
Heerlen o **NL** 92-93 H 3
Heezen Fracture Zone ≊ 14-15 Q 13
Hefa = Haifa ☆ **IL** 130-131 D 1
Hefei ☆ **VRC** 154-155 K 4
Hefeng o **VRC** 156-157 G 2
Heffley Creek o **CDN** 32-33 K 6
Hegang o **VRC** 150-151 H 4
Heggadevankote o **IND** 140-141 G 4

Hegigio River ∼ **PNG** 183 B 4
Hegura-shima ∼ **J** 152-153 G 6
Hehua o **VRC** 154-155 G 6
Heide o **D** 92-93 K 1
Heidelberg o∙∙ **D** 92-93 K 4
Heidelberg o **USA** 48-49 D 4
Heidelberg o **ZA** (CAP) 220-221 E 7
Heidelberg o **ZA** (TRA) 220-221 J 3
Heiden, Port ≈ 22-23 R 4
Hendrina o **ZA** 220-221 J 3
Heihe o **VRC** 150-151 F 2
Hei He ∼ **VRC** 154-155 A 2
Heilbron o **ZA** 220-221 H 3
Heilbronn o∙ **D** 92-93 K 4
Heilongjiang ∼ **VRC** (HUN) 156-157 H 3
Heilong Jiang ∼ **VRC** 150-151 F 3
Heilprin Gletscher **C GRØ** 26-27 S 5
Heilprin Land ⊥ **GRØ** 26-27 h 3
Heilsberg = Lidzbark Warmiński o **PL** 92-93 U 1
Heimaey ∼ **IS** 86-87 c 3
Heimahe o **VRC** 144-145 M 2
Heinola o **FIN** 88-89 J 6
Heinsburg o **CDN** 32-33 P 5
Heinze Chaung ≈ 158-159 D 3
Heirābād o **VRC** 156-157 K 6
Heirane **C DZ** 188-189 L 7
Heishan SK ∼ **VRC** 154-155 J 6
Heist, Knokke- o∙ **B** 92-93 G 3
Heitoral o **BR** 72-73 F 3
Heitske o **RI** 166-167 K 5
Hejaz = Ḩiğāz, al- ▲ **KSA** 130-131 D 4
Hejdžanskij hrebet ▲ **RUS** 120-121 L 4
Hejdžiahe ∼ **RUS** 114-115 L 2
Hejian o **VRC** 154-155 J 3
Hejiang o **VRC** (GDG) 156-157 G 6
Hejiang o **VRC** (SIC) 156-157 D 2
Hejin o **VRC** 154-155 G 4
Hejing o **VRC** 146-147 H 4
Hējjaha ∼ **RUS** 108-109 K 7
Hejsa, ostrov ∼ **RUS** 84-85 e 2
Hēkčekit-Sene ∼ **RUS** 108-109 d 7
Hekimhan ☆ **TR** 128-129 G 3
Hekla ▲ **IS** 86-87 d 2
Hekou o **VRC** 154-155 C 3
Hekou o **VRC** (HUB) 154-155 H 6
Hekou o **VRC** (YUN) 156-157 C 5
Helagsfjället ▲ **S** 86-87 F 5
Helaliturku, ozero o **RUS** 108-109 X 5
Helan o **VRC** 154-155 E 2
Helan Shan ▲ **VRC** 154-155 D 2
Helanshan Z.B. ⋅ **VRC** 154-155 E 2
Helder, Den o **NL** 92-93 H 2
Helen ∼ **USA** 44-45 M 2
Helena o **USA** (AR) 44-45 M 2
Helena ☆ **USA** (MT) 40-41 I 3
Helena Island ∼ **USA** 48-49 H 3
Helen Springs o **AUS** 174-175 B 6
Helensville o **NZ** 182 E 2
Helgoland o **D** 92-93 J 1
Helgöländer Bucht ≈ 92-93 J 1
Helgum o **S** 86-87 H 5
Helheimfjord ≈ 28-29 V 3
Heliopolis ∴∙ **ET** 194-195 E 2
Helleland o **N** 86-87 C 7
Helleristninger ∙∙∙ **N** 86-87 L 2
Hellesvik o **N** 86-87 B 5
Hellin o **E** 98-99 G 5
Hells Canyon ∼ **USA** 40-41 F 3
Hells Gate Airtram ⋅ **CDN** 32-33 K 7
Hells Gate Roadhouse o **AUS** 174-175 E 5
Hellshire Beach ⋅ **JA** 54-55 G 6
Hell Ville = Andoany o **RM** 222-223 F 4
Helmand ⋄ **AFG** 134-135 K 3
Helmand, Rūd-e ∼ **AFG** 134-135 J 4
Helmeringhausen o **NAM** 220-221 C 2
Helmond o **NL** 92-93 H 3
Helmsdale o **GB** 90-91 F 2
Helmstedt o∙ **D** 92-93 L 2
Helong o **VRC** 150-151 G 6
Helper o **USA** 40-41 J 6
Helsingborg o∙ **S** 86-87 F 9
Helsingfors = Helsinki ★∙∙ **FIN** 88-89 H 6
Helsingør o∙ **DK** 86-87 F 8
Helsinki ★∙∙ **FIN** 88-89 H 6
Helska, Mierzeja ∼ **PL** 92-93 P 1
Helvecia o **RA** 76-77 G 6
Hemando o **RA** 78-79 H 2
Hemaruka o **CDN** 32-33 P 6
Hemčik ∼ **RUS** 116-117 I 10
Hemčik ∼ **RUS** 124-125 Q 3
Hemet o **USA** 40-41 F 9
Hemingford o **USA** 42-43 F 4
Heming Lake o **CDN** 34-35 F 3
Hemlo o **CDN** 34-35 O 6
Hemlock Grove o **USA** 46-47 L 5
Hemnesberget o **N** 86-87 F 3
Hemphill, Cape ▲ **CDN** 24-25 O 2
Hempstead o **USA** (NY) 46-47 M 5
Hempstead o **USA** (TX) 44-45 J 4
Hemse o **S** 86-87 J 8
Hemudu Wenhua Yizhi ∴∙ **VRC** 156-157 M 2
Henan o **VRC** 154-155 H 5
Hen and Chicken Islands ∼ **NZ** 182 E 1
Henares, Rio ∼ **E** 98-99 F 4
Henasi-saki ▲ **J** 152-153 H 4
Henbury o **AUS** 178-179 J 4
Henbury Meteorite Craters ⋅ **AUS** 176-177 M 2
Hendek o **TR** 128-129 D 2
Henderson o **RA** 78-79 J 4
Henderson o **USA** (KY) 46-47 E 7
Henderson o **USA** (NC) 48-49 J 2
Henderson o **USA** (NV) 40-41 G 7
Henderson o **USA** (TN) 46-47 K 4
Henderson o **USA** (TX) 48-49 C 4
Henderson o **USA** (TN) 48-49 D 2
Hendersonville o **USA** (NC) 48-49 G 4
Hendersonville o **USA** (TN) 48-49 E 1
Hendiğān o **IR** 134-135 C 3
Hendiğān, Rūdhāne-ye ∼ **IR** 134-135 C 3
Hendon o **CDN** 34-35 E 4

Hendorābī o **IR** 134-135 E 5
Hendorābī, Ğazire-ye ∼ **IR** 134-135 E 5
Hendrik Ø ∼ **GRØ** 26-27 P 3
Hendriksen Strait ≊ 24-25 X 2
Hendrik Verwoerddam ✓ **ZA** 220-221 G 5
Hendrik Verwoerddam Nature Reserve ⊥ **ZA** 220-221 G 5
Hendrina o **ZA** 220-221 J 3
Hengăm, Ğazire-ye ∼ **IR** 134-135 F 5
Ḩengān o **AFG** 136-137 L 7
Henganofi o **PNG** 183 B 4
Hengchun o **RC** 156-157 M 5
Hengduan Shan ▲ **VRC** 144-145 M 7
Hengelo o **NL** 92-93 J 2
Hengshan o **VRC** (HUN) 156-157 H 3
Hengshan o **VRC** (HUN) 156-157 H 3
Hengshan ▲ **VRC** (HUN) 156-157 H 3
Hengshan ∙ **VRC** (SHA) 154-155 H 2
Hengshui o **VRC** 154-155 J 3
Heng Xian o **VRC** 156-157 F 5
Hengyang o **VRC** 156-157 H 3
Heničes'k o **UA** 102-103 H 4
Henley on Klip o **ZA** 220-221 H 3
Hennaya o **DZ** 188-189 L 3
Hennebont o **F** 90-91 F 8
Hennenman o **ZA** 220-221 H 3
Hennessey o **USA** 44-45 J 1
Hennigsdorf o **D** 92-93 M 2
Henrietta o **USA** 44-45 H 2
Henrietta Maria, Cape ▲ **CDN** 34-35 P 4
Henri Pittier, Parque Nacional ⊥ **YV** 60-61 H 2
Henry o **USA** (IL) 46-47 D 5
Henry o **USA** (SD) 42-43 J 3
Henry, Cape ▲ **USA** 48-49 L 1
Henryetta o **USA** 44-45 K 2
Henry Kater, Cape ▲ **CDN** 28-29 G 2
Henry Kater Peninsula ⌣ **CDN** 28-29 F 2
Henry Lawrence Island ∼ **IND** 140-141 J 4
Henry River ∼ **AUS** 176-177 C 1
Henry's Fork ∼ **USA** 40-41 I 4
Hèntèin nurruu ▲ **MAU** 148-149 H 3
Hentiesbaai o **NAM** 216-217 B 9
Hèntij ∼ **MAU** 148-149 J 3
Henvey Inlet Indian Reserve ⋆ **CDN** 38-39 D 6
Henzada o **MYA** 158-159 C 2
Hepburn o **CDN** 34-35 C 4
Hepburn Lake o **CDN** 30-31 M 2
Heping o **VRC** 156-157 J 4
Heppner o **USA** 40-41 E 3
Hepu o **VRC** 156-157 F 6
Heqing o **VRC** 144-145 M 7
Heraclea ∴∙ **MK** 100-101 H 4
Hérádsvötn ∼ **IS** 86-87 d 2
Heralon ∴∙∙ **TR** 128-129 B 4
Ḩerāme o **IR** 134-135 E 4
Heras, Las o **RA** 80 F 3
Herāt ☆ **AFG** 134-135 J 1
Herāt □ **AFG** 134-135 K 1
Heraz, Rüdhāne-ye ∼ **IR** 136-137 B 6
Herbagat o **SUD** 200-201 H 3
Herbang o **BD** 142-143 H 5
Herbert o **CDN** 34-35 C 5
Herbert, Mount ▲ **AUS** 172-173 G 4
Herbert o **NZ** 182 C 6
Herbert Hoover National Historic Site ⋅ **USA** 46-47 C 5
Herbert Island ∼ **USA** 22-23 L 6
Herbert Lake o **CDN** 30-31 R 6
Herbert Ø ∼ **GRØ** 26-27 P 5
Herberton o **AUS** 174-175 H 5
Herbert River ∼ **AUS** 174-175 H 6
Herbert River Falls ⋅ **AUS** 174-175 H 6
Herbertsdale o **ZA** 220-221 E 7
Herbert Vale o **AUS** 174-175 E 6
Herbert Wash ∼ **AUS** 176-177 H 2
Herbiers, les o∙ **F** 90-91 G 8
Herceg-Novi o∙ **YU** 100-101 G 3
Herchmer o **CDN** 34-35 J 2
Hercilio Luz ∙ **BR** 74-75 F 7
Herciliópolis o **BR** 74-75 E 6
Hercules Bay ≈ 183 D 4
Hercules Gemstone Deposit ⋅ **AUS** 176-177 J 3
Herdlak ∼ **GRØ** 28-29 Q 5
Herðubreið ▲ **IS** 86-87 e 2
Hereda, Punta o **PE** 64-65 B 4
Heredia ☆ **CR** 52-53 B 6
Hereford o **GB** 90-91 F 6
Hereford o **USA** (CO) 42-43 F 5
Hereford o **USA** (TX) 44-45 F 2
Hereke o **TR** 128-129 C 2
Herene, In **C LAR** 190-191 G 7
Hereroland ⋅ **NAM** 216-217 E 10
Herford o∙ **D** 92-93 K 2
Hèrgu ∼ **RUS** 122-123 E 2
Herington o **USA** 42-43 J 6
Heriot Bay o **CDN** 32-33 H 6
Heris o∙ **IR** 128-129 M 3
Heritage Range ▲ **ARK** 16 F 28
Hèrlèn o∙ **MAU** 148-149 J 4
Hèrlèn gol ∼ **MAU** 148-149 M 3
Herlen He ∼ **VRC** 148-149 N 3
Herluf Trolles Land ⊥ **GRØ** 26-27 I 2
Herma Ness ▲ **GB** 90-91 G 1
Hermann o **USA** 44-45 M 2
Hermannsburg ⋆ **AUS** 176-177 M 1
Hermannsburg Aboriginal Land ⋆ **AUS** 176-177 M 1
Hermanos, Cerro ▲ **RCH** 80 D 3
Hermanos, Islas Los ∼ **YV** 60-61 J 2
Hermansdorings o **ZA** 220-221 H 2
Hermidale o **AUS** 178-179 J 6
Hermiston o **USA** 40-41 E 3
Hermitage o **USA** 44-45 L 3
Hermitage Bay ≈ 38-39 I Q 5
Hermon o **ZA** 220-221 D 6
Hermopolis ∴∙∙ **ET** 194-195 E 4
Hermosa, La o **CO** 60-61 F 5
Hermosas, Parque Nacional las ⊥ **CO** 60-61 D 6
Hermosillo ★ **MEX** 50-51 D 3
Hernandarias o **RA** 76-77 H 6
Hernán Mejia Miraval o **RA** 76-77 F 4

Herning o **DK** 86-87 D 8
Hérodier, Lac **C CDN** 36-37 P 6
Heroica Zitácuaro o **MEX** 52-53 D 2
Herold o **ZA** 220-221 F 6
Heroldsbaai o **ZA** 220-221 F 7
Heron Island ∼ **AUS** 178-179 L 2
Heron Lake o **USA** 42-43 K 4
Herøy o **N** 86-87 F 4
Herradura o **MEX** 50-51 J 6
Herradura o **RA** 76-77 H 4
Herreid o **USA** 42-43 G 3
Herrera del Duque o∙ **E** 98-99 E 5
Herrera de Pisuerga o **E** 98-99 E 3
Herreras, Las o **MEX** 50-51 G 5
Herreras, Los o **MEX** 50-51 K 5
Herrero, Punta ▲ **MEX** 52-53 L 2
Herries Range ▲ **AUS** 178-179 L 5
Herrin o **USA** 46-47 D 7
Herschel o **CDN** 20-21 W 2
Herschel o **ZA** 220-221 H 5
Herschel Island ∼ **CDN** 20-21 W 2
Hersfeld, Bad o∙ **D** 92-93 K 3
Hertfordshire ☆ **UA** 102-103 H 4
Hertogenbosch, 's- ☆∙∙ **NL** 92-93 H 3
Hertugen of Orleans Land ⊥ **GRØ** 26-27 o 5
Hertzogville o **ZA** 220-221 G 4
Heruarful Trolle, Kap ▲ **GRØ** 28-29 T 6
Herval o **BR** 76-77 K 2
Hervey Bay ≈ 178-179 M 3
Hervey Bay o **AUS** 178-179 M 3
Hervey Junction o **CDN** 38-39 H 5
Herveys Range ▲ **AUS** 180-181 K 2
Herzliyya o **IL** 130-131 D 1
Herzog-Ernst-Bucht ≈ 16 F 33
Hesadi o **IND** 142-143 D 4
Heşārak o **AFG** 138-139 B 2
Heshan o **VRC** 156-157 H 5
Heshun o **VRC** 154-155 H 3
Hesperia o **USA** (CA) 40-41 F 8
Hesperia o **USA** (MI) 46-47 E 4
Hessfjord o **N** 86-87 J 2
Hess Mountains ▲ **CDN** 20-21 Z 5
Hess River ∼ **CDN** 20-21 Z 5
Hester, Peak ▲ **AUS** 172-173 D 7
Hestkjølen ▲ **N** 86-87 F 4
Heta ∼ **RUS** 108-109 c 6
Heta ∼ **RUS** 108-109 c 6
Heta, Bol'šaja ∼ **RUS** 108-109 V 8
Hetagčan ∼ **RUS** 112-113 H 5
Hetagima o **RI** 166-167 K 4
Hetauda o **NEP** 144-145 E 7
Hetch Hetchy Aqueduct < **USA** 40-41 D 7
Het Kruis o **ZA** 220-221 D 6
Hetovo o **RUS** 88-89 R 5
Hettinger o **USA** 42-43 G 2
Hétyfky ∼ **RUS** 114-115 R 2
Heuru o **SOL** 184 I e 4
Heva ☆∙∙ **USA** 136-137 G 4
Héva, Rivière- o **CDN** 38-39 E 4
Hevelándia o **BR** 66-67 G 5
Hevi o∙ **IND** 202-203 L 6
Hevron ☆ **WB** 130-131 D 2
Hewett, Kap ▲ **GRØ** 26-27 p 8
Hewham o∙ **GB** 90-91 F 4
He Xian o **VRC** (ANH) 154-155 L 6
He Xian o **VRC** (GXI) 156-157 G 4
Hexigten Qi o **VRC** 148-149 N 6
Hex River Pass ▲ **ZA** 220-221 D 6
Hexriverberge ▲ **ZA** 220-221 D 6
Heyang o **VRC** 154-155 G 4
Heydon o **ZA** 220-221 G 5
Heyfield o **AUS** 180-181 J 4
Heyu o **VRC** 154-155 J 5
Heyuan o **VRC** 156-157 J 5
Heywood o **AUS** 180-181 F 5
Heywood Islands ∼ **AUS** 172-173 G 3
Heywood Shoal ∼ **AUS** 172-173 G 2
Hezàr, Kūh-e ▲ **IR** 134-135 G 4
Heze o **VRC** 154-155 J 4
Hezhang o **VRC** 156-157 D 3
Ḩezīr o **IR** 134-135 H 1
Hezuozhen o **VRC** 154-155 C 4
Hhohho □ **SD** 220-221 K 2
Hiagtin Gol ∼ **MAU** 144-145 L 2
Hialeah o **USA** 48-49 H 7
Hian o **VRC** 202-203 J 4
Hiawatha o **USA** 42-43 K 6
Ḩibāk, al- ∼ **KSA** 132-133 H 3
Hibarba ∼ **RUS** 108-109 b 7
Hibberdene o **ZA** 220-221 J 5
Hibbing o **USA** 42-43 L 2
Hibbs, Point ▲ **AUS** 180-181 H 7
Hibernia Reef ∼ **AUS** 172-173 F 1
Hibiny ▲ **RUS** 88-89 M 3
Hibis, Temple of ∴∙∙ **ET** 194-195 E 4
Hickman o **USA** 46-47 D 7
Hickman, Mount ▲ **CDN** 32-33 E 3
Hickman o **RA** 76-77 F 2
Hickory o **USA** 48-49 H 2
Hicks, Point ▲ **AUS** 180-181 K 4
Hicks Cays ∼ **BH** 52-53 K 3
Hicks Lake o **CDN** 30-31 T 5
Hickson Lake o **CDN** 34-35 D 2
Hida-gawa ∼ **J** 152-153 F 6
Hidaka o **J** 152-153 H 4
Hidaka-sanmyaku ▲ **J** 152-153 K 3
Hidaldo o **MEX** 50-51 K 5
Hidalgo o **MEX** (DGO) 50-51 G 5
Hidalgo o **MEX** (NL) 50-51 J 5
Hidalgo □ **MEX** 50-51 J 5
Hidalgo del Parral o∙ **MEX** 50-51 G 4
Hida-sanmyaku ▲ **J** 152-153 G 6
Hidden Peak = Gasherbrum I ▲ **PK** 138-139 F 2
Hiddensee ∼ **D** 92-93 N 1
Hidden Valley o **AUS** (NT) 172-173 L 4
Hidden Valley o **AUS** (QLD) 174-175 J 6
Hidden Valley o **AUS** (QLD) 174-175 J 7
Hidden Valley National Park ⊥ **AUS** 172-173 J 3
Hiddensee ≈ 160-161 J 7
Hidrelétrica Curuá-Una o **BR** 66-67 K 4

Hidrolândia o **BR** 68-69 H 4
Hierapolis ∴∙∙ **TR** 128-129 C 4
Hierro ∼ **E** 188-189 B 7
Higashi-Hiroshima ∙ **J** 152-153 E 7
Higashikagura o **J** 152-153 K 3
Higashi-Ōsaka ∙ **J** 152-153 F 7
Higashi Shina Kai = Dong Hai ≈ 154-155 N 6
Higashi-suidō ≈ 152-153 C 8
Ḩiğāz, al- ▲ **KSA** 130-131 D 4
Higbourn Cay ∼ **BS** 54-55 G 2
Highbury o **AUS** (QLD) 174-175 G 5
Highbury o **AUS** (QLD) 178-179 H 2
Highbury o **GUY** 62-63 F 2
Highflats o **ZA** 220-221 J 5
High Hill River o **CDN** 32-33 P 3
High Island o **USA** (TX) 44-45 K 5
High Island ∼ **USA** 22-23 J 3
Highland Park o **USA** 46-47 E 4
Highland Peak ▲ **USA** 40-41 G 7
Highland Plains o **AUS** 174-175 D 6
High Level o **CDN** 30-31 M 4
Highmore o **USA** 42-43 H 3
High Peak ▲ **GB** 90-91 G 5
Hinganghat o∙ **IND** 138-139 G 9
Hinganskij zapovednik ⊥ **RUS** 150-151 G 4
High Plateaus = Hauts Plateaux ⊥ **DZ** 190-191 B 4
High Point o **USA** 48-49 H 2
High Prairie o **CDN** 32-33 M 3
High River o **CDN** 32-33 O 6
High Rock o **BS** 54-55 F 1
High Rolling Mountains ▲ **RP** 160-161 D 3
High Springs o **USA** 48-49 G 5
High Uintas Wilderness Area ⊥ **USA** 40-41 J 5
Highwood River ∼ **CDN** 32-33 N 6
Higiirio, El **C RCH** 76-77 B 5
Higlá o **KSA** 132-133 C 4
Ḩiğr, al- o **KSA** 130-131 C 4
Higuera, La o **RCH** 76-77 B 5
Higuerote o∙ **YV** 60-61 H 2
Higüey o∙ **DOM** 54-55 L 5
Hiiraan □ **SP** 208-209 G 4
Hiiumaa saar ∼ **EST** 94-95 H 2
Hijar o **E** 98-99 G 4
Hikone o **J** 152-153 G 7
Hikurangi ▲ **NZ** 182 G 2
Hikurangi ▲ **NZ** 182 G 2
Hikurangi Trench ≊ 182 F 4
Hila o **RI** (MAL) 166-167 E 3
Hila o **RI** (MAL) 166-167 E 3
Hilakondji o **DY** 202-203 L 6
Ḩilāl, Ğabal ▲ **ET** 194-195 F 2
Hilda o **USA** 48-49 H 3
Hildale o **USA** 40-41 H 7
Hildesheim o∙ **D** 92-93 K 2
Hilger o **USA** 42-43 C 2
Hili o **UAE** 134-135 F 6
Hiliomódi o **GR** 100-101 J 6
Hilismaetano o **RI** 162-163 B 4
Hilla, al- ☆ **IRQ** 128-129 L 5
Hill Air Force Base ★★ **USA** 40-41 H 5
Hill City o **USA** (ID) 40-41 G 4
Hill City o **USA** (KS) 42-43 H 6
Hill City o **USA** (MN) 42-43 L 2
Hill City o **USA** (SD) 42-43 F 4
Hill Creek Extension Uintah and Ouray Indian Reservation ⋆ **USA** 42-43 C 6
Ḩilleket o **TCH** 198-199 K 6
Hill End o∙ **AUS** 180-181 K 2
Hillerød o∙ **DK** 86-87 F 9
Hilli o **IND** 142-143 F 3
Hill Island o **CDN** 36-37 P 3
Hill Island Lake o **CDN** 30-31 P 5
Hillman, Lake o **AUS** 176-177 D 5
Hillsboro o **USA** (IL) 46-47 D 6
Hillsboro o **USA** (ND) 42-43 J 2
Hillsboro o **USA** (NM) 44-45 D 3
Hillsboro o **USA** (OH) 46-47 G 6
Hillsboro o **USA** (OR) 40-41 C 3
Hillsboro o **USA** (TX) 44-45 J 3
Hillsboro Canal < **USA** 48-49 H 6
Hillsborough o **USA** 48-49 J 1
Hillsborough o **WG** 56 K 5
Hillsborough Bay ≈ 38-39 N 5
Hillside o **AUS** 172-173 D 6
Hillside o **AUS** 40-41 H 8
Hillsport o **CDN** 34-35 O 6
Hillston o **AUS** 180-181 H 2
Hillsville o **USA** 46-47 H 7
Hillswick o∙ **GB** 90-91 G 1
Hilo o **USA** 48-49 f 8
Hilok o **RUS** (CTN) 118-119 E 10
Hilok o **RUS** 116-117 O 10
Hilok ∼ **RUS** 118-119 F 10
Hilt o **USA** 40-41 C 5
Hiltaba, Mount ▲ **AUS** 180-181 C 2
Hilton o **USA** 174-175 E 7
Hilton Head Island ∼ **USA** 48-49 H 3
Hilvan ☆ **TR** 128-129 H 4
Hilversum o **NL** 92-93 H 2
Himachal Pradesh □ **IND** 138-139 F 3
Himalaya ▲ **IND** 138-139 F 9
Himalaya = Himalaya Shan ▲ 10-11 G 5
Himalaya = Himalaya Shan ▲ **VRC** 144-145 A 3
Himalaya Shan ▲ **VRC** 144-145 D 6
Himal Chuli ▲ **NEP** 144-145 E 6
Himanka o **FIN** 88-89 G 4
Himatnagar o **IND** 138-139 D 8
Himbirti o∙ **ER** 200-201 J 5
Himeji o **J** 152-153 F 7
Himeji-jo Castle ∴∙∙ **J** 152-153 F 7
Himi o **J** 152-153 G 6
Ḩimki o **RUS** 94-95 P 4
Himora o **ETH** 200-201 H 5
Ḩims ☆ **SYR** 128-129 G 5
Hinatuan Passage ≈ 160-161 F 8
Ḩinceşti ☆ **MD** 102-103 F 4

Hinche ☆ **RH** 54-55 J 5
Hinchinbrook, Cape ▲ **USA** 20-21 R 6
Hinchinbrook Entrance ≈ 20-21 R 6
Hinchinbrook Island ∼ **AUS** 174-175 J 6
Hinchinbrook Island ∼ **USA** 20-21 R 6
Hinchinbrook Island National Park ⊥ **AUS** 174-175 J 6
Hinckley o **USA** 42-43 L 3
Hinckley, Mount ▲ **AUS** 176-177 K 3
Hincks Conservation Park ⊥ **AUS** 180-181 C 2
Hinda o **RCB** 210-211 D 6
Hindan o **IND** 138-139 F 9
Hindiktig-Holʹ ozero o **RUS** 124-125 Q 3
Hindiya, al- ☆ **IRQ** 128-129 L 6
Hindmarsh, Lake o **AUS** 180-181 F 4
Hindubagjo ▲ **PK** 134-135 M 3
Hindu Kush ▲ 138-139 B 2
Hindu Kush = Henдükoş ▲ 10-11 G 6
Hindupur o **IND** 140-141 G 4
Hindustan o **IND** 142-143 B 2
Hines Creek o **CDN** 32-33 L 3
Hinesville o **USA** 48-49 H 4
Hinganghat o∙ **IND** 138-139 G 9
Hinganskij zapovednik ⊥ **RUS** 150-151 G 4
Hinglaj o **PK** (BEL) 134-135 L 6
Hinglaj o∙ **PK** (BEL) 138-139 E 7
Hingol ∼ **PK** 134-135 L 6
Hingoli o∙ **IND** 138-139 F 10
Hingoraja o **PK** 138-139 B 6
Hinisk ∼ **RUS** 134-135 M 6
Hinike ∼ **RUS** 120-121 J 3
Hinis ☆ **TR** 128-129 J 3
Hink Land ⊥ **GRØ** 26-27 I 8
Hinlopenrenna ≈ 84-85 J 2
Hinlopenstretet ≈ 84-85 K 2
Hinnøya ∼ **N** 86-87 G 2
Hinoba-an o **RP** 160-161 E 8
Hino-gawa ∼ **J** 152-153 E 7
Hinogyaung o **MYA** 158-159 C 2
Hinojo o **RA** 78-79 J 4
Hinojosa del Duque o∙ **E** 98-99 E 5
Hinomi-saki ▲ **J** 152-153 E 7
Hinsdale o **USA** 42-43 D 1
Hinton o **CDN** 32-33 M 5
Hinton o **USA** 46-47 H 7
Hios ∼ **GR** 100-101 L 5
Hios o **GR** 100-101 L 5
Hipólito o **MEX** 50-51 J 5
Hir o **IR** ⋅136-137 B 6
Hira o **IND** 140-141 G 2
Hirado o∙ **J** 152-153 C 8
Hirado-shima ∼ **J** 152-153 C 8
Hirafok o **DZ** 190-191 F 9
Hirākūd Reservoir < **IND** 142-143 C 5
Hiraman ∼ **EAK** 212-213 G 4
Hiranai o **J** 152-153 J 4
Hiratsuka o∙ **J** 152-153 H 7
Ḩirbat al-Umbāši ∴∙∙ **SYR** 128-129 G 6
Ḩirbat Isriya o **SYR** 128-129 G 5
Hirehadagalli o **IND** 140-141 F 3
Hiré-Watta o **CI** 202-203 H 6
Hirfanlı Barajı < **TR** 128-129 E 3
Hiripitiya o **CL** 140-141 J 7
Hiriyur o **IND** 140-141 G 4
Ḩirmas, Bir Ibn o **KSA** 130-131 E 3
Hirmil, al- o **RL** 128-129 G 5
Hiroo o **J** 152-153 K 3
Hirosaki o∙ **J** 152-153 J 4
Hiroshima o **J** (HOK) 152-153 J 3
Hiroshima o∙ **J** (HIR) 152-153 E 7
Ḩirr, Wādī ∼ **IRQ** 128-129 K 7
hirs'ka miscevisc' ⋅ **UA** 102-103 G 3
Hirşova o **RO** 102-103 F 5
Hirson o **F** 90-91 J 5
Hirţshals o∙ **DK** 86-87 D 8
Hisaka-shima ∼ **J** 152-153 C 8
Ḩisāna, al- o **KSA** 132-133 B 3
Hisār o **IND** 138-139 E 5
Hisb, Sha'ib ∼ **IRQ** 128-129 K 7
Hišiģ-Öndör o **MAU** 148-149 F 3
Hisiu o **PNG** 183 D 5
Hislavičì o **RUS** 94-95 N 4
Ḩişn, Jabal al- ∼ **SYR** 128-129 G 5
Ḩişn aş Şahābi o **LAR** 192-193 J 2
Hispaniola ∼ 54-55 K 4
Historic Fort Delaware ∴∙∙ **USA** 46-47 L 4
Historic Remains ∴∙∙ **RI** 164-165 K 3
Historic Remains, Forts ∴∙∙ **RI** 164-165 K 3
Historyland ∴∙∙ **USA** 46-47 C 4
Hisw, al- o **KSA** 130-131 G 5
Hit o **IRQ** 128-129 K 6
Hitachi o∙ **J** 152-153 J 6
Hitia Sand Hills ∼ **GUY** 62-63 F 3
Hitoyoshi o∙ **J** 152-153 D 8
Hitra ∼ **N** 86-87 D 5
Hiu = Hiu ile ∼ **VAN** 184 II a 1
Hiu, Ile = Hiu ∼ **VAN** 184 II a 1
Hiuchi-nada ≈ 152-153 E 7
Hiuchi-gawa ∼ **J** 152-153 C 8
Hiva-Oa ∼ **J** 13 P 5
Hiw o **ET** 194-195 F 4
Hiwarkhed o **IND** 138-139 F 9
Hiwassee Lake o **USA** 48-49 F 2
Hixon o **CDN** 32-33 J 5
Hiyoshi o **J** 152-153 F 6
Hiyyon, Náal ∼ **IL** 130-131 D 2
Hizan ☆ **TR** 128-129 K 3
Hjälmaren o **S** 86-87 G 7
Hjälmar Lake o **CDN** 30-31 P 4
Hjartdal ⋅ **N** 86-87 D 7
Hjellset o **N** 86-87 D 5
Hjerkinn o **N** 86-87 D 5
Hjørring o∙ **DK** 86-87 D 8
Hkakabo Razi ▲ **MYA** 142-143 K 1
Hkqingoi o **MYA** 142-143 H 5
Hlabisa o **ZA** 220-221 K 4
Hladiv ∼ **DZ** 190-191 H 7
Hkyenhpa o∙ **MYA** 142-143 H 2
Hlatikulu o **SD** 220-221 K 3

Hlegu o **MYA** 158-159 D 2
Hlobyne o **UA** 102-103 H 3
Hlotse o **LS** 220-221 J 4
Hluchiv o **UA** 102-103 H 2
Hluhluwe o **ZA** 220-221 K 4
Hluhluwe Game Reserve ⊥ **ZA** 220-221 L 4
Hluthi o **SD** 220-221 K 3
Hlybokae o **BY** 94-95 K 4
Hmeľnickij = Chmeľnyc'kyj ☆ **UA** 102-103 E 3
Hmitevskogo, poluostrov ⌣ **RUS** 120-121 N 4
H. N. Andersen, Kap ▲ **GRØ** 26-27 e 7
Hnilij Tikič ∼ **UA** 102-103 G 3
Ho ☆ **GH** 202-203 L 6
Hòa Bình o **VN** 158-159 E 2
Hòa Bình o **VN** 156-157 D 6
Hoài Nhon o **VN** 158-159 K 5
Hoanib ∼ **NAM** 216-217 B 9
Hoar, Lake o **ARK** 176-177 G 2
Hoareau ∼ **NAM** 216-217 B 9
Hoarusib ∼ **NAM** 216-217 B 8
Hoba Meteorite ∙∙ **NAM** 216-217 D 9
Hobart ★∙∙ **AUS** 180-181 J 7
Hobart o **USA** 44-45 H 2
Hobart Island ∼ **CDN** 36-37 N 2
Hobbs o **USA** 44-45 F 3
Hobbs Coast ⌣ **ARK** 16 F 23
Hobetsu o **J** 152-153 K 3
Hobhouse o **ZA** 220-221 H 4
Hobo o **CO** 60-61 D 6
Hobokasar o **VRC** 146-147 G 2
Hobol ∼ **RUS** 110-111 R 6
Hobro o **DK** 86-87 D 8
Hobson, Cape ▲ **CDN** 24-25 X 5
Hobyo o **SP** 208-209 J 4
Hoceima, Al ▲ **MA** 188-189 K 3
Hochalmspitze ▲ **A** 92-93 M 5
Hochfeld ∼ **NAM** 216-217 D 10
Hồ Chí Minh, Thành Phố = Thành Phố Hồ Chí Minh ★∙∙ **VN** 158-159 J 5
Hochstetterbugten ≈ 26-27 p 6
Hochstetter Forland ∼ **GRØ** 26-27 p 6
Hockin o **CDN** 34-35 H 3
Hóc Môn o **VN** 158-159 J 5
Hočo o **RUS** 120-121 D 3
Hočo, Ystannah- o **RUS** 110-111 N 3
Hoctún o **MEX** 52-53 K 1
Hodaδ Afarin o **IR** 128-129 M 3
Hodal o **IND** 138-139 F 6
Hodar, utes ⋅ **RUS** 122-123 H 3
Hodgenville o **USA** 46-47 F 7
Hodges Gardens ⋅ **USA** 44-45 L 4
Hodges Hill ▲ **CDN** 38-39 I R 4
Hodgeville o **CDN** 34-35 C 5
Hodgson River o **AUS** 174-175 C 4
Hodgson River o **AUS** 174-175 C 4
Hodh ∼ **RIM** 196-197 F 6
Hodh ech-Chargui □ **RIM** 196-197 G 5
Hodh el-Gharbi □ **RIM** 196-197 E 6
Hodigere o **IND** 140-141 G 4
Hodma ∼ **SP** 208-209 J 3
Hódmezővásárhely o∙ **H** 92-93 Q 5
Hodna, Plaine du ⌣ **DZ** 190-191 D 2
Hodo Dan ▲ **DVR** 150-151 F 8
Hồ Đo'n Du'o'ng o **VN** 158-159 K 5
Hodonín o∙ **CZ** 92-93 O 4
Hodog Shamo ∼ **VRC** 154-155 E 1
Hodutka, gora ▲ **RUS** 122-123 R 2
Hodžambas o **TM** 136-137 J 5
Hodzana River ∼ 20-21 Q 3
Hodza-Obigarm o **TJ** 136-137 L 5
Hodžejli = Hüdžajli ☆∙ **US** 136-137 F 3
Hoë o **RUS** 122-123 K 3
Hoedspruit o **ZA** 220-221 K 2
Hoë Karoo = Upper Karoo = **ZA** 220-221 E 5
Hoek van Holland o **NL** 92-93 H 3
Hoeryong o **DVR** 150-151 G 6
Hoëveld ⌣ **ZA** 220-221 J 3
Hoeyang o **DVR** 150-151 F 8
Hof o **D** 92-93 L 3
Höfðakaupstaður = Skagaströnd o **IS** 86-87 c 2
Hoffmans Cay ∼ **BS** 54-55 G 2
Hofmark = Odorheiu Secuiesc o **RO** 102-103 F 4
Hofn o **IS** 86-87 f 2
Hofsós o **IS** 86-87 c 2
Höfu o **J** 152-153 D 7
Hoğalák, Kūh-e ▲ **IR** 128-129 M 5
Höganäs o **S** 86-87 F 8
Hogan Group ∼ **AUS** 180-181 J 5
Hogart, Mount ▲ **AUS** 178-179 J 5
Hogatza River ∼ **USA** 20-21 N 4
Hogback Mountain ▲ **USA** 42-43 F 5
Hog Cay ∼ **BS** 54-55 H 3
Høgeloft ▲ **N** 86-87 D 6
Hogem Ranges ▲ **CDN** 32-33 G 4
Hoggar ▲ **DZ** 190-191 E 9
Hoggar, Tassili du ▲ **DZ** 190-191 E 10
Høggia ▲ **N** 86-87 E 5
Hog Harbor o **VAN** 184 II a 2
Hog Landing o **USA** 20-21 N 4
Hogsback o **ZA** 220-221 H 6
Högsby o∙ **S** 86-87 H 8
Høgtuvbreen ▲ **N** 86-87 F 3
Hohenstein = Olsztynek o **PL** 92-93 Q 2
Hohenwald o **USA** 48-49 E 2
Hohe Tatra = Tatry ▲ **SK** 92-93 P 4
Hohe Tauern ▲ **A** 92-93 M 5
Hohhot ★ **VRC** 154-155 G 1
Hohoe ☆ **GH** 202-203 L 6
Hoholitna River ∼ **USA** 20-21 M 6
Hoh Sai Hu o **VRC** 144-145 J 3
Höhük o **J** 152-153 D 7
Hoh Xil Hu o **VRC** 144-145 J 3
Hoh Xil Shan ▲ **VRC** 144-145 F 3
Hội An o **VN** 158-159 K 3
Hoima o **EAU** 212-213 C 3

Hoisington ○ USA 42-43 H 6
Hoj, vozvyšennost' ▲ RUS 108-109 O 7
Hoja Wajeer ○ SP 212-213 H 4
Hojd Tamir gol ~ MAU 148-149 E 4
Hoka ○ RI 166-167 E 5
Hokitika ○ NZ 182 C 5
Hokkaidō ~ J 152-153 K 3
Hokksund ☆ N 86-87 D 7
Hokmābād ○ IR 136-137 E 6
Hokua ○ VAN 184 II a 2
Hola ○ EAK 212-213 H 4
Holalagondi ○ IND 140-141 G 3
Holanda Rous, Reserva Florestal ⊥ RCH 80 F 7
Hola Prystan' ○ UA 102-103 H 4
Holbæk ○ DK 86-87 E 9
Holbox, Isla ~ MEX 52-53 L 1
Holbrook ○ AUS 180-181 J 3
Holbrook (AZ) 44-45 B 2
Holbrook ○ USA (AZ) 44-45 B 2
Holbrook USA ○ 40-41 H 5
Holchit, Punta ▲ MEX 52-53 K 1
Holden ○ USA 32-33 O 5
Holden ○ USA (MO) 42-43 L 6
Holden ○ USA (UT) 40-41 H 6
Holdenville ○ USA 44-45 J 4
Holdrege ○ USA 42-43 H 5
Hold with Hope Halvø ∪ GRØ 26-27 p 7
Hole in the Wall ∴ BS 54-55 G 2
Holejaha ~ RUS 108-109 O 5
Holešov ○ CZ 92-93 O 4
Holger Danskes Tinde ▲ GRØ 26-27 n 4
Holguín ○ C 54-55 G 4
Holhol ○ DJI 208-209 F 3
Holiday Resort · USA 176-177 E 7
Holitna River ~ USA 20-21 M 6
Hollabrunn ○ A 92-93 O 4
Holland ○ CDN 34-35 G 6
Holland ○ · USA 46-47 E 4
Holland Bay ≈ 54-55 G 6
Hollat ○ RI 166-167 G 4
Holleschau = Holešov ○ CZ 92-93 O 4
Hollick-Kenyon Plateau ▲. ARK 16 F 26
Hollis ○ USA (AK) 32-33 D 4
Hollis ○ USA (OK) 44-45 H 2
Hollister ○ USA (CA) 40-41 D 7
Hollister ○ USA (MO) 44-45 L 1
Hollister, Mount ▲ AUS 172-173 B 7
Hollókő = H 92-93 P 4
Hollow Water Indian Reserve ✕ CDN 34-35 H 5
Holly ○ USA 42-43 F 6
Holly Ridge ○ USA 48-49 K 2
Holly Springs ○ USA 48-49 L 2
Hollywood ○ USA (FL) 48-49 H 6
Hollywood ·· USA (CA) 40-41 E 8
Holm ☆ RUS 94-95 M 3
Holma ○ WAN 204-205 K 4
Holman Island ○ CDN 24-25 N 5
Hólmavík ○ IS 86-87 c 2
Holme Park ○ ZA 220-221 J 2
Holmes Reef ∴ AUS 174-175 H 4
Holmes River ~ CDN 32-33 L 5
Holmia ○ GUY 62-63 E 3
Holmogorskaja ○ RUS 88-89 Q 5
Holmsk ○ RUS 122-123 K 5
Holmskj ○ RUS 126-127 C 5
Holms Ø ~ GRØ 26-27 W 6
Holmsund ☆ S 86-87 K 5
Holm-Žirkovskij ○ RUS 94-95 N 4
Holnicote Bay ≈ 183 E 5
Holoj ~ RUS 118-119 F 9
Holokit ~ RUS 108-109 a 7
Holomoloh-Jurjah ~ RUS 118-119 G 4
Holoog ○ NAM 220-221 C 3
Holroyd River ~ AUS 174-175 F 4
Holstebro ○●· DK 86-87 D 8
Holstein ○ USA 42-43 K 4
Holsteinsborg = Sisimiut ○ GRØ 28-29 O 3
Holter Lake ○ USA 40-41 J 2
Holton ○ CDN 36-37 V 4
Holton ○ USA 42-43 K 6
Holt Rock ○ AUS 176-177 E 6
Holuwon ○ RI 166-167 K 4
Holyhead ○ GB 90-91 E 5
Holyoke ○ USA 42-43 F 6
Holyrood ○ CDN 38-39 I S 5
Holyrood ○ USA 42-43 H 6
Hom ~ NAM 220-221 D 4
Homa Bay ○ EAK 212-213 E 4
Homām ○ IR 128-129 N 4
Homand ○ IR 134-135 H 2
Hománe ○ MOC 218-219 H 6
Homathko Icefield ⊏ CDN 32-33 H 6
Homathko River ~ CDN 32-33 H 6
Hombetsu ○ J 152-153 K 3
Hombori ○ RMM 202-203 K 2
Hombori, Monts du ▲ RMM 202-203 J 2
Hombre Muerto, Salar del ○ RA 76-77 D 3
Home Bay ≈ 28-29 G 2
Homedale ○ USA 40-41 F 4
Home Hill ○ AUS 174-175 H 4
Homein ○ IR 134-135 D 2
Homeľ ☆ BY 94-95 M 4
Home of Bullion Mine · AUS 178-179 C 1
Homer ○ USA (AK) 22-23 V 3
Homer ○ USA (LA) 44-45 L 3
Homer Tunnel ☆ NZ 182 A 6
Homerville ○ USA 48-49 G 4
Homestead ○ AUS 174-175 H 7
Homestead ○ USA 48-49 H 4
Homestead National Monument ∴ USA 42-43 J 5
Homewood ○ USA 48-49 E 4
Homi, hrebet ▲. RUS 122-123 H 3
Hominy ○ USA 44-45 J 1
Homnābād ○ IND 140-141 G 4
Homo, Cerro el ▲ HN 52-53 L 4
Homodža ○ RUS 118-119 G 6
Homolha ○ RUS 118-119 G 6
Homolho ○ RUS 118-119 H 6

Homonhon Island ~ RP 160-161 F 7
Homot Tohadar, Čabal ▲ SUD 200-201 H 3
Homustah ○ RUS 118-119 P 4
Homyeľ = Homeľ ☆ BY 94-95 M 4
Honāvar ○ IND 140-141 F 3
Honaz Dağ ▲ TR 128-129 C 4
Honda ○ CO 60-61 D 5
Honda, Chott El ○ DZ 190-191 E 3
Honda, Monts du ▲ DZ 190-191 D 3
Honda Bay ≈ RP 160-161 K 7
Hòn Đất ○ VN 158-159 H 5
Hondekliphaai ○ ZA 220-221 C 5
Hondo ~ C 54-55 D 3
Hondo ○ J 152-153 D 8
Hondo ○ USA (NM) 44-45 E 3
Hondo ○ USA (TX) 44-45 H 5
Hondo, No. ~ BH 52-53 K 3
Hondo River ~ BH 52-53 K 3
Honduras ▪ HN 52-53 A 4
Honduras, Cabo de ▲ HN 52-53 L 3
Hone ○ CDN 34-35 F 2
Hønefoss ☆ N 86-87 E 6
Hone River ~ CDN 36-37 O 2
Honesdale ○ USA 46-47 L 5
Honey Lake ○ USA 40-41 D 5
Hŏng ○ IR 134-135 G 4
Hong'an ○ VRC 154-155 J 6
Hongch'ŏn ○ ROK 150-151 F 9
Hongde ○ VRC 154-155 G 3
Hong Do ~ ROK 150-151 E 10
Hongdong ○ VRC 154-155 G 3
Hongfeng Hu ~ VRC 156-157 E 3
Hông Gai ○ VN 156-157 E 6
Honggun-ri ○ DVR 150-151 G 7
Hongguau ○ VRC 154-155 C 3
Honghu ○ VRC 156-157 H 2
Hong Hu ~ VRC 156-157 H 2
Hongjiang ○ VRC 156-157 F 3
Hongliuyuan ○ VRC (GAN) 146-147 M 5
Hongliuyuan ○ VRC 154-155 B 2
Hongmen ○ VRC 154-155 L 6
Hongmenhe ○ VRC 154-155 F 5
Hŏng Ngụ' ○ VN 158-159 H 5
Hŏn Gŏm, B. D. ≈ VN 158-159 K 4
Hongor ○ MAU (DOG) 148-149 K 5
Hongor ○ MAU (SUH) 148-149 J 5
Hongshan ○ VRC 154-155 H 6
Hongshishan ○ VRC 148-149 C 6
Hongshui He ~ VRC 156-157 E 4
Hongū ○ J 152-153 F 8
Honguedo, Détroit d' ≈ 38-39 M 4
Hongwei ○ VRC 156-157 K 2
Hongwon ○ DVR 150-151 F 7
Hongya ○ VRC 156-157 C 2
Hongyuan ○ VRC 154-155 D 5
Hongze ○ VRC 154-155 L 5
Hongze Hu ~ VRC 154-155 L 5
Honghzi Liang ▲ VRC 154-155 F 4
Honi ○ GE 126-127 E 6
Honiara ★ SOL 184 I d 3
Honiton ○ GB 90-91 F 6
Honjō ○ J 152-153 J 6
Honkawane ○ J 152-153 H 7
Hon Minh Hoa ~ VN 158-159 J 5
Honnali ○ IND 140-141 F 3
Honningsvåg ☆ N 86-87 M 1
Honokaa ○ USA 48-49 E 7
Honokahua ○ USA 48-49 E 7
Honolulu ☆ · USA 48-49 D 7
Honoria ○ PE 64-65 E 4
Hon Rái ~ VN 158-159 H 6
Honshū ~ J 152-153 E 7
Hòn Thị, Mũi ▲ VN 158-159 K 4
Hontorbé ○ SN 202-203 D 2
Honuu ☆ RUS 110-111 Y 6
Hood, Mount ▲ USA 40-41 D 3
Hood Bay ≈ 183 D 6
Hood Point ▲ AUS 176-177 E 7
Hood River ~ CDN 30-31 P 2
Hood River ○ USA 40-41 D 3
Hoogeveen ○ NL 92-93 J 2
Hooghly ~ IND 140-141 J 2
Hooker ○ USA 44-45 G 1
Hooker Creek Aboriginal Land ✕ AUS 172-173 K 5
Hook Island ~ AUS 174-175 K 7
Hook Point ▲ CDN 34-35 P 3
Hool ○ MEX 52-53 K 2
Hoonah ○ USA 32-33 C 2
Hoopa Valley Indian Reservation ✕ USA 40-41 C 5
Hooper ○ USA (CO) 42-43 F 6
Hooper ○ USA (NE) 42-43 J 5
Hooper, Cape ▲ CDN 28-29 G 2
Hooper Bay ○ USA 20-21 G 6
Hooper Bay ≈ 20-21 G 6
Hooper Inlet ≈ 24-25 F 6
Hoopeston ○ USA 46-47 E 5
Hoop Nature Reserve, De ⊥ ZA 220-221 F 7
Hoopstad ○ ZA 220-221 G 3
Hoover Dam ∴ USA 40-41 G 7
Hopa ☆ TR 128-129 J 2
Ho-pang ○ MYA 142-143 L 4
Hope ○ USA 40-41 F 4
Hope < NAM 220-221 C 3
Hope Creek ~ USA 42-43 E 5
Hope ○ USA (AK) 20-21 G 6
Hope ○ USA (AR) 44-45 L 3
Hope, Cape ▲ CDN 24-25 O 6
Hope, Kap ▲ Ittaajimmiit ○ GRØ 26-27 o 8
Hope, Lake ○ AUS 176-177 F 6
Hope, Mount ▲ AUS 180-181 H 2
Hope Campbell Lake ○ AUS 176-177 G 4
Hopefield ○ ZA 220-221 D 6
Hope Island ~ CDN 38-39 D 6
Hopelchén ○· MEX 52-53 K 2
Hopeless, Mount ▲ AUS 178-179 E 5
Hopen ~ N (ROM) 86-87 D 5
Hopen ~ N (SVA) 86-87 O 4
Hopen Radio ○ N 84-85 D 4
Hope or Panda, Lake ○ AUS 178-179 A 6

Hoper ~ RUS 94-95 S 5
Hoper ~ RUS 102-103 N 2
Hope River ~ AUS 176-177 H 7
Hopes Advance Bay ≈ 36-37 P 5
Hopetoun ○ AUS (VIC) 180-181 G 3
Hopetoun ○ AUS (WA) 176-177 F 6
Hopetown ○ ZA 220-221 F 4
Hopewell ○ USA 46-47 J 7
Hopewell Cape ○ CDN 38-39 M 6
Hopewell Islands ~ CDN 36-37 K 5
Hô Phú Ninh ○ VN 158-159 H 5
Hopi Indian Reservation ✕ USA 44-45 B 1
Hopin ○ MYA 142-143 K 3
Hopkins, Lake ○ AUS 176-177 K 2
Hopkinsville ○ USA 46-47 E 7
Hopland ○ USA 40-41 C 6
Ho-pong ○ MYA 142-143 K 3
Hoppner Inlet ≈ 24-25 e 7
Hopton Lake ○ USA 30-31 V 5
Hoque ○ ANG 216-217 B 7
Hoquiam ○ USA 40-41 C 2
Hor ~ RUS 122-123 F 5
Horace Mount ▲ USA 20-21 Q 3
Horana ○ CL 140-141 J 7
Ḩorāsān ▪ IR 134-135 G 2
Horasan ☆ TR 128-129 K 2
Horbusuonka ~ RUS 110-111 P 4
Hörby ☆ S 86-87 F 9
Horcajo de los Montes ○ E 98-99 E 5
Horcones, Río ~ RA 76-77 E 3
Horden River ~ PNG 183 A 2
Hor'dil Sar'dag ▲ MAU 148-149 D 2
Hordogoj ○ RUS 118-119 G 4
Horej-Ver ○ RUS 88-89 Y 3
Horezmskaja oblast' ▪ US 136-137 G 4
Horezu ○ RO 102-103 C 5
Horgo ○ MAU 148-149 D 3
Horgočuma ~ RUS 110-111 N 7
Horincy ○ RUS 118-119 K 5
Horinger ○ VRC 154-155 G 1
Horixontina ○ BR 76-77 E 1
Horki ☆ BY 94-95 M 4
Horlick Mountains ▲. ARK 16 E 0
Horlivka ○ UA 102-103 L 3
Horlog Hu ~ VRC 144-145 L 2
Hormoz ○ IR 134-135 F 5
Hormoz, Ğazīre-ye ~ IR 134-135 G 5
Hormoz, Küh-e ▲ IR 134-135 G 5
Hormozgān ▪ IR 134-135 F 5
Hormūd ○ IR 134-135 F 5
Hormuz, Strait of = Hormoz, Tange-ye ≈ 134-135 G 5
Horn, The ▲ AUS 180-181 J 4
Horn, Van ○ USA 44-45 E 4
Horna ○ RI 166-167 G 2
Homachos ○ E 98-99 D 5
Hornaday River ~ CDN 24-25 K 6
Hornavan ○ S 86-87 H 3
Hornbjarg ▲ IS 86-87 b 1
Hornby Bay ≈ CDN 30-31 L 2
Hornconcitos ○ PA 52-53 C 7
Horndal ○ S 86-87 H 6
Horndean ○ CDN 34-35 H 6
Hornell ○ USA 46-47 K 4
Hornell Lake ○ CDN 30-31 M 3
Hornepayne ○ CDN 34-35 O 6
Hornillos, Punta ▲ PE 70-71 B 6
Horn Island ~ AUS 174-175 G 2
Horn Island ~ USA 48-49 D 4
Horn Mountains ▲ AUS 20-21 L 6
Horn Plateau ▲ CDN 30-31 J 4
Horn River ~ CDN 30-31 K 1
Hornsby ○ AUS 180-181 L 2
Hornslandet ≈ S 86-87 H 6
Hornsund ≈ 84-85 J 4
Horodnja ○ UA 102-103 G 2
Horodok ☆ UA 102-103 C 3
Horog ☆ TJ 136-137 M 6
Horof ○ RUS 122-123 E 6
Horombe ~ RM 222-223 D 9
Horošee ozero ○ RUS 124-125 L 2
Horoshiri-dake ▲ J 152-153 K 3
Horowupotana ○ CL 140-141 J 7
Horqin Youji Zhongqi ○ VRC 150-151 C 5
Horqin Zuoyi Houqi ○ VRC 150-151 D 6
Horqueta ○ PY 76-77 J 2
Horqueta, La ○ YV (BOL) 62-63 D 2
Horqueta, La ○ YV (DAM) 60-61 K 3
Horquetas, Las ○ CR 52-53 C 6
Ḩorramābād ☆· IR 134-135 C 2
Ḩorram Darre ○ IR 128-129 N 4
Ḩorramšahr ○· IR 134-135 C 3
Horrocks ○ AUS 176-177 C 5
Horru ○ VRC 144-145 H 5
Horsburgh Atoll ~ MV 140-141 B 5
Horse (Saint Barbe) Islands ~ CDN 38-39 R 3
Horse Creek ~ USA (WY) 42-43 E 5
Horse Creek ~ USA 42-43 E 5
Horse Creek ~ USA 42-43 G 5
Horsefly ○ CDN 32-33 K 5
Horsefly Lake ○ CDN 32-33 K 5
Horsens ○ DK 86-87 D 9
Horse River ~ CDN 30-31 N 4
Horseshoe Bay ○ CDN (ALB) 32-33 P 4
Horseshoe Bay ○ CDN (BC) 32-33 J 7
Horseshoe Bend ○ USA 40-41 F 4
Horseshoe Bend National Military Park ∴ USA 48-49 F 3
Horsham ○ AUS 180-181 G 3
Horsham ○ GB 32-33 Q 6
Horten ☆ N 86-87 E 7
Hortensias, Las ○ RCH 78-79 C 5
Horti ○ IND 140-141 F 3
Hortobágy ○ H 92-93 Q 5
Hortobágyi Nemzeti Park ⊥ H 92-93 Q 5
Horton Lake ○ CDN 30-31 V 5
Horton River ~ CDN 24-25 H 6

Horumnug-Tajga, hrebet ▲. RUS 116-117 G 10
Horus, Temple of ∴· ET 194-195 F 5
Horuonga ~ RUS 110-111 O 6
Horwakil ~ RUS 200-201 K 5
Horwakil Bay ≈ 200-201 K 5
Horwood Lake ○ CDN 38-39 C 5
Horyn' ~ UA 102-103 E 2
Horyn' ~ UA 102-103 D 3
Horyuji ··· J 152-153 F 7
Hosab Kalesi ·· TR 128-129 K 3
Hoşap Kalesi · TR 128-129 K 3
Hosahalli ○ IND 140-141 F 4
Hosa'ina ○ ETH 208-209 C 5
Hosakote ○ IND 140-141 G 3
Hos-Alas ○ RUS 110-111 S 6
Hosanagara ○ IND 140-141 F 4
Hosato, ozero ○ RUS 108-109 T 6
Hosdrug ○ IND 140-141 F 4
Hosdurga ○ IND 140-141 G 4
Hose, Pegunungan ▲. MAL 162-163 K 3
Hosedaju ~ RUS 108-109 H 8
Hoseinābād ○ IR 128-129 M 5
Hoseinābād ○ IR 134-135 H 3
Hoseinābād ○ IR 134-135 J 3
Hoseinābād, Rūdḫāne-ye ~ IR 134-135 J 3
Hoseiniye-ye Ḩoda Dād ○ IR 134-135 G 2
Hoselaw ○ CDN 32-33 P 4
Hoŝeutovo ○ RUS 96-97 E 10
Hoshāb ○ PK 134-135 I 5
Hoshangābād ○ IND 138-139 F 8
Hoshiārpur ○ IND 138-139 F 3
Hosib ~ SUD 200-201 G 3
Hōsi ○ AFG 138-139 J 3
Hoska ~ RUS 110-111 O 6
Hoskins ○ PNG 183 F 3
Hoskote ○ IND 140-141 G 4
Hōšōōt ○ MAU 146-147 J 1
Hospah ○ USA 44-45 D 2
Hospäs Rüd ~ AFG 134-135 K 3
Hospet ○ IND 140-141 G 3
Hospicio ~ PE 70-71 B 6
Hospicio ○ PE 70-71 B 5
Hospital, Cuchilla del ▲ ROU 78-79 M 2
Hosrovi ○ RUS 108-109 T 6
Hosrovskij zapovednik ⊥ AR 128-129 L 2
Höst ○ AFG 138-139 B 3
Hoste, Isla ~ RCH 80 F 7
Hostomeľ ○ UA 102-103 G 2
Hosūr ○ IND 140-141 G 4
Hoš Yeilāg ○ IR 136-137 D 6
Hot ○ THA 142-143 K 5
Hotaka-dake ▲ J 152-153 G 6
Hotamış Gölü ○ TR 128-129 E 4
Hotan He ~ VRC 144-145 E 6
Hotan ○ VRC 144-145 D 4
Hotan He ~ VRC 146-147 E 6
Hotazel ○ ZA 220-221 F 3
Hotbe Sarā ○ IR 128-129 N 3
Hotchkiss ○ CDN 32-33 M 3
Hotchkiss ○ USA 42-43 D 6
Hotchkiss River ~ CDN 32-33 L 3
Hotel dos Manantiales ○ RA 80 F 4
Hotel el Cerrito ○ RA 80 E 5
Hotel las Horquetas ○ RA 80 E 4
Hotel Río Negro ○ PY 76-77 H 3
Hô Thác Bà ○ VN 158-159 H 1
Hotham, Cape ▲ AUS 172-173 K 2
Hotham, Lake ○ CDN 24-25 Z 3
Hotham River ~ AUS 176-177 D 6
Hotmin Mission ○ PNG 183 A 3
Hotoho ~ RUS 118-119 F 5
Hotpaas ○ RI 166-167 D 5
Hot Springs ○ USA (NC) 48-49 G 3
Hot Springs ○ USA (SD) 42-43 F 4
Hot Springs ○ USA (AR) 44-45 L 2
Hot Springs ○ ZW 218-219 G 4
Hot Springs, Cove · USA 40-41 F 1
Hot Springs National Park ⊥ USA 44-45 L 2
Hotspur Seamount ≃ 72-73 M 4
Hottah Lake ○ CDN 30-31 K 3
Hottentotsbaai ≈ 220-221 B 3
Hottentotskloof ○ ZA 220-221 D 6
Hot Water Beach · NZ 182 E 2
Houëçbo ○ DY 204-205 E 5
Houeiriye ○ RIM 196-197 G 6
Houghton ○ USA 46-47 D 2
Houghton Lake ○ USA (MI) 46-47 F 3
Houghton Lake ○ USA (MI) 46-47 F 3
Houhai ○ VRC 156-157 G 6
Houhora ○ NZ 182 D 1
Houhu ○ VRC 156-157 H 5
Houlton ○ USA 46-47 P 2
Houma ○ TON 184 V 4
Houma ○ USA 44-45 M 5
Houma ○ VRC 154-155 H 4
Houmt Souk ○ TN 190-191 H 4
Houndé ○· BF 202-203 J 4
Hounien, Zouan- ○ CI 202-203 F 6
Hourtin et de Carcans, Lac d' ○ F 90-91 G 9
Housholder Pass ▲ USA 40-41 J 2
Houshui Wan ≈ 156-157 F 7
Houston ○ CDN 32-33 J 4
Houston ○ USA (AK) 20-21 G 6
Houston ○ USA (MS) 48-49 D 3
Houston ○· USA (TX) 44-45 K 5
Houston, Lake ○ USA 44-45 K 4
Houston Point ▲ CDN 34-35 K 3
Houtman Abrolhos ~ AUS 176-177 B 4
Houxia ○ VRC 146-147 H 4
Houʼe-Soltān ○ IR 134-135 D 1
Hova ○ S 86-87 F 7
Hovd ○ MAU (ÖVÖ) 148-149 H 3
Hovd ☆ MAU 146-147 K 1
Hovden ○ N 86-87 D 7
Hoveize ○ IR 134-135 C 3
Hovenweep National Monument · USA 42-43 G 7
Hoverla, hora ▲ UA 102-103 D 3
Hovgaards Ø ~ GRØ 26-27 a 7
Hovoro ○ SOL 184 I c 3
Hövsgöl ○ MAU 148-149 D 3

Hövsgöl nuur ○ MAU 148-149 E 2
Hovsu-Aksy ○ RUS 116-117 F 10
Howakil ~ ER 200-201 K 5
Howakil Bay ≈ 200-201 K 5
Howard ○ USA (SD) 42-43 J 3
Howard ○ USA (WI) 46-47 D 3
Howard City ○ USA 46-47 F 4
Howard Island ~ AUS 174-175 C 3
Howard Junction ○ NZ 182 D 4
Howard Lake ○ CDN 30-31 Q 4
Howard Springs ○· AUS 172-173 K 2
Howe, Cape ▲ AUS 180-181 K 4
Howell ○ USA 46-47 G 4
Howes ○ USA 42-43 F 3
Howick ○ ZA 220-221 J 4
Howick Group ~ AUS 174-175 H 4
Howitt, Lake ○ AUS 178-179 E 4
Howlong ○ AUS 180-181 J 3
Howship, Mount ▲ AUS 174-175 B 3
Hoxie ○ USA (AR) 44-45 M 1
Hoxie ○ USA (KS) 42-43 G 6
Hoxtolgay ○ VRC 146-147 J 3
Hoxud ○ VRC 146-147 H 4
Höy ○· IR 128-129 L 3
Høyanger ☆ N 86-87 C 6
Hoyé, Bin- ○ CI 202-203 F 6
Hoyerswerda ○ D 92-93 N 3
Høylandet ○ N 86-87 E 4
Hoyo, Mont ▲ ZRE 212-213 C 3
Hozier Islands ~ CDN 36-37 R 2
Hpangpai ○ MYA 142-143 L 3
Hpawngtut ○ MYA 142-143 K 3
Hradec Králové ○ CZ 92-93 N 3
Hradyz'k ○ UA 102-103 H 3
Hrami ~ GE 126-127 F 7
Hrebinka ○ UA 102-103 H 2
Hristais ○ BR 68-69 J 4
Hrodna ☆ BY 94-95 H 5
Hroma ~ RUS 110-111 Z 4
Hromskaja guba ≈ 110-111 Z 4
Hromtau ☆ KA 126-127 N 2
Hron ~ SK 92-93 P 4
Hrubieszów ○ PL 92-93 R 3
Hsenwi ○ MYA 142-143 K 4
Hsinchu ○ RC 156-157 M 4
Hsingying ○ RC 156-157 M 5
Hsipaw ○ MYA 142-143 K 4
Hsuen Shan ▲ RC 156-157 M 3
Htingu ○ MYA 142-143 K 3
Hua'an ○ VRC 156-157 L 3
Huab ~ NAM 216-217 C 9
Huabuzhen ○ VRC 156-157 L 2
Huaca ○ EC 64-65 D 1
Huacalera ○ RA 76-77 E 2
Huacaña ○ PE 64-65 E 9
Huacas, Las ∴· CR 52-53 B 6
Huacaya ○ BOL 70-71 F 7
Huacaya, Río ~ BOL 76-77 F 1
Huacaybamba ○ PE 64-65 D 6
Huachacalla ○ BOL 70-71 C 6
Huachi ○ VRC 154-155 G 3
Huachi, Lago ○ BOL 70-71 F 4
Huachinera ○ MEX 50-51 E 2
Huacho ○ PE 64-65 D 7
Huachos ○ PE 64-65 E 8
Huacrachuco ○ PE 64-65 D 6
Huacullani ○ PE 70-71 D 6
Huade ○ VRC 148-149 M 7
Huadian ○ VRC 150-151 F 6
Huaguang Jiao ~ VRC 158-159 L 2
Huahaizi ○ VRC 146-147 M 6
Hua Hin ○ THA 158-159 E 4
Huahua, Río = Río Wawa ~ NIC 52-53 B 4
Huaiá-Miçu, Río ~ BR 68-69 B 7
Huai'an ○ VRC (HEB) 154-155 J 1
Huai'an ○ VRC (JIA) 154-155 L 2
Huaibei ○ VRC 154-155 K 5
Huaibin ○ VRC 154-155 J 5
Huai He ~ VRC 154-155 J 5
Huaihua ○ VRC 156-157 F 3
Huaiji ○ VRC 156-157 H 5
Huailai ○ VRC 154-155 J 1
Huaillas, Cerro ▲ BOL 70-71 D 5
Huai Na ○ THA 158-159 F 2
Huainan ○ VRC 154-155 K 5
Huairen ○ VRC 154-155 H 2
Huaiyang ○ VRC 154-155 J 5
Huaiyin ○ VRC 154-155 L 5
Huai Yot ○ THA 158-159 E 7
Huaiyuan ○ VRC 154-155 K 5
Huajialing ○ VRC 154-155 D 4
Huajianzi ○ VRC 150-151 D 7
Huajuapan ○ MEX 50-51 G 5
Huajuapan de León ○· MEX 52-53 F 3
Huaki ○· RI 166-167 H 4
Hualapai Indian Reservation ✕ USA 40-41 H 7
Hualiangting SK ○ VRC 154-155 J 6
Hualien ○ RC 156-157 N 4
Huallaga, Río ~ PE 64-65 D 6
Huallanca ○ PE 64-65 D 6
Huamachuco ○ PE 64-65 C 6
Huamali ○ PE 64-65 E 7
Huamani ○ PE 64-65 E 8
Huamantla ○ MEX 52-53 F 2
Huambo ○ ANG 216-217 C 6
Huambo ☆ ANG (HBO) 216-217 C 6
Huambo ○ PE 64-65 F 9
Huambos ○ PE 64-65 C 5
Huampami ○ PE 64-65 C 4
Huamuxtitlán ○ MEX 52-53 F 3
Huañamarca ○ PE 70-71 A 5
Huanan ○ VRC 150-151 H 4
Huancabamba ○ PE 64-65 C 5
Huancabamba, Río ~ PE 64-65 C 5
Huancacho, Sierra ▲ RA 78-79 D 7
Huancane ○ PE 70-71 C 4
Huancano ○ PE 64-65 E 8
Huancapi ○ PE 64-65 E 8
Huancas ~ PE 64-65 C 5
Huancavelica ○· PE 64-65 E 8
Huancay ○· PE 64-65 E 8
Huanchaca, Cerro ▲ BOL 70-71 D 7
Huanchaca, Parque Nacional ⊥ BOL 70-71 G 4

Huanchon ○ PE 64-65 E 7
Huangcangyu ○ VRC 154-155 K 5
Huangchuan ○ VRC 154-155 J 5
Huanda Yang ○ VRC 154-155 N 6
Huangdi Ling · VRC 154-155 G 3
Huanggang ○ VRC 154-155 J 6
Huanggangliang ▲ VRC 148-149 N 6
Huangguoshu Pubu ✦ VRC 156-157 D 3
Huang He ~ VRC 154-155 G 3
Huanghe Kou ≈ 154-155 L 3
Huanghua ○ VRC 154-155 K 2
Huanglianyu ▲ VRC 156-157 K 4
Huangling ○ VRC 154-155 G 3
Huanglong ○ VRC 154-155 F 4
Huanglonggong ··· VRC 154-155 M 6
Huanglong Si · VRC 154-155 F 5
Huangmei ○ VRC 154-155 J 6
Huangpi ○ VRC 154-155 J 6
Huangping ○ VRC 156-157 E 3
Huangqi Hai ~ VRC 154-155 H 1
Huangsha ○ VRC 156-157 L 3
Huangshan ○· VRC (ANH) 156-157 L 4
Huangshan ··· VRC (ANH) 154-155 L 6
Huangshi ○ VRC 154-155 J 6
Huang Shui ~ VRC 154-155 C 3
Huangtu Gaoyuan ⊥ VRC 154-155 G 3
Huangyaguan · VRC 154-155 K 5
Huangyan ○ VRC 156-157 N 3
Huangyuan ○ VRC 154-155 B 3
Huangzhong ○ VRC 154-155 C 3
Huaninaoyuan ○ VRC 156-157 G 3
Huaning ○ VRC 156-157 C 4
Huanqueo ○ MEX 52-53 D 2
Huanquén ○ RA 78-79 J 4
Huanquer ○ RA 76-77 D 6
Huanren ○ VRC 150-151 E 7
Huanta ○ PE 64-65 E 8
Huantacero ○ MEX 52-53 C 2
Huantraico, Sierra del ▲ RA 78-79 D 4
Huanuco ○ PE 64-65 D 7
Huanuni ○ BOL 70-71 D 6
Huanuren ○ MEX 50-51 H 7
Huan Xian ○ VRC 154-155 E 3
Huanza ○ PE 64-65 D 7
Huanzo, Cordillera de ▲ PE 64-65 F 9
Huapí, Serranías ▲ NIC 52-53 B 5
Huaping ○ VRC 156-157 B 3
Huaping Yŭ ~ RC 156-157 M 4
Huaping Z.B. ⊥· VRC 156-157 B 3
Huaqiao ○ VRC 154-155 E 6
Huaqién ○ RCH 78-79 D 2
Huaquillas ○ EC 64-65 B 3
Huara ○ RCH 70-71 C 7
Huaral ○ PE 64-65 D 7
Huaraz ☆ PE 64-65 D 6
Huari ○ PE 64-65 D 6
Huarina ○ BOL 70-71 C 5
Huarmey ○ PE 64-65 C 7
Huarochiri ○ PE 64-65 D 8
Huarocondo ○ PE 64-65 F 8
Huarquehue, Parque Nacional ⊥ RCH 78-79 D 3
Huasabas ○ MEX 50-51 E 3
Huasaga ○ EC 64-65 C 3
Huasago, Río ~ PE 64-65 D 3
Hua Sai ○ THA 158-159 F 6
Huascarán, Parque Nacional ⊥··· PE 64-65 D 6
Huasco ○ RCH 76-77 B 5
Huasco, Río ~ RCH 76-77 B 5
Huasco, Salar de ○ RCH 70-71 C 7
Huashan ○ VRC (GXI) 156-157 E 5
Huashan · VRC (SXI) 154-155 G 4
Huashan-Yabihua · VRC 156-157 E 6
Huashaoying ○ VRC 154-155 J 1
Huashixia ○ VRC 144-145 M 3
Huata, Península de ▲ BOL 70-71 C 5
Huatabampo ○ MEX 50-51 E 4
Huatugou ○ VRC 144-145 M 2
Huatunas, Lago ○ BOL 70-71 E 4
Huatusco de Chicuellar ○ MEX 52-53 F 2
Huaura, Río ~ PE 64-65 D 7
Huautla ○ MEX 50-51 K 7
Huautla de Jiménez ○ MEX 52-53 F 2
Huaxi · VRC 156-157 E 3
Hua Xian ○ VRC (GDG) 156-157 H 5
Hua Xian ○ VRC (HEN) 154-155 J 4
Huayabamba, Río ~ PE 64-65 D 5
Huayacocotla ○ MEX 52-53 E 1
Huaying ○ VRC (GDG) 154-155 H 6
Huaying ○ VRC (SXI) 154-155 H 4
Huaylacayan ○ PE 64-65 D 7
Huayllay ○ PE 64-65 D 7
Huaynamota, Río ~ MEX 50-51 G 6
Huayquiña ○ RA 76-77 D 2
Huayuan ○ VRC 156-157 F 2
Huayuachi ○ PE 64-65 E 9
Huazhou ○ VRC 156-157 G 5
Hubar, al- ○ KSA 134-135 C 5
Hubayah, Biʼr ⌑ LAR 192-193 K 2
Hubbard ○ USA 42-43 J 4
Hubbard, Mount ▲ CDN 20-21 V 6
Hubbard, Pointe ▲ CDN 36-37 Q 5
Hubbard Creek Reservoir ◁ USA 44-45 H 4
Hubbard Glacier ⊏ CDN 20-21 V 6
Hubbard Lake ○ USA 46-47 G 3
Hubbards ○ CDN 38-39 M 6
Hubbel Trading Post National Historic Site ∴ USA 44-45 C 2
Hub Chauki ○ PK 134-135 M 6
Hubei ▪ VRC 154-155 G 6
Hubli ○ IND 140-141 F 3
Hubynycha ○ UA 102-103 J 3
Hucal ○ RA 78-79 G 5
Hucal, Valle de ~ RA 78-79 G 5
Hučeto, ozero ○ RUS 108-109 S 6
Huckitta ○ AUS 178-179 C 3
Huckitta Out Station ○ AUS 178-179 C 2
Hudačan, al- ○ Y 132-133 C 6
Hudaida, al- ~ Y 132-133 C 6

Hudan ~ RUS 118-119 E 10
Hudat = Xudat ○ AZ 128-129 N 2
Huddersfield ○ GB 90-91 G 5
Hüdi ○ SUD 200-201 H 3
Hudie Quan ~ VRC 142-143 M 2
Hudiksvall ○ S 86-87 H 6
Hud Mount ▲ USA 20-21 T 3
Hudosej ~ RUS 114-115 S 2
Hudra, Wädi ~ Y 132-133 F 5
Hudson ○ USA (MI) 46-47 F 5
Hudson ○ USA (NY) 46-47 M 4
Hudson ○ USA (WI) 42-43 K 3
Hudson, Cerro ▲ RCH 80 D 3
Hudson Bay ○ CDN 34-35 F 4
Hudson Canyon ≃ 46-47 M 6
Hudson Falls ○ USA 46-47 M 4
Hudson Land ⊥ GRØ 26-27 o 7
Hudson Mountains ▲. ARK 16 F 27
Hudson River ~ USA 46-47 M 4
Hudson's Hope ○ CDN 32-33 K 3
Hudson Strait ≈ CDN 36-37 M 3
Huduk, Naryn- ○ RUS 126-127 G 5
Hudwin Lake ○ CDN 34-35 J 4
Hudžah ~ RUS 120-121 M 2
Hüdžajli ○· US 136-137 F 3
Huê ☆· ··· VN 158-159 J 2
Huechulafquén, Lago ○ RA 78-79 D 5
Hueco ○ USA 44-45 E 4
Huecu, El ○ RA 78-79 D 4
Huedin ○ RO 102-103 C 4
Huehuetenango ☆· GCA 52-53 J 4
Huehuetla ○ MEX 52-53 E 1
Huejotzingo ○ MEX 52-53 E 2
Huejúcar ○ MEX 50-51 H 6
Huejuquilla El Alto ○ MEX 50-51 H 6
Huejutla de Reyes ○ MEX 50-51 K 7
Huelma ○ E 98-99 F 6
Huelva o· E 98-99 D 6
Huenccho Sur ○ RCH 78-79 D 3
Huéneja ○ E 98-99 F 6
Huenque, Río ~ PE 70-71 C 5
Huepil ○ RCH 78-79 D 4
Hueque, Río ~ YV 60-61 G 2
Huequén ○ RCH 78-79 D 4
Huequi, Peninsula ▲ RCH 78-79 C 7
Huequi, Volcán ▲ RCH 78-79 C 7
Huércal-Overa ○ E 98-99 G 6
Huerfano River ~ USA 42-43 E 7
Huerta, La ○ MEX 52-53 D 2
Huerta, La ○ RCH 78-79 D 3
Huerta, Sierra de la ▲ RA 76-77 D 6
Huertecillas ○ MEX 50-51 J 5
Huesca o· E 98-99 G 3
Huéscar ○ E 98-99 F 6
Huesos, Arroyo de los ~ RA 78-79 K 4
Huetamo de Nuñez ○ MEX 52-53 D 2
Huey Yang Waterfall ⊥· THA 158-159 E 5
Hufayyira, al- ○ KSA 130-131 J 5
Hufra, al- ⌑ KSA 130-131 F 3
Huftarøy ~ N 86-87 B 6
Hufūf, al- ○ KSA 130-131 L 5
Hufuma ○ RI 166-167 G 2
Huğand ○ TJ 136-137 L 4
Hugdjakit ~ RUS 108-109 b 7
Hugdjungda, hrebet ▲ RUS 116-117 O 2
Hugh Butler Lake ○ USA 42-43 G 5
Hughenden ○ AUS 174-175 H 7
Hughenden ~ RA 78-79 J 2
Hughes ○ RA 78-79 J 2
Hughes ○ USA 20-21 N 3
Hughesville ○ USA 46-47 K 5
Hugh Glass Monument ∴ USA 42-43 F 3
Hugh River ~ AUS 176-177 M 2
Hugli ~ IND 142-143 E 5
Hugo ○ USA 44-45 K 2
Hugo Reservoir ◁ USA 44-45 K 2
Huguangyan · VRC 156-157 G 6
Huguenot Memorial ∴ ZA 220-221 D 6
Huguo ○ VRC 156-157 D 2
Huia ○ NZ 182 E 2
Huiʼan ○ VRC 156-157 L 4
Huiʼanpu ○ VRC 154-155 E 3
Huib-Hochplato ⊥ NAM 220-221 C 3
Huichang ○ VRC 156-157 J 4
Huichapan ○ MEX 52-53 E 1
Huichon ○ DVR 150-151 F 7
Huidong ○ VRC (GDG) 156-157 J 5
Huidong ○ VRC (SIC) 156-157 C 3
Huila ○ ANG 216-217 C 7
Huilai ○ VRC 156-157 K 5
Huila Plateau ▲ ANG 216-217 C 7
Huili ○ VRC 156-157 C 3
Huillapima ○ RA 76-77 E 5
Huilong ○ VRC 156-157 G 3
Huimbayoc ○ PE 64-65 E 5
Huimilpan ○ MEX 52-53 D 2
Huimin ○ VRC 154-155 K 3
Huiñaimarca, Lago ○ PE 70-71 C 5
Huinan ○ VRC 150-151 F 6
Huinca Renancó ○ RA 78-79 G 3
Huining ○ VRC 154-155 D 4
Huishui ○ VRC 156-157 E 3
Huisne ~ F 90-91 H 7
Huitimbo ○ BR 202-203 J 7
Huitong ○ VRC 156-157 F 3
Huitoto, Raudal ~ CO 64-65 F 1
Huitoyacu, Río ~ PE 64-65 D 3
Huittinen ○ FIN 88-89 G 6
Huitzo ○ MEX 52-53 F 3
Huivulai el Medio ○ MEX 50-51 E 4
Huixtepec ○ MEX 52-53 F 3
Huixtla ○ MEX 52-53 H 4
Huiyang ○ VRC 156-157 J 5
Huize ○ VRC 156-157 C 3
Huizhou ○ VRC 156-157 J 5
Hujra Shāh Meqeem ○ PK 138-139 D 4
Hukeri ○ IND 140-141 F 2
Hukou ○ VRC 156-157 K 2
Hukovo ○ UA 102-103 L 3
Hukuntsi ○ RB 220-221 E 1
Hula ○ PNG 183 D 6
Hulah Lake ○ USA 44-45 J 1

Jasper ○ **USA** (AL) 48-49 E 3
Jasper ○ **USA** (AR) 44-45 L 1
Jasper ○ **USA** (FL) 48-49 G 4
Jasper ○ **USA** (GA) 48-49 F 2
Jasper ○ **USA** (IN) 46-47 E 3
Jasper ○ **USA** (TX) 44-45 K 4
Jasper Lake ○ **CDN** 32-33 M 5
Jasper National Park ⊥ ··· **CDN**
　32-33 L 5
Jasrāna ○ **IND** 138-139 G 6
Jastrow = Jastrowie ○ **PL** 92-93 O 2
Jastrowie ○ **PL** 92-93 O 2
Jasubibeteri ○ **YV** 60-61 J 6
Jataí ○ **BR** 72-73 E 4
Jatapu, Rio ∼ **BR** 66-67 H 4
Jatapu, Serra do ▲ **BR** 62-63 E 6
Jatapuzinho, Rio ∼ **BR** 62-63 E 5
Jateí ○ **BR** 76-77 K 2
Jath ○ **IND** 140-141 F 2
Jāti ○ **IND** 68-69 J 5
Jati ○ **PK** 138-139 D 3
Jati ○ **RI** 168 D 1
Jatibarang ○ **RI** 168 C 3
Jatibonico ○ **C** 54-55 F 4
Jatiluhur, Danau ○ **RI** 168 B 3
Jatirogo ○ **RI** 168 D 3
Jatiwangi ○ **RI** 168 C 3
Jatobá ○ **BR** (MAT) 70-71 K 3
Jatobá ○ **BR** (P) 68-69 B 4
Jaú ○ **BR** 72-73 F 4
Jaú, Parque Nacional do ⊥ **BR**
　66-67 H 4
Jaú, Rio ∼ **BR** 66-67 F 4
Jauaperi, Rio ∼ **BR** 62-63 E 5
Jauaruaú ○ **BR** 66-67 E 4
Jaucha, Arroyo de ∼ **RA** 78-79 E 3
Jauharābād ○ **PK** 138-139 D 3
Jauja ○ · **PE** 64-65 D 7
Jaumave ○ **MEX** 50-51 K 6
Jaunpiebalga ○ · **LV** 94-95 K 3
Jaunpur ○ **IND** 142-143 C 3
Jaupaci ○ **BR** 72-73 E 4
Jauquara, Rio ∼ **BR** 70-71 J 4
Jaurdi ○ **AUS** 176-177 F 5
Jaurin ∼ **RUS** 122-123 D 4
Jauru ○ **BR** (GSU) 70-71 H 4
Jauru ○ **BR** (MAT) 70-71 H 4
Jauru, Rio ∼ **BR** 70-71 H 5
Java Barat □ **RI** 168 B 3
Javaj, poluostrov ∪ **RUS** 108-109 Q 5
Javan ○ **TJ** 136-137 L 5
Javari, Rio ∼ **BR** 62-63 H 6
Javari, Rio ∼ **BR** 64-65 F 4
Java Sea = Java, Laut ≈ **13** C 3
Java Tengah □ **RI** 168 C 3
Java Timur □ **RI** 168 D 4
Java Trench ≃ **168** C 3
Javier, isla ∼ **RCH** 80 C 3
Javier de Viana ○ **ROU** 76-77 J 6
Javieņka ∴ **KA** 124-125 F 1
Jawa ∼ **RI** 168 B 3
Jāwad ○ **IND** 138-139 E 7
Jawi ○ **RI** 162-163 H 5
Jawor ○ · **PL** 92-93 O 3
Jaworzno ○ **PL** 92-93 P 3
Jay ○ **USA** 44-45 K 1
Jayamkondacholapuram ○ **IND**
　140-141 H 5
Jayanca ○ **PE** 64-65 C 5
Jayapura ○ **RI** 166-167 L 3
Jayawijaya, Pegunungan ▲ **RI**
　166-167 K 3
Jayton ○ **USA** 44-45 G 3
Jazā'ir, Al ★··· **DZ** 190-191 D 2
Jaželbicy ○ **RUS** 94-95 N 2
Jazevec ∼ **RUS** 88-89 T 4
Jazira Tarut ∼ **KSA** 134-135 D 5
Jazykovo ○ **RUS** (ULN) 96-97 E 6
Jazykovo ○ **RUS** (BAS) 96-97 J 6
J.B. Thomas, Lake ○ **USA** 44-45 G 3
J. C. Jacobsen, Kap ▲ **GRØ** 28-29 Z 2
Jconha ○ **BR** 72-73 H 6
Jean ○ **USA** 40-41 G 8
Jeanette Bay ≈ **CDN** 36-37 V 7
Jean Rabel ○ **RH** 54-55 J 5
Jeavons, Lake ○ **AUS** 172-173 J 6
Jebala ⊥ **MA** 188-189 D 4
Jebba ○ **WAN** 204-205 F 4
Jeberos ○ **PE** 64-65 D 4
Jebiniana ○ **TN** 190-191 H 3
Jebri ○ **PK** 134-135 L 5
Jeddah = Ğidda ○ **KSA** 132-133 A 3
Jeddore Cape ▲ **CDN** 38-39 N 6
Jędrzejów ○ **PL** 92-93 Q 3
Jeedamya ○ **AUS** 176-177 F 4
Jefawa ○ **SUD** 206-207 F 4
Jefe, Cerro ▲ **PA** 52-53 E 7
Jeffara ⊥ **TN** 190-191 H 4
Jeffers ○ **USA** 42-43 K 3
Jefferson ○ **USA** (AR) 44-45 L 2
Jefferson ○ **USA** (GA) 48-49 G 2
Jefferson ○ **USA** (IN) 46-47 G 2
Jefferson ○ **USA** (TX) 44-45 K 3
Jefferson, Mount ▲ **USA** 40-41 F 6
Jefferson City ○ **USA** (MO) 42-43 L 6
Jefferson City ○ **USA** (MT) 40-41 H 4
Jefferson City ○ **USA** (TN) 48-49 G 1
Jefferson Proving Ground ×× **USA**
　46-47 F 3
Jefferson State Memorial, Fort ∴ **USA**
　46-47 F 5
Jeffersonville ○ **USA** (GA) 48-49 G 3
Jeffersonville ○ **USA** (IN) 46-47 F 4
Jeffersonville ○ **USA** (VT) 46-47 M 3
Jeffrey City ○ **USA** 42-43 D 4
Jeffries, Lake ○ **AUS** 176-177 G 3
Jef-Jef el Kébir ⊥ **TCH** 198-199 K 2
Jega ○ **WAN** 198-199 F 6
Jege ○ **WAN** 204-205 F 4
Jeinemeni, Cerro ▲ **RCH** 80 D 3
Jejekangphu Kang ▲ **BHT** 142-143 F 2
Jejevo ○ **SOL** 184 I d 1
Jejuí-Guazú, Rio ∼ **PY** 76-77 J 3
Jēkabpils ○ · **LV** 94-95 J 3
Jelai ○ **RI** 162-163 J 6
Jelap La ∴ **BHT** 142-143 F 2
Jelgava ○ ·· **LV** 94-95 H 3
Jeli ○ **MAL** 162-163 D 2

Jellico ○ **USA** 48-49 F 1
Jelly Bean Crystals · **AUS** 178-179 L 5
Jelmusibak ○ **RI** 164-165 D 4
Jelsa ○ **HR** 100-101 F 3
Jema ○ **IND** 202-203 K 6
Jemāa-Ida-Oussemlat ○ **MA**
　188-189 G 6
Jemaluang ○ **MAL** 162-163 E 3
Jema Shet' ∼ **ETH** 208-209 D 4
Jembawan, Danau ○ **RI** 162-163 F 6
Jember ○ **RI** 168 E 4
Jemberam ○ **GNB** 202-203 C 4
Jemez Pueblo ○ **USA** 44-45 D 2
Jemil'čyne ○ **UA** 102-103 E 2
Jeminay ○ **VRC** 146-147 G 2
Jemma ○ **WAN** (BAU) 204-205 H 4
Jemma ○ **WAN** (KAD) 204-205 H 4
Jempang, Danau ○ **RI** 164-165 D 4
Jen ○ **WAN** 204-205 J 4
Jena ○ **D** 92-93 L 3
Jenakijeve ○ **UA** 102-103 L 3
Jenda ○ **MW** 214-215 G 7
Jendouba ○ **TN** 190-191 G 3
Jeneien, Oued ∼ **TN** 190-191 G 5
Jenerhodar ○ **UA** 102-103 J 4
Jeneshuaya, Arroyo ∼ **BOL** 70-71 D 7
Jenin ○ **WB** 130-131 D 1
Jenipapo ○ **BR** (AMA) 66-67 G 5
Jenipapo ○ **BR** (P) 62-63 K 6
Jenipapo ○ **BR** (TOC) 68-69 D 5
Jenipapo, Ribeiro ∼ **BR** 68-69 D 5
Jenipapo, Rio ∼ **BR** 68-69 G 4
Jenissej = Enisej ∼ 10-11 H 2
Jenissej = Enisej ∼ **RUS** 10-11 H 2
Jenkins ○ **USA** 46-47 G 7
Jenner ○ **CDN** 32-33 P 6
Jenner ○ **USA** 40-41 C 6
Jennings ○ **CDN** 20-21 Z 7
Jennings ○ **USA** 44-45 L 4
Jenny ○ **VRC** 156-157 H 2
Jenny Lind Island ∼ **CDN** 24-25 V 6
Jenolan Caves · **AUS** 180-181 L 2
Jensen, Cape ▲ **CDN** 24-25 h 6
Jens Munk Island ∼ **CDN** 24-25 g 6
Jens Munk Ø ∼ **GRØ** 28-29 U 4
Jepara ○ **RI** 168 D 3
Jeparit ○ **AUS** 180-181 F 4
Jequié ○ **BR** 72-73 K 2
Jequitinhonha, Rio ∼ **BR** 72-73 L 3
Jequiriçá ○ **BR** 72-73 L 2
Jequitaí ○ **BR** 72-73 H 4
Jequitaí, Rio ∼ **BR** 72-73 H 4
Jequitiba ○ **BR** 72-73 J 5
Jequitinhonha ○ **BR** 72-73 K 4
Jequitinhonha, Rio ∼ **BR** 72-73 J 4
Jerada ○ **MA** 188-189 K 3
Jerangau, Kampung ○ **MAL**
　162-163 E 2
Jerangle ○ **AUS** 180-181 K 3
Jerantut ○ **MAL** 162-163 E 2
Jerba, Île de ∼ **TN** 190-191 G 4
Jerbar ○ **SUD** 206-207 K 6
Jerdera ○ **RI** 166-167 H 5
Jere ○ **RI** 164-165 J 4
Jerecuaro ○ **MEX** 52-53 D 1
Jérémie ∼ **RH** 54-55 H 5
Jeremoabo ○ **BR** 68-69 J 7
Jerer Shet' ∼ **ETH** 208-209 F 4
Jerez, Rio ∼ **MEX** 50-51 H 6
Jerez de García Salinas ○ **MEX**
　50-51 H 6
Jerez de la Frontera ○ **E** 98-99 D 6
Jerez de los Caballeros ○ **E** 98-99 D 5
Jericho ○ **AUS** 178-179 J 4
Jericho ○ **SOL** 184 I c 3
Jericho = Arīḥā ○ **AUT** 130-131 D 2
Jericho Dam < **ZA** 220-221 K 3
Jericoacoara, Ponta ▲ **BR** 68-69 H 3
Jerigu ○ **GH** 202-203 K 5
Jerilderie ○ **AUS** 180-181 H 3
Jerko La ▲ **VRC** 144-145 C 5
Jerome ○ **USA** 40-41 G 4
Jeroní ○ **BOL** 70-71 F 4
Jerramungup ○ **AUS** 176-177 E 6
Jersey ∼ **GBJ** 90-91 F 7
Jersey City ○ **USA** 46-47 L 5
Jerseyville ○ **USA** 46-47 C 6
Jertih ○ **MAL** 162-163 E 2
Jerumenha ○ **BR** 68-69 G 5
Jerusalem = Yěrūshalayim ★ ··· **IL**
　130-131 D 2
Jervis, Monte ▲ **RCH** 80 C 4
Jervis Bay · **AUS** 180-181 L 3
Jervis Inlet ≈ 32-33 J 7
Jervois ○ **AUS** 178-179 D 2
Jesenice ○ **SLO** 100-101 E 1
Jesi ○ **I** 100-101 D 3
Jesi, Monte ▲ **MOC** 214-215 H 7
Jesmond ○ **CDN** 32-33 N 6
Jessamine Creek ∼ **AUS** 178-179 G 2
Jesseltown = Kota Kinabalu ★· **MAL**
　160-161 B 10
Jessheim ○ **N** 86-87 E 6
Jessore ○ **BD** 142-143 F 4
Jesup ○ **USA** 48-49 H 4
Jesús Carranza ○ **MEX** 52-53 G 3
Jesús María ○ **RA** 76-77 G 6
Jesús Menéndez ○ **C** 54-55 G 4
Jet ○ **USA** 44-45 H 1
Jeta, Ilha de ∼ **GNB** 202-203 B 4
Jetmore ○ **USA** 42-43 H 6
Jetpur ○ **IND** 138-139 C 9
Jeudin, Pulau ∼ **RI** 166-167 H 5
Jevargi ○ **IND** 140-141 G 2
Jevlah ○ **AZ** 98-99 G 5
Jevpatorija ○ · **UA** 102-103 H 5
Jewel Cave National Monument · **USA**
　42-43 F 4
Jewish Autonomous Region = Evrejskaja
　avtonomnaja oblast' ∇ **RUS**
　122-123 G 4
Jeypore ○ **IND** 142-143 C 6
Jezercês, maja e ▲ **AL** 100-101 G 3
Jgarassu ∼ **BR** 68-69 L 5
Jhābua ○ **IND** 138-139 E 8
Jhajjar ○ **IND** 138-139 F 5

Jhal ○ **PK** 134-135 M 4
Jhālāwār ○ **IND** 138-139 F 7
Jhālāwār ∼ **IND** 138-139 F 7
Jhamat ○ **PK** 138-139 C 4
Jhang ○ **PK** 138-139 D 3
Jhang Branch < **PK** 138-139 D 4
Jhānsi ○ **IND** 138-139 G 7
Jharol ○ **IND** 138-139 D 7
Jhārsuguda ○ **IND** 142-143 D 5
Jhatpat ○ **PK** 138-139 B 5
Jheerak ○ **PK** 138-139 B 6
Jhelum ∼ **IND** 138-139 E 3
Jhelum ○ **PK** (PU) 138-139 D 3
Jhelum ∼ **PK** (HEI) 138-139 D 3
Jhenida ○ **BD** 142-143 F 4
Jhimpir ○ **PK** 138-139 B 7
Jhudo ○ **PK** 138-139 B 7
Jhunjhunūn ○ **IND** 138-139 F 6
Jiading ○ **VRC** 154-155 M 6
Jiahe ○ **VRC** 156-157 H 4
Jiajiang ○ **VRC** 156-157 C 2
Jialing Jiang ∼ **VRC** 154-155 E 6
Jiamusi ○ **VRC** 150-151 H 4
Ji'an ○ **VRC** (JIL) 150-151 F 7
Ji'an ○ **VRC** (JXI) 156-157 H 3
Jianchang ○ **VRC** 154-155 L 1
Jianchuan ○ **VRC** 142-143 M 4
Jiande ○ **VRC** 154-155 F 3
Jiangaoshan ▲ **MYA** 142-143 L 3
Jiangbai ○ **VRC** 156-157 E 2
Jiangcheng Hanizu Yizu Zizhixian ○ **VRC**
　156-157 B 3
Jiange ○ **VRC** 154-155 D 5
Jianghong ○ **VRC** 156-157 G 4
Jianghua ○ **VRC** 156-157 G 4
Jiangjin ○ **VRC** 156-157 E 2
Jiangjunmiao ○ **VRC** 146-147 J 3
Jiangkou ○ **VRC** (GZH) 156-157 F 3
Jiangkou ○ **VRC** (SIC) 154-155 F 6
Jiangle ○ **VRC** 156-157 K 3
Jiangling ○ **VRC** 154-155 G 6
Jiangmen ○ **VRC** 156-157 H 5
Jiangning ○ **VRC** 154-155 D 4
Jiangpo ○ **VRC** 150-151 G 6
Jiangpo Hu ○ **VRC** 150-151 G 6
Jiangshan ○ **VRC** 154-155 H 6
Jiangtai ○ **VRC** 154-155 L 5
Jiangyin ○ **VRC** 154-155 M 6
Jiangyou ○ **VRC** 156-157 G 4
Jianhe ○ **VRC** 156-157 F 3
Jianli ○ **VRC** 154-155 L 5
Jianmen G. · **VRC** 154-155 D 5
Jianning ○ **VRC** 156-157 K 3
Jian'ou ○ **VRC** 156-157 L 3
Jianping ○ **VRC** 154-155 L 1
Jianshi ○ **VRC** 154-155 F 6
Jianshui ○ **VRC** 156-157 C 5
Jianyang ○ **VRC** (FUJ) 156-157 L 3
Jianyang ○ **VRC** (SIC) 154-155 D 6
Jiaohe ○ **VRC** 150-151 G 6
Jiaohe Gucheng ∵·· **VRC** 146-147 J 4
Jiaojiang ○ **VRC** 156-157 M 2
Jiaokou ○ **VRC** 154-155 G 3
Jiaoling ○ **VRC** 156-157 K 4
Jiaonan ○ **VRC** 154-155 L 4
Jiaotle ○ **VRC** 144-145 F 6
Jiaozhou ○ **VRC** 154-155 L 3
Jiaozuo ○ **VRC** 154-155 H 4
Jiashan ○ **VRC** 154-155 K 5
Jiashi ○ **VRC** 146-147 C 6
Jia Tsuo La ▲ **VRC** 144-145 F 6
Jia Xian ○ **VRC** (HEN) 154-155 H 5
Jia Xian ○ **VRC** (SHA) 154-155 G 4
Jiaxing ○ **VRC** 154-155 M 6
Jiayin ○ **VRC** 150-151 H 3
Jiayu ○ **VRC** 156-157 H 2
Jiayuguan ○ **VRC** 146-147 O 6
Jibaro, El ○ **C** 54-55 F 4
Jibisa ∼ **EAK** 212-213 F 1
Jibiya ○ **WAN** 198-199 G 6
Jibóia ○ **BR** 66-67 C 2
Jibou ○ **RO** 102-103 C 4
Jicarilla Apache Indian Reservation ⊼
　USA 44-45 D 1
Jícaro Galán ○ **HN** 52-53 L 5
Jichang ○ **VRC** 156-157 D 3
Jičín ○ **CZ** 92-93 N 3
Jidali, togga ∼ **SP** 208-209 H 3
Jiddah = Ğidda ○ **KSA** 132-133 A 3
Jidhi ○ **SP** 208-209 H 3
Jiekkevarrebreen ∧ **N** 86-87 J 2
Jieshi ○ **VRC** 156-157 J 5
Jieshi Wan ≈ **VRC** 156-157 J 5
Jieshou ○ **VRC** 154-155 J 5
Jiexi ○ **VRC** 156-157 J 5
Jiexiu ○ **VRC** 154-155 G 3
Jieyang ○ **VRC** 156-157 K 5
Jieznas ○ **LT** 94-95 J 4
Jiga ○ **ETH** 208-209 C 3
Jiggalong ○ **AUS** 176-177 F 1
Jiggalong Aboriginal Land ⊼ **AUS**
　176-177 F 1
Jigongshan · **VRC** 154-155 J 6
Jiguani ○ **C** 54-55 G 4
Jigzhi ○ **VRC** 154-155 D 5
Jishan ○ **VRC** 154-155 G 4
Jishou ○ **VRC** 156-157 F 2
Jishu ○ **VRC** 150-151 F 5
Jitang Gulou ○ **VRC** 156-157 F 3
Jitaúna ○ **BR** 72-73 L 2
Jitra ○ **MAL** 162-163 D 2
Jitschin = Jičín ○ **CZ** 92-93 N 3
Jiu ∼ **RO** 102-103 C 6
Jiucai Ling ▲ **VRC** 156-157 G 4
Jiuhuashan · **VRC** 154-155 K 6
Jiujiang ○ **VRC** 156-157 H 2
Jiuluhu · **VRC** 156-157 L 4
Jiuling Shan ▲ **VRC** 156-157 H 2
Jiulongo ○ **VRC** 156-157 E 2
Jiulongshibatan · **VRC** 156-157 H 4
Jima ∼ **ETH** 208-209 D 4
Jimani ○ **DOM** 54-55 K 5

Jimata ○ **ETH** 208-209 C 4
Jimbe ○ **ANG** 214-215 B 6
Jimei ○ **VRC** 156-157 L 4
Jiménez ○ **MEX** (CHA) 50-51 G 4
Jiménez ○ **MEX** (COA) 50-51 J 4
Jimenez ○ **RP** 160-161 E 8
Jiménez de Teul ○ **MEX** 50-51 H 6
Jimeta ○ **WAN** 204-205 K 4
Jimi River ∼ **PNG** 183 C 3
Jimkar ○ **BHT** 142-143 G 2
Jimna Range ▲ **AUS** 178-179 M 4
Jimo ○ **VRC** (SXI) 150-151 H 5
Jimo ○ **VRC** (HEI) 150-151 L 5
Jimulco ○ **MEX** 50-51 H 5
Jin, Kepulauan ∼ **RI** 166-167 H 5
Jinan ☆· **VRC** 154-155 K 3
Jinchang ○ **VRC** 154-155 C 2
Jincheng ○ **VRC** (SHA) 154-155 H 4
Jincheng ○ **VRC** (YUN) 156-157 C 4
Jinchuan ○ **VRC** 154-155 C 6
Jin Ci · **VRC** 154-155 H 3
Jind ○ **IND** 138-139 F 5
Jindabyne ○ **AUS** 180-181 K 4
Jindare ○ **AUS** 172-173 K 3
Jin Dian · **VRC** 156-157 C 4
Jindřichův Hradec ○ **CZ** 92-93 N 4
Jinfo Shan ▲ **VRC** 156-157 E 2
Jingbian ○ **VRC** 154-155 F 3
Jingchuan ○ **VRC** 154-155 E 4
Jingde ○ **VRC** 154-155 L 6
Jingdezhen ○ **VRC** 156-157 K 2
Jingdong ○ **VRC** 156-157 C 4
Jingellic ○ **AUS** 180-181 J 3
Jinggu ○ **VRC** 156-157 C 4
Jinghai ○ **VRC** 154-155 K 3
Jinghe ○ **VRC** 146-147 F 3
Jing He ∼ **VRC** 154-155 F 4
Jinghong ○ **VRC** 156-157 B 4
Jingjiang ○ **VRC** 154-155 M 5
Jingle ○ **VRC** 154-155 G 3
Jingmen ○ **VRC** 154-155 G 6
Jingning ○ **VRC** 154-155 D 4
Jingpo ○ **VRC** 150-151 G 6
Jingpo Hu ○ **VRC** 150-151 G 6
Jingshan ○ **VRC** 154-155 H 6
Jingtai ○ **VRC** 154-155 D 3
Jingtieshan ○ **VRC** (GAN) 146-147 N 6
Jingtieshan ○ **VRC** (XUZ) 146-147 O 6
Jingtie Shan ▲ **VRC** 146-147 N 6
Jingxi ○ **VRC** 156-157 E 5
Jing Xian ○ **VRC** 154-155 L 6
Jingxing ○ **VRC** 154-155 H 3
Jingyan ○ **VRC** 156-157 D 2
Jingyu ○ **VRC** 150-151 F 6
Jingyuan ○ **VRC** 154-155 D 3
Jingyu Nao ▲ **VRC** 154-155 F 5
Jingzhou ○ **VRC** 156-157 F 3
Jinhe ○ **VRC** 150-151 C 2
Jinhua ○ **VRC** 156-157 L 2
Jining ○ **VRC** (NMZ) 148-149 L 7
Jining ○ **VRC** (SHD) 154-155 K 4
Jinja ○ **EAU** 212-213 D 3
Jinka ∼ **AUS** 178-179 C 2
Jinka ○ **ETH** 208-209 C 6
Jinkou ○ **VRC** 154-155 J 6
Jinning ○ **VRC** 156-157 C 4
Jinniu ○ **VRC** 154-155 J 6
Jinotega ○ **NIC** 52-53 B 5
Jinotepe ☆ **NIC** 52-53 B 5
Jinping ○ **VRC** (GZH) 156-157 F 3
Jinping ○ **VRC** (YUN) 156-157 C 5
Jinqian He ∼ **VRC** 154-155 F 3
Jinsha ○ **VRC** 156-157 E 3
Jinsha Jiang ∼ **VRC** 142-143 L 2
Jinsha Jiang ∼ **VRC** 144-145 M 4
Jinsha Jiang ∼ **VRC** 156-157 C 3
Jinshanlin · **VRC** 154-155 K 1
Jinshi ○ **VRC** 156-157 G 2
Jinshiqiao · **VRC** 156-157 G 3
Jinzū-gawa ∼ **J** 152-153 G 6
Ji-Paraná ○ **BR** 70-71 G 3
Jipe, Lake ○ **EAK** 212-213 F 5
Jipijapa ○ **EC** 64-65 B 2
Jiqui ○ **C** 54-55 F 4
Jiquilpan ○ **MEX** 52-53 C 1
Jiquiriçá, Rio ∼ **BR** 72-73 L 2
Jirau, Salto do ∼ **BR** 66-67 E 7
Jiri ○ **NEP** 144-145 F 2
Jirriban ○ **SP** 208-209 J 5
Jishan ○ **VRC** 154-155 G 4
Jishou ○ **VRC** 156-157 F 2
Jishu ○ **VRC** 150-151 F 5
Jitang Gulou ○ **VRC** 156-157 F 3
Jitaúna ○ **BR** 72-73 L 2
Jitra ○ **MAL** 162-163 D 2
Johannesburg ☆· **ZA** 220-221 J 3
Johan Peninsula ∪ **CDN** 26-27 N 4
Johi ○ **GUY** 62-63 E 5
Johi ○ **PK** 134-135 M 5
John Day Fossil Beds National Monument
　· **USA** (OR) 40-41 D 3
John Day Fossil Beds National Monument
　· **USA** (OR) 40-41 E 3
John Day River ∼ **USA** 40-41 E 3
John D'Or Prairie ○ **CDN** 30-31 M 6
John D'Or Prairie Indian Reserve ⊼ **CDN**
　30-31 M 6
John D. Rockefeller Junior Memorial
　Parkway ⊥ **USA** 40-41 J 4
John Dyer, Cape ▲ **CDN** 24-25 V 4
John Eyre Motel ○ **AUS** 176-177 H 6
John Eyre Telegraph Station ∴ **AUS**
　176-177 H 6
John Fitzgerald Kennedy Space Center
　×× **USA** 48-49 H 5
John Flagler, Lake ▲ **GRØ** 26-27 J 4
John Flynn Memorial · **AUS**
　174-175 C 6
John H. Kerr Reservoir < **USA** 48-49 J 1
John Martin Reservoir < **USA** 42-43 F 6
John Murray Ø ∼ **GRØ** 26-27 J 4
Johnny Hoe River ∼ **CDN** 30-31 J 3
John River ∼ **USA** 20-21 N 4
Johnson ○ **USA** 44-45 G 1
Johnson, Mount ▲ **USA** 176-177 H 2
Johnson, Pico de ▲ **MEX** 50-51 C 3
Johnson City ○ **USA** (TN) 48-49 G 1
Johnson City ○ **USA** (TX) 44-45 H 5
Johnson Dam, Daniel ∴ **CDN** 38-39 K 3
Johnson Island ○ **CDN** 36-37 N 6
Johnson River ○ **CDN** 30-31 G 4
Johnsons Crossing ○ **CDN** 20-21 Y 6
Johnston ○ **USA** 48-49 H 3
Johnston, Chute ∼ **ZRE** 214-215 E 6
Johnstone Hill · **AUS** 176-177 L 1
Johnstone South ○ **AUS** 174-175 J 5
Johnstone Strait ≈ 32-33 G 6
Johnston Islands ∼ **PNG** 183 D 2
Johnston Lakes, The ○ **AUS**
　176-177 F 6
Johnstown ○ **USA** 46-47 J 4
Johnstown Flood National Monument ·
　USA 46-47 J 4
Johor □ **MAL** 162-163 E 3
Johor Baharu ★· **MAL** 162-163 E 3
Jōhvi-Ahtme ○ **EST** 94-95 K 2
Joigny ○ **F** 90-91 J 8
Joinville ○ **BR** 74-75 F 6
Joinville ∼ **ARK** 16 G 31
Jojutla de Juárez ○ **MEX** 52-53 E 2
Jokau ○ **SUD** 208-209 D 3
Jokau ○ **SUD** 208-209 A 4
Jøkel-bugten ≈ 26-27 p 4
Jokkmokk ○ **S** 86-87 J 3
Jōkulsá á Brú ∼ **IS** 86-87 f 2

Jiurongcheng ○ **VRC** 154-155 N 3
Jiusuo ○ **VRC** 156-157 F 7
Jiutai ○ **VRC** 150-151 E 5
Jiuxu ○ **VRC** 156-157 E 4
Jiuyishan · **VRC** 156-157 H 4
Jiuzhaigou ··· **VRC** 154-155 C 5
Jivundu ○ **Z** 218-219 C 1
Jiwā', al- ○ **UAE** 132-133 J 4
Jiwani ○ **PK** 134-135 J 6
Jiwani, Rās ∼ **PK** 134-135 J 6
Jixi ○ **VRC** (ANH) 154-155 L 6
Jixi ○ **VRC** (HEI) 150-151 H 5
Jixian ○ **VRC** 150-151 H 4
Ji Xian ○ **VRC** (SXI) 154-155 G 3
Ji Xian ○ **VRC** (TIA) 154-155 K 1
Jiyang ○ **VRC** 154-155 K 3
Jiyuan ○ **VRC** 154-155 H 4
Jizan ○ **KSA** 132-133 C 4
Jlam ○ **NEP** 144-145 F 7
Jli ∼ **KA** 124-125 K 6
Joaçaba ○ **BR** 74-75 E 6
Joachin ○ **MEX** 52-53 G 3
Joaíma ○ **BR** 72-73 K 4
Joal-Fadiout ○ **SN** 202-203 B 2
Joana Coeli ○ **BR** 62-63 K 6
João, Rio ∼ **BR** 72-73 J 7
João Arregui ○ **BR** 76-77 J 5
João Câmara ○ **BR** 68-69 L 4
João Chagas ○ **ANG** 214-215 B 6
João Fagundes ○ **BR** 76-77 J 6
João Farias ○ **BR** 62-63 E 6
João Lisboa ○ **BR** 68-69 E 4
João Monlevade ○ **BR** 72-73 J 5
João Neiva ○ **BR** 72-73 K 5
João Pessoa ☆ **BR** 68-69 L 5
João Pinheiro ○ **BR** 72-73 G 4
João Vaz ○ **BR** 72-73 K 2
Joaquim ○ **BR** 68-69 G 5
Joáquim Gomes ○ **BR** 68-69 L 5
Joaquim Rios, Salto ∼ **BR** 70-71 H 3
Jobabo ○ **C** 54-55 G 4
Jobele ○ **WAN** 204-205 E 5
Jobillos, Los ○ **DOM** 54-55 K 5
Jordán, El ○ **CO** 60-61 F 5
Jordan, River ∼ 32-33 H 7
Jordan = Urdunn ■ **JOR** 130-131 D 2
Jordania ○ **BR** 72-73 K 4
Jordan Valley ○ **USA** 40-41 F 4
Jorf ○ **MA** 188-189 J 4
Jorge, Cabo ▲ **RCH** 80 C 5
Jorge Montt, Isla ∼ **RCH** 80 C 5
Jorgucat ○ **AL** 100-101 H 5
Jorhát ○ **IND** 142-143 J 2
Joriapani ○ **NEP** 144-145 C 6
Jörm ○ **S** 86-87 H 4
Jorong ○ **RI** 164-165 E 5
Joronga ∼ Pulau Hasil ∼ **RI**
　164-165 L 4
Jorskoe ploskogor'e ▲ **GE** 126-127 F 7
Joru ○ **WAL** 202-203 E 6
Jos ○ **WAN** 204-205 H 4
Josefa Ortiz de Domínguez Estacione,
　Presa < **MEX** 50-51 G 4
Josegun River ○ **CDN** 32-33 M 4
Joselândia ○ **BR** 70-71 J 4
José Pedro Varela ○ **ROU** 78-79 M 2
Joseph ○ **USA** 40-41 F 3
Joseph, Lake ○ **CDN** (NFL) 38-39 M 2
Joseph, Lake ○ **CDN** (ONT) 38-39 H 3
Joseph Bonaparte Gulf ≈ 172-173 J 3
Joseph Henry, Cape ▲ **CDN** 26-27 N 2
Josephine River ∼ **CDN** 30-31 Y 4
Josephstaal ○ **PNG** 183 C 3
José Rodrigues ○ **BR** 68-69 C 4
Joshimath ○ **IND** 138-139 G 4
Joshkar Ola = Joškar-Ola ☆ **RUS**
　96-97 F 5
Joshua Tree National Monument · **USA**
　40-41 G 9
Joškar-Ola ☆ **RUS** 96-97 E 5
Jos Plateau ▲ **WAN** 204-205 H 4
Jostedalsbreen ∧ **N** 86-87 C 6
Jotajana ○ **YV** 60-61 K 3
Jotunheimen ▲ **N** 86-87 D 6
Jotunheimen nasjonalpark ⊥ **N**
　86-87 D 6
Joubertberge ▲ **NAM** 216-217 B 9
Joubertina ○ **ZA** 220-221 F 6
Joulter Cays ∼ **BS** 54-55 F 2
Jourdanton ○ **USA** 44-45 H 5
Joutel ○ **CDN** 38-39 G 4
Joutsa ○ **FIN** 88-89 J 6
Joutsijärvi ○ **FIN** 88-89 L 4
Jovellanos ○ **C** 54-55 E 3
Joviânia ○ **BR** 72-73 F 4
Joy, Mount ▲ **CDN** 20-21 Y 5
Joya de Ceren ·∴··· **ES** 52-53 K 5
Joya de los Sachas, La ○ **EC** 64-65 D 2
Joy Bay ≈ 36-37 M 4
Jreïda ○ **RIM** 196-197 B 5
Jreïf < **RIM** 196-197 E 4
J. Richardson Bay ≈ 26-27 P 3
Juaben ○ **GH** 202-203 K 6
Juami, Rio ∼ **BR** 66-67 D 3
Juami-Japura, Reserva Ecológica ⊥ **BR**
　66-67 C 4
Juanacatlán ○ **MEX** 52-53 C 1
Juan Aldama ○ **MEX** 50-51 H 5
Juan B. Alberdi ○ **RA** 76-77 E 4
Juan Bautista Tuxtepec ○ **MEX**
　52-53 F 2
Juan de Fuca Strait ≈ 40-41 B 1
Juan de Guia, Cabo San ▲ **CO**
　60-61 F 2
Juân de Nova, Île ∼ **F** 222-223 J 5
Jõkulsá á Brú ∼ **IS** 86-87 f 2

Jōkulsá á Fjöllum ∼ **IS** 86-87 e 2
Joli, Mont- ○ **CDN** 38-39 K 4
Joliet ○ **USA** 46-47 D 5
Joliette ○ **CDN** 38-39 H 5
Jolly Lake ○ **CDN** 30-31 N 3
Jolo ○ **RP** 160-161 D 9
Jolo Island ∼ **RP** 160-161 D 9
Jomala ○ **FIN** 88-89 H 6
Jomalig Island ∼ **RP** 160-161 E 5
Jombang ○ **RI** 168 E 3
Jombo ∼ **ANG** 216-217 C 5
Jombo ○ **GH** 202-203 L 5
Jomda ○ **VRC** 144-145 M 5
Jommon ○ **RI** 164-165 J 4
Jomo Lhari ▲ **BHT** 142-143 F 2
Jomonkum kumligi ∡ **US** 136-137 H 4
Jomsom ○ **NEP** 144-145 D 6
Jomu ○ **EAT** 212-213 D 5
Jonava = Ionava ⊥ **LT** 94-95 J 4
Jonē ○ **VRC** 154-155 D 5
Jones ○ **CDN** 34-35 J 6
Jones, Cape ▲ **CDN** 30-31 Y 4
Jones, Kap ▲ **GRØ** 26-27 p 8
Jones, Lake ○ **AUS** 172-173 H 5
Jones, Lake ○ **AUS** 176-177 G 2
Jonesboro ○ **USA** (AR) 44-45 L 2
Jonesboro ○ **USA** (LA) 44-45 L 3
Jones Islands ∼ **USA** 20-21 Q 1
Jones Sound ≈ 24-25 c 2
Jonesville ○ **USA** 44-45 M 4
Jonggol ○ **RI** 168 B 3
Jonglei Canal = Junqoley Canal < **SUD**
　206-207 K 4
Joniškis ○ **LT** 94-95 H 3
Jönköping ○ **S** 86-87 F 8
Jonquière ○ **CDN** 38-39 J 4
Jonuta ○ **MEX** 52-53 H 2
Joowhar ○ **SP** 212-213 K 2
Jopalayo, Cerro ▲ **RA** 76-77 D 5
Joplin ○ **USA** 44-45 K 1
Jordan ○ **RP** 160-161 E 7
Jordan ○ **USA** (MN) 42-43 L 3
Jordan ○ **USA** (MT) 42-43 D 2
Jōshin Etsu Kōgen National Park ⊥ **J**
　152-153 G 6
Júba, Rio ∼ **SUD** 206-207 K 6
Juba, Rio ∼ **BR** 70-71 H 4
Jubaylah, al- ∼ **Y** 132-133 K 5
Jubba, Webi ∼ **SP** 212-213 J 2
Jubbada Dhexe □ **SP** 212-213 H 3
Jubbada Hoose □ **SP** 212-213 H 3
Juberina ○ **YV** 60-61 K 5
Jubilee Island ∼ **CDN** 36-37 N 2
Jubilee Lake ○ **AUS** 176-177 J 4
Jubilee Lake ○ **CDN** 38-39 H 3
Jubni, Bi'r < **LAR** 192-193 L 2
Jucá, Rio ∼ **BR** 68-69 H 5
Júcar, Rio ∼ **E** 98-99 G 5
Juçara ○ **BR** (BAH) 68-69 H 7
Juçara ○ **BR** (GOI) 72-73 E 3
Jucás ○ **BR** 68-69 J 5
Juchipila ○ **MEX** 50-51 H 7
Juchitán ○ **MEX** 52-53 E 3
Juchitán de Zaragoza ○ · **MEX**
　52-53 G 3
Juchusquahuira, Río ∼ **BOL** 70-71 D 5
Juciape ○ **BR** 72-73 K 2
Jucú, Rio ∼ **BR** 72-73 K 5
Jucumarini, Lago ○ **PE** 70-71 D 5
Jucuri ○ **BR** 68-69 K 4
Jucurucu, Rio ∼ **BR** 72-73 L 4
Jucurutu ○ **BR** 68-69 K 4
Judenburg ○ **A** 92-93 N 5
Judèto, ozero ○ **RUS** 108-109 O 8
Judge Daly Promontory ⊥ **CDN**
　26-27 Q 3
Judith River ∼ **USA** 42-43 C 2
Judoma ∼ **RUS** 120-121 H 4
Judoma ∼ **RUS** 120-121 J 4
Judomskij, hrebet ▲ **RUS** 120-121 J 3
Judybaevo ○ **RUS** 96-97 K 7
Juelsminde ○ **DK** 86-87 E 9
Jufrah, Al ⊥ **LAR** 192-193 G 3
Jug ∼ **RUS** 96-97 D 4
Juganskij, zapovednik ⊥ **RUS**
　114-115 N 5
Jugarskaja Ob' ∼ **RUS** 114-115 M 4
Jugiong ○ **AUS** 180-181 K 3
Jugo-Kamskij ○ **RUS** 96-97 J 5
Jugorënok ○ **RUS** 120-121 J 4
Juh ○ **VRC** 154-155 F 3
Juhnov ○ **RUS** 94-95 O 4
Juhovič ○ **RUS** 94-95 L 3
Juhua Dao · **VRC** 150-151 G 7
Juína ○ **BR** 70-71 H 2
Juinamirim, Rio ∼ **BR** 70-71 H 2
Juiná ou Zui-Uina, Rio ∼ **BR** 70-71 H 3
Juist ∼ **D** 92-93 J 2
Juiz de Fora ○ **BR** 72-73 J 6
Juizhou ○ **VRC** 156-157 E 2
Jujun ○ **RI** 162-163 D 6
Jujuy ■ **RA** 76-77 E 2
Jukagirskoe ploskogor'e ▲ **RUS**
　110-111 d 6
Jukamenskoe ○ **RUS** 96-97 H 5
Jukkasjärvi ○ **S** 86-87 K 3
Jukonda ∼ **RUS** 114-115 J 4
Jukseevo ○ **RUS** 96-97 H 4
Jukta ○ **RUS** 116-117 M 4
Juktali ∼ **RUS** 116-117 O 5
Jula ∼ **RUS** 88-89 S 5
Jula, Jasiira ∼ **SP** 212-213 J 4
Julaca ○ **BOL** 70-71 D 7
Juldessa ▲ **ETH** 208-209 D 7
Julesburg ○ **USA** 42-43 G 5
Juli ○ **PE** 70-71 C 5
Júlia ○ **BR** 66-67 C 3
Juliaca ○ **PE** 70-71 B 4
Julia Creek ○ **AUS** 174-175 G 4
Julia-Mabay ○ **C** 54-55 G 4
Julian ○ **USA** 40-41 G 9
Julián, Lac ○ **CDN** 36-37 L 7
Julianatop ▲ **SME** 62-63 G 4
Julianehab = Qaqortoq ○ **GRØ**
　28-29 R 6
Julianehabsfjord ≈ 28-29 R 6
Julião ○ **BR** 66-67 C 2
Julião ○ **ZW** 218-219 G 4
Juliiske Alpe ▲ **SLO** 100-101 D 1
Julio, 9 de ○ **RA** 78-79 J 4
Julio, 16 de ○ **RA** 78-79 J 4
Julio de Castilhos ○ **BR** 74-75 D 7
Julius, Lake ○ **AUS** 174-175 F 4
Juljoma ○ **RUS** 88-89 M 4
Julundur ○ **IND** 138-139 F 4
Julong Shan ▲ **VRC** 154-155 G 6
Julpa, Rio ∼ **BOL** 70-71 D 6
Julwânia ○ **IND** 138-139 E 8
Juma ○ **RUS** 88-89 M 4
Juma, Rio ∼ **BR** 66-67 E 5

Kama ∼ **RUS** 114-115 J 4
Kama ∼ **RUS** 114-115 D 5
Kamada < **TCH** 198-199 G 4
Kamaday o **Z** 152-153 G 6
Kamaishi o **J** 152-153 J 5
Kamakawalar, Danau ∼ **RI** 166-167 H 3
Kamakwie o **WAL** 202-203 D 5
Kamal o **RI** 168 E 3
Kamal o **TCH** 198-199 H 2
Kamál, Abū ☆ **SYR** 128-129 J 5
Kamale Mountain ▲ **WAN** 204-205 K 3
Kamália o **PK** 138-139 D 4
Kamalpur o **IND** 142-143 G 3
Kaman ☆ **TR** 128-129 E 3
Kamanga o **EAT** 212-213 D 5
Kamangu o **Z** 214-215 F 6
Kamanyola o **ZRE** 212-213 B 5
Kamáraj o **IR** 134-135 F 6
Kamarán ∼ **Y** 132-133 C 6
Kamarán ∼ **Y** 132-133 C 6
Kamarang o **GUY** 62-63 D 3
Kámareddi o **IND** 138-139 G 10
Kamaron o **WAL** 202-203 E 5
Kamarsuk o **CDN** 36-37 T 6
Kamaši o **US** 136-137 M 5
Kamativi o **ZW** 218-219 D 4
Kamba o **WAN** 204-205 E 3
Kamba Kota o **RCA** 206-207 C 5
Kambal o **SUD** 208-209 B 3
Kambalda o · **AUS** 176-177 F 5
Kambaʾnaja Sopka, vulkan ▲ **RUS** 122-123 H 4
Kambaľnickie Koški, ostrova ∼ **RUS** 88-89 T 2
Kambaʾnyj, mys ▲ **RUS** 122-123 R 3
Kambang o **RI** 162-163 D 5
Kambarka o **RUS** 96-97 J 5
Kamberatoro o **PNG** 183 A 2
Kambia o **WAL** 202-203 D 5
Kambing, Gunung ▲ **MAL** 162-163 G 2
Kambolé o **RT** 202-203 L 5
Kambot o **PNG** 183 C 3
Kambove o **ZRE** 214-215 D 6
Kambuku o **PNG** 183 D 3
Kambút o **LAR** 192-193 L 2
Kamčátka ∼ **RUS** 120-121 R 6
Kamčatskij, mys ▲ **RUS** 120-121 U 5
Kamčatskij poluostrov ∪ **RUS** 120-121 U 5
Kamčatsk, Ust'- ☆ **RUS** 120-121 U 5
Kamčatskij, Petropavlovsk- ☆ · **RUS** 120-121 S 7
Kamčatskij proliv ≈ 120-121 U 6
Kamčatskij zaliv ≈ 120-121 T 6
Kamchatka Peninsula = Kamčatka, poluostrov ∪ **RUS** 120-121 Q 5
Kámděš o · **AFG** 136-137 M 7
Kameasi o **RI** 164-165 G 4
Kameel o **ZA** 220-221 G 3
Kamélé o **CI** 202-203 J 5
Kamelik o **BY** 94-95 L 4
Kamen' o **BY** 94-95 L 4
Kamen', Serdce-mys ▲ **RUS** 112-113 J 2
Kamende o **ZRE** 214-215 C 4
Kamenec-Podoľskij = Kam'janec'-Podiľskyj ☆ **UA** 102-103 E 3
Kameng o **AFG** 134-135 L 1
Kameng o **IND** 142-143 H 2
Kamenica o **BIH** 100-101 G 3
Kamenka ☆ **RUS** 96-97 G 8
Kamenka o **RUS** (ARH) 88-89 S 4
Kamenka o **RUS** (HBR) 122-123 G 2
Kamenka o **RUS** (KRN) 116-117 G 6
Kamenka o **RUS** (PEN) 96-97 D 7
Kamenka o **RUS** (SML) 94-95 N 4
Kamenka o **RUS** 124-125 O 2
Kamenka o **RUS** 108-109 d 2
Kamenka o **RUS** 110-111 d 6
Kamenka o **RUS** 116-117 G 6
Kamenka o **RUS** 108-109 J 7
Kamennaja, kosa ⊥ **RUS** 108-109 P 7
Kamennaja tundra ∴ **RUS** 108-109 a 7
Kamen'-na-Obi ☆ **RUS** 124-125 M 2
Kamennik, gora ▲ **RUS** 88-89 N 3
Kamennogorsk o **RUS** 94-95 L 1
Kamennyj, mys ▲ **RUS** 110-111 c 2
Kamennyj Dubčes ∼ **RUS** 114-115 T 4
Kamennyj Stolb, mys ▲ **RUS** 110-111 S 4
Kameno o **BG** 102-103 E 6
Kamen'-Rybolov o **RUS** 122-123 F 6
Kamenskoe o **RUS** 112-113 O 5
Kamensk-Šahtinskij o **RUS** 102-103 M 3
Kamensk-Uraľskij o **RUS** 96-97 M 5
Kamensk Uraľskiy = Kamensk-Uraľskij ☆ **RUS** 96-97 M 5
Kamenz o **D** 92-93 N 3
Kameshia o **ZRE** 214-215 D 5
Kameškova ∼ **RUS** 114-115 M 3
Kameškovo o **RUS** 94-95 R 3
Kámet ▲ **IND** 138-139 G 4
Kameur, Bahr ∼ **RCA** 206-207 E 4
Kamiah o **USA** 40-41 F 2
Kamienna, Skarżysko- o **PL** 92-93 Q 3
Kamiesberge ▲▲ **ZA** 220-221 C 5
Kamieskroon o **ZA** 220-221 C 5
Kami-Furano o **J** 152-153 K 3
Kamiiso o **J** 152-153 J 4
Kamiji o **ZRE** 214-215 B 4
Kamikawa o **J** 152-153 K 3
Kami-koshiki-shima ∼ **J** 152-153 C 9
Kámil, al- o **KSA** 130-131 F 6
Kámil, al- o **OM** 132-133 L 2
Kamileroi o **AUS** 174-175 F 6
Kamilukuak Lake o **CDN** 30-31 T 4
Kamilukuak River ∼ **CDN** 30-31 S 5
Kamimbi Fuka, Chute ∼ **ZRE** 214-215 C 5
Kamina o **PNG** 183 C 4
Kamina o **RT** 202-203 L 5
Kamina o **ZRE** (SHA) 210-211 L 6
Kamina o **ZRE** (SHA) 214-215 C 5
Kamina Base o **ZRE** 214-215 C 5
Kaminak Lake o **CDN** 30-31 W 4
Kamin'-Kašyrs'kyj o **UA** 102-103 D 2
Kaminokuni o **J** 152-153 J 4

Kamino-shima ∼ **J** 152-153 C 7
Kaminuriak Lake o **CDN** 30-31 W 4
Kamioka o **J** 152-153 G 6
Kamishak Bay ≈ 22-23 T 3
Kamishak River ∼ **USA** 22-23 T 3
Kami-Shihoro o **J** 152-153 K 3
Kami-shima ∼ **J** 152-153 D 8
Kamitsushima o **J** 152-153 C 7
Kami-Yaku o **J** 152-153 D 9
Kamjana mohyla • **UA** 102-103 J 4
Kam'janec'-Podiľskyj ☆ **UA** 102-103 E 3
Kamjani Mohyly • **UA** 102-103 K 4
Kam'janka o **UA** 102-103 G 4
Kam'janka o **UA** 102-103 H 3
Kam'janske o **UA** 102-103 C 3
Kamjong o **IND** 142-143 J 3
Kamkaly o **KA** 124-125 G 6
Kamloops o **CDN** 32-33 K 6
Kamloops Indian Reserve ⋏ **CDN** 32-33 K 6
Kamloops Plateau ▲ **CDN** 32-33 K 6
Kammanassieberge ▲▲ **ZA** 220-221 F 6
Kamo o **AR** 128-129 L 2
Kamo ∼ **RUS** 116-117 G 6
Kámoke o **PK** 138-139 E 4
Kamola o **ZRE** 214-215 D 4
Kamoro ▲▲ **RM** 222-223 E 6
Kamoro ∼ **RM** 222-223 E 6
Kamoro, Tampoketsan'i ▲▲ **RM** 222-223 E 6
Kamoto o **Z** 218-219 G 1
Kamp 52 o **SME** 62-63 F 3
Kampa, Teluk ≈ 162-163 F 5
Kampa do Rio Amônea, Área Indígena ⋏ **BR** 64-65 F 6
Kampala ★ **EAU** 212-213 D 3
Kampala o **SUD** 206-207 G 4
Kampar o **MAL** 162-163 D 2
Kampar ∼ **RI** 162-163 E 4
Kamparkanan ∼ **RI** 162-163 D 4
Kamparkiri ∼ **RI** 162-163 D 4
Kampene o **ZRE** 210-211 L 5
Kamphaeng Phet o **THA** 158-159 E 2
Kamphambale o **MW** 214-215 G 7
Kampi Katoto o **EAT** 214-215 D 4
Kampi Ya Moto o **EAK** 212-213 E 4
Kampli o **IND** 140-141 G 3
Kampolombo, Lake o **Z** 214-215 E 6
Kâmpóng Cham o **K** 158-159 H 4
Kâmpóng Chhnāng o **K** 158-159 H 4
Kâmpóng Saôm o **K** 158-159 G 5
Kâmpóng Saôm ∼ **K** 158-159 G 5
Kâmpóng Spoe o **K** 158-159 H 5
Kâmpóng Trach o **K** 158-159 H 5
Kâmpôt o **K** 158-159 H 5
Kampti o **BF** 202-203 J 4
Kampumbu o **ZRE** 214-215 G 6
Kampung o **RI** 166-167 K 4
Kampung Ayer Puteh o **MAL** 162-163 E 2
Kampung Balok o **MAL** 162-163 E 3
Kampung Berawan o **MAL** 164-165 D 1
Kampung Buloh o **MAL** 162-163 E 2
Kampung Chenereh o **MAL** 162-163 E 2
Kampung Cherating o **MAL** 162-163 E 2
Kampung Gajah o **MAL** 162-163 D 2
Kampung Jambu Bongkok o **MAL** 162-163 E 2
Kampung Jerangau o **MAL** 162-163 E 2
Kampung Kemara o **MAL** 162-163 E 2
Kampung Koh o **MAL** 162-163 D 2
Kampung Lamir o **MAL** 162-163 E 3
Kampung Laut o **MAL** 162-163 F 4
Kampung Leban Condong o **MAL** 162-163 E 3
Kampung Merang o **MAL** 162-163 E 2
Kampung Merting o **MAL** 162-163 E 3
Kampung Nibong o **MAL** 162-163 D 2
Kampung Penarik o **MAL** 162-163 E 2
Kampung Relok o **MAL** 162-163 E 2
Kampung Sekinchan o **MAL** 162-163 D 3
Kampung Sepat o **MAL** 162-163 E 3
Kampung Sook o **MAL** 160-161 B 10
Kampung Sungai Ayer Deras o **MAL** 162-163 E 2
Kampung Sungai Rengit o **MAL** 162-163 F 4
Kampung Tebingtinggi o **RI** 162-163 H 3
Kampung Tekek o **MAL** 162-163 F 3
Kampung Tengah o **MAL** 162-163 F 4
Kampung Terolak o **MAL** 162-163 F 4
Kamrau, Teluk ≈ 166-167 G 3
Kamsack o **CDN** 34-35 F 5
Kamsar o **RG** 202-203 C 4
Kamskoe Ustʼe o **RUS** 96-97 F 6
Kamskoe vodohranilišče ≈ **RUS** 96-97 K 4
Kamskoye Vodokhranilishche = Kamskoe vodohranilišče ≈ **RUS** 96-97 K 4
Kamsuuma o **SP** 212-213 J 3
Kámthi o **IND** 138-139 G 9
Kamtsha ∼ **ZRE** 210-211 G 5
Kamuchawan Lake o **CDN** 34-35 E 2
Kamudi o **IND** 140-141 H 6
Kamuj, gora ▲ **RUS** 122-123 N 6
Kámuk, Cerro ▲ **CR** 52-53 G 7
Kamuli o **EAU** 212-213 D 3
Kamušnyj ☆ **KA** 124-125 D 5
Kamutambai ∼ **ZRE** 214-215 B 4
Kam'yanets'-Podil'skyy = Kam'janec'- Podiľskyj ☆ **UA** 102-103 E 3
Kamyárán o **IR** 134-135 B 1
Kámysanovka o **RUS** 146-147 B 4
Kamyšet o **RUS** 116-117 U 8
Kamyševatskaja o **RUS** 102-103 K 4
Kamyšin o **RUS** 114-115 H 6
Kamyšin = Kamyšin o **RUS** 96-97 D 8
Kamyšlov o **RUS** 96-97 N 5
Kamyšovyj, Južno-, hrebet ▲ **RUS** 122-123 K 5

Kamyšovyj hrebet ▲ **RUS** 122-123 K 3
Kamys-Samarkólinin kújmasy o **KA** 96-97 G 9
Kamysty-Ajat ∼ **KA** 124-125 G 4
Kamystybas, kól ∼ **KA** 126-127 O 4
Kamyzjak ☆ **RUS** (AST) 96-97 F 10
Kamyzjak ∼ **RUS** 126-127 H 5
Kan ∼ **RUS** 116-117 G 8
Kanaaupscow, Rivière ∼ **CDN** 36-37 M 7
Kanab o **USA** 40-41 H 7
Kanab Creek ∼ **USA** 40-41 H 7
Kanacea ∼ **FJI** 184 III c 2
Kanadej o **RUS** 96-97 E 7
Kanaga Pass ≈ 22-23 H 7
Kanagi o **J** 152-153 J 4
Kanaka o **RI** 166-167 G 3
Kanakapura o **IND** 140-141 G 4
Kanakatte o **IND** 140-141 G 4
Kanakoro o **BF** 202-203 H 4
Kanaktok Mount ▲ **USA** 20-21 L 3
Kanamari do Rio Jurúá, Área Indígena ⋏ **BR** 66-67 C 6
Kananaskis River ∼ **CDN** 32-33 N 6
Kananga ☆ **ZRE** (KOC) 210-211 J 6
Kananggar o **RI** 168 E 8
Kananging, Mount ▲ **PNG** 183 C 3
Kananga Boyd National Park ⊥ **AUS** 180-181 J 2
Kananto o **GH** 202-203 K 4
Kananyga ∼ **RUS** 120-121 Q 3
Kanas o **IND** 138-139 E 8
Kanaš o **RUS** 96-97 E 6
Kanatak o **USA** 22-23 S 4
Kanawha River ∼ **USA** 46-47 H 6
Kanawi, Pulau ∼ **MAL** 160-161 B 10
Kanazawa ☆ · **J** 152-153 G 6
Kanazi o **EAT** 212-213 C 4
Kanbalu o **MYA** 142-143 J 4
Kanbe o **MYA** 158-159 D 2
Kanbi ∼ **BF** 202-203 K 3
Kančalan o **RUS** 112-113 T 4
Kančalan ∼ **RUS** 112-113 T 4
Kanchana Buri o **THA** 158-159 E 3
Kanchanadit o **THA** 158-159 E 6
Kanchanpur o **NEP** 144-145 F 7
Kanchenjunga ▲ **NEP** 144-145 G 7
Kanchibya ∼ **Z** 214-215 F 6
Kánchipuram o · **IND** 140-141 H 4
Kanci o **RI** 168 C 3
Kandahár = Qandahár o · **AFG** 134-135 L 3
Kandahár = Qandahár o · **AFG** 134-135 L 3
Kandalakša o **RUS** 88-89 M 3
Kandalakshskaya Guba = Kandalakšskaja guba ≈ **RUS** 88-89 M 3
Kandalakšskaja guba ≈ 88-89 M 3
Kandalakšskij bereg ∼ **RUS** 88-89 M 3
Kandangan o **RI** 162-163 B 3
Kandangan o **RI** 164-165 D 5
Kandanghaur o **RI** 168 C 3
Kandar o **RI** 166-167 K 5
Kandare o **WAN** 204-205 H 4
Kandarisa o **PNG** 183 A 5
Kandé o **RT** 202-203 L 5
Kandéko ∼ **RCB** 210-211 F 3
Kandep o **PNG** 183 B 3
Kandero o **DY** 204-205 E 3
Kandi o **IND** 142-143 F 4
Kandi, Tanjung o **RI** 164-165 G 3
Kandiadiou o **SN** 202-203 B 3
Kandiáro o **PK** 138-139 B 6
Kandik River ∼ **USA** 20-21 T 4
Kandil Bouzou ∼ **RN** 198-199 E 5
Kandira ☆ **TR** 128-129 D 2
Kandja o **RCA** 206-207 E 6
Kandjhot o **PK** 138-139 B 5
Kándla o **IND** 138-139 C 8
Kando ∼ **ZRE** 214-215 D 6
Kandos o **AUS** 180-181 K 2
Kandreho o **RM** 222-223 E 6
Kandri ∼ **RUS** 96-97 K 5
Kanduanam o **PNG** 183 B 3
Kandukúr o **IND** 140-141 H 3
Kandy o··· **CL** 140-141 J 7
Kane, Kap ▲ **GRØ** 26-27 e 2
Kane Basin ≈ 26-27 P 4
Kane Bassin ≈ 26-27 P 4
Kane Fracture Zone ≃ 6-7 D 6
Kanektok River ∼ **USA** 22-23 Q 3
Kanel o **SN** 202-203 D 2
Kanem ◻ **TCH** 198-199 G 5
Kaneohe o **USA** 48-49 D 7
Kanevka o **RUS** 88-89 P 3
Kanevskaja o **RUS** 102-103 L 4
Kanferandé o **RG** 202-203 C 4
Kang o **RB** 218-219 B 6
Kangaamiut = Gammel Sukkertoppen o **GRØ** 28-29 O 4
Kangaatsiaq o **GRØ** 28-29 O 4
Kangahun o **WAL** 202-203 D 5
Kangal ☆ **TR** 128-129 G 3
Kangalassy o **RUS** 118-119 O 4
Kangalas-Uèle ∼ **RUS** 110-111 L 3
Kangán o **IR** 134-135 E 5
Kangán Čam ∼ **IR** 134-135 B 2
Kangar o **MAL** 162-163 D 2
Kangaré o **RMM** 202-203 F 4
Kangaroo Island ∼ **AUS** 180-181 D 3
Kangaroo Valley ∪ **AUS** 180-181 L 3
Kangasniemi o **FIN** 88-89 J 6
Kangávar o **IR** 134-135 B 1
Kangding o **VRC** 154-155 B 8
Kangean, Kepulauan ∼ **RI** 168 B 6
Kangean, Pulau ∼ **RI** 168 B 6
Kangeeak Point ▲ **CDN** 28-29 H 3

Kangen ∼ **SUD** 208-209 A 5
Kangeq o **GRØ** 26-27 X 7
Kangerdluarssuk ≈ 26-27 Z 8
Kangerdlugssuaq o **GRØ** 26-27 Z 8
Kangerdluluk Fjord ≈ 28-29 T 6
Kangerluarsoruseq = Færingehavn o **GRØ** 28-29 P 5
Kangerluarsuk o **GRØ** 28-29 O 4
Kangerluk = Diskofjord o **GRØ** 28-29 N 2
Kangerlussuaq ≈ 28-27 Z 8
Kangerlussuaq ≈ 28-29 O 3
Kangerlussuaq ≈ 28-29 Y 2
Kangerlussuaq = Søndrestrømfjord o **GRØ** 28-29 P 3
Kangersuatsiaq ≈ 28-29 P 4
Kangertittivaq ≈ 28-29 X 3
Kangertittivaq = Scoresby Sund ≈ 26-27 o 8
Kanghwa o **ROK** 150-151 F 9
Kanghwa Do ∼ **ROK** 150-151 F 9
Kangi o **SUD** 206-207 H 4
Kangik o **USA** 20-21 L 1
Kangikajip Appalia = Brewster, Kap ▲ **GRØ** 26-27 o p 8
Kangilinnguit = Grønnedal o **GRØ** 28-29 O 6
Kangilo Fiord ≈ 28-29 S 2
Kangiqsujuak o **CDN** 36-37 O 4
Kangiwa o **WAN** 204-205 E 2
Kangkir o **VRC** 144-145 B 2
Kang Kra Chan National Park ⊥ · **THA** 158-159 E 4
Kangmar o **VRC** 144-145 G 6
Kangnŭng o **ROK** 150-151 G 9
Kango o **G** 210-211 D 3
Kangole o **EAU** 212-213 E 2
Kangonde o **EAK** 212-213 F 4
Kangoundéni o **BF** 202-203 H 4
Kangping o **VRC** 150-151 E 9
Kangrinbogê Feng ▲ **VRC** 144-145 C 5
Kangro o **VRC** 144-145 E 4
Kangsar, Kuala o **MAL** 162-163 D 2
Kangto ▲ **IND** 142-143 H 2
Kangye ∼ **DVR** 150-151 F 7
Kangz'gyai ▲ **VRC** 146-147 N 6
Kanha National Park ⊥ · **IND** 142-143 B 4
Kanhar ∼ **IND** 142-143 D 3
Kani ∼ **CI** 202-203 G 5
Kani o **J** 152-153 G 7
Kani o **MYA** 142-143 J 4
Kaniama o **ZRE** 214-215 C 4
Kaniasso o **CI** 202-203 G 5
Kanibadam o **TJ** 136-137 M 4
Kanibes ∼ **NAM** 220-221 C 2
Kanigiri o **IND** 140-141 H 3
Kanimeh o **US** 136-137 J 4
Kanin, poluostrov ∪ **RUS** 88-89 S 3
Kanin Kamen' ▲ **RUS** 88-89 R 2
Kanin Nos o **RUS** 88-89 R 2
Kanin Nos, mys ▲ **RUS** 88-89 R 2
Kaninskaja tundra ∴ **RUS** 88-89 S 3
Kanioumé o **RMM** 202-203 J 2
Kanisa o **SUD** 200-201 E 3
Kanita o **J** 152-153 J 4
Kaniva o **AUS** 180-181 G 6
Kanivs'ke vodoschovyšče < **UA** 102-103 G 2
Kaniya o **PNG** 183 B 4
Kanji-dong o **DVR** 150-151 G 7
Kanjirapalli o **IND** 140-141 G 6
Kanjiroba ▲ **NEP** 144-145 E 6
Kankaanpää o **FIN** 88-89 G 6
Kankai ∼ **IND** 142-143 F 4
Kankakee o **USA** 46-47 E 5
Kankalabé o **RG** 202-203 E 4
Kankan ☆ **RG** 202-203 F 4
Kankara o **WAN** 204-205 G 3
Kankelaba ∼ **RMM** 202-203 G 4
Kankesanturai o **CL** 140-141 H 6
Kankiya o **WAN** 198-199 C 6
Kankossa o **RIM** 196-197 E 7
Kankunskij o **RUS** 118-119 N 7
Kanman Kyun ∼ **MYA** 158-159 E 5
Kann o **IR** 136-137 B 7
Kanna o **MYA** 142-143 K 6
Kannad o **IND** 138-139 E 9
Kannapolis o **USA** 48-49 H 2
Kannavam o **IND** 140-141 F 5
Kannoka = Sillamäe o **EST** 94-95 K 2
Kannonkoski o **FIN** 88-89 H 5
Kannonsaha o **FIN** 88-89 H 5
Kannus o **FIN** 88-89 G 5
Kano o **J** 152-153 D 7
Kano o **RMM** 202-203 F 3
Kano o **WAN** 204-205 H 3
Kano ◻ **WAN** 198-199 D 6
Kano, River ∼ **WAN** 204-205 H 3
Kanobe, Pulau ∼ **RI** 166-167 F 1
Kanona o **Z** 218-219 F 1
Kano Nak o **VN** 158-159 J 5
Kanoni o **ZRE** 214-215 D 6
Kanono o **NAM** 218-219 C 3
Kanoroba o **CI** 202-203 G 5
Kanosh o **USA** 40-41 H 6
Kanour ⊥ **RN** 198-199 F 5
Kanovlei o **NAM** 216-217 E 9
Kanowit o **MAL** 162-163 K 3
Kanowna ∴ **AUS** 176-177 F 5
Kanoya o **J** 152-153 D 9
Kanozero o **RUS** 88-89 N 3
Kanpur o **IND** 142-143 B 2
Kansanshi o **Z** 214-215 D 7
Kansas ◻ **USA** (KS) 44-45 K 1
Kansas ∼ **USA** 42-43 G 6
Kansas City o **USA** 44-45 H 6
Kansenia o **ZRE** 214-215 D 6
Kansk ☆ **RUS** 116-117 G 7
Kant o **KS** 136-137 J 5
Kantah o **CDN** 30-31 J 6
Kantang o **THA** 158-159 E 7
Kantang o **RI** 166-167 C 5
Kantchari o **BF** 202-203 L 3
Kantche o **RN** 198-199 D 6

Kantegir ∼ **RUS** 116-117 E 9
Kantemirovka o **KA** 136-137 M 3
Kantemirovka o **RUS** 102-103 L 3
Kantharalak o **THA** 158-159 H 3
Kánthi o **IND** 142-143 E 5
Kantishna o **USA** 20-21 P 5
Kantishna River ∼ **USA** 20-21 P 4
Kanto-sanchi ▲▲ **J** 152-153 H 6
Kanu o **IND** 140-141 G 3
Kanur o **IND** 140-141 G 3
Kanus o **NAM** 220-221 D 3
Kanye ☆ **RB** 220-221 G 2
Kanyemba o **ZW** 218-219 F 2
Kanyilombi o **Z** 214-215 C 7
Kanym Bolšoj, gora ▲ **RUS** 114-115 U 7
Kanyš-Kija o **KS** 136-137 M 4
Kanyu o **RB** 218-219 C 5
Kao o **RN** 198-199 B 5
Kao o **RN** 198-199 B 5
Kaohsiung o **RC** 156-157 M 5
Kaôh Kŏng ∼ **K** 158-159 G 5
Kaôh Rŭng ∼ **K** 158-159 G 5
Kaôh Rŭng Sâmlôem ∼ **K** 158-159 G 5
Kaôh Tang ∼ **K** 158-159 G 5
Kaôh Thmei ∼ **K** 158-159 G 5
Kaoka o **SOL** 184 I e 3
Kaokaona o **SOL** 184 I e 4
Kaokoveld ⊥ **NAM** 216-217 B 8
Kaolack o **SN** 202-203 B 2
Kaolak River ∼ **USA** 20-21 K 2
Kaolé ∼ **RIM** 196-197 F 6
Kaoleni o **EAK** 212-213 G 5
Kaole Ruins = **EAT** 214-215 K 4
Kaolinovo o **BG** 102-103 E 6
Kaolo o **SOL** 184 I d 3
Kaoma o **Z** 218-219 C 2
Kaouadja ∼ **RCA** (Kot) 206-207 F 5
Kaouadja o **RCA** 206-207 G 5
Kaouadja ∼ **RCA** 206-207 F 5
Kapa o **MYA** 158-159 G 10
Kapaa o **USA** 48-49 C 6
Kapadokya = **TR** 128-129 F 4
Kapadvanj o **IND** 138-139 D 8
Kapaimeri o **PNG** 183 B 3
Kapalabuaya o **RI** 164-165 K 4
Kapalala o **Z** 214-215 E 6
Kapandae o **GH** 202-203 K 5
Kapande ∼ **ZRE** 214-215 D 6
Kapanga o **ZRE** 214-215 C 5
Kapangan o **RP** 160-161 D 4
Kapapa o **ZRE** 214-215 E 5
Kapasia o **BD** 142-143 G 3
Kapatu o **EAT** 212-213 E 6
Kapatu o **Z** 214-215 F 5
Kapau River ∼ **PNG** 183 B 4
Kapčagaj = Kapšagaj o **KA** 146-147 C 4
Kapchorwa o **EAU** 212-213 E 3
Kapčiamiestis o **LT** 94-95 H 4
Kapedo o **EAK** 212-213 F 3
Kaperma o **ZRE** 214-215 E 6
Kapenguria o **EAK** 212-213 E 3
Kapia o **ZRE** 210-211 G 6
Kapichira Falls ∼ **MW** 218-219 H 2
Kapini o **LV** 94-95 K 3
Kapip o **PK** 138-139 B 4
Kapiri Mposhi o **Z** 218-219 E 1
Kápisa ◻ **AFG** 138-139 B 2
Kapisillit o **GRØ** 28-29 P 5
Kapiskau River ∼ **CDN** 34-35 O 4
Kapiskong Lake o **CDN** 38-39 D 5
Kapit o **MAL** 162-163 K 3
Kapiti Island ∼ **NZ** 182 E 4
Kapiura River ∼ **PNG** 183 F 3
Kapka, Massif du ▲ **TCH** 198-199 K 5
Kaplamada, Gunung ▲ **RI** 166-167 D 3
Kaplankir, plato ▲ **US** 136-137 E 4
Kaplankyrskij zapovednik ⊥ **TM** 136-137 E 4
Kapoe o **THA** 158-159 D 6
Kapoeta o **SUD** 208-209 A 6
Kapoke o **Z** 214-215 F 5
Kapona o **ZRE** 214-215 E 4
Kapondi, Tanjung ▲ **RI** 166-167 B 6
Kapong o **THA** 158-159 E 6
Kapoposang, Pulau ∼ **RI** 164-165 F 6
Kaporo o **MW** 214-215 G 6
Kaposvár o **H** 92-93 O 5
Kapotakshi ∼ **BD** 142-143 F 4
Kappar o **PK** 134-135 K 6
Kappelskär o **S** 86-87 J 7
Kappelshamn o **S** 86-87 J 8
Kapp Platen ▲ **N** 84-85 N 2
Kapps o **NAM** 220-221 D 11
Kapsabet o **EAK** 212-213 E 3
Kapšagaj o **KA** 146-147 C 4
Kapšagaj su kojmasy < **KA** 146-147 C 4
Kapsan o **DVR** 150-151 G 7
Kapsaoujs, Rivière ∼ **CDN** 36-37 K 7
Kápsi o **IND** 140-141 F 2
Kapski ▲ **CAM** 204-205 D 5
Kaptai o **BD** 142-143 H 4
Kaptai Lake o **BD** 142-143 H 4
Kaptiau o **RI** 166-167 K 3
Kapuas ∼ **RI** 162-163 H 5
Kapuas ∼ **RI** 162-163 H 5
Kapuas Hulu, Banjaran ▲▲ **MAL** 162-163 K 4
Kapur Utara, Pegunungan ▲▲ **RI** 168 D 3
Kapuskasing o **CDN** 34-35 O 6
Kapuskasing River ∼ **CDN** 34-35 P 6
Kapustin Jar o **RUS** 96-97 D 9
Kaputa o **Z** 214-215 D 5
Kaputir o **EAK** 212-213 E 3
Kapuvár o **H** 92-93 O 4
Kapydžik, gora ▲ **AZ** 128-129 L 3
Kapyliušj, ozero ∼ **RUS** 118-119 P 8
Kara o **RI** 166-167 C 5
Kara ∼ **RT** 202-203 L 5
Kara o **RT** (DLK) 202-203 L 5
Kara ◻ **RT** 202-203 L 5

Kara ∼ **RUS** 108-109 L 8
Kara, Ust'- o **RUS** 108-109 L 7
Karaba, Ra's ▲ **KSA** 130-131 E 5
Kara-Balta = Kara-Balty o **KS** 136-137 N 3
Kara-Balty o **KS** 136-137 N 3
Karabaš o **RUS** 96-97 M 6
Karabastau o **KA** 136-137 M 8
Karabau o **KA** 96-97 H 8
Karabaur, pastilgi ▲▲ **KA** 126-127 L 6
Karabekaul o **TM** 136-137 J 5
Karabil', vozvyšennost' ⊥ **TM** 136-137 H 6
Karabuk o **RCB** 210-211 D 3
Karabula ∼ **RUS** 116-117 H 7
Karabulak o **KA** 136-137 L 3
Karabulak o **RUS** 116-117 H 7
Karaburun ☆ **TR** 128-129 B 3
Karabútak o **KA** 126-127 O 3
Karaca Daği ▲▲ **TR** 128-129 H 4
Karačaevsk o **RUS** 126-127 D 6
Karacaköy o **TR** 128-129 C 2
Karacasu ☆ **TR** 128-129 C 3
Karacek, köl o **KA** 126-127 L 6
Karačev o **RUS** 94-95 P 4
Karachay-Cherkessia = Karačaj-Čerkes Respublika ◻ **RUS** 126-127 D 6
Karač o · **PK** 134-135 M 6
Karád o **IND** 140-141 F 2
Kara Deniz ≈ **TR** 128-129 D 1
Karadeniz Boğazi = Bosporus ≈ 128-129 C 2
Karaespe ∼ **KA** 124-125 J 4
Karağ o **IR** 136-137 B 7
Karaga o **GH** 202-203 K 5
Karaga o **RUS** 120-121 U 4
Karaga, buhta o **RUS** 120-121 U 4
Karagaj o **RUS** 96-97 J 4
Karagajly o **KA** 124-125 J 4
Karagajly o **KA** 124-125 J 4
Karagandy = Karaganda ☆ **KA** 124-125 H 4
Karagandyssay o **KA** 126-127 L 2
Karagaz, hrebet ▲▲ **TM** 136-137 D 5
Karaghandy o **KA** 124-125 H 4
Karagie, vpadina ∪ **KA** 126-127 J 6
Karaginskij, ostrov ∼ **RUS** 120-121 V 4
Karaginskij zaliv ≈ 120-121 U 4
Karagoš, gora ▲ **RUS** 124-125 Q 3
Karaguiney Daği ▲▲ **TR** 128-129 C 3
Karahalı ☆ **TR** 128-129 C 3
Kara Hobda ∼ **KA** 126-127 M 2
Karaiaii o **PNG** 183 E 3
Karaidel' o **RUS** 96-97 K 6
Karaisalı ☆ **TR** 128-129 F 4
Karaitem o **PNG** 183 B 2
Karajagi o **IND** 140-141 F 2
Karaja Masefga o **RUS** 88-89 N 5
Karaja ▲ **EAK** 212-213 E 3
Karak, al- ☆ **JOR** 130-131 D 2
Kara-Kala o **TM** 136-137 E 5
Karakamys o **KA** 96-97 H 9
Karakax He ∼ **VRC** 138-139 F 1
Karakax He ∼ **VRC** 144-145 D 2
Karakaya Baraji < **TR** 128-129 H 4
Karakeçi o **TR** 128-129 H 4
Karakeçu ∼ **KA** 124-125 L 4
Karakelong, Kepulauan ∼ **RI** 164-165 K 1
Kara-Kengir ∼ **KA** 124-125 E 4
Karaketang, Pulau ∼ **RI** 164-165 J 2
Karaklis o **AR** 128-129 L 2
Karakoçan o **TR** 128-129 J 3
Karakojyn, köl o **KA** 124-125 F 6
Karaköl o **KA** (GUR) 96-97 N 9
Karaköl o **KA** (KZL) 126-127 O 5
Karaköl o **KA** (KZL) 124-125 D 6
Karakol o **KS** 146-147 C 5
Karaköl, köl o **KA** 126-127 N 5
Karakoram ▲▲ **IND** 138-139 F 1
Karakoram Highway II **PK** 138-139 E 1
Karakojya o **RUS** 120-121 S 6
Karaktau, gory ▲▲ **KA** 124-125 J 6
Kara-Kudzur ∼ **KS** 146-147 C 5
Karakul' o **TJ** 136-137 N 5
Karakul' o **US** 136-137 H 5
Karakul', ozero = **TJ** 136-137 N 5
Karakul'dža o **KS** 136-137 N 4
Karakulino o **RUS** 96-97 H 5
Karakum ⊥ **KA** 126-127 N 5
Karakum ⊥ **KA** 96-97 H 10
Karakum = Garagum ⊥ **TM** 136-137 F 5
Kara Kum = Garagum ⊥ **TM** 136-137 E 4
Karakumskij kanal < **TM** (ASH) 136-137 F 5
Karakumskij kanal < **TM** (MAR) 136-137 H 6
Karal o **TCH** 198-199 H 6
Karalka ∼ **RUS** 114-115 H 3
Karalundi Mission o **AUS** 176-177 E 4
Karam o **RUS** 116-117 N 8
Karamadai o **IND** 140-141 G 5
Karamay o **VRC** 146-147 J 3
Karamba o **VRC** 164-165 E 5
Karamanbeyli Geçidi ▲ **TR** 128-129 D 4
Karamay o **VRC** 146-147 J 3

Kamamor, Pegunungan ▲▲ **RI** 166-167 K 3
Karamyševo o **RUS** 116-117 K 7
Karän ∼ **KSA** 130-131 L 4
Karang o **SN** 202-203 B 3
Karangampel o **RI** 168 C 3
Karanganyar o **RI** 168 D 3
Karangasem o **RI** 168 B 7
Karangboto, Tanjung ▲ **RI** 168 C 3
Karanggede o **RI** 168 D 3
Karangjati o **RI** 168 D 3
Karangnunggal o **RI** 168 C 3
Karangoua o **RCB** 210-211 D 3
Karangpandan o **RI** 168 D 3
Karangua o **Z** 214-215 D 7
Karanguana o **RMM** 202-203 H 3
Karanji o **IND** 138-139 E 9
Karanpur o **IND** 138-139 D 5
Karaoba o **KA** 126-127 M 4
Karaoj o **KA** 124-125 J 4
Karap o **PNG** 183 C 3
Karapınar ☆ **TR** 128-129 E 4
Karapuz ∼ **RUS** 114-115 P 7
Karara o **AUS** 178-179 L 5
Kararaô, Área Indígena ⋏ **BR** 68-69 B 4
Karas, Pulau ∼ **RI** 166-167 G 3
Kara-Saj o **KS** 146-147 C 5
Kara-Sal ∼ **RUS** 102-103 N 4
Karasavon o **FIN** 88-89 G 3
Karasburg ☆ **NAM** 220-221 D 4
Karas'e, ozero Bolšoe o **RUS** 114-115 J 5
Kara Sea = Karskoe more ≈ **RUS** 10-11 F 1
Karasek, Ozero = köl Karacek o **KA** 126-127 L 6
Karasjok o **N** 86-87 M 2
Karašjokka ∼ **N** 86-87 M 2
Karasof, köli o **KA** 124-125 K 3
Karasor, ozero = Köl Karasor o **KA** 124-125 K 3
Karasor, köli o **KA** 124-125 J 4
Karasor, köli o **KA** 124-125 J 4
Karasor, ozero = köli Karasor o **KA** 124-125 J 4
Karasu o **TR** 128-129 D 2
Karasu ∼ **TR** 128-129 H 3
Karasu-Aras Dağları ▲▲ **TR** 128-129 J 3
Karasu Çay ∼ **TR** 128-129 G 4
Karasuk o **RUS** 124-125 L 2
Karasuk Hills ▲▲ **EAK** 212-213 E 2
Kara-Suu o **KS** 136-137 N 4
Karát o **IR** 134-135 J 1
Karatajka o **RUS** 108-109 J 7
Karatal ∼ **KA** 124-125 K 6
Karatas o **KA** 136-137 L 4
Karatas o **KA** 136-137 L 4
Karataş ☆ **TR** 128-129 F 4
Karataš, gora ▲ **RUS** 96-97 L 7
Karatau o **KA** (DZM) 136-137 M 3
Karatau, hrebet ▲▲ **KA** 124-125 E 6
Karatau hrebet ▲▲ **RUS** 96-97 K 6
Karatina o **EAK** 212-213 E 5
Karatogaj o **KA** 124-125 O 4
Karaton o **KA** 96-97 H 10
Karatorgaj ∼ **KA** 124-125 E 4
Karats o **S** 86-87 J 3
Karatsu o **J** 152-153 C 8
Karatu o **EAT** 212-213 E 5
Karatulej, sor ≈ **KA** 126-127 L 5
Karatung, Pulau ∼ **RI** 164-165 K 1
Karaudanawa o **GUY** 62-63 E 4
Karaul o **RUS** 108-109 U 6
Karaul o **RUS** 108-109 U 6
Karaulbazar o **US** 136-137 J 5
Karauli o **IND** 138-139 F 6
Karaungir ⊥ **KA** 124-125 J 5
Karauwi o **PNG** 183 C 4
Karavánsaráy-e Šams o **IR** 134-135 J 1
Karavás o **GR** 100-101 J 6
Karawa o **ZRE** 210-211 J 3
Karawanella o **CL** 140-141 J 7
Karawang o **RI** 168 C 3
Karawang, Tanjung ▲ **RI** 168 B 2
Karawanken ▲▲ **A** 92-93 M 5
Karawari River ∼ **PNG** 183 B 3
Karayaz ☆ **TR** 128-129 K 3
Karaye o **WAN** 204-205 H 3
Karayulgun o **VRC** 146-147 K 3
Karažal o **KA** 124-125 G 4
Karažal o **KA** 124-125 G 4
Karbalá' ☆ **IRQ** (KAR) 128-129 L 6
Kárbóle o **S** 86-87 G 6
Karbulik o **RUS** 116-117 O 9
Karchat o **PK** 134-135 M 6
Karda o **RUS** 116-117 L 8
Kardakáta o **GR** 100-101 H 5
Kardeljevo = Ploče o **HR** 100-101 F 3
Karditsa o **GR** 100-101 H 5
Kardiva Channel ≈ 140-141 B 5
Kärdla ▲ **EST** 94-95 H 2
Kârdžali o **BG** 102-103 D 7
Kârdžali o **BG** 102-103 D 7
Karé, Monts ▲ **RCA** 206-207 C 5
Kareeberge ▲▲ **ZA** 220-221 F 5
Kareebospoort ▲ **ZA** 220-221 F 5
Karegari o **PNG** 183 B 3
Karelia = Karelija, Respublika ◻ **RUS** 88-89 M 5
Karelia = Karelija, Respublika ◻ **RUS** 88-89 M 5
Karelka ∼ **RUS** 108-109 E 5
Karefskij bereg ∼ **RUS** 88-89 M 3
Karema o **EAT** 214-215 F 5
Karema o **EAT** 214-215 E 5
Karenga ∼ **RUS** 118-119 H 8
Karenga, Ust'- o **RUS** 118-119 H 8
Karenni o **WAN** 204-205 F 3
Karera o **RUS** 118-119 H 8
Karesuando o **S** 86-87 L 2
Kärevändar o **IR** 134-135 J 5

Kargal o **IND** 140-141 F 3
Kargala o **RUS** 114-115 R 6
Kargala o **RUS** (ORB) 96-97 J 8
Kargalinskaja o **RUS** 126-127 G 6
Kargalytau ▲ **KA** 126-127 P 2
Kargapofe ☆ **RUS** 96-97 J 8
Kargasok o **RUS** 114-115 Q 5
Kargat ☆ **RUS** 114-115 Q 7
Kargat ~ **RUS** 114-115 Q 7
Kargat, Forpost- o **RUS** 114-115 Q 7
Kargil o **IND** 138-139 F 2
Kargopol ☆ **RUS** 88-89 P 6
Karguéri o **RN** 198-199 E 6
Karhe, Rüd-e ~ **IR** 134-135 C 3
Karhe, Rüdhäne-ye ~ **IR** 134-135 D 3
Kari o **WAN** 204-205 J 3
Karia o **PNG** 183 F 2
Karianga o **RM** 222-223 E 9
Kariba o **ZW** 218-219 E 3
Kariba, Lake < **Z** 218-219 D 3
Kariba-yama ▲ **J** 152-153 H 3
Karibib o **NAM** 216-217 C 10
Karie o **SOL** 184 I 4
Kariega ~ **ZA** 220-221 F 6
Kariés ☆ **GR** 100-101 K 4
Karigasniemi o **FIN** 88-89 H 2
Karikachi-töge ▲ **J** 152-153 K 3
Karikāl o **IND** 140-141 H 5
Karikari, Cape ▲ **NZ** 182 D 1
Karilatsi o **EST** 94-95 K 2
Karima o **SUD** 200-201 E 3
Karimabad o· **IND** 138-139 E 1
Karimama o **DY** 204-205 D 2
Karimata, Pulau ⌒ **RI** 162-163 H 5
Karimata, Kepulauan ⌒ **RI** 162-163 H 5
Karimata Strait = Karimata, Selat ≈ 162-163 G 5
Karimbola ⌊ **RM** 222-223 D 10
Karimganj o **IND** 142-143 H 3
Karimnagar o **IND** 138-139 G 10,
Karimui o **PNG** 183 C 4
Karimui, Mount ▲ **PNG** 183 C 4
Karimun, Pulau ⌒ **RI** 162-163 E 4
Karimunjawa, Kepulaua ⌒ **RI** 168 Q 3
Karin o **SP** 208-209 G 3
Karina o **WAL** 202-203 E 5
Karipuna, Área Indígena X **BR** 66-67 E 7
Karisimbi, Mount ▲ **RWA** 212-213 B 4
Káristos o **GR** 100-101 K 5
Karitiana, Área Indígena X **BR** 66-67 E 7
Kariya o **J** 152-153 H 7
Käriyapatti o **IND** 140-141 H 6
Karjala ⌒ **FIN** 88-89 K 6
Karjat o **IND** 138-139 E 10
Karkabane, Hássi < **RMM** 196-197 K 6
Kärkal o **IND** 140-141 F 5
Karkar o **PNG** 183 C 3
Karkaralinsk = Qarqaraly o **KA** 124-125 J 4
Karkaraly o **KA** 124-125 J 4
Karkar Island ⌒ **PNG** 183 D 3
Karkas, Küh-e ▲ **IR** 134-135 D 2
Karkh o **PK** 134-135 M 5
Karkinits'ka zatoka ≈ 102-103 H 5
Karkonosze ▲ **PL** 92-93 N 3
Karksi-Nuia o ·· **EST** 94-95 J 2
Karla-Aleksandra, ostrov ⌒ **RUS** 84-85 e 2
Kartalarong, Kepulauan ⌒ **RI** 164-165 J 1
Karleby = Kokkola ☆ **FIN** 88-89 G 5
Karlik ▲ **VRC** 146-147 L 4
Karlova ☆ **TR** 128-129 J 3
Karlivka o **UA** 102-103 J 3
Karl-Marx-Stadt = Chemnitz o **D** 92-93 M 3
Karlobag o **HR** 100-101 E 2
Karlo-Libknehtovsk = Soledar o **UA** 102-103 L 3
Karlovac o **HR** 100-101 E 2
Karlovássi o **GR** 100-101 L 6
Karlovo o **BG** 102-103 D 6
Karlovy Vary o **CZ** 92-93 M 3
Karlsbad = Karlovy Vary o **CZ** 92-93 M 3
Karlsborg o **S** 86-87 G 7
Karlsena, mys ▲ **RUS** 108-109 M 3
Karlshamn o **S** 86-87 G 8
Karlskoga o **S** 86-87 G 8
Karlskrona o · **S** 86-87 G 8
Karlsruhe o · **D** 92-93 K 4
Karlsruhe o **USA** 42-43 G 1
Karlstad o· **S** 86-87 F 7
Karlstad o · **S** 86-87 G 1
Karlštejn · **CZ** 92-93 O 4
Karluk o **USA** 22-23 T 4
Karma o **RN** 202-203 D 2
Karma o **TCH** 206-207 C 3
Karmah o· **SUD** 200-201 E 3
Karmála o· **IND** 138-139 E 10
Karmaskaly ☆ **RUS** 96-97 K 6
Karmé o **TCH** 198-199 G 6
Karmelitskyj monastyr · **UA** 102-103 E 3
Karmina o **US** 136-137 J 4
Karmøy ⌒ **N** 86-87 B 7
Karnak, al- o·· **ET** 194-195 F 5
Karnāl o **IND** 138-139 F 3
Karnali ~ **NEP** 144-145 C 6
Karnaou ▲ **TCH** 198-199 H 2
Karnaphuli ~ **BD** 142-143 G 4
Karnataka □ **IND** 140-141 F 3
Karnataka Plateau ▲ **IND** 140-141 F 2
Karnes City o **USA** 44-45 J 5
Karnobat o **BG** 102-103 E 6
Kamprayåp o **RM** 202-203 D 2
Kärnten □ **A** 92-93 M 5
Karo Batak House · **RI** 162-163 C 3
Karoi o **ZW** 218-219 D 3
Karo La ▲ **VRC** 144-145 H 6
Karolinen = **FSM** 156-157 ...
Karoma, Mount ▲ **PNG** 183 B 3
Karonga o **MW** 214-215 G 5
Karoni, Gunung ▲ **RI** 164-165 G 5
Karonie o **AUS** 176-177 G 5
Karoo National Park ⊥ **ZA** 220-221 F 6

Karoonda o **AUS** 180-181 E 3
Karor o **PK** 138-139 C 4
Karora o **SUD** 200-201 J 4
Karosa o **RI** 164-165 F 4
Karoso, Tanjung ▲ **RI** 168 D 7
Kárpathio Pélagos ≈ 100-101 L 6
Kárpathos ⌒ **GR** 100-101 L 7
Kárpathos ☆ **GR** 100-101 H 5
Karpenissi o **GR** 100-101 H 5
Karpinsk o **RUS** 114-115 N 5
Karpinskogo, vulkan ▲ **RUS** 122-123 Q 3
Karpogory o **RUS** 88-89 S 4
Karpuzlu ☆ **TR** 128-129 B 4
Karpysak o **RUS** 114-115 R 7
Karratha o **AUS** 172-173 C 6
Karratha Roadhouse o **AUS** 172-173 C 6
Karrats Fjord ≈ 26-27 Y 8
Karredouw o **ZA** 220-221 E 6
Karridale o **AUS** 176-177 C 7
Kars ☆ · **TR** 128-129 K 2
Karsakbaj o **KA** 124-125 E 5
Kärsämäki o **FIN** 88-89 H 5
Kärsava o **LV** 94-95 K 3
Karshi o **WAN** 204-205 G 4
Karši o **US** 136-137 J 5
Karšinskaja step' = **US** 136-137 J 5
Karsk, Ust'- o **RUS** 118-119 J 9
Karskie Vorota, proliv ≈ 108-109 G 6
Karskive Vorota, Proliv = Karskie Vorota, proliv ≈ 108-109 G 6
Karsnrviervlei o **ZA** 220-221 E 7
Kartabu o **GUY** 62-63 E 2
Kartabuz, ozero o **RUS** 114-115 G 7
Kartaľ o **RUS** 88-89 W 4
Karten o **KA** 124-125 B 2
Karte Conservation Park ⊥ **AUS** 180-181 F 3
Kárthala ▲ **COM** 222-223 C 3
Karti o **IR** 134-135 H 6
Kartosuro o **RI** 168 P 3
Kartuzy o· **PL** 92-93 P 1
Karu o **PNG** 183 G 2
Karubaga o **RI** 166-167 K 3
Karubeamsberge ▲ **NAM** 220-221 C 1
Karufa o **RI** 166-167 G 3
Karumae o **J** 152-153 J 4
Karumba o **AUS** 174-175 F 5
Karumwa o **EAT** 212-213 D 5
Karūn, Küh-e ▲ **IR** 134-135 D 3
Karūn, Rüd-e ~ **IR** 134-135 C 3
Karungu o **EAK** 212-213 E 4
Karur o **IND** 140-141 H 5
Karuzi o **BU** 212-213 C 5
Karvina o **CZ** 92-93 P 4
Karwai o **RI** 164-165 H 6
Kärwär o **IND** 140-141 F 3
Karwin = Karviná o **CZ** 92-93 P 4
Karymskoe o **RUS** 118-119 G 10
Karyngürly ▲ **KA** 126-127 L 6
Karynžaryk = **KA** 126-127 K 6
Kas ~ **RUS** 116-117 E 6
Kaş ☆ ·· **TR** 128-129 C 4
Kasa o **RP** 160-161 D 3
Kasa o **VRC** 154-155 B 6
Kasa o **ZRE** 210-211 G 4
Kasaan Bay ≈ 32-33 D 4
Kasaba o **ZRE** 214-215 E 5
Kasabi o **ZRE** 214-215 E 5
Kasabonika o **CDN** 34-35 M 4
Kašar Rüd ~ **IR** 136-137 G 6
Kasah o **AR** 128-129 L 2
Kasai o **J** 152-153 F 7
Kasai ~ **ZRE** 210-211 G 5
Kasai-Occidental □ **ZRE** 210-211 H 6
Kasai-Oriental □ **ZRE** 210-211 J 5
Kasaji o **ZRE** 214-215 B 6
Kása Khurd o **IND** 138-139 D 10
Kasalú o **Z** 218-219 D 2
Kasama o **Z** 214-215 F 6
Kášán o · **IR** 134-135 D 2
Kašan ~ **TM** 136-137 H 7
Kasane o **RB** 218-219 C 2
Kasanga o **EAT** 214-215 F 5
Kasangulu o **ZRE** 210-211 E 6
Kasansay o **US** 136-137 M 4
Kasanza o **ZRE** 214-215 C 4
Kásaragod o **IND** 140-141 F 4
Kasaro o **SUD** 200-201 F 6
Kasasi o **WAL** 202-203 E 5
Kasatochi Island ⌒ **USA** 22-23 T 4
Kasbahs, Route des · **MA** 188-189 H 5
Kasba Lake o **CDN** 30-31 S 5
Kasba-Tadla o **MA** 188-189 H 4
Kasçjukovičy o **BY** 94-95 N 5
Kasdir < **IR** 188-189 L 4
Kaseda o **J** 152-153 D 10
Kasegaluk Lagoon ≈ 20-21 J 2
Kasei ~ **ZRE** 216-217 F 3
Kasempa o **Z** 218-219 C 1
Katcha o **WAN** 204-205 G 4
Kasenga o **ZRE** (SHA) 214-215 D 8
Kasenga o **ZRE** (SHA) 214-215 B 6
Kasenge o **ZRE** 210-211 G 4
Kasenge o **ZRE** 212-213 C 2
Kasenye o **ZRE** 212-213 C 3
Kasese o **EAU** 212-213 C 3
Kasese o **ZRE** 212-213 A 4
Kaset Wisai o **THA** 158-159 G 3
Kasewe · **RI** 164-165 G 5
Kashabowie o **CDN** 34-35 L 6
Kashechewan o **CDN** 34-35 N 4
Kashega o **USA** 22-23 N 6
Kashi o **VRC** 146-147 C 6
Kashileshi o **ZRE** 214-215 B 6
Kashima o **J** 152-153 J 7
Käshipur o **IND** 138-139 F 4
Kashiwa o **J** 152-153 H 7
Kashiwazaki o **J** 152-153 H 6
Käshmor o **PK** 138-139 B 5

Kashnuk River ~ **USA** 20-21 H 6
Kashwal o **SUD** 206-207 J 5
Kasi o **RI** 166-167 G 2
Kasidishi ~ **ZRE** 214-215 B 5
Kasigau ▲ **EAK** 212-213 G 5
Kasigluk o **USA** 20-21 J 6
Kasimbar o **RI** 166-167 G 4
Kasimov o **RUS** 94-95 R 4
Kasindi o **ZRE** 212-213 B 3
Kasinje o **MW** 218-219 H 2
Kašira ☆ **RUS** 94-95 Q 4
Kasiruta, Pulau ⌒ **RI** 164-165 K 4
Kasiui, Pulau ⌒ **RI** 166-167 F 4
Kasiola ☆ **CI** 202-203 H 6
Kaskabulak o **KA** 124-125 L 4
Kaškadar'inskaja oblast' □ **US** 136-137 J 5
Kaškadar'ja ~ **US** 136-137 J 5
Kaškan, Rüdhäne-ye ~ **IR** 134-135 B 2
Kaškarancy o **RUS** 88-89 O 3
Kaskas o **SN** 196-197 C 6
Kaskaskia River ~ **USA** 46-47 D 6
Kaskaskia State Historic Site, Fort ∴ **USA** 46-47 D 6
Kaškasu o **KS** 146-147 B 5
Kaskattama River ~ **CDN** 34-35 L 2
Kaskinen o **FIN** 88-89 F 5
Kaskö = Kaskinen o **FIN** 88-89 F 5
Kasli ☆ **RUS** 96-97 M 6
Kaslo o **CDN** 32-33 M 7
Kášmar o **IR** 136-137 F 7
Kasmere Lake o **CDN** 30-31 T 6
Kasompe o **Z** 218-219 C 1
Kasongo o **ZRE** 210-211 L 6
Kasongo-Lunda o **ZRE** 216-217 D 3
Kasongo-Lunda, Chutes ~ **ZRE** 216-217 D 3
Kasouga o **ZA** 220-221 H 6
Kasuga o **J** (FKA) 152-153 D 8
Kasuga o **J** (HYO) 152-153 F 7
Kasuku ~ **ZRE** 210-211 K 5
Kasulu o **EAT** 212-213 C 4
Kasumba o **ZRE** 214-215 D 7
Kasumi o **J** 152-153 F 7
Kasumigaura-ura o **J** 152-153 J 6
Kasumkent o **RUS** 126-127 H 7
Kasungu o **MW** 218-219 G 1
Kasungu National Park ⊥ **MW** 214-215 G 7
Kasūr o **PK** 138-139 E 4
Kat o **IR** 134-135 C 3
Kata ~ **RUS** 116-117 L 6
Kataba o **Z** 218-219 C 2
Katabaie o **ZRE** 214-215 D 6
Katagum o **WAN** 198-199 G 6
Katagum, River ~ **WAN** 204-205 H 3
Katajsk ☆ **RUS** 114-115 M 6
Kataka o **IND** 142-143 D 5
Katakakishi o **ZRE** 214-215 B 5
Katako-Kombe o **ZRE** 210-211 K 5
Kataku o **RI** 166-167 E 4
Katakwi o **EAU** 212-213 D 3
Katalah o **RUS** 118-119 N 6
Katamatite o **AUS** 180-181 H 4
Katana o **ZRE** 212-213 B 4
Katanda o **ZRE** 214-215 B 4
Katangi o **IND** 138-139 G 8
Katángi o **IND** 138-139 G 8
Katanning o **AUS** 176-177 D 6
Kataouâne o **RIM** 196-197 E 3
Kataramba o **RIM** 196-197 H 4
Katavi National Park ⊥ **EAT** 214-215 F 4
Katchall Island ⌒ **IND** 140-141 L 6
Katchirga o **BF** 202-203 L 2
Kateel River ~ **USA** 20-21 L 5
Kateman, Pulau o **RI** 162-163 E 4
Katende o **ZRE** 214-215 B 4
Katende, Chutes de ~ **ZRE** 214-215 B 4
Katenga o **ZRE** 214-215 B 4
Katere o **NAM** 216-217 F 9
Katerini o **GR** 100-101 J 4
Katesh o **EAT** 212-213 E 4
Katete o **Z** 218-219 G 2
Kathang o **MYA** 142-143 K 2
Kathangor, Gabal ▲ **SUD** 208-209 A 6
Kathawachaga Lake o **CDN** 30-31 O 2
Katherine o **AUS** 172-173 L 3
Katherine River ~ **AUS** 172-173 K 3
Käthiäwär Peninsula ⌣ **IND**
Kathleen Lake o **CDN** 38-39 C 5

Kathmandu ☆ ··· **NEP** 144-145 E 7
Kathu o **ZA** 220-221 F 3
Kathua o **IND** 138-139 F 2
Kati ~ **NEP** 144-145 C 6
Kati o **RMM** 202-203 F 3
Katiali o **CI** 202-203 G 5
Katiati o **PNG** 183 G 5
Katiéna o **RMM** 202-203 H 3
Katihar o **IND** 142-143 E 3
Katima Mulilo o **NAM** 218-219 C 3
Katimik Lake o **CDN** 34-35 G 4
Katini o **ZRE** 216-217 E 3
Katiola ☆ **CI** 202-203 H 6
Katla o **SUD** 206-207 J 3
Katmai, Mount ▲ **USA** 22-23 T 3
Katmai National Park and Preserve ⊥ **USA** 22-23 T 4
Katmay Bay ≈ 22-23 T 4
Katoa o **GUY** 62-63 E 3
Katoda o **IND** 138-139 E 7
Káto Gliikóvrisi o **GR** 100-101 J 6
Katol o **IND** 138-139 G 8
Katombe o **ZRE** 210-211 H 6
Katompi o **ZRE** 214-215 D 4
Katonga ~ **EAU** 212-213 C 3
Katon-Karagaj o **KA** 146-147 L 4
Katoomba-Wentworth Falls o **AUS** 180-181 L 2
Katoposo, Gunung ▲ **RI** 164-165 G 4
Káto Soúnio o **GR** 100-101 K 6
Katoto o **EAT** 212-213 C 4
Katowice o· **PL** 92-93 P 3
Katoya o **IND** 142-143 F 4
Katranòik Daği ▲ **TR** 128-129 D 4
Katsepy o **RM** 222-223 E 5
Katsina o **WAN** 198-199 C 6
Katsina-Ala o **WAN** 204-205 H 5
Katsina-Ala, River ~ **WAN** 204-205 H 5
Katsumoto o **J** 152-153 C 8
Katsuta o **J** 152-153 J 6
Katsuura o **J** (CHI) 152-153 J 7
Katsuura o **J** (WAK) 152-153 F 8
Kattakisslok o **US** 136-137 K 5
Kattakürgon = Kattakürgon o **US** 136-137 K 5
Kattakürgon o **US** 136-137 K 5
Kattakudi o **CL** 140-141 H 7
Kattamakara o **IND** 140-141 G 6
Kattavia o **GR** 100-101 L 7
Kattawagami Lake o **CDN** 34-35 Q 4
Kattegat ≈ 86-87 E 8
Katterjäkk o **S** 86-87 J 2
Kåttuppuntúr o **IND** 140-141 H 5
Katumbi o **MW** 214-215 G 6
Katun' ~ **RUS** 124-125 P 3
Katung.uru o **EAU** 212-213 C 3
Katunskij hrebet ▲ **RUS** 124-125 O 3
Katupa o **RI** 166-167 E 4
Kátúria o **IND** 142-143 E 3
Katwe o **EAU** 212-213 B 4
Katwe o **ZRE** 214-215 D 6
Katy o **USA** 44-45 K 5
Katym ~ **RUS** 114-115 M 5
Kau o **RI** 164-165 K 3
Kau, Teluk ≈ 164-165 K 3
Kauai ⌒ **USA** 48-49 C 6
Kauai Channel ≈ 48-49 C 7
Kauara o **CI** 202-203 H 4
Kaubi o **PNG** 183 E 3
Kaudom o **NAM** 216-217 F 9
Kaudom Game Park ⊥ **NAM** 216-217 F 9
Kaufbeuren o· **D** 92-93 L 5
Kaugel River ~ **PNG** 183 C 4
Kauhajoki o **FIN** 88-89 G 5
Kauhava o **FIN** 88-89 G 5
Kaukas o **RI** 164-165 H 4
Kaukauna o **USA** 46-47 D 3
Kaukauveld ⌊ **NAM** 216-217 F 9
Kauksi o· **EST** 94-95 K 2
Kaula ⌒ **USA** 48-49 B 7
Kaulakahi Channel ≈ 48-49 B 6
Kaulžur ~ **KA** 126-127 N 3
Kaumalapau Harbor o **USA** 48-49 D 7
Kauman o **RI** 168 E 3
Kaunakakai o **USA** 48-49 D 7
Kaunas ☆ ·· **LT** 94-95 H 4
Kaundy, vpadina ⌊ **KA** 126-127 K 5
Kaup o **PNG** 183 B 2
Kaupanger o **N** 86-87 C 6
Kaupena o **PNG** 183 C 4
Kaupo o **USA** 48-49 D 7
Kaurai o **PNG** 183 G 5
Kauru o **EAK** 212-213 F 4
Kauwa o **WAN** 198-199 F 6
Kau-Ye Kyun ⌒ **MYA** 158-159 E 5
Kava ~ **RUS** 120-121 M 4
Kavadarci o **MK** 100-101 J 4
Kavak ☆ **TR** 128-129 G 2
Kavála o · **GR** 100-101 J 4
Kavali o **IND** 140-141 H 3
Kävali o **IND** 140-141 H 3
Kavaratti o **IND** 140-141 E 5
Kavendu ~ **RG** 202-203 D 4
Kavi o **IND** 138-139 D 8
Kavieng ☆ **PNG** 183 F 2
Kavigyalik Lake o **USA** 20-21 H 7
Kavik River ~ **USA** 20-21 R 2

Kavinga o **Z** 214-215 G 7
Kavir, Dašt-e ⌊ **IR** 134-135 E 1
Kavkazkij zapovednik ⊥ **RUS** 126-127 D 6
Kávos o **GR** 100-101 H 5
Kavrizhka, Cape ▲ **USA** 22-23 N 6
Kavuu ~ **EAT** 214-215 F 4
Kawa ~ **RI** 166-167 E 3
Kawa ~ **RI** 166-167 E 3
Kawa, Temple of · **SUD** 200-201 E 3
Kawagit o **RI** 166-167 L 4
Kawagoe o **J** 152-153 H 7
Kawaguchi o **J** 152-153 H 7
Kawai o **RI** 166-167 L 4
Kawaihae o **USA** 48-49 E 7
Kawaikini ▲ **USA** 48-49 C 6
Kawajena o **SUD** 206-207 J 5
Kawakawa o **NZ** 182 E 1
Kawala ~ **MYA** 142-143 J 2
Kawali o **RI** 168 Q 3
Kawambwa o **Z** 214-215 E 5
Kawana o **Z** 218-219 C 1
Kawangko o **RI** 168 D 7
Kawangkoan o **RI** 164-165 J 3
Kawanoe o **J** 152-153 F 7
Kawant o **IND** 138-139 E 8
Kāwardha o **IND** 142-143 B 8
Kawarga ~ **RI** 166-167 K 5
Kawartha Lakes o **CDN** 38-39 E 6
Kawasa o **ZRE** 214-215 C 5
Kawasaki o **J** 152-153 H 7
Kawatipoli o **MYA** 142-143 K 6
Kawauchi o **J** 152-153 J 4
Kawau Island ⌒ **NZ** 182 E 2
Kawaya o **ZRE** 214-215 C 5
Kawayan o **RP** 160-161 F 7
Kawayu o **J** 152-153 L 3
Kawe, Pulau ⌒ **RI** 166-167 F 2
Kaweka ▲ **NZ** 182 F 3
Kawembwe o **Z** 214-215 F 6
Kawentinkim o **RI** 166-167 L 4
Kawe Rapids ~ **RI** 218-219 F 2
Kawhia o **NZ** 182 E 3
Kawich Peak ▲ **USA** 40-41 F 7
Kawinaw Lake o **CDN** 34-35 G 4
Kawkpalut o **MYA** 158-159 G 2
Kawkwareik o **MYA** 158-159 E 2
Kawlin o **MYA** 142-143 J 4
Kawltang o **MYA** 142-143 J 3
Kaxarari, Área Indígena X **BR** 66-67 D 7
Kaxgar He ~ **VRC** 146-147 C 6
Kax He ~ **VRC** 146-147 J 4
Kaxian D. ∴·· **VRC** 150-151 D 2
Kaxinauá Nova Olinda, Área Indígena X **BR** 66-67 B 7
Kaxinawá do Rio Humaitá, Área Indígena X **BR** 66-67 B 7
Kaxinawá do Rio Jordão, Área Indígena X **BR** 64-65 F 6
Kaya o **BF** 202-203 K 3
Kayaapu o **RI** 162-163 E 7
Kayabi, Área Indígena X **BR** 70-71 J 2
Kayak Island ⌒ **USA** 20-21 S 7
Kayambi o **Z** 214-215 G 5
Kayan ~ **RI** 164-165 E 2
Kayanga ~ **SN** 202-203 C 3
Käyankulam o **IND** 140-141 G 6
Kayanza o **BU** 212-213 B 5
Kayapó, Área Indígena X **BR** 68-69 B 5
Kayar o **SN** 202-203 B 3
Kayasa o **RI** 164-165 K 3
Kayattär o **IND** 140-141 G 6
Kaycee o **USA** 42-43 D 4
Kaye, Mount ▲ **AUS** 180-181 K 4
Kayeli o **RI** 166-167 D 3
Kayembe-Mukulu o **ZRE** 214-215 B 5
Kayenta o **USA** 44-45 B 1
Kayenzi o **EAT** 212-213 D 5
Kayes o **RMM** 202-203 E 2
Kayima o **WAL** 202-203 E 4
Kaymor o **SN** 202-203 C 3
Kaynabayonop o **ZRE** 212-213 B 4
Kayoa, Pulau ⌒ **RI** 164-165 K 3
Kayokwe o **BU** 212-213 B 5
Kayonza o **RWA** 212-213 C 4
Kay Point ▲ **CDN** 20-21 W 2
Kayrunnera o **AUS** 178-179 G 6
Kayseri ☆·· **TR** 128-129 F 3
Kayuadi, Pulau ⌒ **RI** 168 E 6
Kayuagung o **RI** 162-163 F 6
Kayuku o **RI** 164-165 G 4
Kayupangang, Pulau o **RI** 168 D 6
Kayuyu o **ZRE** 210-211 L 5
Kayville o **CDN** 34-35 D 6
Kazabazua o **CDN** 38-39 O 3
Kazača Lopan' o **UA** 102-103 K 2
Kazače o **RUS** 110-111 V 4
Kazan ~ **CDN** 30-31 V 3
Kazandžik = Gazanğuk o **TM** 136-137 D 5
Kazanlák o·· **BG** 102-103 D 6
Kazan River ~ **CDN** 30-31 V 3
Kazanskoe ☆ **RUS** 114-115 K 7
Kazantips'ka zatoka ≈ 102-103 J 5
Kazarman o **KS** 146-147 C 5
Kazaure o **WAN** 198-199 D 6
Kazbegi o **GE** 126-127 F 6
Kazbek, gora ▲ **GE** 126-127 F 6
Kaz Daği ▲ **TR** 128-129 B 3
Kazer ~ **TCH** 198-199 J 3
Kazer, Pico ▲ **RCH** 80 G 7
Käzerün o **IR** 134-135 D 4
Kazi Ahmad o **PK** 138-139 B 6
Kazibna o **BD** 142-143 H 4
Kazîkli Çayı ~ **TR** 128-129 G 3

Kazil'skoe ☆ **RUS** 96-97 L 7
Kazi-Magomed o **AZ** 128-129 N 2
Kazimiya, al- o **IRQ** 128-129 L 6
Kazîranga National Park ⊥ ··· **IND** 142-143 H 2
Kaziza o **ZRE** 214-215 B 6
Kaznakovka o **KA** 124-125 N 4
Kaztalovka o **KA** 126-127 J 3
Kažukas = Marijampole o·· **LT** 94-95 H 4
Kazurna Pan National Park ⊥ **ZW** 218-219 C 3
Kazumba o **ZRE** 214-215 C 5
Kazungula o **Z** 218-219 C 3
Kazuno o **J** 152-153 J 4
Kazym ~ **RUS** 114-115 L 3
Kazyr ~ **RUS** 116-117 G 9
Kbombole o **SN** 202-203 B 3
Kbor Roumia · **DZ** 190-191 D 2
Ké o **G** 210-211 C 3
Ké, Enneri ~ **TCH** 198-199 H 3
Kéa ~ **GR** 100-101 K 6
Keaau o **USA** 48-49 E 8
Keahole Point ▲ **USA** 48-49 D 8
Kearney o **USA** 42-43 H 5
Keating Point ▲ **IND** 140-141 L 5
Keban o **TR** 128-129 H 3
Keban Baraji < **TR** 128-129 H 3
Kébara o **RCB** 210-211 E 5
Kebasen o **RI** 168 C 3
Kebbe o **WAN** 198-199 B 6
Kebbi, Mayo ~ **TCH** 206-207 B 4
Kébémer o **SN** 202-203 B 2
Kébi, Mayo ~ **CAM** 204-205 K 5
Kébila o **RMM** 202-203 G 4
Kebili o **TN** 190-191 G 4
Kebnekaise ▲ **S** 86-87 J 3
Kebock Head ▲ **GB** 90-91 E 3
K'ebri Dehar o **ETH** 208-209 G 5
Kech ~ **PK** 134-135 K 5
K'ech'a Tera'a ▲ **ETH** 208-209 D 5
Kéché o **RCA** 206-207 E 3
Kechika Ranges ▲ **CDN** 30-31 F 6
Kechika River ~ **CDN** 30-31 F 6
Kecskemét o· **H** 92-93 P 5
Keda o **GE** 126-127 G 6
Kedah □ **MAL** 162-163 D 2
Kedarnath o **IND** 138-139 G 2
Kédédéssé o **TCH** 206-207 C 3
Kedgwick o **CDN** 38-39 L 5
Kédia d'Idjil ▲ **RIM** 196-197 E 4
Kediet o **RIM** 196-167 K 3
Kediri o **RI** 168 E 3
Kedon o **RUS** 112-113 K 4
Kedon ~ **RUS** 112-113 K 4
Kedonganan hrebet ▲ **RUS** 112-113 K 4
Kédougou o **SN** 202-203 D 3
Kedrovaja, gora ▲ **RUS** 122-123 D 6
Kedrovyj o **RUS** 114-115 P 6
Kedungwuni o **RI** 168 C 3
Kedva ~ **RUS** 88-89 W 4
Ķędzierzyn o **PL** 92-93 P 3
Ķędzierzyn-Kožle o · **PL** 92-93 P 3
Keekorok Lodge o **EAK** 212-213 E 4
Keel = An Caol o **IRL** 90-91 B 5
Keele River ~ **CDN** 30-31 F 3
Keeley Lake o **CDN** 34-35 Q 4
Keeling o · **RC** 156-157 M 4
Keene o **USA** 46-47 M 4
Keene, Lake o **AUS** 176-177 G 2
Keenjhar Lake o·· **PK** 138-139 B 7
Keepit, Lake < **AUS** 178-179 L 6
Keep River o **AUS** 172-173 J 4
Keep River National Park ⊥ **AUS** 172-173 J 4
Keerweer, Cape ▲ **AUS** 174-175 F 3
Keetmanshoop ☆ **NAM** 220-221 D 3
Keewatin River o **CDN** 34-35 J 2
Keezhik Lake o **CDN** 34-35 M 5
Kefa □ **ETH** 208-209 B 5
Kefalonía ⌒ **GR** 100-101 H 5
Kefamenanu o **RI** 166-167 C 6
Keffi o **WAN** 204-205 G 4
Keflavik o **IS** 86-87 b 2
K'eftya o **ETH** 200-201 H 6
Kegaji ☆ **US** 136-137 F 3
Kégart o **KS** 136-137 N 4
Kegaska o **CDN** 38-39 O 3
Kegdal o **IND** 138-139 F 3
Kegen o **KA** 146-147 E 5
Kegworth o **CDN** 34-35 E 5
Kehihi Indian Reserve X **CDN** 32-33 P 4
Kehl o **D** 92-93 J 4
Keibul-Lamjoa National Park ⊥ **IND** 142-143 H 3
Keikaoko o **RI** 168 E 7
Keila o **RI** 168 E 7
Keila ~ **SOL** 184 I d 1
Keimoes o **ZA** 220-221 E 4
Kei Mouth o **ZA** 220-221 G 6
Keipene o **LV** 94-95 J 3
Kei Road o **ZA** 220-221 G 6
Keiskammarivier ~ **ZA** 220-221 H 6
Keita o **RN** 198-199 B 5
Keita ou Douka, Bahr ~ **TCH** 206-207 D 4
Keitele o **FIN** (KPN) 88-89 J 5
Keitele o **FIN** (KSS) 88-89 H 5
Keith o **AUS** 180-181 F 4
Keith Arm o **CDN** 30-31 H 3
Keithville o **USA** 44-45 J 4
Keiyasi o **FJI** 184 III a 2
Kejimkujik National Park ⊥ **CDN** 38-39 M 6
Kejîng pilgyin, laguna o **RUS** ...
Kejobon o **RI** 168 C 3

Kejvy ▲ **RUS** 88-89 O 3
Kekaha o **USA** 48-49 C 7
Kékajgyr o **KS** 146-147 D 5
Kёk-Art □ **KS** 146-147 B 5
Keke o **PNG** 183 D 5
Kékem o **CAM** 204-205 J 6
Kekertuk o **CDN** 28-29 J 3
Kekesu o **PNG** 184 I b 1
Kekirawa o **CL** 140-141 J 6
Kekneno, Gunung ▲ **RI** 166-167 C 6
Kekova Adasi ⌒ **TR** 128-129 C 4
Kekovandasi ⌒ **TR** 128-129 C 4
Kekri o **IND** 138-139 E 7
Kekurnoi, Cape ▲ **USA** 22-23 T 4
Kekurmyj, zaliv ~ **RUS** 120-121 Q 4
Keku Strait ≈ 32-33 D 3
Kelabo o **PNG** 183 B 3
K'elafo o **ETH** 208-209 G 5
Kelag o **VRC** 154-155 B 6
Kelagay o **AFG** 136-137 L 7
Kelai ~ **RI** 164-165 E 3
Kélakam o **RN** 198-199 G 5
Kelambakkam o **IND** 140-141 J 4
Kelan o **VRC** 154-155 G 2
Kelandic Plateau ≈ 86-87 g 1
Kelang, Pulau ⌒ **RI** 166-167 D 3
Kelankyla o **FIN** 88-89 J 4
Kelanoao o **PNG** 183 D 4
Kelantan □ **MAL** 162-163 D 2
Kelapa o **RI** 162-163 F 5
Kélbo o **BF** 202-203 K 3
Kélcyrë o · **AL** 100-101 H 4
Keľda ~ **RUS** 88-89 P 4
Kele ~ **RUS** 118-119 P 4
Keleft o **AFG** 136-137 K 8
Kelem o **ETH** 208-209 B 6
Kelema o **EAT** 212-213 E 6
Kèlèraš' = Cälärasi o **MD** 102-103 F 4
Keles o **US** 136-137 L 4
Keléya o **RMM** 202-203 G 4
Keleż ~ **RUS** 116-117 F 9
Kelgo Bay ≈ 36-37 C 5
Kelibia o **TN** 190-191 H 2
Kelifskij Uzboj ⌊ **TM** 136-137 H 6
Kelifvun, gora ▲ **RUS** 112-113 O 2
Kelimjar ~ **RUS** 110-111 P 4
Keling o **RI** 168 D 3
Kelkit o **TR** 128-129 H 2
Kelkit Çayı ~ **TR** 128-129 G 2
Kelkit Çayı ~ **TR** 128-129 H 2
Kéllé o **RCB** 210-211 E 5
Kéllé o **RN** 198-199 E 5
Kellerberrin o **AUS** 176-177 D 5
Keller Lake o **CDN** 24-25 H 3
Kellet, Canal de ≈ 50-51 B 4
Kellet, Cape ▲ **CDN** 24-25 H 6
Kellett River ~ **CDN** 24-25 b 5
Kellett River ~ **CDN** 30-31 Y 2
Kellett Strait ≈ 24-25 M 3
Kellog o **RUS** 114-115 S 3
Kellogg o **USA** 40-41 F 2
Kelloselkä o **FIN** 88-89 K 3
Kelly, Mount ▲ **USA** 20-21 J 2
Kelly Range ▲ **AUS** 176-177 F 2
Kelly River ~ **USA** 20-21 J 2
Keľma ~ **RUS** 114-115 U 5
Kelmé o **LT** 94-95 H 4
Kelmet o **ER** 200-201 J 4
Kelo o **TCH** 206-207 B 4
Kelongwa o **Z** 218-219 D 1
Kelowna o **CDN** 32-33 L 7
Kelsey o **CDN** 34-35 H 2
Kelso o· **GB** 90-91 E 4
Kelso o **USA** (CA) 40-41 G 8
Kelso o **USA** (WA) 40-41 C 2
Keltie Bugt ≈ 26-27 Z 2
Kelu o **VRC** 156-157 G 6
Kelua o **RI** 164-165 D 5
Keluang, Tanjung ▲ **RI** 162-163 H 5
Kelume o **RI** 162-163 F 5
Kelvat ~ **RUS** 114-115 N 5
Kelvington o **CDN** 34-35 D 5
Kem' o **RUS** (KAR) 88-89 N 4
Kem' o **RUS** 88-89 M 4
Kem' ~ **RUS** 88-89 M 4
Kemah ☆ **TR** 128-129 H 3
Kemal, Gunung ▲ **RI** 164-165 E 3
Kemáliye o **TR** 128-129 H 3
Kemano o **CDN** 32-33 G 5
Kemara, Kampung o **MAL** 162-163 E 2
Kemasik o **MAL** 162-163 E 2
Kemata I o **TCH** 206-207 D 4
Kemba o **RCA** 206-207 D 4
Kembani o **RI** 166-167 L 6
Kembapi o **RI** 166-167 L 6
Kembé, Chutes de ~ **RCA** 206-207 E 6
Kembéra o **RG** 202-203 D 4
Kembolcha o **ETH** (Wel) 208-209 C 4
Kembolcha o **ETH** (Weo) 208-209 D 3
Kemčug ~ **RUS** 116-117 F 6
Kemčug o **TCH** 206-207 D 4
Kemenagi, Mount ▲ **PNG** 183 B 4
Kemer o **TR** 128-129 D 4
Kemer o **TR** 128-129 D 4
Kemerhisar o **TR** 128-129 F 4
Kemerovo ☆ **RUS** 114-115 T 7
Kemi o **FIN** 88-89 H 4
Kemijärvi o **FIN** (LAP) 88-89 J 3
Kemijärvi o **FIN** (LAP) 88-89 J 3
Kemijoki ~ **FIN** 88-89 H 3
Kemkara o **RUS** 120-121 H 5
Kemľa o **RUS** 96-97 D 6
Kemmerer o **USA** 40-41 J 5
Kémo o **RCA** 206-207 D 6
Kemp, Lake o **USA** 44-45 H 3
Kempasi ~ **RUS** 114-115 P 7
Kempe Fjord ≈ 26-27 m 7
Kempendjaj o **RUS** 118-119 J 4
Kempendjaj ~ **RUS** 118-119 J 4
Kemp Land ⌊ **ARK** 16 G 32
Kemp Peninsula ⌣ **ARK** 16 F 30
Kemps Bay o **BS** 54-55 G 2

King Mountain ▲ USA 44-45 F 4
Kingnait Fiord ≈ 36-37 R 2
Kingnait Range ▲ CDN 36-37 L 2
Kingombe o ZRE 210-211 L 5
Kingoonya o AUS 178-179 C 6
Kingora River ~ CDN 24-25 e 6
Kingri o PK 138-139 B 4
King River ~ AUS 172-173 L 3
King River ~ AUS 180-181 J 4
King Salmon o USA 22-23 S 3
King Salmon River ~ USA 22-23 S 4
King Salmon River ~ USA 22-23 S 3
King's-Bay-Fall o TT 60-61 L 2
Kingsburg o ZA 220-221 K 5
Kings Canyon ∴ USA 176-177 L 2
Kings Canyon National Park ⊥ USA 40-41 E 7
Kingscote o AUS 180-181 D 3
Kings Cove o CDN 38-39 LS 4
Kingslake National Park ⊥ AUS 180-181 H 4
Kings Landing Historical Settlement ∴ CDN 38-39 L 6
Kingsley o ZA 220-221 K 3
King's Lynn o • GB 90-91 H 5
Kings Mountain o USA 48-49 H 2
Kings Mountain National Military Park ∴ USA 48-49 H 2
King Sound ≈ 172-173 F 4
Kings Peak ▲ USA 40-41 J 5
Kingsport o USA 48-49 G 1
Kingston o AUS 180-181 J 7
Kingston o CDN 38-39 F 6
Kingston o • JA 54-55 G 5
Kingston o USA (NY) 46-47 M 5
Kingston o USA (PA) 46-47 L 5
Kingston upon Hull o • GB 90-91 G 5
Kingston S.E. o AUS 180-181 E 4
Kingston-on-Murray o AUS 180-181 F 3
Kingstown ★ WV 56 E 5
Kingstree o USA 48-49 J 3
Kings Trough ≅ 6-7 G 4
Kingsville o USA 44-45 J 6
Kingswood o ZA 220-221 G 3
Kingulube o ZRE 212-213 B 5
Kingungi o ZRE 210-211 F 6
Kingurutik Lake o CDN 36-37 S 6
Kingurutik River ~ CDN 36-37 S 6
Kingussie o GB 90-91 E 3
Kingwaya o ZRE 210-211 G 6
King William Island ∧ CDN 24-25 X 6
King Williams Town o LB 202-203 F 7
King William's Town o • ZA 220-221 H 6
Kingwood o USA 46-47 J 6
Kiniama o ZRE 212-213 C 5
Kinik ☆ TR 128-129 B 3
Kinipaghulghat Mountains ▲ USA 20-21 P 5
Kinirapoort o ZA 220-221 K 5
Kinkala ☆ RCB 210-211 E 6
Kinkasan-shima ∧ J 152-153 J 5
Kinkony, Farihy o RM 222-223 D 6
Kinkosi o ZRE 210-211 E 6
Kinley Point ▲ CDN 26-27 L 3
Kinmundy o USA 46-47 D 6
Kinna o EAK 212-213 G 3
Kinna ☆ S 86-87 F 8
Kinnaird Head ▲ GB 90-91 G 3
Kinnear o USA 42-43 C 4
Kinnegad o IRL 90-91 D 5
Kinnekulle ▲ S 86-87 F 7
Kinniya o CL 140-141 J 6
Kino, Bahía ≈ 50-51 C 3
Kino-gawa ~ J 152-153 F 7
Kinoje River ~ CDN 34-35 Q 5
Kinomoto o J 152-153 G 7
Kinoosao o CDN 34-35 S 2
Kinrara o AUS 174-175 H 6
Kinross o ZA 220-221 J 3
Kinsarvik o N 86-87 C 6
Kinshasa ★ ZRE 210-211 E 6
Kinshasa ★ ZRE (Kin) 210-211 E 6
Kinsley o USA 42-43 H 7
Kinston o USA 48-49 K 2
Kintampo o GH 202-203 K 5
Kintinnian o RG 202-203 F 4
Kintom o RI 164-165 H 4
Kintop o RI 164-165 D 5
Kintore, Mount ▲ AUS 176-177 L 3
Kintore Range ▲ AUS 176-177 K 1
Kintyre ~ GB 90-91 E 4
Kinu-gawa ~ J 152-153 H 6
Kinushao River ~ CDN 34-35 P 3
Kinuso o CDN 32-33 N 4
Kinwat o IND 138-139 G 10
Kinyéran o RG 202-203 F 4
Kinyeti ▲ SUD 212-213 D 2
Kinyinya o BU 212-213 C 5
Kioa ~ FJI 184 III b 2
Kiokluk Mountains ▲ USA 20-21 L 6
Kiosk o CDN 38-39 E 5
Kiowa o USA (CO) 42-43 G 6
Kiowa o USA (KS) 44-45 H 1
Kiowa o USA (OK) 44-45 K 2
Kiowa, Fort ∴ USA 42-43 H 4
Kipaila o ZRE 214-215 E 4
Kipaka o ZRE 210-211 L 6
Kiparissia o GR 100-101 H 6
Kipawa, Lac o CDN 38-39 E 5
Kipemba o ZRE 210-211 L 6
Kipembawe o EAT 214-215 D 5
Kipengere Range ▲ EAT 214-215 G 5
Kipievo o RUS 88-89 X 4
Kipili o EAT 214-215 F 4
Kipini o EAK 212-213 H 5
Kipisa o CDN 36-37 G 2
Kipkelion o EAK 212-213 F 3
Kipnuk o USA 22-23 O 3
Kipti o UA 102-103 G 2
Kipushi o ZRE 214-215 E 4
Kipushia o ZRE (KOR) 214-215 C 4
Kipushia o ZRE (SHA) 214-215 D 6
Kiran ~ RUS 120-121 F 6
Kirana, Tanjung ▲ RI 166-167 G 3
Kirandul o IND 142-143 B 6

Kirané o RMM 202-203 E 2
Kiranomena o RM 222-223 E 7
Kiranur o IND 140-141 H 5
Kiranür o IND 140-141 H 5
Kiraz ☆ TR 128-129 C 3
Kirbej o RUS 110-111 H 5
Kirbikän, Wâdi ~ SUD 200-201 F 3
Kirbyville o USA 44-45 L 4
Kirchhoffer River ~ CDN 36-37 G 2
Kireevsk ☆ RUS 94-95 P 5
Kirej o RUS 116-117 K 9
Kirenga ~ RUS 116-117 N 8
Kirensk o RUS 116-117 O 7
Kirevna o RUS 120-121 T 5
Kirganik o RUS 120-121 S 6
Kirganik ~ RUS 120-121 S 6
Kirgiz-Mijaki ☆ RUS 96-97 J 7
Kirgizskij hrebet ▲ KA 136-137 N 3
Kiri o ZRE 210-211 G 4
Kiriab o RI 166-167 J 2
Kiriaini o EAK 212-213 G 3
Kirikhan o TR 128-129 G 4
Kirikkale o TR 128-129 E 3
Kirillov o RUS 94-95 Q 2
Kirillovo o RUS 122-123 K 5
Kirinda o CL 140-141 J 7
Kirishima-Yaku National Park ⊥ J 152-153 D 9
Kirishima-yama ▲ J 152-153 D 9
Kiriši o RUS 94-95 N 2
Kirit o SP 208-209 H 4
Kiritappu o J 152-153 L 3
Kiritimati Island ~ KIB 13 M 2
Kiritiri o EAK 212-213 F 4
Kiriwa o PNG 183 A 5
Kiriwina Island ~ PNG 183 F 5
Kirjaka-Tas, grjada ▲ RUS 108-109 f 4
Kirkalocka o AUS 176-177 D 4
Kirkcaldy o GB 90-91 F 3
Kirkella o CDN 34-35 F 5
Kirkenes o N 86-87 P 2
Kirkgeçit o TR 128-129 K 3
Kirk Gemstone Deposit, Mount ∴ AUS 176-177 F 6
Kirkimbie o AUS 172-173 J 4
Kirk Lake o CDN 30-31 P 4
Kirkland Lake o CDN 38-39 E 4
Kirklareli ☆ TR 128-129 B 2
Kirksville o USA 42-43 L 5
Kirkük ☆ IRQ 128-129 L 5
Kirkun o RUS 118-119 E 11
Kirkwall o GB 90-91 F 2
Kirkwood o USA 46-47 C 6
Kirkwood o ZA 220-221 G 6
Krobasi o RI 128-129 E 4
Kirov o RUS 94-95 O 4
Kirov ~ RUS (KIR) 94-95 P 4
Kirova, ostrov ~ RUS 108-109 Z 3
Kirovabad = Gandža o • AZ 128-129 N 4
Kirovakan = Karaklis o AR 128-129 L 2
Kirovo o RUS 116-117 L 5
Kirovo-Čepeck ☆ RUS 96-97 G 4
Kirovograd = Kirovohrad o UA 102-103 H 4
Kirovohrad o • UA 102-103 H 3
Kirovsk o RUS (LEN) 94-95 M 2
Kirovsk o RUS (MUR) 88-89 M 3
Kirovsk = Babadayhan o TM 136-137 G 6
Kirov's'ke o UA 102-103 J 5
Kirovskij o RUS 122-123 E 6
Kirovskij o RUS (AMR) 118-119 N 8
Kirovskij o RUS (AST) 126-127 H 5
Kirovskij o RUS (KMC) 120-121 S 6
Kirovskij o RUS (KRN) 116-117 G 6
Kirovskij o TJ 136-137 L 8
Kirovskoe o RUS 136-137 M 3
Kirov su kojmasy ≈ KA 96-97 G 8
Kirpili ~ RUS 102-103 L 5
Kirs ☆ RUS 96-97 H 4
Kirsanov o RUS 94-95 S 5
Kırşehir ☆ TR 128-129 E 3
Kirtachi o RN 204-205 F 2
Kirtäka o AFG 134-135 L 3
Kirtaka ∴ PK 134-135 J 4
Kirthar National Park ⊥ PK 134-135 M 6
Kirthar Range ▲ PK 134-135 M 5
Kiru o WAN 204-205 H 3
Kirundo o BU 212-213 D 4
Kirundu o ZRE 210-211 L 4
Kirwin Reservoir < USA 42-43 H 6
Kiryandongo o EAU 212-213 D 3
Kiryū o J 152-153 H 6
Kiržač ☆ RUS 94-95 Q 3
Kiš o IR 134-135 J 5
Kiš, Ğažire-ye ~ IR 134-135 J 5
Kisa ☆ S 86-87 G 8
Kisaki o EAT 214-215 J 4
Kisanga o EAT 214-215 J 5
Kisangani ☆ ZRE (HAU) 210-211 K 3
Kisangire o EAT 214-215 K 4
Kisantete o ZRE 210-211 F 6
Kisantu o • ZRE 210-211 F 6
Kisar, Pulau ~ RI 166-167 D 6
Kisaralik River ~ USA 20-21 K 6
Kisaran o RI 162-163 C 3
Kisarawe o EAT 214-215 K 4
Kisarazu o J 152-153 H 7
Kisasi o EAT 212-213 G 4
Kiselëva o RUS 122-123 H 3
Kiselëvsk o RUS 124-125 P 1
Kiselëvsk = Kiselëvsk o RUS 124-125 P 1
Kisengi o EAT 212-213 D 6
Kisengwa o ZRE (KOR) 210-211 L 6
Kishanganj o IND 138-139 O 6
Kishangarh o IND 138-139 D 6
Kishangarh o IND (MAP) 138-139 D 6
Kishangarh o IND (RAJ) 138-139 E 6
Kishari o PK 134-135 M 5
Kishiwada o J 152-153 F 7
Kishtwar o IND 138-139 C 4
Kisi o EAT 214-215 F 4
Kisi o WAN 204-205 E 4
Kisigo ~ EAT 214-215 H 5

Kisigo Game Reserve ⊥ EAT 214-215 H 4
Kisii o EAK 212-213 F 4
Kisiju o EAT 214-215 K 4
Kisima o EAT 212-213 F 3
Kišinev = Chişinău ★ MD 102-103 F 4
Kisiwani o EAT 212-213 F 6
Kisiwani, Kilwa •• EAT 214-215 K 5
Kiska Island ~ 22-23 E 7
Kiska Volcan ▲ USA 22-23 E 6
Kiskittogisu Lake o CDN 34-35 G 3
Kiskitto Lake o CDN 34-35 G 3
Kiskörös o H 92-93 P 5
Kiskunfélegyháza o H 92-93 P 5
Kiskunhalas o H 92-93 P 5
Kiskunmajsa o H 92-93 P 5
Kislovodsk o RUS 126-127 E 6
Kismaanyo ☆ SP 212-213 J 4
Kismet o USA 44-45 G 1
Kiso-gawa ~ J 152-153 G 7
Kisogawa o EAT 212-213 C 5
Kisomoro o EAU 212-213 C 3
Kisoro o EAU 212-213 B 4
Kiso-sanmyaku ▲ J 152-153 G 7
Kisose o ZRE 214-215 C 4
Kisoshi o ZRE 212-213 B 6
Kispiox River ~ CDN 32-33 H 4
Kissen ~ RG 202-203 D 4
Kissidougou o RG 202-203 E 5
Kissimmee o USA 48-49 H 6
Kissimmee, Lake o USA 48-49 H 6
Kissimmee River ~ USA 48-49 H 6
Kissingen, Bad o D 92-93 L 3
Kississing Lake o CDN 34-35 F 3
Kistanje o HR 100-101 E 3
Kistigan Lake o CDN 34-35 K 3
Kisuki o J 152-153 E 7
Kisumu o EAK 212-213 E 4
Kisvárda o H 92-93 H 4
Kit, mys ▲ RUS 108-109 d 3
Kita = Vestgrønland ~ GRØ 26-27 X 6
Kita-Daitō-shima ~ J 152-153 D 12
Kitāf ~ Y 132-133 D 5
Kitahiyama o J 152-153 H 3
Kitaibaraki o J 152-153 J 6
Kitakami o J 152-153 J 5
Kitakami-gawa ~ J 152-153 J 5
Kitakami-kōti ▲ J 152-153 J 5
Kitakata o J 152-153 H 6
Kitakyūshū o J 152-153 D 8
Kitale o EAK 212-213 F 3
Kitami o J 152-153 K 2
Kitami-santi ▲ J 152-153 K 2
Kitami-tōge ▲ J 152-153 K 2
Kitami-Yamato-tai ≅ 152-153 L 2
Kita-Nagato Quasi National Park ⊥ J 152-153 D 7
Kitanda o ZRE 214-215 D 4
Kitangari o EAT 214-215 J 6
Kitangiri, Lake o EAT 212-213 E 6
Kitani Safari Camp o EAK 212-213 F 5
Kitava Island ~ PNG 183 F 5
Kitaya o EAT 214-215 K 6
Kit Carson o USA 42-43 F 6
Kitchener o AUS 176-177 H 5
Kitchener o CDN 38-39 D 7
Kitchigama, Rivière ~ CDN 38-39 E 3
Kiteba o ZRE 214-215 C 4
Kitee o FIN 88-89 L 5
Kitendwe o ZRE 214-215 E 4
Kitenga o ZRE 210-211 H 5
Kitengo o ZRE 214-215 C 4
Kiterput qorno ≈ 28-29 R 6
Kitgum o EAU 212-213 D 2
Kithira o GR 100-101 J 6
Kithira ~ GR 100-101 J 6
Kithnos ~ GR 100-101 K 6
Kitika o RCA 206-207 F 6
Kitimat o CDN 32-33 F 4
Kitimat Ranges ▲ CDN 32-33 F 4
Kitinen ~ FIN 88-89 J 3
Kitiwaka o EAT (IRI) 214-215 H 6
Kitilä o FIN 88-89 H 3
Kitlope River ~ CDN 32-33 G 5
Kitob ☆ US 136-137 K 5
Kitobojinyi o RUS 122-123 O 5
Kitoj ~ RUS 116-117 N 9
Kitou o J 152-153 F 8
Kitsamby ~ RM 222-223 E 7
Kitsuki o J 152-153 D 8
Kittakittaooloo, Lake o AUS 178-179 E 5
Kittanning o USA 46-47 J 5
Kittery o USA 46-47 N 4
Kitt Peak National Observatory • USA 40-41 J 9
Kitty Hawk o USA 48-49 L 1
Kitui o EAK 212-213 G 4
Kitumbeine o EAT 212-213 F 4
Kiturnbini o EAT 214-215 K 5
Kitunda o EAT 214-215 G 4
Kitunga o ZRE 214-215 C 5
Kitutu o ZRE 212-213 B 5
Kitwanga o CDN 32-33 F 4
Kitwe o Z 214-215 D 7
Kitzbühel o A 92-93 M 5
Kitzingen o D 92-93 L 4
Kiu o EAK 212-213 F 4
Kiubo, Chute ~ ZRE 214-215 D 5
Kiuga Marine National Reserve ⊥ EAK 212-213 H 4
Kiu Lom Reservoir < THA 142-143 L 6
Kiumbila o EAT 210-211 L 6
Kiunga o EAK 212-213 H 4
Kiunga o PNG 183 A 4
Kiuruvesi o FIN 88-89 J 5
Kivalina o USA 20-21 H 3
Kivalina River ~ USA 20-21 H 3
Kivi o IR 128-129 N 4
Kivijärvi o FIN 88-89 H 5
Kiviõli o EST 94-95 K 2
Kivori-Kui o PNG 183 D 5
Kivu, Lac o ZRE 212-213 B 4
Kiwai Island ~ PNG 183 B 5
Kiwalik o USA 20-21 K 3
Kiwatama o EAT 214-215 J 5
Kiwayuu Bay ≈ 212-213 H 5

Kiwi House • NZ 182 E 3
Kiworo o RI 166-167 K 5
Kiyâmaki Dâġ ▲ IR 128-129 L 3
Kiyâsar o IR 136-137 C 6
Kiyat o KSA 132-133 B 4
Kiyawa o WAN 204-205 H 3
Kiyl ~ KA 96-97 J 9
Kizel o RUS 114-115 D 5
Kizema o RUS 88-89 S 6
Kizhake Chalakudi o IND 140-141 G 5
Kiziba-Baluba ⊥ ZRE 214-215 D 6
Kiži-Hem ~ RUS 116-117 H 9
Kizil ~ RUS 96-97 H 6
Kizilağaç o TR 128-129 J 3
Kizilcahamam ☆ TR 128-129 E 2
Kizilirmak o TR 128-129 E 2
Kizilirmak ~ TR 128-129 G 3
Kizilirmak ~ TR 128-129 F 2
Kizilyurt o RUS 126-127 G 6
Kizilkum ~ US 136-137 G 5
Kizilören o TR 128-129 E 4
Kizil Qianfodonga ∴ VRC 146-147 E 5
Kizittaššskij līman ≈• 102-103 K 5
Kiziltepe o TR 128-129 J 4
Kizimkazi o EAT 214-215 K 4
Kizinga o RUS 118-119 D 10
Kižinga ~ RUS 118-119 D 10
Kiži Pogost ••• RUS 88-89 N 5
Kizir ~ RUS 116-117 G 8
Kizkalesi •• TR 128-129 F 4
Kizljar o RUS 126-127 G 6
Kizner o RUS 96-97 H 3
Kizyl Arvat o TM 136-137 E 5
Kizyl Atrek = Gyzyletrek o TM 136-137 D 6
Kizyl Baudak o TM 136-137 F 3
KizylKaja o TM 136-137 D 4
Kjalvaz o AZ 128-129 N 3
Kjahta o RUS 116-117 N 10
Kjel', Ytyk ★ RUS 120-121 E 2
Kjøllefjord o N 86-87 N 1
Kjøpsvik o N 86-87 H 2
Kjubjainde o RUS 118-119 K 3
Kjubjume ~ RUS 120-121 H 2
Kjueľ, Aleko- o RUS 110-111 c 5
Kjueľ, Bjas'- o RUS 118-119 J 6
Kjueľ, Bjas' o RUS 118-119 J 6
Kjueľ, Kudu- o RUS 118-119 B 9
Kjueľ, Sebjan- o RUS 110-111 P 4
Kjueľ, Segjan- o RUS 118-119 J 4
Kjueľ, Ulahan- o RUS 110-111 V 6
Kjueľ, Us- o RUS 118-119 J 4
Kjueľ, Usun- o RUS 110-111 V 5
Kjuenelëkjan ~ RUS 110-111 G 5
Kjuente ~ RUS 120-121 J 2
Kjuerelejah o RUS 118-119 K 3
Kjulenke ~ RUS 110-111 O 6
Kjundjae ~ RUS 118-119 J 4
Kjundjudej ~ RUS 110-111 P 7
Kjungej Ala-Too', hrebet ▲ KS 146-147 C 4
Kjunkju ~ RUS 118-119 N 5
Kjunkjuj-Rassoha ~ RUS 110-111 G 4
Kjupcy o RUS 120-121 T 3
Kjurdamir = Kürdamir o AZ 128-129 N 2
Kjurjungnekjan ~ RUS 116-117 O 3
Kjusjur o RUS 110-111 Q 4
Kjustendil o • BG 100-101 C 6
Klaarstrom o ZA 220-221 F 6
Klabat, Teluk ≈ 162-163 F 5
Kladanj o BIH 100-101 J 6
Kladno o CZ 92-93 N 3
Klaeng o THA 158-159 F 4
Klagenfurt ☆ A 92-93 N 5
Klaipėda ☆ • LT 94-95 J 3
Klakah o RI 168 E 3
Klamath o USA 40-41 C 4
Klamath Falls o USA 40-41 D 4
Klamath Mountains ▲ USA 40-41 C 5
Klamath River ~ USA 40-41 C 5
Klamono o RI 166-167 F 2
Klang o MAL 162-163 D 3
Klappan River ~ CDN 32-33 F 3
Klarälven ~ S 86-87 F 6
Klark o USA 112-113 V 1
Klaserie Nature Reserve ⊥ ZA 220-221 K 2
Klaten o RI 168 D 2
Klatovy o CZ 92-93 M 4
Klättau = Klatovy o CZ 92-93 M 4
Klawer o ZA 220-221 D 5
Klawock o USA 32-33 D 4
Kle o CI 202-203 H 7
Kleena Kleene o CDN 32-33 H 5
Klein Aub o NAM 220-221 C 1
Kleinbegin o ZA 220-221 E 4
Klein Doringrivier ~ ZA 220-221 D 5
Kleiner Khingan ▲ VRC 150-151 F 2
Klein Karas o NAM 220-221 C 3
Klein Karoo = Little Karoo ~ ZA 220-221 E 6
Klein Letaba ~ ZA 218-219 F 6
Kleinpoort o ZA 220-221 G 6
Klein Rietrivier ~ ZA 220-221 F 5
Klein's Camp o EAT 212-213 E 4
Kleinsee o ZA 220-221 C 4
Klein Swartberge ▲ ZA 220-221 E 6
Klekovača ▲ BIH 100-101 F 2
Kléla o RMM 202-203 H 4
Klerksdorp o ZA 220-221 H 3
Klerkskraal o ZA 220-221 H 3
Klery Creek o USA 20-21 J 3
Klésso o BF 202-203 J 4
Kletnja o RUS 94-95 N 5
Kleve o D 92-93 J 3
Klička o RUS 118-119 H 10
Kličkinskij, hrebet ▲ RUS 118-119 H 10
Klickitat River ~ USA 40-41 D 3
Klimino o RUS 116-117 J 6
Klimpfjäll o S 86-87 G 4
Klina o YU 100-101 H 3
Klinaklini Glacier o CDN 32-33 G 6
Klinaklini River ~ CDN 32-33 H 6
Klincy o RUS 94-95 N 5
Klinovec ▲ CZ 92-93 M 3

Klinsko-Dmitrovskaja grjada ▲ RUS 94-95 O 3
Klintehamn o S 86-87 J 8
Klipfontein o ZA 220-221 G 6
Klipplaat o ZA 220-221 G 6
Kliprand o ZA 220-221 D 5
Kliprivier ~ ZA 220-221 J 3
Klipskool o ZA 220-221 K 2
Klis o RI 166-167 D 6
Klisurski Prohod ▲ BG 102-103 C 6
Kljavino ☆ RUS 96-97 H 6
Kljaz'ma ~ RUS 94-95 Q 3
Ključ o BIH 100-101 F 2
Ključ, Těplyj o RUS 120-121 G 2
Ključevskaja Sopka, vulkan ▲ RUS 120-121 T 5
Ključi o RUS (KMC) 120-121 T 5
Ključi o RUS (ALT) 124-125 L 2
Kljuevka o RUS 108-109 h 5
Klodzko o • PL 102-103 C 2
Klolz, Lac o CDN 36-37 N 4
Klolz, Mount ▲ CDN 20-21 W 5
Klondike Highway II CDN 20-21 U 4
Klondike Plateau ▲ CDN 20-21 U 5
Klondike River ~ CDN 20-21 V 4
Klosterneuburg o A 92-93 O 4
Klotz, Mount ▲ CDN 20-21 W 4
Kluane Lake o CDN 20-21 V 6
Kluang o MAL 162-163 E 3
Kluczbork o PL 92-93 P 3
Kludang o BRU 164-165 D 1
Kluhorskij, pereval ▲ RUS 126-127 D 6
Klunda o IND 138-139 F 2
Klungkung o RI 168 B 7
Klutlan Glacier o USA 20-21 U 6
Klymovo o RUS 94-95 N 5
Km. 60 o PY 76-77 H 4
Km. 100 o RA 76-77 H 4
Km. 145 o PY 76-77 H 2
Kmpóng Thum o K 158-159 H 4
Knarvik o N 86-87 B 6
Knee Lake o CDN (MAN) 34-35 J 3
Knee Lake o CDN (SAS) 34-35 C 3
Knewstubb Lake o CDN 32-33 H 5
Kneža o BG 102-103 D 6
Knidos ••• TR 128-129 B 4
Knifeblade Ridge ▲ USA 20-21 L 2
Knife Delta ~ 30-31 W 6
Knife River ~ USA 42-43 F 2
Knife River Indian Village National Historic Site ∴ USA 42-43 G 2
Knight Inlet ≈ 32-33 H 6
Knight Island ~ USA 20-21 R 6
Knight Islands o CDN 36-37 R 4
Knin o HR 100-101 F 2
Knippa o USA 44-45 H 5
Knivskjelodden ~ N 86-87 M 1
Knjaginino o RUS 96-97 F 3
Knjaze-Bolkonskoe o RUS 122-123 F 4
Knjaže River o CDN 36-37 S 6
Knjazevo o RUS 114-115 N 3
Knjazevo o RUS 122-123 H 2
Knob, Cape ▲ AUS 176-177 C 7
Knobby Head ▲ AUS 176-177 C 4
Knokke-Heist o • B 92-93 G 3
Knolls o USA 40-41 H 5
Knorr, Cape ▲ CDN 26-27 P 4
Knossós ••• GR 100-101 K 7
Knowles, Cape ▲ ARK 16 F 30
Knowles Lake o CDN 30-31 R 5
Knox o USA 46-47 F 5
Knox Land ⊥ ARK 16 G 11
Knoxville o USA (AL) 42-43 L 5
Knoxville o USA (PA) 46-47 K 5
Knoxville o USA (TN) 48-49 G 2
Knuckles ▲ CL 140-141 J 7
Knud Rasmussen Land ⊥ GRØ 26-27 m 8
Knud Rasmussen Land ⊥ GRØ 26-27 V 4
Knysna o ZA 220-221 F 7
Knysna National Lake Area ⊥ ZA 220-221 F 7
Ko, gora ▲ RUS 122-123 G 5
Koaba o DY 202-203 L 4
Koagas o RI 166-167 G 3
Koalla o BF 202-203 K 3
Koamb o CAM 210-211 D 2
Koaties se Pan ⊙ ZA 220-221 D 5
Kob' o RUS 116-117 K 8
Koba o RG 202-203 D 4
Koba o RI (MAL) 166-167 H 5
Koba o RI (SUS) 162-163 G 6
Kobadie o RN 202-203 L 3
Kobadja o RCA 206-207 D 6
Kobayashi o J 152-153 D 9
Kobbermlnebugt ≈ 28-29 Q 6
Kobe ☆ J 152-153 F 7
Kobé o TCH 206-207 C 4
Kobédaigouré o CI 202-203 H 7
Kobefaky o UA 102-103 J 3
Kobenni o RIM 196-197 F 7
Kobi o CAM 206-207 B 2
Kobi o RI 166-167 E 3
Kobi o WAN 204-205 J 3
Koblagué o TCH 206-207 C 4
Koblenz o • D 92-93 J 3
Koble vo o UA 102-103 G 4
Kobli o DY 202-203 K 3
K'obo o ETH 200-201 J 6
Koboko o EAU 212-213 C 2
Kobona o RUS 94-95 M 1
Kobou o RMM 202-203 K 2
Kobroor, Pulau ~ RI 166-167 H 5
Kobryn o BY 94-95 J 5
Kobuk o USA 20-21 M 3
Kobuk River ~ USA 20-21 K 3
Kobuk Valley National Park ⊥ USA 20-21 L 3
Kobuleti o GE 126-127 D 7
Kobyai o RUS 118-119 K 4
Kobylin o PL 92-93 O 3
Koca Deresi ~ TR 128-129 C 3
Kocaköy o TR 128-129 J 3
Kocaöy ~ TR 128-129 C 2
Kočani o MK 100-101 J 4
Koçarli o TR 128-129 B 4
Koçećum ~ RUS 116-117 H 2

Kočegarovo o RUS 118-119 J 6
Kočenevo ☆ RUS 114-115 R 7
Kočenga o RUS 116-117 M 8
Kočerinovo o BG 102-103 C 6
Kočetovka o RUS 94-95 R 5
Kočevo o RUS 96-97 J 4
Kŏch'ang o ROK 150-151 F 10
Koch Bihar o IND 138-139 N 6
Kochel o RUS 124-125 M 1
Kočkorna o RUS 88-89 N 4
Kočkor-Ata o KS 136-137 N 4
Kočkorka o KS 146-147 B 4
Kočubeevskoe o RUS 126-127 D 5
Kočubej o RUS 126-127 G 5
Kočumdek o RUS 116-117 H 4
Koda ~ RUS 116-117 J 6
Kodăr o IND 140-141 G 2
Kodari o NEP 144-145 E 7
Kodarma o IND 142-143 D 3
Kodiak o USA 22-23 U 4
Kodiak Island ~ USA 22-23 U 4
Kodina ~ RUS 88-89 P 5
Kodinär o IND 138-139 C 9
Kodino o RUS 88-89 P 5
Kodiyakkarai o IND 140-141 H 5
Kodjari o BF 202-203 L 4
Kodmo, togga ~ SP 208-209 J 4
Kodok o SUD 206-207 L 4
Kodomuru o IND 140-141 G 3
Kodyma ~ UA 102-103 F 4
Koëbonou o CI 202-203 J 5
Koës o NAM 220-221 D 2
Koettlitz Glacier ∧ ARK 16 F 16
Kofa National Wildlife Refuge ⊥ USA 40-41 G 8
Kofarnihon o TJ 136-137 L 5
Kofelé o ETH 208-209 D 5
Koffiefontein o ZA 220-221 G 4
Kofoidua ☆ GH 202-203 K 6
Kofu o J (TOT) 152-153 E 7
Kōfu o J (YMN) 152-153 H 7
Koga o J 152-153 H 6
Kogalm, Lac o CDN 36-37 L 5
Kogaluc, Rivière ~ CDN 36-37 L 5
Kogaluk Bay ≈ 36-37 K 5
Kogaluk Rive ~ CDN 36-37 S 6
Kogalym o RUS 114-115 N 3
Køge o DK 86-87 F 9
Køge Bugt ≈ 86-87 F 9
Køge Bugt = Pikiutdleq ≈ 28-29 U 4
Kogel ~ RUS 114-115 D 3
Kogmansklocf ▲ ZA 220-221 G 6
Kognak River ~ USA 20-21 M 3
Kogoltuktuk River ~ USA 20-21 M 3
Kogon ~ RG 202-203 C 4
Kogoró o RG 202-203 C 4
Kogrukluk River ~ USA 20-21 L 6
Kogtok River ~ CDN 30-31 V 4
Kogŭr o IR 136-137 B 6
Kogya e Strict Nature Reserve ⊥ GH 202-203 K 6
Kohan o PK 134-135 M 5
Kohăt o PK 138-139 C 3
Kohăt Pass ▲ PK 138-139 C 3
Kohila o EST 94-95 J 2
Kohiľnik ~ UA 102-103 F 4
Kohima ☆• IND 142-143 J 3
Kohinggo ~ AUSOL 184 l c 3
Ko Hinh o LAO 156-157 C 6
Kohi-Patandar ▲ PK 134-135 L 5
Kohler Range ▲ ARK 16 F 25
Kohlu o PK 138-139 C 3
Kohtla-Järve o EST 94-95 K 2
Kohŭng o ROK 150-151 F 10
Kohunlich ∴ MEX 52-53 K 2
Koiama, Jasiira ~ SP 212-213 J 4
Koichab o NAM 220-221 B 2
Koichab Pan ⊙ NAM 220-221 B 3
Koidern o CDN 20-21 U 6
Koidu o WAL 202-203 E 5
Koihoa o IND 140-141 L 5
Koin o EAK 212-213 G 3
Koindu o WAL 202-203 E 5
Koito o EAK 212-213 G 5
Kojbagar, köli o KA 124-125 D 2
Kojda o RUS 88-89 R 3
Kojda ~ RUS 88-89 R 3
Köje Do o ROK 150-151 G 10
Kojgorodok o RUS 96-97 G 3
Kojin o ROK 150-151 X 3
Kojmatdag ▲ TM 136-137 D 4
Kojnatihan, ozero o RUS 112-113 V 4
Kojonup o AUS 176-177 D 6
Kojtaš o RUS 94-95 P 2
Ko'ka Gidib o ETH 208-209 D 4
Ko'ka Häyk' o ETH 208-209 D 4
Kokand o UZ 136-137 M 4
Kokani o EAK 212-213 G 5
Kōkarai o KA 136-137 M 4
Kokari, tubegi ∧ KA 126-127 O 4
Kokas o RI 166-167 G 3
Kokča o US 136-137 L 4
Kökčetaw ☆• KA 124-125 F 2
Kökcegarison köli o KA 124-125 D 2
Kökcetaw Üstirti ▲ KA 124-125 D 2
Kokemäenjoki ~ FIN 88-89 H 6
Kokenau o RI 166-167 J 4
Kokeragi Point ▲ CDN 30-31 H 3

Kokerboomwoud • NAM 220-221 D 3
Kokerit o GUY 62-63 E 2
Ko Kho Khao ~ THA 158-159 E 6
Kokish o CDN 32-33 G 6
Ko-Jangak o KS 136-137 N 4
Kokkola o FIN 88-89 H 5
Kokdapperne o GRØ 28-29 V 4
Koknese o LV 94-95 J 3
Koko o WAN (BEL) 204-205 F 5
Koko o WAN (SOK) 204-205 F 3
Kokoda o PNG 183 D 5
Kokoda Trail • PNG 183 D 5
Kokola o PNG 183 G 2
Kokolik River ~ USA 20-21 K 2
Kokologo o BF 202-203 K 3
Kokomo o USA 46-47 E 5
Kokonselkä o FIN 88-89 H 5
Kokopo o PNG 183 G 3
Kokora, ozero o RUS 108-109 d 5
Kokoro ~ RG 202-203 F 3
Kokosa o ETH 208-209 D 5
Kokoso o GH 202-203 K 6
Kokoti Kouamékro o CI 202-203 H 6
Kokoula ~ RG 202-203 D 4
Kokpek o KA 146-147 D 4
Kokpekty o KA 124-125 L 3
Kokrajhar o IND 142-143 G 2
Kokrines Hills ▲ USA 20-21 N 4
Kokruagarok o USA 20-21 O 1
Koksa ~ RUS 124-125 O 3
Koksan o DVR 150-151 F 8
Köksaraj o KA 136-137 L 5
Köksengir, tau ▲ KA (AKT) 126-127 M 5
Köksengir, tau ▲ KA (KZL) 124-125 D 6
Koksoak, Rivière ~ CDN 36-37 P 6
Kokstad o ZA 220-221 J 5
Köksu o KA 136-137 L 4
Koksu ~ KA 124-125 L 6
Koktac, Rivière ~ CDN 36-37 P 6
Koktal o KA 124-125 L 6
Köktöbe, tau ▲ KA 124-125 E 5
Köktöbe, tau ▲ KA 124-125 E 5
Köktokay o VRC 146-147 J 2
Köktokay ~ VRC 146-147 J 2
Köktymak, tubegi ∧ KA 126-127 O 4
Koku, Tanjung ▲ RI 164-165 G 6
Kokubo o J 152-153 F 8
Kokumbo o CI 202-203 H 6
Kökürm Do ∧ ROK 150-151 F 10
Ko Kut ~ THA 158-159 G 5
Kol o PNG 183 C 3
Kola o RI 166-167 H 4
Kola o RUS 88-89 M 2
Kola, Gorges de o • CAM 204-205 K 4
Kola, Pulau ~ RI 166-167 H 4
Kolachel o IND 140-141 G 6
Koláchi ~ PK 134-135 M 5
Kolahun o LB 202-203 E 5
Kolaka o RI 164-165 G 6
Ko Lanta ~ THA 158-159 E 6
Kola Peninsula = Koľskij poluostrov ∪ RUS 88-89 N 2
Kolár o • IND 140-141 H 4
Kolar Gold Fields o IND 140-141 H 4
Kolari o FIN 88-89 H 3
Kolåsen o S 86-87 F 5
Kolasib o IND 142-143 H 3
Kolašin o • YU 100-101 G 3
Kola Town o LB 202-203 G 6
Kolattupuzha o IND 140-141 G 6
Kolâyat o IND 138-139 D 6
Kölbaj, tau ▲ KA 136-137 K 6
Kolbeinsstaðir o IS 86-87 b 2
Kolbio o EAK 212-213 H 4
Kolčovoe, ozero o RUS 122-123 O 4
Kolčugino o RUS 94-95 Q 3
Kolda ☆ SN 202-203 C 3
Koldaga o TCH 206-207 C 4
Köldenen-Temir ~ KA 126-127 M 5
Kolding o • DK 86-87 D 9
Kole o ZRE (HAU) 210-211 K 3
Kole o ZRE (KOR) 210-211 J 5
Kolebira o IND 142-143 D 4
Kolek"egan ~ RUS 114-115 N 3
Kolendo o RUS 122-123 K 2
Kolendo, Mount ▲ AUS 180-181 D 2
Kolenovskij, Elan'- o RUS 102-103 M 3
Kolenté o RG 202-203 D 4
Kolente o RG 202-203 D 5
Koležma o RUS 88-89 N 4
Kolgompi ~ RUS 122-123 O 4
Kolguev, ostrov ∧ RUS 88-89 U 2
Kolhápur o IND (MAH) 140-141 F 2
Kolhida ⊥ GE 126-127 D 7
Kolhozabad o TJ 136-137 L 6
Koli ∧ FIN 88-89 L 5
Kolia o CI 202-203 G 5
Ko Libong ~ THA 158-159 E 7
Koliganek o USA 22-23 S 3
Kolín o • CZ 92-93 N 3
Kolinbiné ~ RMM 202-203 E 2
K'olito o ETH 208-209 D 5
Koljučaja, gora ▲ RUS 112-113 X 3
Koljučinskaja guba ≈ 112-113 X 3
Kolka o • LV 94-95 H 3
Kolkasrags ▲ LV 94-95 H 3
Kolky o UA 102-103 D 2
Kollegal o IND 140-141 G 4
Kolleru Lake o IND 140-141 J 2
Kollipara o IND 140-141 J 2
Kollo o RN 204-205 E 2
Kolmackij, porog ~ RUS 88-89 P 3
Kolmakovo o RUS 114-115 P 7
Kolmanskop o NAM 220-221 B 3
Kolmar = Chodziez o • PL 92-93 O 2
Kolno o PL 92-93 Q 2
Kolo o EAT 212-213 E 6
Kolo o PL 92-93 P 2
Kolo o WAN 204-205 F 5
Koloa o USA 48-49 G 4
Kolobane o SN 202-203 C 2
Kolobeke o ZRE 210-211 G 4
Kolobrzeg o • PL 92-93 N 1
Kolofata o CAM 206-207 B 3

Ko-lok, Sungai ○ **THA** 158-159 F 7
Kolokani ○ **RMM** 202-203 F 3
Koloko ○ **BF** 202-203 H 4
Kolokol, vulkan ▲ **RUS** 122-123 O 5
Kolokolkova guba ≈ **RUS** 88-89 N 2
Kolomak ○ **UA** 102-103 J 3
Kolomino ○ **RUS** 114-115 R 6
Kolomna ☆•• **RUS** 94-95 G 4
Kolomonyi ○ **ZRE** 210-211 J 6
Kolomyja ○ **UA** 102-103 J 3
Kolondiéba ○ **RMM** 202-203 G 4
Kolondieba ○ **RMM** 202-203 G 4
Kolongotomo ○ **RMM** 202-203 H 3
Kolonia ☆ **FSM** 13 G 2
Kolono ○ **RI** 164-165 H 6
Kolonodale ○ **RI** 164-165 G 4
Kolosovyh, ostrov ∩ **RUS** 108-109 W 4
Kolossa ○ **RMM** 202-203 G 3
Kolotambu = Avu Avu ○ **SOL** 184 I e 3
Kolowana-Watobo, Teluk ≈ **RI** 164-165 H 6
Kolozero ○ **RUS** 88-89 M 2
Kolp' ∼ **RUS** 94-95 O 2
Kolpakova ∼ **RUS** 120-121 R 6
Kolpaševo ○ **RUS** 114-115 R 5
Kolpino ○ **RUS** 94-95 M 2
Kolpny ○ **RUS** 94-95 P 5
Kólpos Hanión ≈ 100-101 J 7
Kólpos Kissámou ≈ 100-101 J 7
Kolpur ○ **PK** 134-135 M 4
Kol'skij zaliv ≈ 88-89 M 2
Kolubara ∼ **YU** 100-101 H 2
Kolumadulu Atoll ∼ **MV** 140-141 B 6
Koluton ∼ **KA** 124-125 F 3
Kolva ∼ **RUS** 88-89 Y 3
Kolva ∼ **RUS** 108-109 H 6
Kolva ∼ **RUS** 114-115 O 4
Kolvavis ∼ **RUS** 108-109 H 8
Kolvereid ○ **N** 86-87 E 4
Kolvica, ozero ○ **RUS** 88-89 M 3
Kolvickoe, ozero ○ **RUS** 88-89 M 3
Kolwa ○ **PK** 134-135 L 5
Kolwezi ○ **ZRE** (SHA) 214-215 C 6
Kolyma ∼ **RUS** 110-111 d 7
Kolyma ∼ **RUS** 110-111 d 6
Kolyma ∼ **RUS** 112-113 L 2
Kolyma ∼ **RUS** 112-113 H 3
Kolyma ∼ **RUS** 120-121 P 2
Kolyma ∼ **RUS** 120-121 M 2
Kolymak ∼ **RUS** 112-113 M 5
Kolymskaja guba ≈ 110-111 d 4
Kolymskaja nizmennost' ∼ **RUS** 110-111 c 5
Kolymskoe ○ **RUS** 112-113 K 2
Kolymskoe, vodohranilišče < **RUS** 120-121 N 3
Kolymskoe nagor'e ▲ **RUS** 120-121 Q 3
Kolymskoye Nagor'ye = Kolymskoe nagor'e ▲ **RUS** 120-121 Q 3
KolyšleJ ○ **RUS** 96-97 D 7
Kolyvan' ○ **RUS** 114-115 R 7
Koľzat ○ **KA** 146-147 E 4
Kom ▲ **BG** 102-103 C 6
Kom ○ **EAT** 212-213 G 3
Kom ∼ **G** 210-211 C 2
Koma ○ **ETH** 208-209 C 4
Komagasberge ∼ **ZA** 220-221 C 4
Komaio ○ **PNG** 183 B 4
Komako ○ **PNG** 183 C 4
Komanda ○ **ZRE** 212-213 B 3
Komandnaja, gora ▲ **RUS** 122-123 H 3
Komandorskaja kotlovina ⊥ **RUS** 120-121 V 5
Komandorskaja Basin ⊥ **RUS** 120-121 V 5
Komandorskie ostrova ∩ **RUS** 120-121 W 6
Komárno ○ **SK** 92-93 P 5
Komárom ○ **H** 92-93 P 5
Komarovka ○ **RUS** 116-117 E 7
Komatipoort ○ **ZA** 220-221 K 2
Komatirivier ∼ **ZA** 220-221 K 2
Komatsu ○ **J** 152-153 G 6
Komba, Pulau ∩ **RI** 166-167 B 5
Kombat ○ **NAM** 216-217 D 9
Kombe ○ **ZRE** 210-211 K 6
Kombile ○ **WAL** 202-203 E 5
Kombissiri ○ **BF** 202-203 K 3
Kombo-Itindi ○ **CAM** 204-205 H 6
Kombone ○ **CAM** 204-205 H 6
Kombongou = Kondio ○ **BF** 204-205 K 3
Koméayo ○ **CI** 202-203 G 6
Kome Island ∩ **EAT** 212-213 D 5
Komenda ○ **GH** 202-203 K 7
Komering ∼ **RI** 162-163 F 6
Komfane ○ **RI** 166-167 H 4
Komga ○ **ZA** 220-221 H 6
Komi = Komi, Respublika ◘ **RUS** 96-97 G 1
Komi-Yanga ○ **BF** 202-203 L 4
Komi-Permyak Autonomous District = Komi-Perm.avt.okrug ◘ **RUS** 96-97 H 3
Kommunarsk = Alčevs'k ○ **UA** 102-103 L 3
Kommunizma, pik ▲ **TJ** 136-137 N 5
Komo ∼ **G** 210-211 C 3
Komo ○ **PNG** 183 B 4
Komodini ∼ **RMM** 202-203 G 3
Komodo ○ **RI** 168 D 7
Komodo, Pulau ∩ **RI** 168 D 7
Komodo National Park ⊥•• **RI** 168 D 7
Komodou ○ **RG** 202-203 H 3
Komono ○ **RCB** 210-211 D 5
Komoran, Pulau ∩ **RI** 166-167 K 6
Komorane ○ **RMM** 202-203 H 3
Komoro ○ **J** 152-153 H 6
Komosi ○ **ZRE** 210-211 K 6
Komotini ○ **GR** 100-101 K 4
Kompa ○ **DY** 204-205 L 5
Komponaone, Pulau ∩ **RI** 164-165 H 6
Kompot ○ **RI** 164-165 J 3
Komrat = Comrat ○ **MD** 102-103 F 4
Komsberge ▲ **ZA** 220-221 D 5
Komsomol ○ **KA** (AKT) 126-127 O 2
Komsomol ○ **KA** (KST) 124-125 B 3
Komsomolabad ○ **TJ** 136-137 M 5
Komsomolec, ostrov ∩ **RUS** 108-109 Z 1
Komsomolec, ostrov ∩ **RUS** 108-109 Z 1
Komsomolec, ostrov ∩ **RUS** 136-137 F 2
Komsomol'sk ☆• **RUS** 94-95 R 3
Komsomol'sk, Ustjurtdagi ○ **US** 136-137 F 2
Komsomol'skij ○ **RUS** (CUK) 112-113 R 2
Komsomol'skij ○ **RUS** (HMN) 114-115 G 4
Komsomol'skij ○ **RUS** (KAR) 88-89 M 4
Komsomol'skij ○ **RUS** (KLM) 126-127 G 5
Komsomol'skij ○ **RUS** (KOM) 108-109 K 8
Komsomol'skij ○ **RUS** (MOR) 96-97 D 6
Komsomol'skij zapovednik ⊥ **RUS** 122-123 G 3
Komsomoľsk na Amure = Komsomoľsk-na-Amure ☆ **RUS** 122-123 G 3
Komsomoľsk-na-Amure ☆ **RUS** 122-123 G 3
Komsomoľsk na Amure ☆ **RUS** 122-123 G 3
Komsomoľsk-na-Pečore ○ **RUS** 114-115 N 4
Komsomoľskoj Pravdy, ostrova ∩ **RUS** 108-109 g 3
Komun Do ∩ **ROK** 150-151 F 11
Kon ○ **CAM** 204-205 J 6
Kōn ∼ **KA** 124-125 F 4
Kona ○ **RMM** 202-203 J 2
Kona ○ **RN** 198-199 D 6
Kona ○ **WAN** 204-205 J 4
Konakovo ☆ **RUS** 94-95 P 3
Konar ○ **AFG** 136-137 M 7
Konar, Darya-ye ∼ **AFG** 138-139 C 2
Konárak ○ **IND** 142-143 E 6
Konárak ○ **IR** 134-135 J 6
Konar-e Hajgir ▲ **AFG** 138-139 C 2
Konar Tahte ○ **IR** 134-135 D 4
Konaweha ∼ **RI** 164-165 G 5
Konda ∼ **RI** 166-167 F 2
Konda ∼ **RUS** 114-115 H 4
Konda ∼ **RUS** 114-115 H 5
Konda ∼ **RUS** 114-115 I 5
Kondagaon ○ **IND** 142-143 B 6
Kondakovskaja vozvyšennost' ▲ **RUS** 110-111 b 4
Kondan, ozero ○ **RUS** 114-115 K 6
Konde ○ **EAT** 212-213 G 4
Kondembaia ○ **WAL** 202-203 E 5
Kondinin ○ **AUS** 176-177 E 6
Kondinskaja nizmennost' ∼ **RUS** 114-115 H 4
Kondinskoe ☆ **RUS** 114-115 J 5
Kondio = Kombongou ○ **BF** 204-205 K 3
Kondoa ○ **EAT** 212-213 F 4
Kondoma ∼ **RUS** 124-125 Q 2
Kondopoga ☆ **RUS** 88-89 N 5
Kondostrov ∩ **RUS** 88-89 O 4
Kondratovskaja ○ **RUS** 88-89 R 5
Kondromo ∼ **RUS** 116-117 G 4
Kondrovo ☆ **RUS** 94-95 O 4
Kondue ○ **ZRE** 210-211 J 6
Konduga ○ **WAN** 204-205 K 3
Konduj-Muhor ○ **RUS** 118-119 F 9
Kondyreva ∼ **RUS** 112-113 O 5
Konecbor ○ **RUS** 114-115 M 4
Konecbor ○ **RUS** (KOM) 88-89 Y 4
Koneng ○ **RI** 162-163 B 2
Koněnmyveem ∼ **RUS** 112-113 V 3
Konergino ○ **RUS** 112-113 V 3
Köneürgenč ☆ **TM** 136-137 F 3
Konevaam ∼ **RUS** 112-113 P 2
Konevo ○ **RUS** 88-89 P 5
Kong ○ **CAM** 204-205 K 6
Kong ○ **CI** 202-203 H 5
Kŏng ∼ **K** 158-159 J 4
Kong, Bandar-e ○ **IR** 134-135 F 5
Kongakut River ∼ **USA** 20-21 J 2
Kongasso ○ **CI** 202-203 G 6
Kongbeng Caves • **RI** 164-165 E 3
Kongbo ○ **RCA** 206-207 F 4
Kong Christian IX Land ⊥ **GRØ** 28-29 V 3
Kong Christian X Land ⊥ **GRØ** 26-27 k 7
Kong Dans Halvø ⊥ **GRØ** 28-29 U 5
Kongelai ○ **EAK** 212-213 E 3
Kong Frederik IX Land ⊥ **GRØ** 28-29 P 3
Kong Frederik VIII Land ⊥ **GRØ** 26-27 m 5
Kong Frederik VI Kyst ∼ **GRØ** 28-29 T 6
Kong Fu ∼ **VRC** 154-155 E 4
Konginskij hrebet ▲ **RUS** 112-113 K 4
Kong Karls Land ∩ **N** 84-85 P 3
Kong Leopold og Dronning Astrid land ⊥ **ARK** 13 G 2
Kongola ○ **NAM** 216-217 F 7
Kongolo ○ **ZRE** 210-211 L 6
Kongor ○ **LB** 202-203 E 6
Kong Oscar Fjord ≈ 26-27 n 7
Kongoussi ○ **BF** 202-203 K 3
Kongsberg ☆ **N** 86-87 D 7
Kongsfjorden ≈ 84-85 G 3
Kongsøya ∩ **N** 84-85 Q 3
Kongsvinger ☆• **N** 86-87 F 4
Kongtongshan ∼ **VRC** 154-155 E 4
Kongur Shan ▲ **VRC** 146-147 B 6
Kongwa ○ **EAT** 214-215 J 4
Kong Wilhelm Land ⊥ **GRØ** 26-27 o 6
Koni ∼ **ZRE** 214-215 D 6
Koni, poluostrov ∼ **RUS** 120-121 Q 6
König, Cape ∼ **CDN** 24-25 q 6
Königgrätz = Hradec Králové ○ **CZ** 92-93 N 3
Konimeh ☆ **US** 136-137 H 4
Konin ☆• **PL** 92-93 P 2
Konina ○ **RMM** 202-203 G 3
Konjed Jān ○ **IR** 134-135 D 2
Konkämäeno ∼ **FIN** 88-89 F 2
Konkan ○ **IND** 138-139 D 9
Konkče, Daryā-ye ∼ **AFG** 136-137 L 6
Konkiep ∼ **NAM** 220-221 C 3
Konko ○ **ZRE** 214-215 D 6
Konkoma ○ **ETH** 208-209 D 6
Konkouré ∼ **RG** (KIN) 202-203 D 4
Konkouré ∼ **RG** 202-203 D 4
Kon'kovaja ∼ **RUS** 112-113 K 2
Kon'kovaja, Boľšaja ∼ **RUS** 112-113 J 2
Konkudera ○ **RUS** 118-119 F 7
K'orahē ○ **ETH** 208-209 C 5
Korakata cukurligi ○ **US** 136-137 J 4
Korakúlka ⊥ **US** 136-137 E 3
Kora National Park ⊥ **EAK** 212-213 G 4
Korangal ○ **IND** 140-141 G 2
Korannaberg ▲ **ZA** 220-221 F 3
Korán-o-Monǧán ○ **AFG** 136-137 M 6
Koraon ○ **IND** 142-143 C 3
Koraput ○ **IND** 142-143 C 6
Korasa ○ **SOL** 184 I c 2
Koratagere ○ **IND** 140-141 G 4
Ko Rawi ∼ **THA** 158-159 E 7
Korbel'naja ∼ **RUS** 108-109 X 7
Korbéndja, hrebet ▲ **RUS** 112-113 K 3
Korbeniči ○ **RUS** 94-95 N 1
Korbol ○ **TCH** 206-207 C 4
Korbol, Bahr ∼ **TCH** 206-207 C 3
Korbu, Gunung ▲ **MAL** 162-163 D 2
Korçë ○ **AL** 100-101 H 4
Korčula ∩ **HR** 100-101 F 3
Korčula ○ **HR** 100-101 F 3
Korda ○ **IND** 138-139 C 8
Kordestan ○ **IR** 134-135 M 5
Kordié ○ **BF** 202-203 J 3
Kord-Kuy ○ **IR** 134-135 G 1
Kord Myriem, Hassi ∼ **DZ** 188-189 K 6
Kordofan = Kurdufān ⊥ **SUD** 200-201 D 6
Kore ○ **RI** 168 D 7
Korea Bay ≈ 150-151 D 8
Korean Folk Village • **ROK** 150-151 F 9
Koreare ○ **RI** 166-167 F 5
Korea Strait ≈ 152-153 O 8
Korec' ∼ **UA** 102-103 E 2
Korem ○ **ETH** 200-201 J 2
Korémalīwa ○ **RN** 204-205 E 2
Korenevo ○ **RUS** 102-103 J 2
Korenovsk ○ **RUS** 102-103 L 5
Korepino ○ **RUS** 114-115 O 4
Korf ○ **RUS** 120-121 V 3
Korfa, zaliv ∼ **RUS** 120-121 V 3
Korgalžyn ○ **KA** 124-125 G 3
Korgas ∼ **VRC** 146-147 E 3
Korgen ○ **N** 86-87 F 3
Korgom ○ **RN** 198-199 D 6
Korhogo ∼• **CI** 202-203 H 5
Koribundu ○ **WAL** 202-203 E 6
Korientze ○ **RMM** 202-203 J 2
Korim ○ **RI** 166-167 J 2
Korinthiakós Kólpos ≈ 100-101 J 5
Kórinthos ○ **GR** 100-101 J 6
Korioume ○ **RMM** 196-197 J 6
Koripobi ○ **PNG** 184 I b 2
Kóris-hegy ▲ • **H** 92-93 O 5
Korissia ○ **GR** 100-101 K 6
Kōriyama ○ **J** 152-153 J 6
Korizo, Passe de ▲ **TCH** 192-193 F 6
Korjaki ○ **RUS** 120-121 S 7
Korjakskaja Sopka, vulkan ▲ **RUS** 120-121 S 7
Korjažma ☆ **RUS** 88-89 U 5
Kosovo Polje ∼ **YU** 100-101 H 3
Kosovska Mitrovica ○ **YU** 100-101 H 3
Kosso ○ **CI** 202-203 H 7
Kossou, Lac de < **CI** 202-203 H 6
Kórkodon ∼ **RUS** 112-113 J 2
Korkodon ∼ **RUS** 112-113 J 5
Korkodonskij hrebet ▲ **RUS** 112-113 J 4
Korkut ☆ **TR** 128-129 J 3
Korkuteli ☆ **TR** 128-129 D 4
Korla ○ **VRC** 146-147 D 4
Korlikí ○ **RUS** 114-115 H 4
Kormakitis, Cape ∼ **TR** 128-129 E 5
Kornake ○ **RN** 198-199 C 5
Kornati ∩ **HR** 100-101 E 3
Korneevka ○ **KA** 124-125 J 3
Kórnik ○ **PL** 92-93 O 2
Koro ○ **FJI** 184 III b 2
Koro ○ **RMM** 202-203 J 3
Koroba ○ **PNG** 183 B 4
Koroc, Rivière ∼ **CDN** 36-37 R 5
Korodiga ○ **EAT** 212-213 F 6
Korodziba ○ **RB** 218-219 D 4
Köroğlu Dağları ▲ **TR** 128-129 E 2
Köroğlu Tepe ▲ **TR** 128-129 D 2
Korogwe ○ **EAT** 212-213 G 6
Korohane ○ **RN** 198-199 C 5
Koroit ○ **AUS** 180-181 J 7
Korolevu ○ **FJI** 184 III a 3
Korom, Bahr ∼ **TCH** 206-207 D 3
Koronadal ○ **RP** 160-161 F 9
Korondougou ○ **CI** 202-203 G 5
Koronga ○ **RMM** 202-203 J 2
Koronga, Mont ▲ **RT** 202-203 L 5
Koróni ○ **GR** 100-101 J 6
Korónia, Límni ∼ **GR** 100-101 J 4
Koroniere ○ **DY** 202-203 L 4
Koror ★ **PAL** (CRO) 13 E 2
Kōrös ∼ **H** 92-93 Q 5
Koro Sea ≈ 184 III b 2
Korosten' ○ **UA** 102-103 F 2
Korostyšiv ○ **UA** 102-103 F 2
Koro Toro ○ **TCH** 198-199 J 4
Korovin Volcan ▲ **USA** 22-23 Q 5
Korovou ○ **SOL** 184 I b 2
Korpilahti ○ **FIN** 88-89 H 5
Korpun ○ **PNG** 183 B 3
Korsakov ○ **RUS** 122-123 K 5
Korsimoro ○ **BF** 202-203 K 3
Korsnäs ○ **FIN** 88-89 F 5
Korsør ○ **DK** 86-87 E 5
Koršunovo ○ **RUS** 118-119 E 6
Kortala ○ **SUD** 200-201 E 6
Kortkeros ○ **RUS** 96-97 G 1
Korumburra ○ **AUS** 180-181 H 5
Korup, Park National de ⊥ **CAM** 204-205 H 6
Köprügay ∼ **TR** 128-129 E 4
Kor, Rūd-e ∼ **IR** 134-135 E 4
Korwai ○ **IND** 138-139 G 7
Korabavur pastligi ⊥ **US** 136-137 E 3
Korača ○ **RUS** 102-103 K 2
Ko Racha Noi ∼ **THA** 158-159 E 7
Ko Racha Yai ∼ **THA** 158-159 E 7
Korakata cukurligi ∼ **US** 136-137 J 4
Koryak Autonomous District = Korjakskij avtonomnyj okrug ◘ **RUS** 112-113 N 5
Koryfky ∼ **RUS** 108-109 T 8
Kós ○ **GR** 100-101 L 6
Kós ∼ **GR** 100-101 L 6
Kosa ○ **ETH** 208-209 C 5
Kosa ☆ **RUS** 96-97 J 4
Kot Kapūra ○ **IND** 138-139 E 4
Kotla Branch ∼ **IND** 138-139 E 4
Kotlas ☆ **RUS** 88-89 T 6
Kotlik ○ **USA** 20-21 D 5
Kot Mümin ○ **PK** 138-139 D 3
Koto ○ **CAM** 204-205 H 6
Kotobi ○ **CI** 202-203 H 6
Kotongoro II ○ **TCH** 206-207 D 4
Koton-Karifi ○ **WAN** 204-205 G 4
Koton-Koro ○ **WAN** 204-205 F 3
Kotopounga ○ **DY** 202-203 L 4
Kotor ○ **YU** 100-101 G 3
Kotor Varoš ○ **BIH** 100-101 F 2
Kotouba ○ **CI** 202-203 J 5
Kotoula ○ **BF** 202-203 J 4
Kotovo ○ **RUS** 96-97 D 8
Kotovs'k ○ **UA** 102-103 F 4
Kotovsk ○ **RUS** 94-95 R 5
Kotovs'k = Hînceşti ○ **MD** 102-103 F 4
Kot Pūtli ○ **IND** 138-139 F 6
Kotri ∼ **IND** 142-143 B 6
Kotri ○ **PK** 138-139 B 7
Kot Shākir ○ **PK** 138-139 D 4
Kottagüdem ○ **IND** 142-143 B 7
Kottakota ○ **IND** 140-141 H 4
Kottayam ○ **IND** 140-141 G 6
Kotto ∼ **RCA** 206-207 E 4
Kottūru ○ **IND** 140-141 G 3
Kotu ∩ **TON** 184 IV a 1
Kotu Group ∩ **TON** 184 IV a 1
Kotuj ∼ **RUS** 108-109 a 7
Kotuj ∼ **RUS** 108-109 e 6
Kotuj ∼ **RUS** 116-117 L 2
Kotujkan ∼ **RUS** 116-117 J 2
Koturdepe ○ **TM** 136-137 C 5
Kotwa ○ **ZW** 218-219 G 3
Kotzebue ○ **USA** 20-21 J 3
Kotzebue Sound ≈ 20-21 J 3
Kouadiokro, Ananda- ○ **CI** 202-203 H 6
Kouadio-Prikro ○ **CI** 202-203 H 6
Kouaga ∼ **RMM** 202-203 E 2
Kouakourou ○ **RMM** 202-203 H 2
Kouandé ○ **DY** 202-203 L 4
Kouandikro ○ **CI** 202-203 H 6
Kouango ○ **RCA** 206-207 D 4
Kouankan ○ **RG** 202-203 F 5
Kouassikro ○ **CI** 202-203 J 6
Kouba Olanga ○ **TCH** 198-199 J 5
Koubia ○ **RG** 202-203 D 4
Koubo Abou Azraq ○ **TCH** 206-207 E 3
Koubouana ∼ **RCB** 210-211 E 5
Kouchibouguac ○ **CDN** 38-39 M 5
Kouchibouguac National Park ⊥ **CDN** 38-39 M 5
Koudou, Cascades de ∼ • **DY** 204-205 L 4
Koudougou ☆ **BF** 202-203 J 3
Kouéré ○ **BF** 202-203 J 4
Koufey ○ **RN** 198-199 F 5
Kouffo ∼ **DY** 204-205 L 5
Kouga ∼ **ZA** 220-221 F 6
Kougnohou ○ **RT** 202-203 L 6
Kougouleu ○ **G** 210-211 B 3
Kouibli ○ **CI** 202-203 G 6
Kouif, El ○ **TN** 190-191 G 3
Kouilou ∼ **RCB** 210-211 C 6
Kouilou ∼ **RCB** 210-211 C 6
Kouka ○ **BF** 202-203 H 4
Koukdjuak, Great Plain of the ⊥ **CDN** 28-29 D 3
Koukdjuak River ∼ **CDN** 28-29 D 3
Kouki ○ **RCA** 206-207 C 4
Kouklia ○ **CY** 128-129 E 5
Koukou ○ **TCH** 206-207 F 3
Koukourou ∼ **RCA** 206-207 E 5
Koukourou-Bamingui, Réserve de faune du ⊥ **RCA** 206-207 D 5
Koula ○ **RMM** 202-203 G 3
Koulamoutou ∼ **G** 210-211 B 4
Koulbo ○ **TCH** 198-199 K 6
Koulbous ○ **SUD** 198-199 L 5
Koulé ○ **RG** 202-203 F 5
Koulé Ekou ∼ **DY** 204-205 L 4
Koulikoro ○ **RMM** 202-203 G 3
Koulouguidi ○ **RMM** 202-203 E 3
Koulountou ∼ **SN** 202-203 D 3
Kouloouoko ○ **BF** 202-203 L 4
Koum ○ **CAM** 206-207 B 4
Koumala ○ **RCA** 206-207 F 4
Kouma ∼ **RCA** 206-207 D 5
Koumantou ∼ **G** 210-211 G 3
Koumban ○ **RMM** 202-203 L 4
Koumbala ○ **RCA** (Bam) 206-207 E 4
Koumbala ∼ **RCA** 206-207 D 5
Koumbia ○ **RG** 202-203 D 4
Koumbia ○ **BF** 202-203 J 4
Koumbri ○ **BF** 202-203 J 3
Koumongou ∼ **RT** 202-203 L 4
Koumpentoum ○ **SN** 202-203 C 2
Koumra ○ **TCH** 206-207 C 4
Koundara ○ **RG** 202-203 C 3
Koundessou ○ **CAM** 206-207 D 5
Koundi ○ **RCA** 206-207 B 5
Koundian ○ **RMM** 202-203 E 3
Koundou ○ **RN** 202-203 L 6
Korumburra ○ **AUS** 180-181 H 5
Koundou ○ **RG** 202-203 E 5
Koundougou ○ **BF** 202-203 H 4
Koun-Fao ○ **CI** 202-203 J 6
Koungheul ○ **SN** 202-203 C 3
Koungouri ○ **TCH** 206-207 C 3
Kouniana ○ **RMM** 202-203 H 3
Kounkané ○ **SN** 202-203 C 3
Kounradskij ○ **KA** 124-125 J 5
Kountouata ○ **SN** 202-203 C 3
Kountze ○ **USA** 44-45 K 4
Kouoro ○ **RMM** 202-203 H 3
Koup ○ **ZA** 220-221 E 6
Koupé, Mont ▲ **CAM** 204-205 H 6
Koupéla ○ **BF** 202-203 K 3
Kouraï ∼ **RG** 202-203 F 5
Kouraqué ○ **RMM** 202-203 E 3
Kourémalé ○ **RMM** 202-203 F 4
Kourgou ○ **TCH** 206-207 B 3
Kourgui ○ **CAM** 206-207 B 3
Kouri ○ **RMM** 202-203 H 3
Kouri Kouri ○ **TCH** 198-199 H 6
Kourion ∼ **CY** 128-129 E 5
Kourkéto ○ **RMM** 202-203 E 2
Kourou ∼ **F** 62-63 H 3
Kourouba ▲ **CI** 202-203 G 5
Kourouba ○ **RMM** 202-203 F 4
Koûroudjel ○ **RIM** 196-197 E 6
Kourougui ∼ **BF** 202-203 J 3
Kouroukoto ○ **RMM** 202-203 E 3
Kourouma ○ **BF** 202-203 H 4
Kourouninkoto ○ **RMM** 202-203 F 3
Kouroussa ○ **RG** 202-203 E 4
Kourtiagou, Réserve de la ⊥ **BF** 202-203 L 4
Kous ○ **NAM** 220-221 C 1
Koussa Arma ○ **RN** 198-199 F 4
Koussanar ∼ **SN** (SO) 202-203 C 3
Koussanar ∼ **SN** 202-203 D 2
Koussané ∼ **SN** 202-203 D 2
Koussané ○ **RMM** 202-203 E 3
Koussane ○ **SN** 202-203 D 2
Kousséri ○ **CAM** 198-199 G 6
Koussi, Emi ▲ **TCH** 198-199 J 3
Koussountou ○ **RT** 202-203 L 5
Koutaba ○ **CAM** 204-205 J 6
Koutia Gaïdi ○ **SN** 202-203 D 2
Koutiala ○ **RMM** 202-203 H 3
Kouto ○ **CI** 202-203 G 5
Kouvola ○ **FIN** 88-89 J 6
Kouyou ∼ **RCB** 210-211 E 4
Kova ∼ **RUS** 116-117 K 6
Kovalam ○ • **IND** 140-141 G 6
Kovalevka ∼ **KA** 124-125 K 2
Kovancolar ☆ **TR** 128-129 H 3
Kovarzino ∼ **RUS** 94-95 Q 1
Kovdor ○ **RUS** 88-89 L 3
Kovdozero ○ **RUS** 88-89 M 3
Kovel' ○ **UA** 102-103 D 2
Kovenskaja ∼ **RUS** 114-115 J 4
Kovernino ○ **RUS** 94-95 S 3
Kovero ○ **FIN** 88-89 L 5
Kovik, Baie ≈ 36-37 L 4
Kovik Bay ≈ 36-37 L 4
Kovillur ○ **IND** 140-141 G 6
Kovilpatti ○ **IND** 140-141 G 6
Kovin ∼ **YU** 100-101 H 2
Kovkula ○ **RUS** 88-89 R 5
Kovran ∼ **RUS** 120-121 R 5
Kovriga, gora ▲ **RUS** 88-89 U 3
Kovrov ∼ **RUS** 94-95 R 3
Kovur ○ **IND** 140-141 H 3
Kovylkino ○ **RUS** 94-95 S 4
Kowanyama ▲ **AUS** 174-175 F 4
Kowares ○ **NAM** 216-217 C 9
Kowloon = Jiulong ○ **HK** 156-157 J 5
Kowyn's Pass ≈ **ZA** 220-221 K 1
Koya ○ **WAN** 198-199 C 6
Koyama ○ **RG** 202-203 D 3
Koyan, Tanjung ▲ **RI** 162-163 D 5
Ko Yao Yai ∼ **THA** 158-159 E 7
Köyceğiz ☆ **TR** 128-129 C 4
Koyna Reservoir ⊙ **IND** 140-141 F 2
Koyuk ○ **USA** 20-21 K 4
Koyuk River ∼ **USA** 20-21 K 4
Koyukuk River ∼ **USA** 20-21 M 4
Koyukuk National Wildlife Refuge ⊥ **USA** 20-21 M 4
Koyweľvèèrgyn ∼ **RUS** 112-113 V 2
Koza ○ **CAM** 204-205 K 3
Kožaköl ○ **KA** 124-125 F 3
Kozan ☆ **TR** 128-129 F 3
Kozáni ☆• **GR** 100-101 H 4
Kozefsk ∼ **RUS** 94-95 O 4
Kozevina, mys ▲ **RUS** 110-111 Z 2
Koževnikova, buhta ≈ 110-111 C 3
Koževnikovo ○ **RUS** 114-115 S 6
Kozhikode = Calicut ○ • **IND** 140-141 F 5
Kozienice ○ **PL** 92-93 Q 3
Kožima, mys ▲ **RUS** 116-117 O 6
Kožle, Kędzierzyn- ○ • **PL** 92-93 P 3
Kozloduj ○ **BG** 102-103 C 6
Kozlova ∼ **RUS** 116-117 M 8
Kozlova, mys ▲ **RUS** 120-121 T 6
Kozlova ○ **RUS** 96-97 F 6
Kozluk ☆ **TR** 128-129 J 3
Koz'modem'jansk ○ **RUS** 96-97 E 5
Kožozero ○ **RUS** 88-89 P 5
Kožuf ▲ **MK** 100-101 J 4
Kõžva-shima ∩ **J** 152-153 H 7
Kožva ∼ **RUS** 88-89 X 4
Kožym ∼ **RUS** 108-109 H 9
Kozyrevskij hrebet ▲ **RUS** 120-121 S 6
Kozyrevsk ○ **RUS** 120-121 S 6
Kpakto ○ **GH** 204-205 K 5
Kpalbusi ○ **GH** 202-203 K 5
Kpalimé ∼ • **RT** 202-203 L 6
Kpandae ○ **GH** 202-203 L 5
Kpandu ○ **GH** 202-203 L 6
Kpassa ∼ **GH** 202-203 L 5
Kpedze ○ **GH** 202-203 L 6
Kpèssi ○ **RT** 202-203 L 6
Kpèssi, Réserve de ⊥ **RT** 202-203 L 5
Kpété Béna ○ **RT** 202-203 L 6

Kpetoe o **GH** 202-203 L 6
Kpimé, Cascade de ~ **RT** 202-203 L 6
Kpong o **GH** 202-203 L 6
Kpungan Pass ◣ **MYA** 142-143 K 2
Kraaifontein o **ZA** 220-221 D 6
Kraairivier ~ **ZA** 220-221 D 6
Kraankuil o **ZA** 220-221 G 4
Krabbé o **RA** 78-79 J 4
Krabi o **THA** 158-159 I 6
Krǎchéh o **K** 158-159 J 4
Krachi, Kete- o **GH** 202-203 K 6
Kracnooskĺs'k vodoschovyšče < **UA** 102-103 K 3
Kragera o **N** 86-87 D 7
Kragujevac o • **YU** 100-101 H 2
Krainij o **RUS** 110-111 X 4
Krajište ◣ **YU** 100-101 J 3
Krajnij, ostrov ◣ **RUS** 120-121 U 3
Krajnovka o **RUS** 126-127 G 6
Kraka hrebet ◣ **RUS** 96-97 K 7
Kraké o **DY** 204-205 E 5
Kraków ☆ •• **PL** 92-93 P 3
Krakurom o **GH** 202-203 J 6
Králanh o **K** 158-159 G 4
Kralendijk o **NL** 60-61 G 1
Kraljevo o **YU** 100-101 H 3
Kramators'k o **UA** 102-103 K 3
Kramatorsk = Kramators'k o **UA** 102-103 K 3
Kramfors o **S** 86-87 H 5
Kranéa o **GR** 100-101 H 5
Kranidi o **GR** 100-101 J 5
Kranj o **SLO** 100-101 E 1
Kransfontein o **ZA** 220-221 J 4
Kranskop o **ZA** 220-221 K 4
Kranuan o **THA** 158-159 G 2
Kranzberg o **NAM** 216-217 C 10
Krãolandia, Área Indigena ✕ **BR** 68-69 E 6
Krapina o **HR** 100-101 E 1
Krapivinskij o **RUS** 114-115 T 7
Krapivnaja o **RUS** 122-121 S 6
Krašeninnikova, mys ◣ **RUS** 120-121 U 4
Krasin, ostrov ∼ **RUS** 108-109 a 3
Krasin, zaliv ≈ **RUS** 112-113 U 1
Krasinka o **RUS** 110-111 U 6
Krasino o **RUS** 108-109 F 6
Kraskino o **RUS** 122-123 D 7
Kráslava •• **LV** 94-95 K 4
Krasnaja Gorka ☆ **RUS** 96-97 K 6
Krasnaja Jaruga o **RUS** 102-103 J 2
Krasnaja Poljana o **RUS** 126-127 D 6
Krasnapolle o **BY** 94-95 M 5
Krasneno o **RUS** 112-113 U 4
Krasnij Luč = Krasnyj Luč o **UA** 102-103 L 3
Krasnik o **PL** 92-93 R 3
Krasni Okny ☆ **UA** 102-103 F 4
Krasnoarmejsk ☆ **KA** 124-125 F 2
Krasnoarmejsk o **RUS** (SAR) 96-97 D 8
Krasnoarmejsk o **RUS** (MOS) 94-95 Q 4
Krasnoarmejsk = Krasnoarmijs'k o **UA** 102-103 K 3
Krasnoarmejskaja o **RUS** 102-103 L 5
Krasnoarmejskij o **RUS** 112-113 Q 2
Krasnoarmejskoe ☆ **RUS** 96-97 G 7
Krasnoarmijs'k o **UA** 102-103 K 3
Krasnoborsk o **RUS** 88-89 S 6
Krasnodar ☆ **RUS** 102-103 L 5
Krasnodarskij kraj o **RUS** 126-127 C 5
Krasnodon o **UA** 102-103 L 3
Krasnoe, ozero o **RUS** 112-113 S 4
Krasnoe Selo o **RUS** 94-95 M 3
Krasnoe Znamja o **TM** 136-137 H 6
Krasnoflotskie, ostrova ∼ **RUS** 108-109 c 2
Krasnogorsk o **RUS** 122-123 K 4
Krasnogorskij o **RUS** (CEL) 96-97 M 6
Krasnogorskij o **RUS** (MAR) 96-97 S 5
Krasnogorskoe o **RUS** 96-97 M 6
Krasnogvardejsk o **US** 136-137 K 5
Krasnoholm o **RUS** 96-97 J 8
Krasnohorivka o **UA** 102-103 K 3
Krasnohrad o **UA** 102-103 J 3
Krasnohvardijs'ke ☆ **UA** 102-103 J 5
Krasnoj Armii, proliv ≈ 108-109 Z 2
Krasnojarovo o **RUS** 122-123 C 3
Krasnojarsk ☆ • **RUS** 116-117 F 7
Krasnojarskoe, vodohranilišče < **RUS** 116-117 E 8
Krasnokamensk ☆ **RUS** 118-119 J 10
Krasnokamsk o **RUS** 96-97 L 6
Krasnokutsk ☆ **KA** 124-125 J 2
Krasnomajskij o **RUS** 94-95 O 3
Krasnoperekops'k ☆ **UA** 102-103 H 5
KrasnopiĺTa o **UA** 102-103 J 2
Krasnopoĺe o **RUS** 122-123 K 4
Krasnoščeĺe o **RUS** 88-89 O 3
Krasnoseĺkup o **RUS** 114-115 O 4
Krasnoslobodsk o **RUS** (MOR) 94-95 S 4
Krasnoslobodsk o **RUS** (VLG) 96-97 D 7
Krasnotur'insk o **RUS** 114-115 F 5
Krasnoufimsk ☆ **RUS** 96-97 L 5
Krasnousoĺskij o **RUS** 96-97 L 5
Krasnova, gora ◣ **RUS** 122-123 K 4
Krasnovišersk o **RUS** 114-115 E 5
Krasnovodsk = Türkmenbaši ☆ **TM** 136-137 C 4
Krasnovodskij zaliv ≈ 136-137 C 5
Krasnovodskij zapovednik ⊥ **TM** 136-137 C 5
Krasnovodskoe plato ◣ **TM** 136-137 C 4
Krasnojarsk = Krasnojarsk ☆ • **RUS** 116-117 F 7
Krasnoznamjans'kyj kanal < **UA** 102-103 H 4
Krasnye Barrikady o **RUS** 96-97 E 10
Krasnyj, liman ≈ **RUS** 96-97 E 10
Krasnyj Aul o **KA** 124-125 M 3
Krasnyj Holm o **RUS** 94-95 P 3
Krasnyj Jar o **RUS** (KMR) 114-115 T 7
Krasnyj Jar o **RUS** (OMS) 114-115 N 3
Krasnyj Jar o **RUS** (VLG) 96-97 D 8
Krasnyj Jar ☆ **RUS** (AST) 96-97 F 10

Krasnyj Jar ☆ **RUS** (SAM) 96-97 G 7
Krasnyj Kut ☆ **RUS** 96-97 E 8
Krasnyj Luč o **UA** 102-103 L 3
Krasnystaw o **PL** 92-93 R 3
Krasnyy Luch = Krasnyj Luč o **UA** 102-103 L 3
Krasuha o **RUS** 94-95 O 2
Kratke Range ◣ **PNG** 183 C 4
Kratovo o • **MK** 100-101 J 3
Krau o **RI** 166-167 J 4
Krečetovo o **RUS** 94-95 Q 1
Krefeld o **D** 92-93 J 3
Kregbé o **CI** 202-203 J 6
Krekatok Island ∼ **USA** 20-21 G 5
Kremenchuk = Kremenčuk o **UA** 102-103 H 3
Kremenčuc'ke vodoschovyšče < **UA** 102-103 H 3
Kremenčug = Kremenčuk o **UA** 102-103 H 3
Kremenčuk o **UA** 102-103 H 3
Kremenec' o **UA** 102-103 D 2
Kremenec'ki hory • **UA** 102-103 D 2
Kreminci o **UA** 102-103 D 3
Kreminna o **UA** 102-103 L 3
Kremĺ o **RUS** 96-97 F 10
Kremling o **USA** 42-43 D 5
Krems an der Donau o • **A** 92-93 N 4
Kremsier = Kroměříž o **CZ** 92-93 O 4
Krenicyna, vulkan ▲ **RUS** 122-123 Q 4
Krenitzin Islands ∼ **USA** 22-23 O 6
Kreščenskoe o **RUS** 114-115 Q 7
Kresik Luway • **RI** 164-165 D 4
Kresta, zaliv ≈ 112-113 V 4
Krestcy ☆ **RUS** 94-95 N 2
Krest-Haĺďžaj o **RUS** 120-121 F 2
Krestijah o **RUS** 118-119 H 4
Krest'janskij o **US** 136-137 L 4
Krestovaja o **RUS** 118-119 F 6
Krestovaja, guba ≈ **RUS** 108-109 F 4
Krestovaja Guba o **RUS** 108-109 F 4
Krestovka o **RUS** 88-89 W 3
Krestovoe o **RUS** 112-113 N 2
Krestovskij, mys ◣ **RUS** 112-113 L 1
Krestovskij, ostrov ∼ **RUS** 112-113 L 1
Krestovyj, pereval ◣ **GE** 126-127 F 6
Krestovyj, mys ◣ **RUS** 122-123 S 3
Krestovyj, ostrov ∼ **RUS** 110-111 c 4
Kresty o **RUS** 108-109 e 6
Kresty o **RUS** (KIR) 96-97 E 5
Kresty o **RUS** (Mos) 94-95 P 4
Kretinga o **LT** 94-95 H 4
Kreuzburg (Oberschlesien) = Kluczbork o **PL** 92-93 P 3
Kreuznach, Bad o **D** 92-93 J 3
Krèva o **BY** 94-95 K 4
Kriam o **RI** 168 C 3
Kribi o **CAM** 210-211 B 2
Kričaĺskaja ∼ **RUS** 112-113 L 3
Krieger Mountains ◣ **CDN** 26-27 J 3
Kriel o **ZA** 220-221 J 3
Krigujgun, mys ◣ **RUS** 112-113 Z 4
KriĬon, mys ◣ **RUS** 122-123 K 6
Krishna ∼ **IND** 140-141 H 2
Krishnagiri o **IND** 140-141 H 4
Krishnarajanagara o **IND** 140-141 G 4
Krishnarajpet o **IND** 140-141 G 4
Kristiansand • **N** 86-87 C 7
Kristianstad o **S** 86-87 G 8
Kristiansund o **N** 86-87 B 6
Kristiinankaupunki = Kristinestad o •• **FIN** 88-89 J 6
Kristinehamn o **S** 86-87 G 7
Kristinestad o •• **FIN** 88-89 J 5
Kristoffer Bay ≈ 24-25 U 1
Kriti ◣ **GR** 100-101 K 7
Kriti o **GR** 100-101 K 7
Kritiko Pelagos ≈ 100-101 K 6
Kriuša o **RUS** 94-95 R 4
Kriva Palanka o **MK** 100-101 J 3
Krivodol o **BG** 102-103 C 6
Krivoj Rog = Kryvyj Rih o **UA** 102-103 H 4
Krivošeino o **RUS** 114-115 R 6
Krivyj Rih o **UA** 102-103 H 4
Križevci o **HR** 100-101 F 1
Krjučkova o **RUS** 96-97 J 8
Krk o **YU** 100-101 M 3
Krka ∼ **HR** 100-101 F 3
Krkonoše ◣ **CZ** 92-93 N 3
Krkonošskƴ národní park ⊥ **CZ** 92-93 N 3
Krohnwodoke o **LB** 202-203 G 7
Krokek o **S** 86-87 H 7
Krokodilrivier ∼ **ZA** 220-221 H 2
Krokom o **S** 86-87 G 5
Krokosua National Park ⊥ **GH** 202-203 J 6
Krôksfjardarnes o **IS** 86-87 c 2
Krolevec' o **UA** 102-103 H 2
Kroměříž o **CZ** 92-93 O 4
Krong Buk o **VN** 158-159 K 4
Kröng Kaôh Kông o **K** 158-159 G 5
Krông Pa o **VN** 158-159 K 4
Kronkel ∼ **RI** 166-167 K 5
Kronockaja ∼ **RUS** 120-121 T 6
Kronockij, mys ◣ **RUS** 120-121 U 6
Kronockij, zaliv ≈ 120-121 T 6
Kronockij poluostrov ∿ **RUS** 120-121 U 6
Kronockij zapovednik ⊥ **RUS** 120-121 T 6
Kronockoe, ozero o **RUS** 120-121 T 6
Kronprins Christian Land ⊥ **GRØ** 26-27 q 4
Kronprinsesse Maertha land ⊥ **ARK** 16 F 35
Kronprins Olav land ⊥ **ARK** 16 G 5
Kronstadt = Kronštadt o **RUS** 94-95 L 2
Kronštadt o **RUS** 94-95 L 2
Kronstad o **ZA** 220-221 H 4
Kropačevo o **RUS** 96-97 K 6
Kropotkin o **RUS** 102-103 M 5
Krośniewice o **PL** 92-93 P 2
Krosno o • **PL** 92-93 Q 4

Krosno Odrzańskie o **PL** 92-93 N 2
Krotoschin = Krotoszyn o **PL** 92-93 O 3
Krotoszyn o **PL** 92-93 O 3
Krotz Springs o **USA** 44-45 M 4
Kroya o **RI** 168 C 3
Krško o **SLO** 100-101 E 2
Kručina ∼ **RUS** 118-119 G 10
Kruet o **RI** 162-163 B 3
Kruger National Park ⊥ •• **ZA** 218-219 J 4
Krugersdorp o **ZA** 220-221 H 3
Kruglyj, ostrov ∼ **RUS** 108-109 V 4
Krui o **RI** 162-163 E 7
Kruidfontein o **ZA** 220-221 E 6
Kruis, Kaap = Cape Cross ◣ **NAM** 216-217 B 10
Krujë ☆ •• **AL** 100-101 G 4
Krumau = Český Krumlov o **CZ** 92-93 N 4
Krumaye o **RI** 166-167 G 2
Krumë o •• **AL** 100-101 H 3
Krumovgrad o **BG** 102-103 D 7
Krung Thep = Bangkok o **THA** 158-159 F 4
Krupanj o **YU** 100-101 G 2
Krusenstern, Cape ◣ **USA** 20-21 H 3
Kruševac o **YU** 100-101 H 3
Kruševo o **MK** 100-101 H 4
Krušné hory ◣ **CZ** 92-93 M 3
Krušņ̆ica ∼ **RUS** 96-97 D 7
Krutinka o **RUS** 114-115 L 7
Krutíška o **RUS** 124-125 M 2
Krutoberegovo o **RUS** 120-121 U 5
Krutogorova ∼ **RUS** 120-121 R 6
Krutoj o **RUS** 112-113 N 2
Kruzenšterna, proliv ≈ 122-123 P 4
Kruzof Island ∼ **USA** 32-33 B 3
Kryčav o **BY** 94-95 M 5
Kryktytau hrebet ◣ **RUS** 96-97 L 7
Krylovo o **RUS** 94-95 G 4
Kryms'ki hory ◣ **UA** 102-103 H 5
Krynica o • **PL** 92-93 Q 4
Kryve Ozero o **UA** 102-103 G 4
Krywyj Rih = Krivyj Rih o **UA** 102-103 H 4
'Ksan Indian Village ∿ **CDN** 32-33 G 4
Ksar Chellala o **DZ** 190-191 D 3
Ksar El Boukhari o **DZ** 190-191 D 3
Ksar El Hirane o **DZ** 190-191 D 4
Ksar Ghilane o **TN** 190-191 J 4
Ksenskij o **RUS** 102-103 K 1
Kshwan Mountain ◣ **CDN** 32-33 F 4
Ksour, Monts des ◣ **DZ** 190-191 C 4
Ksour Essaf o **TN** 190-191 H 4
Ksour Jelidat o **TN** 190-191 H 4
Ktesiphon ·.·•• **IRQ** 128-129 L 6
Kuah o **MAL** 162-163 G 2
Kuala ∼ **RI** 162-163 H 4
Kuala Baram o **MAL** 162-163 K 2
Kuala Belait o **BRU** 164-165 D 1
Kuala Berang o **MAL** 162-163 E 2
Kuala Dungun o **MAL** 162-163 E 2
Kuala Kangsar o **MAL** 162-163 D 2
Kuala Kapuas o **RI** 164-165 D 5
Kuala Kerau o **MAL** 162-163 E 2
Kuala Kerukeriau o **RI** 162-163 K 3
Kuala Lipis o **MAL** 162-163 E 2
Kuala Lumpur ☆ •• **MAL** 162-163 D 3
Kualapembuang o **RI** 162-163 K 4
Kuala Penyu o **MAL** 160-161 A 10
Kuala Pilah o **MAL** 162-163 E 3
Kuala Selangor o **MAL** 162-163 D 3
Kuala Tahan o **MAL** 162-163 E 2
Kualatanjung o **RI** 162-163 C 3
Kuala Terengganu ☆ • **MAL** 162-163 E 2
Kualatungkal o **RI** 162-163 E 5
Kuala Tungkal o **RI** 162-163 E 5
Kuamut o **MAL** 160-161 B 10
Kuamut ∼ **MAL** 160-161 B 10
Kuancheng o **VRC** 154-155 L 1
Kuanda ∼ **RUS** 118-119 H 7
Kuandang o **RI** 164-165 H 4
Kuandian o **VRC** 150-151 E 7
Kuangfu o **RC** 156-157 M 5
Kuantan ☆ • **MAL** 162-163 E 3
Kuba, zaliv o **RUS** 110-111 O 4
Kuba-Aryta, ostrova ∼ **RUS** 110-111 Q 3
Kubalah ∼ **RUS** 108-109 c 5
Kuban' o **RUS** 102-103 M 5
Kuban ∼ **RUS** 126-127 D 5
Kubarâ o **OM** 132-133 K 2
Kubari, Mount ◣ **PNG** 183 C 3
Kubbi o **SUD** 206-207 G 3
Kubbum o **SUD** 206-207 F 3
Kubena ∼ **RUS** 94-95 R 1
Kubenskoe, ozero o **RUS** 94-95 Q 2
Kuberganja o **RUS** 110-111 Z 6
Kubkain o **PNG** 183 B 3
Kubli o **WAN** 204-205 D 5
Kubli Hill ◣ **WAN** 204-205 F 3
Kubokawa o **J** 152-153 E 8
Kubônân o **IR** 134-135 H 4
Kubor Range ◣ **PNG** 183 C 4
Kubumesaai o **RI** 164-165 D 3
Kubuna o **PNG** 183 D 5
Kubupenelokan o **RI** 168 F 7
Kubutambahan o **RI** 168 B 7
Kücek, Rüd -e Zâb -e ∼ **IRQ** 128-129 L 4
Kücesfahân o **IR** 128-129 N 3
Kučevo o **YU** 100-101 H 2
Kuchi o **IND** 140-141 F 2
Kuching ☆ • **MAL** 162-163 H 4
Kuchino-Erabu-shima ∼ **J** 152-153 D 9
Kuchino-shima ∼ **J** 152-153 C 10

Kučukskoe, ozero o **RUS** 124-125 M 2
Kučurhan ∼ **UA** 102-103 F 4
Kuda o **RUS** 116-117 M 9
Kudâl o **IND** 140-141 G 2
Kudan o **WAN** 204-205 G 3
Kudang o **WAG** 202-203 C 5
Kudani o **IND** 202-203 L 8
Kudat o **MAL** 160-161 B 9
Kudayn o **SUD** 200-201 E 4
Kudene o **IND** 166-167 H 5
Kūderu o **IND** 140-141 G 3
Kudever' o **RUS** 94-95 L 3
Kudiakof Islands ∼ **USA** 22-23 P 5
Kudialčaj ∼ **AZ** 128-129 N 2
Kudi-Boma o **ZRE** 210-211 D 6
Kudirkos Naumiestis o •• **LT** 94-95 H 4
Kudjip o **PNG** 183 C 3
Kudligi o **IND** 140-141 G 3
Kudu o **WAN** 204-205 F 4
Kudu-Kjueĺ o **RUS** 118-119 K 6
Kudus o • **RI** 168 D 3
Kudymkar o **RUS** 96-97 J 4
Kueda o **RUS** 96-97 J 5
Kuedemane o **RI** 162-163 B 2
Kuènga ∼ **RUS** 118-119 H 9
Kûfa, al- ☆ **IRQ** 128-129 L 6
Kufrah, Al o **LAR** 192-193 J 5
Kufstein o • **A** 92-93 M 5
Kugaluk River ∼ **CDN** 20-21 Z 2
Kugaluk River ∼ **CDN** 24-25 O 6
Kugaly o **KA** 124-125 L 4
Kuganavolok o **RUS** 88-89 O 5
Kugmallit Bay ≈ 20-21 Y 2
Kugong Island ∼ **CDN** 36-37 K 6
Kugrua River ∼ **USA** 20-21 L 1
Kugruk River ∼ **USA** 20-21 J 4
Kugrurorok River ∼ **USA** 20-21 K 2
Kühak o **IR** (SIS) 134-135 G 5
Kühak o **IR** (SIS) 134-135 K 5
Kühdašt o **IR** 134-135 D 2
Küh-e Banâlūd ◣ **IR** 134-135 G 5
Küh-e Jûrân ◣ **IR** 136-137 H 3
Küh-e Madvâr ◣ **IR** 134-135 F 4
Küh-e Šâfi o **AFG** 138-139 B 2
Küh-e Sah Gûlak ◣ **IR** 128-129 N 5
Küh-e Sâhû ◣ **IR** 128-129 M 5
Küh-e Vâhân ◣ **AFG** 138-139 J 2
Kühgilüye, Büyer Ahmad-o ◣ **IR** 134-135 D 3
Kühin o **IR** 128-129 N 4
Kuhmo o **FIN** 88-89 K 4
Kuhmuh o **RUS** 126-127 G 6
Kuhn ø ∼ **GRØ** 26-27 p 6
Kühpâye o **IR** 134-135 F 2
Kühpâye, Kûhhâ-ye ◣ **IR** 134-135 G 3
Kuhterin Lug o **RUS** 122-123 C 2
Kuhtuj ∼ **RUS** 120-121 Q 5
Kuhtujskij hrebet ◣ **RUS** 120-121 K 3
Kui o **PNG** 183 D 4
Kui, Kivori- o **PNG** 183 D 5
Kui Buri o **THA** 158-159 E 4
Kuilsrivier o **ZA** 220-221 D 6
Kuiseb ∼ **NAM** 220-221 B 1
Kuiseb Canyon ∼ •• **NAM** 220-221 B 1
Kuito o **ANG** 216-217 D 6
Kuiu Island ∼ **USA** 32-33 C 3
Kuiukta Bay ≈ 22-23 R 4
Kuixingyan • **VRC** 156-157 D 3
Kuiyang o **VRC** 156-157 D 3
Kuja ∼ **RUS** 88-89 V 3
Kujama o **WAN** 204-205 G 3
Kujat, Gunung ◣ **RI** 164-165 E 2
Kujbyšev = Bulgar o **RUS** 96-97 F 6
Kujbyšev ∼ **RUS** 114-115 P 7
Kujbyšev = Samara ☆ **RUS** 96-97 G 7
Kujbyševa, mys ◣ **RUS** 108-109 Y 1
Kujbyševskoe < **RUS** 96-97 D 5
Kujdusun o **RUS** 120-121 K 2
Kujdusun ∼ **RUS** 120-121 K 2
Kujgan o **KA** 124-125 J 6
Kujginskij krjaž ◣ **RUS** 110-111 V 4
Kujl o **J** 152-153 J 4
Kujolri o **ROK** 150-151 G 9
Kujši kumlar • **US** 136-137 H 3
Kujtun ☆ **RUS** 116-117 K 8
Kujukuri-nada ≈ 152-153 J 7
Kujul ∼ **RUS** 120-121 V 3
Kujumba o **RUS** 116-117 H 5
Kujü-san ◣ **J** 152-153 D 8
Kujviveem ∼ **RUS** 112-113 R 3
Kujwa o **ROK** 150-151 F 11
Kukalkiek Lake o **USA** 32-23 T 3
Kukariagi o **WAN** 204-205 G 4
Kukawa o **WAN** 198-199 F 6
Kükdarjo ∼ **US** 136-137 G 3
Kuke o **RB** 218-219 D 4
Kukēs ☆ • **AL** 100-101 H 3
Kukipi o **PNG** 183 D 5
Kukmor o **RUS** 96-97 G 6
Kukpowfuk River ∼ **USA** 20-21 J 2
Kukpuk River ∼ **USA** 20-21 H 2
Kukshi o **IND** 138-139 E 8
Kukulbej, reka ∼ **RI** 118-119 H 10
Kukuna o **WAL** 202-203 D 5
Kukup o **MAL** 162-163 E 4
Kukur o **SUD** 208-209 A 3
Kukusunda o **RUS** 110-111 Q 5
Kül, Rüde ∼ **IR** 134-135 G 4
Kula o **BG** 102-103 C 6
Kula ☆ **TR** 128-129 C 3
Kula o **WAN** 204-205 G 6
Kulačhi o **PK** 138-139 C 4
Kulagin o **KA** 96-97 G 9
Kulai o **MAL** 162-163 E 4
Kula Kangri ◣ **BHT** 142-143 G 1
Kulakovo o **RUS** 116-117 G 5
Kulal, Mount ◣ **EAK** 212-213 F 2
Kulaly, ostrov ∼ **KA** 126-127 H 5
Kula Mawe o **EAK** 212-213 G 3
Kulagin o **KA** 96-97 G 9
Kulai o **MAL** 162-163 E 4
Kulazi o **WAN** 204-205 G 3
Kulabjung ∼ **TM** 136-137 G 7
Kúlandy, arcã ∼ **RUS** 116-117 M 9
Kúlandy, tubegi ∼ **KA** 126-127 N 5
Kulankhor o **VRC** 144-145 K 4

Külanötpes ∼ **KA** 124-125 G 4
Kulanutpes ∼ **KA** 124-125 G 3
Kular o **RUS** 110-111 U 4
Kular, hrebet ◣ **RUS** 110-111 S 5
Kulasekarappattinam o **IND** 140-141 H 6
Kulassein Island ∼ **RP** 160-161 D 9
Kulatau o **US** 136-137 G 4
Kulawi o **RI** 164-165 F 4
Kulay o **MAL** 162-163 D 4
Kulaykili o **SUD** 206-207 G 3
Kulčik o **RUS** 122-123 H 2
Kuldiga o • **LV** 94-95 H 3
Kuĺdino o **RUS** 112-113 H 3
Kuĺdur o **RUS** 122-123 D 4
Kule o **RB** 220-221 E 1
Kulebaki o **RUS** 94-95 S 4
Kulegan ∼ **RUS** 114-115 N 4
Kulén o **K** 158-159 H 4
Kulenga ∼ **RUS** 116-117 M 9
Kulgahtah gora ◣ **RUS** 108-109 X 7
Kulgera o **AUS** 176-177 M 2
Kulgeri o **IND** 140-141 G 2
Kulilbi o **ETH** 208-209 E 4
Kulim o **MAL** 162-163 D 2
Kulin o **AUS** 180-181 D 5
Kuljumbe o **RUS** 108-109 X 8
Kulkyne Creek ∼ **AUS** 178-179 H 6
Kullen ∼ **S** 86-87 F 8
Kulliparu Conservation Park ⊥ **AUS** 180-181 C 2
Kullorsuaq o **GRØ** 26-27 W 6
Kulmač Dağları ◣ **TR** 128-129 G 3
Kulmbach o **D** 92-93 L 3
Kulo o **RI** 164-165 K 3
Kuloj o **RUS** 96-97 H 3
Kulp o **TR** 128-129 J 3
Kulpara o **AUS** 180-181 E 3
Kulpawan ∼ **GH** 202-203 K 4
Kulsary ☆ **KA** 96-97 J 10
Kulu ∼ **RUS** 120-121 M 3
Kulu o **RUS** 120-121 L 3
Kulu ☆ **TR** 128-129 E 3
Kulumadau o **PNG** 183 G 5
Kulunda ∼ **RUS** 124-125 L 2
Kulunda ∼ **RUS** 124-125 L 2
Kulundinskaja ravnina ⊥ **RUS** 124-125 L 3
Kulundinskoe, ozero o **RUS** 124-125 L 2
Kulun-Elbjut o **RUS** 110-111 Y 6
Kulungu o **ZRE** 210-211 D 6
Kulu River ∼ **PNG** 183 E 3
Kulusuk o **GRØ** 28-29 W 4
Kulyköl o **KA** 124-125 H 1
Kulusuk Kap Dan o **GRØ** 28-29 W 4
Kulynda o **RUS** 118-119 H 4
Kulyndigol ∼ **KA** 124-125 K 3
Kum, Küh-e ◣ **IR** 134-135 E 3
Kuma ∼ **RI** 164-165 F 4
Kuma ∼ **RUS** 114-115 J 5
Kuma ∼ **RUS** 126-127 F 5
Kumafa, Pegunungan ◣ **RI** 166-167 G 3
Kumagaya o **J** 152-153 H 6
Kumahy o **RUS** 118-119 O 6
Kumai o **RI** 162-163 J 4
Kumai Teluk ≈ 162-163 J 4
Kumari = Gjumri o **AR** 128-129 K 2
Kumak o **RUS** 96-97 L 8
Kumakahi, Cape ◣ **USA** 48-49 E 8
Kumamba, Kepulauan ∼ **RI** 166-167 K 2
Kumamoto ☆ • **J** 152-153 D 8
Kumana o **CL** 140-141 G 2
Kumandan o **RUS** 166-167 G 2
Kumano o **J** 152-153 G 7
Kumano-gawa ∼ **J** 152-153 F 8
Kumano-nada ≈ 152-153 G 7
Kumanovo o • **MK** 100-101 H 3
Kumara o **NZ** 182 C 5
Kumarina Roadhouse o **AUS** 176-177 D 2
Kumari B Fossicking Area • **AUS** 176-177 F 6
Kumashi o **J** 152-153 H 3
Kumasi ☆ •• **GH** 202-203 J 6
K'unzila o **ETH** 208-209 C 4
Kumattur o **IND** 140-141 J 4
Kumba o **CAM** 204-205 H 6
Kumba o **RI** 166-167 J 2
Kumbakonam o **IND** 140-141 H 5
Kumbanikesa o **SOL** 184 I 2
Kumbarilla o **AUS** 178-179 L 4
Kumbe o **RI** 166-167 L 6
Kumbe ∼ **RI** 166-167 L 6
Kumbia o **AUS** 178-179 L 4
Kumbo o **CAM** 204-205 J 5
Kumbwareta o **PNG** 183 B 2
Kum-Dag = Gumdag o **TM** 136-137 D 5
Kümegan o **IR** 134-135 C 1
Kumeny ☆ **RUS** 96-97 J 7
Kumertau o **RUS** 96-97 J 7
Kum Gang ∼ **ROK** 150-151 F 9
Kûmhwa o **ROK** 150-151 F 8
Kumi o **EAU** 212-213 D 3
Kumiai o **IRQ** 128-129 L 4
Kumkurgan o **US** 136-137 K 6
Kumla o **S** 86-87 G 7
Kumlinge o • **FIN** 88-89 H 6
Kumluca ☆ **TR** 128-129 D 4
Kumma o **WAN** 204-205 J 3
Kümo-Manýckij kanal < **RUS** 126-127 F 5
Kumo o **WAN** 204-205 J 3
Kumola ∼ **KA** 124-125 J 3
Kumon Taungdan ◣ **MYA** 142-143 K 2

Kura o **AZ** 128-129 L 2
Kura o **WAN** 204-205 H 3
Kumru ☆ **TR** 128-129 G 2
Kums o **NAM** 220-221 D 3
Kümsaj o **KA** 126-127 N 3
Kumshe o **WAN** 206-207 B 3
Kümsông o **ROK** 150-151 F 10
Kumta o **IND** 140-141 F 3
Kumu o **ZRE** 210-211 K 2
Kumuchuru < **RB** 218-219 B 6
Kümübü o • **ET** 194-195 F 5
Kumusi River ∼ **PNG** 183 E 5
Kumya o **DVR** 150-151 F 8
Kumzâr o **OM** 134-135 G 5
Kuna Cave • **USA** 40-41 F 4
Kunak o **MAL** 160-161 C 10
Kuna River ∼ **USA** 20-21 M 2
Kunašak o **RUS** 96-97 M 6
Kunašir, ostrov ∼ **RUS** 122-123 L 6
Kunaširskij proliv = Nemuro-kaikyô ≈ 152-153 L 3
Kunatata Hill ◣ **WAN** 204-205 J 5
Kunayr, Wâdi ∼ **LAR** 192-193 J 4
Kunda ∼ **RUS** 116-117 F 9
Kunda o •• **EST** 94-95 K 2
Kunda ∼ **ZRE** 210-211 L 5
Kunda ∼ **ZRE** 210-211 L 5
Kundallali Falls ∼ **Z** 218-219 F 1
Kundam o **IND** 142-143 B 4
Kundamturu o **Z** 214-215 E 6
Kundar ∼ **PK** 138-139 B 4
Kundar, Pulau ∼ **RI** 162-163 E 4
Kundara o **IND** 140-141 G 6
Kundelungu, Parc National de ⊥ **ZRE** 214-215 D 6
Kundelungu ouest, Parc National de ⊥ **ZRE** 214-215 D 5
Kundiân o **PK** 138-139 C 3
Kundiawa o **PNG** 183 C 4
Kundichi o **EAT** 214-215 K 4
Kundil Bazar o **IND** 142-143 J 2
Kundla o **IND** 138-139 C 9
Kundurpi o **IND** 140-141 G 3
Kundūz ☆ • **AFG** 136-137 L 6
Kundūz, Daryâ-ye ∼ **AFG** 136-137 L 6
Kunene ∼ **NAM** 216-217 B 8
Künes hu ∼ **VRC** 146-147 K 4
Kungâlv ☆ **S** 86-87 E 8
Kungasalah, ozero o **RUS** 110-111 P 2
Kunghit Island ∼ **CDN** 32-33 E 5
Kungila o **SUD** 208-209 A 3
Küngirod-Müjnçk kanal < **US** 136-137 F 3
Kungsbacka ☆ **S** 86-87 F 8
Kungu o **ZRE** 210-211 G 2
Kungur ☆ **RUS** 96-97 K 5
Kungurtug o **RUS** 116-117 H 10
Kungus ∼ **RUS** 116-117 G 8
Kungyangon o **MYA** 158-159 D 2
Kunhan ∼ **RUS** 138-139 G 9
Kunhâr ∼ **PK** 138-139 D 3
Kunhing o **MYA** 142-143 L 5
Kunigal o **IND** 140-141 G 4
Kunimaipa River ∼ **PNG** 183 D 4
Kuningan o **RI** 168 C 3
Kun'ja ∼ **RUS** 94-95 M 3
Kunjirap Daban = Khunjerab Pass ◣ **VRC** 138-139 E 1
Kunjirop Daban ◣ **KA** 138-139 E 1
Kunka, Bolšaja ∼ **RUS** 120-121 Q 3
Kunlun Shan ◣ **VRC** 144-145 A 1
Kunlun Shankou ◣ **VRC** 144-145 K 3
Kunmarra = Gjumri o **AR** 128-129 K 2
Kun-Man'e ∼ **RUS** 120-121 L 6
Kunming ☆ • **VRC** 156-157 C 4
Kunmunya Aboriginal Land ✕ **AUS** 172-173 G 3
Kunnui o **J** 152-153 J 3
Kunovat ∼ **RUS** 114-115 J 2
Kunsan o **ROK** 150-151 F 10
Kunshan o **VRC** 154-155 N 5
Kuntanase o **GH** 202-203 K 6
Kun-Tas, hrebet ◣ **RUS** 110-111 W 4
Kunthi Kyun ∼ **MYA** 158-159 D 5
Kuntykahy ∼ **RUS** 108-109 c 7
Kunua o **PNG** 184 I b 1
Kununurra o **AUS** 172-173 J 3
Kunya o **WAN** 198-199 D 6
Kunyao o **EAK** 212-213 E 3
K'unzila o **ETH** 208-209 C 4
Kuocang Shan ◣ **VRC** 156-157 M 2
Kuoi o **LB** 202-203 F 7
Kuoka ∼ **RUS** 110-111 M 4
Kuokunu o **RUS** 118-119 H 4
Kuolaji ∼ **RUS** 110-111 U 4
Kuoloma o **RUS** 120-121 F 3
Kuonamka, Boĺšaja ∼ **RUS** 110-111 J 4
Kuonara o **RUS** 110-111 N 6
Kuopio ☆ • **FIN** 88-89 J 5
Kuortane o **FIN** 88-89 J 5
Kupa ∼ **RUS** 116-117 M 7
Kûpâl o **IR** 134-135 C 3
Kupang ☆ **RI** 166-167 B 7
Kupangnunding o **RI** 164-165 D 4
Kup'ans'k o **UA** 102-103 K 3
Kuparuk River ∼ **USA** 20-21 N 2
Kupcino o **RUS** 94-95 M 2
Kupfer Range ◣ **PNG** 183 D 4
Kupiano o **PNG** 183 E 6
Kupino ☆ **RUS** 124-125 K 1
Kupiškis o • **LT** 94-95 K 4
Kuppagallu o **IND** 140-141 G 3
Kupreanof Island ∼ **USA** 32-33 C 3
Kupreanof Point ∼ **USA** 22-23 R 5
Kupreanof Strait ≈ 22-23 Q 4
Kupulima o **GH** 202-203 J 4
Kupuri ∼ **RUS** 120-121 Q 6
Kuputusan o **RI** 164-165 K 4
Kupwara o **IND** 138-139 E 2
Kuqa o **VRC** 146-147 F 4
Kur, Pulau ∼ **RI** 166-167 F 4

Kura ∼ **AZ** 128-129 L 2
Kura o **WAN** 204-205 .H 3
Kurâ o **WAN** 204-205 H 4
Kuragaty o **KA** 124-125 H 4
Kuragino ☆ **RUS** 116-117 F 9
Kuragwi o **WAN** 204-205 H 4
Kurahachi-shima ∼ **J** 152-153 E 7
Kurajlysaj o **KA** 96-97 G 8
Kurali o **IND** 138-139 F 4
Kura Kurk ≈ 94-95 G 3
Kuraminskij hrebet ◣ **TJ** 136-137 L 4
Kuranah-Jurjah ∼ **RUS** 110-111 S 5
Kuranda o **AUS** 174-175 H 5
Kura Nehri ∼ **TR** 128-129 K 2
Kurashiki o • **J** 152-153 E 7
Kurayn ∼ **KSA** 130-131 L 4
Kurayoshi o **J** 152-153 E 7
Kurba ∼ **RUS** 116-117 O 9
Kurbatovo o **RUS** 116-117 E 8
Kurčum o **KA** 124-125 N 4
Kurčum ∼ **KA** 124-125 O 4
Kurdistan ⊥ 128-129 J 4
Kurduvâdi o **IND** 138-139 E 10
Kűrdym, köl o **KA** 126-127 P 4
Kure o **J** 152-153 E 7
Küre Dağları ◣ **TR** 128-129 E 2
Kurejka o **RUS** (KRN) 108-109 W 8
Kurejka ∼ **RUS** 108-109 a 7
Kurejka ∼ **RUS** 116-117 H 2
Kurejskoe vodohranilišče < **RUS** 108-109 X 8
Kurenalus = Pudasjärvi o **FIN** 88-89 J 4
Kuressaare o •• **EST** 94-95 H 2
Kurfil o **WAN** 198-199 C 6
Kurgan o **RUS** 114-115 H 7
Kurganinsk o **RUS** 126-127 D 5
Kurgan-Tjube ☆ **TJ** 136-137 L 4
Kuri ∼ **RI** 166-167 J 3
Küri o **SUD** 200-201 E 3
Kuri Bay o **AUS** 172-173 G 3
Kurichedu o **IND** 140-141 H 3
Kūriĝân o **IR** 128-129 N 5
Kurigram o **BD** 142-143 F 3
Kurik o **RI** 166-167 K 6
Kurikka o **FIN** 88-89 J 5
Kurikoma Quasi National Park ⊥ **J** 152-153 J 5
Kuril Basin ≈ 10-11 O 4
Kuril Islands = Kuriĺskie ostrova ∼ **RUS** 122-123 M 6
Kurilo-Kamčatskij želob ≈ 120-121 T 7
Kuriĺsk o **RUS** 122-123 M 6
Kuriĺsk, Severo- o **RUS** 122-123 Q 4
Kuriĺskoe, ozero o **RUS** 122-123 R 3
Kuril Trench ≈ 10-11 P 4
Kurima o **RI** 166-167 K 4
Kurinelisi Out Station o **AUS** 174-175 C 7
Ku-Ring-Gai Chase National Park ⊥ **AUS** 180-181 L 2
Kur'inskij krjaž ◣ **RUS** 112-113 K 3
Kurinwás, Rio ∼ **NIC** 52-53 B 5
Kuriyama o **J** 152-153 J 3
Kur'ja o **RUS** 124-125 N 3
Kur'ja o **RUS** (KOM) 114-115 D 4
Kur'ja ∼ **RUS** 112-113 L 3
Kurkhera o **IND** 142-143 B 5
Kurkino o **RUS** 94-95 Q 5
Kurkur o **ET** 194-195 F 6
Kurleja o **RUS** 118-119 J 9
Kurlek o **RUS** 114-115 S 6
Kurlin o **RUS** 96-97 G 8
Kurmanaevka o **RUS** 96-97 H 7
Kurmuk o **SUD** 208-209 D 4
Kurmuk o **SUD** 208-209 B 3
Kurmool o **IND** 140-141 H 3
Kuroishi o **J** 152-153 J 4
Kuroiso o **J** 152-153 J 6
Kuroki o **CDN** 34-35 E 5
Kuromatsunai o **J** 152-153 J 4
Kurong, Cape ◣ **RI** 166-167 B 7
Kuror, Ĝabal ◣ **SUD** 200-201 E 4
Kuro-shima ∼ **J** 152-153 C 9
Kurovskoe o **RUS** 94-95 Q 4
Kurovyči o **UA** 102-103 D 3
Kurow o **NZ** 182 C 6
Kurów o **PL** 92-93 R 3
Kurram ∼ **PK** 138-139 C 3
Kurŝab ∼ **KS** 136-137 N 4
Kursavka o **RUS** 126-127 E 5
Kurŝenai o **LT** 94-95 H 3
Kurŝk ☆ • **RUS** 102-103 K 2
Kurŝkaja kosa ∼ **RUS** 94-95 G 4
Kurŝkij zaliv ≈ **RUS** 94-95 G 4
Kurŝunlu ☆ **TR** 128-129 E 2
Kurtamyŝ o **RUS** 114-115 H 7
Kürti o **SUD** 200-201 E 3
Kurtty ∼ **KA** 124-125 K 4
Kuru o **FIN** 88-89 G 6
Kuru o **IND** 142-143 D 4
Kuru ∼ **SUD** 206-207 H 4
Kurubonla o **WAL** 202-203 E 5
Kuruksaj o **TJ** 136-137 L 4
Kuruktag ◣ **VRC** 146-147 H 5
Kuruman o **ZA** (CAP) 220-221 F 4
Kuruman ∼ **ZA** 220-221 F 3
Kuruman Hills ◣ **ZA** 220-221 F 3
Kurume o **J** 152-153 D 8
Kurumkan o **RUS** 118-119 G 8
Kurundi, hrebet ◣ **RUS** 110-111 V 5
Kurunegala o **CL** 140-141 J 7
Kurun-Urjah o **RUS** 120-121 G 4
Kurupa Lake o **USA** 20-21 L 1
Kurupa River ∼ **USA** 20-21 N 2
Kurupukari o **GUY** 62-63 G 4
Kuryk o **KA** 126-127 K 5
Kuržina ∼ **RUS** 114-115 R 5
Kusa o **RUS** 96-97 L 6
Kuşadası ☆ • **TR** 128-129 B 4
Kuşadası Körfezi ≈ 128-129 B 4
Kusagaki-guntô ∼ **J** 152-153 C 9

Kusak ∼ KA 124-125 K 4
Kušalino o RUS 94-95 P 3
Kusawa Lake ⇔ CDN 20-21 W 6
Kuščevskaja o RUS 102-103 L 4
Kus'e-Aleksandrovskij o RUS 96-97 L 4
Kuş Gölü ⇔ TR 128-129 B 2
Kushālgarh o PK 138-139 C 3
Kusheriki o WAN 204-205 G 3
Kushikino o J 152-153 D 9
Kushimoto o J 152-153 F 8
Kushiro o J 152-153 L 3
Kushiro-chō o J 152-153 L 3
Kushiro-gawa ∼ J 152-153 L 3
Kushtagi o IND 140-141 G 3
Kushtia o BD 142-143 F 4
Kušik, Tall o SYR 128-129 K 4
Kusiwigasi, Mount ▲ PNG 183 A 3
Küšk o AFG 134-135 K 1
Kuskokwim Bay ≈ 22-23 P 3
Kuskokwim Mountains ▲ USA 20-21 L 6
Kuskokwim River ∼ USA 20-21 J 6
Kušmurun = Kusmüryn o KA 124-125 D 2
Kušmurun, ozero = Küsmüryn köli ⇔ KA 124-125 D 2
Küsmüryn o KA 124-125 D 2
Küsmüryn köli ⇔ KA 124-125 D 2
Kušnarenkovo ☆ RUS 96-97 J 6
Kusong o DVR 150-151 E 8
Kusova, ostrov ∩ RUS 120-121 H 6
Kustatan o USA 20-21 P 6
Küsti ☆ SUD 200-201 F 6
Kustur o RUS 110-111 S 5
Kusu o RI 164-165 K 3
Kusumkasa o IND 142-143 B 5
Kusuri o RI 164-165 K 3
Kušva o RUS 96-97 L 4
Kus'veem ∼ RUS 112-113 S 2
Küt, al- ☆ IRQ 128-129 L 6
Kuta o RI 168 C 7
Kuta ∼ RUS 116-117 M 7
Kuta o WAN 204-205 G 4
Kutabagok o RI 162-163 B 2
Kutacane o RI 162-163 B 3
Kütahya ☆ TR 128-129 C 3
Kutainang o RI 162-163 A 3
Kutai National Park ⊥ RI 164-165 E 3
Kutaisi o• GE 126-127 E 6
K'ut'aisi = Kutaisi o•• GE 126-127 E 6
Küt al-Ḥayy ☆ IRQ 128-129 M 6
Kutana o RUS 120-121 D 4
Kutanibong o RI 162-163 B 3
Kutaramakan ∼ RUS 108-109 Z 7
Kutchan o J 152-153 J 3
Kutcharo-ko ⇔ J 152-153 L 3
Kutchi Hill ▲ WAN 204-205 H 4
Kute o GH 202-203 L 6
Küt-e Gäpü ∴• IR 134-135 C 2
Kuti o RUS 118-119 J 10
Kutilax o WAN 206-207 B 3
Kutima o RUS 116-117 O 7
Kutima ∼ RUS 118-119 E 7
Kutina o HR 100-101 F 2
Kutiwenji o WAN 204-205 F 4
Kutiyāna o IND 138-139 B 9
Kutná Hora o•• CZ 92-93 N 4
Kutno o PL 92-93 P 2
Kutoarjo o RI 168 C 3
Kutop'jugan o RUS 108-109 O 8
Kutse Game Reserve ⊥ RB 218-219 C 6
Kutse Pan < RB 218-219 C 6
Kutshu o ZRE 210-211 G 2
Kuttenberg = Kutná Hora o•• CZ 92-93 N 4
Kutu o ZRE 210-211 G 5
Kutubdia ∩ BD 142-143 G 5
Kutubu, Lake ⇔ PNG 183 B 4
Kutulo, Lagh ∼ EAK 212-213 H 2
Kutum o SUD 200-201 B 5
Kutu River ∼ PNG 183 E 6
Kuujjuaq o CDN 36-37 P 5
Kuujjua River ∼ CDN 24-25 O 5
Kuuli Majak o TM 136-137 C 4
Kuummiit o GRØ 28-29 W 4
Kuusalu o EST 94-95 J 2
Kuusamo o FIN 88-89 K 4
Kuusankoski o FIN 88-89 J 6
Kuvandyk ☆ RUS 96-97 K 8
Kuvasaj o US 136-137 N 4
Kuvet ∼ RUS 112-113 S 2
Kuvšinovo o RUS 94-95 O 3
Kuvykta o RUS 118-119 M 8
Kuwait o IRQ 128-129 M 6
Kuwait ■ KWT 130-131 K 3
Kuwait, al- ◘ KWT 130-131 K 3
Kuwait, al- ★ KWT (KUW) 130-131 K 3
Kuwait, Ḫalīǧ al- ≈ 130-131 K 3
Kuwait = Kuwait, al- ◘ KWT 128-129 M 6
Kuwana o J 152-153 G 7
Kuwāra o SUD 206-207 J 3
Kuwawin o RI 166-167 G 2
Kuwethluk River ∼ USA 20-21 K 6
Kuybyshevskoye Vodokhranilishche = Samarskoe vodohran. < RUS 96-97 F 7
Küysanǧaq ☆ IRQ 128-129 L 4
Kuytun o VRC 146-147 G 3
Kuyuwini ∼ GUY 62-63 E 4
Kuyuwini Landing o GUY 62-63 E 4
Kužai o LT 94-95 H 4
Kūzarān o IR 134-135 B 1
Kuzedeevo o RUS 124-125 P 2
Kuzema o RUS (KAR) 88-89 N 4
Kuzema ∼ RUS 88-89 M 4
Kuzitrin River ∼ USA 20-21 H 4
Kužka o TM 136-137 H 7
Kužka = Gushgy o TM 136-137 H 7
Küz Konar o AFG 138-139 C 2
Kuzneck o RUS 96-97 E 7
Kuzneckaja guba ≈ 88-89 W 2
Kuzneckij, Leninsk ☆ RUS 114-115 T 7
Kuzneckij Alatau ▲ RUS 114-115 T 7
Kuznezovo o RUS 122-123 J 5
Kuzomen' o RUS 88-89 O 3
Kuzomen o RUS 88-89 R 4
Kuzovatovo ☆ RUS 96-97 E 7
Kuzumaki o J 152-153 J 4
Kvačina, buhta ⇔ RUS 120-121 R 5
Kvænangen ≈ N 86-87 K 1
Kværndrup o DK 86-87 E 9
Kvaløy ∩ N 86-87 J 2
Kvaløya ∩ N 86-87 L 1
Kvalsund o N 86-87 L 1
Kvareli o GE 126-127 F 7
Kvarkeno ☆ RUS 96-97 L 7
Kvarkuš, hrebet ▲ RUS 114-115 E 5
Kvarner ≈ 100-101 E 2
Kvamerič ≈ 100-101 E 2
Kvemo-Ažara o GE 126-127 D 6
Kvichak Bay ≈ 22-23 S 3
Kvichak River ∼ USA 22-23 S 3
Kvikkjokk o S 86-87 H 3
Kvina ∼ N 86-87 C 7
Kvinesdal ☆ N 86-87 C 7
Kvirila ∼ GE 126-127 E 6
Kviteseid ☆ N 86-87 D 7
Kvitøya ∩ N 84-85 R 2
Kwa ∼ ZRE 210-211 F 5
Kwadacha Wilderness Provincial Park ⊥ CDN 32-33 H 3
Kwadwokurom o GH 202-203 K 6
Kwahu Tafo o GH 202-203 K 6
Kwaiawata Island ∩ PNG 183 F 5
Kwa-Ibo o WAN 204-205 G 6
Kwailibesi o SOL 184 I e 3
Kwajok o SUD 206-207 H 4
Kwakwani o GUY 62-63 F 3
Kwale o EAK 212-213 G 6
Kwale o WAN 204-205 G 6
Kwale Game Reserve ⊥ WAN 204-205 G 6
Kwamalasamutu o SME 62-63 F 4
Kwa-Mashu o ZA 220-221 K 4
Kwamedwamenokurom o GH 202-203 K 6
Kwamera o VAN 184 II b 4
Kwamor-Besar o RI 166-167 F 3
Kwamouth o ZRE 210-211 F 5
Kwa Mtoro o EAT 212-213 E 6
Kwandar Rūd ∼ AFG 138-139 B 4
Kwando ∼ RB 218-219 B 4
Kwanga o PNG 183 C 3
Kwanga o ZRE 210-211 K 6
Kwangch'ŏn o ROK 150-151 F 9
Kwangju o ROK 150-151 F 10
Kwango ∼ ZRE 216-217 D 3
Kwanhio o MYA 142-143 L 4
Kwania, Lake ⇔ EAU 212-213 D 3
Kwanmo Bong ▲ DVR 150-151 G 7
Kwapsanek o PNG 183 D 4
Kwara ◘ WAN 204-205 E 4
Kwaraga o RB 218-219 C 5
Kware o WAN 198-199 B 6
Kwashebawa o WAN 198-199 C 6
Kwatisore o RI 166-167 H 3
Kwa Zulu (former Homeland, now part of Kwa Zulu/Natal) ◘ ZA 220-221 K 3
Kwa Zulu/Natal Province ◘ ZA 220-221 K 3
Kwekwe o ZW 218-219 E 4
Kwelkan o AUS 176-177 E 5
Kwendihn o LB 202-203 F 6
Kweneng ◘ RB 218-219 C 6
Kwenge ∼ ZRE 210-211 G 6
Kwiambana Game Reserve ⊥ WAN 204-205 G 3
Kwidzyn o• PL 92-93 P 2
Kwieftim o PNG 183 A 2
Kwigillingok o USA 22-23 P 3
Kwigluk Island ∩ USA 22-23 O 3
Kwiguk o USA 20-21 H 5
Kwihā o ETH 200-201 J 6
Kwikila o PNG 183 D 5
Kwikpak o USA 20-21 H 5
Kwilu ∼ ZRE 210-211 E 6
Kwilu ∼ ZRE 210-211 G 6
Kwilu-Ngongo o ZRE 210-211 E 6
Kwinana o AUS 176-177 C 6
Kwinella o WAG 202-203 C 3
Kwisa ∼ PL 92-93 N 3
Kwoka, Gunung ▲ RI 166-167 G 2
Kwolla o WAN 204-205 H 4
Kyabé o TCH 206-207 D 4
Kyabra o AUS 178-179 G 4
Kyaikkami (Amherst) o MYA 158-159 D 2
Kyaiklat o MYA 158-159 C 2
Kyaikto o MYA 158-159 D 2
Kyaka o EAT 212-213 C 4
Kyancutta o AUS 180-181 C 2
Kyangin o MYA 142-143 J 6
Ky Anh ☆ VN 158-159 J 1
Kyataw o MYA 158-159 E 4
Kyaukme o MYA 142-143 K 4
Kyaukpyu o MYA 142-143 H 6
Kyauksat o MYA 158-159 E 3
Kyaukse o MYA 142-143 K 5
Kyaukt o MYA 142-143 H 6
Kyauktaw o MYA 142-143 H 5
Kyaunggon o MYA 158-159 C 2
Kyawkku o MYA 142-143 K 5
Kybartai o LT 94-95 H 4
Kybeyan Range ▲ AUS 180-181 K 4
Kyčžimit ∼ RUS 118-119 E 9
Kyé ∼ G 210-211 C 2
Kyeburn o NZ 182 C 6
Kyegegwa o EAU 212-213 C 3
Kyeintali o MYA 158-159 C 2
Kyela o EAT 214-215 G 5
Kyenjojo o EAU 212-213 C 3
Kyeryongsan National Park ⊥• ROK 150-151 F 9
Kyidaunggan o MYA 142-143 K 6
Kyjam, gora ▲ RUS 110-111 a 5
Kyjiv ★•• UA 102-103 G 2
Kyjivs'ke vodoschovyšče < UA 102-103 G 2
Kyjy o RUS 120-121 E 2
Kykotsmovi o USA 44-45 B 2
Kyk-over-al • GUY 62-63 E 2
Kylaly o RUS 120-121 E 2
Kylās ▲ IND 142-143 G 3
Kyle o CDN 32-33 Q 6
Kyle, Lake ⇔ ZW 218-219 F 5
Kyll ∼ D 92-93 J 3
Kyllah ∼ RUS 110-111 c 6
Kylvynejveem ∼ RUS 112-113 Q 5
Kyma ∼ RUS 88-89 T 4
Kyneton o AUS 180-181 H 4
Kyngyldyözek ∼ KA 126-127 P 4
Kynquot o CDN 32-33 G 6
Kynuna o AUS 178-179 F 1
Kyoga, Lake ⇔ EAU 212-213 D 3
Kyogami-saki ▲ J 152-153 F 7
Kyogche La ▲ VRC 144-145 H 5
Kyogle o AUS 178-179 M 5
Kyona, Plage ∸• RH 54-55 J 5
Kyŏnggi Man ≈ 150-151 E 9
Kyŏngju o ROK 150-151 G 10
Kyŏngju National Park ⊥• ROK 150-151 G 10
Kyonkadun o MYA 158-159 C 2
Kyōto ☆•• J 152-153 F 7
Kyōwa o J 152-153 J 3
Kypcak, köli ⇔ KA 124-125 F 3
Kyra ☆ RUS (CTN) 118-119 E 11
Kyra ∼ RUS 118-119 E 11
Kyra ∼ RUS 118-119 E 10
Kyren ☆ RUS 116-117 L 10
Kyrgyz o KA 124-125 J 4
Kyrgyzstan ■ KS 136-137 M 4
Kyritz o• D 92-93 M 2
Kyrnyčky o UA 102-103 F 5
Kyrönjoki ∼ FIN 88-89 G 5
Kyrykkeles ∼ KA 136-137 L 4
Kys"egan ∼ RUS 114-115 R 4
Ký So'n o VN 156-157 D 7
Kystatayam o RUS 110-111 O 6
Kyštovka o RUS 114-115 O 6
Kystyk, plato ▲ RUS 110-111 O 4
Kystyktah ∼ RUS 108-109 Y 6
Kyštym o RUS 96-97 M 6
Kysyl-Syr o RUS 118-119 L 4
Kytaj, ozero ⇔ UA 102-103 F 5
Kytépana, gora ▲ RUS 120-121 S 5
Kytepkaj, grjada ▲ RUS 112-113 S 2
Kyttyk, poluostrov ∪ RUS 112-113 O 2
Kytyl, Čumpu o RUS 110-111 Y 7
Kytyl-Djura o RUS 118-119 M 5
Kyungon o MYA 142-143 K 6
Kyunhla o MYA 142-143 J 4
Kyuquot Sound ≈ 32-33 G 6
Kyuroku-shima ∩ J 152-153 H 4
Kyūshū ∩ J 152-153 C 8
Kyushu-Palau Ridge ≃ 152-153 E 10
Kyūshū-sanchi ▲ J 152-153 D 9
Kyvkvyn ∼ RUS 112-113 U 2
Kyvrak o AZ 128-129 L 3
Kywebwe o MYA 142-143 K 6
Kywedatkon o MYA 142-143 K 6
Kyyjärvi o FIN 88-89 H 5
Kyzart o KS 146-147 B 5
Kyzyl ☆ RUS 116-117 G 10
Kyzylagadžskij zapovednik ⊥ AZ 128-129 N 3
Kyzylagaš o KA 124-125 L 6
Kyzyl-Art, pereval ▲ TJ 136-137 N 5
Kyzylbalyk o KA 96-97 G 10
Kyzyl-Hem ∼ RUS 116-117 H 10
Kyzylkajyn ∼ KA 126-127 N 2
Kyzylkak, köli ⇔ KA 124-125 H 2
Kyzyl-Kija o KS 136-137 N 4
Kyzylmazar o US 136-137 L 5
Kyzyl-Oj o KS 146-147 B 5
Kyzyloktjabr o KA 124-125 K 3
Kyzylorda ☆ KA 124-125 D 6
Kyzyl-Ozgërjuš o KS 136-137 N 4
Kyzylsu ∼ TJ 136-137 L 5
Kyzyl-Suu ∼ KS 136-137 N 5
Kyzyltepa o US 136-137 J 4
Kyzyl-Tuu o KS 146-147 C 4
Kyzylžar o KA 124-125 F 4
Kzyltu ☆ KA 124-125 H 2

L

Laa an der Thaya o A 92-93 O 4
Laag, Pulau ∩ RI 166-167 J 4
Laamoro, Danau ⇔ RI 166-167 H 3
Laas Aano o SP 208-209 J 5
Laascaanood o SP 208-209 H 4
Laaso Dawaco o SP 208-209 J 3
Laasqoray o SP 208-209 J 3
Laâyoune = al-'Ayun ☆ MA 188-189 E 7
Laayoune = Al-'Ayun ☆ WSA 188-189 E 7
Laba o BF 202-203 J 4
Laba o RN 198-199 B 5
Laba ∼ RUS 126-127 D 5
Labadie, Plage ∸• RH 54-55 J 5
Labahe Niuling Reserves ⊥ VRC 154-155 C 6
Labakkang o RI 164-165 F 6
Labala o RI 166-167 B 6
Labalama o PNG 183 B 3
Labardén o RA 78-79 K 4
Labasa o FJI 184 III b 2
Labason o RP 160-161 E 8
Labaz, ozero ⇔ RUS 108-109 c 5
Labba o GUY 62-63 E 3
Labbal, al- ∸ KSA 130-131 G 3
Labbezzanga o RMM 202-203 L 2
Labdah ∴•• LAR 192-193 F 1
Labe ∼ CZ 92-93 N 3
Labé ◘ RG 202-203 D 4
Labé ☆ RG 202-203 D 4
Labelle o CDN 38-39 G 5
Labengke, Pulau ∩ RI 164-165 H 5
Laberge, Lake ⇔ CDN 20-21 X 6
Laberinto o CO 60-61 D 6
Laberinto, El o YV 60-61 E 2
Labḥa o KSA 130-131 J 5
Labi o BRU 164-165 D 1
Labin o HR 100-101 E 2
Labinsk o RUS 126-127 D 5
Labinsk, Ust'- o RUS 102-103 L 5
Labis o MAL 162-163 E 3
Lab Lab o PNG 183 E 3
Labná ∴• MEX 52-53 K 1
Labo o RP 160-161 E 5
Labo, Mount ▲ RP 160-161 E 5
Labobo, Pulau ∩ RI 164-165 H 4
Labolatounka o RG 202-203 E 4
Laboulaye o RA 78-79 H 3
Labozhi o WAN 204-205 F 4
Labrador, Cape ▲ CDN 36-37 R 4
Labrador = Labrador Péninsule ∪ CDN 6-7 B 3
Labrador Basin ≃ 6-7 D 3
Labrador City o CDN 38-39 L 2
Labrador Sea ≈ 6-7 D 3
Labrang Si • VRC 154-155 C 4
Labranza Grande o CO 60-61 E 5
Lábrea o BR 66-67 E 6
Labrieville o CDN 38-39 K 4
Labuan o MAL 160-161 A 10
Labuan o RI 168 A 3
Labuan, Pulau ∩ MAL 160-161 A 10
Labuha o RI 164-165 K 4
Labuhanbilik o RI 162-163 D 3
Labuhanhaji o RI (ACE) 162-163 B 3
Labuhanhaji o RI (NBA) 168 C 7
Labuhan Kananga o RI 168 C 7
Labuhanmeringgai o RI 162-163 F 7
Labuhanpandan o RI 168 C 7
Labuhanruku o RI 162-163 C 3
Labuk, Teluk ≈ 160-161 B 9
Labutta o MYA 158-159 C 2
Labynkyr, ozero ⇔ RUS 120-121 K 2
Labyntangi o RUS 108-109 M 8
Labyrinth, Lake ⇔ AUS 178-179 C 6
Labyrinth Lake ⇔ CDN 30-31 Q 5
Laç o•• AL 100-101 G 4
Lac ◘ TCH 198-199 G 6
Lắc o VN 158-159 K 4
Lača, ozero ⇔ RUS 88-89 P 6
Lacadena o CDN 32-33 Q 6
Lacajahuira, Río ∼ BOL 70-71 D 6
Lacanau o F 90-91 G 9
Lacanau-Océan o F 90-91 G 9
Lacandón, Sierra del ▲ MEX 52-53 J 3
Lacanja o MEX (CHI) 52-53 J 3
Lacanja ∴• MEX (CHI) 52-53 J 3
Lacantún, Río ∼ MEX 52-53 J 3
Lacassine National Wildlife Refuge ⊥ USA 44-45 L 5
La Castellana o RP 160-161 E 7
Lacaune o F 90-91 J 10
Laccadive Islands ∩ IND 140-141 E 6
Lac Cardinal o CDN 32-33 M 3
Lac Courte Oreilles Indian Reservation ✗ USA 46-47 C 3
Lac du Bonnet o CDN 34-35 H 5
Lac du Flambeau Indian Reservation ✗ USA 46-47 D 3
Lac-Édouard o CDN 38-39 H 5
Lacepede Bay ≈ 180-181 E 4
Lacepede Islands ∩ AUS 172-173 F 4
Lacey o USA 40-41 C 2
Lachay, Reserva Nacional ⊥ PE 64-65 D 7
Lāchi o PK 138-139 C 3
Lachlan Range ▲ AUS 180-181 H 2
Lachlan River ∼ AUS 180-181 H 3
Lach Truong ≈ 156-157 E 7
Lac-Humqui o CDN 38-39 L 4
Lachute o CDN 38-39 G 6
Lačin o AZ 128-129 M 3
Läckö o•• S 86-87 F 7
Lac la Biche o CDN 32-33 O 4
Lac la Hache o CDN 32-33 K 6
Lac la Martre o CDN 30-31 L 4
Lac la Ronge Provincial Park ⊥ CDN 34-35 D 3
Lac-Mégantic o CDN 38-39 J 6
Lacombe o CDN 32-33 O 5
Laconia o USA 46-47 N 4
Lacrosse o USA 40-41 F 2
La Crosse o USA 46-47 C 4
Lac-Saguay o CDN 38-39 G 5
Lac Seul o CDN 34-35 K 5
La Cueva o USA 44-45 D 2
Lacy, Mount ▲ AUS 172-173 G 4
La Cygnes Lake ⇔ USA 42-43 K 6
Ladakh ∸ IND 138-139 F 2
Ladakh Range ▲ IND 138-139 F 2
Ladar o RI 168 E 7
Ladário o BR 70-71 J 6
Ladder Creek ∼ USA 42-43 G 6
Ladd Reef ≃ 158-159 L 6
Lade o WAN 204-205 F 4
Ládi o GR 100-101 L 4
Lādiqiya, al- ☆ SYR 128-129 F 5
Ladismith o ZA 220-221 E 6
Lādīz o IR 134-135 J 4
Ladongi, Tanjung ▲ RI 164-165 G 5
Ladožskoe ozero ⇔ RUS 88-89 L 6
Ladrillero, Monte ▲ RCH 80 D 6
Ladrones, Islas ∩ PA 52-53 C 8
Ladue River ∼ CDN 20-21 U 5
Laduškin o RUS 94-95 G 4
Lady Ann Strait ≈ 24-25 f 3
Ladybrand o ZA 220-221 H 4
Lady Elliot Island ∩ AUS 178-179 M 3
Lady Evelyn Lake ⇔ CDN 38-39 D 5
Lady Evelyn Smoothwater Provincial Park ⊥ CDN 38-39 D 5
Lady Franklin Point ▲ CDN 24-25 P 6
Lady Frere o ZA 220-221 H 5
Lady Grey o ZA 220-221 H 5
Lady Grey Lake ⇔ CDN 30-31 O 5
Lady Melville Lake ⇔ CDN 24-25 a 6
Lady Newnes Ice Shelf ⊂ ARK 16 F 18
Ladysmith o CDN 32-33 J 7
Ladysmith o ZA 220-221 J 4
Ladyženka o KA 124-125 F 3
Lae ☆ PNG 183 D 4
Laefu o PNG 183 F 2
Lægervallen ▲ GRØ 26-27 q 4
Laela o EAT 214-215 G 5
Laem Ngop o THA 158-159 G 4
Lærdalsøyri ☆• N 86-87 C 6
Læsø ∩ DK 86-87 E 8
Læ̂vvajokgiedde o N 86-87 N 2
Lafayette o USA (CO) 42-43 E 6
Lafayette o USA (IN) 46-47 E 5
Lafayette o USA (TN) 48-49 E 1
Lafayette o• USA (LA) 44-45 L 4
Lafayette, Mount ▲ USA 46-47 N 3
Laferte River ∼ CDN 30-31 K 5
Lafia o WAN 204-205 H 4
Lafiagi o WAN 204-205 F 4
Laflamme, Rivière ∼ CDN 38-39 F 4
Lafoi, Chute de la ∼•• ZRE 214-215 D 6
Läft-e Nou o IR 134-135 F 5
Lagaip River ∼ PNG 183 B 3
Lagamar o BR 72-73 G 5
Lagan' ☆ RUS 126-127 G 5
Lagan ∼ S 86-87 F 8
La Gan, Mũi ▲ VN 158-159 K 5
Lagartero ∴• MEX 52-53 J 4
Lagarto o BR 68-69 K 7
Lagarto, Serra do ▲ BR 72-73 D 7
Lagbar o SN 196-197 C 7
Lagdo o CAM 204-205 K 4
Lagdo, Lac de < CAM 204-205 K 4
Lågen ∼ N 86-87 E 6
Lagernoe o RUS 108-109 F 5
Lages o BR 74-75 E 6
Lage's o USA 40-41 G 5
Lageuen o RI 162-163 A 2
Laǧǧ, Umm o KSA 130-131 E 5
Laghdaria o DZ 190-191 D 2
Laghouart ☆• DZ 190-191 D 4
La Gi o VN 158-159 J 5
l-'Aǧiǧ, Wādī ∼ IRQ 128-129 J 5
Laglan o AUS 178-179 J 2
Laġmān ◘ AFG 136-137 M 7
Lågneset ▲ N 84-85 H 4
Lagoa da Canoa o BR 68-69 K 6
Lagoa da Prata o BR 72-73 H 5
Lagoa do Capim o BR 68-69 K 6
Lagoa do Mato o BR 68-69 J 4
Lagoa Dourada o BR 72-73 H 6
Lagoa Feia o BR 68-69 E 5
Lagoa Grande o BR 68-69 H 6
Lago Agrio o EC 64-65 D 1
Lagoa Nova o MOC 218-219 G 6
Lagoa Preta o BR 72-73 K 3
Lagoa Vermelho o BR 74-75 E 7
Lago Buenos Aires, Meseta del ∸ RA 80 E 3
Lago das Pedras o BR 66-67 K 4
Lago de São Antônio o BR 66-67 F 6
Lago Dilolo o ANG 214-215 B 6
Lago Dorado, El o CO 66-67 B 2
Lago Fontana o RA 80 E 2
Lago Las Torres, Parque Nacional ⊥ RCH 80 D 2
La Gomera ∩ E 188-189 C 6
Lagong, Pulau ∩ RI 162-163 H 3
Lagonoy Gulf ≈ 160-161 E 6
Lagoon Point ▲ USA 22-23 Q 4
Lago Pasadas o RA 80 E 3
Lago Piratuba, Parque Natural do ⊥ BR 62-63 J 5
Lago Puelo, Parque Nacional ⊥ RA 78-79 D 7
Lago Ranco o RCH 78-79 C 6
Lagos o P 98-99 C 6
Lagos o WAN (LAG) 204-205 E 5
Lagos ◘ WAN 204-205 E 5
Lagos, Los o RCH 78-79 C 5
Lagos de Moreno o• MEX 50-51 J 7
Lagos Lagoon ⇔ WAN 204-205 E 5
Lagossa o EAT 212-213 B 6
Lago Verde o BR 68-69 F 3
Lago Verde o RCH 80 E 2
Lago Viedma o RA 80 D 4
Lago Vintter o RA 78-79 D 7
Lågøya ∩ N 84-85 L 2
La Grande-Deux, Réservoir < CDN 38-39 F 2
La Grande-Quatre, Réservoir < CDN 38-39 H 1
La Grande Rivière ∼ CDN 38-39 E 2
La Grande-Trois, Réservoir < CDN 38-39 G 2
La Grange ✗ AUS 172-173 E 5
La Grange o USA (GA) 48-49 F 3
La Grange o USA (KY) 46-47 F 6
La Grange o USA (TX) 44-45 J 5
La Grange Bay ≈ 172-173 E 5
La Guadeloupe o CDN 38-39 J 6
Laguani, Salar del ⇔ BOL 70-71 C 7
Lagudri o RI 162-163 B 4
Laguna o• BR 74-75 F 7
Laguna o USA 44-45 D 2
Laguna, Ilha da ∩ BR 62-63 J 6
Laguna, La o RA 78-79 H 2
Laguna, La = San Cristóbal de la Laguna o E 188-189 C 6
Laguna, Parque Nacionale ⊥ YV 60-61 K 2
Laguna, Río de la ∼ RCH 76-77 B 6
Laguna Blanca o RA 78-79 E 6
Laguna Blanca, Parque Nacional ⊥ RA 78-79 D 5
Laguna Blanca, Sierra ▲ RA 76-77 D 4
Laguna de Bay ⇔ RP 160-161 D 5
Laguna de Chacahua, Parque Natural ⊥ MEX 52-53 F 3
Laguna del Laja, Parque Nacional ⊥ RCH 78-79 D 4
Laguna del Rey o MEX 50-51 H 4
Laguna Grande, Playa ∸• DOM 54-55 L 5
Laguna Grande, Río ∼ RCH 76-77 B 5
Laguna Indian Reservation ✗ USA 44-45 D 2
Laguna Južnaja ⇔ RUS 112-113 U 5
Laguna Lamar o C 54-55 F 4
Laguna Limpia o RA 76-77 H 4
Laguna Paiva o RA 76-77 G 6
Laguna Parillar, Reserva Faunistica ⊥ RCH 80 E 6
Lagunas o PE (LAM) 64-65 C 5
Lagunas o PE (LOR) 64-65 E 4
Lagunas o RCH 70-71 C 7
Laguna Salada o DOM 54-55 K 5
Laguna San Rafael, Parque Nacional ⊥ RCH 80 D 3
Laguna Verde o YV 60-61 H 4
Laguna Verde, Salina de ⇔ RA 76-77 C 4
Laguna Yema o RA 76-77 G 3
Lagundi = Lagudri o RI 162-163 B 4
Lagundu, Tanjung ▲ RI 168 D 7
Lagunes de Montebello, Parque Nacional ⊥ MEX 52-53 J 3
Lagunillas o BOL 70-71 F 6
Lagunillas, Lago ⇔ PE 70-71 B 4
Lagunita Salada o RA 78-79 E 7
Laha o RI 166-167 E 3
La Habana ★••• C 54-55 D 3
Lahad Datu o MAL 160-161 C 10
La Hai o VN 158-159 K 4
Lahaina o• USA 48-49 D 7
Lahār o IND 138-139 G 6
Laharčana ∼ RUS 118-119 D 3
Lahat o RI 162-163 E 6
Lahemaa Rahvuspark ⊥• EST 94-95 J 2
Lahewa o RI 162-163 B 4
Lahiǧ o Y 132-133 D 7
Lāhīǧān o• IR 128-129 N 4
Lahlangubo o ZA 220-221 J 5
Laḥm, Tall al- o IRQ 130-131 K 2
Lahn ∼ D 92-93 K 3
Laholmsbukten ≈ 86-87 F 8
Lahontan Reservoir < USA 40-41 E 6
Lahore ☆••• PK 138-139 E 4
Lahri o PK 138-139 B 5
Lahti o FIN 88-89 H 6
Lahuarpia o PE 64-65 D 5
Laï ☆ TCH 206-207 C 4
Laiagam o PNG 183 B 3
Laiama o PNG 183 E 4
Lai'an o VRC 154-155 L 5
Laibin o VRC 156-157 F 5
Lai Châu ☆ VN 156-157 C 5
Laifeng o VRC 156-157 F 2
Laihia o FIN 88-89 G 5
Lai-hka o MYA 142-143 K 5
Lailā o KSA 130-131 K 6
Laila, Umm ∴• Y 132-133 C 5
Lailaba o WAN 198-199 B 6
Laimu o RI 166-167 E 3
Laingsburg o ZA 220-221 E 6
Laingsnek ▲ ZA 220-221 J 3
Laininir o RI 166-167 H 5
Lainioälven ∼ S 86-87 L 3
Lairg o GB 90-91 E 2
Lai River ∼ PNG 183 B 3
Lais o RI (BEN) 162-163 E 6
Lais o RI (SLT) 164-165 G 3
Laisälven ∼ S 86-87 H 4
Laisamis o EAK 212-213 F 3
Laitila o FIN 88-89 F 6
Laiwu o VRC 154-155 K 3
Laixi o VRC 154-155 M 3
Laiyang o VRC 154-155 M 3
Laiyuan o VRC 154-155 J 2
Laizhou o VRC 154-155 L 3
Laizhou Wan ≈ 154-155 L 3
Laja o BOL 70-71 C 5
Laja ∼ RUS 88-89 X 3
Laja, El Salto del ∼•• RCH 78-79 C 4
Laja, La o MEX 50-51 L 7
Laja, La o RCH (BIO) 78-79 C 4
Laja, La o RCH (COQ) 76-77 B 5
Laja, Laguna de la ⇔ RCH 78-79 D 4
Laja, Le o YV 62-63 D 3
Laja, Río ∼ RCH 78-79 C 4
Laja, La o YV 60-61 H 4
Lajamanu ✗ AUS 172-173 K 5
Lajas o PE 64-65 C 5
Lajas, Las o RA 78-79 D 5
Lajas, Río las ∼ RA 76-77 D 4
Laje o BR (BAH) 72-73 L 2
Laje o BR (MAR) 68-69 F 3
Laje, Cachoeira da ∼ BR 70-71 E 2
Lajeado o BR (MAR) 68-69 E 5
Lajeado o BR (RSU) 74-75 E 7
Lajeado, Serra do ▲ BR 68-69 D 7
Lajeado Grande o BR 74-75 E 7
Lajedão o BR 72-73 K 4
Lajedao, Cachoeira ∼ BR 70-71 H 2
Lajedo o BR 68-69 K 6
Lajedo, Cachoeira de ∼ BR 68-69 B 6
Lajes o BR 68-69 K 4
Lajes, Cachoeira das ∼ BR 68-69 D 5
Lajinha o BR 72-73 K 6
Lajitas o USA 44-45 F 5
Lajitas, Las o RA 76-77 E 3
Lajla, gora ▲ GE 126-127 E 6
Lajma ∼ RUS 114-115 J 5
Lajord o CDN 34-35 D 5
Laka ∼ RUS 88-89 R 4
Lakamané o RMM 202-203 F 2
Lake o USA 40-41 J 3
Lake Alma o CDN 34-35 D 6
Lake Argyle Tourist Village o AUS 172-173 J 4
Lake Arthur o USA 44-45 L 4
Lake Benton o USA 42-43 J 3
Lake Biddy o AUS 176-177 E 6
Lake Boga o AUS 180-181 G 3
Lake Bolac o AUS 180-181 G 4
Lake Cargelligo o AUS 180-181 J 2
Lake Charles o USA 44-45 L 4
Lake City o USA (FL) 48-49 G 4
Lake City o USA (SC) 48-49 J 3
Lake City o USA (SD) 42-43 J 3
Lake Clark National Park and Preserve ⊥ USA 20-21 O 6
Lake Cowichan o CDN 32-33 H 7
Lake Crystal o USA 42-43 K 3
Lake District National Park ⊥ GB 90-91 F 4
Lake Eyre Basin ∼ AUS 178-179 C 4
Lake Eyre National Park ⊥ AUS 178-179 D 5
Lakefield o AUS 174-175 H 4
Lakefield National Park ⊥ AUS 174-175 H 4
Lake Frome Regional Reserve ⊥ AUS 178-179 F 6
Lake Gairdner National Park ⊥ AUS 178-179 C 6
Lake Geneva o USA 46-47 D 4
Lake George o USA 46-47 M 4
Lake Gilles Conservation Park ⊥ AUS 180-181 D 2
Lake Grace o AUS 176-177 E 6
Lakehamu River ∼ PNG 183 D 5
Lake Harbour o CDN 36-37 P 3
Lake Havasu City o USA 40-41 G 8
Lake Hawea o NZ 182 B 6
Lake Hughes o USA 40-41 E 8
Lake Isabella o USA 40-41 E 8
Lake Itasca o USA 42-43 K 2
Lake Jackson o USA 44-45 K 5
Lake Jipe Lodge o EAK 212-213 F 5
Lake King o AUS 176-177 E 6
Lakeland o USA (FL) 48-49 H 5
Lakeland o USA (GA) 48-49 G 4
Lakeland Downs o AUS 174-175 H 4
Lake Louise o CDN 32-33 M 6
Lake Mackay Aboriginal Land ✗ AUS 172-173 J 6
Lake Malawi National Park ⊥••• MW 218-219 H 1
Lake Mason o AUS 176-177 E 3
Lake Mburo National Park ⊥ EAU 212-213 C 4
Lake Mead National Recreation Area ⊥ USA 40-41 G 7
Lake Metigoshe International Peace Garden • USA 42-43 G 1
Lake Mills o USA (IA) 42-43 L 4
Lake Mills o USA (WI) 46-47 D 4
Lake Minchumina o USA 20-21 O 5
Lake Murray o PNG 183 A 4
Lake Nash o AUS 178-179 D 1
Lake Paringa o NZ 182 B 5
Lake Placid o USA (FL) 48-49 H 6
Lake Placid o USA (NY) 46-47 M 3
Lake Providence o USA 44-45 M 3
Lake Rara National Park ⊥ NEP 144-145 C 6
Lakeside o USA (NY) 46-47 J 4
Lakeside o USA (OR) 40-41 B 4
Lakeside o USA (VA) 46-47 K 7
Lakes National Park, The ⊥ AUS 180-181 J 4
Lake Superior Provincial Park ⊥ CDN 34-35 O 7
Lake Tekapo o NZ 182 C 6
Lake Torrens National Park ⊥ AUS 178-179 D 6
Lakeview o USA (MI) 46-47 F 4
Lakeview o USA (OR) 40-41 D 4
Lake Wales o USA 48-49 H 6
Lake Way o AUS 176-177 F 3
Lakewood o USA (CO) 42-43 E 6
Lakewood o USA (NJ) 46-47 L 5
Lakewood o USA (NM) 44-45 E 3
Lake Worth o USA 48-49 H 6
Lākheri o IND 138-139 F 7
Lakhimpur o IND 142-143 B 2
Lakhipur o IND 142-143 H 3
Lakhnādon o IND 138-139 G 8
Lakhpat o IND 138-139 B 8
Lākhra o PK 134-135 M 6
Lakin o USA 42-43 G 7
Lakinsk o RUS 94-95 Q 3
Lakitsuaki River ∼ CDN 34-35 P 3
Lakki o PK 138-139 C 3
Lākkoma o GR 100-101 K 4
Laklo ∼ RI 166-167 C 6
Laklubar o RI 166-167 C 6
Lakohembi o RI 168 E 7
Lakonikós Kólpos ≈ 100-101 J 6
Lakor, Pulau ∩ RI 166-167 E 6
Lakota ☆ CI 202-203 H 7
Lakota o USA (IA) 42-43 K 4
Lakota o USA (ND) 42-43 H 1
Laksefjorden ≈ 86-87 N 1
Lakselv o N 86-87 M 1
Laksfossen ∼•• N 86-87 F 4
Lakshadweep ◘ IND 140-141 E 5
Lakshadweep Sea ≈ 140-141 F 6
Lakshimpur o BD 142-143 G 4
Lakshmipur o IND 140-141 L 3
Laktaši o BIH 100-101 F 2
Lakuan o RI 164-165 G 3
Lakuramau o PNG 183 F 2
Lalafuta ∼ Z 218-219 C 2
Lalago o EAT 212-213 D 5
Lāla Mūsa o PK 138-139 D 3
Lalandai o RI 164-165 H 4
Lalapansi o ZW 218-219 F 4
Lalapaşa ☆ TR 128-129 B 2
Lalara o G 210-211 C 3
Lalaua o MOC 218-219 K 2
Lalaua, Rio ∼ MOC 218-219 K 2
Lalbert o AUS 180-181 G 3
Lalbiti o NEP 144-145 E 7
Laleham o AUS 178-179 K 2
Laleia o RI 166-167 D 6
Lalete, Tanjung ▲ RI 166-167 C 6
Lālezār, Kūh-e ▲ IR 134-135 G 4
Lālezār, Rūd-e ∼ IR 134-135 G 3
Lālganj o IND 142-143 B 2
Lāli o IR 134-135 C 2
Lalibela o••• ETH 200-201 J 6
Laliki o RI 166-167 D 5
Lalik River ∼ PNG 183 F 3
Lalín o E 98-99 C 3
Lalin o VRC 150-151 F 5
Lalindu ∼ RI 164-165 G 5
Lalitpur o IND 138-139 G 7
Lalitpur o•• NEP 144-145 E 7
Lalla Outka ▲ MA 188-189 J 3
l-'Allāqi, Wādī ∼ ET 194-195 F 6
Lalla Rookh o AUS 172-173 D 6
Lal-lo o RP 160-161 D 3
Lalo o DY 202-203 L 6
La'l-ō-Sarǧangal o AFG 134-135 M 1
La'l Pūra o AFG 138-139 C 2
Laluangon o RI 164-165 G 4
Lalung La ▲ VRC 144-145 F 6
Lalyo o SUD 206-207 K 6
Lam o CAM 204-205 J 5
Lama o BD 142-143 H 5
Lama, ozero ⇔ RUS 108-109 Y 7
Lamadongzhao o VRC 154-155 G 2

Kusak — Lamadongzhao 279

Lamainong o RI 162-163 B 3
Lamakera o RI 166-167 B 6
Lamalaga ⩦ MA 196-197 B 3
Lamanai ∴• BH 52-53 K 3
Lamanche Valley Provincial Park ⊥ CDN 38-39 I S 5
Lamanuna o RI 166-167 B 6
Lamap ☆ VAN 184 II a 3
Lamar o USA (CO) 42-43 F 6
Lamar o USA (MO) 44-45 K 1
Lāmard o IR 134-135 E 5
Lamari River ~ PNG 183 C 4
Lamas o PE (LOR) 64-65 F 3
Lamas o PE (MAR) 64-65 D 5
Lamassa o PNG 183 G 3
Lambako o RI 164-165 H 4
Lambale o RI 164-165 H 6
Lamballe o F 90-91 F 7
Lambarene ☆• G 210-211 C 4
Lambari o BR 72-73 H 6
Lambari, Rio ~ BR 72-73 H 5
Lambaro Angan o RI 162-163 A 2
Lambatu o RI 164-165 G 5
Lambayeque o PE 64-65 C 5
Lambell, Mount ▲ AUS 172-173 L 2
Lambert, Cape ▲ AUS 172-173 C 6
Lambert, Cape ▲ PNG 183 F 3
Lambert Glacier ⊂ ARK 16 F 8
Lambert Land ⩦ GRØ 26-27 p 4
Lambertsbaai o ZA 220-221 D 6
Lamberts Bay = Lambertsbaai o ZA 220-221 D 6
Lambi o SOL 184 I d 3
Lamborn o S 86-87 G 6
Lambrama o PE 64-65 F 8
Lambton, Cape ▲ CDN 24-25 K 5
Lambu o PNG 183 F 2
Lambubalano o RI 164-165 H 6
Lambumbu Bay ≈ 184 II a 3
Lambunao o RP 160-161 E 7
Lambuya o RI 164-165 H 5
Lamdesar o RI 166-167 F 5
Lamé o TCH 206-207 B 4
Lame Burra Game Reserve ⊥ WAN 204-205 H 3
Lame Deer o USA 42-43 D 3
Lamego o• 98-99 D 4
Lameguapi o RCH 78-79 C 6
Lameirão, Área Indígena ⚔ BR 66-67 B 5
Lamen Bay o VAN 184 II b 3
Lamentin, Le o F 56 E 4
Lameroo o AUS 180-181 F 3
La Mesa o USA 40-41 F 9
Lamesa o USA 44-45 G 3
Lami o FJI 184 III b 3
Lamía o GR 100-101 J 5
Lamindo o SUD 206-207 K 6
Lamington, Mount ▲ PNG 183 E 5
Lamington National Park ⊥ AUS 178-179 M 5
Lamir, Kampung o MAL 162-163 E 3
Lamitan o RP 160-161 E 9
Lam Kachuan o THA 158-159 F 3
Lammerkop o ZA 220-221 J 2
Lammeulo o RI 162-163 A 2
Lamon Bay ≈ 160-161 D 5
Lamongan o RI 168 E 3
Lamoni o USA 42-43 L 5
Lamont o CDN 32-33 O 5
Lampa o PE 70-71 B 4
Lampa, Rio ~ PE 64-65 F 9
Lampanaih o RI 162-163 A 2
Lampang o THA 142-143 L 6
Lam Pao Reservoir ⊂ THA 158-159 G 2
Lampasas o USA 44-45 H 4
Lampazos de Naranjo o MEX 50-51 J 4
Lampedusa o I 100-101 D 7
Lampedusa, Ísola di ⌒ I 100-101 D 7
Lamper o RI 164-165 E 4
Lamphun o THA 142-143 L 6
Lampione, Ísola di ⌒ I 100-101 D 7
Lam Plaimat o THA 158-159 G 3
Lampman o CDN 34-35 E 6
Lamprey o CDN 30-31 W 6
Lampung ▫ RI 162-163 F 7
Lampung, Teluk ≈ 162-163 F 7
Lamsa, Ksar • TN 190-191 G 2
Lamu o• EAK (COA) 212-213 H 5
Lamud o PE 64-65 D 5
Lamu Island ⌒ EAK 212-213 H 5
Lamutskaja ~ RUS 112-113 R 4
Lamutskoe o RUS 112-113 P 4
Lamy o USA 44-45 E 2
Lan' ~ BY 94-95 K 5
Lana, Rio de la ~ MEX 52-53 G 3
Lanagan, Lake ⊂ AUS 172-173 H 5
Lanai ⌒ USA 48-49 D 7
Lanai City o USA 48-49 D 7
Lanalhué, Lago ⊂ RCH 78-79 C 4
Lanao, Lake ⊂ RP 160-161 F 9
Lanark o GB 90-91 F 4
Lanas o MAL 160-161 B 10
Lanbi Kyun ⌒ MYA 158-159 E 5
Lancang o VRC 142-143 M 4
Lancang Jiang ~ VRC 142-143 M 4
Lancang Jiang ~ VRC 144-145 L 5
Lancaster o• GB 90-91 F 4
Lancaster o USA (CA) 40-41 E 8
Lancaster o USA (NH) 46-47 N 3
Lancaster o USA (OH) 46-47 G 6
Lancaster o USA (PA) 46-47 K 5
Lancaster o USA (SC) 48-49 H 2
Lancaster o USA (WI) 46-47 C 4
Lancaster Sound ≈ 24-25 c 3
Lancaster State Historic Site, Fort ∴ USA 44-45 G 4
Lance Creek o USA 42-43 E 4
Lancelin o AUS 176-177 C 5
Lanciano o I 100-101 E 3
Lanco o RCH 78-79 C 5
Lancones o PE 64-65 B 4
Lancrenon, Chutes de ~• CAM 206-207 B 5
Land, De o USA 48-49 H 5
Landak ~ RI 162-163 H 4
Landana o ANG 210-211 D 6
Land Between The Lakes ⊥ USA 46-47 D 7
Landeck o A 92-93 L 5
Landegode ⌒ N 86-87 G 3
Lander o USA 42-43 C 4
Lander River ~ AUS 172-173 K 6
Lander River ~ AUS 172-173 L 6
Landete o E 98-99 G 5
Landfall Island ⌒ IND 140-141 L 3
Landi o RG 202-203 E 4
Landi Kotal o PK 138-139 C 2
Landing Lake ⊂ CDN 34-35 H 3
Landis o CDN 32-33 Q 5
Landor o AUS 176-177 D 2
Landri Sales o BR 68-69 G 5
Landšaftnyj park "Sofijivka" • UA 102-103 G 3
Land's End ▲•• GB 90-91 E 6
Landshut o D 92-93 M 4
Landskrona o•• S 86-87 F 9
Landštejn • CZ 92-93 N 4
Lanett o USA 48-49 F 3
Lanfiéra o BF 202-203 J 3
Langa o PE 64-65 D 8
Langabou o RT 202-203 L 5
Lan'ga Co ⊂ VRC 144-145 C 5
La'nga Co ⊂ VRC 144-145 C 5
Langadás o GR 100-101 J 4
Langa-Langa o ZRE 210-211 E 5
Langano Häyk' ⊂ ETH 208-209 D 5
Langar o US 136-137 J 4
Langara, Bahía ≈ 80 G 3
Langara Island ⌒ CDN 32-33 D 4
Langarūd o IR 136-137 B 6
Langatabiki o SME 62-63 G 3
Langberg o ZA (CAP) 220-221 E 6
Langberg ▲ ZA 220-221 E 4
Langberge ▲ ZA 220-221 D 6
Langbinsi o GH 202-203 K 4
Lăng Dinh o VN 156-157 D 7
Langdon o USA 42-43 H 1
Langeac o F 90-91 J 9
Langeb, Wādi ~ SUD 200-201 H 3
Langeb, Wādi ~ SUD 200-201 H 4
Langebaan o ZA 220-221 D 6
Langeberg ▲ ZA 220-221 E 6
Langeland ⌒ DK 86-87 E 9
Langenburg o CDN 34-35 F 5
Langeoog ⌒ D 92-93 J 2
Langepas o RUS 114-115 N 4
Langeri o RUS 122-123 K 3
Langfang o VRC 154-155 K 2
Langford o CDN 32-33 J 7
Langgam o RI 162-163 D 4
Langgapayung o RI 162-163 C 4
Langgur o RI 166-167 G 4
Langham o CDN 34-35 C 4
Langjökull ⊂ IS 86-87 c 2
Langka o RI 162-163 B 2
Langkahan o RI 162-163 B 3
Langkawi, Pulau ⌒ MAL 162-163 C 2
Lăng Kè o VN 156-157 D 6
Langkesi, Kepulauan ⌒ RI 164-165 J 6
Langkobale o RI 164-165 G 5
Langkon o MAL 160-161 B 9
Langlade ⌒ F 38-39 I Q 5
Langlade o USA 46-47 D 3
Langley Island ⌒ CDN 20-21 X 2
Langlo Crossing P.O. o AUS 178-179 H 4
Langlo River ~ AUS 178-179 H 3
Langmusi o VRC 154-155 C 4
Langnes o N 86-87 O 1
Lango o G 210-211 E 3
Langō, Tarso ▲ TCH 198-199 J 2
Langogne o F 90-91 J 9
Langon o F 90-91 G 9
Langøya ⌒ N 86-87 G 2
Langqên Zangbo ~ VRC 144-145 C 5
Langres o• F 90-91 K 8
Langruth o CDN 34-35 G 5
Langry ~ RUS 122-123 K 2
Langsa o RI 162-163 B 2
Långseleån ~ S 86-87 G 4
Lang Shan ▲ VRC 148-149 H 7
Lang So'n ☆ VN 156-157 E 6
Lang Suan o THA 158-159 E 6
Langtang o NEP 144-145 E 6
Langtang o WAN 204-205 H 4
Langtang National Park ⊥• NEP 144-145 E 6
Längtans udde ▲ ARK 16 G 31
Langtao o MYA 142-143 K 2
Langton Bay ≈ 24-25 J 6
Långträsk o S 86-87 K 4
Langtry o USA 44-45 G 5
Langu o THA 158-159 E 7
Langudi Rassa National Park ⊥ ETH 208-209 E 3
Languedoc ⩦ F 90-91 J 10
Languedoc-Roussillon ▫ F 90-91 J 10
Languiñeo, Arroyo ~ RA 78-79 K 4
Langui Layo, Lago ⊂ PE 70-71 B 4
Languiñeo o RA 78-79 D 7
Langxi o VRC 154-155 L 6
Langxiang o VRC 150-151 G 4
Langzhong o VRC 154-155 D 6
Laniel o CDN 38-39 E 5
Lanigan o CDN 34-35 D 5
Lanigan Creek ~ CDN 34-35 D 5
Lanín, Parque Nacional ⊥ RA 78-79 D 5
Lanín, Volcán ▲ RA 78-79 D 5
Lanjut o RI 162-163 F 5
Lankao o VRC 154-155 J 4
Lankapatti o IND 142-143 B 3
Lankovaja ~ RUS 120-121 O 4
Lanlacuni Bajo o PE 70-71 B 3
Lannemezan o F 90-91 H 10
Lannes, Cape ▲ AUS 180-181 E 4
Lannion o F 90-91 F 7
Lanquín o• GCA 52-53 K 4
Lansdale o USA 46-47 L 5
Lansdowne o AUS 172-173 H 4
Lansdowne o•• IND 138-139 G 5
Lansdowne House o CDN 34-35 N 4
L'Anse o USA 46-47 D 2
L'Anse aux Meadows National Historic Park ⊥••• CDN 38-39 R 3
L'Anse-Pleureuse o CDN 38-39 M 4
Lansford o USA 42-43 G 1
Lansing o USA (IA) 46-47 C 4
Lansing ☆ USA (MI) 46-47 F 4
Lansjärv o S 86-87 L 3
Lantewa o WAN 198-199 E 6
Lanthenay, Romorantin- o F 90-91 H 8
Lantian o VRC 154-155 F 4
Lantigiang, Pulau ⌒ RI 168 E 6
Lantz Corners o USA 46-47 J 5
Lanu o RI 164-165 G 3
Lanusei o I 100-101 B 5
Lanxi o VRC (HEI) 150-151 F 4
Lanxi o VRC (ZHE) 156-157 L 2
Lan Xian o VRC 154-155 G 2
Lanya o GH 202-203 L 5
Lanyu o RC 156-157 M 5
Lanyu ⌒ RC 156-157 M 5
Lanza o BOL 70-71 D 2
Lanza, Río ~ PE 70-71 C 4
Lanzai o WAN 204-205 J 3
Lanzarote ⌒ E 188-189 E 6
Lanzhou ☆ VRC 154-155 C 3
Laoag ☆ RP 160-161 D 3
Lào Cai ☆ VN 156-157 C 5
Laoguié o CI 202-203 H 7
Laohekou o VRC 154-155 G 5
Laokas o TCH 206-207 B 4
Laon ☆• F 90-91 J 7
Laona o USA 46-47 D 3
Laoong o RP 160-161 F 6
Laora o RI 164-165 H 6
Laos = Lao ■ LAO 156-157 C 7
Laoshan • VRC 154-155 M 3
Laotieshan Shedao Z.B. ⊥• VRC 150-151 C 8
Laouda o CI 202-203 H 6
Laoudi-Ba o CI 202-203 J 5
La'ouelissi o RIM 196-197 D 6
Laouni, Oued ~ DZ 198-199 B 2
Laouridou o CI 202-203 H 7
Lao Xanh, Cũ ⌒ VN 158-159 K 4
Laoye Ling ▲ VRC 150-151 G 6
Lapa o BR 74-75 F 5
Lapachito o RA 76-77 H 4
Lapac Island ⌒ RP 160-161 D 10
Lapai o WAN 204-205 G 4
Lapalisse o F 90-91 J 8
La Palma ⌒ E 188-189 C 6
Laparan Island ⌒ RP 160-161 D 10
Lapata o RA 80 F 7
Lapau o PNG 183 F 3
La Paz ☆• BOL 70-71 C 5
Lape o RI 168 C 7
La Pérade o CDN 38-39 H 5
Lapie River ~ CDN 20-21 Y 6
Lapihunkanan o RI 164-165 D 5
Lapining Island ⌒ RP 160-161 F 7
Lapinlahti o FIN 88-89 J 5
La Plata ☆• RA 78-79 L 3
La Plata o USA 42-43 L 5
La Pocatière o CDN 38-39 K 5
La Poile River ~ CDN 38-39 P 5
La Porte o USA (IN) 46-47 E 5
La Porte o USA (TX) 44-45 K 5
Lappa o RUS 120-121 D 4
Lappajärvi ⊂ FIN 88-89 G 5
Lappeenranta o• FIN 88-89 K 6
Lappland ⩦ 86-87 H 3
Lappy ~ RUS 120-121 D 4
Lapri o RUS 118-119 M 8
Laprida o RA 78-79 J 4
Lapseki ☆ TR 128-129 B 2
Lapševo ☆ RUS 96-97 F 6
Laptev Sea = Laptevyh, more ≈ RUS 110-111 M 2
Lapua o FIN 88-89 G 5
Lapuko o RI 164-165 H 6
La Puntilla ▲ EC 64-65 B 3
Lapus, Muntii ▲ RO 102-103 C 4
Laqiyat Arba'in < SUD 200-201 D 2
Laqiyat 'Umran < SUD 200-201 D 3
L'Áquila ☆•• I 100-101 D 3
Lār o IR 134-135 F 5
Lara o AUS 180-181 H 5
Lara ~ G 210-211 C 3
Larabanga o GH 202-203 K 5
Larache = El Araïch o MA 188-189 H 3
Larache = El-Araïch o MA 188-189 H 3
Laragh = An Láithreach o• IRL 90-91 D 5
Lārak, Ğazire-ye ⌒ IR 134-135 G 5
Laramanay o TCH 206-207 B 4
Laramate o PE 64-65 E 8
Laramie o USA 42-43 E 5
Laramie Mountains ▲ USA 42-43 D 4
Laramie National Historic Site, Fort ∴ USA 42-43 E 4
Laramie Peak ▲ USA 42-43 E 4
Laramie River ~ USA 42-43 E 4
Laranjal o BR (AMA) 66-67 E 3
Laranjal o BR (RSU) 74-75 E 7
Laranjeiras do Sul o BR 74-75 D 5
Laranjinha, Rio ~ BR 72-73 E 7
Larantuka o RI 166-167 B 6
Larat o RI 166-167 F 5
Larat, Pulau ⌒ RI 166-167 F 5
Larba o DZ 190-191 D 2
Larba o RUS 118-119 L 8
Lärbro o S 86-87 J 8
Larde o MOC 218-219 K 3
Lardeau River ~ CDN 32-33 M 6
Larder Lake o CDN 38-39 E 4
Lare o EAK 212-213 F 3
Laredo o E 98-99 F 3
Laredo o USA 44-45 H 6
Laredo Sound ≈ 32-33 F 5
Lar'egan ~ RUS 114-115 O 4
Lār-e Polūr o IR 136-137 C 7
Lares o PE 64-65 F 8
La Réunion ▫ F 224 C 7
Larga, Laguna ⊂ RA 76-77 F 6
Largeau ☆ TCH 198-199 J 4
Largo o BR 68-69 H 7
Largo o USA 48-49 G 6
Largo, Cayo ⌒ C 54-55 E 4
Lariang o RI 164-165 F 4
Lariang ~ RI 164-165 F 4
Larimore o USA 42-43 J 2
Larino o RUS 96-97 L 6
Lario = Lago di Como ⊂ I 100-101 B 2
La Rioja ▫ RA 76-77 C 5
l-'Ariš, Wādi ~ ET 194-195 F 3
Lárissa o GR 100-101 J 5
Lar'jak o RUS 114-115 Q 4
Lārkāna o• PK 138-139 B 6
Lark Harbour o CDN 38-39 P 4
Larkspur o USA 42-43 E 6
Larnaka o• CY 128-129 E 5
Larne o• GB 90-91 E 4
Larned o USA 42-43 H 6
Laro o CAM 204-205 K 4
La Romaine o CDN 38-39 O 3
La Ronge, Lac ⊂ CDN 34-35 D 3
La Ronser, ostrov ⌒ RUS 84-85 g 2
Laropi o EAU 212-213 C 2
Larrainzar o MEX 52-53 H 3
Larrey Point ▲ AUS 172-173 D 5
Larrimah o AUS 174-175 B 4
Larroque o RA 78-79 K 2
Larry's River o CDN 38-39 O 6
Lars Christensen land ⩦ ARK 16 G 7
Larsen is-shelf ⊂ ARK 16 G 30
Laru Mat, Tanjung ▲ RI 166-167 F 5
Larvik ☆ N 86-87 E 7
Lasahata o RI 166-167 E 3
Lasahau o RI 164-165 H 6
La Sal o USA 42-43 C 6
Lasalimu o RI 164-165 H 6
Lasam o RP 160-161 D 3
Lasanga Island ⌒ PNG 183 D 4
Las Animas o USA 42-43 F 6
Lasarat o ETH 208-209 F 3
Lascan, Volcán ▲ RCH 76-77 D 2
Lascano o EC 64-65 B 2
Lascano o ROU 78-79 M 2
Lascaux, Grotte de ••• F 90-91 H 9
Lascelles o AUS 180-181 G 3
Lasem o RI 168 D 3
Lashburn o CDN 32-33 Q 5
Lashio o MYA 142-143 K 4
Łask o PL 92-93 P 3
Laškargāh ☆• AFG 134-135 L 3
Lāš-ō-Ǧovein o AFG 134-135 J 3
Lasolo ~ RI 164-165 G 5
Lasoni, Tanjung ▲ RI 164-165 H 5
Las Palomas o USA 44-45 D 3
La Spézia o•• I 100-101 B 2
Laspur o PK 138-139 D 1
Lassance o BR 72-73 H 4
Lassen Peak ▲ USA 40-41 D 5
Lassen Volcanic National Park ⊥ USA 40-41 D 5
Lasseter Highway II AUS 176-177 M 2
Lassio ~ G 210-211 D 4
Lassul o PNG 183 F 3
Last Chance o USA 42-43 F 6
Last Mountain Lake ⊂ CDN 34-35 D 5
Lastoursville o G 210-211 D 4
Lastovo o HR 100-101 F 3
Lastovo ⌒ HR 100-101 F 3
Lasu o PNG 183 G 3
Las Vegas o USA (NM) 44-45 E 2
Las Vegas o•• USA (NV) 40-41 G 7
Latacunga ☆ EC 64-65 C 2
Latady Island ⌒ ARK 16 F 29
Latah Creek ~ USA 40-41 F 2
Latakia = al-Lādiqīa ☆ SYR 128-129 F 5
Latakia = Lādiqīya, al- ☆ SYR 128-129 F 5
Latalata, Pulau ⌒ RI 164-165 K 4
Lata Papalang, Bukit ▲ MAL 162-163 D 2
Lataro ⌒ VAN 184 II a 2
Latas o RCH 76-77 C 2
Lätäseno ~ FIN 88-89 G 2
Latchford o CDN 38-39 E 5
Late ⌒ TON 184 IV a 1
Lateriquique, Río ~ PY 70-71 H 6
Laterrière o CDN 38-39 J 4
Latham o AUS 176-177 D 4
Lathan o IND 142-143 J 2
Lathi = Île Sakao ⌒ VAN 184 II a 2
Lathu = Île Éléphant ⌒ VAN 184 II a 2
Latifiya, al- o IRQ 128-129 L 6
Latik < RIM 196-197 G 6
Latimojong Mountains Reserve ⊥• RI 164-165 F 5
Latina ☆ I 100-101 D 4
Latinos, Ponta dos ▲ BR 74-75 D 9
Lat'juga o RUS 88-89 U 4
Latodo o RI 168 E 6
Latoma o RI 164-165 G 5
Latorre o RCH 76-77 B 5
Latou o RI 164-165 G 5
Latouche o USA 20-21 R 6
Latouche Island ⌒ USA 20-21 R 6
Latouche Treville, Cape ▲ AUS 172-173 E 5
Látrar o IS 86-87 b 1
Latrobe o AUS 180-181 J 6
Latrobe o USA 46-47 J 5
Latu o RI 166-167 E 3
Lātūr o IND 138-139 F 10
Latura Vati, Tanjung ▲ RI 166-167 D 6
Latvia = Latvija ■ LV 94-95 J 3
Lau o PNG 183 F 3
Lau o WAN 204-205 J 4
Lauca, Parque Nacional ⊥ RCH 70-71 C 6
Laucala ⌒ FJI 184 III c 2
Laudar o Y 132-133 D 7
Lauderdale o USA 48-49 G 3
Lauenburg/Elbe o D 92-93 L 2
Lauge Koch Kyst ⩦ GRØ 26-27 U 5
Laughland Lake ⊂ CDN 30-31 X 2
Laughlen, Mount ▲ AUS 178-179 C 2
Laughlin Peak ▲ USA 44-45 E 1
Lauhkaung o MYA 142-143 L 3
Lauiya Nandangarh o IND 142-143 D 2
Launceston o AUS 180-181 J 6
Launceston o GB 90-91 E 6
Launglen o MYA 158-159 E 4
Laungmasu o IND 142-143 H 4
Launlonbok Islands ⌒ MYA 158-159 D 4
Laupahoehoe o USA 48-49 E 8
Lauqa o KSA 130-131 H 3
Laura o AUS (QLD) 174-175 H 4
Laura o AUS (SA) 180-181 E 2
Laura, Kapp ▲ N 84-85 P 2
Laurel o USA (DE) 46-47 L 6
Laurel o USA (MD) 46-47 K 6
Laurel o USA (MS) 48-49 D 4
Laurel o USA (MT) 42-43 C 3
Laurel, Cerro ▲ MEX 52-53 C 2
Laureles o ROU 76-77 K 6
Laureles Grande, Arroyo ~ ROU 76-77 J 6
Laurens o USA 48-49 G 2
Laurentians ⩦ CDN 38-39 F 5
Laurentides ⩦ CDN 38-39 H 5
Laurentides, Réserve Faunique des ⊥ CDN 38-39 J 5
Lauri o MYA 142-143 J 3
Laurie, Mount ▲ AUS 176-177 G 3
Laurie Island ⌒ ARK 16 G 32
Laurie Lake ⊂ CDN 34-35 E 2
Laurie River o CDN 34-35 F 2
Laurinburg o USA 48-49 J 2
Laurium o USA 46-47 D 2
Lauro de Freitas o BR 72-73 L 2
Lauro Sodré o BR 66-67 F 4
Lausanne ☆• CH 92-93 J 5
Laut, Kampung o MAL 162-163 F 4
Laut, Pulau ⌒ RI 162-163 H 3
Laut, Pulau ⌒ RI 162-163 G 2
Laut, Pulau ⌒ RI (KSE) 164-165 E 5
Laut, Selat ≈ 164-165 E 5
Lautaret, Col du ▲• F 90-91 L 9
Lautaro o RCH 78-79 C 5
Lautem o RI 166-167 D 6
Laut Kecil, Kepulauan ⌒ RI 164-165 D 6
Lautoka o FJI 184 III a 2
Lauttawar, Danau ⊂ RI 162-163 B 2
Lauz, Ğabal al- ▲ KSA 130-131 D 3
Lauzon o CDN 38-39 J 5
Lava Beds National Monument • USA 40-41 D 5
Lavacicle Creek • USA 40-41 D 4
Laval o CDN 38-39 H 6
Laval ☆• F 90-91 G 7
Lavalle o RA 76-77 E 5
Lāvān, Ğazire-ye ⌒ IR 134-135 E 5
Lavapié, Punta ▲ RCH 78-79 C 4
Lavaur o F 90-91 H 10
La Vérendrye, Réserve Faunique ⊥ CDN 38-39 F 5
Laverton o AUS 176-177 G 4
La Veta o USA 44-45 E 1
Laviera < EAT 212-213 F 6
Lavik o N 86-87 B 6
Lavina o USA 42-43 C 2
Lavon, Lake ⊂ USA 44-45 J 3
Lavrador, Ribeiro do ~ BR 70-71 J 3
Lavras o BR 72-73 H 6
Lavrentija o RUS 112-113 Z 4
Lavrio o GR 100-101 K 6
Lavrova, buhta ≈ RUS 112-113 O 6
Lavrova, proliv ≈ 84-85 f 2
Lavumisa o SD 220-221 K 3
Lawang o RI 168 E 3
Lawan Gopeng o MAL 162-163 D 2
Lawas o MAL 164-165 D 1
Lawashi River ~ CDN 34-35 P 4
Lawatu o RI 164-165 G 5
Lawford Islands ⌒ CDN 30-31 N 2
Lawit, Gunung ▲ RI 162-163 K 4
Lawksawk o MYA 142-143 K 5
Lawn Bay ≈ 38-39 I R 5
Lawngngaw o MYA 142-143 J 3
Lawngtlai o IND 142-143 H 4
Lawn Hill o AUS 174-175 E 6
Lawn Hill National Park ⊥ AUS 174-175 E 6
Lawowa o RI 164-165 H 6
Lawra o GH 202-203 J 4
Lawrence o NZ 182 B 6
Lawrence o USA (KS) 42-43 K 6
Lawrence o USA (MA) 46-47 N 4
Lawrenceburg o USA 48-49 E 2
Lawrenceville o USA (GA) 48-49 G 3
Lawrenceville o USA (IL) 46-47 E 6
Lawrenceville o USA (VA) 46-47 K 7
Lawrence Wells, Mount ▲ AUS 176-177 F 3
Lawtha o MYA 142-143 J 4
Lawton o USA (ND) 42-43 H 1
Lawton o USA (TX) 44-45 H 2
Lawushi Manda National Park ⊥ Z 214-215 F 7
Lay o BF 202-203 K 3
Laya o RG 202-203 D 5
Laya Dula o RG 202-203 E 5
Layang Layang o MAL 160-161 A 10
Layar, Tanjung ▲ RI 164-165 E 6
Layarat • MA 188-189 F 7
Layawng Ga o MYA 142-143 K 3
Layo o PE 70-71 B 4
Lazarev o RUS 122-123 J 2
Lazarevac o YU 100-101 H 2
Lazarevskoe o RUS 126-127 C 6
Lázaro Cárdenas o MEX (BCN) 50-51 B 2
Lázaro Cárdenas o MEX (MIC) 52-53 C 3
Lazdijai o LT 94-95 H 4
Lāze o IR 134-135 E 5
Lazio ▫ I 100-101 D 3
Lazo o RUS 110-111 V 6
Lazo o RUS 122-123 E 7
L. Bistrups Bræ ⊂ GRØ 26-27 o 5
Léach o K 158-159 G 4
Leader o CDN 32-33 Q 6
Leading Tickles o CDN 38-39 I R 4
Leadore o USA 40-41 H 3
Leadville o USA 42-43 D 6
Leaf Bay ≈ 36-37 P 5
Leaf Rapids o CDN 34-35 G 2
Leahy o USA 40-41 E 2
Leakey o USA 44-45 H 5
Lea Lea o PNG 183 D 5
Leamington o CDN 38-39 C 7
Leander o USA 44-45 J 4
Leander Point ▲ AUS 176-177 C 4
Leandra o ZA 220-221 J 3
Leandro o BR 68-69 F 5
Leandro N. Alem o RA 76-77 K 4
Learmonth o AUS 172-173 B 7
Leasi, Kepulauan ⌒ RI 166-167 E 3
Leaton State Historic Site, Fort ∴ USA 44-45 E 5
Leavenworth o USA (KS) 42-43 K 6
Leavenworth o USA (WA) 40-41 D 2
Łeba o• PL 92-93 O 1
Lebak o RP 160-161 F 9
Lebamba o G 210-211 C 5
Leban Condong, Kampung o MAL 162-163 E 3
Lébango o RCB 210-211 E 3
Lébango ~ RCB 210-211 E 3
Lebanon o USA (IN) 46-47 E 5
Lebanon o USA (KS) 42-43 H 6
Lebanon o USA (KY) 46-47 F 7
Lebanon o USA (MO) 42-43 L 7
Lebanon o USA (NH) 46-47 M 4
Lebanon o USA (OR) 40-41 C 3
Lebanon o USA (PA) 46-47 K 5
Lebanon o USA (TN) 48-49 E 1
Lebanon = Lubnān, al- ■ RL 128-129 F 5
Lebap o TM 136-137 G 4
Lebbeke o B 92-93 H 3
Lebed' ~ RUS 124-125 P 2
Lebedjan' o RUS 94-95 Q 5
Lebedyn o UA 102-103 J 2
Lebel-sur-Quévillon o CDN 38-39 F 4
Lebida o ZRE 210-211 F 5
Lebiolali < ETH 208-209 H 5
Lébiri ~ G 210-211 D 4
Lebjaž'e ☆• KA 124-125 K 3
Lebjaž'e ☆ RUS 96-97 F 5
Lebjaž'ja ~ RUS 114-115 S 7
Lebo o USA 42-43 K 6
Lebo o ZRE 206-207 F 6
Leboma ~ ZRE 210-211 F 5
Lébombi ~ G 210-211 D 5
Lebombo ▲ SD 220-221 K 2
Lebongtandai o RI 162-163 D 6
Leboni o RI 164-165 G 5
Lebon Régis o BR 74-75 E 6
Lębork o• PL 92-93 O 1
Lebowa o ZA 218-219 E 6
Lebowa (former Homeland, now part of North-Transvaal) ▫ ZA 218-219 D 6
Lebowakgomo ☆ ZA 220-221 J 2
Lebrija o E 98-99 D 6
Lebu o RCH 78-79 C 4
Lebuhanbini, Tanjung ▲ RI 164-165 F 3
Lecce ☆• I 100-101 G 4
Lecco ☆ I 100-101 B 2
Lech ~ D 92-93 L 4
Lechang o VRC 156-157 H 4
Leche, Laguna de la ⊂ MEX 50-51 H 4
Lechiguanas, Islas de las ⌒ RA 78-79 K 2
Lechuguilla, Bahía ≈ 50-51 E 5
Lēči o LV 94-95 G 3
Łęczyca o• PL 92-93 P 2
Ledang, Gunung ▲ MAL (JOH) 162-163 E 3
Ledesma o E 98-99 D 4
Ledge Point o AUS 176-177 C 5
Ledjanaja ~ RUS 108-109 b 6
Ledjanaja gora ▲ RUS 112-113 Q 6
Ledmozero o RUS 88-89 M 4
Ledo o IND 142-143 J 2
Ledong o VRC 156-157 F 7
Ledu o VRC 154-155 C 3
Leduc o CDN 32-33 O 5
Leech Lake ⊂ USA 42-43 K 2
Leech Lake Indian Reservation ⚔ USA 42-43 K 2
Leeds o• GB 90-91 G 5
Leeds o GUY 62-63 F 2
Leeds o USA (AL) 48-49 E 3
Leeds o USA (ND) 42-43 H 1
Leeds, Mount ▲ CDN 26-27 M 4
Leek o GB 90-91 F 5
Leeman o AUS 176-177 C 4
Leer (Ostfriesland) o D 92-93 J 2
Leer, Pulau ⌒ RI 166-167 H 5
Leesburg o USA (FL) 48-49 H 5
Leesburg o USA (VA) 46-47 K 6
Leeston o NZ 182 D 5
Leesville o USA 44-45 L 4
Leeton o AUS 180-181 J 3
Leeudoringstad o ZA 220-221 H 3
Leeu-Gamka o ZA 220-221 E 6
Leeupoort o ZA 220-221 H 2
Leeuwarden ☆• NL 92-93 H 2
Leeuwin, Cape ▲ AUS 176-177 C 7
Leeuwin-Naturaliste National Park ⊥ AUS 176-177 C 6
Leeuwrivier ~ ZA 220-221 F 6
Leeward Islands ⌒ 56 E 2
Leffellier o CDN 34-35 H 6
Léfini ~ RCB 210-211 E 5
Léfini, Réserve de chasse de la ⊥ RCB 210-211 E 5
Lefkáda o GR 100-101 H 5
Lefkáda ⌒ GR 100-101 H 5
Lefkónas o GR 100-101 J 4
Lefkosia ★ CY 128-129 E 5
Lefo, Mont ▲ CAM 204-205 J 6
Lefroy, Lake ⊂ AUS (WA) 176-177 F 5
Lefroy, Lake ⊂ AUS (WA) 176-177 G 5
Legape o RB 220-221 G 2
Legazpi ☆ RP 160-161 E 6
Legendre Island ⌒ AUS 172-173 C 6
Leggett o USA 40-41 C 6
Legion Mine o ZW 218-219 E 5
Legionnaire, Tunnel du • MA 188-189 J 4
Legionowo o PL 92-93 Q 2
Legkraal o ZA 218-219 E 6
Legnica ☆• PL 92-93 O 3
Legokjawa o RI 168 C 3
Le Grand, Mount ▲ AUS 176-177 G 6
Leguan Island ⌒ GUY 62-63 E 2
Legundi, Pulau ⌒ RI 162-163 F 7
Legune o AUS 172-173 J 3
Leh o• IND 138-139 F 2
Le Havre o F 90-91 H 7
Lehena o GR 100-101 H 6
Lehman Caves • USA 40-41 G 6
Lehmann o USA 44-45 F 3
Lehututu o RB 220-221 E 1
Leiah o PK 138-139 C 4
Leibnitz o A 92-93 N 5
Leicester o GB 90-91 G 5
Leichhardt, Mount ▲ AUS 172-173 L 6
Leichhardt Range ▲ AUS 174-175 J 7
Leichhardt River ~ AUS 174-175 E 5
Leiden o• NL 92-93 H 2
Leifs Ø ⌒ GRØ 28-29 W 4
Leigh Creek o AUS 178-179 E 6
Leigh Creek South o AUS 178-179 E 6
Leighton o USA 48-49 E 2
Leigong Shan ▲ VRC 156-157 F 3
Leimebamba o PE 64-65 D 5
Leimus o HN 52-53 B 4
Leine ~ D 92-93 K 2
Leinster o AUS 176-177 F 3
Leiper, Kap ▲ GRØ 26-27 P 4
Leipzig o•• D 92-93 M 3
Leira ☆ N (OPP) 86-87 D 6
Leira ☆ N (ROM) 86-87 D 5
Leiria ☆• P 98-99 C 5
Leirvik ☆ N 86-87 B 7
Leishan o VRC 156-157 F 3
Leisi o EST 94-95 H 2
Leisler, Mount ▲ AUS 176-177 K 1
Leitchfield o USA 46-47 E 7
Leite, Igarapé do ~ BR 66-67 K 5
Leith, Point ▲ CDN 30-31 K 3
Leith Harbour o GB 78-79 O 7
Leith Peninsula ⌣ CDN 30-31 K 3
Leitmeritz = Litoměřice o CZ 92-93 N 3
Leitomischl = Litomyšl o CZ 92-93 O 4
Leitre o PNG 183 A 2
Leiva, Cerro ▲ CO 60-61 D 6
Leiyang o VRC 156-157 H 3
Leizhou Bandao ⌣ VRC 156-157 G 6
Leizhou Wan ≈ 156-157 G 6
Lejone o LS 220-221 J 4
Lek ~ NL 92-93 H 3
Leka ⌒ N 86-87 E 4
Lékana o RCB 210-211 E 5
Lekatero o ZRE 210-211 J 4
Lekeleka ⌒ TON 184 IV a 2
Lékéti ~ RCB 210-211 E 5
Lekhcheb o RIM 196-197 E 5
Lékila o G 210-211 D 4
Lekitobi o RI 164-165 J 4
Lekki Lagoon ⊂ WAN 204-205 F 5
Leknes o N 86-87 F 2
Lekona ~ RCB 210-211 E 4
Lékoni o G (HAU) 210-211 E 4
Lékoni ~ G 210-211 D 4
Lekos ~ RUS 114-115 R 3
Lekoumou ▫ RCB 210-211 D 5
Leksand o S 86-87 G 6
Leksozero o RUS 88-89 L 5
Lekst, Jbel ▲ MA 188-189 G 6
Leksula o RI 166-167 D 3
Leku o ETH 208-209 D 5
Lela o RI 166-167 B 6
Lelai, Tanjung ▲ RI 164-165 L 3
Lélali ~ RCB 210-211 D 5
Leland o USA 44-45 M 3
Lel'čycy o BY 94-95 L 6
Lelehudi o PNG 183 F 6
Lelepa = Île Leleppa ⌒ VAN 184 II b 3
Leleppa, Île = Lelepa ⌒ VAN 184 II b 3
Leleque o RA 78-79 D 7
Leling o VRC 154-155 K 3
Lelinglluang o RI 166-167 F 5
Lelinta o RI 166-167 F 3
Leljuveem ~ RUS 112-113 Q 2
Lelogama o RI 166-167 B 6
Lélouma o RG 202-203 D 4
Lel'vergyrgyn ~ RUS 112-113 M 2
Lelydorp ☆ SME 62-63 G 3
Lelystad o NL 92-93 H 2
Léman, Lac ⊂ CH 92-93 J 5
Lemang o RI 162-163 E 4
Le Mans o• F 90-91 H 8
Lema Shilindi o ETH 208-209 F 6
Lematang ~ RI 162-163 E 6
Lembar o RI 168 C 7
Lembé o CAM 204-205 K 6
Lembeh, Pulau ⌒ RI 164-165 J 3
Lembeni o EAT 212-213 F 5
Lemberg = L'viv ☆• UA 102-103 D 3
Lembing, Sungai o MAL 162-163 E 3
Lembo o RI 164-165 H 5
Lemery o RP 160-161 D 6
Lemesos o• CY 128-129 E 5
Lemfu o ZRE 210-211 E 6
Lemhi, Fort ∴ USA 40-41 H 3
Lemhi Range ▲ USA 40-41 H 3
Lemhi River ~ USA 40-41 H 3
Lemieux o CDN 20-21 Y 7
Lemieux Islands ⌒ CDN 36-37 R 2
Lemin o VRC 156-157 F 5
Lem'ju ~ RUS 88-89 X 4
Lem"junskaja vozvyšennost' ▲ RUS 88-89 X 4
Lemmenjoen kansallispuisto ⊥ FIN 88-89 H 2
Lemmon o USA 42-43 F 3
Lemoenshoek o ZA 220-221 E 6
Lemolemo o RI 164-165 L 4
le Mont Saint-Michel o••• F 90-91 G 7
Lempa, Río ~ ES 52-53 K 5
Lempäälä o FIN 88-89 G 6
Lemsford o CDN 32-33 Q 6
Lemsid o MA 188-189 E 7
Lemtybož o RUS 114-115 D 3
Lemu o WAN 204-205 G 4
Lemukutan, Pulau ⌒ RI 162-163 H 4
Lemva ~ RUS 108-109 J 8
Lemvig o DK 86-87 D 8
Lemyethna o MYA 158-159 C 2
Lena ~ RUS 10-11 M 2
Lena o USA 44-45 L 4
Lenakel ☆ VAN 184 II b 4
Lenangguar o RI 168 C 7

280 Lamainong — Lenangguar

Lena River Delta = Lena Delta ≈ RUS 110-111 P 2
Leñas, Paso de las ▲ RA 78-79 D 3
Lençóis o BR 72-73 K 2
Lençois, Baía dos ≈ 68-69 F 2
Lençóis Maranhenses, Parque Nacional dos ⊥ BR 68-69 G 3
Lençóis Paulista o BR 72-73 F 7
Lenda ~ ZRE 212-213 B 3
Lendaha ~ RUS 116-117 F 6
Lendava o SLO 100-101 F 1
Lende o IR 134-135 D 3
Lendepas o NAM 220-221 D 2
Lendery o RUS 88-89 L 5
Lenge, Bandar-e o • IR 134-135 F 5
Lenger ☆ KA 136-137 L 3
Lengguru ~ RI 166-167 H 3
Lenghu o VRC 146-147 L 6
Lenglong Ling ▲ VRC 154-155 B 3
Lenglong Ling ▲ VRC 154-155 C 3
Lengo o RCA 206-207 F 6
Lengoué ~ RCB 210-211 E 3
Lengshuijiang o VRC 156-157 G 3
Lengshuitan o VRC 156-157 G 3
Leng Su Sin o VN 156-157 C 5
Lengua de Vaca, Punta ▲ RCH 76-77 B 6
Lengulu o ZRE 210-211 L 2
Lengwe National Park ⊥ MW 218-219 H 3
Lenhovda o S 86-87 G 8
Lenin ☆ TM 136-137 F 3
Lenina, kanal imeni < RUS 126-127 F 6
Lenina, pik ▲ KS 136-137 N 5
Lenina, proliv ≈ 108-109 b 3
Leninabad = Hudžand ☆ TJ 136-137 L 4
Leninabadskaja oblast' ◘ TJ 136-137 K 5
Leninakan = Gjumri o AR 128-129 K 2
Lenine o UA 102-103 J 5
Leningrad = Sankt-Peterburg ☆ ••• RUS 94-95 M 2
Leningradskaja o RUS (KRD) 102-103 L 4
Leningradskaja ~ RUS 108-109 d 3
Leningradskij o RUS 112-113 U 2
Leningradskij o TJ 136-137 M 5
Leningradskij, lednik ⊂ RUS 108-109 d 2
Leninogorsk o KA 124-125 N 3
Leninogorsk ☆ RUS 96-97 H 6
Leninsk o KA 126-127 P 5
Leninsk o RUS 96-97 D 9
Leninsk o US 136-137 N 4
Leninskij o KA 124-125 K 2
Leninskij o TJ 136-137 L 5
Leninsk-Kuzneckij ☆ RUS 114-115 T 7
Leninsk-Kuznetskiy = Leninsk-Kuzneckij ☆ RUS 114-115 T 7
Leninskoe o KA (AKT) 126-127 M 2
Leninskoe ☆ KA (KST) 124-125 D 2
Leninskoe o KS 136-137 N 4
Leninskoe o RUS 96-97 E 4
Lenivaja ~ RUS 108-109 X 4
Lenkau o PNG 183 D 2
Lenkivci o UA 102-103 E 2
Lenkoran' = Lankaran o • AZ 128-129 N 3
Lenmalu o RI 166-167 F 2
Lennox o USA 42-43 J 4
Lennox, Isla ⌒ RCH 80 G 7
Leno-Angarskoe, plato ∸ RUS 116-117 L 8
Leno-Angarskoe plato ∸ RUS 116-117 L 8
Lenoir o USA 48-49 H 2
Lenoir City o USA 48-49 F 2
Lenora o USA 42-43 H 6
Lenore Lake ⊖ CDN 34-35 D 4
Lenox o USA 42-43 K 5
Lens o F 90-91 J 6
Lensk ☆ • RUS 118-119 G 5
Lenskie stolby • RUS 118-119 N 5
Lenswood o CDN 34-35 F 4
Lent'evo o RUS 94-95 P 2
Lentiira o FIN 88-89 K 4
Lentini o I 100-101 E 6
Lenya o MYA 158-159 E 5
Léo o BF 202-203 J 4
Leoben o A 92-93 N 5
Léogâne o RH 54-55 J 5
Leok o RI 164-165 G 3
Leola o USA 42-43 H 3
Leominster o • GB 90-91 F 5
León o • E 98-99 E 3
Léon o F 90-91 G 10
León o • MEX 50-51 J 7
León ☆ •• NIC 52-53 L 5
León, Cerro ▲ MEX 52-53 F 3
León, Cerro ▲ PY 70-71 G 7
León, Montes de ▲ E 98-99 D 3
Leona, La o YV 60-61 K 3
Leona, Punta la ▲ EC 64-65 B 2
Leonard o USA (ND) 42-43 J 2
Leonard o USA (TX) 44-45 J 3
Leonardville o NAM 220-221 D 1
Leoncio Prado o PE 64-65 E 3
Leonídio o GR 100-101 J 6
Leonidovka ~ RUS 122-123 K 4
Leonidovo o RUS 122-123 K 4
Leonora o AUS 176-177 F 4
Leon River ~ USA 44-45 H 4
Leont'eva, ostrov ⌒ RUS 112-113 L 1
León Viejo ∴ • NIC 52-53 L 5
Leopold Downs o AUS 172-173 G 4
Leopold II, Lac = Lac Mai-Ndombe ⊖ ZRE 210-211 G 5
Leopoldina o BR 72-73 J 6
Leopold Island ⌒ CDN 36-37 S 2
Leopold M'Clintock, Cape ▲ CDN 24-25 N 2
Leopoldo de Bulhões o BR 72-73 F 4
Leopoldsburg o B 92-93 H 3
Léopoldville = Kinshasa ★ • ZRE 210-211 E 6
Leoti o USA 42-43 G 6
Léoua o RCA 206-207 E 6
Léoura o BF 202-203 L 3
Leova ☆ MD 102-103 F 4
Leovo = Leova ☆ MD 102-103 F 4
Lepar, Pulau ⌒ RI 162-163 G 6
Lepaterique o HN 52-53 L 4
Lepel' ☆ BY 94-95 L 4
Lepellé, Rivière ~ CDN 36-37 N 4
Lephephe o RB 218-219 C 6
Leping o VRC 156-157 K 2
Leplja ~ RUS 114-115 F 4
Lépoura o GR 100-101 K 5
Lepsy o KA 124-125 L 5
Lepsy ~ KA 124-125 M 6
Leptis Magna = Labdah ∴ ••• LAR 192-193 F 1
Leptokariá o GR 100-101 J 4
Leqceiba o RIM (BRA) 196-197 C 6
Leqceiba o RIM (GOR) 196-197 D 6
Lequena o RCH 76-77 C 1
Léraba ~ CI 202-203 H 5
Léraba Occidentale ~ CI 202-203 H 4
Lérabe o SN 196-197 C 6
Lercara Friddi o I 100-101 D 6
Lerdo de Tejada o MEX 52-53 G 2
Léré o RMM 202-203 H 2
Léré o TCH 206-207 B 4
Lere o WAN (BAU) 204-205 H 4
Lere o WAN (KAD) 204-205 H 3
Léré, Lac de ⊖ TCH 206-207 B 4
Lérez, Río ~ E 98-99 C 3
Lérida = Lleida o •• E 98-99 H 4
Lerma o E 98-99 F 3
Lerma o MEX 52-53 J 2
Lermá, Valle de ∸ RA 76-77 E 3
Lerneb o RMM 196-197 H 6
Leron Plains o PNG 183 D 4
Leros ⌒ GR 100-101 L 6
Leross o CDN 34-35 E 5
Lerum ☆ S 86-87 F 8
Lerwick o GB 90-91 G 1
Ler Zerai < SUD 206-207 H 3
Lescoff o F 90-91 E 7
Lesdiguières, Lac ⊖ CDN 36-37 M 4
Leshan o VRC 156-157 C 2
Leshan Dafo • VRC 156-157 C 2
Lesjaskog o N 86-87 D 5
Lesjöfors o S 86-87 G 7
Leskino o RUS 108-109 S 5
Lesko o • PL 92-93 R 4
Leskovac o • YU 100-101 H 3
Leskovik o • AL 100-101 H 4
Leslie o USA (AR) 44-45 L 2
Leslie o USA (ID) 40-41 H 4
Leslie, Kap ▲ GRØ 26-27 n 8
Lesmiegan ~ RUS 114-115 G 2
Lesnaja o RUS 120-121 T 4
Lesnoj Gorodok o RUS 118-119 F 10
Lesnoj Voronež ~ RUS 94-95 R 5
Lesogorsk o RUS 122-123 K 4
Lesosibirsk o RUS 116-117 F 6
Lesotho ■ LS 220-221 H 4
Lesozavodsk o RUS 122-123 E 6
Lesozavodskij o RUS 122-123 M 6
Lesperon o F 90-91 G 10
Lessau o PNG 183 D 2
Léssé ~ RCA 206-207 D 6
Lesser Antilles ∸ 56 B 5
Lesser Hinggan Range = Xiao Hinggan Ling ▲ VRC 150-151 F 2
Lesser Slave Lake ⊖ CDN 32-33 N 4
Lesser Slave Lake Provincial Park ⊥ CDN 32-33 N 4
Lesser Slave River ~ CDN 32-33 N 4
Lesser Sunda, Kepulauan ⌒ RI 168 C 7
Lesser Sunda Islands = Sunda Kecil, Kepulauan ⌒ RI 168 C 6
Lestijärvi o FIN 88-89 H 5
Lesueur, Mount ▲ AUS 176-177 C 5
Lesung, Tanjung ▲ RI 168 A 3
Lesvos ⌒ GR 100-101 L 5
Leszno ☆ • PL 92-93 O 3
Letaba o ZA 218-219 F 6
Letas, Lac = Tes, Lake ⊖ VAN 184 II a 2
Letellier o CDN 34-35 H 6
Letfata o RIM 196-197 D 6
Lethbridge o • CDN 32-33 O 7
Lethem ☆ GUY 62-63 E 4
Leti, Kepulauan ⌒ RI 166-167 D 6
Leti, Pulau ⌒ RI 166-167 D 6
Letiahau ~ RB 218-219 B 5
Leticia o CO 66-67 C 5
Leting o VRC 154-155 L 2
Letka o RUS 96-97 F 4
Letkhokpin o MYA 142-143 K 4
Letlhakeng o RB 220-221 G 2
Letnica o BG 102-103 D 6
Letnij bereg ~ RUS 88-89 O 4
Letniy Bereg = Letnij bereg ~ RUS 88-89 O 4
Letnjaja ~ RUS 112-113 H 3
Letnjaja Zolotica o RUS 88-89 O 4
Letoda o RI 166-167 E 6
Letohatchee o USA 48-49 E 3
Letoon ∴ ••• TR 128-129 C 4
Letpadan o MYA 158-159 C 2
Letpan o MYA 142-143 J 6
Letsitele o ZA 218-219 F 6
Letsok-Aw Kyun ⌒ MYA 158-159 E 5
Letta o CAM 204-205 K 6
Letterkenny o IRL 90-91 D 4
Letwurung o RI 166-167 E 5
Léuá o ANG 216-217 F 5
Leuaniua ⌒ SOL 184 I d 1
Leupp o USA 44-45 B 2
Leura o AUS 178-179 K 2
Leuser, Gunung ▲ RI 162-163 B 3
Leušinskij Tuman, ozero ⊖ RUS 114-115 H 5
Leuven o • B 92-93 H 3
Levaja Avača ~ RUS 120-121 S 7
Levaja Bojarka ~ RUS 108-109 b 6
Levaja Bureja ~ RUS 122-123 F 3
Levaja Hetta ~ RUS 114-115 L 2
Levaja Kamenka ~ RUS 110-111 d 6
Levaja Lesnaja ~ RUS 120-121 T 4
Levaja Mama ~ RUS 118-119 E 7
Levaja Šapina ~ RUS 120-121 T 6
Levaja Vetv', kanal < RUS 102-103 N 5
Levaja Županova ~ RUS 120-121 S 6
Levan o USA 40-41 J 6
Levanger o N 86-87 E 5
Levante, Riviera di ~ I 100-101 B 2
Levantine Basin ≃ 128-129 B 6
Levasi o RUS 126-127 G 6
Levdiev, ostrov ⌒ RUS 108-109 M 7
Level, Isla ⌒ RCH 80 C 2
Levelland o USA 44-45 F 3
Leven o GB 90-91 F 3
Leven ~ GB 90-91 F 3
Leven Bank ≃ 222-223 E 4
Leveque, Cape ▲ AUS 172-173 F 4
Lever, Rio ~ BR 68-69 C 7
Leverett Glacier ⊂ ARK 16 E 0
Leverkusen o D 92-93 J 3
Levick, Mount ▲ ARK 16 F 17
Levídi o GR 100-101 J 6
Levin o NZ 182 E 4
Levinópolis o BR 72-73 H 3
Lévis o CDN 38-39 J 5
Levis, Lac ⊖ CDN 30-31 L 4
Levittown o USA 46-47 L 5
Levkáditi o GR 100-101 J 5
Levkinskaja o RUS 88-89 V 4
Levroux o F 90-91 H 8
Levski o BG 102-103 D 6
Levuka o FJI 184 III b 2
Levyj Hetagčan ~ RUS 112-113 J 5
Levyj Kedon ~ RUS 112-113 K 4
Levyj Mamakan ~ RUS 118-119 F 7
Léwa o CAM 204-205 K 5
Lewa o RI 168 D 7
Lewe o MYA 142-143 K 6
Lewellen o USA 42-43 F 5
Lewes o USA 46-47 L 6
Lewes Plateau ▲ CDN 20-21 W 5
Lewis and Clark Lake ⊖ USA 42-43 J 4
Lewisburg o USA (OR) 40-41 C 3
Lewisburg o USA (TN) 48-49 E 2
Lewisburg o USA (WV) 46-47 H 7
Lewis Hills ▲ CDN 38-39 P 4
Lewis Pass ▲ NZ 182 D 5
Lewis Point o USA 22-23 R 3
Lewisporte o CDN 38-39 R 4
Lewis Range ▲ AUS 172-173 J 6
Lewis Range ▲ USA 40-41 H 1
Lewis River ~ USA 40-41 C 2
Lewis Smith Lake ⊖ USA 48-49 E 3
Lewiston o USA (ID) 40-41 F 2
Lewiston o USA (IN) 46-47 E 5
Lewiston o USA (ME) 46-47 N 3
Lewiston o USA (UT) 40-41 J 5
Lewistown o USA (IL) 46-47 C 5
Lewistown o USA (MT) 42-43 C 2
Lewistown o USA (PA) 46-47 K 5
Lewisville, Lake ⊖ USA 44-45 J 3
Lewoleba o RI 166-167 B 6
Lexington o USA (KY) 46-47 F 6
Lexington o USA (NC) 48-49 H 2
Lexington o USA (NE) 42-43 H 5
Lexington o USA (TN) 48-49 D 2
Lexington o USA (VA) 46-47 J 7
Lexington Park o USA 46-47 K 6
Leybourne Islands ⌒ CDN 36-37 R 2
Leyburn o AUS 178-179 L 5
Leye o VRC 156-157 E 4
Leyson Point ▲ CDN 36-37 J 3
Leyte ⌒ RP 160-161 F 7
Leyte Gulf ≈ 160-161 F 7
Lezama o YV 60-61 H 3
Lezhë ☆ •• AL 100-101 G 4
Lezhi o VRC 154-155 D 6
l-Ġadaf, Wādī ~ IRQ 128-129 J 6
l-Ġaut, Wādī ~ SYR 128-129 J 5
L'gotny, mys ▲ RUS 120-121 H 5
L'gov o RUS 102-103 J 2
L'govskij, Dmitriev o RUS 94-95 O 5
l-Ḥail, Wādī ~ SYR 128-129 H 5
Lhari o VRC 144-145 J 5
L'Haridon Bight ≈ 176-177 B 3
l-Ḥarit, Wādī ~ ET 194-195 F 5
Lhasa ☆ •• VRC 144-145 H 6
Lhasa He ~ VRC 144-145 H 6
Lhazê o • VRC 144-145 F 6
Lhokseumawe o RI 162-163 B 2
Lhoksukon o RI 162-163 B 2
Lhorong o VRC 144-145 K 5
Lhotse ▲ NEP 144-145 F 7
Lhuntsi o BHT 142-143 G 2
Lhünzê o VRC 144-145 J 6
Li o THA 158-159 E 2
Lia, Tanjung ▲ RI 166-167 D 3
Liambezi, Lake ⊖ NAM 218-219 C 3
Liang o RI 164-165 H 4
Liangcheng o VRC (NMZ) 154-155 H 1
Liangcheng o VRC (SHD) 154-155 L 4
Lianghe o VRC (SIC) 156-157 F 2
Lianghe o VRC (YUN) 142-143 L 3
Lianghekou o VRC 154-155 D 5
Liangping o VRC 154-155 E 6
Liangpran, Gunung ▲ RI 164-165 D 3
Liangshan o VRC 154-155 K 4
Lianhua o VRC 156-157 H 3
Lianhua Shan ▲ VRC 156-157 J 5
Lianjiang o VRC (FUJ) 156-157 L 3
Lianjiang o VRC (GDG) 156-157 G 6
Lianping o VRC 156-157 J 4
Lianshan o VRC (GDG) 156-157 H 4
Lianshan o VRC (SHD) 154-155 K 4
Lianshan o VRC (SIC) 154-155 D 6
Lianshui o VRC 154-155 L 5
Liantang o VRC 156-157 G 4
Lian Xian o VRC 156-157 H 4
Lianyuan o VRC 156-157 G 3
Lianyungang o VRC 154-155 L 4
Lianyungang (Xinpu) o VRC 154-155 L 4
Liaocheng o VRC 154-155 J 3
Liao Dao • VRC 144-145 M 2
Liaodong Bandao ∨ VRC 150-151 D 8
Liaodong Wan ≈ 150-151 C 7
Liaodun o VRC 146-147 L 4
Liao He ~ VRC 150-151 D 6
Liaoning ◘ VRC 150-151 C 6
Liao Shangjingcheng Yizhi ∴ • VRC 148-149 O 6
Liaotung, Gulf of = Liaodong Wan ≈ VRC 150-151 C 7
Liaoyang o VRC 150-151 D 7
Liaoyuan o VRC 150-151 E 6
Liaozhong o VRC 150-151 D 7
Liao Zhongjingcheng Yizhi • VRC 148-149 O 7
Liāquatpur o PK 138-139 C 5
Liard Highway II CDN 30-31 H 5
Liard Plateau ▲ CDN 30-31 F 5
Liard River ~ CDN 30-31 H 5
Liat, Pulau ⌒ RI 162-163 G 6
Libano o CO 60-61 D 5
Libano o RA 78-79 J 4
Libanos Gedam, Debre • ETH 208-209 D 4
Libao o VRC 154-155 M 5
Libatemo o RI 164-165 H 5
Libau o CDN 34-35 H 5
Libba o WAN 204-205 F 3
Libby o USA 40-41 G 1
Libenge o ZRE 210-211 G 2
Liberal o USA 44-45 G 1
Liberator Lake ⊖ USA 20-21 L 2
Liberdade, Rio ~ BR 68-69 B 6
Liberec o • CZ 92-93 N 3
Liberia ☆ CR 52-53 B 6
Liberia ■ LB 202-203 E 6
Libertad o RA 76-77 J 6
Libertad o ROU 78-79 L 3
Libertad o YV 60-61 G 3
Libertad, La o ES 52-53 K 5
Libertad, La o HN 52-53 L 4
Libertador General San Martín o RA (JU) 76-77 E 2
Libertador General San Martín o RA (SLU) 78-79 G 2
Liberty o USA (KY) 46-47 F 7
Liberty o USA (NY) 46-47 L 5
Liberty o USA (TX) 44-45 K 4
Libjo o RP 160-161 F 7
Libmanan o RP 160-161 E 6
Libobo, Tanjung ▲ RI 164-165 L 4
Libode o ZA 220-221 J 5
Liboi o EAK 212-213 H 3
Liboko o ZRE 210-211 H 2
Libono o LS 220-221 J 4
Liboumba ~ G 210-211 D 3
Libourne o F 90-91 G 9
Librazhd ☆ • AL 100-101 H 4
Libreville ☆ • G 210-211 B 3
Librija o CO 60-61 E 4
Libro Point ▲ RP 160-161 C 7
Libuganon ~ RP 160-161 F 9
Libya = Libiyā ■ LAR 192-193 D 4
Libyan Desert = as-Sahrā' al-Libiyā ∸ LAR 192-193 K 3
Licancabur, Volcán ▲ RCH 76-77 D 2
Licata o I 100-101 D 6
Lice ☆ TR 128-129 J 3
Licenciado Matienzo o RA 78-79 K 4
Lichang o VRC 154-155 H 6
Licheng o VRC 154-155 H 3
Lichinga ☆ MOC 218-219 H 1
Lichinga, Planalto de ▲ MOC 218-219 H 1
Lichtenburg o ZA 220-221 H 3
Lichteneger, Lac ⊖ CDN 38-39 G 2
Licinio de Almeida o BR 72-73 J 3
Liciro o MOC 218-219 J 3
Licking o USA 46-47 C 7
Licking River ~ USA 46-47 F 6
Licuare, Rio ~ MOC 218-219 J 3
Licungo, Rio ~ MOC 218-219 J 3
Lida ☆ BY 94-95 J 5
Lidan ~ S 86-87 F 7
Liddon Gulf ≈ 24-25 P 3
Liden o S 86-87 H 5
Lidi, Mayo ~ CAM 206-207 B 4
Lidia, Rio ~ PE 70-71 B 2
Lidji ~ ZRE 210-211 F 5
Lidjombo o RCA 210-211 F 2
Lidköping ☆ S 86-87 F 7
Lido o RN 204-205 E 2
Lido di Ostia o I 100-101 D 4
Lidskaja ravnina ▲ 94-95 J 5
Lidzbark Warmiński o • PL 92-93 Q 1
Liebenthal o CDN 32-33 Q 6
Liebenthal o USA 42-43 H 6
Liebig, Mount ▲ AUS 176-177 L 1
Liechtenstein ■ FL 92-93 K 5
Liège ☆ • B 92-93 H 3
Lieksa o FIN 88-89 L 5
Liemianzheng o VRC 154-155 E 6
Lienz o A 92-93 M 5
Liepāja ☆ •• LV 94-95 G 3
Lier o • B 92-93 H 3
Lierre = Lier o • B 92-93 H 3
Lietnik o USA 20-21 F 5
Lièvre, Rivière du ~ CDN 38-39 G 5
Liezen o A 92-93 N 5
Lifamatola, Pulau ⌒ RI 164-165 K 4
Lifford ☆ IRL 90-91 D 4
Lifjell ▲ N 86-87 D 7
Lifuka ⌒ TON 184 IV a 1
Lifune ~ ANG 216-217 C 4
Lifupa Lodge o MW 218-219 G 1
Ligao o RP 160-161 E 6
Ligar o TCH 206-207 C 4
Lightfoot Lake ⊖ AUS 176-177 G 4
Light o RP 160-161 F 7
Light, Cape ▲ ARK 16 F 30
Lighthouse Beach ∸ • BS 54-55 G 2
Lighthouse Reef ⌒ BH 52-53 L 3
Lightning Ridge o AUS 178-179 J 5
Ligonha, Rio ~ MOC 218-219 K 2
Ligonier o USA 46-47 F 5
Ligowola o EAT 214-215 J 6
Ligua, Caleta la ≈ 78-79 D 2
Ligua, La o RCH (COQ) 76-77 B 6
Ligua, La o RCH (VAL) 78-79 D 2
Ligua, Rio la ~ RCH 78-79 D 2
Ligunga o EAT 214-215 J 6
Ligúria ◘ I 100-101 B 2
Ligurian Sea = Ligure, Mar ≈ 100-101 B 3
Ligurta o USA 40-41 G 9
Lihás o GR 100-101 J 5
Lihir, al- o KSA 130-131 F 5
Lihir Group ⌒ PNG 183 G 2
Lihir Island ⌒ PNG 183 G 2
Lihoslavl' ☆ RUS 94-95 O 3
Lihou Reefs and Cays ⌒ AUS 174-175 M 5
Lihovskoj o RUS 102-103 M 3
Lihue o USA 48-49 C 7
Lihuel Calel, Parque Nacional ⊥ RA 78-79 G 4
Lihula o EST 94-95 H 2
Liivi Laht ≈ 94-95 H 2
Lijiang o • VRC (YUN) 142-143 M 2
Lijiang •• VRC (GXI) 156-157 G 4
Lik ~ LAO 156-157 C 7
Lik, Pulau ⌒ RI 166-167 K 2
Likala o ZRE 210-211 G 3
Likame ~ ZRE 210-211 H 2
Likasi o ZRE 214-215 D 6
Likati o ZRE (Hau) 210-211 J 2
Likati ~ ZRE 210-211 J 2
Likely o CDN 32-33 K 5
Likely o USA 40-41 D 5
Likete o ZRE 210-211 H 4
Likisia o RI 166-167 C 6
Likoma Islands ⌒ MW 214-215 H 7
Likoto o ZRE 210-211 J 3
Likouala ◘ RCB 210-211 F 2
Likouala ~ RCB 210-211 E 3
Likouala aux Herbes ~ RCB 210-211 F 3
Likum o PNG 183 D 2
Likuyu o EAT 214-215 J 6
Lilarea o AUS 178-179 H 2
Lilbourn o USA 46-47 D 7
L'Île-d'Entrée o CDN 38-39 O 5
Liliāni o PK 138-139 D 3
Lilikse o GH 202-203 J 4
Liling o VRC 156-157 H 3
Lilla o PK 138-139 D 3
Lille ☆ F 90-91 J 6
Lille Bælt ≈ DK 86-87 D 9
Lillehammer ☆ N 86-87 E 6
Lille Hellefiskebanke ≃ 28-29 N 4
Lilles, Punta ▲ RCH 78-79 D 2
Lillesand ☆ • N 86-87 D 7
Lillestrøm o N 86-87 E 7
Lillico Point ▲ CDN 36-37 K 6
Lillooet o CDN 32-33 K 6
Lillooet River ~ CDN 32-33 J 6
Lilo ~ ZRE 210-211 K 4
Lilongwe ★ • MW 218-219 G 1
Lilo Viego o RA 76-77 F 4
Liloy o RP 160-161 E 8
Lilydale o AUS 180-181 J 6
Lim ~ RCA 206-207 B 5
Lim ~ YU 100-101 G 3
Lima o OM 134-135 G 6
Lima ★ ••• PE 64-65 D 8
Lima o PY 76-77 J 2
Lima o USA 46-47 F 5
Lima, La o • HN 52-53 L 4
Limache o RA 76-77 F 5
Limache o RCH 78-79 D 2
Limal o BOL 76-77 E 2
Liman ☆ RUS 126-127 G 5
Limão, Igarapé do ~ BR 66-67 K 6
Limão do Curuá o BR 62-63 J 5
Limapuluh o RI 162-163 C 3
Limar o RI 166-167 D 5
Limari, Río ~ RCH 76-77 B 6
Limasawa Island ⌒ RP 160-161 F 8
Limassa o RCA 206-207 F 6
Limaubungkuk, Tanjung ▲ RI 162-163 F 6
Limavady o GB 90-91 D 4
Limay, Río ~ RA 78-79 E 5
Limba Limba ~ EAT 214-215 G 4
Limbang o MAL 164-165 D 1
Limbani o PE 70-71 C 4
Limbasa o ZRE 206-207 F 6
Limbaži ☆ •• LV 94-95 J 3
Limbdi o IND 138-139 C 8
Limbe o MW 218-219 H 2
Limbé o RH 54-55 J 5
Limbé = Victoria o • CAM 204-205 H 6
Limbla o AUS 178-179 C 2
Limbo, Pulau ⌒ RI 164-165 J 4
Limboto o RI 164-165 H 3
Limbunan o RP 160-161 E 9
Limbung o RI 164-165 F 5
Limbunya o AUS 172-173 J 4
Limburg an der Lahn o • D 92-93 K 3
Lime Acres o ZA 220-221 F 4
Limeira o BR (MIN) 72-73 H 4
Limeira o BR (PAU) 72-73 G 7
Limerick o CDN 34-35 C 6
Limerick = Luimneach o • IRL 90-91 C 5
Limestone, Lake ⊖ USA 44-45 J 4
Limestone Lake ⊖ CDN 34-35 J 2
Limestone Point ▲ CDN 34-35 G 4
Limestone Rapids ~ CDN 34-35 M 3
Limestone River ~ CDN 34-35 J 2
Limfjorden ≈ 86-87 D 8
Limgytynot ~ RUS 112-113 W 4
Limia, Río ~ E 98-99 D 3
Limingen ⊖ N 86-87 F 4
Liminka o FIN 88-89 H 4
Limmen Bight ≈ 174-175 C 4
Limmen Bight Aboriginal Land ⊼ AUS 174-175 C 4
Limmen Bight River ~ AUS 174-175 C 4
Limnos ⌒ GR 100-101 K 5
Limnu ~ RUS 120-121 E 6
Limoeiro o BR 68-69 L 5
Limoeiro do Ajurú o BR 62-63 K 6
Limoeiro do Norte o BR 68-69 J 4
Limoges ☆ • F 90-91 H 9
Limon o USA 42-43 F 6
Limonar o C 54-55 H 4
Limousin ◘ F 90-91 H 9
Limoux o F 90-91 J 10
Limpio o PY 76-77 J 3
Limpopo o MOC 218-219 G 6
Limpopo ~ ZA 218-219 E 6
Limpopo, Rio ~ MOC 220-221 L 2
Limppityľky ~ RUS 114-115 R 2
Limptèkan ~ RUS 116-117 M 4
Limuri ~ RUS 122-123 H 3
Limuru o EAK 212-213 F 4
Lina o KSA 130-131 H 3
Linaälven ~ S 86-87 K 3
Linahamari o RUS 88-89 L 2
Lin'an o VRC 154-155 L 6
Linao o RP 160-161 D 3
Linao Point ▲ RP 160-161 E 9
Linapacan Island ⌒ RP 160-161 C 7
Linapacan Strait ≈ 160-161 C 7
Linares o E 98-99 F 5
Linares o MEX 50-51 K 5
Linares o RCH 78-79 D 3
Linas, Monte ▲ I 100-101 B 5
Lincang o VRC 142-143 M 4
Linchang o VRC 154-155 F 5
Linchuan o VRC 156-157 K 3
Lincoln ☆ • GB 90-91 G 5
Lincoln o NZ 182 D 5
Lincoln o RA 78-79 J 3
Lincoln o USA (IL) 46-47 D 5
Lincoln o USA (KS) 42-43 H 6
Lincoln o USA (ME) 46-47 O 3
Lincoln o USA (NH) 46-47 N 3
Lincoln ☆ USA (NE) 42-43 J 5
Lincoln Birthplace National Historic Site, Abraham ∴ USA 46-47 F 7
Lincoln Boyhood National Memorial ∴ USA 46-47 E 6
Lincoln Caverns • USA 46-47 J 5
Lincoln City o USA 40-41 C 3
Lincoln Highway II AUS 180-181 D 2
Lincoln National Park ⊥ AUS 180-181 C 3
Lincoln Sea ≈ 26-27 U 2
Lincolnton o USA 48-49 H 2
Lindagadaw o MYA 142-143 J 5
Lindau (Bodensee) o •• D 92-93 K 5
Linde ~ RUS 110-111 N 7
Linde ~ RUS 110-111 M 6
Linde ~ RUS 118-119 M 3
Lindela o MOC 218-219 H 7
Lindeman Group ⌒ AUS 174-175 K 7
Linden o CDN 32-33 O 6
Linden o USA 48-49 E 2
Lindenows Fjord ≈ 28-29 T 6
Lindesnes ▲ N 86-87 C 8
Lindhard Ø ⌒ GRØ 26-27 o 5
Lindi ◘ EAT 214-215 J 5
Lindi ☆ • EAT (LIN) 214-215 K 5
Lindi ~ ZRE 210-211 K 3
Lindian o VRC 150-151 E 4
Lindi Bay ≈ 214-215 K 5
Lindis Pass ▲ NZ 182 B 6
Lindley o ZA 220-221 H 3
Lindleyspoort o ZA 220-221 H 2
Líndos o •• GR 100-101 M 6
Lindsay o CDN 38-39 E 6
Lindsay o USA 42-43 E 2
Lindsay, Mount ▲ AUS 176-177 K 3
Lindsborg o USA 42-43 J 6
Lindström Peninsula ∨ CDN 24-25 e 2
Lindu, Danau ⊖ RI 164-165 G 4
Linduri o VAN 184 II a 2
Línea de la Concepción, La o E 98-99 E 6
Line Islands ⌒ KIB 14-15 N 7
Linejnoe o RUS 96-97 E 10
Linek o RP 160-161 F 9
Lineville o USA 42-43 L 5
Linfen o VRC 154-155 G 3
Linganamakki Reservoir ⊖ IND 140-141 F 3
Lingayen Gulf ≈ 160-161 D 4
Lingbao o VRC 154-155 G 4
Lingbi o VRC 154-155 K 5
Lingbim o CAM 206-207 B 6
Lingen (Ems) o D 92-93 J 2
Lingga o MAL 162-163 J 4
Lingga, Kepulauan ⌒ RI 162-163 F 5
Lingga, Pulau ⌒ RI 162-163 F 5
Lingkeh o RI 164-165 G 4
Lingkobu, Tanjung ▲ RI 164-165 G 5
Lingle o USA 42-43 E 4
Linglingujym, buhta ≈ RUS 112-113 R 6
Lingomo o ZRE (EQU) 210-211 J 4
Lingomo o ZRE (EQU) 210-211 J 3
Lingqi D. • VRC 156-157 L 2
Lingqiu o VRC 154-155 J 2
Lingshan o VRC 156-157 F 5
Lingshan Dao ⌒ VRC 154-155 M 4
Lingshi o VRC 154-155 G 3
Lingshui o VRC 156-157 G 7
Lingsugūr o IND 140-141 G 2
Lingtai o VRC 154-155 E 4
Lingtou o VRC 156-157 F 7
Linguère o SN 202-203 C 2
Lingui o VRC 156-157 G 4
Lingwu o VRC 154-155 E 2
Ling Xian o VRC 156-157 H 3
Lingxiaoyan • VRC 156-157 G 5
Lingyuan o VRC 148-149 O 7
Linh, Ngọc ▲ VN 158-159 J 3
Linhai o VRC (HEI) 150-151 E 2
Linhai o VRC (ZHE) 156-157 M 2
Linhares o BR 72-73 K 5
Linhe o VRC 154-155 E 1
Linhemo o ANG 216-217 D 6
Linjiang o VRC 150-151 F 7
Linke Lakes ⊖ AUS 176-177 G 2
Linkiring o SN 202-203 D 3
Linköping ☆ • S 86-87 G 7
Linkou o VRC 150-151 H 5
Linli o VRC 156-157 G 2
Linlithgow o GB 90-91 F 4
Linn o USA 46-47 C 6
Linpeng o VRC 156-157 F 5
Linqing o VRC 154-155 J 3
Linqu o VRC 154-155 L 3
Linquan o VRC 154-155 J 5
Lins o BR 72-73 F 6
Linsan o RG 202-203 D 4
Linsell o S 86-87 F 5
Linshu o VRC 154-155 L 4
Linshui o VRC 154-155 E 6
Linstead o JA 54-55 G 5
Linta ~ RM 222-223 D 10
Lintao o VRC 154-155 C 4
Linté o CAM 204-205 J 6
Lintea Tiwolu, Pulau ⌒ RI 164-165 H 6
Linthipe o MW 218-219 H 2
Linton o USA (IN) 46-47 E 6
Linton o USA (ND) 42-43 G 2
Lintong o VRC 154-155 F 4
Linville Caverns • USA 48-49 H 2
Linxi o VRC 148-149 O 6
Linxia o VRC 154-155 C 4
Lin Xian o VRC (HEN) 154-155 H 3
Lin Xian o VRC (SHA) 154-155 G 3
Linxiang o VRC 156-157 H 2
Linyanti ~ RB 218-219 B 4
Linyanti Swamp ⊖ NAM 218-219 B 4
Linyi o VRC (SHD) 154-155 K 3
Linyi o VRC (SHD) 154-155 L 4
Linz ☆ A 92-93 N 4
Linze o VRC 154-155 B 2
Linzhen o VRC 154-155 F 3
Linzor o RCH 76-77 D 2
Lioana o RP 160-161 D 4
Lioma o MOC 218-219 J 2
Lion, Golfe du ≈ 90-91 J 10
Lion Camp o Z 218-219 F 1
Liongsong, Tanjung ▲ RI 168 C 7
Lioni, Caño ~ CO 60-61 G 5
Lion Park ⊥ ZA 220-221 H 2
Lions Den o ZW 218-219 F 3
Lioppa o RI 166-167 C 5
Lios Tuathail = Listowel o IRL 90-91 C 5
Lioto o RCA 206-207 E 6
Lioua o TCH 198-199 G 6
Liouesso o RCB 210-211 E 3
Lipa o RP 160-161 D 6
Lipale o MOC 218-219 J 3
Lipantitlan State Historic Site ∴ USA 44-45 J 6
Lipari o I 100-101 E 5
Lipari, Isola ⌒ I 100-101 E 5
Lipcani o MD 102-103 E 3
Lipeck o RUS 94-95 Q 5
Lipeo, Río ~ RA 76-77 E 2
Liperi o FIN 88-89 K 5
Lipetrén, Sierra ▲ RA 78-79 E 6
Lipetsk = Lipeck o RUS 94-95 Q 5
Lipin Bor o RUS 94-95 Q 1
Liping o VRC 156-157 F 3
Lipis, Kuala o • MAL 162-163 E 2
Lipkany = Lipcani o MD 102-103 E 3
Lipki o RUS 94-95 P 5
Lipljan o • YU 100-101 H 3
Lipno o PL 92-93 P 2
Lipno, údolní nádrž ⊖ CZ 92-93 N 4
Lipobane, Ponta ▲ MOC 218-219 K 3
Lipova o RO 102-103 B 4
Lippe ~ D 92-93 K 3
Lippstadt o • D 92-93 K 3
Lipton o CDN 34-35 E 5
Liptougou o BF 202-203 L 3
Liptrap, Cape ▲ AUS 180-181 H 5
Lipu o VRC 156-157 G 4
Liquica = Likisia o RI 166-167 C 6
Lira o EAU 212-213 D 2
Liran, Pulau ⌒ RI 166-167 C 6
Liranga o RCB 210-211 F 4
Lircay o PE 64-65 E 8
Lirung o RI 164-165 K 2
Lisakovsk ☆ KA 124-125 C 2
Lisala o ZRE 210-211 H 2
Lisboa ★ ••• P 98-99 C 5
Lisbon o USA (ND) 42-43 J 2
Lisbon o USA (OH) 46-47 H 5
Lisbon = Lisboa ★ ••• P 98-99 C 5
Lisburn, Cape = Cape Mata'Avea ▲ VAN 184 II a 2
Lisburne, Cape ▲ USA 20-21 G 2
Liscomb Game Sanction ⊥ CDN 38-39 N 6
Lishan o VRC 154-155 E 6
Lishan Z.B. ⊥ • VRC 154-155 G 4
Lishi o VRC (SHA) 154-155 G 3
Lishi o VRC (SIC) 156-157 D 2
Lishu o VRC 154-155 L 6
Lishui o VRC 156-157 L 2
Lisianski Island ⌒ USA 14-15 L 5
Lisica ~ RUS 114-115 S 5
Lisičansk = Lysyčans'k o UA 102-103 L 3
Lisica-Pass ▲ YU 100-101 H 3
Lisieux o • F 90-91 H 7
Lisinskaja buhta ≈ RUS 120-121 W 6
Lisja ~ RUS 112-113 K 3
Lisjanskogo, poluostrov ∨ RUS 120-121 M 4
Liski o RUS 102-103 L 2
Li-Smita, ostrov ⌒ RUS 84-85 d 2
Lismore o AUS (NSW) 178-179 M 5
Lismore o AUS (VIC) 180-181 G 4
Lisnaskea o • GB 90-91 D 4
Lisomu, Tanjung ▲ RI 166-167 C 6
Lissadell o AUS 172-173 J 4
Lister, Mount ▲ ARK 16 F 17
Lištica = Široki Brijeg o BIH 100-101 F 3
Listowel o CDN 38-39 D 7
Listowel = Lios Tuathail o IRL 90-91 C 5
Listvjanka o • RUS 116-117 M 10
Līt, al- o KSA 132-133 B 3
Lita o EC 64-65 C 1
Litang o MAL 160-161 C 10
Litang o VRC (GXI) 156-157 F 5
Litang o VRC (SIC) 154-155 B 6
Lītāni ~ RL 128-129 F 6
Litanirivier ~ BR 62-63 G 4
Litchfield o USA (CA) 40-41 D 5
Litchfield o USA (MN) 42-43 K 3
Litchfield o USA (NE) 42-43 H 5
Litchfield Beach o USA 48-49 J 3
Litchfield Out Station o AUS 172-173 K 2
Litchfield Park ⊥ AUS 172-173 K 2
Litchville o USA 42-43 H 2
Lithgow o AUS 180-181 L 2
Lithuania = Lietuva ■ LT 94-95 G 4

Lena River Delta — Lithuania 281

Litipāra o IND 142-143 E 3
Litke o RUS (ARH) 108-109 F 5
Litke o RUS (HBR) 122-123 J 2
Litke, mys ▲ RUS 112-113 W 1
Litke, proliv ≈ 120-121 U 4
Litoměřice o CZ 92-93 N 3
Litomyšl o CZ 92-93 O 4
Litovko o RUS 122-123 F 4
Little Abaco Island ∩ BS 54-55 G 1
Little Abitibi Lake o CDN 34-35 G 6
Little Abitibi River ∿ CDN 34-35 Q 5
Little Aden o Y 132-133 D 7
Little Andaman ∩ IND 140-141 L 4
Little Barrier Island ∩ NZ 182 E 2
Little Bay Beach ⊥ GB 56 D 3
Little Belt Mountains ▲ USA 40-41 J 2
Little Black River ∿ USA 20-21 T 3
Little Blue River ∿ USA 42-43 H 5
Little Bow River ∿ CDN 32-33 O 6
Little Buffalo River ∿ CDN 30-31 N 5
Little Cadotte River ∿ CDN 32-33 M 4
Little Cayman ∩ GB 54-55 E 3
Little Chicago o CDN 30-31 M 3
Little Churchill River ∿ CDN 34-35 J 2
Little Colorado River ∿ USA 44-45 J 5
Little Corwallis Island ∩ CDN 24-25 Y 3
Littlecote Channel ≈ 36-37 K 2
Little Current o CDN 38-39 D 6
Little Current River ∿ CDN 34-35 O 5
Little Delta River ∿ USA 20-21 R 5
Little Desert ⊥ AUS 180-181 J 7
Little Desert National Park ⊥ AUS 180-181 F 4
Little Diomede Island ∩ USA 20-21 F 4
Little Exuma Island ∩ BS 54-55 H 3
Little Falls o USA (MN) 42-43 K 3
Little Falls o USA (NY) 46-47 L 4
Littlefield o USA (AZ) 40-41 H 7
Littlefield o USA (TX) 44-45 F 3
Little Fork o USA 42-43 L 1
Little Fork River ∿ USA 42-43 L 1
Little Fort o CDN 32-33 K 6
Little Gold River ∿ CDN 172-173 H 4
Little Grand Rapids o CDN 34-35 J 2
Little Harbour o BS 54-55 G 2
Little Humboldt River ∿ USA 40-41 F 5
Little Inagua Island ∩ BS 54-55 J 4
Little Karoo = Klein Karoo ⊥ ZA 220-221 E 6
Little Koniuji Island ∩ USA 22-23 R 5
Little Lake o USA 40-41 F 8
Little Mecatina River ∿ CDN 38-39 N 2
Little Missouri River ∿ USA 42-43 F 2
Little Moose Island ∩ CDN 34-35 H 5
Little Mud River ∿ USA 20-21 O 4
Little Nicobar Island ∩ IND 140-141 L 6
Little Powder River ∿ USA 42-43 E 3
Little Ragged Island ∩ BS 54-55 H 3
Little Rancheria River ∿ CDN 20-21 Z 7
Little Rapid Creek ∿ CDN 30-31 L 6
Little River o CDN 32-33 H 6
Little River ∿ USA 44-45 K 3
Littlerock o USA 40-41 F 8
Little Rock ★ USA 44-45 L 5
Little Ruaha ∿ EAT 214-215 H 5
Little Sable Point ▲ USA 46-47 G 4
Little Sachigo Lake o CDN 34-35 K 3
Little Salmon Lake o CDN 20-21 X 5
Little San Salvador Island ∩ BS 54-55 H 2
Little Scarcies of Kaba ∿ WAL 202-203 D 5
Little Seal River ∿ CDN 30-31 W 6
Little Sioux River ∿ USA 42-43 K 4
Little Sitkin Island ∩ USA 22-23 F 7
Little Smoky River ∿ CDN 32-33 M 4
Little Snake River ∿ USA 42-43 C 5
Little Tanaga Island ∩ USA 22-23 H 7
Littleton o USA (CO) 42-43 E 6
Littleton o USA (NH) 46-47 N 3
Little Wabash River ∿ USA 46-47 D 6
Little White River ∿ CDN 38-39 C 5
Little Yellowstone Park ⊥ USA 42-43 J 2
Littoral ∿ CAM 204-205 H 6
Lituhi o EAT 214-215 H 6
Litunde o MOC 218-219 H 1
Litvinova, mys ▲ RUS 108-109 Y 1
Litvinovo o RUS 96-97 F 3
Liu o RI 164-165 G 5
Liuba o VRC 154-155 E 5
Liuchiu Yü ∿ RC 156-157 M 5
Liuhe o VRC 150-151 E 6
Liuheng Dao ∩ VRC 156-157 N 2
Liujiachang o VRC 154-155 G 6
Liujiang o VRC 156-157 F 4
Liujiaxia Sk o VRC 154-155 C 4
Liujing o VRC 156-157 G 5
Liukanglu, Pulau ∩ RI 164-165 G 6
Liulin o EAT 214-215 H 4
Liupan Shan ▲ VRC 154-155 D 3
Liupanshan Z.B. ⊥ VRC 154-155 E 4
Liupanshui o VRC 156-157 D 3
Liúpo o MOC 218-219 K 2
Liushai o VRC 156-157 F 4
Liushipu o VRC 154-155 J 5
Liuwa Plain National Park ⊥ Z 218-219 B 2
Liuxu o VRC 156-157 F 5
Liuyang o VRC 156-157 H 2
Liuzhao Shan ▲ VRC 156-157 D 5
Liuzhi o VRC 156-157 D 3
Liuzhou o VRC 156-157 F 4
Liuzhuang o VRC 154-155 M 5
Livádi o VRC 100-101 K 6
Livádi o GR 100-101 J 5
Livani o LV 94-95 K 3
Livanovka o KA 124-125 C 2
Lively Island ∩ GB 80 G 7
Livengood o USA 20-21 Q 4
Live Oak o USA 48-49 G 4
Livermore, Mount ▲ USA 44-45 E 4
Livermore Falls o USA 46-47 N 3
Liverpool o AUS 180-181 L 2
Liverpool o CDN 38-39 M 6

Liverpool • GB 90-91 F 5
Liverpool, Cape ▲ CDN 24-25 h 4
Liverpool Bay ≈ 20-21 Y 2
Liverpool Range ▲ AUS 178-179 K 6
Líviko Pélagos ≈ 100-101 J 7
Livingston o USA (AL) 44-45 J 4
Livingston o USA (MT) 40-41 J 3
Livingston o USA (TN) 48-49 D 3
Livingston o USA (TX) 44-45 K 4
Livingston, Lake o USA 44-45 K 4
Livingstone ☆ Z 218-219 C 3
Livingstone Memorial • Z 214-215 H 4
Livingstonia o MW 214-215 H 6
Livingston Island ∩ ARK 16 G 30
Livinston's Cave • RB 220-221 G 2
Livno o BIH 100-101 P 3
Livny o RUS 94-95 P 5
Livonia o USA 46-47 G 4
Livorno o I 100-101 C 3
Livradois-Forez, Parc Naturel Régional ⊥ F 90-91 J 9
Livramento do Brumado o BR 72-73 K 2
Liwa o RI 162-163 F 7
Liwa', al- o OM 132-133 K 1
Liwale o EAT 214-215 J 5
Liwonde o MW 218-219 H 2
Liwonde National Park ⊥ MW 218-219 H 2
Li Xian o VRC (GAN) 154-155 D 4
Li Xian o VRC (SIC) 154-155 C 6
Lixin o VRC 154-155 K 5
Lixouri o GR 100-101 H 6
Liyang o VRC 154-155 L 6
Li Yubu o SUD 206-207 N 6
Lizarda o BR 68-69 E 6
Lizard Head Peak ▲ USA 42-43 C 5
Lizard o AUS 174-175 H 4
Lizard Point ▲ GB 90-91 E 6
Lizard Point Indian Reserve ✕ CDN 34-35 F 5
Lizotte o CDN 38-39 H 4
Lizums o LV 94-95 K 3
Ljadova ∿ UA 102-103 E 3
Ljady o RUS 94-95 L 2
Ljahovskie ostrova ∩ RUS 110-111 U 2
Ljaki o AZ 128-129 M 2
Ljamca o RUS 114-115 L 4
Ljamin, pervyj ∿ RUS 114-115 K 3
Ljamin, vtoroj ∿ RUS 114-115 K 3
Ljangar ▲ RUS 108-109 Y 7
Ljangar o TJ 136-137 N 6
Ljangasovo o RUS 96-97 E 4
Ljantorskij o RUS 114-115 M 4
Ljapin ∿ RUS 114-115 F 3
Ljapiske o RUS 118-119 H 3
Ljig o YU 100-101 H 2
Ljuban' o BY 94-95 L 5
Ljuban' o RUS 94-95 N 2
Ljubanskoe vodohranilišče < BY 94-95 L 5
Ljubar o UA 102-103 E 3
Ljubercy ∿ RUS 94-95 P 4
Ljubertsy = Ljubercy o RUS 94-95 P 4
Ljubinskij o RUS 114-115 M 7
Ljubljana ☆ SLO 100-101 E 1
Ljuboml' o UA 102-103 D 2
Ljubovija o YU 100-101 G 2
Ljubytino o RUS 94-95 O 5
Ljudinovo o RUS 94-95 O 5
Ljugarn o S 86-87 J 8
Ljukkum o KA 124-125 K 5
Ljungby o S 86-87 H 5
Ljungby o S 86-87 G 4
Ljungdalen o S 86-87 F 5
Ljusdal o S 86-87 H 6
Ljusnan ∿ S 86-87 H 6
Ljutoga ∿ RUS 122-123 K 5
Lk. Kambera ∿ RI 168 F 7
Llaima, Volcán ▲ RCH 78-79 D 5
Llallagua o BOL 70-71 F 8
Llalli o PE 70-71 E 4
Llamara, Salar de o RCH 76-77 C 1
Llançà o E 98-99 J 3
Llanddovery o GB 90-91 F 6
Llanes o E 98-99 E 2
Llano o USA 44-45 H 4
Llano, El o PA 52-53 G 7
Llanobajo o CO 60-61 C 6
Llano Estacado ⊥ USA 44-45 F 3
Llano Mariato o PA 52-53 D 8
Llano River ∿ USA 44-45 H 4
Llanos, Sierra de los ▲ RA 76-77 D 6
Llanos de Aridane, Los o E 188-189 C 6
Llanquihué o RCH 78-79 D 5
Llanquihué, Lago o RCH 78-79 D 6
Llao Llao o RA 78-79 D 6
Llaylla o PE 64-65 D 7
Llay-Llay o RCH 78-79 D 2
Lleida o E 98-99 H 4
Llera de Canales o MEX 50-51 K 6
Llerena o E 98-99 D 5
Llewellyn Glacier ☐ CDN 20-21 X 7
Lleyn Peninsula ⊍ GB 90-91 E 5
Llica o BOL 70-71 F 8
Llico o RCH 78-79 C 4
Lliria o E 98-99 G 5
Lliscaya, Cerro ▲ BOL 70-71 C 6
Lloyd Bay ≈ 174-175 G 3
Lloyd Lake o CDN 32-33 Q 3
Lloydminster o CDN 32-33 P 5
Lloyd Rock = The Brothers ∩ BS 54-55 H 3
Lloyd's Camp o RB 218-219 C 4
Llullaillaco, Volcán ▲ RCH 76-77 C 3
Lluta o PE 70-71 A 5
Lluta, Río ∿ RCH 70-71 C 6
l-Miyāh, Wādi ∿ SYR 128-129 H 5
M-Murra, al-Buhaira < EAU 194-195 F 2
Lo, Île = Loh ∿ VAN 184 II a 1
Loa, Caleta ≈ 76-77 B 1

Loa, Río ∿ RCH 76-77 C 1
Loanda ∿ ANG 216-217 D 4
Loandji ∿ ANG 216-217 H 6
Loange ∿ ZRE 210-211 H 6
Loango ∿ ZRE 210-211 D 6
Loanja ∿ Z 218-219 C 3
Loara o RI 164-165 G 5
Loay o RP 160-161 F 8
Loban o RUS 88-89 S 4
Lobatse ☆ RB 220-221 G 3
Lobaye ∿ RCA 206-207 C 6
Lobaye o RCA 206-207 C 6
Lobaye ∿ ZRE 210-211 K 3
Lobé ∿ CAM 210-211 C 2
Lobé, Chutes de la = Lobé Falls ∿ CAM 210-211 B 2
Lobé Falls = Chutes de la Lobé ∿ CAM 210-211 B 2
Lobeke ∿ CAM 210-211 E 2
Lobería o RA 78-79 K 5
Łobez o PL 92-93 N 2
Lobi o MW 218-219 H 2
Lobira o SUD 208-209 A 6
Lobito o ANG (BGU) 216-217 B 6
Lobitos o PE 64-65 B 4
Lobo ∿ ZRE 210-211 D 2
Lobo o RI 164-165 H 4
Loboko o RCB 210-211 F 4
Lobo Lodge o EAT 212-213 E 4
Lobos o RA 78-79 K 3
Lobos, Caño los o CO 64-65 E 1
Lobos, Cayo ∿ MEX 52-53 L 2
Lobos, Isla ∿ MEX 50-51 D 4
Lobos, Islas de ∿ MEX 50-51 L 7
Lobos, Punta ▲ RA 78-79 J 5
Lobos, Punta ▲ RCH (ATA) 76-77 B 5
Lobos, Punta ▲ RCH (LIB) 78-79 C 3
Lobos, Punta ▲ RCH (TAR) 70-71 B 6
Lobos, Río Los ∿ MEX 50-51 F 5
Lobos de Afuera, Islas ∿ PE 64-65 B 5
Lobos de Tierra, Isla ∿ PE 64-65 B 5
Loboto ▲ RT 202-203 L 6
Lobu o RI 164-165 H 4
Lobva o RUS 114-115 H 5
Locas de Cahuinari o CO 66-67 B 3
Locate o USA 42-43 E 2
Loceret o RI 168 D 3
Lochboisdale o GB 90-91 D 3
Lochcarron o GB 90-91 E 3
Lochearn o GB 90-91 F 3
Lochem o NL 92-93 J 2
Loches o F 90-91 H 8
Loch Fyne ≈ 26-27 p 7
Loch Fyne ≈ 90-91 E 4
Loch Garman = Wexford ☆ IRL 90-91 D 5
Lochgilphead o GB 90-91 E 4
Lochiel o ZA 220-221 K 3
Lochinvar National Park ⊥ Z 218-219 C 3
Lochinver o GB 90-91 E 2
Loch Linnhe ≈ 90-91 E 3
Loch Lomond o GB 90-91 E 3
Lochloosa o USA 48-49 G 5
Lochmaddy o GB 90-91 D 3
Lochnagar ▲ GB 90-91 F 3
Loch Ness o GB 90-91 E 3
Łochów o PL 92-93 Q 2
Lochsa River ∿ USA 40-41 G 2
Loch Sport o AUS 180-181 J 5
Lock o AUS 180-181 C 2
Lockart o USA 44-45 J 5
Lockeport o USA 38-39 M 7
Locker Point ▲ CDN 24-25 P 6
Lockhart o USA 44-45 J 5
Lockhart, Lake o AUS 176-177 E 6
Lockhart River ✕ AUS 174-175 G 3
Lockhart River o CDN 30-31 P 4
Lockhart River Aboriginal Land ✕ AUS 174-175 G 3
Lock Haven o USA 46-47 K 5
Lockney o USA 44-45 G 2
Lockport o USA 44-45 J 5
Lockwood o USA (CA) 40-41 D 8
Lockwood o USA (MO) 44-45 L 1
Lockwood Hills ▲ USA 20-21 M 3
Loc Ninh o VN 158-159 J 5
Locri o USA 100-101 F 5
Locumba, Río o PE 70-71 B 5
Locust Creek ∿ USA 42-43 L 5
Lod o IL 130-131 D 2
Loddon River ∿ AUS 180-181 G 3
Lodejnoe Pole o RUS 94-95 N 1
Lodeve o F 90-91 J 10
Lodge Creek ∿ CDN 32-33 P 7
Lodge Grass o USA 42-43 D 3
Lodgepole Creek ∿ USA 42-43 E 5
Lodhrán o PK 138-139 C 5
Lodi o USA (CA) 40-41 D 6
Lodi o USA (OH) 46-47 G 5
Lodi o I 100-101 B 2
Lodié o G 210-211 D 3
Lødingen o N 86-87 G 2
Lodja o ZRE 210-211 J 5
Lod'ma ∿ RUS 88-89 Q 4
Lododrf o CAM 210-211 C 2
Lodoma o RI 164-165 L 3
Lodore o RI 168 E 4
Lodrani o IND 138-139 C 8
Lodungeno o EAK 212-213 F 3
Lodwar o EAK 212-213 E 2
Łódź ☆ PL 92-93 P 3
Loei o THA 158-159 J 5
Loeka o ZRE 210-211 J 2
Loémé o RCB 210-211 D 6
Loeng Nok Tha o THA 158-159 J 5
Loeriesfontein o ZA 220-221 D 5
Lofa ∿ LB 202-203 E 6
Lofanga ∿ SN 202-203 C 2
Log o RUS 102-103 N 3

Loga o RN 204-205 E 2
Loga o SUD 206-207 K 6
Logan o USA (NM) 44-45 F 2
Logan o USA (OH) 46-47 G 6
Logan o USA (UT) 40-41 J 5
Logan o USA (WV) 46-47 H 7
Logan, Mount ▲ ⊶ CDN 20-21 U 6
Logan, Mount ▲ ⊶ USA 40-41 H 1
Logan Mountains ▲ CDN 30-31 E 5
Logansport o USA 46-47 E 5
Logan Pass ▲ USA 40-41 H 1
Lögar ∿ AFG 138-139 B 3
Logas'egan ∿ RUS 114-115 J 4
Logašino o RUS 110-111 d 4
Logata ∿ RUS 108-109 c 5
Loge ∿ ANG 216-217 C 3
Logelcoge o BF 202-203 L 4
Logobou o BF 202-203 L 4
Logoforok o SUD 206-207 L 6
Logone ∿ TCH 206-207 B 3
Logone Birni o TCH 206-207 B 3
Logone Gana o TCH 206-207 B 3
Logone Occidental ∿ TCH 206-207 B 4
Logone Occidental ∿ TCH 206-207 B 4
Logone Oriental ∿ TCH 206-207 C 4
Logone Oriental ∿ TCH 206-207 C 4
Logozone o DY 204-205 E 5
Logroño o E 98-99 F 3
Løgstør o DK 86-87 D 8
Løgstør o DK 86-87 D 8
Loh = Île Lo o VAN 184 II a 1
Lohagara o BD 142-143 F 4
Lohāghāt o IND 144-145 C 6
Lohardaga o IND 142-143 D 4
Lohārghat o IND 142-143 G 3
Lohéac o F 90-91 G 8
Lohiniva o FIN 88-89 H 3
Lohja o FIN 88-89 H 6
Lohjanaan o RI 164-165 E 4
Loh Liang o RI 168 D 7
Loi o PNG 183 D 2
Loiborsoit o EAT 212-213 E 4
Loi-kaw o MYA 142-143 K 6
Loile ∿ ZRE 210-211 H 4
Loilo o RI 210-211 J 3
Loimaa o FIN 88-89 G 6
Loima Hills ▲ EAK 212-213 E 2
Loir ∿ F 90-91 H 8
Loiro Poco o BR 66-67 C 2
Lois ∿ RI 166-167 G 6
Loiš o US 136-137 M 5
Loi Song ▲ MYA 142-143 K 4
Loita Hills ▲ EAK 212-213 E 4
Loita Plains ∿ EAK 212-213 E 4
Loja o EC 64-65 C 3
Lojiš o US 136-137 K 5
Lojmola o RUS 88-89 L 6
Lojno o RUS 96-97 H 4
Lokalema o ZRE 210-211 J 3
Lokandu o ZRE 210-211 K 5
Lokan tekojärvi < FIN 88-89 J 3
Lokata o RI 166-167 C 4
Lokbatan o AZ 128-129 N 2
Lokeli o ZRE 210-211 H 5
Lokichar o EAK 212-213 E 3
Lokichar ∿ EAK 212-213 E 3
Lokichogio o EAK 212-213 E 1
Lokila o ZRE 210-211 H 4
Lokitaung o EAK 212-213 E 1
Loknja ∿ RUS 94-95 M 3
Loko o WAN 204-205 G 4
Lokoja o WAN 204-205 G 4
Lokolama o ZRE 210-211 G 5
Lokolia o ZRE 210-211 H 4
Lokolo ∿ ZRE 210-211 G 4
Lokomby o RM 222-223 E 9
Lokomo o CAM (Est) 210-211 E 2
Lokomo ∿ CAM 210-211 D 2
Lokori o EAK 212-213 F 3
Lokoro ∿ ZRE 210-211 G 4
Lokossa o DY 202-203 L 6
Lokot o RUS 94-95 O 5
Lokoti o CAM 206-207 B 5
Lokoundjé ∿ CAM 210-211 C 2
Loksiati o SME 62-63 G 3
Loks Land ∿ CDN 36-37 R 3
Lokutu o ZRE 210-211 H 4
Loky ∿ RM 222-223 F 6
Lol o SUD (SR) 206-207 J 5
Lol o SUD 206-207 J 4
Lola o RG 202-203 F 6
Lola o RCH 78-79 D 3
Lole ∿ ZRE 210-211 G 5
Lolengi o ZRE 210-211 H 3
Loleta o USA 40-41 B 5
Lolgorien o EAK 212-213 E 4
Lolland ∿ DK 86-87 E 9
Lol Lanok o EAT 212-213 F 6
Lolo o USA 40-41 G 2
Lolobata o RI 164-165 L 3
Lolobau Island ∩ PNG 183 F 3
Lolobo o CI 202-203 H 6
Loloda Utara, Kepulauan ∩ RI 164-165 K 2
Lolodorf o CAM 210-211 C 2
Lolo Hot Springs o USA 40-41 G 2
Lolok o USA 40-41 G 2
Lolol o RCH 78-79 D 3
Lolom o CAM 204-205 K 6
Loloma o FJI 184 III c 2
Lolomi ∿ ZRE 210-211 H 4
Lolua o ETH 208-209 C 9
Loma Alta o USA 44-45 G 4
Loma Arena o CO 60-61 G 4
Loma Bonita o MEX 52-53 M 3
Loma de Cabrera o DOM 54-55 K 5
Loma Mountains ▲ WAL 202-203 E 5

Lomas, Las o PE 64-65 B 4
Lomas, Río de o PE 64-65 E 9
Loma San Martín ∿ RA 78-79 F 5
Lomas de Arena o USA 44-45 E 4
Lomas de Vallejos o RA 76-77 J 4
Lomas de Zamora o RA 78-79 K 3
Lomaum o ANG 216-217 C 6
Lomba ∿ ANG 216-217 E 7
Lombadina ∿ AUS 172-173 F 4
Lombard o USA 40-41 J 3
Lombarda, Serra ▲ BR 62-63 J 4
Lombardia o I 100-101 B 2
Lombe ∿ ANG 216-217 D 4
Lomblen (Kawela), Pulau ∩ RI 166-167 B 6
Lombok o RI (NBA) 168 C 7
Lombok ∿ RI 164-165 F 5
Lombok, Selat ≈ 168 B 7
Lomé ★ RT 202-203 L 6
Lomela o CAM 210-211 D 2
Lomela ∿ ZRE 210-211 H 4
Lometa o USA 44-45 H 4
Lomfjorden ≈ 84-85 K 5
Lomié o CAM 210-211 D 2
Loming o SUD 206-207 L 6
Lomitas, Las o RA 76-77 H 3
Lomond o CDN 32-33 O 6
Lomonosov Ridge ⋍ 16 A 25
Lomovoe o RUS 88-89 Q 4
Lomphät o K 158-159 J 4
Lompobatang, Gunung ▲ RI 164-165 F 6
Lompoc o USA 40-41 D 8
Lompopana, Gunung ▲ RI 164-165 F 4
Lompoul o SN 202-203 B 2
Lom Sak o THA 158-159 F 2
Lo'n ∿ VN 158-159 H 6
Lonambo o EC 64-65 D 2
Lonand o IND 138-139 D 10
Lonāvale o IND 138-139 D 10
Lončákovo o RUS 122-123 G 6
Loncoche o RCH 78-79 D 5
Loncopangue o RCH 78-79 D 4
Loncopue o RA 78-79 D 5
Londa o IND 140-141 F 3
Londéla-Kayes o RCB 210-211 D 6
Londengo o ANG 216-217 E 7
Londiani o EAK 212-213 E 4
Londokomba o EAK 212-213 E 4
Londolovit o PNG 183 G 2
London o CDN 38-39 D 7
London ★ ⊶ GB 90-91 G 5
London o USA (KY) 46-47 F 7
London o USA (OH) 46-47 G 6
Londonderry ☆ GB 90-91 C 4
Londonderry, Cape ▲ AUS 172-173 H 2
Londonderry, Isla ∿ RCH 80 C 7
Londrina o BR 72-73 E 7
Lone Butte o CDN 32-33 K 6
Lone Mine o ZW 218-219 E 4
Lone Rock o USA 46-47 C 4
Long o THA 142-143 L 6
Longa o ANG 216-217 E 7
Longa ∿ ANG 216-217 C 5
Longa, proliv ≈ 112-113 T 1
Longá, Río ∿ BR 68-69 H 3
Longa-Mavinga, Coutada Pública do ⊥ ANG 216-217 E 8
Long'an o VRC 154-155 F 4
Longana o VAN 184 II a 2
Longaví, Río ∿ RCH 78-79 D 4
Longbao Z.B. II VRC 144-145 L 4
Longbow Lake o CDN 34-35 J 6
Long Branch o USA (NJ) 46-47 M 5
Long Branch o USA (NJ) 46-47 M 5
Long Cay ∿ BH 52-53 L 3
Long Cay ∿ BS 54-55 H 3
Longchang o VRC 156-157 D 3
Longchuan o VRC 156-157 H 4
Long Creek o CDN 38-39 L 6
Long Creek ∿ USA 40-41 D 4
Longe ∿ ANG 216-217 C 3
Longfengyan • VRC 156-157 K 3
Long Fjord, De ≈ 26-27 d 2
Longford = An Longfort ☆ IRL 90-91 C 5
Longford o AUS 180-181 J 6
Longgang Shan ▲ VRC 150-151 E 6
Longgang Z.B. ⊥ VRC 156-157 E 5
Longgong o VRC 156-157 E 3
Longguan ∿ VRC 150-151 J 1
Long Harbour o CDN 38-39 I S 5
Longhua o VRC 148-149 N 7
Longhui o VRC 156-157 G 3
Longhushan • VRC 156-157 K 2
Longido o EAT 212-213 F 4
Longikis o RI 164-165 D 4
Longiram o RI 164-165 D 4
Long Island ∿ AUS 178-179 K 2
Long Island ∿ BS 54-55 H 3
Long Island ∿ CDN (NFL) 38-39 I R 4
Long Island ∿ CDN (NS) 38-39 L 6
Long Island ∿ CDN (NWT) 36-37 N 7
Long Island ∿ PNG 183 E 3
Long Island ∿ USA 46-47 M 5
Long Island Sound ≈ 36-37 K 7
Long Island Sound ≈ 46-47 M 5
Longitudinal, Valle ∿ RCH 78-79 D 3
Longkay o RI 164-165 G 5
Longlac o CDN 34-35 N 6
Long Lake o USA 42-43 H 6
Long Lake o USA 42-43 H 6
Long Lake, Indian Reserve ✕ CDN 34-35 N 6
Long Lama o MAL 164-165 D 2

Long Lellang o MAL 164-165 D 2
Longlin o VRC 156-157 D 4
Longling o VRC 142-143 L 3
Long Malinau o RI 164-165 E 2
Longmen o VRC (GDG) 156-157 H 5
Longmen o VRC 156-157 G 6
Longmen Shiku • VRC 154-155 H 4
Longmont o USA 42-43 E 6
Long Mountains, De ▲ USA 20-21 J 2
Long My o VN 158-159 H 6
Longnan o VRC 156-157 H 4
Longnawan o RI 164-165 D 3
Longobardi o I 100-101 D 3
Longo o G 210-211 D 4
Longonjo o ANG 216-217 C 6
Longongot ▲ EAK 212-213 F 4
Longotea o PE 64-65 D 5
Longot'egan ∿ RUS 108-109 M 8
Longozabe o RM 222-223 F 7
Long Palai o MAL 164-165 D 2
Long Pine o USA 42-43 G 5
Long Plain Indian Reserve ✕ CDN 34-35 G 4
Long Point o CDN (ONT) 38-39 D 7
Long Point ∿ CDN (MAN) 34-35 G 3
Long Point ▲ CDN (NFL) 38-39 P 4
Long Point o CDN (ONT) 38-39 D 7
Long Point Bay ≈ CDN 38-39 D 7
Long Prairie o USA 42-43 K 3
Longquan o VRC 156-157 L 2
Long Range Mountains ▲ CDN 38-39 P 5
Longreach o AUS 178-179 H 2
Long Seridar o MAL 164-165 D 1
Longshan o VRC (GDG) 156-157 H 5
Longshan o VRC (HUN) 156-157 F 4
Longsheng o VRC 156-157 F 4
Longshou S'an ▲ VRC 154-155 C 3
Longs Peak ▲ USA 42-43 E 5
Long Thành o VN 158-159 J 5
Longton o USA 174-175 H 7
Longue Pointe ▲ CDN 38-39 E 2
Longueuil o CDN 38-39 H 6
Long Valley Junction o USA 40-41 H 6
Longview o CDN 32-33 N 6
Longview o USA (TX) 44-45 K 3
Longview o USA (WA) 40-41 C 2
Longxi o VRC 154-155 D 4
Long Xian o VRC 154-155 E 4
Long Xuyên o VN 158-159 H 5
Longyan o VRC 156-157 K 4
Longyao o VRC 154-155 J 3
Longyearbyen o 84-85 J 3
Longyou o VRC 156-157 L 2
Longzhou o VRC 156-157 E 5
Loni Kand o VRC 138-139 B 3
Lonkintye o RM 222-223 F 6
Lonoke o USA 210-211 J 3
Lonquimay o RCH 78-79 D 5
Lonsdale o USA 42-43 L 3
Lons-le-Saunier o F 90-91 K 8
Lontar o RI 166-167 G 4
Lontian, Pulau ∩ RI 166-167 E 4
Lontou o RMM 202-203 E 2
Lontra o BR 68-69 C 4
Lontra, Ribeirão ∿ BR 72-73 D 6
Lontra, Rio ∿ BR 68-69 D 5
Lontué, Rio ∿ RCH 78-79 D 3
Lonua ∿ ZRE 210-211 K 4
Looc o RP (BOH) 160-161 E 8
Looc o RP (ROM) 160-161 D 6
Lookout, Cape ▲ CDN 34-35 P 3
Lookout, Cape ▲ USA 40-41 B 3
Lookout, Cape ▲ USA (NC) 48-49 K 2
Lookout, Mount ▲ AUS 174-175 H 6
Lookout Mount o USA 20-21 P 3
Lookout Poirt ▲ AUS 174-175 H 4
Lookout Ridge ▲ USA 20-21 L 2
Look Sembuang o MAL 160-161 C 10
Looma o AUS 172-173 G 5
Loon, Pointe ▲ CDN 38-39 E 1
Loongana o AUS 176-177 J 5
Loon Lake o CDN 32-33 Q 4
Loon River o CDN 32-33 N 3
Loost River o USA 40-41 G 5
Lootsberg Pass ▲ ZA 220-221 G 5
Lop o VRC 144-145 E 3
Lopary o RM 222-223 F 8
Lopatina, gora ▲ RUS 122-123 K 3
Lopatino o RUS 96-97 D 7
Lopatka ∿ RUS 94-95 P 5
Lopatka, poluostrov ⊍ RUS 110-111 c 4
Lopburi o THA 158-159 F 3
Lopča ∿ RUS 118-119 L 8
Lopé-Okanda, Réserve de la ⊥ G 210-211 D 4
Lopevi = Ulveah ∿ VAN 184 II b 3
Lopez o USA 40-41 G 3
Lopez o RP 160-161 E 6
Lopez, Cap ▲ G 210-211 C 5
López Mateos, Ciudad o MEX 52-53 E 2
Lop Nur < VRC 146-147 K 3
Lopori ∿ ZRE 210-211 H 3
Lopphavet ≈ 86-87 K 1
Lopp Lagoon ≈ 20-21 G 4
Loptjuga ∿ RUS 88-89 U 5
Loquilocon o RP 160-161 F 7
Lora o AUS 178-179 D 4
Lora, Río ∿ YV 60-61 G 3
Lora Creek ∿ AUS 178-179 G 5
Lorain o USA 46-47 G 5
Loralāi o PK 138-139 B 4
Loralāi ∿ PK 138-139 B 4
Loranstation = Angisoq o GRØ 28-29 S 7
Lordegān o IR 134-135 D 3
Lord Howe Island ∩ ⊶⊶ AUS 180-181 N 7
Lord Howe Rise ≈ 14-15 L 10
Lord Howe Seamounts ⋍ 13 H 5
Lord Lindsay River ∿ CDN 24-25 Z 5
Lord Loughborough Island ∩ MYA 158-159 D 5
Lord Mayor Bay ≈ 24-25 a 4
Lordsburg o USA 44-45 C 3
Lore o RI 166-167 G 8
Lore Lindu National Park ⊥ RI 164-165 C 4
Loren, Pulau ∩ RI 168 C 7

Lorena o BR (AMA) 66-67 B 6
Lorena o BR (PAU) 72-73 H 7
Lorengau o PNG 183 D 2
Lorentz ∿ RI 166-167 K 4
Lorentz Reserve ⊥ RI 166-167 J 4
Löre Rüd ∿ AFG 134-135 M 2
Lorestān o IR 134-135 B 2
Loreto o BOL 70-71 E 4
Loreto o BR (MAR) 68-69 F 5
Loreto o BR (MAT) 70-71 H 2
Loreto o I 100-101 D 3
Loreto o MEX 50-51 D 4
Loreto o MEX (BCS) 50-51 D 4
Loreto o RP 160-161 F 7
Loreto, Isla ∿ PE 66-67 B 4
Lorian Swamp ∿ EAK 212-213 G 3
Lorica o CO 60-61 E 3
Lorient o F 90-91 F 8
Lorillard River ∿ CDN 30-31 Y 3
Loring, Port o CDN 38-39 E 6
Lorino o RUS 112-113 Z 4
Loriscota, Lago o PE 70-71 B 5
Lorlie o CDN 34-35 E 5
Lormes o F 90-91 J 8
Lorn, Firth of ≈ 90-91 E 3
Loma Downs o AUS (QLD) 178-179 J 3
Lorne o AUS (VIC) 180-181 G 5
Lorneville o CDN 38-39 L 6
Loronyo o SUD 206-207 L 6
Loropéni o BF 202-203 J 4
Loros, Los o RCH 76-77 B 5
Lörrach o D 92-93 J 5
Lorraine o AUS 174-175 E 6
Lorraine ⊥ F 90-91 L 7
Lorsch o ⊶⊶ D (HES) 92-93 K 4
Lort, Cabo o RCH 80 C 2
Loruk o EAK 212-213 F 3
Lorukumu o EAK 212-213 E 2
Lorzot o TN 190-191 H 2
Los o S 86-87 G 6
Los, Îles de o RG 202-203 D 5
Losai National Reserve ⊥ EAK 212-213 F 3
Los Angeles o ⊶ USA 40-41 E 8
Los Angeles Aqueduct ∿ USA 40-41 E 8
Losari o RI 168 C 3
Loseya o EAT 212-213 F 6
Los Mochis o MEX 50-51 E 5
Loso ∿ ZRE 210-211 G 4
Losoni o RI 164-165 H 5
Lospalos o RI 166-167 G 8
Los Reyes Islands ∩ PNG 183 E 1
Lossiemouth o GB 90-91 F 3
Lossogonoi Plateau ▲ EAT 212-213 F 5
Lost Hills o USA 40-41 E 8
Lost River Range ▲ USA 40-41 G 3
Lost Trail Pass ▲ USA 40-41 H 3
Losuia o PNG 183 F 3
Lot ∿ F 90-91 H 9
Lote 15, Cerro ▲ RA 80 C 2
Lotfābād ∿ IR 136-137 F 6
Lothair o USA 40-41 J 1
Lothal o IND 138-139 D 8
Lotikipi Plain ⊍ EAT 212-213 E 1
Lotkipi Plain ⊍ EAK 212-213 E 1
Loto o VRC (KOR) 210-211 J 4
Loto ∿ ZRE 210-211 J 4
Lotoi ∿ ZRE 210-211 G 5
Lotsane ∿ RB 218-219 D 6
Lotshina o RM 222-223 F 8
Lotta ∿ RUS 88-89 K 2
Lotuke ▲ SUD 208-209 A 6
Lötzen = Giżycko o PL 92-93 Q 1
Loualaba, Vallée ou ∿ SN 202-203 E 2
Loubetsi o RCB 210-211 D 6
Loubomo o RCB 210-211 D 6
Loudéac o F 90-91 F 7
Loudi o VRC 156-157 G 3
Loudima o RCB 210-211 D 6
Loudima ∿ RCB 210-211 D 6
Loudun o F 90-91 H 8
Louéssé o RCB 210-211 C 5
Louétsi o G 210-211 C 5
Louga o SN 196-197 B 7
Lougheed Island ∩ CDN 24-25 T 2
Loughrea = Baile Locha Riach o IRL 90-91 C 5
Lougou o DY 204-205 E 3
Louhi o RUS 88-89 M 3
Louingui o RCB 210-211 D 5
Louisa o USA 46-47 G 6
Louisbourg o CDN 38-39 O 6
Louisdale o CDN 38-39 O 6
Louise o USA 44-45 J 5
Louise, Lake o USA 20-21 R 5
Louise Island ∩ CDN 32-33 E 5
Louiseville o CDN 38-39 H 5
Louisiade Archipelago ∩ PNG 183 G 6
Louisiana o USA (MO) 46-47 C 6
Louisiana ☐ USA 44-45 L 4
Lou Island ∿ PNG 183 D 2
Louis Trichardt o ZA 218-219 E 6
Louisville o CDN 38-39 H 5
Louisville o USA (GA) 48-49 G 3
Louisville o USA (KY) 46-47 F 6
Louisville o USA (MS) 48-49 D 3
Louisville o USA (NE) 42-43 J 5
Louisville Ridge ⋍ 14-15 L 10
Louis-XIV, Pointe ▲ CDN 36-37 K 7
Loukoléla o RCB 210-211 F 4
Loukouo o RCB 210-211 F 5
Loulan Gucheng ∴⊶ VRC 146-147 J 3
Loulé o P 98-99 C 6
Louloumi o RMM 202-203 H 4
Lou Lou Park o AUS 178-179 J 4
Loumbi o SN 196-197 D 7
Loumbol, Vallée ou ∿ SN 202-203 D 3
Loumou, Gati-o RMM 202-203 H 2
Loumou o RCB 210-211 E 6

Mabuasehube Game Reserve ⊥ RB 220-221 E 2
Mabuiag Island ∧ AUS 174-175 G 1
Mabuki ○ EAT 212-213 D 5
Mabula ○ ZA 220-221 J 2
Mabur ≈ 166-167 K 5
Mabura ○ GUY 62-63 E 3
Mabuto ○ WAN 204-205 F 3
Mača ○ RUS 118-119 H 6
Macá, Monte ▲ RCH 80 D 2
Macabi, Isla de ∧ PE 64-65 C 5
Maçacara ○ BR 68-69 J 7
Macachin ○ RA 78-79 H 4
Macaco, Cachoeira do ∧ BR 68-69 E 6
Macacos, Ilha dos ∧ BR 62-63 J 6
Macaé ○ BR 72-73 K 7
Macaene ○ MOC 220-221 L 2
Mačah ○ RUS 110-111 T 6
Macaiba ○ BR 68-69 L 4
Macajalar Bay ≈ 160-161 F 8
Macajuba ○ BR 72-73 K 2
Macalister ○ AUS 174-175 F 6
MacAlpine Lake ○ CDN 30-31 S 2
Maçambará ○ BR 76-77 J 5
Macan, Kepulauan ∧ RI 168 E 6
Macanao = Boca de Pozo ○ YV 60-61 J 2
Macandze ○ MOC 218-219 G 6
Maçangana, Rio ∧ BR 66-67 F 7
Macanillal ○ YV 60-61 G 4
Macao ○ P 156-157 H 5
Macao = Aomen ✶∧ P 156-157 H 5
Macao, El ○ DOM 54-55 L 5
Macapá ★ BR 62-63 J 5
Macaparana ○ BR 68-69 L 5
Macapillo ○ RA 76-77 F 3
Macará ○ EC 64-65 C 4
Macaracas ○ PA 52-53 D 8
Maçaranduba, Cachoeira ∧ BR 62-63 H 6
Macarani ○ BR 72-73 K 3
Macarena, La ○ CO 60-61 E 6
Macarena, Parque Nacional La ⊥ CO 60-61 E 6
Macarena, Serranía de la ▲ CO 60-61 E 6
Macareo, Caño ∧ YV 60-61 L 3
Macari ○ PE 70-71 B 4
Maçarico, Cachoeira ∧ BR 66-67 J 3
Macaroni ○ AUS 174-175 F 5
Macarretane ○ MOC 220-221 L 2
Macarthur ○ AUS 180-181 G 5
Macas ○ EC 64-65 C 4
Macatanja ○ MOC 218-219 J 3
Macaú ○ BR 68-69 K 4
Macaú = Macao ✶∧ P 156-157 H 5
Macaúã, Rio ∧ BR 70-71 C 2
Macauari ○ BR 62-63 E 6
Macaúbas ○ BR 72-73 J 2
Macbar, Raas ▲ SP 208-209 K 4
Maccles Lake ○ CDN 38-39 I R 4
Mac Cluer Gulf = Teluk Berau ≈ 166-167 K 3
Macculloch, Cape ▲ CDN 24-25 j 4
Mac Cullochs Range ▲ AUS 178-179 G 6
Macdiarmid ○ CDN 34-35 M 6
MacDonald, Lake ○ AUS 176-177 K 1
Macdonald, Mount ▲ VAN 184 II b 3
Mac Donald Downs ○ AUS 178-179 C 2
MacDonald Island ∧ CDN 36-37 N 3
Mac Donnell, Port ○ AUS 180-181 F 5
Macdonnell Peninsula ∪ AUS 180-181 E 3
Macdonnell Ranges ▲ AUS 176-177 H 4
Macdougall Lake ○ CDN 30-31 U 2
MacDowell Lake ○ CDN 34-35 K 4
Macedo de Cavaleiros ○ P 98-99 D 4
Macedonia = Makedonija ■ MK 100-101 H 4
Maceió ○ BR 68-69 L 6
Macenta ○ RG 202-203 F 5
Macerata ○ I 100-101 D 3
Mačevna, buhta ○ RUS 112-113 Q 6
Macfarlane, Lake ○ AUS 178-179 D 6
Macgillycuddy's Reeks ▲ IRL 90-91 C 6
Mach ○ PK 134-135 M 4
Machacamarca ○ BOL 70-71 D 6
Machachi ○ EC 64-65 C 2
Machadinho ○ BR 66-67 F 7
Machadinho, Rio ∧ BR 66-67 G 7
Machado ○ BR 72-73 H 6
Machado, Rio ∧ BR 70-71 G 2
Machadodorp ○ ZA 220-221 K 2
Machado ou Ji-Paraná, Rio ∧ BR 66-67 F 7
Machagai ○ RA 76-77 G 4
Machala ○ MOC 218-219 G 6
Machakos ○ EAK 212-213 F 4
Machala ○ EC 64-65 C 3
Machalilla, Parque Nacional ⊥ EC 64-65 B 3
Machaneng ○ RB 218-219 D 6
Machang ○ MAL 162-163 E 2
Machang ○ VRC 156-157 E 3
Machanga ○ MOC 218-219 H 5
Machaquilá ∴· GCA 52-53 K 3
Machaquilá, Rio ∧ GCA 52-53 K 3
Machatti, Lake ○ AUS 178-179 E 5
Machawaian Lake ○ CDN 34-35 M 5
Machecoul ○ F 90-91 G 8
Macheke ○ ZW 218-219 F 4
Machemma Ruins ∴·∴ ZA 218-219 E 6
Macheng ○ VRC 154-155 J 6
Macherla ○ IND 140-141 H 2
Machesse ○ MOC 218-219 H 4
Machhlishahr ○ IND 142-143 U 5
Machias ○ USA 46-47 P 3
Machichaco, Cabo ▲ E 98-99 F 3
Machichi River ○ CDN 34-35 L 2
Machile ∧ Z 218-219 C 3
Machilipatnam ○ IND 140-141 J 2
Machina ○ WAN 198-199 E 6
Machinga ○ MW 218-219 H 2
Machiques ○ YV 60-61 E 2

Macho, El ○ C 54-55 G 5
Machu Picchu ∴·∴ PE 64-65 F 8
Machupo, Río ∧ BOL 70-71 E 3
Macia ○ MOC 220-221 L 2
Maciel ○ PY 76-77 J 4
Măcin ○ RO 102-103 P 3
Macintyre River ∧ AUS 178-179 K 5
Mack ○ USA 42-43 G 6
Mackay ○ AUS 178-179 K 1
Mackay, Lake ○ AUS 172-173 J 7
MacKay Lake ○ CDN 30-31 O 4
Mackay River ∧ CDN 32-33 O 3
Mackenzie ○ GUY 62-63 E 2
Mackenzie ∧ CDN 28-29 N 4
Mackenzie, Kap ▲ GRØ 26-27 p 7
Mackenzie Bay ≈ 20-21 W 2
Mackenzie Bison Sanctuary · CDN 30-31 N 3
Mackenzie Delta ·⌣ CDN 20-21 X 2
Mackenzie Highway II (ALB) 32-33 M 3
Mackenzie Highway II (NWT) 30-31 N 4
Mackenzie King Island ∧ CDN 24-25 P 2
Mackenzie Mountains ▲ CDN 30-31 L 3
Mackenzie River ∧ AUS 178-179 K 2
Mackenzie River ∧ CDN 30-31 K 5
Mackinac Bridge · USA 46-47 F 3
Mackinac Island State Park · USA 46-47 F 3
Mackinaw City ○ USA 46-47 F 3
Mackinnon Road ○ EAK 212-213 G 5
Mackkeys ○ USA 48-49 K 2
Macklin ○ CDN 32-33 Q 5
Macks Inn ○ USA 40-41 J 4
Macksville ○ AUS 178-179 M 6
Maclaren River ∧ USA 20-21 R 5
Maclean ○ AUS 178-179 M 5
Maclean Strait ≈ 24-25 T 2
Macleantown ○ ZA 220-221 H 6
Maclear ○ ZA 220-221 H 6
Maclear, Cape ▲·∧ MW 218-219 H 1
Macleay River ∧ AUS 178-179 M 6
Macleod, Fort ○ CDN 32-33 O 7
MacLeod, Lake ○ AUS 172-173 B 4
Macmillan Pass ▲ CDN 30-31 E 4
Macmillan Plateau ▲ CDN 20-21 V 5
Macmillan River ∧ CDN 20-21 X 5
Maco ○ RP 160-161 F 9
Maco, Cerro ▲ CO 60-61 D 3
Maçobere ○ MOC 218-219 G 5
Macocha ▲ CZ 92-93 O 4
Macocola ○ ANG 216-217 C 3
Macomb ○ USA 46-47 C 5
Macomer ○ I 100-101 B 4
Macomia ○ MOC 214-215 L 7
Mâcon ✶· F 90-91 K 8
Macon ○ USA (GA) 48-49 G 3
Macon ○ USA (MO) 42-43 L 6
Macon ○ USA (MS) 48-49 D 3
Macon ○ USA (OH) 46-47 G 6
Macondo ○ ANG 214-215 B 7
Macoppe ○ RI 164-165 G 6
Macossa ○ MOC 218-219 G 5
Macoun Lake ○ CDN 34-35 E 2
Macouria = Tonate ○ F 62-63 H 3
Macovane ○ MOC 218-219 H 5
Macoya ○ BOL 70-71 C 6
Macpès ○ CDN 38-39 K 4
Macquarie, Lake ○ AUS 180-181 L 2
Macquarie Harbour ≈ 180-181 H 7
Macquarie Ridge ≃ 14-15 H 13
Macquarie River ∧ AUS 178-179 J 6
MacQuoid Lake ○ CDN 30-31 W 4
Macroom = Maigh Chromtha ○ IRL 90-91 C 6
Macrorie ○ CDN 32-33 R 6
Mactan Island ∧ RP 160-161 E 7
Macucocha, Lago ○ PE 64-65 F 9
Macuma ○ EC 64-65 D 3
Macumba River ∧ AUS 178-179 D 4
Macuna, Raudal ∧ CO 66-67 B 3
Macururé, Rio ∧ BR 68-69 J 6
Macusani ○ PE 70-71 B 4
Macuto ○ YV 60-61 H 2
Macúzari, Presa ○ MEX 50-51 E 4
Macuze ○ MOC 218-219 J 3
Mada, River ∧ WAN 204-205 H 4
Madabazouma ○ RCA 206-207 F 6
Madadeni ○ ZA 220-221 K 3
Madadi ○ TCH 206-207 E 4
Madagascar = Madagasikara ∧ RM 222-223 E 8
Madagascar = Madagasikara ∧ RM 222-223 E 8
Madagascar Basin ≃ 12 D 7
Madagascar Ridge ≃ 8-9 H 9
Madagali ○ WAN 204-205 K 3
Madagoi ○ SP 212-213 J 3
Ma Đa Gui ○ VN 158-159 J 5
Mada'in Salih ·∴ KSA 130-131 E 4
Madakasira ○ IND 140-141 G 4
Madalena ○ BR 68-69 J 4
Madalena ○ RN 198-199 F 2
Madamba ○ RP 160-161 F 9
Madanapalle ○ IND 140-141 H 4
Madang ·∧ PNG 183 C 3
Madanganj ○ BD 142-143 G 4
Madaniya, al- ○ KSA 132-133 C 5
Madaoua ○ RN 198-199 B 5
Madara Canal · USA 40-41 E 7
Madaorunfa ○ RN 198-199 C 6
Madau ○ TM 136-137 D 5
Madau Island ∧ PNG 183 G 4
Madaya ○ MYA 142-143 K 4
Madavaram ○ IND 140-141 J 2
Madawaska River ∧ CDN 38-39 H 4
Madaya ○ SUD 206-207 K 5
Madden, Lago ○ PA 52-53 U 9
Maddalena, Ísola ∧ I 100-101 B 4

Maddalena, la ○ I 100-101 B 4
Maddūr ○ IND 140-141 G 4
Madeir ○ SUD 206-207 J 5
Madeira ∧ P 188-189 C 4
Madeira, Arquipélago da ∧ P 188-189 C 4
Madeira, Rio ∧ BOL 70-71 G 4
Madeira, Rio ∧ BR 66-67 H 5
Madeira Rise ≃ 6-7 H 5
Madeirinha, Rio ∧ BR 66-67 G 7
Madeleine, Cap-de-la- ○ CDN 38-39 H 5
Madeleine, Îles de la ∧ CDN 38-39 N 5
Madeline Island ∧ USA 46-47 C 2
Maden ✶ TR 128-129 H 3
Madera ○ MEX 50-51 E 3
Madera ○ USA 44-45 D 7
Madero ○ SP 212-213 J 3
Mádhavaram ○ IND 140-141 J 2
Madhuban ○ IND 142-143 D 2
Madhubani ○· IND 142-143 E 2
Madhugiri ○ IND 140-141 G 4
Madhumati ∧ BD 142-143 F 4
Madhupur ○ BD 142-143 G 3
Madhupur ○ IND 142-143 E 3
Madhya Pradesh □ IND 138-139 E 8
Madi, Wādi ∧ OM 132-133 H 5
Madiama ○ EAK 212-213 F 4
Madibira ○ EAT 214-215 H 5
Madibogo ○ ZA 220-221 G 3
Madidi, Río ∧ BOL 70-71 D 3
Madigan Gulf ≈ 178-179 D 5
Madihui ○ VRC 154-155 G 3
Madikeri ○ IND 140-141 F 4
Madill ○ USA 44-45 J 2
Madimba ○ ANG 216-217 C 3
Madimba ○ ZRE 210-211 E 6
Madina ○ RMM (KAY) 202-203 F 3
Madina ○ RMM (SIK) 202-203 G 3
Madina, al- ✶· KSA 130-131 F 5
Madina, al- ✶·· KSA (MAD) 130-131 F 5
Madina, al- ○ Y 132-133 E 6
Madina de Baixo ○ GNB 202-203 C 4
Madina Junction ○ WAL 202-203 D 5
Madina-Oula ○ RG 202-203 E 4
Madina-Salambandé ○ RG 202-203 D 4
Madinat al Abyar ○ LAR 192-193 J 1
Madinat as-Sa'b ○ Y 132-133 D 7
Madinat as-Sādāt ○ ET 194-195 E 2
Madinat aš-Širq ○ Y 132-133 D 6
Madinat at-Taura ○ SYR 128-129 H 5
Madinat Näsir ○ ET 194-195 F 6
Madinat Şahrā' ·∴ ET 194-195 F 6
Madingo-Kayes ○ RCB 210-211 C 6
Madingou ○ RCB 210-211 D 6
Madingrin ○ CAM 206-207 D 2
Madi Opei ○ EAU 212-213 D 2
Madirovalo ○ RM 222-223 E 6
Madison ○ USA (IN) 46-47 F 6
Madison ○ USA (KS) 42-43 J 7
Madison ○ USA (NE) 42-43 J 5
Madison ○ USA (SD) 42-43 J 4
Madison ○ USA (WV) 46-47 H 6
Madison ○ USA (WI) 46-47 D 4
Madison Bird Refuge ⊥ USA 40-41 H 3
Madison Canyon Earthquake Area (1959) · USA 40-41 J 3
Madison River ∧ USA 40-41 J 3
Madisonville ○ USA (KY) 46-47 E 6
Madisonville ○ USA (TX) 44-45 K 4
Madita, Pr. ○ RI 168 E 8
Madiun ○ RI 168 D 3
Madjanga ○ RCA 206-207 F 3
Madjingo ○ G 210-211 E 3
Madley, Mount ▲ AUS 176-177 G 2
Madley Rapids ∧ CDN 30-31 Q 3
Mado Gashi ○ EAK 212-213 G 3
Madoi ○ VRC 144-145 M 3
Madooile ○ SP 212-213 H 2
Madoville ○ SP 212-213 J 2
Madra Dağı ▲ TR 128-129 B 3
Madraka, Ra's ▲ OM 132-133 K 4
Madras ○ USA 40-41 J 4
Madre, Laguna ≈ 44-45 J 6
Madre, Laguna ≈ 50-51 L 5
Madre de Chiapas, Sierra ▲ MEX 52-53 H 3
Madre de Deus de Minas ○ BR 72-73 H 6
Madre de Dios ○ PE 70-71 B 3
Madre de Dios, Isla ∧ RCH 80 C 5
Madre de Dios, Rio ∧ BOL 70-71 D 3
Madre de Dios, Rio ∧ PE 70-71 C 3
Madre del Sur, Sierra ▲ MEX 52-53 D 3
Madre Occidental, Sierra ▲ MEX 50-51 F 4
Madre Oriental, Sierra ▲ MEX 50-51 H 3
Madrid ✶· E 98-99 F 4
Madrid ○ RP 160-161 F 8
Madrid, La ○ RA 76-77 F 4
Madridejos ○ E 98-99 F 5
Madrigal ○ PE 70-71 B 4
Madrona, Sierra ▲ E 98-99 E 5
Madruga ○ C 54-55 E 3
Madrugada, La ○ RA 80 G 3
Madu, Pulau ∧ RI 168 K 3
Maduda ○ ZRE 210-211 D 6
Madula ○ ZRE 210-211 D 6
Madura, Pulau ∧ RI 168 K 3
Madura, Selat ≈ 168 E 3
Madurai ○ IND 140-141 H 6
Madurantakam ○ IND 140-141 H 4
Madurä Pass · AUS 176-177 J 5
Madyan ○ PK 138-139 D 2

Madyl-Tasa, gora ▲ RUS 110-111 U 4
Madžarovo ○ BG 102-103 D 7
Madzilobge ○ RB 218-219 D 5
Madziwadzido ○ ZW 218-219 E 3
Madziwa Mine ○ ZW 218-219 F 3
Maebashi ✶ J 152-153 M 5
Mae Chaem ○ THA 142-143 L 4
Mae Charim ○ THA 142-143 M 6
Mae Hong Son ○ THA 142-143 L 5
Mae Khajan ○ THA 142-143 L 6
Maelang ○ RI 164-165 H 3
Maele ○ RMM 202-203 H 3
Mae Nam Khwae Noi ∧ THA 158-159 E 3
Maenggsan ○ DVR 150-151 F 8
Mae Pok ○ THA 158-159 E 2
Mae Sai ○ THA 142-143 L 5
Mae Sariang ○ THA 142-143 K 6
Mae Sot ○ THA 158-159 E 2
Mae Su ○ THA 142-143 L 6
Mae Suai ○ THA 142-143 L 5
Mae Suya ○ THA 142-143 L 6
Mae Taeng ○ THA 142-143 L 6
Mae Tub Reservoir ○ THA 158-159 E 2
Maevarano ∧ RM 222-223 F 5
Maevatanana ○ RM 222-223 F 6
Maevo ∧ RUS 94-95 L 3
Maewo = Île Aurora ∧ VAN 184 II b 2
Mafa ∧ RI 164-165 K 3
Maféré ○ CI 202-203 J 7
Mafeteng ○ LS 220-221 H 4
Maffin ○ RI 166-167 K 2
Mafia Channel ≈ 214-215 K 4
Mafia Island ∧ EAT 214-215 K 4
Mafikeng ○ ZA 220-221 G 2
Mafil ○ RCH 78-79 C 5
Mafou ∧ RG 202-203 E 4
Mafraq ○ Y 132-133 C 7
Mafraq, al' ∴· JOR 130-131 E 1
Maga ○ CAM 206-207 B 2
Magadan ✶·∧ RUS 120-121 O 4
Magadanskij Kava-Čelomdžinskoe lesničestvo, zapovednik ⊥ RUS 120-121 M 3
Magadanskij Ofskoe lesničestvo, zapovednik ⊥ RUS 120-121 O 4
Magadanskij Sejmčanskoe lesničestvo, zapovednik ⊥ RUS 120-121 P 2
Magadi ○ EAK 212-213 F 4
Magadi, Lake ○ EAK 212-213 F 4
Magága ○ ET 194-195 E 3
Magagnino ○ SP 212-213 K 2
Magalakwin ∧ ZA 218-219 E 6
Magalhães Barata ○ BR 68-69 E 2
Magaliesberg Natural Area ⊥ ZA 220-221 H 2
Magallanes, Estrecho de ≈ 80 E 6
Magamba ○ RCA 206-207 F 6
Magan ○ RUS (SAH) 118-119 O 4
Magandene ○ MOC 218-219 G 6
Magangue ○ CO 60-61 D 3
Maganoy ∧ RP 160-161 F 9
Magan-Tas, gora ▲ RUS 110-111 d 5
Magao ○ TCH 206-207 D 3
Magara ∧ BU 212-213 B 5
Magára, Čabal ▲ ET 194-195 F 2
Magaras ∧ RUS 118-119 O 4
Magarida ∧ PNG 183 E 6
Magárim, al- ∧ Y 132-133 E 6
Magat ∧ RP 160-161 F 7
Magazine Mountain ▲ USA 44-45 L 2
Magba ○ CAM 204-205 J 5
Magbakele ○ ZRE 210-211 J 2
Magbontoso ○ WAL 202-203 D 5
Magburaka ○ WAL 202-203 D 5
Magdad ○ SP 212-213 K 2
Magdagači ∧ RUS 118-119 M 9
Magdal 'Anğar ○ RL 128-129 F 6
Magdalena ○ BOL 70-71 F 3
Magdalena ○ MEX 52-53 C 1
Magdalena ○ RA 78-79 J 3
Magdalena, Isla ∧ MEX 50-51 D 4
Magdalena, Isla ∧ RCH 80 D 7
Magdalena, Punta ▲ CO 60-61 D 6
Magdalena, Río ∧ CO 60-61 D 6
Magdalena, Bahía ≈ 50-51 C 5
Magdalena de Kino ○ MEX 50-51 D 2
Magdalena Tequisistlán ○ MEX 52-53 G 3
Magda Plateau ▲ CDN 24-25 f 4
Magdeburg ✶· D 92-93 M 2
Magedi ○ IND 140-141 G 4
Magej ∧ RUS 120-121 P 5
Magelang ○ RI 168 D 3
Magellan Seamounts ≃ 14-15 H 6
Magenta, Lake ○ AUS 176-177 E 6
Magerøya ∧ N 86-87 M 1
Magetan ○ RI 168 D 3
Magga Range ▲ MAK 16 F 35
Maggieville ○ AUS 174-175 F 5
Maggiore, Lago ○ I 100-101 B 2
Maghama ○ RIM 196-197 D 7
Maghnia ○ DZ 188-189 L 3
Magic Hot Springs ∴· USA 40-41 H 4
Magic Reservoir ∧ USA 40-41 H 4
Magill, Islas ∧ RCH 80 D 7
Maginga ○ EAT 214-215 H 5
Magistraľnyj ○ RUS 116-117 N 7
Magma ○ MS 224 C 7

Magnitogorsk ∧ RUS 96-97 L 7
Magnolia ○ USA 44-45 L 3
Mago ○ FJI 184 III c 2
Mago ○ RUS 122-123 J 2
Mágoé ○ MOC 218-219 F 2
Magog ○ CDN 38-39 H 6
Magou ∧ DY 202-203 L 4
Magoura ○ DZ 188-189 L 3
Magoye ○ Z 218-219 D 3
Magpie, Rivière ∧ CDN 38-39 M 3
Magra ∧ BD 142-143 G 3
Magra ∧ RM 222-223 E 7
Magrath ○ CDN 32-33 O 7
Magta Lahjat ○ RIM 196-197 D 6
Magu, Rio ∧ BR 68-69 G 3
Maguan ○ VRC 156-157 D 5
Maguari ○ BR 66-67 E 3
Maguari, Cabo ▲ BR 62-63 K 6
Magude ○ MOC 220-221 L 2
Magui, Lac ○ RMM 202-203 F 3
Magumeri ○ WAN 198-199 F 6
Magunge ○ ZW 218-219 E 3
Magura ○ BD 142-143 F 4
Maguse Lake ○ CDN 30-31 W 3
Maguse Point ▲ CDN 30-31 X 5
Maguse River ∧ CDN (MWT) 30-31 W 5
Maguse River ∧ CDN 30-31 W 4
Magushan · VRC 156-157 K 3
Magusheni ○ ZA 220-221 J 5
Magwe ✶ MYA 142-143 J 5
Magwegqana ∧ RB 218-219 C 5
Magyichaung ○ MYA 142-143 H 5
Magŷz ∧ Y 132-133 C 5
Mahábád ○ IR 128-129 L 4
Mahábaleshwar ○ IND 140-141 E 2
Mahabe ○ RM 222-223 F 5
Mahabharat Lekh ▲ NEP 144-145 E 7
Mahabharet Lekh ▲ NEP 144-145 C 6
Mahábiša, al- ○ Y 132-133 C 6
Mahabo ○ RM 222-223 E 8
Mahackala ✶ RUS 126-127 G 6
Mahádd ○ IND 138-139 D 10
Mahadday Weeyne ○ SP 212-213 K 2
Mahádeo Hills ▲ IND 138-139 F 8
Mahafalu, Tombeau · RM 222-223 D 10
Mahafaly ⊥ RM 222-223 C 9
Mahafasa ∧ RM 222-223 E 9
Mahagi Port ○ ZRE 212-213 C 2
Mahaicony ○ GUY 62-63 F 2
Mahá'il ○ KSA 132-133 D 5
Mahajamba ∧ RM 222-223 F 6
Mahajamba, Helodrano ≈ 222-223 F 5
Mahajanga ∧ RM 222-223 D 7
Mahajanga ✶ RM 222-223 E 7
Mahajilo ∧ RM 222-223 D 7
Mahakam ∧ RI 164-165 F 5
Mahal ○ IND 140-141 H 4
Mahálāni, al- ○ KSA 130-131 H 4
Mahalapye ○ RB 218-219 D 6
Mahalchari ○ BD 142-143 H 4
Mahalevona ○ RM 222-223 F 6
Mahali Mountains ▲ EAT 214-215 E 4
Mahalla al-Kubrá, al- ○ ET 194-195 E 2
Mahallât ○ IR 134-135 D 2
Mahanoro ○ RM 222-223 F 7
Maha Oya ○ CL 140-141 J 7
Maharágáni ○ IND 138-139 D 10
Maharashtra □ IND 138-139 D 10
Mahari ∧ BD 142-143 G 3
Mahárlú, Daryáče-ye ○ IR 134-135 D 4
Mahásamund ○ IND 142-143 U 9
Maha Sarakham ○ THA 158-159 G 2
Mahasolo ○ RM 222-223 E 7
Mahatalaky ○ RM 222-223 E 10
Mahatsaratsara ○ RM 222-223 E 8
Mahattat 1 ○ SUD 200-201 F 3
Mahattat 2 ○ SUD 200-201 F 3
Mahattat 4 ○ SUD 200-201 F 3
Mahattat 5 ○ SUD 200-201 F 3
Mahattat 6 ○ SUD 200-201 F 3
Mahattat 7 ○ SUD 200-201 F 3
Mahattat 8 ○ SUD 200-201 F 3
Mahattat 9 ○ SUD 200-201 F 3
Mahattat 10 ○ SUD 200-201 F 3
Mahattat Abu Hadriyah ○ KSA 134-135 C 4
Mahattat Talata ○ ET 194-195 F 2
Mahavanona ○ RM 222-223 F 4
Mahavavy ∧ RM 222-223 E 6
Mahavelatota ○ CL 140-141 J 7
Mahaweli Ganga ∧ CL 140-141 J 7
Mahaxai ○ LAO 158-159 H 2
Mahayag ○ RP 160-161 F 8
Mahazoma ○ RM 222-223 E 6
Mahbúb ○ SUD 200-201 D 6
Mahbúbnagar ○ IND 140-141 G 2
Mahda ○ OM 134-135 F 6
Mahd ad-Đahab ○ KSA 130-131 G 6
Mahdia ○ GUY 62-63 E 2
Mahdishár ○ IR 136-137 C 7
Mahe ∧ IND 140-141 H 5
Mahé Island ∧ SY 224 D 2
Mahébourg ○ MS 224 C 7
Mahendragarh ○ IND 138-139 F 5
Mahendra Giri ▲ IND 142-143 D 6
Mahenge ○ EAT 214-215 J 5
Mahéshpur ○ IND 142-143 E 3
Mahéshkhali ∧ BD 142-143 G 5
Mahfar al-Hammám ○ SYR 128-129 H 5

Mahğil, al- ∧ Y 132-133 D 5
Mahi ∧ IND 138-139 E 8
Mahia Peninsula ∪ NZ 182 F 3
Mahila ○ ZRE 212-213 B 4
Mahilëv ∧ BY 94-95 M 5
Mahilyow = Mahilëv ○· BY 94-95 M 5
Mahin ○ WAN 204-205 F 5
Mahina ○ RMM 202-203 F 3
Mahitsy ∧ RM 222-223 E 7
Mahkyetkawng ○ MYA 142-143 K 3
Mahlabatini ○ ZA 220-221 K 4
Mahlaing ○ MYA 142-143 J 5
Mahlake ○ IR 134-135 E 5
Mahmiya ○ SUD 200-201 F 4
Mahmoud, Bir ○ TN 190-191 G 4
Mahmüddábád ○ IR 128-129 M 4
Mahmüdiya, al- ○ IR 128-129 M 4
Mahmür, Jiq ○ IR 128-129 M 3
Mahmür ○ IR 128-129 K 5
Mahne ○ IR 134-135 H 1
Máhnešän ○ IR 128-129 M 4
Mahnja ∧ RUS 114-115 O 5
Mahnomen ○ USA 42-43 K 2
Maho ○ CL 140-141 J 7
Mahoba ○ IND 138-139 G 7
Maho Bay ∧ NA 56 D 2
Mahone Bay ≈ 38-39 M 6
Mahony Lake ○ CDN 30-31 G 3
Mahora ○ E 98-99 G 5
Mahoua ○ TCH 206-207 D 3
Mahrès ○ TN 190-191 H 3
Mährisch Schönberg = Šumperk △ CZ 92-93 O 4
Máhšahr, Bandar-e ○ IR 134-135 C 3
Mahtowa ○ USA 42-43 L 2
Mahúd Budrukh ○ IND 140-141 F 2
Mahulu ○ ZRE 212-213 A 4
Mahur Island ∧ PNG 183 G 2
Mahuva ○ IND 138-139 C 9
Mahwa ○ IND 138-139 F 6
Mahwah ○ IND 138-139 G 7
Mahwit, al- ○ Y 132-133 C 6
Mahya, Wâdi ∧ Y 132-133 F 5
Mahzera, Hassi · DZ 188-189 J 4
Mai, Île = Emae ∧ VAN 184 II b 3
Maiaima ∧ PNG 183 E 4
Maiauatá ○ BR 62-63 K 6
Maibo ○ TCH 206-207 D 4
Maica, Rivière ∧ CDN 38-39 M 3
Maicao ○ CO 60-61 E 2
Maici, Rio ∧ BR 66-67 G 6
Maicillar ○ YV 60-61 G 2
Maicimirim, Rio ∧ BR 66-67 F 6
Maiden, Mount ▲ AUS 176-177 G 3
Maidi ∧ Y 164-165 K 3
Maidstone ○ CDN 32-33 Q 5
Maiduguri ✶ WAN 204-205 K 3
Maidum ·∴ ET 188-189 J 2
Maie ○ ZRE 212-213 C 2
Maiella, la ▲ I 100-101 E 3
Maifa'a ○ Y 132-133 E 6
Maigach Mada ○ SP 212-213 J 2
Maigh Chromtha = Macroom ○ IRL 90-91 C 6
Maigh Nuad = Maynooth ○ IRL 90-91 D 5
Maigualida, Sierra de ▲ YV 60-61 J 5
Mai Gudo ▲ ETH 208-209 C 5
Maihar ○ IND 138-139 G 7
Maiinchi ○ WAN 198-199 C 6
Maijdi ○ BD 142-143 G 4
Maijia ○ YV 60-61 K 5
Maijishan Shiku · VRC 154-155 E 4
Maika ∧ ZRE 212-213 B 2
Maikala Range ▲ IND 142-143 B 4
Maikoor, Pulau ∧ RI 166-167 J 3
Maikoro ○ TCH 206-207 D 2
Mailäni ○ IND 144-145 C 6
Mailepalli ○ IND 140-141 H 2
Mailin, Rio de ∧ RA 76-77 F 3
Mailsi ○ PK 138-139 E 4
Maimana ✶ AFG 136-137 J 7
Maimará ○ RA 76-77 E 2
Maimlja ∧ RUS 120-121 T 5
Maimón ○ DOM 54-55 L 5
Main ○ RP 160-161 E 8
Main à Dieu ○ CDN 38-39 P 5
Mainau · D 92-93 K 5
Main Brook ○ CDN 38-39 Q 3
Main Camp ○ ZW 218-219 D 4
Maine □ USA 46-47 N 3
Maine, Gulf of ≈ 46-47 P 4
Mainé-Soroa ○ RN 198-199 F 6
Mainland ∧ GB 90-91 P 4
Mainoru ○ VRC 144-145 K 6
Mainpuri ○ IND 138-139 G 6
Main River ∧ CDN 38-39 Q 4

Makarov Basin ≃ 16 A 35
Makarov Dvor ○ RUS 88-89 Q 6
Makarovka ○ RUS 122-123 Q 4
Makarovo ○ RUS 116-117 N 7
Makarska ○ HR 100-101 F 3
Makasa ○ Z 214-215 F 5
Makasar = Ujung Pandang ☆ RI 164-165 F 6
Makassar = Ujung Pandang ☆ RI 164-165 F 6
Makassar Strait = Makasar, Selat ≈ RI 164-165 E 5
Makasse ⊂ SP 212-213 J 3
Makat ☆ KA 96-97 H 10
Makedonía ⊥ GR 100-101 H 4
Makeevka = Makijivka ○ UA 102-103 L 3
Makekeda ○ ZRE 212-213 A 2
Makeni ☆ WAL 202-203 D 5
Makere ○ EAT 212-213 C 6
Makgadikgadi ⊥ RB 218-219 C 5
Makgadikgadi Pans Game Park ⊥ RB 218-219 C 5
Makha ○ THA 158-159 E 3
Makhaleng ∼ LS 220-221 H 5
Makhdumnagar ○ IND 142-143 C 2
Makhtal ○ IND 140-141 G 2
Makhu ○ IND 138-139 E 4
Maki ○ RI 166-167 H 3
Makian, Pulau ∼ RI 164-165 K 3
Makijivka ○ UA 102-103 L 3
Makilimbo ○ ZRE 212-213 B 5
Makina ○ SOL 184 I e 3
Maki National Park ⊥ ETH 208-209 C 6
Makinat Šihan ○ OM 132-133 H 5
Makinda ○ EAT 212-213 G 6
Makindu ○ EAK 212-213 F 5
Makinsk ☆ KA 124-125 G 2
Makinson Inlet ≋ 24-25 f 2
Makira, Lembalemban'i ▲ RM 222-223 F 5
Makijivka = Makijivka ○ UA 102-103 L 3
Makka ⊠ KSA 132-133 B 3
Makka ☆ KSA 132-133 A 3
Makkah = Makka ☆ KSA 132-133 A 3
Mak-Klintoka, ostrov ∼ RUS 84-85 e 2
Makkovik ○ CDN 36-37 U 7
Makkovik Bay ≈ 36-37 U 7
Makmin, al- ○ IRQ 128-129 K 7
Makó ○ H 92-93 Q 5
Mako ○ SN 202-203 D 3
Makogai ∼ FJI 184 III b 2
Makokibatan Lake ○ CDN 34-35 N 5
Makokou ∼ G 210-211 D 3
Makonde Plateau ▲ EAT 214-215 K 6
Makongo ○ GH 202-203 K 5
Makongolosi ○ EAT 214-215 K 6
Makoop Lake ○ CDN 34-35 L 4
Makor ○ CAM 204-205 K 5
Makoro ○ ZRE 212-213 E 3
Makosa ○ ZRE 214-215 E 4
Makotipoko ○ RCB 210-211 F 4
Makoua ○ RCB 210-211 E 3
Makoua ○ TCH 206-207 E 4
Makoubi ○ RCB 210-211 D 5
Makovo ○ RUS 96-97 F 10
Makovskaja ∼ RUS 108-109 V 8
Makovskoe, ozero ○ RUS 108-109 V 8
Makrān Coast Range ▲ PK 134-135 K 6
Maks al-Qibli, 'Izbat ○ ET 194-195 E 5
Maksatiha ○ RUS 94-95 O 3
Maksimovca ○ RUS 116-117 M 7
Maksimovka ○ RUS 118-119 E 6
Maksudangarh ○ IND 138-139 F 7
Maktau ○ EAK 212-213 G 5
Makthar ○ TN 190-191 G 3
Mäkü ○ IR 128-129 L 3
Makuende ○ ZRE 214-215 E 4
Makulakubu ○ ZRE 214-215 C 5
Makunduchi ○ EAT 214-215 K 4
Makung ○ RC 156-157 L 5
Makungo ○ SP 212-213 J 3
Makungu ○ EAT 214-215 F 5
Makunguwiro ○ EAT (LIN) 214-215 J 5
Makunudu Atoll ∼ MV 140-141 A 4
Makurazaki ○ J 152-153 D 9
Makurdi ☆ WAN 204-205 H 5
Makuru ∼ VAN 184 II b 3
Makushin Bay ≈ 22-23 N 6
Makushin Volcano ▲ USA 22-23 N 6
Makušino ○ RUS 114-115 U 7
Makutano ○ EAK (EAS) 212-213 F 4
Makutano ○ EAK (RIF) 212-213 F 5
Makuti ○ ZW 218-219 G 4
Makuyuni ○ EAT 212-213 F 5
Makwate ○ RB 218-219 D 6
Makwiro ○ ZW 218-219 F 3
Mal ○ IND 142-143 F 2
Māl ○ RIM 196-197 D 6
Mala ○ PE 64-65 D 8
Mala ○ RI 166-167 F 2
Mala = Mallow ○ IRL 90-91 C 5
Mala, Río de ∼ PE 64-65 D 8
Malabang ○ RP 160-161 F 9
Malabar ∼ SY 222-223 E 2
Malabar Coast ∪ IND 140-141 F 4
Malabo ★ GQ 210-211 B 2
Malabo ○ RI 164-165 F 5
Malabrigo, Punta ▲ PE 64-65 C 5
Malabungan ○ RP 160-161 D 8
Malabwe ○ Z 218-219 O 5
Malaca Beach, Playa ≈ DOM 54-55 L 5
Malacacheta ○ BR 72-73 J 4
Malacca ○ IND 140-141 L 5
Malacca, Strait of ≈ 162-163 D 3
Malacky ○ SK 92-93 O 4
Malad ∼ ER 200-201 J 4
Malaga ○ CO 60-61 E 4
Málaga ○ E 98-99 E 6

Malaga ○ USA 44-45 E 3
Malagarasi ∼ EAT (KIG) 212-213 C 6
Malagarasi ∼ EAT 212-213 C 6
Malagueta, Bahía de ≈ 54-55 G 4
Maláha, al- ○ KSA 132-133 C 5
Malahajtari ○ RUS 108-109 g 4
Malahar ○ IR 168 E 7
Malähit, al- ○ Y 132-133 C 5
Malaimbandy ○ RM 222-223 D 8
Malaita ∼ SOL 184 I e 3
Malaita ○ ZA 220-221 J 2
Malaja Anga ∼ RUS 116-117 N 8
Malaja Balahnja ∼ RUS 108-109 e 5
Malaja Belaja ∼ RUS 116-117 L 9
Malaja Birjusa ∼ RUS 116-117 J 8
Malaja Bykovka ○ RUS 96-97 E 8
Malaja Čažma ∼ RUS 120-121 T 6
Malaja Čuja ∼ RUS 118-119 E 6
Malaja Erëma ∼ RUS 116-117 N 5
Malaja Heta ∼ RUS 108-109 V 7
Malaja Heta ∼ RUS 108-109 V 7
Malaja Ket' ∼ RUS 116-117 E 7
Malaja Kon'kovaja ∼ RUS 112-113 J 2
Malaja Kuonamka ∼ RUS 110-111 J 4
Malaja Kurílʹskaja grjada ∼ RUS 122-123 L 7
Malaja Ob' ∼ RUS 114-115 H 3
Malaja Pera ∼ RUS 122-123 B 3
Malaja Pura ∼ RUS 108-109 V 5
Malaja Purga ○ RUS 96-97 H 6
Malaja Sos'va ∼ RUS 114-115 H 3
Malaja Sos'va, zapovednik ⊥ RUS 114-115 H 4
Malaja Tira ∼ RUS 116-117 N 7
Malaja Usa ∼ RUS 108-109 L 8
Malaja Višera ○ RUS 94-95 N 2
Malakāl ☆ SUD 206-207 K 4
Malakanagiri ○ IND 142-143 B 6
Mälākand ○ PK 138-139 C 2
Mälākand Pass ▲ PK 138-139 C 2
Malakatyn-Tas, gora ▲ RUS 110-111 W 2
Malakula ∼ VAN 184 II a 3
Malakula = Île Mallicolo ∼ VAN 184 II a 3
Malakwa ○ CDN 32-33 L 6
Malakwāl ○ PK 138-139 D 3
Malala ○ PNG (MAD) 183 C 3
Malala ○ PNG (MAD) 183 C 3
Malalamai ○ PNG 183 D 3
Malalaua ○ PNG 183 B 5
Malam ○ PNG 183 B 5
Malamala ○ RI 164-165 G 5
Malambo ○ EAT 212-213 E 5
Malammaduri ○ WAN 198-199 D 6
Malampaka ○ EAT 212-213 D 5
Malän, Räs ▲ PK 134-135 L 6
Malanda ○ AUS 174-175 H 5
Malandji ○ ZRE 210-211 J 6
Malandy Hill ▲ AUS 176-177 D 4
Malang ○ RI 168 E 7
Malanga ○ MOC 218-219 J 1
Malangani ○ EAT 214-215 H 5
Malangbong ○ RI 168 C 3
Malangke ○ RI 164-165 G 5
Malanje ⊡ ANG 216-217 D 4
Malanje ○ ANG (MAL) 216-217 D 4
Malantouen ○ CAM 204-205 J 5
Malanut Bay ≈ 160-161 D 7
Malanville ○ DY 204-205 E 3
Malanzan ○ RA 76-77 D 6
Malanzán, Sierra de ▲ RA 76-77 D 6
Malapatan ○ RP 160-161 F 10
Malapati Safari Area ⊥ ZW 218-219 F 5
Malappuram ○ IND 140-141 G 5
Malär ○ PK 134-135 L 5
Malarba ○ CAM 204-205 K 5
Mälären ⊂ S 86-87 H 7
Malargüe ○ RA 78-79 D 3
Malargüe, Río ∼ RA 78-79 D 3
Malartic, Lac ○ CDN 38-39 F 4
Malasait ○ PNG 183 F 3
Malaso ∼ RI 164-165 F 5
Malaspina Glacier ⊂ USA 20-21 U 7
Malata, Lake ○ AUS 180-181 C 3
Malatayur, Tanjung ▲ RI 162-163 K 6
Malatya ☆ TR 128-129 H 3
Malaulalo Island ∼ SOL 184 I e 4
Malaut ○ IND 138-139 D 4
Malavalli ○ IND 140-141 G 4
Malävi ○ IR 134-135 H 4
Malawali, Pulau ∼ MAL 160-161 B 9
Malawi, Lake ○ MW 214-215 H 6
Malawi = Malawi ■ MW 218-219 G 1
Malay ○ RP 160-161 D 7
Malayagiri ▲ IND 142-143 D 5
Malay Balay ☆ RP 160-161 F 8
Malàyer ○ IR 134-135 C 1
Malàyer, Rüdhäne-ye ∼ IR 134-135 C 1
Malay Peninsula = Semenanjung Malaysia ∼ MAL 162-163 E 2
Malaysia ■ MAL 162-163 E 2
Malazgirt ☆ TR 128-129 K 3
Malbaie, La ○ CDN 38-39 J 5
Malbazza ○ RN 198-199 B 6
Malbhanguwa ○ NEP 144-145 C 6
Malbon ○ AUS 178-179 F 1
Malbon Vale ○ AUS 178-179 E 1
Malbooma ○ AUS 178-179 C 5
Malbork ○⋯ PL 92-93 P 1
Malbrán ○ RA 76-77 F 5
Malcolm ○ AUS 176-177 F 4
Malcolm River ∼ CDN 20-21 V 2
Malcolm, Point ▲ AUS 176-177 G 6
Malden ○ USA 46-47 D 7
Maldives ■ MV 140-141 B 7
Maldives = Maldive Islands ∼ MV 140-141 B 7
Maldonado ○ EC 64-65 C 1
Maldonado ⊡ ROU 78-79 M 3
Maldonado, Punta ▲ MEX 52-53 E 3
Male ★ MV 140-141 B 7
Malea, Gunung ▲ RI 162-163 C 4
Mälegaon ○ IND (MAH) 138-139 F 9
Mälegaon ○ IND (MAH) 138-139 E 9

Malei ○ MOC 218-219 J 3
Maleit ○ SUD 206-207 J 5
Malek ○ SUD 206-207 J 5
Malekkandi ○ IR 128-129 M 4
Malélé ○ RCB 210-211 D 6
Malema ○ MOC 218-219 J 2
Malemba-Nkulu ○ ZRE 214-215 D 5
Malème-Hodar ○ SN 202-203 C 2
Malena ○ RA 78-79 G 2
Malendo, River ∼ WAN 204-205 F 3
Malendok Island ∼ PNG 183 G 2
Malen'ga ○ RUS 88-89 O 5
Male polissja ⊥ UA 102-103 G 2
Maleta ○ RUS 116-117 O 10
Malewära ○ IND 142-143 B 5
Malfa ○ I 100-101 E 7
Malgis ∼ EAK 212-213 F 3
Malgobek ○ RUS 126-127 F 6
Malgrat de Mar ○ E 98-99 J 4
Malha ○ SUD 200-201 C 5
Malhada ○ BR 72-73 J 3
Malheur Lake ○ USA 40-41 E 4
Malheur River ∼ USA 40-41 F 4
Mali ∼ FJI 184 III b 2
Mali ○ LB 202-203 F 6
Mali ○ RG 202-203 D 3
Mali ■ RMM 202-203 G 2
Mali ○ ZRE 210-211 L 5
Maliana ○ RI 166-167 C 6
Maliça ○ BR 68-69 F 6
Malifut ○ RI 164-165 J 5
Maligayo ○ RP 160-161 D 5
Mali K. ∼ MYA 158-159 E 4
Malili ○ RI 164-165 G 5
Malilla ○ S 86-87 G 8
Mali Lošinj ○ HR 100-101 E 2
Malima ∼ FJI 184 III c 2
Malimán de Abajo ○ RA 76-77 C 5
Malimasindi ○ ZW 218-219 E 4
Malinalco ⋅ MEX 52-53 E 2
Malinche, Volcán La ▲ MEX 52-53 E 2
Malindang, Mount ▲ RP 160-161 E 8
Malindi ○⋯ EAK 212-213 H 5
Malindi Marine National Park ⊥ EAK 212-213 H 5
Malines = Mechelen ○⋅ B 92-93 H 3
Malinga ○ RCB 210-211 D 5
Malingping ○ RI 168 C 3
Malin Head ≋ IRL 90-91 D 4
Malinke ∼ SN (SSE) 164-165 C 4
Malino ○ RI (SLT) 164-165 G 4
Malino ∼ RI (SSE) 164-165 F 6
Malino, Gunung ▲ RI 164-165 G 3
Malinovka ∼ RUS (KMR) 124-125 P 2
Malinovka ∼ RUS 122-123 F 6
Malinyi ○ EAT 214-215 J 5
Maliom ∼ PNG 183 G 3
Malipo ○ VRC 156-157 D 5
Maliq ○⋅ AL 100-101 H 5
Mali Rajinac ▲ HR 100-101 E 2
Malita ○ RP 160-161 F 9
Maliva ○ IND 138-139 C 8
Mäliva ○ IND 138-139 C 8
Maljamar ○ USA 44-45 F 3
Malka ∼ RUS 126-127 E 6
Malkara ○ TR 128-129 B 2
Malka Mari ○ EAK 212-213 H 1
Malka Mari National Park ⊥ EAK 212-213 H 1
Malkāpur ○ IND (MAH) 138-139 F 9
Malkāpur ○ IND (MAH) 140-141 G 2
Malkara ☆ TR 128-129 B 2
Malki ○ RUS 120-121 R 7
Malkinskij hrebet ▲ RUS 120-121 R 7
Malko Tărnovo ○ BG 102-103 H 4
Malko Tărnovo ○ BG 102-103 E 7
Malla ○ IND 140-141 G 2
Mallacoota ○ AUS 180-181 K 4
Mallacoota Inlet ≈ AUS 180-181 K 4
Mallaig ○ GB 90-91 E 3
Mallaoua ○ RN 198-199 D 6
Mallapunyah ○ AUS 174-175 C 5
Mallawī ○ ET 194-195 E 4
Mallawīya ○ SUD 200-201 H 5
Malleco, Río ∼ RCH 78-79 C 5
Mallee Cliffs National Park ⊥ AUS 180-181 G 3
Mallen, laguna ○ RUS 112-113 S 6
Malleo, Río ∼ RA 78-79 D 5
Mallery Lake ○ CDN 30-31 U 3
Mallet ○ BR 74-75 E 5
Mallicolo, Île = Malakula ∼ VAN 184 II a 3
Mallig ○ RP 160-161 D 5
Mallina ○ AUS 172-173 D 6
Mallin Grande, Cerro ▲ RA 78-79 D 6
Malloch, Cape ≋ CDN 24-25 Q 1
Mallorca ⊂ E 98-99 J 5
Mallow = Mala ○ IRL 90-91 C 5
Malm ○ N 86-87 E 4
Malmal ○ PNG 183 F 3
Mälmand, Küh-e ▲ AFG 134-135 K 2
Malmberget ○∼ S 86-87 K 3
Malmédy ○ B 92-93 J 3
Malmesbury ○ ZA 220-221 D 6
Malmö ○⋅ S 86-87 F 9
Malmyž ○ RUS 118-119 F 6
Malo ∼ VAN 184 II a 2
Malo, Arroyo ∼ ROU 78-79 M 2
Maloani ○ SOL 184 I e 1
Maloarhangel'sk ○ RUS 116-117 O 10
Maloca ○ BR 62-63 G 5
Maloca do Gonçalo ○ BR 66-67 J 2
Maloca Velha ○ BR 62-63 G 4
Maloca ○ RP 160-161 E 8
Malocu Macu ○ BR 62-63 G 4
Male Hantajskoe, ozero ○ RUS 108-109 X 7
Male Jarovoe ozero ○ RUS 124-125 J 2
Malojaz ☆ RUS 96-97 L 6
Malokurilʹskoe ○ RUS 122-123 M 7
Malolo ∼ Z 214-215 D 5
Malolo ∼ FJI 184 III a 2
Malolo ○ RI 166-167 F 2

Malolotja Nature Reserve ⊥ SD 220-221 K 3
Malom ○ PNG 183 F 2
Malombe ∼ Z 218-219 H 3
Malombe, Lake ○ MW 218-219 H 2
Malonda ○ ZRE 214-215 C 5
Malone ○ USA 46-47 L 3
Malonga ○ ZRE 214-215 D 5
Malŏ ∼ N 86-87 B 6
Malozemelʹskaja tundra ⊥ RUS 88-89 J 3
Maložujka ∼ RUS (ARH) 88-89 O 5
Maložujka ∼ RUS 88-89 O 5
Malpas Hut ○ AUS 174-175 G 6
Malpelo, Isla de ∼ CO 5 C 4
Malpelo, Punta ▲ PE 64-65 B 5
Malpeque Bay ≈ 38-39 N 5
Malpica (Malpica de Bergantiños) ○ E 98-99 C 3
Malprabha ∼ IND 140-141 F 2
Mälpura ○ IND 138-139 E 6
Mälpura ○ IND 138-139 E 6
Malsüniyah, al- ▲ KSA 130-131 L 5
Malta ○ BR 68-69 K 5
Malta ○ LV 94-95 K 3
Malta ○ USA (AR) 44-45 L 2
Malta ⊡ M 100-101 E 7
Malta ☆ M 100-101 E 7
Malta ∼ USA 42-43 D 1
Maltahöhe ○ NAM 220-221 J 2
Maltam ○ CAM 198-199 G 6
Maltan ∼ RUS 120-121 O 3
Maltee ○ AUS 176-177 M 6
Malton ○ GB 90-91 G 4
Maluera ○ MOC 218-219 H 2
Maluku ○ RI 164-165 J 5
Maluku ∼ ZRE 210-211 E 6
Malûli, Rio ∼ MOC 218-219 K 2
Malumfashi ○ WAN 204-205 G 3
Malunda ○ RI 164-165 F 5
Malung ○ S 86-87 F 6
Malungwishi ○ ZRE 214-215 D 6
Malur ○ IND 140-141 G 4
Malüt ○ SUD 206-207 L 5
Maluti Mountains ▲ LS 220-221 J 4
Maluu ○ SOL 184 I e 3
Mälvan ○ IND 140-141 E 1
Malvas ∼ PE 64-65 D 7
Malvern ○ USA (AR) 44-45 L 2
Malvern ○ USA (IA) 42-43 K 5
Malvinas, Islas ⊂ GB 78-79 L 6
Malwa ○ IND 138-139 F 7
Malwal ○ SUD 206-207 K 4
Malya ○ EAT 212-213 E 5
Malye Čany ozero ○ RUS 124-125 K 1
Malye Donki ozero ∼ RUS 114-115 H 7
Malygina, mys ▲ RUS 108-109 O 5
Malygina, proliv ≈ RUS 108-109 O 5
Malyj Abakan ∼ RUS 124-125 Q 2
Malyj Anjui ∼ RUS 112-113 S 6
Malyj Anjui ∼ RUS 112-113 P 3
Malyj Ases"egan ∼ RUS 114-115 S 4
Malyj Begičev, ostrov ∼ RUS 110-111 H 2
Malyj Čaun ∼ RUS 112-113 T 3
Malyj Čaunskyj, proliv ≈ RUS 112-113 O 2
Malyj Enisej ∼ RUS 116-117 H 10
Malyj Hamar-Daban, hrebet ▲ RUS 116-117 L 10
Malyj Jugan ∼ RUS 114-115 N 5
Malyj Karmakuly ○ RUS 108-109 L 5
Malyj Kas ∼ RUS 114-115 U 5
Malyj Kemčug ∼ RUS 116-117 F 7
Malyj Kemčug ∼ RUS 116-117 F 7
Malyj Ljahovskij, ostrov ∼ RUS 110-111 W 2
Malyj Majn ∼ RUS 112-113 Q 4
Malyj Naryn ∼ KS 146-147 C 5
Malyj Nimnyr ○ RUS 118-119 M 7
Malyj Nimnyr ∼ RUS 118-119 M 7
Malyj Ofdoj ∼ RUS 118-119 L 8
Malyj Olër, ozero ○ RUS 112-113 J 2
Malyj Salym ∼ RUS 114-115 L 4
Malyj Šantar, ostrov ∼ RUS 120-121 S 6
Malyj Sarykul ozero ∼ RUS 96-97 M 6
Malyj Semljačik, vulkan ▲ RUS 120-121 S 6
Malyj Tagul ∼ RUS 116-117 H 8
Malyj Turtas ∼ RUS 114-115 L 5
Malyj Urkan ∼ RUS 118-119 M 8
Malyj Uzen' ∼ RUS (SAR) 96-97 E 8
Malyj Uzen' ∼ KA 96-97 F 8
Malyj Van'kin, mys ▲ RUS 110-111 Y 3
Malyj Žemčužnyj, ostrov ∼ RUS 126-127 H 5
Malyk, ozero ○ RUS 120-121 M 2
Malyn ○ UA 102-103 F 2
Malyj Kavkaz = Malyj Kavkaz ▲ GE 126-127 D 7
Mama ∼ RUS (IRK) 118-119 F 6
Mama ∼ RUS 118-119 F 7
Mamad ○ RP 160-161 E 9
Mamadyš ☆ RUS 96-97 G 6
Mamaïe Ana ○ BR 66-67 D 5
Mamaj, köli ∼ KA 124-125 G 2
Mamakan ∼ RUS 118-119 E 7
Mamakan ○ RUS 118-119 F 7
Mamallapuram ○⋯ IND 140-141 J 2
Maman ○ PE 64-65 D 6
Mamana Island = Rum Cay ∼ BS 54-55 H 3
Mamanguape ○ BR 68-69 L 5
Mamanuka Group ∼ FJI 184 III a 2
Mamäri ∼ SN 202-203 D 2
Mamasa ○ RI 164-165 F 5
Mamasiware ○ RI 166-167 H 3
Mamawi Lake ○ CDN 30-31 O 6
Mamba ∼ ZRE 214-215 D 5
Mamba ○ BR 72-73 G 3
Mambajao ○ RP 160-161 F 8
Mambai ○ CAM 204-205 K 5
Mambali ○ EAT 212-213 D 6
Mambare River ∼ PNG 183 D 5
Mambasa ○ ZRE 212-213 B 3

Mambeco ○ MOC 218-219 G 6
Mambenga ∼ ZRE 210-211 G 5
Mamberamo ∼ RI 166-167 K 3
Mamberamo-Foja Mountains-Rouffaer Reserves ⊥ RI 166-167 K 3
Mamberano ○ RI 166-167 E 7
Mambéré ∼ RCA 206-207 B 6
Mambéré-Kadéï ⊡ RCA 206-207 B 6
Mambi ○ RI 164-165 F 5
Mambla ○ RI 164-165 G 5
Mambili ∼ RCB 210-211 E 3
Mambilima Falls ⋅ Z 214-215 E 6
Mambilla Mountains ▲ WAN 204-205 J 5
Mambone ∼ ANG 216-217 C 7
Mamboor, Kepuluaan ∼ RI 166-167 H 3
Mamborê ○ BR 74-75 D 5
Mambova Rapids ∼ Z 218-219 C 3
Mambrui ○ EAK 212-213 H 5
Mamburao ∼ RP 160-161 D 6
Mambusao ○ RP 160-161 E 7
Mambwe ○ Z 214-215 F 5
Mamcai ○ RI 166-167 H 2
Mamčërgyrgyn ∼ RUS 112-113 U 4
Mamdapur ○ IND 140-141 F 2
Mameigwess Lake ○ CDN 34-35 N 4
Mamelodi ○ ZA 220-221 J 2
Ma-Me-O-Beach ○ CDN 32-33 O 5
Mametčinskij, poluostrov ∪ RUS 120-121 U 3
Mametčinskij, zaliv ≈ RUS 120-121 U 3
Mamfé ○ CAM 204-205 J 5
Mämi, Ra's ▲ Y 132-133 J 7
Mamiá, Lago ○ BR 66-67 F 5
Mamiña ○ RCH 76-77 C 7
Mamisi ○ RI 166-167 H 3
Mamisonski, pereval ▲ GE 126-127 E 6
Mamljutka ☆ KA 124-125 F 1
Mammoth ○ USA 44-45 B 3
Mammoth Cave National Park ⊥⋯ USA 46-47 E 7
Mammoth Hot Springs ○ USA 40-41 J 4
Mamoeiro ○ BR 66-67 F 5
Mamonovo ∼ RUS 94-95 F 4
Mamonta ∼ RUS 108-109 V 4
Mamonta, poluostrov ∪ RUS 108-109 R 6
Mamontova gora ∼ RUS 120-121 F 2
Mamontovaja ∼ RUS 112-113 U 1
Mamontovo ○ RUS 114-115 M 4
Mamoré, Río ∼ BOL 70-71 E 3
Mamori ○ BR 66-67 G 4
Mamori, Lago ○ BR 66-67 G 4
Mamori, Paraná do ∼ BR 66-67 H 5
Mamou ☆ RG 202-203 D 4
Mamoriazinho, Rio ∼ BR 66-67 D 6
Mamoun, Lac ∼ RCA 206-207 D 4
Mampikony ○ RM 222-223 E 7
Mampong ∼ GH 202-203 K 6
Ma ∼ VN 158-159 J 5
Mamry, Jezioro ○ PL 92-93 Q 1
Mamu ∼ WAN 204-205 E 5
Mamuil Mulal, Paso ▲ RA 78-79 D 5
Mamuju ○ RI 164-165 F 5
Ma'müniye ○ IR 136-137 B 7
Mamun, al- ○ IR 128-129 L 7
Mamuras ○ AL 100-101 G 4
Mamutzu ○ COM 222-223 D 4
Man ☆⋅ CI 202-203 G 5
Man ∼ RCA 206-207 B 5
Man, al- ∼ RI 168 C 3
Man, Río ∼ PE 64-65 F 7
Mana ∼ RI 162-63 H 3
Mana ∼ RI 162-63 H 3
Mana ∼ FJI 184 III a 2
Mana ∼ RIM 196-197 F 8
Manacacias, Río ∼ CO 60-61 G 6
Manacapurú ○ BR 66-67 G 4
Manacapuru, Río do ∼ BR 66-67 G 4
Manacas ○ C 54-55 E 3
Manacor ○ E 98-99 J 5
Manado ○ RI 164-165 H 3
Manadotari ○ AUS 180-181 G 3
Managua, Lago de ○ NIC 52-53 L 5
Managua ★ Y 132-133 C 6
Manaía ∼ BR 68-69 J 5
Manakana ○ RM 222-223 E 9
Manakara ○ RM 222-223 E 7
Manalapan ○ IND 140-141 H 6
Manalalondo ○ RM 222-223 E 7
Manali ○ IND 138-139 E 3
Manama ○ UAE 134-135 G 6
Manáma, al- ★ BRN 134-135 D 5
Manamadurai ○ IND 140-141 H 6
Manambaru ○ RM 222-223 E 10
Manambolosy ○ RM 222-223 D 7
Manambondro ○ RM 222-223 D 10
Manamgoora ○ AUS 174-175 D 5
Manami ○ RI 166-167 H 3
Manamo, Caño ∼ YV 60-61 K 3
Manampahy ∼ RM 222-223 E 9
Manampatrana ○ RM 222-223 E 9
Mananá, Cachoeira ∼ BR 62-63 D 8
Mananara ∼ RM 222-223 D 8
Mananara Avaratra ○ RM 222-223 E 8
Mananda ○ RM 222-223 E 8
Manandona ∼ RM 222-223 E 8
Manangatang ○ AUS 180-181 G 3
Mananjary ○ RM (FNS) 222-223 E 10
Manankoro ∼ RMM 202-203 G 4
Manantali, Lac de ⊂ RMM 202-203 E 3
Manantenina ○ RM 222-223 E 10
Manántoddy ○ IND 140-141 G 5
Mana Pass ▲ VRC 144-145 B 5
Mana Pools National Park ⊥⋯ ZW 218-219 E 3

Manapouri, Lake ○ NZ 182 A 6
Manappärai ○ IND 140-141 H 5
Manaquiri ○ BR 66-67 G 4
Manaquiri, Lago ○ BR 66-67 G 4
Manari ○ PNG 183 D 5
Manariã ○ BR 66-67 D 6
Manas ○ PE 64-65 D 7
Manas ∼ IND 146-147 H 3
Manas, gora ▲ KS 146-147 C 5
Manasarowar = Mapam Yumco ○ VRC 144-145 C 5
Manas He ∼ VRC 146-147 G 3
Manas Hu ○ VRC 146-147 H 3
Manasu ▲ NEP 144-145 E 6
Manassas ○ USA 46-47 K 6
Manassas National Battlefield Park ⊥⋯ USA 46-47 K 6
Manatí ○ C 54-55 G 4
Manati ○ C 54-55 F 4
Manatlán ○ MEX 52-53 B 2
Manatuto ○ RI 166-167 C 6
Manau ○ PNG 183 D 5
Man'aung ∼ MYA 142-143 H 6
Man'aung Kyûn ∼ MYA 142-143 H 6
Manaure ○ CO 60-61 E 2
Manaus ○ BR (MAR) 68-69 E 2
Manaus ☆ BR (AMA) 66-67 G 4
Manavgat ∼ TR 128-129 D 4
Manavoka, Pulau ∼ RI 166-167 G 4
Manawar ○ IND 138-139 E 8
Mançano ○ I 100-101 C 3
Máncora ○ PE 64-65 B 4
Mancos ○ USA 42-43 C 7
Mand ○ PK 134-135 K 6
Mand, Rüd-e ∼ IR 134-135 D 4
Manda ○ EAT (IRI) 214-215 H 6
Manda ○ EAT (MBE) 214-215 G 4
Manda ○ ETH 200-201 L 6
Manda ∼ RI 166-167 D 4
Manda, Parc National de ⊥ TCH 206-207 C 4
Mandabe ○ RM 222-223 D 8
Mandacaru ○ BR 68-69 G 3
Mandaguari ○ BR 72-73 F 5
Mandah = Töhöm ○ MAU 148-149 J 5
Manda Island ∼ EAK 212-213 H 5
Mandal ☆ N 86-87 C 7
Mandalay ○ MYA 142-143 K 4
Mandalgovĭ ☆ MAU 148-149 H 5
Mandali ○ IRQ 128-129 L 6
Mandal-Ovoo = Šarhulsan ○ MAU 148-149 G 5
Mandalselva ∼ N 86-87 C 7
Mandan ○ USA 42-43 G 2
Mandan ○ RP 160-161 E 6
Mandar, Teluk ≈ RI 164-165 F 5
Mandara Mountains ▲ WAN 204-205 K 3
Mändás ○ I 100-101 B 5
Mandasor ○ IND 138-139 E 7
Mandaue ○ RP 160-161 E 7
Mandélia ○ TCH 206-207 B 4
Mandera ⊡ EAK 212-213 H 2
Mandera ○ EAT 214-215 J 4
Mandera ○ EAK (MBE) 214-215 G 4
Mandeville ○⋅ JA 54-55 G 5
Mandheera ○ SP 208-209 G 4
Mandi ○ IND 138-139 F 4
Mandi, Raudal ∼ CO 66-67 B 2
Mandiakui ○ RMM 202-203 H 3
Mandiangin ○ RI 162-163 G 6
Mandi Bahäuddin ○ PK 138-139 D 3
Mandi Burewala ○ PK 138-139 D 4
Mandié ○ MOC 218-219 G 2
Mandi Langwé ∼ CAM 204-205 J 4
Mandimba ○ MOC 218-219 H 2
Mandingues, Monts ▲ RMM 202-203 F 3
Mandioli, Pulau ∼ RI 164-165 K 4
Mandioré, Lago ○ BOL 70-71 J 6
Mandirituba ○ BR 74-75 F 5
Mandji ○ G 210-211 C 4
Mandla ○ IND 142-143 B 4
Mandleshwar ○ IND 138-139 E 8
Mando ○ RM 222-223 E 8
Mandöl ○ AFG 136-137 M 7
Mandor ○ AUS 172-173 E 5
Mandora ○ AUS 172-173 E 5
Mandouri ○ RT 202-203 L 4
Mandra ○ RI 166-167 H 3
Mandrã ∼ RM 222-223 E 10
Mandrare ∼ RM 222-223 E 10
Mandrikovo ∼ RUS 112-113 K 3

Mandritsara ○ RM 222-223 F 5
Mandronarivo ○ RM 222-223 D 8
Mandrosonoro ○ RM 222-223 E 8
Mandu ○ IND 142-143 D 4
Mandul, Pulau ∼ RI 164-165 E 2
Mandumboa ○ ANG 216-217 F 7
Mandurah ○ AUS 176-177 C 6
Mandúria ○ I 100-101 F 4
Mandúsar ○ AFG 138-139 B 3
Mándvi ○ IND (GUJ) 138-139 D 9
Mándvi ○ IND (GUJ) 138-139 B 8
Mandya ○ IND 140-141 G 4
Mané ○ BF 202-203 K 3
Maneadero ○ C 54-55 E 3
Maneadero ∼ MEX 50-51 A 2
Mané Kondjo ∼ TCH 206-207 D 3
Manengouba, Massif du ▲ CAM 204-205 J 4
Maneromango ○ EAT 214-215 K 4
Manevyči ○ UA 102-103 F 2
Manfalüt ○ ET 194-195 E 4
Manflas, Río ∼ RCH 76-77 C 5
Manfran ○ RG 202-203 F 5
Manfred Downs ○ AUS 174-175 F 7
Manfredónia ○ I 100-101 F 4
Manfredónia, Golfo di ≈ 100-101 F 4
Manga ○ BF 202-203 K 4
Manga ○ BR 72-73 J 3
Manga ▲ CAM 204-205 K 5
Manga ○ PNG 183 G 3
Manga ∼ PN 198-199 F 6
Mangabeiras, Chapada das ▲ BR 68-69 E 6
Mangai ○ PNG 183 G 2
Mangai ○ ZRE 210-211 G 5
Mangaizé ○ RN 202-203 J 2
Mangalia ∼ RO 102-103 J 4
Mangalmé ∼ TCH 198-199 J 6
Mangalore ○ AUS 178-179 J 4
Mangalore ○⋅ IND 140-141 F 4
Mangalwedha ○ IND 140-141 F 2
Mangango ○ Z 218-219 O 2
Mängaon ○ IND 138-139 D 10
Mangangveka ∼ NZ 182 F 3
Mangawan ○ IND 142-143 B 3
Mangaweka ∼ NZ 182 F 3
Mangbwalu ○ ZRE 212-213 C 3
Mangdangshan ∼ VRC 156-157 K 4
Mäng Đen, Đèo ∼ VN 158-159 K 3
Mange ○ PNG 183 D 4
Mange ○ WAL 202-203 D 5
Mangeni, Hamada ∼ RN 192-193 F 4
Manggar ○ RI 162-163 H 6
Manggasi ○ RI 166-167 J 3
Manggawitu ○ RI 166-167 G 4
Mangguar, Tanjung ▲ RI 166-167 H 3
Mangham ○ USA 44-45 M 3
Mangisor, Kôli ○ KA 124-125 F 1
Mangistau, gory ▲ KA 126-127 J 5
Mangit ○ US 136-137 G 5
Mangkalihat, Tanjung ▲ RI 164-165 F 3
Mangkok, Tanjung ▲ RI 164-165 E 5
Mangkutana ○ RI 164-165 G 5
Manglares Cabo ○ CO 60-61 C 5
Manglares, Cabo ▲ CO 64-65 C 1
Manglares, Punta ▲ CO 60-61 C 5
Manglares Churute, Reserva E ⊥ EC 64-65 C 3
Mangla Reservoir < PK 138-139 D 3
Mangnai ○ VRC 144-145 H 2
Mangnai Zhen ○ VRC 146-147 K 6
Mangnuc, Lac ○ CDN 36-37 L 5
Mangoaka ∼ RM 222-223 F 4
Mangochi ○ MW 218-219 H 2
Mango Creek ○ BH 52-53 K 3
Mangodara ○ BF 202-203 H 5
Mangoky ∼ RM 222-223 D 9
Mangole, Pulau ∼ RI 164-165 J 4
Mangole, Selat ≈ 164-165 J 4
Mangom ○ CAM 204-205 K 5
Mangombe ○ ZRE 210-211 L 4
Mangonui ○ NZ 182 D 1
Mangoro ∼ RM 222-223 F 7
Mangowra ○ AUS 174-175 F 5
Mängrol ○ IND 138-139 C 8
Mangrullo, Cuchilla de ▲ ROU 74-75 D 9
Mangrül Pir ○ IND 138-139 F 9
Mangshan ∼ VRC 154-155 H 4
Mangu ○ EAK 212-213 F 4
Manguaurcu ○ EC 64-65 B 3
Mangüchar ○ PK 134-135 M 4
Mangue ○ BR 68-69 F 2
Mangueigne ○ TCH 206-207 E 3
Mangueira, Lagoa ○ BR 74-75 D 9
Mangueirinha ○ BR 74-75 D 5
Manguel Creek ○ AUS 172-173 F 4
Mangues, Rio dos ∼ BR 68-69 D 7
Mangue Seco ○ BR 68-69 K 7
Mangues Secos, Ponta dos ▲ BR 68-69 G 3
Manguin ○ VRC 150-151 D 1
Manguito ○ C 54-55 E 3
Mangum ○ USA 44-45 H 2
Mangunça ○ BR 68-69 F 2
Mangunça, Ilha ∼ BR 68-69 F 2
Mangungu ○ ZRE 210-211 F 6
Manguo ○ Z 218-219 D 3
Manguohe ○ VRC 156-157 O 2
Manguredjipa ○ ZRE 212-213 C 3
Mangut ○ RUS 118-119 F 11
Manguturi, Igarapé ∼ BR 66-67 D 3
Mäng Yang ○ VN 158-159 K 4
Mäng Yang, Đèo ∼ VN 158-159 K 3
Mangyšlak ○ KA 126-127 J 6
Mangyšlakskij zaliv ≈ KA 126-127 J 6
Mangystau, taulary ▲ KA 126-127 J 5
Manhattan ○ USA 42-43 H 4
Manhica ○ MOC 220-221 L 2
Manhuaçu ○ BR 72-73 J 5
Manhumirim ○ BR 72-73 K 6
Mani ○ CO 60-61 E 5

Mani ○ **TCH** 198-199 G 6
Mani ○ **WAN** 198-199 C 6
Mani ○ **ZRE** 214-215 C 4
Mani, Quebrada de ∼ **RCH** 76-77 C 1
Mania ∼ **RM** 222-223 E 8
Maniaçu ○ **BR** 72-73 J 2
Maniamba ○ **MOC** 214-215 H 7
Mania-Muna ○ **ZRE** 214-215 B 5
Manica ○ **MOC** 218-219 G 4
Manica ○ **MOC** 218-219 G 4
Manicaland ▫ **ZW** 218-219 F 4
Manicani Island •• **RP** 160-161 F 7
Manicaragua ○ **C** 54-55 J 5
Maniche ○ **RH** 54-55 J 5
Manico Point ▲ **CDN** 36-37 F 3
Manicoré ○ **BR** 66-67 G 5
Manicoré, Rio ∼ **BR** 66-67 G 6
Manicorézinho, Rio ∼ **BR** 66-67 G 6
Manicouagan ○ **CDN** 38-39 K 3
Manicouagan, Petit Lac ○ **CDN** 38-39 L 3
Manicouagan, Réservoir ⊥ •• **CDN** (QUE) 38-39 K 3
Manicouagan, Réservoir ⪡•• **CDN** (QUE) 38-39 K 3
Manicouagan, Rivière ∼ **CDN** 38-39 K 4
Manic-Trois, Réservoir ⪡ **CDN** 38-39 K 3
Manifold, Cape ▲ **AUS** 178-179 L 2
Maniganggo ○ **VRC** 144-145 M 6
Manigotagan ○ **CDN** 34-35 H 5
Maniitsoq ● **GRØ** 28-29 O 4
Maniitsoq = Sukkertoppen ○ **GRØ** 28-29 O 4
Manika ○ **ZRE** 214-215 C 6
Manila ✶•• **RP** 160-161 D 5
Manila ○ **USA** 42-43 C 5
Manila Bay ≈ 160-161 D 5
Manila ○ **USA** 178-179 L 6
Manily ○ **RUS** 112-113 N 5
Manimbaya, Tanjung ▲ **RI** 164-165 F 4
Maningory ∼ **RM** 222-223 F 6
Maningoza ∼ **RM** 222-223 F 6
Maningrida ⨯ **AUS** 174-175 C 3
Maninjau ○ **RI** 162-163 D 5
Maninjau, Danau ○ **RI** 162-163 D 5
Manipa, Pulau ∧ **RI** 166-167 J 3
Manipa, Selat ≈ 166-167 H 3
Manipur ○ **IND** 142-143 H 3
Manipur ○ **IND** 142-143 H 3
Maniqui, Rio ∼ **BOL** 70-71 D 4
Manisa ✶ **TR** 128-129 B 3
Manisaj ∼ **KA** 126-127 M 4
Manissaua-Miçu, Rio ∼ **BR** 70-71 K 3
Manistee ○ **USA** 46-47 E 3
Manistee River ∼ **USA** 46-47 E 3
Manistique ○ **USA** 46-47 E 3
Manistique Lake ○ **USA** 46-47 F 2
Manistique River ∼ **USA** 46-47 E 2
Manita pećina ∼ **HR** 100-101 E 2
Manitoba ▫ **CDN** 34-35 F 3
Manitoba, Lake ○ **CDN** 34-35 G 5
Manito Lake ○ **CDN** 32-33 Q 5
Manitou ○ **CDN** 34-35 G 6
Manitou, Rivière ∼ **CDN** 38-39 M 3
Manitou Islands ∧ **USA** 46-47 E 3
Manitou Lake ○ **CDN** 38-39 D 6
Manitou Lakes ○ **CDN** 34-35 K 6
Manitoulin Island ∧ **CDN** 38-39 G 6
Manitoumik Sound ≈ 36-37 L 7
Manitou Springs ○ **USA** 42-43 G 4
Manitouwadge ○ **CDN** 34-35 O 6
Manitowoc ○ **USA** 46-47 E 3
Manitsoq ○ **GRØ** 26-27 X 7
Maniwaki ○ **CDN** 38-39 G 5
Maniwaki, Réserve Indienne de ⨯ **CDN** 38-39 F 5
Maniwori ○ **RI** 166-167 H 3
Maniyáchcho ○ **IND** 140-141 G 6
Manizales ✶ **CO** 60-61 D 4
Manja ○ **RM** 222-223 D 8
Manjacaze ○ **MOC** 220-221 L 2
Manjakandriana ○ **RM** 222-223 E 7
Manjakot ○ **PK** 138-139 D 2
Manjeri ○ **IND** 140-141 G 5
Mănjhand ○ **PK** 138-139 B 7
Manjimup ○ **AUS** 176-177 D 7
Manjo ○ **CAM** 204-205 H 6
Manjou ○ **CAM** 204-205 K 6
Manjra ∼ **IND** 138-139 F 10
Mánjra ∼ **IND** 138-139 F 10
Mankarza ○ **ZRE** 210-211 G 3
Mankarigu ○ **GH** 202-203 K 4
Man Kat ○ **MYA** 142-143 L 4
Mankato ○ **USA** (KS) 42-43 H 6
Mankato ○ **USA** (MN) 42-43 L 3
Mankayane ○ **SD** 220-221 K 3
Mankera ○ **PK** 138-139 C 4
Mankessim ○ **GH** 202-203 K 7
Manki II ○ **CAM** 204-205 J 6
Mankim ○ **CAM** 204-205 K 6
Mankins ○ **USA** 44-45 H 5
Mankono ✶ **CI** 202-203 G 5
Mankpan ○ **GH** 202-203 K 6
Mankranso ○ **GH** 202-203 K 6
Mankyclaks, cyganak ≈ 126-127 J 5
Manley Hot Springs ○ **USA** 20-21 P 4
Man Na ○ **MYA** 142-143 K 4
Manna ○ **RI** 162-163 E 7
Mannahill ○ **AUS** 180-181 E 2
Manna Hill Gold Field • **AUS** 180-181 E 2
Mannampitiya ○ **CL** 140-141 J 7
Mannar, Gulf of ≈ 140-141 H 6
Mānnārgudi ○ **IND** 140-141 H 5
Mannar Island ∧ **CL** 140-141 H 6
Mannarkkad ○ **IND** 140-141 G 5
Manners Creek ○ **AUS** 178-179 D 2
Mannheim ○ **D** 92-93 K 4
Manni ○ **VRC** 144-145 M 5
Manning ○ **USA** (IA) 42-43 K 5
Manning ○ **USA** (ND) 42-43 F 2
Manning ○ **USA** (SC) 48-49 H 3
Manning, Cape ∧ 24-25 X 3
Manning Provincial Park ⊥ **CDN** 32-33 K 7
Manning Range, Mount ▲ **AUS** 176-177 E 4
Manning River ∼ **AUS** 178-179 M 6

Manning Strait ≈ 184 I c 2
Mann Ranges ▲ **AUS** 176-177 K 3
Mann River ∼ **AUS** 174-175 C 3
Mannville ○ **CDN** 32-33 P 5
Mano ○ **WAL** 202-203 D 5
Manoã Pium, Área Indígena ⨯ **BR** 62-63 D 4
Mano Junction ○ **WAL** 202-203 D 5
Manokwari ○ **RI** (IRJ) 166-167 H 3
Manokwari ○ **RI** (IRJ) 166-167 H 2
Manolo Fortich ○ **RP** 160-161 F 8
Manoma ∼ **RUS** 122-123 G 4
Manombo Atsimo ○ **RM** 222-223 D 8
Manometimay ○ **RM** 222-223 F 6
Manompana ○ **RM** 222-223 F 6
Manonga ∼ **EAT** 212-213 D 5
Manono ○ **ZRE** 214-215 D 4
Manonwa ○ **ZRE** 214-215 D 4
Mano River ∼ **LB** 202-203 E 6
Manosque ○ **F** 90-91 K 10
Manou ○ **RCA** 206-207 C 4
Manouane ○ **CDN** 38-39 G 5
Manouane, Lac ○ **CDN** (QUE) 38-39 J 3
Manouane, Lac ○ **CDN** (QUE) 38-39 G 5
Manouanis, Lac ○ **CDN** 38-39 J 3
Manovo ○ Tété ∼ **RCA** 206-207 E 4
Manpo ○ **DVR** 150-151 F 7
Manresa ○ **E** 98-99 J 8
Mänsa ∼ **IND** 138-139 E 5
Mansa ✶ **Z** 214-215 F 6
Mansabá ○ **GNB** 202-203 C 3
Mansa Konko ✶ **WAG** 202-203 C 3
Mansalean ○ **RI** 164-165 H 4
Mansavillagra, arroyo ∼ **ROU** 78-79 M 2
Mänsehra ○ **PK** 138-139 D 2
Mansel Island ∧ **CDN** 36-37 K 3
Mansfield ○ **AUS** 180-181 J 4
Mansfield ○ **GB** 90-91 G 5
Mansfield ○ **USA** (AR) 44-45 J 4
Mansfield ○ **USA** (LA) 44-45 L 3
Mansfield ○ **USA** (MO) 44-45 L 1
Mansfield ○ **USA** (OH) 46-47 G 5
Mansfield ○ **USA** (PA) 46-47 J 5
Mansfield ○ **USA** (TX) 44-45 J 3
Mansha ∼ **Z** 214-215 F 6
Mansi ○ **MYA** 142-143 J 3
Mansiari ○ **IND** 144-145 G 5
Mansidão ○ **BR** 68-69 F 7
Mansijsk, Hanty- ✶ **RUS** 114-115 K 4
Mansilla ○ **E** 98-99 F 3
Mansinam, Pulau ∧ **RI** 166-167 H 2
Mansle ○ **F** 90-91 H 9
Manso, Rio ∼ **BR** 70-71 K 4
Mansôa ○ **GNB** 202-203 C 3
Mansôa, Rio ∼ **GNB** 202-203 C 3
Manso au das Mortes, Rio ∼ **BR** 70-71 K 4
Manson ○ **USA** 42-43 K 4
Manson Creek ○ **CDN** 32-33 H 4
Manso-Nkwanta ○ **GH** 202-203 K 6
Mansons Landing ○ **CDN** 32-33 H 6
Mansoura ○ **DZ** 190-191 E 2
Mansourah ○ **DZ** 188-189 L 3
Mansuar, Pulau ∧ **RI** 166-167 F 2
Mansuela ○ **RI** 166-167 E 3
Mansuela Reserve ⊥ ∧ **RI** 166-167 E 3
Mansura ○ **USA** 44-45 L 4
Mansūra, al- ✶ **ET** 194-195 F 2
Mansūriya, al- ○ **Y** 132-133 C 6
Mansurlu ○ **TR** 128-129 F 4
Manta ○ **EC** 64-65 B 2
Manta, Bahía de ≈ 64-65 B 2
Mantaba ∼ **ZRE** 210-211 F 5
Mantalinga ∼ **RI** 164-165 G 5
Mantalingajan, Mount ▲ **RP** 160-161 B 8
Mantantzila, Quebrada ∼ **RCH** 76-77 B 3
Mantaro ∼ **PE** 64-65 E 8
Manteca ○ **USA** 40-41 D 7
Mantecal ○ **YV** (APU) 60-61 G 4
Mantecal ○ **YV** (BOL) 60-61 J 4
Manteco, El ○ **YV** 60-61 K 4
Mantehage, Pulau ∧ **RI** 164-165 J 3
Mantena ○ **BR** 72-73 K 5
Mäpuca ○ **IND** 140-141 E 3
Manteo ○ **USA** 48-49 L 2
Manthani ○ **IND** 138-139 G 10
Mantiqueira, Serra da ▲ **BR** 72-73 G 7
Manto ○ **HN** 52-53 L 4
Manton ○ **USA** 46-47 E 3
Manton Knob ▲ **USA** 176-177 J 3
Mantova ○ **I** 100-101 C 2
Mantralayam ○ **IND** 140-141 G 3
Mäntsälä ○ **FIN** 88-89 H 6
Mantua ○ **C** 54-55 C 3
Mantua ○ **C** 54-55 C 3
Mantuan Downs P.O. ○ **AUS** 178-179 J 3
Manturovo ○ **RUS** 96-97 D 4
Manú ○ **PE** 70-71 B 3
Manu ○ **WAN** 198-199 D 5
Manù, Parque Nacional ⊥••• **PE** 70-71 B 2
Manu'a Islands ∧ **USA** 184 V c 2
Manubepium ○ **RI** 166-167 H 2
Manuel ○ **MEX** 50-51 K 6
Manuela, La ○ **RA** 78-79 J 6
Manuel Alves, Rio ∼ **BR** 68-69 D 7
Manuel Alves Grande, Rio ∼ **BR** 68-69 D 5
Manuel Alves Pequena, Rio ∼ **BR** 68-69 E 6
Manuel Benavides ○ **MEX** 50-51 H 3
Manuel Emidio ○ **BR** 68-69 G 5
Manuel Lake ○ **CDN** 30-31 N 7
Manuel Ribas ○ **BR** 74-75 E 5
Manuel Rodríguez, Isla ∧ **RCH** 80 D 6
Manuel Tames ○ **C** 54-55 H 4
Manuel Urbano ○ **BR** 66-67 C 7
Manuel Viana ○ **BR** 76-77 K 5
Manuel Vitorino ○ **BR** 72-73 K 3
Manûğàn ○ **IR** 134-135 G 5
Manui, Pulau ∧ **RI** 164-165 H 5

Manuk ∼ **RI** 168 C 3
Manuk, Pulau ∧ **RI** 166-167 F 4
Manukan ○ **RP** 160-161 E 8
Manundi, Tanjung ▲ **RI** 166-167 H 2
Manupampi, Pulau ∧ **RI** 166-167 H 2
Manuran, Pulau ∧ **RI** 166-167 F 1
Manurimi, Rio ∼ **PE** 70-71 C 2
Manuripe, Rio ∼ **PE** 70-71 C 2
Manuripi, Rio ∼ **BOL** 70-71 D 2
Manuripi Heath, Natural Reserve ⊥ **BOL** 70-71 C 2
Manus Island ∧ **PNG** 183 D 1
Manvel ○ **USA** 42-43 J 1
Mänvi ○ **IND** 140-141 G 2
Manville ○ **USA** 42-43 E 4
Many ○ **USA** 44-45 L 4
Manyame ∼ **ZW** 218-219 F 3
Manyani ○ **EAK** 212-213 G 5
Manyara, Lake ○ **EAT** 212-213 E 5
Manyara National Park ⊥ **EAT** 212-213 E 5
Manyas ✶ **TR** 128-129 B 2
Manyberries ○ **CDN** 32-33 P 7
Manych ∼ **RUS** 102-103 N 5
Manyémen ○ **CAM** 204-205 H 6
Manyinga ○ **Z** 218-219 C 1
Manyo ○ **EAT** 214-215 F 6
Manyoni ○ **EAT** 212-213 E 6
Manzai ∼ **PK** 138-139 C 3
Mänzai ○ **PK** 138-139 B 4
Manzanares ○ **CO** 60-61 D 4
Manzanares ○ **E** 98-99 F 5
Manzanillo • **MEX** 52-53 G 7
Manzanillo ○ **C** 54-55 G 4
Manzanillo, Punta ▲ **YV** 60-61 G 2
Manzano, El ○ **YV** 60-61 J 2
Manzengele ○ **ZRE** 216-217 D 3
Manzhouli ○ **VRC** 148-149 N 3
Manzini ○ **SD** 220-221 K 3
Manzurka ∼ **RUS** 116-117 N 9
Manzurka ∼ **RUS** 116-117 N 9
Mao ✶ **DOM** 54-55 K 5
Mao ✶ **TCH** 198-199 G 5
Maogong ○ **VRC** 156-157 E 3
Maojing ○ **VRC** 154-155 E 3
Maoke, Pegunungan ▲ **RI** 166-167 J 4
Maolan Z.B. ⊥ **VRC** 156-157 E 4
Mao Ling ∼ **VRC** 154-155 F 4
Maoming ○ **VRC** 156-157 G 6
Maonanzu ○ **VRC** 156-157 E 4
Maopora, Pulau ∧ **RI** 166-167 D 5
Maospati ○ **RI** 168 D 3
Maotou Shan ▲ **VRC** 142-143 M 3
Mao Xian ○ **VRC** 154-155 C 6
Mapagá ○ **RI** 164-165 F 4
Mapai ○ **MOC** 218-219 F 4
Mapam Yumco ○ **VRC** 144-145 C 5
Mapane ○ **RI** 164-165 G 4
Mapangu ○ **ZRE** 210-211 H 6
Mapari, Rio ∼ **BR** 66-67 F 3
Mapastepec ○ **MEX** 52-53 H 4
Mapat, Pulau ∧ **RI** 164-165 E 2
Maphisa ○ **ZW** 218-219 E 4
Mapi ○ **RI** 166-167 K 5
Mapire ○ **YV** 60-61 J 3
Mapiri, Rio ∼ **BOL** 70-71 D 2
Mapiri, Rio ∼ **BOL** 70-71 D 2
Mapiripán ○ **CO** 60-61 F 4
Maple Creek ○ **CDN** 32-33 Q 7
Mapleton ○ **USA** (IA) 42-43 K 5
Mapleton ○ **USA** (OR) 40-41 C 3
Mapmakers Seamount ∼ 14-15 J 5
Mapoon ✶ **AUS** 174-175 G 3
Mapoon Aboriginal Land ⨯ **AUS** 174-175 G 2
Mappsville ○ **USA** 46-47 L 7
Maprik ○ **PNG** 183 B 2
Mapuera, Rio ∼ **BR** 62-63 E 5
Mapulanguene ○ **MOC** 220-221 L 2
Mapunda ○ **ZRE** 214-215 C 5
Mapunga ○ **Z** 218-219 D 1
Maputi, Pulau ∧ **RI** 164-165 F 3
Maputo ○ **MOC** 220-221 L 2
Maputo ✶ **MOC** (MAP) 220-221 L 2
Maputo ⊥ **MOC** (MAP) 220-221 L 2
Maputo, Baía de ≈ 220-221 L 3
Maputo, Reserva de Elefantes do ⊥ **MOC** 220-221 L 3
Maputo, Rio ∼ **MOC** 220-221 L 3
Maputsoe ○ **LS** 220-221 H 4
Maqárijus, Dair ∴ **ET** 194-195 F 2
Maqên ○ **VRC** 154-155 B 4
Maqèn Gangri ▲ **VRC** 144-145 M 3
Maqrat ○ **Y** 132-133 G 6
Maqteir ∴ **RIM** 196-197 E 4
Maqu ○ **VRC** 154-155 B 4
Maquan He (Damqog Zangbo) ∼ **VRC** 144-145 D 3
Maquapit Lake ○ **CDN** 38-39 N 4
Maqueda, Rivière ∼ **CDN** 38-39 N 2
Maqueda Channel ≈ 160-161 E 6
Maquela do Zombo ○ **ANG** 216-217 C 3
Maqueze ○ **MOC** 218-219 G 4
Maquia, Rio ∼ **PE** 64-65 D 5
Maquia, La ○ **C** 54-55 H 4
Maquinchao ○ **RA** 78-79 D 6
Maquinista ○ **BOL** 70-71 D 4
Maquinista Levet ○ **RA** 78-79 F 4
Maquoketa ○ **USA** 46-47 C 4
Mar, La ✶ **RCH** 76-77 C 4
Mar, Serra do ▲ **BR** 72-73 H 7
Mar, Serra do ▲ **BR** 74-75 F 6
Mara ∼ **EAT** 212-213 E 4
Mara ∼ **EAT** 212-213 E 4
Mara ○ **GUY** 62-63 F 2

Mara ○ **ZA** 218-219 E 6
Marabã ○ **BR** 66-67 E 3
Marabadiassa ∼ **CI** 202-203 H 5
Marabahan ○ **RI** 164-165 D 5
Marabatuan, Pulau ∧ **RI** 164-165 D 6
Marabi, al- ○ **KSA** 132-133 C 5
Marabitanas ○ **BR** 62-63 C 5
Maracá ○ **BR** 62-63 J 4
Maracá, Baía de ≈ 62-63 J 4
Maracaçumé ○ **BR** 68-69 F 3
Maracaçumé, Baía do ≈ 68-69 F 2
Maracaçumé, Rio ∼ **BR** 68-69 F 2
Maracaí ○ **BR** 72-73 F 7
Maracaibo ✶ **YV** 60-61 F 2
Maracaibo, Lago de ○ **YV** 60-61 F 2
Maracá-Jipioca, Estação Ecológica ⊥ **BR** 62-63 J 4
Maracaju ○ **BR** 76-77 K 1
Maracaju, Serra de ▲ **BR** 76-77 K 1
Maracaná ○ **BR** 68-69 E 2
Maracanã, Ilha de ≈ 68-69 E 2
Maracanã, Baía de ≈ 68-69 E 2
Maracanaí, Cachoeira ∼ **BR** 62-63 H 6
Maracanaquará, Planalto ▲ **BR** 62-63 H 5
Maracás ○ **BR** 72-73 K 2
Maracas Bay Village ○ **TT** 60-61 K 6
Maracay ✶ **YV** 60-61 H 2
Maracoa ○ **CO** 60-61 G 6
Maracó Grande, Valle ∪ **RA** 78-79 G 4
Maracuni, Rio ∼ **YV** 60-61 J 6
Maradah ○ **LAR** 192-193 H 3
Maradankadawala ○ **CL** 140-141 J 6
Maradi ○ **RN** 198-199 E 5
Maradi ✶ **RN** (MAR) 198-199 C 6
Maradun ○ **WAN** 198-199 C 6
Maraetai ○ **NZ** 182 E 2
Marafa ○ **EAK** 212-213 G 5
Marag ○ **BR** 72-73 J 2
Maragahawewa ○ **CL** 140-141 J 6
Marágže ○ **IR** 128-129 M 4
Maraguay, Punta ▲ **YV** 60-61 F 2
Marahuaca, Cerro ▲ **YV** 60-61 J 6
Marais des Cygnes River ∼ **USA** 42-43 K 6
Marajó, Baía de ≈ 62-63 K 6
Marajó, Ilha de ∧ **BR** 62-63 J 6
Marakabei ○ **LS** 220-221 J 4
Marakalalo Hills ▲ **RB** 218-219 D 5
Marakesa ○ **ZRE** 210-211 L 3
Maralal ○ **EAK** 212-213 G 5
Maralal National Sanctuary ⊥ **EAK** 212-213 F 3
Maraldy, kölí ○ **KA** 124-125 K 2
Marale ○ **HN** 52-53 L 4
Maraleda, Rio ∼ **BR** 72-73 J 2
Maraleda, Canal ≈ 80 D 3
Marali ○ **RCA** 206-207 D 5
Maralinga ○ **AUS** 176-177 L 4
Maralinga -Tjarutja Aboriginal Lands ⨯ **AUS** 176-177 L 4
Maramag ○ **RP** 160-161 F 9
Maramasike = Small Malaita ∧ **SOL** 184 I e 3
Maramec ○ **USA** 44-45 J 1
Marāmiya, al- ○ **KSA** 130-131 C 5
Maramuni ○ **PNG** 183 B 3
Maramuni River ∼ **PNG** 183 B 3
Maran ○ **MAL** 162-163 E 3
Mărán, Köh-i- ▲ **PK** 134-135 M 4
Marana ○ **USA** 40-41 J 9
Maranchón, Puerto de ▲ **E** 98-99 F 4
Marand ○ **IR** 128-129 L 3
Marangu ○ **EAT** (KIL) 212-213 F 5
Maranguape ○ **BR** 68-69 J 3
Maranhão ○ **BR** 66-67 J 4
Maranhão ▫ **BR** 68-69 E 5
Maranhão, Rio ∼ **BR** 72-73 F 3
Maranhoto ○ **BR** 66-67 F 4
Maranoa River ∼ **AUS** 178-179 K 4
Marañón, Rio ∼ **PE** 64-65 C 4
Maransabadi, Pulau ∧ **RI** 166-167 H 3
Marantale ○ **RI** 164-165 G 4
Maranura ○ **PE** 64-65 F 8
Maranura ○ **PE** 64-65 F 8
Marão ○ **MOC** 220-221 M 2
Marapi, Gunung ▲ **RI** 162-163 D 5
Marapi, Rio ∼ **BR** 62-63 F 5
Marapinim ○ **BR** 68-69 E 2
Marapinim, Rio ∼ **BR** 68-69 E 2
Marapiti, Ilha do ∼ **BR** 66-67 E 5
Marari, Rio ∼ **BR** 66-67 E 7
Mara Rosa ○ **BR** 72-73 F 2
Märäğeşti ○ **RO** 102-103 D 5
Marâši, al- ○ **Y** 132-133 D 5
Marasimsim ○ **MAL** 160-161 B 9
Marassu ∼ **RUS** 124-125 Q 2
Mărăşti ○ **RO** 102-103 D 5
Maratea ○ **I** 100-101 F 5
Marathon ○ **USA** 174-175 J 7
Marathon ○ **CDN** 34-35 N 6
Marathon ○ **USA** (FL) 48-49 H 7
Marathon ○ **USA** (TX) 44-45 F 4
Maratua, Pulau ∧ **RI** 164-165 F 3
Marau ○ **BR** 74-75 D 7
Marauiá, Rio ∼ **BR** 66-67 E 2
Marauá ○ **RA** 76-77 G 4
Maravaam ∼ **RUS** 112-113 U 3
Marave ○ **IND** 140-141 D 2
Marávatápée ∼ **IR** 136-137 D 6
Maraval ∼ **RUS** 110-111 J 7
Maravilla ○ **MEX** 52-53 G 4
Maravilha ○ **BR** 72-73 H 5
Maravilha ○ **BOL** 70-71 E 3
Maravillas ○ **MEX** 50-51 G 4
Marawaka ○ **PNG** 183 C 4

Marawi ✶ **RP** 160-161 F 9
Marawi = Merowe ○ **SUD** 200-201 E 3
Marawi'a, al- ○ **Y** 132-133 C 6
Marawih ○ **UAE** 134-135 E 6
Maraxo Patá ○ **BR** 62-63 F 5
Marayes ○ **RA** 76-77 D 6
Maria, El ○ **PA** 52-53 F 7
Maria, El ○ **PA** 52-53 F 7
Marbella ○ **E** 98-99 E 6
Marble Bar ○ **AUS** 172-173 D 6
Marble Falls ○ **USA** 44-45 H 4
Marble Hall ○ **ZA** 220-221 J 2
Marble Hill ○ **USA** 46-47 D 7
Marble Island ∧ **CDN** 30-31 Y 4
Marblethorpe ○ **GB** 90-91 H 5
Marburg (Lahn) ○ **D** 92-93 K 3
Marcbeli ○ **EC** 64-65 D 3
Marcali ○ **H** 92-93 O 5
Marcapata ○ **PE** 70-71 B 3
Marcapomacocha ○ **PE** 64-65 D 7
Marceau, Lac ○ **CDN** 38-39 L 3
Marcel, Lac ○ **CDN** 36-37 Q 6
Marcelândia ○ **BR** 70-71 K 2
Marcelino ○ **BR** (AMA) 66-67 D 3
Marcelino ○ **BR** (AMA) 66-67 D 2
Marcelino Ramos ○ **BR** 74-75 D 6
Marcelo ○ **BR** 68-69 C 3
Marchajanovskij, ostrov ∧ **RUS** 112-113 J 2
Marche ⊥ **F** 90-91 H 9
Marche ▫ **I** 100-101 D 3
Marche-en-Famenne ○ **B** 92-93 H 3
Marchena ○ **E** 98-99 E 6
Marchena, Isla ∧ **EC** 64-65 B 9
Marchinbar Island ∧ **AUS** 174-175 D 3
Marciónilio Sousa ○ **BR** 72-73 K 2
Marco ○ **BR** 68-69 H 3
Marco ○ **USA** 48-49 H 7
Marcoing, gory ▲ **RUS** 112-113 Q 2
Marcona ○ **PE** 64-65 E 9
Marco Rondon ○ **BR** 70-71 E 3
Marcos Juárez ○ **RA** 78-79 J 4
Marcoux ○ **USA** 42-43 J 2
Marcus ○ **USA** 42-43 K 4
Marcus Baker, Mount ▲ **USA** 20-21 R 6
Marcy, Mount ▲ **USA** 46-47 M 3
Mardj, al- ○ **IRQ** 128-129 K 6
Mardakan = Mardakan ○ **AZ** 128-129 O 2
Mardán ○ **PK** 138-139 D 2
Mardie ○ **AUS** 172-173 B 6
Mardin ✶ **TR** 128-129 J 4
Mardin Dağları ▲ **TR** 128-129 J 4
Marea del Portillo ○•• **C** 54-55 G 5
Marechal Deodoro ○ **BR** 68-69 L 6
Mareeba ○ **AUS** 174-175 H 5
Mareeq ○ **SP** 208-209 H 7
Marek ○ **RI** 164-165 G 6
Maremma ⊥ **I** 100-101 C 3
Maréna ○ **RMM** 202-203 F 2
Marendet ○ **RN** 198-199 C 4
Marengâb ○ **IR** 134-135 D 1
Marenge ○ **ZRE** 212-213 B 6
Marengo ○ **CDN** 32-33 Q 6
Marennes ○ **F** 90-91 G 9
Marerano ○ **RM** 222-223 E 8
Mareth ○ **TN** 190-191 H 4
Mar'evka ∼ **RUS** 118-119 M 8
Marewýj ○ **RUS** 118-119 M 8
Marfa ○ **USA** 44-45 E 4
Marfâ, al- ○ **UAE** 134-135 E 6
Marganec = Marhanec' ○ **UA** 102-103 J 4
Margaree Forks ○ **CDN** 38-39 O 5
Margaret, Cape ▲ **CDN** 24-25 d 5
Margaret, Mount ▲ **AUS** (SA) 178-179 F 3
Margaret Creek ∼ **AUS** 178-179 D 5
Margaret Lake ○ **CDN** (ALB) 30-31 M 6
Margaret Lake ○ **CDN** (NWT) 30-31 L 3
Margaret Lake ○ **CDN** (NWT) 30-31 P 4
Margaret River ○ **AUS** (WA) 176-177 C 6
Margaret River ∼ **AUS** 172-173 H 5
Margaridâa, Monte ▲ **BR** 76-77 J 2
Margarima ○ **PNG** 183 B 3
Margarita, Isla de ∧ **YV** 60-61 J 2
Margarita, La ○ **YV** 60-61 G 3
Margaritas, Las ○ **MEX** 52-53 J 3
Margate ○ **USA** 48-49 H 6
Margate ○ **ZA** 220-221 J 5
Marğa'yûn ✶ **RL** 128-129 G 6
Margeride, Monts de la ▲ **F** 90-91 J 9
Margeta, Tanjung ▲ **RI** 166-167 C 6
Marghita ○ **RO** 102-103 C 4
Margie ○ **USA** 42-43 L 1
Margilan ○ **US** 136-137 M 4
Mârgò, Dašte ⊥ **AFG** 134-135 K 3
Margos ○ **PE** 64-65 D 6
Margosatubig ○ **RP** 160-161 E 9
Margua, Rio ∼ **CO** 60-61 F 3
Marguerite ○ **CDN** 32-33 J 5
Marguerite, Baie ≈ 16 G 30
Marguerite River ∼ **CDN** 32-33 J 3
Marha ∼ **RUS** (SAH) 118-119 L 5
Marha ∼ **RUS** 110-111 K 7
Marha ∼ **RUS** 110-111 J 7
Marha ∼ **RUS** 118-119 J 4
Marha ∼ **RUS** 118-119 L 5
Marhamat ○ **US** 136-137 N 4
Marhanec ○ **UA** 102-103 J 4
Marhara ∼ **RUS** 110-111 J 7
Marhoum ○ **DZ** 188-189 L 3

Mari ○ **BR** 68-69 L 5
Mari ○ **PNG** 183 A 5
Maria ○ **BR** 62-63 K 6
Maria, El ○ **PE** 64-65 D 5
Maria, El ○ **PA** 52-53 D 7
María Cleofas, Isla ∧ **MEX** 50-51 E 7
Maria da Fé ○ **BR** 72-73 H 7
María Elena ○ **RCH** 76-77 C 2
María Eugenia ○ **RA** 76-77 G 6
María Grande, Arroyo ∼ **RA** 76-77 H 5
María Ignacia ○ **RA** 78-79 K 4
María Island ∧ **USA** 48-49 F 4
María Island ∧ **AUS** (NT) 174-175 C 4
Mariakani ○ **EAK** 212-213 G 5
María Linda, Rio ∼ **GCA** 52-53 J 4
Marialva ○•• **P** 98-99 D 4
María Madre, Isla ∧ **MEX** 50-51 F 7
María Magdalena, Isla ∧ **MEX** 50-51 F 7
Marian ○ **AUS** 178-179 K 1
Mariana ○ **BR** 72-73 J 6
Mariana, Ilha ⊥ **MOC** 220-221 L 2
Marianao ○ **C** 54-55 D 3
Mariana Trench ∼ 14-15 G 6
Mariani ○ **IND** 142-143 J 2
Marian Lake ○ **CDN** 30-31 L 4
Marianna ○ **USA** (AR) 44-45 M 2
Marianna ○ **USA** (FL) 48-49 F 4
Marianne Nunatakker ▲ **GRØ** 26-27 o 6
Mariannes, Îles ∧ **CDN** 38-39 P 3
Marianno I. Loza ○ **RA** 76-77 H 5
Mariano López ○ **BR** 72-73 H 1
Marian River ∼ **CDN** 30-31 L 4
Mariano ○ **S** 92-93 M 4
Mariapolis ○ **CDN** 34-35 G 6
Mariaqua, Rio ∼ **BR** 66-67 J 4
Mariarano ○ **RM** 222-223 E 6
Marías, Islas ∧ **MEX** 50-51 F 7
Marías Pass ▲ **USA** 40-41 H 1
Marias River ∼ **USA** 40-41 J 1
Maria Teresa ○ **ANG** 216-217 C 4
Maria Teresa ○ **RA** 78-79 J 4
Mariau, Ponta de ▲ **BR** 68-69 E 2
Maria van Diemen, Cape ▲ **NZ** 182 D 1
Mariazell ○ **A** 92-93 N 5
Ma'rib ○ **Y** 132-133 D 6
Maribo ○ **DK** 86-87 D 9
Maribor ○ **SLO** 100-101 F 2
Marica ∼ **BG** 102-103 E 7
Marica ○ **BR** 72-73 J 7
Marico ∼ **RB** 220-221 H 2
Maricopa ○ **USA** (AZ) 40-41 H 9
Maricopa ○ **USA** (CA) 40-41 E 8
Maricunga, Salar de ○ **RCH** 76-77 C 4
Maridi ○ **SUD** (SR) 206-207 J 6
Maridi ∼ **SUD** 206-207 J 6
Marié, Rio ∼ **BR** 66-67 D 3
Marie-Galante ∧ **F** 54-55 Q 4
Mariehamn ✶ **FIN** 88-89 E 6
Mariel ○ **C** 54-55 D 3
Marietta ○ **USA** (GA) 48-49 F 3
Marietta ○ **USA** (OH) 46-47 H 6
Marietta ○ **USA** (OK) 44-45 H 3
Marie Valdemar, Kap ▲ **GRØ** 26-27 q 6
Mariga ∼ **WAN** 204-205 G 3
Mariga, River ∼ **WAN** 204-205 G 3
Marigat ○ **EAK** 212-213 E 3
Marignane ○ **F** 90-91 K 10
Marigot ✶ **F** 56 D 2
Marigot ∼ **RN** 54-55 J 5
Marigot ○ **WD** 56 E 4
Mari, mys ▲ **RUS** 120-121 K 6
Mariinsk ✶ **RUS** 114-115 T 6
Mariinskoe ○ **RUS** 122-123 H 3
Marii Prončiščevoj, buhta ≈ 108-109 k 4
Marijampolė ✶ **LT** 94-95 H 4
Marikal ○ **IND** 140-141 G 2
Marilândia do Sul ○ **BR** 72-73 E 7
Marilia ○ **BR** 72-73 F 7
Marimari, Rio ∼ **BR** 66-67 J 4
Marimba ○ **ANG** 216-217 D 4
Marimbona ∼ **RM** 222-223 F 6
Marimbondo ○ **BR** 68-69 K 6
Marín ○ **E** 98-99 C 3
Marín ○ **MEX** 50-51 J 5
Marina di Léuca ○ **I** 100-101 G 5
Marina Horka ✶ **BY** 94-95 L 5
Marina Plains ○ **AUS** 174-175 G 4
Marinduque Island ∧ **RP** 160-161 D 6
Marine Corps Base Camp Lejeune ⨯⨯ **USA** 48-49 K 2
Marineland cf Florida ∴ **USA** 48-49 H 5
Marine Museum • **USA** 46-47 G 5
Marine National Park ⊥ **ER** 200-201 K 5
Marine National Reserve ⊥ **EAK** 212-213 H 5
Marine Reserve I ⊥ **RI** (SSE) 168 E 6
Marine Reserve I ⊥ **RI** (STG) 164-165 H 6
Marinette ○ **USA** 46-47 E 3
Maringa ∼ **ZRE** 210-211 H 3
Marinheiros, Ilha dos ∧ **BR** 74-75 D 8
Marino Barbareta, Parque Nacional ⊥ **HN** 52-53 L 3
Marino Guanaja, Parque Nacional ⊥ **HN** 54-55 C 6
Marino Punta Sal, Parque Nacional ⊥ **HN** 52-53 L 4
Marinovka ✶ **KA** 124-125 F 3

Marion ○ **USA** (AL) 48-49 E 3
Marion ○ **USA** (IA) 46-47 C 5
Marion ○ **USA** (IL) 46-47 D 7
Marion ○ **USA** (IN) 46-47 F 5
Marion ○ **USA** (KS) 42-43 J 6
Marion ○ **USA** (NC) 48-49 G 2
Marion ○ **USA** (OH) 46-47 G 5
Marion ○ **USA** (SC) 48-49 J 2
Marion ○ **USA** (VA) 46-47 H 7
Marion, Lake ○ **USA** 48-49 H 3
Marion Downs ○ **AUS** 178-179 E 2
Marion Reef ∧ **AUS** 174-175 M 6
Maripa ○ **GUY** 62-63 E 2
Maripasoula ○ **F** 62-63 G 4
Maripa ○ **USA** 40-41 E 7
Mariposa, Sierra ▲ **RCH** 76-77 C 7
Mariquita ○ **BR** 72-73 H 2
Mariquita ○ **CO** 60-61 D 5
Marisa ○ **RI** 164-165 G 4
Mariscal Cáceres ○ **PE** 64-65 E 8
Mariscal de Juárez ○ **MEX** 52-53 G 7
Mariscal Estigarribia ○ **PY** 76-77 G 1
Marismas, Las ⊥ **E** 98-99 D 6
Marita Downs ○ **AUS** 178-179 G 2
Marite ○ **ZA** 220-221 K 2
Mariupol' = Maryupol' ○ **UA** 102-103 K 4
Marivãn ○ **IR** 128-129 M 5
Mariveles ○ **RP** 160-161 D 5
Marj, Al ✶ **LAR** 192-193 J 1
Mârjamaa ○•• **EST** 94-95 J 2
Mar'janovka ∼ **RUS** 124-125 H 1
Marjorie Hills ▲ **USA** 30-31 U 3
Marjorie Lake ○ **CDN** 30-31 U 3
Marka ○ **SP** 212-213 K 3
Markakol', köli ○ **KA** 124-125 O 4
Markala ○ **RMM** 202-203 G 3
Markam ○ **VRC** 144-145 M 6
Markama, proliv ≈ 84-85 d 2
Márkápur ○ **IND** 140-141 H 3
Markara ○ **AR** 128-129 L 2
Markazi ○ **IR** 134-135 C 1
Marked Tree ○ **USA** 44-45 M 2
Marken ○ **ZA** 218-219 E 6
Markham ○ **CDN** 38-39 E 7
Markham, Mount ▲ **ARK** 16 E 0
Markham Bay ≈ 36-37 N 3
Markham Bay ≈ 183 D 4
Markham Lake ○ **CDN** 30-31 S 4
Markham River ∼ **PNG** 183 D 4
Markit ○ **VRC** 146-147 C 6
Markivka ○ **UA** 102-103 L 3
Markley, Fort ∴ **USA** 42-43 J 6
Markos Paz ○ **RA** 78-79 K 4
Markounda ○ **RCA** 206-207 C 5
Markovac ○ **YU** 100-101 H 2
Markovo ○ **RUS** (CUK) 112-113 Q 4
Markovo ○ **RUS** (IRK) 116-117 N 7
Markový ○ **BY** 202-203 L 2
Marks ○ **RUS** 96-97 E 8
Marktredwitz ○ **D** 92-93 M 3
Marktredwitz ○ **D** (BAY) 92-93 M 4
Mark Twain Lake ○ **USA** 46-47 C 6
Markundi ○ **SUD** 206-207 H 6
Markúz, al- ○ **KSA** 130-131 H 2
Markwassie ○ **ZA** 220-221 H 3
Marla ○ **AUS** 176-177 M 3
Marlborough ○ **AUS** 178-179 K 2
Marlborough ○ **GB** 90-91 G 6
Marlborough ○ **GUY** 62-63 G 2
Marlborough ○ **USA** 46-47 N 4
Marlborough Sounds ≈ **NZ** 182 D 4
Marlin ○ **USA** 44-45 J 4
Marlin Coast ∪ **AUS** 174-175 H 5
Marlinton ○ **USA** 46-47 H 6
Marlo ○ **AUS** 180-181 K 4
Marloth Nature Reserve ⊥ **ZA** 220-221 E 6
Marlow ○ **USA** 44-45 H 3
Marmagao ○ **IND** 140-141 E 3
Marmande ○ **F** 90-91 H 9
Marmara Adası ∧ **TR** 128-129 B 2
Marmara Denizi ≈ 128-129 B 2
Marmara Ereğlisi ✶ **TR** 128-129 B 2
Marmaris ○ **TR** 128-129 C 4
Marmarth ○ **USA** 42-43 F 2
Marmelo, Rio ∼ **BR** 66-67 D 7
Marmelos, Rio dos ∼ **BR** 66-67 G 6
Mar Menor ○ **E** 98-99 G 6
Marmion, Lake ○ **AUS** 176-177 F 4
Marmion Lake ○ **CDN** 34-35 L 6
Marmites des géants ∼ **RM** 222-223 E 9
Marmolada ▲ **I** 100-101 C 1
Marmoles, Parque Nacional Los ⊥ **MEX** 50-51 K 7
Marmot Bay ≈ 22-23 U 3
Marmot Island ∧ **USA** 22-23 V 3
Marmul ○ **OM** 132-133 J 4
Marne ∼ **F** 90-91 J 4
Marne-au-Rhin, Canal de la ⪡ **F** 90-91 L 7
Marneuli ○ **GE** 126-127 F 7
Marnoo ○ **AUS** 180-181 G 4
Maro ○ **TCH** 206-207 D 4
Maroa ○ **YV** 60-61 H 5
Maroala ○ **RM** 222-223 E 6
Maroambihy ○ **RM** 222-223 F 5
Marolambo ○ **RM** 222-223 F 7
Marofandilia ○ **RM** 222-223 D 8
Marofototra ○ **RM** 222-223 F 5
Marojejy ▲ **RM** 222-223 F 5
Maroktua ○ **RI** 162-163 F 5
Marolambo ○ **RM** 222-223 F 7
Marolinta ○ **RM** 222-223 D 10
Maromandia ○ **RM** 222-223 F 5
Maromokotro ▲ **RM** 222-223 F 5
Marondera ○ **ZW** 218-219 F 4
Marone ∼ **SME** 62-63 G 3
Maroni ∼ **SME** 62-63 G 3
Maroochydore -Mooloolaba ○ **AUS** 178-179 M 4
Maroon-Village ○ **JA** 54-55 G 5
Maropaika ○ **RM** 222-223 E 8
Maros ∼ **H** 92-93 Q 5
Maros ○ **RI** 164-165 F 6
Maroseranana ○ **RM** 222-223 F 7
Marotandrano ○ **RM** 222-223 F 6
Marotolana ○ **RM** 222-223 F 5

Maroua o • CAM 206-207 B 3
Marova o BR 66-67 F 3
Marovato o RM 222-223 D 10
Marovoalavo, Lembalemban'i ▲ RM 222-223 F 6
Marovoay o RM 222-223 F 7
Marovoay Atsimo o RM 222-223 D 6
Marowijnerivier ~ SME 62-63 G 3
Marowinir ~ F 62-63 G 4
Marqab, al- ∴ IRQ 128-129 F 5
Marqadá o SUD 206-207 K 4
Marqua o AUS 178-179 J 5
Marquard o ZA 220-221 H 4
Marque, La o USA 44-45 M 5
Marquesas Fracture Zone ≃ 14-15 P 8
Marquesas Islands = Marquises, Îles ▲ F 13 N 3
Marquesas Keys ▲ USA 48-49 G 7
Marquette o USA 46-47 E 2
Marquez o USA 44-45 J 4
Marqûq o SUD 206-207 K 4
Marracua o MOC 218-219 J 3
Marrakech = Marrâkush ☆ ••• MA 188-189 H 5
Marraket, Hassi ∴ DZ 190-191 D 5
Marrâkush ☆ ••• MA 188-189 H 5
Marrân o KSA 130-131 G 6
Marrangua, Lagoa o MOC 220-221 M 2
Marrât o KSA 130-131 J 5
Marrawah o AUS 180-181 H 6
Marrecão o BR 66-67 D 6
Marree o AUS 178-179 F 5
Marrero o USA 44-45 M 5
Marresal'skie koški ▲ RUS 108-109 M 7
Marroins, Ilha ▲ BR 66-67 F 7
Marromeu o MOC 218-219 H 4
Marromeu, Reserva de ⊥ MOC 218-219 H 4
Marroonah o AUS 176-177 C 1
Marroquí o Tarifa, Punta ▲ E 98-99 F 2
Marruás o BR 68-69 J 5
Marrupa o MOC 218-219 J 3
Mars, Le o USA 42-43 J 4
Marsá al Burayqah o LAR 192-193 H 2
Marsa, La o TN 190-191 H 2
Marsabit o EAK 212-213 F 2
Marsabit National Reserve ⊥ EAK 212-213 F 2
Marsala o I 100-101 D 6
Marsá l-'Alam o ET 194-195 G 5
Marsá Matrûh o ET 194-195 C 2
Marsá Matrûh • ET 194-195 C 2
Marsá Mubarak o ET 194-195 G 5
Marsassoum o SN 202-203 C 3
Marsden o AUS 180-181 J 2
Marsden, Point ▲ AUS 180-181 D 3
Marseille o F 90-91 K 10
Marsella o CO 60-61 D 5
Mârshenän, Küh-e ▲ IR 134-135 E 2
Marsfjället ▲ S 86-87 G 4
Marsh, Mount ▲ AUS 172-173 D 7
Marshall o LB 202-203 E 6
Marshall o USA (AK) 20-21 J 6
Marshall o USA (AR) 44-45 L 2
Marshall o USA (IL) 46-47 E 3
Marshall o USA (MI) 46-47 F 4
Marshall o USA (MN) 42-43 K 3
Marshall o USA (MO) 42-43 L 6
Marshall o USA (TX) 44-45 K 3
Marshall Islands ■ MAI 14-15 J 6
Marshall River ~ AUS 178-179 D 2
Marshall Seamounts ≃ 14-15 J 6
Marshalltown o USA 42-43 L 5
Marshfield o USA (MO) 44-45 L 1
Marshfield o USA (WI) 46-47 C 3
Marsh Fork ~ USA 20-21 N 2
Marsh Harbour o BS 54-55 G 1
Marsh Hill o USA 46-47 P 2
Marsh Island ▲ USA 44-45 M 5
Marsh Lake o CDN 20-21 X 6
Marsh Pass ▲ USA 44-45 B 1
Marsh Point ▲ CDN 34-35 K 2
Marsiwang o RI 166-167 F 3
Marsiwang, Tanjung ▲ RI (MAL) 166-167 F 3
Marsoui o CDN 38-39 L 4
Märsta o S 86-87 H 7
Martaban o MYA 158-159 D 2
Martaban, Gulf of ≈ 158-159 D 2
Martadi o NEP 144-145 C 6
Martand o • IND 138-139 E 3
Martap o CAM 204-205 K 5
Martapura o RI (KSE) 164-165 D 5
Martapura o RI (SUS) 162-163 F 7
Marte o WAN 198-199 F 6
Marte, Rivière à la ~ CDN 38-39 G 3
Marten River o CDN (ONT) 38-39 E 5
Marten River ~ CDN 30-31 P 5
Martens Falls Indian Reserve ▲ CDN 34-35 O 5
Martensøya ▲ N 84-85 M 2
Marthaguy River ~ AUS 178-179 J 6
Martha's Vineyard ▲ USA 46-47 N 5
Marti o C 54-55 E 3
Martigny o CH 92-93 J 5
Martigues o F 90-91 K 10
Martil o MA 188-189 J 3
Martin o SK 92-93 P 4
Martin o USA (SD) 42-43 G 4
Martin o USA (TN) 48-49 D 1
Martin, Lake < USA 48-49 F 3
Martinas, Las o C 54-55 C 2
Martinborough o NZ 182 E 4
Martinez, Cape ▲ CDN 24-25 J 4
Martineau River ~ CDN 32-33 Q 4
Martinez de la Torre o MEX 52-53 L 1
Martin House o CDN 20-21 Y 3
Martinique ■ F 56 E 4
Martinique = Olapoque o BR 62-63 J 4
Martinique Passage ≈ 56 E 4
Martinópolis o BR 72-73 E 7
Martin Peninsula ∪ ARK 16 F 25
Martin River ~ CDN 30-31 J 5

Martinsburg o USA 46-47 K 6
Martins Drift o RB 218-219 D 6
Martinsville o USA (IN) 46-47 E 6
Martinsville o USA (VA) 46-47 J 7
Martin Vaz Fracture Zone ≃ 6-7 H 10
Martok o KA 126-127 M 2
Marton o NZ 182 E 4
Martos o E 98-99 F 6
Martre, Lac la o CDN 30-31 K 4
Martti o FIN 88-89 K 3
Martuni o AR 128-129 L 2
Martynov o KA 96-97 G 8
Martynovo o RUS 124-125 O 2
Maru o RI 168 E 7
Maru o WAN 198-199 C 6
Maru, Nusa ▲ RI 166-167 F 5
Maruanum o BR 62-63 J 5
Maruchín ∴ MEX 52-53 K 2
Maruda o MAL 164-165 D 1
Marudi, Teluk o RI 160-161 B 9
Ma'rûf o DZ 190-191 D 5
Marum, Mount ▲ VAN 184 II b 3
Marumbi, Pico ▲ BR 74-75 F 5
Marungu ▲ ZRE 214-215 E 4
Marupa o PNG 183 G 3
Marupa, Rio ~ BR 66-67 J 6
Maruteru o IND 140-141 J 2
Maru'ura o SUD 184 I e 3
Marvão o P 98-99 D 5
Marvast o IR 134-135 F 3
Marv Dašt o IR 134-135 K 4
Marvine, Mount ▲ USA 40-41 J 6
Marwân o KSA 130-131 K 6
Marwayne o CDN 32-33 P 5
Mary ▲ TM 136-137 G 6
Maryal Bai o SUD 206-207 H 4
Mary Anne Group ▲ AUS 172-173 B 6
Mary Anne Passage ≈ 172-173 B 6
Mary Ann Point ▲ AUS 176-177 F 6
Maryborough o AUS (QLD) 178-179 M 3
Marydale o ZA 220-221 F 4
Maryfield o AUS 174-175 B 4
Mary Frances Lake o CDN 30-31 M 3
Maryhill o USA 40-41 D 3
Mary Kathleen ∴ AUS 174-175 E 7
Mary Lake o CDN 30-31 S 4
Maryland □ USA 46-47 K 6
Mary River ~ AUS 172-173 K 2
Mary River ~ AUS 172-173 H 5
Mary River ~ AUS 178-179 M 3
Marystown o CDN 38-39 J R 5
Marysvale o USA 40-41 H 6
Marysville o USA (CA) 40-41 D 6
Marysville o USA (KS) 42-43 J 6
Marysville o USA (OH) 46-47 G 5
Maryupol' o UA 102-103 K 4
Maryvale o AUS 174-175 H 5
Maryville o USA (MO) 42-43 K 5
Maryville o USA (TN) 48-49 G 2
Marzagão o BR 72-73 F 4
Marzanábád o IR 134-135 B 6
Marzo, 1 de o PY 76-77 J 3
Marzo, Punta ▲ CO 60-61 C 4
Marzûq o LAR 192-193 E 5
Marzûq ☆ LAR 192-193 E 5
Marzûq, Hamâdat ▲ LAR 192-193 E 4
Marzûq, zSazhrä' ▲ LAR 192-193 F 5
Mas, Tanjung ▲ RI 164-165 D 5
Masagaweyn o SP 208-209 H 7
Masagua o GCA 52-53 J 4
Masaguara o HN 52-53 L 4
Masâhim, Küh-e ▲ IR 134-135 H 4
Masahunga o EAT 212-213 D 5
Masai Mara National Reservat ⊥ EAK 212-213 F 4
Masâî'iqa, al- o OM 132-133 K 2
Masai Steppe ⊥ EAT 214-215 J 3
Masaka o EAU 212-213 C 4
Ma'sal o KSA 130-131 J 5
Masalembobesar, Pulau ▲ RI 164-165 D 5
Masalina, Kepulauau ▲ RI 164-165 C 5
Masally = Masallı o • AZ 128-129 N 3
Masamba o RI 164-165 G 5
Masan o ROK 150-151 G 10
Masanga o ZRE 210-211 J 4
Maşani', al- o Y 132-133 G 7
Masapun o RI 166-167 D 5
Masár, Ĝabal ▲ Y 132-133 G 6
Masasi o EAT 214-215 K 6
Masatepe o NIC 52-53 L 6
Más a Tierra, Isla ▲ RCH 78-79 C 1
Masavi o BOL 70-71 F 5
Masawa o RI 164-165 F 5
Masaya o NIC 52-53 L 6
Masbagik o RI 168 C 7
Masbate o RP (MAS) 160-161 E 6
Masbate ▲ RP (MAS) 160-161 E 6
Mascara ☆ DZ 190-191 C 3
Mascarene Basin ≃ 12 E 6
Mascarene Islands ▲ 224 C 6
Mascarene Plain ≃ 12 E 6
Mascarene Plateau ≃ 12 E 6
Mascasín, Salinas de ⌀ RA 76-77 D 6
Mascota o MEX 52-53 B 1
Masefield o CDN 34-35 Q 6
Masela, Pulau ▲ RI 166-167 E 6
Masel'gskaja o RUS 88-89 N 5
Mášelvfossen ~ N 86-87 J 2
Maseru ☆ LS 220-221 H 4
Masetleng Pan < RB 220-221 E 1
Masęĝde-Abolfazl o IR 134-135 H 4
Mašĝęd-e Soleimân • IR 134-135 C 3
Masha o ETH 208-209 B 5
Mašhad ☆ ••• IR 136-137 F 6
Mashan o VRC 156-157 F 5
Mashansha, Rio ~ PE 64-65 F 7
Mashar o SUD 206-207 J 5
Mashava o ZW 218-219 F 5
Mashhad = Mašhad ☆ ••• IR 136-137 F 6

Mashi o VRC 156-157 G 2
Mashike o J 152-153 J 3
Mäshki ~ PK 134-135 K 5
Mäshkel o PK 134-135 K 5
Mäshkel, Hämün-i o PK 134-135 K 4
Mashkode o CDN 34-35 O 7
Mashonaland Central □ ZW 218-219 F 4
Mashonaland East □ ZW 218-219 F 4
Mashonaland West □ ZW 218-219 F 4
Mashowingrivier ~ ZA 220-221 F 3
Mashra' ar-Raqq o SUD 206-207 J 4
Masi o N 86-87 H 2
Masia-Mbia o ZRE 210-211 F 5
Masian o RI 166-167 H 5
Masica, La o HN 52-53 L 4
Mašigina, guba o RUS 108-109 G 4
Masila, al- ~ Y 132-133 G 6
Masim, gora ▲ RUS 96-97 K 7
Masi-Manimba o ZRE 210-211 F 5
Masinde o EAU 212-213 D 3
Masind Port o EAU 212-213 D 3
Masinga Reservoir < EAK 212-213 F 4
Masingbi o WAL 202-203 E 5
Masinloc o RP 160-161 C 5
Mašira, Ĝazirat ▲ OM 132-133 L 3
Maşīra, Gulf of ≈ 132-133 L 3
Maşīra Channel ≈ 132-133 L 3
Masis o AR 128-129 L 2
Masisea o PE 64-65 E 6
Masisi o ZRE 212-213 B 4
Maskanah o SYR 128-129 H 4
Maskarenen Plateau ≃ 12 E 6
Mašķel, Rūd-e ~ IR 134-135 L 5
Maskelyne Islands ▲ VAN 184 II b 3
Masliya o KSA 132-133 C 5
Masljanino o RUS 114-115 S 7
Mašna'a, al- o OM 132-133 K 2
Masoala, Saikanosy ▲ RM 222-223 G 5
Masoala, Tanjona ▲ RM 222-223 G 6
Masohi o RI 166-167 E 5
Masoko o EAT (MBE) 214-215 G 5
Masomeloka o RM 222-223 F 8
Mason o USA (MI) 46-47 F 4
Mason o USA (TX) 44-45 H 4
Mason, Lake o AUS 176-177 E 3
Mason Bay ≈ 182 A 7
Mason City o USA 42-43 L 5
Masoni, Pulau ▲ RI 164-165 J 4
Mason River ~ CDN 24-25 H 6
Maspalomas o E 188-189 D 7
Masqa, al- o KSA 132-133 C 4
Masqat ☆ ••• OM 132-133 L 2
Massa o I 100-101 D 6
Massa, Oued ~ MA 188-189 G 6
Massaango o ANG 216-217 D 4
Massachusetts □ USA 46-47 M 4
Massachusetts, Fort ∴ USA 48-49 D 4
Massachusetts Bay ≈ 46-47 N 4
Massafra o I 100-101 G 4
Massakory o TCH 198-199 G 6
Massalassef o TCH 206-207 C 3
Massama o WAN 198-199 C 3
Massa Marĭttima o I 100-101 D 6
Massangano o ANG 216-217 C 4
Massangena o MOC 218-219 G 5
Massangulo o MOC 218-219 H 1
Massantola o RMM 202-203 G 3
Massapê o BR 68-69 H 3
Massaranduba o BR 74-75 F 6
Massarole < SP 212-213 H 2
Massau o ANG 216-217 D 3
Massena o USA 46-47 L 3
Massenya o TCH 206-207 C 3
Masset o CDN 30-31 D 6
Masset Inlet ≈ 32-33 D 5
Massey o CDN 38-39 D 5
Massey Island ▲ CDN 24-25 U 3
Massey Sound ≈ 26-27 C 4
Massiac o F 90-91 J 9
Massibi o ANG 214-215 B 6
Massif Central ▲ F 90-91 J 9
Massif Tabulaire ▲ F 62-63 H 4
Massigui o RMM 202-203 G 4
Massili o BF 202-203 K 3
Massillon o USA 46-47 H 5
Massina o RMM 202-203 H 3
Massine, Oued ~ DZ 190-191 D 7
Massinga o MOC 218-219 H 6
Massinger o MOC 218-219 H 6
Massingir, Barragem de < MOC 218-219 F 6
Masson Island ▲ ARK 16 G 10
Massosse o ANG 216-217 D 7
Maštaga o AZ 128-129 O 2
Mastah, ozero o RUS 118-119 L 3
Mastermans Range ▲ AUS 178-179 L 5
Masterton o NZ 182 E 4
Mastic Point o BS 54-55 G 2
Mastigouche, Réserve Faunique ⊥ CDN 38-39 H 4
Mastodonte, Cerro ▲ RCH 76-77 C 2
Mastūj o PK 138-139 D 1
Mastung o • PK 134-135 M 4
Mastūra o KSA 130-131 F 6
Mas'ûd o IRQ 128-129 K 4
Masuda o J 152-153 D 7
Masuguru o EAT 214-215 K 6
Masuika o ZRE 214-215 B 4
Mašuk, gora ▲ RUS 112-113 O 4
Mâsur o IR 134-135 C 2
Mât ~ RUS 120-121 H 4
Mathura o • IND 138-139 F 6
Matia ~ EAK 214-215 J 4
Matiacoali o BF 202-203 L 2
Matiari o PK 138-139 B 7
Matias Cardoso o BR 72-73 J 3
Matias Olímpio o BR 68-69 G 3
Mata (M'bera) ▲ RIM 196-197 C 5
Mata'Avea, Cape = Cape Lisburn ▲ VAN 184 II a 2
Matabeleland North □ ZW 218-219 D 4

Matabeleland South □ ZW 218-219 E 5
Mata Bia, Gunung ▲ RI 166-167 D 6
Matacawa Levu ▲ FJI 184 III a 2
Matachel, Río ~ E 98-99 D 5
Matachewan o CDN 38-39 D 5
Matachic o MEX 50-51 F 3
Matacú o BOL 70-71 F 5
Matad = Zuunbulag o MAU 148-149 M 4
Mata da Corda, Serra da ▲ BR 72-73 H 4
Matadi ☆ ZRE 210-211 D 6
Matador o USA 44-45 G 2
Matagalpa o NIC 52-53 L 5
Matagalpa, Río Grande de ~ NIC 52-53 B 5
Matagami o CDN 38-39 F 4
Matagami, Lac o CDN 38-39 F 4
Matagorda Bay ≈ 44-45 J 5
Matagorda Island ▲ USA 44-45 J 5
Mataj ~ RUS 122-123 F 5
Matak, Pulau ▲ RI 162-163 G 3
Matakana Island ▲ NZ 182 F 2
Matakaoa Point ▲ NZ 182 G 2
Matakawau ▲ NZ 182 E 2
Matakil, Chutes de ~ •• RCA 206-207 A 2
Matala o ANG 216-217 C 7
Matala o GR 100-101 K 7
Mâtala o IND 140-141 G 7
Matala o ZRE 210-211 L 5
Matalaque o PE 70-71 D 4
Matale o CL 140-141 J 7
Matale o ZRE 214-215 B 4
Matam o SN 202-203 D 2
Matamata o NZ 182 E 2
Matamoros o MEX (COA) 50-51 H 5
Matamoros o MEX (TAM) 50-51 L 5
Matana o BU 212-213 B 5
Matana o RI 164-165 G 5
Matana, Danau o RI 164-165 G 5
Matanal Point ▲ RP 160-161 E 8
Matandu ~ EAT 214-215 K 5
Matane o CDN 38-39 L 4
Matane, Réserve Faunique de ⊥ CDN 38-39 K 4
Matanga o RI 164-165 H 4
Matanga o RM 222-223 F 6
Matankari o RN 198-199 B 6
Matantas o VAN 184 II a 2
Matanuska River ~ USA 20-21 Q 6
Matanzas o C 54-55 E 3
Matanzas o MEX 50-51 J 7
Matanzas o YV 60-61 K 3
Matanzilla, Pampa de la ⌀ RA 78-79 E 4
Matão o BR 72-73 F 6
Mataojo o ROU 76-77 J 6
Mataoleo o RI 164-165 H 6
Mata Ortiz o MEX 50-51 F 2
Matapédia, Rivière ~ CDN 38-39 L 4
Matapi, Cachoeira ~ BR 66-67 F 2
Matapi, Rio ~ BR 62-63 J 5
Mataquito, Río ~ RCH 78-79 C 3
Matara o CL 140-141 J 8
Matara o ER 200-201 J 5
Matara o PE 64-65 C 5
Mataró o PE 76-77 F 5
Mataraca o BR 68-69 L 5
Mataram o RI 168 C 7
Mataró o • E 98-99 J 4
Matatiele o ZA 220-221 H 5
Matatindoe Point ▲ RP 160-161 E 8
Mataupu o PNG 183 F 5
Mataura o RI 164-165 H 6
Matawai o NZ 182 F 3
Matawin, Rivière ~ CDN 38-39 H 5
Matâỳ o ET 194-195 E 3
Matayaya o DOM 54-55 K 5
Matechai o ANG 216-217 C 6
Mategua o BOL 70-71 F 3
Matehuala o MEX 50-51 J 6
Mateiros o BR 68-69 E 7
Matekwe o EAT 214-215 K 6
Matela o LS 220-221 H 4
Matelot o TT 60-61 L 4
Matema o EAT 214-215 H 5
Matema o MOC 218-219 J 2
Matenge o MOC 218-219 G 2
Matera ☆ • I 100-101 F 4
Matéri o DY 202-203 L 4
Maternillos, Punta ▲ C 54-55 G 3
Matétszalka o H 92-93 R 5
Matetsi o ZW 218-219 D 4
Matetsi ~ ZW 218-219 D 4
Mateur o TN 190-191 G 2
Matewar o RI 166-167 K 2
Mátherán o • IND 138-139 D 10
Matheson o CDN 34-35 Q 6
Matheson Point ▲ CDN 24-25 L 5
Mathiassen Brook ~ CDN 36-37 H 2
Mathis o USA 44-45 J 5
Mathison o USA 48-49 D 4
Mathoura o AUS 180-181 H 3
Mathura o • IND 138-139 F 6
Mati ~ RUS 120-121 H 4
Matia o EAK 214-215 H 5
Maticora, Río ~ YV 60-61 G 2
Matiguás o NIC 52-53 B 5
Matiló o RCH 78-79 C 3
Matilla o RCH 70-71 C 7
Matima o RB 218-219 C 5
Matina o BR 72-73 J 2
Matinenda Lake o CDN 38-39 C 5
Matinha o BR 74-55 F 5
Matiši o LV 94-95 J 3
Matjiesfontein o ZA 220-221 E 6
Matlabas ~ ZA 218-219 E 7
Matlhaw Point ▲ CDN 32-33 G 7
Mátli o PK 138-139 B 7
Matma o TN 190-191 G 4
Matnog o RP 160-161 F 6
Mato, El o YV 60-61 J 4
Matochkin Shar, Proliv = Matočkin Šar, proliv ≈ RUS 108-109 L 5
Matočkin Šar o RUS 108-109 L 5
Matočkin Šar, proliv ≈ RUS 108-109 F 5
Matōes o BR 68-69 G 4
Matogrossense, Pantanal ~ • BR 70-71 J 3
Matok, Pulau ~ RI 162-163 G 3
Mato Grosso □ BR 70-71 J 3
Mato Grosso, Planalto do ▲ BR 70-71 K 4
Mato Grosso do Sul □ BR 70-71 J 6
Mato Guarojo o CO 60-61 F 5
Matondo o MOC 218-219 H 3
Matong o PNG 183 G 3
Matope o MW 218-219 H 3
Matopo o ZW 218-219 E 5
Matos, Río ~ BOL 70-71 D 4
Matos Costa o BR 74-75 E 6
Matoury o F 62-63 H 3
Mato Verde o BR 72-73 J 3
Matraca o CO 60-61 G 6
Matrah o • OM 132-133 L 2
Matâmah, al- o Y 132-133 D 5
Matras Beach ▲ RI 162-163 G 5
Matroosberg ▲ ZA 220-221 D 6
Matru o WAL 202-203 D 6
Matrûbah o LY 192-193 K 1
Matsalu Riiklik Looduskaitseala ⊥ EST 94-95 H 2
Matsanga o RCB 210-211 D 4
Matsari o CAM 206-207 B 5
Matsiatra ~ RM 222-223 E 8
Matsoandakana o RM 222-223 F 5
Matsue o J 152-153 E 7
Matsuka o G 210-211 B 4
Matsu Liehtao ~ RC 156-157 L 3
Matsumae o J 152-153 J 4
Matsumoto o J 152-153 H 6
Matsu Temple • RC 156-157 M 5
Matsuyama o J 152-153 E 8
Matsuzaka o J 152-153 G 7
Mattagami River ~ CDN 34-35 P 5
Mattawa o CDN 38-39 E 5
Mattawitchewan River ~ CDN 34-35 O 6
Matterhorn ▲ •• CH 92-93 J 5
Matterhorn ▲ USA 40-41 G 5
Mattesalja, mys ▲ RUS 108-109 Q 5
Matthews Ridge o GUY 62-63 D 2
Matthew Town o BS 54-55 J 4
Mattice o CDN 34-35 P 6
Mattili o IND 142-143 C 6
Mattò o J 152-153 G 6
Mattoon o USA 46-47 D 6
Matty Island ~ CDN 24-25 Y 6
Matu o MAL 162-163 H 5
Matuca o PE 64-65 D 7
Matuda, ozero o RUS 108-109 b 5
Matugama o CL 140-141 J 7
Matukar o PNG 183 D 3
Matuku ~ FJI 184 III a 3
Matundu o ZRE 206-207 B 3
Matupi, Igarapé ~ BR 66-67 G 6
Ma'tuq o SUD 200-201 F 5
Maturín ☆ YV 60-61 K 3
Matusadona National Park ⊥ ZW 218-219 E 3
Matusevièa, ford ≈ 108-109 b 2
Matveev, ostrov ~ RUS 108-109 H 7
Matveevka o RUS (ULN) 96-97 F 6
Matveevka ~ RUS (ORB) 96-97 H 7
Matveev Kurgan o RUS 102-103 L 4
Matykit, ostrov ~ RUS 120-121 Q 4
Mau o IND (UTP) 142-143 H 3
Mau o IND (UTP) 142-143 G 3
Mau, Île ~ Emao ~ VAN 184 II b 3
Mauá o BR 72-73 F 5
Maúa o MOC 218-219 J 2
Mauba, Wâdi ~ Y 132-133 G 5
Mauban o RP 160-161 D 5
Maubisse o RI 166-167 E 6
Maude o AUS 180-181 H 3
Maué o ANG 216-217 E 8
Maués o BR 66-67 J 4
Maués-Mirim, Río ~ BR 66-67 J 4
Maugris < RIM 196-197 C 5
Maui ~ USA 48-49 D 7
Maukeli o RI 168 E 7
Maulamyaing o MYA 158-159 D 2
Maulbronn o • D 92-93 K 4
Maule, Laguna del o RCH 78-79 D 4
Maule, Río o RCH 78-79 C 3
Maule o Pehuenche, Paso ▲ RA 78-79 D 4
Maullin o RCH 78-79 C 6
Maulvi, Bahía ~ PE 162-163 D 6
Maumee o USA 46-47 G 5
Maumere o RI 166-167 B 6
Maun ★ RB 218-219 C 5
Mauna Kea ▲ USA 48-49 E 8
Maunaloa o USA 48-49 D 7
Mauneluk River ~ USA 20-21 N 3
Maunggan Islands ~ MYA 158-159 D 3

Maungu o EAK 212-213 G 5
Maunoir, Lac o CDN 30-31 G 2
Maupertuis, Lac o CDN 38-39 J 3
Mauqaq o KSA 130-131 G 4
Maur, Wâdi ~ Y 132-133 C 6
Mau Rânipur o IND 138-139 G 7
Maure, Col de ▲ F 90-91 L 9
Maurelle Islands Wilderness ⊥ USA 32-33 C 4
Maures, Lake o USA 44-45 M 4
Mauri, Río ~ PE 70-71 D 4
Maurice, Lake o AUS 176-177 L 4
Maurice Ewing Bank ≃ 6-7 E 14
Mauricie, Parc National de la ⊥ CDN 38-39 H 4
Mauricio Batista o BR 76-77 K 5
Mauritania = Mawritaniyah ■ RIM 196-197 C 4
Mauritius ■ MS 224 C 7
Maury Channel ≈ 24-25 Y 3
Mausölée o RCA 206-207 D 6
Mauston o USA 46-47 C 4
Mauterndorf o A 92-93 M 5
Mauyama o WAN 204-205 E 2
Mavaca, Río ~ YV 66-67 E 2
Mävelikara o IND 140-141 G 6
Mavengue o ANG 216-217 E 8
Mavila o PE 70-71 C 2
Mavinga o ANG 216-217 F 7
Mavita o MOC 218-219 G 4
Mavua o ZRE 218-219 B 2
Mávuè o MOC 218-219 G 5
Mavunga ~ ANG 216-217 F 6
Mavuradonha ▲ ZW 218-219 F 3
Mawa o ZRE 210-211 L 2
Mawa-Geti o ZRE 210-211 L 2
Mawai o MAL 162-163 E 4
Mawana o ZRE 210-211 J 4
Mawang o VRC 156-157 F 2
Mawangdui Hanmu ∴ VRC 156-157 F 2
Mawara Island ~ PNG 184 I b 2
Mawasangka o RI 164-165 H 6
Mâwat o IRQ 128-129 L 5
Mawdin o MYA 158-159 C 3
Mawefan o RI 166-167 H 3
Mawhun o MYA 142-143 K 3
Mawlaik o MYA 142-143 J 4
Mawson o ARK 16 G 7
Max o USA 42-43 G 2
Maxaans o SP 208-209 H 6
Maxanguape o RB 68-69 L 4
Maxcanú o MEX 52-53 J 1
Máximo Gómez o C 54-55 E 3
Maxixe o MOC 218-219 H 6
Maxville o USA 46-47 O 3
Maxwell Bay ≈ 24-25 Y 3
Maxwell Fracture Zone ≃ 6-7 F 4
Maxwelton o AUS 174-175 G 7
May o PNG 183 A 3
May, Kap ▲ GRØ 26-27 Q 1
Maya, La o C 54-55 H 4
Maya, Pulau ~ RI 162-163 H 5
Mayabander o IND 142-143 G 7
Mayâdin, al- o SYR 128-129 J 5
Mayaguana Island ~ BS 54-55 J 3
Mayaguana Passage ≈ 54-55 J 3
Mayahi o RN 198-199 C 6
Mayala o ZRE 210-211 D 3
Mayama o RCB 210-211 E 5
Mayamba o ZRE 210-211 F 6
Maya Mountains ▲ BH 52-53 K 3
Mayang o VRC 156-157 F 3
Mayanja ~ EAU 212-213 C 3
Mayankwa o ZRE 218-219 B 2
Mayapan ∴ • MEX 52-53 K 1
Mayari o C 54-55 H 4
Mayarí Arriba o C 54-55 H 4
Mayata o RN 198-199 C 5
Maybell o USA 42-43 G 5
Maybelle River ~ CDN 30-31 O 6
Maych'ew o ETH 208-209 D 3
Maydena o AUS 180-181 J 7
Maydh o SP 208-209 H 6
Maydh o SP (San) 208-209 H 3
Mayel-Sarnou o SN 202-203 D 2
Mayenne o F 90-91 G 7
Mayenne ~ F 90-91 G 7
Mayerville o USA 42-43 K 6
Mayerthorpe o CDN 32-33 N 5
Mayfair o CDN 34-35 C 4
Mayfield o USA (ID) 40-41 G 4
Mayfield o USA (KY) 46-47 D 7
Mayhill o USA 44-45 E 3
Mayi, Mbuji- ☆ ZRE 214-215 B 4
May Inlet ≈ 24-25 V 2
Mayi-Jirgui o RN 198-199 D 6
Maymont o CDN 34-35 C 4
Maymyo o MYA 142-143 K 4
Maymūn, Wâdi ▲ LAR 190-191 H 5
Maynas ⊥ PE 64-65 D 3
Mayne River ~ AUS 178-179 F 2
Mayneside o AUS 178-179 G 2
Mâynii o IND 140-141 F 2
Maynooth o CDN 38-39 F 6
Maynooth = Maigh Nuad o IRL 90-91 D 5
Mayo o USA 48-49 G 4
Mayo, 25 de o RA (BUA) 78-79 J 3
Mayo, 25 de o RA (MEN) 78-79 E 3
Mayo, 25 de o ROU 78-79 K 3
Mayo, Río ~ MEX 50-51 E 4
Mayo, Rio ~ PE 64-65 D 5
Mayo o RA 86 G 2
Mayo Belwa o WAN 204-205 J 5
Mayo Butale o WAN 204-205 J 4
Mayo Chehu o WAN 204-205 J 4
Mayo Darlé o CAM 204-205 J 6
Mayo Djoti o CAM 206-207 B 3
Mayo Faran o WAN 204-205 K 4
Mayo Jarandi o WAN 204-205 J 5
Mayo-Kebbi ~ TCH 206-207 B 3

Mayoko o RCB 210-211 D 5
Mayo Lake o CDN 20-21 X 5
Mayombé ▲ G 210-211 C 5
Mayo Ndaga o WAN 204-205 J 5
Mayon Vulcano ▲ RP 160-161 E 6
Mayo Oulo o CAM 204-205 K 4
Mayor Buratovich o RA 78-79 H 5
Mayorga o RP 160-161 F 7
Mayor Island ~ NZ 182 F 2
Mayor Otano o PY 76-77 K 4
Mayototo o WAL 202-203 E 5
Mayotte ■ COM 222-223 D 4
May Pen o JA 54-55 G 6
May Point, Cape ▲ USA 46-47 L 6
Mayǵú' o KSA 130-131 F 3
Mayraira Point ▲ RP 160-161 D 3
Mayran, Desierto de ⌀ MEX 50-51 H 5
May River ~ AUS 172-173 G 4
Mayson o CDN 34-35 C 2
Maysville o USA 46-47 G 6
Maytown ∴ AUS 174-175 H 5
Mayu ~ RI 166-167 K 5
Mayu, Pulau ~ RI 164-165 K 3
Mayumba o G 210-211 C 5
Mayumbe o ZRE 214-215 E 4
Mayum La ▲ VRC 144-145 D 5
Mäyüram o IND 140-141 H 5
Mayville o USA 42-43 J 2
Maywood o USA 42-43 G 5
Maza o RA 78-79 H 4
Maza o WAN 204-205 K 3
Mazabuka o Z 218-219 D 3
Mazagão o BR 62-63 J 6
Mazagão Velho o BR 62-63 H 6
Mazagón o E 98-99 D 6
Mazama o USA 40-41 D 1
Mazamari o PE 64-65 E 7
Mazamet o F 90-91 J 10
Mazan o PE 64-65 F 3
Mazandarán o IR 136-137 B 6
Mazar o VRC 138-139 F 1
Mazâr, Küh-e ▲ AFG 134-135 L 2
Mazara del Vallo o I 100-101 D 6
Mazâr-e Adschaeh o AFG 136-137 K 6
Mazâr-e Šarif ▲ AFG 136-137 K 6
Mazargão o BR 70-71 K 6
mazar Karasopy ∴ KA 136-137 K 3
Mazarredo o RA 80 G 3
Mazartag o VRC 146-147 E 6
Mazar Tag ▲ VRC 146-147 E 6
Mazaruni River ~ GUY 62-63 E 3
Mazarwala o VRC 138-139 F 1
Mazatán o MEX (CHI) 52-53 H 4
Mazatán o MEX (SON) 50-51 D 3
Mazatenango ☆ GCA 52-53 H 4
Mazatlán o • MEX 50-51 F 6
Mazdaĝân, Rüdḫane-ye ~ IR 128-129 N 3
Mažeikiai ~ LT 94-95 H 3
Mazéla o BF 202-203 K 4
Maze Lake o CDN 30-31 N 3
Mazeppa Bay o ZA 220-221 J 6
Mazida ~ TR 128-129 J 4
Mazimechopes, Rio ~ MOC 220-221 L 2
Mazinán o IR 136-137 D 6
Mazocahui o MEX 50-51 D 3
Mazoco o MOC 214-215 H 6
Mazo-Cruz o PE 70-71 C 5
Mazoe, Rio ~ MOC 218-219 G 3
Mazomeno o ZRE 212-213 A 6
Mazomora o EAT 214-215 K 5
Mazong Shan ▲ VRC 148-149 C 7
Mazorca, Isla ~ PE 64-65 C 7
Mazoula o DZ 190-191 F 6
Mazowe o ZW (Mlc) 218-219 F 3
Mazowe ~ ZW 218-219 G 3
Mazra'a, al- o JOR 130-131 D 2
Mazra'eh Akhund o IR 134-135 E 3
Mazrûb o SUD 200-201 D 6
Mazsalaca o LV 94-95 J 3
Mazu Miao o VRC 156-157 L 4
Mazunga o ZW 218-219 E 5
Mazyr o BY 94-95 L 5
Mazzamitla o MEX 52-53 C 2
Mba o CAM 204-205 J 5
Mbabala o Z 218-219 D 3
Mbabane ☆ SD 220-221 K 3
Mbacha o WAN 204-205 J 5
Mbadduna o SOL 184 I c 3
Mbadi o G 210-211 C 5
Mbaéré ~ RCA 206-207 D 6
Mbagne o RIM 196-197 D 6
Mbahiakro o CI 202-203 H 6
Mbaíki ☆ RCA 210-211 F 2
Mbakaou o CAM 204-205 K 5
Mbakaou, Barrage de < CAM 204-205 K 5
Mbaké o SN 202-203 D 2
Mbako o RCA 206-207 B 6
Mbala o Z 214-215 F 5
Mbalabala o ZW 218-219 E 5
Mbalageti ~ EAT 212-213 E 5
Mbalam o CAM 210-211 D 2
Mbalambala o EAK 212-213 G 4
Mbale o • EAU 212-213 E 3
Mbali-Iboma o ZRE 210-211 F 5
Mbalmayo o CAM 210-211 C 2
Mbam ~ CAM 204-205 J 6
Mbam, Massif du ▲ CAM 204-205 J 6
Mbama o CAM 210-211 D 2
Mbama o RCB 210-211 E 4
Mbamba Bay o EAT 214-215 H 6
Mbambanakira o SOL 184 I d 3
Mbam Minkom ▲ CAM 210-211 C 2
Mbandaka ☆ ZRE 210-211 G 5
Mbandza o G 210-211 E 3
Mbandza-Ndounga o RCB 210-211 E 6
Mbane o SN 196-197 D 6
Mbang o CAM 210-211 E 2
Mbanga o CAM 204-205 H 6
Mbanga o SOL 184 I c 5
Mbangala ~ EAT 214-215 K 5
Mbanika Island ~ SOL 184 I d 3

Mesa ○ RI 164-165 L 3
Mesa ○ USA (AZ) 40-41 J 9
Mesa ○ USA (NM) 44-45 E 3
Mesa ○ USA (WA) 40-41 E 2
Mesa, Cerro ▲ RA 78-79 E 5
Mesa, La ○ CO 60-61 D 5
Mesa, La ○ YV 60-61 F 2
Mesabi Range ▲ USA 42-43 L 2
Mesa de las Tablas ○ MEX 50-51 J 5
Mesagrós ○ GR 100-101 J 6
Mesai, Río ~ CO 64-65 F 1
Mešakli ○ US 136-137 G 4
Mesanak, Pulau ⌒ RI 162-163 F 4
Mesaraba ○ ZRE 210-211 L 5
Mesa Verde National Park ⊥ ••• USA 44-45 C 1
Mescalero Apache Indian Reservation ⵅ USA 44-45 E 3
Meščerskaja nizmenost' ▲ RUS 94-95 Q 4
Meschetti ○ SP 212-213 H 3
Meschkakur ▲ MA 188-189 K 4
Mescit Dağları ▲ TR 128-129 J 2
Meseta Baya ▲ RA 78-79 E 5
Meseta de Jaua ▲ YV 60-61 J 5
Meseta de Somuncurá ⩡ RA 78-79 F 6
Meseta el Pedrero ⩡ RA 80 F 3
Mesfinto ○ ETH 200-201 H 6
Meşginšahr ○ IR 128-129 M 3
Mesgouez, Lac ○ CDN 38-39 G 3
Meshik River ~ USA 22-23 R 4
Mesick ○ USA 46-47 F 3
Mesilinka River ~ CDN 32-33 H 3
Mesilla, La ○ GCA 52-53 J 4
Mésima ~ I 100-101 F 5
Mesjagutovo ☆ RUS 96-97 L 6
Mesjid Raya • RI 162-163 C 3
Meškān ○ IR 136-137 F 6
Meski, Source bleue de • MA 188-189 J 5
Meskiana, Oued ~ DZ 190-191 F 3
Mesklip ○ ZA 220-221 C 4
Meslo ○ ETH 208-209 D 5
Mesna ~ RUS 88-89 S 2
Meşndiye ○ TR 128-129 G 2
Mesogi ○ CY 128-129 E 5
Mesopotamia ⩡ IRQ 128-129 J 5
Mesopotamia ⩡ RA 76-77 H 6
Mesquaie Indian Settlement ⵅ USA 42-43 L 5
Mesquita ○ BR 72-73 J 5
Mesquite ○ USA 44-45 J 3
Messaad ○ DZ 190-191 D 3
Messalo ~ MOC 214-215 K 7
Messaména ○ CAM 210-211 D 2
Messaoud, Oued ~ DZ 188-189 L 6
Mess Creek ~ CDN 32-33 E 3
Messeied ○ MA 188-189 F 6
Messejana ○ BR 68-69 J 3
Messelesek ○ RI 164-165 H 4
Messent Conservation Park ⊥ AUS 180-181 E 4
Messier, Canal ≈ 80 C 3
Messina ○ I 100-101 E 5
Messina ○ ZA 218-219 F 6
Messina, Stretto di ≈ 100-101 E 5
Messinge, Rio ~ MOC 214-215 H 7
Messiniakos Kólpos ≈ 100-101 J 6
Messojaha ~ RUS 108-109 T 7
Messolóngi ○ GR 100-101 H 5
Messondo ○ CAM 210-211 C 2
Messum Crater • NAM 216-217 C 10
Mesters Vig ○ GRØ 26-27 n 7
Mestia ○ GE 126-127 E 6
mesto padenija Tungusskogo meteorita • RUS 116-117 L 5
Mesuji ~ RI 162-163 F 7
Mesurado, Cape ▲ LB 202-203 E 6
Meta, Río ~ CO 60-61 E 5
Metaca ○ MOC 214-215 J 7
Metagama ○ CDN 38-39 D 5
Meta Incognita Peninsula ⌣ CDN 36-37 O 3
Metairie ○ USA 44-45 M 5
Métal, Mont du ▲ DZ 198-199 D 2
Meta Lake ○ CDN 34-35 N 5
Metaliferi, Munții ▲ RO 102-103 C 4
Metaline Falls ○ USA 40-41 F 1
Metán ○ RA 76-77 E 3
Metangobalame ○ MOC 218-219 H 2
Metangula ○ MOC 214-215 H 7
Metapán ○ ES 52-53 K 4
Metaponto ○• I 100-101 F 4
Metarica ○ MOC 218-219 J 2
Metchum ~ CAM 204-205 H 5
Meteghan ○ CDN 38-39 L 6
Metema ○ ETH 200-201 H 6
Meteóra ••• GR 100-101 H 5
Meteor Creek ~ AUS 178-179 K 3
Meteorit Ø ⌒ GRØ 26-27 S 5
Meteorologist Peninsula ⌒ CDN 24-25 V 1
Metepec ○ MEX (HGO) 52-53 E 1
Metepec ○ MEX (PUE) 52-53 E 2
Meteran ○ PNG 183 F 2
Métet ○ CAM 210-211 C 2
Meteti ○ PA 52-53 F 7
Methy River ~ CDN 32-33 Q 3
Metil ○ MOC 218-219 K 3
Metionga Lake ○ CDN 34-35 L 6
Metković ○ HR 100-101 F 3
Metlakatla ○ USA 32-33 E 4
Metlaoui ○ TN 190-191 G 3
Metlili, Oued ~ DZ 190-191 D 4
Metlili Chaamba ○ DZ 190-191 D 4
Metohija ⩡ YU 100-101 H 3
Metoro ○ MOC 218-219 K 1
Metro ○ RI 162-163 F 7
Metropolis ○ USA 46-47 D 7
Metsera ○ ZRE 210-211 L 5
Métsovo • GR 100-101 H 5
Mettenpherg Creek ~ USA 20-21 O 3
Mettuppālaiyam ○ IND 140-141 G 5
Mettur ○ IND 140-141 G 5
Metu ☆ ETH 208-209 B 4
Metuge ○ MOC 214-215 L 7
Metz ☆• F 90-91 L 7
Metztitlán ○ MEX 52-53 E 1
Meulaboh ○ RI 162-163 B 2
Meureudu ○ RI 162-163 B 2
Meuse ~ B 92-93 H 3
Meuse ~ F 90-91 K 7
Meuse, Côtes de ⩡ F 90-91 K 7
Mēwār ⩡ IND 138-139 D 7
Mexcaltitán ○ MEX 50-51 G 7
Mexia ○ USA 44-45 J 4
Mexiana, Ilha ⌒ BR 62-63 K 6
Mexicali ☆ MEX 50-51 B 1
Mexican Hat ○ USA 44-45 C 1
Mexicanos, Laguna Los ○ MEX 50-51 F 3
Mexican Plateau = Altiplanicie Mexicana ▲ MEX 50-51 G 4
Mexican Water ○ USA 44-45 C 1
México ■ MEX 52-53 D 2
Mexico ○ USA (ME) 46-47 N 3
Mexico ○ USA (MO) 46-47 C 6
México, Ciudad de = México ★ ••• MEX 52-53 E 2
México, Golfo de = Gulf of Mexico ≈ 4 E 6
Mexico, Gulf of = México, Golfo de ≈ 4 E 6
Mexico = México ■ MEX 52-53 C 1
Mexico City = México, Ciudad de ★ ••• MEX 52-53 E 2
Meyāmei ○ IR 136-137 D 6
Meyanodas ○ RI 166-167 F 5
Meydancık ○ TR 128-129 K 2
Meyersdale ○ USA 46-47 J 6
Méyo Centre ○ CAM 210-211 C 2
Mezada ∴• IL 130-131 D 2
Mezaligon ○ MYA 158-159 C 2
Mezcalapa, Río ~ MEX 52-53 H 3
Mezdra ○ BG 102-103 C 6
Meždurečensk ○ RUS 124-125 Q 2
Meždurečenskij ○ RUS 114-115 H 5
Meždušarskij, ostrov ⌒ RUS 108-109 F 6
Mezen' ○ RUS 88-89 S 4
Mezen' ~ RUS 88-89 T 4
Mézenc, Mont ▲• F 90-91 K 9
Mezenskaja guba ≈ 88-89 R 3
Mezenskaja Pižma ~ RUS 88-89 U 4
Mézessé ○ CAM 210-211 D 2
Mézessé, Rocher du = Mézessé Rock • CAM 210-211 D 2
Mézessé Rock = Rocher du Mézessé • CAM 210-211 D 2
Mežgornoe, ozero ○ RUS 112-113 W 4
Mézier, Charleville ☆ F 90-91 K 7
Mezön ○ BOL 76-77 E 2
Mežozernyj ○ RUS 96-97 L 6
Mezquita Catedral •• E 98-99 E 6
Mezquital ○ MEX (DGO) 50-51 G 6
Mezquital ○ MEX (TAM) 50-51 L 5
Mezquital, Río ~ MEX 50-51 G 6
Mfou ○ CAM 210-211 C 2
Mfouati ○ RCB 210-211 D 6
Mfum ○ WAN 204-205 H 6
Mgači ○ RUS 122-123 K 3
Mgangerabeli Plains ⩡ EAK 212-213 H 4
Mgbidi ○ WAN 204-205 G 6
Mgende ○ EAT 212-213 C 6
Mgeta ~ EAT 214-215 K 4
Mg.Mu'o'n ○ VN 156-157 C 6
Mgneta, Hassi < MA 188-189 K 4
Mgunga ○ EAT 214-215 J 4
Mhamid ○ MA 188-189 J 6
Mhangura ○ ZW 218-219 F 3
Mhasvād ○ IND 140-141 F 2
Mhlatuze ~ ZA 220-221 K 4
Mi, Enneri ~ TCH 198-199 G 2
Miagao ○ RP 160-161 E 7
Miahuatlán ○ MEX 52-53 F 3
Miahuatlán, Sierra de ▲ MEX 52-53 F 3
Miajadas ○ E 98-99 E 5
Miājlār ○ IND 138-139 C 6
Mial, Oued ~ DZ 190-191 D 6
Miamère ○ RCA 206-207 D 4
Miami ○ USA (AZ) 44-45 B 3
Miami ○ USA (OK) 44-45 K 1
Miami ○ USA (TX) 44-45 G 2
Miami ○• USA (FL) 48-49 H 7
Miami Beach ○• USA 48-49 H 7
Miami Canal < USA 48-49 H 6
Miami River ~ USA 46-47 F 6
Miamo, El ○ YV 62-63 D 2
Miān Channūn ○ PK 138-139 D 4
Miandrivazo ○ RM 222-223 D 7
Miangas, Pulau ⌒ RI 164-165 K 1
Miani ○ PK 138-139 D 3
Miani Hor ≈ 134-135 M 6
Mianmian Shan ▲ VRC 156-157 B 2
Mianmin ○ PNG 183 A 3
Mianning ○ VRC 156-157 C 2
Miānwāli ○ PK 138-139 C 3
Mian Xian ○ VRC 154-155 E 5
Mianyang ○ VRC 154-155 D 6
Mianzhu ○ VRC 154-155 D 6
Miao ~ ZRE 214-215 B 4
Miaodao Qundao ⌒ VRC 150-151 C 8
Miaoergou ○ VRC 146-147 F 3
Miao Li ○ RC 156-157 M 4
Miao Ling ▲ VRC 156-157 E 3
Miaozu ○ VRC 156-157 E 4
Miarinarivo ○ RM 222-223 E 7
Miaru ○ PNG 183 D 5
Miass ☆ RUS (CEL) 96-97 M 6
Miass ~ RUS 96-97 L 6
Miass ~ RUS 114-115 H 7
Miasskoe ☆ RUS 96-97 M 6
Miastko ○ PL 92-93 O 1
Miāti ○ IND 138-139 E 8
Mibalaie ○ ZRE 210-211 H 6
Mibenge ○ Z 214-215 E 6
Mibu Island ⌒ PNG 183 B 5
Mica ○ ZA 220-221 K 2
Mica Creek ○ CDN 32-33 L 5
Micaúne ○ MOC 218-219 J 4
Miccosukee Indian Reservation ⵅ USA 48-49 H 6
Michael, Lake ○ CDN 36-37 U 7
Michael, Mount ▲ PNG 183 C 4
Michalovce ○ SK 92-93 Q 4
Michel ○ CDN 32-33 Q 3
Michel, Pointe à ▲ CDN 38-39 K 4
Michelago ○ AUS 180-181 K 3
Michel Peak ▲ CDN 32-33 G 5
Michelsen, Cape ▲ CDN 24-25 U 5
Michelson, Mount ▲ USA 20-21 S 2
Miches ○ DOM 54-55 L 5
Michigan ■ USA 46-47 E 2
Michigan, Lake ○ USA 46-47 E 4
Michigan City ○ USA 46-47 E 5
Michilla ○ RCH 76-77 B 2
Michipicoten Bay ○ CDN 34-35 O 7
Michipicoten Island ⌒ CDN 34-35 O 7
Michoacán ■ MEX 52-53 C 2
Michurinsk = Mičurinsk ○ RUS 94-95 R 5
Mico, Río ~ NIC 52-53 B 5
Micronesia ⌒ 14-15 G 6
Microondas ○ MEX 50-51 C 2
Mičurinsk ○ RUS 94-95 R 5
Midal < RN 198-199 B 4
Midale ○ CDN 34-35 E 6
Midar ○ MA 188-189 K 3
Midas ○ USA 40-41 F 5
Midas Şehri ∴• TR 128-129 D 3
Mid-Atlantic Ridge ≃ 6-7 E 5
Midau, Pulau ⌒ RI 162-163 G 3
Mid Baffin ○ CDN 28-29 E 2
Middelburg ☆ NL 92-93 G 3
Middelburg ○ ZA (CAP) 220-221 G 5
Middelburg ○ ZA (TRA) 220-221 J 2
Middelpos ○ ZA 220-221 E 5
Middelveld ⩡ ZA 220-221 G 3
Middelveld ⩡ ZA 220-221 F 4
Middelwit ○ ZA 220-221 H 2
Middendorfa, zaliv ○ RUS 108-109 Y 4
Middle Alkali Lake ○ USA 40-41 D 5
Middle America Trench ≃ 52-53 F 4
Middle Andaman ⌒ IND 140-141 L 3
Middlebro ○ CDN 34-35 J 6
Middlebury ○ USA 46-47 M 3
Middlecamp ○ AUS 180-181 F 2
Middle Cay ⌒ JA 54-55 G 6
Middle Channel ~ CDN 20-21 X 2
Middle Fiord ≈ 26-27 C 4
Middle Fork ~ USA 20-21 T 4
Middle Fork Chandalar ~ USA 20-21 R 2
Middle Fork John Day River ~ USA 40-41 E 3
Middle Fork Koyukuk ~ USA 20-21 P 3
Middle Fork Kuskokwim River ~ USA 20-21 N 5
Middle Fork River ~ USA 22-23 Q 3
Middle Fork Salmon River ~ USA 40-41 G 3
Middle Gate ○ USA 40-41 E 6
Middle Ground ≈ 54-55 G 2
Middle Hart River ~ CDN 20-21 W 4
Middle Island ⌒ AUS 176-177 G 7
Middle Lake ○ CDN 34-35 D 4
Middle Loup River ~ USA 42-43 H 5
Middlemount ○ AUS 178-179 K 2
Middle Park ○ AUS 174-175 G 6
Middle Rapids ~ CDN 32-33 O 3
Middle Ridge ▲ CDN 38-39 R 4
Middle Sackville ○ CDN 38-39 N 6
Middlesboro ○ USA 46-47 G 7
Middlesbrough ○ GB 90-91 G 4
Middleton ○ AUS 178-179 F 2
Middleton ○ CDN 38-39 M 6
Middleton ○ USA (TN) 48-49 D 2
Middleton ○ USA (WI) 46-47 D 4
Middleton ○ ZA 220-221 G 6
Middleton, Mount ▲ CDN 38-39 F 3
Middleton Island ⌒ USA 20-21 R 7
Middletown ○ USA (CT) 46-47 M 5
Middletown ○ USA (NY) 46-47 L 5
Middletown ○ USA (OH) 46-47 F 6
Midi, Canal du < F 90-91 J 10
Mid-Indian Basin ≃ 12 F 5
Mid-Indian Ridge ≃ 12 E 5
Midi-Pyrénées ■ F 90-91 H 10
Midland ○ AUS 176-177 C 5
Midland ○ CDN 38-39 E 6
Midland ○ USA (MI) 46-47 F 4
Midland ○ USA (SD) 42-43 G 3
Midland ○ USA (TX) 44-45 F 3
Midlander ‖ AUS 178-179 H 2
Midleton ○ IRL 90-91 C 6
Midongy ⩡ RM 222-223 E 9
Midongy Atsimo ○ RM 222-223 E 9
Midouze ~ F 90-91 G 10
Mid-Pacific-Seamounts ≃ 14-15 H 5
Midsandur ○ IS 86-87 c 2
Midsayap ○ RP 160-161 F 9
Midsommersø ○ GRØ 26-27 g 2
Midu ○ VRC 142-143 M 3
Midway ○ CDN 32-33 L 7
Midway ○ USA 48-49 F 3
Midway Island ⌒ USA 14-15 L 5
Midway Islands ⌒ USA 20-21 Q 1
Midway Range ▲ CDN 32-33 L 7
Midwest ○ USA 42-43 D 4
Midwest City ○ USA 44-45 J 2
Midwestern Highway ‖ AUS 180-181 H 3
Midyat ☆• TR 128-129 J 4
Midyobo ○ GQ 210-211 C 3
Midžor ▲•• YU 100-101 J 3
Miechów ○• PL 92-93 Q 3
Międzyrzec Podlaski ○ PL 92-93 R 3
Międzyrzecz ○• PL 92-93 N 2
Mielec ○• PL 92-93 Q 3
Miélékouka ○ RCB 210-211 E 3
Miembwe ○ EAT 214-215 J 5
Mier ○ MEX 50-51 K 4
Miercurea-Ciuc ☆• RO 102-103 D 4
Mieres ○ E 98-99 E 3
Mier y Noriega ○ MEX 50-51 J 6
Mierzeja Wiślana ⌣ PL 92-93 P 1
Mī'ēso ○ ETH 208-209 E 4
Miette Hot Springs • CDN 32-33 M 5
Migdol ○ ZA 220-221 G 3
Migliónico ○• I 100-101 F 4
Migole ○ EAT 214-215 H 4
Migoli ○ EAT (SIN) 212-213 E 6
Migori ○ EAK 212-213 E 4
Migration Lake ○ CDN 30-31 P 3
Miguel Alemán, Presa < MEX 52-53 F 2
Miguel Alves ○ BR 68-69 G 4
Miguel Auza ○ MEX 50-51 H 5
Miguel Calmon ○ BR 68-69 H 7
Miguel Hidalgo, Presa < MEX 50-51 E 4
Miguel Leão ○ BR 68-69 G 4
Miguelópolis ○ BR 72-73 F 6
Miguel Pereira ○ BR 72-73 J 7
Miguel y Alex Tejada, Meteorite craters: • BOL 70-71 D 6
Migues ○ ROU 78-79 M 3
Mihajlov ☆• RUS 94-95 Q 4
Mihajlovgrad = Monatana ☆ BG 102-103 C 6
Mihajlovka ○ KA 136-137 M 3
Mihajlovka ○ RUS 116-117 M 10
Mihajlovka ○ RUS 122-123 D 7
Mihajlovka ○ RUS (SAH) 120-121 E 3
Mihajlovka ○ RUS (VLG) 102-103 N 2
Mihajlovka, Podyem- ○ RUS 96-97 G 7
Mihajlovo ○ BG 102-103 C 6
Mihajlovsk ○ RUS 96-97 L 5
Mihajlovskij ☆ RUS 124-125 L 3
Mihaliççık ○ TR 128-129 D 3
Mihalkino ○ RUS 112-113 L 2
Mihama ○ J 152-153 G 7
Mihintale ○ CL 140-141 J 6
Mihnevo ○ RUS 94-95 P 4
Miho-wan ≈ 152-153 E 7
Mihrād, al- ⩡ KSA 132-133 H 3
Mihuanoyacu ○ EC 64-65 D 2
Mihumo Chini ○ EAT 214-215 K 5
Mijaki, Kirgiz- ☆ RUS 96-97 J 7
Mijaly ☆ KA 96-97 H 9
Mijek ○ MA 196-197 D 3
Mikasa ○ J 152-153 J 3
Mikaševičy ○ BY 94-95 K 5
Mikawa-wan ≈ 152-153 G 7
Mikčangda ~ RUS 108-109 Y 7
Mikese ○ EAT 214-215 J 4
Miki ○ ZRE 212-213 B 5
Mikindani ○ EAT 214-215 L 6
Mikkeli ☆ FIN 88-89 J 6
Mikkwa River ~ CDN 32-33 N 3
Miknās ☆ MA 188-189 J 4
Mikojana, zaliv ○ RUS 108-109 e 2
Mikonos ⌒ GR 100-101 K 6
Mikulkin, mys ▲ RUS 88-89 T 3
Mikumi ○ EAT 214-215 J 4
Mikumi Lodge ○ EAT 214-215 J 4
Mikumi National Park ⊥ EAT 214-215 J 4
Mikumi-sanmyaku ▲ J 152-153 H 6
Mikun' ○ RUS 88-89 V 5
Mikuni ○ J 152-153 G 6
Mil' ~ RUS 120-121 E 3
Mil', Ust'- ○ RUS 120-121 E 4
Mila ☆ DZ 190-191 F 2
Milaca ○ USA 42-43 L 3
Milach, In- < RMM 196-197 K 6
Miladummadulu Atoll ⌒ MV 140-141 B 4
Milagres ○ BR (BAH) 72-73 L 2
Milagres ○ BR (CEA) 68-69 J 5
Milagro ○ EC 64-65 C 3
Milagro, El ○ MEX 50-51 H 3
Milagros ○ RP 160-161 E 6
Milait ⌒ GRØ 28-29 Y 3
Milan ○ USA (MI) 46-47 G 4
Milan ○ USA (MO) 42-43 L 5
Milan ○ USA (TN) 48-49 D 2
Milan = Milano ☆••• I 100-101 B 2
Milando, Reserva Especial do ⊥ ANG 216-217 D 4
Milang ○ AUS 180-181 E 3
Milange ○ MOC 218-219 H 3
Milange ○ ZRE 212-213 A 5
Milango ~ RI 164-165 G 3
Milano ☆••• I 100-101 B 2
Milano ○ USA 44-45 J 4
Milanoa ○ RM 222-223 F 4
Milas ☆• TR 128-129 B 4
Milazzo ○ I 100-101 E 5
Milbank ○ USA 42-43 J 3
Milbanke Sound ≈ 32-33 F 5
Milbridge ○ USA 46-47 P 3
Milden ○ CDN 34-35 C 5
Mildet ○ MA 188-189 J 4
Mildura ○ AUS 180-181 G 3
Mildura Gemstone Deposit • AUS 176-177 F 6
Milē ○ ETH 208-209 E 3
Mile ○ VRC 156-157 C 4
Milepa ○ EAT 214-215 F 5
Miles ○ AUS 178-179 L 4
Miles ○ USA 44-45 G 4
Miles, Cape ▲ CDN 24-25 d 6
Miles City ○ USA (FL) 48-49 H 6
Miles City ○ USA (MT) 42-43 E 2
Milestone ○ CDN 34-35 D 6
Milet ∴•• TR 128-129 B 4
Mileura ○ AUS 176-177 D 3
Milē Wenz ~ ETH 208-209 E 3
Milford ○ USA (DE) 46-47 L 6
Milford ○ USA (IA) 42-43 K 4
Milford ○ USA (PA) 46-47 L 5
Milford ○ USA (UT) 40-41 H 6
Milford Lake ○ USA 42-43 J 6
Milford Sound ≈ 182 A 6
Milford Sound ○ NZ 182 A 6
Milgarra ○ AUS 174-175 F 6
Milgun ○ AUS 176-177 E 2
Mil'guveem ~ RUS 112-113 R 2
Milhana ○ MOC 218-219 K 2
Milhāt ○ IRQ 128-129 K 5
Miliana ○ DZ 190-191 D 2
Milikapiti ⵅ AUS 172-173 K 1
Milim ○ PNG 183 F 3
Milingimbi ⵅ AUS 174-175 C 3
Milijutkějveem ~ RUS 112-113 W 3
Milkengay Lake ○ AUS 180-181 F 2
Mil'kovo ☆ RUS 120-121 S 6
Milk River ~ CDN 32-33 P 7
Milk River ~ USA 32-33 R 7
Millaa Millaa ○• AUS 174-175 H 5
Millaroo ○ AUS 174-175 J 7
Millas ○ F 90-91 J 10
Millau ○ F 90-91 J 9
Mill City ○ USA 40-41 C 3
Milledgeville ○ USA 48-49 G 3
Mille Lacs, Lac des ○ CDN 34-35 L 6
Mille Lacs Lake ○ USA 42-43 L 2
Millen ○ USA 48-49 H 3
Miller ○ USA (NE) 42-43 H 5
Miller ○ USA (SD) 42-43 H 3
Miller ○ ZA 220-221 F 6
Miller, Mount ▲ USA 20-21 T 6
Millerovo ○ RUS 102-103 M 3
Millersburg ○ USA (OH) 46-47 H 5
Millersburg ○ USA (PA) 46-47 K 5
Millers Creek ~ AUS 178-179 C 5
Millers Creek Reservoir < USA 44-45 H 3
Millerton ○ BS 54-55 H 3
Millertown ○ CDN 38-39 I Q 4
Millevaches, Plateau de ▲ F 90-91 H 9
Millicent ○ AUS 180-181 F 4
Millie ○ AUS 178-179 K 5
Milligan Hills ▲ CDN 32-33 K 3
Millington ○ USA 48-49 D 2
Millinocket ○ USA 46-47 O 3
Mill Island ⌒ ARK 16 G 11
Millmerran ○ AUS 178-179 L 4
Millrose ○ AUS 176-177 F 3
Mills Lake ○ CDN 30-31 K 5
Millston ○ USA 46-47 C 3
Millstream ○ AUS 172-173 C 6
Millstream Chichester National Park ⊥ AUS 172-173 C 6
Milltown ○ CDN 38-39 I R 5
Millungera ○ AUS 174-175 F 6
Mill Village ○ CDN 38-39 M 6
Millville ○ USA 46-47 L 6
Millwood Lake ○ USA 44-45 K 3
Millyeewilpa Lake ○ AUS 178-179 D 4
Milly Milly ○ AUS 176-177 D 3
Milne Bay ≈ 183 F 6
Milne Inlet ≈ 24-25 g 4
Milne Land ⩡ GRØ 26-27 m 8
Milner Lake ○ CDN 38-39 L 2
Milnesand ○ USA 44-45 F 3
Milo ○ ETH 208-209 F 3
Milo ~ RG 202-203 F 4
Milodon, Cueva del • RCH 80 D 5
Milogradovo ○ RUS 122-123 F 7
Milos ○ GR 100-101 K 6
Milos ⌒ GR 100-101 K 6
Milot ○ RH 54-55 J 5
Milparinka ○ AUS 178-179 F 5
Mil'skaja ravnina ⌣ AZ 128-129 M 3
Milton ○ NZ 182 B 7
Milton ○ USA (FL) 48-49 E 4
Milton ○ USA (PA) 46-47 K 5
Milton-Freewater ○ USA 40-41 E 3
Milton Lake ○ CDN 30-31 S 6
Miltou ○ TCH 206-207 C 3
Miluo ○ VRC 156-157 H 2
Milwaukee ○• USA 46-47 E 4
Milwaukie ○ USA 40-41 C 3
Mimbelly ○ RCB 210-211 F 2
Mimili (Eyerard Park) ⵅ AUS 176-177
Miminiska Lake ○ CDN 34-35 M 5
Mi Mi Rocks ▲ AUS 176-177 H 3
Mimizan ○ F 90-91 G 9
Mimongo ○ G 210-211 C 4
Mimouna, Kef ▲ DZ 190-191 D 4
Mimpoutou ○ RCB 210-211 F 2
Mina ~ RI 166-167 C 7
Mina ○ USA 40-41 E 6
Minā', al- ○ RL 128-129 F 5
Mina, Oued ~ DZ 190-191 C 3
Mina, Salar de la ○ RA 76-77 D 4
Mināʾ ʿAbdallāh ○ KWT 130-131 L 3
Mināb ○• IR 134-135 G 5
Mina Clavero ○ RA 76-77 E 6
Minaçu ○ BR 72-73 F 2
Mina Exploradora ○ RCH 76-77 C 3
Minahasa Semenao djung ⌣ RI 164-165 G 3
Mina Jebel Ali ○ UAE 134-135 F 6
Minaki ○ CDN 34-35 J 6
Mina la Casualidad ○ RA 76-77 C 3
Mina la Juanita ○ RCH 78-79 D 3
Minami-Alps National Park ⊥ J 152-153 H 7
Minami-Daitō ○ J 152-153 D 12
Minamikayabe ○ J 152-153 J 4
Minami-Tane ○ J 152-153 D 9
Minas ○ C 54-55 G 4
Minas ○ RI 162-163 D 4
Minas ☆ ROU 78-79 M 3
Minas, Cerro las ▲ HN 52-53 K 4
Minas, Sierra de las ▲ GCA 52-53 J 4
Minas Basin ≈ 38-39 M 6
Minas de Barroterán ○ MEX 50-51 J 4
Minas de Corrales ○ ROU 76-77 K 6
Minas del Oro ○ CO 60-61 E 4
Minas de Matahambre ○ C 54-55 D 3
Minas do Mimoso ○ BR 68-69 H 7
Minas Gerais ■ BR 72-73 H 4
Minas Novas ○ BR 72-73 J 4
Mināʾ Suʿud ○ KWT 130-131 L 3
Minatinia Batoche National Historic Park ∴• CDN 34-35 C 4
Minatitlán ○ MEX (COL) 52-53 B 2
Minatitlán ○• MEX (VER) 52-53 G 3
Minbu ○ MYA 142-143 J 5
Min Buri ○ THA 158-159 F 4
Minch, The ≈ 90-91 E 3
Minch, The Little ≈ 90-91 D 3
Minchika ○ WAN 204-205 K 3
Minchinābād ○ PK 138-139 D 4
Minchinmávida, Volcán ▲ RCH 78-79 C 7
Minchumina, Lake ○ USA 20-21 O 5
Mindanao ⌒ RP 160-161 G 8
Mindanao Sea ≈ 160-161 E 10
Mindelo ○• CV 202-203 B 5
Minden ○ CDN 38-39 E 6
Minden ○• D 92-93 K 2
Minden ○ USA (IA) 42-43 K 5
Minden ○ USA (LA) 44-45 L 3
Minden ○ USA (NE) 42-43 H 5
Minderla ○ RUS 116-117 F 7
Mindif ○• CAM 206-207 B 3
Mindif, Dent de ▲• CAM 206-207 B 3
Mindik ○ PNG 183 D 4
Mindiptana ○ RI 166-167 L 4
Mindjik ○ TCH 206-207 E 3
Mindo ○ EC 64-65 C 2
Mindon ○ MYA 142-143 J 6
Mindona Lake ○ AUS 180-181 G 2
Mindoro ⌒ RP 160-161 D 6
Mindoro Strait ≈ 160-161 D 6
Mindouli ○ RCB 210-211 E 6
Mindourou ○ CAM 210-211 D 2
Minduri ○ BR 72-73 H 6
Mindživan ○ AZ 128-129 M 3
Mine ○ J (NAG) 152-153 C 7
Mine ○ J (YMG) 152-153 D 7
Mine Centre ○ CDN 34-35 K 6
Minehead ○ GB 90-91 F 6
Mineiros ○ BR 72-73 D 4
Mineola ○ USA 44-45 K 3
Mineral, Cerro ▲ RCH 80 E 2
Mineral'nye Vody ○ RUS 126-127 E 5
Mineral Wells ○ USA 44-45 H 3
Miner River ~ CDN 20-21 Z 2
Miners Point ▲ USA 22-23 U 4
Minersville ○ USA 40-41 H 6
Minerva, Presa < C 54-55 F 3
Minfeng ○ VRC 144-145 D 2
Minga ○ Z 218-219 F 2
Minga ○ ZRE 214-215 D 6
Mingala ○ RCA 206-207 E 6
Mingan, Îles de ⌒ CDN 38-39 N 3
Minganja ○ ANG 216-217 F 6
Mingao ○ CO 60-61 H 6
Mingary ○ AUS 180-181 F 2
Mingbuloķ ○ US 136-137 H 3
Mingbuloķ cukurligi ⩡ US 136-137 H 3
Mingechevir = Mingaçevir ○• AZ 128-129 M 2
Mingechevirskoe vodohranilišče < AZ 128-129 M 2
Mingela ○ AUS 174-175 J 6
Mingenew ○ AUS 176-177 C 4
Minggang ○ VRC 154-155 J 5
Minghoshan = Dunhuang ○• VRC 146-147 M 5
Mingin ○ MYA 142-143 J 4
Ming Ming ○ PNG 183 D 3
Mingo Lake ○ CDN 36-37 N 2
Mingora ○• PK 138-139 D 2
Mingoyo ○ EAT 214-215 K 6
Mingshui ○ VRC 150-151 E 4
Mingue ○ CAM 204-205 K 6
Mingun ○• MYA 142-143 J 4
Minguri ○ MOC 218-219 L 2
Mingxi ○ VRC 156-157 K 3
Minhe Huizu Tuzu Zizhixian ○ VRC 154-155 C 3
Minh Hải ☆ VN 158-159 H 6
Minh Hòa, Hòn ⌒ VN 158-159 H 5
Minhla ○ MYA 142-143 J 6
Minhla ○ MYA 158-159 C 2
Minho, Rio ~ P 98-99 C 4
Minicoy Island ⌒ IND 140-141 E 6
Minidoka ○ USA 40-41 H 4
Minigwal, Lake ○ AUS 176-177 G 4
Minilya Bridge Roadhouse ○ AUS 176-177 B 1
Minilya River ~ AUS 176-177 C 1
Mininian ○ CI 202-203 G 4
Miniota ○ CDN 34-35 F 5
Minipi Lake ○ CDN 38-39 O 2
Minisiare, Caño ~ CO 60-61 G 6
Minissa ○ BF 202-203 J 3
Miniss Lake ○ CDN 34-35 L 5
Ministro Ramos Mexia ○ RA 78-79 F 6
Minitas, Playa ⩡• DOM 54-55 L 5
Minja ~ RUS 118-119 D 7
Min'jar ○ RUS 96-97 K 6
Min Jiang ~ VRC 154-155 C 6
Min Jiang ~ VRC 156-157 D 2
Min Jiang ~ VRC 156-157 L 3
Minjilang ⵅ AUS 172-173 L 1
Minjip ○ PNG 183 B 3
Minlaton ○ AUS 180-181 D 3
Minle ○ VRC 154-155 B 2
Minna ☆ WAN 204-205 G 4
Minneapolis ○ USA (KS) 42-43 J 6
Minneapolis ○• USA (MN) 42-43 L 3
Minnedosa ○ CDN 34-35 G 5
Minneola ○ USA 44-45 G 1
Minnesota ■ USA 42-43 J 2
Minnesota River ~ USA 42-43 K 3
Minnewaukan ○ USA 42-43 H 1
Minnie Creek ○ AUS 176-177 C 2
Minnies Out Station ○ AUS 174-175 G 5
Minnipa ○ AUS 180-181 C 2
Minnitaki Lake ○ CDN 34-35 L 5
Minnkri ○ RMM 196-197 J 6
Miño, Río ~ E 98-99 D 3
Miñoes ○ RA 76-77 H 6
Minong ○ USA 46-47 C 2
Minot ○ USA 42-43 G 1
Minqin ○ VRC 154-155 C 2
Minqing ○ VRC 156-157 L 3
Minquan ○ VRC 154-155 J 4
Min Shan ▲ VRC 154-155 C 5
Minsk ★ BY 94-95 K 5
Mińsk Mazowiecki ○ PL 92-93 Q 2
Minta ○ CAM 204-205 K 6
Mintabie ○ AUS 176-177 M 3
Minṭaqat ash Shuʿbah ⩡ LAR 192-193 L 2
Minṭaqat Umm Khuwayt ⩡ LAR 192-193 K 2
Mint Hill ○ USA 48-49 H 2
Mintirib, al- ○ OM 132-133 L 2
Minto ○ CDN (MAN) 34-35 G 6
Minto ○ CDN (YT) 20-21 W 5
Minto, Lac ○ CDN 36-37 M 6
Minto Inlet ≈ 24-25 N 5
Mintom II ○ CAM 210-211 D 2
Minton ○ CDN 34-35 D 6
Minturn ○ USA 42-43 D 6
Minūdašt ○ IR 136-137 D 6
Minusinsk ☆ RUS 116-117 E 9
Minvoul ○ G 210-211 D 2
Min Xian ○ VRC 154-155 D 4
Minyā, al- ☆ ET 194-195 E 3
Minzawi, Wādī al- ~ OM 132-133 H 5
Minž gol ~ MAU 148-149 H 3
Miosnum, Pulau ⌒ RI 166-167 H 2
Mipia, Lake ○ AUS 178-179 E 3
Miqdādiya, al- ☆ IRQ 128-129 L 6
Miquelon ○ CDN 38-39 F 4
Miquelon ⌒ F 38-39 I Q 5
Miquihuana ○ MEX 50-51 K 6
Mira ○ EC 64-65 C 1
Mira ○ P 98-99 C 4
Mira, buhta ≈ 110-111 a 2
Mira, Río ~ EC 64-65 C 1
Mirabela ○ BR 72-73 H 4
Miracema ○ BR 72-73 J 6
Miracema de Tocantins ○ BR 68-69 D 6
Miracosta ○ PE 64-65 C 5
Mirador ○ BR (AMA) 64-65 F 4
Mirador ○ BR (MAR) 68-69 F 5
Mirador, El ∴• GCA 52-53 K 3
Mirador, Parque Nacional de ⊥ BR 68-69 F 5
Mirador-Dos Lagunas-Río Azul, Parque Nacional ⊥•• GCA 52-53 K 3
Miradouro ○ BR 72-73 J 6
Miraflores ○ BR 66-67 E 4
Miraflores ○ CO (BOY) 60-61 E 5
Miraflores ○ CO (VAU) 66-67 B 2
Mirage Bay ○ CDN 28-29 E 3
Mirāglia, Portella della ▲ I 100-101 E 6
Miragoâne ○ RH 54-55 J 5
Miraj ○ IND 140-141 F 2
Miramar ○ BR 66-67 G 5
Miramar ○ RA 78-79 L 5
Miramichi Bay ≈ 38-39 M 5
Miramichi River ~ CDN 38-39 L 5
Miram Shāh ○ PK 138-139 C 3
Miran ○ PK 138-139 C 4
Miran ○ VRC 146-147 J 6
Miranda ○ BR (GSU) 70-71 J 7
Miranda ○ BR (MAR) 68-69 F 3
Miranda ○ YV 60-61 G 2
Miranda, Lake ○ AUS 176-177 F 3
Miranda, Rio ~ BR 70-71 J 7
Miranda de Ebro ○ E 98-99 F 3
Miranda do Douro ○ P 98-99 D 4
Miranda Downs ○ AUS 174-175 F 5
Mirandela ○ BR 68-69 J 7
Mirandela ○ P 98-99 D 4
Mirandiba ○ BR 68-69 J 6
Mirandópolis ○ BR 72-73 E 6
Mirani ○ AUS 178-179 K 1
Miranle da Sura ○ BR 70-71 F 2
Mirante ○ BR 68-69 D 6
Mirante ○ BR 72-73 K 3
Mirante do Paranapanema ○ BR 72-73 E 7
Mira por vos Cays ⌒ BS 54-55 H 3
Mira por vos Passage ≈ 54-55 H 3
Mirassol ○ BR 72-73 F 6
Mirassol d'Oeste ○ BR 70-71 H 4
Miratu, Área Indígena ⵅ BR 66-67 E 4
Miratuba, Lago ○ BR 66-67 H 4
Miravalles ▲ E 98-99 D 3
Miravalles, Volcán ▲ CR 52-53 B 6
Mir Bačče Kūt ○ AFG 138-139 B 2
Mir-Bašir = Terter ○ AZ 128-129 M 2
Mirbāṭ ○ OM 132-133 J 5
Mirebalais ○ RH 54-55 J 5
Mirǧāve ○ IR 134-135 J 4
Mirhleft ○ MA 188-189 G 6
Miri ○ MAL 162-163 K 2
Miria ○ RN 198-199 D 6
Miriālgūda ○ IND 140-141 H 2
Miriam Vale ○ AUS 178-179 L 3
Mirim, Lagoa ○ BR 74-75 D 9
Mirim, Lagoa do ○ BR 74-75 F 7
Mirim do Abufari, Paraná ~ BR 66-67 F 5
Mirimire ○ YV 60-61 G 2
Mirina ○ GR 100-101 K 5
Miriñay, Esteros ○ RA 76-77 J 5
Miriñay, Río ~ RA 76-77 J 5
Mirinzal ○ BR 68-69 F 3
Miritiparaná, Río ~ CO 66-67 B 3
Miriye, togga ~ SP 208-209 G 3
Mirjan ○ IND 140-141 F 3
Mirnoe, ozero ○ RUS 114-115 P 6
Mirnyj ○ ARK 16 G 10
Mirnyj ☆• RUS 118-119 F 4
Mirobia ○ RI 166-167 G 3
Mirogi ○ EAK 212-213 E 4
Miroki ○ US 136-137 K 5
Mirond Lake ○ CDN 34-35 E 3
Mirong ○ VRC 156-157 C 5
Mirosławiec ○ PL 92-93 O 2
Mirowāl ○ PK 138-139 E 4
Mirpur Batoro ○ PK 138-139 B 7
Mirpur Khās ○• PK 138-139 B 7
Mirpur Mathelo ○• PK 138-139 B 5
Mirpur Sakro ○ PK 134-135 M 6
Mirra Mitta Bore ○ AUS 178-179 E 4
Mirrngadja Village ⵅ AUS 174-175 C 3
Mirror River ~ CDN 32-33 Q 3
Mirrote ○ MOC 218-219 K 1
Mirsale ○ SP 208-209 H 6
Mirtna ○ AUS 178-179 J 1
Mirtóo Pélagos ≈ 100-101 J 6
Miruro ○ MOC 218-219 F 2
Mirwāh ○ PK 138-139 B 7
Mirzā ʿArab, Kūh-e ▲ IR 134-135 J 2
Mirzapur ○ IND 142-143 C 3
Misāha, Biʾr < ET 194-195 C 6
Misaine Bank ≃ 38-39 P 6
Misaki ○ EAT 212-213 E 6
Misaki ○ J (EHI) 152-153 E 8
Misaki ○ J (OSA) 152-153 F 7
Misantla ○ MEX (VER) 52-53 F 2
Misantla ∴• MEX (VER) 52-53 F 2
Misau ○ WAN 204-205 J 3
Misawa ○ J 152-153 J 4
Misaw Lake ○ CDN 30-31 S 6
Miscou Centre ○ CDN 38-39 M 5
Miscou Island ⌒ CDN 38-39 M 5
Misekumaw Lake ○ CDN 30-31 S 6

Mesa — Misekumaw Lake 289

Misele o **ZRE** 210-211 F 6
Misgund o **ZA** 220-221 F 6
Mishagua, Rio ~ **PE** 64-65 F 7
Mishamo o **EAT** 212-213 C 6
Mishan o **VRC** 150-151 H 5
Mi-shima ~ **J** 152-153 D 7
Misi o **FIN** 88-89 J 3
Misiki o **PNG** 183 B 4
Misión, La o **MEX** 50-51 A 1
Misión de San Fernando o **MEX** 50-51 B 2
Misiones o **RA** 76-77 K 4
Misiones, Sierra de ▲ **RA** 76-77 K 4
Miski o **SUD** 200-201 B 5
Miškino o **RUS** 114-115 G 7
Miškino o **RUS** (BAS) 96-97 J 6
Miskitos, Cayos ~ **NIC** 52-53 C 4
Miskolc o **H** 92-93 U 4
Mismár o **SUD** 200-201 G 3
Misol-Ha Waterfall ~ **MEX** 52-53 H 3
Misool, Pulau ~ **RI** 166-167 K 7
Misouminien o **CI** 202-203 J 6
Mišrafa, al- o **Y** 132-133 C 6
Misrátah ▲ **LAR** 192-193 F 1
Misrátah ✶ **LAR** 192-193 F 1
Misrikh o **IND** 142-143 B 2
Missanabie o **CDN** 34-35 G 2
Misseni o **RMM** 202-203 G 4
Missi Falls ~ **CDN** 34-35 G 2
Missinaibi Lake o **CDN** 34-35 P 6
Missinaibi Lake Provincial Park ⊥ **CDN** 34-35 P 6
Missinaibi River ~ **CDN** 34-35 P 5
Missinipe o **CDN** 34-35 D 3
Mission o **CDN** 32-33 J 7
Mission o **USA** 42-43 G 4
Mission Beach o **AUS** 174-175 J 5
Missión de San Borja o **MEX** 50-51 C 3
Missira o **SN** (SO) 202-203 E 3
Missira o **SN** (SO) 202-203 E 3
Missisagi River ~ **CDN** 38-39 H 3
Missisa Lake o **CDN** 34-35 O 4
Missisicabi, Rivière ~ **CDN** 38-39 E 3
Mississauga o **CDN** 38-39 E 7
Mississippi River ~ **USA** 4 E 5
Mississippi River ~ **USA** 48-49 D 5
Mississippi River Delta ~ **USA** 48-49 D 5
Mississippi Sound ≈ 48-49 D 4
Missoula o **USA** 40-41 H 2
Missour o **MA** 188-189 K 4
Missouri ☐ **USA** 42-43 L 6
Missouri City o **USA** 44-45 K 5
Missouri River ~ **USA** 4 D 4
Missouri Valley o **USA** 42-43 K 5
Mist o **USA** 40-41 C 3
Mistake Creek ~ **AUS** 178-179 G 2
Mistassibi, Rivière ~ **CDN** 38-39 H 3
Mistassini, Lac o **CDN** 38-39 H 3
Mistassini, Réserve de ⊥ **CDN** 38-39 H 3
Mistassini, Rivière ~ **CDN** 38-39 H 4
Mistawak, Rivière ~ **CDN** 38-39 E 4
Mistawasis Indian Reserve ✕ **CDN** 34-35 C 4
Mistelbach an der Zaya o **A** 92-93 U 4
Misterei o **SUD** 198-199 L 6
Misti, Volcán ▲ **PE** 70-71 B 5
Mistinibi Lake o **CDN** 36-37 R 7
Mistoles, Laguna los o **RA** 76-77 F 6
Mistra ~ **GR** 100-101 J 6
Misty Fiords National Monument ⊥ **USA** 32-33 E 4
Misty Fiords National Monument Wilderness ⊥ **USA** 32-33 E 3
Misty Lake o **CDN** 30-31 T 6
Misumba o **ZRE** 210-211 H 6
Misumi o **J** 152-153 D 8
Misvær o **N** 86-87 G 3
Miśwara o **Y** 132-133 D 6
Mita, Punta ▲ **MEX** 52-53 B 1
Mita Hills Dam < **Z** 218-219 E 2
Mitaho • **RM** 222-223 C 10
Mitande o **MOC** 218-219 J 2
Mitare o **YV** 60-61 F 2
Mitau ~ Jelgava o **LV** 94-95 H 3
Mitchell o **AUS** 178-179 J 4
Mitchell o **CDN** 38-39 D 7
Mitchell o **USA** (NE) 42-43 F 4
Mitchell o **USA** (OR) 40-41 D 3
Mitchell o **USA** (SD) 42-43 H 4
Mitchell, Mount ▲ **USA** 48-49 G 2
Mitchell and Alice Rivers National Park ⊥ **AUS** 174-175 G 4
Mitchell Highway ‖ **AUS** 178-179 J 6
Mitchell Lake < **USA** 48-49 G 3
Mitchell River ~ **AUS** 172-173 G 3
Mitchell River ~ **AUS** 174-175 G 4
Mitchell River National Park ⊥ **AUS** 180-181 J 4
Mitchelstown ~ Baile Mhistéala o **IRL** 90-91 C 5
Mitchinamecus, Réservoir o **CDN** 38-39 G 4
Mitémele, Rio ~ **GQ** 210-211 C 3
Mit Ġamr o **ET** 194-195 E 2
Mithankot o **PK** 138-139 C 5
Mitha Tiwána o **PK** 138-139 D 3
Mithi o **PK** 138-139 B 7
Mithimna o **GR** 100-101 L 5
Miti, Pulau ~ **RI** 164-165 L 3
Mitiamo o **AUS** 180-181 H 4
Mitiaro ~ **NZ** 13 M 4
Mitilini ☆ **GR** 100-101 L 5
Mitji o **SN** 202-203 D 3
Mitjušiha, guba o **RUS** 108-109 F 5
Mitla ∴• **MEX** 52-53 F 3
Mitla, Laguna o **MEX** 52-53 D 3
Mitlitkavik o **USA** 20-21 K 1
Mito ☆ **J** 152-153 J 6
Mitoko o **ZRE** 210-211 H 2
Mitole o **EAT** 214-215 K 5
Mitomoni o **EAT** 214-215 H 6
Mitre, Península ◡ **RA** 80 H 7

Mitrofania Island ~ **USA** 22-23 R 5
Mitsamiouli o **COM** 222-223 C 3
Mitsinjo o **RM** 222-223 D 5
Mitsio, Nosy ~ **RM** 222-223 F 4
Mits'iwa ~ **ER** 200-201 J 7
Mits'iwa Channel ≈ 200-201 J 5
Mitsuishi o **J** 152-153 K 3
Mitsushima o **J** 152-153 C 7
Mittagong o **AUS** 180-181 K 3
Mitta Mitta o **AUS** 180-181 J 4
Mittiebah o **AUS** 174-175 D 6
Mitumba, Monts ▲ **ZRE** 212-213 B 5
Mitunguu o **EAK** 212-213 F 4
Mitwaba o **ZRE** 214-215 D 5
Mityana o **EAU** 212-213 D 3
Mitzic o **G** 210-211 C 3
Miura-hanto ◡ **J** 152-153 H 7
Mius ~ **RUS** 102-103 L 4
Mivo River ~ **PNG** 184 I b 2
Mixco o **GCA** 52-53 J 4
Mixquiahuala o **MEX** 52-53 E 1
Mixteco, Rio ~ **MEX** 52-53 E 2
Mixtlán o **MEX** 52-53 B 1
Miya o **WAN** 204-205 H 3
Miya-gawa ~ **J** 152-153 J 5
Miyah, Wādī l- ~ **ET** 194-195 F 5
Miyake-shima ~ **J** 152-153 H 7
Miyako o **J** 152-153 J 5
Miyakonojó o **J** 152-153 D 9
Miyako-jima ~ **J** 148-149 N 3
Miyandoab o **IR** 128-129 M 4
Miyâne o **IR** 128-129 M 4
Miyanoura-dake ▲ **J** 152-153 D 9
Miya-shima ~ **J** 152-153 E 7
Miyazaki ☆ **J** 152-153 D 9
Miyazu o **J** 152-153 J 6
Miyi o **VRC** 156-157 C 3
Miyoshi o **J** 152-153 E 7
Mōco ▲ **ANG** 216-217 C 6
Mocoa o **CO** 64-65 D 1
Mocoduene o **MOC** 218-219 H 5
Moções, Rio ~ **BR** 62-63 K 6
Mocomoco o **BOL** 70-71 C 4
Mocorito o **MEX** 50-51 F 5
Mocotó o **BR** 68-69 E 3
Moctezuma o **MEX** (CHA) 50-51 F 2
Moctezuma o **MEX** (SLP) 50-51 J 6
Moctezuma, Rio ~ **MEX** (SON) 50-51 E 3
Moctezuma, Rio ~ **MEX** 50-51 K 7
Mocuba o **MOC** 218-219 J 3
Mocupe o **PE** 64-65 C 5
Mocimboa da Praia o **MOC** 214-215 L 6
Mocímboa do Rovuma o **MOC** 214-215 K 6
Mocoa ▲ **ANG** 216-217 C 6
Mocoa o **CO** 64-65 D 1
Mocoduene o **MOC** 218-219 H 5
Moçoes, Rio ~ **BR** 62-63 K 6
Mocomoco o **BOL** 70-71 C 4
Mocorito o **MEX** 50-51 F 5
Mocotó o **BR** 68-69 E 3
Moctezuma o **MEX** (CHA) 50-51 F 2
Moctezuma o **MEX** (SLP) 50-51 J 6
Moctezuma, Rio ~ **MEX** (SON) 50-51 E 3
Moctezuma, Rio ~ **MEX** 50-51 K 7
Mocuba o **MOC** 218-219 J 3
Mocupe o **PE** 64-65 C 5
Modan o **RI** 166-167 G 3
Modáša o **IND** 138-139 D 8
Modane o **F** 90-91 L 9
Modasa o **IND** 138-139 D 8
Modderrivier o **ZA** 220-221 G 4
Modena o **I** 100-101 C 2
Modena o **USA** 40-41 H 7
Modesto o **USA** 40-41 D 7
Modesto Méndez o **GCA** 52-53 K 4
Modimolle o **ZA** 220-221 H 2
Modjigo ~ **RN** 198-199 F 4
Modoguhe o **CI** 202-203 G 6
Modot o **MAU** 148-149 J 4
Modriča o **BIH** 100-101 G 2
Moebase o **MOC** 218-219 K 3
Moeiilijk, Pulau ~ **RI** 164-165 L 4
Moeko ~ **ZRE** 210-211 G 2
Moen o **N** 86-87 J 2
Moenkopi Wash ~ **USA** 40-41 J 7
Moeraki Boulders ~ **NZ** 182 C 6
Moerkesung o **VRC** 144-145 L 5
Moero, Lac o **ZRE** 214-215 E 5
Moers o **D** 92-93 J 3
Moe-Yallourn o **AUS** 180-181 J 5
Moffat o **AUS** 180-181 J 5
Moffat Creek ~ **CDN** 32-33 K 5
Moffat, Mount ▲ **USA** 22-23 H 7
Moffat Point ▲ **USA** 22-23 P 5
Moffit o **USA** 42-43 G 2
Mofu o **Z** 218-219 E 4
Moga ~ **RUS** 116-117 O 5
Moga o **IND** 138-139 E 4
Mogadishu ~ Mugdiisho o **SP** 212-213 K 2
Mogadouro o **P** 98-99 D 4
Mogalu o **ZRE** 210-211 H 3
Mogami-gawa ~ **J** 152-153 J 5
Moganshan • **VRC** 154-155 L 6
Mogao Ku ∴• **VRC** 146-147 M 5
Mogapinyana o **RB** 218-219 E 5
Mogaung o **MYA** 142-143 K 3
Mˈlang o **RP** 160-161 F 9
Mˈtawa o **PL** 92-93 U 2
Mˈtelin o **RUS** 112-113 Q 2
Mˈlenganapas ▲ **ZA** 220-221 J 5
Mˈligasˈi ~ **EAT** 212-213 G 6
Mˈljet ~ **HR** 100-101 F 3
Mˈmabatho ☆ **ZA** 220-221 G 2
Mˈmadinare o **RB** 218-219 D 6
Mˈmamabula o **RB** 218-219 D 6
Mˈmashoro o **RB** 218-219 D 5
Mˈmathethe o **RB** 220-221 G 3
Mˈmatshumo o **RB** 218-219 C 5
Mˈnamuk o **RI** 166-167 H 3
Mˈnanzi o **EAT** 212-213 G 5
Mˈnarani ∴• **EAK** 212-213 G 5
Mˈnjoli Dam < **SD** 220-221 J 3
Mˈnogovˈšinnyj o **RUS** 122-123 H 2
Mo ~ **CAM** 204-205 H 6
Mo ~ **GH** 202-203 L 5
Mˈo ~ **RT** 202-203 L 5
Moa o **C** 54-55 H 4
Moa ~ **WAL** 202-203 E 6
Moa, Pulau ~ **RI** 166-167 K 6
Moa, Rio ~ **BR** 64-65 E 5
Moab o **USA** 42-43 C 6
Moabi o **G** 210-211 C 5
Moaco, Rio ~ **BR** 66-67 C 6
Moai ◡◡ **RCH** 78-79 B 9
Moa Island ~ **AUS** 174-175 G 2
Moala ~ **FJI** 184 III b 3
Mo'allem o **IR** 136-137 B 6
Mo'allem Kaláyeh o **IR** 136-137 D 6
Moamba o **MOC** 220-221 L 2
Moanda o **G** 210-211 D 4
Moanda o **ZRE** 210-211 C 5

Moapa o **USA** 40-41 G 7
Móar Bay ≈ 38-39 E 2
Moatize o **MOC** 218-219 H 3
Moba o **ZRE** 214-215 E 4
Mobara o **J** 152-153 J 7
Mobárak, Küh ~ **IR** 134-135 G 6
Mobárak ☆ **IR** 134-135 D 2
Mobaye ☆ **RCA** 206-207 E 6
Mobayi-Mbongi o **ZRE** 206-207 E 6
Mobdoua o **RIM** 196-197 D 7
Mobena o **ZRE** 210-211 G 3
Moberly o **USA** 42-43 L 6
Mobile o **USA** 48-49 D 4
Mobile Bay ≈ 48-49 D 4
Mobridge o **USA** 42-43 G 3
Moca ☆ **USA** 20-21 M 5
Moca ☆ **DOM** 54-55 K 5
Moca, Isla ~ **RCH** 78-79 C 5
Mocajuba o **BR** 68-69 D 3
Moçambicana ⊥ **MOC** 218-219 H 5
Moçâmbique o **MOC** 218-219 J 2
Moçambique, Ilha de ~ **MOC** 218-219 J 2
Moç Châu ☆ **VN** 156-157 D 6
Mocha, Isla ~ **RCH** 78-79 C 5
Mocha = Muhâ, al- o •• **Y** 132-133 D 7
Mochara, Cordillera de ▲ **BOL** 76-77 E 1
Moche Pyramids • **PE** 64-65 C 6
Mochima, Parque Nacional ⊥ **YV** 60-61 J 2
Mochis, Los o **MEX** 50-51 F 5
Moç Hóa o **VN** 158-159 H 5
Mochudi o **RB** 222-223 H 2
Mochumi o **PE** 64-65 C 5
Mocímboa da Praia o **MOC** 214-215 L 6
Mocímboa do Rovuma o **MOC** 214-215 K 6
Mōco ▲ **ANG** 216-217 C 6

Mohammadábád o **IR** (SIS) 134-135 J 3
Mohammadábád o **IR** (YAZ) 134-135 F 3
Mohammad Āgá o **AFG** 138-139 B 2
Mohammadia o **DZ** 190-191 C 3
Mohammedia o **MA** 188-189 H 4
Mohana o **IND** 142-143 H 6
Mohanganj o **BD** 142-143 G 3
Mohania o **IND** 142-143 H 5
Mohanpur o **NEP** 144-145 F 7
Mohawk o **USA** 20-21 K 5
Mohe o **VRC** 150-151 D 1
Mohej o **RUS** 120-121 N 2
Mohenjo Daro ∴• **PK** 138-139 B 6
Mohican, Cape ▲ **USA** 20-21 N 5
Mohol o **IND** 140-141 F 2
Mohon o **EAT** 214-215 K 5
Mohovaja ~ **RUS** 108-109 V 6
Mohovaja, gora ▲ **RUS** 88-89 S 2
Mohrungen ~ Morag o **PL** 92-93 P 2
Mohyliv-Podils'kyj o **UA** 102-103 E 6
Moi o **RI** 166-167 K 7
Moijabana o **RB** 220-221 G 6
Moila Point ▲ **PNG** 184 I b 2
Moili ~ **COM** 222-223 C 4
Moimba o **ANG** 216-217 B 8
Moincêr o **VRC** 144-145 C 5
Moinerie, Lac la o **CDN** 36-37 Q 6
Mo i Rana o **N** 86-87 G 3
Moirang o **IND** 142-143 H 3
Moise ~ **CDN** 38-39 L 3
Moisie, Rivière ~ **CDN** 38-39 L 3
Moison Lake o **CDN** 34-35 H 3
Moissac o **F** 90-91 H 9
Moissala o **TCH** 206-207 C 4
Moitaco o **YV** 60-61 H 3
Moján, El ~ San Rafael o **YV** 60-61 F 2
Mojave o **USA** 40-41 E 8
Mojave Desert ~ **USA** 40-41 F 8
Mojave River ~ **USA** 40-41 F 8
Mojero ~ **RUS** 108-109 f 7
Mojero ~ **RUS** 116-117 I 2
Mojerokan ~ **RUS** 116-117 M 2
Mojiang o **VRC** 156-157 B 5
Moji Guaçu, Rio ~ **BR** 72-73 G 6
Mojiquiçaba o **BR** 72-73 L 4
Mojkovac o **YU** 100-101 G 3
Mojo o **ETH** 208-209 D 4
Mojoagung o **RI** 168 E 3
Mojokerto o **RI** 168 E 3
Mojos, Llanos de ~ **BOL** 70-71 D 4
Mojosari o **RI** 168 E 3
Moju o **BR** 68-69 D 3
Moju dos Campos o **BR** 66-67 K 4
Moj-Urusta o **RUS** 120-121 N 3
Mojylck ~ **KA** 124-125 E 5
Mojynkum ~ **KA** 124-125 E 5
Mojynty o **KA** 124-125 H 6
Mōka ~ **RUS** 96-97 E 8
Mōka o **J** 152-153 J 6
Mokambo o **ZRE** 214-215 E 7
Mokau o **NZ** 182 I 5
Mokelumne Aqueduct < **USA** 40-41 D 6
Mokgomane o **RB** 220-221 G 3
Mokhotlong o **LS** 220-221 J 4
Mokka = al-Muhâ o •• **Y** 132-133 C 7
Mokla ~ **RUS** 118-119 K 8
Moknine o **TN** 190-191 H 3
Mokoan, Lake o **AUS** 180-181 J 4
Mokobela Pan ≈ **RB** 218-219 D 5
Mokokchung o **IND** 142-143 H 3
Mokolo o **CAM** 204-205 K 3
Mokolo ~ **ZA** 220-221 H 2
Mokoreta o **NZ** 182 B 7
Mokp'o o **ROK** 150-151 F 10
Mokrous o **RUS** 96-97 E 8
Mokša ~ **RUS** 96-97 E 8
Mōktama Kwe ≈ 158-159 D 2
Mokwa o **WAN** 204-205 F 4
Mola ~ **GH** 202-203 K 5
Moladjakit, gora ▲ **RUS** 116-117 L 3
Molakalmuru o **IND** 140-141 G 3
Molalatau o **RB** 220-221 G 3
Molalé o **ETH** 208-209 D 3
Molas del Norte, Punta ▲ **MEX** 52-53 L 1
Molat ⊥ **HR** 100-101 E 2
Moldary o **KA** 124-125 L 3
Molde o **N** 86-87 C 5
Moldotau, hrebet ▲ **KS** 146-147 N 5
Moldova ■ **MD** 102-103 F 4
Moldova Nouă o **RO** 102-103 B 5
Molegbe o **ZRE** 206-207 E 6
Mole Island ▲ **EAK** 212-213 E 1
Mole Lake Indian Reservation ✕ **USA** 46-47 D 3
Mole National Park ⊥ **GH** 202-203 K 5
Molepolole o **RB** 218-219 D 6
Moleque, Morro do ▲ **BR** 74-75 F 7
Mole River ~ **AUS** 178-179 L 5
Molétai o **LT** 94-95 J 4
Molfetta o **I** 100-101 F 3
Molibagu o **RI** 164-165 H 3
Molina o **E** 98-99 G 5
Molina o **RCH** 78-79 D 3
Molina de Segura o **E** 98-99 G 5
Moline o **USA** (IL) 46-47 C 5
Moline Mine ∴• **AUS** 172-173 L 2
Molingmol o **RI** 164-165 H 3
Molinillo, Punta ▲ **E** 98-99 C 4
Molinos, Embalse los < **RA** 76-77 E 6
Molinos, Rio ~ **RA** 80 G 2
Moliro o **ZRE** 214-215 E 5
Molise ■ **I** 100-101 E 4
Molkaty, hrebet ▲ **RUS** 112-113 J 4
Mollahˈs Hoek o **LS** 220-221 H 5
Mollah o **USA** 20-21 K 5
Mohamed 5, Barrage < **MA** 188-189 K 3
Mohammadábád o **IR** (ESF) 134-135 E 2
Mohammadábád o **IR** (KER) 134-135 G 4

Molo o **EAK** (RIF) 212-213 E 4
Molo o **EAK** 212-213 E 3
Moló o **MYA** 142-143 K 4
Moločna ~ **UA** 102-103 J 4
Moločnyj lyman ~ **UA** 102-103 J 4
Molocopote o **BR** 62-63 G 5
Molocué ~ **MOC** 218-219 J 2
Molocué, Rio ~ **MOC** 218-219 J 2
Molodečno = Maladzečna o **BY** 94-95 K 4
Molodëznaja o **ARK** 16 G 1
Molodëžnyj o **KA** 124-125 H 3
Molodëžnyj o **RUS** 120-121 N 2
Molodo o **RMM** 202-203 H 2
Molodo ~ **RUS** 110-111 N 5
Mologa ~ **RUS** 94-95 O 2
Molokai ~ **USA** 48-49 D 7
Molokai Fracture Zone ≈ 14-15 O 5
Moloma ~ **RUS** 96-97 E 4
Molong o **AUS** 180-181 K 2
Molongda ~ **RUS** 110-111 V 7
Molongdinskij hrebet ▲ **RUS** 112-113 L 4
Molopo ~ **RB** 220-221 E 3
Moloporivier o **ZA** 220-221 G 2
Moloskovicy o **RUS** 94-95 L 2
Moloundou o **CAM** 210-211 E 2
Molsheim o **F** 90-91 L 7
Molteno o **ZA** 220-221 H 5
Moltenopas ▲ **ZA** 220-221 F 6
Moltke Nunatak ▲ **GRØ** 26-27 o 4
Molu, Pulau ~ **RI** 166-167 J 6
Molucca, Laut ≈ 164-165 J 3
Moluccas = Maluku ~ **RI** 166-167 J 4
Moluccas = Maluku, Kepulauan ~ **RI** 166-167 J 2
Molucca Sea = Maluku, Laut ≈ **RI** 164-165 J 3
Moluki o **AFG** 136-137 G 7
Molumbo o **MOC** 218-219 J 2
Molume o **GR** 202-203 J 5
Molvo ~ **RUS** 116-117 G 3
Molwe o **ZRE** 214-215 C 6
Moma o **MOC** 218-219 K 3
Moma ~ **RUS** 110-111 Y 6
Moma, Ilha de ~ **MOC** 218-219 K 3
Momaligi o **WAL** 202-203 D 6
Momats ~ **RI** 166-167 K 6
Momba o **Z** 218-219 E 2
Mombaça o **BR** 68-69 J 4
Mombaca ~ **EAK** 212-213 G 6
Mombasa Marine National Reserve ⊥ **EAK** 212-213 G 6
Mombenzélé o **RCB** 210-211 F 3
Mombetsu o **J** (HOK) 152-153 K 2
Mombetsu o **J** (HOK) 152-153 K 3
Mombo ~ **RI** 166-167 G 7
Mombo o **EAT** 212-213 G 6
Mombongo o **ZRE** (HAU) 210-211 J 3
Mombongo o **ZRE** 210-211 K 3
Momboyo ~ **ZRE** 210-211 G 4
Mombuca ~ **BR** 72-73 G 6
Mombum o **RI** 166-167 K 6
Momčilgrad o **BG** 100-101 K 4
Momfafa, Tanjung ▲ **RI** 166-167 K 7
Mommon, Tanjung ▲ **RI** 166-167 G 3
Momo o **RI** 164-165 G 4
Momo-Selennjahskaja vpadina ⌣ **RUS** 110-111 W 5
Momote o **PNG** 183 D 2
Mompiche, Ensenada de ≈ 64-65 B 1
Mompog Pass ≈ 160-161 E 6
Mompono o **ZRE** 210-211 H 3
Mompos o **CO** 60-61 D 3
Momskiy Khrebet = Momskij hrebet ▲ **RUS** 110-111 Y 6
Mon o **DK** 86-87 F 9
Møn ▲ **DK** 86-87 F 9
Monaco ■ **MC** 90-91 L 10
Monaco ☆ **MC** 90-91 L 10
Monaco Deep ≃ 6-7 G 5
Monadhliau, Pulau ~ 164-165 J 3
Monadnock o **USA** (IL) 46-47 D 5
Monadyr ~ **KA** 124-125 G 4
Monaghan = Muineachán ☆ **IRL** 90-91 D 4
Monahans o **USA** 44-45 F 4
Monan o **RI** 210-211 D 4
Monapo o **MOC** 218-219 L 2
Monarch o **USA** 40-41 J 2
Monarch Mountain ▲ **CDN** 32-33 H 6
Monashee Mountains ▲ **CDN** 32-33 L 5
Monâši o **UA** 102-103 G 4
Monasterace Marina o **I** 100-101 F 5
Monastery o **CDN** 38-39 O 6
Monastir ☆ **TN** 190-191 H 3
Monastýrišče o **UA** 102-103 F 5
Monastyrščina o **RUS** 94-95 M 4
Monatélé o **CAM** 204-205 J 6
Monati, mys ▲ **RUS** 120-121 W 6
Moncks Corner o **USA** 48-49 H 3
Monclova o **MEX** 50-51 J 4
Monção o **BR** 68-69 F 3
Monção o **P** 98-99 C 4
Monchengladbach ~ **D** 92-93 J 3
Monchy o **CDN** 34-35 C 6
Monroe Lake o **USA** 46-47 E 6
Monçonguê o **RB** 218-219 E 4
Monçonguê ▲ **BR** 74-75 F 7
Monsenhor Gil o **BR** 68-69 H 5
Monsenhor Hipolito o **BR** 68-69 H 5
Monserat, Isla ▲ **MEX** 50-51 E 5
Møns Klint ◡◡ **DK** 86-87 F 9
Monsombougou o **RMM** 202-203 E 2
Montagne dˈAmbre, Parc National de la ⊥ **RM** 222-223 F 4
Montaigu o **F** 90-91 G 8
Montalbán o **E** 98-99 G 4
Montalbo o **E** 98-99 F 5

Molo o **EAK** (RIF) 212-213 E 4
Mondran o **TCH** 198-199 H 2
Montalegre o **ANG** 216-217 D 4
Montalegre o **P** 98-99 D 4
Montalvânia o **BR** 72-73 H 3
Montalvo o **EC** 64-65 D 3
Montana o **BG** 102-103 G 6
Montana ■ **USA** 40-41 J 2
Montaña de Yoro, Parque Nacional ⊥ **HN** 52-53 L 4
Montañas de Oronze ▲ **EC** 64-65 C 1
Montandón o **RCH** 76-77 C 4
Montargis o **F** 90-91 J 8
Montauban o **F** 90-91 H 9
Montauk o **USA** 46-47 N 5
Montauk Point ▲ **USA** 46-47 N 5
Montbard o **F** 90-91 K 8
Mont Bata o **RCA** 206-207 B 6
Montbéliard o **F** 90-91 L 8
Mont Blanc ▲•• **F** 90-91 L 9
Montceau-les-Mines o **F** 90-91 K 8
Mont Darwin o **ZW** 218-219 H 3
Mont-de-Marsan o **F** 90-91 G 10
Mont-Dore, La o **F** 90-91 J 9
Monte, Laguna del o **RA** 78-79 H 4
Monteagle o **AUS** 178-179 J 2
Monteagudo o **BOL** 70-71 F 6
Monteagudo o **RA** 76-77 K 4
Monte Alban ∴••• **MEX** 52-53 F 3
Monte Alegre o **BR** 62-63 G 6
Monte Alegre de Goiás o **BR** 72-73 G 2
Monte Alegre de Minas o **BR** 72-73 F 5
Monte Alegre de Sergipe o **BR** 68-69 K 7
Monte Aprazivel o **BR** 72-73 F 6
Monte Azul o **BR** 72-73 J 3
Montebello o **BR** 38-39 G 6
Montebello Islands ~ **AUS** 172-173 B 6
Monte Belo o **ANG** 216-217 C 6
Monte Bianco = Mont Blanc ▲•• **I** 100-101 A 2
Monte-Carlo o **MC** 90-91 L 10
Monte Carmelo o **BR** 72-73 G 5
Monte Caseros o **RA** 76-77 J 6
Monte Castelo o **BR** 74-75 E 6
Monte Comán o **RA** 78-79 F 3
Monte Creek o **CDN** 32-33 L 6
Monte Cristi o **DOM** 54-55 K 5
Montecristi o **EC** 64-65 B 2
Monte Cristo o **BR** 66-67 D 5
Montecristo, Isola di ▲ **I** 100-101 C 3
Monte Dourado o **BR** 62-63 H 6
Monte Escobedo o **MEX** 50-51 H 6
Montego Bay o **JA** 54-55 G 5
Monte Grande o **BOL** 70-71 F 5
Monte Grande o **NIC** 52-53 B 5
Monte Hermoso o **RA** 78-79 J 5
Monteiro o **BR** 68-69 K 5
Monteiro Lobato o **BR** 72-73 H 7
Monte León, Cerro ▲ **RA** 80 F 5
Montélimar o **F** 90-91 K 9
Monte Lindo, Arroyo ~ **RA** 76-77 H 3
Monte Lindo, Rio ~ **PY** 76-77 J 2
Monte Lindo Grande, Riacho ~ **RA** 76-77 H 3
Montello o **USA** (NV) 40-41 G 5
Montello o **USA** (WI) 46-47 D 4
Montemayor, Meseta de ▲ **RA** 80 G 2
Montemorelos o **MEX** 50-51 K 5
Montemor-o-Novo o **P** 98-99 C 5
Montenegro o **BR** 74-75 E 6
Montenegro = Crna gora ■ **YU** 100-101 G 3
Monte Negro, Quedas de ~ **ANG** 216-217 B 8
Monte Pascoal, Parque Nacional de ⊥ **BR** 72-73 L 4
Monte Patria o **RCH** 76-77 B 6
Monte Peruvia ~ **PE** 64-65 D 4
Montepescali o **I** 100-101 C 3
Montepio o **MEX** 52-53 G 2
Monte Plata ☆ **DOM** 54-55 L 5
Montepuez o **MOC** 218-219 K 1
Montepuez, Rio ~ **MOC** 218-219 K 1
Montepulciano o **I** 100-101 C 3
Monte Quemado o **RA** 76-77 F 3
Monterey o **USA** 40-41 D 7
Monteria o **CO** 60-61 D 3
Montero o **BOL** 70-71 F 5
Monteros o **RA** 76-77 E 4
Monte Rosa ▲ **CH** 92-93 J 6
Monte Rosa ▲ **I** 100-101 A 2
Monterrey ~ **MEX** 50-51 J 5
Monterrey, Parque Nacional de ⊥ **MEX** 50-51 J 5
Monterrey Bay ≈ 40-41 D 7
Monterrico o **GCA** 52-53 J 5
Monterubio o **CO** 60-61 D 2
Montes, Punta ▲ **RA** 80 F 5
Montes Altos o **BR** 68-69 E 4
Montesano sulla Marcellana o **I** 100-101 E 4
Monte SantˈAngelo o **I** 100-101 E 4
Monte Santo o **BR** 68-69 J 6
Monte Santo de Minas o **BR** 72-73 G 6
Montes Claros o **BR** 72-73 J 4
Montes de Oca o **RA** 78-79 H 5
Montesquieu Islands ~ **AUS** 172-173 L 3
Montevideo ★ **ROU** 78-79 L 3
Montevideo o **USA** 42-43 K 3
Monte Vista o **USA** 44-45 D 1
Montezuma o **BR** 72-73 J 4
Montezuma Castle National Monument ∴• **USA** 40-41 J 8
Montezuma Creek o **USA** 44-45 C 1
Montgomery ☆ **USA** (AL) 48-49 E 4
Montgomery ~ Sähiwál o **PK** 138-139 D 4
Montgomery City o **USA** 46-47 C 6

Montgomery Islands ⌒ AUS 172-173 G 3
Monticello o USA (AR) 44-45 M 3
Monticello o USA (GA) 48-49 G 3
Monticello o USA (IA) 46-47 C 4
Monticello o USA (KY) 46-47 F 7
Monticello o USA (MS) 44-45 M 4
Monticello o USA (NM) 44-45 D 3
Monticello o USA (NY) 46-47 L 5
Monticello o USA (UT) 42-43 C 7
Montijo o E 98-99 D 5
Montijo, Golfo de ≈ 52-53 D 8
Montilla o E 98-99 E 6
Montima ~ ZRE 210-211 H 2
Montipa o ANG 216-217 B 7
Montividiu o BR 72-73 E 4
Mont-Laurier o CDN 38-39 G 5
Mont-Louis o F 90-91 J 10
Montluçon o F 90-91 J 8
Montmagny o CDN 38-39 J 5
Montmarault o F 90-91 J 8
Montmartre o CDN 34-35 E 5
Monto o AUS 178-179 L 3
Montoro o• E 98-99 E 5
Montpelier o JA 54-55 G 5
Montpelier o USA (ID) 40-41 J 4
Montpelier ☆ USA (VT) 46-47 M 3
Montpellier ☆• F 90-91 J 10
Montpensier, Kap ▲ GRØ 26-27 r 5
Montréal o• CDN 38-39 H 6
Montreal Lake o CDN (SAS) 34-35 D 3
Montreal Lake ⊖ CDN (SAS) 34-35 D 3
Montreal Lake Indian Reserve ⅩCDN 34-35 D 4
Montreal River ~ CDN 38-39 D 5
Montreux o• CH 92-93 J 5
Montrose o CDN 32-33 M 7
Montrose o GB 90-91 F 3
Montrose o USA (AR) 44-45 M 3
Montrose o USA (CO) 42-43 D 6
Montrose o USA (PA) 46-47 L 5
Montrouis o RH 54-55 J 5
Mont Saint-Michel, le o••• F 90-91 G 7
Mont Sangbé, Parc National du ⊥ CI 202-203 G 5
Mont Selinda o ZW 218-219 G 5
Montserrat Island ⌒ GB 56 D 3
Mont Tremblant, Parc du ⊥ CDN 38-39 G 5
Monturaqui o RCH 76-77 C 3
Monument, The o AUS 178-179 E 1
Monument Hill State Historic Site ∴ USA 44-45 J 5
Monument Pass ▲ USA 44-45 B 1
Monument Rocks • USA 42-43 G 6
Monument Valley Navajo Tribal Park ⊥• USA 44-45 B 1
Monywa o MYA 142-143 J 4
Monza o• I 100-101 B 2
Monza o VRC 144-145 J 4
Monze o Z 218-219 D 3
Monzón o• E 98-99 H 4
Monzon o PE 64-65 D 6
Mooat, Danau ⊖ RI 164-165 J 3
Moodiarrup o AUS 176-177 D 6
Mooirivier ~ ZA 220-221 H 3
Mooirivier ~ ZA 220-221 K 4
Mooketsi o ZA 218-219 F 6
Mooki River ~ AUS 178-179 L 6
Moola, Rio ~ MOC 214-215 H 6
Mooloo Downs o AUS 176-177 D 2
Mooloogool o AUS 176-177 E 3
Moolooloo Out Station o AUS 172-173 K 4
Moomba o AUS 178-179 F 4
Moomin Creek ~ AUS 178-179 K 5
Moonan Flat o AUS 178-179 L 6
Moonaree o AUS 178-179 C 6
Moonbi Range ▲ AUS 178-179 L 6
Moonda Lake ⊖ AUS 178-179 F 3
Moondarra, Lake ⊖ AUS 174-175 E 7
Moonie o AUS 178-179 L 4
Moonie Highway II AUS 178-179 L 4
Moonie River ~ AUS 178-179 K 4
Moonie River ~ AUS 178-179 K 5
Moonlight Head ▲ AUS 180-181 G 5
Moonta Bay o AUS 180-181 D 3
Moonya o AUS 178-179 H 2
Moor, Kepulauan ⌒ RI 166-167 H 3
Moora o AUS 176-177 D 5
Mooraberree o AUS 178-179 F 3
Moorarie o AUS 176-177 D 2
Moorcroft o USA 42-43 E 3
Moordkuil o ZA 220-221 D 6
Moore o USA (MT) 42-43 C 2
Moore o USA (TX) 44-45 H 5
Moore, Lake ⊖ AUS 176-177 D 4
Moore, Mount ▲ AUS 176-177 G 2
Moore Bay ≈ 24-25 N 2
Moore Home State Memorial ∴• USA 46-47 D 6
Moore Park o AUS 178-179 M 3
Moore River ~ AUS 176-177 C 5
Moore River National Park ⊥ AUS 176-177 C 5
Moores Creek National Battlefield • USA 48-49 J 2
Moore's Island ⌒ BS 54-55 G 1
Mooresville o USA 48-49 H 2
Moorhead o USA 42-43 J 2
Moorrivier o ZA 220-221 K 4
Moornanyah Lake ⊖ AUS 180-181 G 2
Moose o USA 40-41 J 4
Moosehead Lake ⊖ USA 46-47 O 3
Moose Island ⌒ CDN 34-35 H 5
Moose Jaw o CDN 34-35 D 5
Moose Jaw Creek ~ CDN 34-35 D 5
Moose Lake o CDN (MAN) 34-35 F 4
Moose Lake ⊖ CDN (MAN) 34-35 G 4
Mooselookmeguntic Lake ⊖ USA 46-47 N 3
Moose Mount ▲ CDN 34-35 E 6
Moose Mountain Creek ~ CDN 34-35 E 5
Moose Mount Provincial Park ⊥ CDN 34-35 E 6
Moose Pass o USA 20-21 Q 6
Moose River o CDN (ONT) 34-35 Q 5
Moose River ~ CDN 34-35 Q 5
Moosomin o CDN 34-35 F 5
Moosonee o CDN 34-35 Q 5
Mootwingee Historic Site • AUS 178-179 G 6
Mootwingee National Park ⊥ AUS 178-179 G 6
Mopádu o IND 140-141 H 3
Mopán, Río ~ GCA 52-53 K 3
Mopane o ZA 218-219 E 6
Mopeia o MOC 218-219 H 3
Mopipi o RB 218-219 C 5
Mopti ◘ RMM 202-203 H 2
Mopti ☆ RMM (MOP) 202-203 H 2
Moqām, Bandar-e o IR 134-135 E 5
Moquegua ☆ PE 70-71 B 5
Moquegua, Río ~ PE 70-71 B 5
Moquehuá o RA 78-79 K 3
Mór o H 92-93 P 5
Mora o CAM 206-207 B 3
Mora o E 98-99 F 5
Mora o P 98-99 C 5
Mora o S 86-87 G 6
Mora o USA (MN) 42-43 L 3
Mora o USA (NM) 44-45 E 2
Mora, La o RA 78-79 F 3
Morab o IND 140-141 F 3
Morača ~ YU 100-101 G 3
Moradabad o IND 138-139 G 5
Morada Nova o BR 68-69 J 4
Morada Nova de Minas o BR 72-73 H 5
Morado, Quebrada del ~ RCH 76-77 B 4
Morado I, Cerro ▲ RA 76-77 E 2
Moraes o BR 74-75 D 8
Morafano o RM 222-223 E 6
Morafenobe o RM 222-223 D 6
Morag o PL 92-93 P 2
Morai o RI 166-167 H 5
Moraine State Park ⊥ USA 46-47 H 5
Morais de Almeida o BR 66-67 K 6
Morajuana o GUY 62-63 E 1
Moraleja o E 98-99 D 4
Moramanga o RM 222-223 F 7
Moran o USA (KS) 42-43 K 7
Moran o USA (WY) 40-41 J 4
Morán, Laguna ⊖ RA 78-79 K 2
Moranbah o AUS 178-179 K 2
Morane Island ~ AUS 172-173 G 3
Morant Bay o JA 54-55 G 6
Morant Cays ⌒ JA 54-55 H 6
Morappur o IND 140-141 H 4
Morarano o RM 222-223 E 8
Morarano-Chrome o RM 222-223 F 6
Mora River ~ USA 44-45 E 2
Moratalla o E 98-99 G 5
Moratuwa o CL 140-141 H 7
Moraújo o BR 68-69 H 3
Morava ⩮ CZ 92-93 O 4
Morava ~ CZ 92-93 O 4
Morávia, Planalto de ▲ MOC 218-219 F 2
Morawa o AUS 176-177 C 4
Moray Downs o AUS 178-179 J 1
Moray Firth ≈ 90-91 E 3
Morazán o HN 52-53 L 4
Morbanipari, Mount ▲ PNG 183 B 3
Morbi o IND 138-139 C 8
Mörbylånga ☆ S 86-87 H 8
Morcego o BR 66-67 F 4
Morden o CDN 34-35 G 6
Mordovo o RUS 94-95 R 5
Mordovskij zopovednik ⊥ RUS 94-95 S 4
Mordvinia = Mordovskaja Respublika ◘ RUS 94-95 S 4
Mordvinof, Cape ▲ USA 22-23 O 5
Mordvinova, zaliv ⊖ RUS 122-123 K 5
Mordyjaha ~ RUS 108-109 N 6
Mor'e o RUS 94-95 M 1
Moreau River ~ USA 42-43 G 3
Morecambe o CDN 32-33 P 5
Morecambe o GB 90-91 F 4
Moree o AUS 178-179 K 5
Moreh o IND 142-143 J 3
Morehead o PNG 183 A 5
Morehead o USA 46-47 G 6
Morehead City o USA 48-49 K 2
Morehead River ~ PNG 183 A 5
Moreira, Arroyo ~ RA 76-77 H 6
More-Ju ~ RUS 108-109 H 8
Morela, Ponta ▲ CV 202-203 C 6
Morelia o CO 64-65 E 1
Morelia ☆••• MEX 52-53 D 2
Morell o CDN 38-39 N 5
Morella o AUS 178-179 G 2
Morella o E 98-99 G 4
Morelos o MEX (COA) 50-51 H 3
Morelos o MEX (COA) 50-51 J 3
Morelos ◘ MEX 52-53 E 2
Morembe o RM 222-223 C 8
Moremi Wildlife Reserve ⊥ RB 218-219 B 4
Morena o IND 138-139 F 6
Morena, Cachoeira ~ BR 66-67 H 4
Morena, Salto da ~ BR 66-67 H 6
Morena, Sierra ▲ E 98-99 E 5
Morenero o YV 60-61 K 3
Moreno o BR 68-69 L 6
Moreno o RA 78-79 K 3
Moreno, Bahía ≈ 76-77 B 2
Moreno, Sierra de ▲ RCH 76-77 C 1
Moreno Chillanes o EC 64-65 C 2
Moresby Island ⌒ CDN 32-33 E 5
Moreton, Cape ▲ AUS 178-179 M 4
Moreton Bay ≈ 178-179 M 4
Moreton Island ⌒ AUS 178-179 M 4
Moreton Post Office o AUS 174-175 G 3
Morfou o TR 128-129 E 5
Morġāb o AFG 136-137 H 7
Morġāb, Daryā-ye ~ AFG 136-137 H 7
Morġābrūd, Daryā-ye ~ AFG 136-137 J 7
Morgan o AUS 180-181 E 3
Morgana, proliv ≈ 84-85 h 2
Morgan City o USA 44-45 M 5
Morgan Creek ~ USA 42-43 D 1
Morganfield o USA 46-47 E 7
Morgan Hill o USA 40-41 D 7
Morgan's Corner o USA 48-49 K 1
Morganton o USA 48-49 H 2
Morgantown o USA (KY) 46-47 E 7
Morgantown o USA (WV) 46-47 J 6
Morgan Vale o AUS 180-181 F 2
Morgenzon o ZA 220-221 J 3
Morgim o IND 140-141 E 3
Morhaja ~ RUS 118-119 D 4
Morhiban, Lac de ⊖ CDN 38-39 N 2
Mori o J 152-153 J 3
Mori o VRC 146-147 K 4
Moriarty o USA 44-45 D 2
Moribaya o RG 202-203 F 5
Morice Lake ⊖ CDN 32-33 G 4
Morice River ~ CDN 32-33 G 4
Moricetown o CDN 32-33 G 4
Morichal Largo, Río ~ YV 60-61 K 3
Morichal Viejo o CO 60-61 F 6
Morigbadougou o RG 202-203 F 5
Morigim o IND 140-141 E 3
Morigio Island ⌒ PNG 183 B 4
Morija o LS 220-221 H 4
Morijo o EAK 212-213 E 4
Moriki o WAN 198-199 C 6
Morin Dawa o VRC 150-151 E 3
Morinville o CDN 32-33 O 5
Morioka ☆• J 152-153 J 5
Morire o MOC 218-219 H 3
Mori River ~ PNG 183 E 5
Moristyj, ostrov ⌒ RUS 126-127 G 5
Morita, La o MEX 50-51 G 3
Moriyama o J 152-153 F 7
Morjakovskij Zaton o RUS 114-115 S 6
Morjen ~ PK 134-135 K 4
Morki ☆ RUS 96-97 F 5
Morkoka ~ RUS 116-117 O 2
Morkoka ~ RUS 118-119 G 3
Morlaix o F 90-91 F 7
Morley o CDN 32-33 N 6
Mormanno o I 100-101 E 5
Mormon Print Shop • USA 46-47 F 3
Morne-à-L'eau o F 56 E 3
Morne Seychellois National Park ⊥ SY 224 D 2
Morney o AUS 178-179 F 3
Mornington, Isla ⌒ RCH 80 C 4
Mornington Abyssal Plain ⩬ 5 C 1
Mornington Island ⌒ AUS 174-175 E 5
Mornington Island Aboriginal Land Trust Ⅹ AUS 174-175 E 5
Moro o PE 64-65 C 6
Moro o PK 138-139 B 6
Moro o USA 40-41 D 3
Moro, Arroyo el ~ RA 78-79 K 5
Moroak o AUS 174-175 B 4
Morobe o PNG 183 D 4
Morobo o SUD 212-213 C 2
Morocco = al-Maghrib ■ MA 188-189 H 4
Morococala, Cerro ▲ BOL 70-71 D 6
Morodougou o RN 202-203 F 4
Morogari ＜ SP 208-209 F 6
Morogoro ◘ EAT 214-215 J 5
Morogoro ☆ EAT 214-215 J 4
Moro Gulf ≈ 160-161 E 9
Moroiemu o RI 166-167 K 5
Morokweng o ZA 220-221 F 3
Moromaho, Pulau ⌒ RI 166-167 C 5
Morón o C 54-55 F 3
Mörön ☆ MAU 148-149 E 3
Morón o RA 78-79 K 3
Morón o YV 60-61 G 2
Morona, Río ~ PE 64-65 D 4
Morondava o RM 222-223 D 8
Morón de la Frontera o E 98-99 E 6
Morondo o CI 202-203 G 5
Moroni ★• COM 222-223 C 3
Moronou o CI 202-203 H 6
Morošečnaja ~ RUS 120-121 R 5
Morotai, Pulau ⌒ RI 164-165 L 2
Morotai, Selat ≈ 164-165 K 2
Moroto ☆ EAU 212-213 E 2
Moroto, Mount ▲ EAU 212-213 E 2
Morouba o RCA 206-207 E 5
Morowali o RI 164-165 G 4
Morowali Reserve ⊥• RI 164-165 G 4
Morozova, mys ▲ RUS 108-109 f 2
Morozovsk o RUS 102-103 M 3
Morpará o BR 68-69 G 7
Morpeth o GB 90-91 G 4
Morrasale o RUS 108-109 M 7
Morreesburg o ZA 220-221 D 6
Morretes o BR 74-75 F 5
Morrilton o USA 44-45 L 2
Morrin o CDN 32-33 O 6
Morrinhos o BR (CEA) 68-69 H 3
Morrinhos o BR (GOI) 72-73 F 4
Morrinhos o BR (MAR) 68-69 E 6
Morrinhos, Cachoeira ~ BR 66-67 E 7
Morrinsville o NZ 182 E 2
Morrión, El o MEX 50-51 G 3
Morris o CDN 34-35 H 6
Morris o USA (IL) 46-47 D 5
Morris o USA (MN) 42-43 K 3
Morris, Mount o AUS 178-179 H 3
Morrisburg o CDN 38-39 G 6
Morris Jesup, Kap ▲ GRØ 26-27 j 2
Morris Jesup Gletscher ⊂ GRØ 26-27 P 5
Morrison Bay ≈ 158-159 E 5
Morristown o USA (SD) 42-43 G 3
Morristown o USA (TN) 48-49 G 1
Morrisville o USA 46-47 M 3
Morro o EC 64-65 B 3
Morro, Canal de ≈ 64-65 B 3
Morro, Punta ▲ MEX 52-53 J 2
Morro, Punta ▲ RCH 76-77 B 4
Morro, Sierra del ▲ RA 78-79 G 2
Morro Agudo o BR 72-73 F 6
Morro Bay o USA 40-41 D 8
Morro Chico o RCH 80 E 6
Morrocoy, Parque Nacional ⊥ YV 60-61 G 2
Morro de Coco o BR 72-73 K 6
Morro do Alvarenga o BR 66-67 D 6
Morro do Chapéu o BR 68-69 H 7
Morro do Pilar o BR 72-73 J 5
Morropón o PE 64-65 C 4
Morro River ~ WAL 202-203 E 6
Morros o BR 68-69 F 3
Morrosquillo, Golfo de ≈ 60-61 D 3
Morrumbala o MOC 218-219 H 3
Morrumbene o MOC 218-219 H 6
Moršank o RUS 94-95 R 5
Morsi o IND 138-139 G 9
Morskoj, aral ⌒ KA 126-127 J 5
Morskoj, ostrov ⌒ KA 126-127 J 5
Morskoj Birjučok, ostrov ⌒ RUS 126-127 G 5
Morsø o DK 86-87 D 8
Morstone o AUS 174-175 E 6
Mørsvikbotn o N 86-87 G 3
Mort, Chutes de la ~ RM 222-223 F 7
Mortandade, Cachoeira ~ BR 68-69 E 5
Mortara o I 100-101 B 2
Morteros o RA 76-77 F 6
Mortes, Rio das ~ BR 72-73 E 3
Mortesoro o SUD 208-209 B 3
Mortimers o• BS 54-55 H 3
Mortlake o AUS 180-181 G 5
Morton o USA (MN) 42-43 K 3
Morton o USA (WA) 40-41 C 2
Morton National Park ⊥ AUS 180-181 L 3
Mort River ~ AUS 178-179 F 1
Mortugaba o BR 72-73 J 3
Moruga o TT 60-61 L 2
Moruita o EAU 212-213 E 3
Morundah o AUS 180-181 J 3
Moruppatti o IND 140-141 H 5
Moruya o AUS 180-181 L 3
Morven o AUS 178-179 J 4
Morvongole ▲ EAU 212-213 E 2
Morwell o AUS 180-181 J 5
Morzhovoi Bay ≈ 22-23 P 5
Moržovec, ostrov ⌒ RUS 88-89 R 3
Mosa o PNG 183 F 3
Moša ~ RUS 88-89 Q 5
Mosby o USA 42-43 D 2
Mosca o USA 44-45 E 1
Moscas, Las o RA 78-79 K 2
Mosconi o RA 78-79 J 3
Moscow o USA (ID) 40-41 F 2
Moscow o USA (KS) 44-45 G 1
Moscow = Moskva ★••• RUS 94-95 P 4
Mosel ~ D 92-93 J 4
Moselebe ~ RB 220-221 F 2
Moselle ~ F 90-91 L 7
Mošens'ka dubrava • UA 102-103 G 3
Mosers River o CDN 38-39 N 6
Moses Lake o• USA 40-41 E 2
Moses Point ▲ USA 20-21 J 4
Mosetse o RB 218-219 D 5
Mošgān o IR 134-135 F 4
Mosgiel o NZ 182 C 6
Moshesh's Ford o ZA 220-221 H 5
Moshi ☆ EAT 212-213 F 5
Moshi, River ~ WAN 204-205 F 4
Moshi Rest Camp o Z 218-219 D 2
Mosi o WAN 204-205 E 4
Mosigo o PNG 184 I b 2
Mosi-Oa-Tunya National Park ⊥ Z 218-219 C 3
Mosite o ZRE 210-211 J 3
Mosjøen o N 86-87 F 4
Moskalenki ☆ RUS 124-125 G 1
Moskal'vo o RUS 122-123 K 2
Moskenesøya ⌒ N 86-87 F 3
Moskosel o S 86-87 J 4
Moškovo ☆ RUS 114-115 R 7
Moskovskij o TJ 136-137 L 6
Moskva ★••• RUS (Mos) 94-95 P 4
Moskva ~ RUS 94-95 O 4
Mosle Creek ~ CDN 32-33 H 6
Moso, Île = Verao ⌒ VAN 184 II b 3
Mošok o RUS 94-95 R 4
Mosomane o RB 220-221 H 2
Mosonmagyaróvár o H 92-93 O 5
Mosopa o RB 220-221 G 2
Mosque o• RI 164-165 G 6
Mosque (Gantarang) • RI 168 E 6
Mosqueiro o BR (P) 62-63 K 6
Mosqueiro o BR (SER) 68-69 K 7
Mosquera o CO 60-61 B 6
Mosquero o USA 44-45 F 2
Mosquitia ⩮ HN 54-55 C 7
Mosquito, Rio ~ PY 76-77 H 2
Mosquito Bay ≈ 36-37 K 4
Mosquito Fork River ~ USA 20-21 T 5
Mosquito Lagoon ≈ 48-49 H 5
Mosquito Lake ⊖ CDN 30-31 S 4
Mosquitos, Costa de ⌣ NIC 52-53 C 5
Mosquitos, Golfo de los ≈ 52-53 D 7
Moss ☆ N 86-87 E 7
Mossaka o RCB 210-211 F 4
Mossbank o CDN 34-35 D 6
Mossburn o NZ 182 B 6
Mosselbaai = Mossel Bay o ZA 220-221 F 7
Mossel Bay = Mosselbaai o ZA 220-221 F 7
Mossendjo o RCB (Nia) 210-211 D 5
Mossgiel o AUS 180-181 H 2
Mossman o AUS 174-175 H 5
Mossoró o BR 68-69 K 4
Mossoró, Rio ~ BR 68-69 K 4
Moss Town o BS 54-55 H 2
Mossuril o MOC 218-219 L 2
Moss Vale o AUS 180-181 L 3
Mossy River ~ CDN 34-35 E 3
Most o CZ 92-93 M 3
Mostaganem ☆ DZ 190-191 C 3
Mostar o• BIH 100-101 F 3
Mostardas o BR 74-75 E 8
Mosteiro de Batalha ••• P 98-99 C 5
Moșteni, Trivalea- o RO 102-103 D 5
Møstling Tvillingøen, Kap ▲ GRØ 28-29 U 5
Móstoles o E 98-99 F 4
Mostovskoj o RUS 126-127 D 5
Mosul = al-Mauṣil ☆ IRQ 128-129 K 4
Mosul = al-Mauṣil ☆ IRQ 128-129 K 4
Møsvatnet ⊖ N 86-87 D 7
Mot'a o ETH 208-209 C 3
Mota ⌒ VAN 184 II a 1
Motaba ~ RCB 210-211 F 2
Motagua, Río ~ GCA 52-53 K 4
Motaha o RI 164-165 H 6
Motala ☆• S 86-87 G 7
Mota Lava ⌒ VAN 184 II a 1
Motengpas ▲ LS 220-221 J 4
Motherwell o GB 90-91 F 4
Moti, Pulau ⌒ RI 164-165 K 3
Motigu o GH 202-203 J 5
Motihari o IND 142-143 D 2
Motilla del Palancar o E 98-99 G 5
Motiti Island ⌒ NZ 182 F 2
Motley o USA 42-43 K 2
Motloutse ~ RB 218-219 E 6
Motloutse Ruins ∴• RB 218-219 E 6
Motobu o J 152-153 B 11
Motorčuna ~ RUS 110-111 N 5
Motozintla de Mendoza o MEX 52-53 H 4
Motril o E 98-99 F 6
Motru o RO 102-103 C 4
Mott o USA 42-43 F 2
Motueka o NZ 182 D 4
Motul o MEX 52-53 K 1
Motupe o PE 64-65 C 5
Motupena Point ▲ PNG 184 I b 2
Moturiki ⌒ FJI 184 III b 2
Motygino ☆• RUS 116-117 G 6
Motyklej o RUS 120-121 N 4
Mouali Gbangba o RCB 210-211 F 2
Mouat, Cape ▲ CDN 24-25 h 2
Moubolo, Mont ▲ RN 198-199 E 3
Moubotsi o RCB 210-211 D 6
Moucha, Île ⌒ DJI 208-209 F 3
Mouchalagane, Rivière ~ CDN 38-39 K 2
Mouchchene, Ibel ▲ MA 188-189 H 4
Mouchoir Passage ≈ 54-55 K 4
Moudjéria o RIM 196-197 D 6
Moúdros o GR 100-101 K 5
Mouenda o G 210-211 C 5
Mougalaba, Reserve de la ⊥ G 210-211 C 5
Mougamou o G 210-211 D 4
Mouila ☆ G 210-211 C 4
Moujia o RN 198-199 B 5
Mouka o RCA 206-207 E 5
Moukoumbi o G 210-211 D 4
Moul ＜ RN 198-199 F 5
Moula ~ TCH 206-207 D 4
Moulamein o AUS 180-181 H 3
Moulares o TN 190-191 G 3
Moulay Bouâzza o MA 188-189 H 4
Moulay-Bousselham o MA 188-189 H 3
Moulay-Idriss o•• MA 188-189 J 3
Mould Bay o CDN 24-25 M 2
Moulèngui Binza o G 210-211 C 5
Moulins ☆• F 90-91 J 8
Mouli Pouli o G 210-211 D 4
Moulmein = Maulamayaing o MYA 158-159 D 2
Moulmein = Maulamyaing o MYA 158-159 D 2
Moulmeingyun o MYA 158-159 C 2
Mouloud o DJI 208-209 F 3
Moulouya, Oued ~ MA 188-189 K 3
Moulton o USA 48-49 E 2
Moultrie o USA 48-49 G 4
Moultrie, Lake ⊖ USA 48-49 H 3
Moulvi Bazar o BD 142-143 G 3
Moulvouday o CAM 206-207 B 3
Mounanko o CAM 210-211 B 2
Mound City Group National Monument • USA 46-47 G 6
Moundhill Point ▲ USA 22-23 K 6
Moundou ☆ TCH 206-207 C 4
Moundsville o USA 46-47 H 6
Moungoun-dou-sud o RCB 210-211 D 5
Moŭng Roessei o K 158-159 G 4
Mounguel o CAM 204-205 K 5
Mountain o USA 46-47 D 3
Mountainair o USA 44-45 D 2
Mountain City o USA (NV) 40-41 G 5
Mountain City o USA (TN) 48-49 H 1
Mountain Gate o USA 40-41 C 5
Mountain Home o USA (AR) 44-45 L 1
Mountain Home o USA (ID) 40-41 G 4
Mountain Lake ⊖ CDN 30-31 U 5
Mountain Lodge o EAK 212-213 F 4
Mountain Point o USA 32-33 E 4
Mountain River ~ CDN 30-31 E 3
Mountain Springs o USA 40-41 G 7
Mountain Valley o AUS 174-175 B 4
Mountain View o USA 44-45 L 2
Mountainview o USA 48-49 E 8
Mountain Village o USA 20-21 J 5
Mount Airy o USA 48-49 H 1
Mount Allan o AUS 172-173 L 7
Mount Amhurst o AUS 172-173 H 5
Mount Aspiring National Park ⊥ NZ 182 B 6
Mount Augustus o AUS 176-177 D 2
Mount Augustus National Park ⊥ AUS 176-177 D 2
Mount Ayliff o ZA 220-221 J 5
Mount Ayr o USA 42-43 K 5
Mount Barker o AUS (SA) 180-181 E 3
Mount Barker o AUS (WA) 176-177 D 7
Mount Barnett o AUS 172-173 H 4
Mountbatten Indian Reserve Ⅹ CDN 38-39 C 5
Mount Baw Baw o• AUS 180-181 J 4
Mount Beauty o AUS 180-181 J 4
Mount Brockman o AUS 172-173 C 7
Mount Buffalo National Park ⊥ AUS 180-181 J 4
Mount Carleton Provincial Park ⊥ CDN 38-39 L 5
Mount Carmel o USA 46-47 E 6
Mount Carmel Junction o USA 40-41 H 7
Mount Carrol o USA 46-47 D 4
Mount Celia o AUS 176-177 G 4
Mount Charleston o USA 40-41 G 7
Mount Clemens o USA 46-47 G 4
Mount Clere o AUS 176-177 D 2
Mount Cook o NZ 182 C 5
Mount Cook National Park ⊥••• NZ 182 C 5
Mount Coolon o AUS 178-179 J 1
Mount Denison o AUS 172-173 L 7
Mount Desert Island ⌒ USA 46-47 O 3
Mount Divide o AUS 172-173 E 7
Mount Dora o USA 48-49 H 5
Mount Doreen o AUS 172-173 K 7
Mount Douglas o AUS 178-179 J 1
Mount Eba o AUS 178-179 C 6
Mount Ebenezer o AUS 176-177 M 2
Mount Eccles National Park ⊥ AUS 180-181 F 5
Mount Edgar o AUS 172-173 E 6
Mount Edziza Provincial Park ⊥ CDN 32-33 E 3
Mount Elizabeth o AUS 172-173 H 4
Mount Everest ▲ NEP 144-145 F 7
Mount Field National Park ⊥ AUS 180-181 J 7
Mount Fletcher o ZA 220-221 J 5
Mount Florance o AUS 172-173 C 6
Mount Forest o CDN 38-39 D 7
Mount Frere o ZA 220-221 J 5
Mount Gambier o AUS 180-181 F 4
Mount Garnet o AUS 174-175 H 5
Mount Hagen ☆•• PNG 183 C 3
Mount Harris Tine Mine Area o AUS 172-173 K 2
Mount Hope o AUS 180-181 C 3
Mount House o AUS 172-173 G 4
Mount Hutt o NZ 182 C 5
Mount Ida o AUS 176-177 F 4
Mount Ida o USA 44-45 L 2
Mountin Zebra National Park ⊥ ZA 220-221 G 6
Mount Isa o•• AUS 174-175 E 7
Mount Jackson o AUS 176-177 E 5
Mount Kaichui ▲ SOL 184 I e 3
Mount Kalourat ▲ SOL 184 I e 3
Mount Kaputar National Park ⊥ AUS 178-179 L 6
Mount Keith o AUS 176-177 F 3
Mount Larcom o AUS 178-179 L 2
Mount Lofty Range ▲ AUS 180-181 E 3
Mount Madden Wheat Bin o AUS 176-177 E 6
Mount Magnet o AUS 176-177 D 4
Mount Maitabi ▲ SOL 184 I c 2
Mount Mary o AUS 180-181 E 3
Mount Molloy o AUS 174-175 H 5
Mount Morgan o• AUS 178-179 L 2
Mount Mulgrave o AUS 174-175 G 5
Mount Mulligan o AUS 174-175 H 5
Mount Narryer o AUS 176-177 C 3
Mountnorris Bay ≈ 172-173 L 1
Mount Padbury o AUS 176-177 E 2
Mount Paget ▲ GB 78-79 O 7
Mount Perry o AUS 178-179 L 3
Mount Pleasant o USA (IA) 46-47 C 5
Mount Pleasant o USA (MI) 46-47 F 4
Mount Pleasant o USA (TX) 44-45 K 3
Mount Pleasant o USA (UT) 40-41 J 6
Mount Rainier National Park ⊥ USA 40-41 D 2
Mount Remarkable National Park ⊥ AUS 180-181 D 2
Mount Revelstoke National Park ⊥ CDN 32-33 L 6
Mount Richmond National Park ⊥ AUS 180-181 F 5
Mount Robson Provincial Park ⊥ CDN 32-33 L 5
Mount Rogers National Recreation Area ⊥ USA 46-47 H 7
Mount Rupert o ZA 220-221 G 4
Mount Rushmore National Memorial ∴ USA 42-43 F 4
Mount Saint Helens National Volcanic Monument ⊥ USA 40-41 C 2
Mount -Sandiman o AUS 176-177 C 2
Mount Sanford o AUS 172-173 K 4
Mount Sasan ▲ SOL 184 I d 3
Mount Skinner o AUS 178-179 C 2
Mount Somers o NZ 182 C 5
Mount Sterling o USA (IL) 46-47 C 6
Mount Sterling o USA (KY) 46-47 G 6
Mount Strzelecki National Park ⊥ AUS 180-181 K 6
Mount Surprise o AUS 174-175 H 6
Mount Swan o AUS 178-179 C 2
Mount Trumbull o USA 40-41 H 7
Mount Union o USA 46-47 K 5
Mount Vernon o AUS 176-177 E 2
Mount Vernon o USA (GA) 48-49 G 3
Mount Vernon o USA (IL) 46-47 D 6
Mount Vernon o USA (IN) 46-47 E 7
Mount Vernon o USA (OH) 46-47 G 5
Mount Vernon o USA (OR) 40-41 E 3
Mount Vernon o USA (WA) 40-41 C 1
Mount Vetters o AUS 176-177 F 5
Mount Walker o AUS 176-177 E 6
Mount Wedge o AUS (NT) 172-173 L 7
Mount Wedge o AUS (SA) 180-181 C 2
Mount William National Park ⊥ AUS 180-181 K 6
Mouping o VRC 154-155 M 3
Moura o AUS 178-179 K 3
Moura o BR 62-63 D 6
Moura o•• P 98-99 D 5
Moura, Cachoeira ~ BR 66-67 H 5
Mourão o P 98-99 D 5
Mouray o TCH 206-207 E 3
Mourdi, Dépression du ⩮ TCH 198-199 K 3
Mourdiah o RMM 202-203 G 2
Mouri Mountains ▲ WAN 204-205 J 4
Mourindi o G 210-211 C 5
Mouroubra o AUS 176-177 D 4
Mourounguolay o TCH 206-207 C 4
Mouscron o B 92-93 G 3
Mousgougou o TCH 206-207 C 3
Mousôayah o RG 202-203 D 5
Moussa, Hassi ＜ DZ 190-191 C 6
Moussadey o RN 204-205 E 2
Moussafoyo o TCH 206-207 D 4
Moussaya o RG 202-203 E 4
Moussoro o TCH 198-199 H 6
Moustiers-Sainte-Marie o F 90-91 L 10
Moutamba o RCB 210-211 D 5
Mouth of the Mekong = Cử'a Sông Cử'u Long ⩮ VN 158-159 J 6
Mouths of the Indus ~ PK 134-135 M 6
Moûtiers o F 90-91 L 9
Moutong o RI 164-165 G 3
Moutourouа o CAM 206-207 B 3
Mouydir, Monts du ▲ DZ 190-191 E 8
Mouyonndzi o RCB 210-211 D 5
Mouzarak o TCH 198-199 G 6
Movila Miresii o RO 102-103 E 5
Moville o USA 42-43 J 4
Mowanjum Ⅹ AUS 172-173 F 4
Mowasi o GUY 62-63 E 3
Moweaqua o USA 46-47 D 6
Mowewe o RI 164-165 G 5
Moxey Town o BS 54-55 G 2
Moxico ◘ ANG 216-217 E 6
Moxotó, Rio ~ BR 68-69 K 6
Moyagee Gemstone Deposit • AUS 176-177 D 3
Moyahua o MEX 50-51 H 7
Moyale o EAK 212-213 G 2
Moyalé o ETH 208-209 D 7
Moyamba o WAL 202-203 D 5
Moyen Atlas ▲ MA 188-189 H 4
Moyen-Chari ◘ TCH 206-207 C 4
Moyeni o LS 220-221 H 5
Moyenne Sido o RCA 206-207 D 4
Moyie o CDN 32-33 N 7
Moyie Springs o USA 40-41 F 1
Moyne, Lac le ⊖ CDN 36-37 P 6
Moyo o EAU 212-213 C 2
Moyo ~ RI 168 C 7
Moyo, Pulau ⌒ RI 168 C 7
Moyobamba ☆ PE 64-65 D 5
Moyogalpa o NIC 52-53 B 6
Moyo Pulau Reserve ⊥• RI 168 C 7
Moyowosi ~ EAT 212-213 C 5
Møysalen ▲ N 86-87 G 2
Moyto o TCH 198-199 H 6
Moyu o VRC 144-145 B 2
Mozaffarābād-e Masileh o IR 134-135 D 1
Možajsk ☆•• RUS 94-95 P 4
Mozambique = Moçambique ■ MOC 218-219 G 6
Mozambique Basin ⩬ 9 G 8
Mozambique Channel ≈ 222-223 A 7
Mozambique Plateau ⩬ 9 G 9
Mozambique Plateau = Natal Ridge ⩬ 220-221 M 6
Mozdok o RUS 126-127 F 6
Mozdūrān o IR 136-137 G 6
Možga ☆ RUS 96-97 H 5
Mozyr' = Mazyr o BY 94-95 L 5
Mpaem o GH 202-203 K 6
Mpaka Station o SD 220-221 K 3
Mpala o ZRE 214-215 E 4
Mpama ~ RCB 210-211 E 5
Mpana o GH 202-203 K 5
Mpanda o EAT 214-215 F 4
Mpandamatenga o RB 218-219 C 4
Mpanga o EAT 214-215 K 4
Mpase o ZRE 210-211 H 4
Mpataba o GH 202-203 J 7
Mpatora o EAT 214-215 K 5
Mpem ~ CAM 204-205 J 6
Mpepayi o EAT (RUV) 214-215 H 6
Mpessoba o RMM 202-203 H 3
Mphaki o LS 220-221 J 5
Mphoengs o ZW 218-219 D 5
Mpiéla o RMM 202-203 G 3
Mpigi o EAU 212-213 D 3
Mpika o Z 214-215 F 6
Mpitimbi o EAT (RUV) 214-215 H 6
Mpo o ZRE 210-211 G 6
Mpoko ~ RCA 206-207 D 6
Mpoko o ZRE 210-211 G 5
Mponde ~ EAT 212-213 E 6
Mponela o MW 218-219 G 1
Mpongwe o Z 218-219 E 1
Mporokoso o Z 214-215 F 5
Mpoukou ~ RCB 210-211 D 5
Mpoumé, Chute ~• CAM 210-211 C 2
Mpouop ~ CAM 210-211 D 2
Mpouya o RCB 210-211 F 5
Mpraeso o GH 202-203 K 6
Mpui o EAT 214-215 F 5
Mpulungu o Z 214-215 F 5
Mpumalanga o ZA 220-221 K 4
Mpume o ZRE 210-211 G 6
M'Pupa, Rápidos ~ ANG 216-217 F 8
Mpwapwa o EAT 214-215 J 4
Mrakovo ☆ RUS 96-97 K 7
Mrara o DZ 190-191 E 4
Mrassu ~ RUS 124-125 Q 2
Mrčajevci o YU 100-101 H 3
Mrezzig ＜ RMM 196-197 K 5
M'saken o TN 190-191 H 3
Msak Millet ▲ LAR 192-193 D 5
Msandile ~ Z 218-219 G 1
Msangasi ~ EAT 212-213 G 6
Msanzara ~ Z 218-219 F 1
Msata o EAT 214-215 K 4
Msembe o EAT 214-215 H 4
M'Sila ☆ DZ 190-191 E 3
Msima ~ EAT 214-215 F 4
Mšinskaja o RUS 94-95 L 2
Msoro o Z 218-219 F 1
Msta ~ RUS 94-95 O 3
Msuna o ZW 218-219 D 4
Mszczonów o PL 92-93 Q 3
Mtakuja o EAT 214-215 F 4
Mtama o EAT 214-215 K 6
Mtambo ~ EAT 214-215 F 4
Mtandikeni o EAT 212-213 G 6
Mtangano Island ⌒ EAT 212-213 D 5
Mtarazi Falls ~ ZW 218-219 G 4
Mtera Dam ＜ EAT 214-215 H 4
Mtina o EAT 214-215 J 6
Mtito Andei o EAK 212-213 G 5
Mto Wa Mbu o EAT 212-213 E 5
Mtubatuba o ZA 220-221 L 4
Mtwara ◘ EAT 214-215 K 6

Montgomery Islands — Mtwara 291

Mtwara ☆ EAT (MTW) 214-215 L 6
Muadiala o ZRE 216-217 F 3
Muaguide o MOC 214-215 L 7
Mualádzi o MOC 218-219 K 3
Mualama o MOC 218-219 K 3
Muaná o BR 62-63 K 6
Muanda o ZRE 210-211 D 6
Muangai o ANG 216-217 E 5
Muang Gnômmarat o LAO 158-159 H 2
Muang Hiam o LAO 156-157 C 6
Muang Hôngsa o LAO 156-157 B 6
Muang Houn o LAO 156-157 B 6
Muang Huang o LAO 156-157 C 7
Muang Khammouan o LAO 158-159 H 2
Muang Không o LAO 158-159 H 3
Muang Khôngxédôn o LAO 158-159 H 3
Muang Khoua o LAO 156-157 C 6
Muang May o LAO 158-159 J 3
Muang Namo o LAO 156-157 B 6
Muang Nan o LAO 156-157 B 7
Muang Ou Thai o LAO 156-157 B 6
Muang Pa o LAO 156-157 B 7
Muang Pakbèng o LAO 156-157 B 7
Muang Pak-Cay o LAO 156-157 B 7
Muang Pakxan o LAO 158-159 H 2
Muang Phalan o LAO 158-159 H 2
Muang Phin o LAO 158-159 J 2
Muang Phôn-Hông o LAO 156-157 C 7
Muang Samsip o THA 158-159 H 3
Muang Souy o LAO 156-157 C 7
Muang Xaigna-bouri o LAO 156-157 B 7
Muang Xay o LAO 156-157 B 6
Muang Xépôn o LAO 158-159 J 2
Muanza o MOC 218-219 H 4
Muanzanza o ZRE 216-217 F 3
Muar o· MAL 162-163 E 3
Muara o BRU 164-165 D 1
Muara o RI 162-163 D 5
Muaraaman o RI 162-163 E 6
Muaraatap o RI 164-165 E 3
Muarabeliti o RI 162-163 E 5
Muarabengkal o RI 164-165 E 3
Muarabinuangeun o RI 168 A 3
Muarabulian o RI 162-163 E 5
Muarabungo o RI 162-163 E 5
Muaradua o RI 162-163 E 7
Muaraenim o RI 162-163 E 6
Muarahalung o RI 164-165 D 5
Muarajawa o RI 164-165 E 4
Muara Koman o RI 164-165 E 4
Muaranayan o RI 164-165 E 4
Muarapayang o RI 164-165 E 4
Muararupit o RI 162-163 E 6
Muarasiberut o RI 162-163 C 5
Muarasimatalu o RI 162-163 C 5
Muarasoma o RI 162-163 D 4
Muaratalang o RI 162-163 E 6
Muaratebo o RI 162-163 E 5
Muaratembesi o RI 162-163 E 5
Muarateweh o RI 164-165 D 4
Muara Tuang o MAL 162-163 J 4
Muarawahau o RI 164-165 E 4
Muari, Pulau ᴖ RI 164-165 K 4
Múari, Rás ▲ PK 134-135 M 6
Muaro Takus Ruins · RI 162-163 D 4
Muatua o MOC 218-219 K 2
Mubambe o ZRE 214-215 D 6
Mubárak, Ĝabal ▲ JOR 130-131 D 2
Mubarek o US 136-137 J 7
Mubarraz o KSA 130-131 L 5
Mubayira o ZW 218-219 F 4
Mubende o EAU 212-213 C 3
Mubi o WAN 204-205 K 3
Mubo o VRC 154-155 E 3
Mubrani o RI 166-167 G 2
Mucajá o BR 62-63 D 4
Mucajaí o BR 62-63 D 4
Mucajaí, Reserva Biológica de ⊥ BR 60-61 K 6
Mucajaí, Rio ~ BR 62-63 D 4
Mucalic, Rivière ~ CDN 36-37 Q 5
Mucanha o MOC 218-219 F 2
Mucari o ANG 216-217 D 4
Muccan o AUS 172-173 E 7
Muchea o AUS 176-177 C 5
Muchena o MOC 214-215 K 6
Muchinga Escarpment ⊥ Z 218-219 E 2
Muchinga Mountains ▲ Z 214-215 F 7
Muchinka o Z 214-215 F 7
Muchuan o VRC 156-157 C 2
Muchuchu Ruins ·:· ZW 218-219 F 4
Mucianyu · VRC 154-155 K 1
Muckadilla o AUS 178-179 K 4
Muckaty o AUS 174-175 J 4
Mučnoj, poluostrov ᴗ RUS 108-109 E 6
Mucojo o MOC 214-215 L 7
Muconda o ANG 216-217 F 3
Mucondo o ANG 216-217 C 4
Mucope o ANG 216-217 C 8
Mucubela o MOC 218-219 J 3
Mucucuaú, Rio ~ BR 62-63 D 5
Mucuim, Rio ~ BR 66-67 F 6
Mucujê o BR 72-73 K 2
Muçum o BR 74-75 E 7
Mucumbura o MOC 218-219 F 3
Mucumbura o ZW 218-219 F 3
Mucupia o MOC 218-219 J 4
Mucur o TR 128-129 F 3
Múcura o YV 60-61 J 3
Mucura, Cachoeira da ~ BR 68-69 B 5
Mucuri o BR 72-73 L 5
Mucuri, Rio ~ BR 72-73 L 5
Mucurici o BR 72-73 K 5
Mucuripe, Ponta de ▲ BR 68-69 J 3
Mucuru, Cachoeira ~ BR 62-63 H 5
Mucusso o ANG 216-217 E 6
Mucusso, Coutada Pública do ⊥ ANG 216-217 F 8
Mucussueje o ANG 216-217 F 5
Müd o IR 134-135 H 2
Mudailif, al- o KSA 132-133 B 4
Mudainib, al- o· OM 132-133 L 2
Mudaisis o OM 132-133 J 2

Mudákim, Bi'r < LAR 192-193 E 1
Mudanjiang o VRC 150-151 G 5
Mudan Jiang ~ VRC 150-151 G 5
Mudanya o TR 128-129 C 2
Mudarraq o KSA 130-131 H 4
Mudawwa o JOR 130-131 E 3
Mudday o OM 132-133 H 5
Müdbidri o IND 140-141 F 4
Muddebihál o IND 140-141 G 2
Mudderbugten ≋ 28-29 P 2
Muddgal o IND 140-141 G 2
Mudgee o· AUS 180-181 K 2
Mudgeeraba o· AUS 178-179 M 5
Mudhol o IND 140-141 F 2
Mudigere o IND 140-141 F 4
Mudigubba o IND 140-141 G 3
Mudimbi o ZRE 218-219 K 5
Mudjatik River ~ CDN 34-35 C 2
Mud Lake o USA 42-43 K 1
Mudon o MYA 158-159 D 2
Mudug ᴑ SP 208-209 J 5
Mudujaha o RUS 108-109 S 7
Mudukulattúr o IND 140-141 H 6
Muecate o MOC 218-219 K 2
Mueda o MOC 214-215 K 6
Muelle de los Bueyes o NIC 52-53 B 5
Mueller Range ▲▲ AUS 172-173 H 5
Muembe o MOC 218-219 H 1
Muende o MOC 218-219 J 2
Muermos, Los o RCH 78-79 C 6
Muerte, Meseta de la ⊥ RA 80 D 4
Muerto, Mar ≋ 52-53 G 3
Muerto, Rio ~ RA 76-77 F 2
Muertos Trough ≃ 56 A 5
Muezerskij o RUS 88-89 M 5
Mufulira o Z 214-215 E 7
Mufu Shan ~ VRC 156-157 H 2
Mufu Shan ▲ VRC 156-157 H 2
Muğanhar, Dár o Y 132-133 D 7
Muğaira o KSA 130-131 F 4
Mugal, Wádi ~ SUD 200-201 G 3
Mugang o VRC 156-157 D 5
Muganga o EAT 212-213 D 4
Muganskaja ravnina ᴗ AZ 128-129 N 3
Mügár o IR 134-135 J 3
Mugdiisho ☆ SP 212-213 K 2
Muger o ETH 208-209 D 4
Muger Falls ~ ETH 208-209 D 4
Muger Wenz ~ ETH 208-209 D 4
Muggon o AUS 176-177 C 3
Mughal Sarai o IND 142-143 C 3
Mughsail o OM 132-133 H 5
Muğib, Wádi l- ~ JOR 130-131 D 2
Mugila, Monts ▲ ZRE 214-215 E 5
Mugina o EAT 212-213 B 6
Mugla ☆ TR 128-129 C 4
Mögödzor, Ayrag ~ RUS 126-127 N 3
Mugur Aksy o RUS 116-117 E 10
Muğa, al- o·· Y 132-133 C 7 ·
Muhabura ▲ EAU 212-213 D 4
Muhágiria o SUD 206-207 Q 3
Muhaiwir o IRQ 128-129 J 6
Muhala o ZRE 212-213 D 4
Muhammad, Ra's ▲ ET 194-195 Q 4
Muhammadábád o IND 142-143 C 2
Muhammadiya o IR 128-129 K 6
Muhammad Qol o SUD 200-201 H 2
Muharraq, al- o BRN 134-135 D 5
Muhazi, Lac o RWA 212-213 C 4
Muheit, Wádi ~ SUD 200-201 F 4
Muheza o EAT 212-213 G 6
Muhino o RUS 118-119 N 9
Mühldorf am Inn o D 92-93 M 4
Mühlhausen/Thüringen o· D 92-93 L 3
Mühlig-Hofmann Mountains = Mühlig-Hofmann-fjella ▲ ARK 16 F 1
Muhorini o EAK 212-213 E 4
Muhor-Konduj o RUS 118-119 F 9
Muhoro o EAK 212-213 E 4
Muhoršibir' o RUS 116-117 N 10
Muhos o FIN 88-89 J 4
Muhu saar ᴖ EST 94-95 H 2
Muhutwe o EAT 212-213 C 4
Muhuwesi ~ EAT (RUV) 214-215 J 4
Mui o ETH 208-209 B 5
Mũi Cà Mau o VN 158-159 H 6
Mũi Chân Mây ▲ VN 158-159 K 2
Mũi Dinh ▲ VN 158-159 K 5
Mũi Đôc ▲ VN 158-159 J 2
Muidumbe o MOC 214-215 K 6
Muié o ANG 216-217 F 7
Mũi Én ▲ VN 158-159 K 4
Mũi Ganh ▲ VN 158-159 K 4
Mũi Kê Gà ▲ VN 158-159 K 5
Mũi Ky Vân ▲ VN 158-159 J 5
Mũi Lach Quèn ▲ VN 156-157 D 7
Mũi La Gàn ▲ VN 158-159 K 5
Mũi Lai ▲ VN 158-159 J 2
Mũi Nai ▲ VN 158-159 H 6
Mũi Nam Trâm ▲ VN 158-159 K 3
Mũi Nay ▲ VN 158-159 K 4
Muine o ANG 216-217 F 8
Muineachán = Monaghan ☆ IRL 90-91 D 4
Muira, Rio ~ MOC 200-201 F 3
Muir Glacier ⊂ USA 20-21 W 7
Muiron Islands ᴖ AUS 172-173 B 6
Muisma ~ RUS 116-117 E 7
Muisne o EC 64-65 B 1
Muite o MOC 218-219 K 2
Muitos Capões o BR 74-75 E 7
Muizenberg o· ZA 220-221 D 7
Muja ~ RUS 118-119 G 7
Mujakan ~ RUS 118-119 F 7
Mujazzam, Sabkhat ᴖ LAR 190-191 G 5
Mujeres, Isla ᴖ MEX 52-53 L 1
Muji o· US 136-137 F 5
Mujnak ~ RUS 118-119 G 9
Muju o ROK 150-151 F 9
Mujunkum ᴗ KA 124-125 H 4

Mukačeva ☆ UA 102-103 C 3
Mukačevo = Mukačeve ᴗ UA 102-103 C 3
Mukah o MAL 162-163 K 3
Muka Head ▲ MAL 162-163 D 2
Mukala o ZRE 210-211 F 6
Mukana o ZRE 214-215 D 5
Mukanga o ZRE 216-217 F 3
Mukarylĵan ~ RUS 112-113 Q 5
Mukawa-gawa ~ J 152-153 K 3
Mukawwa', Ĝazirat ᴖ SUD 200-201 H 2
Mukdahan o THA 158-159 H 2
Mukden = Shenyang o VRC 150-151 D 7
Mukebo o ZRE 214-215 E 4
Mukerián o IND 138-139 E 4
Muke T'uri o ETH 208-209 E 4
Mukinbudin o AUS 176-177 E 5
Mukomuko o RI 162-163 E 6
Mukongo o EAU 212-213 D 3
Mukry o TM 136-137 J 6
Muksu ~ TJ 136-137 M 5
Muksuniha ~ RUS 108-109 V 6
Muksunuoha-Tas, gora ▲ RUS 110-111 X 4
Muktsar o IND 138-139 E 4
Mukuku o Z 214-215 E 7
Mukulu, Kayembe- o ZRE 214-215 B 5
Mukulu, Mutombo- o ZRE 214-215 C 5
Mukulushi o ZRE 214-215 C 6
Mukunsa o Z 214-215 E 5
Mukupa Kaoma o Z 214-215 E 5
Mukurob ᴖ NAM 220-221 D 2
Mukutawa River ~ CDN 34-35 H 4
Mül o IND 138-139 G 9
Mula o VRC 156-157 C 2
Mula ~ D 92-93 M 9
Mula ~ PK 134-135 M 4
Mula, la ▲ I 100-101 E 5
Mulaïlh, al- ᴖ KSA 130-131 F 5
Mulaku Atoll ᴖ MV 140-141 M 6
Mülali cukurligi ᴗ US 136-137 J 4
Mulam ᴖ US 120-121 D 5
Mulamba Gungu, Chute ~ ZRE 214-215 B 5
Mulan o VRC 150-151 G 5
Mulanay o RP 160-161 J 5
Mulanje o MW 218-219 H 2
Mulanje Mountains ▲▲ MW 218-219 H 2
Mulanweichang · VRC 148-149 N 6
Mulatos o CO 60-61 C 3
Mulatupo o PA 52-53 P 7
Mulawa o PK 138-139 D 5
Mulbágal o IND 140-141 H 4
Mulchatna River ~ USA 20-21 N 6
Mulchén o RCH 78-79 C 4
Mulchole o IND 140-141 G 5
Mulde ~ D 92-93 M 3
Muleba o EAT 212-213 C 4
Mule Creek Junction o USA 42-43 E 4
Mulegé o· MEX 50-51 D 4
Mulembe o ZRE 212-213 B 5
Muleshoe o USA 44-45 F 2
Muleta ▲ ETH 208-209 E 4
Muleta ~ RP 160-161 F 9
Mulevala o MOC 218-219 J 3
Mulga Creek ~ AUS 178-179 J 6
Mulgildie o AUS 178-179 L 5
Mulgrave Hills ▲▲ USA 20-21 J 3
Mulhacén ▲ E 98-99 F 6
Mülheim o D 92-93 K 3
Mulhouse · F 90-91 L 8
Muli ≋ 166-167 K 5
Mulia o RI 166-167 J 3
Muli Channel ≋ 166-167 K 5
Mulilansolo o Z 214-215 G 6
Muling o VRC 150-151 H 5
Mulis'ma ~ RUS 118-119 D 6
Mull ᴖ GB 90-91 D 3
Mullaittivu o CL 140-141 J 6
Mullaley o AUS 178-179 K 6
Mullan o USA 40-41 G 2
Mullen o USA 42-43 G 4
Mullens o USA 46-47 H 7
Müller, Pegunungan ▲▲ RI 162-163 K 4
Müller Range ▲▲ PNG 183 B 3
Mullewa o AUS 176-177 C 4
Mulligan River ~ AUS 178-179 G 3
Mullingar = An Muileann -gCearr o IRL 90-91 D 5
Mullins o USA 48-49 J 2
Mulʼmuga ~ RUS 118-119 O 8
Mulobezi o Z 218-219 D 3
Mulondo o ANG 216-217 C 7
Mulonga Plain ⊥ Z 218-219 D 3
Mulongo o ZRE 214-215 D 4
Mulongoie o ZRE 210-211 L 6
Multai o IND 138-139 G 6
Multán o· PK 138-139 M 2
Mulu o ETH 208-209 E 4
Mulu, Gunung ▲ MAL 164-165 D 1
Mulungu o ZRE 214-215 B 5
Mulungushi o Z 218-219 E 2
Mulungushi Dam < Z 218-219 E 2
Mülür o IND 140-141 F 4
Mulurulu Lake o AUS 180-181 G 2
Mulym'ja ~ RUS 114-115 H 4
Mulyungarie o AUS 178-179 F 6
Mumbaï = Bombay ☆ IND 138-139 D 10
Mumballup o AUS 176-177 D 6
Mumbeji o Z 218-219 D 1
Mumbleberry Lake o AUS 178-179 E 3
Mumbondo o ANG 216-217 C 5
Mumbué o ANG 216-217 D 6
Mumbwa o Z 218-219 D 2
Mume, Swana- o ZRE 214-215 D 6
Mumena o ZRE 214-215 D 6
Mumeng o PNG 183 D 4
Mumias o EAK 212-213 C 3
Mumoma o ZRE 214-215 B 4
Mumulusan o RI 166-167 H 4
Muna o RI 166-167 G 4
Muna o MEX 52-53 K 1
Muna ~ RUS 110-111 N 5
Muna ~ RUS 110-111 N 6

Muna, Pulau ~ RI 164-165 H 6
Muna, Selat ≋ 164-165 H 6
Múnajšy o KA 126-127 K 6
Munakan ~ RUS 110-111 M 6
Munarra o AUS 176-177 D 4
Munaya ~ CAM 204-205 H 3
Muncakabau o RI 162-163 F 7
München ☆ D 92-93 L 4
Munchique, Parque Nacional ⊥ CO 60-61 C 6
Muncho Lake o CDN 30-31 L 6
Muncho Lake Provincial Park ⊥ CDN 30-31 L 6
Muncie o USA 46-47 F 5
Muncoonie Lake West o AUS 178-179 E 3
Munda o PK 138-139 C 4
Munda o SOL 184 I 3
Mundabullangana o AUS 172-173 D 6
Mundare o CDN 32-33 O 5
Mundaring o AUS 176-177 D 5
Munday o USA 44-45 H 3
Mundelein o USA 46-47 D 4
Mundemba o CAM 204-205 H 6
Mundgod o IND 140-141 F 3
Mundijong o AUS 176-177 C 6
Mundiwindi o AUS 176-177 F 6
Mundo Novo o BR (BAH) 68-69 H 7
Mundo Novo o BR (GSU) 76-77 K 2
Mundo Nuevo o YV 60-61 J 3
Mundra o IND 138-139 B 8
Mundrabilla o AUS 176-177 J 5
Mundrabilla Motel o AUS 176-177 H 5
Mundubbera o AUS 178-179 L 5
Mundujskoe, ozero o RUS 108-109 X 8
Mundurucânia, Reserva Florestal ⊥ BR (P) 66-67 H 6
Mundurucânia, Área Indígena ✕ BR 66-67 H 6
Mundwa o IND 138-139 D 6
Munenga o ANG 216-217 C 5
Munera o E 98-99 F 5
Munfordville o USA 46-47 E 6
Mungabroom o AUS 174-175 C 5
Mungallala o AUS 178-179 J 4
Mungallala Creek ~ AUS 178-179 J 5
Mungaoli o IND 138-139 G 7
Mungari o MOC 218-219 G 3
Mungbere o ZRE 212-213 B 2
Munger o IND 142-143 E 3
Mungeranie o AUS 178-179 E 5
Mungguresak, Tanjung ▲ RI 162-163 H 4
Mungindi o AUS 178-179 J 5
Munglinup o AUS 176-177 F 6
Mungo o ANG (HBO) 216-217 D 5
Mungo o ANG (LUN) 216-217 E 3
Mungo o SME 62-63 G 3
Mungo National Park ⊥ AUS 180-181 G 2
Mungra Badshahpur o IND 142-143 C 3
Munhango o ANG 216-217 E 6
Munhoz o BR 72-73 H 6
Munich = München o D 92-93 L 4
Muniengashi ~ ZRE 218-219 E 1
Muniesa o E 98-99 G 4
Munikan ~ RUS 122-123 P 2
Munim, Rio ~ BR 68-69 G 4
Munimadugu o IND 140-141 G 3
Muninguo o ZRE 210-211 F 6
Muniz Freire o BR 72-73 K 6
Munkamba ~ RUS 116-117 N 4
Munkumpu o Z 218-219 D 1
Münly, tau ▲ KA 124-125 Q 5
Munnar o IND 140-141 G 5
Munmarlary o AUS 172-173 L 2
Munn, Cape ▲ CDN 36-37 G 2
Munnat o IND 140-141 G 5
Munnikspoort o ZA 220-221 G 6
Munquaz Gameiro, Península ᴗ RCH 80 D 6
Munqati', al- ~ Y 132-133 D 6
Munro, Mount ▲ AUS 180-181 K 6
Munroe o ROK 150-151 F 9
Munse o RI 164-165 H 6
Münster o~ D 92-93 J 3
Münster = Müstair o·· CH 92-93 L 5
Munte o RI 164-165 F 3
Munteme o EAU 212-213 C 3
Muntgatsi o EAK 212-213 E 3
Muntilan o RI 168 D 3
Muntok o RI 162-163 F 6
Muntu o EAU 212-213 D 3
Muntu o ZRE 210-211 G 5
Munukata o J 152-153 D 8
Munyamadzi ~ Z 218-219 F 1
Munyaroo Conservation Park ⊥ AUS 180-181 D 2
Munyati ~ ZW 218-219 E 3
Munzur Vadisi Milli Parkı ⊥ TR 128-129 H 3
Muocco o MOC 218-219 J 1
Muodoslompolo o S 86-87 L 3
Muohyang San ▲ DVR 150-151 F 7
Mu'o'ng Cha o VN 156-157 B 6
Mu'o'ng Het o LAO 156-157 B 6
Mu'o'ng Kim o VN 156-157 C 6
Mu'o'ng Lam o VN 156-157 D 7
Mu'o'ng Loi o VN 156-157 C 6
Mu'o'ng Pôn o VN 156-157 C 6
Mu'o'ng Tè o VN 156-157 B 6
Muonio o FIN 88-89 G 3
Muoniojoki ~ FIN 88-89 G 3
Muor, Pulau ᴖ RI 164-165 H 6
Muostah, mys ▲ RUS 110-111 R 4
Muostah, ostrov ᴖ RUS 110-111 S 4
Mupa o ANG 216-217 D 7
Mupa, Parque Nacional da ⊥ ANG 216-217 C 7
Mupamadzi ~ Z 218-219 F 1
Mupele, Chute ~ ZRE 210-211 K 3

Mupfure ~ ZW 218-219 E 3
Muqaddam, Wádi ~ SUD 200-201 E 5
Muqakoori o SP 208-209 H 6
Muqsim, Ĝabal ▲ ET 194-195 G 6
Muqšin o OM 132-133 J 4
Muqi o BR 72-73 K 6
Muqui, Rio ~ BR 72-73 K 6
Mura o BR 66-67 H 4
Mura ~ RUS 116-117 J 7
Muradiye o TR 128-129 K 2
Muradugar o IND 138-139 F 5
Murafa o UA 102-103 F 5
Murair, Ĝazirat ᴖ ET 194-195 G 6
Murakami o J 152-153 H 5
Murallón, Cerro ▲ RCH 80 D 4
Muramgaon o IND 142-143 B 5
Muranga o EAK 212-213 E 3
Murangering o EAK 212-213 E 2
Muraré, Rio ~ BR 62-63 H 5
Murasi o RUS 96-97 F 4
Murat, Château · F 56 E 4
Murat Çayi ~ TR 128-129 K 3
Murat Daği ▲ TR 128-129 C 3
Murat Nehri ~ TR 128-129 J 3
Muratus, Pegunungan ▲▲ RI 164-165 D 5
Muravera o I 100-101 B 5
Murbád o IND 138-139 D 10
Murça o P 98-99 D 4
Mürče Kúrt o IR 134-135 D 2
Murchinson Range ▲ AUS 174-175 C 7
Murchison o AUS 180-181 H 4
Murchison o NZ 182 D 4
Murchison, Cape ▲ CDN 36-37 R 3
Murchison, Mount ▲ AUS 176-177 D 3
Murchison Falls ~ EAU 212-213 C 2
Murchison Falls National Park ⊥ EAU 212-213 C 2
Murchison Island ᴖ CDN 34-35 M 5
Murchison River ~ AUS 176-177 C 3
Murchison River ~ CDN 24-25 a 6
Murchison Settlement Roadhouse o AUS 176-177 C 3
Murchison Sund ≋ 26-27 P 5
Murchisson, Mount ▲ WAN 204-205 H 4
Murcia o E 98-99 G 6
Murcia ᴑ E 98-99 G 6
Murdo o USA 42-43 G 4
Murdochville o CDN 38-39 M 4
Murehwa o ZW 218-219 F 4
Mureji o WAN 204-205 F 4
Murèn, Zun ~ RUS 116-117 L 10
Mureş ~ RO 102-103 D 4
Muret o F 90-91 H 10
Murfreesboro o USA (AR) 44-45 L 2
Murfreesboro o USA (NC) 48-49 K 1
Murfreesboro o USA (TN) 48-49 E 2
Murgab ~ TJ (GOR) 136-137 N 5
Murgab o TJ 136-137 N 5
Murgab o TM 136-137 H 7
Murgaf ~ RUS 112-113 O 4
Murgenella o AUS 172-173 L 1
Murgenella Wildlife Sanctuary ⊥ AUS 172-173 L 1
Murgha Kibzai o PK 138-139 B 4
Murgho, Hámún-i- o PK 134-135 L 5
Murgon o AUS 178-179 L 4
Murgoo o AUS 176-177 D 3
Murgud o IND 140-141 F 3
Muri o WAN 204-205 F 4
Muriaé o BR 72-73 K 6
Muriaé, Rio ~ BR 72-73 K 6
Murici, Ponta de ▲ BR 68-69 J 5
Muricilândia o BR 68-69 D 5
Muricizal, Rio ~ BR 68-69 D 5
Muridke o PK 138-139 E 4
Muriege o ANG 216-217 F 4
Muriel Lake o CDN 32-33 P 4
Murigñol = Indenpenţa o RO 102-103 F 5
Murinja o RUS 116-117 N 8
Muritiba o BR 72-73 L 2
Müritz ᴑ D 92-93 M 2
Müritz-National-Park ⊥ D 92-93 M 2
Muriwai o NZ 182 E 3
Murizidié Pass ▲ LAR 192-193 F 6
Murman, zaliv ᴗ RUS 108-109 N 3
Murmansk ☆ RUS 88-89 M 2
Murmanskij Bereg = Murmanskij bereg ᴗ RUS 88-89 M 2
Murmanskoye Rise ≃ 10-11 C 1
Murmaši o RUS 88-89 M 2
Murmuro o IND 142-143 D 4
Murnei o SUD 206-207 J 3
Muro Lucano o I 100-101 E 4
Murom ☆ RUS 94-95 S 4
Muroran o· J 152-153 J 3
Muros o E 98-99 C 3
Muroto o J 152-153 F 8
Muroto-saki ▲ J 152-153 F 8
Murphy o USA 48-49 F 2
Murphy Head ▲ CDN 36-37 S 5
Murphy Hot Springs · USA 40-41 G 4
Murphysboro o USA 46-47 D 7
Múrqúm, Kúh-e ▲ IR 134-135 J 3
Murra Murra o AUS 178-179 J 5
Murray o USA 46-47 D 7
Murray, Cape ▲ CDN 24-25 O 2
Murray, Lake o PNG 183 A 4
Murray, Lake o USA 48-49 H 2
Murray Bridge o· AUS 180-181 E 3
Murray Downs o AUS 174-175 C 7
Murray Fracture Zone ≃ 14-15 N 4
Murray Inlet ≋ 24-25 P 3
Murray Islands ᴖ AUS 178-179 H 2
Murray Maxwell Bay ≋ 24-25 f 5
Murray Range ▲ PNG 183 B 3
Murray River ~ AUS 180-181 E 3
Murray River ~ CDN 32-33 K 4
Murray River Basin ᴗ AUS 180-181 G 2
Murraysburg o ZA 220-221 F 5

Murray-Sunset National Park ⊥ AUS 180-181 F 3
Murray Towr o AUS 180-181 F 3
Murrayville o AUS 180-181 F 3
Murree o PK 138-139 E 3
Murrej, mys ▲ RUS 84-85 b 2
Murri, Rio ~ CO 60-61 C 4
Murroa o MOC 218-219 J 3
Murroe Lake o CDN 30-31 U 6
Murrumbidgee River ~ AUS 180-181 H 3
Murrumburrah o AUS 180-181 K 3
Murrupula o MOC 218-219 K 2
Murrurundi o AUS 178-179 L 6
Murshidábác o· IND 142-143 F 3
Murtajápur o IND 138-139 F 5
Murtle Lake o CDN 32-33 L 5
Murtoa o AUS 180-181 G 3
Murtovaara o FIN 88-89 K 4
Muru, Rio ~ BR 66-67 B 7
Murua o PNG 183 D 4
Murua Island = Woodlark Island ᴖ PNG 183 D 5
Muruchachi o YV 60-61 F 3
Murud o· IND 138-139 D 10
Murud, Gunung ▲ MAL 164-165 D 2
Muruken o PNG 183 C 3
Murun, gora ▲ RUS 118-119 J 6
Murupara o NZ 182 F 3
Muruptumatari o BR 108-109 h 4
Murupu o BR 62-63 D 4
Muru, Igarapé ~ BR 68-69 C 6
Mururoa Atcil ᴖ F 13 D 5
Murwára o IND 142-143 B 4
Murwillumbah o AUS 178-179 M 5
Murygino o RUS 96-97 F 4
Mürzzuschlag o A 92-93 N 5
Muş ☆ TR 128-129 J 3
Mûsa, 'Ain ~ ET 194-195 F 3
Mûsa, Ĝaba l- ▲ ET 194-195 F 3
Mûsá, Hör-e ᴗ 134-135 C 5
Mûsa, Wádi ~ JOR 130-131 D 2
Musa Áli Terara ▲ DJI 200-201 L 6
Musadi o ZRE 210-211 J 5
Musa'id ᴗ WAL 202-203 E 5
Musa'id o J 134-135 D 6
Musa River ~ PNG 183 E 5
Musashi o J 152-153 D 8
Mušättä, Qasr al- ·:· JOR 130-131 D 2
Musawa o WAN 198-199 C 6
Musawwarat, Temples of · SUD 200-201 F 4
Musayyib, al- o IRQ 128-129 L 6
Mušbih, Ĝabal al ▲ ET 194-195 G 6
Muscat = Masqat ★·· OM 132-133 L 2
Muscatine o USA 46-47 C 5
Musenge o ZRE (KIV) 212-213 B 4
Musenge o ZRE (SHA) 214-215 B 5
Musengezi ~ ZW 218-219 F 3
Museum o RI 164-165 G 6
Musgrave o AUS 174-175 G 4
Musgrave, Port ≋ 174-175 F 3
Musgrave Fanges ▲▲ AUS 176-177 J 2
Mus-Haja, gora ▲ RUS 120-121 J 2
Mushandike Sanctuary ⊥ ZW 218-219 F 5
Mushayfät o SUD 206-207 K 4
Mushenge o ZRE 210-211 H 5
Mushie o ZRE 210-211 G 5
Mushima o Z 218-219 C 2
Mushipashi o Z 214-215 F 6
Mushota o Z 214-215 F 5
Mushu Island ᴖ PNG 183 B 2
Músi o IND 140-141 H 3
Musi ~ RI 162-163 F 6
Musin o WAN 204-205 E 5
Mūsiyan o IR 134-135 B 2
Muskegon o USA 46-47 E 4
Muskegon River ~ USA 46-47 E 4
Musket River ~ CDN 32-33 L 5
Muskingum River ~ USA 46-47 H 5
Muskö ~ S 86-87 M 2
Muskogee o USA 44-45 K 2
Muskox Lake o CDN 30-31 P 3
Muskratdar's Lake o CDN 34-35 L 4
Muskwa o CDN 30-31 H 6
Muskwa River ~ CDN 30-31 H 6
Muslimiya o SYR 128-129 G 4
Musljumovo o RUS 96-97 H 6
Musoma o EAT 212-213 D 4
Musondweji ~ Z 218-219 C 1
Musono o ZRE 214-215 C 5
Musoshi o ZRE 214-215 D 6
Musquaro, Lac o CDN 38-39 O 3
Musquodoboit o CDN 38-39 N 6
Musselshel River ~ USA 42-43 C 2
Mussende o ANG 216-217 D 5
Musserra o ANG 216-217 D 5
Mussuma o ANG (MOX) 216-217 F 7
Mussuma ~ ANG 216-217 F 7
Mustäfäbác ▲ PK 138-139 D 4
Mustafakemalpaşa o· TR 128-129 C 2
Mustahil o ETH 208-209 G 4
Müstair = Münster o·· CH 92-93 L 5
Mustang o NEP 144-145 D 6
Mustang Island ᴖ USA 44-45 J 6
Musters, Lago o RA 80 F 2
Mustique Island ᴖ WV 56 E 5
Mustjala o EST 94-95 H 2

Mustvee o EST 94-95 K 2
Musu Dan ▲ DVR 150-151 G 7
Musün, Cerro ▲ NIC 52-53 B 5
Muswellbrook o AUS 180-181 L 2
Müt o ET 194-195 D 5
Mut ☆ TR 128-129 E 4
Mutá, Ponta do ▲ BR 72-73 L 2
Mutale o ZA 218-219 F 6
Mutanda o Z 214-215 D 6
Mutanná, al ᴑ IRQ 130-131 J 2
Mutarara o MOC 218-219 H 3
Mutare ☆ ZW 218-219 G 4
Mutemee o AUS 178-179 J 6
Muteba, Xá- o ANG 216-217 D 4
Mutenge o Z 214-215 D 4
Mutha o EAK (EAS) 212-213 G 4
Mutha ▲ EAK (EAS) 212-213 G 4
Mutici o RI 166-167 D 4
Mutiene o ZRE 210-211 E 6
Muting o RI 166-167 L 5
Mutinglupa o RP 160-161 D 5
Mutir o EAU 212-213 C 2
Mutis, Gunung ▲ RI 166-167 C 6
Mutki ☆ TR 128-129 J 3
Mutnaja, buhta ≋ RUS 120-121 S 7
Mutni ~ PK 134-135 M 6
Mutnyj Materik o RUS 88-89 X 4
Mutoko o ZW 218-219 G 3
Mutombo, Bwana- o ZRE 216-217 E 3
Mutombo-Mukulu o ZRE 214-215 C 5
Mutomo o EAK 212-213 G 4
Mutoraj o RUS 116-117 K 5
Mutorashanga o ZW 218-219 F 3
Mutoto o ZRE (KOC) 210-211 J 6
Mutoto o ZRE (SHA) 214-215 C 5
Mutsamudu o· COM 222-223 D 4
Mutshatsha o ZRE 214-215 C 6
Mutsu o J 152-153 J 4
Muttaburra o AUS 178-179 H 2
Mutton Bay o CDN 38-39 P 3
Mutuáli o MOC 218-219 J 2
Mutukula o EAU 212-213 C 4
Mutum o BR (AMA) 66-67 G 6
Mutum o BR (MIN) 72-73 K 5
Mutum, Cachoeira ~ BR 66-67 J 5
Mutum o WAL 202-203 E 5
Mutum, Ilha do ᴖ BR 66-67 C 5
Mutumbi o ZRE 214-215 D 5
Mutum Biyu o WAN 204-205 J 4
Mutumbu o ANG 216-217 D 6
Mutum Daya o WAN 204-205 J 4
Mutum ou Madeira, Rio ~ BR 70-71 K 5
Mutum Paraná o BR 66-67 F 7
Mutungu-Tari o ZRE 216-217 D 3
Mutuoca, Ilha da ᴖ BR 68-69 F 2
Mutur o CL 140-141 J 6
Mututi, Ilha ᴖ BR 66-67 J 5
Mutu-wan ≋ 152-153 J 4
Mutwanga o ZRE 212-213 B 3
Muurola o FIN 88-89 H 3
Mu Us Shamo ⊥ VRC 154-155 E 2
Müvattupula o IND 140-141 G 6
Muwaih, al- o KSA 130-131 G 6
Muwaiha, Ĝabal ▲ UAE 134-135 F 6
Muwailih, al- o KSA 130-131 D 4
Muwassam o KSA 132-133 C 5
Muwo Island ᴖ PNG 183 F 5
Muxima o ANG 216-217 B 4
Muyinga o BU 212-213 C 5
Muy Muy o NIC 52-53 B 5
Muyombe o Z 214-215 G 6
Muyuka o CAM 204-205 H 6
Muyumba o ZRE 214-215 D 4
Muzaffarabád o IND 138-139 D 2
Muzaffargarh o PK 138-139 C 4
Muzaffarnagar o IND 138-139 G 4
Muzaffarpur o IND 142-143 D 2
Muzâhimiya, al- o KSA 130-131 K 5
Muzambinho o BR 72-73 G 6
Muze o MOC 218-219 G 3
Muzej narodnoji architektury i pobutu · UA 102-103 C 2
muzej-usad'ba "Tarhany" · RUS 94-95 S 5
Muzhen o VRC 154-155 K 2
Mužo o RUS 114-115 H 2
Muzizi ~ EAU 212-213 C 3
Muzkol, hrebet ▲▲ TJ 136-137 N 5
Muzo o CO 60-61 D 3
Muzon, Cape ▲ USA 32-33 D 4
Muztag ▲ VRC 144-145 F 2
Muztag ▲ VRC 144-145 C 2
Muztagata ▲ VRC 146-147 B 6
Mvangan o CAM 210-211 D 2
Mveng o CAM 210-211 C 2
Mvengué o CAM 210-211 C 2
Mvera o MW 218-219 H 1
Mvolo o SUD 206-207 J 5
Mvomero o EAT 214-215 J 4
Mvoung ~ G 210-211 D 3
Mvouti o RCB 210-211 D 6
Mvuha o EAT 214-215 J 4
Mvuma o ZW 218-219 F 4
Mvurwi o ZW 218-219 F 3
Mvuye ~ Z 218-219 F 2
Mwabungu o EAK 212-213 G 6
Mwadi-Kalumbu o ZRE 216-217 D 6
Mwadingusha o ZRE 214-215 D 6
Mwafwe ~ Z 218-219 C 1
Mwaga o EAT 214-215 J 5
Mwagaji ~ EAT 214-215 H 3
Mwaleshi ~ Z 214-215 F 6
Mwali o MW 218-219 H 3
Mwanza ☆ EAT 212-213 D 4
Mwanza ~ EAT 212-213 D 5
Mwanza o EAT 214-215 J 4
Mwanza o MW 218-219 H 2
Mwanza o ZRE 214-215 D 4
Mwanza Gulf ≋ EAT 212-213 D 5
Mwanzangoma ~ ZRE 210-211 J 6

Mwaru ~ EAT 212-213 E 6
Mwatasi o EAT (IRI) 214-215 J 4
Mwatate o EAK 212-213 G 5
Mwatate ~ EAK 212-213 G 5
Mwea National Reserve ⊥ EAK 212-213 F 4
Mweka o ZRE 210-211 H 6
Mwembeshi o Z 218-219 D 2
Mwenda o Z 214-215 E 6
Mwene-Biji o ZRE 214-215 B 5
Mwene-Ditu o ZRE 214-215 B 4
Mwenezi o ZW (Mvi) 218-219 F 5
Mwenezi ~ ZW 218-219 F 5
Mwenga o ZRE 212-213 B 5
Mweru, Lake o Z 214-215 E 5
Mweru Wantipa, Lake o Z 214-215 E 5
Mweru Wantipa National Park ⊥ Z 214-215 E 5
Mwilambwe o ZRE 214-215 C 5
Mwimbwi o EAT (RUK) 214-215 F 5
Mwingi o EAK 212-213 G 4
Mwinilunga o Z 214-215 C 6
Mwitika o EAK 212-213 G 4
Mwitikira o EAT (DOD) 214-215 H 4
Mwogo ~ RWA 212-213 B 5
Mwombezhi ~ Z 218-219 C 1
My ~ RUS 122-123 J 2
Mya, Oued ~ DZ 190-191 D 6
Myaing o MYA 142-143 J 5
Myall Lakes National Park ⊥ AUS 180-181 M 2
Myanaung o MYA 142-143 J 6
Myanmar ■ MYA 142-143 J 5
Mychajlivka o UA 102-103 J 4
Mychla o MYA 142-143 K 6
Mye, Mount ▲ CDN 20-21 Y 5
Myingyan o MYA 142-143 J 5
Myinmoletkat Taung ▲ MYA 158-159 E 4
Myitkyina o MYA 142-143 K 3
Myitnge ~ MYA 142-143 K 5
Myittha o MYA 142-143 K 5
Mykenai ∴ GR 100-101 J 6
Mykolajiv o UA 102-103 G 4
Mykolajivs'ka cerkva • UA 102-103 C 3
Mykolayiv = Mykolajiv o UA 102-103 G 4
Myky, Área Indígena ⚔ BR 70-71 H 3
Myla o RUS 88-89 V 4
Myla ~ RUS 88-89 V 4
Mylga ~ RUS 120-121 N 2
Mylius Erichsen Land ⊥ GRØ 26-27 m 3
Mymensingh o BD 142-143 G 3
Mynämäki o FIN 88-89 F 6
Myndagaj o RUS 120-121 E 3
Mynfontein o ZA 220-221 F 5
Mynsualmas ▲ KA 126-127 L 5
Myohaung o MYA 142-143 H 5
Myoko-san ▲ J 152-153 H 6
Myola o AUS 174-175 F 6
Myola o PNG 183 D 5
Myotha o MYA 142-143 J 5
Myra ∴ TR 128-129 D 4
Myre o N 86-87 G 2
Myrhorod o UA 102-103 H 3
Mýri o IS 86-87 e 2
Myronivka ☆ UA 102-103 G 3
Myrtle o CDN 38-39 E 6
Myrtle Beach o • USA 48-49 J 3
Myrtleford o • AUS 180-181 J 4
Myrtle Point o USA 40-41 B 4
Mysen ☆ N 86-87 E 7
Mys-Kamennyj o RUS 108-109 P 7
Myski o RUS 124-125 P 2
Myškin ☆ RUS 94-95 Q 3
Myškino = Myškin ☆ RUS 94-95 Q 3
Myślenice o • PL 92-93 P 4
My So'n • VN 158-159 K 3
Mysore o • IND 140-141 G 4
Mystery Caves • USA 42-43 L 4
Mys Želanija o RUS 108-109 N 3
Myszyniec o PL 92-93 Q 2
My Tho ☆ • VN 158-159 J 5
Mytišči ☆ RUS 94-95 P 4
Mytishchi = Mytišči ☆ RUS 94-95 P 4
Myton o USA 40-41 J 5
Mývatn • IS 86-87 e 2
Myzeqe ~ AL 100-101 G 4
M'Zab ∴ • DZ 190-191 D 4
M'Zab, Oued ~ DZ 190-191 E 4
Mže ~ CZ 92-93 M 4
Mzenga o EAT 214-215 K 4
Mziha o EAT 212-213 F 6
Mzimba o MW 214-215 G 6
Mzimkulwana Nature Reserve ⊥ ZA 220-221 J 4
Mzuzu ☆ MW 214-215 H 6

N

Naab ~ D 92-93 M 4
Naala o TCH 198-199 G 6
Naalehu o USA 48-49 E 8
Na'am o SUD 206-207 J 4
Na'ām ~ SUD 206-207 J 6
Na'ama o ET 194-195 G 4
Na'ān, an- o KSA 130-131 K 6
Naantali o • FIN 88-89 G 6
Naas = An Nás ☆ IRL 90-91 D 5
Nababeep o ZA 220-221 C 4
Naban SK ~ VRC 156-157 F 5
Nabar ‹ TCH 198-199 K 3
Nabarlek o AUS 174-175 B 3
Nabas o RP 160-161 E 7
Nabatiya t-Taḥtā ☆ RL 128-129 F 6
Nabavatu o FJI 184 III b 2
Nabawa o AUS 176-177 C 4
Nabawan o MAL 160-161 B 10
Nabberu, Lake o AUS 176-177 F 2
Nabéré, Réserve Partielle de ⊥ BF 202-203 J 4
Naberera o EAT 212-213 F 6
Naberezhnyye Chelny = Naberežnye Čelny ☆ RUS 96-97 H 6
Naberežnye Čelny ☆ RUS 96-97 H 6
Nabesna River ~ USA 20-21 T 5
Nabeul ☆ TN 190-191 H 2
Nabǧa o UAE 134-135 F 6
Nabhāniya, an- o KSA 130-131 H 5
Nabi, Wādi ~ SUD 200-201 F 2
Nabil' ~ RUS 122-123 K 3
Nabilatuk o EAU 212-213 E 2
Nabileque, Pantanal de o BR 70-71 J 7
Nabileque, Rio ~ BR 70-71 J 7
Nabil'skij, zaliv o RUS 122-123 K 3
Nabingora o EAU 212-213 C 3
Nabire o RI 166-167 H 3
Nabisar o PK 138-139 B 7
Nabi Šu'aib, Ǧabal an- ▲ Y 132-133 C 6
Nabk, an- o KSA 130-131 F 2
Nabljudenij, mys ▲ RUS 120-121 T 3
Naboga o GH 202-203 K 5
Naboomspruit o ZA 220-221 J 2
Nabou o BF 202-203 J 4
Naboulgou o RT 202-203 L 4
Nabouwalu o FJI 184 III b 2
Nabq o ET 194-195 G 3
Nabukjuak Bay ≈ 36-37 L 2
Nābulus = Shekhem ☆ WB 130-131 D 1
Nabuquen, Caño ~ CO 60-61 G 6
Nabusamke o EAU 212-213 D 3
Nabwān o KSA 130-131 G 4
Nacala o MOC 218-219 L 2
Načalovo ☆ RUS 96-97 F 10
Nacaome ☆ HN 52-53 L 5
Nacaroa o MOC 218-219 K 2
Nacebe o BOL 70-71 D 2
Naches River ~ USA 40-41 D 2
Nachicapau, Lac o CDN 36-37 Q 6
Nachingwea o EAT 214-215 K 6
Nāchna o IND 138-139 C 6
Nachtigal, Cap ▲ CAM 210-211 B 2
Nachtigal, Chutes de ~ CAM 204-205 J 6
Nachuge o IND 140-141 L 4
Nachvak Fiord ≈ 36-37 S 5
Načikinskij, mys ▲ RUS 120-121 U 5
Nacionalni park Brioni ⊥ HR 100-101 D 2
Nacionalni park Kornati ⊥ HR 100-101 E 3
Nacionalni park Kozara ⊥ BIH 100-101 F 2
Nacionalni park Mljet ⊥ HR 100-101 F 3
Nacionalni park Orjen ⊥ YU 100-101 G 3
Nacionalni park Paklenica ⊥ • HR 100-101 E 2
Nacionalni park Plitvička Jezera ⊥ ··· HR 100-101 E 2
Nacional'nyj park "Losinyj ostrov" ⊥ RUS 94-95 P 4
Nackara o AUS 180-181 E 2
Naco ∴ HN 52-53 K 4
Nacogdoches o USA 44-45 K 4
Nacori Chico o MEX 50-51 E 3
Nacozari de García o MEX 50-51 E 2
Nacula ⌒ FJI 184 III a 2
Ñacuñán o RA 78-79 F 3
Ñacuñán, Reserva Ecológica ⊥ RA 78-79 E 2
Nacyjanal'ny park Belavežskaja pušča ⊥ ··· BY 94-95 J 5
Nadawli o GH 202-203 J 4
Nād-e 'Ali o AFG 134-135 L 3
Nāder Šāh Kūt o AFG 138-139 C 2
Nadėžnyj, mys ▲ RUS 110-111 Z 2
Nadi o FJI 184 III a 2
Nadi o SUD 200-201 F 3
Nadiād o IND 138-139 D 8
Nadina River o CDN 32-33 G 5
Nadoba o RT 202-203 L 4
Nadojaha ~ RUS 108-109 N 6
Nador o MA 188-189 K 3
Nadudoturku ozero o RUS 108-109 U 5
Nadura, Temple of ∴ • ET 194-195 E 5
Naduri o FJI 184 III b 2
Nadvirna ☆ UA 102-103 D 3
Nadym o RUS 114-115 M 2
Nadym ~ RUS 114-115 L 3
Nadymskaja Ob' ≈ 108-109 N 8
Nadzab o PNG 183 D 4
Nā'ebābād o AFG 136-137 K 6
Naejangsan National Park ⊥ • ROK 150-151 F 10
Nærøyfjorden ∴ • N 86-87 C 6
Næstved o • DK 86-87 E 9
Nafada o WAN 204-205 J 3
Nafadj, Baté- o RG 202-203 F 4
Nafadji o SN 202-203 E 3
Nafaq Ahmad Ḥamdi II ET 194-195 F 2
Nafi o KSA 130-131 H 5
Nafiša o ET 194-195 F 2
Náfpaktos o GR 100-101 H 5
Náfplio o • GR 100-101 J 6
Naft-e Šāh o IR 134-135 A 1
Nafūd ad-Dahi ⊥ KSA 132-133 D 3
Nafūd al-Kubrā, an- ⊥ KSA 130-131 G 3
Nafūd al-'Uraik ⊥ KSA 130-131 H 5
Nafūd as-Sirr ⊥ KSA 130-131 J 5
Nafūsah, Jabal ▲ LAR 192-193 D 2
Näg o PK 134-135 L 5
Naga o RP (CAS) 160-161 E 6
Naga o RP (CEB) 160-161 E 7
Naǧaf, an- o IRQ 128-129 K 7
Naǧaf, an- ☆ IRQ (NAG) 128-129 L 7
Naǧafābād o IR 134-135 D 2
Nagagami Lake o CDN 34-35 O 6
Nagai Island ⌒ USA 22-23 Q 5
Nagaj o IND 140-141 F 2
Nāgāland □ IND 142-143 J 2
Naǧ' al-Ma'mariya o ET 194-195 F 5
Nagamangala o IND 140-141 G 4
Nagambie o AUS 180-181 H 4
Nagam River Mission o PNG 183 B 2
Nagandana o CI 202-203 H 4
Nagano o J 152-153 H 6
Naganuma o J 152-153 J 3
Nagaoka o J 152-153 H 6
Nagaon o IND 142-143 H 2
Nagappattinam o IND 140-141 H 5
Nagara o RMM 202-203 G 2
Nagare Augū ▲ MYA 158-159 C 2
Nagarhole National Park ⊥ IND 140-141 G 4
Nagari o IND 140-141 H 4
Nagarjuna Sāgar o IND 140-141 H 2
Nagar Karnūl o IND 140-141 H 2
Nagarote o NIC 52-53 L 5
Nagar Pārkar o PK 138-139 C 7
Nagarzê o VRC 144-145 H 6
Nagasaki ☆ • J 152-153 C 8
Naga-shima ⌒ J 152-153 D 8
Nāgaur o IND 138-139 D 6
Nagayaman Point ▲ RP 160-161 E 3
Nāgbhir o IND 138-139 G 9
Nagbo o GH 202-203 K 4
Naǧd ⊥ KSA 130-131 G 4
Nage o RI 168 E 7
Nageezi o USA 44-45 D 1
Nagercoil o IND 140-141 G 6
Nageriwāla o PK 138-139 C 4
Naǧ 'Hammādi o ET 194-195 F 4
Nagichot o SUD 208-209 A 6
Nagina o IND 138-139 G 5
Naglějnynvaam ~ RUS 112-113 O 2
Naglějnyn, gora ▲ RUS 112-113 P 2
Naglějnyn, mys ▲ RUS 112-113 P 2
Nago o J 152-153 B 11
Nāgod o IND 142-143 B 3
Nagor'e o RUS 94-95 Q 3
Nagorno-Karabakh = Dağlıq Qarabağ Muxtar Vilayati □ AZ 128-129 M 2
Nagornyj o RUS (SAH) 118-119 M 8
Nagornyj ☆ RUS (KOR) 112-113 U 5
Nagorsk ☆ RUS 96-97 G 4
Nagoya ☆ • J 152-153 G 7
Nāgpur o IND 138-139 G 9
Nagqu o VRC 144-145 J 5
Nāgrāl o IND 140-141 H 2
Naǧrān □ KSA 132-133 D 4
Naǧrān ☆ • KSA (NAG) 132-133 D 5
Naǧrān, Wādi ~ Y 132-133 D 5
Nagslaran o RP 160-161 D 5
Nagua ☆ DOM 54-55 L 5
Nagvaraaluk, Lac o CDN 36-37 O 4
Nagykanizsa o H 92-93 O 5
Naha o J 152-153 B 11
Na Haeo o THA 158-159 F 2
Nāhan o IND 138-139 F 4
Na Hang ☆ VN 156-157 D 5
Nahang, Rūd-e ~ IR 134-135 K 5
Nahanni Butte o CDN 30-31 H 5
Nahanni National Park ⊥ ··· CDN 30-31 G 5
Nahara, Orto- o RUS 118-119 G 5
Nahatta ~ RUS 110-111 X 6
Naheleg ⌒ ER 200-201 K 4
Nahīa Lo ☆ VN 156-157 D 6
Nāhid, Bi'r ‹ ET 194-195 D 2
Nahl, Rūd-e ~ IR 134-135 H 3
Nahlin o CDN 32-33 E 2
Nahlin Plateau ▲ CDN 32-33 D 2
Naho o SOL 184 I e 3
Nahodka o RUS 108-109 R 8
Nahodka o RUS 122-123 E 7
Nahodka, buhta ≈ 108-109 P 8
Nahodka, ostrov ⌒ RUS 112-113 V 1
Nahoi, Cape = Cape Cumberland ▲ VAN 184 II a 2
Nahrin o AFG 136-137 L 6
Nahr Ouessel ~ DZ 190-191 C 3
Nahualate, Río ~ GCA 52-53 J 4
Nahuatzen o MEX 52-53 D 2
Nahuelbuta, Cordillera de ▲ RCH 78-79 C 5
Nahuelbuta, Parque Nacional ⊥ RCH 78-79 C 4
Nahuel Huapi o RA 78-79 D 6
Nahuel Huapi, Lago o RA 78-79 D 6
Nahuel Huapi, Parque Nacional ⊥ RA 78-79 D 6
Nahuel Mapá o RA 78-79 F 3
Nahum, Hefar ∴ • IL 130-131 D 1
Nahunta o USA 48-49 H 4
Nahuo o VRC 156-157 G 6
Nahwitti o CDN 32-33 F 6
Nā'ī, an- o KSA 130-131 H 4
Naiams Fort • NAM 220-221 C 3
Naica o MEX 50-51 G 4
Naicam o CDN 34-35 D 4
Nā'id Abār o KSA 132-133 C 5
Naidi o FJI 184 III b 2
Nā'if al-'Āġil o IRQ 128-129 L 7
Naihbawi o IND 142-143 H 4
Naij Tal o VRC 144-145 K 3
Naikliu o RI 166-167 B 6
Naikoon Provincial Park ⊥ CDN 32-33 E 5
Naila o D 92-93 L 3
Nailaga o FJI 184 III a 2
Naiman Qi o VRC 150-151 C 6
Nain o CDN 36-37 T 6
Nāin o • IR 134-135 E 2
Naini Tāl o • IND 138-139 G 5
Nainpur o IND 142-143 B 4
Naiopue o MOC 218-219 J 2
Nairai ⌒ FJI 184 III b 2
Nairn o GB 90-91 F 3
Nairobi □ EAK 212-213 F 4
Nairobi ★ EAK 212-213 F 4
Nairobi National Park ⊥ ·· EAK 212-213 F 4
Nairoto o MOC 214-215 K 7
Naitaba ⌒ FJI 184 III c 2
Naivasha o EAK 212-213 F 4
Naivasha, Lake o EAK 212-213 F 4
Naiwangaa o EAT 214-215 K 5
Najahan ~ RUS 112-113 K 5
Najahanskaja guba o RUS 120-121 S 3
Najahanskij hrebet ▲ RUS 112-113 K 5
Najasa ~ C 54-55 G 4
Najba o RUS 110-111 S 4
Najba ~ RUS 122-123 K 5
Nājera o • E 98-99 F 3
Najībābād o IND 138-139 G 5
Najtingejl, proliv ≈ 84-85 a 2
Najverga ~ RUS 118-119 G 6
Najzataš, pereval ▲ TJ 136-137 N 6
Nakadori-shima ⌒ J 152-153 C 8
Na Kae o THA 158-159 H 2
Nakagawa o J 152-153 K 2
Naka-gawa ~ J 152-153 J 6
Nakamoéka o RCB 210-211 D 6
Nakamura o J 152-153 E 8
Nakanai Mountains ▲ PNG 183 F 3
Nakanno o RUS 116-117 O 4
Nakano-shima ⌒ J (KGA) 152-153 C 10
Nakano-shima ⌒ J (SHM) 152-153 E 6
Nakasato o J 152-153 J 4
Naka-Shibetsu o J 152-153 L 3
Nakasongola o EAU 212-213 D 3
Naka-Tane o J 152-153 D 9
Nakatsu o J 152-153 D 8
Nakatsugawa o J 152-153 G 7
Nakchamik Island ⌒ USA 22-23 S 4
Naked Island ⌒ USA 20-21 R 6
Nakel = Nakło nad Notecią o PL 92-93 O 2
Nak'fa o ER 200-201 J 4
Nakhchyvan = Naxçıvan ☆ AZ 128-129 L 3
Nakhichevan = Naxçivan Muxtar Respublikası □ AZ 128-129 L 3
Nakhon Nayok o THA 158-159 F 3
Nakhon Pathom o THA 158-159 F 4
Nakhonphanon o THA 158-159 H 2
Nakhon Ratchasima o THA 158-159 G 3
Nakhon Sawan o THA 158-159 F 3
Nakhon Si Thammarat o ·· THA 158-159 E 6
Nakhon Thai o THA 158-159 F 2
Nakhtarāna o IND 138-139 B 8
Naki-Est o RT 202-203 L 4
Nakina o CDN 34-35 N 5
Nakitoma o EAU 212-213 D 3
Nakivali, Lake o EAU 212-213 C 4
Nakkala o CL 140-141 J 7
Naknek o USA 22-23 S 3
Naknek Lake o USA 22-23 S 3
Nako o BF 202-203 J 4
Nakonde o Z 214-215 G 5
Nakong-Atinia o GH 202-203 K 4
Nakop o NAM 220-221 D 4
Nako-Tombetsu o J 152-153 K 2
Nakpanduri o GH 202-203 K 4
Nakpayili o GH 202-203 L 5
Nakskov o DK 86-87 E 9
Nakson, gora ▲ RUS 116-117 G 3
Naktong Gang ~ ROK 150-151 G 10
Nakum ∴ • GCA 52-53 K 3
Nakuru ☆ EAK 212-213 F 4
Nakuru, Lake o EAK 212-213 F 4
Nakusp o CDN 32-33 M 6
Nāl ~ PK 134-135 L 5
Nalagāmula o IND 140-141 J 4
Nālāgarh o IND 138-139 F 4
Nalajh o MAU 148-149 H 4
Nalatale Ruins ∴ • ZW 218-219 E 4
Nālatvād o IND 140-141 G 2
Naláži o MOC 220-221 L 2
Nalbarra o AUS 176-177 D 4
Nalcayes, Isla ⌒ RCH 80 D 3
Nal'čik ☆ RUS 126-127 E 6
Naldrug o IND 140-141 G 2
Nalgonda o IND 140-141 H 2
Nali o VRC 156-157 F 6
Nalim'e, ozero o RUS 108-109 V 8
Nalim-Rassoha ~ RUS 110-111 G 4
Nalimsk o RUS 110-111 d 6
Naliya o IND 138-139 B 8
Nāljānkā o FIN 88-89 K 4
Nalkhera o IND 138-139 F 8
Nallıhan ☆ TR 128-129 D 2
Nalong o MYA 142-143 K 3
Nalusuku Pool ‹ Z 218-219 B 3
Nālūt o LAR 190-191 H 5
Nama ~ RUS 110-111 a 5
Nama o RI 166-167 F 4
Namaa, Tanjung ▲ RI 166-167 E 3
Namaacha o MOC 220-221 L 2
Namacunde o ANG 216-217 C 8
Namacurra o MOC 218-219 J 3
Namadgi National Park ⊥ AUS 180-181 K 3
Namadi, Dağ-e o AFG 134-135 J 2
Namak, Daryā-ye o IR 134-135 D 1
Namak, Kavir-e o IR 134-135 G 1
Namak, Kūh-e ▲ IR 134-135 D 4
Namakan ~ RUS 108-109 a 6
Namak-e Širǧān, Kavir-e o IR 134-135 F 4
Namakia o RM 222-223 D 5
Nāmakkal o IND 140-141 H 5
Namaksār o AFG 134-135 J 2
Namaksar, Kāl-e o IR 134-135 J 1
Namakwaland ⊥ ZA 220-221 C 4
Namaland ⊥ NAM 220-221 C 3
Namana ~ RUS 118-119 K 5
Namanga o EAK 212-213 F 5
Namangan o US 136-137 M 4
Namanganskaja oblast' □ US 136-137 M 4
Namanyere o EAT (RUA) 214-215 F 4
Namapa o MOC 218-219 K 1
Namaponda o MOC 218-219 K 2
Namarrói o MOC 218-219 J 2
Namas o RI 166-167 L 4
Namasagali o EAU 212-213 D 3
Namasale o EAU 212-213 D 3
Namassi o CI 202-203 J 6
Namatanai o PNG 183 G 2
Namatote, Pulau ⌒ RI 166-167 G 3
Namba o ANG 216-217 C 5
Nambazo o MW 218-219 H 2
Nambe Indian Reservation ⚔ USA 44-45 E 2
Namber o RI 166-167 H 2
Nambi o AUS 176-177 F 4
Nambikwara, Área Indígena ⚔ BR 70-71 H 3
Nambima, Tanjung ▲ RI 166-167 H 4
Nambolaki, Pulau ⌒ RI 168 E 6
Namboukaha o CI 202-203 H 5
Nambour o AUS 178-179 M 4
Nambuangongo o ANG 216-217 C 4
Nambucca Heads o AUS 178-179 M 6
Nambung National Park ⊥ AUS 176-177 C 5
Namche Bazar o NEP 144-145 F 7
Namchi o IND 142-143 F 2
Nam Chon Reservoir ‹ THA 158-159 E 3
Nam Co o VRC (XIZ) 144-145 H 5
Nam Co • VRC (XIZ) 144-145 H 5
Namcy ☆ • RUS 118-119 O 4
Nam Du, Quần Đảo ⌒ VN 158-159 H 6
Namen = Namur ☆ • B 92-93 H 3
Namenalala ⌒ FJI 184 III b 2
Nà Mèo o VN 156-157 D 6
Nametil o MOC 218-219 K 2
Namew Lake o CDN 34-35 F 3
Namgorab ▲ NAM 220-221 C 2
Namhae Do ⌒ ROK 150-151 F 10
Namhan Gang ~ ROK 150-151 F 9
Nami o MAL 162-163 D 2
Namialo o MOC 218-219 K 2
Namibe □ ANG 216-217 B 7
Namibe ☆ • ANG 216-217 B 7
Namibe, Deserto de ⊥ ANG 216-217 A 8
Namibe, Reserva de ⊥ ANG 216-217 B 7
Namibia ■ NAM 216-217 C 10
Namib-Naukluft Park ⊥ NAM 220-221 B 2
Namibwoestyn = Namib Desert ⊥ NAM 216-217 B 9
Namidobe o MOC 218-219 J 3
Namie o J 152-153 J 6
Namies o ZA 220-221 D 4
Namin o IR 128-129 N 3
Namina o MOC 218-219 K 2
Namioka o J 152-153 J 4
Namiquipa o MEX 50-51 F 3
Namiroe, Rio ~ MOC 218-219 K 2
Namitete o MW 218-219 G 2
Namjagbarwa Feng ▲ VRC 144-145 K 6
Namlan o MYA 142-143 K 4
Namlea o RI 166-167 D 3
Nam Léa, Mount ▲ K 158-159 J 4
Namling o VRC 144-145 G 6
Nam-mawng o MYA 142-143 L 5
Nam Ngum Reservoir o LAO 156-157 C 7
Namo o RI 164-165 F 4
Namoda, Kaura- o WAN 198-199 C 6
Namoi River ~ AUS 178-179 K 6
Namon o RT 202-203 L 5
Namor o BR 66-67 F 6
Namorona o RM 222-223 F 8
Nam Ou ~ LAO 156-157 C 6
Namounou o BF 202-203 L 4
Namous, Oued ~ DZ 190-191 D 3
Nampa o USA 40-41 F 4
Nampagan o MYA 142-143 J 3
Nampala o RMM 202-203 H 2
Nam Pat o THA 158-159 F 2
Nampevo o MOC 218-219 J 3
Nampo o DVR 150-151 E 8
Nam Poon o THA 142-143 M 6
Nampuecha o MOC 218-219 L 1
Nampula □ MOC 218-219 K 2
Nampula ☆ MOC (Nam) 218-219 K 2
Namrole o RI 166-167 D 3
Namru o VRC 144-145 C 5
Namslau = Namysłów o • PL 92-93 O 3
Namsos o N 86-87 E 4
Namsskogan o N 86-87 F 4
Namtabung o RI 166-167 F 6
Namtha o MYA 142-143 J 3
Nam Theun o LAO 158-159 H 2
Nam Tok Chat Trakan National Park ⊥ THA 158-159 F 2
Namtu o MYA 142-143 K 4
Namtumbo o EAT 214-215 J 6
Namu o CDN 32-33 G 6
Namudi o PNG 183 E 5
Namuiranga o MOC 214-215 L 6
Namukumbo o Z 218-219 D 2
Namuli, Monte ▲ MOC 218-219 J 2
Namuno o MOC 218-219 K 1
Nam Un Reservoir o THA 158-159 G 2
Namur ☆ • B 92-93 H 3
Namur o CDN 38-39 G 6
Namur Lake o CDN 32-33 O 3
Namur Lake Indian Reserve ⚔ CDN 32-33 O 3
Namutoni o NAM 216-217 D 9
Namwaan, Pulau ⌒ RI 166-167 F 5
Namwala o Z 218-219 D 2
Namwera o MW 218-219 H 2
Namwŏn o ROK 150-151 F 10
Namy o RUS 110-111 T 5
Namyldžylah ~ RUS 118-119 K 5
Namyndykan ~ RUS 112-113 K 4
Namysłów o • PL 92-93 O 3
Nan o THA 142-143 M 6
Nan, Sa o THA 142-143 M 6
Nana o CAM 206-207 B 5
Nana ~ RCA 206-207 B 5
Nana Bakassa o RCA (OUH) 206-207 C 5
Nana Bakassa ~ RCA 206-207 C 5
Nana Barya ~ TCH 206-207 C 5
Nana Barya, Réserve de la ⊥ RCA 206-207 C 5
Nana Candundo o ANG 214-215 B 6
Nanae o J 152-153 J 4
Nanafalia o USA 48-49 E 3
Nana-Grébizi □ RCA 206-207 D 5
Nanaimo o CDN 32-33 J 7
Nana-Mambéré □ RCA 206-207 B 6
Nanambinia o AUS 176-177 G 6
Nana Museum of the Arctic • USA 20-21 J 3
Nanango o AUS 178-179 L 4
Nanaru-i-ra ⌒ FJI 184 III b 2
Nanao o J 152-153 G 6
Nan'ao Dao ⌒ VRC 156-157 K 5
Nanase o PNG 183 B 4
Nanay, Rio ~ PE 64-65 F 3
Nanbu o VRC 154-155 E 6
Nancay, Arroyo ~ RA 78-79 K 2
Nancha o VRC 150-151 G 4
Nanchang ☆ • VRC 156-157 J 2
Nancheng o VRC 156-157 K 3
Nanchital o MEX 52-53 G 2
Nanchititla, Parque Natural ⊥ MEX 52-53 D 2
Nanchong o VRC 154-155 E 6
Nanchuan o VRC 156-157 E 2
Nancowry Island ⌒ IND 140-141 L 6
Nancy ☆ ··· F 90-91 L 7
Nanda Devi ▲ ··· IND 144-145 C 5
Nandaime o NIC 52-53 L 6
Nandalūr o IND 140-141 H 3
Nandaly o AUS 180-181 G 3
Nandan o VRC 156-157 E 4
Nanded o IND 138-139 F 10
Nandewar Range ▲ AUS 178-179 L 6
Nāndghāt o IND 142-143 B 5
Nandi o ZW 218-219 F 5
Nandigāma o IND 140-141 J 2
Nandigram o BD 142-143 F 3
Nandi Hills o • IND 140-141 G 4
Nandikotkūr o IND 140-141 H 3
Nanding Hé ~ VRC 142-143 L 4
Nandipadu o IND 140-141 H 3
Nandom o GH 202-203 J 4
Nandouta o RT 202-203 L 5
Nandowrie P.O. o AUS 178-179 J 3
Nāndūra o IND 138-139 F 9
Nandurbār o IND 138-139 E 9
Nandyal o IND 140-141 H 3
Nanfeng o VRC 156-157 K 3
Nangade o MOC 214-215 K 6
Nanga Eboko o CAM 204-205 K 6
Nangah Ketungau o RI 162-163 J 4
Nangah Pinoh o RI 162-163 J 5
Nangah Sokan o RI 162-163 J 5
Nangalala ⚔ AUS 174-175 C 3
Nanganga o EAT 214-215 K 6
Nanga Parbat ▲ PK 138-139 E 2
Nangarhār □ AFG 138-139 C 2
Nangaroro o RI 168 E 7
Nanga Tamin o MAL 162-163 K 3
Nanga Tayap o RI 162-163 J 5
Nangbéto o RT 202-203 L 6
Nangbéto, Retenue de ‹ RT 202-203 L 6
Nang'egan ~ RUS 114-115 L 3
Nangin o MYA 158-159 E 5
Nango o J 152-153 D 8
Nangolet o SUD 208-209 A 6
Nangomba o EAT 214-215 K 6
Nangong o VRC 154-155 J 3
Nangqên o VRC 144-145 L 4
Nang Rong o THA 158-159 G 3
Nānguneri o IND 140-141 G 6
Nangunhe Z.B. ⊥ • VRC 142-143 L 4
Nangurukuru o EAT 214-215 K 5
Nanguruwe o EAT 214-215 L 6
Nang Xian o VRC 144-145 J 6
Nan Hai ≈ 156-157 J 6
Nanhua o RC 156-157 M 5
Nanhua o VRC 156-157 B 4
Nanhui o VRC 154-155 M 6
Nanjangud o • IND 140-141 G 4
Nanjian o VRC 142-143 M 3
Nanjiang o VRC 154-155 E 5
Nanjing ☆ • VRC 154-155 L 5
Nanjirinji o EAT 214-215 K 5
Nankāna Sāhib o PK 138-139 D 4
Nankang o VRC (GXI) 156-157 F 6
Nankang o VRC (JXI) 156-157 J 4
Nanking = Nanjing ☆ • VRC 154-155 L 5
Nankoku o J 152-153 E 8
Nankova o ANG 216-217 E 8
Nankunshan • VRC 156-157 H 5
Nanle o VRC 154-155 J 3
Nanling o VRC 154-155 L 6
Nan Ling ▲ VRC 156-157 G 4
Nanlixa o MOC 218-219 J 1
Nannine o AUS 176-177 E 3
Nanning ☆ VRC 156-157 F 5
Nannup o AUS 176-177 C 6
Nano ~ DY 204-205 E 4
Nanoro o BF 202-203 J 3
Nanortalik o GRØ 28-29 S 6
Nanortalik Banke ≃ 28-29 R 6
Nanosnyj, ostrov ⌒ RUS 110-111 X 1
Nanpan Jiang ~ VRC 156-157 D 4
Nanpara o IND 142-143 B 2
Nanpeng Liedao ⌒ VRC 156-157 K 5
Nanping o VRC (FUJ) 156-157 L 3
Nanping o VRC (HUN) 156-157 H 2
Nansebo o ETH 208-209 D 5
Nansei-shotō ⌒ J 152-153 B 11
Nansen, Kap ▲ GRØ (ØGR) 26-27 r 4
Nansen, Kap ▲ GRØ (ØGR) 28-29 a 2
Nansen, Mount ▲ CDN 20-21 W 5
Nansena, ostrov ⌒ RUS 108-109 Z 3
Nansena, ostrov ⌒ RUS (ARH) 84-85 d 2
Nansen Fjord ≈ 28-29 a 2
Nansen Gletscher ⊂ GRØ 26-27 V 6
Nansen Land ⊥ GRØ 26-27 c 2
Nansen Sound ≈ 26-27 E 3
Nanshui SK ~ VRC 156-157 H 4
Nansio o EAT 212-213 D 5
Nantais, Lac o CDN 36-37 M 4
Nantamba o PNG 183 F 3
Nantes ☆ • F 90-91 G 8
Nanton o CDN 32-33 O 6
Nanton o GH 202-203 K 5
Nantong o VRC 154-155 M 5
Nantong (Jinsha) o VRC 154-155 M 5
Nantou o RC 156-157 M 5
Nantucket o USA 46-47 N 5
Nantucket Island ⌒ USA 46-47 N 5
Nantucket Shoals ≈ 46-47 N 5
Nantulo o MOC 214-215 K 7
Nanuku Passage ≈ FJI 184 III c 2
Nanumea ⌒ TUV 13 J 3
Nanuque o BR 72-73 K 4
Nanūr o IR 128-129 M 5
Nanusa, Kepulauan ⌒ RI 164-165 K 1
Nanutarra Roadhouse o AUS 172-173 B 7
Nan Xian o VRC 156-157 H 2
Nanxiao o VRC 156-157 F 5
Nanxijiang • VRC 156-157 M 2
Nanxiong o VRC 156-157 J 4
Nanxu o VRC 156-157 G 4
Nanyamba o EAT 214-215 K 6
Nanyang o VRC 154-155 H 5
Nanyang Hu ~ VRC 154-155 K 4
Nanyi Hu o VRC 154-155 L 6
Nan-yō o J 152-153 J 5
Nanyuki o EAK 212-213 F 3
Nanzhai o VRC 156-157 F 3
Nanzhang o VRC 154-155 G 6
Nanzhao o VRC 154-155 H 5
Nanzhila o Z (SOU) 218-219 C 3
Nanzhila ~ Z 218-219 D 3
Nao, Cabo de la ▲ E 98-99 H 5
Naococane, Lac o CDN 38-39 J 2
Naogaon o BD 142-143 F 3
Não-me-Toque o BR 74-75 D 7
Náoussa o GR 100-101 J 4
Naozhou Dao ⌒ VRC 156-157 G 6
Napa o USA 40-41 C 6
Napabale Lagoon ⊥ • RI 164-165 H 6
Napacao Point ▲ RP 160-161 F 8
Napadogan o CDN 38-39 L 5
Napaha o MOC 218-219 K 1
Napaiskak o USA 20-21 K 6
Napaleofú, Arroyo ~ RA 78-79 K 4
Napanee o CDN 38-39 F 6
Napanwainami o RI 166-167 H 3
Napan-yaur o RI 166-167 H 3
Napas o RUS 114-115 R 5
Napassorssuaq Fjord ≈ 28-29 T 6
Napatok Bay ≈ 36-37 S 6
Napeitom o EAK 212-213 F 3
Napido o RI 166-167 H 2
Napier o NZ 182 F 3
Napier o ZA 220-221 D 7
Napier, Mount ▲ AUS 172-173 J 4
Napier Broome Bay ≈ 172-173 H 3
Napier Downs o AUS 172-173 G 4
Napier Mountains ▲ ARK 16 G 6
Napier Peninsula ⌣ AUS 174-175 C 3
Napier Range ▲ AUS 172-173 G 4
Naples o USA (FL) 48-49 H 6
Naples o USA (TX) 44-45 K 3
Naples = Nápoli ☆ ·· I 100-101 E 4
Napo o VRC 156-157 D 5
Napo, Río ~ EC 64-65 E 2
Napoca, Cluj- ☆ • RO 102-103 C 4
Napoleon o USA (ND) 42-43 H 2
Napoleon o USA (OH) 46-47 F 5
Nápoli ☆ ·· I 100-101 E 4
Nápoli, Golfo di ≈ 100-101 E 4
Nappa Merrie o AUS 178-179 F 4
Napperby o AUS 172-173 L 7
Naqa, Temples of ·· SUD 200-201 F 4
Naqāda o ET 194-195 F 5
Naqade o • IR 128-129 L 4
Naqb, Ra's an- o JOR 130-131 D 2
Naquen, Serranía de ▲ CO 60-61 G 6
Nār, Umm an- o UAE 134-135 F 6
Nara o AUS 174-175 G 6
Nara ☆ • J 152-153 F 7
Nara o RMM 202-203 G 2
Narač o BY 94-95 K 4
Nāra Canal ‹ PK 138-139 B 7
Naracoorte o AUS 180-181 F 4
Naracoorte Caves Conservation Park ⊥ AUS 180-181 F 4
Naradhan o AUS 180-181 J 2
Naraini o IND 142-143 B 3
Nārāinpur o IND 142-143 B 6
Nārājankher o IND 138-139 F 10
Naran o PK 138-139 D 2
Naran = Hongor o MAU 148-149 L 5
Narandiba o BR 72-73 E 7
Naranjal o EC 64-65 C 3
Naranjas, Punta ▲ PA 52-53 D 8
Naranjito o EC 64-65 C 3
Naranjo ∴ GCA 52-53 K 3
Naranjo o MEX 50-51 E 5
Naranjos o MEX 50-51 L 7
Narao o J 152-153 C 8
Narasannapeta o IND 142-143 D 6
Narasapuram o IND 140-141 J 2
Narasaraopet o IND 140-141 J 2
Narasimharajapura o IND 140-141 F 4
Narataj o RUS 116-117 K 8
Narathiwat ☆ THA 158-159 F 7
Nara Visa o USA 44-45 F 2
Naravuka o FJI 184 III b 2
Narayangadh o NEP 144-145 E 7
Nārāyangaon o IND 138-139 D 10
Narbonne o F 90-91 J 10
Narcondan Island ⌒ IND 158-159 C 4
Narding River ~ CDN 24-25 N 6
Naré o RA 76-77 G 6
Nareči, ostrov ⌒ RUS 108-109 O 8
Narega Island ⌒ PNG 183 E 3
Naregal o IND 140-141 F 3
Narembeen o AUS 176-177 E 6
Naréna o RMM 202-203 F 3
Nares Abyssal Plain ≃ 6-7 F 1
Nares Land ⊥ GRØ 26-27 b 2
Nares Stræde ≈ 26-27 O 4
Nares Strait ≈ 26-27 N 4
Narew o PL 92-93 R 2
Narew ~ PL 92-93 Q 2
Nargund o IND 140-141 F 3
Nari ~ PK 134-135 M 4
Nāri ~ PK 134-135 M 4
Narib o NAM 220-221 C 2
Narijn gol ~ MAU 116-117 F 10
Narijnteel = Čagaan-Ovoo o MAU 148-149 E 5
Narimanov ☆ RUS 96-97 E 10
Narinda, Helodrano ≈ 222-223 E 5
Narin Nur o VRC 154-155 F 2
Narita o J 152-153 J 7
Nar'jan-Mar ☆ RUS 88-89 W 3
Narkatiāganj o IND 142-143 D 2
Narmada ~ IND 138-139 E 8
Narmada ~ IND 138-139 D 9
Narmajaha ~ RUS 108-109 L 7
Nārnaul o IND 138-139 F 5
Narndee o AUS 176-177 E 4
Narob ~ NAM 220-221 C 2
Naroda ~ RUS 114-115 F 2

Mwaru — Naroda 293

Narodnaja, gora ▲ RUS 114-115 F 2
Národní park Šumava ⊥ CZ 92-93 M 4
Naro-Fominsk ☆ • RUS 94-95 P 4
Naro Island ⌒ RP 160-161 E 7
Narok ○ EAK 212-213 E 4
Naro Moru ○ EAK 212-213 F 4
Narooma ○ AUS 180-181 L 4
Närowäl ○ PK 138-139 E 3
Narrabri ○ AUS 178-179 K 6
Narracoota ○ AUS 176-177 E 2
Narragansett Bay ≈ 46-47 N 5
Narrandera ○ AUS 180-181 J 3
Narran Lake ○ AUS 178-179 J 5
Narran River ∼ AUS 178-179 J 5
Narraway River ∼ CDN 32-33 K 4
Narrien Range ▲▲ AUS 178-179 J 2
Narrogin ○ AUS 176-177 D 6
Narromine ○ AUS 180-181 K 2
Narrow Cape ▲ USA 22-23 U 4
Narrows Indian Reserve, The ✗ CDN 34-35 G 5
Narryer, Mount ▲ AUS 176-177 D 3
Narsalik ○ GRØ 28-29 Q 6
Narsampet ○ IND 140-141 H 2
Narsaq Kujalleq = Frederiksdal ○ GRØ 28-29 S 6
Narsarsuaq ○ GRØ 28-29 S 6
Narsimhapur ○ IND 138-139 G 8
Narsinghgarh ○ IND 138-139 F 8
Narsipatnam ○ IND 142-143 C 7
Nart ○ VRC 148-149 M 6
Narubis ○ NAM 220-221 D 3
Naru-shima ⌒ J 152-153 C 8
Naruto ○ J 152-153 F 7
Narva ○ • EST 94-95 L 2
Narva ○ RUS 116-117 F 8
Narva laht ≈ 94-95 K 2
Narvik ○ •• N 86-87 H 2
Narvskoe vodohranilišče < RUS 94-95 L 2
Narwietooma ○ AUS 176-177 M 1
Nary hrebet ▲▲ RUS 96-97 K 6
Naryilco ○ AUS 178-179 F 5
Naryn ∼ KA 124-125 J 6
Naryn ○ KS 146-147 B 5
Naryn ∼ KS 136-137 N 4
Naryn ○ RUS 116-117 G 10
Naryn ∼ RUS 116-117 G 10
Naryn-Huduk ○ RUS 126-127 G 5
Narynkol ○ KA 146-147 E 4
Naryntau, hrebet ▲▲ KS 146-147 C 5
Nasa, Gara ▲ ETH 208-209 B 4
Na'sān, Umm ⌒ BRN 134-135 D 5
Nasanabad ○ IND 138-139 G 10
Nasarawa ○ WAN 198-199 B 6
Năsăud ○ RO 102-103 D 4
Naschitti ○ USA 44-45 C 1
Nashan Island ⌒ 160-161 A 7
Nash Harbor ○ USA 20-21 G 6
Nāshik ○ IND 138-139 D 10
Nashino, Río ∼ EC 64-65 D 2
Nashū', Wādi an ∼ LAR 192-193 E 4
Nashua ○ USA (IA) 42-43 L 4
Nashua ○ USA (MT) 42-43 D 1
Nashua ○ USA (NH) 46-47 N 4
Nashville ☆ • USA 48-49 E 1
Nashwaak Bridge ○ CDN 38-39 L 5
Nashwauk ○ USA 42-43 L 2
Nasia ○ GH 202-203 K 4
Nasia ∼ GH 202-203 K 4
Našice ○ HR 100-101 G 2
Näsijärvi ○ FIN 88-89 G 6
Nasikonis, Tanjung ▲ RI 166-167 B 6
Nasipit ○ RP 160-161 F 8
Nāsir ○ SUD 208-209 A 4
Nāsir, Buhairat < ET 194-195 F 6
Nasirābād ○ IR 136-137 G 7
Nasirābād ○ PK 134-135 K 5
Nasirābād ○ PK 138-139 B 5
Nāşiriyah, Bi'r < LAR 192-193 D 2
Nāsiriya, an- ☆ IRQ 128-129 M 7
Nasiya, Ğabal ▲ ET 194-195 F 6
Naskaupi River ∼ CDN 36-37 T 7
Nasmah ○ LAR 192-193 E 2
Nasolot National Reservoir ⊥ EAK 212-213 E 3
Nasondoye ○ ZRE 214-215 C 6
Nasorolevu ▲ FJI 184 III b 2
Nāsriganj ○ IND 142-143 D 3
Nasriyān ○ IR 134-135 B 2
Nassarawa ○ WAN 204-205 G 4
Nassau ★ •• BS 54-55 G 2
Nassau, Bahía ≈ 80 G 7
Nassau, Fort • GUY 62-63 F 3
Nassau River ∼ AUS 174-175 F 4
Nass Basin ≃ CDN 32-33 F 3
Nasser, Lake = Nāsir, Buhairat < ET 194-195 F 6
Nassian ○ CI (BOA) 202-203 J 5
Nassian ○ CI (FER) 202-203 H 5
Nassoukou ○ DY 202-203 L 4
Nass River ∼ CDN 32-33 F 4
Nastapoka, Rivière ∼ CDN 36-37 L 6
Nastapoka Islands ⌒ CDN 36-37 L 6
Nastapoka Sound ≈ 36-37 L 6
Nasugbu ○ RP 160-161 D 5
Nasuraghena ○ SOL 184 I f 4
Nasva ○ RUS 94-95 M 3
Nata ○ •• PA 52-53 D 7
Nata ○ RB (CEN) 218-219 D 5
Nata ∼ RB 218-219 D 5
Nataboti ○ RI 166-167 D 3
Natal ○ BR (TOC) 68-69 D 4
Natal ☆ BR (RNO) 68-69 L 4
Natal ○ RI 162-163 C 4
Natalia ○ USA 44-45 H 5
Natalii, buhta ○ RUS 112-113 R 6
Natalschwelle ≃ 220-221 M 6
Natal Valley ≃ 9 G 9
Natanz ○ • IR 134-135 D 2
Natar ○ RI 162-163 F 7
Natara ∼ RUS 110-111 P 5
Nataš, Wādi ∼ ET 194-195 F 5
Natashquan ○ CDN 38-39 O 3
Natashquan, Rivière ∼ CDN 38-39 O 3
Natashquan River ∼ CDN 38-39 N 2
Natchamba ○ RT 202-203 L 5
Natchez ○ USA 44-45 M 4
Natchitoches ○ USA 44-45 L 4
Nate ○ IND 140-141 E 2
Natewa Bay ≈ 184 III b 2
Nathahu ○ MYA 158-159 C 2
Nathalia ○ AUS 180-181 H 4
Nathan River ○ AUS 174-175 C 4
Na Thawi ○ THA 158-159 F 7
Nāthdwāra ○ IND 138-139 D 7
Nathenje ○ MW 218-219 G 2
Nathia Gali ○ PK 138-139 D 2
Nathon ○ THA 158-159 E 6
Nathorst Land ⊥ GRØ 26-27 m 7
Nathorst Land ⊥ N 84-85 J 4
Nathrop ○ USA 42-43 D 6
Natiaboani ○ BF 202-203 L 4
Natingui ○ BR 74-75 E 5
Nation ○ USA 20-21 U 4
National Parachute Test Range xx USA 40-41 G 9
National Park ○ NZ 182 E 3
National Park ⊥ PNG 183 B 4
Nationalpark Bayerischer Wald ⊥ D 92-93 M 4
Nationalpark Berchtesgaden ⊥ D 92-93 M 5
Nationalpark Hochharz ⊥ D 92-93 L 3
Nationalpark i Nordgrønland og Østgrønland ⊥ GRØ 26-27 e 5
Nationalpark Niedersächsisches Wattenmeer ⊥ D 92-93 J 2
Nationalpark Sächsische Schweiz ⊥ D 92-93 N 3
Nationalpark Schleswig-Holsteinisches Wattenmeer ⊥ D 92-93 K 1
Nationalpark Vorpommersche Boddenlandschaft ⊥ D 92-93 M 1
National Reactor Testing Station xx USA 40-41 H 4
Nation River ∼ CDN 32-33 H 4
Natitingou ☆ DY 202-203 L 4
Natityay, Ğabal ▲ ET 194-195 G 6
Native Bay ≈ 36-37 H 3
Native Point ▲ CDN 36-37 H 3
Natividade ○ BR 68-69 E 7
Natkusiak Peninsula ⌣ CDN 24-25 R 4
Natla River ∼ CDN 30-31 E 4
Natmauk ○ MYA 142-143 J 5
Natong Kuangqu ○ VRC 156-157 E 2
Nator ○ BD 142-143 F 3
Natovi ○ FJI 184 III b 2
Natron, Lake ○ EAT 212-213 F 5
Natron, Trou du • TCH 198-199 H 2
Nattam ○ IND 140-141 H 5
Nattavaara station ○ S 86-87 K 3
Natukanaoka Pan ○ NAM 216-217 C 9
Natuna Besar, Pulau ⌒ RI 162-163 H 2
Natural Arch • USA 46-47 F 7
Natural Bridge • USA 48-49 E 2
Natural Bridges National Monument • USA 42-43 C 7
Natural Bridge State Monument • USA 40-41 J 3
Naturaliste, Cape ▲ AUS (TAS) 180-181 K 6
Naturaliste, Cape ▲ AUS (WA) 176-177 C 6
Naturaliste Plateau ≃ 176-177 B 6
Naturita ○ USA 42-43 C 6
Nau ○ TJ 136-137 L 4
Nauabu ○ PNG 183 F 6
Nauarai, Bi'r < SUD 200-201 G 2
Naudi ○ BR 62-63 G 5
Naubise ○ NEP 144-145 E 7
Nauchas ○ NAM 220-221 C 1
Naudesberg Pass ▲ ZA 220-221 G 5
Naudesnek ▲ ZA 220-221 J 5
Nauela ○ MOC 218-219 J 2
Naufal le-Chateau ○ IR 134-135 D 1
Naugarh ○ IND 142-143 C 2
Naujan ○ RP 160-161 D 6
Naujan Lake ○ RP 160-161 D 6
Naukot ○ PK 138-139 B 7
Naulila ○ ANG 216-217 C 8
Nauľjaha ∼ RUS 108-109 H 7
Naumatang ○ RI 166-167 D 5
Naumburg (Saale) ○ • D 92-93 L 3
Nauna Island ⌒ PNG 183 E 2
Naungpale ○ MYA 142-143 J 3
Nauru ⌒ NAU 13 H 3
Naushahro Firoz ○ PK 138-139 B 6
Nausori ○ FJI 184 III b 3
Nauta ○ PE 64-65 F 4
Nautanwa ○ IND 142-143 C 2
Nautilus, Selat ≈ 166-167 G 4
Nautimuk ○ AUS 180-181 F 4
Nautla ○ MEX 52-53 F 1
Nautsi ○ RUS 88-89 K 2
Näv ○ IR 128-129 N 4
Nava ○ MEX 50-51 J 3
Nava ∼ ZRE 212-213 A 2
Nava de Ricomalillo, La ○ E 98-99 E 5
Navahrudak ☆ BY 94-95 J 5
Navahrudskae uzvyšša ▲▲ BY 94-95 J 5
Navajo City ○ USA 44-45 D 1
Navajo Indian Reservation ⊥ USA 44-45 B 1
Navajo Mountain ▲ USA 40-41 J 7
Navajo National Monument ∴ USA 44-45 B 1
Navajo Reservoir < USA 44-45 D 1
Naval ○ RP 160-161 F 7
Navalmoral de la Mata ○ E 98-99 E 5
Navalmorales, Los ○ E 98-99 E 5
Navan = An Uaimh ○ IRL 90-91 D 5
Navapara ○ BD 142-143 F 4
Navapolack ☆ •• BY 94-95 L 4
Navapur ○ IND 138-139 D 9
Navarin, mys ▲ RUS 112-113 U 5
Navarino, Isla ⌒ RCH 80 G 7
Navarino, Pico ▲ RCH 80 G 7
Navarra ■ E 98-99 F 3
Navarre ○ AUS 180-181 G 4
Navarro ○ RA 78-79 K 3
Navas, Las ○ RP 160-161 F 6
Navašino ○ RUS 94-95 S 4
Navasota ○ USA 44-45 J 4
Navasota River ∼ USA 44-45 J 4
Navassa Island ⌒ USA 54-55 H 5
Nāve ○ AFG 134-135 M 2
Navere ○ RI 166-167 K 3
Navia ○ E 98-99 D 3
Navidad Bank ≃ 54-55 L 4
Navirai ○ BR 76-77 K 2
Naviti ⌒ FJI 184 III a 2
Naviu Island ⌒ PNG 183 B 5
Navlakhi ○ IND 138-139 C 8
Navlja ○ RUS 94-95 O 5
Nāvodari ○ RO 102-103 F 5
Navoi = Navoij ☆ US 136-137 J 4
Navoij ☆ US 136-137 J 4
Navojoa ○ MEX 50-51 E 4
Na Vong ○ LAO 156-157 C 6
Nāvor ○ AFG (GA) 134-135 M 2
Nāvor ○ AFG (GA) 134-135 M 2
Nāvor, Kōtal-e ▲ AFG 134-135 M 1
Navrongo ○ GH 202-203 K 4
Navsāri ○ IND 138-139 D 9
Navua ○ FJI 184 III b 3
Navua River ∼ FJI 184 III a 3
Navy Board Inlet ≈ 24-25 f 4
Nāwa ○ IND 138-139 E 6
Nawābshāh ○ PK 138-139 B 6
Nawāda ○ IND 142-143 D 3
Na Wai ○ THA 142-143 L 6
Nawa Kot ○ PK 138-139 C 5
Nawākshūt = Nouakchott ★ • RIM 196-197 C 5
Nāwalkal ○ IND 140-141 G 2
Nawalpur ○ NEP 144-145 E 7
Nawāpāra ○ IND 142-143 C 5
Nawar ○ RT 202-203 L 5
Nawinda Kuta ○ Z 218-219 C 3
Nawnghkio ○ MYA 142-143 K 4
Nawngleng ○ MYA 142-143 L 4
Nawuni ○ GH 202-203 K 5
Náxos ○ • GR 100-101 K 6
Náxos ⌒ GR 100-101 K 6
Naya Chor ○ PK 138-139 B 7
Nāyakanhatti ○ IND 140-141 G 3
Nayar ○ MEX 50-51 G 6
Nayarit ■ MEX 50-51 G 6
Nayau ⌒ FJI 184 III c 2
Nāybänd ○ IR 134-135 G 2
Nāyband, Kūh-e ▲ IR 134-135 G 2
Nayé ○ SN 202-203 D 2
Nayoro ○ J 152-153 K 2
Nayorunun River ∼ USA 22-23 Q 3
Nayouri ○ BF 202-203 L 3
Nayuchi ○ MW 218-219 H 2
Nāyudupeta ○ IND 140-141 H 4
Nazaré ○ BR (APA) 62-63 J 4
Nazaré ○ BR (BAH) 72-73 L 2
Nazaré ○ BR (P) 62-63 K 6
Nazaré ○ BR (TOC) 68-69 E 5
Nazaré ○ • P 98-99 C 5
Nazaré, Cachoeira ∼ BR 70-71 G 2
Nazaré da Mata ○ BR 68-69 L 5
Nazaré do Piauí ○ BR 68-69 G 5
Nazareth ○ BOL 70-71 E 4
Nazareth ○ CO 60-61 D 5
Nazareth = Nazerat ☆ IL 130-131 D 1
Nazarovo ☆ RUS 116-117 E 7
Nazas, Río ∼ MEX 50-51 G 5
Nazca ○ • PE 64-65 E 9
Nazca Linea • PE 64-65 E 9
Nazca Ridge ≃ 5 C 7
Naze ○ J 152-153 C 10
Nazerat ☆ IL 130-131 D 1
Nazilli ☆ TR 128-129 C 4
Nazinskaja ∼ RUS 114-115 P 4
Nazirhat ○ BD 142-143 G 4
Nazko ○ CDN 32-33 J 5
Nazko River ∼ CDN 32-33 J 5
Nazombe ○ MOC 214-215 K 6
Nazran ☆ RUS 126-127 F 6
Nazrēt ○ ETH 208-209 D 4
Nazwā ○ • OM 132-133 K 2
Nazym ∼ RUS 114-115 K 4
Nazyvaevsk ☆ RUS 114-115 L 7
Nbâk ○ RIM 196-197 C 6
Nbeiket Dlim < RIM 196-197 G 6
Nbeiket el Ahouâch < RIM 196-197 H 6
Ncamasere ∼ RB 216-217 F 9
Ncanaha ○ ZA 220-221 G 6
Nchalo ○ MW 218-219 H 3
Nchelenge ○ Z 214-215 E 5
Ncojane ○ RB 220-221 E 1
Ncojane Ranches ⊥ RB 216-217 F 11
Ncora Dam < ZA 220-221 H 5
Ncue ○ GQ 210-211 C 2
Ndaki ○ RMM 202-203 K 2
Ndala ○ EAT 212-213 D 6
Ndalambo ○ EAT 214-215 G 5
N'Dalatando ☆ ANG 216-217 C 4
Ndali ○ DY 204-205 E 4
Ndanda ○ EAT 214-215 K 6
Ndanda ○ RCA 206-207 F 6
Ndande ○ SN 202-203 B 2
Ndangane ○ SN 202-203 B 2
Ndao, Pulau ⌒ RI 166-167 B 7
Ndarapo Swamp ○ EAK 212-213 G 5
Ndarassa ○ RCA 206-207 F 5
Ndédu ○ ZRE 212-213 B 2
Ndeji ○ WAN 204-205 F 4
Ndekesha ○ ZRE 214-215 B 4
Ndéko ∼ RCB 210-211 F 4
Ndélé ☆ • RCA 206-207 E 4
Ndélélé ○ CAM 206-207 B 6
Ndemba ○ CAM 204-205 K 6
Ndembera ∼ EAT 214-215 H 5
Ndendé ○ G 210-211 C 5
Ndeyini < EAK 212-213 G 4
Ndia ○ SN 202-203 D 2
Ndian ∼ CAM 204-205 H 6
Ndiékro ○ CI 202-203 H 6
Ndiguina ○ CAM 206-207 B 3
Ndikiniméki ○ CAM 204-205 J 6
Ndikoko ○ CAM 204-205 J 6
Ndim ○ RCA 206-207 B 5
Ndindi ○ G 210-211 C 5
Ndindi ○ SN 202-203 B 2
Ndioum ○ SN 196-197 C 6
Ndioum Guènt ○ SN 202-203 C 2
Nditam ○ CAM 204-205 J 6
Ndiya ○ WAN 204-205 G 4
N'djaména ★ • TCH 198-199 G 6
Ndji ∼ RCA 206-207 F 5
Ndjim ∼ CAM 204-205 J 6
Ndjolé ○ CAM 204-205 J 6
Ndjolé ○ G 210-211 C 4
Ndjoundou ○ RCB 210-211 F 4
Ndjwé ∼ CAM 210-211 E 2
Ndofane ○ SN 202-203 C 3
Ndogo, Lagune ○ G 210-211 B 5
Ndok ○ CAM 206-207 B 5
Ndokama ○ CAM 204-205 J 6
Ndokayo ○ CAM 206-207 B 6
Ndoki ∼ RCB 210-211 F 3
Ndola ☆ Z 214-215 E 7
Ndom ○ CAM 204-205 J 6
Ndondo ○ SOL 184 I e 3
Ndonga ○ NAM 216-217 F 8
Ndongolo ○ G 210-211 C 3
Ndop ○ CAM 204-205 J 5
Ndora Mountains ▲▲ WAN 204-205 J 5
Ndorola ○ BF 202-203 H 4
Ndoto Mountains ▲▲ EAK 212-213 F 3
Ndouci ○ CI 202-203 H 7
Ndoukou ○ RCA 206-207 E 6
Ndoumbou ○ RCA 206-207 C 5
Ndrhamcha, Sebkha ○ RIM 196-197 C 5
Ndu ○ CAM 204-205 J 5
Ndu ○ ZRE 206-207 F 6
Nduluku ○ EAK 212-213 F 4
Ndumbwe ○ EAT 214-215 K 6
Ndumo ○ ZA 220-221 L 3
Ndumo Game Reserve ⊥ ZA 220-221 L 3
Ndurumo ∼ EAT 212-213 E 6
Ndzouani ⌒ COM 222-223 D 4
Neabul Creek ∼ AUS 178-179 J 4
Neagh, Lough ○ GB 90-91 D 4
Neah Bay ○ USA 40-41 B 1
Neakongut Bay ≈ 36-37 K 4
Neale, Lake ○ AUS 176-177 K 2
Neale Junction ○ AUS 176-177 H 4
Neales Creek ∼ AUS 178-179 C 4
Neales River ∼ AUS 178-179 D 4
Néa Moni ⋯ GR 100-101 L 5
Néa Moudania ○ GR 100-101 J 4
Neamt, Piatra- ☆ • RO 102-103 E 4
Neápoli ○ GR 100-101 J 6
Neápoli ○ GR 100-101 H 4
Nearchuss Passage ≈ 158-159 D 5
Near Islands ⌒ USA 22-23 C 6
Nebbou ○ BF 202-203 K 4
Nebe ○ RI 166-167 B 6
Nebelat el Hagana ○ SUD 200-201 D 6
Nebine Creek ∼ AUS 178-179 J 5
Nebitdag ○ TM 136-137 D 5
Neblina, Cerro de la ▲ YV 66-67 E 2
Neblina, Sierra de la ▲▲ YV 66-67 E 2
Nebo ○ AUS 178-179 K 1
Nebraska ■ USA 42-43 F 5
Nebraska City ○ USA 42-43 K 5
Nebrodi, Monti ▲ I 100-101 E 6
Necedah ○ USA 46-47 C 3
Nečera ∼ RUS 118-119 H 6
Nechako Plateau ▲▲ CDN 32-33 G 4
Nechako River ∼ CDN 32-33 H 5
Neche ○ USA 42-43 J 1
Neches River ∼ USA 44-45 K 4
Nechi ○ CO 60-61 D 3
Nechí, Río ∼ CO 60-61 D 4
Nechisar National Park ⊥ ETH 208-209 C 5
Neckarboo Range ▲▲ AUS 180-181 H 2
Necker Island ⌒ USA 14-15 M 5
Necochea ○ RA 78-79 K 5
Necocli ○ CO 60-61 C 3
Necungas ○ MOC 218-219 H 3
Nédéley ○ TCH 198-199 J 5
Nederland ○ USA (CO) 42-43 E 6
Nederland ○ USA (TX) 44-45 L 5
Nedlouc, Lac ○ CDN 36-37 N 6
Nedrata ○ ETH 208-209 D 3
Nedroma ○ DZ 188-189 L 3
Nedryhajliv ○ UA 102-103 H 2
Nedumangad ○ IND 140-141 G 6
Nedunkeni ○ CL 140-141 J 6
Needles ○ CDN 32-33 L 7
Needles ○ USA 40-41 G 8
Neenah ○ USA 46-47 D 3
Neepawa ○ CDN 34-35 G 5
Neergaard Lake ○ CDN 24-25 g 5
Neerim South ○ AUS 180-181 H 5
Nefasit ○ ER 200-201 J 5
Nefas Mewch'a ○ ETH 208-209 D 3
Neffatia ○ TN 190-191 H 4
Nefhi Shet' ∼ ER 200-201 J 5
Nefta ○ TN 190-191 F 4
Neftchala = Neftçala ○ AZ 128-129 N 3
Neftegorsk ○ RUS 122-123 K 2
Neftegorsk ○ RUS (SAM) 96-97 G 7
Neftejugansk ☆ RUS 114-115 M 4
Neftekamsk ☆ RUS 96-97 J 5
Neftekumsk ☆ RUS 126-127 F 5
Nefza ○ TN 190-191 G 2
Negage ○ ANG 216-217 C 3
Négala ○ RMM 202-203 F 3
Negampaha ○ CL 140-141 J 7
Nega Nega ○ Z 218-219 E 2
Négansi ○ DY 204-205 E 3
Negār ○ IR 134-135 G 4
Negara ∼ RI 164-165 D 5
Negaunee ○ USA 46-47 E 2
Negele ○ ETH 208-209 D 5
Negēlē ○ ETH 208-209 D 6
Negerilama ○ RI 164-165 H 3
Negeri Sembilan ■ MAL 162-163 E 3
Negev, ha- ⊥ IL 130-131 D 2
Negiralama ○ RI 162-163 D 3
Negjučej ∼ RUS 118-119 M 6
Negola ○ ANG 216-217 C 7
Negomane ○ MOC 214-215 K 6
Negombo ○ • CL 140-141 H 7
Negotin ○ • YU 100-101 J 2
Negotino ○ MK 100-101 J 4
Negra, Cordillera ▲▲ PE 64-65 C 6
Negra, La ○ RA 78-79 K 4
Negra, La ○ RCH 76-77 B 2
Negra, Ponta ▲ BR 68-69 L 4
Negra, Punta ▲ PE 64-65 B 4
Negra, Punta ▲ RA 78-79 K 5
Negril ○ JA 54-55 F 5
Negril Beach ⊥ • JA 54-55 F 5
Negrine ○ DZ 190-191 F 3
Negri River ∼ AUS 172-173 J 4
Negrito, El ○ HN 52-53 L 4
Negro, Arroyo ∼ ROU 78-79 L 2
Negro, Cerro ▲ PA 52-53 D 7
Negro, Cerro ▲ RA (CHU) 80 F 2
Negro, Cerro ▲ RA (NEU) 78-79 E 5
Negro, Cerro ▲ RCH 76-77 B 4
Negro, Laguna ○ ROU 74-75 D 10
Negro, Riacho ∼ RA 76-77 H 3
Negro, Río ∼ BOL 70-71 D 3
Negro, Río ∼ BOL 70-71 F 4
Negro, Río ∼ BOL 70-71 E 2
Negro, Río ∼ BR 66-67 F 3
Negro, Río ∼ BR 70-71 J 6
Negro, Río ∼ CO 66-67 D 2
Negro, Río ∼ HN 52-53 L 5
Negro, Río ∼ PY 76-77 J 2
Negro, Río ∼ PY 76-77 J 3
Negro, Río ∼ RA 76-77 H 4
Negro, Río ∼ RA 78-79 G 5
Negro, Río ∼ ROU 78-79 L 2
Negro, Río ∼ YV 60-61 E 3
Negros ⌒ RP 160-161 E 8
Negro Urco ○ PE 64-65 F 3
Negru Vodă ○ RO 102-103 F 6
Neguac ○ CDN 38-39 M 5
Nëgus"jah ∼ RUS 114-115 N 5
Nehaevskij ○ RUS 102-103 M 2
Nehalem ○ USA 40-41 C 3
Nehalem River ∼ USA 40-41 C 3
Nehāvand ○ • IR 134-135 C 1
Nehbandān ○ IR 134-135 J 3
Nehe ○ VRC 150-151 E 3
Nehoiu ○ RO 102-103 E 5
Nehone ○ ANG 216-217 D 8
Nehuentue ○ RCH 78-79 C 5
Neiafu ○ TON 184 IV b 1
Neiba ☆ DOM 54-55 K 5
Neiba, Bahía de ≈ 54-55 K 5
Neiba, Sierra de ▲▲ DOM 54-55 K 5
Neiden ○ N 86-87 O 2
Neidenburg = Nidzica ○ • PL 92-93 Q 2
Neidín = Kenmare ○ IRL 90-91 C 6
Neiges, Piton des ▲ F 224 B 7
Neijiang ○ VRC 156-157 D 2
Neilburg ○ CDN 32-33 Q 5
Neilersdrif ○ ZA 220-221 E 4
Neillsville ○ USA 46-47 C 3
Nei Mongol Gaoyuan ⊥ VRC 148-149 G 7
Neinsberg ▲ NAM 216-217 D 9
Neiriz ○ • IR 134-135 F 4
Neiße ∼ D 92-93 N 3
Neiva ☆ CO 60-61 D 6
Neixiang ○ VRC 154-155 G 5
Neizār ○ IR 134-135 D 1
Neizvestnaja ∼ RUS 112-113 V 1
Neja ○ RUS 94-95 S 2
Nejanilin Lake ○ CDN 30-31 V 6
Nejime ○ J 152-153 D 9
Nejo ○ ETH 208-209 B 4
Nëjtajaha ∼ RUS 108-109 Q 6
Nëjto, ozero ○ RUS 108-109 O 6
Nëjto pervoe, ozero ○ RUS 108-109 O 6
Nejva ∼ RUS 96-97 M 5
Nekā ○ IR 136-137 C 6
Nekēkum ∼ RUS 110-111 L 4
Nek'emte ☆ ETH 208-209 C 4
Nekljudovo ○ RUS 94-95 S 3
Nekob ○ MA 188-189 J 5
Nekongdakon, ozero ○ RUS 116-117 L 3
Nekongdokon ∼ RUS 116-117 E 3
Neksø ○ DK 86-87 G 9
Neladero, Sierra del ▲▲ RA 76-77 C 5
Nelamangala ○ IND 140-141 G 4
Nelemnoe ○ RUS 110-111 c 7
Nel'gese ∼ RUS 110-111 T 7
Nel'gjuu ∼ RUS 118-119 N 7
Nelia ○ AUS 174-175 G 7
Nelidovo ☆ RUS 94-95 N 3
Neligh ○ USA 42-43 H 4
Nel'jaty ○ RUS 118-119 G 7
Nel'kan ○ RUS (HBR) 120-121 G 5
Nel'kan ○ RUS (SAH) 110-111 Y 7
Nel'koba ○ RUS 120-121 N 3
Nellie, Mount ▲ AUS 172-173 G 4
Nellikkuppam ○ IND 140-141 H 5
Nellimö ○ FIN 88-89 K 2
Nellipaka ○ IND 142-143 B 7
Nellis Air Force Range xx USA 40-41 F 7
Nelliyālam ○ IND 140-141 F 5
Nellore ○ IND 140-141 H 3
Nel'ma ○ RUS 122-123 H 5
Nelma ○ USA 46-47 D 2
Nëlon ∼ RUS 110-111 Q 5
Nelshoogte ▲ ZA 220-221 K 2
Nelson ○ CDN 32-33 M 7
Nelson ○ NZ 182 D 4
Nelson ○ RA 76-77 G 6
Nelson ○ USA (NE) 42-43 H 5
Nelson ○ USA (WI) 46-47 C 3
Nelson, Cape ▲ AUS 180-181 F 5
Nelson, Cape ▲ PNG 183 E 5
Nelson, Estrecho ≈ 80 C 5
Nelson, Mount ▲ PNG 183 D 5
Nelson, Port ≈ 34-35 K 2
Nelson Forks ○ CDN 30-31 H 6
Nelson House ○ CDN 34-35 G 3
Nelson Island ⌒ USA 20-21 H 6
Nelson Lakes National Park ⊥ NZ 182 D 5
Nelson Museum • KAN 56 D 3
Nelson River ∼ CDN 34-35 J 2
Nelspoort ○ ZA 220-221 F 6
Nelspruit ○ • ZA 220-221 K 2
Nem ∼ RUS 114-115 D 4
Nem, Ust'- ○ RUS 96-97 J 3
Nëma ☆ RIM 196-197 G 6
Nema ☆ RUS 96-97 G 5
Nemaiah Valley ○ CDN 32-33 G 6
Neman ∼ BY 94-95 K 5
Neman ☆ RUS 94-95 H 4
Nembe ○ WAN 204-205 G 6
Nembrala ○ RI 166-167 B 7
Nemenčinė ○ LT 94-95 J 4
Nementcha, Monts des ▲▲ DZ 190-191 F 3
Némiscau, Lac ○ CDN 38-39 F 3
Némiscau, Rivière ∼ CDN 38-39 F 3
Nemkučenskij hrebet ▲▲ RUS 110-111 W 4
Nemnjuga ∼ RUS 88-89 S 4
Nemo, vulkan ▲ RUS 122-123 Q 4
Nemours ○ F 90-91 J 7
Nemrut Dağı ⋯ TR 128-129 H 4
Nemuj ○ RUS 120-121 G 6
Nemunas ∼ LT 94-95 H 4
Nemuro ○ J 152-153 L 3
Nemuro-hantō ⌣ J 152-153 L 3
Nemuro-kaikyō = Kunašírskij proliv ≈ 152-153 L 3
Nemuro-wan ≈ 152-153 L 3
Nemyriv ☆ UA 102-103 F 3
Nenagh = An tAonach ○ IRL 90-91 C 5
Nenana ○ USA 20-21 Q 4
Nenasi ○ MAL 162-163 E 3
Nendel'ginskij, hrebet ▲▲ RUS 110-111 V 6
Nenets Autonomous District = Neneckij avtonomnyj okrug ■ RUS 88-89 T 3
Nenggiri ∼ MAL 162-163 D 2
Nengo ∼ ANG 216-217 F 7
Nenjiang ○ VRC 150-151 E 3
Nen Jiang ∼ VRC 150-151 D 4
Nenoksa ○ RUS 88-89 P 4
Nens"egan ∼ RUS 114-115 K 3
Neo ○ J 152-153 G 7
Neodesha ○ USA 44-45 K 1
Néo Petritsi ○ GR 100-101 J 4
Neópolis ○ BR 68-69 K 7
Neosho ○ USA 44-45 K 1
Neosho River ∼ USA 42-43 K 6
Nepa ○ RUS (IRK) 116-117 O 6
Nepa ∼ RUS 116-117 N 6
Nepa ∼ RUS 116-117 M 6
Nepal ■ NEP 144-145 C 6
Nepalganj ○ NEP 144-145 C 6
Nepara ○ NAM 216-217 E 8
Nepean ○ CDN 38-39 G 6
Nepean Mine • AUS 176-177 F 5
Nepeña ○ PE 64-65 C 6
Nephi ○ USA 40-41 J 6
Nephin Beg Range ▲▲ IRL 90-91 C 4
Nepisiguit Bay ≈ 38-39 M 5
Nepisiguit River ∼ CDN 38-39 L 5
Nepoko ∼ ZRE 212-213 A 2
Nepomuceno ○ BR 72-73 J 6
Neponjatnaja ∼ RUS 108-109 Y 4
Nëptënnë ∼ RUS 116-117 K 4
Neptune Bay ≈ 36-37 R 2
Neptune Islands ⌒ AUS 180-181 D 3
Nera ∼ RUS 110-111 Z 7
Nera, Ust'- ☆ RUS 110-111 Y 7
Nérac ○ F 90-91 H 9
Neragon Island ⌒ USA 20-21 G 6
Nërangda, ozero ∼ RUS 108-109 c 7
Nerča ∼ RUS 118-119 H 8
Nerčinsk ☆ RUS 118-119 H 10
Nerčugan ∼ RUS 118-119 H 9
Nerehta ☆ RUS 94-95 R 3
Nereta ○ •• LV 94-95 J 3
Neretva ∼ HR 100-101 F 3
Neria ≈ 28-29 Q 6
Neria ○ GRØ (VGR) 28-29 Q 6
Neria ⌒ GRØ (VGR) 28-29 Q 6
Nerica ∼ RUS 88-89 W 4
Neriquinha ○ ANG 216-217 F 7
Neris (Vilija) ∼ LT 94-95 J 4
Nerja ○ E 98-99 F 6
Nerjuktjajinsk (Pervyj) ○ RUS 118-119 J 5
Nerjungri ☆ • RUS 118-119 M 7
Nerka, Lake ○ USA 22-23 R 3
Nerl' ∼ RUS 94-95 P 3
Nerla ○ IND 140-141 F 2
Nero, ozero ○ RUS 94-95 Q 3
Nerohi ○ RUS 114-115 F 3
Nerojka, gora ▲ RUS 114-115 E 2
Nerong, Selat ≈ 166-167 G 4
Nerópolis ○ BR 72-73 F 4
Nerpič'e ○ RUS 122-123 L 4
Nerpič'e, ozero ○ RUS (KMC) 120-121 U 5
Nerpič'e, ozero ○ RUS (SAH) 112-113 L 2
Nerpičij, mys ▲ RUS 110-111 Y 2
Nerpo ○ RUS 118-119 G 7
Nerren Nerren ○ AUS 176-177 C 3
Nerrima ○ AUS 172-173 G 5
Nerskoe ploskogor'e ▲▲ RUS 110-111 Z 7
Neruta ∼ RUS 88-89 X 3
Nerutajaha ∼ RUS 108-109 N 7
Nes ○ N 86-87 D 6
Nes' ○ RUS 88-89 S 3
Nes' ∼ RUS 88-89 S 3
Nēšāpūr ○ • IR 136-137 F 6
Nesebăr ○ •• BG 102-103 E 6
Nes'egan ∼ RUS 114-115 G 2
Nesgo ○ PNG 183 F 2
Neškan ○ RUS 112-113 Y 3
Neskaupstaður ○ IS 86-87 g 2
Neskënpil'gyn, laguna ≈ 112-113 Y 3
Nesna ○ N 86-87 F 3
Nesøya ⌒ N 86-87 F 3
Ness City ○ USA 42-43 H 6
Nessona ○ MOC 218-219 H 4
Nestaocano, Rivière ∼ CDN 38-39 H 3
Nesterov = Žovkva ☆ UA 102-103 C 2
Nesterovo ○ RUS 116-117 N 9
Nestiary ○ RUS 96-97 D 5
Nët ∼ RUS 120-121 H 4
Netaar ○ RI 166-167 L 3
Netanya ☆ IL 130-131 D 1
Netap ○ BHT 142-143 F 2
Netarhāt ○ IND 142-143 D 4
Netcong ○ USA 46-47 L 5
Netherlands = Nederland ■ NL 92-93 G 2
Netherlands Antilles = Nederlandse Antillen ■ NA 60-61 G 1
Netia ○ MOC 218-219 K 2
Neto ∼ I 100-101 F 5
Netrakona ○ BD 142-143 G 3
Netsilik Lake ○ CDN 24-25 a 6
Nettilling Lake ○ CDN 28-29 E 3
Nett Lake ○ USA 42-43 L 1
Nett Lake Indian Reservation ✗ USA 42-43 L 1
Nettling Fjord ≈ 28-29 F 3
Neubrandenburg ○ D 92-93 M 2
Neuchâtel ☆ • CH 92-93 J 5
Neuchâtel, Lac de ○ CH 92-93 J 5
Neudač, buhta ○ RUS 108-109 f 2
Neuenahr-Ahrweiler, Bad ○ • D 92-93 J 3
Neuenburg = Neuchâtel ☆ • CH 92-93 J 5
Neuenburger See = Lac de Neuchâtel ○ CH 92-93 J 5
Neufchâteau ○ B 92-93 H 4
Neufchâteau ○ F 90-91 K 7
Neufchâtel-en-Bray ○ F 90-91 H 7
Neuhaus = Jindřichův Hradec ○ CZ 92-93 N 4
Neukaledonien ⌒ F 13 H 5
Neumarkt in der Oberpfalz ○ D 92-93 L 4
Neumünster ○ D 92-93 K 1
Neunkirchen ○ A 92-93 O 5
Neunkirchen ○ D 92-93 J 4
Neupokoeva, mys ▲ RUS 108-109 c 3
Neupokoeva, ostrov ⌒ RUS 108-109 R 5
Neuquén ■ RA 78-79 D 5
Neuquén ☆ RA (NEU) 78-79 E 5
Neuquén, Río ∼ RA 78-79 E 4
Neuruppin ○ • D 92-93 M 2
Neu Sandez = Nowy Sącz ☆ • PL 92-93 Q 4
Neuschwabenland ⊥ ARK 16 F 36
Neuschwanstein •• D 92-93 L 5
Neuse River ∼ USA 48-49 K 2
Neusiedler See ○ A 92-93 O 5
Neusohl = Banská Bystrica ○ SK 92-93 P 4
Neustadt (Orla) ○ D 92-93 L 3
Neustadt an der Aisch ○ D 92-93 L 4
Neustrelitz ○ • D 92-93 M 2
Neutenskij hrebet ▲▲ RUS 112-113 N 4
Neu-Titschein = Nový Jičín ○ CZ 92-93 P 4
Neutral Junction ○ AUS 178-179 C 1
Neuwied ○ D 92-93 J 3
Neva ∼ RUS 94-95 M 2
Nevada ○ USA (MO) 42-43 K 7
Nevada ■ USA 40-41 E 6
Nevada, Sierra ▲▲ RA 78-79 E 7
Nevada, Sierra ▲▲ USA 40-41 D 6
Nevada de Lagunas Bravas, Sierra ▲ RCH 76-77 C 4
Nevada de Santa Marta, Sierra ▲ CO 60-61 E 2
Nevada Test Side xx USA 40-41 F 7
Nevadita, La ○ CO 60-61 E 2
Nevado, Cerro ▲ RCH 78-79 C 7
Nevado, Cerro el ▲ RA 78-79 E 3
Nevado, Sierra del ▲▲ RA 78-79 E 3
Nevado Ampato ▲ PE 70-71 B 4
Nevado Ancohuma ▲ BOL 70-71 C 4
Nevado Cololo Keasani ▲ BOL 70-71 C 4
Nevado Cóndor ▲ RCH 80 D 2
Nevado Coropuna ▲ PE 64-65 F 9
Nevado de Acay ▲ RA 76-77 D 3
Nevado de Cachí ▲ RA 76-77 D 3
Nevado de Chañi ▲ RA 76-77 E 3
Nevado de Colima ▲ MEX 52-53 C 2
Nevado de Cumbal ▲ CO 64-65 D 1
Nevado de Incahuasi ▲ RA 76-77 C 4
Nevado del Huila ▲ CO 60-61 D 6
Nevado del Huila, Parque Nacional ⊥ CO 60-61 D 6
Nevado del Illimani ▲ BOL 70-71 D 5
Nevado de Longaví ▲ RCH 78-79 D 4
Nevado de los Palos ▲ RCH 80 D 2
Nevado del Ruiz ▲ CO 60-61 D 5
Nevado del Tolima ▲ CO 60-61 D 5
Nevado de Putre ▲ RCH 70-71 C 6
Nevado de Sajama ▲ BOL 70-71 C 6
Nevado de Toluca, Parque Nacional ⊥ MEX 52-53 E 2
Nevado Huayasa ▲ PE 70-71 B 5
Nevado Huayna Potosí ▲ BOL 70-71 C 5
Nevado Ojos del Salado ▲ •• RCH 76-77 C 4
Nevado Queva ▲ RA 76-77 D 3
Nevados, Parque Nacional los ⊥ CO 60-61 D 5
Nevado Salcantay ▲ PE 64-65 F 8
Neve, Serra do ▲▲ ANG 216-217 B 6
Nevel' ☆ RUS 94-95 L 3
Nevel'sk ○ RUS 122-123 J 5
Nevel'skogo, proliv ○ RUS 122-123 J 3
Never ○ RUS 118-119 M 8
Nevers ☆ • F 90-91 J 8
Nevertire ○ AUS 178-179 J 6
Neves, Rio ∼ BR 68-69 F 5
Nevesinje ○ BIH 100-101 G 3
Neville ○ CDN 34-35 C 6
Nevinnomyssk ○ RUS 126-127 D 5
Nevis Island ⌒ KAN 56 D 3
Nev'jansk ☆ RUS 96-97 M 5
Nevşehir ☆ • TR 128-129 F 3
Nevskoe, ozero ○ RUS 122-123 K 4
New Aiyansh ○ CDN 32-33 F 4
Newala ○ EAT 214-215 K 6
New Albany ○ USA (IN) 46-47 F 6
New Albany ○ USA (MS) 48-49 D 2
New Alton Downs ○ AUS 178-179 E 4
New Amsterdam ○ GUY 62-63 F 2
Newark ○ USA (DE) 46-47 L 6
Newark ○ USA (NJ) 46-47 L 5
Newark ○ USA (NY) 46-47 K 4
Newark ○ USA (OH) 46-47 G 5
Newark on Trent ○ • GB 90-91 G 5

294 Narodnaja, gora — Newark on Trent

New Athens o USA 46-47 D 6
Newaygo o USA 46-47 F 4
New Bedford o USA 46-47 N 5
Newberg o USA 40-41 C 3
New Bern o USA 48-49 K 2
Newbern o USA 48-49 D 1
Newberry o USA (MI) 46-47 F 2
Newberry o USA (SC) 48-49 H 2
New Bight o BS 54-55 H 2
New Boston o USA (IL) 46-47 C 5
New Boston o USA (TX) 44-45 H 3
New Braunfels o USA 44-45 H 5
New Britain ⌐ PNG 183 E 4
New Britain o USA 46-47 M 5
New Britain Trench o 183 E 4
Newbrook o CDN 32-33 O 4
New Brunswick □ CDN 38-39 L 5
New Buffalo o USA 46-47 E 5
Newburgh o USA 46-47 L 5
Newbury o GB 90-91 G 6
Newburyport o USA 46-47 N 4
New Bussa o WAN 204-205 F 4
Newby River ~ CDN 32-33 P 3
New Caledonia = Nouvelle-Calédonie, Île
  ⌐ F 13 H 5
New Caledonia Basin ≃ 13 H 5
New Caledonian Basin ≃ 182 B 2
Newcastle o AUS 180-181 L 2
Newcastle o CDN (NB) 38-39 M 5
Newcastle o CDN (ONT) 38-39 E 7
Newcastle o GB 90-91 E 4
New Castle o USA (IN) 46-47 F 6
New Castle o USA (PA) 46-47 H 5
Newcastle o USA (TX) 44-45 H 3
Newcastle o USA (WY) 42-43 E 4
Newcastle o ZA 220-221 J 3
Newcastle Creek ~ AUS 174-175 C 5
Newcastle upon Tyne ★ GB 90-91 G 4
Newcastle Waters o AUS 174-175 C 4
Newcastle West = An Caisleán Nua ⌐ IRL
  90-91 C 5
New Cholossa o PNG 183 A 2
Newdale o CDN 34-35 F 5
New Delamere o AUS 172-173 K 3
New Delhi ★ • IND 138-139 F 5
New Denver o CDN 32-33 M 7
New Dixie o USA 174-175 G 4
Newell o USA 42-43 F 3
Newell, Lake o AUS 176-177 J 2
Newell Highway II AUS 178-179 K 6
Newell Lake o CDN 32-33 O 6
New England o USA 42-43 F 2
New England Highway II AUS
  178-179 L 6
New England National Park ⊥ AUS
  178-179 M 6
New England Range ▲ AUS
  178-179 L 6
New England Seamounts ≃ 6-7 E 1
Newenham, Cape ▲ USA 22-23 P 3
New Featherstone o ZW 218-219 F 4
Newfoundland □ CDN 38-39 N 6
Newfoundland o CDN 38-39 I Q 4
Newfoundland, Grand Banks of ≃
  6-7 D 4
Newfoundland Evaporation Basin ⊥ USA
  40-41 H 5
New Gabloi o LB 202-203 F 6
New Galloway o GB 90-91 E 4
New Georgia ⌐ SOL 184 I c 3
New Georgia Group ⌐ SOL 184 I c 3
New Georgia Sound = The Slot ≈
  184 I c 2
New Germany o CDN 38-39 M 6
New Glasgow o CDN 38-39 N 6
New Guinea ⌐ RI 166-167 J 3
New Guinea Trench ≃ 166-167 J 2
Newhalem o USA 40-41 D 1
Newhalen o USA 22-23 T 3
Newhalen River ~ USA 22-23 T 3
New Halfa o SUD 200-201 G 5
New Hamilton o USA 20-21 J 3
New Hampshire □ USA 46-47 N 4
New Hampton o USA 42-43 L 4
New Hanover ⌐ PNG 183 E 2
New Hanover o ZA 220-221 K 4
New Harmony o USA 46-47 E 6
Newhaven o AUS 172-173 K 7
New Haven o USA 46-47 M 5
New Hazelton o CDN 32-33 G 4
New Hebrides ⌐ VAN 184 II a 1
New Iberia o USA 44-45 M 4
New Ireland ⌐ PNG 183 F 2
New Jersey □ USA 46-47 L 6
Newkirk o USA 44-45 E 2
New Knockhock o USA 20-21 N 5
New Leipzig o USA 42-43 G 2
New Liskeard o CDN 38-39 F 6
New London o USA (CT) 46-47 M 5
New London o USA (WI) 46-47 D 4
Newman o AUS 176-177 E 1
Newman o USA 44-45 D 3
Newman Bugt ≈ 26-27 V 3
Newmarket o CDN 38-39 E 6
Newmarket o GB 90-91 H 5
New Market o USA 46-47 J 6
New Martinsville o USA 46-47 H 6
New Meadows o USA 40-41 F 3
New Mexico □ USA 44-45 C 2
New Milford o USA 46-47 M 5
New Mirpur o IND 138-139 D 3
Newnan o USA 48-49 F 3
Newnes ∴ AUS 180-181 L 2
New Norfolk o AUS 180-181 J 7
New Orleans o • USA 44-45 M 4
New Philadelphia o USA 46-47 H 5
New Plymouth o NZ 182 E 3
Newport o CDN 38-39 M 6
Newport o GB (ENG) 90-91 G 6
Newport o GB (WAL) 90-91 F 6
Newport o USA (AR) 44-45 M 2
Newport o USA (KY) 46-47 F 6
Newport o USA (OR) 40-41 B 3
Newport o USA (RI) 46-47 N 5
Newport o USA (TN) 48-49 G 2
Newport o USA (VT) 46-47 M 3
Newport o USA (WA) 40-41 F 1

Newport News o USA 46-47 K 7
New Port Richey o USA 48-49 G 5
New Providence ⌐ BS 54-55 G 2
Newquay o GB 90-91 E 6
New Raymer o USA 42-43 F 5
New Richmond o CDN 38-39 M 4
New Richmond o USA 42-43 L 3
New Ringold o USA 44-45 K 2
New River ~ GUY 62-63 F 4
New River ~ USA 46-47 H 7
New Rochelle o USA 46-47 M 5
New Rockford o USA 42-43 H 2
New Ross = Ros Mhic Thriúin ⌐ IRL
  90-91 D 5
Newry o GB 90-91 E 4
Newry Island ⌐ AUS 174-175 K 7
New Salem o USA 42-43 G 2
New Schwabenland ⊥ ARK 16 F 36
New Siberian Islands = Novosibirskie
  ostrova ⌐ RUS 110-111 Z 2
New Smyrna Beach o USA 48-49 H 5
South Wales ⌐ AUS 180-181 G 2
New Springs o AUS 176-177 F 2
New Stuyahok o USA 22-23 S 3
Newton o USA (IA) 42-43 L 5
Newton o USA (IL) 46-47 D 6
Newton o USA (KS) 42-43 J 6
Newton o USA (MS) 48-49 E 3
Newton o USA (NC) 48-49 H 2
Newton Mills o CDN 38-39 N 6
New Town o USA 42-43 F 2
Newtownabbey o GB 90-91 E 4
Newtown Steward o GB 90-91 D 4
New Ulm o USA 42-43 K 3
New Waterford o CDN 38-39 O 5
New Westminster o CDN 32-33 J 7
New World Island ⌐ CDN 38-39 I R 4
New York □ USA 46-47 J 4
New York o • USA 46-47 M 5
New York State Thruway II USA
  46-47 L 4
New Zealand ■ NZ 182 E 4
New Zealand ⌐ NZ 182 E 4
Nexapa, Río ~ MEX 52-53 E 2
Nexpa, Río ~ MEX 52-53 C 2
Neyyáttinkara o IND 140-141 G 6
Nezahualcóyotl, Ciudad o MEX
  52-53 E 2
Nezahualcóyotl, Presa < MEX 52-53 H 3
Neždaninskoe o RUS 120-121 W 4
Nežin = Nižyn o UA 102-103 G 4
Neznaemyj, zaliv ≈ RUS 108-109 Q 3
Neznanovo o RUS 94-95 R 4
Nez Perce Indian Reservation ✕ USA
  40-41 F 2
Nez Perce National Historic Park ∴ USA
  40-41 F 2
Nfiss, Oued ~ MA 188-189 G 5
Ngabe o RCA 206-207 B 6
Ngabordamlu, Tanjung ▲ RI
  166-167 H 5
Ngabu o MW 218-219 H 3
Ngadiluwih o RI 168 E 3
Ngadda, River ~ WAN 204-205 K 3
Ngadzi o RCA 206-207 E 6
Ngajira o EAT 214-215 H 4
Ngala o WAN 198-199 G 6
Ngalo o ZRE 206-207 F 6
Ngalu o • RI 168 E 8
Ngam o CAM 206-207 B 5
Ngama o TCH 206-207 C 3
Ngama o TCH 198-199 J 6
Ngamakwe o ZA 220-221 H 6
Ngambé o CAM 204-205 J 6
Ngambé Tikar o CAM 204-205 J 6
Ngamdu o WAN 204-205 K 3
Ngamiland o RB 216-217 F 9
Ngamo o ZW 218-219 D 4
Ngamring o VRC 144-145 F 6
Ngarda o RCA 206-207 F 6
Nganga Ringco o VRC 144-145 D 5
Nganglong Kangri ▲ VRC 144-145 D 5
Nganglong Kangri ▲ VRC 144-145 C 4
Ngangzê Co o VRC 144-145 F 5
Nganha, Montagne de ▲ CAM
  206-207 B 5
Nganji o ZRE 212-213 A 5
Nganjuk o RI 168 D 3
Ngantru o RI 168 D 3
Nganzi o ANG 210-211 D 6
Ngao o THA 142-143 L 6
Ngaoui, Mont ▲ CAM 206-207 B 5
Ngaoundal o CAM 204-205 K 5
Ngaoundéré o CAM 204-205 K 5
Ngara o EAT 212-213 C 5
Ngara o MW 214-215 H 1
Ngarama o RWA 212-213 C 4
Ngarangou o TCH 198-199 G 6
Ngaras o RI 162-163 F 7
Ngarimbi o EAT 214-215 N 5
Ngarka-Pyrjajaha ~ RUS 114-115 L 2
Ngarkat Conservation Park ⊥ AUS
  180-181 E 3
Ngaso Plain ~ EAK 212-213 F 2
Ngassau Noum ▲ CAM 206-207 B 4
Ngasumet o EAT 212-213 F 4
Ngathainggyaung o MYA 158-159 C 2
Ngato o CAM 210-211 E 2
Ngawi o RI 168 D 3
Ngawihi o NZ 182 E 4
Ngayu ~ ZRE 212-213 B 3
Ngazidja ⌐ COM 222-223 C 3
Ngazun o MYA 142-143 J 5
Ngbala o RCB 210-211 E 3
Ngerengere o EAT 214-215 K 4
Ngezi ~ ZW 218-219 E 4
Ngatokae ⌐ SOL 184 I d 3
Nggela Pile ⌐ SOL 184 I d 3
Nggela Sule ⌐ SOL 184 I d 3
Nghi Lôc o VN 156-157 D 7
Ngidinga o ZRE 210-211 D 5

Ngilikomba o SOL 184 I e 3
Ngina o ZRE (Ban) 210-211 E 4
Ngina o ZRE (HAU) 212-213 A 2
Ngo o RCB 210-211 F 5
Ngoa o ZRE 212-213 B 2
Ngoassé o CAM 210-211 D 2
Ngoc Hiên o VN 158-159 H 6
Ngofakiaha o RI 164-165 K 3
Ngog Mapubi o CAM 210-211 C 2
Ngoila o CAM 210-211 E 3
Ngoko ~ CAM 210-211 E 3
Ngoko ~ RCB 210-211 E 4
Ngol Kedju ▲ CAM 204-205 H 5
Ngolo o Z 214-215 F 5
Ngolo o ZRE 210-211 G 3
Ngolo, Chutes de ~ RCA 206-207 F 6
Ngoma o NAM 218-219 C 3
Ngoma Bridge o RB 218-219 C 3
Ngoma Tsé-Tsé o RCB 210-211 E 6
Ngomba o EAT 214-215 G 5
Ngomedzap o CAM 210-211 D 2
Ngomeni, Ras ▲ EAK 212-213 H 5
Ngomo o G 210-211 B 4
Ngom Qu ~ VRC 144-145 K 4
Ngong o EAK 212-213 F 4
Ngonga o CAM 204-205 K 4
Ngoni, Tanjung ▲ RI 166-167 H 5
Ngonye Falls ~ Z 218-219 B 3
Ngora o EAU 212-213 E 3
Ngorengore o EAK 212-213 E 4
Ngoring Hu ~ VRC 144-145 L 3
Ngoro o CAM 204-205 J 6
Ngorongoro Conservation Area ⊥ EAT
  (ARV) 212-213 E 5
Ngorongoro Crater ▲ ∴ EAT
  212-213 E 5
Ngorongoro Crater Lodge o EAT
  212-213 E 5
Ngororero o RWA 212-213 B 4
Ngoso o ZRE 210-211 G 6
Ngoto o RCA 206-207 D 7
Ngotwane ~ RB 220-221 H 2
Ngouanga ~ RCA 206-207 F 6
Ngoulemakong o CAM 210-211 D 2
Ngoulonkila o RCB 210-211 E 5
Ngouma o RMM 202-203 J 2
Ngoura o TCH 198-199 J 6
Ngouré o CAM 204-205 J 6
Ngouri o TCH 198-199 H 5
Ngourti o RN 198-199 F 5
Ngoussa o DZ 190-191 K 4
Ngouyo o RCA 206-207 B 6
Ngové-Ndogo, Domaine de chasse de ⊥
  G 210-211 B 5
Ngoyeboma o RCB 210-211 E 3
Ngozi o BU 212-213 B 5
Ngudu o EAT 212-213 D 5
Nguélémendouka o CAM 204-205 K 6
Nguema o ZRE 214-215 B 4
Ngui o RCA 206-207 B 6
Nguia Bouar o RCA 206-207 B 6
Nguigmi o RN 198-199 F 5
Nguila o CAM 204-205 J 6
Nguiu ⌐ AUS 172-173 K 1
Ngukurr ⌐ AUS 174-175 C 4
Nguling o RI 168 E 3
Nguna ~ VAN 184 II b 3
Ngundu o ZW 218-219 F 5
Ngunguru o NZ 182 E 2
Nguni o EAK 212-213 G 4
Ngunju, Tanjung ▲ RI 168 E 8
Ngunut o RI 168 D 4
Nguroje o WAN 204-205 J 5
Ngurore o WAN 204-205 K 4
Ngushi o CAM 204-205 H 6
Nguyên Binh o VN 156-157 D 5
Ngwalulu = Maana'oba ⌐ SOL
  184 I e 3
Ngwedaung o MYA 142-143 K 6
Ngweze ~ Z 218-219 C 3
Ngwo o CAM 204-205 H 5
Ngynesejaha ~ RUS 108-109 R 6
Nhabe ~ RB 218-219 B 3
Nhachengue o MOC 218-219 H 6
Nhacra o GNB 202-203 C 3
Nhamalábue o MOC 218-219 H 3
Nhamatanda o MOC 218-219 H 4
Nhamunda o BR 66-67 J 4
Nhamunda, Rio ~ BR 62-63 F 6
Nhamundá Mapuera, Área Indígena ✕ BR
  62-63 E 6
Nhandeara o BR 72-73 G 4
Nhandu, Rio ~ BR 66-67 K 7
Nhareia o ANG 216-217 D 5
Nhecolândia o BR 70-71 J 6
Nhia ~ ANG 216-217 C 5
Nhill o AUS 180-181 F 4
Nhlangano o SD 220-221 K 3
Nho Quan o VN 156-157 D 6
Nhoquim, Igarapé ~ BR 68-69 C 6
Nhu' Kuân o VN 156-157 D 7
Nhulunbuy (Gove) o AUS 174-175 D 3
Niabayo o CI 202-203 H 7
Niablé o CI 202-203 H 7
Niada o RCA 206-207 D 6
Niafounké o RMM 202-203 H 2
Niagara Falls o CDN (ONT) 38-39 E 7
Niagara Falls o • CDN 38-39 E 7
Niagara Falls o USA 46-47 J 4
Niagara River ~ 46-47 J 4
Niah o CI 202-203 G 7
Niah o MAL 162-163 K 4

Niah Caves • MAL 162-163 K 3
Niah National Park ⊥ MAL 162-163 K 3
Niakaramandougou o CI 202-203 H 5
Niakhar o SN 202-203 B 2
Niaklan o LB 202-203 F 7
Nialaha'u Point = Cape Zele'e ▲ SOL
  184 I e 3
Niambézaria o CI 202-203 H 7
Niamey o RN 204-205 D 3
Niamey ★ • RN (NIA) 204-205 E 2
Niamina o RMM 202-203 G 3
Niampak o RI 164-165 K 1
Niamtougou o RT 202-203 K 4
Niamvoudou o CAM 204-205 K 6
Niandakoro o RG 202-203 F 5
Niandan ~ RG 202-203 F 5
Nianfasa o CI 202-203 G 5
Nianforando o RG 202-203 E 5
Niangara o ZRE 212-213 A 2
Niangay, Lac o RMM 202-203 J 2
Niangoloko o BF 202-203 H 4
Niangyuan o VRC 156-157 G 4
Nia-Nia o ZRE 212-213 A 3
Nianing o SN 202-203 B 2
Niantan ~ RG 202-203 F 4
Niantanina o RN 202-203 F 4
Nianyushan Sk ~ VRC 154-155 J 6
Niaoshu Shan ▲ VRC 154-155 D 4
Niapidou o CI 202-203 F 7
Niapu o ZRE 210-211 L 2
Niaqornaarsuk o GRØ 28-29 O 2
Niaqornat o GRØ 26-27 Y 8
Niara ~ RG 202-203 E 4
Niari □ RCB 210-211 D 5
Niari ~ RCB 210-211 D 5
Niaro o SUD 206-207 M 3
Nias, Pulau ⌐ RI 162-163 B 4
Niassa □ MOC 214-215 H 7
Niassa, Lago o MOC 214-215 H 7
Niassa, Reserva do ⊥ MOC
  214-215 J 7
Niáta o GR 100-101 J 6
Niau ⌐ F 13 N 4
Nibinamik Lake o CDN 34-35 M 4
Nibong, Kampung o MAL 162-163 D 2
Nibong Tebal o MAL 162-163 D 2
Nica ~ RUS 114-115 G 6
Nicaragua ■ NIC 52-53 A 5
Nicaragua, Lago de o NIC 52-53 B 6
Nicasio o PE 70-71 B 4
Nicastro o I 100-101 F 5
Nicatous, Lac o CDN 38-39 M 5
Ničatka, ozero o RUS 118-119 H 7
Nice o • F 90-91 L 6
Nichican o CDN 38-39 J 2
Nichinan o J 152-153 D 9
Nichlaul o IND 142-143 C 4
Nicholas Channel ≈ 54-55 E 3
Nicholasville o USA 46-47 F 7
Nicholson o AUS 174-175 D 3
Nicholson, Mount ▲ AUS 178-179 K 3
Nicholson Lake o CDN 30-31 S 4
Nicholson Peninsula ⌐ 24-25 G 2
Nicholson Range ▲ AUS 176-177 D 3
Nicholson River ~ AUS 174-175 E 5
Nichols Town o BS 54-55 F 2
Nicka o TM 136-137 H 3
Nickerievier ~ SME 62-63 F 3
Nickol Bay ≈ 172-173 C 6
Nicman o CDN 38-39 K 5
Nicola Mameet Indian Reserve ✕ CDN
  32-33 K 6
Nicola River ~ CDN 32-33 K 6
Nicolás Bruzzone o RA 78-79 D 4
Nicolás Levalle o RA 78-79 F 6
Nicondocho, Rio ~ MOC 218-219 K 1
Nicosia o I 100-101 E 6
Nicosia = Lefkosia ★ CY 128-129 E 5
Nicoya o CR 52-53 B 6
Nicoya, Golfo de ≈ 52-53 B 7
Nicoya, Península de ⌐ CR 52-53 B 7
Nictau o CDN 38-39 M 5
Nicuadala o MOC 218-219 J 3
Nicupa o MOC 218-219 K 2
Nida o • LT 94-95 G 4
Nidadavole o IND 140-141 J 2
Nidelva ~ N 86-87 D 7
Nidili, ozero o RUS 118-119 M 4
Nido, El o RP 160-161 C 7
Nidpall o IND 140-141 F 4
Nidri o GR 100-101 H 5
Nidym ~ RUS 116-117 K 4
Nidymkan ~ RUS 116-117 J 4
Nidzica o • PL 92-93 Q 2
Niéboré o RG 202-203 E 4
Niebüll o D 92-93 N 1
Niechorze o PL 92-93 N 1
Niedere Tauern ▲ ▲ A 92-93 M 5
Niederösterreich □ A 92-93 N 4
Niedersachsen □ D 92-93 J 2
Niefang o GQ 210-211 D 2
Niega o BF 202-203 K 3
Niekerkshoop o ZA 220-221 F 4
Niellé o CI 202-203 H 4
Niellim o TCH 206-207 C 4
Niem o RCA 206-207 B 5
Niemba o ZRE 212-213 B 6
Niemba ~ ZRE 214-215 E 4
Niemelane < RIM 196-197 L 5
Niénga ~ RMM 202-203 G 4
Nienburg (Weser) o D 92-93 K 2
Niénokue, Mont ▲ CI 202-203 G 7
Nieu Bethesda o ZA 220-221 G 5
Nieuw Amsterdam o SME 62-63 G 3
Nieuw Nickerie o SME 62-63 F 3
Nieuwoudtville o ZA 220-221 D 5
Nieva, Rio ~ PE 64-65 D 4
Nieves, Las o MEX 50-51 G 4
Niğde ☆ • TR 128-129 F 3
Nigel o ZA 220-221 J 3
Niger ~ 9 D 4
Niger □ RN 198-199 B 4
Niger o WAN 204-205 D 4

Niger Delta ∪ WAN 204-205 F 6
Niger Fan ≃ 9 B 3
Nigeria ■ WAN 204-205 F 4
Night Hawk Lake o CDN 34-35 Q 6
Nightmote o USA 20-21 N 6
Nigu River ~ USA 20-21 M 2
Niha Settlements • RI 162-163 B 4
Nihing o PK 134-135 L 4
Nihing ~ PK 134-135 K 5
Nihoa ~ USA 48-49 B 7
Nihonmatsu o J 152-153 J 6
Nihuil o RA 78-79 E 3
Nihuil, Embalse del < RA 78-79 E 3
Nihuil, Salto ~ RA 78-79 E 3
Niigata ☆ J 152-153 H 6
Niihau ⌐ USA 48-49 B 7
Niijima ⌐ J 152-153 H 7
Niimi o J 152-153 E 7
Niitsu o J 152-153 H 6
Nijadluk Bay ≈ 36-37 T 7
Nijgarh o NEP 144-145 E 7
Nijmegen o • NL 92-93 H 3
Nikel o RUS 88-89 H 5
Nikiniki o RI 166-167 C 6
Nikitinka o KA 134-135 H 4
Nikkaluokta o S 86-87 J 3
Nikki o DY 204-205 E 3
Nikkō o • J 152-153 H 6
Nikko National Park ⊥ J 152-153 H 6
Nikoemvon o CAM 210-211 C 2
Nikolaev = Mykolajiv o UA 102-103 G 4
Nikolaevka o KA 124-125 L 1
Nikolaevo o RUS 94-95 L 2
Nikolaevsk o RUS 96-97 H 6
Nikolaevsk-na-Amure ☆ • RUS
  122-123 J 2
Nikolaja, mys ▲ RUS 108-109 F 4
Nikolaja, zaliv ≈ RUS 108-109 F 4
Nikolka, gora ▲ RUS 120-121 T 6
Nikolo-L'vovskoe o RUS 122-123 D 7
Nikol'sk o RUS 96-97 D 6
Nikol'sk o RUS (PNZ) 96-97 H 5
Nikol'skij = Satpaev ☆ KA 124-125 L 4
Nikol'skoe o RUS (AST) 96-97 E 10
Nikol'skoe o RUS 122-213 C 5
Nikonga ~ EAT 212-213 C 5
Nikopol o BG 102-103 D 6
Nikopol o UA 102-103 J 4
Nikopolis ~ GR 100-101 H 5
Nikšahr o IR 134-135 J 5
Nikšahr, Rūdhāne-ye ~ IR 134-135 J 5
Niksar ☆ • TR 128-129 G 2
Nikšić o YU 100-101 G 3
Nil, an- ~ ET 194-195 E 3
Nila o RI 168 E 7
Nila, Pulau ⌐ RI 166-167 E 5
Nilahué, Estrecho de ≈ RCH 78-79 D 3
Nilakkottai o IND 140-141 G 5
Niland o USA 40-41 G 9
Nilanga o IND 138-139 F 10
Nile □ EAU 212-213 C 2
Nile = an-Nil ~ ET 194-195 E 3
Nile = Nil, an- ~ SUD 194-195 E 3
Niles o USA 46-47 G 8
Nilgvsy ~ RUS 122-123 L 3
Nilka o VRC 146-147 K 4
Nilkötal, Kötal-e ▲ AFG 134-135 M 1
Nilópolis o BR 72-73 J 7
Nilsiä o FIN 88-89 K 5
Nilt o PK 138-139 E 1
Nimach o IND 138-139 E 7
Niman ~ RUS 122-123 E 3
Nimar o IND 138-139 E 9
Nimba □ RG 202-203 F 6
Nimbahera o IND 138-139 E 7
Nimba Range ~ LB 202-203 F 6
Nimbin o AUS 178-179 M 5
Nimbotong o RI 166-167 L 3
Nimburg = Nymburk o • CZ 92-93 N 3
Nimbyan o VRC 150-151 G 5
Nimdé ~ RUS 116-117 E 3
Nimelen ~ RUS 122-123 G 2
Nîmes ☆ • F 90-91 K 10
Nimi ~ RUS 120-121 F 6
Nimingdé ~ RUS 110-111 Q 6
Nimiuktuk River ~ USA 20-21 L 2
Nimjat o RIM 196-197 C 6
Nimmitabel o AUS 180-181 K 4
Nimrōz □ AFG 134-135 K 3
Nimrūd ∴ •• IRQ 128-129 J 4
Nimule o SUD 212-213 D 2
Nimūn, Punta ▲ MEX 52-53 J 1
Nina o NAM 216-217 F 8
Nina, Île = Aniwa Island ⌐ VAN
  184 II b 4
Ninā, Wādi ~ LAR 192-193 F 3
Nina Bang Lake o CDN 24-25 g 5
Ninami-Daitō-shima ⌐ J 152-153 D 12
Ninawā o IRQ 128-129 J 4
Ninawā ✶ IRQ 128-129 K 4
Ninda o ANG 216-217 F 7
Nindigully o AUS 178-179 K 5
Nine Degree Channel ≈ 140-141 D 5
Ninette o CDN 34-35 G 6
Ninetyast Ridge ≃ 12 G 7
Ninety Mile Beach o AUS 180-181 J 5
Ninety Six National Historic Site ∴ • USA
  48-49 G 2
Ninfas, Punta ▲ RA 78-79 G 7
Ningaloo o VRC 172-173 A 7
Ning'an o VRC 150-151 G 3
Ningbi o VRC 156-157 C 3
Ningan o RMM 202-203 J 2
Ningbo • VRC 156-157 M 6
Ningcheng o VRC 148-149 O 7
Ningdu o VRC 156-157 J 5
Ninggu o VRC 156-157 J 3
Ningeehak o USA 20-21 N 5
Ningera o PNG 183 A 3

Ningerum o PNG 183 A 3
Ningguo o VRC 156-157 L 6
Ninghai o VRC 156-157 M 2
Ninghe o VRC 154-155 K 2
Ninghua o VRC 156-157 J 5
Ningi o WAN 204-205 H 3
Ningjin o VRC 154-155 J 5
Ningming o VRC 156-157 E 5
Ningqiang o VRC 154-155 E 5
Ningshan o VRC 154-155 F 5
Ningwu o VRC 154-155 H 4
Ning Xian o VRC (GAN) 154-155 E 4
Ning Xian o VRC (SXI) 154-155 F 4
Ningxiang o VRC 156-157 H 2
Ninh Binh ☆ VN 156-157 D 6
Ninh Hòa o VN 158-159 K 4
Ninh So'n o VN 158-159 K 5
Ninia o RI 166-167 K 4
Ninilchik o USA 20-21 T 4
Nizi o ZRE 212-213 C 3
Nizina Sępolska o PL 92-93 O 1
Nizip o TR 128-129 G 4
Nízke Tatry ▲ SK 92-93 P 4
Nizki Island ⌐ USA 22-23 D 6
Nizkij, mys ▲ RUS (CUK) 112-113 U 4
Nizkij, mys ▲ RUS (KOR) 112-113 R 6
Niž'ma ~ RUS 88-89 T 4
Nižneangarsk o RUS 118-119 G 6
Nižnefouin o RUS 116-117 J 6
Nioghalvfjerdsfjorden ⊂ GRØ 26-27 o 4
Niokolo-Koba o SN 202-203 D 3
Niokolo-Koba, Parc National du ⊥ • •• SN
  202-203 D 3
Niono o RMM 202-203 G 2
Nionsamoridu o RG 202-203 F 5
Niorenge, Rio ~ MOC 218-219 J 1
Nioro du Rip o SN 202-203 C 3
Nioro du Sahel o RMM 202-203 F 2
Niort o • F 90-91 G 8
Niōut o RIM 196-197 G 6
Nipa o PNG 183 B 4
Nipáni o IND 140-141 F 2
Nipanipa, Tanjung ▲ RI 164-165 H 5
Nipawin o CDN 34-35 D 4
Nipawin Provincial Park ⊥ CDN
  34-35 D 4
Nipe, Bahía de ≈ 54-55 H 4
Nipekamev River ~ CDN 34-35 D 3
Nipele ~ NAM 216-217 D 9
Niphad o IND 138-139 E 9
Nipigon o CDN 34-35 N 6
Nipigon, Lake o CDN 34-35 M 6
Nipigon River ~ CDN 34-35 N 6
Nipin River ~ CDN 32-33 Q 4
Nipisi ~ CDN 32-33 N 4
Nipishish Lake o CDN 36-37 T 7
Nipissing, Lake o CDN 38-39 E 5
Nipissing River ~ CDN 38-39 E 6
Nipton o USA 40-41 G 8
Niquelândia o BR 72-73 G 3
Nir o IR (AZS) 128-129 M 3
Nir o IR (YAZ) 134-135 F 3
Nira o IND 138-139 E 10
Ñire-Có o RA 78-79 E 6
Ñireguao o RCH 80 E 2
Nirgua o YV 60-61 G 2
Nirmal o IND 138-139 G 10
Nirmali o IND 138-139 N 5
Nirmoar, Pulau o RI 166-167 K 2
Niš ☆ AFG 134-135 J 3
Niš o YU 100-101 H 3
Nisa o P 98-99 D 5
Nisāb o KSA 130-131 J 3
Nisāb o Y 132-133 E 6
Nišan o S 136-137 J 5
Niseko Shakotan Otaru-kaigan Quasi
  National Park ⊥ J 152-153 J 3
Nishi o VRC 156-157 G 2
Nishibetsu-gawa ~ J 152-153 L 3
Nishi-Chugoku-sanchi Quasi National Park
  ⊥ J 152-153 D 7
Nishi-no-Omote o J 152-153 D 9
Nishino-shima ⌐ J 152-153 K 2
Nishi-Okoppe o J 152-153 K 2
Nishi-suidō ≈ 152-153 C 7
Nisibishu River ~ CAN 42-43 K 5
Nisika River ~ CDN 34-35 M 2
Nisko o PL 92-93 R 3
Nisling River ~ CDN 20-21 V 5
Nissan ~ S 86-87 F 8
Nisséko o BF 202-203 J 4
Nisser o N 86-87 D 7
Nissiros o GR 100-101 L 6
Nissum Bredning ≈ 86-87 D 8
Nistru o MD 102-103 F 4
Nistru ~ MD 102-103 G 4
Ništún o Y 132-133 H 6
Nisutlin Plateau ~ CDN 20-21 Z 6
Nisutlin River ~ CDN 20-21 Y 6
Nita Downs o AUS 172-173 G 5
Nitchequon o CDN 38-39 J 4
Niterói o BR 72-73 J 7
Nith ~ GB 90-91 F 4
Nitija, gora ▲ RUS 120-121 G 4
Nitinat o CDN 32-33 H 7
Niti Pass ▲ VRC 144-145 B 5
Nitmiluk (Katherine Gorge) National Park
  ⊥ AUS 172-173 L 3
Nitra o SK 92-93 P 4
Nitro o USA 46-47 H 6
Nituj ~ RUS 122-123 K 2
Niu' Aunofo Point ▲ TON 184 IV a 2
Niuchang o VRC 156-157 D 3
Niut, Gunung ▲ RI 162-163 H 4
Niutoushan o VRC 154-155 L 6
Niuwudu, Tanjung ▲ RI 168 E 8
Nivala o FIN 88-89 H 5
Niváno o PK 134-135 K 5
Nive River ~ AUS 178-179 J 3
Niviarsiat ▲ GRØ 28-29 T 6

Nivšera o RUS 88-89 W 5
Niwai o IND 138-139 E 6
Niwelin Lake o CDN 30-31 G 2
Nixon o USA 40-41 E 6
Niyrakpak Lagoon ≈ 20-21 E 5
Nizāmábād o IND 138-139 G 10
Nizām Ságar o IND 138-139 F 10
Nizgan, Rūd-e ~ AFG 134-135 L 2
Nižhnekamsk = Nižnekamsk ☆ RUS
  96-97 G 6
Nižhnevartovsk = Nižnevartovsk ☆ RUS
  114-115 O 6
Nižhniy Novgorod = Nižnij Novgorod ☆ ••
  RUS 94-95 S 3
Nižhniy Tagil = Nižnij Tagil ☆ RUS
  96-97 L 5
Nižhnyaya Tunguska = Nižnjaja Tungunska
  ~ RUS 116-117 D 3
Nizina Sępolska o PL 92-93 Q 1
Nizip o TR 128-129 G 4
Nízke Tatry ▲ SK 92-93 P 4
Nizki Island ⌐ USA 22-23 D 6
Nizkij, mys ▲ RUS (CUK) 112-113 U 4
Nizkij, mys ▲ RUS (KOR) 112-113 R 6
Niž'ma ~ RUS 88-89 T 4
Nižneangarsk o RUS 118-119 G 6
Nižnejansk o RUS 110-111 V 4
Nižnekamsk ☆ RUS 96-97 G 6
Nižnekamskoe vodohranilišče < RUS
  96-97 H 6
Nižnekolymsk o RUS 112-113 L 2
Nižnetambovskoe o RUS 122-123 H 3
Nižnevartovsk o RUS 114-115 O 4
Nižnie Sergi o RUS 96-97 L 6
Nižnij Bestjah o RUS 118-119 O 5
Nižnij Časučej o RUS 118-119 G 10
Nižnij Dvojnik ~ RUS 88-89 W 4
Nižnij Imbak o RUS 116-117 H 5
Nižnij Ingaš o RUS 116-117 H 7
Nižnij Lomov o RUS 94-95 S 5
Nižnij Novgorod ☆ •• RUS 94-95 S 3
Nižnij Odes o RUS 88-89 X 5
Nižnij Suzun o RUS 124-125 N 1
Nižnij Viljujkan o RUS 116-117 L 5
Nižnjaja ~ RUS 108-109 T 5
Nižnjaja Agapa ~ RUS 108-109 W 6
Nižnjaja Baiha ~ RUS 114-115 T 5
Nižnjaja Buotankaga ~ RUS
  108-109 W 5
Nižnjaja Cipa ~ RUS 118-119 F 8
Nižnjaja Čunku ~ RUS 116-117 H 4
Nižnjaja Kočoma ~ RUS 116-117 N 4
Nižnjaja Larba ~ RUS 118-119 L 8
Nižnjaja Peša o RUS 88-89 T 3
Nižnjaja Pojma o RUS 116-117 H 6
Nižnjaja Suetka o RUS 124-125 L 2
Nižnjaja Tajmyra ~ RUS 108-109 c 4
Nižnjaja Talovaja o RUS 108-109 X 6
Nižnjaja Tavda o RUS 114-115 K 5
Nižnjaja Tunguska ~ RUS 114-115 U 2
Nižnjaja Tunguska ~ RUS 116-117 H 8
Nižnjaja Tunguska ~ RUS 116-117 N 7
Nižnjaja Tunguska ~ RUS 116-117 H 4
Nižnjaja Tura o RUS 96-97 L 4
Nižyn o UA 102-103 G 2
Nizzana □ IL 130-131 D 2
Njadajaha ~ RUS 108-109 T 7
Njadajama, ozero o RUS 108-109 X 5
Njagan' o RUS 114-115 J 5
Njaiama-Sewafe o WAL 202-203 E 5
Njajs o RUS 114-115 F 3
Njakšìngda, ozero o RUS 116-117 F 2
Njalinskoe o RUS 114-115 K 4
Njamakit, gora ▲ RUS 108-109 f 6
Njandoma o RUS 88-89 Q 6
Njangus'jaha ~ RUS 108-109 T 7
Njanja, gora ▲ RUS 110-111 V 5
Njardvík o IS 86-87 b 3
Njarga ~ RUS 114-115 M 3
Njasviž ☆ BY 94-95 K 5
Njatlongajagun ~ RUS 114-115 M 3
Njau o WAG 202-203 C 3
Njazepetrovsk o RUS 96-97 L 5
Njenje o EAT 214-215 G 5
Njiapanda o EAT (MBE) 214-215 G 5
Njinjo o EAT 214-215 N 5
Njoko ~ Z 218-219 C 3
Njombe o EAT (IRI) 214-215 H 5
Njombe o EAT 214-215 H 4
Njoro o EAK 212-213 E 4
Njuhča o RUS (ARH) 88-89 T 5
Njuhča o RUS 88-89 O 9
Njuja o RUS 118-119 O 6
Njuja ~ RUS 118-119 N 6
Njuja ~ RUS 118-119 O 6
Njuja ~ RUS 118-119 O 6
Njuk, ozero o RUS 88-89 M 5
Njukčorok o RUS 116-117 L 3
Njukža o RUS 118-119 L 8
Njukža ~ RUS 118-119 L 8
Njuksa, Ust'- o RUS 118-119 K 7
Njun'karakutari ~ RUS 108-109 f 4
Njunjaju ▲ RUS 108-109 J 4
Njurba o RUS 118-119 M 5
Njuroľka ~ RUS 114-115 O 5
Nkalagu o WAN 204-205 G 5
Nkam ~ CAM 204-205 J 6
Nkamba Lodge o Z 214-215 F 5
Nkaw o CAM 210-211 D 1
Nkawie o GH 202-203 K 6
Nkayi o RCB 210-211 D 6
Nkayi o ZW 218-219 D 4
Nkeni ~ RCB 210-211 E 4
Nkhilé < RIM 196-197 G 4
Nkhotakota o MW 214-215 H 6
Nkhotakota Game Reserve ⊥ MW
  214-215 G 7
Nkoambang o CAM 204-205 K 6
Nkolabona o G 210-211 C 3

Nkole ○ Z 214-215 F 6
Nkolmengboua ○ G 210-211 C 2
Nkomfap ○ WAN 204-205 H 5
Nkomi ○ G 210-211 B 4
Nkomi, Lagune = Fernan Vaz ○ G 210-211 B 4
Nkondwe ○ EAT 212-213 D 6
Nkongjok ○ CAM 204-205 J 6
Nkongsamba ○ CAM 204-205 H 5
Nkon Ngok ○ CAM 204-205 J 6
Nkoranza ○ GH 202-203 H 6
Nkoteng ○ CAM 204-205 K 6
Nkoué ○ RCB 210-211 E 5
Nkourala ○ RMM 202-203 G 4
Nkula Falls ○ MW 218-219 H 2
Nkuku, Malemba- ○ ZRE 214-215 D 5
Nkundi ○ EAT 214-215 F 4
Nkurenkuru ○ NAM 216-217 E 8
Nkuruman Escarpment ▲ EAK 212-213 F 5
Nkwalini ○ ZA 220-221 H 5
Nkwanta ○ GH (VTA) 202-203 L 5
Nkwanta ○ GH (WTN) 202-203 J 7
Nkwanta, Atasi ○ GH 202-203 K 7
Nkwanta, Manso- ○ GH 202-203 K 6
Nmai Hka ~ MYA 142-143 L 2
n-Natrûn, Wâdi ~ ET 194-195 E 2
Nnewi ○ WAN 204-205 G 5
No.1, Canal < RA 78-79 L 4
No.2, Canal < RA 78-79 L 4
No.5, Canal < RA 78-79 L 4
No.9, Canal < RA 78-79 L 4
No.11, Canal < RA 78-79 K 4
No.12, Canal < RA 78-79 K 4
No.16, Canal < RA 78-79 K 3
Noabanki ○ BD 142-143 F 4
Noakhali ○ BD 142-143 G 4
Noanama ○ CO 60-61 C 5
Noatak ○ USA 20-21 J 3
Noatak National Preserve ⊥ USA 20-21 K 2
Noatak River ~ USA 20-21 M 3
Nobeoka ○ J 152-153 D 8
Nobéré ○ BF 202-203 K 7
Nobles Nob Mine • AUS 174-175 C 6
Noble's Trail Monument ∴ USA 42-43 H 3
Nobokwe ○ ZA 220-221 H 5
Noboribetsu ○ J 152-153 J 3
Nobres ○ BR 70-71 J 4
Nocina ○ E 98-99 F 3
Nockatunga ○ AUS 178-179 G 4
Nocuchich ∴ MEX 52-53 K 2
Noda ○ J 152-153 J 4
Nodaway River ~ USA 42-43 K 5
Noe ○ CI 202-203 J 7
Noefs, Île des ~ SY 224 C 3
Noel ○ CDN 38-39 N 6
Noell Lake ○ CDN 20-21 Y 2
Noenieput ○ ZA 220-221 E 3
Noépé ○ RT 202-203 L 6
Noetinger ○ RA 78-79 H 7
Nogajskaja step ~ RUS 126-127 F 5
Nogales ○ MEX (CHA) 50-51 E 2
Nogales ○ MEX (VER) 52-53 F 2
Nogales ○ • MEX (SON) 50-51 D 2
Nogales ○ RCH 78-79 D 2
Nogales ○ USA 44-45 B 4
Nogamut ○ USA 20-21 M 6
Nogara ○ ETH 200-201 H 6
Nógata ○ J 152-153 D 8
Nogent-le-Rotrou ○ F 90-91 H 7
Nogent-sur-Seine ○ F 90-91 J 7
Noginsk ○ RUS 94-95 Q 4
Nogiri Point ▲ SOL 184 I c 2
Nogliki ☆ RUS 122-123 K 3
Nogoyá ○ RA 78-79 K 2
Nogoyá, Arroyo ~ RA 78-79 K 2
Noguira, Riacho ~ RA 76-77 G 4
Nohar ○ IND 138-139 E 5
Noheji ○ J 152-153 J 4
Nohonč, Kühe ▲ IR 134-135 J 5
Noia ○ E 98-99 C 3
Noice Peninsula ↵ CDN 24-25 T 1
Noire, Rivière ~ CDN 38-39 F 5
Noires, Montagnes ▲▲ RH 54-55 J 4
Noirmoutier, Île de ~ F 90-91 F 8
Noirmoutier-en-l'Île ○ F 90-91 F 8
Nojabr'sk ○ RUS 114-115 N 3
Nojack ○ CDN 32-33 N 5
Nojima-saki ▲ J 152-153 J 4
Nokaneng ○ RB 218-219 E 4
Nokha ○ IND 138-139 D 6
Nokia ○ FIN 88-89 G 6
Nokomis ○ CDN 34-35 D 5
Nokou ○ TCH 198-199 G 5
Nokoué, Lac ○ DY 204-205 E 5
Nokuku ○ VAN 184 II a 2
Nola ○ I 100-101 E 4
Nola ☆ RCA 210-211 F 2
Nol'de guba ○ RUS 112-113 R 1
Noling ○ RI 164-165 G 5
Nolinsk ☆ RUS 96-97 G 5
Noll ○ ZA 220-221 G 6
Nom ○ VRC 146-147 M 4
Nomad River ~ PNG 183 B 4
Noma misaki ▲ J 152-153 D 9
Nomane ○ PNG 183 C 4
Nomansland Point ▲ CDN 34-35 Q 4
Nombre de Dios ○ MEX 50-51 G 6
Nombre de Dios, Cordillera ▲▲ HN 52-53 L 4
Nome ○ USA 20-21 H 4
Nome, Cape ▲ USA 20-21 H 4
Nome-Council-Highway II USA 20-21 H 4
Nome-Taylor-Highway II USA 20-21 H 4
Nomhon ○ VRC 144-145 L 2
Nomtsas ○ NAM 220-221 D 2
Nomuka ○ TON 184 IV a 2
Nomuka Group ~ TON 184 IV a 2
Nona, La ○ MEX 50-51 F 4
Nonacho Lake ○ CDN 30-31 P 5
Nonagama ○ CL 140-141 J 7
Non Champa ○ THA 158-159 G 2
Nondalton ○ USA 20-21 N 6
Nondo ○ Z 214-215 F 5

Nong'an ○ VRC 150-151 E 5
Nong Bua ○ THA 158-159 F 3
Nong Bua Daeng ○ THA 158-159 F 3
Nong Bua Khok ○ THA 158-159 F 3
Nong Bua Lamphu ○ THA 158-159 G 2
Nongchang ○ VRC 154-155 F 3
Nong Khae ○ THA 158-159 F 3
Nong Khai ○ THA 158-159 G 2
Nongoma ○ ZA 220-221 K 3
Nong Phai ○ THA 158-159 F 3
Nong Phok ○ THA 158-159 H 2
Nong Phu ○ THA 158-159 G 2
Nongra Lake ○ AUS 172-173 J 5
Nongsa ○ RI 162-163 F 4
Nonoava ○ MEX 50-51 F 4
Nonogasta ○ RA 78-79 D 5
Non Thai ○ THA 158-159 G 3
Nooleeye ○ SP 208-209 H 6
Noolyeana Lake ○ AUS 178-179 D 4
Noondoonia ○ AUS 176-177 G 6
Noonkanbah ○ AUS 176-177 G 4
Noonthorangee Range ▲▲ AUS 178-179 G 6
Noonyereena Hill ▲ AUS 176-177 G 6
Noordoewer ○ NAM 220-221 D 4
Noordzeekanaal ○ NL 92-93 H 2
Noorvik ○ USA 20-21 K 4
Noosa Heads ○ AUS 178-179 M 4
Nootka Island ~ CDN 32-33 G 7
Nootka Sound ≈ 32-33 G 7
Nopoló ○ MEX 50-51 D 5
Nopoming Provincial Park ⊥ CDN 34-35 J 4
Nóqui ○ ANG 216-217 B 2
Nora ~ RUS 122-123 D 2
Norah ~ ER 200-201 K 4
Norala ○ RP 160-161 F 9
Noranside ○ AUS 178-179 E 2
Norassoba ○ RG 202-203 F 4
Norberg ○ N 86-87 D 6
Norberto de la Riesta ○ RA 78-79 K 3
Norcatur ○ USA 42-43 G 6
Nord, Île du ~ SY 224 C 3
Nord = North ○ CAM 204-205 K 4
Nord, ostrov ~ RUS 108-109 b 3
Nordaustlandet ~ N 84-85 L 3
Nordaust-Svalbard naturreservat ⊥ N 84-85 M 3
Nordbruk, ostrov ~ RUS 84-85 b 3
Nordby ○ DK 86-87 E 9
Nordegg ○ CDN 32-33 M 5
Nordegg River ~ CDN 32-33 N 5
Norden ○ D 92-93 J 2
Nordenšelfa, arhipelag ~ RUS 108-109 Z 3
Nordenšelfa, zaliv ○ RUS 108-109 G 4
Nordenskiöld Islands ~ CDN 24-25 W 6
Nordenskiöld Land ~ N 84-85 J 4
Nordenskiölda River ~ CDN 20-21 W 6
Nordenskiölds Gletscher ⊂ GRØ 28-29 P 2
Nordenskjöld Fjord ≈ 26-27 b 2
Nordgrønland = Avannaarsua ○ GRØ 26-27 V 4
Norderney ○ D 92-93 J 2
Norderstedt ○ D 92-93 K 2
Nordeste ○ ANG 216-217 F 3
Nordfjordeid ○ N 86-87 B 6
Nordfjorden ○ N 84-85 J 3
Nordfold ○ N 86-87 F 4
Nordfriesische Inseln ~ D 92-93 K 1
Nordgrønland = Avannaarsua ○ GRØ 26-27 V 4
Nordhausen ○ D 92-93 L 3
Nordhorn ○ D 92-93 J 2
Nordkapp ▲ N 26-27 w 8
Nordkapp ▲ SVA 84-85 L 2
Nordkapp ▲ • N (FIN) 86-87 M 1
Nordkinnhalvøya ~ N 86-87 N 1
Nordkvaløy ~ N 86-87 J 1
Nordli ○ N 86-87 F 4
Nördlingen ○ D 92-93 L 4
Nordmaling ○ S 86-87 J 5
Nordman ○ USA 40-41 J 1
Nordostrundingen ▲ GRØ 26-27 t 3
Nord-Ostsee-Kanal < D 92-93 K 1
Nord-Ouest = North-West ○ CAM 204-205 J 5
Nord-Pas-de-Calais ○ F 90-91 J 6
Nordre Isortoq ○ GRØ 28-29 O 3
Nordre Strømfjord ○ GRØ 28-29 O 3
Nordrhein-Westfalen ○ D 92-93 J 3
Nordvestfjord ≈ 26-27 m 8
Nordvestinskij, aral ○ KA 96-97 G 10
Nordvik ○ RUS 110-111 H 3
Nordvik, buhta ≈ 110-111 H 3
Norembega ○ CDN 34-35 Q 6
Norheim ○ D 92-93 K 3
Norfolk ○ EAU 212-213 C 2
Norfolk ○ USA (VA) 46-47 J 4
Norfolk, Mount ▲ AUS 180-181 H 6
Norfolk Island ○ AUS 13 H 5
Norfolk Lake ○ USA 44-45 L 1
Norfolk Ridge ≃ 182 B 1
Nor Harberd ○ AR 128-129 L 2
Norias ○ MEX 50-51 H 5
Norikla ~ RUS 108-109 X 7
Norilsk ○ RUS 108-109 X 7
Noring, Gunnung ▲ MAL 162-163 D 2
Noring, Gunnung ▲ MAL 162-163 D 2
Norlina ○ USA 48-49 J 1
Normal ○ USA 44-45 J 2
Norman ○ USA 44-45 J 2
Norman, Lake < USA 48-49 F 7
Normanby Island ~ PNG 183 F 5
Normandia ○ BR 62-63 G 4
Normandie = F 90-91 G 7
Normandin ○ CDN 38-39 H 4
Norman Range ▲▲ CDN 30-31 F 3
Norman's Cay ~ BS 54-55 H 2
Normanton ○ AUS 174-175 F 4
Normanville ○ AUS 180-181 E 5
Normán Wells ○ CDN 30-31 G 4

Normétal ○ CDN 38-39 E 4
Norma, Mount ▲ AUS 174-175 F 7
Norquay ○ CDN 34-35 E 5
Norquinco ○ RA 78-79 D 6
Norråker ○ S 86-87 G 4
Norra Ny ○ S 86-87 F 6
Norra Storfjället ▲▲ S 86-87 G 4
Norris Lake ○ USA 48-49 G 1
Norris Point ○ CDN 38-39 Q 4
Norristown ○ USA 46-47 L 5
Norrköping ☆ • S 86-87 H 7
Norrtälje ○ S 86-87 J 7
Norseman ○ AUS 176-177 F 6
Norsjø ○ N 86-87 D 7
Norsk ○ RUS 122-123 C 2
Norskebanken ≃ 84-85 H 2
Norskehavet ≈ 86-87 E 3
Norske Øer ~ GRØ 26-27 r 4
Norsup ○ VAN 184 II a 3
Norte, Cabo ▲ EC 64-65 C 10
Norte, Cabo do ▲ BR 62-63 K 5
Norte, Canal do ≈ BR 62-63 J 5
Norte, Cayo ~ MEX 52-53 L 2
Norte, Cerro ▲ RA 80 D 4
Norte, Ponta ▲ CV 202-203 C 5
Norte, Punta ▲ MEX 50-51 E 5
Norte, Punta ▲ RA 78-79 H 7
Norte, Serra do ▲ BR 70-71 H 2
Norte de Chiapas, Montañe del ▲ MEX 52-53 H 3
Norte del Cabo San Antonio, Punta ▲ RA 78-79 L 4
Nortelândia ○ BR 70-71 J 4
North ○ USA 48-49 H 3
North, Cape ▲ CDN 38-39 O 5
North = Nord ○ CAM 204-205 K 4
North Adams ○ USA 46-47 M 4
Northam ○ AUS 176-177 D 6
Northam ○ ZA 220-221 H 2
Northampton ○ AUS 176-177 C 4
Northampton ☆ GB 90-91 G 5
Northampton ○ USA 46-47 M 4
North Andaman ~ IND 140-141 L 3
North Arm ~ 24-25 j 5
North Arm ○ CDN 30-31 M 4
North Arm ○ GB 78-79 J 8
North Atlantic Ocean ≈ 6-7 D 6
North Augusta ○ USA 48-49 H 3
North Aulatsivik Island ~ CDN 36-37 S 5
North Australia Basin ≃ 13 C 4
North Balabac Strait ≈ 160-161 B 8
North Banda Basin ≃ 166-167 B 3
North Bannister ○ AUS 176-177 D 6
North Battleford ○ CDN 32-33 Q 5
North Bay ○ S 36-37 P 3
North Bay ~ 140-141 L 5
North Bay ○ CDN (ONT) 38-39 E 5
North Bay ○ CDN (NWT) 36-37 O 2
North Belcher Islands ~ CDN 36-37 K 6
North Bend ○ USA (NE) 42-43 J 5
North Bend ○ USA (OR) 40-41 B 4
North Bimini ~ BS 54-55 F 2
North Bluff ▲ USA 36-37 O 3
North Branch < PK 138-139 D 3
North Branch ○ USA 42-43 L 3
North Caicos ~ GB 54-55 K 4
North Canadian River ~ USA 44-45 H 2
North Cape ▲ CDN 38-39 N 5
North Cape ▲ NZ 182 D 1
North Cape ▲ PNG 183 D 1
North-Cape Province ○ ZA 220-221 D 4
North Caribou Lake ○ CDN 34-35 J 4
North Carolina ○ USA 48-49 G 2
North Cascades National Park ⊥ • USA 40-41 D 1
North Channel ≈ 90-91 E 4
North Channel ○ CDN 38-39 D 5
North Charleston ○ USA 48-49 J 3
North China Plain = Huabei ↵ VRC 154-155 J 3
North Creek ○ USA 178-179 C 5
North Dakota ○ USA 42-43 F 2
North East ○ RB 218-219 D 6
North East ○ USA 46-47 J 4
Northeast Cape ▲ USA 20-21 F 5
Northeast Coast National Scenic Area ⊥ RC 156-157 H 4
North Eastern ○ EAK 212-213 G 3
Northeast Point ~ BS 54-55 J 4
Northeast Point ~ BS 54-55 H 2
Northeast Point ~ BS 54-55 J 3
Northeast Point ○ CDN (NFL) 38-39 R 2
Northeast Point ○ CDN (NWT) 24-25 Z 2
Northeast Point ○ USA 22-23 L 4
Northeast Providence Channel ≈ 54-55 G 2
Northeim ○ D 92-93 K 3
Northern ○ EAU 212-213 C 2
Northern ○ MW 214-215 H 6
Northern ○ Z 214-215 F 6
Northern Cay ~ BZ 52-53 L 3
Northern Cheyenne Indian Reservation X USA 42-43 D 3
Northern Frontier ○ KSA 130-131 H 3
Northern Indian Lake ○ CDN 34-35 H 2
Northern Lau Group ~ FJI 184 III c 2
Northern Light Lake ○ CDN 34-35 L 6
Northern Mariana Islands = Mariana Islands ~ USA 160-161 K 5
Northern Perimeter Highway = Rodovia Perimetral Norte II BR 62-63 F 5
Northern Region ○ GH 202-203 K 5
Northern Region ○ SUD 200-201 B 5
Northern Salwati Pulau Reserve ⊥ • RI 166-167 F 2
Northern Territory ○ AUS 174-175 B 4
Northern Yukon National Park ⊥ CDN 20-21 W 2
Northfield ○ USA 42-43 L 3
North Fiji Basin ≃ 13 J 4
North Fork Chandalar ~ USA 20-21 O 3
North Fork Clearwater River ~ USA 40-41 J 2
North Fork Holston River ~ USA 46-47 G 5

North Fork John Day River ~ USA 40-41 E 3
North Fork Kuskokwim ~ USA 20-21 N 5
North Fork Pavette River ~ USA 40-41 H 3
North Fork Red River ~ USA 44-45 G 2
North Fork Solomon River ~ USA 42-43 G 6
North French River ~ CDN 34-35 Q 5
North Frisian Islands = Nordfriesische Inseln ~ D 92-93 J 1
Northgate ○ CDN 34-35 E 6
North Head ▲ AUS 176-177 C 5
North Head ○ CDN (NB) 38-39 L 6
North Head ○ CDN (NFL) 38-39 Q 4
North Head ▲ NZ 182 E 2
North Heart River ~ CDN 32-33 M 3
North Henik Lake ○ CDN 30-31 V 5
Northhome ○ USA 42-43 K 2
North Horr ○ EAK 212-213 F 2
North Island ~ AUS (NT) 174-175 D 4
North Island ~ AUS (WA) 176-177 C 4
North Island ~ EAK 212-213 F 1
North Island ~ NZ 182 D 2
North Island ~ USA 48-49 J 3
North Kitui National Reserve ⊥ EAK 212-213 G 4
North Knife Lake ○ CDN 30-31 V 6
North Knife River ~ CDN 30-31 V 6
North Korea = Choson M.I.K. ■ DVR 150-151 G 7
North Lakhimpur ○ IND 142-143 J 2
North Land = Severnaja Zemlja ~ RUS 108-109 c 1
North Limington ○ USA 46-47 N 4
North Lincoln Land ~ CDN 24-25 T 2
North Little Rock ○ USA 44-45 L 2
North Loup River ~ USA 42-43 G 4
North Luangwa National Park ⊥ Z 214-215 G 6
North Luconia Shoals ~ 162-163 K 2
North Magnetic Pole = Magnetic Pole Area ARK 24-25 V 3
North Magnetic Pole Area II CDN 24-25 V 3
North Male Atoll ~ MV 140-141 B 5
North Malosmadulu Atoll ~ MV 140-141 B 5
North Milk River ~ CDN 32-33 O 7
North Minch ≈ 90-91 E 2
North Moose Lake ○ CDN 34-35 F 3
North Nahanni River ~ CDN 30-31 G 4
North Nilandu Atoll ~ MV 140-141 B 6
North Ossetia = Cosgat Irystony Respublikoœ ○ RUS 126-127 F 6
North Palisade ▲ USA 40-41 E 7
North Pangnirtung Fjord ≈ 28-29 H 3
North Peninsula ~ 34-35 M 5
North Peron Island ~ AUS 172-173 K 2
North Platte ○ USA 42-43 G 5
North Platte River ~ USA 42-43 D 4
North Point ▲ USA 46-47 G 3
North Point ▲ WAN 204-205 F 6
North Pole · 16 A 28
North Port ○ USA (MI) 46-47 E 3
Northport ○ USA (WA) 40-41 F 1
North Powder ○ USA 40-41 F 3
North Racoon River ~ USA 42-43 K 4
North Redstone River ~ CDN 30-31 F 4
North Reef = Bei Jiao ~ VRC 158-159 L 2
North Rim ○ USA 40-41 H 7
North River ○ CDN 30-31 W 6
North Santiam River ~ USA 40-41 C 3
North Saskatchewan River ~ CDN 32-33 R 5
North Scotia Ridge ≃ 6-7 E 14
North Sea ≈ 90-91 D 3
North Seal River ~ CDN 30-31 T 6
North Sentinel Island ~ IND 140-141 L 4
North Siberian Lowland = Severo-Sibirskaja nizmennost' ↵ RUS 108-109 W 5
North Slope ~ USA 20-21 K 2
North Solitary Island ~ AUS 178-179 M 5
North Spicer Island ~ CDN 24-25 h 6
North Star ○ USA 178-179 L 5
North Star ○ CDN 32-33 M 3
North Stradbroke Island ~ AUS 178-179 M 4
North Sydney ○ CDN 38-39 O 5
North Thompson River ~ CDN 32-33 K 6
North Truchas Peak ▲ USA 44-45 E 2
North Tweedsmuir Island ~ CDN 28-29 C 2
North Twin Island ~ CDN 34-35 Q 4
North Twin Lake ○ CDN 38-39 Q 4
North Uist ~ GB 90-91 D 3
Northumberland Isles ~ AUS 178-179 K 1
Northumberland National Park ⊥ GB 90-91 F 4
Northumberland Ø ~ GRØ 26-27 O 5
Northumberland Strait ≈ 38-39 M 5
North Umpqua River ~ USA 40-41 C 4
North Vancouver ○ CDN 32-33 J 7
North Washagami Lake ○ CDN 34-35 O 3
North-West = Nord-Ouest ○ CAM 204-205 J 5
Northwest Angle Forest Reserve ⊥ CDN 34-35 J 6
North West Basin ~ AUS 176-177 C 3
Northwest Cape ▲ AUS 172-173 B 6
Northwest Cape ▲ USA 20-21 G 5
North West Coastal Highway II AUS 176-177 C 3
North Western ○ Z 218-219 C 1
Northwest Feeder < CDN 38-39 Q 4
North West Frontier Province ○ PK 138-139 D 2

Northwest Gander River ~ CDN 38-39 I R 4
Northwest Highlands ▲▲ GB 90-91 E 3
North West Island ~ AUS 178-179 L 2
Northwest Pacific Basin ≃ 14-15 G 4
Northwest Providence Channel ≈ 54-55 F 1
North-West Province ○ ZA 220-221 G 2
North West River ○ CDN 38-39 O 2
Northwest Territories ○ CDN 30-31 O 2
North Wilkesboro ○ USA 48-49 H 1
North Wind Lake ○ CDN 34-35 N 6
Northwood ○ USA 42-43 L 4
North York Moors National Park ⊥ GB 90-91 G 4
Norton ○ USA (KS) 42-43 H 6
Norton ○ USA (VA) 46-47 G 4
Norton ○ ZW 218-219 F 3
Norton, Cape ▲ CDN 24-25 Y 6
Norton Shaw, Cape ▲ CDN 24-25 g 2
Norton Sound ≈ 20-21 H 5
Nortonville ○ USA (KY) 46-47 M 5
Nortonville ○ USA (ND) 42-43 H 2
Norutak Lake ○ USA 20-21 N 3
Norwalk ○ USA (KY) 46-47 M 5
Norwalk ○ USA (IA) 42-43 L 5
Norwalk ○ USA (OH) 46-47 G 5
Norway = Norge ■ N 86-87 D 7
Norway House ○ CDN 34-35 H 3
Norway, Kapp ▲ ARK 16 F 35
Norwegian Basin ≃ 6-7 J 2
Norwegian Bay ≈ 24-25 Z 2
Norwegian Sea ≈ 8 C 1
Norwegian Trench = Norskerenna ~ N 86-87 B 7
Norwich ○ • GB 90-91 H 5
Norwich ○ USA (CT) 46-47 M 5
Norwich ○ USA (NY) 46-47 L 4
Norwood ○ USA 42-43 L 3
Nosappu-misaki ▲ J 152-153 L 3
Nosara ○ CR 52-53 B 7
Nose Lake ○ CDN 30-31 P 3
Noshiro ○ J 152-153 H 4
Nosive, Farihy ○ RM 222-223 F 7
Nosivka ○ UA 94-95 L 4
Nosok ○ RUS 108-109 X 5
Nosop ~ RB 220-221 F 2
Noşratâbâd ○ IR 134-135 J 4
Nossa Senhora das Dores ○ BR 68-69 K 7
Nossa Senhora do Livramento ○ BR 70-71 J 4
Nossa Senhora do Socorro ○ BR 68-69 K 7
Nossob ~ NAM 220-221 D 1
Nossob Camp ○ ZA 220-221 E 2
Nossombougou ○ RMM 202-203 G 3
Nosy Varika ○ RM 222-223 F 8
Notakwanon River ~ CDN 36-37 S 7
Noté ○ PL 92-93 N 2
Nothaburi ○ THA 158-159 F 4
Nothern Biak Reserve ⊥ RI 166-167 J 2
Notintsila ○ ZA 220-221 J 5
Nótio Egéo ○ GR 100-101 L 6
Noto ○ I 100-101 E 7
Notocote ○ MOC 218-219 K 3
Notodden ☆ N 86-87 D 7
Noto-hantō ↵ J 152-153 F 6
Noto-shima ~ J 152-153 F 6
Notre-Dame, Monts ▲▲ CDN 38-39 J 6
Notre Dame Bay ≈ 38-39 R 4
Notre-Dame-du-Laus ○ CDN 38-39 G 5
Notre-Dame-du-Nord ○ CDN 38-39 E 5
Notre Dame Junction ○ CDN 38-39 R 4
Notsé ○ RT 202-203 L 6
Nottawasaga Bay ≈ 38-39 D 6
Nottaway, Rivière ~ CDN 38-39 F 4
Nottingham ☆ • GB 90-91 G 5
Nottingham Downs ○ AUS 178-179 G 1
Nottingham Island ~ CDN 36-37 K 3
Nottingham Road ○ ZA 220-221 J 4
Nottoway River ~ USA 46-47 K 7
Notukeu Creek ~ CDN 34-35 C 6
Nouâdhibou ○ RIM 196-197 B 4
Nouâdhibou, Râs ▲ RIM 196-197 B 4
Nouakchott = Nawâkshût ★ • RIM 196-197 C 5
Nouâmghâr ○ RIM 196-197 B 4
Nouazereg ○ RIM 196-197 D 5
Noubandégân ○ IR 134-135 G 4
Noubarân ○ IR 128-129 N 5
Nouhao ~ BF 202-203 K 4
Nouméa ★ F 13 H 5
Noumoukiédougou ○ BF 202-203 H 5
Noun ~ CAM 204-205 J 6
Nouna ○ BF 202-203 J 3
Nouport ○ ZA 220-221 G 5
Nourlangie Rock ∴ AUS 172-173 L 2
Nousâhr ○ IR 128-129 M 5
Nousû ○ IR 128-129 M 6
Nouveau-Québec, Cratère du ▲ CDN 36-37 N 4
Nouvelle ○ CDN 38-39 L 4
Nouvelle-France, Cap de ▲ CDN 36-37 N 3
Nouvelles Hébrides = Vanuatu ~ VAN 184 II a 1
Nouzäd ○ AFG 134-135 L 2
Nova Alegria ○ BR 72-73 L 4
Nova Aliança ○ BR 72-73 L 4
Nova Almada ○ MOC 218-219 H 4
Nova Alvorada ○ BR 76-77 K 1
Nova Andradina ○ BR 72-73 D 7
Nova Aurora ○ BR 72-73 J 7
Nova Brasilândia ○ BR (MAT) 70-71 K 4
Nova Brasilândia ○ BR (RON) 70-71 F 3
Nova Caipemba ○ ANG 216-217 C 3

Nova Canaã do Norte ○ BR 70-71 K 3
Nova Coimbra ○ MOC 214-215 H 7
Nova Cruz ○ BR 68-69 L 5
Nova Esperança ○ ANG 216-217 C 3
Nova Esperança ○ BR 72-73 D 7
Nova Floresta ○ BR 68-69 J 4
Nova Friburgo ○ BR 72-73 K 5
Nova Gaia ○ ANG 216-217 D 5
Nova Golegã ○ MOC 218-219 G 5
Nova Gradiška ○ HR 100-101 F 2
Nova Granada ○ BR 72-73 F 5
Nova Iguaçu ○ BR 72-73 J 7
Nova Independência ○ BR 72-73 E 6
Nova Itaipe ○ BR 72-73 K 2
Novaja ○ RUS 108-109 d 6
Novaja ~ RUS 110-111 G 2
Novaja Igirma ○ RUS 116-117 L 7
Novaja Kahovka = Nova Kachovka ○ UA 102-103 H 4
Novaja Ladoga ○ RUS 94-95 N 1
Novaja Ljalja ○ RUS 114-115 F 5
Novaja Sibir', ostrov ~ RUS 110-111 a 2
Nova Jorque ○ BR 68-69 F 5
Nova Kachovka ○ UA (HER) 102-103 H 4
Novales, Punta ▲ RA 80 G 2
Nova Lima ○ BR 72-73 J 5
Novalukoml' ○ BY 94-95 L 4
Nova Macajuba ○ BR 68-69 J 4
Nova Mambone ○ MOC 218-219 H 5
Nova Módica ○ BR 72-73 K 5
Nova Nabúri ○ MOC 218-219 K 3
Nova Olímpia ○ BR 72-73 D 7
Nova Olinda ○ BR 66-67 J 5
Nova Olinda, Riachão ~ BR 68-69 G 6
Nova Olinda do Norte ○ BR 66-67 H 4
Nova Prata ○ BR 74-75 E 7
Novara ☆ I 100-101 B 2
Nova Resende ○ BR 72-73 G 6
Nova Roma ○ BR 72-73 G 4
Nova Russas ○ BR 68-69 J 7
Nova Santarém ○ MOC 218-219 H 1
Nova Scotia ○ CDN 38-39 M 6
Nova Serrana ○ BR 72-73 H 5
Nova Soure ○ BR 68-69 J 7
Nova Timboteua ○ BR 68-69 E 2
Nova Vandúzi ○ MOC 218-219 G 4
Nova Venécia ○ BR 72-73 K 5
Nova Viçosa ○ BR 72-73 L 4
Nova Vida ○ BR 66-67 C 5
Nova Viseu ○ MOC 214-215 J 7
Nova Vodolaha ○ UA 102-103 J 3
Nova Xavantina ○ BR 72-73 C 3
Novaya Zemlya = Novaja Zemlja ~ RUS 108-109 E 6
Nova Zagora ○ BG 102-103 E 6
Nova Zembla Island ~ CDN 26-27 N 7
Nove de Abril, Cachoeira ~ BR 70-71 G 2
Novembro, Cachoeira 15. de ~ BR 70-71 H 2
Nové Zámky ○ SK 92-93 P 5
Novgorod ○ • • • RUS 94-95 M 2
Novgorodka ○ RUS 94-95 L 3
Novhorodka ○ UA 102-103 H 3
Novi Iskâr ○ BG 102-103 C 6
Novikbož ○ RUS 88-89 Y 3
Novikovo ○ RUS 122-123 K 4
Novillero ○ MEX 50-51 G 6
Noville ○ RUS 122-123 J 6
Novi Pazar ○ BG 102-103 E 6
Novi Pazar ☆ YU 100-101 H 3
Novi Sad ○ • YU 100-101 G 3
Novi Sanžary ○ UA 102-103 J 3
Nóvita ○ CO 60-61 C 5
Novo, Lago ○ BR 62-63 J 5
Novo, Rio ~ BR 66-67 J 5
Novo, Rio ~ BR 68-69 B 4
Novo, Rio ~ BR 70-71 E 2
Novo Acordo ○ BR (P) 68-69 B 3
Novo Acordo ○ BR (TOC) 68-69 E 6
Novo Acre ○ BR 72-73 K 2
Novoagansk ○ RUS 114-115 O 4
Novo Airão ○ BR 66-67 E 6
Novoaleksandrovka ○ RUS 116-117 K 8
Novoaleksandrovsk ○ RUS 102-103 M 5
Novoaleksejevka = Karagandysay ☆ KA 126-127 L 2
Novoaltajsk ☆ RUS 124-125 N 2
Novoanninskij ☆ RUS 102-103 N 2
Novo Areal ○ BR 66-67 E 6
Novočeboksarsk ☆ RUS 96-97 E 5
Novočerkassk ○ • RUS 102-103 M 4
Novočerkasskoe ○ KA 124-125 J 5
Novocheboksarsk = Novočeboksarsk ☆ RUS 96-97 E 5
Novocherkassk = Novočerkassk ○ • RUS 102-103 M 4
Novo Cruzeiro ○ BR 72-73 K 4
Novočuguevka ○ RUS 122-123 E 6
Novodvinsk ○ RUS 88-89 Q 4
Novoe ○ RUS 122-123 E 5
Novoe Mašozero ○ RUS 88-89 M 4
Novofedorivka ○ UA 102-103 H 4
Novograd-Volynskij = Novohrad-Volyns'kyj ○ UA 102-103 E 2
Novohopersk ○ RUS 102-103 M 2
Novo Horizonte ○ BR 72-73 F 6
Novohrad-Volyns'kyj ○ UA 102-103 E 2
Novokačalinsk ○ RUS 122-123 E 5
Novokašpirskij ○ RUS 96-97 F 7
Novokazaly ☆ KA 126-127 P 5
Novokievskij Uval ☆ RUS 122-123 C 3
Novokubansk ○ RUS 102-103 M 5
Novokujbyševsk ○ RUS 96-97 F 7
Novokujbyshevsk = Novokujbyševsk ○ RUS 96-97 F 7

Novokuzneck ☆ RUS 124-125 P 2
Novokuznetsk = Novokuzneck ☆ RUS 124-125 P 2
Novolazarevskaja ○ ARK 16 F 1
Novo Mesto ○ SLO 100-101 E 2
Novomičurinsk ○ RUS 94-95 Q 3
Novomihajlovskij ○ RUS 126-127 C 5
Novomoskovsk ☆ RUS 94-95 Q 4
Novomoskovs'k ○ UA 102-103 J 3
Novomuraptalovo ○ RUS 96-97 J 7
Novonadeždinka ○ KA 96-97 N 3
Novonikolaevskij ○ RUS 102-103 N 2
Novooleksijivka ○ UA 102-103 H 4
Novo Oriente ○ BR (CEA) 68-69 H 4
Novo Oriente ○ BR (RON) 66-67 F 7
Novorossijsk ○ RUS 96-97 L 8
Novo Paraíso ○ BR 74-75 D 7
Novo Paraná ○ BR 70-71 J 2
Novopavlovsk ○ RUS 126-127 E 6
Novopetrovskoe ○ RUS 94-95 P 4
Novopokrovka ○ RUS 122-123 F 6
Novopokrovskaja ○ RUS 102-103 M 5
Novopolock = Navapolack ○ • • BY 94-95 L 4
Nôvo Pôrto ○ BR 66-67 B 7
Novopskov ○ UA 102-103 L 3
Novorossijskoe ○ KA 126-127 N 2
Novorybnaja ○ RUS 110-111 F 3
Novoržev ○ RUS 94-95 L 3
Novošahtinsk ○ RUS 102-103 L 4
Novo São Joaquim ○ BR 72-73 D 3
Novoselice ○ RUS 126-127 E 5
Novoselivs'ke ○ UA 102-103 H 5
Novoselycja ○ UA 102-103 E 3
Novosemejkino ○ RUS 96-97 G 7
Novosergievka ○ RUS 96-97 H 7
Novošešminsk ○ RUS 96-97 G 6
Novoshakhtinsk = Novošahtinsk ○ RUS 102-103 L 4
Novosibirsk ☆ • RUS 114-115 R 7
Novosibirskoe vodohranilišče ○ RUS 124-125 M 1
Novosokol'niki ○ RUS 94-95 M 3
Novotroick ○ RUS 96-97 L 8
Novotroickoe ○ RUS 122-123 D 4
Novotroickoe ○ RUS 122-123 D 4
Novotroitsk = Novotroick ○ RUS 96-97 L 8
Novotroji'c'ke ○ UA 102-103 J 4
Novoukrajinka ○ UA 102-103 G 3
Novoul'janovsk ○ RUS 96-97 F 6
Novouzensk ○ RUS 96-97 F 8
Novovjatsk ○ RUS 96-97 F 4
Novovoskresenovka ○ RUS 118-119 N 9
Novovolyns'k = Novovolyns'k ○ UA 102-103 D 2
Novozavidovskij ○ RUS 94-95 P 3
Novozemel'skaja vpadina ≃ 108-109 G 6
Novozybkov ○ BY 94-95 M 5
Novska ○ HR 100-101 F 2
Nový Bor ○ CZ 92-93 N 3
Novye Ljady ○ RUS 96-97 K 4
Novyj Bor ○ RUS 88-89 W 3
Novyj Buh ○ UA 102-103 H 3
Novyj Jič'in ○ CZ 92-93 P 4
Novyj Port ○ RUS 108-109 P 8
Novyj Tartas ○ RUS 114-115 O 7
Novyj Uojan ○ RUS 118-119 J 7
Novyj Urengoj ○ RUS 114-115 O 1
Novyj Uzen' ○ KA 126-127 K 6
Nowashe Lake ○ CDN 34-35 J 4
Nowa Sól ○ PL 92-93 N 3
Nowe ○ PL 92-93 P 2
Nowendoc ○ AUS 178-179 L 6
Nowgong ○ IND 138-139 G 7
Nowitna River ~ USA 20-21 N 4
Nowleye Lake ○ CDN 30-31 T 4
Nowogard ○ PL 92-93 N 2
Nowood Creek ~ USA 42-43 D 3
Nowra-Bomaderry ○ AUS 180-181 L 3
Nowshehrvirkhan ○ PK 138-139 D 4
Nowshera ○ PK 138-139 D 3
Nowy Sącz ☆ • PL 92-93 Q 4
Noxubee National Wildlife Refuge ⊥ USA 48-49 E 3
Noya ~ G 210-211 B 3
Noyabr'sk = Nojabr'sk ○ RUS 114-115 N 3
Noyes Island ~ USA 32-33 H 6
Noyon ○ F 90-91 J 7
Nqadubulu ○ RI 168 D 7
Nritu Ga ○ MYA 142-143 K 2
Nsa ○ RCB 210-211 E 5
Nsadzu ○ Z 218-219 G 2
Nsakaluba ○ Z 214-215 E 6
Nsama ○ Z 214-215 F 5
Nsambi ○ ZRE 210-211 F 4
Nsanje ○ MW 218-219 H 3
Nsawam ○ GH 202-203 K 7
Nsawkaw ○ GH 202-203 J 6
Nsele ~ ZRE 210-211 E 4
Nserm ○ CAM 204-205 K 6
Nsiza ○ ZW 218-219 F 4
Nsog ○ GQ 210-211 C 3
Nsoko ○ SD 220-221 K 3
Nsombo ○ Z 214-215 E 6
Nsontin ○ ZRE 210-211 G 5
Nsukka ○ WAN 204-205 G 5
Ntambu ○ Z 214-215 D 6
Ntatrat < RIM 196-197 C 6
Ntcheu ○ MW 218-219 H 2
Ntchisi ○ MW 218-219 G 1
Nteko ○ Z 214-215 F 6
Ntem ~ CAM 210-211 C 3
Ntemwa ○ Z 218-219 D 2
Nterguent ~ RIM 196-197 D 5
Nthalire ○ MW 214-215 G 6

Nthunga o MW 214-215 H 7
Ntibane o ZA 220-221 J 5
Ntimaru o EAK 212-213 E 4
Ntiona o TCH 198-199 G 5
Ntlenyana, Thabana ▲ LS 220-221 J 4
Ntokou o G 210-211 E 3
Ntomba, Lac o • ZRE 210-211 G 4
Ntoum o G 210-211 E 3
Ntsel, Hassi ⌄ DZ 190-191 F 7
Ntsou o RCB 210-211 E 4
Ntui o CAM 204-205 J 6
Ntungamo o EAU 212-213 C 4
Ntusi o EAU 212-213 C 3
Ntwetwe Pan ⌄ RB 218-219 C 5
Ntyébougou o RMM 202-203 G 2
Nu'airiya, an- o KSA 130-131 L 4
Nuakata Island ⌐ PNG 183 F 6
Nuaneteze, Rio ⌄ MOC 218-219 F 6
Nuangan o RI 164-165 J 3
Nuangola o USA 46-47 L 5
Nûba, Buhairat o SUD 200-201 E 2
Nubarašen o AR 128-129 L 2
Nubeena o AUS 180-181 J 7
Nubia = Nûba, an- ⌐ SUD 200-201 D 3
Nubian Desert = Nûba, Sahrâ' an- ⌐ SUD 200-201 E 2
Nubieber o USA 40-41 D 5
Ñuble, Río ⌄ RCH 78-79 C 4
Nuboai o RI 166-167 J 3
Nučča ⌄ RUS 110-111 W 4
Nucuray, Río ⌄ PE 64-65 D 4
Nudlung Fiord ≈ 28-29 G 2
Nudo Allincapac ▲ PE 70-71 B 4
Nudo Aricoma ▲ PE 70-71 B 3
Nudo Ausangate ▲ PE 70-71 B 3
Nudo Chiclíaraza ▲ PE 64-65 E 8
Nudo de Apolobamba ▲ PE 70-71 C 4
Nudo de Paramillo ▲ CO 60-61 H 3
Nudo de Sunipani ▲ PE 70-71 B 4
Nudyrni ⌄ RUS 120-121 H 4
Nueces River ⌄ USA 44-45 H 5
Nueltin Lake o CDN 30-31 U 5
Nuestra Señora del Rosario de Caá Catí o RA 74-75 E 2
Nueva, Isla ⌐ RCH 80 G 7
Nueva, La o EC 64-65 D 1
Nueva Alejandría o PE 64-65 D 4
Nueva Arcadia o HN 52-53 K 4
Nueva Ciudad Guerrero o MEX 50-51 K 4
Nueva Coahuila o MEX 52-53 J 3
Nueva Constitución o RA 78-79 F 3
Nueva Era o RP 160-161 D 3
Nueva Esperanza o RA (SAE) 76-77 E 4
Nueva Esperanza o RA (SAE) 76-77 F 4
Nueva Florida o YV 60-61 G 3
Nueva Galia o RA 78-79 G 3
Nueva Gerona ☆ C 54-55 D 4
Nueva Granada o CO 60-61 D 3
Nueva Guinea o NIC 52-53 B 6
Nueva Imperial o RCH 78-79 C 5
Nueva Italia o PY 76-77 J 3
Nueva Italia o RA 76-77 G 5
Nueva Italia de Ruíz o MEX 52-53 C 2
Nueva Lubecka o RA 80 E 2
Nueva Ocotepeque o HN 52-53 K 4
Nueva Palmira o ROU 78-79 G 2
Nueva Pompeya o RA 76-77 G 3
Nueva Rosita o MEX 50-51 J 4
Nueva San Salvador = ES 52-53 K 5
Nuevitas o C 54-55 G 4
Nuevo, Cayo ⌐ MEX 52-53 H 1
Nuevo Andoas o PE 64-65 D 3
Nuevo Campechito o MEX 52-53 H 2
Nuevo Casas Grandes o MEX 50-51 F 2
Nuevo Esperanza o RA 76-77 G 3
Nuevo Laredo o MEX 50-51 K 4
Nuevo Leon □ MEX 50-51 K 4
Nuevo Mundo o CO 60-61 F 5
Nuevo Mundo, Cerro ▲ BOL 76-77 D 1
Nuevo Padilla o MEX 50-51 K 5
Nuevo Riaño o E 98-99 E 3
Nuevo Rocafuerte o EC 64-65 E 2
Nuevo Turino o RA 76-77 G 6
Nugaal o SP 208-209 H 4
Nugaal, togga ⌄ SP 208-209 H 4
Nuguçu o BR 68-69 H 7
Nuguškoe vodohranilišče ⌄ RUS 96-97 K 7
Nuhaib o IRQ 128-129 K 6
Nuhaida o OM 132-133 K 2
Nuhaka o NZ 182 F 3
Núi Lang Bian ▲ VN 158-159 K 4
Nuiqsut o USA 20-21 P 1
Núi Thành o VN 158-159 K 3
Nuja = Karksi-Nuja o •• EST 94-95 J 2
Nüjang o VRC 144-145 B 4
Nu Jiang ⌄ VRC 142-143 L 3
Nu Jiang ⌄ VRC 144-145 L 6
Nükäbbäd o IR 134-135 J 4
Nuka Bay ≈ 22-23 V 3
Nuka Island o USA 22-23 V 3
Nuka River ⌄ USA 20-21 V 2
Nukhaylah ⌐ SUD 200-201 C 3
Nukiki o SOL 184 I c 2
Nukshak, Cape ⌐ USA 22-23 U 3
Nuku o PNG 183 B 2
Nuku'alofa ★ TON 184 IV a 2
Nukubasaga ⌐ FJI 184 III c 2
Nuku-Hiva ⌐ F 13 N 3
Nukuhu o PNG 183 E 3
Nukulaelae Atoll ⌐ TUV 13 J 3
Nukus ☆ US 136-137 F 3
Nula, El o YV 60-61 F 4
Nulato o USA 20-21 N 3
Nulato River ⌄ USA 20-21 L 4
Nuli o ZW 218-219 F 6
Nullagine o AUS 172-173 E 6
Nullagine River ⌄ AUS 172-173 E 6
Nulla Nulla o AUS 174-175 H 6
Nullarbor National Park ⊥ AUS 176-177 L 5
Nullarbor Plain ▲ AUS 176-177 J 5

Nullarbor Regional Reserve ⊥ AUS 176-177 K 5
Nullarbor Roadhouse o AUS 176-177 L 5
Nuluk River ⌄ USA 20-21 J 4
Num, Pulau ⌐ RI 166-167 J 3
Numalla, Lake o AUS 178-179 H 5
Numan o WAN 204-205 J 6
Nu'mân, Ĝazirat an- ⌐ KSA 130-131 D 4
Numancia (Ruinas celtibéricas y romanas) ∴ E 98-99 F 4
Numata o J (GUM) 152-153 H 6
Numata o J (HOK) 152-153 J 3
Numatinna ⌄ SUD 206-207 L 4
Numazu o J 152-153 H 7
Number 24 Well o AUS 172-173 F 7
Number 35 Well ⌄ AUS 172-173 G 7
Numbi o ZRE 212-213 B 4
Numbulwar ⌐ AUS 174-175 C 4
Numedal ⌐ N 86-87 D 6
Numfor, Pulau ⌐ RI 166-167 H 3
Numil Downs o AUS 174-175 F 6
Numto o RUS 114-115 L 3
Numto, ozero o RUS 114-115 L 3
Numto, uval ▲ RUS 114-115 K 3
Numurkah o AUS 180-181 H 6
Nunalla (abandoned) o CDN 30-31 W 6
Nunarsuaq ⌐ GRØ 28-29 U 5
Nunarsuit ⌐ GRØ 28-29 Q 6
Nunavakanuk Lake o USA 20-21 H 5
Nunavakpak Lake o USA 20-21 J 5
Nunavaugaluk, Lake o USA 22-23 R 3
Nunavik ⌐ GRØ 26-27 R 8
Nundle o AUS 178-179 L 6
Nundroo o AUS 176-177 M 5
Núñez, Isla ⌐ RCH 80 D 6
Nungesser Lake o CDN 34-35 K 5
Nungwaia o PNG 183 B 2
Nungwe Bay ≈ EAT 212-213 D 5
Nunim Lake o CDN 30-31 S 6
Nunivak Island ⌐ USA 20-21 G 6
Nunjamo o RUS 112-113 Z 4
Nunjamovaam ⌄ RUS 112-113 X 4
Nunligran o RUS (CUK) 112-113 T 3
Nunligran o RUS (CUK) 112-113 X 4
Nunn o USA 42-43 E 5
Ñuñoa o PE 70-71 B 4
Nun River ⌄ WAN 204-205 G 6
Nunukan Timur, Pulau ⌐ RI 164-165 J 1
Nuora ⌄ RUS 118-119 O 3
Nuoraldžyma ⌄ RUS 118-119 M 4
Nuoro ☆ I 100-101 B 4
Nuporanga o BR 72-73 G 6
Nuqay, Jabal ▲ LAR 192-193 H 6
Nuqrus, Ĝabal ▲ ET 194-195 G 5
Nuqūb o Y 132-133 D 6
Nûr o IR 134-135 H 3
Nura ⌄ KA (AKT) 126-127 P 3
Nûra ⌄ KA 124-125 J 4
Nûra ⌄ KA 124-125 J 4
Nûra ⌄ KA 124-125 H 4
Nûra ⌄ KA 124-125 J 4
Nûrâbâd o IR (FAR) 134-135 D 3
Nûrâbâd o IR 134-135 B 1
Nurata ☆ US 136-137 J 4
Nurataldy o KA 124-125 H 4
Nurato tog tizmasi ▲ US 136-137 J 4
Nur Dağlan ▲ TR 128-129 G 4
Nurei o SUD 198-199 L 6
Nurek o TJ 136-137 L 5
Nuremberg = Nürnberg ⚫ D 92-93 L 4
Nürestán □ AFG 138-139 C 2
Nür Gäma o PK 138-139 M 4
Nurhak o TR 128-129 G 4
Nurhak Dağı ▲ TR 128-129 G 3
Nuri o MEX 50-51 E 3
Nuri ⌄ SUD 200-201 E 4
Nuri, Teluk ≈ 162-163 H 5
Nuriootpa o AUS 180-181 E 3
Nurkazat o RI 166-167 F 3
Nurlat ⌐ RUS 96-97 G 6
Nurmes o FIN 88-89 K 5
Nurmijärvi o FIN 88-89 K 5
Nürnberg ⚫ D 92-93 L 4
Nurobod ⌐ UA 136-137 K 4
Núrpur o PK 138-139 C 2
Nusa Barung, Pulau ⌐ RI 168 E 4
Nusa Dua o RI 168 B 7
Nusa Kambangan ⌐ RI 168 C 3
Nusa Laut, Pulau ⌐ RI 166-167 E 3
Nusa Tenggara Timur □ RI 166-167 B 6
Nusawulan o RI 166-167 G 3
Nusaybin o TR 128-129 J 4
Nusela, Kepulauan ⌐ RI 166-167 F 2
Nushagak Bay ≈ 22-23 R 3
Nushagak Peninsula ⌐ USA 22-23 R 3
Nushagak River ⌄ USA 22-23 S 3
Nu Shan ▲ VRC 142-143 L 2
Nushki o PK 134-135 L 4
Nutaarmiut ⌐ GRØ 26-27 X 7
Nutak o CDN 36-37 T 6
Nutauge, laguna ⌄ 112-113 W 3
Nutrias, Las o RA 78-79 K 5
Nutrioso o USA 44-45 C 3
Nuttal o PK 138-139 B 6
Nutuvukti Lake o USA 20-21 N 3
Nutwood Downs o AUS 174-175 C 4
Nuu o EAK 212-213 G 4
Nuugaatsiaq o GRØ 26-27 Y 8
Nuuk = Godthåb ★ GRØ 28-29 P 4
Nuuk, Kangerluaq ≈ 28-29 P 4
Nuurst o MAU 148-149 J 4
Nuussuaq Halvø ⌐ GRØ 28-29 O 1
Nuvuk Point ⌐ USA 20-21 N 1
Nuwaibi' al-Muzayyina o ET 194-195 G 3
Nuwara Eliya o •• CL 140-141 J 7

Nuwefontein o NAM 220-221 D 3
Nuweh o RI 166-167 K 5
Nuwekloof ▲ ZA 220-221 D 6
Nuwerus o ZA 220-221 D 5
Nuweveldberge ▲ ZA 220-221 E 6
Nuy o ZA 220-221 D 6
Nuyakuk Lake o USA 22-23 R 3
Nuyts Archipelago ⌐ AUS 176-177 M 5
Nuyts Reefs ⌐ AUS 176-177 M 6
Nüzvid o IND 140-141 J 2
Nwa o CAM 204-205 J 6
Nwanedi o ZA 220-221 L 2
N.W. Crocodile Island ⌐ AUS 174-175 C 2
Nxai Pan o RB 218-219 C 4
Nxai Pan National Park ⊥ RB 218-219 C 4
Nya ⌄ TCH 206-207 B 4
Nyabarongo ⌄ RWA 212-213 B 4
Nyabisindu o RWA 212-213 B 4
Nyadire ⌄ ZW 218-219 G 3
Nyagassola o RG 202-203 F 3
Nya-Ghezi ⌄ ZRE 212-213 F 5
Nyahanga o EAT 212-213 D 5
Nyahua ⌄ EAT 212-213 D 6
Nyahururu o EAK 212-213 E 3
Nyah West o AUS 180-181 G 6
Nyaingêntanglha Feng ▲ VRC 144-145 H 4
Nyaingêntanglha Shan ▲ VRC 144-145 J 4
Nyainrong o VRC 144-145 J 4
Nyakahura o EAT 212-213 C 5
Nyakanazi o EAT 212-213 C 5
Nyak Co ⌄ VRC 144-145 B 4
Nyalá o SUD 200-201 B 6
Nyalam o VRC 144-145 F 6
Ny Ålesund o N 84-85 G 3
Nyali o RG 210-211 C 5
Nyalikungu o EAT 212-213 D 5
Nyamandhlovu o ZW 218-219 E 4
Nyamapanda o ZW 218-219 G 3
Nyamassila o RT 202-203 L 6
Nyâmati o IND 140-141 F 3
Nyamirembe o EAT 212-213 C 5
Nyamlell o SUD 206-207 H 4
Nyamoko o CAM 204-205 J 6
Nyamuswa o EAT (Ma) 212-213 E 4
Nyanding, Khor ⌄ SUD 206-207 L 4
Nyanga ⌄ G 210-211 D 5
Nyanga o RCB 210-211 C 5
Nyanga o ZW 218-219 G 3
Nyangamara o EAT 214-215 J 4
Nyang Qu ⌄ VRC 144-145 G 5
Nyanza o EAK 212-213 E 4
Nyanza-Lac o BU 212-213 B 5
Nyarling River ⌄ CDN 30-31 P 5
Nyaru o EAK 212-213 E 3
Nyasa o ZRE 210-211 L 6
Nyassar o CAM 204-205 J 6
Nyaungbintho o MYA 142-143 K 4
Nyaungkhashe o MYA 158-159 D 2
Nyaunglebin o MYA 158-159 D 2
Nyaung U o MYA 142-143 J 4
Nyazura o ZW 218-219 G 3
Nyazwidi ⌄ ZW 218-219 F 4
Nybergsund o N 86-87 E 6
Nybor o DK 86-87 E 9
Nyborg o • DK 86-87 E 9
Nyčalah ⌄ RUS 110-111 a 5
Nyda o RUS 108-109 P 8
Nyda ⌄ RUS 108-109 Q 8
Nyé ⌄ G 210-211 C 4
Nyeboe Land ⌐ GRØ 26-27 W 3
Nyegezi o EAT (SHI) 212-213 D 5
Nyêmo o VRC 144-145 G 6
Nyenase o GH 202-203 K 7
Nyensung o GH 202-203 K 5
Nyeri ▲ EAK 212-213 F 4
Nyeri ★ EAU 212-213 C 2
Ny-Friesland ⌐ N 84-85 K 3
Nygčekveem ⌄ RUS 112-113 T 5
Nyğčigen, mys ⌐ RUS 112-113 Y 4
Nyibiam o WAN 204-205 H 4
Nyiel o SUD 206-207 K 5
Nyika o ZW 218-219 F 4
Nyikne o SN 202-203 B 3
Nyima o EAT 212-213 F 4
Nyimba o Z 218-219 F 2
Nyiriniama o RMM 202-203 J 2
Nyingchi o VRC 144-145 K 6
Nyiragongo ▲ ZRE 212-213 B 4
Nyirbátor o H 92-93 R 5
Nyíregyháza o H 92-93 Q 5
Nyiri Desert ⌐ EAK 212-213 F 5
Nyiru Range ▲ EAK 212-213 F 2
Nyjskij, zaliv ≈ RUS 122-123 K 3
Nykarleby o FIN 88-89 G 5
Nyköbing Falster o DK 86-87 E 9
Nyköbing Mors o DK 86-87 D 8
Nyköping o S 86-87 H 7
Nyland = Uusima ⌐ FIN 88-89 H 6
Nyírvier ⌄ ZA 220-221 H 6
Nystroom o ZA 220-221 J 2
Nymagee o AUS 180-181 J 4
Nymburk o CZ 92-93 N 3
Nymphe Bank ≈ 90-91 B 6
Nyngan o AUS 178-179 J 4
Nyoma Rap o IND 138-139 G 3
Nyong ⌄ CAM 204-205 K 6
Nyons o F 90-91 K 9
Nyos, Lac o CAM 204-205 J 5
Nyrud ⌄ RUS 88-89 K 2
Nysa o PL 92-93 O 3
Nysa Kłodzka ⌄ PL 92-93 O 3
Nysa Łużycka ⌄ PL 92-93 N 3
Nyssa o USA 40-41 G 4
Nytva ⌄ RUS 96-97 H 5
Nyudō-saki ⌐ J 152-153 H 4
Nyumba ya Mungu Reservoir ⌄ EAT (ARU) 212-213 F 5
Nyunzu o ZRE 212-213 B 6

Nyvrovo ⌄ RUS 120-121 K 6
Nyžni Sirohozy o UA 102-103 J 4
Nyžni Torhaji o UA 102-103 J 4
Nyžn'ohirs'kyj o UA 102-103 J 5
Nzako o RCA 206-207 E 4
Nzako ⌄ RCA 206-207 F 6
Nzambi o RCB 210-211 C 5
Nzara o SUD 206-207 J 6
Nzassi o RCB 210-211 D 6
Nzébéla o RG 202-203 F 5
Nzega o EAT 212-213 D 5
Nzérékoré □ RG 202-203 F 5
Nzérékoré ▲ RG 202-203 F 5
N'Zeto o ANG 216-217 B 3
Nzi ⌄ CI 202-203 H 6
Nzili, Bahr ⌄ RCA 206-207 F 2
Nzilo, Lac ⌄ ZRE 214-215 C 6
Nzima o EAT 212-213 D 5
Nzo ⌄ CI 202-203 G 6
Nzoia o EAK 212-213 E 3
Nzoro ~ RCA 206-207 B 5
N'zo, Réserve de faune du ⊥ CI 202-203 G 6
Nzoro ⌄ ZRE 212-213 C 2

O

Oä', Wâdi al- ⌄ KSA 130-131 F 4
Oahe, Lake ⌄ USA 42-43 G 3
Oahu ⌐ USA 48-49 D 7
Oakbank o AUS 180-181 F 2
Oakburn o CDN 34-35 F 5
Oak Creek ⌄ USA 42-43 D 5
Oakdale o USA (CA) 40-41 D 7
Oakdale o USA (LA) 44-45 L 4
Oakes o USA 42-43 H 2
Oakey o USA 178-179 L 4
Oakey Creek ⌄ AUS 178-179 J 4
Oak Grove o USA 44-45 M 3
Oak Harbor o USA 40-41 C 1
Oak Hill o USA (FL) 48-49 H 5
Oak Hill o USA (WV) 46-47 H 7
Oak Hills o USA 174-175 H 6
Oakhurst o USA 40-41 E 7
Oak Lake o CDN (MAN) 34-35 F 6
Oak Lake ≈ CDN (MAN) 34-35 F 6
Oakland o USA (CA) 40-41 C 7
Oakland o USA (IA) 42-43 K 5
Oakland o USA (MD) 46-47 J 6
Oakland o USA (MS) 48-49 D 2
Oakland o USA (NE) 42-43 J 5
Oaklands o AUS 180-181 J 3
Oak Lawn o USA 46-47 E 5
Oakley o USA (ID) 40-41 H 4
Oakley o USA (KS) 42-43 G 6
Oakover River ⌄ AUS 172-173 E 6
Oak Point o CDN 34-35 G 5
Oakridge o USA 40-41 C 4
Oak Ridge o USA (TN) 48-49 F 1
Oak Ridge o USA (TX) 44-45 K 4
Oakview o CDN 34-35 G 5
Oakwood o USA 44-45 H 2
Oaky Creek o AUS 178-179 K 2
Oamaru o NZ 182 C 6
Oan o RI 164-165 G 3
Oasis o USA 40-41 G 5
Oates Land ⌐ ARK 16 T 7
Oatlands o AUS 180-181 J 7
Oaxaca □ MEX 52-53 F 3
Oaxaca de Juárez ⚫ MEX 52-53 F 3
Ob' o RUS 114-115 R 7
Ob' ⌄ RUS 10-11 G 2
Oba o CDN 34-35 O 6
Oba o WAN 204-205 F 5
Obaa o RI 166-167 K 5
Obaba o RCB 210-211 E 4
Obaha o PNG 183 E 5
Obala o CAM 204-205 J 6
Obalpuram o IND 140-141 G 3
Obama o J 152-153 F 7
Obamaska, Rivière ⌄ CDN 38-39 E 3
Oban o GB 90-91 E 4
Oban o PNG 183 E 1
Oban o RCB 210-211 E 4
Oban o WAN 204-205 H 6
Obanazawa o J 152-153 J 5
Oban Hills ▲ WAN 204-205 H 6
Obelek-prolaz ▲ MK 100-101 J 4
Obera o RA 76-77 K 4
Oberlin o USA 42-43 G 6
Oberon o AUS 180-181 J 4
Oberon o CDN 34-35 G 5
Oberösterreich ▲ A 92-93 M 4
Oberpfälzer Wald ▲ D 92-93 M 4
Oberstdorf o • D 92-93 L 5
Oberstein, Idar- o D 92-93 J 4
Obhur o KSA 132-133 A 3
Obi o WAN 204-205 H 5
Obi, Kepulauan ⌐ RI 166-167 E 3
Obi, Selat ≈ 164-165 K 4
Obiaruku o WAN 204-205 G 6
Óbidos o BR 62-63 G 6
Óbidos o • P 98-99 C 5
Obigarm o TJ 136-137 L 5
Obihiongou ⌄ J 136-137 M 5
Obihiro o J 152-153 K 3
Obilebit, Riacho ⌄ PY 76-77 H 1
Obispo Trejo o RA 78-79 H 1
Obitočna kosa ⌄ UA 102-103 K 4
Oblačnaja, gora ▲ RUS 122-123 F 3
Oblačnyj Golec, gora ▲ RUS 120-121 Ĝ 5
Obluč'e o RUS 122-123 D 4
Olukovina ⌄ RUS 120-121 R 6
Obninsk o RUS 94-95 O 4
Obo o RCA 206-207 H 6

Obo ▲ VRC 154-155 B 3
Oboa ▲ EAU 212-213 E 3
Obock o DJI 200-201 L 6
Obogu o GH 202-203 K 6
Obojan o RUS 102-103 L 2
Obokote o ZRE 210-211 L 4
Oboli o RCB 210-211 E 4
Obolo o WAN 204-205 G 5
Obonga Lake o CDN 34-35 M 5
Obout o CAM 210-211 C 2
Obouya o RCB 210-211 E 4
Obozerskij o RUS 88-89 O 5
Obra ⌄ PL 92-93 N 2
Obregón, Ciudad o MEX 50-51 E 3
Obrenovac o YU 100-101 H 2
Obrovac o HR 100-101 E 2
Obručeva, vozvyšennosť ▲ RUS 120-121 V 7
Obruchev Rise ≈ 14-15 J 2
Obruk Yaylâsı ▲ TR 128-129 E 3
Obryvistaja, gora ▲ RUS 112-113 S 3
Obryvistj, mys ▲ RUS 108-109 c 2
Obryvistyj, mys ▲ RUS 112-113 M 5
Obščij syrt ▲ RUS 96-97 F 8
Observation Hill ▲ AUS 176-177 M 4
Observatory Inlet ≈ 32-33 E 4
Obskaja Guba = Obskaja guba ≈ RUS 108-109 P 8
Obskaja Guba o 108-109 P 8
Obuasi o CI 202-203 K 6
Obubra o WAN 204-205 H 5
Obuchiv o UA 102-103 G 2
Obudu o WAN 204-205 H 5
Obudu Cattle Ranch o • WAN 204-205 H 5
Obusa o RUS 116-117 L 9
Obusa ⌄ RUS 116-117 M 9
Obytočna zatoka ≈ 102-103 J 4
Očakiv o UA 102-103 G 4
Ocala o USA 48-49 G 5
Ocalli o PE 64-65 D 5
Očarnčira o GE 126-127 D 6
Ocampo o MEX (COA) 50-51 H 4
Ocampo o MEX (TAM) 50-51 K 5
Ocaña o CO 60-61 E 3
Ocaña o E 98-99 F 5
Ocaso o E 64-65 F 1
Ocate o USA 44-45 F 1
Occidental, Cordillera ▲ RCH 64-65 C 5
Occidente o CO 64-65 F 2
Ocean Cape ▲ USA 20-21 U 7
Ocean City o USA 46-47 L 6
Ocean Falls o CDN 32-33 G 5
Ocean Grove-Barwon Heads o AUS 180-181 H 5
Oceanographer Fracture Zone ≃ 6-7 E 5
Ocean Shores o USA 40-41 C 2
Oceanside o USA 40-41 F 9
Ocean Springs o USA 48-49 D 4
Ocenyrd, gora ▲ RUS 108-109 L 7
Očer o RUS 96-97 J 5
Ochiai o J 152-153 E 7
O'Chiese Indian Reserve ⅹ CDN 32-33 N 5
Ochito o PK 134-135 M 6
Ochoa, Sierra de ▲ DOM 54-55 K 5
Ochobo o WAN 204-205 G 5
Ochopee o USA 48-49 H 7
Ocho Rios o JA 54-55 G 4
Ochtyrka o UA 102-103 J 2
Ocilla o USA 48-49 G 3
Ockelbo o S 86-87 H 6
Ocmulgee National Monument ∴ USA 48-49 G 3
Ocmulgee River ⌄ USA 48-49 G 3
Ocoa, Bahía de ≈ 54-55 K 5
Ocoa, Sierra de ▲ DOM 54-55 K 5
Ocoña o PE 70-71 A 5
Ocoña, Río de ⌄ PE 70-71 A 5
Oconee, Lake ⌄ USA 48-49 G 3
Oconee River ⌄ USA 48-49 G 3
Oconto o USA (NE) 42-43 H 5
Oconto o USA (WI) 46-47 D 3
Oconto River ⌄ USA 46-47 D 3
Ocoruro o PE 70-71 B 4
Ocós o GCA 52-53 H 4
Ocosingo o MEX 52-53 H 3
Ocotal ☆ NIC 52-53 L 5
Ocotito, El o MEX 52-53 E 3
Ocotlán o MEX (JAL) 52-53 C 1
Ocotlán o MEX (OAX) 52-53 F 3
Ocozcoautla o MEX 52-53 H 3
Ocracoke o USA 48-49 L 2
Ocreza, Ribeiro do o P 98-99 D 5
Ocros o PE (ANC) 64-65 D 7
Ocros o PE (AYA) 64-65 F 8
Octy, Mount ▲ AUS 178-179 C 1
Ocú o PA 52-53 P 7
Ocua o MOC 218-219 K 1
O'čugnij-Botuobuja ⌄ RUS 118-119 G 4
Ocujal o C 54-55 G 5
Ocumare del Tuy o YV 60-61 H 2
Ocuri o BOL 76-77 D 3
Oda o GH 202-203 K 7
Ódádáhraun ▲ IS 86-87 e 2
Odaejin o DVR 150-151 H 7
Odaesan National Park ⊥ ROK 150-151 G 9
Ödämmun o RI 166-167 J 5
Odate o J 152-153 J 4
Odawara o J 152-153 H 7
Odde, Oke- o WAN 204-205 F 4
Odei River ⌄ CDN 34-35 G 4
Odemira o P 98-99 C 6
Ödemiş o TR 128-129 B 3
Odendaalsrus o ZA 220-221 H 3
Odense o • DK 86-87 E 9
Oder ⌄ D 92-93 N 2
Oderbruch ⌐ D 92-93 N 2
Odesa ☆ UA 102-103 H 4
Odesa ⌄ UA 102-103 H 4
Odessa o USA (TX) 44-45 F 3
Odessa o USA (WA) 40-41 E 2
Odessa = Odesa ★ UA (ODS) 102-103 H 4
Odessa ⌄ UA 120-121 F 5

Odiongan o RP 160-161 D 6
Odjala o G 210-211 D 4
Odjan, zaliv ≈ RUS 120-121 O 4
Odoev o RUS 94-95 P 5
Odomlja ★ RUS 94-95 O 3
Ödöngk o K 158-159 H 6
Odonkawkrom o GH 202-203 K 6
O'Donnell River ⌄ AUS 172-173 H 5
Odorheiu Secuiesc o RO 102-103 D 4
Odra ⌄ PL 92-93 N 2
Odrus o SUD 200-201 H 3
Odžaci o YU 100-101 G 2
Odzala, Parc National d' ⊥ RCB 210-211 E 3
Odzerna o RCB 210-211 D 4
Odzi o ZW 218-219 G 4
Odzi ⌄ ZW 218-219 G 4
Odziba o RCB 210-211 E 5
Oeiras o BR 68-69 J 5
Oeiras do Para o BR 62-63 H 5
Oekussi o RI 166-167 C 6
Oelrichs o USA 42-43 F 4
Oelwein o USA 46-47 C 4
Oenpelli o AUS 174-175 B 3
Oesilo o RI 166-167 C 6
Oever, Den o NL 92-93 H 2
Of ☆ TR 128-129 J 2
Ofa o WAN 204-205 F 5
Öfaerufoss ⌄ IS 86-87 d 3
O'Fallon Creek ⌄ USA 42-43 E 2
Ófanto ⌄ I 100-101 F 4
Ofaqim o JOR 130-131 E 2
Ofcolaco o ZA 220-221 K 2
Ofe, River ⌄ WAN 204-205 F 4
Ofelia, La o RA 78-79 F 3
Offenbach am Main o D 92-93 K 3
Offenburg o D 92-93 J 4
Officer Creek ⌄ AUS 176-177 M 3
Offoué o G 210-211 C 4
Offoué, Réserve de l' ⊥ G 210-211 C 4
Offumpo o CI 202-203 H 7
Ofhidro, Isla ⌐ RCH 80 C 4
Ofhidro, Lago ⌄ RCH 80 F 6
Ofin ⌄ GH 202-203 J 6
Ofinso o GH 202-203 K 6
Ofizina Alemania o RCH 76-77 C 3
Ofjord o 26-27 m 8
Ofoase o GH 202-203 K 6
Ofolanga ⌐ TON 184 IV a 1
Ofotfjorden ≈ 86-87 H 2
Ofu o USA 184 V c 2
Ofunato o J 152-153 J 5
Ôfunato o J 152-153 J 5
Oga o J 152-153 H 5
Oga, zaliv ≈ RUS 108-109 H 4
Ogaden ⌐ ETH 208-209 F 5
Oga-hanto ⌐ J 152-153 H 5
Ogaki-Hachiman-Shrinj · J 152-153 J 5
Ogallala o USA 42-43 F 5
Ogan ⌄ RI 162-163 F 6
Oganda, Parc National de l' ⊥ G 210-211 C 4
Ogani o RI 166-167 G 3
Ogar, Pulau ⌐ RI 166-167 G 3
Ogascanane, Lac o CDN 38-39 E 5
Ogba o WAN 204-205 G 6
Ogbia o WAN 204-205 G 6
Ogbomoso o WAN 204-205 F 5
Ogden o USA (IA) 42-43 K 4
Ogden o USA (UT) 40-41 H 5
Ogdensburg o USA 46-47 L 3
Ogeechee River ⌄ USA 48-49 H 3
Ogema o CDN 34-35 D 6
Ogema o USA 46-47 B 2
Ogembo o EAK 212-213 E 4
Oger = Ogre ☆• LV 94-95 H 3
Ogi o J 152-153 F 7
Ogies o ZA 220-221 J 3
Ogijnuur = Zögstej o MAU 148-149 F 4
Ogilvie o CDN 20-21 V 4
Ogilvie ⌄ CDN 20-21 V 4
Ogilvie Mountains ▲ CDN 20-21 V 4
Ogilvie River ⌄ CDN 20-21 V 4
Oglala Pass ≈ 22-23 F 7
Oglanly o TM 136-137 F 4
Oglat Beraber o MA 188-189 K 5
Oglat el Faci o DZ (TIN) 188-189 J 7
Oglat el Faci ⌄ DZ (TIN) 188-189 J 7
Oglat Khnâchlich o MAUR 196-197 J 4
Oglat Marhboura ⌄ DZ 188-189 L 4
Ogle Point ▲ CDN 24-25 Y 6
Oglethorpe o USA 48-49 G 3
Oglina Island ⌄ USA 22-23 D 5
Ogmore o AUS 178-179 K 2
Ognon ⌄ F 90-91 L 8
Ogodža o RUS 122-123 C 3
Ogoja o WAN 204-205 H 5
Ogoki o CDN 34-35 O 5
Ogoki Reservoir ⌄ CDN 34-35 M 5
Ogoki River ⌄ CDN 34-35 N 5
Ogooué ⌄ G 210-211 D 5
Ogorodtah o RUS 118-119 P 4
Ogoron o RUS 118-119 O 8
Ogosta ⌄ BG 100-101 J 3
Ogoulou ⌄ G 210-211 D 5
Ogr o SUD 200-201 C 6
Ogre ☆• LV 94-95 H 3
Ogulin o HR 100-101 E 2
Ogun □ WAN 204-205 E 5
Ogun ⌄ WAN 204-205 E 5
Ogurčinskij, ostrov = Oğurçaly ⌐ TM 136-137 C 5
Ogurugu o WAN 204-205 G 5
Ogwashi-Uku o WAN 204-205 G 6
Oha • RUS 122-123 K 2
Oha ⌄ RUS 122-123 K 2
Ohafia o WAN 204-205 H 6
Ohai o NZ 182 B 6
Ohakune o NZ 182 E 3
Ohansk o RUS 96-97 J 5
Ohanskaja vozvyšennosť ▲ RUS 96-97 J 5
Ôhata o J 152-153 J 4

Ohau ~ USA 48-49 D 7
Ohau, Lake o NZ 182 B 6
Ōhi ▲ GR 100-101 K 6
O'Higgins, Lago ⌄ RCH 80 D 4
Ohinskij pereśeek ⌄ RUS 122-123 K 2
Ohio □ USA 46-47 G 5
Ohio River ⌄ USA 46-47 F 6
Ohogamut o USA 20-21 K 6
Ohogrigol ~ RUS 114-115 P 3
Ohonua o TON 184 IV a 2
Ohota ⌄ RUS 120-121 K 3
Ohotsk o RUS 120-121 K 3
Ohotsk ☆ RUS 120-121 F 3
Ohotskoe more ≈ RUS 122-123 K 5
Ohře ⌄ CZ 92-93 M 3
Ohrid o ••• MK 100-101 H 4
Ohridsko Ezero ⌄ MK 100-101 H 4
Ohrigstad o ZA 220-221 K 2
Ohrit, Liqeni i ⌄ AL 100-101 H 4
Ohura o NZ 182 E 3
Oiapoque o BR (APA) 62-63 J 4
Oiapoque o BR 62-63 J 3
Oiapoque, Reserva Biológica de ⊥ BR 62-63 H 4
Ōi-gawa ⌄ J 152-153 H 7
Oijärvi o FIN 88-89 H 4
Oil City o USA (LA) 44-45 L 3
Oil City o USA (PA) 46-47 J 5
Oildale o USA 40-41 E 8
Oil Gathering Station o LAR 192-193 G 3
Oilton o USA 44-45 H 6
Oise ⌄ F 90-91 J 7
Ōita ☆ J 152-153 D 8
Oiyug o VRC 144-145 G 6
Oja ~ RUS 116-117 F 9
OjaSinskij, Stancionno- o RUS 114-115 P 7
Oje o WAN 204-205 G 5
Ojibwa o USA 46-47 C 3
Ojinaga o MEX 50-51 G 3
Ojiya o J 152-153 H 6
Ojmauyt o KA 126-127 L 4
Ojmjakon o RUS 120-121 K 2
Ojmjakonskoe nagor'e ▲ RUS 120-121 J 2
Ojmur o RUS 116-117 N 9
Ojnaa o RUS 116-117 H 6
Ojobo o WAN 204-205 G 6
Ojo Caliente o MEX 50-51 H 6
Ojo de Carrizo o MEX 50-51 G 3
Ojo de Liebre, Laguna ≈ RCH 50-51 C 4
Ojokkuduk o US 136-137 J 4
Ojos Negros o MEX 50-51 A 2
Ojotung o RUS 110-111 b 4
Ojsylkara ~ KA 126-127 L 4
Ojtal o KA 136-137 N 3
Oj-Tal o KS 136-137 N 4
Oju o WAN 204-205 H 5
Ojuelos de Jalisco o MEX 50-51 J 7
Ojusardah o RUS 112-113 H 2
Ojusut o RUS 118-119 G 4
Oka ~ RCB 210-211 E 5
Oka ~ RUS 94-95 P 4
Oka ~ RUS 116-117 K 9
Oka o WAN 204-205 G 5
Okaba o RI 166-167 K 6
Okahandja ★ NAM 216-217 D 10
Okakarara o NAM 216-217 D 10
Okak Island ⌐ CDN 36-37 T 6
Okali o RCB 210-211 E 5
Okaliktoks Islands ⌐ CDN 36-37 U 7
Okanagan Falls o CDN 32-33 L 7
Okanagan Indian Reserve ⅹ CDN 32-33 L 6
Okanagan Lake o CDN 32-33 L 7
Okanagan Valley ⌄ CDN 32-33 L 7
Okangobo o NAM 216-217 D 8
Okankolo o NAM 216-217 D 8
Okano ⌄ G 210-211 D 3
Okanogan o USA 40-41 E 1
Okanogan River ⌄ USA 40-41 E 1
Okanono o NAM 216-217 C 10
Okapa o PNG 183 D 3
Okapi, Parc National de la ⊥ ZRE 210-211 L 3
Okâra o PK 138-139 D 4
Okarche o USA 44-45 J 2
Okarem = Ekerem o TM 136-137 C 5
Okata o NAM 204-205 E 4
Okatjoruu o NAM 216-217 C 9
Okatjuru o NAM 216-217 C 9
Okato o NZ 182 D 3
Okaukuejo o NAM 216-217 C 9
Okavango ~ NAM 216-217 F 8
Okavangobecken ⌄ RB 216-217 F 8
Okavango Delta ~ RB 218-219 B 4
Okavango River Lodge o RB 218-219 B 4
Okawa o NAM 216-217 D 10
Okaya o J 152-153 H 6
Okayama ☆ J 152-153 E 7
Okazaki o J 152-153 G 7
Okazie o NAM 216-217 D 7
Okdarjo o US 136-137 J 4
Okeechobee o USA 48-49 H 6
Okeechobee, Lake o USA 48-49 H 6
Okefenokee National Wildlife Refuge ⊥ USA 48-49 G 4
Okefenokee Swamp o USA 48-49 G 4
Oke-Iho o WAN 204-205 E 5
Okélatako o RCB 210-211 E 5
Okemah o USA 44-45 J 2
Okene o WAN 204-205 G 5
Oke-Odde o WAN 204-205 F 4
Oketsew o GH 202-203 K 7
Okha o IND 138-139 B 8
Okha Mâthi o IND 138-139 B 8
Okhotsk, Sea of = Ohotskoe more ≈ RUS 10-11 O 3
Oki o RI 166-167 D 3
Okiep o ZA 220-221 D 4
Okigwe o WAN 204-205 G 6
Oki-Kaikyō ≈ 152-153 E 7
Okinawa ~ J 152-153 B 11
Okinawa-shima ~ J 152-153 C 11

Okinawa-shotō ⌒ J 152-153 B 11
Okinoerabu-shima ⌒ J 152-153 C 11
Okino-shima ⌒ J 152-153 E 8
Oki-shotō ⌒ J 152-153 E 6
Oki-tai ≃ 152-153 F 6
Okitipupa o WAN 204-205 F 5
Okkan o MYA 158-159 C 2
Okkŭrgan ☆ US 136-137 L 4
Okkyn"egan ~ RUS 114-115 R 3
Okla o CDN 34-35 E 4
Oklahoma □ USA 44-45 H 2
Oklahoma City ☆ USA 44-45 J 2
Oklan o RUS 112-113 O 5
Oklan ~ RUS 112-113 N 5
Oklanskoe plato ▲ RUS 112-113 N 5
Okmulgee o USA 44-45 K 2
Oko o WAN 204-205 F 5
Oko, Wādi ~ SUD 200-201 G 2
Ok Ohm River ~ PNG 183 B 3
Okok ~ EAU 212-213 D 2
Okokmilaga River ~ USA 20-21 O 2
Okola o CAM 204-205 J 6
Okolli Island ⌒ CDN 36-37 L 2
Okollo o EAU 212-213 C 2
Okondja o G 210-211 D 4
Okondjatu o NAM 216-217 E 10
Okongo o NAM 216-217 D 8
Okongomba o NAM 216-217 B 9
Okoppe o J 152-153 K 2
Okoppe, Nishi- o J 152-153 K 2
Okora, Mount ▲ WAN 204-205 G 5
Okoruro o BOL 70-71 C 5
Okotoks o CDN 32-33 O 6
Okotusu < NAM 216-217 A 8
Okoyo o RCB 210-211 E 4
Okpala-Ngwa o WAN 204-205 G 6
Okpara ~ DY 204-205 E 4
Okpo o MYA 142-143 J 6
Okrika o WAN 204-205 G 6
Okrouyo o CI 202-203 G 7
Oksaj, gory ▲ TJ 146-147 B 7
Oksapmin o PNG 183 B 3
Øksfjord o N 86-87 L 1
Øksfjordjøkelen ▲·· N 86-87 L 1
Oksibil o RI 166-167 L 4
Oksino o RUS 88-89 W 3
Okskij Gosudarstevennyi zapovednik ⊥ RUS 94-95 R 4
Oksovskij o RUS 88-89 P 5
Okstindan ▲ N 86-87 G 4
Okstindane ▲ N 84-85 J 3
Oksu ~ TJ 146-147 B 6
Oksym ~ RUS 114-115 U 4
Oktemberjan o AR 128-129 L 2
Oktjabrina o RUS 112-113 J 5
Oktjabr'sk ☆ KA 126-127 M 3
Oktjabr'sk o RUS 96-97 F 7
Oktjabr'skaja, gora ▲ RUS 108-109 f 3
Oktjabr'skij o RUS (AMR) 122-123 C 2
Oktjabr'skij o RUS (ARH) 88-89 R 6
Oktjabr'skij o RUS (BAS) 96-97 H 6
Oktjabr'skij o RUS (IRK) 116-117 J 7
Oktjabr'skij o RUS (KMC) 122-123 R 2
Oktjabr'skij o RUS (MUR) 88-89 N 3
Oktjabr'skij o RUS (ULN) 96-97 F 6
Oktjabr'skij o RUS (VOL) 88-89 O 6
Oktjabr'skij ☆ RUS (PRM) 96-97 K 5
Oktjabr'skoe ☆ RUS 96-97 J 7
Oktjabr'skoje ☆ RUS 114-115 G 7
Oktjabr'skoj Revoljucii, ostrov ⌒ RUS 108-109 a 2
Oktoš ☆ US 136-137 J 5
Oktumkum ∸ TM 136-137 C 4
Oktwin o MYA 142-143 K 6
Oktyabr'skiy = Oktjabr'skij o RUS 96-97 H 6
Oku o CAM 204-205 J 5
Oku o J 152-153 C 11
Oku ~ ZRE 210-211 L 4
Oku, Mont ▲ CAM 204-205 J 5
Okubie o WAN 204-205 F 6
Okubie < WAN 204-205 F 6
Ōkuchi o J 152-153 D 8
Okulovka ☆ RUS 94-95 N 2
Okunajka ~ RUS 118-119 D 7
Okundi o WAN 204-205 H 5
Okushiri o J 152-153 H 3
Okushiri-tō ⌒ J 152-153 H 3
Okuta o WAN 204-205 E 4
Okwa ~ RB 216-217 F 11
Okwa, River ~ WAN 204-205 G 4
Ola o PA 52-53 D 7
Ola ☆· RUS 120-121 O 4
Ola ~ RUS 120-121 O 4
Ola o USA 44-45 L 2
Ola, Joškar- o RUS 96-97 E 5
Ola, Zapadnyj Tannu, hrebet ▲ RUS 116-117 E 10
Olaf Prydz bukt ≈ 16 G 8
Ólafsfjörður o IS 86-87 d 1
Ólafsvík o IS 86-87 b 2
Olanchito o HN 52-53 L 4
Öland ⌒· S 86-87 H 8
Olanga ~ RUS 88-89 L 3
Olary o AUS 180-181 F 2
Olathe o USA 42-43 K 6
Olavarría o RA 78-79 J 4
Olav V Land ∸ N 84-85 L 3
Olbernhau o D 92-93 M 3
Olbia o I 100-101 B 4
Ol'čan o RUS 110-111 Y 7
Olcott o USA 46-47 J 4
Old Andado ∴ AUS 178-179 C 3
Old Bahama Channel ≈ 54-55 F 3
Old Bohemia Church ∴ USA 46-47 L 6
Old Brahmaputra ~ BD 142-143 G 3
Old Coralie (Ruins) o AUS 174-175 F 6
Old Cork o AUS 178-179 F 2
Old Crow o CDN 20-21 V 3
Old Crow Mount ▲ CDN 20-21 U 3
Old Crow River ~ CDN 20-21 V 3
Old Delamere o AUS 172-173 K 3
Old Dongola · SUD 200-201 E 3
Old Dutch Capital of Biak ⊥· RI 166-167 J 2
Ol'dë ~ RUS 110-111 V 5
Oldeani o EAT (ARV) 212-213 E 5
Oldeani ▲ EAT (ARU) 212-213 E 5
Oldenburg o D 92-93 K 2
Oldenburg (Holstein) o D 92-93 L 1
Olderdalen o N 86-87 K 2
Olderfjord o N 86-87 M 1
Old Factory Bay ≈ 38-39 E 2
Old Faithful Geyser · USA 40-41 J 3
Oldfield River ~ AUS 176-177 F 6
Old Forge o USA 46-47 L 4
Old Fort Benton ∴· USA 40-41 J 2
Old Fort Dodge ∴ USA 42-43 H 7
Old Fort Henry ∴· CDN 38-39 F 6
Old Fort Parker State Historic Site ∴ USA 44-45 J 4
Old Fort River ~ CDN 30-31 O 6
Old Ghan Route, The ll· AUS 178-179 C 3
Oldham o GB 90-91 F 5
Old Harbor o USA 22-23 U 4
Old Harbour o JA 54-55 G 6
Old Herbert Vale o AUS 174-175 E 6
Old Horse Springs o USA 44-45 C 3
Old Irontown Ruins ∴ USA 40-41 H 7
Old Ivy Mine o AUS 178-179 B 1
Old Limbunya o AUS 172-173 J 4
Oldman River ~ CDN 32-33 O 7
Old Minto o USA 20-21 Q 4
Old Mkushi o Z 218-219 E 2
Old Numery o AUS 178-179 C 2
Oldoiniyo Orok ▲ EAK 212-213 F 5
Ol Doinyo Lengai ▲ EAT 212-213 E 5
Ol Doinyo Lenkiyio ▲ EAK 212-213 F 3
Ol-Doinyo Sabuk National Park ⊥ EAK 212-213 F 4
Ol'doj ~ RUS 118-119 L 9
Oldon ~ RUS 118-119 F 5
Old Oyo Game Reserve ⊥ WAN 204-205 F 4
Old Parakylia o AUS 178-179 D 6
Old Perlican o CDN 38-39 S 4
Old Rampart o USA 20-21 U 3
Olds o CDN 32-33 N 6
Öldsijt gol ~ MAU 148-149 D 4
Old Sitka o USA 32-33 C 3
Old Stock Exchange · ZA 220-221 K 2
Olduvai Gorge · EAT 212-213 E 5
Old Village o USA 20-21 N 6
Old Wives Lake ⊂ CDN 34-35 C 5
Old Woman Mountain ▲ USA 40-41 G 8
Old Woman River ~ USA 20-21 L 5
Olean o USA 46-47 J 4
O'Leary o CDN 38-39 M 5
Oleb o SUD 200-201 H 4
Olecko o PL 92-93 R 1
Oleiros o P 98-99 D 5
Olëkma o RUS (AMR) 118-119 K 7
Olëkma ~ RUS 118-119 H 9
Olëkma ~ RUS 118-119 J 8
Olëkma ~ RUS 118-119 K 8
Olëkma ~ RUS 118-119 K 5
Olëkma ~ RUS 118-119 K 7
Olëkminsk ☆· RUS 118-119 K 5
Olëkminskij stanovik ▲ RUS 118-119 H 9
Olëkminskij zapovednik ⊥ RUS 118-119 L 6
Olëkmo-Čarskoe nagor'e ▲ RUS 118-119 J 6
Oleksandrivka o UA (KRV) 102-103 H 3
Olendi ~ KA 96-97 H 8
Olenegorsk o RUS 88-89 M 2
Olenëk o RUS 110-111 a 5
Olenëk o RUS (SAH) 110-111 J 5
Olenëk ~ RUS 110-111 O 3
Olenëk ~ RUS 110-111 J 6
Olenëk ~ RUS 110-111 M 5
Olenëk ~ RUS 116-117 N 2
Olenëk, Ust'- o RUS 110-111 M 3
Olenëkskaja, protoka ~ RUS 110-111 O 3
Olenëkskij zaliv ≈ 110-111 M 3
Olenguj ~ RUS 118-119 F 10
Olenguruone o EAK 212-213 E 4
Olenica o RUS 88-89 N 3
Olenij, mys ▲ RUS 108-109 R 5
Olenij, ostrov ⌒ RUS (JAN) 108-109 R 5
Olenij, ostrov ⌒ RUS (KAR) 88-89 N 4
Olenij, ostrov ⌒ RUS (TMR) 108-109 V 4
Olenij, proliv ≈ RUS 108-109 S 5
Olenino o RUS 94-95 N 3
Olen'ja ~ RUS 122-123 K 2
Olenogorsk o RUS 88-89 M 2
Olenti ~ KA 124-125 H 3
Olër ~ RUS 112-113 J 2
Ole Rømer Land ∸ GRØ 26-27 n 6
Oléron, Île d' ⌒ F 90-91 G 9
Olesskyj zamok · UA 102-103 D 2
Olevs'k o UA 102-103 E 2
Ølfjellet ▲ N 86-87 G 3
Ol'ga o RUS 122-123 F 7
Ol'ga ~ RUS 118-119 M 9
Olga(Kata Tjuta), Mount ▲ AUS 176-177 L 2
Olga, Lac ⊂ CDN 38-39 F 4
Ol'ga, mys ▲ RUS 120-121 T 6
Olgastretet ≈ 84-85 N 3
Ölgij ☆ MAU 146-147 J 1
Ölgij = Har-Us o MAU 116-117 F 11
Ol'ginsk o RUS 122-123 E 2
Olgujdah o RUS 118-119 F 4
Olgujdah ~ RUS 118-119 F 3
Olhão o P 98-99 D 6
Olho d'Água do Casado o BR 68-69 K 6
Ol'hon, ostrov ⌒ RUS 116-117 N 9
Ol'hovka o RUS 96-97 D 9
Oli ~ DY 204-205 E 3
Oli o WAN 204-205 F 4
Olib ∸ HR 100-101 E 2
Olifants ~ NAM 220-221 D 1
Olifants o ZA 218-219 F 6
Olifantshoek o ZA 220-221 F 3
Olifantsrivier ~ ZA 220-221 D 6
Olifantsrivier ~ ZA 220-221 J 2
Olifantsrivier ~ ZA 220-221 E 6
Oliktok Point ▲ USA 20-21 Q 1
Oli Kültyk, sor ∸ KA 126-127 K 5
Olimarao ⌒ FSM 13 F 2
Olimar Chico, Río ~ ROU 78-79 M 2
Olimbía o GR 100-101 H 6
Olímpia o BR 72-73 F 6
Ólimpos ▲ GR 100-101 J 4
Olinalá o MEX 52-53 E 3
Olinda o··· BR 68-69 L 5
Olindina o BR 68-69 J 7
Olinga o MOC 218-219 J 3
Olio o AUS 178-179 G 1
Oliva o E 98-99 G 5
Oliva o RA 78-79 H 2
Oliva de la Frontera o E 98-99 D 5
Olivares, Cordillera de ▲ RA 76-77 C 6
Olivedos o BR 68-69 K 5
Oliveira o BR 72-73 H 6
Oliveira dos Brejinhos o BR 72-73 J 2
Olivença-a-Nova o ANG 216-217 B 7
Olivenza o E 98-99 D 5
Oliver Lake ⊂ CDN 34-35 E 2
Oliver Sound ≈ 24-25 h 4
Olivet o USA 42-43 J 4
Olivia o USA 42-43 K 3
Olivier Islands ⌒ CDN 20-21 X 2
Ol Joro Orok o EAK 212-213 F 4
Oljoro Wells < EAT 212-213 F 6
Oljutorskij, mys ▲ RUS 112-113 Q 7
Oljutorskij, zaliv ≈ 112-113 O 6
Oljutorskij hrebet ▲ RUS 112-113 Q 6
Oljutorskij poluostrov ⌣ RUS 112-113 Q 6
Ol Keju Ado ~ EAK 212-213 F 5
Olla o USA 44-45 L 4
Ollagüe o RCH 76-77 C 1
Ollagüe, Volcán ▲ BOL 76-77 C 1
Ollita, Cordillera de ▲ RA 76-77 B 6
Ollita, Paso de la ▲ RCH 76-77 C 5
Olmazor o US 136-137 L 4
Olmedo o E 98-99 E 4
Olmesutye o EAK 212-213 E 4
Olmos o PE 64-65 C 4
Olmütz = Olomouc o CZ 92-93 O 4
Olney o USA (IL) 46-47 D 6
Olney o USA (TX) 44-45 H 3
Oloči o RUS 118-119 J 10
Olodio o CI 202-203 G 7
Olofström ☆ S 86-87 G 8
Ologbo Game Reserve ⊥ WAN 204-205 F 5
Ologo, Čapo- o RUS 118-119 J 7
Oloibiri o WAN 204-205 G 6
Oloiserri o EAK 212-213 F 5
Oloitokitok o EAK 212-213 F 5
Oloj ~ RUS 112-113 L 4
Olojčan ~ RUS 112-113 L 3
Olojskij hrebet ▲ RUS 112-113 K 3
Ololdou o SN 202-203 D 2
Olom o RUS 118-119 J 5
Olomane, Rivière ~ CDN 38-39 O 3
Olomburi o SOL 184 I e 3
Olomouc o CZ 92-93 O 4
Olonec o RUS 94-95 N 1
Olongapo o RP 160-161 D 5
Olonki o RUS 116-117 L 9
Olorgasailie National Monument · EAK 212-213 F 4
Oloron-Sainte-Marie o· F 90-91 G 10
Olosega Island ⌒ USA 184 V c 2
Olov, gora ▲ RUS 88-89 O 5
Olovjannaja ☆ RUS 118-119 G 10
Olrik Fjord ≈ 26-27 Q 5
Ol'ša o RUS 94-95 M 4
Olsztyn ☆· PL 92-93 Q 2
Olsztynek o PL 92-93 Q 2
Olt ~ RO 102-103 D 5
Olt, Drăgănești o RO 102-103 D 5
Olta o RA 76-77 D 6
Olten o CH 92-93 J 5
Oltenița o· RO 102-103 E 5
Oltepesi o EAK 212-213 F 4
Oltinkŭl o US 136-137 F 3
Ol'tjan ~ RUS 112-113 R 4
Oltu ☆ TR 128-129 K 2
Oltu Çayı ~ TR 128-129 J 2
Ol Tukai o EAK 212-213 F 5
Oluanpi o RC 156-157 M 6
Oluanpi ▲ RC 156-157 M 6
Oluku o WAN 204-205 F 5
Olu Malua = Three Sisters Islands ⌒ SOL 184 I f 4
Olur ☆ TR 128-129 K 2
Olutange o RP 160-161 E 9
Olutange Island ⌒ RP 160-161 E 9
Olvido, El o CO 60-61 F 6
Ol'vinskij Kamen', gora ▲ RUS 114-115 E 5
Olymp = Ólimpos ▲ GR 100-101 J 4
Olympia ··· GR 100-101 H 6
Olympia ☆ USA 40-41 C 2
Olympic Dam o AUS 178-179 D 6
Olympic Mountains ▲ USA 40-41 C 2
Olympic Mountains National Park ⊥··· USA 40-41 C 2
Olympos ▲ CY 128-129 E 5
Olympus, Mount ▲ USA 40-41 C 2
Olynthos · GR 100-101 J 4
Ölzijm o MAU 148-149 E 3
Om' ~ RUS 114-115 Q 6
Om' ~ RUS 114-115 N 7
Ōma o J 152-153 J 4
Oma o RUS (NAO) 88-89 T 3
Oma ~ RUS 88-89 T 3
Oma o VRC 144-145 D 4
Ōmachi o J 152-153 G 6
Omae-saki ▲ J 152-153 H 7
Ōmagari o J 152-153 J 5
Omagh ☆· GB 90-91 D 4
Omaha o USA (AR) 44-45 L 1
Omaha o USA (NE) 42-43 K 5
Omaha Indian Reservation ⊼ USA 42-43 J 4
Omak o USA 40-41 E 1
Omakau o NZ 182 B 6
Omakwia o GUY 62-63 E 3
Omal ~ RUS 122-123 G 2
Oman, Gulf of ≈ IR 10-11 E 6
Oman = Saltanat 'Umān ■ OM 132-133 J 4
Oman Lake ⊂ CDN (NWT) 30-31 S 4
Oman Lake ⊂ CDN (SAS) 30-31 Q 6
Omapere o NZ 182 D 1
Omarama o NZ 182 B 6
Omar Combon o SP 212-213 K 2
Omarolluk Sound ≈ 36-37 K 7
Omaruru ☆ NAM 216-217 C 10
Omaruru ~ NAM 216-217 D 10
Omas o PE 64-65 D 8
Ōma-saki ▲ J 152-153 J 4
Omatako ▲ NAM (OKA) 216-217 D 10
Omatako ~ NAM 216-217 F 9
Omate o PE 70-71 B 5
Omati o PNG 183 B 4
Omati River ~ PNG 183 B 4
Omawewozonyanda o NAM 216-217 E 10
Ombai = Pulau Alor ⌒ RI 166-167 C 6
Ombai, Selat ≈ 166-167 C 6
Ombalantu o NAM 216-217 C 8
Ombella ~ RCA 206-207 D 6
Ombella-Mpoko □ RCA 206-207 C 6
Ombos · ET 194-195 F 5
Ombotozu ▲ NAM 216-217 D 10
Omboué o G 210-211 B 4
Ombrone ~ I 100-101 C 3
Ombu o RA 76-77 G 6
Ombues de Lavalle o ROU 78-79 L 2
Ombuku ~ NAM 216-217 B 8
Omčak o RUS 120-121 M 3
Omchi o TCH 198-199 H 2
Omčikandja o RUS 110-111 X 5
Omčug, Ust'- ☆ RUS 120-121 N 3
Omdurman = Umm Durmān o·· SUD 200-201 F 5
Ōme o J 152-153 H 7
Omega o USA 44-45 C 2
Omel'dinskij hrebet ▲ RUS 122-123 G 2
Omelič ~ RUS 114-115 Q 5
Omeo o AUS 180-181 J 4
Ometepe, Isla de ⌒ NIC 52-53 B 6
Ometepec o· MEX 52-53 E 3
Omgon, mys ▲ RUS 120-121 R 5
Omi, Río ~ BOL 70-71 E 3
Ōmi-Hachiman o J 152-153 G 7
Omineca Mountains ▲ CDN 32-33 G 3
Omineca River ~ CDN 32-33 H 4
Ominzatov toglari ▲ US 136-137 H 4
Omiš o· HR 100-101 F 3
Ōmi-shima ⌒ J 152-153 E 7
Omitara o NAM 216-217 E 11
Ōmiya o J 152-153 H 7
Ommaney, Cape ▲ USA 32-33 C 3
Ommanney Bay ≈ 24-25 V 4
Omnial o RI 166-167 E 2
Omnja ~ RUS 120-121 F 4
Ömnögov' □ MAU 148-149 F 6
Omoa o· HN 52-53 K 4
Omoku o WAN 204-205 G 6
Omoloj ~ RUS 110-111 S 5
Omolon o RUS 112-113 K 2
Omolon ~ RUS 112-113 L 4
Omo National Park ⊥ ETH 208-209 B 5
Omono-gawa ~ J 152-153 J 5
Omoto-gawa ~ J 152-153 J 5
Omo Wenz ~ ETH 208-209 C 5
Ompah o CDN 38-39 F 6
Ompupa o ANG 216-217 B 8
Omrel'kaj ~ RUS 112-113 Q 2
Omsk ☆· RUS 124-125 H 1
Omskij o RUS 116-117 L 8
Omsukčan ☆ RUS 112-113 H 5
Omsukčanskij hrebet ▲ RUS 112-113 H 4
Ōmu o J 152-153 K 2
Omu-Aran o WAN 204-205 F 4
Omulevka ~ RUS 110-111 c 7
Omulevka ~ RUS 120-121 M 2
Omuljahskaja guba ≈ 110-111 Z 3
Omuo o WAN 204-205 F 5
Omuramba Ovambo ~ NAM 216-217 D 9
Ōmura-wan ≈ 152-153 C 8
Omurtag o BG 102-103 E 6
Ōmuta o J 152-153 D 8
Omutinskij ☆ RUS 114-115 J 6
Omutninsk ☆ RUS 96-97 H 4
Oña o E 98-99 F 3
Oña o EC 64-65 C 3
Ona ~ RUS 118-119 E 9
Ona ~ RUS 124-125 Q 3
Ona = Birjusa ~ RUS 116-117 G 7
Ona Basin ≃ 6-7 O 9
Onaman Lake ⊂ CDN 34-35 N 5
Onamia o USA 42-43 L 2
Onancock o USA 46-47 L 7
Onang o RI 164-165 F 5
Onanganjang o RI 162-163 C 3
Onangué, Lac ⊂ G 210-211 C 4
Onanhasang o RI 162-163 C 4
Onaping Lake ⊂ CDN 38-39 D 5
Onawa o USA 42-43 J 4
Onaway o USA 46-47 F 3
Onça, Cachoeira da ~ BR 62-63 G 6
Onça, Corredeira ~ BR 66-67 H 6
Onça, Travessia da ~ BR 68-69 B 4
Onças, Lago das ⊂ BR 70-71 J 5
Oncativo o RA 76-77 F 6
Oncócua o ANG 216-217 B 8
Onda o E 98-99 G 5
Onda ~ RUS 88-89 M 5
Ondangwa ☆ NAM 216-217 C 8
Ondas, Rio das ~ BR 72-73 H 2
Ondaw o MYA 142-143 J 4
Ondo o WAN 204-205 F 5
Ondo □ WAN 204-205 F 5
Ondores o PE 64-65 D 7
Öndörhaan ☆ MAU 148-149 K 4
Ondozero o RUS (KAR) 88-89 M 5
Ondozero ⊂ RUS (KAR) 88-89 M 5
Onega o RUS 88-89 P 5
Onega ~ RUS 88-89 P 5
Önege o KA 96-97 E 9
One Hundred and Fifty Mile House o CDN 32-33 K 5
One Hundred Mile House o CDN 32-33 K 6
Oneida o USA (NY) 46-47 L 4
Oneida o USA (TN) 48-49 F 1
Oneida Lake ⊂ USA 46-47 L 4
O'Neill o USA 42-43 H 4
Oneko, ozero ⊂ RUS 116-117 E 3
Onekotan, ostrov ⌒ RUS 122-123 Q 4
Onema-Okolo o ZRE 210-211 J 5
Onema Ututu o ZRE 210-211 J 5
Onemen, zaliv ≈ 112-113 T 4
Oneonta o USA 46-47 L 4
Onești o RO 102-103 E 4
Onezhskaya Guba = Onežskaja guba ≈ RUS 88-89 N 4
Onežskaja guba ≈ 88-89 N 4
Onežskij poluostrov ⌣ RUS 88-89 O 4
Onga o G 210-211 E 4
Ongandjera o NAM 216-217 C 8
Ōng Cō, Đèo ▲ VN 158-159 K 5
Ongeri o ZRE 210-211 K 6
Ongersrivier ~ ZA 220-221 F 5
Ongi o MAU 148-149 F 5
Ongi gol ~ MAU 148-149 F 4
Ongjin o DVR 150-151 E 9
Ongka o RI 164-165 G 3
Ongkaw o RI 164-165 J 3
Ongkharak o THA 158-159 F 3
Ongniud Qi o VRC 148-149 O 6
Ongoka o ZRE 210-211 L 4
Ongole o IND 140-141 J 3
Ongon o PE 64-65 D 6
Ongon = Havirga o MAU 148-149 L 5
Ongongoro o NAM 216-217 E 10
Ongonyi o RCB 210-211 F 4
Ongoro Gotjari o NAM 216-217 D 11
Onhne o MYA 158-159 D 2
Oni o GE 126-127 E 6
Oni, River ~ WAN 204-205 F 5
Onibe ~ RM 222-223 F 6
Onie ú Olin, Río ~ RA 80 E 3
Onilahy ~ RM 222-223 D 9
Onin (Fakfak) Peninsula ⌣ RI 166-167 F 3
Onioni o PNG 183 E 6
Onion Lake o CDN 32-33 Q 5
Onitsha ☆ WAN 204-205 G 5
Onive ~ RM 222-223 E 7
Onkamo o FIN 88-89 L 5
Onkivesi ⊂ FIN 88-89 J 5
Onnekon ~ RUS 118-119 O 6
Onnës o RUS 120-121 D 3
Onnë-Siligir ~ RUS 110-111 J 6
Ono ⌒ FJI 184 III b 3
Ōno o J 152-153 G 7
Onoko o TCH 206-207 B 3
Onomichi o J 152-153 E 7
Onon ~ RUS 118-119 G 10
Onon gol ~ MAU 148-149 K 3
Onor o RUS 122-123 K 3
Onor ~ RUS 122-123 K 3
Onor, gora ▲ RUS 122-123 K 3
Onot ~ RUS 116-117 K 9
Onoto o YV 60-61 J 3
Onseepkans o ZA 220-221 D 4
Onslow o AUS 172-173 B 6
Onslow Bay ≈ 48-49 K 2
Ontake-san ▲ J 152-153 G 7
Ontar o VAN 184 II a 2
Ontaratue River ~ CDN 20-21 Z 3
Ontario □ CDN 34-35 L 5
Ontario o USA (CA) 40-41 F 8
Ontario o USA (OR) 40-41 F 3
Ontario o USA (WI) 46-47 C 4
Ontario, Lake ⊂ 46-47 J 4
Ontario Peninsula ⌣ CDN 38-39 D 7
Ontmoeting o ZA 220-221 E 3
Ontonagon o USA 46-47 D 2
Ontong Java ⌒ SOL 184 I d 1
Ōnuma Quasi National Park ⊥ J 152-153 J 4
Onverwacht ☆ SME 62-63 G 3
Onwul River ~ WAN 204-205 H 5
Onyx Cave · USA 44-45 L 1
Oobagooma o AUS 172-173 G 4
Oodnadatta o AUS 178-179 C 4
Oodnadatta Track ll AUS 178-179 C 5
Oodonggo o RI 168 D 7
Oodweyne o SP 208-209 G 4
Ooldea Range ▲ AUS 176-177 L 5
Oolloo o AUS 172-173 K 2
Oologah Lake ⊂ USA 44-45 K 1
Ooratippra o AUS 178-179 D 1
Oorindi o AUS 174-175 F 7
Oos-Londen = East London o· ZA 220-221 H 6
Ooste Lake ⊂ CDN 32-33 G 5
Oostende o· B 92-93 G 3
Oostermoed o ZA 220-221 H 2
Oosterschelde ≈ 92-93 G 3
Ootsa Lake ⊂ CDN 32-33 H 5
Opachuanau Lake ⊂ CDN 34-35 G 2
Opaka o BG 102-103 E 6
Opala ~ RUS 122-123 R 2
Opala o ZRE 210-211 K 4
Opang o RI 164-165 K 4
Opari o SUD 212-213 D 2
Oparino o RUS 96-97 F 4
Opasatika o CDN 34-35 P 6
Opasatika Lake ⊂ CDN 34-35 P 6
Opasnyj, mys ▲ RUS (KMC) 120-121 S 7
Opasnyj, mys ▲ RUS (KOR) 120-121 U 3
Opataca, Lac ⊂ CDN 38-39 G 3
Opatija o HR 100-101 E 2
Opava o CZ 92-93 O 4
Opawica, Lac ⊂ CDN 38-39 G 4
Opelika o USA 48-49 F 3
Opelousas o USA 44-45 L 4
Opémisca, Mont ▲ CDN 38-39 G 4
Open Bay ≈ 183 F 3
Open Bay o PNG 183 F 3
Opeongo Lake ⊂ CDN 38-39 E 6
Opeta, Lake ⊂ EAU 212-213 E 3
Opheim o USA 42-43 D 1
Ophir o USA 20-21 M 5
Ophir, Gunung ▲ RI 162-163 C 4
Ophthalmia Range ▲ AUS 172-173 D 7
Opi o WAN 204-205 G 5
Opichén o MEX 52-53 K 1
Opienge o ZRE 212-213 A 3
Opikeigen Lake ⊂ CDN 34-35 M 5
Opilija ▲ UA 102-103 D 3
Opinaca, Réservoir < CDN 38-39 F 2
Opinaca, Rivière ~ CDN 38-39 E 2
Opinnagau Lake ⊂ CDN 34-35 O 4
Opinnagau River ~ CDN 34-35 P 3
Opiscotéo, Lac ⊂ CDN 38-39 K 2
Opiscotiche, Lac ⊂ CDN 38-39 L 2
Opišn'a o UA 102-103 J 3
Opobo o WAN 204-205 G 6
Opočka ☆ RUS 94-95 L 3
Opocopa, Lac ⊂ CDN 38-39 L 2
Opoczno o PL 92-93 Q 3
Opole ☆· PL 92-93 O 3
Opopeo o MEX 52-53 D 2
Opornyj o KA 96-97 J 10
Opotiki o NZ 182 F 3
Opp o USA 48-49 E 4
Oppa-wan ≈ 152-153 G 3
Oppdal ☆ N 86-87 D 5
Opportunity o USA 40-41 F 2
Opposite Island ⌒ CDN 36-37 H 2
Oppstryn o N 86-87 C 6
Optic Lake ⊂ CDN 34-35 F 3
Opuka ~ RUS 112-113 R 5
Opuka, laguna ⊂ RUS 112-113 S 6
Opunake o NZ 182 D 3
Opuwo ☆ NAM 216-217 B 9
Oquossoc o USA 46-47 N 3
Ör ~ KA 126-127 N 3
Or' ~ RUS 96-97 L 8
Ora o PNG 183 F 3
Ora ~ VAN 184 II a 2
Oraba o EAU 212-213 C 2
Oracle o USA 44-45 B 3
Oracle Junction o USA 44-45 B 3
Oradea ☆· RO 102-103 B 4
Öræfajökull ▲ IS 86-87 e 2
Orah o WAN 204-205 F 5
Orai o IND 138-139 G 7
Oral ☆ KA 96-97 G 8
Oral ~ KA 96-97 G 9
Orami o PNG 184 I b 2
Oran = Wahrān ☆·· DZ 188-189 L 3
Oranapai o GUY 62-63 E 4
Orange o AUS 180-181 K 2
Orange o·· F 90-91 K 9
Orange o USA 44-45 L 4
Orange ~ ZA 220-221 D 4
Orange, Cap ▲ F 62-63 J 3
Orangeburg o USA 48-49 H 3
Orange Cay ⌒ BS 54-55 F 2
Orange Fan ≃ 9 E 9
Orange Free State = Oranje-Vrystaat □ ZA 220-221 G 4
Orange Park o USA 48-49 H 4
Orangerie Bay ≈ 183 E 6
Orangeville o CDN 38-39 D 7
Orange Walk o BH 52-53 K 2
Orangi ~ EAT 212-213 E 5
Orango, Ilha de ⌒ GNB 202-203 B 4
Orangozinho, Ilha de ⌒ GNB 202-203 C 4
Orangutang, mys ▲ RUS 112-113 R 6
Orania o ZA 220-221 G 4
Oranjefontein o ZA 218-219 D 6
Oranjemund o NAM 220-221 C 4
Oranjerivier ~ ZA 220-221 E 4
Oranjestad ☆ ARU 60-61 F 1
Oranjestad ☆·· NA (NA) 56 D 3
Oranjeville o ZA 220-221 J 3
Oranje Vrystaat □ ZA 220-221 G 4
Oransbari o RI 166-167 H 2
Oranžerei o RUS 126-127 G 5
Orapa o RB 218-219 C 5
Oras o RP 160-161 F 6
Oratia, Mount ▲ USA 22-23 Q 3
Oratorio o RA 76-77 D 2
Orattanādu o IND 140-141 H 5
Orava o PNG 184 I b 2
Oravița o RO 102-103 B 5
Orb ~ F 90-91 J 10
Orbata, Jebel ▲ TN 190-191 G 3
Orbetello o I 100-101 C 3
Órbigo, Río ~ E 98-99 E 3
Orbost o AUS 180-181 K 4
Orcadas o ARK 16 G 32
Orchila, Isla ⌒ YV 60-61 H 2
Orco ~ I 100-101 A 2
Orcococha, Lago ⊂ PE 64-65 E 8
Orcopampa o PE 64-65 F 9
Ord o USA 42-43 H 5
Ord, Mount ▲ AUS 172-173 G 4
Orda ☆ RUS 96-97 K 5
Orda < TCH 198-199 H 2
Orderville o USA 40-41 H 7
Ordes o·· E 98-99 C 3
Ordoqui o RA 78-79 J 3
Ordos = Mu Us Shamo ∸ VRC 154-155 E 2
Ord Regeneration Depot o AUS 172-173 J 4
Ord River ~ AUS 172-173 J 4
Ordu ☆ TR 128-129 G 2
Ordubad o AZ 128-129 M 3
Ordway o USA 42-43 F 6
Ordynskoe ☆ RUS 124-125 M 1
Ordženikidze o RUS 124-125 B 2
Ordžonikidze o UA 102-103 J 4
Ordžonikidzeabad = Kofarnihon o TJ 136-137 L 5
Ore o WAN 204-205 F 5
Örebro ☆· S 86-87 G 7
Oredež o RUS 94-95 M 2
Oregon o USA (MO) 42-43 K 6
Oregon o USA (WI) 46-47 D 4
Oregon □ USA 40-41 C 4
Oregon Caves National Monument · USA 40-41 C 4
Orehovo-Zuevo ☆ RUS 94-95 Q 4
Orekhovo-Zuyevo = Orehovo-Zuevo ☆ RUS 94-95 Q 4
Orel' o RUS 94-95 P 5
Orel' ~ UA 102-103 J 3
Orel', ozero ⊂ RUS 122-123 H 2
Orellana o PE (AMA) 64-65 C 4
Orellana o PE (LOR) 64-65 E 5
Orellana la Vieja o E 98-99 E 5
Orem o USA 40-41 J 5
Ören o TR 128-129 B 4
Orenburg ☆ RUS 96-97 J 8
Oreng o RI 162-163 B 2
Orense = Ourense o E 98-99 D 3
Orerokpe o WAN 204-205 F 6
Øresund ≈ 86-87 F 9
Orewa o NZ 182 E 2
Orford, Port o USA 40-41 B 4
Organabo o F 62-63 H 3
Organ Pipe Cactus National Monument · USA 40-41 H 9
Orgeev = Orhei ☆ MD 102-103 F 4
Orgūn o AFG 138-139 B 3
Orhaneli ☆ TR 128-129 C 3
Orhangazi o TR 128-129 C 2
Orhei ☆ MD 102-103 F 4
Orhej = Orhei ☆ MD 102-103 F 4
Orhon o MAU 148-149 G 3
Orhon gol ~ MAU 148-149 F 3
Ori ~ RT 202-203 L 5
Orianda, laguna ⊂ RUS 112-113 U 5
Orica o HN 52-53 L 4
Orichiv o UA 102-103 J 4
Orick o USA 40-41 B 5
Orient o USA 40-41 E 1
Oriental, Cordillera ▲ DOM 54-55 L 5
Oriental, Cordillera ▲ PE 64-65 D 4
Oriental, Llanura ▲ DOM 54-55 L 5
Oriente o RA 78-79 J 5
Oriente, Cachoeira do ~ BR 66-67 E 7
Orihuela o E 98-99 G 5
Orillia o CDN 38-39 E 6
Orin o USA 42-43 E 4
Orinduik o GUY 62-63 D 3
Orinoca o BOL 70-71 D 6
Orinoco, Delta del ≈ 60-61 L 3
Orinoco, Llanos del ∸ 60-61 F 5
Orinoco, Río ~ YV 60-61 J 6
Oriomo o PNG 183 B 5
Orissa □ IND 142-143 C 5
Orissaare o EST 94-95 H 2
Oristano o· I 100-101 B 5
Orito o CO 64-65 D 1
Orituco o YV 60-61 H 3
Orituco, Río ~ YV 60-61 H 3
Oritupano, Río ~ YV 60-61 K 3
Orivesi o FIN 88-89 H 6
Oriximiná o BR 62-63 G 6
Orizaba o· MEX 52-53 F 2
Orizaba, Pico de ▲ MEX 52-53 F 2
Orjahovo o BG 102-103 C 6
Orjen ▲ YU 100-101 G 3
Orjus-Miele ~ RUS 118-119 K 7
Orkadiéré o SN 202-203 D 2
Orkanger o N 86-87 D 5
Örkelljunga o S 86-87 F 8
Orkjule, mys ▲ RUS 110-111 S 4
Orkla ~ N 86-87 D 5
Orkney o ZA 220-221 H 3
Orkney Islands ⌒ GB 90-91 F 2
Orla o USA 44-45 F 4
Orlameš o AFG 136-137 K 6
Orland o USA 40-41 C 6
Orlândia o BR 72-73 G 6
Orlando o· USA 48-49 H 5
Orleães o BR 74-75 F 7
Orléanais ⌒ F 90-91 H 8
Orléans o F 90-91 H 8
Orleans, Île d' ⌒ CDN 38-39 J 5
Orleans Farms o AUS 176-177 G 6
Orle River Game Reserve ⊥ WAN 204-205 G 5
Orlik ☆ RUS 116-117 J 9
Orlinaja gora ▲ RUS 112-113 U 5
Orlinga o RUS 116-117 M 7
Orlinga ~ RUS 116-117 N 8
Orlov Gaj o RUS 96-97 F 8
Orlovka o RUS (NVS) 114-115 O 6
Orlovka ~ RUS 112-113 N 3
Orlovka ~ RUS 112-113 P 4
Orlovka ~ RUS 114-115 T 5
Orlovka ~ RUS 122-123 Q 2
Orlovskij o RUS 102-103 N 4
Orlovskij, mys ▲ RUS 88-89 Q 3
Orlovskij hrebet ▲ RUS 112-113 N 3
Orlovskij zaliv ≈ 88-89 Q 3
Orlu o WAN 204-205 G 6
Ormachea, Bosque Petrificado J. · RA 80 F 2
Ormāra o PK 134-135 L 6
Ormāra, Rās ▲ PK 134-135 L 6
Ormea o·· I 100-101 A 2
Ormiston Gorge National Park ⊥ AUS 176-177 M 1
Ormoc o RP 160-161 F 7
Ormond Beach o USA 48-49 H 5
Ormonde Island ⌒ CDN 24-25 e 6
Ormos Almirou ≈ 100-101 K 7
Ormsby o USA 42-43 K 4
Ormtjørn nasjonalpark ⊥ N 86-87 D 6
Orne ~ F 90-91 G 7
Ørnes o N 86-87 F 3
Örnsköldsvik o S 86-87 J 5
Oro, Lac ⊂ RMM 196-197 J 6
Oro, Museo del · CO 60-61 D 5
Oro, Río de ~ RA 76-77 H 4
Oro, Río del ~ MEX 50-51 G 5
Orobayaya o BOL 70-71 F 3
Orocó o BR 68-69 J 6
Orocue o CO 60-61 F 5
Orodara o BF 202-203 H 4
Orodel o· RO 102-103 C 5
Oroek o RUS 110-111 d 7
Orofino o USA 40-41 F 2
Orog nuur ⊂ MAU 148-149 E 5
Orogrande o USA 44-45 D 3
Orol dengizi = Aral tenizi ⊂ 126-127 N 5
Orom o EAU 212-213 D 2
Oromocto o CDN 38-39 L 6
Oron o RUS 118-119 H 7
Oron o WAN 204-205 H 6
Orondo o USA 40-41 D 2
Oroners Out Station o AUS 174-175 G 4
Oronga o PNG 183 C 3
Orono o USA 46-47 O 3
Oronoquerivier ~ GUY 62-63 F 4
Orope o YV 60-61 E 3

298 Okinawa-shotō — Orope

Oropesa o **E** 98-99 E 5
Oropesa, Río o **PE** 64-65 E 8
Oroqen Zizhiqi o **VRC** 150-151 D 2
Oroquieta o **RP** 160-161 E 8
Orós o **BR** 68-69 J 5
Orós, Açude ⊏ **BR** 68-69 J 5
Orosei o **I** 100-101 B 4
Orosháza o **H** 92-93 Q 5
Orosi o **USA** 40-41 E 7
Orosmayo, Río de o **RA** 76-77 D 2
Orotina o **CR** 52-53 B 7
Orotko, ozero o **RUS** 110-111 W 4
Orotuk o **RUS** 120-121 N 2
Orotukan o **RUS** 120-121 O 2
Orotukan o **RUS** 120-121 O 2
Oroville o **USA** (WA) 40-41 E 1
Oroville o • **USA** (CA) 40-41 D 6
Oroville Reservoir ⊏ **USA** 40-41 D 6
Oroya, La o **PE** 64-65 E 7
Orpheus Lake o **AUS** 180-181 E 2
Orquideas, Parque Nacional las ⊥ **CO** 60-61 C 4
Orroroo o **AUS** 180-181 E 2
Orša o **BY** 94-95 M 4
Orsa o **S** 86-87 G 6
Orsha = Orša ✦ **BY** 94-95 M 4
Orsk o **RUS** 96-97 M 8
Ørstavik o **N** 86-87 C 5
Ortaca o **TR** 128-129 C 4
Ortaköy o **TR** 128-129 F 3
Ortasu o • **KA** 124-125 J 5
Orte o **I** 100-101 D 3
Ortega o **CO** 60-61 D 6
Orteguaza, Río o **CO** 64-65 E 1
Orthez o **F** 90-91 G 10
Ortho, Río o **BOL** 70-71 D 2
Ortigueira o **BR** 74-75 E 5
Ortigueira o **E** 98-99 D 3
Ortit o **GRØ** 28-29 V 4
Ortiz o **MEX** 50-51 D 3
Ort'jagun o **RUS** 114-115 N 4
Ortler = Örtles ▲ **I** 100-101 C 1
Ortona o **I** 100-101 E 3
Orto-Nahara o **RUS** 118-119 G 5
Ortonville o **USA** 42-43 J 3
Orto-Surt o **RUS** 118-119 M 4
Orto-Tokoj o **KS** 146-147 C 4
Oru o **CO** 60-61 E 3
Oruhito o **NAM** 216-217 B 9
Orulgan, hrebet ▲▲ **RUS** 110-111 R 5
Orümiye o ✦ **IR** 128-129 L 4
Orümiye, Daryāče-ye o **IR** 128-129 L 3
Oruro o **BOL** 70-71 D 5
Orust ∩ **S** 86-87 E 7
Örüzgän o **AFG** (OR) 134-135 M 2
Örüzgän o **AFG** 134-135 L 2
Orvieto o **I** 100-101 D 3
Orville Escarpment ⊏ **ARK** 16 F 30
Orwell o **USA** 46-47 H 5
Orzüiye o **IR** 134-135 L 6
Oržycja o **UA** 102-103 H 3
Orzysz o • **PL** 92-93 Q 2
Oš o **KS** 136-137 N 4
Os o **N** 86-87 E 5
Osa o **RUS** 116-117 L 9
Osa ∩ **RUS** (PRM) 96-97 J 3
Oša o **RUS** 114-115 M 6
Osa ∩ **RUS** 116-117 M 9
Osa, Peninsula de o **CR** 52-53 C 7
Osage o **USA** 42-43 L 3
Osage River o **USA** 42-43 L 6
Ōsaka ☆ • **J** 152-153 F 7
Osakarovka = Askarly ✦ **KA** 124-125 H 3
Ōsaka-wan ≈ 152-153 F 7
Osasco o **BR** 72-73 G 7
Osborne o **USA** 42-43 H 6
Osby o **S** 86-87 F 8
Osca, Río o **BOL** 70-71 E 5
Oscar o **F** 62-63 H 4
Oscar II land ∩ **N** 84-85 H 3
Oscar Soto Máynes o **MEX** 50-51 F 3
Osceola o **USA** (AR) 48-49 D 7
Osceola o **USA** (IA) 42-43 L 5
Osceola o **USA** (NE) 42-43 J 5
Óschiri o **I** 100-101 B 4
Oscoda o **USA** 46-47 G 3
Oscura, Punta ▲ **GQ** 210-211 B 2
Osetr o **RUS** 94-95 Q 4
Osh = oš ☆ **KS** 136-137 N 4
Oshakati o **NAM** 216-217 C 8
Oshamambe o **J** 152-153 J 3
Oshawa o **CDN** 38-39 G 6
Oshetna River o **USA** 20-21 R 5
Oshika-hanto ∪ **J** 152-153 J 5
Oshikango o **NAM** 216-217 C 8
Oshikuku o **NAM** 216-217 C 8
Ō-shima ∩ **J** (KGA) 152-153 C 10
Ō-shima ∩ **J** (TOK) 152-153 H 7
Ō-shima ∩ **J** (YMG) 152-153 E 8
Oshima-hantō ∪ **J** 152-153 J 3
Oshivelo o **NAM** 216-217 D 8
Oshkosh o **USA** (NE) 42-43 F 5
Oshkosh o **USA** (WI) 46-47 D 3
Oshun, River ∩ **WAN** 204-205 F 5
Oshwe o **ZRE** 210-211 G 5
Osiān o **IND** 138-139 D 6
Osijek ☆ • **HR** 100-101 G 2
Osilinka River o **CDN** 32-33 N 4
Osinniki o **RUS** 124-125 Q 2
Osinovaja, Bol'šaja o **RUS** 112-113 T 3
Osinovka o **RUS** 116-117 K 7
Osinovo o **RUS** 88-89 R 5
Osinovoe Pleso o **RUS** 114-115 T 7
Osinovskij porog o **RUS** 114-115 U 4
Oskaloosa o **USA** 42-43 L 5
Oskarshamn o **S** 86-87 H 8
Oskélanéo o **CDN** 38-39 G 4
Öskemen o **KA** 124-125 N 4
Os'kino o **RUS** 102-103 L 2
Os'kino o **RUS** 116-117 N 8
Ośkoto, ozero o **RUS** 88-89 Y 3
Oskú o **IR** 128-129 M 4

Osljanka, gora ▲▲ **RUS** 114-115 E 5
Oslo ✦•• **N** 86-87 E 7
Oslofjorden ≈ 86-87 E 7
Osmánābád o **IND** 138-139 F 10
Osmancık o **TR** 128-129 F 2
Osmaneli o **TR** 128-129 D 2
Osmaniye o **TR** 128-129 E 10
Os'mino o **RUS** 94-95 L 2
Ōsmo o **S** 86-87 H 7
Osnabrück o • **D** 92-93 K 2
Ošnüye o • **IR** 128-129 L 3
Oso o **ZRE** 212-213 A 4
Oso, El o **YV** 60-61 G 3
Osogbo o • **WAN** 204-205 F 5
Osogovski pl. ▲▲ **MK** 100-101 J 3
Osório da Fonseca o **BR** 66-67 H 4
Osorno o **E** 98-99 E 3
Osorno o **NZ** 182 E 3
Osorno, Volcán ▲ **RCH** 78-79 C 6
Osoyoos o **CDN** 32-33 L 7
Osoyoos Indian Reserve ⊼ **CDN** 32-33 L 7
Øsøyra o **N** 86-87 B 6
Ospasquia Provincial Park ⊥ **CDN** 34-35 K 4
Ospika River o **CDN** 32-33 H 3
Ospino o **YV** 60-61 G 3
Osprey Reef ∩ **AUS** 174-175 J 3
Ossa ▲ **P** 98-99 D 5
Ossa, Mount ▲ **AUS** 180-181 J 6
Ossabaw Island ∩ **USA** 48-49 H 4
Ossa de Montiel o **E** 98-99 F 5
Ossalinskij krjaž ▲▲ **RUS** 110-111 c 7
Osse, River o **WAN** 204-205 F 5
Ossélé o **RCB** 210-211 E 4
Osseo o **USA** 46-47 C 3
Ossima o **PNG** 183 A 3
Ossining o **USA** 46-47 M 5
Ossokmanuan Lake o **CDN** 38-39 M 2
Ossora ☆ **RUS** 120-121 U 4
Ostapnischer Südpolarbecken ≈ 16 G 27
Ostaškin, kamen' ▲ **RUS** 114-115 T 7
Ostaškov ✦ **RUS** 94-95 N 3
Ostavall o **S** 86-87 G 5
Østby o **N** 86-87 E 6
Oste o **D** 92-93 K 2
Oster ∩ **RUS** 94-95 N 5
Österbotten = Pohjanmaa ∩ **FIN** 88-89 G 5
Österbybruk o **S** 86-87 H 6
Østerdalen ∩ **N** 86-87 E 6
Östergötland ⊥ **S** 86-87 G 7
Østerø = Eysturoy ∩ **FR** 90-91 D 1
Östersund • **S** 86-87 G 5
Ostfriesische Inseln ⊥ **D** 92-93 J 2
Østgrønland = Tunu o **GRØ** 26-27 d 8
Östhammar o **S** 86-87 H 6
Östinskij Pogost o **RUS** 94-95 O 1
Ōstörinán o **IR** 134-135 C 2
Ostraja, gora ▲ **RUS** 112-113 P 5
Ostraja, gora ▲ **RUS** 122-123 O 5
Ostraja, gora ▲ **RUS** (KOR) 120-121 U 4
Ostrava • **CZ** 92-93 P 4
Ostrau = Ostrava o **CZ** 92-93 P 4
Ostrau = Ostrov nad Oslavou o **CZ** 92-93 M 4
Ostrava o **CZ** 92-93 P 4
Ostrjak, gora ▲ **RUS** 112-113 Q 4
Ostróda o • **PL** 92-93 Q 2
Ostrogožsk o **RUS** 102-103 L 2
Ostrołęka o • **PL** 92-93 Q 2
Ostrov o **RO** 102-103 L 2
Ostrov ✦ **RUS** 94-95 L 3
Ostroveršinnyj hrebet ▲▲ **RUS** 112-113 N 2
Ostrovnoe o **RUS** 112-113 N 2
Ostrovnoe o **RUS** (ORB) 96-97 K 8
Ostrovnoj, mys ▲ **RUS** 114-115 M 2
Ostrovnoj, zaliv o **RUS** 120-121 O 1
Ostrovskoe o **RUS** 94-95 S 3
ostrov Vozroždenija ∩ **US** 136-137 F 2
Ostrowiec Świętokrzyski o **PL** 92-93 Q 3
Ostrów Mazowiecka o **PL** 92-93 Q 2
Ostrów Wielkopolski o • **PL** 92-93 O 3
Osttirol ▲ **A** 92-93 M 5
Ostuni o **I** 100-101 F 4
Ošturān, Küh-e ▲▲ **IR** 134-135 C 2
Ōşt Vank • **TR** 128-129 J 2
O'Sullivan Lake o **CDN** 34-35 N 5
Ōsumi-hantō ∪ **J** 152-153 D 9
Ōsumi-kaikyō ≈ 152-153 D 9
Ōsumi-shotō ∩ **J** 152-153 D 9
Osuna o **E** 98-99 E 6
Oswego o **USA** (KS) 44-45 K 1
Oswego o **USA** (NY) 46-47 K 4
Oświęcim o • **PL** 92-93 P 3
Ōta o **J** 152-153 G 7
Otacílio Costa o **BR** 74-75 E 6
Ōta-gawa ∩ **J** 152-153 E 8
Otago Peninsula ∪•• **NZ** 182 C 6
Otajikačanskij hrebet ▲▲ **RUS** 112-113 J 5
Otaki o **NZ** 182 E 4
Otakwa ∩ **RI** 166-167 J 4
Otakwa ∩ **RI** 166-167 J 4
Otaru o **J** 152-153 J 3
Otatal, Cerro ▲ **MEX** 50-51 D 3
Otavalo o **EC** 64-65 C 1
Otavi o **NAM** 216-217 D 9
Otchinjau o **ANG** 216-217 B 8
OTC International Satellite Earth Station • **AUS** 176-177 M 5
O.T.Downs o **AUS** 174-175 D 4
Otelnuk, Lac o **CDN** 36-37 P 6
Oterkpolu o **GH** 202-203 K 6
Otgon Tēngēr ▲ **MAU** 148-149 C 4
Otha ∩ **IND** 138-139 C 9
Othe Cherokees, Lake o **USA** 44-45 K 1
Othello o **USA** 40-41 E 2
Othe Pines, Lake o **USA** 44-45 K 3
Otherside River ∩ **CDN** 30-31 Q 6
Oti ∩ **GH** 202-203 L 5
Oti o **RI** 164-165 F 4

Oti, Réserve de l' ⊥ **RT** 202-203 L 4
Otinolándia o **BR** 72-73 J 3
Otish, Monts ▲▲ **CDN** 38-39 J 2
Otjikondo Lake • **NAM** 216-217 C 9
Otjikoto Lake • **NAM** 216-217 D 11
Otjimbingwe o **NAM** 216-217 B 8
Otjinene o **NAM** 216-217 E 10
Otjinhungwa o **NAM** 216-217 B 8
Otjisemba o **NAM** 216-217 D 10
Otjitanda o **NAM** 216-217 B 8
Otjiwarongo ☆ **NAM** 216-217 D 10
Otjosondjou o **NAM** 216-217 E 10
Otjosondu o **NAM** 216-217 D 10
Otmēk, pereval ▲ **KS** 136-137 N 4
Otoca o **PE** 64-65 E 9
Otog Qi o **VRC** 154-155 E 2
Otog Qian Qi o **VRC** 154-155 E 2
Otoineppu o **J** 152-153 K 2
Otola o **DY** 202-203 L 5
Otorohanga o **NZ** 182 E 3
Ōtoyo o **J** 152-153 E 8
Otra ∩ **N** 86-87 C 7
Otradnaja o **RUS** 126-127 D 5
Otradnyj o **RUS** 96-97 G 7
Otranto o **I** 100-101 G 4
Ótranto, Canale d' ≈ 100-101 G 4
Otrožnyj o **RUS** 112-113 R 4
Otselic o **USA** 46-47 L 4
Ōtsuki o **J** 152-153 H 7
Otta o **N** 86-87 D 6
Ottappidáram o **IND** 140-141 H 6
Ottawa ★• **CDN** 38-39 G 6
Ottawa o **USA** (IL) 46-47 D 5
Ottawa o **USA** (KS) 42-43 K 6
Ottawa o **USA** (OH) 46-47 F 5
Ottawa River ∩ **CDN** 38-39 E 5
Ottawa Islands ∩ **CDN** 36-37 J 5
Otte Krupens Fjord ≈ 28-29 V 3
Otter o **USA** 42-43 D 3
Otter, Peaks of ▲ **USA** 46-47 J 7
Otter Creek o **USA** 48-49 G 5
Otter Island ∩ **USA** 22-23 L 4
Otter Rapids o **CDN** 38-39 S 5
Otter River o **CDN** 34-35 M 4
Otto Fiord ≈ 26-27 F 3
Otto-Sala ∩ **RUS** 110-111 S 7
Ottosdal o **ZA** 220-221 G 3
Ottoshoop o **ZA** 220-221 G 2
Ottuk o **KS** 146-147 C 4
Ottumwa o **USA** 42-43 L 5
Otu o **CAM** 204-205 J 6
Otukamamoan Lake o **CDN** 34-35 K 6
Otukpa o **WAN** 204-205 G 5
Oturmpa o **RA** 76-77 F 4
Otuquis, Bañados de o **BOL** 70-71 H 6
Otuquis, Río ∩ **BOL** 70-71 H 6
Oturkpo o **WAN** 204-205 H 5
Otu Tolu Group ∩ **TON** 184 IV a 2
Otuzco o **PE** 64-65 C 5
Otway, Cape ▲ **AUS** 180-181 G 7
Otway, Seno ≈ 80 E 9
Otway National Park ⊥ **AUS** 180-181 G 5
Oua ∩ **G** 210-211 D 3
Ouachita, Lake o **USA** 44-45 L 2
Ouachita Mountains ▲▲ **USA** 44-45 L 2
Ouachita River ∩ **USA** 44-45 M 4
Ouadda o **RCA** 206-207 F 4
Ouaddaï ▲ **TCH** 198-199 K 6
Ouâd Nâga o **RIM** 196-197 C 6
Ouadou ∩ **RIM** 196-197 E 7
Ouagadougou o ★ **BF** 202-203 K 3
Ouagar, I-n- o **RIM** 196-197 D 4
Ouahabou o **BF** 202-203 J 4
Ouahigouya o **BF** 202-203 J 3
Ouaka o **RCA** 206-207 E 5
Ouaka ∩ **RCA** 206-207 E 6
Ouaké o **DY** 202-203 L 5
Ouala o **RCA** 206-207 F 5
Oualâta o **RIM** 196-197 G 6
Oualâta, Dhar ▲ **RIM** 196-197 G 6
Oualla ▲ **RG** 202-203 F 4
Ouallam o **RN** 204-205 E 1
Ouana ∩ **G** 210-211 D 3
Ouanary o **F** 62-63 J 3
Ouanazein ∩ **TCH** 198-199 H 4
Ouanda Djallé o **RCA** 206-207 G 4
Ouandago o **RCA** 206-207 D 5
Ouandja, Kot) ∩ **RCA** 206-207 F 4
Ouandja-Vakaga, Réserve de faune de la ⊥ **RCA** 206-207 F 4
Ouando o **RCA** 206-207 G 6
Ouango o **RCA** 206-207 G 6
Ouangolodougou o **CI** 202-203 H 5
Ouaninou o • **CI** 202-203 G 5
Ouara ∩ **RCA** 206-207 G 6
Ouarak o **SN** 202-203 B 2
Ouareau, Rivière ∩ **CDN** 38-39 H 5
Ouargaye o **BF** 202-203 L 4
Ouargla • **DZ** 190-191 G 5
Ouaritoufoulout o **RIM** 196-197 M 6
Ouarkla o **CAM** 206-207 B 4
Ouarkziz, Jbel ▲ **MA** 188-189 F 6
Ouarsenis, Massif de l' ▲ **DZ** 190-191 G 3
Ouarzazate o **MA** 188-189 H 5
Ouassa Bamvélé o **CAM** 204-205 K 6
Ouatagouna o **RMM** 202-203 L 2
Ouatcha o **RN** 198-199 D 6
Ouatéré Galafondo o **RCA** 206-207 D 6
Oubangui ∩ **RCA** 210-211 G 3
Oubden o • **RIM** 196-197 H 4
Ouday ∩ **RIM** 196-197 C 4
Oudenaarde o • **B** 92-93 G 3
Oudjila o • **CAM** 206-207 B 3
Oudna • **TN** 190-191 H 2
Oudtshoorn o **ZA** 220-221 F 6
Oued el Abiod o **RIM** 196-197 H 6
Oued el Hajar o **RMM** 196-197 J 5
Ouéden Nsa o **DZ** 190-191 D 4
Oued Mimoun o **DZ** 188-189 J 3

Oued Rhiou o **DZ** 190-191 C 3
Oued Rhir ⊥ **DZ** 190-191 F 4
Oued Tlelat o **DZ** 188-189 J 3
Oued-Zem o **MA** 188-189 H 4
Oued Zenati o **DZ** 190-191 F 2
Ouélélessébougou o **RMM** 202-203 G 4
Ouéllé o **CI** 202-203 H 6
Ouémé o **DY** 204-205 E 4
Ouémé = Affon o **DY** 202-203 L 5
Ouenkoro o **RMM** 202-203 J 3
Ouenza o **DZ** 190-191 F 2
Oué-Oué o **DY** 204-205 E 4
Ouerrha, Oued ∩ **MA** 188-189 J 3
Ouessa o **BF** 202-203 J 4
Ouessant o **F** 90-91 E 7
Ouèssè o **DY** 204-205 E 4
Ouest, Pointe de l' ▲ **CDN** 38-39 M 4
Ouezzane o **MA** 188-189 H 3
Oufrane o **DZ** 190-191 C 6
Ougarou o **BF** 202-203 L 4
Oughterard = Uachtar Ard o **IRL** 90-91 C 5
Ougoué ∩ **RCB** 210-211 D 5
Ouham ∩ **RCA** 206-207 D 5
Ouham-Pendé o **RCA** 206-207 B 5
Ouidah o • **DY** 204-205 E 5
Ouidi o **RN** 198-199 F 5
Ouinardéne o **RMM** 196-197 K 5
Ouinhi o **DY** 204-205 E 5
Oujâf o **RIM** 196-197 G 6
Oujda = Ujdah o **MA** 188-189 K 3
Oujeft o **RIM** 196-197 D 5
Ou Jiang ∩ **VRC** 156-157 M 2
Ouka o **RCA** 206-207 E 5
Oukaimeden o **MA** 188-189 H 5
Oukal o **RFG** 134-135 J 2
Oukraal ∩ **ZA** 220-221 D 7
Oukré o **RIM** 196-197 E 6
Oula, Madina- o **RG** 202-203 D 5
Oulad-Teima o **MA** 188-189 G 5
Oulainen o **FIN** 88-89 H 4
Ould Allenda o **DZ** 190-191 F 4
Ould Yenjé o **RIM** 196-197 E 7
Ouled Djellal o **DZ** 190-191 F 4
Ouled Naïl, Monts de ▲ **DZ** 190-191 E 4
Ouli o **CAM** 206-207 C 5
Oulmes o **MA** 188-189 J 4
Oulnina Hill ▲ **AUS** 180-181 E 2
Oulo, Mayo ∩ **CAM** 204-205 K 4
Oulu ✦ **FIN** 88-89 H 4
Oulu, Bahr ∩ **RCA** 206-207 F 4
Oulujärvi o **FIN** 88-89 J 4
Oulujoki ∩ **FIN** 88-89 J 4
Oum, Bir ∩ **TN** 190-191 F 4
Oumache o **DZ** 190-191 E 3
Oumba ∩ **G** 210-211 C 4
Oum-Chalouba o **TCH** 198-199 K 5
Oum Djerane o **DZ** 190-191 J 3
Oumé o **CI** 202-203 H 6
Oum el Achar o **DZ** 188-189 L 3
Oum el Bouaghi o **DZ** 190-191 F 3
Oum er Rbia, Oued ∩ **MA** 188-189 J 4
Oum-Hadjer o **TCH** 198-199 J 6
Oumm Debua, Sebkha o **MA** 188-189 E 7
Oumm ed Droûs Guebli, Sebkhet o **RIM** 196-197 E 4
Oumm ed Droûs Telli, Sebkhet o **RIM** 196-197 E 2
Oumm el Khezz o **RIM** 196-197 E 7
Ounâne, Bir ∩ **RMM** 196-197 J 6
Ounane, Djebel ▲ **DZ** 190-191 F 8
Ounara o **MA** 188-189 G 5
Ounasjoki ∩ **FIN** 88-89 J 4
Ounay, Kötal-e ▲ **AFG** 138-139 B 2
Oundou o **RG** 202-203 F 4
Ouniamga Kébir o **TCH** 198-199 K 3
Ounianga Sérir o **TCH** 198-199 K 3
Ountivou o **RT** 202-203 L 6
Ouo o **RMM** 202-203 J 2
Ouogo o **RCA** 206-207 D 5
Ouray o **USA** (CO) 42-43 D 6
Ouray o **USA** (UT) 42-43 C 5
Ourei o **RIM** 196-197 E 6
Ouré-Kaba o **RG** 202-203 E 4
Ourém o **BR** 68-69 E 2
Ourense (Orense) o **E** 98-99 D 3
Ouret, Oued ∩ **DZ** 190-191 G 8
Ouricana, Serra da ▲ **BR** 72-73 K 3
Ouricuri o **BR** 68-69 H 5
Ourinhos o **BR** 72-73 G 7
Ourini o **TCH** 198-199 L 4
Ourique o **P** 98-99 C 6
Ourlat o **DZ** 190-191 E 3
Ouro, Rio do ∩ **BR** 72-73 F 2
Ouro Amat o **SN** 202-203 C 2
Ouro Branco o **BR** 68-69 H 7
Ourofane o **RN** 198-199 D 5
Ouro Fino o **BR** 72-73 G 7
Ouro Prêto o •• **BR** 72-73 J 6
Ouro Preto, Rio ∩ **BR** 70-71 E 2
Ouro Preto d'Oeste o **BR** 70-71 F 2
Ouro Sogui o **SN** 202-203 D 2
Ourou Rapids ∩ **WAN** 204-205 F 4
Ouro Velho o **BR** 68-69 K 5
Oursi o **BF** 202-203 K 2
Oursi, Mare de o **BF** 202-203 K 2
Ous o **RUS** 114-115 H 5
Ouse o **USA** 180-181 H 3
Ou-sanmyaku ▲ **J** 152-153 J 5
Oussouye o **SN** 202-203 B 2
Oust, Djebel ▲ **DZ** 188-189 L 4
Oust ∩ **F** 62-63 H 4
Outama-Kilimbi National Park ⊥ **WAL** 202-203 D 5
Outaouais, Rivière des ∩ **CDN** 38-39 E 5
Outardes, Rivière aux ∩ **CDN** 38-39 K 3
Outardes Quatre, Réservoir d' ⊏ **CDN** 38-39 K 3

Outat-Oulad-El-Haj o **MA** 188-189 K 4
Outeid Arkass ⊏ **RMM** 196-197 H 6
Outeniekwaberge ▲ **ZA** 220-221 F 6
Outer Bill Bailey Bank = Outer Bailey Bank ≈ 90-91 A 1
Outer Hebrides ∩ **GB** 90-91 D 3
Outer Island ∩ **USA** 46-47 C 2
Outfene o **RIM** 196-197 F 6
Outjo o **NAM** 216-217 D 10
Outlet Bay o **CDN** 30-31 T 4
Outlook o **CDN** 34-35 C 5
Outokumpu o **FIN** 88-89 K 5
Outoul o **DZ** 190-191 E 9
Ouzarra, Oued ∩ **MA** 188-189 J 3
Ouzefa o **DZ** 190-191 E 4
Ouzouara, Adrar- ⊏ **RMM** 196-197 L 5
Ouzoud, Cascades d' ∩•• **MA** 188-189 H 4
Ouzzele, Adrar- ⊏ **RMM** 196-197 L 5
Ovalau ∩ **FJI** 184 III b 2
Ovalle o **RCH** 76-77 B 4
Ovamboland ⊥ **NAM** 216-217 C 9
Ovan o **G** 210-211 D 3
Ovana, Cerro ▲ **YV** 60-61 H 5
Ovar o **P** 98-99 C 4
Ovau Island ∩ **SOL** 184 I c 2
Ovcyna, proliv ≈ 108-109 S 5
Ovejas, Cerro de las ▲ **RA** 78-79 G 2
Ovejería o **RA** 78-79 F 3
Oveng o **CAM** 210-211 D 4
Ovens, The • **CDN** 38-39 M 6
Ovens Natural Park ⊥ **CDN** 38-39 M 6
Ovens River ∩ **AUS** 180-181 J 4
Overflowing River o **CDN** 34-35 F 4
Øvergård o **N** 86-87 J 2
Øverkalix o **S** 86-87 L 3
Overlander Roadhouse o **AUS** 176-177 C 3
Overland Park o **USA** 42-43 K 6
Overton o **USA** 40-41 G 7
Övertorneå o **S** 86-87 L 3
Överum o **S** 86-87 H 8
Ovgog ∩ **RUS** 116-117 K 3
Oviedo o **DOM** 54-55 K 6
Oviedo = Uviéu o •• **E** 98-99 E 3
Övögdij o **MAU** 148-149 L 5
Övör-Hanga ∩ **MAU** 148-149 F 5
Övzüu ∩ **J** 152-153 E 8
Ozuluama o **MEX** 50-51 L 7
Ozurgeti o **GE** 126-127 E 7

Oyé Yeska o **TCH** 198-199 J 3
Oyo o **RCB** 210-211 E 4
Oyo o **WAN** (OYO) 204-205 E 5
Oyo o **WAN** 204-205 E 5
Oyou Bezzé Denga o **RN** 198-199 F 4
Oyoué o **G** 210-211 D 3
Øyrlandsodden ▲ **N** 84-85 K 4
Øyslebø o **N** 86-87 C 7
Øystervi-Bru o **CDN** 40-41 B 2
Øysterville o **USA** 40-41 B 2
Ožalp o **TR** 128-129 K 3
Ozamiz o **RP** 160-161 E 8
Ozark o **USA** (AL) 48-49 F 4
Ozark o **USA** (AR) 44-45 L 2
Ozark National Scenic Riverways ⊥ **USA** 46-47 C 7
Ozark Plateau ▲ **USA** 44-45 K 1
Ozarks, Lake of the o **USA** 42-43 L 6
Ozark Wonder Cave • **USA** 44-45 K 1
Ozárow o **PL** 92-93 Q 3
Özen o **KA** 126-127 K 6
Ozerki o **RUS** 96-97 E 5
Ozernaja o **RUS** 108-109 b 2
Ozernaja ∩ **RUS** 120-121 T 5
Ozërnoe o **RUS** 102-103 R 3
Ozernovskij o **RUS** 122-123 R 3
Ozërnyj o **RUS** 112-113 V 3
Ozerskij o **RUS** 122-123 K 5
Ozërskoe, Sosnovo ∩ **RUS** 118-119 F 3
Ozery o **RUS** 94-95 Q 4
Ozhiski Lake o **CDN** 34-35 N 4
Ožidaevo o **RUS** 122-123 K 5
Ozieri o **I** 100-101 B 4
Ozimek o **PL** 92-93 P 3
Ozinki o **RUS** 96-97 E 8
Ožogina ∩ **RUS** 110-111 X 6
Ožogino, ozero o **RUS** 118-119 a 5
Ozona o **USA** 44-45 G 4
Ozondati o **NAM** 216-217 C 10
Ozori o **G** 210-211 B 4
Ozorkow o **PL** 92-93 P 3
Ozoro o **WAN** 204-205 G 6

P

Pa o **BF** 202-203 J 4
Paakitsup Nunaa ∪ **GRØ** 28-29 P 2
Paama o **VAN** 184 II b 3
Paama = Île Pau Uma ∩ **VAN** 184 II b 3
Paamiut = Frederikshåb o **GRØ** 28-29 Q 5
Pa-an o **MYA** 158-159 D 3
Paanto o **RI** 164-165 G 4
Paarl o **ZA** 220-221 D 6
Pabal o **IND** 138-139 E 10
Pabbiring, Kepulauan ∩ **RI** 164-165 G 4
Pabean o **RI** 168 B 6
Pabedanã o **IR** 134-135 G 3
Pabellón, El ∩ **MEX** 52-53 J 3
Pabianice o **PL** 92-93 P 3
Pabna o **BD** 142-143 F 4
Pabradé o **LT** 94-95 J 4
Pab Range ▲ **PK** 134-135 M 6
Pacacocha, Río o **PE** 64-65 F 8
Pacaembu o **BR** 72-73 F 6
Pacahuaras, Río o **BOL** 70-71 D 2
Pacajá o **BR** 68-69 C 3
Pacajás, Rio ∩ **BR** 68-69 C 3
Pacajazinho, Rio ∩ **BR** 68-69 C 4
Pacajus o **BR** 68-69 K 4
Pacapausa o **PE** 64-65 E 9
Pacaraima, Sierra ▲▲ **YV** 60-61 K 5
Pacaraos o **PE** 64-65 D 7
Pacasmayo o **PE** 64-65 C 5
Pacatuba o **BR** 68-69 K 4
Pacaya-Samiria, Reserva Nacional ⊥ **PE** 64-65 E 4
Pacbxe o **CDN** 34-35 N 6
Pâc Bó o **VN** 156-157 D 5
Pâc Bo o **VN** 156-157 D 5
Paccha o **EC** 64-65 C 3
Pacchani o **PE** 70-71 D 6
Pacet o **RI** 168 F 7
Pachacámac o **PE** (LIM) 64-65 D 8
Pachacámac • **PE** (LIM) 64-65 D 8
Pachaconas o **PE** 64-65 F 9
Pachia o **PE** 70-71 B 5
Pachino o **I** 100-101 E 6
Pachitea, Río ∩ **PE** 64-65 E 6
Pacho o **CO** 60-61 D 5
Pachón, El ▲ **RA** 76-77 B 6
Pachuca de Soto ☆ **MEX** 52-53 E 1
Paciá o **BR** 66-67 E 6
Paciá, Rio ∩ **BR** 66-67 E 6
Paciencia, Llano de la ⊏ **RCH** 76-77 C 3
Pacific o **USA** 46-47 C 5
Pacific Grove o **USA** 40-41 C 5
Pacific Highway II **AUS** 178-179 M 6
Pacific House o **USA** 40-41 D 6
Pacific Ocean ≈ 14-15 H 4
Pacific Ranges ▲▲ **CDN** 32-33 G 6
Pacific Rim National Park ⊥ **CDN** 32-33 H 7
Pacijan Island ∩ **RP** 160-161 F 7
Paciran o **RI** 168 E 3
Pacitan o **RI** 168 D 7
Packsaddle o **AUS** 178-179 F 6
Packwood o **USA** 40-41 C 2
Pâc Ma o **VN** 156-157 C 5
Pacora o **PA** 52-53 G 7
Pacoval o **BR** 66-67 K 4
Pac Seng o **LAO** 156-157 C 6
Pacuária da Barra do Longa o **ANG** 216-217 B 5

Pacuativa o **CO** 66-67 B 2
Pacuí, Rio ∩ **BR** 72-73 H 4
Pacujá o **BR** 66-67 B 7
Pacuneiro, Rio ∩ **BR** 66-67 H 7
Padag o **PK** 134-135 L 4
Padako o **CI** 202-203 H 7
Padalere o **RI** 164-165 H 5
Padam o **IND** 138-139 F 3
Padamarang, Pulau ∩ **RI** 164-165 G 6
Padang o **RI** 162-163 E 4
Padang, Pulau ∩ **RI** 162-163 E 4
Padang, Selat ≈ 162-163 E 4
Padanganet o **RI** 162-163 G 6
Padangcermin o **RI** 162-163 F 7
Padangguci o **RI** 162-163 F 6
Padangpanjang o **RI** 162-163 D 5
Padang Sidempuan o **RI** 162-163 C 4
Padang Tikar, Tanjung ▲ **RI** 162-163 H 5
Padany o **RUS** 88-89 M 5
Padar, Pulau ∩ **RI** 168 D 7
Padas ∩ **MAL** 162-163 A 10
Padauiri, Rio ∩ **BR** 66-67 E 3
Padawan o **MAL** 162-163 H 3
Padawiya o **CL** 140-141 J 6
Padcaya o **BOL** (HUQ) 70-71 F 4
Padcaya o **BOL** (TAR) 76-77 E 1
Paddig o **RP** 160-161 D 3
Paddington o **AUS** 180-181 H 2
Paddle River o **CDN** 32-33 N 4
Padeabesar, Pulau ∩ **RI** 164-165 H 5
Paden City o **USA** 46-47 H 6
Padeniya o **CL** 140-141 J 7
Paderborn o • **D** 92-93 K 3
Pâderu o **IND** 142-143 C 6
Padibe o **EAU** 212-213 D 2
Padilla o **BOL** 70-71 E 6
Padjelanta nationalpark ⊥ **S** 86-87 H 3
Padlei (abandoned) o **CDN** 30-31 V 5
Padloping Island ∩ **CDN** 28-29 J 3
Padma ∩ **BD** 142-143 F 4
Padmanábhapuram o **IND** 140-141 G 6
Padova ✦• **I** 100-101 D 2
Padrauna o **IND** 142-143 C 3
Padre, Morro do ▲ **BR** 72-73 G 4
Padre Angel Buodo o **RA** 78-79 G 4
Padre Bernardo o **BR** 72-73 F 3
Padre Isla ∩ **PE** 64-65 F 3
Padre Island ∩ **USA** 44-45 J 6
Padre Island National Seashore ⊥ **USA** 44-45 J 6
Padre Paraíso o **BR** 72-73 K 4
Padriya o **NEP** 144-145 J 4
Padrón o **E** 98-99 C 3
Padrone, Cape ▲ **ZA** 220-221 G 6
Paducah o **USA** (KY) 46-47 D 7
Paducah o **USA** (TX) 44-45 G 4
Padun o **RUS** 114-115 J 6
Padun, Vodopad ∩ **RUS** 88-89 O 3
Paegam o **DVR** 150-151 G 7
Paegnyôngdo ∩ **DVR** 150-151 E 9
Paekdu San ▲ **DVR** 150-151 G 8
Paëlavajaha ∩ **RUS** 108-109 T 6
Paeroa o **NZ** 182 E 2
Paestum •• **I** 100-101 E 4
Paete o **RP** 160-161 D 5
Paet Point ▲ **RP** 160-161 F 9
Pafos o **CY** 128-129 D 5
Pafúri o **MOC** 218-219 F 6
Pafuri Gate o **ZA** 218-219 F 6
Pag o **HR** 100-101 E 2
Paga o **RI** 166-167 B 6
Pagadenbaru o **RI** 168 B 3
Pagadian o **RP** 160-161 E 9
Pagadian Bay ≈ 160-161 E 9
Pagai, Kepulauan ∩ **RI** 162-163 C 6
Pagai Selatan, Pulau ∩ **RI** 162-163 D 6
Pagai Utara, Pulau ∩ **RI** 162-163 C 6
Pagalu, Isla de = Annóbon ∩ **GQ** 210-211 a 3
Pagan ∩ **USA** 142-143 J 6
Pagani Bay ≈ 212-213 J 6
Paganzo o **RA** 76-77 D 6
Pagaralam o **RI** 162-163 E 7
Pagas Divisas de **BR** 62-63 H 6
Pagassitikós Kólpos ≈ 100-101 J 5
Pagatan o **RI** 164-165 F 5
Pagatan ✦ **RI** 164-165 H 3
Pagau o **RI** 164-165 H 3
Pagwachuan River ∩ **CDN** 34-35 O 5
Pagwa River o **CDN** 34-35 O 5
Pagwi o **PNG** 183 B 3
Pahača ∩ **RUS** 112-113 P 6
Pahači o **RUS** 112-113 P 6
Pahačinskij hrebet ▲▲ **RUS** 112-113 P 6
Pahala o **USA** 48-49 U 8
Pahang ∩ **MAL** 162-163 E 3
Pahang ∩ **MAL** 162-163 E 3
Paharpur o **PK** 138-139 D 2
Pahāripur o **IND** 142-143 G 3
Pahaska Tepee o **USA** 42-43 C 3
Pahiatua o **NZ** 182 E 4
Pahn Wroal o **LB** 202-203 F 6
Pahoa o **USA** 48-49 V 8
Pahoturi River ∩ **PNG** 183 B 5
Pah River ∩ **USA** 20-21 N 3
Pahrump o **USA** 40-41 G 7
Pahsien Cave • **RC** 156-157 M 5
Pahtaabad o **US** 136-137 N 4

Pardillal ○ YV (ARA) 60-61 H 3
Pardo, Rio ~ BR 64-65 F 4
Pardo, Rio ○ BR 68-69 B 4
Pardo, Rio ~ BR 70-71 F 2
Pardo, Rio ~ BR 72-73 D 6
Pardo, Rio ~ BR 72-73 F 6
Pardubice ○ CZ 92-93 N 3
Pardubitz = Pardubice ○ •• CZ 92-93 N 3
Pare ○ RI 168 E 3
Parece Vela Basin ≃ 14-15 F 6
Parecis ○ BR 70-71 F 4
Parecis, Chapada dos ▲ BR 70-71 F 2
Parecis, Rio ~ BR 70-71 J 3
Paredão de Minas ○ BR 72-73 H 4
Pareditas ○ RA 78-79 E 2
Paredón ○ MEX 52-53 H 3
Paren' ○ RUS 112-113 M 5
Paren' ~ RUS 112-113 M 5
Paren', Verhnij RUS 112-113 M 5
Parenda ○ IND 138-139 E 10
Pareng ○ IND 142-143 J 1
Paren'skoe, ozero ○ RUS 112-113 M 5
Parent ○ CDN 38-39 G 4
Parent, Lac ○ CDN 38-39 F 4
Parepare ○ RI 164-165 F 6
Paresi, Área Indígena ⅄ BR 70-71 H 4
Paresi do Rio Formoso, Área Indígena ⅄ BR 70-71 H 4
Párga ○ GR 100-101 H 5
Pargaon Sudrik ○ IND 138-139 E 10
Pargas = Parainen ○ FIN 88-89 G 6
Pargua ○ RCH 78-79 C 6
Parguaza, Rio ~ YV 60-61 H 5
Parhar ○ TJ 136-137 L 6
Paría ○ BOL 70-71 E 5
Paria, Golfo de ≈ 60-61 K 2
Paria, Península de ◡ YV 60-61 K 2
Pariacoto ○ PE 64-65 D 6
Parlaguán ○ YV 60-61 J 3
Pariaman ○ RI 162-163 C 5
Paricatuba ○ BR 66-67 G 5
Paricutín, Volcán ▲ MEX 52-53 C 2
Parika ○ GUY 62-63 G 2
Parima, Reserva Florestal ⊥ BR 60-61 K 6
Parima, Serra ▲ BR 60-61 J 6
Parinacochas, Lago ○ PE 64-65 F 9
Parinari ○ PE 64-65 E 4
Pariñas, Punta ▲ PE 64-65 B 4
Parintins ○ BR 66-67 J 4
Paripiranga ○ BR 68-69 K 7
Paririque Grande ○ RA 76-77 D 2
Paris ★ •• F 90-91 J 7
Paris ○ USA (AR) 44-45 L 2
Paris ○ USA (IL) 46-47 E 6
Paris ○ USA (KY) 46-47 E 6
Paris ○ USA (MO) 46-47 C 6
Paris ○ USA (TN) 48-49 D 1
Paris ○ USA (TX) 44-45 K 3
Pariserørne ~ GRØ 26-27 q 4
Parish Glacier < CDN 26-27 M 4
Párispea ○ EST 94-95 J 2
Parit ○ MAL 162-163 D 2
Parit ○ RI 162-163 D 4
Parita ○ PA 52-53 D 7
Parita, Golfo de ≈ 52-53 D 7
Parittajungmelayu ○ RI 162-163 E 5
Pariz ○ IR 134-135 H 4
Parkāl ○ IND 138-139 G 10
Parkano ○ FIN 88-89 G 5
Parkbeg ○ CDN 34-35 C 5
Park City ○ USA 46-47 E 7
Parkent ○ US 136-137 L 4
Parker ○ USA (AZ) 40-41 G 8
Parker ○ USA (SD) 42-43 J 4
Parker, Mount ▲ USA 172-173 J 4
Parker Lake ○ CDN 30-31 W 4
Parkersburg ○ USA (IA) 42-43 L 4
Parkersburg ○ USA (WV) 46-47 H 6
Parkers Prairie ○ USA 42-43 J 3
Parkes ○ AUS 180-181 K 2
Park Falls ○ USA 46-47 C 3
Parkman ○ CDN 34-35 F 6
Parkman ○ USA 46-47 H 5
Park Range ▲ USA 42-43 D 5
Park Rapids ○ USA 42-43 K 2
Park River ○ USA 42-43 J 1
Park Rynie ○ ZA 220-221 K 5
Parkston ○ USA 42-43 J 4
Parksville ○ CDN 32-33 H 7
Parlákimidi ○ IND 142-143 D 6
Parli ○ IND 138-139 F 10
Parma ○ •• I 100-101 C 2
Parma ○ USA 46-47 H 5
Parmana ○ YV 60-61 J 4
Parnaíba ○ BR 68-69 H 7
Parnaíba, Rio ~ BR 68-69 H 6
Parnaíba, Serra da ▲ BR 68-69 E 6
Parnamirim ○ BR 68-69 J 6
Parnarama ○ BR 68-69 G 4
Parnassus ○ NZ 182 D 5
Parndana ○ AUS 180-181 D 3
Pärnu ★ •• EST 94-95 J 2
Pärnu-Jaagupi ○ EST 94-95 J 2
Paro ○ BHT 142-143 F 2
Paromang ○ RI 168 E 6
Paroo ○ AUS 176-177 E 3
Paroo River ~ AUS 178-179 H 4
Páros ○ GR 100-101 K 6
Páros ~ GR 100-101 K 6
Parou, Küh-e ▲ IR 134-135 B 1
Parow ○ ZA 220-221 D 6
Parowan ○ USA 40-41 H 7
Parraburdu Mining Area • AUS 176-177 D 3
Parramatta ○ AUS 180-181 L 2
Parramore Island ~ USA 46-47 L 7
Parras de la Fuente ○ MEX 50-51 H 5
Parrita ○ CR 52-53 B 7
Parrsboro ○ CDN 38-39 M 6
Parrs Halt ○ ZA 218-219 D 5
Parry, Cape ▲ CDN 24-25 K 5

Parry, Kap ▲ GRØ (NGR) 26-27 P 5
Parry, Kap ▲ GRØ (OGR) 26-27 p 7
Parry, Lac ○ CDN 36-37 M 5
Parry Bay ≈ 24-25 f 6
Parry Beach ○ AUS 176-177 D 7
Parry Falls ○ CDN 30-31 P 4
Parry Islands ~ CDN 24-25 P 3
Parry Peninsula ◡ CDN 24-25 K 6
Parry Sound ○ CDN 38-39 D 6
Pärsābād ○ IR 128-129 M 3
Parseierspitze ▲ A 92-93 L 5
Parsnip River ~ CDN 32-33 J 4
Parsoburan ○ RI 162-163 C 3
Parsons ○ USA 44-45 K 1
Parsons, Mount ▲ AUS 174-175 C 3
Parsons Lake ○ CDN 20-21 Y 2
Parson's Pond ○ CDN 38-39 Q 3
Parsons Range ▲ AUS 174-175 C 3
Partábpur ○ IND 142-143 C 4
Partago ○ BR 202-203 L 5
Partãwal ○ IND 142-143 C 4
Pärtefjällen ▲ S 86-87 H 3
Parthenay ○ F 90-91 G 8
Pärtibänuir ○ IND 140-141 H 6
Partizanka ○ KA 124-125 G 2
Partizansk ○ RUS 116-117 G 6
Partizansk ○ RUS 122-123 E 7
Partür ○ IND 138-139 F 10
Paru, Ilha ~ BR 62-63 G 6
Paru, Rio ~ BR 62-63 H 5
Paru, Rio ~ YV 60-61 J 5
Paruá ○ BR 68-69 F 3
Paru de Este, Área Indígena ⅄ BR 62-63 G 5
Paru de Este, Rio ~ BR 62-63 G 5
Paruna ○ AUS 180-181 F 3
Parur ○ IND 140-141 G 5
Paruro ○ PE 70-71 B 3
Parusovaja ~ RUS 108-109 U 8
Pärvatipuram ○ IND 142-143 C 6
Parwan ~ IND 138-139 F 7
Paryang ○ VRC 144-145 D 5
Parys ○ ZA 220-221 H 3
Pas, Rivière de ~ CDN 36-37 R 7
Pas, The ○ CDN 34-35 F 4
Paša ○ RUS 94-95 N 1
Pasábánd ○ AFG 134-135 L 2
Pasadena ○ CDN 38-39 Q 4
Pasadena ○ USA (CA) 40-41 D 8
Pasadena ○ USA (TX) 44-45 K 5
Pasaje ○ EC 64-65 C 3
Pasaje o Juramento, Río ~ RA 76-77 E 3
Pasán ○ IND 142-143 C 4
Pasangkayu ○ RI 164-165 F 4
Pasapuat ○ RI 162-163 C 6
Pasaquina ○ ES 52-53 L 5
Pasarbantal ○ RI 162-163 D 6
Pasarbembah ○ RI 162-163 E 6
Pāsárgād ○ •• IR 134-135 E 3
Pasarsibuhuan ○ RI 162-163 C 4
Pasarsorkam = Sorkam ○ RI 162-163 C 4
Pasartalo ○ RI 162-163 E 7
Pasarwajo ○ RI 164-165 H 6
Pasawng ○ MYA 142-143 K 6
Pascagoula ○ USA 48-49 D 4
Pascagoula River ~ USA 48-49 D 4
Pasco ○ USA 40-41 D 2
Pascoe, Mount ▲ AUS 176-177 F 3
Pasco Island ~ AUS 172-173 B 6
Pasewalk ○ D 92-93 M 2
Pasfield Lake ○ CDN 30-31 R 4
Pasi, Pulau ~ RI 168 E 6
Pasiene ○ LV 94-95 L 3
Pasig ☆ RP 160-161 E 7
Pa'sina ○ RUS 116-117 J 6
Pasinler ○ TR 128-129 J 3
Pašino ○ RUS 114-115 R 7
Pasión, Río de la ~ GCA 52-53 J 3
Pasir, Tanjung ▲ MAL 162-163 E 2
Pasir, Tanjung ▲ RI 162-163 H 5
Pasir Panjang ○ MAL 162-163 D 2
Pasirpengarayan ○ RI 162-163 D 4
Pasir Puteh ○ MAL 162-163 E 2
Pasirputih ○ RI 166-167 C 6
Pasitelu, Kepulauan ~ RI 168 E 6
Páskallavik ○ S 86-87 H 8
Pasłęk ○ PL 92-93 P 1
Pasley, Cape ▲ AUS 176-177 G 6
Pasley Bay ≈ 24-25 Y 5
Pašman ~ HR 100-101 F 3
Pasmore River ~ AUS 178-179 E 6
Pasni ○ PK 134-135 K 6
Paso, El ○ USA (IL) 46-47 D 5
Paso, El ○ RI 166-167 D 5
Paso, El ○ USA (TX) 44-45 G 4
Paso de Indios ○ RA 78-79 E 7
Paso de la Laguna ○ RA 76-77 H 6
Paso de las Piedras, Embalse < RA 78-79 J 3
Paso de Lesca ○ C 54-55 G 4
Paso de los Algarrobos ○ RA 78-79 F 4
Paso de los Indios ○ RA 78-79 F 4
Paso de los Libres ○ RA 76-77 J 5
Paso de los Toros ○ ROU 78-79 L 2
Paso del Rey ○ RA 78-79 F 2
Paso del Sapo ○ RA 78-79 E 7
Paso del Toro ○ MEX 52-53 F 2
Paso de Ovejas ○ MEX 52-53 F 2
Paso de Patria ○ PY 76-77 H 4
Paso Flores ○ RA 78-79 D 6
Paso Nacional ○ MEX 50-51 H 5
Paso Nuevo ○ YV 60-61 H 3
Paso Real de Macaira ○ YV 60-61 H 3
Paso Real de San Diego ○ C 54-55 D 3
Paso Robles ○ USA 40-41 D 8
Paso Rodolfo Raballos ○ RA 80 E 3

Pasqua ○ CDN 34-35 D 5
Pasquachai River ~ CDN 34-35 L 3
Pasquia Hills ▲ CDN 34-35 E 4
Pasrur ○ PK 138-139 E 3
Passa ~ RI 210-211 E 4
Passa e Fica ○ BR 68-69 L 5
Passagem ○ BR 68-69 L 5
Passagem Franca ○ BR 68-69 G 5
Passage Point ▲ CDN 24-25 O 4
Passamaquoddy Bay ≈ 38-39 L 6
Passau ○ D 92-93 M 4
Passayten Wilderness Area ⊥ USA 40-41 D 1
Passi ○ RP 160-161 E 7
Passi ○ SN 202-203 B 3
Passira ○ BR 68-69 L 5
Passo da Guarda ○ BR 76-77 J 6
Passo Fundo ○ BR 74-75 D 7
Passo Fundo, Represa de < BR 74-75 D 6
Passo Real, Represa de < BR 74-75 D 7
Passos ○ BR 72-73 G 6
Pastaza, Rio ~ PE 64-65 D 5
Pasteur ○ RA 78-79 H 3
Pasto ○ CO 64-65 D 1
Pastol Bay ≈ 20-21 J 5
Pastor, El ○ MEX 50-51 G 3
Pastos Bons ○ BR 68-69 F 5
Pastos Chicos, Rio ~ RA 76-77 D 2
Pastos Grandes, Sierra de los ▲ RA 76-77 D 3
Pastrana ○ E 98-99 F 4
Pastura ○ USA 44-45 E 2
Pasuruan ○ RI 168 E 5
Pasvalys ○ LT 94-95 J 3
Pasvikelva ~ N 86-87 O 2
Pata ○ BOL 70-71 D 5
Pata ○ CO 64-65 E 4
Pata ○ RCA 206-207 E 4
Pata Island ~ RP 160-161 D 10
Patache, Punta ▲ RCH 76-77 B 7
Patadkal ○ •• IND 140-141 F 3
Pataia ○ IND 138-139 F 10
Patalasang ○ RI 164-165 F 4
Patamba ○ AFG 134-135 L 2
Patambalu ○ ZRE 210-211 D 5
Patambuco ○ PE 70-71 B 3
Patamuté ○ BR 68-69 J 6
Pätan ○ IND (GUJ) 138-139 C 9
Pätan ○ NEP 144-145 F 3
Pätan ○ IND (MAH) 140-141 E 2
Patani ○ RI 164-165 J 4
Patani ○ WAN 204-205 G 6
Patas ○ IND 138-139 E 10
Pataua, Cachoeira do ~ BR 66-67 G 7
Patavila ○ PE 64-65 D 7
Patchogue ○ USA 46-47 M 5
Patea ○ NZ 182 E 3
Pategi ○ WAN 204-205 F 4
Pate Island ~ EAK 212-213 H 5
Patelāo, Rio ~ BR 70-71 J 2
Patensie ○ ZA 220-221 G 6
Paternò ○ I 100-101 E 6
Paterson ○ USA (NJ) 46-47 L 5
Paterson ○ USA (WA) 40-41 E 3
Paterson ○ ZA 220-221 G 6
Paterson Inlet ≈ 182 B 7
Paterson Range ▲ AUS 172-173 F 3
Pathalaia ○ NEP 144-145 E 7
Pathalgaon ○ IND 142-143 C 4
Pathānkot ○ IND 138-139 E 3
Patharkot ○ NEP 144-145 E 3
Pathfinder Reservoir < USA 42-43 D 4
Pathin ○ THA 158-159 F 5
Pathum Thani ○ THA 158-159 F 3
Pathrud ○ IND 138-139 E 10
Pati ○ RI 168 D 3
Patía ○ CO 64-65 D 1
Patía, Río ~ CO 60-61 D 7
Patiala ○ IND 138-139 F 3
Patinti, Selat ≈ 164-165 K 4
Patio Chiquito ○ CO 60-61 F 5
Patiroriolo ○ RI 164-165 G 5
Pativilca ○ PE 64-65 D 7
Pätkai Bum ▲ IND 142-143 J 2
Patlahara ○ NEP 144-145 E 4
Patman, Lake ○ USA 44-45 K 3
Pátmos ~ GR 100-101 L 6
Patna ★ IND 142-143 D 3
Patnanungan Island ~ RP 160-161 E 5
Patnitola ○ BD 142-143 F 3
Patos ○ BR 68-69 L 5
Patoka Lake ○ USA 46-47 E 6
Patomskoe, nagor'e ⊿ RUS 118-119 J 6
Patón, El ○ YV 60-61 H 3
Patonga ○ AUS 172-173 L 2
Patonga ○ EAU 212-213 D 2
Patos ○ BR (CEA) 68-69 K 5
Patos ○ BR (PA) 68-69 K 5
Patos, Cachoeira dos ~ BR 70-71 H 2
Patos, Lagoa dos ○ BR 74-75 E 8
Patos, Rio de los ~ RA 78-79 E 2
Patos de Minas ○ BR 72-73 G 5
Patos ou São José, Rios dos ~ BR 70-71 J 3

Pattani ○ THA 158-159 F 7
Pattaya ○ •• THA 158-159 F 4
Patterson ☆ •• 172-173 K 2
Patterson ○ USA 48-49 G 4
Patterson, Mount ▲ AUS 176-177 D 4
Patterson, Mount ▲ CDN 20-21 X 4
Patti ○ I 100-101 E 5
Pattoki ○ PK 138-139 D 4
Patton Junction ○ USA 46-47 D 7
Pattonsburg ○ USA 42-43 K 5
Pattukkottai ○ IND 140-141 H 5
Patu ○ BR 68-69 K 5
Patuakhali ○ BD 142-143 G 4
Patuanak ○ CDN 34-35 C 3
Patuca, Punta ▲ HN 54-55 C 7
Patuca, Río ~ HN 54-55 C 7
Patugo ○ RI 168 E 6
Patulló, Mount ▲ CDN 32-33 F 3
Paturau River ~ NZ 182 C 4
Patvinsuon kansallispuisto ⊥ FIN 88-89 L 2
Pátzcuaro ○ •• MEX 52-53 D 2
Patzimaro ○ MEX 52-53 C 1
Pau ☆ •• F 90-91 G 10
Pau, Tanjung ▲ RI 166-167 B 6
Pau Alto, Rio ~ BR 72-73 L 4
Paucarbamba ○ PE 64-65 E 8
Paucarcolla ○ PE 70-71 B 4
Paucartambo ○ PE 70-71 B 3
Paucartambo, Rio ~ PE 64-65 E 7
Pau d'Arco, Rio ~ BR 68-69 C 5
Pau de Ferros ○ BR 68-69 J 5
Pauh ○ RI 162-163 G 6
Pauini ○ BR 66-67 D 6
Pauini, Rio ~ BR 66-67 F 3
Pauk ○ MYA 142-143 J 5
Pauksa Taung ▲ MYA 142-143 J 6
Paulatuk ○ CDN 24-25 K 6
Paul Bunyan & Blue Ox Statue • USA 42-43 K 2
Paulina Peak ▲ USA 40-41 D 4
Pauline ○ USA 40-41 H 4
Paul Island ○ CDN 36-37 T 6
Paul Island ~ USA 22-23 R 5
Paulista ○ BR 68-69 L 5
Paulistana ○ BR 68-69 H 6
Paulo Afonso ○ BR 68-69 K 6
Paulo Afonso, Parque Nacional ⊥ BR 68-69 J 6
Paulo de Faria ○ BR 72-73 F 6
Paulo Ramos ○ BR 68-69 F 4
Paulpietersburg ○ ZA 220-221 K 3
Paul Roux ○ ZA 220-221 H 4
Paul Sauer Dam < ZA 220-221 G 6
Paul Spur ○ USA 44-45 C 4
Pauls Valley ○ USA 44-45 J 2
Paungdawthi ○ MYA 158-159 D 2
Paungde ○ MYA 142-143 J 6
Pauni ○ IND 138-139 G 9
Paup ○ PNG 183 B 2
Pauri ○ IND 138-139 F 7
Pausa ○ PE 64-65 E 9
Pauto, Río ~ CO 60-61 F 5
Pau Uma, Île = Paama ~ VAN 184 II b 3
Pauwasi ~ RI 166-167 L 3
Pāvagada ○ IND 140-141 H 6
Pavant Range ▲ USA 40-41 H 6
Pávão ○ BR 72-73 L 4
Pāve ○ IR 128-129 M 5
Pavia ☆ •• I 100-101 B 2
Pavilion ○ CDN 32-33 K 6
Pavilosta ○ LV 94-95 G 3
Pavlikeni ○ BG 102-103 L 7
Pavlodar ○ KA 124-125 K 2
Pavlof Islands ~ USA 22-23 Q 5
Pavlof Volcano ▲ USA 22-23 Q 5
Pavlograd = Pavlohrad ○ UA 102-103 J 3
Pavlohrad ○ UA 102-103 J 3
Pavlogradka ☆ RUS 124-125 H 1
Pavlovac ○ HR 100-101 F 2
Pavlovič, Erofej ○ RUS 118-119 L 8
Pavlovka ○ RUS 96-97 F 2
Pavlovo ○ RUS 94-95 S 4
Pavlovsk ○ RUS 102-103 M 2
Pavlovsk ~ RUS (LEN) 94-95 M 2
Pavlovsk ○ RUS 124-125 J 1
Pavlovskij Posad ☆ RUS 94-95 Q 4
Pavlovskij vodohranilišče < RUS 96-97 K 6
Pavlyš ○ UA 102-103 H 3
Pavon, Arroyo ~ RA 78-79 J 2
Pavullo nel Frignano ○ I 100-101 C 2
Pavylon, ozero ○ RUS 110-111 d 5
Pawaia ○ PNG 183 C 4
Pawan ~ RI 162-163 H 5
Pawáyán ○ IND 144-145 C 3
Pawé ▲ CAM 204-205 J 6
Pawhuska ○ USA 44-45 J 1
Pawnee ○ USA 44-45 J 1
Pawnee City ○ USA 42-43 J 5
Pawnee Indian Village ∴ USA 42-43 J 4
Paw Paw ○ USA 46-47 F 4
Pawtucket ○ USA 46-47 N 5
Pawut ○ MYA 158-159 E 4
Paxi ~ GR 100-101 H 5
Paxiúba, Rio ~ BR 66-67 G 7
Paxson ○ USA 20-21 N 5
Paya, Parque Nacional la ⊥ CO 64-65 E 1
Payagé ○ MYA 158-159 D 2
Payahe ○ RI 164-165 K 3
Payakumbuh ○ RI 162-163 D 5
Payang, Gunung ▲ RI 164-165 D 3
Payar ○ SN 202-203 C 2
Payas ○ TR 128-129 G 3
Payette ○ USA 40-41 F 3
Payette River ~ USA 40-41 F 3

Payne, Lac ○ CDN 36-37 M 5
Payne Bay ≈ 36-37 P 4
Paynes Creek ○ USA 40-41 D 5
Paynesville ○ AUS 180-181 J 4
Paynesville ○ USA 42-43 K 3
Payogasta ○ RA 76-77 D 3
Payong, Tanjung ▲ MAL 162-163 K 3
Paysandú ○ ROU 78-79 K 2
Pays de la Loire ○ F 90-91 G 8
Payson ○ USA (AZ) 40-41 J 8
Payson ○ USA (UT) 40-41 H 6
Payún, Cerro ▲ RA 78-79 E 4
Payung ○ RI 162-163 G 6
Pa Yup ○ THA 158-159 F 4
Payyannur ○ IND 140-141 F 5
Paz, Corredeira da ~ BR 68-69 B 6
Paz, Gruta • BR 66-67 C 8
Paz, La ○ BOL 70-71 D 5
Paz, La ○ CO 60-61 E 2
Paz, La ○ HN 52-53 L 4
Paz, La ★ •• MEX 50-51 D 5
Paz, La ○ RA (COD) 78-79 G 2
Paz, La ○ RA (ERI) 78-79 H 2
Paz, La ○ RA (MEN) 78-79 E 4
Paz, La ○ ROU 78-79 L 3
Paz, Ribeirão da ~ BR 68-69 C 6
Paz, Río de la ~ BOL 70-71 D 5
Pazar ○ TR 128-129 J 2
Pazarbaşı Burnu ▲ TR 128-129 D 2
Pazarcık ○ TR 128-129 G 4
Pazardžik ○ BG 102-103 L 7
Paz Centro, La ○ NIC 52-53 B 5
Pazin ○ HR 100-101 E 2
Pazña ○ BOL 70-71 E 5
Pčić ○ BY 94-95 K 5
Pčinja ~ MK 100-101 H 4
Pe ○ MYA 158-159 E 4
Peabody Bugt ≈ 26-27 R 4
Peace Point ○ CDN 30-31 N 6
Peace River ○ CDN 30-31 L 6
Peace River ~ CDN 32-33 M 3
Peace River ~ USA 48-49 G 6
Peach Springs ○ USA 40-41 H 8
Peacock Bay ≈ 16 F 26
Peacock Hills ▲ CDN 30-31 O 3
Peak Charles National Park ⊥ AUS 176-177 F 6
Peak District National Park ⊥ GB 90-91 K 5
Peak Downs Mine • AUS 178-179 K 2
Peake ○ AUS 180-181 E 3
Peak Creek ~ AUS 178-179 D 4
Peaked Point ▲ RP 160-161 C 7
Peak Hill ○ AUS (NSW) 180-181 K 2
Peak Hill ○ AUS (WA) 176-177 E 2
Peale, Mount ▲ USA 42-43 C 6
Pearce ○ USA 44-45 C 4
Pearce Point ▲ AUS 172-173 J 3
Peard Bay ≈ 20-21 L 1
Pea Ridge National Military Park ✕✕ USA 44-45 K 1
Pearisburg ○ USA 46-47 H 7
Pea River ~ USA 48-49 E 4
Pearland ○ USA 44-45 K 5
Pearl Harbor • USA 48-49 C 7
Pearl River ~ USA 48-49 D 4
Pearsall ○ USA 44-45 H 5
Pearson ○ USA 48-49 G 4
Pearston ○ ZA 220-221 G 6
Peary Channel ≈ 24-25 U 1
Peary Gletscher < GRØ 26-27 U 5
Peary Land ◡ GRØ 26-27 f 2
Pease River ~ USA 44-45 G 2
Peawanuck ○ CDN 34-35 O 3
Peba, Rio ~ BR 68-69 D 5
Pebane ○ MOC 218-219 K 3
Pebas ○ PE 66-67 C 4
Pebble Island ~ GB 78-79 L 6
Pecan Island ○ USA 44-45 L 5
Peças, Ilha das ~ BR 74-75 F 5
Pečenga ○ RUS 88-89 V 2
Peche-Merle, Grotte du • F 90-91 H 9
Pechora = Pečora ○ RUS 88-89 W 3
Pechorskaya Guba = Pečorskaja guba ≈ RUS 88-89 X 2
Pechorskoye More = Pečorskoe more ≈ RUS 88-89 V 2
Pecixe, Ilha ~ GNB 202-203 B 4
Pecnoj tubek ◡ KA 96-97 G 10
Pečora ★ RUS (KOM) 88-89 Y 4
Pečora ~ RUS 114-115 W 3
Pečora ~ RUS 114-115 E 4
Pečoro-Il'yčskij, zapovednik ⊥ RUS 114-115 F 3
Pečoro-Il'yčskij zapovednik ⊥ RUS 114-115 D 4
Pečorsk, Troicko- ☆ RUS 114-115 D 3
Pečorskaja grjada ▲ RUS 88-89 X 3
Pečorskaja guba ≈ 88-89 X 2
Pečorskoe More ≈ 88-89 V 2
Pecos ○ USA 44-45 E 3
Pecos National Monument ∴ USA 44-45 E 2
Pecos Plains ± USA 44-45 E 3
Pecos River ~ USA 44-45 E 3
Pécs ○ •• H 92-93 P 5
Pedda Ahobilam ○ IND 140-141 H 3
Pedder, Lake ○ AUS 180-181 J 7
Pedernales ○ DOM 54-55 K 5
Pedernales ○ RCH 76-77 C 4
Pedernales ○ YV 60-61 K 3
Pedernales ○ EC 64-65 B 1
Pedernales, Punta ▲ RCH 64-65 C 1

Pedernales, Salar de ○ RCH 76-77 C 4
Pedemeira, Cachoeira ~ BR 66-67 E 7
Pedemeiras ○ BR 72-73 F 7
Pé de Serra ○ BR 68-69 J 6
Pedirka ○ AUS 178-179 C 4
Pedra Alta, Cachoeira ~ BR 68-69 C 6
Pedra Azul ○ BR 72-73 K 3
Pedra Azul, Pico ▲ BR 72-73 K 3
Pedra Badejo ○ CV 202-203 L 5
Pedra Branca ○ BR 72-73 G 6
Pedra Corrida ○ BR 72-73 G 6
Pedra de Amolar, Rio ~ BR 68-69 E 6
Pedra do Feitiço, Riachão ~ ANG 216-217 B 2
Pedra-Furada, Riachão ~ BR 68-69 J 5
Pedra Grande ○ BR 72-73 F 3
Pedra Lavrada ○ BR 68-69 K 5
Pedra Lume ○ CV 202-203 C 5
Pedra Preta ○ BR 70-71 K 5
Pedra Preta, Corredeira da ~ BR 68-69 C 5
Pedras, Cachoeira ~ BR 68-69 D 7
Pedras Descobertas ~ BR 70-71 J 3
Pedras Grandes ○ BR 74-75 E 7
Pedras Negras ○ ANG 216-217 C 4
Pedras Negras ○ BR 70-71 F 3
Pedras Tinhosas ~ STP 210-211 a 2
Pedreira, Rio ~ BR 62-63 J 5
Pedreiras ○ BR (MAR) 68-69 F 4
Pedreiras ○ BR (RSU) 74-75 D 7
Pedrera, La ○ CO 66-67 C 3
Pedrinhas ○ BR 68-69 K 7
Pedro Alexandre ○ BR 68-69 K 6
Pedro Alonso ○ BR 68-69 C 6
Pedro Antunes ○ BR 74-75 D 8
Pedro Avelino ○ BR 68-69 K 4
Pedro Barros ○ BR 74-75 G 5
Pedro Canário ○ BR 72-73 L 5
Pedro de Valdivia ○ RCH 76-77 C 2
Pedro Gomes ○ BR 70-71 K 6
Pedro II ○ BR 68-69 H 4
Pedro J. Montero ○ EC 64-65 C 3
Pedro Juan Caballero ○ PY 76-77 H 2
Pedro Luro ○ RA 78-79 H 4
Pedro Montoya ○ MEX 50-51 K 7
Pedroñeras, Las ○ E 98-99 F 5
Pedro Osório ○ BR 74-75 D 8
Pedro Vega ∴ •• MEX 52-53 J 3
Peebinga ○ AUS 180-181 F 3
Peebles ○ GB 90-91 J 4
Peebles ○ USA 46-47 G 6
Peedamulla ○ AUS 172-173 B 6
Peel ○ •• GBM 90-91 H 5
Peel Channel ~ CDN 20-21 X 2
Peel Plateau ▲ CDN 20-21 Y 3
Peel Point ▲ CDN 24-25 P 4
Peel River ~ CDN 20-21 W 4
Peel River Game Reserve ⊥ CDN 20-21 Y 3
Peel Sound ~ CDN 24-25 Y 4
Peene ~ D 92-93 M 2
Peeramudiayeppa Lake ○ AUS 178-179 D 4
Peera Peera Poolanna Lake ○ AUS 178-179 D 4
Peerless ○ CDN 32-33 Q 4
Peerless ○ USA 42-43 E 1
Peerless Lake ○ CDN 32-33 N 3
Peers ○ CDN 32-33 N 5
Peetz ○ USA 42-43 F 5
Pegasus Bay ≈ 182 D 5
Pegatan ○ RI 162-163 K 6
Peg. Müller ▲ RI 162-163 K 4
Pego ○ E 98-99 G 5
Pego ○ P 98-99 C 5
Pegtymel' ~ RUS 112-113 T 2
Pegtymel'skij hrebet ▲ RUS 112-113 S 2
Pehčevo ○ MK 100-101 H 4
Péhonko ○ DY 202-203 L 4
Pehuajó ○ RA 78-79 J 3
Pehuén-Co ○ RA 78-79 J 5
Pei Xian ○ VRC 154-155 K 4
Peinan, Cerro ▲ RA 80 D 5
Peine ○ D 92-93 L 2
Peipus, Lake = Peipsi Järv ○ EST 94-95 K 2
Peïpsi Järv ○ EST 94-95 K 2
Peïxe ○ BR 72-73 F 2
Peixe, Lagoa do ○ BR 74-75 D 8
Peixe, Rio do ~ BR 72-73 D 4
Peixe, Rio do ~ BR 72-73 F 4
Peixe, Rio do ~ BR 72-73 F 5
Peixe, Rio do ~ BR 72-73 H 5
Peixeboi ○ BR 68-69 E 3
Peixe Couro ou Aquinabo, Rio ~ BR 70-71 K 5
Peixes ou do São Francisco, Rio dos ~ BR 70-71 K 2
Peixoto, Represa ○ BR 72-73 G 6
Peixoto de Azevedo ○ BR 70-71 K 2
Peixoto de Azevedo, Rio ~ BR 70-71 H 2
Pejantan, Pulau ~ RI 162-163 F 4
Pekalongan ○ RI 168 C 3
Pekan ○ •• MAL 162-163 E 3
Pekanbaru ○ RI 162-163 D 4
Pekin ○ USA (IL) 46-47 D 5
Pekin ○ USA (ND) 42-43 H 2
Pekin, Pulau ~ RI 164-165 K 2
Peking = Beijing ★ •• VRC 154-155 K 2
Pekinga ○ DY 204-205 E 2
Peklino ○ RUS 94-95 N 5
Peko, Mont ▲ CI 202-203 G 6
Peko, Parc National du Mont ⊥ CI 202-203 G 6
Peko Mine • AUS 174-175 C 6
Pekuľnej, hrebet ▲ RUS 112-113 S 4
Pekuľnejskoe, ozero ○ RUS 112-113 T 5
Péla ○ RG 202-203 F 6
Pelabuhanratu ○ RI 168 C 4
Pelabuhan Ratu, Teluk ≈ 168 B 3
Pelada, Pampa ± RA 80 D 7
Pelagie, Isole = Pelagie, Isole ~ I 100-101 D 8
Pelahatchie ○ USA 48-49 D 3
Pelaihari ○ RI 164-165 D 5
Pelau ○ SOL 184 I d 1
Pélébina ○ DY 202-203 L 5
Pelechuco ○ BOL 70-71 C 4
Peleduj ~ RUS 118-119 F 6
Pelée, Mont ▲ F 56 E 4
Pelee, Point ▲ CDN 46-47 G 5
Pelee Island ~ CDN 46-47 G 5
Pelei ○ RI 164-165 H 4
Pelejo ○ PE 64-65 E 5
Pelekech ▲ EAK 212-213 E 2
Pelencho ○ YV 60-61 L 3
Peleng, Pulau ~ RI 164-165 H 4
Peleng, Selat ≈ 164-165 H 4
Pelézi ○ CI 202-203 G 6
Pelham ○ AUS 174-175 G 6
Pelhřimov ○ CZ 92-93 N 4
Pelican ○ USA 32-33 D 3
Pelican, Lac ○ CDN 36-37 N 5
Pelican Lake ○ CDN 34-35 F 4
Pelicano, Quebrada del ~ RCH 76-77 B 4
Pelican Point (Beach) • AUS 176-177 B 6
Pelican River ~ CDN 32-33 N 3
Pelican Lake ○ USA 42-43 L 1
Pelican Narrows ○ CDN 34-35 E 3
Pelican Rapids ○ USA 42-43 J 2
Pelileo ○ EC 64-65 C 2
Pelindă, Ponta ▲ GNB 202-203 B 4
Pelkosenniemi ○ FIN 88-89 J 3
Pella ○ USA 42-43 L 5
Pelland ○ USA 42-43 L 1
Pellat Lake ○ CDN 30-31 P 3
Pell City ○ USA 48-49 E 3
Pellegrini ○ RA 78-79 H 4
Pellegrini, Lago ○ RA 78-79 F 4
Pell Inlet ≈ 2 C 2
Pello ○ FIN 88-89 G 3
Pellston ○ USA 46-47 F 3
Pellworm ~ D 92-93 K 1
Pelly Bay ≈ 24-25 b 6
Pelly Bay ○ CDN 24-25 a 6
Pelly Crossing ○ CDN 20-21 X 2
Pelly Lake ○ CDN 30-31 T 3
Pelly Mountains ▲ CDN 20-21 Y 6
Pelly Plateau ▲ CDN 20-21 Z 5
Pelly Point ▲ CDN 24-25 W 5
Pelly River ~ CDN 20-21 W 5
Pelmadulla ○ CL 140-141 J 7
Pelokang, Pulau ~ RI 168 D 6
Pelopónnisos □ GR 100-101 J 6
Pelopónnisos ○ GR 100-101 J 6
Peloritani, Monti ▲ I 100-101 E 5
Pelotas ○ BR 74-75 D 8
Pelotas, Rio ~ BR 74-75 E 7
Pelsart Group ~ AUS 176-177 C 4
Pelulutepu ○ SME 62-63 G 4
Pelus ~ MAL 162-163 E 2
Pelym ~ RUS 114-115 F 4
Pelymskij Tuman, ozero ~ RUS 114-115 G 4
Pemadumcook Lake ○ USA 46-47 O 3
Pemalang ○ RI 168 C 3
Pemali, Tanjung ▲ RI (SLT) 164-165 H 4
Pemali, Tanjung ▲ RI (STG) 164-165 H 6
Pemangil, Pulau ~ MAL 162-163 E 4
Pemangkat ○ RI 162-163 H 4
Pematang ○ RI 162-163 D 4
Pematangsiantar ○ RI 162-163 C 3
Pematangtanabjawa ○ RI 162-163 C 3
Pemba ☆ MOC 214-215 L 7
Pemba ○ Z 218-219 E 3
Pemba Channel ≈ 212-213 H 5
Pemba Island ~ EAT 212-213 G 6
Pembe ○ MOC 218-219 K 4
Pemberton ○ AUS 176-177 D 7
Pemberton ○ CDN 32-33 J 6
Pembina River ~ CDN 32-33 M 5
Pembina River ~ CDN 34-35 G 6
Pembine ○ USA 46-47 D 3
Pembre ○ RI 166-167 J 5
Pembroke ○ CDN 38-39 F 6
Pembroke ○ GB 90-91 H 6
Pembroke, Cape ▲ CDN 36-37 J 3
Pembroke Castle •• GB 90-91 E 6
Pembrokeshire Coast National Park ⊥ GB 90-91 E 6
Pemuco ○ RCH 78-79 C 4
Pen ○ IND 138-139 D 10
Peña Blanca ○ RCH 76-77 B 4
Penadoto, ozero ○ RUS 108-109 P 7
Peñafiel ○ E 98-99 E 4
Peñaflor ○ RCH 78-79 D 1
Penalva ○ BR 68-69 F 3
Peña Nevada, Cerro ▲ MEX 50-51 K 6
Penambulai, Pulau ~ RI 166-167 H 5
Penampang ○ MAL 162-163 K 2
Penanjung Game Park ⊥ RI 168 C 3

Penápolis o BR 72-73 E 6
Penarak, Kampung o MAL 162-163 E 2
Peñaranda de Bracamonte o E 98-99 E 4
Peñarroya ▲ E 98-99 G 4
Peñarroya-Pueblonueva o E 98-99 G 4
Peñas, Cabo ▲ RA 80 G 6
Peñas, Golfo de ≈ 80 C 3
Peñas, Las o RA 76-77 D 5
Peñas, Sierra de las ▲ RA 78-79 G 2
Peñas Blancas o NIC 52-53 B 6
Peñas Negras o YV 60-61 J 4
Pench National Park ⊥ IND 138-139 G 9
Penck, Cape ▲ ARK 16 G 9
Pendarves o NZ 182 C 5
Pendé o RCA 206-207 C 5
Pendé ~ RCA 206-207 B 6
Pendembu o WAL (EAS) 202-203 C 5
Pendembu o WAL (NOR) 202-203 D 5
Pendeng o RI 162-163 E 6
Pender o USA 42-43 J 4
Pender Bay ≈ 172-173 F 4
Pendjari ~ DY 202-203 L 5
Pendjari, Parc National de la ⊥ DY 202-203 L 4
Pendjari, Zone Cynégétique de la ⊥ DY 202-203 L 4
Pendjua o ZRE 210-211 G 4
Pendleton o USA (IN) 46-47 F 6
Pendleton o USA (OR) 40-41 D 3
Pendopo o RI 162-163 E 6
Pend Oreille Lake o USA 40-41 F 2
Pend Oreille River ~ USA 40-41 F 1
Pendulium Øer ~ GRØ 26-27 q 6
Penebangan, Pulau ~ RI 162-163 H 5
Penebel o RI 168 B 7
Peneda ▲ P 98-99 C 4
Penedo o BR 68-69 K 7
Pene-Katamba o ZRE 210-211 K 4
Penela o P 98-99 C 4
Pene-Mende o ZRE 212-213 B 6
Pénésoulou o DY 202-203 L 5
Penet, Tanjung ▲ RI 162-163 F 7
Penetanguishene o CDN 38-39 E 6
Penfro = Pembroke o GB 90-91 E 6
Pengalengan o RI 168 B 3
Peng'an o VRC 154-155 L 6
Penganga ~ IND 138-139 G 10
Pengastulan o RI 168 B 7
Pengchia Yü ~ RC 156-157 N 4
Penge o ZRE (HAU) 212-213 A 2
Penge o ZRE (KOR) 210-211 K 6
Penge, Chute ~ ZRE 212-213 B 3
Penghu Islands = RC 156-157 L 5
Pengjie o VRC 154-155 F 6
Pengkalan Kubor, Kampung o MAL 162-163 E 2
Pengkou o VRC 156-157 K 4
Penglai o VRC 154-155 M 3
Penglai o VRC 156-157 G 7
Penglai Ge ~ VRC 154-155 M 3
Pengshan o VRC 154-155 C 6
Pengshui o VRC 156-157 F 2
Penguin o AUS 180-181 H 6
Penguin Island ~ CDN 38-39 I Q 5
Penguin Shoal ≈ AUS 172-173 G 2
Pengxi o VRC 154-155 D 6
Penhalonga o ZW 218-219 G 4
Penhoek Pass ▲ ZA 220-221 H 5
Péni o BF 202-203 H 4
Peniche o P 98-99 C 5
Penida, Nusa ~ RI 168 B 7
Peninga o RUS 88-89 M 5
Peninsular Development Road II AUS 174-175 G 4
Peninsular Lake o CDN 34-35 M 5
Penitente, Serra do ▲ BR 68-69 G 6
Pénjamo o MEX 52-53 D 1
Penmarc'h o F 90-91 E 8
Penmarc'h, Pointe de ▲ · F 90-91 E 8
Pennádam o IND 140-141 H 5
Pennant o CDN 32-33 Q 6
Penner ~ IND 140-141 H 3
Penneshaw o AUS 180-181 D 6
Penn Hills o USA 46-47 J 5
Pennines, The ▲▲ GB 90-91 F 4
Pennsylvania o USA 46-47 J 5
Pennsylvania TPK II USA 46-47 K 5
Penny o CDN 32-33 N 5
Penn Yan o USA 46-47 K 4
Penny Highlands ▲▲ CDN 28-29 G 3
Penny Ice Cap C CDN 28-29 G 3
Penny Strait ≈ 24-25 X 2
Peno ☆ RUS 94-95 N 3
Penobscot River ~ USA 38-39 K 6
Penoka o AUS 180-181 F 4
Penola o · AUS 180-181 E 6
Peñón Blanco o MEX 50-51 H 5
Peñón del Rosario, Cerro ▲ MEX 52-53 E 2
Penong o AUS 176-177 M 5
Peñón Nevada del Falso Azufre ▲ RCH 76-77 C 4
Peñón Nevado del Falso Azufre ▲ RA 76-77 C 4
Penonomé o · PA 52-53 D 7
Penot, Mount ▲ VAN 184 II a 3
Penrhyn, Cape ▲ CDN 24-25 I 7
Penrhyn Basin ≃ 13 M 3
Penrith o GB 90-91 F 4
Pensa o BF 202-203 K 3
Pensacola o USA 48-49 E 4
Pensacola Bay ≈ 48-49 E 4
Pensacola Mountains ▲▲ ARK 16 E 0
Pensamiento, El o BOL 70-71 G 4
Pensepef, mys ▲ RUS 120-121 T 4
Penshurst o AUS 180-181 E 6
Pensilvania o CO 60-61 D 5
Pentálofos o GR 100-101 H 4
Pentecost □ VAN 184 II b 2
Pentecost Downs o AUS 172-173 H 4
Pentecostes o BR 68-69 J 3
Pentecost Island = Île Pentecôte ~ VAN 184 II b 2
Pentecost Range ▲▲ AUS 172-173 H 3
Pentecost River ~ AUS 172-173 H 3

Pentecôte, Île = Pentecost Island ~ VAN 184 II b 2
Pentecôte, Rivière ~ CDN 38-39 L 4
Pentenga o BF 202-203 L 4
Penticton o CDN 32-33 L 7
Penticton Indian Reserve X CDN 32-33 L 7
Pentland o AUS 174-175 H 7
Pentland Firth ≈ 90-91 F 2
Pentwater o USA 46-47 E 4
Penu o RI 164-165 J 4
Penuin, Fiordo ≈ 80 C 4
Penukonda o · IND 140-141 G 4
Penwegon o MYA 142-143 K 6
Penylan Lake o CDN 30-31 Q 5
Penyu, Kepulauan ~ RI 166-167 D 4
Penyu, Teluk ≈ 168 C 3
Penza o RUS 124-125 D 7
Penzance o GB 90-91 E 6
Penzance Lake o CDN 30-31 Q 5
Penze o VRC 156-157 J 2
Penzele o ZRE 210-211 G 4
Penžina ~ RUS 112-113 M 4
Penžinskaja guba ≈ 120-121 T 3
Penžinskij hrebet ▲ RUS 120-121 V 3
Peoria o USA (AZ) 40-41 H 9
Peoria o USA (IL) 46-47 D 5
Pepa o ZRE 214-215 E 4
Pepani ~ ZA 220-221 F 3
Pepita ou Porte Alegre, Rio ~ BR 68-69 B 6
Peque o CO 60-61 D 4
Pequena, Cachoeira ~ BR 68-69 C 3
Pequeri, Rio ~ BR 70-71 K 5
Pequot Lakes o USA 42-43 K 2
Perabumulih o RI 162-163 F 6
Peraguaizinho, Rio ~ BR 70-71 J 4
Perak o MAL 162-163 D 2
Perak o RI 168 E 3
Perambalúr o IND 140-141 H 5
Perämeri ≈ 88-89 K 4
Perapat, Tanjung ▲ RI 164-165 D 6
Perämeri o · 88-89 J 4
Peras-2 ▲ MEX 50-51 G 5
Perbaugan o RI 162-163 C 3
Perbulan o RI 162-163 C 3
Percé o CDN 38-39 M 4
Percival Lakes o AUS 172-173 G 6
Percy, Mount ▲ AUS 172-173 G 4
Percy Isles ~ AUS 178-179 L 1
Perdekop o ZA 220-221 J 3
Perdida, Rio ~ BR 68-69 E 6
Perdido, Arroyo ~ RA 78-79 F 7
Perdidos, Cachoeira dos ~ BR 70-71 H 4
Perdizes o BR 72-73 G 5
Perdões o BR 72-73 H 6
Perdón, Puerto del ▲ E 98-99 G 3
Perdue o CDN 34-35 C 4
Perehins'ke o UA 102-103 J 3
Pereira ☆ CO 60-61 D 5
Pereira, Cachoeira ~ BR 66-67 J 3
Pereira Barreto o BR 72-73 E 6
Pereirinha o BR 66-67 J 7
Perejaslav-Chmel'nyc'kyj o UA 102-103 Q 2
Perejastavka o RUS 122-123 F 5
Pereljub ☆ RUS 96-97 G 8
Pereljubovka ▲ RUS 126-127 M 3
Peremetnoe ☆ KA 96-97 G 8
Peremul Par o IND 140-141 E 7
Perené, Rio ~ PE 64-65 E 7
Perenjori o AUS 176-177 D 4
Pererère o DY 204-205 E 4
Perešcepyne o UA 102-103 J 3
Pereslavl-Zalesskij o · RUS 94-95 Q 3
pereval Kajtezek ▲ TJ 136-137 N 6
Perevolockij o RUS 96-97 J 8
Perevoz o RUS 118-119 H 6
Perevoz o RUS (GOR) 96-97 S 4
Perevoznaja, guba ≈ RUS 108-109 H 7
Perez o RA 78-79 J 2
Pergamino o RA 78-79 J 2
Pergamon ·.··= TR 128-129 B 3
Pérgola o I 100-101 D 3
Perge ·.··= TR 128-129 D 4
Perhentian Besar, Pulau ~ MAL (TER) 162-163 E 2
Perho o FIN 88-89 H 5
Perhonjoki ~ FIN 88-89 H 5
Periá, Rio ~ BR 68-69 G 3
Péribonka de Ramos o MEX 52-53 C 2
Péribonka, Lac o CDN 38-39 J 3
Péribonka, Rivière ~ CDN 38-39 J 3
Perico o C 54-55 E 3
Pericos o MEX 50-51 F 5
Périgban o BF 202-203 J 4
Perigosa, Cachoeira ~ BR 70-71 H 2
Perigoso, Canal ≈ BR 62-63 K 6
Périgueux o · F 90-91 G 7
Perijá, Parque Nacional ⊥ YV 60-61 E 3
Perijá, Sierra de ▲ YV 60-61 E 3
Peri Lake o AUS 178-179 G 6
Peril Strait ≈ 32-33 Q 3
Perim = Barim, Ǧazīrat ~ Y 132-133 C 7
Peringat o RI 162-163 E 2
Periptaveto, porto ~ RUS 108-109 S 6
Periquen o YV 62-63 D 2
Periquito, Cachoeira ~ BR 66-67 K 6
Periquito, Cachoeira do ~ BR 66-67 G 6
Peristrema · TR 128-129 F 3
Peri Suyu ~ TR 128-129 H 3
Perito Moreno o RA 80 E 3
Peritoro o BR 68-69 F 4
Periyar Lake o IND 140-141 G 6
Perkat, Tanjung ▲ RI 162-163 F 5
Perla, La o MEX 50-51 G 3
Perlah ▲ MAL 162-163 E 2
Perlas, Archipiélago de las ~ PA 52-53 D 7
Perlas, Cayos de ~ NIC 52-53 C 5
Perlas, Laguna de ≈ NIC 52-53 C 5
Perlas, Punta de ▲ NIC 52-53 C 5
Perleporten ~ N 84-85 L 5
Perley Island ~ CDN 36-37 J 5

Perlis □ MAL 162-163 D 2
Perlis, Kuala o MAL 162-163 D 2
Perm' ☆ RUS 96-97 K 4
Perma o DY 202-203 L 4
Pèrmet o AL 100-101 H 4
Pernambuco o BR 68-69 J 6
Pernambuco Abyssal Plain ≃ 6-7 G 9
Pernatti Lagoon ≈ AUS 178-179 D 6
Pernik o BG 102-103 C 6
Perniö o FIN 88-89 H 6
Pernštejn · CZ 92-93 O 4
Perola o BR 72-73 D 6
Peron North, Cape ▲ AUS 176-177 B 2
Peron Peninsula ~ AUS 176-177 B 2
Perote o MEX 52-53 F 2
Peroto o BOL 70-71 G 4
Perouse Strait, La = Laperuza, proliv ≈ 122-123 J 4
Perow o CDN 32-33 J 4
Perpignan o · F 90-91 J 10
Perquilauquén, Rio ~ RCH 78-79 D 4
Perret, Punta ▲ YV 60-61 F 2
Perrine o USA 48-49 H 7
Perrin Vale o AUS 174-175 F 4
Perrival o AUS 174-175 G 4
Perry o CDN 34-35 O 7
Perry o USA (FL) 48-49 G 4
Perry o USA (GA) 48-49 G 3
Perry o USA (IA) 42-43 K 5
Perry o USA (ME) 38-39 L 6
Perry o USA (MO) 46-47 C 6
Perry o USA (OK) 44-45 J 1
Perry Island ~ USA 20-21 R 6
Perry Lake o USA 42-43 K 6
Perry River ~ CDN 30-31 T 2
Perryton o USA 44-45 G 1
Perryville o USA (AK) 22-23 R 2
Perryville o USA (MO) 46-47 D 7
Persepolis ·.··= IR 134-135 E 4
Perseverancia o BOL 70-71 F 4
Perseverance, Île ~ BR 66-67 E 3
Perseveranza o BR 68-69 E 2
Persian Gulf ≈ 10-11 E 6
Pertek ☆ TR 128-129 H 3
Perth o AUS (TAS) 180-181 J 6
Perth ☆ · AUS (WA) 176-177 C 5
Perth o CDN 38-39 F 6
Perth o GB 90-91 F 3
Perth Amboy o USA 46-47 L 5
Perth-Andover o CDN 38-39 L 5
Perth Basin ≃ 176-177 A 5
Pertominsk o RUS 88-89 P 4
Pertuis Breton ≈ 90-91 G 8
Pertuis d'Antioche ≈ 90-91 G 8
Pertusato, Capo ▲ F 98-99 M 4
Perú o BOL 70-71 D 3
Perú = PE 64-65 D 4
Peru o USA (IL) 46-47 D 5
Peru o USA (IN) 46-47 E 5
Peru, El o YV 62-63 D 2
Peru Basin ≃ 5 C 6
Perúgia o · I 100-101 D 3
Perugorría o RA 76-77 H 5
Peruibe o BR 74-75 G 5
Peruípe, Rio ~ BR 72-73 L 4
Perumpávúr o IND 140-141 G 5
Perunduraí o IND 140-141 G 5
Perupuk, Tanjung ▲ RI 164-165 F 3
Pervari ☆ TR 128-129 K 4
Perves, Alt de ▲ E 98-99 H 3
Pervomaevka o RUS 116-117 O 9
Pervomaiskyj o UA 102-103 K 3
Pervomajsk o UA (LUG) 102-103 L 3
Pervomajsk o UA (NIK) 102-103 J 3
Pervomajsk = Pervomajs'k ☆ UA 102-103 Q 3
Pervomajs'ke o UA 102-103 H 5
Pervomajskij o KA 124-125 N 3
Pervomajskij o RUS 94-95 R 5
Pervomajskij o RUS 118-119 Q 10
Pervomajskij o RUS (CEL) 96-97 M 6
Pervomajskij o RUS (ORB) 96-97 K 7
Pervomajskoe o RUS 122-123 K 4
Pervomajskoe o RUS (LEN) 94-95 L 1
Pervosovetsk o KA 96-97 G 8
Pervouralsk o RUS 96-97 L 5
Pervyj Kuril'skij proliv o RUS 122-123 R 3
Pervyj Mindej o RUS 116-117 L 7
Peša ~ RUS 88-89 T 3
Pesalai o CL 140-141 H 6
Pésaro o · I 100-101 D 3
Pesca, La o MEX 50-51 L 6
Pesca, Punta ▲ RCH 78-79 C 4
Pescada, Ponta da ▲ BR 62-63 J 4
Pescado Castigado, Arroyo el ~ RA 78-79 K 4
Pescadores = Penghu Islands ~ RC 156-157 L 5
Pescanaja ~ RUS 124-125 O 2
Pescanaja ~ RUS 124-125 O 2
Pescanoe ~ RUS 88-89 U 2
Pescanoe o RUS 88-89 N 5
Pescanoe, ozero ~ RUS 88-89 W 2
Pescanoe ozero ~ RUS 124-125 L 2
Pescanokopskoe o RUS 102-103 M 4
Pescanyj, mys ▲ RUS 108-109 e 4
Pescanyj, mys ▲ KA 126-127 J 6
Pescara o · I 100-101 E 3
Pescara Cassiano o MOC 218-219 H 2
Pescara, Rio ~ RA 80 G 2
Pescodo, Rio ~ BR 72-73 C 4
Pescoaja, buhta ≈ 112-113 U 1
Peshāwar o · PK 138-139 C 3
Pesqueria, Rio ~ MEX 50-51 J 4

Peštera o BG 102-103 D 6
Pestovo o RUS 94-95 O 2
Pestravka o RUS 96-97 F 7
Petah Tiqwa ☆ IL 130-131 D 1
Petäjävesi o FIN 88-89 H 5
Petak, Tanjung ▲ RI 164-165 L 3
Petaling Jaya o MAL 162-163 D 3
Petaluma o USA 40-41 C 6
Petani, Sungai o MAL 162-163 D 2
Petaquillas o MEX 52-53 E 3
Petatbar o IND 142-143 D 4
Petare o YV 60-61 H 2
Petas, Rio Las ~ BOL 70-71 H 5
Petatlán o MEX 52-53 D 3
Petatlán, Rio ~ MEX 50-51 F 4
Petauke o Z 218-219 F 2
Petawanga Lake o CDN 34-35 M 5
Petawawa o CDN 38-39 F 6
Petcacab o MEX 52-53 K 2
Petchaburi o THA 158-159 E 4
Pété o CAM 206-207 D 4
Pétel, Djoutou- o RG 202-203 D 4
Petén Itzá, Lago o GCA 52-53 K 3
Peterborough o AUS (SA) 180-181 E 2
Peterborough o AUS (VIC) 180-181 C 5
Peterborough o · CDN 38-39 E 6
Peterborough o · GB 90-91 G 5
Peterbell o CDN 34-35 P 6
Peterhead o GB 90-91 G 3
Peter Lake o CDN 30-31 X 4
Peter Pond Lake o CDN 32-33 Q 3
Peter Pond Lake Indian Reserve X CDN 32-33 Q 4
Peter Richards, Cape ▲ CDN 24-25 M 5
Petermann Aboriginal Land X AUS 176-177 K 2
Petermann Bjerg ▲ GRØ 26-27 I 7
Petermann Fjord ≈ 26-27 H 2
Petermann Gletscher C GRØ 26-27 H 2
Petermann Ranges ▲▲ AUS 176-177 K 2
Peteroa, Volcán ▲ RA 78-79 D 3
Peter Pond Lake o CDN 32-33 Q 3
Peter Pond Lake Indian Reserve X CDN 32-33 Q 4
Petersburg o USA (AK) 32-33 Q 3
Petersburg o USA (ND) 42-43 J 1
Petersburg o USA (OK) 44-45 J 3
Petersburg o USA (VA) 46-47 K 7
Petersburg Creek-Duncan Salt Chuck Wilderness ⊥ USA 32-33 Q 3
Peter's Mine o GUY 62-63 E 2
Peterson, ostrov ~ RUS 108-109 b 3
Petersfield o · GB 90-91 G 6
Petersville o USA 20-21 P 5
Pethel Peninsula ~ CDN 30-31 O 4
Petifu Junction o WAL 202-203 D 5
Petin o E 98-99 D 3
Pétionville o · RH 54-55 J 5
Petit-Bourg o F 56 E 3
Petit Forte o CDN 38-39 I R 5
Petite Kabylie = DZ 190-191 E 2
Petite Rivière de la Baleine ~ CDN 36-37 L 7
Petite Rivière de Povungnituk ~ CDN 36-37 M 4
Petit Goâve o RH 54-55 J 5
Petit Jardin o CDN 38-39 P 4
Petit Lac des Loups Marins o CDN 36-37 N 6
Petit Lac Opinaca o CDN 38-39 F 2
Petit Loango, Parc National du ⊥ G 210-211 B 5
Petit Mécatina, Rio du ~ CDN 38-39 P 3
Petit Mécatina, Rivière du ~ CDN 38-39 O 3
Petit Mont Cameroun ▲ CAM 204-205 H 6
Petitot River ~ CDN 30-31 J 6
Petit Point ▲ AUS 176-177 B 2
Petit-Rocher o CDN 38-39 M 5
Petit-Saguenay o CDN 38-39 J 4
Petitsikapau Lake o CDN 36-37 O 7
Petlad o IND 138-139 D 8
Peto o MAL 162-163 E 3
Petorca, Rio ~ RCH 78-79 D 7
Petoskey o USA 46-47 F 3
Petra ·.··= JOR 130-131 D 2
Petra o USA 42-43 G 3
Petra I, ostrov ~ ARK 16 G 27
Petra Velikogo, zaliv ≈ 122-123 D 7
Petrel Bank ≃ 22-23 F 6
Petrič o BG 102-103 C 7
Petrila o RO 102-103 C 5
Petrohué o RCH 78-79 C 6
Petrokrepost' = Šlisselburg o RUS 94-95 M 2
Petrolândia o BR 68-69 J 6
Petrolia o CDN 38-39 D 6
Petrolina o BR 68-69 H 6
Petrolina de Goiás o BR 72-73 F 4
Petropavl ☆ KA 124-125 F 1
Petropavlovka o UA 102-103 K 3
Petropavlovka o RUS 126-127 M 2
Petropavlovka o RUS (IRK) 116-117 J 7
Petropavlovka o RUS (BUR) 116-117 M 10
Petropavlovsk-Kamčatskij ☆ · RUS 120-121 S 7
Petropavlovsk Kamchatskiy = Petropavlovsk-Kamčatskij ☆ · RUS 120-121 S 7
Petropavlovskoe, ozero ~ RUS 122-123 F 4
Petrópolis o · BR 72-73 J 6
Petroqímica o RA 80 G 2
Petrovka o RUS 124-125 D 8
Petrovka o RUS 96-97 G 7
Petrovsk-Zabajkal'skij ☆ RUS 116-117 O 10
Petrov Val o RUS 96-97 D 8

Petrozavodsk ☆ RUS 88-89 N 6
Petrusburg o ZA 220-221 G 4
Petrus Steyn o ZA 220-221 J 3
Petrusdal o NAM 220-221 C 1
Petrusville o ZA 220-221 G 5
Petrykau o BY 94-95 L 5
Petuhovo, Bahía de ≈ 52-53 C 3
Petuhovo o RUS 114-115 J 3
Petušinki o RUS 112-113 L 2
Petuški ☆ RUS (VL) 94-95 Q 4
Peumo o RCH 78-79 C 6
Peuno, ozero ~ RUS 108-109 O 7
Peureula o RI 162-163 B 2
Peureula ▲ RI 162-163 B 3
Peusangan o RI 162-163 B 2
Pevek o RUS 112-113 Q 2
Peyumi, Sierra ▲ YV 60-61 K 5
Peza ~ RUS 88-89 S 4
Pezas o RUS 112-113 M 7
Pezenka ~ RUS 112-113 M 5
Pézenas o F 90-91 J 10
Pezu o PK 138-139 C 3
Pfarrkirchen o D 92-93 M 4
Pfizner, Mount ▲ AUS 178-179 C 2
Pforzheim o D 92-93 K 4
Phaileng o IND 142-143 H 4
Phalaborwa o ZA 218-219 F 6
Phá Lai o VN 156-157 E 6
Phalodi o IND 138-139 D 6
Phalombe o MW 218-219 H 2
Phältan o IND 140-141 F 2
Phan o THA 142-143 L 6
Phang Khon o THA 158-159 G 2
Phangnga o THA 158-159 E 6
Phanom o THA 158-159 E 6
Phanom Dong Rak ▲▲ THA 158-159 G 3
Phanom Sarakham o THA 158-159 F 4
Phan Rang Tháp Chàm o VN 158-159 K 5
Phan Ri, Vũng ~ VN 158-159 K 5
Phan Thiết o VN 158-159 K 5
Phantoms Cave = Trou des Fantomes · CAM 210-211 C 2
Pharenda o IND 142-143 C 2
Pharping o NEP 144-145 E 7
Pharr o USA 44-45 H 6
Phaselis ·.··= TR 128-129 D 4
Phatthalung o THA 158-159 F 7
Phayakhaphun Phiasi o THA 158-159 G 3
Phayao o THA 142-143 L 6
Phayuha Khiri o THA 158-159 F 3
Phedra o SME 62-63 G 3
Phelp River ~ AUS 174-175 C 3
Phelps Lake o CDN 30-31 S 6
Phen o THA 158-159 F 2
Phenix City o USA 48-49 F 3
Phetchabun o THA 158-159 F 2
Phibun Mangsahan o THA 158-159 H 3
Phichit o THA 158-159 F 2
Phikwe, Selebi- o RB 218-219 D 6
Philadelphia o USA (MS) 48-49 D 3
Philadelphia o USA (PA) 46-47 L 6
Philae ·.··= ET 194-195 F 5
Philip o USA 42-43 G 3
Philip Broke, Kap ▲ GRØ 26-27 r 6
Philippeville o B 92-93 H 3
Philippi, Lake o AUS 178-179 E 3
Philippi, Monte ▲ RA 80 E 5
Philippine Basin ≃ 14-15 C 5
Philippines = Pilipinas ■ RP 160-161 D 5
Philippines = Pilipinas ~ RP 160-161 D 5
Philippine Trench ≃ 160-161 G 6
Philippolis o ZA 220-221 G 5
Philipsburg o NA 56 D 2
Philip Smith Mountains ▲ USA 20-21 O 4
Philipstown o ZA 220-221 G 5
Phil Kearny, Fort ·.· USA 42-43 D 3
Phillip Bay, Port o AUS 180-181 H 5
Phillip Creek o AUS 174-175 C 6
Phillip Creek Station o AUS 174-175 C 6
Phillip Island o AUS 180-181 H 5
Phillips o USA (ME) 46-47 N 3
Phillips o USA (WI) 46-47 C 3
Phillipsburg o USA (KS) 42-43 H 6
Phillipsburg o USA (MO) 44-45 L 1
Phillips Inlet ≈ 26-27 G 2
Phillips Mountains ▲ ARK 16 F 23
Phillips Point ▲ CDN 24-25 N 2
Phillips Range ▲▲ AUS 172-173 G 4
Philpots Island ~ CDN 24-25 g 3
Phippsøya ~ N 84-85 M 2
Phitsanulok o THA 158-159 F 2
Phitshane o RB 220-221 G 2
Phnom Penh = Phnum Pénh ★· K 158-159 H 5
Phoenix ☆ · USA 40-41 H 9
Phon o THA 158-159 H 2
Phon o THA 158-159 F 2
Phoncharoen o THA 158-159 G 2
Phonda o IND 140-141 F 2
Phongota o IND 138-139 H 3
Phôngsali o LAO 156-157 C 6
Phong Thô o VN 156-157 C 6
Phong Thong o THA 158-159 G 2
Phôn Sa Van o LAO 156-157 C 7
Phoque, Rivière au ~ CDN 36-37 K 7
Phou Khoun o LAO 156-157 C 7
Phrae o THA 142-143 M 6
Phranakhon Si Ayutthaya o ··· THA 158-159 F 3
Phran Kratai o THA 158-159 E 2
Phra Pathom Chedi · THA 158-159 E 4
Phú Bài o VN 158-159 K 3
Phú Cát o VN 158-159 K 3
Phú Ðen Ðin ▲ VN 156-157 C 5
Phú Hung o VN 158-159 J 5

Phuket o · THA 158-159 E 7
Phukradung o THA 158-159 F 2
Phulbari o IND 142-143 F 3
Phulchari o BD 142-143 F 3
Phuldu o IND 142-143 H 4
Phú Lộc o VN 158-159 J 2
Phú Luông ▲ VN 156-157 D 6
Phumi Ântôât o K 158-159 G 6
Phumi Bahm o K 158-159 H 5
Phumi Banam o K 158-159 H 5
Phumi Chhlong o K 158-159 H 5
Phumi Chôâm Sla o K 158-159 G 5
Phumi Kâmpóng Trâbêk o K 158-159 H 4
Phumi Kôki Kraôm o K 158-159 G 4
Phumi Khley o K 158-159 H 5
Phumi Khna o K 158-159 H 5
Phumi Krêk o K 158-159 H 5
Phumi Labang Siêk o K 158-159 J 4
Phumi Mlu Prey o K 158-159 H 4
Phumi Prêk Sândêk o K 158-159 H 5
Phumi Pring o K 158-159 H 4
Phumi Sala Vichey o K 158-159 H 4
Phumi Sâmraông o K 158-159 G 3
Phumi Spoe Tbong o K 158-159 H 5
Phumi Taêk Sôk o K 158-159 G 4
Phumi Thmâ Pôk o K 158-159 G 3
Phumi Véal Rénh o K 158-159 G 5
Phumiphon Reservoir o THA 158-159 F 2
Phumi Phsa Rôméas o K 158-159 H 4
Phun Phin o THA 156-157 D 6
Phu Ninh o VN 158-159 K 3
Phú Nhon o VN 158-159 K 4
Phunphin o THA 158-159 E 6
Phuntsholing o BHT 142-143 F 2
Phu'ớc Long o VN 158-159 H 6
Phu'ớc So'n o VN 158-159 J 4
Phú Quốc, Ðảo ~ VN 158-159 H 5
Phú Qúy ~ VN 158-159 K 5
Phurkia o IND 138-139 G 4
Phu Sa Phin ~ VN 156-157 D 6
Phu Tho o VN 156-157 D 6
Phutnadītjhaba o ZA 220-221 J 4
Phutthaisong o THA 158-159 G 3
Phu Yen o THA 158-159 F 2
Piaçabuçu o BR 68-69 K 7
Piaca dos Mineiros o BR 72-73 D 5
Piacenza ☆ · I 100-101 B 2
Piamonte o CO 60-61 D 5
Pianaj o RP 160-161 D 6
Pianco o BR 68-69 K 5
Piancó, Rio ~ BR 68-69 J 5
Pian Creek ~ AUS 178-179 K 5
Piandang, Tarijung o MAL 162-163 D 2
Piangil o AUS 180-181 G 3
Pianguan o VRC 154-155 G 2
Piankana o ZRE 210-211 G 5
Pianosa, Isola ~ I 100-101 C 3
Piapot o CDN 32-33 Q 7
Piardí, Rio ~ BR 68-69 F 2
Piauí, Rio ~ BR 68-69 G 5
Piauí, Rio ~ BR 68-69 G 5
Piave ~ I 100-101 D 2
Piaxtla, Punta ▲ MEX 50-51 F 5
Piaxtla, Rio ~ MEX 50-51 G 5
Pibor o SUD 208-209 A 5
Pibor Post o SUD 208-209 A 5
Pibrans = Pribram o CZ 92-93 N 4
Pica o RCH 70-71 C 7
Pica, La o YV 60-61 G 3
Picacho de la Laguna ▲ MEX 50-51 E 6
Picada o BR 70-71 K 5
Picão, Ponta do ▲ BR 72-73 J 7
Pica-Pau, Cachoeira ~ BR 62-63 F 6
Picard o SY 222-223 E 2
Picardie o F 90-91 H 6
Picayune o USA 48-49 D 4
Picentini, Monti ▲ I 100-101 E 4
Pich o MEX 52-53 J 2
Pichalo, Punta ▲ RCH 70-71 C 7
Pichaman o RCH 78-79 C 6
Pichana, Rio ~ RA 76-77 C 6
Pichanal o RA 76-77 E 2
Picher o USA 44-45 K 1
Picheregua, Paso ▲ RA 76-77 C 6
Pichilemu o RCH 78-79 C 6
Pichileufu, Cerro ▲ RA 78-79 D 6
Pichilingue o MEX 50-51 D 5
Pichi Mahuida o RA 78-79 G 5
Pichincha, Volcán ▲ EC 64-65 C 2
Pichi Richi Railway · AUS 180-181 D 2
Pichis, Rio ~ PE 64-65 E 7
Pichor o IND 138-139 G 7
Pichucalco o MEX 52-53 H 3
Pichuchén, Volcán ▲ PE 70-71 B 5
Pickerel Lake o CDN 34-35 L 6
Pickertaramoor X AUS 172-173 K 1
Pickstown o USA 42-43 H 4
Pickwick Lake o USA 48-49 D 2
Pico o YV 60-61 F 4
Pico da Neblina, Parque Nacional do ⊥ BR 66-67 D 2
Pico de Orizaba, Parque Nacional ⊥ MEX 52-53 F 2
Pico de Salamanca o RA 80 G 2
Pico Fracture Zone ≃ 6-7 E 5
Pico Negro, Cerro ▲ RCH 70-71 C 7
Picos o BR 68-69 H 5
Picos, Los o MEX 50-51 H 3
Picota o PE 64-65 D 5
Picton o CDN 38-39 F 6
Picton o NZ 182 E 4
Picton, Isla ~ RCH 80 E 8
Pictou o CDN 38-39 N 6
Pictou Island ~ CDN 38-39 N 6
Pictured Rocks National Lakeshore ⊥ USA 46-47 E 2
Picturesque Site ·.· RI 166-167 H 2

Picudo, Cerro ▲ RA 80 F 3
Picuí o BR 68-69 K 5
Picunda o GE 126-127 D 6
Picunda, mys ▲ GE 126-127 D 6
Picún Leufú o RA 78-79 E 5
Picúnleufú, Arroyo ~ RA 78-79 D 5
Picúnleufú, Cerro ▲ RA 78-79 D 5
Pidando ~ DVR 150-151 J 8
Pidarak o PK 134-135 K 6
Pidie, Ujung ▲ RI 162-163 A 2
Pidurutalagala ▲ CL 140-141 J 7
Piebli o CI 202-203 G 6
Piedad de Cavadas, La o MEX 52-53 C 1
Piedade o BR 72-73 G 7
Pié de Palo, Sierra ▲ RA 76-77 C 6
Piedmont o USA 48-49 F 3
Piedra, Cerro ▲ RCH 78-79 D 6
Piedrabuena o E 98-99 E 5
Piedra del Águila o RA 78-79 D 6
Piedra de la Virgen · YV 62-63 D 3
Piedra de Olla, Cerro ▲ MEX 52-53 F 3
Piedra Echada o RA 78-79 H 5
Piedrahita o E 98-99 E 4
Piedras, Las o PE 70-71 C 3
Piedras, Las o ROU 78-79 L 3
Piedras, Punta ▲ RA 78-79 L 3
Piedras, Rio de las ~ PE 70-71 B 2
Piedras Altas o BR 74-75 D 8
Piedras Blancas o CR 52-53 C 7
Piedras Negras ·.· GCA 52-53 J 3
Piedras Negras o MEX 50-51 J 3
Piedra Sola o ROU 78-79 L 2
Piedras Point ▲ RP 160-161 C 7
Piedritas o RA 78-79 H 3
Pie Island ~ CDN 34-35 M 6
Piekenaarskloof ▲ ZA 220-221 D 6
Pieksämäki o FIN 88-89 J 5
Piélá o BF 202-203 K 4
Pielavesi o FIN 88-89 J 5
Pielinen o FIN 88-89 K 5
Pieljekaise nationalpark ⊥ S 86-87 H 3
Pieman River ~ AUS 180-181 H 6
Piemonte = I 100-101 A 2
Pienaarsrivier o ZA 220-221 J 2
Piendamo o CO 60-61 C 5
Pieniężno o PL 92-93 Q 1
Pienza o I 100-101 C 3
Pierce Lake o CDN 34-35 K 3
Pierceland o CDN 32-33 Q 4
Pieres o RA 78-79 K 4
Pierowall o GB 90-91 F 2
Pierre ☆ · USA 42-43 G 3
Pierre Hoho o F 62-63 H 4
Pierre Lake o CDN 34-35 Q 6
Pierrette o F 62-63 H 3
Pierre Verendrye Monument, Fort ·.· USA 42-43 G 3
Pierreville o TT 60-61 L 2
Pierson o CDN 34-35 F 6
Pierson o USA 48-49 H 7
Piešťany o SK 92-93 O 4
Pietarsaari = Jakobstad o FIN 88-89 G 5
Pietermaritzburg o ☆·· ZA 220-221 K 4
Pietersburg o ZA 218-219 E 6
Pietlo o LB 202-203 F 7
Piet Plessis o ZA 220-221 G 3
Piet Retief o · ZA 220-221 K 3
Pietroşani o RO 102-103 D 6
Pifo o EC 64-65 C 2
Pigeon Hole o AUS 172-173 K 4
Pigeon Lake o CDN 32-33 N 5
Piggott o USA 44-45 M 1
Piggs Peak o SD 220-221 K 3
Pigu o GH 202-203 K 5
Pigüé o RA 78-79 H 4
Pigüé, Arroyo ~ RA 78-79 H 4
Pigüm Do ~ ROK 150-151 E 10
Pihtipudas o FIN 88-89 H 5
Pihtovyj greben', gora ▲ RUS 114-115 S 7
Pijijiapan o MEX 52-53 H 4
Pikalevo o RUS 94-95 O 2
Pikangikum o CDN 34-35 K 5
Pikangikum Lake o CDN 34-35 J 5
Pikas', hrebet ▲ RUS 112-113 Q 5
Pikasilla o EST 94-95 K 2
Pikas'vajat ~ RUS 112-113 R 5
Pike Island ~ CDN 36-37 J 3
Pike Lake o CDN 34-35 J 5
Pikes Peak ▲ USA 42-43 E 6
Piketberg o ZA 220-221 D 6
Piketon o USA 46-47 G 6
Pikeville o USA (KY) 46-47 G 7
Pikeville o USA (TN) 48-49 F 2
Pikin Rio ~ SME 62-63 G 3
Pikiutdleq = Køge Bugt ≈ 28-29 U 4
Pikmiktalik o USA 20-21 J 5
Pikounda o RCB 210-211 D 3
Pikovka, Buhta ≈ RUS 114-115 R 5
Pila ☆ · PL 92-93 O 2
Pila, La o MEX 50-51 J 4
Pilaga, Riacho ~ RA 76-77 H 3
Pilah, Kuala o MAL 162-163 E 3
Pila Kyun ~ MYA 158-159 D 5
Pilane o RB 220-221 H 2
Pilani o IND 138-139 F 5
Pilão Arcado o BR 68-69 G 6
Pilar o · IND 140-141 J 7
Pilar ☆ PY 78-79 K 2
Pilar, La o RA (BUA) 78-79 K 3
Pilar, La o RA (COD) 76-77 F 4
Pilar, El o YV 60-61 K 2
Pilar de Goiás o BR 72-73 F 3
Pilas Group ~ RP 160-161 D 9
Pilas Island ~ RP 160-161 D 9
Pilaya, Rio ~ BOL 76-77 E 1
Pilbara ☆ AUS 172-173 D 4
Pilcaniyeu o RA 78-79 D 6
Pilcomayo, Rio ~ PY 76-77 F 2
Pilcopata o PE 70-71 B 3

Pol-e Safīd ○ **IR** 136-137 C 6
Polessk ☆ **RUS** 94-95 G 4
Polevskoj ☆ **RUS** 96-97 M 5
Polewali ○ **RI** 164-165 F 5
Polgahawela ○ **CL** 140-141 J 7
Poli ○ **CAM** 204-205 K 4
Poli ○ **CY** 128-129 E 5
Policastro, Golfo di ≈ 100-101 E 5
Police, Pointe ▲ **SY** 224 D 2
Policemans Point ○ **AUS** 180-181 E 4
Policoro ○ **I** 100-101 F 4
Poligiros ○ **GR** 100-101 J 4
Polihnitos ○ **GR** 100-101 L 5
Polikastro ○ **GR** 100-101 J 4
Poliny Osipenko, imeni ☆ **RUS** 122-123 G 2
Polis'ke ○ **UA** 102-103 F 2
Politovo ○ **RUS** 88-89 U 4
Poliva ∼ **RUS** 116-117 L 6
Polja ∼ **RUS** 94-95 Q 4
Poljakovskij ○ **RUS** 118-119 N 9
Poljana ○ **UA** 102-103 C 3
Poljamoe ○ **RUS** 110-111 b 4
Poljarnyj ○ **RUS** (CUK) 112-113 U 2
Poljarnyj ○ **RUS** (MUR) 88-89 M 2
Poljarnyj ○ **RUS** (SAH) 110-111 H 6
Poljarnyj hrebet ▲ **RUS** 120-121 O 2
Poljarnyj Ural ▲ **RUS** 114-115 E 2
Polk, Fort ✕✕ **USA** 44-45 L 4
Pollāchi ○ **IND** 140-141 G 5
Pollença ○ **E** 98-99 J 5
Pollilo ○ **RP** 160-161 D 5
Pollilo Island ⌒ **RP** 160-161 D 5
Pollilo Islands ⌒ **RP** 160-161 E 5
Pollilo Strait ≈ 160-161 D 5
Pollino, Parco del ⊥ **I** 100-101 F 5
Pollock ○ **USA** 44-45 L 4
Pollock Hills ▲ **AUS** 172-173 H 7
Pol'noj Voronež ∼ **RUS** 94-95 R 5
Polo ○ **USA** 46-47 D 5
Polobaya Grande ○ **PE** 70-71 B 5
Polochic, Río ∼ **GCA** 52-53 K 4
Polock = Polack ☆ •• **BY** 94-95 L 4
Pologij-Sergeeva, ostrov ⌒ **RUS** 108-109 T 4
Pologoe Zajmišče ○ **RUS** 96-97 E 9
Polohy ○ **UA** 102-103 K 4
Polom ○ **RUS** 96-97 G 4
Polomolok ○ **RP** 160-161 F 9
Polonina-Runa hora ▲ **UA** 102-103 C 3
Polonnaruwa ○ ••• **CL** 140-141 J 7
Polousnyj krjaž ▲ **RUS** 110-111 X 5
Polovinnoe, ozero ○ **RUS** 108-109 W 6
Poltava ☆ **UA** 102-103 J 3
Poltavka ☆ **RUS** 124-125 G 1
Põltsamaa ○ • **EST** 94-95 J 2
Poluj ∼ **RUS** 108-109 M 8
Poluj ∼ **RUS** 114-115 K 2
Polujskaja vozvyšennost' ▲ **RUS** 114-115 J 2
Polūr ○ **IND** 140-141 H 4
Põlva ☆ **EST** 94-95 K 2
Polvār, Rūd-e ∼ **IR** 134-135 E 3
Polvaredas ○ **RA** 78-79 K 3
Polvora ○ **PE** 64-65 D 5
Põlwe = Põlva ☆ **EST** 94-95 K 2
Polyarnyy Ural = Poljarnyj Ural ▲ **RUS** 114-115 E 2
Polynesia ⌒ 14-15 M 7
Polyuc ○ **MEX** 52-53 K 2
Poma ○ **ZRE** 210-211 K 4
Pomabamba ○ **PE** 64-65 D 6
Pomacanchi ○ **PE** 70-71 B 3
Pomahuaca ○ **PE** 64-65 C 4
Pomarkku ○ **FIN** 88-89 F 6
Pomasi, Cerro de ▲ **PE** 70-71 B 4
Pombal ○ **BR** (PA) 68-69 K 5
Pombal ○ **BR** (RON) 70-71 F 2
Pombal ○ **P** 98-99 C 5
Pombal, Igarapé do ∼ **BR** 68-69 B 5
Pombangi ○ **RI** 164-165 G 5
Pombas ○ **BR** 66-67 F 3
Pombas, Rio das ∼ **BR** 66-67 G 6
Pombuige ∼ **ANG** 216-217 C 5
Pomene ○ **MOC** 218-219 H 6
Pomeroy ○ **USA** (OH) 46-47 G 6
Pomeroy ○ **USA** (WA) 40-41 F 2
Pomeroy ○ **ZA** 220-221 K 4
Pomfret ○ **ZA** 220-221 F 2
Pomio ○ **PNG** 183 F 3
Pomona ○ **RA** 78-79 G 5
Pomona ○ **USA** 42-43 K 6
Pomona Lake ○ **USA** 42-43 K 6
Pomorska, Zatoka ≈ 92-93 N 1
Pomorskij proliv ≈ 88-89 U 2
Pomorskoe ○ **RUS** 108-109 E 5
Pomos ○ **CY** 128-129 E 5
Pompano Beach ○ **USA** 48-49 H 6
Pompei •• **I** 100-101 E 4
Pompéia ○ **BR** 72-73 E 7
Pompeu ○ **BR** 72-73 H 5
Pompeys Pillar ○ **USA** (MT) 42-43 D 3
Pompeys Pillar • **USA** (MT) 42-43 D 3
Pom Phra Chunlachomkiao ○ **THA** 158-159 F 4
Pompué, Rio ∼ **MOC** 200-201 F 3
Pomr', zaliv ○ **RUS** 122-123 K 2
Pomut ∼ **RUS** 114-115 K 3
Ponape ⌒ **FSM** 13 G 2
Ponass Lake ○ **CDN** 34-35 D 4
Ponazyrevo ○ **RUS** 96-97 E 4
Ponca ○ **USA** 42-43 J 4
Ponca City ○ **USA** 44-45 J 1
Poncha Springs ○ **USA** 42-43 D 6
Ponchatoula ○ **USA** 44-45 M 4
Poncheville, Lac ○ **CDN** 38-39 F 3
Pond Creek ○ **USA** 44-45 J 1
Ponderosa ○ **USA** 40-41 E 7
Pondicherry □ **IND** 140-141 H 5
Pondicherry ☆ •• **IND** 140-141 H 5
Pond Inlet ≈ 24-25 h 4
Pond Inlet ○ **CDN** 24-25 h 4
Pondosa ○ **USA** 40-41 D 5
Ponds, Isle of ⌒ **CDN** 38-39 R 2
Pondung Lamanggang ○ **RI** 162-163 D 6
Poneloya ○ **NIC** 52-53 L 5
Ponente, Riviera di ◡ **I** 100-101 A 3
Ponerečnyj Algan ∼ **RUS** 112-113 R 4
Ponferrada ○ • **E** 98-99 D 3
Pônfi ∼ **MOC** 218-219 G 2
Pongaí ○ **BR** 72-73 F 6
Pongara, Pointe ▲ **G** 210-211 B 3
Pong Chi ○ **THA** 158-159 F 2
Pong Nam Ron ○ **THA** 158-159 G 4
Pongo ∼ **SUD** 206-207 H 5
Pongo de Cumbinama ∼ **PE** 64-65 C 4
Pongo de Paquipachango ∼ **PE** 64-65 E 7
Pongola ○ **ZA** 220-221 K 3
Pongola ∼ **ZA** 220-221 K 3
Pongolapoortdam < **ZA** 220-221 L 3
Pongore ○ **ZW** 218-219 D 4
Poni ∼ **BF** 202-203 J 4
Ponindilisa, Tanjung ▲ **RI** 164-165 G 4
Ponio ○ **RT** 202-203 L 4
Ponio, Río ∼ **RCH** 76-77 B 6
Ponna ○ **MYA** 142-143 J 5
Ponnaiyar ∼ **IND** 140-141 H 4
Ponnāni ○ **IND** 140-141 F 5
Ponneri ○ **IND** 140-141 J 4
Ponnūru Nidubrolu ○ **IND** 140-141 J 2
Ponoj ○ **RUS** (MUR) 88-89 Q 3
Ponoj ∼ **RUS** 88-89 N 3
Ponoka ○ **CDN** 32-33 O 5
Ponomarevka ○ **RUS** 114-115 R 6
Ponomarevka ☆ **RUS** (ORB) 96-97 J 7
Ponondougou ○ **CI** 202-203 G 5
Ponorogo ○ **RI** 168 D 3
Ponrang ○ **RI** 164-165 G 5
Ponson Island ⌒ **RP** 160-161 F 7
Ponta ○ **BR** 66-67 E 3
Ponta Delgada ⌒ **P** 6-7 E 6
Ponta de Mata ○ **YV** 60-61 K 3
Ponta de Pedras ○ **BR** 62-63 K 6
Ponta dos Índios ○ **BR** 62-63 J 3
Ponta do Sol ○ **CV** 202-203 B 5
Ponta do Zumbi ○ **BR** 68-69 F 2
Ponta Freitas Morna ○ **ANG** 216-217 B 3
Ponta Grande ▲ **BR** 72-73 L 4
Ponta Grossa ○ **BR** 74-75 E 5
Pontal ○ **BR** 72-73 F 6
Pontal, Rio do ∼ **BR** 68-69 H 6
Pontalina ○ **BR** 72-73 F 4
Pontan River ∼ **CDN** 30-31 L 6
Ponta Porã ○ **BR** 76-77 K 2
Pontarlier ○ • **F** 90-91 L 8
Pontas de Pedras ○ **BR** 68-69 L 5
Pont-Audemer ○ **F** 90-91 H 7
Pontchartrain, Lake ○ **USA** 44-45 M 4
Pontchâteau ○ **F** 90-91 F 8
Pont de Suert, el ○ **E** 98-99 H 3
Pont du Gard ••• **F** 90-91 K 10
Ponte Alta, Rio ∼ **BR** 68-69 E 7
Ponte Alta do Tocantins ○ **BR** 68-69 E 7
Ponteareas ○ **E** 98-99 C 3
Ponte Branca ○ **BR** 72-73 D 4
Ponte da Barca ○ **P** 98-99 C 4
Ponte de Itabapoana ○ **BR** 72-73 K 6
Ponte de Sor ○ **P** 98-99 C 5
Ponte Firme ○ **BR** 72-73 G 5
Ponte Nova ○ **BR** 72-73 J 6
Ponte Ribeiro, Lago ○ **BR** 70-71 H 4
Pontes e Lacerda ○ **BR** 70-71 H 4
Ponte Serrada ○ **BR** 74-75 D 6
Pontevedra ○ **E** 98-99 C 3
Pontiac ○ **USA** (IL) 46-47 D 5
Pontiac ○ **USA** (MI) 46-47 G 4
Pontianak ☆ **RI** 162-163 H 5
Pontian Kecil ○ **MAL** 162-163 E 4
Pontic Mountains = Kuzey Anadolu Dağları ▲ **TR** 10-11 C 4
Pontivy ○ **F** 90-91 F 7
Ponto Arari ○ **BR** 62-63 J 5
Ponto Busch ○ **BOL** 70-71 J 6
Pontoise ☆ **F** 90-91 J 7
Pontokerasía ○ **GR** 100-101 J 4
Ponton ○ **CDN** 34-35 G 3
Ponton Creek ∼ **AUS** 176-177 G 5
Pontorson ○ **F** 90-91 G 7
Pontotoc ○ **USA** 48-49 D 2
Pontrémoli ○ • **I** 100-101 B 2
Ponts ○ **E** 98-99 H 4
Ponuga ○ **PA** 52-53 D 8
Pony Express Station ∴ **USA** 42-43 J 6
Ponza ○ **I** 100-101 D 4
Ponziane, Ìsole ⌒ **I** 100-101 D 4
Poochera ○ **AUS** 180-181 C 2
Pool □ **RCB** 210-211 E 5
Poole ○ **GB** 90-91 G 6
Poole's Monument • **AUS** 178-179 F 5
Pool Malebo ○ **ZRE** 210-211 E 6
Poolowanna Lake ○ **AUS** 178-179 D 4
Pools Cove ○ **CDN** 38-39 R 5
Poonamallee ○ **IND** 140-141 J 4
Pooncarie ○ **AUS** 180-181 G 2
Pooneryn ○ **CL** 140-141 J 6
Poopó ○ **BOL** 70-71 D 6
Poopó, Lago de ○ **BOL** 70-71 D 6
Pooppelloe Lake ○ **AUS** 178-179 G 6
Poorman ○ **USA** 20-21 N 4
Poor Man Indian Reserve ✕ **CDN** 34-35 D 5
Popa Falls ∼ • **NAM** 216-217 F 9
Popayán ☆ •• **CO** 60-61 C 6
Popča ○ **RUS** 88-89 W 5
Pope ○ • **LV** 94-95 G 3
Popenguine ○ • **SN** 202-203 B 2
Poperechnoi Island ⌒ **USA** 22-23 Q 5
Poperinge ○ **B** 92-93 G 3
Popham Bay ≈ 36-37 R 2
Popigaj ○ **RUS** (TMR) 110-111 H 4
Popigaj ∼ **RUS** 110-111 F 3
Popigaj ∼ **RUS** 110-111 H 4
Popilta Lake ○ **AUS** 180-181 F 2
Poplar ○ **USA** (MT) 42-43 E 1
Poplar ○ **USA** (WI) 46-47 C 2
Poplar Bluff ○ **USA** 44-45 M 1
Poplarfield ○ **CDN** 34-35 H 5
Poplar Point ○ **CDN** 34-35 H 5
Poplar River ∼ **CDN** 30-31 J 5
Poplar River ∼ **CDN** 34-35 D 6
Poplar River ∼ **CDN** 34-35 H 4
Poplarville ○ **USA** 48-49 D 4
Popocatépetl, Volcán ▲ •• **MEX** 52-53 E 2
Popof Island ⌒ **USA** 22-23 Q 5
Popoh ○ **RI** 168 D 4
Popokabaka ○ **ZRE** 210-211 F 6
Pópoli ○ **I** 100-101 D 3
Popomanaseu, Mount = Makarakombu ▲ **SOL** 184 I e 3
Popondetta ☆ **PNG** 183 E 5
Popovka ○ **RUS** (ROS) 102-103 M 3
Popovka ∼ **RUS** 110-111 c 7
Popovka ∼ **RUS** 120-121 P 2
Popovo ○ **BG** 102-103 E 6
Popov Porog ○ **RUS** 88-89 N 5
Poprad ○ **SK** 92-93 Q 4
Poptún ○ **GCA** 52-53 K 3
Porāli ∼ **PK** 134-135 M 5
Porangatu ○ **BR** 72-73 F 2
Porbandar ○ • **IND** 138-139 B 9
Porčaman ○ **AFG** 134-135 K 2
Porção, Cachoeira do ∼ **BR** 68-69 B 3
Porcher Island ⌒ **CDN** 32-33 E 5
Porciúngula ○ **BR** 72-73 J 6
Porcos, Riacho dos ∼ **BR** 68-69 J 5
Porcos, Rio dos ∼ **BR** 72-73 H 2
Porcupine ○ **USA** 20-21 W 7
Porcupine Abyssal Plain ≃ 6-7 H 3
Porcupine Forest Reserve ⊥ **CDN** 34-35 F 4
Porcupine Gorge National Park ⊥ **AUS** 174-175 H 7
Porcupine Hills ▲ **CDN** 34-35 E 4
Porcupine Plain ○ **CDN** (SAS) 34-35 E 4
Porcupine Plain ≛ **CDN** 20-21 V 2
Porcupine Plateau ▲ **CDN** 20-21 U 3
Porcupine River ∼ **CDN** 30-31 R 6
Porcupine River ∼ **USA** 20-21 U 3
Pordenone ☆ • **I** 100-101 D 2
Pore ○ **CO** 60-61 F 5
Porebada ○ **PNG** 183 D 5
Porecatu ○ **BR** 72-73 E 7
Poreckoe ○ **RUS** 96-97 E 6
Porédaka ○ **RG** 202-203 D 4
Porekautimbu, Gunung ▲ **RI** 164-165 G 4
Porga ○ **DY** 202-203 L 4
Porgera ○ **PNG** 183 B 3
Porhov ☆ **RUS** 94-95 L 3
Pori ○ **FIN** 88-89 F 6
Porirua ○ **NZ** 182 E 4
Porjus ○ **S** 86-87 J 3
Pork Peninsula ◡ **CDN** 30-31 X 4
Porlakshöfn ○ **IS** 86-87 c 3
Porlamar ○ **YV** 60-61 K 2
Porog ○ **RUS** 88-89 P 5
Poro Island ⌒ **RP** 160-161 F 7
Poro Island ⌒ **SOL** 184 I c 2
Poroma ○ **PNG** 183 B 4
Poronaj ∼ **RUS** 122-123 K 4
Poronajsk ○ **RUS** 122-123 K 4
Porong ○ **RI** 168 E 3
Póros ○ **GR** 100-101 H 5
Porosozero ○ **RUS** 88-89 M 5
Porotos, Punta ▲ **RCH** 76-77 B 5
Porožsk ○ **RUS** 88-89 W 5
Porpoise Bay ≈ 16 G 13
Porquis Junction ○ **CDN** 34-35 Q 6
Porsangen ≈ 86-87 M 1
Porsangerhalvøya ◡ **N** 86-87 M 1
Porsea ○ **RI** 162-163 C 3
Porsgrunn ☆ **N** 86-87 D 7
Porsild Mountains ▲ **CDN** 36-37 H 2
Porsuk Çayı ∼ **TR** 128-129 D 3
Port, Le ○ **F** 224 B 7
Porta, Rio da ∼ **BR** 68-69 C 5
Porta Ascotan ó del Jardin ▲ **BOL** 76-77 C 1
Port Adelaide ○ **AUS** 180-181 E 3
Portage ○ **CDN** 38-39 M 5
Portage ○ **USA** (AK) 20-21 Q 6
Portage ○ **USA** (WI) 46-47 D 4
Portage Bay ≈ 22-23 T 4
Portage la Prairie ○ **CDN** 34-35 G 6
Portageville ○ **USA** 46-47 J 4
Portal ○ **USA** 42-43 F 1
Port Alberni ○ **CDN** 32-33 H 7
Portalegre ○ • **P** 98-99 D 5
Portales ○ **USA** 44-45 F 2
Port Alexander ○ **USA** 32-33 C 3
Port Alfred ○ **ZA** 220-221 H 6
Port Alice ○ **CDN** 32-33 G 6
Port Allegany ○ **USA** 46-47 J 5
Port Alma ○ **AUS** 178-179 L 2
Port Angeles ○ **USA** 40-41 C 1
Port Antonio ○ • **JA** 54-55 G 5
Portão de Baixo, Cachoeira ∼ **BR** 66-67 K 5
Port Arthur ○ **USA** 44-45 L 5
Port Arthur = Lüshun ○ **VRC** 150-151 C 8
Port Askaig ○ **GB** 90-91 D 4
Port au Choix ○ **CDN** 38-39 Q 3
Port Augusta ○ • **AUS** 180-181 D 2
Port au Port Bay ≈ 38-39 P 4
Port au Port Peninsula ◡ **CDN** 38-39 P 4
Port-au-Prince ★ • **RH** 54-55 J 5
Port Austin ○ **USA** 46-47 G 3
Port aux Choix National Historic Park ∴ **CDN** 38-39 Q 3
Port Bell ○ **EAU** 212-213 D 3
Port-Bergé = Boriziny ○ **RM** 222-223 E 5
Port Blair ☆ **IND** 140-141 L 4
Port Blandford ○ **CDN** 38-39 R 4
Port Bolivar ○ **USA** 44-45 K 5
Port Broughton ○ **AUS** 180-181 D 2
Port Burwell ○ **CDN** 38-39 D 7
Port Campbell ○ **AUS** 180-181 G 5
Port Campbell National Park ⊥ **AUS** 180-181 G 5
Port Cartier Sept Îles, Parc Provencial de ⊥ **CDN** 38-39 L 3
Port Charlotte ○ **USA** 48-49 G 6
Port Chilkoot ○ **USA** 20-21 X 7
Port Clements ○ **CDN** 32-33 D 5
Port Clinton ○ **USA** 46-47 G 5
Port Clyde ○ **USA** 46-47 O 4
Port-Daniel ○ **CDN** 38-39 M 4
Port-de-Paix ☆ **RH** 54-55 J 5
Port Dickson ○ • **MAL** 162-163 D 3
Port Douglas ○ • **AUS** 174-175 H 5
Port Edward ○ **CDN** 32-33 E 4
Port Edward ○ **ZA** 220-221 K 5
Porteira, Cachoeira da ∼ **BR** 66-67 H 7
Porteiras ○ **BR** 62-63 F 6
Porteirinha ○ **BR** 72-73 J 3
Portel ○ **BR** 62-63 J 6
Portel ○ **P** 98-99 D 5
Portelândia ○ **BR** 72-73 D 4
Port Elizabeth ○ **ZA** 220-221 G 6
Port Ellen ○ **GB** 90-91 D 4
Porteno, Río ∼ **RA** 76-77 H 3
Porters Corner ○ **USA** 40-41 H 2
Porterville ○ **USA** 40-41 E 7
Porterville ○ **ZA** 220-221 D 6
Portezuela ▲ **BOL** 76-77 C 1
Portezuela del Huaytiquina ▲ **RCH** 76-77 D 2
Portezuela Llullaillaco Norte ▲ **RCH** 76-77 C 3
Portezuela Pasto Ventura ▲ **RA** 76-77 D 4
Portezuelo ○ **RCH** 78-79 C 4
Portezuelo, El ○ **RA** 76-77 E 5
Port Fitzroy ○ **NZ** 182 E 2
Port Fourchon ○ **USA** 44-45 M 5
Port Gentil ☆ **G** 210-211 B 4
Port Germein ○ **AUS** 180-181 D 2
Port Gibson ○ **USA** 44-45 M 4
Port Grosvenor ○ **ZA** 220-221 J 5
Port-Harcourt ☆ **WAN** 204-205 G 6
Port Hardy ○ **CDN** 32-33 G 6
Port Harrison = Inukjuak ○ **CDN** 36-37 K 5
Port Hedland ○ **AUS** 172-173 D 6
Port Heiden ○ **USA** 22-23 R 4
Port Hope ○ **CDN** 38-39 E 7
Port Hope Simpson ○ **CDN** 38-39 Q 2
Port Howard ○ **GB** 78-79 L 6
Port Howe ○ **BS** 54-55 H 2
Port Huron ○ **USA** 46-47 G 4
Portillo, Paso del ▲ **RA** 76-77 B 6
Portimão ○ **P** 98-99 C 6
Portimo ○ **FIN** 88-89 J 3
Port Isabel ○ **USA** 44-45 J 6
Port Isabel Lighthouse State Historic Site ∴ **USA** 44-45 J 6
Port Jackson ≈ 180-181 L 2
Port Jackson ○ **NZ** 182 E 2
Port Jefferson ○ **USA** 46-47 M 5
Port Jervis ○ **USA** 46-47 L 5
Port Kenny ○ **AUS** 180-181 C 2
Port Láirge = Waterford ○ • **IRL** 90-91 D 5
Portland ○ **AUS** 180-181 F 5
Portland ○ **USA** (IN) 46-47 F 5
Portland ○ **USA** (ME) 46-47 N 4
Portland ○ **USA** (OR) 40-41 C 3
Portland ○ **USA** (TX) 44-45 J 6
Portland, Cape ▲ **AUS** 180-181 J 6
Portland Bay ≈ 180-181 F 5
Portland Bight ≈ 54-55 G 6
Portland Canal ≈ 32-33 E 4
Portland Creek Pond ○ **CDN** 38-39 Q 3
Portland Inlet ≈ 32-33 E 4
Portland Island ⌒ **NZ** 182 F 3
Portland Point ▲ **JA** 54-55 G 6
Port Langdon ≈ 174-175 D 3
Port Laoise ○ **IRL** 90-91 D 5
Port Lavaca ○ **USA** 44-45 J 5
Port Lincoln ○ •• **AUS** 180-181 C 3
Port Lions ○ **USA** 22-23 U 4
Portlock Reefs ⌒ **PNG** 183 C 5
Port Loko ○ **WAL** 202-203 D 5
Port-Louis ○ **F** 56 E 3
Port Louis ★ • **MS** 224 C 7
Port Mac Donnell ○ **AUS** 180-181 F 5
Port Macquarie ○ • **AUS** 178-179 M 6
Port Maria ○ **JA** 54-55 G 5
Port Mathurin ○ **MS** 224 F 6
Port Maurant ○ **GUY** 62-63 F 2
Port Mayaca ○ **USA** 48-49 H 6
Port Mc Arthur ≈ 174-175 D 4
Port-Menier ○ **CDN** 38-39 M 4
Port Menier ○ **CDN** 38-39 M 4
Port Moller ○ **USA** 22-23 Q 5
Portmore ○ **JA** 54-55 G 6
Port Moresby ★ **PNG** 183 D 5
Port Neill ○ **AUS** 180-181 D 3
Port Nelson ○ **BS** 54-55 H 3
Port Nelson ○ **CDN** 34-35 K 2
Portneuf, Rivière ∼ **CDN** 38-39 K 4
Port Neville ○ **CDN** 32-33 G 6
Portnjagino, ozero ○ **RUS** 110-111 F 2
Port Nolloth ○ **ZA** 220-221 C 4
Port-Nouveau-Québec ○ **CDN** 36-37 R 5
Porto ○ **BR** 68-69 G 3
Porto ○ **BR** 72-73 M 3
Porto ☆ •• **P** 98-99 C 4
Pôrto Acre ○ **BR** 66-67 D 7
Porto Alegre ○ **BR** 70-71 J 5
Porto Alegre ○ **BR** (BAH) 72-73 K 2
Porto Alegre ○ **BR** (P) 66-67 J 5
Porto Alegre ☆ **BR** (RSU) 74-75 E 8
Porto-Alegre ○ **STP** 210-211 b 2
Porto Alegre do Norte ○ **BR** 68-69 C 7
Porto Amazonas ○ **BR** 74-75 F 5
Porto Amboim ○ **ANG** 216-217 B 5
Porto Antunes ○ **BR** 66-67 D 4
Porto Azzurro ○ **I** 100-101 C 3
Portobelo ○ ••• **PA** 52-53 E 7
Porto Belo, Baía de ≈ 74-75 F 6
Porto Belo, Ponta do ▲ **BR** 74-75 F 6
Porto Bicentenário ○ **BR** 70-71 F 2
Porto Braga ○ **BR** (AMA) 66-67 E 4
Porto Braga ○ **BR** (GSU) 70-71 J 7
Porto Cabello ○ **YV** 60-61 G 2
Porto Camargo ○ **BR** 72-73 D 7
Porto Cristo ○ **E** 98-99 J 5
Porto da Soledade ○ **BR** 72-73 G 4
Pôrto de Fora ○ **BR** 70-71 K 5
Porto de Pedras ○ **BR** 68-69 L 6
Porto do Caititu ○ **BR** 68-69 F 4
Porto do Mangue ○ **BR** 68-69 K 4
Porto do Moz ○ **BR** 62-63 H 6
Porto dos Gaúchos ○ **BR** 70-71 J 2
Porto dos Mosteiros ○ **CV** 202-203 B 6
Porto Esperanza ○ **RA** 76-77 K 4
Porto Esperidião ○ **BR** 70-71 H 4
Porto Estrela ○ **BR** 70-71 J 4
Porto Euchdes da Cunha ○ **BR** 72-73 D 7
Portoferráio ○ **I** 100-101 C 3
Porto Ferreira ○ **BR** 72-73 G 6
Port of Ness ○ **GB** 90-91 D 2
Porto Franco ○ **BR** 68-69 E 5
Port of Spain ★ **TT** 60-61 L 2
Porto Gen. Nac. el Portillo ▲ **RA** 78-79 E 2
Porto Grande ○ **BR** 62-63 J 5
Portogruaro ○ • **I** 100-101 D 2
Porto Henrique ○ **MOC** 220-221 L 3
Pôrto Jofre ○ **BR** 70-71 J 5
Porto Levante ○ **I** 100-101 E 5
Port-Olry ○ **VAN** 184 II a 2
Porto Lucena ○ **BR** 76-77 K 4
Porto Omna = Portumna ○ **IRL** 90-91 C 5
Porto Moniz ○ **P** 188-189 C 4
Porto Mosquito ○ **CV** 202-203 C 6
Pôrto Murtinho ○ **BR** 76-77 J 1
Porto Nacional ○ **BR** 68-69 D 7
Porto Novo ○ **BR** 72-73 J 2
Porto-Novo ★ • **DY** 204-205 E 5
Portonovo ○ **IND** 140-141 H 5
Porto Novo, Vila de ○ **CV** 202-203 B 5
Porto Quebra ○ **BR** 66-67 F 4
Port Orchard ○ **USA** 40-41 C 2
Porto Reis ○ **BR** 66-67 E 4
Porto Rico ○ **BR** 70-71 D 2
Porto Rolha ○ **BR** 70-71 D 2
Porto Santo ⌒ **P** 188-189 C 4
Porto São José ○ **BR** 72-73 D 7
Portoscuso ○ **I** 100-101 B 5
Porto Seguro ○ • **BR** 72-73 L 4
Porto Seguro, Corredeira ∼ **BR** 68-69 B 5
Porto Tolle ○ **I** 100-101 D 2
Porto Tórres ○ **I** 100-101 B 4
Porto União ○ **BR** 74-75 E 6
Pôrto Valter ○ **BR** 64-65 F 6
Porto-Vecchio ○ **F** 98-99 M 4
Porto Velho ☆ **BR** 66-67 F 7
Portovelo ○ **EC** 64-65 C 3
Portoviejo ☆ **EC** 64-65 B 2
Portpatrick ○ **GB** 90-91 E 4
Port Pirie ○ **AUS** 180-181 D 2
Port Radium ○ **CDN** 30-31 L 2
Portree ○ **GB** 90-91 D 3
Port Rowan ○ **CDN** 38-39 D 7
Port Royal National Historic Park ∴ **CDN** 38-39 M 6
Port Royal Sound ≈ 48-49 H 3
Port Said = Būr Sa'īd ☆ **ET** 194-195 F 2
Port Saint Joe ○ **USA** 48-49 F 5
Port Saint Johns ○ **ZA** 220-221 J 5
Port-Saint-Louis-du-Rhône ○ **F** 90-91 K 10
Portsalon ○ **IRL** 90-91 D 4
Port Salut ○ **RH** 54-55 J 5
Port Salut, Plage ≛ • **RH** 54-55 H 5
Port Sanilac ○ **USA** 46-47 G 4
Port Shepstone ○ **ZA** 220-221 K 5
Port Simpson ○ **CDN** 32-33 E 4
Portsmouth ○ **GB** 90-91 G 6
Portsmouth ○ **USA** (IA) 42-43 K 5
Portsmouth ○ **USA** (NH) 46-47 N 4
Portsmouth ○ **USA** (OH) 46-47 G 6
Portsmouth ○ **USA** (VA) 46-47 K 7
Portsmouth ○ **WD** 56 E 4
Port Stephens ○ **GB** 78-79 K 7
Port Sudan = Būr Sūdān ☆ • **SUD** 200-201 H 3
Port Sulphur ○ **USA** 48-49 D 5
Porttipahdan tekojärvi ○ **FIN** 88-89 J 2
Port Townsend ○ • **USA** 40-41 C 1
Portugais, Grotte des = Tenika • **RM** 222-223 D 9
Portugal ■ **P** 98-99 B 4
Portugal, Cachoeira ∼ **BR** 66-67 E 7
Portuguesa, Río ∼ **YV** 60-61 H 3
Portumna = Port Omna ○ **IRL** 90-91 C 5
Port-Vato ○ **VAN** 184 II b 3
Port-Vendres ○ **F** 90-91 J 10
Port Victoria ○ **AUS** 180-181 D 3
Port Victoria ○ **EAK** 212-213 D 3
Port-Vila ★ • **VAN** 184 II b 3
Port Vincent ○ **AUS** 180-181 D 3
Port Wakefield ○ **AUS** 180-181 E 3
Port Washington ○ **USA** 46-47 E 4
Port Wing ○ **USA** 46-47 C 2
Poruj, mys ▲ **RUS** 108-109 P 6
Poruk Çayı ∼ **TR** 128-129 D 3
Porumamilla ○ **IND** 140-141 H 3
Porvenir ○ 64-65 B 10
Porvenir ○ **BOL** 70-71 C 2
Porvenir ○ **PE** 64-65 D 3
Porvenir ○ **RCH** 80 E 6
Porvenir, El ○ **MEX** 50-51 G 2
Porvenir, El ☆ **PA** 52-53 E 7
Porvenir, El ○ **YV** (APU) 60-61 G 4
Porvenir, El ○ **YV** (BAR) 60-61 F 4
Posadas ☆ **RA** 76-77 K 4
Pošegda ○ **RUS** 88-89 R 5
Pošehon'e ○ **RUS** 94-95 Q 2
Pošehon'e-Volodarsk = Pošehon'e ○ **RUS** 94-95 Q 2
Poseidon, Temple of •• **GR** 100-101 K 6
Posesión, Bahía ≈ 80 F 6
Posevnaja ○ **RUS** 124-125 N 1
Posik, Pulau ⌒ **RI** 162-163 F 5
Posio ○ **FIN** 88-89 K 3
Posiposi ○ **RI** 164-165 L 2
Posito, El ∴ **BH** 52-53 K 3
Poso ○ **RI** 164-165 G 4
Poso, Danau ○ **RI** 164-165 G 4
Posof ☆ **TR** 128-129 K 2
Posŏng ○ **ROK** 150-151 F 10
Posorja ○ **EC** 64-65 B 3
Pospeliha ○ **RUS** 124-125 M 3
Posse ○ **BR** 72-73 G 3
Possel ○ **RCA** 206-207 D 6
Possession, Point ▲ **USA** 20-21 P 6
Possessioneiland ⌒ **NAM** 220-221 B 3
Possoš' ○ **RUS** 102-103 L 2
Possum Kingdom Lake ○ **USA** 44-45 H 3
Post ○ **USA** 44-45 G 3
Posta Cambio a Zalazar ○ **RA** 76-77 G 3
Posta Km. 45 ○ **RA** 76-77 G 3
Posta Lencina ○ **RA** 76-77 G 3
Post Arinda ○ **GUY** 62-63 E 3
Poste-de-la-Baleine ○ **CDN** 36-37 L 7
Post Falls ○ **USA** 40-41 F 2
Postmasburg ○ **ZA** 220-221 F 4
Posto Ajuricaba ○ **BR** 66-67 F 2
Post Oak ○ **USA** 42-43 L 6
Posto Cocraimore ○ **BR** 68-69 B 5
Post Office Tree • **ZA** 220-221 F 7
Posto Funai ○ **BR** (AMA) 62-63 D 6
Posto Funai ○ **BR** (AMA) 62-63 E 6
Posto Funai ○ **BR** (AMA) 64-65 F 4
Posto Funai ○ **BR** (APA) 62-63 J 4
Postojna ○ **SLO** 100-101 E 2
Postojnska jama •• **SLO** 100-101 E 2
Posto Uaçá ○ **BR** 62-63 J 4
Postrervalle ○ **BOL** 70-71 F 6
Postville ○ **USA** 46-47 C 4
Pota ○ **RI** 168 E 7
Potawatomi Indian Reservation ✕ **USA** 42-43 K 6
Potchefstroom ○ **ZA** 220-221 H 3
Potčurk, gora ▲ **RUS** 88-89 W 5
Poté ○ **BR** 72-73 K 4
Poteau ○ **USA** 44-45 K 2
Poteet ○ **USA** 44-45 H 5
Potengi ○ **BR** 68-69 H 5
Potenji, Rio ∼ **BR** 68-69 K 4
Potenza ☆ • **I** 100-101 E 4
Potfontein ○ **ZA** 220-221 G 5
Potgietersrus ○ **ZA** 220-221 J 2
Potherie, Lac la ○ **CDN** 36-37 N 5
Potholes Reservoir ○ **USA** 40-41 E 2
Poti ○ • **GE** 126-127 D 6
Poti, Rio ∼ **BR** 68-69 G 4
Potidaia • **GR** 100-101 J 4
Potiguara, Área Indígena ✕ **BR** 68-69 L 5
Potimalal, Río ∼ **RA** 78-79 D 4
Potin ○ **IND** 142-143 H 2
Potiragua ○ **BR** 72-73 L 3
Potiskum ○ **WAN** 204-205 J 3
Pot Jostler Creek ∼ **AUS** 178-179 F 2
Pot Mountain ▲ **USA** 40-41 G 2
Potol Point ▲ **RP** 160-161 D 7
Potomac River ∼ **USA** 46-47 K 6
Potoru ○ **WAL** 202-203 E 6
Potosí ☆ ••• **BOL** 70-71 E 6
Potosí ○ **NIC** 52-53 L 5
Potosi ○ **USA** 46-47 C 7
Potosi, Río ∼ **MEX** 50-51 K 5
Pototan ○ **RP** 160-161 E 7
Potrerillos ○ **RA** 78-79 E 2
Potrerillos, Río ∼ **RCH** 76-77 B 5
Potrero de Gallegos ○ **MEX** 50-51 H 6
Potrero del Llano ○ **MEX** 50-51 G 3
Potrero Grance ○ **CR** 52-53 C 7
Potrero Quemado ○ **BOL** 70-71 H 6
Potrero Seco ○ **RCH** 76-77 B 4
Potro, Cerro del ▲ **RCH** 76-77 C 5
Potro, Río ∼ **PE** 64-65 D 4
Potronillos Abajo ○ **PA** 52-53 C 7
Potsdam ☆ ••• **D** 92-93 M 2
Potsdam ○ **USA** 46-47 L 3
Potter Island ⌒ **CDN** 36-37 R 3
Pottstown ○ **USA** 46-47 L 5
Pottsville ○ **USA** 46-47 K 5
Pottuvil ○ **CL** 140-141 J 7
Pötürge ☆ **TR** 128-129 H 3
Pouch Cove ○ **CDN** 38-39 I S 5
Pouéré ○ **RCB** 210-211 E 4
Poughkeepsie ○ **USA** 46-47 M 5
Pougol ○ **RCA** 206-207 C 5
Poularies ○ **CDN** 38-39 E 4
Poultney ○ **USA** 46-47 M 4
Pouma ○ **CAM** 210-211 C 2
Poumalé ○ **RCA** 206-207 D 6
Pound Maker Indian Reserve ✕ **CDN** 32-33 Q 5
Poura ○ **BF** 202-203 J 4
Pourerere ○ **NZ** 182 F 4
Pouso Alegre ○ **BR** 72-73 H 7
Pouso Grande ○ **BR** 66-67 J 5
Pouss ○ • **CAM** 206-207 B 3
Poŭthĭsăt ○ **K** 158-159 G 4
Pouto ○ **NZ** 182 E 2
Pouytenga ○ **BF** 202-203 K 3
Poveneckij zaliv ≈ 88-89 N 5
Poverty Bay ≈ 182 F 3
Póvoa de Varzim ○ **P** 98-99 C 4
Povorot ○ **RUS** 116-117 N 10
Povorotnyj, mys ▲ **RUS** (CUK) 112-113 V 4
Povorotnyj, mys ▲ **RUS** (MAG) 120-121 T 3
Povorotnyj, mys ▲ **RUS** (SAH) 110-111 V 3
Povorotnyj, mys ▲ **RUS** (TMR) 108-109 X 4
Povungnituk ○ **CDN** 36-37 L 4
Povungnituk, Lac de ○ **CDN** 36-37 L 4
Povungnituk, Monts de ▲ **CDN** 36-37 M 4
Povungnituk, Rivière de ∼ **CDN** 36-37 M 4
Povungnituk Bay ≈ 36-37 L 5
Powder River ○ **USA** (WY) 42-43 D 4
Powder River ∼ **USA** 40-41 F 3
Powder River ∼ **USA** 42-43 E 3
Powder River Pass ▲ **USA** 42-43 D 3
Powell ○ **USA** 42-43 C 3
Powell, Lake < **USA** 40-41 J 7
Powell Creek ∼ **AUS** 178-179 G 3
Powell Point ▲ **BS** 54-55 G 2
Powell River ○ **CDN** 32-33 H 7
Powers ○ **USA** 46-47 E 3
Powhatan ○ **USA** 44-45 L 4
Powlathanga ○ **AUS** 174-175 H 7
Powlett, Kap ▲ **GRØ** 26-27 P 5
Powoollak Camp ○ **USA** 20-21 E 5
Poxoréo ○ **BR** 70-71 K 4
Poyang Hu ○ **VRC** 156-157 K 2
Poyanghu Z.B. ⊥ • **VRC** 156-157 K 2
Poyata, La ○ **CO** 60-61 E 5
Poygan, Lake ○ **USA** 46-47 D 3
Pozantı ☆ **TR** 128-129 F 4
Požarevac ○ • **YU** 100-101 H 2
Poza Rica ○ **MEX** 52-53 F 1
Poza Rica de Hidalgo = Poza Rica ○ **MEX** 52-53 F 1
Pozas de Santa Ana ○ **MEX** 50-51 J 6
Pozdeevka ○ **RUS** 122-123 C 3
Požeg ○ **RUS** 96-97 J 3
Požega ○ **YU** 100-101 H 3
Poznań ☆ •• **PL** 92-93 O 2
Pozo, Río del ∼ **RA** 76-77 D 4
Pozo Alcón ○ **E** 98-99 F 6
Pozo Almonte ○ **RCH** 70-71 C 7
Pozo Colorado ☆ **PY** 76-77 H 2
Pozo del Molle ○ **RA** 76-77 F 6
Pozo del Tigre ○ **BOL** 70-71 G 5
Pozo del Tigre ○ **RA** 76-77 G 3
Pozo del Zorro ○ **RA** 76-77 F 2
Pozo de Maza ○ **RA** 76-77 G 2
Pozo Dulce ○ **RA** 76-77 F 5
Pozo Herrera ○ **RA** 76-77 F 5
Pozo Hondo ○ **RA** 76-77 E 4
Pozón ○ **YV** 60-61 H 4
Pozos, Los ○ **PA** 52-53 D 8
Pozos, Punta ▲ **RA** 80 H 3
Pozuelos ○ **YV** 60-61 J 2
Pozuelos, Laguna de ○ •• **RA** 76-77 D 2
Pozuzo ○ **PE** 64-65 E 7
Pozuzo, Río ∼ **PE** 64-65 E 6
Pozzuoli ○ • **I** 100-101 E 4
P. Pelapis, Pulau ⌒ **RI** 162-163 H 5
Pra ∼ **GH** 202-203 K 7
Prachin Buri ○ **THA** 158-159 F 3
Prachuap Khirikhan ○ **THA** 158-159 E 5
Pracupi, Rio ∼ **BR** 68-69 C 3
Praděd ▲ **CZ** 92-93 O 3
Prado ○ **BR** 72-73 L 4
Pradópolis ○ **BR** 72-73 F 6
Prague = Praha ★ ••• **CZ** 92-93 N 3
Praha ★ ••• **CZ** 92-93 N 3
Praia ○ **BR** 66-67 K 5
Praia ★ **CV** 202-203 C 6
Praia da Barata ○ **BR** 66-67 D 3
Praia de Vaca ○ **BR** 66-67 C 7
Praia do Bilene ○ **MOC** 220-221 L 2
Praia do Maçarico ○ **BR** 66-67 D 3
Praia do Tofo ○ **MOC** 218-219 H 6
Praia do Xai-Xai ○ **MOC** 220-221 L 2
Praia Grande ○ **BR** (CAT) 74-75 F 7
Praia Grande ○ **BR** (PAU) 74-75 G 5
Praikalogu ○ **RI** 168 D 7
Prailiu ○ • **RI** 168 E 7
Prainha ○ **BR** 66-67 D 6
Prainha ○ **BR** (P) 62-63 H 6
Prainha ○ **BR** (P) 68-69 C 3
Prainha Nova ○ **BR** 66-67 G 6
Prairie ○ **AUS** 174-175 H 7
Prairie ○ **USA** 42-43 L 3
Prairie City ○ **USA** 40-41 E 3
Prairie Dog Creek ∼ **USA** 42-43 G 6
Prairie Dog Town Fork of the Red River ∼ **USA** 44-45 G 2
Prairie Downs ○ **AUS** 176-177 E 1
Prairie du Chien ○ **USA** 46-47 C 4
Prairie River ○ **CDN** 34-35 E 4
Prairie Village ∴ **USA** 42-43 J 4
Prajyawang ○ • **RI** 168 E 7
Prakhon Chai ○ **THA** 158-159 G 3
Prambanan ○ ••• **RI** 168 D 3
Prampram ○ **GH** 202-203 L 7
Pran Buri ○ **THA** 158-159 E 4
Pran Buri Reservoir < **THA** 158-159 E 4
Prāntij ○ **IND** 138-139 D 8
Prapat ○ **RI** 162-163 C 3
Prasat ○ **THA** 158-159 G 3
Praslin Island ⌒ **SY** 224 D 2
Prasokuma ○ **GH** 202-203 K 6
Prat ○ **RCH** 76-77 B 2
Prat, Cerro ▲ **RCH** 80 F 6
Prat, Isla ⌒ **RCH** 80 C 4
Prata ○ **BR** 68-69 H 3
Prata, Igarapé ∼ **BR** 66-67 J 5
Prata, Rio ∼ **BR** 72-73 F 5
Prata, Rio da ∼ **BR** 72-73 G 4
Prathai ○ **THA** 158-159 G 3
Prato ○ **I** 100-101 C 3
Prats-de-Mollo-la-Preste ○ **F** 90-91 J 10
Pratt ○ **USA** 44-45 H 1
Prattville ○ **USA** 48-49 E 3
Pratudão, Rio ∼ **BR** 72-73 H 2
Pravaja Bojarka ∼ **RUS** 108-109 b 6
Pravaja Bureja ∼ **RUS** 122-123 F 3
Pravaja Hetta ∼ **RUS** 114-115 M 2
Pravaja Hodutka ∼ **RUS** 122-123 R 3
Pravaja Kamenka ∼ **RUS** 110-111 d 6
Pravaja Mama ∼ **RUS** 118-119 E 7
Pravaja Šapina ∼ **RUS** 120-121 S 6
Pravdinsk ○ • **RUS** 94-95 G 4
Pravyj Kihčik ∼ **RUS** 120-121 R 7
Pravyj Mamakan ∼ **RUS** 118-119 G 7
Prawn Fishing Base • **AUS** 174-175 C 4
Praya ○ **RI** 168 C 7
Prazaroki ○ **BY** 94-95 L 4
Preacher Creek ∼ **USA** 20-21 S 4
Preăh Vihéar ○ **K** 158-159 H 3
Precipice National Park ⊥ **AUS** 178-179 L 3
Prečistoe ○ **RUS** 94-95 N 4
Precordillera ▲ **RA** 76-77 C 6
Predaltajskaja ravnina ≛ **RUS** 124-125 M 3
Predbajkal'skaja vpadina ≛ **RUS** 116-117 M 9
Predporožnyj ○ **RUS** 110-111 Y 7
Preeceville ○ **CDN** 34-35 E 5
Preguiça ○ **CV** 202-203 B 5
Prehistoric Mounds ∴ • **CDN** 34-35 F 6
Prekestolen •• **N** 86-87 C 7
Prekonosta pećina •• **YU** 100-101 J 3
Prele Ranger Station, La ○ **USA** 42-43 E 4
Premier Diamond Mine • **ZA** 220-221 J 2
Premier Downs ○ **AUS** 176-177 H 5
Premio ○ **CDN** 38-39 M 3

304 Pol-e Safīd — Premio

Remboken o • RI 164-165 J 3
Remedios o C 54-55 F 3
Remedios o PA 52-53 D 7
Remedios, Río Los ~ MEX 50-51 F 5
Remel El Abiod ▲ TN 190-191 G 5
Remennikovo o RUS 94-95 L 3
Remer o USA 42-43 L 2
Remešk o IR 134-135 H 5
Remígio o BR 68-69 L 5
Remire o F 62-63 H 3
Remiremont o F 90-91 L 7
Remolino, El o MEX 50-51 J 3
Remolino, Puerto o RA 80 G 7
Rena ☆ N 86-87 E 6
Renaico, Río ~ RCH 78-79 C 4
Renard, Rivière-au- o CDN 38-39 M 4
Renca o RA 78-79 G 2
Rencēni o LV 94-95 J 3
Renčin humbe = Zöölön o MAU 148-149 E 2
Rencontre East o CDN 38-39 R 5
Rencoret o RCH 76-77 C 2
Rende o • RI 168 E 7
Rend Lake o USA 46-47 D 6
Rendova ⌒ SOL 184 I c 3
Rendsburg o • D 92-93 K 1
Renfrew o CDN 38-39 F 6
Rengas, Tanjung ▲ RI 164-165 F 5
Rengat o RI 162-163 E 5
Rengel o RI 168 E 3
Rengleng River ~ CDN 20-21 Y 3
Rengo o RCH 78-79 D 3
Renhe o VRC 154-155 E 6
Renhua o VRC 156-157 H 4
Renhuai o VRC 156-157 E 3
Reni ☆ UA 102-103 F 5
Reni, Pulau ⌒ RI 166-167 F 1
Renigunta o IND 140-141 H 4
Reñihue, Fiordo ≈ 78-79 C 7
Reninjauan o RI 162-163 D 4
Renland ⊥ GRØ 26-27 m 8
Renmark o AUS 180-181 F 3
Renmei o VRC 154-155 B 6
Rennell, Islas ⌒ RCH 80 C 5
Renner Springs o AUS 174-175 B 6
Rennes ☆ • F 90-91 G 7
Rennick Glacier ⊂ ARK 16 F 17
Rennie o CDN 34-35 J 6
Rennie Lake o CDN 30-31 R 5
Reno o • USA 40-41 E 6
Reno, El o USA 44-45 J 2
Renosterrivier ~ ZA 220-221 E 5
Renosterrivier ~ ZA 220-221 H 3
Renous o CDN 38-39 M 5
Renovo o USA 46-47 K 5
Renqiu o VRC 154-155 K 2
Rens Fiord ≈ 26-27 C 3
Renshi o VRC 154-155 E 6
Renton o USA 40-41 C 2
Rentoul River ~ PNG 183 B 4
Réo o • BF 202-203 J 3
Reo o RI 168 E 7
Reodhar o IND 138-139 D 7
Réole, la o F 90-91 G 9
Repalle o IND 140-141 J 2
Repartimento o BR (AMA) 66-67 G 4
Repartimento o BR (AMA) 66-67 J 4
Repartimento, Corredeira do ~ BR 68-69 C 5
Repentigny o CDN 38-39 H 6
Repetekskij zapovednik ⊥ TM 136-137 H 5
Represa da Boa Esperança < BR 68-69 F 5
Represa de São Simão < BR 72-73 E 5
Republic o USA 40-41 E 1
Republican River ~ USA 42-43 H 5
Repulse Bay ≈ 24-25 c 7
Repulse Bay o CDN 24-25 c 7
Repununi River ~ GUY 62-63 E 4
Reque o PE 64-65 C 5
Requena o • E 98-99 G 5
Requena o PE 64-65 F 4
Requena o YV 60-61 J 3
Rera o BR 62-63 D 3
Reriutaba o BR 68-69 H 4
Reşadiye o TR 128-129 B 4
Reşadiye ☆ TR 128-129 G 2
Reşadiye Yarımadası ⌒ TR 128-129 B 4
Reschenpass = Passo di Rèsia ▲ I 100-101 C 1
Reseida, Wâdi ~ SUD 200-201 F 2
Resen o MK 100-101 H 4
Resende o BR 72-73 H 7
Reserva o BR 74-75 E 5
Reserva o CO 64-65 F 2
Reserva Natural de Ria Formosa ⊥ P 98-99 D 6
Reserva Natural do Estuário do Sado ⊥ P 98-99 C 5
Reserve o CDN 34-35 E 4
Rèsia, Passo di = Reschenpass ▲ I 100-101 C 1
Resistencia ☆ RA 76-77 H 4
Reşiţa ☆ RO 102-103 B 5
Resolute o CDN 24-25 Y 3
Resolution Island o CDN (NWT) 36-37 R 4
Resolution Island ⌒ CDN (NWT) 36-37 R 4
Resolution Island ⌒ NZ 182 A 6
Respiro, El o YV 60-61 G 4
Resplendor o BR 72-73 K 5
Restauração o BR 62-63 D 5
Restauración o DOM 54-55 K 5
Restigouche Indian Reserve X CDN 38-39 L 4
Restigouche River ~ CDN 38-39 L 5
Restin, Punta ▲ PE 64-65 B 4
Restinga de Marambaia ⌒ BR 72-73 J 7
Restinga Seca o BR 74-75 D 7
Resurrection, Cape ▲ USA 20-21 Q 7
Retalhuleu ☆ GCA 52-53 J 4
Retamo, El o RA 78-79 F 2
Retchel Head ▲ CDN 36-37 S 5
Retem, Oued ~ DZ 190-191 E 4
Retén Atalaya o RCH 78-79 D 2
Reten Laguna o RA 78-79 D 3
Rethel o F 90-91 K 7
Réthimno o GR 100-101 K 7
Reting • VRC 144-145 H 5
Retiro o BR (AMA) 66-67 D 4
Retiro o BR (MAT) 72-73 D 3
Retiro, El o YV 60-61 H 3
Retiro Baia Grande o BR 70-71 K 5
Retiro São Benedito o BR 70-71 J 5
Retra o PK 138-139 C 4
Retreat o AUS 178-179 G 3
Return Islands ⌒ USA 20-21 Q 1
Réunion ⌒ F 224 B 7
Réunion, La ▫ F 224 C 7
Reus o E 98-99 H 4
Reutlingen o • D 92-93 K 4
Reva o USA 42-43 F 3
Reval = Tallinn ☆ •• EST 94-95 J 2
Revda ☆ RUS 96-97 L 5
Reveca o RCH 76-77 B 2
Revello Channel ≈ 140-141 L 6
Revelstoke o CDN 32-33 L 6
Reventon, El o MEX 50-51 J 6
Revés, El o MEX 50-51 H 4
Révia o MOC 218-219 J 1
Revilla Gigedo, Islas ⌒ MEX 50-51 A 7
Revillagigedo Channel ≈ 32-33 E 4
Revillagigedo Island ⌒ USA 32-33 E 4
Revillo o USA 42-43 J 3
Revoljucii, pik ▲ TJ 136-137 N 5
Revué ~ MOC 218-219 G 4
Rewa o IND 142-143 B 3
Rewari o IND 138-139 F 5
Rewa River ~ FJI 184 III b 2
Rex, Mount ▲ ARK 16 F 29
Rexburg o USA 40-41 J 4
Rey, Arroyo del ~ RA 76-77 H 5
Rey, El o RA 76-77 E 3
Rey, Isla de ⌒ PA 52-53 E 7
Rey, Laguna del o MEX 50-51 H 4
Rey, Mayo ~ CAM 206-207 B 4
Rey, Parque Nacional el ⊥ RA 76-77 E 3
Reyābād o IR 136-137 D 6
Rey Bouba o CAM 206-207 B 4
Reyes o BOL 70-71 D 4
Reyes, Point ▲ USA 40-41 C 6
Reyes, Punta ▲ CO 60-61 B 6
Reyes, Punta das ▲ RCH 76-77 B 3
Reyes Salgado, Los o MEX 52-53 C 2
Reyhanlı ☆ TR 128-129 G 4
Reykjanes Ridge ≃ 6-7 F 3
Reykjanestá ▲ IS 86-87 b 3
Reykjavík ★ • IS 86-87 c 2
Reynaud o CDN 34-35 D 4
Reynolds o USA 46-47 E 5
Reynoldsburg o USA 46-47 G 6
Reynolds Range ▲ AUS 172-173 L 7
Reynosa o MEX 50-51 K 4
Reyy o • IR 136-137 B 7
Rež ☆ RUS 96-97 M 5
Reza, gora ▲ TM 136-137 F 6
Rēzekne ☆ •• LV 94-95 K 3
Rezina ☆ MD 102-103 F 4
Rēznas ezers o • LV 94-95 K 3
Rezovo o BG 102-103 E 6
Režvān Šahr o IR 128-129 N 4
Rharb ⊥ MA 188-189 H 3
Rharous ☆ RMM 196-197 L 5
Rhea o USA 44-45 H 2
Rhein ~ D 92-93 J 3
Rheine o D 92-93 J 2
Rheinfall ~ •• CH 92-93 K 5
Rheinland-Pfalz ▫ D 92-93 J 3
Rheinwaldhorn ▲ CH 92-93 K 5
Rhemilès < DZ 188-189 J 6
Rheris, Oued ~ MA 188-189 J 5
Rhine = Rhein ~ D 92-93 K 4
Rhinelander o USA 46-47 D 3
Rhino Camp o EAU 212-213 C 2
Rhiou, Oued ~ DZ 190-191 C 3
Rhir, Cap ▲ MA 188-189 G 5
Rhode Island ▫ USA 46-47 N 5
Rhode Island ⌒ USA (RI) 46-47 N 5
Rhodes Inyangani National Park ⊥ ZW 218-219 G 4
Rhodes Matopos National Park ⊥ ZW 218-219 E 5
Rhodope Mountains = Rodopi ▲ BG 102-103 C 7
Rhön ▲ D 92-93 K 3
Rhondda o GB 90-91 F 6
Rhône ~ CH 92-93 J 5
Rhône ~ F 90-91 K 10
Rhône-Alpes ▫ F 90-91 K 9
Rhoraffa, Bir < DZ 190-191 G 5
Rhoufi o DZ 190-191 F 3
Rhourd El Baguel o DZ 190-191 F 5
Rhum ⌒ GB 90-91 D 3
Rhumel, Oued ~ DZ 190-191 F 2
Riaba o GQ 210-211 B 2
Ria Celestún Parque Natural ⊥ MEX 52-53 J 1
Riachão o BR 68-69 E 5
Riachão, Rio ~ BR 68-69 G 5
Riachão das Neves o BR 68-69 F 7
Riachão do Banabuiú o BR 68-69 J 4
Riachão do Jacuípe o BR 68-69 J 7
Riacho de Santana o BR 72-73 J 2
Riacho do Sal o BR 68-69 J 6
Riacho dos Machados o BR 72-73 J 3
Riachos, Isla de los ⌒ RA 78-79 H 6
Riacho Seco o BR 68-69 J 6
Riákia o GR 100-101 J 4
Riamkanan, Danau o RI 164-165 D 5
Rianápolis o BR 72-73 F 3
Riangnom o SUD 206-207 K 4
Riaño, Embalse de < E 98-99 E 3
Riau ▫ RI 162-163 D 5
Riau, Kepulauan ⌒ RI 162-163 F 4
Ribadavia o • E 98-99 C 3
Ribadeo o E 98-99 D 3
Ribadesella o E 98-99 E 3
Ribah o WAN 204-205 F 3
Ribanʹi Manamby ▲ RM 222-223 D 9
Ribariće o YU 100-101 H 3
Ribas do Rio Pardo o BR 72-73 D 6
Ribāt, ar- o IRQ 128-129 J 5
Ribatejo ⊥ P 98-99 C 5
Ribāt Qila o PK 134-135 J 4
Ribáuè o MOC 218-219 K 2
Ribe o •• DK 86-87 D 9
Ribeira Brava, Vila de o CV 202-203 B 5
Ribeira Grande o CV 202-203 B 5
Ribeira do Pombal o BR 68-69 J 7
Ribeira do Pombal, Rio ~ BR 68-69 J 7
Ribeirão o BR 68-69 L 6
Ribeirão, Área Indígena X BR 70-71 E 2
Ribeirão, Rio ~ BR 70-71 E 2
Ribeirão das Neves o BR 72-73 H 5
Ribeirão do Pinhal o BR 72-73 E 7
Ribeirão Preto o BR 72-73 G 6
Ribeiro Gonçalves o BR 68-69 F 5
Ribera o I 100-101 D 6
Ribérac o F 90-91 H 9
Riberalta o BOL 70-71 D 2
Rîbniţa ☆ MD 102-103 F 4
Ribnitz-Damgarten o D 92-93 M 1
Ribo Escale o SN 202-203 C 2
Ribstone Creek ~ CDN 32-33 P 5
Rica, Cañada ~ RA 76-77 F 2
Ricardo Flores Magón o MEX 50-51 F 3
Ricaute o CO 60-61 D 6
Rice o USA 40-41 G 8
Rice Historic Site, Fort ∴ USA 42-43 G 2
Rice Lake o CDN 38-39 E 6
Rice Lake o USA 46-47 C 3
Rice Terraces •• RP 160-161 D 4
Rich o MA 188-189 J 4
Richan o CDN 34-35 K 6
Richão do Dantas o BR 68-69 K 7
Richão dos Paulos o BR 68-69 F 6
Richard Collinson Inlet ≈ 24-25 P 4
Richardsbaai = Richards Bay o ZA 220-221 L 4
Richards Bay = Richardsbaai o ZA 220-221 L 4
Richards Island ⌒ CDN 20-21 Y 2
Richardson o USA 44-45 J 3
Richardson, Cape ▲ CDN 24-25 d 6
Richardson Bay ≈ 30-31 M 2
Richardson Island ⌒ CDN 30-31 L 3
Richardson Islands ⌒ CDN 24-25 R 6
Richardson Lake o CDN 30-31 O 6
Richardson Mountains ▲ CDN 20-21 W 2
Richardson Point ▲ AUS 180-181 H 6
Richardson River ~ CDN 30-31 L 2
Richardson River ~ CDN 32-33 P 3
Richards Trench ≃ 76-77 B 4
Richard Toll o SN 196-197 C 6
Richardton o USA 42-43 F 2
Riche, Cape ▲ AUS 176-177 E 7
Richfield o USA (ID) 40-41 G 4
Richfield o USA (KS) 44-45 G 1
Richfield o USA (UT) 40-41 H 6
Richgrove o USA 40-41 E 8
Richibucto o CDN 38-39 M 5
Richibucto 15 Indian Reserve X CDN 38-39 M 5
Richland o USA (MO) 42-43 L 7
Richland o USA (WA) 40-41 E 2
Richland Center o USA 46-47 C 4
Richlands o USA 46-47 H 7
Richmond o AUS 174-175 G 7
Richmond o CDN (BC) 32-33 J 7
Richmond o CDN (QUE) 38-39 H 6
Richmond o NZ 182 D 4
Richmond o USA (AR) 40-41 C 7
Richmond o USA (IN) 46-47 F 6
Richmond o USA (KS) 42-43 K 6
Richmond o USA (KY) 46-47 F 7
Richmond ☆ USA (VA) 46-47 K 7
Richmond o ZA (CAP) 220-221 F 5
Richmond o ZA (NTL) 220-221 K 4
Richmond Hills o AUS 178-179 H 2
Richmond River ~ AUS 178-179 M 5
Rich Mountain ▲ USA 44-45 K 2
Richtersveld National Park ⊥ ZA 220-221 C 4
Richthofen, Mount ▲ AUS 172-173 C 6
Richton o USA 48-49 D 4
Richwood o USA 46-47 H 6
Ricketts, Cape ▲ CDN 24-25 a 3
Ricrah o PE 64-65 E 7
Ridder, De o USA 44-45 L 4
Riddersprenget • N 86-87 D 6
Riddle o USA (ID) 40-41 G 4
Riddle o USA (OR) 40-41 C 4
Ridge Crest o USA 40-41 F 8
Ridgeland o USA 44-45 M 3
Ridgeway o USA 48-49 H 2
Ridgway o USA (CO) 42-43 D 6
Ridgway o USA (PA) 46-47 J 5
Riding Mountain ▲ CDN 34-35 F 5
Riding Mountain National Park ⊥ CDN 34-35 F 5
Riding Rock Point ▲ BS 54-55 H 2
Riebeck Bay ≈ 183 E 3
Riebeek Kasteel o ZA 220-221 D 6
Riebeek-Oos o ZA 220-221 H 6
Riebeekstaad o ZA 220-221 H 3
Riecito o YV 60-61 G 2
Riecito, Río ~ YV 60-61 G 4
Rieppe ▲ N 86-87 K 2
Riesa o D 92-93 M 3
Riesco, Isla ⌒ RCH 80 D 6
Rietavas o LT 94-95 G 4
Rietbron o ZA 220-221 F 6
Rietfontein o NAM 216-217 F 10
Rietfontein ~ NAM 216-217 F 10
Rietfontein o ZA 220-221 E 3
Rieti ☆ I 100-101 D 3
Rietrivier ~ ZA 220-221 G 4
Rietse Vloer o ZA 220-221 E 5
Rietvlei o ZA 220-221 K 4
Rievaulx Abbey •• GB 90-91 G 4
Rifāʿī, ar- ☆ IRQ 128-129 M 7
Rifaina o BR 72-73 G 6
Rifle o USA 42-43 D 6
Rifleman Bank ≃ 158-159 L 7
Rift Valley ⊥ EAK 212-213 F 2
Rift Valley ⊥ •• EAK 212-213 F 4
Rift Valley National Park ⊥ ETH 208-209 D 5
Rīg, Bandar-e o IR 134-135 D 4
Riga, Gulf of = Rigas Jūras Līcis ≈ LV 94-95 H 3
Rīga = Riga ★ •• LV 94-95 J 3
Rigāʾ, Umm o Y 132-133 D 7
Rigacikun o WAN 204-205 G 3
Rigal Almaʾ o KSA 132-133 C 4
Rigas Jūras Līcis ≈ 94-95 H 3
Rigby o USA 40-41 J 4
Riggins o USA 40-41 F 3
Rigolet o CDN 36-37 U 7
Rig Rig o TCH 198-199 G 5
Rigsdagen, Kap ▲ GRØ 26-27 o 2
Riguldi o EST 94-95 H 2
Rihab, ar- ⊥ IRQ 128-129 L 7
Riihimäki o FIN 88-89 H 6
Riiser-Larsen halvøy ⊥ ARK 16 G 4
Riisitunturin kansallispuisto ⊥ FIN 88-89 K 3
Riistina o FIN 88-89 J 6
Rijau o WAN 204-205 F 3
Rijeka o HR 100-101 E 2
Rijpfjorden ≈ 84-85 N 2
Rīkām Panchū, Gardaneh-ye ▲ IR 134-135 J 5
Rikbaktsa, Área Indígena X BR 70-71 H 2
Rikorda, mys ▲ RUS 122-123 M 6
Rikorda, proliv o RUS 122-123 P 5
Rikuchū-Kaigan National Park ⊥ J 152-153 K 5
Rikumbetsu o J 152-153 K 3
Rila o • BG 102-103 C 6
Rila ▲ BG 102-103 C 6
Riley o USA (KS) 42-43 J 6
Riley o USA (OR) 40-41 E 4
Rilski Manastir ••• BG 102-103 C 6
Rima ~ WAN 198-199 B 6
Rima, Wādī ar- ~ KSA 130-131 H 5
Rimac, Río ~ PE 64-65 D 8
Rimbey o CDN 32-33 N 5
Rime ~ TCH 198-199 J 5
Rimé, Ouadi ~ TCH 198-199 J 6
Rimini o I 100-101 D 2
Rîmnicu Sărat o RO 102-103 E 5
Rîmnicu Vîlcea ☆ • RO 102-103 D 5
Rimouski o CDN 38-39 K 4
Rimouski, Réserve Faunique de ⊥ CDN 38-39 K 4
Rimsko-Korsakovka o RUS 96-97 F 8
Rinaré o BR 68-69 J 4
Rinbung o VRC 144-145 G 6
Rinca, Pulau ⌒ RI 168 D 7
Rincão o BR 72-73 F 6
Rincón o CR 52-53 C 7
Rincón o DOM 54-55 K 5
Rincon o USA 44-45 D 3
Rincon, Cerro ▲ RA 76-77 D 3
Rincón, Salina del o RA 76-77 D 3
Rinconada o RA 76-77 D 2
Rincón de la Vieja, Parque Nacional ⊥ CR 52-53 B 6
Rincón de la Vieja, Volcán ▲ CR 52-53 B 6
Rincón del Guanal o C 54-55 D 4
Rincon de Palometas o BOL 70-71 F 5
Rincos de Romos o MEX 50-51 H 6
Rind ~ IND 142-143 B 2
Rindal ☆ N 86-87 D 5
Ringba o VRC 154-155 H 6
Ringgi o SOL 184 I c 3
Ringgold o USA 44-45 L 3
Ringgold Isles ⌒ FJI 184 III c 2
Ringim o WAN 198-199 D 6
Ringkøbing o DK 86-87 D 8
Ringkøbing Fjord o DK 86-87 D 8
Ringling o USA 40-41 J 2
Ring of Kerry • IRL 90-91 B 6
Ringoma o ANG 216-217 D 6
Ringvassøy ⌒ N 86-87 J 2
Ringwood o AUS 178-179 C 2
Riñihue, Lago o RCH 78-79 C 5
Riñinahue o RCH 78-79 C 6
Riniquiarí o CO 60-61 F 6
Rinjani, Gunung ▲ RI 168 C 7
Rintala o RUS 88-89 K 6
Rio o GR 100-101 H 5
Río, El o DOM 54-55 K 5
Río Abiseo, Parque Nacional ⊥ ••• PE 64-65 D 5
Rio Acre, Estação Ecologica ⊥ BR 70-71 B 2
Rio Amazonas, Estuário do ~ BR 62-63 K 5
Rio Ariapo o BR 66-67 E 2
Rio Ariguaisa o YV 60-61 E 3
Río Azul ∴ • GCA 52-53 K 3
Riobamba o EC 64-65 C 2
Rio Bananal o BR 72-73 K 5
Río Bermejo, Valle del ⌒ RA 76-77 C 6
Rio-Biá, Áreas Indígenas X BR 66-67 D 5
Ríoblanco o CO 60-61 D 6
Río Blanco o CO 60-61 C 6
Rio Bonito o BR (PAR) 74-75 E 5
Rio Bonito o BR (RIO) 72-73 J 7
Rio Branco o BR (ACR) 64-65 F 6
Rio Branco o BR (MAT) 70-71 H 4
Rio Branco ☆ BR (ACR) 66-67 D 7
Río Branco o ROU 74-75 D 9
Rio Branco, Área Indígena X BR 70-71 F 3
Rio Branco, Parque Nacional do ⊥ BR 66-67 F 2
Rio Branco do Sul o BR 74-75 F 5
Rio Bravo o GCA 52-53 J 4
Rio Bravo o MEX 50-51 K 5
Río Bravo, Parque Internacional del ⊥ MEX 50-51 H 3
Rio Brilhante o BR 76-77 K 1
Río Bueno o JA 54-55 G 5
Río Bueno o RCH 78-79 C 6
Río Caribe o YV 60-61 K 2
Río Casca o BR 72-73 J 6
Río Cauto o C 54-55 G 4
Río Ceballos o RA 76-77 E 6
Río Chico o YV 60-61 J 2
Río Chiquito o HN 54-55 C 7
Río Clarillo, Parque Nacional ⊥ RCH 78-79 D 2
Rio Claro o BR 72-73 G 7
Rio Claro o TT 60-61 L 2
Río Colorado o RA 78-79 G 5
Rio Conchas o BR (MAT) 70-71 K 4
Rio Conchas o BR (MAT) 70-71 K 3
Río Cuarto o RA 78-79 G 2
Rio das Pedras o MOC 218-219 H 6
Rio de Janeiro ▫ BR 72-73 J 7
Rio de Janeiro ☆ • BR 72-73 J 7
Rio de Janeiro, Serra do ▲ BR 72-73 H 4
Río de la Plata ≈ 78-79 L 3
Río Deseado, Valle del ⊥ RA 80 F 3
Rio do Pires o BR 72-73 J 2
Rio do Prado o BR 72-73 K 4
Rio do Sul o BR 74-75 F 6
Río Dulce, Parque Nacional ⊥ GCA 52-53 K 4
Río Gallegos ☆ RA 80 F 5
Rio Grande o BOL 70-71 D 7
Rio Grande o BR 74-75 D 9
Río Grande o MEX 50-51 H 6
Río Grande o RA 80 G 6
Rio Grande ~ USA 44-45 G 5
Río Grande, Ciudad de = Río Grande o MEX 50-51 H 6
Río Grande, Salar de o RA 76-77 C 3
Rio Grande do Norte ▫ BR 68-69 K 4
Rio Grande do Sul ▫ BR 76-77 K 5
Rio Grande Fracture Zone ≃ 6-7 H 11
Rio Grande Plateau ≃ 6-7 F 12
Rio Gregorio, Área Indígena X BR 66-67 B 7
Rio Guaporé, Área Indígena X BR 70-71 E 2
Río Guengue o RA 80 E 2
Riohacha ☆ CO 60-61 E 2
Río Hato o PA 52-53 D 7
Río Hondo o GCA 52-53 K 4
Río Hondo, Embalse < RA 76-77 E 4
Río Hondo, Termas de o • RA 76-77 E 4
Río Ichilo o BOL 70-71 E 5
Rioja o PE 64-65 D 5
Rioja, La ▫ E 98-99 F 3
Rioja, La ▫ RA 76-77 C 5
Rioja, La ☆ • RA (LAR) 76-77 D 5
Rioja, Llanos de la ⊥ RA 76-77 D 5
Rio Lagartos o • MEX 52-53 K 1
Río Lagartos, Parque Natural ⊥ MEX 52-53 L 1
Rio Largo o BR 68-69 L 6
Riom o F 90-91 J 9
Rio Maior o P 98-99 C 5
Río Malo o RCH 78-79 D 3
Río Mayo o RA 80 E 2
Rio Mequens, Área Indígena X BR 70-71 G 3
Río Mulatos o BOL 70-71 D 6
Riondel o CDN 32-33 M 7
Rio Negrinho o BR 74-75 F 6
Rio Negro o BR (GSU) 70-71 J 6
Rio Negro o BR (GSU) 70-71 K 6
Rio Negro o BR (PAR) 74-75 F 6
Rionegro o CO 60-61 E 4
Río Negro ▫ RA 78-79 E 6
Río Negro o RCH 78-79 C 6
Rio Negro, Pantanal do o BR 70-71 J 6
Río Negro, Represa del < ROU 78-79 L 2
Rio Negro, Reserva Florestal do ⊥ BR 66-67 C 2
Rio Negro Ocaiai, Área Indígena X BR 70-71 E 2
Rioni ~ GE 126-127 E 5
Rio Pardo o BR 74-75 D 7
Rio Pardo de Minas o BR 72-73 J 3
Río Pilcomayo, Parque Nacional ⊥ RA 76-77 H 3
Río Plátano, Parque Nacional ⊥ ••• HN 54-55 C 7
Rio Pomba o BR 72-73 J 6
Rio Preto o BR 72-73 J 7
Rio Prêto, Serra do ▲ BR 72-73 G 4
Rio Preto da Eva o BR 66-67 H 4
Río Primero o RA 76-77 F 6
Río Queguay, Cascadas del ~ ROU 78-79 K 2
Rio Quente • BR 72-73 F 4
Río San Juan o DOM 54-55 K 5
Río Seco o RA 76-77 E 2
Río Seco o YV 60-61 F 2
Río Segundo o RA 76-77 F 6
Río Simpsom, Parque Nacional ⊥ RCH 80 D 2
Rio Sono o BR 68-69 E 6
Riosucio o CO 60-61 D 5
Río Sucio o CO 60-61 D 4
Ríosucio o CO 60-61 C 4
Rio Telha o BR 74-75 E 7
Río Tercero, Embalse del < RA 78-79 G 2
Rio Tinto o BR 68-69 L 5
Río Tocuyo o YV 60-61 G 2
Rio Trombetas, Reserva Biológica do ⊥ BR 62-63 F 6
Riou, Point ▲ USA 20-21 U 7
Rioug < RIM 196-197 E 6
Riou Lake o CDN 30-31 Q 6
Rio Verde o BR 72-73 E 4
Río Verde o MEX 50-51 K 7
Río Verde o YV 60-61 H 3
Rio Verde de Mato Grosso o BR 70-71 K 6
Rio Verde Grande ~ BR 72-73 J 3
Rio Vermelho o BR 72-73 J 5
Río Villegas o RA 78-79 D 6
Riozinho ~ BR 66-67 D 6
Riozinho ~ BR 68-69 F 6
Riozinho, Rio ~ BR 66-67 D 4
Riozinho, Rio ~ BR 68-69 B 5
Riozinho do Anfrísio ~ BR 66-67 K 5
Riozinho ou Rio Verde, Rio ~ BR 72-73 E 2
Ripky o UA 102-103 G 2
Ripley o USA (KY) 46-47 G 6
Ripley o USA (MS) 48-49 D 2
Ripley o USA (WV) 46-47 H 6
Ripoll o • E 98-99 J 3
Rišāʿ, Wādī ar- ~ KSA 130-131 H 5
Risālpur o PK 138-139 D 2
Risasa o ZRE 210-211 K 4
Rishikesh o IND 138-139 G 4
Rishiri o J 152-153 J 2
Rishirifuji o J 152-153 J 2
Rishiri-Rebun National Park ⊥ J 152-153 J 2
Rishiri-suidō ≈ 152-153 J 2
Rishiri-tō ⌒ J 152-153 J 2
Rishon le Ẕiyyon ☆ IL 130-131 D 2
Rising Star o USA 44-45 H 3
Rising Sun o USA 46-47 F 6
Riske Creek o CDN 32-33 J 6
Risør ☆ • N 86-87 D 7
Risøyhamn o N 86-87 G 2
Rissa o N 86-87 E 5
Rissani o MA 188-189 J 5
Rištan o US 136-137 M 4
Risti o EST 94-95 J 2
Ritchie o ZA 220-221 G 4
Ritch Island ⌒ CDN 30-31 K 2
Rithi o IND 142-143 B 4
Rito o ANG 216-217 E 8
Ritter, Mount ▲ USA 40-41 E 7
Ritzville o USA 40-41 E 2
Riv ~ UA 102-103 F 3
Rivadavia o RA (BUA) 78-79 J 3
Rivadavia o RA (MEN) 78-79 E 2
Rivadavia o RA (SAJ) 76-77 C 6
Rivadavia o RA (SAL) 76-77 F 3
Rivadavia o RCH 76-77 B 5
Riva del Garda o I 100-101 C 2
Rivalensundet ≈ 84-85 P 3
Rivaš o IR 136-137 F 7
Rivas ☆ NIC 52-53 B 6
Rivera o EC 64-65 C 3
Rivera o RA 78-79 H 4
Rivera ☆ ROU 76-77 K 6
Riverboat Cruise • AUS 180-181 H 4
River Cess o LB 202-203 F 7
Riverdale o USA 42-43 G 2
Riverhead o USA 46-47 M 5
Riverina ⌒ AUS 180-181 H 3
Rivero, Isla ⌒ RCH 80 C 2
River of No Return Wilderness ⊥ USA 40-41 G 3
Rivers o CDN 34-35 F 5
Rivers ▫ WAN 204-205 G 6
Riversdal = Riversdale o ZA 220-221 E 7
Riversdale o BH 52-53 K 3
Riversdale o CDN 38-39 D 6
Riversdale = Riversdal o ZA 220-221 E 7
Riversdale Beach o NZ 182 F 4
Riverside o AUS 178-179 K 1
Riverside o USA (CA) 40-41 F 9
Riverside o USA (IA) 46-47 C 5
Riverside o USA (WY) 42-43 D 5
Rivers Inlet ≈ 32-33 G 6
Riversleigh o AUS 174-175 E 6
Riverton o CDN 34-35 H 5
Riverton o NZ 182 B 7
Riverton o USA 42-43 C 4
Rivesaltes o F 90-91 J 10
Riviera o USA 44-45 J 6
Rivière, George ~ CDN 36-37 Q 5
Rivière-à-Pierre o CDN 38-39 H 5
Rivière-aux-Saumons o CDN 38-39 N 4
Rivière-Bleue o CDN 38-39 K 5
Rivière-du-Loup o CDN 38-39 K 5
Rivière Saint-Jean o CDN 38-39 M 3
Rivière-Saint-Paul o CDN 38-39 Q 3
Riviersonderend o ZA 220-221 D 7
Rivne o UA 102-103 E 2
Rivoli o I 100-101 A 2
Rivungo o ANG 218-219 B 3
Riwat o PK 138-139 D 3
Riwoqê o VRC 144-145 L 5
Riyād, ar- ▫ KSA 130-131 J 6
Riyād, ar- ★ •• KSA 130-131 K 5
Riyād al-Ḫabra o KSA 130-131 H 4
Riyadh = Riyād, ar- ★ •• KSA 130-131 K 5
Rize ☆ TR 128-129 J 2
Rizhao o VRC 154-155 L 4
Rizokarpaso o TR 128-129 F 5
Rizzuto, Capo ▲ I 100-101 F 5
Rjabovskij o RUS 102-103 M 2
Rjazanʾ ☆ •• RUS 94-95 Q 4
Rjažsk ☆ • RUS 94-95 R 5
Rjukan ☆ N 86-87 D 7
Rkîz o RIM 196-197 C 6
Rkîz, Lac o RIM 196-197 C 6
Roadhouse o AUS 174-175 B 5
Road River ~ CDN 20-21 X 3
Road Town ☆ •• GB 56 C 2
Roan Cliffs ▲ USA 42-43 C 6
Roanne o F 90-91 K 8
Roanoke o USA (AL) 48-49 F 3
Roanoke o USA (VA) 46-47 J 7
Roanoke Island ⌒ USA 48-49 L 2
Roanoke Rapids o USA 48-49 K 1
Roanoke River ~ USA 46-47 J 7
Roaring Springs o USA 44-45 G 3
Roatán ☆ HN 52-53 L 3
Roatán, Isla de ⌒ HN 52-53 L 3
Robalo, Cachoeira do ~ BR 70-71 K 6
Roban o MAL 162-163 J 4
Robanda o EAT 212-213 E 5
Robāṭak o AFG 136-137 L 6
Robāṭ-e Čaʾlī o AFG 134-135 J 4
Robāṭ-e Hān o IR 134-135 G 2
Robāṭe Ḥošāb o IR 134-135 G 2
Robāṭ-e Hošk o AFG 134-135 K 2
Robāṭ-e-Mīrzā, Kōtal-e ▲ AFG 134-135 K 1
Robāṭ-e Pošt Badām o IR 134-135 F 2
Robāṭ-e Sang o IR 136-137 F 7
Robāṭ-e Sangī-ye Pāīn o AFG 134-135 K 1
Robāṭkarīm o IR 136-137 B 7
Robbeneiland ⌒ ZA 220-221 D 6
Robbies Pass ▲ NAM 216-217 B 9
Robbins Island ⌒ AUS 180-181 H 6
Robe o AUS 180-181 E 4
Robē o ETH (Ars) 208-209 D 5
Robē o ETH (Bal) 208-209 E 5
Robe, Mount ▲ AUS 178-179 F 6
Robe River ~ AUS 172-173 B 6
Robert, Le o F 56 E 4
Roberta o USA 48-49 F 3
Robert's Arm o CDN 38-39 R 4
Roberts Creek Montain ▲ USA 40-41 F 6
Robertsganj o IND 142-143 C 3
Robert S. Kerr Lake < USA 44-45 K 2
Robertson o ZA 220-221 D 6
Robertson, Kap ▲ GRØ 26-27 O 5
Robertson, Lake < ZW 218-219 F 3
Robertson Bay ≈ 16 F 18
Robertson Bay ≈ 36-37 K 7
Robertson Fjord ≈ 26-27 P 5
Robertson Range ▲ AUS 172-173 E 7
Robertson River ~ CDN 24-25 e 5
Robertsons Øy ⌒ ARK 16 G 31
Roberts Port ☆ LB 202-203 E 6
Roberval o CDN 38-39 H 4
Robi o ETH 208-209 D 4
Robin Falls • AUS 172-173 K 2
Robins Camp o ZW 218-219 C 4
Robinson o USA 46-47 E 6
Robinson, Mount ▲ AUS 172-173 D 7
Robinson Island ⌒ ARK 16 G 30
Robinson Pass ▲ ZA 220-221 F 6
Robinson Range ▲ AUS 176-177 E 2
Robinson River o AUS 174-175 D 5
Robinson River ~ AUS 174-175 D 5
Robinson River o PNG 183 E 6
Robinson Sound ≈ 36-37 R 3
Robinsons River ~ CDN 38-39 P 4
Robinvale o AUS 180-181 G 3
Robla, La o E 98-99 E 3
Roble Alto, Cerro ▲ RCH 78-79 D 2
Robles Junction o USA 40-41 J 9
Roblin o CDN 34-35 F 5
Robooksibia o RI 166-167 H 2
Rob Roy Island ⌒ SOL 184 I c 2
Robsart o CDN 32-33 Q 7
Robson, Mount ▲ CDN 32-33 L 5
Robstown o USA 44-45 J 6
Roby o USA (MO) 44-45 L 1
Roby o USA (TX) 44-45 G 3
Roca, Cabo da ▲ •• P 98-99 C 5
Roca, Peninsula ⌒ RCH 80 D 5
Roça de Bruno o BR 68-69 E 2
Roca de la Sierra, La o E 98-99 D 5
Rocafuerte o EC 64-65 B 2
Rocanville o CDN 34-35 F 5
Roca Partida, Isla ⌒ MEX 50-51 B 7
Roca Redonda ⌒ EC 64-65 B 9
Rocas, Atol das ⌒ BR 68-69 L 1
Rocas Alijos ⌒ MEX 50-51 B 5
Roça Tapirapé o BR 68-69 C 6
Rocha ☆ ROU 78-79 M 3
Rocha, Laguna de o ROU 78-79 M 3
Roche Cabrit o F 62-63 H 3
Rochedo o BR 70-71 K 6
Rochefort o F 90-91 G 9
Rochelle o USA (IL) 46-47 D 5
Rochelle o USA (TX) 44-45 H 4
Rochelle, la o CDN 34-35 H 6
Rochelle, la ☆ • F 90-91 G 8
Roche River, La ~ CDN 30-31 O 5
Rocher River o CDN 30-31 N 5
Rochester o USA (IN) 46-47 E 5
Rochester o USA (MI) 46-47 G 4
Rochester o USA (NH) 46-47 N 4
Rochester o USA (NY) 46-47 K 4
Rochester o USA (MN) 42-43 L 3
Roche-sur-Yon, la ☆ • F 90-91 G 8
Rock, The o AUS 180-181 J 3
Rockall Plateau ≃ 6-7 H 3
Rockall Trough ≃ 6-7 H 3
Rock Creek o CDN 32-33 L 7
Rockdale o USA 44-45 J 4
Rockefeller National Wildlife Refuge ⊥ USA 44-45 L 5
Rockefeller Plateau ▲ ARK 16 F 24
Rock Engravings Music Stones • NAM 220-221 C 3
Rock Falls o USA 46-47 D 5
Rockford o USA (AL) 48-49 E 3
Rockford o USA (IL) 46-47 D 4
Rockglen o CDN 34-35 D 6
Rockhampton o • AUS 178-179 L 2
Rockhampton Downs o AUS 174-175 C 6
Rock Hill o USA 48-49 H 2
Rockhouse Island ⌒ CDN 30-31 Y 4
Rockingham o USA 48-49 J 2
Rockingham Bay ≈ 174-175 J 6
Rock Island o CDN 38-39 H 6
Rockland o USA 42-43 H 1
Rock Lake o USA 40-41 F 2
Rockland o CDN 38-39 G 6
Rockland o USA 46-47 O 3
Rocklands Reservoir < AUS 180-181 G 4
Rocklea o AUS 172-173 C 7
Rock of Cashel •• IRL 90-91 D 5
Rockport o USA (IN) 46-47 E 7
Rockport o USA (TX) 44-45 J 5
Rockport o USA (WA) 40-41 D 1
Rock Rapids o USA 42-43 J 4
Rock River ~ CDN 20-21 X 3
Rock River ~ CDN 30-31 F 5
Rock River o USA (WY) 42-43 E 5
Rock River ~ USA 42-43 J 4
Rock Sound o • BS 54-55 G 2
Rocksprings o USA 44-45 G 4
Rock Springs o USA (AZ) 40-41 H 8
Rock Springs o USA (MT) 42-43 D 2
Rock Springs o USA (WY) 42-43 C 5
Rockstone o GUY 62-63 E 2
Rockton o AUS 180-181 K 4
Rockville o USA (IN) 46-47 E 6
Rockville o USA (MD) 46-47 K 6
Rockwall o USA 44-45 J 3
Rockwell City o USA 42-43 K 4
Rockwood o USA 48-49 F 2
Rocky Boy's Indian Reservation X USA 42-43 C 1

308 Remboken — Rocky Boy's Indian Reservation

Rocky Ford o USA 42-43 F 6
Rocky Gully o AUS 176-177 D 7
Rocky Island Lake o CDN 38-39 C 5
Rocky Lake o CDN 34-35 F 3
Rocky Mount o USA (NC) 48-49 K 2
Rocky Mount o USA (VA) 46-47 J 7
Rocky Mountain House o CDN 32-33 N 5
Rocky Mountain House National Historic Park ∴ • CDN 32-33 N 5
Rocky Mountain National Park ⊥ ••• USA 42-43 E 5
Rocky Mountains ▲ 4 B 3
Rocky Point ▲ NAM 216-217 B 9
Rocky Point ▲ USA 20-21 J 4
Rocky River ∼ CDN 32-33 M 5
Roda, La o E 98-99 F 5
Roda Velha o BR 72-73 H 2
Rōdbār o AFG 134-135 K 3
Rødberg o N 86-87 D 6
Rødbyhavn o DK 86-87 E 9
Roddickton o CDN 38-39 Q 3
Rodds Bay ≈ 178-179 L 2
Røde Fjord ≈ 26-27 I 8
Rodel o GB 90-91 D 3
Rodelas o BR 68-69 J 6
Rodeo o USA 44-45 C 4
Rodeo Viejo o PA 52-53 D 7
Rodez ★ • F 90-91 J 9
Rodgers Bank ≃ 72-73 M 4
Rodi, Tanjung ▲ RI 166-167 B 7
Rodino ★ RUS 124-125 M 2
Rodnei, Munţii ▲ RO 102-103 D 4
Rodney, Cape ▲ NZ 182 E 2
Rodniki o RUS 94-95 R 3
Rodnikovskoe o KA 124-125 H 3
Rododero-Playa, El • CO 60-61 D 2
Ródos ★ •• GR 100-101 M 6
Ródos ⌒ GR 100-101 M 6
Rodovia Perimetral Norte II BR 62-63 F 5
Rodrigo Arenas Betancourt, Monumento • CO 60-61 E 5
Rodrigues ⌒ MS 12 E 6
Rodrigues ⌒ MS 224 F 6
Rodrigues Ridge ≃ 224 E 6
Rodríguez, Los o MEX 50-51 J 4
Rodžers, buhta ≈ 112-113 V 1
Roe, Lake o AUS 176-177 G 5
Roebourne o AUS 172-173 C 6
Roebuck Bay ≈ 172-173 F 5
Roebuck Roadhouse o AUS 172-173 F 4
Roedtan o ZA 220-221 J 2
Roe River ∼ AUS 172-173 G 3
Roermond o NL 92-93 J 3
Roeselare o B 92-93 G 3
Roes Welcome Sound ≈ 36-37 F 3
Rofia o WAN 204-205 F 3
Rogačeva ∼ RUS 108-109 E 6
Rogačevka o RUS 102-103 L 2
Rogačevo o RUS 94-95 P 3
Rogagua, Lago o BOL 70-71 D 3
Rogaguado o BOL 70-71 E 3
Rogasen = Rogoźno o PL 92-93 O 2
Rogatica o BIH 100-101 G 3
Rogberi o WAL 202-203 D 5
Rogeia Island ⌒ PNG 183 F 6
Rogers o USA 44-45 K 1
Rogers, Mount ▲ USA 46-47 H 7
Rogers City o USA 46-47 G 3
Rogerson o USA 40-41 G 4
Rogers Pass o CDN 32-33 M 6
Rogersville o CDN 38-39 M 5
Roggeveen Basin ≃ 5 B 8
Roggeveldberge ▲ ZA 220-221 E 5
Rognan o N 86-87 G 3
Rogo o WAN 204-205 G 3
Rogoaguado, Lago o BOL 70-71 E 3
Rogovaja, Bol'šaja ∼ RUS 108-109 J 8
Rogoźno o PL 92-93 O 2
Rogue River ∼ USA 40-41 B 4
Rogun o WAN 204-205 F 4
Roha o IND 138-139 D 10
Rohat o IND 138-139 D 7
Rohatyn ★ UA 102-103 D 3
Rohault, Lac o CDN 38-39 G 4
Rohmojva, gora ▲ RUS 88-89 K 3
Rohri o PK 138-139 B 6
Rohri Canal < PK 138-139 B 6
Rohru o IND 138-139 F 4
Rohtak o IND 138-139 F 5
Rohtak, Rūdḫāne-ye ∼ IR 134-135 K 5
Rohtas Fort • PK 138-139 D 3
Rohuküla o EST 94-95 H 2
Roi Et o THA 158-159 G 2
Roja o •• LV 94-95 H 3
Roja, Punta ▲ RA 80 H 2
Rojas o RA 78-79 J 3
Rojhān o PK 138-139 B 5
Rojo, Cabo ▲ MEX 50-51 L 7
Rokan o RI 162-163 D 4
Rokan-Kanan ∼ RI 162-163 D 4
Rokan-Kiri ∼ RI 162-163 D 4
Rokeby o AUS 174-175 G 3
Rokeby-Croll Creek National Park ⊥ AUS 174-175 G 3
Rokiškis ★ •• LT 94-95 J 4
Rokkasho o J 152-153 J 4
Rokom o SUD 206-207 K 6
Rokskij, pereval ▲ RUS 126-127 F 6
Roland o CDN 34-35 H 6
Rolândia o BR 72-73 E 7
Røldal o N 86-87 C 7
Roldán o RA 78-79 J 2
Rolim de Moura o BR (RON) 70-71 G 2
Rolim de Moura o BR (RON) 70-71 F 3
Roll o USA 44-45 H 2
Rolla ⌒ N 86-87 H 2
Rolla o USA (KS) 44-45 G 1
Rolla o USA (MO) 46-47 C 7
Rolla o USA (ND) 42-43 H 1
Rollapenta o IND 140-141 H 3
Rolleston o AUS 178-179 K 3
Rolleston o NZ 182 D 5
Rolleville o • BS 54-55 H 3
Rolling Fork o USA 44-45 M 3
Rolling Hills o CDN 32-33 P 6
Rolling River Indian Reserve ✗ CDN 34-35 G 5
Rolvsøya ⌒ N 86-87 M 1
Roma o AUS 178-179 K 4
Roma ★ ••• I 100-101 D 4
Roma o LS 220-221 H 4
Roma o S 86-87 J 8
Roma o USA 44-45 H 6
Roma, Pulau ⌒ RI 166-167 D 5
Romain, Cape ▲ USA 48-49 J 3
Romaine, Rivière ∼ CDN 38-39 N 3
Roman o BG 102-103 C 6
Roman o • RO 102-103 E 4
Romana, La ★ DOM 54-55 L 5
Romanche Fracture Zone ≃ 6-7 G 9
Romanek, Lac o CDN 36-37 Q 6
Romang, Selat ≈ 166-167 D 5
Romania = România ■ RO 102-103 C 5
Romanina, Bol'šaja ∼ RUS 108-109 c 6
Roman-Koš, hora ▲ UA 102-103 J 5
Romano, Cape ▲ USA 48-49 H 7
Romano, Cayo ⌒ C 54-55 F 3
Romanovka o RUS 118-119 F 9
Romans-sur-Isère o F 90-91 K 9
Romanzof, Cape ▲ USA 20-21 G 6
Romanzof Mountains ▲ USA 20-21 S 2
Romblon ★ RP 160-161 E 6
Romblon Island ⌒ RP 160-161 E 6
Romblon Strait ≈ 160-161 E 6
Rome o USA (GA) 48-49 F 2
Rome o USA (NY) 46-47 L 4
Rome = Roma ★ ••• I 100-101 D 4
Romero o USA 44-45 F 2
Romero, Isla ⌒ RCH 80 C 2
Romer Sø o GRØ 26-27 q 3
Romita o MEX 52-53 D 1
Rommani o MA 188-189 H 4
Romney o USA (IN) 46-47 E 5
Romney o USA (WV) 46-47 J 6
Romny o RUS 122-123 C 3
Romny o UA 102-103 H 2
Rømø ⌒ DK 86-87 D 9
Romodan o UA 102-103 H 2
Romorantin-Lanthenay o F 90-91 H 8
Rompía o YV 60-61 H 4
Rompin ∼ MAL 162-163 E 3
Romsdalen ∼ N 86-87 C 5
Ronan o USA 40-41 G 2
Roncador o BR 74-75 D 5
Roncador, Serra do ▲ BR 72-73 E 2
Roncador Reef ⌒ SOL 184 I d 2
Roncesvalles o • E 98-99 G 3
Roncière Falls, La ∼ CDN 24-25 L 6
Ronda o E 98-99 E 6
Ronda, Serranía de ▲ E 98-99 E 6
Rønde o DK 86-87 E 8
Ronde, Rivière la ∼ CDN 38-39 L 2
Ronde Island ⌒ WG 56 E 5
Rondon o BR 72-73 D 7
Rondon, Pico ▲ BR 66-67 F 2
Rondon Dopara o BR 68-69 D 4
Rondônia ◘ BR 70-71 F 2
Rondonópolis o BR 70-71 K 5
Rond-Point de Gaulle ▲ TCH 198-199 H 3
Rondslottet ▲ N 86-87 D 6
Rondu o IND 138-139 E 2
Rong'an o VRC 156-157 F 4
Rongbuk o VRC 144-145 F 6
Rongchang o VRC 156-157 D 2
Rongcheng o VRC 154-155 N 3
Ronge, La o CDN 34-35 D 3
Rongjiang o VRC 156-157 F 4
Rongkong ∼ RI 164-165 G 5
Rong Kwang o THA 142-143 M 6
Rongo o EAK 212-213 E 4
Rongshui o VRC 156-157 F 4
Rõngu o EST 94-95 K 2
Rongxar o VRC 144-145 F 6
Rong Xian o VRC (GXI) 156-157 G 5
Rong Xian o VRC (SIC) 156-157 D 2
Rønne o DK 86-87 G 9
Ronne Bay ≈ 16 F 29
Ronneby ★ S 86-87 G 8
Rönnöfors o S 86-87 F 5
Ron Phibun o THA 158-159 E 6
Ronsard, Cape ▲ AUS 176-177 B 2
Ronuro, Rio ∼ BR 70-71 K 3
Roodepoort o ZA 220-221 H 3
Roof Butte ▲ USA 44-45 C 1
Rooiberge ▲ ZA 220-221 J 4
Rooibokkraal o ZA 220-221 H 2
Rooikloof ▲ ZA 220-221 E 6
Rooipoort o NAM 216-217 C 11
Rooikraal o ZA 220-221 J 2
Rooirand ▲ NAM 220-221 C 2
Room, Pulau ⌒ RI 166-167 H 3
Rooney Point ▲ AUS 178-179 M 3
Roosendaal o NL 92-93 H 3
Roosevelt o USA (AZ) 40-41 J 9
Roosevelt o USA (OK) 44-45 H 2
Roosevelt, Área Indígena ✗ BR 70-71 G 2
Roosevelt, Mount ▲ CDN 30-31 G 6
Roosevelt, Rio ∼ BR 66-67 G 7
Roosevelt Campobello International Park ⊥ CDN 38-39 L 6
Roosevelt Fjelde ▲ GRØ 26-27 g 2
Roosevelt Island ⌒ ARK 16 F 21
Roossenekal o ZA 220-221 J 2
Roosville o CDN 32-33 N 7
Rootok Island ⌒ USA 22-23 O 5
Root River ∼ CDN 30-31 G 4
Root River ∼ USA 46-47 C 4
Roper Bar o AUS 174-175 C 4
Roper River ∼ AUS 174-175 C 4
Roper Valley o AUS 174-175 C 4
Roquefort o F 90-91 G 9
Roques, Islas los ⌒ YV 60-61 H 2
Roques, Los o YV 60-61 H 2
Roquetas de Mar o E 98-99 F 6
Roraima ◘ BR 62-63 D 5
Roraima, Mount ▲ GUY 62-63 D 3
Roraya ∼ RI 164-165 H 6
Rorey Lake o CDN 30-31 F 2
Rori o RI 166-167 J 2
Røros ★ •• N 86-87 E 5
Rørvik o N 86-87 E 4
Ros' ∼ UA 102-103 G 3
Rosa, La o YV 60-61 G 3
Rosa, Lake o BS 54-55 J 4
Rosa, Río Santa ∼ BOL 70-71 D 5
Rosal o BR 72-73 K 6
Rosal' o RUS 94-95 Q 4
Rosal, El o CO 60-61 D 5
Rosal de la Frontera o E 98-99 D 6
Rosalia o USA 40-41 F 2
Rosamoraga o MEX 50-51 G 6
Rosana o BR 72-73 D 7
Rosário o BR 68-69 F 3
Rosario o DOM 54-55 K 5
Rosario o MEX 50-51 E 4
Rosario o PE 70-71 B 4
Rosario o PY 76-77 J 3
Rosario o RA (BUA) 78-79 J 2
Rosario o RA (JU) 76-77 D 2
Rosario o • RA (COD) 78-79 J 2
Rosario o RCH 76-77 B 4
Rosario o RP (BTG) 160-161 D 6
Rosario o RP (LUN) 160-161 D 4
Rosario, Cayo del ⌒ C 54-55 E 4
Rosario, El o MEX (BCN) 50-51 B 2
Rosario, El o MEX (SIN) 50-51 G 6
Rosario, El o YV (BOL) 60-61 J 4
Rosario, El o YV (MON) 60-61 K 3
Rosario, Río ∼ RA 76-77 D 2
Rosario, Río ∼ RA 76-77 E 3
Rosario de la Frontera o • RA 76-77 E 3
Rosario de Lerma o RA 76-77 E 3
Rosario del Ingre o BOL 70-71 F 7
Rosario del Tala o RA 78-79 K 2
Rosário do Catete o BR 68-69 K 7
Rosário do Sul o BR 76-77 K 6
Rosário Oeste o BR 70-71 J 4
Rosarito o MEX (BCN) 50-51 B 3
Rosarito o MEX (BCS) 50-51 D 4
Rosarito o • MEX (BCN) 50-51 A 1
Rosas o CO 60-61 C 6
Rosas, Las o MEX 52-53 H 3
Rosas, Las o RA 78-79 J 2
Rosaspata o PE 70-71 C 4
Rosa Zárate o EC 64-65 C 1
Rosburg o USA 40-41 C 2
Roscoe River ∼ CDN 24-25 M 6
Roscoff o F 90-91 F 7
Ros Comáin = Roscommon ★ IRL 90-91 C 5
Roscommon o USA 46-47 F 3
Roscommon = Ros Comáin ★ IRL 90-91 C 5
Ros Cré = Roscrea o IRL 90-91 D 5
Roscrea = Ros Cré o IRL 90-91 D 5
Roseau o USA 42-43 K 1
Roseau ★ WD 56 E 4
Roseau River ∼ USA 42-43 J 1
Roseaux o RH 54-55 H 5
Rose Belle o MS 224 C 7
Rosebery o AUS 180-181 H 6
Roseblade Lake o CDN 30-31 V 5
Rose-Blanche o CDN 38-39 P 5
Rose Bud o USA 44-45 L 2
Rosebud o USA (SD) 42-43 G 4
Rosebud o USA (TX) 44-45 J 4
Rosebud Creek ∼ USA 42-43 D 3
Rosebud Indian Reservation ✗ USA 42-43 G 4
Rosebud River ∼ CDN 32-33 O 6
Roseburg o USA 40-41 C 4
Rose Creek ∼ CDN 32-33 N 5
Rosedale o AUS 178-179 J 2
Rose Harbour o CDN 32-33 E 5
Rose Hill o MS 224 C 7
Rose Island ⌒ BS 54-55 G 2
Rose Lake o CDN 32-33 G 4
Rosemount o USA 42-43 L 3
Rosenberg o USA 44-45 K 5
Rosenberg = Ružomberok o SK 92-93 P 4
Rosenberg, Sulzbach- o D 92-93 L 4
Rosenburg o CDN 34-35 H 5
Rosendal ★ N 86-87 C 7
Rosendal o ZA 220-221 H 4
Rosenheim o D 92-93 M 5
Rose Point ▲ CDN 32-33 E 4
Rose Prairie o CDN 32-33 K 3
Rose River ∼ AUS 174-175 C 3
Roses o USA 46-47 J 5
Rosetilla o MEX 50-51 G 3
Rosetown o CDN 34-35 C 5
Rosetta = Rašīd o • ET 194-195 E 2
Rose Valley o CDN 34-35 E 4
Roseveltpiek ▲ SME 62-63 G 4
Rosewood o AUS 172-173 J 4
Rosh Pinah o NAM 220-221 C 3
Rosi ∼ IND 138-139 G 5
Rosie Creek o AUS 174-175 C 4
Rosiers, Cap-des- o CDN 38-39 M 4
Rosignano Marittima o I 100-101 C 3
Rosignol o GUY 62-63 F 2
Rosillo, Cañada el ∼ RA 76-77 F 2
Roșiori de Vede o RO 102-103 D 5
Rosita, La o CO 60-61 F 5
Rosita, La o NIC 52-53 B 5
Roskilde o •• DK 86-87 F 9
Roslavl' o RUS 94-95 N 5
Rosmead o ZA 220-221 G 5
Ros Mhic Thriúin = New Ross o IRL 90-91 D 5
Ross, Cape ▲ RP 160-161 C 7
Rossano o I 100-101 F 5
Ross Barnett Reservoir < USA 48-49 D 3
Ross Bay ≈ 24-25 d 7
Ross Bay Junction o CDN 38-39 L 2
Ross-Béthio o SN 196-197 B 6
Rossburn o CDN 34-35 F 5
Rosseau, Lake o CDN 38-39 E 6
Ross Ice Shelf ⊂ ARK 16 E 0
Rossignol, Lac o CDN 38-39 H 2
Rossignol, Lake o CDN 38-39 M 6
Rössing o NAM 216-217 C 11
Ross Inlet ≈ 24-25 c 7
Ross Island ⌒ ARK 16 G 31
Ross Island ⌒ ARK 16 F 17
Ross Island ⌒ CDN 34-35 H 3
Ross Lake o USA 40-41 D 1
Rossland o CDN 32-33 M 7
Rosslare = Ros Láir o IRL 90-91 D 5
Rosso ★ RIM 196-197 C 6
Rossomaha ∼ RUS 114-115 T 5
Rossošino o RUS 118-119 G 8
Rossouw o ZA 220-221 H 5
Rossport o CDN 34-35 N 6
Ross River o AUS 178-179 C 2
Ross River o CDN (NWT) 20-21 Y 6
Ross River ∼ CDN 20-21 Z 5
Ross Sea ≈ 16 F 19
Rosston o USA 44-45 H 1
Røssvatnet o N 86-87 F 4
Rossville o AUS 174-175 H 4
Rossville Mission • CDN 34-35 H 4
Rosswood o CDN 32-33 F 4
Røst o N 86-87 F 3
Rostāq o AFG 136-137 L 6
Rostāq o IR 134-135 E 5
Rosthern o CDN 34-35 C 4
Rostock o • D 92-93 M 1
Rostov ★ •• RUS 94-95 Q 3
Rostov-na-Donu ★ RUS 102-103 L 4
Rostraver o USA 46-47 J 5
Rostrenen o F 90-91 F 7
Roswell o USA (GA) 48-49 F 2
Roswell o USA (NM) 44-45 E 3
Rote = Pulau Roti ⌒ RI 166-167 B 7
Rothenburg ob der Tauber o • D 92-93 L 4
Rotherham o GB 90-91 G 5
Rothesay o • GB 90-91 E 4
Rothsay o USA 42-43 J 2
Roti o RI 166-167 B 7
Roti, Pulau ⌒ RI 166-167 B 7
Roti, Selat ≈ 166-167 B 7
Rotifunk o WAL 202-203 D 5
Roto o AUS 180-181 H 2
Rotondo, Monte ▲ F 98-99 M 3
Rotorua o •• NZ 182 F 3
Rotterdam o • NL 92-93 H 3
Rottnest Island o • AUS (WA) 176-177 C 6
Rottnest Island ⌒ AUS (WA) 176-177 C 6
Rottweil o • D 92-93 K 4
Roualist Bank ≃ 158-159 H 6
Roubaix o F 90-91 J 6
Rouen ★ • F 90-91 H 7
Rouge, P.K. o RCB 210-211 E 5
Rouge-Matawin, Réserve Faunique ⊥ CDN 38-39 G 5
Rough Rock o USA 44-45 C 1
Rouhia o TN 190-191 G 3
Roumsiki o • CAM 204-205 K 3
Roundeyed, Lac o CDN 38-39 J 2
Round Hill o CDN 32-33 O 5
Round Mountain ▲ AUS 178-179 M 6
Round Mountain o USA 40-41 F 6
Round Pond o CDN 38-39 I R 4
Round Rock o USA (AZ) 44-45 C 1
Round Rock o USA (TX) 44-45 J 4
Round Spring o USA 46-47 C 7
Roundup o USA 42-43 C 2
Round Valley Indian Reservation ✗ USA 40-41 C 6
Roura o F 62-63 H 3
Rourkela = Raurkela o • IND 142-143 D 4
Route 66 II USA 44-45 C 2
Rouxdam, P.K. le < ZA 220-221 G 5
Rouxville o ZA 220-221 H 5
Rouyn-Noranda o CDN 38-39 E 4
Rovdino o RUS 88-89 R 6
Roven'ky o UA 102-103 L 3
Rover, Mount ▲ CDN 20-21 U 3
Rovereto o • I 100-101 C 2
Roversi o RA 76-77 G 4
Rovigo ★ • I 100-101 C 2
Rovinari o RO 102-103 C 5
Rovinj o • HR 100-101 D 2
Rovno = Rivne o UA 102-103 E 2
Rovnoe o RUS 96-97 E 8
Rovnyj, mys ▲ RUS 120-121 V 4
Rovnyj, ostrov ⌒ RUS 120-121 U 3
Rovubo ∼ EAT (KAG) 212-213 C 5
Rovuma ∼ MOC 214-215 K 6
Rowala Kot o IND 138-139 D 3
Rowan, Port o CDN 38-39 D 7
Rowena o AUS 178-179 K 5
Rowley o CDN 24-25 g 6
Rowley Island ⌒ CDN 24-25 h 6
Rowley Lake o CDN 30-31 R 5
Rowley River ∼ CDN 24-25 j 5
Rowley Shelf ≃ 172-173 C 5
Rowley Shoals ⌒ AUS 172-173 D 4
Roxa, Ilha ⌒ GNB 202-203 C 4
Roxas o RP (ISA) 160-161 D 4
Roxas o RP (MIO) 160-161 D 6
Roxas o RP (PAL) 160-161 C 7
Roxas ★ RP (CAP) 160-161 E 7
Roxboro o USA 48-49 J 1
Roxborough Downs o AUS 178-179 E 2
Roxby Downs o AUS 178-179 D 6
Roxo, Cap ▲ GNB 202-203 B 3
Roy o USA (MT) 42-43 C 2
Roy o USA (NM) 44-45 E 2
Roy o USA (UT) 40-41 H 5
Roy, Lac le o CDN 36-37 M 5
Royal, Mount ▲ CDN 34-35 M 6
Royal Charlotte, Bank ≃ 72-73 L 4
Royal Chitawan National Park ⊥ ••• NEP 144-145 E 7
Royale, Isle ⌒ USA 46-47 D 2
Royal Geographical Society Islands ⌒ CDN 24-25 W 6
Royal Gorge ∴ USA 42-43 E 6
Royal Island ⌒ BS 54-55 G 2
Royal Natal National Park ⊥ ZA 220-221 J 4
Royal National Park ⊥ AUS 180-181 L 3
Royal Palace o • RI 168 D 7
Royal Society Range ▲ ARK 16 F 16
Royalton o USA 42-43 K 3
Royan o • F 90-91 G 9
Roye o F 90-91 J 7
Roy Hill o AUS (WA) 172-173 D 7
Roy Hill ▲ AUS (WA) 172-173 D 7
Røyrvik o N 86-87 F 4
Royston o USA 48-49 G 2
Rožaje o • YU 100-101 H 3
Różan o PL 92-93 Q 2
Rozdol'ne ★ UA 102-103 H 5
Rozivka o UA 102-103 K 4
Rožňava o SK 92-93 Q 4
Rozy Ljuksemburga, mys ▲ RUS 108-109 c 1
r-Raṭqa, Wādī ∼ IRQ 128-129 J 6
Rtiščevo o RUS 94-95 S 5
Ruacana o NAM 216-217 C 8
Ruacaná, Quedas do ∼ •• ANG 216-217 C 8
Ruacana Falls ∼ •• NAM 216-217 C 8
Ruaha National Park ⊥ EAT 214-215 H 4
Ruahine Range ▲ NZ 182 F 3
Ru'ais o UAE 134-135 E 6
Ruangwa o EAT 214-215 K 6
Ruapehu, Mount ▲ NZ 182 E 3
Ruapuke Island ⌒ NZ 182 B 7
Ruarwe o MW 214-215 H 6
Ruatahuna o NZ 182 F 3
Ruatoria o NZ 182 G 2
Ruawai o NZ 182 E 2
Rubafu o EAT 212-213 C 4
Rubai'iya, ar- o KSA 130-131 J 4
Rub' al-Ḫālī, ar- ∸ KSA 132-133 D 4
Rubcovsk o RUS 124-125 M 3
Rubeho Mountains ▲ EAT 214-215 J 4
Rubens, Río ∼ RCH 80 D 6
Ruberong ▲ IND 138-139 F 3
Rubeshibe o J 152-153 K 3
Rubi o ZRE 210-211 K 2
Rubi ∼ ZRE 210-211 K 2
Rubiataba o BR 72-73 F 3
Rubicon River ∼ USA 40-41 D 6
Rubikon, mys ▲ RUS 112-113 S 6
Rubim o BR 72-73 K 4
Rubinéia o BR 72-73 E 6
Rubio o YV 60-61 E 4
Rubondo Island ⌒ EAT 212-213 C 5
Rubondo National Park ⊥ EAT 212-213 C 5
Ruby o USA 20-21 N 4
Ruby Dome ▲ USA 40-41 G 5
Ruby Lake o USA 40-41 G 5
Ruby Mountains ▲ USA 40-41 G 5
Ruby Plains o AUS 172-173 H 5
Ruby Range ▲ CDN 20-21 V 6
Ruby River ∼ USA 40-41 H 3
Rubyvale o AUS 178-179 J 2
Rucachoroi, Cerro ▲ RA 78-79 D 5
Rucava o LV 94-95 G 3
Ruči o RUS 88-89 Q 3
Rucio, El o MEX 50-51 H 6
Rūd o IR 134-135 J 1
Rudal o AUS 180-181 D 2
Rudall River National Park ⊥ AUS 172-173 E 7
Rūdbār o IR 128-129 N 4
Ruddera, buhta ≈ 112-113 W 4
Rūd-e Čalūs ∼ IR 136-137 B 6
Rūd-e Hellē ∼ IR 134-135 D 4
Rūdehen o IR 136-137 B 7
Rūd-e Mārūn ∼ IR 134-135 C 3
Rūd-e Šindand ∼ AFG 134-135 K 2
Rudewa o EAT 214-215 H 6
Rūdḫāne-ye 'Aliābād ∼ IR 134-135 J 3
Rūdḫāne-ye Ğarrāhī ∼ IR 134-135 C 3
Rūdḫāne-ye Nekā ∼ IR 136-137 C 6
Rudkøbing o • DK 86-87 E 9
Rudnaja Pristan' o RUS 122-123 G 6
Rudnik ▲ • YU 100-101 H 2
Rudnja ★ RUS 94-95 M 4
Rudnyj o KA 124-125 C 2
Rudnyy = Rudnyj o KA 124-125 C 2
Rud Ø ⌒ GRØ 28-29 T 6
Rudolf, Lake = Turkana, Lake o EAK 212-213 F 2
Rudoľfa o RUS 84-85 e 2
Rudoľfa, ostrov ⌒ RUS 84-85 f 2
Rudong o VRC 154-155 M 5
Rūdsar o IR 136-137 B 6
Rudyard o USA 40-41 J 1
Ruente Nacional o CO 60-61 E 5
Ruenya ∼ ZW 218-219 G 3
Rufā'ah o SUD 200-201 F 5
Rufiji ∼ EAT 214-215 J 5
Rufino o BR 62-63 F 6
Rufino o RA 78-79 H 3
Rufisque o SN 202-203 B 2
Rufrufua o RI 166-167 G 3
Rufunsa o Z 218-219 E 2
Rufunsa ∼ Z 218-219 E 2
Rufus Lake o CDN 20-21 Z 2
Rugāji o LV 94-95 K 3
Rugao o VRC 154-155 M 5
Rugby o USA 42-43 G 1
Rügen ⌒ D 92-93 M 1
Rugenwalde = Darłowo o • PL 92-93 O 1
Rugged Island ⌒ USA 20-21 Q 7
Rugheiwa < SUD 200-201 E 4
Rugufu ∼ EAT 212-213 C 6
Ruḫaimiya, ar- o IRQ 130-131 J 3
Ruḫayyah, Ğabal ar- ▲ KSA 130-131 L 4
Ruhengeri o RWA 212-213 B 4
Ruhnu saar ⌒ • EST 94-95 H 3
Ruhudji ∼ EAT 214-215 H 5
Ruhuhu ∼ EAT 214-215 H 6
Rui'an o VRC 156-157 M 3
Rui Barbosa o BR 72-73 K 2
Ruichang o VRC 156-157 J 2
Ruicheng o VRC 154-155 G 4
Ruidosa o USA 44-45 E 4
Ruidoso o USA 44-45 E 3
Ruijin o VRC 156-157 J 4
Ruiki ∼ ZRE 210-211 K 4
Ruili o VRC 142-143 K 3
Ruimte o NAM 220-221 B 1
Ruin Point ▲ CDN 36-37 H 3
Ruins ∴ AUS 176-177 L 5
Ruins of Sambor • K 158-159 H 4
Ruipa o EAT (MOR) 214-215 J 5
Ruiru o EAK 212-213 F 4
Ruitersbos o ZA 220-221 F 6
Rūjiena o •• LV 94-95 J 3
Ruka o FIN 88-89 K 3
Rukanga o EAK 212-213 G 5
Rukarara ∼ RWA 212-213 B 5
Ruki ∼ ZRE 210-211 G 4
Rukua o RI 164-165 J 6
Rukubji o BHT 142-143 G 2
Rukutama ∼ RUS 122-123 K 4
Rukwa ◘ EAT 214-215 F 4
Rukwa, Lake o EAT 214-215 F 4
Rule o USA 44-45 H 3
Rulenge o EAT 212-213 C 5
Ruleville o USA 44-45 M 3
Ruma o WAN 198-199 C 6
Ruma o YU 100-101 G 2
Rumāh o KSA 130-131 K 5
Rumahbaru o RI 162-163 B 2
Rumahkai o RI 166-167 E 3
Rumah Kulit o MAL 164-165 D 2
Rumahtinggih o RI 166-167 L 5
Rumaila o IRQ 130-131 K 2
Ruma National Park ⊥ EAK 212-213 E 4
Rumbek o SUD 206-207 J 5
Rumberpon, Pulau ⌒ RI 166-167 H 2
Rum Cay = Mamana Island ⌒ BS 54-55 H 3
Rum Jungle o AUS 172-173 K 2
Rummāna o ET 194-195 F 2
Rumo o BR 68-69 F 2
Rumoi o J 152-153 J 3
Rumonge o BU 212-213 B 5
Rumorosa, La o • MEX 50-51 A 1
Rumphi o MW 214-215 G 6
Rumpi Hills ▲ CAM 204-205 H 6
Rum River ∼ USA 42-43 L 3
Rumuruti o EAK 212-213 F 3
Run, Pulau ⌒ RI 166-167 E 4
Runan o VRC 154-155 J 5
Runaway, Cape ▲ NZ 182 F 2
Runaway Bay o JA 54-55 G 5
Runazi o EAT 212-213 C 5
Runde ∼ ZW 218-219 F 5
Rundeng o RI 162-163 B 3
Rundu ★ NAM (KV1) 216-217 E 8
Runduma, Pulau ⌒ RI 164-165 J 6
Rungu o ZRE 212-213 A 2
Rungwa o EAT (RUK) 214-215 F 4
Rungwa o EAT (SIN) 214-215 G 4
Rungwa ∼ EAT 214-215 G 4
Rungwa Game Reserve ⊥ EAT 214-215 G 4
Runmarö ⌒ S 86-87 J 7
Runnymede o AUS 174-175 G 7
Runton Range ▲ AUS 176-177 G 1
Ruokolahti o FIN 88-89 K 6
Ruoqiang o VRC 146-147 J 6
Ruo Shui ∼ VRC 148-149 D 7
Ruo Shui ∼ VRC 154-155 B 2
Ruovesi o FIN 88-89 H 6
Rupanco, Lago o RCH 78-79 C 6
Rupanyup o AUS 180-181 G 4
Rupat, Pulau ⌒ RI 162-163 D 4
Rupat, Selat ≈ 162-163 D 4
Rupert o USA (ID) 40-41 H 4
Rupert o USA (WV) 46-47 H 7
Rupert, Baie de o CDN 38-39 E 3
Rupert, Rivière de ∼ CDN 38-39 F 3
Rupisi o ZW 218-219 G 5
Ruponda o EAT 214-215 K 6
Ruppert Coast ∸ ARK 16 F 22
Ruqa'i', ar- o KSA 130-131 K 3
Ruqayba o SUD 200-201 E 5
Rurópolis Presidente Médici o BR 66-67 K 5
Rurutu Island ⌒ F 13 M 5
Rušāfa, ar- o •• SYR 128-129 H 5
Rušan o TJ 136-137 M 6
Rusanova, lednik ⊂ RUS 108-109 b 2
Rusanova, zaliv o RUS 108-109 J 4
Rusanovo o RUS 108-109 G 6
Rusape o ZW 218-219 G 4
Ruṣayris Dam < SUD 208-209 B 3
Ruse o BG 102-103 D 6
Rushan o VRC 154-155 M 3
Rush Center o USA 42-43 H 6
Rush Creek ∼ USA 42-43 F 6
Rushford o USA 46-47 C 4
Rush Springs o USA 44-45 J 2
Rushville o USA (IL) 46-47 C 5
Rushville o USA (IN) 46-47 F 6
Rushville o USA (NE) 42-43 F 4
Rushworth o AUS 180-181 H 4
Rusizi ∼ BU 212-213 B 5
Rus'ka o UA 102-103 D 4
Rus'ka, Rava- o UA 102-103 C 2
Ruskeala o RUS 88-89 L 6
Rusksele o S 86-87 J 4
Rusnė o •• LT 94-95 G 4
Rus Rus o HN 52-53 B 4
Russas o BR 68-69 K 4
Russel o CDN 34-35 F 5
Russell o USA 42-43 H 6
Russell, Cape ▲ CDN 24-25 N 3
Russell, Kap ▲ GRØ 26-27 Q 4
Russell, Mount ▲ AUS 176-177 L 1
Russell, Mount ▲ USA 20-21 P 5
Russel Lake o CDN 30-31 M 4
Russell Cave National Monument ∴ • USA 48-49 F 2
Russell Fiord ≈ 20-21 V 7
Russell Fiord Wilderness ⊥ USA 20-21 V 7
Russell Gletscher ⊂ GRØ 28-29 P 3
Russell Inlet ≈ 20-21 Z 2
Russell Island ⌒ CDN 24-25 W 4
Russell Islands ⌒ SOL 184 I d 3
Russell Lake o CDN 34-35 F 2
Russell Lake < USA 48-49 G 2
Russellville o USA (AL) 48-49 E 2
Russellville o USA (AR) 44-45 L 2
Russellville o USA (KY) 46-47 E 7
Russel Springs o USA 42-43 G 6
Russia = Rossija ■ RUS 114-115 H 4
Russian River ∼ USA 40-41 C 6
Russkaja Gavan, zaliv o RUS 108-109 K 3
Russkaja Lučajaha ∼ RUS 108-109 T 8
Russkaja Rečka o RUS 118-119 K 5
Russkaja Tavra o RUS 96-97 K 5
Russkie gory ▲ RUS 112-113 P 4
Russkij, ostrov ⌒ RUS 108-109 b 3
Russkij Zavorot, poluostrov ∪ RUS 88-89 W 2
Rust, De o ZA 220-221 F 6
Rustāq, ar- o OM 132-133 K 2
Rustavi o GE 126-127 F 7
Rust de Winter o ZA 220-221 J 2
Rust de Winterdam < ZA 220-221 J 2
Rustefjelbma o N 86-87 O 1
Rustenburg o ZA 220-221 H 2
Rustfontein Dam < ZA 220-221 H 4
Rustic o USA 42-43 E 5
Ruston o USA 44-45 L 3
Rusumo Falls ∼ • EAT (KAG) 212-213 C 5
Ruta o RI 164-165 K 4
Rutaimi, ar- o IRQ 128-129 J 5
Rutana o BU 212-213 C 5
Ruṭba, ar- o IRQ 128-129 J 6
Ruten ▲ N (OPP) 86-87 D 6
Ruten ▲ N (STR) 86-87 D 5
Ruteng o • RI 168 E 7
Rutenga o ZW 218-219 F 5
Rutherglen o AUS 180-181 J 4
Ruti o PNG 183 C 3
Rutland o USA 46-47 M 4
Rutland Island ⌒ IND 140-141 L 4
Rutland Plains o AUS 174-175 F 4
Rutledge Lake o CDN 30-31 O 5
Rutledge River ∼ CDN 30-31 O 5
Rutog o VRC 144-145 B 4
Rutshuru o ZRE 212-213 B 4
Rutukira ∼ EAT 214-215 H 6
Rutul o RUS 126-127 G 7
Ruvu ∼ EAT 214-215 K 4
Ruvubu, Parc National de la ⊥ BU 212-213 C 5
Ruvuma ◘ EAT 214-215 H 6
Ruvuma ∼ EAT 214-215 K 6
Ruwaiḍa, ar- o KSA (RIY) 130-131 J 6
Ruwaiḍa, ar- o KSA (RIY) 130-131 J 5
Ruwais, ar- o Q 134-135 D 5
Ruwaišid, Wādī r- ∼ JOR 130-131 F 1
Ruwāq, Ğabal ar- ▲ SYR 128-129 G 5
Ruwenzori ▲ ZRE 212-213 B 3
Ruwi o OM 132-133 L 2
Ruya ∼ ZW 218-219 F 3
Ruyang o VRC 154-155 H 4
Rū-ye Dōāb o AFG 136-137 K 7
Ruyigi o BU 212-213 C 5
Ruyuan o VRC 156-157 H 4
Ruza ★ RUS 94-95 P 4
Ruzaevka o RUS 96-97 D 6
Ružany o BY 94-95 J 5
Ruzhou o VRC 154-155 H 4
Ružomberok o SK 92-93 P 4
Rwamagana o RWA 212-213 C 4
Rwanda ■ RWA 212-213 B 5
Rwashamaire o EAU 212-213 C 4
Rweru, Lac o BU 212-213 C 5
Ryan, Mount ▲ AUS (NSW) 180-181 K 2
Ryan, Mount ▲ AUS (QLD) 174-175 G 4
Ryazan' = Rjazan' ★ •• RUS 94-95 Q 4
Rybač'e = Ysyk-Köl o KS 146-147 C 4
Rybacij, aral ⌒ KA 126-127 J 5
Rybačij, poluostrov ∪ RUS 88-89 M 2
Ryberg Fjord ≈ 28-29 Z 2
Rybinsk ★ RUS 94-95 Q 2
Rybinskoe vodohranilišče < RUS 94-95 Q 2
Rybinskoye Vodokhranilishche = Rybinskoe vodohranilišče < RUS 94-95 Q 2
Rybnaja ∼ RUS 108-109 h 3
Rybnaja ∼ RUS 116-117 G 8
Rybnaja ∼ RUS 116-117 E 5
Rybnaja Sloboda ★ RUS 96-97 G 6
Rybnica = Rîbniţa ★ MD 102-103 F 4
Rybnik o • PL 92-93 P 3
Rybnoe o RUS 116-117 G 8
Rybnoe o RUS (RZN) 94-95 Q 4
Rybnovsk o RUS 122-123 J 2
Ryčkovo o RUS 96-97 M 4
Rycroft o CDN 32-33 L 4
Ryder Gletscher ⊂ GRØ 26-27 a 3
Ryder Øer ⌒ GRØ 26-27 V 6
Ryegate o USA 42-43 C 2
Rye Patch Reservoir < USA 40-41 E 5
Ryjanranot, ostrov ⌒ RUS 112-113 P 1
Rykerts o CDN 32-33 M 7
Ryki o PL 92-93 Q 3
Ryl'sk o RUS 102-103 J 2
Rylstone o AUS 180-181 K 2
Rynda ∼ RUS 88-89 O 2
Ryn-kum ∸ KA 96-97 E 9
Ryohaku-sanchi ▲ J 152-153 G 6
Ryōhū-kaizan ≃ 152-153 L 5
Ryōtsu o J 152-153 H 5
Rypin o PL 92-93 P 2
Rys'ja ★ RUS 118-119 E 6
Rytkuči o RUS 112-113 Q 2
Ryukyu Islands = Nansei-shotō ⌒ J 152-153 B 1
Ryūkyū-shotō ⌒ J 152-153 C 12
Ryukyu Trench = Ryūkyū Trench ≃ 152-153 C 12
Rzeszów ★ PL 92-93 R 3
Ržev ★ RUS 94-95 O 3

S

Sa o PNG 183 C 3
Saa o CAM 204-205 J 6
Sa'a o SOL 184 I e 3
Sa'ādatābād o IR 134-135 E 3
Sa'ādatābād o IR 134-135 F 4
Saale ∼ D 92-93 L 3
Saalfeld o • D 92-93 L 3
Saanich o CDN 32-33 J 7
Saarbrücken ★ • D 92-93 J 4
Sääre o EST 94-95 H 3
Saaremaa ⌒ EST 94-95 G 2
Saarijärvi o FIN 88-89 H 5
Saariselkä o FIN 88-89 J 2

Rocky Ford — Saariselkä 309

Santa Cruz de Campezo = Santi Kurutze
 Kanpezu ○ E 98-99 F 3
Santa Cruz de la Palma ○ E
 188-189 C 6
Santa Cruz de la Sierra ☆ BOL
 70-71 F 4
Santa Cruz del Norte ○ C 54-55 E 3
Santa Cruz del Quiché ☆ GCA
 52-53 J 4
Santa Cruz del Sur ○ C 54-55 G 4
Santa Cruz de Mudela ○ E 98-99 F 5
Santa Cruz de Tenerife ○ E
 188-189 C 6
Santa Cruz do Arari ○ BR 62-63 K 6
Santa Cruz do Capibaribe ○ BR
 68-69 K 5
Santa Cruz do Sul ○ BR 74-75 D 7
Santa Cruz Island ∧ USA 40-41 E 8
Santa Cruz Verapaz ○ GCA 52-53 J 4
Santa de Ayes Laguna Colorada, Parque
 Nacional ⊥ BOL 76-77 D 2
Santa Doménica Talão ○ I 100-101 E 5
Santa Elena ○ EC 64-65 B 3
Santa Elena ○ MEX 50-51 H 4
Santa Elena ○ RA 76-77 H 6
Santa Elena ○ YV 60-61 K 3
Santa Elena, Bahía de ≈ 52-53 B 6
Santa Elena, Bahía de ≈ 64-65 B 3
Santa Elena, Cabo ▲ CR 52-53 B 6
Santa Elena, Cerro ▲ RA 80 H 2
Santa Elena, Paso de ▲ RA 78-79 D 3
Santa Elena de Arenales ○ YV
 60-61 F 3
Santa Elena de Uairén ○ YV 62-63 D 3
Santa Eleodora ○ RA 78-79 H 3
Santa Eugenia (Ribeira) ○ E 98-99 C 3
Santa Eulalia ○ MEX 50-51 D 2
Santa Eulària del Riu ○ E 98-99 H 5
Santa Fé ○ BR 68-69 J 5
Santa Fé ○ C 54-55 D 3
Santa Fé ○ CO 60-61 D 2
Santa Fé ○ E 98-99 F 6
Santa Fé ○ PA (Dar) 52-53 E 7
Santa Fé ○ PA (Ver) 52-53 D 7
Santa Fé ○ PE 64-65 F 4
Santa Fe ○ RA 76-77 H 5
Santa Fe ★ RA (SAF) 76-77 G 6
Santa Fe ○ RP 160-161 E 9
Santa Fe ○ RP 160-161 D 6
Santa Fe ○ USA 44-45 E 2
Santa Fe, Isla ∧ EC 64-65 B 10
Santa Fé de Minas ○ BR 72-73 H 4
Santa Fé do Sul ○ BR 72-73 E 6
Santa Filomena ○ BR 68-69 F 6
Santa Helena ○ BR (MAR) 68-69 F 3
Santa Helena ○ BR (PAR) 76-77 K 3
Santa Helena ○ CO 60-61 E 6
Santa Helena de Cusima ○ CO
 60-61 F 5
Santa Helena de Goiás ○ BR 72-73 E 4
Santai ○ VRC 154-155 D 6
Santa Inês ○ BR (BAH) 72-73 L 2
Santa Inês ○ BR (MAR) 68-69 F 3
Santa Inés ○ YV 60-61 G 2
Santa Ines ○ YV 60-61 H 2
Santa Ines, Bahía ≈ 50-51 D 4
Santa Inés, Isla ∧ RCH 80 D 8
Santa Isabel ○ MEX 52-53 H 3
Santa Isabel ○ PA 52-53 E 7
Santa Isabel ○ PE 64-65 E 4
Santa Isabel ○ RA 78-79 F 4
Santa Isabel ○ SOL 184 I d 2
Santa Isabel, Cachoeira ∼ BR 68-69 D 5
Santa Isabel, Río ∼ GCA 52-53 K 4
Santa Isabel do Araguaia ○ BR
 68-69 D 5
Santa Isabel d'Oeste ○ BR 74-75 D 5
Santa Isabel do Pará ○ BR 62-63 K 6
Santa Isabel do Preto ○ BR 72-73 H 7
Santa Isabel do Rio Negro ○ BR
 66-67 E 3
Santa Júlia ○ BR 66-67 G 6
Santa Lucía ○ C 54-55 D 3
Santa Lucía ○ EC 64-65 C 2
Santa Lucía ○ PE 70-71 B 4
Santa Lucía ○ RA (CO) 76-77 H 5
Santa Lucía ○ RA (SAJ) 76-77 C 6
Santa Lucía ○ ROU 78-79 L 3
Santa Lucía, Río ∼ RA 76-77 H 5
Santa Lucía, Río ∼ ROU 78-79 L 3
Santa Lucía, Sierra de ▲ MEX
 50-51 C 4
Santa Lucia Cotzumalguapa ○ GCA
 52-53 J 4
Santa Lucia la Reforma ○ GCA
 52-53 J 4
Santa Lucia Range ▲ USA 40-41 D 7
Santa Lugarda, Punta ▲ MEX 50-51 E 4
Santa Luisa ○ RCH 76-77 B 5
Santa Luz ○ BR (BAH) 68-69 J 7
Santa Luz ○ BR (PIA) 68-69 F 6
Santa Luzia ○ BR (BAH) 72-73 L 3
Santa Luzia ○ BR (MAR) 68-69 F 3
Santa Luzia ○ BR (MIN) 72-73 J 5
Santa Luzia ○ BR (PA) 68-69 K 5
Santa Luzia ○ BR (ROR) 62-63 D 5
Santa Luzia, Ilha de ∧ CV 202-203 B 5
Santa Luzia do Pacuí ○ BR 62-63 J 5
Santa Magdalena ○ RA 78-79 H 3
Santa Margarita, Isla ∧ MEX 50-51 D 5
Santa Maria ○ ANG 216-217 B 3
Santa Maria ○ BR (AMA) 66-67 H 5
Santa María ○ BR (PJ) 62-63 J 4
Santa María ○ BR (RSU) 74-75 D 7
Santa María ○ CO 60-61 E 5
Santa María ○ CR 52-53 C 7
Santa María ○ CV 202-203 C 5
Santa María ○ HN 52-53 D 7
Santa María ○ PA 52-53 D 7
Santa María ○ RA 76-77 G 5
Santa María ○ RP 160-161 F 9
Santa María ○ USA 40-41 D 8
Santa María ○ YV 60-61 F 3
Santa Maria ○ YV (APU) 60-61 H 4
Santa María ○ YV (SUC) 60-61 K 2
Santa María, Bahía ≈ 50-51 C 3
Santa María, Boca ≈ 50-51 L 5
Santa Maria, Cabo de ▲ P 98-99 D 6

Santa Maria, Cape ▲ BS 54-55 H 3
Santa Maria, Corredeira ∼ BR
 66-67 H 6
Santa Maria, Isla ∧ EC 64-65 B 10
Santa María, Isla ∧ RCH 78-79 C 4
Santa María, Laguna de ○ MEX
 50-51 F 2
Santa Maria, Punta ▲ ROU 78-79 M 3
Santa María, Ribeiro ∼ BR 68-69 D 5
Santa Maria, Rio ∼ BR 72-73 G 3
Santa María, Rio ∼ MEX 50-51 J 7
Santa Maria, Rio ∼ RA 76-77 E 4
Santa Maria da Vitória ○ BR 72-73 H 2
Santa Maria da Vitória, Mosteiro de ↔ P
 98-99 C 5
Santa María de Ipire ○ YV 60-61 J 3
Santa María de Itabira ○ BR 72-73 J 5
Santa María de Jebitá ○ BR 72-73 K 6
Santa María del Camí ○ E 98-99 J 5
Santa María del Oro ○ MEX 50-51 G 5
Santa María de los Guaicas ○ YV
 60-61 J 4
Santa María del Valle ○ PE 64-65 D 6
Santa María de Nanay ○ PE 64-65 F 3
Santa María de Nieva ○ PE 64-65 D 4
Santa María di Léuca, Capo ▲ I
 100-101 G 5
Santa María do Para ○ BR 68-69 E 2
Santa María do Suaçui ○ BR 72-73 J 5
Santa María Ecatepec ○ MEX 52-53 G 3
Santa María Eterna ○ BR 72-73 L 3
Santa Maria Island ∼ Île Gaua ∧ VAN
 184 II a 2
Santa María Zacatepec ○ MEX
 52-53 F 3
Santa María Zoquitlán ○ MEX 52-53 F 3
Santa Marta ○ ANG 216-217 B 6
Santa Marta ○ C 54-55 E 3
Santa Marta ★ CO 60-61 D 2
Santa Marta, Cabo de ▲ BR 74-75 F 7
Santa Monica ○ USA 40-41 E 8
Santan ○ RI 164-165 E 4
Santan, Tanjung ▲ RI 164-165 E 3
Santana ○ BR (AMA) 66-67 F 3
Santana ○ BR (APA) 62-63 J 6
Santana ○ BR (BAH) 72-73 H 2
Santana ○ BR (PJ) 68-69 E 3
Santana ○ CO (MET) 60-61 D 6
Santana ○ CO 60-61 G 4
Santana ○ P 98-99 B 2
Santana, Área Indígena ⋇ BR 70-71 H 4
Santana, Cachoeira ∼ BR 72-73 F 3
Santana, Caverna de • BR 74-75 F 5
Santana, Ilha ∧ BR 68-69 G 3
Santana, Ribeiro ∼ BR 68-69 C 6
Santana, Rio ∼ BR 68-69 G 6
Santana da Boa Vista ○ BR 74-75 D 8
Santana da Vargem ○ BR 72-73 H 6
Santana de Pirapama ○ BR 72-73 H 5
Santana do Acaraú ○ BR 68-69 H 5
Santana do Araguaia ○ BR 68-69 C 6
Santana do Garambeu ○ BR 72-73 H 6
Santana do Ipanema ○ BR 68-69 K 6
Santana do Itararé ○ BR 72-73 F 7
Santana do Livramento ○ BR 76-77 K 6
Santana do Manhuaçu ○ BR 72-73 J 6
Santana do Matos ○ BR 68-69 K 4
Santander ○ E 98-99 F 3
Santander ○ RP 160-161 E 8
Santander Jiménez ○ MEX 50-51 K 5
Santanilla, Islas = Islas del Cisne ∧ HN
 54-55 D 6
Sant'Antíoco ○ I 100-101 B 5
Sant'Antíoco, Ísola di ∧ I 100-1C1 B 5
Sant Antoni Abat ○ E 98-99 H 5
Santa Olalla del Cala ○ E 98-99 D 6
Santa Paula ○ USA 40-41 E 8
Santa Pola ○ E 98-99 G 5
Santa Quitéria ○ BR 68-69 H 4
Santa Quitéria do Maranhão ○ BR
 68-69 G 3
Sant'Arcángelo ○ I 100-101 F 4
Santarém ○ BR 66-67 K 4
Santarém ○ P 98-99 C 5
Santarém, Ponta de ▲ BR 62-63 J 5
Santarém Novo ○ BR 68-69 E 2
Santaren Channel ≈ 54-55 F 2
Santa Rita ∴• BH 52-53 K 2
Santa Rita ○ BR (AMA) 66-67 C 4
Santa Rita ○ BR (PA) 68-69 L 5
Santa Rita ○ CO (CA) 64-65 F 1
Santa Rita ○ CO (VIC) 60-61 G 5
Santa Rita ○ HN 52-53 L 4
Santa Rita ○ MEX 50-51 D 5
Santa Rita ○ YV (BOL) 60-61 K 3
Santa Rita ○ YV (GUA) 60-61 H 3
Santa Rita ○ YV (ZUL) 60-61 F 2
Santa Rita, Arroyo ∼ RA 76-77 E 2
Santa Rita, Ilha de ∧ BR 62-63 F 6
Santa Rita de Caldas ○ BR 72-73 H 6
Santa Rita de Cássia ○ BR 68-69 F 7
Santa Rita do Araguaia ○ BR 72-73 D 4
Santa Rita do Sul ○ BR 74-75 E 8
Santa Rosa ○ BOL (BEN) 70-71 D 4
Santa Rosa ○ BOL (PAN) 70-71 D 4
Santa Rosa ○ BR (CAT) 74-75 F 7
Santa Rosa ○ BR (RON) 70-71 G 3
Santa Rosa ○ BR (ROR) 60-61 K 6
Santa Rosa ○ BR (RSU) 76-77 K 6
Santa Rosa ○ BR (TOC) 68-69 D 7
Santa Rosa ○ CO (CAU) 64-65 D 1
Santa Rosa ○ CO (GU) 60-61 D 5
Santa Rosa ○ CO (VAU) 60-61 F 6
Santa Rosa ○ EC (ELO) 64-65 C 3
Santa Rosa ○ EC (LOJ) 64-65 B 3
Santa Rosa ○ EC (PAS) 64-65 D 2
Santa Rosa ○ MEX (BCS) 50-51 E 6
Santa Rosa ○ MEX (QR) 52-53 K 2
Santa Rosa ○ PE (LOR) 64-65 F 3
Santa Rosa ○ PE (PUN) 70-71° B 4
Santa Rosa ∼ RA (LAP) 78-79 G 4
Santa Rosa ○ USA (CA) 40-41 D 6
Santa Rosa ○ USA (NM) 44-45 E 2
Santa Rosa ○ YV (ANZ) 60-61 J 3
Santa Rosa ○ YV (APU) 60-61 G 4

Santa Rosa ○ YV (BOL) 60-61 K 4
Santa Rosa, Baja de ≈ 62-63 K 5
Santa Rosa, Cordillera de ▲ RA
 76-77 C 2
Santa Rosa, Isla ∧ EC 64-65 C 1
Santa Rosa, Lago ○ BOL 70-71 H 6
Santa Rosa Aboriginal Land ⋇ AUS
 178-179 Z 4
Santa Rosa de Amonadona ○ YV
 66-67 D 2
Santa Rosa de Copán ○ HN 52-53 K 4
Santa Rosa de Cusubamba ○ EC
 64-65 C 2
Santa Rosa del Conlara ○ RA 78-79 G 2
Santa Rosa de los Pastos Grandes ○ RA
 76-77 D 3
Santa Rosa de Ocopa • PE 64-65 E 7
Santa Rosa de Quijos ○ EC 64-65 D 2
Santa Rosa de Sucumbís ○ EC
 64-65 D 1
Santa Rosa de Viterbo ○ BR 72-73 G 6
Santa Rosa dos Dourados ○ BR
 72-73 G 5
Santa Rosa Island ∧ USA (CA)
 40-41 D 9
Santa Rosa Island ∧ USA (FL)
 48-49 E 4
Santa Rosalia ○• MEX 50-51 C 4
Santa Rosalia ○ YV 60-61 J 4
Šantarskie, ostrova ∧ RUS 120-121 G 6
Šantarskoe more ≈ 120-121 G 6
Santa Si ∼ VRC 142-143 M 3
Santa Sylvina ○ RA 76-77 H 4
Santa Tecla = Nueva San Salvador ○ ES
 52-53 K 5
Santa Teresa ⋇ AUS 178-179 C 3
Santa Teresa ○ MEX 50-51 D 2
Santa Teresa ○ RA 78-79 J 2
Santa Teresa, Fortaleza • ROU
 74-75 D 10
Santa Teresa, Parque Nacional de ⊥ ROU
 74-75 D 10
Santa Teresa, Punta ▲ MEX 50-51 C 4
Santa Teresa, Rio ∼ BR 72-73 F 2
Santa Teresa de Goiás ○ BR 72-73 F 2
Santa Teresa di Gallura ○ I 100-101 B 4
Santa Teresinha de Goiás ○ BR
 72-73 F 3
Santa Teresita ○ RA 78-79 L 4
Santa Terezinha ○ BR 68-69 C 7
Santa Ursula, Cachoeira ∼ BR
 66-67 H 7
Sant' Auta ○ BR 74-75 E 8
Santa Victoria ○ RA 76-77 E 2
Santa Victoria, Río ∼ RA 76-77 E 2
Santa Victoria, Sierra ▲ RA 76-77 E 2
Santa Vitória do Palmar ○ BR 74-75 D 9
San-ta-Wani Safari Lodge ∼ RB
 218-219 B 4
Sant Carles de la Rápita ○ E 98-99 H 4
Sant Celoni ○ E 98-99 J 4
Santchou ○ CAM 204-205 H 5
Santee Indian Reservation ⋇ USA
 42-43 J 4
Santee River ∼ USA 48-49 J 3
Sante Marie Among the Hurons Historic
 Park • CDN 38-39 E 6
San Tempo, Sierra de ▲ BOL 76-77 E 2
Sant Feliu de Guíxols ○ E 98-99 J 4
Sant Francesc de Formentera ○ E
 98-99 H 5
Santhe ○ MW 218-219 G 1
Santiago ○ BOL 70-71 H 6
Santiago ○ BR 76-77 K 5
Santiago ○ CO 60-61 E 4
Santiago ○ EC 64-65 C 3
Santiago ○ MEX (BCS) 50-51 E 6
Santiago ○ MEX (NL) 50-51 J 5
Santiago ○ PA 52-53 D 7
Santiago ○ RP 160-161 F 4
Santiago, Cabo ▲ RCH 80 C 4
Santiago, Cerro ▲ PA 52-53 D 7
Santiago, Ilha de ∧ CV 202-203 C 6
Santiago, Punta ▲ GQ 210-211 B 2
Santiago, Río ∼ PE 64-65 D 3
Santiago, Rio ∼ MEX 50-51 H 5
Santiago Atitlán ○ GCA 52-53 J 4
Santiago Chazumba ○ MEX 52-53 F 2
Santiago de Cao ○ PE 64-65 C 5
Santiago de Choeorvos ○ PE 64-65 D 8
Santiago de Chuco ○ PE 64-65 C 6
Santiago de Compostela ○••• E
 98-99 C 3
Santiago de Cuba ★☆ C 54-55 H 4
Santiago de Guba, Bahía de ≈
 54-55 G 5
Santiago del Estero ○ RA 76-77 F 4
Santiago del Estero ☆ RA (SAE)
 76-77 E 4
Santiago de Los Caballeros ○ MEX
 50-51 F 5
Santiago de los Cabelloros ☆• DOM
 54-55 K 5
Santiago de Machaca ○ BOL 70-71 C 5
Santiago de Pacaguaras ○ BOL
 70-71 C 3
Santiago Ixcuintla ○ MEX 50-51 G 7
Santiago Jamiltepec ○ MEX 52-53 F 3
Santiago Maior ○ CV 202-203 C 6
Santiago Maravatío ○ MEX 52-53 D 2
Santiago Mountains ▲ USA 44-45 F 4
Santiago Papasquiaro, Río ∼ MEX
 50-51 G 5
Santiago Tamazola ○ MEX 52-53 F 2
Santiago Tuxtla ○ MEX 52-53 G 2
Santiago Yosondúa ○ MEX 52-53 F 3
Santianna Point ▲ CDN 36-37 G 3
San Tiburcio ○ MEX 50-51 J 5
Santig ○ RI 164-165 G 3
Santigi, Tanjung ▲ RI (SLT)
 164-165 H 4
Santig, Tanjung ▲ RI (SLT)
 164-165 H 4
Santiguila ○ RMM 202-203 G 3
Santipur ○ IND 142-143 B 5
Säntis ▲ CH 92-93 K 5

Santíssima Trinità di Saccárgia •• I
 100-101 B 4
Sant Joan de Labritja ○ E 98-99 H 5
Sant Jordi, Golf de ≈ 98-99 H 4
Santo/Malo ∼ VAN 184 II a 2
Sao Amaro ○ BR 72-73 L 2
Santo Agostinho ○ BR 66-67 B 6
Santo Amaro ○ BR 66-67 K 6
Santo Amore, Ilha de ∼ BR 72-73 H 7
Santo André ○ ANG 216-217 C 6
Santo André ○ BR 72-73 G 4
Santo André ○ BR (P) 62-63 H 7
Santo André ∼ PAU 72-73 G 7
Santo Ângelo ○ BR 76-77 K 5
Santo Antão, Ilha de ∧• CV
 202-203 B 5
Santo Antônio ○ BR 62-63 F 6
Santo Antônio ○ BR 66-67 G 4
Santo Antônio ○ BR 68-69 L 5
Santo Antônio ○ CV 202-203 C 6
Santo Antônio ○ STP 210-211 b 2
Santo Antônio, Ponta de ▲ BR
 68-69 L 3
Santo Antonio, Rio ∼ BR 68-69 D 7
Santo Antônio da Platina ○ BR 72-73 F 7
Santo Antônio das Missões ○ BR
 76-77 K 5
Santo Antônio de Jesus ○ BR 72-73 L 2
Santo Antônio de Pádua ○ BR 72-73 J 6
Santo Antônio de Posse ○ BR 72-73 G 6
Santo Antônio do Amparo ○ BR
 72-73 H 6
Santo Antônio do Içá ○ BR 66-67 D 4
Santo Antônio do Jacinto ○ BR 72-73 K 4
Santo Antônio do Leverger ○ BR
 74-75 E 2
Santo Antonio de Lisboa ○ BR
 68-69 F 5
Santo Antônio Desejado ○ BR
 66-67 F 7
Santo Antônio do Içá ○ BR 66-67 D 4
Santo Antônio do Monte ○ BR
 72-73 H 6
Santo Antônio dos Lopes ○ BR
 68-69 F 4
Santo Antônio do Sudoeste ○ BR
 74-75 D 6
Santo Corazón ○ BOL 70-71 H 5
Santo Domingo ○ C 54-55 F 3
Santo Domingo ○ CO 60-61 D 4
Santo Domingo ○ NIC 52-53 B 5
Santo Domingo ○ RA 76-77 F 4
Santo Domingo ★ DOM 54-55 L 5
Santo Domingo ○ MEX (BCS)
 50-51 D 5
Santo Domingo ○ MEX (JAL) 50-51 G 7
Santo Domingo ○ MEX (SLP) 50-51 J 6
Santo Domingo ○ NIC 52-53 B 5
Santo Domingo, Cay ∧ BS 54-55 H 4
Santo Domingo, Rio ∼ MEX 52-53 G 3
Santo Domingo, Rio ∼ MEX 52-53 H 3
Santo Domingo, Río ∼ MEX 52-53 F 3
Santo Domingo, Río ∼ YV 60-61 F 3
Santo Domingo de Acobamba ○ PE
 64-65 E 7
Santo Domingo da Maranhão ○ BR
 68-69 F 4
Santo Domingo de los Colerados ○ EC
 64-65 C 2
Santo Domingo Tehuantepec ○ MEX
 52-53 G 3
Santo Inácio do Piauí ○ BR 68-69 F 6
San Tomé ○ YV 60-61 J 3
Santoméri ○ GR 100-101 H 6
Santoña ○ E 98-99 F 3
Santonia ○ F 62-63 G 3
Santop ▲ VAN 184 II b 4
Santópolis do Aguapeí ○ BR 72-73 F 6
Santorini = Thíra ∧ GR 100-101 K 6
Santos ○ AUS 178-179 F 5
Santos ○ BR 72-73 G 7
Santos, Baía de ≈ 72-73 G 7
Santos, Ilha ∧ C 54-55 F 3
Santos, General ★ RP 160-161 F 9
Santos, Los ○•• PA 52-53 D 8
Santos Dumont ○ BR 72-73 J 6
Santos Lugares ○ RA 76-77 F 4
Santos Mercado ○ BOL 66-67 D 7
Santos Plateau ≃ 2-F 11
Santo Tirso ○ P 98-99 C 4
Santo Tomás ○ MEX 50-51 A 2
Santo Tomás ○ MEX 50-51 J 5
Santo Tomás ○ NIC 52-53 B 5
Santo Tomas ○ PA 52-53 C 7
Santo Tomás ○ RP 160-161 F 9
Santo Tomas, Rio ∼ PE 64-65 F 9
Santo Tomé ○ RA 76-77 J 4
Santo Tomé ○ RA (CO) 76-77 G 4
Santo Tomé ○ RA (SAF) 76-77 H 4
Santo Tomé, Volcán ▲ RA 52-53 J 4
Santu Antine, Nuraghe • I 100-101 B 4
Santuario Nacional de Ampay ⊥ PE
 64-65 F 8
Santuario de Flora y Fauna Arauca ⊥ CO
 60-61 F 4
Santuario de la Coromoto ○• YV
 60-61 G 3
Santuario Nacional Huayllay ⊥ PE
 64-65 D 7
Santuario Nacional Pampas del Heath ⊥
 BOL 70-71 C 3
Santubong ○ MAL 162-163 J 4
Santu Lussúrgiu ○ I 100-101 B 4
San Vicente ○ ES 52-53 K 5
San Vicente ○ RA 76-77 D 1
San Vicente ○ YV (AMA) 60-61 H 5
San Vicente ○ YV (ANZ) 60-61 J 3
San Vicente ○ YV (SUC) 60-61 K 2
San Vicente, Bahía ≈ 78-79 C 4
San Vicente de Tagua ○ RCH 78-79 D 3
San Vicente Tancuayalab ○ MEX
 50-51 K 7
San Víctor ○ GUY 62-63 D 2
San Victor ○ RA 76-77 H 6
San Vicente de Caguan ○ CO
 60-61 D 6
San Vicente de Cañete ○ PE
 64-65 D 8
San Vito ○ CR 52-53 C 7
San Vito, Capo ▲ I 100-101 F 4
San Vito, Capo ▲ I 100-101 D 5
San Xavier Indian Reservation ⋇ USA
 40-41 J 9
Sanya ○ VRC 156-157 F 7
Sanya Juu ○ EAT 212-213 F 5
Sanyat ad Daffah ○ LAR 192-193 L 2
Sanyati ○ ZW (Mlw) 218-219 E 3
Sanyati ∼ ZW 218-219 E 3
Sanying ○ VRC 154-155 E 3
San Ysidro ○ USA 44-45 D 2

Sanyuan ○ VRC 154-155 F 4
Sanza Pombo ○ ANG 216-217 C 3
São Agostinho, Cabo de ▲ BR
 68-69 L 6
Sao João de Labritja ∼
São João do Caiuá ○ BR 72-73 D 7
São João do Paraíso ○ BR 72-73 J 3
São João do Paraná ○ BR 66-67 J 7
São João do Piauí ○ BR 68-69 G 6
São João do Sabuji ○ BR 68-69 K 5
São João do Tigre ○ BR 68-69 K 5
São João Evangelista ○ BR 72-73 J 5
São Joaquim ○ BR (CAT) 74-75 F 7
São Joaquim ○ BR (AMA) 66-67 D 7
São Joaquim, Parque Nacional de ⊥ BR
 74-75 F 7
São Joaquim da Barra ○ BR 72-73 G 6
São Jorge, Ilha ∧ BR 68-69 F 2
São Jorge do Jvaí ○ BR 72-73 E 7
São José ○ BR (ACR) 66-67 C 7
São José ○ BR (CAT) 74-75 F 7
São José ○ BR (P) 68-69 D 3
São José, Baía ≈ 68-69 G 3
São José, Igarapé ∼ BR 68-69 B 4
São José de Piranhas ○ BR 68-69 J 5
São José de Ribamar ○ BR 68-69 F 3
São José do Anauá ○ BR 62-63 D 5
São José do Barreiro ○ BR 72-73 H 7
São José do Belmonte ○ BR 68-69 J 5
São José do Caciporé ○ BR 62-63 J 4
São José do Calcado ○ BR 72-73 J 6
São José do Cedro ○ BR 74-75 D 6
São José do Cerrito ○ BR 74-75 F 6
São José do Egito ○ BR 68-69 K 5
São José do Norte ○ BR 74-75 D 9
São José do Peixe ○ BR 68-69 G 5
São José do Prado ○ BR 72-73 L 4
São José do Rio Claro ○ BR 70-71 J 3
São José do Rio Pardo ○ BR 72-73 F 6
São José dos Campos ○ BR 72-73 H 7
São José dos Cordeiros ○ BR
 68-69 K 5
São José dos Dourados, Rio ∼ BR
 72-73 E 6
São José dos Martírios ○ BR 68-69 D 5
São José dos Pinhais ○ BR 74-75 F 7
São José do Xingu ○ BR 68-69 B 7
São Julia do Jurupari ○ BR 62-63 J 5
São Juliana ○ BR 72-73 G 5
São Lourenço ○ BR 72-73 H 6
São Lourenço, Pantanal do ∼ BR
 70-71 J 5
São Lourenço, Riachão ∼ BR 68-69 G 6
São Lourenço, Rio ∼ BR 70-71 K 5
São Lourenço do Sul ○ BR 74-75 E 8
São Lucas ▲ ANG 216-217 D 5
São Lucas, Cachoeira ∼ BR 66-67 H 7
São Luís ☆ BR (AMA) 66-67 E 3
São Luís ☆ BR (MAR) 68-69 F 3
São Luís, Cachoeira ∼ BR 66-67 H 7
São Luís, Ilha de ∧ BR 68-69 F 3
São Luís de Montes Belos ○ BR
 72-73 E 4
São Luís do Curu ○ BR 68-69 J 4
São Luís do Paraitinga ○ BR 72-73 H 7
São Luís do Purunã ○ BR 74-75 F 5
São Luís do Quitunde ○ BR 68-69 L 6
São Luís do Tapajós ○ BR 66-67 J 5
São Luís Gonzaga ○ BR 76-77 K 5
São Luís Gonzaga do Maranhão ○ BR
 68-69 F 4
São Manuel ○ BR (MAT) 70-71 K 4
São Manuel ○ BR (PAU) 72-73 F 7
São Manuel ou Teles Pires, Rio ∼ BR
 70-71 K 2
São Marcos, Área Indígena ⋇ BR (MAT)
 72-73 D 3
São Marcos, Área Indígena ⋇ BR (ROR)
 62-63 D 3
São Marcos, Baía de ≈ 68-69 F 3
São Martinho ○ BR 74-75 F 7
São Mateus ○ BR 72-73 L 5
São Mateus, Pico ▲ BR 72-73 J 5
São Mateus do Sul ○ BR 74-75 E 6
São Miguel ○ BR (APA) 62-63 J 4
São Miguel ○ BR (MAT) 72-73 D 2
São Miguel ○ BR (RNO) 68-69 K 4
São Miguel ○ P 6-7 G 6
São Miguel, Rio ∼ BR 70-71 J 3
São Miguel, Rio ∼ BR 70-71 F 3
São Miguel Arcanjo ○ BR 72-73 G 7
São Miguel das Missões •• BR
 76-77 K 5
São Miguel do Araguaia ○ BR
 72-73 E 3
São Miguel d'Oeste ○ BR 74-75 D 6
São Miguel do Guama ○ BR 68-69 E 2
São Miguel do Iguaçu ○ BR 76-77 K 3
São Miguel dos Campos ○ BR
 68-69 K 6
São Miguel dos Macacos ○ BR
 62-63 J 6
São Miguel do Tapuio ○ BR 68-69 H 4
Saona, Isla ∧ DOM 54-55 L 5
Saône ∼ F 90-91 L 7
São Nicolau ▲ ANG 216-217 B 7
São Nicolau ○ BR 76-77 K 5
São Nicolau, Ilha de ∧ CV 202-203 B 6
São Nicolau, Rio ∼ BR 68-69 H 4
São Onofre, Rio ∼ BR 72-73 J 2
São Paulo ★ BR (PAU) 72-73 G 7
São Paulo ○ BR 72-73 E 6
São João, Ilha de ∧ BR 68-69 G 3
São João, Ribeiro ∼ BR 72-73 G 2
São João, Rio ∼ BR 72-73 G 2
São João, Serra de ▲ BR 74-75 G 5
São João Batista ○ BR 68-69 F 3
São João Batista da Gloria ○ BR
 72-73 G 6
São João da Aliança ○ BR 72-73 G 3
São João da Barra ○ BR 72-73 K 6
São João da Barra, Cachoeira ∼ BR
 66-67 H 7
São João da Barra, Rio ∼ BR 68-69 H 7
São João da Ponte ○ BR 72-73 H 3
São João da Pracajuba ○ BR 62-63 J 6
São João do Branco, Igarapé ∼ BR
 70-71 F 2

São Pedro dos Crentes ○ BR 68-69 E 5
São Pedro do Sul ○ BR 76-77 K 5
São Raimundo das Mangabeiras ○ BR
 68-69 F 5
São Raimundo Nonato ○ BR 68-69 G 6
São Ramão ○ BR 72-73 H 4
São Romão ○ BR 66-67 D 5
São Roque, Cabo de ▲ BR 68-69 L 4
São Roque, Cachoeira ∼ BR 70-71 F 2
São Sebastião ○ BR 72-73 H 7
São Sebastião, Ilha de ∧ BR 72-73 H 7
São Sebastião, Ponta ▲ MOC
 218-219 H 4
São Sebastião da Amoreira ○ BR
 72-73 F 7
São Sebastião da Boa Vista ○ BR
 62-63 K 6
São Sebastião da Gama ○ BR
 72-73 G 6
São Sebastião do Caí ○ BR 74-75 E 7
São Sebastião do Maranhão ○ BR
 72-73 J 5
São Sebastião do Paraíso ○ BR
 72-73 G 6
São Sebastião do Rio Verde ○ BR
 72-73 H 7
São Sebastião dos Poções ○ BR
 72-73 H 3
São Sebastião do Tocantins ○ BR
 68-69 D 4
São Sepé ○ BR 74-75 D 8
São Timóteo ○ BR 72-73 J 6
São Simão, Cachoeira ∼ BR 66-67 H 7
São Simão, Ponta ▲ BR 74-75 E 8
São Simão ou Branco, Rio ∼ BR
 70-71 F 3
São Teotónio ○ P 98-99 C 6
São Timóteo ○ BR 72-73 J 6
São Tomé ○ BR (APA) 62-63 J 6
São Tomé ○ BR (RIO) 72-73 K 7
São Tomé ★ STP 210-211 b 2
São Tomé ∼ STP 210-211 b 2
São Tomé and Príncipe = São Tomé e
 Príncipe ■ STP 210-211 B 5
Saouyane, Pointe ▲ CDN 38-39 E 3
Saoura, Oued ∼ DZ 188-189 L 6
São Valentim ○ BR 74-75 D 6
São Vendelino ○ BR 74-75 E 7
São Vice ○ BR 76-77 K 5
São Vicente ○ BR (ACR) 66-67 B 6
São Vicente ○ BR (GOI) 72-73 G 6
São Vicente ○ BR (GSU) 70-71 J 6
São Vicente ○ BR (MAT) 70-71 K 4
São Vicente ○ BR (P) 62-63 J 6
São Vicente ○ BR (PAU) 72-73 G 7
São Vicente, Cabo de ▲ P 98-99 C 6
São Vicente, Ilha de ∧ CV 202-203 B 5
São Vicente, Rio ∼ BR 68-69 G 5
Sapang ○ MAL 160-161 C 10
Sapão, Rio ∼ BR 68-69 E 6
Saparua ○ RI 166-167 E 3
Saparua, Pulau ∧ RI 166-167 E 3
Sapé ○ BR 68-69 L 5
Sape ○ RI 168 D 7
Sapeaçu ○ BR 72-73 L 2
Sapele ○ WAN 204-205 F 6
Sapelo Island ∧ USA 48-49 H 4
Sapèmone ∼ RUS 94-95 L 1
Sápes ○ GR 100-101 K 4
Šaphane Daği ▲ TR 128-129 C 3
Šapina ∼ RUS 120-121 S 6
Sapiranga ○ BR 74-75 E 7
Sapiranga do Sul ○ BR 74-75 D 6
Sapi Safari Area ⊥ ZW 218-219 E 2
Šapki ∼ RUS 94-95 M 2
Šapkina ∼ RUS 88-89 X 3
Sap Malua ○ THA 158-159 G 3
Sapo, Serrania del ▲ PA 52-53 E 8
Sapoba ○ WAN 204-205 F 5
Sapočani ••• RUS 94-95 L 5
Sapocoy, Mount ▲ RP 160-161 D 4
Sapodilla Cays ∧ BH 52-53 K 3
Saponé ○ BF 202-203 K 4
Sapo Sapo ○ ZRE 210-211 J 6
Saposoa ○ PE 64-65 D 5
Sapouy ○ BF 202-203 K 4
Sappa Creek ∼ USA 42-43 G 6
Sapphire Mountains ▲ USA 40-41 H 2
Sappho ○ USA 40-41 B 1
Sapporo ○• J 152-153 J 3
Sapri ○ I 100-101 F 4
Šapšaľskij hrebet ▲ RUS 124-125 Q 3
Sapucaí, Rio ∼ BR 72-73 H 6
Sapucaia ○ BR (AMA) 66-67 J 4
Sapucaia ○ BR (MIN) 72-73 J 6
Sapucaia ○ BR (RIO) 72-73 J 7
Sapudi, Pulau ∧ RI 168 B 6
Sapuka-Besar, Pulau ∧ RI 168 D 6
Sapulpa ○ USA 44-45 J 1
Sapulut ○ MAL 160-161 B 10
Saputing Lake ∼ CDN 24-25 d 5
Saqadi ○ SUD 200-201 F 6
Sâqain ∼ Y 132-133 E 5
Sãqiya ○ IRQ 128-129 K 5
Šaqlawa ∼ ET 128-129 L 4
Saqqaq ○ GRØ 28-29 P 1
Saqqãra ∼ ET 194-195 E 3
Saqqara, Pyramids of ∴•• ET
 194-195 E 3
Saqqat al-Harita ∼ KSA 132-133 D 5
Saqqez ∼ IR 128-129 M 4
Saqr ○ Y 132-133 G 6
Šaqrã' ○ KSA 130-131 J 4
Šaqrä' ∼ KSA 132-133 B 3
Ša'rä', aš ∼ KSA 130-131 J 4
Sara ○ BF 202-203 J 4
Sara ○ RI 166-167 G 3
Sara ○ RP 160-161 E 7
Ša'rã', aš ∼ KSA 132-133 B 3
Sara, Col de ▲ RN 198-199 F 2
Saraar, Bannaanka ≃ SP 208-209 G 4
Sãráb ∼ IR 128-129 M 4
Sãráb Dôre ∼ IR 134-135 C 2
Saraburi ○ THA 158-159 F 3

Šaraf al-Ba'l ○ **KSA** 130-131 D 3
Sarafara ○ **SUD** 206-207 K 3
Saraf Doungnoun ○ **TCH** 198-199 J 6
Saraféré ○ **RMM** 202-203 J 2
Sarafgegän ○ **IR** 134-135 D 1
Šarafhäne ○ **IR** 128-129 L 3
Šarafiya, aš- ○ **KSA** 132-133 B 3
Saraguro ○ **EC** 64-65 C 3
Sarah Lake ○ **CDN** 30-31 L 4
Sarahs ○ **IR** 136-137 G 6
Sarai ○ **RUS** 94-95 P 5
Šaräʼï, aš- ○ **KSA** 132-133 A 3
Sarai Gambila ○ **PK** 138-139 C 3
Saraipali ○ **IND** 142-143 C 5
Sarajevo ★ **BIH** 100-101 J 3
Saraj-Ôrdasy ansambli · **KA** 136-137 L 3
Sara-Kawa ○ **RT** 202-203 L 5
Saraktaš ☆ **RUS** 96-97 K 8
Sarala ○ **CI** 202-203 D 5
Saraland ○ **USA** 48-49 D 4
Saramaccarivier ∼ **SME** 62-63 G 3
Saramaguacán ∼ **C** 54-55 G 4
Saranʼ ○ **KA** 124-125 H 4
Saran, Gunung ▲ **RI** 162-163 J 5
Saranda ○ **EAT** 212-213 E 6
Sarandê ☆ **AL** 100-101 H 5
Sarandi ○ **BR** 74-75 D 6
Sarandi, Arroyo ∼ **RA** 76-77 H 6
Sarandi del Yí ○ **ROU** 78-79 M 2
Sarandi de Navarro ○ **ROU** 78-79 L 2
Sarandi Grande ○ **ROU** 78-79 L 2
Šaranga ○ **RUS** 96-97 G 4
Sarangani Bay ≈ 160-161 F 10
Sarangani Island ∼ **RP** 160-161 F 10
Saranglayang, Tanjung ▲ **RI** 162-163 G 6
Särangpur ○ **IND** 138-139 F 8
Sarannoe, ozero ○ **RUS** 120-121 W 6
Saranpaulʼ ○ **RUS** 114-115 P 2
Saransk ○ **RUS** 96-97 D 6
Saranzal ○ **BR** 68-69 D 4
Šarapov Šar, zaliv ○ **RUS** 108-109 M 6
Šarapovy koški, ostrova ∼ **RUS** 108-109 M 6
Sarapul ○ **RUS** 96-97 H 5
Sarapulʼskaja vozvyšennostʼ ▲ **RUS** 96-97 H 5
Šaraqraq ○ **SYR** 128-129 H 4
Sarär ○ **Y** 132-133 G 6
Sarare, Área Indigena ⚿ **BR** 70-71 H 4
Sarare, Rio ∼ **BR** 70-71 H 4
Sarare, Rio ∼ **YV** 60-61 F 4
Sarasota ○ **USA** 48-49 G 6
Sarata ∼ **UA** 102-103 F 4
Saratoga Hot Springs · **USA** 42-43 D 5
Saratoga National Historic Park ∴ **USA** 46-47 M 4
Saratoga Springs ○ **USA** 46-47 M 4
Saratok ○ **MAL** 162-163 J 4
Saratov ○ **RUS** 96-97 E 8
Saratovskoe vodohranilišče < **RUS** 96-97 F 7
Saratovskoye Vodokhranilishche =
Saratovskoe vodohranil. < **RUS** 96-97 F 7
Šaraura, aš- ○ **KSA** 132-133 E 5
Saräván ○ **IR** 134-135 K 5
Saravan ○ **LAO** 158-159 J 3
Sarawak ☐ **MAL** 162-163 J 3
Saray ☆ **TR** 128-129 B 2
Saraya ○ **SN** 202-203 E 3
Saräyän ○ **IR** 134-135 H 2
Sarayköy ☆ **TR** 128-129 C 4
Šarbakty ○ **KA** 124-125 L 5
Sar Bandar ○ **IR** 134-135 C 3
Sarbäz ○ **IR** (SIS) 134-135 J 5
Sarbäz ∼ **IR** 134-135 J 5
Sarbäz, Rüdhäne-ye ∼ **IR** 134-135 J 5
Sarbiše ○ **IR** 134-135 H 2
Šarbität ○ **OM** 132-133 K 5
Šarbität, Ra's ▲ **OM** 132-133 K 5
Sarbulak ○ **VRC** 146-147 J 2
Sarco ○ **RCH** 76-77 B 5
Sarda ∼ **NEP** 144-145 C 6
Sardanga ○ **RUS** 118-119 H 4
Šardara ○ **KA** 136-137 L 4
Šardara, küm ▲ **KA** 136-137 K 4
Šardara sukojmasy < **KA** 136-137 L 4
Sardärshahr ○ **IND** 138-139 E 6
Sardastʼ ○ **IR** (HUZ) 134-135 D 3
Sarde Band ○ **AFG** 138-139 B 3
Sardegna ▯ **I** 100-101 B 4
Sardegna, Mar di ≈ 98-99 L 4
Sardegna, Punta ∼ **I** 100-101 B 4
Sardes ∴ **TR** 128-129 C 3
Sardinas ○ **EC** 64-65 D 2
Sardinata ○ **CO** 60-61 E 3
Sardinia = Sardegna ▯ **I** 100-101 B 4
Sardinia = Sardegna ∼ **I** 100-101 B 4
Sardis Lake ○ **USA** (MS) 48-49 D 2
Sardis Lake ○ **USA** (OK) 44-45 K 2
Šardonemʼ ○ **RUS** 88-89 S 5
Sare, Rumah ○ **MAL** 164-165 D 1
Sarege, Pulau ∼ **RI** 168 D 6
Sarʼein o · **IR** 128-129 N 3
Saré Kali ○ **RG** 202-203 D 4
Sareks nationalpark ⊥ **S** 86-87 H 3
Saré Ndiaye ○ **SN** 202-203 C 3
Sar-e Pol ○ **AFG** 136-137 J 6
Sar-e-Pol, Daryä-ye ∼ **AFG** 136-137 J 6
Sar-e Pol-e Zahäb ○ **IR** 134-135 A 1
Saréyamou ○ **RMM** 196-197 J 6
Sarezckoe, ozero ○ **TJ** 136-137 N 5
Sarfanngua ○ **GRØ** 28-29 O 3
Šarga (GAL) 146-147 M 2
Šarga ○ **MAU** (HÖG) 148-149 J 3
Šargalant ○ **MAU** 146-147 K 2
Sargapur ○ **IND** 140-141 G 2
Sargasso Sea ≈ 4 G 5
Sargent Icefield ⊂ **USA** 20-21 Q 6
Sargento, Bahia ≈ 50-51 C 3
Sargento Ayte Victor Sanabria ○ **RA** 76-77 H 2
Sargents ○ **AUS** 172-173 K 2
Sargodha ○ **PK** 138-139 D 3

Sarguʼ, ozero ○ **RUS** 124-125 L 1
Sarh ∼ **TCH** 206-207 D 4
Sarhäd ∴ **IR** 134-135 J 4
Sarhro, Jbel ▲ **MA** 188-189 H 5
Šarhulsan ○ **MAU** 148-149 G 5
Sári ☆ · **IR** 136-137 H 4
Šari ○ **RUS** 130-131 H 4
Šári, Buhairat < **IRQ** 128-129 L 6
Saria ∼ **GR** 100-101 L 7
Saria ○ **IND** 138-139 H 5
Sariä, Rio ∼ **BR** 66-67 E 6
Sariba Island ∼ **PNG** 183 F 6
Saribi, Tanjung ▲ **RI** 166-167 H 2
Saric ○ **MEX** 50-51 D 2
Sarichef, Cape ▲ **USA** 22-23 O 5
Sarichʼ, Gazirat ∼ **KSA** 132-133 B 3
Šarifa, Gazirat ∼ **KSA** 132-133 B 3
Sariga, Kepulauan ∼ **RI** 166-167 G 3
Sangöl ☆ **TR** 128-129 C 3
Sankamiş ☆ **TR** 128-129 F 3
Sankaya ☆ **TR** 128-129 F 3
Sarikei ○ **MAL** 162-163 J 3
Sarina ○ **AUS** 178-179 K 1
Sariñena ○ **E** 98-99 G 4
Saripai ○ **RI** 164-165 D 4
Sari-i-Parom ○ **PK** 134-135 K 5
Šáriqa, Aš- ○ **UAE** 134-135 F 6
Sariri ○ **PNG** 183 F 5
Sariwon ○ **DVR** 150-151 E 8
Šarjah ○ **RUS** 96-97 D 4
Sark ∼ **GBG** 90-91 F 7
Šarkan ☆ **RUS** 96-97 H 5
Sarkand ○ **KA** 124-125 L 6
Sarkari Tala ○ **IND** 138-139 C 6
Šarkavščyna ○ **BY** 94-95 K 4
Šarkikaraağaç ☆ **TR** 128-129 D 3
Šarkin ○ **KA** 96-97 M 9
Sarkin Kudin ○ **WAN** 204-205 H 4
Šarköy ☆ **TR** 128-129 B 2
Sarlat Ghar ▲ **PK** 134-135 M 4
Sarlat-la-Canéda ○ **F** 90-91 H 7
Šarlauk = Šarlawuk ○ **TM** 136-137 D 5
Šarlawuk = Šarlauk ○ **TM** 136-137 D 5
Šarlyk ☆ **RUS** 96-97 J 7
Šarma ○ **KSA** 130-131 D 3
Sarmanovo ☆ **RUS** 96-97 H 6
Särmäşel Garä ○ **RO** 102-103 D 4
Šarm aš-Šaih ○ · **ET** 194-195 G 4
Sarmette ○ **VAN** 184 II a 3
Sarmi ○ **RI** 166-167 K 2
Sarmiento (CHU) 80 F 2
Sarmiento ○ **RA** (COD) 76-77 E 6
Sarmiento, Monte ▲ **RCH** 80 E 7
Sarmsabun ○ **RUS** 114-115 Q 3
Šarmuhiya ○ **IRQ** 128-129 M 7
Särna ○ **S** 86-87 F 6
Samako ○ **RI** 164-165 G 5
Samia ○ **CDN** 38-39 C 7
Samy ○ **UA** 102-103 E 2
Saröbi ○ **AFG** 138-139 B 2
Sarolangun ○ **RI** 162-163 E 6
Saroma ○ **J** 152-153 K 2
Saroma-ko ○ **J** 152-153 K 2
Šaromy ○ **RUS** 120-121 S 6
Saronikós Kólpos ≈ 100-101 J 6
Sarore ○ **RI** 166-167 L 6
Saros Körfezi ≈ 128-129 B 2
Sarovce ☆ **SK** 92-93 P 4
Sarpinske ozera ○ **RUS** 96-97 D 9
Sarpsborg ☆ **N** 86-87 E 7
Sarqardlit ▲ **GRØ** 28-29 O 2
Šarrär, aş ○ **KSA** 130-131 L 4
Sarre ∼ **F** 90-91 L 7
Sarre, La ○ **CDN** 38-39 D 4
Sarrebourg ○ **F** 90-91 L 7
Sarria ○ **E** 98-99 D 3
Sarro ○ **RMM** 202-203 H 3
Sarstoon River ∼ **BH** 52-53 K 4
Sartang ∼ **RUS** 110-111 T 7
Sartang ∼ **RUS** 110-111 T 6
Sarthe ∼ **F** 90-91 G 8
Sartlan, ozero ○ **RUS** 114-115 P 7
Saru, Kaffin- ○ **WAN** 204-205 G 4
Sarubetsu ○ **J** 152-153 K 3
Sarufutsu ○ **J** 152-153 K 2
Saru-gawa ∼ **J** 152-153 K 3
Saruwaged Range ▲ **PNG** 183 D 4
Sárvár ○ **H** 92-93 O 5
Sarvestan ○ **IR** 134-135 E 4
Šarwain, Ra's ▲ **Y** 132-133 G 6
Saryagaš ☆ **KA** 136-137 L 4
Sary-Bulak ○ **KS** 146-147 B 5
Sarybylak ○ **KA** 136-137 M 3
Saryčevo ☆ **RUS** 122-123 P 4
Sary-Džaz ∼ **KA** 146-147 H 4
Saryesik-Atyrau ⊥ **KA** 124-125 J 6
Saryg-Sep ☆ **RUS** 116-117 G 10
Sary Hobda ∼ **KA** 126-127 M 3
Saryjazinskoe vodohranilišče < **TM** 136-137 H 6
Sarykamysskaja kotlorina ∪ **US** 136-137 E 3
Sarykamysskoe ozero ○ **US** 136-137 E 3
Sarykamysskoye ozero = Sarygamyš kôli ○ **TM** 136-137 E 4
Sarykôl ○ **KA** 124-125 D 2
Sarykopa, köli ○ **KA** 124-125 D 3
Sarykudyk ○ **KA** 96-97 F 9
Sarykulʼ ○ **RUS** 110-111 Y 7
Sarymojyn, köli ○ **KA** 124-125 D 3
Saryozen ∼ **KA** 124-125 K 6
Šaryповo ☆ **RUS** 114-115 U 7
Sarysu ∼ **KA** 124-125 H 5
Sary syganak köli ○ **KA** 96-97 F 9
Sary-Tash ○ **KS** 146-147 D 5
Sary-Torgaj ∼ **KA** 124-125 E 4
Sarzal ○ **KA** 124-125 L 4
Saržo, kuduk ○ **US** 136-137 E 3
Sasa ○ **PNG** 183 D 4
Sasabe ○ **USA** 40-41 J 10

Sasabeneh ○ **ETH** 208-209 F 4
Sasan, Mount ▲ **SOL** 184 I d 3
Sasar, Tanjung ▲ **RI** 168 D 7
Sasarâm ○ **IND** 142-143 D 3
Sasebo ○ **J** 152-153 C 8
Šašgâv, Kôtal-e ▲ **AFG** 138-139 B 3
Saskaf ○ **RUS** 122-123 B 3
Saskatchewan ▯ **CDN** 32-33 Q 4
Saskatchewan, Fort ○ **CDN** 32-33 O 4
Saria ○ **IND** 138-139 G 9
Saskatchewan Landing Provincial Park ⊥ **CDN** 34-35 Q 5
Saskatchewan River ∼ **CDN** 34-35 D 4
Saskatchewan River Crossing ○ **CDN** 32-33 M 6
Saskatoon ○ **CDN** 34-35 C 4
Saskylah ○ **RUS** 110-111 K 4
Saslaya, Cerro ▲ **NIC** 52-53 B 5
Saslaya, Parque Nacional ⊥ **NIC** 52-53 B 5
Sasmik, Cape ▲ **USA** 22-23 H 7
Sasolburg ○ **ZA** 220-221 H 3
Sasoma ○ **IND** 138-139 F 2
Sasovo ○ **RUS** 94-95 R 4
Sassafras Mountain ▲ **USA** 48-49 G 2
Sassandra ☆ **CI** (SAS) 202-203 G 7
Sassandra ∼ **CI** 202-203 G 7
Sässari ☆ · **I** 100-101 B 4
Sassélé ○ **RCA** 206-207 C 6
Sassi ○ **I** 100-101 C 2
Sassie Island ∼ **AUS** 174-175 G 1
Sassnitz ○ **D** 92-93 M 1
Saßnitz = Sassnitz ○ **D** 92-93 M 1
Sassoumbouroum ○ **RN** 198-199 D 6
Sass River ∼ **CDN** 30-31 N 5
Sass Town ○ **LB** 202-203 F 7
Sastre ○ **RA** 76-77 G 6
Sastyg-Hem ○ **RUS** 116-117 G 9
Sâsvad ○ **IND** 138-139 E 10
Sasykköl ○ **KA** 124-125 B 2
Sasykköl, köli ○ **KA** 124-125 M 5
Sasyk ozero ○ **UA** 102-103 H 5
Sasyr ○ **RUS** 110-111 a 7
Sata ○ **J** 152-153 M 4
Satadougou ○ **RMM** 202-203 E 3
Satagai ○ **RUS** 118-119 L 3
Satama-Sokoro ○ **CI** 202-203 H 6
Satama-Sokoura ○ **CI** 202-203 H 6
Sata misaki ▲ **J** 152-153 D 9
Satâna ○ **IND** 138-139 E 9
Sâtâra ○ **IND** 140-141 E 2
Satara ○ **ZA** 220-221 K 2
Satellite Bay ≈ 24-25 N 2
Satéma ○ **RCA** 206-207 E 6
Satengar, Kepulauau ∼ **RI** 168 C 6
Satengar, Pulau ∼ **RI** 168 C 6
Sathing Phra ○ **THA** 158-159 F 7
Satilla River ∼ **USA** 48-49 H 4
Satipo ○ **PE** 64-65 E 7
Satiri ○ **BF** 202-203 H 4
Satiwála ○ **PK** 138-139 D 4
Satka ○ **RUS** 96-97 L 6
Satluj ○ **IND** 138-139 E 4
Satluj ∼ **IND** 138-139 E 4
Satna ○ **IND** 142-143 B 3
Sato ○ **J** 152-153 C 9
Sátoraljaujhely ○ **H** 92-93 Q 4
Satpaev ○ **KA** 124-125 F 4
Sâtpura Range ▲ **IND** 138-139 E 9
Šatra, aš- ☆ **IRQ** 128-129 M 7
Satrokala ○ **RM** 222-223 D 9
Šatrovo ○ **RUS** 114-115 H 6
Satsuma-hantô ∠ **J** 152-153 D 9
Sattahip ○ **THA** 158-159 F 4
Satymangalam ○ **IND** 140-141 G 5
Šatt al-'Arab ∼ **IRQ** 130-131 K 2
Šatt al-Hilla ∼ **IRQ** 128-129 L 6
Sattenapalle ○ **IND** 140-141 J 2
Šatt-e Šur ∼ **IR** 134-135 E 1
Satti ○ **IND** 138-139 F 2
Šâtû, Kôtal-e ▲ **AFG** 134-135 M 1
Sätuimalufilufi ○ **WS** 184 V a 1
Satuk ○ **THA** 158-159 G 3
Satu Mare ○ **RO** 102-103 C 4
Satang ∼ **RUS** 110-111 T 6
Sartène ○ · **F** 98-99 M 4
Satun ○ **THA** 158-159 F 7
Satunan-shotô ∠ **J** 152-153 C 11
Šatura ○ **RUS** 94-95 Q 4
Saty ○ **KA** 146-147 D 4
Satyg-Hem ○ **RUS** 116-117 G 9
Satymangalam ○ **IND** 140-141 G 5
Šaubak ⊙ **JOR** 130-131 D 2
Sauce ○ **RA** 76-77 H 6
Sauce, El ○ **NIC** 52-53 L 5
Sauce Blanco ○ **RA** 78-79 H 5
Sauce Chico, Rio ∼ **RA** 78-79 H 5
Sauce Corto, Arroyo ∼ **RA** 78-79 J 5
Sauces, Los ○ **RCH** 78-79 C 4
Saucier ○ **USA** 48-49 D 4
Saucillo ○ **MEX** 50-51 G 3
Sauda ☆ **N** 86-87 C 7
Saudá', as- ∼ **Y** 132-133 J 5
Saudade ○ **BR** 66-67 E 5
Saudade, Cachoeira de ∼ **BR** 72-73 D 3
Saudade, Serra da ▲ **BR** 72-73 H 5
Saudárkrkur ☆ **IS** 86-87 d 2
Saudavel ○ **BR** 72-73 J 2
Saúde ○ **BR** 68-69 H 7
Saudi Arabia = al-Mamlaka al-'Arabiya as-Sa'ûdiya ■ **KSA** 130-131 D 4
Sawu ○ **RI** 168 E 8
Sauenina ou Papagaio, Rio ∼ **BR** 70-71 H 4
Šauildir ○ **KA** 136-137 L 3
Saujil ○ **RA** 76-77 D 5
Sauk Centre ○ **USA** 42-43 K 3
Sauk City ○ **USA** 46-47 D 4
Saukorem ○ **RI** 166-167 G 2
Sauk Rapids ○ **USA** 42-43 K 3
Saûl ○ **F** 62-63 H 4
Sauldre ∼ **F** 90-91 J 8
Saulieu ○ **F** 90-91 K 8
Saulkrasti ○ **LV** 94-95 J 3
Sault, Rivière du ∼ **CDN** 34-35 O 7
Sault Sainte-Marie ○ **CDN** 34-35 O 7
Sault Sainte Marie ○ **USA** 46-47 G 2
Saum, as- ○ **Y** 132-133 H 5
Saumarez Reef ∼ **AUS** 178-179 M 1
Saumlakki · **RI** 166-167 F 5
Saumur o · **F** 90-91 G 8

Say Tha Ni ○ **LAO** 156-157 C 7
Sayula ○ **MEX** 52-53 C 2
Saunders Ø ∼ **GRØ** 26-27 P 5
Saunders Point ▲ **AUS** 176-177 H 3
Sayula de Alemán ○ **MEX** 52-53 G 3
Saunryi ○ **EAT** 212-213 E 6
Sayward ○ **CDN** 32-33 H 6
Sauqira ○ **OM** 132-133 K 4
Sayyâni, as- ○ **Y** 132-133 D 7
Sauqira Bay ≈ 132-133 K 4
Sauri Hill ▲ **ANG** 204-205 G 3
Šazand ○ **IR** 134-135 C 2
Saurimo ○ **ANG** 216-217 F 4
Sázava ∼ **CZ** 92-93 N 4
Sauriwauwana ○ **GUY** 62-63 E 4
Sazin ○ **PK** 138-139 D 2
Sausalito o · **USA** 40-41 C 7
Sazonovo ○ **RUS** 94-95 O 2
Sausar ○ **IND** 138-139 G 9
Saztöbe ○ **KA** 136-137 M 3
Sausu ○ **PNG** 183 C 3
Sazykulʼ, ozero ○ **RUS** 114-115 J 7
Sautar ○ **ANG** 216-217 E 5
Sbaa ○ **DZ** 188-189 L 6
Sautatá ○ **CO** 60-61 C 4
Sbeitla ○ **TN** 190-191 G 3
Saut Macague ∼ **F** 62-63 H 4
Scaër ○ **F** 90-91 F 7
Sauvage, Lac du ○ **CDN** 30-31 P 3
Scafell Pike ▲ **GB** 90-91 F 4
Sauvolles, Lac ○ **CDN** 38-39 H 2
Scammon Bay ∼ **USA** 20-21 G 6
Sauz, El ○ **MEX** 50-51 F 3
Scammon Bay ○ **USA** 20-21 H 6
Sauzal ○ **RCH** 78-79 C 3
Scamp Hill ▲ **AUS** 176-177 J 2
Sava ∼ **BIH** 100-101 G 2
Scandia ○ **CDN** 32-33 O 6
Sava ∼ **HN** 52-53 L 4
Scandia ○ **USA** 44-45 J 5
Sava ∼ **HR** 100-101 F 2
Scandola, La ∪ · · · **F** 98-99 M 3
Sava ∼ **SLO** 100-101 E 1
Ščara ∼ **BY** 94-95 J 5
Savage ○ **USA** 42-43 E 2
Scarborough ∪ **GB** 90-91 F 4
Savage Cove ○ **CDN** 38-39 Q 3
Scarborough Shoal ∼ **RP** 160-161 B 5
Savage Islands ∼ **CDN** 30-31 Z 3
Ščastʼja, zaliv ○ **RUS** 122-123 J 2
Savage River ○ **AUS** 180-181 H 6
Scawfell Bank ≈ 158-159 J 7
Savaiʼi Island ∼ **WS** 184 V a 1
Scawfell Island ∼ **AUS** 174-175 K 7
Savalou ○ **DY** 202-203 L 6
Sceccai Reba ▲ **ER** 200-201 H 4
Savan ∼ **DY** 202-203 L 6
Ščekino ☆ **RUS** 94-95 P 5
Savane ○ **MOC** 218-219 H 4
Ščéfjabož ○ **RUS** 88-89 Y 3
Savane Bissainthe ○ **RH** 54-55 J 5
Ščéljajur ○ **RUS** 88-89 W 4
Savane Zombi ○ **RH** 54-55 K 5
Ščelkovo ○ **RUS** 94-95 Q 4
Savanna ○ **USA** 46-47 C 4
Ščérbakovo ○ **KA** 124-125 D 2
Savannah ○ **USA** (TN) 48-49 D 2
Seal Island ∼ **AUS** 22-23 R 4
Savannah ○ **USA** (GA) 48-49 H 3
Seal Cove ○ **CDN** 38-39 Q 4
Savannah Downs ○ **AUS** 174-175 F 6
Seale ○ **USA** 48-49 F 3
Savannah River ∼ **USA** 48-49 H 3
Sealhole Lake ○ **CDN** 30-31 U 5
Savannah River Plant x x **USA** 48-49 G 3
Sea Lion Islands ∼ **GB** 78-79 L 7
Savannakhet ○ **LAO** 158-159 H 2
Seal Islands ∼ **USA** 22-23 R 4
Savanna-la-Mar ○ **JA** 54-55 F 5
Seal Reserve · **NAM** 216-217 B 10
Savant Lake ○ **CDN** 34-35 J 5
Seal River ∼ **CDN** 30-31 W 6
Savant Lake ○ **CDN** 34-35 L 5
Sealy ○ **USA** 44-45 J 5
Savanûr ○ **IND** 140-141 F 3
Sea Otter Sound ≈ 32-33 D 4
Savastepe ☆ **TR** 128-129 B 3
Sea Park ○ **ZA** 220-221 K 5
Savate ○ **ANG** 216-217 D 8
Searo ○ **BR** 74-75 D 6
Savatili Bay ≈ 162-163 K 2
Searchlight ○ **USA** 40-41 G 8
Savè ○ **DY** 204-205 E 4
Searchmont ○ **CDN** 34-35 O 7
Säve o · **IN** 136-137 B 7
Searcy ○ **USA** 44-45 M 2
Save ○ **MOC** 218-219 G 5
Seashore Shoal ≈ 162-163 K 2
Save ∼ **ZW** 218-219 G 5
Seaside ○ **USA** 40-41 C 3
Säveni ○ **RO** 102-103 E 4
Seaspray ○ **AUS** 180-181 J 5
Savigliano ○ **I** 100-101 A 2
Seattle ○ **USA** 40-41 C 3
Savina ∼ **RUS** 108-109 F 6
Seaward Kaikoura Range ▲ **NZ** 182 D 5
Savinobor ○ **RUS** 114-115 D 3
Seba ○ **RI** 168 E 8
Savinskij ○ **RUS** 88-89 Q 5
Sébaco ○ **NIC** 52-53 L 5
Savitaipale ○ **FIN** 88-89 J 6
Sebago Lake ○ **USA** 46-47 N 4
Savnik ○ **YU** 100-101 G 3
Sebakor, Teluk ○ **RI** 166-167 G 3
Savoie ∠ **F** 90-91 L 9
Šebalino ○ **RUS** 124-125 O 3
Savo Island ∼ **SOL** 184 I d 3
Sebamban ○ **RI** 164-165 D 5
Savona ○ **CDN** 32-33 K 6
Sebangang Teluk ○ **RI** 162-163 K 6
Savona ○ · **I** 100-101 B 2
Sebangka, Pulau ∼ **RI** 162-163 F 4
Savonlinna o ∼ **FIN** 88-89 K 6
Sebapala ○ **LS** 220-221 H 5
Savoonga ○ **USA** 20-21 C 5
Sebarak ○ **RI** 166-167 G 3
Savory River ○ **AUS** 176-177 F 1
Sebastián Vizcaíno, Bahía de ≈ 50-51 B 3
Savot ○ **US** 136-137 G 4
Sebatik, Pulau ∼ **RI** 164-165 E 1
Savukoski ○ **FIN** 88-89 J 3
Sebauh ○ **MAL** 162-163 K 3
Savusavu ○ **FJI** 184 III b 2
Sebayan, Gunung ▲ **RI** 162-163 J 5
Savusavu Bay ≈ 184 III b 2
Sebes, Pulau ∼ **RI** 162-163 F 7
Savu Sea = Sawu, Laut ≈ **RI** 166-167 A 6
Sebesi, Pulau ∼ **RI** 162-163 E 7
Savute ∼ **RB** 218-219 B 4
Sebež ☆ **RUS** 94-95 L 3
Saw ○ **MYA** 142-143 J 5
Šebinkarahisar ☆ **TR** 128-129 H 2
Sawädiya, as- ○ **Y** 132-133 D 6
Sebino = Lago dʼIseo ○ **I** 100-101 C 2
Sawadori ○ **RI** 166-167 J 2
Sebis ○ **RO** 102-103 C 4
Sawahlunto ○ **RI** 162-163 D 5
Sebjaki ∼ **RUS** 108-109 D 7
Sawai ○ **RI** 166-167 E 3
Sebian-Kjuélʼ ○ **RUS** 110-111 R 7
Sawai Mâdhopur ○ **IND** 138-139 F 7
Sebiat, Gunung ▲ **RI** 162-163 E 6
Sawaleke ○ **FJI** 184 III b 2
Sebol ○ **GCA** 52-53 K 4
Sawang Dan Din ○ **THA** 158-159 G 2
Sebonpopo ○ **RI** 164-165 L 3
Sawäq ○ **KSA** 130-131 E 4
Seboto Point ▲ **RP** 160-161 E 9
Sawara ○ **J** 152-153 K 7
Sebou, Oued ∼ **MA** 188-189 J 3
Sawäri ○ **RI** 128-129 K 5
Sebree ○ **USA** 46-47 E 7
Sawatch Mountains ▲ **USA** 42-43 D 6
Sebring ○ **USA** 48-49 H 6
Sawbill ○ **CDN** 38-39 G 4
Sebta = Ceuta ○ **E** 98-99 E 7
Sawfajjin = Wâdi ∼ **LAR** 192-193 D 2
Sebu, Pulau ∼ **RI** (KSE) 164-165 G 5
Sawfajjin, Wâdi ∼ **LAR** 192-193 P 2
Sebuku, Pulau ∼ **RI** (LAM) 162-163 F 7
Sawi ○ **THA** 158-159 E 5
Sebuku Teluk ○ **RI** 164-165 E 2
Sawia ○ **RI** 166-167 J 3
Sebunino ○ **RUS** 122-123 J 5
Šâwiya, aš- ○ **IRQ** 130-131 J 2
Sebuyau ○ **MAL** 162-163 J 4
Šöit, gora ▲ **RUS** 112-113 R 3
Sebyar ∼ **RI** 166-167 G 2
Sclater ○ **CDN** 34-35 F 5
Sėbys' ∼ **RUS** 88-89 W 4
Scobey ○ **USA** 42-43 E 1
Seča, Cachoeira ∼ **BR** 66-67 K 5
Scone ○ **AUS** 180-181 L 2
Seca, Pampa ⊥ **RA** 78-79 F 3
Scoresby Land · **GRØ** 26-27 n 8
Secang ○ **RI** 168 D 3
Scoresbysund = Ittoqqortoormiit ○ **GRØ** 26-27 p 8
Secca Abú el-cnus ∼ **ER** 200-201 K 5
Scotia ○ **USA** 40-41 B 5
Sechura ○ **PE** 64-65 B 4
Scotia Bay ○ **CDN** 20-21 Y 7
Sechura, Bahía de ≈ 64-65 B 4
Scotia Sea ≈ 6-7 E 14
Sechura, Desierto de ⊥ **PE** 64-65 B 4
Scotstour Lake ○ **CDN** 30-31 M 3
Seco, Rio ∼ **RCH** 78-79 C 3
Scotstown ○ **CDN** 38-39 J 4
Seco de las Peñas, Rio ∼ **RA** 78-79 D 3
Scioto River ∼ **USA** 46-47 G 6
Seco ○ Yaminué, Arroyo ∼ **RA** 78-79 F 6
Scipio ○ **USA** 40-41 D 4
Scott, Cape ▲ **USA** 172-173 J 2
Secos ou do Rombo, Ilheus ∼ **CV** 202-203 B 6
Scott, Cape ▲ **CDN** (BC) 32-33 F 6
Second Mesa ○ **USA** 44-45 B 2
Scott, Cape ▲ **CDN** (NWT) 24-25 O 2
Secretary Island ∼ **NZ** 182 A 6
Scott, Mount ▲ **AUS** 176-177 H 3
Secunderâbâd ○ **IND** 140-141 P 2
Scott Channel ≈ 32-33 F 6
Sécure, Rio ∼ **BOL** 70-71 E 4
Scott City ○ **USA** 42-43 G 6
Seda ∼ **LT** 94-95 H 4
Scott Glacier ⊂ **ARK** 16 G 11
Sedalia ○ **USA** 44-45 L 2
Scott Glacier ⊂ **ARK** 16 E 10
Sedan ○ **AUS** (QLD) 178-179 G 3
Scott Lake ○ **CDN** 30-31 Q 6
Sedan ○ **AUS** (SA) 180-181 G 5
Scott National Historic Site, Fort ∴ **USA** 42-43 K 7
Sedan ○ **F** 90-91 K 7
Scott Point ▲ **AUS** 174-175 D 3
Sedan ○ **USA** 44-45 J 1
Scott Range ▲ **ARK** 16 B 6
Sedanka ○ **RUS** 120-121 S 5
Scott Reef ∼ **AUS** 172-173 F 5
Sedanka Island ∼ **USA** 22-23 N 5
Scottsbluff ○ **USA** 42-43 F 5
Sedano ○ **E** 98-99 F 3
Scotts Bluff National Monument · **USA** 42-43 F 5
Sedati ○ **RI** 168 E 3
Scottsboro ○ **USA** 48-49 E 2
Seddenga, Temple of · **SUD** 200-201 E 2

Scottsburg ○ **USA** 46-47 F 6
Seddon, Kap ▲ **GRØ** 26-27 V 6
Scottsdale ○ **AUS** 180-181 J 6
Seddonville ○ **NZ** 182 C 4
Scottsdale ○ **USA** 40-41 J 9
Sedederna ○ **RUS** 110-111 b 6
Scottsville ○ **USA** 46-47 E 7
Sedeh ○ **IR** 134-135 H 2
Scottville ○ **USA** 46-47 E 4
Sedefnikovo ○ **RUS** 114-115 N 6
Scotty's Junction ○ **USA** 40-41 F 7
Sederberge ▲ **ZA** 220-221 D 6
Scranton ○ **USA** 46-47 L 5
Sedgefield ○ **ZA** 220-221 F 7
Šču'e ○ **RUS** (JAN) 108-109 N 8
Sedgwick ○ **USA** 42-43 J 7
Šču'e ☆ **RUS** (KRG) 114-115 G 7
Sédhiou ○ **SN** 202-203 C 3
Šču'e, ozero ○ **RUS** 114-115 G 7
Sedič ○ **IR** 134-135 H 6
Šču'e Ozero ○ **RUS** 96-97 K 5
Sedič, Rüdhäne-ye ∼ **IR** 134-135 H 6
Ščučij hrebe: ▲ **RUS** 112-113 P 3
Sed'ju ○ **RUS** 88-89 W 5
Ščučinsk ☆ **KA** 124-125 G 2
Sedoa ○ **RI** 164-165 G 4
Ščuč'ja ∼ **RUS** 108-109 M 8
Sedom o · **IL** 130-131 D 2
Ščučyn ○ **BY** 94-95 J 5
Sedona ○ **USA** 40-41 J 8
Ščugor ∼ **RUS** 114-115 E 3
Sedova, pik ▲ **RUS** 108-109 F 5
Scuol/Schuls ○ **CH** 92-93 L 5
Sedova, zaliv ○ **RUS** 108-109 H 4
Seabird Restng Pulau ⊥ · **RI** 166-167 G 3
Sedrata ○ **DZ** 190-191 F 2
Seabra ○ **BR** 72-73 K 2
Sedro Woolley ○ **USA** 40-41 C 1
Seabrook, Lake ○ **AUS** 176-177 E 5
Šeduva ○ · **LT** 94-95 H 4
Seaford ○ **USA** 46-47 L 6
Seebe ○ **CDN** 32-33 N 6
Seaforth ○ **AUS** 174-175 K 7
Seeber ○ **RA** 76-77 G 6
Sea Islands ∼ **USA** 48-49 H 4
Seeheim ○ **NAM** 220-221 C 3
Sea Lake ○ **AUS** 180-181 G 3
Seekaskootch Indian Reserve ⚿ **CDN** 32-33 Q 5
Sea Lion Island ∼ **GB** 78-79 L 7
Seekoegat ○ **ZA** 220-221 F 6
Seemore Downs ○ **AUS** 176-177 H 5
Seekoerivier ∼ **ZA** 220-221 G 5
Sèèr ○ **MAU** 146-147 L 1
Šefaatli ☆ **TR** 128-129 F 3
Sefenhisar ☆ **TR** 128-129 B 3
Séfeto ○ **RMM** 202-203 F 2
Sefidâbe ○ **IR** 134-135 J 3
Sefidan, Rüdhäne-ye ∼ **IR** 134-135 F 3
Sefid Rüd ∼ **IR** 128-129 N 4
Sefophe ○ **RB** 218-219 D 5
Sefrou ○ **MA** 188-189 J 4
Sefton, Mount ▲ **AUS** 176-177 G 4
Segag ○ **ETH** 208-209 F 5
Segala ○ **RMM** 202-203 E 2
Ségala ∼ **DY** 204-205 E 3
Segbwema ○ **WAL** 202-203 E 6
Segen Wenz ∼ **ETH** 208-209 C 6
Segera ○ **EAT** 212-213 G 6
Seget ○ **RI** 166-167 F 2
Segeža ○ **RUS** 88-89 N 5
Seghe ○ **SOL** 184 I c 3
Segian-Kjuélʼ ○ **RUS** 118-119 P 4
Šegmas ○ **RUS** 88-89 U 4
Segnän ○ **AFG** 136-137 M 6
Segoch, Küh-e ▲ **IR** 134-135 G 3
Ségou ○ **RMM** 202-203 G 2
Ségou ○ **RMM** (SÉ) 202-203 G 3
Segovia ○ **CO** 60-61 D 4
Segovia ∼ · · · **E** 98-99 E 4
Segozero ○ **RUS** 88-89 M 5
Segré ○ **F** 90-91 G 8
Segre, el ∼ **E** 98-99 H 4
Seguam Island ∼ **USA** 22-23 K 6
Seguam Pass ≈ 22-23 K 6
Ségué ○ **RMM** 202-203 J 3
Seguedine ○ **RN** 198-199 F 2
Séguéla ☆ **CI** 202-203 G 6
Séguéla ○ **RMM** 202-203 G 3
Séguéla ○ **RMM** 202-203 G 3
Séguénéga ○ **BF** 202-203 K 3
Seguin ○ **USA** 44-45 J 5
Segula Island ∼ **USA** 22-23 H 6
Segunda, Rio ∼ **RA** 76-77 F 6
Segura ○ **RA** 98-99 D 5
Segura, Sierra de ▲ **E** 98-99 F 5
Seguro ○ **BR** 68-69 G 2
Sehän ○ **PK** 138-139 B 4
Sehesteds Fjord ≈ 28-29 T 5
Sehithwa ○ **RB** 218-219 B 5
Sehnkwehn River ∼ **LB** 202-203 F 6
Seho, Pulau ∼ **RI** 166-167 G 3
Sehonghong ○ **LS** 220-221 J 4
Sehore ○ **IND** 138-139 F 8
Sehulea ○ **PNG** 183 F 5
Sehwän ○ · **PK** 134-135 M 5
Seia ○ **P** 98-99 D 4
Seibert ○ **USA** 42-43 F 6
Seibo, El ○ **DOM** 54-55 L 5
Seigals Creek ○ **AUS** 174-175 D 5
Šeih 'Ali ○ **AFG** 138-139 B 2
Seikan Tunnel ↔ **J** 152-153 J 4
Šeikpyu ○ **MYA** 142-143 J 5
Seila ∼ **N** 86-87 L 1
Seiland ∼ **N** 86-87 L 1
Seiling ○ **USA** 44-45 H 1
Seille ∼ **F** 90-91 K 8
Seinäjoki ○ **FIN** 88-89 G 5
Seine ∼ **F** 90-91 H 7
Seine, Baie de la ≈ 90-91 G 7
Seine Bank ≈ 188-189 D 4
Seinma ○ **RI** 166-167 K 4
Seira, Pulau ∼ **RI** 166-167 F 5
Seis de Julho, Cachoeira ∼ **BR** 66-67 F 7
Seival ○ **BR** 74-75 D 8
Šeja ○ **RUS** 118-119 H 4
Sêjahä ○ **RUS** (JAN) 108-109 P 6
Sêjahä ∼ **RUS** 108-109 N 6
Sêjahä ∼ **RUS** 108-109 O 7
Sejaka ○ **RI** 164-165 E 5
Sejenane ○ **TN** 190-191 G 2
Sejm ∼ **RUS** 102-103 K 2
Sejm ∼ **UA** 102-103 H 2
Sejmčan ○ **RUS** 120-121 P 2
Sejmčan ∼ **RUS** 120-121 O 2
Sejmžän ○ **RUS** 118-119 N 7
Sejmkan ∼ **RUS** 120-121 N 3
Sejorong ○ **RI** 168 C 7
Seka ○ **ETH** 208-209 C 5
Seka Banza ○ **ZRE** 210-211 D 4
Sekak ○ **RI** 166-167 G 2

Spokane o • USA 40-41 F 2
Spokane House ∴ USA 40-41 F 2
Spokane Indian Reservation ✗ USA 40-41 F 2
Spokane River ~ USA 40-41 F 2
Špola o UA 102-103 G 3
Spoleto o • I 100-101 D 3
Spooner o USA 46-47 C 3
Spoon River ~ USA 46-47 C 5
Sporades = Sporádes, Notioi ⌒ GR 100-101 K 6
Sporádes, Vóries ⌣ GR 100-101 J 5
Sporavskoe, vozero ⊖ BY 94-95 J 5
Spornoe o RUS 120-121 O 2
Sporyj Navolok, mys ▲ RUS 108-109 N 3
Spotted House o USA 42-43 E 3
Spotted Island ⌒ CDN (NFL) 38-39 R 2
Spotted Island ⌒ CDN (NFL) 38-39 R 2
Sprague o USA 40-41 F 2
Sprague River ~ USA 40-41 D 4
Spray o USA 40-41 E 3
Spree ~ D 92-93 M 2
Sprenger, Lake ⊖ AUS 176-177 H 2
Sprengisandur ▲ IS 86-87 d 2
Springbok o ZA 220-221 C 4
Spring Creek ~ AUS 174-175 H 6
Spring Creek ~ AUS 178-179 F 2
Springdale o CDN 38-39 Q 4
Springdale o USA (AR) 44-45 K 1
Springdale o USA (WA) 40-41 F 1
Springer o USA 44-45 E 1
Springerville o USA 44-45 C 2
Springfield o USA (CO) 44-45 F 1
Springfield o USA (IL) 46-47 D 6
Springfield o USA (MO) 44-45 L 1
Springfield o USA (OH) 46-47 G 6
Springfield o USA (OR) 40-41 C 3
Springfield o USA (TN) 48-49 E 1
Springfontein o ZA 220-221 G 5
Spring Garden o GUY 62-63 E 2
Springhill o CDN 38-39 M 6
Springhill o USA 44-45 L 3
Spring Hill o USA 48-49 G 5
Springlake o USA 44-45 F 2
Spring Lake o USA 48-49 J 2
Spring Mill State Park • USA 46-47 E 6
Springrale o AUS 178-179 F 2
Springs o ZA 220-221 J 3
Springs Junction o NZ 182 D 5
Springsure o AUS 178-179 K 3
Springvale o AUS 172-173 H 4
Spring Vale o AUS 174-175 D 6
Springvale Homestead o • AUS 172-173 L 3
Spring Valley o ZA 220-221 H 6
Springview o USA 42-43 H 4
Springville o USA (AL) 48-49 E 3
Springville o USA (NY) 46-47 J 4
Springville o USA (UT) 40-41 J 5
Springwater o CDN 32-33 Q 6
Sprova o N 86-87 E 4
Sprucedale o CDN 38-39 E 6
Spruce Grove o CDN 32-33 O 5
Spruce Home o CDN 34-35 D 4
Spruce Island ⌒ USA 22-23 U 4
Spruce Knob ▲ USA 46-47 J 6
Spruce Mountain ▲ USA 40-41 G 5
Spruce Pine o USA 48-49 G 2
Spruce River ~ CDN 30-31 V 6
Spruce Woods Forest Reserve ⊥ CDN 34-35 G 6
Spruce Woods Provincial Park ⊥ CDN 34-35 G 6
Spur o USA 44-45 G 3
Spurn Head ▲ GB 90-91 H 5
Squamish o CDN 32-33 J 7
Square Hill ▲ AUS 176-177 H 3
Square Ilands o CDN 38-39 R 2
Squamish River ~ CDN 32-33 J 6
Squilax o CDN 32-33 L 6
Squillace, Golfo di ≈ 100-101 F 5
Squires, Mount ▲ AUS 176-177 J 3
Squirrel River ~ USA 20-21 K 3
Sragen o RI 168 D 3
Srbica o YU 100-101 H 3
Srbobran o YU 100-101 G 2
Srebărna, Naroden Park ⊥ ••• BG 102-103 E 5
Sredec o BG 102-103 E 6
Srednij hrebet ▲ RUS 120-121 R 7
Srednebelaja o RUS 122-123 C 3
Srednee Kujto, ozero ⊖ RUS 88-89 L 4
Srednekan, Ust'- o RUS 120-121 P 2
Srednekolymsk o RUS 110-111 d 6
Sredneobskaja nizmennost' ⌣ RUS 114-115 L 3
Sredne russkaja vozvyšennost' ▲ RUS 94-95 Q 5
Srednij, ostrov ⌒ RUS 108-109 Y 3
Srednij, proliv ≈ 112-113 P 2
Srednij, zaliv o RUS 120-121 S 3
Srednij Ikorec o RUS 102-103 L 2
Srednij Kalar o RUS 118-119 H 8
Srednij Mamakan ~ RUS 118-119 G 7
Srednij Ural ▲ RUS 114-115 E 5
Srednij Viljujkan ~ RUS 116-117 N 3
Sredny Ural = Srednij Ural ▲ RUS 114-115 E 5
Srednjaja ~ RUS 110-111 K 3
Srednjaja, gora ▲ RUS 108-109 a 4
Srednjaja Kočoma ~ RUS 116-117 N 4
Srednjaja Mokla ~ RUS 118-119 J 8
Srednjaja Olëkma o RUS 118-119 K 8
Srednogorie = Pirdop + Zlatica o BG 102-103 D 6
Šrenk ~ RUS 108-109 Z 4
Srê Noy o K 158-159 H 4
Srê Sbov o K 158-159 J 4
Sretensk ☆ RUS 118-119 H 9
Sribne o UA 102-103 H 2
Sribordi o BD 142-143 F 3
Sri Dungargarh o IND 138-139 E 5
Srikākulam o IND 142-143 C 6
Sri Kālahasti o • IND 140-141 H 4
Sri Lanka ■ CL 140-141 J 6
Srinagar ☆ • IND 138-139 E 2
Srinakarin National Park ⊥ • THA 158-159 E 3
Srinakarin Reservoir < THA 158-159 E 3
Sringeri o IND 140-141 F 4
Sriniväspur o IND 140-141 H 4
Sriparumbudur o IND 140-141 H 4
Srirämapura o IND 140-141 G 4
Srirämpur o IND 138-139 E 10
Srirangam o • IND 140-141 H 5
Srirangapatnam o • IND 140-141 G 4
Srirangaräjupuram o IND 140-141 H 3
Srisailam o IND 140-141 H 2
Sri Toi o PK 138-139 B 4
Srivaikuntam o IND 140-141 G 6
Srivardhan o IND 138-139 D 10
Srivilliputtür o • IND 140-141 G 6
Środa Wielkopolska o PL 92-93 O 2
Srostki o RUS 124-125 O 2
Srungavarapukota o IND 142-143 C 6
ş-Şawāb, Wādī ~ SYR 128-129 J 5
s-Sibū', Wādi ∴ • ET 194-195 F 6
Staaten River ~ AUS 174-175 G 5
Staaten River National Park ⊥ AUS 174-175 G 5
Stabbursdalen nasjonalpark ⊥ N 86-87 M 1
Stabkirche Urnes ••• N 86-87 C 6
Stackpool o CDN 38-39 D 5
Stack Skerry ⌒ GB 90-91 E 2
Stade o • D 92-93 K 2
Staduhino o RUS 112-113 O 3
Stafford ☆ GB 90-91 F 5
Stahanov = Kadijivka o UA 102-103 L 3
Staines, Península ⌣ RCH 80 D 5
Staked Plain = Llano Estacado ⌣ USA 44-45 F 3
Stalingrad = Zarizyn ☆ • RUS 96-97 D 9
Stamberg, gora ▲ RUS 122-123 K 5
Stamford o AUS 178-179 G 1
Stamford o GB 90-91 G 5
Stamford o USA 46-47 M 5
Stamford, Lake < USA 44-45 H 3
Stampriet o NAM 220-221 D 2
Stamps o USA 44-45 L 3
Stamsund o N 86-87 F 2
Stanberry o USA 42-43 K 5
Stancionno-Ojašinskij o RUS 114-115 R 7
Standerton o ZA 220-221 J 3
Standing Rock Indian Reservation ✗ USA 42-43 G 3
Standish o USA 46-47 G 3
Stanford o USA (KY) 46-47 F 7
Stanford o USA (MT) 40-41 J 2
Stang, Cape ▲ CDN 24-25 U 5
Stanger o ZA 220-221 K 4
Stanhope o AUS 180-181 H 4
Stanhope o GB 90-91 F 4
Staniard Creek o BS 54-55 G 2
stanica Bagaevskaja o RUS 102-103 M 4
Staniel Cay Beach ∸ • BS 54-55 G 2
Stanislaus River ~ USA 40-41 D 6
Stanke Dimitrov = Dupnica o BG 102-103 C 6
Stanley o AUS 180-181 H 6
Stanley ☆ GB 78-79 M 6
Stanley o USA (ID) 40-41 G 3
Stanley o USA (ND) 42-43 F 1
Stanley, Mount ▲ ZRE 212-213 B 3
Stanley, Port o CDN 38-39 D 7
Stanley Mission o CDN 34-35 D 3
Stanley Pool ⊖ ZRE 210-211 E 6
Stanley Reservoir ⊖ IND 140-141 G 5
Stanleyville = Kisangani ☆ ZRE 210-211 K 3
Stanmore o ZW 218-219 E 5
Stanovik, hrebet ▲ RUS 118-119 F 11
Stanovoe köli ⊖ KA 124-125 F 1
Stanovoe nagor'e ▲ RUS 118-119 E 7
Stanovoj hrebet ▲ RUS 118-119 L 7
Stanovoye Nagor'ye = Stanovoe nagor'e ▲ RUS 118-119 E 7
Stanovoy Khrebet = Stanovoj hrebet ▲ RUS 118-119 L 7
Stansmore Range ▲ AUS 172-173 H 6
Stanthorpe o AUS 178-179 L 5
Stanton o USA (ND) 42-43 G 2
Stanton o USA (TX) 44-45 G 3
Stanwell o AUS 178-179 L 2
Stanwell Fletcher Lake ⊖ CDN 24-25 Y 4
Stanwix National Monument, Fort ∴ USA 46-47 L 4
Stanwood o USA 40-41 C 1
Stanyčno-Luhans'ke o UA 102-103 L 3
Stapleford o ZW 218-219 G 4
Stapleton o USA 42-43 G 5
Stapylton Bay ≈ 24-25 O 6
Staraja Kulatka ☆ RUS 96-97 E 7
Staraja Majna ☆ RUS 96-97 F 6
Staraja Poltavka ☆ RUS 96-97 E 8
Staraja Russa ☆ RUS 94-95 M 3
Staraja Toropa o RUS 94-95 M 3
Stará Ľubovňa o SK 92-93 Q 4
Staravina o MK 100-101 H 4
Stara Zagora o BG 102-103 D 6
Starbuck o USA 42-43 K 3
Starbuck Island ⌒ 13 M 3
Star City o USA 44-45 M 3
Starcke National Park ⊥ AUS 174-175 H 4
Stargard Szczeciński o PL 92-93 N 2
Starica o RUS (AST) 96-97 D 9
Starica o RUS (TVR) 94-95 O 3
Starigrad-Paklenica o HR 100-101 E 2
Starke o USA 48-49 G 5
Stark Lake ⊖ CDN 30-31 O 4
Starkville o USA 48-49 D 3
Stamberg o D 92-93 L 4
Stamberger See ⊖ D 92-93 L 5
Starobaltačevo ☆ RUS 96-97 J 5
Starobeševe o UA 102-103 L 4
Starobil's'k o UA 102-103 L 3
Starokostjantyniv ☆ UA 102-103 E 3
Starominskaja o RUS 102-103 L 4
Staro Orjahovo o BG 102-103 E 6
Staroščerbinovskaja o RUS 102-103 L 4
Starosubhangulovo o RUS 96-97 K 7
Starting Point to Baliem Valley ⊥ •• RI 166-167 K 4
Start Point ▲ GB 90-91 F 6
Start Point to Torajaland ⊥ •• RI 164-165 G 5
Staryi Oskol o RUS 102-103 K 2
Staryja Darohi o BY 94-95 L 5
State College o USA 46-47 K 5
State Line o USA 48-49 D 4
Staten Island ⌒ USA 46-47 L 5
Statesboro o USA 48-49 H 3
Statesville o USA 48-49 H 2
Station Nord o GRØ 26-27 r 3
Statue of Liberty ••• USA 46-47 M 5
Stauing Alper ▲ GRØ 26-27 n 7
Staunton o USA 46-47 J 6
Stavanger ☆ • N 86-87 B 7
Stave Lake ⊖ CDN 32-33 J 7
Stavropol' ☆ RUS 102-103 M 5
Stavropol'skij kraj □ RUS 126-127 E 5
Stawell o • AUS 180-181 G 4
Steamboat o USA 40-41 C 4
Steamboat Springs o USA 42-43 D 5
Stebbins o USA 20-21 J 5
Steele, Fort o CDN 32-33 N 7
Steele, Mount ▲ CDN 20-21 U 6
Steele Island ⌒ ARK 16 F 30
Steelpoortrivier ~ ZA 220-221 J 2
Steenkampsberge ▲ ZA 220-221 J 2
Steen River ~ CDN 30-31 L 6
Steensby Gletscher ⊂ GRØ 26-27 Y 3
Steensby Inlet ≈ 24-25 h 5
Steensby Land ∸ GRØ 26-27 P 5
Steensby Peninsula ⌣ CDN 24-25 d 4
Steens Mountain ▲ USA 40-41 E 4
Steenstrup Gletscher ⊂ GRØ 26-27 V 6
Steenwijk o NL 92-93 J 2
Steepbank River ~ CDN 32-33 P 3
Steep Cape ▲ USA 22-23 U 3
Steephill Lake ⊖ CDN 34-35 E 3
Steep Point ▲ AUS 176-177 B 3
Steeprock o CDN 34-35 G 5
Steese Highway II USA 20-21 R 4
Stefansson Island ⌒ CDN 24-25 T 4
Steffen, Cerro ▲ RA 80 E 2
Ştei o RO 102-103 C 4
Steiermark □ A 92-93 N 5
Steilloopsbrug o ZA 218-219 E 6
Steilrand o ZA 220-221 K 3
Steilrandberge ▲ NAM 216-217 B 8
Stein am Rhein o •• CH 92-93 K 5
Steinbach o CDN 34-35 H 6
Steine o N 86-87 G 2
Steinen, Rio ~ BR 70-71 K 3
Steinhausen o NAM 216-217 E 10
Steinkjer ☆ N 86-87 E 4
Steinkopf o ZA 220-221 C 4
Steinsland o N 86-87 H 2
Stella o ZA 220-221 G 3
Stellarton o CDN 38-39 N 6
Stellenbosch o • ZA 220-221 D 6
Stellera, gora ▲ RUS 120-121 W 6
Stèlvio, Parco Nazionale d. = Nationalpark Stilfser Joch ⊥ I 100-101 C 1
Stendal o • D 92-93 L 2
Steneby o S 86-87 F 7
Stenen o CDN 34-35 E 5
Stenón Elafonissou ≈ 100-101 J 6
Stenón Kásu ≈ 100-101 L 7
Stenón Kimolou Sifnou ≈ 100-101 K 6
Stenón Kithéron ≈ 100-101 J 6
Stenón Kithnou ≈ 100-101 K 6
Stenón Serifou ≈ 100-101 K 6
Stenón Sifnou ≈ 100-101 K 6
Stenungsund ☆ S 86-87 E 7
Stepanakert = Khankendi ☆ AZ 128-129 M 3
Stepanavan o AR 128-129 L 2
Stepan Razin o AZ 128-129 O 2
Stephanie Wildlife Reserve ⊥ ETH 208-209 C 6
Stephan Strait ≈ 183 C 3
Stephen o USA 42-43 J 1
Stephens o USA 44-45 L 3
Stephens, Cape ▲ NZ 182 D 4
Stephens Creek ~ AUS 180-181 F 2
Stephens Island ⌒ CDN 32-33 E 4
Stephenson Ø ⌒ GRØ 26-27 a 2
Stephens Passage ≈ 32-33 C 2
Stephenville o CDN 38-39 P 4
Stephenville o USA 44-45 H 3
Stephenville Crossing o CDN 38-39 P 4
Stepnoe o RUS (CEL) 96-97 M 6
Stepnoe ☆ RUS (SAR) 96-97 E 8
Stepovak Bay ≈ 22-23 R 5
Steppe, The = Kazahskij melkosopočnik ∸ KA 124-125 F 3
Sterkfonteindam < ZA 220-221 J 4
Sterkspruit o ZA 220-221 H 5
Sterkstroom o ZA 220-221 H 5
Sterlibaševo ☆ RUS 96-97 J 7
Sterling o USA (CO) 42-43 F 5
Sterling o USA (KS) 42-43 H 6
Sterling o USA (ND) 42-43 G 2
Sterling o ZA 220-221 E 5
Sterling City o USA 44-45 G 4
Sterling Heights o USA 46-47 G 4
Sterling Highway II USA 22-23 V 3
Sterling Landing o USA 20-21 N 5
Sterlitamak ☆ RUS 96-97 J 7
Stérnes o GR 100-101 K 7
Steroh o Y 132-133 H 7
Stettin Bay ≈ 183 F 3
Stettiner Haff ⊖ D 92-93 N 2
Stettler o CDN 32-33 O 5
Steubenville o USA 46-47 H 5
Stevenage o GB 90-91 G 6
Stevenson o USA 40-41 D 3
Stevenson Creek ~ AUS 178-179 C 4
Stevenson Lake ⊖ CDN 34-35 J 4
Stevensons Peak ▲ AUS 176-177 L 2
Stevens Pass ▲ USA 40-41 D 2
Stevens Point o USA 46-47 D 3
Stevens Village o USA 20-21 Q 3
Stevensville o USA 40-41 G 2
Stewart o CDN 32-33 F 4
Stewart o USA 42-43 K 3
Stewart, Cape ▲ AUS 174-175 C 2
Stewart, Isla ⌒ RCH 80 E 7
Stewart, Monte ▲ RCH 80 E 7
Stewart, Mount ▲ AUS 174-175 H 7
Stewart, Mount ▲ CDN 20-21 V 5
Stewart Crossing o CDN 20-21 W 5
Stewart Island ⌒ NZ 182 A 7
Stewart Islands ⌒ SOL 184 I f 3
Stewart Lake ⊖ CDN 30-31 Z 2
Stewart Plateau ▲ CDN 20-21 W 4
Stewart River ~ CDN 20-21 V 5
Stewart Valley o CDN 34-35 C 5
Stewartville o USA 42-43 L 4
Steynsburg o ZA 220-221 G 5
Steynsrus o ZA 220-221 H 3
Steyr o • A 92-93 N 4
Steytlerville o ZA 220-221 G 6
Stickney Corner o USA 46-47 O 3
Stiegler's Gorge • EAT 214-215 K 4
Stigler o USA 44-45 K 2
Stikine-Leconte Wilderness ⊥ • USA 32-33 D 3
Stikine Plateau ▲ CDN 32-33 D 2
Stikine Ranges ▲ CDN 20-21 Z 7
Stikine River ~ CDN 32-33 E 3
Stikine Strait ≈ 32-33 D 3
Stilbaai-Wes o ZA 220-221 E 7
Stile o DZ 190-191 E 3
Stilfontein o ZA 220-221 H 3
Stilfser Joch = Passo dello Stèlvio ▲ I 100-101 C 1
Stillwater o USA (MN) 42-43 L 3
Stillwater o USA (OK) 44-45 J 1
Stillwater River ~ USA 42-43 C 3
Stilo o I 100-101 F 5
Stilo, Punta ▲ I 100-101 F 5
Stinear Nunataks ▲ ARK 16 F 7
Stinnett o USA 44-45 G 2
Stintino o I 100-101 B 4
Štip o MK 100-101 J 4
Stirling o AUS (NT) 178-179 B 1
Stirling o AUS (QLD) 174-175 F 5
Stirling o CDN 38-39 F 6
Stirling o • GB 90-91 F 3
Stirling Creek ~ AUS 172-173 J 4
Stirling North o AUS 180-181 D 2
Stirling Range National Park ⊥ AUS 176-177 D 7
Stjørdalshalsen o N 86-87 E 5
St. Kitts = Saint Christopher Island ⌒ KAN 56 D 3
Stockach o D 92-93 K 5
Stockbridge o USA 48-49 F 3
Stockbridge Indian Reservation ✗ USA 46-47 D 3
Stockdale o USA 44-45 J 5
Stockerau o A 92-93 O 4
Stockholm o CDN 34-35 E 5
Stockholm ☆ •• S 86-87 J 7
Stockman's Hall of Fame • AUS 178-179 H 2
Stockport o AUS 178-179 E 2
Stockport o GB 90-91 F 5
Stockton o USA (CA) 40-41 D 7
Stockton o USA (FL) 48-49 G 4
Stockton o USA (IL) 46-47 C 4
Stockton o USA (KS) 42-43 H 6
Stockton o USA (MO) 44-45 L 1
Stockton Island ⌒ USA 46-47 C 2
Stockton Islands ⌒ USA 20-21 R 1
Stockton Lake ⊖ USA 44-45 L 1
Stockton Plateau ▲ USA 44-45 F 4
Stockville o USA 42-43 G 5
Stöde o S 86-87 H 5
Stœng Trêng o K 158-159 H 4
Stoffberg o ZA 220-221 J 2
Stohid ~ UA 102-103 D 2
Stojba o RUS 122-123 D 2
Stokan, gora ▲ RUS 122-123 M 6
Stoke-on-Trent o GB 90-91 F 5
Stokes, Bahía ≈ 80 D 7
Stokes Point ▲ AUS 180-181 G 6
Stokes Range ▲ AUS 172-173 K 3
Stokkvågen o N 86-87 F 3
Stokmarknes o N 86-87 G 2
Stolac o BIH 100-101 F 3
Stolbovaja ~ RUS 116-117 E 4
Stolbovoe, ozero ⊖ RUS 120-121 U 5
Stolbovoj, mys ▲ RUS 120-121 U 5
Stolbovoj, ostrov ⌒ RUS 110-111 V 2
Stolby o RUS 110-111 U 6
Stolby, zapovednik ⊥ RUS 116-117 F 8
Stole, Mountain ▲ PNG 183 A 3
Stolin o BY 94-95 K 6
Stompneuspunt ▲ ZA 220-221 C 6
Ston o HR 100-101 F 3
Stone Forest ••• VRC 156-157 C 4
Stonehaven o GB 90-91 F 3
Stonehenge o AUS 178-179 G 3
Stonehenge ••• GB 90-91 G 6
Stone Indian Reserve ✗ CDN 32-33 J 5
Stonepynten ▲ N 84-85 O 4
Stone Rondavel • NAM 220-221 D 3
Stones River National Battlefield ∴ • USA 48-49 E 2
Stonewall o CDN 34-35 H 5
Stoney Point ▲ AUS 178-179 F 4
Stonington o ARK 16 G 30
Stonington o USA 46-47 O 3
Stony, Pointe ▲ CDN 36-37 P 5
Stony Creek o USA 46-47 K 7
Stony Creek Indian Reserve ✗ CDN 32-33 H 5
Stony Indian Reserve ✗ CDN 32-33 N 6
Stony Island ⌒ CDN 38-39 R 2
Stony Lake ⊖ CDN 30-31 U 6
Stony Point ▲ CDN 34-35 H 5
Stony Rapids o CDN 30-31 R 6
Stony River o USA 20-21 M 6
Stony River ~ USA 20-21 M 6
Stooping River ~ CDN 34-35 P 5
Stopem Blockem Range ▲ AUS 174-175 H 6
Storå ~ DK 86-87 D 8
Stora Bläsjön ⊖ S 86-87 G 4
Stora Lulevatten ⊖ S 86-87 J 3
Stora Sjöfallets nationalpark ⊥ •• S 86-87 H 3
Storavan ⊖ S 86-87 J 4
Storby o FIN 88-89 E 6
Stord ⌒ N 86-87 B 7
Store Bælt ≈ DK 86-87 E 9
Store Hellefiskebanke ≃ 28-29 N 3
Store Koldewey ⌒ GRØ 26-27 q 5
Støren ☆ N 86-87 E 5
Store Sotra ⌒ N 86-87 B 6
Storfjordbanken ≃ 84-85 M 4
Storfjorden ≈ 84-85 L 4
Storfjordrenna ≃ 84-85 K 4
Storfors ☆ S 86-87 G 7
Storforsen ~ •• S 86-87 K 4
Storforshei o N 86-87 G 3
Storis Passage ≈ 24-25 W 6
Storjord o N 86-87 G 3
Storkerson, Cape ▲ CDN 24-25 T 4
Storkerson Bay ≈ 24-25 J 4
Storkerson Peninsula ⌣ CDN 24-25 S 4
Storlien o S 86-87 F 5
Storm Bay ≈ 180-181 J 7
Stormberg o ZA 220-221 H 5
Stormberg ▲ ZA 220-221 H 5
Storm Lake o USA 42-43 K 4
Stormrivier o ZA 220-221 F 6
Stormsvlei o ZA 220-221 E 7
Stornoway o CDN 38-39 J 6
Stornoway o GB 90-91 D 2
Stør Ø ⌒ GRØ 26-27 m 8
Storø ⌒ GRØ 28-29 X 3
Storøen ⌒ GRØ 26-27 q 4
Storøya ⌒ N 84-85 Q 2
Storož ~ RUS 120-121 T 6
Storoževoj, mys ▲ RUS 120-121 S 3
Storoževsk o RUS 88-89 W 5
Storsätern o S 86-87 F 5
Storsjö o S 86-87 F 5
Storsjøen ~ N 86-87 E 6
Storsjön ⊖ S 86-87 G 5
Storsteinhalvøya ⌣ N 84-85 L 2
Storstrømmen ≈ 26-27 o 5
Stortoppen ▲ S 86-87 H 3
Storuman o S (AC) 86-87 H 4
Storuman ⊖ S (AC) 86-87 H 4
Storvik o S 86-87 H 6
Story City o USA 42-43 L 4
Stöttingfjället ▲ S 86-87 H 4
Stoughton o CDN 34-35 E 6
Stoughton o USA 46-47 D 4
Stoŭng o K 158-159 H 4
Stout Lake ⊖ CDN 34-35 J 4
Strabane o GB 90-91 D 4
Strahan o AUS 180-181 H 7
Straight Lake ⊖ CDN 34-35 N 4
Strait of Malacca = Melaka, Selat ≈ RI 162-163 C 2
Strakonice o CZ 92-93 M 4
Strakonitz = Strakonice o CZ 92-93 M 4
Stralki o BY 94-95 L 4
Stralsund o • D 92-93 M 1
Strand o ZA 220-221 D 7
Strandfontein o ZA (CAP) 220-221 D 5
Strandfontein o ZA (CAP) 220-221 D 7
Strangford o • GB 90-91 E 4
Stranraer o GB 90-91 E 4
Strasbourg o CDN 34-35 D 5
Strasbourg ☆ ••• F 90-91 L 7
Strasburg o USA (CO) 42-43 E 6
Strasburg o USA (ND) 42-43 G 2
Stratford o CDN 46-47 H 4
Stratford o NZ 182 E 3
Stratford o USA (CA) 40-41 E 7
Stratford o USA (TX) 44-45 F 1
Stratford-upon-Avon o • GB 90-91 G 5
Strathburn o AUS 174-175 G 4
Strathcoma Provincial Park ⊥ CDN 32-33 H 7
Strathcona Sound ≈ 24-25 d 4
Strathfillan o AUS 178-179 G 2
Strathgordon o AUS (QLD) 174-175 G 4
Strathgordon o AUS (TAS) 180-181 J 7
Strathhaven o AUS 174-175 G 4
Strathleven o AUS 174-175 G 4
Strathmore o AUS (QLD) 174-175 J 7
Strathmore o AUS (QLD) 174-175 G 5
Strathmore o CDN 32-33 O 6
Strathnaver o CDN 32-33 J 5
Strathroy o CDN 38-39 D 7
Stratóni o GR 100-101 J 4
Stratton o USA (CO) 42-43 F 6
Stratton o USA (ME) 46-47 N 3
Stratton Mountain ▲ USA 46-47 M 4
Straubing o D 92-93 M 4
Stravropol'-na-Volgi ☆ RUS 96-97 F 7
Strawberry, Cape ▲ CDN 36-37 U 7
Strawberry Mountain ▲ USA 40-41 E 3
Strawberry Reservoir < USA 40-41 J 5
Strawberry River ~ USA 40-41 J 5
Strawn o USA 44-45 H 3
Streaky Bay ≈ 180-181 C 2
Streaky Bay o AUS 180-181 C 2
Streatfield Lake ⊖ CDN 34-35 O 4
Streatham o AUS 180-181 G 4
Streator o USA 46-47 D 5
Street o GB 90-91 F 6
Strehaia o RO 102-103 C 5
Streich Mound ▲ AUS 176-177 G 5
Strelka o RUS (KRN) 116-117 F 6
Strelka o RUS (MAG) 120-121 P 3
Strelka-Čunja o RUS 116-117 L 5
Strelley o AUS 172-173 D 6
Strelna o RUS (MUR) 88-89 P 3
Strelna ~ RUS 88-89 P 3
Strenči o LV 94-95 J 3
Stresa o • I 100-101 B 2
Stretch Range ▲ AUS 172-173 H 6
Strevell o USA 40-41 H 4
Streymoy ⌒ FR 90-91 D 1
Strezelecki Track • AUS 178-179 E 6
Streževoj o RUS 114-115 O 4
Strickland River ~ PNG 183 B 3
Striding River ~ CDN 30-31 S 5
Strindberg Land ∸ GRØ 26-27 n 6
Strizament, gora ▲ RUS 126-127 E 5
Strobel, Lago ⊖ RA 80 E 4
Stroeder o RA 78-79 H 6
Strofiliá o GR 100-101 J 5
Strogonof Point ▲ USA 22-23 R 4
Strokkurgeysir •• IS 86-87 c 2
Strómboli, Ísola ⌒ •• I 100-101 E 5
Stromness o GB 90-91 F 2
Strømø = Streymoy ⌒ FR 90-91 D 1
Strömstad ☆ S 86-87 E 7
Strömsund o S 86-87 G 5
Ströms vattudal ∸ S 86-87 G 4
Strong o USA 44-45 L 3
Strong, Mount ▲ PNG 183 D 4
Strong City o USA 42-43 J 6
Stronsay ⌒ GB 90-91 F 2
Stroud o AUS 180-181 L 2
Stroudsburg o USA 46-47 L 5
Struan o CDN 34-35 C 4
Struer o DK 86-87 D 8
Struga o • MK 100-101 H 4
Struisbaai ≈ 220-221 E 7
Strumešnica ~ MK 100-101 J 4
Strumica o • MK 100-101 J 4
Strydenburg o ZA 220-221 F 4
Strydpoolberge ▲ ZA 220-221 J 2
Stryj ☆ UA 102-103 C 3
Stryj ~ UA 102-103 C 3
Stryker o USA 40-41 G 1
Strymón ~ GR 100-101 J 4
Strypa ~ UA 102-103 D 3
Strzelce Krajeńskie o PL 92-93 N 2
Strzelecki Creek ~ AUS 178-179 F 5
Strzelecki Regional Reserve ⊥ AUS 178-179 E 5
Stuart o USA (FL) 48-49 H 6
Stuart o USA (IA) 42-43 K 5
Stuart o USA (NE) 42-43 H 4
Stuart o USA (VA) 46-47 H 7
Stuart, Mount o AUS 172-173 C 7
Stuart Bluff Range ▲ AUS 172-173 L 7
Stuartburn o CDN 34-35 H 6
Stuart Highway II AUS 178-179 C 5
Stuart Island ⌒ USA 20-21 J 5
Stuart Lake ⊖ CDN 32-33 H 4
Stuart Memorial • AUS 174-175 C 6
Stuart Ranges ▲ AUS 178-179 C 5
Stuart River ~ CDN 32-33 J 4
Stubbenkammer ▲ •• D 92-93 M 1
Studenčeskoe o KA 126-127 M 2
Studenica o ••• YU 100-101 H 3
Studina o RO 102-103 D 6
Stugun o S 86-87 G 5
Stuie o CDN 32-33 G 5
Stull Lake ⊖ CDN 34-35 K 3
Stupino ☆ RUS 94-95 Q 4
Sturgeon Bay o CDN 34-35 G 4
Sturgeon Bay o USA 46-47 E 3
Sturgeon Falls o CDN 38-39 E 5
Sturgeon Lake ⊖ CDN (ALB) 32-33 M 4
Sturgeon Lake ⊖ CDN (ONT) 34-35 L 6
Sturgeon Lake ⊖ CDN (ONT) 38-39 E 6
Sturgeon Lake Indian Reserve ✗ CDN 32-33 M 4
Sturgeon River ~ CDN 34-35 L 3
Sturgeon River ~ CDN 34-35 C 4
Sturges Islands ⌒ CDN 24-25 e 7
Sturgis o USA (MI) 46-47 F 5
Sturgis o USA (SD) 42-43 F 3
Šturmovoj o RUS 120-121 N 2
Štúrovo o SK 92-93 P 5
Sturt, Mount ▲ AUS 178-179 F 5
Sturt Bay ≈ 180-181 D 3
Sturt Creek o AUS (WA) 172-173 J 5
Sturt Creek ~ AUS 172-173 J 5
Sturt Highway II AUS 180-181 H 3
Sturt National Park ⊥ AUS 178-179 F 5
Sturt Stony Desert ⌣ AUS 178-179 E 4
Stutterheim o ZA 220-221 H 6
Stuttgart ☆ • D 92-93 K 4
Stuttgart o USA 44-45 M 2
Stuyahok o USA 20-21 K 5
Styal o CDN 32-33 N 5
Stygge Glacier ⊂ CDN 26-27 L 4
Stykkishólmsbær ☆ IS 86-87 b 2
Styr ~ UA 102-103 D 2
Šu ~ KA 124-125 F 6
Suai o MAL 162-163 K 3
Suai o RI 166-167 C 6
Su'aiba, aš- o KSA 130-131 H 4
Suain o PNG 183 B 2
Suakin o • SUD 200-201 H 3
Suakin Archipelago ⌒ SUD 200-201 J 3
Suakoko o LB 202-203 F 6
Suam ~ EAK 212-213 E 3
Suana o ZRE 216-217 F 3
Suao o RC 156-157 M 4
Sua Phung o THA 158-159 E 4
Suapi o BOL 70-71 D 4
Suapure, Río ~ YV 60-61 H 4
Suaruru, Cordillera de ▲ BOL 76-77 E 1
Suasúa o YV 62-63 D 2
Suavanao o SOL 184 I d 2
Suay Riêng o K 158-159 H 5
Šu'b, Ra's ▲ Y 132-133 H 7
Šu'ba, aš- o KSA 130-131 J 3
Šubaihi, aš- ∸ Y 132-133 C 7
Šubaikiya, aš- o KSA 130-131 H 5
Subang o RI 168 B 3
Suban Point ▲ RP 160-161 E 6
Suban Siri ~ IND 142-143 H 2
Šubarkūdyk ☆ KA 126-127 M 3
Šubaršy o KA 126-127 M 3
Subate o • LV 94-95 J 3
Subei o VRC 146-147 M 6
Šuberta, mys ▲ RUS 108-109 O 5
Šuberta, zaliv ⊖ RUS 108-109 F 5
Subi Besar, Pulau ⌒ RI 162-163 H 3
Subiya, al- o KWT 130-131 L 3
Sublett o USA 40-41 H 4
Sublette o USA 44-45 G 1
Subotica ☆ • YU 100-101 G 1
Šubrā al-Ḫaima o ET 194-195 E 2
Subrahmanya o IND 140-141 F 4
Subway Caves • USA 40-41 D 5
Sucatinga o BR 68-69 J 4
Suceava ☆ ••• RO 102-103 E 4
Suches, Lago ⊖ PE 70-71 B 4
Suches, Río ~ PE 70-71 C 4
Suchiapa, Río ~ MEX 52-53 H 3
Suchil o MEX 50-51 H 6
Suchumi ☆ GE 126-127 D 6
Sucio, Río ~ CO 60-61 C 4
Suckling, Mount ▲ PNG 183 E 5
Sucre ☆ ••• BOL 70-71 E 6
Sucre o CO 60-61 D 3
Sucre o EC 64-65 B 2
Sucúa o EC 64-65 C 3
Suçuarana o BR 72-73 K 3
Suçuarana, Serra do ▲ BR 72-73 H 3
Sucunduri, Rio ~ BR 66-67 H 6
Sucupira do Norte o BR 68-69 F 5
Sucuriju o BR 62-63 K 5
Sucuriú, Cachoeira ~ BR 68-69 F 5
Sucuriú, Rio ~ BR 72-73 D 6
Sud, Île du ⌒ SY 224 B 5
Sud = South □ CAM 210-211 C 2
Suda ~ RUS 94-95 P 2
Sudaira, as- o KSA 132-133 B 3
Sudak ☆ • UA 102-103 J 5
Sudan ∸ 200-201 C 4
Sudan o USA 44-45 F 2
Sudan = As-Sūdān ■ SUD 200-201 D 4
Sudbury o • CDN 38-39 D 5
Sud-Camerounais, Plateau ▲ CAM 204-205 K 6
Sudd ∸ SUD 206-207 K 4
Suddie o GUY 62-63 E 2
Sudeten = Sudety ∸ CZ 92-93 N 3
Sudety ∸ CZ 92-93 N 3
Süd Gān o IR 134-135 D 2
Sudirman, Pegunungan ▲ RI 166-167 J 3
Sudislavl' o RUS 94-95 R 3
Sud ou de la Hotte, Massif du ▲ RH 54-55 H 5
Sud-Ouest = South-West □ CAM 204-205 H 6
Südpol ∸ ARK 16 E 0
Sudskoe, Borisovo- o RUS 94-95 P 2
Suduci, kŭli ⊖ US 136-137 F 3
Suðureyri o IS 86-87 b 1
Sudwala Caves • ZA 220-221 K 2
Sudža o RUS 102-103 J 2
Sudžensk, Anžero- o RUS 114-115 T 6
Sue ~ SUD 206-207 J 5
Sueca o E 98-99 G 5
Sueco, El o MEX 50-51 F 3
Suehn, Big o LB 202-203 F 7
Suemez Island ⌒ USA 32-33 D 4
Suess Land ∸ GRØ 26-27 m 7
Sueur, Le o USA 42-43 L 3
Suez, Gulf of = Suwais, Ḫalīǧ as- ≈ ET 194-195 F 3
Suez = Suwais, as- ☆ ET 194-195 F 3
Suez Canal = Suwais, Qanāt as- < ET 194-195 F 2
Šūf, Darre-ye ~ AFG 136-137 K 7
Sufetula • TN 190-191 G 3
Suffern o USA 46-47 L 5
Suffield o CDN 32-33 P 6
Suffolk o USA 46-47 K 7
Sūfijon mašiti • US 136-137 J 4
Šūfiyān o IR 128-129 L 3
Šuga ~ RUS 108-109 O 8
Sugaing o • MYA 142-143 J 5
Sugal o RP 160-161 F 10
Sūg al Kharis o LAR 192-193 E 1
Sugar Land o USA 44-45 K 5
Sugarloaf Mount ▲ USA 46-47 N 3
Sugarloaf Mountain ▲ AUS 180-181 K 2
Sugarloaf Mountain ▲ USA 22-23 S 3
Sugar Mill = Château Murat • F 56 E 4
Sugar River ~ USA 46-47 D 4
Sugar Town • AUS 174-175 J 5
Sugbongkogon o RP 160-161 F 8
Suge La ▲ VRC 144-145 H 6
Suggan Buggan o AUS 180-181 K 4
Suggi Lake ⊖ CDN 34-35 E 3
Sugi, Pulau ⌒ RI 162-163 E 4
Sugihwaras o RI 162-163 E 7
Suğla Gölü ⊖ TR 128-129 E 4
Suguk Inlet ≈ 36-37 M 3
Sugmutun"egan ~ RUS 114-115 R 4
Šugoj ~ RUS 112-113 H 4
Sugu o WAN 204-205 K 4
Sugun o VRC 146-147 C 6
Šugur o RUS 114-115 J 4
Sugut, Tanjung ▲ MAL 160-161 B 9
Suguta ~ EAK 212-213 F 3
Šugža ~ RUS 120-121 G 2
Sūhāğ ☆ • ET 194-195 E 4
Šuhair, Abū ☆ IRQ 128-129 L 7
Šuhair, aš- o Y 132-133 F 6
Suhait o VRC 154-155 D 2
Suhaja Bahta ~ RUS 114-115 U 3
Suhaja Tunguska ~ RUS 114-115 U 2
Šuhār ☆ • OM 132-133 K 1
Suhariha ~ RUS 108-109 W 8
Suharnyj, ostrov ⌒ RUS 112-113 L 2
Suhbaatar □ MAU 148-149 L 4
Suheli Par ∸ IND 140-141 E 5
Suhiniči o RUS 94-95 O 4
Suhl o D 92-93 L 3
Suhmiten"jah ~ RUS 114-115 M 5
Suhna, as- o SYR 128-129 H 5
Suhna, as- o Y 132-133 C 6
Suhodol o RUS 96-97 G 7
Suhoj Log ☆ RUS 96-97 M 5
Suhoj Nos, mys ▲ RUS 108-109 E 5
Suhoj Pit ~ RUS 116-117 F 6
Suhoj Poluj ~ RUS 114-115 K 2
Suhona ~ RUS 94-95 S 1
Suhum o GH 202-203 K 6
Şuhut ☆ TR 128-129 D 3
Sui ~ DY 204-205 E 4
Sui o PK 138-139 B 5
Sui o PNG 183 B 5
Suiá-Miçu, Rio ~ BR 68-69 B 7
Suiá Missu, Rio ~ BR 72-73 D 2
Suibin o VRC 150-151 H 4
Suichang o VRC 156-157 L 2
Suichuan o VRC 156-157 J 3
Suide o VRC 154-155 G 3
Suifenhe o VRC 150-151 H 5
Suigam o IND 138-139 C 7
Suihua o VRC 150-151 F 4
Suijiang o VRC 156-157 C 2
Suileng o VRC 150-151 F 4
Suining o VRC (HUN) 156-157 G 3
Suining o VRC (JIA) 154-155 K 5

Spokane — Suining 319

Suining ○ **VRC** (SIC) 154-155 D 6
Suir ~ **IRL** 90-91 D 5
Suixi ○ **VRC** 156-157 G 6
Sui Xian ○ **VRC** 154-155 J 4
Suiyang ○ **VRC** (GZH) 156-157 E 3
Suiyang ○ **VRC** (HEI) 150-151 H 5
Suizhou ○ **VRC** 154-155 H 6
Šuja ○ **RUS** 94-95 R 3
Šuja ~ **RUS** 88-89 M 6
Sujálpur ○ **IND** 138-139 F 8
Sujáwal ○ **PK** 138-139 B 7
Sujawal ○ **PK** 138-139 B 6
Šujostrov ~ **RUS** 88-89 N 4
Šujutkina Kosa, mys ▲ **RUS** 126-127 Q 5
Šukābad ○ **IR** 134-135 C 2
Sukaburni ○ **RI** 168 B 3
Sukadana ○ **RI** (KBA) 162-163 H 5
Sukadana ○ **RI** (LAM) 162-163 F 7
Sukadana Teluk ≈ 162-163 H 5
Sukagawa ○ **J** 152-153 J 6
Sukamenang ○ **RI** 162-163 E 6
Sukaraja ○ **RI** (JTE) 168 C 3
Sukaraja ○ **RI** (KBA) 162-163 J 6
Sukauegara ○ **RI** 168 B 3
Sukeva ○ **FIN** 88-89 J 5
Sukhothai ○ •••• **THA** 158-159 E 2
Sukkar,as- ○ **SYR** 128-129 J 5
Sukkur, Qal'at ☆ **IRQ** 128-129 M 7
Sukkertoppen = Maniitsoq ○ **GRØ** 28-29 O 4
Sukkertoppen Isflade ⊂ **GRØ** 28-29 O 3
Sukkozero ○ **RUS** 88-89 M 5
Sukkur ○ •• **PK** 138-139 B 6
Sukkwan Island ▲ **USA** 32-33 D 4
Sukodadi ○ **RI** 168 E 3
Sukoharjo ○ **RI** 168 D 3
Sukopuro ○ **RI** 168 E 3
Sukorejo ○ **RI** 168 D 3
Sukpai ~ **RUS** 122-123 G 5
Sukri ~ **IND** 138-139 D 7
Suksun ○ **RUS** 96-97 K 5
Sukunka River ~ **CDN** 32-33 M 3
Sul, Canal do ~ **BR** 62-63 K 6
Sula ~ **N** 86-87 B 6
Sula ~ **RUS** 88-89 U 4
Sula ~ **RUS** 88-89 U 3
Sula ~ **UA** 102-103 H 3
Sula ○ **USA** 40-41 H 3
Sula, Kepulauan ▲ **RI** 164-165 J 5
Sülagiri ○ **IND** 140-141 H 4
Sulaib at-Ṭarfâ' ▲ **KSA** 130-131 G 3
Sulaimāniya, as- ○ **IRQ** 128-129 L 5
Sulaimāniya, as- ☆ **IRQ** 128-129 L 5
Sulaiman Range ▲ **PK** 138-139 B 5
Sulak ~ **RUS** 126-127 N 4
Sulakkan ~ **RUS** 110-111 a 6
Sulakyurt ○ **TR** 128-129 E 2
Sulamu ○ **RI** 166-167 B 7
Sulat ~ **RP** 160-161 F 7
Sulatna River ~ **USA** 20-21 N 4
Sulawesi ▲ **RI** 164-165 F 5
Sulawesi Selatan □ **RI** 164-165 F 5
Sulawesi Tengah □ **RI** 164-165 F 4
Sulawesi Tenggara □ **RI** 164-165 G 5
Sulawesi Utara □ **RI** 164-165 H 4
Šulb, as- ▲ **KSA** 130-131 K 4
Sulb, Temple of • **SUD** 200-201 E 2
Sulechów ○ **PL** 92-93 N 2
Suleja ○ **WAN** 204-205 G 4
Sulejów ○ **PL** 92-93 P 3
Sulen, Mount ▲ **PNG** 183 B 2
Sule Skerry ▲ **GB** 90-91 L 2
Šuľgan-Taš zapovednik ⊥ **RUS** 96-97 K 7
Sülíč ○ **AFG** 136-137 K 7
Suliki ○ **RI** 162-163 D 5
Sulina ○ **RO** 102-103 F 5
Sulina, Braţul ~ **RO** 102-103 F 5
Sulitjelma ▲ **S** 86-87 H 3
Sulitjelma ○ **N** 86-87 H 3
Suljukta ○ **KS** 136-137 L 5
Suľkovskogo, mys ▲ **RUS** 120-121 W 6
Sullana ○ **PE** 64-65 B 4
Sulligent ○ **USA** 48-49 D 3
Sullivan ○ **USA** (IN) 46-47 E 6
Sullivan ○ **USA** (MO) 46-47 C 6
Sullivan Lake ○ **CDN** 32-33 P 6
Sullorsuaq Vaigat ≈ 28-29 N 1
Sully-sur-Loire ○ **F** 90-91 J 4
Sulmona ○ **I** 100-101 D 3
Sulop ○ **RP** 160-161 F 9
Sulphur ○ **USA** (LA) 44-45 L 4
Sulphur ○ **USA** (NV) 40-41 E 5
Sulphur ○ **USA** (OK) 44-45 J 2
Sulphur Bank ≃ 72-73 M 4
Sulphur River ~ **USA** 44-45 K 3
Sulphur Springs ○ **USA** 44-45 K 3
Sultan ○ **CDN** 38-39 C 5
Sultán ○ **IRQ** 128-129 L 6
Sultandağı ○ **TR** 128-129 D 3
Sultan Dağları ▲ **TR** 128-129 D 3
Sultan Hamud ○ **EAK** 212-213 F 5
Sultanhanı ○ **TR** 128-129 E 3
Sultan Kudarat ○ **RP** 160-161 F 9
Sultánpur ○ **IND** 142-143 C 2
Sultánpur = Kulu ○ •• **IND** 138-139 F 4
Sultan-Ubajs ▲ **US** 136-137 D 2
Sultepec, Rio ~ **MEX** 52-53 J 4
Sulu ○ **ZRE** 210-211 K 6
Sulu, Laut ≈ 160-161 E 9
Sulúova ○ **TR** 128-129 G 2
Sulu Sea ≈ 160-161 C 8

Sülütöbe ○ **KA** 124-125 E 6
Sulzbach-Rosenberg ○ **D** 92-93 L 4
Sumaco ○ **EC** 64-65 D 2
Sumaco, Volcán ▲ **EC** 64-65 D 2
Sumahode ○ **RI** 164-165 K 3
Sumaianyar ○ **RI** 164-165 E 5
Sumair, Ǧazirat ▲ **KSA** 132-133 C 5
Šumanaj ○ **US** 136-137 F 3
Sümár ○ **IR** 134-135 D 6
Sumara, Naqil ▲ **Y** 132-133 D 6
Sumaroto ○ **RI** 168 D 3
Sumas ○ **USA** 40-41 C 1
Sumatera Barat □ **RI** 162-163 C 5
Sumatera Selatan □ **RI** 162-163 E 6
Sumatera Utara □ **RI** 162-163 C 5
Sumatra ○ **USA** 48-49 F 4
Sumatra = Sumatera ▲ **RI** 162-163 B 2
Sumaúma ○ **BR** 66-67 G 6
Šumava ▲ **CZ** 92-93 M 4
Sumba ~ **RI** 168 F 2
Sumba, Ile ▲ **RI** 166-167 B 5
Sumba, Selat ≈ 168 D 7
Šumbar ~ **TM** 136-137 E 5
Sumbawa ▲ **RI** 168 C 7
Sumbawa Besar ○ **RI** 168 C 7
Sumbawanga ● **EAT** 214-215 F 4
Sumbe ○ **ANG** 216-217 B 5
Sumbèr ~ **MAU** 146-147 E 4
Sumbèr = Čojr ○ **MAU** 148-149 J 4
Sumbi ○ **ZRE** 210-211 D 6
Sumbu ○ **Z** 214-215 F 5
Sumbu National Park ⊥ **Z** 214-215 F 5
Sumburgh ○ **GB** 90-91 G 2
Sumbuya ○ **WAL** 202-203 E 6
Sumé ○ **BR** 68-69 K 5
Sumedang ○ **RI** 168 B 3
Sumelas ~ **TR** 128-129 H 2
Šumen ○ **BG** 102-103 E 6
Sumenep ○ **RI** 168 E 3
Šumerlja ○ **RUS** 96-97 E 6
Sumidouro Grande, Rio ~ **BR** 70-71 J 4
Šumiha ○ **RUS** 114-115 G 7
Šumilina ▲ **BY** 94-95 L 4
Šummän, as- ▲ **KSA** 130-131 J 4
Summer ○ **USA** 44-45 M 3
Summer Creek ~ **CDN** 32-33 K 7
Summerdown ○ **NAM** 216-217 E 10
Summerfield ○ **USA** 42-43 J 6
Summer Lake ○ **USA** 40-41 D 4
Summerland ○ **CDN** 32-33 L 7
Summerside ○ **CDN** 38-39 N 5
Summerstrand ○ **ZA** 220-221 G 6
Summersville ○ **USA** (MO) 46-47 C 7
Summersville ○ **USA** (WV) 46-47 H 6
Summerville ○ **USA** (GA) 48-49 F 2
Summerville ○ **USA** (SC) 48-49 H 3
Summit ○ **SUD** 200-201 H 3
Summit ○ **USA** (MS) 44-45 M 4
Summit ○ **USA** (SD) 42-43 J 3
Summit Lake ○ **CDN** (BC) 30-31 G 6
Summit Lake ○ **CDN** (BC) 32-33 J 4
Summit Peak ▲ **USA** 44-45 D 1
Sumner ○ **USA** 42-43 L 6
Sumner, Lake ○ **USA** 44-45 E 2
Sumner State Memorial, Fort ∴• **USA** 44-45 E 2
Sumoto ○ **J** 152-153 F 7
Sumozero ○ **RUS** 88-89 N 4
Sumpangbinangae ○ **RI** 164-165 F 6
Šumperk ○ **CZ** 92-93 O 4
Sumpiuh ○ **RI** 168 C 3
Sumpul, Rio ~ **HN** 52-53 K 4
Sumqayıt ○ **AZ** 128-129 N 2
Sumqayıt = Sumqayıt ○ **AZ** 128-129 N 2
Šumskij Posad ○ **RUS** 88-89 N 4
Šumšu, ostrov ▲ **RUS** 122-123 R 3
Sumter ○ **USA** 48-49 H 3
Sumter National Monument, Fort ∴• **USA** 48-49 J 3
Sumuna ○ **PNG** 183 F 2
Sumur ○ **RI** 168 A 3
Sumoi ○ **VRC** 144-145 C 3
Sumy ○ **UA** 102-103 J 2
Sumysker ○ **KA** 96-97 G 5
Suna ☆ **RUS** 96-97 G 5
Suna ~ **Y** 132-133 F 6
Sunaisila ○ **IRQ** 128-129 J 5
Sunamganj ○ **BD** 142-143 G 3
Sunan ○ **DVR** 150-151 E 8
Sunan ○ **VRC** 154-155 A 2
Sunáo ○ **IND** 138-139 D 8
Sunburst ○ **USA** 40-41 J 1
Sunbury ○ **AUS** 180-181 H 4
Sunbury ○ **USA** 46-47 J 5
Sunchales ○ **RA** 76-77 G 6
Suncho Corral ○ **RA** 76-77 F 4
Sunchon ○ **DVR** 150-151 E 8
Sunch'ŏn ○ **ROK** 150-151 F 10
Sun City ○ **USA** 40-41 H 9
Sun City ○ •• **ZA** 220-221 H 2
Suncun ○ **VRC** 154-155 K 4
Sunda, Kepulauan ▲ **RI** 168 B 2
Sunda, Selat ≈ 168 A 3
Sundarbans ~ **IND** 142-143 F 5
Sundarbans National Park ⊥ •••• **IND** 142-143 F 4
Sundargarh ○ **IND** 142-143 D 4
Sunda Shelf ≃ 12 J 4
Sunda Trench ≂ 12 J 4
Sunday Strait ≈ 172-173 H 4
Sundby ○ **GB** 90-91 G 4
Sündiken Dağları ▲ **TR** 128-129 D 3
Sundi-Lutete ○ **ZRE** 210-211 D 6
Sundown National Park ⊥ **AUS** 178-179 L 5
Sundozero, ozero ~ **RUS** 88-89 N 5
Sundre ○ **CDN** 32-33 N 6
Sundsvall ○ **S** 86-87 H 5
Sunduki, peski ~ **TM** 136-137 H 5
Sunel ○ **IND** 138-139 F 7
Sunflower, Mount ▲ **USA** 42-43 F 6
Sungaibamban ○ **RI** 162-163 C 3
Sungaibelidah ○ **RI** 162-163 F 6

Sungaibenkal ○ **RI** 162-163 E 5
Sungai Buloh ○ **MAL** 162-163 D 3
Sungaibuluh ○ **RI** 164-165 D 5
Sungaidareh ○ **RI** 162-163 D 5
Sungaigerung ○ **RI** 162-163 E 4
Sungaiguntung ○ **RI** 162-163 E 4
Sungai Ko-lok ○ **THA** 158-159 F 7
Sungai Lembing ○ **MAL** 162-163 E 3
Sungai Penuh ○ **RI** 162-163 D 6
Sungai Pin ○ **MAL** 160-161 K 6
Sungaiparaya ○ **RI** 162-163 H 4
Sungai Rengit, Kampung ○ **MAL** 162-163 F 4
Sungaiselan ○ **RI** 162-163 F 6
Sungai Siput ○ **MAL** 162-163 D 2
Sungguminasa ○ **RI** 164-165 F 6
Sunggai ○ **SUD** 200-201 D 6
Sung Noen ○ **THA** 158-159 F 3
Sungsang ○ **RI** 162-163 F 6
Sungurlu ○ **TR** 128-129 F 2
Suni ○ **SUD** 200-201 B 6
Sun Kosi ~ **NEP** 144-145 E 7
Sunlander II **AUS** 174-175 K 7
Sun Moon Lake ○ **RC** 156-157 M 5
Sunndalsøra ▲ **N** 86-87 D 5
Sunne ○ **S** 86-87 F 7
Sunnyside ○ **USA** 40-41 E 2
Sunnyvale ○ **USA** 40-41 C 7
Sun Prairie ○ **USA** 46-47 D 4
Sun River ~ **USA** 40-41 J 2
Sunrise Beach ○ **USA** 40-41 B 2
Sunset Country ▲ **AUS** 180-181 F 3
Sunset Crater National Monument • **USA** 40-41 J 8
Sunshine Coast ▲ **AUS** 178-179 M 4
Suntai ○ **WAN** 204-205 J 5
Suntai, River ~ **WAN** 204-205 J 5
Suntar ○ **RUS** 118-119 H 4
Suntar ~ **RUS** 120-121 J 2
Suntar-Hajata, hrebet ▲ **RUS** 110-111 V 7
Suntsar ○ **PK** 134-135 K 6
Suntu ○ **ETH** 208-209 C 4
Sun Valley ○ **USA** 40-41 G 5
Sunwi Do ~ **DVR** 150-151 E 9
Sunwu ○ **VRC** 150-151 N 1
Sunyani ○ **GH** 202-203 H 6
Sun Zhongshan Guju • **VRC** 156-157 H 6
Suŏi Rut ~ **VN** 156-157 D 4
Suojarvi ○ **RUS** 88-89 M 5
Suojarvi, ozero ~ **RUS** 88-89 M 5
Suola ~ **RUS** 120-121 D 3
Suolama ~ **RUS** 110-111 H 3
Suomenlinna = Sveaborg ••• **FIN** 88-89 H 6
Suomenselkä ▲ **FIN** 88-89 H 5
Suó-nada ≈ 152-153 D 8
Suonenjoki ○ **FIN** 88-89 J 5
Suon-Tit ○ **RUS** 118-119 L 6
Suot-Ujala, hrebet ▲ **RUS** 110-111 d 5
Suowenna Shan ▲ **VRC** 144-145 E 4
Supamo, Rio ~ **YV** 60-61 K 4
Supe'é ○ **ETH** 208-209 B 4
Superagui, Parque Nacional do ⊥ **BR** 74-75 F 5
Superior ○ **USA** (AZ) 40-41 J 9
Superior ○ **USA** (NE) 42-43 H 5
Superior ○ **USA** (WI) 42-43 L 2
Superior, Laguna ≈ 52-53 G 3
Superior, Lake ~ 46-47 C 2
Supetar ○ **HR** 100-101 F 3
Suphan Buri ○ **THA** 158-159 F 3
Süphan Dağı ▲ **TR** 128-129 K 3
Supia ○ **CO** 60-61 D 5
Supiori, Pulau ▲ **RI** 166-167 H 2
Supiori Pulau Reserve ⊥• **RI** 166-167 H 2
Supplejack Downs ○ **AUS** 172-173 K 5
Supris ○ **USA** 112-113 J 3
Suqailibiya ○ **SYR** 128-129 J 5
Šuqaiq, aš- ○ **KSA** 132-133 C 5
Süq al-Ğarráhi ○ **Y** 132-133 C 6
Süq al-Inán ○ **Y** 132-133 D 5
Süq aš-Šuyúh ○ **IRQ** 130-131 K 2
Suqian ○ **VRC** 154-155 L 5
Šuqqán, aš- ▲ **KSA** 132-133 F 3
Šüq Suwaiq ○ **KSA** 130-131 F 5
Suqu ○ **VRC** 156-157 J 5
Šür ○ **OM** 132-133 L 2
Šür ~ **RL** 128-129 F 7
Šür, Káfe ~ **IR** 136-137 E 7
Šur, Point ▲ **USA** 40-41 C 7
Šür, Rüd-e ~ **IR** 134-135 H 3
Šür, Rüd-e ~ **IR** 134-135 D 4
Šür, Rüd-e ~ **IR** 134-135 G 3
Šür, Rüd-e ~ **IR** 134-135 H 5
Šür, Rüd-e ~ **IR** 134-135 J 2
Šür, Rüd-e ~ **IR** 134-135 E 4
Šür, Rüdhâne-ye ~ **IR** 134-135 F 3
Šür, Rüdhâne-ye ~ **IR** 134-135 B 7
Sutherland ○ **AUS** 178-179 H 1
Sutherland ○ **ZA** 220-221 E 5
Sutherland Range ▲ **AUS** 176-177 H 3
Sutherlin ○ **USA** 40-41 C 4
Sutti ○ **WAN** 198-199 B 6
Sutton ○ **CDN** 38-39 N 6
Sutton ○ **USA** (NE) 42-43 H 5
Sutton ○ **USA** (WV) 46-47 H 6
Sutton Downs ○ **AUS** 178-179 H 1
Sutton Lake ~ **CDN** 34-35 P 3
Sutton River ~ **CDN** 34-35 P 3
Suttor River ~ **AUS** 178-179 J 1
Suttsu ○ **J** 152-153 J 3
Suțukoba ○ **WAG** 202-203 C 3
Suturuoba ○ **RUS** 110-111 a 5
Sutvik Island ~ **USA** 22-23 S 4
Suṭyr' ~ **RUS** 122-123 E 6
Suugaant ○ **MAU** 148-149 H 5
Suuhanny ○ **GRØ** 28-29 V 4
Suuraho ○ **FIN** 88-89 K 5
Suva, Mount ▲ **AUS** 172-173 G 4
Suva ★• **FJI** 184 III b 3
Suvadiva Atoll ~ **MV** 140-141 B 7
Suva ★ **IND** 138-139 D 9
Suva Reka ○ **YU** 100-101 H 3
Suvorov ○ **RUS** 94-95 P 4

Surrey ○ **CDN** 32-33 J 7
Surrey ○ **USA** 42-43 G 1
Surske ~ **RUS** 96-97 E 6
Surt ○ **LAR** 192-193 G 2
Surt, Orto- ○ **RUS** 118-119 M 4
Surtsey ▲ **IS** 86-87 c 3
Šürtugaj ○ **TJ** 136-137 L 6
Suru ○ **ZRE** 212-213 J 2
Surubim ○ **BR** 68-69 L 5
Surubim, Rio ~ **BR** 66-67 J 6
Surubin, Rio ~ **BR** 68-69 D 7
Surubin, Rio ~ **BR** 68-69 D 7
Surumu, Rio ~ **BR** 62-63 D 4
Sur Vajo, Salar ~ **RCH** 70-71 C 7
Survílle, Cape ▲ **SOL** 184 I f 4
Šurygino ○ **KA** 124-125 N 1
Šuryškarskij Sor, ozero ~ **RUS** 114-115 H 2
Šüš ○ •• **IR** 134-135 C 2
Susa ○ **CO** 60-61 E 5
Susa ○ **I** 100-101 A 2
Susa ○ **J** 152-153 D 7
Šuša = Şuşa ○ **AZ** 128-129 M 3
Süsah ○ **LAR** 192-193 J 1
Susaki ○ **J** 152-153 E 8
Susang ○ **VRC** 154-155 K 6
Süsangerd ○ **IR** 134-135 C 3
Susanino ○ **RUS** 122-123 R 3
Susanville ○ **USA** 40-41 D 5
Susapampa, Sierra de ▲ **RA** 76-77 D 4
Susehri ○ **TR** 128-129 H 2
Šušenskoe ○ **RUS** 116-117 E 4
Šušenskoe-Sajano, vodohranilišče ~ **RUS** 116-117 E 9
Sušin ○ **IRQ** 128-129 L 4
Susitna River ~ **USA** 20-21 N 5
Suspiro ○ **BR** 76-77 K 6
Susquehanna River ~ **USA** 46-47 K 6
Sussex ○ **CDN** 38-39 M 6
Šuštar ○ **IR** 134-135 C 2
Sustut Peak ▲ **CDN** 32-33 H 3
Sustut River ~ **CDN** 32-33 H 3
Susua ○ **RI** 164-165 G 5
Susuka ○ **SOL** 184 I c 2
Susulatna River ~ **USA** 20-21 N 5
Susuman ○ **RUS** 120-121 N 2
Susunu ○ **RI** 166-167 G 3
Susupu ○ **RI** 164-165 K 2
Susuwruk ○ **TR** 128-129 C 3
Sutamo-Gonamskij, hrebet ▲ **RUS** 118-119 N 8
Sutara ○ **ETH** 208-209 E 5
Sutara ~ **RUS** 88-89 S 5
Suța, as- ○ **IRQ** 128-129 K 5
Šüra, Rüd-e ~ **IR** 136-137 E 7
Sütav ▲ **MAU** 146-147 L 2
Sutam ~ **RUS** 118-119 N 8

Suvorovskaja ○ **RUS** 126-127 E 5
Suvut ○ **PNG** 183 F 2
Suwaida', as- ○ **SYR** 128-129 G 6
Suwaida, as- ☆ **SYR** 128-129 G 6
Suwaihán ○ **UAE** 134-135 F 6
Suwailih ○ **JOR** 130-131 D 1
Šuwaihitiya, as- ○ **KSA** 130-131 G 2
Šuwaimiya, as- ○ **OM** 132-133 J 5
Šuwair, Haur as- ○ **KSA** 130-131 L 6
Šuwair, as- ○ **KSA** 130-131 G 2
Suwaiqa, as- ▲ **KSA** 130-131 G 6
Suwais, as- ○ **IRQ** 128-129 L 6
Suwais, as- ☆ **ET** 194-195 F 3
Suwa-ko ○ **J** 152-153 H 6
Suwałki ○ **PL** 92-93 R 1
Suwannaphum ○ **THA** 158-159 F 3
Suwannee River ~ **USA** 48-49 G 5
Suwanose-shima ~ **J** 152-153 C 10
Šuwár, as- ○ **SYR** 128-129 J 5
Šuwayyir, Abú ○ **IRQ** 130-131 K 2
Suwŏn ○ **ROK** 150-151 F 9
Suxianling ○ **VRC** 156-157 H 4
Suyckutambo ○ **PE** 70-71 D 7
Suyo ○ **PE** 64-65 C 4
Süzä ○ **IR** 134-135 G 5
Suzak ○ **KS** 136-137 N 4
Suzaka ○ **J** 152-153 H 6
Suzdaľ ○ •••• **RUS** 94-95 R 5
Suzhou ○ **VRC** (ANH) 154-155 K 5
Suzhou ○ **VRC** (JIA) 154-155 M 6
Suzu ○ **J** 152-153 G 6
Suzuka ○ **J** 152-153 G 7
Suzuka Quasi National Park ⊥ **J** 152-153 G 7
Suzu-misaki ▲ **J** 152-153 G 6
Suzun ○ **RUS** 124-125 N 2
Svalbard ◻ **N** 30-31 f 5
Svappavaara ○ **S** 86-87 K 3
Svärdsjö ○ **S** 86-87 G 6
Svartisen ▲•• ▲ **N** 86-87 F 3
Svatava ○ **RUS** 102-103 N 3
Svatove ○ **UA** 102-103 L 3
Svaty Kopeček ▲ **CZ** 92-93 O 4
Sveagruva ○ **N** 84-85 K 4
Svealand ⌐ **S** 86-87 F 7
Sveg ○ **S** 86-87 G 5
Švenčionys ○ **LT** 94-95 K 4
Svendborg ○ **DK** 86-87 E 9
Svenskoøya ▲ **N** 84-85 N 4
Svenstavik ○ **S** 86-87 F 5
Šventoji ○ **LT** 94-95 G 3
Sverdlova, mys ▲ **RUS** 108-109 b 2
Sverdlovs'k ○ **UA** 102-103 L 3
Sverdlovsk = Ekaterinburg ☆ **RUS** 96-97 M 5
Sverdlovsk = Sverdlovs'k ○ **UA** 102-103 L 3
Sverdrup, ostrov ~ **RUS** 108-109 S 4
Sverdrup Islet ~ **CDN** 24-25 c 3
Sverdrup Islands ▲ **CDN** 24-25 U 1
Sverdrup Pass ⊂ **CDN** 26-27 A 2
Sverre, Cape ▲ **CDN** 24-25 X 1
Svešťari ○ **BG** 102-103 E 6
Sveti Nikole ○ **MK** 100-101 H 4
Sveti Stefan ○ **YU** 100-101 G 3
Svetlograd ○ **RUS** 102-103 N 5
Svetlovodnaja ○ **RUS** 122-123 G 5
Svetlovodsk = Svitlovods'k ○ **UA** 102-103 H 3
Svetlyj ○ **RUS** (IRK) 118-119 G 6
Svetlyj ○ **RUS** (SAH) 118-119 F 4
Svetlyj ○ **RUS** (ORB) 126-127 O 2
Svetogorsk ○ **RUS** 88-89 K 6
Sviča ~ **UA** 102-103 G 3
Svidnik ○ **SK** 92-93 Q 4
Svilaja ~ **RUS** 96-97 F 6
Svilaga ~ **RUS** 96-97 F 6
Svilengrad ○ **BG** 102-103 E 7
Svincovyj Rudnik ○ **TM** 136-137 K 6
Svir ○ **BY** 94-95 K 4
Svir' ~ **RUS** 94-95 N 1
Svirsk ○ **RUS** 116-117 L 9
Svislač ~ **BY** 94-95 L 5
Svištov ○ **BG** 102-103 D 6
Svitlovods'k ○ **UA** 102-103 H 3
Svobodnyj ○ **RUS** 122-123 C 3
Svoge ○ **BG** 102-103 C 6
Svolvær ○ **N** 86-87 G 2
Svyataya Anna Trough = Svjataja Anna, Žolob ≂ 84-85 I 2
Syr, Kysyl ○ **RUS** 118-119 L 5
Syr, Kysyl ○ **RUS** 118-119 J 4
Syracuse ○ **USA** (NE) 42-43 J 5
Syracuse ○ **USA** (NY) 46-47 K 4
Syradasaj ~ **RUS** 108-109 U 5
Syrdarija ○ **KA** 124-125 D 6
Syrdarija ~ **KA** 124-125 D 6
Syrdarija ~ **KA** 136-137 L 4
Syrdarija ~ **KA** 136-137 L 4
Syren ○ **RI** 166-167 J 5
Sygynah ~ **RUS** 110-111 Q 6
Syhtymtor, ozero ~ **RUS** 114-115 M 4
Sykes Bluff ▲ **AUS** 176-177 M 3
Sykotu-gawa ~ **J** 152-153 K 2
Sylacauga ○ **USA** 48-49 E 3
Sylgy-Ytar ○ **RUS** 112-113 H 3
Sylhet ○ **BD** 142-143 G 3
Sylt ~ **D** 92-93 K 1
Sylva ~ **RUS** 96-97 K 5
Sylva ~ **RUS** 96-97 K 5
Sylva ○ **USA** 48-49 G 2
Sylvania ○ **USA** (GA) 48-49 H 3
Sylvania ○ **USA** (OH) 46-47 G 5
Sylvan Lake ○ **CDN** 32-33 N 5
Sylvan Pass ⊂ **USA** 40-41 J 4
Sylvester ○ **USA** 48-49 G 4
Sylvia ○ **USA** 42-43 H 7
Sylvia Grinnell Lake ○ **CDN** 36-37 P 2
Sylvinskij krjaž ▲ **RUS** 96-97 K 5
Sym ~ **RUS** 114-115 U 4
Sym ○ **RUS** 114-115 U 4
Symbeget ○ **KA** 124-125 D 6
Symkent ★ **KA** 136-137 L 3
Synča ~ **RUS** 110-111 Q 6
Syndassko ○ **RUS** 110-111 Q 3
Synder ○ **USA** 44-45 G 3
Synel'nykove ○ **UA** 102-103 J 3
Šyngyrlau ○ **KA** 96-97 J 8
Synja ~ **RUS** (KÖM) 88-89 Y 4
Synja ~ **RUS** 114-115 K 4
Synja, Boľšaja ~ **RUS** 108-109 H 9
Synjaha ~ **RUS** 114-115 K 4
Synnfjell ▲ **N** 86-87 D 6
Synnott Range ▲ **AUS** 172-173 G 4
Synnyr, hrebet ▲ **RUS** 118-119 E 7
Syó-gawa ~ **J** 152-153 G 6
Syowa ○ **ARK** 16 F 2
Sypaľky ~ **RUS** 114-115 R 2
Syr ~ **RUS** 114-115 U 4
Syria = Sûriya ■ **SYR** 128-129 G 5
Syrian Desert = Bādiyat aš-Šām ⌐ **SYR** 128-129 H 6

Swan Lake ○ **CDN** 34-35 F 4
Swannell Ranges ▲ **CDN** 32-33 G 3
Swan Plain ○ **CDN** 34-35 E 4
Swanquarter ○ **USA** 48-49 K 2
Swan Reach ○ **AUS** 180-181 F 3
Swan River ○ **CDN** 32-33 N 4
Swan River ~ **CDN** 34-35 N 4
Swan River ~ **CDN** 34-35 D 4
Swan River ○ **USA** 42-43 L 2
Swan River ○ **CDN** (MAN) 34-35 F 4
Swanquarter ○ **USA** 48-49 K 2
Swansea ○ **GB** 90-91 F 6
Swansea ○ **USA** 48-49 H 3
Swan Valley ○ **USA** 40-41 J 4
Swartberg ○ **ZA** 220-221 J 5
Swart Kei ~ **ZA** 220-221 H 6
Swartkolkvloer ○ **ZA** 220-221 E 5
Swartkops ○ **ZA** 220-221 G 6
Swartmodder ○ **ZA** 220-221 E 4
Swartplaas ○ **ZA** 220-221 E 4
Swartruggens ○ **ZA** 220-221 J 5
Swartruggens ▲ **ZA** 220-221 D 6
Swartz Bay ○ **CDN** 32-33 J 7
Swat ~ **PK** 138-139 D 2
Swate ○ **WAN** 204-205 E 3
Swaziland ■ **SD** 220-221 K 3
Sweden = Sverige ■ **S** 86-87 G 7
Swedru ○ **GH** 202-203 H 7
Sweers Island ▲ **AUS** 174-175 E 5
Sweetgrass ○ **USA** 40-41 J 1
Sweet Grass Indian Reserve ✗ **CDN** 32-33 Q 5
Sweet Home ○ **USA** 40-41 C 3
Sweetwater ○ **USA** 44-45 G 3
Sweetwater Fiver ~ **USA** 42-43 C 4
Sweetwater Station ○ **USA** 42-43 C 4
Swellendam ○ **ZA** 220-221 E 7
Swett, Peninsula ~ **RCH** 80 C 4
Świdnica ○ **PL** 92-93 O 3
Świebodzin ○ **PL** 92-93 N 2
Świecie ○ **PL** 92-93 O 2
Świft Current ○ **CDN** 34-35 D 5
Swift Current ○ **CDN** 32-33 Q 7
Swift Fork Kuskokwim River ~ **USA** 20-21 O 5
Swift River ~ **USA** 20-21 N 6
Swifts Creek ○ **AUS** 180-181 J 4
Swinburne, Cape ▲ **CDN** 24-25 X 5
Swindon ○ **GB** 90-91 G 6
Świnoujście ○ **PL** 92-93 N 1
Swiss Historic Village • **USA** 46-47 D 4
Switzerland = Schweiz ■ **CH** 92-93 K 5
Swords Range ▲ **AUS** 174-175 G 6
Syaburbensi ○ **NEP** 144-145 E 6
Syagannah ○ **RUS** 110-111 Y 5
Syakotan-hantō ▲ **J** 152-153 J 3
Syalysardah ~ **RUS** 118-119 L 6
Syari-dake ▲ **J** 152-153 L 3
Syč evka ○ **RUS** 94-95 O 4
Syderø = Suðuroy ~ **FR** 90-91 D 1
Sydkap ▲ **GRØ** 26-27 n 8
Sydkap Fiord ≈ 24-25 d 2
Sydney ★• **AUS** 180-181 L 2
Sydney ○ **CDN** 38-39 O 5
Sydney Lake ○ **CDN** 34-35 J 5
Sydostbugten ≈ 28-29 P 2
Sydyjaha ~ **RUS** 108-109 Q 7
Sydykta ~ **RUS** 118-119 H 7
Syeri ○ **RI** 166-167 J 5
Sygynah ~ **RUS** 110-111 Q 6

Šyrjajeve ○ **UA** 102-103 G 4
Šyrkala, tizbek ▲ **KA** 126-127 M 4
Syrkovo, ozero ~ **RUS** 114-115 N 4
Syroke ○ **UA** 102-103 H 4
Syruta, ozero ~ **RUS** 108-109 X 5
Sysčyčy ○ **BY** 94-95 K 5
Sysert' ○ **RUS** 96-97 M 5
Syskonsyn"ja ~ **RUS** 114-115 M 4
Sysmä ○ **FIN** 88-89 H 6
Sysola ~ **RUS** 96-97 G 3
Sytygan-Syylba ~ **RUS** 120-121 L 2
Syväjärvi ○ **FIN** 88-89 H 3
Syverma ~ **RUS** 116-117 G 3
Syvtuga ~ **RUS** 88-89 P 5
Šyža vtoroi ○ **RUS** 96-97 F 8
Syzran' ○ **RUS** 96-97 F 7
Szaga, Lake ○ **PNG** 183 A 4
Szamotuły ○ **PL** 92-93 O 2
Szarvas ○ **H** 92-93 Q 5
Szczecin ○ **PL** 92-93 N 2
Szczecinek ○ **PL** 92-93 O 2
Szczeciński, Zalew ~ **PL** 92-93 N 2
Szczekociny ○ **PL** 92-93 P 3
Szczytno ○ **PL** 92-93 Q 2
Szechwan = Sichuan ◻ **VRC** 154-155 C 6
Szeged ○ **H** 92-93 Q 5
Székesfehérvár ○ **H** 92-93 P 5
Szekszárd ○ **H** 92-93 P 5
Szentes ○ **H** 92-93 Q 5
Szolnok ○ **H** 92-93 Q 5
Szombathely ○ **H** 92-93 O 5

T

T1 ○ **IRQ** 128-129 J 5
Ta, 108 • **VRC** 154-155 D 3
Taabo, Lac de ○ **CI** 202-203 H 6
Taal, Lake ○ **RP** 160-161 D 5
Taam, Pulau ▲ **RI** 166-167 G 4
Tâba ○ **KSA** 130-131 H 4
Tabaco ○ **RP** 160-161 E 6
Tabaconas ○ **PE** 64-65 C 4
Tabagbuǧ, 'Ain ○ **ET** 194-195 C 3
Tabahanyar ○ **RI** 162-163 E 6
Tabajara ○ **BR** 66-67 G 6
Tabakkentatyr ○ **KA** 124-125 J 5
Tabála ○ **KSA** 132-133 C 3
Tabala ○ **MEX** 50-51 F 5
Tabalosos ○ **PE** 64-65 C 5
Tabanan ○ **RI** 168 B 7
Tabankort ○ **RMM** 196-197 L 6
Tabankort, Hassi • **DZ** 190-191 F 4
Tábanos, Los ○ **RA** 76-77 H 5
Tabaquén ○ **CO** 60-61 G 6
Tábara ○ **E** 98-99 E 8
Tabarano ○ **RI** 164-165 G 5
Tabar Island ~ **PNG** 183 G 2
Tabar Islands ▲ **PNG** 183 G 2
Tabarka ○ **TN** 190-191 G 2
Tabas ○ **IR** 134-135 G 2
Tabasco ◻ **MEX** 52-53 H 2
Tabaskwia Channel ~ **CDN** 34-35 N 4
Tabatinga ○ **BR** 66-67 C 5
Tabatinga, Pico ▲ **BR** 66-67 F 2
Tabatinga, Serra da ▲ **BR** 68-69 F 7
Tabayog, Mount ▲ **RP** 160-161 D 4
Tabbowa ○ **CL** 140-141 H 6
Tabelbala ○ **DZ** 188-189 K 6
Tabelbalet, Hassi • **DZ** 190-191 F 7
Taber ○ **CDN** 32-33 O 7
Taberdga ○ **DZ** 190-191 F 3
Taberfane ○ **RI** 166-167 H 5
Tabernas ○ **E** 98-99 F 6
Tabibuga ○ **PNG** 183 C 3
Tabina ○ **RP** 160-161 E 9
Tabingbulang ○ **RI** 162-163 E 6
Tab'jah ~ **RUS** 108-109 L 7
Tabkin Kouka ○ **RN** 204-205 E 5
Tabla ○ **RN** 204-205 D 2
Tablas ○ **BOL** 70-71 D 5
Tablas, Cabo ▲ **RCH** 76-77 C 4
Tablas, Las ○ **PA** 52-53 O 8
Tablas Island ▲ **RP** 160-161 D 6
Tablas Strait ~ **RP** 160-161 D 6
Tablazo de Ica ⌐ **PE** 64-65 D 9
Table Bay ~ **ZA** 183 E 6
Table Cape ▲ **NZ** 182 F 3
Table Head ▲ **CDN** 38-39 R 4
Tableland ○ **AUS** 172-173 H 4
Tableland Highway II **AUS** 174-175 D 6
Table Mountain ▲ **ZA** 220-221 D 6
Table Rock Lake ○ **USA** 44-45 L 1
Tabletop ▲ **AUS** (WA) 172-173 F 7
Tabletop ▲ **AUS** (WA) 176-177 E 4
Tabletop, Mount ▲ **AUS** 178-179 J 2
Tabligbo ○ **RT** 202-203 L 6
Taboada ○ **RA** 76-77 F 5
Taboca ○ **BR** 66-67 D 7
Tabocal ○ **BR** (AMA) 66-67 D 7
Tabocal ○ **BR** (AMA) 66-67 E 3
Tabocal, Igarapé ~ **BR** 66-67 D 7
Tabocas ○ **BR** 72-73 H 3
Taboco, Rio ~ **BR** 70-71 K 7
Taboleiro ○ **BR** 68-69 J 6
Tabon Caves • **RP** 160-161 C 8
Tabone ○ **RI** 164-165 F 5
Tabong ○ **MYA** 142-143 K 2
Tabor ○ **BF** 202-203 J 4
Tábor ○ **CZ** 92-93 N 4
Tabora ◻ **EAT** 212-213 D 6
Tabora ● **EAT** (TAB) 212-213 D 6
Tabor City ○ **USA** 48-49 J 2
Tabora ☆ **EAT** 212-213 D 6
Tabou ○ **BF** 202-203 J 4
Tabou ○ **CI** 202-203 G 8
Tabrinkout ○ **RIM** 196-197 C 5
Tabriz ○ •• **IR** 128-129 M 3
Tábua, Riachão ~ **BR** 68-69 F 6
Tabuaeran ▲ **KIB** 13 J 2
Tabuan, Pulau ▲ **RI** 162-163 F 7
Tabubil ○ **PNG** 183 A 3
Tabuenan ○ **RI** 164-165 D 5
Tabūk ◻ **KSA** 130-131 F 4

Tabūk ✩ KSA 130-131 E 3
Tabuk ✩ RP 160-161 D 4
Tabulerinho, Cachoeira do ∿ BR 62-63 F 6
Tabulo o RUS 124-125 K 1
Tabūr o SUD 206-207 F 3
Tabusintac Nine Indian Reserve ⅄ CDN 38-39 M 5
Tabwemasana ▲ VAN 184 II a 2
Tacabamba o PE 64-65 C 5
Tacajó o C 54-55 H 4
Tacalaya o PE 70-71 B 5
Tacana, Volcán ▲ GCA 52-53 H 4
Tacañitas o RA 76-77 F 5
Tacarembó, Rio ∿ ROU 78-79 M 2
Tacarigua o YV 60-61 H 2
Tacarigua, Parque Nacional Laguna de ⊥ YV 60-61 J 2
Tacarutu o BR 68-69 J 6
Tacbolubu o RP 160-161 B 8
Tachakou o VRC 146-147 G 3
Tachdalt, Adrar ▲ RMM 196-197 L 5
Tacheng o VRC 146-147 F 2
Tachibana-wan ≋ 152-153 D 8
Tachilek o MYA 142-143 L 5
Tachiumet < LAR 190-191 H 7
Tacima o BR 68-69 L 6
Tacinskij o RUS 102-103 M 6
Taciuã, Lago o BR 66-67 G 5
Tacloban ✩ RP 160-161 F 7
Tacna ✩ PE 70-71 B 6
Tacoma o USA 40-41 C 2
Tacora, Volcán ▲ RCH 70-71 C 5
Taco Taco o C 54-55 D 3
Tacuane o MOC 218-219 J 3
Tacuaras o PY 76-77 J 4
Tacuarembo o ROU 76-77 K 6
Tacuato o YV 60-61 J 2
Tácume • PE 64-65 C 5
Tacunara, Rio ∿ BR 68-69 C 7
Tacupare, Cachoeira ∿ BR 66-67 K 5
Tacurong o RP 160-161 F 9
Tacuru o RP 76-77 K 2
Tacutu, Rio ∿ ROU 76-77 K 6
Tadadahi o SOL 184 I e 4
Tadami-gawa ∿ J 152-153 H 6
Tadant, Oued ∿ DZ 190-191 D 4
Tadao o RP 160-161 C 8
Taddert o MA 188-189 H 5
Taddert, Tizi-n ▲ MA 188-189 J 5
Tadebjajaha ∿ RUS 108-109 Q 6
Tadek Lake o CDN 30-31 F 2
Tadélako < RN 198-199 D 5
Tademait, Plateau du ▲ DZ 190-191 D 4
Tadenet Lake o CDN 24-25 J 6
Tādepallegūdem o IND 140-141 J 2
Tadéra, I-n- < RN 198-199 D 2
Tadio, Lagune ≋ 202-203 H 7
Tadjemout o DZ 190-191 D 4
Tadjentourt ▲ DZ 190-191 F 8
Tadjetaret, Oued ∿ DZ 190-191 F 9
Tadjmout o DZ 190-191 D 4
Tadjoura, Golfe de ≋ 208-209 F 3
Tadjrouna o DZ 190-191 D 4
Tadmur Palmyra ✩∴ SYR 128-129 H 5
Tadoba National Park ⊥ IND 138-139 G 9
Tadohae Haesang National Park ⊥ ROK 150-151 F 10
Tadoule Lake o CDN 30-31 U 6
Tadoussac o CDN 38-39 K 4
Tadpatri o IND 140-141 H 3
Tadrart, Jabal ▲ DZ 190-191 H 8
Taduna o RI 166-167 C 5
Taduno o RI 164-165 H 4
Taech'ōn o ROK 150-151 F 9
Taech'ŏngdo ∿ DVR 150-151 E 8
Taedong Gang ∿ DVR 150-151 E 8
Taegu o ROK 150-151 G 10
Taehan Haehyŏp ≋ 150-151 F 11
Taehūksan Do ∿ ROK 150-151 E 10
Taejŏn o ROK 150-151 F 9
Taejŏng o ROK 150-151 F 11
Taejŏnpyŏngdo ∿ ROK 150-151 E 9
T'aepaek o ROK 150-151 G 9
Ta'er Si • VRC 154-155 D 4
Taёžnyj o RUS 116-117 G 7
Tafalla o E 98-99 G 3
Tafarit, Rās ▲ RIM 196-197 B 4
Tafassasset ∿ RN 198-199 D 2
Tafassasset, Oued ∿ DZ 190-191 G 9
Tafea ◻ VAN 184 II b 4
Tafédek < RN 198-199 C 4
Tafelberg ▲ SME 62-63 F 4
Tafelberg, National Reservaat ⊥ SME 62-63 F 4
Tafermaar o RI 166-167 H 5
Tafí del Valle o • RA 76-77 E 4
Tafila, aṭ- ✩ JOR 130-131 D 2
Tafilalt ± MA 188-189 J 5
Tafinkar < RMM 196-197 M 7
Tafiré o CI 202-203 H 6
Tafraoute o • MA 188-189 G 6
Tafreš o IR 134-135 D 1
Taft o IR 134-135 J 4
Taftān, Kūh-e ▲ IR 134-135 J 4
Tāga o WS 184 V a 1
Tagab o AFG 138-139 B 2
Tagab o SUD 200-201 E 3
Tagagawik River ∿ USA 20-21 L 4
Tagakal Island ∿ USA 22-23 J 7
Taganét Keyna ≋ RMM 196-197 J 5
Taganito o RP 160-161 F 8
Taganrog o ✩ RUS 102-103 H 4
Taganrogskij zaliv ≋ 102-103 K 4
Tagant ▲ RIM 196-197 B 5
Tagapula Island ∿ RP 160-161 F 6
Tagarev, gora ▲ TM 136-137 F 5
Tagari River ∿ PNG 183 B 3
Tagaung o MYA 142-143 K 4

Tagaytay o RP 160-161 D 5
Tagbalé o RCA 206-207 E 6
Tagbara o RCA 206-207 E 6
Tagbilaran ✩ RP 160-161 E 8
Tage, Danau o RI 166-167 J 3
Tagelajiabo o VRC 144-145 F 4
Taghit o DZ 188-189 K 5
Taghouaji, Massif de ▲ RN 198-199 D 4
Tăğiābād, Rūdẖāne-ye ∿ IR 134-135 H 4
Tagish Lake o CDN 20-21 X 6
Taglo Point ▲ RP 160-161 E 8
Tagna ∿ RUS 116-117 K 9
Tagopah, Tanjung ▲ RI 166-167 G 3
Tagou o BF 202-203 L 4
Tagoûraret < RIM 196-197 G 3
Tagpait o RP 160-161 C 8
Tagrina, Oued ∿ DZ 198-199 C 2
Tagrīs, El o IR 136-137 B 7
Taguá o BR 68-69 F 7
Tagua, Rio ∿ CO 60-61 D 6
Taguaruçu, Ribeiro ∿ BR 70-71 K 7
Taguas, Rio de las ∿ RA 76-77 C 5
Taguatinga o BR (FED) 72-73 F 3
Taguatinga o BR (TOC) 72-73 G 2
Taguay o YV 60-61 H 3
Tagum o RP 160-161 F 9
Tah, Sebkha o MA 188-189 E 7
Tahafo o RI 164-165 K 3
Tahala ± DZ 190-191 E 9
Tahalupu o RI 166-167 D 3
Tahamiyam o SUD 200-201 H 3
Tahan, Gunung ▲ MAL 162-163 L 2
Tahan, Kuala o MAL 162-163 E 2
Tāhār o AFG 136-137 L 6
Taharoa o NZ 182 E 3
Tahar-Souk o MA 188-189 J 3
Tahat ▲ DZ 190-191 E 9
Tahe o VRC 150-151 E 1
Tāheri, Bandar-e o IR 134-135 E 5
Tahifet o DZ 190-191 F 9
Tahifet, Oued ∿ DZ 190-191 F 9
Tahilt o MAU 148-149 C 5
Tahiryuak Lake o CDN 24-25 Q 5
Tahiti ∿ F 13 N 4
Tahlāb ∿ PK 134-135 K 4
Tahláb, Dasht-i- ± PK 134-135 J 4
Tahoe, Lake o USA 40-41 D 6
Tahoe Lake o CDN 24-25 R 5
Tahoka o USA 44-45 G 3
Taholah o USA 40-41 B 2
Tahome o LB 202-203 F 7
Tahoua o RN 198-199 B 5
Tahoua ∿ RN (TAH) 198-199 B 5
Tahquamenon Falls State Park ⊥ USA 46-47 F 2
Tahrami o LAR 192-193 F 5
Tahr-e Ğamšid o•• IR 134-135 E 4
Tahrou, Oued ∿ DZ 190-191 D 2
Tahsis o CDN 32-33 G 7
Tahta o ET 194-195 E 4
Tahta o RUS 122-123 H 2
Tahta o TM 136-137 H 7
Tahta-Bazar o TM 136-137 H 7
Tahtaköprü ▲ US 136-137 G 3
Tahtakupyr o US 136-137 G 3
Tahtalı Dağları ▲ TR 128-129 F 3
Tahtamygda o RUS 118-119 L B
Taht-e Soleiman, Kūh-e ▲ IR 136-137 B 6
Taht-e Suleimān o•• IR 128-129 M 4
Tahtojama ∿ RUS 120-121 Q 3
Tahtsa Lake o CDN 32-33 G 7
Tahuamanu, Rio ∿ PE 70-71 B 2
Tahulandang o RI 164-165 J 2
Tahulandang, Pulau ∿ RI 164-165 J 2
Tahuna o RI 164-165 J 2
Tai o CI 202-203 G 7
Tai, Parc National de ⊥ •••• CI 202-203 G 7
Taiama o WAL 202-203 D 7
Tai'an o VRC 154-155 K 3
Taibai o VRC 154-155 H 4
Taibai Shan ▲ VRC 154-155 E 5
Taibao Z.B. ⊥ • VRC 154-155 E 5
Taibet o DZ 190-191 F 4
Taibique o E 188-189 C 7
Taibus Qi o VRC 148-149 M 7
Taichung o VRC 156-157 M 4
Taidatt o MA 188-189 G 6
Ta'if, aṭ o KSA 132-133 B 3
Taigetos ▲ GR 100-101 J 6
Taigu o VRC 154-155 H 3
Taihang Shan ▲ VRC 154-155 H 4
Taihape o NZ 182 E 3
Taihe o VRC (ANH) 154-155 J 5
Taihe o VRC (JXI) 156-157 J 3
Taihu o VRC (ANH) 154-155 K 6
Tai Hu o VRC (JIA) 154-155 M 6
Taijiang o VRC 156-157 F 2
Taikang o VRC 154-155 J 4
Taikkyi o MYA 158-159 C 2
Tailai o VRC 150-151 D 4
Tailako o RI 166-167 C 6
Tailem Bend o AUS 180-181 G 6
Tailing o GUY 62-63 G 2
Taim o BR 74-75 D 9
Taimá' o • KSA 130-131 F 4
Taimana o RMM 202-203 G 3
Taimba o RUS 116-117 U 5
Taimushan • VRC 156-157 M 3
Tain o GB 90-91 G 3
Tainan o VRC 156-157 M 5
Tainhas o BR 74-75 E 7
Taining o VRC 156-157 K 3
Taino, Plage ∿ RH 54-55 J 5
Taió o BR 74-75 E 6
Taioibeiras o BR 72-73 J 3
Taiof Island ∿ PNG 184 I b 1
Taipei ★ VRC 156-157 M 4
Taiping o• MAL 162-163 L 2
Taiping o VRC (GXI) 156-157 F 5
Taiping o VRC (GXI) 156-157 F 5
Taipingchuan o VRC 150-151 D 5

Taiping L. ▲ VRC 150-151 C 4
Taipong o GUY 62-63 E 3
Taipur o IND 142-143 D 3
Tair, Ǧabal at- ∿ Y 132-133 B 6
Tairhemt, Tizi-n ▲ MA 188-189 J 4
Tairona, Parque Nacional ⊥•• CO 60-61 D 2
Tais o RI 162-163 E 7
Taisha o EC 64-65 D 3
Taisi o VRC (GDG) 156-157 H 5
Taishan ▲ • VRC (SHD) 154-155 K 3
Taishi o RC 156-157 M 5
Taishun o VRC 156-157 L 3
Taisiya ± KSA 130-131 H 3
Taita Hills ▲ EAK 212-213 G 5
Taitaitanopo, Pulau ∿ RI 162-163 D 6
Taitao, Península de ∿ RCH 80 C 3
Taititu o BR 66-67 D 5
Taitna Lake o CDN 30-31 S 5
Taitung o RC 156-157 M 5
Taivalkoski o FIN 88-89 K 4
Taiwan ◻ RC 156-157 M 5
Taiwan Banks ≈ 156-157 L 5
Taiwan Strait ≈ 156-157 L 5
Tai Xian o VRC 154-155 M 5
Taiyang Dao • VRC 150-151 F 5
Taiyuan ✩ • VRC 154-155 H 3
Taizhou o VRC 154-155 L 5
Taizhou Liedao ∿ VRC 156-157 M 2
Taizhou Wan ≈ VRC 156-157 M 2
Ta'izz ✩ Y 132-133 D 7
Tajdon ∿ RUS 114-115 T 7
Tajen o RC 156-157 M 5
Tajga o RUS 114-115 S 6
Tajga o RUS (SHL) 122-123 K 4
Tajga ∿ RUS 116-117 H 6
Tajgan o MAU 148-149 C 4
Tajgonos, mys ▲ RUS 120-121 T 3
Tajgonos, poluostrov ∪ RUS 120-121 T 3
Tajicaringa o MEX 50-51 G 6
Tajin, El ∴•• MEX 52-53 F 1
Tajkanskij, hrebet ▲ RUS 122-123 F 2
Tajlan, köl ∿ KA 96-97 G 10
Taj Mahal ∴•• IND 138-139 G 6
Tajmendra, Bol'šaja ∿ RUS 118-119 H 6
Tajmura ∿ RUS 116-117 V 6
Tajmylyr o RUS 110-111 N 3
Tajmyr, ostrov ∿ RUS 108-109 a 3
Tajmyr, ozero o RUS 108-109 e 2
Tajmyra, mys ▲ RUS 108-109 b 3
Tajmyrskij zaliv ≈ RUS 108-109 b 3
Tajnnynotskij hrebet ▲ RUS 120-121 T 3
Tajo, Río ∿ E 98-99 F 4
Tajšet o RUS 116-117 J 8
Tajumulco, Volcán ▲ GCA 52-53 J 4
Tajuña, Río ∿ E 98-99 F 4
Tajūrā' o LAR 192-193 F 1
Tajura ∿ RUS 116-117 N 7
Tak o THA 158-159 E 5
Takāb o IR 128-129 M 4
Takaba o EAK 212-213 H 2
Takachiho o J 152-153 D 8
Takahashi o J 152-153 E 7
Takahashi-gawa ∿ J 152-153 E 7
Takahe, Mount ▲ ARK 16 F 26
Takaka o NZ 182 D 4
Takalala o RI 164-165 F 6
Takalar o RI 164-165 F 6
Takalou o TCH 206-207 D 3
Takalous, Oued ∿ DZ 190-191 F 9
Takamaka o SY 224 D 2
Takamatsu ✩ J (EHI) 152-153 E 8
Takamatsu ✩ • J (KAG) 152-153 F 7
Takan, Gunung ▲ RI 168 C 7
Takanabe o J 152-153 D 8
Takanosu o J 152-153 J 4
Takaoka o J 152-153 G 6
Takapuna o NZ 182 E 2
Takara o RCA 206-207 E 4
Takara-shima ∿ J 152-153 D 9
Takasaki o J 152-153 H 6
Takatokwane o RB 220-221 G 2
Takatsuki o J 152-153 F 7
Takatu hrebet ▲ RUS 96-97 K 7
Takaungu o EAK 212-213 G 5
Takayama o J 152-153 G 6
Takefu o J 152-153 G 7
Takengon (Takingeun) o RI 162-163 B 2
Takeo o J 152-153 C 8
Takeo o K 158-159 H 5
Tákestān o IR 128-129 N 4
Taketa o J 152-153 D 8
Tak Fa o THA 158-159 F 3
Takhini River ∿ CDN 20-21 W 6
Takhro o THA 158-159 G 5
Takht-i-Bahi ∴ PK 138-139 C 2
Takht-i-Sulaiman ▲ PK 138-139 B 4
Takiéta o RN 198-199 D 6
Takikawa o J 152-153 J 3
Takino ue o J 152-153 K 2
Takis o PNG 183 F 3
Takisset, Oued ∿ DZ 190-191 H 8
Takiyoki, Pointe ▲ CDN 36-37 P 5
Takiyuak Lake o CDN 30-31 O 2
Takla Landing o CDN 32-33 H 4
Takla Makan Desert = Taklimakan Shamo ± VRC 146-147 E 6
Takli Dhokeshwar o IND 138-139 E 10
Taklimakan Shamo ± VRC 146-147 E 6
Taknis o LAR 192-193 J 1
Takobanda o RCA 206-207 E 5
Takoradi o• GH 202-203 K 7
Takorka o RN 198-199 C 6
Takoutala o SN 202-203 C 3
Takrit o IRQ 128-129 K 5
Takpamba o RT 202-203 L 5
Takpouma o LB 202-203 G 8
Taksagerbej, grjada ▲ RUS 108-109 a 5
Taksimo o RUS 118-119 G 7

Takslesluk Lake o USA 20-21 J 6
Taku Arm ∿ CDN 20-21 X 7
Takum o WAN 204-205 H 7
Takundi o ZRE 210-211 X 7
Taku Plateau ⊥ CDN 20-21 Y 7
Taku River ∿ CDN 32-33 D 2
Takwa ∴ EAK 212-213 H 5
Tāl o IND 138-139 F 8
Tala o EAK 212-213 G 5
Tala o MEX 52-53 C 1
Tala o ROU 78-79 M 3
Tala, Ćubuka-gora ▲ RUS 110-111 a 7
Tala, El o RA 76-77 E 4
Tala, El ∿ RA 76-77 C 6
Talagang o PK 138-139 D 4
Talagante o RCH 78-79 D 2
Talāhāt, Ša'īb at- ∿ IRQ 128-129 L 7
Talahini o CI 202-203 J 5
Talahini-Tomora o CI 202-203 J 5
Talaimannar o CL 140-141 H 6
Talaivasal o IND 140-141 H 5
Talaja o RUS (MAG) 120-121 P 3
Talaja o IND 138-139 D 8
Talakalla o IND 140-141 J 6
Talakan o RUS (AMR) 122-123 D 3
Talakan o RUS (HBR) 122-123 E 4
Talali o RUS 122-123 D 3
Talamanca, Cordillera de ▲ CR 52-53 C 7
Talamba o PK 138-139 D 4
Talanga o RN 52-53 L 4
Talangbetutu o RI 162-163 F 6
Talangjauh o RI 162-163 F 6
Talangpadung o RI 162-163 F 7
Talara o PE 64-65 B 4
Talaroo o AUS 174-175 G 6
Talas ∿ KA 124-125 G 6
Talas ∿ KA 124-125 F 6
Talas o KS 136-137 N 3
Talasea o PNG 183 E 3
Talasskij Alatau, hrebet ▲ KA 136-137 M 3
Talata-Ampano o RM 222-223 E 8
Talatakoh, Pulau ∿ RI 164-165 H 4
Talata Mafara o WAN 198-199 C 6
Talat at-Timiat o KSA 130-131 H 4
Tal'at Damya o KSA 130-131 E 4
Talaud, Kepulauan ∿ RI 164-165 K 1
Talavera, Ilha ∿ PY 76-77 J 4
Talavera de la Reina o • E 98-99 E 5
Talawana o AUS 172-173 E 7
Talawanta o AUS 174-175 F 6
Talawdi o SUD 206-207 K 3
Talawe, Mount ▲ PNG 183 E 3
Talawi o RI 162-163 D 5
Talbot ∿ AUS 176-177 J 3
Talbot, Mount ▲ AUS 176-177 J 3
Talbot Glacier ⊂ CDN 24-25 g 2
Talbot Inlet ≈ 24-25 b 2
Talbot Lake o CDN 34-35 G 3
Talbotton o USA 48-49 F 3
Talbragar River ∿ AUS 180-181 K 2
Talca ✩ RCH 78-79 D 3
Talcahuano o RCH 78-79 C 4
Talcan, Isla ∿ RCH 78-79 C 7
Tālcher o IND 142-143 D 5
Talcho o RN 198-199 B 5
Taldom o RUS 94-95 P 3
Taldy ∿ KA 124-125 J 4
Taldy-Bulak o VRC 146-147 F 2
Taldyk, pereval ▲ KS 136-137 N 5
Taldykorgan o KA 124-125 L 6
Taldygorghan = Taldykorgan ✩ KA 124-125 L 6
Taleb, Bir < RMM 196-197 F 6
Taleex o SP 208-209 J 4
Talegaon o IND 138-139 G 9
Tālem o IR 128-129 N 4
Talence o F 90-91 G 9
Taléqān o AFG 136-137 L 6
Taléqān Rūd ∿ AFG 136-137 L 6
Talequah o USA 44-45 K 2
Tāleš, Kūhhā-ye ▲ IR 128-129 N 4
Taley o RCA 206-207 D 3
Talgar o KA 146-147 C 4
Talgar, pik ▲ KA 124-125 L 6
Talguharai o SUD 200-201 G 3
Talḥah, Kōtal-e ▲ AFG 134-135 L 1
Taliabu, Pulau ∿ RI 164-165 J 4
Talibon o RP 160-161 F 7
Talibura o RI 166-167 G 6
Talica ✩ RUS 114-115 G 6
Talicherla o IND 140-141 H 3
Talihina o USA 44-45 K 2
Talikota o IND 140-141 G 2
Talimã o BR 62-63 G 6
Talina, Río ∿ BOL 76-77 E 1
Taling Chan o THA 158-159 F 4
Taliouine o MA 188-189 H 5
Taliparamba o IND 140-141 F 4
Talipaw o RP 160-161 D 10
Talipolo, Tanjung ▲ RI 164-165 F 5
Tali Post o SUD 206-207 K 6
Talisayan o RP 160-161 D 6
Talisei, Pulau ∿ RI 164-165 J 3
Taliwang o RI 168 C 7
Taljain ∿ RUS 112-113 S 4
Taljany ∿ RUS 116-117 L 9
Talkeetna o USA 20-21 P 5
Talkeetna Mountains ▲ USA 20-21 Q 6
Talkeetna River ∿ USA 20-21 P 5
Tall, at- o SYR 128-129 G 6

Talladega o USA 48-49 E 3
Tall 'Afar o IRQ 128-129 K 4
Tallahassee ✩ USA 48-49 F 4
Tall al-Abyaḍ ✩ SYR 128-129 H 4
Tallangatta o AUS 180-181 J 4
Tallaringa Conservation Park ⊥ AUS 176-177 M 4
Tall Birāk o SYR 128-129 J 4
Tallering Peak ▲ AUS 176-177 C 4
Tall Ğudaida ∴ IRQ 130-131 K 2
Tall Ḥarīri ∴ SYR 128-129 J 5
Tall Ḥugna o IRQ 128-129 K 4
Tallin = Tallinn ★ EST 94-95 J 2
Tallinn ★•• EST 94-95 J 2
Tallkalā o SYR 128-129 G 5
Tall-Kalah o SYR 128-129 G 5
Tall Kūšik o SYR 128-129 K 4
Tallorutīt ∿ GRØ 26-27 d 4
Tall Sāğir Bāzār o • SYR 128-129 J 4
Tall Tamr o SYR 128-129 J 4
Tallulah o USA 44-45 M 3
Tall 'Uwainát o IRQ 128-129 K 4
Talmassah o MA 188-189 G 5
Talnah o RUS 108-109 X 7
Taloard o IR 134-135 D 3
Taloda o IND 138-139 E 9
Talokan o RUS (AMR) 122-123 D 3
Talokan o RUS (HBR) 122-123 E 4
Talali o RUS 122-123 D 3
Talovskoe, ozero o RUS 120-121 V 3
Talovka o RUS 122-123 B 3
Talovka o RUS 112-113 O 5
Talovka o RUS 112-113 N 5
Talovka, ozero o RUS 120-121 V 3
Talras < RN 198-199 D 3
Talšānd o MAU 148-149 C 5
Talsen = Talsi o• LV 94-95 H 3
Talsi o• LV 94-95 H 3
Talsint o MA 188-189 K 4
Taltal o RCH 76-77 B 4
Taltal, Quebrada de ∿ RCH 76-77 B 3
Taltson River ∿ CDN 30-31 N 5
Talu o RI 162-163 C 4
Taludaa o RI 164-165 H 3
Talvár, Rūdẖāne-ye ∿ IR 128-129 N 4
Talwood o AUS 178-179 K 5
Talyawalka Anabranch ∿ AUS 180-181 G 4
Tama o RN 198-199 D 3
Tama o USA 42-43 K 5
Tama, Parque Nacional el ⊥ YV 60-61 F 4
Tama Abu, Banjaran ▲ MAL 164-165 D 2
Tamacuari, Pico ▲ BR 66-67 E 2
Tamad, aṭ- o RUS 166-167 G 4
Tamafupae o J 152-153 F 6
Tama-gawa ∿ J 152-153 J 5
Tamako o RI 164-165 J 2
Tamala = Yopei o GH 202-203 K 5
Tamale ✩ GH 202-203 K 5
Taman o IR 168 C 3
Tamaná, Cerro ▲ CO 60-61 C 5
Tamanaco, Embalse ∿ YV 60-61 J 3
Tamanar o MA 188-189 G 5
Tamanco o PE 64-65 E 4
Tamandouririt < RMM 196-197 K 5
Tamanduá o BR (AMA) 66-67 D 5
Tamanduá o BR (MIN) 72-73 J 4
Tamaneke o SOL 184 I c 3
Tamango, Parque Nacional ⊥ RCH 80 D 3
Tamanhint o LAR 192-193 F 4
Tamani o RMM 202-203 G 3
Tamaniquá o BR 66-67 E 4
Taman Negara National Park ⊥ •• MAL 162-163 E 2
Tamano o J 152-153 E 7
Tamanrasset ✩ •• DZ 190-191 E 9
Tamanrasset, Oued ∿ DZ 190-191 D 9
Tamanredjo o SME 62-63 G 3
Tamanskij zaliv ≈ 102-103 K 5
Tamaquillo o PE 64-65 D 6
Tamar, Alto de ▲ CO 60-61 D 4
Tamarack Island ∿ CDN 34-35 H 5
Tamaraná o BR 72-73 E 7
Tamarike o RI 166-167 L 6
Tamarit o OM 132-133 J 5
Tamarou o DY 204-205 E 4
Tamarugal, Pampa del ± RCH 70-71 C 6
Tamaruz, Pampa del ∿ RCH 76-77 C 1
Tamási o H 92-93 P 5
Tamaso o SUD 200-201 F 6
Tamassoumit o RIM 196-197 E 3
Tamat, Wādi ∿ LAR 192-193 G 2
Tamatama o YV 60-61 H 5
Tamatave = Toamasina ✩ RM 222-223 F 7
Tamaulipas ◻ MEX 50-51 K 6
Tama Wildlife Reserve ⊥ ETH 208-209 C 5
Tamaya, Rio ∿ PE 64-65 F 6
Tamazula de Gordiano o MEX 52-53 C 2
Tamazulapán o MEX 52-53 F 3
Tamazunchale o• MEX 50-51 K 7
Tamba ∿ RI 168 C 3
Tambach o EAK 212-213 F 4
Tambacounda o SN 202-203 D 3
Tambakara o RMM 202-203 D 3
Tamba Kosi ∿ NEP 144-145 F 7
Tambalongang, Pulau ∿ RI 168 C 8
Tamban o RP 160-161 E 6
Tambapui o BR 66-67 E 7
Tambara o BR 202-203 J 4
Tambarga ◻ BR 202-203 J 4
Tambar Springs o AUS 178-179 K 6
Tambaur o IND 142-143 J 7
Tambawel o WAN 198-199 B 6
Tambelan ≈ 216-217 G 6
Tambea o SOL 184 I d 3
Tämbelbui o IND 140-141 L 4

Tambej o RUS 108-109 O 6
Tambelan Besar, Pulau ∿ RI 162-163 G 4
Tambelan Kepulauan ∿ RI 162-163 G 4
Tambellup o AUS 176-177 D 7
Tamberu o RI 168 E 3
Tambillo o EC 64-65 C 3
Tambillo, Quebrada ∿ RCH 76-77 C 1
Tambisan, Pulau ∿ MAL 160-161 C 10
Tambo o AUS 178-179 J 3
Tambo o PE 64-65 C 5
Tambo, El o CO 60-61 C 6
Tambo, Rio ∿ PE 64-65 F 7
Tambo, Rio ∿ PE 70-71 B 4
Tambobamba o PE 64-65 F 8
Tambo Colorado ∴ PE 64-65 E 8
Tambo Grande o PE 64-65 B 4
Tambohorano o RM 222-223 C 6
Tamboli o RI 164-165 G 5
Tambopata, Rio ∿ PE 70-71 C 3
Tambo Ponciano o PE 66-67 B 4
Tambo Pucacuro o PE 64-65 E 3
Tambor o ANG 216-217 B 8
Tambor o BR 66-67 F 4
Tambora, Gunung ▲ RI 168 C 7
Tambores o ROU 76-77 J 6
Tamboril o BR 68-69 H 4
Tamboritha, Mount ▲ AUS 180-181 J 4
Tambo Tambillo o BOL 70-71 D 6
Tamboura o RCA 206-207 G 6
Tambov o ✩ RUS 94-95 R 5
Tambovka o RUS 122-123 B 3
Tambo Yacu, Rio ∿ PE 64-65 F 4
Tambrey ∴ AUS 172-173 C 6
Tambu, Teluk ≈ RI 164-165 G 4
Tambugo o RP 160-161 D 4
Tambul o PNG 183 B 3
Tambunan o MAL 160-161 B 10
Tambura o SUD 206-207 H 6
Tambuttegama o CL 140-141 J 6
Tamc dabaa ▲ MAU 146-147 L 3
Tāmchakett o RIM 196-197 G 6
Tamdibulak o US 136-137 J 4
Tamdy o KA 124-125 E 4
Tam Điệp o VN 156-157 D 6
Tāndárei o RO 102-103 E 5
Tanderiouel ∿ RMM 202-203 K 2
Tandil o RA 78-79 K 4
Tamdytov, toglari ▲ US 136-137 J 4
Tame o CO 60-61 F 4
Tämega, Rio ∿ P 98-99 C 4
Tamegroute o MA 188-189 J 5
Tamelelt o MA 188-189 H 5
Tamelhat o DZ 190-191 F 4
Tamenglong o IND 142-143 H 3
Tamesi, Rio ∿ MEX 50-51 K 6
Tamesna ± RN 198-199 B 3
Tamewali = Khairpur o PK 138-139 D 5
Tamezret o TN 190-191 H 4
Tamghas o NEP 144-145 D 6
Tamiahua o MEX 50-51 L 7
Tamiahua, Laguna de ≈ MEX 50-51 L 7
Tamiang ∿ RI 162-163 B 2
Tamica o RUS 88-89 P 4
Tami Islands ∿ PNG 183 D 4
Tamil Nādu ◻ IND 140-141 G 5
Tamiš ∿ YU 158-159 K 3
Tamiwa o VN 158-159 K 3
Tamky o VN 158-159 K 3
Tamlelt, Plaine de ± MA 188-189 K 4
Tamluk o IND 142-143 E 4
Tamma ∿ RUS 118-119 O 5
Tammisaari = Ekenäs o• FIN 88-89 G 7
Tammū, Jabal ▲ LAR 192-193 F 6
Tamou o RN 204-205 E 2
Tampa o ANG (NAM) 216-217 D 7
Tampa ∿ RMM 216-217 B 7
Tampa o USA 48-49 G 6
Tampang, Rio ∿ RI 168 C 3
Tampa Bay ≈ 48-49 G 6
Tampang o RI 162-163 N 6
Tampa Hill ▲ AUS 176-177 C 6
Tampia Hill ▲ AUS 176-177 C 6
Tampico o• MEX 50-51 L 6
Tampin o MEX 50-51 L 6
Tampoko ≈ ...
Tampoko o RF 224 B 7
Tampomá ▲ BF 202-203 L 4
Tampon, Le o F 224 B 7
Tampué, Massif du ▲ RG 202-203 D 3
Tamsá o H 92-93 P 5
Tamsagbulag o RIM 196-197 K 3
Tamsaomit o RIM 196-197 E 3
Tamri o MA 188-189 G 5
Tamshiyacu o PE 64-65 F 5
Tamsweg o • A 92-93 M 5
Tamu o MYA 142-143 H 6
Tamuin o• MEX 50-51 K 7
Tamul o NEP 144-145 F 7
Tamur ∿ NEP 144-145 F 7
Tamuratvam ∿ RUS 112-113 S 6
Tamworth o AUS 178-179 L 6
Tana ∿ N 86-87 O 1
Tana ∿ EAK 212-213 G 4
Tana = Île Tanna ∿ VAN 184 II b 4
Tana, Lake = T'ana Hayk' o ETH 200-201 H 6
Tanabe o J 152-153 F 8
Tanabi o BR 72-73 F 6
Tanacross o USA 20-21 U 5
Tanadak Island ∿ USA 22-23 G 7
Tanafjorden ≈ 86-87 O 1
Tanaga Island ∿ USA 22-23 G 7
Tanah, Danau o RI 166-167 G 2
Tanahbala, Pulau ∿ RI 162-163 C 5
Tanahgrogot o RI 164-165 G 5
Tanahjampea, Pulau ∿ RI 168 C 8
Tanahmasa, Pulau ∿ RI 162-163 C 5
Tanahmerah o RI (IRJ) 166-167 G 3
Tanahmerah o RI (KTI) 164-165 G 4
Tanahmolala, Pulau ∿ RI 168 C 6
Tanah Rata o MAL 162-163 D 2

Tanahwangko o RI 164-165 J 3
Tänai o PK 138-139 B 3
Tanakeke o RI 164-165 F 6
Tanakeke, Pulau ∿ RI 164-165 F 6
Tanakpur o RMM 144-145 C 6
Tanal o RMM 202-203 J 2
Tanama o BF 202-203 K 3
Tanama ∿ RUS 108-109 S 7
Tanamalwila o CL 140-141 J 7
Tanami, Mount ▲ AUS 176-177 J 3
Tanami Desert ± AUS 172-173 K 5
Tanami Desert Wildlife Sanctuary ⊥ AUS 172-173 K 6
Tanami Mine ∴ AUS 172-173 J 6
Tanami Road II AUS 172-173 J 6
Tân An ✩ VN 158-159 J 5
Tanana o USA 20-21 O 4
Tanana River ∿ USA 20-21 S 4
Tanandava o RM 222-223 C 8
Tanani o USA 20-21 X 7
Tanantou o RG 202-203 F 5
Tan-ó Camiña, Quebrada de ∿ RCH 70-71 B 6
Tana River Primate National Reserve ⊥ EAK 212-213 H 4
Tanārut, Wādi ∿ LAR 190-191 H 6
Tanatar, ozera o RUS 124-125 L 3
Tanba-kochi ▲ J 152-153 F 7
Tanbaoura, Falaise de ▲ RMM 202-203 E 3
Tancheng o VRC 154-155 L 4
Tanchon o DVR 150-151 G 7
Tanchon Karang o MAL 162-163 D 3
Tancítaro, Cerro ▲ MEX 52-53 C 2
Tancítaro, Parque Nacional ⊥ MEX 52-53 C 2
Tancuime o MEX 50-51 K 7
Tanda o CI 202-203 J 6
Tanda ∿ RUS 120-121 P 4
Tanda, Lac o RMM 202-203 H 2
Tandako o RG 202-203 G 4
Tandalti o SUD 200-201 E 6
Tāndárei o RO 102-103 E 5
Tanderiouel ∿ RMM 202-203 K 2
Tandil o RA 78-79 K 4
Tandil, Sierra del ▲ RA 78-79 K 4
Tandjilé ∿ TCH 206-207 C 4
Tandjilé ∿ TCH 206-207 C 4
Tandjouaré o RT 202-203 L 4
Tāndliänwāla o PK 138-139 D 4
Tando Ādam o PK 138-139 B 7
Tando Allāhyār o PK 138-139 B 7
Tando Bāgo o PK 138-139 B 7
Tando Ikram o PK 138-139 B 7
Tando Jam o PK 138-139 B 7
Tando Muhammad Khān o PK 138-139 B 7
Tandou Lake o AUS 180-181 G 4
Tandovo, ozero o RUS 114-115 O 7
Tando Zinze o ANG 210-211 D 6
Tandubatu Island ∿ RP 160-161 D 10
Tandung o RI 164-165 F 5
Tandür o IND 140-141 G 2
Tanega-shima ∿ J 152-153 D 9
Taneichi o J 152-153 J 4
Tan Emellet o DZ 190-191 G 7
Tanetze, Danau o RI 166-167 G 2
Tanete o RI 164-165 G 6
Taneti, Pulau ∿ RI 164-165 K 4
Tanezrouft ± DZ 196-197 K 3
Tanezrouft-Tan-Ahenet ∿ DZ 190-191 O 9
Tanezzruft, Wādi ∿ LAR 190-191 H 8
Tanf, at- o SYR 128-129 H 6
Tanga ✩ EAT 212-213 G 6
Tanga o RUS 118-119 E 10
Tanga < TCH 198-199 J 4
Tangail o BD 142-143 F 3
Tanga Islands ∿ PNG 183 G 2
Tangalle o CL 140-141 J 7
Tanganyika, Lac = Lake Tanganyika o ZRE 214-215 J 3
Tanganyika, Lake = Lac Tanganyika o BU 214-215 J 3
Tangara o BR 68-69 L 5
Tangará da Serra o BR 70-71 J 4
Tangarana, Rio ∿ PE 64-65 E 3
Tangarare o SOL 184 I d 3
Tangaye o BF 202-203 L 4
Tangent Point ▲ USA 20-21 N 1
Tanger = Tanjah ✩ • MA 188-189 J 3
Tangerang o RI 168 B 3
Tangermünde o • D 92-93 L 2
Tanggu o VRC 154-155 K 2
Tangguantun o VRC 154-155 K 2
Tanggula (Dangla) Shan ▲ VRC 144-145 G 4
Tanggulangin o RI 168 E 3
Tanggula Shankou ▲ VRC 144-145 H 4
Tangha ∿ RUS 120-121 D 3
Tangi o PK 138-139 C 2
Tangiahe Z.B. ⊥ • VRC 154-155 D 5
Tangkak o MAL 162-163 E 3
Tangkoto-Batuangus-Dua Saudara Reserves ⊥ RI 164-165 J 3
Tangmai o VRC 144-145 G 5
Tangmai o VRC 144-145 G 5
Tangnay ∿ RUS 118-119 G 5
Tangorin o AUS 178-179 H 1
Tangoûnan = Ti-n-Aguelhaj < RMM 196-197 J 6
Tangra Yumco o VRC 144-145 F 5
Tangse o RI 162-163 A 2
Tangshan o VRC 154-155 L 2
Tangu o PNG 183 C 3
Tangue River Reservoir < USA 42-43 D 4
Tanguieta o DY 202-203 L 4
Tanguin-Dassouri o BF 202-203 K 3

Tangulbei ○ **EAK** 212-213 F 3
Tangyuan ○ **VRC** 150-151 G 4
Tân Hiep ○ **VN** 158-159 H 5
Tánh Linh ○ **VN** 158-159 J 5
Tanhoj ○ **RUS** 116-117 M 10
Tanhuijo, Arrecife ∧ **MEX** 50-51 L 7
Tani ○ **AFG** 138-139 B 3
Taniantaweng Shan ▲ **VRC** 144-145 N 5
Tanichuchi ○ **EC** 64-65 C 2
Taniga ○ **MOC** 220-221 L 2
Tanimbar, Kepulauan ⌒ **RI** 166-167 F 6
Taninga ○ **MOC** 220-221 L 2
Taninthari ○ **MYA** 158-159 E 4
Taninthari ∧ **MYA** 158-159 E 4
Tanipaddi ○ **IND** 140-141 H 4
Tanis ∴· **ET** 194-195 E 2
Tanisapata ○ **RI** 166-167 G 3
Tãniya, Ģabal at- ▲ **Y** 132-133 E 2
Tanjah ☆ **MA** 188-189 J 3
Tanjay ○ **RP** 160-161 E 8
Tan'ju ∧ **RUS** 108-109 L 8
Tanjung ○ **RI** (JTE) 168 C 3
Tanjung ○ **RI** (KSE) 164-165 D 5
Tanjung ○ **RI** (NBA) 168 C 7
Tanjung Api Reserve ⊥· **RI** 164-165 G 4
Tanjungbalai ○ **RI** 162-163 C 2
Tanjungbatu ○ **RI** 164-165 F 2
Tanjungbaya, Pulau ∧ **RI** 164-165 F 3
Tanjungenim ○ **RI** 162-163 E 6
Tanjungkarang = Bandar Lampung ○ **RI** 162-163 F 7
Tanjunglolo ○ **RI** 162-163 D 5
Tanjung Malim ○ **MAL** 162-163 C 2
Tanjungmangil ○ **RI** 162-163 C 2
Tanjungmarcang ○ **RI** 162-163 F 6
Tanjungniur ○ **RI** 162-163 D 5
Tanjungpandan ○ **RI** 162-163 G 6
Tanjung Panjang Reserve ⊥· **RI** 164-165 G 3
Tanjungpinang ○ **RI** 162-163 E 5
Tanjungpura ○ **RI** 162-163 C 3
Tanjungraja ○ **RI** 162-163 F 6
Tanjungraya ○ **RI** 162-163 E 7
Tanjungredeb ○ **RI** 164-165 F 2
Tanjungsaleh, Pulau ∧ **RI** 162-163 H 5
Tanjungselor ○ **RI** 164-165 E 2
Tanjung Sepat ○ **MAL** 162-163 D 3
Tanjunguban ○ **RI** 162-163 G 6
Tanjungwaringin ○ **RI** 162-163 G 6
Tanjurer ∧ **RUS** 112-113 S 4
Tãnk ○ **PK** 138-139 C 3
Tank ○ **USA** 44-45 J 4
Tankse ○ **IND** 138-139 G 2
Tankses ∧ **RUS** 114-115 T 4
Tankwa ○ **ZA** 220-221 D 6
Tankwa-Karoo National Park ⊥ **ZA** 220-221 D 6
Tân Ky ○ **VN** 156-157 D 7
Tanlova ∧ **RUS** 116-117 N 2
Tanlovajaha ∧ **RUS** 108-109 N 8
Tân Minh ○ **VN** 158-159 J 5
Tanna, Île = Tana ∧ **VAN** 184 II b 4
Tannakallu ○ **IND** 140-141 H 4
Tannin ○ **CDN** 34-35 L 6
Tannum Sands ○ **AUS** 178-179 L 2
Tannûra, Ra's ○ **KSA** 134-135 D 5
Tano ○ **GH** 202-203 J 6
Tano, Tanjung ▲ **RI** 168 C 7
Tanon Strait ≋ 160-161 E 8
Tanot ○ **IND** 138-139 C 6
Tanougou ○ **DY** 202-203 L 4
Tanougou, Cascades de ∼··∨ **DY** 202-203 L 4
Tanout ○ **RN** 198-199 D 5
Tanouzkka, Sebkhet ∽ **MA** 196-197 C 3
Tân Phú ○ **VN** 158-159 J 5
Tanquary Fiord ≋ 26-27 L 3
Tanque Novo ○ **BR** 72-73 J 2
Tanque Nuevo ○ **MEX** 50-51 H 4
Tanquinho ○ **BR** 68-69 J 7
Tansarga ○ **BF** 202-203 L 4
Tansen ○ **NEP** 144-145 D 7
Tanshui · **RC** 156-157 M 4
Tansilla ○ **BF** 202-203 H 4
Tanşulôkh ○ **LAR** 192-193 J 1
Tantã ○ **ET** 194-195 E 2
Tantamayo ○ **PE** 64-65 D 6
Tan-Tan ☆ **MA** 188-189 D 6
Tan-Tan-Plage ○ **MA** 188-189 F 6
Tân Thu'o'ng ○ **VN** 158-159 J 5
Tan Ti-m-Missaou, Tassili ▲ **DZ** 196-197 M 4
Tantoyuca ○ **MEX** 50-51 K 7
Tanūma ○ **KSA** 132-133 C 4
Tanumbirini ○ **AUS** 174-175 C 5
Tanumshede ○ **S** 86-87 E 7
Tanxi ○ **VRC** 156-157 F 7
Tanyan ○ **MYA** 142-143 L 4
Tanzania ○ **EAT** 214-215 F 3
Tanzilla Plateau ▲ **CDN** 32-33 E 2
Tanzilla River ∧ **CDN** 32-33 E 2
Taocun ○ **VRC** 154-155 M 3
Tao He ∧ **VRC** 154-155 C 4
Taohua Dao ∧ **VRC** 156-157 N 2
Taohuayuan · **VRC** 156-157 G 2
Taojiang ○ **VRC** 156-157 H 2
Taonan ○ **VRC** 150-151 D 5
Taopa ○ **RI** 164-165 G 3
Taora ○ **SOL** 184 I c 2
Taormina ○ **I** 100-101 H 4
Taos, Pueblo ∴··· **USA** 44-45 J 3
Taoshan Shouliechang · **VRC** 150-151 G 4
Taouârdei ∧ **RMM** 196-197 L 6
Taoudenni ○ **RMM** 196-197 L 6
Taounate ☆ **MA** 188-189 J 3
Taourirt ○ **MA** (Ojd) 188-189 K 3
Taourirt ○ **MA** (Orz) 188-189 H 5
Taouz ○ **MA** 188-189 J 5
Taoyuan ○ **RC** 156-157 M 4
Taoyuan ○ **VRC** 156-157 G 2
Tapachula ○ **MEX** 52-53 H 4
Tapah ○ **MAL** 162-163 D 2
Tapah, Tanjung ▲ **RI** 162-163 F 6

Tapaiuna, Cachoeira ∽ **BR** 66-67 K 6
Tapaiuna, Ribeiro ∧ **BR** 70-71 J 2
Tapajos, Rio ∧ **BR** 66-67 K 5
Tapajós, Rio ∧ **BR** 66-67 K 4
Tapaktuan ○ **RI** 162-163 B 3
Tapalpa ○· **MEX** 52-53 C 2
Tapalqué ○ **RA** 78-79 J 4
Tapalqué, Arroyo ∧ **RA** 78-79 J 4
Tapan ○ **RI** 162-163 D 5
Tapanahonirivier ∧ **SME** 62-63 G 4
Tapandulu ○ **RI** 164-165 F 5
Tapanuli, Teluk ≋ 162-163 C 4
Tapat, Pulau ∧ **RI** 164-165 K 4
Tapauá ○ **BR** 66-67 F 5
Tapauá, Rio ∧ **BR** 66-67 E 5
Tapauá, Rio ∧ **BR** 66-67 D 5
Tapaulama, Tanjung ▲ **RI** 164-165 H 5
Tapawera ○ **NZ** 182 E 2
Tapebicuá ○ **RA** 76-77 J 5
Tapejara ○ **BR** 74-75 E 7
Tapena ○ **BOL** 70-71 C 5
Tapenaga, Rio ∧ **RA** 76-77 H 4
Tapera ○ **BR** 60-61 J 5
Tapera, La ○ **RCH** 80 E 2
Tapera, Rio ∧ **BR** 72-73 G 4
Taperaba ○ **BR** 62-63 J 5
Taperoá ○ **BR** 68-69 K 5
Tapes ○ **BR** 74-75 E 8
Tapes, Ponta de ▲ **BR** 74-75 E 8
Tapeta ○ **LB** 202-203 F 6
Taphan Hin ○ **THA** 158-159 F 2
Tapi ○ **IND** 138-139 E 4
Tãpi ∧ **IND** 138-139 E 9
Tapian ○ **RI** 164-165 E 1
Tapiantana Channel ≋ 160-161 D 9
Tapiantana Group ⌒ **RP** 160-161 D 9
Tapiche, Rio ∧ **PE** 64-65 E 5
Tapini ○ **PNG** 183 D 5
Tapiocanga, Chapada do ▲ **BR** 72-73 G 4
Tapira ○ **BR** 72-73 G 5
Tapirabe ○ **BR** 72-73 K 2
Tapirapecó, Sierra ▲ **YV** 66-67 E 2
Tapirapé Karajá, Área Indígena ⊥ **BR** 68-69 C 7
Tapiruçu, Cachoeira ∽ **BR** 68-69 E 3
Tapis, Gunung ▲ **MAL** 162-163 D 2
Tapiù, Cachoeira do ∽ **BR** 62-63 F 6
Tapkaluk Islands ⌒ **USA** 20-21 M 1
Taplejung ○ **NEP** 144-145 F 7
Tapoa, La ○ **BF** (DOS) 204-205 E 2
Tapoa, La ∧ **BF** 202-203 L 3
Tapol ○ **PNG** 183 B 5
Tappahannock ○ **USA** 46-47 K 7
Tappalang ○ **RI** 164-165 F 5
Tapsuj ∧ **RUS** 114-115 T 5
Taptugary ∧ **RUS** 118-119 K 9
Tapul ○ **RP** 160-161 D 10
Tapul Group ⌒ **RP** 160-161 D 10
Tapul Island ∧ **RP** 160-161 D 10
Tãqa ○ **OM** 132-133 J 5
Taq-e Bostán ○· **IR** 128-129 M 4
Taqtaq ○ **IRQ** 128-129 K 6
Taqtaqâna, at- ○ **IRQ** 128-129 K 6
Taquara ○ **BR** 74-75 E 7
Taquari ○ **BR** 74-75 E 7
Taquari, Pantanal do ≃ **BR** 70-71 J 4
Taquari, Rio ∧ **BR** 72-73 J 4
Taquari, Rio ∧ **BR** 72-73 G 3
Taquaritinga ○ **BR** 72-73 F 6
Taquarituba ○ **BR** 72-73 F 7
Taques, Los ○ **YV** 60-61 F 2
Taquili, Isla ∧ **PE** 70-71 C 4
Tara ○ **AUS** 178-179 L 4
Tará ○ **BR** 68-69 K 6
Tara ☆ **RUS** (OMS) 114-115 N 6
Tara ∧ **RUS** 114-115 P 6
Tara ∧ **RUS** 114-115 N 6
Tara ∧ **YU** 100-101 G 3
Tara ∧ **Z** 218-219 D 3
Tarã, Ģaziart ∧ **KSA** 132-133 B 4
Taraba, River ∧ **WAN** 204-205 J 4
Tarabuco ○ **BOL** 70-71 E 6
Tarãbulus ○ **LAR** 192-193 E 1
Tarãbulus ★ **LAR** 192-193 E 1
Tarãbulus ○ **RL** 128-129 F 5
Tarãbulus ∽ **RL** 128-129 F 5
Taraca, Golfo de ≋ **BOL** 70-71 C 5
Taraco ○ **PE** 70-71 C 4
Tarãd al-Kahf ○ **IRQ** 128-129 L 7
Taraf, at- ○ **KSA** 130-131 L 5
Tarafiya, at- ○ **KSA** 130-131 J 4
Tarag ○ **IND** 140-141 F 2
Tarãghin ○ **LAR** 192-193 F 3
Tarahumara, Sierra ▲ **MEX** 50-51 E 3
Taraira, Rio ∧ **CO** 66-67 C 3
Tarairi ○ **BOL** 76-77 F 1
Tarajim ○ **WAN** 204-205 J 3
Taraka, Mount ▲ **PNG** 184 I b 2
Tarakan ○ **RI** 164-165 E 2
Tarakan, Pulau ∧ **RI** 164-165 E 2
Tarakbits ○ **PNG** 183 A 3
Taralga ○ **AUS** 180-181 K 3
Taramana ○ **RI** 166-167 C 6
Taranaki Bight, North ≋ 182 E 2
Taranaki Bight, South ≋ 182 E 4
Tarancón ○ **E** 98-99 F 4
Tarangara ○ **TCH** 206-207 D 4
Tarangire ∧ **EAT** 212-213 F 6
Tarangire National Park ⊥ **EAT** 212-213 F 6
Tarangire Safari Camp ○ **EAT** (ARV) 212-213 F 6
Taranköl, köli ∽ **KA** 124-125 F 1
Taranovskij ∧ **KA** 124-125 C 2
Táranto ☆· **I** 100-101 G 4
Táranto, Golfo di ≋ 100-101 F 4
Tarapacá ○ **CO** 66-67 C 4
Tarapacá ○ **RCH** 70-71 C 4
Tarapoa ○ **EC** 64-65 D 2
Tarapoto ○ **PE** 64-65 D 5
Tarãpur ○ **IND** 138-139 D 10
Taraquá ○ **BR** 66-67 E 3
Tarara ○ **CU** 54-55 D 3
Táranto, Golfo di ≋·· **I** 100-101 F 4
Tárapur ○ **IND** 138-139 D 10
Tarare ○ **F** 90-91 K 9

Taras ○ **BD** 142-143 F 3
Tarasa Dwip Island ∧ **IND** 140-141 L 5
Tarascon ∽· **F** 90-91 K 10
Tarasovo ○ **RUS** 116-117 N 8
Tarasovo ○ **RUS** (NAO) 88-89 T 3
Tarasovsk ○ **RUS** 116-117 L 8
Tarat ○ **DZ** 190-191 G 7
Tarata ○ **PE** 70-71 B 5
Taruacá ○ **BR** 66-67 B 7
Tarauacá, Rio ∧ **BR** 66-67 B 6
Tarazona ○ **E** 98-99 G 4
Tarbagatai ∧ **RUS** 116-117 N 10
Tarbagataj Range = Tarbagataj žotasy ▲ **KA** 124-125 M 5
Tarbaj ○ **EAK** 212-213 G 4
Tarbela Reservoir ≋ **PK** 138-139 D 2
Tarbes ☆ **F** 90-91 H 10
Tarboro ○ **USA** 48-49 K 2
Tarcoola ○ **AUS** 178-179 C 6
Tardie ○ **AUS** 176-177 D 3
Tardoki-Jani, gora ▲ **RUS** 122-123 H 4
Tardun ○ **AUS** 176-177 C 4
Targhee Pass ∧ **USA** 40-41 J 3
Tãrgovište ○ **BG** 102-103 E 6
Targuist ○ **MA** 188-189 J 3
Tarhaouhaout ∴· **DZ** 190-191 E 9
Tarhatine, Tizi-n ▲ **MA** 188-189 H 5
Tarhovo ○ **RUS** 116-117 E 7
Tarhûnah ○ **LAR** 192-193 E 1
Tarhûnah ∽· **LAR** 192-193 E 1
Tari ○ **PNG** 183 B 3
Tari, Mutungu- ○ **ZRE** 216-217 D 3
Tariat = Horgo ○ **MAU** 148-149 D 3
Tarib ○ **KSA** 132-133 C 4
Tãriba ○ **YV** 60-61 E 4
Tarica ○ **PE** 64-65 D 6
Tarif ○ **UAE** 134-135 E 6
Tarifa ○ **E** 98-99 E 6
Tarija ○ **BOL** 76-77 E 1
Tarija, Rio ∧ **BOL** 76-77 F 1
Tarikere ○ **IND** 140-141 F 4
Tariku ∧ **RI** 166-167 J 3
Tariku (Rouffaer) ∧ **RI** 166-167 J 3
Tarim ○· **Y** 132-133 F 5
Tarim Basin = Tarim Pendi ≃ **VRC** 146-147 E 6
Tarime ○ **EAT** 212-213 E 4
Tarimoro ○ **MEX** 52-53 D 1
Tanmi Milli Parki ⊥ **TR** 128-129 F 3
Tarim Pendi ≃ **VRC** 146-147 E 6
Taring ○ **RI** 162-163 B 3
Taripa ○ **RI** 164-165 G 4
Tarira ○ **BR** 66-67 C 2
Tarit, Oued ∽ **DZ** 190-191 D 8
Taritatu (Idenburg) ∧ **RI** 166-167 K 3
Tarka ∧ **ZA** 220-221 G 6
Tarkastad ○ **ZA** 220-221 H 6
Tarkio ○ **USA** (MO) 42-43 H 5
Tarkio ∧ **USA** (MT) 40-41 G 2
Tarkio River ∧ **USA** 42-43 H 5
Tarko-Sale ○ **RUS** 114-115 O 2
Tarkwa ○ **GH** 202-203 K 7
Tarlac ☆ **RP** 160-161 D 5
Tarlton Downs ○ **AUS** 178-179 D 2
Tarma ○ **PE** 64-65 E 7
Tarmaber Pass ∧ **ETH** 208-209 D 4
Tarmidã ○ **KSA** 130-131 J 5
Tarn ∧· **F** 90-91 J 10
Tarn, Gorges du ∼··∨ **F** 90-91 J 9
Tärnaby ○ **S** 86-87 G 4
Tarnak Rūd ∧ **AFG** 134-135 M 2
Tarnogskij Gorodok ○ **RUS** 94-95 S 1
Tarnów ★· **PL** 92-93 Q 3
Taroa ○ **CO** 60-61 F 1
Taro Co ∽ **VRC** 144-145 E 5
Tarobi ○ **PNG** 183 F 3
Taroko National Park ⊥· **RC** 156-157 M 4
Taron ○ **PNG** 183 G 3
Taronggo ○ **RI** 164-165 G 4
Taroom ○ **AUS** 178-179 K 3
Taroudant ☆· **MA** 188-189 G 5
Taroum ○ **RN** 204-205 J 1
Tarpon Springs ○ **USA** 48-49 G 5
Tarquinia ○ **I** 100-101 D 3
Tarrafal ○ **CV** 202-203 C 6
Tarrafal ○ **CV** 202-203 B 5
Tarrafol ○ **CV** 202-203 B 5
Tarragona ○ **AUS** 178-179 H 2
Tarragona ○· **E** 98-99 H 4
Tarrajäkkå ∧ **S** 86-87 H 3
Tarraleah ○ **AUS** 180-181 J 7
Tarras ○ **NZ** 182 B 6
Tàrrega ○ **E** 98-99 H 4
Tar River ∧ **USA** 48-49 J 2
Tarso Emissi ▲ **TCH** 198-199 J 2
Tarsu Musa ▲ **TCH** 198-199 J 2
Tarsus ☆· **TR** 128-129 F 4
Tartagal ○ **RA** 76-77 F 2
Tartagal, Rio ∧ **RA** 76-77 F 2
Tartãr, Buhairat at- ≋ **IRQ** 128-129 K 5
Tartãr, Nahr at- ∧ **IRQ** 128-129 K 6
Tartaruga ○ **BR** 72-73 L 2
Tartarugalzinho ○ **BR** 62-63 J 5
Tartarugas, Cachoeira das ∽ **BR** 68-69 D 4
Tartas ∧ **RUS** 114-115 O 7
Tartrat, Hassi ○ **DZ** 188-189 H 7
Tartu ☆· **EST** 94-95 K 2
Tartüs ★· **SYR** 128-129 F 5
Taruca ○ **PE** 70-71 C 5

Tarucani ○ **PE** 70-71 B 5
Tarum ∧ **RI** 168 B 3
Tarusa ☆· **RUS** 94-95 P 4
Tarutung ○ **RI** 162-163 C 3
Tärüt, Wädi ∧ **LAR** 192-193 E 4
Tatkon ○ **MYA** 142-143 K 5
Tarvagatajn Nuruu ▲ **MAU** 148-149 D 3
Tarves ○ **AUS** 178-179 H 3
Tarvo, Rio ∧ **BOL** 70-71 G 4
Ţarwãniya ○ **UAE** 132-133 J 2
Taryng-Ėfge ∧ **RUS** 120-121 E 4
Tasabo ∽ **WAN** 204-205 G 6
Tašãk, Küh-e ▲ **IR** 134-135 F 3
Tãšanta ○ **RUS** 124-125 Q 4
Tašauz = Dašoguz ☆ **TM** 136-137 F 4
Tašauzskja oblast' = Dašoguz ▫ **TM** 136-137 F 4
Tasböget ☆ **KA** 124-125 G 6
Tase ○ **VRC** 144-145 F 6
Tas-Ėekit ∧ **RUS** 110-111 P 4
Taseeva ∧ **RUS** 114-115 P 6
Tareja ∧ **RUS** 108-109 Z 4
Tasendjerft, Erg ⊥ **DZ** 190-191 D 8
Taseko Lake ∽ **CDN** 32-33 K 6
Taseko River ∧ **CDN** 32-33 J 6
Tasermiut ≋ 28-29 S 6
Tasersiaq ≋ 28-29 P 3
Tasersiaq ≋ 28-29 P 3
Tasersuaq (VGR) ∽ **GRØ** 28-29 P 3
Tasersuaq (VGR) ∽ **GRØ** 28-29 O 5
Tasersuatsiaq ∽ **GRØ** 28-29 P 4
Tãsgaon ○ **IND** 140-141 F 3
Taš Guzar ○ **AFG** 136-137 K 6
Tashiding ∧· **IND** 144-145 G 7
Tashigang ○ **BHT** 142-143 G 2
Tashkent = Toškent ★ ··∨ **US** 136-137 L 4
Tashota ○ **CDN** 34-35 N 5
Tasiaalujjuaq, Lac ∽ **CDN** 36-37 O 5
Tasiat, Lac ∽ **CDN** 36-37 M 5
Tasik Bera ∽ **MAL** 162-163 E 3
Tasik Chini ∽ **MAL** 162-163 E 3
Tasik Kenyir ∽ **MAL** 162-163 E 2
Tasikmalaya ○ **RI** 168 C 3
Tasik Temengur ∽ **MAL** 162-163 D 2
Tašina ∧ **RUS** 122-123 D 3
Tašir* ∧ **AR** 128-129 L 2
Tasiussaq ○ **GRØ** 26-27 X 7
Tasiussuaq ≋ 28-29 P 4
Taskan ○ **RUS** 120-121 O 2
Taskan ∧ **RUS** 120-121 O 2
Taškent = Toškent ★ ··∨ **US** 136-137 L 4
Taškentskaja oblast' ▫ **US** 136-137 L 4
Taškepri ○ **TM** 136-137 H 6
Taškepri ∽ **TM** 136-137 H 6
Taškeprinskoe vodohranilišče ∽ **TM** 136-137 H 6
Tasker ○ **RN** 198-199 E 5
Taskeskan ○ **KA** 124-125 M 5
Taşköprü ☆ **TR** 128-129 F 2
Taskul ○ **PNG** 183 F 2
Tas-Kystabyt, hrebet ▲ **RUS** 110-111 Y 7
Tašla ∧ **RUS** 96-97 H 8
Tasman Abyssal Plain ≃ 13 G 6
Tasman Basin ≃ 13 G 7
Tasman Bay ≋ 182 D 4
Tasman Head ▲ **AUS** 180-181 J 7
Tasman Highway II **AUS** 180-181 K 6
Tasmania ○ **AUS** 180-181 H 6
Tasman Mountains ▲ **NZ** 182 D 4
Tasman Peninsula ∪··· **AUS** 180-181 J 7
Tasman Point ▲ **AUS** 174-175 D 4
Tasman Sea ≋ 13 G 6
Tasmate ○ **VAN** 184 II a 2
Tåsgnad ○ **RO** 102-103 C 4
Tagova ☆ **TR** 128-129 G 2
Tãšqorğan = Hülm ∽· **AFG** 136-137 K 6
Tassara ○ **RN** 198-199 B 4
Tassa-Takorat ∧ **RN** 198-199 B 4
Tassedjefit, Erg ⊥ **DZ** 190-191 D 8
Tasserest ○ **RMM** 196-197 M 7
Tassialouc, Lac ∽ **CDN** 36-37 N 5
Tassiné ∽ **DY** 204-205 E 3
Tasso Fragoso ○ **BR** 68-69 F 6
Taštagol ○ **RUS** 114-115 Q 7
Tastau, gora ▲ **KA** 124-125 N 5
Tastöp ○ **KA** 136-137 K 3
Tastop ○ **KA** 136-137 K 3
Tastuba ○ **RUS** 96-97 K 6
Taštyp ☆ **RUS** 124-125 Q 4
Tasty-Taldy ∧ **KA** 124-125 E 3
Tasüğ ○ **IR** 128-129 L 3
Tãsüki ∽· **IR** 134-135 J 3
Tata ☆ **H** 92-93 O 5
Tata ☆ **MA** 188-189 H 6
Tatabánya ○ **H** 92-93 O 5
Ta Ta Creek ○ **CDN** 32-33 N 7
Tata d'Albouri Ndiaye ∴··· **SN** 196-197 C 4
Tataguine ○ **SN** 202-203 C 6
Tatajachura, Cerro ▲ **RCH** 70-71 C 6
Tatajuba ○ **BR** 64-65 F 5
Tatali ○ **GH** 202-203 L 5
Tatam ○ **RI** 164-165 L 3
Tatamagouche ○ **CDN** 38-39 N 6
Tata Mailau, Gunung ▲ **RI** 166-167 C 6
Tatan ○ **KA** 124-125 K 4
Tataouine ☆· **TN** 190-191 H 4
Tatarbunary ☆ **UA** 102-103 F 5
Tatarsk ○ **RUS** 114-115 N 7
Tatarskij proliv ≋ 122-123 J 3
Tatarskij Proliv = Tatarskij proliv ≋ **RUS** 122-123 J 3
Tatau ○ **MAL** 162-163 K 3
Tatau Island ∧ **PNG** 183 F 3
Tatawa ○ **RI** 166-167 H 3
Tatéma ○ **RG** 202-203 D 5
Tateyama ○ **J** 152-153 H 7
Tate-yama ▲ **J** 152-153 G 6
Tathlina Lake ∽ **CDN** 30-31 L 5
Tathra ○ **AUS** 180-181 K 4

Tathra National Park ⊥ **AUS** 176-177 C 4
Tati ∧ **RB** 218-219 D 5
Tatinnai Lake ∽ **CDN** 30-31 V 5
Tatištčevo ○ **RUS** 96-97 D 8
Tatitlek ○ **USA** 20-21 R 6
Tat Kha ○ **THA** 158-159 F 2
Tatkon ○ **MYA** 142-143 K 5
Tatla Lake ○ **CDN** 32-33 H 6
Tatlanika Creek ∧ **USA** 20-21 Q 4
Tatlatui Provincial Park ⊥ **CDN** 32-33 G 5
Tatlayoko Lake ∽ **CDN** 32-33 H 6
Taţlit ○ **KSA** 132-133 C 4
Taţlit, Wãdi ∧ **KSA** 132-133 K 3
Tatlmain Lake ∽ **CDN** 20-21 X 5
Tatnam, Cape ▲ **CDN** 34-35 L 2
Tatokou ○ **RN** 198-199 D 5
Tatra = Tatry ▲ **SK** 92-93 P 4
Tatry ∧ **SK** 92-93 P 4
Tatta ○ **VRC** 120-121 E 4
Tattakarai ○ **IND** 140-141 G 5
Tattannagaripalli ○ **IND** 140-141 G 4
Tatu, Cachoeira do ∽ **BR** 62-63 H 5
Tatui ○ **BR** 72-73 G 7
Tatul, Sierra de ▲ **RCH** 76-77 B 5
Tatum ○ **USA** 44-45 F 3
Taturgou ○ **VRC** 138-139 F 1
Tatvan ☆· **TR** 128-129 K 3
Tau ○ **N** 86-87 B 7
Ta'u ○ **USA** 184 V c 2
Tauá ○ **BR** 68-69 K 5
Tauari ○ **BR** 68-69 E 2
Taubaté ○ **BR** 72-73 H 7
Tauberbischofsheim ○· **D** 92-93 K 4
Tauca ○ **PE** 64-65 C 6
Taufikia ○ **SUD** 206-207 K 4
Ta'u Island ∧ **USA** 184 V c 2
Tauj ∧ **RUS** 120-121 N 4
Taujskaja guba ≋ 120-121 N 4
Taukum ∼ **KA** 124-125 J 6
Taulihawa ○ **NEP** 144-145 D 7
Tauliya ○ **IRQ** 128-129 J 6
Taumarunui ○ **NZ** 182 E 3
Taum Sauk Mountain ▲ **USA** 46-47 G 2
Taunay, Cachoeira ∽ **BR** 70-71 J 3
Taung ○ **ZA** 220-221 G 5
Taungbon ○ **MYA** 142-143 J 4
Taungdwingyi ○ **MYA** 142-143 J 3
Taunggyi ★ **MYA** 142-143 K 5
Taungtha ○ **MYA** 142-143 J 5
Taungthônlôn ▲ **MYA** 142-143 J 3
Taungup ○ **MYA** 142-143 J 4
Taunsa ○ **PK** 138-139 C 4
Taunton ○ **GB** 90-91 F 6
Taunton ○ **USA** 46-47 N 5
Taupo ○ **NZ** 182 F 3
Taupo, Lake ∽ **NZ** 182 E 3
Tauragė ☆ ··∨ **LT** 94-95 H 4
Tauranga ○ **NZ** 182 F 2
Taureau, Réservoir ∽ **CDN** 38-39 H 3
Tauria ○ **USA** 44-45 J 5
Tauri River ∧ **PNG** 183 C 4
Tauroa Point ▲ **NZ** 182 D 1
Taurova ○ **RUS** 114-115 M 5
Taurus Mountains = Toros Dağları ▲ **TR** 128-129 D 4
Taus = Domažlice ○ **CZ** 92-93 M 4
Tau Šalkamrãp ▲ **KA** 126-127 P 3
Tauste ○ **E** 98-99 G 4
Taušyk ○ **KA** 126-127 J 5
Taušyk ∧ **KA** 126-127 P 2
Tauta ○ **PNG** 183 C 3
Tavai ○ **PY** 76-77 K 4
Tavda ☆ **RUS** 112-113 T 4
Tavda ○ **RUS** (SVR) 114-115 H 5
Tavda ∧ **RUS** 115-116 J 6
Tavda ∧ **RUS** 114-115 H 5
Taverner Bay ≋ 28-29 D 3
Taveta ○ **EAK** 212-213 F 5
Taveta ○ **EAT** 214-215 H 5
Taveuni ∧ **FJI** 184 III c 2
Tavira ○· **P** 98-99 D 6
Tavoliere ∪ **I** 100-101 E 4
Távora, Rio ∧ **P** 98-99 D 4
Tavoy ○ **MYA** 158-159 E 3
Tavrīčeskoe ○ **RUS** 124-125 H 5
Tavşanlı ☆ **TR** 128-129 C 3
Tavua ○ **FJI** 184 III a 2
Tavuki ○ **FJI** 184 III b 3
Tavul Point ▲ **PNG** 183 G 3
Tavu Na Sici ∧ **FJI** 184 III c 3
Tawaeli ○ **RI** 164-165 F 4
Tawakoni, Lake ∽ **USA** 44-45 J 3
Tawali ○ **RI** 168 D 7
Tawallah ○ **AUS** 174-175 C 5
Tawallah Range ▲ **AUS** 174-175 C 5
Tawang ∨ **IND** 142-143 G 2
Tawa Reservoir ∽ **IND** 138-139 F 8
Tawargeni ○ **IND** 140-141 G 3
Tawas City ○ **USA** 46-47 M 3
Tawau ○ **MAL** 160-161 G 5
Tawau Hills Park ⊥ **MAL** 160-161 B 10
Tawil, at- ∼ **KSA** 130-131 F 3
Tawilla, at- ∽ **Y** 132-133 G 5
Tawilah ○ **SUD** 200-201 B 6
Tawitawi Island ∧ **RP** 160-161 C 10
Tawlokehn ○ **LB** 202-203 F 7
Tawu ○ **RC** 156-157 M 5
Tãwûqo ∧ **IRQ** 128-129 L 5
Tãwûğ Çãy ∧ **IRQ** 128-129 L 5
Tawurghã' ○ **LAR** 192-193 F 1
Tawurghã', Sabkhat ∽ **LAR** 192-193 F 1
Taxco ○ **MEX** 52-53 E 2
Taxco de Alarcon = Taxco ○· **MEX** 52-53 E 2

Taxi ○ **VRC** 150-151 F 3
Taxila ○···· **PK** 138-139 D 3
Taxkorgan ○ **VRC** 146-147 B 7
Tay, Lake ∽ **AUS** 176-177 E 4
Tay, Loch ∽ **GB** 90-91 F 3
Tayabamba ○ **PE** 64-65 D 6
Tayabas Bay ≋ 160-161 D 6
Tayahua ○ **MEX** 50-51 H 6
Tayan ○ **RI** 162-163 J 5
Tayandu, Keоulauan ∧ **RI** 166-167 G 4
Tayandu, Pulau ∧ **RI** 166-167 G 4
Tãyebãd ○ **IR** 134-135 J 1
Tayeeglow ○ **SP** 208-209 G 6
Tãyin, Wãdi ∽ **OM** 132-133 J 2
Taykah ○ **LAR** 192-193 J 2
Taylor ○ **CDN** 32-33 K 3
Taylor ○ **USA** (AK) 20-21 H 4
Taylor ○ **USA** (NE) 42-43 H 5
Taylor ○ **USA** (TX) 44-45 J 4
Taylor, Mount ▲ **USA** 44-45 D 2
Taylor Highway II **USA** 20-21 T 5
Taylor Lake ∽ **CDN** 20-21 T 3
Taylor Mountains ▲ **USA** 20-21 M 6
Taylor Park ∽ **USA** 42-43 D 6
Taylor River ∧ **USA** 42-43 D 6
Taylorville ○ **USA** 46-47 D 6
Taymyr, Ozero = Tajmyr, ozero ∽ **RUS** 108-109 d 4
Taymyr Autonomous District = Tajmyrskij avtonomnyj okrug ▫ **RUS** 108-109 a 4
Taymyr Peninsula = Tajmyr, poluostrov ∪ **RUS** 108-109 Y 4
Tãy Ninh ○ **VN** 158-159 J 5
Tayoltita ○ **MEX** 50-51 G 5
Tayota, Rio ∧ **BOL** 70-71 F 4
Tay River ∧ **CDN** 20-21 Y 5
Tãy So'n ○ **VN** 158-159 K 4
Tay Sound ≋ 24-25 g 4
Taytay ○ **RP** 160-161 C 7
Taytay ○ **RP** 160-161 C 7
Taytay Bay ≋ 160-161 C 7
Tayu ○ **RI** 168 D 3
Tayuling ○ **RC** 156-157 M 4
Tayyãl, Wãdi ∧ **KSA** 130-131 F 3
Tayyãra ○ **SYR** 128-129 J 5
Tayyibah ○ **SUD** 200-201 F 5
Taz ∧ **RUS** 108-109 S 8
Taz ∧ **RUS** 116-117 S 9
Tãzah = Taza ☆ **MA** 188-189 J 3
Tazawa-ko ∽ **J** 152-153 J 5
Tazenakht ○ **MA** 188-189 H 5
Tazerzait ∽ **RN** 198-199 E 5
Tazewell ○ **USA** (TN) 48-49 G 1
Tazewell ○ **USA** (VA) 46-47 H 7
Tazgun ○ **VRC** 146-147 E 6
Tazirt, Bir ∼ **LAR** 192-193 E 5
Tazin Lake ∽ **CDN** 30-31 P 6
Tazin River ∧ **CDN** 30-31 O 5
Tãzirbü ∧ **LAR** 192-193 J 5
Tazlina Lake ∽ **USA** 20-21 R 6
Tazna, Cerro ▲ **BOL** 70-71 D 7
Tazolé ∧ **RN** 198-199 D 4
Tazovskaja guba ≋ 108-109 Q 7
Tazovskij ○ **RUS** 108-109 Q 7
Tazovskij poluostrov ∪ **RUS** 108-109 Q 7
Tazrouk ○ **DZ** 190-191 F 9
Tazzarine, Oued ∧ **MA** 188-189 J 5
Tazzeka, Jbel ▲ **MA** 188-189 J 3
Tbilisi ★· **GE** 126-127 F 6
Tchabal Gangdaba ▲ **CAM** 204-205 K 5
Tchabal Mbabo ▲ **CAM** 204-205 K 5
Tchad, Lac ∽ **CAM** 198-199 F 6
Tchad, Plaine du ≃ **CAM** 206-207 B 3
Tchadaoua ○ **RN** 198-199 C 6
Tchamba ○ **CAM** 204-205 K 4
Tchamba ○ **RT** 202-203 L 5
Tchangsou ○ **TCH** 206-207 B 4
Tchaourou ○ **DY** 204-205 E 4
Tchatchou ○ **DY** 204-205 E 4
Tchentlo Lake ∽ **CDN** 32-33 H 4
Tchériba ○ **BF** 202-203 J 3
Tchetti ○ **DY** 202-203 L 6
Tchibanga ☆· **G** 210-211 C 5
Tchibemba ○ **ANG** 216-217 C 7
Tchie ∧ **TCH** 198-199 J 4
Tchigaï, Plateau du ▲ **RN** 198-199 G 2
Tchilounga ○ **RCB** 210-211 C 6
Tchin-Tabaradene ○ **RN** 198-199 B 5
Tchissakata ○ **RCB** 210-211 C 6
Tchizalamou ○ **RCB** 210-211 C 6
Tchollirè ○ **CAM** 206-207 B 4
Tchula ○ **USA** 44-45 M 3
Tczew ○· **PL** 92-93 P 1
Teá, Rio ∧ **BR** 66-67 E 3
Teacapan ○ **MEX** 50-51 G 6
Teague, Lake ∽ **AUS** 176-177 F 2
Te Anau ○ **NZ** 182 A 6
Te Anau, Lake ∽ **NZ** 182 A 6
Teano Range ▲ **AUS** 176-177 D 2
Teapa ○ **MEX** 52-53 H 3
Te Araroa ○ **NZ** 182 G 2
Te Aroha ○ **NZ** 182 F 2
Te Awamutu ○ **NZ** 182 E 3
Teba ○ **RI** 166-167 J 2
Tebaga, Jebel ▲ **TN** 190-191 G 4
Tebaram ○ **RN** 198-199 B 5
Tébé ○ **G** 210-211 D 4
Tebedu ○ **MAL** 162-163 J 4
Tebel, Kampung ○ **MAL** 162-163 G 3
Teboli ○ **KA** 124-125 L 6
Tékélit, I-n- ∽ **BF** 202-203 L 3
Tekes ○ **VRC** 146-147 E 4
Tekes He ∼ **VRC** 146-147 E 4
Teketau ▲ **KA** 126-127 P 2
Tekezê Wenz ∧ **ETH** 200-201 J 6
Tekhammat, Oued ∼ **DZ** 190-191 D 9
Tékirat, Oued ∼ **DZ** 190-191 G 7
Tekirdağ ☆ **TR** 128-129 B 2
Tekit ○ **MEX** 52-53 K 1
Tekkali ∼ **IND** 142-143 D 6
Teklatnika River ∧ **USA** 20-21 Q 4
Tekman ○ **TR** 128-129 J 3
Teknaf ○ **BD** 142-143 H 5
Tekoa ∨ **USA** 40-41 G 2
Tèkodeřka ∧ **RUS** 114-115 Q 2
Tekomaj ○ **MEX** 52-53 K 1
Tekouiat, Oued ∼ **DZ** 190-191 D 9

Tibana o CO 60-61 E 5
Tibati o CAM 204-205 K 5
Tibaú o BR 68-69 K 4
Tibau, Gunung ▲ RI 164-165 D 3
Tibaú do Sul o BR 68-69 L 5
Tibba o PK 138-139 C 5
Tibooburra o AUS 178-179 F 5
Tiberghamine o DZ 190-191 C 6
Tibesti ▲ TCH 198-199 H 2
Tibesti, Sarir ± LAR 192-193 G 5
Tibet = Xizang Zizhiqu □ VRC 144-145 E 5
Tibi, Pulau ∼ RI 164-165 E 2
Tibiri o RN (DOS) 198-199 B 6
Tibiri o RN (MAR) 198-199 C 6
Tibirica, Rio ∼ BR 72-73 E 6
Tibles, Munţii ▲ RO 102-103 C 4
Tibni o SYR 128-129 D 6
Tibo o BF 202-203 J 2
Tibo o RI 164-165 F 5
Tibo o ZRE 212-213 A 2
Tibung o RI 164-165 F 5
Tiburon o ••• RH 54-55 H 5
Tiburón, Isla ▲ MEX 50-51 C 3
Tica o MOC 218-219 H 4
Ticao Island ∼ RP 160-161 E 6
Ticao Pass o RP 160-161 E 6
Ticatica o BOL 70-71 D 7
Tichet < RMM 196-197 L 5
Tichît o RIM 196-197 F 5
Tichît, Dahr ∴ RMM 196-197 F 5
Tichka, Tizi-n- ▲ MA 188-189 H 5
Tichkatine, Oued ∼ DZ 198-199 B 2
Ticho o ETH 208-209 D 5
Ticho Brahe, Kap ▲ GRØ 28-29 V 4
Tickera o AUS 180-181 G 2
Ticonderoga o USA 46-47 M 4
Ticonderoga, Fort ∴ USA 46-47 M 4
Ticsani, Volcán ▲ PE 70-71 D 8
Ticul o MEX 52-53 K 1
Tidal River ∼ AUS 180-181 J 5
Tidangpala o RI 164-165 D 2
Tiddim o MYA 142-143 H 4
Tiddis ∴• DZ 190-191 F 2
Tiderjaouine, Adrar ▲ DZ 190-191 D 7
Tidermené o RMM 196-197 M 6
Tidi Dunes ∴ RN 198-199 G 2
Tidikelt, Plaine du ± DZ 190-191 C 7
Tidirhine, Ibel ▲ MA 188-189 J 3
Tidjidit, Erg ∴ DZ 190-191 C 9
Tidjikdja o RIM 196-197 E 5
Tidore, Pulau ∼ •• RI 164-165 K 3
Tidore = Soa-Siu o RI 164-165 K 3
Tidra, Île ∼ RIM 196-197 B 5
Tidsit, Sebkhet o MA 196-197 C 3
Tiébissou o CI 202-203 H 5
Tiéblé o• BF 202-203 K 4
Tiéboro o TCH 198-199 H 3
Tiefa o MOC 150-151 D 6
Tiéfora o BF 202-203 H 4
Tiegba o CI 202-203 H 7
Tiel o SN 202-203 C 2
Tiel, Mayo ∼ CAM 204-205 K 4
Tieli o VRC 150-151 G 4
Tieling o VRC 150-151 D 6
Tielong o VRC 144-145 B 3
Tielongtan o VRC 144-145 B 3
Tielt o B 92-93 G 3
Tiéma o CI 202-203 G 5
Tiemba ∼ CI 202-203 G 5
Tiémé o CI 202-203 G 5
Tiémélékro o CI 202-203 H 6
Tiene o LB 202-203 H 5
Tiéningboué o CI 202-203 H 5
Tienko o CI 202-203 G 4
Tientsin = Tianjin ☆ VRC 154-155 K 2
Tiên Yên ∼ VN 156-157 E 6
Tiéré o RMM 202-203 H 3
Tierfontein o ZA 220-221 H 3
Tieri o AUS 178-179 K 2
Tierra Amarilla o USA 44-45 D 1
Tierra Blanca o MEX 52-53 F 3
Tierra Colorada o MEX 52-53 E 3
Tierra Colorada, Bajo de la ± RA 78-79 F 7
Tierra del Fuego ∼ 5 E 10
Tierra del Fuego o RA 80 F 6
Tierra del Fuego, Isla Grande del ∼ 80 F 6
Tierra del Fuego, Parque Nacional ⊥ RA 80 F 7
Tierradentro, Parque Archipiélago • CO 60-61 C 6
Tierralta o CO 60-61 C 3
Tiétar, Rio ∼ E 98-99 E 5
Tietê o BR 72-73 G 4
Tietê, Rio ∼ BR 72-73 G 7
Tie-Tree Roadhouse o AUS 178-179 E 2
Tiev, Shangev- o WAN 204-205 H 5
Tieyon o AUS 176-177 H 3
Tifernine, Erg ∴ DZ 190-191 F 7
Tiffin o USA 46-47 G 5
Tiflèt o MA 188-189 H 4
Tiflis = Tbilisi ★ GE 126-127 F 7
Tifore, Pulau ∼ RI 164-165 K 3
Tifton o USA 48-49 G 4
Tifu o RI 166-167 G 2
Tiga, Pulau ∼ MAL 160-161 A 10
Tigalda Island ∼ USA 22-23 O 5
Tigapulan, Pegunungan ▲ RI 162-163 E 5
Tiga Reservoir ∼ WAN 204-205 H 3
Tiga Tarok o MAL 160-161 B 9
Tiger o USA 40-41 F 1
Tiger Island ∼ GUY 62-63 G 4
Tighanimines, Gorges de • DZ 190-191 F 3
Tigherif o DZ 190-191 C 3
Tigi, Danau ∼ RI 166-167 J 4
Tiglî ★ RUS 120-121 S 5
Tigil' ∼ RUS 120-121 S 5
Tignère o CAM 204-205 K 5
Tigniré < RMM 196-197 F 5
Tignish o CDN 38-39 M 5
Tignuan o RP 160-161 D 5
Tigray □ ETH 200-201 J 6

Tigre o RA 78-79 K 3
Tigre, Arroyo el ∼ RA 76-77 H 6
Tigre, Cordillera del ▲ RA 78-79 E 2
Tigre, El o CO 60-61 D 4
Tigre, El o YV 60-61 J 2
Tigre, El ∴• MEX 52-53 J 2
Tigre, Isla ∼ PE 66-67 B 4
Tigre, Laguna del o GCA 52-53 J 3
Tigre, Río ∼ PE 64-65 D 3
Tigre, Río ∼ PE 66-67 K 3
Tigre, Sierra del ▲ RA 76-77 C 6
Tigre de San Lorenzo, El o PA 52-53 D 8
Tigres, Península dos ∪ ANG 216-217 A 8
Tigris ∼ 134-135 B 2
Tigris = Dijla ∼ IRQ 128-129 M 6
Tigrito, El = San José de Guanipa o YV 60-61 J 3
Tiguent o RIM 196-197 C 6
Tiguézéfene o RN 196-197 M 7
Tiguili o TCH 206-207 D 3
Tigzerte, Oued ∼ MA 188-189 G 6
Tigzirt o DZ 190-191 E 2
Tihaja ∼ RUS 120-121 R 5
Tihäma ± Y 132-133 C 6
Tihämat aš-Šäm ∼ KSA 132-133 B 4
Tihodaine, Erg ± DZ 190-191 F 8
Tihoreck o RUS 102-103 M 5
Tihosuco o MEX 52-53 K 1
Tihuatlán o• MEX 52-53 F 1
Tihvin ★ RUS 94-95 N 2
Tihvinskaja grjada ▲ RUS 94-95 N 2
Tijamuchi, Rio ∼ BOL 70-71 E 4
Tijära o IND 138-139 F 6
Tijeras o USA 44-45 D 2
Tiji o LAR 192-193 G 3
Tijo, Tanjung ▲ RI 162-163 F 5
Tijoca, Ilha ∼ BR 68-69 E 2
Tijuana o• MEX 50-51 A 1
Tijucas o BR 74-75 F 6
Tijucas, Ensenada de ≈ 74-75 F 6
Tijucu, Rio ∼ BR 72-73 F 5
Tika o CDN 38-39 K 4
Tikal o GCA (ELP) 52-53 K 3
Tikal ∴•• GCA 52-53 K 3
Tikal, Parque Nacional ⊥••• GCA 52-53 K 3
Tikamgarh o IND 138-139 G 7
Tikanlik o VRC 146-147 H 5
Tikaré o BF 202-203 K 3
Tikem o TCH 206-207 B 4
Tiki Basin ≃ 14-15 P 9
Tikiklut o USA 20-21 M 1
Tikkerutuk, Lac o CDN 36-37 L 6
Tiko o CAM 204-205 H 6
Tikota o IND 140-141 F 2
Tiksa o RUS 88-89 M 4
Tikšeozero o RUS 88-89 L 3
Tiksi ★ RUS 110-111 R 4
Tiksi, buhta ≈ RUS 110-111 R 4
Tiku o RI 162-163 C 5
Tikuna de Feijoal, Área Indígena ⊥ BR 66-67 C 5
Tikuna São Leopoldo, Área Indígena ⊥ BR 66-67 C 5
Tiladummati Atoll ∼ MV 140-141 B 4
Tilaiya o IND 138-139 D 9
Tilakvåda o IND 138-139 E 7
Tilama o RCH 78-79 D 2
Tilamuta o RI 164-165 H 3
Tilantongo o MEX (OAX) 52-53 F 3
Tilantongo ∴• MEX (OAX) 52-53 F 3
Tilarán o CR 52-53 B 6
Tilburg o NL 92-93 H 3
Tilbury o CDN 38-39 D 7
Tilchuse River ∼ CDN 30-31 L 2
Tilden o USA (NE) 42-43 J 4
Tilden o USA (TX) 44-45 H 5
Tilemsen o MA 188-189 F 6
Tilemsi, Vallée du ∼ RMM 196-197 L 5
Tilia, Oued ∼ DZ 190-191 C 7
Tilichiki ★ RUS 112-113 O 6 *
Tiljuga ∼ IND 142-143 D 3
Tillabéri ★ RN 202-203 L 2
Tillamook o USA 40-41 C 3
Tillamook Bay ≈ 40-41 C 3
Tillanchang Dwip ∼ IND 140-141 L 5
Tiller o USA 40-41 C 4
Tillsonburg o CDN 38-39 D 7
Tilly, Lac o CDN 38-39 G 2
Tiloa o RN 204-205 E 1
Tilopozo o RCH 76-77 C 2
Tilos ∼ GR 100-101 L 6
Tilpa o AUS 178-179 H 6
Tilrempt o DZ 190-191 D 4
Tittil o RCH 78-79 D 2
Timä o ET 194-195 E 4
Timahdite o MA 188-189 J 4
Timalchara o RCH 70-71 C 6
Timampuu o RI 164-165 G 5
Timane, Río ∼ PY 70-71 G 7
Timanfaya, Parque Nacional de ⊥ E 188-189 D 5
Timanskij bereg ∪ RUS 88-89 U 3
Timanskij krjaž ▲ RUS 88-89 U 3
Timanskiy Kryazh = Timanskij krjaž ▲ RUS 88-89 U 3
Timare o RI 166-167 J 4
Timargarha o• PK 138-139 C 2
Timaru o NZ 182 D 6
Timaševsk o RUS 102-103 L 5
Timau o EAK 212-213 F 3
Timba o CO 60-61 C 5
Timbalier Bay ≈ 44-45 M 5
Timbang, Pulau ∼ MAL 160-161 C 10
Timbaúba o BR 68-69 L 6
Timbavati Game Reserve ⊥ ZA 220-221 K 2
Timbedgha o RIM 196-197 F 6
Timber o USA 40-41 C 3
Timber Creek o AUS 172-173 K 3
Timber Mill o AUS 172-173 K 4
Timber Mountain ▲ USA 40-41 G 6
Timbiras o BR 68-69 G 4
Timbó o BR 74-75 F 6
Timbó o RG 202-203 E 4

Timboon o AUS 180-181 G 5
Timboroa o EAK 212-213 E 3
Timbotuba, Ilha do ∼ BR 66-67 D 4
Timboy o BOL 76-77 E 1
Timbuktu = Tombouctou o ••• RMM 196-197 K 4
Timbulun o RI 162-163 D 5
Timbuni ∼ RI 166-167 G 2
Timbunke o PNG 183 B 3
Timbun Mata, Pulau ∼ MAL 160-161 C 10
Timeldjame, Oued ∼ DZ 190-191 D 6
Timelloutine o DZ 190-191 G 6
Timétrine, Djebel ▲ RMM 196-197 K 5
Timgad o••• DZ 190-191 F 3
Timia o RN 198-199 D 3
Timiaouine o RMM 196-197 L 4
Timimoun o DZ 190-191 C 6
Timimoun, Sebkha de o DZ 188-189 L 6
Timirist, Râs ▲ RIM 196-197 B 5
Timiş ∼ RO 102-103 C 5
Timimoara ☆• RO 102-103 B 5
Timissit, Oued ∼ DZ 190-191 E 9
Timkinskaja ∼ RUS 112-113 K 2
Timmiarmiut o GRØ 28-29 U 5
Timmins o CDN 34-35 Q 6
Timms Hill ▲ USA 46-47 C 3
Timna' ∴• IL 130-131 D 3
Timoforo ∼ RI 166-167 G 2
Timok ∼ YU 100-101 J 2
Timon o BR 68-69 G 4
Timonha, Rio ∼ BR 68-69 H 3
Timor ∼ RI 166-167 G 6
Timor, Laut ≈ 166-167 D 7
Timor Sea ≈ 172-173 H 2
Timor Trough ≈ 166-167 C 7
Timote o RA 78-79 H 3
Timóteo o BR 72-73 J 5
Timoudi o DZ 188-189 L 6
Timpanogos Cave National Monument • USA 40-41 J 5
Timpas o USA 42-43 F 7
Timpaus, Pulau ∼ RI 164-165 H 4
Timpton o RUS 118-119 N 6
Timra o S 86-87 H 5
Tim Raré o RMM 196-197 J 6
Tims Ford Lake o USA 48-49 E 2
Timun o RI 162-163 E 4
Timur, Banjaran ▲ MAL 162-163 E 2
Timur Digul ∼ RI 166-167 L 4
Timurni o IND 138-139 F 8
Timur Timor ∼ RI 166-167 C 8
Tina ∼ ZA 220-221 J 5
Tin Abunda, Bi'r < LAR 192-193 E 4
Tinaca Point ▲ RP 160-161 F 10
Tinaco o YV 60-61 G 3
Ti-n-Aguelhaj o RMM 196-197 J 6
Tinaja, La o MEX 52-53 F 2
Tinaja, Punta ▲ PE 70-71 A 5
Ti-n-Akof o BF 202-203 K 2
Tin Alkoum < DZ 190-191 H 8
Tinambung o RI 164-165 F 5
Ti-n-Amzag < RMM 196-197 H 6
Tin Amzi, Oued ∼ DZ 198-199 B 2
Tinangkong o RI 164-165 H 4
Tinaroo Falls Reservoir < AUS 174-175 H 3
Ti-n-Azaoa o RMM 196-197 L 6
Ti-n-Bessais < RIM 196-197 D 3
Ti-n-Brahim < RMM 196-197 C 5
Tindangou o BF 202-203 L 4
Tinderry Range ▲ AUS 180-181 K 3
Tindila o RG 202-203 F 4
Tindivanam o IND 140-141 H 4
Tindjassé o RT 202-203 L 5
Tindouf ☆• DZ 188-189 G 7
Tindouf, Hamada de ± DZ 188-189 G 7
Tindouf, Sebkha de o DZ 188-189 G 7
Tineba, Pegunungan ▲ RI 164-165 G 4
Ti-n-Eguelai o RMM 196-197 J 6
Tineo o Tinéu o E 98-99 D 3
Ti-n-Essako o RMM 196-197 M 5
Tinfouchy o DZ 188-189 J 6
Tin Fouye o DZ 190-191 F 6
Tingal ▲ SUD 200-201 E 6
Tingambato o MEX 52-53 D 2
Tinggi, Pulau ∼ MAL (KED) 162-163 F 3
Tinghert, Hamádat ± DZ 190-191 F 6
Tinglayan o RP 160-161 D 4
Tingmiarmiut o GRØ 28-29 U 5
Tingmiarmiut Fjord ≈ 28-29 T 5
Tingo Maria, Parque Nacional ⊥ PE 64-65 D 6
Tingong o VRC 156-157 F 4
Tingri o VRC 144-145 F 6
Tingsryd o S 86-87 G 8
Tingstäde o S 86-87 J 8
Tinguá, Parque Nacional de ⊥ BR 72-73 J 7
Tingvoll ☆ N 86-87 D 5
Tingwon Group ∼ PNG 183 C 2
Tingya o SUD 206-207 L 3
Tinharé, Ilha de ∼ BR 72-73 L 2
Tinher o MA 188-189 J 5
Tinh Gia o VN 156-157 D 7
Tini o SUD 198-199 L 5
Ti-n-Idnàne < RMM 196-197 J 6
Tinigart < RMM 196-197 F 3
Tiniroto o NZ 182 F 3
Tinis, Wádi ∼ LAR 192-193 D 5
Tintan o RP 160-161 C 7
Tinitéquilaaq o GRØ 28-29 W 4
Tiniton Bay ≈ 36-37 N 2
Tinjil, Pulau ∼ RI 168 A 3
Tinkisso ∼ RG 202-203 F 4
Ti-n-Medjouf < RMM 196-197 C 5
Tinnoset o N 86-87 D 7
Tinogasta o RA 76-77 D 5
Tinombó o RI 164-165 G 3
Tinompo o RI 164-165 G 4

Tinos o GR 100-101 K 6
Tinos ∼ GR 100-101 K 6
Ti-n-Oufart < RMM 196-197 K 6
Tinputz o PNG 184 I b 1
Tin Rerhoch < DZ 198-199 B 2
Tinrhert, Hamada de ± DZ 190-191 F 6
Tinrhert, Plateau du ▲ DZ 190-191 F 6
Tin Tadjant ∼ DZ 190-191 E 10
Tintâne o RIM 196-197 E 6
Tin Tarabine, Oued ∼ DZ 190-191 F 9
Ti-n-Tehoun < RMM 196-197 J 6
Tintejert, Adrar ▲ DZ 190-191 D 8
Tintern Abbey •• GB 90-91 H 6
Ti-n-Tijot < RMM 196-197 H 6
Tintina o RA 76-77 F 4
Tintinara o AUS 180-181 F 3
Tintioulen o RG 202-203 F 4
Tin Toumma ∼ RN 198-199 F 4
Ti-n-Zaouâtene o RMM 196-197 M 5
Tin-Zawatine o DZ 196-197 M 5
Ti'o o ER 200-201 K 6
Tiobraid Árann = Tipperary o IRL 90-91 C 5
Tioman, Pulau ∼ MAL 162-163 F 3
Tionesta o USA 46-47 J 5
Tioor, Pulau ∼ RI 166-167 F 4
Tiop o RI 162-163 D 4
Tioribougou o RMM 202-203 H 2
Tioroniaradougou o CI 202-203 H 5
Tiou o BF 202-203 J 3
Tiouilît o RIM 196-197 B 5
Tiouki o RMM 202-203 H 2
Tioussiana o BF 202-203 H 4
Tipaza ∼••• DZ 190-191 D 2
Tipitapa o• NIC 52-53 L 5
Tipitapa, Río ∼ NIC 52-53 L 5
Tipolo o RP 160-161 F 7
Tipperary o AUS 172-173 K 2
Tipperary = Tiobraid Árann o IRL 90-91 C 5
Tipton o USA (CA) 40-41 F 6
Tipton o USA (IA) 46-47 C 5
Tipton o USA (MO) 42-43 L 6
Tipton, Mount ▲ USA 40-41 G 8
Tiptonville o USA 48-49 D 1
Tip Top Mountain ▲ CDN 34-35 N 6
Tipuani, Río ∼ BOL 70-71 E 4
Tipuini o EC 64-65 E 2
Tiquaracup o BR 72-73 L 2
Tiquicheo o MEX 52-53 D 2
Tiquié, Rio ∼ BR 66-67 C 2
Tiquillaca o PE 70-71 B 4
Tira, Bol'šaja ∼ RUS 116-117 M 7
Tiracambu, Serra do ▲ BR 68-69 E 4
Tiradentes o BR 72-73 H 6
Tirahart, Oued ∼ DZ 190-191 D 9
Tîrân, Ğazirat ∼ KSA 130-131 D 4
Tirana, La o RCH 76-77 C 7
Tirane ★• AL 100-101 Q 4
Tirangole o SUD 206-207 L 3
Tiraouene o RN 198-199 C 3
T'irarê Shet' ∼ ETH 200-201 J 6
Tirari Desert ± AUS 178-179 E 5
Tirasberge ▲ NAM 220-221 C 2
Tiraspol ☆ MD 102-103 E 4
Tirau o NZ 182 E 2
Tirband-e Torkestân, Selsele-ye Küh-e ▲ AFG 136-137 H 7
Tire o TR 128-129 B 3
Tire, Kôtal-e ▲ AFG 138-139 B 3
Tirebolu o TR 128-129 H 2
Tirecatinga, Área Indígena ⊥ BR 70-71 H 3
Tiree ∼ GB 90-91 D 3
Tirehtjah ∼ RUS 110-111 a 7
Tirehtjah ∼ RUS 110-111 P 6
Tirere o PNG 183 B 5
Tîrgovişte ☆• RO 102-103 D 5
Tîrgu Frumos o RO 102-103 E 4
Tîrgu Jiu o RO 102-103 C 5
Tîrgu Mureş ★ RO 102-103 D 4
Tîrgu Secuiesc o RO 102-103 E 4
Tirhatimene < DZ 190-191 D 8
Tirhemar, Oued ∼ DZ 190-191 F 7
Tiri Aguge ∼ TCH 192-193 H 6
Tiriri o EAU 212-213 D 3
Tiririca o BR 68-69 G 7
Tiririne, Oued ∼ DZ 190-191 G 9
Tiririo o RG 202-203 F 4
Tiris Zemour □ RIM 196-197 D 4
Tirnâveni o RO 102-103 D 4
Tiro o RG 202-203 G 3
Tirourgouloy o RCA 206-207 F 4
Tirreno, Mar ≈ 100-101 D 5
Tirso ∼ I 100-101 B 4
Tirthahalli o IND 140-141 F 4
Tiruchchendũr o IND 140-141 H 6
Tiruchchiräppalli o• IND 140-141 H 5
Tiruchengodu o IND 140-141 G 5
Tiruganna o IND 140-141 F 4
Tirukkalukkunram o IND 140-141 J 4
Tirukkoyilũr o IND 140-141 H 5
Tirumakudal o IND 140-141 G 4
Tirumala o IND 140-141 H 4
Tirumangalam o IND 140-141 H 5
Tirumullaivâsal o IND 140-141 H 5
Tirunelveli o IND 140-141 G 6
Tiruntan o PE 64-65 E 5
Tirupati o• IND 140-141 H 4
Tirupparangunram • IND 140-141 H 5
Tiruppattũr o IND 140-141 H 5
Tiruppattũr o IND 140-141 H 5
Tiruppur o IND 140-141 G 5
Tirupuvanam o IND 140-141 H 6
Tiruturaippūndi o IND 140-141 H 5
Tiruvalaru o IND 140-141 H 5
Tiruvalla o IND 140-141 G 6
Tiruvannámalai o• IND 140-141 H 4
Tiruvattiyur o• IND 140-141 J 4
Tiruvűru o IND 142-143 D 7

Tirvyjaha ∼ RUS 108-109 O 6
Tis o IR 134-135 J 6
Tis ∼ RUS 116-117 E 6
Tisa ∼ UA 102-103 C 3
Tisa ∼ YU 100-101 H 2
Tisaiyanvilai o IND 140-141 G 6
Tisdale o CDN 34-35 D 4
Tisgaon o IND 138-139 E 10
Tisgui-Remz o MA 188-189 G 6
Tishomingo o USA 44-45 J 2
Tišina ∼ RUS 122-123 D 3
T'is Isat Fwafwatë = Blue Nile Falls ∼•• ETH 208-209 C 3
Tiska, Pic ▲ DZ 190-191 E 9
Tisnaiet, Oued ∼ DZ 190-191 E 6
Tissa ∼ RUS 116-117 J 9
Tissamaharama o CL 140-141 J 7
Tissán, Hasy < LAR 192-193 E 3
Tissemsilt o DZ 190-191 C 3
Tista ∼ BD 142-143 F 2
Tisuf ∼ RUS 114-115 U 7
Tisza ∼ H 92-93 Q 5
Tit o DZ (ADR) 190-191 C 7
Tit o DZ (TAM) 190-191 E 9
Tit, Suon- o RI 118-119 L 6
Tit-Ary o RUS (SAH) 110-111 Q 3
Tit-Ary o RUS (SAH) 118-119 N 5
Tite o GNB 202-203 D 4
Titicaca, Lago o PE 70-71 C 4
Titicaca, Reserva Nacional ⊥ PE 70-71 B 4
Titigading o RI 162-163 D 4
Titiwaifuru o RI 166-167 K 3
Titiwan, Banjaran ▲ MAL 162-163 D 3
Titograd = Podgorica ☆• YU 100-101 G 3
Titova Mitrovica = Kosovska Mitrovica o YU 100-101 H 3
Titov Drvar o BIH 100-101 F 2
Titovo Užice = Užice o YU 100-101 H 3
Titov Veles o• MK 100-101 H 4
Ti-Tree o AUS 178-179 B 2
Titu o RO 102-103 D 5
Titule o ZRE 210-211 K 2
Titumate o CO 60-61 C 3
Titusville o USA (FL) 48-49 H 5
Titusville o USA (PA) 46-47 J 5
Titwân ☆• MA 188-189 J 3
Tiung, Tanjung ▲ RI 162-163 G 5
Tiva ∼ EAK 212-213 G 4
Tivaouane o SN 202-203 B 2
Tivoli o I 100-101 D 4
Tivoli o USA 44-45 J 5
Tivtejjaha ∼ RUS 108-109 N 6
Tiwâl, at- o KSA 132-133 C 5
Tiwi o EAK 212-213 G 6
Tiwori, Teluk ≈ 164-165 G 4
Tiworo, Kepulauan ∼ RI 164-165 H 4
Tiworo, Selat ≈ 164-165 H 5
Tixmul ∼• MEX 52-53 K 2
Tixtla de Guerrero o MEX 52-53 E 3
Tiya o••• ETH 208-209 C 5
Tiyâb o IR 134-135 J 5
Tiyo, Pegunungan ▲ RI 166-167 H 4
Tizayuca o MEX 52-53 E 2
Tizi, Mare de o MEX 206-207 F 3
Tizí, Mare de o RCA 206-207 F 3
Tizi Ouzou ☆ DZ 190-191 J 2
Tizimin o MEX 52-53 K 1
Tiznados, Río ∼ YV 60-61 H 3
Tiznit o MA 188-189 G 6
Tižtiž o IR 128-129 M 5
Tjaneni o SD 220-221 K 2
Tjanja o RUS 118-119 J 6
Tjanja ∼ RUS 118-119 K 6
Tjater ∼ RUS 96-97 J 7
Tjatino o RUS 122-123 M 6
Tjatja, vulkan ▲ RUS 122-123 M 6
Tjažin ∼ RUS 114-115 U 6
Tjažinskij ∼ RUS 114-115 U 6
Tjeggelvas o S 86-87 H 3
Tjera o BF 202-203 H 4
Tjibjon ∼ S 86-87 E 8
Tjugêl'saj o KS 146-147 E 5
Tjuguène ∼ RUS 118-119 N 4
Tjuhtet o RUS 114-115 U 6
Tjukalinsk ★ RUS 114-115 M 7
Tjukjan o RUS 110-111 M 7
Tjukjan ∼ RUS 118-119 L 7
Tjukjan ∼ RUS 118-119 L 4
Tjulender araly ∼ KA 126-127 J 5
Tjulenij, mys ▲ AZ 128-129 O 2
Tjul'gan ★ RUS 96-97 K 7
Tjuli o RUS 114-115 K 4
Tjumen' ★ RUS 114-115 H 6
Tjung ∼ RUS 110-111 K 6
Tjung ∼ RUS 110-111 M 6
Tjung ∼ RUS 110-111 M 7
Tjungjulju o RUS 118-119 P 4
Tjup o KS 146-147 M 4
Tjup ∼ KS 146-147 M 4
Tjuvfjorden ≈ 84-85 M 4
Tkacoapa o MEX 52-53 E 3
Tkibuli o GE 126-127 F 7
Tkvarčeli o GE 126-127 D 6
Tlacoachistlahuaca o MEX 52-53 E 3
Tlacolula o MEX 52-53 F 3
Tlacotalpan o• MEX 52-53 G 2
Tlacotepec o MEX 52-53 F 3
Tlacuilotepec o MEX 52-53 E 1
Tlahuac o MEX 52-53 E 2
Tlahuiltepa o MEX 52-53 E 1
Tläkshín, Bi'r < LAR 192-193 E 2
Tlalchapa o MEX 52-53 E 2
Tlalnepantla o MEX 52-53 E 2
Tlalpan = Tlalnepantla o MEX 52-53 E 2
Tlaltenango o MEX 50-51 H 7
Tlapa o MEX 52-53 E 3
Tlapa del Comonfort o MEX 52-53 E 3
Tlapaneco, Río ∼ MEX 52-53 E 3
Tlaquepaque o• MEX 52-53 C 1
Tlaxcala □ MEX 52-53 E 2
Tlaxcala ☆• MEX (TLA) 52-53 E 2
Tlaxiaco o MEX 52-53 F 3
Tlell o CDN 32-33 E 5
Toga, Île = Île Toga ∼ VAN 184 II a 1
Togafo o RI 164-165 K 3
Toganaly o AZ 128-129 M 2
Tõgane o J 152-153 J 7
Togba < RIM 196-197 E 6

Tleta-de-Sidi-Bouguedra o MA 188-189 H 4
Tlevak Strait ≈ 32-33 D 4
Tlhakgameng o ZA 220-221 G 3
Tlhakoeng o LS 220-221 J 4
Tmassah o LAR 192-193 F 4
Tmeimichât o RIM 196-197 D 4
Tne Haven o ZA 220-221 J 6
Tô o BF 2C2-203 J 4
Toade, Kepulauan ∼ RI 164-165 J 2
Toad River ∼ CDN 30-31 G 6
Toak o VAN 184 II b 3
Toamasina □ RM 222-223 F 6
Toamasina ★ RM (TMA) 222-223 F 7
Toari o BR 66-67 D 6
Toaupulai o IND 140-141 G 6
Toaya o RI 164-165 F 4
Toba o CDN 32-33 H 6
Toba o J 152-153 G 7
Toba o VRC 144-145 D 3
Toba, Arroyo el ∼ RA 76-77 G 5
Toba, Isla ∼ RA 80 H 2
Tobacco Range ▲ BH 52-53 K 3
Tobago o TT 60-61 L 2
Toba Inlet ≈ 32-33 H 6
Toba Kâkar Fange ▲ PK 134-135 M 3
Tobalai, Pulau ∼ RI 164-165 L 4
Tobalai, Selat ≈ 164-165 L 4
Tobamawu o RI 164-165 L 6
Tobarra o E 98-99 G 5
Toba Tek Singh o PK 138-139 D 4
Tobejuba, Isla ∼ YV 60-61 L 3
Tobelo o RI 164-165 K 3
Tobelombang o RI 164-165 G 4
Tobermorey o AUS 178-179 D 2
Tobermory o• CDN 46-47 H 3
Tobermory ∼ GB 90-91 D 3
Tobias Barreto o BR 68-69 J 7
Tobin, Kap = Uunarteq o GRØ 26-27 p 8
Tobin, Mount ▲ USA 40-41 F 4
Tobin Lake o AUS 172-173 G 6
Tobin Lake o CDN 34-35 E 4
Tobique 20 Indian Reserve ✕ CDN 38-39 L 5
Tobique River ∼ CDN 46-47 M 3
Tobishima ∼ J 152-153 H 5
Toboali o RI 162-163 G 6
Tobol o KA 124-125 C 2
Tobol ∼ RUS 114-115 J 6
Tobol ∼ RUS 114-115 H 7
Tobol ∼ RUS 124-125 B 3
Tobol o RI 164-165 G 4
Tobol'sk ★• RUS 114-115 K 5
Tobol'skij malerik, vozvyšennost' ▲ RUS 114-115 K 6
Tobseda o RUS 88-89 W 2
Toby = Moramano o RM 222-223 E 8
Tobyčan ∼ RUS 110-111 X 7
Tobys' ∼ RUS 88-89 W 5
Tobyš ∼ RUS 88-89 V 4
Tobyšskaja vozvyšennost' ▲ RUS 88-89 V 3
Toca o CO 60-61 E 5
Tocache Nuevo o PE 64-65 D 5
Tocaima o CO 60-61 D 5
Tocancipá o CO 60-61 E 5
Tocantínia o BR 68-69 D 6
Tocantinópolis o BR 68-69 E 5
Tocantins □ BR 68-69 D 7
Tocantins, Rio ∼ BR 62-63 K 6
Tocantins, Rio ∼ BR 68-69 E 5
Toccoa o USA 48-49 G 3
Točes ∼ RUS 114-115 U 4
Tochatwi Bay o CDN 30-31 O 4
Tochi ∼ PK 138-139 B 3
Toch'o Do ∼ ROK 150-151 E 10
Toco o ANG 216-217 B 7
Toco o RCH 76-77 C 2
Toco o TT 60-61 L 2
Toconao o RCH 76-77 B 2
Tocopilla o• RCH 76-77 B 2
Tocopuri, Cerros de ▲ BOL 76-77 D 2
Tocota o RA 76-77 C 6
Tocumwal o AUS 180-181 H 3
Tocuyito o YV 60-61 G 3
Tocuyo, El o YV 60-61 G 3
Tocuyo, Río ∼ YV 60-61 G 2
Toda-saki ▲ J 152-153 K 5
Todd River ∼ AUS 178-179 C 3
Todeli o RI 164-165 J 4
Todenyang o EAK 212-213 E 1
Tõdi ▲ CH 92-93 K 5
Todi o I 100-101 D 3
Todin o RI 166-167 F 2
Todmorden o AUS 178-179 C 4
Todos los Santos, Lago o RCH 78-79 D 6
Todos os Santos, Baia de ≈ 72-73 L 2
Todos os Santos, Bir ∼ BR 72-73 K 4
Todos Santos o BOL 70-71 E 5
Todos Santos o MEX 50-51 D 6
Todra, Gorges du • MA 188-189 J 5
Todža, onyri = ozero Azas o RUS 116-117 H 9
Tõdžinskaja kotlovina ± RUS 116-117 H 9
Toéguin o BF 202-203 K 3
Toèni o BF 202-203 J 3
Toéssé o BF 202-203 K 4
Toez o CO 60-61 C 5
Toffo o DY 204-205 E 5
Tofield o CDN 32-33 N 5
Tofino o CDN 32-33 G 7
Töfsingdalens nationalpark ⊥ S 86-87 F 5

Togdheer □ SP 208-209 G 4
Tog Dheer, togga ∼ SP 208-209 H 4
Togi o J 152-153 G 6
Togiak Bay ≈ 22-23 Q 3
Togian, Kepulauan ∼ RI 164-165 G 4
Togian, Pulau ∼ RI 164-165 G 4
Togme o VRC 144-145 H 4
Togo o SUD 200-201 G 3
Togo o PNG 183 B 5
Togo ■ RT 204-205 D 4
Togo, USA 42-43 L 2
Togo, Lago o PNG 183 L 6
Togobala o PNG 183 J 6
Togo Hills ▲ GH 202-203 L 6
Togolîka ∼ RUS 114-115 T 5
Togoromã o CO 60-61 C 5
Togou o RMM 202-203 H 3
Tögrög o MAU 146-147 J 3
Togtoh o VRC 154-155 G 1
Toguéré-Koumbé o RMM 202-203 H 2
Togul o RUS 124-125 P 2
Tog Wajaale o SP 208-209 F 4
Togwotee Pass ▲ USA 40-41 J 4
Togyzak ∼ KA 124-125 C 2
Tohâna o IND 138-139 E 5
Tohareu, poluostrov ∼ RUS 122-123 H 2
Tohiatoš o US 136-137 F 3
Tohma Çayı ∼ TR 128-129 H 3
Tõhoku o J 152-153 J 4
Töhörn o MAU 148-149 J 5
Tohomo ∼ RUS 116-117 G 5
Tohopekaliga, Lake o USA 48-49 H 5
Tohoun o RT 202-203 L 6
Toibalewe o IND 140-141 L 4
Toili o RI 164-165 H 4
Toineke o RI 166-167 C 7
Toison, La o RH 54-55 K 5
Toivala o FIN 88-89 J 5
Tojo o J 152-153 F 7
Tojoku o RUS 118-119 K 4
Tojtepa o US 136-137 L 4
Tok ∼ RUS 96-97 H 7
Tok o RUS 118-119 H 4
Toka o GUY 62-63 E 4
Tokachi-dake ▲ J 152-153 K 3
Tokachi-gawa ∼ J 152-153 K 3
Tôkamachi o J 152-153 H 6
Tokapalle o IND 140-141 H 3
Tokar o SUD 200-201 H 3
Tokara-kaikyõ ≈ 152-153 C 9
Tokara-rettõ ∼ J 152-153 C 10
Tokat ☆• TR 128-129 G 2
Tõkchõkto ∼ ROK 150-151 E 9
Tokchon o DVR 150-151 F 8
Tok Do ∼ ROK 150-151 H 9
Tokelau Islands ∼ NZ 13 K 3
Toki o TCH 206-207 C 4
Tokio o RUS (SAH) 118-119 K 6
Tokko o RUS 118-119 J 6
Tokko ∼ RUS 118-119 J 7
Toklat River ∼ USA 20-21 N 4
Tokma o RUS 116-117 M 6
Tokmak o KS 146-147 L 4
Tokmak o UA 102-103 J 4
Tokoro o J 152-153 L 2
Tokoroa o NZ 182 E 3
Tokounou o RG 202-203 F 4
Tokrau ∼ KA 124-125 J 4
Toksovo o RUS 94-95 M 1
Toksum o VRC 146-147 J 4
Toktogul o KS 136-137 L 4
Toktogul'skoje vodohranilišče < KS 136-137 N 4
Tokuma o RUS 110-111 U 6
Tokunoshima o J 152-153 C 11
Tokuno-shima ∼ J 152-153 C 11
Tokur-Jurjah ∼ RUS 112-113 J 4
Tokushima o J 152-153 F 7
Tokuyama o J 152-153 D 7
Tokwe ∼ ZW 218-219 F 6
Toky, Chute ∼ RM 222-223 B 3
Tōkyō ★• J 152-153 H 7
Tõkyô-wan ≈ 152-153 H 7
Tõkyusan National Park ⊥ ROK 150-151 F 10
Tol o PNG 183 G 3
Tola, La o EC 64-65 C 1
Tolabit o RI 164-165 K 3
Tolaga Bay ∼ NZ 182 G 3
Tolar, Cerro ▲ RCH 76-77 B 1
Tolbazy ∼ RUS 96-97 J 6
Tolbo o RUS 94-95 H 4
Tolbo nuur o MAU 146-147 J 1
Tolbuhin = Dobrič o BG 102-103 E 6
Tolbuzino o RUS 118-119 M 9
Toldi o GH 202-203 K 5
Tolé o RCA 206-207 B 5
Toledo o BOL 70-71 D 5
Toledo o BR 74-75 D 5
Toledo o•• E 98-99 E 5
Toledo o USA (OH) 46-47 G 5
Toledo □ USA
Toledo, Montes de ▲ E 98-99 E 5
Toledo Bend Reservoir < USA 44-45 L 3
Toledo City o RP 160-161 E 7
Toliara □ RM 222-223 C 9
Toliara ★• RM (Tla) 222-223 C 9
Tolima □ CO 60-61 C 5
Tolimán o MEX 52-53 E 1
Tolisäin o NEP 144-145 C 6
Tolitoli o RI 164-165 G 3

Tol'jatti = Stavropol'-na-Volgi ☆ RUS 96-97 F 7
Tol'ka ~ RUS 114-115 Q 3
Tollja, zaliv ≈ 108-109 d 3
Tolmačovo o RUS 94-95 L 2
Tolo o ZRE 210-211 G 5
Tolo, Teluk ≈ 164-165 G 5
Tolode o LB 202-203 F 6
Tolofu o RI 164-165 K 3
Tolokiwa Island ⌒ PNG 183 D 3
Tololai (Muslim Tombs) ∴ RI 168 D 7
Tolon o• RUS 120-121 E 3
Tolongoina o RM 222-223 E 8
Tolono o USA 46-47 D 6
Tolonuu, Pulau ⌒ RI 164-165 L 3
Tolosa o E 98-99 F 3
Tolovana River ~ USA 20-21 Q 4
Tolsan Do ⌒ ROK 150-151 F 10
Tolstova, mys ▲ RUS 110-111 V 2
Tolstyj, mys ▲ RUS 120-121 W 6
Toltén o RCH 78-79 C 5
Toltén, Río ~ RCH 78-79 C 5
Tolu o CO 60-61 D 3
Toluca ☆• MEX 52-53 E 2
Toluca de Lerdo = Toluca ☆• MEX 52-53 E 2
Toluk o KS 136-137 N 4
Toluviejo o CO 60-61 D 3
Tolwe o ZA 218-219 E 6
Tol'yatti = Stavropol'-na-Volgi ☆ RUS 96-97 F 7
Tölz, Bad o D 92-93 L 5
Tom' ~ RUS 114-115 S 7
Tom ~ RUS 122-123 D 3
Tom' ~ RUS 122-123 D 3
Tom' ~ RUS 124-125 P 1
Tom o US 136-137 J 5
Toma o BF 202-203 J 3
Toma, La o RA 78-79 G 2
Toma, Río la ~ RA 76-77 D 4
Tomah o USA 46-47 C 4
Tomahawk o USA 46-47 D 3
Tomakomai o J 152-153 J 3
Tomales Bay ≈ 40-41 C 6
Tomali o RI 164-165 G 4
Tomani o MAL 160-161 A 10
Tomanivi ▲ FJI 184 III b 2
Tomar o BR 66-67 F 3
Tomar o••• P 98-99 C 5
Tomara, Talahini- o CI 202-203 J 5
Tomari o RUS 122-123 K 5
Tomarovka o RUS 102-103 K 2
Tomarza ☆ TR 128-129 F 3
Tomas o PE 64-65 E 8
Tomás Garrido o MEX 52-53 K 2
Tomásia o BR 68-69 E 6
Tomaszów Lubelski o PL 92-93 R 3
Tomaszów Mazowiecki o PL 92-93 P 3
Tomat o SUD (Kas) 200-201 G 5
Tomat o SUD (NR) 206-207 H 3
Tomatán o MEX 50-51 B 3
Tomatlán o MEX 52-53 B 2
Tombador, Serra do ▲ BR 70-71 J 2
Tombali, Rio ~ GNB 202-203 C 4
Tombe o ANG 216-217 D 6
Tombe du Camerounais ▲ TCH 198-199 H 3
Tombel o CAM 204-205 H 6
Tombetsu, Hama- o J 152-153 K 2
Tombetsu, Nako- o J 152-153 K 2
Tombetsu, Shō- o J 152-153 K 2
Tombigbee River ~ USA 48-49 D 3
Tombo, Punta ▲•• RA 80 H 2
Tomboco o ANG 216-217 B 3
Tombokro o CI 202-203 H 6
Tombolo o RI 164-165 F 6
Tombouctou o••• RMM 196-197 J 6
Tombstone o USA 44-45 B 4
Tombua o ANG 216-217 A 7
Tomé o RCH 78-79 C 4
Tomea, Pulau ⌒ RI 164-165 H 6
Tomé-Açu o BR 68-69 D 3
Tomelloso o E 98-99 F 5
Tomi ~ RCA 206-207 D 6
Tomiko o CDN 38-39 E 5
Tomina, Río ~ BOL 70-71 E 6
Tominé ~ RG 202-203 D 4
Tomingley o AUS 180-181 K 2
Tomini o RI 164-165 G 3
Tomini, Teluk ≈ 164-165 G 4
Tominián o RMM 202-203 H 3
Tomioka o J 152-153 H 6
Tomkinson Ranges ▲ AUS 176-177 K 3
Tomma ⌒ N 86-87 F 3
Tommot o RUS 118-119 N 6
Tommotskij massiv ▲ RUS 110-111 W 5
Tomo, Río ~ CO 60-61 G 5
Tomochic o MEX 50-51 F 3
Tomohon o RI 164-165 J 3
Tomori o RCA 210-211 E 2
Tomorrit, Mali i ▲ AL 100-101 H 4
Tompira o RI 164-165 G 5
Tompi Seleka o ZA 220-221 J 2
Tompo o RI 164-165 G 3
Tompo o RUS 120-121 F 2
Tompo ~ RUS 120-121 H 1
Tom Price o AUS 172-173 C 7
Tom Price, Mount ▲ AUS 172-173 C 7
Tompuda ~ RUS 118-119 E 8
Tomsk ☆• RUS 114-115 S 6
Toms River o USA 46-47 L 6
Tomtor o RUS (SAH) 110-111 T 6
Tomtor o RUS (SAH) 120-121 E 2
Tomu o RI 166-167 G 3
Tomur Feng ▲ VRC 146-147 E 4
Tomu River ~ PNG 183 B 4
Tom White, Mount ▲ USA 20-21 T 6
Tonalá o MEX (JAL) 52-53 C 1
Tonalá o• MEX (CHI) 52-53 H 3
Tonami o J 152-153 G 6
Tonantins o BR 66-67 D 4
Tonasket o USA 40-41 E 1
Tonate o F 62-63 H 3
Tonawanda Indian Reservation ⚔ USA 46-47 J 4
Tonb-e Bozorg, Ğazire-ye ⌒ IR 134-135 F 5
Tonb-e Kučak, Ğazire-ye ⌒ IR 134-135 F 5
Tonda o PNG 183 A 5
Tondano o RI 164-165 J 3
Tondano, Danau ⊖ RI 164-165 J 3
Tonde o Z 218-219 E 1
Tønder o• DK 86-87 D 9
Tondi o IND 140-141 H 6
Tondibi o RMM 196-197 K 6
Tondidji o RMM 202-203 E 3
Tondigamé Goulbi ~ RN 204-205 E 2
Tondi Kiwidi o RN 204-205 E 1
Tondon o RG 202-203 D 4
Tondong o RI 164-165 F 5
Toné o BF 202-203 J 4
Tone-gawa ~ J 152-153 H 6
Tonekābon o IR 136-137 B 6
Tong o SUD 206-207 J 5
Tong ~ SUD 206-207 J 5
Tonga o CAM 204-205 J 6
Tonga o SUD 206-207 K 4
Tonga ■ TON 184 IV a 1
Tongaat o ZA 220-221 K 4
Tongaland ⌒ ZA 220-221 L 3
Tong'an o VRC 156-157 L 4
Tonga Ridge ≃ 184 IV a 2
Tongariki ⌒ VAN 184 II b 3
Tongariro National Park ⊥••• NZ 182 E 3
Tongatapu ⌒ TON 184 IV a 2
Tongatapu Group ⌒ TON 184 IV a 2
Tonga Trench ≃ 13 K 4
Tongbai o VRC 154-155 H 5
Tongbai Shan ▲ VRC 154-155 H 5
Tongcheng o VRC (ANH) 154-155 K 6
Tongcheng o VRC (HUB) 156-157 H 2
Tongchon o DVR 150-151 F 8
Tongchuan o VRC 154-155 F 4
Tongdao o VRC 156-157 F 3
Tongde o VRC 154-155 B 4
T'ongdo Sa • ROK 150-151 G 10
Tongehatan Point ▲ RP 160-161 D 10
Tongerai, Tanjung ▲ RI 166-167 G 3
Tonggu o VRC 156-157 J 2
Tongguan o VRC 154-155 G 4
Tongguzbasti o VRC 146-147 E 6
Tonggu Zhang ▲ VRC 156-157 K 4
Tonghae o ROK 150-151 G 9
Tonghai o VRC 156-157 C 4
Tonghaiko o VRC 154-155 H 6
Tonghe o VRC 150-151 G 5
Tonghua o VRC 150-151 E 7
Tong Island ⌒ PNG 183 D 2
Tongjiang o VRC (HEI) 150-151 J 4
Tongjiang o VRC (SIC) 154-155 E 6
Tongjosŏn Man ≈ 150-151 F 8
Tongko o RI 164-165 G 4
Tongkomanino o RI 164-165 G 5
Tongku o RI 164-165 G 4
Tongliang o VRC 156-157 E 2
Tongliao o VRC 150-151 D 6
Tongling o VRC 154-155 K 6
Tonglu o VRC 156-157 L 2
Tongmu o VRC 156-157 H 3
Tongnan o VRC 154-155 D 6
Tongo o RCB 210-211 F 4
Tongoa ⌒ VAN 184 II b 3
Tongobory o RM 222-223 D 9
Tongomayél o BF 202-203 K 2
Tongren o VRC (GZH) 156-157 F 3
Tongren o VRC (QIN) 154-155 B 4
Tongsa o BHT 142-143 G 2
Tongshan o VRC 156-157 J 2
Tongshi o• VRC 156-157 F 7
Tongtian He ~ VRC 144-145 L 4
Tongue o• GB 90-91 E 2
Tongue River ~ USA 42-43 D 3
Tonguo ~ RUS 118-119 K 4
Tonguro, Rio ~ BR 72-73 D 2
Tongxiang o VRC 154-155 M 6
Tongxin o VRC 154-155 D 3
Tongyu o VRC (JIL) 150-151 D 5
Tongyu o VRC (SHA) 154-155 H 3
Tongzi o VRC 156-157 E 2
Tonhil = Zujl o MAU 146-147 L 2
Tonichi o MEX 50-51 E 3
Tonila o MEX 52-53 C 2
Tonimuca, Raudal ~ CO 66-67 B 3
Tonina o CO 60-61 H 6
Toniná ∴• MEX 52-53 H 3
Tonk o IND 138-139 E 6
Tonka o RMM 196-197 J 6
Tonkawa o USA 44-45 J 1
Tonkensval ~ SME 62-63 F 3
Tonki Cape ▲ USA 22-23 V 3
Tonkin, Gulf of ≈ 156-157 E 6
Tonkui, Mont ▲ CI 202-203 G 6
Tônlé Sab ⊖ K 158-159 H 4
Tonnerre o F 90-91 J 8
Tōno o J 152-153 J 5
Tonoda ~ RUS 118-119 G 6
Tonono o RA 76-77 F 2
Tonopah o USA 40-41 F 6
Tonopah Test Range Atomic Energy Commission xx USA 40-41 F 7
Tonoro o YV 60-61 K 3
Tonosí o PA 52-53 D 8
Tonosyō o J 152-153 F 7
Tonotha o RB 218-219 D 5
Tonquil Island ⌒ RP 160-161 D 10
Ton Sai o THA 158-159 F 7
Tønsberg ☆ N 86-87 E 7
Tonsina o USA 20-21 S 6
Tonstad ☆ N 86-87 C 7
Tontado, Caleta ≈ 76-77 B 5
Tontal, Sierra del ▲ RA 76-77 C 6
Tontelbos o ZA 220-221 E 5
Tonto, Río ~ MEX 52-53 F 2
Tonto National Monument ∴• USA 40-41 J 9
Tonumea ⌒ TON 184 IV a 2
Tonya ☆ TR 128-129 H 2
Tonzona River ~ USA 20-21 O 5
Toobanna o AUS 174-175 J 6
Toobli o LB 202-203 F 6
Toodyay o AUS 176-177 D 5
Tooele o USA 40-41 H 5
To Okena o PNG 183 D 4
Toolebuc o AUS 178-179 F 2
Toolik River ~ USA 20-21 Q 2
Toolondo o AUS 180-181 F 4
Tooloombilla o AUS 178-179 K 3
Toompine o AUS 178-179 H 4
Toomula o AUS 174-175 J 6
Tooncatchyin Creek ~ AUS 178-179 E 5
Toora-Hem ☆ RUS 116-117 H 9
Toormt o MAU 116-117 F 10
Toornaarsuk ⌒ GRØ 28-29 Q 6
Toowoomba o AUS 178-179 L 4
Top, Ozero = Topozero ⊖ RUS 88-89 M 4
Topagoruk River ~ USA 20-21 N 1
Topar o KA 124-125 J 6
Topasoėj, ostrov ⌒ RUS 108-109 M 7
Topaz Lake o USA 40-41 E 6
Topeka ☆ USA 42-43 K 6
Topia o MEX 50-51 F 5
Topia ~ RCA 206-207 C 6
Topia, Quebrada ~ MEX 50-51 F 5
Topko, gora ▲ RUS 120-121 G 5
Toplița o• RO 102-103 D 4
Topocalma, Punta ▲ RCH 78-79 C 3
Topografičeskaja, grjada ▲ RUS 108-109 Z 4
Topol o RUS 116-117 G 7
Topola o• YU 100-101 H 2
Topoli o ZRE 212-213 A 2
Topolinoe o RUS 120-121 F 1
Topolobampo o MEX 50-51 E 5
Topolovgrad o BG 102-103 E 6
Topolovka o RUS 120-121 T 3
Topozero ⊖ RUS 88-89 M 4
Toppenish o USA 40-41 D 2
Toppi-misaki ▲ J 152-153 J 4
Toprakkale ∴• TR 128-129 K 3
Tops, Mount ▲ AUS 178-179 B 1
Topsfield o USA 46-47 P 3
Top Springs o AUS (NT) 172-173 K 4
Top Springs o AUS (NT) 174-175 C 5
Topura o PNG 183 F 6
Topyrakkala • US 136-137 G 4
Toquerville o USA 40-41 H 7
Tor o ETH 208-209 A 5
Toramarkog o VRC 144-145 L 4
Torata o PE 70-71 B 5
Torbanlea o AUS 178-179 M 3
Torbat-e Ğām o• IR 136-137 G 7
Torbat-e Heidariye o• IR 136-137 F 7
Torbay o AUS 176-177 D 7
Torbay o CDN 38-39 S 5
Torbay o GB 90-91 F 6
Tordenskjøld, Kap ▲ GRØ 28-29 T 6
Tordesillas o E 98-99 E 4
Töre o S 86-87 L 4
Torej, Zun, ozero ⊖ RUS 118-119 H 10
Torell Land ∸ N 84-85 K 4
Torelló o E 98-99 J 3
Torenur o IND 140-141 F 4
Toreo Bugis o RI 164-165 H 5
Torgaj o KA (KST) 126-127 P 3
Torgaj ~ KA 124-125 D 3
Torgaj ~ KA 126-127 P 3
Torgaj kolaty ⊍ KA 126-127 P 3
Torgaj üstirti ▲ KA 124-125 B 3
Torgau o• D 92-93 M 3
Torgun ~ RUS 96-97 E 8
Torhout o B 92-93 G 3
Tori o RMM 202-203 J 3
Toribio o CO 60-61 C 6
Tori-Bossito o DY 204-205 E 5
Torino ☆• I 100-101 A 2
Torino, Cachoeira do ~ BR 62-63 F 6
Tori-shima ⌒ J 152-153 C 11
Torit o SUD 206-207 L 6
Toritama o BR 68-69 K 6
Toriu o PNG 183 F 3
Toriud o IR 136-137 D 7
Torje, Barun, ozero ⊖ RUS 118-119 G 10
Torkamān o IR 128-129 M 4
Torkemān, Bandar-e o IR 136-137 D 6
Torlu River ~ PNG 183 F 3
Tormentor, ozero ⊖ RUS 114-115 P 4
Torment, Point ▲ AUS 172-173 F 4
Tormes, Río ~ E 98-99 E 4
Tormosin o RUS 102-103 N 3
Tornado Mountain ▲ CDN 32-33 N 7
Torneälven ~ S 86-87 L 3
Torneträsk ⊖• S 86-87 J 2
Torngat Mountains ▲ CDN 36-37 R 5
Tornik ▲ YU 100-101 G 3
Tornio o FIN 88-89 H 4
Tornionjoki ~ FIN 88-89 G 3
Tornquist o RA 78-79 H 5
Toro o E 98-99 E 4
Toro o EAU 212-213 C 3
Toro, Cerro del ▲ RA 76-77 C 5
Toro, Isla del ⌒ MEX 50-51 L 7
Toro, Lago del ⊖ RCH 80 D 5
Toro, Punta ▲ RCH 78-79 D 2
Torobuku o RI 164-165 H 6
Torodi o RN 202-203 L 3
Toro Doum < TCH 198-199 H 4
Toro Game Reservat ⊥ EAU 212-213 C 3
Torokina o PNG 184 I b 2
Toro Kinkéné o CI 202-203 H 5
Torokoroba o RMM 202-203 G 3
Törökszentmiklós o H 92-93 Q 5
Torola, Río ~ ES 52-53 K 5
Torom o RUS 120-121 F 6
Torom ~ RUS 120-121 F 6
Toro Negro, Sierra del ▲ RA 76-77 C 5
Toronto ☆• CDN 38-39 E 7
Toronto o USA 44-45 K 1
Toropec ☆ RUS 94-95 M 3
Toroq o IR 136-137 F 6
Tororo o EAU 212-213 E 3
Torqabe o IR 136-137 F 6
Torquato Severo o BR 76-77 K 6
Torquay o CDN 34-35 E 6
Torquinie, Lake ⊖ AUS 178-179 E 3
Torrabaai o NAM 216-217 B 10
Torrance o USA 40-41 E 9
Torrão o P 98-99 C 5
Torrealba o YV 60-61 J 3
Torre del Greco o I 100-101 E 4
Torre de Moncorvo o P 98-99 D 4
Torrelaguna o E 98-99 F 4
Torrelavega o E 98-99 E 3
Torremolinos o E 98-99 E 6
Torrens, Cape ▲ CDN 24-25 a 2
Torrens, Lake ⊖ AUS 178-179 D 6
Torrens Creek o AUS 174-175 H 7
Torrens Creek ~ AUS 178-179 H 2
Torreón o MEX 50-51 H 5
Torreon o USA 44-45 D 2
Torre-Pacheco o E 98-99 G 6
Torres o• BR 74-75 F 7
Torres, Îles = Torres Islands ⌒ VAN 184 II a 1
Torres del Paine o RCH 80 D 5
Torres del Paine, Parque Nacional ⊥•• RCH 80 D 5
Torres Islands = Îles Torres ⌒ VAN 184 II a 1
Torres Novas o P 98-99 C 5
Torres Selat ≈ 183 A 5
Torres Strait ≈ 174-175 F 1
Torres Vedras o P 98-99 C 5
Torrevieja o E 98-99 G 6
Torrey o USA 40-41 J 6
Torricelli Mountains ▲ PNG 183 B 2
Torrijos o E 98-99 E 5
Torrington o USA (CT) 46-47 M 5
Torrington o USA (WY) 42-43 E 4
Torrock o TCH 206-207 B 4
Torrön ⊖ S 86-87 F 5
Torsås ☆ S 86-87 H 8
Torsby ☆• S 86-87 F 6
Torset, Oued ~ DZ 190-191 G 8
Tórshavn ☆ FR 90-91 D 1
Torsö ⌒ S 86-87 F 7
Torssugatak ≈ 28-29 P 2
Tortas, Cachoeira das ~ BR 70-71 J 4
Tortel o RCH 80 D 3
Tortiya o• CI 202-203 H 5
Törtköl o KA 136-137 L 3
Tortola ⌒ GB 56 C 2
Tórtoles de Esgueva o E 98-99 E 4
Tortona o I 100-101 B 2
Tortosa o E 98-99 H 4
Tortosa, Cabo de ▲ E 98-99 H 4
Tortue, Ile de la ⌒ RH 54-55 J 4
Tortuga, Isla ⌒ MEX 50-51 D 4
Tortuga, Isla La ⌒ YV 60-61 J 2
Tortuguero, Parque Nacional ⊥ CR 52-53 C 6
Tortuguilla o C 54-55 H 5
Tortum ☆ TR 128-129 J 2
Torue o RI 164-165 G 4
Torul ☆ TR 128-129 H 2
Toruń ☆•• PL 92-93 P 2
Torup o S 86-87 F 8
Tōrva o•• EST 94-95 J 2
Torwood o AUS 174-175 G 5
Tory o RUS 116-117 L 10
Tory Hill o CDN 38-39 E 6
Toržkovskaja grjada ▲ RUS 94-95 O 3
Toržok ☆ RUS 94-95 O 3
Torzym o PL 92-93 N 2
Tosagua o EC 64-65 B 2
Tosari o RI 168 E 3
Tosa-shimizu o J 152-153 E 8
Tosa-wan ≈ 152-153 E 8
Tosca o ZA 220-221 F 2
Toscana ◘ I 100-101 C 3
Toscas, Las o RA (BUA) 78-79 J 3
Toscas, Las o RA (SAF) 76-77 H 5
Toscas, Las o ROU 78-79 M 2
Toshām o IND 138-139 E 5
Toshima ⌒ J 152-153 H 7
Toshino-Kumano National Park ⊥ J 152-153 G 7
Tosi o SUD 206-207 K 3
Toškent ☆•• US 136-137 L 4
Toškuduk, kumlik ∸ US 136-137 G 3
Toškürgon o US 136-137 K 5
Tosno ☆ RUS 94-95 M 2
Tosoncengel o MAU 148-149 D 3
Toson Hu ⊖ VRC 144-145 L 2
Tostado o RA 76-77 G 5
Tõstamaa o EST 94-95 H 2
Toston o USA 40-41 J 2
Tošviska o RUS 88-89 W 3
Tosya ☆ TR 128-129 F 2
Tot o EAK 212-213 E 3
Totaranui o NZ 182 D 4
Toteng o RB 218-219 B 5
Tôtes o F 90-91 H 7
Totias o SP 212-213 J 2
Tot'ma o RUS 94-95 S 2
Totnes Fiord ≈ 28-29 J 3
Totness ☆ SME 62-63 F 3
Toto o ANG 216-217 C 3
Toto o WAN 204-205 G 4
Totoglag o VAN 184 II a 1
Totok o RI 164-165 J 3
Totolán o MEX 52-53 C 1
Totolapan o MEX 52-53 F 3
Totomai, Monts ▲ RN 198-199 G 2
Totonicapán ☆• GCA 52-53 J 4
Totora o BOL (COC) 70-71 E 5
Totora o BOL (ORU) 70-71 C 5
Totoral o RCH 76-77 B 4
Totoral, Quebrada del ~ RCH 76-77 B 5
Totoralejos o RA 76-77 E 5
Totoras o RA 78-79 J 2
Totota o LB 202-203 F 6
Totoya ⌒ FJI 184 III c 3
Totta ~ RUS 120-121 G 5
Tottan Range ▲ ARK 16 F 35
Totten Glacier ⊂ ARK 16 G 12
Tottenham o AUS 180-181 J 2
Tottori ☆ J 152-153 F 7
Totumito o YV 60-61 F 4
Totydėottajaha, Boľšaja ~ RUS 108-109 T 8
Touājil o RIM 196-197 D 3
Touak Fiord ≈ 36-37 S 2
Touâret < RN 198-199 C 2
Touaris, Djebel ▲ DZ 188-189 K 6
Touat ∸ DZ 188-189 L 7
Touba o CI 202-203 G 5
Touba o• SN 202-203 C 2
Toubacouta o SN 202-203 B 3
Toubéré Bafal o SN 202-203 D 2
Toubkal, Ibel ▲ MA 188-189 H 5
Touboro o CAM 206-207 B 5
Touboutou, Chutes de ~• RCA 206-207 B 6
Toucha, Djebel ▲ DZ 188-189 L 5
Toucy o F 90-91 J 8
Toueyyirât < RMM 196-197 J 5
Tougan o BF 202-203 J 3
Tougé o RG 202-203 E 4
Touggourt o• DZ 190-191 F 4
Tougnifili o RG 202-203 C 4
Tougouri o BF 202-203 K 3
Tougoutaou < RN 198-199 C 5
Touijinet < RIM 196-197 F 5
Touil, Hâssi < RIM 196-197 H 6
Touila, Bir < TN 190-191 G 4
Toujil o RIM 196-197 E 7
Toukoto o RMM 202-203 F 3
Toukountouna o DY 202-203 L 4
Toul o F 90-91 K 7
Touléplеu o CI 202-203 F 6
Touliu o RC 156-157 M 5
Toulnustouc, Rivière ~ CDN 38-39 K 4
Toulon ☆ F 90-91 K 10
Toulou, Abri des • RCA 206-207 E 4
Toulounga o TCH 206-207 D 3
Toulouse ☆•• F 90-91 H 10
Toumbélaga < RN 198-199 C 5
Toumodi o CI 202-203 H 6
Toumoundjila o RN 202-203 F 4
Tounassine, Hamada ∸ DZ 188-189 H 6
Tounfafi o RN 198-199 B 5
Toungo o WAN 204-205 K 4
Toungoo o MYA 142-143 K 6
Toungour < TCH 198-199 J 4
Toura ~ BF 202-203 K 3
Toura o DY 204-205 E 3
Tourağondi o AFG 136-137 H 7
Tourassinne < RIM 196-197 E 2
Tourba o TCH 198-199 G 6
Tourcoing o F 90-91 J 6
Touré Kounda o SN 202-203 D 3
Tour Ham o AFG 138-139 C 2
Tourińán, Cabo ▲ E 98-99 C 3
Tourîne o RIM 196-197 E 3
Tournai o• B 92-93 G 3
Tournavista o PE 64-65 E 6
Tournde, Oued ~ DZ 190-191 H 9
Tourni o BF 202-203 H 4
Tournus o F 90-91 K 8
Touros o BR 68-69 L 4
Tourou ▲ CAM 204-205 K 3
Tourou o CAM 204-205 K 4
Touroug o MA 188-189 J 5
Tourougoumbé o RMM 202-203 F 2
Tourouko o BF 202-203 H 4
Tours o F 90-91 H 8
Tour Village, The o USA 46-47 G 3
Touside, Pic ▲ TCH 198-199 H 2
Toussoro, Mont ▲ RCA 206-207 F 4
Toutes Aides o CDN 34-35 G 5
Toutoukro o CI 202-203 H 5
Touwsrivier o ZA 220-221 E 6
Touwsrivier ~ ZA 220-221 E 6
Töv ◘ MAU 148-149 G 4
Tovar o YV 60-61 F 3
Tovar Donoso o EC 64-65 C 1
Tovarkovskij o RUS 94-95 Q 5
Tovdalselva ~ N 86-87 D 7
Tovuz o AZ 128-129 L 2
Towada o J 152-153 J 4
Towada Hachimantai National Park ⊥ J 152-153 J 5
Towada-Hachimantai National Park ⊥ J 152-153 J 4
Towada-ko • J 152-153 J 4
Towakaima o GUY 62-63 D 2
Towanda o USA 46-47 K 5
Towari o RI 164-165 G 6
Towe o LB 202-203 F 6
Tower o USA 42-43 L 2
Towera o AUS 176-177 C 1
Towerhill Creek ~ AUS 178-179 H 1
Tower Peak ▲ AUS 176-177 G 6
Towla o ZW 218-219 E 5
Towner o USA 42-43 G 1
Townsend o USA 40-41 J 2
Townsend Lake ⊖ CDN 30-31 W 4
Townsend Ridges ▲ AUS 176-177 J 3
Townshend Island ⌒ AUS 178-179 L 2
Towns River ~ AUS 174-175 C 4
Townsville o•• AUS 174-175 J 6
Towson o USA 46-47 K 6
Towuti, Danau ⊖ RI 164-165 G 5
Toxkan He ~ VRC 146-147 D 5
Toyah o USA 44-45 F 4
Tōya-ko ⊖ J 152-153 J 3
Toyama ☆ J 152-153 G 6
Toyama-wan ≈ 152-153 G 6
Toyo o J 152-153 F 8
Toyohashi o J 152-153 G 7
Toyokawa o J 152-153 G 7
Toyooka o J 152-153 F 7
Toyota o J 152-153 G 7
Toyotomi o J 152-153 J 2
Tozer, Mount ▲ AUS 174-175 G 3
Tozeur ☆• TN 190-191 G 4
Tozitna River ~ USA 20-21 O 4
Trabária, Bocca ▲ I 100-101 D 3
Trà Bông o VN 158-159 K 3
Trabzon ☆•• TR 128-129 H 2
Tracadie o CDN 38-39 M 5
Trácino o I 100-101 D 6
Tracy o USA (CA) 40-41 D 7
Tracy o USA (MN) 42-43 K 3
Tracy Arm Fords Terror Wilderness ⊥• USA 32-33 D 3
Traditional Villages • RI 168 D 7
Tradit. Villages o• RI 168 D 7
Traela, Punta de ▲ RCH 78-79 D 2
Trænstaven ⌒ N 86-87 E 3
Traer o USA 42-43 L 4
Tragacete o E 98-99 G 4
Traiguén o RCH 78-79 C 5
Traiguen, Isla ⌒ RCH 80 D 2
Trail o CDN 32-33 M 7
Traill Ø ⌒ GRØ 26-27 o 7
Traine River ~ AUS 172-173 H 4
Traipu o BR 68-69 K 6
Traíra, Serra do ▲ BR 66-67 C 3
Trairão, Rio ~ BR 68-69 C 5
Trairi o BR 68-69 J 3
Trajgorodskaja ~ RUS 114-115 P 4
Trakai ☆ LT 94-95 J 4
Trakan Phut Phon o THA 158-159 H 3
Trakošćan • HR 100-101 E 1
Trakt o RUS 88-89 V 5
Tralee = Trá Lí ☆ IRL 90-91 C 5
Trá Lí = Tralee ☆ IRL 90-91 C 5
Trallwng = Welshpool o• GB 90-91 F 5
Tramandaí o BR 74-75 E 7
Tramanu ~ RI 166-167 B 6
Trampa, La o PE 64-65 B 5
Tramping Lake o CDN 32-33 Q 5
Trà My o VN 158-159 K 3
Trăn o BG 102-103 C 6
Tranås ☆ S 86-87 G 7
Tranche-sur-Mer, la o F 90-91 G 8
Trang o THA 158-159 E 7
Trangan, Pulau ⌒ RI 166-167 H 5
Trảng Bàng o VN 158-159 J 5
Trangie o AUS 180-181 J 2
Tranomaro o RM 222-223 E 10
Tranoroa o RM 222-223 D 10
Tranqui, Isla ⌒ RCH 78-79 C 7
Trans Africa Route = Route transafricaine II WAN 204-205 G 5
Trānsāh o IR 128-129 M 4
Trans-Amazon Highway = Transamazônica II BR 66-67 H 6
Transamazônica II BR 66-67 H 6
Trans-Australian-Railway II AUS 176-177 K 5
Trans-Canada-Highway II CDN 32-33 K 7
Transhimalaya = Gangdisê Shan ▲ 144-145 C 5
Transkei (former Homeland, now part of East-Cape) ◘ ZA 220-221 H 5
Transsib II• RUS 118-119 E 10
Transsua o CI 202-203 J 6
Transylvania = Transilvani, Podișul ⊍ RO 102-103 C 4
Transylvanian Alps = Carpații Meridionali ▲ RO 100-101 J 2
Tranum o MAL 162-163 D 3
Tranzitnyj o RUS 112-113 V 3
Trà Ôn o VN 158-159 H 6
Trapalco, Cerro ▲ RA 78-79 E 5
Trapalcó, Salinas ⊖ RA 78-79 F 5
Trápani o I 100-101 D 5
Traralgon o AUS 180-181 J 5
Traras, Monts des ▲ DZ 188-189 L 3
Trarza ∸ RIM 196-197 C 5
Trârza ∸ RIM 196-197 C 6
Trasimeno, Lago ⊖ I 100-101 D 3
Trás os Montes e Alto Douro ∸ P 98-99 D 4
Trat o THA 158-159 G 4
Trautenau = Trutnov o CZ 92-93 N 3
Trautfetter ~ RUS 108-109 d 4
Travaillant Lake ⊖ CDN 20-21 Z 3
Travellers Lake ⊖ AUS 180-181 F 2
Travellers Rest ∴ USA 40-41 G 2
Travemünde o D 92-93 L 2
Traverse, Lake ⊖ USA 42-43 J 3
Traverse City o USA 46-47 F 3
Traverse Peak ▲ USA 20-21 L 4
Travesía del Tunuyán ∸ RA 78-79 F 2
Travesía Puntana ∸ RA 78-79 F 3
Travessia de Caju ~ BR 68-69 D 5
Travessia do Jacuzao ~ BR 68-69 D 5
Trà Vinh o VN 158-159 J 6
Travis, Lake ⊖ USA 44-45 H 4
Travka ~ RUS 112-113 P 4
Trawas o RI 162-163 E 6
Trayning o AUS 176-177 D 5
Trbovlje o SLO 100-101 E 1
Tre ⌒ VN 158-159 K 4
Treasure Beach o JA 54-55 G 6
Treasury Islands ⌒ SOL 184 I b 2
Třebíč o CZ 92-93 N 4
Trebinje o BIH 100-101 G 3
Trebisacce o I 100-101 F 5
Trebitsch = Třebíč o CZ 92-93 N 4
Tree River ~ CDN 20-21 Y 3
Tree River ~ CDN 30-31 O 2
Treesbank o CDN 34-35 G 6
Trees Point ▲ CDN 26-27 J 3
Trego o USA 46-47 C 3
Trehbugornyj, mys ▲ RUS 108-109 P 7
Treherne o CDN 34-35 G 6
Treinta y Tres ☆ ROU 78-79 M 2
Trelew o RA 78-79 G 7
Trelleborg o S 86-87 F 9
Tremblant, Mont ▲ CDN 38-39 G 5
Trembleur Lake ⊖ CDN 32-33 H 4
Tremen, Volcán ▲ RA 78-79 D 4
Trémiti, Ísole ⌒ I 100-101 E 3
Tremonton o USA 40-41 H 5
Tremp o E 98-99 H 3
Trena o ETH 208-209 E 3
Trenary o USA 46-47 E 2
Trenche, Rivière ~ CDN 38-39 H 4
Trenčín o SK 92-93 P 4
Trenčín = Trentschin o SK 92-93 P 4
Trenggalek o RI 168 D 4
Trenque Lauquen o RA 78-79 H 3
Trent ~ GB 90-91 F 5
Trent o USA 44-45 G 3
Trentino -Alto Àdige ◘ I 100-101 C 1
Trento ☆• I 100-101 C 1
Trenton o CDN 38-39 F 6
Trenton o USA (MI) 46-47 G 4
Trenton o USA (MO) 42-43 L 5
Trenton o USA (NE) 42-43 G 5
Trenton ☆ USA (NJ) 46-47 L 5
Trepassey o CDN 38-39 S 5
Trepassey Bay ≈ 38-39 S 5
Trephina Gorge ⊥ AUS 178-179 C 2
Tréport, Le o F 90-91 H 6
Tres Altilos, Cerro ▲ RA 78-79 E 2
Tres Arboles o• ROU 78-79 L 2
Tres Arroyos o RA 78-79 J 5
Três Barracas, Cachoeira ~ BR 66-67 G 7
Três Bicos o BR 74-75 E 5
Tres Bocas o RA 78-79 K 2
Três Casas o BR 66-67 F 6
Tres Cerros ▲ RA 78-79 D 7
Três Corações o BR 72-73 H 6
Tres Cruces o BOL 70-71 F 5
Tres Cruces, Arroyo ~ ROU 76-77 J 6
Tres Cruces, Cerro ▲ MEX 52-53 H 4
Tres Cruces, Cerro ▲ RCH 76-77 C 4
Três de Maio o BR 76-77 K 4
Tres Esquinas o CO 64-65 E 1
Três Ilhas, Cachoeira das ~ BR 66-67 J 7
Três Irmãos, Cachoeira dos ~ BR 70-71 H 2
Três Irmãos, Serra dos ▲ BR 66-67 E 7
Tres Isletas o RA 76-77 G 4
Treska ~ MK 100-101 H 4
Três Lagoas o BR 72-73 E 6
Tres Lagos o RA 80 E 4
Tres Mapejos o BOL 70-71 E 2
Três Marias o BR 72-73 H 5
Três Marias, Represa < BR 72-73 H 5
Tres Matas, Las o YV 60-61 J 3
Tres Mojones o RA 76-77 G 4
Tres Montes, Cabo ▲ RCH 80 C 3
Tres Montes, Península ⊍ RCH 80 C 3
Tres Morros o RA 76-77 E 2
Tres Palmas o CO 60-61 D 3
Três Palmeiras o BR 74-75 D 6
Tres Palos, Laguna ⊖ MEX 52-53 E 3
Três Passos o BR 74-75 D 6
Tres Picos, Cerro ▲ RA 78-79 J 5
Tres Piedras o USA 44-45 E 1
Três Praias o BR 66-67 D 7
Tres Puntas ▲ GCA 52-53 K 4
Tres Puntas, Cabo ▲ RA 80 H 3
Três Ranchos o BR 72-73 G 5
Três Rios o BR 72-73 J 7
Tres Unidos o PE 64-65 E 4
Tres Valles o MEX 52-53 F 2
Três Vendas o BR 76-77 K 6
Tres Virgenes, Volcán de las ▲ MEX 50-51 C 4
Tres Zapotes ∴• MEX 52-53 G 2
Tretes o• RI 168 E 3
Tretij, ostrov ⌒ RUS 120-121 U 3
Tret'jakovo o RUS 124-125 M 3
Treuburg = Olecko o PL 92-93 R 1
Treuenbrietzen o D 92-93 M 2
Treuer Range ▲ AUS 172-173 K 7
Trevelín o RA 78-79 D 7
Treviglio o I 100-101 B 2
Treviso o BR 74-75 F 7
Treviso ☆ I 100-101 D 2
Trewdate o CDN 34-35 C 5
Triabunna o AUS 180-181 J 7
Triang o MAL 162-163 E 3
Triangle o CDN 32-33 M 4
Triangle o ZW 218-219 F 5
Triángulos, Arrecifes ⌒ MEX 52-53 H 1
Trianon o RH 54-55 J 5
Tribugá o CO 60-61 C 5
Tribugá, Golfo de ≈ 60-61 C 5
Tribune o USA 42-43 G 6
Tricase o I 100-101 G 5
Trichur o• IND 140-141 G 5
Trici o BR 68-69 H 4
Trida o AUS 180-181 H 2
Trident Peak ▲ USA 40-41 E 5
Trier o•• D 92-93 J 4
Trieste ☆• I 100-101 D 2
Trieste, Golfo di ≈ 100-101 D 2
Trieste, Gulf of = Trieste, Golfo di ≈ I 100-101 D 2
Triglav ▲ SLO 100-101 D 1
Triglavski Narodni Park ⊥ SLO 100-101 D 1
Trigo, El o RA 78-79 K 3
Trigonon o GR 100-101 H 4
Tríkala o• GR 100-101 H 5
Trikkandiyur o IND 140-141 F 5
Trikonamadu o CL 140-141 J 6
Trillbar o AUS 176-177 D 2
Trilsbeck Lake ⊖ CDN 34-35 O 5
Trim = Baile Átha Troim ☆• IRL 90-91 D 5
Trincheras, Las o YV 60-61 J 4
Trincomalee o• CL 140-141 J 6
Trindade o BR (GOI) 72-73 F 4
Trindade o BR (PER) 68-69 H 5
Trindade o BR (ROR) 62-63 D 5
Tring o PNG 183 B 2
Trinidad ☆ BOL 70-71 E 4
Trinidad o••• C 54-55 F 4
Trinidad o CO 60-61 F 5
Trinidad o••• PY 76-77 K 4
Trinidad ☆ ROU 78-79 L 2
Trinidad ⌒ TT 60-61 L 2
Trinidad o USA 44-45 E 1
Trinidad, Golfo ≈ 80 C 4
Trinidad, Isla ⌒ RA 78-79 J 5
Trinidad, Laguna ⊖ PY 70-71 G 7
Trinidad and Tobago ■ TT 60-61 L 2
Trinidad de Arauca, La o YV 60-61 G 4
Trinidade o BR 68-69 D 3
Trinidade, Ilha da ⌒ BR 66-67 H 4
Trinitaria, La o MEX 52-53 H 3
Trinity o CDN 38-39 I S 4
Trinity o USA 44-45 K 4
Trinity Bay ≈ 38-39 I S 5
Trinity Islands ⌒ USA 22-23 T 4
Trinity Range ⌒ USA 40-41 E 6
Trinity River ~ USA 40-41 C 5
Trinity River ~ USA 44-45 J 3
Trinkat Island ⌒ IND 140-141 L 5
Triolet o MS 224 C 7
Trios o BR 62-63 G 4
Trípoli o GR 100-101 J 6
Tripoli = Tarābulus o• RL 128-129 F 5
Tripolis = Tarābulus ★ LAR 192-193 E 1

Tol'jatti — Tripolis 325

Tripolitania = Tarābulus ⊥ **LAR** 192-193 D 2
Tripp o **USA** 42-43 J 4
Tripura □ **IND** 142-143 G 6
Tristan da Cunha Fracture Zone ≃ 6-7 G 12
Tristao, Iles ∼ **RG** 202-203 C 4
Triste, Golfo ≋ 60-61 H 2
Triste, Monte ▲ **RA** 78-79 G 7
Tristeza, Cuchilla de la ▲▲ **RA** 78-79 H 3
Trisul ▲ **IND** 138-139 G 4
Trisuli ∼ **NEP** 144-145 E 7
Trisuli Bazar o **NEP** 144-145 E 7
Triton, Teluk ≋ 166-167 H 3
Triton Island = Zhongjian Dao ∼ **VRC** 158-159 L 3
Triunfo o **BR** 74-75 E 7
Triunfo, El o **MEX** 52-53 E 3
Triunfo, Igarapé ∼ **BR** 68-69 B 5
Triunvirato o **RA** 78-79 J 3
Trivalea-Moşteni o **RO** 102-103 D 5
Trivandrum ✶ **IND** 140-141 G 6
Trnava o **SK** 92-93 O 4
Trobriand Islands ∼ **PNG** 183 F 5
Trocana, Ilha ∼ **BR** 68-69 D 8
Trocará, Área Indigena ⅄ **BR** 68-69 D 8
Trochu o **CDN** 32-33 O 6
Trocoman, Rio ∼ **RA** 78-79 D 4
Troebratskij o **RUS** 124-125 E 1
Trofors o **N** 86-87 F 4
Trogir o··· **HR** 100-101 F 3
Troick o **RUS** 116-117 G 7
Troick ✶ **RUS** (CEL) 96-97 M 6
Troickij o **RUS** 114-115 D 3
Troicko-Pečorsk ✶ **RUS** 114-115 D 3
Trois Fourches, Cap des ▲ **MA** 188-189 K 3
Trois-Ilets, Les o **F** 56 E 4
Trois-Pistoles o **CDN** 38-39 K 4
Trois-Rivières o **CDN** 38-39 H 5
Trois Rivières, des o **RCA** 206-207 G 3
Trois Rivières, Les ∼ **RH** 54-55 J 5
Trois Sauts o **F** 62-63 H 4
Trojan o **BG** 102-103 D 6
Trojes, Las o **HN** 52-53 D 4
Trojnoj, ostrov ∼ **RUS** 108-109 U 4
Trolla ◁ **TCH** 198-199 G 5
Trollhättan ✶ **S** 86-87 F 7
Trolltindane ▲▲·· **N** 86-87 C 5
Tromai, Baía do ≋ 68-69 F 2
Tromai, Rio ∼ **BR** 68-69 F 2
Trombetas, Rio ∼ **BR** 62-63 F 5
Trom"egan ∼ **RUS** 114-115 M 3
Tromelin, Île ∼ **F** 12 D 6
Tromsberg o **N** 86-87 J 2
Tromsø ✶ **N** 86-87 J 2
Trona o **USA** 40-41 F 8
Tronador, Cerro ▲ **RCH** 78-79 C 6
Troncal, Lo o **BOL** 70-71 F 5
Troncos, Los o **BOL** 70-71 F 5
Trondheim ✶✶··· **N** 86-87 E 6
Trondheimsfjorden ≋ 86-87 D 5
Troodos ▲ **CY** 128-129 C 3
Troodos, Kirchen von = Ekklisía ··· **CY** 128-129 E 5
Tropas, Rio das ∼ **BR** 66-67 J 6
Tropea o **I** 100-101 E 5
Tropeço Grande, Cachoeira do ∼ **BR** 72-73 F 2
Tropia, Ponta ▲ **BR** 68-69 H 3
Tropico, El o **C** 54-55 E 3
Tropic of Cancer 6-7 D 6
Tropic of Cancer Monument · **MEX** 50-51 G 6
Tropic of Capricorn 6-7 H 11
Tropojë o **AL** 100-101 H 3
Troppau = Opava o **CZ** 92-93 O 4
Trosna o **RUS** 94-95 O 5
Trostjanec' o **UA** 102-103 J 2
Trotters o **USA** 42-43 F 2
Troubador Shoal ≃ 166-167 E 6
Trouin o **RH** 54-55 J 5
Troutbeck o **ZW** 218-219 G 4
Trout Creek o **CDN** 38-39 E 6
Trout Creek o **USA** 40-41 G 2
Trout Lake o **CDN** (NWT) 30-31 J 5
Trout Lake o **CDN** (NWT) 30-31 J 5
Trout Lake o **CDN** (ONT) 34-35 K 5
Trout Lake o **USA** (MI) 46-47 F 2
Trout Lake o **USA** (WA) 40-41 D 3
Trout Lake o **CDN** (NFL) 38-39 P 4
Trout River ∼ **CDN** 30-31 G 6
Trout River ∼ **CDN** 30-31 J 5
Trout River o **CDN** 32-33 N 3
Troux aux Cerfs · **MS** 224 C 7
Trovoada, Cachoeira da ∼ **BR** 66-67 K 5
Trowulan o **RI** 168 E 9
Troy o **USA** (AL) 48-49 G 4
Troy o **USA** (KS) 42-43 K 6
Troy o **USA** (MO) 46-47 O 4
Troy o **USA** (MT) 40-41 G 1
Troy o **USA** (NY) 46-47 M 4
Troy o **USA** (OH) 46-47 F 5
Troya, Rio de la ∼ **RA** 76-77 C 5
Troya, Rio la ∼ **RA** 76-77 C 4
Troyes ✶✶· **F** 90-91 K 7
Troy Peak ▲ **USA** 40-41 G 6
Trpanj o **HR** 100-101 F 3
Trstenik o **YU** 100-101 H 4
Truandó, Rio ∼ **CO** 60-61 C 4
Truant Island ∼ **AUS** 174-175 D 2
Trubčevsk o **RUS** 94-95 N 5
Truckee o **USA** 40-41 D 6
Truckee River ∼ **USA** 40-41 E 6
Truck Island ∼ **FSM** 13 G 2
Trucu o **BR** 68-69 J 3
True, Cape ▲ **USA** 36-37 R 3
Trufanova o **RUS** 88-89 S 4
Trujillo o **E** 98-99 E 5
Trujillo o **HN** 54-55 C 7
Trujillo ✶ **PE** 64-65 C 6
Trujillo ✶ **YV** 60-61 F 2
Trumon o **RI** 162-163 B 3

Trừng Lớn, Hòn ∼ **VN** 158-159 J 6
Trunkey Creek o **AUS** 180-181 K 2
Truro o **CDN** 38-39 N 6
Trusan o **MAL** 164-165 D 1
Trus Madi, Gunung ▲ **MAL** 160-161 B 10
Trutch o **CDN** 32-33 J 3
Truth or Consequences o **USA** 44-45 D 3
Trutnov o **CZ** 92-93 N 3
Truva (Troja) ∴· **TR** 128-129 B 3
Tryon o **USA** 42-43 G 5
Tryon Island ∼ **AUS** 178-179 L 2
Tryphena o **NZ** 182 E 1
Trzebnica o **PL** 92-93 O 3
Trzemeszno o **PL** 92-93 O 2
Tsadumu o **IND** 140-141 H 4
Tsagaan ▲ **MAU** 148-149 E 2
Tsala Apopka Lake o **USA** 48-49 G 5
Tsalwor Lake o **CDN** 30-31 P 6
Tsama I o **RCB** 210-211 C 4
Tsarnai o **WAN** 198-199 B 6
Tsandi o **NAM** 216-217 C 8
Tsangano o **MOC** 218-219 H 3
Tsanyawa o **WAN** 198-199 C 6
Tsaramandroso o **RM** 222-223 E 6
Tsaranonenana o **RM** 222-223 E 7
Tsaratanana o **RM** (MJG) 222-223 E 6
Tsaratanana ▲▲ **RM** 222-223 F 4
Tsarisberge ▲ **NAM** 220-221 C 2
Tsarishoogte Pass ▲ **NAM** 220-221 C 2
Tsau o **RB** 218-219 B 5
Tsauchab ∼ **NAM** 220-221 B 2
Tsavo o **EAK** 212-213 G 5
Tsavo ∼ **EAK** 212-213 G 5
Tsavo East National Park ⊥ **EAK** 212-213 G 5
Tsavo Safari Camp o **EAK** 212-213 G 5
Tsavo West National Park ⊥ **EAK** 212-213 F 5
Tsawah o **LAR** 192-193 E 4
Tsawwassen o **CDN** 32-33 J 7
Tsazar o **IND** 138-139 F 3
Tschida, Lake o **USA** 42-43 G 2
Tseikuru o **EAK** 212-213 G 4
Tselinograd = Akmola o **KA** 124-125 F 3
Tsembo o **RCB** 210-211 D 5
Tseminyu o **IND** 142-143 J 3
Tses o **NAM** 220-221 D 2
Tsévié o **RT** 202-203 L 6
Tshabong o **RB** 220-221 F 3
Tshako o **ZRE** 214-215 B 5
Tshala o **ZRE** 214-215 B 5
Tshane o **RB** 220-221 E 2
Tshela o **ZRE** 210-211 D 6
Tshenga-Oshwe o **ZRE** 210-211 J 5
Tshesebe o **RB** 218-219 D 5
Tshibala o **ZRE** 214-215 D 7
Tshibamba o **ZRE** 214-215 B 5
Tshibamba o **ZRE** 210-211 J 6
Tshibeke o **ZRE** 212-213 B 5
Tshibuka o **ZRE** 216-217 F 3
Tshibwika o **ZRE** 216-217 F 4
Tshidilamolomo o **ZA** 220-221 G 2
Tshie o **ZRE** 214-215 B 5
Tshikapa o **ZRE** 216-217 F 3
Tshikapa ∼ **ZRE** 216-217 F 3
Tshikula o **ZRE** 214-215 B 4
Tshilenge o **ZRE** 214-215 D 4
Tshimbalanga o **ZRE** 214-215 B 5
Tshimboko o **ZRE** 214-215 C 4
Tshimbulu o **ZRE** 214-215 B 5
Tshimbungu o **ZRE** 214-215 B 5
Tshintshanku o **ZRE** 214-215 B 4
Tshipise o **ZA** 218-219 F 6
Tshisenda o **ZRE** 214-215 D 7
Tshisenge o **ZRE** 216-217 F 3
Tshisonge o **ZRE** 214-215 B 5
Tshitadi o **ZRE** 216-217 F 3
Tshitanzu o **ZRE** 214-215 B 5
Tshofa o **ZRE** 210-211 H 5
Tshokwane o **ZA** 220-221 K 2
Tsholotsho o **ZW** 218-219 D 4
Tshongwe o **ZRE** 214-215 C 4
Tshootsha = Kalkfontein o **RB** 216-217 F 11
Tshopo ∼ **ZRE** 210-211 J 3
Tshuapa ∼ **ZRE** 210-211 H 4
Tshunga, Chutes ∼ **ZRE** 210-211 K 3
Tsiafajavona ▲ **RM** 222-223 E 7
Tsiaki o **RCB** 210-211 D 5
Tsianaloka o **RM** 222-223 D 8
Tsiazompaniry o **RM** 222-223 E 7
Tsimafana o **RM** 222-223 D 7
Tsimanampetsotsa, Farihy o **RM** 222-223 C 10
Tsimazava o **RM** 222-223 D 8
Tsimeloule-Skoye Vodokhranilishche = Cimljanskoe vodohranil. ◁ **RUS** 102-103 N 4
Tsimpsean Indian Reserve ⅄ **CDN** 32-33 E 4
Tsineng o **ZA** 220-221 F 3
Tsingtao = Qingdao ✶ **VRC** 154-155 M 3
Tsingy de Bamaraha Strict Nature Reserve ⊥··· **RM** 222-223 D 7
Tsiningia o **RM** 222-223 E 5
Tsinjoariyo o **RM** 222-223 E 7
Tsinjomitondraka o **RM** 222-223 E 6
Tsinjomorona ∼ **RM** 222-223 E 7
Tsintsabis o **NAM** 216-217 D 9
Tsiombe o **RM** 222-223 D 10
Tsiribihina ∼ **RM** 222-223 D 7
Tsiroanomandidy o **RM** 222-223 E 7
Tsitondroina o **RM** 222-223 E 8
Tsitsikamma National Park ⊥ **ZA** 220-221 F 7
Tsivory o **RM** 222-223 E 9
Tsoe o **RB** 218-219 C 5
Tsogtsetii o **MAU** 148-149 H 3
Tsogtsalu o **MAU** 138-139 G 2
Tsolo o **ZA** 220-221 H 5
Tsomo ∼ **ZA** 220-221 H 5
Tsomo ∼ **ZA** 220-221 G 6
Tsu ∼ **J** 152-153 Q 7
Tsubata o **J** 152-153 G 6

Tsuchiura o **J** 152-153 J 6
Tsugaru Quasi National Park ⊥ **J** 152-153 J 4
Tsugaru Strait = Tsugaru-kaikyō ≋ **J** 152-153 J 4
Tsu Lake o **CDN** 30-31 N 5
Tsuli o **RB** 218-219 D 4
Tsumbiri o **ZRE** 210-211 F 5
Tsumeb ✶ **NAM** 216-217 C 8
Tsumkwe ✶ **NAM** 216-217 F 9
Tsuruga o **J** 152-153 G 7
Tsurugi-san ▲ **J** 152-153 F 8
Tsurui o **J** 152-153 L 3
Tsuruoka o **J** 152-153 H 5
Tsushima ∼ **J** 152-153 C 7
Tsuyama o **J** 152-153 F 7
Tswaane o **RB** (GHA) 216-217 F 11
Tswaane o **RB** (KWE) 218-219 B 5
t-Tarfa, Wādi ∼ **ET** 194-195 E 3
t-Tartar, Wādi ∼ **IRQ** 128-129 K 5
t-Tartār, Wādi ∼ **IRQ** 128-129 K 5
t-Tawil, Wādi ∼ **IRQ** 128-129 J 1
t-Tūbal, Wādi ∼ **IRQ** 128-129 K 6
Tu ∼ **RUS** 118-119 N 9
Tua, Tanjung ∼ **RI** 162-163 F 7
Tuaim = Tuaim o **IRL** 90-91 C 5
Tual o **RI** 166-167 J 4
Tuam = Tuaim o **IRL** 90-91 C 5
Tuambli o **CI** 202-203 H 6
Tuamese h, Tanjung ▲ **RI** 166-167 C 6
Tuam Island ∼ **PNG** 183 E 3
Tuamotu Archipel ∼ **F** 13 N 4
Tuamotu Archipelago = Tuamotu, Îles ∼ **F** 13 N 4
Tuần Giáo ✶ **VN** 156-157 C 6
Tuangku, Pulau ∼ **RI** 162-163 B 3
Tuanxi o **VRC** 156-157 E 3
Tuapse o **RUS** 126-127 C 5
Tuaran o **MAL** 160-161 B 9
Tuare o **RI** 164-165 G 4
Tua River ∼ **PNG** 183 C 2
Tuba ∼ **RUS** 116-117 F 9
Tūbā, Qaşr at- ·∴· **JOR** 130-131 E 2
Tubac o **USA** 40-41 J 10
Tuba City o **USA** 40-41 J 7
Tubaiq, Ğabal at- ▲ **KSA** 130-131 E 2
Tuban o **RI** 168 E 9
Tubarão o **BR** 74-75 F 7
Tubarão Latunde, Área Indigena ⅄ **BR** 70-71 G 3
Tubas o **WB** 130-131 D 1
Tubau o **MAL** 162-163 K 3
Tubbataha Reefs ≃··· **RP** 160-161 C 8
Tubek Büzacký o **KA** 96-97 G 10
Tubek Büzacký o **KA** 126-127 J 1
Tubek Tub-Karagan o **KA** 126-127 J 1
Tubeya o **ZRE** 214-215 B 4
Tubğa, Wādi ∼ **RI** 130-131 F 5
Tubili Point ▲ **RP** 160-161 D 6
Tübingen o··· **D** 92-93 K 4
Tubisyimita o **RI** 166-167 K 2
Tubkaragan, mujisi ▲ **KA** 126-127 J 5
Tubmanburg o **LB** 202-203 E 6
Tubo, River ∼ **WAN** 204-205 G 3
Tuborg Fondets Land ⊥ **GRØ** 26-27 o 4
Tubruq o **LAR** 192-193 K 2
Tubruq ✶ **LAR** 192-193 K 1
Tubukia-Inseln ∼ **F** 13 M 5
Tubuai-Inseln ∼ **F** 13 M 5
Tubuai Islands ∼ **F** 13 M 5
Tubuai Islands = Australes, Îles ∼ **F** 13 M 5
Tuburan o **RP** 160-161 E 7
Tucacas o **YV** 60-61 G 2
Tucano o **BR** 68-69 J 7
Tucapel, Punta ▲ **RCH** 78-79 C 4
Tucavaca, Rio ∼ **BOL** 70-71 H 6
Tucha River ∼ **CDN** 30-31 E 6
Tucheng o **VRC** 156-157 D 3
Tuchitua o **CDN** 30-31 E 5
Tuchola o **PL** 92-93 O 2
Tuchołka o **UA** 102-103 D 2
Tuckanarra o **AUS** 176-177 E 3
Tucker Bay ≋ 16 F 18
Tuckerton o **USA** 46-47 L 6
Tuckfield, Mount ▲ **AUS** 172-173 G 5
Tucson o **USA** 44-45 B 3
Tucuco, Rio ∼ **YV** 60-61 E 3
Tucum, Corredeira do ∼ **BR** 70-71 J 4
Tucumá o **BR** 66-67 H 6
Tucumán o **RA** 76-77 E 4
Tucumcari o **USA** 44-45 F 2
Tucuña o **CO** 66-67 B 2
Tucunare, Raudal ∼ **CO** 66-67 B 2
Tucupido o **YV** 60-61 H 3
Tucupita ✶ **YV** 60-61 K 3
Tucuriba o **BR** 66-67 H 5
Tucuriba, Corredeira ∼ **BR** 66-67 H 5
Tucurui o **BR** 68-69 D 3
Tucurui, Represa de ◁ **BR** 68-69 D 4
Tucutibapo o **CO** 66-67 D 2
Tucu-Tucu o **RA** 80 E 4
Tüdakūl, Kūli o **US** 136-137 J 5
Tudela o **E** 98-99 G 3
Tudela o **RP** 160-161 E 8
Tudu o **EST** 94-95 K 2
Tudun Wada o **WAN** 204-205 H 3
Tuekta o **RUS** 124-125 O 3
Tuena o **AUS** 180-181 K 3
Tueré, Rio ∼ **BR** 68-69 C 4
Tuetue o **RI** 164-165 H 6
Tufanbeyli ✶ **TR** 128-129 G 3
Tufi o **PNG** 183 E 5
Tug o **VRC** 154-155 F 2
Tugela ∼ **ZA** 220-221 K 4
Tugela Ferry o **ZA** 220-221 K 4
Tugidak Island ∼ **USA** 22-23 T 4
Tugtorqurtôq o **GRØ** 26-27 W 7
Tugtutik o **GRØ** 26-27 Y 5
Tugu o **GH** 202-203 K 4
Tuguegarao ✶ **RP** 160-161 D 4
Tugulym o **RUS** 114-115 H 6
Tugur o **RUS** 122-123 G 2
Tugur o **RUS** 122-123 G 2
Tugurskij poluostrov ∼ **RUS** 122-123 G 2
Tugurskij zaliv ≋ 122-123 G 2
Tuguttur o **RUS** 110-111 F 4

Tugyi o **MYA** 158-159 C 2
Tuhan, Wādi ∼ **Y** 132-133 D 7
Tuhsigat ∼ **RUS** 114-115 O 5
Tui ∼ **E** 98-99 C 3
Tuichi, Rio ∼ **BOL** 70-71 C 4
Tuina o **RCH** 76-77 C 2
Tuineje o **E** 188-189 D 6
Tuisen o **IND** 142-143 H 4
Tuitán o **MEX** 50-51 G 5
Tuiué o **BR** 66-67 F 5
Tuj ∼ **RUS** 114-115 M 6
Tujala, Tanjung ▲ **RI** 166-167 D 5
Tujamay ∼ **RUS** 96-97 H 6
Tujin gol ∼ **MAU** 148-149 E 5
Tukalan ∼ **RUS** 120-121 G 3
Tukan ∼ **RUS** 114-115 M 6
Tukangbesi, Kepuluan ∼ **RI** 164-165 H 6
Tukarak Island ∼ **CDN** 36-37 K 6
Tukayel o **ETH** 208-209 G 4
Tuki o **SOL** 184 I c 2
Tukola Tolha o **VRC** 144-145 K 3
Tukosmera ▲ **VAN** 184 II b 4
Tükrah o **LAR** 192-193 J 1
Tuktoyaktuk o **CDN** 20-21 Y 2
Tukulan ∼ **RUS** 120-121 G 2
Tukums o **LV** 94-95 H 3
Tukuringra, hrebet ▲▲ **RUS** 118-119 M 8
Tukuyu o **EAT** 214-215 G 5
Tula o **EAK** (COA) 212-213 G 4
Tula ∼ **EAK** 212-213 G 4
Tula o **MEX** 50-51 K 6
Tula ∼ **RUS** 94-95 P 4
Tulä o **Y** 132-133 C 6
Tula Yiri o **WAN** 204-205 J 4
Tula de Allende o · **MEX** 52-53 E 1
Tuladenggi o **RI** 164-165 G 3
Tula Hill ▲· **WAN** 204-205 J 4
Tūlak ▲ **AFG** 134-135 K 2
Tulalip Indian Reservation ⅄ **USA** 40-41 C 1
Tulameen o **CDN** 32-33 K 7
Tulancingo o **MEX** 52-53 F 1
Tulare o **USA** 40-41 E 7
Tulare Lake o **USA** 40-41 E 8
Tularosa o **USA** 44-45 D 3
Tulate o **GCA** 52-53 J 4
Tula Yiri o **WAN** 204-205 J 4
Tulbagh o **ZA** 220-221 D 6
Tulcan ✶ **EC** 64-65 D 1
Tulcea ✶ **RO** 102-103 F 5
Tul'čyn o **UA** 102-103 F 3
Tule, El o **MEX** 50-51 J 5
Tule, Estero del ∼ **MEX** 50-51 F 5
Tuléar = Toliara ✶ · **RM** 222-223 C 9
Tulebaevo o **KA** 124-125 L 2
Tulehu o **RI** 166-167 E 3
Tulema Lake o **CDN** 30-31 H 4
Tulen' o **RUS** 110-111 F 9
Tule River Indian Reservation ⅄ **USA** 40-41 E 7
Tulia o **USA** 44-45 G 2
Tuli Block Farms ⅄ **RB** 218-219 D 6
Tulik Volcano ▲ **USA** 22-23 M 6
Tulipan o **MEX** 52-53 J 3
Tuljāpur o **IND** 140-141 G 2
Tullahoma o **USA** 48-49 E 2
Tullamore o **AUS** 180-181 J 3
Tullamore = Tulach Mhór o **IRL** 90-91 D 5
Tulle ✶· **F** 90-91 H 9
Tullibigeal o **AUS** 180-181 J 2
Tullos o **USA** 44-45 L 4
Tullus o **SUD** 206-207 G 3
Tully o **AUS** 174-175 H 5
Tully Range ▲ **AUS** 178-179 G 2
Tuloma ∼ **RUS** 88-89 M 3
Tulppio o **FIN** 88-89 K 3
Tulsa · o **USA** 44-45 K 1
Tulsequah o **CDN** 32-33 D 2
Tulsipur o **IND** 142-143 C 2
Tulu o **CO** 60-61 C 4
Tulua o **CO** 60-61 C 4
Tulu Āmara Terara ▲ **ETH** 208-209 G 4
Tulu Bolo o **ETH** 208-209 D 4
Tuluca o **BR** 66-67 C 2
Tulukskak o **USA** 20-21 K 6
Tulum o **MEX** (QR) 52-53 J 1
Tulum ·∴· **MEX** (QR) 52-53 L 1
Tulumayo, Rio ∼ **PE** 64-65 E 7
Tulume o **ZRE** 214-215 B 4
Tulun o **RUS** 116-117 K 8
Tulungagung o **RI** 168 D 9
Tulungselapan o **RI** 162-163 F 6
Tulu Welel ▲ **ETH** 208-209 H 4
Tulvinskaja vozvyšennost' ▲▲ **RUS** 96-97 K 5
Tuma ∼ **RUS** 94-95 R 4
Tuma, Rio ∼ **NIC** 54-55 D 5
Tūma, Wādi ∼ **IRQ** 128-129 K 6
Tumacacori National Monument ∴· **USA** 40-41 J 10
Tumaco o **CO** 60-61 B 7
Tumaco, Ensenada de ≋ 60-61 B 7
Tumagabok o **RP** 160-161 D 6
Tumair o **KSA** 130-131 J 5
Tumalin o **RP** 160-161 D 5
Tuma Island ∼ **PNG** 183 F 5
Tumalin o **RP** 160-161 D 5
Tuman Gang ∼ **DVR** 150-151 G 6
Tuman, Rio ∼ **RP** 160-161 D 5
Tumannyj o **RUS** 88-89 N 2
TumanSet o **RUS** 116-117 H 8
Tumanskij hrebet ▲▲ **RUS** 120-121 Q 3
Tumara ∼ **RUS** 118-119 P 3
Tumat o **RUS** 118-119 L 4
Tuo Jiang ∼ **VRC** 156-157 D 2
Tuokechikemili o **VRC** 144-145 E 4
Tuolba ∼ **RUS** 118-119 L 5
Tuolbačan ∼ **RUS** 118-119 L 5
Tuöl Kruös o **K** 158-159 H 4
Tuolumne River ∼ **USA** 40-41 D 7
Tu'o'ng Du'o'ng ∼ **VN** 156-157 D 7
Tumkmeskij zaliv ≋ 136-137 C 5
Türkoğlu ∼ **TR** 129-129 G 4
Tuora ∼ **RUS** 118-119 M 6
Tuora-Sis, hrebet ▲▲ **RUS** 110-111 Q 4
Tuostah ∼ **RUS** 110-111 V 6
Tuotuo He ∼ **VRC** 144-145 H 3

Tumbes, Península de ∼ **RCH** 78-79 C 4
Tumbes, Punta ▲ **RCH** 78-79 C 4
Tumbler Ridge o **CDN** 32-33 K 4
Tumbu o **RI** 164-165 F 5
Tumbwe o **ZRE** 214-215 D 6
Tumby Bay o **AUS** 180-181 D 3
Tumd Youqi o **VRC** 154-155 G 1
Tumd Zuoqi o **VRC** 154-155 G 1
Tumen o **VRC** 150-151 G 6
Tumen Jiang ∼ **VRC** 150-151 G 6
Tumereno o **YV** 62-63 D 2
Tumgaon o **IND** 142-143 C 5
Tumindao Island ∼ **RP** 160-161 C 10
Tumkūr o **IND** 140-141 G 4
Tumlingtar o **NEP** 144-145 F 7
Tumnin ∼ **RUS** 122-123 H 4
Tumoiscatio del Ruiz o **MEX** 52-53 C 2
Tumpang o · **RI** 168 E 9
Tumpu, Gunung ▲ **RI** 164-165 H 4
Tumputiga, Gunung ▲ **RI** 164-165 H 4
Tumrok, hrebet ▲▲ **RUS** 120-121 S 6
Tumsar o **IND** 138-139 G 9
Tumu o **GH** 202-203 K 4
Tumucumaque, Parque Indigena do ⅄ **BR** 62-63 G 4
Tumucumaque, Serra do ▲▲ **BR** 62-63 G 4
Tumul o **RUS** 118-119 P 4
Tumupasa o **BOL** 70-71 D 4
Tumurong o **GUY** 62-63 D 2
Tumut o **AUS** 180-181 K 3
Tuna o **GH** 202-203 J 5
Tuna Lake o **CDN** 30-31 J 2
Tunago Lake o **CDN** 30-31 J 2
Tunaida o **ET** 194-195 D 5
Tunaįča, ozero o **RUS** 122-123 K 5
Tünali Sälang · **AFG** 136-137 L 7
Tunapa, Cerro ▲ **BOL** 70-71 D 6
Tunapuna o **TT** 60-61 L 2
Tunas, Las o **C** 54-55 G 4
Tunas, Sierra de las ▲▲ **RA** 78-79 J 4
Tunas de Zaza o **C** 54-55 F 4
Tunas Grandes, Lagunas las o **RA** 78-79 H 3
Tunayadibah o **SUD** 200-201 G 3
Tunceli ✶ **TR** 128-129 H 3
Tunchang o **VRC** 156-157 G 7
Tuncurry o **AUS** 180-181 M 2
Tunda, Pulau ∼ **RI** 168 B 2
Tund las Raices o **RCH** 78-79 D 5
Tundulu o **Z** 214-215 H 7
Tunduma o **EAT** 214-215 G 5
Tunduru o **EAT** 214-215 J 6
Tundyk ∼ **KA** 124-125 K 4
Tundža ∼ **BG** 102-103 E 6
Tunertooq ∼ **GRØ** 28-29 P 2
Tunga o **WAN** 204-205 H 4
Tungabhadra o **IND** 140-141 G 3
Tungabhadra Reservoir o **IND** 140-141 G 3
Tungaru o **SUD** 206-207 K 3
Tungawan o **RP** 160-161 E 8
Tungaztarim o **VRC** 144-145 D 2
Tungho o **RC** 156-157 M 5
Tungi o **BD** 142-143 G 4
Tungir ∼ **RUS** 118-119 K 8
Tungirskij, hrebet ▲▲ **RUS** 118-119 J 8
Tungkaranasam o **RI** 164-165 G 5
Tungku o **MAL** (SAB) 160-161 C 10
Tungku o **MAL** (SAR) 162-163 K 3
Tungkočen o **RUS** 118-119 G 9
Tungor o **RUS** 122-123 K 2
Tungshih o **RC** 156-157 M 4
Tungsten o **CDN** 30-31 E 5
Tungurahua, Volcán ▲ **EC** 64-65 C 2
Tungurča ∼ **RUS** 118-119 K 7
Tunguru o **EAT** 212-213 D 5
Tungusskaja vozvyšennost' ▲▲ **RUS** 116-117 K 5
Tungusskoe-Centraľno, plato ⊥ **RUS** 116-117 K 5
Tungwatu o **RI** 166-167 H 4
Tunhèl o **MAU** 148-149 H 3
Tuni o **IND** 142-143 D 7
Tunia, La o **CO** 64-65 F 1
Tunis ✶··· **TN** 190-191 H 2
Tunis, Golfe de ≋ 190-191 H 2
Tunisia = Tunisiyah ■ **TN** 190-191 G 4
Tunja ✶ **CO** 60-61 E 5
Tunkal ∼ **RI** 162-163 E 5
Tunkhannock o **USA** 46-47 L 5
Tunku Abdul Rahman National Park ⊥ **MAL** 160-161 A 9
Tunnel Creek National Park ⊥ **AUS** 172-173 G 4
Tunnsjøen o **N** 86-87 F 5
Tunqui o **VRC** 156-157 F 4
Tuntum o **BR** 68-69 F 4
Tuntutuliak o **USA** 20-21 J 6
Tunu ∼ **GRØ** 26-27 o 8
Tunú, Cachoeira ∼ **BR** 66-67 C 2
Tunulic, Rivière ∼ **CDN** 36-37 O 5
Tunulliarfik ≋ 28-29 R 6
Tununak o **USA** 20-21 J 6
Tunungayualok Island ∼ **CDN** 36-37 T 6
Tunuyan o **RA** 78-79 E 2
Tunuyan, Sierra de ▲▲ **RA** 78-79 F 2
Tunuyánvieijo, Rio ∼ **RA** 78-79 F 2
Tuoa Creek ∼ **PNG** 183 C 4
Tuobuja o **RUS** 118-119 L 4

Tuotuo Heyan o **VRC** 144-145 J 3
Tupā o **BR** 72-73 F 5
Tupacaguara o **BR** 72-73 F 5
Tupambaéo o **ROU** 78-79 M 2
Tupana, Rio ∼ **BR** 66-67 G 5
Tupanaci o **BR** 68-69 J 6
Tupanatinga o **BR** 68-69 K 6
Tupanciretã o **BR** 74-75 D 7
Tuparetá, Caño ∼ **CO** 60-61 G 5
Tuparro, Caño ∼ **CO** 60-61 G 5
Tuparrito, Rio ∼ **CO** 60-61 G 5
Tupé o **BR** 66-67 D 2
Tumèncogt = Hanhöhij o **MAU** 148-149 L 4
Tupelo o **USA** 48-49 D 2
Tupelo National Battlefield ∴· **USA** 48-49 D 2
Tupik ✶ **RUS** 118-119 J 8
Tupilco o **MEX** 52-53 H 2
Tupim, Rio de ∼ **BR** 72-73 K 2
Tupinambarana, Ilha ∼ **BR** 66-67 J 4
Tupinier, Kap ▲ **GRØ** 28-29 b 2
Tupiratins o **BR** 68-69 D 6
Tupitina o **MEX** 52-53 C 2
Tupiza o **BOL** 76-77 E 1
Tupiza, Rio ∼ **BOL** 76-77 E 1
Tupper o **CDN** 32-33 K 4
Tupper Lake o **USA** 46-47 L 3
Tupungato o **RA** 78-79 E 2
Tupungato, Cerro ▲ **RA** 78-79 E 2
Tupure o **YV** 60-61 F 2
Tuquan o **VRC** 150-151 C 5
Tuque, La o **CDN** 38-39 H 5
Tuquerres o **CO** 64-65 C 1
Tuqu Gang ≋ 156-157 F 7
Tür, at- o **Y** 132-133 C 6
Tura o **IND** 142-143 G 3
Tura ∼ **RUS** 96-97 L 4
Tura o **RUS** 114-115 J 6
Tura o **RUS** 114-115 J 6
Tura ∼ **RUS** 118-119 F 10
Tura o **VRC** 144-145 E 2
Turaba o **KSA** (HAI) 130-131 H 3
Turaba o **KSA** (MAK) 132-133 B 3
Turagua, Serraria ▲ **YV** 60-61 J 4
Turaif o **KSA** 130-131 F 2
Turaif o **SYR** 128-129 H 5
Turakurgan o **US** 136-137 M 4
Turama ∼ **RUS** 116-117 F 9
Turama River ∼ **PNG** 183 B 4
Turan ✶ **RUS** 116-117 F 9
Turangi o **NZ** 182 E 3
Turan Lowland = Turanskaja nizmennost' ∪ 136-137 F 4
Turan Lowland = Turanskaja nizmennost' ∪ 136-137 F 4
Türan ojlety = Turan persligi = Turon Pasttekisligi ∪ **KA** 136-137 F 5
Turanskaja nizmennost' ∪ **RUS** 114-115 T 2
Turanskaja nizmennost' ∪ **RUS** 114-115 T 2
Türan ojlety = Turan persligi = Turon ojlety ∪ **TM** 136-137 F 5
Turäq al-'Ilab ▲ **SYR** 128-129 H 6
Turba o **BR** 72-73 E 4
Turba, at- o **Y** 132-133 D 7
Turba, at- o **Y** 132-133 C 7
Turbaco o **CO** 60-61 D 2
Turbat o **PK** 134-135 K 6
Turbo o **CO** 60-61 C 3
Turbón, Raudal el ∼ **CO** 66-67 B 2
Turčo o **BOL** 70-71 C 6
Turco, Rio o **BOL** 70-71 C 6
Turda o **RO** 102-103 D 5
Türda ◁ **SUD** 206-207 J 3
Turee Creek o **AUS** 176-177 D 1
Turek o **PL** 92-93 P 2
Turen o **RI** 168 E 9
Turgen ∼ **KA** 146-147 C 4
Türgen ▲ **MAU** 146-147 E 4
Turgeon, Rivière ∼ **CDN** 38-39 E 4
Turgut o **TR** 128-129 B 3
Turgutlu ✶ **TR** 128-129 B 3
Turhal ✶ **TR** 128-129 G 2
Türi o **EST** 94-95 J 2
Turi, Igarapé ∼ **BR** 66-67 D 3
Turia, Rio ∼ **E** 93-99 G 4
Türiaçu o **BR** 68-69 F 2
Türiaçu, Rio ∼ **BR** 68-69 F 3
Turiamo o **YV** 60-61 H 2
Türiançaj ∼ **AZ** 128-129 M 2
Turiani o **EAT** 214-215 J 4
Türiba o **YV** 60-61 H 4
Turin = Torino ✶ · **I** 100-101 A 3
Turinsk ✶ **RUS** 114-115 G 5
Turinskaja ravnina ∪ **RUS** 114-115 G 5
Turinskaja Sloboda o **RUS** 114-115 H 6
Tur'ja o **RUS** 88-89 V 5
Turka ∼ **RUS** 116-117 G 9
Turka o **UA** 102-103 C 3
Turka ∼ **UA** 102-103 C 3
Turka ∼ **RUS** 113-119 G 9
Türkan o **AZ** 128-129 N 2
Turkana ⊥ **EAK** 212-213 G 3
Turkana, Lake o **EAK** (Eas) 212-213 F 2
Turkestan o **KA** 136-137 L 3
Turkestanskij hrebet ▲▲ **US** 136-137 K 5
Turkestanskij kanal ◁ **KA** 136-137 L 3
Turkey o **USA** 44-45 G 2
Turkey Creek ∼ **AUS** 172-173 J 4
Turkey Mountain ▲ **AUS** 178-179 L 4
Turkey Mountain ▲ **USA** 46-47 C 4
Turkistan ✶ **KA** 136-137 L 3
Türkmen Dağı ▲ **TR** 128-129 C 3
Turkmenistan = Türkmenistan ■ **TM** 136-137 D 5
Turkmen-Kala o **TM** 136-137 H 6
Turkmenskij zaliv ≋ 136-137 C 5
Türks and Caicos Islands ∼ **GB** 54-55 K 3
Turks Islands ∼ **GB** 54-55 K 4

Turku = Åbo ✶ · **FIN** 88-89 G 6
Turkwel ∼ **EAK** 212-213 E 2
Turkwel Gorge Reservoir ◁ **EAK** 212-213 E 2
Turlock o **USA** 40-41 D 7
Turmalina o **BR** 72-73 J 4
Turmantas o **LT** 94-95 K 4
Turnagain, Cape ▲ **NZ** 182 F 4
Turnagain Arm ≋ 20-21 O 6
Turnagain Island ∼ **AUS** 174-175 G 1
Turnagain Point ▲ **CDN** 24-25 P 6
Turnagain River ∼ **CDN** 30-31 E 6
Turneffe Islands ∼ **BH** 52-53 L 3
Turner ∼ **GB** 42-43 C 1
Turner Lake o **CDN** 32-33 O 3
Turner Ø ∼ **GRØ** 28-29 d 2
Turner River o **AUS** 172-173 D 6
Turners Peninsula ∼ **WAL** 202-203 D 6
Turnhout o **B** 92-93 H 3
Turnu Măgurele o **RO** 102-103 D 6
Turočak ✶ **RUS** 124-125 P 2
Turon Pasttekisligi = Turan persligi = Türan ojlety ∪ **US** 136-137 F 5
Turpan o **VRC** 146-147 J 4
Turpan Pendi ∪ **VRC** 146-147 J 4
Türpsal = Järve ✶ **EST** 94-95 K 2
Turra ∼ **SUD** 200-201 B 6
Turrialba o **CR** 52-53 E 7
Tursaq o **IRQ** 128-129 L 6
Tursuntskij Tuman, ozero o **RUS** 114-115 G 4
Tursunzade o **TJ** 136-137 L 5
Turt o **MAU** 148-149 E 2
Turt (Hanh) o **MAU** 148-149 E 2
Turtas ∼ **RUS** 114-115 K 5
Türtkül ✶ **US** 136-137 G 4
Turtle Farm · **GB** 54-55 E 5
Turtleford o **CDN** 32-33 O 5
Turtle Head Island ∼ **AUS** 183 B 6
Turtle Islands ∼ **RP** 160-161 C 9
Turtle Islands Marine Park ⊥ **MAL** 160-161 C 9
Turtle Lake o **CDN** 32-33 O 5
Turtle Lake o **USA** 42-43 L 3
Turtle Mountain ▲ **CDN** 34-35 F 6
Turtle Mountain Indian Reservation ⅄ **USA** 42-43 H 1
Turton Lake o **CDN** 30-31 G 3
Turu ∼ **RUS** 116-117 M 3
Turu, Wangasi- o **ZRE** 202-203 N 5
Turu Cay Island ∼ **AUS** 183 A 5
Turuchipa, Rio ∼ **BOL** 76-77 E 1
Turugart Shankou ▲ **VRC** 146-147 B 5
Turuhan ∼ **RUS** 108-109 V 8
Turuhan ∼ **RUS** 114-115 T 2
Turuhansk o **RUS** 114-115 T 2
Turuhanskaja nizmennost' ∪ **RUS** 114-115 T 2
Turuklah, mys ▲ **RUS** 110-111 W 4
Turuna, Rio ∼ **BR** 62-63 F 5
Turuntaevo o **RUS** (TOM) 114-115 T 6
Turuntaevo o **RUS** (BUR) 116-117 N 9
Turvânia o **BR** 72-73 E 4
Turvo, Rio ∼ **BR** 72-73 H 6
Turvo, Rio o **BR** 72-73 H 6
Turvolândia o **BR** 72-73 H 6
Turwi ∼ **ZW** 218-219 F 5
Tüs o **IR** 136-137 H 6
Tušarna ∼ **RUS** 116-117 K 7
Tuscania o · **I** 100-101 C 3
Tuscaloosa o **USA** 48-49 E 3
Tuscola o **USA** (IL) 46-47 E 3
Tuscola o **USA** (TX) 44-45 H 3
Tusenøyane ∼ **N** 84-85 M 4
Tušig-Zeltēr o **MAU** 148-149 G 2
Tuskegee o **USA** 48-49 F 3
Tuskegee Institute National Historic Site ∴· **USA** 48-49 F 3
Tustumena Lake o **USA** 20-21 P 6
Tutaev ∼ **RUS** 94-95 Q 3
Tutak ✶ **TR** 128-129 J 3
Tuticorin o **IND** 140-141 H 6
Tutóia o **BR** 68-69 G 3
Tutoko, Mount ▲ **NZ** 182 B 6
Tutonchana o **RUS** 116-117 J 3
Tutong o **BRU** 164-165 D 1
Tutrakan o **BG** 102-103 E 5
Tuttle o **USA** 42-43 H 2
Tuttle Creek Lake o **USA** 42-43 J 6
Tuttosoni, Nuraghe · **I** 100-101 B 4
Tutuaca o **MEX** 50-51 F 3
Tutuala o **RI** 166-167 H 6
Tutuila Island ∼ **USA** 184 V b 2
Tutukpene o **GH** 202-203 L 5
Tutume o **RB** 218-219 D 5
Tutup, Tanjung ▲ **MAL** 160-161 C 10
Tutupa o **RI** 164-165 K 4
Tutura ∼ **RUS** 116-117 M 8
Tutura ∼ **RUS** 116-117 M 8
Tuul gol ∼ **MAU** 148-149 G 4
Tuusniemi o **FIN** 88-89 K 5
Tuva = Tuva, Respublika □ **RUS** 116-117 F 10
Tuvšinširèè = Sèrgèlèn o **MAU** 148-149 K 4
Tuwaiq, Ğabal ▲ **KSA** 130-131 J 5
Tuwaiq, Ğabal ▲ **KSA** 132-133 D 3
Tūwal o **KSA** 130-131 F 6
Tuxcueca o **MEX** 52-53 C 1
Tuxedni Bay ≋ 20-21 O 6
Tuxford o **CDN** 34-35 D 5
Tuxpan o **MEX** (NAY) 50-51 G 7
Tuxpan o · **MEX** (JAL) 52-53 C 2
Tuxpan, Rio ∼ **MEX** 52-53 F 1
Tuxpan de Rodriguez Cano o **MEX** 52-53 F 1
Tuxtla, Sierra de las ▲▲ **MEX** 52-53 G 2
Tuxtla Gutierrez ✶ **MEX** 52-53 H 3
Tuy, Rio ∼ **YV** 60-61 H 2
Tuya River ∼ **CDN** 32-33 E 2
Tuyên Quang ✶ **VN** 156-157 D 6
Tuy Hòa o **VN** 158-159 K 4
Tuy Phong o **VN** 158-159 K 4
Tüyserkân o · **IR** 134-135 C 1
Tüzdyköl o **KA** 136-137 M 3
Tuz Gölü o **TR** 128-129 E 3
Ṭūz Ḫūrmātū o **IRQ** 128-129 L 5

Tuzigoot National Monument ∴ USA 40-41 J 8
Tuzla ○ BIH 100-101 G 2
Tuzla Çayı ~ TR 128-129 J 3
Tuzlov ~ RUS 102-103 L 4
Tuzule ○ ZRE 214-215 B 4
Tværá ○ FR 90-91 D 1
Tveitsund ○ N 86-87 D 7
Tver ☆☆ RUS 94-95 P 3
Tverrfjelli ▲ N 86-87 D 5
TV Tower · USA 42-43 J 2
Tweed ~ GB 90-91 F 4
Tweed Heads ○ AUS 178-179 M 5
Tweedsmuir Provincial Park ⊥ CDN 32-33 J 5
Tweefontein ○ ZA 220-221 D 6
Tweeling ○ ZA 220-221 J 3
Twee Rivier ○ NAM 220-221 D 2
Twee Rivieren ○ ZA 220-221 E 3
Tweespruit ○ ZA 220-221 H 4
Twelve Apostles, The ~ AUS 180-181 G 5
Twentynine Palms ○ USA 40-41 F 8
Twentynine Palms Marine Corps Base ✕✕ USA 40-41 F 8
Twilight Cove ~ 176-177 H 6
Twillingate ○ CDN 38-39 I R 4
Twin Bridges ○ USA 40-41 H 3
Twin Buttes Reservoir < USA 44-45 G 4
Twin Falls ○ USA 40-41 G 4
Twingge ○ MYA 142-143 K 4
Twingi ○ Z 214-215 E 6
Twin Mount ▲ USA 20-21 T 4
Twin Peak ▲ USA 40-41 G 3
Twin Peaks ○ USA 176-177 C 3
Twitya River ~ CDN 30-31 J 4
Twizel ○ NZ 182 C 6
Two Brothers ~ CDN 36-37 J 5
Twofold Bay ≈ 180-181 K 4
Two Harbors ○ USA 46-47 C 2
Two Hills ○ CDN 32-33 P 5
Twopete Mountain ▲ CDN 20-21 Y 5
Two Rivers ○ USA 46-47 E 3
Two Rocks ○ AUS 176-177 C 5
Twyfelfontein · NAM 216-217 C 10
Tyara, Cayo △ NIC 52-53 C 5
Tyčany ~ RUS 116-117 H 5
Tychy ○ PL 92-93 P 3
Tydyotta ~ RUS 116-117 I O 2
Tyélé ○ RMM 202-203 G 3
Tygda ○ RUS 118-119 N 9
Tygda ~ RUS 118-119 N 9
Tygh Valley ○ USA 40-41 D 2
Tyiebas, cyganak ≈ 126-127 N 4
Tyf ~ RUS 120-121 F 6
Tylawa ○ PL 92-93 Q 4
Tyler ○ USA 44-45 K 3
Tylertown ○ USA 44-45 M 4
Tylgovajam ~ RUS 112-113 O 6
Tylihul ~ UA 102-103 F 4
Tylihul's'kyj lyman ~ 102-103 G 4
Tylnoj ~ RUS 112-113 M 5
Tym ~ RUS 114-115 T 4
Tym ~ RUS 114-115 Q 5
Tym' ~ RUS 122-123 K 3
Tym, Ust'- ○ RUS 114-115 Q 5
Tymerokan ~ RUS 116-117 F 2
Tymlat ☆ RUS 120-121 U 4
Tymna ~ RUS 118-119 O 8
Tymna, laguna ≈ 112-113 U 4
Tymovskoe ☆ RUS 122-123 K 3
Tympyčan, Uёl' ~ RUS 118-119 E 5
Tymtej ~ RUS 120-121 L 2
Tynda ☆ RUS 118-119 M 8
Tynda ~ RUS 118-119 N 9
Tyndall ○ CDN 34-35 H 5
Tyndall ○ USA 42-43 J 4
Tyndik ~ KA 124-125 K 3
Tyndrum ○ GB 90-91 E 3
Tyne ~ GB 90-91 G 4
Tynep ~ RUS 114-115 U 3
Tyner ○ USA 46-47 G 7
Tynset ○ N 86-87 E 5
Typical Torajan Villages ✕ ○ RI 164-165 F 5
Typtygir, köli ○ KA 124-125 D 2
Tyr ~ RL 128-129 F 6
Tyrifjorden ○ N 86-87 E 4
Tyrkan ~ RUS 120-121 H 7
Tyrma ○ RUS (HBR) 122-123 E 3
Tyrma ~ RUS 122-123 D 3
Tyrma ~ RUS 122-123 E 4
Tyrnavaz ○ RUS 126-127 E 6
Tyrone ○ USA (NM) 40-41 J 5
Tyrone ○ USA (PA) 46-47 J 5
Tyrrell, Lake ○ AUS 180-181 G 3
Tyrrell Lake ○ CDN 30-31 Q 4
Tyrrhenian Basin ≃ 100-101 C 5
Tyrrhenian Sea ≈ 100-101 C 5
Tyrs Bjerge ▲ GRØ 28-29 Q 7
Tyrtova, ostrov ∧ RUS 108-109 b 3
Tyry ~ RUS 120-121 H 2
Tyškanbaj ○ KA 126-127 P 2
Tysnesøy ∧ N 86-87 B 6
Tytyľ, ozero ○ RUS 112-113 P 3
Tyumen' = Tjumen' ☆ RUS 114-115 H 9
Tzaneen ○ ZA 218-219 F 6
Tzinteel ○ MEX 52-53 H 3
Tziscao ○ MEX 52-53 J 3
Tzonconejo, Río ~ MEX 52-53 J 3
Tzucacab ○ MEX 52-53 K 1

U

Uaçá, Área Indígena ✕ BR 62-63 J 4
Uacaca, Cachoeira ~ CO 66-67 C 2
Uachtar Ard = Oughterard ○ IRL 90-91 C 5
Uaco Cungo ○ ANG 216-217 C 5
Uacurí, Cachoeira ~ BR 70-71 G 2
Ua'ili, Wādī al- ~ KSA 130-131 F 2
Uala, zaliv ≈ RUS 120-121 V 3
Uamba ○ ANG 216-217 D 3
Uanda ○ AUS 178-179 H 1

Uanga ~ RUS 122-123 K 2
Uangando ~ ANG 216-217 D 8
Uape ○ MOC 218-219 K 3
Uapuí, Cachoeira ~ BR 66-67 C 2
Uarges ▲ SP 212-213 J 3
Uar Igarore < SP 212-213 J 3
Uarini ○ BR 66-67 E 4
Uarini, Rio ~ BR 66-67 D 5
Uaroo ○ AUS 172-173 A 3
Uauá ○ BR 68-69 J 6
Uauaretê ○ BR 66-67 C 2
Uaupés, Rio ~ BR 66-67 D 2
Uaus, Ra's ▲ OM 132-133 J 5
Uavala ○ ANG 216-217 D 8
Uaxactún ∴ Ucar ○ AZ 128-129 M 2
Ub ○ YU 100-101 H 2
Ubá ○ BR 72-73 J 6
Uba ○ KA 124-125 N 3
Ubaxaan ~ KA 124-125 D 2
Ubaí ○ BR 72-73 H 4
Ubai ○ PNG 183 F 3
'Ubaid < SUD 200-201 B 6
Ubaila ○ IRQ 128-129 J 6
'Ubaila, al- ○ KSA 132-133 G 2
Ubaitaba ○ BR 72-73 L 3
Ubajay ○ RA 76-77 H 6
Ubaldino Taques ○ BR 74-75 E 6
Ubangi ~ BR 210-211 F 3
Ubangui ○ ZRE 206-207 D 6
Ubaporanga ○ BR 72-73 J 5
Ubar ∴ OM 132-133 H 4
Ubarc' ~ BY 94-95 K 6
Ubatã ○ BR 72-73 L 3
Ubate ○ CO 60-61 E 5
Ubatuba ○ BR 72-73 H 7
Ubauro ○ PK 138-139 B 5
'Ubayyid, Wādī I- ~ IRQ 128-129 J 7
Ube ○ J 152-153 D 8
Úbeda ○ E 98-99 F 5
Ubekendt Ejland ∧ GRØ 26-27 Y 8
Uberaba ○ BR 72-73 G 5
Uberaba, Lago ○ BR 70-71 J 5
Uberaba, Rio ~ BR 72-73 G 5
Uberlândia ○ BR (MIN) 72-73 F 5
Uberlândia ○ BR (ROR) 62-63 G 5
Ubia, Gunung (Gunung Leonard Darwin) ▲ RI 166-167 J 4
Ubiaja ○ WAN 204-205 G 5
Ubina ○ BOL 70-71 F 7
Ubinskoe ○ RUS 114-115 P 7
Ubinskoe, ozero ○ RUS 114-115 P 7
Ubirajara ○ BR 72-73 F 7
Ubirr · AUS 172-173 L 2
Ubit < WAN 204-205 H 6
Ubojnaja ~ RUS 108-109 J 6
Ubol Rat Reservoir ○ THA 158-159 G 2
Ubombo ▲ ZA 220-221 L 3
Ubon Ratchathani ○ THA 158-159 H 3
Ubovka ~ RUS 122-123 F 6
Ubundu ○ ZRE 210-211 K 4
Uč-Adži ○ TM 136-137 H 4
Učaly ~ RUS 96-97 L 6
Učami ~ RUS 116-117 F 4
Ucapinima ○ CO 66-67 C 2
Ucaral ○ KA 124-125 M 5
Ucayali, Río ~ PE 64-65 F 4
Učdepe ~ RUS 116-117 H 6
Uch ○ PK 138-139 C 5
Ucharonidge ○ AUS 174-175 C 5
Uchiura-wan ≈ 152-153 J 3
Uchiza ○ PE 64-65 D 6
Učkeken ○ RUS 126-127 E 6
Učkuduk ○ US 136-137 H 3
Učkurgan ○ US 136-137 N 4
Ucluelet ○ CDN 32-33 H 7
Učničhilja ~ RUS 112-113 P 5
Ucross ○ USA 42-43 D 3
Učsaj ○ US 136-137 F 3
Učtagankum ⊥ TM 136-137 E 4
Úcua ○ ANG 216-217 C 4
Učur ~ RUS 120-121 F 6
Uda ~ RUS 116-117 O 10
Uda ~ RUS 116-117 J 8
Uda ~ RUS 118-119 E 9
Uda ~ RUS 120-121 D 6
Udačnyj ~ RUS 110-111 J 6
Udagamandalam ○ IND 140-141 G 5
Udaia ○ RUS 142-143 K 5
'Udaib, al- ○ KSA 130-131 E 4
'Udaiba, 'Uqlat al- ○ IRQ 130-131 K 3
'Udaid, al- ○ UAE 134-135 D 6
Udaipur ○ IND (RAJ) 138-139 D 7
Udaipur ○ IND (TRI) 142-143 J 4
Udaiyarpalaiyam ○ IND 140-141 H 5
Udaquiola ○ RA 78-79 K 4
Udayagiri ○ IND 140-141 H 3
Udbina ○ HR 100-101 D 2
Uddeholm ○ S 86-87 F 6
Uddevalla ○ S 86-87 E 6
Uddjaure ○ S 86-87 H 4
Udě, Ulan ☆ RUS 116-117 N 10
Udegi ○ WAN 204-205 G 4
Udgir ○ IND 138-139 F 10
Udhampur ○ IND 138-139 E 3
Udi ○ WAN 204-205 G 5
Údine · I 100-101 D 1
Udinsk ○ RUS 122-123 H 2
Udintsev Fracture Zone ≃ 14-15 N 13
Udispattu ○ CL 140-141 J 7
Udja ~ RUS 110-111 L 4
Udmurtia = Udmurtskaja Respublika ▫ RUS 96-97 H 5
Udobnaja ~ RUS 126-127 D 5
Udobnaja, buhta ≈ RUS 108-109 b 2
Udokan, hrebet ▲ RUS 118-119 J 7
Udon Thani ○ THA 158-159 G 2
Udova ~ RUS 120-121 R 6
Udpüdi ○ IND 140-141 F 2
Udskaja guba ≈ RUS 120-121 J 6
Udskoe ○ RUS 120-121 H 6
Ududbaddawa ○ CL 140-141 H 7
Udumalaippettai ○ IND 140-141 G 5
Udupi ○ IND 140-141 F 6

Udu Point ▲ FJI 184 III c 2
Udy ~ RUS 102-103 K 2
Udyhyn ~ RUS 120-121 D 6
Udyl', ozero ○ RUS 122-123 H 2
Udzhar = Ucar ○ AZ 128-129 M 2
Ueca ▲ SUD 208-209 C 4
Ueda ○ J 152-153 H 6
Uedineniia, ostrov ∧ RUS 108-109 U 3
Uekuli ○ RI 164-165 G 4
Uele ~ RUS 110-111 K 3
Uele ~ ZRE 210-211 J 4
Uélen ○ RUS 112-113 a 3
Uelgi, ozero ○ RUS 96-97 M 6
Uélkal ○ RUS 110-111 P 5
Uéf-Siktjah ~ RUS 110-111 P 5
Uél'-Tympyčan ~ RUS 118-119 E 5
Uelzen ○ D 92-93 L 7
Uembje, Lagoa ○ MOC 220-221 L 2
Ueno ○ J 152-153 H 7
Uere ~ ZRE 206-207 H 6
Ueré, Rio ~ BR 66-67 D 5
Ufa ○ RUS (BAS) 96-97 J 6
Ufa ~ RUS 96-97 K 5
Ufeyn ○ SP 208-209 J 3
Ufimskoe plato ▲ RUS 96-97 K 4
Uftjuga ~ RUS 88-89 T 6
Ugab ~ NAM 216-217 D 9
Ugahan ○ RUS 118-119 G 6
Ugak Island ∧ USA 22-23 U 4
Ugále ~ LV 94-95 H 5
Ugalla ~ EAT 212-213 E 5
Ugalla ~ EAT 212-213 D 5
Ugalla River Game Reserve ⊥ EAT (TAB) 212-213 D 5
Ugamak Island ∧ USA 22-23 O 5
Uganda ▪ EAU 212-213 C 4
Uganik Island ∧ USA 22-23 U 4
Ugarit ∴ · SYR 128-129 F 5
Ugashik Bay ≈ 22-23 R 4
Ugashik Lake ○ USA 22-23 S 4
Ugatkyn ~ RUS 112-113 Q 3
Ugba ○ WAN 204-205 H 5
Ugbala ○ WAN 204-205 H 5
Ugbenu ~ WAN 204-205 F 5
Ugep ~ WAN 204-205 H 5
Ughelli ○ WAN 204-205 F 6
Ugie ~ ZA 220-221 J 5
Ugíjar ○ E 98-99 F 6
Uglič ☆ RUS 94-95 Q 3
Uglovoe, ozero ○ RUS 108-109 J 1
Uglovoe, ozero ○ RUS 122-123 C 3
Ugo ○ RUS 204-205 G 5
Ugojan ○ RUS 118-119 M 6
Ugol'naja, buhta ≈ RUS 112-113 U 5
Ugol'noe ○ RUS 110-111 b 7
Ugol'nye Kopi ~ RUS 112-113 T 4
Ugol'nyj, mys ▲ RUS 118-119 M 7
Ugol'nyj, mys ▲ RUS 120-121 L 3
Ugra ~ RUS 94-95 O 4
Ugssugtussoq ≈ 28-29 V 4
Uḫaidir ∴ · IRQ 128-129 K 6
Uhen ~ WAN 204-205 F 5
Uherské Hradiště ○ CZ 92-93 O 4
Uhi ~ WAN 204-205 G 5
Uhiere ~ WAN 204-205 F 5
Úhlava ~ CZ 92-93 M 4
Uhlenhorst ~ NAM 220-221 C 1
Uhma ~ RUS 88-89 W 5
Uholovo ~ RUS 94-95 R 5
Uhrichsville ○ USA 46-47 H 5
Uhta ~ RUS (KOM) 88-89 W 5
Uhta ~ RUS 88-89 W 5
Uhuru Peak ▲ EAT 212-213 F 5
Uib ○ NAM 216-217 D 9
Uige ○ ANG 216-217 C 3
Uige ▫ ANG (UIG) 216-217 C 3
Uíha ~ TON 184 IV a 1
üijönbu ○ ROK 150-151 F 9
Uiju ○ DVR 150-151 E 7
Uinskoe ~ RUS 96-97 J 5
Uintah and Ouray Indian Reservation ✕ USA 40-41 J 5
Uinta Mountains ▲ USA 40-41 J 5
Uinta River ~ USA 42-43 B 5
Uirapuru ○ BR 70-71 H 4
Uísôes Myn ~ NAM 216-217 C 10
Uísongo ○ RUS 150-151 G 9
Uitenhage ○ ZA 220-221 G 6
Uivak, Cape ▲ CDN 36-37 S 5
Uivaq ~ GRØ 28-29 U 5
Uizën ○ MAU 148-149 C 4
Uj ~ RUS 96-97 L 6
Uj ~ RUS 114-115 G 7
Uj ~ RUS 114-115 N 6
Ujali ○ WAN 204-205 G 5
Ujaly ○ KA (KZL) 120-121 O 5
Ujaly ○ KA (MNG) 126-127 L 3
Ujaly ○ TJ 136-137 L 5
Ujan ~ RUS 120-121 L 5
Ujana ~ RUS 120-121 F 7
Ujandina ~ RUS 110-111 Z 5
Ujar ☆ RUS 116-117 H 9
Ujdah ☆ MA 188-189 L 3
Ujelang ~ MAI 13 H 2
Uji ○ J 152-153 F 7
Uji-guntō ∧ J 152-153 C 9
Ujjii ○ EAT 212-213 D 5
Ujjil ○ KA 96-97 H 9
Ujil ~ KA 124-125 L 3
Ujjain ○ IND 138-139 E 8
Újjmen' ~ RUS 124-125 P 3
Ujjobilang ○ RI 164-165 D 3
Újskoe ~ RUS 96-97 M 6
Ujuk ○ KA 136-137 M 3
Újuksij, hrebet ▲ RUS 116-117 F 10
Újungberung ○ RI 168 B 3
Ujung Kulon Game Park ⊥ RI 168 A 3
Ujung Kulon National Park ⊥ · RI 168 A 3
Ujunglamuru ○ RI 164-165 F 6

Ujung Pandang ★ RI 164-165 F 6
Ujvirvyvajam ~ RUS 120-121 V 3
Üüyk ○ KA 136-137 M 3
Uka ~ RUS 120-121 T 5
Ukara Island ∧ EAT 212-213 D 4
'Ukāš, Tulūl al- ▲ IRQ 128-129 K 7
Ukata ○ WAN 204-205 F 3
Ukatnyj, ostrov ∧ RUS 126-127 H 5
Ukehe ○ WAN 204-205 G 5
Ukélajat ~ RUS 112-113 Q 3
Ukerewe Island ∧ EAT 212-213 D 5
Ukhrul ○ IND 142-143 K 3
Ukholovo ~ RUS 94-95 R 5
Ukiah ○ USA (CA) 40-41 C 6
Ukiah ○ USA (OR) 40-41 E 3
Uki Ni Masi Island ∧ SOL 184 I e 4
Ukinskaja guba ≈ RUS 120-121 U 5
Ukkusissat ○ GRØ 26-27 Z 8
Ukláná ○ IND 138-139 E 5
Ukmergė ○ LT 94-95 J 4
Ukolnoi Island ∧ USA 22-23 Q 4
Ukraina = Ukrajina ▪ UA 102-103 E 3
Ukšum ~ RUS 118-119 G 8
Uktyrm ~ RUS 88-89 U 5
Ukuit ~ RUS 114-115 T 6
Uku-shima ∧ J 152-153 C 8
Ukwatutu ~ ZRE 206-207 H 6
Ul ~ RUS 122-123 H 2
Ulaa, Rio ~ HN 52-53 K 4
Ulaanbaatar ▲ MAU 148-149 H 4
Ulaan-Ereg ○ MAU 148-149 J 4
Ulaangom ☆ MAU 116-117 F 11
Ulaanhudag ○ MAU 148-149 G 4
Ulaan nuur ○ MAU 148-149 J 4
Ulaanšiveelt ○ MAU 148-149 G 4
Ulaan Tajga ⊥ MAU 148-149 J 4
Ulagan, Ust'- ○ RUS 124-125 Q 3
Ulah-An ○ RUS 118-119 G 8
Ulahan-Bom, hrebet ▲ RUS 120-121 G 2
Ulahan-Botuobuja ~ RUS 118-119 L 5
Ulahan-Jurjah ~ RUS 110-111 O 3
Ulahan-Küüel'gjuljur ~ RUS 110-111 U 3
Ulahan-Küüel' ~ RUS (SAH) 110-111 V 6
Ulahan-Küüel' ~ RUS (SAH) 110-111 a 7
Ulahan-Murbajy ~ RUS 118-119 F 6
Ulahan-Siligile ~ RUS 120-121 D 4
Ulahan-Sis, hrebet ▲ RUS 110-111 b 6
Ulahan Taryn ~ RUS 110-111 Z 7
Ulahan-Taryn-Jurjah ~ RUS 110-111 Y 7
Ulahan-Tirentjah ~ RUS 110-111 P 5
Ulahan-Vava ~ RUS 116-117 J 3
Ulah-Tas, gora ▲ RUS 110-111 d 4
'Ulaim az-Zarna ~ KSA 130-131 G 3
Ulak Island ∧ USA 22-23 G 7
Ulamona ○ PNG 183 F 3
Ulan ~ RUS 120-121 H 3
Ulan Bator = Ulaanbaatar ★ MAU 148-149 H 4
Ulánbel ○ KA 124-125 G 6
Ulan-Burgasy, hrebet ▲ RUS 116-117 O 9
Ulanhot ○ VRC 150-151 D 4
Ulanlinggi ○ VRC 146-147 H 4
Ulansuhai Nur ○ VRC 154-155 F 1
Ulan Tohoi ○ VRC 148-149 E 7
Ulan Ul Hu ○ VRC 144-145 H 3
Ulapara ○ BD 142-143 F 3
Ulapes, Sierra de ▲ RA 76-77 D 6
Ularbemban ○ RI 162-163 E 4
Ulas ☆ TR 128-129 G 3
Ulawa Island ∧ SOL 184 I e 3
Ulawun, Mount ▲ PNG 183 F 3
Ulaya ○ EAT 214-215 J 4
Ulcinj ○ YU 100-101 G 4
Ulco ○ ZA 220-221 G 4
Ul'durga ~ RUS 118-119 J 8
Uleåborg ☆ FIN 88-89 J 4
Ulefoss ○ N 86-87 D 7
Ulemariirvier ~ SME 62-63 G 4
Ulete ○ EAT 214-215 H 5
Uliaga Island ∧ USA 22-23 M 6
Uliastaj ☆ MAU 148-149 C 4
Uliga ▲ MAI 13 J 2
Ulindi ~ ZRE 210-211 L 4
Ulinta ~ RUS 122-123 F 6
Uīrínskij, hrebet ▲ RUS 120-121 H 5
Uljagan ~ RUS 112-113 L 4
Uljanivka ~ UA 102-103 G 3
Ul'janovka ~ RUS 94-95 M 2
Ul'janovo ~ RUS 94-95 N 4
Ul'janovsk ○ KA 124-125 H 3
Ul'janovskij ○ KA 124-125 H 3
Ul'janovsk = Simbirsk ☆ RUS 96-97 F 6
Uljatuj ○ RUS 118-119 H 10
Uljin ○ ROK 150-151 G 9
Ulken ○ KA 124-125 G 6
Ul'ken Acbolat, köli ○ KA 124-125 K 2
Ul'ken-Aktau, tau ▲ KA 136-137 L 3
Ul'ken Borsyk, kúm ⊥ KA 124-125 K 2
Ülken Cobda ~ KA 124-125 L 2
Ülken-Karoj, köli ○ KA 124-125 G 2
Ülken Özen ~ KA 96-97 G 9
Ülken sor ~ KA 126-127 J 5

Ullah-Kjuel', ozero ○ RUS 110-111 P 6
Ullål ○ IND 140-141 F 4
Ullånger ○ S 86-87 J 5
Ullapool ○ GB 90-91 E 3
Ulla Ulla, Reserva Faunística ⊥ BOL 70-71 C 4
Ullawarra ○ AUS 176-177 D 1
Ulloma ○ BOL 70-71 C 6
Ullsfjorden ≈ 86-87 J 2
Ulléung Do ∧ ROK 150-151 H 9
Ulléung ○ ROK 150-151 G 10
Ulm ○ D 92-93 K 4
Ulm ○ USA (MT) 40-41 J 2
Ulm ○ USA (WY) 42-43 D 3
Ulma ~ RUS 122-123 D 3
Ul'ma ~ RUS 122-123 D 3
Ulongwé ○ MOC 218-219 H 2
Uloowaranie, Lake ○ AUS 178-179 E 4
Ulricehamn ○ S 86-87 F 6
Ulsan ○ ROK 150-151 G 10
Ultima ○ AUS 180-181 G 3
Ulu ○ MYA 158-159 E 5
Ulu ○ RI 164-165 J 2
Ulu ~ RUS (SAH) 118-119 N 5
Ulu ~ RUS 118-119 N 5
Ulu ○ SUD 208-209 A 3
Uluaa ○ GRØ (VGR) 26-27 X 7
Uluaa ~ GRØ (VGR) 26-27 X 7
Ulubat Gölü ○ TR 128-129 C 2
Uluçinar ○ TR 128-129 F 4
Uludağ ▲ TR 128-129 C 2
Uludere ○ TR 128-129 K 4
Uludoruk Tepe ▲ TR 128-129 K 4
Ulugqat ○ VRC 146-147 B 6
Uluguru Mountains ▲ EAT 214-215 J 4
Ului Island ∧ AUS 183 B 6
Uluinggalau ▲ FJI 184 III b 2
Ulujami ○ RI 168 C 3
Ulujul ~ RUS 114-115 T 6
Uluksan Peninsula ◡ CDN 24-25 d 4
Ulung Hu ○ VRC (XUZ) 146-147 H 2
Ulungur He ~ VRC 146-147 H 3
Ulungur Hu ○ VRC (XUZ) 146-147 H 2
Ulupalakua ○ USA 48-49 D 7
Uluputur ○ PNG 183 D 3
Uluru National Park ⊥ · AUS 176-177 L 2
Ulut ~ RP 160-161 F 7
Ulu Tiram ○ MAL 162-163 E 4
Ulva ○ AUS 178-179 H 1
Ulveah = Lopevi ∧ VAN 184 II b 3
Ulverstone ○ AUS 180-181 H 6
'Ulyá, Wādī I- ○ OM 132-133 K 2
Ulysses ○ USA 44-45 G 1
Umadam ○ SUD 200-201 H 4
Umair ○ KSA 132-133 C 3
Umaish ○ WAN 204-205 G 4
Umaki ○ CO 60-61 F 2
Umak Island ∧ USA 22-23 J 7
Umala ○ BOL 70-71 C 5
Umafia, Ust'- ○ RUS 122-123 E 3
Umán ○ MEX 52-53 K 1
Uman' ☆ UA 102-103 G 3
Umaí ○ BR 72-73 G 4
Umanak Fjord ≈ 26-27 Y 8
Umanaq ○ GRØ 28-29 P 4
Umangcinang, Tanjung ▲ RI 164-165 J 5
Umari, Rio ~ BR 66-67 E 7
Umaria ○ IND 142-143 B 4
Umarkhed ○ IND 138-139 F 10
Umarkot ○ PK 138-139 C 7
Umaroo ○ AUS 178-179 D 4
Umarooma Lake ○ AUS 178-179 D 4
Umatilla Indian Reservation ✕ USA 40-41 E 3
Umatilla River ~ USA 40-41 E 3
Umba ○ EAT 212-213 G 5
Umba ~ RUS 88-89 N 3
Umbakumba ✕ AUS 174-175 D 3
Umbarger ○ USA 44-45 F 2
Umbe ○ PE 64-65 D 6
Umbelasha ~ SUD 206-207 F 4
Umboi Island ∧ PNG 183 D 3
Umbozero ○ RUS 88-89 N 3
Umbraj ○ IND 140-141 F 2
Umbria ▫ I 100-101 C 3
Umbukul ○ PNG 183 E 2
Umbulan Gayohpecoh ○ RI 162-163 F 6
Umbuluzi ~ MOC 220-221 L 3
Umbumbulu ○ ZA 220-221 K 5
Umburanas ○ BR 68-69 H 7
Umbuzeiro ○ BR 68-69 K 6
Ume ~ ZW 218-219 E 3
Umeå ☆ S 86-87 K 5
Umeälven ~ S 86-87 J 4
Umfolozi Game Reserve ⊥ ZA 220-221 L 4
Umgababa ○ ZA 220-221 K 5
Umiat ○ USA 20-21 O 2
Umiivik Bugt ≈ 28-29 U 4
Umirim ○ BR 68-69 J 3
Umitaka Spur ≃ 13 E 3
Umkomaas ○ ZA (NTL) 220-221 K 5
Umkomaas ~ ZA 220-221 K 5
Umlekan ○ RUS 118-119 N 9
Umm al 'Abid ○ LAR 192-193 F 4
Umm al Aranib ○ LAR 192-193 F 4
Umm al-Hait, Wādī = Ibn Hautar, Wādī ~ OM 132-133 J 4
Umm al 'tzam, Sabkhat ○ LAR 192-193 F 2
Ummannannarsuaq = Kap Farvel ▲ GRØ 28-29 T 7
Umm ar Rizam ○ LAR 192-193 K 1
Umm Ašar aš-Šarqíyá ○ KSA 130-131 J 4

Umm Badr ○ SUD 200-201 C 5
Umm Barbit ○ SUD 206-207 L 3
Umm Bel ○ SUD 200-201 D 6
Umm Buru ○ SUD 198-199 L 5
Umm Dafag ○ SUD 206-207 F 3
Umm Dam ○ SUD 200-201 E 6
Umm Defeis ○ SUD 206-207 F 3
Umm Digulgulaya ○ SUD 206-207 G 3
Umm Dubban ○ SUD 200-201 F 5
Umm Durmān = Omdurman ★ · SUD 200-201 F 5
Umm Gamāla ○ SUD 206-207 G 3
Umm Gederni ○ SUD 206-207 F 3
Umm Harāz ○ SUD 206-207 G 3
Umm Hawsh ○ SUD 200-201 D 5
Umm Hibāl, Bi'r < ET 194-195 F 6
Umm Hitan ○ SUD 206-207 K 3
Ummi, Godār-e ▲ IR 134-135 H 1
Umm Inderaba ○ SUD 200-201 E 5
Umm Kaddādah ○ SUD 200-201 C 6
Umm Marahik ○ SUD 200-201 C 6
Umm Mirdi ○ SUD 200-201 F 3
Umm Naqqāt, Gabal ▲ ET 194-195 G 5
Umm Oozein ○ SUD 200-201 C 5
Umm Qasr ○ IRQ 130-131 K 2
Umm Qurein ○ SUD 200-201 D 4
Umm Ruwābah ○ SUD 200-201 E 6
Umm Sa'ad ○ LAR 192-193 L 2
Umm Sagura ○ SUD 206-207 J 4
Umm Sayyálah ○ SUD 200-201 E 6
Umm Segelti ○ SUD 200-201 C 6
Umnak ○ USA 22-23 M 6
Umnak Island ∧ USA 22-23 M 6
Umnak Pass ≈ 22-23 M 6
Umniati ○ ZW 218-219 E 4
Umpaqua River ~ USA 40-41 C 4
Umphua ○ MOC 218-219 K 3
Umran ○ KSA 130-131 L 5
Umrer ○ IND 138-139 G 10
Umsini, Gunung ▲ RI 166-167 J 3
Umtata ☆ ZA 220-221 J 5
Umtentu ○ ZA 220-221 K 5
Umuahia ○ WAN 204-205 G 5
Umuarama ○ BR 72-73 D 7
Umuda Island ∧ PNG 183 B 5
Umu-Duru ○ WAN 204-205 G 5
Umunede ○ WAN 204-205 G 6
Umutina, Área Indígena ✕ BR 70-71 J 4
Umutu ○ WAN 204-205 G 6
Umvukwe Range ▲ ZW 218-219 F 3
Umurudzi Safari Area ⊥ ZW 218-219 F 3
Umzimkulu ○ ZA 220-221 J 5
Umzimkuluʼ ○ ZA 220-221 J 5
Umzimvubu ~ ZA 220-221 J 5
Umzingwani ~ ZW 218-219 E 5
Umzinto ○ ZA 220-221 K 5
Una ○ IND 138-139 F 4
Una, Rio ~ BR 68-69 K 6
Unadilla ○ USA 48-49 G 3
Unaha ~ RUS 118-119 N 8
Unaí ○ BR 72-73 G 4
Unaiza ○ JOR 130-131 D 2
'Unaiza ○ KSA 130-131 J 4
Unalakleet ○ USA 20-21 K 5
Unalakleet River ~ USA 20-21 K 5
Unalaska ○ USA 22-23 N 6
Unalaska Island ∧ USA 22-23 N 6
Unalga Island ∧ USA 22-23 N 6
Unango ○ MOC 218-219 J 2
Unare, Río ~ YV 60-61 J 5
Unari, Corredeira ~ BR 66-67 C 2
Unauna ∧ RI 164-165 G 4
Unauna, Pulau ∧ RI 164-165 G 4
Unawari ○ RI 166-167 H 3
Unbunmaroo, Mount ▲ AUS 178-179 F 2
Unčeny = Ungheni ○ MD 102-103 E 4
Uncompahgre Peak ▲ USA 42-43 D 6
Uncompahgre Plateau ▲ USA 42-43 C 6
Unda ~ RUS 118-119 H 10
Undandita ✕ AUS 176-177 M 1
Underberg ○ ZA 220-221 J 5
Underbool ○ AUS 180-181 F 3
Underground River · RP 160-161 C 7
Underwood ○ USA 42-43 G 2
Undjulinga ~ RUS 110-111 P 6
Undozero, ozero ○ RUS 88-89 P 5
Undu, Tanjung ▲ RI 168 E 4
Unduma, Río ~ BOL 70-71 D 3
Unduri ○ RI 166-167 F 3
Unea Island ∧ PNG 183 E 3
Uneča ○ RUS 94-95 N 5
Unel, Igarapé ~ BR 66-67 D 3
Uneiuxi, Área Indígena ✕ BR 66-67 D 3
Uneiuxi, Rio ~ BR 66-67 D 3
Uneiuxi, Serra de ▲ BR 66-67 D 3
Unga Island ∧ USA 22-23 Q 5
Ungalik ○ USA 20-21 K 4
Ungalik River ~ USA 20-21 K 4
Ungarie ○ AUS 180-181 J 2
Ungava ○ AUS 180-181 G 2
Ungava, Péninsule d' ◡ CDN 36-37 L 4
Ungava Bay ≈ 36-37 O 5
Ungerem ○ PNG 183 A 4
Ungheni ☆ MD 102-103 E 4
Ungie ~ RUS 118-119 D 10
Ungra ~ RUS 118-119 L 7
Ungra ~ TM 136-137 G 5
Ungwana Bay ≈ 212-213 H 5
Uni ☆ RUS 96-97 G 5
Unia, Lac ○ ZRE 210-211 K 5
Uniab ~ NAM 216-217 B 9

União ○ BR (AMA) 66-67 C 4
União ○ BR (BHA) 68-69 H 6
União ○ BR (GSU) 70-71 K 5
União ○ BR (PIA) 68-69 G 4
União da Vitória ○ BR 74-75 E 6
União dos Palmares ○ BR 68-69 K 6
Uniára ○ BR 138-139 I R 4
Unimak ○ USA 22-23 O 5
Unimak Bigh ≈ 22-23 O 5
Unimak Island ∧ USA 22-23 O 5
Unimak Pass ≈ 22-23 O 5
Unini, Rio ~ BR 66-67 F 3
Unión ○ RA 78-79 G 3
Unión ○ USA (SC) 48-49 G 3
Unión ○ USA (WV) 46-47 H 7
Union, Bahía ≈ 78-79 H 5
Union, La ○ CO (NAR) 64-65 D 1
Union, La ○ CO (VCA) 60-61 C 5
Union, La ○ ES 98-99 G 6
Union, La ○ EC 64-65 B 2
Union, La ○ HN 52-53 L 4
Union, La ○ MEX 52-53 D 3
Union, La ○ MEX 52-53 K 3
Union, La ○ PE 64-65 C 5
Union, La ○ RCH 78-79 C 6
Union, Mount ▲ USA 40-41 H 8
Unión, Río La ~ MEX 52-53 D 2
Union City ○ USA (PA) 46-47 J 5
Union City ○ USA (TN) 48-49 D 1
Union Creek ○ USA 40-41 C 4
Uniondale ○ ZA 220-221 F 6
Unión de Tula ○ MEX 52-53 B 2
Unión Hidalgo ○ MEX 52-53 G 3
Union Point ○ USA 48-49 G 3
Union Springs ○ USA 48-49 F 3
Uniontown ○ USA 46-47 J 6
Unionville ○ USA 42-43 L 5
Unipouheos Indian Reserve ✕ CDN 32-33 P 5
Unita ○ PE 64-65 D 3
United Arab Emirates = Daul.al-Imal-'Ara. Al-Muttahida ▪ UAE 132-133 H 4
United Kingdom ▪ GB 90-91 H 4
United States ▪ 38-39 F 7
United States Air Force Academy ✕✕ USA 42-43 E 4
United States Atomic Energy Reserve ✕✕ USA 42-43 D 4
United States Military Academy ✕✕ USA 46-47 L 5
United States Naval Weapons Center ✕✕ USA 40-41 F 7
United States Range ▲ CDN 26-27 J 3
Unity ○ CDN 32-33 Q 5
Universal City ○ USA 44-45 H 5
Universitetskij, lednik ⊏ RUS 108-109 c 2
University Park ○ USA 44-45 D 3
Unmet ○ VAN 184 II a 3
Unnáo ○ IND 142-143 B 2
Unnejvajam ~ RUS 112-113 O 6
Uno ○ GNB 202-203 B 4
Uno, Ilha de ∧ GNB 202-203 B 4
Unpongkor ∧ VAN 184 II b 4
Unsan ○ DVR 150-151 E 7
Unša ~ RUS 94-95 S 3
Unža ~ RUS 96-97 D 4
Ünye ☆ TR 128-129 G 2
Unzen Amakusa National Park ⊥ · J 152-153 D 8
Uojan, Novyj ○ RUS 118-119 E 7
Uoʼcan ~ RUS 110-111 Y 7
Uông Bí ○ VN 156-157 E 6
Uoro ○ Mbini, Río ~ GQ 210-211 C 3
Uozo ○ J 152-153 G 6
Upata ○ YV 60-61 K 3
Upemba, Lac ○ ZRE 214-215 D 5
Upemba, Parc National de l' ⊥ ZRE 214-215 D 5
Upernagssivik ○ GRØ 28-29 U 4
Upernavik ○ GRØ (VGR) 26-27 W 7
Upernavik ○ GRØ (VGR) 26-27 X 7
Upernavik Kujalleq = Søndre Upernavik ○ GRØ 26-27 X 7
Uphan ○ USA 42-43 G 1
Upi ○ RP 160-161 F 9
Upington ○ ZA 220-221 E 4
Upoloksa ○ RUS 88-89 L 3
'Upolu Island ∧ WS 184 V b 1
Upolu Point ▲ USA 48-49 E 7
Uporovo ○ RUS 114-115 J 6
Upper Arrow Lake ○ CDN 32-33 M 6
Upper Canada Village ∴ · CDN 38-39 G 4
Upper East Region ▫ GH 202-203 K 4
Upper Forster Lake ○ CDN 34-35 D 2
Upper Humber River ~ CDN 38-39 Q 4
Upper Indian Pond ○ CDN 38-39 Q 4
Upper Karoo = Hoë Karoo ⊥ ZA 220-221 D 5
Upper Klamath Lake ○ USA 40-41 D 4
Upper Lake ○ USA (CA) 40-41 C 5
Upper Lake ○ USA (CA) 40-41 D 5
Upper May ○ PNG 183 A 3
Upper Musquodoboit ○ CDN 38-39 N 6
Upper Peninsula ◡ USA 46-47 E 2
Upper Red Lake ○ USA 42-43 K 1
Upper Sioux Indian Reservation ✕ USA 42-43 K 3
Upper Twin Lake ○ CDN 34-35 N 5
Upper West Region ▫ GH 202-203 J 4
Uppland ▫ S 86-87 H 7
Uppsala ☆ S 86-87 H 7
Upright, Cape ▲ USA 112-113 Y 6
Upsala ○ CDN 34-35 L 4
Upshi ○ IND 138-139 F 3
Upstart, Cape ▲ AUS 174-175 J 6

Varberg ☆ • S 86-87 F 8
Varčato, ozero o RUS 108-109 K 8
Vardar ~ MK 100-101 H 4
Vardård o IR 136-137 B 7
Varde o DK 86-87 D 9
Vardenis o AR 128-129 L 2
Vardenis, gora ▲ AR 128-129 L 3
Vardin o IR 128-129 M 3
Vardø o N 86-87 P 1
Varejonal, El o MEX 50-51 F 5
Varela o GNB 202-203 B 3
Varela o RA 78-79 F 3
Varela, Baía de ≈ 202-203 B 3
Varela, Sierra de ▲▲ RA 78-79 F 3
Varéna o LT 94-95 J 4
Varese ☆ I 100-101 B 2
Vårgårda o S 86-87 F 7
Vargem Alegre o BR 72-73 J 5
Vargem Alta o BR 72-73 K 6
Vargem Bonita o BR 72-73 G 6
Vargem Grande o BR 68-69 G 3
Varginha o BR 72-73 H 6
Varhalamskaja guba ≈ RUS 120-121 S 3
Varhalamskij, mys ▲ RUS 120-121 S 3
Variata National Park ⊥ PNG 183 D 5
Varillas o RCH (ANT) 76-77 C 3
Varillas o RCH (ANT) 76-77 B 3
Varillas, Las o RA 76-77 F 6
Varita, Pampa de la ▲ RA 78-79 F 3
Varka-Syfky ~ RUS 114-115 Q 2
Varkaus o FIN 88-89 H 5
Varmahlíð o IS 86-87 d 2
Värmland ⊥ S 86-87 F 7
Varna o BG 102-103 E 6
Varna ☆ RUS 124-125 B 2
Värnamo ☆ S 86-87 G 8
Varnek o RUS 108-109 J 7
Varnjany o BY 94-95 K 4
Varón, Cerro de ▲ MEX 52-53 B 2
Varsaĝ o AFG 136-137 M 6
Varsinais Suomi ⊥ FIN 88-89 F 6
Varto o TR 128-129 J 3
Varvarco o RA 78-79 D 4
Varvarinskij o RUS 118-119 F 8
Varžane o IR 134-135 L 2
Várzea Alegre o BR 68-69 J 5
Várzea da Ema o BR 68-69 J 6
Várzea da Palma o BR 72-73 H 4
Várzea do Poço o BR 68-69 H 7
Varzea Grande o BR 68-69 G 5
Várzea Grande o BR 70-71 J 4
Varzeão o BR 74-75 F 5
Varzelândia o BR 72-73 H 3
Várzeo o BR 68-69 H 3
Varzuga ~ RUS 88-89 O 3
Varzuga, Bolšaja ~ RUS 88-89 O 3
Vasa = Vaasa o FIN 88-89 F 5
Väsad o IND 138-139 D 10
Vasai o IND 138-139 D 10
Vasconcelos o MEX 52-53 G 3
Vasiľeva, zaliv ≈ RUS 122-123 Q 3
Vasiľevka o RUS 122-123 F 5
Vasilija, mys ▲ RUS 112-113 U 4
Vašir o AFG 134-135 K 2
Vasjugan ~ RUS 114-115 Q 5
Vasjuganskaja ravnina ⌄ RUS 114-115 N 6
Vaška ~ RUS 88-89 T 5
Vaslui ☆ RO 102-103 E 4
Vassako o RCA 206-207 D 4
Vassar o USA 46-47 G 4
Vassouras o BR 72-73 J 7
Västbacka o S 86-87 H 6
Västerås o S 86-87 H 7
Västerbotten ⊥ S 86-87 H 4
Västerhaninge o S 86-87 J 7
Västervik o S 86-87 H 8
Vasto o I 100-101 E 3
Vašutkiny jezera o RUS 108-109 J 7
Vasvár o H 92-93 O 5
Vasyľkiva o UA 102-103 J 4
Vasyľkiv o UA 102-103 K 3
Vaté, île = État0 o VAN 184 II b 3
Vat'ngan ~ RUS 114-115 N 3
Vatican City = Città del Vaticano ☆ •••
SCV 100-101 C 4
Vaticano, Capo ▲ I 100-101 E 5
Vatilau Island = Buena Vista Island ~ SOL 184 I d 3
Vatinskij Egan ~ RUS 114-115 N 4
Vat Luang Temple • LAO 158-159 H 3
Vatolatsaka o RM 222-223 D 9
Vatomandry o RM 222-223 F 7
Vatondrangy ▲ RM 222-223 E 8
Vat Phu Temple • LAO 158-159 H 3
Vatra Dornei o RO 102-103 D 4
Vatrak ~ IND 138-139 D 8
Vattaikundu o IND 140-141 H 5
Vättern o S 86-87 G 7
Vatu-I-ra Channel ≈ 184 III b 2
Vatukoula o FJI 184 III a 2
Vatulele ~ FJI 184 III a 3
Vatu Vara ~ FJI 184 III c 2
Vatyfka ~ RUS 114-115 Q 3
Vatyna ~ RUS 112-113 R 6
Vaughan Springs o AUS 172-173 K 7
Vaughn o USA (MT) 40-41 J 7
Vaughn o USA (NM) 44-45 G 2
Vaupés, Río ~ CO 66-67 C 2
Vauxhall o CDN 32-33 O 6
Vavatenina o RM 222-223 F 6
Vava'u ~ TON 184 IV a 1
Vava'u Group ~ TON 184 IV a 1
Vavilova, lednik ▲ CDN 108-109 a 2
Vavkavysk o BY 94-95 J 5
Vavkavyskoe vozvyšša ▲ BY 94-95 J 5
Vavoua o CI 202-203 G 5
Vavož ☆ RUS 96-97 G 5
Vavuniya o CL 140-141 J 6
Växjö ☆ S 86-87 G 8

Vaygach, Ostrov = Vajgač, ostrov ~ RUS 108-109 H 6
Vaza Barris, Rio ~ BR 68-69 J 6
Väzažhā o AFG 138-139 B 3
Vazante o BR 72-73 G 4
Vazante Grande ou Funda ~ BR 70-71 J 6
Važgort o RUS 88-89 T 4
Vazobe ▲ RM 222-223 E 7
Vázquez o C 54-55 G 4
Veado, Cachoeira ~ BR 72-73 F 3
Vecumnieki o LV 94-95 J 3
Vedaranniyam o IND 140-141 H 5
Vedel, Kap ▲ GRØ 28-29 b 2
Vedel Fjord ≈ 28-29 b 2
Vedia o RA 78-79 J 4
Vedrovo o RUS 94-95 S 3
Vefsna ~ N 86-87 E 4
Vega ~ N 86-87 E 4
Vega o USA 44-45 F 2
Vega, La o CO 60-61 C 6
Vega, La ☆ DOM 54-55 K 5
Vega, mys ▲ RUS 108-109 e 3
Vega de Alatorre o MEX 52-53 F 1
Vega de Coro, La o YV 60-61 G 2
Velápur o IND 140-141 F 2
Veguita, La o YV 60-61 F 3
Vehowa o PK 138-139 C 4
Veimandu Channel ≈ 140-141 B 7
Veintiocho de Mayo o EC 64-65 C 3
Veiru o PNG 183 C 4
Veis o IR 134-135 C 3
Vejer de la Frontera o E 98-99 E 3
Vejle o DK 86-87 D 9
Vekšino o RUS 94-95 M 3
Vela, Cabo de la o CO (GUA) 60-61 G 1
Vela, Cabo de la ▲ CO (GUA) 60-61 F 1
Vela de Coro, La o YV 60-61 G 2
Vela Luka o HR 100-101 F 3
Velbert o D 90-91 J 3
Velázquez o ROU 78-79 M 3
Velcho, Río ~ MEX 50-51 H 4
Velddrif o ZA 220-221 D 6
Velebitski kanal ≈ 100-101 E 2
Vélez o CO 60-61 E 4
Vélez Rubio o E 98-99 F 6
Velha Boipeba o BR 72-73 L 2
Velha Goa o ••• IND 140-141 E 3
Velhas, Rio das ~ BR 72-73 H 4
Vélia • I 100-101 E 4
Velikaja ~ RUS (NAO) 88-89 T 3
Velikaja ~ RUS 112-113 S 5
Velikaja Guba o RUS 88-89 N 5
Velikaja Kema o RUS 122-123 G 6
Velikan, gora ▲ RUS 112-113 P 2
Veliki Đerdap • YU 100-101 J 2
Velikie Luki ☆ RUS 94-95 M 3
Velikij, ostrov ~ RUS 88-89 M 3
Velikij Ustjug o RUS 88-89 T 4
Velikie Luki = Velikie Luki ☆ RUS 94-95 M 3
Velikoe, ozero o RUS 94-95 P 3
Velikonda Range ▲ IND 140-141 H 4
Veliko Plana o YU 100-101 H 2
Veliko Tărnovo o BG 102-103 D 6
Velile o PE 70-71 B 4
Velimlje o YU 100-101 G 2
Vélingara o SN (CAS) 202-203 C 3
Vélingara o SN (DIO) 202-203 C 2
Velingrad o BG 102-103 C 6
Veliž ☆ RUS 94-95 M 4
Vefju ~ RUS 88-89 X 5
Věr Kaľ o RUS 112-113 V 4
Vella Lavella ~ SOL 184 I c 2
Vellankulam o CL 140-141 H 4
Velloor o NAM 220-221 H 4
Vellore o IND 140-141 H 4
Velloso o RA 78-79 K 4
Veľmaj ~ RUS 112-113 U 3
Vefmo ~ RUS 116-117 Q 5
Velo Troglav ▲ YU 100-101 F 3
Velsen o NL 92-93 H 2
Veľsk o RUS 88-89 R 6
Veľt'' ~ RUS 88-89 V 4
Velva o USA 42-43 G 1
Velyka Lepetycha o UA 102-103 H 4
Velyka Pysarivka o UA 102-103 J 2
Velykij Bereznyj o UA 102-103 C 3
Velykij Byčkiv o UA 102-103 D 3
Velykij Dobron' = Dobron' o UA 102-103 C 3
Vema Fracture Zone ≃ 5 G 3
Vembanad Lake o IND 140-141 G 6
Vempalle o IND 140-141 H 3
Vemsdalen o S 86-87 F 6
Venado, El o CO 60-61 H 6
Venado, Isla del ~ NIC 52-53 C 6
Venado Tuerto o RA 78-79 J 2
Venamo, Río ~ YV 62-63 D 2
Venâncio Aires o BR 74-75 D 7
Venancia o PNG 183 A 4
Vencelas Brás o BR 72-73 H 7
Venda (former Homeland, now part of North-Transvaal) ▲ ZA 218-219 D 6
Venda do Imigrante o BR 72-73 K 6
Vendas Novas o P 98-99 C 5
Vendôme o F 90-91 H 8
Vendom Fiord ≈ 24-25 a 4
Veneral o CO 60-61 C 6
Venetie o USA 20-21 R 3
Véneto o I 100-101 C 2
Venézia ☆ ••• I 100-101 D 2
Venézia, Golfo di ≈ 100-101 D 2
Venezuela ■ YV 60-61 F 3
Venezuela, Golfo de ≈ 60-61 F 2
Venezuela Basin ≃ 5 E 3
Vengurla o IND 140-141 E 3
Veniaminof Volcano ▲ USA 22-23 R 4

Venice o USA (FL) 48-49 G 6
Venice o USA (LA) 48-49 D 5
Venice, Gulf of = Venézia, Golfo di ≈ I 100-101 D 2
Venice = Venézia ☆ ••• I 100-101 D 2
Venjan o S 86-87 F 6
Venkatagiri o IND 140-141 H 4
Venlo o NL 92-93 J 3
Venray o NL 92-93 H 3
Venta o LT 94-95 H 3
Venta, La ☆• MEX (TAB) 52-53 G 2
Venta, La .∴. MEX (TAB) 52-53 G 2
Venta de Baños o E 98-99 E 4
Ventana, La o YV 60-61 H 4
Ventanas o EC 64-65 C 2
Ventanas, Las o YV 60-61 H 4
Ventania o BR 74-75 E 5
Ventas con Peña Aguilera, Las o E 98-99 E 5
Ventersburg o ZA 220-221 H 4
Ventersdorp o ZA 220-221 H 3
Venterstad o ZA 220-221 G 5
Ventisquero, Cerro ▲ RA 78-79 D 6
Ventosa, La o MEX 52-53 G 3
Ventoux, Mont ▲ F 90-91 K 9
Ventspils ☆ LV 94-95 G 3
Venturari, Río ~ YV 60-61 H 5
Ventura ☆ USA 40-41 H 4
Venujeoo o RUS 108-109 O 6
Venustiano Carranza o MEX 52-53 H 3
Venustiano Carranza, Presa o MEX 50-51 J 4
Venustiano Carranza o MEX 52-53 C 2
Veppur o IND 140-141 H 5
Ver, Horej- o RUS 88-89 Y 3
Vera ▲ RR 70-71 K 3
Vera o RA 78-79 J 1
Vera, Bahía ≈ 80 H 2
Vera, Cape ▲ CDN 24-25 b 2
Vera, Laguna o PY 76-77 J 4
Veracruz ▲ MEX (BCN) 50-51 B 1
Veracruz ☆ MEX 52-53 F 1
Veracruz □ MEX 52-53 E 1
Verada da Redençao ~ BR 68-69 G 7
Verada do Buriti ~ BR 72-73 F 3
Verada Tábua ou Rio Grande o BR 68-69 H 7
Verado de Cócos ~ BR 72-73 H 2
Veranópolis o BR 74-75 E 7
Verao = Moso ~ VAN 184 II b 3
Veráival o IND 138-139 C 9
Verbano = Lago Maggiore o I 100-101 B 2
Verbljud, ozero o RUS 108-109 I 3
Verbrande Berg ▲ NAM 216-217 C 10
Verchiveeve o UA 102-103 J 3
Verchnie Jamki o RUS 112-113 L 2
Verchnjadzvinsk ▲ BY 94-95 K 4
Verchn'odniprovs'k o UA 102-103 J 3
Verdalsøra o N 86-87 E 5
Verde, Arroyo ~ RA 78-79 G 6
Verde, Bahía ≈ 78-79 H 5
Verde, Cay ~ BS 54-55 H 3
Verde, Laguna o RA 78-79 E 7
Verde, Península ~ RA 78-79 H 5
Verde, Punta ▲ EC 64-65 C 1
Verde, Río ~ BR 70-71 K 3
Verde, Río ~ BR 72-73 G 4
Verde, Río ~ BR 72-73 E 5
Verde, Río ~ MEX 50-51 K 5
Verde, Río ~ MEX 52-53 K 3
Verde, Río ~ MEX 52-53 C 1
Verde, Río ~ PY 70-71 J 6
Verde, Río ~ PY 76-77 H 2
Verde Island ~ RP 160-161 D 6
Verde Island Passage ≈ 160-161 D 6
Verde River ~ USA 40-41 J 8
Verdigre o USA 42-43 H 4
Verdinho, Rio ~ BR 72-73 E 4
Verdon ~ F 90-91 L 10
Verdon-sur-Mer, le o F 90-91 G 9
Verdun o F 90-91 K 7
Verdun o ROU 78-79 H 5
Verdun, Pampa o RA 80 E 3
Vereda Pimenteira ~ BR 68-69 G 6
Vereeniging o ZA 220-221 H 3
Verena o ZA 220-221 J 2
Vereščagino o RUS 114-115 T 2
Vereščagino o RUS (PRM) 96-97 J 4
Verestovo, ozero o RUS 94-95 P 3
Vergara o ROU 74-75 D 9
Vergareña, La o YV 60-61 K 4
Vergel, El o MEX 50-51 H 4
Vergeleë o ZA 220-221 G 2
Vergement o AUS 178-179 G 2
Vergi o EST 94-95 K 2
Verhalen o USA 44-45 F 4
Verhnee Ondomozero o RUS 88-89 P 3
Verhneimbatsk o RUS 114-115 U 3
Verhnejarkovo ▲ RUS 96-97 H 4
Verhnekamskaja vozvyšennost' ▲ RUS 96-97 H 4
Verhnekarahbahskij kanal ≺ AZ 128-129 M 2
Verhnekolymskoe, nagor'e ▲▲ RUS 120-121 M 2
Verhnespasskoe o RUS 88-89 T 4
Verhne tazovskaja vozvyšennost' ▲ RUS 114-115 Q 3
Verhnetazovskij, zapovednik ⊥ RUS 114-115 R 3
Verhnetulomsk o RUS 88-89 L 2
Verhnetulomskoe Vodohranilišče ≺ RUS 88-89 L 2
Verhneuraľsk ☆ RUS 96-97 L 7
Verhnevilujsk ▲ RUS 118-119 K 4
Verhnevym'skaja grada ▲ RUS 88-89 V 4
Verhnezejskaja ravnina ⌄ RUS 118-119 N 8
Verhnie Kigi o RUS 96-97 L 6

Verhnie Tatyšly ☆ RUS 96-97 J 5
Verhnie Usugli ~ RUS 118-119 G 9
Verhnij Balygyčan o RUS 112-113 H 5
Verhnij Baskunčak o RUS 96-97 E 8
Verhnij Enisej ~ RUS 116-117 F 10
Verhnij Kužebar o RUS 116-117 F 9
Verhnij Meľgin o RUS 122-123 D 3
Verhnij Paren' o RUS 112-113 M 5
Verhnij Suzun o RUS 124-125 N 2
Verhnij Toguzak ~ RUS 124-125 B 2
Verhnij Turukan ~ RUS 116-117 L 3
Verhnij Ufalej o RUS 96-97 F 6
Verhnjaja Agapa ~ RUS 108-109 W 6
Verhnjaja Amga o RUS 118-119 N 6
Verhnjaja Angara ~ RUS 118-119 E 7
Verhnjaja Baiha ~ RUS 114-115 U 3
Verhnjaja Čunku ~ RUS 116-117 J 4
Verhnjaja Kočoma ~ RUS 116-117 N 5
Verhnjaja Kuěnga o RUS 118-119 H 9
Verhnjaja Larba ~ RUS 118-119 M 8
Verhnjaja Mokla ~ RUS 118-119 J 8
Verhnjaja Pyšma o RUS 96-97 M 5
Verhnjaja Sarčina ~ RUS 114-115 U 3
Verhnjaja Salda ~ RUS 96-97 M 4
Verhnjaja Tajmyra ~ RUS 108-109 a 4
Verhnjaja Tomba ~ RUS 116-117 N 4
Verhnjaja Vilujka ~ RUS 116-117 M 2
Verhnjaja Zolotica o RUS 88-89 R 3
Verhojansk o RUS 110-111 T 6
Verhojanskij hrebet ▲▲ RUS 110-111 R 5
Verhotupova, ostrov ~ RUS 120-121 V 4
Verhotur'e o RUS 96-97 M 4
Véria o GR 100-101 J 4
Verín o E 98-99 D 3
Verkhoyanskiy Khrebet = Verhojanskij hrebet ▲ RUS 110-111 Q 5
Verkola o RUS 88-89 S 5
Verkykerskop o ZA 220-221 J 3
Verlegenhuken ▲ N 84-85 K 2
Vermasse o RI 166-167 J 4
Vermelha, Serra ▲ BR 68-69 G 6
Vermelha, Serra ▲ BR 72-73 F 3
Vermelho, Rio ~ BR 68-69 G 6
Vermelho, Rio ~ BR 68-69 D 5
Vermelho, Rio ~ BR 68-69 G 5
Vermelho, Rio ~ BR 68-69 J 7
Vermelho, Rio ~ BR 72-73 E 3
Vermillion o CDN 32-33 P 5
Vermillion ~ USA 46-47 G 5
Vermillion Bay ≈ 44-45 L 5
Vermillion Lake o CDN 34-35 K 5
Vermillion Lake o CDN 42-43 L 2
Vermillion River ~ CDN 32-33 P 5
Vermillion River ~ USA 42-43 J 4
Vermillion, Rivière ~ CDN 38-39 H 5
Vermont □ USA 46-47 M 4
Vernal o USA 42-43 C 5
Verner o CDN 38-39 H 5
Verneuil-sur-Avre o F 90-91 H 7
Verneuk Pan o ZA 220-221 E 4
Vernia, La o USA 44-45 H 5
Vernoe o RUS 122-123 C 3
Vernon o CDN 32-33 N 6
Vernon o F 90-91 H 7
Vernon o USA (TX) 44-45 H 2
Vernon o USA (UT) 40-41 J 6
Vernon Center o USA 42-43 K 4
Vernon Islands ~ AUS 172-173 K 2
Vero Beach o USA 48-49 H 6
Verona o ••• I 100-101 C 2
Verónica o RA 78-79 L 3
Veron Range ▲ PNG 183 G 3
Versailles o ••• F 90-91 J 7
Versailles o USA (MO) 42-43 L 4
Versalles o CO 60-61 C 6
Veršina-Tuojdah, gora ▲ RUS 110-111 W 7
Veršino-Darasunskij o RUS 118-119 G 9
Veršiny, Čelno ~ RUS 96-97 G 6
Versteende Woud ▲ NAM 216-217 C 10
Vert, Cap ▲ SN 202-203 B 2
Vertentes o BR 68-69 G 6
Vertientes o C 54-55 F 4
Vertijievka o UA 102-103 G 2
Vértiz o RA 78-79 H 4
Verulam o ZA 220-221 K 4
Verviers o B 92-93 H 3
Verwoert Tunnels ‖ ZA 218-219 E 6
Vesali, Ruins of • MYA 142-143 H 5
Ves'egonsk o RUS 94-95 P 3
Vesele o UA 102-103 J 4
Veselovskoe vodohranilišče ≺ RUS 102-103 M 4
Vesenniji o RUS 112-113 N 3
Vešenskaja o RUS 102-103 M 3
Vesiljana o RUS 88-89 V 5
Vesoul ☆ F 90-91 L 8
Vestbygd o N 86-87 C 7
Vesterålen ~ N 86-87 F 4
Vesterø Havn o DK 86-87 E 8
Vestfjorden ≈ 86-87 F 3
Vestgrønland = Kitaa □ GRØ 26-27 b 5
Vestmannaeyjar o IS (RAN) 86-87 c 3
Vestmannaeyjar ~ IS (RAN) 86-87 c 3
Vestnik, buhta ≈ RUS 122-123 R 3
Vestvågøy ~ N 86-87 F 2
Vesúvio ▲ I 100-101 E 4
Veszprém ☆ H 92-93 O 5
Vetauua ▲ FJI 184 III c 1
Vetlanda • S 86-87 G 8
Vetluga o RUS (GOR) 96-97 D 5
Vetluga ~ RUS 96-97 E 5
Vetovo o BG 102-103 E 6
Vetrennyj pojas, kraž ▲ RUS 88-89 N 5
Vetrivier o BY 94-95 L 4
Vetryna o BY 94-95 L 4
Vetvejskij hrebet ▲ RUS 120-121 V 3
Vévi o GR 100-101 J 4

Veyo o USA 40-41 H 7
Vezdehodnaja ~ RUS 108-109 j 4
Vézelay o ••• F 90-91 J 8
Vežen ▲ BG 102-103 D 6
Vézère ~ F 90-91 H 9
V. Gradište o YU 100-101 H 2
Vi o S 86-87 H 5
Viacha o BOL 70-71 C 5
Viahtu o RUS 122-123 K 3
Viahtu ~ RUS 122-123 K 3
Viai Island ~ PNG 183 C 2
Vialdougou o CI 202-203 G 5
Viale o RA 76-77 H 6
Viamão o BR 74-75 E 8
Viana o ANG 216-217 B 4
Viana o BR (ESP) 72-73 K 6
Viana o BR (MAR) 68-69 F 3
Viana o BR (PI) 62-63 J 6
Viana do Castelo o P 98-99 C 4
Viangchan ☆ LAO 158-159 G 2
Viangphoukha o LAO 156-157 B 6
Viánopolis o BR 72-73 F 4
Viar, Río ~ E 98-99 E 5
Viaréggio o I 100-101 C 3
Via River ~ PNG 183 A 4
Vibora, La o MEX 50-51 H 4
Viboras, Las o RA 76-77 E 3
Viborg o DK 86-87 D 8
Vic o E 98-99 J 4
Vicebck o BY 94-95 M 4
Vic-en-Bigorre o F 90-91 H 10
Vicência o BR 68-69 L 5
Vicente Franco o BR 68-69 E 3
Vicente Guerrero o MEX 52-53 L 1
Vicente Guerrero o MEX (DGO) 50-51 H 4
Vicente Guerrero o MEX (TLA) 52-53 E 2
Vicente Noble o DOM 54-55 K 5
Vicenza ☆• I 100-101 C 2
Vicertópolis o BR 72-73 E 6
Vichada, Río ~ CO 60-61 G 5
Vichadero o ROU 76-77 K 6
Vichy o F 90-91 J 8
Vici o USA 44-45 H 1
Vicksburg o USA 44-45 M 3
Vicksburg National Military Park ∴ USA 44-45 M 3
Viçosa o BR (ALA) 68-69 K 6
Viçosa o BR (MIN) 72-73 J 6
Victor o USA (ID) 40-41 J 4
Victor o USA (NY) 46-47 K 4
Victor o USA (SD) 42-43 J 3
Victor, Lac o CDN 38-39 O 3
Victor, Mount ▲ USA 180-181 E 2
Victor Emanuel Range ▲▲ PNG 183 A 3
Victor Harbor o AUS 180-181 E 3
Victoria □ AUS 180-181 H 4
Victoria o BOL 70-71 D 5
Victoria • CDN 32-33 J 7
Victoria o CO 60-61 D 5
Victoria o HK 156-157 L 5
Victoria o M 100-101 E 6
Victoria o RA 78-79 J 2
Victoria o RCH 78-79 C 5
Victoria o SME 62-63 G 3
Victoria ▲ SY 224 D 2
Victoria o USA 44-45 J 5
Victoria, Isla ~ RCH 80 C 2
Victoria, La o YV (APU) 60-61 F 4
Victoria, La o YV (ARA) 60-61 H 3
Victoria, Lake o AUS 180-181 F 3
Victoria, Lake o EAT 212-213 D 4
Victoria, Mount ▲ MYA 142-143 H 5
Victoria, Mount ▲ PNG 183 D 5
Victoria, Sierra de la ▲▲ RA 76-77 K 3
Victoria and Albert Mountains ▲ CDN 26-27 L 4
Victoria Beach o CDN 34-35 H 5
Victoria de Durango = Durango ☆• MEX 50-51 G 5
Victoria Falls ~••• Z 218-219 C 3
Victoria Falls National Park ⊥ ZW 218-219 C 3
Victoria Fjord ≈ 26-27 a 2
Victoria Head o CDN 26-27 N 4
Victoria Hill o BS 54-55 H 2
Victoria Lake o CDN 24-25 O 5
Victoria Land ⟍ ARK 16 F 16
Victoria Nile ~ EAU 212-213 C 2
Victoria Peak ▲ BH 52-53 K 3
Victoria River o AUS (NT) 172-173 K 3
Victoria River ~ AUS 172-173 K 3
Victoria River o CDN 38-39 I Q 4
Victoria River Downs o AUS 172-173 K 4
Victorias o RP 160-161 E 7
Victoria Strait ≈ 24-25 Z 3
Victoria Valle o AUS 174-175 G 6
Victoriaville o CDN 38-39 N 5
Victorica o RA 78-79 G 4
Victorino o C 54-55 G 4
Victor Rosales o MEX 50-51 H 6
Victorville o USA 40-41 H 4
Victory, Mount ▲ PNG 183 E 5
Vícus • PE 64-65 B 4
Vicuña o RCH (COQ) 76-77 B 6
Vicuña o RCH (MAC) 80 F 7
Vicuña Mackenna o RA 78-79 G 3
Vida o USA 42-43 G 1
Vidal o PE 64-65 F 3
Vidal o USA 40-41 G 8
Vidalia o USA (GA) 48-49 G 3
Vidalia o USA (LA) 44-45 M 4
Vidamilp o PY 76-77 J 3
Vidapanakallu o IND 140-141 G 3
Videira o BR 74-75 D 7
Vidhareidhi = Viðareiði ▲ FR 90-91 D 1
Vidim o RUS 116-117 L 7
Vidisha o IND 138-139 F 8
Vidor o USA 44-45 L 4
Vidzy o BY 94-95 K 4

Viedgesville o ZA 220-221 J 5
Viedma o RA 78-79 H 6
Viedma, Lago o RA 80 D 4
Vieira Grande, Canal do o ~ BR 62-63 G 4
Viejitas, Caño las o CO 60-61 F 6
Viejo, El o NIC 52-53 L 5
Viejo, Rio ~ NIC 52-53 L 5
Vielha e Mijaran o E 98-99 H 3
Vielha-Mitg Arán = Vielha e Mijaran o E 98-99 H 3
Vienna o USA (IL) 46-47 D 7
Vienna o USA (MO) 46-47 C 6
Vienna o USA (WV) 46-47 H 5
Vienna = Wien ☆ A 92-93 O 4
Vienne o F 90-91 K 9
Vienne ~ F 90-91 H 8
Vientiane = Viangchan ☆ LAO 158-159 G 2
Viento, Cordillera del ▲ RA 78-79 D 4
Viento, Puerto del ▲ RA 78-79 D 4
Vientos, Los o RCH 76-77 C 3
Vientos, Paso de los ≈ 54-55 H 5
Vieremä o FIN 88-89 H 5
Vierwaldstätter See o CH 92-93 K 5
Vierzon o F 90-91 J 8
Viesca o MEX 50-51 H 5
Viesite o LV 94-95 J 3
Vieste o I 100-101 F 4
Vietas o S 86-87 J 3
Vietnam = Viet Nam ■ VN 158-159 K 2
Viet Tri o VN 156-157 D 5
Vieux-Comptoir, Lac du o CDN 38-39 F 2
Vieux-Comptoir, Rivière du ~ CDN 38-39 F 2
Vieux Fort o WL 56 E 5
Vieytes o RA 78-79 L 3
Vigan o RP 160-161 D 4
Vigan, le o F 90-91 J 10
Vigia o BR 62-63 K 6
Vigia, El o YV 60-61 F 3
Vigia Chico o MEX 52-53 L 2
Vigia de Curvaradó o CO 60-61 C 4
Vigia del Fuerta o CO 60-61 C 4
Vigo o E 98-99 C 3
Vihanti o FIN 88-89 H 5
Vihári o PK 138-139 D 4
Vihorevka o RUS 116-117 K 7
Vihren ▲ BG 102-103 C 7
Vihti o FIN 88-89 G 6
Viisanmäki o FIN 88-89 H 5
Viitasaari o FIN 88-89 H 5
Vitna o FIN 88-89 H 5
Vijayadurg o IND 140-141 E 3
Vijayanagar o IND 138-139 G 7
Vijayápati o IND 140-141 G 6
Vijayapura o IND 140-141 G 4
Vijayapuri o IND 140-141 H 3
Vijayawada o IND 140-141 J 2
Vik o IS 86-87 d 3
Vikajärvi o FIN 88-89 J 3
Vikárábád o IND 140-141 G 2
Vikeke o RI 166-167 D 6
Vikenara Point ▲ SOL 184 I d 3
Vikersund o N 86-87 D 7
Viking o CDN 32-33 P 5
Vikna ~ N 86-87 E 4
Viksøyri o N 86-87 C 6
Viktoria = Labuan o MAL 160-161 A 10
Viktoria ▲ USA 84-85 U 2
Viktorija, ostrov ~ RUS 84-85 U 2
Vikulova, mys ▲ RUS 108-109 H 4
Vila Aurora o BR 68-69 G 4
Vila Bela da Santíssima Trindade o BR 70-71 H 4
Vila Coutinho o MOC 218-219 H 4
Vila de Ribeira Brava o CV 202-203 B 5
Vila de Sal-Rei o CV 202-203 C 5
Vila de Sena o MOC 218-219 H 4
Vila do Maio o CV 202-203 C 6
Vila dos Remédios o BR 68-69 L 1
Vila Flor o ANG 216-217 C 6
Vila Franca de Xira o P 98-99 C 5
Vila Gomes da Costa o MOC 220-221 L 2
Vilaine ~ F 90-91 G 8
Vila Ipixuna o BR 68-69 E 3
Vila Maria Pia o CV 202-203 B 5
Vila Martins o BR 66-67 C 6
Vila Meriti o BR 72-73 J 7
Vila Nova o ANG 216-217 D 6
Vila Nova o BR (PAR) 74-75 D 5
Vila Nova o BR (RSU) 74-75 D 8
Vila Nova da Fronteira o MOC 218-219 H 3
Vila Nova de Foz Côa o P 98-99 D 4
Vila Nova do Seles o ANG 216-217 C 5
Vila Nova Sintra o CV 202-203 B 6
Vila Porto Franco o BR 66-67 H 6
Vila-real o E 98-99 G 5
Vila Real ☆ P 98-99 D 4
Vila Real de Santo António o P 98-99 D 6
Vilar Formoso o P 98-99 D 4
Vila Rica o BR 68-69 D 8
Vilarinho do Monte o BR 62-63 H 5
Vilas, Los o RCH 76-77 B 6
Vila Sagrada Coração de Jesus o BR 66-67 H 5
Vila Tambaqui o BR 66-67 E 4
Vila Tepequem o BR 62-63 D 4
Vila Velha o BR 72-73 K 6
Vila Velha de Rónda o PE 70-71 B 4
Vilavila o PE 70-71 B 4
Vilcabamba o EC 64-65 C 4
Vilcabamba • PE 64-65 F 8

Vilcabamba, Cordillera de ▲ PE 64-65 F 8
Vilcanota, Cordillera de ▲ PE 70-71 B 3
Vilcas Huaman o PE 64-65 F 7
Vilčeka, Zemlja ~ RUS 84-85 f 2
Vilches o E 98-99 F 5
Vilcún o RCH 78-79 C 5
Vilcún, Río ~ RCH 78-79 C 5
Vilejka o BY 94-95 K 4
Vilelas o RA 78-79 J 3
Vilhelmina o S 86-87 H 4
Vilhena o BR 70-71 G 3
Viliga ~ RUS 120-121 R 3
Viliginskij, mys ▲ RUS 120-121 R 3
Viljandi ☆•• EST 94-95 J 2
Viljoenskroen o ZA 220-221 H 3
Viljučinskaja buhta o RUS 120-121 S 7
Viluj ~ RUS 116-117 M 3
Viluj ~ RUS 118-119 O 3
Viluj ~ RUS 118-119 G 4
Vilujčan ~ RUS 118-119 G 4
Vilujsk ☆• RUS 118-119 K 4
Vilujskoe vodohranilišče o RUS 118-119 E 4
Vilvockogo, ostrov ~ RUS 108-109 Q 5
Viľkickogo, proliv ≈ 108-109 J 3
Vilkija o LT 94-95 H 4
Viľkitskogo, Proliv = Viľkickogo, proliv ≈ RUS 108-109 d 3
Villa Abecia o BOL 70-71 E 7
Villa Ahumada o MEX 50-51 F 2
Villa Alcaraz o RA 76-77 H 6
Villa Alemana o RCH 78-79 D 2
Villa Ana o RA 76-77 G 4
Villa Angela o RA 76-77 G 4
Villa Atuel o RA 78-79 E 3
Villa Azueta o MEX 52-53 G 2
Villaba o RP 160-161 F 7
Villa Berthet o RA 76-77 G 4
Villablino o E 98-99 D 3
Villa Brana o RA 76-77 F 4
Villa Bruzual o YV 60-61 G 3
Villacañas o E 98-99 F 5
Villa Cañas o RA 78-79 J 3
Villacarrillo o E 98-99 F 5
Villa Candelaria o RA 76-77 G 4
Villa Carlos Paz o RA 76-77 G 6
Villacarrito o E 98-99 F 5
Villach o A 92-93 M 5
Villa Constitución o RA 78-79 J 2
Villa Corona o MEX 52-53 C 1
Villa Coronado o MEX 50-51 G 4
Villa de Cazones o MEX 52-53 F 1
Villa de Cos o MEX 50-51 H 6
Villa de Cura o YV 60-61 H 2
Villa de García o MEX 50-51 J 5
Villa de Leiva o•• CO 60-61 E 5
Villa del Rosario o RA 76-77 H 6
Villa del Rosario o YV 60-61 E 2
Villa de Orestes o MEX 50-51 G 4
Villa de Reyes o MEX 50-51 J 7
Villa de Sari o MEX 50-51 D 3
Villadiego o E 98-99 E 3
Villa Dolores o RA 76-77 E 6
Villa Figueroa o RA 76-77 F 4
Villa Flores o MEX 52-53 H 3
Villafranca del Bierzo o E 98-99 D 3
Village Cove o CDN 38-39 I H 4
Villa General Belgrano o RA 76-77 E 6
Villa General Güemes o RA 76-77 H 3
Villa General Roca o RA 78-79 F 2
Villa General San Martín o RA 76-77 C 6
Village of Yesteryear ∴ USA 42-43 L 4
Villa Gesell o RA 78-79 L 4
Villa Gobernador Gálvez o RA 78-79 J 2
Villagran o MEX 52-53 D 1
Villaguay o RA 76-77 H 6
Villaguay Grande, Arroyo o RA 76-77 H 6
Villa Hermosa o MEX 52-53 C 1
Villahermosa ☆• MEX (TAB) 52-53 H 3
Villa Hidalgo o MEX (DGO) 50-51 G 4
Villa Hidalgo o MEX (JAL) 50-51 H 7
Villa Hidalgo o MEX (SON) 50-51 E 2
Villa Huidobra o RA 78-79 H 3
Villa Insurgentes o MEX 50-51 D 5
Villa Joyosa o E 98-99 G 5
Villa Juárez o MEX 50-51 J 6
Villa Larca o RA 78-79 G 2
Villalba o E 98-99 D 3
Villalbín o PY 76-77 H 4
Villa Lola o YV 60-61 J 4
Villalonga o RA 78-79 H 4
Villalpando o E 98-99 E 3
Villa Mainero o MEX 50-51 K 6
Villa María o RA 78-79 H 2
Villamartín o E 98-99 E 6
Villa Mascardi o RA 78-79 D 6
Villa Mazán o RA 76-77 D 5
Villa Media Agua o RA 76-77 D 6
Villa Mercedes o RA 76-77 F 6
Villa Mills o CR 52-53 C 7
Villamontes o BOL 76-77 H 2
Villanueva o CO 60-61 F 2
Villanueva o RA 76-77 G 6
Villanueva o MEX 50-51 H 6
Villa Nueva o RA 76-77 C 6
Villanueva de Córdoba o E 98-99 E 5
Villanueva de los Castillejos o E 98-99 D 5
Villanueva de los Infantes o E 98-99 F 5
Villanueva y Geltrú = Vilanova i la Geltrú o E 98-99 H 4
Villa Ocampo o MEX 50-51 G 4
Villa Ocampo o RA 76-77 H 4
Villa Ojo de Agua o RA 76-77 F 5
Villa Oliva o PY 76-77 H 4
Villa Oliva o PY (NEE) 76-77 J 4
Villa Ortega o RCH 80 E 2
Villapinzon o CO 60-61 E 5
Villarcayo o E 98-99 F 3
Villard o RA 54-55 J 5
Villardeciervos o E 98-99 D 4
Villa Reducción o RA 78-79 H 2
Villa Regina o RA 78-79 F 5

Villarpando o DOM 54-55 K 5
Villarreal de los Infantes = Vila-real o E 98-99 G 5
Villarrica ☆ PY 76-77 J 3
Villarrica o RCH 78-79 C 5
Villarrica, Lago ⊖ RCH 78-79 C 5
Villarrica, Parque Nacional ⊥ RCH 78-79 C 5
Villarrica, Volcán ▲ RCH 78-79 D 5
Villarrobledo o E 98-99 F 5
Villa Salvadorita o NIC 52-53 L 5
Villa San Martin o RA 76-77 E 5
Villa Santa Rita de Catuna o RA 76-77 D 6
Villasimius o I 100-101 B 5
Villa Talavera o BOL 70-71 E 6
Villa Toquepala o PE 70-71 B 5
Villatoya o E 98-99 G 5
Villa Tunari o BOL 70-71 E 5
Villa Unión o MEX 50-51 J 3
Villa Unión o MEX (DGO) 50-51 G 6
Villa Unión o MEX (SIN) 50-51 F 6
Villa Unión o RA 76-77 C 5
Villa Valeria o RA 78-79 G 3
Villa Vásquez o DOM 54-55 K 5
Villavicencio ☆ CO 60-61 E 5
Villaviciosa o• E 98-99 E 3
Villazon o RA 76-77 E 2
Villefranche-de-Rouergue o F 90-91 J 9
Villefranche-sur-Saône o F 90-91 K 9
Villeguera, La o YV 60-61 H 4
Ville-Marie o CDN 38-39 E 5
Villena o E 98-99 G 5
Villeneuve-sur-Lot o F 90-91 H 9
Villeroy o CDN 38-39 J 5
Villeurbanne o F 90-91 K 9
Villicún, Sierra de ▲ RA 76-77 C 6
Villiers o ZA 220-221 J 3
Villisca o USA 42-43 K 5
Vilnes o N 86-87 B 6
Vilnius ★•• LT 94-95 J 4
Vil'njans'k o UA 102-103 J 4
Vil'nohirs'k o UA 102-103 J 3
Vils ~ D 92-93 L 4
Vil'šany o UA 102-103 J 2
Vilyuyskoye Vodokhranilishche = Viljujskoe vodohranilišče < RUS 118-119 E 4
Vimieiro o P 98-99 D 5
Vimioso o P 98-99 D 4
Vimmerby ☆• S 86-87 G 8
Vina ~ CAM 204-205 K 5
Vina, Chute de la ~• CAM 204-205 K 5
Viña, La o RA (CAT) 76-77 E 5
Viña, La o RA (SAL) 76-77 E 3
Viña del Mar o RCH 78-79 D 2
Vinalhaven o USA 46-47 O 3
Vinalhaven Island ⌒ USA 46-47 O 3
Vinanivao o RM 222-223 G 5
Vinaròs o E 98-99 H 4
Vînători o RO 102-103 C 5
Vincelotte, Lac ⊖ CDN 36-37 N 7
Vincennes o USA 46-47 E 6
Vincennes Bay ≈ 16 G 11
Vinces o EC 64-65 C 2
Vinchina o RA 76-77 C 5
Vinchina, Río ~ RA 76-77 C 5
Vindelälven ~ S 86-87 J 4
Vindeln o S 86-87 J 4
Vindhya Range ▲ IND 138-139 E 8
Vineland o USA 46-47 L 6
Viner Nejstadt, ostrov ⌒ RUS 84-85 f 2
Vingåker ☆ S 86-87 G 7
Vingerklip • NAM 216-217 C 10
Vinh ☆ VN 156-157 D 7
Vinhais o P 98-99 D 4
Vinh Bắc Bộ ≈ 156-157 E 6
Vinh Cam Ranh ≈ 158-159 K 5
Vinh Cây Du'o'ng ≈ 158-159 H 5
Vinh Diên Châu ≈ 156-157 D 7
Vinhedo o BR 72-73 G 7
Vinh Hy o VN 158-159 K 5
Vinh Kim o VN 158-159 K 3
Vinh Lộc ☆ VN 156-157 D 6
Vinh Long o VN 158-159 H 5
Vinh Pham Thiêy ≈ 158-159 K 5
Vinh Yên ☆ VN 156-157 D 6
Vinita o USA 44-45 K 1
Vinju Mare o RO 102-103 C 5
Vinkovci o HR 100-101 G 2
Vinnica = Vinnycja ☆ UA 102-103 F 3
Vinnycja ☆ UA 102-103 F 3
Vinnytsya = Vinnycja ☆ UA 102-103 F 3
Vinson, Mount ▲ ARK 16 F 28
Vinstra ☆ N 86-87 D 6
Vinter Øer ⌒ GRØ 26-27 W 6
Vinton o USA 42-43 L 4
Vinukonda o IND 140-141 H 2
Vinza o RCB 210-211 E 5
Vinzili o RUS 114-115 H 6
Viola o USA (IL) 46-47 C 5
Viola o USA (KS) 44-45 J 1
Violaineville o G 210-211 C 3
Violeta, La o RA 78-79 J 2
Vioolsdrif o ZA 220-221 C 4
Viphya Mountains ▲ MW 214-215 G 7
Vipos, Río ~ RA 76-77 E 4
Vir o TJ 136-137 M 6
Virac ☆ RP 160-161 F 6
Viração, Cachoeira da ~ BR 62-63 G 6
Virac Point ▲ RP 160-161 F 6
Viradouro o BR 72-73 F 6
Vira-e-Volta, Cachoeira ~ BR 68-69 C 3
Viraganur o IND 140-141 H 5
Viramgām o IND 138-139 D 8
Viranşehir ☆ TR 128-129 H 4
Virapalle o IND 140-141 H 3
Virār o IND 138-139 D 10
Virarājendrapet o IND 140-141 F 4
Virāwah o PK 138-139 C 7
Virden o CDN 34-35 F 6
Virden o USA 46-47 D 6
Vire o F 90-91 G 7
Virei o ANG 216-217 B 7
Virgem da Lapa o BR 72-73 J 4
Virgen, La o NIC 52-53 B 6
Virgen de las Lajas, Santuario • CO 64-65 D 1
Virgen del Carmen, Canal < RA 76-77 F 3
Virgin Gorda ⌒ GB 56 C 2
Virginia o AUS 180-181 E 3
Virginia o USA (MN) 42-43 L 2
Virginia ▫ USA 46-47 J 7
Virginia o ZA 220-221 H 4
Virginia Beach o USA 46-47 K 7
Virginia Dale o USA 42-43 E 5
Virginia Falls ~ CDN 30-31 F 5
Virgin Islands ⌒ GB 56 C 3
Virgin Passage ≈ 56 C 2
Virgin River ~ USA 40-41 G 7
Virgolândia o BR 72-73 J 5
Virihaure ⊖ S 86-87 H 3
Virojoki = Virolahti o FIN 88-89 J 6
Virolahti o FIN 88-89 J 6
Virovitica o HR 100-101 F 2
Virrat o FIN 88-89 G 5
Virtsu o EST 94-95 H 2
Viru o PE 64-65 C 6
Virudó o CO 60-61 C 5
Virudunagar o IND 140-141 G 6
Virunga, Parc National des ⊥••• ZRE 212-213 B 4
Vis o HR 100-101 F 3
Vis ⌒ HR 100-101 F 3
Vis ~ NAM 220-221 C 2
Visaginas ☆ LT 94-95 K 4
Visalia o USA 40-41 E 7
Visayan Sea ≈ 160-161 E 7
Visayas ⌒ RP 160-161 F 7
Visby ☆•• S 86-87 J 8
Viscount Melville Sound ≈ 24-25 P 3
Višegrad o• BIH 100-101 G 3
Višera ~ RUS 88-89 V 5
Višera ~ RUS 114-115 D 4
Viseu ☆• P 98-99 D 4
Vishākhapatnam o•• IND 142-143 C 7
Visicsa, Río ~ BOL 70-71 D 6
Visim ~ RUS 114-115 F 3
Visimskij zapovednik ⊥ RUS 96-97 L 5
Visita o BR 66-67 H 6
Visite, La o RH 54-55 J 5
Višneva o BY 94-95 K 4
Višnevka ☆ KA 124-125 H 3
Visočica ▲ HR 100-101 E 2
Visoko o BIH 100-101 G 3
Visrivier o ZA (CAP) 220-221 G 5
Visrivier ~ ZA 220-221 E 5
Visrivierafgronde Park ⊥ NAM 220-221 D 3
Visriviercanyon •• NAM 220-221 C 3
Visrivier Canyon Park, Ai-Ais and ⊥ NAM 220-221 C 3
Vista Alegre o ANG 216-217 C 4
Vista Alegre o BR (AMA) 66-67 E 3
Vista Alegre o BR (AMA) 66-67 C 6
Vista River ~ CDN 24-25 c 4
Visuvisu Point ▲ SOL 184 I c 2
Visviri o RCH 70-71 C 5
Vit ~ BG 102-103 D 6
Vita o IND 140-141 F 2
Vitberget ▲ S 86-87 L 3
Vitebsk = Vicebsk o BY 94-95 M 4
Viterbo ☆• I 100-101 D 3
Vitgenštejna, mys ▲ RUS 112-113 R 6
Vithalapur o IND 138-139 D 8
Vị Thanh o VN 158-159 H 6
Vitiaz Strait ≈ 183 D 3
Vitigudino o E 98-99 D 4
Viti Levu ⌒ FJI 184 III a 2
Vitim o RUS (SAH) 118-119 F 6
Vitim ~ RUS 118-119 F 6
Vitimkan ~ RUS 118-119 E 8
Vitimskij o RUS 118-119 F 6
Vitimskij zapovednik ⊥ RUS 118-119 H 7
Vitimskoe ploskogor'e ⩦ RUS 118-119 F 9
Vitimskoye Ploskogor'ye = Vitimskoe ploskogor'e ⩦ RUS 118-119 F 9
Vitiones, Lago de los ⊖ BOL 70-71 H 6
Vitolište o MK 100-101 H 4
Vitória o BR 76-77 K 5
Vitor o PE 70-71 B 5
Vitoria o BR 68-69 B 3
Vitória ☆ BR 72-73 K 6
Vitória da Conquista o BR 72-73 K 3
Vitória de Santo Antão o BR 68-69 L 6
Vitória do Mearim o BR 68-69 F 3
Vitoria-Gasteiz o• E 98-99 F 3
Vitória Seamount ⩦ 72-73 M 6
Vitorino o BR 74-75 D 6
Vitorino Freire o BR 68-69 F 4
Vitoša, Naroden Park ⊥ BG 102-103 C 6
Vitré o F 90-91 G 7
Vitry-le-François o F 90-91 K 7
Vitshumbi o• ZRE 212-213 B 4
Vitsyebsk = Vicebsk o BY 94-95 M 4
Vittangi o S 86-87 K 3
Vittel o• F 90-91 K 7
Vitichi, Río ~ BOL 70-71 E 7
Vittória o I 100-101 E 6
Vittorio Vèneto o I 100-101 D 1
Vityaz Depth ⩦ 122-123 O 6
Viuda, Isla La ⌒ PE 64-65 C 6
Viuda, La o YV 60-61 K 3
Viudas de Oriente o MEX 50-51 H 6
Vivario o F 98-99 M 3
Viveiro o E 98-99 D 3
Vivero, El o YV 60-61 H 4
Vivi ~ RUS 116-117 H 4
Vivi ~ RUS 116-117 G 2
Vivi, ozero ⊖ RUS 116-117 G 2
Vivian o CDN 34-35 H 6
Vivian o USA 42-43 G 4
Vivo o ZA 218-219 E 6
Vivonne Bay ≈ 180-181 D 4
Vivoratá, Arroyo ~ RA 78-79 L 4
Vivorillo, Cayos ⌒ HN 54-55 D 7
Viwa ⌒ FJI 184 III a 2
Vižas ~ RUS 88-89 S 3
Vizcachas, Meseta de las ⩦ RCH 80 D 5
Vizcachillas, Cerro ▲ BOL 76-77 D 2
Vizcaino, Desierto de ⩦ MEX 50-51 C 4
Vizcaino, Peninsula de ⌣ MEX 50-51 B 4
Vizcaíno, Reserva de la Biósfera El ⊥••• MEX 50-51 B 4
Vizcaya, Golfo de ≈ 90-91 G 10
Vizcaya, Golfo de ≈ 98-99 G 3
Vize, ostrov ⌒ RUS 84-85 p 3
Vizeu o BR 68-69 E 2
Vizianagaram o IND 142-143 C 6
Vizien, Rivière ~ CDN 36-37 N 5
Vizille o F 90-91 K 9
Vizinga o RUS 96-97 G 3
Vizzini o I 100-101 E 6
Vjalozero ⊖ RUS 88-89 N 3
Vjartsilja o RUS 88-89 L 5
Vjatka ~ RUS 96-97 H 4
Vjatskie Poljany ☆ RUS 96-97 G 5
Vjazemskij o RUS 122-123 F 5
Vjaz'ma ☆ RUS 94-95 O 4
Vjazniki o RUS 94-95 S 3
Vjosës, Lumi i ~ AL 100-101 G 4
Vlaanderen ▫ B 92-93 H 3
Vladičin Han o YU 100-101 J 3
Vladikavkaz ☆ RUS 126-127 F 6
Vladimir ☆••• RUS 94-95 R 3
Vladimirovka o KA 124-125 F 2
Vladimirovka o RUS 122-123 K 3
Vladimirovo o RUS 122-123 K 4
Vladivostok o RUS 122-123 D 7
Vlaşca, Drăgăneşti- o RO 102-103 D 5
Vlasenica o BIH 100-101 G 2
Vlas'evo o RUS 122-123 J 2
Vlasovo o RUS 110-111 U 4
V. Lelija ▲ BIH 100-101 G 3
Vlieland ⌒ NL 92-93 H 2
Vlissingen o NL 92-93 G 3
Vlkolínec o••• SK 92-93 P 4
Vlorë ☆•• AL 100-101 G 4
Vltava ~ CZ 92-93 N 4
Vnutrennjaja guba ⊖ RUS 120-121 T 3
Vobkent o US 136-137 J 4
Voč' ~ RUS 96-97 J 3
Vodla ~ RUS 88-89 O 6
Vodlozero, ozero ⊖ RUS 88-89 O 5
Vodnyj o RUS 88-89 W 5
Vodopadnyj, mys ▲ RUS 120-121 U 3
Vogan o RT 202-203 L 6
Vogelkop = Doberai Peninsula ⌣ RI 166-167 F 2
Vogulka ~ RUS 114-115 G 3
Vogul'skij Kamen', gora ▲ RUS 114-115 E 4
Vogvazdino o RUS 88-89 V 5
Vohémar = Iharana o RM 222-223 G 4
Vohilava o RM 222-223 F 8
Vohilengo o RM 222-223 F 6
Vohimena o RM 222-223 F 6
Vohimena ▲ RM 222-223 E 10
Vohimena, Tanjona ▲ RM 222-223 D 10
Vohipeno o RM 222-223 E 9
Vohitra ~ RM 222-223 F 7
Vohitraivo o RM 222-223 F 6
Võhma o EST 94-95 H 2
Võhma o•• EST 94-95 J 2
Vohma o RUS 96-97 E 4
Voi o EAK 212-213 G 5
Voi ~ EAK 212-213 G 5
Voi o VN 156-157 E 7
Voinjama ☆ LB 202-203 F 5
Voiron o F 90-91 K 9
Voisey Bay ≈ 36-37 T 6
Voja, Ust'- o RUS 114-115 D 2
Voja, Ust'- o RUS (KOM) 88-89 Y 4
Vojampolka o RUS 120-121 S 4
Vojampolka (Matëraja) ~ RUS 120-121 S 4
Vojampolka (Žilovaja) ~ RUS 120-121 S 4
Vojejkov šel'fovyj lednik ⌒ ARK 16 G 13
Vojkarsyn'inskij massiv ▲ RUS 114-115 F 2
Vojkor ~ RUS 114-115 G 2
Vojnica o RUS 88-89 L 4
Vojvareto, ozero ⊖ RUS 108-109 P 7
Vojvož o RUS 88-89 X 5
Vokeo Island ⌒ PNG 183 C 2
Vokre, Hosséré ▲ CAM 204-205 K 4
Vol' ~ RUS 88-89 W 5
Volborg o USA 42-43 E 3
Volcán o PA 52-53 C 7
Volcán o RA 76-77 E 2
Volcán, El o RCH 78-79 D 2
Volcán Barú, Parque Nacionale ⊥•• PA 52-53 C 7
Volcán de Colima, Parque Nacional ⊥ MEX 52-53 C 2
Volčanka ~ RUS 108-109 Z 6
Volcano o USA 48-49 E 8
Volcans, Parc National des ⊥ ZRE 212-213 B 4
Volčansk o RUS 114-115 F 5
Volcán Tupungato, Parque Provincial ⊥ RA 78-79 E 2
Volčiha ☆ RUS 124-125 M 3
Volda ☆ N 86-87 C 5
Vol'dino o RUS 88-89 X 5
Volga ~ RUS 94-95 N 3
Volga ~ RUS 96-97 E 10
Volga ~ RUS 96-97 F 10
Volga ~ RUS 96-97 E 8
Volga ~ RUS 126-127 G 5
Volga-Baltic Waterway = Volgo-Baltijskij kanal < RUS 94-95 P 1
Volgo-Baltijskij kanal < RUS 94-95 P 1
Volgodonsk o RUS 102-103 N 4
Volgo-Donskoi kanal < RUS 102-103 N 3
Volgograd = Zarizyn ☆• RUS 96-97 D 9
Volgogradskoe vodohranilišče < RUS (SAR) 96-97 E 8
Volgogradskoe vodohranilišče < RUS (VLG) 96-97 D 9
Volgogradskoye Vodokhranilishche = Volgogradskoe vodohranil. < RUS 96-97 D 9
Volhov o RUS (LEN) 94-95 N 2
Volhov ~ RUS 94-95 N 2
Volimes o GR 100-101 H 6
Volksrust o ZA 220-221 J 3
Volna, gora ▲ RUS 112-113 H 5
Volnovacha o UA 102-103 K 4
Voločanka o RUS 108-109 a 6
Voločys'k ☆ UA 102-103 E 3
Volodarsk ☆ KA 124-125 F 2
Volodarsk o RUS 94-95 S 3
Volodarskij ☆ RUS 96-97 F 10
Volodino o RUS 114-115 S 6
Volodymyr-Volyns'kyj o UA 102-103 D 2
Vologda ☆• RUS 94-95 Q 2
Volokolamsk o• RUS 94-95 O 3
Volokonovka o RUS 102-103 K 2
Volokovaja o RUS 88-89 U 3
Volokvynejtkon, gora ▲ RUS 112-113 R 5
Volop o ZA 220-221 F 4
Vólos o• GR 100-101 J 5
Volosovo ☆ RUS 94-95 L 2
Volot o RUS 94-95 M 3
Volquart Boon Kyst ⩦ GRØ 26-27 o 8
Volšepahk, gora ▲ RUS 88-89 M 2
Vol'sk ☆ RUS 96-97 E 7
Volstruisleegte o ZA 220-221 F 6
Volta ~ GH 202-203 L 7
Volta Blanche ~ BF 202-203 K 3
Voltaire, Cape ▲ AUS 172-173 G 3
Volta Lake < GH 202-203 K 5
Volta Noire ~ BF 202-203 J 4
Volta Redonda o BR 72-73 H 7
Volta Region ▫ GH 202-203 L 5
Volta Rouge ~ BF 202-203 K 4
Volterra o I 100-101 C 3
Volturino, Monte ▲ I 100-101 E 4
Volturno ~ I 100-101 E 4
Voltzberg ▲ SME 62-63 F 3
Volubilis ∴•• MA 188-189 J 3
Vólvi, Límni ⊖ GR 100-101 J 4
Volyns'ka vysočyna ▲ UA 102-103 D 2
Volyns'kyj, Novohrad- o UA 102-103 E 2
Volyns'kyj, Volodymyr- o UA 102-103 D 2
Volzhskiy = Volžskij o RUS 96-97 D 9
Volžsk o RUS 96-97 F 6
Volžskij o RUS 96-97 D 9
Volžsko-Kamskij zapovednik ⊥ RUS 96-97 F 6
Vom o WAN 204-205 H 4
Vonavona = Parara ⌒ SOL 184 I c 3
Vondanka o RUS 96-97 E 4
Vondrove o RM 222-223 D 8
Vondrozo o RM 222-223 E 9
Von Frank Mountain ▲ USA 20-21 N 5
Vónitsa o GR 100-101 H 5
Von Lindequist Gate < NAM 216-217 D 9
Vontimitta o IND 140-141 H 3
Voon, Tarso ▲ TCH 198-199 H 2
Voortrekker fort • ZA 220-221 K 2
Vopnafjarðargrunn ⩦ 86-87 g 1
Vopnafjörður ≈ 86-87 f 2
Vopnafjörður o IS 86-87 f 2
Voranava ☆ BY 94-95 J 4
Voranga ~ RUS 118-119 L 3
Vorarlberg ▫ A 92-93 K 5
Vordingborg o• DK 86-87 E 9
Vóreio Egéo ▫ GR 100-101 K 5
Vorenža o RUS 88-89 N 5
Vorgašor o RUS 108-109 K 8
Vóries Sporádes ⌣ GR 100-101 J 5
Vøringfossen •• N 86-87 C 6
Vøring Plateau ⩦ 6-7 K 2
Vor'ja ~ RUS 114-115 G 3
Vorkuta ☆ RUS 108-109 K 8
Vorkuta ~ RUS 108-109 K 8
Vorma ~ N 86-87 E 6
Vormamay o AFG 138-139 B 3
Vormsi saar ⌒ EST 94-95 H 2
Vorob'evo o RUS 114-115 O 6
Vorogovka ~ RUS 116-117 E 5
Vorona ~ RUS 94-95 S 5
Vorona ~ RUS 102-103 N 2
Voroncovka o RUS 118-119 F 6
Voroncovo o RUS 108-109 U 6
Voronet o••• RO 102-103 D 4
Voronež o RUS 102-103 L 2
Voronež ~ RUS 94-95 Q 5
Voronezh = Voronež o RUS 102-103 L 2
Voronina, ostrov ⌒ RUS 108-109 a 2
Voron'ja ~ RUS 88-89 N 2
Voronov, mys ▲ RUS 88-89 R 3
Vorošilovgrad = Luhans'k ☆ UA 102-103 L 3
Vorotan ~ AR 128-129 L 3
Vorotynec o RUS 96-97 D 5
Vorožba o UA 102-103 J 2
Vorskla ~ RUS 102-103 J 2
Vorsma o RUS 94-95 S 4
Vorstershoop o ZA 220-221 F 2
Vörtsjärv järv ⊖ EST 94-95 K 2
Võru ☆•• EST 94-95 K 3
Vosburg o ZA 220-221 F 5
Vose o TJ 136-137 L 6
Vosges ▲ F 90-91 K 8
Voskopojë o• AL 100-101 H 4
Voskresenovka o RUS 122-123 C 3
Voskresensk ☆• RUS 94-95 Q 4
Voskresenskoe o RUS 94-95 P 3
Voskresenskoo, buhta ⊖ RUS 108-109 X 4
Vossavangen o• N 86-87 C 6
Vostočnaja, kosa ⌒ RUS 108-109 R 5
Vostočnaja Handyga ~ RUS 120-121 G 2
Vostočnoe Munozero ⊖ RUS 88-89 N 3
Vostočno-Sahalinskie gory ▲ RUS 122-123 K 3
Vostočnyj, proliv ≈ 110-111 H 2
Vostočnyj o RUS (CUK) 112-113 W 3
Vostočnyj o RUS (SHL) 122-123 K 4
Vostočnyj hrebet ▲ RUS 120-121 S 7
Vostočnyj Kamennyj, ostrov ⌒ RUS 108-109 U 4
Vostočnyj Sinij, hrebet ▲ RUS 122-123 E 7
Vostočnyj Tannu-Ola, hrebet ▲ RUS 116-117 F 10
Vostok o ARK 16 F 11
Vostok o RUS 122-123 F 5
Votkinsk ☆ RUS 96-97 J 5
Votkinskoe vodohranilišče < RUS 96-97 J 5
Votkinskoye Vodokhranilishche = Votkinskoe vodohranilišče < RUS 96-97 J 5
Vot Tande ⌒ VAN 184 II a 1
Votuporanga o BR 72-73 F 6
Vouga o ANG 216-217 D 6
Vouga, Rio ~ P 98-99 C 4
Vouka o RCB 210-211 D 5
Vouliagméni o GR 100-101 J 6
Vouzela o P 98-99 C 4
Vovča ~ UA 102-103 K 3
Vovča ~ UA 102-103 J 3
Vovčans'k o UA 102-103 K 2
Vovodo ~ RCA 206-207 G 5
Voxna o S 86-87 G 6
Voyageurs National Park ⊥ USA 42-43 L 1
Vože, ozero ⊖ RUS 94-95 Q 1
Vožega o RUS 94-95 R 1
Vožgora o RUS 88-89 U 4
Voznesens'k o UA 102-103 G 4
Voznesenskoe o RUS 94-95 S 4
Vozroždenie o RUS 96-97 F 7
Vozroždenija otasi ⌒ US 136-137 F 2
Vozvraščenija, gora ▲ RUS 122-123 K 4
vpadina Assake-Audan ⌣ US 136-137 E 3
Vraca o BG 102-103 C 6
Vrangelja, mys ▲ RUS 120-121 H 6
Vrangelja, ostrov ⌒ RUS 112-113 U 1
Vranica ▲ BIH 100-101 F 2
Vraška čuka, Prohod ▲ BG 102-103 C 6
Vrbas ~ BIH 100-101 F 2
Vrede o ZA 220-221 J 3
Vredefort o ZA 220-221 H 3
Vredenburg o ZA 220-221 C 6
Vredendal o ZA 220-221 D 5
Vredeshoop o NAM 220-221 D 3
Vreed-en-Hoop o GUY 62-63 E 2
Vreede Stein o GUY 62-63 E 2
Vriddhāchalam o IND 140-141 H 5
Vrigstad o S 86-87 G 8
Vrissa o GR 100-101 L 5
Vroolijk, Pulau ⌒ RI 164-165 L 4
Vršac o• YU 100-101 H 2
Vryburg o ZA 220-221 G 3
Vryheid o ZA 220-221 K 3
Vsesvjats'kyj kostel • UA 102-103 C 3
Vsevidof, Mount ▲ USA 22-23 M 6
Vsevidof Island ⌒ USA 22-23 M 6
Vsevoložsk ☆ RUS 94-95 M 1
Vstrečnyj o RUS 112-113 N 3
Vtoroj Kuril'skij proliv ⊖ RUS 122-123 R 3
Vuadil' o US 136-137 M 4
Vube o ZRE 212-213 A 2
Vui-Uata Nova Itália, Área Indígena ⚔ BR 66-67 C 4
Vuka ~ HR 100-101 G 2
Vukovar o• HR 100-101 G 2
Vuktyl ☆ RUS 114-115 D 3
Vulavu o SOL 184 I d 3
Vulcan o CDN 32-33 O 6
Vulcano, Ísola ⌒ I 100-101 E 5
Vulcan Shoal ⌒ AUS 172-173 G 2
Vulkannyj hrebet ▲ RUS 112-113 N 3
Vulsinio = Lago di Bolsena ⊖ I 100-101 C 3
Vulture, Monte ▲ I 100-101 E 4
Vul'vyveem ~ RUS 112-113 T 3
Vumba Gardens ⊥ ZW 218-219 G 4
Vumba Mountains ▲ ZW 218-219 G 4
Vũng Hòn Khói ≈ 158-159 K 4
Vũng Lăng Mai ≈ 158-159 K 4
Vũng Tàu ☆• VN 158-159 J 5
Vunisea o FJI 184 III b 3
Vuokatti o FIN 88-89 K 4
Vuolijoki o FIN 88-89 J 4
Vuollerim o S 86-87 K 3
Vuolvojaure ⊖ S 86-87 J 3
Vuotso o FIN 88-89 J 2
Vuranggo o SOL 184 I c 2
Vurnary o RUS 96-97 E 6
Vuxikou o VRC 154-155 L 6
Vwaza Game Reserve ⊥ MW 214-215 G 6
Vyaparla o IND 140-141 H 2
Vybor o RUS 94-95 L 3
Vyborg ☆• RUS 94-95 L 1
Vyčegda ~ RUS 88-89 W 6
Vydrino o RUS 116-117 M 10
Vydropužsk o RUS 94-95 O 3
Vyezžij Log o RUS 116-117 F 8
Vygoniči o RUS 94-95 O 5
Vygozero ⊖ RUS 88-89 N 5
Vyhanaščanskoe, vozero ⊖ BY 94-95 J 5
Vyhodnoj, mys ▲ RUS 108-109 G 5
Vyja ~ RUS 88-89 S 5
Vyksa ☆ RUS 94-95 S 4
Vylkove o UA 102-103 F 5
Vym' ~ RUS 88-89 V 5
Vym' ~ RUS 88-89 V 4
Vyngajaha ~ RUS 114-115 O 2
Vyngapurovskij o RUS 114-115 O 3
Vyra o RUS 94-95 L 2
Vys', gora ▲ RUS 112-113 H 5
Vyšhorod o UA 102-103 G 2
Vyšnij Voloček ☆ RUS 94-95 O 3
Vysoke o BY 94-95 H 5
Vysokaja, gora ▲ RUS 122-123 N 6
Vysokaja Gora ☆ RUS 96-97 F 6
Vysokaja gora ▲ RUS 120-121 V 4
Vysokaja Parma vozvyšennost' ▲ RUS 114-115 E 4
Vysokij, mys ▲ RUS (KOR) 112-113 R 6
Vysokij, mys ▲ RUS (SAH) 110-111 a 2
Vysokogornyj o RUS 122-123 H 3
Vytegra ☆• RUS 88-89 O 6
Vyvenka o RUS (KOR) 120-121 V 3
Vyvenka ~ RUS 112-113 P 6
Vyvenka ~ RUS 120-121 V 3

W

Wa o GH 202-203 F 6
Wa ☆• GH 202-203 J 4
Waaheen, togga ~ SP 208-209 G 3
Waajid o SP 212-213 J 2
Waal ~ NL 92-93 H 3
Waangyi-Garawa Aboriginal Land ⚔ AUS 174-175 D 6
Waar, Pulau ⌒ RI 166-167 H 3
Waara o RI 164-165 H 6
Waarlangier, Tanjung ▲ RI 166-167 G 5
Waat o SUD 206-207 L 4
Wabag ☆• PNG 183 B 3
Wabakimi Lake ⊖ CDN 34-35 M 5
Wabakimi Provincial Park ⊥ CDN 34-35 M 5
Wabamun Lake ~ CDN 32-33 N 5
Wabasca Indian Reserve ⚔ CDN 32-33 O 4
Wabasca River ~ CDN 32-33 N 3
Wabash o USA 46-47 F 5
Wabasha o USA 42-43 L 3
Wabash River ~ USA 46-47 F 5
Wabassi River ~ CDN 34-35 N 5
Wabē Shebelē Wenz ~ ETH 208-209 E 5
Wabigoon Lake ⊖ CDN 34-35 K 6
Wabimeig Lake ⊖ CDN 34-35 O 5
Wabinosh Lake ⊖ CDN 34-35 M 5
Wabo o PNG 183 C 4
Wabowden o CDN 34-35 G 3
Wabuda o PNG 183 B 5
Wabuda Island ⌒ PNG 183 B 5
Wabuk Point ▲ CDN 34-35 O 3
Waburton Bay o CDN 30-31 N 4
Waccasassa Bay ≈ 48-49 G 5
Wach'īlē o ETH 208-209 D 6
Waci o RI 164-165 L 3
Waco o CDN 38-39 M 3
Waco o USA 44-45 J 4
Wacuach, Lac ⊖ CDN 36-37 Q 7
Wad o PK 134-135 M 5
Wada'ah o SUD 200-201 B 6
Wadalai o PNG 183 F 5
Wadamago o SP 208-209 H 4
Wad an-Nail o SUD 200-201 G 6
Wadau o PNG 183 D 3
Wadayama o J 152-153 F 7
Wad Bandah o SUD 200-201 C 6
Wad Ban Naqa o SUD 200-201 F 4
Wadbilliga National Park ⊥ AUS 180-181 K 4
Waddān o• LAR 192-193 G 3
Waddān, Jabal ▲ LAR 192-193 G 3
Waddell Bay ≈ 36-37 Q 3
Waddenzee ≈ 92-93 H 2
Waddikee o AUS 180-181 D 2
Waddington, Mount ▲ CDN 32-33 H 6
Waddy Point ▲ AUS 178-179 M 3
Wade Lake ⊖ CDN 36-37 R 7
Wadena o CDN 34-35 E 5
Wadena o USA 42-43 K 2
Wadesboro o USA 48-49 H 2
Wadeye o AUS 172-173 J 3
Wad Hāmid o SUD 200-201 F 4
Wadham Islands ⌒ CDN 38-39 I S 4
Wad Hassib o SUD 206-207 H 3
Wadhope o CDN 34-35 J 5
Wadi o IND 140-141 G 2
Wādi Gimal, Gazirat ⌒ ET 194-195 G 5
Wādi Halfā o SUD 200-201 E 2
Wādi Seidna o SUD 200-201 F 5
Wadley o USA 48-49 G 3
Wad Madani ☆ SUD 200-201 F 5
Wad Nafarein o SUD 200-201 F 6
Wadomari o J 152-153 C 11
Wad Rāwah o SUD 200-201 F 5
Wadsworth o USA 40-41 E 6
Waenhuiskrans o ZA 220-221 E 7
Waeplau o RI 166-167 D 3
Waeputih o RI 166-167 D 3
Waerana o RI 168 E 7
Wafangdian o VRC 150-151 C 8
Wafra, al- o KWT 130-131 K 3
Wagait Aboriginal Land ⚔ AUS 172-173 K 2
Wagan o PNG 183 D 4
Waga River ~ PNG 183 B 4
Wagau o PNG 183 D 4
Wagdari o IND 140-141 G 2
Wageningen o SME 62-63 F 3
Wager, Isla ⌒ RCH 80 C 3
Wager Bay ≈ 30-31 Z 3
Wageseri o RI 166-167 K 2
Wagga Wagga o AUS 180-181 J 3
Wağh, al- o KSA 130-131 E 4
Waghai o IND 138-139 D 9
Waghete o RI 166-167 J 4
Waǧid, Ǧabal al- ▲ KSA 132-133 D 4
Wagin o AUS 176-177 D 6
Wagner o BR 72-73 K 2
Wagner o USA 42-43 H 4
Wagny = Ouana ~ G 210-211 D 4
Wagon Mound o USA 44-45 E 1
Wagontire o USA 40-41 E 4
Wagrowiec o• PL 92-93 O 2
Waha o RI 164-165 H 6
Wahabu o GH 202-203 J 4
Wahai o RI 166-167 E 3
Wahala o RT 202-203 L 6
Wah Cantonment o PK 138-139 D 3
Wahi o PK 134-135 M 6
Wahiawa o USA 48-49 C 7
Wahlbergøya ⌒ N 84-85 L 3
Wahlebone Cape ▲ USA 22-23 N 6
Wahlenbergfjorden ≈ 84-85 L 3
Wahoo o USA 42-43 J 5
Wahpeton o USA 42-43 J 2
Wahrān ☆ DZ 138-189 L 3
Wahroonga o AUS 176-177 C 2
Wai o IND 140-141 E 2
Waialua o USA (HI) 48-49 C 7
Waialua o USA (HI) 48-49 D 7
Waian o RC 156-157 L 5
Waianae o USA 48-49 C 7
Waiãpi, Área Indígena ⚔ BR 62-63 H 5
Waiau o NZ 182 D 5
Waibula o PNG 183 F 5
Waidhān o IND 142-143 C 3
Waidhofen an der Thaya o A 92-93 N 4
Waidu o WAL 202-203 E 5
Waigen Lakes ⊖ AUS 176-177 K 3
Waigeo, Pulau ⌒ RI 166-167 F 2
Waihau Bay o NZ 182 F 2
Waihi o NZ 182 E 2
Waiji, Pulau ⌒ RI 166-167 F 2
Waikabubak o• RI 168 D 7
Waikaia o NZ 182 B 6
Waikaremoana o NZ 182 F 3
Waikawa o NZ 182 B 7
Waikelo o RI 168 D 7
Waikerie o AUS 180-181 E 3
Waikiki Beach <• USA 48-49 D 7
Wailapa o VAN 184 II a 2
Wailebe o RI 166-167 B 6
Wailuku o USA 48-49 D 7
Waimanguar o RI 168 D 7
Waimate o NZ 182 C 6
Waimea o USA 48-49 E 7
Waimenda o RI 164-165 G 5
Waimiri Atroari, Área Indígena ⚔ BR 62-63 D 6
Wainganga ~ IND 138-139 G 9
Waingapu o RI 168 E 7
Waini River ~ GUY 62-63 E 1
Wainwright o CDN 32-33 P 5
Wainwright o USA 20-21 L 1
Waiouru o NZ 182 E 3
Waipa o RI 166-167 J 3
Waipara o NZ 182 D 5
Waipawa o NZ 182 F 3
Waipoua Kauri Forest • NZ 182 D 1
Waipukang o RI 166-167 B 6
Waipukurau o NZ 182 F 4
Wair o RI 166-167 G 4
Waira o PNG (GUL) 183 B 4
Waira o PNG (GUL) 183 C 4
Wairaha ~ SOL 184 I e 3
Wairoa o NZ 182 F 3
Wairunu o RI 166-167 B 6
Waisa o PNG 183 C 4
Waitakaruru o NZ 182 E 2
Waitaki o NZ 182 C 6
Waitaki River ~ NZ 182 C 6
Waitangi o•• NZ 182 E 1
Waitara o NZ 182 E 3
Waitati o NZ 182 C 6
Waitomo Caves • NZ 182 E 3
Waitsburg o USA 40-41 E 2
Waiuku o NZ 182 E 2
Waiwa o PNG 183 E 5
Waiwai o GUY 62-63 E 5
Waiwerang o RI 166-167 B 6
Waje o WAN 204-205 G 4
Wajima o J 152-153 G 6
Wajir o EAK 212-213 H 3
Waka o ETH 208-209 C 5
Waka o RI 168 E 7
Waka o ZRE (EQU) 210-211 H 4
Waka o ZRE (EQU) 210-211 H 3
Waka, Tanjung ▲ RI 166-167 D 3
Wakaf Tapai o MAL 162-163 E 2
Wakamoek o RI 166-167 F 2
Wakasa-wan ≈ 152-153 F 7
Wakasawan Quasi National Park ⊥ J 152-153 F 7
Wakatin o RI 166-167 D 3
Wakatipu, Lake ⊖ NZ 182 B 6
Wakaw o CDN 34-35 D 4
Wakay o SME 62-63 F 3
Wakaya ⌒ FJI 184 III b 2
Wakayama ☆ J 152-153 F 7
Wakde, Pulau ⌒ RI 166-167 K 2
WaKeeney o USA 42-43 H 6
Wakefield o CDN 38-39 G 6
Wakefield o NZ 182 D 4
Wakefield o USA (MI) 46-47 D 2
Wakefield o USA (RI) 46-47 N 5
Wakefield River ~ AUS 180-181 E 3
Wakeham, Rivière ~ CDN 36-37 N 4
Wakingku o RI 164-165 H 6
Wakinosawa o J 152-153 J 4
Wakkanai o J 152-153 J 2
Wakkerstroom o ZA 220-221 K 3
Waklarok o USA 20-21 H 5
Wako o PNG 183 E 4
Wakomata Lake ⊖ CDN 38-39 C 5
Wakooo o AUS 180-181 H 3
Wakool River ~ AUS 180-181 G 3
Wakulla Springs • USA 48-49 F 4
Wakunai o PNG 184 I b 1
Wala ~ EAT 212-213 D 6
Walachia ⩦ RO 102-103 D 5
Wālājāpet o IND 140-141 H 4
Walakpa o USA 20-21 M 1
Walambele o GH 202-203 K 4
Walamo, El o MEX 50-51 F 6
Walanae ~ RI 164-165 G 6
Wal Athiang o SUD 206-207 J 5
Wałbrzych ☆• PL 92-93 O 3
Walbundrie o AUS 180-181 J 3
Walcha o AUS 178-179 L 6
Walckenaer, Teluk ≈ 166-167 K 3
Walcott o CDN 32-33 G 4
Walcott o USA 42-43 D 5
Walcott Inlet ≈ 172-173 G 4
Wałcz o• PL 92-93 O 2
Waldburg o AUS 176-177 D 2
Waldburg Range ▲ AUS 176-177 D 2
Walden o USA 42-43 D 5
Waldenburg o USA 44-45 M 2
Walden Ridge ▲ USA 48-49 F 2
Waldersee o CDN 34-35 G 5
Waldo o USA 48-49 G 5
Waldorf o USA 46-47 K 6
Waldport o USA 40-41 B 3
Waldron o USA 44-45 K 2
Walea, Selat ≈ 164-165 H 4
Waleabahi, Pulau ⌒ RI 164-165 H 4
Waleakodi, Pulau ⌒ RI 164-165 H 4
Waleri o RI 168 D 3
Wales ▫ GB 90-91 E 5
Wales o USA 20-21 F 4
Wales Island ⌒ CDN 24-25 c 6

330 Villarpando — Wales Island

Walewale ○ GH 202-203 K 4
Walfe, Chute ∼ ZRE 210-211 J 6
Walgett ○ AUS 178-179 K 6
Walgra ○ AUS 178-179 E 1
Walgreen Coast ⌣ ARK 16 F 26
Walhalla ○ USA 42-43 J 1
Walhalla Historic Site ∴ USA 42-43 H 1
Walikale ○ ZRE 212-213 B 4
Walir, Pulau ⌒ RI 166-167 G 4
Walis Island ⌒ PNG 183 B 2
Walk = Valga ☆ ·· EST 94-95 K 3
Walker ○ USA (MI) 46-47 F 4
Walker ○ USA (MN) 42-43 K 2
Walker, Mount ▲ CDN 24-25 Z 4
Walker Baldwin Range ▲ CDN 24-25 S 3
Walker Bay ≈ 24-25 N 5
Walker Bay ≈ 220-221 D 7
Walker Creek ∼ AUS 176-177 M 2
Walker Lake ○ CDN (MAN) 34-35 H 3
Walker Lake ○ CDN (NWT) 30-31 Y 2
Walker Lake ○ USA (AK) 20-21 N 3
Walker Lake ○ USA (NV) 40-41 E 6
Walker Mountains ▲ ARK 16 F 26
Walker River ∼ AUS 174-175 C 3
Walker River ∼ USA 40-41 E 6
Walker River Indian Reservation X USA 40-41 E 6
Walkerston ○ AUS 178-179 K 1
Walkerville ○ AUS 180-181 H 5
Wall ○ USA 42-43 F 3
Wall, Mount ▲ AUS 172-173 C 7
Wallabi Group ⌒ AUS 176-177 B 4
Wallace ○ USA (ID) 40-41 G 2
Wallace ○ USA (NE) 42-43 G 5
Wallaceburg ○ CDN 38-39 C 7
Wallace River ○ CDN 30-31 W 5
Wallachisch Meseritsch = Valašské Meziříčí ○ CZ 92-93 O 4
Wallal Downs ○ AUS 172-173 E 5
Wallambin, L. ○ AUS 176-177 D 5
Wallam Creek ∼ AUS 178-179 J 5
Wallareenya ○ AUS 172-173 D 6
Wallaroo ○ AUS 180-181 D 2
Walla Walla ○ USA 40-41 E 2
Wallekraal ○ ZA 220-221 C 5
Wallhallow ○ AUS 174-175 C 5
Walliser Alpen ▲ CH 92-93 J 5
Wallis Lake ○ AUS 180-181 M 2
Walløe, Kap ▲ GRØ 28-29 T 6
Wallonie □ B 92-93 H 3
Wallowa Mountains ▲ USA 40-41 F 3
Walls of China, The · AUS 180-181 G 2
Wallula ○ USA 40-41 E 2
Wallumbilla ○ AUS 178-179 K 4
Walmanpa-Warlpiri Aboriginal Land X AUS 172-173 K 5
Walnut ○ USA 48-49 D 2
Walnut Canyon National Monument · USA 40-41 J 8
Walnut Cove ○ USA 48-49 H 1
Walnut Creek ∼ USA 42-43 G 6
Walnut Grove ○ USA 42-43 K 3
Walpeup ○ AUS 180-181 G 3
Walpole ○ AUS 176-177 D 7
Walpole Island Indian Reserve X CDN 38-39 C 7
Walrus Island ⌒ USA 22-23 Q 4
Walrus Islands ⌒ USA 22-23 Q 3
Walrus Islands State Game Sanctuary ⊥ USA 22-23 Q 3
Walsall ○ GB 90-91 G 5
Walsenburg ○ USA 44-45 E 1
Walsh ○ USA 44-45 F 1
Walsh River ∼ AUS 174-175 H 5
Walsingham, Cape ▲ CDN 28-29 K 3
Walsrode ○ D 92-93 K 2
Walt Disney World ·· USA 48-49 H 5
Walterboro ○ USA 48-49 H 3
Walter James Range ▲ AUS 176-177 K 2
Waltershausen Gletscher ⊂ GRØ 26-27 n 6
Waltham Station ○ CDN 38-39 F 6
Walthill ○ USA 42-43 J 4
Walton ○ CDN 38-39 M 6
Walton ○ USA 46-47 F 6
Walton, Mount ▲ AUS 176-177 F 5
Walue ○ RI 164-165 H 6
Walungu ○ ZRE 212-213 B 5
Walvisbaai ≈ 220-221 B 1
Walvisbaai = Walvis Bay ☆ · NAM 220-221 B 1
Walvis Bay ☆ · NAM 220-221 B 1
Walvis Ridge ≃ 6-7 K 11
Wamal ○ RI 166-167 K 6
Wamala, Lake ○ EAU 212-213 C 3
Wamanfo ○ GH 202-203 J 6
Wamar, Pulau ⌒ RI 166-167 H 4
Wamaza ○ ZRE 210-211 L 6
Wamba ○ EAK 212-213 F 3
Wamba ∸ WAN 204-205 H 4
Wamba ○ ZRE 212-213 B 2
Wamba ∼ ZRE 216-217 D 3
Wamba-Luadi ○ ZRE 216-217 D 3
Wamba Mountains ▲ WAN 204-205 J 5
Wamdé Tabal ▲ BF 202-203 K 2
Wamena ○ RI 166-167 K 4
Wamera Island ⌒ PNG 183 F 5
Wami ∼ EAT 214-215 K 4
Wamis ○ LAR 192-193 E 2
Wamoi Falls ∼ PNG 183 B 4
Wamonket, Tanjung ▲ RI 166-167 F 2
Wampembe ○ EAT 214-215 F 4
Wamtakin, Mount ▲ PNG 183 A 3
Wāna ○ PK 138-139 B 3
Wanaaring ○ AUS 178-179 H 5
Wanaka ○ NZ 182 B 6
Wanaka, Lake ○ NZ 182 B 6
Wanapitae Lake ○ CDN 38-39 D 5
Wanapitei ○ CDN 38-39 D 5
Wanapitei River ∼ CDN 38-39 D 5
Wanasabari ○ RI 164-165 H 6
Wanau ○ RI 166-167 G 2
Wanbu ○ VRC 156-157 J 2
Wanci ○ RI 164-165 H 6
Wandagee ○ AUS 176-177 C 1
Wandai (Homeyo) ○ RI 166-167 J 3
Wandamen, Teluk ≈ 166-167 H 3
Wandamen Peninsula ⌒ RI 166-167 H 3
Wanda Shan ▲ VRC 150-151 H 5
Wandel, Kap ▲ GRØ 28-29 X 3
Wandering River ∼ CDN 32-33 O 4
Wanderlândia ○ BR 68-69 E 5
Wanding ○ VRC 142-143 L 3
Wando ○ PNG 183 A 5
Wando ○ ROK 150-151 F 10
Wandoan ○ AUS 178-179 K 4
Wandokai ○ PNG 183 D 4
Wanesabe ○ RI 168 C 7
Wanfotang Shiku · VRC 150-151 C 7
Wang ○ PNG 183 G 2
Wanga ○ ZRE 212-213 B 2
Wanga Mountains ▲ WAN 204-205 J 5
Wanganui ○ NZ 182 E 3
Wanganui River ∼ NZ 182 E 3
Wangaratta ○ AUS 180-181 J 4
Wangary ○ AUS 180-181 C 3
Wangasi-Turu ○ GH 202-203 K 5
Wangcang ○ VRC 154-155 E 5
Wangcheng ○ VRC 156-157 H 2
Wangdi Phodrang ○ BHT 142-143 F 2
Wangerooge ⌒ D 92-93 J 2
Wanggamet, Gunung ▲ RI 168 E 8
Wanggao ○ VRC 156-157 G 4
Wanggar ○ RI 166-167 H 3
Wanggar ∼ RI 166-167 H 3
Wangi ○ AUS 172-173 K 2
Wāngi ○ IND 138-139 E 10
Wangianna ○ AUS 178-179 D 5
Wangiwangi, Pulau ⌒ RI 164-165 H 6
Wangjiang ○ VRC 154-155 K 6
Wangjie ○ VRC 156-157 B 5
Wangkí, Río = Coco o Segovia ∼ HN 52-53 B 4
Wangmo ○ VRC 156-157 E 4
Wang Nam Yen ○ THA 158-159 G 4
Wangon ○ RI 168 C 3
Wangpan Yang ≈ 154-155 M 6
Wang Sam Mo ○ THA 158-159 G 2
Wang Saphung ○ THA 158-159 F 2
Wang Thong ○ THA 158-159 F 2
Wang Wiset ○ THA 158-159 E 7
Wangziguan ○ VRC 154-155 D 5
Wanham ○ CDN 32-33 L 4
Wan Hsa-la ○ MYA 142-143 L 5
Wanhuayan · VRC 156-157 H 4
Wani ○ IND 138-139 G 9
Wanie-Rukula ○ ZRE 210-211 K 3
Wanigela ○ PNG 183 E 5
Wānkāner ○ IND 138-139 C 8
Wanless ○ CDN 34-35 F 3
Wanleweeyn ○ SP 212-213 K 2
Wan Long ○ MYA 142-143 L 4
Wanlong ○ VRC 154-155 E 6
Wanna ○ AUS 176-177 D 1
Wanna Lakes ○ AUS 176-177 K 4
Wannarra ○ AUS 176-177 D 4
Wannian ○ VRC 156-157 K 2
Wannian Temple ○ VRC 156-157 C 2
Wannianxue ▲ VRC 154-155 C 6
Wanning ○ VRC 156-157 G 7
Wannon River ∼ AUS 180-181 F 4
Wannoo ○ AUS 176-177 C 3
Wanparti ○ IND 140-141 H 2
Wan Pong ○ MYA 142-143 L 5
Wanqing ○ VRC 150-151 G 6
Wanshan Qundao ⌒ VRC 156-157 J 6
Wansra ○ RI 166-167 H 2
Wantang ○ VRC 156-157 C 5
Wantoat ○ PNG 183 D 4
Wan Xian ○ VRC 154-155 F 6
Wanyuan ○ VRC 154-155 F 5
Wanzai ○ VRC 156-157 J 2
Waogena ○ RI 164-165 H 6
Wapanucka ○ USA 44-45 J 2
Wapaseese River ∼ CDN 34-35 L 3
Wapato ○ USA 40-41 D 2
Wapawekka Hills ▲ CDN 34-35 D 3
Wapawekka Lake ○ CDN 34-35 D 3
Wapella ○ CDN 34-35 F 5
Wapello ○ USA 46-47 C 5
Wapenamanda ○ PNG 183 B 3
Wapet Camp ○ AUS 172-173 B 6
Wāpi ○ IND 138-139 D 9
Wapikopa Lake ○ CDN 34-35 M 4
Wapi Pathum ○ THA 158-159 G 3
Wapoga ∼ RI 166-167 J 3
Wapomaru ○ RI 164-165 H 6
Wapotih ○ RI 166-167 D 3
Wappapello ○ USA 46-47 C 7
Wappapello, Lake ○ USA 44-45 M 1
Waprak ○ RI 166-167 H 3
Wapuli ○ GH 202-203 L 5
Wapumba Island ⌒ PNG 183 B 5
Wara ○ WAN 204-205 F 3
Waradi ‹ EAK 212-213 H 3
Warakaraket, Pulau ⌒ RI 166-167 F 3
Warakurna X AUS 176-177 K 2
Warambif ○ PNG 183 G 3
Warandab ○ ETH 208-209 G 5
Waranga Basin ‹ AUS 180-181 H 4
Warangal ○ · IND 138-139 G 10
Wararisbari, Tanjung ▲ RI 166-167 J 2
Waratah ○ AUS 180-181 H 6
Wara Wara Mountains. ▲ WAL 202-203 E 5
Warbreccan ○ AUS 178-179 G 3
Warburg ○ CDN 32-33 N 5
Warburton ○ AUS (VIC) 180-181 H 4
Warburton X AUS (WA) 176-177 J 3
Warburton ○ ZA 220-221 K 3
Warburton Creek ∼ AUS 178-179 E 4
Warburton Range ▲ AUS 176-177 J 3
Warburton Range Aboriginal Land X AUS 176-177 J 2
Ward ○ NZ 182 E 4
Wardak □ AFG 138-139 B 2
Wardang Island ⌒ AUS 180-181 D 3
Ward Cove ○ USA 32-33 E 4
Wardé ○ RMM 202-203 G 2
Warden ○ ZA 220-221 J 3
Wardha ○ IND (MAH) 138-139 G 9
Wardha ∼ IND 138-139 G 10
Wardha ∼ IND 138-139 G 9
War Dhugulle ‹ SP 212-213 K 2
Ward Hunt, Cape ▲ PNG 183 E 5
Ward Hunt Island ⌒ CDN 26-27 N 2
Ward Hunt Strait ≈ 183 F 5
Ward Inlet ≈ 36-37 Q 3
Wardlaw, Kap ▲ GRØ 26-27 p 8
Wardo ○ RI 166-167 H 2
Ware ○ CDN 32-33 H 3
Waren ○ RI 166-167 J 3
Waren ∼ RI 166-167 J 3
Waren (Müritz) ○ · D 92-93 M 2
Warenda ○ AUS 178-179 F 2
Warfallah, Ra's ▲ LAR 192-193 F 3
War Galoh ○ SP 208-209 H 5
Wariai, Tanjung ▲ RI 166-167 F 2
Warialda ○ AUS 178-179 L 5
Waria River ∼ PNG 183 D 4
Wāri Godri ○ IND 138-139 E 10
Wari Island ⌒ PNG 183 F 6
Warilau ○ RI 166-167 H 4
Warilau, Pulau ⌒ RI 166-167 H 4
Warin Chamrap ○ THA 158-159 H 3
Waring Mountains ▲ USA 20-21 K 3
Wario River ∼ PNG 183 B 3
Wāris Aliganj ○ IND 142-143 D 3
Warkopi ○ RI 166-167 H 2
Warkworth ○ NZ 182 E 2
Warman ○ CDN 34-35 C 4
Warmandi ○ RI 166-167 G 2
Warmbad ○ NAM 220-221 D 4
Warmbad ○ ZA 220-221 J 2
Warm Baths = Warmbad ○ ZA 220-221 J 2
Warming Land ∸ GRØ 26-27 Y 3
Warm Springs ○ USA (NV) 40-41 F 6
Warm Springs ○ USA (OR) 40-41 D 3
Warm Springs Indian Reservation X USA 40-41 D 3
Warnemünde ○ D 92-93 M 1
Warner ○ CDN 32-33 O 7
Warner ○ USA 44-45 K 2
Warner Mountains ▲ USA 40-41 D 4
Warner Range ▲ USA 40-41 D 5
Warner Robins ○ USA 48-49 G 3
Warnes ○ RA 78-79 J 3
Warning, Mount ▲ AUS 178-179 M 5
Warnow ∼ D 92-93 L 2
Waromge, Teluk ≈ 166-167 F 2
Warooka ○ AUS 180-181 D 3
Waroona ○ AUS 176-177 C 6
Waropen, Teluk ≈ 166-167 J 2
Waropko ○ RI 166-167 L 4
Warora ○ IND 138-139 G 9
Warra ○ AUS 178-179 L 4
Warrabri X AUS 178-179 C 1
Warracknabeal ○ AUS 180-181 G 4
Warragul ○ AUS 180-181 H 5
Warrakalanna, Lake ○ AUS 178-179 E 5
Warrakunta Point ▲ AUS 174-175 C 4
Warralakin ○ AUS 176-177 E 5
Warral Island ⌒ AUS 183 B 6
Warrandirinna, Lake ○ AUS 178-179 D 4
Warrawagine ○ AUS 172-173 E 6
Warrego Highway II AUS 178-179 J 4
Warrego Mine · AUS 174-175 B 6
Warrego Range ▲ AUS 178-179 H 3
Warrego River ∼ AUS 178-179 H 4
Warren ○ AUS 178-179 J 6
Warren ○ CDN 34-35 H 5
Warren ○ USA (AR) 44-45 L 3
Warren ○ USA (MI) 46-47 G 4
Warren ○ USA (MN) 42-43 J 1
Warren ○ USA (MT) 42-43 C 3
Warren ○ USA (NH) 46-47 N 4
Warren ○ USA (OH) 46-47 H 5
Warren ○ USA (PA) 46-47 J 5
Warrendale ○ USA 46-47 H 5
Warrender, Port ○ AUS 172-173 G 3
Warren Point ▲ CDN 20-21 Y 2
Warrensburg ○ USA 42-43 L 6
Warrens Landing ○ CDN 34-35 H 4
Warrenton ○ USA (GA) 48-49 G 3
Warrenton ○ USA (VA) 46-47 K 6
Warrenton ○ ZA 220-221 G 4
Warren Vale ○ AUS 174-175 F 6
Warri ○ WAN 204-205 F 6
Warriedar ○ AUS 176-177 D 4
Warriedar Hill ▲ AUS 176-177 D 4
Warriner Creek ∼ AUS 178-179 D 5
Warrington ○ USA 48-49 E 4
Warrington Bay ≈ 24-25 N 3
Warrior ○ USA 48-49 E 3
Warrior Reefs ⌒ AUS 174-175 G 2
Warri River ∼ WAN 204-205 F 6
Warri Warri Creek ∼ AUS 178-179 F 5
Warrnambool ○ AUS 180-181 G 5
Warroad ○ USA 42-43 K 1
Warrumbungle National Park ⊥ AUS 178-179 K 6
Warrumbungle Range ▲ AUS 178-179 K 6
Warruwi X AUS 174-175 B 2
Warsa ○ RI 166-167 H 2
Warsaw ○ USA (IN) 46-47 F 5
Warsaw ○ USA (MO) 42-43 L 6
Warsaw ○ USA (NC) 48-49 J 2
Warsaw = Warszawa ★ ··· PL 92-93 Q 2
Warshi ○ IND 138-139 F 10
Warshiikh ○ SP 212-213 K 2
Warszawa ★ ··· PL 92-93 Q 2
Warta ∼ PL 92-93 O 2
Warton, Monte ▲ RCH 80 D 6
Waru ○ RI (JTI) 168 E 3
Waru ○ RI (KTI) 164-165 E 4
Waru ○ RI (MAL) 166-167 F 3
Warud ○ IND 138-139 G 9
Waruta ∼ RI 166-167 L 3
Warwick ○ AUS 178-179 L 5
Warwick ☆ · GB 90-91 G 5
Warwick ○ USA (GA) 48-49 G 4
Warwick ○ USA (OK) 44-45 J 2
Warwick Channel ≈ 174-175 D 4
Warwick Downs O.S. ○ AUS 178-179 E 1
Waryori ∼ RI 166-167 G 2
Warzazāt = Ouarzazate ☆ MA 188-189 H 5
Wasagaming ○ CDN 34-35 G 5
Wasagu ○ WAN 204-205 F 3
Wasai ○ RI 166-167 F 2
Wasalangka ○ RI 164-165 H 6
Wasatch Plateau ▲ USA 40-41 J 6
Wasatch Range ▲ USA 40-41 J 4
Wasco ○ USA 40-41 E 8
Wase ○ WAN 204-205 H 4
Wase, River ∼ WAN 204-205 H 4
Waseca ○ USA 42-43 L 3
Washackie Wilderness Area ⊥ USA 42-43 C 4
Washago ○ CDN 38-39 E 6
Washāp ○ PK 134-135 K 5
Washburn ○ USA 42-43 G 2
Washburne Lake ○ CDN 24-25 S 5
Washi Lake ○ CDN 34-35 N 5
Wāshim ○ IND 138-139 F 9
Washington ○ USA (GA) 48-49 G 3
Washington ○ USA (IA) 46-47 C 5
Washington ○ USA (IN) 46-47 E 6
Washington ○ USA (KS) 42-43 J 6
Washington ○ USA (MO) 46-47 C 6
Washington ○ USA (NC) 48-49 K 2
Washington ○ USA (OH) 46-47 G 6
Washington ○ USA (PA) 46-47 H 5
Washington ○ USA (WI) 46-47 E 3
Washington □ USA 40-41 C 2
Washington, Mount ▲ USA 46-47 N 3
Washington/Slagbaai, National Reservaat ⊥ NL 60-61 G 1
Washington Birthplace National Monument, George ∴ USA 46-47 K 6
Washington D.C. ★ · USA 46-47 K 6
Washington Island ⌒ USA 46-47 E 3
Washington Land ∸ GRØ 26-27 R 3
Washington National Monument, Booker T. ∴ USA 46-47 J 7
Washita, Fort ∴ USA 44-45 J 2
Washita River ∼ USA 44-45 J 2
Washow Bay ○ CDN 34-35 H 5
Washowng ☆ MYA 142-143 K 3
Washpool National Park ⊥ AUS 178-179 M 5
Washtucna ○ USA 40-41 E 2
Wāshūk ○ PK 134-135 L 5
Wasian ○ RI 166-167 G 2
Wasile ○ RI 164-165 K 3
Wasilla ○ USA 20-21 Q 6
Wasimi ○ WAN 204-205 E 4
Wasini Island ⌒ EAK 212-213 G 6
Wasini Marine National Park ⊥ EAK 212-213 G 6
Wāsiqa, al- ○ KSA 132-133 B 4
Wasir, Pulau ⌒ RI 166-167 H 4
Wāsiṭ □ IRQ 128-129 L 6
Wāsit ∴ · IRQ 128-129 M 6
Wāsiṭa, al- ○ KSA 130-131 F 6
Waskaganish ○ CDN 38-39 E 3
Waskahigan River ∼ CDN 32-33 M 4
Waskaiowaka Lake ○ CDN 34-35 H 2
Waskesiu Lake ○ CDN 34-35 C 4
Waskom ○ USA 44-45 K 3
Wasletan ○ RI 166-167 F 5
Waspam ○ NIC 52-53 B 4
Waspuk, Río ∼ NIC 52-53 B 4
Wassadou ○ SN 202-203 C 3
Wassamu ○ J 152-153 K 2
Wasserburg am Inn ○ D 92-93 M 4
Wassou ○ RG 202-203 D 4
Wasta ○ USA 42-43 F 3
Wasu ○ PNG 183 D 3
Wasua ○ PNG 183 B 5
Wasum ○ PNG 183 E 4
Waswanipi, Lac ○ CDN 38-39 F 4
Waswanipi, Réserve de X CDN 38-39 G 4
Waswanipi, Rivière ∼ CDN 38-39 F 4
Wata ○ RI 164-165 G 5
Waṭā, al- ∸ OM 132-133 K 3
Watalgan ○ AUS 178-179 M 3
Watam ○ PNG 183 C 2
Watam ○ RI 164-165 L 3
Watambayoli ○ RI 164-165 G 4
Watampone ○ RI 164-165 G 6
Watamu Marine National Park ⊥ EAK 212-213 G 5
Watansoppeng ○ RI 164-165 F 6
Watar ○ IND 140-141 F 2
Watarais ○ PNG 183 D 4
Watarrka National Park ⊥ ·· AUS 176-177 L 2
Watawa ○ RI 166-167 D 3
Watee ○ SOL 184 I f 4
Waterberge ▲ ZA 220-221 H 2
Waterberg Plateau Park ⊥ NAM 216-217 D 10
Waterbury ○ USA 46-47 M 5
Waterbury Lake ○ CDN 30-31 R 6
Water Cay ⌒ BS 54-55 H 3
Water Cay ⌒ GB 54-55 J 4
Wateree River ∼ USA 48-49 H 3
Waterford ○ AUS 178-179 E 2
Waterford ○ ZA 220-221 G 6
Waterford = Port Láirge ☆ · IRL 90-91 D 5
Waterfound River ∼ CDN 30-31 R 6
Watergap ○ USA 46-47 G 7
Waterhen ○ CDN 34-35 G 5
Waterhen Indian Reserve X CDN 34-35 G 5
Waterhen Lake ○ CDN (MAN) 34-35 G 4
Waterhen Lake ○ CDN (SAS) 32-33 Q 4
Waterhen River ∼ CDN 32-33 Q 4
Waterhouse River ∼ AUS 174-175 B 4
Waterloo ○ AUS 172-173 J 4
Waterloo ○ B 92-93 H 3
Waterloo ○ CDN 38-39 D 7
Waterloo ○ USA 42-43 L 4
Waterloo ○ WAL 202-203 D 5
Waterpoort ○ ZA 218-219 E 6
Watersmeet ○ USA 46-47 D 2
Waterton Glacier International Peace Park ⊥ ··· USA 40-41 G 1
Waterton Lakes National Park ⊥ ··· CDN 32-33 N 7
Waterton Park ○ CDN 32-33 O 7
Watertown ○ USA (NY) 46-47 L 4
Watertown ○ USA (SD) 42-43 J 3
Watertown ○ USA (WI) 46-47 D 4
Waterval-Boven ○ · ZA 220-221 K 2
Water Valley ○ USA 48-49 D 2
Waterville ○ USA (KS) 42-43 J 6
Waterville ○ USA (ME) 46-47 O 3
Waterville = An Coireán ○ IRL 90-91 B 6
Watford ○ GB 90-91 G 6
Watford City ○ USA 42-43 F 2
Wathaman Lake ○ CDN 34-35 D 2
Watheroo ○ AUS 176-177 D 5
Watheroo National Park ⊥ AUS 176-177 C 5
Watino ○ CDN 32-33 M 4
Watkin Bjerge ▲ GRØ 28-29 a 2
Watkins Woolen Mill State Historic Site ∴ USA 42-43 K 6
Watmuri ○ RI 166-167 F 5
Watnil ○ RI 166-167 G 4
Watoa Island ⌒ PNG 183 F 5
Watom Island ⌒ PNG 183 G 3
Watonga ○ USA 44-45 H 2
Watpi ○ PNG 183 G 3
Watri ○ RMM 202-203 F 2
Watrous ○ CDN 34-35 D 5
Watrous ○ USA 44-45 E 2
Watrupun ○ RI 166-167 E 5
Watsa ○ ZRE 212-213 B 2
Watseka ○ USA 46-47 E 5
Watsi ○ ZRE 210-211 H 4
Watsikengo ○ ZRE 210-211 H 4
Watson ○ AUS 176-177 L 5
Watson ○ CDN 34-35 D 4
Watson Lake ○ CDN 30-31 E 5
Watson River ∼ AUS 174-175 F 3
Watsonville ○ USA 40-41 D 7
Watta, Hiré- ○ CI 202-203 H 6
Wattegama ○ CL 140-141 J 7
Watterson Lake ○ CDN 30-31 U 5
Watt Hills ▲ AUS 176-177 F 5
Wattiwarriganna Creek ∼ AUS 178-179 C 5
Watts Bar Lake ○ USA 48-49 F 2
Watubela, Kepulauan ⌒ RI 166-167 F 4
Watukebo, Tanjung ▲ RI 166-167 G 4
Watumanuk, Tanjung ▲ RI 168 E 7
Watumohai, Gunung ▲ RI 164-165 H 6
Watunea ○ RI 164-165 H 6
Watupati, Tanjung ▲ RI 166-167 E 6
Watutau ○ RI 164-165 G 4
Wau ○ PNG 183 D 4
Wau ○ RI 166-167 G 2
Wāu ○ SUD 206-207 H 5
Wāu ∼ SUD 206-207 H 5
Waubaushene ○ CDN 38-39 E 6
Waubra ○ AUS 180-181 G 4
Wauchope ○ AUS (NSW) 178-179 M 6
Wauchope ○ AUS (NT) 174-175 C 7
Waukaringa ○ AUS 180-181 E 2
Waukarlycarly, Lake ○ AUS 172-173 E 6
Waukegan ○ USA 46-47 E 4
Waukesha ○ USA 46-47 D 4
Waupaca ○ USA 46-47 D 3
Waupun ○ USA 46-47 D 4
Waurika ○ USA 44-45 H 2
Waurika Lake ○ USA 44-45 H 2
Wausau ○ USA 46-47 D 3
Wausaukee ○ USA 46-47 E 3
Wauwatosa ○ USA 46-47 D 4
Wave Hill ○ AUS 172-173 K 4
Waverly ○ USA (IA) 42-43 L 4
Waverly ○ USA (MO) 42-43 L 6
Waverly ○ USA (NY) 46-47 K 4
Waverly ○ USA (TN) 48-49 E 1
Waverly ○ USA (VA) 46-47 K 7
Wave Rock ·· AUS 176-177 E 6
Wawa ○ CDN 34-35 O 7
Wawa ○ WAN 204-205 F 4
Wawa, Río = Río Huahua ∼ NIC 52-53 B 4
Wawalalindu ○ RI 164-165 H 5
Wāw al Kabīr ○ LAR 192-193 G 5
Wawan ○ RP 160-161 D 6
Wawanesa ○ CDN 34-35 G 6
Wawiwa Island ⌒ PNG 183 F 5
Wawo ○ RI 164-165 G 5
Wawoi River ∼ PNG 183 B 4
Wawolandawe ○ RI 164-165 H 5
Waworada ○ RI 168 D 7
Waworada, Teluk ≈ 168 D 7
Wawotobi ○ RI 164-165 H 5
Wawousu ○ RI 164-165 H 6
Waxahachie ○ USA 44-45 J 3
Waxxari ○ VRC 146-147 H 6
Way, Lake ○ AUS 176-177 F 3
Waya ⌒ FJI 184 III a 2
Wayabula ○ RI 164-165 L 2
Wayag, Pulau ⌒ RI 166-167 F 1
Wayamli ○ RI 164-165 L 3
Wayamli, Tanjung ▲ RI 164-165 L 3
Wayaua ○ RI 164-165 K 4
Waycross ○ USA 48-49 G 4
Wayerton ○ CDN 38-39 M 5
Waygay ○ RI (MAL) 164-165 J 4
Waygay ○ RI (MAL) 164-165 J 5
Wayhaya ○ RI 164-165 J 4
Waykadai ○ RI 164-165 J 4
Waykilo ○ RI 164-165 J 4
Wayne ○ USA 42-43 J 4
Waynesboro ○ USA (GA) 48-49 G 3
Waynesboro ○ USA (MS) 48-49 D 4
Waynesboro ○ USA (TN) 48-49 E 2
Waynesboro ○ USA (VA) 46-47 J 6
Waynesburg ○ USA 46-47 H 6
Waynesville ○ USA 48-49 G 2
Waynoka ○ USA 44-45 H 1
Wayongon ○ MYA 142-143 J 3
Waza ○ CAM 206-207 B 3
Waza, Parc National de ⊥ CAM 206-207 B 3
Wāzaḥwa = Vāzaḥā ○ AFG 138-139 B 3
Wazān = Ouezzane ○ MA 188-189 J 3
Wāzin ○ LAR 190-191 H 5
Wazīrābād ○ PK 138-139 E 3
W du Niger, Parc National du ⊥ BF 204-205 E 2
We ○ CAM 204-205 J 5
Weagamow Lake ○ CDN 34-35 L 4
Weagomow Lake ○ CDN 34-35 L 4
Weam ○ PNG 183 A 5
Weasua ○ LB 202-203 E 6
Weatherall Bay ≈ 24-25 S 2
Weatherford ○ USA (OK) 44-45 H 2
Weatherford ○ USA (TX) 44-45 J 3
Weaverville ○ USA 40-41 C 5
Webb, Mount ▲ AUS 172-173 J 7
Webb Gemstone Deposit · AUS 176-177 E 3
Webequie ○ CDN 34-35 N 4
Weber ○ NZ 182 F 4
Webster ○ USA 42-43 J 3
Webster City ○ USA 42-43 L 4
Webster Springs ○ USA 46-47 H 6
Webuye ○ EAK 212-213 E 3
Wech'echa ▲ ETH 208-209 D 4
Wecho Lake ○ CDN 30-31 N 4
Wecho River ∼ CDN 30-31 M 4
Weda ○ RI 164-165 K 3
Weda, Teluk ≈ 164-165 L 3
Wedangkau ○ RI 166-167 F 5
Weddell Island ⌒ GB 78-79 K 6
Weddell Sea ≈ ARK 16 F 32
Wedderburn ○ AUS 180-181 G 4
Weddin Mountain National Park ⊥ AUS 180-181 K 2
Wedel Jarlsberg Land ∸ N 84-85 J 4
Wedge Island ⌒ AUS 176-177 C 5
Wednesday Island ⌒ AUS 183 B 6
Wedowee ○ USA 48-49 F 3
Weduar ○ RI 166-167 G 4
Weduar, Tanjung ▲ RI 166-167 G 4
Wedweil ○ SUD 206-207 H 4
Weebubbie Caves ⊥ AUS 176-177 K 5
Weed ○ USA 40-41 C 5
Weeim, Pulau ⌒ RI 166-167 F 2
Weeki Wachee Spring · USA 48-49 G 5
Weelarrana ○ AUS 176-177 F 1
Weelhamby Lake ○ AUS 176-177 D 4
Weemarie, Lake ○ AUS 178-179 E 3
Weenen ○ ZA 220-221 K 4
Weethalle ○ AUS 180-181 J 2
Wee Waa ○ AUS 178-179 K 6
Wegdraai ○ ZA 220-221 E 4
Wegener-Inlandeis ⊂ ARK 16 F 36
Węgorzewo ○ · PL 92-93 Q 1
Weh, Pulau ⌒ RI 162-163 A 2
Wehnī ○ ETH 200-201 H 6
Weichang ○ VRC 148-149 N 7
Weiden in der Oberpfalz ○ D 92-93 M 4
Weifang ○ VRC 154-155 L 3
Weihai ○ VRC 154-155 N 3
Wei He ∼ VRC 154-155 J 4
Wei He ∼ VRC 154-155 E 4
Weihui ○ VRC 154-155 J 4
Weila ○ GH 202-203 K 5
Weilmoringle ○ AUS 178-179 J 5
Weimar ○ ·· D 92-93 L 3
Wein, Bur ▲ EAK 212-213 H 2
Weinan ○ VRC 154-155 F 4
Weining ○ VRC 156-157 D 3
Weipa ○ AUS 174-175 F 3
Weipa South X AUS 174-175 F 3
Weir River ∼ AUS 178-179 K 5
Weir River ○ CDN (MAN) 34-35 J 2
Weir River ∼ CDN 34-35 K 2
Weirton ○ USA 46-47 H 5
Weiser ○ USA 40-41 F 3
Weiser River ∼ USA 40-41 F 3
Weishan ○ VRC 154-155 K 4
Weishan Hu ∼ VRC 154-155 K 4
Weishi ○ VRC 154-155 J 4
Weiss Lake ‹ USA 48-49 F 2
Weitchpec ○ USA 40-41 C 5
Weitou ○ VRC 156-157 L 4
Weixi ○ VRC 142-143 L 2
Wei Xian ○ VRC 154-155 J 3
Weixin ○ VRC 156-157 D 3
Weiya ○ VRC 146-147 M 5
Weiyuan ○ VRC (GAN) 154-155 D 4
Weiyuan ○ VRC (SIC) 156-157 D 2
Weizhou Dao ⌒ VRC 156-157 F 6
Wekakura Point ▲ NZ 182 D 4
Weko ○ ZRE 210-211 K 3
Wekusko ○ CDN 34-35 G 3
Wekusko Lake ○ CDN 34-35 G 3
Welab ○ RI 166-167 K 6
Welanpela ○ CL 140-141 J 7
Welatam ○ MYA 142-143 L 2
Welbedacht Dam ‹ ZA 220-221 H 4
Welch ○ USA 46-47 H 7
Welchman Hall Gully · BDS 56 F 5
Weldiya ○ ETH 208-209 D 3
Weldon ○ USA 48-49 K 1
Weld Range ▲ AUS 176-177 D 3
Welega □ ETH 208-209 B 4
Welench'ītī ○ ETH 208-209 D 4
Weligama ○ · CL 140-141 J 8
Welisara ○ CL 140-141 H 7
Wel Jara ‹ EAK 212-213 H 4
Welk'ītē ○ ETH 208-209 C 4
Welkom ○ ZA 220-221 H 3
Welland ○ CDN 38-39 E 7
Wella-Sofon-Gari ○ RN 204-205 E 1
Wellawaya ○ CL 140-141 J 7
Wellesley Basin ∸ CDN 20-21 U 5
Wellesley Islands ⌒ AUS 174-175 E 5
Wellesley Lake ○ CDN 20-21 V 5
Wellington ○ AUS 180-181 K 2
Wellington ○ CDN 38-39 F 7
Wellington ★ NZ 182 E 4
Wellington ○ USA (CO) 42-43 E 5
Wellington ○ USA (KS) 44-45 J 1
Wellington ○ USA (UT) 40-41 J 6
Wellington ○ ZA 220-221 D 6
Wellington, Isla ⌒ RCH 80 C 4
Wellington, Lake ○ AUS 180-181 J 5
Wellington Bay ≈ 24-25 S 6
Wellington Caves · AUS 180-181 K 2
Wellington Channel ≈ 24-25 Z 3
Wellington Range ▲ AUS 176-177 F 3
Wellman ○ USA 44-45 F 3
Wells ○ USA 40-41 G 5
Wells, Lake ○ AUS 176-177 G 3
Wellsford ○ NZ 182 E 2
Wells Gray Provincial Park ⊥ CDN 32-33 K 5
Wells Lake ○ CDN 34-35 F 2
Wellstead ○ AUS 176-177 E 7
Wellston ○ USA 46-47 G 6
Wellsville ○ USA (MO) 46-47 C 6
Wellsville ○ USA (NY) 46-47 K 4
Welmel Shet' ∼ ETH 208-209 E 6
Wel Meret ‹ EAK 212-213 H 2
Wels ○ A 92-93 N 4
Welsford ○ CDN 38-39 L 6
Welsford, Cape ▲ CDN 36-37 G 2
Welshpool ○ · GB 90-91 F 5
Welshpool, Port ○ AUS 180-181 J 5
Welutu ○ RI 166-167 F 5
Welwel ○ ETH 208-209 G 5
Wema ○ ZRE 210-211 H 4
Wembere ∼ EAT 212-213 E 6
Wembi ○ RI 166-167 L 3
Wembley ○ CDN 32-33 L 4
Wemindji ○ CDN 38-39 E 2
Wen ○ SUD 206-207 H 4
Wenago ○ ETH 208-209 D 5
Wenasaga River ∼ CDN 34-35 K 5
Wenatchee ○ USA 40-41 D 2
Wenatchee Mountains ▲ USA 40-41 D 2
Wenceslao Escalante ○ RA 78-79 H 2
Wenchang ○ VRC (HAI) 156-157 G 7
Wenchang ○ VRC (SIC) 154-155 E 6
Wenchi ○ GH 202-203 J 6
Wenchiki ○ GH 202-203 L 4
Wench'it Shet' ∼ ETH 208-209 D 3
Wenchuan ○ VRC 154-155 C 6
Wenden ○ USA 40-41 H 9
Wendeng ○ VRC 154-155 N 3
Wendesi ○ RI 166-167 H 3
Wendi ○ RI 164-165 J 4
Wendi ○ VRC 156-157 G 6
Wendo ○ ETH 208-209 D 5
Wendou Borou ○ RG 202-203 D 4
Wendover ○ USA 40-41 H 5
Wendover Range xx USA 40-41 H 5
Wenga ○ ZRE 210-211 G 3
Weng'an ○ VRC 156-157 E 3
Wenge ○ ZRE 210-211 K 3
Weni ○ NEP 144-145 D 6
Wenlock ∴ AUS 174-175 G 3
Wenlock River ∼ AUS 174-175 F 3
Wenquan ○ VRC 144-145 H 4
Wenshan ○ VRC 156-157 D 5
Wen Shang ○ VRC 154-155 K 4
Wenshui ○ VRC (GZH) 156-157 E 2
Wenshui ○ VRC (SHA) 154-155 G 3
Wentworth ○ AUS 180-181 F 3
Wentworth Centre ○ CDN 38-39 N 6
Wentzel Lake ○ CDN (ALB) 30-31 M 6
Wentzel Lake ○ CDN (NWT) 30-31 M 2
Wentzel River ∼ CDN 30-31 M 6
Wentzville ○ USA 46-47 C 6
Wenxi ○ VRC 154-155 G 4
Wen Xian ○ VRC 154-155 D 5
Wenzhen ○ VRC 156-157 K 2
Wenzhou ○ VRC 156-157 M 2
Wenzhou Wan ≈ 156-157 M 3
Wepener ○ ZA 220-221 H 4
Wer ○ IND 138-139 F 6
Werda ○ RB 220-221 F 2
Werdēr ○ ETH 208-209 G 5
Were Īlu ○ ETH 208-209 D 3
Wernadinga ○ AUS 174-175 E 6
Werner Lake ○ CDN 34-35 J 5
Werota ○ ETH 208-209 C 3
Wer Ping ○ SUD 206-207 J 4
Werra ∼ D 92-93 L 3
Werribee ○ AUS 180-181 H 4
Werrikimbie National Park ⊥ AUS 178-179 M 6
Werris Creek ○ AUS 178-179 L 6
Wertach ∼ D 92-93 L 4
Wesel ○ D 92-93 J 3
Weser ∼ D 92-93 K 2
Weslaco ○ USA 44-45 H 6
Wesley ○ USA 46-47 P 3
Wesleyville ○ CDN 38-39 I S 4
Wessel, Cape ▲ AUS 174-175 D 2
Wessel Islands ⌒ AUS 174-175 D 2
Wesselsbron ○ ZA 220-221 H 3
Wessington Springs ○ USA 42-43 H 3
West = Ouest □ CAM 204-205 J 6
West Amatuli Island ⌒ USA 22-23 V 3
West Baines River ∼ AUS 172-173 J 4
West Bay ≈ 48-49 D 5
West Bay ○ · GB 54-55 E 5
West Bend ○ CDN 34-35 E 5
West Bend ○ USA 46-47 D 4
West Bengal □ IND 142-143 E 4
Westboro ○ USA 46-47 C 3
Westbourne ○ CDN 34-35 G 5
West Branch ○ USA 46-47 F 3
Westbrook ○ USA 46-47 N 4
Westbury ○ AUS 178-179 H 2
Westby ○ USA (MT) 42-43 E 1
Westby ○ USA (WI) 46-47 C 4
West Caicos ⌒ GB 54-55 J 4
West Cape Howe ▲ AUS 176-177 D 7
West-Cape Province □ ZA 220-221 D 6
West Channel ∼ CDN 20-21 X 2
West Chichagof Yakobi Wilderness ⊥ · USA 32-33 B 3
Westcliffe ○ USA 42-43 E 6
West Coast National Park ⊥ ZA 220-221 D 6
West Columbia ○ USA 44-45 K 5
West End ○ BS 54-55 F 1
West End ○ GB 54-55 F 5
Westerberg ○ ZA 220-221 F 4
Westerland ○ D 92-93 K 1
Westerly ○ USA 46-47 N 5
Western □ EAK 212-213 E 3
Western □ EAU 212-213 C 3
Western □ PNG 183 A 4
Western ○ USA 42-43 J 5
Western □ Z 218-219 B 2

Walewale — Western 331

Western Australia ◻ AUS 176-177 F 1
Western Creek ~ AUS 178-179 L 4
Western Desert = Ṣaḥrā' al-Ġarbīa, aṣ- ⚊ ET 194-195 B 4
Western Entrance ≈ 184 I b 2
Western Ghāts ⚊ IND 10-11 G 7
Western Island ⌒ PNG 183 C 2
Western Kentucky Parkway II USA 46-47 E 7
Western Plains Zoo • AUS 180-181 K 2
Western Region ◻ GH 202-203 J 6
Western River ~ CDN 30-31 Q 2
Western Sahara ■ WSA 196-197 C 2
Western Samoa ⌒ WS 184 V a 1
Western Samoa = Sāmoa-i-Sisifo ■ WS 184 V b 1
Western Sayan Mountains = Zapadnyj Sajan ▲▲ RUS 116-117 D 9
Western Tasmania National Parks ⊥••• AUS 180-181 H 7
Western Thebes ∴•• ET 194-195 F 5
Western Waigeo Pulau Reserve ⊥• RI 166-167 F 2
Western Yamuna Canal < IND 138-139 F 5
Westerschelde ≈ 92-93 G 3
Westerville o USA 46-47 G 5
Westerwald ▲▲ D 92-93 J 3
West Falkland ⌒ GB 78-79 L 6
Westfield o USA (MA) 46-47 M 4
Westfield o USA (NY) 46-47 J 4
West Fork ~ USA 42-43 D 1
West Fork des Moines ~ USA 42-43 K 4
West Frankfort o USA 46-47 D 7
West Frisian Islands = Waddeneilanden ⚊ NL 92-93 H 2
Westgate o AUS 178-179 J 4
West Glacier o USA 40-41 H 1
West Gletscher ⊂ GRØ 26-27 I 8
West Group ⌒ AUS 176-177 F 6
West Hamlin o USA 46-47 G 6
West Holothuria Reef ⌒ AUS 172-173 G 2
Westhope o USA 42-43 G 1
West Ice Shelf ⊂ ARK 16 G 9
West Indies ⚊ 4 G 6
West Island ⌒ AUS (NT) 174-175 D 4
West Island ⌒ AUS (WA) 176-177 F 7
West Kettle River ~ CDN 32-33 L 7
Westland National Park ⊥••• NZ 182 C 5
West Liberty o USA 46-47 G 7
Westlock o CDN 32-33 O 4
West Lunga ~ Z 214-215 C 7
West Lunga National Park ⊥ Z 214-215 C 7
Westmar o AUS 178-179 K 4
West Memphis o USA 44-45 M 2
Westminster o ZA 220-221 H 4
Westmoreland o AUS 174-175 E 5
Westmorland o USA 40-41 G 9
West Mount Barren ▲ AUS 176-177 E 7
West Nicholson o ZW 218-219 E 5
Weston o USA (ID) 40-41 J 4
Weston o USA (WV) 46-47 H 6
Weston-Super-Mare o GB 90-91 F 6
West Ossipee o USA 46-47 N 4
West Palm Beach o•• USA 48-49 H 6
West Plains o USA 44-45 M 1
West Point ▲ AUS (SA) 180-181 C 3
West Point ▲ AUS (TAS) 180-181 H 6
West Point o CDN 38-39 M 5
Westpoint o GB 78-79 K 6
West Point o USA (NE) 42-43 J 5
West Point o USA (VA) 46-47 K 7
West Point ▲ USA (AK) 20-21 S 4
West Point ▲ WAN 204-205 H 6
West Point Lake < USA 48-49 F 3
West Poplar o CDN 34-35 C 6
Westport o CDN 38-39 Q 4
Westport o NZ 182 C 4
Westport o USA (OR) 40-41 C 2
Westport o USA (WA) 40-41 B 2
Westport = Cathair na Mart o• IRL 90-91 C 5
West Prairie River ~ CDN 32-33 M 4
Westpunt o NL 60-61 G 1
Westray o CDN 34-35 F 4
Westray ⌒ GB 90-91 F 2
West River ~ CDN 24-25 H 6
West Road River ~ CDN 32-33 H 5
West Scotia Ridge ≃ 6-7 D 14
West Sepik ◻ PNG 183 A 2
West Siberian Plain = Zapadno-Sibirskaja ravnina ⌣ RUS 114-115 J 2
West Springfield o USA 46-47 H 5
West Thumb o USA 40-41 J 3
West Travaputs Plateau ▲▲ USA 40-41 J 6
West Union o USA 46-47 C 4
West Virginia ◻ USA 46-47 H 6
Westwood o AUS 178-179 L 2
Westwood o USA 40-41 D 5
West Wyalong o AUS 180-181 J 2
West Yellowstone o USA 40-41 J 3
West York Island ⌒ 160-161 A 7
Wetalltok Bay ≈ 36-37 K 7
Wetan, Pulau ⌒ RI 166-167 E 5
Wetar, Pulau ⌒ RI 166-167 D 5
Wetar, Selat ≈ 166-167 C 6
Wetaskiwin o CDN 32-33 O 5
Wete o EAT 212-213 G 6
Wete o ZRE 210-211 K 6
Wetherell, Lake ⊖ AUS 180-181 G 2
Wet Mountains ▲▲ USA 42-43 E 6
Weto o WAN 204-205 G 5
Wettlet o MYA 142-143 J 4
Wet Tropics of Queensland ⊥••• AUS 174-175 H 5
Wetzlar o• D 92-93 K 3
Wevok o USA 20-21 G 2
Wewak ☆ PNG 183 B 2
Wexford = Loch Garman ☆ IRL 90-91 D 5
Weyakwin o CDN 34-35 D 3
Weyburn o CDN 34-35 E 6
Weyland, Point ▲ AUS 180-181 C 2
Weymouth o CDN 38-39 M 6
Weymouth o• GB 90-91 F 6
Weymouth, Cape ▲ AUS 174-175 G 3
Weymouth Bay ≈ 174-175 G 3
Whakatane o NZ 182 F 2
Whalan Creek ~ AUS 178-179 K 5
Whaleback Mining Area, Mount • AUS 176-177 E 1
Whale Bay ≈ 32-33 C 3
Whale Bay ≈ 158-159 E 5
Whale Cay ⌒ BS 54-55 G 2
Whale Cove o CDN 30-31 X 4
Whale Island ⌒ USA 22-23 U 4
Whale Point ▲ CDN 36-37 F 2
Whangamata o NZ 182 E 2
Whanganui National Park • NZ 182 E 3
Whangarei o NZ 182 E 1
Wharfe ~ GB 90-91 F 4
Wharton o USA 44-45 J 5
Wharton, Península ⌣ RCH 80 C 4
Wharton Lake ⊖ CDN 30-31 T 3
Wheatland o CDN 34-35 F 5
Wheatland o USA (CA) 40-41 D 6
Wheatland o USA (WY) 42-43 E 4
Wheatland Reservoir No.2 < USA 42-43 E 5
Wheaton o USA 42-43 J 3
Wheeler o USA 44-45 G 2
Wheeler Lake < USA 48-49 E 2
Wheeler Peak ▲ USA (NM) 44-45 E 1
Wheeler Peak ▲ USA (NV) 40-41 G 6
Wheeler Ridge o USA 40-41 E 8
Wheeler River ~ CDN 34-35 D 2
Wheelers Point o USA 42-43 K 1
Wheeling o USA 46-47 H 5
Whela Creek ~ AUS 176-177 D 3
Whelan, Mount ▲ AUS 178-179 E 2
Whewell, Mount ▲ ARK 16 F 17
Whidbey Island ⌒ USA 40-41 C 1
Whidbey Isles ⌒ AUS 180-181 C 3
Whim Creek o AUS 172-173 C 6
Whirlwind Lake ⊖ CDN 30-31 P 5
Whiskey Jack Lake ⊖ CDN 30-31 T 6
Whitbourne o CDN 38-39 S 5
Whitby o CDN 38-39 E 7
Whitby o• GB 90-91 G 4
Whitchurch o GB 90-91 F 5
White, Lake ⊖ AUS 172-173 J 6
White, Mount ▲ AUS 176-177 F 3
White Bay ≈ 38-39 Q 3
Whitebear Point ▲ CDN 24-25 U 6
White Bear River ~ CDN 38-39 Q 4
White Butte ▲ USA 42-43 F 2
White Cape Mount ▲ USA 46-47 O 3
White Cay ⌒ BS 54-55 H 2
White City o CDN 34-35 D 5
Whiteclay o USA 42-43 F 4
Whiteclay Lake ⊖ CDN 34-35 M 5
White Cliff ▲ BS 54-55 J 3
White Cliffs o• AUS 178-179 G 6
Whitecourt o CDN 32-33 N 4
White crowned pigeons • BS 54-55 G 2
Whitedog o CDN 34-35 J 5
White Earth o USA (MN) 42-43 K 2
White Earth o USA (ND) 42-43 F 1
White Earth Indian Reservation ✗ USA 42-43 K 2
Whitefish o CDN 38-39 D 5
Whitefish o USA 40-41 G 1
Whitefish Bay o USA 46-47 F 2
Whitefish Lake ⊖ CDN 30-31 Q 4
Whitefish Lake ⊖ USA (AK) 20-21 L 6
Whitefish Lake ⊖ USA (MN) 42-43 K 2
Whitefish Lake Indian Reserve ✗ CDN 38-39 D 5
Whitefish Point o USA 46-47 F 2
Whitefish River ~ CDN 30-31 H 3
Whitegull, Lac ⊖ CDN 36-37 R 7
Whitehall o USA (MT) 40-41 H 3
Whitehall o USA (NY) 46-47 M 4
Whitehall o USA (WI) 46-47 C 3
White Hall State Historic Site • USA 46-47 F 7
White Handkerchief, Cape ▲ CDN 36-37 S 5
White Hills ▲ USA 20-21 Q 2
Whitehills Lake ⊖ CDN 30-31 W 3
Whitehorse ☆• CDN 20-21 X 6
Whitehorse o USA 42-43 G 3
White Horse Pass ▲ USA 40-41 G 5
White Island ⌒ CDN 36-37 G 2
White Island ⌒ NZ 182 F 2
White Lady • NAM 216-217 C 10
White Lake ⊖ AUS 176-177 F 2
White Lake ⊖ CDN 34-35 O 6
White Lake o USA (SD) 42-43 H 4
White Lake ⊖ USA (WI) 46-47 D 3
White Lake o USA (LA) 44-45 L 5
Whitelaw o CDN 32-33 L 3
Whiteman Range ▲▲ PNG 183 E 3
Whitemark o AUS 180-181 K 6
White Mountain o USA 20-21 J 4
White Mountains ▲▲ USA 20-21 R 4
White Mountains ▲▲ USA 40-41 E 7
White Mountains ▲▲ USA 46-47 N 3
Whitemouth o CDN 34-35 J 6
Whitemud River ~ CDN 32-33 L 3
White Nile = al-Baḥr al-Abyaḍ ~ SUD 206-207 K 4
White Otter Lake ⊖ CDN 34-35 L 6
White Pass ▲ CDN 20-21 X 7
White Pass ▲ USA 40-41 D 2
White Plains o LB 202-203 E 6
White River o CDN (ONT) 34-35 O 6
White River ~ CDN 20-21 U 5
White River ~ CDN 32-33 N 6
White River ~ CDN 34-35 N 6
White River o USA (SD) 42-43 G 4
White River ~ USA 40-41 G 6
White River ~ USA 40-41 D 2
White River ~ USA 42-43 C 5
White River ~ USA 42-43 H 4
White River ~ USA 44-45 M 2
White River ~ USA 44-45 G 3
White River ~ USA 46-47 E 6
White River Junction o USA 46-47 M 4
White River National Wildlife Refuge ⊥ USA 44-45 M 2
Whitesail Lake ⊖ CDN 32-33 G 5
White Salmon o USA 40-41 D 3
Whitesand River ~ CDN 34-35 E 5
White Sands Missile Range ✕✕ USA 44-45 D 3
White Sands National Monument • USA 44-45 D 3
White Sands Space Harbor ✕✕ USA 44-45 D 3
White Sea = Beloe more ≈ RUS 88-89 O 4
White Sea-Baltic Canal = Belomorsko-Baltijskij kanal < RUS 88-89 N 4
White Settlement o USA 44-45 J 3
Whiteshell Provincial Park ⊥•• CDN 34-35 J 5
Whiteside, Canal ≈ 80 E 6
Whitespruce Rapids ~ CDN 30-31 T 6
White Star o USA 46-47 F 4
Whitestone River ~ CDN 20-21 V 4
White Strait ≈ 36-37 O 3
White Sulphur Springs o USA (MT) 40-41 J 2
White Sulphur Springs o USA (WV) 46-47 H 7
White Umfolozi ~ ZA 220-221 K 4
Whiteville o USA 48-49 J 2
White Volta ~ GH 202-203 K 5
Whitewater o USA (CO) 42-43 C 6
Whitewater o USA (WI) 46-47 D 4
Whitewater Baldy ▲ USA 44-45 C 3
Whitewater Bay ≈ 48-49 H 7
Whitewater Lake ⊖ CDN 34-35 M 5
Whitewood o AUS 178-179 G 1
Whitewood o CDN 34-35 E 5
Whitfield o AUS 180-181 J 4
Whitianga o NZ 182 E 2
Whiting River ~ USA 32-33 D 2
Whitlash o USA 40-41 J 1
Whitley City o USA 46-47 F 7
Whitman o USA 42-43 G 4
Whitmann Mission National Historic Site ∴ USA 40-41 E 2
Whitmore Mountains ▲▲ ARK 16 E 0
Whitney o CDN 38-39 E 6
Whitney, Lake ⊖ USA 44-45 J 4
Whitney, Mount ▲ USA 40-41 E 7
Whitney Point o USA 46-47 L 4
Whitney Turn o JA 54-55 G 5
Whitsunday Island ⌒ AUS 174-175 K 7
Whitsunday Island National Park ⊥ AUS 174-175 K 7
Whitsunday Passage ≈ 174-175 K 7
Whittier o USA 20-21 Q 6
Whittle, Cap ▲ CDN 38-39 O 3
Whittlesea o AUS 180-181 H 4
Whittlesea o ZA 220-221 H 6
Whitula Creek ~ AUS 178-179 G 3
Whitworth o CDN 38-39 K 5
Wholdaia Lake ⊖ CDN 30-31 R 5
Why o USA 40-41 H 9
Whyalla o AUS 180-181 D 2
Whycocomagh o CDN 38-39 O 6
Whycocomagh Indian Reserve ✗ CDN 38-39 O 6
Whycocomagh Provincial Park ⊥ CDN 38-39 O 5
Wiang Chai o THA 142-143 L 6
Wiang Sa o THA 142-143 M 6
Wiang Sa o THA 158-159 E 6
Wiarton o CDN 38-39 D 6
Wiawer o EAU 212-213 D 2
Wia-Wia, National Reservaat ⊥ SME 62-63 G 2
Wiawso o GH 202-203 J 6
Wichaway Nunataks ▲▲ ARK 16 E 0
Wichita o USA 44-45 J 1
Wichita Falls o USA 44-45 H 3
Wichita Mountains ▲▲ USA 44-45 H 2
Wichita Mountains National Wildlife Refuge • USA 44-45 H 2
Wick o GB 90-91 F 2
Wickenburg o• USA 40-41 H 9
Wickepin o AUS 176-177 D 6
Wickersham Dome ▲ USA 20-21 Q 4
Wickes o USA 44-45 K 2
Wickham o AUS 172-173 C 6
Wickham, Cape ▲ AUS 180-181 G 5
Wickham River ~ AUS 172-173 K 4
Wickliffe o USA 46-47 D 7
Wicklow = Cill Mhantáin ☆ IRL 90-91 D 5
Wicklow Mountains ▲▲ IRL 90-91 D 5
Wide Bay ≈ 22-23 S 4
Wide Bay ≈ 183 G 3
Wide Opening ≈ 54-55 F 2
Widgeegoara Creek ~ AUS 178-179 J 5
Widgee Mountain ▲ AUS 178-179 M 4
Widi, Kepulauan ⌒ RI 164-165 L 4
Widjefjorden ≈ 84-85 J 3
Wi Do ⌒ ROK 150-151 F 10
Widyān, al- ⚊ IRQ 128-129 J 6
Widyan, al- ▲▲ KSA 130-131 G 2
Wielbark o PL 92-93 Q 2
Wieliczka o•• PL 92-93 Q 4
Wieluń o• PL 92-93 P 3
Wien ☆•• A 92-93 O 4
Wiener Neustadt o A 92-93 O 5
Wieprz ~ PL 92-93 R 3
Wierden o NL 92-93 J 2
Wiesbaden ☆• D 92-93 K 3
Wieskirche •• D 92-93 L 5
Wiga Hill ▲ WAN 204-205 K 3
Wiggins o USA (CO) 42-43 E 5
Wiggins o USA (MS) 48-49 D 4
Wignes Lake ⊖ CDN 30-31 R 5
Wikieup o USA 40-41 H 8
Wikki warm Spring ~• WAN 204-205 J 4
Wik'ro o ETH 200-201 J 6
Wikwemikong Indian Reserve ✗ CDN 38-39 D 6
Wilber o USA 42-43 J 5
Wilberforce, Cape ▲ AUS 174-175 D 2
Wilbert o CDN 32-33 Q 5
Wilbrunga Range ▲▲ AUS 172-173 J 6
Wilbur o USA 40-41 E 2
Wilburton o USA 44-45 K 2
Wilcannia o AUS 178-179 G 6
Wilcock, Peninsula ⌣ RCH 80 C 5
Wildcat Hill ▲ CDN 34-35 E 4
Wildcat Hill Wilderness Area ⊥ CDN 34-35 E 4
Wilde o CDN 34-35 H 3
Wilderness National Park ⊥ ZA 220-221 F 6
Wildhay River ~ CDN 32-33 L 5
Wild Horse o CDN 32-33 P 7
Wild Lake ⊖ USA 20-21 P 3
Wildman Lagoon o AUS 172-173 K 2
Wild Rice River ~ USA 42-43 J 2
Wildwood o USA 46-47 L 6
Wilge ~ ZA 220-221 J 3
Wilhelm, Mount ▲ PNG 183 C 3
Wilhelmina Gebergte ▲▲ SME 62-63 F 4
Wilhelmøya ⌒ N 84-85 M 3
Wilhelm-Pieck-Stadt Guben = Guben o D 92-93 N 3
Wilhelmshaven o D 92-93 K 2
Wilhelmstal o NAM 216-217 D 10
Wilkes o ARK 16 G 12
Wilkes-Barre o USA 46-47 L 5
Wilkes Fracture Zone ≃ 14-15 R 8
Wilkes Land ⚊ ARK 16 F 12
Wilkes Rise ≃ 222-223 E 2
Wilkie o CDN 32-33 Q 5
Wilkinson Lakes ⊖ AUS 176-177 M 4
Wilkins Strait ≈ 24-25 P 1
Will, Mount ▲ CDN 32-33 F 3
Willamette River ~ USA 40-41 C 4
Willandra Creek ~ AUS 180-181 H 2
Willandra Lakes Region ⊥••• AUS 180-181 H 2
Willandra National Park ⊥ AUS 180-181 H 2
Willapa Bay ≈ 40-41 B 2
Willapa Hills ▲▲ USA 40-41 C 2
Willard o USA 44-45 D 2
Willare Bridge Roadhouse o AUS 172-173 F 4
Willcox o USA 44-45 C 3
Willem Pretorius Wildtuin ⊥ ZA 220-221 H 4
Willemstad ☆ NL 60-61 G 1
Willen o CDN 34-35 F 5
Willenberg o PL 92-93 Q 2
Willeroo o AUS 172-173 K 3
William, Mount ▲ AUS 180-181 G 4
William "Bill" Dannelly Reservoir < USA 48-49 E 3
Williambury o AUS 176-177 C 1
William Creek o AUS 178-179 D 5
Williamez Peninsula ⌣ PNG 183 F 3
William Lake ⊖ CDN 34-35 G 3
William Lambert, Mount ▲ AUS 176-177 H 2
William Point ▲ CDN 30-31 P 6
William River ~ CDN 30-31 P 6
Williams o AUS 176-177 D 6
Williams o USA (AZ) 40-41 H 8
Williams o USA (CA) 40-41 C 6
Williamsburg o USA (IA) 46-47 C 5
Williamsburg o USA (VA) 46-47 K 7
Williams Island ⌒ BS 54-55 F 2
Williams Lake o CDN 32-33 J 5
Williamson o USA 46-47 G 7
Williams Peninsula ⌣ CDN 36-37 R 3
Williamsport o USA (AK) 22-23 U 3
Williamsport o USA (PA) 46-47 K 5
Williams River ~ AUS 174-175 F 7
Williamston o USA 48-49 K 2
William's Town o BS 54-55 H 3
Williamstown o USA 46-47 F 6
Williamsville o USA 44-45 M 1
Willibert, Mount ▲ CDN 32-33 E 3
Willimantic o USA 46-47 M 5
Willis Group ⌒ AUS 174-175 L 5
Williston o USA (FL) 48-49 G 5
Williston o USA (ND) 42-43 F 1
Williston o USA (SC) 48-49 H 3
Williston o ZA 220-221 E 5
Williston Lake ⊖ CDN 32-33 J 4
Willmar o CDN 34-35 E 6
Willmar o USA 42-43 K 3
Willmore Wilderness Provincial Park ⊥ CDN 32-33 L 5
Willochra ∴ AUS 180-181 E 2
Willochra Creek ~ AUS 178-179 D 6
Willow o USA 20-21 Q 6
Willowbrook o CDN 34-35 E 5
Willow Bunch o CDN 34-35 D 6
Willow Creek o CDN (SAS) 32-33 Q 7
Willow Creek ~ CDN 32-33 O 6
Willow Creek ~ USA 40-41 E 3
Willow Lake ⊖ CDN 30-31 K 4
Willowlake River ~ CDN 30-31 H 4
Willowmore o ZA 220-221 F 6
Willowra o AUS 172-173 L 6
Willowra Aboriginal Land Trust ✗ AUS 172-173 L 6
Willow Ranch o USA 40-41 D 5
Willow River ~ CDN 32-33 J 5
Willow River ~ CDN 32-33 N 4
Willow River o USA 42-43 L 2
Willows o USA 40-41 C 6
Willow Springs o USA 44-45 M 1
Willowvale o ZA 220-221 J 6
Willsboro o USA 46-47 M 3
Wills, Lake ⊖ AUS 172-173 J 6
Wills Creek ~ AUS 178-179 E 2
Wilmer o USA 48-49 D 4
Wilmington o AUS 180-181 E 2
Wilmington o USA (DE) 46-47 L 6
Wilmington o USA (OH) 46-47 G 6
Wilmington o• USA (NC) 48-49 K 2
Wilmot o USA 46-47 H 5
Wilpattu National Park ⊥ CL 140-141 H 6
Wilpena Creek ~ AUS 178-179 E 6
Wilpena Pound • AUS 178-179 E 6
Wilshaw Ridge ≃ 224 B 7
Wilson ∴ AUS 178-179 E 6
Wilson o USA 48-49 K 2
Wilson, Monte ▲ PE 64-65 D 9
Wilson, Mount ▲ CDN 30-31 E 4
Wilson Bay ≈ 30-31 X 4
Wilson Buff Old Telegraph Station • AUS 176-177 K 5
Wilson Creek ~ USA 40-41 E 2
Wilson Island ⌒ IND 140-141 L 3
Wilson Lake < USA (KS) 42-43 H 6
Wilson Lake < USA (AL) 48-49 E 2
Wilson River ~ AUS 172-173 H 4
Wilson River ~ AUS 178-179 G 4
Wilson River ~ CDN 30-31 X 4
Wilson's Creek National Battlefield Park ∴• USA 44-45 L 1
Wilsons Promontory National Park ⊥ AUS 180-181 J 5
Wilton o USA 42-43 G 2
Wiltondale o CDN 38-39 Q 4
Wilton River ~ AUS 174-175 C 4
Wiluna o AUS 176-177 F 3
Wimborne o CDN 32-33 O 6
Wimmera ⌣ AUS 180-181 G 4
Wimmera River ~ AUS 180-181 F 4
Winamac o USA 46-47 E 5
Winam Bay ≈ 212-213 E 4
Winburg o ZA 220-221 H 4
Winchelsea o• AUS 180-181 G 5
Winchester o CDN 38-39 G 6
Winchester o• GB 90-91 G 6
Winchester o USA (ID) 40-41 F 2
Winchester o USA (KY) 46-47 F 6
Winchester o USA (TN) 48-49 E 2
Winchester o USA (VA) 46-47 J 6
Winchester o USA (WY) 42-43 C 4
Winchester Inlet ≈ 30-31 Z 4
Windabout Lake ⊖ AUS 178-179 D 6
Windamere, Lake < AUS 180-181 K 2
Windarra Mine, Mount • AUS 176-177 G 4
Wind Cave National Park ⊥ USA 42-43 F 4
Winder o USA 48-49 G 3
Winderie o AUS 176-177 C 2
Windermere Lake ⊖ CDN 38-39 C 5
Windham o USA 32-33 D 3
Windhoek ★ NAM 216-217 D 11
Windidda o AUS 176-177 G 3
Windigo Lake ⊖ CDN 34-35 L 4
Windigo River ~ CDN 34-35 L 4
Windjana Gorge National Park ⊥ AUS 172-173 G 4
Windom o USA 42-43 K 4
Windorah o AUS 178-179 G 3
Window on China • RC 156-157 M 4
Wind River ~ CDN 20-21 X 4
Wind River ~ USA (WY) 42-43 C 4
Wind River ~ USA 42-43 C 4
Wind River Indian Reservation ✗ USA 42-43 C 4
Wind River Range ▲▲ USA 42-43 C 4
Windsor o AUS 176-177 E 4
Windsor o CDN (NFL) 38-39 R 4
Windsor o CDN (NS) 38-39 M 6
Windsor o CDN (ONT) 38-39 C 7
Windsor o GB 90-91 G 6
Windsor o USA 48-49 K 1
Windsor, Mount o AUS 178-179 F 2
Windsorton o ZA 220-221 G 4
Windsorton Road o ZA 220-221 G 4
Windthorst o USA 44-45 H 3
Windward Islands ⌒ 56 E 4
Windward Passage = Vent, Passe du ≈ 54-55 H 5
Windy Bay o CDN 30-31 M 5
Windy Corner ▲ AUS 176-177 H 1
Windygates o CDN 34-35 G 6
Windy Harbour o AUS 176-177 D 7
Windy Lake ⊖ CDN 30-31 T 5
Windy River ~ CDN 30-31 T 5
Winefred Lake ⊖ CDN 32-33 P 4
Winefred River ~ CDN 32-33 P 3
Winejok o SUD 206-207 H 4
Winfield o CDN 32-33 N 5
Winfield o USA (AL) 48-49 E 3
Winfield o USA (KS) 44-45 J 1
Wing o USA 42-43 G 2
Wingate Mountains ▲▲ AUS 172-173 K 3
Wingfield Petroglyphs ⚊ KAN 56 D 3
Wingham o AUS 178-179 M 6
Wingham o CDN 38-39 D 7
Wingham Island ⌒ USA 20-21 S 6
Wingon o MYA 142-143 J 4
Winifred o USA 42-43 C 2
Winifred, Lake ⊖ AUS 172-173 F 7
Winiperu o GUY 62-63 E 2
Winisk o CDN 34-35 O 3
Winisk River ~ CDN 34-35 O 3
Winisk River Provincial Park ⊥ CDN 34-35 N 4
Winkelmann o USA 44-45 B 3
Winkler o CDN 34-35 H 6
Winneba o GH 202-203 K 7
Winnebago o USA 42-43 K 4
Winnebago, Lake ⊖ USA 46-47 D 3
Winnebago Indian Reservation ✗ USA 42-43 J 4
Winnecke Creek ~ AUS 172-173 K 5
Winnemucca o USA 40-41 F 5
Winnemucca Lake ⊖ USA 40-41 E 5
Winnepegosis o CDN 34-35 G 5
Winner o USA 42-43 H 4
Winnfield o USA 44-45 L 4
Winnibigoshish Lake ⊖ USA 42-43 K 2
Winnie o USA 44-45 K 5
Winning o AUS 176-177 C 1
Winnipeg ☆ CDN 34-35 H 6
Winnipeg, Lake ⊖ CDN 34-35 G 4
Winnipeg Beach o CDN 34-35 H 5
Winnipegosis, Lake ⊖ CDN 34-35 F 4
Winnipesaukee, Lake ⊖ USA 46-47 N 4
Winnsboro o USA (LA) 44-45 M 3
Winnsboro o USA (TX) 44-45 K 3
Winona o USA (AZ) 40-41 J 8
Winona o USA (MI) 46-47 D 2
Winona o USA (MN) 46-47 C 3
Winona o USA (MO) 46-47 C 7
Winona o USA (MS) 48-49 D 3
Winschoten o NL 92-93 J 2
Winslow o USA (AR) 44-45 K 2
Winslow o USA (AZ) 44-45 B 2
Winston o USA 40-41 C 4
Winston-Salem o USA 48-49 H 1
Winterberg o D 92-93 K 3
Winterberge ▲▲ ZA 220-221 G 6
Winter Harbour ≈ 24-25 R 3
Winter Harbour o CDN 32-33 F 6
Winter Haven o USA 48-49 H 5
Wintering Lake ⊖ CDN 34-35 H 3
Winter Island ⌒ CDN 24-25 e 7
Winter Lake ⊖ CDN 30-31 N 3
Winters o USA 44-45 H 4
Winterset o USA 42-43 K 5
Winterthur o CH 92-93 K 5
Winterton o ZA 220-221 J 4
Winterveld ⚊ ZA 220-221 F 5
Winterville State Historic Site ∴ USA 44-45 M 3
Winthrop o USA (MN) 42-43 K 3
Winthrop o USA (WA) 40-41 D 1
Winton o AUS 178-179 G 2
Winton o NZ 182 B 7
Wintua o VAN 184 II a 3
Winyaw o MYA 158-159 E 3
Wipim o PNG 183 B 5
Wiradesa o RI 168 C 3
Wirawila o CL 140-141 J 7
Wiriagar ~ RI 166-167 G 2
Wirliyajarrayi Aboriginal Land ✗ AUS 172-173 L 6
Wirmaf o RI 166-167 F 4
Wirrabara o AUS 180-181 E 2
Wirrulla o AUS 180-181 C 2
Wiscasset o USA 46-47 O 3
Wisconsin ◻ USA 46-47 C 3
Wisconsin Dells o• USA 46-47 D 4
Wisconsin Rapids o USA 46-47 D 3
Wisconsin River ~ USA 46-47 C 4
Wisdom o USA 40-41 H 3
Wisdom, Lake ⊖ PNG 183 D 3
Wisemans Ferry o AUS 180-181 L 2
Wisemen o USA 20-21 P 3
Wishart o CDN 34-35 E 5
Wishaw o GB 90-91 F 4
Wishek o USA 42-43 H 2
Wisil o SP 208-209 J 6
Wisła o PL (BIE) 92-93 P 4
Wisła ~ PL 92-93 P 1
Wiślany, Zalew ≈ 92-93 P 1
Wisłoka ~ PL 92-93 Q 3
Wismar o• D 92-93 L 2
Wismar o GUY 62-63 E 2
Wisner o USA 42-43 J 5
Witagron o SME 62-63 F 3
Witbank o ZA 220-221 J 2
Witbooisvlei o NAM 220-221 D 2
Witchecan Lake ⊖ CDN 34-35 C 4
Witfonteinrand ▲▲ ZA 220-221 H 2
Witjira National Park ⊥ AUS 178-179 C 4
Wit Kei ~ ZA 220-221 H 5
Witkoppies ▲ ZA 220-221 J 3
Witkransnek ▲ ZA 220-221 G 5
Witney o GB 90-91 G 6
Witputz < NAM 220-221 C 3
Witrivier o ZA 220-221 K 2
Witsand o ZA 220-221 E 7
Witt, De o USA (AR) 44-45 M 2
Witt, De o USA (IA) 46-47 C 5
Wittabrenna Creek ~ AUS 178-179 F 5
Witteberge ▲▲ ZA 220-221 F 6
Witteberge ▲▲ ZA 220-221 H 4
Witteberge ▲▲ ZA 220-221 E 6
Witteklip o ZA 220-221 G 6
Wittenberg o USA 46-47 D 3
Wittenberge o D 92-93 L 2
Wittenoom o AUS 172-173 D 7
Wittenoom Gorge • AUS 172-173 D 7
Wittingen o D 92-93 L 2
Wittlich o D 92-93 J 4
Wittman o USA 40-41 H 9
Wittstock o• D 92-93 M 2
Witu o EAK 212-213 H 5
Witu o PNG 183 E 3
Witu Islands ⌒ PNG 183 E 3
Witvlei o NAM 216-217 E 11
Witwater o NAM 220-221 B 2
Witwater o ZA 220-221 D 5
Witwatersberge ▲ NAM 216-217 C 11
Witwatersrand ▲ ZA 220-221 H 2
Wivenhoe, Lake < AUS 178-179 M 4
Wizzard Breakers ~ SY 224 B 4
Wladiwostok = Vladivostok o RUS 122-123 J 2
Władysławowo o• PL 92-93 P 1
Wlingi o RI 168 E 4
Włocławek ☆• PL 92-93 P 2
Włodawa o PL 92-93 R 3
Włoszczowa o PL 92-93 P 3
Woburn o CDN 38-39 J 6
Woe o GH 202-203 L 7
Woëvre ⚊ F 90-91 K 7
Wofikehn o LB 202-203 G 7
Wogadjina Hill ▲ AUS 176-177 F 1
Woganakai o PNG 183 F 3
Wogerlin Hill ▲ AUS 176-177 D 6
Wohlthat Mountains = Wohlthatmassivet ▲▲ ARK 16 F 2
Woinui, Selat ≈ 166-167 H 2
Woitape o PNG 183 D 5
Wokam, Pulau ⌒ RI 166-167 H 4
Woko National Park ⊥ AUS 178-179 L 6
Wolcott o USA (CO) 42-43 D 6
Wolcott o USA (NY) 46-47 K 4
Woleai ⌒ FSM 13 F 2
Woleu ~ G 210-211 C 3
Wolf, Isla ⌒ EC 64-65 B 9
Wolf, Volcán ▲ EC 64-65 B 9
Wolf Creek ~ AUS 172-173 H 5
Wolf Creek o USA (MT) 40-41 H 2
Wolf Creek o USA (OR) 40-41 C 4
Wolf Creek Meteorite Crater National Park ⊥ AUS 172-173 H 5
Wolf Creek Pass ▲ USA 44-45 D 1
Wolfe Island ⌒ CDN 38-39 F 6
Wolfenbüttel o•• D 92-93 L 2
Wolf Lake ⊖ CDN 20-21 Z 6
Wolf Point o USA 42-43 E 1
Wolf Rapids ~ CDN 30-31 V 2
Wolf River ~ CDN 20-21 Y 6
Wolf River ~ CDN 32-33 P 4
Wolf River ~ USA 46-47 D 3
Wolf Rock, Pulau ⌒ RI 164-165 K 3
Wolfsburg o D 92-93 L 2
Wolgast o D 92-93 M 1
Wolgograd = Zarizyn ☆• RUS 96-97 D 9
Wolin ⌒ PL 92-93 N 2
Wolkefit Pass ▲ ETH 200-201 H 6
Wollaston, Islas ⌒ RCH 80 G 7
Wollaston Forland ⚊ GRØ 26-27 p 6
Wollaston Lake o CDN (SAS) 30-31 S 6
Wollaston Lake ⊖ CDN (SAS) 34-35 E 2
Wollaston Peninsula ⌣ CDN 24-25 O 6
Wollemi National Park ⊥ AUS 180-181 L 2
Wollogorang o AUS 174-175 D 5
Wollomombi o AUS 178-179 M 6
Wollondilly River ~ AUS 180-181 L 3
Wollongong o AUS 180-181 L 3
Wolmaransstad o ZA 220-221 G 3
Wolo o• RI 166-167 K 3
Wologizi Range ⚊ LB 202-203 F 5
Wolong Daxiongmao Reserves ⊥ VRC 154-155 C 6
Wolong Xiongmao Baohuqu ⊥• VRC 154-155 C 6
Wołów o PL 92-93 O 3
Wolowaru o RI 168 E 7
Wolseley o CDN 34-35 E 5
Wolseley o ZA 220-221 D 6
Wolsey o USA 42-43 H 3
Wolstenholme, Cap ▲ CDN 36-37 L 3
Wolstenholme Fjord ≈ 26-27 Q 5
Wolstenholme Ø ⌒ GRØ 26-27 P 5
Wolsztyn o• PL 92-93 O 2
Wolverhampton o GB 90-91 F 5
Wolverine River ~ CDN 20-21 a 2
Wolverine River ~ CDN 30-31 V 6
Wolvefontein o ZA 220-221 G 6
Woman River o CDN 38-39 C 5
Wombil Downs o AUS 178-179 J 5
Wonderfontein o ZA 220-221 J 2
Wonder Gorge ⌣• Z 218-219 E 2
Wondinong o AUS 176-177 E 3
Wondiwoi, Pegunungan ▲▲ RI 166-167 H 3
Wonegizi Mountain ▲▲ LB 202-203 F 6
Wonenara o PNG 183 C 4
Wongalarroo Lake ⊖ AUS 178-179 H 6
Wongan Hills o AUS 176-177 D 5
Wonganoo o AUS 176-177 F 3
Wonga Wongué o G 210-211 B 4
Wonga-Wongué, Parc National du ⊥ G 210-211 B 4
Wonga Wongué, Réserve de ⊥ G 210-211 B 4
Wongoondy Wheat Bin o AUS 176-177 C 4
Wŏnju o ROK 150-151 F 9
Wonnangatta River ~ AUS 180-181 J 4
Wono o RI 164-165 F 5
Wonogiri o RI 168 D 3
Wonoka o AUS 178-179 E 6
Wonosari o RI 168 D 3
Wonosobo o RI 168 C 3
Wonreli o RI 166-167 D 6
Wonsan o DVR 150-151 F 8
Wonthaggi o AUS 180-181 H 5
Wonyulgunna Hill ▲ AUS 176-177 E 2
Wood, Isla ⌒ RA 78-79 H 5
Wood, Islas ⌒ RCH 80 F 7
Wood, Mount ▲ USA 42-43 C 3
Woodanilling o AUS 176-177 E 6
Wood Bay ≈ 16 F 17
Wood Bay ≈ 24-25 G 6
Woodbine o USA 48-49 H 4
Woodbridge o AUS 180-181 J 7
Woodbridge o• GB 90-91 H 5
Wood Buffalo National Park ⊥••• CDN 30-31 N 6
Wood Buffalo River ~ CDN 32-33 O 3
Woodburn o AUS 178-179 M 5
Woodburn o USA 40-41 C 3
Woodbury o USA 48-49 F 3
Wood Creek ~ CDN 34-35 N 3
Woodenbong o AUS 178-179 M 5
Woodfjorden ≈ 84-85 H 3
Woodford o AUS 178-179 M 4
Woodgate o AUS 178-179 M 3
Woodgreen o AUS 178-179 C 2
Wood Islands ⌒ AUS 172-173 G 4
Wood Islands o CDN 38-39 N 6
Woodi Woodi Mining Centre • AUS 172-173 E 6
Wood Lake o USA 42-43 G 4
Woodland o USA (CA) 40-41 D 6
Woodland o USA (WA) 40-41 C 3
Woodland Caribou Provincial Park ⊥ CDN 34-35 J 5
Woodland Park o USA 42-43 E 6
Woodlands o AUS 176-177 E 2
Woodlark Island = Murua Island ⌒ PNG 183 G 5
Woodleigh (Old Homestead) o AUS 176-177 C 3
Wood Mountain o CDN 34-35 C 6
Woodridge o CDN 34-35 H 6
Wood River ~ CDN 32-33 L 5
Wood River ~ CDN 34-35 C 6
Wood River ~ USA 20-21 Q 4
Woodroffe, Mount ▲ AUS 176-177 L 3
Woodrow o USA 20-21 Q 6
Woodruff o USA (UT) 40-41 J 5
Woodruff o USA (WI) 46-47 D 3
Woodruff Lake ⊖ CDN 30-31 R 5
Woods, Cape ▲ CDN 26-27 G 2
Woods, Lake ⊖ AUS 174-175 B 5
Woods, Lake of the ⊖ CDN 34-35 J 6
Woodsboro o USA 44-45 J 5
Woodsfield o USA 46-47 H 6
Woods Lake ⊖ CDN 36-37 R 7
Woods Landing o USA 42-43 D 5
Woodson o USA 44-45 H 3

332 Western Australia — Woodson

Woods Peak ~ AUS 174-175 H 5
Woodstock o AUS (QLD) 174-175 J 6
Woodstock o AUS (QLD) 178-179 F 2
Woodstock o CDN (NB) 38-39 L 5
Woodstock o CDN (ONT) 38-39 H 4
Woodstock o USA (IL) 46-47 D 4
Woodstock o USA (VA) 46-47 J 6
Woodstock 23 Indian Reserve X CDN 38-39 L 5
Woodstock Dam < ZA 220-221 J 4
Woodsville o USA 46-47 M 3
Woodville o NZ 182 E 4
Woodville o USA (MS) 44-45 M 4
Woodville o USA (TX) 44-45 K 4
Woodward o USA 44-45 H 1
Woody Island ~ USA 22-23 U 4
Woody Point ○ CDN 38-39 Q 4
Woogi o RI 166-167 K 3
Woolfield o AUS 178-179 G 1
Woolgoolga o AUS 178-179 M 6
Wooli o AUS 178-179 N 5
Woollett, Lac o CDN 38-39 H 3
Woolner o AUS 172-173 K 2
Woolnorth Point ▲ AUS 180-181 H 6
Woolocutty o AUS 176-177 E 6
Woolyeenyer Hill ▲ AUS 176-177 F 6
Woomera o AUS 178-179 D 6
Woomerangee Hill ▲ AUS 176-177 B 3
Woomera Prohibited Area X AUS 178-179 D 6
Woonsocket o USA 46-47 N 5
Woorabinda X AUS 178-179 L 2
Wooramel Raodhouse o AUS 176-177 C 2
Wooramel River ~ AUS 176-177 C 2
Woorkabing Hill ▲ AUS 176-177 D 6
Woomdoo o AUS 180-181 G 4
Wooster o USA 46-47 H 5
Wopasali o PNG 183 C 4
Wopmay Lake o CDN 30-31 L 3
Wopmay River ~ CDN 30-31 L 3
Woqooyi Galbeed ★ SP 208-209 F 3
Woraksan National Park ⊥ ROK 150-151 G 9
Worcester ★ GB 90-91 F 5
Worcester o USA 46-47 N 4
Worcester o ZA 220-221 D 6
Worcester Range ▲ ARK 16 F 17
Worden o USA 40-41 O 4
Wordie Bay ≈ 28-29 D 2
Wordie Gletscher ⊂ GRØ 26-27 o 6
Wori o RI 166-167 J 5
Worin o PNG 183 D 4
Workai, Pulau ~ RI 166-167 H 5
Workington o GB 90-91 F 4
Worland o USA 42-43 D 3
World's Largest Mineral Hot Springs • USA 42-43 C 4
Worms o D 92-93 K 4
Worthington o USA 42-43 K 4
Wosi o RI 164-165 J 4
Wosimi o RI 166-167 H 3
Wosnesenski Island ~ USA 22-23 Q 5
Wosu o RI 164-165 G 4
Wotap, Pulau ~ RI 166-167 F 6
Wotu o RI 164-165 G 4
Woumbou o CAM 206-207 B 6
Wounded Knee Battlefield • USA 42-43 F 4
Wour o TCH 198-199 G 2
Wouri ~ CAM 198-199 G 2
Wouri, Wâdi ~ TCH 198-199 G 2
Wowoni, Pulau ~ RI 164-165 H 6
Woyamdero Plain ⊥ EAK 212-213 G 3
Wozhang Shan ▲ VRC 156-157 C 4
Wrangel Island = Vrangelja, ostrov ~ RUS 112-113 U 1
Wrangell o USA 32-33 D 3
Wrangell, Cape ▲ USA 22-23 C 6
Wrangell Island ~ USA 32-33 D 3
Wrangell Mountains ▲ USA 20-21 T 6
Wrangell-St. Elias N.P. & Preserve & Glacier Bay N.P. ⊥ ··· USA 20-21 T 6
Wray o USA 42-43 F 5
Wrens o USA 48-49 G 3
Wrentham o CDN 32-33 O 7
Wrexham o GB 90-91 F 5
Wriedijk o SME 62-63 G 3
Wright o RP 160-161 F 7
Wright o USA 42-43 E 4
Wright Brothers National Memorial ∴ USA 48-49 L 2
Wrightsville o USA 48-49 G 3
Wrigley o CDN 30-31 H 4
Wrigley Gulf ≈ 16 F 24
Writing Rock • USA 42-43 F 1
Wrocław ☆ ·· PL 92-93 O 3
Wrotham Park o AUS 174-175 G 5
Wrottesley, Cap o CDN 24-25 L 3
Wrottesley Inlet ≈ 24-25 Y 5
Wroxton o CDN 34-35 F 5
Września o PL 92-93 O 2
Wschowa o PL 92-93 O 3
Wu'an o PL 92-93 J 3
Wuasa o RI 164-165 G 4
Wubin o AUS 176-177 D 5
Wubu o VRC 154-155 G 3
Wuchang o VRC (HEI) 150-151 F 3
Wuchang o VRC (HUB) 154-155 J 6
Wuchiu Yü ~ RC 156-157 K 5
Wuchuan o VRC (GDG) 156-157 G 6
Wuchuan o VRC (GZH) 156-157 E 5
Wuchuan o VRC (NMZ) 148-149 K 7
Wuda o VRC 154-155 E 2
Wudalianchi o VRC (HEI) 150-151 F 3
Wudalianchi ⊥ VRC (HEI) 150-151 F 3
Wudang Shan ▲ VRC 154-155 G 5
Wudangshan • VRC 154-155 G 5
Wudang Zhao • VRC 154-155 G 1
Wudan Shan ▲ VRC 154-155 G 1
Wuday'ah o KSA 132-133 E 5
Wudil o WAN 204-205 H 3
Wuding o VRC 156-157 C 4
Wuding He ~ VRC 154-155 F 2
Wudu o VRC 154-155 D 5

Wufeng o VRC 154-155 G 6
Wugang o VRC 156-157 G 3
Wugong o VRC 154-155 F 4
Wugong Ci • VRC 156-157 J 3
Wugong Shan ▲ VRC 156-157 J 3
Wuhai o VRC 154-155 E 2
Wuhan ☆ VRC 154-155 J 6
Wuhe o VRC 154-155 K 5
Wuhu o VRC 154-155 L 6
Wuhua o VRC 156-157 J 5
Wiijang o VRC 144-145 B 4
Wuji o VRC 154-155 J 2
Wu Jiang ~ VRC 156-157 F 2
Wukari o WAN 204-205 H 5
Wulai • RC 156-157 M 4
Wulff Land ∴ GRØ 26-27 a 2
Wulgo o WAN 198-199 G 6
Wuli o VRC 144-145 J 3
Wulian o VRC 154-155 L 4
Wulian Feng ▲ VRC 156-157 C 3
Wuliaru, Pulau ~ RI 166-167 F 5
Wulichuan o VRC 154-155 G 5
Wulik River ~ USA 20-21 J 3
Wuling Shan ▲ VRC 156-157 F 3
Wulingshan Z.B. ⊥ · VRC 156-157 K 1
Wulingyuan ··· VRC 156-157 G 2
Wulo Kode o ETH 208-209 C 5
Wulong o VRC 156-157 E 2
Wuluhan o RI 168 E 4
Wulur o RI 166-167 E 5
Wum o CAM 204-205 J 5
Wumeng Shan ▲ VRC 156-157 C 4
Wuming o VRC 156-157 F 5
Wundanyi o EAK 212-213 G 5
Wundowie o AUS 176-177 D 5
Wunen o RI 166-167 K 3
Wuning o VRC 154-155 J 6
Wunna ~ IND 138-139 G 9
Wunnummin Lake o CDN 34-35 M 4
Wun Rog o SUD 206-207 J 4
Wun Shwai o SUD 206-207 J 4
Wuntau o SUD 206-207 J 4
Wuntho o MYA 142-143 J 4
Wuping o VRC 156-157 K 4
Wuppertal ☆ D 92-93 J 3
Wuppertal o ZA 220-221 D 6
Wuqi o VRC 154-155 F 3
Wuqia o VRC 146-147 B 6
Wurarga o AUS 176-177 D 4
Wurno o WAN 198-199 B 6
Wuruma Reservation < AUS 178-179 L 3
Würzburg ☆ ·· D 92-93 K 4
Wuse o WAN 204-205 H 4
Wushan o VRC (ANH) 154-155 K 5
Wushan o VRC (GAN) 154-155 D 4
Wushan o VRC (SIC) 156-157 F 1
Wushan Ling ▲ VRC 154-155 C 3
Wusheng Guan ▲ VRC 154-155 J 6
Wushi o VRC (GDG) 156-157 F 6
Wushi o VRC (XUZ) 146-147 D 5
Wushishi o WAN 204-205 G 4
Wushizen o VRC 156-157 F 6
Wuskwatim Lake o CDN 34-35 G 3
Wusuli Jiang ~ VRC 150-151 K 4
Wutai o VRC 154-155 H 2
Wutaishan ▲ VRC 154-155 H 2
Wutan o VRC 156-157 G 2
Wutongqiao o VRC 156-157 C 2
Wutung o PNG 183 A 2
Wuwei o VRC (ANH) 154-155 K 6
Wuwei o VRC (GAN) 154-155 C 3
Wuwu o PNG 183 D 4
Wuxi o VRC (JIA) 154-155 M 6
Wuxi o VRC (SIC) 154-155 F 6
Wuxu o VRC 156-157 F 5
Wuxuan o VRC 156-157 F 5
Wuxue o VRC 156-157 J 2
Wuyang o VRC 154-155 H 5
Wuyi o VRC 156-157 L 3
Wuyiling o VRC (FUJ) 156-157 L 3
Wuyi Shan ▲ VRC 156-157 K 3
Wuyishan o VRC (FUJ) 156-157 K 3
Wuyishan Z.B. ⊥· VRC 156-157 K 3
Wuyunan o VRC 148-149 J 7
Wuzhai o VRC 154-155 H 4
Wuzhi o VRC 154-155 H 4
Wuzhi Shan ▲ VRC 156-157 G 2
Wuzhi Shan ▲ VRC 156-157 F 7
Wuzhong o VRC 154-155 E 2
Wuzhou o VRC 156-157 G 5
Wyaaba Creek ~ AUS 174-175 G 5
Wyabing o AUS 176-177 E 6
Wyalkatchem o AUS 176-177 D 5
Wyandotte Caves • USA 46-47 F 6
Wyandra o AUS 178-179 H 4
Wyangala, Lake o AUS 180-181 K 2
Wyara, Lake o AUS 178-179 H 5
Wycheproof o AUS 180-181 G 5
Wyemandoo Hill ▲ AUS 176-177 E 4
Wyena o AUS 178-179 J 1
Wylie Scarp ⊥ AUS 176-177 G 6
Wyllie's Poort o ZA 218-219 G 6
Wyloo o AUS 172-173 C 7
Wymore o USA 42-43 J 5
Wynbring o AUS 176-177 M 5
Wyndham o AUS 172-173 J 3
Wyndmere o USA 42-43 J 2
Wynne o USA 44-45 M 2
Wynniatt Bay ≈ 24-25 Q 4
Wynyard o AUS 180-181 H 6
Wyola o USA 42-43 D 3
Wyola Lake o AUS 176-177 L 4
Wyoming o USA (MI) 46-47 F 4
Wyoming □ USA (WY) 42-43 E 3
Wyoming Peak ▲ USA 40-41 J 4
Wyoming Range ▲ USA 40-41 J 4
Wyperfeld National Park ⊥ AUS 180-181 G 5
Wyralinu Hill ▲ AUS 176-177 D 4
Wyseby o AUS 178-179 K 3
Wyszków o PL 92-93 Q 2
Wytheville o USA 46-47 H 7
Wyżyna Małopolska ⊾ PL 92-93 Q 3

X

Xaafuun = Dante o SP 208-209 K 3
Xaafuun, Raas ▲ SP 208-209 K 3
Xagquka o VRC 144-145 J 5
Xaidulla o VRC 138-139 F 1
Xainza o VRC 144-145 G 5
Xai-Xai ☆ MOC 218-219 F 1
Xakriabá, Área Indígena X BR 72-73 H 3
Xalin o SP 208-209 J 4
Xalpatláhuac o MEX 52-53 E 3
Xa Mát o VN 158-159 J 5
Xambioiá o BR 68-69 D 5
Xambrê, Rio ~ BR 72-73 D 7
Xam Hua o LAO 156-157 D 7
Xamindele o ANG 216-217 B 3
Xá-Muteba o ANG 216-217 D 4
Xandel o ANG 216-217 D 4
Xangongo o ANG 216-217 C 8
Xánthi o GR 100-101 K 4
Xanthos ∴ TR 128-129 C 4
Xanxerê o BR 74-75 D 6
Xapuri o BR 70-71 C 2
Xapuri, Rio ~ BR 70-71 C 2
Xarar < SP 208-209 J 6
Xarardheere o SP 208-209 H 6
Xarlag o VRC 154-155 F 2
Xar Obot o VRC 148-149 O 5
Xarrama, Rio ~ P 98-99 C 5
Xassengue o ANG 216-217 E 5
Xátiva o E 98-99 G 5
Xaudum ~ RB 218-219 C 5
Xavante ou Rio das Vertentes, Rio ~ BR 68-69 C 7
Xavantes, Represa de < BR 72-73 F 7
Xavantes, Serra dos ▲ BR 72-73 F 7
Xavantina o BR 72-73 D 6
Xavantinho, Rio ~ BR 68-69 C 7
Xayar o VRC 146-147 F 5
Xêgar o VRC 144-145 F 6
Xeitongmoin o VRC 144-145 G 6
Xel-Há ∴· MEX 52-53 K 2
Xenia o USA 46-47 G 6
Xerente, Área Indígena X BR 68-69 D 6
Xeriuni, Rio ~ BR 66-67 F 3
Xerokambos o GR 100-101 L 7
Xert o E 98-99 H 4
Xeruá, Rio ~ BR 66-67 C 6
Xiabande o VRC 150-151 E 5
Xiachuan Dao ~ VRC 156-157 H 6
Xiahe o VRC 154-155 C 4
Xi'an ☆ ·· VRC 154-155 F 4
Xianfen o VRC 154-155 G 4
Xianfeng o VRC 156-157 F 2
Xiangcheng o VRC (HEN) 154-155 H 5
Xiangcheng o VRC (SIC) 144-145 M 6
Xianger Shan ▲ VRC 154-155 G 4
Xiangfan o VRC 154-155 H 5
Xiangcheng Qi o VRC 148-149 L 6
Xiang Jiang ~ VRC 156-157 H 3
Xiangkhoang o LAO 156-157 C 7
Xiangmihu • VRC 156-157 H 5
Xiang Ngeun o LAO 156-157 C 7
Xiangning o VRC 154-155 G 4
Xiangshan o VRC 156-157 M 2
Xiangsha Wan • VRC 154-155 F 1
Xiangshui o VRC 154-155 L 4
Xiangtan o VRC 156-157 H 3
Xiangtangshan Shiku • VRC 154-155 J 3
Xiangxiang o VRC 156-157 H 3
Xiangyin o VRC 156-157 H 2
Xiangzhou o VRC 156-157 F 5
Xianju o VRC 156-157 M 2
Xianning o VRC 156-157 J 2
Xianshan Gang ~ VRC 156-157 M 2
Xiantao o VRC 154-155 H 6
Xianxia Ling ▲ VRC 156-157 L 3
Xianyang o VRC 154-155 F 4
Xianyou o VRC 156-157 L 4
Xianzhao Shan ▲ VRC 154-155 E 2
Xinzhelin SK o VRC 156-157 L 2
Xianzheng o VRC 154-155 H 4
Xianzhou o VRC 156-157 L 2
Xinzuotang o VRC 156-157 J 5
Xiongyuecheng o VRC 150-151 D 7
Xipamanu, Rio ~ BR 70-71 C 2
Xipaotai • VRC 150-151 D 7
Xipembe, Rio ~ MOC 218-219 G 5
Xiping o VRC (HEN) 154-155 H 5
Xiping o VRC (HEN) 156-157 G 5
Xique-Xique o BR 68-69 G 6
Xiaochi o VRC 154-155 J 4
Xiaogan o VRC 154-155 H 6
Xiaohe o VRC 154-155 F 5
Xiaojiahe o VRC 156-157 L 2
Xiaojin o VRC 154-155 C 6
Xiaokouzi • VRC 154-155 G 1
Xiaomei Guan ▲ VRC 156-157 J 4
Xiaonanchuan o VRC 144-145 K 3
Xiaoniao Tiantang • VRC 156-157 H 3
Xiaoshan o VRC 154-155 M 6
Xiao Shan ▲ VRC 154-155 G 4
Xiaowutai Shan ▲ VRC 154-155 J 2
Xiao Xian o VRC 154-155 L 3
Xiapu o VRC 156-157 L 3
Xiawa o VRC 150-151 C 6
Xiayi o VRC 154-155 K 4
Xiazhai o VRC 156-157 H 3
Xiazhifu o VRC 144-145 C 5
Xiazhuang o VRC 172-173 C 7
Xiazi o VRC 156-157 F 3
Xichang o VRC (GXI) 156-157 F 5
Xichang o VRC (SIC) 156-157 C 3
Xichou o VRC 156-157 D 5
Xichuan o VRC 154-155 G 5
Xicoténcatl o MEX 50-51 K 6
Xicotepec de Juárez o MEX 52-53 F 1
Xide o VRC 156-157 C 2
Xie, Rio ~ BR 66-67 D 2
Xiezhou Guandi Miao • VRC 154-155 G 4
Xifeng o VRC (GAN) 154-155 E 3
Xifeng o VRC (GZH) 156-157 E 3
Xigang o VRC 150-151 F 3
Xigazê o VRC 144-145 G 6
Xigaze Shannan ▲ VRC 144-145 H 6
Xihua o VRC 154-155 J 5

Xiis o SP 208-209 H 3
Xiji o VRC 154-155 D 4
Xi Jiang ~ VRC 156-157 G 5
Xijin SK o VRC 156-157 F 5
Xijir Ulan Hu o VRC 144-145 H 3
Xijishui o VRC 156-157 D 3
Xikou o VRC (JXI) 156-157 J 2
Xikou o VRC (ZHE) 156-157 M 2
Xilamuren Caoyuan • VRC 148-149 K 7
Xi Liao He ~ VRC 150-151 D 6
Xilin o VRC 156-157 D 4
Xilinhot o VRC 148-149 N 6
Xilinji = Mohe o VRC 150-151 D 1
Xilitla o MEX 52-53 E 1
Xime o GNB 202-203 C 4
Xin'anjiang Sk o VRC 156-157 L 2
Xin Barag Youqi o VRC 148-149 N 3
Xin Barag Zuoqi o VRC 150-151 B 3
Xinbin o VRC 150-151 E 7
Xincai o VRC 154-155 J 5
Xincheng o VRC 156-157 M 2
Xinchang o VRC 156-157 J 2
Xinchuan o VRC 154-155 M 5
Xindeng o VRC 156-157 L 2
Xindong o VRC 156-157 G 5
Xinduqiao o VRC 154-155 B 6
Xinfeng o VRC 156-157 J 4
Xinfengjiang SK < VRC 156-157 J 5
Xingan o VRC 156-157 J 3
Xing'an o VRC 156-157 G 4
Xingcheng o VRC 150-151 C 7
Xinge o ANG 216-217 D 4
Xingguo o VRC 156-157 J 3
Xinghua o VRC 154-155 L 5
Xingjiejie o VRC 156-157 E 5
Xingkai Hu o VRC 150-151 J 5
Xinglong o VRC 154-155 K 1
Xinglong-Shan Z.B. ⊥· VRC 154-155 C 4
Xingning o VRC 156-157 J 4
Xingod o SP 208-209 J 5
Xingpan o VRC 156-157 E 5
Xingren o VRC 156-157 D 4
Xingrenbu o VRC 154-155 D 3
Xingshan o VRC 154-155 H 6
Xingtai o VRC 154-155 J 3
Xingu, Parque Indígena do X BR 68-69 D 7
Xingu, Rio ~ BR 68-69 B 5
Xingu, Rio ~ BR 72-73 D 2
Xinguara o BR 68-69 D 5
Xingwen o VRC 156-157 D 2
Xing Xian o VRC 154-155 G 3
Xingxingxia o VRC 146-147 M 5
Xingyi o VRC 156-157 D 4
Xinhe o VRC 146-147 F 5
Xinhuang o VRC 156-157 F 3
Xinhui o VRC 156-157 H 6
Xining ☆ VRC 154-155 B 3
Xiniujiao o VRC 156-157 L 8
Xinji o VRC 154-155 J 3
Xinjie o VRC 156-157 D 5
Xinjin o VRC (LIA) 150-151 C 8
Xinjin o VRC (SIC) 156-157 C 2
Xinlong o VRC 154-155 B 6
Xinmin o VRC 150-151 D 7
Xinning o VRC 156-157 G 3
Xinping o VRC 156-157 C 4
Xinshao o VRC 156-157 G 3
Xintai o VRC 154-155 K 4
Xintian o VRC 156-157 H 4
Xinxiang o VRC 154-155 H 4
Xinxim, Rio ~ BR 68-69 B 6
Xinyang o VRC 154-155 H 5
Xinye o VRC 154-155 H 5
Xinyi o VRC (GDG) 156-157 G 5
Xinyi o VRC (JIA) 154-155 L 4
Xinyu o VRC 156-157 J 3
Xinzheng o VRC 154-155 H 4
Xinzhou o VRC 154-155 H 3
Xiongyuecheng o VRC 146-147 H 2
Xi Ujimqin Qi o VRC 148-149 N 5
Xiushan o VRC 156-157 F 2
Xiushui o VRC 156-157 J 2
Xiuwen o VRC 156-157 E 3
Xiuyan o VRC 150-151 D 7
Xiuying o VRC 156-157 G 7
Xiwu o VRC 144-145 L 4
Xixabangma Feng ▲ VRC 144-145 E 6
Xi Xian o VRC 154-155 H 5
Xixiang o VRC 154-155 E 5
Xixia Wangling • VRC 154-155 E 2
Xixón = Gijón o E 98-99 E 3
Xixona o E 98-99 G 5
Xiyang o VRC 154-155 H 3
Xifeng o VRC (GZH) 156-157 E 3
Xizhou Guandi Miao • VRC 154-155 G 4
Xiyang o VRC 150-151 F 3
Xizang o VRC 144-145 G 5
Xigaze Shannan ▲ VRC 144-145 H 6
Xihua o VRC 154-155 J 5

Xochicalco ∴ MEX 52-53 E 2
Xochimilco •·· MEX 52-53 E 2
Xochob ∴·· MEX 52-53 K 2
Xom Don o VN 158-159 J 4
Xom Thôn o VN 158-159 J 5
Xopoto, Rio ~ BR 72-73 J 2
Xpujil o MEX 52-53 K 2
Xpujil ∴·· MEX 52-53 K 2
Xuan Đài, Vũng ≈ VN 158-159 K 4
Xuan'en o VRC 156-157 F 2
Xuanhan o VRC 154-155 E 6
Xuanhua o VRC 154-155 J 1
Xuankong Si • VRC 154-155 H 3
Xuân Lộc o VN 158-159 J 5
Xuanwei o VRC 156-157 D 3
Xuanzhong Si • VRC 154-155 H 3
Xuanzhou o VRC 154-155 L 6
Xuchang o VRC 154-155 H 4
Xuddur o SP 208-209 F 6
Xudun o SP 208-209 H 4
Xuebao Ding ▲ VRC 154-155 C 5
Xuefeng Shan ▲ VRC 156-157 G 3
Xueshan ▲ VRC 154-155 D 3
Xufeng Shan ▲ VRC 156-157 G 3
Xugana Lodge o RB 218-219 B 4
Xumishan Shiku • VRC 154-155 D 3
Xunantunich ∴· BH 52-53 K 3
Xungru o VRC 144-145 E 6
Xun He ~ VRC 154-155 F 5
Xunhua o VRC 154-155 C 4
Xun Jiang ~ VRC 156-157 G 5
Xunke o VRC 150-151 G 3
Xunwu o VRC 156-157 J 4
Xun Xian o VRC 154-155 J 4
Xunyi o VRC 154-155 F 4
Xupu o VRC 156-157 G 3
Xuro Co o VRC 144-145 F 5
Xushui o VRC 154-155 J 3
Xuwen o VRC 156-157 G 6
Xuyi o VRC 154-155 L 5
Xuyong o VRC 156-157 D 2
Xuzhou o VRC 154-155 K 4

Y

Yaak o USA 40-41 G 1
Yaamba o AUS 178-179 L 2
Ya'an o VRC 154-155 C 2
Yaaq Braaway o SP 212-213 J 3
Yaba-Hita-Hikosan Quasi National Park ⊥ J 152-153 D 8
Yabassi o CAM 204-205 H 6
Yabayo o CI 202-203 G 7
Yabe o J 152-153 D 8
Yabebyry o PY 76-77 J 4
Yabebyry, Arroyo ~ PY 76-77 J 4
Yabelo o ETH 208-209 D 6
Yabelo Wildlife Sanctuary ⊥ ETH 208-209 D 6
Yabia o ZRE 210-211 J 2
Yabiti o DY 202-203 L 4
Yabo o YV 60-61 K 3
Yabrin o KSA 130-131 L 6
Yabuli o VRC 150-151 G 5
Yabus ~ ETH 208-209 B 4
Yabuyanos o PE 64-65 F 2
Yacambú, Parque Nacional ⊥ YV 60-61 J 2
Yacaré Norte, Riacho ~ PY 76-77 H 2
Yacheng o VRC 156-157 F 7
Yachi ~ VRC 156-157 E 3
Yacimiento Río Turbio o RA 80 D 5
Yaciretá, Ilha ~ PY 76-77 J 4
Yacoraite, Río ~ RA 76-77 E 2
Yacuiba o BOL 70-71 G 8
Yacuma, Río ~ BOL 70-71 D 4
Yadat, Wâdi ~ SUD 200-201 G 4
Yadé, Massif du ▲ RCA 206-207 B 5
Yadgir o IND 140-141 G 2
Yadibikro o CI 202-203 H 6
Yadiki o IND 140-141 G 3
Yadma o KSA 132-133 D 4
Yadong o VRC 144-145 G 6
Yadua o FJI 184 III b 2
Yaeng o THA 158-159 F 5
Yafase o RI 166-167 L 3
Yafo, Tel Aviv- ☆ IL 130-131 D 1
Yafran o LAR 192-193 E 1
Yagati o IND 140-141 G 4
Yaghan Basin ≃ 5 E 10
Yagishiri-tô ~ J 152-153 J 2
Yagoua o CAM 206-207 B 3
Yagradagzê Shan ▲ VRC 144-145 K 3
Yaguajay o C 54-55 F 3
Yagual, El o YV 60-61 G 4
Yaguarapro o YV 60-61 K 2
Yaguari, Arroyo ~ RA 76-77 H 5
Yaguarón, Río ~ ROU 74-75 D 9
Yaguas o CO 66-67 B 4
Yaguas, Río ~ PE 66-67 B 4
Yahekou o VRC 154-155 H 5
Yahk o CDN 32-33 M 7
Yahualica o MEX 50-51 H 7
Yahuma o ZRE 210-211 J 3
Yahyalı o TR 128-129 E 3
Yaibrai o VRC 156-157 L 2
Yaita o J 152-153 H 6
Yajalón o MEX 52-53 H 3
Yajiang o VRC 154-155 B 6
Yaka o RCA 206-207 D 6
Yakabindie o AUS 176-177 F 3
Yakak, Cape ▲ USA 22-23 H 7
Yakana o ZRE 210-211 J 3
Yakassé-Attobrou o CI 202-203 J 6
Yakatograd o VRC 146-147 H 6
Yakeshi o VRC 150-151 C 5
Yakima ☆ USA 40-41 D 2
Yakima Indian Reservation X USA 40-41 D 2

Yakima River ~ USA 40-41 D 2
Yakmach o PK 134-135 K 4
Yako o BF 202-203 J 4
Yakobi Island ~ USA 32-33 B 2
Yakoma o ZRE 206-207 F 6
Yaku o J 152-153 D 9
Yaku-shima ~ J 152-153 D 9
Yaku-shima National Park ⊥ J 152-153 D 9
Yakutat o USA 20-21 V 7
Yakutat Bay ≈ 20-21 V 7
Yakutsk = Jakutsk ☆ ·· RUS 118-119 O 4
Yala o EAK 212-213 E 3
Yala o EAK 212-213 E 4
Yala o GH 202-203 K 6
Yala o THA 158-159 F 7
Yalaki o ZRE 210-211 J 2
Yalape ∴ PE 64-65 D 5
Yalata o AUS 176-177 L 5
Yalata Aboriginal Lands X AUS 176-177 L 5
Yalbalgo o AUS 176-177 C 2
Yalbyn ~ RUS 118-119 O 7
Yale o CDN 32-33 K 7
Yale o USA 40-41 O 2
Yaleko o ZRE 210-211 K 3
Yalewa Kalou ~ FJI 184 III a 2
Yalgoo o AUS 176-177 D 4
Yalgorup National Park ⊥ AUS 176-177 C 6
Yali ~ BF 202-203 L 3
Yali o CO 60-61 D 4
Yali o NIC 52-53 L 5
Yaligimba o ZRE 210-211 J 2
Yalinga o RCA 206-207 F 5
Yallahs o JAM 54-55 H 5
Yalleroi o AUS 178-179 K 3
Yallingup Caves • AUS 176-177 C 6
Yallo ▲ BF 202-203 K 3
Yalogo o BF 202-203 K 3
Yaloké o RCA 206-207 C 6
Yalong Jiang ~ VRC 144-145 M 4
Yalong Jiang ~ VRC 156-157 B 2
Yalongwa o ZRE 210-211 K 3
Yalova o TR 128-129 C 2
Yaltubung o RI 166-167 E 5
Yalu Jiang ~ VRC 150-151 E 7
Ya'lujiang Kou ≈ 150-151 E 8
Yâlür ▲ AFG 136-137 M 1
Yamada o J 152-153 J 5
Yamagata ☆ J 152-153 J 5
Yamaguchi ☆ J 152-153 D 7
Yamakawa o J 152-153 D 8
Yamal, Poluostrov = Jamal, poluostrov ◡ RUS 108-109 N 7
Yamal Nenets Autonomous District = Jam.-Neneckij avt.okrug ◻ RUS 108-109 N 7
Yamanashi □ J 152-153 H 7
Yamama ▲ AUS 176-177 G 4
Yamarna Aboriginal Land X AUS 176-177 G 3
Yamasá o DOM 54-55 K 5
Yamasaki o J 152-153 F 7
Yamato Rise ≃ 152-153 F 5
Yamatosammyaku ▲ ARK 16 F 4
Yamatsuri o J 152-153 J 6
Yamba o AUS 178-179 M 5
Yambah o AUS 176-177 M 1
Yambacoona o AUS 180-181 G 5
Yambah o AUS 206-207 M 1
Yambala o RCA 206-207 E 5
Yamba Lake o CDN 30-31 O 3
Yambala Koudouvelé o RCA 206-207 E 5
Yambata o ZRE 210-211 H 2
Yamba-Yamba o ZRE 210-211 L 6
Yambéring o RG 202-203 D 4
Yambio o SUD 206-207 J 6
Yambuya o ZRE 210-211 J 3
Yamdena, Pulau ~ RI 166-167 F 5
Yame o J 152-153 D 8
Yamethin o MYA 142-143 K 5
Yam Hamelah = Bahrēt Lut ◡ JOR 130-131 D 2
Yamin o IRQ 130-131 J 2
Yam Kinneret ◡ IL 130-131 D 1
Yamma Yamma Lake o AUS 178-179 H 4
Yamon o PE 64-65 C 5
Yamoussoukro ★ CI 202-203 H 6
Yampa o USA 42-43 D 4
Yampa River ~ USA 42-43 C 5
Yampi Sound Mining Area • AUS 172-173 F 4
Yamtu, Cape ▲ RI 166-167 F 2
Yamuna ~ IND 138-139 G 5
Yamuna ~ IND 138-139 G 4
Yamuna ~ IND 142-143 B 3
Yamunanagar o IND 138-139 F 4
Yamur, Danau o RI 166-167 H 3
Yamzho Yumco o VRC 144-145 H 6
Yan o MAL 162-163 D 9
Yana o WAL 202-203 D 5
Yanaba Island ~ PNG 183 F 5
Yanac o AUS 180-181 G 4
Yanachaga-Chemillén, Parque Nacional ⊥ PE 64-65 C 6
Yanacu Grande, Río ~ PE 64-65 C 5
Yanadani o J 152-153 E 8
Yanagawa o J 152-153 D 8
Yanahuanca o PE 64-65 D 7
Yanam o J 152-153 E 8
Yanam o IND 140-141 K 2
Yanaoca o PE 70-71 B 4
Yanatili, Río ~ PE 64-65 E 7
Yanayacu o PE 64-65 D 5
Yanbū o KSA 130-131 F 5
Yanbū' an-Naḥl o KSA 130-131 F 5
Yancannia o AUS 178-179 H 6
Yancannia Creek ~ AUS 178-179 G 6

Yancannia Range ▲ AUS 178-179 G 6
Yanchang o VRC 154-155 G 3
Yancheng o VRC 154-155 M 5
Yanchep Beach o AUS 176-177 C 5
Yanchep National Park ⊥ AUS 176-177 C 5
Yanchi o VRC 154-155 E 3
Yanco Creek ~ AUS 180-181 H 3
Yanco Glen o AUS 178-179 H 6
Yanda Creek ~ AUS 178-179 J 5
Yandama Creek ~ AUS 178-179 F 5
Yandang Shan ▲ VRC 156-157 L 3
Yandangshan • VRC 156-157 M 2
Yandakadi o AUS 146-147 D 6
Yandeearra o AUS 172-173 D 5
Yandeearra Aboriginal Land X AUS 172-173 D 5
Yandev o WAN 204-205 H 5
Yandina o SOL 184 I d 3
Yandon o MYA 158-159 C 2
Yandongi o ZRE 210-211 J 2
Yandun o VRC 146-147 M 4
Yanfeng o VRC 156-157 C 4
Yanfolia o RMM 202-203 F 4
Yang o THA 158-159 F 3
Yanga o CAM 210-211 E 2
Yanga o TCH 206-207 D 4
Yanga, Komin- o BF 202-203 L 4
Yangalia o RCA 206-207 E 5
Yangambi o ZRE 210-211 K 3
Yangara ~ TCH 198-199 J 2
Yangas o PE 64-65 D 7
Yangasso o RMM 202-203 F 4
Yangbajain o VRC (XIZ) 144-145 H 5
Yangbajain • VRC (XIZ) 144-145 H 5
Yangcheng o VRC 154-155 H 4
Yangchun o VRC 156-157 G 5
Yangcun o VRC 156-157 L 4
Yangdok o DVR 150-151 F 8
Yanggandu o RI 166-167 L 6
Yangjiang o VRC 156-157 G 6
Yanglin o VRC 156-157 C 4
Yangliu o VRC 154-155 J 4
Yangmingshan National Park ⊥ RC 156-157 M 4
Yangon o PNG 183 B 4
Yangoru o PNG 183 B 4
Yangouali, Mare o DY 202-203 L 4
Yangqi Gang ~ VRC 154-155 H 3
Yangquan o VRC 154-155 H 3
Yanguanguiu o VRC 154-155 G 3
Yangqu Shan ▲ VRC 154-155 H 3
Yangshan o VRC 156-157 H 4
Yangshaocun Yizhi ∴· VRC 154-155 G 4
Yangshuo o VRC 156-157 G 4
Yangtze = Chang Jiang ~ VRC 154-155 L 6
Yangxi o VRC 156-157 G 6
Yangxin o VRC 154-155 J 6
Yangzhou o VRC 154-155 L 5
Yang'e Z.B. ⊥· VRC 156-157 L 6
Yanhe o VRC 156-157 F 2
Yanhu o VRC 144-145 D 4
Yanhuqu o VRC 144-145 D 4
Yanji o VRC 150-151 G 6
Yanjin o VRC 156-157 D 2
Yankari Game Reserve ⊥ WAN 204-205 J 4
Yankoman o GH 202-203 J 7
Yankton o USA 42-43 J 4
Yankton Indian Reservation X USA 42-43 J 4
Yanmen ▲ VRC 154-155 H 2
Yannarie River ~ AUS 176-177 C 1
Yanomami, Parque Indígena X BR 60-61 K 6
Yanonge o ZRE 210-211 K 3
Yan Oya ~ CL 140-141 J 6
Yanqi o VRC 146-147 H 4
Yanqing o VRC 154-155 J 1
Yanqul o OM 132-133 K 2
Yanrey o AUS 172-173 B 7
Yanshan o VRC (HEB) 154-155 K 2
Yanshan o VRC (YUN) 156-157 D 5
Yanshiping o VRC 144-145 J 4
Yanshou o VRC 150-151 G 5
Yansoribo o RI 166-167 G 2
Yantai o VRC 154-155 M 3
Yantakkeqik o VRC 146-147 J 6
Yantara, Lake o AUS 178-179 G 5
Yanting o VRC 154-155 D 6
Yantou o VRC 156-157 M 2
Yantzaza o EC 64-65 C 3
Yanuca o FJI 184 III a 2
Yanwodao • VRC 150-151 J 4
Yanzikou o VRC 154-155 D 3
Yaodian o VRC (GAN) 154-155 E 3
Yaodian o VRC (SXI) 154-155 F 3
Yaolin D. • VRC 156-157 L 2
Yaoundé ★ CAM 210-211 C 2
Yaowang Gang o VRC 154-155 M 5
Yaowang Hill o VRC 154-155 F 4
Yao Xian o VRC 154-155 F 4
Yapacana, Parque Nacional ⊥ YV 60-61 H 6
Yapacani o BOL 70-71 F 6
Yapacani ~ BOL 70-71 F 6
Yapacaraí o PY 76-77 J 3
Yapen, Pulau ~ RI 166-167 J 2
Yapen, Selat ≈ 166-167 J 2
Yapero o RI 166-167 K 3
Yapeyú o RA 76-77 J 5
Yappar River ~ AUS 174-175 F 6
Yappirala o IND 140-141 J 4
Yapui o BOL 70-71 E 4
Yaputih o RI 166-167 E 3
Yaqeta ~ FJI 184 III a 2
Yaque del Norte, Río ~ DOM 54-55 K 5
Yaqui, Boca del ≈ 50-51 D 4
Yaqui, Río ~ MEX 50-51 E 3
Yar ≈ 166-167 H 5
Yara o RN 198-199 J 7
Yara o C 54-55 G 4
Yaraka o AUS 178-179 H 3
Yaralıgöz Dağı ▲ TR 128-129 F 2

Contributors/Credits

Cartography

Editors-in-Chief/Project Directors
Dieter Meinhardt and Eberhard Schäfer, Stuttgart

Editor, Coordinator
Rüdiger Werr, Stuttgart

Editorial Staff
Ralf van den Berg, Stuttgart
Klaus Dorenburg, Leipzig
Marion Kästner, Leipzig
Karl-Heinz Klimpel, Leipzig

Cartography Relief Artists
Kai Gründler, Leipzig
Eberhard von Harsdorf, Siegsdorf
Prof. Dr. Christian Herrmann, Karlsruhe
Bruno Witzky, Stuttgart

Computer Cartographers
Director: Jörg Wagner, Stuttgart
Natascha Fischer, Stuttgart
Margot Graf, Leipzig
Doris Kordisch, Leipzig
Hannelore Kühsel, Leipzig
Helga Michel, Leipzig
Karin Oelzner, Leipzig

Technology
Director: Joachim Drück, Stuttgart
Elke Bellstedt, Stuttgart
Bernd Hlawatsch, Stuttgart
Erika Rieger, Stuttgart
Walter Zimmermann, Stuttgart

Index
Gabriele Kiechle, Stuttgart

Typesetting
Director: Jörg Wulfes, Stuttgart
Frank Barchet, Stuttgart

Final Checking
Bernd Hilberer, Stuttgart

Independent Contributors and Consultants
Institut für Angewandte Geodäsie, Frankfurt/M.
UNESCO, World Heritage Center, Paris, Vesna Vujicic
Moscow Aerogeodetic Enterprise, Moscow,
Dr. Alexander Borodko
Academia Sinica, Nanking,
Prof. Zhang Longsheng
Mrs. Liu Xiaomei
Kartografie Praha A.S., Prague,
Jirí Kucera
Cartographia Ltd, Sofia, Ivan Petrov
Maplan Warszawa, Warsaw,
H. Michal Siwicki
Prof. Dr. Christian Herrmann, Karlsruhe
Prof. Dr. Wilfried Fiedler, Munich
Prof. Dr. Heinrich Lamping, Frankfurt/M.
Kartographisches Büro Messer, Pfungstadt
Internationales Landkartenhaus, Stuttgart
Birgit Kapper-Wichtler, Buhlenberg
Beate Siewert-Mayer, Tübingen
Dr. Martin Coy, Tübingen
Dr. Wolfgang Frank, Remshalden
Martin Friedrich, Tübingen
Henryk Gorski, Warsaw
Jörg Haas, Rottenburg
Ernst-Dieter Zeidler, Potsdam
Peter Krause, Regensburg
Studio für Landkartentechnik, Norderstedt
Jochen Layer, Fellbach
Maryland Cartographics, Columbia MD
European Map Graphics, Finchampstead (Berkshire)
GeoSystems, Lancaster PA
Timothy J. Carter, Comfort TX

Text and Photo Division

Editor-in-Chief/Project Director
Armin Sinnwell, Munich

Editorial Staff
Raphaela Moczynski, Munich
Karola Pfennig, Munich

Photo Editor
Sabine Geese, Munich

Texts
Dr. Ambros Brucker, Gräfelfing

Translation
GAIA Text, Munich

Illustrations

Satellite Imagery
GEOSPACE-Beckel Satellitenbilddaten, Bad Ischl, Salzburg
© Satellite images:
GEOSPACE/EURIMAGE/EOSAT
© Original data: EOSAT 1994

Photographers
Abbreviations: AKG – Archiv für Kunst und Geschichte; B&U – B&U International Picture Service; IFA – IFA-Bilderteam; TG – Transglobe Agency; TIB – The Image Bank; TSW – Tony Stone Worldwide

Photo credits
I NASA; 1 (center left/cl) AKG; 1 (top to bottom) Hans Wolf/TIB, David W. Hamilton/TIB, Ben Simmons/TG, TIB, Albrecht G. Schaefer, Luis Castaneda/TIB), Rauh/PhotoPress, B&U, Magnus Reitz/TIB, Eric Meola/TIB; 17 (cl) AKG, 17 (left column: top to bottom) Zefa, J. Gnass/Zefa, Norbert Rosing/Silvestris, Hansgeorg Arndt/Silvestris, W. Allgöwer/TG, Norbert Rosing/Silvestris, TSW, Derek Trask/TG, 17 (right column: top to bottom) Scholz/Bavaria, Hunter/IFA, Kokta/IFA, Fuhrmann/PhotoPress, Donovan Reese/TSW, Glen Allison/TSW, A. Schein/Zefa, John J. Wood/PhotoPress, Cosmo Condina/TSW, Chris Haigh/ TSW, Rob Boudreau/TSW; 57 (cl) AKG, 57 (top to bottom) Koene/TG, Diaf/IFA, Michael Scott/TSW, Martin Wendler/Silvestris, R. McLeod/TG, TIB, L. Veiga/TIB, Giuliano Colliva/TIB, A.N.T./Silvestris, R. McLeod/TG, A.N.T./Silvestris; 81 (cl) AKG, 81 (top to bottom) Damm/Zefa, Magnus Rietz/TIB, Jürgens Ost+Europa Photo, UPA/IFA, Jeff Hunter/TIB, Wolfgang Korall/Silvestris, Konrad Wothe/Silvestris, Everts/IFA, A. Gallant/TIB, Backhaus/Zefa, Jürgens Ost+ Europa Photo; 105 (cl) AKG, 105 (left column: top to bottom) Jürgens Ost+Europa Photo, Jürgens Ost+ Europa Photo, Hubert Manfred/Bavaria, Aberham/IFA, Ben Simmons/TG, Jürgens Ost+Europa Photo, A. Filatow/APN/Nowosti, Hubert Manfred/Bavaria, Gerd Ludwig/Visum, 105 (center column: top to bottom) Jürgens Ost+Europa Photo, M. Theis/TG, Richard Elliott/TSW, Ben Edwards/TSW, Rolf Richardson/TG, Everts/IFA, David Sutherland/TSW, Hoa-Qui/Silvestris, Roland Birke/Agentur Hilleke, Alex Stewart/TIB, Andreas Gruschke/Agentur Hilleke, 105 (right column: top to bottom) B&U, Terry Madison/TIB, K. Stration/TG, Romilly Lockyer/TIB, IFA, Glen Hillson/TSW, Paul Chesley/TSW, Chris Haigh/TSW, Nigel Dickinson/TSW, Bail/IFA, Paul Chesley/TSW; 169 (cl) Interfoto, 169 (top to bottom) Clemens Emmler, Gottschalk/IFA, Vollmer/IFA, Albrecht G. Schaefer, Albrecht G. Schaefer, Siebig/IFA, P. Arnold/IFA, BCI/IFA; 185 (cl) AKG, 185 (left column: top to bottom) Kiepke/PhotoPress, Werner Gartung, Diaf/IFA, Erika Graddock/Silvestris, Hoa-Qui/Silvestris, Werner Gartung, Werner Gartung, Obremski/TIB, 185 (right column: top to bottom) Diaf/IFA, Aberham/IFA, Fiedler/IFA, Sally Mayman/TSW, Herbert Schaible/TIB, Nicholas Parfitt/TSW, Stefan Meyers/Silvestrsi, Chris Harvey/TSW, Aberham/IFA, Konrad Wothe/Silvestris, Hoa-Qui/Silvestris.

Production

Design, Layout
Pro Design, Munich
Typographischer Betrieb
Walter Biering & Hans Numberger, Munich

Reproduction
Worldscan, Munich

Repro Director
Wolfgang Mudrak, Munich

Manufacture
Bernhard Mörk, Stuttgart

General Manufacture
Graficas Estella, Estella, Spain

Printed in Spain